JOEL WHITBURN PRESENTS THE

Billboard® POP Charts

1955-1959

Reproductions of *Billboard's* Pop singles charts (*Best Sellers in Stores, Most Played by Jockeys, Most Played in Juke Boxes, Top 100,* and *Hot 100*) from 1955 through 1959.

Record Research Inc.
P.O. Box 200
Menomonee Falls, Wisconsin 53052-0200
U.S.A.

ISBN 0-89820-092-X

Published independently by Record Research Inc.
P.O. Box 200, Menomonee Falls, Wisconsin 53052-0200 U.S.A.

AUTHOR'S NOTE

Nineteen hundred fifty-five through 1959 — the first definitive chapter in the history of rock 'n' roll. This explosive half decade in American pop music has been a favorite subject of musicologists worldwide who have devoted much ink to its musical events. In this book, the *Billboard* pop singles charts will present a detailed week-by-week account of those dynamic five years.

Rock 'n' roll's exciting infancy is evident on the multiple charts of 1955 through 1958. The *Best Sellers, Jockey, Juke Box* and *Top 100* charts each tell the story of the pop music explosion in a different way. The *Most Played in Juke Boxes* and the *Best Sellers in Stores* charts reveal early on that the Fifties teenagers spent their earnings on rock 'n' roll. The *Most Played by Jockeys* reflect the reluctance of radio stations to add rock (the rebellious new teen music that fueled parental ire) to their playlists. Artists such as Johnny Mathis and Frank Sinatra usually did not match their notable Jockeys chart success on the *Best Sellers* or *Juke Box* charts. On the flip side, rockers like Little Richard and Jerry Lee Lewis ranked higher on the *Best Sellers* and *Juke Box* charts than on the *Jockeys.* The *Top 100 Sides* chart seemed to be less of a combination of dealer, disc jockey and juke box operator reports than a potpourri of everything.

The multiple charts ushered in the legacies of Elvis Presley, Buddy Holly, Chuck Berry, Jerry Lee Lewis and The Everly Brothers, and, reinforced pop music's "old guard" influence of Perry Como, Frank Sinatra, Patti Page, Teresa Brewer and Nat "King" Cole. The four charts presented a wide array of pop music — Rockabilly, R&B, Country, Rock 'n Roll, Ballads, Orchestrations and more.

The rock revolution was a few years old when the multiple charts were discontinued in favor of the all-encompassing *Hot 100.* The *Hot 100* maintained the variety of pop music previously displayed by multiple charts, from Tommy Edwards and The Fleetwoods to Conway Twitty and Lloyd Price. This new chart proved successful as it continues to be the nation's leading ranking of popular music 34 years later.

In the pages to follow, the swift and complete transformation of pop music will unfold, week by week. The stage will be set and the lead characters introduced. This is where the story begins.

Joel Whitburn

THE POP CHARTS 1955-1959

Reproductions, in weekly chronological order, of every *Billboard Best Sellers in Stores, Most Played by Jockeys, Most Played in Juke Boxes, Top 100* and *Hot 100* pop singles chart published from January 1, 1955 through December 28, 1959.

The following is a synopsis of the pop singles charts reproduced in this book:

Chart Title	Chart Dates	# of Positions
Best Sellers in Stores	1/1/55 - 10/13/58 (chart ended)	25-50
Most Played by Jockeys	1/1/55 - 7/28/58 (chart ended)	20-25
Most Played in Juke Boxes	1/1/55 - 6/17/57 (chart ended)	20
Top 100	11/12/55 - 7/28/58 (chart ended)	100
Hot 100	8/4/58 - 12/28/59	100

The charts were reproduced by taking photos of the original charts. Most charts reproduced beautifully, but you will note some imperfections due to slight printing flaws on the actual *Billboard* charts.

In most cases, the complete, original page has been reproduced, even though many charts were less than a full page in size, and therefore, you are treated to additional material – such as record ads, record reviews, and more. From November 11, 1957 through July 28, 1958 the *Most Played by Jockeys* chart and the *Top 100* chart were published on separate pages; however, in order to retain the weekly continuity of this book, those charts were spliced together onto one page. From August 4, 1958 to October 13, 1958 the *Hot 100* chart was published as a double-page spread.

During this time period we selected one full-page ad from each week's issue and displayed it next to the *Best Sellers* chart of that week.

ISSUE / WEEK ENDING DATES

Throughout the '50s, both an issue date and week ending date appeared at the top of each chart. Please refer to the *issue date* as the date of reference. (All Record Research books use the issue date.) Also, in one instance, *Billboard's* issue date did not adhere to a seven-day week: April 27, 1957 to April 29, 1957 (*Billboard* went from a Saturday to a Monday issue date).

The Billboard Music Popularity Charts — POPULAR RECORDS

• Best Sellers in Stores

For survey week ending December 22

RECORDS are ranked in order of their current national selling importance at the retail level. Results are based on The Billboard's weekly survey among the nation's top volume pop record dealers representing every important market area. The reverse side of each record is also listed. When a figure is given in parenthesis after the flip title it indicates what position it occupies on the chart.

This Week		Last Week	Weeks on Chart
1.	MR. SANDMAN—Chordettes I Don't Wanna See You Cryin'—Cadence 1247—ASCAP	1	10
2.	LET ME GO, LOVER—J. Weber Marionette—Col 40366—BMI	2	5
3.	NAUGHTY LADY OF SHADY LANE—Ames Brothers Addio—V 20-5897—ASCAP	6	6
4.	THIS OLE HOUSE—R. Clooney Hey, There—(21)—Col 40266—BMI	4	22
5.	COUNT YOUR BLESSINGS—E. Fisher Fanny—(40)—V 20-5871—ASCAP	7	10
6.	I NEED YOU NOW—E. Fisher Heaven Was Never Like This—V 20-5830—ASCAP	5	18
7.	TEACH ME TONIGHT—DeCastro Sisters It's Love—Abbott 3001—ASCAP	3	13
8.	HEARTS OF STONE—Fontane Sisters Bless Your Heart—Dot 15265—BMI	10	4
9.	PAPA LOVES MAMBO—P. Como Things I Didn't Do—V 20-5857—ASCAP	8	14
10.	LET ME GO, LOVER—T. Brewer Moon Is on Fire—Coral 61315—BMI	12	3
11.	MR. SANDMAN—Four Aces I'll Be With You in Apple Blossom Time—Dec 29344—ASCAP	9	6
12.	SHAKE, RATTLE AND ROLL—B. Haley ABC Boogie—Dec 29204—BMI	14	20
13.	MAKE YOURSELF COMFORTABLE—S. Vaughan Crazy 'Bout Lollipop—Mercury 70432—ASCAP	11	6
14.	DIM, DIM THE LIGHTS—B. Haley Happy Baby—Dec 29317—BMI	15	7
15.	HEARTS OF STONE—Charms Who Knows—DeLuxe 6062—BMI	17	6
16.	THAT'S ALL I WANT FROM YOU—J. P. Morgan Dawn—V 20-5896—BMI	16	6
17.	MAMBO ITALIANO—R. Clooney We'll Be Together Again—Col 40361—ASCAP	13	8
18.	HOME FOR THE HOLIDAYS—P. Como Silk Stockings—V 20-5950—ASCAP	22	2
19.	NO MORE—DeJohn Sisters Theresa—Epic 9085—BMI	—	1
20.	MELODY OF LOVE—B. Vaughn Joy Ride—Dot 15247—ASCAP	24	4
21.	HEY, THERE—R. Clooney This Ole House—(4)—Col 40266—ASCAP	18	25
22.	OPEN UP YOUR HEART—Cowboy Church Sunday School The Lord Is Counting on You—Dec 29367—BMI	—	1
23.	IF I GIVE MY HEART TO YOU—Doris Day Anyone Can Fall in Love—Col 40300—ASCAP	19	17
24.	WHITE CHRISTMAS—B. Crosby God Rest Ye Merry Gentlemen—Dec 23778—ASCAP	21	2
25.	LET ME GO, LOVER—P. Page Hocus Pocus—Mercury 70511—BMI	24	3
25.	HOLD MY HAND—D. Cornell I'm Blessed—Coral 61206—ASCAP	20	17
27.	EARTH ANGEL—Penguins Hey, Senorita—Dootone 348—BMI	28	2
27.	RUNAROUND—Chuckles At Last You Understand—X 0066—BMI	—	7
29.	HAJJI BABA—Nat (King) Cole Unbelievable—Cap 2949—ASCAP	—	7
30.	SANTO NATALE—D. Whitfield Adeste Fideles—Lon 1508—ASCAP	—	1

• This Week's Best Buys

According to sales reports in key markets, the following recent releases are recommended for extra profits:

MY LOVE SONG TO YOU (Songsmiths, ASCAP)—Bob Manning—Capitol 3014

The television medium has again given a disk an unusually strong initial push. Since time of release this record has shown good to strong sales in Los Angeles, St. Louis, Chicago, Milwaukee, Cleveland, Pittsburgh, Philadelphia and New York. Flip is "After My Laughter Came Tears" (Shapiro-Bernstein, ASCAP).

MELODY OF LOVE (Shapiro - Bernstein, ASCAP)—Four Aces—Decca 29395

In the furious competitive scramble now going on over this tune, the Aces seem to be emerging with the strongest of the vocal versions. While not all parts of the country have received first shipments, in most of those that have, sales reaction was immediate and positive, particularly in Philadelphia, Providence, Pittsburgh, Cincinnati, Cleveland, Milwaukee and St. Louis. An instrumental version of "Melody of Love" that is off to a good start is that by David Carroll. The Four Aces' disk was a previous Billboard "Spotlight" pick. The flip side is "There Is a Tavern in the Town" (Halsey, ASCAP).

• Most Played in Juke Boxes

For survey week ending December 22

RECORDS are ranked in order of the greatest number of plays in juke boxes thruout the country. Results are based on The Billboard's weekly survey among the nation's juke box operators. The reverse side of each record is also listed. When a figure is given in parenthesis after the flip title it indicates what position it occupies on the chart.

This Week		Last Week	Weeks on Chart
1.	MR. SANDMAN—Chordettes I Don't Wanna See You Cryin'—Cadence 1247—ASCAP	1	8
2.	LET ME GO, LOVER—J. Weber Marionette—Col 40366—BMI	6	4
2.	TEACH ME TONIGHT—DeCastro Sisters It's Love—Abbott 3001—ASCAP	3	12
4.	I NEED YOU NOW—E. Fisher Heaven Was Never Like This—V 20-5830—ASCAP	2	18
5.	NAUGHTY LADY OF SHADY LANE—Ames Brothers Addio—V 20-5897—ASCAP	8	4
6.	THIS OLE HOUSE—R. Clooney Hey, There—(20)—Col 40266—BMI	4	21
7.	PAPA LOVES MAMBO—P. Como Things I Didn't Do—V 20-5857—ASCAP	5	12
8.	IF I GIVE MY HEART TO YOU—Doris Day Anyone Can Fall in Love—Col 40300—ASCAP	9	14
9.	MR. SANDMAN—Four Aces I'll Be With You in Apple Blossom Time—Dec 29344—ASCAP	7	5
10.	COUNT YOUR BLESSINGS—E. Fisher Fanny—V 20-5871—ASCAP	11	7
11.	HOLD MY HAND—D. Cornell I'm Blessed—Coral 61206—ASCAP	10	13
12.	LET ME GO, LOVER—T Brewer Moon Is on Fire—Coral 61315—BMI	19	2
13.	SHAKE, RATTLE AND ROLL—B. Haley ABC Boogie—Dec 29204—BMI	12	15
14.	HEARTS OF STONE—Fontane Sisters Bless Your Heart—Dot 15265—BMI	15	3
15.	THAT'S ALL I WANT FROM YOU—J. P. Morgan Dawn—V 20-5896—BMI	17	2
16.	TEACH ME TONIGHT—J. Stafford Suddenly—Col 40351—ASCAP	18	2
16.	MAMBO ITALIANO—R. Clooney We'll Be Together Again—Col 40361—ASCAP	13	7
16.	LET ME GO, LOVER—P. Page Hocus Pocus—Mercury 70511—BMI	—	1
19.	MAKE YOURSELF COMFORTABLE—S. Vaughn Idle Gossip—Mercury 70469—ASCAP	—	1
20.	HEY THERE—R. Clooney This Ole House—(6)—Col 40266—ASCAP	14	22

• Most Played by Jockeys

For survey week ending December 22

RECORDS are ranked in order of the greatest number of plays on disk jockey radio shows thruout the country. Results are based on The Billboard's weekly survey among the nation's disk jockeys. The reverse side of each record is also listed.

This Week		Last Week	Weeks on Chart
1.	LET ME GO, LOVER—J. Weber Marionette—Col 40366—BMI	2	4
2.	MR. SANDMAN—Chordettes I Don't Wanna See You Cryin'—Cadence 1247—ASCAP	1	10
3.	TEACH ME TONIGHT—DeCastro Sisters It's Love—Abbott 3001—ASCAP	4	12
4.	NAUGHTY LADY OF SHADY LANE—Ames Brothers Addio—V 20-5897—ASCAP	3	7
5.	MR. SANDMAN—Four Aces I'll Be With You in Apple Blossom Time—Dec 29344—ASCAP	6	6
6.	I NEED YOU NOW—E. Fisher Heaven Was Never Like This—V 20-5830—ASCAP	5	17
7.	LET ME GO, LOVER—T. Brewer Moon Is on Fire—Coral 61315—BMI	10	3
8.	HEARTS OF STONE—Fontane Sisters Bless Your Heart—Dot 15265—BMI	9	4
9.	MAKE YOURSELF COMFORTABLE—S. Vaughn Idle Gossip—Mercury 70469—ASCAP	7	6
10.	COUNT YOUR BLESSINGS—E. Fisher Fanny—V 20-5871—ASCAP	13	10
11.	LET ME GO, LOVER—P. Page Hocus Pocus—Mercury 70511—BMI	8	3
12.	HOME FOR THE HOLIDAYS—P. Como Silk Stockings—V 20-5950—ASCAP	15	2
13.	THAT'S ALL I WANT FROM YOU—J. P. Morgan Dawn—V 20-5896—BMI	14	4
14.	HOLD MY HAND—D. Cornell I'm Blessed—Coral 61206—ASCAP	11	15
15.	NO MORE—DeJohn Sisters Theresa—Epic 9085—BMI	20	2
16.	PAPA LOVES MAMBO—P. Como Things I Didn't Do—V 20-5857—ASCAP	12	13
17.	MAMBO ITALIANO—R. Clooney We'll Be Togther Again—Col 40361—ASCAP	16	5
17.	IF I GIVE MY HEART TO YOU—Doris Day Anyone Can Fall in Love—Col 40300—ASCAP	17	16
19.	NAUGHTY LADY OF SHADY LANE—A. Bleyer While the Vesper Bells Were Ringing—Cadence 1254—ASCAP	19	4
19.	WHITE CHRISTMAS—B. Crosby God Rest Ye Merry, Gentleman—Dec 23778—ASCAP	—	1

The Billboard Music Popularity Charts — POPULAR RECORDS

• Best Sellers in Stores

For survey week ending December 29

RECORDS are ranked in order of their current national selling importance at the retail level. Results are based on The Billboard's weekly survey among the nation's top volume pop record dealers representing every important market area. The reverse side of each record is also listed. When a figure is given in parenthesis after the flip title it indicates what position it occupies on the chart.

This Week		Last Week	Weeks on Chart
1.	MR. SANDMAN—Chordettes — I Don't Wanna See You Cryin'—Cadence 1247—ASCAP	1	11
2.	LET ME GO, LOVER—J. Weber — Marionette—Col 40366—BMI	2	6
3.	NAUGHTY LADY OF SHADY LANE—Ames Brothers — Addio—V 20-5897—ASCAP	3	7
4.	I NEED YOU NOW—E. Fisher — Heaven Was Never Like This—V 20-5830—ASCAP	6	19
5.	THIS OLE HOUSE—R. Clooney — Hey, There—(23)—Col 40266—BMI	4	23
6.	TEACH ME TONIGHT—DeCastro Sisters — It's Love—Abbott 3001—ASCAP	7	14
7.	HEARTS OF STONE—Fontane Sisters — Bless Your Heart—Dot 15265—BMI	8	5
8.	COUNT YOUR BLESSINGS—E. Fisher — Fanny—V 20-5871—ASCAP	5	11
9.	LET ME GO, LOVER—T. Brewer — Moon Is on Fire—Coral 61315—BMI	10	4
10.	MR. SANDMAN—Four Aces — I'll Be With You in Apple Blossom Time—Dec 29344—ASCAP	11	7
11.	PAPA LOVES MAMBO—P. Como — Things I Didn't Do—V 20-5857—ASCAP	9	15
11.	SHAKE, RATTLE AND ROLL—B. Haley — ABC Boogie—Dec 29204—BMI	12	21
13.	MAKE YOURSELF COMFORTABLE—S. Vaughan — Crazy 'Bout Lollipop—Mercury 70432—ASCAP	13	7
14.	DIM, DIM THE LIGHTS—B. Haley — Happy Baby—Dec 29317—BMI	14	8
15.	MELODY OF LOVE—B. Vaughn — Joy Ride—Dot 15247—ASCAP	20	5
16.	NO MORE—DeJohn Sisters — Theresa—Epic 9085—BMI	19	2
17.	THAT'S ALL I WANT FROM YOU—J. P. Morgan — Dawn—V 20-5896—BMI	16	7
18.	HOME FOR THE HOLIDAYS—P. Como — Silk Stockings—V 20-5950—ASCAP	18	3
19.	OPEN UP YOUR HEART—Cowboy Church Sunday School — The Lord Is Counting on You—Dec 29367—BMI	22	2
20.	HEARTS OF STONE—Charms — Who Knows—DeLuxe 6062—BMI	15	7
21.	MAMBO ITALIANO—R. Clooney — We'll Be Togther Again—Col 40361—ASCAP	17	9
22.	EARTH ANGEL—Penguins — Hey, Senorita—Dootone 348—BMI	27	3
23.	HEY, THERE—R. Clooney — This Ole House—(5)—Col 40266—ASCAP	21	26
24.	SINCERELY—McGuire Sisters — No More—Coral 61323—BMI	—	1
25.	LET ME GO, LOVER—P. Page — Hocus Pocus—Mercury 70511—BMI	25	4
26.	CARA MIA—D. Whitfield — How, When or Where?—London 1486—ASCAP	—	18
27.	WHITE CHRISTMAS—B. Crosby — God Rest Ye, Merry Gentlemen—Dec 23778—ASCAP	24	3
27.	SANTO NATALE—D. Whitfield — Adeste Fideles—London 1508—ASCAP	30	2
29.	MELODY OF LOVE—D. Carroll — La Golonerina—Mercury 70516—ASCAP	—	1
30.	HOLD MY HAND—D. Cornell — I'm Blessed—Coral 61206—ASCAP	25	18

• This Week's Best Buys

According to sales reports in key markets, the following recent releases are recommended for extra profits:

MELODY OF LOVE (Presser, ASCAP)—David Carroll Ork—Mercury 70516

This instrumental version of this successfully revived standard has been coming up quickly and now holds the No. 29 position on the national retail chart. Its strength was concentrated in the Buffalo, Pittsburgh, Cincinnati, Chicago, Milwaukee, Detroit and St. Louis trade territories. Boston and Providence reports indicate that it is beginning to break in New England as well.

I LOVE YOU MADLY (Angel, BMI)—The Four Coins—Epic 9082

The label is scoring with still another new group. Operators, in particular, have been enthusiastic about this r.&b.-derived material that is reported strong in Detroit, St. Louis, Kansas City, Pittsburgh, Cleveland, Cincinnati and Chicago. Retail sales are also good in Boston, Providence, Philadelphia and Durham. Flip is "Maybe" (Berkshire, BMI). A previous Billboard "Talent Spotlight" pick.

• Most Played in Juke Boxes

For survey week ending December 29

RECORDS are ranked in order of the greatest number of plays in juke boxes thruout the country. Results are based on The Billboard's weekly survey among the nation's juke box operators. The reverse side of each record is also listed. When a figure is given in parenthesis after the flip title it indicates what position it occupies on the chart.

This Week		Last Week	Weeks on Chart
1.	MR. SANDMAN—Chordettes — I Don't Wanna See You Cryin'—Cadence 1247—ASCAP	1	9
2.	LET ME GO, LOVER—J. Weber — Marionette—Col 40366—BMI	2	5
3.	TEACH ME TONIGHT—DeCastro Sisters — It's Love—Abbott 3001—ASCAP	2	13
4.	NAUGHTY LADY OF SHADY LANE—Ames Brothers — Addio—V 20-5897—ASCAP	5	5
5.	I NEED YOU NOW—E. Fisher — Heaven Was Never Like This—V 20-5830—ASCAP	4	19
6.	LET ME GO, LOVER—T. Brewer — Moon Is on Fire—Coral 61315—BMI	12	3
7.	HEARTS OF STONE—Fontane Sisters — Bless Your Heart—Dot 15265—BMI	14	4
7.	PAPA LOVES MAMBO—P. Como — Things I Didn't Do—V 20-5857—ASCAP	7	13
9.	THIS OLE HOUSE—R. Clooney — Hey, There—(21)—Col 40266—BMI	6	22
10.	MR. SANDMAN—Four Aces — I'll Be With You in Apple Blossom Time—Dec 29344—ASCAP	9	6
11.	HOLD MY HAND—D. Cornell — I'm Blessed—Coral 61206—ASCAP	11	14
12.	IF I GIVE MY HEART TO YOU—Doris Day — Anyone Can Fall in Love—Col 40300—ASCAP	8	15
12.	MAKE YOURSELF COMFORTABLE—S. Vaughan — Idle Gossip—Mercury 70469—ASCAP	19	2
14.	COUNT YOUR BLESSINGS—E. Fisher — Fanny—V 20-5871—ASCAP	10	8
14.	THAT'S ALL I WANT FROM YOU—J. P. Morgan — Dawn—V 20-5896—BMI	15	3
14.	SHAKE, RATTLE AND ROLL—B. Haley — ABC Boogie—Dec 29204—BMI	13	16
17.	MAMBO ITALIANO—R. Clooney — We'll Be Together Again—Col 40361—ASCAP	16	8
18.	TEACH ME TONIGHT—J. Stafford — Suddenly—Col 40351—ASCAP	16	3
19.	WHITE CHRISTMAS—B. Crosby — God Rest Ye, Merry Gentlemen—Dec 23778—ASCAP	—	1
19.	MELODY OF LOVE—B. Vaughn — Joy Ride—Dot 15247—ASCAP	—	1

• Most Played by Jockeys

For survey week ending December 29

RECORDS are ranked in order of the greatest number of plays on disk jockey radio shows thruout the country. Results are based on The Billboard's weekly survey among the nation's disk jockeys. The reverse side of each record is also listed.

This Week		Last Week	Weeks on Chart
1.	MR. SANDMAN—Chordettes — I Don't Wanna See You Cryin'—Cadence 1247—ASCAP	2	11
2.	LET ME GO, LOVER—J. Weber — Marionette—Col 40366—BMI	1	5
3.	NAUGHTY LADY OF SHADY LANE—Ames Brothers — Addio—V 20-5897—ASCAP	4	8
4.	TEACH ME TONIGHT—DeCastro Sisters — It's Love—Abbott 3001—ASCAP	3	13
5.	MR. SANDMAN—Four Aces — I'll Be With You in Apple Blossom Time—Dec 29344—ASCAP	5	7
6.	MAKE YOURSELF COMFORTABLE—S. Vaughan — Idle Gossip—Mercury 70469—ASCAP	9	7
7.	HEARTS OF STONE—Fontane Sisters — Bless Your Heart—Dot 15265—BMI	8	5
8.	HOME FOR THE HOLIDAYS—P. Como — Silk Stockings—V 20-5950—ASCAP	12	3
9.	I NEED YOU NOW—E. Fisher — Heaven Was Never Like This—V 20-5830—ASCAP	6	18
10.	LET ME GO, LOVER—T. Brewer — Moon Is on Fire—Coral 61315—BMI	7	4
11.	THAT'S ALL I WANT FROM YOU—J. P. Morgan — Dawn—V 20-5896—BMI	13	5
12.	LET ME GO, LOVER—P. Page — Hocus Pocus—Mercury 70511—BMI	11	4
13.	WHITE CHRISTMAS—B. Crosby — God Rest Ye, Merry Gentlemen—Dec 23778—ASCAP	19	2
14.	COUNT YOUR BLESSINGS—E. Fisher — Fanny—V 20-5871—ASCAP	10	11
15.	NO MORE—DeJohn Sisters — Theresa—Epic 9085—BMI	15	3
15.	TEACH ME TONIGHT—J. Stafford — Suddenly—Col 40351—ASCAP	—	4
17.	LET ME GO, LOVER—S. Gale — Unsuspecting Heart—V 20-5952	—	1
18.	PAPA LOVES MAMBO—P. Como — Things I Didn't Do—V 20-5857—ASCAP	16	14
19.	SANTO NATALE—E. Whitfield — Adeste Fideles—London 1508—ASCAP	—	1
20.	NAUGHTY LADY OF SHADY LANE—A. Bleyer — While the Vesper Bells Were Ringing—Cadence 1254—ASCAP	19	5

The Billboard Music Popularity Charts — POPULAR RECORDS

• Best Sellers in Stores

For survey week ending January 5

RECORDS are ranked in order of their current national selling importance at the retail level. Results are based on The Billboard's weekly survey among the nation's top volume pop record dealers representing every important market area. The reverse side of each record is also listed. When a figure is given in parenthesis after the flip title it indicates what position it occupies on the chart.

This Week	Record	Last Week	Weeks on Chart
1.	MR. SANDMAN—Chordettes — I Don't Wanna See You Cryin'—Cadence 1247—ASCAP	1	12
2.	LET ME GO, LOVER—J. Weber — Marionette—Col 40366—BMI	2	7
3.	NAUGHTY LADY OF SHADY LANE—Ames Brothers — Addio—V 20-5897—ASCAP	3	8
4.	HEARTS OF STONE—Fontane Sisters — Bless Your Heart—Dot 15265—BMI	7	6
5.	TEACH ME TONIGHT—DeCastro Sisters — It's Love—Abbott 3001—ASCAP	6	15
6.	THIS OLE HOUSE—R. Clooney — Hey, There—(25)—Col 40266—BMI	5	24
7.	COUNT YOUR BLESSINGS—E. Fisher — Fanny—V 20-5871—ASCAP	8	12
8.	LET ME GO, LOVER—T. Brewer — Moon Is on Fire—Coral 61315—BMI	9	5
9.	I NEED YOU NOW—E. Fisher — Heaven Was Never Like This—V 20-5830—ASCAP	4	20
10.	MAKE YOURSELF COMFORTABLE—S. Vaughan — Crazy 'Bout Lollipop—Mercury 70432—ASCAP	13	8
11.	MR. SANDMAN—Four Aces — I'll Be With You in Apple Blossom Time—Dec 29344—ASCAP	10	8
12.	DIM, DIM THE LIGHTS—B. Haley — Happy Baby—Dec 29317—BMI	14	9
13.	SHAKE, RATTLE AND ROLL—B. Haley — ABC Boogie—Dec 29204—BMI	11	22
14.	MELODY OF LOVE—B. Vaughn — Joy Ride—Dot 15247—ASCAP	15	6
15.	THAT'S ALL I WANT FROM YOU—J. P. Morgan — Dawn—V 20-5896—BMI	17	8
16.	PAPA LOVES MAMBO—P. Como — Things I Didn't Do—V 20-5857—ASCAP	11	16
17.	NO MORE—DeJohn Sisters — Theresa—Epic 9085—BMI	16	3
18.	HEARTS OF STONE—Charms — Who Knows—DeLuxe 6062—BMI	20	8
19.	SINCERELY—McGuire Sisters — No More—Coral 61323—BMI	24	2
20.	EARTH ANGEL—Penguins — Hey, Senorita—Dootone 348—BMI	22	4
21.	OPEN UP YOUR HEART—Cowboy Church Sunday School — The Lord Is Counting on You—Dec 29367—BMI	19	3
22.	MELODY OF LOVE—D. Carroll — Golondrina, La—Mercury 70516—ASCAP	29	2
22.	MAMBO ITALIANO—R. Clooney — We'll Be Together Again—Col 40361—ASCAP	21	10
24.	LET ME GO, LOVER—P. Page — Hocus Pocus—Mercury 70511—BMI	25	5
25.	HEY, THERE—R. Clooney — This Ole House—(6)—Col 40266—ASCAP	23	27
26.	NAUGHTY LADY OF SHADY LANE—A. Bleyer — While the Vesper Bells Were Ringing—Cadence 1254—ASCAP	—	5
27.	TWEEDLE DEE—L. Baker — Tomorrow Night—Atlantic 1047—BMI	—	1
28.	I LOVE YOU MADLY—Four Coins — Maybe—Epic 9082—BMI	—	1
29.	LING TING TONG—Charms — Bazoom (I Need Your Lovin')—DeLuxe 6076—BMI	—	1
30.	THIS OLE HOUSE—S. Hamblen — When My Lord Picks Up the Phone—V 20-5739—BMI	—	4

• This Week's Best Buys

According to sales reports in key markets, the following recent releases are recommended for extra profits:

TWEEDLE DEE (Progressive, BMI) — Georgia Gibbs —Mercury 70517

While La Vern Baker's recording of this tune is now on both the national pop and rhythm and blues retail charts, Georgia Gibbs is also making a fine showing in many pop markets, and is coming up rapidly. Best sales have been reported in Philadelphia and major Midwestern markets like St. Louis, Chicago, Milwaukee, Detroit, Cleveland and Cincinnati. Two other pop versions of the tune showing better than average sales are by the Lancers and Vicki Young. Flip of the Gibbs record is "You're Wrong, All Wrong." It was a previous Billboard "Spotlight" pick.

• Most Played in Juke Boxes

For survey week ending January 5

RECORDS are ranked in order of the greatest number of plays in juke boxes thruout the country. Results are based on The Billboard's weekly survey among the nation's juke box operators. The reverse side of each record is also listed. When a figure is given in parenthesis after the flip title it indicates what position it occupies on the chart.

This Week	Record	Last Week	Weeks on Chart
1.	LET ME GO, LOVER—J. Weber — Marionette—Col 40366—BMI	2	6
2.	MR. SANDMAN—Chordettes — I Don't Wanna See You Cryin'—Cadence 1247—ASCAP	1	10
3.	TEACH ME TONIGHT—DeCastro Sisters — It's Love—Abbott 3001—ASCAP	3	14
3.	NAUGHTY LADY OF SHADY LANE—Ames Brothers — Addio—V 20-5897—ASCAP	4	6
5.	HEARTS OF STONE—Fontane Sisters — Bless Your Heart—Dot 15265—BMI	7	5
6.	I NEED YOU NOW—E. Fisher — Heaven Was Never Like This—V 20-5830—ASCAP	5	20
7.	MR. SANDMAN—Four Aces — I'll Be With You in Apple Blossom Time—Dec 29344—ASCAP	10	7
8.	LET ME GO, LOVER—T. Brewer — Moon Is on Fire—Coral 61315—BMI	6	4
9.	THIS OLE HOUSE—R. Clooney — Hey, There—(22)—Col 40266—BMI	9	23
10.	PAPA LOVES MAMBO—P. Como — Things I Didn't Do—V 20-5857—ASCAP	7	14
10.	MAKE YOURSELF COMFORTABLE—S. Vaughan — Idle Gossip—Mercury 70469—ASCAP	12	3
12.	COUNT YOUR BLESSINGS—E. Fisher — Fanny—V 20-5871—ASCAP	14	9
13.	IF I GIVE MY HEART TO YOU—Doris Day — Anyone Can Fall in Love—Col 40300—ASCAP	12	16
13.	THAT'S ALL I WANT FROM YOU—J. P. Morgan — Dawn—V 20-5896—BMI	14	4
15.	HOLD MY HAND—D. Cornell — I'm Blessed—Coral 61206—ASCAP	11	15
16.	MELODY OF LOVE—B. Vaughn — Joy Ride—Dot 15247—ASCAP	19	2
17.	SHAKE, RATTLE AND ROLL—B. Haley — A.B.C. Boogie—Dec 29204—BMI	14	17
17.	MAMBO ITALIANO—R. Clooney — We'll Be Together Again—Col 40361—ASCAP	17	9
17.	TEACH ME TONIGHT—J. Stafford — Suddenly—Col 40351—ASCAP	18	4
20.	NAUGHTY LADY OF SHADY LANE—A. Bleyer — While the Vesper Bells Were Ringing—Cadence 1254—ASCAP	—	1
20.	MELODY OF LOVE—Four Aces — There's a Tavern in the Town—Dec 29395—ASCAP	—	1

• Most Played by Jockeys

For survey week ending January 5

RECORDS are ranked in order of the greatest number of plays on disk jockey radio shows thruout the country. Results are based on The Billboard's weekly survey among the nation's disk jockeys. The reverse side of each record is also listed.

This Week	Record	Last Week	Weeks on Chart
1.	LET ME GO, LOVER—J. Weber — Marionette—Col 40366—BMI	2	6
2.	MR. SANDMAN—Chordettes — I Don't Wanna See You Cryin'—Cadence 1247—ASCAP	1	12
3.	NAUGHTY LADY OF SHADY LANE—Ames Brothers — Addio—V 20-5897—ASCAP	3	9
4.	HEARTS OF STONE—Fontane Sisters — Bless Your Heart—Dot 15265—BMI	7	6
5.	MR. SANDMAN—Four Aces — I'll Be With You in Apple Blossom Time—Dec 29344—ASCAP	5	8
6.	TEACH ME TONIGHT—DeCastro Sisters — It's Love—Abbott 3001—ASCAP	4	14
7.	MAKE YOURSELF COMFORTABLE—S. Vaughan — Idle Gossip—Mercury 70469—ASCAP	6	8
8.	LET ME GO, LOVER—T. Brewer — Moon Is on Fire—Coral 61315—BMI	10	5
9.	NO MORE—DeJohn Sisters — Theresa—Epic 9085—BMI	15	4
10.	THAT'S ALL I WANT FROM YOU—J. P. Morgan — Dawn—V 20-5896—BMI	11	6
11.	I NEED YOU NOW—E. Fisher — Heaven Was Never Like This—V 20-5830—ASCAP	9	19
12.	COUNT YOUR BLESSINGS—E. Fisher — Fanny—V 20-5871—ASCAP	14	12
13.	MELODY OF LOVE—B. Vaughn — Joy Ride—Dot 15247—ASCAP	—	1
14.	LET ME GO, LOVER—P. Page — Hocus Pocus—Mercury 70511—BMI	12	5
15.	SINCERELY—McGuire Sisters — No More—Coral 61323—BMI	—	1
16.	DIM, DIM THE LIGHTS—B. Haley — Happy Baby—Dec 29317—BMI	—	1
17.	NAUGHTY LADY OF SHADY LANE—A. Bleyer — While the Vesper Bells Were Ringing—Cadence 1254—ASCAP	20	6
18.	PAPA LOVES MAMBO—P. Como — Things I Didn't Do—V 20-5857—ASCAP	18	15
19.	TEACH ME TONIGHT—J. Stafford — Suddenly—Col 40351—ASCAP	15	5
20.	MAMBO ITALIANO—R. Clooney — We'll Be Together Again—Col 40361—ASCAP	—	6

The Billboard Music Popularity Charts — POPULAR RECORDS

• Best Sellers in Stores

For survey week ending January 12

RECORDS are ranked in order of their current national selling importance at the retail level. Results are based on The Billboard's weekly survey among the nation's top volume pop record dealers representing every important market area. The reverse side of each record is also listed. When a figure is given in parenthesis after the flip title it indicates what position it occupies on the chart.

This Week	Record	Last Week	Weeks on Chart
1.	LET ME GO, LOVER—J. Weber — Marionette—Col 40366—BMI	2	8
2.	MR. SANDMAN—Chordettes — I Don't Wanna See You Cryin'—Cadence 1247—ASCAP	1	13
3.	NAUGHTY LADY OF SHADY LANE—Ames Brothers — Addio—V -5897—ASCAP	3	9
4.	HEARTS OF STONE—Fontane Sisters — Bless Your Heart—Dot 15265—BMI	4	7
5.	TEACH ME TONIGHT—DeCastro Sisters — It's Love—Abbott 3001—ASCAP	5	16
6.	SINCERELY—McGuire Sisters — No More—(36)—Coral 61323—BMI	19	3
7.	MELODY OF LOVE—B. Vaughn — Joy Ride—Dot 15247—ASCAP	14	7
8.	MAKE YOURSELF COMFORTABLE—S. Vaughan — Crazy 'Bout Lollipop—Mercury 70432—ASCAP	10	9
9.	LET ME GO, LOVER—T. Brewer — Moon Is on Fire—Coral 61315—BMI	8	6
10.	THAT'S ALL I WANT FROM YOU—J. P. Morgan — Dawn—V 20-5896—BMI	15	9
11.	DIM, DIM THE LIGHTS—B. Haley — Happy Baby—Dec 29317—BMI	12	10
12.	MR. SANDMAN—Four Aces — I'll Be With You in Apple Blossom Time—Dec 29344—ASCAP	11	9
13.	NO MORE—DeJohn Sisters — Theresa—Epic 9085—BMI	17	4
14.	SHAKE, RATTLE AND ROLL—B. Haley — ABC Boogie—Dec 29204—BMI	13	23
15.	THIS OLE HOUSE—R. Clooney — Hey, There—(36)—Col 40266—BMI	6	25
16.	COUNT YOUR BLESSINGS—E. Fisher — Fanny—V 20-5871—ASCAP	7	13
17.	I NEED YOU NOW—E. Fisher — Heaven Was Never Like This—V 20-5830—ASCAP	9	21
18.	EARTH ANGEL—Penguins — Hey Senorita—Dootone 348—BMI	20	5
19.	PAPA LOVES MAMBO—P. Como — Things I Didn't Do—V 20-5857—ASCAP	16	17
20.	HEARTS OF STONE—Charms — Who Knows—DeLuxe 6062—BMI	18	9
21.	MELODY OF LOVE—D. Carroll — Golondrina, La—Mercury 70516—ASCAP	22	3
22.	MELODY OF LOVE—Four Aces — There's a Tavern in the Town—Dec 29395—ASCAP	—	1
23.	OPEN UP YOUR HEART—Cowboy Church Sunday School — The Lord Is Counting on You—Dec 29367—BMI	21	4
24.	MAMBO ITALIANO—R. Clooney — We'll Be Together Again—Col 40361—ASCAP	22	11
25.	TWEEDLE DEE—L. Baker — Tomorrow Night—Atlantic 1047—BMI	27	2
26.	LING, TING, TONG—Charms — Bazoom (I Need Your Lovin')—DeLuxe 6076—BMI	29	2
27.	LET ME GO, LOVER—P. Page — Hocus Pocus—Mercury 70511—BMI	24	6
27.	TEACH ME TONIGHT—J. Stafford — Suddenly—Col 40351—ASCAP	—	6
27.	SONG OF THE BAREFOOT CONTESSA—H. Winterhalter — Land of Dreams—(33)—V 20-5888—ASCAP	—	2
30.	RUNAROUND—Chuckles — At Last You Understand—X 0066—BMI	—	8

• This Week's Best Buys

According to sales reports in key markets, the following recent releases are recommended for extra profits:

KO KO MO (Meridian, BMI)
EARTH ANGEL (Dootsie Williams, BMI)—The Crew Cuts—Mercury 70529

KO KO MO (Meridian, BMI)—Perry Como—RCA Victor 20-5994

Out of the numerous competing versions of this tune, these two have taken decisive leads. The Crew Cuts enjoyed a head start in several areas, but Como's TV shot earlier in the week narrowed down the group's margin. Both disks are getting excellent initial reaction. The Mercury record, with another top rhythm & blues tune on the coupling, is proving to have potent appeal for operators. Flip of the Como disk is "You'll Always Be My Lifteime Sweetheart" (Wizell & Day, ASCAP). Both records were previous Billboard "Spotlight" picks.

I GOTTA GO GET MY BABY (Four Star, BMI)—Teresa Brewer—Coral 61339

Tho available in most territories little more than a week, the singer's latest release has garnered a collection of fine sales reports. Rated as a good or strong seller in Boston, Providence, Philadelphia, Pittsburgh, Cincinnati, Cleveland, Milwaukee, Nashville and Atlanta. Flip is "What More Is There to Say" (Mellin, ASCAP). A previous Billboard "Spotlight" pick.

DARLIN' (Tee Pee, ASCAP)—The Hilltoppers—Dot 15318

Middle Western markets like St. Louis, Milwaukee, Cincinnati and Cleveland have been doing good business with this disk the past few weeks. Its popularity has spread now to Buffalo, Philadelphia, Boston, Durham and Nashville as well, with prospects good that it will soon include most of the remaining parts of the country. Flip is "Frivolette" (Randy-Smith, ASCAP). A previous Billboard "Spotlight" pick.

• Most Played in Juke Boxes

For survey week ending January 12

RECORDS are ranked in order of the greatest number of plays in juke boxes thruout the country. Results are based on The Billboard's weekly survey among the nation's juke box operators. The reverse side of each record is also listed. When a figure is given in parenthesis after the flip title it indicates what position it occupies on the chart.

This Week	Record	Last Week	Weeks on Chart
1.	LET ME GO, LOVER—J. Weber — Marionette—Col 40366—BMI	1	7
2.	MR. SANDMAN—Chordettes — I Don't Wanna See You Cryin'—Cadence 1247—ASCAP	2	11
3.	NAUGHTY LADY OF SHADY LANE—Ames Brothers — Addio—V 20-5897—ASCAP	3	7
4.	HEARTS OF STONE—Fontane Sisters — Bless Your Heart—Dot 15265—BMI	5	6
5.	TEACH ME TONIGHT—DeCastro Sisters — It's Love—Abbott 3001—ASCAP	3	15
6.	MR. SANDMAN—Four Aces — I'll Be With You in Apple Blossom Time—Dec 29344—ASCAP	7	8
7.	I NEED YOU NOW—E. Fisher — Heaven Was Never Like This—V 20-5830—ASCAP	6	21
8.	LET ME GO, LOVER—T. Brewer — Moon Is on Fire—Coral 61315—BMI	8	5
9.	COUNT YOUR BLESSINGS—E. Fisher — Fanny—V 20-5871—ASCAP	12	10
10.	MAKE YOURSELF COMFORTABLE—S. Vaughan — Idle Gossip—Mercury 70469—ASCAP	10	4
11.	THIS OLE HOUSE—R. Clooney — Hey, There—(39)—Col 40266—BMI	9	24
11.	THAT'S ALL I WANT FROM YOU—J. P. Morgan — Dawn—V 20-5896—BMI	13	5
13.	MELODY OF LOVE—B. Vaughn — Joy Ride—Dot 15247—ASCAP	16	3
14.	LET ME GO, LOVER—P. Page — Hocus Pocus—Mercury 70511—BMI	—	2
15.	PAPA LOVES MAMBO—P. Como — Things I Didn't Do—V 20-5857—ASCAP	10	15
16.	IF I GIVE MY HEART TO YOU—Doris Day — Anyone Can Fall in Love—Col 40300—ASCAP	13	17
17.	MELODY OF LOVE—Four Aces — There's a Tavern in the Town—Dec 29395—ASCAP	20	2
17.	SINCERELY—McGuire Sisters — No More—(27)—Coral 61323—BMI	—	1
19.	TEACH ME TONIGHT—J. Stafford — Suddenly—Col 40351—ASCAP	17	5
19.	SHAKE, RATTLE AND ROLL—B. Haley — ABC Boogie—Dec 29204—BMI	17	18

• Most Played by Jockeys

For survey week ending January 12

RECORDS are ranked in order of the greatest number of plays on disk jockey radio shows thruout the country. Results are based on The Billboard's weekly survey among the nation's disk jockeys. The reverse side of each record is also listed.

This Week	Record	Last Week	Weeks on Chart
1.	MR. SANDMAN—Chordettes — I Don't Wanna See You Cryin'—Cadence 1247—ASCAP	2	13
2.	LET ME GO, LOVER—J. Weber — Marionette—Col 40366—BMI	1	7
3.	NAUGHTY LADY OF SHADY LANE—Ames Brothers — Addio—V 20-5897—ASCAP	3	10
4.	HEARTS OF STONE—Fontane Sisters — Bless Your Heart—Dot 15265—BMI	4	7
5.	TEACH ME TONIGHT—DeCastro Sisters — It's Love—Abbott 3001—ASCAP	6	15
6.	MAKE YOURSELF COMFORTABLE—S. Vaughan — Idle Gossip—Mercury 70469—ASCAP	7	9
7.	MR. SANDMAN—Four Aces — I'll Be With You in Apple Blossom Time—Dec 29344—ASCAP	5	9
8.	NO MORE—DeJohn Sisters — Theresa—Epic 9085—BMI	9	5
9.	THAT'S ALL I WANT FROM YOU—J. P. Morgan — Dawn—V 20-5896—BMI	10	7
10.	SINCERELY—McGuire Sisters — No More—Coral 61323—BMI	15	2
11.	LET ME GO, LOVER—T. Brewer — Moon Is on Fire—Coral 61315—BMI	8	6
12.	MELODY OF LOVE—B. Vaughn — Joy Ride—Dot 15247—ASCAP	13	2
13.	I NEED YOU NOW—E. Fisher — Heaven Was Never Like This—V 20-5830—ASCAP	11	20
14.	MELODY OF LOVE—D. Carroll — Golondrina, La—Mercury 70516—ASCAP	—	1
15.	MELODY OF LOVE—Four Aces — There's a Tavern in the Town—Dec 29395—ASCAP	—	1
16.	LET ME GO, LOVER—P. Page — Hocus Pocus—Mercury 70511—BMI	14	6
17.	COUNT YOUR BLESSINGS—E. Fisher — Fanny—V 20-5871—ASCAP	12	13
18.	DIM, DIM THE LIGHTS—B. Haley — Happy Baby—Dec 29317—BMI	16	2
19.	MELODY OF LOVE—F. Sinatra & R. Anthony — I'm Gonna Live Till I Die—Cap 3018—ASCAP	—	1
20.	HEARTS OF STONE—Charms — Who Knows—DeLuxe 6062—BMI	—	1

The Billboard Music Popularity Charts

POPULAR RECORDS

• Best Sellers in Stores

For survey week ending January 19

RECORDS are ranked in order of their current national selling importance at the retail level. Results are based on The Billboard's weekly survey among the nation's top volume pop record dealers representing every important market area. The reverse side of each record is also listed. When a figure is given in parenthesis after the flip title it indicates what position it occupies on the chart.

This Week		Last Week	Weeks on Chart
1.	LET ME GO, LOVER—J. Weber Marionette—Col 40366—BMI	1	9
2.	MR. SANDMAN—Chordettes I Don't Wanna See You Cryin'—Cadence 1247—ASCAP	2	14
3.	HEARTS OF STONE—Fontane Sisters Bless Your Heart—Dot 15265—BMI	4	8
4.	NAUGHTY LADY OF SHADY LANE—Ames Brothers Addio—V 20-5897—ASCAP	3	10
5.	SINCERELY—McGuire Sisters No More—(27)—Coral 61323—BMI	6	4
6.	MELODY OF LOVE—B. Vaughn Joy Ride—Dot 15247—ASCAP	7	8
7.	THAT'S ALL I WANT FROM YOU—J. P. Morgan Dawn—V 20-5896—BMI	10	10
8.	NO MORE—DeJohn Sisters Theresa—Epic 9085—BMI	13	5
9.	MAKE YOURSELF COMFORTABLE—S. Vaughan Idle Gossip—Mercury 70469—ASCAP	8	10
10.	TEACH ME TONIGHT—DeCastro Sisters It's Love—Abbott 3001—ASCAP	5	17
11.	LET ME GO, LOVER—T. Brewer Moon Is on Fire—Coral 61315—BMI	9	7
12.	MELODY OF LOVE—D. Carroll La Golondrina—Mercury 70516—ASCAP	21	4
13.	EARTH ANGEL—Penguins Hey Senorita—Dootone 348—BMI	18	6
14.	MR. SANDMAN—Four Aces I'll Be With You In Apple Blossom Time—Dec 29344—ASCAP	12	10
15.	DIM, DIM THE LIGHTS—B. Haley Happy Baby—Dec 29317—BMI	11	11
16.	I NEED YOU NOW—E. Fisher Heaven Was Never Like This—V 20-5830—ASCAP	17	22
17.	MELODY OF LOVE—Four Aces There's a Tavern in the Town—Dec 29395—ASCAP	22	2
18.	OPEN UP YOUR HEART—Cowboy Church Sunday School The Lord Is Counting on You—Dec 29367—BMI	23	5
19.	COUNT YOUR BLESSINGS—E. Fisher Fanny—V 20-5871—ASCAP	16	14
20.	THIS OLE HOUSE—R. Clooney Hey, There—Col 40266—BMI	15	26
20.	HEARTS OF STONE—Charms Who Knows—DeLuxe 6062—BMI	20	10
22.	TWEEDLE DEE—G. Gibbs You're Wrong, All Wrong—Mercury 70517—BMI	—	1
23.	SHAKE, RATTLE AND ROLL—B. Haley A B C Boogie—Dec 29204—BMI	14	24
24.	KO KO MO—Crew Cuts Earth Angel—Mercury 70529—BMI	—	1
25.	TWEEDLE DEE—L. Baker Tomorrow Night—Atlantic 1047—BMI	25	3
26.	SONG OF THE BAREFOOT CONTESSA—H. Winterhalter Land of Dreams—(39)—V 20-5888—ASCAP	27	3
27.	NO MORE—McGuire Sisters Sincerely—(5)—Coral 61323—BMI	—	1
27.	PAPA LOVES MAMBO—P. Como Things I Didn't Do—V 20-5857—ASCAP	19	18
29.	LING, TING, TONG—Five Keys I'm Alone—Cap 2945—BMI	—	1
30.	MAMBO ITALIANO—R. Clooney We'll Be Together Again—Col 40361—ASCAP	24	12

• This Week's Best Buys

According to sales reports in key markets, the following recent releases are recommended for extra profits:

THE CRAZY OTTO — Johnny Maddox — Dot 15325
In this zany novelty, Maddox is enjoying one of his biggest records in quite a while. Boston, New York, Philadelphia, Buffalo, Pittsburgh, Chicago, Milwaukee, Nashville, Durham, Atlanta, Richmond and St. Louis were among the territories that reported strong sales this week. Flip is "Humoresque." A previous Billboard "Spotlight" pick.

EVERLOVIN' (Tannen, BMI)—Patti Page—Mercury 70528
The singer is maintaining her high batting average, from all indications of early sales reports on this most recent release of hers. The disk moved out quickly and with accelerating speed in New England, Philadelphia, Pittsburgh, Buffalo, Cincinnati, Cleveland, Milwaukee, Nashville, Richmond, Durham and St. Louis. Flip is "You Too Can Be a Dreamer" (Mills, ASCAP). A previous Billboard "Spotlight" pick.

HOW IMPORTANT CAN IT BE? (Laurel, ASCAP)—Joni James—M-G-M 11919
Tho the competition on this tune is heavy, Joni James has taken a decisive early lead. Territories where this disk was delivered first and sent off in a big way included New York, Providence, Philadelphia; Buffalo and Pittsburgh. Initial sales reaction was also good in St. Louis and Cincinnati. Some areas received the Sarah Vaughan and Lou Monte versions of this tune at about the same time as the James disk and were giving it competition. The flip is "This Is My Confession" (Miller, ASCAP). A previous Billboard "Spotlight" pick.

MALAGUENA (E. B. Marks, BMI)—Caterina Valente—Decca 29394
In the past two weeks this German language disk has gained coast-to-coast acceptance and has achieved an unusually good spread of enthusiastic sales reports. Los Angeles, St. Louis, Milwaukee, Pittsburgh, Chicago, Cincinnati, Buffalo and New York were among them. Flip is "Mambo from Chile" (Copar, BMI). A previous Billboard "Spotlight" pick.

• Most Played in Juke Boxes

For survey week ending January 19

RECORDS are ranked in order of the greatest number of plays in juke boxes thruout the country. Results are based on The Billboard's weekly survey among the nation's juke box operators. The reverse side of each record is also listed. When a figure is given in parenthesis after the flip title it indicates what position it occupies on the chart.

This Week		Last Week	Weeks on Chart
1.	LET ME GO, LOVER—J. Weber Marionette—Col 40366—BMI	1	8
2.	MR. SANDMAN—Chordettes I Don't Wanna See You Cryin'—Cadence 1247—ASCAP	2	12
3.	HEARTS OF STONE—Fontane Sisters Bless Your Heart—Dot 15265—BMI	4	7
4.	NAUGHTY LADY OF SHADY LANE—Ames Brothers Addio—V 20-5897—ASCAP	3	8
5.	TEACH ME TONIGHT—DeCastro Sisters It's Love—Abbott 3001—ASCAP	5	16
6.	MR. SANDMAN—Four Aces I'll Be With You in Apple Blossom Time—Dec 29344—ASCAP	6	9
7.	LET ME GO, LOVER—T. Brewer Moon Is on Fire—Coral 61315—BMI	8	6
8.	I NEED YOU NOW—E. Fisher Heaven Was Never Like This—V 20-5830—ASCAP	7	22
9.	MAKE YOURSELF COMFORTABLE—S. Vaughan Idle Gossip—Mercury 70469—ASCAP	10	5
9.	SINCERELY—McGuire Sisters No More—(20)—Coral 61323—BMI	17	2
11.	THAT'S ALL I WANT FROM YOU—J. P. Morgan Dawn—V 20-5896—BMI	11	6
12.	MELODY OF LOVE—B. Vaughn Joy Ride—Dot 15247—ASCAP	13	4
13.	COUNT YOUR BLESSINGS—E. Fisher Fanny—V 20-5871—ASCAP	9	11
13.	THIS OLE HOUSE—R. Clooney Hey, There—Col 40266—BMI	11	25
15.	MELODY OF LOVE—Four Aces There's a Tavern in the Town—Dec 29395—ASCAP	17	3
16.	LET ME GO, LOVER—P. Page Hocus Pocus—Mercury 70511—BMI	14	3
16.	SHAKE, RATTLE AND ROLL—B. Haley ABC Boogie—Dec 29204—BMI	19	19
18.	TEACH ME TONIGHT—J. Stafford Suddenly—Col 40351—ASCAP	19	6
18.	NO MORE—DeJohn Sisters Theresa—Epic 9085—BMI	—	1
20.	NO MORE—McGuire Sisters Sincerely—(9)—Coral 61323—BMI	—	1
20.	HEARTS OF STONE—Charms Who Knows—DeLuxe 6062—BMI	—	1

• Most Played by Jockeys

For survey week ending January 19

RECORDS are ranked in order of the greatest number of plays on disk jockey radio shows thruout the country. Results are based on The Billboard's weekly survey among the nation's disk jockeys. The reverse side of each record is also listed.

This Week		Last Week	Weeks on Chart
1.	LET ME GO, LOVER—J. Weber Marionette—Col 40366—BMI	2	8
2.	MR. SANDMAN—Chordettes I Don't Wanna See You Cryin'—Cadence 1247—ASCAP	1	14
3.	HEARTS OF STONE—Fontane Sisters Bless Your Heart—Dot 15265—BMI	4	8
4.	NAUGHTY LADY OF SHADY LANE—Ames Brothers Addio—V 20-5897—ASCAP	3	11
5.	SINCERELY—McGuire Sisters No More—Coral 61323—BMI	10	3
6.	MAKE YOURSELF COMFORTABLE—S. Vaughan Idle Gossip—Mercury 70469—ASCAP	6	10
7.	THAT'S ALL I WANT FROM YOU—J. P. Morgan Dawn—V 20-5896—BMI	9	8
8.	NO MORE—DeJohn Sisters Theresa—Epic 9085—BMI	8	6
9.	MR. SANDMAN—Four Aces I'll Be With You in Apple Blossom Time—Dec 29344—ASCAP	7	10
10.	TEACH ME TONIGHT—DeCastro Sisters It's Love—Abbott 3001—ASCAP	5	16
11.	MELODY OF LOVE—B. Vaughn Joy Ride—Dot 15247—ASCAP	12	3
12.	MELODY OF LOVE—D. Carroll Golondrina, La—Mercury 70516—ASCAP	14	2
13.	LET ME GO, LOVER—T. Brewer Moon Is on Fire—Coral 61315—BMI	11	7
14.	LET ME GO, LOVER—P. Page Hocus Pocus—Mercury 70511—BMI	16	7
15.	MELODY OF LOVE—Four Aces There's a Tavern in the Town—Dec 29395—ASCAP	15	2
16.	I NEED YOU NOW—E. Fisher Heaven Was Never Like This—V 20-5830—ASCAP	13	21
17.	EARTH ANGEL—Penguins Hey, Senorita—Dootone 348—BMI	—	1
18.	OPEN UP YOUR HEART—Cowboy Church Sunday School Lord Is Counting on You—Dec 29367—BMI	—	1
19.	TWEEDLE DEE—G. Gibbs You're Wrong, All Wrong—Mercury 70517—BMI	—	1
20.	NO MORE—McGuire Sisters Sincerely—Coral 61323—BMI	—	1

The Billboard Music Popularity Charts — POPULAR RECORDS

• Best Sellers in Stores

For survey week ending January 26

RECORDS are ranked in order of their current national selling importance at the retail level. Results are based on The Billboard's weekly survey among the nation's top volume pop record dealers representing every important market area. The reverse side of each record is also listed. When a figure is given in parenthesis after the flip title it indicates what position it occupies on the chart.

This Week		Last Week	Weeks on Chart
1.	HEARTS OF STONE—Fontane Sisters. Bless Your Heart—Dot 15265—BMI	3	9
2.	SINCERELY—McGuire Sisters. No More—(26)—Coral 61323—BMI	5	5
3.	LET ME GO, LOVER—J. Weber. Marionette—Col 40366—BMI	1	10
4.	MR. SANDMAN—Chordettes. I Don't Wanna See You Cryin'—Cadence 1247—ASCAP	2	15
5.	NAUGHTY LADY OF SHADY LANE—Ames Brothers. Addio—V 20-5897—ASCAP	4	11
6.	MELODY OF LOVE—B. Vaughn. Joy Ride—Dot 15247—ASCAP	6	9
7.	THAT'S ALL I WANT FROM YOU—J. P. Morgan. Dawn—V 20-5896—BMI	7	11
8.	EARTH ANGEL—Penguins. Hey, Senorita—Dootone 348—BMI	13	7
9.	LET ME GO, LOVER—T. Brewer. Moon Is on Fire—Coral 61315—BMI	11	8
9.	NO MORE—DeJohn Sisters. Theresa—Epic 9085—BMI	8	6
11.	KO KO MO—P. Como. You'll Always Be My Lifetime Stweetheart—V 20-5994—BMI	—	1
12.	MAKE YOURSELF COMFORTABLE—S. Vaughan. Idle Gossip—Mercury 70469—ASCAP	9	11
13.	MR. SANDMAN—Four Aces. I'll Be With You in Apple Blossom Time—Dec 29344—ASCAP	14	11
14.	TEACH ME TONIGHT—DeCastro Sisters. It's Love—Abbott 3001—ASCAP	10	18
15.	MELODY OF LOVE—D. Carroll. La Golondrina—Mercury 70516—ASCAP	12	5
16.	OPEN UP YOUR HEART—Cowboy Church Sunday School. The Lord Is Counting on You—Dec 29367—BMI	18	6
17.	TWEEDLE DEE—G. Gibbs. You're Wrong, All Wrong—Mercury 70517—BMI	22	2
18.	MELODY OF LOVE—Four Aces. There's a Tavern in the Town—Dec 29395—ASCAP	17	3
19.	EARTH ANGEL—Crew Cuts. Ko Ko Mo—(21)—Mercury 70529—BMI	—	1
20.	DIM, DIM THE LIGHTS—B. Haley. Happy Baby—Dec 29317—BMI	15	12
21.	KO KO MO—Crew Cuts. Earth Angel—(19)—Mercury 70529—BMI	24	2
22.	COUNT YOUR BLESSINGS—E. Fisher. Fanny—V 20-5871—ASCAP	19	15
23.	SHAKE, RATTLE AND ROLL—B. Haley. ABC Boogie—Dec 29204—BMI	23	25
24.	CRAZY OTTO MEDLEY—J. Maddox. Humoresque—Dot 15325—	—	1
25.	HEARTS OF STONE—Charms. Who Knows—DeLuxe 6062—BMI	20	11
26.	NO MORE—McGuire Sisters. Sincerely—(2)—Coral 61323—BMI	27	2
27.	THIS OLE HOUSE—R. Clooney. Hey, There—Col 40266—BMI	20	27
28.	I NEED YOU NOW—E. Fisher. Heaven Was Never Like This—V 20-5830—ASCAP	16	23
29.	TWEEDLE DEE—L. Baker. Tomorrow Night—Atlantic 1047—BMI	25	4
30.	MAKE YOURSELF COMFORTABLE—P. King. Gentleman in the Next Apartment—Col 40363—ASCAP	—	1

• This Week's Best Buys

According to sales reports in key markets, the following recent releases are recommended for extra profits:

SMILES (Remick, ASCAP)
GLAD RAG DOLL (Advance, ASCAP)—**Happy Otto—Decca 29403**

The German piano-player who created a sensation with a medley released originally on a Polydor import is getting a far larger audience on this waxing of two familiar standards. This week the disk appears on the Pittsburgh, Cleveland and Detroit territorial charts and also was reported to be selling well in Buffalo, Providence, Durham, Atlanta, Chicago, Milwaukee, St. Louis and Cincinnati. A previous Billboard "Spotlight" pick.

ROCK LOVE (Jay & Cee, BMI)—**Fontane Sisters—Dot 8570**

Of the many versions (pop and r.&b.) of this tune competing for sales, the one by the Fontane Sisters is moving out ahead of the field. In its first week, highly favorable sales reports were returned from Boston, Providence, New York, Philadelphia, Baltimore, Chicago, Detroit, Nashville, Durham and St. Louis. In many instances, the disk was reported to be racking up equally good r.&b. and pop sales. Flip is "You're Mine" (Arc, BMI). A previous Billboard "Spotlight" pick.

HOW IMPORTANT CAN IT BE? (Laurel, ASCAP)—**Sarah Vaughan—Mercury 70534**

The second version of this tune to take off. While the Joni James record still holds the edge nationally, good volume on the Mercury disk was reported this week in Los Angeles, St. Louis, Durham, Baltimore, New York, Providence, Cincinnati, Cleveland and Chicago. Flip is "Waltzing Down the Aisle" (Golden Bell, ASCAP). A previous Billboard "Spotlight" pick.

• Most Played in Juke Boxes

For survey week ending January 26

RECORDS are ranked in order of the greatest number of plays in juke boxes throut the country. Results are based on The Billboard's weekly survey among the nation's juke box operators. The reverse side of each record is also listed. When a figure is given in parenthesis after the flip title it indicates what position it occupies on the chart.

This Week		Last Week	Weeks on Chart
1.	LET ME GO, LOVER—J. Weber. Marionette—Col 40366—BMI	1	9
2.	MR. SANDMAN—Chordettes. I Don't Wanna See You Cryin'—Cadence 1247—ASCAP	2	13
3.	HEARTS OF STONE—Fontane Sisters. Bless Your Heart—Dot 15265—BMI	3	8
4.	NAUGHTY LADY OF SHADY LANE—Ames Brothers. Addio—V 20-5397—ASCAP	4	9
5.	TEACH ME TONIGHT—DeCastro Sisters. It's Love—Abbott 3001—ASCAP	5	17
6.	MELODY OF LOVE—B. Vaughn. Joy Ride—Dot 15247—ASCAP	12	5
7.	SINCERELY—McGuire Sisters. No More—(19)—Coral 61323—BMI	9	3
8.	MAKE YOURSELF COMFORTABLE—S. Vaughan. Idle Gossip—Mercury 70469—ASCAP	9	6
9.	MELODY OF LOVE—Four Aces. There's a Tavern in the Town—Dec 29395—ASCAP	15	4
10.	THAT'S ALL I WANT FROM YOU—J. P. Morgan. Dawn—V 20-5896—BMI	11	7
11.	LET ME GO, LOVER—T. Brewer. Moon Is on Fire—Coral 61315—BMI	7	7
12.	MR. SANDMAN—Four Aces. I'll Be With You in Apple Blossom Time—Dec 29344—ASCAP	6	10
13.	I NEED YOU NOW—E. Fisher. Heaven Was Never Like This—V 20-5830—ASCAP	8	23
13.	NO MORE—DeJohn Sisters. Theresa—Epic 9085—BMI	18	2
15.	LET ME GO, LOVER—P. Page. Hocus Pocus—Mercury 70511—BMI	16	4
16.	SHAKE, RATTLE AND ROLL—B. Haley. ABC Boogie—Dec 29204—BMI	16	20
17.	HEARTS OF STONE—Charms. Who Knows—DeLuxe 6062—BMI	20	2
18.	THIS OLE HOUSE—R. Clooney. Hey, There—Col 40266—BMI	13	26
19.	NO MORE—McGuire Sisters. Sincerely—(7)—Coral 61323—BMI	20	2
20.	DIM, DIM THE LIGHTS—B. Haley. Happy Baby—(28)—Dec 29317—BMI	—	4

• Most Played by Jockeys

For survey week ending January 26

RECORDS are ranked in order of the greatest number of plays on disk jockey radio shows throut the country. Results are based on The Billboard's weekly survey among the nation's disk jockeys. The reverse side of each record is also listed.

This Week		Last Week	Weeks on Chart
1.	LET ME GO, LOVER—J. Weber. Marionette—Col 40366—BMI	1	9
2.	HEARTS OF STONE—Fontane Sisters. Bless Your Heart—Dot 15265—BMI	3	9
3.	SINCERELY—McGuire Sisters. No More—Coral 61323—BMI	5	4
4.	MR. SANDMAN—Chordettes. I Don't Wanna See You Cryin'—Cadence 1247—ASCAP	2	15
5.	NAUGHTY LADY OF SHADY LANE—Ames Brothers. Addio—V 20-5897—ASCAP	4	12
6.	THAT'S ALL I WANT FROM YOU—J. P. Morgan. Dawn—V 20-5896—BMI	7	9
7.	MELODY OF LOVE—B. Vaughn. Joy Ride—Dot 15247—ASCAP	11	4
8.	NO MORE—DeJohn Sisters. Theresa—Epic 9085—BMI	8	7
9.	MAKE YOURSELF COMFORTABLE—S. Vaughan. Idle Gossip—Mercury 70469—ASCAP	6	11
10.	MELODY OF LOVE—D. Carroll. Golondrina, La—Mercury 70516—ASCAP	12	3
11.	MR. SANDMAN—Four Aces. I'll Be With You in Apple Blossom Time—Dec 29344—ASCAP	9	11
12.	MELODY OF LOVE—Four Aces. There's a Tavern in the Town—Dec 29395—ASCAP	15	3
13.	TEACH ME TONIGHT—DeCastro Sisters. It's Love—Abbott 3001—ASCAP	10	17
14.	TWEEDLE DEE—G. Gibbs. You're Wrong, All Wrong—Mercury 70517—BMI	19	2
15.	LET ME GO, LOVER—T. Brewer. Moon Is on Fire—Coral 61315—BMI	13	8
15.	KO KO MO—Crew Cuts. Earth Angel—Mercury 70529—BMI	—	1
17.	KO KO MO—P. Como. You'll Always Be My Liftime Sweetheart—V 20-5994—BMI	—	1
18.	EARTH ANGEL—Penguins. Hey, Senorita—Dootone 348—BMI	17	2
19.	EARTH ANGEL—Crew Cuts. Ko Ko Mo—Mercury 70529—BMI	—	1
20.	MELODY OF LOVE—F. Sinatra & R. Anthony. I'm Gonna Live Till I Die—Cap 3018—ASCAP	—	2

The Billboard Music Popularity Charts — POPULAR RECORDS

• Best Sellers in Stores

For survey week ending February 2

RECORDS are ranked in order of their current national selling importance at the retail level. Results are based on The Billboard's weekly survey among the nation's top volume pop record dealers representing every important market area. The reverse side of each record is also listed. When a figure is given in parenthesis after the flip title it indicates what position it occupies on the chart.

This Week		Last Week	Weeks on Chart
1.	SINCERELY—McGuire Sisters No More—(23)—Coral 61323—BMI	2	6
2.	HEARTS OF STONE—Fontane Sisters Bless Your Heart—Dot 15265—BMI	1	10
3.	LET ME GO, LOVER—J. Weber Marionette—Col 40366—BMI	3	11
4.	MR. SANDMAN—Chordettes I Don't Wanna See You Cryin'—Cadence 1247—ASCAP	4	16
5.	MELODY OF LOVE—B. Vaughn Joy Ride—Dot 15247—ASCAP	6	10
6.	THAT'S ALL I WANT FROM YOU—J. P. Morgan Dawn—V 20-5896—BMI	7	12
7.	NAUGHTY LADY OF SHADY LANE—Ames Brothers Addio—V 20-5897—ASCAP	5	12
8.	EARTH ANGEL—Penguins Hey, Senorita—Dootone 348—BMI	8	8
9.	KO KO MO—P. Como You'll Always Be My Lifetime Sweetheart—V 20-5994—BMI	11	2
10.	MAKE YOURSELF COMFORTABLE—S. Vaughan Idle Gossip—Mercury 70469—ASCAP	12	12
11.	MELODY OF LOVE—Four Aces There's a Tavern in the Town—Dec 29395—ASCAP	18	4
12.	TWEEDLE DEE—G. Gibbs You're Wrong, All Wrong—Mercury 70517—BMI	17	3
13.	MELODY OF LOVE—D. Carroll La Golondrina—Mercury 70516—ASCAP	15	6
14.	EARTH ANGEL—Crew Cuts Ko Ko Mo—(15)—Mercury 70529—BMI	19	2
15.	KO KO MO—Crew Cuts Earth Angel—(14)—Mercury 70529—BMI	21	3
16.	NO MORE—DeJohn Sisters Theresa—Epic 9085—BMI	9	7
17.	LET ME GO, LOVER—T. Brewer Moon Is on Fire—Coral 61315—BMI	9	9
18.	OPEN UP YOUR HEART—Cowboy Church Sunday School The Lord Is Counting on You—Dec 29367—BMI	16	7
18.	CRAZY OTTO MEDLEY—J. Maddox Humoresque—Dot 15325	24	2
20.	DIM, DIM THE LIGHTS—B. Haley Happy Baby—Dec 29317—BMI	20	13
21.	MR. SANDMAN—Four Aces I'll Be With You in Apple Blossom Time—Dec 29344—ASCAP	13	12
22.	TEACH ME TONIGHT—DeCastro Sisters It's Love—Abbott 3001—ASCAP	14	19
23.	NO MORE—McGuire Sisters Sincerely—(1)—Coral 61323—BMI	26	3
24.	HEARTS OF STONE—Charms Who Knows—DeLuxe 6062—BMI	25	12
24.	TWEEDLE DEE—L. Baker Tomorrow Night—Atlantic 1047—BMI	29	5
24.	PLANTATION BOOGIE—L. Dee Birth of the Blues—Dec 29360—BMI	—	1
27.	EARTH ANGEL—G. Mann I Love You So—Sound 108—BMI	—	1
28.	SONG OF THE BAREFOOT CONTESSA—H. Winterhalter Land of Dreams—V 20-5888—ASCAP	—	3
29.	SHAKE, RATTLE AND ROLL—B. Haley A B C Boogie—Dec 29204—BMI	23	26
30.	LING TING TONG—Charms Bazoom (I Need Your Lovin')—DeLuxe 6076—BMI	—	3

• This Week's Best Buys

According to sales reports in key markets, the following recent releases are recommended for extra profits:

THE SAND AND THE SEA (Winneton, BMI)
DARLING, JE VOUS AIME BEAUCOUP (Chappell, ASCAP)—**Nat (King) Cole—Capitol 3027**

In the past two weeks, the popular singer has racked up enviable sales in almost every key market. Los Angeles, St. Louis, Chicago, Milwaukee, Pittsburgh, Buffalo and Durham reported the disk to be a strong seller. It was also rated good in Baltimore, Providence, Philadelphia, Detroit and Atlanta. Preference for side was almost evenly split, with "Sand and the Sea" holding a slight edge.

PLANTATION BOOGIE (Copar, BMI)—**Lenny Dee—Decca 29360**

Midwestern sources report a surprise hit in this recently released instrumental. This week it appears on the Cleveland, Milwaukee and Detroit territorial charts and it garnered enough points from other Midwestern areas to make the national retail list. Good reports were also received from St. Louis, Nashville and Buffalo. While little action has been reported so far on either the East or West Coast, it could come up quickly and dealers and operators should be prepared. Flip is "The Birth of the Blues" (Harms, ASCAP).

ALL OF YOU (Chappell, ASCAP)
SIX BRIDGES TO CROSS (Leeds, ASCAP)—**Sammy Davis Jr.—Decca 29402**

Davis' most recent record is shaping up into a solid seller. From Los Angeles to New York, good sales reports have been received, indicating national acceptance. Buffalo, Pittsburgh, Cleveland, Chicago, Nashville, St. Louis and Philadelphia were among the territories that are showing heavy volume. Both sides are seeing good action, with "All of You" leading at this time.

• Most Played in Juke Boxes

For survey week ending February 2

RECORDS are ranked in order of the greatest number of plays in juke boxes thruout the country. Results are based on The Billboard's weekly survey among the nation's juke box operators. The reverse side of each record is also listed. When a figure is given in parenthesis after the flip title it indicates what position it occupies on the chart.

This Week		Last Week	Weeks on Chart
1.	HEARTS OF STONE—Fontane Sisters Bless Your Heart—Dot 15265—BMI	3	9
2.	LET ME GO, LOVER—J. Weber Marionette—Col 40366—BMI	1	10
3.	MR. SANDMAN—Chordettes I Don't Wanna See You Cryin'—Cadence 1247—ASCAP	2	14
4.	NAUGHTY LADY OF SHADY LANE—Ames Brothers Addio—V 20-5897—ASCAP	4	10
5.	MELODY OF LOVE—Four Aces There's a Tavern in the Town—Dec 29395—ASCAP	9	5
6.	MELODY OF LOVE—B. Vaughn Joy Ride—Dot 15247—ASCAP	6	6
6.	SINCERELY—McGuire Sisters No More—(17)—Coral 61323—BMI	7	4
8.	THAT'S ALL I WANT FROM YOU—J. P. Morgan Dawn—V 20-5896—BMI	10	8
9.	TEACH ME TONIGHT—DeCastro Sisters It's Love—Abbott 3001—ASCAP	5	18
9.	MAKE YOURSELF COMFORTABLE—S. Vaughan Idle Gossip—Mercury 70469—ASCAP	8	7
11.	NO MORE—DeJohn Sisters Theresa—Epic 9085—BMI	13	3
12.	LET ME GO, LOVER—P. Page Hocus Pocus—Mercury 70511—BMI	15	5
13.	LET ME GO, LOVER—T. Brewer Moon Is on Fire—Coral 61315—BMI	11	8
13.	MR. SANDMAN—Four Aces I'll Be With You in Apple Blossom Time—Dec 29344—ASCAP	12	11
15.	TWEEDLE DEE—G. Gibbs You're Wrong, All Wrong—Mercury 70517—BMI	—	1
16.	EARTH ANGEL—Penguins Hey, Senorita—Dootone 348—BMI	—	1
17.	HEARTS OF STONE—Charms Who Knows—DeLuxe 6062—BMI	17	3
17.	NO MORE—McGuire Sisters Sincerely—(6)—Coral 61323—BMI	19	3
17.	KO KO MO—P. Como You'll Always Be a Lifetime Sweetheart—V 20-5994—BMI	—	1
20.	I NEED YOU NOW—E. Fisher Heaven Was Never Like This—V 20-5830—ASCAP	13	24
20.	EARTH ANGEL—Crew Cuts Ko Ko Mo—(20)—Mercury 70529—BMI	—	1
20.	KO KO MO—Crew Cuts Earth Angel—(20)—Mercury 70529—BMI	—	1

• Most Played by Jockeys

For survey week ending February 2

RECORDS are ranked in order of the greatest number of plays on disk jockey radio shows thruout the country. Results are based on The Billboard's weekly survey among the nation's disk jockeys. The reverse side of each record is also listed.

This Week		Last Week	Weeks on Chart
1.	SINCERELY—McGuire Sisters No More—Coral 61323—BMI	3	5
2.	HEARTS OF STONE—Fontane Sisters Bless Your Heart—Dot 15265—BMI	2	10
3.	LET ME GO, LOVER—J. Weber Marionette—Col 40366—BMI	1	10
4.	THAT'S ALL I WANT FROM YOU—J. P. Morgan Dawn—V 20-5896—BMI	6	10
5.	MR. SANDMAN—Chordettes I Don't Wanna See You Cryin'—Cadence 1247—ASCAP	4	16
6.	NO MORE—DeJohn Sisters Theresa—Epic 9085—BMI	8	8
7.	MAKE YOURSELF COMFORTABLE—S. Vaughan Idle Gossip—Mercury 70469—ASCAP	19	12
8.	MELODY OF LOVE—B. Vaughn Joy Ride—Dot 15247—ASCAP	7	5
9.	KO KO MO—P. Como You'll Always Be My Lifetime Sweetheart—V 20-5994—BMI	17	2
10.	NAUGHTY LADY OF SHADY LANE—Ames Brothers Addio—V 20-5897—ASCAP	5	13
11.	MELODY OF LOVE—D. Carroll Golondrina, La—Mercury 70516—ASCAP	10	4
12.	KO KO MO—Crew Cuts Earth Angel—Mercury 70529—BMI	15	2
13.	EARTH ANGEL—Crew Cuts Ko Ko Mo—Mercury 70529—BMI	19	2
14.	TWEEDLE DEE—G. Gibbs You're Wrong, All Wrong—Mercury 70517—BMI	14	3
15.	MR. SANDMAN—Four Aces I'll Be With You in Apple Blossom Time—Dec 29344—ASCAP	11	12
16.	MELODY OF LOVE—Four Aces There's a Tavern in the Town—Dec 29395—ASCAP	12	4
17.	NO MORE—McGuire Sisters Sincerely—Coral 61323—BMI	—	1
18.	LET ME GO, LOVER—T. Brewer Moon Is on Fire—Coral 61315—BMI	15	9
19.	EARTH ANGEL—Penguins Hey, Senorita—Dootone 348—BMI	18	3
20.	CRAZY OTTO MEDLEY—J. Maddox Humoresque—Dot 15325—	—	1

The Billboard Music Popularity Charts — POPULAR RECORDS

• Best Sellers in Stores

For survey week ending February 9

RECORDS are ranked in order of their current national selling importance at the retail level. Results are based on The Billboard's weekly survey among the nation's top volume pop record dealers representing every important market area. The reverse side of each record is also listed. When a figure is given in parenthesis after the flip title it indicates what position it occupies on the chart.

This Week		Last Week	Weeks on Chart
1.	SINCERELY—McGuire Sisters No More—(28)—Coral 61323—BMI	1	7
2.	HEARTS OF STONE—Fontane Sisters Bless Your Heart—Dot 15265—BMI	2	11
3.	MELODY OF LOVE—B. Vaughn Joy Ride—Dot 15247—ASCAP	5	11
4.	KO KO MO—P. Como You'll Always Be My Lifetime Sweetheart—V 20-5994—BMI	9	3
5.	THAT'S ALL I WANT FROM YOU—J. P. Morgan Dawn—V 20-5896—BMI	6	13
6.	LET ME GO, LOVER—J. Weber Marionette—Col 40366—BMI	3	12
7.	TWEEDLEE DEE—G. Gibbs You're Wrong, All Wrong—Mercury 70517—BMI	12	4
8.	EARTH ANGEL—Penguins Hey, Senorita—Dootone 348—BMI	8	9
9.	MR. SANDMAN—Chordettes I Don't Wanna See You Cryin'—Cadence 1247—ASCAP	4	17
10.	MELODY OF LOVE—D. Carroll La Golondrina—Mercury 70516—ASCAP	13	7
10.	KO KO MO—Crew Cuts Earth Angel—(14)—Mercury 70529—BMI	15	4
10.	CRAZY OTTO MEDLEY—J. Maddox Humoresque—Dot 15325—	18	3
13.	NAUGHTY LADY OF SHADY LANE—Ames Brothers Addio—V 20-5897—ASCAP	7	13
14.	EARTH ANGEL—Crew Cuts Ko Ko Mo—(10)—Mercury 70529—BMI	14	3
15.	MAKE YOURSELF COMFORTABLE—S. Vaughan Idle Gossip—Mercury 70469—ASCAP	10	13
16.	MELODY OF LOVE—Four Aces There's a Tavern in the Town—Dec 29395—ASCAP	11	5
17.	OPEN UP YOUR HEART—Cowboy Church Sunday School The Lord Is Counting on You—Dec 29367—BMI	18	8
18.	NO MORE—DeJohn Sisters Theresa—Epic 9085—BMI	16	8
19.	HOW IMPORTANT CAN IT BE—J. James This Is My Confession—M-G-M 11919—ASCAP	—	1
20.	MR. SANDMAN—Four Aces I'll Be With You in Apple Blossom Time—Dec 29344—ASCAP	21	13
21.	HEARTS OF STONE—Charms Who Knows—DeLuxe 6062—BMI	24	13
22.	LET ME GO, LOVER—T. Brewer Moon Is on Fire—Coral 61315—BMI	17	10
23.	DIM, DIM THE LIGHTS—B. Haley Happy Baby—Dec 29317—BMI	20	14
24.	EARTH ANGEL—G. Mann I Love You So—Sound 108—BMI	27	2
25.	SONG OF THE BAREFOOT CONTESSA—H. Winterhalter Land of Dreams—V 20-5888—ASCAP	28	4
26.	TWEEDLE DEE—L. Baker Tomorrow Night—Atlantic 1047—BMI	24	6
26.	PLANTATION BOOGIE—L. Dee Birth of the Blues—Dec 29360—BMI	24	2
28.	NO MORE—McGuire Sisters Sincerely—(1)—Coral 61323—BMI	23	4
29.	SHAKE, RATTLE AND ROLL—B. Haley ABC Boogie—Dec 29204—BMI	29	27
30.	MELODY OF LOVE—L. Diamond Phantom Gaucho—V 20-5973—ASCAP	—	1
30.	PLEDGING MY LOVE—J. Ace No Money—Duke 136—BMI	—	1

• This Week's Best Buys

According to sales reports in key markets, the following recent releases are recommended for extra profits:

THE BALLAD OF DAVY CROCKETT (Wonderland, BMI)—**Bill Hayes—Cadence 1256**
Not since Joan Weber's "Let Me Go, Lover" has a record taken off with the excitement sparked by this disk since being introduced on a recent TV show. This week already it is on the Cincinnati and Cleveland charts and considering the unanimous strong sales reports from all parts of the country, should hit the national lists shortly. Flip is "Farewell" (Wonderland, BMI). A previous Billboard "Spotlight" pick.

WEDDING BELLS (Mellin, BMI)
A MAN CHASES A GIRL (Berlin, ASCAP)—**Eddie Fisher—RCA Victor 20-6015**
Solid sales in most key markets is the picture here also. "Wedding Bells" had the edge at the outset, but since singing the tune on the flip on the Ed Sullivan show, action on both sides has been good. "Wedding Bells in the Frankie Lester version has also been selling well in several Middle Western territories, including Chicago, Cleveland, Kansas City, Milwaukee and Detroit. The Fisher disk was a previous Billboard "Spotlight" pick.

CLOSE YOUR EYES (Miller, ASCAP) — **Tony Bennett—Columbia 40427**
This record has been generally available three weeks now and has been growing steadily. In Los Angeles last week, it spurted forward with renewed strength and was also reported a good seller in New York, Philadelphia, Chicago, Buffalo, Pittsburgh, Milwaukee, St. Louis, Detroit, Durham, Baltimore and Atlanta. Flip is "It's Too Soon to Know" (E. H. Morris, ASCAP). A previous Billboard "Spotlight" pick.

MAMBO ROCK (Myers, ASCAP)
BIRTH OF THE BOOGIE (Sea Breeze, ASCAP) —**Bill Haley—Decca 29418**
Initial reaction to Haley's latest has been, with few exceptions, highly positive. Operators and dealers across the country report that sales have been easy and daily increasing in volume. Both sides are liked and, at this stage, it is not easy to predict which will win out. A previous Billboard "Spotlight" pick.

• Most Played in Juke Boxes

For survey week ending February 9

RECORDS are ranked in order of the greatest number of plays in juke boxes thruout the country. Results are based on The Billboard's weekly survey among the nation's juke box operators. The reverse side of each record is also listed. When a figure is given in parenthesis after the flip title it indicates what position it occupies on the chart.

This Week		Last Week	Weeks on Chart
1.	HEARTS OF STONE—Fontane Sisters Bless Your Heart—Dot 15265—BMI	1	10
2.	LET ME GO, LOVER—J. Weber Marionette—Col 40366—BMI	2	11
2.	SINCERELY—McGuire Sisters No More—Coral 61323—BMI	6	5
4.	MR. SANDMAN—Chordettes I Don't Wanna See You Cryin'—Cadence 1247—ASCAP	3	15
5.	MELODY OF LOVE—Four Aces There's a Tavern in the Town—Dec 29395—ASCAP	5	6
6.	NAUGHTY LADY OF SHADY LANE—Ames Brothers Addio—V 20-5897—ASCAP	4	11
7.	MELODY OF LOVE—B. Vaughn Joy Ride—Dot 15247—ASCAP	6	7
8.	THAT'S ALL I WANT FROM YOU—J. P. Morgan Dawn—V 20-5896—BMI	8	9
9.	MAKE YOURSELF COMFORTABLE—S. Vaughan Idle Gossip—Mercury 70469—ASCAP	9	8
10.	TEACH ME TONIGHT—DeCastro Sisters It's Love—Abbott 3001—ASCAP	9	19
11.	LET ME GO, LOVER—T. Brewer Moon Is On Fire—Coral 61315—BMI	13	9
11.	KO KO MO—P. Como You'll Always Be My Lifetime Sweetheart—V 20-5994—BMI	17	2
13.	TWEEDLE DEE—G. Gibbs You're Wrong, All Wrong—Mercury 70517—BMI	15	2
14.	EARTH ANGEL—Penguins Hey, Senorita—Dootone 348—BMI	16	2
15.	MELODY OF LOVE—D. Carroll La Golondrina—Mercury 70516—ASCAP	—	1
15.	CRAZY OTTO MEDLEY—J. Maddox Humoresque—Dot 15325—	—	1
17.	MR. SANDMAN—Four Aces I'll Be With You in Apple Blossom Time—Dec 29344—ASCAP	13	12
18.	LET ME GO, LOVER—P. Page Hocus Pocus—Mercury 70511—BMI	12	6
19.	NO MORE—DeJohn Sisters Theresa—Epic 9085—BMI	11	4
19.	EARTH ANGEL—Crew Cuts Ko Ko Mo—Mercury 70529—BMI	20	2
19.	NO MORE—McGuire Sisters Sincerely—Coral 61323—BMI	17	4

• Most Played by Jockeys

For survey week ending February 9

RECORDS are ranked in order of the greatest number of plays on disk jockey radio shows thruout the country. Results are based on The Billboard's weekly survey among the nation's disk jockeys. The reverse side of each record is also listed.

This Week		Last Week	Weeks on Chart
1.	SINCERELY—McGuire Sisters No More—Coral 61323—BMI	1	6
2.	HEARTS OF STONE—Fontane Sisters Bless Your Heart—Dot 15265—BMI	2	11
3.	LET ME GO, LOVER—J. Weber Marionette—Col 40366—BMI	3	11
4.	THAT'S ALL I WANT FROM YOU—J. P. Morgan Dawn—V 20-5896—BMI	4	11
5.	MELODY OF LOVE—B. Vaughn Joy Ride—Dot 15247—ASCAP	8	6
6.	NO MORE—DeJohn Sisters Theresa—Epic 9085—BMI	6	9
7.	KO KO MO—P. Como You'll Always Be My Lifetime Sweetheart—V 20-5994—BMI	9	3
8.	MR. SANDMAN—Chordettes I Don't Wanna See You Cryin'—Cadence 1247—ASCAP	5	17
9.	EARTH ANGEL—Crew Cuts Ko Ko Mo—Mercury 70529—BMI	13	3
10.	TWEEDLE DEE—G. Gibbs You're Wrong, All Wrong—Mercury 70517—BMI	14	4
11.	KO KO MO—Crew Cuts Earth Angel—Mercury 70529—BMI	12	3
12.	NAUGHTY LADY OF SHADY LANE—Ames Brothers Addio—V 20-5897—ASCAP	10	14
13.	MAKE YOURSELF COMFORTABLE—S. Vaughan Idle Gossip—Mercury 70469—ASCAP	7	13
14.	MELODY OF LOVE—Four Aces There's a Tavern in the Town—Dec 29395—ASCAP	16	5
15.	EARTH ANGEL—Penguins Hey, Senorita—Dootone 348—BMI	19	4
16.	MELODY OF LOVE—D. Carroll Golondrina, La—Mercury 70516—ASCAP	11	5
17.	CRAZY OTTO MEDLEY—J. Maddox Humoresque—Dot 15325—	20	2
18.	MR. SANDMAN—Four Aces I'll Be With You in Apple Blossom Time—Dec 29344—ASCAP	15	13
19.	NO MORE—McGuire Sisters Sincerely—Coral 61323—BMI	17	2
20.	MELODY OF LOVE—F. Sinatra & R. Anthony I'm Gonna Live Till I Die—Cap 3018—ASCAP	—	3

The Billboard Music Popularity Charts POPULAR RECORDS

• Best Sellers in Stores

For survey week ending February 16

RECORDS are ranked in order of their current national selling importance at the retail level. Results are based on The Billboard's weekly survey among the nation's top volume pop record dealers representing every important market area. The reverse side of each record is also listed. When a figure is given in parenthesis after the flip title it indicates what position it occupies on the chart.

This Week	Record	Last Week	Weeks on Chart
1.	SINCERELY—McGuire Sisters No More—(23)—Coral 61323—BMI	1	8
2.	HEARTS OF STONE—Fontane Sisters Bless Your Heart—Dot 15265—BMI	2	12
3.	MELODY OF LOVE—B. Vaughn Joy Ride—Dot 15247—ASCAP	3	12
4.	KO KO MO—P. Como You'll Always Be My Lifetime Sweetheart—V 20-5994—BMI	4	4
5.	TWEEDLE DEE—G. Gibbs You're Wrong, All Wrong—Mercury 70517—BMI	7	5
6.	CRAZY OTTO MEDLEY—J. Maddox Humoresque—Dot 15325	10	4
7.	THAT'S ALL I WANT FROM YOU—J. P. Morgan Dawn—V 20-5896—BMI	5	14
8.	EARTH ANGEL—Crew Cuts Ko Ko Mo—(10)—Mercury 70529—BMI	14	4
9.	EARTH ANGEL—Penguins Hey, Senorita—Dootone 348—BMI	8	10
10.	KO KO MO—Crew Cuts Earth Angel—(8)—Mercury 70529—BMI	10	5
11.	MELODY OF LOVE—D. Carroll La Golondrina—Mercury 70516—ASCAP	10	8
12.	LET ME GO, LOVER—J. Weber Marionette—Col 40366—BMI	6	13
12.	MELODY OF LOVE—Four Aces There's a Tavern in the Town—Dec 29395—ASCAP	16	6
14.	MR. SANDMAN—Chordettes I Don't Wanna See You Cryin'—Cadence 1247—ASCAP	9	18
15.	OPEN UP YOUR HEART—Cowboy Church Sunday School The Lord Is Counting on You—Dec 29367—BMI	17	9
16.	BALLAD OF DAVY CROCKETT—B. Hayes Farewell—Cadence 1256—BMI	—	1
17.	NO MORE—DeJohn Sisters Theresa—Epic 9085—BMI	18	9
18.	HOW IMPORTANT CAN IT BE?—J. James This Is My Confession—M-G-M 11919—ASCAP	19	2
19.	MAKE YOURSELF COMFORTABLE—S. Vaughan Idle Gossip—Mercury 70469—ASCAP	15	14
20.	NAUGHTY LADY OF SHADY LANE—Ames Brothers Addio—V 20-5897—ASCAP	13	14
21.	SMILES—Crazy Otto Glad Rag Doll—Dec 20403—ASCAP	—	1
22.	TWEEDLE DEE—L. Baker Tomorrow Night—Atlantic 1047—BMI	26	7
23.	LET ME GO, LOVER—T. Brewer Moon Is on Fire—Coral 61315—BMI	22	11
24.	NO MORE—McGuire Sisters Sincerely—(1)—Coral 61323—BMI	28	5
25.	HEARTS OF STONE—Charms Who Knows—DeLuxe 6062—BMI	21	14
26.	MR. SANDMAN—Four Aces I'll Be With You In Apple Blossom Time—Dec 29344—ASCAP	20	14
27.	ROCK LOVE—Fontane Sisters You're Mine—Dot 8570—BMI	—	1
27.	HOW IMPORTANT CAN IT BE?—S. Vaughan Waltzing Down the Aisle—Mercury 70534—ASCAP	—	1
29.	DIM, DIM THE LIGHTS—B. Haley Happy Baby—Dec 29317—BMI	23	15
29.	PLANTATION BOOGIE—L. Dee Birth of the Blues—Dec 29360—BMI	26	3

• This Week's Best Buys

According to sales reports in key markets, the following recent releases are recommended for extra profits:

CHERRY PINI AND APPLE BLOSSOM WHITE (Chappelll, ASCAP)—**Perez Prado—RCA Victor 20-5965**

A surprise Latin record that is doing well in a wide variety of pop and rhythm & blues stores and locations—in addition to traditional Latin outlets. Areas reporting strong sales this week included Boston, New York, Philadelphia, Buffalo, Pittsburgh, Cleveland, Detroit, St. Louis and Los Angeles. Flip is "Marie Elena Rumba" (Peer, BMI).

PLEDGING MY LOVE (Lion, BMI) — **Teresa Brewer—Coral 61362**

This is shaping up as the most important pop-styled version of Johnny Ace's great r.&b. hit. With the exception of those territories where the Ace record is firmly entrenched and pop customers will have no substitute, the Brewer disk is doing extremely well. Good markets for Brewer included Los Angeles, St. Louis, Atlanta, Richmond, Baltimore, Nashville, Milwaukee, Detroit, Pittsburgh, Buffalo and Providence. Flip is "How Important Can It Be?" (Laurel, ASCAP).

THERE GOES MY HEART (Feist, ASCAP)—**Four Aces—Decca 29435**

The group has lost none of its grip, from the appearance of first week reports from the nation's key markets. An immediate affirmative reaction was indicated in Boston, Providence, Philadelphia, Buffalo, Pittsburgh, Cleveland, Detroit, Nashville, Durham and St. Louis. Flip is "You'll Always Be the One" (Jack Gold, ASCAP). A previous Billboard "Spotlight" pick.

DANGER! HEARTBREAK AHEAD (Robbins, ASCAP)—**Jaye P. Morgan—RCA Victor 20-6016**

A good steady seller since time of release, this disk has been coming up slowly but surely. Territories that reported it selling in a good or strong category included Boston, Baltimore, Richmond, Buffalo, Pittsburgh, Chicago, Milwaukee, Detroit, Durham, Baltimore, Richmond, Buffalo, Pittsburgh, Chicago, Milwaukee, Detroit, and St. Louis. Some areas reported action was also good on the flip "Softly, Softly" (Sherwin, ASCAP). A previous Billboard "Spotlight" pick.

• Most Played in Juke Boxes

For survey week ending February 16

RECORDS are ranked in order of the greatest number of plays in juke boxes thruout the country. Results are based on The Billboard's weekly survey among the nation's top volume juke box operators. The reverse side of each record is also listed. When a figure is given in parenthesis after the flip title it indicates what position it occupies on the chart.

This Week	Record	Last Week	Weeks on Chart
1.	HEARTS OF STONE—Fontane Sisters Bless Your Heart—Dot 15265—BMI	1	11
2.	SINCERELY—McGuire Sisters No More—(20)—Coral 61323—BMI	2	6
3.	LET ME GO, LOVER—J. Weber Marionette—Col 40366—BMI	2	12
4.	MELODY OF LOVE—B. Vaughn Joy Ride—Dot 15247—ASCAP	7	8
5.	MR. SANDMAN—Chordettes I Don't Wanna See You Cryin'—Cadence 1247—ASCAP	4	16
6.	MELODY OF LOVE—Four Aces There's a Tavern in the Town—Dec 29395—ASCAP	5	7
7.	THAT'S ALL I WANT FROM YOU—J. P. Morgan Dawn—V 20-5896—BMI	8	10
8.	CRAZY OTTO MEDLEY—J. Maddox Humoresque—Dot 15325—	15	2
9.	KO KO MO—P. Como You'll Always Be My Lifetime Sweetheart—V 20-5994—BMI	11	3
10.	NAUGHTY LADY OF SHADY LANE—Ames Brothers Addio—V 20-5897—ASCAP	6	12
11.	TWEEDLE DEE—G. Gibbs You're Wrong, All Wrong—Mercury 70517—BMI	13	3
12.	LET ME GO, LOVER—T. Brewer Moon Is on Fire—Coral 61315—BMI	11	10
13.	EARTH ANGEL—Penguins Hey, Senorita—Dootone 348—BMI	14	3
13.	MELODY OF LOVE—D. Carroll Golondrina, La—Mercury 70516—ASCAP	15	2
15.	MAKE YOURSELF COMFORTABLE—S. Vaughan Idle Gossip—Mercury 70469—ASCAP	9	9
16.	KO KO MO—Crew Cuts Earth Angel—(17)—Mercury 70529—BMI	—	2
17.	EARTH ANGEL—Crew Cuts Ko Ko Mo—(16)—Mercury 70529—BMI	19	3
18.	TEACH ME TONIGHT—DeCastro Sisters It's Love—Abbott 3001—ASCAP	10	20
19.	HEARTS OF STONE—Charms Who Knows—DeLuxe 6062—BMI	—	4
20.	NO MORE—McGuire Sisters Sincerely—(2)—Coral 61323—BMI	19	5
20.	HOW IMPORTANT CAN IT BE—J. James This Is My Confession—M-G-M 11919—ASCAP	—	1

• Most Played by Jockeys

For survey week ending February 16

RECORDS are ranked in order of the greatest number of plays on disk jockey radio shows thruout the country. Results are based on The Billboard's weekly survey among the nation's disk jockeys. The reverse side of each record is also listed.

This Week	Record	Last Week	Weeks on Chart
1.	SINCERELY—McGuire Sisters No More—Coral 61323—BMI	1	7
2.	HEARTS OF STONE—Fontane Sisters Bless Your Heart—Dot 15265—BMI	2	12
3.	THAT'S ALL I WANT FROM YOU—J. P. Morgan Dawn—V 20-5896—BMI	4	12
4.	KO KO MO—P. Como You'll Always Be My Lifetime Sweetheart—V 20-5994—BMI	7	4
5.	MELODY OF LOVE—B. Vaughn Joy Ride—Dot 15247—ASCAP	5	7
6.	NO MORE—DeJohn Sisters Theresa—Epic 9085—BMI	6	10
7.	EARTH ANGEL—Crew Cuts Ko Ko Mo—Mercury 70529—BMI	9	4
8.	TWEEDLE DEE—G. Gibbs You're Wrong, All Wrong—Mercury 70517—BMI	10	5
9.	LET ME GO, LOVER—J. Weber Marionette—Col 40366—BMI	3	12
10.	MELODY OF LOVE—D. Carroll Golondrina, La—Mercury 70516—ASCAP	16	6
11.	KO KO MO—Crew Cuts Earth Angel—Mercury 70529—BMI	11	4
12.	MELODY OF LOVE—Four Aces There's a Tavern in the Town—Dec 29395—ASCAP	14	6
13.	MAKE YOURSELF COMFORTABLE—S. Vaughan Idle Gossip—Mercury 70469—ASCAP	13	14
14.	MR. SANDMAN—Chordettes I Don't Wanna See You Cryin'—Cadence 1247—ASCAP	8	18
15.	EARTH ANGEL—Penguins Hey, Senorita—Dootone 348—BMI	15	5
16.	CRAZY OTTO MEDLEY—J. Maddox Humoresque—Dot 15323—	17	3
17.	HOW IMPORTANT CAN IT BE—J. James This Is My Confession—M-G-M 11919—ASCAP	—	1
18.	NAUGHTY LADY OF SHADY LANE—Ames Brothers Addio—V 20-5897—ASCAP	12	15
19.	HOW IMPORTANT CAN IT BE—S. Vaughan Waltzing Down the Aisle—Mercury 70534—ASCAP	—	1
20.	NO MORE—McGuire Sisters Sincerely—Coral 61323—BMI	19	3

The Billboard Music Popularity Charts POPULAR RECORDS

• Best Sellers in Stores

For survey week ending February 23

RECORDS are ranked in order of their current national selling importance at the retail level. Results are based on The Billboard's weekly survey among the nation's top volume pop record dealers representing every important market area. The reverse side of each record is also listed. When a figure is given in parenthesis after the flip title it indicates what position it occupies on the chart.

This Week		Last Week	Weeks on Chart
1.	SINCERELY—McGuire Sisters. No More—(24)—Coral 61323—BMI	1	9
2.	MELODY OF LOVE—B. Vaughn. Joy Ride—Dot 15247—ASCAP	3	13
3.	CRAZY OTTO MEDLEY—J. Maddox. Humoresque—Dot 15325—	6	5
4.	HEARTS OF STONE—Fontane Sisters. Bless Your Heart—Dot 15265—BMI	2	13
5.	KO KO MO—P. Como. You'll Always Be My Lifetime Sweetheart—V 20-5994—BMI	4	5
6.	TWEEDLE DEE—G. Gibbs. You're Wrong, All Wrong—Mercury 70517—BMI	5	6
7.	THAT'S ALL I WANT FROM YOU—J. P. Morgan. Dawn—V 20-5896—BMI	7	15
8.	EARTH ANGEL—Crew Cuts. Ko Ko Mo—(11)—Mercury 70529—BMI	8	5
9.	BALLAD OF DAVY CROCKETT—B. Hayes. Farewell—Cadence 1256—BMI	16	2
10.	EARTH ANGEL—Penguins. Hey, Senorita—Dootone 348—BMI	9	11
11.	KO KO MO—Crew Cuts. Earth Angel—(8)—Mercury 70529—BMI	10	6
12.	MELODY OF LOVE—D. Carroll. La Golondrina—Mercury 70516—ASCAP	11	9
13.	HOW IMPORTANT CAN IT BE?—J. James. This Is My Confession—M-G-M 11919—ASCAP	18	3
14.	MELODY OF LOVE—Four Aces. There's a Tavern in the Town—Dec 29395—ASCAP	12	7
15.	OPEN UP YOUR HEART—Cowboy Church Sunday School. The Lord Is Counting on You—Dec 29367—BMI	15	10
16.	LET ME GO, LOVER—J. Weber. Marionette—Col 40366—BMI	12	14
17.	MR. SANDMAN—Chordettes. I Don't Wanna See You Cryin'—Cadence 1247—ASCAP	14	19
18.	HOW IMPORTANT CAN IT BE?—S. Vaughan. Waltzing Down the Aisle—Mercury 70534—ASCAP	27	2
19.	GLAD RAG DOLL—Crazy Otto. Smiles—Dec 29403—ASCAP	—	1
20.	DARLING JE VOUS AIME BEAUCOUP—Nat (King) Cole. Sand and the Sea—(28)—Cap 3027—ASCAP	—	1
21.	PLEDGING MY LOVE—J. Ace. No Money—Duke 136—BMI	—	2
22.	NAUGHTY LADY OF SHADY LANE—Ames Brothers. Addio—V 20-5897—ASCAP	20	15
23.	HEARTS OF STONE—Charms. Who Knows—DeLuxe 6062—BMI	25	15
24.	NO MORE—McGuire Sisters. Sincerely—(1)—Coral 61323—BMI	24	6
24.	PLANTATION BOOGIE—L. Dee. Birth of the Blues—Dec 29360—BMI	29	4
24.	MAMBO ROCK—B. Haley. Birth of the Boogie—Dec 29418—ASCAP	—	1
27.	CHERRY PINK AND APPLE BLOSSOM WHITE—P. Prado. Marie Elena Rumba—V 20-5965—ASCAP	—	1
28.	MAN CHASES A GIRL—E. Fisher. Wedding Bells—V 20-6015—ASCAP	—	1
28.	SAND AND THE SEA—Nat (King) Cole. Darling Je Vous Aime Beaucoup—(20)—Cap 3027—BMI	—	1
30.	TWEEDLE DEE—L. Baker. Tomorrow Night—Atlantic 1047—BMI	22	8

• This Week's Best Buys

According to sales reports in key markets, the following recent releases are recommended for extra profits:

THE BALLAD OF DAVY CROCKETT (Wonderland, BMI)—**Fess Parker—Columbia 40449**

Despite the fact that Bill Hayes' version of this tune got off to an early lead, the demand for the "original" (Parker's record) has continued to be so strong that it seems likely to follow the Cadence disk on to the charts. Even now, in some territories, like Los Angeles and Milwaukee, the Columbia record is selling better than any of the competitive versions. Dealers, in most cases, are stocking both the Parker and Hayes records to good profit. Flip is "I Gave My Love." A previous Billboard 'Spotlight" pick.

IT MAY SOUND SILLY (Progressive, BMI) **McGuire Sisters—Coral 61369**

This disk has been snowballing strength in the past week and now appears to have the potential of other big records in recent months by the sisters. Territories reporting good and strong sales included Boston, Providence, New York, Philadelphia, Buffalo, Pittsburgh, Baltimore, Durham, St. Louis and Milwaukee. Flip is "Doesn't Anybody Love Me?" A previous Billboard "Spotlight" pick.

• Most Played in Juke Boxes

For survey week ending February 23

RECORDS are ranked in order of the greatest number of plays in juke boxes thruout the country. Results are based on The Billboard's weekly survey among the nation's juke box operators. The reverse side of each record is also listed. When a figure is given in parenthesis after the flip title it indicates what position it occupies on the chart.

This Week		Last Week	Weeks on Chart
1.	SINCERELY—McGuire Sisters. No More—(24)—Coral 61323—BMI	2	7
2.	HEARTS OF STONE—Fontane Sisters. Bless Your Heart—Dot 15265—BMI	1	12
3.	MELODY OF LOVE—B. Vaughn. Joy Ride—Dot 15247—ASCAP	4	9
4.	MELODY OF LOVE—Four Aces. There's a Tavern in the Town—Dec 29395—ASCAP	6	8
5.	THAT'S ALL I WANT FROM YOU—J. P. Morgan. Dawn—V 20-5896—BMI	7	11
6.	LET ME GO, LOVER—J. Weber. Marionette—Col 40366—BMI	3	13
7.	KO KO MO—P. Como. You'll Always Be My Lifetime Sweetheart—V 20-5994—BMI	9	4
8.	CRAZY OTTO MEDLEY—J. Maddox. Humoresque—Dot 15325—	8	3
9.	TWEEDLE DEE—G. Gibbs. You're Wrong, All Wrong—Mercury 70517—BMI	11	4
10.	MR. SANDMAN—Chordettes. I Don't Wanna See You Cryin'—Cadence 1247—ASCAP	5	17
11.	EARTH ANGEL—Penguins. Hey, Senorita—Dootone 348—BMI	13	4
12.	MELODY OF LOVE—D. Carroll. Golondrina, La—Mercury 70516—ASCAP	13	3
13.	KO KO MO—Crew Cuts. Earth Angel—(14)—Mercury 70529—BMI	16	3
14.	EARTH ANGEL—Crew Cuts. Ko Ko Mo—(13)—Mercury 70529—BMI	17	4
15.	HEARTS OF STONE—Charms. Who Knows—DeLuxe 6062—BMI	19	5
16.	MAKE YOURSELF COMFORTABLE—S. Vaughan. Idle Gossip—Mercury 70469—ASCAP	15	10
17.	NAUGHTY LADY OF SHADY LANE—Ames Brothers. Addio—V 20-5897—ASCAP	10	13
18.	LET ME GO, LOVER—T. Brewer. Moon Is on Fire—Coral 61315—BMI	12	11
18.	HOW IMPORTANT CAN IT BE?—J. James. This Is My Confession—M-G-M 11919—ASCAP	20	2
20.	ROCK LOVE—Fontane Sisters. You're Mine—Dot 8570—BMI	—	1

• Most Played by Jockeys

For survey week ending February 23

RECORDS are ranked in order of the greatest number of plays on disk jockey radio shows thruout the country. Results are based on The Billboard's weekly survey among the nation's disk jockeys. The reverse side of each record is also listed.

This Week		Last Week	Weeks on Chart
1.	SINCERELY—McGuire Sisters. No More—Coral 61323—BMI	1	8
2.	KO KO MO—P. Como. You'll Always Be My Lifetime Sweetheart—V 20-5994—BMI	4	5
3.	HEARTS OF STONE—Fontane Sisters. Bless Your Heart—Dot 15265—BMI	2	13
4.	THAT'S ALL I WANT FROM YOU—J. P. Morgan. Dawn—V 20-5896—BMI	3	13
5.	MELODY OF LOVE—B. Vaughn. Joy Ride—Dot 15247—ASCAP	5	8
6.	EARTH ANGEL—Crew Cuts. Ko Ko Mo—Mercury 70529—BMI	7	5
7.	TWEEDLE DEE—G. Gibbs. You're Wrong, All Wrong—Mercury 70517—BMI	8	6
8.	MELODY OF LOVE—D. Carroll. Golondrina, La—Mercury 70516—ASCAP	10	7
9.	MELODY OF LOVE—Four Aces. There's a Tavern in the Town—Dec 29395—ASCAP	12	7
10.	NO MORE—DeJohn Sisters. Theresa—Epic 9085—BMI	6	11
11.	KO KO MO—Crew Cuts. Earth Angel—Mercury 70529—BMI	11	5
12.	CRAZY OTTO MEDLEY—J. Maddox. Humoresque—Dot 15325—	16	4
13.	EARTH ANGEL—Penguins. Hey, Senorita—Dootone 348—BMI	15	6
14.	HOW IMPORTANT CAN IT BE?—J. James. This Is My Confession—M-G-M 11919—ASCAP	17	2
15.	HOW IMPORTANT CAN IT BE?—S. Vaughan. Waltzing Down the Aisle—Mercury 70534—ASCAP	19	2
16.	LET ME GO, LOVER—J. Weber. Marionette—Col 40366—BMI	9	13
17.	MR. SANDMAN—Chordettes. I Don't Wanna See You Cryin'—Cadence 1247—ASCAP	14	19
18.	NO MORE—McGuire Sisters. Sincerely—Coral 61323—BMI	20	4
19.	DARLING JE VOUS AIME BEAUCOUP—Nat (King) Cole. Sand and the Sea—Cap 3027—ASCAP	—	1
20.	MELODY OF LOVE—F. Sinatra & R. Anthony. I'm Gonna Live Till I Die—Cap 3018—ASCAP	—	4

The Billboard Music Popularity Charts — POPULAR RECORDS

Best Sellers in Stores

For survey week ending March 2

RECORDS are ranked in order of their current national selling importance at the retail level. Results are based on The Billboard's weekly survey among the nation's top volume pop record dealers representing every important market area. The reverse side of each record is also listed. When a figure is given in parenthesis after the flip title it indicates what position it occupies on the chart.

This Week		Last Week	Weeks on Chart
1.	SINCERELY—McGuire Sisters No More—(31)—Coral 61323—BMI	1	10
2.	CRAZY OTTO MEDLEY—J. Maddox Humoresque—Dot 15325—	3	6
3.	TWEEDLE DEE—G. Gibbs You're Wrong, All Wrong—Mercury 70517—BMI	6	7
4.	MELODY OF LOVE—B. Vaughn Joy Ride—Dot 15247—ASCAP	2	14
5.	KO KO MO—P. Como You'll Always Be My Lifetime Sweetheart—V 20-5994—BMI	5	6
6.	BALLAD OF DAVY CROCKETT—B. Hayes Farewell—Cadence 1256—BMI	9	3
7.	HEARTS OF STONE—Fontane Sisters Bless Your Heart—Dot 15265—BMI	4	14
8.	EARTH ANGEL—Crew Cuts Ko Ko Mo—(10)—Mercury 70529—BMI	8	6
9.	MELODY OF LOVE—D. Carroll La Golondrina—Mercury 70516—ASCAP	12	10
10.	KO KO MO—Crew Cuts Earth Angel—(8)—Mercury 70529—BMI	11	7
11.	THAT'S ALL I WANT FROM YOU—J. P. Morgan Dawn—V 20-5896—BMI	7	16
12.	HOW IMPORTANT CAN IT BE?—J. James This Is My Confession—M-G-M 11919—ASCAP	13	4
13.	EARTH ANGEL—Penguins Hey, Senorita—Dootone 348—BMI	10	12
14.	OPEN UP YOUR HEART—Cowboy Church Sunday School The Lord Is Counting on You—Dec 29367—BMI	15	11
15.	MELODY OF LOVE—Four Aces There's a Tavern in the Town—Dec 29395—ASCAP	14	8
16.	BALLAD OF DAVY CROCKETT—F. Parker I Gave My Love—Col 40449—BMI	—	1
17.	DARLING JE VOUS AIME BEAUCOUP—Nat (King) Cole Sand and the Sea—(23)—Cap 3027—ASCAP	20	2
18.	PLEDGING MY LOVE—J. Ace No Money—Duke 136—BMI	21	3
19.	ROCK LOVE—Fontane Sisters You're Mine—Dot 8570—BMI	—	2
20.	MR. SANDMAN—Chordettes I Don't Wanna See You Cryin'—Cadence 1247—ASCAP	17	20
21.	GLAD RAG DOLL—Crazy Otto Smiles—Dec 29403—ASCAP	19	2
22.	CHERRY PINK AND APPLE BLOSSOM WHITE—P. Prado Marie Elena Rumba—V 20-5965—ASCAP	27	2
23.	MAMBO ROCK—B. Haley Birth of the Boogie—(35)—Dec 29418—ASCAP	24	2
23.	SAND AND THE SEA—Nat (King) Cole Darling Je Vous Aime Beaucoup—(17)—Cap 3027—BMI	28	2
25.	HOW IMPORTANT CAN IT BE?—S. Vaughan Waltzing Down the Aisle—Mercury 70534—ASCAP	18	3
26.	TWEEDLE DEE—L. Baker Tomorrow Night—Atlantic 1047—BMI	30	9
27.	MAKE YOURSELF COMFORTABLE—S. Vaughan Idle Gossip—Mercury 70469—ASCAP	—	15
28.	LET ME GO, LOVER—J. Weber Marionette—Col 40366—BMI	16	15
29.	PLANTATION BOOGIE—L. Dee Birth of the Blues—Dec 29360—BMI	24	5
30.	NO MORE—DeJohn Sisters Theresa—Epic 9085—BMI	—	10

This Week's Best Buys

According to sales reports in key markets, the following recent releases are recommended for extra profits:

DANCE WITH ME, HENRY (Modern, BMI)—Georgia Gibbs—Mercury 70572

The songstress is hitting a profitable groove in her stylings of rhythm & blues hits. Her latest one moved out this week in a way that suggested "Tweedle Dee" in its initial stages. Good sales reports came in from Boston, New York, Philadelphia, Baltimore, Buffalo, Pittsburgh, Cincinnati, Milwaukee, Detroit, Richmond and Durham. Flip is "Ballin' the Jack" (Jerry Vogel-E. B. Marks, ASCAP). A previous Billboard "Spotlight" pick.

WHERE WILL THE DIMPLE BE? (Roger, ASCAP)—Rosemary Clooney—Columbia 40434

The sales curve on this disk is also showing a fine upward slope after little more than 10 days in the field. Los Angeles, Atlanta, Pittsburgh, Cleveland, Chicago, Cincinnati, Buffalo and St. Louis were among the territories indicating good action. Flip is "Brahms' Lullaby." A previous Billboard "Spotlight" pick.

Most Played in Juke Boxes

For survey week ending March 2

RECORDS are ranked in order of the greatest number of plays in juke boxes thruout the country. Results are based on The Billboard's weekly survey among the nation's juke box operators. The reverse side of each record is also listed. When a figure is given in parenthesis after the flip title it indicates what position it occupies on the chart.

This Week		Last Week	Weeks on Chart
1.	SINCERELY—McGuire Sisters No More—(34)—Coral 61323—BMI	1	8
2.	HEARTS OF STONE—Fontane Sisters Bless Your Heart—Dot 15265—BMI	2	13
3.	MELODY OF LOVE—Four Aces There's a Tavern in the Town—Dec 29395—ASCAP	4	9
4.	CRAZY OTTO MEDLEY—J. Maddox Humoresque—Dot 15325—	8	4
5.	KO KO MO—P. Como You'll Always Be My Lifetime Sweetheart—V 20-5994—BMI	7	5
6.	TWEEDLE DEE—G. Gibbs You're Wrong, All Wrong—Mercury 70517—BMI	9	5
7.	MELODY OF LOVE—B. Vaughn Joy Ride—Dot 15247—ASCAP	3	10
7.	THAT'S ALL I WANT FROM YOU—J. P. Morgan Dawn—V 20-5896—BMI	5	12
9.	EARTH ANGEL—Crew Cuts Ko Ko Mo—(11)—Mercury 70529—BMI	14	5
10.	EARTH ANGEL—Penguins Hey, Senorita—Dootone 348—BMI	11	5
11.	KO KO MO—Crew Cuts Earth Angel—(9)—Mercury 70529—BMI	13	4
12.	LET ME GO, LOVER—J. Weber Marionette—Col 40366—BMI	6	14
13.	MELODY OF LOVE—D. Carroll La Golondrina—Mercury 70516—ASCAP	12	4
13.	HOW IMPORTANT CAN IT BE?—J. James This Is My Confession—M-G-M 11919—ASCAP	18	3
15.	MR. SANDMAN—Chordettes I Don't Wanna See You Cryin'—Cadence 1247—ASCAP	10	18
16.	HEARTS OF STONE—Charms Who Knows—DeLuxe 6062—BMI	15	6
17.	LET ME GO, LOVER—T. Brewer Moon Is on Fire—Coral 61315—BMI	18	12
18.	ROCK LOVE—Fontane Sisters You're Mine—Dot 8570—BMI	20	2
18.	TWEEDLE DEE—L. Baker Tomorrow Night—Atlantic 1047—BMI	—	1
18.	BALLAD OF DAVY CROCKETT—B. Hayes Farewell—Cadence 1256—BMI	—	1

Most Played by Jockeys

For survey week ending March 2

RECORDS are ranked in order of the greatest number of plays on disk jockey radio shows thruout the country. Results are based on The Billboard's weekly survey among the nation's disk jockeys. The reverse side of each record is also listed.

This Week		Last Week	Weeks on Chart
1.	SINCERELY—McGuire Sisters No More—Coral 61323—BMI	1	9
2.	KO KO MO—P. Como You'll Always Be My Lifetime Sweetheart—V 20-5994—BMI	2	6
3.	EARTH ANGEL—Crew Cuts Ko Ko Mo—Mercury 70529—BMI	6	6
4.	HEARTS OF STONE—Fontane Sisters Bless Your Heart—Dot 15265—BMI	3	14
5.	MELODY OF LOVE—B. Vaughn Joy Ride—Dot 15247—ASCAP	5	9
6.	TWEEDLE DEE—G. Gibbs You're Wrong, All Wrong—Mercury 70517—BMI	7	7
7.	THAT'S ALL I WANT FROM YOU—J. P. Morgan Dawn—V 20-5896—BMI	4	14
8.	HOW IMPORTANT CAN IT BE?—J. James This Is My Confession—M-G-M 11919—ASCAP	14	3
9.	MELODY OF LOVE—D. Carroll La Golondrina—Mercury 70516—ASCAP	8	8
10.	NO MORE—DeJohn Sisters Theresa—Epic 9085—BMI	10	12
11.	CRAZY OTTO MEDLEY—J. Maddox Humoresque—Dot 15325—	12	5
12.	MELODY OF LOVE—Four Aces There's a Tavern in the Town—Dec 29395—ASCAP	9	8
13.	EARTH ANGEL—Penguins Hey, Senorita—Dootone 348—BMI	13	7
14.	KO KO MO—Crew Cuts Earth Angel—Mercury 70529—BMI	11	6
15.	HOW IMPORTANT CAN IT BE—S. Vaughan Waltzing Down the Aisle—Mercury 70534—ASCAP	15	3
16.	BALLAD OF DAVY CROCKETT—B. Hayes Farewell—Cadence 1256—BMI	—	1
17.	DARLING JE VOUS AIME BEAUCOUP—Nat (King) Cole Sand and the Sea—Cap 3027—ASCAP	19	2
18.	MR. SANDMAN—Chordettes I Don't Wanna See You Cryin'—Cadence 1247—ASCAP	17	20
19.	PLEDGING MY LOVE—J. Ace No Money—Duke 136—BMI	—	1
20.	DANGER, HEARTBREAK AHEAD—J. P. Morgan Softly, Softly—V 20-6016—ASCAP	—	1

The Billboard Music Popularity Charts

POPULAR RECORDS

• Best Sellers in Stores

For survey week ending March 9

RECORDS are ranked in order of their current national selling importance at the retail level. Results are based on The Billboard's weekly survey among the nation's top volume pop record dealers representing every important market area. The reverse side of each record is also listed. When a figure is given in parenthesis after the flip title it indicates what position it occupies on the chart.

This Week		Last Week	Weeks on Chart
1.	SINCERELY—McGuire Sisters No More—Coral 61323—BMI	1	11
2.	CRAZY OTTO MEDLEY—J. Maddox Humoresque—Dot 15325	2	7
3.	BALLAD OF DAVY CROCKETT—B. Hayes Farewell—Cadence 1256—BMI	6	4
4.	TWEEDLE DEE—G. Gibbs You're Wrong, All Wrong—Mercury 70517—BMI	3	8
5.	MELODY OF LOVE—B. Vaughn Joy Ride—Dot 15247—ASCAP	4	15
6.	KO KO MO—P. Como You'll Always Be My Lifetime Sweetheart—V 20-5994—BMI	5	7
7.	HEARTS OF STONE—Fontane Sisters Bless Your Heart—Dot 15265—BMI	7	15
8.	EARTH ANGEL—Crew Cuts Ko Ko Mo—(16)—Mercury 70529—BMI	8	7
9.	HOW IMPORTANT CAN IT BE?—J. James This Is My Confession—M-G-M 11919—ASCAP	12	5
10.	THAT'S ALL I WANT FROM YOU—J. P. Morgan Dawn—V 20-5896—BMI	11	17
11.	BALLAD OF DAVY CROCKETT—F. Parker I Gave My Love—Col 40449—BMI	16	2
12.	MELODY OF LOVE—D. Carroll La Golondrina—Mercury 70516—ASCAP	9	11
13.	EARTH ANGEL—Penguins Hey, Senorita—Dootone 348—BMI	13	13
14.	OPEN UP YOUR HEART—Cowboy Church Sunday School The Lord Is Counting on You—Dec 29367—BMI	14	12
15.	MELODY OF LOVE—Four Aces There's a Tavern in the Town—Dec 29395—ASCAP	15	9
16.	KO KO MO—Crew Cuts Earth Angel—(8)—Mercury 70529—BMI	10	8
17.	PLEDGING MY LOVE—J. Ace No Money—Duke 136—BMI	18	4
18.	MAMBO ROCK—B. Haley Birth of the Boogie—(27)—Dec 29418—ASCAP	23	3
19.	BALLAD OF DAVY CROCKETT—Tennessee Ernie Ford Farewell—Cap 3058—BMI	—	1
20.	GLAD RAG DOLL—Crazy Otto Smiles—(31)—Dec 29403—ASCAP	21	3
21.	CHERRY PINK AND APPLE BLOSSOM WHITE—P. Prado Marie Elena Rumba—V 20-5965—ASCAP	22	3
22.	ROCK LOVE—Fontane Sisters You're Mine—Dot 8570—BMI	19	3
23.	DARLING JE VOUS AIME BEAUCOUP—Nat (King) Cole Sand and the Sea—Cap 3027—ASCAP	17	3
24.	PLANTATION BOOGIE—L. Dee Birth of the Blues—Dec 29360—BMI	29	6
25.	SAND AND THE SEA—Nat (King) Cole Darling Je Vous Aime Beaucoup—Cap 3027—BMI	23	3
26.	HOW IMPORTANT CAN IT BE?—S. Vaughan Waltzing Down the Aisle—Mercury 70534—ASCAP	25	4
27.	TWEEDLE DEE—L. Baker Tomorrow Night—Atlantic 1047—BMI	26	10
27.	BIRTH OF THE BOOGIE—B. Haley Mambo Rock—(18)—Dec 29418—ASCAP	—	1
27.	MAN CHASES A GIRL—E. Fisher Wedding Bells—(31)—V 20-6015—ASCAP	—	1
30.	PLEDGING MY LOVE—T. Brewer How Important Can It Be?—Coral 61362—BMI	—	1

• This Week's Best Buys

According to sales reports in key markets, the following recent releases are recommended for extra profits:

PLAY ME HEARTS AND FLOWERS (Advanced, ASCAP) — Johnny Desmond — Coral 61379

Desmond's showcasing of this tune on a recent television show skyrocketed it to sensational sales, particularly in the retail market. Operator action thruout the country has been good, too, but was not immediately as heavy as in stores. At its present rate of speed, this disk should not be long in hitting the national charts. Flip is "I'm So Ashamed" (Studio, BMI).

TWO HEARTS (St. Louis, BMI)—Pat Boone—Dot 15338

The singer's version of the r.&b. hit is making ground quickly, particularly in the Middle West and in the South. The disk already appears on the Cleveland and Dallas territorial charts this week. Other areas where sales were reported good included Atlanta, Durham, Baltimore, Nashville, St. Louis, Cincinnati and Buffalo. Flip is "Tra-La-La."

• Most Played in Juke Boxes

For survey week ending March 9

RECORDS are ranked in order of the greatest number of plays in juke boxes thruout the country. Results are based on The Billboard's weekly survey among the nation's juke box operators. The reverse side of each record is also listed. When a figure is given in parenthesis after the flip title it indicates what position it occupies on the chart.

This Week		Last Week	Weeks on Chart
1.	SINCERELY—McGuire Sisters No More—Coral 61323—BMI	1	9
2.	HEARTS OF STONE—Fontane Sisters Bless Your Heart—Dot 15265—BMI	2	14
3.	CRAZY OTTO MEDLEY—J. Maddox Humoresque—Dot 15325	4	5
4.	MELODY OF LOVE—Four Aces There's a Tavern in the Town—Dec 29395—ASCAP	3	10
5.	MELODY OF LOVE—B. Vaughn Joy Ride—Dot 15247—ASCAP	7	11
6.	KO KO MO—P. Como You'll Always Be My Lifetime Sweetheart—V 20-5994—BMI	5	6
7.	TWEEDLE DEE—G. Gibbs You're Wrong, All Wrong—Mercury 70517—BMI	6	6
8.	THAT'S ALL I WANT FROM YOU—J. P. Morgan Dawn—V 20-5896—BMI	7	13
8.	EARTH ANGEL—Crew Cuts Ko Ko Mo—(11)—Mercury 70529—BMI	9	6
10.	HOW IMPORTANT CAN IT BE?—J. James This Is My Confession—M-G-M 11919—ASCAP	13	4
11.	KO KO MO—Crew Cuts Earth Angel—(8)—Mercury 70529—BMI	11	5
12.	EARTH ANGEL—Penguins Hey, Senorita—Dootone 348—BMI	10	6
13.	BALLAD OF DAVY CROCKETT—B. Hayes Farewell—Cadence 1256—BMI	18	2
14.	MELODY OF LOVE—D. Carroll Golondrina,La—Mercury 70516—ASCAP	13	5
15.	LET ME GO, LOVER—J. Weber Marionette—Col 40366—BMI	12	15
16.	ROCK LOVE—Fontane Sisters You're Mine—Dot 8570—BMI	18	3
17.	TWEEDLE DEE—L. Baker Tomorrow Night—Atlantic 1047—BMI	18	2
18.	MR. SANDMAN—Chordettes I Don't Wanna See You Cryin'—Cadence 1247—ASCAP	15	19
18.	EARTH ANGEL—G. Mann I Love You So—Sound 108—BMI	—	1
20.	MAN CHASES A GIRL—E. Fisher Wedding Bells—(39)—V 20-6015—ASCAP	—	1
20.	HOW IMPORTANT CAN IT BE?—S. Vaughan Waltzing Down the Aisle—Mercury 70534—ASCAP	—	1

• Most Played by Jockeys

For survey week ending March 9

RECORDS are ranked in order of the greatest number of plays on disk jockey radio shows thruout the country. Results are based on The Billboard's weekly survey among the nation's disk jockeys. The reverse side of each record is also listed.

This Week		Last Week	Weeks on Chart
1.	SINCERELY—McGuire Sisters No More—Coral 61323—BMI	1	10
2.	MELODY OF LOVE—B. Vaughn Joy Ride—Dot 15247—ASCAP	5	10
3.	KO KO MO—P. Como You'll Always Be My Lifetime Sweetheart—(34)—V 20-5994—BMI	2	7
4.	TWEEDLE DEE—G. Gibbs You're Wrong, All Wrong—Mercury 70517—BMI	6	8
5.	EARTH ANGEL—Crew Cuts Ko Ko Mo—(16)—Mercury 70529—BMI	3	7
6.	HOW IMPORTANT CAN IT BE?—J. James This Is My Confession—M-G-M 11919—ASCAP	8	4
7.	THAT'S ALL I WANT FROM YOU—J. P. Morgan Dawn—V 20-5896—BMI	7	15
8.	CRAZY OTTO MEDLEY—J. Maddox Humoresque—Dot 15325	11	6
9.	HEARTS OF STONE—Fontane Sisters Bless Your Heart—Dot 15265—BMI	4	15
10.	BALLAD OF DAVY CROCKETT—B. Hayes Farewell—Cadence 1256—BMI	16	2
11.	MELODY OF LOVE—Four Aces There's a Tavern in the Town—Dec 29395—ASCAP	12	9
12.	MELODY OF LOVE—D. Carroll Golondrina, La—Mercury 70516—ASCAP	9	9
13.	HOW IMPORTANT CAN IT BE?—S. Vaughan Waltzing Down the Aisle—Mercury 70534—ASCAP	15	4
14.	NO MORE—DeJohn Sisters Theresa—Epic 9085—BMI	10	13
15.	EARTH ANGEL—Penguins Hey, Senorita—Dootone 348—BMI	13	8
16.	KO KO MO—Crew Cuts Earth Angel—(5)—Mercury 70529—BMI	14	7
17.	DANGER, HEARTBREAK AHEAD—J. P. Morgan Softly, Softly—V 20-6016—ASCAP	20	2
18.	DARLING JE VOUS AIME BEAUCOUP—Nat (King) Cole Sand and the Sea—Cap 3027—ASCAP	17	3
19.	PLEDGING MY LOVE—J. Ace No Money—Duke 136—BMI	19	2
20.	PLEDGING MY LOVE—T. Brewer How Important Can It Be?—(37)—Coral 61362—BMI	—	1

The Billboard Music Popularity Charts — POPULAR RECORDS

• Best Sellers in Stores

For survey week ending March 16

RECORDS are ranked in order of their current national selling importance at the retail level. Results are based on The Billboard's weekly survey among the nation's top volume pop record dealers representing every important market area. The reverse side of each record is also listed. When a figure is given in parenthesis after the flip title it indicates what position it occupies on the chart.

This Week		Last Week	Weeks on Chart
1.	BALLAD OF DAVY CROCKETT—B. Hayes Farewell—Cadence 1256—BMI	3	5
2.	CRAZY OTTO MEDLEY—J. Maddox Humoresque—Dot 15325	2	8
3.	SINCERELY—McGuire Sisters No More—Coral 61323—BMI	1	12
4.	TWEEDLE DEE—G. Gibbs You're Wrong, All Wrong—Mercury 70517—BMI	4	9
5.	MELODY OF LOVE—B. Vaughn Joy Ride—Dot 15247—ASCAP	5	16
6.	KO KO MO—P. Como You'll Always Be My Lifetime Sweetheart—V 20-5994—BMI	6	8
7.	BALLAD OF DAVY CROCKETT—F. Parker I Gave My Love—Col 40449—BMI	11	3
8.	HOW IMPORTANT CAN IT BE?—J. James This Is My Confession—M-G-M 11919—ASCAP	9	6
9.	OPEN UP YOUR HEART—Cowboy Church Sunday School The Lord Is Counting on You—Dec 29367—BMI	14	13
10.	EARTH ANGEL—Crew Cuts Ko Ko Mo—(14)—Mercury 70529—BMI	8	8
11.	HEARTS OF STONE—Fontane Sisters Bless Your Heart—Dot 15265—BMI	7	16
12.	MELODY OF LOVE—Four Aces There's a Tavern in the Town—Dec 29395—ASCAP	15	10
13.	MELODY OF LOVE—D. Carroll La Golondrina—Mercury 70516—ASCAP	12	12
14.	KO KO MO—Crew Cuts Earth Angel—(10)—Mercury 70529—BMI	16	9
15.	THAT'S ALL I WANT FROM YOU—J. P. Morgan Dawn—V 20-5896—BMI	10	18
15.	CHERRY PINK AND APPLE BLOSSOM WHITE—P. Prado Marie Elena Rumba—V 20-5965—ASCAP	21	4
17.	BALLAD OF DAVY CROCKETT—Tennessee Ernie Ford Farewell—Cap 3058—BMI	19	2
17.	EARTH ANGEL—Penguins Hey, Senorita—Dootone 348—BMI	13	14
19.	DARLING JE VOUS AIME BEAUCOUP—Nat (King) Cole Sand and the Sea—(32)—Cap 3027—ASCAP	23	4
20.	PLEDGING MY LOVE—J. Ace No Money—Duke 136—BMI	17	5
21.	DANCE WITH ME HENRY—G. Gibbs Every Road Must Have a Turning—Mercury 70572—BMI	—	1
22.	ROCK LOVE—Fontane Sisters You're Mine—Dot 8570—BMI	22	4
23.	PLANTATION BOOGIE—L. Dee Birth of the Blues—Dec 29360—BMI	24	7
24.	TWEEDLE DEE—L. Baker Tomorrow Night—Atlantic 1047—BMI	27	11
25.	MAMBO ROCK—B. Haley Birth of the Boogie—(26)—Dec 29418—ASCAP	18	4
26.	HOW IMPORTANT CAN IT BE?—S. Vaughan Waltzing Down the Aisle—Mercury 70534—ASCAP	26	5
26.	BIRTH OF THE BOOGIE—B. Haley Mambo Rock—(25)—Dec 29418—ASCAP	27	2
28.	IT MAY SOUND SILLY—McGuire Sisters Doesn't Anybody Love Me?—Coral 61369—BMI	—	1
29.	PLAY ME HEARTS AND FLOWERS—J. Desmond I'm So Ashamed—Coral 61379—ASCAP	—	1
30.	DANCER, HEARTBREAK AHEAD—J. P. Morgan Softly, Softly—V 20-6016—ASCAP	—	1

• This Week's Best Buys

According to sales reports in key markets, the following recent releases are recommended for extra profits:

UNCHAINED MELODY (Frank, ASCAP) — **Al Hibbler— Decca 29441**
Initial reaction to this movie tune has been quite strong. Al Hibbler's version already has jumped on the Cleveland and Detroit territorial charts and is a big seller in New York, Pittsburgh and Los Angeles, as well. This disk is also doing nicely in the r. & b. market. Several other versions are sparking considerable action but have not yet gained the acceptance that the Decca record has. Flip is "Daybreak" (Feist, ASCAP).

SILVER MOON (Harms, ASCAP)—**Billy Vaughn —Dot 15347**
This is another recent release that has taken little time to hit pay dirt. Operators have been particularly enthusiastic about this record. Good sales reports were returned from a wide range of territories that included Philadelphia, Buffalo, Pittsburgh, Cleveland, Chicago, Milwaukee, Nashville, St. Louis, Atlanta and Baltimore. Flip is "Baby O' Mine" (Randy-Smith, ASCAP). A previous Billboard "Spotlight" pick.

NOBODY (Jerry Vogel, ASCAP)
DOOR OF DREAMS (Roncom, ASCAP)—**Perry Como—RCA Victor 6059**
While this has been a slow starter for Como, it is beginning to pick up nicely in various parts of the country. This disk is moving at a good rate in Chicago, Milwaukee, St. Louis, Cincinnati, Pittsburgh and Buffalo. Preference as to side is almost evenly split. A previous Billboard "Spotlight" pick.

MAKE YOURSELF COMFORTABLE (Rylan, ASCAP)—**Deacon Andy Griffith—Capitol 3057**
Southern dealers have been having a field day with this humorous disk. Retailers in the Carolinas, Atlanta, Nashville, Dallas, Baltimore, St. Louis and Kansas City have found a ready response to it. The concentration of strong reports in those territories may put the Griffith record on the national charts in the near future. Flip is "Ko Ko Mo" (Meridian, BMI). A previous Billboard "Spotlight" pick.

• Most Played in Juke Boxes

For survey week ending March 16

RECORDS are ranked in order of the greatest number of plays in juke boxes thruout the country. Results are based on The Billboard's weekly survey among the nation's juke box operators. The reverse side of each record is also listed. When a figure is given in parenthesis after the flip title it indicates what position it occupies on the chart.

This Week		Last Week	Weeks on Chart
1.	SINCERELY—McGuire Sisters No More—Coral 61323—BMI	1	10
2.	CRAZY OTTO MEDLEY—J. Maddox Humoresque—Dot 15325	3	6
3.	HEARTS OF STONE—Fontane Sisters Bless Your Heart—Dot 15265—BMI	2	15
4.	MELODY OF LOVE—B. Vaughn Joy Ride—Dot 15247—ASCAP	5	12
5.	TWEEDLE DEE—G. Gibbs You're Wrong, All Wrong—Mercury 70517—BMI	7	7
6.	MELODY OF LOVE—Four Aces There's a Tavern in the Town—Dec 29395—ASCAP	4	11
7.	KO KO MO—P. Como You'll Always Be My Lifetime Sweetheart—V 20-5994—BMI	6	7
8.	BALLAD OF DAVY CROCKETT—B. Hayes Farewell—Cadence 1256—BMI	13	3
9.	HOW IMPORTANT CAN IT BE?—J. James This Is My Confession—M-G-M 11919—ASCAP	10	5
10.	KO KO MO—Crew Cuts Earth Angel—(12)—Mercury 70529—BMI	11	6
11.	THAT'S ALL I WANT FROM YOU—J. P. Morgan Dawn—V 20-5896—BMI	8	14
12.	EARTH ANGEL—Crew Cuts Ko Ko Mo—(10)—Mercury 70529—BMI	8	7
13.	EARTH ANGEL—Penguins Hey, Senorita—Dootone 348—BMI	12	7
13.	MELODY OF LOVE—D. Carroll Golondrina, La—Mercury 70516—ASCAP	14	6
15.	ROCK LOVE—Fontane Sisters You're Mine—Dot 8570—BMI	16	4
16.	TWEEDLE DEE—L. Baker Tomorrow Night—Atlantic 1047—BMI	17	3
17.	LET ME GO, LOVER—J. Weber Marionette—Col 40366—BMI	15	16
17.	DARLING JE VOUS AIME BEAUCOUP—Nat (King) Cole Sand and the Sea—Cap 3027—ASCAP	—	1
19.	OPEN UP YOUR HEART—Cowboy Church Sunday School Lord Is Counting on You—Dec 29367—BMI	—	1
20.	SINCERELY—Moonglows Tempting—Chess 1581—BMI	—	1

• Most Played by Jockeys

For survey week ending March 16

RECORDS are ranked in order of the greatest number of plays on disk jockey radio shows thruout the country. Results are based on The Billboard's weekly survey among the nation's disk jockeys. The reverse side of each record is also listed.

This Week		Last Week	Weeks on Chart
1.	SINCERELY—McGuire Sisters No More—Coral 61323—BMI	1	11
2.	KO KO MO—P. Como You'll Always Be My Lifetime Sweetheart—V 20-5994—BMI	3	8
3.	HOW IMPORTANT CAN IT BE?—J. James This Is My Confession—M-G-M 11919—ASCAP	6	5
4.	TWEEDLE DEE—G. Gibbs You're Wrong, All Wrong—Mercury 70517—BMI	4	9
5.	MELODY OF LOVE—B. Vaughn Joy Ride—Dot 15247—ASCAP	2	11
6.	EARTH ANGEL—Crew Cuts Ko Ko Mo—Mercury 70529—BMI	5	8
7.	CRAZY OTTO MEDLEY—J. Maddox Humoresque—Dot 15325	8	7
8.	BALLAD OF DAVY CROCKETT—B. Hayes Farewell—Cadence 1256—BMI	10	3
9.	HEARTS OF STONE—Fontane Sisters Bless Your Heart—Dot 15265—BMI	9	16
9.	MELODY OF LOVE—D. Carroll Golondrina, La—Mercury 70516—ASCAP	12	10
11.	THAT'S ALL I WANT FROM YOU—J. P. Morgan Dawn—V 20-5896—BMI	7	16
12.	HOW IMPORTANT CAN IT BE?—S. Vaughan Waltzing Down the Aisle—Mercury 70534—ASCAP	13	5
13.	MELODY OF LOVE—Four Aces There's a Tavern in the Town—Dec 29395—ASCAP	11	10
14.	EARTH ANGEL—Penguins Hey, Senorita—Dootone 348—BMI	15	9
15.	DARLING JE VOUS AIME BEAUCOUP—Nat (King) Cole Sand and the Sea—Cap 3027—ASCAP	18	4
16.	MAN CHASES A GIRL—E. Fisher Wedding Bells—V 20-6015—ASCAP	—	1
17.	PLEDGING MY LOVE—T. Brewer How Important Can It Be?—Coral 61362—BMI	20	2
18.	DANCER, HEARTBREAK AHEAD—J. P. Morgan Softly, Softly—V 20-6016—ASCAP	17	3
19.	BALLAD OF DAVY CROCKETT—Tennessee Ernie Farewell—Cap 3058—BMI	—	1
20.	IT MAY SOUND SILLY—McGuire Sisters Doesn't Anybody Love Me?—Coral 61369—BMI	—	1

The Billboard Music Popularity Charts — POPULAR RECORDS

• Best Sellers in Stores

For survey week ending March 23

RECORDS are ranked in order of their current national selling importance at the retail level. Results are based on The Billboard's weekly survey among the nation's top volume pop record dealers representing every important market area. The reverse side of each record is also listed. When a figure is given in parenthesis after the flip title it indicates what position it occupies on the chart.

This Week		Last Week	Weeks on Chart
1.	BALLAD OF DAVY CROCKETT—B. Hayes — Farewell—Cadence 1256—BMI	1	6
2.	CRAZY OTTO MEDLEY—J. Maddox — Humoresque—Dot 15325	2	9
3.	TWEEDLE DEE—G. Gibbs — You're Wrong, All Wrong—Mercury 70517—BMI	4	10
4.	SINCERELY—McGuire Sisters — No More—Coral 61323—BMI	3	13
5.	MELODY OF LOVE—B. Vaughn — Joy Ride—Dot 15247—ASCAP	5	17
6.	BALLAD OF DAVY CROCKETT—F. Parker — I Gave My Love—Col 40449—BMI	7	4
7.	KO KO MO—P. Como — You'll Always Be My Lifetime Sweetheart—Vic 20-5994—BMI	6	9
8.	OPEN UP YOUR HEART—Cowboy Church Sunday School — The Lord Is Counting on You—Dec 29367—BMI	9	14
9.	HOW IMPORTANT CAN IT BE?—J. James — This Is My Confession—M-G-M 11919—ASCAP	8	7
10.	BALLAD OF DAVY CROCKETT—Tennessee Ernie Ford — Farewell—Cap 3058—BMI	17	3
11.	CHERRY PINK AND APPLE BLOSSOM WHITE—P. Prado — Marie Elena Rumba—Vic 20-5965—ASCAP	15	5
12.	EARTH ANGEL—Crew Cuts — Ko Ko Mo—(16)—Mercury 70529—BMI	10	9
13.	MELODY OF LOVE—Four Aces — There's a Tavern in the Town—Dec 29395—ASCAP	12	11
14.	MELODY OF LOVE—D. Carroll — Golondrina, La—Mercury 70516—ASCAP	13	13
15.	DANCE WITH ME, HENRY—G. Gibbs — Every Road Must Have a Turning—Mercury 70572—BMI	21	2
16.	KO KO MO—Crew Cuts — Earth Angel—(12)—Mercury 70529—BMI	14	10
17.	THAT'S ALL I WANT FROM YOU—J. P. Morgan — Dawn—Vic 20-5896—BMI	15	19
18.	DARLING JE VOUS AIME BEAUCOUP—Nat (King) Cole — Sand and the Sea—(27)—Cap 3027—ASCAP	19	5
19.	HEARTS OF STONE—Fontane Sisters — Bless Your Heart—Dot 15265—BMI	11	17
20.	PLAY ME HEARTS AND FLOWERS—J. Desmond — I'm So Ashamed—Coral 61379—ASCAP	29	2
21.	PLEDGING MY LOVE—J. Ace — No Money—Duke 136—BMI	20	6
22.	EARTH ANGEL—Penguins — Hey, Senorita—Dootone 348—BMI	17	15
23.	DANGER, HEARTBREAK AHEAD—J. P. Morgan — Softly, Softly—Vic 20-6016—ASCAP	30	2
24.	TWO HEARTS—P. Boone — Tra-La-La—Dot 15338—BMI	—	1
25.	MAMBO ROCK—B. Haley — Birth of the Boogie—Dec 29418—ASCAP	25	5
26.	MAKE YOURSELF COMFORTABLE—A. Griffith — Ko Ko Mo—Cap 3057—ASCAP	—	1
27.	SAND AND THE SEA—Nat (King) Cole — Darling Je Vous Aime Beaucoup—(18)—Cap 3027—BMI	—	4
28.	IT'S A SIN TO TELL A LIE—S. Smith and the Redheads — My Baby Just Cares for Me—Epic 9093—ASCAP	—	1
29.	PLANTATION BOOGIE—L. Dee — Birth of the Blues—Dec 29360—BMI	23	8
30.	IT MAY SOUND SILLY—McGuire Sisters — Doesn't Anybody Love Me?—Coral 61369 BMI	28	2

• This Week's Best Buys

According to sales reports in key markets, the following recent releases are recommended for extra profits:

UNCHAINED MELODY (Frank, ASCAP)—**Les Baxter—Capitol 3055**

This instrumental is making a big impression in almost all sales areas. Already on the Cleveland territorial chart, the Baxter disk is also selling well in Pittsburgh, Baltimore, Chicago, Milwaukee, Detroit, St. Louis, Atlanta, Durham and Nashville. Flip is "Medic" (Young, ASCAP), which is also showing good action in some parts of the country.

IN THE MOOD (Shapiro-Bernstein, ASCAP)
MY MELANCHOLY BABY (Shapiro-Bernstein, ASCAP)—**Crazy Otto—Decca 29449**

The mania for souped-up piano disks is far from over, judging from the good reception given Crazy Otto's latest record. Operators, in particular, have found it a profitable item. Areas returning best reports include Boston, Buffalo, Pittsburgh, Cleveland, Milwaukee, St. Louis and Nashville. A previous Billboard "Spotlight" pick.

TAKE MY LOVE (Feist, ASCAP)—**Eddie Fisher—RCA Victor 6071**

While this record has not taken off with the dazzling speed of some of the big Fisher hits, it has moved out nicely this past week. Philadelphia, Buffalo, Pittsburgh, Chicago, Milwaukee, St. Louis, Baltimore, and Nashville sales reports indicated it was off to a fine start and moving out quickly. Flip is "Just One More Time" (Paxton, ASCAP). A previous Billboard "Spotlight" pick.

• Most Played in Juke Boxes

For survey week ending March 23

RECORDS are ranked in order of the greatest number of plays in juke boxes thruout the country. Results are based on The Billboard's weekly survey among the nation's juke box operators. The reverse side of each record is also listed. When a figure is given in parenthesis after the flip title it indicates what position it occupies on the chart.

This Week		Last Week	Weeks on Chart
1.	SINCERELY—McGuire Sisters — No More—(30)—Coral 61323—BMI	1	11
2.	CRAZY OTTO MEDLEY—J. Maddox — Humoresque—Dot 15325	2	7
3.	HEARTS OF STONE—Fontane Sisters — Bless Your Heart—Dot 15265—BMI	3	16
4.	TWEEDLE DEE—G. Gibbs — You're Wrong, All Wrong—Mercury 70517—BMI	5	8
4.	BALLAD OF DAVY CROCKETT—B. Hayes — Farewell—Cadence 1256—BMI	8	4
6.	MELODY OF LOVE—B. Vaughn — Joy Ride—Dot 15247—ASCAP	3	16
7.	MELODY OF LOVE—Four Aces — There's a Tavern in the Town—Dec 29395—ASCAP	6	12
8.	HOW IMPORTANT CAN IT BE?—J. James — This Is My Confession—M-G-M 11919—ASCAP	9	6
9.	KO KO MO—P. Como — You'll Always Be My Lifetime Sweetheart—(26)—Vic 20-5994—BMI	7	8
10.	KO KO MO—Crew Cuts — Earth Angel—(12)—Mercury 70529—BMI	10	7
11.	THAT'S ALL I WANT FROM YOU—J. P. Morgan — Dawn—Vic 20-5896—BMI	11	15
12.	EARTH ANGEL—Crew Cuts — Ko Ko Mo—(10)—Mercury 70529—BMI	12	8
13.	MELODY OF LOVE—D. Carroll — Golondrina, La—Mercury 70516—ASCAP	13	7
14.	TWEEDLE DEE—L. Baker — Tomorrow Night—Atlantic 1047—BMI	16	4
15.	EARTH ANGEL—Penguins — Hey Senorita—Dootone 348—BMI	13	8
16.	ROCK LOVE—Fontane Sisters — You're Mine—Dot 8570—BMI	15	5
17.	PLEDGING MY LOVE—J. Ace — No Money—Duke 136—BMI	—	1
17.	DANCE WITH ME HENRY—G. Gibbs — Every Road Must Have a Turning—Mercury 70572—BMI	—	1
19.	TWO HEARTS—P. Boone — Tra-La-La—Dot 15338—BMI	—	1
20.	WEDDING BELLS—E. Fisher — Man Chases a Girl—Vic 20-6015—BMI	—	1

• Most Played by Jockeys

For survey week ending March 23

RECORDS are ranked in order of the greatest number of plays on disk jockey radio shows thruout the country. Results are based on The Billboard's weekly survey among the nation's disk jockeys. The reverse side of each record is also listed.

This Week		Last Week	Weeks on Chart
1.	SINCERELY—McGuire Sisters — No More—Coral 61323—BMI	1	12
2.	TWEEDLE DEE—G. Gibbs — You're Wrong, All Wrong—Mercury 70517—BMI	4	10
3.	HOW IMPORTANT CAN IT BE?—J. James — This Is My Confession—M-G-M 11919—ASCAP	3	6
4.	KO KO MO—P. Como — You'll Always Be My Lifetime Sweetheart—Vic 20-5994—BMI	2	9
5.	BALLAD OF DAVY CROCKETT—B. Hayes — Farewell—Cadence 1256—BMI	8	4
6.	MELODY OF LOVE—B. Vaughn — Joy Ride—Dot 15247—ASCAP	5	12
7.	EARTH ANGEL—Crew Cuts — Ko Ko Mo—Mercury 70529—BMI	6	9
8.	CRAZY OTTO MEDLEY—J. Maddox — Humoresque—Dot 15325	7	8
9.	MELODY OF LOVE—Four Aces — There's a Tavern in the Town—Dec 29395—ASCAP	13	11
10.	DARLING JE VOUS AIME BEAUCOUP—Nat (King) Cole — Sand and the Sea—Cap 3027—ASCAP	15	5
11.	THAT'S ALL I WANT FROM YOU—J. P. Morgan — Dawn—Vic 20-5896—BMI	11	17
12.	MELODY OF LOVE—D. Carroll — Golondrina, La—Mercury 70516—ASCAP	9	11
13.	HOW IMPORTANT CAN IT BE?—S. Vaughan — Waltzing Down the Aisle—Mercury 70534—ASCAP	12	6
13.	BALLAD OF DAVY CROCKETT—F. Parker — I Gave My Love—Col 40449—BMI	—	1
15.	DANGER, HEARTBREAK AHEAD—J. P. Morgan — Softly Softly—Vic 20-6016—ASCAP	18	4
16.	IT MAY SOUND SILLY—McGuire Sisters — Doesn't Anybody Love Me?—Coral 61369—BMI	20	2
17.	BALLAD OF DAVY CROCKETT—Tennessee Ernie — Farewell—Cap 3058—BMI	19	2
18.	HEARTS OF STONE—Fontane Sisters — Bless Your Heart—Dot 15265—BMI	9	17
19.	PLAY ME HEARTS AND FLOWERS—J. Desmond — I'm So Ashamed—Coral 61379—ASCAP	—	1
20.	PLEDGING MY LOVE—T. Brewer — How Important Can It Be?—Coral 61362—BMI	17	3

The Billboard Music Popularity Charts — POPULAR RECORDS

• Best Sellers in Stores

For survey week ending March 30

RECORDS are ranked in order of their current national selling importance at the retail level, as determined by The Billboard's weekly survey of the top volume dealers in every important market area. When significant action is reported on both sides of a record, points are combined to determine position on the chart. In such a case, both sides are listed in bold type, the leading side on top.

This Week	Record	Last Week	Weeks on Chart
1.	**BALLAD OF DAVY CROCKETT** (BMI)—B. Hayes. Farewell (BMI)—Cadence 1256	1	7
2.	**CRAZY OTTO MEDLEY**—J. Maddox. Humoresque (BMI)—Dot 15325	2	10
3.	**SINCERELY** (BMI)—McGuire Sisters. No More (BMI)—Coral 61323	4	14
4.	**TWEEDLE DEE** (BMI)—G. Gibbs. You're Wrong, All Wrong (ASCAP)—Mercury 70517	3	11
5.	**MELODY OF LOVE** (ASCAP)—B. Vaughn. Joy Ride (ASCAP)—Dot 15247	5	18
6.	**CHERRY PINK AND APPLE BLOSSOM WHITE** (ASCAP)—P. Prado. Marie Elena Rumba (ASCAP)—Vic 20-5965	11	6
7.	**BALLAD OF DAVY CROCKETT** (BMI)—F. Parker. I Gave My Love (BMI)—Col 40449	6	5
8.	**DANCE WITH ME HENRY** (BMI)—G. Gibbs. Every Road Must Have a Turning—Mercury 70572	15	3
9.	**BALLAD OF DAVY CROCKETT** (BMI)—Tennessee Ernie Ford. Farewell (BMI)—Cap 3058	10	4
10.	**HOW IMPORTANT CAN IT BE?** (ASCAP)—J. James. This Is My Confession (ASCAP)—M-G-M 11919	9	8
11.	**DARLING JE VOUS AIME BEAUCOUP** (ASCAP)—Nat (King) Cole / **SAND AND THE SEA** (BMI)—Cap 3027	18	6
12.	**KO KO MO** (BMI)—P. Como. You'll Always Be My Lifetime Sweetheart (ASCAP)—Vic 20-5094	7	10
13.	**OPEN UP YOUR HEART** (BMI)—Cowboy Church Sunday School. The Lord Is Counting on You (BMI)—Dec 29367	8	15
14.	**EARTH ANGEL** (BMI)—Crew Cuts / **KO KO MO** (BMI)—Mercury 70529	12	11
15.	**MELODY OF LOVE** (ASCAP)—Four Aces. There's a Tavern in the Town (ASCAP)—Dec 29395	13	12
16.	**PLAY ME HEARTS AND FLOWERS** (ASCAP)—J. Desmond. I'm So Ashamed (ASCAP)—Coral 61379	20	3
17.	**MELODY OF LOVE** (ASCAP)—D. Carroll. La Golondrina—Mercury 70516	14	14
18.	**DANGER, HEARTBREAK AHEAD** (ASCAP)—J. P. Morgan / **SOFTLY, SOFTLY**—Vic 20-6016	23	3
19.	**UNCHAINED MELODY** (ASCAP)—A. Hibbler. Daybreak—Dec 29441	—	1
20.	**UNCHAINED MELODY** (ASCAP)—L. Baxter. Medic—Cap 3055	—	1
21.	**TWO HEARTS** (BMI)—P. Boone. Tra-La-La—Dot 15338	24	2
22.	**HEARTS OF STONE** (BMI)—Fontane Sisters. Bless Your Heart (ASCAP)—Dot 15265	19	18
23.	**GLAD RAG DOLL** (ASCAP)—Crazy Otto / **SMILES** (ASCAP)—Dec 29403	—	4
24.	**PLEDGING MY LOVE** (BMI)—J. Ace. No Money (BMI)—Duke 136	21	7
25.	**IT MAY SOUND SILLY** (BMI)—McGuire Sisters. Doesn't Anybody Love Me (BMI)—Coral 61369	30	3
26.	**THAT'S ALL I WANT FROM YOU** (BMI)—J. P. Morgan. Dawn (ASCAP)—Vic 20-5896	17	20
27.	**MAMBO ROCK** (ASCAP)—B. Haley. Birth of the Boogie (ASCAP)—Dec 29418	25	6
28.	**BREEZE AND I** (BMI)—C. Valente. Jalousie—Dec 29467	—	1
29.	**IT'S A SIN TO TELL A LIE** (ASCAP)—S. Smith & the Redheads. My Baby Just Cares for Me—Epic 9093	28	2
30.	**PLANTATION BOOGIE** (BMI)—L. Dee. Birth of the Blues (ASCAP)—Dec 29360	29	9

• This Week's Best Buys

According to sales reports in key markets, the following recent releases are recommended for extra profits:

THE BREEZE AND I (E. B. Marks, BMI)—**Caterina Valente—Decca 29467**
There seems to be nothing flash-in-the-pan about the appeal of this singer, whose "Malaguena" first introduced her to the American public. Action has been even quicker on this second release, which this week zoomed into the No. 28 slot on the national retail chart, and occupies a place on many territorial charts as well. Flip is "Jalousie" (Harms, ASCAP). A previous Billboard "Spotlight" pick.

WHATEVER LOLA WANTS (Frank, ASCAP)
OH YEAH (Ross Jungnickel, ASCAP) — **Sarah Vaughan—Mercury 70595**
Miss Vaughan also seems to be in solid with the customers these days. In most stores little more than a week, this disk has moved out speedily, chalking up good and strong sales in Boston, Providence, New York, Baltimore, Buffalo, Pittsburgh, Cleveland, Chicago, Milwaukee, Detroit and St. Louis. While "Lola" leads, "Oh Yeah" shows good action, too, and the promise of more. A previous Billboard "Spotlight" pick.

UNCHAINED MELODY (Frank, ASCAP)—**Roy Hamilton—Epic 9102**
This disk is forging ahead with growing power in both the pop and r.&b. fields. While the Al Hibbler record has a good headstart, and is also doing well in both categories, Hamilton is making an impressive showing, particularly in Boston, New York, Providence, Baltimore, Philadelphia, Buffalo, Pittsburgh, Cleveland, St. Louis, Durham, Atlanta and Nashville. Flip is "From Here to Eternity" (Barton, ASCAP). A previous Billboard "Spotlight" pick.

Beginning With This Issue...

All national retail and juke box charts now list records in positions earned by combining survey reports on both sides of the disk, whenever significant action is reported on both sides. "TWO-SIDED" RECORDS have both sides listed in bold type, with the leading side on top. The Chart Comments feature this week describes relative changes in chart positions due to this innovation. A story on the first music page explains the move in detail.

• Most Played in Juke Boxes

For survey week ending March 30

RECORDS are ranked in order of the greatest number of plays in juke boxes thruout the country, as determined by The Billboard's weekly survey of the nation's juke box operators. When significant play is reported on both sides of a record, points are combined to determine position on the chart. In such a case, both sides are listed in bold type, the leading side on top.

This Week	Record	Last Week	Weeks on Chart
1.	**SINCERELY** (BMI)—McGuire Sisters. No More (BMI)—Coral 61323	1	12
2.	**CRAZY OTTO MEDLEY** (BMI)—J. Maddox. Humoresque (BMI)—Dot 15325	2	8
3.	**TWEEDLE DEE** (BMI)—G. Gibbs. You're Wrong, All Wrong (ASCAP)—Mercury 70517	4	9
4.	**BALLAD OF DAVY CROCKETT** (BMI)—B. Hayes. Farewell (BMI)—Cadence 1256	4	5
5.	**MELODY OF LOVE** (ASCAP)—B. Vaughn. Joy Ride (ASCAP)—Dot 15247	6	17
6.	**KO KO MO** (BMI)—Crew Cuts / **EARTH ANGEL** (BMI)—Mercury 70529	10	9
7.	**MELODY OF LOVE** (ASCAP)—Four Aces. There's a Tavern in the Town (ASCAP)—Dec 29395	7	13
8.	**HOW IMPORTANT CAN IT BE?** (ASCAP)—J. James. This Is My Confession (ASCAP)—M-G-M 11919	8	7
9.	**HEARTS OF STONE** (BMI)—Fontane Sisters. Bless Your Heart (ASCAP)—Dot 15265	3	17
10.	**KO KO MO** (BMI)—P. Como. You'll Always Be My Lifetime Sweetheart (ASCAP)—Vic 20-5994	9	9
10.	**THAT'S ALL I WANT FROM YOU** (BMI)—J. P. Morgan. Dawn (ASCAP)—Vic 20-5896	11	16
12.	**DANCE WITH ME HENRY** (BMI)—G. Gibbs. Every Road Must Have a Turning—Mercury 70572	17	2
13.	**ROCK LOVE** (BMI)—Fontane Sisters. You're Mine (BMI)—Dot 8570	16	6
13.	**MELODY OF LOVE** (ASCAP)—D. Carroll. La Golondrina (ASCAP)—Mercury 70516	13	8
15.	**CHERRY PINK AND APPLE BLOSSOM WHITE** (ASCAP)—P. Prado. Marie Elena Rumba (ASCAP)—Vic 20-5965	—	1
16.	**DANGER, HEARTBREAK AHEAD** (ASCAP)—J. P. Morgan. Softly, Softly (ASCAP)—Vic 20-6016	—	1
17.	**TWO HEARTS** (BMI)—P. Boone. Tra-La-La—Dot 15338	19	2
18.	**EARTH ANGEL** (BMI)—Penguins. Hey, Senorita (BMI)—Dootone 348	15	9
18.	**PLAY ME HEARTS AND FLOWERS** (ASCAP)—J. Desmond. I'm So Ashamed (ASCAP)—Coral 61379	—	1
20.	**DARLING JE VOUS AIME BEAUCOUP** (ASCAP)—Nat (King) Cole. Sand and the Sea (BMI)—Cap 3027	—	2

• Most Played by Jockeys

For survey week ending March 30

SIDES are ranked in order of the greatest number of plays on disk jockey radio shows thruout the country. Results are based on The Billboard's weekly survey among the nation's disk jockeys. The reverse side of each record is also listed.

This Week	Record	Last Week	Weeks on Chart
1.	**SINCERELY**—McGuire Sisters. No More—Coral 61323—BMI	1	13
2.	**HOW IMPORTANT CAN IT BE?**—J. James. This Is My Confession—M-G-M 11919—ASCAP	3	7
3.	**BALLAD OF DAVY CROCKETT**—B. Hayes. Farewell—Cadence 1256—BMI	5	5
4.	**MELODY OF LOVE**—B. Vaughn. Joy Ride—Dot 15247—ASCAP	6	13
5.	**TWEEDLE DEE**—G. Gibbs. You're Wrong, All Wrong—Mercury 70517—BMI	2	11
6.	**KO KO MO**—P. Como. You'll Always Be My Lifetime Sweetheart—Vic 20-5994—BMI	4	10
7.	**CRAZY OTTO MEDLEY**—J. Maddox. Humoresque—Dot 15325	8	9
8.	**BALLAD OF DAVY CROCKETT**—Tennessee Ernie. Farewell—Cap 3058—BMI	17	3
9.	**EARTH ANGEL**—Crew Cuts. Ko Ko Mo—Mercury 70529—BMI	7	10
10.	**DARLING JE VOUS AIME BEAUCOUP**—Nat (King) Cole. Sand and the Sea—Cap 3027—ASCAP	10	6
11.	**IT MAY SOUND SILLY**—McGuire Sisters. Doesn't Anybody Love Me?—Coral 61369—BMI	16	3
12.	**DANGER, HEARTBREAK AHEAD**—J. P. Morgan. Softly, Softly—Vic 20-6016—ASCAP	15	5
13.	**DANCE WITH ME HENRY**—G. Gibbs. Every Road Must Have a Turning—Mercury 70572—BMI	—	1
14.	**BALLAD OF DAVY CROCKETT**—W. Schumann. Let's Make Up—Vic 20-6014—BMI	—	1
15.	**PLAY ME HEARTS AND FLOWERS**—J. Desmond. I'm So Ashamed—Coral 61379—ASCAP	19	2
16.	**MELODY OF LOVE**—D. Carroll. Golondrina, La—Mercury 70516—ASCAP	12	12
17.	**HOW IMPORTANT CAN IT BE?**—S. Vaughan. Waltzing Down the Aisle—Mercury 70534—ASCAP	13	7
18.	**MELODY OF LOVE**—Four Aces. There's a Tavern in the Town—Dec 29395—ASCAP	9	12
19.	**THAT'S ALL I WANT FROM YOU**—J. P. Morgan. Dawn—Vic 20-5896—BMI	11	18
20.	**UNCHAINED MELODY**—L. Baxter. Medic—Cap 3055—ASCAP	—	1

The Billboard Music Popularity Charts — POPULAR RECORDS

• Best Sellers in Stores

For survey week ending April 6

RECORDS are ranked in order of their current national selling importance at the retail level, as determined by The Billboard's weekly survey of the top volume dealers in every important market area. When significant action is reported on both sides of a record, points are combined to determine position on the chart. In such a case, both sides are listed in bold type, the leading side on top.

This Week	Record	Last Week	Weeks on Chart
1.	**BALLAD OF DAVY CROCKETT** (BMI)—B. Hayes Farewell (BMI)—Cadence 1256	1	8
2.	**CRAZY OTTO MEDLEY** (BMI)—J. Maddox Humoresque (BMI)—Dot 15325	2	11
3.	**TWEEDLE DEE** (BMI)—G. Gibbs You're Wrong, All Wrong (ASCAP)—Mercury 70517	4	12
4.	**CHERRY PINK AND APPLE BLOSSOM WHITE** (ASCAP)—P. Prado Marie Elena Rumba (ASCAP)—Vic 20-5965	6	7
5.	**SINCERELY** (BMI)—McGuire Sisters No More (BMI)—Coral 61323	3	15
6.	**BALLAD OF DAVY CROCKETT** (BMI)—F. Parker I Gave My Love (BMI)—Col 40449	7	6
7.	**MELODY OF LOVE** (ASCAP)—B. Vaughn Joy Ride (ASCAP)—Dot 15247	5	19
8.	**DANCE WITH ME HENRY** (BMI)—G. Gibbs Every Road Must Have a Turning (BMI)—Mercury 70572	8	4
9.	**HOW IMPORTANT CAN IT BE?** (ASCAP)—J. James This Is My Confession (ASCAP)—M-G-M 11919	10	9
10.	**BALLAD OF DAVY CROCKETT** (BMI)—Tennessee Ernie Ford Farewell (BMI)—Cap 3058	9	5
11.	**DARLING JE VOUS AIME BEAUCOUP** (ASCAP)—Nat (King) Cole **SAND AND THE SEA** (BMI)—Cap 3027	11	7
12.	**UNCHAINED MELODY** (ASCAP)—L. Baxter Medic—Cap 3055	20	2
13.	**OPEN UP YOUR HEART** (BMI)—Cowboy Church Sunday School The Lord Is Counting on You (BMI)—Dec 29367	13	16
14.	**UNCHAINED MELODY** (ASCAP)—A. Hibbler Daybreak—Dec 29441	19	2
15.	**EARTH ANGEL** (BMI)—Crew Cuts **KO KO MO** (BMI)—Mercury 70529	14	12
16.	**KO KO MO** (BMI)—P. Como You'll Always Be My Lifetime Sweetheart (ASCAP)—Vic 20-5994	12	11
17.	**MELODY OF LOVE** (ASCAP)—Four Aces There's a Tavern in the Town (ASCAP)—Dec 29395	15	13
18.	**TWO HEARTS** (BMI)—P. Boone Tra-La-La—Dot 15338	21	3
19.	**BREEZE AND I** (BMI)—C. Valente Jalousie—Dec 29467	28	2
20.	**PLAY ME HEARTS AND FLOWERS** (ASCAP)—J. Desmond I'm So Ashamed (ASCAP)—Coral 61379	16	4
21.	**MELODY OF LOVE** (ASCAP)—D. Carroll La Golondrina (ASCAP)—Mercury 70516	17	15
22.	**MAMBO ROCK** (ASCAP)—B. Haley **BIRTH OF THE BOOGIE** (ASCAP)—Dec 29418	27	7
23.	**IT MAY SOUND SILLY** (BMI)—McGuire Sisters Doesn't Anybody Love Me? (BMI)—Coral 61369	25	4
24.	**THAT'S ALL I WANT FROM YOU** (BMI)—J. P. Morgan Dawn (ASCAP)—Vic 20-5896	26	21
25.	**DANGER, HEARTBREAK AHEAD** (ASCAP)—J. P. Morgan Softly, Softly (ASCAP)—Vic 20-6016	18	4
26.	**PLEDGING MY LOVE** (BMI)—J. Ace No Money (BMI)—Duke 136	24	8
27.	**SMILES** (ASCAP)—Crazy Otto **GLAD RAG DOLL** (ASCAP)—Dec 29403	23	5
27.	**PLANTATION BOOGIE** (BMI)—L. Dee Birth of the Blues (ASCAP)—Dec 29360	30	10
29.	**IT'S A SIN TO TELL A LIE** (ASCAP)—S. Smith & the Redheads My Baby Just Cares for Me—Epic 9093	29	3
30.	**DIXIE DANNY** (ASCAP)—Laurie Sisters No Chance (ASCAP)—Mercury 70548	—	1

• This Week's Best Buys

According to sales reports in key markets, the following recent releases are recommended for extra profits:

HONEY BABE (Witmark, ASCAP)—**Art Mooney—M-G-M 11900**

Tho this disk has been out for several months, it is only now that the movie "Battle Cry" is getting around to local theaters that it is stirring up unusually strong reaction. This week the record appears on the Atlanta and Boston territorial charts and was a potent seller in Chicago, Providence and enough other sales areas to make it a national chart threat. Dealers and operators should not be caught unawares. Flip is "No Regrets" (Miller, ASCAP).

BOOM BOOM BOOMERANG (Dandelion, BMI) **—De Castro Sisters—Abbott 3003**

In the past two weeks this record has shown excellent growth and placed on the Cleveland and Dallas territorial listings. Good sales were also reported in Philadelphia, New England, Buffalo, Pittsburgh, Chicago, Milwaukee, Durham, Nashville, Atlanta and St. Louis. Flip is "Let Your Love Walk In" (Teri, ASCAP).

CHOP CHOP BOOM (Lee, BMI)
Don't Be Angry (Republic, BMI)—**The Crew Cuts—Mercury 70597**

The Crew Cuts' latest release has moved out quickly, showing especially good form in Detroit, Chicago, Milwaukee, St. Louis, Pittsburgh, Buffalo and Boston. Action was reported on both sides, but with an edge at this stage on "Chop Chop Boom." A previous Billboard "Spotlight" pick.

Now in The Billboard...

All national retail and juke box charts now list records in positions earned by combining survey reports on both sides of the disk, whenever significant action is reported on both sides. "TWO-SIDED" RECORDS have both sides listed in bold type, with the leading side on top. The Chart Comments feature this week describes relative changes in chart positions due to this innovation.

• Most Played in Juke Boxes

For survey week ending April 6

RECORDS are ranked in order of the greatest number of plays in juke boxes thruout the country, as determined by The Billboard's weekly survey of the nation's juke box operators. When significant play is reported on both sides of a record, points are combined to determine position on the chart. In such a case, both sides are listed in bold type, the leading side on top.

This Week	Record	Last Week	Weeks on Chart
1.	**SINCERELY** (BMI)—McGuire Sisters No More (BMI)—Coral 61323	1	13
2.	**CRAZY OTTO MEDLEY** (BMI)—J. Maddox Humoresque (BMI)—Dot 15325	2	9
3.	**BALLAD OF DAVY CROCKETT** (BMI)—B. Hayes Farewell (BMI)—Cadence 1256	4	6
4.	**TWEEDLE DEE** (BMI)—G. Gibbs You Wrong, All Wrong (ASCAP)—Mercury 70517	3	10
5.	**MELODY OF LOVE** (ASCAP)—B. Vaughn Joy Ride (ASCAP)—Dot 15247	5	18
6.	**MELODY OF LOVE** (ASCAP)—Four Aces There's a Tavern in the Town (ASCAP)—Dec 29395	7	14
7.	**KO KO MO** (BMI)—Crew Cuts **EARTH ANGEL** (BMI)—Mercury 70529	6	10
7.	**DANCE WITH ME HENRY** (BMI)—G. Gibbs Every Road Must Have a Turning—Mercury 70572	12	3
9.	**HOW IMPORTANT CAN IT BE?** (ASCAP)—J. James This Is My Confession (ASCAP)—M-G-M 11919	8	8
10.	**CHERRY PINK AND APPLE BLOSSOM WHITE** (ASCAP)—P. Prado Marie Elena Rumba (ASCAP)—Vic 20-5965	15	2
11.	**KO KO MO** (BMI)—P. Como You'll Always Be My Lifetime Sweetheart (ASCAP)—Vic 20-5994	10	10
12.	**BALLAD OF DAVY CROCKETT** (BMI)—Tennessee Ernie Farewell (BMI)—Cap 3058	—	1
13.	**HEARTS OF STONE** (BMI)—Fontane Sisters Bless Your Heart (ASCAP)—Dot 15265	9	18
14.	**ROCK LOVE** (BMI)—Fontane Sisters You're Mine (BMI)—Dot 8570	13	7
15.	**IT MAY SOUND SILLY** (BMI)—McGuire Sisters **DOESN'T ANYBODY LOVE ME?** (BMI)—Coral 61369	—	1
16.	**MELODY OF LOVE** (ASCAP)—D. Carroll La Golondrina (ASCAP)—Mercury 70516	13	9
17.	**DANGER, HEARTBREAK AHEAD** (ASCAP)—J. P. Morgan Softly, Softly (ASCAP)—Vic 20-6016	16	2
18.	**DARLING JE VOUS AIME BEAUCOUP** (ASCAP)—Nat (King) Cole **SAND AND THE SEA** (BMI)—Cap 3027	20	3
19.	**PLEDGING MY LOVE** (BMI)—T. Brewer How Important Can It Be? (ASCAP)—Coral 61362	—	1
20.	**PLAY ME HEARTS AND FLOWERS** (ASCAP)—J. Desmond I'm So Ashamed (ASCAP)—Coral 61379	18	2

• Most Played by Jockeys

For survey week ending April 6

SIDES are ranked in order of the greatest number of plays on disk jockey radio shows thruout the country. Results are based on The Billboard's weekly survey among the nation's disk jockeys. The reverse side of each record is also listed.

This Week	Record	Last Week	Weeks on Chart
1.	**SINCERELY**—McGuire Sisters No More (BMI)—Coral 61323	1	14
2.	**BALLAD OF DAVY CROCKETT**—B. Hayes Farewell (BMI)—Cadence 1256	3	6
3.	**HOW IMPORTANT CAN IT BE?**—J. James This Is My Confession (ASCAP)—M-G-M 11919	2	8
4.	**MELODY OF LOVE**—B. Vaughn Joy Ride (ASCAP)—Dot 15247	4	14
5.	**TWEEDLE DEE**—G. Gibbs You're Wrong, All Wrong (BMI)—Mercury 70517	5	12
6.	**DANCE WITH ME, HENRY**—G. Gibbs Every Road Must Have a Turning (BMI)—Mercury 70572	13	2
7.	**DARLING JE VOUS AIME BEAUCOUP**—Nat (King) Cole Sand and the Sea (ASCAP)—Cap 3027	10	7
8.	**PLAY ME HEARTS AND FLOWERS**—J. Desmond I'm So Ashamed (ASCAP)—Coral 61379	15	3
9.	**CHERRY PINK AND APPLE BLOSSOM WHITE**—P. Prado Marie Elena Rumba (ASCAP)—Vic 20-5965	—	1
10.	**BALLAD OF DAVY CROCKETT**—F. Parker I Gave My Love (BMI)—Col 40449	—	2
11.	**UNCHAINED MELODY**—L. Baxter Medic (ASCAP)—Cap 3055	20	2
12.	**BALLAD OF DAVY CROCKETT**—Tennessee Ernie Farewell (BMI)—Cap 3058	8	4
13.	**KO KO MO**—P. Como You'll Always Be My Lifetime Sweetheart (BMI)—Vic 20-5994	6	11
14.	**CRAZY OTTO MEDLEY**—J. Maddox Humoresque—Dot 15325	7	10
15.	**HOW IMPORTANT CAN IT BE?**—S. Vaughan Waltzing Down the Aisle (ASCAP)—Mercury 70534	17	8
16.	**DANGER, HEARTBREAK AHEAD**—J. P. Morgan Softly, Softly (ASCAP)—Vic 20-6016	12	6
17.	**BALLAD OF DAVY CROCKETT**—W. Schumann Let's Make Up (BMI)—Vic 20-6014	14	2
18.	**IT MAY SOUND SILLY**—McGuire Sisters Doesn't Anybody Love Me? (BMI)—Coral 61369	11	4
19.	**MELODY OF LOVE**—D. Carroll La Golondrina (ASCAP)—Mercury 70516	16	13
20.	**EARTH ANGEL**—Crew Cuts Ko Ko Mo (BMI)—Mercury 70529	9	11

The Billboard Music Popularity Charts — POPULAR RECORDS

• Best Sellers in Stores

For survey week ending April 13

RECORDS are ranked in order of their current national selling importance at the retail level, as determined by The Billboard's weekly survey of the top volume dealers in every important market area. When significant action is reported on both sides of a record, points are combined to determine position on the chart. In such a case, both sides are listed in bold type, the leading side on top.

This Week		Last Week	Weeks on Chart
1.	**BALLAD OF DAVY CROCKETT** (BMI)—B. Hayes Farewell (BMI)—Cadence 1256	1	9
2.	**CHERRY PINK AND APPLE BLOSSOM WHITE** (ASCAP)—P. Prado Marie Elena Rumba (ASCAP)—Vic 20-5965	4	8
3.	**DANCE WITH ME HENRY** (BMI)—G. Gibbs Every Road Must Have a Turning (BMI)—Mercury 70572	8	5
4.	**CRAZY OTTO MEDLEY** (BMI)—J. Maddox Humoresque (BMI)—Dot 15325	2	12
5.	**TWEEDLE DEE** (BMI)—G. Gibbs You're Wrong, All Wrong (ASCAP)—Mercury 70517	3	13
6.	**BALLAD OF DAVY CROCKETT** (BMI)—F. Parker I Gave My Love (BMI)—Col 40449	6	7
7.	**BALLAD OF DAVY CROCKETT** (BMI)—Tennessee Ernie Ford Farewell (BMI)—Cap 3058	10	6
8.	**UNCHAINED MELODY** (ASCAP)—L. Baxter Medic (ASCAP)—Cap 3055	12	3
9.	**MELODY OF LOVE** (ASCAP)—B. Vaughn Joy Ride (ASCAP)—Dot 15247	7	20
10.	**HOW IMPORTANT CAN IT BE?** (ASCAP)—J. James This Is My Confession (ASCAP)—M-G-M 11919	9	10
11.	**SINCERELY** (BMI)—McGuire Sisters No More (BMI)—Coral 61323	5	16
12.	**UNCHAINED MELODY** (ASCAP)—A. Hibbler Daybreak (ASCAP)—Dec 29441	14	3
13.	**DARLING JE VOUS AIME BEAUCOUP** (ASCAP)—Nat (King) Cole **SAND AND THE SEA** (BMI)—Cap 3027	11	8
14.	**BREEZE AND I** (BMI)—C. Valente Jalousie (ASCAP)—Dec 29467	19	3
15.	**OPEN UP YOUR HEART** (BMI)—Cowboy Church Sunday School The Lord Is Counting on You (BMI)—Dec 29367	13	17
16.	**MELODY OF LOVE** (ASCAP)—Four Aces There's a Tavern in the Town (ASCAP)—Dec 29395	17	14
17.	**PLAY ME HEARTS AND FLOWERS** (ASCAP)—J. Desmond I'm So Ashamed (ASCAP)—Coral 61379	20	5
18.	**TWO HEARTS** (BMI)—P. Boone Tra-La-La—Dot 15338	18	4
18.	**WHATEVER LOLA WANTS** (ASCAP)—S. Vaughan Oh Yeah (ASCAP)—Mercury 70595	—	1
20.	**KO KO MO** (BMI)—P. Como You'll Always Be My Lifetime Sweetheart (ASCAP)—Vic 20-5994	16	12
21.	**IT'S A SIN TO TELL A LIE** (ASCAP)—S. Smith & the Redheads My Baby Just Cares for Me—Epic 9093	29	4
22.	**UNCHAINED MELODY** (ASCAP)—R. Hamilton From Here to Eternity (ASCAP)—Epic 9102	—	1
23.	**IT MAY SOUND SILLY** (BMI)—McGuire Sisters Doesn't Anybody Love Me (BMI)—Coral 61369	23	5
24.	**EARTH ANGEL** (BMI)—Crew Cuts **KO KO MO** (BMI)—Mercury 70529	15	13
24.	**DANGER, HEARTBREAK AHEAD** (ASCAP)—J. P. Morgan Softly, Softly (ASCAP)—Vic 20-6016	25	5
26.	**MELODY OF LOVE** (ASCAP)—D. Carroll La Golondrina (ASCAP)—Mercury 70516	21	16
27.	**MAMBO ROCK** (ASCAP)—B. Haley **BIRTH OF THE BOOGIE** (ASCAP)—Dec 29418	22	8
28.	**PLANTATION BOOGIE** (BMI)—L. Dee Birth of the Blues (ASCAP)—Dec 29360	27	11
29.	**PLEDGING MY LOVE** (BMI)—J. Ace No Money (BMI)—Duke 136	26	9
29.	**HONEY BABE** (ASCAP)—A. Mooney No Regrets (ASCAP)—M-G-M 11900	—	1

• This Week's Best Buys

According to sales reports in key markets, the following recent releases are recommended for extra profits:

MOST OF ALL (Arc, BMI)
THE DOOR IS STILL OPEN (Berkshire, BMI)
—Don Cornell—Coral 61393

The singer has been making steady progress these past weeks with his latest release, and despite the competition on "Door" is beginning to show good action on both sides. The disk is currently on the Buffalo territorial chart and reported to be selling well in Baltimore, Pittsburgh, Cleveland, Milwaukee, Detroit, Nashville, Durham and St. Louis. A previous Billboard "Spotlight" pick.

THE DOOR IS STILL OPEN (Berkshire, BMI)
—The Hilltoppers—Dot 15351

Competition on this tune is keen, and it is still too early to predict the eventual victor. The Hilltoppers have been showing good form so far and are getting their share of the loot. Listed this week on the Cleveland territorial chart, the record is also a good seller in Cincinnati, Nashville, St. Louis, Milwaukee, Pittsburgh, Buffalo and Baltimore. Flip is "Teardrops From My Eyes" (Simon House, BMI). A previous Billboard "Spotlight" pick.

LEARNIN' THE BLUES (Barton, ASCAP) —
Frank Sinatra—Capitol 3102

Moving out far more quickly than the last few Sinatra releases, this disk is shaping up as one of the outstanding sellers of the past several weeks. Both juke box and retail reports from Philadelphia, Buffalo, Cleveland, St. Louis, Milwaukee and Baltimore have been in the good to strong categories. Flip is "If I Had Three Wishes" (Shaw, ASCAP).

• Most Played in Juke Boxes

For survey week ending April 13

RECORDS are ranked in order of the greatest number of plays in juke boxes thruout the country, as determined by The Billboard's weekly survey of the nation's juke box operators. When significant play is reported on both sides of a record, points are combined to determine position on the chart. In such a case, both sides are listed in bold type, the leading side on top.

This Week		Last Week	Weeks on Chart
1.	**BALLAD OF DAVY CROCKETT**—(BMI)—B. Hayes Farewell (BMI)—Cadence 1256	3	7
2.	**CRAZY OTTO MEDLEY** (BMI)—J. Maddox Humoresque (BMI)—Dot 15325	2	10
3.	**SINCERELY** (BMI)—McGuire Sisters No More (BMI)—Coral 61323	1	14
4.	**DANCE WITH ME HENRY** (BMI)—G. Gibbs Every Road Must Have a Turning (BMI)—Mercury 70572	7	4
5.	**TWEEDLE DEE** (BMI)—G. Gibbs You're Wrong, All Wrong (ASCAP)—Mercury 70517	4	11
6.	**MELODY OF LOVE** (ASCAP)—B. Vaughn Joy Ride (ASCAP)—Dot 15247	5	19
7.	**HOW IMPORTANT CAN IT BE?** (ASCAP)—J. James This Is My Confession (ASCAP)—M-G-M 11919	9	9
8.	**MELODY OF LOVE** (ASCAP)—Four Aces There's a Tavern in the Town (ASCAP)—Dec 29395	6	15
9.	**KO KO MO** (BMI)—Crew Cuts **EARTH ANGEL** (BMI)—Mercury 70529	7	11
10.	**CHERRY PINK AND APPLE BLOSSOM WHITE** (ASCAP)—P. Prado Marie Elena Rumba (ASCAP)—Vic 20-5965	10	3
11.	**BALLAD OF DAVY CROCKETT** (BMI)—Tennessee Ernie Farewell (BMI)—Cap 3058	12	2
12.	**HEARTS OF STONE** (BMI)—Fontane Sisters Bless Your Heart (ASCAP)—Dot 15265	13	19
13.	**DANGER, HEARTBREAK AHEAD** (ASCAP)—J. P. Morgan Softly, Softly (ASCAP)—Vic 20-6016	17	3
14.	**KO KO MO** (BMI)—P. Como You'll Always Be My Lifetime Sweetheart (ASCAP)—Vic 20-5994	11	11
15.	**IT MAY SOUND SILLY** (BMI)—McGuire Sisters **DOESN'T ANYBODY LOVE ME?** (BMI)—Coral 61369	15	2
16.	**MELODY OF LOVE** (ASCAP)—D. Carroll La Golondrina (ASCAP)—Mercury 70516	16	10
17.	**PLAY ME HEARTS AND FLOWERS** (ASCAP)—J. Desmond I'm So Ashamed (ASCAP)—Coral 61379	20	3
18.	**TWEEDLE DEE**—L. Baker Tomorrow Night (BMI)—Atlantic 1047	—	5
18.	**THAT'S ALL I WANT FROM YOU** (BMI)—J. P. Morgan Dawn (ASCAP)—Vic 20-5896	—	17
18.	**ROCK LOVE** (BMI)—Fontane Sisters You're Mine (BMI)—Dot 15333	14	8

• Most Played by Jockeys

For survey week ending April 13

SIDES are ranked in order of the greatest number of plays on disk jockey radio shows thruout the country. Results are based on The Billboard's weekly survey among the nation's disk jockeys. The reverse side of each record is also listed.

This Week		Last Week	Weeks on Chart
1.	**BALLAD OF DAVY CROCKETT**—B. Hayes Farewell (BMI)—Cadence 1256	2	7
2.	**SINCERELY**—McGuire Sisters No More (BMI)—Coral 61323	1	15
3.	**DANCE WITH ME, HENRY**—G. Gibbs Every Road Must Have a Turning (BMI)—Mercury 70572	6	3
4.	**HOW IMPORTANT CAN IT BE?**—J. James This Is My Confession (ASCAP)—M-G-M 11919	3	9
5.	**TWEEDLE DEE**—G. Gibbs You're Wrong, All Wrong (BMI)—Mercury 70517	5	13
6.	**UNCHAINED MELODY**—A Hibbler Daybreak (ASCAP)—Dec 29441	—	1
7.	**UNCHAINED MELODY**—L. Baxter Medic (ASCAP)—Cap 3055	11	3
8.	**BALLAD OF DAVY CROCKETT**—Tennessee Ernie Farewell (BMI)—Cap 3058	12	5
9.	**PLAY ME HEARTS AND FLOWERS**—J. Desmond I'm So Ashamed (ASCAP)—Coral 61379	8	4
10.	**MELODY OF LOVE**—B. Vaughn Joy Ride (ASCAP)—Dot 15247	4	15
11.	**CHERRY PINK AND APPLE BLOSSOM WHITE**—P. Prado Marie Elena Rumba (ASCAP)—Vic 20-5965	9	2
12.	**IT MAY SOUND SILLY**—McGuire Sisters Doesn't Anybody Love Me? (BMI)—Coral 61369	18	5
13.	**DARLING JE VOUS AIME BEAUCOUP**—Nat (King) Cole Sand and the Sea (ASCAP)—Cap 3027	7	8
14.	**BALLAD OF DAVY CROCKETT**—F. Parker I Gave My Love (BMI)—Col 40449	10	3
15.	**CRAZY OTTO MEDLEY**—J. Maddox Humoresque (BMI)—Dot 15325	14	11
16.	**HOW IMPORTANT CAN IT BE?**—S. Vaughan Waltzing Down the Aisle (ASCAP)—Mercury 70534	15	9
17.	**BALLAD OF DAVY CROCKETT**—W. Schumann Let's Make Up (BMI) Vic 20-6014	17	3
18.	**KO KO MO**—P. Como You'll Always Be My Lifetime Sweetheart (BMI)—Vic 20-5994	13	12
18.	**BREEZE AND I**—C. Valente Jalousie (BMI)—Dec 29467	—	1
20.	**DANGER, HEARTBREAK AHEAD**—J. P. Morgan Softly, Softly (ASCAP)—Vic 20-6016	16	7

The Billboard Music Popularity Charts — POPULAR RECORDS

• Best Sellers in Stores

For survey week ending April 20

RECORDS are ranked in order of their current national selling importance at the retail level, as determined by The Billboard's weekly survey of the top volume dealers in every important market area. When significant action is reported on both sides of a record, points are combined to determine position on the chart. In such a case, both sides are listed in bold type, the leading side on top.

This Week	Record	Last Week	Weeks on Chart
1.	CHERRY PINK AND APPLE BLOSSOM WHITE (ASCAP)—P. Prado Marie Elena Rumba (ASCAP)—Vic 20-5965	2	9
2.	BALLAD OF DAVY CROCKETT (BMI)—B. Hayes Farewell (BMI)—Cadence 1256	1	10
3.	DANCE WITH ME, HENRY (BMI)—G. Gibbs Every Road Must Have a Turning (BMI)—Mercury 70572	3	21
4.	CRAZY OTTO MEDLEY (ASCAP)—J. Maddox Humoresque (BMI)—Dot 15325	4	13
5.	UNCHAINED MELODY (ASCAP)—L. Baxter MEDIC (ASCAP)—Cap 3055	8	4
6.	BALLAD OF DAVY CROCKETT (BMI)—Tennessee Ernie Ford Farewell (BMI)—Cap 3058	7	7
7.	BALLAD OF DAVY CROCKETT F. Parker I Gave My Love (BMI)—Col 40449	6	8
8.	UNCHAINED MELODY (ASCAP)—A. Hibbler Daybreak—Dec 29441	12	4
9.	TWEEDLE DEE (BMI)—G. Gibbs You're Wrong, All Wrong (ASCAP)—Mercury 70517	5	14
10.	DARLING JE VOUS AIME BEAUCOUP (ASCAP)—Nat (King) Cole SAND AND THE SEA (BMI)—Cap 3027	13	9
11.	SINCERELY (BMI)—McGuire Sisters No More (BMI)—Coral 61323	11	17
12.	HOW IMPORTANT CAN IT BE? (ASCAP)—J. James This Is My Confession (ASCAP)—M-G-M 11919	10	11
13.	MELODY OF LOVE (ASCAP)—B. Vaughn Joy Ride (ASCAP)—Dot 15247	9	21
14.	UNCHAINED MELODY (ASCAP)—R. Hamilton From Here to Eternity (ASCAP)—Epic 9102	22	2
15.	BREEZE AND I (BMI)—C. Valente Jalousie (ASCAP)—Dec 29467	14	4
16.	TWO HEARTS (BMI)—P. Boone Tra-La-La—Dot 15338	18	5
17.	OPEN UP YOUR HEART (BMI)—Cowboy Church Sunday School The Lord Is Counting on You (BMI)—Dec 29367	15	18
18.	WHATEVER LOLA WANTS (ASCAP)—S. Vaughan Oh, Yeah (ASCAP)—Mercury 70595	18	2
19.	HONEY BABE (ASCAP)—A. Mooney No Regrets (ASCAP)—M-G-M 11900	29	2
20.	PLAY ME HEARTS AND FLOWERS J. Desmond I'm So Ashamed (ASCAP)—Coral 61379	17	6
21.	IT'S A SIN TO TELL A LIE (ASCAP)—S. Smith & the Redheads My Baby Just Cares for Me—Epic 9093	21	5
22.	DON'T BE ANGRY (BMI)—Crew Cuts CHOP CHOP BOOM (BMI)—Mercury 70597	—	1
23.	PLANTATION BOOGIE (BMI)—L. Dee Birth of the Blues (ASCAP)—Dec 29360	28	12
24.	MELODY OF LOVE (ASCAP)—Four Aces There's a Tavern in the Town (ASCAP)—Dec 29395	16	15
24.	KO KO MO—Crew Cuts EARTH ANGEL (BMI)—Mercury 70529	24	14
26.	IT MAY SOUND SILLY (BMI)—McGuire Sisters Doesn't Anybody Love Me? (ASCAP)—Coral 61369	23	6
27.	MELODY OF LOVE (ASCAP)—D. Carroll La Golondrina (ASCAP)—Mercury 70516	26	17
28.	DON'T BE ANGRY (BMI)—N. Brown It's Really You (BMI)—Savoy 1155	—	1
29.	KO KO MO (BMI)—P. Como You'll Always Be My Lifetime Sweetheart (ASCAP)—Vic 20-5994	20	13
29.	DANGER, HEARTBREAK AHEAD (ASCAP)—J. P. Morgan Softly, Softly (ASCAP)—Vic 20-6016	24	6

• This Week's Best Buys

According to sales reports in key markets, the following recent releases are recommended for extra profits:

A BLOSSOM FELL (Shapiro, Bernstein, ASCAP)

IF I MAY (Roosevelt, BMI)—Nat (King) Cole—Capitol 3095

The singer is once more receiving the solid reception that has greeted his recent releases. New York, Philadelphia, Buffalo, Baltimore, Cleveland, Chicago, Milwaukee, St. Louis, Nashville and Atlanta were among the territories reporting the disk selling well and moving up at a fast clip. "Blossom" has the edge, altho some territories report keen action on the flip. A previous Billboard "Spotlight" pick.

HEY, MR. BANJO (Mills, ASCAP)—The Sunnysiders—Kapp 113

This bright novelty has moved out of the sleeper category into that of a chart contender. Good sales were reported this past week in Boston, New York, Philadelphia, Baltimore, Buffalo, Cleveland, Chicago, Milwaukee, Detroit, Nashville and Durham. Flip is "Zoom, Zoom, Zoom" (Mills, ASCAP).

HEART (Frank, ASCAP)—The Four Aces—Decca 29476

HEART (Frank, ASCAP) — Eddie Fisher — RCA Victor 6097

Competition on this tune has been lively. The Four Aces are benefiting from a slight edge in timing, but both records are now doing well and both could easily make the charts. The Decca disk is doing especially well in Philadelphia, Providence, Buffalo, Cleveland, Milwaukee, Detroit, Nashville, Durham, Baltimore and St. Louis. The Victor record has a slight edge in Los Angeles, Chicago, Buffalo and is also a good seller in Baltimore, St. Louis, Durham, Nashville, Detroit and Philadelphia. The flip of the Four Aces record is "Sluefoot" (Robbins, ASCAP), while that of the Fisher record is "Near to You" (Frank, ASCAP). Both were previous Billboard "Spotlight" picks.

• Most Played in Juke Boxes

For survey week ending April 20

RECORDS are ranked in order of the greatest number of plays in juke boxes throut the country, as determined by The Billboard's weekly survey of the nation's juke box operators. When significant play is reported on both sides of a record, points are combined to determine position on the chart. In such a case, both sides are listed in bold type, the leading side on top.

This Week	Record	Last Week	Weeks on Chart
1.	BALLAD OF DAVY CROCKETT (BMI)—B. Hayes Farewell (BMI)—Cadence 1256	1	8
2.	CRAZY OTTO MEDLEY (ASCAP)—J. Maddox Humoresque (BMI)—Dot 15325	2	11
3.	SINCERELY (BMI)—McGuire Sisters No More (BMI)—Coral 61323	3	15
4.	DANCE WITH ME HENRY (BMI)—G. Gibbs Every Road Must Have a Turning—Mercury 70572	4	5
5.	TWEEDLE DEE (BMI)—G. Gibbs You're Wrong, All Wrong (ASCAP)—Mercury 70517	5	12
6.	HOW IMPORTANT CAN IT BE? (ASCAP)—J. James This Is My Confession (ASCAP)—M-G-M 11919	7	10
7.	MELODY OF LOVE (ASCAP)—B. Vaughn Joy Ride (ASCAP)—Dot 15247	6	20
8.	BALLAD OF DAVY CROCKETT (BMI)—Tennessee Ernie Farewell (BMI)—Cap 3058	11	3
9.	CHERRY PINK AND APPLE BLOSSOM WHITE (ASCAP)—P. Prado Marie Elena Rumba (ASCAP)—Vic 20-5965	10	4
10.	KO KO MO (BMI)—Crew Cuts EARTH ANGEL (BMI)—Mercury 70529	9	12
11.	MELODY OF LOVE (ASCAP)—Four Aces There's a Tavern in the Town (ASCAP)—Dec 29395	8	16
12.	HEARTS OF STONE (BMI)—Fontane Sisters Bless Your Heart (ASCAP)—Dot 15265	12	20
13.	PLAY ME HEARTS AND FLOWERS (ASCAP)—J. Desmond I'm So Ashamed (ASCAP)—Coral 61379	17	4
14.	DANGER, HEARTBREAK AHEAD (ASCAP)—J. P. Morgan Softly, Softly (ASCAP)—Vic 20-6016	13	4
14.	KO KO MO (BMI)—P. Como You'll Always Be Lifetime Sweetheart (ASCAP)—Vic 20-5994	14	12
16.	THAT'S ALL I WANT FROM YOU (BMI)—J. P. Morgan Dawn (ASCAP—Vic 20-5896	18	18
17.	DARLING JE VOUS AIME BEAUCOUP (ASCAP)—Nat (King) Cole SAND AND THE SEA (BMI)—Cap 3027	—	18
17.	BIRTH OF THE BOOGIE (ASCAP)—B. Haley MAMBO ROCK—Dec 29418	—	1
19.	IT MAY SOUND SILLY (BMI)—McGuire Sisters Doesn't Anybody Love Me? (ASCAP)—Coral 61369	15	3
20.	TWO HEARTS (BMI)—P. Boone Tra-La-La—Dot 15338	—	3
20.	TWEEDLE DEE—L. Baker Tomorrow Night (BMI)—Atlantic 1047	18	6
20.	UNCHAINED MELODY (ASCAP)—A. Hibbler Daybreak (ASCAP)—Dec 29441	—	1

• Most Played by Jockeys

For survey week ending April 20

SIDES are ranked in order of the greatest number of plays on disk jockey radio shows throut the country. Results are based on The Billboard's weekly survey among the nation's disk jockeys. The reverse side of each record is also listed.

This Week	Record	Last Week	Weeks on Chart
1.	BALLAD OF DAVY CROCKETT—B. Hayes Farewell (BMI)—Cadence 1256	1	8
2.	CHERRY PINK AND APPLE BLOSSOM WHITE—P. Prado Marie Elena Rumba (ASCAP)—Vic 20-5965	11	3
3.	DANCE WITH ME HENRY—G. Gibbs Every Road Must Have a Turning (BMI)—Mercury 70572	3	4
4.	HOW IMPORTANT CAN IT BE?—J. James This Is My Confession (ASCAP)—M-G-M 11919	4	10
5.	UNCHAINED MELODY—L. Baxter Medic (ASCAP)—Cap 3055	7	4
6.	PLAY ME HEARTS AND FLOWERS—J. Desmond I'm So Ashamed (ASCAP)—Coral 61379	9	5
7.	SINCERELY—McGuire Sisters No More (BMI)—Coral 61323	2	16
8.	UNCHAINED MELODY—A. Hibbler Daybreak (ASCAP)—Dec 29441	6	2
9.	TWEEDLE DEE—G. Gibbs You're Wrong, All Wrong (BMI)—Mercury 70517	5	14
10.	BALLAD OF DAVY CROCKETT—Tennessee Ernie Farewell (BMI)—Cap 3058	8	6
11.	DARLING JE VOUS AIME BEAUCOUP—Nat (King) Cole Sand and the Sea (ASCAP)—Cap 3027	13	9
12.	CRAZY OTTO MEDLEY—(ASCAP)—J. Maddox Humoresque (BMI)—Dot 15325	15	12
13.	MELODY OF LOVE—B. Vaughn Joy Ride (ASCAP)—Dot 15247	10	16
13.	BALLAD OF DAVY CROCKETT—F. Parker I Gave My Love (BMI)—Col 40449	14	4
15.	BREEZE AND I—C. Valente Jalousie (BMI)—Dec 29467	18	2
16.	BALLAD OF DAVY CROCKETT—W. Schumann Let's Make Up (BMI)—Vic 20-6014	17	4
17.	WHATEVER LOLA WANTS—S. Vaughan Oh, Yeah (ASCAP)—Mercury 70595	—	1
18.	IT MAY SOUND SILLY—McGuire Sisters Doesn't Anybody Love Me? (ASCAP)—Coral 61369	12	6
19.	CHERRY PINK AND APPLE BLOSSOM WHITE—A. Dale I'm Sincere (ASCAP)—Coral 61373	—	1
20.	DANGER, HEARTBREAK AHEAD—J. P. Morgan Softly, Softly (ASCAP)—Vic 20-6016	20	8

The Billboard Music Popularity Charts — POPULAR RECORDS

• Best Sellers in Stores

For survey week ending April 27

RECORDS are ranked in order of their current national selling importance at the retail level, as determined by The Billboard's weekly survey of the top volume dealers in every important market area. When significant action is reported on both sides of a record, points are combined to determine position on the chart. In such a case, both sides are listed in bold type, the leading side on top.

This Week		Last Week	Weeks on Chart
1.	**CHERRY PINK AND APPLE BLOSSOM WHITE** (ASCAP)—P. Prado... Marie Elena Rumba (ASCAP)—Vic 20-5965	1	10
2.	**BALLAD OF DAVY CROCKETT** (BMI)—B. Hayes... Farewell (BMI)—Cadence 1256	2	11
3.	**DANCE WITH ME HENRY** (BMI)—G. Gibbs... Every Road Must Have a Turning (BMI)—Mercury 70572	3	22
4.	**UNCHAINED MELODY** (ASCAP)—L. Baxter... Medic (ASCAP)—Cap 3055	5	5
5.	**CRAZY OTTO MEDLEY** (ASCAP)—J. Maddox... Humoresque (BMI)—Dot 15325	4	14
6.	**UNCHAINED MELODY** (ASCAP)—A. Hibbler... Daybreak—Dec 29441	8	5
7.	**BALLAD OF DAVY CROCKETT** (BMI)—F. Parker... I Gave My Love (BMI)—Col 40449	7	9
8.	**BALLAD OF DAVY CROCKETT** (BMI)—Tennessee Ernie Ford... Farewell (BMI)—Cap 3058	6	8
9.	**TWEEDLE DEE** (BMI)—G. Gibbs... You're Wrong, All Wrong (ASCAP)—Mercury 70517	9	15
10.	**DARLING JE VOUS AIME BEAUCOUP** (ASCAP)—Nat (King) Cole ... **SAND AND THE SEA** (BMI)—Cap 3027	10	10
11.	**MELODY OF LOVE** (ASCAP)—B. Vaughn... Joy Ride (ASCAP)—Dot 15247	13	22
12.	**UNCHAINED MELODY** (ASCAP)—R. Hamilton... From Here to Eternity (ASCAP)—Epic 9102	14	3
13.	**BREEZE AND I** (BMI)—C. Valente... Jalousie—Dec 29467	15	5
14.	**SINCERELY** (BMI)—McGuire Sisters.. No More (BMI)—Coral 61323	11	18
15.	**WHATEVER LOLA WANTS** (ASCAP)—S. Vaughan... Oh, Yeah (ASCAP)—Mercury 70595	18	3
16.	**HOW IMPORTANT CAN IT BE?** (ASCAP)—J. James... This Is My Confession (ASCAP)—M-G-M 11919	12	12
17.	**HONEY BABE** (ASCAP)—A. Mooney.. No Regrets (ASCAP)—M-G-M 11900	19	3
18.	**DON'T BE ANGRY** (BMI)—Crew Cuts **CHOP CHOP BOOM** (BMI)—Mercury 70597	22	2
19.	**TWO HEARTS** (BMI)—P. Boone..... Tra-La-La—Dot 15338	16	6
20.	**OPEN UP YOUR HEART** (BMI)—Cowboy Church Sunday School.... The Lord Is Counting on You (BMI)—Dec 29367	17	19
21.	**PLAY ME HEARTS AND FLOWERS** (ASCAP)—J. Desmond... I'm So Ashamed (ASCAP)—Coral 61379	20	7
22.	**IT'S A SIN TO TELL A LIE** (ASCAP)—S. Smith & the Redheads... My Baby Just Cares for Me—Epic 9093	21	6
23.	**MELODY OF LOVE** (ASCAP)—Four Aces... There's a Tavern in the Town (ASCAP)—Dec 29395	24	16
24.	**BOOM BOOM BOOMERANG** (BMI)—DeCastro Sisters... Let Your Love Walk In (ASCAP)—Abbott 3003	—	1
25.	**DON'T BE ANGRY** (BMI)—N. Brown. It's Really You (BMI)—Savoy 1155	28	2
26.	**PLANTATION BOOGIE** (BMI)—L. Dee... Birth of the Blues (ASCAP)—Dec 29360	23	13
27.	**BLOSSOM FELL** (ASCAP)—Nat (King) Cole... If I May (BMI)—Cap 3095	—	1
28.	**CHERRY PINK AND APPLE BLOSSOM WHITE** (ASCAP)—A. Dale... I'm Sincere (BMI)—Coral 61373	—	1
29.	**BALLAD OF DAVY CROCKETT** (BMI)—W. Schumann... Let's Make Up—Vic 20-6041	—	1
30.	**KO KO MO** (BMI)—P. Como... You'll Always Be My Lifetime Sweetheart (ASCAP)—Vic 20-5994	29	14
30.	**PLEDGING MY LOVE** (BMI)—T. Brewer... How Important Can It Be? (ASCAP)—Coral 61362	—	2

• This Week's Best Buys

According to sales reports in key markets, the following recent releases are recommended for extra profits:

NO LETTER TODAY (Peer, BMI)
GENUINE LOVE (Roosevelt, BMI)—**Les Paul and Mary Ford—Capitol 3108**

The duo's latest release is shaping up as a potent two-sided coin-grabber. Because of the country flavor of "No Letter Today," Southern territories have noted particularly favorable reaction on that side. While most Northern territories have been generally slower in moving the disk, action is becoming more lively, especially in New England, Philadelphia, Baltimore, Buffalo, Milwaukee and St. Louis. In time, "Genuine Love" may overcome the edge of "No Letter Today." A previous Billboard "Spotlight" selection.

LOVE ME OR LEAVE ME (B, V & C, ASCAP)
SOMETHING'S GOTTA GIVE (Robbins, ASCAP)—**Sammy Davis Jr.—Decca 29484**

Almost all sections of the country are now reporting good to strong action on this disk. In the past two weeks, in particular, the record has moved out in Los Angeles, New York, Boston, Chicago, Detroit, Cleveland and Baltimore. Several areas are doing well with the Lena Horne version of "Love Me." It is on the Los Angeles territorial chart, for example, and also doing nicely in New York. The Sammy Davis Jr. disk was a previous Billboard "Spotlight" selection.

• Most Played in Juke Boxes

For survey week ending April 27

RECORDS are ranked in order of the greatest number of plays in juke boxes thruout the country, as determined by The Billboard's weekly survey of the nation's juke box operators. When significant play is reported on both sides of a record, points are combined to determine position on the chart. In such a case, both sides are listed in bold type, the leading side on top.

This Week		Last Week	Weeks on Chart
1.	**BALLAD OF DAVY CROCKETT** (BMI)—B. Hayes... Farewell (BMI)—Cadence 1256	1	9
2.	**CRAZY OTTO MEDLEY** (ASCAP)—J. Maddox... Humoresque (BMI)—Dot 15325	2	12
3.	**DANCE WITH ME, HENRY** (BMI)—G. Gibbs... Every Road Must Have a Turning—Mercury 70572	4	6
4.	**CHERRY PINK AND APPLE BLOSSOM WHITE** (ASCAP)—P. Prado.. Marie Elena Rumba (ASCAP)—Vic 20-5965	9	5
5.	**SINCERELY** (BMI)—McGuire Sisters.. No More (BMI)—Coral 61323	3	16
6.	**BALLAD OF DAVY CROCKETT** (BMI)—Tennessee Ernie... Farewell (BMI)—Cap 3058	8	4
7.	**TWEEDLE DEE** (BMI)—G. Gibbs.... You're Wrong, All Wrong (ASCAP)—Mercury 70517	5	13
7.	**HOW IMPORTANT CAN IT BE?** (ASCAP)—J. James... This Is My Confession (ASCAP)—M-G-M 11919	6	11
9.	**MELODY OF LOVE** (ASCAP)—B. Vaughn... Joy Ride (ASCAP)—Dot 15247	7	21
10.	**MELODY OF LOVE** (ASCAP)—Four Aces... There's a Tavern in the Town (ASCAP)—Dec 29395	11	17
11.	**UNCHAINED MELODY** (ASCAP)—A. Hibbler... Daybreak (ASCAP)—Dec 29441	20	2
12.	**KO KO MO** (BMI)—Crew Cuts...... **EARTH ANGEL** (BMI)—Mercury 70529	10	13
13.	**PLAY ME HEARTS AND FLOWERS** (ASCAP)—J. Desmond... I'm So Ashamed (ASCAP)—Coral 61379	13	5
14.	**DARLING JE VOUS AIME BEAUCOUP** (ASCAP)—Nat (King) Cole ... Sand and the Sea (BMI)—Cap 3027	17	19
14.	**IT MAY SOUND SILLY** (BMI)—McGuire Sisters... Doesn't Anybody Love Me? (ASCAP)—Coral 61369	19	4
14.	**UNCHAINED MELODY** (ASCAP)—L. Baxter... Medic (ASCAP)—Cap 3055	—	1
14.	**CHERRY PINK AND APPLE BLOSSOM WHITE** (ASCAP)—A. Dale... I'm Sincere—Coral 61373	—	1
18.	**UNCHAINED MELODY** (ASCAP)—R. Hamilton... From Here to Eternity (ASCAP)—Epic 9102	—	1
18.	**PLEDGING MY LOVE** (BMI)—T. Brewer... **HOW IMPORTANT CAN IT BE?** (ASCAP)—Coral 61362	—	1
20.	**KO KO MO** (BMI)—P. Como... You'll Always Be My Lifetime Sweetheart (ASCAP)—Vic 20-5994	14	13
20.	**TWO HEARTS** (BMI)—P. Boone.... Tra-La-La—Dot 15338	20	4

• Most Played by Jockeys

For survey week ending April 27

SIDES are ranked in order of the greatest number of plays on disk jockey radio shows thruout the country. Results are based on The Billboard's weekly survey among the nation's disk jockeys. The reverse side of each record is also listed.

This Week		Last Week	Weeks on Chart
1.	**BALLAD OF DAVY CROCKETT**—B. Hayes... Farewell (BMI)—Cadence 1256	1	9
2.	**UNCHAINED MELODY**—L. Baxter.. Medic (ASCAP)—Cap 3055	5	5
3.	**DANCE WITH ME, HENRY**—G. Gibbs... Every Road Must Have a Turning (BMI)—Mercury 70572	3	5
4.	**CHERRY PINK AND APPLE BLOSSOM WHITE**—P. Prado... Marie Elena Rumba (ASCAP)—Vic 20-5965	2	4
5.	**UNCHAINED MELODY**—A. Hibbler. Daybreak (ASCAP)—Dec 29441	8	3
6.	**SINCERELY**—McGuire Sisters... No More (BMI)—Coral 61323	7	17
7.	**BALLAD OF DAVY CROCKETT**—Tennessee Ernie... Farewell (BMI)—Cap 3058	10	7
8.	**PLAY ME HEARTS AND FLOWERS**—J. Desmond... I'm So Ashamed (ASCAP)—Coral 61379	6	6
9.	**HOW IMPORTANT CAN IT BE?**—J. James... This Is My Confession (ASCAP)—M-G-M 11919	4	11
10.	**TWEEDLE DEE**—G. Gibbs... You're Wrong, All Wrong (BMI)—Mercury 70517	9	15
11.	**MELODY OF LOVE**—B. Vaughn.... Joy Ride (ASCAP)—Dot 15247	13	17
12.	**BALLAD OF DAVY CROCKETT**—F. Parker... I Gave My Love (BMI)—Col 40449	13	5
13.	**CRAZY OTTO MEDLEY**—J. Maddox... Humoresque (ASCAP)—Dot 15325	12	13
14.	**BREEZE AND I**—C. Valente... Jalousie (BMI)—Dec 29467	15	3
14.	**BALLAD OF DAVY CROCKETT**—W. Schumann... Let's Make Up (BMI)—Vic 20-6014	16	5
16.	**WHATEVER LOLA WANTS**—S. Vaughan... Oh, Yeah (BMI)—Mercury 70595	17	2
17.	**DARLING JE VOUS AIME BEAUCOUP**—Nat (King) Cole..... Sand and the Sea (ASCAP)—Cap 3027	11	10
18.	**UNCHAINED MELODY**—R. Hamilton... From Here to Eternity (ASCAP)— Epic 9102	—	1
19.	**LEARNING THE BLUES**—F. Sinatra. If I Had Three Wishes (ASCAP)—Cap 3102	—	1
20.	**IT MAY SOUND SILLY**—McGuire Sisters... Doesn't Anybody Love Me? (ASCAP)—Coral 61369	18	7

The Billboard Music Popularity Charts — POPULAR RECORDS

• Best Sellers in Stores

For survey week ending May 4

RECORDS are ranked in order of their current national selling importance at the retail level, as determined by The Billboard's weekly survey of the top volume dealers in every important market area. When significant action is reported on both sides of a record, points are combined to determine position on the chart. In such a case, both sides are listed in bold type, the leading side on top.

This Week		Last Week	Weeks on Chart
1.	**CHERRY PINK AND APPLE BLOSSOM WHITE** (ASCAP)—P. Prado — Marie Elena Rumba (ASCAP)—Vic 20-5965	1	11
2.	**UNCHAINED MELODY** (ASCAP)—L. Baxter — Medic (ASCAP)—Cap 3055	4	6
3.	**DANCE WITH ME, HENRY** (BMI)—G. Gibbs — Every Road Must Have a Turning (BMI)—Mercury 70572	3	23
4.	**BALLAD OF DAVY CROCKETT** (BMI)—B. Hayes — Farewell (BMI)—Cadence 1256	2	12
5.	**UNCHAINED MELODY** (ASCAP)—A. Hibbler — Daybreak (ASCAP)—Dec 29441	6	6
6.	**BALLAD OF DAVY CROCKETT** (BMI)—F. Parker — I Gave My Love (BMI)—Col 40449	7	10
7.	**BALLAD OF DAVY CROCKETT** (BMI)—Tennessee Ernie Ford — Farewell (BMI)—Cap 3058	8	9
8.	**CRAZY OTTO MEDLEY** (ASCAP)—J. Maddox — Humoresque (BMI)—Dot 15325	5	15
9.	**UNCHAINED MELODY** (ASCAP)—R. Hamilton — From Here to Eternity (ASCAP)—Epic 9102	12	4
10.	**DARLING JE VOUS AIME BEAUCOUP** (ASCAP)—Nat (King) Cole / **SAND AND THE SEA** (BMI)—Cap 3027	10	11
11.	**HONEY BABE** (ASCAP)—A. Mooney — No Regrets (ASCAP)—M-G-M 11900	17	4
12.	**TWEEDLE DEE** (BMI)—G. Gibbs — You're Wrong, All Wrong (ASCAP)—Mercury 70517	9	16
13.	**WHATEVER LOLA WANTS** (ASCAP)—S. Vaughan — Oh Yeah (ASCAP)—Mercury 70595	15	4
14.	**DON'T BE ANGRY** (BMI)—Crew Cuts / **CHOP CHOP BOOM** (BMI)—Mercury 70597	18	3
15.	**BREEZE AND I** (BMI)—C. Valente — Jalousie (ASCAP)—Dec 29467	13	6
16.	**TWO HEARTS** (BMI)—P. Boone — Tra-La-La—Dot 15338	19	7
17.	**MELODY OF LOVE** (ASCAP)—B. Vaughn — Joy Ride (ASCAP)—Dot 15247	11	23
18.	**IT'S A SIN TO TELL A LIE** (ASCAP)—S. Smith & the Redheads — My Baby Just Cares for Me—Epic 9093	22	7
19.	**HOW IMPORTANT CAN IT BE?** (ASCAP)—J. James — This Is My Confession (ASCAP)—M-G-M 11919	16	13
20.	**BLOSSOM FELL** (ASCAP)—Nat (King) Cole — If I May (BMI)—Cap 3095	27	2
21.	**PLAY ME HEARTS AND FLOWERS** (ASCAP)—J. Desmond — I'm So Ashamed (ASCAP)—Coral 61379	21	8
22.	**ROCK AROUND THE CLOCK** (ASCAP)—B. Haley — Thirteen Women (BMI)—Dec 29124	—	1
23.	**SINCERELY** (BMI)—McGuire Sisters — No More (BMI)—Coral 61323	14	19
23.	**OPEN UP YOUR HEART** (BMI)—Cowboy Church Sunday School — The Lord Is Counting on You (BMI)—Dec 29367	20	20
25.	**LEARNIN' THE BLUES** (ASCAP)—F. Sinatra — If I Had Three Wishes (ASCAP)—Cap 3102	—	1
26.	**MOST OF ALL** (BMI)—D. Cornell — Door Is Still Open (BMI)—Coral 61393	—	1
27.	**MELODY OF LOVE** (ASCAP)—Four Aces — There's a Tavern in the Town (ASCAP)—Dec 29395	23	17
28.	**DON'T BE ANGRY** (BMI)—N. Brown — It's Really You (BMI)—Savoy 1155	25	3
29.	**UNCHAINED MELODY** (ASCAP)—J. Valli — Tomorrow—Vic 20-6078	—	1
30.	**BALLAD OF DAVY CROCKETT** (BMI)—W. Schumann — Let's Make Up—Vic 20-6041	29	2

• This Week's Best Buys

According to sales reports in key markets, the following recent releases are recommended for extra profits:

SOMETHING'S GOTTA GIVE (Robbins, ASCAP)—The McGuire Sisters—Coral 61423

The generally quiet market conditions that have made it difficult for many recently released disks to get off the ground quickly have not had much effect on this record. Strong sales reports were returned from most parts of the country, including Philadelphia, Baltimore, Chicago, Milwaukee and St. Louis. It also is doing well in Boston, Cleveland, Nashville and Durham. Flip is "Rhythm 'n' Blues" (Tee-Kay, BMI). A previous Billboard "Spotlight" pick.

ROLLIN' STONE (Excellorec, BMI)—The Fontaine Sisters—Dot 15370

The immediate pick-up of this record shows solid dealer and operator confidence. Good and strong sales were indicated in Boston, Philadelphia, Baltimore, Buffalo, Pittsburgh, Chicago, Atlanta and St. Louis. While "Rollin' Stone" is the preferred side in the majority of territories, several reported good action on the flip "Playmates" (Santly-Joy, ASCAP). A previous Billboard "Spotlight" pick.

• Most Played in Juke Boxes

For survey week ending May 4

RECORDS are ranked in order of the greatest number of plays in juke boxes thruout the country, as determined by The Billboard's weekly survey of the nation's juke box operators. When significant play is reported on both sides of a record, points are combined to determine position on the chart. In such a case, both sides are listed in bold type, the leading side on top.

This Week		Last Week	Weeks on Chart
1.	**DANCE WITH ME HENRY** (BMI)—G. Gibbs — Every Road Must Have a Turning (BMI)—Mercury 70572	3	7
2.	**BALLAD OF DAVY CROCKETT** (BMI)—B. Hayes — Farewell (BMI)—Cadence 1256	1	10
3.	**CHERRY PINK AND APPLE BLOSSOM WHITE** (ASCAP)—P. Prado — Marie Elena Rumba (ASCAP)—Vic 20-5965	4	6
4.	**CRAZY OTTO MEDLEY** (ASCAP)—J. Maddox — Humoresque (BMI)—Dot 15325	2	13
5.	**BALLAD OF DAVY CROCKETT** (BMI)—Tennessee Ernie — Farewell (BMI)—Cap 3058	6	5
6.	**SINCERELY** (BMI)—McGuire Sisters — No More (BMI)—Coral 61323	5	17
7.	**MELODY OF LOVE** (ASCAP)—Four Aces — There's a Tavern in the Town (ASCAP)—Dec 29395	10	18
7.	**UNCHAINED MELODY** (ASCAP)—A. Hibbler — Daybreak (ASCAP)—Dec 29441	11	3
9.	**HOW IMPORTANT CAN IT BE?** (ASCAP)—J. James — This Is My Confession (ASCAP)—M-G-M 11919	7	12
10.	**MELODY OF LOVE** (ASCAP)—B. Vaughn — Joy Ride (ASCAP)—Dot 15247	9	22
11.	**PLAY ME HEARTS AND FLOWERS** (ASCAP)—J. Desmond — I'm So Ashamed (ASCAP)—Coral 61379	13	6
12.	**TWEEDLE DEE** (BMI)—G. Gibbs — You're Wrong, All Wrong (ASCAP)—Mercury 70517	7	14
13.	**UNCHAINED MELODY** (ASCAP)—R. Hamilton — From Here to Eternity (ASCAP)—Epic 9102	18	2
14.	**WHATEVER LOLA WANTS** (ASCAP)—S. Vaughan — Oh, Yeah (ASCAP)—Mercury 70595	—	1
15.	**UNCHAINED MELODY** (ASCAP)—L. Baxter — Medic (ASCAP)—Cap 3055	14	2
15.	**IT MAY SOUND SILLY** (BMI)—McGuire Sisters — Doesn't Anybody Love Me? (ASCAP)—Coral 61369	14	5
17.	**CHERRY PINK AND APPLE BLOSSOM WHITE** (ASCAP)—A. Dale — I'm Sincere—Coral 61373	14	2
18.	**DARLING JE VOUS AIME BEAUCOUP** (ASCAP)—Nat (King) Cole — Sand and the Sea (BMI)—Cap 3027	14	20
19.	**TWO HEARTS** (BMI)—P. Boone — Tra-La-La—Dot 15338	20	5
19.	**PLANTATION BOOGIE** (BMI)—L. Dee — Birth of the Blues (ASCAP)—Dec 29360	—	1

• Most Played by Jockeys

For survey week ending May 4

SIDES are ranked in order of the greatest number of plays on disk jockey radio shows thruout the country. Results are based on The Billboard's weekly survey among the nation's disk jockeys. The reverse side of each record is also listed.

This Week		Last Week	Weeks on Chart
1.	**UNCHAINED MELODY**—L. Baxter — Medic (ASCAP)—Cap 3055	2	6
2.	**CHERRY PINK AND APPLE BLOSSOM WHITE**—P. Prado — Marie Elena Rumba (ASCAP)—Vic 20-5965	4	5
3.	**DANCE WITH ME HENRY**—G. Gibbs — Every Road Must Have a Turning (BMI)—Mercury 70572	3	6
4.	**BALLAD OF DAVY CROCKETT**—B. Hayes — Farewell (BMI)—Cadence 1256	1	10
5.	**UNCHAINED MELODY**—A. Hibbler — Daybreak (ASCAP)—Dec 29441	5	4
6.	**PLAY ME HEARTS AND FLOWERS**—J. Desmond — I'm So Ashamed (ASCAP)—Coral 61379	8	7
7.	**WHATEVER LOLA WANTS**—S. Vaughan — Oh Yeah (ASCAP)—Mercury 70595	16	3
8.	**BREEZE AND I**—C. Valente — Jalousie (BMI)—Dec 29467	14	4
9.	**BALLAD OF DAVY CROCKETT**—Tennessee Ernie — Farewell (BMI)—Cap 3058	7	8
10.	**BALLAD OF DAVY CROCKETT**—F. Parker — I Gave My Love (BMI)—Col 40449	12	6
11.	**UNCHAINED MELODY**—R. Hamilton — From Here to Eternity (ASCAP)—Epic 9102	18	2
12.	**SINCERELY**—McGuire Sisters — No More (BMI)—Coral 61323	6	18
13.	**HOW IMPORTANT CAN IT BE?**—J. James — This Is My Confession (ASCAP)—M-G-M 11919	9	12
14.	**MELODY OF LOVE**—B. Vaughn — Joy Ride (ASCAP)—Dot 15247	11	18
15.	**LEARNING THE BLUES**—F. Sinatra — If I Had Three Wishes (ASCAP)—Cap 3102	19	2
16.	**HEART**—E. Fisher — Near to You (ASCAP)—Vic 20-6097	—	1
17.	**CRAZY OTTO MEDLEY**—J. Maddox — Humoresque (ASCAP)—Dot 15325	13	14
18.	**DARLING JE VOUS AIME BEAUCOUP**—Nat (King) Cole — Sand and the Sea (ASCAP)—Cap 3027	17	11
19.	**BLOSSOM FELL**—Nat (King) Cole — If I May (ASCAP)—Cap 3095	—	1
20.	**WHATEVER LOLA WANTS**—D Shore — Church Twice on Sunday (ASCAP)—Vic 20-6077	—	1

The Billboard Music Popularity Charts — POPULAR RECORDS

• Best Sellers in Stores

For survey week ending May 11

RECORDS are ranked in order of their current national selling importance at the retail level, as determined by The Billboard's weekly survey of the top volume dealers in every important market area. When significant action is reported on both sides of a record, points are combined to determine position on the chart. In such a case, both sides are listed in bold type, the leading side on top.

This Week		Last Week	Weeks on Chart
1.	**CHERRY PINK AND APPLE BLOSSOM WHITE** (ASCAP)—P. Prado Marie Elena Rumba (ASCAP)—Vic 20-5965	1	12
2.	**DANCE WITH ME, HENRY** (BMI)—G. Gibbs Every Road Must Have a Turning (BMI)—Mercury 70572	3	9
3.	**UNCHAINED MELODY** (ASCAP)—L. Baxter Medic (ASCAP)—Cap 3055	2	7
4.	**BALLAD OF DAVY CROCKETT** (BMI)—B. Hayes Farewell (BMI)—Cadence 1256	4	13
5.	**BALLAD OF DAVY CROCKETT** (BMI)—F. Parker I Gave My Love (BMI)—Col 40449	6	11
6.	**UNCHAINED MELODY** (ASCAP)—A. Hibbler Daybreak (ASCAP)—Dec 29441	5	7
7.	**BALLAD OF DAVY CROCKETT** (BMI)—Tennessee Ernie Ford Farewell (BMI)—Cap 3058	7	10
8.	**CRAZY OTTO MEDLEY** (ASCAP)—J. Maddox Humoresque (BMI)—Dot 15325	8	16
9.	**UNCHAINED MELODY** (ASCAP)—R. Hamilton From Here to Eternity (ASCAP)—Epic 9102	9	5
10.	**HONEY BABE** (ASCAP)—A. Mooney No Regrets (ASCAP)—M-G-M 11900	11	5
11.	**BLOSSOM FELL** (ASCAP)—Nat (King) Cole **IF I MAY** (BMI)—Cap 3095	20	3
12.	**DARLING JE VOUS AIME BEAUCOUP** (ASCAP)—Nat (King) Cole **SAND AND THE SEA** (BMI)—Cap 3027	10	12
12.	**WHATEVER LOLA WANTS** (ASCAP)—S. Vaughan Oh Yeah (ASCAP)—Mercury 70595	13	5
14.	**ROCK AROUND THE CLOCK** (ASCAP)—B. Haley Thirteen Women (BMI)—Dec 29124	22	2
15.	**TWEEDLE DEE** (BMI)—G. Gibbs You're Wrong, All Wrong (ASCAP)—Mercury 70517	12	17
15.	**DON'T BE ANGRY** (BMI)—Crew Cuts **CHOP CHOP BOOM** (BMI)—Mercury 70597	14	4
17.	**BREEZE AND I** (BMI)—C. Valente Jalousie (ASCAP)—Dec 29467	15	7
18.	**MELODY OF LOVE** (ASCAP)—B. Vaughn Joy Ride (ASCAP)—Dot 15247	17	24
19.	**TWO HEARTS** (BMI)—P. Boone Tra-La-La—Dot 15338	16	8
20.	**IT'S A SIN TO TELL A LIE** (ASCAP)—S. Smith & the Redheads My Baby Just Cares for Me—Epic 9093	18	8
21.	**LEARNIN' THE BLUES** (ASCAP)—F. Sinatra If I Had Three Wishes (ASCAP)—Cap 3102	25	2
22.	**MOST OF ALL** (BMI)—D. Cornell **DOOR IS STILL OPEN** (BMI)—Coral 61393	26	2
23.	**HOW IMPORTANT CAN IT BE?**—(ASCAP)—J. James This Is My Confession (ASCAP)—M-G-M 11919	19	14
24.	**HEY, MR. BANJO** (ASCAP)—Sunnysiders Zoom, Zoom, Zoom (ASCAP)—Kapp 113	—	1
25.	**PLAY ME HEARTS AND FLOWERS** (ASCAP)—J. Desmond I'm So Ashamed (ASCAP)—Coral 61379	21	9
26.	**HEART** (ASCAP)—E. Fisher Near to You (ASCAP)—Vic 20-6097	—	1
27.	**DON'T BE ANGRY** (BMI)—N. Brown It's Really You (BMI)—Savoy 1155	28	4
28.	**OPEN UP YOUR HEART** (BMI)—Cowboy Church Sunday School The Lord Is Counting on You (BMI)—Dec 29367	23	21
29.	**PLANTATION BOOGIE** (BMI)—L. Dee Birth of the Blues (ASCAP)—Dec 29360	—	14
30.	**CHERRY PINK AND APPLE BLOSSOM WHITE** (ASCAP)—A. Dale I'm Sincere (BMI)—Coral 61373	—	2
30.	**SINCERELY** (BMI)—McGuire Sisters No More (BMI)—Coral 61323	—	19

• This Week's Best Buys

According to sales reports in key markets, the following recent releases are recommended for extra profits:

JOHNNY'S MEDLEY — Johnny Maddox — Dot 15365

The pianist's latest release is shaping up nicely in quite a few Midwestern markets and is beginning to spill over into adjacent territories. This past week, sales were reported good to strong in Chicago, Milwaukee, Cincinnati, Pittsburgh, Baltimore, Buffalo, Durham, Nashville and St. Louis. Juke box sales generally were excellent. Flip is "The Whistlin' Piano Man" (Randy-Smith, ASCAP). A previous Billboard "Spotlight" pick.

• Most Played in Juke Boxes

For survey week ending May 11

RECORDS are ranked in order of the greatest number of plays in juke boxes thruout the country, as determined by The Billboard's weekly survey of the nation's juke box operators. When significant play is reported on both sides of a record, points are combined to determine position on the chart. In such a case, both sides are listed in bold type, the leading side on top.

This Week		Last Week	Weeks on Chart
1.	**DANCE WITH ME, HENRY** (BMI)—G. Gibbs Every Road Must Have a Turning (BMI)—Mercury 70572	1	8
2.	**CHERRY PINK AND APPLE BLOSSOM WHITE** (ASCAP)—P. Prado Marie Elena Rumba (ASCAP)—Vic 20-5965	3	7
3.	**BALLAD OF DAVY CROCKETT** (BMI)—B. Hayes Farewell (BMI)—Cadence 1256	2	11
4.	**CRAZY OTTO MEDLEY** (ASCAP)—J. Maddox Humoresque (BMI)—Dot 15325	4	14
5.	**BALLAD OF DAVY CROCKETT** (BMI)—Tennessee Ernie Farewell (BMI)—Cap 3058	5	6
6.	**UNCHAINED MELODY** (ASCAP)—L. Baxter Medic (ASCAP)—Cap 3055	15	3
7.	**SINCERELY** (BMI)—McGuire Sisters No More (BMI)—Coral 61323	6	18
7.	**UNCHAINED MELODY** (ASCAP)—A. Hibbler Daybreak (ASCAP)—Dec 29441	7	4
9.	**UNCHAINED MELODY** (ASCAP)—R. Hamilton From Here to Eternity (ASCAP)—Epic 9102	13	3
10.	**HOW IMPORTANT CAN IT BE?** (ASCAP)—J. James This Is My Confession (ASCAP)—M-G-M 11919	9	13
11.	**PLAY ME HEARTS AND FLOWERS** (ASCAP)—J. Desmond I'm So Ashamed (ASCAP)—Coral 61379	11	7
12.	**WHATEVER LOLA WANTS** (ASCAP)—S. Vaughan Oh Yeah (ASCAP)—Mercury 70595	14	2
13.	**MELODY OF LOVE** (ASCAP)—B. Vaughn Joy Ride (ASCAP)—Dot 15247	12	15
13.	**TWEEDLE DEE** (BMI)—G. Gibbs You're Wrong, All Wrong (ASCAP)—Mercury 70517	10	23
15.	**MELODY OF LOVE** (ASCAP)—Four Aces There's a Tavern in the Town (ASCAP)—Dec 29395	7	19
16.	**TWO HEARTS** (BMI)—P. Boone Tra-La-La—Dot 15338	19	6
17.	**IT MAY SOUND SILLY** (BMI)—McGuire Sisters Doesn't Anybody Love Me? (ASCAP) Coral 61369	15	6
17.	**DARLING JE VOUS AIME BEAUCOUP** (ASCAP)—Nat (King) Cole Sand and the Sea (BMI)—Cap 3027	18	21
17.	**HONEY BABE**—(ASCAP)—A. Mooney No Regrets (ASCAP)—M-G-M 11900	—	1
17.	**BOOM BOOM BOOMERANG** (BMI)—DeCastro Sisters Let Your Love Walk In (ASCAP)—Abbott 3003	—	1

• Most Played by Jockeys

For survey week ending May 11

SIDES are ranked in order of the greatest number of plays on disk jockey radio shows thruout the country. Results are based on The Billboard's weekly survey among the nation's disk jockeys. The reverse side of each record is also listed.

This Week		Last Week	Weeks on Chart
1.	**CHERRY PINK AND APPLE BLOSSOM WHITE**—P. Prado Marie Elena Rumba (ASCAP)—Vic 20-5965	2	6
2.	**UNCHAINED MELODY**—L. Baxter Medic (ASCAP)—Cap 3055	1	7
3.	**DANCE WITH ME HENRY**—G. Gibbs Every Road Must Have a Turning (BMI)—Mercury 70572	3	7
4.	**BALLAD OF DAVY CROCKETT**—B. Hayes Farewell (BMI)—Cadence 1256	4	11
5.	**UNCHAINED MELODY**—A. Hibbler Daybreak (ASCAP)—Dec 29441	5	5
6.	**UNCHAINED MELODY**—R. Hamilton From Here to Eternity (ASCAP)—Epic 9102	11	3
7.	**WHATEVER LOLA WANTS**—S. Vaughan Oh Yeah (BMI)—Mercury 70595	7	4
8.	**BREEZE AND I**—C. Valente Jalousie (BMI)—Dec 29467	8	5
9.	**PLAY ME HEARTS AND FLOWERS**—J. Desmond I'm So Ashamed (ASCAP)—Coral 61379	6	8
10.	**LEARNIN' THE BLUES**—F. Sinatra If I Had Three Wishes (ASCAP)—Cap 3102	15	3
11.	**BALLAD OF DAVY CROCKETT**—Tennessee Ernie Farewell (BMI)—Cap 3058	9	9
12.	**BLOSSOM FELL**—Nat (King) Cole If I May (ASCAP)—Cap 3095	19	2
13.	**HEART**—E. Fisher Near to You (ASCAP)—Vic 20-6097	16	2
14.	**MOST OF ALL**—D. Cornell Door Is Still Open (BMI)—Coral 61393	—	1
15.	**DARLING JE VOUS AIME BEAUCOUP**—Nat (King) Cole Sand and the Sea (ASCAP)—Cap 3027	18	12
16.	**SINCERELY**—McGuire Sisters No More (BMI)—Coral 61323	12	19
17.	**BALLAD OF DAVY CROCKETT**—F. Parker I Gave My Love (BMI)—Col 40449	10	7
18.	**MELODY OF LOVE**—B. Vaughn Joy Ride (ASCAP)—Dot 15247	14	19
19.	**CHERRY PINK AND APPLE BLOSSOM WHITE**—A. Dale I'm Sincere (ASCAP)—Coral 61373	—	2
20.	**WHATEVER LOLA WANTS**—D. Shore Church Twice on Sunday (ASCAP)—Vic 20-6077	20	2

The Billboard Music Popularity Charts POPULAR RECORDS

• Best Sellers in Stores

For survey week ending May 18

RECORDS are ranked in order of their current national selling importance at the retail level, as determined by The Billboard's weekly survey of the top volume dealers in every important market area. When significant action is reported on both sides of a record, points are combined to determine position on the chart. In such a case, both sides are listed in bold type, the leading side on top.

This Week		Last Week	Weeks on Chart
1.	CHERRY PINK AND APPLE BLOSSOM WHITE (ASCAP)—P. Prado Marie Elena Rumba (ASCAP)—Vic 20-5965	1	13
2.	UNCHAINED MELODY (ASCAP)—L. Baxter Medic (ASCAP)—Cap 3055	3	8
3.	DANCE WITH ME, HENRY (BMI)—G. Gibbs Every Road Must Have a Turning (BMI)—Mercury 70572	2	10
4.	BALLAD OF DAVY CROCKETT (BMI)—B. Hayes Farewell (BMI)—Cadence 1256	4	14
5.	UNCHAINED MELODY (ASCAP)—A. Hibbler Daybreak (ASCAP)—Dec 29441	6	8
6.	BALLAD OF DAVY CROCKETT (BMI)—F. Parker I Gave My Love (BMI)—Col 40449	5	12
7.	BALLAD OF DAVY CROCKETT (BMI)—Tennessee Ernie Ford Farewell (BMI)—Cap 3058	7	11
8.	BLOSSOM FELL (ASCAP)—Nat (King) Cole IF I MAY (BMI)—Cap 3095	11	4
9.	UNCHAINED MELODY (ASCAP)—R. Hamilton From Here to Eternity (ASCAP)—Epic 9102	9	6
10.	ROCK AROUND THE CLOCK (ASCAP)—B. Haley Thirteen Women (BMI)—Dec 29124	14	3
11.	HONEY BABE (ASCAP)—A. Mooney No Regrets (ASCAP)—M-G-M 11900	10	6
12.	CRAZY OTTO MEDLEY (ASCAP)—J. Maddox Humoresque (BMI)—Dot 15325	8	17
13.	WHATEVER LOLA WANTS (ASCAP) S. Vaughan Oh, Yeah (ASCAP)—Mercury 70595	12	6
14.	DARLING JE VOUS AIME BEAUCOUP (ASCAP)—Nat (King) Cole SAND AND THE SEA (BMI)—Cap 3027	12	13
15.	BREEZE AND I (BMI)—C. Valente Jalousie (ASCAP)—Dec 29467	17	8
16.	LEARNIN' THE BLUES (ASCAP)—F. Sinatra If I Had Three Wishes (ASCAP)—Cap 3102	21	3
17.	TWEEDLE DEE (BMI)—G. Gibbs You're Wrong, All Wrong (ASCAP)—Mercury 70517	15	18
17.	DON'T BE ANGRY (BMI)—Crew Cuts CHOP CHOP BOOM (BMI)—Mercury 70597	15	5
19.	IT'S A SIN TO TELL A LIE (ASCAP)—S. Smith & The Redheads My Baby Just Cares for Me—Epic 9093	20	9
20.	MOST OF ALL (BMI)—D. Cornell DOOR IS STILL OPEN (BMI)—Coral 61393	22	3
21.	HEART (ASCAP)—E. Fisher Near to You (ASCAP)—Vic 20-6097	26	2
21.	HEY, MR. BANJO (ASCAP)—Sunnysiders Zoom, Zoom, Zoom (ASCAP)—Kapp 113	24	2
23.	TWO HEARTS (BMI)—P. Boone Tra-La-La—Dot 15338	19	9
24.	LOVE ME OR LEAVE ME (ASCAP) S. Davis Jr. Something's Gotta Give (ASCAP)—Dec 29484	—	1
25.	MELODY OF LOVE (ASCAP)—B. Vaughn Joy Ride (ASCAP)—Dot 15247	18	25
26.	HOW IMPORTANT CAN IT BE (ASCAP)—J. James This Is My Confession (ASCAP)—M-G-M 11919	23	15
27.	CHERRY PINK AND APPLE BLOSSOM WHITE (ASCAP)—A. Dale I'm Sincere (BMI)—Coral 61373	30	3
28.	PLAY ME HEARTS AND FLOWERS (ASCAP)—J. Desmond I'm So Ashamed (ASCAP)—Coral 61379	25	10
29.	HEART (ASCAP)—Four Aces Sluefoot (ASCAP)—Dec 29476	—	1
30.	BLUE STAR (ASCAP)—F. Sanders My Love's a Gentle Man—Col 40508—BMI	—	1

• This Week's Best Buys

According to sales reports in key markets, the following recent releases are recommended for extra profits:

CHEE CHEE-OO CHEE (Hill & Range, BMI) TWO LOST SOULS (Frank, ASCAP) — Perry Como and Jaye P. Morgan—RCA Victor 6137

The Victor version of the much recorded "Chee Chee-oo Chee" has been profiting from the head start in distribution that it enjoyed in many areas. The Como-Morgan disk has taken a definite lead over its competitors and is now selling well in Philadelphia, Baltimore, Buffalo, Pittsburgh, Chicago, Milwaukee, Detroit, St. Louis, Durham and Atlanta. Action is primarily on "Chee Chee-oo Chee," but with some significant reports on the flip as well. A previous Billboard "Spotlight" pick.

BLUE STAR (Chappell, ASCAP)—Felicia Sanders—Columbia 40508

This vocal version of the "Medic" theme has begun kicking up a lot of action in widely scattered territories. New Orleans, Denver and Kansas City are currently reporting it in their top ten, and the combined national reports place the record in the No. 30 position of the national retail chart. Dealers and operators not yet on this disk ought to be aware of the untapped potential here. Flip is "My Love's a Gentle Man" (Montauk, BMI)

SMACK DAB IN THE MIDDLE (Roosevelt, BMI)—Mills Brothers—Decca 29511

With "Opus One" still a good, steady seller, this more recent release is coming up nicely, too. Currently on the Dallas-Fort Worth chart, the disk is also showing good sales in Los Angeles, St. Louis, Nashville, Charlotte, Detroit, Milwaukee, Cleveland, Pittsburgh, Buffalo, Baltimore and Philadelphia. Flip is "Kiss Me and Kill Me With Love" (Chappell, ASCAP). A previous Billboard "Spotlight" pick.

• Most Played in Juke Boxes

For survey week ending May 18

RECORDS are ranked in order of the greatest number of plays in juke boxes thruout the country, as determined by The Billboard's weekly survey of the nation's juke box operators. When significant play is reported on both sides of a record, points are combined to determine position on the chart. In such a case, both sides are listed in bold type, the leading side on top.

This Week		Last Week	Weeks on Chart
1.	DANCE WITH ME, HENRY (BMI)—G. Gibbs Every Road Must Have a Turning (BMI)—Mercury 70572	1	9
2.	CHERRY PINK AND APPLE BLOSSOM WHITE (ASCAP)—P. Prado Marie Elena Rumba (ASCAP)—Vic 20-5965	2	8
3.	BALLAD OF DAVY CROCKETT (BMI)—B. Hayes Farewell (BMI)—Cadence 1256	3	12
4.	CRAZY OTTO MEDLEY (ASCAP)—J. Maddox Humoresque (BMI)—Dot 15325	4	15
5.	BALLAD OF DAVY CROCKETT (BMI)—Tennessee Ernie Farewell (BMI)—Cap 3058	5	7
6.	UNCHAINED MELODY (ASCAP)—L. Baxter Medic (ASCAP)—Cap 3055	6	4
7.	UNCHAINED MELODY (ASCAP)—A. Hibbler Daybreak (ASCAP)—Dec 29441	7	5
8.	UNCHAINED MELODY (ASCAP)—R. Hamilton From Here to Eternity (ASCAP)—Epic 9102	9	4
9.	SINCERELY (BMI)—McGuire Sisters No More (BMI)—Coral 61323	7	19
10.	WHATEVER LOLA WANTS (ASCAP)—S. Vaughan Oh, Yeah (ASCAP)—Mercury 70595	12	3
11.	HOW IMPORTANT CAN IT BE? (ASCAP)—J. James This Is My Confession (ASCAP)—M-G-M 11919	10	14
12.	BLOSSOM FELL (ASCAP)—Nat (King) Cole If I May (BMI)—Cap 3095	—	1
13.	TWEEDLE DEE (BMI)—G. Gibbs You're Wrong, All Wrong (ASCAP)—Mercury 70517	13	24
14.	MELODY OF LOVE (ASCAP)—Four Aces There's a Tavern in the Town (ASCAP)—Dec 29395	15	20
14.	PLAY ME HEARTS AND FLOWERS (ASCAP)—J. Desmond I'm So Ashamed (ASCAP)—Coral 61379	11	8
14.	HONEY BABE (ASCAP)—A. Mooney No Regrets (ASCAP)—M-G-M 11900	17	2
17.	CHERRY PINK AND APPLE BLOSSOM WHITE (ASCAP)—A. Dale I'm Sincere—Coral 61373	—	3
17.	HEY, MR. BANJO (ASCAP)—Sunnysiders Zoom, Zoom, Zoom (ASCAP)—Kapp 113	—	1
19.	MELODY OF LOVE (ASCAP)—B. Vaughn Joy Ride (ASCAP)—Dot 15247	13	16
20.	BOOM BOOM BOOMERANG (BMI)—DeCastro Sisters Let Your Love Walk In (ASCAP)—Abbott 3003	17	2
20.	IT'S A SIN TO TELL A LIE (ASCAP)—S. Smith & The Redheads My Baby Just Cares for Me—Epic 9093	—	1

• Most Played by Jockeys

For survey week ending May 18

SIDES are ranked in order of the greatest number of plays on disk jockey radio shows thruout the country. Results are based on The Billboard's weekly survey among the nation's disk jockeys. The reverse side of each record is also listed.

This Week		Last Week	Weeks on Chart
1.	CHERRY PINK AND APPLE BLOSSOM WHITE—P. Prado Marie Elena Rumba (ASCAP)—Vic 20-5965	1	7
2.	UNCHAINED MELODY—L. Baxter Medic (ASCAP)—Cap 3055	2	8
3.	DANCE WITH ME, HENRY—G. Gibbs Every Road Must Have a Turning (BMI)—Mercury 70572	3	8
4.	UNCHAINED MELODY—A. Hibbler Daybreak (ASCAP)—Dec 29441	5	6
5.	BALLAD OF DAVY CROCKETT—B. Hayes Farewell (BMI)—Cadence 1256	4	12
6.	WHATEVER LOLA WANTS—S. Vaughan Oh, Yeah (BMI)—Mercury 70595	7	5
7.	UNCHAINED MELODY—R. Hamilton From Here to Eternity (ASCAP)—Epic 9102	6	4
8.	BREEZE AND I—C. Valente Jalousie (BMI)—Dec 29467	8	6
9.	HEART—E. Fisher Near to You (ASCAP)—Vic 20-6097	13	3
10.	LEARNIN' THE BLUES—F. Sinatra If I Had Three Wishes (ASCAP)—Cap 3102	10	4
11.	BLOSSOM FELL—Nat (King) Cole If I May (ASCAP)—Cap 3095	12	3
12.	WHATEVER LOLA WANTS—D. Shore Church Twice on Sunday (ASCAP)—Vic 20-6077	20	3
13.	PLAY ME HEARTS AND FLOWERS—J. Desmond I'm So Ashamed (ASCAP)—Coral 61379	9	9
14.	DON'T BE ANGRY—Crew Cuts Chop Chop Boom (BMI)—Mercury 70597	—	1
15.	BALLAD OF DAVY CROCKETT—Tennessee Ernie Farewell (BMI)—Cap 3058	11	10
16.	BALLAD OF DAVY CROCKETT—W. Schumann Let's Make Up (BMI)—Vic 20-6014	—	6
17.	BALLAD OF DAVY CROCKETT—F. Parker I Gave My Love (BMI)—Col 40449	17	8
18.	HEART—Four Aces Sluefoot (ASCAP)—Dec 29476	—	1
19.	HOW IMPORTANT CAN IT BE—J. James This Is My Confession (ASCAP)—M-G-M 11919	—	13
20.	ROCK AROUND THE CLOCK—B. Haley Thirteen Women (ASCAP)—Dec 29124	—	1

The Billboard Music Popularity Charts — POPULAR RECORDS

• Best Sellers in Stores

For survey week ending May 25

RECORDS are ranked in order of their current national selling importance at the retail level, as determined by The Billboard's weekly survey of the top volume dealers in every important market area. When significant action is reported on both sides of a record, points are combined to determine position on the chart. In such a case, both sides are listed in bold type, the leading side on top.

This Week	Record	Last Week	Weeks on Chart
1.	**CHERRY PINK AND APPLE BLOSSOM WHITE** (ASCAP)—P. Prado Marie Elena Rumba (ASCAP)—Vic 20-5965	1	14
2.	**UNCHAINED MELODY** (ASCAP)—L. Baxter Medic (ASCAP)—Cap 3055	2	9
3.	**DANCE WITH ME HENRY** (BMI)—G. Gibbs Every Road Must Have a Turning (BMI)—Mercury 70572	3	11
4.	**BALLAD OF DAVY CROCKETT** (BMI)—B. Hayes Farewell (BMI)—Cadence 1256	4	15
5.	**UNCHAINED MELODY** (ASCAP)—A. Hibbler Daybreak (ASCAP)—Dec 29441	5	9
6.	**BLOSSOM FELL** (ASCAP)—Nat (King) Cole **IF I MAY** (BMI)—Cap 3095	8	5
7.	**BALLAD OF DAVY CROCKETT** (BMI)—F. Parker I Gave My Love (BMI)—Col 40449	6	13
8.	**HONEY BABE** (ASCAP)—A. Mooney No Regrets (ASCAP)—M-G-M 11900	11	7
9.	**ROCK AROUND THE CLOCK** (ASCAP)—B. Haley Thirteen Women (BMI)—Dec 29124	10	4
10.	**LEARNIN' THE BLUES** (ASCAP)—F. Sinatra If I Had Three Wishes (ASCAP)—Cap 3102	16	4
11.	**BALLAD OF DAVY CROCKETT** (BMI)—Tennessee Ernie Ford Farewell (BMI)—Cap 3058	7	12
12.	**UNCHAINED MELODY** (ASCAP)—R. Hamilton From Here to Eternity (ASCAP)—Epic 9102	9	7
13.	**WHATEVER LOLA WANTS** (ASCAP)—S. Vaughan Oh, Yeah (ASCAP)—Mercury 70595	13	7
14.	**BREEZE AND I** (BMI)—C. Valente Jalousie (ASCAP)—Dec 29467	15	9
15.	**DON'T BE ANGRY** (BMI)—Crew Cuts **CHOP CHOP BOOM** (BMI)—Mercury 70597	17	6
16.	**LOVE ME OR LEAVE ME** (ASCAP)—S. Davis Jr. **SOMETHING'S GOTTA GIVE** (ASCAP)—Dec 29484	24	2
17.	**IT'S A SIN TO TELL A LIE** (ASCAP)—S. Smith & the Redheads My Baby Just Cares for Me—Epic 9093	19	10
18.	**DARLING JE VOUS AIME BEAUCOUP** (ASCAP)—Nat (King) Cole **SAND AND THE SEA** (BMI)—Cap 3027	14	14
19.	**HEART** (ASCAP)—E. Fisher Near to You (ASCAP)—Vic 20-6097	21	3
20.	**HEY, MR. BANJO** (ASCAP)—Sunnysiders Zoom, Zoom, Zoom (ASCAP)—Kapp 113	21	3
21.	**MOST OF ALL** (BMI)—D. Cornell Door Is Still Open (BMI)—Coral 61393	20	4
22.	**CRAZY OTTO MEDLEY** (ASCAP)—J. Maddox Humoresque (BMI)—Dot 15325	12	18
23.	**SOMETHING'S GOTTA GIVE** (ASCAP)—McGuire Sisters Rhythm 'n' Blues (BMI)—Coral 61423	—	1
24.	**HEART** (ASCAP)—Four Aces Sluefoot (ASCAP)—Dec 29476	29	2
25.	**TWO HEARTS** (BMI)—P. Boone Tra-La-La—Dot 15338	23	10
26.	**HARD TO GET** (ASCAP)—G. MacKenzie Boston Fancy (BMI)—X 0137	—	1
27.	**TWEEDLE DEE** (BMI)—G. Gibbs You're Wrong, All Wrong (ASCAP)—Mercury 70517	17	19
28.	**CHERRY PINK AND APPLE BLOSSOM WHITE** (ASCAP)—A. Dale I'm Sincere (BMI)—Coral 61373	27	4
29.	**MELODY OF LOVE** (ASCAP)—B. Vaughn Joy Ride (ASCAP)—Dot 15247	25	26
29.	**BLUE STAR** (ASCAP)—F. Sanders My Love's a Gentle Man (BMI)—Col 40508	30	2

• This Week's Best Buys

According to sales reports in key markets, the following recent releases are recommended for extra profits:

HARD TO GET (Witmark, ASCAP) — **Gisele MacKenzie—"X" 137**

In the most recent crop of releases, this has been easily one of the fastest moving. During the short time that it has been available, it has established itself firmly in Boston, New York, Buffalo, Pittsburgh, Cleveland, St. Louis, Kansas City, Milwaukee, Chicago, Atlanta and Durham. It is clear that the singer has a good possibility of going very high on the charts with this one. Flip is "Boston Fancy" (Sheldon, BMI). A previous Billboard "Spotlight" pick.

STORY UNTOLD (Rush, BMI) — **Crew Cuts — Mercury 70634**

Top rhythm and blues material still seems to be the key to easy success for this group. The sales pattern of this disk is falling into the familiar groove of other recent Crew Cuts' releases. In the past two weeks, the record has been reported good and strong in Los Angeles, St. Louis, Chicago, Milwaukee, Detroit, Cleveland, Pittsburgh, Buffalo, New York and Boston. Some territories also report excellent sales on the flip side, "Carmen's Boogie" (Broadcast, BMI). A previous Billboard "Spotlight" pick.

• Most Played in Juke Boxes

For survey week ending May 25

RECORDS are ranked in order of the greatest number of plays in juke boxes thruout the country, as determined by The Billboard's weekly survey of the nation's juke box operators. When significant play is reported on both sides of a record, points are combined to determine position on the chart. In such a case, both sides are listed in bold type, the leading side on top.

This Week	Record	Last Week	Weeks on Chart
1.	**CHERRY PINK AND APPLE BLOSSOM WHITE** (ASCAP)—P. Prado Marie Elena Rumba (ASCAP)—Vic 20-5965	2	9
2.	**DANCE WITH ME HENRY** (BMI)—G. Gibbs Every Road Must Have a Turning (BMI)—Mercury 70572	1	10
3.	**BALLAD OF DAVY CROCKETT** (BMI)—B. Hayes Farewell (BMI)—Cadence 1256	3	13
4.	**UNCHAINED MELODY** (ASCAP)—A. Hibbler Daybreak (ASCAP)—Dec 29441	7	6
5.	**BALLAD OF DAVY CROCKETT** (BMI)—Tennessee Ernie Farewell (BMI)—Cap 3058	5	8
6.	**UNCHAINED MELODY** (ASCAP)—L. Baxter Medic (ASCAP)—Cap 3055	6	5
7.	**CRAZY OTTO MEDLEY** (ASCAP)—J. Maddox Humoresque (BMI)—Dot 15325	4	16
8.	**UNCHAINED MELODY** (ASCAP)—R. Hamilton From Here to Eternity (ASCAP)—Epic 9102	8	5
9.	**WHATEVER LOLA WANTS** (ASCAP)—S. Vaughan Oh Yeah (ASCAP)—Mercury 70595	10	4
10.	**TWEEDLE DEE** (BMI)—G. Gibbs You're Wrong, All Wrong (ASCAP)—Mercury 70517	13	25
11.	**SINCERELY** (BMI)—McGuire Sisters No More (BMI)—Coral 61323	9	20
12.	**HONEY BABE** (ASCAP)—A. Mooney No Regrets (ASCAP)—M-G-M 11900	14	3
13.	**BLOSSOM FELL** (ASCAP)—Nat (King) Cole If I May (BMI)—Cap 3095	12	2
13.	**HEY, MR. BANJO** (ASCAP)—Sunnysiders Zoom, Zoom, Zoom (ASCAP)—Kapp 113	17	2
15.	**HOW IMPORTANT CAN IT BE?** (ASCAP)—J. James This Is My Confession (ASCAP)—M-G-M 11919	11	15
16.	**PLAY ME HEARTS AND FLOWERS**—J. Desmond I'm So Ashamed (ASCAP)—Coral 61379	14	9
17.	**HEART** (ASCAP)—E. Fisher Near to You (ASCAP)—Vic 20-6097	—	1
18.	**MELODY OF LOVE** (ASCAP)—Four Aces There's a Tavern in the Town (ASCAP)—Dec 29395	14	21
18.	**ROLLIN' STONE** (BMI)—Fontane Sisters Playmates (ASCAP)—Dot 15370	—	1
20.	**CHERRY PINK AND APPLE BLOSSOM WHITE** (ASCAP)—A. Dale I'm Sincere (BMI)—Coral 61373	17	4
20.	**SILVER DOLLAR** (ASCAP)—T. Brewer I Don't Want to Be Lonely Tonight (ASCAP)—Coral 61394	—	1

• Most Played by Jockeys

For survey week ending May 25

SIDES are ranked in order of the greatest number of plays on disk jockey radio shows thruout the country. Results are based on The Billboard's weekly survey among the nation's disk jockeys. The reverse side of each record is also listed.

This Week	Record	Last Week	Weeks on Chart
1.	**UNCHAINED MELODY**—L. Baxter Medic (ASCAP)—Cap 3055	2	9
2.	**CHERRY PINK AND APPLE BLOSSOM WHITE**—P. Prado Marie Elena Rumba (ASCAP)—Vic 20-5965	1	8
3.	**UNCHAINED MELODY**—A. Hibbler Daybreak (ASCAP)—Dec 29441	4	7
4.	**DANCE WITH ME HENRY**—G. Gibbs Every Road Must Have a Turning (BMI)—Mercury 70572	3	9
5.	**BALLAD OF DAVY CROCKETT**—B. Hayes Farewell (BMI)—Cadence 1256	5	13
6.	**LEARNIN' THE BLUES**—F. Sinatra If I Had Three Wishes (ASCAP)—Cap 3102	10	5
7.	**UNCHAINED MELODY**—R. Hamilton From Here to Eternity (ASCAP)—Epic 9102	7	5
8.	**WHATEVER LOLA WANTS**—S. Vaughan Oh Yeah (BMI)—Mercury 70595	6	6
9.	**HEART**—E. Fisher Near to You (ASCAP)—Vic 20-6097	9	4
10.	**BREEZE AND I**—C. Valente Jalousie (BMI)—Dec 29467	8	7
11.	**BALLAD OF DAVY CROCKETT**—Tennessee Ernie Farewell (BMI)—Cap 3058	15	11
12.	**BLOSSOM FELL**—Nat (King) Cole If I May (ASCAP)—Cap 3095	11	4
13.	**BALLAD OF DAVY CROCKETT**—F. Parker I Gave My Love (BMI)—Col 40449	17	9
14.	**PLAY ME HEARTS AND FLOWERS**—J. Desmond I'm So Ashamed (ASCAP)—Coral 61379	13	10
15.	**IF I MAY**—Nat (King) Cole Blossom Fell (BMI)—Cap 3095	—	1
16.	**ROCK AROUND THE CLOCK**—B. Haley Thirteen Women (ASCAP)—Dec 29124	20	2
16.	**MOST OF ALL**—D. Cornell Door Is Still Open (BMI)—Coral 61393	—	2
18.	**DON'T BE ANGRY**—Crew Cuts Chop, Chop, Boom (BMI)—Mercury 70597	14	2
19.	**CHERRY PINK AND APPLE BLOSSOM WHITE**—A. Dale I'm Sincere (ASCAP)—Coral 61373	—	3
20.	**SOMETHING'S GOTTA GIVE**—McGuire Sisters Rhythm 'n' Blues (ASCAP)—Coral 61423	—	1

The Billboard Music Popularity Charts — POPULAR RECORDS

• Best Sellers in Stores

For survey week ending June 1

RECORDS are ranked in order of their current national selling importance at the retail level as determined by The Billboard's weekly survey of the top volume dealers in every important market area. When significant action is reported on both sides of a record, points are combined to determine position on the chart. In such a case, both sides are listed in bold type, the leading side on top.

This Week		Last Week	Weeks on Chart
1.	CHERRY PINK AND APPLE BLOSSOM WHITE (ASCAP)—P. Prado Marie Elena Rumba (ASCAP)—Vic 20-5965	1	15
2.	UNCHAINED MELODY (ASCAP)—L. Baxter Medic (ASCAP)—Cap 3055	2	10
3.	DANCE WITH ME, HENRY (BMI)—G. Gibbs Every Road Must Have a Turning (BMI)—Mercury 70572	3	12
4.	BLOSSOM FELL (ASCAP)—Nat (King) Cole IF I MAY (BMI)—Cap 3095	6	6
5.	UNCHAINED MELODY (ASCAP)—A. Hibbler Daybreak (ASCAP)—Dec 29441	5	10
6.	BALLAD OF DAVY CROCKETT (BMI)—B. Hayes Farewell (BMI)—Cadence 1256	4	16
7.	ROCK AROUND THE CLOCK (ASCAP)—B. Haley Thirteen Women (BMI)—Dec 29124	9	5
8.	HONEY BABE (ASCAP)—A. Mooney No Regrets (ASCAP)—M-G-M 11900	8	8
9.	LEARNIN' THE BLUES (ASCAP)—F. Sinatra If I Had Three Wishes (ASCAP)—Cap 3102	10	5
10.	BALLAD OF DAVY CROCKETT (BMI)—F. Parker I Gave My Love (BMI)—Col 40449	7	14
11.	BALLAD OF DAVY CROCKETT (BMI)—Tennessee Ernie Ford Farewell (BMI)—Cap 3058	11	13
11.	UNCHAINED MELODY (ASCAP)—R. Hamilton From Here to Eternity (ASCAP)—Epic 9102	12	8
13.	WHATEVER LOLA WANTS (ASCAP)—S. Vaughan Oh, Yeah (ASCAP)—Mercury 70595	13	8
14.	BREEZE AND I (BMI)—C. Valente Jalousie (ASCAP)—Dec 29467	14	10
15.	LOVE ME OR LEAVE ME (ASCAP)—S. Davis Jr. SOMETHING'S GOTTA GIVE (ASCAP)—Dec 29484	16	3
16.	IT'S A SIN TO TELL A LIE (ASCAP)—S. Smith & the Redheads My Baby Just Cares for Me—Epic 9093	17	11
17.	DON'T BE ANGRY (BMI)—Crew Cuts CHOP CHOP BOOM (BMI)—Mercury 70597	15	7
18.	HEART (ASCAP)—E. Fisher Near to You (ASCAP)—Vic 20-6097	19	4
19.	SOMETHING'S GOTTA GIVE (ASCAP)—McGuire Sisters Rhythm 'n' Blues (BMI)—Coral 61423	23	2
20.	HEY, MR. BANJO (ASCAP)—Sunnysiders Zoom, Zoom, Zoom (ASCAP)—Kapp 113	20	4
21.	MOST OF ALL (BMI)—D. Cornell Door Is Still Open (BMI)—Coral 61393	21	5
22.	DARLING JE VOUS AIME BEAUCOUP (ASCAP)—Nat (King) Cole Sand and the Sea (BMI)—Cap 3027	18	15
23.	HEART (ASCAP)—Four Aces Sluefoot (ASCAP)—Dec 29476	24	3
24.	TWO HEARTS (BMI)—P. Boone Tra-La-La—Dot 15338	25	11
25.	HARD TO GET (ASCAP)—G. MacKenzie Boston Fancy (BMI)—X 0137	26	2
26.	CRAZY OTTO MEDLEY (ASCAP)—J. Maddox Humoresque (BMI)—Dot 15325	22	19
26.	MELODY OF LOVE (ASCAP)—B. Vaughn Joy Ride (ASCAP)—Dot 15247	29	27
28.	CHERRY PINK AND APPLE BLOSSOM WHITE (ASCAP)—A. Dale I'm Sincere (BMI)—Coral 61373	28	5
29.	BLUE STAR (ASCAP)—F. Sanders My Love's a Gentle Man (BMI)—Col 40508	29	3
30.	WHATEVER LOLA WANTS (ASCAP)—D. Shore Church Twice on Sunday (ASCAP)—Vic 20-6077	—	1

• This Week's Best Buys

According to sales reports in key markets, the following recent releases are recommended for extra profits:

SWEET AND GENTLE (Peer, BMI)—Alan Dale—Coral 61435

Dale's most recent release has lost little time in gaining a firm hold in the market. New York, Philadelphia, Buffalo, Baltimore, Milwaukee, Detroit and St. Louis are among the areas in which action is reported strong. Good sales reports also were returned from Cleveland, Chicago, Providence and Durham. Flip is "You Still Mean the Same to Me." A previous Billboard "Spotlight" pick.

NOT AS A STRANGER (Maraville, ASCAP)—Frank Sinatra—Capitol 3130

Without the movie from which the theme of this music has been taken having opened, interest in it has already reached an intense pitch. Undoubtedly, it will still go much higher. Sinatra's vocal version is now selling well in Philadelphia, Buffalo, Pittsburgh, Baltimore, Richmond, Durham, Chicago, Milwaukee and St. Louis. Flip is "How Could You Do a Thing Like That to Me?" (United, ASCAP). A previous Billboard "Spotlight pick.

ALABAMA JUBILEE (Remick, ASCAP)—Ferko String Band—Media 1010

Competition on this tune has been rugged, but at this point this disk enjoys a comfortable lead. Appearing on the Detroit territorial chart, it has also been reported a good seller in Boston, Providence, Philadelphia, Buffalo, Baltimore, Chicago, Milwaukee, St. Louis, Durham and Richmond. In some territories, the Art Mooney version is now coming up very fast. On the flip of the Media disk is "Sing a Little Melody" (Eastwick, BMI).

SACRED

HIS HANDS—Tennessee Ernie—Capitol 3135

It is not often that a sacred record makes such a quick and deep impression on both the pop and country markets as this one. In the Carolinas, Atlanta, Richmond and Nashville, the sales response is unusually good for either a regular pop or country disk. It is not just the South, however, that is taking to this record in a big way; New York and Los Angeles are also in the van. Flip is "I'm a Pilgrim." A previous Billboard "Spotlight" pick.

• Most Played in Juke Boxes

For survey week ending June 1

RECORDS are ranked in order of the greatest number of plays in juke boxes thruout the country, as determined by The Billboard's weekly survey of the nation's juke box operators. When significant play is reported on both sides of a record, points are combined to determine position on the chart. In such a case, both sides are listed in bold type, the leading side on top.

This Week		Last Week	Weeks on Chart
1.	CHERRY PINK AND APPLE BLOSSOM WHITE (ASCAP)—P. Prado Marie Elena Rumba (ASCAP)—Vic 20-5965	1	10
2.	DANCE WITH ME HENRY (BMI)—G. Gibbs Every Road Must Have a Turning (BMI)—Mercury 70572	2	11
3.	UNCHAINED MELODY (ASCAP)—L. Baxter Medic (ASCAP)—Cap 3055	6	6
4.	BALLAD OF DAVY CROCKETT (BMI)—B. Hayes Farewell (BMI)—Cadence 1256	3	14
5.	UNCHAINED MELODY (ASCAP)—A. Hibbler Daybreak (ASCAP)—Dec 29441	4	7
6.	UNCHAINED MELODY (ASCAP)—R. Hamilton From Here to Eternity (ASCAP)—Epic 9102	8	6
7.	BALLAD OF DAVY CROCKETT (BMI)—Tennessee Ernie Farewell (BMI)—Cap 3058	5	9
7.	CRAZY OTTO MEDLEY (ASCAP)—J. Maddox Humoresque (BMI)—Dot 15325	7	17
7.	BLOSSOM FELL (ASCAP)—Nat (King) Cole IF I MAY (BMI)—Cap 3095	13	3
10.	HONEY BABE (ASCAP)—A. Mooney No Regrets (ASCAP)—M-G-M 11900	12	4
11.	IT'S A SIN TO TELL A LIE (ASCAP)—S. Smith & the Redheads My Baby Just Cares for Me—Epic 9093	—	2
12.	WHATEVER LOLA WANTS (ASCAP)—S. Vaughan Oh Yeah (ASCAP)—Mercury 70595	9	5
13.	HEY, MR. BANJO (ASCAP)—Sunnysiders Zoom, Zoom, Zoom (ASCAP)—Kapp 113	13	3
14.	TWEEDLE DEE (BMI)—G. Gibbs You're Wrong, All Wrong (ASCAP)—Mercury 70517	10	26
15.	SINCERELY (BMI)—McGuire Sisters No More (BMI)—Coral 61323	11	21
15.	ROLLIN' STONE (BMI)—Fontane Sisters Playmates (ASCAP)—Dot 15370	18	2
17.	PLAY ME HEARTS AND FLOWERS (ASCAP)—J. Desmond I'm So Ashamed (ASCAP)—Coral 61379	16	10
18.	BOOM BOOM BOOMERANG (BMI)—DeCastro Sisters Let Your Love Walk In (ASCAP)—Abbott 3003	—	3
18.	SOMETHING'S GOTTA GIVE (ASCAP)—McGuire Sisters Rhythm 'n' Blues (BMI)—Coral 61423	—	1
20.	HEART (ASCAP)—E. Fisher Near to You (ASCAP)—Vic 20-6097	17	2
20.	HOW IMPORTANT CAN IT BE?—J. James This Is My Confession (ASCAP)—M-G-M 11919	15	16

• Most Played by Jockeys

For survey week ending June 1

SIDES are ranked in order of the greatest number of plays on disk jockey radio shows thruout the country. Results are based on The Billboard's weekly survey among the nation's disk jockeys. The reverse side of each record is also listed.

This Week		Last Week	Weeks on Chart
1.	CHERRY PINK AND APPLE BLOSSOM WHITE—P. Prado Marie Elena Rumba (ASCAP)—Vic 20-5965	2	9
2.	UNCHAINED MELODY—L. Baxter Medic (ASCAP)—Cap 3055	1	10
3.	DANCE WITH ME HENRY—G. Gibbs Every Road Must Have a Turning (BMI)—Mercury 70572	4	10
4.	UNCHAINED MELODY—A. Hibbler Daybreak (ASCAP)—Dec 29441	3	8
5.	LEARNIN' THE BLUES—F. Sinatra If I Had Three Wishes (ASCAP)—Cap 3102	6	6
6.	BLOSSOM FELL—Nat (King) Cole If I May (ASCAP)—Cap 3095	12	5
7.	HEART—E. Fisher Near to You (ASCAP)—Vic 20-6097	9	5
8.	WHATEVER LOLA WANTS—S. Vaughan Oh, Yeah (BMI)—Mercury 70595	8	7
9.	BALLAD OF DAVY CROCKETT—B. Hayes Farewell (BMI)—Cadence 1256	5	14
10.	UNCHAINED MELODY—R. Hamilton From Here to Eternity (ASCAP)—Epic 9102	7	6
11.	BREEZE AND I—C. Valente Jalousie (BMI)—Dec 29467	10	8
12.	ROCK AROUND THE CLOCK—B. Haley Thirteen Women (ASCAP)—Dec 29124	16	3
13.	HEART—Four Aces Sluefoot (ASCAP)—Dec 29476	—	2
14.	SOMETHING'S GOTTA GIVE—McGuire Sisters Rhythm 'n' Blues (ASCAP)—Coral 61423	20	2
15.	BALLAD OF DAVY CROCKETT—F. Parker I Gave My Love (BMI)—Col 40449	13	10
16.	MOST OF ALL—D. Cornell Door Is Still Open (BMI)—Coral 61393	16	3
17.	IF I MAY—Nat (King) Cole Blossom Fell (BMI)—Cap 3095	15	2
18.	HONEY BABE—A. Mooney No Regrets (ASCAP)—M-G-M 11900	—	1
19.	PLAY ME HEARTS AND FLOWERS—J. Desmond I'm So Ashamed (ASCAP)—Coral 61379	14	11
20.	CHEE CHEE OO CHEE—P. Como & J. P. Morgan Two Lost Souls (BMI)—Vic 20-6137	—	1

The Billboard Music Popularity Charts — POPULAR RECORDS

• Best Sellers in Stores

For survey week ending June 8

RECORDS are ranked in order of their current national selling importance at the retail level, as determined by The Billboard's weekly survey of the top volume dealers in every important market area. When significant action is reported on both sides of a record, points are combined to determine position on the chart. In such a case, both sides are listed in bold type, the leading side on top.

This Week	Record	Last Week	Weeks on Chart
1.	**CHERRY PINK AND APPLE BLOSSOM WHITE** (ASCAP)—P. Prado Marie Elena Rumba (ASCAP)—Vic 20-5965	1	16
2.	**UNCHAINED MELODY** (ASCAP)—L. Baxter Medic (ASCAP)—Cap 3055	2	11
3.	**BLOSSOM FELL** (ASCAP)—Nat (King) Cole **IF I MAY** (BMI)—Cap 3095	4	7
4.	**ROCK AROUND THE CLOCK** (ASCAP)—B. Haley Thirteen Women (BMI)—Dec 29124	7	6
5.	**DANCE WITH ME HENRY** (BMI)—G. Gibbs Every Road Must Have a Turning (BMI)—Mercury 70572	3	13
6.	**LEARNIN' THE BLUES** (ASCAP)—F. Sinatra If I Had Three Wishes (ASCAP)—Cap 3102	9	6
7.	**UNCHAINED MELODY** (ASCAP)—A. Hibbler Daybreak (ASCAP)—Dec 29441	5	11
8.	**HONEY BABE** (ASCAP)—A. Mooney No Regrets (ASCAP)—M-G-M 11900	8	9
9.	**BALLAD OF DAVY CROCKETT** (BMI)—B. Hayes Farewell (BMI)—Cadence 1256	6	17
10.	**BALLAD OF DAVY CROCKETT** (BMI)—F. Parker I Gave My Love (BMI)—Col 40449	10	15
11.	**SOMETHING'S GOTTA GIVE** (ASCAP)—McGuire Sisters Rhythm 'n' Blues (BMI)—Coral 61423	19	3
12.	**UNCHAINED MELODY** (ASCAP)—R. Hamilton From Here to Eternity (ASCAP)—Epic 9102	11	9
13.	**IT'S A SIN TO TELL A LIE** (ASCAP)—S. Smith & the Redheads My Baby Just Cares for Me—Epic 9093	16	12
14.	**LOVE ME OR LEAVE ME** (ASCAP)—S. Davis Jr. **SOMETHING'S GOTTA GIVE** (ASCAP)—Dec 29484	15	4
15.	**WHATEVER LOLA WANTS** (ASCAP)—S. Vaughan Oh, Yeah (ASCAP)—Mercury 70595	13	9
16.	**BALLAD OF DAVY CROCKETT** (BMI)—Tennessee Ernie Ford Farewell (BMI)—Cap 3058	11	14
17.	**HEART** (ASCAP)—E. Fisher Near to You (ASCAP)—Vic 20-6097	18	5
18.	**BREEZE AND I** (BMI)—C. Valente Jalousie (ASCAP)—Dec 29467	14	11
19.	**DON'T BE ANGRY** (BMI)—Crew Cuts **CHOP CHOP BOOM** (BMI)—Mercury 70597	17	8
20.	**HEY, MR. BANJO** (ASCAP)—Sunnysiders Zoom, Zoom, Zoom (ASCAP)—Kapp 113	20	5
21.	**HARD TO GET** (ASCAP)—G. MacKenzie Boston Fancy (BMI)—X 0137	25	3
22.	**TWO HEARTS** (BMI)—P. Boone Tra-La-La—Dot 15338	24	12
23.	**ALABAMA JUBILEE** (ASCAP)—Ferko String Band Sing a Little Melody (BMI)—Media 1010	—	1
24.	**DARLING JE VOUS AIME BEAUCOUP** (ASCAP)—Nat (King) Cole Sand and the Sea (BMI)—Cap 3027	22	16
25.	**CHEE CHEE OO CHEE** (BMI)—P. Como & J. P. Morgan Two Lost Souls (ASCAP)—Vic 20-6137	—	1
26.	**MOST OF ALL** (BMI)—D. Cornell Door Is Still Open (BMI)—Coral 61393	21	6
27.	**CRAZY OTTO MEDLEY** (ASCAP)—J. Maddox Humoresque (BMI)—Dot 15325	26	20
28.	**WHATEVER LOLA WANTS** (ASCAP)—D. Shore Church Twice on Sunday (ASCAP)—Vic 20-6077	30	2
28.	**PLANTATION BOOGIE** (BMI)—L. Dee Birth of the Blues (ASCAP)—Dec 29360	—	15
30.	**HOUSE OF BLUE LIGHTS** (ASCAP)—C. Miller Can't Help Wonderin' (ASCAP)—Mercury 70627	—	1

• This Week's Best Buys

According to sales reports in key markets, the following recent releases are recommended for extra profits:

HOUSE OF BLUE LIGHTS (Robbins, ASCAP) —**Chuck Miller—Mercury 70627**

A sleeper that has been taking several Middle Western areas by storm has garnered enough strength to rate the No. 30 slot on the national retail chart. Detroit shoved the disk off, and Milwaukee, Cleveland, St. Louis, Nashville and Seattle were among other cities to catch the spark. Many territories have not even begun to tap the record's potential yet. Flip is "Can't Help Wonderin'" (Robbins, ASCAP).

THAT OLD BLACK MAGIC (Famous, ASCAP) —**Sammy Davis Jr.—Decca 29541**

This artist has built himself an enviable following with his last few releases, and his fans are gobbling up supplies of this latest offering with avidity. From Los Angeles to Boston, a solid belt of enthusiastic sales territories almost unanimously indicated good to strong volume. Flip is "A Man With a Dream" (Chappell, ASCAP). A previous Billboard "Spotlight" pick.

MY ONE SIN (Mellin, BMI)
THE BLUES FROM "KISS ME DEADLY" (Winneton, BMI) — **Nat (King) Cole — Capitol 3136**

Nat Cole has been churning out hits longer than Sammy Davis Jr., and he lets the newcomers know that he hasn't lost his touch by any means. In the second week since release, action on his new record was reported good in New York, Philadelphia, Providence, Baltimore, Buffalo, Cleveland, Milwaukee, St. Louis, Nashville and Durham. Both sides are doing well, with an edge on "Sin." A previous Billboard "Spotlight" pick.

THE MAN IN THE RAINCOAT — Priscilla Wright—Unique 303

This Canadian import has been making progress steadily and is now becoming a chart threat. Reported this week on both the Detroit and Minneapolis territorial charts, various other Northern cities like Buffalo, St. Louis and Milwaukee were also beginning to register significant cash register success. Many areas have not yet gotten deliveries; when they do, the young singer may find herself with an American hit. Flip is "Please Have Mercy."

CATTLE CALL (Forster, ASCAP)
THE KENTUCKIAN SONG (Frank, ASCAP)—**Eddy Arnold—RCA Victor 6139**

See Country & Western Best Buys.

• Most Played in Juke Boxes

For survey week ending June 8

RECORDS are ranked in order of the greatest number of plays in juke boxes thruout the country, as determined by The Billboard's weekly survey of the nation's juke box operators. When significant play is reported on both sides of a record, points are combined to determine position on the chart. In such a case, both sides are listed in bold type, the leading side on top.

This Week	Record	Last Week	Weeks on Chart
1.	**CHERRY PINK AND APPLE BLOSSOM WHITE** (ASCAP)—P. Prado Marie Elena Rumba (ASCAP)—Vic 20-5965	1	11
2.	**DANCE WITH ME HENRY** (BMI)—G. Gibbs Every Road Must Have a Turning (BMI) Mercury 70572	2	12
3.	**UNCHAINED MELODY** (ASCAP)—L. Baxter Medic (ASCAP)—Cap 3055	3	7
4.	**BLOSSOM FELL** (ASCAP)—Nat (King) Cole **IF I MAY** (BMI)—Cap 3095	7	4
5.	**UNCHAINED MELODY** (ASCAP)—A. Hibbler Daybreak (ASCAP)—Dec 29441	5	8
6.	**BALLAD OF DAVY CROCKETT** (BMI)—B. Hayes Farewell (BMI)—Cadence 1256	4	15
7.	**UNCHAINED MELODY** (ASCAP)—R. Hamilton From Here to Eternity (ASCAP)—Epic 9102	6	7
8.	**HONEY BABE** (ASCAP)—A. Mooney No Regrets (ASCAP)—M-G-M 11900	10	5
9.	**IT'S A SIN TO TELL A LIE** (ASCAP)—S. Smith & The Redheads My Baby Just Cares for Me—Epic 9093	11	3
10.	**WHATEVER LOLA WANTS** (ASCAP)—S. Vaughan Oh Yeah (ASCAP)—Mercury 70595	12	6
11.	**CRAZY OTTO MEDLEY** (ASCAP)—J. Maddox Humoresque (BMI)—Dot 15325	7	18
12.	**HEY, MR. BANJO** (ASCAP)—Sunnysiders Zoom, Zoom, Zoom (ASCAP)—Kapp 113	13	4
13.	**BALLAD OF DAVY CROCKETT** (BMI)—Tennessee Ernie Farewell (BMI)—Cap 3058	7	10
13.	**ROLLING STONE** (BMI)—Fontane Sisters **PLAYMATES** (ASCAP)—Dot 15370	15	3
15.	**SOMETHING'S GOTTA GIVE** (ASCAP)—McGuire Sisters Rhythm 'n' Blues (BMI)—Coral 61423	18	2
16.	**LEARNIN' THE BLUES** (ASCAP)—F. Sinatra If I Had Three Wishes (ASCAP)—Cap 3102	—	1
17.	**HEART** (ASCAP)—E. Fisher Near to You (ASCAP)—Vic 20-6097	20	3
18.	**CHERRY PINK AND APPLE BLOSSOM WHITE** (ASCAP)—A. Dale I'm Sincere (BMI)—Coral 61373	—	4
18.	**ROCK AROUND THE CLOCK** (ASCAP)—B. Haley Thirteen Women (BMI)—Dec 29124	—	1
20.	**BOOM BOOM BOOMERANG** (BMI)—DeCastro Sisters Let Your Love Walk In (ASCAP)—Abbott 3003	18	4

• Most Played by Jockeys

For survey week ending June 8

SIDES are ranked in order of the greatest number of plays on disk jockey radio shows thruout the country. Results are based on The Billboard's weekly survey among the nation's disk jockeys. The reverse side of each record is also listed.

This Week	Record	Last Week	Weeks on Chart
1.	**CHERRY PINK AND APPLE BLOSSOM WHITE**—P. Prado Marie Elena Rumba (ASCAP)—Vic 20-5965	1	10
2.	**UNCHAINED MELODY**—L. Baxter Medic (ASCAP)—Cap 3055	2	11
3.	**LEARNING THE BLUES**—F. Sinatra If I Had Three Wishes (ASCAP)—Cap 3102	5	7
4.	**UNCHAINED MELODY**—A. Hibbler Daybreak (ASCAP)—Dec 29441	4	9
5.	**BLOSSOM FELL**—Nat (King) Cole If I May (ASCAP)—Cap 3095	6	6
6.	**DANCE WITH ME HENRY**—G. Gibbs Every Road Must Have a Turning (BMI)—Mercury 70572	3	11
7.	**UNCHAINED MELODY**—R. Hamilton From Here to Eternity (ASCAP)—Epic 9102	10	7
8.	**HEART**—E. Fisher Near to You (ASCAP)—Vic 20-6097	7	6
9.	**WHATEVER LOLA WANTS**—S. Vaughan Oh Yeah (BMI)—Mercury 70595	8	8
10.	**ROCK AROUND THE CLOCK**—B. Haley Thirteen Women (ASCAP)—Dec 29124	12	4
11.	**BALLAD OF DAVY CROCKETT**—B. Hayes Farewell (BMI)—Cadence 1256	9	15
12.	**SOMETHING'S GOTTA GIVE**—McGuire Sisters Rhythm 'n' Blues (ASCAP)—Coral 61423	14	3
13.	**BREEZE AND I**—C. Valente Jalousie (BMI)—Dec 29467	11	9
14.	**IF I MAY**—Nat (King) Cole Blossom Fell (BMI)—Cap 3095	17	3
15.	**HEART**—Four Aces Sluefoot (ASCAP)—Dec 29476	13	3
16.	**HONEY BABE**—A. Mooney No Regrets (ASCAP)—M-G-M 11900	18	2
17.	**CHEE CHEE OO CHEE**—P. Como & J. P. Morgan Two Lost Souls (BMI)—Vic 20-6137	20	2
18.	**IT'S A SIN TO TELL A LIE**—S. Smith & The Redheads My Baby Just Cares for Me (ASCAP)—Epic 9093	—	1
19.	**MOST OF ALL**—D. Cornell Door Is Still Open (BMI)—Coral 61393	16	4
20.	**SOMETHING'S GOTTA GIVE**—S. Davis Jr. Love Me Or Leave Me (ASCAP)—Dec 2948	—	1

The Billboard Music Popularity Charts — POPULAR RECORDS

• Best Sellers in Stores

For survey week ending June 15

RECORDS are ranked in order of their current national selling importance at the retail level, as determined by The Billboard's weekly survey of the top volume dealers in every important market area. When significant action is reported on both sides of a record, points are combined to determine position on the chart. In such a case, both sides are listed in bold type, the leading side on top.

This Week	Record	Last Week	Weeks on Chart
1.	**CHERRY PINK AND APPLE BLOSSOM WHITE** (ASCAP)—P. Prado — Marie Elna Rumba (ASCAP)—Vic 20-5965	1	17
2.	**UNCHAINED MELODY** (ASCAP)—L. Baxter — Medic (ASCAP)—Cap 3055	2	12
3.	**ROCK AROUND THE CLOCK** (ASCAP)—B. Haley — Thirteen Women (BMI)—Dec 29124	4	7
4.	**BLOSSOM FELL** (ASCAP)—Nat (King) Cole — **IF I MAY** (BMI)—Cap 3095	3	8
5.	**LEARNIN' THE BLUES** (ASCAP)—F. Sinatra — If I Had Three Wishes (ASCAP)—Cap 3102	6	7
6.	**HONEY BABE** (ASCAP)—A. Mooney — No Regrets (ASCAP)—M-G-M 11900	8	10
7.	**DANCE WITH ME HENRY** (BMI)—G. Gibbs — Every Road Must Have a Turning (BMI)—Mercury 70572	5	14
8.	**UNCHAINED MELODY** (ASCAP)—A. Hibbler — Daybreak (ASCAP)—Dec 29441	7	12
9.	**SOMETHING'S GOTTA GIVE** (ASCAP)—McGuire Sisters — **RHYTHM 'N' BLUES** (BMI)—Coral 61423	11	4
10.	**SOMETHING'S GOTTA GIVE** (ASCAP)—S. Davis Jr. — **LOVE ME OR LEAVE ME** (ASCAP)—Dec 29484	14	5
11.	**IT'S A SIN TO TELL A LIE** (ASCAP)—S. Smith & the Redheads — My Baby Just Cares for Me—Epic 9093	13	13
12.	**BALLAD OF DAVY CROCKETT** (BMI)—B. Hayes — Farewell (BMI)—Cadence 1256	9	18
13.	**BALLAD OF DAVY CROCKETT** (BMI)—F. Parker — I Gave My Love (BMI)—Col 40449	10	16
14.	**HARD TO GET** (ASCAP)—G. MacKenzie — Boston Fancy (BMI)—X 0137	21	4
15.	**WHATEVER LOLA WANTS** (ASCAP)—S. Vaughan — Oh, Yeah (ASCAP)—Mercury 70595	15	10
15.	**UNCHAINED MELODY** (ASCAP)—R. Hamilton — From Here to Eternity (ASCAP)—Epic 9102	12	10
17.	**BREEZE AND I** (BMI)—C. Valente — Jalousie (ASCAP)—Dec 29467	18	12
18.	**HEART** (ASCAP)—E. Fisher — Near to You (ASCAP)—Vic 20-6097	17	6
19.	**BALLAD OF DAVY CROCKETT** (BMI)—Tennessee Ernie Ford — Farewell (BMI)—Cap 3058	16	15
20.	**HEY, MR. BANJO** (ASCAP)—Sunnysiders — Zoom, Zoom, Zoom (ASCAP)—Kapp 113	20	6
21.	**MAN IN THE RAINCOAT** (BMI)—P. Wright — Please Have Mercy (BMI)—Unique 303	—	1
22.	**HOUSE OF BLUE LIGHTS** (ASCAP)—C. Miller — Can't Help Wonderin' (ASCAP)—Mercury 70627	30	2
23.	**ALABAMA JUBILEE** (ASCAP)—Ferko String Band — Sing a Little Melody (BMI)—Media 1010	23	2
24.	**CHEE CHEE OO CHEE** (BMI)—P. Como-J. P. Morgan — **TWO LOST SOULS** (ASCAP)—Vic 20-6137	25	2
25.	**STORY UNTOLD** (BMI)—Crew Cuts — Carmen's Boogie (BMI)—Mercury 70634	—	1

• This Week's Best Buys

According to sales reports in key markets, the following recent releases are recommended for extra profits:

AIN'T THAT A SHAME (Commodore, BMI) —**Pat Boone—Dot 15377**

Boone seems all set to better the mark he made with "Two Hearts." In 10 days time, his latest release was rated good to strong in most Middle Western markets, including Chicago, Cincinnati, Cleveland, Milwaukee and St. Louis. Other areas in which it is selling well are Baltimore, Buffalo, Pittsburgh and Nashville. Flip is "Tennessee Saturday Night" (Hill & Range, BMI). A previous Billboard "Spotlight" pick.

DAVY CROCKETT (Wonderland, BMI)—**Mickey Katz—Capitol 3144**

This humorous novelty is showing far more than the specialized appeal that most of Katz' recent disks have had. For two weeks it has been on Boston's territorial chart and has been rated one of the stronger new records in New York and Cleveland. Sales have also been good in Pittsburgh, Chicago, Milwaukee, St. Louis and Atlanta. Flip is "Tweedle Dee" (Progressive, BMI).

I'LL NEVER STOP LOVING YOU (Feist, ASCAP)—**Doris Day—Columbia 40505**

Now that the movie from which this song originates is being exhibited all over the country, Doris Day's waxing of the tune is picking up momentum. Now on the Cleveland territorial chart, strong sales are also indicated in St. Louis, Chicago, Milwaukee, Atlanta, Buffalo, New York and Providence. Flip is "Never Look Back" (Daywin, BMI). A previous Billboard "Spotlight" pick.

SWEET AND GENTLE (Peer, BMI)
•
BLUEBERRIES (Gil, BMI) — **Georgia Gibbs — Mercury 70647**

Despite Alan Dale's head start on this tune, the singer has been doing nicely with her version. Territories that are reporting excellent sales reaction include Boston, Providence, Buffalo, Baltimore, Pittsburgh, Chicago, Milwaukee, Durham, Atlanta and St. Louis. Some areas report a preference for "Blueberries," tho "Sweet and Gentle" has the edge. A previous Billboard "Spotlight" pick.

• Most Played in Juke Boxes

For survey week ending June 15

RECORDS are ranked in order of the greatest number of plays in juke boxes thruout the country, as determined by The Billboard's weekly survey of the nation's juke box operators. When significant play is reported on both sides of a record, points are combined to determine position on the chart. In such a case, both sides are listed in bold type, the leading side on top.

This Week	Record	Last Week	Weeks on Chart
1.	**CHERRY PINK AND APPLE BLOSSOM WHITE** (ASCAP)—P. Prado — Marie Elena Rumba (ASCAP)—Vic 20-5965	1	12
2.	**DANCE WITH ME, HENRY** (BMI)—G. Gibbs — Every Road Must Have a Turning (BMI)—Mercury 70572	2	13
3.	**UNCHAINED MELODY** (ASCAP)—A. Hibbler — Daybreak (ASCAP)—Dec 29441	5	9
4.	**BLOSSOM FELL** (ASCAP)—Nat (King) Cole — **IF I MAY** (BMI)—Cap 3095	4	5
5.	**UNCHAINED MELODY** (ASCAP)—L. Baxter — Medic (ASCAP)—Cap 3055	3	8
6.	**HONEY BABE** (ASCAP)—A. Mooney — No Regrets (ASCAP)—M-G-M 11900	8	6
7.	**BALLAD OF DAVY CROCKETT** (BMI)—B. Hayes — Farewell (BMI)—Cadence 1256	6	16
8.	**IT'S A SIN TO TELL A LIE** (ASCAP)—S. Smith & the Redheads — My Baby Just Care for Me—Epic 9093	9	4
9.	**UNCHAINED MELODY** (ASCAP)—R. Hamilton — From Here to Eternity (ASCAP)—Epic 9102	7	8
9.	**ROCK AROUND THE CLOCK** (ASCAP)—B. Haley — Thirteen Women (BMI)—Dec 29124	18	2
11.	**LEARNIN' THE BLUES** (ASCAP)—F. Sinatra — If I Had Three Wishes (ASCAP)—Cap 3102	16	2
12.	**HEY, MR. BANJO** (ASCAP)—Sunnysiders — Zoom, Zoom, Zoom (ASCAP)—Kapp 113	12	5
13.	**WHATEVER LOLA WANTS** (ASCAP)—S. Vaughan — Oh, Yeah (ASCAP)—Mercury 70595	10	7
13.	**SOMETHING'S GOTTA GIVE** (ASCAP)—McGuire Sisters — Rhythm 'n' Blues (BMI)—Coral 61423	15	3
15.	**BALLAD OF DAVY CROCKETT** (BMI)—Tennessee Ernie — Farewell (BMI)—Cap 3058	13	11
16.	**ROLLIN' STONE** (BMI)—Fontane Sisters — **PLAYMATES** (ASCAP)—Dot 15370	13	4
17.	**CRAZY OTTO MEDLEY** (ASCAP)—J. Maddox — Humoresque (BMI)—Dot 15325	11	19
17.	**HEART** (ASCAP)—E. Fisher — Near to You (ASCAP)—Vic 20-6097	17	4
19.	**CHERRY PINK AND APPLE BLOSSOM WHITE** (ASCAP)—A. Dale — I'm Sincere—Coral 61373	18	5
19.	**DON'T BE ANGRY** (BMI)—Crew Cuts — Chop Chop Boom (BMI)—Mercury 70597	—	1

• Most Played by Jockeys

For survey week ending June 15

SIDES are ranked in order of the greatest number of plays on disk jockey radio shows thruout the country. Results are based on The Billboard's weekly survey among the nation's disk jockeys. The reverse side of each record is also listed.

This Week	Record	Last Week	Weeks on Chart
1.	**CHERRY PINK AND APPLE BLOSSOM WHITE**—P. Prado — Marie Elena Rumba ASCAP—Vic 20-5965	1	11
2.	**UNCHAINED MELODY**—L. Baxter — Medic (ASCAP)—Cap 3055	2	12
3.	**LEARNIN' THE BLUES**—F. Sinatra — If I Had Three Wishes ASCAP—Cap 3102	3	8
4.	**BLOSSOM FELL**—Nat (King) Cole — If I May (ASCAP)—Cap 3095	5	7
5.	**UNCHAINED MELODY**—A. Hibbler — Daybreak (ASCAP)—Dec 29441	4	10
6.	**HEART**—E. Fisher — Near to You (ASCAP)—Vic 20-6097	8	7
7.	**DANCE WITH ME, HENRY**—G. Gibbs — Every Road Must Have a Turning (BMI)—Mercury 70572	6	12
8.	**ROCK AROUND THE CLOCK**—B. Haley — Thirteen Women (ASCAP)—Dec 29124	10	5
9.	**SOMETHING'S GOTTA GIVE**—McGuire Sisters — Rhythm 'n' Blues ASCAP—Coral 61423	12	4
10.	**UNCHAINED MELODY**—R. Hamilton — From Here to Eternity (ASCAP)—Epic 9102	7	8
11.	**WHATEVER LOLA WANTS**—S. Vaughan — Oh, Yeah (BMI)—Mercury 70595	9	9
12.	**HONEY BABE**—A. Mooney — No Regrets (ASCAP)—M-G-M 11900	16	3
13.	**BREEZE AND I**—C. Valente — Jalousie (BMI)—Dec 29467	13	10
14.	**HEART**—Four Aces — Sluefoot (ASCAP)—Dec 29476	15	4
15.	**IF I MAY**—Nat (King) Cole — Blossom Fell (BMI)—Cap 3095	14	4
16.	**CHEE CHEE OO CHEE**—P. Como & J. P. Morgan — Two Lost Souls (BMI)—Vic 20-6137	17	3
17.	**BALLAD OF DAVY CROCKETT**—B. Hayes — Farewell (BMI)—Cadence 1256	11	16
18.	**TWO LOST SOULS**—P. Como & J. P. Morgan — Chee Chee-oo-chee (ASCAP)—Vic 20-6137	—	1
19.	**HEY, MR. BANJO**—Sunnysiders — Zoom, Zoom, Zoom (ASCAP)—Kapp 113	—	1
20.	**MOST OF ALL**—D. Cornell — Door Is Still Open (BMI)—Coral 61393	19	5

The Billboard Music Popularity Charts — POPULAR RECORDS

• Best Sellers in Stores

For survey week ending June 22

RECORDS are ranked in order of their current national selling importance at the retail level, as determined by The Billboard's weekly survey of the top volume dealers in every important market area. When significant action is reported on both sides of a record, points are combined to determine position on the chart. In such a case, both sides are listed in bold type, the leading side on top.

This Week	Record	Last Week	Weeks on Chart
1.	**CHERRY PINK AND APPLE BLOSSOM WHITE** (ASCAP)—P. Prado Marie Elena Rumba (ASCAP)—Vic 20-5965	1	18
2.	**ROCK AROUND THE CLOCK** (ASCAP)—B. Haley Thirteen Women (BMI)—Dec 29124	3	8
3.	**BLOSSOM FELL** (ASCAP)—Nat (King) Cole **IF I MAY** (BMI)—Cap 3095	4	9
4.	**UNCHAINED MELODY** (ASCAP)—L. Baxter Medic (ASCAP)—Cap 3055	2	13
5.	**LEARNIN' THE BLUES** (ASCAP)—F. Sinatra If I Had Three Wishes (ASCAP)—Cap 3102	5	8
6.	**HONEY BABE** (ASCAP)—A. Mooney No Regrets (ASCAP)—M-G-M 11900	6	11
7.	**UNCHAINED MELODY** (ASCAP)—A. Hibbler Daybreak (ASCAP)—Dec 29441	8	13
8.	**SOMETHING'S GOTTA GIVE** (ASCAP)—McGuire Sisters Rhythm 'n' Blues (BMI)—Coral 61423	9	5
9.	**DANCE WITH ME HENRY** (BMI)—G. Gibbs Every Road Must Have a Turning (BMI)—Mercury 70572	7	15
10.	**IT'S A SIN TO TELL A LIE** (ASCAP)—S. Smith & the Redheads My Baby Just Cares for Me—Epic 9093	11	14
11.	**HARD TO GET** (ASCAP)—G. MacKenzie Boston Fancy (BMI)—X 0137	14	5
12.	**LOVE ME OR LEAVE ME** (ASCAP)—S. Davis Jr. **SOMETHING'S GOTTA GIVE** (ASCAP)—Dec 29484	10	6
13.	**UNCHAINED MELODY** (ASCAP)—R. Hamilton From Here to Eternity (ASCAP)—Epic 9102	15	11
14.	**BALLAD OF DAVY CROCKETT** (BMI)—B. Hayes Farewell (BMI)—Cadence 1256	12	19
15.	**HEART** (ASCAP)—E. Fisher Near to You (ASCAP)—Vic 20-6097	18	7
16.	**BALLAD OF DAVY CROCKET** (BMI)—F. Parker I Gave My Love (BMI)—Col 40449	13	17
17.	**SWEET AND GENTLE** (BMI)—A. Dale You Still Mean the Same to Me (ASCAP)—Coral 61435	—	1
18.	**ALABAMA JUBILEE** (ASCAP)—Ferko String Band Sing a Little Melody (BMI)—Media 1010	23	3
19.	**WHATEVER LOLA WANTS** (ASCAP)—S. Vaughan Oh, Yeah (ASCAP)—Mercury 70595	15	11
20.	**HOUSE OF BLUE LIGHTS** (ASCAP)—C. Miller Can't Help Wonderin' (ASCAP)—Mercury 70627	22	3
21.	**BALLAD OF DAVY CROCKETT** (BMI)—Tennessee Ernie Ford Farewell (BMI)—Cap 3058	19	16
22.	**MAN IN THE RAINCOAT** (BMI)—P. Wright Please Have Mercy (BMI)—Unique 303	21	2
23.	**HEY, MR. BANJO** (ASCAP)—Sunnysiders Zoom, Zoom, Zoom (ASCAP)—Kapp 113	20	7
24.	**THAT OLD BLACK MAGIC** (ASCAP)—S. Davis Jr. Man With a Dream (ASCAP)—Dec 29541	—	2
24.	**STORY UNTOLD** (BMI)—Crew Cuts Carmen's Boogie (BMI)—Mercury 70634	25	2

The Best-Selling Retail Chart published essentially as a buying guide, now carries 25 listings as compared with 30 carried in recent months. Several months ago the listing was extended from 20 to 30 because of the stability of the general record market and because listings between the 20th and 30th positions represented disks with established public acceptance. Such is not the case in the present pop singles market. Fluctuations below the 25th position are too violent to be considered reliable buying information. Thus it is considered in the best interests of dealers and operators that the chart be confined to 25 listings at this time.

In an early issue The Billboard will feature a new service exposing record activity among disks pushing up toward the chart.

• This Week's Best Buys

According to sales reports in key markets, the following recent releases are recommended for extra profits:

HUMMINGBIRD (Ross Jungnickel, ASCAP)—**Les Paul & Mary Ford—Capitol 3165**

HUMMINGBIRD (Ross Jungnickel, ASCAP)—**Frankie Laine—Columbia 40526**

The several versions of this tune have seen considerable competitive action in the past two weeks, with the above mentioned two emerging as early leaders. The Capitol disk has the edge at this point but by no overwhelming margin. Among territories reporting sizeable sales were Baltimore, Buffalo, Pittsburgh, St. Louis, Richmond, Durham, Nashville, Cleveland and Detroit. Excellent reports on the Laine record were also received from Philadelphia, Milwaukee, and Atlanta. The flip of the Paul-Ford record, which was a previous Billboard "Spotlight" pick, is "Goodbye, My Love." On the back of Laine's disk is "My Little One."

RAZZLE-DAZZLE (Roosevelt, BMI)

TWO HOUND DOGS (Valleybrook, ASCAP)—**Bill Haley—Decca 29552**

The enthusiasm of the youngsters for Haley seems to be irrepressible. From the outset, this latest release has stormed one territory after the other and encountered little resistance. Top volume was reported in many areas, including New York, Philadelphia, Buffalo, Pittsburgh, Cincinnati, Cleveland, Detroit, St. Louis and numerous Southern cities. "Razzle-Dazzle" is moving out faster than the flip, tho action has been heavy on both sides, and both could easily make the charts. A previous Billboard "Spotlight" pick.

DOMANI (Montauk, BMI)

MAMA ROSA (Shapiro-Bernstein, ASCAP) — **Julius LaRosa—Cadence 1265**

Without losing much time, this disk is increasing its pace to the point where it is beginning to look like a winner. This week, it appears for the first time on the Chicago territorial chart, and is also reported selling well in New York, Philadelphia, Buffalo, Pittsburgh, Cleveland, Milwaukee, Detroit, St. Louis and Baltimore. "Domani" is the favored side, but some areas also find the reverse quite potent. A previous Billboard "Spotlight" pick.

• Most Played in Juke Boxes

For survey week ending June 22

RECORDS are ranked in order of the greatest number of plays in juke boxes thruout the country, as determined by The Billboard's weekly survey of the nation's juke box operators. When significant play is reported on both sides of a record, points are combined to determine position on the chart. In such a case, both sides are listed in bold type, the leading side on top.

This Week	Record	Last Week	Weeks on Chart
1.	**CHERRY PINK AND APPLE BLOSSOM WHITE** (ASCAP)—P. Prado Marie Elena Rumba (ASCAP)—Vic 20-5965	1	13
2.	**DANCE WITH ME HENRY** (BMI)—G. Gibbs Every Road Must Have a Turning (BMI)—Mercury 70572	2	14
3.	**BLOSSOM FELL** (ASCAP)—Nat (King) Cole **IF I MAY** (BMI)—Cap 3095	4	6
4.	**UNCHAINED MELODY** (ASCAP)—A. Hibbler Daybreak (ASCAP)—Dec 29441	3	10
4.	**UNCHAINED MELODY** (ASCAP)—L. Baxter Medic (ASCAP)—Cap 3055	5	9
6.	**ROCK AROUND THE CLOCK** (ASCAP)—B. Haley Thirteen Women (BMI)—Dec 29124	9	3
7.	**LEARNIN' THE BLUES** (ASCAP)—F. Sinatra If I Had Three Wishes (ASCAP)—Cap 3102	11	3
8.	**HONEY BABE** (ASCAP)—A. Mooney No Regrets (ASCAP)—M-G-M 11900	6	7
9.	**SOMETHING'S GOTTA GIVE** (ASCAP)—McGuire Sisters **RHYTHM 'N' BLUES** (BMI)—Coral 61423	13	4
10.	**UNCHAINED MELODY** (ASCAP)—R. Hamilton From Here to Eternity (ASCAP)—Epic 9102	9	9
11.	**IT'S A SIN TO TELL A LIE** (ASCAP)—S. Smith & the Redheads My Baby Just Cares for Me—Epic 9093	8	5
12.	**BALLAD OF DAVY CROCKETT** (BMI)—B. Hayes Farewell (BMI)—Cadence 1256	7	17
13.	**BALLAD OF DAVY CROCKETT** Tennessee Ernie Farewell (BMI)—Cap 3058	15	12
14.	**HEART** (ASCAP)—E. Fisher Near to You (ASCAP)—Vic 20-6097	17	5
15.	**WHATEVER LOLA WANTS** (ASCAP)—S. Vaughan Oh, Yeah (ASCAP)—Mercury 70595	13	8
16.	**HEY, MR. BANJO** (ASCAP)—Sunnysiders Zoom, Zoom, Zoom (ASCAP)—Kapp 113	12	6
17.	**CRAZY OTTO MEDLEY** (ASCAP)—J. Maddox Humoresque (BMI)—Dot 15325	17	20
17.	**CHERRY PINK AND APPLE BLOSSOM WHITE** (ASCAP)—A. Dale I'm Sincere—Coral 61373	19	6
19.	**CHEE CHEE OO CHEE** P. Como & J. P. Morgan Two Lost Souls (BMI)—Vic 20-6137	—	1
20.	**DON'T BE ANGRY** (BMI)—Crew Cuts Chop Chop Boom (BMI)—Mercury 70597	19	2
20.	**TWO HEARTS** (BMI)—P. Boone Tra-La-La—Dot 15338	—	7
20.	**HEART**—Four Aces Sluefoot (ASCAP)—Dec 29476	—	1

• Most Played by Jockeys

For survey week ending June 22

SIDES are ranked in order of the greatest number of plays on disk jockey radio shows thruout the country. Results are based on The Billboard's weekly survey among the nation's disk jockeys. The reverse side of each record is also listed.

This Week	Record	Last Week	Weeks on Chart
1.	**CHERRY PINK AND APPLE BLOSSOM WHITE**—P. Prado Marie Elena Rumba (ASCAP)—Vic 20-5965	1	12
2.	**LEARNIN' THE BLUES**—F. Sinatra If I Had Three Wishes (ASCAP)—Cap 3102	3	9
3.	**UNCHAINED MELODY**—L. Baxter Medic (ASCAP)—Cap 3055	2	13
4.	**ROCK AROUND THE CLOCK**—B. Haley Thirteen Women (ASCAP)—Dec 29124	8	6
5.	**BLOSSOM FELL**—Nat (King) Cole If I May (ASCAP)—Cap 3095	4	8
6.	**UNCHAINED MELODY**—A. Hibbler Daybreak (ASCAP)—Dec 29441	5	11
7.	**SOMETHING'S GOTTA GIVE**—McGuire Sisters Rhythm 'n' Blues (ASCAP)—Coral 61423	9	5
8.	**HEART**—E. Fisher Near to You (ASCAP)—Vic 20-6097	6	8
9.	**DANCE WITH ME HENRY**—G. Gibbs Every Road Must Have a Turning (BMI)—Mercury 70572	7	13
10.	**HONEY BABE**—A. Mooney No Regrets (ASCAP)—M-G-M 11900	12	4
11.	**UNCHAINED MELODY**—R. Hamilton From Here to Eternity (ASCAP)—Epic 9102	10	9
12.	**IF I MAY**—Nat (King) Cole Blossom Fell (BMI)—Cap 3095	15	5
13.	**CHEE CHEE OO CHEE**—P. Como & J. P. Morgan Two Lost Souls (BMI)—Vic 20-6137	16	4
14.	**WHATEVER LOLA WANTS**—S. Vaughan Oh, Yeah (BMI)—Mercury 70595	11	10
15.	**IT'S A SIN TO TELL A LIE**—S. Smith & the Redheads My Baby Just Cares for Me (ASCAP)—Epic 9093	—	2
16.	**HEART**—Four Aces Sluefoot (ASCAP)—Dec 29476	14	5
17.	**HARD TO GET**—G. MacKenzie Boston Fancy (ASCAP)—X 0137	—	1
18.	**BREEZE AND I**—C. Valente Jalousie (BMI)—Dec 29467	13	11
19.	**BALLAD OF DAVY CROCKETT**—B. Hayes Farewell (BMI)—Cadence 1256	17	17
20.	**LOVE ME OR LEAVE ME**—S. Davis Jr. Something's Gotta Give (ASCAP)—Dec 29484	—	1

The Billboard Music Popularity Charts — POPULAR RECORDS

• Best Sellers in Stores

For survey week ending June 29

RECORDS are ranked in order of their current national selling importance at the retail level, as determined by The Billboard's weekly survey of the top volume dealers in every important market area. When significant action is reported on both sides of a record, points are combined to determine position on the chart. In such a case, both sides are listed in bold type, the leading side on top.

This Week		Last Week	Weeks on Chart
1.	**ROCK AROUND THE CLOCK** (ASCAP)—B. Haley Thirteen Women (BMI)—Dec 29124	2	9
2.	**CHERRY PINK AND APPLE BLOSSOM WHITE** (ASCAP)—P. Prado Marie Elena Rumba (ASCAP)—Vic 20-5965	1	19
3.	**BLOSSOM FELL** (ASCAP)—Nat (King) Cole **IF I MAY** (BMI)—Cap 3095	3	10
4.	**UNCHAINED MELODY** (ASCAP)—L. Baxter Medic (ASCAP)—Cap 3055	4	14
5.	**LEARNIN' THE BLUES** (ASCAP)—F. Sinatra If I Had Three Wishes (ASCAP)—Cap 3102	5	9
6.	**HONEY BABE** (ASCAP)—A. Mooney No Regrets (ASCAP)—M-G-M 11900	6	12
7.	**SOMETHING'S GOTTA GIVE** (ASCAP)—McGuire Sisters Rhythm 'n' Blues (BMI)—Coral 61423	8	6
8.	**HARD TO GET** (ASCAP)—G. MacKenzie Boston Fancy (BMI)—"X" 0137	11	6
9.	**UNCHAINED MELODY** (ASCAP)—A. Hibbler Daybreak (ASCAP)—Dec 29441	7	14
10.	**SOMETHING'S GOTTA GIVE** (ASCAP)—S. Davis Jr. **LOVE ME OR LEAVE ME** (ASCAP) Dec 29484	12	7
11.	**DANCE WITH ME, HENRY** (BMI)—G. Gibbs Every Road Must Have a Turning (BMI)—Mercury 70572	9	16
12.	**IT'S A SIN TO TELL A LIE** (ASCAP)—S. Smith & The Redheads My Baby Just Cares for Me (ASCAP)—Epic 9093	10	15
13.	**UNCHAINED MELODY** (ASCAP)—R. Hamilton From Here to Eternity (ASCAP)—Epic 9102	13	12
14.	**SWEET AND GENTLE** (BMI)—A. Dale You Still Mean the Same to Me (ASCAP)—Coral 61435	17	2
15.	**BALLAD OF DAVY CROCKETT** (BMI)—B. Hayes Farewell (BMI)—Cadence 1256	14	20
16.	**THAT OLD BLACK MAGIC** (ASCAP)—S. Davis Jr. Man With a Dream (ASCAP)—Dec 29541	24	3
17.	**HEART** (ASCAP)—E. Fisher Near to You (ASCAP)—Vic 20-6097	15	8
18.	**MAN IN THE RAINCOAT** (BMI)—P. Wright Please Have Mercy (BMI)—Unique 303	22	3
19.	**AIN'T IT A SHAME** (BMI)—P. Boone Tennessee Saturday Night (BMI)—Dot 15377	—	1
20.	**STORY UNTOLD** (BMI)—Crew Cuts Carmen's Boogie (BMI)—Mercury 70634	24	3
21.	**ALABAMA JUBILEE** (ASCAP)—Ferko String Band Sing a Little Melody (BMI)—Media 1010	18	4
22.	**HOUSE OF BLUE LIGHTS** (ASCAP)—C. Miller Can't Help Wonderin' (ASCAP)—Mercury 70627	20	4
23.	**HEY, MR. BANJO** (ASCAP)—Sunnysiders Zoom, Zoom, Zoom (ASCAP)—Kapp 113	23	8
24.	**SEVENTEEN** (BMI)—B. Bennett Little Old You-All (BMI)—King 1470	—	1
25.	**BALLAD OF DAVY CROCKETT** (BMI)—Tennessee Ernie Ford Farewell (BMI)—Cap 3058	21	17
25.	**BREEZE AND I** (BMI)—C. Valente Jalousie (ASCAP)—Dec 29467	—	13

• This Week's Best Buys

According to sales reports in key markets, the following recent releases are recommended for extra profits:

SEVENTEEN (Lois, BMI)—**Boyd Bennett—King 1470**

A sleeper that emerged this week as one of the country's hottest new disks. Now No. 24 on the national retail chart, the record also placed on the Pittsburgh, Cincinnati and Cleveland territorial listings with excellent sales ratings in many other cities to its credit. Flip is "Little Ole You-All" (Lois, BMI).

THE POPCORN SONG (Central, BMI)—**Cliffie Stone—Capitol 3131**

This novelty has also been a left-field surprise in many areas, appealing to customers in both the pop and hillbilly markets. Currently the top record in Kansas City, "Popcorn Song," is also a good seller in New York, Buffalo, Pittsburgh, Milwaukee, Richmond, Nashville, Durham, Atlanta, St. Louis and Baltimore. Flip is "Barracuda."

THE BANJO'S BACK IN TOWN (World, ASCAP)—**Teresa Brewer—Coral 61448**

In the past 10 days this disk has taken off with almost all territories catching the spark at once. Sales are good to strong and growing rapidly in Boston, Providence, Philadelphia, Baltimore, Buffalo, Pittsburgh, Cleveland, Chicago, Milwaukee, St. Louis, Durham, Nashville and Atlanta. Flip is "How to Be Very, Very Popular." A previous Billboard "Spotlight" pick.

EXPERIENCE UNNECESSARY (Pincus, ASCAP)—**Sarah Vaughan—Mercury 70646**

While this has not been one of the thrush's fastest moving disks, it is now beginning to show a fine spread of good sales reports and is shaping up as a record with chart potential. Best areas for Miss Vaughan so far have been Philadelphia, Buffalo, Baltimore, Providence, Pittsburgh, Cleveland, Chicago, Milwaukee, St. Louis, Detroit and Nashville. Flip is "Slowly With Feeling" (Planetary, ASCAP). A previous Billboard "Spotlight" pick.

• Most Played in Juke Boxes

For survey week ending June 29

RECORDS are ranked in order of the greatest number of plays in juke boxes thruout the country, as determined by The Billboard's weekly survey of the nation's juke box operators. When significant play is reported on both sides of a record, points are combined to determine position on the chart. In such a case, both sides are listed in bold type, the leading side on top.

This Week		Last Week	Weeks on Chart
1.	**CHERRY PINK AND APPLE BLOSSOM WHITE** (ASCAP)—P. Prado Marie Elena Rumba (ASCAP)—Vic 20-5965	1	14
2.	**BLOSSOM FELL** (ASCAP)—Nat (King) Cole If I May (BMI)—Cap 3095	3	7
3.	**DANCE WITH ME HENRY** (BMI)—G. Gibbs Every Road Must Have a Turning (BMI)—Mercury 70572	2	15
4.	**UNCHAINED MELODY** (ASCAP)—L. Baxter Medic (ASCAP)—Cap 3055	4	10
5.	**ROCK AROUND THE CLOCK** (ASCAP)—B. Haley Thirteen Women (BMI)—Dec 29124	6	4
6.	**LEARNIN' THE BLUES** (ASCAP)—F. Sinatra If I Had Three Wishes (ASCAP)—Cap 3102	7	4
7.	**UNCHAINED MELODY** (ASCAP)—A. Hibbler Daybreak (ASCAP)—Dec 29441	4	11
7.	**HONEY BABE** (ASCAP)—A. Mooney No Regrets (ASCAP)—M-G-M 11900	8	8
9.	**SOMETHING'S GOTTA GIVE** (ASCAP)—McGuire Sisters Rhythm 'n' Blues (BMI)—Coral 61423	9	5
10.	**UNCHAINED MELODY** (ASCAP)—R. Hamilton From Here to Eternity (ASCAP)—Epic 9102	10	10
11.	**HARD TO GET** (ASCAP)—G. MacKenzie Boston Fancy (BMI)—"X" 0137	—	1
12.	**IT'S A SIN TO TELL A LIE** (ASCAP)—S. Smith & th Redheads My Baby Just Cares for Me—Epic 9093	11	6
13.	**HEART** (ASCAP)—E. Fisher Near to You (ASCAP)—Vic 20-6097	14	6
14.	**BALLAD OF DAVY CROCKETT** (BMI)—B. Hayes Farewell (BMI)—Cadence 1256	12	18
15.	**BALLAD OF DAVY CROCKETT** (BMI)—Tennessee Ernie Farewell (BMI)—Cap 3058	13	13
16.	**SWEET AND GENTLE** (BMI)—A. Dale You Still Mean the Same to Me (ASCAP)—Coral 61435	—	1
17.	**WHATEVER LOLA WANTS** (ASCAP)—S. Vaughan Oh Yeah (ASCAP)—Mercury 70595	15	9
18.	**HEY, MR. BANJO** (ASCAP)—Sunnysiders Zoom, Zoom, Zoom (ASCAP)—Kapp 113	16	7
18.	**CHEE CHEE OO CHEE**—P. Como & J. P. Morgan Two Lost Souls (BMI)—Vic 20-6137	19	2
18.	**SOMETHING'S GOTTA GIVE** (ASCAP)—S. Davis Jr. Love Me or Leave Me (ASCAP)—Dec 29484	—	1

• Most Played by Jockeys

For survey week ending June 29

SIDES are ranked in order of the greatest number of plays on disk jockey radio shows thruout the country. Results are based on The Billboard's weekly survey among the nation's disk jockeys. The reverse side of each record is also listed.

This Week		Last Week	Weeks on Chart
1.	**LEARNING THE BLUES**—F. Sinatra If I Had Three Wishes (ASCAP)—Cap 3102	2	10
2.	**UNCHAINED MELODY**—L. Baxter Medic (ASCAP)—Cap 3055	3	14
3.	**ROCK AROUND THE CLOCK**—B. Haley Thirteen Women (ASCAP)—Dec 29124	4	7
4.	**BLOSSOM FELL**—Nat (King) Cole If I May (ASCAP)—Cap 3095	5	9
5.	**CHERRY PINK AND APPLE BLOSSOM WHITE**—P. Prado Marie Elena Rumba (ASCAP)—Vic 20-5965	1	13
6.	**SOMETHING'S GOTTA GIVE**—McGuire Sisters Rhythm 'n' Blues (BMI)—Coral 61423	7	6
7.	**UNCHAINED MELODY**—A. Hibbler Daybreak (ASCAP)—Dec 29441	6	12
8.	**HEART**—E. Fisher Near to You (ASCAP)—Vic 20-6097	8	9
9.	**UNCHAINED MELODY**—R. Hamilton From Here to Eternity (ASCAP)—Epic 9102	11	10
10.	**SWEET AND GENTLE**—A. Dale You Still Mean the Same to Me (BMI)—Coral 61435	—	1
11.	**HONEY BABE**—A. Mooney No Regrets (ASCAP)—M-G-M 11900	10	5
12.	**CHEE CHEE OO CHEE**—P. Como & J. P. Morgan Two Lost Souls (BMI)—Vic 20-6137	13	5
13.	**DANCE WITH ME HENRY**—G. Gibbs Every Road Must Have a Turning (BMI)—Mercury 70572	9	14
14.	**IF I MAY**—Nat (King) Cole Blossom Fell (BMI)—Cap 3095	12	6
15.	**THAT OLD BLACK MAGIC** (ASCAP)—S. Davis Jr. Man With a Dream (ASCAP)—Dec 29541	—	1
16.	**HARD TO GET**—G. MacKenzie Boston Fancy (ASCAP)—"X" 0137	17	2
17.	**HEART**—Four Aces Stuefoot (ASCAP)—Dec 29476	16	6
18.	**HUMMINGBIRD SONG** (ASCAP)—L. Paul & Mary Ford Goodbye My Love (ASCAP)—Cap 3165	—	1
19.	**LOVE ME OR LEAVE ME**—L. Horne I Love to Love (ASCAP)—Vic 20-6073	—	1
20.	**SWEET AND GENTLE**—G. Gibbs Blueberries (BMI)—Mercury 70647	—	1

The Billboard Music Popularity Charts — POPULAR RECORDS

• Best Sellers in Stores

For survey week ending July 6

RECORDS are ranked in order of their current national selling importance at the retail level, as determined by The Billboard's weekly survey of the top volume dealers in every important market area. When significant action is reported on both sides of a record, points are combined to determine position on the chart. In such a case, both sides are listed in bold type, the leading side on top.

This Week	Title	Last Week	Weeks on Chart
1.	ROCK AROUND THE CLOCK (ASCAP)—B. Haley — Thirteen Women (BMI)—Dec 29124	1	10
2.	CHERRY PINK AND APPLE BLOSSOM WHITE (ASCAP)—P. Prado — Marie Elena Rumba (ASCAP)—Vic 20-5965	2	20
3.	BLOSSOM FELL (ASCAP)—Nat (King) Cole / IF I MAY (BMI)—Cap 3095	3	11
4.	UNCHAINED MELODY (ASCAP)—L. Baxter — Medic (ASCAP)—Cap 3055	4	15
5.	LEARNIN' THE BLUES (ASCAP)—F. Sinatra — If I Had Three Wishes (ASCAP)—Cap 3102	5	10
6.	HONEY BABE (ASCAP)—A. Mooney — No Regrets (ASCAP)—M-G-M 11900	6	13
7.	SOMETHING'S GOTTA GIVE (ASCAP)—McGuire Sisters — Rhythm 'n' Blues (BMI)—Coral 61423	7	7
8.	HARD TO GET (ASCAP)—G. MacKenzie — Boston Fancy (BMI)—X 0137	8	7
9.	SOMETHING'S GOTTA GIVE (ASCAP)—S. Davis Jr. / LOVE ME OR LEAVE ME (ASCAP)—Dec 29484	10	8
10.	IT'S A SIN TO TELL A LIE (ASCAP)—S. Smith & the Redheads — My Baby Just Cares for Me (ASCAP)—Epic 9093	12	16
11.	UNCHAINED MELODY (ASCAP)—A. Hibbler — Daybreak (ASCAP)—Dec 29441	9	15
12.	SWEET AND GENTLE (BMI)—A. Dale — You Still Mean the Same to Me (ASCAP)—Coral 61435	14	3
13.	UNCHAINED MELODY (ASCAP)—R. Hamilton — From Here to Eternity (ASCAP)—Epic 9102	13	13
14.	DANCE WITH ME HENRY (BMI)—G. Gibbs — Every Road Must Have a Turning (BMI)—Mercury 70572	11	17
15.	HEART (ASCAP)—E. Fisher — Near to You (ASCAP)—Vic 20-6097	17	9
16.	AIN'T IT A SHAME? (BMI)—P. Boone — Tennessee Saturday Night (BMI)—Dot 15377	19	2
17.	HOUSE OF BLUE LIGHTS (ASCAP)—C. Miller — Can't Help Wonderin' (ASCAP)—Mercury 70627	22	5
18.	STORY UNTOLD (BMI)—Crew Cuts — Carmen's Boogie (BMI)—Mercury 70634	20	4
19.	ALABAMA JUBILEE (ASCAP)—Ferko String Band — Sing a Little Melody (BMI)—Media 1010	21	5
20.	AIN'T IT A SHAME? (BMI)—F. Domino — La, La (BMI)—Imperial 5348	—	1
21.	THAT OLD BLACK MAGIC (ASCAP)—S. Davis Jr. — Man With a Dream (ASCAP)—Dec 29541	16	4
22.	SEVENTEEN (BMI)—B. Bennett — Little Old You-All (BMI)—King 1470	24	2
23.	BREEZE AND I (BMI)—C. Valente — Jalousie (ASCAP)—Dec 29467	25	14
24.	MAN IN THE RAINCOAT (BMI)—P. Wright — Please Have Mercy (BMI)—Unique 303	18	4
24.	MY ONE SIN (BMI)—Nat (King) Cole — Blues From "Kiss Me Deadly" (BMI)—Cap 3136	—	1

DEALERS AND OPERATORS . . .

Top Ten Tunes Poster
is on page 38
Tomorrow's Hits . . . Today
Poster is on page 40

• THIS WEEK'S BEST BUYS

According to sales reports in key markets, the following recent releases are recommended for extra profits:

THE KENTUCKIAN SONG (Frank, ASCAP)—**The Hilltoppers—Dot 15375**

While the film, "The Kentuckian," has not yet been released, this theme has gradually been building into a powerful tune in its own right. This week, the Hilltoppers appear on the Cleveland and Minneapolis-St. Paul territorial charts and were also selling well in Cincinnati, Detroit, Nashville, Atlanta, St. Louis, Richmond, Milwaukee, Pittsburgh and Philadelphia. The Eddy Arnold version of the tune is also experiencing easy acceptance in many areas. The flip of the Dot record is "I Must Be Dreaming" (Quintet, BMI). A previous Billboard "Spotlight" pick.

FORGIVE THIS FOOL (Sheldon, BMI)—**Roy Hamilton—Epic 9111**

Hamilton's latest release is stepping out quickly in both the pop and the rhythm & blues markets, and threatens to be a chart contender in both categories. With each release, however, Hamilton shows more rapid take-off in the pop field, indicating that acceptance as a pop artist is now almost complete. Areas that were seeing particularly good action on this disk included Boston, Providence, Baltimore, Philadelphia, Detroit, St. Louis, Durham and Nashville. Flip is "You Wanted to Change Me" (Kahl, BMI). A previous Billboard "Spotlight" pick.

CLOSE THE DOOR—Jim Lowe—Dot 15381

This novelty has been breezing merrily thru a number of Middle Western areas and has now built up a solid core of devotees there. Cleveland, Kansas City, St. Louis and Chicago have witnessed strong sales to date. The disk is now also moving out handsomely in New York, Baltimore, Nashville and the Carolinas. Flip is "Nuevo Laredo."

• Most Played in Juke Boxes

For survey week ending July 6

RECORDS are ranked in order of the greatest number of plays in juke boxes thruout the country, as determined by The Billboard's weekly survey of the nation's juke box operators. When significant play is reported on both sides of a record, points are combined to determine position on the chart. In such a case, both sides are listed in bold type, the leading side on top.

This Week	Title	Last Week	Weeks on Chart
1.	CHERRY PINK AND APPLE BLOSSOM WHITE (ASCAP)—P. Prado — Marie Elena Rumba (ASCAP)—Vic 20-5965	1	15
2.	ROCK AROUND THE CLOCK (ASCAP)—B. Haley — Thirteen Women (BMI)—Dec 29124	5	5
3.	BLOSSOM FELL (ASCAP)—Nat (King) Cole / IF I MAY (BMI)—Cap 3095	2	8
4.	DANCE WITH ME HENRY (BMI)—G. Gibbs — Every Road Must Have a Turning (BMI)—Mercury 70572	3	16
5.	LEARNIN' THE BLUES (ASCAP)—F. Sinatra — If I Had Three Wishes (ASCAP)—Cap 3102	6	5
6.	UNCHAINED MELODY (ASCAP)—L. Baxter — Medic (ASCAP)—Cap 3055	4	11
7.	HONEY BABE (ASCAP)—A. Mooney — No Regrets (ASCAP)—M-G-M 11900	7	9
8.	UNCHAINED MELODY (ASCAP)—A. Hibbler — Daybreak (ASCAP)—Dec 29441	7	12
9.	SOMETHING'S GOTTA GIVE (ASCAP)—McGuire Sisters — Rhythm 'n' Blues (BMI)—Coral 61423	9	6
10.	HARD TO GET (ASCAP)—G. MacKenzie — Boston Fancy (BMI)—X 0137	11	2
11.	UNCHAINED MELODY (ASCAP)—R. Hamilton — From Here to Eternity (ASCAP)—Epic 9102	10	11
12.	IT'S A SIN TO TELL A LIE (ASCAP)—S. Smith & The Redheads — My Baby Just Cares for Me (ASCAP)—Epic 9093	12	7
13.	BALLAD OF DAVY CROCKETT (BMI)—Tennessee Ernie — Farewell (BMI)—Cap 3058	15	14
14.	SWEET AND GENTLE (BMI)—A. Dale — You Still Mean the Same to Me (ASCAP)—Coral 61435	16	2
14.	CHEE CHEE OO CHEE—P. Como & J. P. Morgan — Two Lost Souls (BMI)—Vic 20-6137	18	3
14.	ROLLIN' STONE (BMI)—Fontane Sisters — Playmates (ASCAP)—Dot 15370	—	4
17.	HEART (ASCAP)—E. Fisher — Near to You (ASCAP)—Vic 20-6097	13	7
18.	BANDIT (ASCAP)—E. Barclay — Neu Piao—Tico 249	—	1
18.	AIN'T IT A SHAME (BMI)—P. Boone — Tennessee Saturday Night (BMI)—Dot 15377	—	1
20.	HEY, MR. BANJO (ASCAP)—Sunnysiders — Zoom, Zoom, Zoom (ASCAP)—Kapp 113	18	8

• Most Played by Jockeys

For survey week ending July 6

SIDES are ranked in order of the greatest number of plays on disk jockey radio shows thruout the country. Results are based on The Billboard's weekly survey among the nation's disk jockeys. The reverse side of each record is also listed.

This Week	Title	Last Week	Weeks on Chart
1.	ROCK AROUND THE CLOCK—B. Haley — Thirteen Women—Dec 29124—ASCAP	3	8
2.	LEARNIN' THE BLUES—F. Sinatra — If I Had Three Wishes—Cap 3102—ASCAP	1	11
3.	UNCHAINED MELODY—L. Baxter — Medic—Cap 3055—ASCAP	2	15
4.	CHERRY PINK AND APPLE BLOSSOM WHITE—P. Prado — Marie Elena Rumba—Vic 20-5965—ASCAP	5	14
5.	BLOSSOM FELL—Nat (King) Cole — If I May—Cap 3095—ASCAP	4	10
6.	SOMETHING'S GOTTA GIVE—McGuire Sisters — Rhythm 'n' Blues—Coral 61423—ASCAP	6	7
7.	UNCHAINED MELODY—A. Hibbler — Daybreak—Dec 29441—ASCAP	7	13
8.	IF I MAY—Nat (King) Cole — Blossom Fell—Cap 3095—BMI	14	7
9.	HARD TO GET—G. MacKenzie — Boston Fancy—X 0137—ASCAP	16	3
10.	UNCHAINED MELODY—R. Hamilton — From Here to Eternity—Epic 9102—ASCAP	9	11
11.	SWEET AND GENTLE—A. Dale — You Still Mean the Same to Me—Coral 61435—BMI	10	2
12.	SWEET AND GENTLE—G. Gibbs — Blueberries—Mercury 70647—BMI	20	2
13.	HEART—E. Fisher — Near to You—Vic 20-6097—ASCAP	8	10
14.	EXPERIENCE UNNECESSARY—S. Vaughan — Slowly With Feeling—Mercury 70646—ASCAP	—	1
15.	IT'S A SIN TO TELL A LIE—S. Smith & The Redheads — My Baby Just Cares for Me—Epic 9093—ASCAP	—	3
16.	AIN'T IT A SHAME—P. Boone — Tennessee Saturday Night—Dot 15377—BMI	—	1
17.	DANCE WITH ME HENRY—G. Gibbs — Every Road Must Have a Turning—Mercury 70572—BMI	13	15
18.	HUMMINGBIRD—L. Paul & M. Ford — Goodbye My Love—Cap 3165—ASCAP	18	2
19.	THAT OLD BLACK MAGIC—S. Davis Jr. — Man With a Dream—Dec 29541—ASCAP	15	2
20.	HONEY BABE—A. Mooney — No Regrets—M-G-M 11900—ASCAP	11	6
20.	MAN IN THE RAINCOAT—M. Marlowe — Heartbeat—Cadence 1266—BMI	—	1

The Billboard Music Popularity Charts — POPULAR RECORDS

• Best Sellers in Stores

For survey week ending July 13

RECORDS are ranked in order of their current national selling importance at the retail level, as determined by The Billboard's weekly survey of the top volume dealers in every important market area. When significant action is reported on both sides of a record, points are combined to determine position on the chart. In such a case, both sides are listed in bold type, the leading side on top.

This Week	Record	Last Week	Weeks on Chart
1.	**ROCK AROUND THE CLOCK** (ASCAP)—B. Haley Thirteen Women (BMI)—Dec 29124	1	11
2.	**LEARNIN' THE BLUES** (ASCAP)—F. Sinatra If I Had Three Wishes (ASCAP)—Cap 3102	5	11
3.	**CHERRY PINK AND APPLE BLOSSOM WHITE** (ASCAP)—P. Prado Marie Elena Rumba (ASCAP)—Vic 20-5965	2	21
4.	**BLOSSOM FELL** (ASCAP)—Nat (King) Cole **IF I MAY** (BMI)—Cap 3095	3	12
5.	**UNCHAINED MELODY** (ASCAP)—L. Baxter Medic (ASCAP)—Cap 3055	4	16
6.	**SOMETHING'S GOTTA GIVE** (ASCAP)—McGuire Sisters Rhythm n' Blues (BMI)—Coral 61423	7	8
7.	**HARD TO GET** (ASCAP)—G. MacKenzie Boston Fancy (BMI)—X 0137	8	8
8.	**AIN'T IT A SHAME?** (BMI)—P. Boone Tennessee Saturday Night (BMI)—Dot 15377	16	3
9.	**HONEY BABE** (ASCAP)—A. Mooney No Regrets (ASCAP)—M-G-M 11900	6	14
10.	**IT'S A SIN TO TELL A LIE** (ASCAP)—S. Smith & the Redheads My Baby Just Cares for Me (ASCAP)—Epic 9093	10	17
11.	**SOMETHING'S GOTTA GIVE** (ASCAP)—S. Davis Jr. **LOVE ME OR LEAVE ME** (ASCAP)—Dec 29484	9	9
12.	**UNCHAINED MELODY** (ASCAP)—A. Hibbler Daybreak (ASCAP)—Dec 29441	11	16
13.	**SWEET AND GENTLE** (BMI)—A. Dale You Still Mean the Same to Me (ASCAP)—Coral 61435	12	4
14.	**SEVENTEEN** (BMI)—B. Bennett Little Old You-All (BMI)—King 1470	22	3
15.	**RAZZLE DAZZLE** (BMI)—B. Haley **TWO HOUND DOGS** (ASCAP)—Dec 29552	—	1
16.	**STORY UNTOLD** (BMI)—Crew Cuts Carmen's Boogie (BMI)—Mercury 70634	18	5
17.	**HUMMINGBIRD** (ASCAP)—L. Paul & M. Ford Goodbye My Love—Cap 3165	—	1
18.	**HOUSE OF BLUE LIGHTS** (ASCAP)—C. Miller Can't Help Wonderin' (ASCAP)—Mercury 70627	17	6
19.	**MAN IN THE RAINCOAT** (BMI)—P. Wright Please Have Mercy (BMI)—Unique 303	24	5
20.	**UNCHAINED MELODY** (ASCAP)—R. Hamilton From Here to Eternity (ASCAP)—Epic 9102	13	14
21.	**DANCE WITH ME HENRY** (BMI)—G. Gibbs Every Road Must Have a Turning (BMI)—Mercury 70572	14	18
22.	**THAT OLD BLACK MAGIC** (ASCAP)—S. Davis Jr. Man With a Dream (ASCAP)—Dec 29541	21	5
23.	**AIN'T IT A SHAME?** (BMI)—F. Domino La La (BMI)—Imperial 5348	20	2
23	**I'LL NEVER STOP LOVING YOU** (ASCAP)—Doris Day Never Look Back (BMI)—Col 40505	—	1
25	**ALABAMA JUBILEE** (ASCAP)—Ferko String Band Sing a Little Melody (BMI)—Media 1010	19	6
25.	**DOMANI** (BMI)—J. La Rosa Mama Rosa (ASCAP)—Cadence 1265	—	1

DEALERS AND OPERATORS...

Top Ten Tunes Poster is on page 84

Tomorrow's Hits . . . Today Poster is on Page 86

• THIS WEEK'S BEST BUYS

According to sales reports in key markets, the following recent releases are recommended for extra profits:

FOOLED (Harms, ASCAP)

TINA MARIE (Roncom, ASCAP)—**Perry Como—RCA Victor 6192**

Both sides of Como's latest record have been kicking up considerable action these past two weeks, with considerable territorial variation as to side preference. The disk itself is now selling very well in New York, Philadelphia, Baltimore, Buffalo, Pittsburgh, Milwaukee, Detroit, Atlanta and St. Louis. A previous Billboard "Spotlight" pick.

PIDDILY PATTER PATTER (E. B. Marks, BMI)—**Patti Page—Mercury 70657**

The songstress appears to have a timely piece of material in this rhythm & blues hit, for pop customers in almost all territories checked were reported buying it in sizable quantities. The Nappy Brown version is also seeing good pop action in some areas, but this has not been much of an obstacle to Patti Page in Boston, New York, Baltimore, Philadelphia, Buffalo, Pittsburgh, Chicago, Milwaukee, Detroit, St. Louis and Cincinnati. Flip is "Every Day" (Golden State, BMI).

THE LONGEST WALK (Advanced, ASCAP)

SWANEE (New World, ASCAP)—**Jaye P. Morgan—RCA Victor 6182**

The fast way this disk is shaping up indicates that it may very well be one of the thrush's strongest powerhouses to date. Available little more than 10 days, this record is now solidly entrenched in Philadelphia, Baltimore, Buffalo, Milwaukee, Detroit, St. Louis and Pittsburgh. It is also beginning to move well in Atlanta, Boston, Providence and Chicago. Action on the two sides is fairly evenly split at this point, with the edge on "Walk." A previous Billboard "Spotlight" pick.

• Most Played in Juke Boxes

For survey week ending July 13

RECORDS are ranked in order of the greatest number of plays in juke boxes thruout the country, as determined by The Billboard's weekly survey of the nation's juke box operators. When significant play is reported on both sides of a record, points are combined to determine position on the chart. In such a case, both sides are listed in bold type, the leading side on top.

This Week	Record	Last Week	Weeks on Chart
1.	**CHERRY PINK AND APPLE BLOSSOM WHITE** (ASCAP)—P. Prado Marie Elena Rumba (ASCAP)—Vic 20-5965	1	16
2.	**ROCK AROUND THE CLOCK** (ASCAP)—B. Haley Thirteen Women (BMI)—Dec 29124	2	6
3.	**BLOSSOM FELL** (ASCAP)—Nat (King) Cole **IF I MAY** (BMI)—Cap 3095	3	9
4.	**LEARNIN' THE BLUES** (ASCAP)—F. Sinatra If I Had Three Wishes (ASCAP)—Cap 3102	5	6
5.	**UNCHAINED MELODY** (ASCAP)—L. Baxter Medic (ASCAP)—Cap 3055	6	12
6.	**DANCE WITH ME HENRY** (BMI)—G. Gibbs Every Road Must Have a Turning (BMI)—Mercury 70572	4	17
7.	**HONEY BABE** (ASCAP)—A. Mooney No Regrets (ASCAP)—M-G-M 11900	7	10
7.	**HARD TO GET** (ASCAP)—G. MacKenzie Boston Fancy (BMI)—X 0137	10	3
9.	**UNCHAINED MELODY** (ASCAP)—A. Hibbler Daybreak (ASCAP)—Dec 29441	8	13
10.	**SOMETHING'S GOTTA GIVE** (ASCAP)—McGuire Sisters Rhythm 'n' Blues (BMI)—Coral 61423	9	7
11.	**IT'S A SIN TO TELL A LIE** (ASCAP)—S. Smith & the Redheads My Baby Just Cares for Me (ASCAP)—Epic 9093	12	8
12.	**UNCHAINED MELODY** (ASCAP)—R. Hamilton From Here to Eternity (ASCAP)—Epic 9102	11	12
13.	**HEART** (ASCAP)—E. Fisher Near to You (ASCAP)—Vic 20-6097	17	8
14.	**ROLLIN' STONE** (BMI)—Fontane Sisters Playmates (ASCAP)—Dot 15370	14	5
15.	**HEY, MR. BANJO** (ASCAP)—Sunnysiders Zoom, Zoom, Zoom (ASCAP)—Kapp 113	20	9
16.	**AIN'T IT A SHAME?** (BMI)—P. Boone Tennessee Saturday Night (BMI)—Dot 15377	18	2
16.	**BALLAD OF DAVY CROCKETT** (BMI)—Tennessee Ernie Farewell (BMI)—Cap 3058	13	15
18.	**SWEET AND GENTLE** (BMI)—A. Dale You Still Mean the Same to Me (ASCAP)—Coral 61435	14	3
18.	**CHEE CHEE OO CHEE** P. Como & J. P. Morgan Two Lost Souls (BMI)—Vic 20-6137	14	4
20.	**THAT OLD BLACK MAGIC** (ASCAP)—S. Davis Jr. Man With a Dream (ASCAP)—Dec 29541	—	1

• Most Played by Jockeys

For survey week ending July 13

SIDES are ranked in order of the greatest number of plays on disk jockey radio shows thruout the country. Results are based on The Billboard's weekly survey among the nation's disk jockeys. The reverse side of each record is also listed.

This Week	Record	Last Week	Weeks on Chart
1.	**ROCK AROUND THE CLOCK**—B. Haley Thirteen Women (ASCAP)—Dec 29124	1	9
2.	**LEARNIN' THE BLUES**—F. Sinatra If I Had Three Wishes (ASCAP)—Cap 3102	2	12
3.	**BLOSSOM FELL**—Nat (King) Cole If I May (ASCAP)—Cap 3095	5	11
4.	**CHERRY PINK AND APPLE BLOSSOM WHITE**—P. Prado Marie Elena Rumba (ASCAP)—Vic 20-5965	4	15
5.	**SOMETHING'S GOTTA GIVE**—McGuire Sisters Rhythm 'n' Blues (ASCAP)—Coral 61423	6	8
6.	**UNCHAINED MELODY**—L. Baxter Medic (ASCAP)—Cap 3055	3	16
7.	**HARD TO GET**—G. MacKenzie Boston Fancy (ASCAP)—X 0137	9	4
8.	**UNCHAINED MELODY**—A. Hibbler Daybreak (ASCAP)—Dec 29441	7	14
9.	**IF I MAY**—Nat (King) Cole Blossom Fell (BMI)—Cap 3095	8	8
10.	**SWEET AND GENTLE**—A. Dale You Still Mean the Same to Me (BMI)—Coral 61435	11	3
11.	**UNCHAINED MELODY**—R. Hamilton From Here to Eternity (ASCAP)—Epic 9102	10	12
12.	**HUMMINGBIRD**—L. Paul & M. Ford Goodbye My Love (ASCAP)—Cap 3165	18	3
13.	**IT'S A SIN TO TELL A LIE**—S. Smith & the Redheads My Baby Just Cares for Me (ASCAP)—Epic 9093	15	4
14.	**AIN'T IT A SHAME?**—P. Boone Tennessee Saturday Night (BMI)—Dot 15377	16	2
15.	**HONEY BABE**—A. Mooney No Regrets (ASCAP)—M-G-M 11900	20	7
16.	**HEART**—E. Fisher Near to You (ASCAP)—Vic 20-6097	13	11
17.	**SWEET AND GENTLE**—G. Gibbs Blueberries (BMI)—Mercury 70647	12	3
18.	**THAT OLD BLACK MAGIC**—S. Davis Jr. Man With a Dream (ASCAP)—Dec 29541	19	3
19.	**HOUSE OF BLUE LIGHTS**—C. Miller Can't Help Wonderin' (ASCAP)—Mercury 70627	—	1
20.	**SOMETHING'S GOTTA GIVE**—S. Davis Jr. Love Me Or Leave Me (ASCAP)—Dec 2948	—	2

The Billboard Music Popularity Charts — POPULAR RECORDS

• Best Sellers in Stores

For survey week ending July 20

RECORDS are ranked in order of their current national selling importance at the retail level, as determined by The Billboard's weekly survey of the top volume dealers in every important market area. When significant action is reported on both sides of a record, points are combined to determine position on the chart. In such a case, both sides are listed in bold type, the leading side on top.

This Week		Last Week	Weeks on Chart
1.	ROCK AROUND THE CLOCK (ASCAP)—B. Haley Thirteen Women (BMI)—Dec 29124	1	12
2.	BLOSSOM FELL (ASCAP)—Nat (King) Cole IF I MAY (BMI)—Cap 3095	4	13
3.	LEARNIN' THE BLUES (ASCAP)—F. Sinatra If I Had Three Wishes (ASCAP)—Cap 3102	2	12
4.	CHERRY PINK AND APPLE BLOSSOM WHITE (ASCAP)—P. Prado Marie Elena Rumba (ASCAP)—Vic 20-5965	3	22
5.	AIN'T IT A SHAME? (BMI)—P. Boone Tennessee Saturday Night (BMI)—Dot 15377	8	4
6.	HARD TO GET (ASCAP)—G. MacKenzie Boston Fancy (BMI)—X 0137	7	9
7.	UNCHAINED MELODY (ASCAP)—L. Baxter Medic (ASCAP)—Cap 3055	5	17
8.	SOMETHING'S GOTTA GIVE (ASCAP)—McGuire Sisters RHYTHM 'N' BLUES (BMI)—Coral 61423	6	9
9.	IT'S A SIN TO TELL A LIE (ASCAP)—S. Smith & the Redheads My Baby Just Cares for Me (ASCAP)—Epic 9093	10	18
10.	SOMETHING'S GOTTA GIVE (ASCAP)—S. Davis Jr. LOVE ME OR LEAVE ME (ASCAP)—Dec 29484	12	17
11.	HONEY BABE (ASCAP)—A. Mooney No Regrets (ASCAP)—M-G-M 11900	9	15
12.	UNCHAINED MELODY (ASCAP)—A. Hibbler Daybreak (ASCAP)—Dec 29441	12	17
13.	HUMMINGBIRD (ASCAP)—L. Paul & M. Ford Goodbye My Love (ASCAP)—Cap 3165	17	2
14.	HOUSE OF BLUE LIGHTS (ASCAP)—C. Miller Can't Help Wonderin' (ASCAP)—Mercury 70627	18	7
15.	SWEET AND GENTLE (BMI)—A. Dale You Still Mean the Same to Me (ASCAP)—Coral 61435	13	5
16.	SEVENTEEN (BMI)—B. Bennett Little Old You-All (BMI)—King 1470	14	4
17.	STORY UNTOLD (BMI)—Crew Cuts Carmen's Boogie (BMI)—Mercury 70634	16	6
18.	DOMANI (BMI)—J. La Rosa Mama Rosa (ASCAP)—Cadence 1265	25	2
19.	THAT OLD BLACK MAGIC (ASCAP)—S. Davis Jr. Man With a Dream (ASCAP)—Dec 29541	22	6
19.	I'LL NEVER STOP LOVING YOU (ASCAP)—Doris Day Never Look Back (BMI)—Col 40505	23	2
21.	RAZZLE DAZZLE (BMI)—B. Haley TWO HOUND DOGS (ASCAP)—Dec 29552	15	2
22.	AIN'T IT A SHAME? (BMI)—F. Domino La, La (BMI)—Imperial 5348	23	3
23.	MAN IN THE RAINCOAT (BMI)—P. Wright Please Have Mercy (BMI)—Unique 303	19	6
24.	KENTUCKIAN SONG—Hilltoppers I Must Be Dreaming—Dot 15375	—	1
25.	MY ONE SIN (BMI)—Nat (King) Cole Blues From "Kiss Me Deadly" (BMI)—Cap 3136	—	2

DEALERS AND OPERATORS...

Tomorrow's Hits . . . Today Poster is on page 37

Top Ten Tunes Poster is on page 39

• THIS WEEK'S BEST BUYS

According to sales reports in key markets, the following recent releases are recommended for extra profits:

YELLOW ROSE OF TEXAS (Planetary, ASCAP) —**Mitch Miller—Columbia 40540—Johnny Desmond—Coral 61476**

In this tune at least two record companies have hit gushers. The Miller waxing is leading on an over-all national basis, but both versions listed above bid fair to crash the national charts at an early date. The Milwaukee and Cleveland territorial charts already list the Columbia disk, but in those two areas, as in many others, Desmond is also doing a very healthy volume. Flip of the Miller record is "Blackberry Winter" (Acuff-Rose, BMI), while that of Desmond's is "You're in Love With Someone" (Supreme, ASCAP). Both previously were Billboard "Spotlight" picks.

WAKE THE TOWN (Joy, ASCAP)—**Les Baxter—Capitol 3120**

While the flip side of this record, "I'll Never Stop Loving You" (Robbins, ASCAP) did nicely from the time of release two months ago, it has taken the last two weeks to kick off the reverse side on really big scale. Territories that are selling it in especially large quantities include New York, Pittsburgh, Cleveland, Cincinnati, Milwaukee, Detroit, St. Louis and the Carolinas. Some areas report the Mindy Carson version also to be shaping up nicely. The Baxter record was a Billboard "Spotlight" pick.

SONG OF THE DREAMER (Ludlow, ASCAP)—**Eddie Fisher—RCA Victor 6196**

Skeptics that thought Eddie Fisher would have a tough time breaking thru with a rhythm & blues piece of material seem doomed to disappointment, for this record is coming up quite fast now. Philadelphia, Buffalo, Pittsburgh, Baltimore, Durham, St. Louis, Boston, Providence, Cleveland and Milwaukee were among the areas enjoying sizable volume. More than casual interest is being expressed in the flip side, "Don't Stay Away Too Long" (Bourne, ASCAP). A previous Billboard "Spotlight" pick.

LOVE IS A MANY-SPLENDORED THING (Robbins, ASCAP)—**The Four Aces—Decca 29625**

While dealers have not had deliveries of this disk more than 10 days, interest has been so spontaneous that it looks set for a quick transit to the charts. Best areas for it so far have been Philadelphia, Buffalo, Pittsburgh, Boston, Providence, Baltimore, Cleveland, Detroit and St. Louis. Flip is "Shine On, Harvest Moon." A previous Billboard "Spotlight" pick.

• Most Played in Juke Boxes

For survey week ending July 20

RECORDS are ranked in order of the greatest number of plays in juke boxes thruout the country, as determined by The Billboard's weekly survey of the nation's juke box operators. When significant play is reported on both sides of a record, points are combined to determine position on the chart. In such a case, both sides are listed in bold type, the leading side on top.

This Week		Last Week	Weeks on Chart
1.	ROCK AROUND THE CLOCK (ASCAP)—B. Haley Thirteen Women (BMI)—Dec 29124	2	7
2.	CHERRY PINK AND APPLE BLOSSOM WHITE (ASCAP)—P. Prado Marie Elena Rumba (ASCAP)—Vic 20-5965	1	17
3.	BLOSSOM FELL (ASCAP)—Nat (King) Cole If I May (BMI)—Cap 3095	3	10
4.	LEARNIN' THE BLUES (ASCAP)—F. Sinatra If I Had Three Wishes (ASCAP)—Cap 3102	4	7
5.	UNCHAINED MELODY (ASCAP)—L. Baxter Medic (ASCAP)—Cap 3055	5	13
6.	HARD TO GET (ASCAP)—G. MacKenzie Boston Fancy (BMI)—X 0137	7	4
7.	HONEY BABE (ASCAP)—A. Mooney No Regrets (ASCAP)—M-G-M 11900	7	11
8.	DANCE WITH ME HENRY (BMI)—G. Gibbs Every Road Must Have a Turning (BMI)—Mercury 70572	6	18
9.	SOMETHING'S GOTTA GIVE (ASCAP)—McGuire Sisters Rhythm 'n' Blues (BMI)—Coral 61423	10	8
10.	IT'S A SIN TO TELL A LIE (ASCAP)—S. Smith & the Redheads My Baby Just Cares for Me (ASCAP)—Epic 9093	11	9
11.	UNCHAINED MELODY (ASCAP)—A. Hibbler Daybreak (ASCAP)—Dec 29441	9	14
12.	UNCHAINED MELODY (ASCAP)—R. Hamilton From Here to Eternity (ASCAP)—Epic 9102	12	13
13.	AIN'T IT A SHAME? (BMI)—P. Boone Tennessee Saturday Night (BMI)—Dot 15377	16	3
14.	HEART (ASCAP)—E. Fisher Near to You (ASCAP)—Vic 20-6097	13	9
14.	ALABAMA JUBILEE (ASCAP)—Ferko String Band Sing a Little Melody (BMI)—Media 1010	—	1
16.	AIN'T IT A SHAME? (BMI)—Fats Domino La, La (BMI)—Imperial 5348	—	1
16.	HUMMINGBIRD (ASCAP)—L. Paul & M. Ford Goodbye My Love (ASCAP)—Cap 3165	—	1
18.	HEY, MR. BANJO (ASCAP)—Sunnysiders Zoom, Zoom, Zoom (ASCAP)—Kapp 113	15	10
18.	THAT OLD BLACK MAGIC (ASCAP)—S. Davis Jr. Man With a Dream (ASCAP)—Dec 29541	20	2
18.	BANJO'S BACK IN TOWN (ASCAP)—T. Brewer How to Be Very, Very Popular (ASCAP)—Coral 61448	—	1

• Most Played by Jockeys

For survey week ending July 20

SIDES are ranked in order of the greatest number of plays on disk jockey radio shows thruout the country. Results are based on The Billboard's weekly survey among the nation's disk jockeys. The reverse side of each record is also listed.

This Week		Last Week	Weeks on Chart
1.	LEARNIN' THE BLUES—F. Sinatra If I Had Three Wishes (ASCAP)—Cap 3102	2	13
2.	ROCK AROUND THE CLOCK—B. Haley Thirteen Women (ASCAP)—Dec 29124	1	10
3.	BLOSSOM FELL—Nat (King) Cole If I May (ASCAP)—Cap 3095	3	12
4.	UNCHAINED MELODY—L. Baxter Medic (ASCAP)—Cap 3055	6	17
5.	HARD TO GET—G. MacKenzie Boston Fancy (ASCAP)—X 0137	7	5
6.	SOMETHING'S GOTTA GIVE—McGuire Sisters Rhythm 'n' Blues (ASCAP)—Coral 61423	5	9
7.	AIN'T IT A SHAME?—P. Boone Tennessee Saturday Night (BMI)—Dot 15377	14	3
8.	CHERRY PINK AND APPLE BLOSSOM WHITE—P. Prado Marie Elena Rumba (ASCAP)—Vic 20-5965	4	16
9.	UNCHAINED MELODY—A. Hibbler Daybreak (ASCAP)—Dec 29441	8	15
10.	IF I MAY—Nat (King) Cole Blossom Fell (BMI)—Cap 3095	9	9
11.	HEART—E. Fisher Near to You (ASCAP)—Vic 20-6097	16	12
12.	HUMMINGBIRD—L. Paul & M. Ford Goodbye My Love—Cap 3165	12	4
13.	SWEET AND GENTLE—A. Dale You Still Mean the Same to Me—Coral 61435	10	4
14.	UNCHAINED MELODY—R. Hamilton From Here to Eternity (ASCAP)—Epic 9102	11	13
15.	THAT OLD BLACK MAGIC—S. Davis Jr. Man With a Dream (ASCAP)—Dec 29541	18	4
16.	SWEET AND GENTLE—G. Gibbs Blueberries (BMI)—Mercury 70647	17	4
17.	IT'S A SIN TO TELL A LIE—S. Smith & the Redheads My Baby Just Cares for Me (ASCAP)—Epic 9093	13	5
18.	HONEY BABE—A. Mooney No Regrets (ASCAP)—M-G-M 11900	15	8
19.	DOMANI—J. La Rosa Mama Rosa (BMI)—Cadence 1265	—	1
20.	I'LL NEVER STOP LOVING YOU—Doris Day Never Look Back (ASCAP)—Col 40505	—	1

The Billboard Music Popularity Charts — POPULAR RECORDS

• Best Sellers in Stores

For survey week ending July 27

RECORDS are ranked in order of their current national selling importance at the retail level, as determined by The Billboard's weekly survey of the top volume dealers in every important market area. When significant action is reported on both sides of a record, points are combined to determine position on the chart. In such a case, both sides are listed in bold type, the leading side on top.

This Week		Last Week	Weeks on Chart
1.	**ROCK AROUND THE CLOCK** (ASCAP)—B. Haley Thirteen Women (BMI)—Dec 29124	1	13
2.	**LEARNIN' THE BLUES** (ASCAP)—F. Sinatra If I Had Three Wishes (ASCAP)—Cap 3102	3	13
3.	**BLOSSOM FELL** (ASCAP)—Nat (King) Cole **IF I MAY** (BMI)—Cap 3095	2	14
4.	**AIN'T IT A SHAME?** BMI)—P. Boone Tennessee Saturday Night (BMI)—Dot 15377	5	5
5.	**CHERRY PINK AND APPLE BLOSSOM WHITE** ASCAP)—P. Prado Marie Elena Rumba (ASCAP)—V 20-5965	4	23
6.	**HARD TO GET** (ASCAP)—G. MacKenzie Boston Fancy (BMI)—X 0137	6	10
7.	**UNCHAINED MELODY** (ASCAP)—L. Baxter Medic (ASCAP)—Cap 3055	7	18
8.	**IT'S A SIN TO TELL A LIE** (ASCAP)—S. Smith & the Redheads My Baby Just Cares for Me (ASCAP)—Epic 9093	9	19
9.	**SOMETHING'S GOTTA GIVE** (ASCAP)—McGuire Sisters Rhythm 'n' Blues (BMI)—Coral 61423	8	10
10.	**SOMETHING'S GOTTA GIVE** (ASCAP) S. Davis Jr. **LOVE ME OR LEAVE ME** (ASCAP)—	10	18
11.	**HUMMINGBIRD** (ASCAP)—L. Paul & M. Ford Goodbye My Love (ASCAP)—Cap 3165	13	3
12.	**SWEET AND GENTLE** (BMI)—A. Dale You Still Mean the Same to Me (ASCAP)—Coral 61435	15	6
13.	**DOMANI** (BMI)—J. La Rosa Mama Rosa (ASCAP)—Cadence 1265	18	3
14.	**SEVENTEEN** (BMI)—B. Bennett Little Old You-All (BMI)—King 1470	16	5
15.	**HONEY BABE** (ASCAP)—A. Mooney No Regrets (ASCAP)—M-G-M 11900	11	16
16.	**HOUSE OF BLUE LIGHTS** (ASCAP)—C. Miller Can't Help Wonderin' (ASCAP)—Mercury 70627	14	8
17.	**YELLOW ROSE OF TEXAS** (ASCAP)—M. Miller Blackberry Winter (BMI)—Col 40540	—	1
18.	**MAN IN THE RAINCOAT** (BMI)—P. Wright Please Have Mercy (BMI)—Unique 303	23	7
19.	**AIN'T IT A SHAME?** (BMI)—F. Domino La La (BMI)—Imperial 5348	22	4
20.	**UNCHAINED MELODY** (ASCAP)—A. Hibbler Daybreak (ASCAP)—Dec 29441	12	18
21.	**STORY UNTOLD** (BMI)—Crew Cuts Carmen's Boogie (BMI)—Mercury 70634	17	7
22.	**KENTUCKIAN SONG** (ASCAP)—Hilltoppers I Must Be Dreaming (BMI)—Dot 15375	24	2
23.	**THAT OLD BLACK MAGIC** (ASCAP)—S. Davis Jr. Man With a Dream (ASCAP)—Dec 29541	19	7
24.	**RAZZLE DAZZLE** (BMI)—B. Haley Two Hound Dogs (ASCAP)—Dec 29552	21	3
25.	**I'LL NEVER STOP LOVING YOU** (ASCAP)—Doris Day Never Look Back (BMI)—Col 40505	19	3

DEALERS AND OPERATORS...

Top Ten Tunes Poster is on page 60

Tomorrow's Hits . . . Today Poster is on page 62

• THIS WEEK'S BEST BUYS

According to sales reports in key markets, the following recent releases are recommended for extra profits:

THE BIBLE TELLS ME SO (Paramount, ASCAP)—Nick Noble—Wing 90003

LOVE IS A MANY SPLENDORED THING (Robbins, ASCAP—Don Cornell—Coral 61467

Nick Noble's version of "Bible" has been available for a number of weeks and has gradually built up a solid core of strength. Currently it appears on the Detroit, Chicago and Cleveland territorial charts. Cornell has come up from behind to give Noble stiff competition in many areas. It has a good spread of favorable sales reports thruout the country. Both are now shaping up as chart threats. The flip side of the Cornell disk is showing good action, too, but the Four Aces have a decided edge on that tune. The Coral record was a previous Billboard "Spotlight" pick.

AUTUMN LEAVES (Ardmore, ASCAP)—Roger Williams—Kapp 16

One of the biggest records to hit New York, Cleveland and Detroit in the past few weeks has been this instrumental featuring piano and strings. The record is now beginning to take off in Boston, Buffalo and Milwaukee, and promises to be a big seller in other territories once delivered and more thoroly exploited. The potential of this disk is burgeoning quite rapidly. Flip is "Take Care" (Ashland, BMI).

SEVENTEEN (Lois, BMI)—Fontane Sisters—Dot 15386

The Fontane Sisters are coming up fast with their recently released cover of this hit. While the Boyd Bennett waxing is still far ahead, reports from Boston, New York, Philadelphia, Baltimore, Buffalo, Providence, Nashville, St. Louis and Durham indicate that this has not prevented the girls from racking up very good sales in those areas. Flip is "If I Could Be With You" (Remick, ASCAP). A previous Billboard "Spotlight" pick.

• Most Played in Juke Boxes

For survey week ending July 27

RECORDS are ranked in order of the greatest number of plays in juke boxes thruout the country, as determined by The Billboard's weekly survey of the nation's juke box operators. When significant play is reported on both sides of a record, points are combined to determine position on the chart. In such a case, both sides are listed in bold type, the leading side on top.

This Week		Last Week	Weeks on Chart
1.	**ROCK AROUND THE CLOCK** (ASCAP)—B. Haley Thirteen Women (BMI)—Dec 29124	1	8
2.	**CHERRY PINK AND APPLE BLOSSOM WHITE**—(ASCAP)—P. Prado Marie Elena Rumba (ASCAP)—Vic 20-5965	2	18
3.	**BLOSSOM FELL** (ASCAP)—Nat (King) Cole **IF I MAY**—Cap 3095	3	11
4.	**LEARNIN' THE BLUES** (ASCAP)—F. Sinatra If I Had Three Wishes (ASCAP)—Cap 3102	4	8
5.	**HARD TO GET** (ASCAP)—G. MacKenzie Boston Fancy (BMI)—X 0137	6	5
6.	**SOMETHING'S GOTTA GIVE** (ASCAP)—McGuire Sisters Rhythm 'n' Blues (BMI)—Coral 61423	9	9
7.	**AIN'T IT A SHAME?** (BMI)—P. Boone Tennessee Saturday Night (BMI)—Dot 15377	13	4
8.	**UNCHAINED MELODY** (ASCAP)—L. Baxter Medic (ASCAP)—Cap 3055	5	14
8.	**HONEY BABE** (ASCAP)—A. Mooney No Regrets (ASCAP)—M-G-M 11900	7	12
10.	**IT'S A SIN TO TELL A LIE** (ASCAP)—S. Smith & the Redheads My Baby Just Cares for Me (ASCAP)—Epic 9093	10	10
11.	**UNCHAINED MELODY** (ASCAP)—A. Hibbler Daybreak (ASCAP)—Dec 29441	11	15
12.	**DANCE WITH ME HENRY** (BMI)—G. Gibbs Every Road Must Have a Turning (BMI)—Mercury 70572	8	19
13.	**HUMMINGBIRD** (ASCAP)—L. Paul & M. Ford Goodbye My Love—Cap 3165	16	2
14.	**UNCHAINED MELODY** (ASCAP)—R. Hamilton From Here to Eternity (ASCAP)—Epic 9102	12	14
15.	**BANJO'S BACK IN TOWN** (ASCAP)—T. Brewer How to Be Very, Very Popular—Coral 61448	18	2
16.	**AIN'T IT A SHAME?** (BMI)—F. Domino La, La (BMI)—Imperial 5348	16	2
17.	**GOOD AND LONESOME**—K. Starr Where, What or When?—Vic 20-6146	—	1
18.	**ALABAMA JUBILEE** (ASCAP)—Ferko String Band Sing a Little Melody (BMI)—Media 1010	14	2
18.	**SOMETHING'S GOTTA GIVE** S. Davis Jr. Love Me or Leave Me (ASCAP)—Dec 29484	—	2
18.	**MAN IN THE RAINCOAT** (BMI)—M. Marlowe Heartbeat—Cadence 1266	—	1

• Most Played by Jockeys

For survey week ending July 27

SIDES are ranked in order of the greatest number of plays on disk jockey radio shows thruout the country. Results are based on The Billboard's weekly survey among the nation's disk jockeys. The reverse side of each record is also listed.

This Week		Last Week	Weeks on Chart
1.	**ROCK AROUND THE CLOCK**—B. Haley Thirteen Women—Dec 29124—ASCAP	2	11
2.	**LEARNIN' THE BLUES**—F. Sinatra If I Had Three Wishes—Cap 3102—ASCAP	1	14
3.	**AIN'T IT A SHAME?**—P. Boone Tennessee Saturday Night—Dot 15377—BMI	3	13
4.	**BLOSSOM FELL**—Nat (King) Cole If I May—Cap 3095—ASCAP	7	4
5.	**HARD TO GET**—G. MacKenzie Boston Fancy—X 0137—ASCAP	5	6
6.	**SOMETHING'S GOTTA GIVE**—McGuire Sisters Rhythm 'n' Blues—Coral 61423—ASCAP	6	10
7.	**UNCHAINED MELODY**—L. Baxter Medic—Cap 3055—ASCAP	4	18
8.	**CHERRY PINK AND APPLE BLOSSOM WHITE**—P. Prado Marie Elena Rumba—Vic 20-5965—ASCAP	8	17
9.	**HUMMINGBIRD**—L. Paul & M. Ford Goodbye My Love—Cap 3165—ASCAP	12	5
10.	**SWEET AND GENTLE**—A. Dale You Still Mean the Same to Me—Coral 61435—BMI	13	5
11.	**IT'S A SIN TO TELL A LIE**—S. Smith & the Redheads My Baby Just Care for Me—Epic 9093—ASCAP	17	6
12.	**UNCHAINED MELODY**—A. Hibbler Daybreak—Dec 29441—ASCAP	9	16
13.	**THAT OLD BLACK MAGIC**—S. Davis Jr. Man With a Dream—Dec 29541—ASCAP	15	5
14.	**MAN IN THE RAINCOAT**—M. Marlowe Heartbreak—Cadence 1266—BMI	—	2
15.	**I'LL NEVER STOP LOVING YOU**—D. Day Never Look Back—Col 40505—ASCAP	20	2
16.	**MAN IN THE RAINCOAT**—P. Wright Please Have Mercy—Unique 303—BMI	—	1
17.	**YELLOW ROSE OF TEXAS**—M. Miller Blackberry Winter—Col 40540—ASCAP	—	1
18.	**IF I MAY**—Nat (King) Cole Blossom Fell—Cap 3095—BMI	10	10
18.	**DOMANI**—J. La Rosa Mama Rosa—Cadence 1265—BMI	19	2
20.	**HOUSE OF BLUE LIGHTS**—C. Miller Can't Help Wonderin'—Mercury 70627—ASCAP	—	1
20.	**HEART**—E. Fisher Near to You—Vic 20-6097—ASCAP	11	13

The Billboard Music Popularity Charts — POPULAR RECORDS

• Best Sellers in Stores

For survey week ending August 3

RECORDS are ranked in order of their current national selling importance at the retail level, as determined by The Billboard's weekly survey of the top volume dealers in every important market area. When significant action is reported on both sides of a record, points are combined to determine position on the chart. In such a case, both sides are listed in bold type, the leading side on top.

This Week		Last Week	Weeks on Chart
1.	ROCK AROUND THE CLOCK (ASCAP)—B. Haley — Thirteen Women (BMI)—Dec 29124	1	14
2.	AIN'T IT A SHAME? (BMI)—P. Boone — Tennessee Saturday Night (BMI)—Dot 15377	4	6
3.	LEARNIN' THE BLUES (ASCAP)—F. Sinatra — If I Had Three Wishes (ASCAP)	2	14
4.	BLOSSOM FELL (ASCAP)—Nat (King) Cole — IF I MAY (BMI)—Cap 3095	3	15
5.	YELLOW ROSE OF TEXAS (ASCAP)—M. Miller — Blackberry Winter (BMI)—Col 45040	17	2
6.	HARD TO GET (ASCAP)—G. MacKenzie — Boston Fancy (BMI)—X 0137	6	11
7.	IT'S A SIN TO TELL A LIE (ASCAP)—S. Smith & the Redheads — My Baby Just Cares for Me (ASCAP)—Epic 9093	8	20
8.	HUMMINGBIRD (ASCAP)—L. Paul & M. Ford — Goodbye My Love (ASCAP)—Cap 3165	11	4
9.	CHERRY PINK AND APPLE BLOSSOM WHITE (ASCAP)—P. Prado — Marie Elena Rumba (ASCAP)—Vic 20-5965	5	24
10.	UNCHAINED MELODY (ASCAP)—L. Baxter — Medic (ASCAP)—Cap 3055	7	19
11.	SEVENTEEN (BMI)—B. Bennett — Little Old You-All (BMI)—King 1470	14	6
12.	HOUSE OF BLUE LIGHTS (ASCAP)—C. Miller — Can't Help Wonderin' (ASCAP)—Mercury 70627	16	9
13.	DOMANI (BMI)—J. La Rosa — Mama Rosa (ASCAP)—Cadence 1265	13	4
14.	SOMETHING'S GOTTA GIVE (ASCAP)—McGuire Sisters — Rhythm 'n' Blues (ASCAP)—Coral 61423	9	11
15	YELLOW ROSE OF TEXAS (ASCAP)—J. Desmond — You're in Love With Someone (ASCAP)—Coral 61476	—	1
16.	SOMETHING'S GOTTA GIVE (ASCAP)—S. Davis Jr. — LOVE ME OR LEAVE ME (ASCAP)—Dec 29484	10	19
17.	RAZZLE DAZZLE (BMI)—B. Haley — Two Hound Dogs (ASCAP)—Dec 29552	24	4
18.	SWEET AND GENTLE (BMI)—A. Dale — You Still Mean the Same to Me (ASCAP)—Coral 61435	12	7
19.	HONEY BABE (ASCAP)—A. Mooney — No Regrets (ASCAP)—M-G-M 11900	15	17
20.	KENTUCKIAN SONG (ASCAP)—Hilltoppers — I Must Be Dreaming—Dot 15375	22	3
21.	I'LL NEVER STOP LOVING YOU (ASCAP)—Doris Day — Never Look Back (BMI)—Col 40505	25	4
22.	TINA MARIE (ASCAP)—P. Como — FOOLED (ASCAP)—Vic 20-6192	—	1
23.	WAKE THE TOWN AND TELL THE PEOPLE (ASCAP)—L. Baxter — I'll Never Stop Loving You (ASCAP)—Cap 3120	—	1
23.	MAN IN THE RAINCOAT (BMI)—P. Wright — Please Have Mercy (BMI)—Unique 303	18	8
25.	AIN'T IT A SHAME? (BMI)—F. Domino — La La (BMI)—Imperial 5348	19	5

• THIS WEEK'S BEST BUYS

According to sales reports in key markets, the following recent releases are recommended for extra profits:

GUM DROP (Toombs, BMI)—Crew Cuts—Mercury 70668

The Crew Cuts' version of this item out of the rhythm and blues ranks is shaping up quickly as a national chart threat. This week it hit the territorial charts in Cincinnati and Cleveland, and it's a top favorite among dealers in many areas. There's particularly good action also reported this week in Boston, Pittsburgh and St. Louis, and it's showing good strength in Chicago, Milwaukee, Philadelphia and several other important markets. The flip is "Present Arms" (Bourne, ASCAP). "Gum Drop" was a previous Billboard "Spotlight" pick.

WAKE THE TOWN AND TELL THE PEOPLE (Joy, ASCAP)—Mindy Carson—Columbia 40537

The Les Baxter Capitol version made the charts this week, and there are better than strong indications that this solo vocal version soon will follow suit. It's close behind in dealer preference, and made its first territorial chart breakthru in Philadelphia. In addition, it's showing heavy action in Milwaukee, Atlanta, St. Louis, Providence and Baltimore. Strong sales in Philadelphia, Boston, Chicago, Pittsburgh, Buffalo and Durham. Flip is "Hold Me Tight" (Joy, ASCAP).

• Most Played in Juke Boxes

For survey week ending August 3

RECORDS are ranked in order of the greatest number of plays in juke boxes thruout the country, as determined by The Billboard's weekly survey of the nation's juke box operators. When significant play is reported on both sides of a record, points are combined to determine position on the chart. In such a case, both sides are listed in bold type, the leading side on top.

This Week		Last Week	Weeks on Chart
1.	ROCK AROUND THE CLOCK (ASCAP)—B. Haley — Thirteen Women (BMI)—Dec 29124	1	9
2.	LEARNIN' THE BLUES (ASCAP)—F. Sinatra — If I Had Three Wishes (ASCAP)—Cap 3102	4	9
3.	BLOSSOM FELL (ASCAP)—Nat (King) Cole — IF I MAY (BMI)—Cap 3095	3	12
4.	CHERRY PINK AND APPLE BLOSSOM WHITE (ASCAP)—P. Prado — Marie Elena Rumba (ASCAP)—Vic 20-5965	2	19
5.	AIN'T IT A SHAME? (BMI)—P. Boone — Tennessee Saturday Night (BMI)—Dot 15377	7	5
6.	HARD TO GET (ASCAP)—G. MacKenzie — Boston Fancy (BMI)—X 0137	5	6
7.	SOMETHING'S GOTTA GIVE (ASCAP)—McGuire Sisters — Rhythm 'n' Blues (ASCAP)—Coral 61423	6	10
8.	IT'S A SIN TO TELL A LIE (ASCAP)—S. Smith & the Redheads — My Baby Just Cares for Me (ASCAP)—Epic 9093	10	11
9.	HONEY BABE (ASCAP)—A. Mooney — No Regrets (ASCAP)—M-G-M 11900	8	13
10.	UNCHAINED MELODY (ASCAP)—A. Hibbler — Daybreak (ASCAP)—Dec 29441	11	16
11.	HUMMINGBIRD (ASCAP)—L. Paul & M. Ford — Goodbye My Love—Cap 3165	13	3
12.	UNCHAINED MELODY (ASCAP)—L. Baxter — Medic (ASCAP)—Cap 3055	8	15
12.	UNCHAINED MELODY (ASCAP)—R. Hamilton — From Here to Eternity (ASCAP)—Epic 9102	14	15
14.	AIN'T IT A SHAME? (BMI)—Fats Domino — LaLa (BMI)—Imperial 5348	16	3
14.	DANCE WITH ME HENRY (BMI)—G. Gibbs — Every Road Must Have a Turning (BMI)—Mercury 70572	12	20
16.	SOMETHING'S GOTTA GIVE (ASCAP)—S. Davis Jr. — Love Me Or Leave Me (ASCAP)—Dec 29484	18	3
16.	DOMANI (BMI)—J. La Rosa — Mama Rosa (ASCAP)—Cadence 1265	—	1
18.	BANJO'S BACK IN TOWN (ASCAP)—T. Brewer — How to Be Very, Very Popular—Coral 61448	15	3
18.	POPCORN SONG (BMI)—C. Stone — Barracuda—Cap 3131	—	1
20.	SWEET AND GENTLE (BMI)—A. Dale — You Still Mean the Same to Me (ASCAP)—Coral 61435	—	4
20.	MAN IN THE RAINCOAT (BMI)—P. Wright — Please Have Mercy (BMI)—Unique 303	—	1

• Most Played by Jockeys

For survey week ending August 3

SIDES are ranked in order of the greatest number of plays on disk jockey radio shows thruout the country. Results are based on The Billboard's weekly survey among the nation's disk jockeys. The reverse side of each record is also listed.

This Week		Last Week	Weeks on Chart
1.	ROCK AROUND THE CLOCK—B. Haley — Thirteen Women (ASCAP)—Dec 29124	1	12
2.	LEARNIN' THE BLUES—F. Sinatra — If I Had Three Wishes (ASCAP)—Cap 3102	2	15
3.	AIN'T IT A SHAME?—P. Boone — Tennessee Saturday Night (BMI)—Dot 15377	3	14
4.	HARD TO GET—G. MacKenzie — Boston Fancy (ASCAP)—X 0137	5	7
5.	YELLOW ROSE OF TEXAS—M. Miller — Blackberry Winter (ASCAP)—Col 40540	17	2
6.	BLOSSOM FELL—Nat (King) Cole — If I May (ASCAP)—Cap 3095	4	5
7	SOMETHING'S GOTTA GIVE—McGuire Sisters — Rhythm 'n' Blues (ASCAP)—Coral 61423	6	11
8.	UNCHAINED MELODY—L. Baxter — Medic (ASCAP)—Cap 3055	7	19
9.	IT'S A SIN TO TELL A LIE—S. Smith & the Redhead — My Baby Just Cares for Me (ASCAP)—Epic 9093	11	7
10.	HUMMINGBIRD—L. Paul & M. Ford — Goodbye My Love—Cap 3165	9	6
11.	UNCHAINED MELODY—A. Hibbler — Daybreak (ASCAP)—Dec 29441	12	17
12.	SWEET AND GENTLE—A. Dale — You Still Mean the Same to Me (BMI)—Coral 61435	10	6
13.	CHERRY PINK AND APPLE BLOSSOM WHITE—P. Prado — Marie Elena Rumba (ASCAP)—Vic 20-5965	8	18
13.	I'LL NEVER STOP LOVING YOU—D. Day — Never Look Back (ASCAP)—Col 40505	15	3
15.	SEVENTEEN—B. Bennett — Little Old You-All (BMI)—King 1470	—	1
16.	MAN IN THE RAINCOAT—P. Wright — Please Have Mercy (BMI)—Unique 303	16	2
16.	DOMANI—J. La Rosa — Mama Rosa (BMI)—Cadence 1265	18	3
18.	HOUSE OF BLUE LIGHTS—C. Miller — Can't Help Wonderin' (ASCAP)—Mercury 70627	20	2
18.	WAKE THE TOWN AND TELL THE PEOPLE—L. Baxter — I'll Never Stop Loving You (ASCAP)—Cap 3120	—	1
20.	THAT OLD BLACK MAGIC—S. Davis Jr. — Man With a Dream (ASCAP)—Dec 29541	13	6

The Billboard Music Popularity Charts — POPULAR RECORDS

• Best Sellers in Stores

For survey week ending August 10

RECORDS are ranked in order of their current national selling importance at the retail level, as determined by The Billboard's weekly survey of the top volume dealers in every important market area. When significant action is reported on both sides of a record, points are combined to determine position on the chart. In such a case, both sides are listed in bold type, the leading side on top.

This Week		Last Week	Weeks on Chart
1.	ROCK AROUND THE CLOCK (ASCAP)—B. Haley — Thirteen Women (BMI)—Dec 29124	1	15
2.	AIN'T THAT A SHAME? (BMI)—P. Boone — Tennessee Saturday Night (BMI)—Dot 15377	2	7
3.	YELLOW ROSE OF TEXAS (ASCAP)—M. Miller — Blackberry Winter (BMI)—Col 40540	5	3
4.	LEARNIN' THE BLUES (ASCAP)—F. Sinatra — If I Had Three Wishes (ASCAP)—Cap 3102	3	15
5.	BLOSSOM FELL (ASCAP)—Nat (King) Cole — IF I MAY (BMI)—Cap 3095	4	16
6.	SEVENTEEN (BMI)—B. Bennett — Little Old You-All (BMI)—King 1470	11	7
7.	HARD TO GET (ASCAP)—G. MacKenzie — Boston Fancy (BMI)—X 0137	6	12
8.	IT'S A SIN TO TELL A LIE (ASCAP)—S. Smith & the Redheads — My Baby Just Cares for Me (ASCAP)—Epic 9093	7	21
9.	HUMMINGBIRD (ASCAP)—L. Paul & M. Ford — Goodbye, My Love (ASCAP)—Cap 3165	8	5
10.	HOUSE OF BLUE LIGHTS (ASCAP)—C. Miller — Can't Help Wonderin' (ASCAP)—Mercury 70627	12	10
11.	YELLOW ROSE OF TEXAS (ASCAP)—J. Desmond — You're in Love With Someone (ASCAP)—Coral 61476	15	2
12.	UNCHAINED MELODY (ASCAP)—L. Baxter — Medic (ASCAP)—Cap 3055	10	20
13.	MAYBELLENE (BMI)—C. Berry — Wee Wee Hours (BMI)—Chess 1604	—	1
14.	CHERRY PINK AND APPLE BLOSSOM WHITE (ASCAP)—P. Prado — Marie Elena Rumba (ASCAP)—Vic 20-5965	9	25
15.	I'LL NEVER STOP LOVING YOU (ASCAP)—Doris Day — Never Look Back (BMI)—Col 40505	21	5
16.	WAKE THE TOWN AND TELL THE PEOPLE (ASCAP)—L. Baxter — I'll Never Stop Loving You (ASCAP)—Cap 3120	23	2
17.	DOMANI (BMI)—J. La Rosa — Mama Rosa (ASCAP)—Cadence 1265	13	5
18.	AIN'T THAT A SHAME? (BMI)—F. Domino — La La (BMI)—Imperial 5348	25	6
19.	MAN IN THE RAINCOAT (BMI)—P. Wright — Please Have Mercy (BMI)—Unique 303	23	9
20.	SOMETHING'S GOTTA GIVE (ASCAP)—McGuire Sisters — Rhythm 'n' Blues (ASCAP)—Coral 61423	14	12
21.	AUTUMN LEAVES (ASCAP)—R. Williams — Take Care (BMI)—Kapp 16	—	1
22.	KENTUCKIAN SONG (ASCAP) Hilltoppers — I Must Be Dreaming (BMI)—Dot 15575	20	4
23.	BIBLE TELLS ME SO (ASCAP)—N. Noble — Army of the Lord (BMI)—Wing 90003	—	1
23.	SEVENTEEN (BMI)—R. Draper — Can't Live With 'Em, Can't Live Without Them (BMI)—Mercury 70651	—	1
25.	POPCORN SONG (BMI)—C. Stone — Barracuda (BMI)—Cap 3131	—	1

DEALERS AND OPERATORS . . .

Tomorrow's Hits . . . Today
Poster is on page 42

Top Ten Tunes Poster
is on page 43

• THIS WEEK'S BEST BUYS

According to sales reports in key markets, the following recent releases are recommended for extra profits:

DAY BY DAY (Barton, ASCAP) — The Four Freshmen—Capitol 3154

A side that has been building slowly but steadily for some weeks, this now looms as an imminent chart entry. This week it appears on four territorial charts—Buffalo, Dallas-Fort Worth, Detroit and New Orleans. It's also reported strong in such scattered sectors as Pittsburgh, Atlanta, St. Louis, Milwaukee, New York, Baltimore, Durham and Los Angeles. Flip side is "How Can I Tell Her" (Famous, ASCAP).

YOU ARE MY SUNSHINE (Peer, BMI)—Ferko String Band—Media 1013

The follow-up to this gang's smash, "Alabama Jubilee," this version of the perennial is off to a fast start in the Midwest, with special strength reported in Milwaukee, St. Louis and Chicago. There's Eastern action in Providence, Philadelphia and Buffalo, and noticeable stirrings in Boston and Baltimore. A previous Billboard "Spotlight" pick. Flip is "Ma, He's Making Eyes at Me," (Mills, ASCAP).

• Most Played in Juke Boxes

For survey week ending August 10

RECORDS are ranked in order of the greatest number of plays in juke boxes thruout the country, as determined by The Billboard's weekly survey of the nation's juke box operators. When significant play is reported on both sides of a record, points are combined to determine position on the chart. In such a case, both sides are listed in bold type, the leading side on top.

This Week		Last Week	Weeks on Chart
1.	ROCK AROUND THE CLOCK (ASCAP)—B. Haley — Thirteen Women (BMI)—Dec 29124	1	10
2.	LEARNIN' THE BLUES (ASCAP)—F. Sinatra — If I Had Three Wishes (ASCAP)—Cap 3102	2	10
3.	AIN'T THAT A SHAME? (BMI)—P. Boone — Tennessee Saturday Night (BMI)—Dot 15377	5	6
4.	BLOSSOM FELL (ASCAP)—Nat (King) Cole — IF I MAY—Cap 3095	3	13
5.	HARD TO GET (ASCAP)—G. MacKenzie — Boston Fancy (BMI)—X 0137	6	7
6.	CHERRY PINK AND APPLE BLOSSOM WHITE (ASCAP)—P. Prado — Marie Elena Rumba (ASCAP)—Vic 20-5965	4	20
7.	HONEY BABE (ASCAP)—A. Mooney — No Regrets (ASCAP)—M-G-M 11900	9	14
8.	SOMETHING'S GOTTA GIVE (ASCAP)—McGuire Sisters — Rhythm 'n' Blues (ASCAP)—Coral 61423	7	11
8.	IT'S A SIN TO TELL A LIE (ASCAP)—S. Smith & the Redheads — My Baby Just Cares for Me (ASCAP)—Epic 9093	8	12
10.	UNCHAINED MELODY (ASCAP)—A. Hibbler — Daybreak (ASCAP)—Dec 29441	10	17
11.	HUMMINGBIRD (ASCAP)—L. Paul & M. Ford — Goodbye My Love—Cap 3165	11	4
12.	AIN'T IT A SHAME? (BMI)—Fats Domino — La, La (BMI)—Imperial 5348	14	4
13.	DOMANI (BMI)—J. La Rosa — Mama Rosa (ASCAP)—Cadence 1265	16	2
14.	POPCORN SONG (BMI)—C. Stone — Barracuda (BMI)—Cap 3131	18	2
14.	YELLOW ROSE OF TEXAS (ASCAP)—M. Miller — Blackberry Winter (BMI)—Col 40540	—	1
16.	UNCHAINED MELODY (ASCAP)—L. Baxter — Medic (ASCAP)—Cap 3055	12	16
16.	UNCHAINED MELODY (ASCAP)—R. Hamilton — From Here to Eternity (ASCAP)—Epic 9102	12	16
18.	SOMETHING'S GOTTA GIVE (ASCAP)—S. Davis Jr. — Love Me or Leave Me (ASCAP)—Dec 29484	16	4
18.	MAN IN THE RAINCOAT (BMI)—M. Marlowe — Heartbeat—Cadence 1266	20	2
18.	SEVENTEEN (BMI)—Fontane Sisters — If I Could Be With You (ASCAP)—Dot 15386	—	1

• Most Played by Jockeys

For survey week ending August 10

SIDES are ranked in order of the greatest number of plays on disk jockey radio shows thruout the country. Results are based on The Billboard's weekly survey among the nation's disk jockeys. The reverse side of each record is also listed.

This Week		Last Week	Weeks on Chart
1.	ROCK AROUND THE CLOCK—B. Haley — Thirteen Women—Dec 29124—ASCAP	1	13
2.	LEARNIN' THE BLUES—F. Sinatra — If I Had Three Wishes—Cap 3102—ASCAP	2	16
3.	YELLOW ROSE OF TEXAS—M. Miller — Blackberry Winter—Col 40540—ASCAP	5	3
4.	AIN'T THAT A SHAME?—P. Boone — Tennessee Saturday Night—Dot 15377—BMI	3	15
5.	HARD TO GET—G. MacKenzie — Boston Fancy—X 0137—ASCAP	4	8
6.	UNCHAINED MELODY—L. Baxter — Medic—Cap 3055—ASCAP	8	20
7.	BLOSSOM FELL—Nat (King) Cole — If I May—Cap 3095—ASCAP	6	6
8.	HUMMINGBIRD—L. Paul & M. Ford — Goodbye My Love—Cap 3165—ASCAP	10	7
9.	YELLOW ROSE OF TEXAS—J. Desmond — You're in Love With Someone—Coral 61476—ASCAP	—	1
10.	SEVENTEEN—B. Bennett — Little Old You-All—King 1470—BMI	15	2
11.	IT'S A SIN TO TELL A LIE—S. Smith & the Redheads — My Baby Just Cares for Me—Epic 9093—ASCAP	9	8
12.	TINA MARIE—P. Como — Fooled—Vic 20-6192—ASCAP	—	1
13.	SOMETHING'S GOTTA GIVE—McGuire Sisters — Rhythm 'n' Blues—Coral 61423—ASCAP	7	12
14.	I'LL NEVER STOP LOVING YOU—D. Day — Never Look Back—Col 40505—ASCAP	13	4
15.	LONGEST WALK—J. P. Morgan — Swanee—Vic 20-6182—ASCAP	—	1
16.	SWEET AND GENTLE—A. Dale — You Still Mean the Same to Me—Coral 61435	12	7
17.	WAKE THE TOWN AND TELL THE PEOPLE—L. Baxter — I'll Never Stop Loving You—Cap 3120—ASCAP	18	2
18.	SEVENTEEN—Fontane Sisters — If I Could Be With You—Dot 15386—BMI	—	1
19.	DOMANI—J. La Rosa — Mama Rosa—Cadence 1265—BMI	16	4
20.	FOOLED—P. Como — Tina Marie—Vic 20-6192—ASCAP	—	1

The Billboard Music Popularity Charts — POPULAR RECORDS

• Best Sellers in Stores

For survey week ending August 17

RECORDS are ranked in order of their current national selling importance at the retail level, as determined by The Billboard's weekly survey of the top volume dealers in every important market area. When significant action is reported on both sides of a record, points are combined to determine position on the chart. In such a case, both sides are listed in bold type, the leading side on top.

This Week		Last Week	Weeks on Chart
1.	ROCK AROUND THE CLOCK (ASCAP)—B. Haley Thirteen Women (BMI)—Dec 29124	1	16
2.	AIN'T THAT A SHAME? (BMI)—P. Boone Tennessee Saturday Night (BMI)—Dot 15377	2	7
3.	YELLOW ROSE OF TEXAS (ASCAP)—M. Miller Blackberry Winter (BMI)—Col 40540	3	4
4.	LEARNIN' THE BLUES (ASCAP)—F. Sinatra If I Had Three Wishes (ASCAP)—Cap 3102	4	16
5.	HARD TO GET (ASCAP)—G. MacKenzie Boston Fancy (BMI)—X 0137	7	13
6.	YELLOW ROSE OF TEXAS (ASCAP)—J. Desmond You're in Love With Someone (ASCAP)—Coral 61476	11	3
7.	SEVENTEEN (BMI)—B. Bennett Little Old You-All (BMI)—King 1470	6	8
8.	BLOSSOM FELL (ASCAP)—Nat (King) Cole IF I MAY (BMI)—Cap 3095	5	17
9.	HOUSE OF BLUE LIGHTS (ASCAP)—C. Miller Can't Help Wonderin' (ASCAP)—Mercury 70627	10	11
10.	MAYBELLENE (BMI)—C. Berry Wee Wee Hours (BMI)—Chess 1604	13	2
11.	IT'S A SIN TO TELL A LIE (ASCAP)—S. Smith & the Redheads My Baby Just Cares for Me (ASCAP)—Epic 9093	8	22
12.	HUMMINGBIRD (ASCAP)—L. Paul & M. Ford Goodbye My Love (ASCAP)—Cap 3165	9	6
13.	TINA MARIE (ASCAP)—P. Como FOOLED (ASCAP)—Vic 20-6192	—	2
14.	WAKE THE TOWN AND TELL THE PEOPLE (ASCAP)—L. Baxter I'll Never Stop Loving You (ASCAP)—Cap 3120	16	3
15.	SEVENTEEN (BMI)—Fontane Sisters If I Could Be With You (ASCAP)—Dot 15386	—	1
16.	AIN'T THAT A SHAME? (BMI)—F. Domino La, La (BMI)—Imperial 5348	18	7
17.	I'LL NEVER STOP LOVING YOU (ASCAP)—Doris Day Never Look Back (BMI)—Col 40505	15	6
18.	SEVENTEEN (BMI)—R. Draper Can't Live With 'Em, Can't Live Without Them (BMI)—Mercury 70651	23	2
19.	GUM DROP (BMI)—Crew Cuts Present Arms (ASCAP)—Mercury 70668	—	1
20.	AUTUMN LEAVES (ASCAP)—R. Williams Take Care (BMI)—Kapp 16	21	2
21.	DOMANI (BMI)—J. La Rosa Mama Rosa (ASCAP)—Cadence 1265	17	6
22.	UNCHAINED MELODY (ASCAP)—L. Baxter Medic (ASCAP)—Cap 3055	11	21
23.	WAKE THE TOWN AND TELL THE PEOPLE (ASCAP)—M. Carson Hold Me Tight (ASCAP)—Col 40537	—	1
24.	SONG OF THE DREAMER (BMI)—E. Fisher Don't Stay Away Too Long (ASCAP)—Vic 20-6196	—	1
25.	CHERRY PINK AND APPLE BLOSSOM WHITE (ASCAP)—P. Prado Marie Elena Rumba (ASCAP)—Vic 20-5965	14	26

DEALERS AND OPERATORS . . .

Top Ten Tunes Poster is on page 48

Tomorrow's Hits . . . Today Poster is on page 50

• THIS WEEK'S BEST BUYS

According to sales reports in key markets, the following recent releases are recommended for extra profits:

I WANT YOU TO BE MY BABY (Victory, BMI) —Lillian Briggs—Epic 9115

I WANT YOU TO BE MY BABY (Victory, BMI) —Georgia Gibbs—Mercury 70685

A nip-and-tuck struggle for top position has been going on the past two weeks between these two competitive versions. Timing and solid promotion by the manufacturer has helped Miss Briggs to hold her own up to this point, tho Georgia Gibbs is a formidable opponent and is beginning to make her weight felt. The Epic record appears on the St. Louis territorial chart this week and is doing nicely in Boston, Philadelphia, Cleveland, Baltimore and Durham. In some areas the Mercury disk is starting to pull ahead. The Briggs record has "Don't Stay Away Too Long" (Meridian, BMI) on the flip; the Gibbs record is coupled with "Come Rain or Come Shine" (A-M, ASCAP). Both versions were Billboard "Spotlight" picks, the former in the "Talent" category.

• Most Played in Juke Boxes

For survey week ending August 17

RECORDS are ranked in order of the greatest number of plays in juke boxes thruout the country, as determined by The Billboard's weekly survey of the nation's juke box operators. When significant play is reported on both sides of a record, points are combined to determine position on the chart. In such a case, both sides are listed in bold type, the leading side on top.

This Week		Last Week	Weeks on Chart
1.	ROCK AROUND THE CLOCK (ASCAP)—B. Haley Thirteen Women (BMI)—Dec 29124	1	11
2.	LEARNIN' THE BLUES (ASCAP) F. Sinatra If I Had Three Wishes (ASCAP)—Cap 3102	2	11
2.	AIN'T THAT A SHAME? (ASCAP)—P. Boone Tennessee Saturday Night (BMI)—Dot 15377	3	7
4.	BLOSSOM FELL (ASCAP)—Nat (King) Cole IF I MAY (BMI)—Cap 3095	4	14
5.	HARD TO GET (ASCAP)—G. MacKenzie Boston Fancy (BMI)—X 0137	5	8
6.	YELLOW ROSE OF TEXAS (ASCAP)—M. Miller Blackberry Winter (BMI)—Col 40540	14	2
7.	HUMMINGBIRD (ASCAP)—L. Paul & M. Ford Goodbye My Love (ASCAP)—Cap 3165	11	5
8.	CHERRY PINK AND APPLE BLOSSOM WHITE (ASCAP)—P. Prado Marie Elena Rumba (ASCAP)—Vic 20-5965	6	21
9.	HONEY BABE (ASCAP)—A. Mooney No Regrets (ASCAP)—M-G-M 11900	7	15
10.	IT'S A SIN TO TELL A LIE (ASCAP)—S. Smith & the Redheads My Baby Just Cares for Me (ASCAP)—Epic 9093	8	13
10.	AIN'T THAT A SHAME? (BMI)—Fats Domino La, La (BMI)—Imperial 5348	12	5
12.	SOMETHING'S GOTTA GIVE (ASCAP)—McGuire Sisters Rhythm 'n' Blues (ASCAP)—Coral 61423	8	12
12.	SEVENTEEN (BMI)—Fontane Sisters If I Could Be With You (ASCAP)—Dot 15386	18	2
14.	UNCHAINED MELODY (ASCAP)—L. Baxter Medic (ASCAP)—Cap 3055	16	17
14.	YELLOW ROSE OF TEXAS (ASCAP)—J. Desmond You're in Love With Someone (ASCAP)—Coral 61476	—	1
16.	POPCORN SONG (BMI)—C. Stone Barracuda (BMI)—Cap 3131	14	3
16.	SEVENTEEN (BMI)—B. Bennett Little Ole You-All (BMI)—King 1470	—	1
18.	UNCHAINED MELODY (ASCAP)—A. Hibbler Daybreak (ASCAP)—Dec 29441	10	18
18.	BANJO'S BACK IN TOWN (ASCAP)—T. Brewer How to Be Very, Very Popular—Coral 61448	—	4
18.	LONGEST WALK (ASCAP)—J. P. Morgan Swanee (ASCAP)—Vic 20-6182	—	1

• Most Played by Jockeys

For survey week ending August 17

SIDES are ranked in order of the greatest number of plays on disk jockey radio shows thruout the country. Results are based on The Billboard's weekly survey among the nation's disk jockeys. The reverse side of each record is also listed.

This Week		Last Week	Weeks on Chart
1.	ROCK AROUND THE CLOCK B. Haley Thirteen Women—Dec 29124—ASCAP	1	14
2.	YELLOW ROSE OF TEXAS—M. Miller Blackberry Winter—Col 40540—ASCAP	3	4
3.	AIN'T THAT A SHAME?—P. Boone Tennessee Saturday Night—Dot 15377—BMI	4	16
4.	LEARNIN' THE BLUES—F. Sinatra If I Had Three Wishes—Cap 3102—ASCAP	2	17
5.	HARD TO GET—G. MacKenzie Boston Fancy—X 0137—ASCAP	5	9
6.	TINA MARIE—P. Como Fooled—Vic 20-6192—ASCAP	12	2
7.	YELLOW ROSE OF TEXAS—J. Desmond You're in Love With Someone—Coral 61476—ASCAP	9	2
8.	HUMMINGBIRD (ASCAP)—L. Paul & M. Ford Goodbye My Love—Cap 3165	8	8
9.	SEVENTEEN—Fontane Sisters If I Could Be With You—Dot 15386—BMI	18	2
9.	WAKE THE TOWN AND TELL THE PEOPLE—L. Baxter I'll Never Stop Loving You—Cap 3120—ASCAP	17	3
11.	BLOSSOM FELL—Nat (King) Cole If I May—Cap 3095—ASCAP	7	7
12.	LONGEST WALK—J. P. Morgan Swanee—Vic 20-6182—ASCAP	15	2
13.	SEVENTEEN—B. Bennett Little Old You-All—King 1470—BMI	10	3
14.	I'LL NEVER STOP LOVING YOU—D. Day Never Look Back—Col 40505—ASCAP	14	5
15.	UNCHAINED MELODY—L. Baxter Medic—Cap 3055—ASCAP	6	21
16.	IT'S A SIN TO TELL A LIE—S. Smith & the Redheads My Baby Just Cares for Me—Epic 9093—ASCAP	11	9
17.	LOVE IS A MANY-SPLENDORED THING—Four Aces Shine On, Harvest Moon—Dec 29625—ASCAP	—	1
18.	DOMANI—J. La Rosa Mama Rosa—Cadence 1265—BMI	19	5
19.	MAN IN THE RAINCOAT—P. Wright Please Have Mercy—Unique 303—BMI	—	3
20.	SOMETHING'S GOTTA GIVE—McGuire Sisters Rhythm 'n' Blues—Coral 61423—ASCAP	13	13

The Billboard Music Popularity Charts — POPULAR RECORDS

• Best Sellers in Stores

For survey week ending August 24

RECORDS are ranked in order of their current national selling importance at the retail level, as determined by The Billboard's weekly survey of the top volume dealers in every important market area. When significant action is reported on both sides of a record, points are combined to determine position on the chart. In such a case, both sides are listed in bold type, the leading side on top.

This Week		Last Week	Weeks on Chart
1.	**YELLOW ROSE OF TEXAS** (ASCAP)—M. Miller Blackberry Winter (BMI)—Col 40540	3	5
2.	**AIN'T THAT A SHAME?** (BMI)—P. Boone Tennessee Saturday Night (BMI)—Dot 15377	2	8
3.	**ROCK AROUND THE CLOCK** (ASCAP)—B. Haley Thirteen Women (BMI)—Dec 29124	1	17
4.	**LEARNIN' THE BLUES** (ASCAP)—F. Sinatra If I Had Three Wishes (ASCAP)—Cap 3102	4	17
5.	**SEVENTEEN** (BMI)—B. Bennett Little Old You-All (BMI)—King 1470	7	9
6.	**YELLOW ROSE OF TEXAS** (ASCAP)—J. Desmond You're In Love With Someone (ASCAP)—Coral 61476	6	4
7.	**MAYBELLENE** (BMI)—C. Berry Wee Wee Hours (BMI)—Chess 1604	10	3
8.	**HARD TO GET** (ASCAP)—G. MacKenzie Boston Fancy (BMI)—X 0137	5	14
9.	**SEVENTEEN** (BMI)—Fontane Sisters If I Could Be With You (ASCAP)—Dot 15386	15	2
10.	**WAKE THE TOWN AND TELL THE PEOPLE** (ASCAP)—L. Baxter I'll Never Stop Loving You (ASCAP)—Cap 3120	14	4
11.	**AUTUMN LEAVES** (ASCAP)—R. Williams Take Care (BMI)—Kapp 16	20	3
12.	**BLOSSOM FELL** (ASCAP)—Nat (King) Cole **IF I MAY** (BMI)—Cap. 3095	8	18
13.	**HUMMINGBIRD** (ASCAP)—L. Paul & M. Ford Goodbye My Love (ASCAP)—Cap 3165	12	7
14.	**TINA MARIE** (ASCAP)—P. Como **FOOLED** (ASCAP)—Vic. 20-6192	13	3
15.	**GUM DROP** (BMI)—Crew Cuts Present Arms (ASCAP)—Mercury 70668	19	2
16.	**HOUSE OF BLUE LIGHTS** (ASCAP)—C. Miller Can't Help Wonderin' (ASCAP)—Mercury 70627	9	12
17.	**LOVE IS A MANY-SPLENDORED THING** (ASCAP)—Four Aces Shine On Harvest Moon (ASCAP)—Dec 29625	—	1
18.	**SONG OF THE DREAMER** (BMI)—E. Fisher **DON'T STAY AWAY TOO LONG** (ASCAP)—Vic. 20-6196	24	2
19.	**I'LL NEVER STOP LOVING YOU** (ASCAP)—Doris Day Never Look Back (BMI)—Col 40505	17	7
20.	**WAKE THE TOWN AND TELL THE PEOPLE** (ASCAP)—M. Carson Hold Me Tight (ASCAP)—Col 40537	23	2
21.	**MOMENTS TO REMEMBER** (ASCAP)—Four Lads Dream On, My Love, Dream On (ASCAP)—Col 40539	—	1
22.	**DOMANI** (BMI)—J. LaRosa Mama Rosa (ASCAP)—Cadence 1265	21	7
23.	**SEVENTEEN** (BMI)—R. Draper Can't Live With Em, Can't Live Without Them (BMI)—Mercury 70651	18	3
24.	**IT'S A SIN TO TELL A LIE** (ASCAP)—S. Smith & The Redheads My Baby Just Cares for Me (ASCAP)—Epic 9093	11	23
24.	**BIBLE TELLS ME SO** (ASCAP)—N. Noble Army of the Lord (BMI)—Wing 90003	—	2

DEALERS AND OPERATORS . . .

Top Ten Tunes Poster is on page 36

Tomorrow's Hits . . . Today Poster is on page 40

• THIS WEEK'S BEST BUYS

According to sales reports in key markets, the following recent releases are recommended for extra profits:

MOMENTS TO REMEMBER (Beaver, ASCAP) **—The Four Lads—Columbia 40539**

The outstanding sales performance among the newer disks this week was chalked up by this quartet. Now showing on the Boston, Cleveland, Chicago, and Detroit territorial listings, this tune has corralled enough strength to hit the national retail chart as well. Pittsburgh, Milwaukee and St. Louis were other areas reporting unusually heavy action on the disk. Flip is "Dream On, My Love, Dream On" (Evans, ASCAP).

SAME OLE SATURDAY NIGHT (Barton, ASCAP)

FAIRY TALE (Sands, ASCAP—**Frank Sinatra—Capitol 3218**

Tho this disk has not been on most retailers' shelves more than a week or 10 days, initial action has been so good in almost every area checked as to leave little doubt that it will shape up quickly as a big seller. "Saturday Night" is the preferred side, but enough activity on "Fairy Tale" has been reported to indicate that this could very well be a two-side hit. A previous Billboard "Spotlight" pick.

GOODNIGHT SWEET DREAMS (Roger, ASCAP)—**Gordon Jenkins—"X" 159**

One of the late summer sleepers now shaping up fast. Pittsburgh, Cleveland, Chicago, Milwaukee, St. Louis and Philadelphia reported the disk up and away, with great potential for further growth. Flip is "Young Ideas" (Harms, ASCAP). A previous Billboard "Spotlight" pick.

• Most Played in Juke Boxes

For survey week ending August 24

RECORDS are ranked in order of the greatest number of plays in juke boxes thruout the country, as determined by The Billboard's weekly survey of the nation's juke box operators. When significant play is reported on both sides of a record, points are combined to determine position on the chart. In such a case, both sides are listed in bold type, the leading side on top.

This Week		Last Week	Weeks on Chart
1.	**ROCK AROUND THE CLOCK** (ASCAP)—B. Haley Thirteen Women (BMI)—Dec 29124	1	12
2.	**AIN'T THAT A SHAME?** (BMI)—P. Boone Tennessee Saturday Night (BMI)—Dot 15377	2	8
3.	**LEARNIN' THE BLUES** (ASCAP)—F. Sinatra If I Had Three Wishes (ASCAP)—Cap 3102	2	12
4.	**YELLOW ROSE OF TEXAS** (ASCAP)—M. Miller Blackberry Winter (BMI)—Col. 40540	6	3
5.	**HARD TO GET** (ASCAP)—G. MacKenzie Boston Fancy (BMI)—X 0137	5	9
6.	**BLOSSOM FELL** (ASCAP)—Nat King Cole **IF I MAY** (BMI)—Cap 3095	4	15
7.	**HUMMINGBIRD** (ASCAP)—L. Paul & M. Ford Goodbye My Love (ASCAP)—Cap 3165	7	6
8.	**YELLOW ROSE OF TEXAS** (ASCAP)—J. Desmond You're in Love With Someone (ASCAP)—Coral 61476	14	2
9.	**IT'S A SIN TO TELL A LIE** (ASCAP)—S. Smith & the Redheads My Baby Just Cares for Me (ASCAP)—Epic 9093	10	14
10.	**SEVENTEEN** (BMI)—B. Bennett Little Ole You-All (BMI)—King 1470	16	2
11.	**AIN'T THAT A SHAME?** (BMI)—Fats Domino LaLa (BMI)—Imperial 5348	10	6
11.	**MAYBELLENE** (BMI)—C. Berry Wee Wee Hours (BMI)—Chess 1604	—	1
13.	**CHERRY PINK AND APPLE BLOSSOM WHITE** (ASCAP)—P. Prado Marie Elena Rumba (ASCAP)—Vic 20-5965	8	22
14.	**SOMETHING'S GOTTA GIVE** (ASCAP)—McGuire Sisters Rhythm 'N' Blues (ASCAP)—Coral 61423	12	13
15.	**SEVENTEEN** (BMI)—Fontane Sisters If I Could Be With You (ASCAP)—Dot 15386	12	3
16.	**LONGEST WALK** (ASCAP)—J. P. Morgan Swanee (ASCAP)—Vic. 20-6182	18	2
17.	**TINA MARIE** (ASCAP)—P. Como Fooled (ASCAP)—Vic 20-6192	—	1
18.	**HUMMINGBIRD** (ASCAP)—F. Laine My Little One (BMI)—Col 40526	—	1
19.	**POPCORN SONG** (BMI) C. Stone Barracuda (BMI)—Cap. 3131	16	4
19.	**UNCHAINED MELODY** (ASCAP)—L. Baxter Medic (ASCAP)—Cap 3055	[illegible]	18

• Most Played by Jockeys

For survey week ending August 24

SIDES are ranked in order of the greatest number of plays on disk jockey radio shows thruout the country. Results are based on The Billboard's weekly survey among the nation's disk jockeys. The reverse side of each record is also listed.

This Week		Last Week	Weeks on Chart
1.	**YELLOW ROSE OF TEXAS**—M. Miller Blackberry Winter—Col 40540—ASCAP	2	5
2.	**ROCK AROUND THE CLOCK**—B. Haley Thirteen Women—Dec 29124—ASCAP	1	15
3.	**AIN'T THAT A SHAME?**—P. Boone Tennessee Saturday Night—Dot 15377—BMI	3	17
4.	**YELLOW ROSE OF TEXAS**—J. Desmond You're in Love With Someone—Coral 61476—ASCAP	7	3
5.	**LEARNIN' THE BLUES**—F. Sinatra If I Had Three Wishes—Cap 3102—ASCAP	4	18
6.	**HARD TO GET**—G. MacKenzie Boston Fancy—X 0137—ASCAP	5	10
7.	**LONGEST WALK**—J. P. Morgan Swanee—Vic 20-6182—ASCAP	12	3
8.	**TINA MARIE**—P. Como Fooled—Vic 20-6192—ASCAP	6	3
9.	**SEVENTEEN**—B. Bennett Little Old You-All—King 1470—BMI	13	4
10.	**SEVENTEEN**—Fontane Sisters If I Could Be With You—Dot 15386—BMI	9	3
11.	**LOVE IS A MANY SPLENDORED THING**—Four Aces Shine On Harvest Moon—Dec 29625—ASCAP	17	2
12.	**HUMMINGBIRD**—L. Paul & M. Ford Goodbye My Love—Cap. 3165—ASCAP	8	9
13.	**MAYBELLENE**—C. Berry Wee Wee Hours—Chess 1604—BMI	—	1
14.	**WAKE THE TOWN AND TELL THE PEOPLE**—L. Baxter I'll Never Stop Loving You—Cap 3120—ASCAP	9	4
15.	**DOMANI**—J. LaRosa Mama Rosa—Cadence 1265—BMI	18	6
16.	**SONG OF THE DREAMER**—E. Fisher Don't Stay Away Too Long—Vic 20-6196—ASCAP	—	1
17.	**IT'S A SIN TO TELL A LIE**—S. Smith & The Redheads My Baby Just Cares for Me—Epic 9093—ASCAP	16	10
18.	**GUM DROP**—Crew Cuts Present Arms—Mercury 70668—BMI	—	1
19.	**I'LL NEVER STOP LOVING YOU**—D. Day Never Look Back—Col 40505—ASCAP	14	6
20.	**WAKE THE TOWN AND TELL THE PEOPLE**—M. Carson Hold Me Tight—Col 40537—ASCAP	—	1

The Billboard Music Popularity Charts — POPULAR RECORDS

• Best Sellers in Stores

For survey week ending August 31

RECORDS are ranked in order of their current national selling importance at the retail level, as determined by The Billboard's weekly survey of the top volume dealers in every important market area. When significant action is reported on both sides of a record, points are combined to determine position on the chart. In such a case, both sides are listed in bold type, the leading side on top.

This Week		Last Week	Weeks on Chart
1.	YELLOW ROSE OF TEXAS (ASCAP)—M. Miller Blackberry Winter (BMI)—Col 40540	1	6
2.	AIN'T THAT A SHAME (BMI)—P. Boone Tennessee Saturday Night (BMI)—Dot 15377	2	9
3.	ROCK AROUND THE CLOCK (ASCAP)—B. Haley Thirteen Women (BMI)—Dec 29124	3	18
4.	LOVE IS A MANY-SPLENDORED THING (ASCAP)—Four Aces Shine On, Harvest Moon—Dec 29625	17	2
5.	MAYBELLENE (BMI)—C. Berry Wee Wee Hours (BMI)—Chess 1604	7	4
6.	YELLOW ROSE OF TEXAS (ASCAP)—J. Desmond You're in Love With Someone (ASCAP)—Coral 61476	6	5
7.	AUTUMN LEAVES (ASCAP)—R. Williams Take Care (BMI)—Kapp 16	11	4
8.	SEVENTEEN (BMI)—Fontane Sisters If I Could Be With You (ASCAP)—Dot 15386	9	3
9.	SEVENTEEN (BMI)—B. Bennett Little Old You-All (BMI)—King 1470	5	10
10.	HARD TO GET (ASCAP)—G. MacKenzie Boston Fancy (BMI)—X 0137	8	15
11.	WAKE THE TOWN AND TELL THE PEOPLE (ASCAP)—L. Baxter I'll Never Stop Loving You (ASCAP)—Cap 3120	10	5
12.	TINA MARIE (ASCAP)—P. Como **FOOLED (ASCAP)—Vic 20-6192**	14	4
13.	LEARNIN' THE BLUES (ASCAP)—F. Sinatra If I Had Three Wishes (ASCAP)—Cap 3102	4	18
14.	GUM DROP (BMI)—Crew Cuts Present Arms (ASCAP)—Mercury 70668	15	3
15.	HUMMINGBIRD (ASCAP)—L. Paul & M. Ford Goodbye My Love (ASCAP)—Cap 3165	13	8
16.	BLOSSOM FELL (ASCAP)—Nat (King) Cole **IF I MAY (BMI)—Cap 3095**	12	19
17.	LONGEST WALK (ASCAP)—J. P. Morgan Swanee (ASCAP)—Vic 20-6182	—	1
18.	SONG OF THE DREAMER (BMI)—E. Fisher **DON'T STAY AWAY TOO LONG (ASCAP)—Vic 20-6196**	18	3
19.	MOMENTS TO REMEMBER (ASCAP)—Four Lads Dream On, My Love, Dream On (ASCAP)—Col 40539	21	2
20.	BIBLE TELLS ME SO (ASCAP)—D. Cornell Love Is a Many-Splendored Thing (ASCAP)—Coral 61467	—	1
21.	WAKE THE TOWN AND TELL THE PEOPLE (ASCAP)—M. Carson Hold Me Tight (ASCAP)—Col 40537	20	3
22.	HOUSE OF BLUE LIGHTS (ASCAP)—C. Miller Can't Help Wonderin' (ASCAP)—Mercury 70627	16	13
23.	I'LL NEVER STOP LOVING YOU (ASCAP)—Doris Day Never Look Back (BMI)—Col 40505	19	8
24.	AIN'T THAT A SHAME (BMI)—F. Domino La La (BMI)—Imperial 5348	—	8
25.	SEVENTEEN (BMI)—R. Draper Can't Live With 'Em, Can't Live Without Them (BMI)—Mercury 70651	23	4

DEALERS AND OPERATORS . . .

Top Ten Tunes Poster is on page 38

Tomorrow's Hits . . . Today Poster is on page 44

• THIS WEEK'S BEST BUYS

According to sales reports in key markets, the following recent releases are recommended for extra profits:

THE SHIFTING, WHISPERING SANDS (Gallatin, BMI)—Billy Vaughan Ork—Dot 15409

Many were the skeptics when this two-sided talking disk first appeared, but most of them are keeping quiet now that it is developing into a very big seller. Now appearing on the Seattle and Cleveland territorial charts, the disk is also spurring unusually heavy sales in Boston, New York, Philadelphia, Pittsburgh, Chicago, Milwaukee, St. Louis, Durham and Nashville. A previous Billboard "Spotlight" pick.

HAWK-EYE (Showcase, BMI)—Frankie Laine—Columbia 40558

In this tune Laine seems to have found some congenial material, and his following is rallying quickly to put it over. First week sales found an exceptionally wide-spread acceptance of this record, and this will give him an initial edge over other versions of the tune now available. Boston, Philadelphia, Pittsburgh, Cleveland, Chicago, Milwaukee, St. Louis, Atlanta were among the areas reporting good sales. Flip is "Your Love" (Evergreen, BMI). A previous Billboard "Spotlight" pick.

GIVE ME LOVE (Hill & Range, BMI)
Sweet Song of India (BVC, ASCAP) — McGuire Sisters—Coral 61494

With the kind of batting average that these girls have, it is no surprise to find this disk taking off with the speed that it is. Wherever it has been delivered, little time was lost in selling the customers on it. Best reports this week were received from Boston, Philadelphia, Cleveland, Chicago, and St. Louis. Initial preference is for "Give Me Love," but in some areas "Song of India" is also coming in for a good share of attention. A previous Billboard "Spotlight" pick.

• Most Played in Juke Boxes

For survey week ending August 31

RECORDS are ranked in order of the greatest number of plays in juke boxes thruout the country, as determined by The Billboard's weekly survey of the nation's juke box operators. When significant play is reported on both sides of a record, points are combined to determine position on the chart. In such a case, both sides are listed in bold type, the leading side on top.

This Week		Last Week	Weeks on Chart
1.	ROCK AROUND THE CLOCK (ASCAP)—B. Haley Thirteen Women (BMI)—Dec 29124	1	13
2.	AIN'T THAT A SHAME (BMI)—P. Boone Tennessee Saturday Night (BMI)—Dot 15377	2	9
3.	YELLOW ROSE OF TEXAS (ASCAP)—M. Miller Blackberry Winter (BMI)—Col 40540	4	4
4.	LEARNIN' THE BLUES (ASCAP)—F. Sinatra If I Had Three Wishes (ASCAP)—Cap 3102	3	13
5.	HARD TO GET (ASCAP)—G. MacKenzie Boston Fancy (BMI)—X 0137	5	10
6.	YELLOW ROSE OF TEXAS (ASCAP)—J. Desmond You're in Love With Someone (ASCAP)—Coral 61476	8	3
7.	BLOSSOM FELL (ASCAP)—Nat (King) Cole **IF I MAY—Cap 3095**	6	16
8.	SEVENTEEN (BMI)—Fontane Sisters If I Could Be With You (ASCAP)—Dot 15386	15	4
8.	MAYBELLENE (BMI)—C. Berry Wee Wee Hours (BMI)—Chess 1604	11	2
10.	HUMMINGBIRD (ASCAP)—L. Paul & M. Ford Goodbye My Love (ASCAP)—Cap 3165	7	7
11.	SEVENTEEN (BMI)—B. Bennett Little Ole You-All (BMI)—King 1470	10	3
12.	TINA MARIE (ASCAP)—P. Como Fooled (ASCAP)—Vic 20-6192	17	2
13.	AIN'T THAT A SHAME (BMI)—Fats Domino La, La (BMI)—Imperial 5348	11	7
14.	LONGEST WALK (ASCAP)—J. P. Morgan Swanee (ASCAP)—Vic 20-6182	16	3
15.	IT'S A SIN TO TELL A LIE (ASCAP)—S. Smith & the Redheads My Baby Just Cares for Me (ASCAP)—Epic 9093	9	15
16.	CHERRY PINK AND APPLE BLOSSOM WHITE (ASCAP)—P. Prado Marie Elena Rumba (ASCAP)—Vic 20-5965	13	23
17.	HUMMINGBIRD (ASCAP)—F. Laine My Little One (BMI)—Col 40526	18	2
17.	SOMETHING'S GOTTA GIVE (ASCAP)—McGuire Sisters Rhythm 'n' Blues (ASCAP)—Coral 61423	14	14
19.	HOUSE OF BLUE LIGHTS (ASCAP)—C. Miller Can't Help Wonderin' (ASCAP)—Mercury 70627	—	1
20.	UNCHAINED MELODY (ASCAP)—A. Hibbler Daybreak (ASCAP)—Dec 29441	—	19

• Most Played by Jockeys

For survey week ending August 31

SIDES are ranked in order of the greatest number of plays on disk jockey radio shows thruout the country. Results are based on The Billboard's weekly survey among the nation's disk jockeys. The reverse side of each record is also listed.

This Week		Last Week	Weeks on Chart
1.	YELLOW ROSE OF TEXAS—M. Miller Blackberry Winter—Col 40540—ASCAP	1	6
2.	AIN'T THAT A SHAME—P. Boone Tennessee Saturday Night—Dot 15377—BMI	3	18
3.	ROCK AROUND THE CLOCK—B. Haley Thirteen Women—Dec 29124—ASCAP	2	16
4.	YELLOW ROSE OF TEXAS—J. Desmond You're in Love With Someone—Coral 61476—ASCAP	4	4
5.	LEARNIN' THE BLUES—F. Sinatra If I Had Three Wishes—Cap 3102—ASCAP	5	19
6.	TINA MARIE—P. Como Fooled—Vic 20-6192—ASCAP	8	4
7.	HARD TO GET—G. MacKenzie Boston Fancy—X 0137—ASCAP	6	11
8.	SEVENTEEN—Fontane Sisters If I Could Be With You—Dot 15386—BMI	10	4
9.	LONGEST WALK—J. P. Morgan Swanne—Vic 20-6182—ASCAP	7	4
10.	WAKE THE TOWN AND TELL THE PEOPLE—L. Baxter I'll Never Stop Loving You—Cap 3120—ASCAP	14	5
11.	LOVE IS A MANY-SPLENDORED THING—Four Aces Shine On, Harvest Moon—Dec 29625—ASCAP	11	3
12.	SEVENTEEN—B. Bennett Little Old You-All—King 1470—BMI	9	5
13.	HUMMINGBIRD—L. Paul & M. Ford Goodbye My Love—Cap 3165	12	10
14.	GUM DROP—Crew Cuts Present Arms—Mer 70668—BMI	18	2
15.	MAYBELLENE—C. Berry Wee Wee Hours—Chess 1604—BMI	13	2
16.	SONG OF THE DREAMER—E. Fisher Don't Stay Away Too Long—Vic 20-6196	16	2
17.	DOMANI—J. LaRosa Mama Rosa—Cadence 1265—BMI	15	7
18.	WAKE THE TOWN AND TELL THE PEOPLE—M. Carson Hold Me Tight—Col 40537—ASCAP	20	2
19.	BIBLE TELLS ME SO—D. Cornell Love Is a Many-Splendored Thing—Coral 61467—ASCAP	—	1
20.	AUTUMN LEAVES—R. Williams Take Care—Kapp 16—ASCAP	—	1

The Billboard Music Popularity Charts — POPULAR RECORDS

• Best Sellers in Stores

For survey week ending September 7

RECORDS are ranked in order of their current national selling importance at the retail level, as determined by The Billboard's weekly survey of the top volume dealers in every important market area. When significant action is reported on both sides of a record, points are combined to determine position on the chart. In such a case, both sides are listed in bold type, the leading side on top.

This Week	Record	Last Week	Weeks on Chart
1.	YELLOW ROSE OF TEXAS (ASCAP)—M. Miller Blackberry Winter (BMI)—Col 40540	1	7
2.	AIN'T THAT A SHAME (BMI)—P. Boone Tennessee Saturday Night (BMI)—Dot 15377	2	10
3.	LOVE IS A MANY-SPLENDORED THING (ASCAP)—Four Aces Shine On, Harvest Moon—Dec 29625	4	3
4.	ROCK AROUND THE CLOCK (ASCAP)—B. Haley Thirteen Women (BMI)—Dec 29124	3	19
5.	AUTUMN LEAVES (ASCAP)—R. Williams Take Care (BMI)—Kapp 116	7	5
6.	SEVENTEEN (BMI)—B. Bennett Little Old You-All (BMI)—King 1470	9	11
7.	MAYBELLENE (BMI)—C. Berry Wee Wee Hours (BMI) Chess 1604	5	5
8.	YELLOW ROSE OF TEXAS (ASCAP)—J. Desmond You're In Love With Someone (ASCAP)—Coral 61476	6	6
9.	MOMENTS TO REMEMBER (ASCAP)—Four Lads Dream On, My Love, Dream On (ASCAP)—Col 40539	19	3
10.	GUM DROP (BMI)—Crew Cuts Present Arms (ASCAP) Mercury 70668	14	4
11.	SEVENTEEN (BMI)—Fontane Sisters If I Could Be With You (ASCAP)—Dot 15386	8	4
12.	TINA MARIE (ASCAP)—P. Como FOOLED (ASCAP)—Vic 20-6192	12	5
13.	LONGEST WALK (ASCAP)—J. P. Morgan Swanee (ASCAP)—Vic 20-6182	17	2
14.	WAKE THE TOWN AND TELL THE PEOPLE (ASCAP)—L. Baxter I'll Never Stop Loving You (ASCAP)—Cap 3120	11	6
14.	LEARNIN' THE BLUES (ASCAP)—F. Sinatra If I Had Three Wishes (ASCAP)—Cap 3102	13	19
16.	HARD TO GET (ASCAP)—G. MacKenzie Boston Fancy (BMI)—X 0137	10	16
16.	SONG OF THE DREAMER (BMI)—E. Fisher DON'T STAY AWAY TOO LONG—(ASCAP)—Vic 20-6196	18	4
18.	HOUSE OF BLUE LIGHTS (ASCAP)—C. Miller Can't Help Wonderin' (ASCAP)—Mercury 70627	22	14
19.	BIBLE TELLS ME SO (ASCAP)—D. Cornell Love Is a Many-Splendored Thing (ASCAP)—Coral 61467	20	2
20.	WAKE THE TOWN AND TELL THE PEOPLE (ASCAP)—M. Carson Hold Me Tight (ASCAP)—Col 40537	21	4
21.	HUMMINGBIRD (ASCAP)—L. Paul & M. Ford Goodbye, My Love (ASCAP)—Cap 3165	15	9
22.	BIBLE TELLS ME SO (ASCAP)—N. Noble Army of the Lord (BMI)—Wing 90003	—	3
23.	I WANT YOU TO BE MY BABY (BMI)—L. Briggs Don't Stay Away Too Long (BMI)—Epic 9115	—	1
24.	BLOSSOM FELL (ASCAP)—Nat (King) Cole IF I MAY (BMI)—Cap 3095	16	20
25.	I WANT YOU TO BE MY BABY (BMI)—G. Gibbs Come Rain or Come Shine (ASCAP)—Mercury 70685	—	1

DEALERS AND OPERATORS . . .

Top Ten Tunes Poster
is on page 44

Tomorrow's Hits . . . Today
Poster is on page 46

• THIS WEEK'S BEST BUYS

According to sales reports in key markets, the following recent releases are recommended for extra profits:

BLACK DENIM TROUSERS (Quintet-Hill & Range, BMI)—**The Cheers—Capitol 3219**

The group has found a piece of material here that has quickly fired the imagination of the youngsters. They are buying this disk in increasingly large quantities in New York, Los Angeles, Baltimore, St. Louis, Pittsburgh, Philadelphia, Milwaukee and Chicago. In Cleveland the record is already on the territorial chart. Flip is "Some Night in Alaska" (Simon House, BMI). A previous Billboard "Spotlight" pick.

HE (Avas, BMI)—**Al Hibbler—Decca 29660**

Once more a semi-sacred tune is carrying the field. Hibbler is selling up a storm in New York, Philadelphia, Cleveland, Detroit, Milwaukee, Providence, St. Louis, Nashville, Atlanta, and Durham. Flip is "Breeze" (Shapiro-Bernstein, ASCAP), on which some action is also reported. The disk was a previous Billboard "Spotlight" pick.

• Most Played in Juke Boxes

For survey week ending September 7

RECORDS are ranked in order of the greatest number of plays in juke boxes thruout the country, as determined by The Billboard's weekly survey of the nation's juke box operators. When significant play is reported on both sides of a record, points are combined to determine position on the chart. In such a case, both sides are listed in bold type, the leading side on top.

This Week	Record	Last Week	Weeks on Chart
1.	AIN'T THAT A SHAME (BMI)—P. Boone Tennessee Saturday Night (BMI)—Dot 15377	2	10
2.	YELLOW ROSE OF TEXAS (ASCAP)—M. Miller Blackberry Winter (BMI)—Col 40540	3	5
3.	ROCK AROUND THE CLOCK (ASCAP)—B. Haley Thirteen Women (BMI)—Dec 29124	1	14
4.	YELLOW ROSE OF TEXAS (ASCAP)—J. Desmond You're in Love With Someone (ASCAP)—Coral 61476	6	4
5.	SEVENTEEN (BMI)—Fontane Sisters If I Could Be With You (ASCAP)—Dot 15386	8	5
6.	LEARNIN' THE BLUES (ASCAP)—F. Sinatra If I Had Three Wishes (ASCAP)—Cap 3102	4	14
6.	HARD TO GET (ASCAP)—G. MacKenzie Boston Fancy (BMI)—X 0137	5	11
8.	MAYBELLENE (BMI)—C. Berry Wee Wee Hours (BMI)—Chess 1604	8	3
9.	TINA MARIE (ASCAP)—P. Como Fooled (ASCAP)—Vic 20-6192	12	3
10.	SEVENTEEN (BMI)—B. Bennett Little Ole You-All (BMI)—King 1470	11	4
11.	LONGEST WALK (ASCAP)—J. P Morgan Swanee (ASCAP)—Vic 20-6182	14	4
12.	HUMMINGBIRD (ASCAP)—L. Paul & M. Ford Goodbye, My Love (ASCAP)—Cap 3165	10	8
13.	BLOSSOM FELL (ASCAP)—Nat (King) Cole If I May—(BMI)—Cap 3095	7	17
14.	WAKE THE TOWN AND TELL THE PEOPLE (ASCAP)—M. Carson Hold Me Tight (ASCAP)—Col 40537	—	1
15.	AUTUMN LEAVES (ASCAP)—R. Williams Take Care (BMI)—Kapp 116	—	1
16.	AIN'T THAT A SHAME (BMI)—Fats Domino La, La (BMI)—Imperial 5348	13	8
17.	IT'S A SIN TO TELL A LIE (ASCAP)—S. Smith & The Redheads My Baby Just Cares for Me (ASCAP)—Epic 9093	15	16
17.	SONG OF THE DREAMER (BMI)—E. Fisher DON'T STAY AWAY TOO LONG (ASCAP)—Vic. 20-6196	—	1
19.	WAKE THE TOWN AND TELL THE PEOPLE (ASCAP)—L. Baxter I'll Never Stop Loving You (ASCAP)—Cap 3120	—	1
20.	GUM DROP (BMI)—Crew Cuts Present Arms (ASCAP)—Mercury 70668	—	1

• Most Played by Jockeys

For survey week ending September 7

SIDES are ranked in order of the greatest number of plays on disk jockey radio shows thruout the country. Results are based on The Billboard's weekly survey among the nation's disk jockeys. The reverse side of each record is also listed.

This Week	Record	Last Week	Weeks on Chart
1.	YELLOW ROSE OF TEXAS—M. Miller Blackberry Winter—Col 40540—ASCAP	1	7
2.	AIN'T THAT A SHAME—P. Boone Tennessee Saturday Night—Dot 15377—BMI	2	19
3.	YELLOW ROSE OF TEXAS—J. Desmond You're in Love With Someone—Coral 61476—ASCAP	4	5
4.	LOVE IS A MANY-SPLENDORED THING—Four Aces Shine On, Harvest Moon—Dec 29625—ASCAP	11	4
5.	ROCK AROUND THE CLOCK—B. Haley Thirteen Women—Dec 29124—ASCAP	3	17
6.	LONGEST WALK—J. P. Morgan Swanee—Vic 20-6182—ASCAP	9	5
7.	SEVENTEEN—Fontane Sisters If I Could Be With You—Dot 15386—BMI	8	5
8.	TINA MARIE—P. Como Fooled—Vic 20-6192—ASCAP	6	5
9.	LEARNIN' THE BLUES—F. Sinatra If I Had Three Wishes—Cap 3102—ASCAP	5	20
10.	WAKE THE TOWN AND TELL THE PEOPLE—L. Baxter I'll Never Stop Loving You—Cap 3120—ASCAP	10	6
11.	HARD TO GET—G. MacKenzie Boston Fancy—X 0137—ASCAP	7	12
12.	SEVENTEEN—B. Bennett Little Old You-All—King 1470—BMI	12	6
13.	MAYBELLENE—C. Berry Wee Wee Hours—Chess 1604—BMI	15	3
14.	GUM DROP—Crew Cuts Present Arms—Mer 70668—BMI	14	3
15.	AUTUMN LEAVES—R. Williams Take Care—Kapp 116—ASCAP	20	2
16.	HUMMINGBIRD—L. Paul & M. Ford Goodbye, My Love—Cap 3165	13	11
17.	MOMENTS TO REMEMBER—Four Lads Dream On, My Love, Dream On—Col 40539	—	1
18.	I'LL NEVER STOP LOVING YOU—D. Day Never Look Back—Col 40505—ASCAP	—	7
19.	WAKE THE TOWN AND TELL THE PEOPLE—M. Carson Hold Me Tight—Col 40537—ASCAP	18	3
20.	BIBLE TELLS ME SO—D. Cornell Love Is a Many-Splendored Thing—Coral 61467	19	2

The Billboard Music Popularity Charts — POPULAR RECORDS

• Best Sellers in Stores

For survey week ending September 14

RECORDS are ranked in order of their current national selling importance at the retail level, as determined by The Billboard's weekly survey of the top volume dealers in every important market area. When significant action is reported on both sides of a record, points are combined to determine position on the chart. In such a case, both sides are listed in bold type, the leading side on top.

This Week	Record	Last Week	Weeks on Chart
1.	YELLOW ROSE OF TEXAS (ASCAP)—M. Miller. Blackberry Winter (BMI)—Col 40540	1	8
2.	LOVE IS A MANY-SPLENDORED THING (ASCAP)—Four Aces. Shine On, Harvest Moon—Dec. 29625	3	4
3.	AIN'T THAT A SHAME (BMI)—P. Boone. Tennessee Saturday Night (BMI)—Dot 15377	2	11
4.	AUTUMN LEAVES (ASCAP)—R. Williams. Take Care (BMI)—Kapp 116	5	6
5.	ROCK AROUND THE CLOCK (ASCAP)—B. Haley. Thirteen Women (BMI)—Dec. 29124	4	20
6.	SEVENTEEN (BMI)—Fontane Sisters. If I Could Be With You (ASCAP)—Dot 15386	11	5
7.	MAYBELLENE (BMI)—C. Berry. Wee Wee Hours (BMI)—Chess 1604	7	6
8.	MOMENTS TO REMEMBER—Four Lads. Dream On, My Love, Dream On (ASCAP)—Col. 40539	9	4
9.	YELLOW ROSE OF TEXAS (ASCAP)—J. Desmond. You're In Love With Someone (ASCAP)—Coral 61476	8	7
10.	TINA MARIE (ASCAP)—P. Como / FOOLED (ASCAP)—Vic 20-6192	12	6
11.	SEVENTEEN (BMI)—B. Bennett. Little Old You-All (BMI) King 1470	6	12
12.	GUM DROP (BMI)—Crew Cuts. Present Arms (ASCAP)—Mercury 70668	10	5
13.	WAKE THE TOWN AND TELL THE PEOPLE (ASCAP)—L. Baxter. I'll Never Stop Loving You (ASCAP)—Cap 3120	14	7
14.	BIBLE TELLS ME SO (ASCAP)—D. Cornell / LOVE IS A MANY-SPLENDORED THING (ASCAP)—Coral 61467	19	3
15.	LONGEST WALK (ASCAP)—J. P. Morgan. Swanee (ASCAP)—Vic 20-6182	13	3
16.	SONG OF THE DREAMER (BMI)—E. Fisher / DON'T STAY AWAY TOO LONG (ASCAP)—Vic 20-6196	16	5
17.	HARD TO GET (ASCAP)—G. MacKenzie. Boston Fancy (BMI)—X 0137	16	17
18.	LEARNIN' THE BLUES (ASCAP)—F. Sinatra. If I Had Three Wishes (ASCAP)—Cap 3102	14	20
18.	SHIFTING WHISPERING SANDS (Parts I & II) (BMI)—B. Vaughn. Dot 15409	—	1
20.	HUMMINGBIRD (ASCAP)—L. Paul & M. Ford. Goodbye My Love (ASCAP)—Cap 3165	21	10
21.	WAKE THE TOWN AND TELL THE PEOPLE (ASCAP)—M. Carson. Hold Me Tight (ASCAP)—Col 40537	20	5
22.	I WANT YOU TO BE MY BABY (BMI)—G. Gibbs. Come Rain or Come Shine (ASCAP)—Mercury 70685	25	2
23.	BLACK DENIM TROUSERS (BMI)—Cheers. Some Night In Alaska (BMI)—Cap 3219	—	1
24.	I WANT YOU TO BE MY BABY—L. Briggs. Don't Stay Away Too Long (BMI)—Epic 9115	23	2
25.	I'LL NEVER STOP LOVING YOU (ASCAP)—Doris Day. Never Look Back (BMI)—Col. 40505	—	9

DEALERS AND OPERATORS . . .

Tomorrow's Hits . . . Today Poster is on page 32

Top Ten Tunes Poster is on page 38

• THIS WEEK'S BEST BUYS

According to sales reports in key markets, the following recent releases are recommended for extra profits:

THE SHIFTING, WHISPERING SANDS (Gallatin, BMI)—Rusty Draper—Mercury 70696

While the Billy Vaughn version of this tune is now on the national retail chart, the Draper one-side treatment is coming up from behind to give it vigorous competition over the counter, and more importantly, with the juke box trade. Already on the Pittsburgh, Milwaukee and St. Louis territorial charts, the Draper record also appears slated for early listing on the national charts. Flip is "Last Frontier" (Columbia Pictures, ASCAP). A previous Billboard "Spotlight" pick.

MY BONNIE LASSIE (Blossom, ASCAP)—Ames Brothers—RCA Victor 6208

This disk has been available for over a month, but it's only during the past two weeks that it has begun to take off in a really big way. The most impressive spurts of new sales activity took place in Los Angeles, New York, Detroit, Milwaukee, Atlanta, Pittsburgh, Providence, Boston and Philadelphia. Flip is "So Will I" (Roosevelt, BMI). A previous Billboard "Spotlight" pick.

SUDDENLY THERE'S A VALLEY (Warman-Hill & Range, BMI)—Gogi Grant—Era 1003

SUDDENLY THERE'S A VALLEY (Warman-Hill & Range, BMI)—Julius LaRosa—Cadence 1270

The past few weeks have witnessed a lively struggle between numerous competing versions of this tune. The original recording by Gogi Grant has not only held its own, but is still at the top of the heap. In such key markets as Los Angeles, Chicago, Philadelphia and New York, the Era disk is leading all other versions. Julius LaRosa is the strongest competitor at this point, and is rated good to strong in almost every key national market, so that he may also place on the national charts along with Miss Grant. The flip side of her record is "Love Is" (Warman, BMI); that of LaRosa's is "Every Time That I Kiss Carrie" (Cadence, BMI). The latter was a previous Billboard "Spotlight" pick.

MY BOY FLAT-TOP (Lois, BMI)—Boyd Bennett Ork—King 1494

With "Seventeen" still riding high in the charts, the band has come up with another record that is fast becoming a hit of sizable proportions. Buffalo, Baltimore, Pittsburgh, Cincinnati, Cleveland, Chicago, Milwaukee, Detroit, St. Louis and Durham were among the cities that indicated this disk to be a big local seller. Flip is "Banjo Rock and Roll" (Lois, BMI). A previous Billboard "Spotlight" pick.

• Most Played in Juke Boxes

For survey week ending September 14

RECORDS are ranked in order of the greatest number of plays in juke boxes thruout the country, as determined by The Billboard's weekly survey of the nation's juke box operators. When significant play is reported on both sides of a record, points are combined to determine position on the chart. In such a case, both sides are listed in bold type, the leading side on top.

This Week	Record	Last Week	Weeks on Chart
1.	AIN'T THAT A SHAME (BMI)—P. Boone. Tennessee Saturday Night (BMI)—Dot 15377	1	11
2.	YELLOW ROSE OF TEXAS (ASCAP)—M. Miller. Blackberry Winter (BMI)—Col 40540	2	6
3.	ROCK AROUND THE CLOCK (ASCAP)—B. Haley. Thirteen Women (BMI)—Dec 29124	3	15
4.	YELLOW ROSE OF TEXAS (ASCAP)—J. Desmond. You're in Love With Someone (ASCAP)—Coral 61476	4	5
5.	SEVENTEEN (BMI)—Fontane Sisters. If I Could Be With You (ASCAP)—Dot 15386	5	6
6.	HARD TO GET (ASCAP)—G. MacKenzie. Boston Fancy (BMI)—X 0137	6	12
7.	MAYBELLENE (BMI)—C. Berry. Wee Wee Hours (BMI)—Chess 1604	8	4
8.	SEVENTEEN (BMI)—B. Bennett. Little Ole You-All (BMI)—King 1470	10	5
9.	LONGEST WALK (ASCAP)—J. P. Morgan. Swanee (ASCAP)—Vic 20-6182	11	5
10.	LEARNIN' THE BLUES (ASCAP)—F. Sinatra. If I Had Three Wishes (ASCAP)—Cap 3102	6	15
10.	WAKE THE TOWN AND TELL THE PEOPLE (ASCAP)—L. Baxter. I'll Never Stop Loving You (ASCAP)—Cap 3120	19	2
12.	TINA MARIE (ASCAP)—P. Como. Fooled (ASCAP)—Vic 20-6192	9	4
13.	WAKE THE TOWN AND TELL THE PEOPLE (ASCAP)—M. Carson. Hold Me Tight (ASCAP)—Col 40537	14	2
14.	AUTUMN LEAVES (ASCAP)—R. Williams. Take Care (BMI)—Kapp 116	15	2
15.	HUMMINGBIRD (ASCAP)—L. Paul & M. Ford. Goodbye My Love (ASCAP)—Cap 3165	12	9
16.	SONG OF THE DREAMER—E. Fisher / DON'T STAY AWAY TOO LONG (ASCAP)—Vic 20-6196	17	2
17.	LOVE IS A MANY-SPLENDORED THING (ASCAP)—Four Aces. Shine On, Harvest Moon (ASCAP)—Dec 29625	—	1
18.	BLOSSOM FELL (ASCAP)—Nat (King) Cole. If I May (BMI)—Cap 3095	13	18
19.	HUMMINGBIRD (ASCAP)—F. Laine. My Little One—Col 40526	—	3
20.	AIN'T THAT A SHAME (BMI)—Fats Domino. La La (BMI)—Imperial 5348	16	9
20.	BIBLE TELLS ME SO (ASCAP)—D. Cornell. Love Is a Many Splendored Thing (ASCAP)—Coral 61467	—	1

• Most Played by Jockeys

For survey week ending September 14

SIDES are ranked in order of the greatest number of plays on disk jockey radio shows thruout the country. Results are based on The Billboard's weekly survey among the nation's disk jockeys. The reverse side of each record is also listed.

This Week	Record	Last Week	Weeks on Chart
1.	YELLOW ROSE OF TEXAS—M. Miller. Blackberry Winter (ASCAP)—Col 40540	1	8
2.	AIN'T THAT A SHAME—P. Boone. Tennessee Saturday Night (BMI)—Dot 15377	2	20
3.	LOVE IS A MANY-SPLENDORED THING—Four Aces. Shine On, Harvest Moon (ASCAP)—Dec 29625	4	5
4.	YELLOW ROSE OF TEXAS—J. Desmond. You're in Love With Someone (ASCAP)—Coral 61476	3	6
5.	WAKE THE TOWN AND TELL THE PEOPLE—L. Baxter. I'll Never Stop Loving You (ASCAP)—Cap 3120	10	7
6.	TINA MARIE—P. Como. Fooled (ASCAP)—Vic 20-6192	8	6
7.	SEVENTEEN—Fontane Sisters. If I Could Be With You (BMI)—Dot 15386	7	6
8.	AUTUMN LEAVES—R. Williams. Take Care (ASCAP)—Kapp 116	15	3
9.	LONGEST WALK—J. P. Morgan. Swanne (ASCAP)—Vic 20-6182	6	6
10.	ROCK AROUND THE CLOCK—B. Haley. Thirteen Women (ASCAP)—Dec 29124	5	18
11.	MOMENTS TO REMEMBER—Four Lads. Dream On, My Love, Dream On (ASCAP)—Col 40539	17	2
12.	LEARNING THE BLUES—F. Sinatra. If I Had Three Wishes (ASCAP)—Cap 3102	9	21
13.	WAKE THE TOWN AND TELL THE PEOPLE—M. Carson. Hold Me Tight (ASCAP)—Col 40537	19	4
14.	SHIFTING, WHISPERING SANDS—(Parts I & II)—B. Vaughn. (BMI)—Dot 15509	—	1
15.	HARD TO GET—G. MacKenzie. Boston Fancy (ASCAP)—X 0137	11	13
16.	MY BONNIE LASSIE—Ames Brothers. So Will I (ASCAP)—Vic 20-6208	—	1
17.	I WANT YOU TO BE MY BABY—G. Gibbs. Come Rain or Come Shine (BMI)—Mercury 70685	—	1
18.	I'LL NEVER STOP LOVING YOU—D. Day. Never Look Back (ASCAP)—Col 40505	18	8
19.	SEVENTEEN—B. Bennett. Little Old You-All (BMI)—King 1470	12	7
20.	SAME OLE SATURDAY NIGHT—F. Sinatra. Fairy Tale (ASCAP)—Cap 3218	—	1

The Billboard Music Popularity Charts — POPULAR RECORDS

• Best Sellers in Stores

For survey week ending September 21

RECORDS are ranked in order of their current national selling importance at the retail level, as determined by The Billboard's weekly survey of the top volume dealers in every important market area. When significant action is reported on both sides of a record, points are combined to determine position on the chart. In such a case, both sides are listed in bold type, the leading side on top.

This Week		Last Week	Weeks on Chart
1.	YELLOW ROSE OF TEXAS (ASCAP)—M. Miller Blackberry Winter (BMI)—Col 40540	1	9
2.	LOVE IS A MANY-SPLENDORED THING (ASCAP)—Four Aces Shine On, Harvest Moon—Dec 29625	2	5
3.	AUTUMN LEAVES (ASCAP)—R. Williams Take Care (BMI)—Kapp 116	4	7
4.	AIN'T THAT A SHAME (BMI)—P. Boone Tennessee Saturday Night (BMI)—Dot 15377	3	12
5.	MOMENTS TO REMEMBER (ASCAP)—Four Lads Dream On, My Love, Dream On (ASCAP)—Col 40539	8	5
6.	YELLOW ROSE OF TEXAS (ASCAP)—J. Desmond You're in Love With Someone (ASCAP)—Coral 61476	9	8
7.	TINA MARIE (ASCAP)—P. Como FOOLED (ASCAP)—Vic 20-6192	10	7
8.	ROCK AROUND THE CLOCK (ASCAP)—B. Haley Thirteen Women (BMI)—Dec 29124	5	21
9.	SEVENTEEN (BMI)—Fontane Sisters If I Could Be With You (ASCAP)—Dot 15386	6	6
9.	MAYBELLENE (BMI)—C. Berry Wee Wee Hours (BMI)—Chess 1604	7	7
11.	BIBLE TELLS ME SO (ASCAP)—D. Cornell Love Is a Many-Splendored Thing (ASCAP)—Coral 61467	14	4
12.	SEVENTEEN (BMI)—B. Bennett Little Old You-All (BMI)—King 1470	11	13
13.	SHIFTING, WHISPERING SANDS (Parts I & II) (BMI)—B. Vaughn Dot 15409	18	2
14.	WAKE THE TOWN AND TELL THE PEOPLE (ASCAP)—L. Baxter I'll Never Stop Loving You (ASCAP)—Cap 3120	13	8
15.	LONGEST WALK (ASCAP)—J. P. Morgan Swanee (ASCAP)—Vic 20-6182	15	4
16.	GUM DROP (BMI)—Crew Cuts Present Arms (ASCAP)—Mercury 70668	12	6
17.	SONG OF THE DREAMER (BMI)—E. Fisher Don't Stay Away Too Long (ASCAP)—Vic 20-6196	16	6
17.	BLACK DENIM TROUSERS (BMI)—Cheers Some Night in Alaska (BMI)—Cap 3219	23	2
19.	HE (BMI)—A. Hibbler Breeze (ASCAP)—Dec 29660	—	1
20.	HARD TO GET (ASCAP)—G. MacKenzie Boston Fancy (BMI)—X 0137	17	18
21.	ONLY YOU (BMI)—Platters Bark, Battle and Ball (BMI)—Mercury 70633	—	1
22.	SHIFTING, WHISPERING SANDS (BMI)—R. Draper Last Frontier (ASCAP)—Mercury 70696	—	1
23.	I WANT YOU TO BE MY BABY (BMI)—G. Gibbs Come Rain or Come Shine (ASCAP)—Mercury 70685	22	3
24.	WAKE THE TOWN AND TELL THE PEOPLE (ASCAP)—M. Carson Hold Me Tight (ASCAP)—Col 40537	21	6
25.	I WANT YOU TO BE MY BABY (BMI)—L. Briggs Don't Stay Away Too Long (BMI)—Epic 9115	24	3

DEALERS AND OPERATORS . . .

Tomorrow's Hits . . . Today
Poster is on page 52
Top Ten Tunes Poster is on page 56

• THIS WEEK'S BEST BUYS

According to sales reports in key markets, the following recent releases are recommended for extra profits:

YOU ARE MY LOVE (Jubilee, ASCAP)—Joni James—M-G-M 12066

In an impressive show of power, this disk swept on to the New York and Buffalo territorial charts this week, and was also reported strong in Boston, Providence, Philadelphia, Pittsburgh and St. Louis. Other cities that indicated good and growing volume included Milwaukee, Nashville, Baltimore and Chicago. Flip is "I Lay Me Down to Sleep" (Meridian, BMI).

SOMEONE YOU LOVE (Bradshaw, BMI)
FORGIVE MY HEART (Bregman, Vocco & Conn, ASCAP)—Nat (King) Cole—Capitol 3234

Cole often is a slow starter, but invariably strong at the finish line. With this record he has moved out unusually fast, however, and bids fair to break into the charts with little delay. Territories that already report good to strong sales include Baltimore, Philadelphia, Pittsburgh, Buffalo, Atlanta, St. Louis, Milwaukee, Durham, Cleveland and Detroit. Like many other Cole disks, both sides have attracted favorable reaction, with the majority preferring "Someone You Love" at this point. A previous Billboard "Spotlight" pick.

• Most Played in Juke Boxes

For survey week ending September 21

RECORDS are ranked in order of the greatest number of plays in juke boxes thruout the country, as determined by The Billboard's weekly survey of the nation's juke box operators. When significant play is reported on both sides of a record, points are combined to determine position on the chart. In such a case, both sides are listed in bold type, the leading side on top.

This Week		Last Week	Weeks on Chart
1.	YELLOW ROSE OF TEXAS—M. Miller Blackberry Winter (BMI)—Col 40540	2	7
2.	AIN'T THAT A SHAME (BMI)—P. Boone Tennessee Saturday Night (BMI)—Dot 15377	1	12
3.	ROCK AROUND THE CLOCK (ASCAP)—B. Haley Thirteen Women (BMI)—Dec 29124	3	16
4.	SEVENTEEN (BMI)—Fontane Sisters If I Could Be With You (ASCAP)—Dot 15386	5	7
5.	YELLOW ROSE OF TEXAS (ASCAP) J. Desmond You're in Love With Someone (ASCAP)—Coral 61476	4	6
6.	HARD TO GET (ASCAP)—G. MacKenzie Boston Fancy (BMI)—X 0137	6	13
7.	MAYBELLENE (BMI)—C. Berry Wee Wee Hours (BMI)—Chess 1604	7	5
8.	TINA MARIE (ASCAP)—P. Como Fooled (ASCAP)—Vic 20-6192	12	5
9.	WAKE THE TOWN AND TELL THE PEOPLE (ASCAP)—L. Baxter I'll Never Stop Loving You (ASCAP)—Cap 3120	10	3
10	SEVENTEEN (BMI)—B. Bennett Little Ole You-All (BMI)—King 1470	8	6
11.	LONGEST WALK (ASCAP)—J. P. Morgan Swanee (ASCAP)—Vic 20-6182	9	6
11.	SONG OF THE DREAMER—E. Fisher DON'T STAY AWAY TOO LONG (ASCAP)—Vic 20-6196	16	3
13.	HUMMINGBIRD (ASCAP)—L. Paul & M. Ford Goodbye My Love (ASCAP)—Cap 3165	15	10
13.	LOVE IS A MANY-SPLENDORED THING (ASCAP)—Four Aces Shine On, Harvest Moon (ASCAP)—Dec 29625	17	2
15.	LEARNIN' THE BLUES (ASCAP)—F. Sinatra If I Had Three Wishes (ASCAP)—Cap 3102	10	16
16.	WAKE THE TOWN AND TELL THE PEOPLE (ASCAP)—M. Carson Hold Me Tight (ASCAP)—Col 40537	13	3
16.	AUTUMN LEAVES (ASCAP)—R. Williams Take Care (BMI)—Kapp 116	14	3
18.	AIN'T THAT A SHAME (BMI)—Fats Domino La La (BMI)—Imperial 5348	20	10
19.	BIBLE TELLS ME SO (ASCAP)—D. Cornell LOVE IS A MANY-SPLENDORED THING (ASCAP)—Coral 61467	20	2
20.	SHIFTING, WHISPERING SANDS (Parts I & II)—B. Vaughn (BMI)—Dot 15409	—	1

• Most Played by Jockeys

For survey week ending September 21

SIDES are ranked in order of the greatest number of plays on disk jockey radio shows thruout the country. Results are based on The Billboard's weekly survey among the nation's disk jockeys. The reverse side of each record is also listed.

This Week		Last Week	Weeks on Chart
1.	YELLOW ROSE OF TEXAS—M. Miller Blackberry Winter (ASCAP)—Col 40540	1	9
2.	LOVE IS A MANY-SPLENDORED THING—Four Aces Shine On Harvest Moon (ASCAP)—Dec 29625	3	6
3.	AIN'T THAT A SHAME—P. Boone Tennessee Saturday Night (BMI)—Dot 15377	2	21
4.	AUTUMN LEAVES—R. Williams Take Care (ASCAP)—Kapp 116	8	4
5.	YELLOW ROSE OF TEXAS—J. Desmond You're in Love With Someone (ASCAP)—Coral 61476	4	7
6.	WAKE THE TOWN AND TELL THE PEOPLE—L. Baxter I'll Never Stop Loving You (ASCAP)—Cap 3120	5	8
7.	TINA MARIE—P. Como Fooled (ASCAP)—Vic 20-6192	6	7
8.	SEVENTEEN—Fontane Sisters If I Could Be With You (BMI)—Dot 15386	7	7
9.	MOMENTS TO REMEMBER (ASCAP)—Four Lads Dream On, My Love, Dream On—Col 40539	11	3
10.	LONGEST WALK—J. P. Morgan Swanee (ASCAP)—Vic 20-6182	9	7
11.	SHIFTING, WHISPERING SANDS (Parts I & II)—B. Vaughn (BMI)—Dot 15409	14	2
12.	ROCK AROUND THE CLOCK—B. Haley Thirteen Women (ASCAP)—Dec 29124	10	19
13.	SEVENTEEN—B. Bennett Little Old You-All (BMI)—King 1470	19	8
14.	I WANT YOU TO BE MY BABY—G. Gibbs Come Rain or Come Shine (BMI)—Mercury 70685	17	2
15.	SAME OLE SATURDAY NIGHT—F. Sinatra Fairy Tale (ASCAP)—Cap 3218	20	2
16.	HARD TO GET—G. MacKenzie Boston Fancy (ASCAP)—X 0137	15	14
17.	MAYBELLENE—C. Berry Wee Wee Hours (BMI)—Chess 1604	—	4
18.	I WANT YOU TO BE MY BABY—L. Briggs Don't Stay Away Too Long (BMI)—Epic 9115	—	1
19.	SUDDENLY THERE'S A VALLEY—G. Grant Love Is (BMI)—Era 1003	—	1
20.	BIBLE TELLS ME SO—D. Cornell Love Is a Many-Splendored Thing (ASCAP)—Coral 61467	—	3

The Billboard Music Popularity Charts — POPULAR RECORDS

• Best Sellers in Stores

For survey week ending September 28

RECORDS are ranked in order of their current national selling importance at the retail level, as determined by The Billboard's weekly survey of the top volume dealers in every important market area. When significant action is reported on both sides of a record, points are combined to determine position on the chart. In such a case, both sides are listed in bold type, the leading side on top.

This Week		Last Week	Weeks on Chart
1.	LOVE IS A MANY-SPLENDORED THING (ASCAP)—Four Aces Shine On, Harvest Moon (ASCAP)—Dec 29625	2	6
2.	YELLOW ROSE OF TEXAS (ASCAP)—M. Miller Blackberry Winter (BMI)—Col 40540	1	10
3.	AUTUMN LEAVES (ASCAP)—R. Williams Take Care (BMI)—Kapp 116	3	8
4.	AIN'T THAT A SHAME (BMI)—P. Boone Tennessee Saturday Night (BMI)—Dot 15377	4	13
5.	MOMENTS TO REMEMBER—(ASCAP)—Four Lads Dream On, My Love, Dream On (ASCAP)—Col 40539	5	6
6.	YELLOW ROSE OF TEXAS (ASCAP)—J. Desmond You're in Love With Someone (ASCAP)—Coral 61476	6	9
7.	SEVENTEEN (BMI)—Fontane Sisters. If I Could Be With You (ASCAP)—Dot 15386	9	7
8.	TINA MARIE (ASCAP)—P. Como Fooled (ASCAP)—Vic 20-6192	7	8
9.	SHIFTING, WHISPERING SANDS (Parts I & II) (BMI)—B. Vaughn Dot 15409	13	3
10.	BIBLE TELLS ME SO (ASCAP)—D. Cornell LOVE IS A MANY-SPLENDORED THING (ASCAP)—Coral 61467	11	5
11.	MAYBELLENE (BMI)—C. Berry Wee Wee Hours (BMI)—Chess 1604	9	8
12.	BLACK DENIM TROUSERS (BMI)—Cheers Some Night in Alaska (BMI)—Cap 3219	17	3
13.	ROCK AROUND THE CLOCK (ASCAP)—B. Haley Thirteen Women (BMI)—Dec 29124	8	22
14.	SHIFTING, WHISPERING SANDS (BMI)—R. Draper Last Frontier (ASCAP)—Mercury 70696	22	2
15.	SEVENTEEN (BMI)—B. Bennett Little Old You-All (BMI)—King 1470	12	14
16.	GUM DROP (BMI)—Crew Cuts Present Arms (ASCAP)—Mercury 70668	16	7
17.	WAKE THE TOWN AND TELL THE PEOPLE (ASCAP)—L. Baxter I'll Never Stop Loving You (ASCAP)—Cap 3120	14	9
18.	ONLY YOU (BMI)—Platters Bark, Battle and Ball (BMI)—Mercury 70633	21	2
19.	HE (BMI)—A. Hibbler Breeze (ASCAP)—Dec 29660	19	2
20.	LONGEST WALK (ASCAP)—J. P. Morgan Swanee (ASCAP)—Vic 20-6182	15	5
21.	SUDDENLY THERE'S A VALLEY (BMI)—G. Grant Love Is (BMI)—Era 1003	—	1
22.	MY BONNIE LASSIE (ASCAP)—Ames Brothers So Will I (BMI)—Vic 20-6208	—	1
23.	WAKE THE TOWN AND TELL THE PEOPLE (ASCAP)—M. Carson Hold Me Tight (ASCAP)—Col 40537	24	7
24.	SONG OF THE DREAMER (BMI)—E. Fisher Don't Stay Away Too Long (ASCAP)—Vic 20-6196	17	7
25.	HARD TO GET (ASCAP)—G. MacKenzie Boston Fancy (BMI)—X 0137	20	19

DEALERS AND OPERATORS . . .

Top Ten Tunes Poster is on page 31

Tomorrow's Hits . . . Today Poster is on page 48

• THIS WEEK'S BEST BUYS

According to sales reports in key markets, the following recent releases are recommended for extra profits:

AT MY FRONT DOOR (Tollie, BMI)

NO ARMS CAN EVER HOLD YOU (Gil, BMI) **—Pat Boone—Dot 15422**

Boone has taken over another r.&b. tune, with impressive commercial results. "At My Front Door" has moved out especially fast in Southern and Midwest areas. Chicago, Cincinnati, Milwaukee, Kansas City, St. Louis, Richmond, Durham, Nashville report outstanding volume. On the Eastern Seaboard, best reports were received from Providence, Baltimore and Philadelphia. "No Arms" is the preferred side at this time, but enough action on the flip has been indicated to make it a threat. A previous Billboard "Spotlight" pick.

HE (Avas, BMI)**—The McGuire Sisters—Coral 61501**

With two records by the McGuire Sisters released within a short time, the public has had a chance to choose a favorite. "He" clearly is it. The disk has taken over the steam that "Give Me Love" worked up, and is now snowballing into a leading chart threat. The majority of sales areas checked indicated good to strong volume. Flip is "If You Believe" (Chappell, ASCAP). A previous Billboard "Spotlight" pick.

AMUKIRIKI (Famous, ASCAP)

MAGIC MELODY (Iris-Trojan, BMI)**—Les Paul and Mary Ford—Capitol 3248**

The duo is following up "Hummingbird" with another fast seller. In the boxes and over the counter, this disk is pulling in a heap of coin. Territories reporting particularly keen action included Philadelphia, Buffalo, Pittsburgh, Cleveland, Milwaukee, Detroit, Providence, Richmond, Baltimore and St. Louis. "Amukiriki" is the leading side by a considerable margin, but the flip is doing nicely in many areas and could be a sleeper. A previous Billboard "Spotlight" pick.

SUDDENLY THERE'S A VALLEY (Warman-Hill & Range, BMI)**—Jo Stafford—Columbia 40559**

As this tune continues to climb up the "Honor Roll of Hits," all versions keep on growing. Records by Gogi Grant and Julius LaRosa were previously picked as Best Buys, and still lead Stafford. The latter thrush has a strong following, however, and they are now bringing their forces forward. The Columbia disk is selling nicely in Providence, Pittsburgh, Milwaukee, Detroit, Nashville, Durham, Atlanta and St. Louis. Flip is "Night Watch" (Copar, BMI). A previous Billboard "Spotlight" pick.

• Most Played in Juke Boxes

For survey week ending September 28

RECORDS are ranked in order of the greatest number of plays in juke boxes thruout the country, as determined by The Billboard's weekly survey of the nation's juke box operators. When significant play is reported on both sides of a record, points are combined to determine position on the chart. In such a case, both sides are listed in bold type, the leading side on top.

This Week		Last Week	Weeks on Chart
1.	YELLOW ROSE OF TEXAS (ASCAP)—M. Miller Blackberry Winter (BMI)—Col 40540	1	8
2.	AIN'T THAT A SHAME (BMI)—P. Boone Tennessee Saturday Night (BMI)—Dot 15377	2	13
3.	SEVENTEEN (BMI)—Fontane Sisters If I Could Be With You (ASCAP)—Dot 15386	4	8
4.	YELLOW ROSE OF TEXAS (ASCAP)—J. Desmond You're in Love With Someone (ASCAP)—Coral 61476	5	7
5.	ROCK AROUND THE CLOCK (ASCAP)—B. Haley Thirteen Women (BMI)—Dec 29124	3	17
6.	MAYBELLENE (BMI)—C. Berry Wee Wee Hours (BMI)—Chess 1604	7	6
7.	LONGEST WALK (ASCAP)—J. P. Morgan SWANEE (ASCAP)—Vic 20-6182	11	7
8.	LOVE IS A MANY-SPLENDORED THING (ASCAP)—Four Aces Shine On, Harvest Moon (ASCAP—Dec 29625	13	3
9.	WAKE THE TOWN AND TELL THE PEOPLE (ASCAP)—L. Baxter I'll Never Stop Loving You (ASCAP)—Cap 3120	9	4
9.	AUTUMN LEAVES (ASCAP)—R. Williams Take Care (BMI)—Kapp 116	16	4
11.	TINA MARIE (ASCAP)—P. Como Fooled (ASCAP)—Vic 20-6192	8	6
12.	HARD TO GET (ASCAP)—G. MacKenzie Boston Fancy (BMI)—X 0137	6	14
13.	SEVENTEEN (BMI)—B. Bennett Little Ole You-All (BMI)—King 1470	10	7
14.	HUMMINGBIRD (ASCAP)—L. Paul & M. Ford Goodbye, My Love (ASCAP)—Cap 3165	13	11
15.	SONG OF THE DREAMER—E. Fisher DON'T STAY AWAY TOO LONG (ASCAP)—Vic 20-6196	11	4
16.	WAKE THE TOWN AND TELL THE PEOPLE (ASCAP)—M. Carson Hold Me Tight (ASCAP)—Col 40537	16	4
17.	AIN'T THAT A SHAME (BMI)—Fats Domino La La (BMI)—Imperial 5348	18	11
17.	BIBLE TELLS ME SO (ASCAP)—D. Cornell LOVE IS A MANY-SPLENDORED THING (ASCAP)—Coral 61467	19	3
19.	LEARNIN' THE BLUES (ASCAP)—F. Sinatra If I Had Three Wishes (ASCAP)—Cap 3102	15	17
19.	I WANT YOU TO BE MY BABY (BMI)—L. Briggs Don't Stay Away Too Long (BMI)—Epic 9115	—	1

• Most Played by Jockeys

For survey week ending September 28

SIDES are ranked in order of the greatest number of plays on disk jockey radio shows thruout the country. Results are based on The Billboard's weekly survey among the nation's disk jockeys. The reverse side of each record is also listed.

This Week		Last Week	Weeks on Chart
1.	YELLOW ROSE OF TEXAS—M. Miller Blackberry Winter (ASCAP)—Col 40540	1	10
2.	LOVE IS A MANY-SPLENDORED THING—Four Aces Shine On, Harvest Moon (ASCAP)—Dec 29625	2	7
3.	AUTUMN LEAVES—R. Williams Take Care (ASCAP)—Kapp 116	4	5
4.	AIN'T THAT A SHAME—P. Boone Tennessee Saturday Night (BMI)—Dot 15377	3	22
5.	YELLOW ROSE OF TEXAS—J. Desmond You're in Love With Someone (ASCAP)—Coral 61476	5	8
6.	WAKE THE TOWN AND TELL THE PEOPLE—L. Baxter I'll Never Stop Loving You (ASCAP)—Cap 3120	6	9
7.	MOMENTS TO REMEMBER (ASCAP)—Four Lads Dream On, My Love, Dream On—Col 40539	9	4
8.	TINA MARIE—P. Como Fooled (ASCAP)—Vic 20-6192	7	8
9.	SEVENTEEN—Fontane Sisters If I Could Be With You (BMI)—Dot 15386	8	8
10.	SHIFTING, WHISPERING SANDS (Parts I & II) (BMI)—B. Vaughn Dot 15409—BMI	11	3
11.	LONGEST WALK—J. P. Morgan Swanee (ASCAP)—Vic 20-6182	10	8
12.	BLACK DENIM TROUSERS—Cheers Some Night in Alaska (BMI)—Cap 3219	—	1
13.	SAME OLE SATURDAY NIGHT—F. Sinatra Fairy Tale (ASCAP)—Cap 3218	15	3
14.	WAKE THE TOWN AND TELL THE PEOPLE—M. Carson Hold Me Tight (ASCAP)—Col 40537	—	-
15.	SUDDENLY THERE'S A VALLY—G. Grant Love Is (BMI)—Era 1003	19	2
16.	MY BONNIE LASSIE—Ames Bros. So Will I (ASCAP)—Vic 20-6208	—	2
17.	I WANT YOU TO BE MY BABY—G. Gibbs Come Rain or Come Shine (BMI)—Mercury 70685	14	3
18.	BIBLE TELLS ME SO—D. Cornell Love Is a Many-Splendored Thing (ASCAP)—Coral 61467	20	4
19.	I WANT YOU TO BE MY BABY—L. Briggs Don't Stay Away Too Long (BMI)—Epic 9115	18	2
20.	SUDDENLY THERE'S A VALLEY—J. LaRosa Every Time That I Kiss Carrie (BMI)—Cadence 1270	—	1

The Billboard Music Popularity Charts — POPULAR RECORDS

• Best Sellers in Stores

For survey week ending October 5

RECORDS are ranked in order of their current national selling importance at the retail level, as determined by The Billboard's weekly survey of the top volume dealers in every important market area. When significant action is reported on both sides of a record, points are combined to determine position on the chart. In such a case, both sides are listed in bold type, the leading side on top.

This Week	Record	Last Week	Weeks on Chart
1.	**YELLOW ROSE OF TEXAS** (ASCAP)—M. Miller Blackberry Winter (BMI)—Col 40540	2	11
2.	**LOVE IS A MANY-SPLENDORED THING** (ASCAP)—Four Aces Shine On Harvest Moon—Dec 29625	1	7
3.	**AUTUMN LEAVES** (ASCAP)—R. Williams Take Care (BMI)—Kapp 116	3	9
4.	**MOMENTS TO REMEMBER** (ASCAP)—Four Lads Dream On, My Love, Dream On (ASCAP) Col 40539	5	7
5.	**AIN'T THAT A SHAME** (BMI)—P. Boone Tennessee Saturday Night (BMI)—Dot 15377	4	14
6.	**TINA MARIE** (ASCAP)—Perry Como Fooled (ASCAP)—Vic 20-6192	8	9
7.	**SHIFTING, WHISPERING SANDS** (BMI)—(Parts I & II) B. Vaughn Dot 15409	9	4
8.	**BIBLE TELLS ME SO** (ASCAP)—D. Cornell **LOVE IS A MANY-SPLENDORED THING** (ASCAP)—Coral 61467	10	6
9.	**BLACK DENIM TROUSERS** (BMI)—Cheers Some Night in Alaska (BMI)—Cap 3219	12	4
10.	**SEVENTEEN** (BMI)—Fontane Sisters If I Could be With You (ASCAP)—Dot 15386	7	8
11.	**YELLOW ROSE OF TEXAS** (ASCAP)—J. Desmond You're in Love With Someone (ASCAP)—Coral 61476	6	10
12.	**HE** (BMI)—A. Hibbler Breeze (ASCAP)—Dec 29660	19	3
13.	**SHIFTING, WHISPERING SANDS** (BMI)—R. Draper Last Frontier (ASCAP)—Mercury 70696	14	3
14.	**ONLY YOU** (BMI)—Platters Bark, Battle and Ball (BMI)—Mercury 70633	18	3
15.	**SEVENTEEN** (BMI)—B. Bennett Little Old You-All (BMI)—King 1470	15	15
16.	**WAKE THE TOWN AND TELL THE PEOPLE** (ASCAP)—L. Baxter I'll Never Stop Loving You (ASCAP)—Cap 3120	17	10
17.	**MAYBELLENE** (BMI)—C. Berry Wee Wee Hours (BMI)—Chess 1604	11	9
18.	**ROCK AROUND THE CLOCK** (ASCAP)—B. Haley Thirteen Women (BMI)—Dec 29124	13	23
19.	**MY BONNIE LASSIE** (ASCAP)—Ames Brothers So Will I (BMI)—Vic 20-6208	22	2
20.	**SUDDENLY THERE'S A VALLEY** (BMI)—G. Grant Love Is (BMI)—Era 1003	21	2
21.	**LONGEST WALK** (ASCAP)—J. P. Morgan Swanee (ASCAP)—Vic 0-6182	20	6
22.	**SONG OF THE DREAMER** (BMI)—E. Fisher Don't Stay Away Too Long (ASCAP)—Vic 20-6196	24	8
23.	**AT MY FRONT DOOR** (BMI)—El Dorados What's Buggin' You, Baby (BMI)—Vee Jay 147	—	1
24.	**GUM DROP** (BMI)—Crew Cuts Present Arms (ASCAP)—Mercury 70668	16	8
25.	**WAKE THE TOWN AND TELL THE PEOPLE** (ASCAP)—M. Carson Hold Me Tight (ASCAP)—Col 40537	23	8

• THIS WEEK'S BEST BUYS

According to sales reports in key markets, the following recent releases are recommended for extra profits:

I HEAR YOU KNOCKING (Commodore, BMI)
NEVER LEAVE ME (Hometown, ASCAP)—**Gale Storm—Dot 15412**

The thrush's first release on the label is stirring considerable excitement among deejays, dealers and operators. This week Buffalo and Seattle report the disk on their territorial charts. Good sales are also reported in Pittsburgh, Cincinnati, Cleveland, Nashville, St. Louis, Milwaukee, Chicago, Los Angeles and Baltimore. The majority of territories prefer the rhythm and blues tunes, but in some areas the flip is receiving better-than-average attention.

NO ARMS CAN EVER HOLD YOU (Gil, BMI) —**Georgie Shaw—Decca 29679**

With this record, Shaw is turning in one of his best sales performances in several recent tries. On the Detroit territorial chart this week, the disk is also taking off in Philadelphia, St. Louis, Milwaukee and Cincinnati in a big way, and appears to have strong chart potential. On the reverse of Shaw's disk is "Look to Your Heart" (Barton, ASCAP). A previous Billboard "Spotlight" pick.

MAGIC FINGERS (Ross-Jungnickel, ASCAP)
I WANNA GO WHERE YOU GO (Bourne, ASCAP)—**Eddie Fisher—RCA Victor 6264**

While this disk has not taken off with the speed of some of the big Fisher hits of the last few years, in the past three weeks it has garnered an impressive set of sales reports from most parts of the country. Among these were Providence, Philadelphia, Baltimore, Richmond, Durham, Buffalo, Pittsburgh, Chicago, Milwaukee, Nashville, Atlanta and St. Louis. Action is almost evenly divided between the two sides. A previous Billboard "Spotlight" pick.

• Most Played in Juke Boxes

For survey week ending October 5

RECORDS are ranked in order of the greatest number of plays in juke boxes thruout the country, as determined by The Billboard's weekly survey of the nation's juke box operators. When significant play is reported on both sides of a record, points are combined to determine position on the chart. In such a case, both sides are listed in bold type, the leading side on top.

This Week	Record	Last Week	Weeks on Chart
1.	**YELLOW ROSE OF TEXAS** (ASCAP)—M. Miller Blackberry Winter (BMI)—Col 40540	1	9
2.	**AIN'T THAT A SHAME** (BMI)—P. Boone Tennessee Saturday Night (BMI)—Dot 15377	2	14
3.	**AUTUMN LEAVES** (ASCAP)—R. Williams Take Care (BMI)—Kapp 116	9	5
4.	**LOVE IS A MANY-SPLENDORED THING** (ASCAP)—Four Aces Shine On, Harvest Moon (ASCAP)—Dec 29625	8	4
5.	**SEVENTEEN** (BMI)—Fontane Sisters If I Could Be With You (ASCAP)—Dot 15386	3	9
6.	**YELLOW ROSE OF TEXAS** (ASCAP)—J. Desmond You're in Love With Someone (ASCAP)—Coral 61476	4	8
7.	**LONGEST WALK** (ASCAP)—J. P. Morgan Swanee (ASCAP)—Vic 20-6182	7	8
8.	**MAYBELLLENE** (BMI)—C. Berry Wee Wee Hours (BMI)—Chess 1604	6	7
9.	**ROCK AROUND THE CLOCK** (ASCAP)—B. Haley Thirteen Women (BMI)—Dec 29124	5	18
10.	**TINA MARIE** (ASCAP)—P. Como Fooled (ASCAP)—Vic 20-6192	11	7
11.	**WAKE THE TOWN AND TELL THE PEOPLE** (ASCAP)—L. Baxter I'll Never Stop Loving You (ASCAP)—Cap 3120	9	5
12.	**SEVENTEEN** (BMI)—B. Bennett Little Ole You-All (BMI)—King 1470	13	8
13.	**HARD TO GET** (ASCAP)—G. MacKenzie Boston Fancy (BMI)—X 0137	12	15
14.	**WAKE THE TOWN AND TELL THE PEOPLE** (ASCAP)—M. Carson Hold Me Tight (ASCAP)—Col 40537	16	5
15.	**SHIFTING, WHISPERING SANDS** (Parts I & II) (BMI)—B. Vaughn Dot 15409 (BMI)	—	2
16.	**BIBLE TELLS ME SO** (ASCAP)—D. Cornell Love Is a Many-Splendored Thing (ASCAP)—Coral 61467	17	4
17.	**AIN'T IT A SHAME** (BMI)—Fats Domino La La (BMI)—Imperial 5348	17	4
18.	**HUMMINGBIRD** (ASCAP)—L. Paul & M. Ford Goodbye My Love (ASCAP)—Cap 3165	14	12
19.	**MOMENTS TO REMEMBER** (ASCAP)—Four Lads Dream On, My Love, Dream On (ASCAP)—Col 40539	—	1
20.	**I WANT YOU TO BE MY BABY**—L. Briggs Don't Stay Away Too Long (BMI)—Epic 9115	19	2
20.	**SUDDENLY THERE'S A VALLEY** (BMI)—G. Grant Love Is (BMI)—Era 1003	—	1
20.	**ONLY YOU** (BMI)—Platters Bark, Battle and Ball (BMI)—Mercury 70633	—	1

• Most Played by Jockeys

For survey week ending October 5

SIDES are ranked in order of the greatest number of plays on disk jockey radio shows thruout the country. Results are based on The Billboard's weekly survey among the nation's disk jockeys. The reverse side of each record is also listed.

This Week	Record	Last Week	Weeks on Chart
1.	**LOVE IS A MANY-SPLENDORED THING**—Four Aces Shine On, Harvest Moon (ASCAP)—Dec 29625	2	8
2.	**YELLOW ROSE OF TEXAS**—M. Miller Blackberry Winter (ASCAP)—Col 40540	1	11
3.	**AUTUMN LEAVES**—R. Williams Take Care (ASCAP)—Kapp 116	3	6
4.	**MOMENTS TO REMEMBER**—Four Lads Dream On, My Love, Dream On (ASCAP)—Col 40539	7	5
5.	**TINA MARIE**—P. Como Fooled (ASCAP)—Vic 20-6192	8	9
6.	**AIN'T THAT A SHAME**—P. Boone Tennessee Saturday Night (BMI)—Dot 15377	4	23
7.	**SEVENTEEN**—Fontane Sisters If I Could Be With You (BMI)—Dot 15386	9	9
8.	**SHIFTING, WHISPERING SANDS**—(Parts I & II)—B. Vaughn (BMI)—Dot 15409	10	4
9.	**WAKE THE TOWN AND TELL THE PEOPLE**—L. Baxter I'll Never Stop Loving You (ASCAP)—Cap 3120	6	10
10.	**YELLOW ROSE OF TEXAS**—J. Desmond You're in Love With Someone (ASCAP)—Coral 61476	5	9
11.	**BLACK DENIM TROUSERS**—Cheers Some Night in Alaska (BMI)—Cap 3219	12	2
12.	**LONGEST WALK**—J. P. Morgan Swanee (ASCAP)—Vic 20-6182	11	9
13.	**SAME OLE SATURDAY NIGHT**—F. Sinatra Fairy Tale (ASCAP)—Cap 3218	13	4
14.	**SUDDENLY THERE'S A VALLEY**—G. Grant Love Is (BMI)—Era 1003	15	3
15.	**MY BONNIE LASSIE**—Ames Bros. So Will I (ASCAP)—Vic 20-6208	16	3
16.	**HE**—A. Hibbler Breeze (BMI)—Dec 29660	—	1
17.	**SHIFTING, WHISPERING SANDS**—R. Draper Last Frontier (BMI)—Mercury 70696	—	1
18.	**SUDDENLY THERE'S A VALLEY**—J. Stafford Night Watch (BMI)—Col 40559	—	1
19.	**BIBLE TELLS ME SO**—D. Cornell Love Is a Many-Splendored Thing (ASCAP)—Coral 61467	18	5
20.	**HARD TO GET**—G. MacKenzie Boston Fancy (ASCAP)—X 0137	—	15

The Billboard Music Popularity Charts

POPULAR RECORDS

• Best Sellers in Stores

For survey week ending October 12

RECORDS are ranked in order of their current national selling importance at the retail level, as determined by The Billboard's weekly survey of the top volume dealers in every important market area. When significant action is reported on both sides of a record, points are combined to determine position on the chart. In such a case, both sides are listed in bold type, the leading side on top.

This Week		Last Week	Weeks on Chart
1.	LOVE IS A MANY-SPLENDORED THING (ASCAP)—Four Aces Shine On, Harvest Moon—Dec 29625	2	8
2.	AUTUMN LEAVES (ASCAP)—R. Williams Take Care (BMI)—Kapp 116	3	10
3.	YELLOW ROSE OF TEXAS (ASCAP)—M. Miller Blackberry Winter (BMI)—Col 40540	1	12
4.	MOMENTS TO REMEMBER (ASCAP) Four Lads Dream On, My Love Dream On (ASCAP)—Col 40539	4	8
5.	SHIFTING, WHISPERING SANDS (BMI) (PARTS I & II)—B. Vaughn Dot 15409	7	5
6.	AIN'T THAT A SHAME (BMI)—P. Boone Tennessee Saturday Night (BMI)—Dot 15377	5	15
7.	BIBLE TELLS ME SO (ASCAP)—D. Cornell LOVE IS A MANY-SPLENDORED THING—Coral 61467	8	7
8.	TINA MARIE (ASCAP)—P. Como Fooled (ASCAP)—Vic 20-6192	6	10
9.	SHIFTING, WHISPERING SANDS (BMI)—R. Draper Last Frontier (ASCAP)—Mercury 70696	13	4
10.	ONLY YOU (BMI)—Platters Bark, Battle and Ball (BMI)—Mercury 70633	14	4
11.	YELLOW ROSE OF TEXAS (ASCAP)—J. Desmond You're in Love With Someone (ASCAP)—Coral 61476	11	11
12.	HE (BMI)—A. Hibbler Breeze (ASCAP)—Dec 29660	12	4
13.	BLACK DENIM TROUSERS (BMI)—Cheers Some Night in Alaska (BMI)—Cap 3219	9	5
14.	SEVENTEEN (BMI)—Fontane Sisters If I Could Be With You (ASCAP)—Dot 15386	10	9
15.	MY BONNIE LASSIE (ASCAP)—Ames Brothers So Will I (BMI)—Vic 20-6208	19	3
16.	WAKE THE TOWN AND TELL THE PEOPLE (ASCAP)—L. Baxter I'll Never Stop Loving You (ASCAP)—Cap 3120	16	11
17.	SUDDENLY THERE'S A VALLEY (BMI)—G. Grant Love Is (BMI)—Era 1003	20	3
18.	LONGEST WALK (ASCAP)—J. P. Morgan Swanee (ASCAP)—Vic 20-6182	21	7
19.	MAYBELLENE (BMI)—C. Berry Wee Wee Hours (BMI)—Chess 1604	17	10
20.	SOMEONE YOU LOVE (BMI)—Nat (King) Cole FORGIVE MY HEART (ASCAP)—Cap 3234	—	1
21.	AT MY FRONT DOOR (BMI)—El Dorados What's Buggin' You, Baby (BMI)—Vee Jay 147	23	2
22.	YOU ARE MY LOVE (ASCAP)—J. James I Lay Me Down to Sleep (BMI)—M-G-M 12066	—	1
23.	SUDDENLY THERE'S A VALLEY (BMI)—J. Stafford Night Watch (BMI)—Col 40559	—	1
24.	SEVENTEEN (BMI)—B. Bennett Little Old You-All (BMI)—King 1470	15	16
25.	ROCK AROUND THE CLOCK (ASCAP)—B. Haley Thirteen Women (BMI)—Dec 29124	18	24
25.	I HEAR YOU KNOCKIN' (BMI)—G. Storm Never Leave Me (ASCAP)—Dot 15412	—	1

DEALERS AND OPERATORS . . .

Top Ten Tunes Poster
is on page 32

Tomorrow's Hits . . . Today
Poster is on page 36

• THIS WEEK'S BEST BUYS

According to sales reports in key markets, the following recent releases are recommended for extra profits:

LOVE AND MARRIAGE (Barton, ASCAP)—Frank Sinatra—Capitol 3260

Since Sinatra's TV appearance, this record has been selling steadily and at an ever increasing pace. Boston and New York now rate the disk among their top 10, and it is also reported to be a strong seller in Los Angeles, Providence, Philadelphia, Buffalo, Pittsburgh, Atlanta, St. Louis and Cleveland. Flip is "The Impatient Years" (Barton, ASCAP). A previous Billboard "Spotlight" pick.

CROCE DI ORO (Shapiro-Bernstein, ASCAP)—Patti Page—Mercury 70713

The thrush is moving out with this disk in a big way, indications being that this will be her biggest record in recent months. Best commercial reports come from Philadelphia, Baltimore, Pittsburgh, Milwaukee, Providence, Cleveland, St. Louis and Durham. In some cities, the Joan Regan version of this tune is also seeing good action. Flip of the Page disk is "Search My Heart" (Berkshire, BMI). A previous Billboard "Spotlight" pick.

DOGFACE SOLDIER (Shawnee, ASCAP)—Russ MORGAN—Decca 29703

This tune, featured in the film "To Hell and Back," is getting a send-off that smacks a bit of "Honey Babe." With the pic still in the early part of its run, this record figures to keep on building far beyond the already substantial proportions it has acheived. New York, Providence, Philadelphia, Los Angeles, Cleveland, Detroit, Milwaukee, St. Louis, Baltimore and Cincinnati are among the cities indicating excellent sales reaction this past week. Flip is "Don't Cry, Sweetheart."

• Most Played in Juke Boxes

For survey week ending October 12

RECORDS are ranked in order of the greatest number of plays in juke boxes thruout the country, as determined by The Billboard's weekly survey of the nation's juke box operators. When significant play is reported on both sides of a record, points are combined to determine position on the chart. In such a case, both sides are listed in bold type, the leading side on top.

This Week		Last Week	Weeks on Chart
1.	YELLOW ROSE OF TEXAS (ASCAP)—M. Miller Blackberry Winter (BMI)—Col 40540	1	10
2.	AIN'T THAT A SHAME (BMI)—P. Boone Tennessee Saturday Night (BMI)—Dot 15377	2	15
3.	LOVE IS A MANY-SPLENDORED THING (ASCAP)—Four Aces Shine On, Harvest Moon (ASCAP)—Dec 29625	4	5
4.	SEVENTEEN (BMI)—Fontane Sisters If I Could Be With You (ASCAP)—Dot 15386	5	10
5.	YELLOW ROSE OF TEXAS (ASCAP)—J. Desmond You're in Love With Someone (ASCAP)—Coral 61476	6	9
6.	AUTUMN LEAVES (ASCAP)—R. Williams Take Care (BMI)—Kapp 116	3	6
7.	MAYBELLENE (BMI)—C. Berry Wee Wee Hours (BMI)—Chess 1604	8	8
8.	WAKE THE TOWN AND TELL THE PEOPLE (ASCAP)—L. Baxter I'll Never Stop Loving You (ASCAP)—Cap 3120	11	6
9.	LONGEST WALK (ASCAP)—J. P. Morgan Swanee (ASCAP)—Vic 20-6182	7	9
10.	ROCK AROUND THE CLOCK (ASCAP)—B. Haley Thirteen Women (BMI)—Dec 29124	9	19
11.	SEVENTEEN (BMI)—B. Bennett Little Ole You-All (BMI)—King 1470	12	9
12.	TINA MARIE (ASCAP)—P. Como Fooled (ASCAP)—Vic 20-6192	10	8
13.	HARD TO GET (ASCAP)—G. MacKenzie Boston Fancy (BMI)—X 0137	13	16
14.	BIBLE TELLS ME SO (ASCAP)—D. Cornell Love Is a Many-Splendored Thing (ASCAP)—Coral 61467	16	5
15.	WAKE THE TOWN AND TELL THE PEOPLE (ASCAP)—M. Carson Hold Me Tight (ASCAP)—Col 40537	14	6
16.	SHIFTING, WHISPERING SANDS—(Parts I & II) B. Vaughn Dot 15409 (BMI)	15	3
17.	MOMENTS TO REMEMBER (ASCAP)—Four Lads Dream On, My Love, Dream On (ASCAP)—Col 40539	19	2
18.	AIN'T THAT A SHAME (BMI)—Fats Domino La La (BMI)—Imperial 5348	17	5
19.	HUMMINGBIRD (ASCAP)—L. Paul & M. Ford Goodbye, My Love (ASCAP)—Cap 3165	18	13
19.	SUDDENLY THERE'S A VALLEY (BMI)—G. Grant Love Is (BMI)—Era 1003	20	2
19.	SONG OF THE DREAMER E. Fisher Don't Stay Away Too Long (ASCAP)—Vic 20-6196	—	5
19.	SHIFTING, WHISPERING SANDS (BMI)—R. Draper Last Frontier (ASCAP)—Mercury 70696	—	1

• Most Played by Jockeys

For survey week ending October 12

SIDES are ranked in order of the greatest number of plays on disk jockey radio shows thruout the country. Results are based on The Billboard's weekly survey among the nation's disk jockeys. The reverse side of each record is also listed.

This Week		Last Week	Weeks on Chart
1.	LOVE IS A MANY-SPLENDORED THING—Four Aces Shine On, Harvest Moon (ASCAP)—Dec 29625	1	9
2.	YELLOW ROSE OF TEXAS—M. Miller Blackberry Winter (ASCAP)—Col 40540	2	12
3.	MOMENTS TO REMEMBER—Four Lads Dream On, My Love, Dream On (ASCAP)—Col 40539	4	6
4.	AUTUMN LEAVES—R. Williams Take Care (ASCAP)—Kapp 116	3	7
5.	SHIFTING, WHISPERING SANDS—(Parts I & II) B. Vaughn Dot 15409 (BMI)	8	5
6.	YELLOW ROSE OF TEXAS—J. Desmond You're in Love With Someone (ASCAP)—Coral 61476	10	10
7.	BLACK DENIM TROUSERS—Cheers Some Night in Alaska (BMI)—Cap 3219	11	3
8.	AIN'T THAT A SHAME—P. Boone Tennessee Saturday Night (BMI)—Dot 15377	6	24
9.	LONGEST WALK—J. P. Morgan Swanee (ASCAP)—Vic 20-6182	12	10
10.	TINA MARIE—P. Como Fooled (ASCAP)—Vic 20-6192	5	10
11.	SEVENTEEN—Fontane Sisters If I Could Be With You (BMI)—Dot 15386	7	10
12.	WAKE THE TOWN AND TELL THE PEOPLE—L. Baxter I'll Never Stop Loving You (ASCAP)—Cap 3120	9	11
13.	HE—A. Hibbler Breeze (BMI)—Dec 29660	16	2
14.	SUDDENLY THERE'S A VALLEY—J. Stafford Night Watch (BMI)—Col 40559	18	2
15.	SUDDENLY THERE'S A VALLEY—G. Grant Love Is (BMI)—Era 1003	14	4
16.	YELLOW ROSE OF TEXAS—S. Freberg Rock Around Stephen Foster (ASCAP)—Cap 3249	—	1
17.	I WANT YOU TO BE MY BABY—G. Gibbs Come Rain or Come Shine (BMI)—Mercury 70685	—	3
18.	MY BONNIE LASSIE—Ames Bros. So Will I (ASCAP)—Vic 20-6208	15	4
19.	SOMEONE YOU LOVE—Nat (King) Cole Forgive My Heart (BMI)—Cap 3234	—	1
20.	YOU ARE MY LOVE—J. James I Lay Me Down to Sleep (ASCAP)—M-G-M 12066	—	1

The Billboard Music Popularity Charts — POPULAR RECORDS

• Best Sellers in Stores

For survey week ending October 19

RECORDS are ranked in order of their current national selling importance at the retail level, as determined by The Billboard's weekly survey of the top volume dealers in every important market area. When significant action is reported on both sides of a record, points are combined to determine position on the chart. In such a case, both sides are listed in bold type, the leading side on top.

This Week		Last Week	Weeks on Chart
1.	AUTUMN LEAVES (ASCAP)—R. Williams Take Care (BMI)—Kapp 116	2	11
2.	LOVE IS A MANY-SPLENDORED THING (ASCAP)—Four Aces Shine On, Harvest Moon (ASCAP)—Dec 29625	1	9
3.	YELLOW ROSE OF TEXAS (ASCAP)—M. Miller Blackberry Winter (BMI)—Col 40540	3	13
4.	MOMENTS TO REMEMBER (ASCAP)—Four Lads Dream On, My Love, Dream On (ASCAP)—Col 40539	4	9
5.	SHIFTING, WHISPERING SANDS (PARTS I & II) (BMI)—B. Vaughn Dot 15409	5	6
6.	BLACK DENIM TROUSERS (BMI)—Cheers Some Night in Alaska (BMI)—Cap 3219	13	6
7.	BIBLE TELLS ME SO (ASCAP)—D. Cornell LOVE IS A MANY-SPLENDORED THING (ASCAP)—Coral 61467	7	8
8.	SHIFTING, WHISPERING SANDS (BMI)—R. Draper Time (ASCAP)—Mercury 70696	9	5
9.	ONLY YOU (BMI)—Platters Bark, Battle and Ball (BMI)—Mercury 70633	10	5
10.	HE (BMI)—A. Hibbler Breeze (ASCAP)—Dec 29660	12	5
11.	AIN'T THAT A SHAME (BMI)—P. Boone Tennessee Saturday Night (BMI)—Dot 15377	6	16
12.	TINA MARIE (ASCAP)—P. Como Fooled (ASCAP)—Vic 20-6192	8	11
13.	YELLOW ROSE OF TEXAS (ASCAP)—J. Desmond You're in Love With Someone (ASCAP)—Coral 61476	11	12
14.	SEVENTEEN (BMI)—Fontane Sisters If I Could Be With You (ASCAP)—Dot 15386	14	10
15.	SUDDENLY THERE'S A VALLEY (BMI)—G. Grant Love Is (BMI)—Era 1003	17	4
16.	MY BONNIE LASSIE (ASCAP)—Ames Brothers So Will I (BMI)—Vic 20-6208	15	4
17.	AT MY FRONT DOOR (BMI)—P. Boone No Arms Can Ever Hold You (BMI)—Dot 15422	—	1
18.	SOMEONE YOU LOVE (BMI)—Nat (King) Cole FORGIVE MY HEART (ASCAP)—Cap 3234	20	2
19.	WAKE THE TOWN AND TELL THE PEOPLE (ASCAP)—L. Baxter I'll Never Stop Loving You (ASCAP)—Cap 3120	16	12
20.	I HEAR YOU KNOCKIN' (BMI)—G. Storm Never Leave Me (ASCAP)—Dot 15412	25	2
21.	YOU ARE MY LOVE (ASCAP)—J. James I Lay Me Down to Sleep (BMI)—M-G-M 12066	22	2
22.	SUDDENLY THERE'S A VALLEY—J. La Rosa Everytime That I Kiss Carrie (BMI)—Cadence 1270	—	1
23.	LONGEST WALK (ASCAP)—J. P. Morgan Swanee (ASCAP)—Vic 20-6182	18	8
24.	AT MY FRONT DOOR (BMI)—El Dorados What's Buggin' You Baby (BMI)—Vee Jay 147	21	3
25.	HE (BMI)—McGuire Sisters If You Believe (ASCAP)—Coral 61501	—	1

DEALERS AND OPERATORS . . .

Top Ten Tunes Poster is on page 40

Tomorrow's Hits . . . Today Poster is on page 42

• THIS WEEKS BEST BUYS

According to sales reports in key markets, the following recent releases are recommended for extra profits:

PEPPER-HOT BABY (Sheldon, BMI)
IF YOU DON'T WANT MY LOVE (Von Tilzer, ASCAP)—**Jaye P. Morgan—RCA Victor 6282**

A solid blanket of good sales reports has been won by this disk in less than three weeks. From Los Angeles to Boston come enthusiastic reports of quick and mounting sales, with few territories holding back. The jump tune is enjoying most action now, but the ballad is also doing nicely and could pull ahead in the long run. Some areas, incidentally, are also doing well with Gisele MacKenzie's version of "Pepper-Hot Baby." Miss Morgan's record was a previous Billboard "Spotlight" pick.

ROCK-A-BEATIN' BOOGIE (Myers, ASCAP)
BURN THAT CANDLE (Roosevelt, BMI)—**Bill Haley & His Comets—Decca 29713**

For speedy take-off, Haley is still the man to beat. Most sales territories have had this disk only a week, but the immediate response in the stores and in juke boxes has been solid. Best reports this week came from Baltimore, Providence, Boston, New York, Philadelphia, Buffalo, Chicago, Nashville, Durham, St. Louis and Milwaukee. Customers, eager for the record, so far have not indicated a clear preference for top side, tho the "Boogie" does have an early edge. A previous Billboard "Spotlight" pick.

THE RICHEST MAN (Showcase, BMI)—**Eddy Arnold—RCA Victor 6290**

See Country & Western "Best Buys" this week.

• Most Played in Juke Boxes

For survey week ending October 19

RECORDS are ranked in order of the greatest number of plays in juke boxes thruout the country, as determined by The Billboard's weekly survey of the nation's juke box operators. When significant play is reported on both sides of a record, points are combined to determine position on the chart. In such a case, both sides are listed in bold type, the leading side on top.

This Week		Last Week	Weeks on Chart
1.	YELLOW ROSE OF TEXAS (ASCAP)—M. Miller Blackberry Winter (BMI)—Col 40540	1	11
2.	LOVE IS A MANY-SPLENDORED THING (ASCAP)—Four Aces Shine On, Harvest Moon (ASCAP)—Dec 29625	3	6
3.	AIN'T THAT A SHAME (BMI)—P. Boone Tennessee Saturday Night (BMI)—Dot 15377	2	16
4.	AUTUMN LEAVES (ASCAP)—R. Williams Take Care (BMI)—Kapp 116	6	7
5.	SEVENTEEN (BMI)—Fontane Sisters If I Could Be With You (ASCAP)—Dot 15386	4	11
5.	YELLOW ROSE OF TEXAS (ASCAP)—J. Desmond You're in Love With Someone (ASCAP)—Coral 61476	5	10
7.	MAYBELLENE (BMI)—C. Berry Wee Wee Hours (BMI)—Chess 1604	7	9
7.	LONGEST WALK (ASCAP)—J. P. Morgan Swanee (ASCAP)—Vic 20-6182	9	10
9.	WAKE THE TOWN AND TELL THE PEOPLE (ASCAP)—L. Baxter I'll Never Stop Loving You (ASCAP) Cap 3120	8	7
9.	MOMENTS TO REMEMBER (ASCAP)—Four Lads Dream On, My Love, Dream On (ASCAP)—Col 40539	17	3
11.	SEVENTEEN (BMI)—B. Bennett Little Old You-All (BMI)—King 1470	11	10
11.	BIBLE TELLS ME SO (ASCAP)—D. Cornell LOVE IS A MANY SPLENDORED THING (ASCAP)—Coral 61467	14	6
13.	SHIFTING, WHISPERING SANDS (BMI)—R. Draper Time (ASCAP)—Mercury 70696	19	2
14.	TINA MARIE (ASCAP)—P. Como Fooled (ASCAP)—Vic 20-6192	12	9
14.	SHIFTING, WHISPERING SANDS (PARTS I & II)—B. Vaughn Dot 15409 (BMI)	16	4
16.	I HEAR YOU KNOCKING (BMI)—G. Storm Never Leave Me (ASCAP)—Dot 15412	—	1
17.	ONLY YOU (BMI)—Platters Bark, Battle and Ball (BMI)—Mercury 70623	—	2
18.	HE (BMI)—McGuire Sisters If You Believe (ASCAP)—Coral 61501	—	1
19.	SUDDENLY THERE'S A VALLEY (BMI)—G. Grant Love Is (BMI)—Era 1003	19	3
20.	WAKE THE TOWN AND TELL THE PEOPLE (ASCAP)—M. Carson Hold Me Tight (ASCAP)—Col 40537	15	7
20.	SONG OF THE DREAMER—E. Fisher Don't Stay Away Too Long (ASCAP)—Vic 20-6196	19	6
20.	BLACK DENIM TROUSERS (BMI)—Cheers Some Night in Alaska (BMI)—Cap 3219	—	1
20.	HE (BMI)—A. Hibbler Breeze (ASCAP)—Dec 29660	—	1

• Most Played by Jockeys

For survey week ending October 19

SIDES are ranked in order of the greatest number of plays on disk jockey radio shows thruout the country. Results are based on The Billboard's weekly survey among the nation's disk jockeys. The reverse side of each record is also listed.

This Week		Last Week	Weeks on Chart
1.	LOVE IS A MANY-SPLENDORED THING—Four Aces Shine On, Harvest Moon (ASCAP)—Dec 29625	1	10
2.	MOMENTS TO REMEMBER—Four Lads Dream On, My Love, Dream On (ASCAP)—Col 40539	3	7
3.	YELLOW ROSE OF TEXAS—M. Miller Blackberry Winter (ASCAP)—Col 40540	2	13
4.	AUTUMN LEAVES—R. Williams Take Care (ASCAP)—Kapp 116	4	8
5.	SHIFTING, WHISPERING SANDS (PARTS I & II)—B. Vaughn Dot 15409 (BMI)	5	6
6.	BLACK DENIM TROUSERS—Cheers Some Night in Alaska (BMI)—Cap 3219	7	4
7.	TINA MARIE—P. Como Fooled (ASCAP)—Vic 20-6192	10	11
8.	YOU ARE MY LOVE—J. James I Lay Me Down to Sleep (ASCAP) M-G-M 12066	20	2
9.	SUDDENLY THERE'S A VALLEY—G. Grant Love Is (BMI) Era 1003	15	5
10.	SEVENTEEN—Fontane Sisters If I Could Be With You (BMI)—Dot 15386	11	11
11.	AIN'T THAT A SHAME—P. Boone Tennessee Saturday Night (BMI) Dot 15377	8	25
12.	LONGEST WALK—J. P. Morgan Swanee (ASCAP)—Vic 20-6182	9	11
13.	SAME OLE SATURDAY NIGHT—F. Sinatra Fairy Tale (ASCAP)—Cap 3218	—	1
14.	I HEAR YOU KNOCKIN'—G. Storm Never Leave Me (BMI)—Dot 15412	—	1
15.	MY BONNIE LASSIE—Ames Bros. So Will I (ASCAP)—Vic 20-6208	18	5
16.	YELLOW ROSE OF TEXAS—J. Desmond You're in Love With Someone (ASCAP)—Coral 61476	6	11
16.	YELLOW ROSE OF TEXAS—S. Freberg Rock Around Stephen Foster (ASCAP)—Cap 3249	16	2
18.	ONLY YOU—Platters Bark, Battle and Ball (BMI)—Mercury 70633	—	1
19.	SOMEONE YOU LOVE—Nat (King) Cole Forgive My Heart (BMI)—Cap 3234	19	2
19.	HE—A. Hibbler Breeze (BMI)—Dec 29660	13	3

The Billboard Music Popularity Charts — POPULAR RECORDS

• Best Sellers in Stores

For survey week ending October 26

RECORDS are ranked in order of their current national selling importance at the retail level, as determined by The Billboard's weekly survey of the top volume dealers in every important market area. When significant action is reported on both sides of a record, points are combined to determine position on the chart. In such a case, both sides are listed in bold type, the leading side on top.

This Week		Last Week	Weeks on Chart
1.	AUTUMN LEAVES (ASCAP)—R. Williams — Take Care (BMI)—Kapp 116	1	12
2.	LOVE IS A MANY-SPLENDORED THING (ASCAP)—Four Aces — Shine On, Harvest Moon—Dec 29625	2	10
3.	YELLOW ROSE OF TEXAS (ASCAP)—M. Miller — Blackberry Winter (BMI)—Col 40540	3	14
4.	MOMENTS TO REMEMBER (ASCAP)—Four Lads — Dream On, My Love, Dream On (ASCAP)—Col 40539	4	10
5.	ONLY YOU (BMI)—Platters — Bark, Battle and Ball (BMI)—Mercury 70633	9	6
6.	SHIFTING, WHISPERING SANDS (BMI)—R. Draper — Time (BMI)—Mercury 70696	8	6
7.	HE (BMI)—A. Hibbler — Breeze (ASCAP)—Dec 29660	10	6
8.	SHIFTING, WHISPERING SANDS—Parts I & II (BMI)—B. Vaughn — Dot 15409	5	7
9.	BLACK DENIM TROUSERS (BMI)—Cheers — Some Night in Alaska (BMI)—Cap 3219	6	7
10.	BIBLE TELLS ME SO (ASCAP)—D. Cornell — LOVE IS A MANY-SPLENDORED THING (ASCAP)—Coral 61467	7	9
11.	MY BONNIE LASSIE (ASCAP)—Ames Brothers — So Will I (BMI)—Vic 20-6208	16	5
12.	I HEAR YOU KNOCKIN' (BMI)—G. Storm — Never Leave Me (ASCAP)—Dot 15412	20	3
13.	AT MY FRONT DOOR (BMI)—P. Boone — No Arms Can Ever Hold You (BMI)—Dot 15422	17	2
14.	SUDDENLY THERE'S A VALLEY (BMI)—G. Grant — Love Is (BMI)—Era 1003	15	5
15.	TINA MARIE (ASCAP)—P. Como — Fooled (ASCAP)—Vic 20-6192	12	12
16.	FORGIVE MY HEART (ASCAP)—Nat (King) Cole — SOMEONE YOU LOVE (BMI)—Cap 3234	18	3
17.	YELLOW ROSE OF TEXAS J. Desmond — You're In Love With Someone (ASCAP)—Coral 61476	13	13
18.	AIN'T THAT A SHAME (BMI)—P. Boone — Tennessee Saturday Night (BMI)—Dot 15377	11	17
19.	SEVENTEEN (BMI)—Fontane Sisters — If I Could Be With You (ASCAP)—Dot 15386	14	11
19.	YOU ARE MY LOVE (ASCAP)—J. James — I Lay Me Down to Sleep (BMI)—M-G-M 12066	21	3
21.	AT MY FRONT DOOR (BMI)—El Dorados — What's Buggin' You, Baby (BMI)—Vee Jay 147	24	4
22.	HE (BMI)—McGuire Sisters — If You Believe (ASCAP)—Coral 61501	25	2
22.	SUDDENLY THERE'S A VALLEY (BMI)—J. Stafford — Night Watch (BMI)—Col 40559	—	2
24.	SEVENTEEN (BMI)—B. Bennett — Little Old You-All (BMI)—King 1470	—	17
25.	LONGEST WALK (ASCAP)—J. P. Morgan — Swanee (ASCAP)—Vic 20-6182	23	9

• THIS WEEKS BEST BUYS

According to sales reports in key markets, the following recent releases are recommended for extra profits:

SIXTEEN TONS (American, BMI)—**Tennessee Ernie Ford—Capitol 3262**

This week's territorial charts show Ford bustin' out all over; Minneapolis-St. Paul, Milwaukee, Pittsburgh and Dallas-Fort Worth are the cities that number this disk in their top 10. In addition to these, however, there was hardly a major market in the entire country that did not report the record a strong seller. The singer's many country fans are not overlooking this record; sales to them are also reported to be unusually good. Flip is "You Don't Have to Be a Baby to Cry" (Frank, ASCAP).

IT'S ALMOST TOMORROW (Northern, ASCAP) —**The Dream Weavers—Decca 29683**

Each week this disk has taken a big step in the direction of the charts and is now well established in many markets. Now appearing on the Cleveland and Atlanta territorial charts, the record is also enjoying excellent volume in Boston, New York, Baltimore, Chicago, St. Louis and Durham. Flip is "You Got Me Wondering" (Northern, ASCAP).

DADDY-OH (Mar-Kay, BMI)
ADORABLE (Panther, BMI)—**Fontane Sisters—Dot 15428**

DADDY-OH (Mar-Kay, BMI)—**Bonnie Lou—King 4835**

Bonnie Lou is currently enjoying one of her biggest records to date in "Daddy-Oh," and is breaking out in areas as widely scattered as Baltimore, New York, Pittsburgh, Cleveland, Cincinnati and Chicago. The Fontanes' version has not been available quite so long, but is coming up quickly, with best reports coming from Boston, Philadelphia, Baltimore, St. Louis, Pittsburgh, Providence, Chicago, Nashville and Los Angeles. The Dot record is helped by the fact that "Adorable" is as popular as the flip in many areas. The Fontane Sisters disk was a previous Billboard "Spotlight" pick.

WHEN YOU DANCE (Angel, BMI)—**The Turbans—Herald 458**

A rhythm and blues record that has been attracting a larger and larger pop audience. Its appearances high on the Detroit and Pittsburgh pop territorial charts this week are warning signals for other areas that have not yet picked up this disk. Pop sales are also reported good in Philadelphia, Cleveland, Milwaukee, Nashville, Atlanta and Durham. Flip is "Let Me Show You" (Angel, BMI).

NOTE: One side of Eddy Arnold's recent record, "I Walked Alone Last Night" (Reis, ASCAP), RCA Victor 6290, was erroneously omitted under last week's list of pop Best Buys. Pop action on this tune has been very good in many areas, and it merited listing along with "The Richest Man."

• Most Played in Juke Boxes

For survey week ending October 26

RECORDS are ranked in order of the greatest number of plays in juke boxes thruout the country, as determined by The Billboard's weekly survey of the nation's juke box operators. When significant play is reported on both sides of a record, points are combined to determine position on the chart. In such a case, both sides are listed in bold type, the leading side on top.

This Week		Last Week	Weeks on Chart
1.	YELLOW ROSE OF TEXAS (ASCAP)—M. Miller — Blackberry Winter (BMI)—Col 40540	1	12
2.	LOVE IS A MANY-SPLENDORED THING (ASCAP)—Four Aces — Shine On, Harvest Moon (ASCAP)—Dec 29625	2	7
3.	AUTUMN LEAVES (ASCAP)—R. Williams — Take Care (BMI)—Kapp 116	4	8
4.	AIN'T THAT A SHAME (BMI)—P. Boone — Tennessee Saturday Night (BMI)—Dot 15377	3	17
5.	MOMENTS TO REMEMBER (ASCAP)—Four Lads — Dream On, My Love, Dream On (ASCAP)—Col 40539	9	4
6.	SEVENTEEN (BMI)—Fontane Sisters — If I Could Be With You (ASCAP)—Dot 15386	5	12
7.	SHIFTING, WHISPERING SANDS (BMI)—R. Draper — Time (ASCAP)—Mercury 70696	13	3
8.	YELLOW ROSE OF TEXAS (ASCAP)—J. Desmond — You're in Love With Someone (ASCAP)—Coral 61476	5	11
9.	LONGEST WALK (ASCAP)—J. P. Morgan — Swanee (ASCAP)—Vic 20-6182	7	11
10.	SEVENTEEN (BMI)—B. Bennett — Little Ole You-All (BMI)—King 1470	11	11
11.	SHIFTING, WHISPERING SANDS (PARTS I & II) (BMI)—B. Vaughn — Dot 15409	14	5
12.	BIBLE TELLS ME SO (ASCAP)—D. Cornell — LOVE IS A MANY-SPLENDORED THING (ASCAP)—Coral 61467	11	7
12.	I HEAR YOU KNOCKIN' (BMI)—G. Storm — Never Leave Me (ASCAP)—Dot 15412	16	2
14.	MAYBELLENE (BMI)—C. Berry — Wee Wee Hours (BMI)—Chess 1604	7	10
15.	TINA MARIE (ASCAP)—P. Como — Fooled (ASCAP)—Vic 20-6192	14	10
16.	WAKE THE TOWN AND TELL THE PEOPLE (ASCAP)—L. Baxter — I'll Never Stop Loving You (ASCAP)—Cap 3120	9	8
17.	HE (BMI)—McGuire Sisters — If You Believe (ASCAP)—Coral 51501	18	2
18.	ONLY YOU (BMI)—Platters — Bark, Battle and Ball (BMI)—Mercury 70623	17	3
19.	HE (BMI)—A. Hibbler — Breeze (ASCAP)—Dec 29660	20	2
20.	AT MY FRONT DOOR (BMI)—P. Boone — No Arms Can Ever Hold You (BMI)—Dot 15422	—	1

• Most Played by Jockeys

For survey week ending October 26

SIDES are ranked in order of the greatest number of plays on disk jockey radio shows thruout the country. Results are based on The Billboard's weekly survey among the nation's disk jockeys. The reverse side of each record is also listed.

This Week		Last Week	Weeks on Chart
1.	LOVE IS A MANY-SPLENDORED THING —Four Aces — Shine On, Harvest Moon (ASCAP)—Dec 29625	1	11
2.	MOMENTS TO REMEMBER (ASCAP)—Four Lads — Dream On, My Love, Dream On (ASCAP)—Col 40539	2	8
3.	YELLOW ROSE OF TEXAS—M. Miller — Blackberry Winter (ASCAP)—Col 40540	3	14
4.	AUTUMN LEAVES—R. Williams — Take Care (ASCAP)—Kapp 116	4	9
5.	SHIFTING, WHISPERING SANDS—PARTS I & II—B. Vaughn — Dot 15409 (BMI)	5	7
6.	YOU ARE MY LOVE—J. James — I Lay Me Down to Sleep (ASCAP)—M-G-M 12066	8	3
7	BLACK DENIM TROUSERS—Cheers — Some Night in Alaska (BMI)—Cap 3219	6	5
8.	LOVE AND MARRIAGE—F. Sinatra — Impatient Years (ASCAP)—Cap 3260	—	1
9.	AIN'T THAT A SHAME—P. Boone — Tennessee Saturday Night (BMI)—Dot 15377	11	26
10.	HE—A. Hibbler — Breeze (BMI)—Dec 29660	19	4
11.	ONLY YOU—Platters — Bark, Battle and Ball (BMI)—Mercury 70633	18	2
12.	YELLOW ROSE OF TEXAS—J. Desmond — You're in Love With Someone (ASCAP)—Coral 61476	16	12
13.	SUDDENLY THERE'S A VALLEY—J. Stafford — Night Watch (BMI)—Col 40559	—	3
14.	I HEAR YOU KNOCKIN'—G. Storm — Never Leave Me (BMI)—Dot 15412	14	2
15.	SHIFTING, WHISPERING SANDS (BMI)—R. Draper — Time (ASCAP)—Mercury 70696	—	2
16.	LONGEST WALK—J. P. Morgan — Swanee (ASCAP)—Vic 20-6182	12	12
17.	AT MY FRONT DOOR—P. Boone — No Arms Can Ever Hold You (BMI)—Dot 15422	—	1
18.	MY BONNIE LASSIE—Ames Bros. — So Will I (ASCAP)—Vic 20-6208	15	6
19.	TINA MARIE—P. Como — Fooled (ASCAP)—Vic 20-6192	7	12
20.	SUDDENLY THERE'S A VALLEY—G. Grant — Love Is (BMI)—Era 1003	9	6

The Billboard Music Popularity Charts — POPULAR RECORDS

• Best Sellers in Stores

For survey week ending November 2

RECORDS are ranked in order of their current national selling importance at the retail level, as determined by The Billboard's weekly survey of the top volume dealers in every important market area. When significant action is reported on both sides of a record, points are combined to determine position on the chart. In such a case, both sides are listed in bold type, the leading side on top.

This Week	Record	Last Week	Weeks on Chart
1.	AUTUMN LEAVES (ASCAP)—R. Williams ... Take Care (BMI)—Kapp 116	1	13
2.	LOVE IS A MANY-SPLENDORED THING (ASCAP)—Four Aces ... Shine On, Harvest Moon—Dec 29625	2	11
3.	MOMENTS TO REMEMBER—Four Lads ... Dream On, My Love, Dream On (ASCAP)—Col 40539	4	11
4.	YELLOW ROSE OF TEXAS (ASCAP)—M. Miller ... Blackberry Winter (BMI)—Col 40540	3	15
5.	SIXTEEN TONS (BMI)—Tennessee Ernie ... You Don't Have to Be a Baby. (ASCAP)—Cap 3262	—	1
6.	ONLY YOU (BMI)—Platters ... Bark, Battle and Ball (BMI)—Mercury 70633	5	7
7.	SHIFTING, WHISPERING SANDS (BMI)—R. Draper ... Time (ASCAP)—Mercury 70696	6	7
8.	I HEAR YOU KNOCKIN' (BMI)—G. Storm ... Never Leave Me (ASCAP)—Dot 15412	12	4
9.	AT MY FRONT DOOR (BMI)—P. Boone ... No Arms Can Ever Hold You (BMI)—Dot 15422	13	3
10.	SHIFTING, WHISPERING SANDS (PARTS I & II) (BMI)—B. Vaughn ... Dot 15409	8	8
11.	HE (BMI)—A. Hibbler ... Breeze (ASCAP)—Dec 29660	7	7
12.	BLACK DENIM TROUSERS (BMI)—Cheers ... Some Night in Alaska (BMI)—Cap 3219	9	8
13.	FORGIVE MY HEART (ASCAP)—Nat (King) Cole ... SOMEONE YOU LOVE (BMI)—Cap 3234	16	4
14.	SUDDENLY THERE'S A VALLEY (BMI)—G. Grant ... Love Is (BMI)—Era 1003	14	6
15.	MY BONNIE LASSIE (ASCAP)—Ames Brothers ... So Will I (BMI)—Vic 20-6208	11	6
16.	HE (BMI)—McGuire Sisters ... If You Believe (ASCAP)—Coral 61501	22	3
17.	AT MY FRONT DOOR (BMI)—El Dorados ... What's Buggin' You, Baby (BMI)—Vee Jay 147	21	5
18.	BIBLE TELLS ME SO (ASCAP)—D. Cornell ... Love Is a Many-Splendored Thing (ASCAP)—Coral 61467	10	10
19.	LOVE AND MARRIAGE (ASCAP)—F. Sinatra ... Impatient Years (ASCAP)—Cap 3260	—	1
20.	TINA MARIE (ASCAP)—P. Como ... Fooled (ASCAP)—Vic 20-6192	15	13
21.	SUDDENLY THERE'S A VALLEY (BMI)—J. Stafford ... Night Watch (BMI)—Col 40559	22	3
22.	SEVENTEEN (BMI)—Fontane Sisters ... If I Could Be With You (ASCAP)—Dot 15386	19	12
23.	ONLY YOU (BMI)—Hilltoppers ... Until the Real Thing Comes Along (ASCAP)—Dot 15423	—	1
24.	IT'S ALMOST TOMORROW (ASCAP)—Dream Weavers ... You Got Me Wondering (ASCAP)—Dec 29683	—	1
25.	YOU ARE MY LOVE (ASCAP)—J. James ... I Lay Me Down to Sleep (BMI)—M-G-M 12066	19	4

• THIS WEEKS BEST BUYS

According to sales reports in key markets, the following recent releases are recommended for extra profits:

ONLY YOU (Wildwood, BMI)—The Hilltoppers—Dot 15423

While the Platters' version of this tune continues to hold a secure place near the top of the charts, the Hilltoppers have come up with a solid second contender that is now also on the national retail chart. Minneapolis-St. Paul, Chicago, Kansas City, St. Louis, Pittsburgh, Baltimore, Providence are among the territories reporting strong sales. Flip is "Until the Real Thing Comes Along" (Chappell, ASCAP)

A WOMAN IN LOVE (Frank, ASCAP)—The Four Aces—Decca 29725

Competition is keen on this tune, but the Aces are establishing a comfortable early lead. Strong sales reports were returned this past week from Providence, Philadephia, Baltimore, Pittsburgh, Milwaukee, Detroit, St. Louis, Durham and Cleveland. Frankie Laine is selling well in some of these territories, too. The flip of the Decca record is "Of This I'm Sure" (Chappell, ASCAP). A previous Billboard "Spotlight" pick.

ALL AT ONCE YOU LOVE HER (Chappell, ASCAP)

ROSE TATTOO (Paramount, ASCAP)—Perry Como—RCA Victor 6294

Como's latest release is now gathering steam, and pushing ahead for what may be a big doubleheader. The following territories indicated good action: Chicago, Milwaukee, St. Louis, Cleveland, Pittsburgh, Providence, Philadelphia, Buffalo and Baltimore. "Rose Tattoo" is gaining steadily, after a slow start, and with increasing movie publicity may show real strength. A previous Billboard "Spotlight pick.

C'EST LA VIE (Planetary, ASCAP)—Sarah Vaughan—Mercury 70727

Both pop and rhythm and blues stores are reporting sizable volume on this recently released disk. It is off to an excellent start in Boston, Philadelphia, Providence, Baltimore, New York, Pittsburgh, St. Louis, Nashville, Cleveland and Milwaukee. Flip is "Never" (Laurel, ASCAP). A previous Billboard "Spotlight" pick.

MY BOY—FLAT TOP (Lois, BMI)—Dorothy Collins—Coral 61510

Available for a month, this record keeps growing and growing. By now it is a definite chart threat. Strong in Buffalo, New York, Philadelphia, Boston, Pittsburgh, Providence, Chicago, St. Louis and Nashville, Miss Collins is competing vigorously with Boyd Bennett for top honors. Flip is "In Love".

• Most Played in Juke Boxes

For survey week ending November 2

RECORDS are ranked in order of the greatest number of plays in juke boxes thruout the country, as determined by The Billboard's weekly survey of the nation's juke box operators. When significant play is reported on both sides of a record, points are combined to determine position on the chart. In such a case, both sides are listed in bold type, the leading side on top.

This Week	Record	Last Week	Weeks on Chart
1.	LOVE IS A MANY-SPLENDORED THING (ASCAP)—Four Aces ... Shine On Harvest Moon (ASCAP)—Dec 29625	2	8
2.	YELLOW ROSE OF TEXAS (ASCAP)—M. Miller ... Blackberry Winter (BMI)—Col 40540	1	13
3.	AUTUMN LEAVES (ASCAP)—R. Williams ... Take Care (BMI)—Kapp 116	3	9
4.	MOMENTS TO REMEMBER (ASCAP)—Four Lads ... Dream On, My Love, Dream On (ASCAP)—Col 40539	5	5
5.	SHIFTING, WHISPERING SANDS (BMI)—R. Draper ... Time (ASCAP)—Mercury 70696	7	4
6.	SEVENTEEN (BMI)—Fontane Sisters ... If I Could Be With You (ASCAP)—Dot 15386	6	13
7.	YELLOW ROSE OF TEXAS (ASCAP)—J. Desmond ... You're in Love With Someone (ASCAP)—Coral 61476	8	12
8.	I HEAR YOU KNOCKIN' (BMI)—G. Storm ... Never Leave Me (ASCAP)—Dot 15412	12	3
9.	AIN'T THAT A SHAME (BMI)—P. Boone ... Tennessee Saturday Night (BMI)—Dot 15377	4	18
10.	TINA MARIE (ASCAP)—P. Como ... Fooled (ASCAP)—Vic 20-6192	15	11
10.	AT MY FRONT DOOR (BMI)—P. Boone ... No Arms Can Ever Hold You (BMI)—Dot 15422	20	2
12.	LONGEST WALK (ASCAP)—J. P. Morgan ... Swanee (ASCAP)—Vic 20-6182	9	12
13.	ONLY YOU (BMI)—Platters ... Bark, Battle and Ball (BMI)—Mercury 70623	18	4
14.	SHIFTING, WHISPERING SANDS (PARTS I & II)—B. Vaughn ... BMI—Dot 15409	11	6
14.	BIBLE TELLS ME SO (ASCAP)—D. Cornell ... LOVE IS A MANY-SPLENDORED THING—Coral 61467	12	8
16.	SEVENTEEN (BMI)—B. Bennett ... Little Ole You-All (BMI)—King 1470	10	12
17.	MAYBELLENE (BMI)—C. Berry ... Wee Wee Hours (BMI)—Chess 1604	14	11
18.	WAKE THE TOWN AND TELL THE PEOPLE (ASCAP)—L. Baxter ... I'll Never Stop Loving You (ASCAP)—Cap 3120	16	9
19.	HE (BMI)—McGuire Sisters ... If You Believe (ASCAP)—Coral 51501	17	3
19.	HE (BMI)—A. Hibbler ... Breeze (ASCAP)—Dec 29660	19	3

• Most Played by Jockeys

For survey week ending November 2

SIDES are ranked in order of the greatest number of plays on disk jockey radio shows thruout the country. Results are based on The Billboard's weekly survey among the nation's disk jockeys. The reverse side of each record is also listed.

This Week	Record	Last Week	Weeks on Chart
1.	LOVE IS A MANY-SPLENDORED THING—Four Aces ... Shine On Harvest Moon (ASCAP)—Dec 29625	1	12
2.	MOMENTS TO REMEMBER (ASCAP)—Four Lads ... Dream On, My Love, Dream On (ASCAP)—Col 40539	2	9
3.	AUTUMN LEAVES—R. Williams ... Take Care (ASCAP)—Kapp 116	4	10
4.	YELLOW ROSE OF TEXAS—M. Miller ... Blackberry Winter (ASCAP)—Col 40540	3	15
5.	SHIFTING, WHISPERING SANDS (PARTS I & II)—B. Vaughn ... BMI—Dot 15409	5	8
6.	I HEAR YOU KNOCKIN'—G. Storm ... Never Leave Me (BMI)—Dot 15412	14	3
7.	SIXTEEN TONS—Tennessee Ernie ... You Don't Have to Be a Baby to Cry (BMI)—Cap 3262	—	1
8.	YOU ARE MY LOVE—J. James ... I Lay Me Down to Sleep (ASCAP)—M-G-M 12066	6	4
9.	LOVE AND MARRIAGE—F Sinatra ... Impatient Years (ASCAP)—Cap 3260	8	2
10.	ONLY YOU—Platters ... Bark, Battle and Ball (BMI)—Mercury 70633	11	3
11.	HE—A. Hibbler ... Breeze (BMI)—Dec 29660	10	5
12.	BLACK DENIM TROUSERS—Cheers ... Some Night in Alaska (BMI)—Cap 3219	7	6
13.	AT MY FRONT DOOR—P. Boone ... No Arms Can Ever Hold You—Dot 15422	17	2
14.	MY BONNIE LASSIE—Ames Brothers ... So Will I (ASCAP)—Vic 20-6208	18	7
15.	SUDDENLY THERE'S A VALLEY—G. Grant ... Love Is (BMI)—Era 1003	20	7
16.	SHIFTING, WHISPERING SANDS (BMI)—R. Draper ... Time (ASCAP)—Mercury 70696	15	3
17.	ONLY YOU—Hilltoppers ... Until the Real Thing Comes Along (BMI)—Dot 15423	—	1
18.	HE—McGuire Sisters ... If You Believe (BMI)—Coral 61501	—	1
19.	SOMEONE YOU LOVE—Nat (King) Cole ... Forgive My Heart (BMI)—Cap 3234	—	3
20.	TINA MARIE—P. Como ... Fooled (ASCAP)—Vic 20-6192	19	13

The Billboard Music Popularity Charts POPULAR RECORDS

THE TOP 100

For survey week ending November 2

A list of the **TOP 100 RECORD SIDES** in the nation according to a **COMBINED TABULATION** of Dealer, Disk Jockey and Juke Box Operator replies to The Billboard's weekly popular record Best Seller and Most Played surveys. Its purpose is to provide Disk Jockeys with additional programming material and to give trade exposure to NEWER records just beginning to show action in the field.

CAUTION TO DEALERS AND JUKE BOX OPERATORS!

The Billboard's Top 100 is NOT designed to provide tested information for buying purposes. This function is most reliably served by other regular weekly features: Best Sellers in Stores, Most Played in Juke Boxes, Coming Up Strong and Best Buys.

Last Week	This Week	Title	Artist	Label
1	1	LOVE IS A MANY-SPLENDORED THING	Four Aces	Decca
3	2	AUTUMN LEAVES	R. Williams	Kapp
4	3	MOMENTS TO REMEMBER	Four Lads	Columbia
2	4	YELLOW ROSE OF TEXAS	M. Miller	Columbia
5	5	SHIFTING, WHISPERING SANDS	B. Vaughn	Dot
11	6	I HEAR YOU KNOCKIN'	G. Storm	Dot
6	7	SHIFTING, WHISPERING SANDS	R. Draper	Mercury
13	8	AT MY FRONT DOOR	P. Boone	Dot
10	9	ONLY YOU	Platters	Mercury
8	10	HE	A. Hibbler	Decca
17	11	MY BONNIE LASSIE	Ames Brothers	Victor
15	12	TINA MARIA	P. Como	Victor
12	13	BLACK DENIM TROUSERS	Cheers	Capitol
18	14	SUDDENLY THERE'S A VALLEY	G. Grant	Era
14	15	SEVENTEEN	Fontane Sisters	Dot
23	16	LOVE AND MARRIAGE	F. Sinatra	Capitol
9	17	YELLOW ROSE OF TEXAS	J. Desmond	Coral
31	18	ONLY YOU	Hilltoppers	Dot
16	19	LONGEST WALK	J. P. Morgan	Victor
19	20	SUDDENLY THERE'S A VALLEY	J. Stafford	Columbia
7	21	AIN'T THAT A SHAME	P. Boone	Dot
22	22	YOU ARE MY LOVE	J. James	M-G-M
23	23	SOMEONE YOU LOVE	Nat (King) Cole	Capitol
21	24	WAKE THE TOWN AND TELL THE PEOPLE	L. Baxter	Capitol
—	25	YOUNG ABE LINCOLN	D. Cornell	Coral
29	26	FORGIVE MY HEART	Nat (King) Cole	Capitol
47	27	SIXTEEN TONS	Tennessee Ernie	Capitol
28	28	SEVENTEEN	B. Bennett	King
43	29	IT'S ALMOST TOMORROW	Dream Weavers	Decca
27	30	LOVE IS A MANY-SPLENDORED THING	D. Cornell	Coral
25	31	SUDDENLY THERE'S A VALLEY	J. LaRosa	Cadence
25	32	BIBLE TELLS ME SO	D. Cornell	Coral
29	33	WAKE THE TOWN AND TELL THE PEOPLE	M. Carson	Columbia
37	34	CROCE DI ORO (CROSS OF GOLD)	P. Page	Mercury
36	35	NO ARMS CAN EVER HOLD YOU	G. Shaw	Decca
57	36	DOG FACED SOLDIER	R. Morgan	Decca
56	37	PEPPER-HOT BABY	J. P. Morgan	Victor
35	38	BLACK DENIM TROUSERS	V. Monroe	Victor
44	39	MY BOY FLAT TOP	B. Bennett	King
46	40	AMUKIRIKI	L. Paul & M. Ford	Capitol
33	41	AT MY FRONT DOOR	El Dorados	Vee Jay
41	42	MAYBELLENE	C. Berry	Chess
38	43	SONG OF THE DREAMER	E. Fisher	Victor
40	44	AUTUMN LEAVES	S. Allen	Coral
19	45	HE	McGuire Sisters	Coral
—	46	BURN THAT CANDLE	B. Haley	Decca
42	47	YELLOW ROSE OF TEXAS	S. Freberg	Capitol
39	48	I WANT YOU TO BE MY BABY	G. Gibbs	Mercury
51	49	MY BOY FLAT TOP	D. Collins	Coral
72	50	DADDY-O	B. Lou	King
53	51	BONNIE BLUE GAL	M. Miller	Columbia
59	52	NO ARMS CAN EVER HOLD YOU	P. Boone	Dot
61	53	I WANT YOU TO BE MY BABY	L. Briggs	Epic
54	54	AUTUMN LEAVES	V. Young	Decca
62	55	LOVE AND MARRIAGE	D. Shore	Victor
31	56	ROCK AROUND THE CLOCK	B. Haley	Decca
64	57	REMEMB'RING	P. L. Hayes & M. Healy	Columbia
91	58	CRY ME A RIVER	J. London	Liberty
50	59	SUDDENLY THERE'S A VALLEY	Mills Brothers	Decca
71	60	LOVE IS A MANY-SPLENDORED THING	D. Rose	M-G-M
66	61	LEARNIN' TO LOVE	P. King	Columbia
—	62	ROCK-A-BEATIN' BOOGIE	B. Haley	Decca
52	63	CROCE DI ORO (CROSS OF GOLD)	J. Regan	London
34	64	AUTUMN LEAVES	M. Miller	Columbia
62	65	SAME OLE SATURDAY NIGHT	F. Sinatra	Capitol
54	66	MAGIC FINGERS	E. Fisher	Victor
49	67	AUTUMN LEAVES	J. Gleason	Capitol
56	68	IF YOU DON'T WANT MY LOVE	J. P. Morgan	Victor
73	69	SUDDENLY THERE'S A VALLEY	P. Andrews	Capitol
—	70	ALL AT ONCE YOU LOVE HER	P. Como	Victor
78	71	TIMES TWO I LOVE YOU	Chuckles	"X"
—	72	PAPER ROSES	L. Dee	Wing
45	73	HAWK-EYE	F. Laine	Columbia
67	74	BIBLE TELLS ME SO	N. Noble	Wing
91	75	I WANNA GO WHERE YOU GO	E. Fisher	Victor
48	76	DAY BY DAY	Four Freshmen	Capitol
100	77	AUTUMN LEAVES	R. Charles Singers	M-G-M
97	78	PET ME, PAPA	R. Clooney	Columbia
84	79	LOVE IS A MANY-SPLENDORED THING	W. Herman	Capitol
—	80	DADDY-O	Fontane Sisters	Dot
—	81	ROSE TATTOO	P. Como	Victor
77	82	WHY DON'T YOU WRITE ME?	Jacks	RPM
58	83	GUM DROP	Crew Cuts	Mercury
75	84	HARD TO GET	G. MacKenzie	"X"
—	85	SWEET KENTUCKY ROSE	K. Kallen	Decca
69	86	AIN'T THAT A SHAME	Fats Domino	Imperial
79	87	NO ARMS CAN EVER HOLD YOU	Gaylords	Mercury
70	88	SEVENTEEN	R. Draper	Mercury
—	89	OCCASIONAL MAN	J. Southern	Decca
84	90	WHEN ALL THE STREETS ARE DARK	S. Smith	Epic
—	91	YOU'RE SO NICE TO BE NEAR	Loreleis	Spotlight
—	92	COME HOME	B. Johnson	King
80	93	I'LL NEVER STOP LOVING YOU	Doris Day	Columbia
—	94	IT'S OBDACIOUS	B. Johnson	Mercury
82	95	GIVE ME YOUR LOVE	McGuire Sisters	Coral
—	96	MAGIC MELODY	L. Paul & M. Ford	Capitol
—	97	IT'S ALMOST TOMORROW	S. Lanson	Dot
87	98	WHEN YOU DANCE	Turbans	Herald
—	99	SEARCHING	Hilltoppers	Dot
86	100	JOHNNIE'S COMIN' HOME	J. Ray	Columbia

The Billboard Music Popularity Charts — POPULAR RECORDS

• Best Sellers in Stores

For survey week ending November 9

RECORDS are ranked in order of their current national selling importance at the retail level, as determined by The Billboard's weekly survey of the top volume dealers in every important market area. When significant action is reported on both sides of a record, points are combined to determine position on the chart. In such a case, both sides are listed in bold type, the leading side on top.

This Week		Last Week	Weeks on Chart
1.	AUTUMN LEAVES (ASCAP)—R. Williams Take Care (BMI)—Kapp 116	1	14
2.	LOVE IS A MANY-SPLENDORED THING (ASCAP)—Four Aces Shine On, Harvest Moon—Dec 29625	2	12
3.	SIXTEEN TONS (BMI)—Tennessee Ernie You Don't Have to Be a Baby to Cry (ASCAP)—Cap 3262	5	2
4.	MOMENTS TO REMEMBER (ASCAP)—Four Lads Dream On, My Love, Dream On (ASCAP)—Col 40539	3	12
5.	YELLOW ROSE OF TEXAS (ASCAP)—M. Miller Blackberry Winter (BMI)—Col 40540	4	16
6.	I HEAR YOU KNOCKIN' (BMI)—G. Storm Never Leave Me (ASCAP)—Dot 15412	8	5
7.	ONLY YOU (BMI)—Platters Bark, Battle and Ball (BMI)—Mercury 70633	6	8
8.	SHIFTING, WHISPERING SANDS (BMI)—R. Draper Time (ASCAP)—Mercury 70696	7	8
9.	AT MY FRONT DOOR (BMI)—P. Boone No Arms Can Ever Hold You (BMI)—Dot 15422	9	4
10.	HE (BMI)—A. Hibbler Breeze (ASCAP)—Dec 29660	11	8
11.	SHIFTING, WHISPERING SANDS (PARTS I & II) (BMI)—B. Vaughn Dot 15409	10	9
12.	LOVE AND MARRIAGE (ASCAP)—F. Sinatra Impatient Years (ASCAP)—Cap 3260	19	2
13.	SOMEONE YOU LOVE (BMI)—Nat (King) Cole FORGIVE MY HEART (ASCAP)—Cap 3234	13	5
14.	MY BONNIE LASSIE (ASCAP)—Ames Brothers So Will I (BMI)—Vic 20-6208	15	7
15.	HE (BMI)—McGuire Sisters If You Believe (ASCAP)—Coral 61501	16	4
16.	BLACK DENIM TROUSERS (BMI)—Cheers Some Night in Alaska (BMI)—Cap 3219	12	9
17.	TINA MARIE (ASCAP)—P. Como Fooled (ASCAP)—Vic 20-6192	20	14
18.	SUDDENLY THERE'S A VALLEY (BMI)—G. Grant Love Is (BMI)—Era 1003	14	7
19.	BIBLE TELLS ME SO (ASCAP)—D. Cornell LOVE IS A MANY-SPLENDORED THING (ASCAP)—Coral 61467	18	11
20.	YELLOW ROSE OF TEXAS (ASCAP)—J. Desmond You're in Love With Someone (ASCAP)—Coral 61476	—	14
21.	YOU ARE MY LOVE (ASCAP)—J. James I Lay Me Down to Sleep (BMI)—M-G-M 12066	25	5
22.	ONLY YOU (BMI)—Hilltoppers Until the Real Thing Comes Along (ASCAP)—Dot 15423	23	2
23.	ROCK-A-BEATIN' BOOGIE (ASCAP)—B. Haley BURN THAT CANDLE (BMI)—Dec 29713	—	1
24.	SUDDENLY THERE'S A VALLEY (BMI)—J. Stafford Night Watch (BMI)—Col 40559	21	4
25.	IT'S ALMOST TOMORROW (ASCAP)—Dream Weavers You Got Me Wondering (ASCAP)—Dec 29683	24	2

• THIS WEEKS BEST BUYS

According to sales reports in key markets, the following recent releases are recommended for extra profits:

CRY ME A RIVER (Frank, ASCAP)—**Julie London—Liberty 55006**

Sales have been snowballing on this unusual record. Territory after territory has reported great consumer reaction. The New York, Los Angeles, Milwaukee and Dallas-Ft. Worth sales areas now list the disk in their top ten, and it is also an outstanding seller in Boston, Philadelphia, Baltimore, Chicago, Cleveland and St. Louis. Flip is "S'Wonderful" (New World, ASCAP). A previous Billboard "Spotlight" pick.

MEMORIES OF YOU (Shapiro - Bernstein, ASCAP)—**Four Coins—Epic 9129**

Excitement on this record has been at high pitch ever since release. Strong volume has been reported the past ten days in Boston, New York, Philadelphia, Baltimore, Pittsburgh, Cleveland, Milwaukee, St. Louis, and Cincinnati. The Coins have taken a decisive early lead over the competitive versions of the tune now on the market. Flip is "Tear Down the Fence" (Shapiro - Bernstein, ASCAP). A previous Billboard "Spotlight" pick.

TWENTY FOUR HOURS A DAY (RT, BMI)

GOODBYE TO ROME (Campbell, Connelly, ASCAP)—**Georiga Gibbs—Mercury 70743**

The songstress has come up with a solid two-sided seller, a survey of the country's key markets reveals. The rhythm side started off quickly, but now the ballad is showing strength, too. The record is selling impressively in Philadelphia, Buffalo, St. Louis, Baltimore, Milwaukee, Boston, Pittsburgh, and Cincinnati. A previous Billboard "Spotlight" pick.

• Most Played in Juke Boxes

For survey week ending November 9

RECORDS are ranked in order of the greatest number of plays in juke boxes thruout the country, as determined by The Billboard's weekly survey of the nation's juke box operators. When significant play is reported on both sides of a record, points are combined to determine position on the chart. In such a case, both sides are listed in bold type, the leading side on top.

This Week		Last Week	Weeks on Chart
1.	LOVE IS A MANY-SPLENDORED THING (ASCAP)—Four Aces Shine On Harvest Moon (ASCAP)—Dec 29625	1	9
2.	AUTUMN LEAVES (ASCAP)—R. Williams Take Care (BMI)—Kapp 116	3	10
3.	YELLOW ROSE OF TEXAS (ASCAP)—M. Miller Blackberry Winter (BMI)—Col 40540	2	14
4.	MOMENTS TO REMEMBER (ASCAP)—Four Lads Dream On, My Love, Dream On (ASCAP)—Col 40539	4	6
5.	SHIFTING, WHISPERING SANDS (BMI)—R. Draper Time (ASCAP)—Mercury 70696	5	5
6.	I HEAR YOU KNOCKIN' (BMI)—G. Storm Never Leave Me (ASCAP)—Dot 15412	8	4
7.	AT MY FRONT DOOR (BMI)—P. Boone NO ARMS CAN EVER HOLD YOU (BMI)—Dot 15422	10	3
8.	BIBLE TELLS ME SO (ASCAP)—D. Cornell LOVE IS A MANY-SPLENDORED THING (ASCAP)—Coral 61467	14	9
9.	SEVENTEEN (BMI)—Fontane Sisters If I Could Be With You (ASCAP)—Dot 15386	6	14
10.	ONLY YOU (BMI)—Platters Bark, Battle and Ball (BMI)—Mercury 70623	13	5
10.	HE (BMI)—McGuire Sisters If You Believe (ASCAP)—Coral 51051	19	4
12.	YELLOW ROSE OF TEXAS (ASCAP)—J. Desmond You're in Love With Someone (ASCAP)—Coral 61476	7	13
13.	AIN'T THAT A SHAME (BMI)—P. Boone Tennessee Saturday Night (BMI)—Dot 15377	9	19
14.	SHIFTING, WHISPERING SANDS (PARTS I & II)—B. Vaughn Dot 15409 (BMI)	14	7
15	TINA MARIE (ASCAP)—P. Como Fooled (ASCAP)—Vic 20-6192	10	12
16.	SIXTEEN TONS (BMI)—Tennessee Ernie You Don't Have to Be a Baby to Cry (ASCAP)—Cap 3262	—	1
17.	LONGEST WALK (ASCAP)—J. P. Morgan Swanee (ASCAP)—Vic 20-6182	12	13
18.	ONLY YOU (BMI)—Hilltoppers Until the Real Thing Comes Along (ASCAP)—Dot 15423	—	1
19.	HE (BMI)—A. Hibbler Breeze (ASCAP)—Dec 29660	19	4
20.	SEVENTEEN (BMI)—B. Bennett Little Ole You-All (BMI)—King 1470	16	13
20.	MY BONNIE LASSIE (ASCAP)—Ames Brothers So Will I (BMI)—Vic 20-6208	—	1

• Most Played by Jockeys

For survey week ending November 9

SIDES are ranked in order of the greatest number of plays on disk jockey radio shows thruout the country. Results are based on The Billboard's weekly survey among the nation's disk jockeys. The reverse side of each record is also listed.

This Week		Last Week	Weeks on Chart
1.	LOVE IS A MANY-SPLENDORED THING (ASCAP)—Four Aces Shine On Harvest Moon (ASCAP)—Dec 29625	1	13
2.	MOMENTS TO REMEMBER (ASCAP)—Four Lads Dream On, My Love, Dream On (ASCAP)—Col 40539	2	10
3.	SIXTEEN TONS (BMI)—Tennessee Ernie You Don't Have to Be a Baby to Cry (ASCAP)—Cap 3262	7	2
4.	AUTUMN LEAVES (ASCAP)—R. Williams Take Care (BMI)—Kapp 116	3	11
5.	YELLOW ROSE OF TEXAS (ASCAP)—M. Miller Blackberry Winter (BMI)—Col 40540	4	16
6.	ONLY YOU (BMI)—Platters Bark, Battle and Ball (BMI)—Mercury 70633	10	4
7.	SHIFTING, WHISPERING SANDS (PARTS I & II)—B. Vaughn Dot 15409 (BMI)	5	9
8.	YOU ARE MY LOVE (ASCAP)—J. James I Lay Me Down to Sleep (BMI)—M-G-M 12066	8	5
9.	LOVE AND MARRIAGE (ASCAP)—F. Sinatra Impatient Years (ASCAP)—Cap 3260	9	3
10.	AT MY FRONT DOOR (BMI)—P. Boone No Arms Can Ever Hold You (BMI)—Dot 15422	13	3
11.	I HEAR YOU KNOCKIN' (BMI)—G. Storm Never Leave Me (ASCAP)—Dot 15412	6	4
12.	HE (BMI)—A. Hibbler Breeze (ASCAP)—Dec 29660	11	6
13.	ONLY YOU (BMI)—Hilltoppers Until the Real Thing Comes Along (ASCAP)—Dot 15423	17	2
14.	SHIFTING, WHISPERING SANDS (BMI)—R. Draper Time (BMI)—Mercury 70696	16	4
15.	BLACK DENIM TROUSERS (BMI)—Cheers Some Night in Alaska (BMI)—Cap 3129	12	7
16.	SUDDENLY THERE'S A VALLEY (BMI)—G. Frant Love Is (BMI)—Era 1003	15	8
17.	IT'S ALMOST TOMORROW (ASCAP)—Dream Weavers You Got Me Wondering (ASCAP)—Dec 29683	—	1
18.	TINA MARIE (ASCAP)—P. Como Fooled (ASCAP)—Vic 20-6192	20	14
19.	SOMEONE YOU LOVE (BMI)—Nat (King) Cole Forgive My Heart (BMI)—Cap 3234	19	4
20.	SUDDENLY THERE'S A VALLEY (BMI)—J. Stafford Night Watch (BMI)—Col 40559	—	3

The Billboard Music Popularity Charts

POPULAR RECORDS

THE TOP 100

For survey week ending November 9

A list of the TOP 100 RECORD SIDES in the nation according to a COMBINED TABULATION of Dealer, Disk Jockey and Juke Box Operator replies to The Billboard's weekly popular record Best Seller and Most Played surveys. Its purpose is to provide Disk Jockeys with additional programming material and to give trade exposure to NEWER records just beginning to show action in the field.

This Week	Song	Artist	Label	Last Week
1.	LOVE IS A MANY-SPLENDORED THING	Four Aces	Decca	1
2.	AUTUMN LEAVES	R. Williams	Kapp	2
3.	MOMENTS TO REMEMBER	Four Lads	Columbia	3
4.	YELLOW ROSE OF TEXAS	M. Miller	Columbia	4
5.	ONLY YOU	Platters	Mercury	9
6.	SIXTEEN TONS	T. Ernie	Capitol	27
7.	I HEAR YOU KNOCKIN'	G. Storm	Dot	6
8.	SHIFTING, WHISPERING SANDS	R. Draper	Mercury	7
9.	AT MY FRONT DOOR	P. Boone	Dot	8
10.	SHIFTING, WHISPERING SANDS	B. Vaughn	Dot	5
11.	HE	A. Hibbler	Decca	10
12.	HE	McGuire Sisters	Coral	45
13.	LOVE AND MARRIAGE	F. Sinatra	Capitol	16
14.	TINA MARIE	P. Como	Victor	12
15.	ONLY YOU	Hilltoppers	Dot	18
16.	YOU ARE MY LOVE	J. James	M-G-M	22
16.	YELLOW ROSE OF TEXAS	J. Desmond	Coral	17
18.	BLACK DENIM TROUSERS	Cheers	Capitol	13
18.	SUDDENLY THERE'S A VALLEY	G. Grant	Era	14
20.	SEVENTEEN	Fontane Sisters	Dot	15
21.	MY BONNIE LASSIE	Ames Brothers	Victor	11
22.	SUDDENLY THERE'S A VALLEY	J. Stafford	Columbia	20
23.	IT'S ALMOST TOMORROW	Dream Weavers	Decca	29
24.	SOMEONE YOU LOVE	Nat (King) Cole	Capitol	23
25.	CROCE DI ORO (CROSS OF GOLD)	P. Page	Mercury	34
26.	AIN'T THAT A SHAME	P. Boone	Dot	21
27.	LONGEST WALK	J. P. Morgan	Victor	19
28.	PEPPER-HOT BABY	J. P. Morgan	Victor	37
29.	SUDDENLY THERE'S A VALLEY	J. La Rosa	Cadence	31
30.	DOG FACED SOLDIER	R. Morgan	Decca	36
31.	BIBLE TELLS ME SO	D. Cornell	Coral	32
32.	LOVE IS A MANY-SPLENDORED THING	D. Cornell	Coral	30
33.	WAKE THE TOWN AND TELL THE PEOPLE	L. Baxter	Capitol	24
34.	FORGIVE MY HEART	Nat (King) Cole	Capitol	24
35.	SEVENTEEN	B. Bennett	King	28
36.	NO ARMS CAN EVER HOLD YOU	G. Shaw	Decca	35
37.	NO ARMS CAN EVER HOLD YOU	P. Boone	Dot	52
38.	AMUKIRIKI	L. Paul & M. Ford	Capitol	40
39.	ALL AT ONCE YOU LOVE HER	P. Como	Victor	70
39.	BURN THAT CANDLE	B. Haley	Decca	46
41.	AUTUMN LEAVES	M. Miller	Columbia	64
42.	BLACK DENIM TROUSERS	V. Monroe	Victor	38
42.	CRY ME A RIVER	J. London	Liberty	58
44.	WAKE THE TOWN AND TELL THE PEOPLE	M. Carson	Columbia	33
45.	AT MY FRONT DOOR	El Dorados	Vee Jay	41
46.	MY BOY FLAT TOP	D. Collins	Coral	49
47.	DADDY-O	B. Lou	King	50
40.	IF YOU DON'T WANT MY LOVE	J. P. Morgan	Victor	68
49.	AUTUMN LEAVES	S. Allen	Coral	44
50.	AUTUMN LEAVES	J. Gleason	Capitol	67
51.	SUDDENLY THERE'S A VALLEY	Mills Brothers	Decca	59
52.	AUTUMN LEAVES	V. Young	Decca	54
52.	MAGIC FINGERS	E. Fisher	Victor	66
54.	LOVE IS A MANY-SPLENDORED THING	D. Rose	M-G-M	60
55.	AUTUMN LEAVES	R. Charles	M-G-M	77
56.	BONNIE BLUE GAL	M. Miller	Columbia	51
57.	MY BOY FLAT TOP	B. Bennett	King	39
57.	ROCK AROUND THE CLOCK	B. Haley	Decca	56
57.	CROCE DI ORO (CROSS OF GOLD)	J. Regan	London	63
60.	DADDY-O	Fontane Sisters	Dot	80
60.	PEPPER-HOT BABY	G. MacKenzie	X	—
60.	YELLOW ROSE OF TEXAS	S. Freberg	Capitol	47
63.	ROCK A BEATIN' BABY	B. Haley	Decca	—
64.	LOVE AND MARRIAGE	D. Shore	Victor	55
65.	LEARNIN' TO LOVE	P. King	Columbia	61
66.	C'EST LA VIE	S. Vaughan	Mercury	—
67.	IT'S ALMOST TOMORROW	S. Lanson	Dot	97
68.	WOMAN IN LOVE	Four Aces	Decca	—
69.	NO ARMS CAN EVER HOLD YOU	Gaylords	Mercury	87
69.	CATTLE CALL	E. Arnold & H. Winterhalter	Victor	—
70.	SAME OLD SATURDAY NIGHT	F. Sinatra	Capitol	65
71.	MAYBELLENE	C. Berry	Chess	42
71.	SIXTEEN TONS	J. Desmond	Coral	—
73.	POR FAVOR	V. Damone	Mercury	—
73.	BIBLE TELLS ME SO	N. Noble	Wing	74
73.	REMEMB'RING	P. L. Hayes & M. Healy	Columbia	57
76.	SWEET KENTUCKY ROSE	K. Kallen	Decca	85
77.	I WANNA GO WHERE YOU GO	E. Fisher	Victor	75
77.	ADORABLE	Fontane Sisters	Dot	—
79.	I WANT YOU TO BE MY BABY	G. Gibbs	Mercury	48
80.	GUM DROPS	Crew Cuts	Mercury	—
80.	BAND OF GOLD	K. Carson	Capitol	—
82.	I WANT YOU TO BE MY BABY	L. Briggs	Epic	53
82.	THERE SHOULD BE RULES	B. Madigan	M-G-M	—
84.	PAPER ROSES	L. Dee	Wing	72
85.	HAWK-EYE	F. Laine	Columbia	73
86.	BURN THAT CANDLE	Cues	Capitol	—
87.	LOVE IS A MANY-SPLENDORED THING	W. Herman	Capitol	79
87.	SHOOT IT AGAIN	T. Brewer	Coral	—
87.	WHY DON'T YOU WRITE ME	Jacks	RPM	82
91.	DAY BY DAY	Four Freshmen	Capitol	76
92.	YOU WIN AGAIN	Paulette Sisters	Capitol	—
93.	SOMEONE ON YOUR MIND	C. Butler	Coral	—
94.	SONG OF THE DREAMER	E. Fisher	Victor	43
95.	NUMBER ONE STREET	B. Corley	Stars	—
96.	WHEN YOU DANCE	Turbans	Herald	98
97.	SUDDENLY THERE'S A VALLEY	P. Andrews	Capitol	69
98.	ROSE TATTOO	P. Como	Victor	81
99.	OCCASIONAL MAN	J. Southern	Decca	89
100.	PET ME POPPA	R. Clooney	Columbia	78

CAUTION TO DEALERS AND JUKE BOX OPERATORS

The Billboard's Top 100 is NOT designed to provide tested information for buying purposes. This function is most reliably served by other regular weekly features: Best Sellers in Stores, Most Played in Juke Boxes, Coming Up Strong and Best Buys.

The Billboard Music Popularity Charts — POPULAR RECORDS

• Best Sellers in Stores

For survey week ending November 16

RECORDS are ranked in order of their current national selling importance at the retail level, as determined by The Billboard's weekly survey of the top volume dealers in every important market area. When significant action is reported on both sides of a record, points are combined to determine position on the chart. In such a case, both sides are listed in bold type, the leading side on top.

This Week	Record	Last Week	Weeks on Chart
1.	**SIXTEEN TONS** (BMI)—Tennessee Ernie You Don't Have to Be a Baby to Cry (ASCAP)—Cap 3262	3	3
2.	**AUTUMN LEAVES** (ASCAP)—R. Williams Take Care (BMI)—Kapp 116	1	15
3.	**LOVE IS A MANY-SPLENDORED THING** (ASCAP)—Four Aces Shine On, Harvest Moon (ASCAP)—Dec 29625	2	13
4.	**MOMENTS TO REMEMBER** (ASCAP)—Four Lads Dream On, My Love, Dream On (ASCAP)—Col 40539	4	13
5.	**I HEAR YOU KNOCKIN'** (BMI)—G. Storm Never Leave Me (ASCAP)—Dot 15412	6	6
6.	**ONLY YOU** (BMI)—Platters Bark, Battle and Ball (BMI)—Mercury 70633	7	9
7.	**HE** (BMI)—A. Hibbler Breeze (ASCAP)—Dec 29660	10	9
8.	**AT MY FRONT DOOR** (BMI)—P. Boone **NO ARMS CAN EVER HOLD YOU** (BMI)—Dot 15422	9	5
9.	**YELLOW ROSE OF TEXAS** (ASCAP)—M. Miller Blackberry Winter (BMI)—Col 40540	5	17
10.	**SHIFTING, WHISPERING SANDS** (BMI)—R. Draper Time (ASCAP)—Mercury 70696	8	9
11.	**LOVE AND MARRIAGE** (ASCAP)—F. Sinatra Impatient Years (ASCAP)—Cap 3260	12	3
12.	**SHIFTING, WHISPERING SANDS (PARTS I & II)** (BMI)—B. Vaughn Dot 15409	11	10
13.	**SOMEONE YOU LOVE** (BMI)—Nat (King) Cole **FORGIVE MY HEART** (ASCAP)—Cap 3234	13	6
14.	**IT'S ALMOST TOMORROW** (ASCAP)—Dream Weavers You Got Me Wondering (ASCAP)—Dec 29683	25	3
15.	**MY BONNIE LASSIE** (ASCAP)—Ames Brothers So Will I (BMI)—Vic 20-6208	14	8
16.	**HE** (BMI)—McGuire Sisters If You Believe (ASCAP)—Coral 61501	15	5
16.	**ONLY YOU** (BMI)—Hilltoppers Until the Real Thing Comes Along (ASCAP)—Dot 15423	22	3
18.	**YOU ARE MY LOVE** (ASCAP)—J. James I Lay Me Down to Sleep (BMI)—M-G-M 12066	21	6
19.	**SUDDENLY THERE'S A VALLEY** (BMI)—G. Grant Love Is (BMI)—Era 1003	18	8
20.	**BIBLE TELLS ME SO** (ASCAP)—D. Cornell **LOVE IS A MANY-SPLENDORED THING** (ASCAP)—Coral 61467	19	12
21.	**BLACK DENIM TROUSERS** (BMI)—Cheers Some Night In Alaska (BMI)—Cap 3219	16	10
21.	**SUDDENLY THERE'S A VALLEY** (BMI)—J. Stafford Night Watch (BMI)—Col 40559	24	5
23.	**ROCK-A-BEATIN' BOOGIE** (ASCAP)—B. Haley **BURN THAT CANDLE** (BMI)—Dec 29713	23	2
24.	**AT MY FRONT DOOR** (BMI)—El Dorados What's Buggin You Baby (BMI)—Vee Jay 147	—	6
25.	**DADDY-O** (BMI)—B. Lou Dancin' In My Socks (BMI)—King 4835	—	1

• THIS WEEKS BEST BUYS

According to sales reports in key markets, the following recent releases are recommended for extra profits:

BAND OF GOLD (Ludlow, BMI)—**Kit Carson—Capitol 3283**
Don Cherry—Columbia 40597

This tune is beginning to shape up strongly, with Kit Carson and Don Cherry competing for top position. The Capitol record is on the Cincinnati territorial chart this week and is leading in Baltimore, Buffalo, St. Louis and other markets. Cherry is doing exceptionally well in New York, Chicago, Providence and Atlanta, among others. Both disks exhibit strong chart potential. The flip of the Carson record is "Cast Your Bread Upon the Waters" (Hollis, BMI), while that of the Cherry record is "Rumble Boogie" (Ludlow, BMI).

MEMORIES ARE MADE OF THIS (Montclare, BMI)—**Dean Martin—Capitol 3295**

The combination of Martin and an outstanding piece of material still seems to add up to commercial dynamite. First week sales on this record were so heavy in Los Angeles, Pittsburgh, Philadelphia, Cleveland and Boston that early chart action is threatened. While some areas received only small shipments, these were quickly exhausted, with buyers clamoring for more. Flip is "Change of Heart." A previous Billboard "Spotlight" pick.

• Most Played in Juke Boxes

For survey week ending November 16

RECORDS are ranked in order of the greatest number of plays in juke boxes thruout the country, as determined by The Billboard's weekly survey of the nation's juke box operators. When significant play is reported on both sides of a record, points are combined to determine position on the chart. In such a case, both sides are listed in bold type, the leading side on top.

This Week	Record	Last Week	Weeks on Chart
1.	**LOVE IS A MANY-SPLENDORED THING** (ASCAP)—Four Aces Shine On, Harvest Moon (ASCAP)—Dec 29625	1	10
2.	**AUTUMN LEAVES** (ASCAP)—R. Williams Take Care (BMI)—Kapp 116	2	11
3.	**SHIFTING, WHISPERING SANDS** R. Draper Time (ASCAP)—Mercury 70696	5	6
4.	**MOMENTS TO REMEMBER** (ASCAP)—Four Lads Dream On, My Love, Dream On (ASCAP)—Col 40539	4	7
5.	**YELLOW ROSE OF TEXAS** (ASCAP)—M. Miller Blackberry Winter (BMI)—Col 40540	3	15
6.	**I HEAR YOU KNOCKIN'** (BMI)—G. Storm Never Leave Me (ASCAP)—Dot 15412	6	5
7.	**SIXTEEN TONS** (BMI)—Tennessee Ernie You Don't Have to Be a Baby to Cry (ASCAP)—Cap 3262	16	2
8.	**AT MY FRONT DOOR** (BMI)—P. Boone **NO ARMS CAN EVER HOLD YOU** (BMI)—Dot 15422	7	4
9.	**ONLY YOU** (BMI)—Platters Bark, Battle and Ball (BMI)—Mercury 70623	10	6
10.	**HE** (BMI)—McGuire Sisters If You Believe (ASCAP)—Coral 51501	10	5
11.	**BIBLE TELLS ME SO** (ASCAP)—D. Cornell **LOVE IS A MANY-SPLENDORED THING** (ASCAP)—Coral 61467	8	10
12.	**SHIFTING, WHISPERING SANDS (Parts I & II)**—B. Vaughn Dot 1540—BMI	14	8
13.	**SEVENTEEN** (BMI)—Fontane Sisters If I Could Be With You (ASCAP)—Dot 15386	9	15
14.	**YELLOW ROSE OF TEXAS** (ASCAP)—J. Desmond You're in Love With Someone (ASCAP) Coral 61476	12	14
15.	**AIN'T THAT A SHAME** (BMI)—P. Boone Tennessee Saturday Night (BMI)—Dot 15377	13	20
16.	**ONLY YOU** (BMI)—Hilltoppers Until the Real Thing Comes Along (ASCAP)—Dot 15423	18	2
16.	**HE** (BMI)—A. Hibbler Breeze (ASCAP)—Dec 29660	19	5
18.	**LONGEST WALK** (ASCAP)—J. P. Morgan Swanee (ASCAP)—Vic 20-6182	17	14
19.	**TINA MARIE** (ASCAP)—P. Como Fooled (ASCAP)—Vic 20-6192	15	13
19.	**SUDDENLY THERE'S A VALLEY** (BMI)—G. Grant Love Is (BMI)—Era 1003	—	4
19.	**PEPPER-HOT BABY** (BMI)—J. P. Morgan If You Don't Want My Love (ASCAP)—Vic 20-6282	—	1

• Most Played by Jockeys

For survey week ending November 16

SIDES are ranked in order of the greatest number of plays on disk jockey radio shows thruout the country. Results are based on The Billboard's weekly survey among the nation's disk jockeys. The reverse side of each record is also listed.

This Week	Record	Last Week	Weeks on Chart
1.	**SIXTEEN TONS** (BMI)—Tennessee Ernie You Don't Have to Be a Baby to Cry (ASCAP)—Cap 3262	3	3
2.	**LOVE IS A MANY-SPLENDORED THING** (ASCAP)—Four Aces Shine On, Harvest Moon (ASCAP)—Dec 29625	1	14
3.	**MOMENTS TO REMEMBER** (ASCAP)—Four Lads Dream On, My Love, Dream On (ASCAP)—Col 40539	2	11
4.	**AUTUMN LEAVES** (ASCAP)—R. Williams Take Care (BMI)—Kapp 116	4	12
5.	**LOVE AND MARRIAGE** (ASCAP)—F. Sinatra Impatient Years (ASCAP)—Cap 3260	9	4
6.	**ONLY YOU** (BMI)—Platters Bark, Battle and Ball (BMI)—Mercury 70633	6	5
7.	**HE** (BMI)—A. Hibbler Breeze (ASCAP)—Dec 29660	12	7
8.	**I HEAR YOU KNOCKIN'** (BMI)—G. Storm Never Leave Me (ASCAP)—Dot 15412	11	5
9.	**SHIFTING, WHISPERING SANDS (Parts I & II)**—B. Vaughn Dot 15409 (BMI)	7	10
10.	**AT MY FRONT DOOR** (BMI)—P. Boone No Arms Can Ever Hold You (BMI)—Dot 15422	10	4
11.	**YELLOW ROSE OF TEXAS** (ASCAP)—M. Miller Blackberry Winter (BMI)—Col 40540	5	17
12.	**YOU ARE MY LOVE** (ASCAP)—J. James I Lay Me Down to Sleep (BMI)—M-G-M 12066	8	6
13.	**SUDDENLY THERE'S A VALLEY** (BMI)—G. Grant Love Is (BMI)—Era 1003	16	9
14.	**ONLY YOU** (BMI)—Hilltoppers Until the Real Thing Comes Along (ASCAP)—Dot 15423	13	3
15.	**SUDDENLY THERE'S A VALLEY** (BMI)—J. Stafford Night Watch (BMI)—Col 40559	20	4
16.	**HE** (BMI)—McGuire Sisters If You Believe (BMI)—Coral 61501	—	2
17.	**MY BONNIE LASSIE** (ASCAP)—Ames Brothers So Will I (BMI)—Vic 20-6208	—	8
18.	**DADDY O** (BMI)—Fontane Sisters Adorable (BMI)—Dot 15428	—	1
19.	**BLACK DENIM TROUSERS** (BMI)—Cheers Some Night In Alaska (BMI)—Cap 3219	15	8
20.	**ALL AT ONCE YOU LOVE HER** (ASCAP)—P. Como Rose Tattoo (ASCAP)—Vic 20-6294	—	1

The Billboard Music Popularity Charts

POPULAR RECORDS

THE TOP 100

For survey week ending November 16

A list of the **TOP 100 RECORD SIDES** in the nation according to a **COMBINED TABULATION** of Dealer, Disk Jockey and Juke Box Operator replies to The Billboard's weekly popular record Best Seller and Most Played surveys. Its purpose is to provide Disk Jockeys with additional programming material and to give trade exposure to NEWER records just beginning to show action in the field.

This Week	Song	Artist	Label	Last Week
1.	LOVE IS A MANY-SPLENDORED THING	Four Aces	Decca	1
2.	AUTUMN LEAVES	R. Williams	Kapp	2
3.	SIXTEEN TONS	T. Ernie	Capitol	6
4.	MOMENTS TO REMEMBER	Four Lads	Columbia	3
5.	I HEAR YOU KNOCKIN'	G. Storm	Dot	7
6.	ONLY YOU	Platters	Mercury	5
7.	YELLOW ROSE OF TEXAS	M. Miller	Columbia	4
8.	AT MY FRONT DOOR	P. Boone	Dot	9
9.	HE	A. Hibbler	Decca	11
10.	SHIFTING, WHISPERING SANDS	B. Vaughn	Dot	10
11.	SHIFTING, WHISPERING SANDS	R. Draper	Mercury	8
12.	HE	McGuire Sisters	Coral	12
13.	LOVE AND MARRIAGE	F. Sinatra	Capitol	13
14.	ONLY YOU	Hilltoppers	Dot	15
15.	SUDDENLY THERE'S A VALLEY	G. Grant	Era	18
16.	MY BONNIE LASSIE	Ames Brothers	Victor	21
17.	YOU ARE MY LOVE	J. James	M-G-M	16
18.	SUDDENLY THERE'S A VALLEY	J. Stafford	Columbia	22
19.	BLACK DENIM TROUSERS	Cheers	Capitol	18
20.	TINA MARIE	P. Como	Victor	14
21.	SOMEONE YOU LOVE	Nat (King) Cole	Capitol	24
22.	CROCE DI ORO (CROSS OF GOLD)	P. Page	Mercury	25
23.	YELLOW ROSE OF TEXAS	J. Desmond	Coral	16
24.	PEPPER-HOT BABY	J. P. Morgan	Victor	28
25.	DADDY-O	Fontane Sisters	Dot	60
26.	LOVE IS A MANY-SPLENDORED THING	D. Cornell	Coral	32
27.	IT'S ALMOST TOMORROW	Dream Weavers	Decca	23
28.	SEVENTEEN	Fontane Sisters	Dot	20
28.	DADDY-O	B. Lou	King	47
30.	FORGIVE MY HEART	Nat (King) Cole	Capitol	34
30.	LONGEST WALK	J. P. Morgan	Victor	27
32.	AIN'T THAT A SHAME	P. Boone	Dot	26
33.	SUDDENLY THERE'S A VALLEY	J. La Rosa	Cadence	29
34.	ALL AT ONCE YOU LOVE HER	P. Como	Victor	39
35.	AT MY FRONT DOOR	El Dorados	Vee Jay	45
36.	NO ARMS CAN EVER HOLD YOU	G. Shaw	Decca	36
37.	DOG FACED SOLDIER	R. Morgan	Decca	30
38.	BURN THAT CANDLE	B. Haley	Decca	39
39.	NO ARMS CAN EVER HOLD YOU	P. Boone	Dot	37
40.	SEVENTEEN	B. Bennett	King	35
41.	ROCK-A-BEATIN' BOOGIE	B. Haley	Decca	63
42.	WOMAN IN LOVE	Four Aces	Decca	68
43.	IT'S ALMOST TOMORROW	S. Lanson	Dot	67
44.	CRY ME A RIVER	J. London	Liberty	42
45.	SUDDENLY THERE'S A VALLEY	Mills Brothers	Decca	51
45.	AUTUMN LEAVES	S. Allen	Coral	49
47.	BIBLE TELLS ME SO	D. Cornell	Coral	31
48.	MY BOY FLAT TOP	D. Collins	Coral	46
49.	AMUKIRIKI	L. Paul & M. Ford	Capitol	38
50.	IF YOU DON'T WANT MY LOVE	J. P. Morgan	Victor	48
51.	C'EST LA VIE	S. Vaughan	Mercury	66
51.	MEMORIES OF YOU	Four Coins	Epic	—
53.	LOVE AND MARRIAGE	D. Shore	Victor	64
53.	YELLOW ROSE OF TEXAS	S. Freeberg	Capitol	60
55.	AUTUMN LEAVES	M. Miller	Columbia	41
55.	CROCE DI ORO (CROSS OF GOLD)	J. Regan	London	57
57.	BONNIE BLUE GAL	M. Miller	Columbia	56
58.	AUTUMN LEAVES	V. Young	Decca	52
59.	WAKE THE TOWN AND TELL THE PEOPLE	L. Baxter	Capitol	33
60.	LOVE IS A MANY-SPLENDORED THING	D. Rose	M-G-M	54
61.	AUTUMN LEAVES	J. Gleason	Capitol	50
61.	BIBLE TELLS ME SO	N. Noble	Wing	73
63.	MY BOY FLAT TOP	B. Bennett	King	57
63.	WHEN YOU DANCE	Turbans	Herald	96
65.	IT'S ALMOST TOMORROW	D. Carroll	Mercury	—
66.	SHOOT IT AGAIN	T. Brewer	Coral	87
67.	NO ARMS CAN EVER HOLD YOU	Gaylords	Mercury	69
68.	WOMAN IN LOVE	F. Laine	Columbia	—
69.	IT'S ALMOST TOMORROW	J. Stafford	Columbia	—
70.	WAKE THE TOWN AND TELL THE PEOPLE	M. Carson	Columbia	44
71.	ADORABLE	Fontane Sisters	Dot	77
72.	SAME OLE SATURDAY NIGHT	F. Sinatra	Capitol	70
73.	MAGIC FINGERS	E. Fisher	Victor	52
74.	BAND OF GOLD	K. Carson	Capitol	80
75.	THERE SHOULD BE RULES	B. Madigan	M-G-M	82
76.	PEPPER-HOT BABY	G. MacKenzie	X	60
77.	PET ME PAPA	R. Clooney	Columbia	99
78.	SUDDENLY THERE'S A VALLEY	P. Andrews	Capitol	97
79.	I WANT YOU TO BE MY BABY	G. Gibbs	Mercury	79
80.	LEARNIN' TO LOVE	P. King	Columbia	65
81.	HAWK-EYE	F. Laine	Columbia	85
81.	TIMES TWO I LOVE YOU	Chuckles	X	—
83.	AUTUMN LEAVES	R. Charles	M-G-M	55
83.	OO BANG	Doris Day	Columbia	—
83.	LOVE IS A MANY-SPLENDORED THING	W. Herman	Capitol	87
86.	BLACK DENIM TROUSERS	V. Monroe	Victor	42
87.	MAYBELLENE	C. Berry	Chess	71
88.	C'EST LA VIE	S. Gale	Victor	—
89.	DAY BY DAY	Four Freshmen	Capitol	91
90.	I'LL KNOW	S. Davis Jr.	Decca	—
90.	SOMEONE ON YOUR MIND	C. Butler	Coral	93
92.	YOU WIN AGAIN	Paulette Sisters	Capitol	92
93.	WITHOUT A SONG	R. Hamilton	Epic	—
94.	WHY DON'T YOU WRITE ME	Jacks	RPM	87
95.	I'LL NEVER STOP LOVING YOU	Doris Day	Columbia	—
95.	REMEMB'RING	P. L. Hayes-M. Healy	Columbia	73
97.	C'EST LA VIE	De John Sisters	Epic	—
98.	GUM DROP	Crew Cuts	Mercury	80
99.	SEVENTEEN	R. Draper	Mercury	—
100.	SONG OF THE DREAMER	E. Fisher	Victor	94

CAUTION TO DEALERS AND JUKE BOX OPERATORS

The Billboard's Top 100 is NOT designed to provide tested information for buying purposes. This function is most reliably served by other regular weekly features: Best Sellers in Stores, Most Played in Juke Boxes, Coming Up Strong and Best Buys.

The Billboard Music Popularity Charts — POPULAR RECORDS

• Best Sellers in Stores

For survey week ending November 23

RECORDS are ranked in order of their current national selling importance at the retail level, as determined by The Billboard's weekly survey of the top volume dealers in every important market area. When significant action is reported on both sides of a record, points are combined to determine position on the chart. In such a case, both sides are listed in bold type, the leading side on top.

This Week		Last Week	Weeks on Chart
1.	SIXTEEN TONS (BMI)—Tennessee Ernie You Don't Have to Be a Baby to Cry (ASCAP)—Cap 3262	1	4
2.	AUTUMN LEAVES (ASCAP)—(ASCAP)—R. Williams Take Care (BMI)—Kapp 116	2	16
3.	LOVE IS A MANY-SPLENDORED THING (ASCAP)—Four Aces Shine On, Harvest Moon (ASCAP)—Dec 29625	3	14
4.	MOMENTS TO REMEMBER—(ASCAP) Four Lads Dream On, My Love, Dream On (ASCAP)—Col 40539	4	14
5.	ONLY YOU (BMI)—Platters Bark, Battle and Ball (BMI)—Mercury 70633	6	10
6.	I HEAR YOU KNOCKIN' (BMI)—G. Storm Never Leave Me (ASCAP)—Dot 15412	5	7
7.	HE (BMI)—A. Hibbler Breeze (ASCAP)—Dec 29660	7	10
8.	LOVE AND MARRIAGE (ASCAP)—(ASCAP)—F. Sinatra Impatient Years (ASCAP)—Cap 3260	11	4
9.	SHIFTING, WHISPERING SANDS R. Draper Time (ASCAP)—Mercury 70696	10	10
10.	AT MY FRONT DOOR (BMI)—P. Boone NO ARMS CAN EVER HOLD YOU (BMI)—Dot 15422	8	6
11.	YELLOW ROSE OF TEXAS (ASCAP)—M. Miller Blackberry Winter (BMI)—Col 40540	9	18
12.	HE (BMI)—McGuire Sisters If You Believe (ASCAP)—Coral 61501	16	6
13.	SHIFTING, WHISPERING SANDS (PARTS I & II)—(BMI)B. Vaughn Dot 15409	12	11
14.	IT'S ALMOST TOMORROW (ASCAP)—Dream Weavers You Got Me Wondering (ASCAP)—Dec 29683	14	4
15.	SOMEONE YOU LOVE (BMI)—Nat (King) Cole FORGIVE MY HEART (ASCAP)—Cap 3234	13	7
16.	SUDDENLY THERE'S A VALLEY (BMI)—G. Grant Love Is (BMI)—Era 1003	19	9
17.	ONLY YOU (BMI)—Hilltoppers Until the Real Thing Comes Along (ASCAP)—Dot 15423	16	4
18.	BURN THAT CANDLE (BMI)—B. Haley ROCK-A-BEATIN' BOOGIE (ASCAP)—Dec 29713	23	3
19.	YOU ARE MY LOVE (ASCAP)—J. James I Lay Me Down to Sleep (BMI)—M-G-M 12066	18	7
20.	MY BONNIE LASSIE (ASCAP)—Ames Brothers So Will I (BMI)—Vic 20-6208	15	9
20.	CROCE DI ORO (Cross of Gold) (ASCAP)—P. Page Search My Heart (BMI)—Mercury 70713	—	1
22.	SUDDENLY THERE'S A VALLEY (BMI)—J. Stafford Night Watch (BMI)—Col 40559	21	6
23.	MEMORIES ARE MADE OF THIS—(BMI)—D. Martin Change of Heart (BMI)—Cap 3295	—	1
24.	BIBLE TELLS ME SO (ASCAP)—D. Cornell Love Is a Many-Splendored Thing (ASCAP)—Coral 61467	20	13
24.	BLACK DENIM TROUSERS (BMI)—Cheers Some Night in Alaska (BMI)—Cap 3219	21	11

• THIS WEEKS BEST BUYS

According to sales reports in key markets, the following recent releases are recommended for extra profits:

GEE WHITTAKERS! (Lowell, BMI)—**Pat Boone—Dot 15435**

Boone has captured the imagination of the teen-age audience once more with this congenial material. First-week sales in Philadelphia, Buffalo, Milwaukee, Baltimore, Cleveland, Richmond and Nashville have been exceptionally good and are rising rapidly. Flip is "Take the Time" (Tee Pee, ASCAP). A previous Billboard "Spotlight" pick.

A WOMAN IN LOVE (Frank, ASCAP)—**Frankie Laine—Columbia 40583**

With this tune getting stronger all the time, both the Four Aces (previously picked as a "Best Buy") and the Frankie Laine versions are shaping up as disks with strong chart potential. While the former still is leading Laine, the latter has also begun to swing considerable volume in Providence, Baltimore, Pittsburgh, Atlanta, Milwaukee, Chicago, Durham and Cleveland, among others. Flip is "Walking the Night Away."

WANTING YOU (Harms, ASCAP)—**Roger Williams—Kapp 127**

This disk is a strong follow-up to "Autumn Leaves." Initial sales reaction in New York, Philadelphia, Buffalo, Cleveland, Chicago, St. Louis, Baltimore and Milwaukee has been excellent; juke box operators in all these territories are buying particularly heavily. Flip is "Night Wind."

MY BELIEVING HEART (Valando, ASCAP)

YOU NEVER FALL IN LOVE AGAIN (Hub-Leeds, ASCAP)—**Joni James—M-G-M 12126**

An unusually fast take-off has been reported in a majority of territories where this disk was delivered last week. While the side has not been determined yet, interest at this point is keen on both. Providence, Baltimore, St. Louis, Buffalo, Philadelphia, Durham and New York are among the territories that indicated good to strong sales. A previous Billboard "Spotlight" pick.

• Most Played in Juke Boxes

For survey week ending November 23

RECORDS are ranked in order of the greatest number of plays in juke boxes thruout the country, as determined by The Billboard's weekly survey of the nation's juke box operators. When significant play is reported on both sides of a record, points are combined to determine position on the chart. In such a case, both sides are listed in bold type, the leading side on top.

This Week		Last Week	Weeks on Chart
1.	SIXTEEN TONS (BMI)—Tennessee Ernie You Don't Have to Be a Baby to Cry (ASCAP)—Cap 3262	7	3
2.	AUTUMN LEAVES (ASCAP)—R. Williams Take Care (BMI)—Kapp 116	2	12
3.	SHIFTING, WHISPERING SANDS (BMI)—R. Draper Time (ASCAP)—Mercury 70696	3	7
4.	LOVE IS A MANY-SPLENDORED THING (ASCAP)—Four Aces Shine On, Harvest Moon (ASCAP)—Dec 29625	1	11
5.	I HEAR YOU KNOCKIN' (BMI)—G. Storm Never Leave Me (ASCAP)—Dot 15412	6	6
6.	MOMENTS TO REMEMBER (ASCAP)—Four Lads Dream On, My Love, Dream On (ASCAP)—Col 40539	4	8
7.	YELLOW ROSE OF TEXAS (ASCAP)—M. Miller Blackberry Winter (BMI)—Col 40540	5	16
7.	AT MY FRONT DOOR (BMI)—P. Boone NO ARMS CAN EVER HOLD YOU (BMI)—Dot 15422	8	5
9.	ONLY YOU (BMI)—Platters Bark, Battle and Ball (BMI)—Mercury 70623	9	7
10.	ONLY YOU (BMI)—Hilltoppers Until the Real Thing Comes Along (ASCAP)—Dot 15423	16	3
11.	HE (BMI)—McGuire Sisters If You Believe (ASCAP)—Coral 51501	10	6
12.	SHIFTING, WHISPERING SANDS (PARTS I & II)—B. Vaughn (BMI)—Dot 15409	12	9
13.	YELLOW ROSE OF TEXAS (ASCAP)—J. Desmond You're in Love With Someone (ASCAP)—Coral 61476	14	15
14.	DADDY-O (BMI)—B. Lou Dancin' in My Socks (BMI)—King 4835	—	1
15.	PEPPER HOT BABY (BMI)—J. P. Morgan IF YOU DON'T WANT MY LOVE (ASCAP)—Vic 20-6282	19	2
16.	BIBLE TELLS ME SO (ASCAP) D. Cornell Love Is a Many-Splendored Thing (ASCAP)—Coral 61467	11	11
16.	MY BOY FLAT TOP (BMI)—D Collins In Love (BMI)—Coral 61510	—	1
16.	MY BONNIE LASSIE (ASCAP)—Ames Brothers So Will I (BMI)—Vic 20-6208	—	8
19.	SUDDENLY THERE'S A VALLEY (BMI)—G. Grant Love Is (BMI)—Era 1003	19	5
20.	HE (BMI)—A. Hibbler Breeze (ASCAP)—Dec 29660	16	6

• Most Played by Jockeys

For survey week ending November 23

SIDES are ranked in order of the greatest number of plays on disk jockey radio shows thruout the country. Results are based on The Billboard's weekly survey among the nation's disk jockeys. The reverse side of each record is also listed.

This Week		Last Week	Weeks on Chart
1.	SIXTEEN TONS—Tennessee Ernie You Don't Have to Be a Baby to Cry (ASCAP)—Cap 3262	1	4
2.	MOMENTS TO REMEMBER—Four Lads Dream On, My Love, Dream On (ASCAP)—Col 40539	3	12
3.	LOVE IS A MANY-SPLENDORED THING—Four Aces Shine On, Harvest Moon (ASCAP)—Dec 29625	2	15
4.	AUTUMN LEAVES—R. Williams Take Care (BMI)—Kapp 116	4	13
5.	I HEAR YOU KNOCKIN'—G. Storm Never Leave Me (ASCAP)—Dot 15412	8	6
6.	LOVE AND MARRIAGE—F. Sinatra Impatient Years (ASCAP)—Cap 3260	5	5
7.	ONLY YOU—Platters Bark, Battle and Ball (BMI)—Mercury 70633	6	6
8.	HE—A. Hibbler Breeze (ASCAP)—Dec 29660	7	8
9.	ONLY YOU—Hilltoppers Until the Real Thing Comes Along (ASCAP)—Dot 15423	14	4
10.	AT MY FRONT DOOR—P. Boone No Arms Can Ever Hold You (BMI)—Dot 15422	10	5
11.	YOU ARE MY LOVE—J. James I Lay Me Down to Sleep (BMI)—M-G-M 12066	12	7
12.	C'EST LA VIE—S. Vaughan Never (ASCAP)—Mercury 70727	—	1
13.	CRY ME A RIVER—J. London S'Wonderful (ASCAP)—Liberty 55006	—	1
14.	SHIFTING, WHISPERING SANDS (PARTS I & II)—B. Vaughn Dot 15409 (BMI)—	9	11
15.	ALL AT ONCE YOU LOVE HER—P. Como Rost Tattoo (ASCAP)—Vic 20-6294	20	2
16.	YELLOW ROSE OF TEXAS—M. Miller Blackberry Winter (BMI)—Col 40540	11	18
17.	SIXTEEN TONS—J. Desmond Ballo Italiano (BMI)—Coral 61529	—	1
18.	HE—McGuire Sisters If You Believe (BMI)—Coral 61501	16	3
19.	SUDDENLY THERE'S A VALLEY—J. Stafford Night Watch (BMI)—Col 40559	15	5
20.	IT'S ALMOST TOMORROW—S. Lanson Stop (ASCAP)—Dot 15424	—	1

The Billboard Music Popularity Charts

POPULAR RECORDS

THE TOP 100

For survey week ending November 23

A list of the **TOP 100 RECORD SIDES** in the nation according to a **COMBINED TABULATION** of Dealer, Disk Jockey and Juke Box Operator replies to The Billboard's weekly popular record Best Seller and Most Played surveys. Its purpose is to provide Disk Jockeys with additional programming material and to give trade exposure to NEWER records just beginning to show action in the field.

This Week	Song	Artist	Label	Last Week
1.	SIXTEEN TONS	T. Ernie	Capitol	3
2.	AUTUMN LEAVES	R. Williams	Kapp	2
3.	LOVE IS A MANY-SPLENDORED THING	Four Aces	Decca	1
4.	MOMENTS TO REMEMBER	Four Lads	Columbia	4
5.	I HEAR YOU KNOCKIN'	G. Storm	Dot	5
6.	ONLY YOU	Platters	Mercury	6
7.	AT MY FRONT DOOR	P. Boone	Dot	8
8.	HE	A. Hibbler	Decca	9
9.	LOVE AND MARRIAGE	F. Sinatra	Capitol	13
9.	ONLY YOU	Hilltoppers	Dot	14
11.	SHIFTING, WHISPERING SANDS	B. Vaughn	Dot	10
12.	HE	McGuire Sisters	Coral	12
13.	SHIFTING, WHISPERING SANDS	R. Draper	Mercury	11
14.	SUDDENLY THERE'S A VALLEY	G. Grant	Era	15
15.	YOU ARE MY LOVE	J. James	M-G-M	17
16.	SUDDENLY THERE'S A VALLEY	J. Stafford	Columbia	18
17.	MY BONNIE LASSIE	Ames Brothers	Coral	16
18.	CROCE DI ORO (CROSS OF GOLD)	P. Page	Mercury	22
19.	DADDY-O	Fontane Sisters	Dot	25
20.	IT'S ALMOST TOMORROW	Dreamweavers	Decca	27
21.	FORGIVE MY HEART	Nat (King) Cole	Capitol	30
22.	MY BOY FLAT TOP	D. Collins	Coral	48
23.	CRY ME A RIVER	J. London	Liberty	44
24.	IT'S ALMOST TOMORROW	S. Lanson	Dot	43
25.	YELLOW ROSE OF TEXAS	J. Desmond	Coral	23
26.	NO ARMS CAN EVER HOLD YOU	P. Boone	Dot	39
26.	WOMAN IN LOVE	Four Aces	Decca	42
28.	BURN THAT CANDLE	B. Haley	Decca	38
29.	BLACK DENIM TROUSERS	Cheers	Capitol	19
30.	ALL AT ONCE YOU LOVE HER	P. Como	Victor	34
31.	PEPPER-HOT BABY	J. P. Morgan	Victor	24
32.	IT'S ALMOST TOMORROW	J. Stafford	Columbia	69
33.	SUDDENLY THERE'S A VALLEY	J. La Rosa	Cadence	33
33.	BIBLE TELLS ME SO	D. Cornell	Coral	47
35.	NO ARMS CAN EVER HOLD YOU	G. Shaw	Decca	36
36.	DADDY-O	B. Lou	King	28
37.	SEVENTEEN	Fontane Sisters	Dot	28
38.	C'EST LA VIE	S. Vaughan	Mercury	51
38.	SOMEONE IN LOVE	Nat (King) Cole	Capitol	21
40.	AUTUMN LEAVES	S. Allen	Coral	45
41.	MEMORIES OF YOU	Four Coins	Epi	51
42.	ROCK A BEATIN' BOOGIE	B. Haley	Decca	41
42.	DOG-FACED SOLDIER	R. Morgan	Decca	37
44.	MEMORIES ARE MADE OF THIS	D. Martin	Capitol	—
45.	BAND OF GOLD	D. Cherry	Columbia	—
46.	AIN'T THAT A SHAME	P. Boone	Dot	32
47.	TINA MARIE	P. Como	Victor	20
48.	LOVE AND MARRIAGE	D. Shore	Victor	53
48.	IF YOU DON'T WANT MY LOVE	J. P. Morgan	Victor	50
50.	WOMAN IN LOVE	F. Laine	Columbia	60
51.	AT MY FRONT DOOR	El Dorados	Vee Jay	35
52.	MY BOY FLAT TOP	B. Bennett	King	63
53.	AMUKIRIKI	L. Paul & M. Ford	Capitol	49
54.	THERE SHOULD BE RULES	B. Madigan	M-G-M	75
55.	AUTUMN LEAVES	V. Young	Decca	58
55.	LOVE IS A MANY-SPLENDORED THING	D. Cornell	Coral	26
55.	LOVE IS A MANY-SPLENDORED THING	D. Rose	M-G-M	60
58.	LONGEST WALK	J. P. Morgan	Victor	30
59.	WAKE THE TOWN AND TELL THE PEOPLE	L. Baxter	Capitol	59
60.	CROCE DI ORO (CROSS OF GOLD)	J. Regan	London	55
61.	SEVENTEEN	B. Bennett	King	40
62.	AUTUMN LEAVES	M. Miller	Columbia	55
62.	MAGIC FINGERS	E. Fisher	Victor	73
64.	JAPANESE FAREWELL SONG	K. C. Jones	Mrq.	—
65.	SIXTEEN TONS	J. Desmond	Coral	—
65.	WHEN YOU DANCE	Turbans	Herald	63
67.	BAND OF GOLD	K. Carson	Capitol	74
67.	BLACK DENIM TROUSERS	V. Monroe	Victor	86
67.	IT'S ALMOST TOMORROW	D. Carroll	Mercury	65
70.	SUDDENLY THERE'S A VALLEY	Mills Brothers	Decca	45
71.	OF THIS I'M SURE	Four Aces	Decca	—
72.	DAY BY DAY	Four Freshmen	Capitol	89
73.	AUTUMN LEAVES	J. Gleason	Capitol	61
74.	HAWK-EYE	F. Laine	Columbia	81
75.	GOODBYE TO ROME	G. Gibbs	Mercury	—
76.	PEPPER-HOT BABY	G. MacKenzie	X	76
77.	WITHOUT A SONG	R. Hamilton	Epic	93
78.	BONNIE BLUE GAL	M. Miller	Columbia	57
79.	ROSE TATTOO	P. Como	Victor	—
80.	WAKE THE TOWN AND TELL THE PEOPLE	M. Carson	Columbia	70
81.	ROCK AROUND THE CLOCK	B. Haley	Decca	—
82.	YELLOW ROSE OF TEXAS	S. Freberg	Capitol	53
83.	TIMES TWO I LOVE YOU	Chuckles	X	81
84.	LOVE IS A MANY-SPLENDORED THING	W. Herman	Capitol	83
85.	C'EST LA VIE	S. Gale	Victor	88
86.	SHOOT IT AGAIN	T. Brewer	Coral	66
87.	LEARNIN' TO LOVE	P. King	Columbia	80
87.	MAYBELLENE	C. Berry	Chess	87
89.	ADORABLE	Fontane Sisters	Dot	71
90.	SONG OF THE DREAMER	E. Fisher	Victor	100
91.	NO ARMS CAN EVER HOLD YOU	Gaylords	Mercury	67
92.	BIBLE TELLS ME SO	N. Noble	Wing	61
93.	SAME OLE SATURDAY NIGHT	F. Sinatra	Capitol	72
94.	PET ME PAPA	R. Clooney	Columbia	77
94.	SWEET KENTUCKY ROSE	K. Kallen	Decca	—
94.	YOUNG ABE LINCOLN	D. Cornell	Coral	—
97.	AUTUMN LEAVES	R. Charles	M-G-M	83
98.	LOVE IS A MANY-SPLENDORED THING	Don, Dick & Jimmy	Cwn.	—
99.	POR FAVOR	V. Damone	Mercury	—
100.	OO BANG	Doris Day	Columbia	83

CAUTION TO DEALERS AND JUKE BOX OPERATORS

The Billboard's Top 100 is NOT designed to provide tested information for buying purposes. This function is most reliably served by other regular weekly features: Best Sellers in Stores, Most Played in Juke Boxes, Coming Up Strong and Best Buys.

The Billboard Music Popularity Charts

POPULAR RECORDS

• Best Sellers in Stores

For survey week ending November 30

RECORDS are ranked in order of their current national selling importance at the retail level, as determined by The Billboard's weekly survey of the top volume dealers in every important market area. When significant action is reported on both sides of a record, points are combined to determine position on the chart. In such a case, both sides are listed in bold type, the leading side on top.

This Week		Last Week	Weeks on Chart
1.	**SIXTEEN TONS** (BMI)—Tennessee Ernie You Don't Have to Be a Baby to Cry (ASCAP)—Cap 3262	1	5
2.	**AUTUMN LEAVES** (ASCAP)—R. Williams Take Care (BMI)—Kapp 116	2	17
3.	**LOVE IS A MANY-SPLENDORED THING** (ASCAP)—Four Aces Shine On, Harvest Moon—Dec 29625	3	15
4.	**MOMENTS TO REMEMBER** (ASCAP)—Four Lads Dream On, My Love, Dream On (ASCAP)—Col 40539	4	15
5.	**MEMORIES ARE MADE OF THIS**—(BMI)—D. Martin Change of Heart (BMI)—Cap 3295	23	2
6.	**I HEAR YOU KNOCKIN'** (BMI)—G. Storm Never Leave Me (ASCAP)—Dot 15412	6	8
7.	**ONLY YOU** (BMI)—Platters Bark, Battle and Ball (BMI)—Mercury 70633	5	11
8.	**HE** (BMI)—A. Hibbler Breeze (ASCAP)—Dec 29660	7	11
9.	**LOVE AND MARRIAGE** (ASCAP)—F. Sinatra Impatient Years (ASCAP)—Cap 3260	8	5
10.	**SHIFTING, WHISPERING SANDS** R. Draper Time (ASCAP)—Mercury 70696	9	11
11.	**IT'S ALMOST TOMORROW** (ASCAP)—Dream Weavers You Got Me Wondering (ASCAP)—Dec 29683	14	5
12.	**AT MY FRONT DOOR** (BMI)—P. Boone No Arms Can Ever Hold You (BMI)—Dot 15422	10	7
13.	**SHIFTING, WHISPERING SANDS (PARTS I & II)**—B. Vaughn Dot 15409	13	12
14.	**HE** (BMI)—McGuire Sisters If You Believe (ASCAP)—Coral 61501	12	7
15.	**ONLY YOU** (BMI)—Hilltoppers Until the Real Thing Comes Along (ASCAP)—Dot 15423	17	5
16.	**YELLOW ROSE OF TEXAS** (ASCAP)—M. Miller Blackberry Winter (BMI)—Col 40540	11	19
17.	**BURN THAT CANDLE** (BMI)—B. Haley **ROCK-A-BEATIN' BOOGIE** (ASCAP)—Dec 29713	18	4
18.	**SUDDENLY THERE'S A VALLEY** (BMI)—G. Grant Love Is (BMI)—Era 1003	16	10
19.	**BAND OF GOLD** (BMI)—D. Cherry Rumble Boogie—Col 40597	—	1
20.	**FORGIVE MY HEART** (ASCAP)—Nat (King) Cole **SOMEONE YOU LOVE** (BMI)—Cap 3234	15	8
20.	**DADDY-O** (BMI)—Fontane Sisters Adorable (BMI)—Dot 15428	—	1
22.	**MY BONNIE LASSIE** (ASCAP)—Ames Brothers So Will I (BMI)—Vic 20-6208	20	10
22.	**MEMORIES OF YOU** (ASCAP)—Four Coins Tear Down the Fence (ASCAP)—Epic 9129	—	1
24.	**YOU ARE MY LOVE** (ASCAP)—J. James I Lay Me Down to Sleep (BMI)—M-G-M 12066	19	8
25.	**CROCE DI ORO (CROSS OF GOLD)**—P. Page Search My Heart (BMI)—Mercury 70713	20	2
25.	**NO ARMS CAN EVER HOLD YOU** (BMI)—G. Shaw Look to Your Heart (ASCAP)—Dec 29679	—	1

• THIS WEEKS BEST BUYS

According to sales reports in key markets, the following recent releases are recommended for extra profits:

DOLLY'S OH! SUSANNA (Springfield, BMI)—**Don Charles' Singing Dogs—RCA Victor 6344**

Not many novelties have gotten the enthusiastic reception that this one has. Out only a short time, it is already on the St. Louis, Milwaukee and Seattle territorial charts and very close to the top 10 in many other market areas checked. The flip is a medley: Pearl's "Jingle Bells," King's "Three Blind Mice," Caesar's "Pat-a-Cake" (Springfield, BMI). A previous Billboard Novelty "Spotlight."

ANGELS IN THE SKY (Ridgeway, BMI)—**The Crewcuts—Mercury 70741**

Little by little this tune has been coming toward the top. Listed this week on the Cleveland and Minneapolis-St. Paul territorial charts, it is also a strong seller in Pittsburgh, Buffalo, Milwaukee and other important markets. Flip is "Mostly Martha" (Hill & Range, BMI). A previous Billboard "Spotlight" pick.

THE TENDER TRAP (Barton, ASCAP)—**Frank Sinatra—Capitol 3290**

With the film now garnering lush box-office receipts, this theme song is shaping up as a big one for Sinatra. Atlanta, Baltimore, Pittsburgh, Philadelphia, Providence, Buffalo and Chicago are typical areas returning strong and mounting sales reports. Flip is "Weep They Will." A previous Billboard "Spotlight" pick.

TEEN-AGE PRAYER (Peer, BMI)—**Gloria Mann—Sound 126**

The competition is keen on this tune, but Miss Mann had the advantage of a head start and is holding on to a comfortable lead. Strongest originally in Eastern cities—New York, Boston, Baltimore, Philadelphia—it is now coming up fast in Chicago, St. Louis, Cleveland and other Midwestern territories. Flip is "Gypsy Lady" (Peer, BMI). A previous Billboard "Spotlight" pick.

ARE YOU SATISFIED? (Cordial, BMI)—**Rusty Draper—Mercury 70757**

The singer is following up his hit disk with another strong seller. "Are You Satisfied?" is selling nicely in Pittsburgh, Nashville, St. Louis, Baltimore, Philadelphia, Milwaukee, Cleveland and Chicago. In some areas, Sheb Wooley's competitive version has been taking a profitable slice of the melon. Flip of the Draper disk is "Wabash Cannonball."

THE GREAT PRETENDER (Pera, BMI)—**The Platters—Mercury 70753**

(See this week's Rhythm and Blues "Best Buys.")

SPEEDO (Rush, BMI)—**The Cadillacs—Josie 785**

(See this week's Rhythm and Blues "Best Buys.")

Christmas

NUTTIN' FOR CHRISTMAS (Ross Jungnickel, ASCAP) — **Art Mooney - Barry Gordon — M-G-M 12092 — Ricky Zahnd — Columbia 40576**

Early reports indicate that "Nuttin'" is the strong Christmas tune this year. A fierce competitive situation exists, but M-G-M was leading the field at the end of the week, with Columbia coming up with enough strength to challenge it seriously in many key territories. Both have strong chance of hitting the charts in the next weeks. Good regional support for the Joe Ward, Fontane Sisters and Stan Freberg versions also was reported.

• Most Played in Juke Boxes

For survey week ending November 30

RECORDS are ranked in order of the greatest number of plays in juke boxes thruout the country, as determined by The Billboard's weekly survey of the nation's juke box operators. When significant play is reported on both sides of a record, points are combined to determine position on the chart. In such a case, both sides are listed in bold type, the leading side on top.

This Week		Last Week	Weeks on Chart
1.	**SIXTEEN TONS** (BMI)—Tennessee Ernie You Don't Have to Be a Baby to Cry (ASCAP)—Cap 3262	1	4
2.	**I HEAR YOU KNOCKIN'** (BMI)—G. Storm Never Leave Me (ASCAP)—Dot 15412	5	7
3.	**AUTUMN LEAVES** (ASCAP)—R. Williams Take Care (BMI)—Kapp 116	2	13
4.	**MOMENTS TO REMEMBER** (ASCAP)—Four Lads Dream On, My Love, Dream On (ASCAP)—Col 40539	6	9
5.	**SHIFTING, WHISPERING SANDS** (BMI)—R. Draper Time (ASCAP)—Mercury 70696	3	8
6.	**LOVE IS A MANY-SPLENDORED THING** (ASCAP)—Four Aces Shine On, Harvest Moon (ASCAP)—Dec 29625	4	12
7.	**ONLY YOU** (BMI)—Platters Bark, Battle and Ball (BMI)—Mercury 70623	9	8
8.	**AT MY FRONT DOOR** (BMI)—P. Boone **NO ARMS CAN EVER HOLD YOU** (BMI)—Dot 15422	7	6
9.	**HE** (BMI)—A. Hibbler Breeze (ASCAP)—Dec 29660	20	7
10.	**SHIFTING, WHISPERING SANDS (PARTS I & II)**—B. Vaughn Dot 15409	12	10
11.	**ONLY YOU** (BMI)—Hilltoppers Until the Real Thing Comes Along (ASCAP)—Dot 15423	10	4
12.	**YELLOW ROSE OF TEXAS** (ASCAP)—J. Desmond You're in Love With Someone (ASCAP)—Coral 61476	13	16
12.	**IF YOU DON'T WANT MY LOVE** (ASCAP)—J. P. Morgan **PEPPER HOT BABY** (BMI)—Vic 20-6282	15	3
14.	**HE** (BMI)—McGuire Sisters If You Believe (ASCAP)—Coral 51501	11	7
15.	**YELLOW ROSE OF TEXAS** (ASCAP)—M. Miller Blackberry Winter (BMI)—Col 40540	7	17
16.	**LOVE AND MARRIAGE** (ASCAP)—F. Sinatra Impatient Years (ASCAP)—Cap 3260	—	1
17.	**DADDY-O** (BMI)—Fontane Sisters Adorable (BMI)—Dot 15428	—	1
18.	**CROCE DI ORO (CROSS OF GOLD)** (ASCAP)—P. Page Search My Heart (BMI)—Mercury 70713	—	1
19.	**IT'S ALMOST TOMORROW** (ASCAP)—Dream Weavers You Got Me Wondering (ASCAP)—Dec 29683	—	1
20.	**BURN THAT CANDLE** (BMI)—B. Haley Rock-A-Beatin' Boogie (BMI)—Dec 29713	—	1

• Most Played by Jockeys

For survey week ending November 30

SIDES are ranked in order of the greatest number of plays on disk jockey radio shows thruout the country. Results are based on The Billboard's weekly survey among the nation's disk jockeys. The reverse side of each record is also listed.

This Week		Last Week	Weeks on Chart
1.	**SIXTEEN TONS** (BMI)—Tennessee Ernie You Don't Have to Be a Baby to Cry (ASCAP)—Cap 3262	1	5
2.	**MOMENTS TO REMEMBER** (ASCAP)—Four Lads Dream On, My Love, Dream On (ASCAP)—Col 40539	2	13
3.	**LOVE IS A MANY-SPLENDORED THING** (ASCAP)—Four Aces Shine On, Harvest Moon (ASCAP)—Dec 29625	3	16
4.	**AUTUMN LEAVES** (ASCAP)—R. Williams Take Care (BMI)—Kapp 116	4	14
5.	**ONLY YOU** (BMI)—Platters Bark, Battle and Ball (BMI)—Mercury 70633	7	7
6.	**LOVE AND MARRIAGE** (ASCAP)—F. Sinatra Impatient Years (ASCAP)—Cap 3260	6	6
7.	**MEMORIES ARE MADE OF THIS** (BMI)—D. Martin Change of Heart (BMI)—Cap 3295	—	1
8.	**I HEAR YOU KNOCKIN'** (BMI)—G. Storm Never Leave Me (ASCAP)—Dot 15412	5	7
9.	**HE** (BMI)—A. Hibbler Breeze (ASCAP)—Dec 29660	8	9
10.	**ONLY YOU** (BMI)—Hilltoppers Until the Real Thing Comes Along (ASCAP)—Dot 15423	9	5
10.	**IT'S ALMOST TOMORROW** (ASCAP)—Dream Weavers You Got Me Wondering (ASCAP)—Dec 29683	—	2
12.	**AT MY FRONT DOOR** (BMI)—P. Boone No Arms Can Ever Hold You (BMI)—Dot 15422	10	6
13.	**YOU ARE MY LOVE** (ASCAP)—J. James I Lay Me Down to Sleep (BMI)—M-G-M 12066	11	8
14.	**ALL AT ONCE YOU LOVE HER** (ASCAP)—P. Como Rose Tattoo (ASCAP)—Vic 20-6294	15	3
15.	**CRY ME A RIVER** (ASCAP)—J. London S' Wonderful (ASCAP)—Liberty 55006	13	2
16.	**C'EST LA VIE** (ASCAP)—S. Vaughan Never (ASCAP)—Mercury 70727	12	2
17.	**CROCE DI ORO (CROSS OF GOLD)** (ASCAP)—P. Page Search My Heart (BMI)—Mercury 70713	—	1
18.	**SHIFTING, WHISPERING SANDS (PARTS I & II)**—B. Vaughn Dot 15409	14	12
19.	**DADDY-O** (BMI)—Fontane Sisters Adorable (BMI)—Dot 15428	—	1
20.	**IT'S ALMOST TOMORROW** (ASCAP)—J. Stafford If You Want to Love (ASCAP)—Col 40595	—	1
20.	**LOVE AND MARRIAGE** (ASCAP)—D. Shore Compare (ASCAP)—Vic 20-6266	—	1

The Billboard Music Popularity Charts

POPULAR RECORDS

THE TOP 100

For survey week ending November 23

A list of the TOP 100 RECORD SIDES in the nation according to a COMBINED TABULATION of Dealer, Disk Jockey and Juke Box Operator replies to The Billboard's weekly popular record Best Seller and Most Played surveys. Its purpose is to provide Disk Jockeys with additional programming material and to give trade exposure to NEWER records just beginning to show action in the field.

This Wk.	Song	Artist	Label	Last Wk.
1.	SIXTEEN TONS	T. Ernie	Capitol	1
2.	AUTUMN LEAVES	R. Williams	Kapp	2
3.	MOMENTS TO REMEMBER	Four Lads	Columbia	4
4.	LOVE IS A MANY-SPLENDORED THING	Four Aces	Decca	3
5.	I HEAR YOU KNOCKIN'	G. Storm	Dot	5
6.	ONLY YOU	Platters	Mercury	6
7.	HE	A. Hibbler	Decca	8
8.	LOVE AND MARRIAGE	F. Sinatra	Capitol	9
9.	AT MY FRONT DOOR	P. Boone	Dot	7
10.	ONLY YOU	Hilltoppers	Dot	9
11.	IT'S ALMOST TOMORROW	Dream Weavers	Decca	20
12.	SHIFTING, WHISPERING SANDS	B. Vaughn	Dot	11
13.	SHIFTING, WHISPERING SANDS	R. Draper	Mercury	13
14.	HE	McGuire Sisters	Coral	12
15.	DADDY-O	Fontane Sisters	Dot	19
16.	CROCE DI ORO (CROSS OF GOLD)	P. Page	Mercury	18
17.	YOU ARE MY LOVE	J. James	M-G-M	15
18.	YELLOW ROSE OF TEXAS	M. Miller	Columbia	10
19.	CRY ME A RIVER	J. London	Liberty	23
20.	SUDDENLY THERE'S A VALLEY	G. Grant	Era	14
21.	PEPPER HOT BABY	J. P. Morgan	Victor	31
22.	SUDDENLY THERE'S A VALLEY	J. Stafford	Columbia	16
23.	NO ARMS CAN EVER HOLD YOU	G. Shaw	Decca	35
24.	ALL AT ONCE YOU LOVE HER	P. Como	Victor	30
25.	MY BONNIE LASSIE	Ames Brothers	Victor	17
26.	C'EST LA VIE	S. Vaughan	Mercury	38
26.	MEMORIES ARE MADE OF THIS	D. Martin	Capitol	44
28.	MEMORIES OF YOU	Four Coins	Epic	41
28.	WOMAN IN LOVE	Four Aces	Decca	26
30.	IT'S ALMOST TOMORROW	J. Stafford	Columbia	32
31.	BURN THAT CANDLE	B. Haley	Decca	28
32.	MY BOY—FLAT TOP	T. Collins	Coral	22
33.	DADDY-O	B. Lou	King	36
34.	DOG-FACED SOLDIER	R. Morgan	Decca	42
35.	AUTUMN LEAVES	S. Allen	Coral	40
35.	NO ARMS CAN EVER HOLD YOU	P. Boone	Dot	26
37.	SUDDENLY THERE'S A VALLEY	J. La Rosa	Cadence	33
38.	SOMEONE YOU LOVE	Nat (King) Cole	Capitol	38
38.	IT'S ALMOST TOMORROW	S. Lanson	Dot	24
40.	IF YOU DON'T WANT MY LOVE	J. P. Morgan	Victor	48
41.	FORGIVE MY HEART	Nat (King) Cole	Capitol	21
42.	BAND OF GOLD	K. Carson	Capitol	67
43.	WOMAN IN LOVE	F. Laine	Columbia	50
44.	ANGELS IN THE SKY	Crew Cuts	Mercury	—
45.	BAND OF GOLD	D. Cherry	Columbia	45
45.	TINA MARIE	P. Como	Victor	47
47.	LOVE AND MARRIAGE	D. Shore	Victor	48
48.	ROCK-A-BEATIN' BOOGIE	B. Haley	Decca	42
48.	BLACK DENIM TROUSERS	Cheers	Capitol	29
50.	AUTUMN LEAVES	M. Miller	Columbia	62
51.	SEVENTEEN	Fontane Sisters	Dot	37
51.	IT'S ALMOST TOMORROW	D. Carroll	Mercury	67
53.	YELLOW ROSE OF TEXAS	J. Desmond	Coral	25
54.	LOVE IS A MANY-SPLENDORED THING	D. Cornell	Coral	55
55.	BIBLE TELLS ME SO	D. Cornell	Coral	33
56.	AT MY FRONT DOOR	El Dorados	Vee Jay	51
56.	OF THIS I'M SURE	Four Aces	Decca	71
58.	DOLLY'S OH SUSANNA	D. Charles-Singing Dogs	Victor	—
59.	SIXTEEN TONS	J. Desmond	Coral	65
59.	LONGEST WALK	J. P. Morgan	Victor	58
61.	AUTUMN LEAVES	J. Gleason	Capitol	73
61.	LISBON ANTIGUA	N. Riddle	Capitol	—
63.	TENDER TRAP	F. Sinatra	Capitol	—
64.	MY BOY—FLAT TOP	B. Bennett	King	52
65.	AMUKIRIKI	L. Paul & M. Ford	Capitol	53
66.	YELLOW ROSE OF TEXAS	S. Freberg	Capitol	82
67.	TIMES TWO I LOVE YOU	Chuckles	X	83
68.	LOVE IS A MANY-SPLENDORED THING	D. Rose	M-G-M	55
69.	WHEN YOU DANCE	Turbans	Herald	65
70.	WAKE THE TOWN AND TELL THE PEOPLE	L. Baxter	Capitol	59
70.	CROCE DI ORO (CROSS OF GOLD)	J. Regan	London	60
70.	GOODBYE TO ROME	G. Gibbs	Mercury	75
73.	THERE SHOULD BE RULES	B. Madigan	M-G-M	54
74.	TWENTY-FOUR HOURS A DAY	G. Gibbs	Mercury	—
75.	SPEEDO	Cadilliacs	Herald	—
76.	SEVENTEEN	B. Bennett	King	61
77.	AIN'T THAT A SHAME	P. Boone	Dot	46
77.	YOU TICKLE ME BABY	Royal Jokers	Atco	—
79.	PET ME PAPA	R. Clooney	Columbia	94
79.	SMOKEY JOE'S CAFE	Robins	Atco	—
79.	SUDDENLY THERE'S A VALLEY	Mills Brothers	Decca	70
82.	JAPANESE FAREWELL SONG	K. C. Jones	Marquee	64
83.	WANTING YOU	R. Williams	Kapp	—
84.	AUTUMN LEAVES	V. Young	Decca	55
85.	PEPPER HOT BABY	G. MacKenzie	X	76
86.	AUTUMN LEAVES	R. Charles Singers	M-G-M	97
87.	TEENAGE PRAYER	G. Mann	Sound	—
87.	ADORABLE	Fontane Sisters	Dot	89
89.	LOVE IS A MANY-SPLENDORED THING	W. Herman	Capitol	84
90.	YOUNG ABE LINCOLN	Hugo & Luigi	Mercury	—
91.	ROSE TATTOO	P. Como	Victor	79
92.	CHARMAINE	Four Freshman	Capitol	—
92.	OO BANG	Doris Day	Columbia	100
92.	I'LL KNOW	S. Davis, Jr.	Decca	—
95.	I WANT YOU TO BE MY BABY	G. Gibbs	Mercury	—
96.	POR FAVOR	V. Damone	Mercury	99
97.	NO ARMS CAN EVER HOLD YOU	Gaylords	Mercury	91
97.	DAY BY DAY	Four Freshman	Capitol	72
99.	HEARTLESS	T. Leonetti	Capitol	—
99.	MY BELIEVING HEART	J. James	M-G-M	—
99.	RICHEST MAN	E. Arnold	Victor	—

CAUTION TO DEALERS AND JUKE BOX OPERATORS

The Billboard's Top 100 is NOT designed to provide tested information for buying purposes. This function is most reliably served by other regular weekly features: Best Sellers in Stores, Most Played in Juke Boxes, Coming Up Strong and Best Buys.

The Billboard Music Popularity Charts

POPULAR RECORDS

• Best Sellers in Stores

For survey week ending December 7

RECORDS are ranked in order of their current national selling importance at the retail level, as determined by The Billboard's weekly survey of the top volume dealers in every important market area. When significant action is reported on both sides of a record, points are combined to determine position on the chart. In such a case, both sides are listed in bold type, the leading side on top.

This Week		Last Week	Weeks on Chart
1.	**SIXTEEN TONS** (BMI)—Tennessee Ernie You Don't Have to Be a Baby to Cry (ASCAP)—Cap 3262	1	6
2.	**MEMORIES ARE MADE OF THIS** D. Martin Change of Heart (BMI)—Cap 3295	5	3
3.	**AUTUMN LEAVES** (ASCAP)—R. Williams Take Care (BMI)—Kapp 116	2	18
4.	**I HEAR YOU KNOCKIN'** (BMI)—G. Storm Never Leave Me (ASCAP)—Dot 15412	6	9
5.	**MOMENTS TO REMEMBER** (ASCAP)—Four Lads Dream On, My Love, Dream On (ASCAP)—Col 40539	4	16
6.	**LOVE IS A MANY-SPLENDORED THING** (ASCAP)—Four Aces Shine On, Harvest Moon (ASCAP)—Dec 29625	3	16
7.	**ONLY YOU** (BMI)—Platters Bark, Battle and Ball (BMI)—Mercury 70633	7	12
8.	**LOVE AND MARRIAGE** (ASCAP)—F. Sinatra Impatient Years (ASCAP)—Cap 3260	9	6
9.	**HE** (BMI)—A. Hibbler Breeze (ASCAP)—Dec 29660	8	12
10.	**IT'S ALMOST TOMORROW** (ASCAP)—Dream Weavers You Got Me Wondering (ASCAP)—Dec 29683	11	6
11.	**AT MY FRONT DOOR** (BMI)—P. Boone **NO ARMS CAN EVER HOLD YOU** (BMI)—Dot 15422	12	8
12.	**SHIFTING, WHISPERING SANDS** (BMI)—R. Draper Time (ASCAP)—Mercury 70696	10	12
13.	**HE** (BMI)—McGuire Sisters If You Believe (ASCAP)—Coral 61501	14	8
14.	**BAND OF GOLD** (BMI)—D. Cherry Rumble Boogie (BMI)—Col 40597	19	2
15.	**DADDY-O** (BMI)—Fontane Sisters Adorable (BMI)—Dot 15428	20	2
16.	**ONLY YOU** (BMI)—Hilltoppers Until the Real Thing Comes Along (ASCAP)—Dot 15423	15	6
17.	**SHIFTING, WHISPERING SANDS (PARTS I & II)** (BMI)—B. Vaughn Dot 15409	13	13
18.	**BURN THAT CANDLE** (BMI)—B. Haley **ROCK-A-BEATIN' BOOGIE** (ASCAP)—Dec 29713	17	5
19.	**WOMAN IN LOVE** (ASCAP)—F. Laine Walking the Night Away (ASCAP)—Col 40583	—	1
20.	**ANGELS IN THE SKY** (BMI)—Crew Cuts Mostly Martha (BMI)—Mercury 70741	—	1
21.	**YOU ARE MY LOVE** (ASCAP)—J. James I Lay Me Down to Sleep (BMI)—M-G-M 12066	24	9
22.	**MY BONNIE LASSIE** (ASCAP)—Ames Brothers So Will I (BMI)—Vic 20-6208	22	11
22.	**DOLLY'S OH SUSANNA (PARTS I & II)** (BMI)—D. Charles-Singing Dogs Vic 20-6344	—	1
24.	**SUDDENLY THERE'S A VALLEY** (BMI)—J. Stafford Night Watch (BMI)—Col 40559	—	7
25.	**IT'S ALMOST TOMORROW** (ASCAP)—J. Stafford If You Want to Love (ASCAP)—Col 40595	—	1
25.	**NUTTIN' FOR CHRISTMAS** (ASCAP)—B. Gordon-A. Mooney Santa Claus Looks Just Like Daddy (ASCAP)—M-G-M 12092	—	1

• THIS WEEK'S BEST BUYS

According to sales reports in key markets, the following recent releases are recommended for extra profits:

EVERYBODY'S GOT A HOME BUT ME (Chappel, ASCAP)—**Roy Hamilton—Epic 9132**

This tune from the new musical "Pipe Dream" is getting extensive play, and customers are buying both the Fisher and the Hamilton versions in impressive amounts. If the tune continues to gain in popularity, both versions stand to make the charts. The Epic record was reported selling well in Boston, New York, Buffalo, Pittsburgh, Cleveland, Milwaukee, Nashville, Durham, Providence, St. Louis and Baltimore. Flip is "Take Me With You" (Pincus, ASCAP).

DUNGAREE DOLL (E. B. Marks, BMI)

EVERYBODY'S GOT A HOME BUT ME (Chappel, ASCAP)—**Eddie Fisher—RCA Victor 6337**

Fisher's latest has not wasted much time in breaking out in most sales areas. Strong sales reports came in from Boston, Providence, New York, Philadelphia, Buffalo, Pittsburgh, Baltimore, St. Louis and Milwaukee, among others. "Dungaree Doll" is the favored side at this time, tho the flip also has territorial strength. A previous Billboard "Spotlight" pick.

TEEN-AGE PRAYER (Peer, BMI)

MEMORIES ARE MADE OF THIS (Montclare, BMI)—**Gale Storm—Dot 15436**

Out two weeks, Miss Storm's new record is showing impressive form, even tho both of her tunes are covers of disks available some time before hers. "Teen-Age Prayer" is doing best, and is racking up most volume in Baltimore, Providence, Atlanta, Pittsburgh, Chicago, Nashville, Kansas City, Buffalo and Durham. "Memories" is reported to have great appeal in several of the territories. A previous Billboard "Spotlight" pick.

LISBON ANTIGUA (Southern, ASCAP)—**Nelson Riddle Ork—Capitol 3287**

This instrumental is a "sleeper" that gradually has come to be an outstanding coin-puller in the juke boxes and a fast over-the-counter seller. The Riddle disk appears on Pittsburgh's and Atlanta's top 10 list this week, and is also doing excellent business in Chicago, Milwaukee, Durham, Detroit, Buffalo, Philadelphia and Cleveland. Flip is "Robin Hood" (Official, ASCAP)

• Most Played in Juke Boxes

For survey week ending December 7

RECORDS are ranked in order of the greatest number of plays in juke boxes thruout the country, as determined by The Billboard's weekly survey of the nation's juke box operators. When significant play is reported on both sides of a record, points are combined to determine position on the chart. In such a case, both sides are listed in bold type, the leading side on top.

This Week		Last Week	Weeks on Chart
1.	**SIXTEEN TONS** (BMI)—Tennessee Ernie You Don't Have to Be a Baby to Cry (ASCAP)—Cap 3262	1	5
2.	**I HEAR YOU KNOCKIN'** (BMI)—G. Storm Never Leave Me (ASCAP)—Dot 15412	2	8
3.	**AUTUMN LEAVES** (ASCAP) R. Williams Take Care (BMI)—Kapp 116	3	14
4.	**MOMENTS TO REMEMBER** (ASCAP)—Four Lads Dream On, My Love, Dream On (ASCAP)—Col 40539	4	10
5.	**SHIFTING, WHISPERING SANDS** (BMI)—R. Draper Time (ASCAP)—Mercury 70696	5	9
6.	**ONLY YOU** (BMI)—Platters Bark, Battle and Ball (BMI)—Mercury 70623	7	9
7.	**LOVE IS A MANY-SPLENDORED THING** (ASCAP)—Four Aces Shine On, Harvest Moon (ASCAP)—Dec 29625	6	13
8.	**HE** (BMI)—A. Hibbler Breeze (ASCAP)—Dec 29660	9	8
9.	**AT MY FRONT DOOR** (BMI)—P. Boone **NO ARMS CAN EVER HOLD YOU** (BMI)—Dot 15422	8	7
10.	**LOVE AND MARRIAGE** (ASCAP)—F. Sinatra Impatient Years (ASCAP)—Cap 3260	16	2
11.	**ONLY YOU** (BMI)—Hilltoppers Until the Real Thing Comes Along (ASCAP)—Dot 15423	11	5
12.	**SHIFTING, WHISPERING SANDS (PARTS I & II)**—B. Vaughn Dot 15409 (BMI)	10	11
13.	**HE** (BMI)—McGuire Sisters If You Believe (ASCAP)—Coral 51501	14	8
14.	**CRY ME A RIVER** (ASCAP)—J. London S'Wonderful (ASCAP)—Liberty 55006	—	1
15.	**DADDY-O** (BMI)—Fontane Sisters Adorable (BMI)—Dot 15428	17	2
16.	**CROCE DI ORO (Cross of Gold)** (ASCAP)—P. Page Search My Heart (BMI)—Mercury 70713	18	2
16.	**IF YOU DON'T WANT MY LOVE** (ASCAP)—J. P. Morgan **PEPPER HOT BABY** (BMI)—Vic 20-6282	12	4
18.	**IT'S ALMOST TOMORROW** (ASCAP)—Dream Weavers You Got Me Wondering (ASCAP)—Dec 29683	19	2
18.	**SUDDENLY THERE'S A VALLEY** (BMI)—J. Stafford Night Watch (BMI)—Col 40559	—	1
20.	**BURN THAT CANDLE** (BMI)—B. Haley Rock-A-Beatin' Boogie (ASCAP)—Dec 29713	20	2
20.	**YELLOW ROSE OF TEXAS** (ASCAP)—M. Miller Blackberry Winter (BMI)—Col 40540	15	18

• Most Played by Jockeys

For survey week ending December 7

SIDES are ranked in order of the greatest number of plays on disk jockey radio shows thruout the country. Results are based on The Billboard's weekly survey among the nation's disk jockeys. The reverse side of each record is also listed.

This Week		Last Week	Weeks on Chart
1.	**SIXTEEN TONS** (BMI)—Tennessee Ernie You Don't Have to Be a Baby to Cry (ASCAP)—Cap 3262	1	6
2.	**MEMORIES ARE MADE OF THIS** (BMI)—D. Martin Change of Heart (BMI)—Cap 3295	7	2
3.	**MOMENTS TO REMEMBER** (ASCAP)—Four Lads Dream On, My Love, Dream On (ASCAP)—Col 40539	2	14
4.	**LOVE IS A MANY-SPLENDORED THING** (ASCAP)—Four Aces Shine On, Harvest Moon (ASCAP)—Dec 29625	3	17
5.	**AUTUMN LEAVES** (ASCAP)—R. Williams Take Care (BMI)—Kapp 116	4	15
6.	**LOVE AND MARRIAGE** (ASCAP)—F. Sinatra Impatient Years (ASCAP)—Cap 3260	6	7
7.	**I HEAR YOU KNOCKIN'** (BMI)—G. Storm Never Leave Me (ASCAP)—Dot 15412	8	8
8.	**ONLY YOU** (BMI)—Platters Bark, Battle and Ball (BMI)—Mercury 70633	5	8
9.	**CRY ME A RIVER** (ASCAP)—J. London S' Wonderful (ASCAP)—Liberty 55006	15	3
10.	**ONLY YOU** (BMI)—Hilltoppers Until the Real Thing Comes Along (ASCAP)—Dot 15423	10	6
11.	**He** (BMI)—A. Hibbler Breeze (ASCAP)—Dec 29660	9	10
12.	**IT'S ALMOST TOMORROW** (ASCAP)—Dream Weavers You Got Me Wondering (ASCAP)—Dec 29683	10	3
13.	**ALL AT ONCE YOU LOVE HER** (ASCAP)—P. Como Rose Tattoo (ASCAP)—Vic 20-6294	14	4
14.	**C'EST LA VIE** (ASCAP)—S. Vaughn Never (ASCAP)—Mercury 70727	16	3
15.	**WOMAN IN LOVE** (ASCAP)—Four Aces Of This I'm Sure (ASCAP)—Dec 29725	—	1
16.	**YOU ARE MY LOVE** (ASCAP)—J. James I Lay Me Down to Sleep (BMI)—M-G-M 12066	13	9
17.	**TENDER TRAP** (ASCAP)—F. Sinatra Weep They Will (ASCAP)—Cap 3290	—	1
18.	**BAND OF GOLD** (BMI)—D. Cherry Rumble Boogie (BMI)—Col 40597	—	1
19.	**AT MY FRONT DOOR** (BMI)—P. Boone No Arms Can Ever Hold You (BMI)—Dot 15422	12	7
20.	**DADDY-O** (BMI)—Fontane Sisters Adorable (BMI)—Dot 15428	19	2

The Billboard Music Popularity Charts

POPULAR RECORDS

THE TOP 100

For survey week ending November 30

A list of the Top 100 RECORD SIDES in the nation according to a COMBINED TABULATION of Dealer, Disk Jockey and Juke Box Operator replies to The Billboard's weekly popular record Best Seller and Most Played surveys. Its purpose is to provide Disk Jockeys with additional programming material and to give trade exposure to NEWER records just beginning to show action in the field.

This Week	Song	Artist	Label	Last Week
1.	SIXTEEN TONS	T. Ernie	Capitol	1
2.	AUTUMN LEAVES	R. Williams	Kapp	2
3.	MOMENTS TO REMEMBER	Four Lads	Columbia	3
4.	I HEAR YOU KNOCKIN'	G. Storm	Dot	5
5.	LOVE IS A MANY-SPLENDORED THING	Four Aces	Decca	4
6.	ONLY YOU	Platters	Mercury	6
7.	LOVE AND MARRIAGE	F. Sinatra	Capitol	8
8.	MEMORIES ARE MADE OF THIS	D. Martin	Capitol	26
9.	HE	A. Hibbler	Decca	7
10.	ONLY YOU	Hilltoppers	Dot	10
11.	IT'S ALMOST TOMORROW	Dream Weavers	Decca	11
12.	AT MY FRONT DOOR	P. Boone	Dot	9
13.	DADDY-O	Fontane Sisters	Dot	15
13.	SHIFTING, WHISPERING SANDS	R. Draper	Mercury	13
15.	SHIFTING, WHISPERING SANDS	B. Vaughn	Dot	12
16.	HE	McGuire Sisters	Coral	14
17.	CRY ME A RIVER	J. London	Liberty	19
18.	YOU ARE MY LOVE	J. James	M-G-M	17
19.	CROCE DI ORO (CROSS OF GOLD)	P. Page	Mercury	16
20.	IT'S ALMOST TOMORROW	S. Lanson	Dot	38
20.	IT'S ALMOST TOMORROW	J. Stafford	Columbia	30
22.	C'EST LA VIE	S. Vaughan	Mercury	26
23.	WOMAN IN LOVE	Four Aces	Decca	28
24.	ALL AT ONCE YOU LOVE HER	P. Como	Victor	24
25.	SUDDENLY THERE'S A VALLEY	G. Grant	Era	20
26.	SUDDENLY THERE'S A VALLEY	J. Stafford	Columbia	22
27.	BURN THAT CANDLE	B. Haley	Columbia	31
28.	NO ARMS CAN EVER HOLD YOU	G. Shaw	Decca	23
29.	BAND OF GOLD	D. Cherry	Columbia	45
30.	NO ARMS CAN EVER HOLD YOU	P. Boone	Dot	35
30.	MEMORIES OF YOU	Four Coins	Epic	28
32.	ANGELS IN THE SKY	Crew Cuts	Mercury	44
33.	WOMAN IN LOVE	F. Laine	Columbia	43
34.	PEPPER-HOT BABY	J. P. Morgan	Victor	21
34.	IT'S ALMOST TOMORROW	D. Carroll	Mercury	51
34.	YELLOW ROSE OF TEXAS	M. Miller	Columbia	18
37.	MY BONNIE LASSIE	Ames Brothers	Victor	25
38.	SOMEONE YOU LOVE	Nat (King) Cole	Capitol	38
39.	FORGIVE MY HEART	Nat (King) Cole	Capitol	41
40.	DOLLY'S OH! SUSANNA	D. Charles-Singing Dogs	Victor	58
41.	GREAT PRETENDER	Platters	Mercury	—
42.	WHEN YOU DANCE	Turbans	Herald	69
43.	LISBON ANTIQUA	N. Riddle	Capitol	61
44.	MY BOY—FLAT TOP	D. Collins	Coral	32
45.	SUDDENLY THERE'S A VALLEY	J. La Rosa	Cadence	37
45.	TENDER TRAP	F. Sinatra	Capitol	63
47.	LOVE AND MARRIAGE	D. Shore	Victor	47
48.	BAND OF GOLD	K. Carson	Capitol	42
49.	TINA MARIE	P. Como	Victor	45
50.	AUTUMN LEAVES	M. Miller	Columbia	50
51.	SEVENTEEN	Fontane Sisters	Dot	51
51.	GOODBYE TO ROME	G. Gibbs	Mercury	70
53.	BLACK DENIM TROUSERS	Cheers	Capitol	48
54.	TEEN AGE PRAYER	G. Mann	Sound	87
55.	SUDDENLY THERE'S A VALLEY	Mills Brothers	Decca	79
56.	AUTUMN LEAVES	S. Allen	Coral	35
57.	ROCK A BEATIN' BOOGIE	B. Haley	Decca	48
57.	LOVE IS A MANY-SPLENDORED THING	D. Cornell	Coral	54
57.	DOG-FACED SOLDIER	R. Morgan	Decca	34
57.	MY BELIEVING HEART	J. James	M-G-M	99
57.	WANTING YOU	R. Williams	Kapp	83
62.	NUTTIN' FOR CHRISTMAS	B. Gordon-A. Mooney	M-G-M	—
63.	DUNGAREE DOLL	E. Fisher	Victor	—
64.	DADDY-O	B. Lou	King	33
64.	AT MY FRONT DOOR	El Dorados	Vee Jay	56
66.	IF YOU DON'T WANT MY LOVE	J. P. Morgan	Victor	40
67.	GEE WHITTAKERS	P. Boone	Dot	—
68.	THERE SHOULD BE RULES	B. Madigan	M-G-M	73
69.	AUTUMN LEAVES	J. Gleason	Capitol	61
69.	YELLOW ROSE OF TEXAS	J. Desmond	Coral	53
71.	NUTTIN' FOR CHRISTMAS	J. Ward	King	—
72.	BIBLE TELLS ME SO	D. Cornell	Coral	55
73.	MY BOY—FLAT TOP	B. Bennett	King	64
74.	TOO LATE NOW	DeCastro Sisters	Abbott	—
75.	LULLABY OF BIRDLAND	Blue Stars	Mercury	—
76.	TWENTY-FOUR HOURS A DAY	G. Gibbs	Mercury	74
77.	TIMES TWO I LOVE YOU	Chuckles	X	67
78.	AUTUMN LEAVES	V. Young	Decca	84
78.	MEMORIES ARE MADE OF THIS	M. Carson	Columbia	—
78.	NUTTIN' FOR CHRISTMAS	Fontane Sisters	Dot	—
81	SEARCHING	Hilltoppers	Dot	—
82.	NUTTIN' FOR CHRISTMAS	R. Zahnd	Columbia	—
83.	LOVE IS A MANY-SPLENDORED THING	D. Rose	M-G-M	68
84.	EVERYBODY'S GOT A HOME BUT ME	E. Fisher	Victor	—
84.	JAPANESE FAREWELL SONG	K. C. Jones	Marquee	82
86.	ARE YOU SATISFIED?	R. Draper	Mercury	—
86.	YELLOW ROSE OF TEXAS	S. Freberg	Capitol	66
88.	LEARNIN' TO LOVE	P. King	Columbia	—
89.	DAY BY DAY	Four Freshmen	Capitol	97
90.	SIXTEEN TONS	J. Desmond	Coral	59
90.	TEENAGERS WALTZ	E. Howard	Mercury	—
92.	PET ME PAPA	R. Clooney	Columbia	79
93.	SPEEDO	Cadillacs	Josie	75
93.	WHAT IS A WIFE	S. Allen	Coral	—
95.	ARE YOU SATISFIED?	S. Wooley	M-G-M	—
96.	LOVE IS A MANY-SPLENDORED THING	Don, Dick and Jimmy	Crown	—
96.	AMUKIRIKI	L. Paul & M. Ford	Capitol	65
98.	OF THIS I'M SURE	Four Aces	Decca	56
99.	SOMEONE ON YOUR MIND	C. Butler	Coral	—
100.	OO BANG	Doris Day	Columbia	92

CAUTION TO DEALERS AND JUKE BOX OPERATORS

The Billboard's Top 100 is NOT designed to provide tested information for buying purposes. This function is most reliably served by other regular weekly features: Best Sellers in Stores, Most Played in Juke Boxes, Coming Up Strong and Best Buys.

The Billboard Music Popularity Charts

POPULAR RECORDS

• Best Sellers in Stores

For survey week ending December 14

RECORDS are ranked in order of their current national selling importance at the retail level, as determined by The Billboard's weekly survey of the top volume dealers in every important market area. When significant action is reported on both sides of a record, points are combined to determine position on the chart. In such a case, both sides are listed in bold type, the leading side on top.

This Week	Record	Last Week	Weeks on Chart
1.	**SIXTEEN TONS** (BMI)—Tennessee Ernie You Don't Have to Be a Baby to Cry (ASCAP)—Cap 3262	1	7
2.	**MEMORIES ARE MADE OF THIS** (BMI)—D. Martin Change of Heart (BMI)—Cap 3295	2	4
3.	**I HEAR YOU KNOCKIN'** (BMI)—G. Storm Never Leave Me (ASCAP)—Dot 15412	4	10
4.	**MOMENTS TO REMEMBER** (ASCAP)—Four Lads Dream On, My Love, Dream On (ASCAP)—Col 40539	5	17
5.	**AUTUMN LEAVES** (ASCAP)—R. Williams Take Care (BMI)—Kapp 116	3	19
6.	**HE** (BMI)—A. Hibbler Breeze (ASCAP)—Dec 29660	9	13
7.	**ONLY YOU** (BMI)—Platters Bark, Battle and Ball (BMI)—Mercury 70633	7	13
7.	**LOVE AND MARRIAGE** (ASCAP)—F. Sinatra Impatient Years (ASCAP)—Cap 3260	8	7
9.	**LOVE IS A MANY-SPLENDORED THING** (ASCAP)—Four Aces Shine On, Harvest Moon (ASCAP)—Dec 29625	6	17
10.	**NUTTIN' FOR CHRISTMAS** (ASCAP)—B. Gordon-A. Mooney Santa Claus Looks Just Like Daddy (ASCAP)—M-G-M 12092	25	2
11.	**IT'S ALMOST TOMORROW** (ASCAP)—Dream Weavers You Got Me Wondering (ASCAP)—Dec 29683	10	7
12.	**SHIFTING, WHISPERING SANDS** (BMI)—R. Draper Time (ASCAP)—Mercury 70696	12	13
13.	**DADDY-O** (BMI)—Fontane Sisters Adorable (BMI)—Dot 15428	15	3
14.	**BAND OF GOLD** (BMI)—D. Cherry Rumble Boogie (BMI)—Col 40597	14	3
15.	**GREAT PRETENDER** (ASCAP)—Platters I'm Just a Dancing Partner (ASCAP)—Mercury 70753	—	1
16.	**ONLY YOU** (BMI)—Hilltoppers Until the Real Thing Comes Along (ASCAP)—Dot 15423	16	7
17.	**HE** (BMI)—McGuire Sisters If You Believe (ASCAP)—Coral 61501	13	9
18.	**ANGELS IN THE SKY** (BMI)—Crew Cuts Mostly Martha (BMI)—Mercury 70741	20	2
19.	**AT MY FRONT DOOR** (BMI)—P. Boone No Arms Can Ever Hold You (BMI)—Dot 15422	11	9
20.	**WOMAN IN LOVE** (ASCAP)—Four Aces Of This I'm Sure (ASCAP)—Dec 29725	—	1
21.	**NUTTIN' FOR CHRISTMAS** (ASCAP)—R. Zahnd Something Barked on Christmas (ASCAP)—Col 40576	—	1
22.	**NUTTIN' FOR CHRISTMAS** (ASCAP)—J. Ward Christmas Questions (BMI)—King 4854	—	1
22.	**BURN THAT CANDLE** (BMI)—B. Haley Rock-a-Beatin' Boogie (ASCAP)—Dec 29713	18	6
24.	**SHIFTING, WHISPERING SANDS (PARTS I & II)** (BMI)—B. Vaughn Dot 15409	17	14
25.	**WOMAN IN LOVE** (ASCAP)—F. Laine **Walking the Night Away—Col 40583**	19	2

• THIS WEEK'S BEST BUYS

According to sales reports in key markets, the following recent releases are recommended for extra profits:

TAKE ME BACK TO TOYLAND (Harvard, BMI)

I'M GONNA LAUGH YOU RIGHT OUT OF MY LIFE (Redd Evans, ASCAP)—**Nat (King) Cole—Capitol 3305**

While not a Christmas tune, "Toyland" has an aptness that is registering in a big way juke box-wise and in retail sales. At present it is the top side, but action on the flip is substantial enough to throw out the possibility that in time it might equal the acceptance of "Toyland." The disk was selling best in Los Anugeles, Cleveland, Milwaukee, St. Louis, Baltimore, Buffalo, Philadelphia, Pittsburgh, Nashville, Atlanta, Durham. A previous Billboard "Spotlight" pick.

THE ROCK AND ROLL WALTZ (Sheldon, BMI)—**Kay Starr—RCA Victor 6359**

The fastest breaking record for the thrush since she has been on the Victor label. In addition to being on the Los Angeles territorial chart this week, it is reported strong in Baltimore, Providence, Buffalo, Atlanta, St. Louis and Pittsburgh. "Waltz" is also a good seller in Philadelphia, Cleveland, Milwaukee and elsewhere. Flip is "I've Changed My Mind a Thousand Times" (Shapiro-Bernstein, ASCAP). A previous Billboard "Spotlight" pick.

• Most Played in Juke Boxes

For survey week ending December 14

RECORDS are ranked in order of the greatest number of plays in juke boxes thruout the country, as determined by The Billboard's weekly survey of the nation's juke box operators. When significant play is reported on both sides of a record, points are combined to determine position on the chart. In such a case, both sides are listed in bold type, the leading side on top.

This Week	Record	Last Week	Weeks on Chart
1.	**SIXTEEN TONS** (BMI)—Tennessee Ernie You Don't Have to Be a Baby to Cry (ASCAP)—Cap 3262	1	6
2.	**I HEAR YOU KNOCKIN'** (BMI)—G. Storm Never Leave Me (ASCAP)—Dot 15412	2	9
3.	**AUTUMN LEAVES** (ASCAP)—R. Williams Take Care (BMI)—Kapp 116	3	15
4.	**MOMENTS TO REMEMBER** (ASCAP)—Four Lads Dream On, My Love, Dream On (ASCAP)—Col 40539	4	11
4.	**SHIFTING, WHISPERING SANDS** (BMI)—R. Draper Time (ASCAP)—Mercury 70696	5	10
6.	**ONLY YOU** (BMI)—Platters Bark, Battle and Ball (BMI)—Mercury 70623	6	10
7.	**MEMORIES ARE MADE OF THIS** (BMI)—D. Martin Change of Heart (BMI)—Cap 3295	—	1
8.	**HE** (BMI)—A. Hibbler Breeze (ASCAP)—Dec 29660	8	9
8.	**LOVE AND MARRIAGE** (ASCAP)—F. Sinatra Impatient Years (ASCAP)—Cap 3260	10	3
10.	**LOVE IS A MANY-SPLENDORED THING** (ASCAP)—Four Aces Shine On, Harvest Moon (ASCAP)—Dec 29625	7	14
11.	**DADDY-O** (BMI)—Fontane Sisters Adorable (BMI)—Dot 15428	15	3
12.	**ONLY YOU** (BMI)—Hilltoppers Until the Real Thing Comes Along (ASCAP)—Dot 15423	11	6
13.	**AT MY FRONT DOOR** (BMI)—P. Boone No Arms Can Ever Hold You (BMI)—Dot 15422	9	8
14.	**HE** (BMI)—McGuire Sisters If You Believe (ASCAP)—Coral 51501	13	9
15.	**CRY ME A RIVER** (ASCAP)—J. London S'Wonderful (ASCAP)—Liberty 55006	14	2
15.	**BURN THAT CANDLE** (BMI)—B. Haley Rock-A-Beatin' Boogie (ASCAP)—Dec. 29713	20	3
17.	**SHIFTING, WHISPERING SANDS (PARTS I & II)**—B. Vaughn Dot 15409—BMI	12	12
17.	**PEPPER-HOT BABY** (BMI)—J. P. Morgan If You Don't Want My Love (ASCAP)—Vic 20-6282	—	4
19.	**IT'S ALMOST TOMORROW** (ASCAP)—Dream Weavers You Got Me Wondering (ASCAP)—Dec 29683	18	3
20.	**IT'S ALMOST TOMORROW** (ASCAP)—S. Lanson Stop—Dot 15424	—	1

• Most Played by Jockeys

For survey week ending December 14

SIDES are ranked in order of the greatest number of plays on disk jockey radio shows thruout the country. Results are based on The Billboard's weekly survey among the nation's disk jockeys. The reverse side of each record is also listed.

This Week	Record	Last Week	Weeks on Chart
1.	**SIXTEEN TONS** (BMI)—Tennessee Ernie You Don't Have to Be a Baby to Cry (ASCAP)—Cap 3262	1	7
2.	**MEMORIES ARE MADE OF THIS** (BMI)—D. Martin Change of Heart (BMI)—Cap 3295	2	3
3.	**MOMENTS TO REMEMBER** (ASCAP)—Four Lads Dream On, My Love, Dream On (ASCAP)—Col 40539	3	15
4.	**I HEAR YOU KNOCKIN'** (BMI)—G. Storm Never Leave Me (ASCAP)—Dot 15412	7	9
5.	**ONLY YOU** (BMI)—Platters Bark, Battle and Ball (BMI)—Mercury 70633	8	9
6.	**LOVE AND MARRIAGE** (ASCAP)—F. Sinatra Impatient Years (ASCAP)—Cap 3260	6	8
7.	**AUTUMN LEAVES** (ASCAP)—R. Williams Take Care (BMI)—Kapp 116	5	16
8.	**LOVE IS A MANY-SPLENDORED THING** (ASCAP)—Four Aces Shine On, Harvest Moon (ASCAP)—Dec 29625	4	18
9.	**ONLY YOU** (BMI)—Hilltoppers Until the Real Thing Comes Along (ASCAP)—Dot 15423	10	7
10.	**HE** (BMI)—A. Hibbler Breeze (ASCAP)—Dec 29660	11	11
11.	**C'EST LA VIE** (ASCAP)—S. Vaughan Never (ASCAP)—Mercury 70727	14	4
12.	**BAND OF GOLD** (BMI)—D. Cherry Rumble Boogie (BMI)—Col 40597	18	2
13.	**CRY ME A RIVER** (ASCAP)—J. London S'Wonderful (ASCAP)—Liberty 55006	9	4
14.	**WOMAN IN LOVE** (ASCAP)—Four Aces Of This I'm Sure (ASCAP)—Dec 29725	15	2
15.	**ALL AT ONCE YOU LOVE HER** (ASCAP)—P. Como Rose Tattoo (ASCAP)—Vic 20-6294	13	5
16.	**TENDER TRAP** (ASCAP)—F. Sinatra Weep They Will—Cap. 3290	17	2
17.	**YOU ARE MY LOVE** (ASCAP)—J. James I Lay Me Down to Sleep (BMI)—M-G-M 12066	16	10
18.	**DADDY-O** (BMI)—Fontane Sisters Adorable (BMI)—Dot 15428	20	3
19.	**IT'S ALMOST TOMORROW** (ASCAP)—Dream Weavers You Got Me Wondering (ASCAP)—Dec 29683	12	4
20.	**IT'S ALMOST TOMORROW** (ASCAP)—D. Carroll You Are Mine (BMI)—Mercury 70717	—	1

The Billboard Music Popularity Charts

• Reviews of New Pop Records

• *Continued from page 28*

by the Young strings. Good program wax. **(Northern, ASCAP)**

The Last Round-up....69
Another tasteful rendition of familiar material. Disk could double as moppet wax. **(Shapiro-Bernstein, ASCAP)**

CAROLE BENNETT

If You Have Faith in Me 70
RAMA 179—A pretty ballad with a strong lyric that makes an attractive vehicle for Miss Bennett. She has a fine voices; with it she socks home the emotional message of this tune impressively. **(Shale, ASCAP)**

Someday You'll Want Me to Want You....68
Again, with solid choral backing, the singer sings out uninhibitedly, this time on a standard. Her rendition is rather stylized, but pleasantly listenable. **(Duchess, BMI)**

EDDIE (LOCKJAW) DAVIS TRIO

A Foggy Day 69
KING 4863—Davis is a wailing tenor man, and he has a bawl with this oldie. Backed by organ and drums, he gives operators a swinging dance instrumental that all can use. **(Chappell, ASCAP)**

Together....68
Slowing the tempo a bit, Davis expertly styles another standard with taste here. Two good instrumentals that ought to enjoy long, steady sales. **(De Sylva, Brown and Henderson, ASCAP)**

THE FIVE ENCORES

Double Date 68
RAMA 180—Teen-agers should get some kicks from this side. It could pull occasional coin on the boxes.

Whistlin' Willie....66
Bouncy ditty is chanted pleasantly by the group. Makes for easy listening.

THE FIVE KINGS

The Story of Grand Central 68
PARKER 114—Jazz buyers and deejays in that field will find this of mild interest. The gal vocalist is Carrie Phillips. **(Parker, ASCAP)**

Holiday From the Blues....63
Routine performance of this bluesy item. A gal takes the vocal. **(Parker, ASCAP)**

PAT BOLTON

Don't Ask Me Why I Love You 67
JUBILEE 5229 — Elaborate ballad fails to impress in an over-expressive reading by Pat Bolton. **(Essex, ASCAP)**

The More I Go Out With Somebody Else....65
The songstress puts her all behind this heartfelt rendition. Small potential, tho. **(Barton, ASCAP)**

PHIL LUPINO

Chit-Chi-Chi-Chit 66
JESTER 2—Deejays in search of out-of-the-way material have a ready-made "discovery" in this pretty, gay Philippine folk song. The simple, catchy riff, with piano and flute playing tag with each other, could stir a lot of noise.

My Broken Guitar....62
A melancholy ballad, also picked up in the Philippines, is listenable material, but Lupino does only a fair job with it.

BARBARA McRITCHIE

You Wrote the Words 64
FULTON 111—A soprano with silver in her pipes, Miss McRitchie has a knowing way with a ballad. Her phrasing and sense of beat are noteworthy.

THE MELLOWMEN

Marseillaise....61
The French national anthem is not too likely a piece of material, but the quartet almost succeeds in making a fair case for it here. The drums and brass in the backing at least give it a festive, martial air.

THE MELLOWMEN

San Francisco 63
FULTON 114—A hymn of praise to the California city that is appealing in this bright arrangement. The male quartet turns in a competent harmony job.

Daddy's Lullaby....60
The baritone lead is featured in a quiet, tasteful slumber tune. Pretty, but has limited commercial potential.

• Reviews of New Pop-Christmas Records

LYNNE RICHARDS

Christmas Lullaby 71
STYLECRAFT 5043—This Christmas song is a finely written piece, and it is excellently sung by Lynne Richards. Should get deejay play and will appeal to adults. **(BMI)**

You'll Find Santa There....70
This one, also a good ditty, is slanted to the kiddies. Makes a nice coupling. **(BMI)**

• Reviews of New Sacred Records

THE STAMPS QUARTET

The Road That Leads to Tomorrow (Is the Road That Leads to God)....74
COLUMBIA 21476—A strong group vocal reading on a moving sacred item. **(Stamps Quartet, SESAC)**

It Won't Be Very Long Now....72
The quartet registers decisively on a good-natured spiritual with an infectious beat. **(Stamps Quartet, SESAC)**

• Reviews of New Childrens Records

ROBERT EMERICKS, GWEN DAVIES AND GILBERT MACK

The Three Little Pigs (Parts 1 and 2)...79
MERCURY MP 31 — A well-packaged, well-performed, well-recorded version of the standard favorite, pressed on a good quality disk, has to do excellent business at Christmas and most other times when kidisks move. One of the comparatively few new platters suitable for pre-school tots.

JUNE WINTERS

The Good Ship Lollipop; Tootles the Tug 76
MERCURY MP 32 — Attractive, glossy package houses two nautical themes. The first side is a durable standard, and the flip is a song story that barely does justice to a favorite moppet theme. The sort of stuff bachelor uncles will pick out for Christmas.

JUNE WINTERS

Little Willie, the Leader of the Band (Parts 1 and 2)........76
MERCURY MP 30—In simplified form, this duplicates the lesson of "Sparky's Magic Piano," but on one 78 r.p.m. disk. Actually for musical beginners, some pre-school tots will take to it also.

JUNE WINTERS

The Little White Duck; Hatchy Milatchy 76
MERCURY MP 33 — Two kiddie tunes that have been around, with the former now established as a big standard via the Burl Ives and Danny Kaye versions. The sock packaging of this issue will attract Christmas buyers. For all ages.

• Reviews of New Polka Records

LI'L WALLY

Roll Out the Barrell Polka...........70
JAY JAY 147—Rather weak group vocalizing on the gay old polka standard. Instrumentally, tho, the disk has plenty of verve and should do well juke-wise.

Happy Anniversary Waltz....70
A sentimental, old-fashioned waxing with a strong dancing tempo.

• Reviews of New Spiritual Records

THE PROGRESSIVEAIRES

The Bongos Are Beating Out Salvation 70
D-C 228—This is a new wrinkle for this type of music: Bongos introduce and punctuate this spiritual, undeniably adding considerable excitement. Not all will approve, but plenty of interest will be shown nonetheless. **(Four Star Sales, BMI)**

When We All Get Together With the Lord....65
A more conventionally arranged spiritual sung with good harmony but faltering beat. **(Four Star Sales, BMI)**

THE RADIO FOUR

Sending Up a Prayer Parts 1 & 2 67
NASHBORO 568—Excellent warbling stint by the Radio Four on a moving two-part spiritual, with a particularly warm, sincere job by the lead singer. **(BMI)**

POPULAR RECORDS

THE TOP 100

For survey week ending December 7

A list of the Top 100 **RECORD SIDES** in the nation according to a **COMBINED TABULATION** of Dealer, Disk Jockey and Juke Box Operator replies to The Billboard's weekly popular record Best Seller and Most Played surveys. Its purpose is to provide Disk Jockeys with additional programming material and to give trade exposure to NEWER records just beginning to show action in the field.

This Week	Song	Artist	Label	Week Last
1.	SIXTEEN TONS	T. Ernie	Capitol	1
2.	I HEAR YOU KNOCKIN'	G. Storm	Dot	4
3.	MOMENTS TO REMEMBER	Four Lads	Columbia	3
3.	MEMORIES ARE MADE OF THIS	D. Martin	Capitol	8
5.	AUTUMN LEAVES	R. Williams	Kapp	2
6.	ONLY YOU	Platters	Mercury	6
7.	LOVE AND MARRIAGE	F. Sinatra	Capitol	7
8.	HE	A. Hibbler	Decca	9
9.	LOVE IS A MANY-SPLENDORED THING	Four Aces	Decca	5
10.	ONLY YOU	Hilltoppers	Dot	10
11.	DADDY-O	Fontane Sisters	Dot	13
12.	IT'S ALMOST TOMORROW	Dream Weavers	Decca	11
13.	HE	McGuire Sisters	Coral	16
13.	CRY ME A RIVER	J. London	Liberty	17
15.	SHIFTING, WHISPERING SANDS	R. Draper	Mercury	13
16.	SHIFTING, WHISPERING SANDS	B. Vaughn	Dot	15
17.	AT MY FRONT DOOR	P. Boone	Dot	12
18.	NUTTIN' FOR CHRISTMAS	B. Gordon-A. Mooney	M-G-M	62
19.	WOMAN IN LOVE	Four Aces	Decca	23
20.	BAND OF GOLD	D. Cherry	Columbia	29
21.	ANGELS IN THE SKY	Crew Cuts	Mercury	32
21.	GREAT PRETENDER	Platters	Mercury	41
23.	C'EST LA VIE	S. Vaughan	Mercury	22
24.	ALL AT ONCE YOU LOVE HER	P. Como	Victor	24
24.	YOU ARE MY LOVE	J. James	M-G-M	18
26.	IT'S ALMOST TOMORROW	S. Lanson	Dot	20
26.	NUTTIN' FOR CHRISTMAS	J. Ward	King	71
28.	IT'S ALMOST TOMORROW	J. Stafford	Columbia	20
29.	SUDDENLY THERE'S A VALLEY	J. Stafford	Columbia	26
29.	BURN THAT CANDLE	B. Haley	Decca	27
31.	CROCE DI ORO (CROSS OF GOLD)	P. Page	Mercury	19
31.	WOMAN IN LOVE	F. Laine	Columbia	33
33.	MEMORIES OF YOU	Four Coins	Epic	30
34.	PEPPER HOT BABY	J. P. Morgan	Victor	34
35.	TEEN-AGE PRAYER	G. Storm	Dot	—
36.	DUNGAREE DOLL	E. Fisher	Victor	63
37.	DOLLY'S OH SUSANNA	D. Charles-Singing Dogs	Victor	40
38.	GEE WHITTAKERS	P. Boone	Dot	67
38.	SUDDENLY THERE'S A VALLEY	G. Grant	Era	25
40.	TEEN-AGE PRAYER	G. Mann	Sound	54
40.	TENDER TRAP	F. Sinatra	Capitol	45
42.	IT'S ALMOST TOMORROW	D. Carroll	Mercury	34
43.	NO ARMS CAN EVER HOLD YOU	P. Boone	Dot	30
44.	MY BOY FLAT TOP	D. Collins	Coral	44
45.	FORGIVE MY HEART	Nat (King) Cole	Capitol	39
46.	LISBON ANTIGUA	N. Riddle	Capitol	43
47.	BAND OF GOLD	K. Carson	Capitol	48
48.	ROCK-A-BEATIN' BOOGIE	B. Haley	Decca	57
48.	MY BONNIE LASSIE	Ames Brothers	Victor	37
50.	YELLOW ROSE OF TEXAS	M. Miller	Columbia	34
51.	IF YOU DON'T WANT MY LOVE	J. P. Morgan	Victor	66
52.	WHEN YOU DANCE	Turbans	Herald	42
53.	WHITE CHRISTMAS	Bing Crosby	Decca	—
54.	MOSTLY MARTHA	Crew Cuts	Mercury	—
54.	MEMORIES ARE MADE OF THIS	G. Storm	Dot	—
56.	NO ARMS CAN EVER HOLD YOU	G. Shaw	Decca	28
57.	AUTUMN LEAVES	V. Young	Decca	78
58.	ARE YOU SATISFIED	R. Draper	Mercury	86
58.	NUTTIN' FOR CHRISTMAS	Fontane Sisters	Dot	78
58.	NUTTIN' FOR CHRISTMAS	R. Zahnd	Columbia	82
61.	AUTUMN LEAVES	J. Gleason	Capitol	69
62.	PET ME POPPA	R. Clooney	Columbia	92
63.	THERE SHOULD BE RULES	B. Madigan	M-G-M	68
63.	WANTING YOU	R. Williams	Kapp	57
65.	LOVE AND MARRIAGE	D. Shore	Victor	47
65.	MY BELIEVING HEART	J. James	M-G-M	57
67.	LOVE IS A MANY-SPLENDORED THING	D. Cornell	Coral	57
68.	EVERYBODY'S GOT A HOME BUT ME	E. Fisher	Victor	84
69.	SIXTEEN TONS	J. Desmond	Coral	90
70.	AUTUMN LEAVES	M. Miller	Columbia	50
71.	NUTTIN' FOR CHRISTMAS	S. Freberg	Capitol	—
71.	GOODBYE TO ROME	G. Gibbs	Mercury	51
73.	SOMEONE YOU LOVE	Nat (King) Cole	Capitol	38
74.	BIBLE TELLS ME SO	D. Cornell	Coral	72
75.	DADDY-O	B. Lou	King	64
76.	AUTUMN LEAVES	S. Allen	Coral	56
77.	SOMEONE ON YOUR MIND	C. Butler	Coral	99
78.	WHAT IS A WIFE	S. Allen	Coral	93
79.	SEVENTEEN	Fontane Sisters	Dot	51
80.	TOO LATE NOW	De Castro Sisters	Abbott	74
81.	SUDDENLY THERE'S A VALLEY	Mills Brothers	Decca	55
82.	NOT ONE GOODBYE	J. P. Morgan	Victor	—
82.	CHARMAINE	Four Freshmen	Capitol	—
84.	LULLABY OF BIRDLAND	Blue Stars	Mercury	75
85.	ZAMBESI	L. Busch	Capitol	—
86.	EVERYBODY'S GOT A HOME BUT ME	R. Hamilton	Epic	—
86.	SUDDENLY THERE'S A VALLEY	J. La Rosa	Cadence	45
86.	CROCE DI ORO (CROSS OF GOLD)	J. Regan	London	—
89.	YELLOW ROSE OF TEXAS	S. Freberg	Capitol	86
90.	SUDDENLY THERE'S A VALLEY	P. Andrews	Capitol	—
91.	JAPANESE FAREWELL SONG	K. C. Jones	Marquee	84
91.	TWENTY-FOUR HOURS A DAY	G. Gibbs	Mercury	76
93.	SPEEDOO	Cadillacs	Josie	93
94.	C'EST LA VIE	S. Gale	Victor	—
95.	AUTUMN LEAVES	R. Charles Singers	M-G-M	—
95.	MEMORIES ARE MADE OF THIS	M. Carson	Columbia	78
97.	LOVE IS A MANY-SPLENDORED THING	D. Rose	M-G-M	83
98.	BLACK DENIM TROUSERS	Cheers	Capitol	53
98.	AIN'T THAT A SHAME	P. Boone	Dot	—
100.	OO BANG	Doris Day	Columbia	100

CAUTION TO DEALERS AND JUKE BOX OPERATORS

The Billboard's Top 100 is NOT designed to provide tested information for buying purposes. This function is most reliably served by other regular weekly features: Best Sellers in Stores, Most Played in Juke Boxes, Coming Up Strong and Best Buys.

The Billboard Music Popularity Charts — POPULAR RECORDS

• Best Sellers in Stores

For survey week ending December 21

RECORDS are ranked in order of their current national selling importance at the retail level, as determined by The Billboard's weekly survey of the top volume dealers in every important market area. When significant action is reported on both sides of a record, points are combined to determine position on the chart. In such a case, both sides are listed in bold type, the leading side on top.

This Week	Record	Last Week	Weeks on Chart
1.	SIXTEEN TONS (BMI)—Tennessee Ernie You Don't Have to Be a Baby to Cry (ASCAP)—Cap 3262	1	8
2.	MEMORIES ARE MADE OF THIS (BMI)—D. Martin Change of Heart (BMI)—Cap 3295	2	5
3.	I HEAR YOU KNOCKIN' (BMI)—G. Storm Never Leave Me (ASCAP)—Dot 15412	3	11
4.	HE (BMI)—A. Hibbler Breeze (ASCAP)—Dec 29660	6	14
5.	MOMENTS TO REMEMBER—(ASCAP)—Four Lads Dream On, My Love, Dream On (ASCAP)—Col 40539	4	18
6.	AUTUMN LEAVES (ASCAP)—R. Williams Take Care (BMI)—Kapp 116	5	20
7.	LOVE AND MARRIAGE (ASCAP)—F. Sinatra Impatient Years (ASCAP)—Cap 3260	7	8
8.	NUTTIN' FOR CHRISTMAS (ASCAP)—B. Gordon-A. Mooney Santa Claus Looks Just Like Daddy (ASCAP)—M-G-M 12092	10	3
9.	ONLY YOU (BMI)—Platters Bark, Battle and Ball (BMI)—Mercury 70633	7	14
10.	LOVE IS A MANY-SPLENDORED THING (ASCAP)—Four Aces Shine On, Harvest Moon (ASCAP)—Dec. 29625	9	18
11.	GREAT PRETENDER (ASCAP)—Platters I'm Just a Dancing Partner (ASCAP)—Mercury 70753	15	2
12.	IT'S ALMOST TOMORROW (ASCAP)—Dream Weavers You Got Me Wondering (ASCAP)—Dec 29683	11	8
13.	BAND OF GOLD (BMI)—D. Cherry Rumble Boogie (BMI)—Col 40597	14	4
14.	HE (BMI)—McGuire Sisters If You Believe (ASCAP)—Coral 61501	17	10
15.	DUNGAREE DOLL (BMI)—E. Fisher Everybody's Got a Home But Me (ASCAP)—Vic 20-6337	—	1
16.	SHIFTING, WHISPERING SANDS (BMI)—R. Draper Time (ASCAP)—Mercury 70696	12	14
17.	ANGELS IN THE SKY (BMI)—Crew Cuts Mostly Martha (BMI)—Mercury 70741	18	3
18.	DADDY-O (BMI)—Fontane Sisters Adorable (BMI)—Dot 15428	13	4
19.	ONLY YOU (BMI)—Hilltoppers Until the Real Thing Comes Along (ASCAP)—Dot 15423	16	8
20.	TEEN-AGE PRAYER (ASCAP)—G. Storm **MEMORIES ARE MADE OF THIS** (BMI)—Dot 15436	—	1
21.	LISBON ANTIGUA (ASCAP) N. Riddle Robin Hood (ASCAP)—Cap 3287	—	1
22.	BURN THAT CANDLE (BMI)—B. Haley Rock-A-Beatin' Boogie (ASCAP)—Dec 29713	22	7
23.	NUTTIN' FOR CHRISTMAS (ASCAP)—R. Zahnd Something Barked on Christmas (ASCAP)—Col 40576	21	2
23.	CRY ME A RIVER (ASCAP)—J. London S'Wonderful (ASCAP)—Liberty 55006	—	1
25.	SHIFTING, WHISPERING SANDS (PARTS I & II) (BMI)—B. Vaughn Dot 15409	24	15

• THIS WEEK'S BEST BUYS

According to sales reports in key markets, the following recent releases are recommended for extra profits:

MY TREASURE (Song Smiths, ASCAP)—**The Hilltoppers—Dot 15437**

The early appearance of this disk on the Minneapolis-St. Paul chart is indicative of the fast progress the Hilltoppers' latest release has been making. Strength of the disk was centered in various Midwestern areas like St. Louis, Kansas City, Milwaukee, Cincinnati and Cleveland. On the East Coast, Baltimore, Providence, Boston and Philadelphia also reported excellent volume. Flip is "The Last Word in Love" (Randy-Smith, ASCAP).

BE GOOD TO ME (Bregman, Vocco & Conn, ASCAP)

MY BABY'S GOT SUCH LOVIN' WAYS (Pincus, ASCAP)—**McGuire Sisters—Coral 61532**

The solid string of hits that the McGuires have to their credit should be extended with their most recent issue. It has taken off in Chicago, Milwaukee, Nashville, Durham, St. Louis, Pittsburgh, Buffalo, Philadelphia, Boston and other cities. So far action has been good on both sides, with no clear-cut preference at this point. A previous Billboard "Spotlight" pick.

GO ON WITH THE WEDDING (Pincus, ASCAP)—**Patti Page—Mercury 70766**

GO ON WITH THE WEDDING (Pincus, ASCAP) — **Kitty Kallen and Georgie Shaw — Decca 29776**

One of the most active tunes this past week. Patti Page's version was the leading seller in most territories; it racked up in usually good sales on both the retail and juke box levels in Boston, Philadelphia, Providence, Baltimore, St. Louis, Cleveland, Buffalo and Pittsburgh. The Decca record showed a similarly wide spread of acceptance in territories thruout the country, but generally was a shade under the Page disk sales-wise. Both have excellent chart potential. "The Voice Inside" (Laurel, ASCAP) is the reverse of Miss Page's record; "The Second Greatest Sex" (Northern, ASCAP) is the flip of the Kallen-Shaw wax.

• Most Played in Juke Boxes

For survey week ending December 21

RECORDS are ranked in order of the greatest number of plays in juke boxes thruout the country, as determined by The Billboard's weekly survey of the nation's juke box operators. When significant play is reported on both sides of a record, points are combined to determine position on the chart. In such a case, both sides are listed in bold type, the leading side on top.

This Week	Record	Last Week	Weeks on Chart
1.	SIXTEEN TONS (BMI)—Tennessee Ernie You Don't Have to Be a Baby to Cry (ASCAP)—Cap 3262	1	7
2.	MEMORIES ARE MADE OF THIS (BMI)—D. Martin Change of Heart (BMI)—Cap 3295	7	2
3.	I HEAR YOU KNOCKIN' (BMI)—G. Storm Never Leave Me (ASCAP)—Dot 15412	2	10
4.	MOMENTS TO REMEMBER (ASCAP)—Four Lads Dream On, My Love, Dream On (ASCAP)—Col 40539	4	12
5.	AUTUMN LEAVES (ASCAP)—R. Williams Take Care (BMI)—Kapp 116	3	16
6.	ONLY YOU (BMI)—Platters Bark, Battle and Ball (BMI)—Mercury 70623	6	11
7.	SHIFTING, WHISPERING SANDS (BMI)—R. Draper Time (ASCAP)—Mercury 70696	4	11
8.	HE (BMI)—A. Hibbler Breeze (ASCAP)—Dec 29660	8	10
9.	LOVE AND MARRIAGE (ASCAP)—F. Sinatra Impatient Years (ASCAP)—Cap 3260	8	4
9.	LOVE IS A MANY-SPLENDORED THING (ASCAP)—Four Aces Shine On Harvest Moon (ASCAP)—Dec 29625	10	15
11.	DADDY-O (BMI)—Fontane Sisters Adorable (BMI)—Dot 15428	11	4
12.	BURN THAT CANDLE (BMI)—B. Haley **ROCK-A-BEATIN' BOOGIE** (ASCAP)—Dec 29713	15	4
13.	IT'S ALMOST TOMORROW (ASCAP)—Dream Weavers You Got Me Wondering (ASCAP)—Dec 29683	19	4
14.	NUTTIN' FOR CHRISTMAS (ASCAP)—B. Gordon-A. Mooney Santa Claus Looks Just Like Daddy (ASCAP)—M-G-M 12092	—	1
15.	ONLY YOU (BMI)—Hilltoppers Until the Real Thing Comes Along (ASCAP)—Dot 15423	12	7
16.	PEPPER HOT BABY (BMI)—J. P. Morgan If You Don't Want My Love (ASCAP)—Vic 20-6282	17	5
17.	HE (BMI)—McGuire Sisters If You Believe (ASCAP)—Coral 51501	14	10
18.	TEEN-AGE PRAYER (ASCAP)—G. Storm Memories Are Made of This (BMI)—Dot 15436	—	1
19.	CRY ME A RIVER (ASCAP)—J. London S'Wonderful (ASCAP)—Liberty 55006	15	3
20.	AT MY FRONT DOOR (BMI)—P. Boone No Arms Can Ever Hold You (BMI)—Dot 15422	13	9
20.	NUTTIN' FOR CHRISTMAS (ASCAP)—J. Ward Christmas Questions (ASCAP)—King 4854	—	1

• Most Played by Jockeys

For survey week ending December 21

SIDES are ranked in order of the greatest number of plays on disk jockey radio shows thruout the country. Results are based on The Billboard's weekly survey among the nation's disk jockeys. The reverse side of each record is also listed.

This Week	Record	Last Week	Weeks on Chart
1.	SIXTEEN TONS (BMI)—Tennessee Ernie You Don't Have to Be a Baby to Cry (ASCAP)—Cap 3262	1	8
2.	MEMORIES ARE MADE OF THIS (BMI)—D. Martin Change of Heart (BMI)—Cap 3295	2	4
3.	MOMENTS TO REMEMBER (ASCAP)—Four Lads Dream on, My Love, Dream On (ASCAP)—Col 40539	3	16
4.	I HEAR YOU KNOCKIN' (BMI)—G. Storm Never Leave Me (ASCAP)—Dot 15412	4	10
5.	LOVE AND MARRIAGE (ASCAP)—F. Sinatra Impatient Years (ASCAP)—Cap 3260	6	9
6.	ONLY YOU (BMI)—Platters Bark, Battle and Ball (BMI)—Mercury 70633	5	10
7.	GREAT PRETENDER (ASCAP)—Platters I'm Just a Dancing Partner (ASCAP)—Mercury 70753	—	1
8.	ONLY YOU (BMI)—Hilltoppers Until the Real Thing Comes Along (ASCAP)—Dot 15423	9	8
9.	BAND OF GOLD (BMI)—D. Cherry Rumble Boogie (BMI)—Col 40597	12	3
10.	NUTTIN' FOR CHRISTMAS (ASCAP)—B. Gordon-A. Mooney Santa Claus Looks Just Like Daddy (ASCAP)—M-G-M 12092	—	1
11.	BAND OF GOLD (BMI)—K. Carson Cast Your Bread Upon the Waters—Cap 3283	—	1
12.	AUTUMN LEAVES (ASCAP)—R. Williams Take Care (BMI)—Kapp 116	7	17
13.	MEMORIES ARE MADE OF THIS (BMI)—G. Storm Teen-Age Prayer (ASCAP)—Dot 15436	—	1
14.	TENDER TRAP (ASCAP)—F. Sinatra Weep They Will—Cap 3290	16	3
15.	IT'S ALMOST TOMORROW (ASCAP)—Dream Weavers You Got Me Wondering (ASCAP)—Dec 29683	19	5
16.	LOVE IS A MANY-SPLENDORED THING (ASCAP)—Four Aces Shine On Harvest Moon (ASCAP)—Dec 29625	8	19
17.	HE (BMI)—A. Hibbler Breeze (ASCAP)—Dec 29660	10	12
18.	CRY ME A RIVER (ASCAP)—J. London S'Wonderful (ASCAP)—Liberty 55006	13	5
19.	C'EST LA VIE (ASCAP)—S. Vaughan Never (ASCAP)—Mercury 70727	11	5
20.	EVERYBODY'S GOT A HOME BUT ME (ASCAP)—E. Fisher Dungaree Doll (BMI)—Vic 20-6337	—	1

The Billboard Music Popularity Charts

POPULAR RECORDS

THE TOP 100

For survey week ending December 14

A list of the **Top 100 RECORD SIDES** in the nation according to a **COMBINED TABULATION** of Dealer, Disk Jockey and Juke Box Operator replies to The Billboard's weekly popular record Best Seller and Most Played surveys. Its purpose is to provide Disk Jockeys with additional programming material and to give trade exposure to NEWER records just beginning to show action in the field.

This Week	Song	Artist	Label	Week Last
1.	SIXTEEN TONS	T. Ernie	Capitol	1
2.	MEMORIES ARE MADE OF THIS	D. Martin	Capitol	3
3.	I HEAR YOU KNOCKIN'	G. Storm	Dot	2
4.	MOMENTS TO REMEMBER	Four Lads	Columbia	3
5.	ONLY YOU	Platters	Mercury	6
5.	LOVE AND MARRIAGE	F. Sinatra	Capitol	7
7.	AUTUMN LEAVES	R. Williams	Kapp	5
8.	HE	A. Hibbler	Decca	8
9.	NUTTIN' FOR CHRISTMAS	B. Gordon & A. Mooney	M-G-M	18
10.	LOVE IS A MANY-SPLENDORED THING	Four Aces	Decca	9
11.	IT'S ALMOST TOMORROW	Dream Weavers	Decca	12
12.	GREAT PRETENDER	Platters	Mercury	21
13.	ONLY YOU	Hilltoppers	Dot	10
14.	CRY ME A RIVER	J. London	Liberty	13
15.	DADDY-O	Fontane Sisters	Dot	11
16.	DUNGAREE DOLL	E. Fisher	Victor	37
17.	HE	McGuire Sisters	Coral	13
18.	BAND OF GOLD	D. Cherry	Columbia	20
19.	TEEN-AGE PRAYER	G. Storm	Dot	35
20.	BURN THAT CANDLE	B. Haley	Decca	29
21.	ANGELS IN THE SKY	Crew Cuts	Mercury	21
22.	NUTTIN' FOR CHRISTMAS	J. Ward	King	26
23.	SHIFTING, WHISPERING SANDS	R. Draper	Mercury	15
24.	WHITE CHRISTMAS	Bing Crosby	Decca	53
25.	ARE YOU SATISFIED?	R. Draper	Mercury	58
26.	MEMORIES ARE MADE OF THIS	G. Storm	Dot	54
27.	YOU ARE MY LOVE	J. James	M-G-M	24
28.	AT MY FRONT DOOR	P. Boone	Dot	17
29.	SHIFTING, WHISPERING SANDS	B. Vaughn	Dot	16
30.	IT'S ALMOST TOMORROW	S. Lanson	Dot	26
31.	WOMAN IN LOVE	Four Aces	Decca	19
32.	PEPPER-HOT BABY	J. P. Morgan	Victor	34
33.	GEE WHITTAKERS	P. Boone	Dot	38
34.	LISBON ANTIGUA	N. Riddle	Capitol	46
35.	MEMORIES OF YOU	Four Coins	Epic	33
36.	NUTTIN' FOR CHRISTMAS	Fontane Sisters	Dot	58
37.	TEEN-AGE PRAYER	G. Mann	Sound	40
38.	WOMAN IN LOVE	F. Laine	Columbia	31
39.	BAND OF GOLD	K. Carson	Capitol	47
40.	IT'S ALMOST TOMORROW	J. Stafford	Columbia	28
41.	C'EST LA VIE	S. Vaughan	Mercury	23
42.	ALL AT ONCE YOU LOVE HER	P. Como	Victor	24
43.	TENDER TRAP	F. Sinatra	Capitol	40
43.	DOLLY'S OH! SUZANNA	D. Charles-Singing Dogs	Victor	37
45.	NUTTIN' FOR CHRISTMAS	R. Zahnd	Columbia	58
46.	CROCE DI ORO (CROSS OF GOLD)	P. Page	Mercury	31
47.	ROCK AND ROLL WALTZ	K. Starr	Capitol	—
48.	WANTING YOU	R. Williams	Kapp	63
49.	MOSTLY MARTHA	Crew Cuts	Mercury	54
50.	SIXTEEN TONS	J. Desmond	Coral	69
51.	IT'S ALMOST TOMORROW	D. Carroll	Mercury	42
51.	LOVE AND MARRIAGE	D. Shore	Victor	65
53.	NO ARMS CAN EVER HOLD YOU	P. Boone	Dot	43
54.	GOODBYE TO ROME	G. Gibbs	Mercury	71
55.	DADDY-O	B. Lou	King	75
56.	MY BOY—FLAT TOP	D. Collins	Coral	44
57.	WHEN YOU DANCE	Turbans	Herald	52
58.	EVERYBODY'S GOT A HOME BUT ME	E. Fisher	Victor	58
59.	NUTTIN' FOR CHRISTMAS	S. Freberg	Capitol	71
60.	MY BONNIE LASSIE	Ames Brothers	Victor	48
61.	SUDDENLY THERE'S A VALLEY	J. Stafford	Columbia	29
62.	AUTUMN LEAVES	M. Miller	Columbia	70
63.	ROCK-A-BEATIN BOOGIE	B. Haley	Decca	48
64.	NO ARMS CAN EVER HOLD YOU	G. Shaw	Decca	56
65.	FORGIVE MY HEART	Nat (King) Cole	Capitol	45
66.	LULLABY OF BIRDLAND	Blue Stars	Mercury	84
67.	AUTUMN LEAVES	S. Allen	Coral	76
68.	YELLOW ROSE OF TEXAS	M. Miller	Columbia	50
68.	AUTUMN LEAVES	J. Gleason	Capitol	61
68.	EVERYBODY'S GOT A HOME BUT ME	R. Hamilton	Epic	86
71.	SOMEONE YOU LOVE	Nat (King) Cole	Capitol	73
72.	BIBLE TELLS ME SO	D. Cornell	Coral	74
72.	MEMORIES ARE MADE OF THIS	M. Carson	Columbia	95
72.	NOT ONE GOODBYE	J. P. Morgan	Victor	82
75.	SUDDENLY THERE'S A VALLEY	G. Grant	Era	38
76.	CROCE DI ORO (CROSS OF GOLD)	J. Regan	London	86
77.	TOYLAND	Nat (King) Cole	Capitol	—
78.	DOG-FACED SOLDIER	R. Morgan	Decca	—
79.	ADORABLE	Fontane Sisters	Dot	—
80.	WHITE CHRISTMAS	Drifters	Atlantic	—
81.	THERE SHOULD BE RULES	B. Madigan	M-G-M	63
82.	TEEN-AGE PRAYER	K. White	Mercury	—
83.	MY BOY—FLAT TOP	B. Bennett	King	—
84.	SNOWBOUND FOR CHRISTMAS	DeCastro Sisters	Abbott	—
85.	MY BELIEVING HEART	J. James	M-G-M	65
85.	YELLOW ROSE OF TEXAS	J. Desmond	Coral	—
87.	AT MY FRONT DOOR	El Dorados	Vee Jay	—
88.	C'EST LA VIE	S. Gale	Victor	94
88.	SEVENTEEN	Fontane Sisters	Dot	79
90.	TWENTY-FOUR HOURS A DAY	G. Gibbs	Mercury	—
90.	PET ME POPPA	R. Clooney	Columbia	62
92.	JAPANESE FAREWELL SONG	K. C. Jones	Marquee	91
93.	OF THIS I'M SURE	Four Aces	Decca	—
95.	IF YOU DON'T WANT MY LOVE	J. P. Morgan	Victor	51
96.	AMUKIRIKI	L. Paul & M. Ford	Capitol	—
97.	NO ARMS CAN EVER HOLD YOU	Gaylords	Mercury	—
98.	WHAT IS A WIFE	S. Allen	Coral	78
99.	LOVE IS A MANY-SPLENDORED THING	D. Rose	M-G-M	97
99.	MY TREASURE	Hilltoppers	Dot	—
99.	AUTUMN LEAVES	V. Young	Decca	57

CAUTION TO DEALERS AND JUKE BOX OPERATORS

The Billboard's Top 100 is NOT designed to provide tested information for buying purposes. This function is most reliably served by other regular weekly features: Best Sellers in Stores, Most Played in Juke Boxes, Coming Up Strong and Best Buys.

Col-LP Plan

• *Continued from page 10*

selling items to grab off sales on slower selling LP's which they may not carry in stock.

About 400 LP's have been placed in a "great standard album" category, any one of which may be "sold" by dealers, beginning February 2, by a coupon set-up. Established dealers will be given, at no cost, a binder liisting all LP's available under the plan. Quantities of coupons will also be supplied which the dealer will use to complete the sale with his customer.

Coupons will be sent to a new Columbia facility at Terre Haute, Ind., which will mail the ordered album direct to the consumer or to the store, whichever is indicated. Tho dealers will collect from consumers when the sale is made at the counter, stores will be billed later.

On sales completed in this manner, distributors will bill dealers at 25 per cent off the list price, rather than the normal discount. If the dealer elects to stock sets in this category, he may place orders twice a year, in March and in September. In this case, of course, the full discount is allowed.

85 Cents Each

The third major facet of "Operation Quicksilver" will provide for delivery of an ample supply of demonstration LP's to dealers at low cost. Cost per 12-incher to dealers subscribing to the plan will be 85 cents each.

To come into the plan, dealers may order a basic library of demonstration material consisting of 100 pre-selected LP's in all repertoire categories for $85. This catalog material will be supplemented at the rate of three to five LP's a month at an additional cost of 85 cents per 12-incher. Disks will be regular pressings in commercial jackets, but will sport a "not for sale" slug on labels.

With the debuting of the new merchandising program, Columbia will also promote heavily a bumper crop of new packages in the classical, pop, jazz and children's categories. Heaviest push will be given a set of Benny Goodman LP's in a two-month promotion commemorating the 25th year since the orkster first recorded for the label. This program, described in an earlier story, will be accompanied by the availability of a large number of dealer selling aids.

On the new artist line-up, major stress will be placed on three new pianist acquisitions—Glenn Gould, Villegas, and Leon Fleisher.

Single Sales

Singles sales will also come in for special attention, with first plug releases to include new sides by Jill Corey, Jack Paar and Vic Damone. The Corey release will be kicked off by a U. S. Steel Hour drama over CBS-TV January 4, in which the disk, featuring the ditty "Wait for Tomorrow," will be played in its entirety three times. The platter figures as integral part of the seg.

Columbia merchandising and sales execs who will introduce "Quicksilver" to the diskery's 37 distributors next week include Hal Cook, Bill Gallagher, Jack Loetz, Stan Kavan, Jack Fuller, Art Schwartz, Peter Munves, Gil McKean and Irv Towsend. They will be joined by Columbia district men Paul Peppin, Gene Block, Tom Cade, Warner Pagliara, Ken Glancy, Gene Weiss, Arnold Klein, Fred Wilmot and Jim Turnbull.

Mercury Plans

• *Continued from page 10*

searchist-publicist Eileen Mack to conduct a special survey of the album field, and her findings will be incorporated into the label's over-all LP production plan for 1956. Mercury's new subsidiary Wing will also put special emphasis on package goods next year.

Cincinnati

RCA Victor's **Al Calders** was in from New York for several days last week to contact the local deejays on **Kay Starr's** "Rock 'n' Roll Waltz" He left here **Thursday** (22) for **Pittsburgh.**

The Billboard Music Popularity Charts

COUNTRY & WESTERN RECORDS

• Best Sellers in Stores

For survey week ending December 21

RECORDS are ranked in order of their current national selling importance at the retail level, as determined by The Billboard's weekly survey of dealers thruout the nation with a high volume of sales in country and western records. When significant action is reported on both sides of a record, points are combined to determine position on the chart. In such a case, both sides are listed in bold type, the leading side on top.

This Week	Record	Last Week	Weeks on Chart
1.	**SIXTEEN TONS** (BMI)—Tennessee Ernie You Don't Have to Be a Baby to Cry (ASCAP)—Cap 3262	1	8
2.	**LOVE, LOVE, LOVE** (BMI)—W. Pierce If You Were Me (BMI)—Dec 29662	2	15
3.	**JUST CALL ME LONESOME** (BMI)—E. Arnold That Do Make It Nice (BMI)—Vic 20-6198	3	20
4.	**EAT, DRINK AND BE MERRY** (BMI)—P. Wagoner Let's Squiggle (BMI)—Vic 20-6289	6	5
5.	**I FORGOT TO REMEMBER TO FORGET** (BMI)—E. Presley Mystery Train (BMI)—Vic 20-6357; Sun 223	4	16
6.	**ALL RIGHT** (BMI)—F. Young Go Back, You Fool (BMI)—Cap 3169	5	22
7.	**WHY, BABY, WHY?** (BMI)—G. Jones Seasons of My Heart (BMI)—Starday 202	—	3
8.	**IT'S A GREAT LIFE** (BMI)—F. Young For the Love of a Woman Like You (BMI)—Cap 3258	7	6
9.	**BEAUTIFUL LIES** (BMI)—J. Shepard I Thought of You (BMI)—Cap 3222	10	8
10.	**I'VE KISSED YOU MY LAST TIME** (BMI)—K. Wells Lonely Side of Town (BMI)—Dec 29728	7	3
10.	**RICHEST MAN** (BMI)—E. Arnold **I WALKED ALONE LAST NIGHT** (ASCAP)—Vic 20-6290	10	8
12.	**WHY, BABY, WHY?** (BMI)—R. Sovine & W. Pierce Missing You (BMI)—Dec 29755	12	2
13.	**DON'T TAKE IT OUT ON ME** (BMI)—H. Thompson **HONEY, HONEY BEE BALL** (BMI)—Cap 3275	9	4
14.	**I FEEL LIKE CRYIN'** (BMI)—C. Smith **YOU'RE FREE TO GO** (ASCAP)—Col 21462	—	3
15.	**I DON'T CARE** (BMI)—W. Pierce Your Good for Nothing Heart (BMI)—Dec 29480	13	27

• Most Played in Juke Boxes

For survey week ending December 21

RECORDS are ranked in order of the greatest number of plays in juke boxes thruout the country, as determined by The Billboard's weekly survey of operators using a high proportion of country and western records. When significant action is reported on both sides of a record, points are combined to determine positon on the chart.

This Week	Record	Last Week	Weeks on Chart
1.	**SIXTEEN TONS** (BMI)—Tennessee Ernie You Don't Have to Be a Baby to Cry (ASCAP)— Cap 3262	2	6
2.	**LOVE, LOVE, LOVE** (BMI)—W. Pierce **IF YOU WERE ME** (BMI)—Dec 29662	1	13
3.	**JUST CALL ME LONESOME** (BMI)—E. Arnold That Do Make It Nice (BMI)—Vic 20-2198	3	18
4.	**I FORGOT TO REMEMBER TO FORGET** (BMI)—E. Presley **MYSTERY TRAIN** (BMI)—Vic 20-6357; Sun 223	6	7
5.	**EAT, DRINK AND BE MERRY** (BMI)—P. Wagoner Let's Squiggle (BMI)—Vic 20-5289	8	3
6.	**IT'S A GREAT LIFE** (BMI)—F. Young For the Love of a Woman Like You (BMI)—Cap 3258	10	5
7.	**WHY, BABY, WHY?** (BMI)—G. Jones Seasons of My Heart (BMI)—Starday 202	4	7
8.	**THIRTY DAYS** (BMI)—E. Tubbs Answer the Phone (BMI)—Dec 29731	7	3
8.	**BORN TO BE HAPPY** (BMI)—H. Snow Mainliner (BMI)—Vic 20-6269	5	7
10.	**YONDER COMES A SUCKER** (BMI)—J. Reeves I'm Hurtin' Inside (ASCAP)—Vic 20-6200	9	14

• Most Played by Jockeys

For survey week ending December 21

SIDES are ranked in order of the greatest number of plays on disk jockey radio shows thruout the country according to The Billboard's weekly survey of top disk jockey shows in all key markets.

This Week	Record	Last Week	Weeks on Chart
1.	**LOVE, LOVE, LOVE**—W. Pierce Dec 29662—BMI	1	14
2.	**SIXTEEN TONS**—Tennessee Ernie Cap 3262—BMI	2	7
3.	**WHY, BABY, WHY?**—R. Sovine & W. Pierce Dec 29739—BMI	4	3
4.	**I FORGOT TO REMEMBER TO FORGET**—E. Presley Vic 20-6357; Sun 223—BMI	8	12
5.	**JUST CALL ME LONESOME**—E. Arnold Vic 20-6198—BMI	3	18
6.	**EAT, DRINK AND BE MERRY**—P. Wagoner Vic 20-6289—BMI	5	5
6.	**IT'S A GREAT LIFE**—F. Young Cap 3258—BMI	6	5
8.	**ALL RIGHT**—F. Young Cap 3169—BMI	15	21
9.	**YOU'RE FREE TO GO**—C. Smith Col 21462—ASCAP	7	4
10.	**WHY, BABY, WHY?**—G. Jones Starday 202—BMI	9	5
11.	**HERE TODAY AND GONE TOMORROW**—J. E. & Maxine Brown Fabor 126—BMI	10	7
11.	**I FEEL LIKE CRYIN'**—C. Smith Col 21462—BMI	—	1
13.	**YONDER COMES A SUCKER**—J. Reeves Vic 20-6200—BMI	11	19
13.	**MYSTERY TRAIN**—E. Presley Sun 223—BMI	—	1
15.	**BEAUTIFUL LIES**—J. Shepard Cap 3222—BMI	12	2
15.	**BORN TO BE HAPPY**—H. Snow Vic 20-6269—BMI	14	4
15.	**THIRTY DAYS**—E. Tubb Dec 29731—BMI	—	1

The Billboard Music Popularity Charts — POPULAR RECORDS

• Best Sellers in Stores

For survey week ending December 28

RECORDS are ranked in order of their current national selling importance at the retail level, as determined by The Billboard's weekly survey of the top volume dealers in every important market area. When significant action is reported on both sides of a record, points are combined to determine position on the chart. In such a case, both sides are listed in bold type, the leading side on top.

This Week	Record	Last Week	Weeks on Chart
1.	**SIXTEEN TONS (BMI)**—Tennessee Ernie You Don't Have to Be a Baby to Cry (ASCAP)—Cap 3262	1	9
2.	**MEMORIES ARE MADE OF THIS** (BMI)—D. Martin Change of Heart (BMI)—Cap 3295	2	6
3.	**I HEAR YOU KNOCKIN'** (BMI)—G. Storm Never Leave Me (ASCAP)—Dot 15412	3	12
4.	**GREAT PRETENDER** (ASCAP)—Platters I'm Just a Dancing Partner (ASCAP)—Mercury 70753	11	3
5.	**MOMENTS TO REMEMBER** (ASCAP)—Four Lads Dream On, My Love, Dream On (ASCAP)—Col 40539	5	19
6.	**NUTTIN' FOR CHRISTMAS** (ASCAP)—B. Gordon-A. Mooney M-G-M 12092	8	4
7.	**AUTUMN LEAVES** (ASCAP)—R. Williams Take Care (BMI)—Kapp 116	6	21
8.	**LOVE AND MARRIAGE** (ASCAP)—F. Sinatra Impatient Years (ASCAP)—Cap 3260	7	9
9.	**BAND OF GOLD** (BMI)—D. Cherry Rumble Boogie (BMI)—Col 40597	13	5
10.	**HE** (BMI)—A. Hibbler Breeze (ASCAP)—Dec 29660	4	15
11.	**LOVE IS A MANY-SPLENDORED THING** (ASCAP)—Four Aces Shine On, Harvest Moon (ASCAP)—Dec 29625	10	19
12.	**IT'S ALMOST TOMORROW** (ASCAP)—Dream Weavers You Got Me Wondering (ASCAP)—Dec 29683	12	9
13.	**ONLY YOU** (BMI)—Platters Bark, Battle and Ball (BMI)—Mercury 70633	9	15
14.	**ANGELS IN THE SKY** (BMI)—Crew Cuts Mostly Martha (BMI)—Mercury 70741	17	4
15.	**LISBON ANTIGUA** (ASCAP)—N. Riddle Robin Hood (ASCAP)—Cap 3287	21	2
16.	**TEEN-AGE PRAYER** (ASCAP)—G. Storm **MEMORIES ARE MADE OF THIS** (BMI)—Dot 15436	20	2
17.	**HE** (BMI)—McGuire Sisters If You Believe (ASCAP)—Coral 61501	14	11
18.	**DUNGAREE DOLL** (BMI)—E. Fisher Everybody's Got a Home But Me (ASCAP)—Vic 20-6337	15	2
19.	**TEEN-AGE PRAYER** (ASCAP)—G. Mann Gypsy Lady (BMI)—Sound 126	—	1
20.	**SHIFTING, WHISPERING SANDS** (BMI)—R. Draper Time (ASCAP)—Mercury 70696	16	15
21.	**DADDY-O** (BMI)—Fontane Sisters Adorable (BMI)—Dot 15428	18	5
21.	**ROCK AND ROLL WALTZ** (BMI)—K. Starr I've Changed My Mind a Thousand Times (ASCAP)—Vic 20-6359	—	1
23.	**ARE YOU SATISFIED?** (BMI)—R. Draper Wabash Cannonball (BMI)—Mercury 70757	—	1
24.	**ONLY YOU** (BMI)—Hilltoppers Until the Real Thing Comes Along (ASCAP)—Dot 15423	19	9
25.	**BURN THAT CANDLE** (BMI)—B. Haley **ROCK-A-BEATIN' BOOGIE** (ASCAP)—Dec 29713	22	8

• THIS WEEK'S BEST BUYS

According to sales reports in key markets, the following recent releases are recommended for extra profits:

SEE YOU LATER, ALLIGATOR (Arc, BMI)—**Bill Haley—Decca 29791**

Haley's popularity remains at high ebb. All parts of the country were resoundingly unanimous in strong first week sales reports. At the speed it is going, chart action can be expected without delay. Flip is "The Paper Boy" (Valleybrook, ASCAP). A previous Billboard "Spotlight" pick.

CHAIN GANG (Pincus, ASCAP)—**Bobby Scott—ABC-Paramount 9658**

In Bobby Scott the new label has found its strongest entry in the lists to date. Volume in the first week since release has been especially heavy in Boston, New York, Philadelphia, Baltimore, Buffalo, Cleveland, Chicago and Milwaukee. An unusually fast mover. Flip is "Shadrach" (Carl Fischer, ASCAP). Scott was a Billboard Talent "Spotlight."

WHAT IS A WIFE?—Steve Allen—Coral 61554

This novelty is showing real staying power, with solid weekly growth, especially on the retail level. Good to strong sales reports were received this week from Los Angeles, St. Louis, Chicago, Boston, New York, Providence, Philadelphia, Buffalo, Pittsburgh, Cleveland and Milwaukee. Flip is Jayne Meadows' reading of "What Is a Husband?"

LULLABY OF BIRDLAND (Patricia, BMI) — **Blue Stars—Mercury 70742**

A sleeper that has begun making big strides in the past two weeks, French lyrics notwithstanding. Big city dealers and operators, in particular, report snowballing action. Boston, New York, Philadelphia, Buffalo, Pittsburgh, Cleveland, Milwaukee, St. Louis and Los Angeles were in the van. Flip is "That's My Girl" (Crestview, ASCAP).

• Most Played in Juke Boxes

For survey week ending December 28

RECORDS are ranked in order of the greatest number of plays in juke boxes thruout the country, as determined by The Billboard's weekly survey of the nation's juke box operators. When significant play is reported on both sides of a record, points are combined to determine position on the chart. In such a case, both sides are listed in bold type, the leading side on top.

This Week	Record	Last Week	Weeks on Chart
1.	**SIXTEEN TONS** (BMI)—Tennessee Ernie You Don't Have to Be a Baby to Cry (ASCAP)—Cap 3262	1	8
2.	**MEMORIES ARE MADE OF THIS** (BMI)—D. Martin Change of Heart (BMI)—Cap 3295	2	3
3.	**I HEAR YOU KNOCKIN'** (BMI)—G. Storm Never Leave Me (ASCAP)—Dot 15412	3	11
4.	**MOMENTS TO REMEMBER** (ASCAP) Four Lads Dream On, My Love, Dream On (ASCAP)—Col 40539	4	13
5.	**ONLY YOU** (BMI)—Platters Bark, Battle and Ball (BMI)—Mercury 70633	6	12
6.	**AUTUMN LEAVES** (ASCAP)—R. Williams Take Care (BMI)—Kapp 116	5	17
7.	**SHIFTING, WHISPERING SANDS** (BMI)—R. Draper Time (ASCAP)—Mercury 70696	7	12
8.	**TEEN-AGE PRAYER** (ASCAP)—G. Storm Memories Are Made of This (BMI)—Dot 15436	18	2
9.	**NUTTIN' FOR CHRISTMAS** (ASCAP)—B. Gordon-A. Mooney Santa Claus Looks Just Like Daddy (ASCAP)—M-G-M 12092	14	2
10.	**LOVE AND MARRIAGE** (ASCAP)—F. Sinatra Impatient Years (ASCAP)—Cap 3260	9	5
11.	**HE** (BMI)—A. Hibbler Breeze (ASCAP)—Dec 29660	8	11
12.	**IT'S ALMOST TOMORROW** (ASCAP)—Dream Weavers You Got Me Wondering (ASCAP)—Dec 29683	13	5
13.	**LOVE IS A MANY-SPLENDORED THING** (ASCAP)—Four Aces Shine On Harvest Moon (ASCAP)—Dec 29625	9	16
14.	**ONLY YOU** (BMI)—Hilltoppers Until the Real Thing Comes Along (ASCAP)—Dot 15423	15	8
14.	**PEPPER HOT BABY** (BMI)—J. P. Morgan If You Don't Want My Love (ASCAP)—Vic 20-6282	16	6
14.	**GREAT PRETENDER** (ASCAP)—Platters I'm Just a Dancing Partner (ASCAP)—Mercury 70753	—	1
17.	**DADDY-O** (BMI)—Fontane Sisters Adorable (BMI)—Dot 15428	11	5
18.	**BURN THAT CANDLE** (BMI)—B. Haley Rock-A-Beatin' Boogie (ASCAP)—Dec 29713	12	5
18.	**HE** (BMI)—McGuire Sisters If You Believe (ASCAP)—Coral 61501	17	11
20.	**CRY ME A RIVER** (ASCAP)—J. London S'Wonderful (ASCAP)—Liberty 55006	19	4

• Most Played by Jockeys

For survey week ending December 28

SIDES are ranked in order of the greatest number of plays on disk jockey radio shows thruout the country. Results are based on The Billboard's weekly survey among the nation's disk jockeys. The reverse side of each record is also listed.

This Week	Record	Last Week	Weeks on Chart
1.	**MEMORIES ARE MADE OF THIS** (BMI)—D. Martin Change of Heart (BMI)—Cap 3295	2	5
2.	**SIXTEEN TONS** (BMI)—Tennessee Ernie You Don't Have to Be a Baby to Cry (ASCAP)—Cap 3262	1	9
3.	**MOMENTS TO REMEMBER** (ASCAP)—Four Lads Dream On, My Love, Dream On (ASCAP)—Col 40539	3	17
4.	**BAND OF GOLD** (BMI)—D. Cherry Rumble Boogie (BMI)—Col 40597	9	4
5.	**GREAT PRETENDER**—Platters I'm Just a Dancing Partner (ASCAP)—Mercury 70753	7	2
6.	**LOVE AND MARRIAGE** (ASCAP)—F. Sinatra Impatient Years (ASCAP)—Cap 3260	5	10
7.	**WHITE CHRISTMAS** (ASCAP)—Bing Crosby God Rest Ye Merry, Gentlemen—Dec 23778	—	1
8.	**ONLY YOU** (BMI)—Platters Bark, Battle and Ball (BMI)—Mercury 70633	6	11
9.	**I HEAR YOU KNOCKIN'** (BMI)—G. Storm Never Leave Me (ASCAP)—Dot 15412	4	11
10.	**NUTTIN' FOR CHRISTMAS** (ASCAP)—B. Gordon-A. Mooney Santa Claus Looks Just Like Daddy (ASCAP)—M-G-M 12092	10	2
11.	**ROCK AND ROLL WALTZ** (BMI)—K. Starr I've Changed My Mind a Thousand Times (ASCAP)—Vic 20-6359	—	1
12.	**C'EST LA VIE** (ASCAP)—S. Vaughan Never (ASCAP)—Mercury 70727	19	6
13.	**MEMORIES ARE MADE OF THIS** (BMI)—G. Storm Teen-Age Prayer (ASCAP)—Dot 15436	13	2
14.	**AUTUMN LEAVES** (ASCAP)—R. Williams Take Care (BMI)—Kapp 116	12	18
15.	**TEEN-AGE PRAYER** (ASCAP)—G. Storm Memories Are Made of This (BMI)—Dot 15436	—	1
16.	**BAND OF GOLD** (BMI)—K. Carson Cast Your Bread Upon the Waters—Cap 3283	11	2
16.	**TENDER TRAP** (ASCAP)—F. Sinatra Weep They Will—Cap 3290	14	4
18.	**HE** (BMI)—A. Hibbler Breeze (ASCAP)—Dec 29660	17	13
19.	**CRY ME A RIVER** (ASCAP)—J. London S'Wonderful (ASCAP)—Liberty 55006	18	6
20.	**LISBON ANTIGUA** (ASCAP)—N. Riddle Robin Hood (ASCAP)—Cap 3287	—	1

The Billboard Music Popularity Charts

POPULAR RECORDS

THE TOP 100

For survey week ending December 21

A list of the **TOP 100 RECORD SIDES** in the nation according to a **COMBINED TABULATION** of Dealer Disk Jockey and Juke Box Operator replies to The Billboard's weekly popular record Best Seller and Most Played surveys. Its purpos is to provide Disk Jockeys with additional programming material and to give trade exposure to NEWER records just beginning to show action in the field.

This Week	Song	Artist	Label	Last Week
1.	SIXTEEN TONS	T. Ernie	Capitol	1
2.	MEMORIES ARE MADE OF THIS	D. Martin	Capitol	2
3.	MOMENTS TO REMEMBER	Four Lads	Columbia	4
4.	I HEAR YOU KNOCKIN'	G. Storm	Dot	3
5.	LOVE AND MARRIAGE	F. Sinatra	Capitol	5
5.	GREAT PRETENDER	Platters	Mercury	12
7.	NUTTIN' FOR CHRISTMAS	B. Gordon-A. Mooney	M-G-M	9
8.	ONLY YOU	Platters	Mercury	5
9.	AUTUMN LEAVES	R. Williams	Kapp	7
10.	HE	A. Hibbler	Decca	8
11.	TEEN-AGE PRAYER	G. Storm	Dot	19
12.	IT'S ALMOST TOMORROW	Dream Weavers	Decca	11
13.	LOVE IS A MANY-SPLENDORED THING	Four Aces	Decca	10
14.	ROCK AND ROLL WALTZ	K. Starr	Victor	47
15.	ONLY YOU	Hilltoppers	Dot	13
16.	BAND OF GOLD	D. Cherry	Columbia	18
17.	HE	McGuire Sisters	Coral	17
18.	WHITE CHRISTMAS	Bing Crosby	Decca	24
19.	CRY ME A RIVER	J. London	Liberty	14
20.	MEMORIES ARE MADE OF THIS	G. Storm	Dot	26
21.	DUNGAREE DOLL	E. Fisher	Victor	16
21.	ARE YOU SATISFIED?	R. Draper	Mercury	25
23.	DADDY-O	Fontane Sisters	Dot	15
24.	BAND OF GOLD	K. Carson	Capitol	39
25.	NUTTIN' FOR CHRISTMAS	J. Ward	King	22
26.	SHIFTING, WHISPERING SANDS	R. Draper	Mercury	23
26.	TEEN-AGE PRAYER	G. Mann	Sound	37
26.	BURN THAT CANDLE	B. Haley	Decca	20
29.	LISBON ANTIGUA	N. Riddle	Capitol	34
29.	ALL AT ONCE YOU LOVE HER	P. Como	Victor	42
31.	MEMORIES OF YOU	Four Coins	Epic	35
32.	WOMAN IN LOVE	F. Laine	Columbia	38
33.	IT'S ALMOST TOMORROW	S. Lanson	Dot	30
34.	WOMAN IN LOVE	Four Aces	Decca	31
35.	ANGELS IN THE SKY	Crew Cuts	Mercury	21
36.	AT MY FRONT DOOR	P. Boone	Dot	27
37.	MOSTLY MARTHA	Crew Cuts	Mercury	49
38.	MY BOY—FLAT TOP	D. Collins	Coral	56
39.	CROCE DI ORO (CROSS OF GOLD)	P. Page	Mercury	46
40.	NUTTIN' FOR CHRISTMAS	R. Zahnd	Columbia	45
41.	GEE WHITTAKERS	P. Boone	Dot	33
42.	EVERYBODY'S GOT A HOME BUT ME	R. Hamilton	Epic	68
43.	ROCK A BEATIN' BOOGIE	B. Haley	Decca	47
44.	TENDER TRAP	F. Sinatra	Capitol	43
45.	NUTTIN' FOR CHRISTMAS	Fontane Sisters	Dot	36
46.	IT'S ALMOST TOMORROW	J. Stafford	Columbia	40
47.	SHIFTING, WHISPERING SANDS	B. Vaughn	Dot	29
48.	YOU ARE MY LOVE	J. James	M-G-M	27
49.	DADDY-O	B. Lou	King	55
49.	AUTUMN LEAVES	M. Miller	Columbia	62
51.	GO ON WITH THE WEDDING	P. Page	Mercury	—
51.	DOLLY'S OH SUSANNA	D. Charles-Singing Dogs	Victor	43
53.	NUTTIN' FOR CHRISTMAS	S. Freberg	Capitol	59
53.	MY BELIEVING HEART	J. James	M-G-M	85
55.	PEPPER HOT BABY	J. P. Morgan	Victor	32
56.	WANTING YOU	R. Williams	Kapp	48
57.	TOYLAND	Nat King Cole	Capitol	77
57.	FORGIVE MY HEART	Nat King Cole	Capitol	65
59.	MEMORIES ARE MADE OF THIS	M. Carson	Columbia	72
60.	IT'S ALMOST TOMORROW	D. Carroll	Mercury	51
61.	MY TREASURE	Hilltoppers	Dot	99
61.	SOMEONE YOU LOVE	Nat King Cole	Capitol	71
63.	C'EST LA VIE	S. Vaughan	Mercury	4[illegible]
64.	NO ARMS CAN EVER HOLD YOU	G. Shaw	Decca	64
65.	GOODBYE TO ROME	G. Gibbs	Mercury	54
65.	EVERYBODY'S GOT A HOME BUT ME	E. Fisher	Victor	58
67.	WHEN YOU DANCE	Turbans	Herald	57
68.	LOVE AND MARRIAGE	D. Shore	Victor	51
69.	SPEEDOO	Cadillacs	Josie	—
69.	SIXTEEN TONS	J. Desmond	Coral	50
71.	ADORABLE	Fontane Sisters	Dot	79
71.	BIBLE TELLS ME SO	D. Cornell	Coral	72
73.	LULLABY OF BIRDLAND	Blue Stars	Mercury	66
74.	NOT ONE GOODBYE	J. P. Morgan	Victor	72
75.	SUDDENLY THERE'S A VALLEY	J. Stafford	Columbia	61
75.	SEVENTEEN	Fontane Sisters	Dot	88
77.	LET IT RING	D. Day	Columbia	—
77.	NO ARMS CAN EVER HOLD YOU	P. Boone	Dot	53
79.	ZAMBESI	L. Busch	Capitol	—
80.	MY BONNIE LASSIE	Ames Brothers	Victor	60
80.	AUTUMN LEAVES	V. Young	Decca	99
82.	LOVE IS A MANY-SPLENDORED THING	D. Rose	M-G-M	99
83.	SUDDENLY THERE'S A VALLEY	G. Grant	Era	75
83.	AUTUMN LEAVES	S. Allen	Coral	67
85.	GO ON WITH THE WEDDING	K. Kallen-G. Shaw	Decca	—
85.	C'EST LA VIE	S. Gale	Victor	88
87.	YELLOW ROSE OF TEXAS	J. Desmond	Coral	85
88.	THERE SHOULD BE RULES	B. Madigan	M-G-M	81
89.	SUDDENLY THERE'S A VALLEY	J. La Rosa	Cadence	—
90.	CHARMAINE	Four Freshmen	Capitol	—
91.	YELLOW ROSE OF TEXAS	M. Miller	Columbia	68
91.	YELLOW ROSE OF TEXAS	S. Freberg	Capitol	—
91.	TOO LATE NOW	De Castro Sisters	Abbott	—
91.	DOG-FACED SOLDIER	R. Morgan	Decca	78
95.	JAPANESE FAREWELL SONG	K. C. Jones	Marquee	92
96.	AMUKIRKI	L. Paul & M. Ford	Capitol	96
97.	NO ARMS CAN EVER HOLD YOU	Gaylords	Mercury	97
98.	AT MY FRONT DOOR	El Dorados	Vee Jay	87
98.	TINA MARIE	P. Como	Victor	—
100.	LOVE IS A MANY-SPLENDORED THING	W. Herman	Capitol	—
100.	POR FAVOR	V. Damone	Mercury	—
100.	AUTUMN LEAVES	J. Gleason	Capitol	68

CAUTION TO DEALERS AND JUKE BOX OPERATORS

The Billboard's Top 100 is NOT designed to provide tested information for buying purposes. This function is most reliably served by other regular weekly features: Best Sellers in Stores, Most Played in Juke Boxes, Coming Up Strong and Best Buys.

The Billboard Music Popularity Charts — POPULAR RECORDS

• Best Sellers in Stores

For survey week ending January 4

RECORDS are ranked in order of their current national selling importance at the retail level, as determined by The Billboard's weekly survey of the top volume dealers in every important market area. When significant action is reported on both sides of a record, points are combined to determine position on the chart. In such a case, both sides are listed in bold type, the leading side on top.

This Week		Last Week	Weeks on Chart
1.	**MEMORIES ARE MADE OF THIS** (BMI)—D. Martin Change of Heart (BMI)—Cap 3295	2	7
2.	**SIXTEEN TONS** (BMI)—Tennessee Ernie You Don't Have to Be a Baby to Cry (ASCAP)—Cap 3262	1	10
3.	**GREAT PRETENDER** (ASCAP)—Platters I'm Just a Dancing Partner (ASCAP)—Mercury 70753	4	4
4.	**I HEAR YOU KNOCKIN'** (BMI)—G. Storm Never Leave Me (ASCAP)—Dot 15412	3	13
5.	**BAND OF GOLD** (BMI)—D. Cherry Rumble Boogie (BMI)—Col 40597	9	6
6.	**LOVE AND MARRIAGE** (ASCAP)—F. Sinatra Impatient Years (ASCAP)—Cap 3260	8	10
7.	**He** (BMI)—A. Hibbler Breeze (ASCAP)—Dec 29660	10	16
8.	**MOMENTS TO REMEMBER** (ASCAP)—Four Lads Dream On, My Love, Dream On (ASCAP)—Col 40539	5	20
9.	**ROCK AND ROLL WALTZ** (BMI)—K. Starr I've Changed My Mind a Thousand Times (ASCAP)—Vic 20-6359	21	2
10.	**ONLY YOU** (BMI)—Platters Bark, Battle and Ball (BMI)—Mercury 70633	13	16
11.	**LISBON ANTIGUA** (ASCAP)—N. Riddle Robin Hood (ASCAP)—Cap 3287	15	3
12.	**AUTUMN LEAVES** (ASCAP)—R. Williams Take Care (BMI)—Kapp 116	7	22
13.	**ANGELS IN THE SKY** (BMI)—Crew Cuts **MOSTLY MARTHA** (BMI)—Mercury 70741	14	5
14.	**IT'S ALMOST TOMORROW** (ASCAP)—Dream Weavers You Got Me Wondering (ASCAP)—Dec 29683	12	10
15.	**DUNGAREE DOLL** (BMI)—E. Fisher Everybody's Got a Home But Me (ASCAP)—Vic 20-6337	18	3
16.	**BURN THAT CANDLE** (BMI)—B. Haley **ROCK-A-BEATIN' BOOGIE** (ASCAP)—Dec 29713	25	9
17.	**TEEN-AGE PRAYER** (ASCAP)—G. Storm **MEMORIES ARE MADE OF THIS** (BMI)—Dot 15436	16	3
18.	**ARE YOU SATISFIED?** (BMI)—R. Draper Wabash Cannonball (BMI)—Mercury 70757	23	2
19.	**LOVE IS A MANY-SPLENDORED THING** (ASCAP)—Four Aces Shine On, Harvest Moon (ASCAP)—Dec 29625	11	20
20.	**DADDY-O** (BMI)—Fontane Sisters Adorable (BMI)—Dot 15428	21	6
21.	**HE** (BMI)—McGuire Sisters If You Believe (ASCAP)—Coral 61501	17	12
21.	**TEEN-AGE PRAYER** (ASCAP)—G. Mann Gypsy Lady (BMI)—Sound 126	19	2
23.	**SHIFTING, WHISPERING SANDS** (BMI)—R. Draper Time (ASCAP)—Mercury 70696	20	16
24.	**TENDER TRAP** (ASCAP)—F. Sinatra Weep They Will—Cap 3290	—	1
25.	**SEE YOU LATER, ALLIGATOR** (BMI)—B. Haley Paper Boy (ASCAP)—Dec 29791	—	1

• THIS WEEK'S BEST BUYS

According to sales reports in key markets, the following recent releases are recommended for extra profits:

NO, NOT MUCH (Beaver, ASCAP)—The Four Lads—Columbia 40629

The Lads are following up "Moments to Remember," one of the big records of 1955, with a fast mover that may win some 1956 laurels for the group. Ten days after release, it was showing outstanding sales volume in Boston, New York, Baltimore, Pittsburgh, Cleveland, Milwaukee, St. Louis. Reports from Chicago and Philadelphia also were good. Flip is "I'll Never Know" (Montauk, BMI). A previous Billboard "Spotlight" pick.

• Most Played in Juke Boxes

For survey week ending January 4

RECORDS are ranked in order of the greatest number of plays in juke boxes thruout the country, as determined by The Billboard's weekly survey of the nation's juke box operators. When significant play is reported on both sides of a record, points are combined to determine position on the chart. In such a case, both sides are listed in bold type, the leading side on top.

This Week		Last Week	Weeks on Chart
1.	**SIXTEEN TONS** (BMI)—Tennessee Ernie You Don't Have to Be a Baby to Cry (ASCAP)—Cap 3262	1	9
2.	**MEMORIES ARE MADE OF THIS** (BMI)—D. Martin Change of Heart (BMI)—Cap 3295	2	4
3.	**I HEAR YOU KNOCKIN'** (BMI)—G. Storm Never Leave Me (ASCAP)—Dot 15412	3	12
4.	**MOMENTS TO REMEMBER** (ASCAP)—Four Lads Dream On My Love, Dream On (ASCAP)—Col 40539	4	14
5.	**ONLY YOU** (BMI)—Platters Bark, Battle and Ball (BMI)—Mercury 70623	5	13
6.	**TEEN-AGE PRAYER** (ASCAP)—G. Storm **MEMORIES ARE MADE OF THIS** (BMI)—Dot 15436	8	3
7.	**LOVE AND MARRIAGE** (ASCAP)—F. Sinatra Impatient Years (ASCAP)—Cap 3260	10	6
8.	**IT'S ALMOST TOMORROW** (ASCAP)—Dream Weavers You Got Me Wondering (ASCAP)—Dec 29683	12	6
9.	**HE** (BMI)—A. Hibbler Breeze (ASCAP)—Dec 29660	11	12
9.	**BURN THAT CANDLE** (BMI)—B. Haley **ROCK-A-BEATIN' BOOGIE** (ASCAP)—Dec 29713	18	6
11.	**AUTUMN LEAVES** (ASCAP)—R. Williams Take Care (BMI)—Kapp 116	6	18
11.	**DUNGAREE DOLL** (BMI)—E. Fisher Everybody's Got a Home But Me (ASCAP)—Vic 20-6337	—	1
13.	**SHIFTING, WHISPERING SANDS** (BMI)—R. Draper Time (ASCAP)—Mercury 70696	7	13
13.	**ONLY YOU** (BMI)—Hilltoppers Until the Real Thing Comes Along (ASCAP)—Dot 15423	14	9
15.	**PEPPER HOT BABY** (BMI)—J. P. Morgan It You Don't Want My Love (ASCAP)—Vic 20-6282	14	7
15.	**GREAT PRETENDER** (ASCAP)—Platters I'm Just a Dancing Partner (ASCAP)—Mercury 70753	14	2
15.	**CRY ME A RIVER** (ASCAP)—J. London S'Wonderful (ASCAP)—Liberty 55006	20	5
18.	**ROCK AND ROLL WALTZ** (BMI)—K. Starr I've Changed My Mind a Thousand Times (ASCAP)—Vic 20-6359	—	1
19.	**DADDY-O** (BMI)—Fontane Sisters Adorable (BMI)—Dot 15428	17	6
20.	**LOVE IS A MANY-SPLENDORED THING** (ASCAP)—Four Aces Shine On, Harvest Moon (ASCAP)—Dec 29625	13	17

• Most Played by Jockeys

For survey week ending January 4

SIDES are ranked in order of the greatest number of plays on disk jockey radio shows thruout the country. Results are based on The Billboard's weekly survey among the nation's disk jockeys. The reverse side of each record is also listed.

This Week		Last Week	Weeks on Chart
1.	**MEMORIES ARE MADE OF THIS** (BMI)—D. Martin Change of Heart (BMI)—Cap 3295	1	6
2.	**SIXTEEN TONS** (BMI)—Tennessee Ernie You Don't Have to Be a Baby to Cry (ASCAP)—Cap 3262	2	10
3.	**GREAT PRETENDER**—Platters I'm Just a Dancing Partner (ASCAP)—Mercury 70753	5	3
4.	**MOMENTS TO REMEMBER** (ASCAP)—Four Lads Dream On, My Love, Dream On (ASCAP)—Col 40539	3	18
5.	**MEMORIES ARE MADE OF THIS** (BMI)—G. Storm Teen-Age Prayer (ASCAP)—Dot 15436	13	3
6.	**LOVE AND MARRIAGE** (ASCAP)—F. Sinatra Impatient Years (ASCAP)—Cap 3260	6	11
7.	**I HEAR YOU KNOCKIN'** (BMI)—G. Storm Never Leave Me (ASCAP)—Dot 15412	9	12
8.	**ROCK AND ROLL WALTZ** (BMI)—K. Starr I've Changed My Mind a Thousand Times (ASCAP)—Vic 20-6359	11	2
9.	**BAND OF GOLD** (BMI)—D. Cherry Rumble Boogie (BMI)—Col 40597	16	3
10.	**ONLY YOU** (BMI)—Platters Bark, Battle and Ball (BMI)—Mercury 70633	8	12
11.	**TENDER TRAP** (ASCAP)—F. Sinatra Weep They Will—Cap 3290	16	5
12.	**LISBON ANTIGUA** (ASCAP)—N. Riddle Robin Hood (ASCAP)—Cap 3287	20	2
13.	**ONLY YOU** (BMI)—Hilltoppers Until the Real Thing Comes Along (ASCAP)—Dot 15423	—	9
14.	**BAND OF GOLD** (BMI)—K. Carson Cast Your Bread Upon the Waters—Cap 3283	4	5
15.	**CRY ME A RIVER** (ASCAP)—J. London S'Wonderful (ASCAP)—Liberty 55006	19	7
16.	**TEEN-AGE PRAYER** (ASCAP)—G. Storm Memories Are Made of This (BMI)—Dot 15436	15	2
17.	**ALL AT ONCE YOU LOVE HER** (ASCAP)—P. Como Rose Tattoo (ASCAP)—Vic 20-6294	—	6
18.	**HE** (BMI)—A. Hibbler Breeze (ASCAP)—Dec 29660	18	14
19.	**ANGELS IN THE SKY** (BMI)—Crew Cuts Mostly Martha (BMI)—Mercury 70741	—	1
19.	**WOMAN IN LOVE** (ASCAP)—Four Aces Of This I'm Sure (ASCAP)—Dec 29725	—	3

The Billboard Music Popularity Charts

POPULAR RECORDS

THE TOP 100

For survey week ending December 28

A list of the TOP 100 RECORD SIDES in the nation according to a COMBINED TABULATION of Dealer Disk Jockey and Juke Box Operator replies to The Billboard's weekly popular record Best Seller and Most Played surveys. Its purpose is to provide Disk Jockeys with additional programming material and to give trade exposure to NEWER records just beginning to show action in the field.

This Week	Song	Artist	Label	Last Week
1.	MEMORIES ARE MADE OF THIS	D. Martin	Capitol	2
2.	SIXTEEN TONS	T. Ernie	Capitol	1
3.	I HEAR YOU KNOCKIN'	G. Storm	Dot	4
4.	MOMENTS TO REMEMBER	Four Lads	Columbia	3
5.	LOVE AND MARRIAGE	F. Sinatra	Capitol	5
6.	GREAT PRETENDER	Platters	Mercury	5
7.	ONLY YOU	Platters	Mercury	8
8.	HE	A. Hibbler	Decca	10
8.	ROCK AND ROLL WALTZ	K. Starr	Victor	14
10.	BAND OF GOLD	D. Cherry	Columbia	16
11.	IT'S ALMOST TOMORROW	Dream Weavers	Decca	12
12.	TEEN-AGE PRAYER	G. Storm	Dot	11
13.	AUTUMN LEAVES	R. Williams	Dot	9
13.	DUNGAREE DOLL	E. Fisher	Victor	21
15.	ONLY YOU	Hilltoppers	Dot	15
16.	MEMORIES ARE MADE OF THIS	G. Storm	Dot	20
17.	LOVE IS A MANY-SPLENDORED THING	Four Aces	Decca	13
18.	ANGELS IN THE SKY	Crew Cuts	Mercury	35
19.	ARE YOU SATISFIED?	R. Draper	Mercury	21
20.	BURN THAT CANDLE	B. Haley	Decca	26
21.	HE	McGuire Sisters	Coral	17
22.	WOMAN IN LOVE	Four Aces	Decca	34
23.	DADDY-O	Fontane Sisters	Dot	23
24.	CRY ME A RIVER	J. London	Liberty	19
25.	TEEN-AGE PRAYER	G. Mann	Sound	26
26.	TENDER TRAP	F. Sinatra	Capitol	44
27.	ALL AT ONCE YOU LOVE HER	P. Como	Victor	29
28.	BAND OF GOLD	K. Carson	Capitol	24
29.	IT'S ALMOST TOMORROW	J. Stafford	Columbia	46
30.	LISBON ANTIGUA	N. Riddle	Capitol	29
31.	MOSTLY MARTHA	Crew Cuts	Mercury	37
32.	WOMAN IN LOVE	F. Laine	Columbia	32
33.	WHEN YOU DANCE	Turbans	Herald	67
34.	MEMORIES OF YOU	Four Coins	Capitol	31
35.	GEE WHITTAKERS	P. Boone	Dot	41
36.	AT MY FRONT DOOR	P. Boone	Dot	36
37.	SHIFTING, WHISPERING SANDS	R. Draper	Mercury	26
38.	GO ON WITH THE WEDDING	P. Page	Mercury	51
38.	YOU ARE MY LOVE	J. James	M-G-M	48
38.	WANTING YOU	R. Williams	Kapp	56
41.	IT'S ALMOST TOMORROW	D. Carroll	Mercury	60
42.	CROCE DI ORO (CROSS OF GOLD)	P. Page	Mercury	39
43.	EVERYBODY'S GOT A HOME BUT ME	R. Hamilton	Epic	42
44.	IT'S ALMOST TOMORROW	S. Lanson	Dot	33
45.	AUTUMN LEAVES	S. Allen	Coral	83
45.	SHIFTING, WHISPERING SANDS	B. Vaughn	Dot	47
47.	C'EST LA VIE	S. Vaughan	Mercury	63
48.	NOT ONE GOODBYE	J. P. Morgan	Victor	74
49.	MY BELIEVING HEART	J. James	M-G-M	53
50.	EVERYBODY'S GOT A HOME BUT ME	E. Fisher	Victor	65
50.	LULLABY OF BIRDLAND	Blue Stars	Mercury	73
52.	MY TREASURE	Hilltoppers	Dot	61
53.	AUTUMN LEAVES	M. Miller	Columbia	49
53.	DADDY-O	B. Lou	King	49
55.	SUDDENLY THERE'S A VALLEY	J. Stafford	Columbia	75
56.	LOVE AND MARRIAGE	D. Shore	Victor	68
56.	SOMEONE YOU LOVE	Nat (King) Cole	Capitol	61
56.	SEE YOU LATER, ALLIGATOR	B. Haley	Decca	—
56.	THERE SHOULD BE RULES	B. Madigan	M-G-M	88
60.	MY BOY—FLAT TOP	D. Collins	Coral	38
61.	ROCK A BEATIN' BOOGIE	B. Haley	Decca	43
62.	DOLLY'S OH SUSANNA	D. Charles-Singing Dogs	Victor	51
62.	GO ON WITH THE WEDDING	K. Kallen-G. Shaw	Decca	85
64.	NO ARMS CAN EVER HOLD YOU	G. Shaw	Decca	64
65.	NO ARMS CAN EVER HOLD YOU	P. Boone	Dot	77
66.	TOO LATE NOW	DeCastro Sisters	Abbott	91
67.	PEPPER-HOT BABY	J. P. Morgan	Victor	55
68.	TUTTI FRUTTI	Little Richard	Specialty	—
69.	SIXTEEN TONS	J. Desmond	Coral	69
70.	MEMORIES ARE MADE OF THIS	M. Carson	Columbia	59
71.	AT MY FRONT DOOR	El Dorados	Vee Jay	98
72.	BIBLE TELLS ME SO	D. Cornell	Coral	71
73.	WHAT IS A WIFE?	S. Allen	Coral	—
74.	TAKE ME BACK TO TOYLAND	Nat (King) Cole	Capitol	57
75.	ZAMBESI	L. Busch	Capitol	79
76.	LET IT RING	Doris Day	Columbia	77
77.	SUDDENLY THERE'S A VALLEY	G. Grant	Era	83
78.	APRIL IN PARIS	C. Basie	Clef	—
78.	ADORABLE	Fontane Sisters	Dot	71
80.	CHARMAINE	Four Freshmen	Capitol	90
81.	CHAIN GANG	B. Scott	Paramount	—
82.	SPEEDOO	Cadillacs	Josie	69
83.	TWENTY-FOUR HOURS A DAY	G. Gibbs	Mercury	—
84.	SUDDENLY THERE'S A VALLEY	Mills Brothers	Decca	—
84.	MY BONNIE LASSIE	Ames Brothers	Victor	80
86.	CROCE DI ORO (CROSS OF GOLD)	J. Regan	London	—
87.	LOVE IS A MANY-SPLENDORED THING	D. Cornell	Coral	—
87.	GOODBYE TO ROME	G. Gibbs	Mercury	65
89.	AUTUMN LEAVES	V. Young	Decca	80
90.	I'M GONNA LAUGH YOU RIGHT OUT OF MY LIFE	Nat (King) Cole	Capitol	—
91.	SEVENTEEN	Fontane Sisters	Dot	75
91.	YELLOW ROSE OF TEXAS	M. Miller	Columbia	91
93.	WEDDING	Chordettes	Cadence	—
94.	LOVE IS A MANY-SPLENDORED THING	D. Rose	M-G-M	82
94.	AMUKIRIKI	L. Paul & M. Ford	Capitol	96
96.	AUTUMN LEAVES	R. Charles	M-G-M	—
97.	C'EST LA VIE	S. Gale	Victor	85
97.	NO ARMS CAN EVER HOLD YOU	Gaylords	Mercury	97
97.	DAY BY DAY	Four Freshmen	Capitol	—
97.	YELLOW ROSE OF TEXAS	J. Desmond	Coral	87
97.	YELLOW ROSE OF TEXAS	S. Freberg	Capitol	91

CAUTION TO DEALERS AND JUKE BOX OPERATORS

The Billboard's Top 100 is NOT designed to provide tested information for buying purposes. This function is most reliably served by other regular weekly features: Best Sellers in Stores, Most Played in Juke Boxes, Coming Up Strong and Best Buys.

The Billboard Music Popularity Charts — POPULAR RECORDS

• Best Sellers in Stores

For survey week ending January 11

RECORDS are ranked in order of their current national selling importance at the retail level, as determined by The Billboard's weekly survey of the top volume dealers in very important market area. When significant action is reported on both sides of a record, points are combined to determine position on the chart. In such a case, both sides are listed in bold type, the leading side on top.

This Week		Last Week	Weeks on Chart
1.	MEMORIES ARE MADE OF THIS (BMI)—D. Martin Change of Heart (BMI)—Cap 3295	1	8
2.	SIXTEEN TONS (BMI)—Tennessee Ernie You Don't Have to Be a Baby to Cry (ASCAP)—Cap 3262	2	11
3.	GREAT PRETENDER (ASCAP)—Platters I'm Just a Dancing Partner (ASCAP)—Mercury 70753	3	5
4.	LISBON ANTIGUA (ASCAP) N. Riddle Robin Hood (ASCAP)—Cap 3287	11	4
5.	BAND OF GOLD (BMI)—D. Cherry Rumble Boogie (BMI)—Col 40597	5	7
6.	ROCK AND ROLL WALTZ (BMI)—K. Starr I've Changed My Mind a Thousand Times (ASCAP)—Vic 20-6359	9	3
7.	I HEAR YOU KNOCKIN' (BMI)—G. Storm Never Leave Me (ASCAP)—Dot 15412	4	14
8.	DUNGAREE DOLL (BMI)—E. Fisher Everybody's Got a Home But Me (ASCAP)—Vic 20-6337	15	4
9.	IT'S ALMOST TOMORROW (ASCAP)—Dream Weavers You Got Me Wondering (ASCAP)—Dec 29683	14	11
10.	LOVE AND MARRIAGE (ASCAP)—F. Sinatra Impatient Years (ASCAP)—Cap 3260	6	11
11.	MOMENTS TO REMEMBER (ASCAP)—Four Lads Dream On, My Love, Dream On (ASCAP)—Col 40539	8	21
12.	AUTUMN LEAVES (ASCAP)—R. Williams Take Care (BMI)—Kapp 116	12	23
13.	HE (BMI)—A. Hibbler Breeze (ASCAP)—Dec 29660	7	17
14.	ANGELS IN THE SKY (BMI)—Crew Cuts MOSTLY MARTHA (BMI)—Mercury 70741	13	6
15.	ONLY YOU (BMI)—Platters Bark, Battle and Ball (BMI)—Mercury 70633	10	17
16.	ARE YOU SATISFIED (BMI)—R. Draper Wabash Cannonball (BMI)—Mercury 70757	18	3
17.	TEEN-AGE PRAYER (ASCAP)—G. Storm MEMORIES ARE MADE OF THIS (BMI)—Dot 15436	17	4
17.	SEE YOU LATER, ALLIGATOR (BMI)—B. Haley Paper Boy (ASCAP)—Dec 29791	25	2
19.	TEEN-AGE PRAYER (ASCAP)—G. Mann Gypsy Lady (BMI)—Sound 126	21	3
20.	HE (BMI)—McGuire Sisters If You Believe (ASCAP)—Coral 61501	21	13
21.	CHAIN GANG (ASCAP)—B. Scott Shadrack (ASCAP)—ABS-Paramount 9658	—	1
22.	ONLY YOU (BMI)—Hilltoppers Until the Real Thing Comes Along (ASCAP)—Dot 15423	—	10
23.	LOVE IS A MANY-SPLENDORED THING (ASCAP)—Four Aces Shine On, Harvest Moon—Dec 29625	19	21
23.	WOMAN IN LOVE (ASCAP)—F. Laine Walking the Night Away (ASCAP)—Col 40583	—	3
25.	WOMAN IN LOVE (ASCAP)—Four Aces Of This I'm Sure (ASCAP)—Dec 29725	—	2

• THIS WEEK'S BEST BUYS

According to sales reports in key markets, the following recent releases are recommended for extra profits:

THEME FROM "THE THREE-PENNY OPERA" ("MORITAT") Harms, ASCAP — Dick Hyman Trio—M-G-M 12149

It was this version of "Moritat" that occasioned the wave of competing covers of the tune, and Hyman has been reaping the benefits of his time handicap. The M-G-M disk is now rated strong in New York, Philadelphia, Providence, Cleveland, Milwaukee, Detroit and Baltimore. It is also selling well in Boston, Atlanta, St. Louis and Chicago. Considering the current excitement over the tune, some of the other versions that are now beginning to establish themselves may also become strong chart contenders. Flip of the Hyman record is "Baubles, Bangles and Beads" (Frank, ASCAP). A previous Billboard "Spotlight" pick.

NINETY-NINE YEARS (Oxford, ASCAP) — Guy Mitchell—Columbia 40631

Mitchell's latest record has taken off with remarkable speed, and easily shapes up commercially as his most potent entry in a long time. Among the territories indicating strong sales are Pittsburgh, St. Louis, Chicago, Milwaukee and Cleveland. Good reports were received from Baltimore, Boston, Detroit, Durham and Atlanta. Operators and one-stops have been particularly pleased with the disk's performance in the boxes. Flip is "Perfume, Candy and Flowers" (Hawthorne, ASCAP).

EXTENDED PLAY

SONGS FROM "GUYS AND DOLLS"—Marlon Brando—Decca EB 2332

This EP has intrigued enough of the legion of Brando admirers to make it a surprisingly big seller in the first weeks it has been available. Retailers sampled in New York, Chicago, Cleveland, St. Louis, Milwaukee, Philadelphia and Durham reported exceptional volume. Tunes in the set are: "Luck Be a Lady," "If I Were a Bell," "Woman in Love" and "I'll Know." These are also available as two single records.

• Most Played in Juke Boxes

For survey week ending January 11

RECORDS are ranked in order of the greatest number of plays in juke boxes thruout the country, as determined by The Billboard's weekly survey of the nation's juke box operators. When significant play is reported on both sides of a record, points are combined to determine position on the chart. In such a case, both sides are listed in bold type, the leading side on top.

This Week		Last Week	Weeks on Chart
1.	SIXTEEN TONS (BMI)—Tennessee Ernie You Don't Have to Be a Baby to Cry (ASCAP)—Cap 3262	1	10
2.	MEMORIES ARE MADE OF THIS (BMI)—D. Martin Change of Heart (BMI)—Cap 3295	2	5
3.	I HEAR YOU KNOCKIN' (BMI)—G. Storm Never Leave Me (ASCAP)—Dot 15412	3	13
4.	MOMENTS TO REMEMBER (ASCAP)—Four Lads Dream On, My Love, Dream On (ASCAP)—Col 40539	4	15
5.	ONLY YOU (BMI)—Platters Bark, Battle and Ball (BMI)—Mercury 70623	5	14
6.	TEEN-AGE PRAYER (ASCAP)—G. Storm MEMORIES ARE MADE OF THIS (BMI)—Dot 15436	6	4
7.	IT'S ALMOST TOMORROW (ASCAP)—Dream Weavers You Got Me Wondering (ASCAP)—Dec 29683	8	7
8.	GREAT PRETENDER (ASCAP)—Platters I'm Just a Dancing Partner (ASCAP)—Mercury 70753	15	3
9.	LOVE AND MARRIAGE (ASCAP)—F. Sinatra Impatient Years (ASCAP)—Cap 3260	7	7
10.	HE (BMI)—A. Hibbler Breeze (ASCAP)—Dec 29660	9	13
11.	DUNGAREE DOLL (BMI)—E. Fisher Everybody's Got a Home But Me (ASCAP)—Vic 20-6337	11	2
12.	ROCK AND ROLL WALTZ (BMI)—K. Starr I've Changed My Mind a Thousand Times (ASCAP)—Vic 20-6359	18	2
13.	AUTUMN LEAVES (ASCAP)—R. Williams Take Care (BMI)—Kapp 116	11	19
14.	BURN THAT CANDLE (BMI) B. Haley ROCK-A-BEATIN' BOOGIE (ASCAP)—Dec 29713	9	7
14.	ONLY YOU (BMI)—Hilltoppers Until the Real Thing Comes Along (ASCAP)—Dot 15423	13	10
16.	CRY ME A RIVER (ASCAP)—J. London S'Wonderful (ASCAP)—Liberty 55006	15	6
16.	DADDY-O (BMI)—Fontane Sisters Adorable (BMI)—Dot 15428	19	7
16.	BAND OF GOLD (BMI)—D. Cherry Rumble Boogie (BMI)—Col 40597	—	1
19.	SHIFTING, WHISPERING SANDS (BMI)—R. Draper Time (ASCAP)—Mercury 70696	13	14
19.	ANGELS IN THE SKY (BMI)—Crew Cuts MOSTLY MARTHA (BMI)—Mercury 70741	—	1

• Most Played by Jockeys

For survey week ending January 11

SIDES are ranked in order of the greatest number of plays on disk jockey radio shows thruout the country. Results are based on The Billboard's weekly survey among the nation's disk jockeys. The reverse side of each record is also listed.

This Week		Last Week	Weeks on Chart
1.	MEMORIES ARE MADE OF THIS (BMI)—D. Martin Change of Heart (BMI)—Cap 3295	1	7
2.	SIXTEEN TONS (BMI)—Tennessee Ernie You Don't Have to Be a Baby to Cry (ASCAP)—Cap 3262	2	11
3.	GREAT PRETENDER (ASCAP)—Platters I'm Just a Dancing Partner (ASCAP)—Mercury 70753	3	4
4.	ROCK AND ROLL WALTZ (BMI)—K. Starr I've Changed My Mind a Thousand Times (ASCAP)—Vic 20-6359	8	3
5.	LISBON ANTIGUA (ASCAP)—N Riddle Robin Hood (ASCAP)—Cap 3287	12	3
6.	TEEN-AGE PRAYER (ASCAP)—G. Storm Memories Are Made of This (BMI)—Dot 15436	16	3
7.	LOVE AND MARRIAGE (ASCAP)—F. Sinatra Impatient Years (ASCAP)—Cap 3260	6	12
8.	BAND OF GOLD (BMI)—D. Cherry Rumble Boogie (BMI)—Col 40597	9	4
9.	MOMENTS TO REMEMBER (ASCAP)—Four Lads Dream On, My Love, Dream On (ASCAP) Col 40539	4	19
10.	I HEAR YOU KNOCKIN' (BMI)—G. Storm Never Leave Me (ASCAP)—Dot 15412	7	13
11.	TENDER TRAP (ASCAP)—F. Sinatra Weep They Will—Cap 3290	11	6
12.	MEMORIES ARE MADE OF THIS (BMI)—G. Storm Teen-Age Prayer (ASCAP)—Dot 15436	5	4
13.	HE (BMI)—A. Hibbler Breeze (ASCAP)—Dec 29660	18	15
14.	ONLY YOU (BMI)—Platters Bark, Battle and Ball (BMI)—Mercury 70633	10	13
15.	DUNGAREE DOLL (BMI)—E. Fisher Everybody's Got a Home But Me (ASCAP)—Vic 20-6337	—	1
16.	BAND OF GOLD (BMI)—K. Carson Cast Your Bread Upon the Waters (ASCAP)—Cap 3283	14	6
17.	CRY ME A RIVER (ASCAP)—J. London S'Wonderful (ASCAP)—Liberty 55006	15	8
18.	ALL AT ONCE YOU LOVE HER (ASCAP)—P. Como Rose Tattoo (ASCAP)—Vic 20-6294	17	7
19.	ANGELS IN THE SKY (BMI)—Crew Cuts Mostly Martha (BMI)—Mercury 70741	19	2
20.	IT'S ALMOST TOMORROW (ASCAP)—Dream Weavers You Got Me Wondering (ASCAP)—Dec 29683	—	6

The Billboard Music Popularity Charts

POPULAR RECORDS

THE TOP 100

For survey week ending January 11

A list of the Top 100 RECORD SIDES in the nation according to a COMBINED TABULATION of Dealer, Disk Jockey and Juke Box Operator replies to The Billboard's weekly popular record Best Seller and Most Played surveys. Its purpose is to provide Disk Jockeys with additional programming material and to give trade exposure to NEWER records just beginning to show action in the field.

Pos.	Song	Artist	Label	Last Week
1.	MEMORIES ARE MADE OF THIS	D. Martin	Capitol	1
2.	SIXTEEN TONS	T. Ernie	Capitol	2
3.	GREAT PRETENDER	Platters	Mercury	6
4.	I HEAR YOU KNOCKIN'	G. Storm	Dot	3
5.	ROCK AND ROLL WALTZ	K. Starr	Victor	8
6.	MOMENTS TO REMEMBER	Four Lads	Columbia	4
7.	LOVE AND MARRIAGE	F. Sinatra	Capitol	5
8.	BAND OF GOLD	D. Cherry	Columbia	10
9.	TEEN-AGE PRAYER	G. Storm	Dot	12
10.	ONLY YOU	Platters	Mercury	7
11.	DUNGAREE DOLL	E. Fisher	Victor	13
12.	IT'S ALMOST TOMORROW	Dream Weavers	Decca	11
13.	HE	A. Hibbler	Decca	8
14.	AUTUMN LEAVES	R. Williams	Kapp	13
15.	LISBON ANTIGUA	N. Riddle	Capitol	30
16.	ANGELS IN THE SKY	Crew Cuts	Mercury	18
17.	ONLY YOU	Hilltoppers	Dot	15
18.	CRY ME A RIVER	J. London	Liberty	24
19.	ARE YOU SATISFIED?	R. Draper	Mercury	19
19.	IT'S ALMOST TOMORROW	J. Stafford	Columbia	29
21.	TEEN-AGE PRAYER	G. Mann	Sound	25
22.	HE	McGuire Sisters	Coral	21
22.	LOVE IS A MANY-SPLENDORED THING	Four Aces	Decca	17
24.	DADDY-O	Fontane Sisters	Dot	23
25.	TENDER TRAP	F. Sinatra	Capitol	26
26.	WOMAN IN LOVE	Four Aces	Decca	22
27.	MEMORIES ARE MADE OF THIS	G. Storm	Dot	16
28.	BAND OF GOLD	K. Carson	Capitol	28
29.	ALL AT ONCE YOU LOVE HER	P. Como	Victor	27
30.	BURN THAT CANDLE	B. Haley	Decca	20
31.	GO ON WITH THE WEDDING	P. Page	Mercury	38
31.	MY TREASURE	Hilltoppers	Dot	52
33.	MOSTLY MARTHA	Crew Cuts	Mercury	31
34.	MEMORIES OF YOU	Four Coins	Capitol	34
35.	GEE WHITTAKERS	P. Boone	Dot	35
35.	YOU ARE MY LOVE	J. James	M-G-M	38
35.	WOMAN IN LOVE	F. Laine	Columbia	32
38.	C'EST LA VIE	S. Vaughan	Mercury	47
39.	SHIFTING, WHISPERING SANDS	R. Draper	Mercury	37
40.	CHAIN GANG	B. Scott	ABC-Paramount	81
41.	SEE YOU LATER, ALLIGATOR	B. Haley	Decca	56
42.	EVERYBODY'S GOT A HOME BUT ME	R. Hamilton	Epic	43
43.	AT MY FRONT DOOR	P. Boone	Dot	36
44.	CROCE DI ORO (CROSS OF GOLD)	P. Page	Mercury	42
44.	WANTING YOU	R. Williams	Kapp	36
46.	LOVE AND MARRIAGE	D. Shore	Victor	56
47.	EVERYBODY'S GOT A HOME BUT ME	E. Fisher	Victor	50
48.	LULLABY OF BIRDLAND	Blue Stars	Mercury	50
49.	WHEN YOU DANCE	Turbans	Herald	33
50.	FORGIVE MY HEART	Nat (King) Cole	Capitol	—
50.	SPEEDOO	Cadillacs	Josie	82
52.	PEPPER-HOT BABY	J. P. Morgan	Victor	67
52.	JAPANESE FAREWELL SONG	K. C. Jones	Marquee	—
54.	AUTUMN LEAVES	S. Allen	Coral	45
54.	NO, NO, NOT MUCH	Four Lads	Columbia	—
56.	IT'S ALMOST TOMORROW	S. Lanson	Dot	44
56.	WHAT IS A WIFE	S. Allen	Coral	73
58.	MY BOY—FLAT TOP	D. Collins	Coral	60
59.	APRIL IN PARIS	C. Basie	Clef	78
60.	NOT ONE GOODBYE	J. P. Morgan	Victor	48
60.	SHIFTING, WHISPERING SANDS	B. Vaughn	Dot	45
62.	AUTUMN LEAVES	M. Miller	Columbia	53
63.	AUTUMN LEAVES	V. Young	Decca	89
64.	TAKE ME BACK TO TOYLAND	Nat (King) Cole	Capitol	74
65.	SIXTEEN TONS	J. Desmond	Coral	69
66.	NINETY-NINE YEARS	G. Mitchell	Columbia	—
67.	ROCK A BEATIN' BOOGIE	B. Haley	Decca	61
67.	I'M GONNA LAUGH YOU RIGHT OUT OF MY LIFE	Nat (King) Cole	Capitol	90
67.	IT'S ALMOST TOMORROW	D. Carroll	Mercury	41
70.	THEME FROM THE THREE PENNY OPERA	D. Hyman	M-G-M	—
71.	GO ON WITH THE WEDDING	K. Kallen-G. Shaw	Decca	62
71.	SOMEONE YOU LOVE	Nat (King) Cole	Capitol	56
73.	TOO LATE NOW	De Castro Sisters	Abbott	66
73.	DON'T GO TO STRANGERS	V. Monroe	Victor	—
75.	MEMORIES ARE MADE OF THIS	M. Carson	Columbia	70
76.	CHARMAINE	Four Freshmen	Capitol	80
77.	SUDDENLY THERE'S A VALLEY	J. Stafford	Columbia	55
78.	YOU DON'T HAVE TO BE A BABY TO CRY	T. Ernie	Capitol	—
79.	NO ARMS CAN EVER HOLD YOU	P. Boone	Dot	65
80.	SUDDENLY THERE'S A VALLEY	G. Grant	Era	77
81.	MY BELIEVING HEART	J. James	M-G-M	49
82.	KEY TO MY HEART	R. Clooney	Columbia	—
83.	NO ARMS CAN EVER HOLD YOU	G. Shaw	Decca	64
83.	LET IT RING	Doris Day	Columbia	76
85.	SUDDENLY THERE'S A VALLEY	Mills Brothers	Decca	84
86.	GOODBYE TO ROME	G. Gibbs	Mercury	87
87.	I'LL KNOW	S. Davis Jr.	Decca	—
88.	DADDY-O	B. Lou	King	53
88.	THERE SHOULD BE RULES	B. Madigan	M-G-M	56
90.	DOLLY'S OH SUSANNA	D. Charles-Singing Dogs	Victor	62
91.	LOVE IS A MANY-SPLENDORED THING	D. Cornell	Coral	87
91.	ADORABLE	Fontane Sisters	Dot	78
91.	TEEN-AGERS WALTZ	E. Howard	Mercury	—
94.	SUDDENLY THERE'S A VALLEY	J. LaRosa	Cadence	—
94.	IF YOU DON'T WANT MY LOVE	J. P. Morgan	Victor	—
94.	TWENTY-FOUR HOURS A DAY	G. Gibbs	Mercury	83
97.	MY BOY—FLAT TOP	B. Bennett	King	—
98.	WAKE THE TOWN AND TELL THE PEOPLE	L. Baxter	Capitol	—
99.	C'EST LA VIE	S. Gale	Victor	97
99.	SUDDENLY THERE'S A VALLEY	P. Andrews	Capitol	—
99.	BIBLE TELLS ME SO	D. Cornell	Coral	72
99.	WITHOUT A SONG	R. Hamilton	Epic	—
99.	YELLOW ROSE OF TEXAS	J. Desmond	Coral	97

CAUTION TO DEALERS AND JUKE BOX OPERATORS

The Billboard's Top 100 is NOT designed to provide tested information for buying purposes. This function is most reliably served by other regular weekly features: Best Sellers in Stores, Most Played in Juke Boxes, Coming Up Strong and Best Buys.

The Billboard Music Popularity Charts

POPULAR RECORDS

• Best Sellers in Stores

For survey week ending January 18

RECORDS are ranked in order of their current national selling importance at the retail level, as determined by The Billboard's weekly survey of the top volume dealers in very important market area. When significant action is reported on both sides of a record, points are combined to determine position on the chart. In such a case, both sides are listed in bold type, the leading side on top.

This Week		Last Week	Weeks on Chart
1.	**MEMORIES ARE MADE OF THIS** (BMI)—D. Martin Change of Heart (BMI)—Cap 3295	1	9
2.	**GREAT PRETENDER** (ASCAP)—Platters I'm Just a Dancing Partner (ASCAP)—Mercury 70753	3	6
3.	**SIXTEEN TONS** (BMI)—Tennessee Ernie You Don't Have to Be a Baby to Cry (ASCAP)—Cap 3262	2	12
4.	**LISBON ANTIGUA** (ASCAP)—N. Riddle Robin Hood (ASCAP)—Cap 3287	4	5
5.	**ROCK AND ROLL WALTZ** (BMI)—K. Starr I've Changed My Mind a Thousand Times (ASCAP)—Vic 20-6359	6	4
6.	**BAND OF GOLD** (BMI)—D. Cherry Rumble Boogie (BMI)—Col 40597	5	8
7.	**SEE YOU LATER, ALLIGATOR** (BMI)—B. Haley Paper Boy (ASCAP)—Dec 29791	17	3
8.	**IT'S ALMOST TOMORROW** (ASCAP)—Dream Weavers You Got Me Wondering (ASCAP)—Dec 29683	9	12
9.	**DUNGAREE DOLL** (BMI)—E. Fisher Everybody's Got a Home But Me (ASCAP)—Vic 20-6337	8	5
10.	**I HEAR YOU KNOCKIN'** (BMI)—G. Storm Never Leave Me (ASCAP)—Dot 15412	7	15
11.	**ANGELS IN THE SKY** (BMI)—Crew Cuts **MOSTLY MARTHA** (BMI)—Mercury 70741	14	7
12.	**LOVE AND MARRIAGE** (ASCAP)—F. Sinatra Impatient Years (ASCAP)—Cap 3260	10	12
13.	**MOMENTS TO REMEMBER**—Four Lads Dream On, My Love, Dream On (ASCAP)—Col 40539	11	22
14.	**HE** (BMI)—A. Hibbler Breeze (ASCAP)—Dec 29660	13	18
15.	**AUTUMN LEAVES** (ASCAP)—R. Williams Take Care (BMI)—Kapp 116	12	24
16.	**ARE YOU SATISFIED?** (BMI)— Wabash Cannonball (BMI)—Mercury 70757	16	4
17.	**TEEN-AGE PRAYER** (ASCAP)—G. Storm **MEMORIES ARE MADE OF THIS** (BMI)—Dot 15436	17	5
18.	**CHAIN GANG** (ASCAP)—B. Scott Shadrach (ASCAP)—ABC-Paramount 9658	21	2
19.	**NO, NOT MUCH** (ASCAP)—Four Lads I'll Never Know (BMI)—Col 40629	—	1
20.	**ONLY YOU** (BMI)—Platters Bark, Battle and Ball (BMI)—Mercury 70633	15	18
21.	**THEME FROM "THE THREE PENNY OPERA" ("MORITAT")** (ASCAP)—D. Hyman Baubles, Bangles and Beads (ASCAP)—M-G-M 12149	—	1
22.	**TEEN-AGE PRAYER** (ASCAP)—G. Mann Gypsy Lady (BMI)—Sound 126	19	4
23.	**WOMAN IN LOVE** (ASCAP)—F. Laine Walking the Night Away (ASCAP)—Col 40583	23	4
24.	**BURN THAT CANDLE** (BMI)—B. Haley Rock-a-Beatin' Boogie (ASCAP)—Dec 29713	—	10
24.	**TUTTI FRUTTI** (BMI)—Little Richard I'm Just a Lonely Guy (BMI)—Specialty 561	—	1

• THIS WEEK'S BEST BUYS

According to sales reports in key markets, the following recent releases are recommended for extra profits:

TUTTI FRUTTI (Venice, BMI)

I'LL BE HOME (Arc, BMI) — Pat Boone — Dot 15443

Boone's new issue is catching on quickly. The original r.&b. version of "Tutti Frutti" is now on the national pop retail chart; if anything, this seems to have made the path of the Boone record all the easier. Already this week it was reported a strong seller in Baltimore, Richmond, St. Louis, Cleveland, Milwaukee, Cincinnati, Buffalo, Providence and Chicago. Several territories indicated excellent action on "I'll Be Home" as well. A previous Billboard "Spotlight" pick.

11TH HOUR MELODY (Paxton, ASCAP) — Al Hibbler—Decca 29789

The wide national spread of favorable sales reports on this record prove it is hitting quickly and spontaneously. New York, Philadelphia, Buffalo, Pittsburgh, Cleveland, Chicago, St. Louis, Baltimore, Nashville and Durham were among the localities that turned over sizable quantities of the disk at the retail and one-stop level. Flip is "Let's Try Again" (Paco, ASCAP). A previous Billboard "Spotlight" pick.

• Most Played in Juke Boxes

For survey week ending January 18

RECORDS are ranked in order of the greatest number of plays in juke boxes thruout the country, as determined by The Billboard's weekly survey of the nation's juke box operators. When significant play is reported on both sides of a record, points are combined to determine position on the chart. In such a case, both sides are listed in bold type, the leading side on top.

This Week		Last Week	Weeks on Chart
1.	**MEMORIES ARE MADE OF THIS** (BMI)—D. Martin Change of Heart (BMI)—Cap 3295	2	6
2.	**SIXTEEN TONS** (BMI)—Tennessee Ernie You Don't Have to Be a Baby to Cry (ASCAP)—Cap 3262	1	11
3.	**GREAT PRETENDER** (ASCAP)—Platters I'm Just a Dancing Partner (ASCAP)—Mercury 70753	8	4
4.	**I HEAR YOU KNOCKIN'** (BMI)—G. Storm Never Leave Me (ASCAP)—Dot 15412	3	14
5.	**ROCK AND ROLL WALTZ** (BMI)—K. Starr I've Changed My Mind a Thousand Times (ASCAP)—Vic 20-6359	12	3
6.	**MOMENTS TO REMEMBER** (ASCAP)—Four Lads Dream On, My Love, Dream On (ASCAP)—Col 40539	4	16
7.	**TEEN-AGE PRAYER** (ASCAP)—G. Storm Memories Are Made of This (BMI)—Dot 15436	6	5
7.	**BAND OF GOLD** (BMI)—D. Cherry Rumble Boogie (BMI)—Col 40597	16	2
9.	**IT'S ALMOST TOMORROW** (ASCAP)—Dream Weavers You Got Me Wondering (ASCAP) Dec 29683	7	8
10.	**ONLY YOU** (BMI)—Platters Bark, Battle and Ball (BMI)—Mercury 70623	5	15
11.	**DUNGAREE DOLL** (BMI)—E. Fisher Everybody's Got a Home But Me (ASCAP)—Vic 20-6337	11	3
12.	**LOVE AND MARRIAGE** (ASCAP)—F. Sinatra Impatient Years (ASCAP)—Cap 3260	9	8
12.	**ONLY YOU** (BMI)—Hilltoppers Until the Real Thing Comes Along (ASCAP)—Dot 15423	14	11
14.	**HE** (BMI)—A. Hibbler Breeze (ASCAP)—Dec 29660	10	14
15.	**AUTUMN LEAVES** (ASCAP)—R. Williams Take Care (BMI)—Kapp 116	13	20
16.	**DADDY-O** (BMI)—Fontane Sisters Adorable (BMI)—Dot 15428	16	8
17.	**CRY ME A RIVER** (ASCAP)—J. London S'Wonderful (ASCAP)—Liberty 55006	16	7
17.	**ANGELS IN THE SKY** (BMI)—Crew Cuts **MOSTLY MARTHA** (BMI)—Mercury 70741	19	2
19.	**He** (BMI)—McGuire Sisters If You Believe (ASCAP)—Coral 51501	—	11
19.	**GEE WHITTAKERS** (BMI)—P. Boone Take the Time (ASCAP)—Dot 15435	—	1

• Most Played by Jockeys

For survey week ending January 18

SIDES are ranked in order of the greatest number of plays on disk jockey radio shows thruout the country. Results are based on The Billboard's weekly survey among the nation's disk jockeys. The reverse side of each record is also listed.

This Week		Last Week	Weeks on Chart
1.	**MEMORIES ARE MADE OF THIS** (BMI)—D. Martin Change of Heart (BMI)—Cap 3295	1	8
2.	**SIXTEEN TONS** (BMI)—Tennessee Ernie You Don't Have to Be a Baby to Cry (ASCAP—Cap 3262	2	12
3.	**GREAT PRETENDER** (ASCAP)—Platters I'm Just a Dancing Partner (ASCAP)—Mercury 70753	3	5
4.	**LIBSON ANTIGUA** (ASCAP)—N. Riddle Robin Hood (ASCAP)—Cap 3287	5	4
5.	**ROCK AND ROLL WALTZ** (BMI)—Kay Starr I've Changed My Mind a Thousand Times (ASCAP)—Vic 20-6359	4	4
6.	**BAND OF GOLD** (BMI)—D. Cherry Rumble Boogie (BMI)—Col 40597	8	5
7.	**TENDER TRAP** (ASCAP)—F. Sinatra Weep They Will (ASCAP)—Cap 3290	11	7
8.	**TEEN-AGE PRAYER** (ASCAP)—G. Storm Memories Are Made of This (BMI)—Dot 15436	6	4
9.	**DUNGAREE DOLL** (BMI)—E. Fisher Everybody's Got a Home But Me (ASCAP)—Vic 20-6337	15	2
10.	**MOMENTS TO REMEMBER** (ASCAP)—Four Lads Dream On, My Love, Dream On (ASCAP)—Col 40539	9	20
11.	**ALL AT ONCE YOU LOVE HER** (ASCAP)—P. Como Rose Tattoo (ASCAP)—Vic 20-6294	18	8
12.	**LOVE AND MARRIAGE** (ASCAP)—F. Sinatra Impatient Years (ASCAP)—Cap 3260	7	13
13.	**I HEAR YOU KNOCKIN'** (BMI)—G. Storm Never Leave Me (ASCAP)—Dot 15412	10	14
14.	**IT'S ALMOST TOMORROW** (ASCAP)—Dream Weavers You Got Me Wondering (ASCAP)—Dec 29683	20	7
15.	**CRY ME A RIVER** (ASCAP)—J. London S'Wonderful (ASCAP)—Liberty 55006	17	9
16.	**ANGELS IN THE SKY** (BMI)—Crew Cuts Mostly Martha (BMI)—Mercury 70741	19	3
17.	**BAND OF GOLD** (BMI)—K. Carson Cast Your Bread Upon the Waters (ASCAP)—Cap 3283	16	7
17.	**AUTUMN LEAVES** (ASCAP)—R. Williams Take Care (BMI)—Kapp 116	—	19
19.	**MEMORIES ARE MADE OF THIS** (BMI)—G. Storm Teen-Age Prayer (ASCAP)—Dot 15436	12	5
19.	**C'EST LA VIE** (ASCAP)—S. Vaughan Never (ASCAP)—Mercury 70727	—	7
19.	**ONLY YOU** (BMI)—Hilltoppers Until the Real Thing Comes Along (ASCAP)—Dot 15423	—	10

The Billboard Music Popularity Charts
POPULAR RECORDS

THE TOP 100

For survey week ending January 18

A list of the **Top 100 RECORD SIDES** in the nation according to a **COMBINED TABULATION** of Dealer, Disk Jockey and Juke Box Operator replies to The Billboard's weekly popular record Best Seller and Most Played surveys. Its purpose is to provide Disk Jockeys with additional programming material and to give trade exposure to NEWER records just beginning to show action in the field.

Pos.	Song	Artist	Label	Last Week
1.	MEMORIES ARE MADE OF THIS	D. Martin	Capitol	1
2.	SIXTEEN TONS	T. Ernie	Capitol	2
3.	GREAT PRETENDER	Platters	Mercury	3
4.	ROCK AND ROLL WALTZ	K. Starr	Victor	5
5.	BAND OF GOLD	D. Cherry	Columbia	8
6.	I HEAR YOU KNOCKIN'	G. Storm	Dot	4
7.	MOMENTS TO REMEMBER	Four Lads	Columbia	6
8.	DUNGAREE DOLL	E. Fisher	Victor	11
9.	IT'S ALMOST TOMORROW	Dream Weavers	Decca	12
10.	LISBON ANTIGUA	N. Riddle	Capitol	15
10.	TEEN-AGE PRAYER	G. Storm	Dot	9
12.	LOVE AND MARRIAGE	F. Sinatra	Capitol	7
13.	AUTUMN LEAVES	R. Williams	Kapp	14
14.	HE	A. Hibbler	Decca	13
15.	ANGELS IN THE SKY	Crew Cuts	Mercury	16
16.	ONLY YOU	Platters	Mercury	10
17.	CRY ME A RIVER	J. London	Liberty	18
18.	ARE YOU SATISFIED?	R. Draper	Mercury	19
19.	ONLY YOU	Hilltoppers	Dot	17
20.	SEE YOU LATER, ALLIGATOR	B. Haley	Decca	41
21.	BAND OF GOLD	K. Carson	Capitol	28
22.	TEEN-AGE PRAYER	G. Mann	Sound	21
23.	TENDER TRAP	F. Sinatra	Capitol	25
24.	GO ON WITH THE WEDDING	P. Page	Mercury	31
24.	WOMAN IN LOVE	F. Laine	Columbia	35
26.	HE	McGuire Sisters	Coral	22
27.	GEE WHITTAKERS	P. Boone	Dot	35
27.	MEMORIES ARE MADE OF THIS	G. Storm	Dot	27
29.	BURN THAT CANDLE	B. Haley	Decca	30
29.	WOMAN IN LOVE	Four Aces	Decca	26
31.	ALL AT ONCE YOU LOVE HER	P. Como	Victor	29
32.	C'EST LA VIE	S. Vaughn	Mercury	38
33.	DADDY-O	Fontane Sisters	Dot	24
34.	MEMORIES OF YOU	Four Coins	Epic	34
35.	IT'S ALMOST TOMORROW	J. Stafford	Columbia	19
35.	MOSTLY MARTHA	Crew Cuts	Mercury	33
37.	THEME FROM THE THREE-PENNY OPERA (MORITAT)	D. Hyman	M-G-M	70
38.	NO, NOT MUCH	Four Lads	Columbia	54
39	CHAIN GANG	B. Scott	ABC-Paramount	40
40.	LOVE IS A MANY-SPLENDORED THING	Four Aces	Decca	22
40.	SHIFTING, WHISPERING SANDS	R. Draper	Mercury	39
42.	WHEN YOU DANCE	Turbans	Herald	49
43.	SPEEDOO	Cadillacs	Josie	50
44.	LOVE AND MARRIAGE	D. Shore	Victor	46
45.	AT MY FRONT DOOR	P. Boone	Dot	43
46.	TUTTI FRUTTI	Little Wichard	Specialty	—
47.	TAKE ME BACK TO TOYLAND	Nat (King) Cole	Capitol	64
48.	IT'S ALMOST TOMORROW	D. Carroll	Mercury	67
49.	LULLABY OF BIRDLAND	Blue Stars	Mercury	48
50.	TROUBLE WITH HARRY	Alfi & Harry	Liberty	—
51.	LET IT RING	Doris Day	Columbia	83
52.	DON'T GO TO STRANGERS	V. Monroe	Victor	73
53.	APRIL IN PARIS	C. Basie	Clef	59
54.	IT'S ALMOST TOMORROW	S. Lanson	Dot	56
55.	EVERYBODY'S GOT A HOME BUT ME	E. Fisher	Victor	47
56.	TUTTI FRUTTI	P. Boone	Dot	—
57.	I'M GONNA LAUGH YOU RIGHT OUT OF MY LIFE	Nat (King) Cole	Capitol	67
58.	WANTING YOU	R. Williams	Kapp	44
59.	MEMORIES ARE MADE OF THIS	M. Carson	Columbia	75
60.	MY TREASURE	Hilltoppers	Dot	31
60.	NINETY-NINE YEARS	G. Mitchell	Columbia	66
62.	YOU ARE MY LOVE	J. James	M-G-M	35
63.	ALL THE WAY AROUND THE WORLD	Mills Brothers	Decca	—
63.	MY BOY FLAT TOP	D. Collins	Coral	58
63.	MEMORIES OF YOU	R. Clooney-B. Goodman	Columbia	—
66.	NOT ONE GOODBYE	J. P. Morgan	Victor	60
67.	EVERYBODY'S GOT A HOME BUT ME	R. Hamilton	Epic	42
68.	MEMORIES OF YOU	H. Winterhalter	Victor	—
69.	CHARMAINE	Four Freshmen	Capitol	76
70.	WHAT IS A WIFE?	S. Allen	Coral	56
71.	GO ON WITH THE WEDDING	K. Kallen-G. Shaw	Decca	71
71.	SOMEONE YOU LOVE	Nat (King) Cole	Capitol	71
71.	THERE SHOULD BE RULES	B. Madigan	M-G-M	88
74.	AUTUMN LEAVES	M. Miller	Columbia	62
74	FORGIVE MY HEART	Nat (King) Cole	Capitol	50
74.	PEPPER HOT BABY	J. P. Morgan	Victor	52
74.	MY BELIEVING HEART	J. James	M-G-M	81
78.	THAT'S YOUR MISTAKE	O. Williams	DeLuxe	—
79.	ADORABLE	Fontane Sisters	Dot	91
79.	SEVEN DAYS	D. Collins	Coral	—
79.	TEEN-AGE PRAYER	K. White	Mercury	—
82.	PET ME, PAPA	R. Clooney	Columbia	—
82.	DADDY-O	B. Lou	King	88
84.	AT MY FRONT DOOR	El Dorados	Vee Jay	—
84.	SHIFTING, WHISPERING SANDS	B. Vaughn	Dot	60
86.	AUTUMN LEAVES	R. Charles	M-G-M	—
86.	GOODBYE TO ROME	G. Gibbs	Mercury	—
88.	SIXTEEN TONS	J. Desmond	Coral	65
88.	OO BANG	Doris Day	Columbia	—
88.	ROCK AROUND THE CLOCK	B. Haley	Decca	—
91.	WEDDING	Chordettes	Cadence	—
91.	TEXAS LADY	L. Paul & M. Ford	Capitol	—
93.	ROCK A BEATIN' BOOGIE	B. Haley	Decca	67
93.	SUDDENLY THERE'S A VALLEY	J. Stafford	Columbia	77
93.	IF YOU DON'T WANT MY LOVE	J. P. Morgan	Victor	94
93.	CROCE DI ORO (CROSS OF GOLD)	P. Page	Mercury	44
93.	KEY TO MY HEART	R. Clooney	Columbia	82
93.	AIN'T THAT A SHAME?	P. Boone	Dot	—
93.	TEEN-AGERS WALTZ	E. Howard	Mercury	91
93.	C'EST LA VIE	S. Gale	Victor	99
93.	ZAMBESI	L. Busch	Capitol	—

CAUTION TO DEALERS AND JUKE BOX OPERATORS

The Billboard's Top 100 is NOT designed to provide tested information for buying purposes. This function is most reliably served by other regular weekly features: Best Sellers in Stores, Most Played in Juke Boxes, Coming Up Strong and Best Buys.

The Billboard Music Popularity Charts — POPULAR RECORDS

• Best Sellers in Stores

For survey week ending January 25

RECORDS are ranked in order of their current national selling importance at the retail level, as determined by The Billboard's weekly survey of the top volume dealers in very important market area. When significant action is reported on both sides of a record, points are combined to determine position on the chart. In such a case, both sides are listed in bold type, the leading side on top.

This Week	Title	Last Week	Weeks on Chart
1.	**MEMORIES ARE MADE OF THIS** (BMI)—D. Martin; Change of Heart (BMI)—Cap 3295	1	10
2.	**GREAT PRETENDER** (ASCAP)—Platters; I'm Just a Dancing Partner (ASCAP)—Mercury 70753	2	7
3.	**ROCK AND ROLL WALTZ** (BMI)—K. Starr; I've Changed My Mind a Thousand Times (ASCAP)—Vic 20-6359	5	5
4.	**SIXTEEN TONS** (BMI)—Tennessee Ernie; You Don't Have to Be a Baby to Cry (ASCAP)—Cap 3262	3	13
5.	**LISBON ANTIGUA** (ASCAP)—N. Riddle; Robin Hood (ASCAP)—Cap 3287	4	6
6.	**BAND OF GOLD** (BMI)—D. Cherry; Rumble Boogie (BMI)—Col 40597	6	9
7.	**SEE YOU LATER, ALLIGATOR** (BMI)—B. Haley; Paper Boy (ASCAP)—Dec 29791	7	4
8.	**IT'S ALMOST TOMORROW** (ASCAP)—Dream Weavers; You Got Me Wondering (ASCAP)—Dec 29683	8	13
9.	**DUNGAREE DOLL** (BMI)—E. Fisher; Everybody's Got a Home But Me (ASCAP)—Vic 20-6337	9	6
10.	**NO, NOT MUCH** (ASCAP)—Four Lads; I'll Never Know (BMI)—Col 40629	19	2
11.	**ARE YOU SATISFIED?** (BMI)—R. Draper; Wabash Cannonball (BMI)—Mercury 70757	16	5
12.	**ANGELS IN THE SKY** (BMI)—Crew Cuts; **MOSTLY MARTHA** (BMI)—Mercury 70741	11	8
13.	**HE** (BMI)—A. Hibbler; Breeze (ASCAP)—Dec 29660	14	19
14.	**I HEAR YOU KNOCKIN'** (BMI)—G. Storm; Never Leave Me (ASCAP)—Dot 15412	10	16
15.	**LOVE AND MARRIAGE** (ASCAP)—F. Sinatra; Impatient Years (ASCAP)—Cap 3260	12	13
16.	**MOMENTS TO REMEMBER** (ASCAP)—Four Lads; Dream On, My Love, Dream On (ASCAP)—Col 40539	13	23
17.	**ONLY YOU** (BMI)—Platters; Bark, Battle and Ball (BMI)—Mercury 70633	20	19
18.	**TEEN-AGE PRAYER** (ASCAP)—G. Storm; Memories Are Made of This (BMI)—Dot 15436	17	6
19.	**CHAIN GANG** (ASCAP)—B. Scott; Shadrach (ASCAP)—ABC-Paramount 9654	18	3
20.	**THEME FROM "THE THREE PENNY OPERA" ("MORITAT")** (ASCAP)—D. Hyman; Baubles, Bangles and Beads (ASCAP)—M-G-M 12149	21	2
21.	**GO ON WITH THE WEDDING** (ASCAP)—P. Page; Voice Inside (ASCAP)—Mercury 70766	—	1
22.	**AUTUMN LEAVES** (ASCAP)—R. Williams; Take Care (BMI)—Kapp 116	15	25
23.	**BURN THAT CANDLE** (BMI)—B. Haley; Rock-a-Beatin' Boogie (ASCAP)—Dec 29713	24	11
24.	**TUTTI FRUTTI** (BMI)—Little Richard; I'm Just a Lonely Guy (BMI)—Specialty 561	24	2
25.	**TENDER TRAP** (ASCAP)—F. Sinatra; Weep They Will (ASCAP)—Cap 3290	—	2

• THIS WEEK'S BEST BUYS

According to sales reports in key markets, the following recent releases are recommended for extra profits:

ASK ME (ABC, ASCAP)

NOTHING EVER CHANGES MY LOVE FOR YOU (Marvin, ASCAP)—Nat (King) Cole—Capitol 3328

Cole's latest release has taken little more than a week to make its presence felt. As has often been the case previously, action has been good on both sides, tho "Ask Me" has registered most strongly at the outset. Very good sales reports at the retail and one-stop levels have been returned from Boston, New York, Philadelphia, Buffalo, Baltimore, Detroit, Cleveland, Atlanta, St. Louis, Nashville and Durham. A previous Billboard "Spotlight" pick.

THAT'S YOUR MISTAKE (R-T, BMI)—Otis Williams—Deluxe 6091

See this week's Rhythm & Blues Best Buys.

• Most Played in Juke Boxes

For survey week ending January 25

RECORDS are ranked in order of the greatest number of plays in juke boxes thruout the country, as determined by The Billboard's weekly survey of the nation's juke box operators. When significant play is reported on both sides of a record, points are combined to determine position on the chart. In such a case, both sides are listed in bold type, the leading side on top.

This Week	Title	Last Week	Weeks on Chart
1.	**MEMORIES ARE MADE OF THIS** (BMI)—D. Martin; Change of Heart (BMI)—Cap 3295	1	7
2.	**SIXTEEN TONS** (BMI)—Tennessee Ernie; You Don't Have to Be a Baby to Cry (ASCAP)—Cap 3262	2	12
3.	**GREAT PRETENDER** (ASCAP)—Platters; I'm Just a Dancing Partner (ASCAP)—Mercury 70753	3	5
4.	**ROCK AND ROLL WALTZ** (BMI)—K. Starr; I've Changed My Mind a Thousand Times (ASCAP)—Vic 20-6359	5	4
5.	**I HEAR YOU KNOCKIN'** (BMI)—G. Storm; Never Leave Me (ASCAP)—Dot 15412	4	15
6.	**BAND OF GOLD** (BMI)—D. Cherry; Rumble Boogie (BMI)—Col 40597	7	3
7.	**LISBON ANTIGUA** (ASCAP)—N. Riddle; Robin Hood (ASCAP)—Cap 3287	—	1
8.	**IT'S ALMOST TOMORROW** (ASCAP)—Dream Weavers; You Got Me Wondering (ASCAP)—Dec 29683	9	9
9.	**TEEN-AGE PRAYER** (ASCAP)—G. Storm; Memories Are Made of This (BMI)—Dot 15436	7	6
10.	**MOMENTS TO REMEMBER** (ASCAP)—Four Lads; Dream On, My Love, Dream On (ASCAP)—Col 40539	6	17
10.	**DUNGAREE DOLL** (BMI)—E. Fisher; Everybody's Got a Home But Me (ASCAP)—Vic 20-6337	11	4
12.	**LOVE AND MARRIAGE** (ASCAP)—F. Sinatra; Impatient Years (ASCAP)—Cap 3260	12	9
13.	**ARE YOU SATISFIED?** (BMI)—R. Draper; Wabash Cannonball (BMI)—Mercury 70757	—	1
14.	**ONLY YOU** (BMI)—Platters; Bark, Battle and Ball (BMI)—Mercury 70623	10	16
15.	**ANGELS IN THE SKY** (BMI)—Crew Cuts; **MOSTLY MARTHA** (BMI)—Mercury 70741	17	3
15.	**HE** (BMI)—McGuire Sisters; If You Believe (ASCAP)—Coral 51501	19	12
17.	**ONLY YOU** (BMI)—Hilltoppers; Until the Real Thing Comes Along (ASCAP)—Dot 15423	12	12
17.	**AUTUMN LEAVES** (ASCAP)—R. Williams; Take Care (BMI)—Kapp 116	15	21
17.	**GO ON WITH THE WEDDING** (ASCAP)—P. Page; Voice Inside (ASCAP)—Mercury 70766	—	1
17.	**TUTTI FRUTTI** (BMI)—Little Richard; I'm Just a Lonely Guy (BMI)—Specialty 561	—	1

• Most Played by Jockeys

For survey week ending January 25

SIDES are ranked in order of the greatest number of plays on disk jockey radio shows thruout the country. Results are based on The Billboard's weekly survey among the nation's disk jockeys. The reverse side of each record is also listed.

This Week	Title	Last Week	Weeks on Chart
1.	**MEMORIES ARE MADE OF THIS** (BMI)—D. Martin; Change of Heart (BMI)—Cap 3295	1	9
2.	**GREAT PRETENDER**—Platters; I'm Just a Dancing Partner (ASCAP)—Mercury 70753	3	6
3.	**SIXTEEN TONS** (BMI)—Tennessee Ernie; You Don't Have to Be a Baby to Cry (ASCAP)—Cap 3262	2	13
4.	**ROCK AND ROLL WALTZ** (BMI)—K. Starr; I've Changed My Mind a Thousand Times (ASCAP)—Vic 20-6359	5	5
5.	**LISBON ANTIGUA** (ASCAP)—N. Riddle; Robin Hood (ASCAP)—Cap 3287	4	5
6.	**BAND OF GOLD** (BMI)—D. Cherry; Rumble Boogie (BMI)—Col 40597	6	6
7.	**MEMORIES ARE MADE OF THIS** (BMI)—G. Storm; Teen-Age Prayer (ASCAP)—Dot 15436	19	6
8.	**TEEN-AGE PRAYER** (ASCAP)—G. Storm; Memories Are Made of This (BMI)—Dot 15436	8	5
9.	**MOMENTS TO REMEMBER** (ASCAP)—Four Lads; Dream On, My Love, Dream On (ASCAP)—Col 40539	10	21
10.	**TENDER TRAP** (ASCAP)—F. Sinatra; Weep They Will (ASCAP)—Cap 3290	7	8
11.	**DUNGAREE DOLL** (BMI)—E. Fisher; Everybody's Got a Home But Me (ASCAP)—Vic 20-6337	9	3
12.	**LOVE AND MARRIAGE** (ASCAP)—F. Sinatra; Impatient Years (ASCAP)—Cap 3260	12	14
13.	**SEE YOU LATER, ALLIGATOR** (BMI)—B. Haley; Paper Boy (ASCAP)—Dec 29791	—	1
14.	**NO, NOT MUCH** (ASCAP)—Four Lads; I'll Never Know (BMI)—Col 40629	—	1
15.	**ALL AT ONCE YOU LOVE HER** (ASCAP)—P. Como; Rose Tattoo (ASCAP)—Vic 20-6294	14	9
16.	**CRY ME A RIVER** (ASCAP)—J. London; S'Wonderful (ASCAP)—Liberty 55006	15	10
17.	**IT'S ALMOST TOMORROW** (ASCAP)—Dream Weavers; You Got Me Wondering (ASCAP)—Dec 29683	14	8
18.	**ANGELS IN THE SKY** (BMI)—Crew Cuts; Mostly Martha (BMI)—Mercury 70741	16	4
19.	**I HEAR YOU KNOCKIN'** (BMI)—G. Storm; Never Leave Me (ASCAP)—Dot 15412	13	15
20.	**BAND OF GOLD** (BMI)—K. Carson; Cast Your Bread Upon the Waters—(ASCAP)—Cap 3283	17	8

The Billboard Music Popularity Charts

POPULAR RECORDS

THE TOP 100

For survey week ending January 25

A list of the Top 100 RECORD SIDES in the nation according to a COMBINED TABULATION of Dealer, Disk Jockey and Juke Box Operator replies to The Billboard's weekly popular record Best Seller and Most Played surveys. Its purpose is to provide Disk Jockeys with additional programming material and to give trade exposure to NEWER records just beginning to show action in the field.

Pos.	Song	Artist	Label	Last Week
1.	MEMORIES ARE MADE OF THIS	D. Martin	Capitol	1
2.	GREAT PRETENDER	Platters	Mercury	3
3.	SIXTEEN TONS	T. Ernie	Capitol	2
4.	ROCK AND ROLL WALTZ	K. Starr	Victor	4
5.	LISBON ANTIGUA	N. Riddle	Capitol	10
6.	BAND OF GOLD	D. Cherry	Columbia	5
7.	DUNGAREE DOLL	E. Fisher	Victor	8
8.	IT'S ALMOST TOMORROW	Dream Weavers	Decca	9
9.	MOMENTS TO REMEMBER	Four Lads	Columbia	7
9.	TEEN-AGE PRAYER	G. Storm	Dot	10
11.	I HEAR YOU KNOCKIN'	G. Storm	Dot	6
12.	LOVE AND MARRIAGE	F. Sinatra	Capitol	12
13.	SEE YOU LATER, ALLIGATOR	B. Haley	Decca	20
14.	ARE YOU SATISFIED?	R. Draper	Mercury	18
15.	HE	A. Hibbler	Decca	14
15.	ONLY YOU	Platters	Mercury	16
17.	ANGELS IN THE SKY	Crew Cuts	Mercury	15
18.	GO ON WITH THE WEDDING	P. Page	Mercury	24
19.	AUTUMN LEAVES	R. Williams	Kapp	13
20.	CRY ME A RIVER	J. London	Liberty	17
20.	THEME FROM THE THREE PENNY OPERA (MORITAT)	R. Hyman	M-G-M	37
22.	CHAIN GANG	B. Scott	ABC-Paramount	39
23.	ONLY YOU	Hilltoppers	Dot	19
24.	BAND OF GOLD	K. Carson	Capitol	21
25.	TEEN-AGE PRAYER	G. Mann	Sound	22
26.	NO, NOT MUCH	Four Lads	Columbia	38
27.	TUTTI FRUTTI	P. Boone	Dot	56
28.	IT'S ALMOST TOMORROW	J. Stafford	Columbia	35
29.	HE	McGuire Sisters	Coral	26
30.	TUTTI FRUTTI	Little Richard	Specialty	46
31.	MOSTLY MARTHA	Crew Cuts	Mercury	35
32.	TENDER TRAP	F. Sinatra	Capitol	23
33.	SPEEDOO	Cadillacs	Josie	43
34.	DADDY-O	Fontane Sisters	Dot	33
35.	LULLABY OF BIRDLAND	Blue Stars	Mercury	49
35.	BURN THAT CANDLE	B. Haley	Decca	29
37.	WOMAN IN LOVE	Four Aces	Decca	29
38.	ALL AT ONCE YOU LOVE HER	P. Como	Victor	31
38.	WOMAN IN LOVE	F. Laine	Columbia	24
40.	APRIL IN PARIS	C. Basie	Clef	53
41.	EVERYBODY'S GOT A HOME BUT ME	E. Fisher	Victor	55
42.	LOVE AND MARRIAGE	D. Shore	Victor	44
43.	MEMORIES ARE MADE OF THIS	G. Storm	Dot	27
44.	GO ON WITH THE WEDDING	K. Kallen-G. Shaw	Decca	71
44.	SEVEN DAYS	C. McPhatter	Atlantic	—
44.	TROUBLE WITH HARRY	Alfi & Harry	Liberty	50
47.	WHEN YOU DANCE	Turbans	Herald	42
48.	SEVEN DAYS	D. Collins	Coral	79
49.	GEE WHITTAKERS	P. Boone	Dot	27
49.	YOU ARE MY LOVE	J. James	M-G-M	62
51.	NINETY-NINE YEARS	G. Mitchell	Columbia	60
52.	MEMORIES OF YOU	Four Coins	Epic	34
53.	MEMORIES ARE MADE OF THIS	M. Carson	Columbia	59
54.	DON'T GO TO STRANGERS	V. Monroe	Victor	52
54.	AT MY FRONT DOOR	P. Boone	Dot	45
56.	MY BELIEVING HEART	J. James	M-G-M	74
57.	PEPPER HOT BABY	J. P. Morgan	Victor	74
57.	WANTING YOU	R. Williams	Kapp	58
59.	MEMORIES OF YOU	R. Clooney-B. Goodman	Columbia	63
60.	THEME FROM THE THREE PENNY OPERA (MORITAT)	R. Hayman-J. August	Mercury	—
60.	IT'S ALMOST TOMORROW	D. Carroll	Mercury	48
60.	LOVE IS A MANY-SPLENDORED THING	Four Aces	Decca	40
63.	THAT'S YOUR MISTAKE	O. Williams	De Luxe	78
63.	SHIFTING, WHISPERING SANDS	B. Vaughn	Dot	84
65.	C'EST LA VIE	S. Vaughan	Mercury	32
66.	LET IT RING	Doris Day	Columbia	51
67.	AUTUMN LEAVES	M. Miller	Columbia	74
68.	SEVEN DAYS	Crew Cuts	Mercury	—
68.	TAKE ME BACK TO TOYLAND	Nat (King) Cole	Capitol	47
70.	THEME FROM THE THREE PENNY OPERA (MORITAT)	B. Vaughn	Dot	—
71.	ALL THE WAY AROUND THE WORLD	Mills Brothers	Decca	63
72.	I'LL BE HOME	P. Boone	Dot	—
72.	IT'S ALMOST TOMORROW	S. Lanson	Dot	54
74.	WHO ARE WE	G. Grant	Era	—
75.	ROCK A-BEATIN' BOOGIE	B. Haley	Decca	93
75.	NEXT TIME IT HAPPENS	C. McRae	Decca	—
75.	I'VE CHANGED MY MIND A THOUSAND TIMES	K. Starr	Victor	—
78.	ARE YOU SATISFIED?	T. Arden	Victor	—
78.	I'M GONNA LAUGH YOU RIGHT OUT OF MY LIFE	Nat (King) Cole	Capitol	57
80.	NOT ONE GOODBYE	J. P. Morgan	Victor	66
81.	EVERYBODY'S GOT A HOME BUT ME	R. Hamilton	Epic	67
81.	NO ARMS CAN EVER HOLD YOU	G. Shaw	Decca	—
81.	TEEN-AGE PRAYER	K. White	Mercury	79
84.	AT MY FRONT DOOR	El Dorados	Vee Jay	84
85.	LISBON ANTIGUA	M. Miller	Columbia	—
86.	ADORABLE	Fontane Sisters	Dot	79
87.	SOMEONE YOU LOVE	Nat (King) Cole	Capitol	71
87.	DADDY-O	B. Lou	King	82
87.	TWENTY FOUR HOURS A DAY	G. Gibbs	Mercury	86
87.	WHAT IS A WIFE?	S. Allen	Coral	70
91.	MY BOY—FLAT TOP	D. Collins	Coral	63
92.	AIN'T THAT A SHAME	P. Boone	Dot	93
93.	MEMORIES OF YOU	H. Winterhalter	Victor	68
94.	AUTUMN LEAVES	S. Allen	Coral	—
94.	ELEVENTH HOUR MELODY	A. Hibbler	Decca	—
96.	GOODBYE TO ROME	G. Gibbs	Mercury	86
96.	WHEN YOU LOSE THE ONE YOU LOVE	D. Whitfield	London	—
98.	MAGIC MELODY	L. Paul & M. Ford	Capitol	—
98.	CROCE DI ORO (CROSS OF GOLD)	P. Page	Mercury	93
98.	TEXAS LADY	L. Paul & M. Ford	Capitol	91
98.	ZAMBESI	L. Busch	Capitol	93

CAUTION TO DEALERS AND JUKE BOX OPERATORS

The Billboard's Top 100 is NOT designed to provide tested information for buying purposes. This function is most reliably served by other regular weekly features: Best Sellers in Stores, Most Played in Juke Boxes, Coming Up Strong and Best Buys.

The Billboard Music Popularity Charts

POPULAR RECORDS

• Best Sellers in Stores

For survey week ending February 1

RECORDS are ranked in order of their current national selling importance at the retail level, as determined by The Billboard's weekly survey of the top volume dealers in very important market area. When significant action is reported on both sides of a record, points are combined to determine position on the chart. In such a case, both sides are listed in bold type, the leading side on top.

This Week		Last Week	Weeks on Chart
1.	**MEMORIES ARE MADE OF THIS** (BMI)—D. Martin Change of Heart (BMI)—Cap 3295	1	11
2.	**GREAT PRETENDER** (ASCAP)—Platters I'm Just a Dancing Partner (ASCAP) Mercury 70753	2	8
3.	**ROCK AND ROLL WALTZ** (BMI)—K. Starr I've Changed My Mind a Thousand Times (ASCAP)—Vic 20-6359	3	6
4.	**LISBON ANTIGUA** (ASCAP)—N. Riddle Robin Hood (ASCAP)—Cap 3287	5	7
5.	**SIXTEEN TONS** (BMI)—Tennessee Ernie You Don't Have to Be a Baby to Cry (ASCAP)—Cap 3262	4	14
6.	**SEE YOU LATER, ALLIGATOR** (BMI)—B. Haley Paper Boy (ASCAP)—Dec 29791	7	5
7.	**BAND OF GOLD** (BMI)—D. Cherry Rumble Boogie (BMI)—Col 40597	6	10
8.	**NO, NOT MUCH** (ASCAP)—Four Lads I'll Never Know (BMI)—Col 40629	10	3
9.	**IT'S ALMOST TOMORROW** (ASCAP)—Dream Weavers You Got Me Wondering (ASCAP)—Dec 29683	8	14
10.	**DUNGAREE DOLL** (BMI)—E. Fisher Everybody's Got a Home But Me (ASCAP—Vic 20-6337	9	7
11.	**THEME FROM "THE THREE PENNY OPERA" (MORITAT)** (ASCAP)—D. Hyman Baubles, Bangles and Beads (ASCAP)—M-G-M 12149	20	3
12.	**ANGELS IN THE SKY** (BMI)—Crew Cuts Mostly Martha (BMI)—Mercury 70741	12	9
13.	**TEEN-AGE PRAYER** (ASCAP)—G. Storm **MEMORIES ARE MADE OF THIS** (BMI)—Dot 15436	18	7
14.	**ARE YOU SATISFIED?** (BMI)—R. Draper Wabash Cannonball (BMI)—Mercury 70757	11	6
15.	**TUTTI FRUTTI** (BMI)—P. Boone **I'LL BE HOME** (BMI)—Dot 15443	—	1
16.	**HE** (BMI)—A. Hibbler Breeze (ASCAP)—Dec 29660	13	20
17.	**GO ON WITH THE WEDDING** (ASCAP)—P. Page Voice Inside (ASCAP)—Mercury 70766	21	2
18.	**I HEAR YOU KNOCKIN'** (BMI)—G. Storm Never Leave Me (ASCAP)—Dot 15412	14	17
19.	**MOMENTS TO REMEMBER** (ASCAP)—Four Lads Dream On, My Love, Dream On (ASCAP)—Col 40539	16	24
20.	**CHAIN GANG** (ASCAP)—B. Scott Shadrach (ASCAP)—ABC-Paramount 9658	19	4
21.	**TUTTI FRUTTI** (BMI)—Little Richard I'm Just a Lonely Guy (BMI)—Specialty 561	24	3
22.	**LOVE AND MARRIAGE** (ASCAP)—F. Sinatra Impatient Years (ASCAP)—Cap 3260	15	14
23.	**AUTUMN LEAVES** (ASCAP)—R. Williams Take Care (BMI)—Kapp 116	22	26
24.	**ONLY YOU** (BMI)—Platters Bark, Battle and Ball (BMI)—Mercury 70633	17	20
25.	**SPEEDOO** (BMI)—Cadillacs Let Me Explain (BMI)—Josie 785	—	1

• THIS WEEK'S BEST BUYS

According to sales reports in key markets, the following recent releases are recommended for extra profits:

THE POOR PEOPLE OF PARIS (Connelly, ASCAP)—**Les Baxter Ork—Capitol 3336**

When it comes to instrumentals, Baxter has a batting average that other conductors can only envy. Here again, two weeks after release, he has taken a tune a long way up the hit trail. Already on the Cleveland and Milwaukee territorial charts, "Poor People of Paris" is also rated a strong seller in New York, Chicago, Los Angeles, Philadelphia, Baltimore, Boston, Buffalo, St. Louis and other key markets. Flip is "Theme From Helen of Troy" (Harms, ASCAP). A previous Billboard "Spotlight" pick.

WHY DO FOOLS FALL IN LOVE? (Patricia, BMI)—**The Teenagers—Gee 1002**

The inroads that this disk has made in both the pop and r.&b. fields in the past week prove it to be a two-front threat on the order of "The Great Pretender." The Teenagers are now showing on both pop and r.&b. territorial charts and are moving up toward both national charts. Unusually good volume was reported in Cleveland, Cincinnati, Detroit, St. Louis, Nashville, Baltimore, Philadelphia, New York and Boston. Flip is "Please Be Mine" (Kahl, BMI). A previous Billboard "Spotlight" pick.

IF YOU CAN DREAM (Feist, ASCAP)
THE GAL WITH THE YALLER SHOES (Miller, ASCAP)—**Four Aces—Decca 29809**

Both these tunes from the pic "Meet Me in Las Vegas" are getting an excellent reception from disk jockeys, operators and retail customers, from all early indications. Shortly after being delivered, the disk was reported winging its way upward at a good clip in Philadelphia, Providence, Baltimore, Milwaukee, St. Louis, Pittsburgh and in several important Southern markets. Competition between sides is keen, with the ultimate "top side" unclear at this stage. A previous Billboard "Spotlight" pick.

• Most Played in Juke Boxes

For survey week ending February 1

RECORDS are ranked in order of the greatest number of plays in juke boxes thruout the country, as determined by The Billboard's weekly survey of the nation's juke box operators. When significant play is reported on both sides of a record, points are combined to determine position on the chart. In such a case, both sides are listed in bold type, the leading side on top.

This Week		Last Week	Weeks on Chart
1.	**MEMORIES ARE MADE OF THIS** (BMI)—D. Martin Change of Heart (BMI)—Cap 3295	1	8
2.	**GREAT PRETENDER** (ASCAP)—Platters I'm Just a Dancing Partner (ASCAP)—Mercury 70753	3	6
3.	**SIXTEEN TONS** (BMI)—Tennessee Ernie You Don't Have to Be a Baby to Cry (ASCAP)—Cap 3262	2	13
4.	**ROCK AND ROLL WALTZ** (BMI)—K. Starr I've Changed My Mind a Thousand Times (ASCAP)—Vic 20-6359	4	5
5.	**LISBON ANTIGUA** (ASCAP)—N. Riddle Robin Hood (ASCAP)—Cap 3287	7	2
6.	**BAND OF GOLD** (BMI)—D. Cherry Rumble Boogie (BMI)—Col 40597	6	4
7.	**I HEAR YOU KNOCKIN'** (BMI)—G. Storm Never Leave Me (ASCAP)—Dot 15412	5	16
8.	**DUNGAREE DOLL** (BMI)—E. Fisher Everybody's Got a Home But Me (ASCAP)—Vic 20-6337	10	5
9.	**IT'S ALMOST TOMORROW** (ASCAP)—Dream Weavers You Got Me Wondering (ASCAP)—Dec 29683	8	10
10.	**TEEN-AGE PRAYER** (ASCAP)—G. Storm **MEMORIES ARE MADE OF THIS** (BMI)—Dot 15436	9	7
10.	**SEE YOU LATER, ALLIGATOR** (BMI)—B. Haley Paper Boy (ASCAP)—Dec 29791	—	1
12.	**ARE YOU SATISFIED?** (BMI)—R. Draper Wabash Cannonball (BMI)—Mercury 70757	13	2
13.	**MOMENTS TO REMEMBER** (ASCAP)—Four Lads Dream On, My Love, Dream On (ASCAP)—Col 40539	10	18
13.	**ANGELS IN THE SKY** (BMI)—Crew Cuts **MOSTLY MARTHA** (BMI)—Mercury 70741	15	4
13.	**GO ON WITH THE WEDDING** (ASCAP)—P. Page Voice Inside (ASCAP)—Mercury 70766	17	2
16.	**LOVE AND MARRIAGE** (ASCAP)—F. Sinatra Impatient Years (ASCAP)—Cap 3260	12	10
17.	**ONLY YOU** (BMI)—Platters Bark, Battle and Ball (BMI)—Mercury 70623	14	17
17.	**CRY ME A RIVER** (ASCAP)—J. London S'Wonderful (ASCAP)—Liberty 55006	—	8
17.	**IT'S ALMOST TOMORROW** (ASCAP)—J. Stafford If You Want to Love (ASCAP)—Col 40595	—	1
17.	**SEVEN DAYS** (BMI)—D. Collins Manuello (BMI)—Cor 61562	—	1

• Most Played by Jockeys

For survey week ending February 1

SIDES are ranked in order of the greatest number of plays on disk jockey radio shows thruout the country. Results are based on The Billboard's weekly survey among the nation's disk jockeys. The reverse side of each record is also listed.

This Week		Last Week	Weeks on Chart
1.	**MEMORIES ARE MADE OF THIS** (BMI)—D. Martin Change of Heart (BMI)—Cap 3295	1	10
2.	**GREAT PRETENDER**—Platters I'm Just a Dancing Partner (ASCAP)—Mercury 70753	2	7
3.	**ROCK AND ROLL WALTZ** (BMI)—K. Starr I've Changed My Mind a Thousand Times (ASCAP)—Vic 20-6359	4	6
4.	**LISBON ANTIGUA** (ASCAP)—N. Riddle Robin Hood (ASCAP)—Cap 3287	5	6
5.	**SIXTEEN TONS** (BMI)—Tennessee Ernie You Don't Have to Be a Baby to Cry (ASCAP)—Cap 3262	3	14
6	**BAND OF GOLD** (BMI)—D. Cherry Rumble Boogie (BMI)—Col 40597	6	7
7.	**TEEN-AGE PRAYER** (ASCAP)—G. Storm Memories Are Made of This (BMI)—Dot 15436	8	6
8.	**NO, NOT MUCH** (ASCAP)—Four Lads I'll Never Know (BMI)—Col 40629	14	2
9.	**SEE YOU LATER, ALLIGATOR** (BMI)—B. Haley Paper Boy (ASCAP)—Dec 29791	13	2
10.	**DUNGAREE DOLL** (BMI)—E. Fisher Everybody's Got a Home But Me (ASCAP)—Vic 20-6337	11	4
11.	**THEME FROM THE THREE PENNY OPERA (MORITAT)** (ASCAP)—B. Hyman Baubles, Bangles and Beads (ASCAP)—M-G-M 12149	—	1
12.	**MEMORIES ARE MADE OF THIS** (BMI)—G. Storm Teen-Age Prayer (ASCAP)—Dot 15436	7	7
13.	**TENDER TRAP** (ASCAP)—F. Sinatra Weep They Will (ASCAP)—Cap 3290	10	9
14.	**CHAIN GANG** (ASCAP)—B. Scott Shadrack (ASCAP)—ABC-Paramount 9658	—	1
15.	**IT'S ALMOST TOMORROW** (ASCAP)—Dream Weavers You Got Me Wondering (ASCAP)—Dec 29683	17	9
16.	**GO ON WITH THE WEDDING** (ASCAP)—P. Page Voice Inside (ASCAP)—Mercury 70766	—	1
17.	**ANGELS IN THE SKY** (BMI)—Crew Cuts Mostly Martha (BMI)—Mercury 70741	18	5
18.	**BAND OF GOLD** (BMI)—K. Carson Cast Your Bread Upon the Waters (ASCAP)—Cap 3283	20	9
19.	**CRY ME A RIVER** (ASCAP)—J. London S'Wonderful (ASCAP)—Liberty 55006	16	11
20.	**I'LL BE HOME** (BMI)—P. Boone Tutti Frutti (BMI)—Dot 15443	—	1

when answering ads . . .
SAY YOU SAW IT IN THE BILLBOARD!

The Billboard Music Popularity Charts

POPULAR RECORDS

THE TOP 100

For survey week ending February 1

A list of the Top 100 **RECORD SIDES** in the nation according to a **COMBINED TABULATION** of Dealer, Disk Jockey and Juke Box Operator replies to The Billboard's weekly popular record Best Seller and Most Played surveys. Its purpose is to provide Disk Jockeys with additional programming material and to give trade exposure to NEWER records just beginning to show action in the field.

Pos.	Song	Artist	Label	Last Week
1.	MEMORIES ARE MADE OF THIS	D. Martin	Capitol	1
2.	GREAT PRETENDER	Platters	Mercury	2
3.	ROCK AND ROLL WALTZ	K. Starr	Victor	4
4.	SIXTEEN TONS	T. Ernie	Capitol	3
4.	LISBON ANTIGUA	N. Riddle	Capitol	3
6.	BAND OF GOLD	D. Cherry	Columbia	6
7.	SEE YOU LATER, ALLIGATOR	B. Haley	Decca	13
8.	DUNGAREE DOLL	E. Fisher	Victor	7
9.	IT'S ALMOST TOMORROW	Dream Weavers	Decca	8
9.	TEEN-AGE PRAYER	G. Storm	Dot	9
11.	GO ON WITH THE WEDDING	P. Page	Mercury	18
12.	ARE YOU SATISFIED?	R. Draper	Mercury	14
13.	ANGELS IN THE SKY	Crew Cuts	Mercury	17
13.	NO, NOT MUCH	Four Lads	Columbia	26
15.	MOMENTS TO REMEMBER	Four Lads	Columbia	9
16.	I HEAR YOU KNOCKIN'	G. Storm	Dot	11
17.	LOVE AND MARRIAGE	F. Sinatra	Capitol	12
18.	CHAIN GANG	B. Scott	ABC Paramount	22
19.	THEME FROM THE THREE PENNY OPERA (Moritat)	D. Hyman	M-G-M	20
20.	HE	A. Hibbler	Decca	15
21.	IT'S ALMOST TOMORROW	J. Stafford	Columbia	28
22.	ONLY YOU	Platters	Mercury	15
23.	BAND OF GOLD	K. Carson	Capitol	24
23.	TUTTI FRUTTI	P. Boone	Dot	27
25.	CRY ME A RIVER	J. London	Liberty	20
26.	MEMORIES ARE MADE OF THIS	G. Storm	Dot	43
27.	TUTTI FRUTTI	Little Richard	Specialty	30
28.	TENDER TRAP	F. Sinatra	Capitol	32
29.	WOMAN IN LOVE	F. Laine	Columbia	38
30.	SPEEDOO	Cadillacs	Josie	33
31.	HE	McGuire Sisters	Coral	29
32.	SEVEN DAYS	D. Collins	Coral	48
33.	THEME FROM THE THREE PENNY OPERA (Moritat)	R. Hayman-J. August	Mercury	60
34.	LULLABY OF BIRDLAND	Blue Stars	Mercury	35
35.	I'LL BE HOME	P. Boone	Dot	72
36.	WOMAN IN LOVE	Four Aces	Decca	37
37.	TEEN-AGE PRAYER	G. Mann	Sound	25
38.	BURN THAT CANDLE	B. Haley	Decca	35
39.	GO ON WITH THE WEDDING	K. Kallen-G. Shaw	Decca	44
39.	MOSTLY MARTHA	Crew Cuts	Mercury	31
41.	WHEN YOU DANCE	Turbans	Herald	47
42.	GEE WHITTAKERS	P. Boone	Dot	49
42.	MEMORIES OF YOU	Four Coins	Epic	52
44.	ONLY YOU	Hilltoppers	Dot	23
45.	AUTUMN LEAVES	R. Williams	Kapp	19
46.	DADDY-O	Fontane Sisters	Dot	34
46.	ALL AT ONCE YOU LOVE HER	P. Como	Victor	38
46.	POOR PEOPLE OF PARIS	L. Baxter	Capitol	—
49.	DON'T GO TO STRANGERS	V. Monroe	Victor	54
49.	EVERYBODY'S GOT A HOME BUT ME	E. Fisher	Victor	41
51.	APRIL IN PARIS	C. Basie	Clef	40
51.	NINETY-NINE YEARS	C. Mitchell	Columbia	51
53.	THEME FROM THE THREE PENNY OPERA (Moritat)	B. Vaughn	Dot	70
54.	IT'S ALMOST TOMORROW	S. Lanson	Dot	72
55.	IT'S ALMOST TOMORROW	D. Carroll	Mercury	60
55.	SEVEN DAYS	C. McPhatter	Atlantic	44
57.	ELEVENTH HOUR MELODY	A. Hibbler	Decca	94
58.	SEVEN DAYS	Crew Cuts	Mercury	68
59.	LIPSTICK CANDY AND RUBBER SOLED SHOES	J. La Rosa	Victor	—
60.	TROUBLE WITH HARRY	Alfi & Harry	Liberty	44
60.	MACK THE KNIFE	L. Armstrong	Decca	—
62.	C'EST LA VIE	S. Vaughan	Mercury	65
62.	MEMORIES OF YOU	H. Winterhalter	Victor	93
64.	MR. WONDERFUL	S. Vaughan	Mercury	—
65.	MEMORIES ARE MADE OF THIS	M. Carson	Columbia	53
66.	WHO ARE WE?	G. Grant	Era	74
67.	ROCK AROUND MOTHER GOOSE	B. Gordon	M-G-M	—
68.	TAKE ME BACK TO TOYLAND	Nat (King) Cole	Capitol	68
69.	LET IT RING	Doris Day	Columbia	66
69.	MEMORIES ARE MADE OF THIS	B. Goodman-R. Clooney	Columbia	59
71.	MY BELIEVING HEART	J. James	M-G-M	56
72.	LOVE AND MARRIAGE	D. Shore	Victor	42
73.	STOLEN LOVE	D. Shore	Victor	—
74.	ASK ME	Nat (King) Cole	Capitol	—
74.	LOVE IS A MANY-SPLENDORED THING	Four Aces	Decca	60
76.	NOT ONE GOODBYE	J. P. Morgan	Victor	80
76.	WANTING YOU	R. Williams	Kapp	57
76.	LITTLE BOY BLUE	B. Vaughn	Dot	—
79.	AUTUMN LEAVES	M. Miller	Columbia	67
80.	DADDY-O	B. Lou	King	87
80.	TROUBLE WITH HARRY	L. Baxter	Capitol	—
80.	OUR LOVE AFFAIR	T. Charles	Decca	—
83.	TWENTY-FOUR HOURS A DAY	G. Gibbs	Mercury	87
84.	I'M GONNA LAUGH YOU RIGHT OUT OF MY LIFE	Nat (King) Cole	Capitol	78
84.	THAT'S YOUR MISTAKE	O. Williams	De Luxe	63
86.	WHY DO FOOLS FALL IN LOVE?	Teen-Agers	Gee	—
87.	ROCK A BEATIN BOOGIE	B. Haley	Decca	75
87.	MY BOY FLAT TOP	D. Collins	Coral	91
87.	I'M JUST A DANCING PARTNER	Platters	Mercury	—
90.	AT MY FRONT DOOR	P. Boone	Dot	54
90.	TEEN-AGE PRAYER	K. White	Mercury	81
92.	CHARMAINE	Four Freshmen	Capitol	—
93.	MY TREASURE	Hilltoppers	Dot	—
93.	GOODBYE TO ROME	G. Gibbs	Mercury	96
95.	THEME FROM THE THREE PENNY OPERA (MORITAT)	L. Paul & M. Ford	Capitol	—
95.	NEXT TIME IT HAPPENS	G. Mac Rae	Decca	75
97.	SIXTEEN TONS	J. Desmond	Coral	—
97.	KEY TO MY HEART	R. Clooney	Columbia	—
97.	WHAT IS A WIFE?	S. Allen	Coral	87
100.	SHIFTING, WHISPERING SANDS	B. Vaughn	Dot	63

CAUTION TO DEALERS AND JUKE BOX OPERATORS

The Billboard's Top 100 is NOT designed to provide tested information for buying purposes. This function is most reliably served by other regular weekly features: Best Sellers in Stores, Most Played in Juke Boxes, Coming Up Strong and Best Buys.

The Billboard Music Popularity Charts — POPULAR RECORDS

• Best Sellers in Stores

For survey week ending February 8

RECORDS are ranked in order of their current national selling importance at the retail level, as determined by The Billboard's weekly survey of the top volume dealers in very important market area. When significant action is reported on both sides of a record, points are combined to determine position on the chart. In such a case, both sides are listed in bold type, the leading side on top.

This Week	Record	Last Week	Weeks on Chart
1.	**ROCK AND ROLL WALTZ** (BMI)—K. Starr I've Changed My Mind a Thousand Times (ASCAP)—Vic 20-6359	3	7
2.	**LISBON ANTIGUA** (ASCAP)—N. Riddle Robin Hood (ASCAP)—Cap 3287	4	8
3.	**GREAT PRETENDER** (ASCAP)—Platters I'm Just a Dancing Partner (ASCAP)—Mercury 70753	2	9
4.	**MEMORIES ARE MADE OF THIS** (BMI)—D. Martin Change of Heart (BMI)—Cap 3295	1	12
5.	**NO, NOT MUCH** (ASCAP)—Four Lads I'll Never Know (BMI)—Col 40629	8	4
6.	**SEE YOU LATER, ALLIGATOR** (BMI)—B. Haley Paper Boy (ASCAP)—Dec 29791	6	6
7.	**BAND OF GOLD** (BMI)—D. Cherry Rumble Boogie (BMI)—Col 40597	7	11
8.	**SIXTEEN TONS** (BMI)—Tennessee Ernie You Don't Have to Be a Baby to Cry (ASCAP)—Cap 3262	5	15
9.	**POOR PEOPLE OF PARIS** (ASCAP)—L. Baxter Theme From Helen of Troy (ASCAP)—Cap 3336	—	1
10.	**I'LL BE HOME** (BMI)—P. Boone **TUTTI FRUTTI** (BMI)—Dot 15443	15	2
11.	**IT'S ALMOST TOMORROW** (ASCAP)—Dream Weavers You Got Me Wondering (ASCAP)—Dec 29683	9	15
12.	**DUNGAREE DOLL** (BMI)—E. Fisher Everybody's Got a Home But Me (ASCAP)—Vic 20-6337	10	8
13.	**THEME FROM "THE THREE PENNY OPERA" ("MORITAT")** (ASCAP)—D. Hyman Baubles, Bangles and Beads (ASCAP)—M-G-M 12149	11	4
14.	**ANGELS IN THE SKY** (BMI)—Crew Cuts **MOSTLY MARTHA** (BMI)—Mercury 70741	12	10
15.	**TEEN-AGE PRAYER** (ASCAP)—G. Storm Memories Are Made of This (BMI)—Dot 15436	13	8
15.	**WHY DO FOOLS FALL IN LOVE?** (BMI)—Teen Agers Please Be Mine (BMI)—Gee 1002	—	1
17.	**GO ON WITH THE WEDDING** (ASCAP)—P. Page Voice Inside (ASCAP)—Mercury 70766	17	3
18.	**TUTTI FRUTTI** (BMI)—Little Richard I'm Just a Lonely Guy (BMI)—Specialty 561	21	4
19.	**THEME FROM "THE THREE PENNY OPERA" ("MORITAT")**—R. Hayman-J. August I'll Be With You in Apple-Blossom Time (ASCAP)—Mercury 12159	—	1
20.	**CHAIN GANG** (ASCAP)—B. Scott Shadrach (ASCAP)—ABC-Paramount 9658	20	5
21.	**SPEEDOO** (BMI)—Cadillacs Let Me Explain (BMI)—Josie 785	25	2
22.	**LOVE AND MARRIAGE** (ASCAP)—F. Sinatra Impatient Years (ASCAP)—Cap 3260	22	15
23.	**MOMENTS TO REMEMBER**—Four Lads Dream On, My Love, Dream On (ASCAP)—Col 40539	19	25
24.	**HE** (BMI)—A. Hibbler Breeze (ASCAP)—Dec 29660	16	21
25.	**WOMAN IN LOVE** (ASCAP)—Four Aces Of This I'm Sure (ASCAP)—Dec 29725	—	3

• THIS WEEK'S BEST BUYS

According to sales reports in key markets, the following recent releases are recommended for extra profits:

THAT'S ALL (American, BMI)—Tennessee Ernie Ford—Capitol 3343

Bucking the persistent appeal of his previous hit release, "Sixteen Tons," Tennessee Ernie's latest release has taken a while to get started. Now it has achieved general distribution and is sailing smoothly. Reports from Los Angeles, St. Louis, Milwaukee, Atlanta, Baltimore, Nashville, Durham, Buffalo, Philadelphia, Cleveland and Boston indicated the disk is selling well and increasing velocity. Flip is "Bright Lights and Blonde-Haired Women" (Century, BMI). A previous Billboard "Spotlight" pick.

A TEAR FELL (Progressive, BMI)

BO WEEVIL (Reeve, BMI)—Teresa Brewer—Coral 61590

The chantress has hit upon some potent material in these two r.&b. tunes. Sales in the first 10 days were unusually good in most key markets. Providence, Baltimore, Philadelphia, Cleveland, Chicago, Milwaukee, St. Louis, Atlanta, Nashville and Los Angeles had particularly good results with the disk. Action is reported on both sides, but with a majority preferring "A Tear Fell." A previous Billboard "Spotlight" pick.

• Most Played in Juke Boxes

For survey week ending February 8

RECORDS are ranked in order of the greatest number of plays in juke boxes thruout the country, as determined by The Billboard's weekly survey of the nation's juke box operators. When significant play is reported on both sides of a record, points are combined to determine position on the chart. In such a case, both sides are listed in bold type, the leading side on top.

This Week	Record	Last Week	Weeks on Chart
1.	**MEMORIES ARE MADE OF THIS** (BMI)—D. Martin Change of Heart (BMI)—Cap 3295	1	9
2.	**GREAT PRETENDER** (ASCAP)—Platters I'm Just a Dancing Partner (ASCAP)—Mercury 70753	2	7
3.	**ROCK AND ROLL WALTZ** (BMI)—K. Starr I've Changed My Mind a Thousand Times (ASCAP)—Vic 20-6359	4	6
4.	**SIXTEEN TONS** (BMI)—Tennessee Ernie You Don't Have to Be a Baby to Cry (ASCAP)—Cap 3262	3	14
5.	**LISBON ANTIGUA** (ASCAP)—N. Riddle Robin Hood (ASCAP)—Cap 3287	5	3
6.	**BAND OF GOLD** (BMI)—D. Cherry Rumble Boogie (BMI)—Col 40597	6	5
7	**DUNGAREE DOLL** (BMI)—E. Fisher Everybody's Got a Home But Me (ASCAP)—Vic 20-6337	8	6
8.	**SEE YOU LATER, ALLIGATOR** (BMI)—B. Haley Paper Boy (ASCAP)—Dec 29791	10	2
9.	**IT'S ALMOST TOMORROW** (ASCAP)—Dream Weavers You Got Me Wondering (ASCAP)—Dec 29683	9	11
10.	**TEEN-AGE PRAYER** (ASCAP)—G. Storm **MEMORIES ARE MADE OF THIS** (BMI)—Dot 15436	10	8
11.	**I HEAR YOU KNOCKIN'** (BMI)—G Storm Never Leave Me (ASCAP)—Dot 15412	7	17
12.	**GO ON WITH THE WEDDING** (ASCAP)—P. Page Voice Inside (ASCAP)—Mercury 70766	13	3
13.	**ARE YOU SATISFIED?** (BMI)—R. Draper Wabash Cannonball (BMI)—Mercury 70757	12	3
13.	**MOMENTS TO REMEMBER** (ASCAP)—Four Lads Dream On, My Love, Dream On (ASCAP)—Col 40539	13	19
13.	**TUTTI FRUTTI** (BMI)—P. Boone I'll Be Home (BMI)—Dot 15443	—	1
16.	**NO, NOT MUCH** (ASCAP)—Four Lads I'll Never Know (BMI)—Col 40629	—	1
17.	**ANGELS IN THE SKY** (BMI)—Crew Cuts Mostly Martha (BMI)—Mercury 70741	13	5
17.	**SEVEN DAYS** (BMI)—D. Collins Manuello (BMI)—Coral 61562	17	2
19.	**CHAIN GANG** (ASCAP)—B. Scott Shadrach (ASCAP)—ABC Paramount 9658	—	1
20.	**IT'S ALMOST TOMORROW** (ASCAP)—J. Stafford If You Want to Love (ASCAP)—Col 40595	17	2

• Most Played by Jockeys

For survey week ending February 8

SIDES are ranked in order of the greatest number of plays on disk jockey radio shows thruout the country. Results are based on The Billboard's weekly survey among the nation's disk jockeys. The reverse side of each record is also listed.

This Week	Record	Last Week	Weeks on Chart
1.	**GREAT PRETENDER**—Platters I'm Just a Dancing Partner (ASCAP)—Mercury 70753	2	8
2.	**MEMORIES ARE MADE OF THIS** (BMI)—D. Martin Change of Heart (BMI)—Cap 3295	1	11
3.	**ROCK AND ROLL WALTZ** (BMI)—K. Starr I've Changed My Mind a Thousand Times (ASCAP)—Vic 20-6359	3	7
4.	**LISBON ANTIGUA** (ASCAP)—N. Riddle Robin Hood (ASCAP)—Cap 3287	4	7
5.	**NO, NOT MUCH** (ASCAP)—Four Lads I'll Never Know (BMI)—Col 40629	8	3
6.	**SEE YOU LATER, ALLIGATOR** (BMI)—B. Haley Paper Boy (ASCAP)—Dec 29791	9	3
7.	**SIXTEEN TONS** (BMI)—Tennessee Ernie You Don't Have to Be a Baby to Cry (ASCAP)—Cap 3262	5	15
8.	**BAND OF GOLD** (BMI)—D. Cherry Rumble Boogie (BMI)—Col 40597	6	8
9.	**POOR PEOPLE OF PARIS** (ASCAP)—L. Baxter Theme From Helen of Troy (ASCAP)—Cap 3336	—	1
10.	**THEME FROM THE "THREE PENNY OPERA" (MORITAT)** (ASCAP)—D. Hyman Baubles, Bangles, and Beads (ASCAP)—M-G-M 12149	11	2
11.	**DUNGAREE DOLL** (BMI)—E. Fisher Everybody's Got a Home But Me (ASCAP)—Vic 20-6337	10	5
12.	**I'LL BE HOME** (BMI)—P. Boone Tutti Frutti (BMI)—Dot 15443	20	2
13.	**TEEN-AGE PRAYER** (ASCAP)—G. Storm Memories Are Made of This (BMI)—Dot 15436	7	7
13.	**CHAIN GANG** (ASCAP)—B. Scott Shadrach (ASCAP)—ABC-Paramount 9658	14	2
15.	**IT'S ALMOST TOMORROW** (ASCAP)—Dream Weavers You Got Me Wondering (ASCAP)—Dec 29683	15	10
16.	**BAND OF GOLD** (BMI)—K. Carson Cast Your Bread Upon the Waters (ASCAP)—Cap 3283	18	10
17.	**THEME FROM "THE THREE PENNY OPERA" (MORITAT)** (ASCAP)—R. Hayman-J. August I'll Be With You in Apple Blossom Time (ASCAP)—Mercury 12159	—	1
18.	**TUTTI FRUTTI** (BMI)—P. Boone I'll Be Home (BMI)—Dot 15443	—	1
19.	**LISBON ANTIGUA** (ASCAP)—M. Miller Willy Can (BMI)—Col 40635	—	1
20.	**ANGELS IN THE SKY** (BMI)—Crew Cuts Mostly Martha (BMI)—Mercury 70741	17	6

The Billboard Music Popularity Charts

POPULAR RECORDS

THE TOP 100

For survey week ending February 8

A list of the **Top 100 RECORD SIDES** in the nation according to a **COMBINED TABULATION** of Dealer, Disk Jockey and Juke Box Operator replies to The Billboard's weekly popular record Best Seller and Most Played surveys. Its purpose is to provide Disk Jockeys with additional programming material and to give trade exposure to NEWER records just beginning to show action in the field.

Pos.	Song	Artist	Label	Last Week
1.	GREAT PRETENDER	Platters	Mercury	2
2.	MEMORIES ARE MADE OF THIS	D. Martin	Capitol	1
2.	ROCK AND ROLL WALTZ	K. Starr	Victor	3
4.	LISBON ANTIGUA	N. Riddle	Capitol	4
5.	SIXTEEN TONS	T. Ernie	Capitol	4
6.	SEE YOU LATER, ALLIGATOR	B. Haley	Decca	7
7.	BAND OF GOLD	D. Cherry	Columbia	6
8.	NO, NOT MUCH	Four Lads	Columbia	13
9.	DUNGAREE DOLL	E. Fisher	Victor	8
10.	IT'S ALMOST TOMORROW	Dream Weavers	Decca	9
11.	TEEN-AGE PRAYER	G. Storm	Dot	9
12.	TUTTI FRUTTI	P. Boone	Dot	23
13.	GO ON WITH THE WEDDING	P. Page	Mercury	11
13.	THEME FROM THE THREE PENNY OPERA (MORITAT)	D. Hyman	M-G-M	19
15.	CHAIN GANG	B. Scott	ABC Paramount	18
16.	ANGELS IN THE SKY	Crew Cuts	Mercury	13
17.	BAND OF GOLD	K. Carson	Capitol	23
18.	I HEAR YOU KNOCKIN'	G. Storm	Dot	16
19.	I'LL BE HOME	P. Boone	Dot	35
20.	IT'S ALMOST TOMORROW	J. Stafford	Columbia	21
21.	TUTTI FRUTTI	Little Richard	Specialty	27
22.	CRY ME A RIVER	J. London	Liberty	25
23.	THEME FROM THE THREE PENNY OPERA (MORITAT)	R. Hayman-J. August	Mercury	33
24.	HE	A. Hibbler	Decca	20
25.	POOR PEOPLE OF PARIS	L. Baxter	Capitol	46
25.	SEVEN DAYS	D. Collins	Coral	32
27.	ONLY YOU	Platters	Mercury	22
27.	MOMENTS TO REMEMBER	Four Lads	Columbia	15
29.	MEMORIES ARE MADE OF THIS	G. Storm	Dot	26
30.	SEVEN DAYS	Crew Cuts	Mercury	58
31.	LULLABY OF BIRDLAND	Blue Stars	Mercury	34
32.	WOMAN IN LOVE	F. Laine	Columbia	29
33.	TENDER TRAP	F. Sinatra	Capitol	28
34.	SPEEDOO	Cadillacs	Josie	30
35.	ARE YOU SATISFIED	R. Draper	Mercury	12
35.	APRIL IN PARIS	C. Basie	Clef	51
37.	WOMAN IN LOVE	Four Aces	Decca	36
38.	DON'T GO TO STRANGERS	V. Monroe	Victor	49
39.	LIPSTICK, CANDY AND RUBBER SOLED SHOES	J. La Rosa	Victor	59
39.	MOSTLY MARTHA	Crew Cuts	Mercury	39
41.	MEMORIES OF YOU	Four Coins	Epic	42
42.	ELEVENTH HOUR MELODY	A. Hibbler	Decca	57
43.	LOVE AND MARRIAGE	F. Sinatra	Capitol	17
44.	GEE WHITTAKERS	P. Boone	Dot	42
45.	HE	McGuire Sisters	Coral	31
46.	ONLY YOU	Hilltoppers	Dot	44
47.	WHY DO FOOLS FALL IN LOVE?	Teen-Agers	Gee	86
48.	LISBON ANTIGUA	M. Miller	Columbia	-
49.	NINETY-NINE YEARS	G. Mitchell	Columbia	51
50.	IT'S ALMOST TOMORROW	S. Lanson	Dot	54
50.	BURN THAT CANDLE	B. Haley	Decca	38
52.	ROCK AROUND MOTHER GOOSE	B. Gordon	M-G-M	67
53.	GO ON WITH THE WEDDING	K. Kallen-G. Shaw	Decca	39
54.	THEME FROM THE THREE PENNY OPERA (MORITAT)	L. Paul & M. Ford	Capitol	95
55.	IT'S ALMOST TOMORROW	D. Carroll	Mercury	55
55.	WHEN YOU DANCE	Turbans	Herald	41
57.	THEME FROM THE THREE PENNY OPERA (MORITAT)	B. Vaughn	Dot	53
58.	MR. WONDERFUL	T. King	Victor	—
59.	LITTLE CHILD	E. Albert	Kapp	—
60.	TEEN-AGE PRAYER	G. Mann	Sound	37
61.	THEME FROM THE THREE PENNY OPERA (MACK THE KNIFE)	L. Armstrong	Columbia	60
62.	WHO ARE WE?	G. Grant	Era	66
63.	ALL AT ONCE YOU LOVE HER	P. Como	Victor	46
64.	THEME FROM THE THREE PENNY OPERA (MORITAT)	L. Welk	Coral	-
65.	AUTUMN LEAVES	R. Williams	Kapp	45
66.	SHIFTING, WHISPERING SANDS	R. Draper	Mercury	--
66.	OUR LOVE AFFAIR	T. Charles	Decca	80
68.	ASK ME	Nat (King) Cole	Capitol	74
68.	TEEN-AGE PRAYER	K. White	Mercury	90
70.	C'EST LA VIE	S. Vaughan	Mercury	62
71.	MEMORIES ARE MADE OF THIS	M. Carson	Columbia	65
72.	EVERYBODY'S GOT A HOME BUT ME	E. Fisher	Victor	49
72.	TROUBLE WITH HARRY	Alfie & Harry	Liberty	60
74.	MR. WONDERFUL	S. Vaughan	Mercury	64
74.	MY BELIEVING HEART	J. James	M-G-M	71
76.	DADDY-O	Fontane Sisters	Dot	46
76.	MEMORIES OF YOU	R. Clooney-B. Goodman	Columbia	69
78.	CHAIN GANG	L. Dressler	Mercury	—
78.	YOU, BABY, YOU	Cleftones	Gee	—
80.	LOVE IS A MANY-SPLENDORED THING	Four Aces	Decca	74
81.	CRY BABY	Bonnie Sisters	Rainbow	—
81.	WHY DO FOOLS FALL IN LOVE?	Diamonds	Mercury	—
81.	LITTLE CHILD	C. Calloway	ABC Paramount	—
81.	THESE HANDS	L. Dressler	Mercury	—
85.	THAT'S YOUR MISTAKE	O. Williams	De Luxe	84
85.	WHEN YOU LOSE THE ONE YOU LOVE	D. Whitfield	London	—
87.	YOU ARE MY LOVE	J. James	M-G-M	—
87.	MEMORIES OF YOU	H. Winterhalter	Victor	62
89.	SUCH A DAY	R. Raines	Deed	—
90.	I'VE CHANGED MY MIND A THOUSAND TIMES	K. Starr	Victor	—
91.	LET IT RING	Doris Day	Columbia	—
91.	NUEVO LAREDO	L. Paul & M. Ford	Capitol	—
93.	TROUBLE WITH HARRY	L. Baxter	Capitol	80
93.	BAND OF GOLD	Hi-Fi Four	King	—
95.	SEVEN DAYS	C. McPhatter	Atlantic	55
96.	GOODBYE TO ROME	G. Gibbs	Mercury	93
96.	TEEN-AGE MEETING	D. Cornell	Coral	—
98.	MY BOY FLAT TOP	D. Collins	Coral	87
98.	IF YOU CAN DREAM	Four Aces	Decca	—
100.	ADORABLE	Fontane, Sisters	Dot	—
100.	MY TREASURE	Hilltoppers	Dot	—
100.	VALLEY VALPARAISO	P. Faith	Columbia	

CAUTION TO DEALERS AND JUKE BOX OPERATORS

The Billboard's Top 100 is NOT designed to provide tested information for buying purposes. This function is most reliably served by other regular weekly features: Best Sellers in Stores, Most Played in Juke Boxes, Coming Up Strong and Best Buys.

The Billboard Music Popularity Charts — POPULAR RECORDS

• Best Sellers in Stores

For survey week ending February 15

RECORDS are ranked in order of their current national selling importance at the retail level, as determined by The Billboard's weekly survey of the top volume dealers in very important market area. When significant action is reported on both sides of a record, points are combined to determine position on the chart. In such a case, both sides are listed in bold type, the leading side on top.

This Week	Title	Last Week	Weeks on Chart
1.	LISBON ANTIGUA (ASCAP)—N. Riddle. Robin Hood (ASCAP)—Cap 3287	2	9
2.	ROCK AND ROLL WALTZ (BMI)—K. Starr. I've Changed My Mind a Thousand Times (ASCAP)—Vic 20-6359	1	8
3.	GREAT PRETENDER (ASCAP)—Platters. I'm Just a Dancing Partner (ASCAP)—Mercury 70753	3	10
4.	MEMORIES ARE MADE OF THIS (BMI)—D. Martin. Change of Heart (BMI)—Cap 3295	4	13
5.	NO, NOT MUCH (ASCAP)—Four Lads. I'll Never Know (BMI)—Col 40629	5	5
6.	SEE YOU LATER, ALLIGATOR (BMI)—B. Haley. Paper Boy (ASCAP)—Dec 29791	6	7
7.	POOR PEOPLE OF PARIS (ASCAP)—L. Baxter. Theme From Helen of Troy (ASCAP)—Cap 3336	9	2
8.	BAND OF GOLD (BMI)—D. Cherry. Rumble Boogie (BMI)—Col 40597	7	12
9.	I'LL BE HOME (BMI)—P. Boone. Tutti Frutti (BMI)—Dot 15443	10	3
10.	SIXTEEN TONS (BMI)—Tennessee Ernie. You Don't Have to Be a Baby to Cry (ASCAP)—Cap 3262	8	16
11.	IT'S ALMOST TOMORROW (ASCAP)—Dream Weavers. You Got Me Wondering (ASCAP)—Dec 29683	11	16
12.	DUNGAREE DOLL (BMI)—E. Fisher. Everybody's Got a Home But Me (ASCAP)—Vic 20-6337	12	9
13.	WHY DO FOOLS FALL IN LOVE? (BMI)—Teen-Agers. Please Be Mine (BMI)—Gee 1002	15	2
14.	THEME FROM "THE THREE PENNY OPERA" (MORITAT) (ASCAP)—D. Hyman. Baubles, Bangles and Beads (ASCAP)—M-G-M 12149	13	5
15.	ANGELS IN THE SKY (BMI)—Crew Cuts. **MOSTLY MARTHA (BMI)—Mercury 70741**	14	11
16.	THEME FROM "THE THREE PENNY OPERA" (MORITAT) (ASCAP)—R. Hayman-J. August. I'll Be With You in Apple Blossom Time—(ASCAP)—Mercury 12159	19	2
17.	SPEEDOO (BMI)—Cadillacs. Let Me Explain (BMI)—Josie 785	21	3
18.	CHAIN GANG (ASCAP)—B. Scott. Shadrach (ASCAP)—ABC-Paramount 9658	20	6
19.	TEEN-AGE PRAYER (ASCAP)—G. Storm. Memories Are Made of This (BMI)—Dot 15436	15	9
20.	GO ON WITH THE WEDDING (ASCAP)—P. Page. Voice Inside (ASCAP)—Mercury 70766	17	4
21.	LULLABY OF BIRDLAND (BMI)—Blue Stars. That's My Girl (ASCAP)—Mercury 70742	—	1
22.	CRY BABY (BMI)—Bonnie Sisters. I Saw Mommy Cha Cha Cha With You Know Who (ASCAP)—Rainbow 328	—	1
23.	ARE YOU SATISFIED? (BMI)—R. Draper. Wabash Cannonball (BMI)—Mercury 70757	—	7
24.	TUTTI FRUTTI (BMI)—Little Richard. I'm Just a Lonely Guy (BMI)—Specialty 561	18	5
25.	HE (BMI)—A. Hibbler. Breeze (ASCAP)—Dec 29660	24	22

• THIS WEEK'S BEST BUYS

According to sales reports in key markets, the following recent releases are recommended for extra profits:

FLOWERS MEAN FORGIVENESS (Barton, ASCAP)—Frank **Sinatra—Capitol 3350**

In the past two weeks, this new release has been making good headway in most major markets. Now it is reported an excellent seller in Boston, Providence, New York, Philadelphia, Baltimore, Buffalo, Cleveland, Milwaukee, Atlanta, St. Louis, Nashville and other cities. "Flowers" seems headed for early placement in the charts. Flip is "You'll Get Yours" (Barton, ASCAP).

LIPSTICK AND CANDY AND RUBBERSOLE SHOES (Jimskip, BMI)—**Julius La Rosa—RCA Victor 6416**

Action on La Rosa's first Victor release has been good from almost the very beginning and continues to mount. Among the areas indicating outstanding sales were St. Louis, Baltimore, Milwaukee, Philadelphia, Providence, Boston, Durham, Nashville and Buffalo. Flip is "Winter in New England" (Bourne, ASCAP). A previous Billboard "Spotlight" pick.

• Most Played in Juke Boxes

For survey week ending February 15

RECORDS are ranked in order of the greatest number of plays in juke boxes thruout the country, as determined by The Billboard's weekly survey of the nation's juke box operators. When significant play is reported on both sides of a record, points are combined to determine position on the chart. In such a case, both sides are listed in bold type, the leading side on top.

This Week	Title	Last Week	Weeks on Chart
1.	GREAT PRETENDER (ASCAP)—Platters. I'm Just a Dancing Partner (ASCAP)—Mercury 70753	2	8
1.	ROCK AND ROLL WALTZ (BMI)—K. Starr. I've Changed My Mind a Thousand Times (ASCAP)—Vic 20-6359	3	7
3.	MEMORIES ARE MADE OF THIS (BMI)—D. Martin. Change of Heart (BMI)—Cap 3295	1	10
4.	LISBON ANTIGUA (ASCAP)—N. Riddle. Robin Hood (ASCAP)—Cap 3287	5	4
5.	SIXTEEN TONS (BMI)—Tennessee Ernie. You Don't Have to Be a Baby to Cry (ASCAP)—Cap 3262	4	15
6.	BAND OF GOLD (BMI)—D. Cherry. Rumble Boogie (BMI)—Col 40597	6	6
7.	SEE YOU LATER, ALLIGATOR (BMI)—B. Haley. Paper Boy (ASCAP)—Dec 29791	8	3
8.	I'LL BE HOME (BMI)—P. Boone. **TUTTI FRUTTI (BMI)—Dot 15443**	13	2
9.	DUNGAREE DOLL (BMI)—E. Fisher. Everybody's Got a Home But Me (ASCAP)—Vic 20-6337	7	7
10.	NO, NOT MUCH (ASCAP)—Four Lads. I'll Never Know (BMI)—Col 40629	16	2
11.	IT'S ALMOST TOMORROW (ASCAP)—Dream Weavers. You Got Me Wondering (ASCAP)—Dec 29683	9	12
12.	TEEN-AGE PRAYER (ASCAP)—G. Storm. Memories Are Made of This (BMI)—Dot 15436	10	9
13.	CHAIN GANG (ASCAP)—B. Scott. Shadrach (ASCAP)—ABC-Paramount 9658	19	2
14.	ARE YOU SATISFIED? (BMI)—R. Draper. Wabash Cannonball (BMI)—Mercury 70757	13	4
15.	GO ON WITH THE WEDDING (ASCAP)—P. Page. Voice Inside (ASCAP)—Mercury 70766	12	4
15.	IT'S ALMOST TOMORROW (ASCAP)—J. Stafford. If You Want to Love (ASCAP)—Col 40595	20	3
17.	THEME FROM THE THREE PENNY OPERA (MORITAT) (ASCAP)—D. Hyman. Baubles, Bangles and Beads (ASCAP)—M-G-M 12149	—	1
18.	MOMENTS TO REMEMBER (ASCAP)—Four Lads. Dream On My Love, Dream On (ASCAP)—Col 40539	13	20
18.	POOR PEOPLE OF PARIS (ASCAP)—L. Baxter. Theme From Helen of Troy (ASCAP)—Cap 3336	—	1
20.	ANGELS IN THE SKY (BMI)—Crew Cuts. Mostly Martha (BMI)—Mercury 70741	17	6

• Most Played by Jockeys

For survey week ending February 15

SIDES are ranked in order of the greatest number of plays on disk jockey radio shows thruout the country. Results are based on The Billboard's weekly survey among the nation's disk jockeys. The reverse side of each record is also listed.

This Week	Title	Last Week	Weeks on Chart
1.	GREAT PRETENDER (ASCAP)—Platters. I'm Just a Dancing Partner (ASCAP)—Mercury 70753	1	9
2.	ROCK AND ROLL WALTZ (BMI)—K. Starr. I've Changed My Mind a Thousand Times (ASCAP)—Vic 20-6359	3	8
3.	LISBON ANTIGUA (ASCAP)—N. Riddle. Robin Hood (ASCAP)—Cap 3287	4	8
4.	MEMORIES ARE MADE OF THIS (BMI)—D. Martin. Change of Heart (BMI)—Cap 3295	2	12
5.	NO, NOT MUCH (ASCAP)—Four Lads. I'll Never Know (BMI)—Col 40629	5	4
6.	POOR PEOPLE OF PARIS (ASCAP)—L. Baxter. Theme From Helen of Troy (ASCAP)—Cap 3336	9	2
7.	SEE YOU LATER, ALLIGATOR B. Haley. Paper Boy (ASCAP)—Dec 29791	6	4
8.	I'LL BE HOME (BMI)—P. Boone. Tutti Frutti (BMI)—Dot 15443	12	3
9.	BAND OF GOLD (BMI)—D. Cherry. Rumble Boogie (BMI)—Col 40597	8	9
10.	THEME FROM THE "THREE PENNY OPERA" (MORITAT) (ASCAP)—D. Hyman. Baubles, Bangles and Beads (ASCAP)—M-G-M 12149	10	3
11.	DUNGAREE DOLL (BMI)—E. Fisher. Everybody's Got a Home But Me (ASCAP) Vic 20-6337	11	6
12.	TEEN-AGE PRAYER (ASCAP)—G. Storm. Memories Are Made of This (BMI)—Dot 15436	13	8
13.	SIXTEEN TONS (BMI)—Tennessee Ernie. You Don't Have to Be a Baby to Cry (ASCAP)—Cap 3262	7	16
14.	THEME FROM "THE THREE PENNY OPERA (MORITAT) (ASCAP)—R. Hayman-J. August. I'll Be With You in Apple Blossom Time (ASCAP)—Mercury 12159	17	2
15.	CHAIN GANG (ASCAP)—B. Scott. Shadrack (ASCAP)—ABC-Paramount 9658	13	3
16.	BAND OF GOLD (BMI)—K. Carson. Cast Your Bread Upon the Waters—Cap 3283	16	11
17.	IT'S ALMOST TOMORROW (ASCAP)—Dream Weavers. You Got Me Wondering (ASCAP)—Dec 29683	15	11
17.	GO ON WITH THE WEDDING (ASCAP)—P. Page. Voice Inside (ASCAP)—Mercury 70766	—	2
19.	MEMORIES ARE MADE OF THIS (BMI)—G. Storm. Teen-Agre Prayer (ASCAP)—Dot 15436	—	8
20.	LULLABY OF BIRDLAND (BMI)—Blue Stars. That's My Girl (ASCAP)—Mercury 70742	—	1

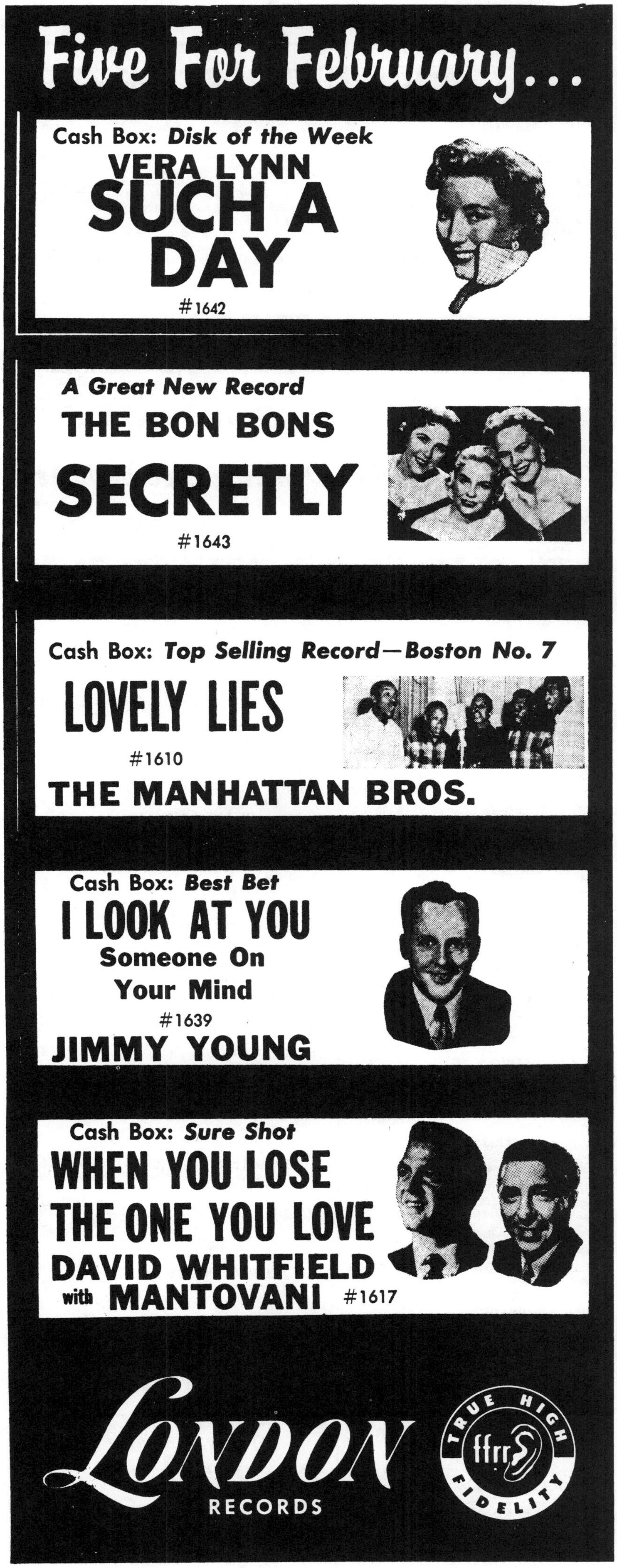

The Billboard Music Popularity Charts

POPULAR RECORDS

THE TOP 100

For survey week ending February 15

A list of the Top 100 RECORD SIDES in the nation according to a **COMBINED TABULATION** of Dealer, Disk Jockey and Juke Box Operator replies to The Billboard's weekly popular record Best Seller and Most Played surveys. Its purpose is to provide Disk Jockeys with additional programming material and to give trade exposure to NEWER records just beginning to show action in the field.

Pos.	Song	Artist	Label	Last Week
1.	GREAT PRETENDER	Platters	Mercury	1
1.	ROCK AND ROLL WALTZ	K. Starr	Victor	2
3.	LISBON ANTIGUA	N. Riddle	Capitol	4
4.	MEMORIES ARE MADE OF THIS	D. Martin	Capitol	2
5.	NO, NOT MUCH	Four Lads	Columbia	8
6.	SEE YOU LATER, ALLIGATOR	B. Haley	Decca	6
7.	BAND OF GOLD	D. Cherry	Columbia	7
8.	SIXTEEN TONS	T. Ernie	Capitol	5
9.	DUNGAREE DOLL	E. Fisher	Victor	9
10.	POOR PEOPLE OF PARIS	L. Baxter	Capitol	25
11.	I'LL BE HOME	P. Boone	Dot	19
12.	IT'S ALMOST TOMORROW	Dream Weavers	Decca	10
13.	THEME FROM THE THREE PENNY OPERA (MORITAT)	D. Hyman	M-G-M	13
14.	TEEN-AGE PRAYER	G. Storm	Dot	11
15.	CHAIN GANG	B. Scott	ABC-Paramount	15
16.	TUTTI FRUTTI	P. Boone	Dot	12
17.	GO ON WITH THE WEDDING	P. Page	Mercury	13
18.	ANGELS IN THE SKY	Crew Cuts	Mercury	16
19.	THEME FROM THE THREE PENNY OPERA (MORITAT)	R. Hayman-J. August	Mercury	23
20.	LULLABY OF BIRDLAND	Blue Stars	Mercury	31
21.	ARE YOU SATISFIED	R. Draper	Mercury	35
22.	BAND OF GOLD	K. Carson	Capitol	17
23.	NINETY-NINE YEARS	G. Mitchell	Columbia	49
23.	SEVEN DAYS	Crew Cuts	Mercury	30
25.	TENDER TRAP	F. Sinatra	Capitol	33
26.	WHY DO FOOLS FALL IN LOVE	Teen-Agers	Gee	47
27.	IT'S ALMOST TOMORROW	J. Stafford	Columbia	20
28.	APRIL IN PARIS	C. Basie	Clef	35
29.	MEMORIES ARE MADE OF THIS	G. Storm	Dot	29
30.	SPEEDOO	Cadillacs	Josie	34
31.	HE	A. Hibbler	Decca	24
31.	LOVE AND MARRIAGE	F. Sinatra	Capitol	43
33.	ELEVENTH HOUR MELODY	A. Hibbler	Decca	42
34.	MOMENTS TO REMEMBER	Four Lads	Columbia	27
34.	LIPSTICK CANDY AND RUBBER SOLED SHOES	J. La Rosa	Victor	39
34.	MOSTLY MARTHA	Crew Cuts	Mercury	39
34.	THEME FROM THE THREE PENNY OPERA (MACK THE KNIFE)	L. Armstrong	Columbia	61
38.	I HEAR YOU KNOCKING	G. Storm	Dot	18
39.	THEME FROM THE THREE PENNY OPERA (MORITAT)	B. Vaughn	Dot	57
40.	CRY BABY	Bonnie Sisters	Rainbow	81
41.	LISBON ANTIGUA	M. Miller	Columbia	48
42.	ONLY YOU	Hilltoppers	Dot	46
43.	TUTTI FRUTTI	Little Richard	Specialty	21
43.	SEVEN DAYS	D. Collins	Coral	25
45.	ONLY YOU	Platters	Mercury	27
46.	WOMAN IN LOVE	Four Aces	Decca	37
47.	WOMAN IN LOVE	F. Laine	Columbia	32
48.	THAT'S YOUR MISTAKE	O. Williams	Deluxe	85
49.	OUR LOVE AFFAIR	T. Charles	Decca	66
50.	BURN THAT CANDLE	B. Haley	Decca	50
51.	ASK ME	Nat (King) Cole	Capitol	68
51.	THEME FROM THE THREE PENNY OPERA (MORITAT)	L. Paul & M. Ford	Capitol	54
53.	CRY ME A RIVER	J. London	Liberty	22
54.	TEAR FELL	T. Brewer	Coral	—
55.	THEME FROM THE THREE PENNY OPERA (MORITAT)	L. Welk	Coral	64
56.	MR. WONDERFUL	S. Vaughan	Mercury	74
56.	THAT'S ALL	T. Ernie	Capitol	—
58.	MEMORIES OF YOU	Four Coins	Epic	41
59.	LITTLE CHILD	E. Albert	Kapp	59
60.	WHEN YOU DANCE	Turbans	Herald	55
61.	ALL AT ONCE YOU LOVE HER	P. Como	Victor	63
62.	LITTLE CHILD	C. Calloway	ABC-Paramount	81
62.	LONELY LIES	Manhattan Brothers	London	—
64.	IT'S ALMOST TOMORROW	S. Lanson	Dot	50
65.	MR. WONDERFUL	T. King	Victor	58
65.	JEAN'S SONG	C. Atkins	Victor	—
67.	GO ON WITH THE WEDDING	K. Kallen-G. Shaw	Decca	53
68.	TEEN-AGE PRAYER	G. Mann	Sound	60
69.	DON'T GO TO STRANGER	V. Monroe	Victor	38
70.	HE	McGuire Sisters	Coral	45
70.	ELEVENTH HOUR MELODY	L. Busch	Capitol	—
72.	NOTHING EVER CHANGES MY LOVE FOR YOU	Nat (King) Cole	Capitol	—
73.	MY BELIEVING HEART	J. James	M-G-M	74
74.	FLOWERS MEAN FORGIVENESS	F. Sinatra	Capitol	—
74.	ROCK AROUND MOTHER GOOSE	B. Gordon	M-G-M	52
76.	TAKE ME BACK TO TOYLAND	Nat (King) Cole	Capitol	—
77.	MEMORIES ARE MADE OF THIS	M. Carson	Columbia	71
78.	TO YOU MY LOVE	N. Noble	Wing	—
79.	IF YOU CAN DREAM	Four Aces	Decca	98
79.	YOU ARE MY LOVE	J. James	M-G-M	87
79.	VALLEY VALPARAISO	P. Faith	Columbia	100
82.	I'LL NEVER KNOW	Four Lads	Columbia	—
82.	ZAMBESI	L. Busch	Capitol	—
84.	WHO ARE WE?	G. Grant	Era	62
85.	DADDY-O	Fontane Sisters	Dot	76
86.	EVERYBODY'S GOT A HOME BUT ME	E. Fisher	Victor	72
87.	MEMORIES OF YOU	R. Clooney & B. Goodman	Columbia	76
88.	SEVEN DAYS	C. McPhatter	Atlantic	95
89.	FOREVER DARLING	Ames Brothers	Victor	—
89.	ROCK A BEATIN' BOOGIE	B. Haley	Decca	—
89.	TEEN-AGE MEETING	D. Cornell	Coral	96
89.	WHEN YOU LOSE THE ONE YOU LOVE	D. Whitfield	London	85
93.	TOO LATE NOW	De Castro Sisters	Abbott	—
94.	MEMORIES OF YOU	H. Winterhalter	Victor	87
95.	TROUBLE WITH HARRY	Alfi & Harry	Liberty	72
95.	SHIFTING, WHISPERING SANDS	R. Draper	Mercury	66
97.	C'EST LA VIE	S. Vaughan	Mercury	70
97.	DADDY-O	B. Lou	King	—
97.	ROCK AROUND THE CLOCK	B. Haley	Decca	—
97.	TEEN-AGE PRAYER	K. White	Mercury	68

CAUTION TO DEALERS AND JUKE BOX OPERATORS

The Billboard's Top 100 is NOT designed to provide tested information for buying purposes. This function is most reliably served by other regular weekly features: Best Sellers in Stores, Most Played in Juke Boxes, Coming Up Strong and Best Buys.

The Billboard Music Popularity Charts — POPULAR RECORDS

• Best Sellers in Stores

For survey week ending February 22

RECORDS are ranked in order of their current national selling importance at the retail level, as determined by The Billboard's weekly survey of the top volume dealers in every important market area. When significant action is reported on both sides of a record, points are combined to determine position on the chart. In such a case, both sides are listed in bold type, the leading side on top.

This Week	Title	Last Week	Weeks on Chart
1.	**LISBON ANTIGUA** (ASCAP)—N. Riddle — Robin Hood (ASCAP) Cap. 3287	1	10
2.	**ROCK AND ROLL WALTZ** (BMI)—K. Starr — I've Changed My Mind a Thousand Times (ASCAP) Vic. 20-6359	2	9
3.	**GREAT PRETENDER** (ASCAP)—Platters — I'm Just a Dancing Partner (ASCAP) Mercury 70753	3	11
4.	**NO, NOT MUCH** (ASCAP)—Four Lads — I'll Never Know (BMI) Col 40629	5	6
5.	**POOR PEOPLE OF PARIS** (ASCAP)—L. Baxter — Theme From Helen of Troy (ASCAP) Cap 3336	7	3
6.	**MEMORIES ARE MADE OF THIS** (BMI)—D. Martin — Change of Heart (BMI) Cap 3295	4	14
7.	**SEE YOU LATER, ALLIGATOR** (BMI)—B. Haley — Paper Boy (ASCAP) Dec 29791	6	8
8.	**I'LL BE HOME** (BMI)—P. Boone / **TUTTI FRUTTI** (BMI)—Dot 15443	9	4
9.	**BAND OF GOLD** (BMI)—D. Cherry — Rumble Boogie (BMI) Col 40597	8	13
10.	**THEME FROM "THE THREE PENNY OPERA" (MORITAT)** (ASCAP)—D. Hyman — Baubles, Bangles and Beads (ASCAP) MGM 12149	14	6
11.	**WHY DO FOOLS FALL IN LOVE?** (BMI)—Teen-Agers — Please Be Mine (BMI) Gee 1002	13	3
12.	**IT'S ALMOST TOMORROW** (ASCAP)—R. Hayman-J. August — You Got Me Wondering (ASCAP) Dec 29683	16	3
13.	**DUNGAREE DOLL** (BMI)—E. Fisher — Everybody's Got a Home But Me (ASCAP) Vic 20-6337	12	10
14.	**SIXTEEN TONS** (BMI)—Tennessee Ernie — You Don't Have to Be a Baby to Cry (ASCAP) Cap 3262	10	17
15.	**THEME FROM "THE THREE PENNY OPERA" (MORITAT)** (ASCAP)—R. Hayman-J. August — I'll Be With You in Apple Blossom Time (ASCAP) Mercury 12159	16	3
16.	**ANGELS IN THE SKY** (BMI)—Crew Cuts — Mostly Martha (BMI) Mercury 70741	15	12
17.	**CHAIN GANG** (ASCAP)—B. Scott — Shadrach (ASCAP) ABC-Paramount 9658	18	7
18.	**CRY BABY** (BMI)—Bonnie Sisters — I Saw Mommy Cha Cha Cha With You Know Who (ASCAP) Rainbow 328	22	2
18.	**TEAR FELL** (BMI)—T. Brewer / **BO WEEVIL** (BMI)—Coral 61590	—	1
20.	**LULLABY OF BIRDLAND** (BMI)—Blue Stars — That's My Girl (ASCAP) Mercury 70742	21	2

• THIS WEEK'S BEST BUYS

According to sales reports in key markets, the following recent releases are recommended for extra profits:

JUKE BOX BABY (Winneton, BMI)

HOT DIGGITY (Roncom, ASCAP)—**Perry Como—RCA Victor 6427**

In two weeks this disk has snowballed into a mighty big record. With "Juke Box Baby" getting most attention, Como's latest has racked up impressive sales in Boston, New York, Philadelphia, Buffalo, Cleveland, St. Louis, Baltimore and Milwaukee, to mention just a few cities. Some areas indicated that "Hot Diggity" was also seeing excellent activity. A previous Billboard "Spotlight" pick.

WHEN YOU LOSE THE ONE YOU LOVE (Chappell, ASCAP)—**David Whitfield—London 1617**

This is shaping up as Whitfield's most successful disk in some time. In St. Louis it is already on the territorial chart and is a very good seller in number of markets. Flip is "Angelus."

MR. WONDERFUL (Laurel, ASCAP)—**Sarah Vaughan—Mercury 70777**

Competition is still fierce between the various versions of this tune, but Sarah Vaughan has now achieved a strong lead. Her placing on this week's national disk jockey chart indicates that she has had top exposure so far, and dealers in most areas confirm that this been paralleled on the customer level. Flip is "You Ought to Have a Wife" (E. H. Morris, ASCAP). A previous Billboard "Spotlight" pick.

BEYOND THE SEA (Harms, ASCAP—**Roger Williams—Kapp 138**

Starting quietly, this instrumental has gradually gained strength, so that now operators and dealers must recognize the side as a potent sleeper. In the past week it took significant steps forward in Los Angeles, Chicago, Cleveland, Milwaukee, Detroit. St. Louis, Baltimore, New York and Boston. Flip is "Song of Devotion" (Garland, ASCAP).

• Most Played in Juke Boxes

For survey week ending February 22

RECORDS are ranked in order of the greatest number of plays in juke boxes thruout the country, as determined by The Billboard's weekly survey of the nation's juke box operators. When significant play is reported on both sides of a record, points are combined to determine position on the chart. In such a case, both sides are listed in bold type, the leading side on top.

This Week	Title	Last Week	Weeks on Chart
1.	**ROCK AND ROLL WALTZ** (BMI)—K. Starr — I've Changed My Mind a Thousand Times (ASCAP)—Vic 20-6359	2	8
2.	**GREAT PRETENDER** (ASCAP)—Platters — I'm Just a Dancing Partner (ASCAP)—Mercury 70753	1	9
3.	**MEMORIES ARE MADE OF THIS** (BMI)—D. Martin — Change of Heart (BMI)—Cap 3295	3	11
4.	**LISBON ANTIGUA** (ASCAP)—N. Riddle — Robin Hood (ASCAP)—Cap 3287	4	5
5.	**BAND OF GOLD** (BMI)—D. Cherry — Rumble Boogie (BMI)—Col 40597	6	7
6.	**SEE YOU LATER, ALLIGATOR** (BMI)—B. Haley — Paper Boy (ASCAP)—Dec 29791	7	4
7.	**NO, NOT MUCH** (ASCAP)—Four Lads — I'll Never Know (BMI)—Col 40629	10	3
8.	**SIXTEEN TONS** (BMI)—Tennessee Ernie — You Don't Have to Be a Baby to Cry (ASCAP)—Cap 3262	5	16
9.	**I'LL BE HOME** (BMI)—P. Boone — Tutti Frutti (BMI)—Dot 15443	8	3
10.	**TEEN-AGE PRAYER** (ASCAP)—G. Storm / **MEMORIES ARE MADE OF THIS** (BMI)—Dot 15436	12	10
11.	**DUNGAREE DOLL** (BMI)—E. Fisher — Everybody's Got a Home But Me (ASCAP)—Vic 20-6337	9	8
12.	**POOR PEOPLE OF PARIS** (ASCAP)—L. Baxter — Theme From Helen of Troy (ASCAP)—Cap 3336	18	2
13.	**ARE YOU SATISFIED?** (BMI)—R. Draper — Wabash Cannonball (BMI)—Mercury 70757	14	5
14.	**CHAIN GANG** (ASCAP)—B. Scott — Shadrach (ASCAP)—ABC-Paramount 9658	13	3
14.	**IT'S ALMOST TOMORROW** (ASCAP)—J. Stafford — If You Want to Love (ASCAP)—Col 40595	15	4
16.	**IT'S ALMOST TOMORROW** (ASCAP)—Dream Weavers — You Got Me Wondering (ASCAP)— Dec 29683	11	13
17.	**THEME FROM THE "THREE PENNY OPERA" (MORITAT)** (ASCAP)—R. Hayman-J. August — I'll Be With You in Apple Blossom Time (ASCAP)—Mercury 70781	—	1
18.	**GO ON WITH THE WEDDING** (ASCAP)—P. Page — Voice Inside (ASCAP)—Mercury 70766	15	5
19.	**THEME FROM THE "THREE PENNY OPERA" (MORITAT)** (ASCAP)—D. Hyman — Baubles, Bangles, and Beads (ASCAP)—M-G-M 12149	17	2
20.	**WHY DO FOOLS FALL IN LOVE?** (BMI)—Teen-Agers — Please Be Mine (BMI)—Gee 1002	—	1

• Most Played by Jockeys

For survey week ending February 22

SIDES are ranked in order of the greatest number of plays on disk jockey radio shows thruout the country. Results are based on The Billboard's weekly survey among the nation's disk jockeys. The reverse side of each record is also listed.

This Week	Title	Last Week	Weeks on Chart
1.	**LISBON ANTIGUA** (ASCAP)—N. Riddle — Robin Hood (ASCAP)—Cap 3287	3	9
2.	**ROCK AND ROLL WALTZ** (BMI)—K. Starr — I've Changed My Mind a Thousand Times (ASCAP)—Vic 20-6359	2	9
3.	**GREAT PRETENDER**—Platters — I'm Just a Dancing Partner (ASCAP)—Mercury 70753	1	10
4.	**POOR PEOPLE OF PARIS** (ASCAP)—L. Baxter — Theme From Helen of Troy (ASCAP)—Cap 3336	6	3
5.	**NO, NOT MUCH** (ASCAP)—Four Lads — I'll Never Know (BMI)—Col 40629	5	5
6.	**MEMORIES ARE MADE OF THIS** (BMI)—D. Martin — Change of Heart (BMI)—Cap 3295	4	13
7.	**I'LL BE HOME** (BMI)—P. Boone — Tutti Frutti (BMI)—Dot 15443	8	4
8.	**SEE YOU LATER, ALLIGATOR** (BMI)—B. Haley — Paper Boy (ASCAP)—Dec 29791	7	5
8.	**THEME FROM THE "THREE PENNY OPERA" (MORITAT)** (ASCAP) D. Hyman — Baubles, Bangles, and Beads (ASCAP)—M-G-M 12149	10	4
10.	**BAND OF GOLD** (BMI)—D. Cherry — Rumble Boogie (BMI)—Col 40597	9	10
11.	**THEME FROM "THE THREE PENNY OPERA" (MORITAT)** (ASCAP)—R. Hayman-J. August — I'll Be With You in Apple Blossom Time (ASCAP)—Mercury 12159	14	3
12.	**DUNGAREE DOLL** (BMI)—E. Fisher — Everybody's Got a Home But Me (ASCAP)—Vic 20-6337	11	7
13.	**MR. WONDERFUL** (ASCAP)—S. Vaughan — You Ought to Have a Wife (ASCAP)—Mercury 70700	—	1
14.	**TEEN-AGE PRAYER** (ASCAP)—G. Storm — Memories Are Made of This (BMI)—Dot 15436	12	9
15.	**LIPSTICK, CANDY AND RUBBER SOLED SHOES** (BMI)—J. La Rosa — Winter in New England (ASCAP)—Vic 20-6416	—	1
16.	**TUTTI FRUTTI** (BMI)—P. Boone — I'll Be Home (BMI)—Dot 15443	—	2
16.	**SIXTEEN TONS** (BMI)—Tennessee Ernie — You Don't Have to Be a Baby to Cry (ASCAP)—Cap 3262	13	17
18.	**SEVEN DAYS** (BMI)—Crew Cuts — That's Your Mistake (BMI)—Mercury 70782	—	1
19.	**BAND OF GOLD** (BMI)—K. Carson — Cast Your Bread Upon the Waters—Cap 3283	16	12
20.	**MEMORIES ARE MADE OF THIS**—G. Storm — Teen-Age Prayer (ASCAP)—Dot 15436	19	9

The Billboard Music Popularity Charts
POPULAR RECORDS

THE TOP 100

For survey week ending February 22

A list of the **Top 100 RECORD SIDES** in the nation according to a **COMBINED TABULATION** of Dealer, Disk Jockey and Juke Box Operator replies to The Billboard's weekly popular record Best Seller and Most Played surveys. Its purpose is to provide Disk Jockeys with additional programming material and to give trade exposure to NEWER records just beginning to show action in the field.

Pos.	Song	Artist	Label	Last Week
1.	ROCK AND ROLL WALTZ	K. Starr	Victor	1
2.	LISBON ANTIGUA	N. Riddle	Capitol	3
3.	GREAT PRETENDER	Platters	Mercury	1
4.	MEMORIES ARE MADE OF THIS	D. Martin	Capitol	4
5.	NO, NOT MUCH	Four Lads	Columbia	5
6.	POOR PEOPLE OF PARIS	L. Baxter	Capitol	10
7.	SEE YOU LATER, ALLIGATOR	B. Haley	Decca	6
8.	BAND OF GOLD	D. Cherry	Columbia	7
9.	I'LL BE HOME	P. Boone	Dot	11
10.	THEME FROM THE THREE PENNY OPERA (MORITAT)	D. Hyman	M-G-M	13
11.	SIXTEEN TONS	T. Ernie	Capitol	8
12.	DUNGAREE DOLL	E. Fisher	Victor	9
13.	THEME FROM THE THREE PENNY OPERA (MORITAT)	R. Hayman-J. August	Mercury	19
14.	TEEN-AGE PRAYER	G. Storm	Dot	14
15.	WHY DO FOOLS FALL IN LOVE?	Teen Agers	Gee	26
16.	CHAIN GANG	B. Scott	ABC-Paramount	15
16.	IT'S ALMOST TOMORROW	Dream Weavers	Decca	27
18.	ARE YOU SATISFIED?	R. Draper	Mercury	21
19.	ANGELS IN THE SKY	Crew Cuts	Mercury	18
20.	SEVEN DAYS	Crew Cuts	Mercury	23
21.	LIPSTICK, CANDY AND RUBBER SOLED SHOES	J. La Rosa	Victor	34
21.	THEME FROM THE THREE PENNY OPERA (MACK THE KNIFE)	L. Armstrong	Columbia	34
23.	BAND OF GOLD	K. Carson	Capitol	22
24.	LULLABY OF BIRDLAND	Blue Stars	Mercury	20
25.	ASK ME	Nat (King) Cole	Capitol	51
27.	TENDER TRAP	F. Sinatra	Capitol	25
28.	HE	A. Hibbler	Decca	31
28.	IT'S ALMOST TOMORROW	J. Stafford	Columbia	27
30.	ELEVENTH HOUR MELODY	A. Hibbler	Decca	33
31	NINETY-NINE YEARS	G. Mitchell	Columbia	23
32.	MR. WONDERFUL	T. King	Victor	65
33.	TUTTI FRUTTI	Little Richard	Specialty	43
33.	SPEEDOO	Cadillacs	Josie	30
35.	CRY BABY	Bonnie Sisters	Rainbow	40
35.	CRY ME A RIVER	J. London	Liberty	53
37.	THEME FROM THE THREE PENNY OPERA (MORITAT)	B. Vaughn	Dot	39
37.	WHY DO FOOLS FALL IN LOVE?	G. Storm	Dot	—
39.	THEME FROM THE THREE PENNY OPERA (MORITAT)	L. Welk	Coral	55
40.	LISBON ANTIGUA	M. Miller	Columbia	41
41.	BEYOND THE SEA	R. Williams	Kapp	—
42.	TUTTI FRUTTI	P. Boone	Dot	16
43.	MEMORIES ARE MADE OF THIS	G. Storm	Dot	29
44.	MOSTLY MARTHA	Crew Cuts	Mercury	34
44.	THAT'S ALL	T. Ernie	Capitol	56
46.	ONLY YOU	Platters	Mercury	45
47.	WOMAN IN LOVE	Four Aces	Decca	46
48.	WHY DO FOOLS FALL IN LOVE?	Diamonds	Mercury	—
49.	FLOWERS MEAN FORGIVENESS	F. Sinatra	Capitol	74
50.	MOMENTS TO REMEMBER	Four Lads	Columbia	34
51.	LOVE AND MARRIAGE	F. Sinatra	Capitol	31
52.	I'LL NEVER KNOW	Four Lads	Columbia	82
52.	MEMORIES OF YOU	R. Clooney-B. Goodman	Columbia	87
54.	BO WEEVIL	T. Brewer	Coral	—
55.	THEME FROM THE THREE PENNY OPERA (MORITAT)	L. Paul & M. Ford	Capitol	51
56.	ELEVENTH HOUR MELODY	L. Busch	Capitol	70
56.	LITTLE CHILD	E. Albert	Kapp	59
56.	MR. WONDERFUL	S. Vaughan	Mercury	56
59.	FOREVER DARLING	Ames Brothers	Victor	89
59.	VALLEY VALPARAISO	P. Faith	Columbia	79
61.	TEAR FELL	T. Brewer	Coral	54
62.	APRIL IN PARIS	C. Basie	Clef	28
62.	IF YOU CAN DREAM	Four Aces	Decca	79
62.	WHEN YOU LOSE THE ONE YOU LOVE	D. Whitfield	London	89
65.	IT'S ALMOST TOMORROW	D. Carroll	Mercury	—
66.	ALL AT ONCE YOU LOVE HER	P. Como	Victor	61
67.	YOU'LL GET YOURS	F. Sinatra	Capitol	—
68.	HEARTBREAK HOTEL	E. Presley	Victor	—
69.	LOVELY LIES	Manhattan Brothers	London	62
70.	MEMORIES OF YOU	Four Coins	Epic	58
71.	ONLY YOU	Hilltoppers	Dot	42
72.	EVERYBODY'S GOT A HOME BUT ME	E. Fisher	Victor	86
73.	SEVEN DAYS	D. Collins	Coral	43
73.	I'VE CHANGED MY MIND A THOUSAND TIMES	K. Starr	Victor	—
75.	MEMORIES ARE MADE OF THIS	M. Carson	Columbia	77
75.	SEVEN DAYS	C. McPhatter	Atlantic	88
77.	HE	McGuire Sisters	Coral	70
77.	TROUBLE WITH HARRY	Alfi & Harry	Liberty	95
79.	NOTHING EVER CHANGES MY LOVE FOR YOU	Nat (King) Cole	Capitol	72
80.	TEEN-AGE MEETING	D. Cornell	Coral	89
81.	MY BELIEVING HEART	J. James	M-G-M	73
82.	MR. WONDERFUL	P. Lee	Decca	—
83.	BLUE SUEDE SHOES	C. Perkins	Sun	—
84.	I'M GONNA LOVE YOU	Ames Brothers	Victor	—
85.	GO ON WITH THE WEDDING	K. Kallen-G. Shaw	Decca	67
86.	TO YOU MY LOVE	N. Noble	Wing	78
87.	WHO ARE WE?	G. Grant	Era	84
88.	KISS AND RUN	P. King	Columbia	—
88.	POOR PEOPLE OF PARIS	R. Morgan	Decca	—
90.	DON'T GO TO STRANGERS	V. Monroe	Victor	69
91.	I HEAR YOU KNOCKIN'	G. Storm	Dot	38
91.	BO WEEVIL	F. Domino	Imperial	—
93.	EDDIE MY LOVE	Teen Queens	Gee	—
94.	WHEN YOU DANCE	Turbans	Herald	60
94.	I'LL WAIT	B. Johnson	Bally	—
96.	TROUBLE WITH HARRY	L. Baxter	Capitol	—
96.	WOMAN IN LOVE	F. Laine	Columbia	47
96.	SUCH A DAY	V. Lynn	London	—
99.	BURN THAT CANDLE	B. Haley	Decca	50
100.	ROCK AROUND MOTHER GOOSE	B. Gordon	M-G-M	74

CAUTION TO DEALERS AND JUKE BOX OPERATORS

The Billboard's Top 100 is NOT designed to provide tested information for buying purposes. This function is most reliably served by other regular weekly features: Best Sellers in Stores, Most Played in Juke Boxes, Coming Up Strong and Best Buys.

The Billboard Music Popularity Charts — POPULAR RECORDS

• Best Sellers in Stores

For survey week ending February 29

RECORDS are ranked in order of their current national selling importance at the retail level, as determined by The Billboard's weekly survey of the top volume dealers in every important market area. When significant action is reported on both sides of a record, points are combined to determine position on the chart. In such a case, both sides are listed in bold type, the leading side on top.

This Week		Last Week	Weeks on Chart
1.	**LISBON ANTIGUA (ASCAP)—N. Riddle** Robin Hood (ASCAP)—Cap 3287	1	11
2.	**ROCK AND ROLL WALTZ (BMI)—K. Starr** I've Changed My Mind a Thousand Times (ASCAP)—Vic 20-6359	2	10
3.	**POOR PEOPLE OF PARIS (ASCAP)—L. Baxter** Helen of Troy (ASCAP)—Cap 3336	5	4
4.	**NO, NOT MUCH (ASCAP)—Four Lads** I'll Never Know (BMI)—Col 40629	4	7
5.	**GREAT PRETENDER (ASCAP)—Platters** I'm Just a Dancing Partner (ASCAP)—Mercury 70553	3	12
6.	**SEE YOU LATER, ALLIGATOR (BMI)—B. Haley** Paper Boy (ASCAP)—Dec 29791	7	9
7.	**I'LL BE HOME (BMI)—P. Boone** **TUTTI FRUTTI (BMI)—Dot 15443**	8	5
8.	**MEMORIES ARE MADE OF THIS (BMI)—D. Martin** Change of Heart (BMI)—Cap 3295	6	15
9.	**WHY DO FOOLS FALL IN LOVE? (BMI)—Teen-Agers** Please Be Mine (BMI)—Gee 1002	11	4
10.	**BAND OF GOLD (BMI)—D. Cherry** Rumble Boogie (BMI)—Col 40597	9	14
11.	**THEME FROM THE "THREE PENNY OPERA" (MORITA) (ASCAP)—D. Hyman** Baubles, Bangles, and Beads (ASCAP)—M-G-M 12149	10	7
12.	**HOT DIGGITY (ASCAP)—P. Como** **JUKE BOX BABY (ASCAP)—Vic 20-6427**	—	1
13.	**IT'S ALMOST TOMORROW (ASCAP)—Dream Weavers** You Got Me Wondering (ASCAP)—Dec 29683	12	18
14.	**BLUE SUEDE SHOES (BMI)—C. Perkins** Honey, Don't (BMI)—Sun 234	—	1
15.	**DUNGAREE DOLL (BMI)—E. Fisher** Everybody's Got a Home But Me (ASCAP)—Vic 20-6337	13	11
16.	**TEAR FELL (BMI)—T. Brewer** **BO WEEVIL (BMI)—Coral 61590**	18	2
17.	**THEME FROM THE "THREE PENNY OPERA" (MORITAT) (ASCAP)—R. Hayman-J. August** I'll Be With You in Apple Blossom Time—Mercury 70781	15	4
18.	**EDDIE, MY LOVE (BMI)—Teen Queens** Just Goofed (BMI)—RPM 453	—	1
19.	**HEARTBREAK HOTEL (BMI)—E. Presley** I Was the One (ASCAP)—Vic 20-6420	—	1
20.	**ANGELS IN THE SKY (BMI)—Crew Cuts** Mostly Martha (BMI)—Mercury 70741	16	13
20.	**CRY BABY (BMI)—Bonnie Sisters** I Saw Mommy Cha, Cha, Cha With You Know Who (ASCAP)—Rainbow 328	18	3

• THIS WEEK'S BEST BUYS

According to sales reports in key markets, the following recent releases are recommended for extra profits:

INNAMORATA (Paramount, ASCAP—**Jerry Vale—Columbia 40634—Dean Martin—Capitol 3352**)

Jerry Vale was out first with his version of this tune from "Artists and Models" and has entrenched himself well, particularly on the East Coast. Currently he is listed on the Boston territorial chart, and is selling extremely well in New York, Baltimore, Providence and Buffalo, among others. Martin has come up from behind to give Vale strong competition, and is doing best in Los Angeles, Cleveland, Milwaukee, St. Louis, Nashville, Richmond, Philadelphia, Chicago and Cincinnati. The Martin version was a Billboard "Spotlight" pick.

FOREVER DARLING (Feist, ASCAP) — **The Ames Brothers—RCA Victor 6400**

This tune has been coming up quietly these past weeks, and is now shaping as a strong contender for chart honors. Already on the Baltimore territorial chart, "Forever Darling" is also rated a strong seller in St. Louis, Buffalo, Nashville, Milwaukee, and Philadelphia. It is also coming along nicely in Cleveland, Pittsburgh, Detroit, Providence, and Durham. Flip is "I'm Gonna Love You" (Winneton, BMI). A previous Billboard "Spotlight" pick.

ROCK RIGHT (E. B. Marks, BMI)

THE GREATEST THING (Ross Jungnickel, ASCAP)—**Georgia Gibbs—Mercury 70811**

With "Rock Right" sparking most initial action, this record has moved out quickly. Good sales were reported in a wide variety of areas from Coast to Coast. They included Los Angeles, Philadelphia, Chicago, St. Louis, Cleveland, Baltimore, Buffalo, Providence, Pittsburgh and Nashville. Some cities showed a strong preference for "Greatest Thing." A previous Billboard "Spotlight" pick.

• Most Played in Juke Boxes

For survey week ending February 29

RECORDS are ranked in order of the greatest number of plays in juke boxes thruout the country, as determined by The Billboard's weekly survey of the nation's juke box operators. When significant play is reported on both sides of a record, points are combined to determine position on the chart. In such a case, both sides are listed in bold type, the leading side on top.

This Week		Last Week	Weeks on Chart
1.	**ROCK AND ROLL WALTZ (BMI)—K. Starr** I've Changed My Mind a Thousand Times (ASCAP)—Vic 20-6359	1	9
2.	**GREAT PRETENDER (ASCAP)—Platters** I'm Just a Dancing Partner (ASCAP)—Mercury 70753	2	10
3.	**MEMORIES ARE MADE OF THIS (BMI)—D. Martin** Change of Heart (BMI)—Cap 3295	3	12
4.	**LISBON ANTIGUA (ASCAP)—N. Riddle** Robin Hood (ASCAP)—Cap 3287	4	6
5.	**I'LL BE HOME (BMI)—P. Boone** **TUTTI FRUTTI (BMI)—Dot 15443**	9	4
6.	**NO, NOT MUCH (ASCAP)—Four Lads** I'll Never Know (BMI)—Col 40629	7	4
7.	**SEE YOU LATER, ALLIGATOR (BMI)—B. Haley** Paper Boy (ASCAP)—Dec 29791	6	5
8.	**BAND OF GOLD (BMI)—D. Cherry** Rumble Boogie (BMI)—Col 40597	5	8
9.	**POOR PEOPLE OF PARIS (ASCAP)—L. Baxter** Theme From Helen of Troy (ASCAP)—Cap 3336	12	3
10.	**SIXTEEN TONS (BMI)—Tennessee Ernie** You Don't Have to Be a Baby to Cry (ASCAP)—Cap 3262	8	17
11.	**ARE YOU SATISFIED? (BMI)—R. Draper** Wabash Cannonball (BMI)—Mercury 70757	13	6
12.	**WHY DO FOOLS FALL IN LOVE? (BMI)—Tenn-Agers** Please Be Mine (BMI)—Gee 1002	20	2
13.	**THEME FROM "THE THREE PENNY OPERA" (MORITAT) (ASCAP)—R. Hayman-J. August** I'll Be With You in Apple Blossom Time (ASCAP)—Mercury 70781	17	2
13.	**TEEN-AGE PRAYER (ASCAP)—G. Storm** Memories Are Made of This (BMI)—Dot 15436	10	11
15.	**THEME FROM "THE THREE PENNY OPERA" (MORITAT) (ASCAP)—D. Hyman** Baubles, Bangles and Beads (ASCAP)—MGM 12149	19	3
16.	**IT'S ALMOST TOMORROW (ASCAP)—Dream Weavers** You Got Me Wondering (ASCAP)—Dec 29683	16	14
17.	**DUNGAREE DOLL (BMI)—E. Fisher** Everybody's Got a Home But Me (ASCAP)—Vic 20-6337	11	9
18.	**IT'S ALMOST TOMORROW (ASCAP)—J. Stafford** If You Want to Love (ASCAP)—Col 40595	14	5
19.	**WHY DO FOOLS FALL IN LOVE? (BMI)—G. Storm** I Walk Alone (BMI)—Dot 15448	—	1
20.	**CHAIN GANG (ASCAP)—B. Scott** Shadrach (ASCAP)—ABC-Paramount 9658	14	4

• Most Played by Jockeys

For survey week ending February 29

SIDES are ranked in order of the greatest number of plays on disk jockey radio shows thruout the country. Results are based on The Billboard's weekly survey among the nation's disk jockeys. The reverse side of each record is also listed.

This Week		Last Week	Weeks on Chart
1.	**ROCK AND ROLL WALTZ (BMI)—K. Starr** I've Changed My Mind a Thousand Times (ASCAP)—Vic 20-6359	2	10
2.	**POOR PEOPLE OF PARIS (ASCAP)—L. Baxter** Theme From Helen of Troy (ASCAP)—Cap 3336	4	4
3.	**NO, NOT MUCH (ASCAP)—Four Lads** I'll Never Know (BMI)—Col 40629	5	6
4.	**GREAT PRETENDER—Platters** I'm Just a Dancing Partner (ASCAP)—Mercury 70753	3	11
5.	**LISBON ANTIGUA (ASCAP)—N. Riddle** Robin Hood (ASCAP)—Cap 3287	1	10
6.	**MEMORIES ARE MADE OF THIS (BMI)—D. Martin** Change of Heart (BMI)—Cap 3295	6	14
7.	**I'LL BE HOME (BMI)—P. Boone** Tutti Frutti (BMI)—Dot 15443	7	5
8.	**SEE YOU LATER, ALLIGATOR (BMI)—B. Haley** Paper Boy (ASCAP)—Dec 29791	8	6
9.	**THEME FROM "THE THREE PENNY OPERA" (MORITAT) (ASCAP)—D. Hyman** Baubles, Bangles and Beads (ASCAP)—MGM 12149	8	5
10.	**BAND OF GOLD (BMI)—D. Cherry** Rumble Boogie (BMI)—Col 40597	10	11
11.	**WHY DO FOOLS FALL IN LOVE? (BMI)—Teen-Agers** Please Be Mine (BMI)—Gee 1002	—	1
12.	**DUNGAREE DOLL (BMI)—E. Fisher** Everybody's Got a Home But Me (ASCAP)—Vic 20-6337	12	8
13.	**THEME FROM "THE THREE PENNY OPERA" (MORITAT) (ASCAP)—R. Hayman-J. August** I'll Be With You in Apple Blossom Time (ASCAP)—Mercury 70781	11	4
14.	**HEARTBREAK HOTEL (BMI)—E. Presley** I Was the One (BMI)—Vic 20-6420	—	1
15.	**TUTTI FRUTTI (BMI)—P. Boone** I'll Be Home (BMI)—Dot 15443	16	3
16.	**MR. WONDERFUL (ASCAP)—S. Vaughan** You Ought to Have a Wife (ASCAP)—Mercury 70777	13	2
17.	**THAT'S ALL (BMI)—T. Ernie** Bright Lights and Blond Haired Women (ASCAP)—Cap 3343	—	1
18.	**SEVEN DAYS (BMI)—Crew Cuts** That's Your Mistake (BMI)—Mercury 70782	18	2
19.	**LULLABY OF BIRDLAND (BMI)—Blue Stars** That's My Girl (ASCAP)—Mercury 70742	—	2
20.	**LIPSTICK, CANDY AND RUBBER SOLED SHOES (BMI)—J. La Rosa** Winter in New England (ASCAP)—Vic 20-6416	15	2

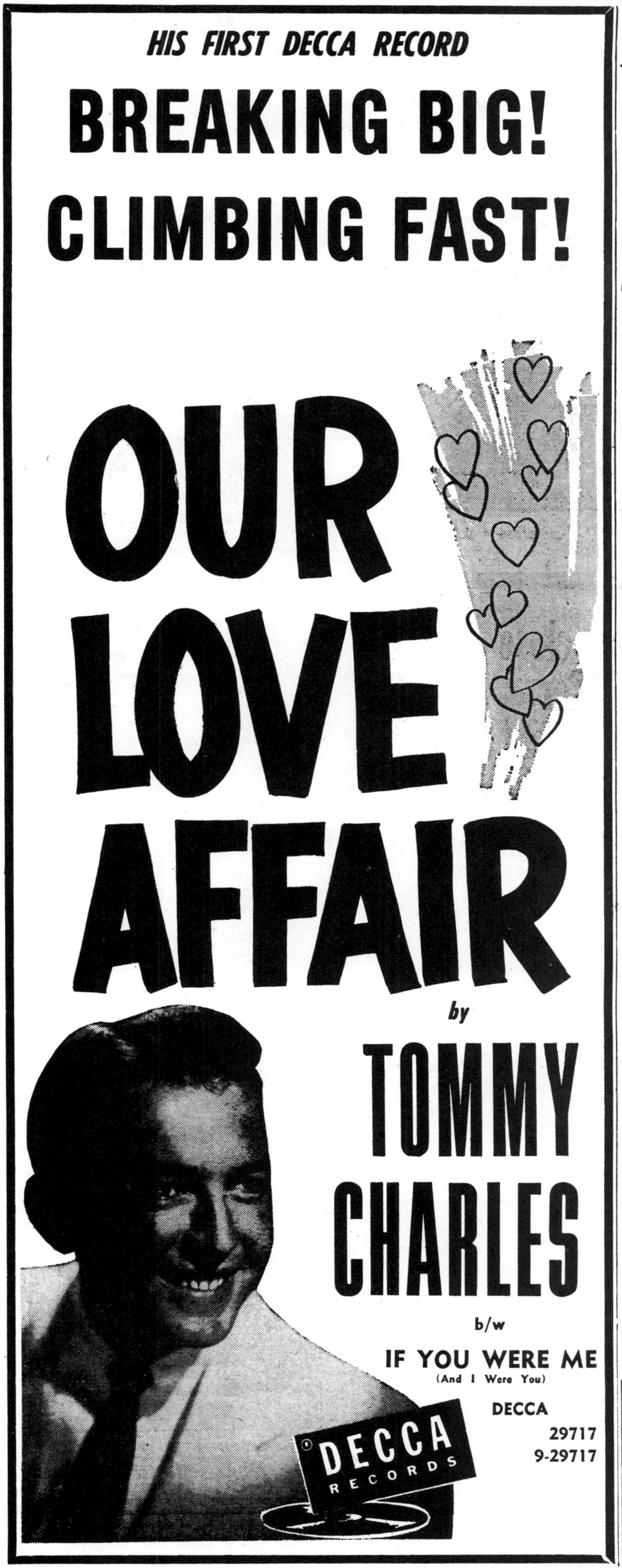

The Billboard Music Popularity Charts
POPULAR RECORDS

THE TOP 100

For survey week ending February 29

A list of the Top 100 RECORD SIDES in the nation according to a COMBINED TABULATION of Dealer, Disk Jockey and Juke Box Operator replies to The Billboard's weekly popular record Best Seller and Most Played surveys. Its purpose is to provide Disk Jockeys with additional programming material and to give trade exposure to NEWER records just beginning to show action in the field.

Pos.	Song	Artist	Label	Last Week
1.	ROCK AND ROLL WALTZ	K. Starr	Victor	1
2.	LISBON ANTIGUA	N. Riddle	Capitol	2
3.	GREAT PRETENDER	Platters	Mercury	3
4.	NO, NOT MUCH	Four Lads	Columbia	5
5.	POOR PEOPLE OF PARIS	L. Baxter	Capitol	6
6.	MEMORIES ARE MADE OF THIS	D. Martin	Capitol	4
7.	SEE YOU LATER, ALLIGATOR	B. Haley	Decca	7
8.	I'LL BE HOME	P. Boone	Dot	9
9.	BAND OF GOLD	D. Cherry	Columbia	8
10.	WHY DO FOOLS FALL IN LOVE?	Teen Agers	Gee	15
11.	THEME FROM "THE THREE PENNY OPERA" (MORITAT)	D. Hyman	M-G-M	10
12.	TUTTI FRUTTI	P. Boone	Dot	42
13.	THEME FROM "THE THREE PENNY OPERA" (MORITAT)	R. Hayman-J. August	Mercury	13
14.	DUNGAREE DOLL	E. Fisher	Victor	12
15.	IT'S ALMOST TOMORROW	Dream Weavers	Decca	16
15.	TEEN-AGE PRAYER	G. Storm	Dot	14
17.	SIXTEEN TONS	T. Ernie	Capitol	11
18.	TEAR FELL	T. Brewer	Coral	61
18.	WHY DO FOOLS FALL IN LOVE?	G. Storm	Dot	37
20.	ANGELS IN THE SKY	Crew Cuts	Mercury	19
21.	ELEVENTH HOUR MELODY	A. Hibbler	Decca	30
22.	THEME FROM "THE THREE PENNY OPERA" (MACK THE KNIFE)	L. Armstrong	Columbia	21
23.	BLUE SUEDE SHOES	C. Perkins	Sun	83
24.	BAND OF GOLD	K. Carson	Capitol	23
25.	GO ON WITH THE WEDDING	P. Page	Mercury	—
26.	SEVEN DAYS	Crew Cuts	Mercury	20
27.	NINETY-NINE YEARS	G. Mitchell	Columbia	31
28.	CHAIN GANG	B. Scott	ABC-Paramount	16
28.	HEARTBREAK HOTEL	E. Presley	Victor	68
30.	LIPSTICK, CANDY AND RUBBER SOLED SHOES	J. La Rosa	Victor	21
31.	ARE YOU SATISFIED?	R. Draper	Mercury	18
32.	IT'S ALMOST TOMORROW	J. Stafford	Columbia	28
33.	ASK ME	Nat (King) Cole	Capitol	25
34.	JUKE BOX BABY	P. Como	Victor	—
35.	HOT DIGGITY	P. Como	Victor	—
36.	LULLABY OF BIRDLAND	Blue Stars	Mercury	24
37.	HE	A. Hibbler	Decca	28
38.	EDDIE MY LOVE	Chordettes	Cadence	—
39.	EDDIE MY LOVE	Teen Queens	RPM	93
40.	BO WEEVIL	T. Brewer	Coral	54
41.	WHY DO FOOLS FALL IN LOVE?	Diamonds	Mercury	48
42.	TUTTI FRUTTI	Little Richard	Specialty	33
43.	OUR LOVE AFFAIR	T. Charles	Decca	—
44.	LISBON ANTIGUA	M. Miller	Columbia	40
45.	BEYOND THE SEA	R. Williams	Kapp	41
46.	INNAMORATA	J. Vale	Columbia	—
46.	ELOISE	K. Thompson	Cadence	—
48.	CRY ME A RIVER	J. London	Liberty	35
49.	SPEEDOO	Cadillacs	Josie	33
50.	THAT'S ALL	T. Ernie	Capitol	44
51.	FOREVER DARLING	Ames Brothers	Victor	59
52.	CRY BABY	Bonnie Sisters	Rainbow	35
53.	MR. WONDERFUL	T. King	Victor	32
53.	VALLEY VALPARAISO	P. Faith	Columbia	59
55.	MR. WONDERFUL	S. Vaughan	Mercury	56
56.	MEMORIES ARE MADE OF THIS	G. Storm	Dot	43
57.	ELEVENTH HOUR MELODY	L. Busch	Capitol	56
57.	FLOWERS MEAN FORGIVENESS	F. Sinatra	Capitol	49
57.	THEME FROM "THE THREE PENNY OPERA" (MORITAT)	L. Paul & M. Ford	Capitol	55
60.	TO YOU MY LOVE	N. Noble	Mercury	86
61.	ONLY YOU	Platters	Mercury	46
63.	WHEN YOU DANCE	Turbans	Herald	94
64.	MADERIA	M. Miller	Columbia	—
65.	APRIL IN PARIS	C. Basie	Clef	62
65.	MISSING	McGuire Sisters	Coral	—
67.	THEME FROM "THE THREE PENNY OPERA" (MORITAT)	B. Vaughn	Dot	37
67.	POOR PEOPLE OF PARIS	R. Morgan	Decca	88
69.	SEVEN DAYS	D. Collins	Coral	73
69.	TENDER TRAP	F. Sinatra	Capitol	27
71.	THEME FROM "THE THREE PENNY OPERA" (MORITAT)	L. Welk	Coral	39
72.	NOTHING EVER CHANGES MY LOVE FOR YOU	Nat (King) Cole	Capitol	79
73.	MR. WONDERFUL	P. Lee	Decca	82
74.	EDDIE MY LOVE	Fontane Sisters	Dot	—
74.	INNAMORATA	D. Martin	Capitol	—
76.	I'LL NEVER KNOW	Four Lads	Columbia	52
77.	MEMORIES OF YOU	Four Coins	Epic	70
78.	LOVELY ONE	Four Voices	Columbia	—
79.	WOMAN IN LOVE	F. Laine	Columbia	96
80.	WHEN YOU LOSE THE ONE YOU LOVE	D. Whitfield	London	62
81.	YOU'LL GET YOURS	F. Sinatra	Capitol	67
82.	INTO THE NIGHT	Dream Weavers	Decca	—
83.	DON'T TELL ME NOT TO LOVE YOU	J. James	MGM	—
84.	I'VE CHANGED MY MIND A THOUSAND TIMES	K. Starr	Victor	73
84.	I WAS THE ONE	E. Presley	Victor	—
86.	HE	McGuire Sisters	Coral	77
87.	ONLY YOU	Hilltoppers	Dot	71
87.	IT'S ALMOST TOMORROW	D. Carroll	Mercury	65
87.	WHY DO FOOLS FALL IN LOVE?	G. Mann	Sound	—
87.	MOSTLY MARTHA	Crew Cuts	Mercury	44
91.	BITTER WITH THE SWEET	B. Eckstine	Victor	—
92.	LITTLE CHILD	E. Albert	Kapp	56
93.	BUTTERNUT	J. Heap	Capitol	—
93.	KISS AND RUN	P. King	Columbia	88
93.	THESE HANDS	L. Dressler	Mercury	—
96.	I HEAR YOU KNOCKIN'	G. Storm	Dot	91
96.	MOMENTS TO REMEMBER	Four Lads	Columbia	50
96.	WHO ARE WE?	G. Grant	Era	87
99.	BO WEEVIL	F. Domino	Imperial	91
99.	ALL NIGHT LONG	J. Stafford	Columbia	—
99.	ROCK A BEATIN' BOOGIE	B. Haley	Decca	—

CAUTION TO DEALERS AND JUKE BOX OPERATORS

The Billboard's Top 100 is NOT designed to provide tested information for buying purposes. This function is most reliably served by other regular weekly features: Best Sellers in Stores, Most Played in Juke Boxes, Coming Up Strong and Best Buys.

The Billboard Music Popularity Charts — POPULAR RECORDS

• Best Sellers in Stores

For survey week ending March 7

RECORDS are ranked in order of their current national selling importance at the retail level, as determined by The Billboard's weekly survey of the top volume dealers in every important market area. When significant action is reported on both sides of a record, points are combined to determine position on the chart. In such a case, both sides are listed in bold type, the leading side on top.

This Week	Record	Last Week	Weeks on Chart
1.	**LISBON ANTIGUA** (ASCAP)—N. Riddle — Robin Hood (ASCAP)—Cap 3287	1	12
2.	**POOR PEOPLE OF PARIS** (ASCAP)—L. Baxter — Theme From Helen of Troy (ASCAP)—Cap 3336	3	5
3.	**ROCK AND ROLL WALTZ** (BMI)—K. Starr — I've Changed My Mind a Thousand Times (ASCAP)—Vic 20-6359	2	11
4.	**NO, NOT MUCH** (ASCAP)—Four Lads — I'll Never Know (BMI)—Col 40629	4	8
5.	**GREAT PRETENDER** (ASCAP)—Platters — I'm Just a Dancing Partner (ASCAP)—Mercury 70753	5	13
6.	**I'LL BE HOME** (BMI)—P. Boone / **TUTTI FRUTTI** (BMI)—Dot 15443	7	6
7.	**SEE YOU LATER, ALLIGATOR** (BMI)—B. Haley — Paper Boy (ASCAP)—Dec 29791	6	10
8.	**WHY DO FOOLS FALL IN LOVE?** (BMI)—Teen-Agers — Please Be Mine (BMI)—Gee 1002	9	5
9.	**HOT DIGGITY** (ASCAP)—P. Como / **JUKE BOX BABY** (ASCAP)—Vic 20-6427	12	2
10.	**MEMORIES ARE MADE OF THIS** (BMI)—D. Martin — Change of Heart (BMI)—Cap 3295	8	16
11.	**BAND OF GOLD** (BMI)—D. Cherry — Rumble Boogie (BMI)—Col 40597	10	15
12.	**THEME FROM "THE THREE PENNY OPERA" (MORITAT)** (ASCAP)—D. Hyman — Baubles, Bangles and Beads (ASCAP)—M-G-M 12149	11	8
13.	**THEME FROM "THE THREE PENNY OPERA" (MORITAT)** (ASCAP)—R. Hayman-J. August — I'll Be With You in Apple Blossom Time (ASCAP)—Mercury 12159	17	5
14.	**BLUE SUEDE SHOES** (BMI)—C. Perkins — Honey, Don't (BMI)—Sun 234	14	2
15.	**HEARTBREAK HOTEL** (BMI)—E. Presley / **I WAS THE ONE** (BMI)—Vic 20-6420	19	2
16.	**TEAR FELL** (BMI)—T. Brewer / **BO WEEVIL** (BMI)—Coral 61590	16	3
17.	**DUNGAREE DOLL** (BMI)—E. Fisher — Everybody's Got a Home But Me (ASCAP)—Victor 20-6337	15	12
18.	**IT'S ALMOST TOMORROW** (ASCAP)—Dream Weavers — You Got Me Wondering (ASCAP)—Decca 29683	13	19
19.	**WHY DO FOOLS FALL IN LOVE?** (BMI)—Diamonds — You, Baby, You (BMI)—Mercury 70790	—	1
20.	**LOVELY ONE** (BMI)—Four Voices — Geronimo (BMI)—Columbia 40643	—	1

• THIS WEEK'S BEST BUYS

According to sales reports in key markets, the following recent releases are recommended for extra profits:

EDDIE, MY LOVE (Modern-Roosevelt, BMI)—**The Chordettes—Cadence 1284—The Fontane Sisters—Dot 15450**

These cover records of the r.&b.-pop hit, cut originally by the Teen Queens, are now carving off big slices of the melon. The Cadence disk now appears on the Baltimore and Milwaukee territorial charts and is coming close to the national board also. The Fontanes are only a little behind, and have a wide spread of excellent retail showings, particularly in the Northeastern and Middle West. The latter was a Billboard "Spotlight" pick.

LOVELY ONE (Blackwood, BMI)—**The Four Voices—Columbia 40643**

A "sleeper" that made a fast play for chart scores this week, and edged into the No. 20 slot. A top record in Baltimore and Minneapolis, "Lovely One" was also reported showing strong action in Atlanta, Buffalo, St. Louis, Milwaukee and New York. Flip is "Geronimo" (Stratton, BMI).

WHY DO FOOLS FALL IN LOVE? (Patricia, BMI)—**The Diamonds—Mercury 70790—Gale Storm—Dot 15448**

The Teen-Agers' original version of this tune has been in the national listings over a month. The two covers above are now beginning to figure in the national charts, too. The Diamonds placed in the top 20 national retail list this week; Gale Storm is on the national juke box chart, and is within a stone's throw of the retail chart as well. The Storm record was a previous Billboard "Spotlight" pick.

TO YOU, MY LOVE (Leeds, ASCAP)—**Nick Noble—Mercury 70821**

This disk has been slowly showing its power, and at this point looks like a champ. The Chicago, Milwaukee and New Orleans territorial charts have it listed, and Boston, Providence, Baltimore, Buffalo, Cleveland, St. Louis, Durham, and Atlanta also indicated top-notch sales. Flip is "You Are My Only Love" (Meridian, BMI)

• Most Played in Juke Boxes

For survey week ending March 7

RECORDS are ranked in order of the greatest number of plays in juke boxes thruout the country, as determined by The Billboard's weekly survey of the nation's juke box operators. When significant play is reported on both sides of a record, points are combined to determine position on the chart. In such a case, both sides are listed in bold type, the leading side on top

This Week	Record	Last Week	Weeks on Chart
1.	**ROCK AND WALTZ** (BMI)—K. Starr — I've Changed My Mind a Thousand Times (ASCAP)—Vic 20-6359	1	10
2.	**GREAT PRETENDER** (ASCAP)—Platters — I'm Just a Dancing Partner (ASCAP)—Mercury 70753	2	11
3.	**LISBON ANTIGUA** (ASCAP)—N. Riddle — Robin Hood (ASCAP)—Cap 3287	4	7
4.	**NO, NOT MUCH** (ASCAP)—Four Lads — I'll Never Know (BMI)—Col 40629	6	5
5.	**MEMORIES ARE MADE OF THIS** (BMI)—D. Martin — Change of Heart (BMI)—Cap 3295	3	13
6.	**I'LL BE HOME** (BMI)—P. Boone / **TUTTI FRUTTI** (BMI)—Dot 15443	5	5
7.	**POOR PEOPLE OF PARIS** (ASCAP)—L. Baxter — Theme From Helen of Troy (ASCAP)—Cap 3336	9	4
8.	**SEE YOU LATER, ALLIGATOR** (BMI)—B. Haley — Paper Boy (ASCAP)—Dec 29791	7	6
9.	**BAND OF GOLD** (BMI)—D. Cherry — Rumble Boogie (BMI)—Col 40597	8	9
10.	**WHY DO FOOLS FALL IN LOVE?** (BMI)—Teen-Agers — Please Be Mine (BMI)—Gee 1002	12	3
11.	**TEAR FELL** (BMI)—T. Brewer / **BO WEEVIL** (BMI)—Coral 61590	—	1
12.	**DUNGAREE DOLL** (BMI)—E. Fisher — Everybody's Got a Home But Me (ASCAP)—Vic 20-6337	17	10
12.	**ARE YOU SATISFIED?** (BMI)—R. Draper — Wabash Cannonball (BMI)—Mercury 70757	11	7
14.	**SIXTEEN TONS** (BMI)—Tennessee Ernie — You Don't Have to Be a Baby to Cry (ASCAP)—Cap 3262	10	18
15.	**THEME FROM THE "THREE PENNY OPERA" (MORITAT)** (ASCAP)—R. Hayman-J. August — I'll Be With You in Apple Blossom Time (ASCAP)—Mercury 70781	13	3
16.	**WHY DO FOOLS FALL IN LOVE?** (BMI)—G. Storm — I Walk Alone (BMI)—Dot 15448	19	2
17.	**IT'S ALMOST TOMORROW** (ASCAP)—Dream Weavers — You Got Me Wondering (ASCAP)—Dec 29683	16	15
18.	**THEME FROM THE "THREE PENNY OPERA" (MORITAT)** (ASCAP)—D. Hyman — Baubles, Bangles and Beads (ASCAP)—M-G-M 12149	15	4
19.	**TEEN-AGE PRAYER** (ASCAP)—G. Storm — Memories Are Made of This (BMI)—Dot 15436	13	12
20.	**CHAIN GANG** (ASCAP)—B. Scott — Shadrach (ASCAP)—ABC-Paramount 9658	20	5
20.	**MEMORIES OF YOU** (ASCAP)—R. Clooney & B. Goodman — It's Bad for Me (ASCAP)—Col 40616	—	1

• Most Played by Jockeys

For survey week ending March 7

SIDES are ranked in order of the greatest number of plays on disk jockey radio shows thruout the country. Results are based on The Billboard's weekly survey among the nation's disk jockeys. The reverse side of each record is also listed.

This Week	Record	Last Week	Weeks on Chart
1.	**POOR PEOPLE OF PARIS** (ASCAP)—L. Baxter — Theme From Helen of Troy (ASCAP)—Cap 3336	2	5
2.	**NO, NOT MUCH** (ASCAP)—Four Lads — I'll Never Know (BMI)—Col 40629	3	7
3.	**ROCK AND ROLL WALTZ** (BMI)—K. Starr — I've Changed My Mind a Thousand Times (ASCAP)—Vic 20-6359	1	11
4.	**LISBON ANTIGUA** (ASCAP)—N. Riddle — Robin Hood (ASCAP)—Cap 3287	5	11
5.	**GREAT PRETENDER**—Platters — I'm Just a Dancing Partner (ASCAP)—Mercury 70753	4	12
6.	**I'LL BE HOME** (BMI)—P. Boone — Tutti Frutti (BMI)—Dot 15443	7	6
7.	**SEE YOU LATER, ALLIGATOR** (BMI)—B. Haley — Paper Boy (ASCAP)—Dec 29791	8	7
8.	**THEME FROM THE "THREE PENNY OPERA" (MORITAT)** (ASCAP)—D. Hyman — Baubles, Bangles and Beads (ASCAP)—M-G-M 12149	9	6
9.	**WHY DO FOOLS FALL IN LOVE?** (BMI)—Teen-Agers — Please Be Mine (BMI)—Gee 1002	11	2
10.	**MEMORIES ARE MADE OF THIS** (BMI)—D. Martin — Change of Heart (BMI)—Cap 3295	6	15
11.	**THEME FROM THE "THREE PENNY OPERA" (MORITAT)** (ASCAP)—R. Hayman-J. August — I'll Be With You in Apple Blossom Time (ASCAP)—Mercury 12159	13	5
12.	**HEARTBREAK HOTEL** (BMI)—E. Presley — I Was the One (BMI)—Vic 20-6420	14	2
13.	**HOT DIGGITY** (ASCAP)—P. Como — Juke Box Baby (BMI)—Vic 20-6427	—	1
14.	**BAND OF GOLD** (BMI)—D. Cherry — Rumble Boogie (BMI)—Col 40597	10	12
15.	**JUKE BOX BABY** (BMI)—P. Como — Hot Diggity (ASCAP)—Vic 20-6427	—	1
16.	**MR. WONDERFUL** (ASCAP)—S. Vaughan — You Ought to Have a Wife (ASCAP)—Mercury 70777	16	3
17.	**WHY DO FOOLS FALL IN LOVE?** (BMI)—Diamonds — You, Baby, You (BMI)—Mercury 70790	—	1
18.	**ASK ME** (ASCAP)—Nat (King) Cole — Nothing Ever Changes My Love for You (ASCAP)—Cap 3328	—	1
19.	**LULLABY OF BIRDLAND** (BMI)—Blue Stars — That's My Girl (ASCAP)—Mercury 70742	19	3
20.	**LIPSTICK, CANDY AND RUBBER SOLED SHOES** (BMI)—J. La Rosa — Winter in New England (ASCAP)—Vic 20-6416	20	3

The Billboard Music Popularity Charts

POPULAR RECORDS

THE TOP 100

For survey week ending March 7

A list of the **TOP 100 RECORD SIDES** in the nation according to a **COMBINED TABULATION** of Dealer, Disk Jockey and Juke Box Operator replies to The Billboard's weekly popular record Best Seller and Most Played surveys. Its purpose is to provide Disk Jockeys with additional programming material and to give trade exposure to NEWER records just beginning to show action in the field.

Pos.	Song	Artist	Label	Last Week
1.	ROCK AND ROLL WALTZ	K. Starr	Victor	1
2.	LISBON ANTIGUA	N. Riddle	Capitol	2
3.	POOR PEOPLE OF PARIS	L. Baxter	Capitol	5
4.	NO, NOT MUCH	Four Lads	Columbia	4
5.	GREAT PRETENDER	Platters	Mercury	3
6.	I'LL BE HOME	P. Boone	Dot	8
6.	SEE YOU LATER, ALLIGATOR	B. Haley	Decca	7
8.	MEMORIES ARE MADE OF THIS	D. Martin	Capitol	6
9.	WHY DO FOOLS FALL IN LOVE?	Teen-Agers	Gee	10
10.	BAND OF GOLD	D. Cherry	Columbia	9
11.	THEME FROM "THE THREE PENNY OPERA" (MORITAT)	D. Hyman	M-G-M	11
12.	THEME FROM "THE THREE PENNY OPERA" (MORITAT)	R. Hayman-J. August	Mercury	13
13.	TUTTI FRUTTI	P. Boone	Dot	12
14.	JUKE BOX BABY	P. Como	Victor	34
15.	BLUE SUEDE SHOES	C. Perkins	Sun	23
16.	TEAR FELL	T. Brewer	Coral	18
17.	WHY DO FOOLS FALL IN LOVE?	G. Storm	Dot	18
18.	DUNGAREE DOLL	E. Fisher	Victor	14
19.	IT'S ALMOST TOMORROW	Dream Weavers	Decca	15
20.	THEME FROM "THE THREE PENNY OPERA" (MACK THE KNIFE)	L. Armstrong	Columbia	22
21.	BO WEEVIL	T. Brewer	Coral	40
21.	HOT DIGGITY	P. Como	Victor	35
21.	HEARTBREAK HOTEL	E. Presley	Victor	28
24.	EDDIE, MY LOVE	Chordettes	Cadence	39
25.	SEVEN DAYS	Crew Cuts	Mercury	26
26.	WHY DO FOOLS FALL IN LOVE?	Diamonds	Mercury	41
27.	ANGELS IN THE SKY	Crew Cuts	Mercury	20
27.	CHAIN GANG	B. Scott	ABC-Paramount	28
29.	EDDIE, MY LOVE	Fontane Sisters	Dot	74
30.	ASK ME	Nat (King) Cole	Capitol	33
31.	ELEVENTH HOUR MELODY	A. Hibbler	Decca	21
31.	I WAS THE ONE	E. Presley	Victor	84
33.	LISBON ANTIGUA	M. Miller	Columbia	44
34.	ARE YOU SATISFIED?	R. Draper	Mercury	31
34.	EDDIE, MY LOVE	Teen Queens	RPM	39
36.	NINETY-NINE YEARS	G. Mitchell	Columbia	27
37.	POOR PEOPLE OF PARIS	R. Morgan	Decca	67
38.	LIPSTICK CANDY AND RUBBER-SOLED SHOES	J. La Rosa	Victor	30
39.	ELOISE	K. Thompson	Cadence	46
40.	SIXTEEN TONS	T. Ernie	Capitol	17
41.	FLOWERS MEAN FORGIVENESS	F. Sinatra	Capitol	57
42.	TUTTI FRUTTI	Little Richard	Specialty	42
43.	MR. WONDERFUL	T. King	Victor	53
44.	LOVELY ONE	Four Voices	Columbia	78
45.	LULLABY OF BIRDLAND	Blue Stars	Mercury	36
46.	TEEN-AGE PRAYER	G. Storm	Dot	15
47.	THEME FROM "THE THREE PENNY OPERA" (MORITAT)	L. Welk	Coral	71
48.	CRY BABY	Bonnie Sisters	Rainbow	52
49.	THEME FROM "THE THREE PENNY OPERA" (MORITAT)	L. Paul & M. Ford	Capitol	57
50.	MADERIA	M. Miller	Columbia	64
51.	THAT'S YOUR MISTAKE	O. Williams	DeLuxe	—
52.	POOR PEOPLE OF PARIS (JEAN'S SONG)	C. Atkins	Victor	—
53.	BAND OF GOLD	K. Carson	Capitol	24
53.	THEME FROM "THE THREE PENNY OPERA" (MORITAT)	B. Vaughn	Dot	67
55.	MR. WONDERFUL	S. Vaughan	Mercury	55
56.	GO ON WITH THE WEDDING	P. Page	Mercury	25
56.	INNAMORATA	D. Martin	Capitol	74
58.	ELEVENTH HOUR MELODY	L. Busch	Capitol	57
59.	WHY DO FOOLS FALL IN LOVE?	G. Mann	Sound	87
60.	MEMORIES OF YOU	R. Clooney-B. Goodman	Columbia	—
60.	THAT'S ALL	T. Ernie	Capitol	50
62.	MISSING	McGuire Sisters	Coral	65
63.	TO YOU, MY LOVE	N. Noble	Mercury	60
64.	INNAMORATA	J. Vale	Columbia	46
65.	POOR PEOPLE OF PARIS	L. Welk	Coral	—
66.	APRIL IN PARIS	C. Basie	Clef	65
67.	BEYOND THE SEA	R. Williams	Kapp	45
67.	LOVELY LIES	Manhattan Brothers	London	—
69.	MR. WONDERFUL	P. Lee	Decca	73
70.	BO WEEVIL	F. Domino	Imperial	99
70.	OUR LOVE AFFAIR	T. Charles	Decca	43
72.	FOREVER, DARLING	Ames Brothers	Victor	51
73.	HE	A. Hibbler	Decca	37
73.	WHEN YOU LOSE THE ONE YOU LOVE	D. Whitfield	London	80
75.	TENDER TRAP	F. Sinatra	Capitol	69
76.	ROCK RIGHT	G. Gibbs	Mercury	—
77.	YOU'LL GET YOURS	F. Sinatra	Capitol	81
78.	TEEN-AGE PRAYER	G. Mann	Sound	—
79.	LARGE, LARGE HOUSE	M. Pedicin	Victor	—
80.	WHEN YOU DANCE	Turbans	Herald	—
81.	ONLY YOU	Platters	Mercury	61
82.	ROCK AROUND MOTHER GOOSE	B. Gordon	M-G-M	—
82.	WOMAN IN LOVE	Four Aces	Decca	—
84.	MAN WITH THE GOLDEN ARM	R. Maltby	X	—
84.	CRY ME A RIVER	J. London	Liberty	48
86.	AND THE ANGELS SING	Chuckles	X	—
87.	NOTHING EVER CHANGES MY LOVE FOR YOU	Nat (King) Cole	Capitol	72
87.	SEVEN DAYS	D. Collins	Coral	69
89.	IF YOU CAN DREAM	Four Aces	Decca	—
90.	MEMORIES ARE MADE OF THIS	M. Carson	Columbia	—
91.	VALLEY VALPARAISO	P. Faith	Columbia	53
92.	IT'S ALMOST TOMORROW	D. Carroll	Mercury	87
93.	IT'S ALMOST TOMORROW	J. Stafford	Columbia	32
93.	MEMORIES ARE MADE OF THIS	G. Storm	Dot	56
95.	I'LL NEVER KNOW	Four Lads	Columbia	76
96.	BITTER WITH THE SWEET	B. Eckstine	Victor	91
97.	WHO ARE WE?	G. Grant	Era	96
98.	TEEN-AGE MEETING	D. Cornell	Coral	—
99.	SPEEDOO	Cadillacs	Josie	49
100.	I'M GONNA LOVE YOU	Ames Brothers	Victor	—

CAUTION TO DEALERS AND JUKE BOX OPERATORS

The Billboard's Top 100 is NOT designed to provide tested information for buying purposes. This function is most reliably served by other regular weekly features: Best Sellers in Stores, Most Played in Juke Boxes, Coming Up Strong and Best Buys.

• Best Sellers in Stores

For survey week ending March 14

RECORDS are ranked in order of their current national selling importance at the retail level, as determined by The Billboard's weekly survey of the top volume dealers in every important market area. When significant action is reported on both sides of a record, points are combined to determine position on the chart. In such a case, both sides are listed in bold type, the leading side on top.

This Week		Last Week	Weeks on Chart
1.	**POOR PEOPLE OF PARIS** (ASCAP)—L. Baxter Helen of Troy (ASCAP)—Cap 3336	2	6
2.	**LISBON ANTIGUA** (ASCAP)—N. Riddle Robin Hood (ASCAP)—Cap 3287	1	13
3.	**ROCK AND ROLL WALTZ** (BMI)—K. Starr I've Changed My Mind a Thousand Times (ASCAP)—Vic 20-6359	3	12
4.	**NO, NOT MUCH** (ASCAP)—Four Lads I'll Never Know (BMI)—Col 40629	4	9
5.	**GREAT PRETENDER** (ASCAP)—Platters I'm Just a Dancing Partner (ASCAP)—Mercury 70753	5	14
6.	**I'LL BE HOME** (BMI)—P. Boone **TUTTI FRUTTI** (BMI)—Dot 15443	6	7
7.	**HOT DIGGITY** (ASCAP)—P. Como **JUKE BOX BABY** (ASCAP)—Vic 20-6427	9	3
8.	**WHY DO FOOLS FALL IN LOVE?** Teen-Agers Please Be Mine (BMI)—Gee 1002	8	6
9.	**BLUE SUEDE SHOES** (BMI)—C. Perkins Honey, Don't (BMI)—Sun 234	14	3
10.	**SEE YOU LATER, ALLIGATOR** B. Haley Paper Boy (ASCAP)—Dec 29791	7	11
11.	**HEARTBREAK HOTEL** (BMI)—E. Presley **I WAS THE ONE** (BMI)—Vic 20-6420	15	3
12.	**THEME FROM "THE THREE PENNY OPERA" (MORITAT)** (ASCAP)—D. Hyman Baubies, Bangles and Beads (ASCAP)—M-G-M 12149	12	9
13.	**MEMORIES ARE MADE OF THIS** (BMI)—D. Martin Change of Heart (BMI)—Cap 3295	10	17
14.	**A TEAR FELL** (BMI)—T. Brewer **BO WEEVIL** (BMI)—Coral 61590	16	4
15.	**BAND OF GOLD** (BMI)—D. Cherry Rumble Boogie (BMI)—Col 40597	11	16
16.	**THEME FROM "THE THREE PENNY OPERA" (MORITAT)** (ASCAP)—R. Hayman-J. August I'll Be With You in Apple Blossom Time—Mercury 12159	13	6
17.	**EDDIE, MY LOVE** (BMI)—Teen Queens Just Goofed (BMI)—RPM 453	22	3
18.	**WHY DO FOOLS FALL IN LOVE?** (BMI)—Diamonds You, Baby, You (BMI)—Mercury 70790	19	2
19.	**WHY DO FOOLS FALL IN LOVE?** G. Storm I Walk Alone (BMI)—Dot 15448	—	1
20.	**IT'S ALMOST TOMORROW** (ASCAP)—Dream Weavers You Got Me Wondering (ASCAP)—Dec 29683	18	20

• Most Played in Juke Boxes

For survey week ending March 14

RECORDS are ranked in order of the greatest number of plays in juke boxes thruout the country, as determined by The Billboard's weekly survey of the nation's juke box operators. When significant play is reported on both sides of a record, points are combined to determine position on the chart. In such a case, both sides are listed in bold type, the leading side on top.

This Week		Last Week	Weeks on Chart
1.	**ROCK AND ROLL WALTZ** (BMI)—K. Starr I've Changed My Mind a Thousand Times (ASCAP)—Vic 20-6359	1	11
2.	**GREAT PRETENDER** (ASCAP)—Platters I'm Just a Dancing Partner (ASCAP)—Mercury 70753	2	12
3.	**LISBON ANTIGUA** (ASCAP)—N. Riddle Robin Hood (ASCAP)—Cap 3287	3	8
4.	**NO, NOT MUCH** (ASCAP)—Four Lads I'll Never Know (BMI)—Col 40629	4	6
5.	**POOR PEOPLE OF PARIS** (ASCAP)—L. Baxter Theme From Helen of Troy (ASCAP)—Cap 3336	7	5
6.	**I'LL BE HOME** (BMI)—P. Boone **TUTTI FRUTTI** (BMI)—Dot 15443	6	6
7.	**MEMORIES ARE MADE OF THIS** (BMI)—D. Martin Change of Heart (BMI)— Cap 3295	5	14
8.	**SEE YOU LATER, ALLIGATOR** (BMI)—B. Haley Paper Boy (ASCAP)—Dec 29791	8	7
9.	**BAND OF GOLD** (BMI)—D. Cherry Rumble Boogie (BMI)—Col 40597	9	10
10.	**WHY DO FOOLS FALL IN LOVE?** (BMI)—Teen-Agers Please Be Mine (BMI)—Gee 1002	10	4
10.	**A TEAR FELL** (BMI)—T. Brewer **BO WEEVIL** (BMI)—Coral 61590	11	2
12.	**ARE YOU SATISFIED?** (BMI)—R. Draper Wabash Cannonball (BMI)—Mercury 70757	12	8
13.	**DUNGAREE DOLL** (BMI)—E. Fisher Everybody's Got a Home But Me (ASCAP)—Vic 20-6337	12	11
14.	**THEME FROM "THE THREE PENNY OPERA" (MORITAT)** (ASCAP)—D. Hyman Baubles, Bangles and Beads (ASCAP)—M-G-M 12149	18	5
15.	**WHY DO FOOLS FALL IN LOVE?** (BMI)—G. Storm I Walk Alone (BMI)—Dot	16	3
16.	**SIXTEEN TONS** (BMI)—Tennessee Ernie You Don't Have to Be a Baby to Cry (ASCAP)—Cap 3262	14	19
17.	**THEME FROM "THE THREE PENNY OPERA" (MORITAT)** (ASCAP)—R. Hayman-J. August I'll Be With You in Apple Blossom Time (ASCAP)—Mercury 70781	15	4
17.	**IT'S ALMOST TOMORROW** (ASCAP)—Dream Weavers You Got Me Wondering (ASCAP)—Dec 29683	17	16
19.	**HOT DIGGITY** (BMI)—P. Como **JUKE BOX BABY** (BMI)—Vic 20-6427	—	1
20.	**BLUE SUEDE SHOES** (BMI)—C. Perkins Honey, Don't (BMI)—Sun 234	—	1

• Best Selling Sheet Music

Tunes are ranked in order of their current national selling importance at the sheet music jobber level.

This Week		Last Week	Weeks on Chart
1.	**Rock and Roll Waltz** (Sheldon)	1	10
2.	**Poor People of Paris** (Connelly)	4	5
3.	**HE** (Avas)	3	26
4.	**Lisbon Antigua** (Southern)	2	10
5.	**No, Not Much** (Beaver)	6	6
6.	**Theme From The Three Penny Opera** (Moritat) (Harms)	8	5
7.	**It's Almost Tomorrow** (Northern)	7	15
8.	**Memories Are Made of This** (Mont Clare)	9	14
9.	**Great Pretender** (Southern)	5	10
10.	**Eleventh Hour Melody** (Paxton)	11	6
11.	**I'll Be Home** (Arc)	13	2
12.	**Hot Diggity** (Roncom)	14	2
12.	**Band of Gold** (Ludlow)	10	13
14.	**Dungaree Doll** (E. B. Marks)	12	10
15.	**See You Later, Alligator** (Arc)	15	2

• Most Played by Jockeys

For survey week ending March 14

SIDES are ranked in order of the greatest number of plays on disk jockey radio shows thruout the country. Results are based on The Billboard's weekly survey among the nation's disk jockeys. The reverse side of each record is also listed.

This Week		Last Week	Weeks on Chart
1.	**POOR PEOPLE OF PARIS** (ASCAP)—L. Baxter Theme From Helen of Troy (ASCAP)—Cap 3336	1	6
2.	**NO, NOT MUCH** (ASCAP)—Four Lads I'll Never Know (BMI)—Col 40629	2	8
3.	**LISBON ANTIGUA** (ASCAP)—N. Riddle Robin Hood (ASCAP)—Cap 3287	4	12
4.	**ROCK AND ROLL WALTZ** (BMI) K. Starr I've Changed My Mind a Thousand Times (ASCAP)—Vic 20-6359	3	12
5.	**I'LL BE HOME** (BMI)—P. Boone Tutti Frutti (BMI)—Dot 15443	6	7
6.	**GREAT PRETENDER**—Platters I'm Just a Dancing Partner (ASCAP)—Mercury 70753	5	13
7.	**HEARTBREAK HOTEL** (BMI)—E. Presley I Was the One (BMI)—Vic 20-6420	12	3
8.	**HOT DIGGITY** (ASCAP)—P. Como Juke Box Baby (BMI)—Vic 20-6427	13	2
9.	**WHY DO FOOLS FALL IN LOVE?** (BMI)—G. Storm I Walk Alone (BMI)—Dot 15448	—	1
10.	**WHY DO FOOLS FALL IN, LOVE?** (BMI)—Teen-Agers Please Be Mine (BMI)—Gee 1002	9	3
11.	**SEE YOU LATER, ALLIGATOR** (BMI)—B. Haley Paper Boy (ASCAP)—Dec 29791	7	8
12.	**THEME FROM "THE THREE PENNY OPERA" (MORITAT)** (ASCAP)—D. Hyman Baubles, Bangles and Beads (ASCAP)—M-G-M 12149	8	7
13.	**JUKE BOX BABY** (BMI)—P. Como Hot Diggity (BMI)—Vic 20-6427	15	2
14.	**BLUE SUEDE SHOES** (BMI)—C Perkins Honey, Don't (BMI)—Sun 234	—	1
15.	**MEMORIES ARE MADE OF THIS** (BMI)—D. Martin Change of Heart (BMI)—Cap 3295	10	16
16.	**LULLABY OF BIRDLAND** (BMI)—Blue Stars That's My Girl (ASCAP)—Mercury 70742	19	4
17.	**THEME FROM "THE THREE PENNY OPERA" (MORITAT)** (ASCAP)—R. Hayman-J. August I'll Be With You in Apple Blossom Time (ASCAP)—Mercury 12159	11	6
18.	**BAND OF GOLD** (BMI)—D. Cherry Rumble Boogie (BMI)—Col 40597	14	13
18.	**MR. WONDERFUL** (ASCAP)—T. King Are You Slipping Through My Fingers? (BMI)—Vic 20-6392	—	1
20.	**LIPSTICK, CANDY AND RUBBER SOLED SHOES** (BMI)— J. La Rosa Winter in New England (ASCAP)—Vic 20-6416	20	4
21.	**MR. WONDERFUL** (ASCAP)—P. Lee Crazy in the Heart (BMI)—Dec 29834	—	1
22.	**EDDIE, MY LOVE** (BMI)—Fontane Sisters Yum Yum (BMI)—Dot 15450	—	1
23.	**WHY DO FOOLS FALL IN LOVE?** (BMI)—Diamonds You, Baby, You (BMI)—Mercury 70790	—	1
23.	**EDDIE, MY LOVE** (BMI)—Chordettes Whistling Willie (ASCAP)—Cadence 1084	—	1
25.	**A TEAR FELL** (BMI)—T. Brewer Bo Weevil (BMI)—Coral 61590	—	1

THE TOP 100

For survey week ending March 7

A list of the **TOP 100 RECORD SIDES** in the nation according to a **COMBINED TABULATION** of Dealer, Disk Jockey and Juke Box Operator replies to The Billboard's weekly popular record Best Seller and Most Played surveys. Its purpose is to provide Disk Jockeys with additional programming material and to give trade exposure to NEWER records just beginning to show action in the field.

Pos.	Song	Artist	Label	Last Week
1.	POOR PEOPLE OF PARIS	L. Baxter	Capitol	3
2.	LISBON ANTIGUA	N. Riddle	Capitol	2
2.	ROCK AND ROLL WALTZ	K. Starr	Victor	1
4.	NO, NOT MUCH	Four Lads	Columbia	4
5.	GREAT PRETENDER	Platters	Mercury	5
6.	I'LL BE HOME	P. Boone	Dot	6
7.	WHY DO FOOLS FALL IN LOVE?	Teen-Agers	Gee	9
8.	SEE YOU LATER, ALLIGATOR	B. Haley	Decca	6
9.	MEMORIES ARE MADE OF THIS	D. Martin	Capitol	8
9.	THEME FROM "THE THREE PENNY OPERA" (MORITAT)	D. Hyman	M-G-M	11
11.	HEARTBREAK HOTEL	E. Presley	Victor	21
12.	BLUE SUEDE SHOES	C. Perkins	Sun	15
13.	BAND OF GOLD	D. Cherry	Columbia	10
14.	HOT DIGGITY	P. Como	Victor	21
15.	WHY DO FOOLS FALL IN LOVE?	G. Storm	Dot	17
16.	THEME FROM "THE THREE PENNY OPERA" (MORITAT)	R. Hayman-J. August	Mercury	12
17.	A TEAR FELL	T. Brewer	Coral	16
18.	JUKE BOX BABY	P. Como	Victor	14
19.	TUTTI FRUTTI	P. Boone	Dot	13
20.	EDDIE MY LOVE	Fontane Sisters	Dot	29
21.	EDDIE MY LOVE	Chordettes	Cadence	24
22.	THEME FROM "THE THREE PENNY OPERA" (MACK THE KNIFE)	L. Armstrong	Columbia	20
23.	BO WEEVIL	T. Brewer	Coral	21
23.	WHY DO FOOLS FALL IN LOVE?	Diamonds	Mercury	26
25.	DUNGAREE DOLL	E. Fisher	Victor	18
26.	EDDIE MY LOVE	Teen Queens	RPM	34
27.	IT'S ALMOST TOMORROW	Dream Weavers	Decca	19
27.	TO YOU MY LOVE	N. Noble	Mercury	63
29.	I WAS THE ONE	E. Presley	Victor	31
30.	LISBON ANTIGUA	M. Miller	Columbia	33
31.	THEME FROM "THE THREE PENNY OPERA" (MORITAT)	L. Welk	Coral	47
32.	ANGELS IN THE SKY	Crew Cuts	Mercury	27
32.	INNAMORATA	J. Vale	Columbia	64
34.	LIPSTICK, CANDY AND RUBBER SOLED SHOES	J. La Rosa	Victor	38
35.	ELEVENTH HOUR MELODY	L. Busch	Capitol	58
35.	FLOWERS MEAN FORGIVENESS	F. Sinatra	Capitol	41
37.	BEYOND THE SEA	R. Williams	Kapp	67
38.	CHAIN GANG	B. Scott	ABC-Paramount	27
39.	ELOISE	K. Thompson	Cadence	39
40.	FOREVER DARLING	Ames Brothers	Victor	72
41.	MR. WONDERFUL	P. Lee	Decca	69
41.	POOR PEOPLE OF PARIS	R. Morgan	Decca	37
43.	ELEVENTH HOUR MELODY	A. Hibbler	Decca	31
44.	ASK ME	Nat (King) Cole	Capitol	30
44.	MISSING	McGuire Sisters	Coral	62
46.	SEVEN DAYS	Crew Cuts	Mercury	25
47.	LULLABY OF BIRDLAND	Blue Stars	Mercury	45
48.	BO WEEVIL	F. Domino	Imperial	70
49.	OUR LOVE AFFAIR	T. Charles	Decca	70
50.	MR. WONDERFUL	T. King	Victor	43
51.	LOVELY ONE	Four Voices	Columbia	44
52.	ARE YOU SATISFIED?	R. Draper	Mercury	34
53.	POOR PEOPLE OF PARIS	L. Welk	Coral	65
54.	SIXTEEN TONS	T. Ernie	Capitol	40
55.	NINETY-NINE YEARS	G. Mitchell	Columbia	36
56.	TUTTI FRUTTI	Little Richard	Specialty	42
57.	THEME FROM "THE THREE PENNY OPERA" (MORITAT)	L. Paul & M. Ford	Capitol	49
58.	BAND OF GOLD	K. Carson	Capitol	53
58.	ROCK RIGHT	G. Gibbs	Mercury	76
58.	SPEEDOO	Cadillacs	Josie	99
61.	INNAMORATA	D. Martin	Capitol	56
61.	MR. WONDERFUL	S. Vaughan	Mercury	55
63.	THEME FROM "THE THREE PENNY OPERA" (MORITAT)	B. Vaughn	Dot	53
64.	LOVELY LIES	Manhattan Brothers	London	67
65.	TEEN-AGE PRAYER	G. Storm	Dot	46
66.	MAIN TITLE (MAN WITH THE GOLDEN ARM)	R. Maltby	Vik	84
67.	CRY BABY	Bonnie Sisters	Rainbow	48
67.	MAIN TITLE MOLLY-O (MAN WITH THE GOLDEN ARM)	D. Jacobs	Coral	—
67.	THAT'S ALL	T. Ernie	Capitol	60
70.	AND THE ANGELS SING	Chuckles	Vik	86
71.	IF YOU CAN DREAM	Four Aces	Decca	89
72.	WHEN YOU LOSE THE ONE YOU LOVE	D. Whitfield	London	73
73.	HE	A. Hibbler	Decca	73
74.	GO ON WITH THE WEDDING	P. Page	Mercury	56
75.	NOTHING EVER CHANGES MY LOVE FOR YOU	Nat (King) Cole	Capitol	87
76.	MAGIC TOUCH	Platters	Mercury	—
77.	MAIN TITLE (MAN WITH THE GOLDEN ARM)	E. Bernstein	Decca	—
78.	MAIN TITLE (MAN WITH THE GOLDEN ARM)	B. May	Capitol	—
78.	MADEIRA	M. Miller	Columbia	50
80.	PORT AU PRINCE	N. Riddle	Capitol	—
81.	IVORY TOWER	C. Carr	Fraternity	—
81.	ROCK ISLAND LINE	L. Donegan	London	—
83.	IT'S ALMOST TOMORROW	J. Stafford	Columbia	93
84.	SEVEN DAYS	D. Collins	Coral	87
85.	BITTER WITH THE SWEET	B. Eckstine	Victor	96
86.	ROCK A BEATIN' BOOGIE	B. Haley	Decca	—
86.	WHY DO FOOLS FALL IN LOVE?	G. Mann	Sound	59
88.	THAT'S YOUR MISTAKE	O. Williams	De Luxe	51
89.	MEMORIES ARE MADE OF THIS	G. Storm	Dot	93
90.	APRIL IN PARIS	C. Basie	Clef	66
91.	GAL WITH THE YALLER SHOES	Four Aces	Decca	—
92.	CRY ME A RIVER	J. London	Liberty	84
92.	SWEET LIPS	J. P. Morgan	Victor	—
94.	INTO THE NIGHT	Dream Weavers	Decca	—
95.	ONLY YOU	Platters	Mercury	81
95.	POOR PEOPLE OF PARIS (JEAN'S SONG)	C. Atkins	Victor	52
97.	WHEN YOU DANCE	Turbans	Herald	80
97.	MEMORIES OF YOU	R. Clooney-B. Goodman	Columbia	60
99.	TEEN-AGE MEETING	D. Cornell	Coral	98
100.	WOMAN IN LOVE	F, Laine	Columbia	—

CAUTION TO DEALERS AND JUKE BOX OPERATORS

The Billboard's Top 100 is NOT designed to provide tested information for buying purposes. This function is most reliably served by other regular weekly features: Best Sellers in Stores, Most Played in Juke Boxes, Coming Up Strong and Best Buys.

• Best Sellers in Stores

For survey week ending March 21

RECORDS are ranked in order of their current national selling importance at the retail level, as determined by The Billboard's weekly survey of the top volume dealers in every important market area. When significant action is reported on both sides of a record, points are combined to determine position on the chart. In such a case, both sides are listed in bold type, the leading side on top.

This Week	Record	Last Week	Weeks on Chart
1.	**POOR PEOPLE OF PARIS** (ASCAP)—L. Baxter. Theme From "Helen of Troy" (ASCAP)—Cap 3336	1	7
2.	**LISBON ANTIGUA** (ASCAP)—N. Riddle. Robin Hood (ASCAP)—Cap 3287	2	14
3.	**ROCK AND ROLL WALTZ** (BMI)—K. Starr. I've Changed My Mind a Thousand Times (ASCAP)—Vic 20-6359	3	13
4.	**NO, NOT MUCH** (ASCAP)—Four Lads. I'll Never Know (BMI)—Col 40629	4	10
5.	**HOT DIGGITY** (ASCAP)—P. Como. **JUKE BOX BABY** (ASCAP)—Vic 20-6427	7	4
6.	**I'LL BE HOME** (BMI)—P. Boone. **TUTTI FRUTTI** (BMI)—Dot 15443	6	8
7.	**BLUE SUEDE SHOES** (BMI)—C. Perkins. Honey, Don't (BMI)—Sun 234	9	4
8.	**WHY DO FOOLS FALL IN LOVE?** (BMI)—Teen-Agers. Please Be Mine (BMI)—Gee 1002	8	7
8.	**HEARTBREAK HOTEL** (BMI)—E. Presley. **I WAS THE ONE** (BMI)—Vic 20-6420	11	4
10.	**GREAT PRETENDER** (ASCAP)—Platters. I'm Just a Dancing Partner (ASCAP)—Mercury 70753	5	15
11.	**A TEAR FELL** (BMI)—T. Brewer. **BO WEEVIL** (BMI)—Coral 61590	14	5
12.	**SEE YOU LATER, ALLIGATOR** (BMI)—B. Haley. Paper Boy (ASCAP)—Dec 29791	10	12
13.	**THEME FROM "THE THREE PENNY OPERA" (MORITAT)** (ASCAP)—D. Hyman. Baubles, Bangles and Beads (ASCAP)—M-G-M 12149	12	10
14.	**EDDIE, MY LOVE** (BMI)—Teen Queens. Just Goofed (BMI)—RPM 453	17	4
15.	**BAND OF GOLD** (BMI)—D. Cherry. Rumble Boogie (BMI)—Col 40597	15	17
15.	**WHY DO FOOLS FALL IN LOVE?** (BMI)—G. Storm. I Walk Alone (BMI)—Dot 15448	19	2
17.	**EDDIE, MY LOVE** (BMI)—Chordettes. Whistlin' Willie (BMI)—Cadence 1284	—	1
18.	**WHY DO FOOLS FALL IN LOVE?** (BMI)—Diamonds. You, Baby, You (BMI)—Mercury 70790	18	3
19.	**MEMORIES ARE MADE OF THIS** (BMI)—D. Martin. Change of Heart (BMI)—Cap 3295	13	18
20.	**MAIN TITLE (MAN WITH THE GOLDEN ARM)** (ASCAP)—R. Maltby. Heart of Paris (ASCAP)—Vik 0196	25	1
21.	**EDDIE, MY LOVE** (BMI)—Fontane Sisters. Yum, Yum (BMI)—Dot 15450	—	1
21.	**ROCK ISLAND LINE** (BMI)—L. Donegan. John Henry (BMI)—London 1650	—	1
23.	**THEME FROM "THE THREE PENNY OPERA" (MORITAT)** (ASCAP)—R. Hayman-J. August. I'll Be With You in Apple Blossom Time (ASCAP)—Mercury 12159	16	7
24.	**MAGIC TOUCH** (BMI)—Platters. Winner Take All (ASCAP)—Mercury 70819	—	1
25.	**MR. WONDERFUL** (ASCAP)—P. Lee. Crazy in the Heart (BMI)—Dec 29834	—	1

• Most Played in Juke Boxes

For survey week ending March 21

RECORDS are ranked in order of the greatest number of plays in juke boxes thruout the country, as determined by The Billboard's weekly survey of the nation's juke box operators. When significant play is reported on both sides of a record, points are combined to determine position on the chart. In such a case, both sides are listed in bold type, the leading side on top.

This Week	Record	Last Week	Weeks on Chart
1.	**ROCK AND ROLL WALTZ** (BMI)—K. Starr. I've Changed My Mind a Thousand Times (ASCAP)—Vic 20-6359	1	12
2.	**LISBON ANTIGUA** (ASCAP)—N. Riddle. Robin Hood (ASCAP)—Cap 3287	3	9
2.	**POOR PEOPLE OF PARIS** (ASCAP)—L. Baxter. Theme From "Helen of Troy" (ASCAP)—Cap 3336	5	6
4.	**GREAT PRETENDER** (ASCAP)—Platters. I'm Just a Dancing Partner (ASCAP)—Mercury 70753	2	13
5.	**NO, NOT MUCH** (ASCAP)—Four Lads. I'll Never Know (BMI)—Col 40629	4	7
6.	**I'LL BE HOME** (BMI)—P. Boone. **TUTTI FRUTTI** (BMI)—Dot 15443	6	7
7.	**SEE YOU LATER, ALLIGATOR** (BMI)—B. Haley. Paper Boy (ASCAP)—Dec 29791	8	8
8.	**HOT DIGGITY** (BMI)—P. Como. **JUKE BOX BABY** (BMI)—Vic 20-6427	19	2
9.	**MEMORIES ARE MADE OF THIS** (BMI)—D. Martin. Change of Heart (BMI)—Cap 3295	7	15
9.	**TEAR FELL** (BMI)—T. Brewer. **BO WEEVIL** (BMI)—Coral 61590	10	3
11.	**BAND OF GOLD** (BMI)—D. Cherry. Rumble Boogie (BMI)—Col 40597	9	11
12.	**WHY DO FOOLS FALL IN LOVE?** (BMI)—Teen Agers. Please Be Mine (BMI)—Gee 1002	10	5
13.	**BLUE SUEDE SHOES** (BMI)—C. Perkins. Honey, Don't (BMI)—Sun 234	20	2
14.	**THEME FROM "THE THREE PENNY OPERA" (MORITAT)** (ASCAP)—D. Hyman. Baubles, Bangles and Beads (ASCAP)—M-G-M 12149	14	6
15.	**HEARTBREAK HOTEL** (BMI)—E. Presley. I Was the One (BMI)—Vic 20-6420	—	1
16.	**EDDIE, MY LOVE** (BMI)—Fontane Sisters. Yum, Yum (BMI)—Dot 15450	—	1
17.	**THEME FROM "THE THREE PENNY OPERA" (MORITAT)** (ASCAP)—L. Welk. Stompin' at the Savoy (ASCAP)—Coral 61574	—	1
18.	**WHY DO FOOLS FALL IN LOVE?** (BMI) G. Storm. I Walk Alone (BMI)—Dot 15448	15	4
19.	**DUNGAREE DOLL** (BMI)—E. Fisher. Everbody's Got a Home But Me (ASCAP)—Vic 20-6337	13	12
19.	**POOR PEOPLE OF PARIS** (ASCAP)—R. Morgan. Annabelle (BMI)—Dec 29836	—	1

• Best Selling Sheet Music

Tunes are ranked in order of their current national selling importance at the sheet music jobber level.

This Week	Title	Last Week	Weeks on Chart
1.	**Rock and Roll Waltz** (Sheldon)	1	10
2.	**He** (Avas)	3	27
3.	**Lisbon Antigua** (Southern)	4	11
4.	**Poor People of Paris** (Connelly)	2	6
5.	**No, Not Much** (Beaver)	5	7
6.	**Theme From "The Three Penny Opera" (Moritat)** (Harms)	6	6
7.	**Eleventh Hour Melody** (Paxton)	10	7
8.	**Memories Are Made of This** (Montclare)	8	15
9.	**Hot Diggity** (Roncom)	12	3
10.	**Great Pretender** (Southern)	9	11
11.	**Why Do Fools Fall in Love?** (Patricia)	—	1
12.	**Mr. Wonderful** (Laurel)	—	1
13.	**I'll Be Home** (Arc)	11	3
14.	**It's Almost Tomorrow** (Northern)	7	16
15.	**Dungaree Doll** (E. B. Marks)	14	11

• Most Played by Jockeys

For survey week ending March 21

SIDES are ranked in order of the greatest number of plays on disk jockey radio shows thruout the country. Results are based on The Billboard's weekly survey among the nation's disk jockeys. The reverse side of each record is also listed.

This Week	Record	Last Week	Weeks on Chart
1.	**POOR PEOPLE OF PARIS** (ASCAP)—L. Baxter. Theme From "Helen of Troy" (ASCAP)—Cap 3336	1	7
2.	**NO, NOT MUCH** (ASCAP)—Four Lads. I'll Never Know (BMI)—Col. 40629	2	9
3.	**LISBON ANTIGUA** (ASCAP)—N. Riddle. Robin Hood (ASCAP)—Cap 3287	3	13
4.	**ROCK AND ROLL WALTZ** (BMI)—K. Starr. I've Changed My Mind a Thousand Times (ASCAP)—Vic 20-6359	4	13
5.	**I'LL BE HOME** (BMI)—P. Boone. Tutti Frutti (BMI)—Dot 15443	5	8
6.	**HEARTBREAK HOTEL** (BMI)—E. Presley. I Was the One (BMI)—Vic 20-6420	7	4
7.	**GREAT PRETENDER**—Platters. I'm Just a Dancing Partner (ASCAP)—Mercury 70753	6	14
8.	**HOT DIGGITY** (ASCAP)—P. Como. Juke Box Baby (BMI)—Vic 20-6427	8	3
9.	**WHY DO FOOLS FALL IN LOVE?** (BMI)—Teen Agers. Please Be Mine (BMI)—Gee 1002	10	4
10.	**SEE YOU LATER, ALLIGATOR** (BMI)—B. Haley. Paper Boy (ASCAP)—Dec 29791	11	9
11.	**THEME FROM "THE THREE PENNY OPERA" (MORITAT)** (ASCAP)—D. Hyman. Baubles, Bangles and Beads (ASCAP)—M-G-M 12149	12	8
12.	**WHY DO FOOLS FALL IN LOVE?** (BMI)—G. Storm. I Walk Alone (BMI)—Dot 15448	9	2
13.	**BLUE SUEDE SHOES** (BMI)—C. Perkins. Honey, Don't (BMI)—Sun 234	14	2
14.	**EDDIE, MY LOVE** (BMI)—Chordettes. Whistling Willie (ASCAP)—Cadence 1084	23	2
15.	**JUKE BOX BABY** (BMI)—P. Como. Hot Diggity (BMI)—Vic 20-6427	13	3
16.	**WHY DO FOOLS FALL IN LOVE?** (BMI)—Diamonds. You, Baby, You (BMI)—Mercury 70790	23	2
17.	**MR. WONDERFUL** (ASCAP)—S. Vaughan. You Ought to Have a Wife (ASCAP)—Mercury 70777	—	4
18.	**A TEAR FELL** (BMI)—T. Brewer. Bo Weevil (BMI)—Coral 61590	25	2
19.	**EDDIE, MY LOVE** (BMI)—Fontane Sisters. Yum, Yum (BMI)—Dot 15450	22	2
20.	**MR. WONDERFUL** (ASCAP)—P. Lee. Crazy in the Heart (BMI)—Dec 29834	21	2
21.	**FLOWERS MEAN FORGIVENESS** (ASCAP)—F. Sinatra. You'll Get Yours (ASCAP)—Cap 3350	—	1
22.	**BAND OF GOLD** (BMI)—D Cherry. Rumble Boogie (BMI)—Col 40597	18	14
23.	**MEMORIES ARE MADE OF THIS** (BMI)—D. Martin. Change of Heart (BMI)—Cap 3295	15	17
24.	**I WAS THE ONE** (BMI)—E. Presley. Heartbreak Hotel (BMI)—Vic 20-6420	—	1
25.	**THEME FROM "THE THREE PENNY OPERA" (MORITAT)** (ASCAP)—R. Hyman-J. August. I'll Be With You in Apple Blossom Time (ASCAP)—Mercury 12159	17	7

THE TOP 100

For survey week ending March 14

A list of the **TOP 100 RECORD SIDES** in the nation according to a **COMBINED TABULATION** of Dealer, Disk Jockey and Juke Box Operator replies to The Billboard's weekly popular record Best Seller and Most Played surveys. Its purpose is to provide Disk Jockeys with additional programming material and to give trade exposure to NEWER records just beginning to show action in the field.

Pos.	Song	Artist	Label	Last Week
1.	POOR PEOPLE OF PARIS	L. Baxter	Capitol	1
2.	LISBON ANTIGUA	N. Riddle	Capitol	2
3.	ROCK AND ROLL WALTZ	K. Starr	Victor	2
4.	NO, NOT MUCH	Four Lads	Columbia	4
5.	I'LL BE HOME	P. Boone	Dot	6
6.	GREAT PRETENDER	Platters	Mercury	5
7.	WHY DO FOOLS FALL IN LOVE?	Teen-Agers	Gee	7
8.	SEE YOU LATER, ALLIGATOR	B. Haley	Decca	8
9.	BLUE SUEDE SHOES	K. C. Perkins	Sun	12
9.	HEARTBREAK HOTEL	E. Presley	Victor	11
11.	HOT DIGGITY	P. Como	Victor	14
12.	THEME FROM "THE THREE PENNY OPERA" (MORITAT)	D. Hyman	M-G-M	9
13.	JUKE BOX BABY	P. Como	Victor	18
14.	A TEAR FELL	T. Brewer	Coral	17
15.	BAND OF GOLD	D. Cherry	Columbia	13
16.	WHY DO FOOLS FALL IN LOVE?	G. Storm	Dot	15
17.	MEMORIES ARE MADE OF THIS	D. Martin	Capitol	9
18.	EDDIE, MY LOVE	Chordettes	Cadence	21
18.	EDDIE, MY LOVE	Fontane Sisters	Dot	20
20.	WHY DO FOOLS FALL IN LOVE?	Diamonds	Mercury	23
21.	TUTTI FRUTTI	P. Boone	Dot	19
22.	BO WEEVIL	T. Brewer	Coral	23
23.	THEME FROM "THE THREE PENNY OPERA" (MORITAT)	R. Hayman-J. August	Mercury	16
24.	EDDIE, MY LOVE	Teen Queens	RPM	26
25.	I WAS THE ONE	E. Presley	Victor	29
26.	POOR PEOPLE OF PARIS	R. Morgan	Decca	41
27.	DUNGAREE DOLL	E. Fisher	Victor	25
28.	MR. WONDERFUL	P. Lee	Decca	41
29.	LIP STICK, CANDY AND RUBBER SOLED SHOES	J. La Rosa	Victor	34
30.	INNAMORATA	J. Vale	Columbia	32
31.	MAGIC TOUCH	Platters	Mercury	76
32.	PORT-AU-PRINCE	N. Riddle	Capitol	80
33.	ELEVENTH HOUR MELODY	A. Hibbler	Decca	43
34.	THEME FROM "THE THREE PENNY OPERA" (MACK THE KNIFE)	L. Armstrong	Columbia	22
35.	FOREVER DARLING	Ames Brothers	Victor	40
35.	LULLABY OF BIRDLAND	Blue Stars	Mercury	47
35.	TO YOU, MY LOVE	N. Noble	Mercury	27
38.	ELEVENTH HOUR MELODY	L. Busch	Capitol	35
38.	IT'S ALMOST TOMORROW	Dream Weavers	Decca	27
40.	FLOWERS MEAN FORGIVENESS	F. Sinatra	Capitol	35
41.	MAIN TITLE ("MAN WITH THE GOLDEN ARM")	R. Maltby	Vik	66
42.	IVORY TOWER	C. Carr	Fraternity	81
43.	LOVELY ONE	Four Voices	Columbia	51
44.	INNAMORATA	D. Martin	Capitol	61
45.	LOVELY LIES	Manhattan Brothers	London	64
46.	MISSING	McGuire Sisters	Coral	44
47.	BO WEEVIL	F. Domino	Imperial	48
48.	ASK ME	Nat (King) Cole	Capitol	44
48.	MR. WONDERFUL	S. Vaughan	Mercury	61
50.	ROCK ISLAND LINE	L. Donegan	London	81
50.	THEME FROM "THE THREE PENNY OPERA" (MORITAT)	L. Welk	Coral	31
52.	OUR LOVE AFFAIR	T. Charles	Decca	49
53.	THAT'S ALL	T. Ernie	Capitol	67
54.	POOR PEOPLE OF PARIS	L. Welk	Coral	53
55.	THEME FROM "THE THREE PENNY OPERA" (MORITAT)	L. Paul & M. Ford	Capitol	57
56.	ELOISE	K. Thompson	Cadence	39
57.	MAIN TITLE MOLLY-O (MAN WITH THE GOLDEN ARM)	D. Jacobs	Coral	67
58.	LISBON ANTIGUA	M. Miller	Columbia	30
59.	MR. WONDERFUL	T. King	Victor	50
60.	ARE YOU SATISFIED?	R. Draper	Mercury	52
61.	ANGELS IN THE SKY	Crew Cuts	Mercury	32
62.	ROCK RIGHT	G. Gibbs	Mercury	58
63.	BEYOND THE SEA	R. Williams	Kapp	37
64.	MAIN TITLE (MAN WITH THE GOLDEN ARM)	B. May	Capitol	78
65.	SEVEN DAYS	Crew Cuts	Mercury	46
66.	GO ON WITH THE WEDDING	P. Page	Mercury	74
66.	TUTTI FRUTTI	Little Richard	Specialty	56
68.	POOR PEOPLE OF PARIS (JEAN'S SONG)	C. Atkins	Victor	95
69.	IVORY TOWER	O. Williams	De Luxe	—
70.	THEME FROM "THE THREE PENNY OPERA" (MORITAT)	B. Vaughn	Dot	63
71.	MAIN TITLE (MAN WITH THE GOLDEN ARM)	E. Bernstein	Decca	77
72.	HE	A. Hibbler	Decca	73
73.	NOTHING EVER CHANGES MY LOVE FOR YOU	Nat (King) Cole	Capitol	75
74.	CRY BABY	Bonnie Sisters	Rainbow	67
74.	CHAIN GANG	B. Scott	ABC-Paramount	38
76.	BITTER WITH THE SWEET	B. Eckstine	Victor	85
77.	AND THE ANGELS SING	Chuckles	Vik	70
78.	BAND OF GOLD	K. Carson	Capitol	58
79.	MEMORIES ARE MADE OF THIS	G. Storm	Dot	89
79.	WHY DO FOOLS FALL IN LOVE?	G. Mann	Decca	86
81.	TEEN-AGE PRAYER	G. Storm	Dot	65
82.	SIXTEEN TONS	T. Ernie	Capitol	54
83.	GET UP, GET UP	J. P. Morgan	Victor	—
84.	IT'S ALMOST TOMORROW	J. Stafford	Columbia	83
85.	IF YOU CAN DREAM	Four Aces	Decca	71
85.	SWEET LIPS	J. P. Morgan	Victor	92
87.	WHEN YOU LOSE THE ONE YOU LOVE	D Whitfield	London	72
88.	INTO THE NIGHT	Dream Weavers	Decca	94
89.	NINETY-NINE YEARS	G. Mitchell	Columbia	55
90.	YOU'LL GET YOURS	F. Sinatra	Capitol	—
91.	APRIL IN PARIS	C. Basie	Clef	90
91.	MADEIRA	M. Miller	Columbia	78
93.	WHEN YOU DANCE	Turbans	Herald	97
93.	SPEEDOO	Cadillacs	Josie	58
95.	I'LL NEVER KNOW	Four Lads	Columbia	—
95.	MY FIRST FORMAL GOWN	P. Page	Mercury	—
97.	APRIL IN PARIS	Modernaires	Coral	—
98.	SEVEN DAYS	D. Collins	Coral	84
99.	ONLY YOU	Hilltoppers	Dot	—
100.	HE	McGuire Sisters	Coral	—

CAUTION TO DEALERS AND JUKE BOX OPERATORS

The Billboard's Top 100 is NOT designed to provide tested information for buying purposes. This function is most reliably served by other regular weekly features: Best Sellers in Stores, Most Played in Juke Boxes, Coming Up Strong and Best Buys.

• Best Sellers in Stores

For survey week ending March 28

RECORDS are ranked in order of their current national selling importance at the retail level, as determined by The Billboard's weekly survey of the top volume dealers in every important market area. When significant action is reported on both sides of a record, points are combined to determine position on the chart. In such a case, both sides are listed in bold type, the leading side on top.

This Week		Last Week	Weeks on Chart
1.	**POOR PEOPLE OF PARIS** (ASCAP)—L. Baxter Theme From "Helen of Troy" (ASCAP)—Cap 3336	1	8
2.	**LISBON ANTIGUA** (ASCAP)—N. Riddle Robin Hood (ASCAP)—Cap 3287	2	15
3.	**BLUE SUEDE SHOES** (BMI)—C. Perkins Honey, Don't (BMI)—Sun 234	7	5
4.	**HOT DIGGITY** (ASCAP)—P. Como **JUKE BOX BABY** (ASCAP)—Vic 20-6427	5	5
5.	**HEARTBREAK HOTEL** (BMI)—E. Presley **I WAS THE ONE** (BMI)—Vic 20-6420	8	5
6.	**ROCK AND ROLL WALTZ** (BMI)—K. Starr I've Changed My Mind a Thousand Times (ASCAP)—Vic 20-6359	3	14
7.	**I'LL BE HOME** (BMI)—P. Boone **TUTTI FRUTTI** (BMI)—Dot 15443	6	9
8.	**NO, NOT MUCH** (ASCAP)—Four Lads I'll Never Know (BMI)—Col 40629	4	11
9.	**WHY DO FOOLS FALL IN LOVE?** (BMI)—Teen-Agers Please Be Mine (BMI)—Gee 1002	8	8
10.	**GREAT PRETENDER** (ASCAP)—Platters I'm Just a Dancing Partner (ASCAP)—Mercury 70753	10	16
11.	**A TEAR FELL** (BMI)—T. Brewer Bo Weevil (BMI)—Coral 61590	11	6
12.	**ROCK ISLAND LINE** (BMI)—L. Donegan John Henry (BMI)—London 1650	21	2
13.	**THEME FROM "THE THREE PENNY OPERA" ("MORITAT")** (ASCAP)—D. Hyman Baubles, Bangles and Beads (ASCAP)—M-G-M 12149	13	11
14.	**SEE YOU LATER, ALLIGATOR** (BMI)—B. Haley Paper Boy (ASCAP)—Dec 29791	12	13
15.	**EDDIE MY LOVE** (BMI)—Fontane Sisters Yum, Yum (BMI)—Dot 15450	21	2
16.	**EDDIE MY LOVE** (BMI)—Teen Queens Just Goofed (BMI)—RPM 453	14	5
17.	**MAIN TITLE (MAN WITH THE GOLDEN ARM)** (ASCAP)—E. Bernstein Clark Street (ASCAP)—Dec 29869	—	1
18.	**WHY DO FOOLS FALL IN LOVE?** (BMI)—Diamonds You, Baby, You (BMI)—Mercury 70790	18	4
19.	**MAGIC TOUCH** (BMI)—Platters Winner Take All (ASCAP)—Mercury 70819	24	2
20.	**WHY DO FOOLS FALL IN LOVE?** (BMI)—G. Storm I Walk Alone (BMI)—Dot 15448	15	3
21.	**SAINTS ROCK AND ROLL** (ASCAP)—B. Haley **R-O-C-K** (ASCAP)—Dec 29870	—	1
22.	**EDDIE MY LOVE** (BMI)—Chordettes Whistlin' Willie (BMI)—Cadence 1284	17	2
23.	**LONG TALL SALLY** (BMI)—Little Richard Slippin' and Slidin' (BMI)—Specialty 572	—	1
24.	**THEME FROM THE "THREE PENNY OPERA" (MORITAT)** (ASCAP)—R. Hayman I'll Be With You in Apple Blossom Time (ASCAP)—Mercury 12159	23	8
25.	**MAIN TITLE (MAN WITH THE GOLDEN ARM)**—R. Maltby Heart of Paris (ASCAP)—Vik 0196	20	2
25.	**IVORY TOWER** (ASCAP)—C. Carr Please, Please, Believe Me (ASCAP)—Fraternity 734	—	1

• Most Played in Juke Boxes

For survey week ending March 28

RECORDS are ranked in order of the greatest number of plays in juke boxes thruout the country, as determined by The Billboard's weekly survey of the nation's juke box operators. When significant play is reported on both sides of a record, points are combined to determine position on the chart. In such a case, both sides are listed in bold type, the leading side on top.

This Week		Last Week	Weeks on Chart
1.	**ROCK AND ROLL WALTZ** (BMI)—K. Starr I've Changed My Mind a Thousand Times (ASCAP)—Vic 20-6359	1	13
2.	**POOR PEOPLE OF PARIS** (ASCAP)—L. Baxter Theme From "Helen of Troy" (ASCAP)—Cap 3336	2	7
3.	**LISBON ANTIGUA** (ASCAP) N. Riddle Robin Hood (ASCAP)—Cap 3287	2	10
4.	**NO, NOT MUCH** (ASCAP)—Four Lads I'll Never Know (BMI)—Col 40629	5	8
5.	**GREAT PRETENDER** (ASCAP)—Platters I'm Just a Dancing Partner (ASCAP)—Mercury 70753	4	14
6.	**I'LL BE HOME** (BMI)—P. Boone **TUTTI FRUTTI** (BMI)—Dot 15443	6	8
7.	**HOT DIGGITY** (BMI)—P. Como **JUKE BOX BABY** (BMI)—Vic 20-6427	8	3
8.	**SEE YOU LATER, ALLIGATOR** (BMI)—B. Haley Paper Boy (ASCAP)—Dec 29791	7	9
9.	**A TEAR FELL** (BMI)—T. Brewer **BO WEEVIL** (BMI)—Coral 61590	9	4
10.	**WHY DO FOOLS FALL IN LOVE?** (BMI)—Teen-Agers Please Be Mine (BMI)—Gee 1002	12	6
11.	**BLUE SUEDE SHOES** (BMI)—C. Perkins Honey, Don't (BMI)—Sun 234	13	3
12.	**EDDIE, MY LOVE** (BMI)—Fontane Sisters Yum, Yum (BMI)—Dot 15450	16	2
13.	**HEARTBREAK HOTEL** (BMI)—E. Presley **I WAS THE ONE** (BMI)—Vic 20-6420	15	2
14.	**BAND OF GOLD** (BMI)—D. Cherry Rumble Boogie (BMI)—Col 40597	11	12
15.	**MEMORIES ARE MADE OF THIS** (BMI)—D. Martin Change of Heart (BMI)—Cap 3295	9	16
16.	**THEME FROM "THE THREE PENNY OPERA" (MORITAT)** (ASCAP)—D. Hyman Baubles, Bangles, and Beads (ASCAP)—M-G-M 12149	14	7
17.	**WHY DO FOOLS FALL IN LOVE?** (BMI)—G. Storm I Walk Alone—Dot 15448	18	5
18.	**THEME FROM "THE THREE PENNY OPERA" (MORITAT)** (ASCAP)—R. Hyman-J. August I'll Be With You in Apple Blossom Time (ASCAP)—Mercury 70781	—	5
18.	**POOR PEOPLE OF PARIS** (ASCAP)—L. Welk Nobody Knows But the Lord (ASCAP)—Coral 61592	—	1
20.	**THEME FROM "THE THREE PENNY OPERA" (MORITAT)**—L. Welk Stompin' at the Savoy (ASCAP)—Coral 61574	17	2

• Best Selling Sheet Music

Tunes are ranked in order of their current national selling importance at the sheet music jobber level.

This Week		Last Week	Weeks on Chart
1.	**Rock and Roll Waltz** (Sheldon)	1	12
2.	**Poor People of Paris** (Connelly)	4	7
3.	**Lisbon Antigua** (Southern)	3	12
3.	**No, Not Much** (Beaver)	5	8
5.	**Hot Diggity** (Roncom)	9	4
6.	**Theme From "The Three Penny Opera" (Moritat)** Harms)	6	7
7.	**Eleventh Hour Melody** (Paxton)	7	8
8.	**He** (Avas)	2	28
9.	**Mr. Wonderful** (Laurel)	12	2
10.	**I'll Be Home** (Arc)	13	4
11.	**Memories Are Made of This** (Montclare)	8	16
12.	**Why Do Fools Fall in Love?** (Patricia)	11	2
13.	**Eddie, My Love** (Modern-Roosevelt)	—	1
14.	**Little Child** (E. H. Morris)	—	1
15.	**Juke Box Baby** (Winneton)	—	1

• Most Played by Jockeys

For survey week ending March 28

SIDES are ranked in order of the greatest number of plays on disk jockey radio shows thruout the country. Results are based on The Billboard's weekly survey among the nation's disk jockeys. The reverse side of each record is also listed.

This Week		Last Week	Weeks on Chart
1.	**POOR PEOPLE OF PARIS** (ASCAP)—L. Baxter Theme From "Helen of Troy" (ASCAP)—Cap 3336	1	8
2.	**NO, NOT MUCH** (ASCAP)—Four Lads I'll Never Know (BMI)—Col 40629	2	10
3.	**LISBON ANTIGUA** (ASCAP)—N. Riddle Robin Hood (ASCAP)—Cap 3287	3	14
4.	**I'LL BE HOME** (BMI)—P. Boone Tutti Frutti (BMI)—Dot 15443	5	9
5.	**ROCK AND ROLL WALTZ** (BMI)—K. Starr I've Changed My Mind a Thousand Times (ASCAP)—Vic 20-6359	4	14
6.	**HOT DIGGITY** (ASCAP)—P. Como Juke Box Baby (BMI)—Vic 20-6427	8	4
7.	**HEARTBREAK HOTEL** (BMI)—E. Presley I Was the One (BMI)—Vic 20-6420	6	5
8.	**BLUE SUEDE SHOES** (BMI)—C. Perkins Honey, Don't (BMI)—Sun 234	13	3
9.	**WHY DO FOOLS FALL IN LOVE?** (BMI)—Teen-Agers Please Be Mine (BMI)—Gee 1002	9	5
10.	**WHY DO FOOLS FALL IN LOVE?** (BMI)—G. Storm I Walk Alone (BMI)—Dot 15448	12	3
11.	**GREAT PRETENDER**—Platters I'm Just a Dancing Partner (ASCAP)—Mercury 70753	7	15
12.	**JUKE BOX BABY** (BMI)—P. Como Hot Diggity (BMI)—Vic 20-6427	15	4
13.	**A TEAR FELL** (BMI)—T. Brewer Bo Weevil (BMI)—Coral 61590	18	3
14.	**EDDIE, MY LOVE** (BMI)—Fontane Sisters Yum, Yum (BMI)—Dot 15450	19	3
15.	**WHY DO FOOLS FALL IN LOVE?** (BMI)—Diamonds You, Baby, You (BMI)—Mercury 70790	16	3
16.	**THEME FROM "THE THREE PENNY OPERA" (MORITAT)** (ASCAP)—D. Hyman Baubles, Bangles and Beads (ASCAP)—M-G-M 12149	11	9
17.	**MR. WONDERFUL** (ASCAP)—P. Lee Crazy in the Heart (BMI)—Dec 29834	20	3
18.	**EDDIE, MY LOVE** (BMI)—Chordettes Whistling Willie (ASCAP)—Cadence 1084	14	3
19.	**I WAS THE ONE** (BMI)—E. Presley Heartbreak Hotel (BMI)—Vic 20-6420	24	2
20.	**BO WEEVIL** (BMI)—T. Brewer A Tear Fell (BMI)—Coral 61590	—	1
21.	**SEE YOU LATER, ALLIGATOR** (BMI)—B. Haley Paper Boy (ASCAP)—Dec 29791	10	10
22.	**MR. WONDERFUL** (ASCAP) S. Vaughan You Ought to Have a Wife (ASCAP)—Mercury 70777	17	5
23.	**POOR PEOPLE OF PARIS** (ASCAP)—R. Morgan Annabelle (BMI)—Dec 29836	—	1
24.	**FLOWERS MEAN FORGIVENESS** (ASCAP)—F. Sinatra You'll Get Yours (ASCAP)—Cap 3350	21	2
25.	**MEMORIES ARE MADE OF THIS** D. Martin Change of Heart (BMI)—Cap 3295	23	18

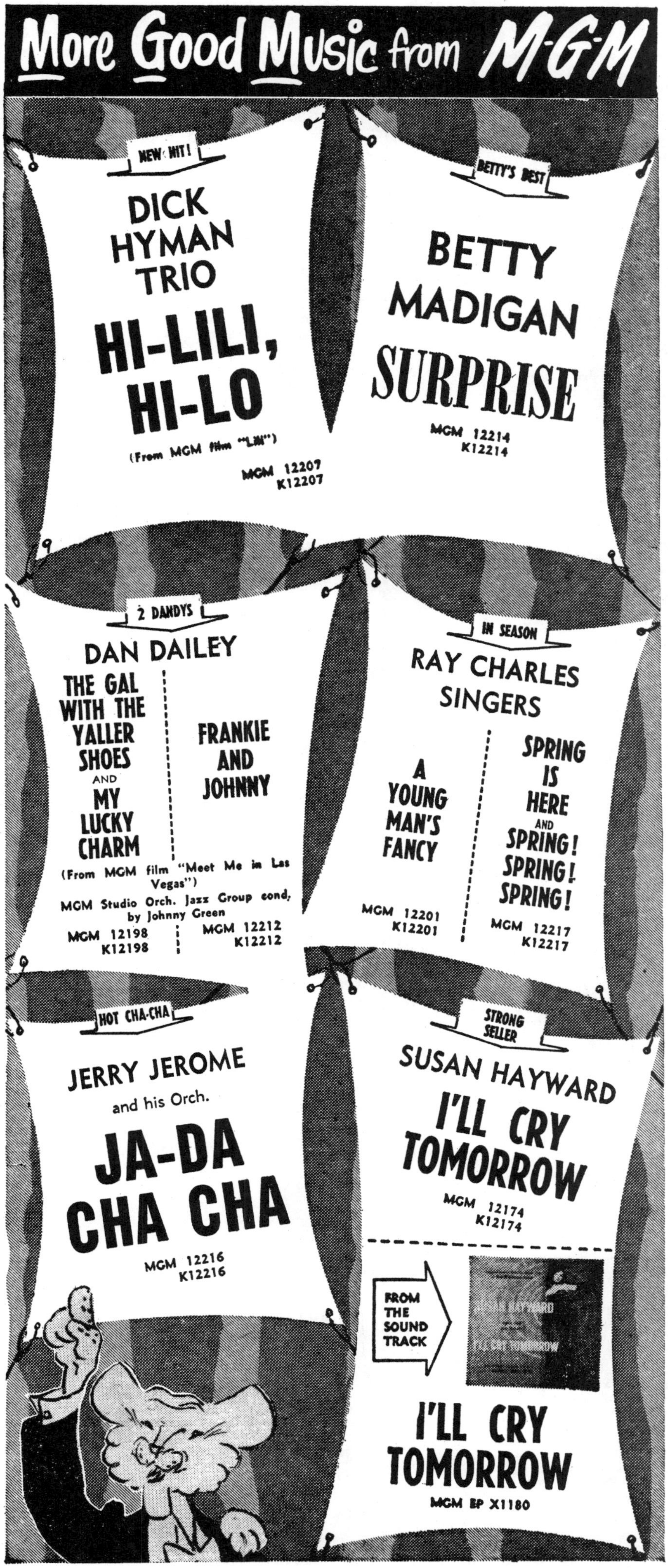

THE TOP 100

Week ending March 28

A list of the **TOP 100 RECORD SIDES** in the nation according to a **COMBINED TABULATION** of Dealer, Disk Jockey and Juke Box Operator replies to The Billboard's weekly popular record Best Seller and Most Played surveys. Its purpose is to provide Disk Jockeys with additional programming material and to give trade exposure to NEWER records just beginning to show action in the field.

Pos.	Song	Artist	Label	Last Week
1.	POOR PEOPLE OF PARIS	L. Baxter	Capitol	1
2.	LISBON ANTIGUA	N. Riddle	Capitol	2
3.	ROCK AND ROLL WALTZ	K. Starr	Victor	3
4.	NO, NOT MUCH	Four Lads	Columbia	4
5.	I'LL BE HOME	P. Boone	Dot	5
6.	BLUE SUEDE SHOES	C. Perkins	Sun	9
7.	WHY DO FOOLS FALL IN LOVE?	Teen Agers	Gee	7
8.	GREAT PRETENDER	Platters	Mercury	6
8.	HEARTBREAK HOTEL	E. Presley	Victor	9
10.	JUKE BOX BABY	P. Como	Victor	13
11.	A TEAR FELL	T. Brewer	Coral	14
12.	EDDIE, MY LOVE	Fontane Sisters	Dot	18
12.	SEE YOU LATER, ALLIGATOR	B. Haley	Decca	8
14.	THEME FROM "THE THREE PENNY OPERA" (MORITAT)	D. Hyman	M-G-M	12
15.	WHY DO FOOLS FALL IN LOVE?	G. Storm	Dot	16
17.	BO WEEVIL	T. Brewer	Coral	22
18.	EDDIE, MY LOVE	Chordettes	Cadence	18
19.	MAGIC TOUCH	Platters	Mercury	31
20.	THEME FROM "THE THREE PENNY OPERA" (MORITAT)	R. Hayman-J. August	Mercury	23
21.	BAND OF GOLD	D. Cherry	Columbia	15
22.	EDDIE, MY LOVE	Teen Queens	RPM	24
23.	I WAS THE ONE	E. Presley	Victor	25
24.	MEMORIES ARE MADE OF THIS	D. Martin	Capitol	17
25.	TUTTI FRUTTI	P. Boone	Dot	21
26.	ROCK ISLAND LINE	L. Donegan	London	50
27.	HOT DIGGITY	P. Como	Victor	11
27.	TO YOU, MY LOVE	N. Noble	Mercury	35
29.	POOR PEOPLE OF PARIS	R. Morgan	Decca	26
30.	IVORY TOWER	C. Carr	Fraternity	42
31.	INNAMORATA	D. Martin	Capitol	44
32.	INNAMORATA	J. Vale	Columbia	30
33.	MR. WONDERFUL	P. Lee	Decca	28
34.	DUNGAREE DOLL	E. Fisher	Victor	27
35.	BO WEEVIL	F. Domino	Imperial	47
36.	MR. WONDERFUL	T. King	Victor	59
37.	MAIN TITLE, MOLLY-O ("MAN WITH THE GOLDEN ARM")	D. Jacobs	Coral	57
38.	MR. WONDERFUL	S. Vaughan	Mercury	48
38.	PORT-AU-PRINCE	N. Riddle	Capitol	32
40.	THEME FROM "THE THREE PENNY OPERA" (MACK THE KNIFE)	L. Armstrong	Columbia	34
41.	MAIN TITLE ("MAN WITH THE GOLDEN ARM")	R. Maltby	Vik	41
42.	LIPSTICK, CANDY AND RUBBER SOLED SHOES	J. La Rosa	Victor	29
43.	IVORY TOWER	O. Williams	De Luxe	69
44.	LOVELY ONE	Four Voices	Columbia	43
44.	OUR LOVE AFFAIR	T. Charles	Decca	52
46.	ELEVENTH HOUR MELODY	A. Hibbler	Decca	33
47	FLOWERS MEAN FORGIVENESS	F. Sinatra	Capitol	40
48.	ROCK RIGHT	G. Gibbs	Mercury	62
49	CRAZY LITTLE PALACE	B. Williams	Coral	—
50.	ASK ME	Nat (King) Cole	Capitol	48
50.	MAIN TITLE ("MAN WITH THE GOLDEN ARM")	E. Bernstein	Decca	71
52.	FOREVER DARLING	Ames Brothers	Victor	35
52.	MAIN TITLE ("MAN WITH THE GOLDEN ARM")	B. May	Capitol	64
54.	IT'S ALMOST TOMORROW	Dream Weavers	Decca	38
55.	ELEVENTH HOUR MELODY	L. Busch	Capitol	38
56.	THEME FROM "THE THREE PENNY OPERA" (MORITAT)	B. Vaughn	Dot	70
57.	LOVELY LIES	Manhattan Brothers	London	45
58.	ANGELS IN THE SKY	Crew Cuts	Mercury	61
59.	THEME FROM "THE THREE PENNY OPERA" (MORITAT)	L. Paul & M. Ford	Capitol	55
60.	LULLABY OF BIRDLAND	Blue Stars	Mercury	35
61.	ELOISE	K. Thompson	Cadence	56
61.	POOR PEOPLE OF PARIS (JEAN'S SONG)	C. Atkins	Victor	68
63.	SEVEN DAYS	Crew Cuts	Mercury	65
63.	THEME FROM "THE THREE PENNY OPERA" (MORITAT)	L. Welk	Coral	50
63.	WITHOUT YOU	E. Fisher	Victor	—
66.	LONG TALL SALLY	Little Richard	Specialty	—
67.	SAINTS ROCK AND ROLL	B. Haley	Decca	—
68.	LISBON ANTIGUA	M. Miller	Columbia	58
68.	WINNER TAKE ALL	Platters	Mercury	—
68.	WILD CHERRY	D. Cherry	Columbia	—
71.	BEYOND THE SEA	R. Williams	Kapp	63
72.	POOR PEOPLE OF PARIS	L. Welk	Coral	54
73.	LITTLE MUSICIANS	H. Winterhalter	Victor	—
74.	CHURCH BELLS MAY RING	Willows	Melba	—
74.	SIXTEEN TONS	Tennessee Ernie	Capitol	82
76.	HELD FOR QUESTIONING	R. Draper	Mercury	—
77.	APRIL IN PARIS	C. Basie	Clef	91
78.	MADERIA	M. Miller	Columbia	91
79.	R-O-C-K	B. Haley	Decca	—
80.	THAT'S ALL	Tennessee Ernie	Capitol	53
81.	MAIN TITLE (MAN WITH THE GOLDEN ARM)	L. Elgart	Columbia	—
82.	IN A LITTLE SPANISH TOWN	Bing Crosby	Decca	—
83.	MISSING	McGuire Sisters	Coral	46
84.	BAND OF GOLD	K. Carson	Capitol	78
84.	TUTTI FRUTTI	Little Richard	Specialty	66
86.	IF YOU CAN DREAM	Four Aces	Decca	85
87.	INTO THE NIGHT	Dream Weavers	Decca	88
88.	BLUE SUEDE SHOES	E. Presley	Victor	—
88.	GO ON WITH THE WEDDING	P. Page	Mercury	66
90.	THAT'S YOUR MISTAKE	O. Williams	De Luxe	—
91.	ANGEL PIE	P. King	Columbia	—
91.	TOO YOUNG TO GO STEADY	Nat (King) Cole	Capitol	—
93.	ARE YOU SATISFIED?	R. Draper	Mercury	60
94.	CHINESE ROCK AND EGG ROLL	B. Hackett	Coral	—
94.	IT'S ALMOST TOMORROW	J. Stafford	Columbia	84
96.	ONLY YOU	Platters	Mercury	—
96.	WHY DO FOOLS FALL IN LOVE?	G. Mann	Decca	79
98.	CHAIN GANG	B. Scott	ABC-Paramount	74
98.	MEMORIES ARE MADE OF THIS	G. Storm	Dot	79
100.	MY FIRST FORMAL GOWN	P. Page	Mercury	95
100.	YOU'RE MINE	Dream Weavers	Decca	—

CAUTION TO DEALERS AND JUKE BOX OPERATORS

The Billboard's Top 100 is NOT designed to provide tested information for buying purposes. This function is most reliably served by other regular weekly features: Best Sellers in Stores, Most Played in Juke Boxes, Coming Up Strong and Best Buys.

• Best Sellers in Stores

For survey week ending April 4

RECORDS are ranked in order of their current national selling importance at the retail level, as determined by The Billboard's weekly survey of the top volume dealers in every important market area. When significant action is reported on both sides of a record, points are combined to determine position on the chart. In such a case, both sides are listed in bold type, the leading side on top.

This Week		Last Week	Weeks on Chart
1.	POOR PEOPLE OF PARIS (ASCAP)—L. Baxter Theme From "Helen of Troy (ASCAP)—Cap 3336	1	9
2.	HEARTBREAK HOTEL (BMI)—E. Presley I WAS THE ONE (BMI)—Vic 20-6420	5	6
3.	HOT DIGGITY (ASCAP)—P. Como JUKE BOX BABY (ASCAP)—Vic 20-6427	4	6
4.	BLUE SUEDE SHOES (BMI)—C. Perkins Honey, Don't (BMI)—Sun 234	3	6
5.	LISBON ANTIGUA (ASCAP)—N. Riddle Robin Hood (ASCAP)—Cap 3287	2	16
6.	WHY DO FOOLS FALL IN LOVE? (BMI)—Teen-Agers Please Be Mine (BMI)—Gee 1002	9	9
7.	I'LL BE HOME (BMI)—P. Boone TUTTI FRUTTI (BMI)—Dot 15443	7	10
8.	ROCK AND ROLL WALTZ (BMI)—K. Starr I've Changed My Mind a Thousand Times (ASCAP)—Vic 20-6359	6	15
9.	NO, NOT MUCH (ASCAP)—Four Lads I'll Never Know (BMI)—Col 40629	8	12
10.	A TEAR FELL (BMI)—T. Brewer BO WEEVIL (BMI)—Coral 61590	11	7
11.	ROCK ISLAND LINE (BMI)—L. Donegan John Henry (BMI)—London 1650	12	3
12.	MAGIC TOUCH (BMI)—Platters Winner Take All (ASCAP)—Mercury 70819	19	3
13.	LONG, TALL, SALLY (BMI)—Little Richard Slippin' and Slidin' (BMI)—Specialty 572	23	2
14.	THEME FROM "THE THREE PENNY OPERA" (MORITAT) (ASCAP)—D. Hyman Baubles, Bangles anad Beads (ASCAP)—M-G-M 12149	13	12
15.	GREAT PRETENDER (ASCAP)—Platters I'm Just a Dancing Partner (ASCAP)—Mercury 70753	10	17
16.	EDDIE, MY LOVE (BMI)—Fontane Sisters Yum, Yum (BMI)—Dot 15450	15	3
17.	MAIN TITLE (MAN WITH THE GOLDEN ARM) (ASCAP)—R. Maltby Heart of Paris (ASCAP)—Vik 0196	25	3
18.	SEE YOU LATER, ALLIGATOR (BMI)—B. Haley Paper Boy (ASCAP)—Dec 29791	14	14
19.	WHY DO FOOLS FALL IN LOVE? (BMI)—Diamonds You, Baby, You (BMI)—Mercury 70790	18	5
20.	MAIN TITLE (MAN WITH THE GOLDEN ARM) (ASCAP)—E. Bernstein Clark Street (ASCAP)—Dec 29869	17	2
21.	IVORY TOWER (ASCAP)—O. Williams In Paradise (BMI)—De Luxe 6093	—	1
22.	WHY DO FOOLS FALL IN LOVE? (BMI)—G. Storm I Walk Alone (BMI)—Dot 15448	20	4
23.	EDDIE, MY LOVE (BMI)—Teen Queens Just Goofed (BMI)—RPM 453	16	6
23.	SAINTS ROCK AND ROLL (ASCAP)—B. Haley R-O-C-K (ASCAP)—Dec 29870	21	2
25.	EDDIE, MY LOVE (BMI)—Chordettes Whistlin' Willie (BMI)—Cadence 1284	22	8

• Most Played in Juke Boxes

For survey week ending April 4

RECORDS are ranked in order of the greatest number of plays in juke boxes thruout the country, as determined by The Billboard's weekly survey of the nation's juke box operators. When significant play is reported on both sides of a record, points are combined to determine position on the chart. In such a case, both sides are listed in bold type, the leading side on top.

This Week		Last Week	Weeks on Chart
1.	POOR PEOPLE OF PARIS (ASCAP)—L. Baxter Theme From "Helen of Troy" (ASCAP)—Cap 3336	2	8
2.	ROCK AND ROLL WALTZ (BMI)—K. Starr I've Changed My Mind a Thousand Times (ASCAP)—Vic 20-6359	1	14
3.	LISBON ANTIQUA (ASCAP)—N. Riddle Robin Hood (ASCAP)—Cap 3287	3	11
4.	I'LL BE HOME (BMI)—P. Boone TUTTI FRUTTI (BMI)—Dot 15443	6	9
5.	HOT DIGGITY (BMI)—P. Como JUKE BOX BABY (BMI)—Vic 20-6427	7	4
6.	NO NOT MUCH (ASCAP)—Four Lads I'll Never Know (BMI)—Col 40629	4	9
7.	A TEAR FELL (BMI)—T. Brewer BO WEEVIL (BMI)—Coral 61590	9	5
8.	GREAT PRETENDER (ASCAP) Platters I'm Just a Dancing Partner (ASCAP)—Mercury 70753	5	15
8.	BLUE SUEDE SHOES (BMI)—C. Perkins Honey, Don't (BMI)—Sun 234	11	4
10.	HEARTBREAK HOTEL (BMI)—E. Presley I WAS THE ONE (BMI)—Vic 20-6420	13	3
10.	WHY DO FOOLS FALL IN LOVE? (BMI)—Teen-Agers Please Be Mine (BMI)—Gee 1002	10	7
12.	EDDIE, MY LOVE (BMI)—Fontane Sisters Yum, Yum (BMI)—Dot 15450	12	3
13.	SEE YOU LATER, ALLIGATOR (BMI)—B. Haley Paper Boy (ASCAP)—Dec 29791	8	10
14.	WHY DO FOOLS FALL IN LOVE? (BMI)—G. Storm I Walk Alone (BMI)—Dot 15448	17	6
15.	MAGIC TOUCH (ASCAP)—Platters WINNER TAKE ALL (ASCAP)—Mercury 70819	—	1
16.	BAND OF GOLD (BMI)—D. Cherry Rumble Boogie (BMI)—Col 40597	14	13
17.	MEMORIES ARE MADE OF THIS (BMI)—D. Martin Change of Heart (BMI)—Cap 3295	15	17
17.	THEME FROM "THE THREE PENNY OPERA" (MORITAT)—R. Hyman-J. August I'll Be With You in Apple Blossom Time (ASCAP)—Mercury 70781	18	6
19.	THEME FROM "THE THREE PENNY OPERA" (MORITAT) (ASCAP)—D. Hyman Baubles, Bangles and Beads (ASCAP)—M-G-M 12149	16	8
20.	EDDIE, MY LOVE (BMI)—Teen Queens Just Goofed (BMI)—RPM 453	—	1

• Best Selling Sheet Music

Tunes are ranked in order of their current national selling importance at the sheet music jobber level.

This Week		Last Week	Weeks on Chart
1.	Rock aand Roll Waltz (Sheldon)	1	13
2.	Poor People of Paris (Connelly)	2	8
3.	Lisbon Antigua (Southern)	3	13
4.	He (Avas)	8	29
5.	Hot Diggity (Roncom)	5	5
6.	No, Not Much (Beaver)	3	9
7.	Eleventh Hour Melody (Paxton)	7	9
8.	Theme From "The Three Penny Opera" (Moritat) (Harms)	6	8
9.	Mr. Wonderful (Laurel)	9	3
10.	I'll Be Home (Arc)	10	5
11.	Why Do Fools Fall in Love? (Patricia)	12	3
12.	Blue Suede Shoes (Hi-Lo)	—	1
13.	Eddie, My Love (Modern-Roosevelt)	13	2
14.	Memories Are Made of This (Montclare)	11	17
15.	To You, My Love (Leeds)	—	1

• Most Played by Jockeys

For survey week ending April 4

SIDES are ranked in order of the greatest number of plays on disk jockey radio shows thruout the country. Results are based on The Billboard's weekly survey among the nation's disk jockeys. The reverse side of each record is also listed.

This Week		Last Week	Weeks on Chart
1.	LISBON ANTIQUA (ASCAP)—N. Riddle Robin Hood (ASCAP)—Cap 3287	3	15
2.	POOR PEOPLE OF PARIS (ASCAP)—L. Baxter Theme From "Helen of Troy" (ASCAP)—Cap 3336	1	9
3.	NO, NOT MUCH (ASCAP)—Four Lads I'll Never Know (BMI)—Col 40629	2	11
4.	HOT DIGGITY (ASCAP)—P. Como Juke Box Baby (BMI)—Vic 20-6427	6	5
5.	HEARTBREAK HOTEL (BMI)—E. Presley I Was the One (BMI)—Vic 20-6420	7	6
6.	ROCK AND ROLL WALTZ (BMI)—K. Starr I've Changed My Mind a Thousand Times (ASCAP)—Vic 20-6359	5	15
7.	I'LL BE HOME (BMI)—P. Boone Tutti Frutti (BMI)—Dot 15443	4	10
8.	BLUE SUEDE SHOES (BMI)—C. Perkins Honey' Don't (BMI)—Sun 234	8	4
9.	WHY DO FOOLS FALL IN LOVE? (BMI)—Teen-Agers Please Be Mine (BMI)—Gee 1002	9	6
10.	WHY DO FOOLS FALL IN LOVE? (BMI)—G. Storm I Walk Alone (BMI)—Dot 15448	10	4
11.	JUKE BOX BABY (BMI)—P. Como Hot Diggity (BMI)—Vic 20-6427	12	5
12.	A TEAR FELL (BMI)—T. Brewer Bo Weevil (BMI)—Coral 61590	13	4
13.	EDDIE, MY LOVE (BMI)—Fontane Sisters Yum, Yum (BMI)—Dot 15450	14	4
14.	MR. WONDERFUL (ASCAP)—P. Lee Crazy in the Heart (BMI)—Dec 29834	17	4
15.	EDDIE, MY LOVE (BMI)—Chordettes Whistling Willie (ASCAP)—Cadence 1084	18	4
16.	GREAT PRETENDER—Platters I'm Just a Dancing Partner (ASCAP)—Mercury 70753	11	16
17.	MAGIC TOUCH—Platters Winner Take All (ASCAP)—Mercury 70819	—	1
18.	THEME FROM "THE THREE PENNY OPERA" (MORITAT) (ASCAP)—D. Hyman Baubles, Bangles and Beads (ASCAP)—M-G-M 12149	16	10
19.	ROCK ISLAND LINE—L. Donegan John Henry (BMI)—London 1650	—	1
20.	PORT-AU-PRINCE (BMI)—N. Riddle Midnight Blues (BMI)—Cap 3374	—	1
21.	MR. WONDERFUL (ASCAP)—S. Vaughan You Ought to Have a Wife (ASCAP)—Mercury 70777	22	6
22.	WHY DO FOOLS FALL IN LOVE? Diamonds You, Baby, You (BMI)—Mercury 70790	15	4
23.	I WAS THE ONE (BMI)—E. Presley Heartbreak Hotel (BMI)—Vic 20-6420	19	3
24.	BO WEEVIL (BMI)—T. Brewer A Tear Fell (BMI)—Coral 61590	20	2
25.	SEE YOU LATER, ALLIGATOR (BMI)—B. Haley Paper Boy (ASCAP)—Dec 29791	21	11

THE TOP 100

For survey week ending April 4

A list of the **Top 100 RECORD SIDES** in the nation according to a **COMBINED TABULATION** of Dealer, Disk Jockey and Juke Box Operator replies to The Billboard's weekly popular record Best Seller and Most Played surveys. Its purpose is to provide Disk Jockeys with additional programming material and to give trade exposure to NEWER records just beginning to show action in the field.

Pos.	Song	Artist	Label	Last Week
1.	POOR PEOPLE OF PARIS	L. Baxter	Capitol	1
2.	LISBON ANTIGUA	N. Riddle	Capitol	2
3.	HOT DIGGITY	P. Como	Victor	27
3.	NO, NOT MUCH	Four Lads	Columbia	4
3.	ROCK AND ROLL WALTZ	K. Starr	Victor	3
6.	HEARTBREAK HOTEL	E. Presley	Victor	8
7.	BLUE SUEDE SHOES	C. Perkins	Sun	6
8.	I'LL BE HOME	P. Boone	Dot	5
9.	WHY DO FOOLS FALL IN LOVE?	Teen-Agers	Gee	7
10.	JUKE BOX BABY	P. Como	Victor	10
11.	A TEAR FELL	T. Brewer	Coral	11
12.	GREAT PRETENDER	Platters	Mercury	8
13.	EDDIE, MY LOVE	Fontane Sisters	Dot	12
14.	MAGIC TOUCH	Platters	Mercury	19
15.	WHY DO FOOLS FALL IN LOVE?	G. Storm	Dot	15
16.	THEME FROM "THE THREE PENNY OPERA" (MORITAT)	D. Hyman	M-G-M	14
17.	SEE YOU LATER, ALLIGATOR	B. Haley	Decca	12
18.	ROCK ISLAND LINE	L. Donegan	London	26
19.	BO WEEVIL	T. Brewer	Coral	17
20.	EDDIE, MY LOVE	Chordettes	Cadence	18
21.	WHY DO FOOLS FALL IN LOVE?	Diamonds	Mercury	16
22.	THEME FROM "THE THREE PENNY OPERA" (MORITAT)	R. Hayman-J. August	Mercury	20
23.	EDDIE, MY LOVE	Teen Queens	RPM	22
23.	I WAS THE ONE	E. Presley	Victor	23
25.	IVORY TOWER	C. Carr	Fraternity	30
26.	MAIN TITLE MOLLY-O ("MAN WITH THE GOLDEN ARM")	D. Jacobs	Coral	37
27.	INNAMORATA	D. Martin	Capitol	31
28.	TO YOU, MY LOVE	N. Noble	Mercury	27
29.	MAIN TITLE ("MAN WITH THE GOLDEN ARM")	R. Maltby	Vik	31
30.	BAND OF GOLD	D. Cherry	Columbia	21
31.	IVORY TOWER	O. Williams	De Luxe	43
31.	LOVELY ONE	Four Voices	Columbia	44
33.	LONG TALL SALLY	Little Richard	Specialty	66
34.	TUTTI FRUTTI	P. Boone	Dot	25
35.	MEMORIES ARE MADE OF THIS	D. Martin	Capitol	24
36.	ROCK RIGHT	G. Gibbs	Mercury	48
37.	PORT-AU-PRINCE	N. Riddle	Capitol	38
38.	FOREVER, DARLING	Ames Brothers	Victor	52
39.	WILD CHERRY	D. Cherry	Columbia	68
40.	MR. WONDERFUL	S. Vaughan	Mercury	38
40.	ROCK	B. Haley	Decca	79
42.	INNAMORATA	J. Vale	Columbia	32
42.	MR. WONDERFUL	P. Lee	Decca	33
44.	WITHOUT YOU	E. Fisher	Victor	63
45.	ELEVENTH HOUR MELODY	A. Hibbler	Decca	46
46.	MR. WONDERFUL	T. King	Victor	36
47.	POOR PEOPLE OF PARIS	L. Welk	Coral	72
48.	FLOWERS MEAN FORGIVENESS	F. Sinatra	Capitol	47
49.	SAINTS ROCK AND ROLL	B. Haley	Decca	67
50.	POOR PEOPLE OF PARIS	R. Morgan	Decca	29
50.	WINNER TAKE ALL	Platters	Mercury	68
52.	MAIN TITLE ("MAN WITH THE GOLDEN ARM")	E. Bernstein	Decca	50
53.	IN A LITTLE SPANISH TOWN	B. Crosby	Decca	82
54.	CRAZY LITTLE PALACE	B. Williams	Coral	49
54.	HELD FOR QUESTIONING	R. Draper	Mercury	76
56.	ASK ME	Nat (King) Cole	Capitol	50
57.	BLUE SUEDE SHOES	E. Presley	Victor	88
58.	THEME FROM "THE THREE PENNY OPERA" (MORITAT)	L. Welk	Coral	63
59.	LISBON ANTIGUA	M. Miller	Columbia	68
60.	MAIN TITLE ("MAN WITH THE GOLDEN ARM")	B. May	Capitol	52
60.	MOONGLOW AND THEME FROM "PICNIC"	M. Stoloff	Decca	—
62.	TOO YOUNG TO GO STEADY	Nat (King) Cole	Capitol	91
63.	THEME FROM "THE THREE PENNY OPERA" (MORITAT)	L. Paul & M. Ford	Capitol	59
64.	BEYOND THE SEA	R. Williams	Kapp	71
65.	ELEVENTH HOUR MELODY	L. Busch	Capitol	55
66.	MOONGLOW AND THEME FROM "PICNIC"	G. Cates	Coral	—
66.	OUR LOVE AFFAIR	T. Charles	Decca	44
68.	BLUE SUEDE SHOES	B. Bennet	King	—
68.	ROCK ISLAND LINE	D. Cornell	Coral	—
68.	THEME FROM "THE THREE PENNY OPERA" (MORITAT)	B. Vaughn	Dot	56
71.	LIPSTICK, CANDY AND RUBBER-SOLED SHOES	J. La Rosa	Victor	72
72.	ELOISE	K. Thompson	Cadence	61
73.	LOVELY LIES	Manhattan Brothers	London	57
74.	BO WEEVIL	Fats Domino	Imperial	35
75.	DUNGAREE DOLL	E. Fisher	Victor	34
76.	NO OTHER ONE	E. Fisher	Victor	—
77.	LULLABY OF BIRDLAND	Blue Stars	Mercury	60
78.	IT'S ALMOST TOMORROW	Dream Weavers	Decca	54
79.	CAN YOU FIND IT IN YOUR HEART?	T. Bennett	Columbia	—
80.	MY FIRST FORMAL GOWN	P. Page	Mercury	100
81.	CHURCH BELLS MAY RING	Willows	Melba	74
82.	THEME FROM "THE THREE PENNY OPERA" (MACK THE KNIFE)	L. Armstrong	Decca	40
83.	POOR PEOPLE OF PARIS (JEAN'S SONG)	C. Atkins	Victor	61
84.	LONG TALL SALLY	P. Boone	Dot	—
85.	MISSING	McGuire Sisters	Coral	83
86.	ONLY YOU	Platters	Mercury	96
87.	ARE YOU SATISFIED?	R. Draper	Mercury	93
87.	CHINESE ROCK AND ROLL	B. Hackett	Coral	94
87.	SWEET LIPS	J. P. Morgan	Victor	—
90.	BAND OF GOLD	K. Carson	Capitol	84
91.	SEVEN DAYS	Crew Cuts	Mercury	63
92.	THAT'S ALL	T. Ernie	Capitol	80
93.	WE ALL NEED LOVE	P. Faith	Columbia	—
94.	MAIN TITLE ("MAN WITH THE GOLDEN ARM")	L. Elgart	Columbia	—
94.	YOU'LL GET YOURS	F. Sinatra	Capitol	—
96.	LITTLE MUSICIANS	H. Winterhalter	Victor	73
97.	TOO YOUNG TO GO STEADY	P. Page	Mercury	—
98.	GET UP, GET UP	J. P. Morgan	Victor	—
99.	INTO THE NIGHT	Dream Weavers	Decca	87
99.	MADERIA	M. Miller	Columbia	78

CAUTION TO DEALERS AND JUKE BOX OPERATORS

The Billboard's Top 100 is NOT designed to provide tested information for buying purposes. This function is most reliably served by other regular weekly features: Best Sellers in Stores, Most Played in Juke Boxes, Coming Up Strong and Best Buys.

Reviews of New Pop Records

Continued from page 56

MIYOSHI UMEKI

Why Talk? 73
MERCURY 70838 — Here the gal opens with a little Japanese before warbling the sexy ballad. Miss Umeki is recorded close and intimate and her sighs help the effect. **(E. B. Marks, BMI)**

How Deep Is the Ocean?....71
Nice phrasing and an intriguing remnant of exotic accent make a listenable entry. Should get spins. **(Berlin, ASCAP)**

RAY MARTIN ORK

Tickled Pink 73
CAPITOL 3393 — Lots of pizzicato string here in a fetching little bounce job. Jockeys might well latch on to this. **(Francis, Day & Hunter, ASCAP)**

If Hearts Could Talk....70
Here's a slow, romantic, dreamer's type of dance fare with a unison vocal by a male group. Flip has more spin appeal. **(Hill & Range, BMI)**

MONCHITO

The Ice Cream Man 72
FIESTA 064—A hip-swinging instrumental in cha-cha rhythm and an infectious danceable tempo.

The Secretary's Cha Cha Cha....72
Same comment.

FRANK YORK ORK

Cavaquinho 72
CORAL 61615—Fast and fancy fiddling highlight this orchestral job. Current instrumental trend being what it is, this has a chance. **(Robbins, ASCAP)**

I Can't Win....70
A much more conventional side, this is a romance ballad with pleasant work by singer Connie Mitchell and violinist York. **(Paco, ASCAP)**

LUCY ROBERTS

Leap Year Red 72
VIK 0201 — Sock thrushing on a bouncy rock and roll rhythm ditty with a solid beat. **(Malvern, ASCAP)**

Supper on the Table....69
The canary half talks, half sings her way thru a familiar blues item. Her delivery is more effective on the flip. **(General, ASCAP)**

HELEN MERRILL

Anything Goes 71
MERCURY 70844—The chick sings the great standard from her album with a fine jazz feeling and a unique style; and she's backed by a subtle instrumental group. Watch it, for a lot o' deejays will like it. **(Harms, ASCAP)**

End of a Love Affair....71
Miss Merrill does this pretty ballad with the same fine phrasing and style revealed on the flip. Nice deejay programming. **(Duchess, BMI)**

JOE MAIZE

The Donkey Serenade 71
DECCA 29848—Here's a bright and rollicking treatment of the famous operetta novelty. Organ, accordion-guitar line-up makes its bow on the label with a possible juke entry. **(Schirmer, ASCAP)**

Lonely Lovers Rhapsody....68
Maize and his Cordsmen offer a slow, dance-styled instrumental. Will take more distinctive efforts to catch spinners' fancy. Flip has a big edge. **(Arthur, ASCAP)**

JERRY JEROME ORK

Ja-Da Cha Cha 70
M-G-M 12216—An amusing version of the oldie in cha cha rhythm, with grunt and groan chorus by the band. Good juke material.

Christopher Columbus....70
Tasteful instrumental treatment of the standard with a swingy beat and a danceable tempo.

DAVE APPELL

The Rock and Roll Story 70
PRESIDENT 1011—Appell and his Applejacks contribute an enthusiastic vocal to a happy rhythm song with swingy r.&b. pacing. **(Wemar, BMI)**

Rainbow of Love....68
Acceptable vocal treatment of a pretty ballad with a strong rock and roll beat. **(Grand, ASCAP)**

JEAN (TOOTS) THIELEMANS

Jack of Hearts 70
COLUMBIA 40677—A flashy showpiece for Thielemans, who is master both of vibes and harmonica, and gets a chance to shine on both here. Deejays on the look-out for a tuneful instrumental, have a dazzler here. **(Zodiac, BMI)**

Sleepy Lagoon....68
Thielemans gives a nostalgic reading of this lovely oldie that will provide enjoyable listening to a wide circle. The harmonica is his featured instrument thruout. **(Chappell, ASCAP)**

SYLVIA SYMS

The World in My Corner 69
DECCA 29903—Title ballad from a forthcoming flick doesn't provide the fine jazz thrush with real coin bait, but some jocks will like her "different" sound. **(Northern, ASCAP)**

I Could Have Danced All Night....68
Matching the stylist to this "My Fair

• Best Sellers in Stores

For survey week ending April 11

RECORDS are ranked in order of their current national selling importance at the retail level, as determined by The Billboard's weekly survey of the top volume dealers in every important market area. When significant action is reported on both sides of a record, points are combined to determine position on the chart. In such a case, both sides are listed in bold type, the leading side on top.

This Week		Last Week	Weeks on Chart
1.	**HEARTBREAK HOTEL** (BMI)—E. Presley **I WAS THE ONE** (BMI)—Vic 20-6420	2	7
2.	**HOT DIGGITY** (ASCAP)—P. Como **JUKE BOX BABY** (ASCAP)—Vic 20-6427	3	7
3.	**POOR PEOPLE OF PARIS** (ASCAP)—L. Baxter Theme From "Helen of Troy" (ASCAP)—Cap 3336	1	10
4.	**BLUE SUEDE SHOES** (BMI)—C. Perkins Honey, Don't (BMI)—Sun 234	4	7
5.	**LISBON ANTIGUA** (ASCAP)—N. Riddle Robin Hood (ASCAP)—Cap 3287	5	17
6.	**WHY DO FOOLS FALL IN LOVE?** (BMI)—Teen-Agers Please Be Mine (BMI)—Gee 1002	6	10
7.	**I'LL BE HOME** (BMI)—P. Boone Tutti Frutti (BMI)—Dot 15443	7	11
8.	**ROCK ISLAND LINE** (BMI)—L. Donegan John Henry (BMI)—London 1650	11	4
9.	**A TEAR FELL** (BMI)—T. Brewer **BO WEEVIL** (BMI)—Coral 61590	10	8
10.	**NO, NOT MUCH** (ASCAP)—Four Lads I'll Never Know (BMI)—Col 40629	9	13
11.	**MAGIC TOUCH** (ASCAP)—Platters Winner Take All (ASCAP)—Mercury 70819	12	4
12.	**LONG, TALL SALLY** (BMI)—Little Richard Slippin' and Slidin' (BMI)—Specialty 572	13	3
13.	**ROCK AND ROLL WALTZ** (BMI)—K. Starr I've Changed My Mind a Thousand Times (ASCAP)—Vic 20-6359	8	16
14.	**MOONGLOW AND THEME FROM "PICNIC"** (ASCAP)—M. Stoloff Theme From "Picnic" (ASCAP)—Dec 29888	—	1
15.	**IVORY TOWER** (ASCAP)—O. Williams In Paradise (BMI)—DeLuxe 6093	21	2
16.	**IVORY TOWER** (ASCAP)—C. Carr Please Believe Me (ASCAP)—Fraternity 734	—	2
17.	**MAIN TITLE (MAN WITH THE GOLDEN ARM)**—R. Maltby Heart of Paris (ASCAP)—Vik 0196	17	4
18.	**SAINTS ROCK AND ROLL** (ASCAP)—B. Haley **R-O-C-K** (ASCAP)—Dec 29870	23	3
19.	**MAIN TITLE (MAN WITH THE GOLDEN ARM)** (ASCAP)—E. Bernstein Clark Street (ASCAP)—Dec 29869	20	3
20.	**EDDIE, MY LOVE** (BMI)—Fontane Sisters Yum Yum (BMI)—Dot 15450	16	4
21.	**THEME FROM "THE THREE PENNY OPERA" (MORITAT)** (ASCAP)—D. Hyman Baubles, Bangles and Beads (ASCAP)—M-G-M 12149	14	13
22.	**GREAT PRETENDER** (ASCAP)—Platters I'm Just a Dancing Partner (ASCAP)—Mercury 70753	15	18
22.	**MOONGLOW AND THEME FROM "PICNIC"** (ASCAP)—G. Cates Rio Batucada (ASCAP)—Coral 61618	—	1
24.	**WHY DO FOOLS FALL IN LOVE?** (BMI)—G. Storm I Walk Alone (BMI)—Dot 15448	22	5
25.	**WHY DO FOOLS FALL IN LOVE?** Diamonds You, Baby, You (BMI)—Mercury 70790	19	6

• Most Played in Juke Boxes

For survey week ending April 11

RECORDS are ranked in order of the greatest number of plays in juke boxes thruout the country, as determined by The Billboard's weekly survey of the nation's juke box operators. When significant play is reported on both sides of a record, points are combined to determine position on the chart. In such a case, both sides are listed in bold type, the leading side on top.

This Week		Last Week	Weeks on Chart
1.	**POOR PEOPLE OF PARIS** (ASCAP)—L. Baxter Theme From "Helen of Troy" (ASCAP)—Cap 3336	1	9
2.	**HOT DIGGITY** (BMI)—P. Como **JUKE BOX BABY** (BMI)—Vic 20-6427	5	5
3.	**LISBON ANTIGUA** (ASCAP)—N. Riddle Robin Hood (ASCAP)—Cap 3287	3	12
4.	**ROCK AND ROLL WALTZ** (BMI)—K. Starr I've Changed My Mind a Thousand Times (ASCAP)—Vic 20-6359	2	15
5.	**I'LL BE HOME** (BMI)—P. Boone **TUTTI FRUTTI** (BMI)—Dot 15443	4	10
5.	**BLUE SUEDE SHOES** (BMI)—C. Perkins Honey, Don't (BMI)—Sun 234	8	5
7.	**HEARTBREAK HOTEL** (BMI)—E. Presley **I WAS THE ONE** (BMI)—Vic 20-6420	10	4
8.	**A TEAR FELL** (BMI)—T. Brewer **BO WEEVIL** (BMI)—Coral 61590	5	5
9.	**NO, NOT MUCH** (ASCAP)—Four Lads I'll Never Know (BMI)—Col 40629	6	10
10.	**WHY DO FOOLS FALL IN LOVE?** (BMI)—Teen-Agers Please Be Mine (BMI)—Gee 1002	10	8
11.	**EDDIE, MY LOVE** (BMI)—Fontane Sisters Yum, Yum (BMI)—Dot 15450	12	4
12.	**GREAT PRETENDER** (ASCAP)—Platters I'm Just a Dancing Partner (ASCAP)—Mercury 70753	8	16
13.	**MAGIC TOUCH** (ASCAP)—Platters Winner Take All (ASCAP)—Mercury 70819	15	2
14.	**SEE YOU LATER, ALLIGATOR** (BMI)—B. Haley Paper Boy (ASCAP)—Dec 29791	13	11
15.	**WHY DO FOOLS FALL IN LOVE?** (BMI)—G. Storm I Walk Alone (BMI)—Dot 15448	14	7
16.	**EDDIE, MY LOVE** (BMI)—Teen Queens Just Goofed (BMI)—RPM 453	20	2
17.	**LONG TALL SALLY** (BMI)—Little Richard Slippin' and Slidin' (BMI)—Specialty 572	—	1
18.	**ROCK ISLAND LINE** (BMI)—L. Donegan John Henry (BMI)—London 1650	—	1
19.	**THEME FROM "THE THREE PENNY OPERA" (MORITAT)** (ASCAP)—D. Hyman Baubles, Bangles and Beads (ASCAP)—M-G-M 12149	19	9
19.	**BAND OF GOLD** (BMI)—D. Cherry Rumble Boogie (BMI)—Col 40597	16	14

• Best Selling Sheet Music

Tunes are ranked in order of their current national selling importance at the sheet music jobber level.

This Week Last Week Weeks on Chart

This Week		Last Week	Weeks on Chart
1.	**Poor People of Paris** (Connelly)	2	9
2.	**Rock and Roll Waltz** (Sheldon)	1	14
3.	**Lisbon Antigua** (Southern)	3	14
4.	**Hot Diggity** (Roncom)	5	6
5.	**Mr. Wonderful** (Laurel)	9	4
6.	**Theme From "The Three Penny Opera" (Moritat)** (Harms)	8	9
7.	**Blue Suede Shoes** (Hi-Lo)	12	2
8.	**He** (Avas)	4	30
9.	**Eddie, My Love** (Modern-Roosevelt)	13	3
10.	**No, Not Much** (Beaver)	6	10
11.	**Why Do Fools Fall in Love?** (Patricia)	11	4
11.	**Heartbreak Hotel** (Tree)	—	1
13.	**Eleventh Hour Melody** (Paxton)	7	10
14.	**I'll Be Home** (Arc)	10	6
15.	**To You My Love** (Leeds)	15	2

• Most Played by Jockeys

For survey week ending April 11

SIDES are ranked in order of the greatest number of plays on disk jockey radio shows thruout the country. Results are based on The Billboard's weekly survey among the nation's disk jockeys. The reverse side of each record is also listed.

This Week		Last Week	Weeks on Chart
1.	**POOR PEOPLE OF PARIS** (ASCAP)—L. Baxter Theme From "Helen of Troy" (ASCAP)—Cap 3336	2	10
2.	**HOT DIGGITY** (ASCAP)—P. Como Juke Box Baby (BMI)—Vic 20-6427	4	6
3.	**NO, NOT MUCH** (ASCAP)—Four Lads I'll Never Know (BMI)—Col 40629	3	12
4.	**HEARTBREAK HOTEL** (BMI)—E. Presley I Was the One (BMI)—Vic 20-6420	5	7
5.	**LISBON ANTIGUA** (ASCAP)—N. Riddle Robin Hood (ASCAP)—Cap 3287	1	16
6.	**I'LL BE HOME** (BMI)—P. Boone Tutti Frutti (BMI)—Dot 15443	7	11
7.	**BLUE SUEDE SHOES** (BMI)—C. Perkins Honey, Don't (BMI)—Sun 234	8	5
8.	**ROCK AND ROLL WALTZ** (BMI)—K. Starr I've Changed My Mind a Thousand Times (ASCAP)—Vic 20-6359	6	16
9.	**WHY DO FOOLS FALL IN LOVE?** (BMI)—Teen-Agers Please Be Mine (BMI)—Gee 1002	9	7
10.	**A TEAR FELL** (BMI)—T. Brewer Bo Weevil (BMI)—Coral 61590	12	5
11.	**WHY DO FOOLS FALL IN LOVE?** (BMI)—G. Storm I Walk Alone (BMI)—Dot 15448	10	5
12.	**WHY DO FOOLS FALL IN LOVE?** (BMI)—Diamonds You, Baby, You (BMI)—Mercury 70790	22	5
13.	**MAGIC TOUCH** (ASCAP)—Platters Winner Take All (ASCAP)—Mercury 70819	17	2
14.	**JUKE BOX BABY** (BMI)—P. Como Hot Diggity (BMI)—Vic 20-6427	11	6
15.	**ROCK ISLAND LINE** (BMI)—L. Donegan John Henry (BMI)—London 1650	19	2
16.	**EDDIE, MY LOVE** (BMI)—Fontane Sisters Yum, Yum (BMI)—Dot 15450	13	5
17.	**MR. WONDERFUL** (ASCAP)—P. Lee Crazy in the Heart (BMI)—Dec 29834	14	5
18.	**GREAT PRETENDER**—Platters I'm Just a Dancing Partner (ASCAP)—Mercury 70753	16	17
19.	**MR. WONDERFUL** (ASCAP)—S. Vaughan You Ought to Have a Wife (ASCAP)—Mercury 70777	21	7
20.	**I WAS THE ONE** (BMI)—E. Presley Heartbreak Hotel (BMI)—Vic 20-6420	23	4
21.	**MOONGLOW AND THEME FROM "PICNIC"** (ASCAP)—G. Cates Rio Batucada (ASCAP)—Coral 61618	—	1
22.	**MAIN TITLE AND MOLLY-O ("MAN WITH THE GOLDEN ARM")** (ASCAP)—D. Jacobs Butternut (BMI)—Coral 61606	—	1
23.	**EDDIE, MY LOVE** (BMI)—Chordettes Whistling Willie (ASCAP)—Cadence 1084	15	5
24.	**MOONGLOW AND THEME FROM "PICNIC"** (ASCAP)—M. Stoloff Theme From "Picnic" (ASCAP)—Dec 29888	—	1
25.	**FLOWERS MEAN FORGIVENESS** (ASCAP)—F. Sinatra You'll Get Yours (ASCAP)—Cap 3350	—	3
25.	**TOO YOUNG TO GO STEADY** (ASCAP)—Nat (King) Cole Never Let Me Go (ASCAP)—Cap 3390	—	1

THE TOP 100

For survey week ending April 11

A list of the Top 100 **RECORD SIDES** in the nation according to a **COMBINED TABULATION** of Dealer, Disk Jockey and Juke Box Operator replies to The Billboard's weekly popular record Best Seller and Most Played surveys. Its purpose is to provide Disk Jockeys with additional programming material and to give trade exposure to NEWER records just beginning to show action in the field.

Pos.	Song	Artist	Label	Last Week
1.	POOR PEOPLE OF PARIS	L. Baxter	Capitol	1
2.	HOT DIGGITY	P. Como	Victor	3
2.	HEARTBREAK HOTEL	E. Presley	Victor	6
4.	LISBON ANTIGUA	N. Riddle	Capitol	2
5.	BLUE SUEDE SHOES	C. Perkins	Sun	7
6.	I'LL BE HOME	P. Boone	Dot	8
6.	NO, NOT MUCH	Four Lads	Columbia	3
8.	ROCK AND ROLL WALTZ	K. Starr	Victor	3
9.	WHY DO FOOLS FALL IN LOVE?	Teen Agers	Gee	9
10.	A TEAR FELL	T. Brewer	Coral	11
11.	MAGIC TOUCH	Platters	Mercury	14
12.	JUKE BOX BABY	P. Como	Victor	10
13.	ROCK ISLAND LINE	L. Donegan	London	18
14.	EDDIE MY LOVE	Fontane Sisters	Dot	13
15.	WHY DO FOOLS FALL IN LOVE?	G. Storm	Dot	15
16.	GREAT PRETENDER	Platters	Mercury	12
17.	LONG TALL SALLY	Little Richard	Specialty	33
18.	WHY DO FOOLS FALL IN LOVE?	Diamonds	Mercury	21
19.	THEME FROM "THE THREE PENNY OPERA" (MORITAT)	D. Hyman	M-G-M	16
20.	BO WEEVIL	T. Brewer	Coral	19
21.	IVORY TOWER	O. Williams	De Luxe	31
22.	IVORY TOWER	C. Carr	Fraternity	25
23.	I WAS THE ONE	E. Presley	Victor	23
24.	MOONGLOW AND THEME FROM "PICNIC"	G. Cates	Coral	66
25.	SEE YOU LATER, ALLIGATOR	B. Haley	Decca	17
26.	MAIN TITLE MOLLY-O ("MAN WITH THE GOLDEN ARM")	D. Jacobs	Coral	26
27.	EDDIE MY LOVE	Teen Queens	RPM	23
28.	MAIN TITLE ("MAN WITH THE GOLDEN ARM")	R. Maltby	Vik	29
29.	R-O-C-K	B. Haley	Decca	40
30.	LOVELY ONE	Four Voices	Columbia	31
31.	TOO YOUNG TO GO STEADY	Nat (King) Cole	Capitol	62
32.	THEME FROM "THE THREE PENNY OPERA" (MORITAT)	R. Hayman	Mercury	22
33.	INNAMORATA	D. Martin	Capitol	27
33.	MR. WONDERFUL	P. Lee	Decca	42
35.	WILD CHERRY	D. Cherry	Columbia	39
36.	MOONGLOW AND THEME FROM "PICNIC"	M. Stoloff	Decca	60
37.	EDDIE, MY LOVE	Chordettes	Cadence	20
37.	PORT AU PRINCE	N. Riddle	Capitol	37
37.	TO YOU, MY LOVE	N. Noble	Mercury	28
40.	INNAMORATA	J. Vale	Columbia	42
41.	LITTLE MUSICIANS	H. Winterhalter	Victor	96
42.	SAINTS ROCK AND ROLL	B. Haley	Decca	49
43.	MAIN TITLE ("MAN WITH THE GOLDEN ARM")	E. Bernstein	Decca	52
44.	BAND OF GOLD	D. Cherry	Columbia	30
45.	MEMORIES ARE MADE OF THIS	D. Martin	Capitol	35
45.	POOR PEOPLE OF PARIS	L. Welk	Coral	47
45.	ROCK RIGHT	G. Gibbs	Mercury	36
48.	MR. WONDERFUL	S. Vaughan	Mercury	40
49.	IN A LITTLE SPANISH TOWN	Bing Crosby	Decca	53
50.	MAIN TITLE ("MAN WITH THE GOLDEN ARM")	B. May	Capitol	60
51.	HELD FOR QUESTIONING	R. Draper	Mercury	54
52.	LONG TALL SALLY	P. Boone	Dot	84
53.	CRAZY LITTLE PALACE	B. Williams	Coral	54
54.	BLUE SUEDE SHOES	E. Presley	Victor	57
55.	FLOWERS MEAN FORGIVENESS	F. Sinatra	Capitol	48
56.	DUNGAREE DOLL	E. Fisher	Victor	75
56.	MR. WONDERFUL	T. King	Victor	46
58.	WITHOUT YOU	E. Fisher	Victor	44
59.	TUTTI FRUTTI	P. Boone	Dot	34
60.	FOREVER DARLING	Ames Brothers	Victor	38
61.	THEME FROM "THE THREE PENNY OPERA" (MORITAT)	L. Welk	Coral	58
62.	CAN YOU FIND IT IN YOUR HEART?	T. Bennett	Columbia	79
63.	BLUE SUEDE SHOES	B. Bennett	King	68
64.	LIPSTICK, CANDY AND RUBBER-SOLED SHOES	J. La Rosa	Victor	71
65.	NO OTHER ONE	E. Fisher	Victor	76
66.	ROCK AND ROLL WEDDING	S. Gale	Victor	—
66.	WINNER TAKE ALL	Platters	Mercury	50
68.	BEYOND THE SEA	R. Williams	Kapp	64
69.	ELOISE	K. Thompson	Cadence	72
70.	TO YOU, MY LOVE	G. Shaw	Decca	—
71.	ELEVENTH HOUR MELODY	A. Hibbler	Decca	45
72.	I'M STILL A KING TO YOU	D. Cherry	Columbia	—
73.	TOO CLOSE FOR COMFORT	E. Gorme	ABC-Paramount	—
74.	ELEVENTH HOUR MELODY	L. Busch	Capitol	65
75.	BO WEEVIL	F. Domino	Imperial	74
75.	CHURCH BELLS MAY RING	Willows	Melba	81
75.	ROCK ISLAND LINE	D. Cornell	Coral	68
78.	ASK ME	Nat (King) Cole	Capitol	56
78.	MAIN TITLE ("MAN WITH THE GOLDEN ARM")	L. Elgart	Columbia	94
80.	THEME FROM "THE THREE PENNY OPERA" (MORITAT)	B. Vaughn	Dot	68
81.	SLIPPIN' AND SLIDIN'	Little Richard	Specialty	—
82.	ON THE STREET WHERE YOU LIVE	V. Damone	Mercury	—
83.	THEME FROM "THE THREE PENNY OPERA" ("MACK THE KNIFE")	L. Armstrong	Decca	82
84.	MAIN TITLE ("MAN WITH THE GOLDEN ARM")	B. Morrow	Wing	—
84.	OUR LOVE AFFAIR	T. Charles	Decca	66
86.	LISBON ANTIGUA	M. Miller	Columbia	59
87.	SPEEDOO	Cadillacs	Josie	—
88.	HI LILI HI LO	D. Hyman	M-G-M	—
89.	TOO YOUNG TO GO STEADY	P. Page	Mercury	97
90.	LOVELY LIES	Manhattan Brothers	London	73
91.	WALK HAND IN HAND	T. Martin	Victor	—
92.	CHURCH BELLS MAY RING	Diamonds	Mercury	—
92.	LULLABY OF BIRDLAND	Blue Stars	Mercury	77
94.	WE ALL NEED LOVE	P. Faith	Columbia	93
95.	THEME FROM "THE THREE PENNY OPERA" (MORITAT)	L. Paul & M. Ford	Capitol	63
96.	POOR PEOPLE OF PARIS (JEAN'S SONG)	C. Atkins	Victor	83
96.	WALK HAND IN HAND	A. Williams	Cadence	—
98.	NEVER LET ME GO	Nat (King) Cole	Capitol	—
98.	THAT'S YOUR MISTAKE	O. Williams	De Luxe	—
100.	MADERIA	M. Miller	Columbia	99

CAUTION TO DEALERS AND JUKE BOX OPERATORS

The Billboard's Top 100 is NOT designed to provide tested information for buying purposes. This function is most reliably served by other regular weekly features: **Best Sellers in Stores, Most Played in Juke Boxes, Coming Up Strong and Best Buys.**

• Best Sellers in Stores

For survey week ending April 18

RECORDS are ranked in order of their current national selling importance at the retail level, as determined by The Billboard's weekly survey of the top volume dealers in every important market area. When significant action is reported on both sides of a record, points are combined to determine position on the chart. In such a case, both sides are listed in bold type, the leading side on top.

This Week	Record	Last Week	Weeks on Chart
1.	HEARTBREAK HOTEL (BMI)—E. Presley I WAS THE ONE (BMI)—Vic 20-6420	1	8
2.	HOT DIGGITY (ASCAP)—P. Como JUKE BOX BABY (ASCAP)—Vic 20-6427	2	8
3.	POOR PEOPLE OF PARIS (ASCAP)—L. Baxter Theme From "Helen of Troy" (ASCAP)—Cap 3336	3	11
4.	BLUE SUEDE SHOES (BMI)—C. Perkins Honey, Don't (BMI)—Sun 234	4	8
5.	LISBON ANTIGUA (ASCAP)—N. Riddle Robin Hood (ASCAP)—Cap 3287	5	18
6.	WHY DO FOOLS FALL IN LOVE? (BMI)—Teen-Agers Please Be Mine (BMI)—Gee 1002	6	11
7.	MOONGLOW AND THEME FROM "PICNIC" (ASCAP)—M. Stoloff Theme From "Picnic" (ASCAP)—Dec 29888	14	2
8.	MAGIC TOUCH (BMI)—Platters Winner Take All (ASCAP)—Mercury 70819	11	5
9.	ROCK ISLAND LINE (BMI)—L. Donegan John Henry (BMI)—London 1650	8	5
10.	A TEAR FELL (BMI)—T. Brewer BO WEEVIL (BMI)—Coral 61590	9	9
11.	I'LL BE HOME (BMI)—P. Boone Tutti Frutti (BMI)—Dot 15443	7	12
12.	LONG, TALL SALLY (BMI)—Little Richard Slippin' and Slidin' (BMI)—Specialty 572	12	4
13.	NO, NOT MUCH (ASCAP) I'll Never Know (BMI)—Col 40629	10	14
14.	IVORY TOWER (ASCAP)—C. Carr Please, Please, Believe Me (ASCAP)—Fraternity 734	16	3
15.	MAIN TITLE ("MAN WITH THE GOLDEN ARM")—R. Maltby Heart of Paris (ASCAP)—Vik 0196	17	5
16.	MAIN TITLE ("MAN WITH THE GOLDEN ARM")—E. Bernstein Clark Street (ASCAP)—Dec 29869	19	4
17.	MOONGLOW AND THEME FROM "PICNIC" (ASCAP)—G. Cates Rio Batucada (ASCAP)—Coral 61618	22	2
18.	ROCK AND ROLL WALTZ (BMI)—K. Starr I've Changed My Mind a Thousand Times (ASCAP)—Vic 20-6359	13	17
19.	IVORY TOWER (ASCAP)—O. Williams In Paradise (BMI)—De Luxe 6093	15	3
20.	*BLUE SUEDE SHOES (BMI)—E. Presley Vic EPA-747, EPB-1254	—	1
21.	EDDIE, MY LOVE (BMI)—Fontane Sisters Yum, Yum (BMI)—Dot 15450	20	5
22.	WHY DO FOOLS FALL IN LOVE? Diamonds You, Baby, You (BMI)—Mercury 70790	25	7
22.	MY LITTLE ANGEL (BMI)—Four Lads STANDING ON THE CORNER (ASCAP)—Col 40674	—	1
24.	SAINTS ROCK AND ROLL (ASCAP)—B. Haley R-O-C-K (ASCAP)—Dec 29870	18	4
25.	WHY DO FOOLS FALL IN LOVE? (BMI)—G. Storm I Walk Alone (BMI)—Dot 15448	24	6

*This is an EP. However, action is of sufficient strength to warrant the present rank on this chart.

• Most Played in Juke Boxes

For survey week ending April 18

RECORDS are ranked in order of the greatest number of plays in juke boxes thruout the country, as determined by The Billboard's weekly survey of the nation's juke box operators. When significant play is reported on both sides of a record, points are combined to determine position on the chart. In such a case, both sides are listed in bold type, the leading side on top.

This Week	Record	Last Week	Weeks on Chart
1.	POOR PEOPLE OF PARIS (ASCAP)—L. Baxter Theme From "Helen of Troy" (ASCAP)—Cap 3336	1	10
2.	HOT DIGGITY (BMI)—P. Como Juke Box Baby (BMI)—Vic 20-6427	2	6
3.	HEARTBREAK HOTEL (BMI)—E. Presley I Was the One (BMI)—Vic 20-6420	7	5
4.	LISBON ANTIGUA (ASCAP)—N. Riddle Robin Hood (ASCAP)—Cap 3287	3	13
5.	ROCK AND ROLL WALTZ (BMI)—K. Starr I've Changed My Mind a Thousand Times (ASCAP)—Vic 20-6359	4	16
6.	BLUE SUEDE SHOES (BMI)—C. Perkins Honey, Don't (BMI)—Sun 234	5	6
7.	I'LL BE HOME (BMI)—P. Boone Tutti Frutti (BMI)—Dot 15443	5	11
8.	NO, NOT MUCH (ASCAP)—Four Lads I'll Never Know (BMI)—Col 40629	9	11
9.	A TEAR FELL (BMI)—T. Brewer Bo Weevil (BMI)—Coral 61590	8	6
10.	WHY DO FOOLS FALL IN LOVE? (BMI)—Teen-Agers Please Be Mine (BMI)—Gee 1002	10	9
11.	EDDIE, MY LOVE (BMI)—Fontane Sisters Yum, Yum (BMI)—Dot 15450	11	5
12.	GREAT PRETENDER (ASCAP)—Platters I'm Just a Dancing Partner (ASCAP)—Mercury 70753	12	17
13.	MAGIC TOUCH (ASCAP)—Platters Winneer Take All (ASCAP)—Mercury 70819	13	3
14.	WHY DO FOOLS FALL IN LOVE? (BMI)—G. Storm I Walk Alone (BMI)—Dot 15448	15	8
15.	SEE YOU LATER, ALLIGATOR (BMI)—B. Haley Paper Boy (ASCAP)—Dec 29791	14	12
16.	ROCK ISLAND LINE (BMI)—L. Donegan John Henry (BMI)—London 1650	18	2
17.	EDDIE, MY LOVE (BMI)—Teen Queens Just Goofed (BMI)—RPM 453	16	3
17.	POOR PEOPLE OF PARIS (ASCAP)—L. Welk Nobody Knows But the Lord (???)—Coral 61592	—	1
19.	THEME FROM "THE THREE PENNY OPERA" (MORITAT) (ASCAP)—D. Hyman Baubles, Bangles and Beads (ASCAP)—M-G-M 12149	19	10
19.	MAIN TITLE (MAN WITH THE GOLDEN ARM) (ASCAP)—R. Maltby Heart of Paris (ASCAP)—Vik 0196	—	1

• Best Selling Sheet Music

Tunes are ranked in order of their current national selling importance at the sheet music jobber level.

This Week	Title	Last Week	Weeks on Chart
1.	**Poor People of Paris** (Connelly)	1	10
2.	**Hot Diggity** (Roncom)	4	7
3.	**Rock and Roll Waltz** (Sheldon)	2	15
4.	**Blue Suede Shoes** (Hi Lo)	7	3
5.	**Theme From "The Three Penny Opera" (Moritat)**, (Harms)	6	10
6.	**Lisbon Antigua** (Southern)	3	15
7.	**Mr. Wonderful** (Laurel)	5	8
8.	**Heartbreak Hotel** (Tree)	11	2
9.	**He** (Avas)	8	31
10.	**No, Not Much** (Beaver)	10	11
11.	**A Tear Fell** (Progressive)	—	1
12.	**Rock Island Line** (Hollis)	—	1
13.	**Eddie, My Love** (Modern-Roosevelt)	9	4
14.	**Ivory Tower** (E. H. Morris)	—	1
15.	**I'll Be Home** (Arc)	14	7
15.	**To You, My Love** (Leeds)	15	3

• Most Played by Jockeys

For survey week ending April 18

SIDES are ranked in order of the greatest number of plays on disk jockey radio shows thruout the country. Results are based on The Billboard's weekly survey among the nation's disk jockeys. The reverse side of each record is also listed.

This Week	Record	Last Week	Weeks on Chart
1.	POOR PEOPLE OF PARIS (ASCAP)—L. Baxter Theme From "Helen of Troy" (ASCAP)—Cap 3336	1	11
2.	HOT DIGGITY (ASCAP)—P. Como Juke Box Baby (BMI)—Vic 20-6427	2	7
3.	HEARTBREAK HOTEL (BMI)—E. Presley I Was the One (BMI)—Vic 20-6420	4	8
4.	NO, NOT MUCH (ASCAP)—Four Lads I'll Never Know (BMI)—Col 40629	3	13
5.	LISBON ANTIGUA (ASCAP)—N. Riddle Robin Hood (ASCAP)—Cap 3287	5	17
6.	BLUE SUEDE SHOES (BMI)—C. Perkins Honey, Don't (BMI)—Sun 234	7	6
7.	I'LL BE HOME (BMI)—P. Boone Tutti Frutti (BMI)—Dot 15443	6	12
8.	MAGIC TOUCH (BMI)—Platters Winner Take All (ASCAP)—Mercury 70819	13	3
9.	A TEAR FELL (BMI)—T. Brewer Bo Weevil (BMI)—Coral 61590	10	6
10.	ROCK ISLAND LINE (BMI)—L. Donegan John Henry (BMI)—London 1650	15	3
11.	WHY DO FOOLS FALL IN LOVE? (BMI)—Teen-Agers Please Be Mine (BMI)—Gee 1002	9	8
12.	WHY DO FOOLS FALL IN LOVE? (BMI)—Diamonds You, Baby, You (BMI)—Mercury 70790	12	6
13.	ROCK AND ROLL WALTZ (BMI)—K. Starr I've Changed My Mind a Thousand Times (ASCAP)—Vic 20-6359	8	17
14.	MOONGLOW AND THEME FROM "PICNIC" (ASCAP)—M. Stoloff Theme From "Picnic" (ASCAP)—Dec 29888	24	2
15.	IVORY TOWER (ASCAP)—C. Carr Please, Please, Believe Me (ASCAP)—Fraternity 734	—	1
16.	IVORY TOWER (ASCAP)—O. Williams In Paradise (BMI)—De Luxe 6093	—	1
17.	JUKE BOX BABY (BMI)—P. Como Hot Diggity (BMI)—Vic 20-6427	14	7
19.	WHY DO FOOLS FALL IN LOVE? (BMI)—G. Storm I Walk Alone (BMI)—Dot 15448	11	6
20.	MAIN TITLE (MAN WITH THE GOLDEN ARM) (ASCAP)—R. Maltby Heart of Paris (ASCAP)—Vik 0196	—	1
21.	TOO YOUNG TO GO STEADY (ASCAP)—Nat (King) Cole Never Let Me Go (ASCAP)—Cap 3390	25	2
22.	MR. WONDERFUL (ASCAP)—P. Lee Crazy in the Heart (BMI)—Dec 29834	17	6
23.	EDDIE, MY LOVE (BMI)—Fontane Sisters Yum, Yum (BMI)—Dot 15450	16	6
24.	*BLUE SUEDE SHOES—E. Presley Vic EPA-747; EPB-1254	—	1
25.	PORT AU PRINCE (BMI)—N. Riddle Midnight Blues (BMI)—Cap 3374	—	2

*This is an EP. However, action on this side is of sufficient strength to warrant the present rank on this chart.

THE TOP 100

For survey week ending April 18

A list of the **Top 100 RECORD SIDES** in the nation according to a **COMBINED TABULATION** of Dealer, Disk Jockey and Juke Box Operator replies to The Billboard's weekly popular record Best Seller and Most Played surveys. Its purpose is to provide Disk Jockeys with additional programming material and to give trade exposure to NEWER records just beginning to show action in the field.

Pos.	Song	Artist	Label	Last Week
1.	POOR PEOPLE OF PARIS	L. Baxter	Capitol	1
2.	HEARTBREAK HOTEL	E. Presley	Victor	2
3.	HOT DIGGITY	P. Como	Victor	2
4.	LISBON ANTIGUA	N. Riddle	Capitol	4
5.	BLUE SUEDE SHOES	C. Perkins	Sun	5
6.	NO, NOT MUCH	Four Lads	Columbia	6
7.	I'LL BE HOME	P. Boone	Dot	6
8.	WHY DO FOOLS FALL IN LOVE?	Teen Agers	Gee	9
9.	MAGIC TOUCH	Platters	Mercury	11
9.	A TEAR FELL	T. Brewer	Coral	10
11.	ROCK AND ROLL WALTZ	K. Starr	Victor	8
12.	ROCK ISLAND LINE	L. Donegan	London	13
13.	JUKE BOX BABY	P. Como	Victor	12
14.	EDDIE, MY LOVE	Fontane Sisters	Dot	14
14.	MAIN TITLE ("MAN WITH THE GOLDEN ARM")	R. Maltby	Vik	28
16.	WHY DO FOOLS FALL IN LOVE?	G. Storm	Dot	15
17.	WHY DO FOOLS FALL IN LOVE?	Diamonds	Mercury	18
18.	IVORY TOWER	O. Williams	De Luxe	21
19.	IVORY TOWER	C. Carr	Fraternity	22
20.	LONG, TALL SALLY	Little Richard	Specialty	17
21.	MOONGLOW AND THEME FROM "PICNIC"	M. Stoloff	Decca	36
22.	THEME FROM "THE THREE PENNY OPERA" (MORITAT)	D. Hyman	M-G-M	19
23.	I WAS THE ONE	E. Presley	Victor	23
24.	BO WEEVIL	T. Brewer	Coral	20
25.	BLUE SUEDE SHOES	E. Presley	Victor	54
26.	MAIN TITLE MOLLY-O ("MAN WITH THE GOLDEN ARM")	D. Jacobs	Coral	26
27.	GREAT PRETENDER	Platters	Mercury	16
28.	MR. WONDERFUL	P. Lee	Decca	33
29.	WILD CHERRY	D. Cherry	Columbia	35
30.	LOVELY ONE	Four Voices	Columbia	30
31.	LONG, TALL SALLY	P. Boone	Dot	52
32.	MAIN TITLE ("MAN WITH THE GOLDEN ARM")	E. Berstein	Decca	43
33.	EDDIE, MY LOVE	Chordettes	Cadence	37
34.	EDDIE, MY LOVE	Teen Queens	RPM	27
35.	MOONGLOW AND THEME FROM "PICNIC"	G. Cates	Coral	24
35.	SEE YOU LATER, ALLIGATOR	B. Haley	Decca	25
35.	TOO YOUNG TO GO STEADY	Nat (King) Cole	Capitol	31
38.	INNAMORATA	J. Vale	Columbia	40
39.	INNAMORATA	D. Martin	Capitol	33
39.	STANDING ON THE CORNER	Four Lads	Columbia	—
41.	CHURCH BELLS MAY RING	Diamonds	Mercury	92
42.	TO YOU, MY LOVE	N. Noble	Mercury	37
43.	POOR PEOPLE OF PARIS	R. Morgan	Decca	—
44.	R-O-C-K	B. Haley	Decca	29
44.	WITHOUT YOU	E. Fisher	Victor	58
46.	IVORY TOWER	G. Storm	Dot	—
46.	THEME FROM "THE THREE PENNY OPERA" (MORITAT)	R. Hayman-J. August	Mercury	32
48.	SAINTS ROCK AND ROLL	B. Haley	Decca	42
49.	MAIN TITLE ("MAN WITH THE GOLDEN ARM")	B. May	Capitol	50
49.	PORT-AU-PRINCE	N. Riddle	Capitol	37
51.	HAPPY WHISTLER	D. Robertson	Capitol	—
52.	CAN YOU FIND IT IN YOUR HEART?	T. Bennett	Columbia	62
53.	CRAZY LITTLE PALACE	B. Williams	Coral	53
54.	IN A LITTLE SPANISH TOWN	Bing Crosby	Decca	49
55.	BAND OF GOLD	D. Cherry	Columbia	44
56.	LISBON ANTIGUA	M. Miller	Columbia	86
56.	THEME FROM "THE THREE PENNY OPERA" (MACK THE KNIFE)	L. Armstrong	Columbia	83
56.	WAYWARD WIND	G. Grant	Era	—
59.	OUR LOVE AFFAIR	T. Charles	Decca	84
59.	POOR PEOPLE OF PARIS	L. Welk	Coral	45
59.	ROCK ISLAND LINE	D. Cornell	Coral	75
62.	ELEVENTH HOUR MELODY	A. Hibbler	Decca	71
63.	HELD FOR QUESTIONING	R. Draper	Mercury	71
64.	MR. WONDERFUL	S. Vaughan	Mercury	48
65.	MR. WONDERFUL	T. King	Victor	56
66.	I WANT YOU TO BE MY GIRL	Teen Agers	Gee	—
67.	CHURCH BELLS MAY RING	Willows	Melba	75
67.	NO OTHER ONE	E. Fisher	Victor	65
69.	FLOWERS MEAN FORGIVENESS	F. Sinatra	Capitol	55
69.	MY LITTLE ANGEL	Four Lads	Columbia	—
71.	ROCK RIGHT	G. Gibbs	Mercury	45
71.	WALK HAND IN HAND	T. Martin	Victor	91
73.	BLUE SUEDE SHOES	B. Bennett	King	63
74.	ON THE STREET WHERE YOU LIVE	V. Damone	Columbia	82
75.	TOO CLOSE FOR COMFORT	E. Gorme	ABC-Paramount	73
76.	TUTTI FRUTTI	P. Boone	Dot	59
77.	THEME FROM "THE THREE PENNY OPERA" (MORITAT)	B. Vaughn	Dot	80
78.	HI LILI HI LO	D. Hyman	M-G-M	88
78.	WINNER TAKE ALL	Platters	Mercury	66
80.	THEME FROM "THE THREE PENNY OPERA" (MORITAT)	L. Welk	Coral	61
81.	MAIN TITLE ("MAN WITH THE GOLDEN ARM")	L. Elgart	Columbia	78
81.	ANGEL PIE	P. King	Columbia	—
83.	I'M IN LOVE AGAIN	F. Domino	Imperial	—
84.	FOREVER, DARLING	Ames Brothers	Victor	60
84.	LITTLE GIRL OF MINE	Cleftones	Gee	—
86.	MEMORIES ARE MADE OF THIS	D. Martin	Capitol	45
87.	LOVELY LIES	Manhattan Brothers	London	90
88.	SLIPPIN' AND SLIDIN'	Little Richard	Specialty	81
89.	LIPSTICK, CANDY AND RUBBER-SOLED SHOES	J. La Rosa	Victor	64
89.	THEME FROM "THE THREE PENNY OPERA" (MORITAT)	L. Paul & M. Ford	Capitol	95
91.	TO YOU, MY LOVE	G. Shaw	Decca	70
92.	ELEVENTH HOUR MELODY	L. Busch	Capitol	74
93.	ELOISE	K. Thompson	Cadence	69
94.	I COULD HAVE DANCED ALL NIGHT	D. Shore	Victor	—
95.	MY BLUE HEAVEN	F. Domino	Imperial	—
96.	WE ALL NEED LOVE	P. Faith	Columbia	94
97.	JUST AS LONG AS I'M WITH YOU	P. Boone	Dot	—
98.	I WOKE UP CRYING	J. James	M-G-M	—
99.	LULLABY OF BIRDLAND	Blue Stars	Mercury	92
100.	BEYOND THE SEA	R. Williams	Kapp	68

CAUTION TO DEALERS AND JUKE BOX OPERATORS

The Billboard's Top 100 is NOT designed to provide tested information for buying purposes. This function is most reliably served by other regular weekly features: Best Sellers in Stores, Most Played in Juke Boxes, Coming Up Strong and Best Buys.

• Best Sellers in Stores

For survey week ending April 25

RECORDS are ranked in order of their current national selling importance at the retail level, as determined by The Billboard's weekly survey of the top volume dealers in every important market area. When significant action is reported on both sides of a record, points are combined to determine position on the chart. In such a case, both sides are listed in bold type, the leading side on top.

This Week		Last Week	Weeks on Chart
1.	**HEARTBREAK HOTEL** (BMI)—E. Presley I Was the One (BMI)—Vic 20-6420	1	9
2.	**HOT DIGGITY** (ASCAP)—P. Como **JUKE BOX BABY** (ASCAP)—Vic 20-6427	2	9
3.	**POOR PEOPLE OF PARIS** (ASCAP)—L. Baxter Theme From Helen of Troy (ASCAP)—Cap 3336	3	12
4.	**BLUE SUEDE SHOES** (BMI)—C. Perkins Honey, Don't (BMI)—Sun 234	4	9
5.	**MAGIC TOUCH** (BMI)—Platters Winner Take All (ASCAP)—Mercury 70819	9	6
6.	**MOONGLOW AND THEME FROM "PICNIC"** (ASCAP)—M. Stoloff Theme From "Picnic" (ASCAP)—Dec 29888	7	3
7.	**WHY DO FOOLS FALL IN LOVE?** (BMI)—Teen-Agers Please Be Mine (BMI)—Gee 1002	6	12
8.	**LISBON ANTIGUA** (ASCAP)—N. Riddle Robin Hood (ASCAP)—Cap 3287	5	19
9.	**A TEAR FELL** (BMI)—T. Brewer **BO WEEVIL** (BMI)—Coral 61590	10	10
10.	**ROCK ISLAND LINE** (BMI)—L. Donegan John Henry (BMI)—London 1650	9	6
11.	**MOONGLOW AND THEME FROM "PICNIC"** (ASCAP)—G. Cates Rio Batucada (ASCAP)—Coral 61618	17	3
12.	**I'LL BE HOME** (BMI)—P. Boone Tutti Frutti (BMI)—Dot 15443	11	13
13.	**LONG, TALL SALLY** (BMI)—Little Richard Slippin' and Slidin' (BMI)—Specialty 572	12	5
14.	**IVORY TOWER** (ASCAP)—C. Carr Please, Please Believe Me (ASCAP)—Fraternity 734	14	4
15.	**STANDING ON THE CORNER** (ASCAP)—Four Lads **MY LITTLE ANGEL** (BMI)—Col 40674	22	2
16.	**NO, NOT MUCH** (ASCAP)—Four Lads I'll Never Know (BMI)—Col 40629	13	15
17.	**MAIN TITLE (MAN WITH THE GOLDEN ARM)**—R. Maltby Heart of Paris (ASCAP)—Vik 0196	15	6
17.	**IVORY TOWER** (ASCAP)—O. Williams In Paradise (BMI)—De Luxe 6093	19	4
19.	**MAIN TITLE (MAN WITH THE GOLDEN ARM)**—E. Bernstein Clark Street (ASCAP)—Dec 29869	16	5
20.	**R-O-C-K** (ASCAP)—B. Haley **SAINTS ROCK AND ROLL** (ASCAP)—Dec 29870	24	5
21.	**HAPPY WHISTLER** (ASCAP)—D. Robertson You're Free to Go (ASCAP)—Cap 3391	—	1
22.	**I'M IN LOVE AGAIN** (BMI)—F. Domino **MY BLUE HEAVEN** (ASCAP)—Imperial 964	—	1
23.	**WAYWARD WIND** (BMI)—G. Grant No More Than Forever (ASCAP)—Era 1013	—	1
23.	**CAN YOU FIND IT IN YOUR HEART?** (ASCAP)—T. Bennett Forget Her (ASCAP)—Col 49667	—	1
25.	**EDDIE, MY LOVE** (BMI)—Fontane Sisters Yum Yum (BMI)—Dot 15450	21	6

• Most Played in Juke Boxes

For survey week ending April 25

RECORDS are ranked in order of the greatest number of plays in juke boxes thruout the country, as determined by The Billboard's weekly survey of the nation's juke box operators. When significant play is reported on both sides of a record, points are combined to determine position on the chart. In such a case, both sides are listed in bold type, the leading side on top.

This Week		Last Week	Weeks on Chart
1.	**HEARTBREAK HOTEL** (BMI)—E. Presley **I WAS THE ONE** (BMI)—Vic 20-6420	3	6
2.	**HOT DIGGITY** (BMI)—P. Como **JUKE BOX BABY** (BMI)—Vic 20-6427	2	7
3.	**POOR PEOPLE OF PARIS** (ASCAP)—L. Baxter Theme From "Helen of Troy" (ASCAP)—Cap 3336	1	11
4.	**BLUE SUEDE SHOES** (BMI)—C. Perkins Honey, Don't (BMI)—Sun 234	6	7
5.	**I'LL BE HOME** (BMI)—P. Boone **TUTTI FRUTTI** (BMI)—Dot 15443	7	12
6.	**LISBON ANTIGUA** (ASCAP)—N. Riddle Robin Hood (ASCAP)—Cap 3287	4	14
7.	**A TEAR FELL** (BMI)—T. Brewer Bo Weevil (BMI)—Coral 61590	9	7
8.	**ROCK AND ROLL WALTZ** (BMI)—K. Starr I've Changed My Mind a Thousand Times (ASCAP)—Vic 20-6359	5	17
9.	**NO, NOT MUCH** (ASCAP)—Four Lads I'll Never Know (BMI)—Col 40629	8	12
10.	**MAGIC TOUCH** (ASCAP)—Platters Winner Take All (ASCAP)—Mercury 70819	13	4
11.	**WHY DO FOOLS FALL IN LOVE?** (BMI)—Teen-Agers Pleease Be Mine (BMI)—Gee 1002	10	10
12.	**EDDIE, MY LOVE** (BMI)—Fontane Sisters Yum, Yum (BMI)—Dot 15450	11	6
13.	**ROCK ISLAND LINE** (BMI)—L. Donegan John Henry (BMI)—London 1650	16	3
14.	**IVORY TOWER** (ASCAP)—C. Carr Please Believe Me (ASCAP)—Fraternity 734	—	1
15.	**LONG, TALL SALLY** (BMI)—P. Boone Any Place in Heaven (ASCAP)—Dot 15457	—	1
16.	**WHY DO FOOLS FALL IN LOVE?** (BMI)—G. Storm I Walk Alone (BMI)—Dot 15448	14	9
17.	**R-O-C-K** (ASCAP)—B. Haley **SAINTS ROCK AND ROLL** (ASCAP)—Dec 29870	—	1
18.	**GREAT PRETENDER** (ASCAP)—Platters I'm Just a Dancing Partner (ASCAP)—Mercury 70753	12	18
19.	**MAIN TITLE ("MAN WITH THE GOLDEN ARM")** (ASCAP)—R. Maltby Heart of Paris (ASCAP)—Vik 0196	19	2
19.	**WHY DO FOOLS FALL IN LOVE?** (BMI)—Diamonds You, Baby, You (BMI)—Mercury 70790	—	1

• Best Selling Sheet Music

Tunes are ranked in order of their current national selling importance at the sheet music jobber level.

This Week		Last Week	Weeks on Chart
1.	**Poor People of Paris** (Connelly)	1	11
2.	**Hot Diggity** (Roncom)	2	8
3.	**Theme From "The Three Penny Opera" (Moritat)** (Harms)	5	11
4.	**Blue Suede Shoes** (Hi Lo)	4	4
5.	**Rock and Roll Waltz** (Sheldon)	3	16
6.	**Lisbon Antigua** (Southern)	6	16
7.	**Mr. Wonderful** (Laurel)	7	6
8.	**Heartbreak Hotel** (Tree)	8	3
9.	**Ivory Tower** (E. H. Morris)	14	2
10.	**He** (Avas)	9	32
11.	**No, Not Much** (Beaver)	10	12
11.	**A Tear Fell** (Progressive)	11	2
13.	**Rock Island Line** (Hollis)	12	2
14.	**On the Street Where You Live** (Chappell)	—	1
14.	**Why Do Fools Fall in Love?** (Patricia)	—	8

• Most Played by Jockeys

For survey week ending April 25

SIDES are ranked in order of the greatest number of plays on disk jockey radio shows thruout the country. Results are based on The Billboard's weekly survey among the nation's disk jockeys. The reverse side of each record is also listed.

This Week		Last Week	Weeks on Chart
1.	**HOT DIGGITY** (ASCAP)—P. Como Juke Box Baby (BMI)—Vic 20-6427	2	8
2.	**HEARTBREAK HOTEL** (BMI)—E. Presley I Was the One (BMI)—Vic 20-6420	3	9
3.	**POOR PEOPLE OF PARIS** (ASCAP)—L. Baxter Theme From "Helen of Troy" (ASCAP)—Cap 3336	1	12
4.	**NO, NOT MUCH** (ASCAP)—Four Lads I'll Never Know (BMI)—Col 40629	4	14
5.	**BLUE SUEDE SHOES** (BMI)—C. Perkins Honey, Don't (BMI)—Sun 234	6	7
6.	**MAGIC TOUCH** (BMI)—Platters Winner Take All (ASCAP)—Mercury 70819	8	4
7.	**MOONGLOW AND THEME FROM "PICNIC"** (ASCAP)—M. Stoloff Theme From "Picnic" (ASCAP)—Dec 29888	—	1
8.	**LISBON ANTIGUA** (ASCAP) N. Riddle Robin Hood (ASCAP)—Cap 3287	5	18
9.	**I'LL BE HOME** (BMI)—P. Boone Tutti Frutti (BMI)—Dot 15443	7	13
10.	**ROCK ISLAND LINE** (BMI)—L. Donegan John Henry (BMI)—London 1650	10	4
11.	**A TEAR FELL** (BMI)—T. Brewer Bo Weevil (BMI)—Coral 61590	9	7
12.	**IVORY TOWER** (ASCAP)—C. Carr Please, Please, Believe Me (ASCAP)—Fraternity 734	15	2
13.	**IVORY TOWER** (ASCAP)—O. Williams In Paradise (BMI)—DeLuxe 6093	16	2
14.	**MOONGLOW AND THEME FROM "PICNIC"** (ASCAP)—M. Stololff Theme From "Picnic" (ASCAP)—Dec 29888	14	3
14.	**MOONGLOW AND THEME FROM "PICNIC"** (ASCAP)—G. Gates Rio Batucada (ASCAP)—Coral 61618	18	3
16.	**WHY DO FOOLS FALL IN LOVE?** Teen-Agers Please Be Mine (BMI)—Gee 1002	11	9
16.	**LONG TALL SALLY** (BMI)—Little Richard Slippin' and Slidin' (BMI)—Specialty 572	—	1
18.	**STANDING ON THE CORNER** (ASCAP)—Four Lads My Little Angel (BMI)—Col 40674	—	1
19.	**WHY DO FOOLS FALL IN LOVE?** (BMI)—Diamonds You, Baby, You (BMI)—Mercury 70790	12	7
20.	**HAPPY WHISTLER** (ASCAP)—D. Robertson You're Free to Go (ASCAP)—Cap 3391	—	1
21.	**WHY DO FOOLS FALL IN LOVE?** (BMI)—G. Storm I Walk Alone (BMI)—Dot 15448	19	7
22.	**EDDIE, MY LOVE** (BMI)—Chordettes Whistling Willie (ASCAP)—Cadence 1084	—	6
23.	**MR. WONDERFUL** (ASCAP)—P. Lee Crazy in the Heart—Dec 29834	22	7
24.	**MAIN TITLE ("MAN WITH THE GOLDEN ARM")** (ASCAP)—R. Maltby Heart of Paris (ASCAP)—Vik 0196	20	2
25.	**BLUE SUEDE SHOES**—E. Presley Vic EPA-747; EPB-1254	24	2

THE TOP 100

For survey week ending April 25

A list of the Top 100 **RECORD SIDES** in the nation according to a **COMBINED TABULATION** of Dealer, Disk Jockey and Juke Box Operator replies to The Billboard's weekly popular record Best Seller and Most Played surveys. Its purpose is to provide Disk Jockeys with additional programming material and to give trade exposure to NEWER records just beginning to show action in the field.

Pos.	Song	Artist	Label	Last Week
1.	HEARTBREAK HOTEL	E. Presley	Victor	2
2.	HOT DIGGITY	P. Como	Victor	3
3.	POOR PEOPLE OF PARIS	L. Baxter	Capitol	1
4.	BLUE SUEDE SHOES	C. Perkins	Sun	5
5.	LISBON ANTIGUA	N. Riddle	Capitol	4
5.	MAGIC TOUCH	Platters	Mercury	9
7.	A TEAR FELL	T. Brewer	Coral	9
8.	NO, NOT MUCH	Four Lads	Columbia	6
9.	I'LL BE HOME	P. Boone	Dot	7
10.	ROCK ISLAND LINE	L. Donegan	London	12
11.	WHY DO FOOLS FALL IN LOVE?	Teen-Agers	Gee	8
12.	IVORY TOWER	C. Carr	Fraternity	19
13.	MOONGLOW AND THEME FROM "PICNIC"	M. Stoloff	Decca	21
14.	IVORY TOWER	O. Williams	De Luxe	18
14.	LONG, TALL SALLY	Little Richard	Specialty	20
16.	MOONGLOW AND THEME FROM "PICNIC"	G. Cates	Coral	35
17.	MAIN TITLE ("MAN WITH THE GOLDEN ARM")	R. Maltby	Vik	14
17.	ROCK AND ROLL WALTZ	K. Starr	Victor	11
19.	EDDIE MY LOVE	Fontane Sisters	Dot	14
20.	WHY DO FOOLS FALL IN LOVE?	G. Storm	Dot	16
21.	JUKE BOX BABY	P. Como	Victor	13
22.	WHY DO FOOLS FALL IN LOVE?	Diamonds	Mercury	17
23.	LONG, TALL SALLY	P. Boone	Dot	31
24.	BLUE SUEDE SHOES	E. Presley	Victor	25
25.	HAPPY WHISTLER	D. Robertson	Capitol	51
26.	IVORY TOWER	G. Storm	Dot	46
27.	MR. WONDERFUL	P. Lee	Decca	28
28.	EDDIE, MY LOVE	Chordettes	Cadence	33
28.	MAIN TITLE MOLLY-O ("MAN WITH THE GOLDEN ARM")	D. Jacobs	Coral	26
30.	STANDING ON THE CORNER	Four Lads	Columbia	39
31.	R-O-C-K	B. Haley	Decca	44
32.	I WAS THE ONE	E. Presley	Victor	23
33.	WILD CHERRY	D. Cherry	Columbia	29
34.	BO WEEVIL	T. Brewer	Coral	24
35.	THEME FROM "THE THREE PENNY OPERA" (MORITAT)	D. Hyman	M-G-M	22
35.	TOO YOUNG TO GO STEADY	Nat (King) Cole	Capitol	35
37.	SEE YOU LATER, ALLIGATOR	B. Haley	Decca	35
38.	MAIN TITLE ("MAN WITH THE GOLDEN ARM")	E. Bernstein	Decca	32
39.	LOVELY ONE	Four Voices	Columbia	30
40.	TO YOU, MY LOVE	N. Noble	Mercury	42
41.	WITHOUT YOU	E. Fisher	Victor	44
42.	I'M IN LOVE AGAIN	F. Domino	Imperial	83
43.	POOR PEOPLE OF PARIS	R. Morgan	Decca	43
44.	I WANT YOU TO BE MY GIRL	Teen-Agers	Gee	66
44.	INNAMORATA	D. Martin	Capitol	39
46.	EDDIE, MY LOVE	Teen Queens	RPM	34
47.	CAN YOU FIND IT IN YOUR HEART?	T. Bennett	Columbia	52
47.	CHURCH BELLS MAY RING	Diamonds	Mercury	41
47.	GREAT PRETENDER	Platters	Mercury	27
50.	HELD FOR QUESTIONING	R. Draper	Mercury	63
50.	PORT-AU-PRINCE	N. Riddle	Capitol	49
50.	SAINTS ROCK AND ROLL	B. Haley	Decca	48
50.	WAYWARD WIND	G. Grant	Era	56
54.	SLIPPIN' AND SLIDIN'	Little Richard	Specialty	88
55.	LOOK HOMEWARD, ANGEL	Four Esquires	Epic	—
56.	MAIN TITLE ("MAN WITH THE GOLDEN ARM")	L. Elgart	Columbia	81
57.	WALK HAND IN HAND	A. Williams	Cadence	—
58.	MR. WONDERFUL	S. Vaughan	Mercury	64
58.	TOO CLOSE FOR COMFORT	E. Gorme	ABC-Paramount	75
60.	CRAZY TITLE PALACE	B. Williams	Coral	53
61.	LITTLE GIRL OF MINE	Cleftones	Gee	84
62.	WALK HAND IN HAND	T. Martin	Victor	71
63.	MY LITTLE ANGEL	Four Lads	Columbia	69
64.	ON THE STREET WHERE YOU LIVE	V. Damone	Columbia	74
64.	ROCK ISLAND LINE	D. Cornell	Coral	59
64.	TO LOVE AGAIN	Four Aces	Decca	—
67.	NO OTHER ONE	E. Fisher	Victor	67
68.	MAIN TITLE ("MAN WITH THE GOLDEN ARM")	B. May	Capitol	49
69.	DELILAH JONES	McGuire Sisters	Coral	—
69.	TUTTI FRUTTI	P. Boone	Dot	76
71.	ROCK RIGHT	G. Gibbs	Mercury	71
72.	LISBON ANTIGUA	M. Miller	Columbia	56
73.	WINNER TAKE ALL	Platters	Mercury	78
74.	FLOWERS MEAN FORGIVENESS	F. Sinatra	Capitol	69
75.	MR. WONDERFUL	T. King	Victor	65
76.	IT ONLY HURTS FOR A LITTLE WHILE	Ames Brothers	Victor	—
76.	MEMORIES ARE MADE OF THIS	D. Martin	Capitol	86
78.	ROCK AND ROLL WEDDING	S. Gale	Victor	—
79.	FOREVER DARLING	Ames Brothers	Victor	84
79.	MY BLUE HEAVEN	F. Domino	Imperial	95
81.	INNAMORATA	J. Vale	Columbia	38
82.	IN A LITTLE SPANISH TOWN	Bing Crosby	Decca	54
83.	I WOKE UP CRYING	J. James	M-G-M	98
84.	CHURCH BELLS MAY RING	Willows	Melba	67
85.	JUST AS LONG AS I'M WITH YOU	P. Boone	Dot	97
86.	ELEVENTH HOUR MELODY	L. Busch	Capitol	92
87.	OUR LOVE AFFAIR	T. Charles	Decca	59
88.	NEVER LET ME GO	Nat (King) Cole	Capitol	—
88.	THEME FROM "THE THREE PENNY OPERA" (MACK THE KNIFE)	L. Armstrong	Columbia	56
90.	A LITTLE LONG CAN GO A LONG, LONG WAY	Dream Weavers	Decca	—
90.	BLUE SUEDE SHOES	B. Bennett	King	73
90.	ELEVENTH HOUR MELODY	A. Hibbler	Decca	62
93.	HI LILI HI LO	D. Hyman	M-G-M	78
94.	I COULD HAVE DANCED ALL NIGHT	D. Shore	Victor	94
94.	MY FIRST FORMAL GOWN	P. Page	Mercury	—
96.	POOR PEOPLE OF PARIS (JEAN'S SONG)	C. Atkins	Victor	—
97.	MAIN TITLE ("MAN WITH THE GOLDEN ARM")	B. Morrow	Wing	—
98.	BO WEEVIL	F. Domino	Imperial	—
99.	IF YOU CAN DREAM	Four Aces	Decca	—
100.	PICNIC	McGuire Sisters	Coral	—
100.	JOEY, JOEY, JOEY	P. Lee	Decca	—

CAUTION TO DEALERS AND JUKE BOX OPERATORS

The Billboard's Top 100 is NOT designed to provide tested information for buying purposes. This function is most reliably served by other regular weekly features: Best Sellers in Stores, Most Played in Juke Boxes, Coming Up Strong and Best Buys.

• Best Sellers in Stores

For survey week ending May 2

RECORDS are ranked in order of their current national selling importance at the retail level, as determined by The Billboard's weekly survey of the top volume dealers in every important market area. When significant action is reported on both sides of a record, points are combined to determine position on the chart. In such a case, both sides are listed in bold type, the leading side on top.

This Week		Last Week	Weeks on Chart
1.	**HEARTBREAK HOTEL** (BMI)—E. Presley I Was the One (BMI)—Vic 20-6420	1	10
2.	**HOT DIGGITY** (ASCAP)—P. Como **JUKE BOX BABY** (ASCAP)—Vic 20-6427	2	10
3.	**BLUE SUEDE SHOES** (BMI)—C. Perkins Honey, Don't (BMI)—Sun 234	4	10
4.	**MOONGLOW AND THE THEME FROM "PICNIC"** (ASCAP)—M. Stoloff Theme From "Picnic" (ASCAP)—Dec 29888	6	4
5.	**POOR PEOPLE OF PARIS** (ASCAP)—L. Baxter Theme From "Helen of Troy" (ASCAP)—Cap 3336	3	13
6.	**LONG, TALL SALLY** (BMI)—Little Richard **SLIPPIN' AND SLIDIN'** (BMI)—Specialty 572	13	6
7.	**MAGIC TOUCH** (BMI)—Platters Winner Take All (ASCAP)—Mercury 70819	5	7
8.	**MOONGLOW AND THE THEME FROM "PICNIC"** (ASCAP)—G. Cates Rio Batucada (ASCAP)—Coral 61618	11	4
9.	**WHY DO FOOLS FALL IN LOVE?** (BMI)—Teen-Agers Please Be Mine, (BMI)—Gee 1002	7	13
10.	**IVORY TOWER** (ASCAP)—C. Carr Please, Please, Believe Me (ASCAP)—Fraternity 734	14	5
11.	**A TEAR FELL** (BMI)—T. Brewer **BO WEEVIL** (BMI)—Coral 61590	9	11
12.	**LISBON ANTIGUA** (ASCAP)—N. Riddle Robin Hood (ASCAP)—Cap 3287	8	20
13.	**IVORY TOWER** (ASCAP)—O. Williams In Paradise (BMI)—De Luxe 6093	17	5
14.	**I'M IN LOVE AGAIN** (BMI)—F. Domino **MY BLUE HEAVEN** (ASCAP)—Imperial 964	22	2
15.	**ROCK ISLAND LINE** (BMI)—L. Donegan John Henry (BMI)—London 1650	10	7
16.	**WAYWARD WIND** (BMI)—G. Grant No More Than Forever (ASCAP)—Era 1013	23	2
17.	**STANDING ON THE CORNER** (ASCAP)—Four Lads **MY LITTLE ANGEL** (BMI)—Col 40674	15	3
18.	**HAPPY WHISTLER** (ASCAP)—D. Robertson You're Free to Go (ASCAP)—Dec 29870	21	2
19.	**MAIN TITLE (MAN WITH THE GOLDEN ARM)**—R. Maltby Heart of Paris (ASCAP)—Vik 0196	17	7
20.	**I'LL BE HOME** (BMI)—P. Boone Tutti Frutti (BMI)—Dot 15443	12	14
21.	**MAIN TITLE (MAN WITH THE GOLDEN ARM)** (ASCAP)—E. Bernstein Clark Street (ASCAP)—Dec 29869	19	6
22.	**I WANT YOU TO BE MY GIRL** (BMI)—Teen-Agers I'm Not a Know-It-All (ASCAP)—Gee 1012	—	1
23.	**LONG, TALL SALLY** (BMI)—P. Boone Any Place in Heaven (ASCAP)—Dot 15457	—	1
24.	**CHURCH BELLS MAY RING** (BMI)—Diamonds Little Girl of Mine (BMI)—Mercury 70835	—	1
25.	**CAN YOU FIND IT IN YOUR HEART?** (ASCAP)—T. Bennett Forget Her (ASCAP)—Col 49667	23	2

• Most Played in Juke Boxes

For survey week ending May 2

RECORDS are ranked in order of the greatest number of plays in juke boxes thruout the country, as determined by The Billboard's weekly survey of the nation's juke box operators. When significant play is reported on both sides of a record, points are combined to determine position on the chart. In such a case, both sides are listed in bold type, the leading side on top.

This Week		Last Week	Weeks on Chart
1.	**HEARTBREAK HOTEL** (BMI)—E. Presley I Was the One (BMI)—Vic 20-6420	1	7
2.	**POOR PEOPLE OF PARIS** (ASCAP)—L. Baxter Theme From "Helen of Troy" (ASCAP)—Cap 3336	3	12
3.	**BLUE SUEDE SHOES** (BMI)—C. Perkins Honey Don't (BMI)—Sun 234	4	8
4.	**HOT DIGGITY** (BMI)—P. Como **JUKE BOX BABY** (BMI)—Vic 20-6427	2	8
5.	**A TEAR FELL** (BMI)—T. Brewer **BO WEEVIL** (BMI)—Coral 61590	7	8
6.	**MAGIC TOUCH** (ASCAP)—Platters Winner Take All (ASCAP)—Mercury 70819	10	5
7.	**IVORY TOWER** (ASCAP)—C. Carr Please Believe Me (ASCAP)—Fraternity 734	14	2
8.	**I'LL BE HOME** (BMI)—P. Boone **TUTTI FRUTTI** (BMI)—Dot 15443	5	13
9.	**LISBON ANTIGUA** (ASCAP)—N. Riddle Robin Hood (ASCAP)—Cap 3287	6	15
9.	**ROCK AND ROLL WALTZ** (BMI)—K. Starr I've Changed My Mind a Thousand Times (ASCAP)—Vic 20-6359	8	18
11.	**WHY DO FOOLS FALL IN LOVE?** (BMI)—Teen-Agers Please Be Mine (BMI)—Gee 1002	11	11
12.	**NO, NOT MUCH** (ASCAP)—Four Lads I'll Never Know (ASCAP)—Col 40629	9	13
13.	**EDDIE, MY LOVE** (BMI)—Fontane Sisters Yum, Yum (BMI)—Dot 15450	12	7
14.	**LONG, TALL SALLY** (BMI)—P. Boone Any Place in Heaven (ASCAP)—Dot 15457	15	2
15.	**ROCK ISLAND LINE** (BMI)—L. Donegan John Henry (BMI)—London 1650	13	4
16.	**R-O-C-K** (ASCAP)—B. Haley **SAINTS ROCK AND ROLL** (ASCAP)—Dec 29870	17	2
17.	**LONG, TALL SALLY** (BMI)—Little Richard Slippin' and Slidin' (BMI)—Specialty 572	—	2
18.	**MOONGLOW AND THEME FROM "PICNIC"** (ASCAP)—G. Cates Rio Batucada (ASCAP)—Coral 61618	—	1
19.	**WHY DO FOOLS FALL IN LOVE?** (BMI)—G. Storm I Walk Alone—Dot 15448	16	10
19.	**GREAT PRETENDER** (ASCAP)—Platters I'm Just a Dancing Partner (ASCAP)—Mercury 70753	18	19
19.	**IVORY TOWER** (ASCAP)—O. Williams In Paradise (BMI)—DeLuxe 6093	—	1

• Best Selling Sheet Music

Tunes are ranked in order of their current national selling importance at the sheet music jobber level.

This Week		Last Week	Weeks on Chart
1.	**Hot Diggity** (Roncom)	2	9
2.	**Poor People of Paris** (Connelly)	1	12
3.	**Blue Suede Shoes** (Hi-Lo)	4	5
4.	**Lisbon Antigua** (Southern)	6	17
5.	**Theme From "The Three Penny Opera"** (Moritat) (Harms)	3	12
6.	**Rock and Roll Waltz** (Sheldon)	5	17
7.	**Mr. Wonderful** (Laurel)	7	7
8.	**Ivory Tower** (E. H. Morris)	9	3
9.	**A Tear Fell** (Progressive)	11	3
10.	**Heartbreak Hotel** (Tree)	8	4
11.	**Walk Hand in Hand** (Republic)	—	1
12.	**He** (Avas)	10	33
13.	**No, Not Much** (Beaver)	11	13
14.	**Rock Island Line** (Hollis)	13	3
15.	**On the Street Where You Live** (Chappell)	14	2

• Most Played by Jockeys

For survey week ending May 2

SIDES are ranked in order of the greatest number of plays on disk jockey radio shows thruout the country. Results are based on The Billboard's weekly survey among the nation's disk jockeys. The reverse side of each record is also listed.

This Week		Last Week	Weeks on Chart
1.	**HEARTBREAK HOTEL** (BMI)—E. Presley I Was the One (BMI)—Vic 20-6420	2	10
2.	**HOT DIGGITY** (ASCAP)—P. Como Juke Box Baby (BMI)—Vic 20-6427	1	9
3.	**POOR PEOPLE OF PARIS** (ASCAP)—L. Baxter Theme From "Helen of Troy" (ASCAP)—Cap 3336	3	13
4.	**MOONGLOW AND THEME FROM "PICNIC"** (ASCAP)—M. Stoloff Theme From "Picnic" (ASCAP)—Dec 29888	7	4
5.	**MAGIC TOUCH** (BMI)—Platters Winner Take All (ASCAP)—Mercury 70819	6	5
6.	**BLUE SUEDE SHOES** (BMI)—C. Perkins Honey Don't (BMI)—Sun 234	5	8
7.	**MOONGLOW AND THEME FROM "PICNIC"** (ASCAP)—G. Cates Rio Batucada (ASCAP)—Coral 61618	14	4
8.	**LISBON ANTIGUA** (ASCAP) N. Riddle Robin Hood (ASCAP)—Cap 3287	8	19
9.	**NO, NOT MUCH** (ASCAP)—Four Lads I'll Never Know (BMI)—Col 40629	4	15
10.	**STANDING ON THE CORNER** (ASCAP)—Four Lads My Little Angel (BMI)—Col 40674	18	2
11.	**IVORY TOWER** (ASCAP)—O. Williams In Paradise (BMI)—DeLuxe 6093	13	3
12.	**IVORY TOWER** (ASCAP)—C. Carr Please, Please Believe Me (ASCAP)—Fraternity 734	12	3
13.	**IVORY TOWER** (ASCAP)—G. Storm I Ain't Gonna Worry (BMI)—Dot 15458	—	1
14.	**A TEAR FELL** (BMI)—T. Brewer Bo Weevil (BMI)—Coral 61590	11	8
15.	**ROCK ISLAND LINE** (BMI)—L. Donegan John Henry (BMI)—London 1650	10	5
16.	**HAPPY WHISTLER** (ASCAP)—D. Robertson You're Free to Go (ASCAP)—Cap 3391	20	2
17.	**I'LL BE HOME** (BMI)—P. Boone Tutti Frutti (BMI)—Dot 15443	9	14
18.	**WHY DO FOOLS FALL IN LOVE?** (BMI)—Teen-Agers Please Be Mine (BMI)—Gee 1002	16	10
19.	**WHY DO FOOLS FALL IN LOVE?** (BMI)—G. Storm I Walk Alone (BMI)—Dot 15448	21	8
20.	**WHY DO FOOLS FALL IN LOVE?** (BMI)—Diamonds You, Baby, You (BMI)—Mercury 70790	19	8
21.	**LONG, TALL SALLY** (BMI)—Little Richard Slippin' and Slidin' (BMI)—Specialty 572	16	2
22.	**MR. WONDERFUL** (ASCAP)—P. Lee Crazy in the Heart—Dec 29834	23	8
23.	**TOO YOUNG TO GO STEADY** (ASCAP)—Nat (King) Cole Never Let Me Go (ASCAP)—Cap 3390	—	2
24.	**WAYWARD WIND** (BMI)—G. Grant No More Than Forever (ASCAP)—Era 1013	—	1
*25.	**BLUE SUEDE SHOES**—E. Presley Vic EPA-747; EPB-1254	23	3

*This is an EP. However, action on this side is of sufficient strength to warrant the present rank on this chart.

THE TOP 100

For survey week ending May 2

A list of the Top 100 RECORD SIDES in the nation according to a COMBINED TABULATION of Dealer, Disk Jockey and Juke Box Operator replies to The Billboard's weekly popular record Best Seller and Most Played surveys. Its purpose is to provide Disk Jockeys with additional programming material and to give trade exposure to NEWER records just beginning to show action in the field.

Pos.	Song	Artist	Label	Last Week
1.	HEARTBREAK HOTEL	E. Presley	Victor	1
2.	HOT DIGGITY	P. Como	Victor	2
3.	POOR PEOPLE OF PARIS	L. Baxter	Capitol	3
4.	BLUE SUEDE SHOES	C. Perkins	Sun	4
5.	MAGIC TOUCH	Platters	Mercury	5
6.	LIBSON ANTIGUA	N. Riddle	Capitol	5
7.	IVORY TOWER	C. Carr	Fraternity	12
8.	MOONGLOW AND THEME FROM "PICNIC"	G. Cates	Coral	16
8.	MOONGLOW AND THEME FROM "PICNIC"	M. Stoloff	Decca	13
10.	A TEAR FELL	T. Brewer	Coral	7
11.	WHY DO FOOLS FALL IN LOVE?	Teen-Agers	Gee	11
12.	IVORY TOWER	Williams	DeLuxe	14
13.	LONG TALL SALLY	Little Richard	Specialty	14
13.	ROCK ISLAND LINE	L. Donegan	London	10
15.	I'LL BE HOME	P. Boone	Dot	9
16.	NO, NOT MUCH	Four Lads	Columbia	8
17.	HAPPY WHISTLER	D. Robertson	Capitol	25
18.	LONG, TALL SALLY	P. Boone	Dot	23
19.	MAIN TITLE (MAN WITH THE GOLDEN ARM")	R. Maltby	Vik	17
20.	IVORY TOWER	G. Storm	Dot	26
20.	WHY DO FOOLS FALL IN LOVE?	Diamonds	Mercury	22
22.	WHY DO FOOLS FALL IN LOVE?	G. Storm	Dot	20
23.	EDDIE, MY LOVE	Fontane Sisters	Dot	19
24.	JUKE BOX BABY	P. Como	Victor	21
25.	STANDING ON THE CORNER	Four Lads	Columbia	30
26.	I'M IN LOVE AGAIN	F. Domino	Imperial	42
27.	BLUE SUEDE SHOES	E. Presley	Victor	24
28.	ROCK AND ROLL WALTZ	K. Starr	Victor	17
28.	CAN YOU FIND IT IN YOUR HEART	T. Bennett	Columbia	47
30.	WAYWARD WIND	G. Grant	Era	50
31.	MAIN TITLE MOLLY-O ("MAN WITH GOLDEN ARM")	D. Jacobs	Coral	28
32.	MR. WONDERFUL	P. Lee	Decca	27
33.	WILD CHERRY	D. Cherry	Columbia	33
34.	MAIN TITLE ("MAN WITH THE GOLDEN ARM")	E. Bernstein	Decca	38
35.	R-O-C-K	B. Haley	Decca	31
36.	CHURCH BELLS MAY RING	Diamonds	Mercury	47
37.	BO WEEVIL	T .Brewer	Coral	34
38.	TOO YOUNG TO GO STEADY	Nat (King) Cole	Capitol	35
38.	I WANT YOU TO BE MY GIRL	Teen-Agers	Gee	44
40.	I WAS THE ONE	E. Presley	Victor	32
41.	THEME FROM "THE THREE PENNY OPERA" (MORITAT)	D. Hyman	M-G-M	35
42.	GRADUATION DAY	Four Freshmen	Capitol	—
43.	TO LOVE AGAIN	Four Aces	Decca	64
44.	PICNIC	McGuire Sisters	Coral	100
44.	SLIPPIN' AND SLIDIN'	Little Richard	Specialty	54
46.	MR. WONDERFUL	S. Vaughn	Mercury	58
47.	MY LITTLE ANGEL	Four Lads	Columbia	63
48.	IT ONLY HURTS FOR A LITTLE WHILE	Ames Brothers	Victor	77
49.	WALK HAND IN HAND	T. Martin	Victor	62
50.	TO YOU MY LOVE	N. Noble	Mercury	40
51.	PORT-AU-PRINCE	N. Riddle	Capitol	50
52.	ON THE STREET WHERE YOU LIVE	V. Damone	Columbia	64
53.	MAIN TITLE ("MAN WITH THE GOLDEN ARM")	B. May	Capitol	68
54.	EDDIE, MY LOVE	Teen Queens	RPM	46
54.	EDDIE, MY LOVE	Chordettes	Cadence	28
56.	GREAT PRETENDER	Platters	Mercury	47
57.	SAINTS ROCK AND ROLL	B. Haley	Decca	50
58.	SEE YOU LATER, ALLIGATOR	B. Haley	Decca	37
59.	WITHOUT YOU	E. Fisher	Victor	41
60.	INNAMORATA	D. Martin	Capitol	44
61.	POOR PEOPLE OF PARIS	R. Morgan	Decca	43
62.	MAIN TITLE ("MAN WITH THE GOLDEN ARM"	L. Elgart	Columbia	56
63.	HELD FOR QUESTIONING	R. Draper	Mercury	50
64.	LOVELY ONE	Four Voices	Columbia	39
65.	CORRINE, CORRINA	J. Turner	Atlantic	—
66.	WINNER TAKE ALL	Platters	Mercury	73
67.	LITTLE GIRL OF MINE	Cleftones	Gee	61
68.	POOR PEOPLE OF PARIS (JEAN'S SONG)	C. Atkins	Victor	96
69.	MY BLUE HEAVEN	F. Domino	Imperial	79
70.	NO OTHER ONE	E. Fisher	Victor	67
70.	TOO CLOSE FOR COMFORT	E. Gorme	ABC-Paramount	58
72.	POOR PEOPLE OF PARIS	L. Welk	Coral	—
73.	BLUE SUEDE SHOES	B. Bennett	King	90
74.	IN A LITTLE SPANISH TOWN	Bing Crosby	Decca	82
75.	CRAZY LITTLE PALACE	B. Williams	Coral	60
76.	JUST AS LONG AS I'M WITH YOU	P. Boone	Dot	85
76.	OUR LOVE AFFAIR	T. Charles	Decca	87
78.	ROCK ISLAND LINE	D. Cornell	Coral	64
79.	NEVER LET ME GO	Nat (King) Cole	Capitol	88
80.	FLOWERS MEAN FORGIVENESS	F. Sinatra	Capitol	74
81.	INNAMORATA	J. Vale	Columbia	81
81.	I COULD HAVE DANCED ALL NIGHT	S. Syms	Decca	—
83.	HI-LILI HI-LO	D. Hyman	M-G-M	93
84.	A LITTLE LOVE CAN GO A LONG, LONG WAY	Dream Weavers	Decca	90
84.	MONEY, HONEY	E. Presley	Victor	—
86.	ELEVENTH HOUR MELODY	A. Hibbler	Decca	90
86.	TUTTI FRUTTI	P. Boone	Dot	69
86.	GRADUATION DAY	Rover Boys	ABC-Paramount	—
89.	CHURCH BELLS MAY RING	Willows	Melba	84
90.	LOOK HOMEWARD, ANGEL	Four Esquires	London	55
91.	WALK HAND IN HAND	A. Williams	Cadence	57
92.	DELILAH JONES	McGuire Sisters	Coral	69
93.	MEMORIES ARE MADE OF THIS	D. Martin	Capitol	76
94.	JOEY, JOEY, JOEY	P. Lee	Decca	100
95.	KISS ME ANOTHER	G. Gibbs	Mercury	—
96.	I'VE GROWN ACCUSTOMED TO YOUR FACE	G. MacRae	Capitol	—
97.	ROCK AND ROLL WEDDING	S. Gale	Victor	78
98.	I COULD DANCE ALL NIGHT	D. Shore	Victor	94
98.	THEME FROM "THE THREE PENNY OPERA" (MACK THE KNIFE)	L. Armstrong	Columbia	88
98.	THEME FROM "THE THREE PENNY OPERA" (MORITAT)	R. Hayman-J. August	Mercury	—

CAUTION TO DEALERS AND JUKE BOX OPERATORS

The Billboard's Top 100 is NOT designed to provide tested information for buying purposes. This function is most reliably served by other regular weekly features: Best Sellers in Stores, Most Played in Juke Boxes, Coming Up Strong and Best Buys.

• Best Sellers in Stores

For survey week ending May 9

RECORDS are ranked in order of their current national selling importance at the retail level, as determined by The Billboard's weekly survey of the top volume dealers in every important market area. When significant action is reported on both sides of a record, points are combined to determine position on the chart. In such a case, both sides are listed in bold type, the leading side on top.

This Week		Last Week	Weeks on Chart
1.	HEARTBREAK HOTEL (BMI)—E. Presley I Was the One (BMI)—Vic 20-6420	1	11
2.	HOT DIGGITY (ASCAP)—P. Como JUKE BOX BABY (ASCAP)—Vic 20-6427	2	11
3.	BLUE SUEDE SHOES (BMI)—C. Perkins Honey, Don't (BMI)—Sun 234	3	11
4.	MOONGLOW AND THEME FROM PICNIC (ASCAP)—M. Stoloff Theme From "Picnic" (ASCAP)—Dec 29888	4	5
5.	POOR PEOPLE OF PARIS (ASCAP)—L. Baxter Theme From Helen of Troy (ASCAP)—Cap 3336	5	14
6.	MAGIC TOUCH (BMI)—Platters Winner Take All (ASCAP)—Mercury 70819	7	8
7.	MOONGLOW AND THEME FROM PICNIC (ASCAP)—G. Cates Rio Batucada (ASCAP)—Coral 61618	8	5
8.	IVORY TOWER (ASCAP)—C. Carr Please Believe Me (ASCAP)—Fraternity 734	10	6
9.	WHY DO FOOLS FALL IN LOVE? (BMI)—Teen-Agers Please Be Mine (BMI)—Gee 1002	9	14
10.	STANDING ON THE CORNER (ASCAP)—Four Lads MY LITTLE ANGEL (BMI)—Col 40674	17	4
11.	WAYWARD WIND (BMI)—G. Grant No More Than Forever (ASCAP)—Era 1013	16	3
12.	I'M IN LOVE AGAIN (BMI)—F. Domino MY BLUE HEAVEN (ASCAP)—Imperial 964	14	3
13.	I WANT YOU TO BE MY GIRL (BMI)—Teen-Agers I'm Not a Know-It-All (ASCAP)—Gee 1012	22	2
14.	ROCK ISLAND LINE (BMI)—L. Donegan John Henry (BMI)—London 1650	15	8
15.	LONG, TALL SALLY (BMI)—Little Richard Slippin' and Slidin' (BMI)—Specialty 572	6	7
16.	HAPPY WHISTLER (ASCAP)—D. Robertson You're Free to Go (ASCAP)—Dec 29870	18	3
17.	LISBON ANTIGUA (ASCAP)—N. Riddle Robin Hood (ASCAP)—Cap 3287	12	21
18.	A TEAR FELL (BMI)—T. Brewer Bo Weevil (BMI)—Coral 61590	11	12
19.	IVORY TOWER (ASCAP)—O. Williams In Paradise (BMI)—DeLuxe 6093	13	6
20.	MAIN TITLE ("MAN WITH THE GOLDEN ARM") (ASCAP)—E. Bernstein Clark Street (ASCAP)—Dec 29869	21	7
21.	I'LL BE HOME (BMI)—P. Boone Tutti Frutti (BMI)—Dot 15443	20	15
22.	MAIN TITLE ("MAN WITH THE GOLDEN ARM")—R. Maltby Heart of Paris (ASCAP)—Vik 0196	19	8
23.	CHURCH BELLS MAY RING (BMI)—Diamonds Little Girl of Mine (BMI)—Mercury 70835	24	2
24.	CAN YOU FIND IT IN YOUR HEART? (ASCAP)—T. Bennett Forget Her (ASCAP)—Col 49667	25	3
25.	LONG, TALL SALLY (BMI)—P. Boone Any Place in Heaven (ASCAP)—Dot 15457	23	2

• Most Played in Juke Boxes

For survey week ending May 9

RECORDS are ranked in order of the greatest number of plays in juke boxes thruout the country, as determined by The Billboard's weekly survey of the nation's juke box operators. When significant play is reported on both sides of a record, points are combined to determine position on the chart. In such a case, both sides are listed in bold type, the leading side on top.

This Week		Last Week	Weeks on Chart
1.	HEARTBREAK HOTEL (BMI)—E. Presley I Was the One (BMI)—Vic 20-6420	1	8
2.	BLUE SUEDE SHOES (BMI)—C. Perkins Honey, Don't (BMI)—Sun 234	3	9
3.	POOR PEOPLE OF PARIS (ASCAP)—L. Baxter Theme From "Helen of Troy" (ASCAP)—Cap 3336	2	13
4.	HOT DIGGITY (BMI)—P. Como JUKE BOX BABY (BMI)—Vic 20-6427	4	9
5.	A TEAR FELL (BMI)—T. Brewer Bo Weevil (BMI)—Coral 61590	5	9
6.	MAGIC TOUCH (ASCAP)—Platters Winner Take All (ASCAP)—Mercury 70819	6	6
7.	IVORY TOWER (ASCAP)—C. Carr Please Believe Me (ASCAP)—Fraternity 734	7	3
8.	WHY DO FOOLS FALL IN LOVE? (BMI)—Teen-Agers Please Be Mine (BMI)—Gee 1002	11	12
9.	I'LL BE HOME (BMI)—P. Boone Tutti Frutti (BMI)—Dot 15443	8	14
10.	LISBON ANTIGUA (ASCAP)—N. Riddle Robin Hood (ASCAP)—Cap 3287	9	16
11.	MOONGLOW AND THEME FROM "PICNIC" (ASCAP)—G. Gates Rio Batucada (ASCAP)—Coral 61618	18	2
12.	LONG, TALL SALLY (BMI)—P. Boone Any Place in Heaven (ASCAP)—Dot 15457	14	3
13.	NO, NOT MUCH (ASCAP)—Four Lads I'll Never Know (BMI)—Col 40629	12	14
14.	ROCK AND ROLL WALTZ (BMI)—K. Starr I've Changed My Mind a Thousand Times (ASCAP)—Vic 20-6359	9	19
15.	EDDIE, MY LOVE (BMI)—Fontane Sisters Yum Yum (BMI)—Dot 15450	13	8
16.	IVORY TOWER (ASCAP)—G. Storm I Ain't Gonna Worry (BMI)—Dot 15458	—	1
17.	ROCK ISLAND LINE (BMI)—L. Donegan John Henry (BMI)—London 1650	15	5
17	MOONGLOW AND THEME FROM "PICNIC" (ASCAP)—M. Stoloff Theme From "Picnic" (ASCAP)—Dec 29888	—	1
17.	I'M IN LOVE AGAIN (BMI)—F. Domino MY BLUE HEAVEN (ASCAP)—Imperial 964	—	1
20.	WHY DO FOOLS FALL IN LOVE? (BMI)—G. Storm I Walk Alone (BMI)—Dot 15448	19	11

• Best Selling Sheet Music

Tunes are ranked in order of their current national selling importance at the sheet music jobber level.

This Week		Last Week	Weeks on Chart
1.	**Hot Diggity** (Roncom)	1	10
2.	**Poor People of Paris** (Connelly)	2	13
3.	**Ivory Tower** (E. H. Morris)	8	4
4.	**Heartbreak Hotel** (Tree)	10	5
5.	**Rock and Roll Waltz** (Sheldon)	6	18
6.	**Blue Suede Shoes** (Hi-Lo)	3	6
7.	**Walk Hand in Hand** (Republic)	11	2
8.	**Moonglow** (Mills-Columbia Pictures)	—	1
9.	**Mr. Wonderful** (Laurel)	7	8
10.	**Picnic** (Shapiro-Bernstein)	—	1
11.	**A Tear Fell** (Progressive)	9	4
12.	**Theme From the "Three Penny Opera" (Moritat)** (Harms)	5	13
13.	**Lisbon Antigua** (Southern)	4	18
14.	**Standing On the Corner** (Frank)	—	1
15.	**He** (Avas)	12	34

• Most Played by Jockeys

For survey week ending May 9

SIDES are ranked in order of the greatest number of plays on disk jockey radio shows thruout the country. Results are based on The Billboard's weekly survey among the nation's disk jockeys. The reverse side of each record is also listed.

This Week		Last Week	Weeks on Chart
1.	HEARTBREAK HOTEL (BMI)—E. Presley I Was the One (BMI)—Vic 20-6420	1	11
2.	HOT DIGGITY (ASCAP)—P. Como Juke Box Baby (BMI)—Vic 20-6427	2	10
3.	POOR PEOPLE OF PARIS (ASCAP)—L. Baxter Theme From "Helen of Troy" (ASCAP—Cap 3336	3	14
4.	MOONGLOW AND THEME FROM "PICNIC" (ASCAP)—M. Stoloff Theme From "Picnic" (ASCAP)—Dec 29888	4	5
5.	MAGIC TOUCH (BMI)—Platters Winner Take All (ASCAP)—Mercury 70819	5	6
6.	IVORY TOWER (ASCAP)—G. Storm I Ain't Gonna Worry (BMI)—Dot 15458	13	2
7.	STANDING ON THE CORNER (ASCAP)—Four Lads My Little Angel (BMI)—Col 40674	10	3
8.	MOONGLOW AND THEME FROM "PICNIC" (ASCAP)—G. Cates Rio Batucada (ASCAP)—Coral 61618	7	5
9.	HAPPY WHISTLER (ASCAP)—D. Robertson You're Free to Go (ASCAP)—Cap 3391	16	3
10.	IVORY TOWER (ASCAP)—C. Carr Please Believe Me (ASCAP)—Fraternity 734	12	4
11.	IVORY TOWER (ASCAP)—O. Williams In Paradise (BMI)—DeLuxe 6093	11	4
12.	WAYWARD WIND (BMI)—G. Grant No More Than Forever (ASCAP)—Era 1013	24	2
13.	BLUE SUEDE SHOES (BMI)—C. Perkins Honey, Don't (BMI)—Sun 234	6	9
14.	LISBON ANTIGUA (ASCAP)—N. Riddle Robin Hood (ASCAP)—Cap 3287	8	20
15.	A TEAR FELL (BMI)—T. Brewer Bo Weevil (BMI)—Coral 61590	14	9
16.	MR. WONDERFUL (ASCAP) P. Lee Crazy in the Heart—Dec 29834	22	9
17.	NO, NOT MUCH (ASCAP)—Four Lads I'll Never Know (BMI)—Col 40629	9	16
18.	LONG, TALL SALLY (BMI)—Little Richard Slippin' and Slidin' (BMI)—Specialty 572	21	3
19.	I'M IN LOVE AGAIN (BMI)—F. Domino My Blue Heaven (ASCAP)—Imperial 5386	—	1
20.	I'LL BE HOME (BMI)—P. Boone Tutti Frutti (BMI)—Dot 15443	17	15
21.	ROCK ISLAND LINE (BMI)—L. Donegan John Henry (BMI)—London 1650	15	6
22.	I WAS THE ONE (BMI)—E. Presley Heartbreak Hotel (BMI)—Vic 20-6420	—	5
23.	WHY DO FOOLS FALL IN LOVE? (BMI)—Diamonds You, Baby You (BMI)—Mercury 70790	20	9
24.	TOO YOUNG TO GO STEADY (ASCAP)—Nat (King) Cole Never Let Me Go (ASCAP)—Cap 3390	23	3
25.	GRADUATION DAY (BMI)—Rover Boys I Hear Music (BMI)—ABC-Paramount 9700	—	1

VOX JOX

By JUNE BUNDY

DESERVING DEEJAYS: Disk jockeys, in search of a worthy cause with human interest appeal for their listeners, would be well advised to contact the Save the Children Federation, New York, a non-profit organization which helps underprivileged youngsters here and overseas. Bish Thompson, WGBF, Evansville, Ind., for instance, and his fans are currently sponsoring four Navajo Indian children. It all started a few years ago when Thompson plugged the Federation on the air and invited listeners to contribute to the cause. The audience responded with such enthusiasm that Thompson's listeners now support four "sons." The deejay corresponds with the youngsters and reads their letters on the air to the collective "family." Sponsoring a child under the Federation costs $96 a year, and provides money for clothes, school supplies, food and even a little spending money.

ROCK 'N' ROLL ANYBODY?: Controversy continues to swirl around rock and roll. This week WDOK, Cleveland, reported that in answer to its recent listeners poll on r.&r., 1,968 people voted against it, as compared to 564 in favor. The results, WDOK deejay-program director Norman Wain said, "will certainly influence future programming," both by himself and the station's other jocks, Bill Reid and Wayne Mack. . . . On the other hand, Barry Kaye, WJAS, Pittsburgh, recently conducted what is believed to be the first rock and roll radio telephone poll with considerably different results. During a two-hour air interview with Bill Haley, Kaye asked listeners to phone him and give their age, and state whether or not they liked rock and roll music. Out of a total 639 calls, 625 people voted "yes" and only nine "no." Average age of those voting "yes" was 32, while the average of those voting "no" was 26. Ages ranged from 7 to 82.

GIMMIX: Manhattan indie, WNEW, celebrated National Music Week (May 6-13) by presenting five unpublished songs — "which merit recognition as better examples of popular music" — on the station's daily noon to 1 p.m. recorded and live music show with Bill Harrington, Bill Williams, and Roy Ross' orchestra. The tunes were selected by a panel of judges, including artist and repertoire chiefs Mitch Miller and Joe Carlton, WNEW music Manager Al Trilling, BMI musical director Julie Stearns and Harrington and Ross. Efforts will be made by the station to have the winner's song recorded by a major disk artist. . . . Chicago disk jockeys are literally living up to their names these days. Every Tuesday evening of this month top jocks from the Chicago area are competing in a series of special harness races at Maywood Park, with winners of the heats scheduled to compete for top honors in the derby May 29. Racing spinners include Jim Mills, WIND; Dan Sorkin, WCFL; Bob Carpenter, WAAF; Steve Schickel (ex-Billboard scribe), WGN; Paul Saliner, WGN; Chuck Francisco, Dick Harley, WHFC; Jack Stilwill, WLS; Dick Elliott, WHFC; Spider Webb, WAIT; Magnificent Montague, WAAF; Jim Daris, WEDC; Jim Lounsbury, WGN; Tony Ford, WGES, and Bill O'Connor, WIND.

YESTERYEAR'S TOPS—

The nation's top tunes on records as reported in The Billboard

MAY 18, 1946

1. Laughing on the Outside (Crying on the Inside)
2. The Gypsy
3. Oh! What It Seemed to Be!
4. Shoo-Fly Pie and Apple Pan Dowdy
5. Prisoner of Love
6. I'm a Big Girl Now
7. They Say It's Wonderful
8. One-Zy, Two-Zy (I Love You-Zy)
9. Day by Day
10. You Won't Be Satisfied (Until You Break My Heart)
11. Seems Like Old Times
12. Full Moon and Empty Arms
13. Atlanta
14. Personality
15. Cement Mixer

MAY 19, 1951

1. Mocking Bird Hill
2. How High the Moon
3. On Top of Old Smoky
4. Too Young
5. If
6. Be My Love
7. I Apologize
8. Would I Love You?
9. Sparrow in the Tree Top
10. Beautiful Brown Eyes

Alexander Agency

● *Continued from page 13*

rick, the Lennie Hambro Quintet, Oscar Pettiford, Joe Venuto Trio, Charlie Mingus Jazz Workshop Quintet, Urbie Green Quartet and the Art-Farmer-Gigi Gryce Quintet.

Maxine Sullivan, who is essaying a comeback after several years out of the business, will begin her first booking on the Coast June 27. Millie Vernon formerly sang under the name of Pat Cameron. She has been inked by Storyville Records.

The demise of Universal's special jazz department, after only a couple of month's operation, has been attributed to the agency's inability to come up with real "leader" attractions in the field. On the other hand, the mushrooming of Alexander's jazz wing is credited to the fact that this office books both Benny Goodman and Count Basie.

Donegan Dates

● *Continued from page 14*

other "A Showcase of British Jazz." He is also talking up ace jazz trumpet man, Humphry Littleton, whom he hopes to bring over here for personal appearances this fall, in conjunction with the U.S. publication of Littleton's book "I Play as I Please," a best seller in England.

Meanwhile Manny Greenfield, who manages Donegan in the U.S., has arranged for the "Rock Island" warbler to appear on the Perry Como show Saturday (19). Donegan arrives here Wednesday (16) to rehearse for the NBC-TV show, then planes out to Cleveland Sunday (20) where he will guest on Bill Randle's local TV show. He opens at the Town and Country nitery here May 22 for two weeks, following which he plays a three-day (June 15, 16 and 17) run at a local Cleveland theater.

Altho Donegan's big U.S. hit was waxed for London, he will be ushered around to deejays, under the auspices of Mercury, since Donegan records for PYE-Nixa in England, and Mercury has a reciprocal distribution deal with Nixa under its new contract with the British firm. Donegan's first Mercury disk here—"Lost John" and "Stewball" — is currently riding high on the British best seller charts.

THE TOP 100

For survey week ending May 9

A list of the Top 100 **RECORD SIDES** in the nation according to a **COMBINED TABULATION** of Dealer, Disk Jockey and Juke Box Operator replies to The Billboard's weekly popular record Best Seller and Most Played surveys. Its purpose is to provide Disk Jockeys with additional programming material and to give trade exposure to NEWER records just beginning to show action in the field.

Pos.	Song	Artist	Label	Last Week
1.	HEARTBREAK HOTEL	E. Presley	Victor	1
2.	HOT DIGGITY	P. Como	Victor	2
3.	POOR PEOPLE OF PARIS	L. Baxter	Capitol	3
4.	MAGIC TOUCH	Platters	Mercury	5
5.	BLUE SUEDE SHOES	C. Perkins	Sun	4
6.	IVORY TOWER	C. Carr	Fraternity	7
7.	MOONGLOW AND THEME FROM "PICNIC"	G. Cates	Coral	8
7.	MOONGLOW AND THEME FROM "PICNIC"	M. Stoloff	Decca	8
9.	A TEAR FELL	T. Brewer	Coral	10
10.	LISBON ANTIGUA	N. Riddle	Capitol	6
11.	WHY DO FOOLS FALL IN LOVE?	Teen-Agers	Gee	11
12.	HAPPY WHISTLER	D. Robertson	Capitol	17
13.	ROCK ISLAND LINE	L. Donegan	London	13
14.	IVORY TOWER	O. Williams	De Luxe	12
15.	I'LL BE HOME	P. Boone	Dot	15
16.	IVORY TOWER	G. Storm	Dot	20
16.	LONG, TALL SALLY	Little Richard	Specialty	13
18.	WAYWARD WIND	G. Grant	Era	30
19.	STANDING ON THE CORNER	Four Lads	Columbia	25
20.	NO, NOT MUCH	Four Lads	Columbia	16
21.	I'M IN LOVE AGAIN	F. Domino	Imperial	26
21.	LONG, TALL SALLY	P. Boone	Dot	18
23.	MR. WONDERFUL	P. Leé	Decca	32
24.	CAN YOU FIND IT IN YOUR HEART?	T. Bennett	Columbia	28
25.	I WANT YOU TO BE MY GIRL	Teen-Agers	Gee	38
26.	CHURCH BELLS MAY RING	Diamonds	Mercury	36
26.	MAIN TITLE ("MAN WITH THE GOLDEN ARM")	R. Maltby	Vik	19
26.	PICNIC	McGuire Sisters	Coral	44
29.	WHY DO FOOLS FALL IN LOVE?	G. Storm	Dot	22
30.	WHY DO FOOLS FALL IN LOVE?	Diamonds	Mercury	20
31.	ROCK AND ROLL WALTZ	K. Starr	Victor	28
32.	IT ONLY HURTS FOR A LITTLE WHILE	Ames Brothers	Victor	48
33.	EDDIE, MY LOVE	Fontane Sisters	Dot	23
33.	LITTLE LOVE CAN GO A LONG WAY	Dream Weavers	Decca	84
35.	WILD CHERRY	D. Cherry	Columbia	33
36.	MAIN TITLE & MOLLY-O ("MAN WITH THE GOLDEN ARM")	D. Jacobs	Coral	31
37.	BLUE SUEDE SHOES	E. Presley	Victor	27
38.	MAIN TITLE ("MAN WITH THE GOLDEN ARM")	E. Bernstein	Decca	34
39.	R-O-C-K	B. Haley	Decca	35
40.	I WAS THE ONE	E. Presley	Victor	40
40.	MY BLUE HEAVEN	F. Domino	Imperial	69
42.	WALK HAND IN HAND	T. Martin	Victor	49
43.	MY LITTLE ANGEL	Four Lads	Columbia	47
43.	TOO YOUNG TO GO STEADY	Nat King Cole	Capitol	38
45.	GIRL IN MY DREAMS	Cliques	Modern	—
46.	ON THE STREET WHERE YOU LIVE	V. Damone	Columbia	52
47.	TO LOVE AGAIN	Four Aces	Decca	43
47.	BO WEEVIL	T. Brewer	Coral	37
49.	LOVELY ONE	Four Voices	Columbia	64
50.	JUKE BOX BABY	P. Como	Victor	24
51.	STANDING ON THE CORNER	D. Martin	Capitol	—
52.	THEME FROM "THE THREE PENNY OPERA" (MORITAT)	D. Hyman	M-G-M	41
53.	SLIPPIN' AND SLIDIN'	Little Richard	Specialty	44
54.	KISS ME ANOTHER	G. Gibbs	Mercury	95
54.	TOO CLOSE FOR COMFORT	E. Gorme	ABC-Paramount	70
56.	I COULD HAVE DANCED ALL NIGHT	S. Syms	Decca	81
57.	LITTLE GIRL OF MINE	Cleftone	Gee	67
58.	GRADUATION DAY	Four Freshmen	Capitol	42
59.	WITHOUT YOU	E. Fisher	Victor	59
60.	DELILAH JONES	McGuire Sisters	Coral	92
61.	PORTUGUESE WASHERWOMAN	J. (Fingers) Carr	Capitol	—
61.	PORT-AU-PRINCE	N. Riddle	Capitol	51
63.	CORRINE CORRINA	J. Turner	Atlantic	65
64.	TO YOU MY LOVE	N. Noble	Mercury	50
65.	SAINTS ROCK AND ROLL	B. Haley	Decca	57
65.	WINNER TAKE ALL	Platters	Mercury	66
67.	MR. WONDERFUL	S. Vaughan	Mercury	46
68.	TANGO OF THE DRUMS	L. Baxter	Capitol	—
68.	WALK HAND IN HAND	A. Williams	Cadence	91
70.	MAIN TITLE ("MAN WITH THE GOLDEN ARM")	B. May	Capitol	53
71.	POOR PEOPLE OF PARIS	R. Morgan	Decca	61
72.	INNAMORATA	D. Martin	Capitol	60
72.	I WOKE UP CRYING	J. James	M-G-M	—
74.	HELD FOR QUESTIONING	R. Draper	Mercury	63
74.	PICNIC	R. Marterie	Mercury	—
74.	WALK HAND IN HAND	D. Vaughan	Kapp	—
77.	ROVING GAMBLER	T. Ernie	Capitol	—
78.	BLUE SUEDE SHOES	B. Bennett	King	73
78.	CHURCH BELLS MAY RING	Willows	Melba	89
80.	MONEY HONEY	E. Presley	Victor	84
81.	EDDIE, MY LOVE	Chordettes	Cadence	54
82.	GREAT PRETENDER	Platters	Mercury	56
84.	ROCK ISLAND LINE	D. Cornell	Coral	78
85.	MAIN TITLE ("MAN WITH THE GOLDEN ARM")	L. Elgart	Columbia	62
85.	SEE YOU LATER, ALLIGATOR	B. Haley	Decca	58
87.	HOW LITTLE WE KNOW	F. Sinatra	Capitol	—
88.	INNAMORATA	J. Vale	Columbia	81
89.	MAIN TITLE ("MAN WITH THE GOLDEN ARM")	B. Morrow	Wing	—
90.	EDDIE, MY LOVE	Teen Queens	RPM	54
90.	JOEY, JOEY, JOEY	P. Lee	Decca	94
90.	NO OTHER ONE	E. Fisher	Victor	70
93.	THEME FROM "THE THREE PENNY OPERA" (MORITAT)	R. Hayman-J. August	Mercury	98
94.	MOCKING BIRD	Four Lads	Columbia	—
95.	FLOWERS MEAN FORGIVENESS	F. Sinatra	Capitol	80
96.	THEME FROM "THE THREE PENNY OPERA" (MACK THE KNIFE)	L. Armstrong	Columbia	98
97.	POOR PEOPLE OF PARIS	L. Welk	Coral	72
98.	IS THERE SOMEBODY ELSE?	Dream Weavers	Decca	—
99.	I COULD HAVE DANCED ALL NIGHT	R. Clooney	Columbia	—
100.	NEVER LET ME GO	Nat King Cole	Capitol	79

CAUTION TO DEALERS AND JUKE BOX OPERATORS

The Billboard's Top 100 is NOT designed to provide tested information for buying purposes. This function is most reliably served by other regular weekly features: Best Sellers in Stores, Most Played in Juke Boxes, Coming Up Strong and Best Buys.

• Best Sellers in Stores

For survey week ending May 16

RECORDS are ranked in order of their current national selling importance at the retail level, as determined by The Billboard's weekly survey of the top volume dealers in every important market area. When significant action is reported on both sides of a record, points are combined to determine position on the chart. In such a case, both sides are listed in bold type, the leading side on top.

This Week		Last Week	Weeks on Chart
1.	**HEARTBREAK HOTEL** (BMI)—E. Presley I Was the One (BMI)—Vic 20-6420	1	12
2.	**MOONGLOW AND THEME FROM "PICNIC"** (ASCAP)—M. Stoloff Theme From "Picnic" (ASCAP)—Dec 29888	4	6
3.	**HOT DIGGITY** (ASCAP)—P. Como Juke Box Baby (ASCAP)—Vic 20-6427	2	12
4.	**WAYWARD WIND** (BMI)—G. Grant No More Than Forever (ASCAP)—Era 1013	11	4
5.	**MOONGLOW AND THEME FROM "PICNIC"** (ASCAP)—G. Cates Rio Batucada (ASCAP)—Coral 61618	7	6
6.	**I'M IN LOVE AGAIN** (BMI)—F. Domino **MY BLUE HEAVEN** (ASCAP)—Imperial 964	12	4
7.	**IVORY TOWER** (ASCAP)—C. Carr Please Believe Me (ASCAP)—Fraternity 734	8	7
7.	**STANDING ON THE CORNER** (ASCAP)—Four Lads **MY LITTLE ANGEL** (BMI)—Col 40674	10	5
9.	**BLUE SUEDE SHOES** (BMI)—C. Perkins Honey, Don't (BMI)—Sun 234	3	12
10.	**MAGIC TOUCH** (BMI)—Platters Winner Take All (ASCAP)—Mercury 70819	6	9
11.	**POOR PEOPLE OF PARIS** (ASCAP)—L. Baxter Theme From "Helen of Troy" (ASCAP)—Cap 3336	5	15
12.	**HAPPY WHISTLER** (ASCAP)—D. Robertson You're Free to Go (ASCAP)—Dec 29870	16	4
13.	**LONG, TALL, SALLY** (BMI)—Little Richard Slippin' and Slidin' (BMI)—Specialty 572	15	8
14.	**CHURCH BELLS MAY RING** (BMI)—Diamonds Little Girl of Mine (BMI)—Mercury 70835	23	3
15.	**A TEAR FELL** (BMI)—T. Brewer Bo Weevil (BMI)—Coral 61590	18	13
16.	**I WANT YOU TO BE MY GIRL** (BMI)—Teen-Agers I'm Not a Know-It-All (ASCAP)—Gee 1012	13	3
17.	**WHY DO FOOLS FALL IN LOVE?** (BMI)—Teen-Agers Please Be Mine (BMI)—Gee 1002	9	15
18.	**ROCK ISLAND LINE** (BMI)—L. Donegan John Henry (BMI)—London 1650	14	9
18.	**PICNIC** (ASCAP)—McGuire Sisters Delilah Jones (ASCAP)—Coral 61627	—	1
20.	**IVORY TOWER** (ASCAP)—O. Williams In Paradise (BMI)—DeLuxe 6093	19	7
21.	**IVORY TOWER** (ASCAP)—G. Storm I Ain't Gonna Worry (BMI)—Dot 15458	—	1
22.	**MAIN TITLE ("MAN WITH THE GOLDEN ARM")** (ASCAP)—E. Bernstein Clark Street (ASCAP)—Dec 29869	20	8
23.	**CAN YOU FIND IT IN YOUR HEART?** (ASCAP)—T. Bennett Forget Her (ASCAP)—Col 49667	24	4
24.	**LISBON ANTIGUA** (ASCAP)—N. Riddle Robin Hood (ASCAP)—Cap 3287	17	22
25.	**WALK HAND IN HAND** (BMI)—T. Martin Flamanco Love (ASCAP)—Vic 20-6493	—	1

• Most Played in Juke Boxes

For survey week ending May 16

RECORDS are ranked in order of the greatest number of plays in juke boxes thruout the country, as determined by The Billboard's weekly survey of the nation's juke box operators. When significant play is reported on both sides of a record, points are combined to determine position on the chart. In such a case, both sides are listed in bold type, the leading side on top.

This Week		Last Week	Weeks on Chart
1.	**HEARTBREAK HOTEL** (BMI)—E. Presley **I WAS THE ONE** (BMI)—Vic 20-6420	1	9
2.	**BLUE SUEDE SHOES** (BMI)—C. Perkins Honey, Don't (BMI)—Sun 234	2	10
3.	**HOT DIGGITY** (BMI)—P. Como **JUKE BOX BABY** (BMI)—Vic 20-6427	4	10
4.	**MAGIC TOUCH** (ASCAP)—Platters Winner Take All (ASCAP)—Mercury 70819	6	7
5.	**IVORY TOWER** (ASCAP)—C. Carr Please Believe Me (ASCAP)—Fraternity 734	7	4
6.	**POOR PEOPLE OF PARIS** (ASCAP)—L. Baxter Theme From "Helen of Troy" (ASCAP)—Cap 3336	3	14
7.	**A TEAR FELL** (BMI)—T. Brewer Bo Weevil (BMI)—Coral 61590	5	10
8.	**WHY DO FOOLS FALL IN LOVE?** (BMI)—Teen-Agers Please Be Mine (BMI)—Gee 1002	8	13
9.	**MOONGLOW AND THEME FROM "PICNIC"** (ASCAP)—G. Cates Rio Batucada (ASCAP)—Coral 61618	11	3
9.	**IVORY TOWER** (ASCAP)—G. Storm I Ain't Gonna Worry (BMI)—Dot 15458	16	2
11.	**LONG, TALL SALLY** (BMI) P. Boone Any Place in Heaven (ASCAP)—Dot 15457	12	4
12.	**I'LL BE HOME** (BMI)—P. Boone Tutti Frutti (BMI)—Dot 15443	9	15
13.	**ROCK ISLAND LINE** (BMI)—L. Donegan John Henry (BMI)—London 1650	17	6
14.	**MOONGLOW AND THEME FROM "PICNIC"** (ASCAP)—M. Stoloff Theme From "Picnic" (ASCAP)—Dec 29888	17	2
15.	**LISBON ANTIGUA** (ASCAP)—N. Riddle Robin Hood (ASCAP)—Cap 3287	10	17
16.	**LONG, TALL SALLY** (BMI) Little Richard Slippin' and Slidin' (BMI)—Specialty 572	—	3
17	**ROCK AND ROLL WALTZ** (BMI)—K. Starr I've Changed My Mind a Thousand Times (ASCAP)—Vic 20-6359	14	20
17.	**WHY DO FOOLS FALL IN LOVE?** (BMI)—G. Storm I Walk Alone (BMI)—Dot 15448	20	12
19.	**MY BLUE HEAVEN** (ASCAP)—F. Domino **I'M IN LOVE AGAIN** (BMI)—Imperial 964	17	2
19.	**STANDING ON THE CORNER** (ASCAP)—Four Lads My Little Angel (BMI)—Col 40674	—	1

• Best Selling Sheet Music

Tunes are ranked in order of their current national selling importance at the sheet music jobber level.

This Week		Last Week	Weeks on Chart
1.	**Hot Diggity** (Roncom)	1	11
2.	**Poor People of Paris** (Connelly)	2	14
3.	**Ivory Tower** (E. H. Morris)	3	5
4.	**Moonglow** (Mills-Columbia Pictures)	8	2
5.	**Standing on the Corner** (Frank)	14	2
6.	**Walk Hand in Hand** (Republic)	7	3
7.	**Heartbreak Hotel** (Tree)	4	6
8.	**Blue Suede Shoes** (Hi Lo)	6	7
9.	**Rock and Roll Waltz** (Sheldon)	5	19
10.	**Mr. Wonderful** (Laurel)	9	9
11.	**Picnic** (Shapiro-Bernstein)	10	2
12.	**On the Street Where You Live** (Chappell)	—	3
13.	**A Tear Fell** (Progressive)	11	5
14.	**Theme From "The Three Penny Opera"** (Moritat) (Harms)	12	14
15.	**Lisbon Antigua** (Southern)	13	19

• Most Played by Jockeys

For survey week ending May 16

SIDES are ranked in order of the greatest number of plays on disk jockey radio shows thruout the country. Results are based on The Billboard's weekly survey among the nation's disk jockeys. The reverse side of each record is also listed.

This Week		Last Week	Weeks on Chart
1.	**HEARTBREAK HOTEL** (BMI)—E. Presley I Was the One (BMI)—Vic 20-6420	1	12
2.	**HOT DIGGITY** (ASCAP)—P. Como Juke Box Baby (BMI)—Vic 20-6427	2	11
3.	**MOONGLOW AND THEME FROM "PICNIC"** (ASCAP)—M. Stoloff Theme From "Picnic" (ASCAP)—Dec 29888	4	6
4.	**POOR PEOPLE OF PARIS** (ASCAP)—L. Baxter Theme From "Helen of Troy" (ASCAP)—Cap 3336	3	15
5.	**STANDING ON THE CORNER** (ASCAP)—Four Lads My Little Angel (BMI)—Col 40674	7	4
6.	**IVORY TOWER** (ASCAP)—G. Storm I Ain't Gonna Worry (BMI)—Dot 15458	6	3
7.	**WAYWARD WIND** (BMI)—G. Grant No More Than Forever (ASCAP)—Era 1013	12	3
8.	**HAPPY WHISTLER** (ASCAP)—D. Robertson You're Free to Go (ASCAP)—Cap 3391	9	4
9.	**MOONGLOW AND THEME FROM "PICNIC"** (ASCAP)—G. Cates Rio Batucada (ASCAP)—Coral 61618	8	6
10.	**MAGIC TOUCH** (BMI)—Platters Winner Take All (ASCAP)—Mercury 70819	5	7
11.	**BLUE SUEDE SHOES** (BMI)—C. Perkins Honey, Don't (BMI)—Sun 234	13	10
12.	**IVORY TOWER** (ASCAP)—C. Carr Please Believe Me (ASCAP)—Fraternity 734	10	5
13.	**IVORY TOWER** (ASCAP)—O. Williams In Paradise (BMI)—DeLuxe 6093	11	5
14.	**A TEAR FELL** (BMI)—T. Brewer Bo Weevil (BMI)—Coral 61590	15	10
15.	**PICNIC** (ASCAP)—McGuire Sisters Delilah Jones (ASCAP)—Coral 61627	—	1
16.	**WALK HAND IN HAND** (BMI)—T. Martin Flamenco Love (ASCAP)—Vic 20-6493	—	1
17.	**GRADUATION DAY** (BMI)—Rover Boys I Hear Music (BMI)—ABC-Paramount 9700	25	2
18.	**MR. WONDERFUL** (ASCAP)—P. Lee Crazy in the Heart (BMI)—Dec 29834	16	10
19.	**LISBON ANTIGUA** (ASCAP)—N. Riddle Robin Hood (ASCAP)—Cap 3287	14	21
20.	**CAN YOU FIND IT IN YOUR HEART** (ASCAP)—T. Bennett Forget Her (ASCAP)—Col 49667	—	1
21.	**CHURCH BELLS MAY RING** (BMI)—Diamonds Little Girl of Mine (BMI)—Mercury 70835	—	1
22.	**ROCK ISLAND LINE** (BMI)—L. Donegan John Henry (BMI)—London 1650	21	7
23.	**STANDING ON THE CORNER** (ASCAP)—D. Martin Watching the World Go By (ASCAP)—Cap 3414	—	1
24.	**TOO YOUNG TO GO STEADY** (ASCAP)—Nat (King) Cole Never Let Me Go (ASCAP)—Cap 3390	24	4
25.	**NO, NOT MUCH** (ASCAP)—Four Lads I'll Never Know (BMI)—Col 40629	17	17

THE TOP 100

For survey week ending May 16

A list of the **Top 100 RECORD SIDES** in the nation according to a **COMBINED TABULATION** of Dealer, Disk Jockey and Juke Box Operator replies to The Billboard's weekly popular record Best Seller and Most Played surveys. Its purpose is to provide Disk Jockeys with additional programming material and to give trade exposure to NEWER records just beginning to show action in the field.

Pos.	Song	Artist	Label	Last Week
1.	HEARTBREAK HOTEL	E. Presley	Victor	1
2.	HOT DIGGITY	P. Como	Victor	2
3.	MOONGLOW AND THEME FROM PICNIC	M. Stoloff	Decca	7
3.	POOR PEOPLE OF PARIS	L. Baxter	Capitol	3
5.	BLUE SUEDE SHOES	C. Perkins	Sun	5
6.	MAGIC TOUCH	Platters	Mercury	4
7.	IVORY TOWER	C. Carr	Fraternity	6
7.	MOONGLOW AND THEME FROM PICNIC	G. Cates	Coral	7
9.	STANDING ON THE CORNER	Four Lads	Columbia	19
10.	IVORY TOWER	G. Storm	Dot	16
11.	A TEAR FELL	T. Brewer	Coral	9
12.	WAYWARD WIND	G. Grant	Era	18
13.	HAPPY WHISTLER	D. Robertson	Capitol	12
14.	IVORY TOWER	O. Williams	De Luxe	14
15.	ROCK ISLAND LINE	L. Donegan	London	13
16.	WHY DO FOOLS FALL IN LOVE	Teen-Agers	Gee	11
17.	LISBON ANTIGUA	N. Riddle	Capitol	10
18.	PICNIC	McGuire Sisters	Coral	26
19.	I'M IN LOVE AGAIN	F. Domino	Imperial	21
20.	I'LL BE HOME	P. Boone	Dot	15
21.	CHURCH BELLS MAY RING	Diamonds	Mercury	26
21.	LONG, TALL SALLY	Little Richard	Specialty	16
23.	CAN YOU FIND IT IN YOUR HEART?	T. Bennett	Columbia	24
24.	MR. WONDERFUL	P. Lee	Decca	23
25.	I WANT YOU TO BE MY GIRL	Teen-Agers	Gee	25
26.	WALK HAND IN HAND	T. Martin	Victor	42
27.	LONG, TALL SALLY	P. Boone	Dot	21
28.	NO, NOT MUCH	Four Lads	Columbia	20
29.	WHY DO FOOLS FALL IN LOVE?	G. Storm	Dot	29
30.	WHY DO FOOLS FALL IN LOVE?	Diamonds	Mercury	30
31.	GRADUATION DAY	Rover Boys	ABC Paramount	—
32.	TOO YOUNG TO GO STEADY	Nat (King) Cole	Capitol	43
33.	MAIN TITLE (MAN WITH THE GOLDEN ARM)	R. Maltby	Vik	26
34.	IT ONLY HURTS FOR A LITTLE WHILE	Ames Brothers	Victor	32
35.	MAIN TITLE (MAN WITH THE GOLDEN ARM)	E. Bernstein	Decca	38
36.	EDDIE, MY LOVE	Fontane Sisters	Dot	33
36.	MY LITTLE ANGEL	Four Lads	Columbia	43
38.	MY BLUE HEAVEN	F. Domino	Imperial	40
39.	STANDING ON THE CORNER	D. Martin	Capitol	51
40.	KISS ME ANOTHER	G. Gibbs	Mercury	54
41.	BLUE SUEDE SHOES	E. Presley	Victor	37
42.	MAIN TITLE, MOLLY O (MAN WITH THE GOLDEN ARM)	D. Jacobs	Coral	36
42.	MR. WONDERFUL	S. Vaughan	Mercury	67
44.	R-O-C-K	B. Haley	Decca	39
45.	WILD CHERRY	D. Cherry	Columbia	35
46.	LOVELY ONE	Four Voices	Columbia	49
47.	ROCK AND ROLL WALTZ	K. Starr	Victor	31
48.	CORRINE, CORRINA	J. Turner	Atlantic	63
49.	TOO CLOSE FOR COMFORT	E. Gorme	ABC Paramount	54
50.	ON THE STREET WHERE YOU LIVE	V. Damone	Columbia	46
51.	I COULD HAVE DANCED ALL NIGHT	S. Syms	Decca	56
52.	DELILAH JONES	McGuire Sisters	Coral	60
52.	PORTUGUESE WASHERWOMAN	J. (Fingers) Carr	Capitol	61
54.	WALK HAND IN HAND	A. Williams	Cadence	68
55.	TO LOVE AGAIN	Four Aces	Decca	47
56.	GRADUATION DAY	Four Freshmen	Capitol	58
56.	HOW LITTLE WE KNOW	F. Sinatra	Capitol	87
58.	I WAS THE ONE	E. Presley	Victor	40
58.	LITTLE GIRL OF MINE	Cleftones	Gee	57
60.	JUKE BOX BABY	P. Como	Victor	50
61.	LITTLE LOVE CAN GO A LONG, LONG WAY	Dream Weavers	Decca	33
62.	SLIPPIN' AND SLIDIN'	Little Richard	Specialty	53
63.	ROVIN' GAMBLER	T. Ernie	Capitol	77
64.	BLUE SUEDE SHOES	B. Bennett	King	78
64.	I'M IN LOVE AGAIN	Fontane Sisters	Dot	—
64.	MAIN TITLE (MAN WITH THE GOLDEN ARM	B. May	Capitol	70
67.	TO YOU MY LOVE	N. Noble	Mercury	64
68.	MAIN TITLE (MAN WITH THE GOLDEN ARM	L. Elgart	Columbia	85
68.	MY BABY LEFT ME	E. Presley	Victor	—
70.	PORT-AU-PRINCE	N. Riddle	Capitol	61
71.	PICNIC	R. Marterie	Mercury	74
72.	WALK HAND IN HAND	D. Vaughan	Kapp	74
73.	POOR PEOPLE OF PARIS	R. Morgan	Decca	71
73.	THEME FROM THE THREE PENNY OPERA (MORITAT)	D. Hyman	M-G-M	52
75.	ROCK ISLAND LINE	D. Cornell	Coral	84
76.	MONEY HONEY	E. Presley	Victor	80
77.	TANGO OF THE DRUMS	L. Baxter	Capitol	68
78.	POOR PEOPLE OF PARIS	L. Welk	Coral	97
79.	LOOK HOMEWARD ANGEL	Four Esquires	London	—
80.	NO OTHER ONE	E. Fisher	Victor	90
81.	PLAY FOR KEEPS	J. P. Morgan	Victor	—
82.	I WOKE UP CRYING	J. James	M-G-M	72
82.	MAIN TITLE (MAN WITH THE GOLDEN ARM)	B. Morrow	Wing	89
84.	CHURCH BELLS MAY RING	Willows	Melba	78
84.	EDDIE, MY LOVE	Chordettes	Cadence	81
86.	TREASURE OF LOVE	C. McPhatter	Atlantic	—
87.	HELD FOR QUESTIONING	R. Draper	Mercury	74
88.	STANDING ON THE CORNER	Mills Brothers	Decca	—
89.	SAINTS ROCK AND ROLL	B. Haley	Decca	65
90.	I WANT YOU, I NEED YOU, I LOVE YOU	E. Presley	Victor	—
90.	YOU'RE THE APPLE OF MY EYE	Four Lovers	Victor	—
92.	INNAMORTA	J. Vale	Columbia	88
92.	LOST IN THE SHUFFLE	J. P. Morgan	Victor	—
92.	HI LILI HI LO	R. Williams	Kapp	—
95.	MOCKING BIRD	Four Lads	Columbia	94
97.	JOEY JOEY JOEY	P. Lee	Decca	90
98.	I'M GROWN ACCUSTOMED TO YOUR FACE	R. Clooney	Columbia	—
98.	OUR LOVE AFFAIR	T. Charles	Decca	—
100.	INNAMORATA	D. Martin	Capitol	72

CAUTION TO DEALERS AND JUKE BOX OPERATORS

The Billboard's Top 100 is NOT designed to provide tested information for buying purposes. This function is most reliably served by other regular weekly features: Best Sellers in Stores, Most Played in Juke Boxes, Coming Up Strong and Best Buys.

• Best Sellers in Stores

For survey week ending May 23

RECORDS are ranked in order of their current national selling importance at the retail level, as determined by The Billboard's weekly survey of the top volume dealers in every important market area. When significant action is reported on both sides of a record, points are combined to determine position on the chart. In such a case, both sides are listed in bold type, the leading side on top.

This Week		Last Week	Weeks on Chart
1.	HEARTBREAK HOTEL (BMI)–E. Presley I Was the One (BMI)—Vic 20-6420	1	13
2.	MOONGLOW AND THEME FROM "PICNIC" (ASCAP)–M. Stoloff Theme From "Picnic" (BMI)—Dec 29888	2	7
3.	WAYWARD WIND (BMI)–G. Grant No More Than Forever (ASCAP)—Era 1013	4	5
4.	HOT DIGGITY ASCAP)–P. Como JUKE BOX BABY (ASCAP)–Vic 20-6427	3	13
5.	STANDING ON THE CORNER (ASCAP)–Four Lads MY LITTLE ANGEL (BMI)–Col 40674	7	6
6.	MOONGLOW AND THEME FROM "PICNIC" (ASCAP)–G. Cates Rio Batucada (ASCAP)—Coral 61618	5	7
7.	I'M IN LOVE AGAIN (BMI)–F. Domino MY BLUE HEAVEN (ASCAP)–Imperial 5386	6	5
8.	IVORY TOWER (ASCAP)–C. Carr Please, Please Believe Me (ASCAP)—Fraternity 734	7	8
9.	MAGIC TOUCH (BMI)–Platters Winner Take All (ASCAP)—Mercury 70819	10	10
10.	HAPPY WHISTLER (ASCAP)–D. Robertson You're Free to Go (ASCAP)—Cap 3391	12	5
11.	BLUE SUEDE SHOES (BMI)–C. Perkins Honey, Don't (BMI)—Sun 234	9	13
12.	POOR PEOPLE OF PARIS (ASCAP)–L. Baxter Theme From "Helen of Troy" (ASCAP)—Cap 3336	11	16
13.	LONG, TALL SALLY (BMI)–Little Richard Slippin' and Slidin' (BMI)—Specialty 572	13	9
14.	CHURCH BELLS MAY RING (BMI)–Diamonds Little Girl of Mine (BMI)—Mercury 70835	14	4
15.	A TEAR FELL (BMI)–T. Brewer Bo Weevil (BMI)—Coral 61590	15	14
16.	I WANT YOU TO BE MY GIRL (BMI)–Teen-Agers I'm Not A Know-It-All (ASCAP)—Gee 1012	16	4
17.	PICNIC (ASCAP)–McGuire Sisters DELILAH JONES (ASCAP)–Coral 61627	18	2
18.	IVORY TOWER (ASCAP)–O. Williams In Paradise (BMI)—De Luxe 6093	20	8
19.	I WANT YOU, I NEED YOU, I LOVE YOU (BMI)–E. Presley MY BABY LEFT ME (BMI)–Vic 20-6540	—	1
20.	IVORY TOWER (ASCAP)–G. Storm I Ain't Gonna Worry (BMI)—Dot 15458	21	2
21.	WHY DO FOOLS FALL IN LOVE? (BMI)–Teen-Agers Please Be Mine (BMI)—Gee 1002	17	16
22.	WALK HAND IN HAND (BMI)–T. Martin Flamenco Love (ASCAP)—Vic 20-6493	25	2
23.	CAN YOU FIND IT IN YOUR HEART? (ASCAP)–T. Bennett Forget Her (ASCAP)—Col 49667	23	5
24.	MAIN TITLE ("MAN WITH THE GOLDEN ARM") (ASCAP)–E. Bernstein Clark Street (ASCAP)—Dec 29869	22	9
25.	IT ONLY HURTS FOR A LITTLE WHILE (ASCAP)–Ames Brothers If You Wanna See Mamie Tonight (ASCAP)—Vic 20-6481	—	1

• Most Played in Juke Boxes

For survey week ending May 23

RECORDS are ranked in order of the greatest number of plays in juke boxes thruout the country, as determined by The Billboard's weekly survey of the nation's juke box operators. When significant play is reported on both sides of a record, points are combined to determine position on the chart. In such a case, both sides are listed in bold type, the leading side on top.

This Week		Last Week	Weeks on Chart
1.	HEARTBREAK HOTEL (BMI)–E. Presley I Was the One (BMI)—Vic 20-6420	1	10
2.	BLUE SUEDE SHOES (BMI)–C. Perkins Honey, Don't (BMI)—Sun 234	2	11
3.	HOT DIGGITY (BMI)–P. Como JUKE BOX BABY (BMI)–Vic 20-6427	3	11
4.	MAGIC TOUCH (ASCAP)–Platters Winner Take All (ASCAP)—Mercury 70819	4	8
5.	IVORY TOWER (ASCAP)–C. Carr Please Believe Me (ASCAP)—Fraternity 734	5	5
6.	IVORY TOWER (ASCAP)–G. Storm I Ain't Gonna Worry (BMI)—Dot 15458	9	3
7.	MOONGLOW AND THEME FROM "PICNIC" (ASCAP)–G. Cates Rio Batucada (ASCAP)—Coral 61618	9	4
8.	POOR PEOPLE OF PARIS (ASCAP)–L. Baxter Theme From "Helen of Troy" (ASCAP)—Cap 3336	6	15
8.	TEAR FELL (BMI)–T. Brewer Bo Weevil (BMI)—Coral 61590	7	11
8.	LONG, TALL SALLY (BMI)–P. Boone Any Place in Heaven (ASCAP)—Dot 15457	11	5
11.	MOONGOW AND THEME FROM "PICNIC" (ASCAP)–M. Stoloff Theme From "Picnic" (ASCAP)—Dec 29888	14	3
12.	HAPPY WHISTLER (ASCAP)–D. Robertson You're Free to Go (ASCAP)—Cap 3391	—	1
13.	STANDING ON THE CORNER (ASCAP)–Four Lads My Little Angel (BMI)—Col 40674	19	2
14.	LONG, TALL SALLY (BMI)–Little Richard Slippin' and Slidin' (BMI)—Specialty 572	16	4
14.	WAYWARD WIND (BMI)–G. Grant No More Than Forever (ASCAP)—Era 1013	—	1
16.	ROCK ISLAND LINE (BMI)–L. Donegan John Henry (BMI)—London 1650	13	7
17.	WHY DO FOOLS FALL IN LOVE? (BMI)–Teen-Agers Please Be Mine (BMI)—Gee 1002	8	14
18.	I'M IN LOVE AGAIN (BMI)–F. Domino MY BLUE HEAVEN (ASCAP)–Imperial 5386	19	3
19.	I'LL BE HOME (BMI)–P. Boone Tutti Frutti (BMI)—Dot 15443	12	16
19.	IVORY TOWER (ASCAP)–O. Williams In Paradise (BMI)—De Luxe 6093	—	2

• Best Selling Sheet Music

Tunes are ranked in order of their current national selling importance at the sheet music jobber level.

This Week		Last Week	Weeks on Chart
1.	Ivory Tower (E. H. Morris)	3	6
2.	Standing On the Corner (Frank)	5	3
3.	Walk Hand in Hand (Republic)	6	4
4.	Moonglow (Mills-Columbia Pictures)	4	3
5.	Hot Diggity (Roncom)	1	12
6.	Picnic (Shapiro-Bernstein)	11	3
7.	Poor People of Paris (Connelly)	2	15
8.	Heartbreak Hotel (Tree)	7	7
9.	Blue Suede Shoes (Hi-Lo)	8	8
10.	Mr. Wonderful (Laurel)	10	10
11.	To Love Again (Columbia Pictures)	—	1
12.	I Could Have Danced All Night (Chappell)	—	1
13.	On the Street Where You Live (Chappell)	12	4
14.	Wayward Wind (Warman)	—	1
15.	A Tear Fell (Progressive)	13	6

• Most Played by Jockeys

For survey week ending May 23

SIDES are ranked in order of the greatest number of plays on disk jockey radio shows thruout the country. Results are based on The Billboard's weekly survey among the nation's disk jockeys. The reverse side of each record is also listed.

This Week		Last Week	Weeks on Chart
1.	MOONGLOW AND THEME FROM "PICNIC" (ASCAP)–M. Stoloff Theme From "Picnic" (ASCAP)—Dec 29888	3	7
2.	HEARTBREAK HOTEL (BMI)–E. Presley I Was the One (BMI)—Vic 20-6420	1	13
3.	WAYWARD WIND (BMI)–G. Grant No More Than Forever (ASCAP)—Era 1013	7	4
4.	HOT DIGGITY (ASCAP)–P. Como Juke Box Baby (BMI)—Vic 20-6427	2	12
5.	STANDING ON THE CORNER (ASCAP)–Four Lads My Little Angel (BMI)—Col 40674	5	5
6.	HAPPY WHISTLER (ASCAP)–D. Robertson You're Free to Go (ASCAP)—Cap 3391	8	5
7.	MOONGLOW AND THEME FROM "PICNIC" (ASCAP)–G. Cates Rio Batucada (ASCAP)—Coral 61618	9	7
8.	IVORY TOWER (ASCAP)–G. Storm I Ain't Gonna Worry (BMI)—Dot 15458	6	4
9.	POOR PEOPLE OF PARIS (ASCAP)–L. Baxter Theme From "Helen of Troy" (ASCAP)—Cap 3336	4	16
10.	MAGIC TOUCH (BMI)–Platters Winner Take All (ASCAP)—Mercury 70819	10	8
11.	IVORY TOWER (ASCAP)–C. Carr Please Believe Me (ASCAP)—Fraternity 734	12	6
12.	IVORY TOWER (ASCAP)–O. Williams In Paradise (BMI)—De Luxe 6093	13	6
13.	I'M IN LOVE AGAIN (BMI)–F. Domino My Blue Heaven (ASCAP)—Imperial 5386	—	2
14.	PICNIC (ASCAP)–McGuire Sisters Delilah Jones (ASCAP)—Coral 61627	15	2
15.	HOW LITTLE WE KNOW (ASCAP)–F. Sinatra Five Hundred Guys (ASCAP)—Cap 3423	—	1
16.	WALK HAND IN HAND (BMI)–T. Martin Flamenco Love (ASCAP)—Vic 20-6493	16	2
17.	CHURCH BELLS MAY RING (BMI)–Diamonds Little Girl of Mine (BMI)—Mercury 70835	21	2
18.	ON THE STREET WHERE YOU LIVE (ASCAP)–V. Damone We All Need Love (ASCAP)—Col 40654	—	1
19.	BLUE SUEDE SHOES (BMI)–C. Perkins Honey, Don't (BMI)—Sun 234	11	11
20.	A TEAR FELL (BMI)–T. Brewer Bo Weevil (BMI)—Coral 61590	14	11
21.	CAN YOU FIND IT IN YOUR HEART? (ASCAP)–T. Bennett Forget Her (ASCAP)—Col 49667	20	2
22.	IT ONLY HURTS A LITTLE WHILE (ASCAP)–Ames Brothers If You Want to See Mamie Tonight (ASCAP)—Vic 20-6481	—	1
23.	LONG, TALL SALLY (BMI)–P. Boone Any Place in Heaven (ASCAP)—Dot 15457	—	1
24.	LONG, TALL SALLY (BMI)–Little Richard Slippin' and Slidin' (BMI)—Specialty 572	—	4
24.	GRADUATION DAY (BMI)–Rover Boys I Hear Music (BMI)—ABC-Paramount 9700	17	3
24.	MY LITTLE ANGEL (BMI)–Four Lads Standing On the Corner (ASCAP)—Col 40674	—	1

THE TOP 100

For survey week ending May 23

A list of the Top 100 **RECORD SIDES** in the nation according to a **COMBINED TABULATION** of Dealer, Disk Jockey and Juke Box Operator replies to The Billboard's weekly popular record Best Seller and Most Played surveys. Its purpose is to provide Disk Jockeys with additional programming material and to give trade exposure to NEWER records just beginning to show action in the field.

Pos.	Song	Artist	Label	Last Week
1.	HEARTBREAK HOTEL	E. Presley	Victor	1
2.	HOT DIGGITY	P. Como	Victor	2
3.	MOONGLOW AND THEME FROM "PICNIC"	M. Stoloff	Decca	3
4.	MOONGLOW AND THEME FROM "PICNIC"	G. Cates	Coral	7
5.	WAYWARD WIND	G. Grant	Era	12
6.	MAGIC TOUCH	Platters	Mercury	6
7.	IVORY TOWER	C. Carr	Fraternity	7
8.	STANDING ON THE CORNER	Four Lads	Columbia	9
9.	HAPPY WHISTLER	D. Robertson	Capitol	13
10.	POOR PEOPLE OF PARIS	L. Baxter	Capitol	3
11.	BLUE SUEDE SHOES	C. Perkins	Sun	5
12.	IVORY TOWER	G. Storm	Dot	10
13.	A TEAR FELL	T. Brewer	Coral	11
14.	I'M IN LOVE AGAIN	F. Domino	Imperial	19
15.	IVORY TOWER	O. Williams	De Luxe	14
16.	LONG, TALL SALLY	Little Richard	Specialty	21
17.	PICNIC	McGuire Sisters	Coral	18
18.	LONG, TALL SALLY	P. Boone	Dot	27
19.	CAN YOU FIND IT IN YOUR HEART?	T. Bennett	Columbia	23
20.	CHURCH BELLS MAY RING	Diamonds	Mercury	21
21.	IT ONLY HURTS FOR A LITTLE WHILE	Ames Brothers	Victor	34
22.	WALK HAND IN HAND	T. Martin	Victor	26
23.	I WANT YOU TO BE MY GIRL	Teen-Agers	Gee	23
24.	ROCK ISLAND LINE	L. Donegan	London	15
25.	LISBON ANTIGUA	N. Riddle	Capitol	17
26.	WHY DO FOOLS FALL IN LOVE?	Teen-Agers	Gee	16
27.	GRADUATION DAY	Rover Boys	ABC-Paramount	31
28.	I'LL BE HOME	P. Boone	Dot	20
29.	MY BLUE HEAVEN	F. Domino	Imperial	38
30.	KISS ME ANOTHER	G. Gibbs	Mercury	40
31.	I WANT YOU, I NEED YOU, I LOVE YOU	E. Presley	Victor	90
32.	ON THE STREET WHERE YOU LIVE	V. Damone	Columbia	50
33.	MY LITTLE ANGEL	Four Lads	Columbia	36
34.	MR. WONDERFUL	P. Lee	Decca	24
35.	WHY DO FOOLS FALL IN LOVE?	G. Storm	Dot	29
36.	MAIN TITLE ("MAN WITH THE GOLDEN ARM")	R. Maltby	Vik	33
37.	DELILAH JONES	McGuire Sisters	Coral	52
38.	BLUE SUEDE SHOES	E. Presley	Victor	41
39.	TOO YOUNG TO GO STEADY	N. (King) Cole	Capitol	32
40.	NO, NOT MUCH	Four Lads	Columbia	28
41.	CORRINE, CORRINA	J. Turner	Atlantic	48
41.	R-O-C-K	B. Haley	Decca	44
43.	STANDING ON THE CORNER	D. Martin	Capitol	39
44.	TANGO OF THE DRUMS	L. Baxter	Capitol	77
45.	I'M IN LOVE AGAIN	Fontane Sisters	Dot	64
46.	I COULD HAVE DANCED ALL NIGHT	S. Syms	Decca	51
47.	A LITTLE LOVE CAN GO A LONG, LONG WAY	Dream Weavers	Decca	61
48.	PORTUGUESE WASHERWOMAN	J. (Fingers) Carr	Capitol	52
49.	JUKE BOX BABY	P. Como	Victor	60
50.	WILD CHERRY	D. Cherry	Columbia	45
51.	MAIN TITLE & MOLLY-O ("MAN WITH THE GOLDEN ARM")	D. Jacobs	Coral	42
52.	HOW LITTLE WE KNOW	F. Sinatra	Capitol	56
52.	I WAS THE ONE	E. Presley	Victor	58
52.	TREASURE OF LOVE	C. McPhatter	Atlantic	86
52.	TOO CLOSE FOR COMFORT	E. Gorme	ABC-Paramount	49
56.	MR. WONDERFUL	S. Vaughan	Mercury	42
57.	GRADUATION DAY	Four Freshmen	Capitol	56
58.	WHY DO FOOLS FALL IN LOVE?	Diamonds	Mercury	30
59	TO LOVE AGAIN	Four Aces	Decca	55
60.	ROVIN' GAMBLER	T. Ernie	Capitol	63
61.	BORN TO BE WITH YOU	Chordettes	Cadence	—
62.	SLIPPIN' AND SLIDIN'	Little Richard	Specialty	62
63.	EDDIE, MY LOVE	Fontane Sisters	Dot	36
63.	MAIN TITLE ("MAN WITH THE GOLDEN ARM")	E. Bernstein	Decca	35
65.	LITTLE GIRL OF MINE	Cleftones	Gee	58
66.	WALK HAND IN HAND	A. Williams	Cadence	54
67.	LOVELY ONE	Four Voices	Columbia	46
68.	I ALMOST LOST MY MIND	P. Boone	Dot	—
69.	TRANSFUSION	N. Norvis	Dot	—
70.	CRAZY LITTLE PALACE	B. Williams	Coral	—
71.	STANDING ON THE CORNER	Mills Brothers	Decca	88
72.	MY BABY LEFT ME	E. Presley	Victor	68
73.	FIVE HUNDRED GUYS	F. Sinatra	Capitol	—
73.	TO YOU, MY LOVE	N. Noble	Mercury	67
73.	TOO YOUNG TO GO STEADY	P. Page	Mercury	—
76.	ROCK AND ROLL WALTZ	K. Starr	Victor	47
77.	MAIN TITLE ("MAN WITH THE GOLDEN ARM")	B. May	Capitol	64
78.	PORT-AU-PRINCE	N. Riddle	Capitol	70
79.	PLAY FOR KEEPS	J. P. Morgan	Victor	81
80.	I COULD HAVE DANCED ALL NIGHT	R. Clooney	Columbia	—
81.	POOR PEOPLE OF PARIS	L. Welk	Coral	78
82.	LOOK HOMEWARD, ANGEL	Four Esquires	London	79
83.	SWEET HEARTACHES	E. Fisher	Victor	—
83.	WATCHING THE WORLD GO BY	D. Martin	Capitol	—
85.	HI LILI HI LO	R. Williams	Kapp	92
86.	I WOKE UP CRYING	J. James	M-G-M	82
87.	IS THERE SOMEBODY ELSE?	Dream Weavers	Decca	—
87	POOR PEOPLE OF PARIS	L. Welk	Coral	73
89.	MAIN TITLE ("MAN WITH THE GOLDEN ARM")	L. Elgart	Columbia	68
90.	BO WEEVIL	T. Brewer	Coral	—
91.	CHURCH BELLS MAY RING	Willows	Melba	84
92.	I'VE GROWN ACCUSTOMED TO YOUR FACE	R. Clooney	Columbia	98
93.	ROCK ISLAND LINE	D. Cornell	Coral	75
94.	IN A SHANTY IN OLD SHANTY TOWN	S. Smith	Epic	—
95.	MONEY HONEY	E. Presley	Victor	76
95.	THEME FROM THE THREE PENNY OPERA (MORITAT)	D. Hyman	M-G-M	73
97.	PICNIC	R. Marterie	Mercury	71
97.	SAINTS ROCK AND ROLL	B. Haley	Decca	89
99.	I'VE GROWN ACCUSTOMED TO YOUR FACE	G. MacRae	Capitol	—
100.	LOST IN THE SHUFFLE	J. P. Morgan	Victor	92
100.	NEVER LET ME GO	N. (King) Cole	Capitol	—

CAUTION TO DEALERS AND JUKE BOX OPERATORS

The Billboard's Top 100 is NOT designed to provide tested information for buying purposes. This function is most reliably served by other regular weekly features: Best Sellers in Stores, Most Played in Juke Boxes, Coming Up Strong and Best Buys.

• Best Sellers in Stores

For survey week ending May 30

RECORDS are ranked in order of their current national selling importance at the retail level, as determined by The Billboard's weekly survey of the top volume dealers in every important market area. When significant action is reported on both sides of a record, points are combined to determine position on the chart. In such a case, both sides are listed in bold type, the leading side on top.

This Week		Last Week	Weeks on Chart
1.	**HEARTBREAK HOTEL** (BMI)—E. Presley I Was the One (BMI)—Vic 20-6420	1	14
2.	**MOONGLOW AND THEME FROM PICNIC** (ASCAP)—M. Stoloff Theme From "Picnic" (ASCAP)—Dec 29888	2	8
3.	**WAYWARD WIND** (BMI)—G. Grant No More Than Forever (ASCAP)—Era 1013	3	6
4.	**STANDING ON THE CORNER** (ASCAP)—Four Lads **MY LITTLE ANGEL** (BMI)—Col 40674	5	7
5.	**I'M IN LOVE AGAIN** (BMI)—F. Domino **MY BLUE HEAVEN** (ASCAP)—Imperial 5386	7	6
6.	**HOT DIGGITY** (ASCAP)—P. Como Juke Box Baby (ASCAP)—Vic 20-6427	4	14
7.	**MOONGLOW AND THEME FROM PICNIC** (ASCAP)—G. Cates Rio Batucada (ASCAP)—Coral 61618	6	8
8.	**IVORY TOWER** (ASCAP)—C. Carr Please, Please Believe Me (ASCAP)—Fraternty 734	8	9
9.	**MAGIC TOUCH** (BMI)—Platters Winner Take All (ASCAP)—Mercury 70819	9	11
9.	**I WANT YOU, I NEED YOU, I LOVE YOU** (BMI)—E. Presley **MY BABY LEFT ME** (BMI)—Vic 20-6540	19	2
11.	**HAPPY WHISTLER** (ASCAP)—D. Robertson You're Free to Go (ASCAP)—Cap 3391	10	6
12.	**BLUE SUEDE SHOES** (BMI)—C. Perkins Honey, Don't (BMI)—Sun 234	11	14
13.	**LONG, TALL SALLY** (BMI)—Little Richard **SLIPPIN' AND SLIDIN'** (BMI)—Specialty 572	13	10
14.	**I WANT YOU TO BE MY GIRL** (BMI)—Teen Agers I'm Not a Know-It-All (ASCAP)—Gee 1012	16	5
15.	**IVORY TOWER** (ASCAP)—G. Storm I Ain't Gonna Worry (BMI)—Dot 15458	20	3
16.	**PICNIC** (ASCAP)—McGuire Sisters Delilah Jones (ASCAP)—Coral 61627	17	3
17.	**POOR PEOPLE OF PARIS** (ASCAP)—L. Baxter Theme From "Helen of Troy" (ASCAP)—Cap 3336	12	17
18.	**CHURCH BELLS MAY RING** (BMI)—Diamonds Little Girl of Mine (BMI)—Mercury 70835	14	5
19.	**A TEAR FELL** (BMI)—T. Brewer Bo Weevil (BMI)—Coral 61590	15	15
20.	**ON THE STREET WHERE YOU LIVE** (ASCAP)—V. Damone We All Need Love (ASCAP)—Col 40654	—	1
21.	**IT ONLY HURTS FOR A LITTLE WHILE** (ASCAP)—Ames Brothers If You Want to See Mamie Tonight (ASCAP)—Vic 20-6481	25	2
22.	**IVORY TOWER** (ASCAP)—O. Williams In Paradise (BMI)—De Luxe 6093	18	9
23.	**TRANSFUSION** (BMI)—Nervous Norvus Dig (BMI)—Dot 15470	—	1
24.	**CAN YOU FIND IT IN YOUR HEART?** (ASCAP)—T. Bennett Forget Her (ASCAP)—Col 49667	23	6
25.	**WALK HAND IN HAND** (BMI) T. Martin Flamenco Love (ASCAP)—Vic 20-6493	22	3

• Most Played in Juke Boxes

For survey week ending May 30

RECORDS are ranked in order of the greatest number of plays in juke boxes thruout the country, as determined by The Billboard's weekly survey of the nation's juke box operators. When significant play is reported on both sides of a record, points are combined to determine position on the chart. In such a case, both sides are listed in bold type, the leading side on top.

This Week		Last Week	Weeks on Chart
1.	**HEARTBREAK HOTEL** (BMI)—E. Presley I Was the One (BMI)—Vic 20-6420	1	11
2.	**BLUE SUEDE SHOES** (BMI)—C. Perkins Honey, Don't (BMI)—Sun 234	2	12
3.	**HOT DIGGITY** (BMI)—P. Como **JUKE BOX BABY** (BMI)—Vic 20-6427	3	12
4.	**MAGIC TOUCH** (BMI)—Platters Winner Take All (ASCAP)—Mercury 70819	4	9
4.	**IVORY TOWER** (ASCAP)—C. Carr Please Believe Me (ASCAP)—Fraternity 734	5	6
6.	**WAYWARD WIND** (BMI)—G. Grant No More Than Forever (ASCAP)—Era 1013	14	2
7.	**MOONGLOW AND THEME FROM "PICNIC"** (ASCAP)—M. Stoloff Theme From "Picnic" (ASCAP)—Dec 29888	11	4
8.	**MOONGLOW AND THEME FROM "PICNIC"** (ASCAP)—G. Cates Rio Batucada (ASCAP)—Coral 61618	7	5
9.	**STANDING ON THE CORNER** (ASCAP)—Four Lads My Little Angel (BMI)—Col 40674	13	3
10.	**LONG, TALL SALLY** (BMI)—P. Boone Any Place in Heaven (ASCAP)—Dot 15457	8	6
11.	**IVORY TOWER** (ASCAP)—G. Storm I Ain't Gonna Worry (BMI)—Dot 15458	6	4
12.	**TEAR FELL** (BMI)—T. Brewer Bo Weevil (BMI)—Coral 61590	8	12
13.	**HAPPY WHISTLER** (ASCAP)—D. Robertson You're Free to Go (ASCAP)—Cap 3391	12	2
14.	**POOR PEOPLE OF PARIS** (ASCAP)—L. Baxter Theme From "Helen of Troy" (ASCAP)—Cap 3336	8	16
15.	**I'M IN LOVE AGAIN** (BMI)—F. Domino **MY BLUE HEAVEN** (ASCAP)—Imperial 5396	18	4
16.	**LONG, TALL SALLY** (BMI)—Little Richard Slippin' and Slidin' (BMI)—Specialty 572	14	5
17.	**WHY DO FOOLS FALL IN LOVE?** (BMI)—Teen Agers Please Be Mine (BMI)—Gee 1002	17	15
17.	**I WANT YOU, I NEED YOU, I LOVE YOU** (BMI)—E. Presley **MY BABY LEFT ME** (BMI)—Vic 20-6540	—	1
19.	**PICNIC** (ASCAP)—McGuire Sisters Delilah Jones (ASCAP)—Coral 61627	—	1
20.	**I WANT YOU TO BE MY GIRL** (BMI)—Teen Agers I'm Not a Know-It-All (ASCAP)—Gee 1012	—	1

• Best Selling Sheet Music

Tunes are ranked in order of their current national selling importance at the sheet music jobber level.

This Week		Last Week	Weeks on Chart
1.	**Ivory Tower** (E. H. Morris)	1	7
2.	**Walk Hand in Hand** (Republic)	3	5
3.	**Hot Diggity** (Roncom)	5	13
4.	**Standing On the Corner** (Frank)	2	4
4.	**Moonglow** (Mills-Columbia Pictures)	4	4
6.	**Poor People of Paris** (Connelly)	7	16
7.	**Picnic** (Shapiro-Bernstein)	6	4
8.	**Heartbreak Hotel** (Tree)	8	8
9.	**Wayward Wind** (Warman)	14	2
10.	**Mr. Wonderful** (Laurel)	10	11
11.	**On the Street Where You Live** (Chappell)	13	5
12.	**Blue Suede Shoes** (Hi-Lo)	8	9
13.	**Graduation Day** (Sheldon)	—	1
14.	**Magic Touch** (Panter)	—	1
15.	**I Could Have Danced All Night** (Chappell)	12	2

• Most Played by Jockeys

For survey week ending May 30

SIDES are ranked in order of the greatest number of plays on disk jockey radio shows thruout the country. Results are based on The Billboard's weekly survey among the nation's disk jockeys. The reverse side of each record is also listed.

This Week		Last Week	Weeks on Chart
1.	**MOONGLOW AND THEME FROM "PICNIC"** (ASCAP)—M. Stoloff Theme From "Picnic" (ASCAP)—Dec 29888	1	8
2.	**WAYWARD WIND** (BMI)—G. Grant No More Than Forever (ASCAP)—Era 1013	3	5
3.	**HEARTBREAK HOTEL** (BMI)—E. Presley I Was the One (BMI)—Vic 20-6420	2	14
4.	**STANDING ON THE CORNER** (ASCAP)—Four Lads My Little Angel (BMI)—Col 40674	5	6
5.	**HOT DIGGITY** (ASCAP)—P. Como Juke Box Baby (BMI)—Vic 20-6427	4	13
6.	**HAPPY WHISTLER** (ASCAP)—D. Robertson You're Free to Go (ASCAP)—Cap 3391	6	6
7.	**MOONGLOW AND THEME FROM "PICNIC"** (ASCAP)—G. Cates Rio Batucada (ASCAP)—Coral 61618	7	8
8.	**IVORY TOWER** (ASCAP)—G. Storm I Ain't Gonna Worry (BMI)—Dot 15458	8	5
9.	**MAGIC TOUCH** (BMI)—Platters Winner Take All (ASCAP)—Mercury 70819	10	9
10.	**I'M IN LOVE AGAIN** (BMI)—F. Domino My Blue Heaven (ASCAP)—Imperial 5386	13	3
11.	**IVORY TOWER** (ASCAP)—C. Carr Please, Please Believe Me (ASCAP)—Fraternity 734	11	7
12.	**ON THE STREET WHERE YOU LIVE** (ASCAP)—V. Damone We All Need Love (ASCAP)—Col 40654	18	2
13.	**IVORY TOWER** (ASCAP)—O. Williams In Paradise (BMI)—De Luxe 6093	12	7
14.	**POOR PEOPLE OF PARIS** (ASCAP)—L. Baxter Theme From "Helen of Troy" (ASCAP)—Cap 3336	9	17
15.	**PICNIC** (ASCAP)—McGuire Sisters Delilah Jones (ASCAP)—Coral 61627	14	3
15.	**WALK HAND IN HAND** (BMI)—T. Martin Flamenco Love (ASCAP)—Vic 20-6493	16	3
17.	**A TEAR FELL** (BMI)—T. Brewer Bo Weevil (BMI)—Coral 61590	20	12
18.	**HOW LITTLE WE KNOW** (ASCAP)—F. Sinatra Five Hundred Guys (ASCAP)—Cap 3423	15	2
19.	**GRADUATION DAY** (BMI)—Four Freshmen Lonely Night in Paris (ASCAP)—Cap 3410	—	1
20.	**BLUE SUEDE SHOES** (BMI)—C. Perkins Honey, Don't (BMI)—Sun 234	19	12
21.	**GRADUATION DAY** (BMI)—Rover Boys I Hear Music (BMI)—ABC-Paramount 9700	24	4
22.	**STANDING ON THE CORNER** (ASCAP)—D. Martin Watching the World Go By (ASCAP)—Cap 3414	—	2
23.	**CHURCH BELLS MAY RING** (BMI)—Diamonds Little Girl of Mine (BMI)—Mercury 70835	17	3
23.	**BORN TO BE WITH YOU** (ASCAP)—Chordettes Love Never Changes (ASCAP)—Cadence 1291	—	1
25.	**I WANT YOU TO BE MY GIRL** (BMI)—Teen Agers I'm Not a Know-It-All (ASCAP)—Gee 1012	—	1

THE TOP 100

For survey week ending May 30

A list of the **Top 100 RECORD SIDES** in the nation according to a **COMBINED TABULATION** of Dealer, Disk Jockey and Juke Box Operator replies to The Billboard's weekly popular record Best Seller and Most Played surveys. Its purpose is to provide Disk Jockeys with additional programming material and to give trade exposure to NEWER records just beginning to show action in the field.

Pos.	Song	Artist	Label	Last Week
1.	HEARTBREAK HOTEL	E. Presley	Victor	1
2.	MOONGLOW AND THEME FROM "PICNIC"	M. Stoloff	Decca	3
2.	WAYWARD WIND	G. Grant	Era	5
4.	HOT DIGGITY	P. Como	Victor	2
5.	STANDING ON THE CORNER	Four Lads	Columbia	8
6.	MOONGLOW AND THEME FROM "PICNIC"	G. Cates	Coral	4
7.	MAGIC TOUCH	Platters	Mercury	6
8.	IVORY TOWER	C. Carr	Fraternity	7
9.	HAPPY WHISTLER	D. Robertson	Capitol	9
10.	IVORY TOWER	G. Storm	Dot	12
11.	BLUE SUEDE SHOES	C. Perkins	Sun	11
12.	I'M IN LOVE AGAIN	F. Domino	Imperial	14
13.	POOR PEOPLE OF PARIS	L. Baxter	Capitol	10
14.	A TEAR FELL	T. Brewer	Coral	13
15.	PICNIC	McGuire Sisters	Coral	17
16.	IVORY TOWER	O. Williams	De Luxe	15
17.	I WANT YOU TO BE MY GIRL	Teen-Agers	Gee	23
18.	LONG, TALL SALLY	Little Richard	Specialty	16
19.	I WANT YOU, I NEED YOU, I LOVE YOU	E. Presley	Victor	31
20.	IT ONLY HURTS FOR A LITTLE WHILE	Ames Brothers	Victor	21
21.	CAN YOU FIND IT IN YOUR HEART?	T. Bennett	Columbia	19
22.	CHURCH BELLS MAY RING	Diamonds	Mercury	20
23.	GRADUATION DAY	Rover Boys	ABC-Paramount	27
24.	WALK HAND IN HAND	T. Martin	Victor	22
25.	I ALMOST LOST MY MIND	P. Boone	Dot	68
25.	ON THE STREET WHERE YOU LIVE	V. Damone	Columbia	32
27.	BORN TO BE WITH YOU	Chordettes	Cadence	61
27.	LONG, TALL SALLY	P. Boone	Dot	18
29.	TRANSFUSION	N. Norvis	Dot	69
30.	STANDING ON THE CORNER	D. Martin	Capitol	43
31.	MY BLUE HEAVEN	F. Domino	Imperial	29
32.	ROCK ISLAND LINE	L. Donegan	London	24
33.	MY LITTLE ANGEL	Four Lads	Columbia	23
34.	MY BABY LEFT ME	E. Presley	Victor	72
35.	LISBON ANTIGUA	N. Riddle	Capitol	25
36.	WHY DO FOOLS FALL IN LOVE?	Teen-Agers	Gee	26
37.	TREASURE OF LOVE	C. McPhatter	Atlantic	52
38.	GRADUATION DAY	Four Freshmen	Capitol	57
39.	KISS ME ANOTHER	G. Gibbs	Mercury	30
40.	I'LL BE HOME	P. Boone	Dot	28
41.	MR. WONDERFUL	P. Lee	Decca	34
41.	TOO YOUNG TO GO STEADY	N. (King) Cole	Capitol	39
43.	SLIPPIN' AND SLIDIN'	Little Richard	Specialty	62
44.	R-O-C-K	B. Haley	Decca	41
45.	DELILAH JONES	McGuire Sisters	Coral	37
46.	MAIN TITLE ("MAN WITH THE GOLDEN ARM")	R. Maltby	Vik	36
47.	CORRINE, CORRINA	J. Turner	Atlantic	41
48.	TO LOVE AGAIN	Four Aces	Decca	59
48.	WHY DO FOOLS FALL IN LOVE?	G. Storm	Dot	35
50.	TOO CLOSE FOR COMFORT	E. Gorme	ABC-Paramount	52
51.	LITTLE LOVE CAN GO A LONG, LONG WAY	Dream Weavers	Decca	47
52.	HOW LITTLE WE KNOW	F. Sinatra	Capitol	52
53.	WILD CHERRY	D. Cherry	Columbia	50
54.	I'M IN LOVE AGAIN	Fontane Sisters	Dot	45
55.	PORTUGUESE WASHERWOMAN	J. (Fingers) Carr	Capitol	48
56.	TANGO OF THE DRUMS	L. Baxter	Capitol	44
57.	LITTLE GIRL OF MINE	Cleftones	Gee	65
58.	LOST JOHN	L. Donegan	London	—
58.	MAIN TITLE "(MAN WITH THE GOLDEN ARM")	E. Bernstein	Decca	63
60.	I COULD HAVE DANCED ALL NIGHT	S. Syms	Decca	46
61.	WHY DO FOOLS FALL IN LOVE?	Diamonds	Mercury	58
62.	LOVELY ONE	Four Voices	Columbia	67
63.	JUKE BOX BABY	P. Como	Victor	49
63.	MAIN TITLE MOLLY-O ("MAN WITH THE GOLDEN ARM")	D. Jacobs	Coral	51
65.	MR. WONDERFUL	S. Vaughan	Mercury	56
66.	WALK HAND IN HAND	A. Williams	Cadence	66
67.	I WAS THE ONE	E. Presley	Victor	52
68.	BLUE SUEDE SHOES	E. Presley	Victor	38
69.	LOST IN THE SHUFFLE	J. P. Morgan	Victor	100
70.	SWEET OLD-FASHIONED GIRL	T. Brewer	Coral	—
71.	IN A SHANTY IN OLD SHANTY TOWN	S. Smith	Epic	94
72.	POOR PEOPLE OF PARIS	R. Morgan	Decca	—
73.	FREE	T. Leonetti	Capitol	—
74.	BO WEEVIL	T. Brewer	Coral	90
75.	SAINTS ROCK AND ROLL	B. Haley	Decca	97
75.	SWEET HEARTACHES	E. Fisher	Victor	83
77.	NO, NOT MUCH	Four Lads	Columbia	40
78.	YOU'RE THE APPLE OF MY EYE	Four Lovers	Victor	—
79.	ROVIN' GAMBLER	T. Ernie	Capitol	60
80.	I COULD HAVE DANCED ALL NIGHT	R. Clooney	Columbia	80
81.	I WOKE UP CRYING	J. James	M-G-M	86
82.	NO OTHER ONE	E. Fisher	Victor	—
83.	LOOK HOMEWARD ANGEL	Four Esquires	London	82
84.	EDDIE, MY LOVE	Fontane Sisters	Dot	63
85.	I'M IN LOVE WITH YOU	P. Boone	Dot	—
86.	ROCK AND ROLL WALTZ	K. Starr	Victor	76
87.	HI LILI HI LO	R. Williams	Kapp	85
88.	WINNER TAKE ALL	Platters	Mercury	—
89.	PORT-AU-PRINCE	N. Riddle	Capitol	78
90.	SECOND FIDDLE	K. Starr	Victor	—
91.	LAZY RIVER	R. Sherwood	Decca	—
92.	HOT AND COLD RUNNING TEARS	S. Vaughan	Mercury	—
92.	STANDING ON THE CORNER	Mills Brothers	Decca	71
94.	MAIN TITLE ("MAN WITH THE GOLDEN ARM")	B. May	Capitol	77
95.	PLAY FOR KEEPS	J. P. Morgan	Victor	79
95.	TO YOU MY LOVE	N. Noble	Mercury	73
97.	ON THE STREET WHERE YOU LIVE	E. Fisher	Victor	—
98.	PICNIC	R. Marterie	Mercury	97
99.	GLENDORA	P. Como	Victor	—
160.	I'VE GROWN ACCUSTOMED TO YOUR FACE	G. MacRae	Capitol	99

CAUTION TO DEALERS AND JUKE BOX OPERATORS

The Billboard's Top 100 is NOT designed to provide tested information for buying purposes. This function is most reliably served by other regular weekly features: Best Sellers in Stores, Most Played in Juke Boxes, Coming Up Strong and Best Buys.

• Best Sellers in Stores

For survey week ending June 6

RECORDS are ranked in order of their current national selling importance at the retail level, as determined by The Billboard's weekly survey of the top volume dealers in every important market area. When significant action is reported on both sides of a record, points are combined to determine position on the chart. In such a case, both sides are listed in bold type, the leading side on top.

This Week		Last Week	Weeks on Chart
1.	WAYWARD WIND (BMI)—G. Grant No More Than Forever (ASCAP)—Era 1013	3	7
2.	MOONGLOW AND THEME FROM "PICNIC" (ASCAP)—M. Stoloff Theme From "Picnic" (ASCAP)—Dec 29888	2	9
3.	HEARTBREAK HOTEL (BMI) E. Presley I Was the One (BMI)—Vic 20-6420	1	15
4.	STANDING ON THE CORNER (ASCAP)—Four Lads MY LITTLE ANGEL (BMI)—Col 40574	4	8
5.	I'M IN LOVE AGAIN (BMI)—F. Domino MY BLUE HEAVEN (ASCAP)—Imperial 5386	5	7
6.	MOONGLOW AND THEME FROM "PICNIC" (ASCAP)—G. Cates Rio Batucada (ASCAP)—Coral 61618	7	9
7.	IVORY TOWER (ASCAP)—C. Carr Please, Please Believe Me (ASCAP)—Fraternity 734	8	10
8.	HOT DIGGITY (ASCAP)—P. Como Juke Box Baby (ASCAP)—Vic 20-6427	6	15
9.	HAPPY WHISTLER (ASCAP)—D. Robertson You're Free to Go (ASCAP)—Cap 3391	11	7
10.	I ALMOST LOST MY MIND (BMI)—P. Boone I'm in Love With You (BMI)—Dot 15427	—	1
11.	TRANSFUSION (BMI)— Dig (BMI)—Dot 15470	23	2
12.	I WANT YOU, I NEED YOU, I LOVE YOU (BMI)—E. Presley MY BABY LEFT ME (BMI)—Vic 20-6540	9	3
13.	ON THE STREET WHERE YOU LIVE (ASCAP)—V. Damone We All Need Love (ASCAP)—Col 40654	20	2
14.	MAGIC TOUCH (BMI)—Platters Winner Take All (ASCAP)—Mercury 70819	9	12
15.	PICNIC (ASCAP)—McGuire Sisters Delilah Jones (ASCAP)—Coral 61627	16	4
16.	CAN YOU FIND IT IN YOUR HEART? (ASCAP)—T. Bennett Forget Her (ASCAP)—Col 49667	24	7
17.	CHURCH BELLS MAY RING (BMI)—Diamonds Little Girl of Mine (BMI)—Mercury 70835	18	6
18.	IVORY TOWER (ASCAP)—G. Storm I Ain't Gonna Worry (BMI)—Dot 15458	15	4
19.	I WANT YOU TO BE MY GIRL (BMI)—Teen-Agers I'm Not a Know-It-All (ASCAP)—Gee 1012	14	6
20.	IT ONLY HURTS FOR A LITTLE WHILE (ASCAP)—Ames Brothers If You Want to See Mamie Tonight (ASCAP)—Vic 20-6481	21	3
21.	GRADUATION DAY (BMI)—Rover Boys I Hear Music (BMI)—ABC-Paramount 9700	—	1
22.	LONG, TALL SALLY (BMI)—Little Richard Slippin' and Slidin' (BMI)—Specialty 572	13	11
22.	MORE (ASCAP)—P. Como GLENDORA (BMI)—Vic 20-6554	—	1
24.	POOR PEOPLE OF PARIS (ASCAP)—L. Baxter Theme From "Helen of Troy" (ASCAP)—Cap 3336	17	18
25.	BLUE SUEDE SHOES (BMI)—C. Perkins Honey, Don't (BMI)—Sun 234	12	15

• Most Played in Juke Boxes

For survey week ending June 6

RECORDS are ranked in order of the greatest number of plays in juke boxes thruout the country, as determined by The Billboard's weekly survey of the nation's juke box operators. When significant play is reported on both sides of a record, points are combined to determine position on the chart. In such a case, both sides are listed in bold type, the leading side on top.

This Week		Last Week	Weeks on Chart
1.	HEARTBREAK HOTEL (BMI)—E. Presley I Was the One (BMI)—Vic 20-6420	1	12
2.	IVORY TOWER (ASCAP)—C. Carr Please, Please Believe Me (ASCAP)—Fraternity 734	4	7
3.	HOT DIGGITY (BMI)—P. Como JUKE BOX BABY (BMI)—Vic 20-6427	3	13
4.	BLUE SUEDE SHOES (BMI)—C. Perkins Honey, Don't (BMI)—Sun 234	2	13
5.	WAYWARD WIND (BMI)—G. Grant No More Than Forever (ASCAP)—Era 1013	6	3
6.	MOONGLOW AND THEME FROM "PICNIC" (ASCAP)—M. Stoloff Theme From "Picnic" (ASCAP)—Dec 29888	7	5
7.	MAGIC TOUCH (ASCAP)—Platters Winner Take All (ASCAP)—Mercury 70819	4	10
8.	MOONGLOW AND THEME FROM "PICNIC" (ASCAP)—G. Cates Rio Batucada (ASCAP)—Coral 61618	8	6
9.	STANDING ON THE CORNER (ASCAP)—Four Lads My Little Angel (BMI)—Col 40674	9	4
10.	IVORY TOWER (ASCAP)—G. Storm I Ain't Gonna Worry (BMI)—Dot 15458	11	5
11.	A TEAR FELL (BMI)—T. Brewer Bo Weevil (BMI)—Coral 61590	12	13
12.	I'M IN LOVE AGAIN (BMI)—F. Domino My Blue Heaven (ASCAP)—Imperial 5386	15	5
13.	HAPPPY WHISTLER (ASCAP)—D. Robertson You're Free to Go (ASCAP)—Cap 3391	13	3
14.	LONG, TALL SALLY (BMI) P. Boone Any Place in Heaven (ASCAP)—Dot 15457	10	7
15.	I WANT YOU, I NEED YOU, I LOVE YOU (BMI)—E. Presley MY BABY LEFT ME (BMI)—Vic 20-6540	17	2
16.	WHY DO FOOLS FALL IN LOVE? (BMI)—Teen-Agers Please Be Mine (BMI)—Gee 1002	17	16
16.	I ALMOST LOST MY MIND (BMI)—P. Boone I'm In Love With You (BMI)—Dot 15472	—	1
18.	POOR PEOPLE OF PARIS (ASCAP)—L. Baxter Theme From "Helen of Troy" (ASCAP)—Cap 3336	14	17
19.	LONG, TALL SALLY (BMI) Little Richard Slippin' and Slidin' (BMI)—Specialty 572	16	6
20.	PICNIC (ASCAP)—McGuire Sisters Delilah Jones (ASCAP)—Coral 61627	19	2

• Best Selling Sheet Music

Tunes are ranked in order of their current national selling importance at the sheet music jobber level.

This Week		Last Week	Weeks on Chart
1.	**Ivory Tower** (E. H. Morris)	1	8
2.	**Walk Hand in Hand** (Republic)	2	6
3.	**Standing On the Corner** (Frank)	4	5
4.	**Wayward Wind** (Warman)	9	3
5.	**Moonglow** (Mills-Columbia Pictures)	4	5
6.	**Picnic** (Shapiro-Bernstein)	7	5
7.	**Hot Diggity** (Roncom)	3	14
8.	**On the Street Where You Live** (Chappell)	11	6
9.	**Heartbreak Hotel** (Tree)	8	9
10.	**Graduation Day** (Sheldon)	13	2
11.	**Poor People of Paris** (Connelly)	6	17
12.	**Mr. Wonderful** (Laurel)	10	12
13.	**I Could Have Danced All Night** (Chappell)	15	3
14.	**Rock and Roll Waltz** (Sheldon)	—	20
15.	**Blue Suede Shoes** (Hi-Lo)	12	10

• Most Played by Jockeys

For survey week ending June 6

SIDES are ranked in order of the greatest number of plays on disk jockey radio shows thruout the country. Results are based on The Billboard's weekly survey among the nation's disk jockeys. The reverse side of each record is also listed.

This Week		Last Week	Weeks on Chart
1.	MOONGLOW AND THEME FROM "PICNIC" (ASCAP)—M. Stoloff Theme From "Picnic" (ASCAP)—Dec 29888	1	9
2.	WAYWARD WIND (BMI)—G. Grant No More Than Forever (ASCAP)—Era 1013	2	6
3.	STANDING ON THE CORNER (ASCAP)—Four Lads My Little Angel (BMI)—Col 40674	4	7
4.	HEARTBREAK HOTEL (BMI)—E. Presley I Was the One (BMI)—Vic 20-6420	3	15
5.	HOT DIGGITY (ASCAP)—P. Como Juke Box Baby (BMI)—Vic 20-6427	5	14
6.	HAPPY WHISTLER (ASCAP)—D. Robertson You're Free to Go (ASCAP)—Cap 3391	6	7
7.	I'M IN LOVE AGAIN (BMI)—F. Domino My Blue Heaven (ASCAP)—Imperial 5386	10	4
8.	MOONGLOW AND THEME FROM "PICNIC" (ASCAP)—G. Cates Rio Batucada (ASCAP)—Coral 61618	7	9
9.	ON THE STREET WHERE YOU LIVE (ASCAP)—V. Damone We All Need Love (ASCAP)—Col 40654	12	3
10.	IVORY TOWER (ASCAP)—G. Storm I Ain't Gonna Worry—Dot 15458	8	6
11.	MAGIC TOUCH (BMI)—Platters Winner Take All (ASCAP)—Mercury 70819	9	10
12.	IVORY TOWER (ASCAP)—C. Carr Please, Please Believe Me (ASCAP)—Fraternity 734	11	8
13.	HOW LITTLE WE KNOW (ASCAP)—F. Sinatra Five Hundred Guys (ASCAP)—Cap 3423	18	3
14.	IVORY TOWER (ASCAP)—O. Williams In Paradise (BMI)—De Luxe 6093	13	8
15.	BORN TO BE WITH YOU (ASCAP)—Chordettes Love Never Changes (ASCAP)—Cadence 1291	23	2
16.	PICNIC (ASCAP)—McGuire Sisters Delilah Jones (ASCAP)—Coral 61627	15	4
17.	I ALMOST LOST MY MIND (BMI)—P. Boone I'm In Love With You (BMI)—Dot 15472	—	1
18.	WALK HAND IN HAND (BMI)—T. Martin Flamenco Love (ASCAP)—Vic 20-6493	15	4
19.	GRADUATION DAY (BMI)—Rover Boys I Hear Music (BMI)—ABC-Paramount 9700	21	5
20.	I COULD HAVE DANCED ALL NIGHT (ASCAP)—S. Syms World in My Corner (ASCAP)—Dec 29903	—	1
21.	TRANSFUSION (BMI)—Nervous Norvus Dig (BMI)—Dot 15470	—	1
22.	BLUE SUEDE SHOES (BMI)—C. Perkins Honey, Don't (BMI)—Sun 234	20	13
23.	POOR PEOPLE OF PARIS (ASCAP)—L. Baxter Theme From "Helen of Troy" (ASCAP)—Cap 3336	14	18
23.	I WANT YOU, I NEED YOU, I LOVE YOU (BMI)—E. Presley My Baby Left Me (BMI) (ASCAP)—Vic 20-6540	—	1
25.	GRADUATION DAY (BMI)—Four Freshmen Lonely Night in Paris (ASCAP)—Cap 3410	19	2
25.	PORTUGUESE WASHERWOMAN (ASCAP)—J. (Fingers) Carr Lucky Pierre (ASCAP)—Cap 3418	—	1

THE TOP 100

For survey week ending June 6

A list of the **TOP 100 RECORD SIDES** in the nation according to a **COMBINED TABULATION** of Dealer Disk Jockey and Juke Box Operator replies to The Billboard's weekly popular record Best Seller and Most Played surveys. Its purpose is to provide Disk Jockeys with additional programming material and to give trade exposure to NEWER records just beginning to show action in the field.

Pos.	Song	Artist	Label	Last Week
1.	HEARTBREAK HOTEL	E. Presley	Victor	1
1.	WAYWARD WIND	G. Grant	Era	2
3.	MOONGLOW AND THEME FROM "PICNIC"	M. Stoloff	Decca	2
4.	HOT DIGGITY	P. Como	Victor	4
4.	STANDING ON THE CORNER	Four Lads	Columbia	5
6.	IVORY TOWER	C. Carr	Fraternity	8
7.	MOONGLOW AND THEME FROM "PICNIC"	G. Cates	Coral	6
8.	I'M IN LOVE AGAIN	F. Domino	Imperial	12
9.	HAPPY WHISTLER	D. Robertson	Capitol	9
10.	MAGIC TOUCH	Platters	Mercury	7
11.	IVORY TOWER	G. Storm	Dot	10
12.	I ALMOST LOST MY MIND	P. Boone	Dot	25
13.	PICNIC	McGuire Sisters	Coral	15
14.	BLUE SUEDE SHOES	C. Perkins	Sun	11
15.	TRANSFUSION	N. Norvus	Dot	29
16.	I WANT YOU, I NEED YOU, I LOVE YOU	E. Presley	Victor	19
17.	ON THE STREET WHERE YOU LIVE	V. Damone	Columbia	25
18.	POOR PEOPLE OF PARIS	L. Baxter	Capitol	13
19.	IVORY TOWER	O. Williams	De Luxe	16
20.	BORN TO BE WITH YOU	Chordettes	Cadence	27
21.	IT ONLY HURTS FOR A LITTLE WHILE	Ames Brothers	Victor	20
21.	A TEAR FELL	T. Brewer	Coral	14
23.	GRADUATION DAY	Rover Boys	ABC-Paramount	23
23.	LONG, TALL SALLY	Little Richard	Specialty	18
25.	CAN YOU FIND IT IN YOUR HEART?	T. Bennett	Columbia	21
26.	CHURCH BELLS MAY RING	Diamonds	Mercury	22
26.	I WANT YOU TO BE MY GIRL	Teen-Agers	Gee	17
28.	WALK HAND IN HAND	T. Martin	Victor	24
29.	MY BLUE HEAVEN	F. Domino	Imperial	31
30.	MY LITTLE ANGEL	Four Lads	Columbia	33
31.	MY BABY LEFT ME	E. Presley	Victor	34
32.	STANDING ON THE CORNER	D. Martin	Capitol	30
33.	GRADUATION DAY	Four Freshmen	Capitol	38
34.	SWEET OLD-FASHIONED GIRL	T. Brewer	Coral	70
34.	TREASURE OF LOVE	C. McPhatter	Atlantic	37
36.	LONG, TALL SALLY	P. Boone	Dot	27
37.	ALLEGHENY MOON	P. Page	Mercury	—
38.	ROCK ISLAND LINE	L. Donegan	London	32
39.	TOO CLOSE FOR COMFORT	E. Gorme	ABC-Paramount	50
40.	KISS ME ANOTHER	G. Gibbs	Mercury	39
40.	PORTUGUESE WASHERWOMAN	J. (Fingers) Carr	Capitol	55
42.	LISBON ANTIGUA	N. Riddle	Capitol	35
43.	HOW LITTLE WE KNOW	F. Sinatra	Capitol	52
44.	I'M IN LOVE AGAIN	Fontane Sisters	Dot	54
45.	I COULD HAVE DANCED ALL NIGHT	S. Syms	Decca	60
45.	MORE	P. Como	Victor	—
47.	IN A SHANTY IN OLD SHANTY TOWN	S. Smith	Epic	71
48.	TOO YOUNG TO GO STEADY	N. (King) Cole	Capitol	41
49.	MAIN TITLE (" MAN WITH THE GOLDEN ARM")	R. Maltby	Vik	46
49.	MR. WONDERFUL	P. Lee	Decca	41
51.	I COULD HAVE DANCED ALL NIGHT	R. Clooney	Columbia	80
51.	WHY DO FOOLS FALL IN LOVE?	Teen-Agers	Gee	36
53.	WHY DO FOOLS FALL IN LOVE?	G. Storm	Dot	48
54.	GLENDORA	P. Como	Victor	99
55.	I'LL BE HOME	P. Boone	Dot	40
56.	WILD CHERRY	D. Cherry	Columbia	53
57.	TO LOVE AGAIN	Four Aces	Decca	48
58.	SLIPPIN' AND SLIDIN'	Little Richard	Specialty	43
59.	MAIN TITLE ("MAN WITH THE GOLDEN ARM")	E. Bernstein	Decca	58
60.	DELILAH JONES	McGuire Sisters	Coral	45
61.	CORRINE, CORRINA	J. Turner	Atlantic	47
62.	YOU'RE THE APPLE OF MY EYE	Four Lovers	Victor	78
63.	WHY DO FOOLS FALL IN LOVE?	Diamonds	Mercury	61
64.	ROVIN' GAMBLER	T. Ernie	Capitol	79
65.	WALK HAND IN HAND	A. Williams	Cadence	66
66.	BLUE SUEDE SHOES	E. Presley	Victor	68
66.	NO, NOT MUCH	Four Lads	Columbia	77
68.	LITTLE GIRL OF MINE	Cleftones	Gee	—
69.	ON THE STREET WHERE YOU LIVE	E. Fisher	Victor	97
70.	I'VE GROWN ACCUSTOMED TO YOUR FACE	R. Clooney	Columbia	—
71.	SECOND FIDDLE	K. Starr	Victor	90
72.	R-O-C-K	B. Haley	Decca	44
73.	BLUE SUEDE SHOES	B. Bennett	King	—
73.	FREE	T. Leonetti	Capitol	73
75.	MAIN TITLE MOLLY-O ("MAN WITH THE GOLDEN ARM")	D. Jacobs	Coral	63
75.	NEVER TURN BACK	A. Hibbler	Decca	—
77.	OOBY DOOBY	R. Orbison	Spn	—
78.	LITTLE LOVE CAN GO A LONG, LONG WAY	Dream Weavers	Decca	51
78.	MR. WONDERFUL	S. Vaughan	Mercury	65
78.	BE BOP A LULA	G. Vincent	Cap	—
81.	STANDING ON THE CORNER	Mills Brothers	Decca	92
82.	HOT DOG BUDDY BUDDY	B. Haley	Decca	—
82.	MAIN TITLE ("MAN WITH THE GOLDEN ARM")	B. May	Capitol	94
84.	CHURCH BELLS MAY RING	Willows	Melba	—
84.	SWEET HEARTACHES	E. Fisher	Victor	75
86.	PORT-AU-PRINCE	N. Riddle	Capitol	89
87.	LOST JOHN	L. Donegan	London	58
88.	LOST IN THE SHUFFLE	J. P. Morgan	Victor	69
89.	LOOK HOMEWARD, ANGEL	Four Esquires	London	83
89.	POOR PEOPLE OF PARIS	L. Welk	Coral	—
91.	LOVELY ONE	Four Voices	Columbia	62
92.	EDDIE, MY LOVE	Fontane Sisters	Dot	84
93.	MONEY, HONEY	E. Presley	Victor	—
94.	CRAZY LITTLE PALACE	B. Williams	Coral	—
95.	I'M IN LOVE WITH YOU	P. Boone	Dot	85
95.	MAIN TITLE ("MAN WITH THE GOLDEN ARM"	L. Elgart	Columbia	—
97.	JOEY, JOEY, JOEY	P. Lee	Decca	—
97.	JUKE BOX BABY	P. Como	Victor	63
97.	POOR PEOPLE OF PARIS (JEAN'S SONG)	C. Atkins	Victor	—
100.	ROCK AND ROLL WALTZ	K. Starr	Victor	86

CAUTION TO DEALERS AND JUKE BOX OPERATORS

The Billboard's Top 100 is NOT designed to provide tested information for buying purposes. This function is most reliably served by other regular weekly features: Best Sellers in Stores, Most Played in Juke Boxes, Coming Up Strong and Best Buys.

• Best Sellers in Stores

For survey week ending June 13

RECORDS are ranked in order of their current national selling importance at the retail level, as determined by The Billboard's weekly survey of the top volume dealers in every important market area. When significant action is reported on both sides of a record, points are combined to determine position on the chart. In such a case, both sides are listed in bold type, the leading side on top.

This Week		Last Week	Weeks on Chart
1.	WAYWARD WIND (BMI)—G. Grant No More Than Forever (ASCAP)—Era 1013	1	8
2.	MOONGLOW AND THEME FROM "PICNIC" (ASCAP)—M. Stoloff Theme From "Picnic" (ASCAP)—Dec 29888	2	10
3.	STANDING ON THE CORNER (ASCAP)—Four Lads MY LITTLE ANGEL (BMI)—Col 40574	4	9
4.	I'M IN LOVE AGAIN (BMI)—F. Domino MY BLUE HEAVEN (ASCAP)—Imperial 5386	5	8
5.	I ALMOST LOST MY MIND (BMI)—P. Boone I'M IN LOVE WITH YOU (BMI)—Dot 15472	10	2
6.	HEARTBREAK HOTEL (BMI)—E. Presley I Was the One (BMI)—Vic 20-6420	3	16
7.	I WANT YOU, I NEED YOU, I LOVE YOU (BMI)—E. Presley MY BABY LEFT ME (BMI)—Vic 20-6540	12	4
8.	TRANSFUSION (BMI)—Nervous Norvus Dig (BMI)—Dot 15470	11	3
9.	IVORY TOWER (ASCAP)—C. Carr Please, Please Believe Me (ASCAP)—Fraternity 734	7	11
10.	MOONGLOW AND THEME FROM "PICNIC" (ASCAP)—G. Cates Rio Batucada (ASCAP)—Coral 61618	6	10
11.	HAPPY WHISTLER (ASCAP)—D. Robertson You're Free to Go (ASCAP)—Cap 3391	9	8
12.	ON THE STREET WHERE YOU LIVE (ASCAP)—V. Damone We All Need Love (ASCAP)—Col 40654	13	3
13.	MORE (ASCAP)—P. Como GLENDORA (BMI)—Vic 20-6554	22	2
14.	HOT DIGGITY (ASCAP)—P. Como Juke Box Baby (ASCAP)—Vic 20-6427	8	16
15.	BORN TO BE WITH YOU (ASCAP)—Chordettes Love Never Changes (ASCAP)—Cadence 1291	—	1
16.	IT ONLY HURTS FOR A LITTLE WHILE (ASCAP)—Ames Brothers If You Want to See Mamie Tonight (ASCAP)—Vic 20-6481	20	4
17.	PICNIC (ASCAP)—McGuire Sisters Delilah Jones (ASCAP)—Coral 61627	15	5
18.	TREASURE OF LOVE (BMI)—C. McPhatter When You're Sincere (BMI)—Atlantic 1092	—	1
19.	GRADUATION DAY (BMI)—Rover Boys I Hear Music (ASCAP)—ABC-Paramount 9700	21	2
20.	I WANT YOU TO BE MY GIRL (BMI)—Teen-Agers I'm Not a Know-It-All (ASCAP)—Gee 1012	19	7
21.	IVORY TOWER (ASCAP)—G. Storm I Ain't Gonna Worry (BMI)—Dot 15458	18	5
22.	MAGIC TOUCH (BMI)—Platters Winner Take All (ASCAP)—Mercury 70819	14	13
22.	WALK HAND IN HAND (BMI)—T. Martin Flamenco Love (ASCAP)—Vic 20-6493	—	4
24.	BE-BOP-A-LULA (BMI)—G. Vincent Woman Love (BMI)—Cap 3450	—	1
25.	SWEET OLD-FASHIONED GIRL (ASCAP)—T. Brewer Goodbye, John (BMI)—Coral 61636	—	1

• Most Played in Juke Boxes

For survey week ending June 13

RECORDS are ranked in order of the greatest number of plays in juke boxes thruout the country, as determined by The Billboard's weekly survey of the nation's juke box operators. When significant play is reported on both sides of a record, points are combined to determine position on the chart. In such a case, both sides are listed in bold type, the leading side on top.

This Week		Last Week	Weeks on Chart
1.	HEARTBREAK HOTEL (BMI)—E. Presley I Was the One (BMI)—Vic 20-6420	1	13
2.	WAYWARD WIND (BMI)—G. Grant No More Than Forever (ASCAP)—Era 1013	5	4
3.	IVORY TOWER (ASCAP)—C. Carr Please, Please Believe Me (ASCAP)—Fraternity 734	2	8
4.	MOONGLOW AND THEME FROM "PICNIC" (ASCAP)—M. Stoloff Theme From "Picnic" (ASCAP)—Dec 29888	6	6
5.	STANDING ON THE CORNER (ASCAP)—Four Lads MY LITTLE ANGEL (BMI)—Col 40674	9	5
6.	I'M IN LOVE AGAIN (BMI)—F. Domino MY BLUE HEAVEN (ASCAP)—Imperial 5386	12	6
7.	BLUE SUEDE SHOES (BMI)—C. Perkins Honey, Don't (BMI)—Sun 234	4	14
7.	IVORY TOWER (ASCAP)—G. Storm I Ain't Gonna Worry (BMI)—Dot 15458	10	6
9.	MOONGLOW AND THEME FROM "PICNIC" (ASCAP)—G. Cates Rio Batucada (ASCAP)—Coral 61618	8	7
10.	HOT DIGGITY (BMI)—P. Como Juke Box Baby (BMI)—Vic 20-6427	3	14
11.	MAGIC TOUCH (ASCAP)—Platters Winner Take All (ASCAP)—Mercury 70819	7	11
12.	HAPPY WHISTLER (ASCAP)—D. Robertson You're Free to Go (ASCAP)—Cap 3391	13	4
13.	I WANT YOU, I NEED YOU, I LOVE YOU (BMI)—E. Presley MY BABY LEFT ME (BMI)—Vic 20-6540	15	3
14.	I ALMOST LOST MY MIND (BMI)—P. Boone I'm in Love With You (BMI)—Dot 15472	16	2
15.	A TEAR FELL (BMI)—T. Brewer Bo Weevil (BMI)—Coral 61590	11	14
16.	LONG, TALL SALLY (BMI)—P. Boone Any Place in Heaven (ASCAP)—Dot 15457	14	8
17.	IT ONLY HURTS A LITTLE WHILE (ASCAP)—Ames Brothers If You Want to See Mamie Tonight (ASCAP)—Vic 20-6481	—	1
18.	TRANSFUSION (BMI)—Nervous Norvus Dig (BMI)—Dot 15470	—	1
19.	LONG, TALL SALLY (BMI)—Little Richard Slippin' and Slidin' (BMI)—Specialty 572	19	7
20.	PICNIC (ASCAP)—McGuire Sisters Delilah Jones (ASCAP)—Coral 61627	20	3

• Best Selling Sheet Music

Tunes are ranked in order of their current national selling importance at the sheet music jobber level.

This Week		Last Week	Weeks on Chart
1.	Ivory Tower (E. H. Morris)	1	9
2.	Walk Hand in Hand (Republic)	2	7
3.	Wayward Wind (Warman)	4	4
4.	Standing On the Corner (Frank)	3	6
4.	Moonglow (Mills-Columbia Pictures)	5	6
6.	Picnic (Shapiro-Bernstein)	6	6
7.	On the Street Where You Live (Chappell)	8	7
8.	Hot Diggity (Roncom)	7	15
9.	Graduation Day (Sheldon)	10	3
10.	I Could Have Danced All Night (Chappell)	12	4
11.	Heartbreak Hotel (Tree)	9	10
12.	Poor People of Paris (Connelly)	11	18
13.	Mr. Wonderful (Laurel)	12	13
14.	Rock and Roll Waltz (Sheldon)	14	21
15.	Happy Whistler (Birchwood)	—	1

• Most Played by Jockeys

For survey week ending June 13

SIDES are ranked in order of the greatest number of plays on disk jockey radio shows thruout the country. Results are based on The Billboard's weekly survey among the nation's disk jockeys. The reverse side of each record is also listed.

This Week		Last Week	Weeks on Chart
1.	WAYWARD WIND (BMI)—G. Grant No More Than Forever (ASCAP)—Era 1013	2	7
2.	MOONGLOW AND THEME FROM "PICNIC" (ASCAP)—M. Stoloff Theme From "Picnic" (ASCAP)—Dec 29888	1	10
3.	STANDING ON THE CORNER (ASCAP)—Four Lads My Little Angel (BMI)—Col 40674	3	8
4.	MOONGLOW AND THEME FROM "PICNIC" (ASCAP)—G. Cates Rio Batucada (ASCAP)—Coral 61618	8	10
5.	ON THE STREET WHERE YOU LIVE (ASCAP)—V. Damone We All Need Love (ASCAP)—Col 40654	9	4
6.	I'M IN LOVE AGAIN (BMI)—F. Domino My Blue Heaven (ASCAP)—Imperial 5386	7	5
7.	HEARTBREAK HOTEL (BMI)—E. Presley I Was the One (BMI)—Vic 20-6420	4	16
8.	I ALMOST LOST MY MIND (BMI)—P. Boone I'm in Love With You (BMI)—Dot 15472	17	2
9.	HOT DIGGITY (ASCAP)—P. Como Juke Box Baby (BMI)—Vic 20-6427	5	15
10.	HAPPY WHISTLER (ASCAP)—D. Robertson You're Free to Go (ASCAP)—Cap 3391	6	8
11.	IVORY TOWER (ASCAP)—G. Storm I Ain't Gonna Worry—Dot 15458	10	7
12.	IVORY TOWER (ASCAP)—C. Carr Please, Please Believe Me (ASCAP)—Fraternity 734	12	9
13.	WALK HAND IN HAND (BMI)—T. Martin Flamenco Love—Vic 20-6493	18	5
14.	BORN TO BE WITH YOU (ASCAP)—Chordettes Love Never Changes (ASCAP)—Cadence 1291	15	3
15.	I WANT YOU, I NEED YOU, I LOVE YOU (BMI)—E. Presley My Baby Left Me (BMI)—Vic 20-6540	23	2
16.	GRADUATION DAY (BMI)—Rover Boys I Hear Music (BMI)—ABC-Paramount 9700	19	6
17.	GRADUATION DAY (BMI)—Four Freshmen Lonely Night in Paris (ASCAP)—Cap 3410	25	3
18.	HOW LITTLE WE KNOW (ASCAP)—F. Sinatra Five Hundred Guys (ASCAP)—Cap 3423	13	4
19.	GLENDORA (BMI)—P. Como More (ASCAP)—Viv 20-6554	—	1
20.	PICNIC (ASCAP)—McGuire Sisters Delilah Jones (ASCAP)—Coral 61627	16	5
21.	TRANSFUSION (BMI)—Nervous Norvus Dig (BMI)—Dot 15470	21	2
22.	IT ONLY HURTS FOR A LITTLE WHILE (ASCAP)—Ames Brothers See Mamie Tonight (ASCAP)—Vic 20-6481	—	2
23.	POOR PEOPLE OF PARIS (ASCAP)—L. Baxter Helen of Troy (ASCAP)—Cap 3336	23	19
23.	MAGIC TOUCH (BMI)—Platters Winner Take All (ASCAP)—Mercury 70819	11	11
25.	I COULD HAVE DANCED ALL NIGHT (ASCAP)—S. Syms World in My Corner (ASCAP)—Dec 29903	20	2

VOX JOX

By JUNE BUNDY

JOCK'S JUKES: Johnny Harper show, "The Juke Box," is expanding its time on KRLD, Dallas. Show will now be heard 12:30 to 5 p.m. Saturdays and will feature interviews with celebs and round-ups of the Dallas entertainment picture. . . . (Did) Dwyer of KAMO, Rogers, Ark., makes a tie-in with the boxes too, with his new show, "Juke Box of the Air," 6:30 to 7 p.m. daily. Dwyer now spins 38 and a half hours of disks each week.

WKAL, Rome, N. Y., jockey, Lou Barile, lifts his hat to the Nervous Norvous disking of "Transfusion," for "a terrific plug for safe driving . . . aimed right at the age group the National Safety Council has been trying so desperately to reach." . . . WAYB in Waynesboro, Va., on the other hand, banned the disk. "We consider the lyrics in poor taste," said jockey Frank Bleam. . . . WSKY, Asheville, is bringing the jockeys and the music to the people—in person. A German Volkswagen has been equipped with two turntables and record storage compartments. It's used to bring jockeys to the merchants' doors.

Harold Gann, who hosts the Spinnersanctum show on KDEN, Denver, up-dated the old Scavenger Hunt game on a recent airing. Gimmick offered a 1950 Pontiac to the first listener to show at the studio with a May 7 copy of Time magazine, a set of ice cubes, plastic wrapped, a photo of Mamie Eisenhower, a tire from a midget auto and a live pigeon. The winner arrived 50 minutes later.

Latest fem jockey entry is "The Girl Upstairs," who plays music in the soft light vein on a late evening show on KVOD, Denver. The lady is Merrie Lynn, announcer and gal Friday at the station. Teen-ager Candy Lee, on the other hand, who celebrates her fifth year at Green's Hotel, Pleasantdale, N. J., will run weekly deejay salutes during its entire summer season. On salute days, guests will receive autographed albums of favorite artists of the jock being honored.

ALBUM PLAYS: Jim Aylward, of WHIL, Malden, Mass., is including a 15-minute album exposure seg on his morning and afternoon shows, highlighting increasing use of packages by jocks. . . . Deejay Joe Ryan, of WALL, Middleton, N. Y., does a 55-minute slotting called "Album Time" on his daily airer. Ryan says that diskeries sending out LP excerpts of album releases are missing the boat. Ryan claims that companies cannot tell which album selections individual jockeys will play and that those who send complete al-

(Continued on page 56)

YESTERYEAR'S TOPS—

The nation's top tunes on records as reported in The Billboard

JUNE 22, 1946:

1. The Gypsy
2. Laughing on the Outside (Crying on the Inside)
3. They Say It's Wonderful
4. Prisoner of Love
5. All Through the Day
6. Doin' What Comes Natur'lly
7. Sioux City Sue
8. Full Moon and Empty Arms
9. I Don't Know Enough About You
10. Do You Love Me?
11. I'm a Big Girl Now
12. Cement Mixer
13. In Love in Vain
14. In the Moon Mist
15. Shoo-Fly Pie and Apple Pan Dowdy

JUNE 23, 1951:

1. Too Young
2. How High the Moon
3. On Top of Old Smoky
4. My Truly, Truly Fair
5. Mockin' Bird Hill
6. Jezebel
7. Rose, Rose I Love You
8. Mister and Mississippi
9. Sound Off
10. Loveliest Night of the Year

THE TOP 100

For survey week ending June 13

A list of the **TOP 100 RECORD SIDES** in the nation according to a **COMBINED TABULATION** of Dealer Disk Jockey and Juke Box Operator replies to The Billboard's weekly popular record Best Seller and Most Played surveys. Its purpose is to provide Disk Jockeys with additional programming material and to give trade exposure to NEWER records just beginning to show action in the field.

Pos.	Song	Artist	Label	Last Week
1.	WAYWARD WIND	G. Grant	Era	1
2.	MOONGLOW AND THEME FROM "PICNIC"	M. Stoloff	Decca	3
3.	STANDING ON THE CORNER	Four Lads	Columbia	4
4.	HEARTBREAK HOTEL	E. Presley	Victor	1
5.	MOONGLOW AND THEME FROM "PICNIC"	G. Cates	Coral	7
6.	I'M IN LOVE AGAIN	Fats Domino	Imperial	8
7.	IVORY TOWER	C. Carr	Fraternity	6
7.	I ALMOST LOST MY MIND	P. Boone	Dot	12
9.	HOT DIGGITY	P. Como	Victor	4
10.	HAPPY WHISTLER	D. Robertson	Capitol	9
11.	I WANT YOU, I NEED YOU, I LOVE YOU	E. Presley	Victor	16
12.	IVORY TOWER	G. Storm	Dot	11
13.	TRANSFUSION	N. Norvus	Dot	15
14.	BORN TO BE WITH YOU	Chordettes	Cadence	20
15.	IT ONLY HURTS FOR A LITTLE WHILE	Ames Brothers	Victor	21
16.	ON THE STREET WHERE YOU LIVE	V. Damone	Columbia	17
17.	MAGIC TOUCH	Platters	Mercury	10
18.	PICNIC	McGuire Sisters	Coral	13
18.	WALK HAND IN HAND	T. Martin	Victor	28
20.	GRADUATION DAY	Rover Boys	ABC-Paramount	23
21.	MY BLUE HEAVEN	Fats Domino	Imperial	29
22.	BLUE SUEDE SHOES	C. Perkins	Sun	14
22.	I WANT YOU TO BE MY GIRL	Teen-Agers	Gee	26
24.	MORE	P. Como	Victor	45
25.	CHURCH BELLS MAY RING	Diamonds	Mercury	26
26.	IVORY TOWER	O. Williams	De Luxe	19
27.	CAN YOU FIND IT IN YOUR HEART?	T. Bennett	Columbia	25
28.	SWEET OLD-FASHIONED GIRL	T. Brewer	Coral	34
28.	A TEAR FELL	T. Brewer	Coral	21
30.	GLENDORA	P. Como	Victor	54
31.	POOR PEOPLE OF PARIS	L. Baxter	Capitol	18
32.	MY LITTLE ANGEL	Four Lads	Columbia	30
33.	ALLEGHENY MOON	P. Page	Mercury	37
34.	STANDING ON THE CORNER	D. Martin	Capitol	32
35.	GRADUATION DAY	Four Freshmen	Capitol	33
36.	LONG, TALL SALLY	P. Boone	Dot	36
37.	MY BABY LEFT ME	E. Presley	Victor	31
38.	TREASURE OF LOVE	C. McPhatter	Atlantic	34
39.	PORTUGUESE WASHERWOMAN	J. (Fingers) Carr	Capitol	40
40.	LONG, TALL SALLY	Little Richard	Specialty	23
41.	IN A SHANTY IN OLD SHANTY TOWN	Somethin' Smith	Epic	47
42.	SWEET HEARTACHES	E. Fisher	Victor	84
43.	BE-BOP-A-LULA	G. Vincent	Capitol	78
43.	ON THE STREET WHERE YOU LIVE	E. Fisher	Victor	69
45.	KISS ME ANOTHER	G. Gibbs	Mercury	40
46.	I'M IN LOVE AGAIN	Fontane Sisters	Dot	44
47.	SECOND FIDDLE	K. Starr	Victor	71
48.	TOO CLOSE FOR COMFORT	E. Gorme	ABC-Paramount	39
49.	I COULD HAVE DANCED ALL NIGHT	R. Clooney	Columbia	51
49.	ROCK ISLAND LINE	L. Donegan	London	38
51.	LISBON ANTIGUA	N. Riddle	Capitol	42
52.	CORRINE, CORRINA	J. Turner	Atlantic	61
53.	HOW LITTLE WE KNOW	F. Sinatra	Capitol	43
53.	WHY DO FOOLS FALL IN LOVE?	Teen-Agers	Gee	51
55.	MR. WONDERFUL	P. Lee	Decca	49
56.	SLIPPIN' AND SLIDIN'	Little Richard	Specialty	58
57.	DELILAH JONES	McGuire Sisters	Coral	60
57.	I COULD HAVE DANCED ALL NIGHT	S. Syms	Decca	45
57.	STANDING ON THE CORNER	Mills Brothers	Decca	81
57.	I'M IN LOVE WITH YOU	P. Boone	Dot	95
61.	NEVER LOOK BACK	A. Hibbler	Decca	75
62.	CHURCH BELLS MAY RING	Willows	Melba	84
63.	LITTLE GIRL OF MINE	Cleftones	Gee	68
64.	TOO YOUNG TO GO STEADY	Nat (King) Cole	Capitol	48
65.	NO, NOT MUCH	Four Lads	Columbia	66
66.	I LOOK AT YOU	Lassies	Decca	—
67.	ROVIN' GAMBLER	T. Ernie	Capitol	64
67.	TANGO OF THE DRUMS	L. Baxter	Capitol	—
69.	FREE	T. Leonetti	Capitol	73
70.	OOBY DOOBY	R. Orbison	Sun	77
70.	WALK HAND IN HAND	D. Vaughan	Kapp	—
72.	LOVE, LOVE, LOVE	Diamonds	Mercury	—
73.	TO LOVE AGAIN	Four Aces	Decca	57
74.	LOVE, LOVE, LOVE	Clovers	Atlantic	—
75.	MAIN TITLE (MAN WITH THE GOLDEN ARM)	R. Maltby	Vik	49
76.	LAZY RIVER	R. Sherwood	Decca	—
77.	I'VE GROWN ACCUSTOMED TO YOU FACE	R. Clooney	Columbia	70
78.	WHATEVER WILL BE, WILL BE	Doris Day	Columbia	—
78.	WHY DO FOOLS FALL IN LOVE?	G. Storm	Dot	53
80.	MAIN TITLE (MAN WITH THE GOLD ARM)	E. Bernstein	Decca	59
81.	MAIN TITLE MOLLY-O (MAN WITH THE GOLDEN ARM)	D. Jacobs	Coral	75
82.	POOR PEOPLE OF PARIS	L. Welk	Coral	89
83.	A LITTLE LOVE CAN GO A LONG, LONG WAY	Dream Weavers	Decca	78
84.	GREAT PRETENDER	Platters	Mercury	—
85.	WILD CHERRY	D. Cherry	Columbia	56
86.	I'LL BE HOME	P. Boone	Dot	55
87.	BO WEEVIL	T. Brewer	Coral	—
87.	BLUE SUEDE SHOES	B. Bennett	King	73
89.	YOU'RE THE APPLE OF MY EYE	Four Lovers	Victor	62
90.	WALK HAND IN HAND	A. Williams	Cadence	65
91.	CANADIAN SUNSET	H. Winterhalter	Victor	—
91.	EDDIE MY LOVE	Fontane Sisters	Dot	92
93.	JUKE BOX BABY	P. Como	Victor	97
94.	POOR PEOPLE OF PARIS	R. Morgan	Decca	—
95.	HOT DOG BUDDY BUDDY	B. Haley	Decca	82
96.	TUTTI FRUTTI	P. Boone	Dot	—
96.	ROCK RIGHT	G. Gibbs	Mercury	—
96.	ON THE STREET WHERE YOU LIVE	L. Welk	Coral	—
99.	WHY DO FOOLS FALL IN LOVE?	Diamonds	Mercury	63
100.	PICNIC	R. Marterie	Mercury	—

CAUTION TO DEALERS AND JUKE BOX OPERATORS

The Billboard's Top 100 is NOT designed to provide tested information for buying purposes. This function is most reliably served by other regular weekly features: Best Sellers in Stores, Most Played in Juke Boxes, Coming Up Strong and Best Buys.

• Best Sellers in Stores

For survey week ending June 20

RECORDS are ranked in order of their current national selling importance at the retail level, as determined by The Billboard's weekly survey of the top volume dealers in every important market area. When significant action is reported on both sides of a record, points are combined to determine position on the chart. In such a case, both sides are listed in bold type, the leading side on top.

This Week		Last Week	Weeks on Chart
1.	**WAYWARD WIND** (BMI)—G. Grant No More Than Forever (ASCAP)—Era 1013	1	9
2.	**MOONGLOW AND THEME FROM "PICNIC"** (ASCAP)—M. Stoloff Theme From "Picnic" (ASCAP)—Dec 29888	2	11
3.	**I ALMOST LOST MY MIND** (BMI)—P. Boone I'm In Love With You (BMI)—Dot 15472	5	3
4.	**STANDING ON THE CORNER** (ASCAP)—Four Lads **MY LITTLE ANGEL** (BMI)—Col 40574	3	10
5.	**I'M IN LOVE AGAIN** (BMI)—F. Domino **MY BLUE HEAVEN** (ASCAP)—Imperial 5386	4	9
6.	**I WANT YOU, I NEED YOU, I LOVE YOU** (BMI)—E. Presley **MY BABY LEFT ME** (BMI)—Vic 20-6540	7	5
7.	**MORE** (ASCAP)—P. Como **GLENDORA** (BMI)—Vic 20-6554	13	3
8.	**HEARTBREAK HOTEL** (BMI)—E. Presley I Was the One (BMI)—Vic 20-6420	6	17
9.	**IVORY TOWER** (ASCAP)—C. Carr Please, Please Believe Me (ASCAP)—Fraternity 734	9	12
10.	**ON THE STREET WHERE YOU LIVE** (ASCAP)—V. Damone We All Need Love (ASCAP)—Col 40654	12	4
11.	**TRANSFUSION** (BMI)—Nervous Norvus Dig (BMI)—Dot 15470	8	4
12.	**MOONGLOW AND THEME FROM "PICNIC"** (ASCAP)—G. Cates Rio Batucada (ASCAP)—Coral 61618	10	11
13.	**HAPPY WHISTLER** (ASCAP)—D. Robertson You're Free to Go (ASCAP)—Cap 3391	11	9
14.	**BORN TO BE WITH YOU** (ASCAP)—Chordettes Love Never Changes (ASCAP)—Cadence 1291	15	2
15.	**BE-BOP-A-LULA** (BMI)—G. Vincent Woman Love (BMI)—Cap 3450	24	2
16.	**TREASURE OF LOVE** (BMI)—C. McPhatter When You're Sincere (BMI)—Atlantic 1092	18	2
17.	**SWEET OLD-FASHIONED GIRL** (ASCAP)—T. Brewer Goodbye, John (BMI)—Coral 61636	25	2
18.	**HOT DIGGITY** (ASCAP)—P. Como Juke Box Baby (ASCAP)—Vic 20-6427	14	17
19.	**IT ONLY HURTS FOR A LITTLE WHILE** (ASCAP)—Ames Brothers If You Want to See Mamie Tonight (ASCAP)—Vic 20-6481	16	5
20.	**PICNIC** (ASCAP)—McGuire Sisters Delilah Jones (ASCAP)—Coral 61627	17	6
21.	**WALK HAND IN HAND** (BMI)—T. Martin Flamenco Love (ASCAP)—Vic 20-6493	22	5
22.	**I WANT YOU TO BE MY GIRL** (BMI)—Teen-Agers I'm Not a Know-It-All (ASCAP)—Gee 1012	20	8
23.	**GRADUATION DAY** (BMI)—Rover Boys I Hear Music (ASCAP)—ABC-Paramount 9700	19	3
24.	**IVORY TOWER** (ASCAP)—G. Storm I Ain't Gonna Worry (BMI)—Dot 15458	21	6
25.	**GRADUATION DAY** (BMI)—Four Freshmen Lonely Night in Paris (ASCAP)—Cap 3410	—	1

• Most Played in Juke Boxes

For survey week ending June 20

RECORDS are ranked in order of the greatest number of plays in juke boxes thruout the country, as determined by The Billboard's weekly survey of the nation's juke box operators. When significant play is reported on both sides of a record, points are combined to determine position on the chart. In such a case, both sides are listed in bold type, the leading side on top.

This Week		Last Week	Weeks on Chart
1.	**WAYWARD WIND** (BMI)—G. Grant No More Than Forever (ASCAP)—Era 1013	2	5
2.	**HEARTBREAK HOTEL** (BMI)—E. Presley I Was the One (BMI)—Vic 20-6420	1	14
3.	**STANDING ON THE CORNER** (ASCAP)—Four Lads **MY LITTLE ANGEL** (BMI)—Col 40674	5	6
4.	**MOONGLOW AND THEME FROM "PICNIC"** (ASCAP)—M. Stoloff Theme From "Picnic" (ASCAP)—Dec 29888	4	7
5.	**IVORY TOWER** (ASCAP)—C. Carr Please, Please Believe Me (ASCAP)—Fraternity 734	3	9
5.	**I'M IN LOVE AGAIN** (BMI)—F. Domino **MY BLUE HEAVEN** (ASCAP)—Imperial 5386	6	7
7.	**MOONGLOW AND THEME FROM "PICNIC"** (ASCAP)—G. Cates Rio Batucada (ASCAP)—Coral 61618	9	8
8.	**I ALMOST LOST MY MIND** (BMI)—P. Boone I'm In Love With You (BMI)—Dot 15472	14	3
9.	**I WANT YOU, I NEED YOU, I LOVE YOU** (BMI)—E. Presley **MY BABY LEFT ME** (BMI)—Vic 20-6540	13	4
10.	**IVORY TOWER** (ASCAP)—G. Storm I Ain't Gonna Worry (BMI)—Dot 15458	7	7
11.	**BLUE SUEDE SHOES** (BMI)—C. Perkins Honey, Don't (BMI)—Sun 234	7	15
12.	**MAGIC TOUCH** (ASCAP)—Platters Winner Take All (ASCAP)—Mercury 70819	11	12
13.	**HAPPY WHISTLER** (ASCAP)—D. Robertson You're Free to Go (ASCAP)—Cap 3391	12	5
14.	**HOT DIGGITY** (BMI)—P. Como Juke Box Baby (BMI)—Vic 20-6427	10	15
15.	**CHURCH BELLS MAY RING** (BMI)—Diamonds Little Girl of Mine (BMI)—Mercury 70835	—	1
16.	**WALK HAND IN HAND** (BMI)—T. Martin Flamenco Love (ASCAP)—Vic 20-6493	—	1
17.	**A TEAR FELL** (BMI)—T. Brewer Bo Weevil (BMI)—Coral 61590	15	15
17.	**LONG, TALL SALLY** (BMI)—Little Richard Slippin' and Slidin' (BMI)—Specialty 572	19	8
19.	**IT ONLY HURTS FOR A LITTLE WHILE** (ASCAP)—Ames Brothers If You Want to See Mamie Tonight (ASCAP)—Vic 20-6481	17	2
20.	**BORN TO BE WITH YOU** (ASCAP)—Chordettes Love Never Changes (ASCAP)—Cadence 1291	—	1

• Best Selling Sheet Music

Tunes are ranked in order of their current national selling importance at the sheet music jobber level.

This Week		Last Week	Weeks on Chart
1.	**Ivory Tower** (E. H. Morris)	1	10
2.	**Moonglow** (Mills-Columbia Pictures)	5	7
3.	**Wayward Wind** (Warman)	3	5
4.	**On the Street Where You Live** (Chappell)	7	8
5.	**Picnic** (Shapiro-Bernstein)	6	7
6.	**Walk Hand in Hand** (Republic)	2	8
7.	**Standing On the Corner** (Frank)	4	7
8.	**Graduation Day** (Sheldon)	9	4
9.	**Hot Diggity** (Roncom)	8	16
10.	**Allegheny Moon** (Oxford)	—	1
11.	**More** (Shapiro-Bernstein)	—	1
12.	**It Only Hurts for a Little While** (Advanced)	—	1
12.	**Poor People of Paris** (Connelly)	12	19
14.	**Heartbreak Hotel** (Tree)	11	11
15.	**I Almost Lost My Mind** (Hill & Range)	—	1

• Most Played by Jockeys

For survey week ending June 20

SIDES are ranked in order of the greatest number of plays on disk jockey radio shows thruout the country. Results are based on The Billboard's weekly survey among the nation's disk jockeys. The reverse side of each record is also listed.

This Week		Last Week	Weeks on Chart
1.	**WAYWARD WIND** (BMI)—G. Grant No More Than Forever (ASCAP)—Era 1013	1	8
2.	**MOONGLOW AND THEME FROM "PICNIC"** (ASCAP)—M. Stoloff Theme From "Picnic" (ASCAP)—Dec 29888	2	11
3.	**STANDING ON THE CORNER** (ASCAP)—Four Lads My Little Angel (BMI)—Col 40674	3	9
4.	**I ALMOST LOST MY MIND** (BMI)—P. Boone I'm In Love With You (BMI)—Dot 15472	8	3
5.	**ON THE STREET WHERE YOU LIVE** (ASCAP)—V. Damone We All Need Love (ASCAP)—Col 40654	5	5
6.	**MOONGLOW AND THEME FROM "PICNIC"** (ASCAP)—G. Cates Rio Batucada (ASCAP)—Coral 61618	4	11
7.	**BORN TO BE WITH YOU** (ASCAP)—Chordettes Love Never Changes (ASCAP)—Cadence 1291	14	4
8.	**I WANT YOU, I NEED YOU, I LOVE YOU** (BMI)—E. Presley My Baby Left Me (BMI)—Vic 20-6540	15	3
9.	**I'M IN LOVE AGAIN** (BMI)—F. Domino My Blue Heaven (ASCAP)—Imperial 5386	6	6
10.	**GLENDORA** (BMI)—P. Como More (ASCAP)—Vic 20-6554	19	2
11.	**IVORY TOWER** (ASCAP)—G. Storm I Ain't Gonna Worry (BMI)—Dot 15458	11	8
12.	**HEARTBREAK HOTEL** (BMI)—E. Presley I Was the One (BMI)—Vic 20-6420	7	17
13.	**IVORY TOWER** (ASCAP)—C. Carr Please, Please Believe Me (ASCAP)—Fraternity 734	12	10
14.	**TRANSFUSION** (BMI)—Nervous Norvus Dig (BMI)—Dot 15470	21	3
15.	**HAPPY WHISTLER** (ASCAP)—D. Robertson You're Free to Go (ASCAP)—Cap 3391	10	9
16.	**GRADUATION DAY** (BMI)—Rover Boys I Hear Music (BMI)—ABC-Paramount 9700	16	7
17.	**MORE** (ASCAP)—P. Como Glendora (BMI)—Vic 20-6554	—	1
18.	**ALLEGHENY MOON** (ASCAP)—P. Page Strangest Romance (ASCAP)—Mercury 70878	—	1
19.	**WALK HAND IN HAND** (BMI)—T. Martin Flamenco Love (ASCAP)—Vic 20-6493	13	6
20.	**PICNIC** (ASCAP)—McGuire Sisters Delilah Jones (ASCAP)—Coral 61627	20	6
21.	**IT ONLY HURTS FOR A LITTLE WHILE** (ASCAP)—Ames Brothers If You Want to See Mamie Tonight (ASCAP)—Vic 20-6481	22	3
22.	**HOW LITTLE WE KNOW** (ASCAP)—F. Sinatra Five Hundred Guys (ASCAP)—Cap 3423	18	5
23.	**GRADUATION DAY** (BMI)—Four Freshmen Lonely Night in Paris (ASCAP)—Cap 3410	17	4
24.	**BE-BOP-A-LULA** (BMI)—G. Vincent Woman Love (BMI)—Cap 3450	—	1
25.	**HOT DIGGITY** (ASCAP)—P. Como Juke Box Baby (BMI)—Vic 20-6427	9	16

THE TOP 100

For survey week ending June 20

A list of the **TOP 100 RECORD SIDES** in the nation according to a **COMBINED TABULATION** of Dealer Disk Jockey and Juke Box Operator replies to The Billboard's weekly popular record Best Seller and Most Played surveys. Its purpose is to provide Disk Jockeys with additional programming material and to give trade exposure to NEWER records just beginning to show action in the field.

Pos.	Song	Artist	Label	Last Week
1.	WAYWARD WIND	G. Grant	Era	1
2.	MOONGLOW AND THEME FROM "PICNIC"	M. Stoloff	Decca	2
3.	STANDING ON THE CORNER	Four Lads	Columbia	3
4.	I ALMOST LOST MY MIND	P. Boone	Dot	7
5.	HEARTBREAK HOTEL	E. Presley	Victor	4
6.	I'M IN LOVE AGAIN	F. Domino	Imperial	6
7.	I WANT YOU, I NEED YOU, I LOVE YOU	E. Presley	Victor	11
8.	IVORY TOWER	C. Carr	Fraternity	7
9.	MOONGLOW AND THEME FROM "PICNIC"	G. Cates	Coral	5
10.	WALK HAND IN HAND	T. Martin	Victor	18
11.	HAPPY WHISTLER	D. Robertson	Capitol	10
12.	BORN TO BE WITH YOU	Chordettes	Cadence	14
12.	ON THE STREET WHERE YOU LIVE	V. Damone	Columbia	16
14.	IVORY TOWER	G. Storm	Dot	12
15.	TRANSFUSION	N. Norvus	Dot	13
16.	HOT DIGGITY	P. Como	Victor	9
17.	IT ONLY HURTS FOR A LITTLE WHILE	Ames Brothers	Victor	15
17.	MORE	P. Como	Victor	24
19.	PICNIC	McGuire Sisters	Coral	18
20.	GLENDORA	P. Como	Victor	30
21.	GRADUATION DAY	Rover Boys	ABC-Paramount	21
22.	MY BLUE HEAVEN	F. Domino	Imperial	21
23.	BE-BOP-A-LULA	G. Vincent	Capitol	43
24.	I WANT YOU TO BE MY GIRL	Teen-Agers	Gee	22
25.	TREASURE OF LOVE	C. McPhatter	Atlantic	38
26.	SWEET, OLD-FASHIONED GIRL	T. Brewer	Coral	28
27.	ALLEGHENY MOON	P. Page	Mercury	33
28.	MAGIC TOUCH	Platters	Mercury	17
29.	ROLL OVER, BEETHOVEN	C. Berry	Chess	—
30.	CHURCH BELLS MAY RING	Diamonds	Mercury	25
31.	CAN YOU FIND IT IN YOUR HEART?	T. Bennett	Columbia	27
32.	IVORY TOWER	O. Williams	De Luxe	26
33.	SLIPPIN' AND SLIDIN'	Little Richard	Specialty	56
33.	HOW LITTLE WE KNOW	F. Sinatra	Capitol	53
35.	A TEAR FELL	T. Brewer	Coral	28
36.	MY LITTLE ANGEL	Four Lads	Columbia	32
37.	BLUE SUEDE SHOES	C. Perkins	Sun	22
38.	POOR PEOPLE OF PARIS	L. Baxter	Capitol	31
39.	LONG, TALL SALLY	Little Richard	Specialty	40
40.	SECOND FIDDLE	K. Starr	Victor	47
40.	STANDING ON THE CORNER	D. Martin	Capitol	34
40.	ON THE STREET WHERE YOU LIVE	E. Fisher	Victor	43
43.	CORRINE, CORRINA	J. Turner	Atlantic	52
44.	I COULD HAVE DANCED ALL NIGHT	S. Syms	Decca	57
45.	TELL ME WHY	Crew Cuts	Mercury	—
46.	KISS ME ANOTHER	G. Gibbs	Mercury	45
47.	WAYWARD WIND	T. Ritter	Capitol	—
48.	GRADUATION DAY	Four Freshmen	Capitol	35
48.	MY BABY LEFT ME	E. Presley	Victor	37
50.	TOO CLOSE FOR COMFORT	E. Gorme	ABC-Paramount	20
51.	SOFT SUMMER BREEZE	E. Heywood	Mercury	—
52.	TELL ME WHY	G. Storm	Dot	—
52.	LONG, TALL SALLY	P. Boone	Dot	36
54.	CANADIAN SUNSET	H. Winterhalter	Victor	91
55.	SWEET HEARTACHES	E. Fisher	Victor	42
55.	PORTUGUESE WASHERWOMAN	J. (Fingers) Carr	Capitol	39
57.	LAZY RIVER	R. Sherwood	Decca	76
57.	I COULD HAVE DANCED ALL NIGHT	R. Clooney	Columbia	49
59.	IN A SHANTY IN OLD SHANTY TOWN	S. Smith	Epic	41
60.	STRANDED IN THE JUNGLE	Jay Hawks	Flash	—
61.	ROCKIN' GHOST	A. Bleyer	Cadence	—
62.	NO, NOT MUCH	Four Lads	Columbia	65
62.	OOBY DOOBY	R. Orbison	Sun	70
64.	LOVE, LOVE, LOVE	Clovers	Atlantic	74
64.	PICNIC	R. Marterie	Mercury	100
66.	WHATEVER WILL BE, WILL BE	Doris Day	Columbia	78
67.	WE ALL NEED LOVE	P. Faith	Columbia	—
67.	WHY DO FOOLS FALL IN LOVE?	G. Storm	Dot	78
69.	WHY DO FOOLS FALL IN LOVE?	Diamonds	Mercury	99
70.	I WAS THE ONE	E. Presley	Victor	—
71.	JUKE BOX BABY	P. Como	Victor	93
72.	I'M IN LOVE AGAIN	Fontane Sisters	Dot	46
73.	STANDING ON THE CORNER	Mills Brothers	Decca	57
74.	CRAZY LITTLE PALACE	B. Williams	Coral	—
74.	LOST IN THE SHUFFLE	J. P. Morgan	Victor	—
76.	FOREVER DARLING	Ames Brothers	Victor	—
76.	HOT DOG BUDDY BUDDY	B. Haley	Decca	95
76.	JOEY, JOEY, JOEY	P. Lee	Decca	—
76.	NEVER TURN BACK	A. Hibbler	Decca	61
80.	TUTTI FRUTTI	P. Boone	Dot	96
81.	FREE	T. Leonetti	Capitol	69
82.	SINNER MAN	L. Baxter	Capitol	—
82.	ELEVENTH HOUR MELODY	A. Hibbler	Decca	—
82.	HI LILI HI LO	D. Hyman	M-G-M	—
82.	NEVER LET ME GO	N. (King) Cole	Capitol	—
82.	PLAY FOR KEEPS	J. P. Morgan	Victor	—
87.	BLUE SUEDE SHOES	B. Bennett	King	87
88.	TANGO OF THE DRUMS	L. Baxter	Capitol	67
89.	IF YOU WANNA SEE MAMIE TONIGHT	Ames Brothers	Victor	—
89.	LOOK HOMEWARD, ANGEL	Four Esquires	London	—
91.	WINNER TAKE ALL	Platters	Mercury	—
92.	TO LOVE AGAIN	Four Aces	Decca	73
93.	WATCHING THE WORLD GO BY	D. Martin	Capitol	—
93.	EDDIE, MY LOVE	Fontane Sisters	Dot	91
93.	FIVE HUNDRED GUYS	F. Sinatra	Capitol	—
93.	HOT AND COLD RUNNING TEARS	S. Vaughan	Mercury	—
93.	I'VE GOT LOVE	J. La Rosa	Victor	—
93.	IN A LITTLE SPANISH TOWN	Bing Crosby	Decca	—
99.	LITTLE GIRL OF MINE	Cleftones	Gee	63
99.	MR. WONDERFUL	P. Lee	Decca	55

CAUTION TO DEALERS AND JUKE BOX OPERATORS

The Billboard's Top 100 is NOT designed to provide tested information for buying purposes. This function is most reliably served by other regular weekly features: Best Sellers in Stores, Most Played in Juke Boxes, Coming Up Strong and Best Buys.

• Best Sellers in Stores

For survey week ending June 27

RECORDS are ranked in order of their current national selling importance at the retail level, as determined by The Billboard's weekly survey of the top volume dealers in every important market area. When significant action is reported on both sides of a record, points are combined to determine position on the chart. In such a case, both sides are listed in bold type, the leading side on top.

This Week	Record	Last Week	Weeks on Chart
1.	**WAYWARD WIND** (BMI)—G. Grant No More Than Forever (ASCAP)—Era 1013	1	10
2.	**I ALMOST LOST MY MIND** (BMI)—P. Boone I'm in Love With You (BMI)—Dot 15472	3	4
3.	**MOONGLOW AND THEME FROM "PICNIC"** (ASCAP)—M. Stoloff Theme From "Picnic" (ASCAP)—Dec 29888	2	12
4.	**I WANT YOU, I NEED YOU, I LOVE YOU** (BMI)—E. Presley **MY BABY LEFT ME** (BMI)—Vic 20-6540	6	6
5.	**I'M IN LOVE AGAIN** (BMI)—F. Domino My Blue Heaven (ASCAP)—Imperial 5386	5	10
6.	**MORE** (ASCAP)—P. Como **GLENDORA** (BMI)—Vic 20-6554	7	4
7.	**STANDING ON THE CORNER** (ASCAP)—Four Lads **MY LITTLE ANGEL** (BMI)—Col 40574	4	11
8.	**ON THE STREET WHERE YOU LIVE** (ASCAP)—V. Damone We All Need Love (ASCAP)—Col 40654	10	5
9.	**BORN TO BE WITH YOU** (ASCAP)—Chordettes Love Never Changes (ASCAP)—Cadence 1291-1019	14	3
10.	**TRANSFUSION** (BMI)—Nervous Norvus Dig (BMI)—Dot 15470	11	5
11.	**BE-BOP-A-LULA** (BMI)—G. Vincent Woman Love (BMI)—Cap 3450	15	3
12.	**HEARTBREAK HOTEL** (BMI)—E. Presley I Was the One (BMI)—Vic 20-6420	8	18
13.	**SWEET OLD-FASHIONED GIRL** (ASCAP)—T. Brewer Goodbye, John (BMI)—Coral 61636	17	3
14.	**IVORY TOWER** (ASCAP)—C. Carr Please, Please Believe Me (ASCAP)—Fraternity 734	9	13
15.	**MOONGLOW AND THEME FROM "PICNIC"** (ASCAP)—G. Cates Rio Batucada (ASCAP)—Coral 61618	12	12
16.	**ALLEGHENY MOON** (ASCAP)—P. Page Strangest Romance (ASCAP)—Mercury 70878	—	1
17.	**HAPPY WHISTLER** (ASCAP)—D. Robertson You're Free to Go (ASCAP)—Cap 3391	13	10
18.	**PICNIC** (ASCAP)—McGuire Sisters Delilah Jones (ASCAP)—Coral 61627	20	7
19.	**IVORY TOWER** (ASCAP)—G. Storm I Ain't Gonna Worry (BMI)—Dot 15458	24	7
20.	**WHATEVER WILL BE, WILL BE** (ASCAP)—Doris Day I Gotta Sing Away These Blues (BMI)—Col 40740	—	1
21.	**WALK HAND IN HAND** (BMI)—T. Martin Flamenco Love (ASCAP)—Vic 20-6493	21	6
22.	**TREASURE OF LOVE** (BMI)—C. McPhatter When You're Sincere (BMI)—Atlantic 1092	16	3
23.	**IT ONLY HURTS FOR A LITTLE WHILE** (ASCAP)—Ames Brothers If You Want to See Mamie Tonight (ASCAP)—Vic 20-6481	19	6
24.	**HOT DIGGITY** (ASCAP)—P. Como Juke Box Baby (ASCAP)—Vic 20-6427	18	18
25.	**GRADUATION DAY** (BMI)—Rover Boys I Hear Music (ASCAP)—ABC-Paramount 9700	23	4

• Most Played in Juke Boxes

For survey week ending June 27

RECORDS are ranked in order of the greatest number of plays in juke boxes thruout the country, as determined by The Billboard's weekly survey of the nation's juke box operators. When significant play is reported on both sides of a record, points are combined to determine position on the chart. In such a case, both sides are listed in bold type, the leading side on top.

This Week	Record	Last Week	Weeks on Chart
1.	**WAYWARD WIND** (BMI)—G. Grant No More Than Forever (ASCAP)—Era 1013	1	6
2.	**HEARTBREAK HOTEL** (BMI)—E. Presley I Was the One (BMI)—Vic 20-6420	2	15
3.	**I ALMOST LOST MY MIND** (BMI)—P. Boone I'm In Love With You (BMI)—Dot 15472	8	4
4.	**IVORY TOWER** (ASCAP)—C. Carr Please, Please Believe Me (ASCAP)—Fraternity 734	5	10
5.	**STANDING ON THE CORNER** (ASCAP)—Four Lads My Little Angel (BMI)—Col 40674	3	7
6.	**I'M IN LOVE AGAIN** (BMI)—F. Domino **MY BLUE HEAVEN** (ASCAP)—Imperial 5386	5	8
7.	**MOONGLOW AND THEME FROM "PICNIC"**—G. Cates Rio Batucada (ASCAP)—Coral 61618	7	9
8.	**MOONGLOW AND THEME FROM "PICNIC"** (ASCAP)—M. Stoloff Theme From "Picnic" (ASCAP)—Dec 29888	4	8
9.	**I WANT YOU, I NEED YOU, I LOVE YOU** (BMI)—E. Presley **MY BABY LEFT ME** (BMI)—Vic 20-6540	9	5
10.	**IVORY TOWER** (ASCAP)—G. Storm I Ain't Gonna Worry (BMI)—Dot 15458	10	8
11.	**MORE** (ASCAP)—P. Como **GLENDORA** (BMI)—Vic 20-6554	—	1
12.	**HAPPY WHISTLER** (ASCAP)—D. Robertson You're Free to Go (ASCAP)—Cap 3391	13	6
13.	**MAGIC TOUCH** (ASCAP)—Platters Winner Take All (ASCAP)—Mercury 70819	12	13
14.	**BLUE SUEDE SHOES** (BMI)—C. Perkins Honey, Don't (BMI)—Sun 234	11	16
15.	**HOT DIGGITY** (BMI)—P. Como Juke Box Baby (BMI)—Vic 20-6427	14	16
16.	**BORN TO BE WITH YOU** (ASCAP)—Chordettes Love Never Changes (ASCAP)—Cadence 1291	20	2
17.	**IT ONLY HURTS FOR A LITTLE WHILE** (ASCAP)—Ames Brothers If You Want to See Mamie Tonight (ASCAP)—Vic 20-6481	19	3
18.	**ON THE STREET WHERE YOU LIVE** (ASCAP)—V. Damone We All Need Love (ASCAP)—Col 40654	—	1
19.	**ALLEGHENY MOON** (ASCAP)—P. Page Strangest Romance (ASCAP)—Mercury 70878	—	1
20.	**ON THE STREET WHERE YOU LIVE** (ASCAP)—E. Fisher **SWEET HEARTACHES** (ASCAP)—Vic 20-6529	—	1

• Best Selling Sheet Music

Tunes are ranked in order of their current national selling importance at the sheet music jobber level.

This Week	Title	Last Week	Weeks on Chart
1.	**Ivory Tower** (E. H. Morris)	1	11
2.	**Wayward Wind** (Warman)	3	6
3.	**Walk Hand in Hand** (Republic)	6	9
4.	**Picnic** (Shapiro-Bernstein)	5	8
5.	**Moonglow** (Mills-Columbia Pictures)	2	8
6.	**On the Street Where You Live** (Chappell)	4	9
7.	**Standing On the Corner** (Frank)	7	8
8.	**Allegheny Moon** (Oxford)	10	2
9.	**Graduation Day** (Sheldon)	8	8
10.	**I Almost Lost My Mind** (Hill & Range)	15	2
11.	**Hot Diggity** (Roncom)	9	17
12.	**I Could Have Danced All Night** (Chappell)	—	5
13.	**Poor People of Paris** (Connelly)	12	20
14.	**Happy Whistler** (Birchwood)	—	2
15.	**Heartbreak Hotel** (Tree)	14	13

• Most Played by Jockeys

For survey week ending June 27

SIDES are ranked in order of the greatest number of plays on disk jockey radio shows thruout the country. Results are based on The Billboard's weekly survey among the nation's disk jockeys. The reverse side of each record is also listed.

This Week	Record	Last Week	Weeks on Chart
1.	**WAYWARD WIND** (BMI)—G. Grant No More Than Forever (ASCAP)—Era 1013	1	9
2.	**MOONGLOW AND THEME FROM "PICNIC"** (ASCAP)—M. Stoloff Theme From "Picnic" (ASCAP)—Dec 29888	2	12
3.	**I ALMOST LOST MY MIND** (BMI)—P. Boone I'm In Love With You (BMI)—Dot 15472	4	4
4.	**ON THE STREET WHERE YOU LIVE** (ASCAP)—V. Damone We All Need Love (ASCAP)—Col 40654	5	6
5.	**STANDING ON THE CORNER** (ASCAP)—Four Lads My Little Angel (BMI)—Col 40674	3	10
6.	**BORN TO BE WITH YOU** (ASCAP)—Chordettes Love Never Changes (ASCAP)—Cadence 1291	7	5
7.	**I WANT YOU, I NEED YOU, I LOVE YOU** (BMI)—E. Presley My Baby Left Me (BMI)—Vic 20-6540	8	4
8.	**MOONGIOW AND THEME FROM "PICNIC"** (ASCAP)—G. Cates Rio Batucada (ASCAP)—Coral 61618	6	12
9.	**IVORY TOWER** (ASCAP)—C. Carr Please, Please Believe Me (ASCAP)—Fraternity 734	13	11
10.	**MORE** (ASCAP)—P. Como Glendora (BMI)—Vic 20-6554	17	2
11.	**I'M IN LOVE AGAIN** (BMI)—F. Domino My Blue Heaven (ASCAP)—Imperial 5386	9	7
12.	**GLENDORA** (BMI)—P. Como More (ASCAP)—Vic 20-6554	10	3
13.	**ALLEGHENY MOON** (ASCAP)—P. Page Strangest Romance (ASCAP)—Mercury 70878	18	2
14.	**IVORY TOWER** (ASCAP)—G. Storm I Ain't Gonna Worry (BMI)—Dot 15458	11	9
15.	**HAPPY WHISTLER** (ASCAP)—D. Robertson You're Free to Go (ASCAP)—Cap 3391	15	10
16.	**BE-BOP-A-LULA** (BMI)—G. Vincent Woman Love (BMI)—Cap 3450	24	2
17.	**PICNIC** (ASCAP)—McGuire Sisters Delilah Jones (ASCAP)—Coral 61627	20	7
18.	**TRANSFUSION** (BMI)—Nervous Norvus Dig (BMI)—Dot 15470	14	4
19.	**HEARTBREAK HOTEL** (BMI)—E. Presley I Was the One (BMI)—Vic 20-6420	12	18
20.	**WHATEVER WILL BE, WILL BE** (ASCAP)—Doris Day I Gotta Sing Away These Blues (BMI)—Col 40704	—	1
21.	**IT ONLY HURTS A LITTLE WHILE** (ASCAP)—Ames Brothers If You Want to See Mamie Tonight (ASCAP)—Vic 20-6481	21	4
22.	**SWEET OLD-FASHIONEL GIRL** (ASCAP)—T. Brewer Goodbye, John (BMI)—Coral 61636	—	1
23.	**WALK HAND IN HAND** (BMI)—T. Martin Flamenco Love (ASCAP)—Vic 20-6493	19	7
24.	**GRADUATION DAY** (BMI)—Four Freshmen Lonely Night in Paris (ASCAP)—Cap 3410	23	5
25.	**PORTUGUESE WASHERWOMAN** (ASCAP)—J. (Fingers) Carr Lucky Pierre (ASCAP)—Cap 3418	—	2

THE TOP 100

For survey week ending June 27

A list of the Top 100 RECORD SIDES in the nation according to a COMBINED TABULATION of Dealer, Disk Jockey and Juke Box Operator replies to The Billboard's weekly popular record Best Seller and Most Played surveys. Its purpose is to provide Disk Jockeys with additional programming material and to give trade exposure to NEWER records just beginning to show action in the field.

Pos.	Song	Artist	Label	Last Week
1.	WAYWARD WIND	G. Grant	Era	1
2.	I ALMOST LOST MY MIND	P. Boone	Dot	4
3.	MOONGLOW AND THEME FROM "PICNIC"	M. Stoloff	Decca	2
4.	STANDING ON THE CORNER	Four Lads	Columbia	3
5.	I WANT YOU, I NEED YOU, I LOVE YOU	E. Presley	Victor	7
6.	I'M IN LOVE AGAIN	F. Domino	Imperial	6
7.	IVORY TOWER	C. Carr	Fraternity	8
8.	BORN TO BE WITH YOU	Chordettes	Cadence	12
9.	MOONGLOW AND THEME FROM "PICNIC"	G. Cates	Coral	9
9.	ON THE STREET WHERE YOU LIVE	V. Damone	Columbia	12
11.	HEARTBREAK HOTEL	E. Presley	Victor	5
12.	MORE	P. Como	Victor	17
13.	HAPPY WHISTLER	D. Robertson	Capitol	11
14.	IVORY TOWER	G. Storm	Dot	14
15.	ALLEGHENY MOON	P. Page	Mercury	27
16.	TRANSFUSION	N. Norvus	Dot	15
17.	SWEET OLD-FASHIONED GIRL	T. Brewer	Coral	26
18.	PICNIC	McGuire Sisters	Coral	19
19.	GLENDORA	P. Como	Victor	20
20.	IT ONLY HURTS FOR A LITTLE WHILE	Ames Brothers	Victor	17
21.	WALK HAND IN HAND	T. Martin	Victor	10
21.	HOT DIGGITY	P, Como	Victor	16
23.	BE-BOP-A-LULA	G. Vincent	Capitol	23
24.	MAGIC TOUCH	Platters	Mercury	28
25.	CHURCH BELLS MAY RING	Diamonds	Mercury	30
26.	WHATEVER WILL BE, WILL BE	Doris Day	Columbia	66
27.	GRADUATION DAY	Four Freshmen	Capitol	48
28.	TREASURE OF LOVE	C. McPhatter	Atlantic	25
29.	STANDING ON THE CORNER	D. Martin	Capitol	40
30.	GRADUATION DAY	Rover Boys	ABC-Paramount	21
31.	IVORY TOWER	O. Williams	De Luxe	32
31.	MY BLUE HEAVEN	F. Domino	Imperial	22
31.	ON THE STREET WHERE YOU LIVE	E. Fisher	Victor	40
34.	I WANT YOU TO BE MY GIRL	Teen-Agers	Gee	24
35.	HOW LITTLE WE KNOW	F. Sinatra	Capitol	33
36.	CAN YOU FIND IT IN YOUR HEART?	T. Bennett	Columbia	31
37.	WAYWARD WIND	T. Ritter	Capitol	47
38.	MY PRAYER	Platters	Mercury	—
39.	I COULD HAVE DANCED ALL NIGHT	S. Syms	Decca	44
40.	FREE	T. Leoetti	Capitol	81
40.	PORTUGUESE WASHERWOMAN	J. (Fingers) Carr	Capitol	55
42.	BLUE SUEDE SHOES	C. Perkins	Sun	37
42.	MY BABY LEFT ME	E. Presley	Victor	48
43.	A TEAR FELL	T. Brewer	Coral	35
44.	LONG, TALL SALLY	P. Boone	Dot	52
45.	SECOND FIDDLE	K. Starr	Victor	40
46.	IN A SHANTY IN OLD SHANTY TOWN	S. Smith	Epic	59
47.	POOR PEOPLE OF PARIS	L. Baxter	Capitol	38
47.	KISS ME ANOTHER	G. Gibbs	Mercury	46
49.	LONG, TALL SALLY	Little Richard	Specialty	39
50.	FEVER	L. W. John	King	—
51.	NEVER TURN BACK	A. Hibbler	Decca	76
52.	LOVE, LOVE, LOVE	Clovers	Atlantic	64
53.	TELL ME WHY	Crew Cuts	Mercury	45
54.	I COULD HAVE DANCED ALL NIGHT	R. Clooney	Columbia	57
55.	TOO CLOSE FOR COMFORT	E. Gorme	ABC-Paramount	50
56.	RIP IT UP	Little Richard	Specialty	—
57.	I'M IN LOVE AGAIN	Fontane Sisters	Dot	72
58.	LOVE, LOVE, LOVE	Diamonds	Mercury	—
59.	OOBY DOOBY	R. Orbison	Sun	62
60.	HOT DOG BUDDY, BUDDY	B. Haley	Decca	76
61.	SWEET HEARTACHES	E. Fisher	Victor	55
61.	YOU DON'T KNOW ME	J. Vale	Columbia	—
63.	STANDING ON THE CORNER	Mills Brothers	Decca	73
64.	THAT'S ALL THERE IS TO THAT	N. (King) Cole	Capitol	—
65.	WALK HAND IN HAND	A. Williams	Cadence	—
65.	STRANDED IN THE JUNGLE	Jay Hawks	Flash	60
67.	MR. WONDERFUL	P. Lee	Decca	99
67.	MOCKING BIRD	Four Lads	Columbia	—
69.	TO LOVE AGAIN	Four Aces	Decca	92
70.	ROCK ISLAND LINE	L. Donegan	London	—
70.	SLIPPIN' AND SLIDIN'	Little Richard	Specialty	33
70.	SOFT SUMMER BREEZE	E. Heywood	Mercury	51
73.	DAYDREAMS	A. Mooney	M-G-M	—
73.	I'LL BE HOME	P. Boone	Dot	—
75.	TE AMO	D. Jacobs	Coral	—
76.	CORRINE, CORRINA	J. Turner	Atlantic	43
77.	TELL ME WHY	G. Storm	Dot	52
77.	MY DREAM SONATA	N. (King) Cole	Capitol	—
79.	I WAS THE ONE	E. Presley	Victor	70
80.	READY TEDDY	Little Richard	Specialty	—
80.	CRAZY LITTLE PALACE	B. Williams	Coral	74
82.	I WOKE UP CRYING	J. James	M-G-M	—
83.	MAIN TITLE ("MAN WITH THE GOLDEN ARM")	R. Maltby	Vik	—
84.	PORT-AU-PRINCE	N. Riddle	Capitol	—
85.	LITTLE GIRL OF MINE	Cleftones	Gee	99
86.	TANGO OF THE DRUMS	L. Baxter	Capitol	88
87.	ROLL OVER BEETHOVEN	C. Berry	Chess	—
88.	BLUE SUEDE SHOES	E. Presley	Victor	—
89.	ROCKIN' GHOST	A. Bleyer	Cadence	61
89.	INTO THE NIGHT	Dream Weavers	Decca	—
91.	DELILAH JONES	McGuire Sisters	Coral	—
92.	WHY DO FOOLS FALL IN LOVE?	Teen-Agers	Gee	—
93.	STRANGEST ROMANCE	P. Page	Mercury	—
93.	I COULD HAVE DANCED ALL NIGHT	D. Shore	Victor	—
95.	LOVELY ONE	Four Voices	Columbia	—
96.	FIVE HUNDRED GUYS	F. Sinatra	Capitol	93
96.	LITTLE LOVE CAN GO A LONG WAY	Dream Weavers	Decca	—
98.	PICNIC	R. Marterie	Mercury	64
99.	DON'T CRY	F. Laine	Columbia	—
99.	MAIN TITLE ("MAN WITH THE GOLDEN ARM")	B. May	Capitol	—

CAUTION TO DEALERS AND JUKE BOX OPERATORS

The Billboard's Top 100 is NOT designed to provide tested information for buying purposes. This function is most reliably served by other regular weekly features: Best Sellers in Stores, Most Played in Juke Boxes, Coming Up Strong and Best Buys.

• Best Sellers in Stores

For survey week ending July 4

RECORDS are ranked in order of their current national selling importance at the retail level, as determined by The Billboard's weekly survey of the top volume dealers in every important market area. When significant action is reported on both sides of a record, points are combined to determine position on the chart. In such a case, both sides are listed in bold type, the leading side on top.

This Week		Last Week	Weeks on Chart
1.	**WAYWARD WIND** (BMI)—G. Grant No More Than Forever (ASCAP)—Era 1013	1	11
2.	**I ALMOST LOST MY MIND** (BMI)—P. Boone I'm In Love With You (BMI)—Dot 15472	2	5
3.	**MOONGLOW AND THEME FROM "PICNIC"** (ASCAP)—M. Stoloff Theme From "Picnic" (ASCAP)—Dec 29888	3	13
4.	**I WANT YOU, I NEED YOU, I LOVE YOU** (BMI)—E. Presley My Baby Left Me (BMI)—Vic 20-6540	4	7
5.	**I'M IN LOVE AGAIN** (BMI)—F. Domino **MY BLUE HEAVEN** (ASCAP)—Imperial 5386	5	11
6.	**MORE** (ASCAP)—P. Como Glendora (BMI)—Vic 20-6554	6	5
7.	**STANDING ON THE CORNER** (ASCAP)—Four Lads My Little Angel (BMI)—Col 40574	7	12
7.	**BORN TO BE WITH YOU** (ASCAP)—Chordettes Love Never Changes (ASCAP)—Cadence 1291-1019	9	4
9.	**ON THE STREET WHERE YOU LIVE** (ASCAP)—V. Damone We All Need Love (ASCAP)—Col 40654	8	6
10.	**BE-BOP-A-LULA** (BMI)—G. Vincent Woman Love (BMI)—Cap 3450	11	4
11.	**ALLEGHENY MOON** (ASCAP)—P. Page Strangest Romance (ASCAP)—Mercury 70878	16	2
12.	**SWEET OLD-FASHIONED GIRL** (ASCAP)—T. Brewer Goodbye, John (BMI)—Coral 61636	13	4
13.	**TRANSFUSION** (BMI)—Nervous Norvus Dig (BMI)—Dot 15470	10	6
14.	**MOONGLOW AND THEME FROM "PICNIC"** (ASCAP)—G. Cates Rio Batucada (ASCAP)—Coral 61618	15	13
15.	**WHATEVER WILL BE, WILL BE** (ASCAP)—Doris Day I' Gotta Sing Away These Blues (BMI)—Col 40740	20	2
16.	**HEARTBREAK HOTEL** (BMI)—E. Presley I Was the One (BMI)—Vic 20-6420	12	19
17.	**MY PRAYER** (ASCAP)—Platters Heaven on Earth (ASCAP)—Mercury 70893	—	1
18.	**IVORY TOWER** (ASCAP)—C. Carr Please, Please, Believe Me (ASCAP)—Fraternity 734	14	14
19.	**IT ONLY HURTS FOR A LITTLE WHILE** (ASCAP)—Ames Brothers If You Want to See Mamie Tonight (ASCAP)—Vic 20-6481	23	7
20.	**HAPPY WHISTLER** (ASCAP)—D. Robertson You're Free to Go (ASCAP)—Cap 3391	17	11
21.	**TREASURE OF LOVE** (BMI)—C. McPhatter When You're Sincere (BMI)—Atlantic 1092	22	4
22.	**WALK HAND IN HAND** (BMI)—T. Martin Flamenco Love (ASCAP)—Vic 20-6493	21	7
23.	**IVORY TOWER** (ASCAP)—G. Storm I Ain't Gonna Worry (BMI)—Dot 15458	19	8
24.	**PICNIC** (ASCAP)—McGuire Sisters Delilah Jones (ASCAP)—Coral 61627	18	8
25.	**PORTUGUESE WASHERWOMAN** (ASCAP)—J. (Fingers) Carr Lucky Pierre (ASCAP)—Cap 3418	—	1

• Most Played in Juke Boxes

For survey week ending July 4

RECORDS are ranked in order of the greatest number of plays in juke boxes thruout the country, as determined by The Billboard's weekly survey of the nation's juke box operators. When significant play is reported on both sides of a record, points are combined to determine position on the chart. In such a case, both sides are listed in bold type, the leading side on top.

This Week		Last Week	Weeks on Chart
1.	**WAYWARD WIND** (BMI)—G. Grant No More Than Forever (ASCAP)—Era 1013	1	7
2.	**I ALMOST LOST MY MIND** (BMI)—P. Boone I'm in Love With You (BMI)—Dot 15472	3	5
3.	**I'M IN LOVE AGAIN** (BMI)—F. Domino **MY BLUE HEAVEN** (ASCAP)—Imperial 5386	6	9
4.	**I WANT YOU, I NEED YOU, I LOVE YOU** (BMI)—E. Presley My Baby Left Me (BMI)—Vic 20-6540	9	6
5.	**HEARTBREAK HOTEL** (BMI)—E. Presley I Was the One (BMI)—Vic 20-6420	2	16
6.	**IVORY TOWER** (ASCAP)—C. Carr Please, Please Believe Me (ASCAP)—Fraternity 734	4	11
7.	**MOONGLOW AND THEME FROM "PICNIC"** (ASCAP)—M. Stoloff Theme From "Picnic" (ASCAP)—Dec 29888	8	9
8.	**STANDING ON THE CORNER** (ASCAP)—Four Lads My Little Angel (BMI)—Col 40674	5	8
9.	**MORE** (ASCAP)—P. Como **GLENDORA** (BMI)—Vic 20-6554	11	2
10.	**MOONGLOW AND THEME FROM "PICNIC"** (ASCAP)—G. Cates Rio Batucada (ASCAP)—Coral 61618	7	10
11.	**IVORY TOWER** (ASCAP)—G. Storm I Ain't Gonna Worry (BMI)—Dot 15458	10	9
12.	**BORN TO BE WITH YOU** (ASCAP)—Chordettes Love Never Changes (ASCAP)—Cadence 1291	16	3
13.	**IT ONLY HURTS FOR A LITTLE WHILE** (ASCAP)—Ames Brothers If You Want to See Mamie Tonight (ASCAP)—Vic 20-6481	17	4
14.	**ALLEGHENY MOON** (ASCAP)—P. Page Strangest Romance (ASCAP)—Mercury 70878	19	2
15.	**ON THE STREET WHERE YOU LIVE** (ASCAP)—V. Damone We All Need Love (ASCAP)—Col 40654	18	2
16.	**HAPPY WHISTLER** (ASCAP)—D. Robertson You're Free to Go (ASCAP)—Cap 3391	12	7
17.	**BE-BOP-A-LULA** (BMI)—G. Vincent Woman Love (BMI)—Cap 3450	—	1
18.	**ON THE STREET WHERE YOU LIVE** (ASCAP)—E. Fisher Sweet Heartaches (ASCAP)—Vic 20-6529	20	2
19.	**SWEET OLD-FASHIONED GIRL** (ASCAP)—T. Brewer Goodbye, John (BMI)—Coral 61636	—	1
20.	**MAGIC TOUCH** (ASCAP)—Platters Winner Take All (ASCAP)—Mercury 70819	13	14

• Best Selling Sheet Music

Tunes are ranked in order of their current national selling importance at the sheet music jobber level.

This Week		Last Week	Weeks on Chart
1.	**Wayward Wind** (Warman)	2	7
2.	**Ivory Tower** (E. H. Morris)	1	12
3.	**Allegheny Moon** (Oxford)	8	3
4.	**Picnic** (Shapiro-Bernstein)	4	9
5.	**On the Street Where You Live** (Chappell)	6	10
6.	**Moonglow** (Mills-Columbia Pictures)	5	9
7.	**Walk Hand in Hand** (Republic)	3	10
8.	**Standing On the Corner** (Frank)	7	9
9.	**I Almost Lost My Mind** (Hill & Range)	10	3
10.	**More** (Shapiro-Bernstein)	—	2
11.	**Graduation Day** (Sheldon)	9	6
12.	**Whatever Will Be, Will Be** (Che Sera, Sera Artists)	—	1
13.	**Heartbreak Hotel** (Tree)	15	2
14.	**I Could Have Danced All Night** (Chappell)	12	6
15.	**Hot Diggity** (Roncom)	11	18

• Most Played by Jockeys

For survey week ending July 4

SIDES are ranked in order of the greatest number of plays on disk jockey radio shows thruout the country. Results are based on The Billboard's weekly survey among the nation's disk jockeys. The reverse side of each record is also listed.

This Week		Last Week	Weeks on Chart
1.	**WAYWARD WIND** (BMI)—G. Grant No More Than Forever (ASCAP)—Era 1013	1	10
2.	**MOONGLOW AND THEME FROM "PICNIC"** (ASCAP)—M. Stoloff Theme From "Picnic" (ASCAP)—Dec 29888	2	13
3.	**I ALMOST LOST MY MIND** (BMI)—P. Boone I'm In Love With You (BMI)—Dot 15472	3	5
4.	**ON THE STREET WHERE YOU LIVE** (ASCAP)—V. Damone We All Need Love (ASCAP)—Col 40654	4	7
5.	**BORN TO BE WITH YOU** (ASCAP)—Chordettes Love Never Changes (ASCAP)—Cadence 1291	6	6
6.	**STANDING ON THE CORNER** (ASCAP)—Four Lads My Little Angel (BMI)—Col 40674	5	11
7.	**I WANT YOU, I NEED YOU, I LOVE YOU** (BMI)—E. Presley My Baby Left Me (BMI)—Vic 20-6540	7	5
8.	**GLENDORA** (BMI)—P. Como More (ASCAP)—Vic 20-6554	12	4
9.	**MORE** (ASCAP)—P. Como Glendora (BMI)—Vic 20-6554	10	3
10.	**I'M IN LOVE AGAIN** (BMI)—F. Domino My Blue Heaven (ASCAP)—Imperial 5386	11	8
11.	**MOONGLOW AND THEME FROM "PICNIC"** (ASCAP)—G. Cates Rio Batucada (ASCAP)—Coral 61618	8	13
12.	**ALLEGHENY MOON** (ASCAP)—P. Page Strangest Romance (ASCAP)—Mercury 70878	13	3
13.	**BE-BOP-A-LULA** (BMI)—G. Vincent Woman Love (BMI)—Cap 3450	16	3
14.	**SWEET OLD-FASHIONED GIRL** (ASCAP)—T. Brewer Goodbye, John (BMI)—Coral 61636	22	2
15.	**IT ONLY HURTS FOR A LITTLE WHILE** (ASCAP)—Ames Brothers If You Want to See Mamie Tonight (ASCAP)—Vic 20-6481	21	5
16.	**WHATEVER WILL BE, WILL BE** (ASCAP)—Doris Day I Gotta Sing Away These Blues (BMI)—Col 40704	20	2
17.	**IVORY TOWER** (ASCAP)—G. Storm I Ain't Gonna Worry (BMI)—Dot 15458	14	10
18.	**WALK HAND IN HAND** (BMI)—T. Martin Flamenco Love (ASCAP)—Vic 20-6493	23	8
19.	**IVORY TOWER** (ASCAP)—C. Carr Please, Please Believe Me (ASCAP)—Fraternity 734	9	12
20.	**PICNIC** (ASCAP)—McGuire Sisters Delilah Jones (ASCAP)—Coral 61627	17	8
21.	**GRADUATION DAY** (BMI)—Four Freshmen Lonely Night in Paris (ASCAP)—Cap 3410	24	6
22.	**NEVER TURN BACK** (BMI)—A. Hibbler Away All Boats (ASCAP)—Dec 29950	—	1
23.	**FREE** (ASCAP)—T. Leonetti It's Wild (BMI)—Cap 3442	—	1
24.	**PORTUGUESE WASHERWOMAN** (ASCAP)—J. (Fingers) Carr Lucky Pierre (ASCAP)—Cap 3418	25	3
25.	**MY PRAYER** (ASCAP)—Platters Heaven on Earth (ASCAP)—Mercury 70893	—	1

THE TOP 100

For survey week ending July 4

A list of the Top 100 RECORD SIDES in the nation according to a COMBINED TABULATION of Dealer, Disk Jockey and Juke Box Operator replies to The Billboard's weekly popular record Best Seller and Most Played surveys. Its purpose is to provide Disk Jockeys with additional programming material and to give trade exposure to NEWER records just beginning to show action in the field.

Pos.	Song	Artist	Label	Last Week
1.	WAYWARD WIND	G. Grant	Era	1
2.	I ALMOST LOST MY MIND	P. Boone	Dot	2
3.	MOONGLOW AND THEME FROM "PICNIC"	M. Stoloff	Decca	3
4.	I WANT YOU, I NEED YOU, I LOVE YOU	E. Presley	Victor	5
5.	I'M IN LOVE AGAIN	F. Domino	Imperial	6
6.	BORN TO BE WITH YOU	Chordettes	Cadence	8
7.	STANDING ON THE CORNER	Four Lads	Columbia	4
8.	ON THE STREET WHERE YOU LIVE	V. Damone	Columbia	9
9.	MORE	P. Como	Victor	12
10.	MOONGLOW AND THEME FROM "PICNIC"	G. Cates	Coral	9
11.	ALLEGHENY MOON	P. Page	Mercury	15
12.	BE-BOP-A-LULA	G. Vincent	Capitol	23
13.	IVORY TOWER	C. Carr	Fraternity	7
13.	SWEET OLD-FASHIONED GIRL	T. Brewer	Coral	17
15.	GLENDORA	P. Como	Victor	19
16.	IT ONLY HURTS A LITTLE WHILE	Ames Brothers	Victor	20
17.	HEARTBREAK HOTEL	E. Presley	Victor	11
18.	IVORY TOWER	G. Storm	Dot	14
19.	HAPPY WHISTLER	D. Robertson	Capitol	13
20.	PICNIC	McGuire Sisters	Coral	18
20.	WHATEVER WILL BE, WILL BE (QUE SERA, SERA)	Doris Day	Columbia	26
22.	TRANSFUSION	N. Norvas	Dot	16
23.	WALK HAND IN HAND	T. Martin	Victor	21
24.	MY PRAYER	Platters	Mercury	38
25.	HOT DIGGITY	P. Como	Victor	21
26.	TREASURE OF LOVE	C. McPhatter	Atlantic	28
27.	PORTUGUESE WASHERWOMAN	J. (Fingers) Carr	Capitol	40
28.	I WANT YOU TO BE MY GIRL	Teen-Agers	Gee	34
28.	MY BLUE HEAVEN	F. Domino	Imperial	31
30.	GRADUATION DAY	Four Freshmen	Capitol	27
31.	ON THE STREET WHERE YOU LIVE	E. Fisher	Victor	31
32.	WAYWARD WIND	T. Ritter	Capitol	37
33.	CHURCH BELLS MAY RING	Diamonds	Mercury	25
34.	IVORY TOWER	O. Williams	De Luxe	31
35.	I COULD HAVE DANCED ALL NIGHT	S. Syms	Decca	39
36.	CAN YOU FIND IT IN YOUR HEART	T. Bennett	Columbia	36
37.	FEVER	L. W. John	King	50
38.	I'M IN LOVE AGAIN	Fontane Sisters	Dot	57
39.	IN A SHANTY IN OLD SHANTY TOWN	S. Smith	Epic	46
40.	RIP IT UP	Little Richard	Specialty	56
41.	HOW LITTLE WE KNOW	F. Sinatra	Capitol	35
42.	MY BABY LEFT ME	E. Presley	Victor	42
43.	THAT'S ALL THERE IS TO THAT	Nat (King) Cole	Capitol	64
44.	STANDING ON THE CORNER	D. Martin	Capitol	29
45.	BLUE SUEDE SHOES	C. Perkins	Sun	42
46.	MAGIC TOUCH	Platters	Mercury	24
47.	STRANDED IN THE JUNGLE	Cadets	Modern	—
48.	LOVE, LOVE, LOVE	Clovers	Atlantic	52
48.	NEVER TURN BACK	A. Hibbler	Decca	51
50.	SWEET HEARTACHES	E. Fisher	Victor	61
51.	I COULD HAVE DANCED ALL NIGHT	R. Clooney	Columbia	54
52.	MY LITTLE ANGEL	Four Lads	Columbia	—
52.	STRANDED IN THE JUNGLE	Jayhawks	Flash	65
54.	GRADUATION DAY	Rover Boys	ABC-Paramount	30
54.	A TEAR FELL	T. Brewer	Coral	43
56.	SECOND FIDDLE	K. Starr	Victor	45
57.	HEAVEN ON EARTH	Platters	Mercury	—
58.	KISS ME ANOTHER	G. Gibbs	Mercury	47
59.	LONG, TALL SALLY	Little Richard	Specialty	49
60.	FREE	T. Leonetti	Capitol	40
61.	LOVE, LOVE, LOVE	Diamonds	Mercury	58
62.	READY TEDDY	Little Richard	Specialty	80
62.	CANADIAN SUNSET	H. Winterhalter	Victor	—
64.	YOU DON'T KNOW ME	J. Vale	Columbia	61
65.	HOT DOG, BUDDY BUDDY	B. Haley	Decca	60
65.	TELL ME WHY	G. Storm	Dot	77
67.	CORRINE, CORRINA	J. Turner	Atlantic	76
68.	POOR PEOPLE OF PARIS	L. Baxter	Capitol	47
69.	TANGO OF THE DRUMS	L. Baxter	Capitol	86
70.	BOPPIN' THE BLUES	C. Perkins	Sun	—
71.	THEME FROM "THE PROUD ONE"	N. Riddle	Capitol	—
72.	LONG, TALL SALLY	P. Boone	Dot	44
73.	TOO CLOSE FOR COMFORT	E. Gorme	ABC-Paramount	55
74.	MY DREAM SONATA	Nat (King) Cole	Capitol	77
75.	TE AMO	D. Jacobs	Coral	75
75.	SOFT SUMMER BREEZE	E. Heywood	Mercury	70
75.	GHOST TOWN	D. Cherry	Columbia	—
78.	ROLL OVER, BEETHOVEN	C. Berry	Chess	87
79.	FABULOUS CHARACTER	S. Vaughan	Mercury	—
80.	TELL ME WHY	Crew Cuts	Mercury	53
81.	OOBY DOOBY	R. Orbison	Sun	59
82.	MARIMBA CHARLESTON	M. Chiapas	Capitol	—
82.	WALK HAND IN HAND	A. Williams	Cadence	65
84.	STANDING ON THE CORNER	Mills Brothers	Decca	63
85.	ROCKIN' THROUGH THE RYE	B. Haley	Decca	—
86.	I'VE GROWN ACCUSTOMED TO YOUR FACE	R. Clooney	Columbia	—
87.	DREAMER	Four Aces	Decca	—
87.	ROCKIN' GHOST	A. Bleyer	Cadence	89
89.	DELILAH JONES	McGuire Sisters	Coral	91
90.	MR. WONDERFUL	P. Lee	Decca	67
91.	CASUAL LOOK	Six Teens	Flip	—
91.	GET ME TO THE CHURCH ON TIME	J. La Rosa	Cadence	—
93.	SLIPPIN' AND SLIDIN'	Little Richard	Specialty	70
94.	I'M IN LOVE WITH YOU	P. Boone	Dot	—
95.	R-O-C-K	B. Haley	Decca	—
96.	I COULD HAVE DANCED ALL NIGHT	D. Shore	Victor	93
96.	FIVE	S. Davis Jr.	Decca	—
98.	ROCK ISLAND LINE	L. Donegan	London	70
99.	YOU'RE SENSATIONAL	F. Sinatra	Capitol	—
99.	TO LOVE AGAIN	Four Aces	Decca	69

CAUTION TO DEALERS AND JUKE BOX OPERATORS

The Billboard's Top 100 is NOT designed to provide tested information for buying purposes. This function is most reliably served by other regular weekly features: Best Sellers in Stores, Most Played in Juke Boxes, Coming Up Strong and Best Buys.

• Best Sellers in Stores

For survey week ending July 11

RECORDS are ranked in order of their current national selling importance at the retail level, as determined by The Billboard's weekly survey of the top volume dealers in every important market area. When significant action is reported on both sides of a record, points are combined to determine position on the chart. In such a case, both sides are listed in bold type, the leading side on top.

This Week		Last Week	Weeks on Chart
1.	**WAYWARD WIND** (BMI)—G. Grant No More Than Forever (ASCAP)—Era 1013	1	12
2.	**I ALMOST LOST MY MIND** (BMI)—P. Boone I'm In Love With You (BMI)—Dot 15472	2	6
3.	**I WANT YOU, I NEED YOU, I LOVE YOU** (BMI)—E. Presley **MY BABY LEFT ME** (BMI)—Vic 20-6450	4	8
4.	**MORE** (ASCAP)—P. Como **GLENDORA** (BMI)—Vic 20-6554	6	6
5.	**MY PRAYER** (ASCAP)—Platters **HEAVEN ON EARTH** (ASCAP)—Mercury 70893	17	2
6.	**MOONGLOW AND THEME FROM "PICNIC"** (ASCAP)—M. Stoloff Theme From "Picnic" (ASCAP)—Dec 29888	3	14
7.	**I'M IN LOVE AGAIN** (BMI)—F. Domino **MY BLUE HEAVEN** (ASCAP)—Imperial 5386	5	12
8.	**BE-BOP-A-LULA** (BMI)—G. Vincent Woman Love (BMI)—Cap 3450	10	5
9.	**WHATEVER WILL BE, WILL BE** (ASCAP)—Doris Day I Gotta Sing Away These Blues (BMI)—Col 40704	15	3
10.	**BORN TO BE WITH YOU** (ASCAP)—Chordettes Love Never Changes (ASCAP)—Cadence 1291-1091	7	5
11.	**ON THE STREET WHERE YOU LIVE** (ASCAP)—V. Damone We All Need Love (ASCAP)—Col 40654	9	7
12.	**ALLEGHENY MOON** (ASCAP)—P. Page Strangest Romance (ASCAP)—Mercury 70878	11	3
13.	**STANDING ON THE CORNER** (ASCAP)—Four Lads My Little Angel (BMI)—Col 40574	7	13
14.	**SWEET OLD-FASHIONED GIRL** (ASCAP)—T. Brewer Goodbye, John (BMI)—Coral 61636	12	5
15.	**TRANSFUSION** (BMI)—Nervous Norvus Dig (BMI)—Dot 15470	13	7
16.	**MOONGLOW AND THEME FROM "PICNIC"** (ASCAP)—G. Cates Rio Batucada (ASCAP)—Coral 61618	14	14
17.	**IT ONLY HURTS FOR A LITTLE WHILE** (ASCAP)—Ames Brothers If You Want to See Mamie Tonight (ASCAP)—Vic 20-6481	19	8
18.	**HEARTBREAK HOTEL** (BMI)—E. Presley I Was the One (BMI)—Vic 20-6420	16	20
19.	**RIP IT UP** (BMI)—Little Richard **READY TEDDY** (BMI)—Specialty 579	—	1
20.	**IVORY TOWER** (ASCAP)—C. Carr Please, Please, Believe Me (ASCAP)—Fraternity 734	18	15
21.	**STRANDED IN THE JUNGLE** (BMI) Cadets I Want You (BMI)—Modern 994	—	1
22.	**TREASURE OF LOVE** (BMI)—C. McPhatter When You're Sincere (BMI)—Atlantic 1092	21	5
23.	**THAT'S ALL THERE IS TO THAT** (BMI)—Nat (King) Cole My Dream Sonata (ASCAP)—Cap 3456	—	1
24.	**SOFT SUMMER BREEZE** (BMI)—E. Heywood Heywood's Bounce (BMI)—Mercury 70863	—	1
25.	**HAPPY WHISTLER** (ASCAP)—D. Robertson You're Free to Go (ASCAP)—Cap 3391	20	12

• Most Played in Juke Boxes

For survey week ending July 11

RECORDS are ranked in order of the greatest number of plays in juke boxes thruout the country, as determined by The Billboard's weekly survey of the nation's juke box operators. When significant play is reported on both sides of a record, points are combined to determine position on the chart. In such a case, both sides are listed in bold type, the leading side on top.

This Week		Last Week	Weeks on Chart
1.	**WAYWARD WIND** (BMI)—G. Grant No More Than Forever (ASCAP)—Era 1013	1	8
2.	**I ALMOST LOST MY MIND** (BMI)—P. Boone I'm In Love With You (BMI)—Dot 15472	2	6
3.	**I'M IN LOVE AGAIN** (BMI)—F. Domino **MY BLUE HEAVEN** (ASCAP)—Imperial 5386	3	10
4.	**I WANT YOU, I NEED YOU, I LOVE YOU** (BMI)—E. Presley My Baby Left Me (BMI)—Vic 20-6540	4	7
5.	**MOONGLOW AND THEME FROM "PICNIC"** (ASCAP)—M. Stoloff Theme From "Picnic" (ASCAP)—Dec 29888	7	10
6.	**STANDING ON THE CORNER** (ASCAP)—Four Lads My Little Angel (BMI)—Col 40674	8	9
7.	**HEARTBREAK HOTEL** (BMI)—E. Presley I Was the One (BMI)—Vic 20-6420	5	17
8.	**IVORY TOWER** (ASCAP)—C. Carr Please Believe Me (ASCAP)—Fraternity 734	6	12
9.	**MORE** (ASCAP)—P. Como **GLENDORA** (BMI)—Vic 20-6554	9	3
9.	**BORN TO BE WITH YOU** (ASCAP)—Chordettes Love Never Changes (ASCAP)—Cadence 1291	12	4
11.	**ALLEGHENY MOON** (ASCAP)—P. Page Strangest Romance (ASCAP)—Mercury 70878	14	3
12.	**MOONGLOW AND THEME FROM "PICNIC"** (ASCAP)—G. Cates Rio Batucada (ASCAP)—Coral 61618	10	11
13.	**BE-BOP-A-LULA** (BMI)—G. Vincent Woman Love (BMI)—Cap 3450	17	2
14.	**SWEET OLD-FASHIONED GIRL** (ASCAP)—T. Brewer Goodbye, John (BMI)—Coral 61636	19	2
15.	**ON THE STREET WHERE YOU LIVE** (ASCAP)—V. Damone We All Need Love (ASCAP)—Col 40654	15	3
16.	**IVORY TOWER** (ASCAP)—G. Storm I Ain't Gonna Worry (BMI)—Dot 15458	11	10
17.	**IT ONLY HURTS FOR A LITTLE WHILE** (ASCAP)—Ames Brothers If You Want to See Mamie Tonight (ASCAP)—Vic 20-6481	13	5
18.	**HAPPY WHISTLER** (ASCAP)—D. Robertson You're Free to Go (ASCAP)—Cap 3391	16	8
19.	**TRANSFUSION** (BMI)—Nervous Norvus Dig (BMI)—Dot 15470	—	1
20.	**MY PRAYER** (ASCAP)—Platters Heaven On Earth (ASCAP)—Mercury 70893	—	1

• Best Selling Sheet Music

Tunes are ranked in order of their current national selling importance at the sheet music jobber level.

This Week		Last Week	Weeks on Chart
1.	**Wayward Wind** (Warman)	1	8
2.	**Allegheny Moon** (Oxford)	3	4
3.	**Ivory Tower** (E. H. Morris)	2	13
4.	**Picnic** (Shapiro-Bernstein)	4	10
5.	**On the Street Where You Live** (Chappell)	5	11
6.	**Moonglow** (Mills-Columbia Pictures)	6	10
7.	**Walk Hand in Hand** (Republic)	7	11
8.	**Whatever Will Be, Will Be** (Che Sera, Sera Artists)	12	2
9.	**I Almost Lost My Mind** (Hill & Range)	9	4
10.	**More** (Shapiro-Bernstein)	10	3
11.	**Standing On the Corner** (Frank)	8	10
12.	**Sweet Old-Fashioned Girl** (Valor)	—	1
13.	**My Prayer** (Shapiro-Bernstein)	—	1
14.	**It Only Hurts for a Little While** (Advanced)	—	2
14.	**Graduation Day** (Sheldon)	11	7
14.	**Heartbreak Hotel** (Tree)	13	14

• Most Played by Jockeys

For survey week ending July 11

SIDES are ranked in order of the greatest number of plays on disk jockey radio shows thruout the country. Results are based on The Billboard's weekly survey among the nation's disk jockeys. The reverse side of each record is also listed.

This Week		Last Week	Weeks on Chart
1.	**WAYWARD WIND** (BMI)—G. Grant No More Than Forever (ASCAP)—Era 1013	1	11
2.	**I ALMOST LOST MY MIND** (BMI)—P. Boone I'm In Love With You (BMI)—Dot 15472	3	6
3.	**MOONGLOW AND THEME FROM "PICNIC"** (ASCAP)—M. Stoloff Theme From "Picnic" (ASCAP)—Dec 29888	2	14
4.	**ON THE STREET WHERE YOU LIVE** (ASCAP)—V. Damone We All Need Love (ASCAP)—Col 40654	4	8
5.	**BORN TO BE WITH YOU** (ASCAP)—Chordettes Love Never Changes (ASCAP)—Cadence 1291	5	7
6.	**ALLEGHENY MOON** (ASCAP)—P. Page Strangest Romance (ASCAP)—Mercury 70878	12	4
7.	**I WANT YOU, I NEED YOU, I LOVE YOU** (BMI)—E. Presley My Baby Left Me (BMI)—Vic 20-6540	7	6
8.	**STANDING ON THE CORNER** (ASCAP)—Four Lads My Little Angel (BMI)—Col 40674	6	12
9.	**GLENDORA** (BMI)—P. Como More (ASCAP)—Vic 20-6554	8	5
10.	**WHATEVER WILL BE, WILL BE** (ASCAP)—Doris Day I Gotta Sing Away These Blues (BMI)—Col 40704	16	3
11.	**MORE** (ASCAP)—P. Como Glendora (BMI)—Vic 20-6554	9	4
12.	**MOONGLOW AND THEME FROM "PICNIC"** (ASCAP)—G. Cates Rio Batucada (ASCAP)—Coral 61618	11	14
13.	**BE-BOP-A-LULA** (BMI)—G. Vincent Woman Love (BMI)—Cap 3450	13	4
14.	**I'M IN LOVE AGAIN** (BMI)—F. Domino My Blue Heaven (ASCAP)—Imperial 5386	10	9
15.	**SWEET OLD-FASHIONED GIRL** (ASCAP)—T. Brewer Goodbye, John (BMI)—Coral 61636	14	3
16.	**MY PRAYER** (ASCAP)—Platters Heaven On Earth (ASCAP)—Mercury 70893	25	2
17.	**IT ONLY HURTS FOR A LITTLE WHILE** (ASCAP)—Ames Brothers If You Want to See Mamie Tonight (ASCAP)—Vic 20-6481	15	6
18.	**WALK HAND IN HAND** (BMI)—T. Martin Flamenco Love (ASCAP)—Vic 20-6493	18	9
19.	**PICNIC** (ASCAP)—McGuire Sisters Delilah Jones (ASCAP)—Coral 61627	20	9
20.	**HAPPY WHISTLER** (ASCAP)—D. Robertson You're Free to Go (ASCAP)—Cap 3391	—	11
21.	**IVORY TOWER** (ASCAP)—G. Storm I Ain't Gonna Worry (BMI)—Dot 15458	17	11
22.	**NEVER TURN BACK** (BMI)—A. Hibbler Away All Boats (ASCAP)—Dec 29950	22	2
23.	**GRADUATION DAY** (BMI)—Four Freshmen Lonely Night In Paris (ASCAP)—Cap 3410	21	7
24.	**FABULOUS CHARACTER**—S. Vaughan Other Woman (ASCAP)—Mercury 70885	—	1
25.	**FREE** (ASCAP)—T. Leonetti It's Wild (BMI)—Cap 3442	23	2

THE TOP 100

For survey week ending July 11

A list of the Top 100 **RECORD SIDES** in the nation according to a **COMBINED TABULATION** of Dealer, Disk Jockey and Juke Box Operator replies to The Billboard's weekly popular record Best Seller and Most Played surveys. Its purpose is to provide Disk Jockeys with additional programming material and to give trade exposure to NEWER records just beginning to show action in the field.

Pos.	Song	Artist	Label	Last Week
1.	WAYWARD WIND	G. Grant	Era	1
2.	I ALMOST LOST MY MIND	P. Boone	Dot	2
3.	MOONGLOW AND THEME FROM "PICNIC"	M. Stoloff	Decca	3
4.	I WANT YOU, I NEED YOU, I LOVE YOU	E. Presley	Victor	4
5.	BORN TO BE WITH YOU	Chordettes	Cadence	6
6.	I'M IN LOVE AGAIN	F. Domino	Imperial	5
7.	STANDING ON THE CORNER	Four Lads	Columbia	7
8.	ALLEGHENY MOON	P. Page	Mercury	11
9.	ON THE STREET WHERE YOU LIVE	V. Damone	Columbia	8
10.	BE-BOP-A-LULA	G. Vincent	Capitol	12
11.	MORE	P. Como	Victor	9
12.	MOONGLOW AND THEME FROM "PICNIC"	G. Cates	Coral	10
12.	WHATEVER WILL BE, WILL BE	Doris Day	Columbia	20
14.	MY PRAYER	Platters	Mercury	24
15.	SWEET OLD-FASHIONED GIRL	T. Brewer	Coral	13
16.	GLENDORA	P. Como	Victor	15
17.	IT ONLY HURTS FOR A LITTLE WHILE	Ames Brothers	Victor	16
18.	IVORY TOWER	C. Carr	Fraternity	13
19.	HEARTBREAK HOTEL	E. Presley	Victor	17
20.	HAPPY WHISTLER	D. Robertson	Capitol	19
21.	IVORY TOWER	G. Storm	Dot	18
21.	TRANSFUSION	N. Norvus	Dot	22
23.	PICNIC	McGuire Sisters	Coral	20
24.	WALK HAND IN HAND	T. Martin	Victor	23
25.	TREASURE OF LOVE	C. McPhatter	Atlantic	26
26.	STRANDED IN THE JUNGLE	Cadets	Modern	47
27.	PORTUGUESE WASHERWOMAN	J. (Fingers) Carr	Capitol	27
28.	ON THE STREET WHERE YOU LIVE	E. Fisher	Victor	31
29.	CHURCH BELLS MAY RING	Diamonds	Mercury	33
30.	HOW LITTLE WE KNOW	F. Sinatra	Capitol	41
31.	GRADUATION DAY	Four Freshmen	Capitol	30
31.	HOT DIGGITY	P. Como	Victor	25
31.	WAYWARD WIND	T. Ritter	Capitol	32
34.	FEVER	L. W. John	King	37
34.	MY BLUE HEAVEN	F. Domino	Imperial	28
36.	I WANT YOU TO BE MY GIRL	Teen-Agers	Gee	28
37.	MAGIC TOUCH	Platters	Mercury	46
38.	THAT'S ALL THERE IS TO THAT	Nat (King) Cole	Capitol	43
39.	RIP IT UP	Little Richard	Specialty	40
40.	IVORY TOWER	O. Williams	De Luxe	34
41.	I COULD HAVE DANCED ALL NIGHT	S. Syms	Decca	35
42.	STRANDED IN THE JUNGLE	Jayhawks	Flash	52
42.	YOU DON'T KNOW ME	J. Vale	Columbia	64
44.	READY TEDDY	Little Richard	Specialty	62
45.	STANDING ON THE CORNER	D. Martin	Capitol	44
46.	CANADIAN SUNSET	H. Winterhalter	Victor	62
47.	LOVE, LOVE, LOVE	Clovers	Atlantic	48
48.	IN A SHANTY IN OLD SHANTY TOWN	S. Smith	Epic	39
48.	I'M IN LOVE AGAIN	Fontane Sisters	Dot	38
50.	GRADUATION DAY	Rover Boys	ABC-Paramount	54
51.	SWEET HEARTACHES	E. Fisher	Victor	50
51.	SECOND FIDDLE	K. Starr	Victor	56
53.	LOVE, LOVE, LOVE	Diamonds	Mercury	61
54.	SOFT SUMMER BREEZE	E. Heywood	Mercury	75
55.	I COULD HAVE DANCED ALL NIGHT	R. Clooney	Columbia	51
56.	POOR PEOPLE OF PARIS	L. Baxter	Capitol	68
57.	NEVER TURN BACK	A. Hibbler	Decca	48
58.	TELL ME WHY	G. Storm	Dot	65
59.	GHOST TOWN	D. Cherry	Columbia	75
60.	FREE	T. Leonetti	Capitol	60
61.	HEAVEN ON EARTH	Platters	Mercury	57
61.	THEME FROM "THE PROUD ONE"	N. Riddle	Capitol	71
63.	FABULOUS CHARACTER	S. Vaughan	Mercury	79
63.	MY BABY LEFT ME	E. Presley	Victor	42
65.	CAN YOU FIND IT IN YOUR HEART	T. Bennett	Columbia	36
65.	A TEAR FELL	T. Brewer	Coral	54
67.	KISS ME ANOTHER	G. Gibbs	Mercury	58
68.	LONG, TALL SALLY	Little Richard	Specialty	59
69.	BLUE SUEDE SHOES	C. Perkins	Sun	45
70.	TE AMO	D. Jacobs	Coral	75
71.	ROLL OVER BEETHOVEN	C. Berry	Chess	78
72.	STRANDED IN THE JUNGLE	Gadabouts	Mercury	—
72.	TOO CLOSE FOR COMFORT	E. Gorme	ABC-Paramount	73
74.	MY LITTLE ANGEL	Four Lads	Columbia	52
75.	HOW LUCKY YOU ARE	J. James	M-G-M	—
76.	YOU'RE SENSATIONAL	F. Sinatra	Capitol	99
77.	YOUR THE APPLE OF MY EYE	Four Lovers	Victor	—
78.	ROCKIN' THROUGH THE RYE	B. Haley	Decca	85
79.	HEARTBREAK HOTEL	S. Freberg	Capitol	—
80.	OOBY DOOBY	R. Orbison	Sun	81
81.	JOHNNY CASANOVA	J. P. Morgan	Victor	—
81.	TELL ME WHY	Crew Cuts	Mercury	80
83.	I'M IN LOVE WITH YOU	P. Boone	Dot	94
84.	DELILAH JONES	McGuire Sisters	Coral	89
84.	WITH A LITTLE BIT OF LUCK	P. Faith	Columbia	—
86.	TO LOVE AGAIN	Four Aces	Decca	99
87.	HOT DOG BUDDY BUDDY	B. Haley	Decca	65
88.	PRESIDENT ON THE DOLLAR	M. Miller	Columbia	—
89.	GET ME TO THE CHURCH ON TIME	J. La Rosa	Victor	91
89.	SLIPPIN' AND SLIDIN'	Little Richard	Specialty	93
91.	CASUAL LOOK	Six Teens	Flip	91
92.	AFTER SCHOOL	T. Charles	Decca	—
92.	MARIMBA CHARLESTON	M. Chiapas	Capitol	82
92.	MY DREAM SONATA	Nat (King) Cole	Capitol	74
92.	STANDING ON THE CORNER	Mills Brothers	Decca	84
96.	LAZY RIVER	R. Sherwood	Decca	—
97.	LITTLE GIRL OF MINE	Cleftones	Gee	—
98.	LONG, TALL SALLY	P. Boone	Dot	72
99.	ROCK ISLAND LINE	L. Donegan	London	98
100.	TANGO OF THE DRUMS	L. Baxter	Capitol	69

CAUTION TO DEALERS AND JUKE BOX OPERATORS

The Billboard's Top 100 is NOT designed to provide tested information for buying purposes. This function is most reliably served by other regular weekly features: Best Sellers in Stores, Most Played in Juke Boxes, Coming Up Strong and Best Buys.

• Best Sellers in Stores

For survey week ending July 18

RECORDS are ranked in order of their current national selling importance at the retail level, as determined by The Billboard's weekly survey of the top volume dealers in every important market area. When significant action is reported on both sides of a record, points are combined to determine position on the chart. In such a case, both sides are listed in bold type, the leading side on top.

This Week		Last Week	Weeks on Chart
1.	I WANT YOU, I NEED YOU, I LOVE YOU (BMI)—E. Presley / MY BABY LEFT ME (BMI)—Vic 20-6540	3	9
2.	WAYWARD WIND (BMI)—G. Grant / No More Than Forever (ASCAP)—Era 1013	1	13
3.	I ALMOST LOST MY MIND (BMI)—P. Boone / I'm in Love With You (BMI)—Dot 15472	2	7
4.	MY PRAYER (ASCAP)—Platters / HEAVEN ON EARTH (ASCAP)—Mercury 70893	5	3
5.	MORE (ASCAP)—P. Como / GLENDORA (BMI)—Vic 20-6554	4	7
6.	WHATEVER WILL BE, WILL BE (ASCAP)—Doris Day / I Gotta Sing Away These Blues (BMI)—Col 40704	9	4
7.	BE-BOP-A-LULA (BMI)—G. Vincent / Woman Love (BMI)—Cap 3450	8	6
8.	I'M IN LOVE AGAIN (BMI)—F. Domino / MY BLUE HEAVEN (ASCAP)—Imperial 5386	7	13
9.	ALLEGHENY MOON (ASCAP)—P. Page / Strangest Romance (ASCAP)—Mercury 70878	12	4
10.	BORN TO BE WITH YOU (ASCAP)—Chordettes / Love Never Changes (ASCAP)—Cadence 1291	10	6
11.	MOONGLOW AND THEME FROM "PICNIC" (ASCAP)—M. Stoloff / Theme From "Picnic" (ASCAP)—Dec 29888	6	15
12.	ON THE STREET WHERE YOU LIVE (ASCAP)—V. Damone / We All Need Love (ASCAP)—Col 40654	11	8
13.	SWEET OLD-FASHIONED GIRL (ASCAP)—T. Brewer / Goodbye, John (BMI)—Coral 61636	14	6
14.	STANDING ON THE CORNER (ASCAP)—Four Lads / MY LITTLE ANGEL (BMI)—Col 40574	13	14
15.	TRANSFUSION (BMI)—Nervous Norvus / Dig (BMI)—Dot 15470	15	8
16.	STRANDED IN THE JUNGLE (BMI)—Cadets / I Want You (BMI)—Modern 994	21	2
17.	IT ONLY HURTS FOR A LITTLE WHILE (ASCAP)—Ames Brothers / If You Want to See Mamie Tonight (ASCAP)—Vic 20-6481	17	9
18.	STRANDED IN THE JUNGLE (BMI)—Jayhawks / My Only Darling (BMI)—Flash 109	—	1
19.	CANADIAN SUNSET (BMI)—H. Winterhalter / This Is Real (ASCAP)—Vic 20-6537	—	1
20.	RIP IT UP (BMI)—Little Richard / READY TEDDY (BMI)—Specialty 579	19	2
21.	MOONGLOW AND THEME FROM "PICNIC" (ASCAP)—G. Cates / Rio Batucada (ASCAP)—Coral 61618	16	15
22.	IVORY TOWER (ASCAP)—C. Carr / Please, Please Believe Me (ASCAP)—Fraternity 734	20	16
23.	SOFT SUMMER BREEZE (BMI)—E. Heywood / Heywood's Bounce (BMI)—Mercury 70863	24	2
24.	THAT'S ALL THERE IS TO THAT (BMI)—Nat (King) Cole / My Dream Sonata (ASCAP)—Cap 3456	23	2
25.	WHEN MY DREAM BOAT COMES HOME (ASCAP)—F. Domino / SO-LONG (BMI)—Imperial 5396	—	1

• Most Played in Juke Boxes

For survey week ending July 18

RECORDS are ranked in order of the greatest number of plays in juke-boxes thruout the country, as determined by The Billboard's weekly survey of the nation's juke box operators. When significant play is reported on both sides of a record, points are combined to determine position on the chart. In such a case, both sides are listed in bold type, the leading side on top.

This Week		Last Week	Weeks on Chart
1.	I ALMOST LOST MY MIND (BMI)—P. Boone / I'm In Love With You (BMI)—Dot 15472	2	7
2.	WAYWARD WIND (BMI)—G. Grant / No More Than Forever (ASCAP)—Era 1013	1	9
3.	I WANT YOU, I NEED YOU, I LOVE YOU (BMI)—E. Presley / My Baby Left Me (BMI)—Vic 20-6540	4	8
4.	I'M IN LOVE AGAIN (BMI)—F. Domino / MY BLUE HEAVEN (ASCAP)—Imperial 5386	3	11
5.	MOONGLOW AND THEME FROM "PICNIC" (ASCAP)—M. Stoloff / Theme From "Picnic" (ASCAP)—Dec 29888	5	11
6.	BORN TO BE WITH YOU (ASCAP)—Chordettes / Love Never Changes (ASCAP)—Cadence 1291	9	5
7.	MORE (ASCAP)—P. Como / GLENDORA (BMI)—Vic 20-6554	9	4
8.	ALLEGHENY MOON (ASCAP)—P. Page / Strangest Romance (ASCAP)—Mercury 70878	11	4
9.	SWEET OLD-FASHIONED GIRL (ASCAP)—T. Brewer / Goodbye, John (BMI)—Coral 61636	14	3
10.	IVORY TOWER (ASCAP)—C. Carr / Please Believe Me (ASCAP)—Fraternity 734	8	13
11.	STANDING ON THE CORNER (ASCAP)—Four Lads / My Little Angel (BMI)—Col 40674	6	10
12.	MOONGLOW AND THEME FROM "PICNIC" (ASCAP)—G. Cates / Rio Batucada (ASCAP)—Coral 61618	12	12
13.	MY PRAYER (ASCAP)—Platters / Heaven On Earth (ASCAP)—Mercury 70893	20	2
14.	HEARTBREAK HOTEL (BMI)—E. Presley / I Was the One (BMI)—Vic 20-6420	7	18
15.	WHATEVER WILL BE, WILL BE (ASCAP)—Doris Day / I Gotta Sing Away These Blues (BMI)—Col 40704	—	1
16.	IVORY TOWER (ASCAP)—G. Storm / I Ain't Gonna Worry (BMI)—Dot 15458	16	11
16.	IT ONLY HURTS A LITTLE WHILE (ASCAP)—Ames Brothers / If You Want to See Mamie Tonight (ASCAP)—Vic 20-6481	17	6
18.	ON THE STREET WHERE YOU LIVE (ASCAP)—V. Damone / We All Need Love (ASCAP)—Col 40654	15	4
19.	TRANSFUSION (BMI)—Nervous Norvus / Dig (BMI)—Dot 15470	19	2
20.	BE-BOP-A-LULA (BMI)—G. Vincent / Woman Love (BMI)—Cap 3450	13	3

• Best Selling Sheet Music

Tunes are ranked in order of their current national selling importance at the sheet music jobber level.

This Week		Last Week	Weeks on Chart
1.	**Wayward Wind** (Warman)	1	9
2.	**Allegheny Moon** (Oxford)	2	5
3.	**Whatever Will Be, Will Be** (Che Sera, Sera Artist)	8	3
4.	**On the Street Where You Live** (Chappell)	5	12
5.	**Moonglow** (Mills-Columbia Pictures	6	11
6.	**Ivory Tower** (E. H. Morris)	3	14
7.	**Picnic** (Shapiro-Bernstein)	4	11
8.	**I Almost Lost My Mind** (Hill & Range)	9	5
9.	**Walk Hand in Hand** (Republic)	7	12
10.	**Sweet Old-Fashioned Girl** (Valor)	12	2
11.	**More** (Shapiro-Bernstein)	10	4
11.	**I Want You, I Need You, I Love You** (Presley)	—	1
13.	**My Prayer** (Shapiro-Bernstein)	13	2
14.	**Standing On the Corner** (Frank)	11	11
15.	**Born to Be With You** (E. H. Morris)	—	1

• Most Played by Jockeys

For survey week ending July 18

SIDES are ranked in order of the greatest number of plays on disk jockey radio shows thruout the country. Results are based on The Billboard's weekly survey among the nation's disk jockeys. The reverse side of each record is also listed.

This Week		Last Week	Weeks on Chart
1.	WAYWARD WIND (BMI)—G. Grant / No More Than Forever (ASCAP)—Era 1013	1	12
2.	I ALMOST LOST MY MIND (BMI)—P. Boone / I'm in Love With You (BMI)—Dot 15472	2	7
3.	MOONGLOW AND THEME FROM "PICNIC" (ASCAP)—M. Stoloff / Theme From "Picnic" (ASCAP)—Dec 29888	3	15
4.	ALLEGHENY MOON (ASCAP)—P. Page / Strangest Romance (ASCAP)—Mercury 70878	6	5
5.	ON THE STREET WHERE YOU LIVE (ASCAP)—V. Damone / We All Need Love (ASCAP)—Col 40654	4	9
6.	I WANT YOU, I NEED YOU, I LOVE YOU (BMI)—E. Presley / My Baby Left Me (BMI)—Vic 20-6540	7	7
7.	BORN TO BE WITH YOU (ASCAP)—Chordettes / Love Never Changes (ASCAP)—Cadence 1291	5	8
8.	MORE (ASCAP)—P. Como / Glendora (BMI)—Vic 20-6554	11	5
9.	MY PRAYER (ASCAP)—Platters / Heaven On Earth (ASCAP)—Mercury 70893	16	3
10.	WHATEVER WILL BE, WILL BE (ASCAP)—Doris Day / I Gotta Sing Away These Blues (BMI)—Col 40704	10	4
11.	BE-BOP-A-LULA (BMI)—G. Vincent / Woman Love (BMI)—Cap 3450	13	5
12.	STANDING ON THE CORNER (ASCAP)—Four Lads / My Little Angel (BMI)—Col 40674	8	13
13.	I'M IN LOVE AGAIN (BMI)—F. Domino / My Blue Heaven (ASCAP)—Imperial 5386	14	10
14.	SWEET OLD-FASHIONED GIRL (ASCAP)—T. Brewer / Goodbye, John (BMI)—Coral 61636	15	4
15.	GLENDORA (BMI)—P. Como / More (ASCAP)—Vic 20-6554	9	6
16.	MOONGLOW AND THEME FROM "PICNIC" (ASCAP)—G. Cates / Rio Batucada (ASCAP)—Coral 61618	12	15
17.	CANADIAN SUNSET (BMI)—H. Winterhalter / This Is Real (ASCAP)—Vic 20-6537	—	1
18.	THAT'S ALL THERE IS TO THAT (BMI)—Nat (King) Cole / My Dream Sonata (ASCAP)—Cap 3456	—	1
19.	PORTUGUESE WASHERWOMAN (ASCAP)—J. (Fingers) Carr / Lucky Pierre—Cap 3418	—	4
20.	STRANDED IN THE JUNGLE (BMI)—Cadets / I Want You (BMI)—Modern 994	—	1
21.	FABULOUS CHARACTER—S. Vaughan / Other Woman (ASCAP)—Mercury 70885	24	2
22.	IT ONLY HURTS FOR A LITTLE WHILE (ASCAP)—Ames Brothers / If You Want to See Mamie Tonight (ASCAP)—Vic 20-6481	17	7
23.	IVORY TOWER (ASCAP)—G. Storm / I Ain't Gonna Worry (BMI)—Dot 15458	21	12
24.	WALK HAND IN HAND (BMI)—T. Martin / Flamenco Love (ASCAP)—Vic 20-6493	18	10
24.	PICNIC (ASCAP)—McGuire Sisters / Delilah Jones (ASCAP)—Coral 61627	19	10

THE TOP 100

For survey week ending July 18

A list of the Top 100 RECORD SIDES in the nation according to a COMBINED TABULATION of Dealer, Disk Jockey and Juke Box Operator replies to The Billboard's weekly popular record Best Seller and Most Played surveys. Its purpose is to provide Disk Jockeys with additional programming material and to give trade exposure to NEWER records just beginning to show action in the field.

Pos.	Song	Artist	Label	Last Week
1.	WAYWARD WIND	G. Grant	Era	1
2.	I ALMOST LOST MY MIND	P. Boone	Dot	2
3.	I WANT YOU, I NEED YOU, I LOVE YOU	E. Presley	Victor	4
4.	ALLEGHENY MOON	P. Page	Mercury	8
4.	MOONGLOW AND THEME FROM "PICNIC"	M. Stoloff	Decca	3
6.	BORN TO BE WITH YOU	Chordettes	Cadence	5
7.	MY PRAYER	Platters	Mercury	14
8.	I'M IN LOVE AGAIN	F. Domino	Imperial	6
9.	WHATEVER WILL BE, WILL BE	Doris Day	Columbia	12
10.	MORE	P. Como	Victor	11
11.	SWEET OLD-FASHIONED GIRL	T. Brewer	Coral	15
12.	ON THE STREET WHERE YOU LIVE	V. Damone	Columbia	9
13.	STANDING ON THE CORNER	Four Lads	Columbia	7
14.	BE-BOP-A-LULA	G. Vincent	Capitol	10
15.	MOONGLOW AND THEME FROM "PICNIC"	G. Cates	Coral	12
16.	GLENDORA	P. Como	Victor	16
17.	IT ONLY HURTS FOR A LITTLE WHILE	Ames Brothers	Victor	17
18.	IVORY TOWER	G. Storm	Dot	21
18.	STRANDED IN THE JUNGLE	Cadets	Modern	26
20.	THAT'S ALL THERE IS TO THAT	Nat (King) Cole	Capitol	38
20.	TRANSFUSION	N. Norvus	Dot	21
22.	IVORY TOWER	C. Carr	Fraternity	18
23.	HAPPY WHISTLER	D. Robertson	Capitol	20
24.	PICNIC	McGuire Sisters	Coral	23
25.	WALK HAND IN HAND	T. Martin	Victor	24
26.	TREASURE OF LOVE	C. McPhatter	Atlantic	25
27.	PORTUGUESE WASHERWOMAN	J. (Fingers) Carr	Capitol	27
28.	HEARTBREAK HOTEL	E. Presley	Victor	19
29.	FEVER	L. W. John	King	34
30.	LOVE, LOVE, LOVE	Clovers	Atlantic	47
30.	LOVE, LOVE, LOVE	Diamonds	Mercury	53
32.	YOU DON'T KNOW ME	J. Vale	Columbia	42
33.	ON THE STREET WHERE YOU LIVE	E. Fisher	Victor	28
34.	STRANDED IN THE JUNGLE	Jayhawks	Flash	42
35.	RIP IT UP	Little Richard	Specialty	39
36.	IN A SHANTY IN OLD SHANTY TOWN	S. Smith	Epic	48
37.	CAN YOU FIND IT IN YOUR HEART?	T. Bennett	Columbia	65
37.	CANADIAN SUNSET	H. Winterhalter	Victor	46
39.	HOW LITTLE WE KNOW	F. Sinatra	Capitol	30
40.	SOFT SUMMER BREEZE	E. Heywood	Mercury	54
41.	I COULD HAVE DANCED ALL NIGHT	S. Syms	Decca	41
42.	FABULOUS CHARACTER	S. Vaughan	Mercury	63
43.	STANDING ON THE CORNER	D. Martin	Capitol	45
44.	CHURCH BELLS MAY RING	Diamonds	Mercury	29
45.	IVORY TOWER	O. Williams	De Luxe	40
46.	STRANDED IN THE JUNGLE	Gadabouts	Mercury	72
46.	THEME FROM "THE PROUD ONES"	N. Riddle	Capitol	61
48.	MY LITTLE ANGEL	Four Lads	Columbia	74
49.	VOICES	Fontane Sisters	Dot	—
50.	MY BABY LEFT ME	E. Presley	Victor	63
51.	MAGIC TOUCH	Platters	Mercury	37
52.	MY BLUE HEAVEN	F. Domino	Imperial	34
52.	READY TEDDY	Little Richard	Specialty	44
54.	GHOST TOWN	D. Cherry	Columbia	59
55.	I WANT YOU TO BE MY GIRL	Teen-Agers	Gee	36
56.	HOT DIGGITY	P. Como	Victor	31
57.	I'M IN LOVE AGAIN	Fontane Sisters	Dot	48
58.	FOOL	S. Clark	Dot	—
59.	LONG, TALL SALLY	Little Richard	Specialty	68
59.	MY DREAM SONATA	Nat (King) Cole	Capitol	92
61.	NEVER TURN BACK	A. Hibbler	Decca	57
62.	KISS ME ANOTHER	G. Gibbs	Mercury	67
63.	HEAVEN ON EARTH	Platters	Mercury	61
63.	I ONLY KNOW I LOVE YOU	Four Aces	Decca	—
65.	WAYWARD WIND	T. Ritter	Capitol	31
65.	YOU'RE SENSATIONAL	F. Sinatra	Capitol	76
67.	HEART HIDEWAY	C. Carr	Fraternity	—
68.	CASUAL LOOK	Six Teens	Flip	91
68.	WEARY BLUES	McGuire Sisters	Coral	—
70.	HOW LUCKY YOU ARE	J. James	M-G-M	75
71.	A TEAR FELL	T. Brewer	Coral	65
72.	I COULD HAVE DANCED ALL NIGHT	R. Clooney	Columbia	75
73.	SECOND FIDDLE	K. Starr	Victor	51
74.	GRADUATION DAY	Rover Boys	ABC Paramount	50
75.	JOHNNY CONCHO THEME	F. Sinatra	Capitol	—
75.	SOMEBODY UP THERE LIKES ME	P. Como	Victor	—
77.	R-O-C-K	B. Haley	Decca	—
78.	FREE	T. Leonetti	Capitol	60
79.	GRADUATION DAY	Four Freshmen	Capitol	31
80.	APE CALL	N. Norvus	Dot	—
81.	TO LOVE AGAIN	Four Aces	Decca	86
82.	TELL ME WHY	G. Storm	Dot	58
83.	ROLL OVER BEETHOVEN	C. Berry	Chess	71
84.	MAMA TEACH ME TO DANCE	E. Gorme	ABC Paramount	—
85.	BOPPIN' THE BLUES	C. Perkins	Sun	—
86.	TELL ME WHY	Crew Cuts	Mercury	81
87.	I'M IN LOVE WITH YOU	P. Boone	Dot	83
87.	ROCKIN' THROUGH THE RYE	B. Haley	Decca	78
89.	BEAUTIFUL FRIENDSHIP	E. Fitzgerald	Decca	—
90.	MARIMBA CHARLESTON	M. Chiapas	Capitol	92
91.	PRESIDENT ON THE DOLLAR	M. Miller	Columbia	88
92.	FIVE	S. Davis Jr.	Decca	—
93.	SWEET HEARTACHES	E. Fisher	Victor	51
94.	I PROMISE TO REMEMBER	Teen-Agers	Gee	—
95.	WHEN MY DREAMBOAT COMES HOME	F. Domino	Imperial	—
96.	SO-LONG	F. Domino	Imperial	—
97.	KA DING DONG	G-Clefs	Pilgrim	—
98.	DREAM ALONG WITH ME	P. Como	Victor	—
99.	MAIN TITLE (MAN WITH THE GOLDEN ARM)	E. Bernstein	Decca	—
99.	WITH A LITTLE BIT OF LUCK	P. Faith	Columbia	84

CAUTION TO DEALERS AND JUKE BOX OPERATORS

The Billboard's Top 100 is NOT designed to provide tested information for buying purposes. This function is most reliably served by other regular weekly features: Best Sellers in Stores, Most Played in Juke Boxes, Coming Up Strong and Best Buys.

• Best Sellers in Stores

For survey week ending July 25

RECORDS are ranked in order of their current national selling importance at the retail level, as determined by The Billboard's weekly survey of the top volume dealers in every important market area. When significant action is reported on both sides of a record, points are combined to determine position on the chart. In such a case, both sides are listed in bold type, the leading side on top.

This Week		Last Week	Weeks on Chart
1.	**MY PRAYER** (ASCAP)—Platters **HEAVEN ON EARTH** (ASCAP)—Mercury 70893	4	4
2.	**I WANT YOU, I NEED YOU, I LOVE YOU** (BMI)—E. Presley **MY BABY LEFT ME** (BMI)—Vic 20-6540	1	10
3.	**I ALMOST LOST MY MIND** (BMI)—P. Boone I'm in Love With You (BMI)—Dot 15472	3	8
4.	**WAYWARD WIND** (BMI)—G. Grant No More Than Forever (ASCAP)—Era 1013	2	14
5.	**WHATEVER WILL BE, WILL BE** (ASCAP)—Doris Day I Gotta Sing Away These Blues (BMI)—Col 40704	6	5
6.	**ALLEGHENY MOON** (ASCAP)—P. Page Strangest Romance (ASCAP)—Mercury 70878	9	5
7.	**BE-BOP-A-LULA** (BMI)—G. Vincent Woman Love (BMI)—Cap 3450	7	7
8.	**MORE** (ASCAP)—P. Como **GLENDORA** (BMI)—Vic 20-6554	5	8
9.	**HOUND DOG** (BMI)—E. Presley Don't Be Cruel (BMI)—Vic 6604	—	1
10.	**MOONGLOW AND THEME FROM "PICNIC"** (ASCAP)—M. Stoloff Theme From "Picnic" (ASCAP)—Dec 29888	11	16
11.	**BORN TO BE WITH YOU** (ASCAP)—Chordettes Love Never Changes (ASCAP)—Cadence 1291	10	7
12.	**I'M IN LOVE AGAIN** (BMI)—F. Domino **MY BLUE HEAVEN** (ASCAP)—Imperial 5386	8	14
13.	**ON THE STREET WHERE YOU LIVE** (ASCAP)—V. Damone We All Need Love (ASCAP)—Col 40654	12	9
14.	**SWEET OLD-FASHIONED GIRL** (ASCAP)—T. Brewer Goodbye, John (BMI)—Coral 61636	13	7
15.	**STRANDED IN THE JUNGLE** (BMI)—Cadets I Want You (BMI)—Modern 994	16	3
16.	**CANADIAN SUNSET** (BMI)—H. Winterhaler & E. Heywood This Is Real (ASCAP)—Vic 20-6537	19	2
17.	**RIP IT UP** (BMI)—Little Richard **READY TEDDY** (BMI)—Specialty 579	20	3
18.	**TRANSFUSION** (BMI)—Nervous Norvus Dig (BMI)—Dot 15470	15	9
18.	**IT ONLY HURTS FOR A LITTLE WHILE** (ASCAP)—Ames Brothers If You Want to See Mamie Tonight (ASCAP) Vic 20-6481	17	10
20.	**STANDING ON THE CORNER** (ASCAP)—Four Lads My Little Angel (BMI)—Col 40574	14	15
21.	**SOFT SUMMER BREEZE** (BMI)—E. Heywood Heywood's Bounce (BMI)—Mercury 70863	23	3
22.	**YOU DON'T KNOW ME** (BMI)—J. Vale Dream Along With Me (ASCAP)—Col 40710	—	1
23.	**MOONGLOW AND THEME FROM "PICNIC"** (ASCAP)—G. Cates Rio Batucada (ASCAP)—Coral 61618	21	16
24.	**STRANDED IN THE JUNGLE** (BMI)—Jayhawks My Only Darling (BMI)—Flash 109	18	2
25.	**THAT'S ALL THERE IS TO THAT** (BMI)—Nat (King) Cole My Dream Sonata (ASCAP)—Cap 3456	24	3

• Most Played in Juke Boxes

For survey week ending July 25

RECORDS are ranked in order of the greatest number of plays in juke boxes throut the country, as determined by The Billboard's weekly survey of the nation's juke box operators. When significant play is reported on both sides of a record, points are combined to determine position on the chart. In such a case, both sides are listed in bold type, the leading side on top.

This Week		Last Week	Weeks on Chart
1.	**I ALMOST LOST MY MIND** (BMI)—P. Boone I'm in Love With You (BMI)—Dot 15472	1	8
2.	**WAYWARD WIND** (BMI)—G. Grant No More Than Forever (ASCAP)—Era 1013	2	10
3.	**I WANT YOU, I NEED YOU, I LOVE YOU** (BMI)—E. Presley **MY BABY LEFT ME** (BMI)—Vic 20-6540	3	9
4.	**ALLEGHENY MOON** (ASCAP)—P. Page Strangest Romance (ASCAP)—Mercury 70878	8	5
5.	**BORN TO BE WITH YOU** (ASCAP)—Chordettes Love Never Changes (ASCAP)—Cadence 1291	6	6
6.	**MORE** (ASCAP)—P. Como **GLENDORA** (BMI)—Vic 20-6554	7	5
7.	**I'M IN LOVE AGAIN** (BMI)—F. Domino **MY BLUE HEAVEN** (ASCAP)—Imperial 5386	4	12
8.	**SWEET OLD-FASHIONED GIRL** (ASCAP)—T. Brewer Goodbye, John (BMI)—Coral 61636	9	4
9.	**MY PRAYER** (ASCAP)—Platters Heaven on Earth (ASCAP)—Mercury 70893	13	3
10.	**MOONGLOW AND THEME FROM "PICNIC"** (ASCAP)—M. Stoloff Theme From "Picnic" (ASCAP)—Dec 29888	5	12
11.	**WHATEVER WILL BE, WILL BE** (ASCAP)—Doris Day I Gotta Sing Away These Blues (BMI)—Col 40704	15	2
12.	**BE-BOP-A-LULA** (BMI)—G. Vincent Woman Love (BMI)—Cap 3450	20	4
13.	**IVORY TOWER** (ASCAP)—C. Carr Please Believe Me (ASCAP)—Fraternity 734	10	14
14.	**MOONGLOW AND THEME FROM "PICNIC"** (ASCAP)—G. Cates Rio Batucada (ASCAP)—Coral 61618	12	13
15.	**STANDING ON THE CORNER** (ASCAP)—Four Lads My Little Angel (BMI)—Col 40674	11	11
16.	**ON THE STREET WHERE YOU LIVE** (ASCAP)—V. Damone We All Need Love (ASCAP)—Col 40654	18	5
17.	**IT ONLY HURTS FOR A LITTLE WHILE** (ASCAP)—Ames Brothers If You Want to See Mamie Tonight (ASCAP)—Vic 20-6481	16	7
18.	**PICNIC** (ASCAP)—McGuire Sisters Delilah Jones (ASCAP)—Coral 61627	—	3
19.	**TRANSFUSION** (BMI)—Nervous Norvus Dig (BMI)—Dot 15470	19	3
20.	**TREASURE OF LOVE** (BMI)—C. McPhatter When You're Sincere (BMI)—Atlantic 1092	—	1

• Best Selling Sheet Music

Tunes are ranked in order of their current national selling importance at the sheet music jobber level.

This Week		Last Week	Weeks on Chart
1.	**Wayward Wind** (Warman)	1	10
2.	**Allegheny Moon** (Oxford)	2	6
3.	**Whatever Will Be, Will Be** (Che Sera, Sera Artists)	3	4
4.	**On the Street Where You Live** (Chappell)	4	13
5.	**Sweet Old-Fashioned Girl** (Valor)	10	3
6.	**Ivory Tower** (E. H. Morris)	6	15
7.	**Moonglow** (Mills-Columbia Pictures)	5	12
8.	**Picnic** (Shapiro-Bernstein)	7	12
9.	**My Prayer** (Shapiro-Bernstein)	13	3
10.	**More** (Shapiro-Bernstein)	11	5
11.	**I Almost Lost My Mind** (Hill & Range)	8	6
12.	**Walk Hand in Hand** (Republic)	9	13
13.	**I Want You, I Need You, I Love You** (Presley)	11	2
14.	**Born to Be With You** (E. H. Morris)	15	2
15.	**Standing On the Corner** (Frank)	14	12

• Most Played by Jockeys

For survey week ending July 25

SIDES are ranked in order of the greatest number of plays on disk jockey radio shows throut the country. Results are based on The Billboard's weekly survey among the nation's disk jockeys. The reverse side of each record is also listed.

This Week		Last Week	Weeks on Chart
1.	**WAYWARD WIND** (BMI)—G. Grant No More Than Forever (ASCAP)—Era 1013	1	13
2.	**I ALMOST LOST MY MIND** (BMI)—P. Boone I'm in Love With You (BMI)—Dot 15472	2	8
3.	**ALLEGHENY MOON** (ASCAP)—P. Page Strangest Romance (ASCAP)—Mercury 70878	4	6
4.	**ON THE STREET WHERE YOU LIVE** (ASCAP)—V. Damone We All Need Love (ASCAP)—Col 40654	5	10
5	**MOONGLOW AND THEME FROM "PICNIC"** (ASCAP)—M. Stoloff Theme From "Picnic" (ASCAP)—Dec 29888	3	16
6.	**BORN TO BE WITH YOU** (ASCAP)—Chordettes Love Never Changes (ASCAP)—Cadence 1291	7	9
7.	**WHATEVER WILL BE, WILL BE** (ASCAP)—Doris Day I Gotta Sing Away These Blues (BMI)—Col 40704	10	5
8.	**I WANT YOU, I NEED YOU, I LOVE YOU** (BMI)—E. Presley My Baby Left Me (BMI)—Vic 20-6540	6	8
9.	**MORE** (ASCAP)—P. Como Glendora (BMI)—Vic 20-6554	8	6
10.	**MY PRAYER** (ASCAP)—Platters Heaven on Earth (ASCAP)—Mercury 70893	9	4
11.	**BE-BOP-A-LULA** (BMI)—G. Vincent Woman Love (BMI)—Cap 3450	11	6
12.	**GLENDORA** (BMI)—P. Como More (ASCAP)—Vic 20-6554	15	7
13.	**SWEET OLD-FASHIONED GIRL** (ASCAP)—T. Brewer Goodbye, John (BMI)—Coral 61636	14	5
14.	**STANDING ON THE CORNER** (ASCAP)—Four Lads My Little Angel (BMI)—Col 40674	12	14
15.	**CANADIAN SUNSET** (BMI)—H. Winterhalter This Is Real (ASCAP)—Vic 20-6537	17	2
16.	**STRANDED IN THE JUNGLE** (BMI) Cadets I Want You (BMI)—Modern 994	20	2
17.	**IT ONLY HURTS FOR A LITTLE WHILE** (ASCAP)—Ames Brothers If You Want to See Mamie Tonight (ASCAP)—Vic 20-6481	22	8
18.	**I'M IN LOVE AGAIN** (BMI)—F. Domino My Blue Heaven (ASCAP)—Imperial 5386	13	11
19.	**THAT'S ALL THERE IS TO THAT** (BMI)—Nat (King) Cole My Dream Sonata (ASCAP)—Cap 3456	18	2
20.	**MOONGLOW AND THEME FROM "PICNIC"** (ASCAP)—G. Cates Rio Batucada (ASCAP)—Coral 61618	16	16
21.	**YOU DON'T KNOW ME** (BMI)—J. Vale Enchanted (ASCAP)—Columbia 40710	—	1
22.	**I ONLY KNOW I LOVE YOU** (ASCAP)—Four Aces Dreamer (ASCAP)—Dec 29989	—	1
23.	**PORTUGUESE WASHERWOMAN** (ASCAP)—J. (Fingers) Carr Lucky Pierre—Cap 3418	19	5
24.	**IVORY TOWER** (ASCAP)—G. Storm I Ain't Gonna Worry (BMI)—Dot 15458	23	13
25.	**HOUND DOG** (BMI)—E. Presley Don't Be Cruel (BMI)—Vic 20-6604	—	1

THE TOP 100

For survey week ending July 25

A list of the Top 100 **RECORD SIDES** in the nation according to a **COMBINED TABULATION** of Dealer, Disk Jockey and Juke Box Operator replies to The Billboard's weekly popular record Best Seller and Most Played surveys. Its purpose is to provide Disk Jockeys with additional programming material and to give trade exposure to NEWER records just beginning to show action in the field.

Pos.	Song	Artist	Label	Last Week
1.	I ALMOST LOST MY MIND	P. Boone	Dot	2
2.	WAYWARD WIND	G. Grant	Era	1
3.	I WANT YOU, I NEED YOU, I LOVE YOU	E. Presley	Victor	3
4.	ALLEGHENY MOON	P. Page	Mercury	4
5.	BORN TO BE WITH YOU	Chordettes	Cadence	6
5.	MY PRAYER	Platters	Mercury	7
7.	WHATEVER WILL BE, WILL BE	Doris Day	Columbia	9
8.	MOONGLOW AND THEME FROM "PICNIC"	M. Stoloff	Decca	4
9.	BE-BOP-A-LULA	G. Vincent	Capitol	14
10.	MORE	P. Como	Victor	10
11.	ON THE STREET WHERE YOU LIVE	V. Damone	Columbia	12
11.	SWEET OLD FASHIONED GIRL	T. Brewer	Coral	11
13.	I'M IN LOVE AGAIN	F. Domino	Imperial	8
14.	GLENDORA	P. Como	Victor	16
15.	STANDING ON THE CORNER	Four Lads	Columbia	13
16.	IT ONLY HURTS FOR A LITTLE WHILE	Ames Brothers	Victor	17
17.	MOONGLOW AND THEME FROM "PICNIC"	G. Cates	Coral	15
18.	THAT'S ALL THERE IS TO THAT	Nat (King) Cole	Capitol	20
19.	STRANDED IN THE JUNGLE	Cadets	Modern	18
20.	SOFT SUMMER BREEZE	E. Heywood	Mercury	40
21.	TRANSFUSION	N. Norvus	Dot	20
22.	IVORY TOWER	G. Storm	Dot	18
23.	TREASURE OF LOVE	C. McPhatter	Atlantic	26
24.	HOUND DOG	E. Presley	Victor	—
25.	IVORY TOWER	C. Carr	Fraternity	22
26.	PORTUGUESE WASHERWOMAN	J. Fingers Carr	Capitol	27
27.	IN A SHANTY IN OLD SHANTY TOWN	S. Smith	Epic	36
27.	FEVER	L. W. John	King	29
29.	CANADIAN SUNSET	H. Winterhalter-E. Heywood	Victor	37
30.	PICNIC	McGuire Sisters	Coral	24
31.	WALK HAND IN HAND	T. Martin	Victor	25
32.	LOVE, LOVE, LOVE	Clovers	Atlantic	30
33.	YOU DON'T KNOW ME	J. Vale	Columbia	32
34.	HAPPY WHISTLER	D. Robertson	Capitol	23
35.	ON THE STREET WHERE YOU LIVE	E. Fisher	Victor	33
36.	HOW LITTLE WE KNOW	F. Sinatra	Capitol	39
37.	I ONLY KNOW I LOVE YOU	Four Aces	Decca	63
38.	HEARTBREAK HOTEL	E. Presley	Victor	28
39.	STRANDED IN THE JUNGLE	Gadabouts	Mercury	46
39.	THEME FROM "THE PROUD ONE"	N. Riddle	Capitol	46
41.	FOOL	S. Clark	Dot	58
41.	MY BLUE HEAVEN	F. Domino	Imperial	52
41.	STRANDED IN THE JUNGLE	Jayhawks	Flash	44
44.	I COULD HAVE DANCED ALL NIGHT	S. Syms	Decca	41
45.	LOVE, LOVE, LOVE	Diamonds	Mercury	30
46.	APE CALL	N. Norvus	Dot	80
47.	I'M IN LOVE AGAIN	Fontane Sisters	Dot	57
47.	STANDING ON THE CORNER	D. Martin	Capitol	43
49.	FABULOUS CHARACTER	S. Vaughan	Mercury	42
49.	RIP IT UP	Little Richard	Specialty	35
51.	VOICES	Fontane Sisters	Dot	49
52.	READY TEDDY	Little Richard	Specialty	52
53.	SONG FOR A SUMMER NIGHT	M. Miller	Columbia	—
54.	CAN YOU FIND IT IN YOUR HEART?	T. Bennett	Columbia	37
55.	HOT DIGGITY	P. Como	Victor	56
56.	GHOST TOWN	D. Cherry	Columbia	54
57.	I PROMISE TO REMEMBER	Teen-Agers	Gee	94
58.	WEARY BLUES	McGuire Sisters	Coral	68
59.	MY BABY LEFT ME	E. Presley	Victor	50
60.	GIVE US THIS DAY	J. James	M-G-M	70
61.	CHURCH BELLS MAY RING	Diamonds	Mercury	44
61.	SOMEBODY UP THERE LIKES ME	P. Como	Victor	75
63.	WAYWARD WIND	T. Ritter	Capitol	65
64.	IVORY TOWER	O. Williams	De Luxe	45
65.	MY DREAM SONATA	Nat (King) Cole	Capitol	59
66.	I WANT YOU TO BE MY GIRL	Teen-Agers	Gee	55
67.	LONG, TALL SALLY	Little Richard	Specialty	59
68.	TONIGHT YOU BELONG TO ME	Patience & Prudence	Lbt	—
69.	YOU'RE SENSATIONAL	F. Sinatra	Capitol	65
70.	MY LITTLE ANGEL	Four Lads	Columbia	48
71.	FIVE	S. Davis Jr.	Decca	92
72.	THEME FROM "THE PROUD ONE"	L. Newman	Columbia	—
73.	SWEET HEARTACHES	E. Fisher	Victor	93
74.	OOBY DOOBY	R. Orbison	Sun	—
75.	AFTER THE LIGHTS ARE DOWN LOW	A. Hibbler	Decca	—
76.	HEART HIDEAWAY	C. Carr	Fraternity	67
77.	BEAUTIFUL FRIENDSHIP	E. Fitzgerald	Decca	89
77.	WHEN MY DREAMBOAT COMES HOME	F. Domino	Imperial	95
79.	MAGIC TOUCH	Platters	Mercury	51
79.	GRADUATION DAY	Four Freshmen	Capitol	79
81.	FREE	T. Leonetti	Capitol	78
82.	WITH A LITTLE BIT OF LUCK	P. Faith	Columbia	99
83.	SECOND FIDDLE	K. Starr	Victor	73
84.	FLYING SAUCER	Buchanan & Goodman	Universe	—
85.	DREAM ALONG WITH ME	P. Como	Victor	98
86.	DREAMER	Four Aces	Decca	—
86.	I COULD HAVE DANCED ALL NIGHT	R. Clooney	Columbia	72
86.	OTHER WOMAN	S. Vaughan	Mercury	—
86.	WITH A LITTLE BIT OF LUCK	J. Stafford	Columbia	—
90.	JOHNNY CONCHO THEME	F. Sinatra	Capitol	75
90.	LOLA'S THEME	M. Matheison	Columbia	—
92.	TO LOVE AGAIN	Four Aces	Decca	81
93.	SO-LONG	F. Domino	Imperial	96
94.	GET ME TO THE CHURCH ON TIME	J. La Rosa	Victor	—
95.	MARIMBA CHARLESTON	M. Chiapas	Capitol	90
95.	MAMA TEACH ME TO DANCE	E. Gorme	ABC-Paramount	84
97.	HOW LUCKY YOU ARE	J. James	M-G-M	70
98.	IN THE ALPS	McGuire Sisters-L. Welk	Coral	—
99.	STANDING ON THE CORNER	Mills Brothers	Decca	—
99.	WALK HAND IN HAND	D. Vaughan	Kapp	—

CAUTION TO DEALERS AND JUKE BOX OPERATORS

The Billboard's Top 100 is NOT designed to provide tested information for buying purposes. This function is most reliably served by other regular weekly features: Best Sellers in Stores, Most Played in Juke Boxes, Coming Up Strong and Best Buys.

• Best Sellers in Stores

For survey week ending August 1

RECORDS are ranked in order of their current national selling importance at the retail level, as determined by The Billboard's weekly survey of the top volume dealers in every important market area. When significant action is reported on both sides of a record, points are combined to determine position on the chart. In such a case, both sides are listed in bold type, the leading side on top.

This Week		Last Week	Weeks on Chart
1.	**MY PRAYER** (ASCAP)—Platters; **HEAVEN ON EARTH** (ASCAP)—Mercury 70893	1	5
2.	**HOUND DOG** (BMI)—E. Presley; **DON'T BE CRUEL** (BMI)—Vic 20-6604	11	2
3.	**WHATEVER WILL BE, WILL BE** (ASCAP)—Doris Day; I Gotta Sing Away These Blues (BMI)—Col 40704	5	6
4.	**I WANT YOU, I NEED YOU, I LOVE YOU** (BMI)—E. Presley; My Baby Left Me (BMI)—Vic 20-6540	2	11
5.	**I ALMOST LOST MY MIND** (BMI)—P. Boone; I'm in Love With You (BMI)—Dot 15472	3	9
6.	**WAYWARD WIND** (BMI)—G. Grant; No More Than Forever (ASCAP)—Era 1013	4	15
7.	**ALLEGHENY MOON** (ASCAP)—P. Page; Strangest Romance (ASCAP)—Mercury 70878	6	6
8.	**BE-BOP-A-LULA** (BMI)—G. Vincent; Woman Love (BMI)—Cap 3450	7	8
9.	**FLYING SAUCER (PARTS I & II)**—Buchanan & Goodman; Luniverse 101	—	1
10.	**MORE** (ASCAP)—P. Como; **GLENDORA** (BMI)—Vic 20-6554	8	9
11.	**BORN TO BE WITH YOU** (ASCAP)—Chordettes; Love Never Changes (ASCAP)—Cadence 1291, 1019	11	8
12.	**ON THE STREET WHERE YOU LIVE** (ASCAP)—V. Damone; We All Need Love (ASCAP)—Col 40654	13	10
13.	**MOONGLOW AND THEME FROM "PICNIC"** (ASCAP)—M. Stoloff; Theme From "Picnic" (ASCAP)—Dec 29888	10	17
14.	**CANADIAN SUNSET** (BMI)—H. Winterhalter; This Is Real (ASCAP)—Vic 20-6537	16	3
15.	**SWEET OLD-FASHIONED GIRL** (ASCAP)—T. Brewer; Goodbye, John (BMI)—Coral 61636	14	8
16.	**I'M IN LOVE AGAIN** (BMI)—F. Domino; My Blue Heaven (ASCAP)—Imperial 5386	12	15
17.	**SONG FOR A SUMMER NIGHT (PARTS I & II)** (ASCAP)—M. Miller; Col 40730	—	1
18.	**IT ONLY HURTS FOR A LITTLE WHILE** (ASCAP)—Ames Brothers; If You Want to See Mamie Tonight (ASCAP)—Vic 20-6481	18	11
19.	**STRANDED IN THE JUNGLE** (BMI)—Cadets; I Want You (BMI)—Modern 994	15	4
20.	**THAT'S ALL THERE IS TO THAT** (BMI)—Nat (King) Cole; My Dream Sonata (ASCAP)—Cap 3456	25	4
21.	**FOOL** (BMI)—S. Clark; Lonesome for a Letter (BMI)—Dot 15481	—	1
22.	**STANDING ON THE CORNER** (ASCAP)—Four Lads; My Little Angel (BMI)—Col 40574	20	16
23.	**YOU DON'T KNOW ME** (BMI)—J. Vale; Dream Along With Me (ASCAP)—Col 40710	22	2
24.	**SOFT SUMMER BREEZE** (BMI)—E. Heywood; Heywood's Bounce (BMI)—Mercury 70863	21	4
24.	**WHEN MY DREAMBOAT COMES HOME** (ASCAP)—F. Domino; **SO LONG** (BMI)—Imperial 5396	—	2

• Most Played in Juke Boxes

For survey week ending August 1

RECORDS are ranked in order of the greatest number of plays in juke boxes thruout the country, as determined by The Billboard's weekly survey of the nation's juke box operators. When significant play is reported on both sides of a record, points are combined to determine position on the chart. In such a case, both sides are listed in bold type, the leading side on top.

This Week		Last Week	Weeks on Chart
1.	**I ALMOST LOST MY MIND** (BMI)—P. Boone; I'm In Love With You (BMI)—Dot 15472	1	9
2.	**ALLEGHENY MOON** (ASCAP)—P. Page; Strangest Romance (ASCAP)—Mercury 70878	4	6
3.	**WAYWARD WIND** (BMI)—G. Grant; No More Than Forever (ASCAP)—Era 1013	2	11
4.	**I WANT YOU, I NEED YOU, I LOVE YOU** (BMI)—E. Presley; **MY BABY LEFT ME** (BMI)—Vic 20-6540	3	10
5.	**MY PRAYER** (ASCAP)—Platters; Heaven on Earth (ASCAP)—Mercury 70893	9	4
6.	**WHATEVER WILL BE, WILL BE** (ASCAP)—Doris Day; I Gotta Sing Away These Blues (BMI)—Col 40704	11	3
7.	**SWEET OLD-FASHIONED GIRL** (ASCAP)—T. Brewer; Goodbye, John (BMI)—Coral 61636	8	5
8.	**MORE** (ASCAP)—P. Como; **GLENDORA** (BMI)—Vic 20-6554	6	6
9.	**BORN TO BE WITH YOU** (ASCAP)—Chordettes; Love Never Changes (ASCAP)—Cadence 1291	5	7
10.	**BE-BOP-A-LULA** (BMI)—G. Vincent; Woman Love (BMI)—Cap 3450	12	5
11.	**I'M IN LOVE AGAIN** (BMI)—F. Domino; **MY BLUE HEAVEN** (ASCAP)—Imperial 5386	7	13
12.	**IT ONLY HURTS FOR A LITTLE WHILE** (ASCAP)—Ames Brothers; If You Want to See Mamie Tonight (ASCAP)—Vic 20-6481	17	8
13.	**ON THE STREET WHERE YOU LIVE** (ASCAP)—V. Damone; We All Need Love (ASCAP)—Col 40654	16	6
14.	**MOONGLOW AND THEME FROM "PICNIC"** (ASCAP)—M. Stoloff; Theme From "Picnic" (ASCAP)—Dec 29888	10	13
15.	**MOONGLOW AND THEME FROM "PICNIC"** (ASCAP)—G. Cates; Rio Batucada (ASCAP)—Coral 61618	14	14
16.	**STANDING ON THE CORNER** (ASCAP)—Four Lads; My Little Angel (BMI)—Col 40674	15	12
16.	**THAT'S ALL THERE IS TO THAT** (BMI)—Nat (King) Cole; My Dream Sonata (ASCAP)—Cap 3456	—	1
18.	**TREASURE OF LOVE** (BMI)—C. McPhatter; When You're Sincere (BMI)—Atlantic 1092	20	2
18.	**PICNIC** (ASCAP)—McGuire Sisters; Delilah Jones (ASCAP)—Coral 61627	18	4
20.	**ON THE STREET WHERE YOU LIVE** (ASCAP)—E. Fisher; Sweet Heartaches (ASCAP)—Vic 20-6529	—	3
20.	**HOUND DOG** (BMI)—E. Presley; Don't Be Cruel (BMI)—Vic 20-6604	—	1

• Best Selling Sheet Music

Tunes are ranked in order of their current national selling importance at the sheet music jobber level.

This Week		Last Week	Weeks on Chart
1.	**Allegheny Moon** (Oxford)	2	7
2.	**Whatever Will Be, Will Be** (Che Sera, Sera Artists)	3	5
3.	**Wayward Wind** (Warman)	1	11
4.	**On the Street Where You Live** (Chappell)	4	14
5.	**Sweet, Old-Fashioned Girl** (Valor)	5	4
6.	**My Prayer** (Shapiro-Bernstein)	9	4
7.	**Canadian Sunset** (Meridian)	—	1
8.	**More** (Shapiro-Bernstein)	10	6
9.	**I Almost Lost My Mind** (Hill & Range)	11	7
10.	**Walk Hand in Hand** (Republic)	12	14
10.	**I Want You, I Need You, I Love You** (Presley)	13	3
12.	**I Could Have Danced All Night** (Chappell)	—	7
13.	**Ivory Tower** (E. H. Morris)	6	16
14.	**Picnic** (Shapiro-Bernstein)	8	13
15.	**Moonglow** (Mills-Columbia Pictures)	7	13

• Most Played by Jockeys

For survey week ending August 1

SIDES are ranked in order of the greatest number of plays on disk jockey radio shows thruout the country. Results are based on The Billboard's weekly survey among the nation's disk jockeys. The reverse side of each record is also listed.

This Week		Last Week	Weeks on Chart
1.	**WAYWARD WIND** (BMI)—G. Grant; No More Than Forever (ASCAP)—Era 1013	1	14
2.	**I ALMOST LOST MY MIND** (BMI)—P. Boone; I'm in Love With You (BMI)—Dot 15472	2	9
3.	**WHATEVER WILL BE, WILL BE** (ASCAP)—Doris Day; I Gotta Sing Away These Blues (BMI)—Col 40704	7	6
4.	**MY PRAYER** (ASCAP)—Platters; Heaven on Earth (ASCAP)—Mercury 70893	10	5
5.	**ALLEGHENY MOON** (ASCAP)—P. Page; Strangest Romance (ASCAP)—Mercury 70878	3	7
6.	**ON THE STREET WHERE YOU LIVE** (ASCAP)—V. Damone; We All Need Love (ASCAP)—Col 40654	5	17
7.	**I WANT YOU, I NEED YOU, I LOVE YOU** (BMI)—E. Presley; My Baby Left Me (BMI)—Vic 20-6540	8	9
8.	**MOONGLOW AND THEME FROM "PICNIC"** (ASCAP)—M. Stoloff; Theme From "Picnic" (ASCAP)—Dec 29888	5	17
9.	**MORE** (ASCAP)—P. Como; Glendora (BMI)—Vic 20-6554	9	7
10.	**BORN TO BE WITH YOU** (ASCAP)—Chordettes; Love Never Changes (ASCAP)—Cadence 1291	6	10
11.	**CANADIAN SUNSET** (BMI)—H. Winterhalter-E. Heywood; This Is Real (ASCAP)—Vic 20-6537	15	3
12.	**HOUND DOG** (BMI)—E. Presley; Don't Be Cruel (BMI)—Vic 20-6604	25	2
13.	**I'M IN LOVE AGAIN** (BMI)—F. Domino; My Blue Heaven (ASCAP)—Imperial 5386	18	12
14.	**STANDING ON THE CORNER** (ASCAP)—Four Lads; My Little Angel (BMI)—Col 40674	14	15
15.	**SWEET OLD-FASHIONED GIRL** (ASCAP)—T. Brewer; Goodbye, John (BMI)—Coral 61636	13	6
16.	**BE-BOP-A-LULA** (BMI)—G. Vincent; Woman Love (BMI)—Cap 3450	11	7
17.	**MOONGLOW AND THEME FROM "PICNIC"** (ASCAP)—G. Cates; Rio Batucada (ASCAP)—Coral 61618	20	17
18.	**GLENDORA** (BMI)—P. Como; More (ASCAP)—Vic 20-6554	12	8
19.	**DON'T BE CRUEL**—E. Presley; Hound Dog (BMI)—Vic 20-6604	—	1
20.	**FABULOUS CHARACTER** (ASCAP)—S. Vaughan; Other Woman (ASCAP)—Mercury 70885	—	1
21.	**FLYING SAUCER** (Parts I & II)—Buchanan & Goodman; Luniverse 101	—	1
22.	**GHOST TOWN** (ASCAP)—D. Cherry; I'll Be Around (BMI)—Col 40705	—	1
23.	**SONG OF THE SUMMER NIGHT** (Parts I & II)—M. Miller; (ASCAP)—Col 40730	—	1
24.	**IT ONLY HURTS FOR A LITTLE WHILE** (ASCAP)—Ames Brothers; If You Want to See Mamie Tonight (ASCAP)—Vic 20-6481	17	9
24.	**PORTUGUESE WASHERWOMAN** (ASCAP)—J. (Fingers) Carr; Lucky Pierre (ASCAP)—Cap 3418	23	6

THE TOP 100

For survey week ending August 1

A list of the Top 100 **RECORD SIDES** in the nation according to a **COMBINED TABULATION** of Dealer, Disk Jockey and Juke Box Operator replies to The Billboard's weekly popular record Best Seller and Most Played surveys. Its purpose is to provide Disk Jockeys with additional programming material and to give trade exposure to NEWER records just beginning to show action in the field.

Pos.	Song	Artist	Label	Last Week
1.	I ALMOST LOST MY MIND	P. Boone	Dot	1
2.	MY PRAYER	Platters	Mercury	5
2.	WAYWARD WIND	Grant	Era	2
4.	WHATEVER WILL BE, WILL BE	Doris Day	Columbia	7
5.	ALLEGHENY MOON	P. Page	Mercury	4
6.	I WANT YOU, I NEED YOU, I LOVE YOU	E. Presley	Victor	3
7.	BORN TO BE WITH YOU	Chordettes	Cadence	5
8.	ON THE STREET WHERE YOU LIVE	V. Damone	Columbia	11
9.	MORE	P. Como	Victor	10
10.	BE-BOP-A-LULA	G. Vincent	Capitol	9
11.	HOUND DOG	E. Presley	Victor	24
12.	MOONGLOW AND THEME FROM "PICNIC"	M. Stoloff	Decca	8
13.	SWEET OLD-FASHIONED GIRL	T. Brewer	Coral	11
14.	I'M IN LOVE AGAIN	F. Domino	Imperial	13
15.	STANDING ON THE CORNER	Four Lads	Columbia	15
15.	IT ONLY HURTS A LITTLE WHILE	Ames Brothers	Victor	16
17.	GLENDORA	P. Como	Victor	14
18.	CANADIAN SUNSET	H. Winterhalter-E. Heywood	Victor	29
18.	MOONGLOW AND THEME FROM "PICNIC"	G. Cates	Coral	17
20.	THAT'S ALL THERE IS TO THAT	N. (King) Cole	Capitol	18
21.	STRANDED IN THE JUNGLE	Cadets	Modern	19
22.	TREASURE OF LOVE	C. McPhatter	Atlantic	23
23.	SOFT SUMMER BREEZE	E. Heywood	Mercury	20
23.	YOU DON'T KNOW ME	J. Vale	Columbia	33
25.	PORTUGUESE WASHERWOMAN	J. (Fingers) Carr	Capitol	26
26.	FOOL	S. Clark	Dot	41
26.	GHOST TOWN	D. Cherry	Columbia	56
28.	DON'T BE CRUEL	E. Presley	Victor	—
29.	APE CALL	N. Norvus	Dot	46
29.	STRANDED IN THE JUNGLE	Jayhawks	Flash	41
31.	WHEN MY DREAMBOAT COMES HOME	F. Domino	Imperial	77
32.	WEARY BLUES	McGuire Sisters	Coral	58
33.	FLYING SAUCER	Buchanan & Goodman	Luniverse	84
33.	GIVE US THIS DAY	J. James	M-G-M	60
35.	I ONLY KNOW I LOVE YOU	Four Aces	Decca	37
36.	HOW LITTLE WE KNOW	F. Sinatra	Capitol	36
37.	LOVE, LOVE, LOVE	Clovers	Atlantic	32
38.	WAYWARD WIND	T. Ritter	Capitol	63
39.	FEVER	L. W. John	King	27
39.	HEAVEN ON EARTH	Platters	Mercury	—
39.	THEME FROM "THE PROUD ONES"	N. Riddle	Capitol	39
42.	CAN YOU FIND IT IN YOUR HEART?	T. Bennett	Columbia	54
42.	SONG FOR A SUMMER NIGHT	M. Miller	Columbia	53
44.	HAPPY WHISTLER	D. Robertson	Capitol	34
45.	FABULOUS CHARACTER	S. Vaughan	Mercury	49
46.	LOVE, LOVE, LOVE	Diamonds	Mercury	45
46.	SOMEBODY UP THERE LIKES ME	P. Como	Victor	61
46.	TRANSFUSION	N. Norvus	Dot	21
49.	ON THE STREET WHERE YOU LIVE	E. Fisher	Victor	45
50.	WALK HAND IN HAND	T. Martin	Victor	31
51.	IVORY TOWER	C. Carr	Fraternity	25
52.	PICNIC	McGuire Sisters	Coral	30
53.	I'M IN LOVE AGAIN	Fontane Sisters	Dot	47
54.	MY BLUE HEAVEN	F. Domino	Imperial	41
55.	OLD PHILOSOPHER	E. Lawrence	Coral	—
56.	YOU'RE SENSATIONAL	F. Sinatra	Capitol	69
57.	I COULD HAVE DANCED ALL NIGHT	S. Syms	Decca	44
58.	RIP IT UP	Little Richard	Specialty	49
59.	IVORY TOWER	G. Storm	Dot	22
60.	TONIGHT BELONGS TO ME	Patience and Prudence	Liberty	68
60.	STRANDED IN THE JUNGLE	Gadabouts	Mercury	39
62.	IN A SHANTY IN OLD SHANTY TOWN	S. Smith	Epic	27
63.	IN THE ALPS	McGuire Sisters & L. Welk	Coral	98
63.	MY BABY LEFT ME	E. Presley	Victor	59
65.	HEARTBREAK HOTEL	E. Presley	Victor	38
65.	ST. THERESE OF THE ROSES	B. Ward	Decca	—
67.	LOLA'S THEME	M. Mathieson	Columbia	90
68.	AFTER THE LIGHTS GO DOWN LOW	A. Hibbler	Decca	75
69.	STANDING ON THE CORNER	D. Martin	Capitol	47
70.	RIP IT UP	B. Haley	Decca	—
71.	MAMA, TEACH ME TO DANCE	E. Gorme	ABC-Paramount	95
71.	VOICES	Fontane Sisters	Dot	51
73.	IVORY TOWER	O. Williams	De Luxe	64
74.	MY LITTLE ANGEL	Four Lads	Columbia	70
75.	FREE	T. Leonetti	Capitol	81
76.	CASUAL LOOK	Six Teens	Flip	—
77.	CANADIAN SUNSET	A. Williams	Cadence	—
78.	MY DREAM SONATA	N. (King) Cole	Capitol	65
79.	SWEET HEARTACHES	E. Fisher	Victor	73
80.	READY TEDDY	Little Richard	Specialty	52
81.	SO-LONG	F. Domino	Imperial	93
82.	ENGLISH MUFFINS AND IRISH STEW	S. Syms	Decca	—
83.	HEART HIDEAWAY	C. Carr	Fraternity	76
84.	TO LOVE AGAIN	Four Aces	Decca	92
85.	WITH A LITTLE BIT OF LUCK	J. Stafford	Columbia	86
86.	BEAUTIFUL FRIENDSHIP	E. Fitzgerald	Decca	77
87.	DREAM ALONG WITH ME	P. Como	Victor	85
88.	HOT DIGGITY	P. Como	Victor	55
89.	LOVE AIN'T RIGHT	K. Starr	Victor	—
89.	TELL ME WHY	G. Storm	Dot	—
91.	JOHNNY CONCHO THEME	F. Sinatra	Capitol	90
92.	SECOND FIDDLE	K. Starr	Victor	83
93.	LET THE GOOD TIMES ROLL	Shirley & Lee	Aladdin	—
93.	LONESOME LOVER BLUES	Fontane Sisters	Dot	—
95.	I'M IN LOVE WITH YOU	P. Boone	Dot	—
95.	THEME FROM "THE PROUD ONES"	L. Holmes	M-G-M	—
97.	LONG, TALL SALLY	Little Richard	Specialty	67
98.	GET ME TO THE CHURCH ON TIME	J. La Rosa	Victor	94
98.	I'VE GROWN ACCUSTOMED TO YOUR FACE	R. Clooney	Columbia	—
100.	I PROMISE TO REMEMBER	Teen-Agers	Gee	57

CAUTION TO DEALERS AND JUKE BOX OPERATORS

The Billboard's Top 100 is NOT designed to provide tested information for buying purposes. This function is most reliably served by other regular weekly features: Best Sellers in Stores, Most Played in Juke Boxes, Coming Up Strong and Best Buys.

• Best Sellers in Stores

For survey week ending August 8

RECORDS are ranked in order of their current national selling importance at the retail level, as determined by The Billboard's weekly survey of the top volume dealers in every important market area. When significant action is reported on both sides of a record, points are combined to determine position on the chart. In such a case, both sides are listed in bold type, the leading side on top.

This Week	Record	Last Week	Weeks on Chart
1.	**HOUND DOG** (BMI)—E. Presley; **DON'T BE CRUEL** (BMI)—Vic 20-6604	2	3
2.	**MY PRAYER** (ASCAP)—Platters; Heaven on Earth (ASCAP)—Mercury 70893	1	6
3.	**WHATEVER WILL BE, WILL BE** (ASCAP)—Doris Day; I Gotta Sing Away These Blues (BMI)—Col 40704	3	7
4.	**FLYING SAUCER (PARTS I & II)**—Buchanan & Goodman; Luniverse 101	9	2
5.	**I WANT YOU, I NEED YOU, I LOVE YOU** (BMI)—E. Presley; My Baby Left Me (BMI)—Vic 20-6540	4	12
6.	**I ALMOST LOST MY MIND** (BMI)—P. Boone; I'm in Love With You (BMI)—Dot 15472	5	10
7.	**ALLEGHENY MOON** (ASCAP)—P. Page; Strangest Romance (ASCAP)—Mercury 70878	7	7
8.	**BE-BOP-A-LULA** (BMI)—G. Vincent; Woman Love (BMI)—Cap 3450	8	9
9.	**WAYWARD WIND** (BMI)—G. Grant; No More Than Forever (ASCAP)—Era 1013	6	16
10.	**CANADIAN SUNSET** (BMI)—H. Winterhalter-E. Heywood; This Is Real (ASCAP)—Vic 20-6537	14	4
11.	**MORE** (ASCAP)—P. Como; **GLENDORA** (BMI)—Vic 20-6554	10	10
12.	**BORN TO BE WITH YOU** (ASCAP)—Chordettes; Love Never Changes (ASCAP)—Cadence 1291, 1019	11	9
13.	**SWEET OLD-FASHIONED GIRL** (ASCAP)—T. Brewer; Goodbye, John (BMI)—Coral 61636	15	9
14.	**FOOL** (BMI)—S. Clark; Lonesome for a Letter (BMI)—Dot 15481	21	2
15.	**ON THE STREET WHERE YOU LIVE** (ASCAP)—V. Damone; We All Need Love (ASCAP)—Col 40654	12	11
16.	**SONG FOR A SUMMER NIGHT (PARTS I & II)** (ASCAP)—M. Miller; Col 40730	17	2
17.	**IT ONLY HURTS FOR A LITTLE WHILE** (ASCAP)—Ames Brothers; If You Want to See Mamie Tonight (ASCAP) Vic 20-6481	18	12
17.	**MOONGLOW AND THEME FROM "PICNIC"** (ASCAP)—M. Stoloff; Theme From "Picnic" (ASCAP)—Dec 29888	13	18
19.	**THAT'S ALL THERE IS TO THAT** (BMI)—Nat (King) Cole; My Dream Sonata (ASCAP)—Cap 3456	20	5
20.	**I'M IN LOVE AGAIN** (BMI)—F. Domino; My Blue Heaven (ASCAP)—Imperial 5386	16	16
21.	**SOFT SUMMER BREEZE** (BMI)—E. Heywood; Heywood's Bounce (BMI)—Mercury 70863	24	5
22.	**YOU DON'T KNOW ME** (BMI)—J. Vale; Enchanted (ASCAP)—Col 40710	23	3
23.	**STRANDED IN THE JUNGLE** (BMI)—Cadets; I Want You (BMI)—Modern 994	19	5
24.	**FEVER** (BMI)—L. W. John; Letter From My Darling (BMI)—King 4935	—	1
25.	**WHEN MY DREAMBOAT COMES HOME** (ASCAP)—F. Domino; **SO-LONG** (BMI)—Imperial 5396	24	3

• Most Played in Juke Boxes

For survey week ending August 8

RECORDS are ranked in order of the greatest number of plays in juke boxes thruout the country, as determined by The Billboard's weekly survey of the nation's juke box operators. When significant play is reported on both sides of a record, points are combined to determine position on the chart. In such a case, both sides are listed in bold type, the leading side on top.

This Week	Record	Last Week	Weeks on Chart
1.	**I ALMOST LOST MY MIND** (BMI)—P. Boone; I'm in Love With You (BMI)—Dot 15472	1	10
2.	**ALLEGHENY MOON** (ASCAP)—P. Page; Strangest Romance (ASCAP)—Mercury 70878	2	7
3.	**WAYWARD WIND** (BMI); No More Than Forever (ASCAP)—Era 1013	3	12
4.	**MY PRAYER** (ASCAP)—Platters; Heaven on Earth (ASCAP)—Mercury 70893	5	5
5.	**WHATEVER WILL BE, WILL BE** (ASCAP)—Doris Day; I Gotta Sing Away These Blues (BMI)—Col 40704	6	4
6.	**I WANT YOU, I NEED YOU, I LOVE YOU** (BMI)—E. Presley; My Baby Left Me (BMI)—Vic 20-6540	4	11
7.	**SWEET OLD-FASHIONED GIRL** (ASCAP)—T. Brewer; Goodbye, John (BMI)—Coral 61636	7	6
8.	**MORE** (ASCAP)—P. Como; **GLENDORA** (BMI)—Vic 20-6554	8	7
9.	**BORN TO BE WITH YOU** (ASCAP)—Chordettes; Love Never Changes (ASCAP)—Cadence 1291	9	8
10.	**HOUND DOG** (BMI)—E. Presley; **DON'T BE CRUEL** (BMI)—Vic 20-6604	20	2
11.	**BE-BOP-A-LULA** (BMI)—G. Vincent; Woman Love (BMI)—Cap 3450	10	6
12.	**IT ONLY HURTS FOR A LITTLE WHILE** (ASCAP)—Ames Brothers; If You Want to See Mamie Tonight (ASCAP)—Vic 20-6481	12	9
13.	**I'M IN LOVE AGAIN** (BMI)—F. Domino; **MY BLUE HEAVEN** (ASCAP)—Imperial 5386	11	14
14.	**ON THE STREET WHERE YOU LIVE** (ASCAP)—V. Damone; We All Need Love (ASCAP)—Col 40654	13	7
15.	**MOONGLOW AND THEME FROM "PICNIC"** (ASCAP)—M. Stoloff; Theme From "Picnic" (ASCAP)—Dec 29888	14	14
16.	**STRANDED IN THE JUNGLE** (BMI)—Cadets; I Want You (BMI)—Modern 994	—	1
17.	**CANADIAN SUNSET** (BMI)—H. Winterhalter-E. Heywood; This Is Real (ASCAP)—Vic 20-6537	—	1
18.	**CAN YOU FIND IT IN YOUR HEART?** (ASCAP)—T. Bennett; Forget Her (ASCAP)—Col 40667	—	1
19.	**SOFT SUMMER BREEZE** (BMI)—E. Heywood; Heywood's Bounce (BMI)—Mercury 70863	—	1
20.	**THAT'S ALL THERE IS TO THAT** (BMI)—Nat (King) Cole; My Dream Sonata (ASCAP)—Cap 3456	16	2

• Best Selling Sheet Music

Tunes are ranked in order of their current national selling importance at the sheet music jobber level.

This Week	Tune	Last Week	Weeks on Chart
1.	**Allegheny Moon** (Oxford)	1	8
2.	**Whatever Will Be, Will Be** (Che Sera, Sera Artist)	2	6
3.	**Wayward Wind** (Warman)	3	12
4.	**On the Street Where You Live** (Chappell)	4	15
5.	**My Prayer** (Shapiro-Bernstein)	6	5
6.	**Canadian Sunset** (Meridian)	7	2
7.	**Ivory Tower** (E. H. Morris)	13	17
8.	**I Almost Lost My Mind** (Hill & Range)	9	8
9.	**I Want You, I Need You, I Love You** (Presley)	10	4
10.	**Moonglow** (Mills-Columbia Pictures)	15	14
11.	**Walk Hand in Hand** (Republic)	10	15
12.	**Picnic** (Shapiro-Bernstein)	14	14
12.	**It Only Hurts for a Little While** (Advanced)	—	3
14.	**Sweet Old-Fashioned Girl** (Valor)	5	5
15.	**More** (Shapiro-Bernstein)	8	7

• Most Played by Jockeys

For survey week ending August 8

SIDES are ranked in order of the greatest number of plays on disk jockey radio shows thruout the country. Results are based on The Billboard's weekly survey among the nation's disk jockeys. The reverse side of each record is also listed.

This Week	Record	Last Week	Weeks on Chart
1.	**MY PRAYER** (ASCAP)—Platters; Heaven on Earth (ASCAP)—Mercury 70893	4	6
2.	**ALLEGHENY MOON** (ASCAP)—P. Page; Strangest Romance (ASCAP)—Mercury 70878	5	8
3.	**WHATEVER WILL BE, WILL BE** (ASCAP)—Doris Day; I Gotta Sing Away These Blues (BMI)—Col 40704	3	7
4.	**WAYWARD WIND** (BMI)—G. Grant; No More Than Forever (ASCAP)—Era 1013	1	15
5.	**I ALMOST LOST MY MIND** (BMI)—P. Boone; I'm in Love With You (BMI)—Dot 15472	2	10
6.	**HOUND DOG** (BMI)—E. Presley; Don't Be Cruel (BMI)—Vic 20-6604	12	3
7.	**DON'T BE CRUEL** (BMI)—E. Presley; Hound Dog (BMI)—Vic 20-6604	19	2
8.	**BORN TO BE WITH YOU** (ASCAP)—Chordettes; Love Never Changes (ASCAP)—Cadence 1291	10	11
9.	**ON THE STREET WHERE YOU LIVE** (ASCAP)—V. Damone; We All Need Love (ASCAP)—Col 40654	6	18
10.	**I WANT YOU, I NEED YOU, I LOVE YOU** (BMI)—E. Presley; My Baby Left Me (BMI)—Vic 20-6540	7	10
11.	**MORE** (ASCAP)—P. Como; Glendora (BMI)—Vic 20-6554	9	8
12.	**CANADIAN SUNSET** (BMI)—H. Winterhalter-E. Heywood; This Is Real (ASCAP)—Vic 20-6537	11	4
13.	**SWEET OLD-FASHIONED GIRL** (ASCAP)—T. Brewer; Goodbye, John (BMI)—Coral 61636	15	7
14.	**MOONGLOW AND THEME FROM "PICNIC"** (ASCAP)—M. Stoloff; Theme From "Picnic" (ASCAP)—Dec 29888	8	18
15.	**CANADIAN SUNSET** (BMI)—A. Williams; High Upon a Mountain (ASCAP)—Cadence 1297	—	1
16.	**YOU DON'T KNOW ME** (BMI)—J. Vale; Enchanted (ASCAP)—Col 40710	—	2
17.	**FLYING SAUCER (PARTS I & II)**—Buchanan & Goodman; Luniverse 101	21	2
18.	**IT ONLY HURTS FOR A LITTLE WHILE** (ASCAP)—Ames Brothers; If You Want to See Mamie Tonight (ASCAP)—Vic 20-6481	24	10
19.	**FROM THE CANDY STORE ON THE CORNER** (ASCAP)—T. Bennett; Happiness Street (ASCAP)—Col 40726	—	1
20.	**SONG FOR A SUMMER NIGHT (PARTS I & II)**—M. Miller; Col 40730—ASCAP	23	2
21.	**SOFT SUMMER BREEZE** (BMI)—E. Heywood; Heywood's Bounce (BMI)—Mercury 70863	—	1
22.	**FABULOUS CHARACTER** (ASCAP)—S. Vaughan; Other Woman (ASCAP)—Mercury 70885	20	2
23.	**THAT'S ALL THERE IS TO THAT** (BMI)—Nat (King) Cole; My Dream Sonata (ASCAP)—Cap 3456	—	3
24.	**GLENDORA** (BMI)—P. Como; More (ASCAP)—Vic 20-6554	18	9
25.	**PORTUGUESE WASHERWOMAN** (ASCAP)—J. (Fingers) Carr; Lucky Pierre (ASCAP)—Cap 3418	24	7

THE TOP 100

For survey week ending August 8

A list of the **Top 100 RECORD SIDES** in the nation according to a **COMBINED TABULATION** of Dealer, Disk Jockey and Juke Box Operator replies to The Billboard's weekly popular record Best Seller and Most Played surveys. Its purpose is to provide Disk Jockeys with additional programming material and to give trade exposure to NEWER records just beginning to show action in the field.

Pos.	Song	Artist	Label	Last Week
1.	MY PRAYER	Platters	Mercury	2
2.	ALLEGHENY MOON	P. Page	Mercury	5
2.	WHATEVER WILL BE, WILL BE	Doris Day	Columbia	4
4.	I ALMOST LOST MY MIND	P. Boone	Dot	1
5.	WAYWARD WIND	G. Grant	Era	2
6.	HOUND DOG	E. Presley	Victor	11
7.	I WANT YOU, I NEED, YOU, I LOVE YOU	E. Presley	Victor	6
8.	BORN TO BE WITH YOU	Chordettes	Cadence	7
9.	SWEET OLD-FASHIONED GIRL	T. Brewer	Coral	13
10.	MORE	P. Como	Victor	9
11.	ON THE STREET WHERE YOU LIVE	V. Damone	Columbia	8
12.	CANADIAN SUNSET	H. Winterhalter-E. Heywood	Victor	18
13.	FLYING SAUCER	Buchanan & Goodman	Luniverse	33
13.	BE-BOP-A-LULA	G. Vincent	Capitol	10
15.	MOONGLOW AND THEME FROM "PICNIC"	M. Stoloff	Decca	12
16.	IT ONLY HURTS FOR A LITTLE WHILE	Ames Brothers	Victor	15
17.	DON'T BE CRUEL	E. Presley	Victor	28
18.	SOFT SUMMER BREEZE	E. Heywood	Mercury	23
18.	THAT'S ALL THERE IS TO THAT	N. (King) Cole	Capitol	20
20.	YOU DON'T KNOW ME	J. Vale	Columbia	23
21.	I'M IN LOVE AGAIN	F. Domino	Imperial	14
22.	GLENDORA	P. Como	Victor	17
23.	STRANDED IN THE JUNGLE	Cadets	Modern	21
24.	SONG FOR A SUMMER NIGHT	M. Miller	Columbia	42
25.	STANDING ON THE CORNER	Four Lads	Columbia	15
25.	TREASURE OF LOVE	C. McPhatter	Atlantic	22
27.	FOOL	S. Clark	Dot	26
28.	FABULOUS CHARACTER	S. Vaughan	Mercury	45
28.	MOONGLOW AND THEME FROM "PICNIC"	G. Cates	Coral	18
30.	GIVE US THIS DAY	J. James	M-G-M	33
31.	GHOST TOWN	D. Cherry	Columbia	26
32.	FEVER	L. W. John	King	39
32.	WHEN MY DREAMBOAT COMES HOME	F. Domino	Imperial	31
34.	CANADIAN SUNSET	A. Williams	Cadence	77
35.	APE CALL	N. Norvus	Dot	29
36.	I ONLY KNOW I LOVE YOU	Four Aces	Decca	35
37.	PORTUGUESE WASHERWOMAN	J. (Fingers) Carr	Capitol	25
38.	WAYWARD WIND	T. Ritter	Capitol	38
39.	LOVE, LOVE, LOVE	Diamonds	Mercury	46
40.	ON THE STREET WHERE YOU LIVE	E. Fisher	Victor	49
41.	LOVE, LOVE, LOVE	Clovers	Atlantic	37
42.	SOMEBODY UP THERE LIKES ME	P. Como	Victor	46
43.	RIP IT UP	Little Richard	Specialty	58
44.	WEARY BLUES	McGuire Sisters	Coral	32
45.	STRANDED IN THE JUNGLE	Jayhawks	Flash	29
46.	PICNIC	McGuire Sisters	Coral	52
47.	VOICES	Fontane Sisters	Dot	71
48.	RIP IT UP	B. Haley	Decca	70
48.	TONIGHT YOU BELONG TO ME	Patience & Prudence	Liberty	60
50.	IVORY TOWER	G. Storm	Dot	59
50.	STRANDED IN THE JUNGLE	Gadabouts	Mercury	60
52.	YOU'RE SENSATIONAL	F. Sinatra	Capitol	56
53.	CAN YOU FIND IT IN YOUR HEART?	T. Bennett	Columbia	42
54.	HONKY TONK	B. Doggett	King	—
55.	OLD PHILOSOPHER	E. Lawrence	Coral	55
56.	TRANSFUSION	N. Norvus	Dot	46
57.	THEME FROM "THE PROUD ONES"	N. Riddle	Capitol	39
58.	MY BLUE HEAVEN	F. Domino	Imperial	54
59.	AFTER THE LIGHTS GO DOWN LOW	A. Hibbler	Decca	68
60.	HAPPINESS STREET	T. Bennett	Columbia	—
60.	MAMA, TEACH ME TO DANCE	E. Gorme	ABC-Paramount	71
62.	IN A SHANTY IN OLD SHANTY TOWN	S. Smith	Epic	62
63.	HAPPY WHISTLER	D. Robertson	Capitol	44
64.	HOW LITTLE WE KNOW	F. Sinatra	Capitol	36
64.	IVORY TOWER	C. Carr	Fraternity	51
66.	STANDING ON THE CORNER	D. Martin	Capitol	69
67.	READY TEDDY	Little Richard	Specialty	80
68.	MIRACLE OF LOVE	E. Rogers	Columbia	—
69.	HEAVEN ON EARTH	Platters	Mercury	39
69.	I COULD HAVE DANCED ALL NIGHT	R. Clooney	Columbia	—
69.	KA DING DONG	G. Clefs	Pilgrim	—
72.	ENGLISH MUFFINS AND IRISH STEW	S. Syms	Decca	82
72.	WALK HAND IN HAND	T. Martin	Victor	50
74.	FROM THE CANDY STORE ON THE CORNER	T. Bennett	Columbia	—
74.	IN THE ALPS	McGuire Sisters-L. Welk	Coral	6
74.	MY LITTLE ANGEL	Four Lads	Columbia	74
77.	MY BABY LEFT ME	E. Presley	Victor	63
78.	SO LONG	F. Domino	Imperial	81
79.	SWEET HEARTACHES	E. Fisher	Victor	79
80.	FOOL	Gallahads	Jubilee	—
81.	LOLA'S THEME	S. Allen	Coral	—
82.	LOLA'S THEME	M. Mathieson	Columbia	67
83.	CLAY IDOL	B. Johnson	Bally	—
84.	CASUAL LOOK	Six Teens	Flip	76
85.	KISS ME ANOTHER	G. Gibbs	Mercury	—
86.	I PROMISE TO REMEMBER	Teen-Agers	Gee	100
86.	I'M IN LOVE AGAIN	Fontane Sisters	Dot	33
88.	DREAMER	Four Aces	Decca	—
88.	HAPPINESS STREET	G. Gibbs	Mercury	—
90.	I DON'T WANT NOBODY	W. Herman	Capitol	—
90.	WITH A LITTLE BIT OF LUCK	J. Stafford	Columbia	85
92.	HEARTBREAK HOTEL	E. Presley	Victor	65
93.	CHURCH BELLS MAY RING	Diamonds	Mercury	—
93.	HOW LUCKY YOU ARE	J. James	M-G-M	—
93.	R-O-C-K	B. Haley	Decca	—
96.	IVORY TOWER	O. Williams	De Luxe	73
97.	OOBY DOOBY	R. Orbison	Sun	—
98.	DREAM ALONG WITH ME	P. Como	Victor	87
99.	AWAY ALL BOATS	A. Hibbler	Decca	—
100.	LONESOME LOVER BLUES	Fontane Sisters	Dot	93

CAUTION TO DEALERS AND JUKE BOX OPERATORS

The Billboard's Top 100 is NOT designed to provide tested information for buying purposes. This function is most reliably served by other regular weekly features: Best Sellers in Stores, Most Played in Juke Boxes, Coming Up Strong and Best Buys.

• Best Sellers in Stores

For survey week ending August 15

RECORDS are ranked in order of their current national selling importance at the retail level, as determined by The Billboard's weekly survey of the top volume dealers in every important market area. When significant action is reported on both sides of a record, points are combined to determine position on the chart. In such a case, both sides are listed in bold type, the leading side on top.

This Week		Last Week	Weeks on Chart
1.	**HOUND DOG** (BMI)—E. Presley **DON'T BE CRUEL** (BMI)— Vic 20-6604	1	4
2.	**MY PRAYER** (ASCAP)—Platters Heaven on Earth (ASCAP)—Mercury 70893	2	7
3.	**FLYING SAUCER**— Buchannan & Goodman Luniverse 101	4	3
4.	**WHATEVER WILL BE, WILL BE** (ASCAP)—Doris Day I Gotta Sing Away These Blues (BMI)—Col 40704	3	8
5.	**I WANT YOU, I NEED YOU, I LOVE YOU** (BMI)—E. Presley My Baby Left Me (BMI)—Vic 20-6540	5	13
5.	**ALLEGHENY MOON** (ASCAP)— P. Page Strangest Romance (ASCAP)—Mercury 70878	7	8
7.	**BE-BOP-A-LULA** (BMI)—G. Vincent Woman Love (BMI)—Cap 3450	8	10
8.	**CANADIAN SUNSET** (BMI)— H. Winterhalter This Is Real (ASCAP)—Vic 20-6537	10	5
9.	**I ALMOST LOST MY MIND** (BMI)— P. Boone I'm in Love With You (BMI)—Dot 15472	6	11
10.	**WAYWARD WIND** (BMI)—G. Grant No More Than Forever (ASCAP)—Era 1013	9	17
11.	**MORE** (ASCAP)—P. Como **GLENDORA** (BMI)—Vic 20-6554	11	11
12.	**SONG FOR A SUMMER NIGHT (PARTS I & II)** (ASCAP)—M. Miller Col 40730	16	3
13.	**FOOL** (BMI)—S. Clark Lonesome for a Letter (BMI)—Dot 15481	14	3
14.	**BORN TO BE WITH YOU** (ASCAP)— Chordettes Love Never Changes (ASCAP)—Cadence 1291	12	10
15.	**TONIGHT YOU BELONG TO ME** (ASCAP)—Patience & Prudence A Smile and a Ribbon (ASCAP)—Liberty 55022	—	1
16.	**SWEET OLD-FASHIONED GIRL** (ASCAP)—T. Brewer Goodbye, John (BMI)—Coral 61636	13	10
17.	**IT ONLY HURTS FOR A LITTLE WHILE** (ASCAP)—Ames Brothers If You Want to See Mamie Tonight (ASCAP)—Vic 20-6481	17	13
18.	**HONKY TONK (PARTS I & II)** (BMI)—B. Doggett King 4950	—	1
19.	**YOU DON'T KNOW ME** (BMI)— J. Vale Enchanted (ASCAP)—Col 40710	22	4
20.	**ON THE STREET WHERE YOU LIVE** (ASCAP)—V. Damone We All Need Love (ASCAP)—Col 40654	15	12
21.	**WHEN MY DREAMBOAT COMES HOME** (ASCAP)—F. Domino **SO-LONG** (BMI)—Imperial 5396	25	4
21.	**SOFT SUMMER BREEZE** (BMI)— E. Heywood Heywood's Bounce (BMI)—Mercury 70863	21	6
23.	**THAT'S ALL THERE IS TO THAT** (BMI)—Nat (King) Cole My Dream Sonata (ASCAP)—Cap 3456	19	6
24.	**APE CALL** (ASCAP)—N. Norvus Wild Dog of Kentucky (BMI)—Dot 15485	—	1
25.	**MOONGLOW AND THEME FROM "PICNIC"** (ASCAP)—M. Stoloff Theme From "Picnic" (ASCAP)—Dec 29888	17	19

• Most Played in Juke Boxes

For survey week ending August 15

RECORDS are ranked in order of the greatest number of plays in juke boxes thruout the country, as determined by The Billboard's weekly survey of the nation's juke box operators. When significant play is reported on both sides of a record, points are combined to determine position on the chart. In such a case, both sides are listed in bold type, the leading side on top.

This Week		Last Week	Weeks on Chart
1.	**MY PRAYER** (ASCAP)—Platters Heaven on Earth (ASCAP)—Mercury 70893	4	6
2.	**I ALMOST LOST MY MIND** (BMI)— P. Boone I'm in Love With You (BMI)—Dot 15472	1	11
3.	**WHATEVER WILL BE, WILL BE** (ASCAP)—Doris Day I Gotta Sing Away These Blues (BMI)—Col 40704	5	5
4.	**HOUND DOG** (BMI)—E. Presley **DON'T BE CRUEL** (BMI)— Vic 20-6604	10	3
5.	**ALLEGHENY MOON** (ASCAP)— P. Page Strangest Romance (ASCAP)—Mercury 70878	2	8
6.	**WAYWARD WIND** (BMI)—G. Grant No More Than Forever (ASCAP)—Era 1013	3	13
7.	**I WANT YOU, I NEED YOU, I LOVE YOU** (BMI)—E. Presley My Baby Left Me (BMI)—Vic 20-6540	6	12
8.	**SWEET OLD-FASHIONED GIRL** (ASCAP)—T. Brewer Goodbye, John (BMI)—Coral 61636	7	7
8.	**MORE** (ASCAP)—P. Como **GLENDORA** (BMI)—Vic 20-6554	8	8
10.	**BORN TO BE WITH YOU** (ASCAP)— Chordettes Love Never Changes (ASCAP)—Cadence 1291	9	9
11.	**IT ONLY HURTS FOR A LITTLE WHILE** (ASCAP)—Ames Brothers If You Want to See Mamie Tonight (ASCAP)—Vic 6481	12	10
12.	**BE-BOP-A-LULA** (BMI)— G. Vincent Woman Love (BMI)—Cap 3450	11	7
12.	**FLYING SAUCER (PARTS I & II)**— Buchanan & Goodman Luniverse 101	—	1
14.	**I'M IN LOVE AGAIN** (BMI)— F. Domino My Blue Heaven (ASCAP)—Imperial 5386	13	15
15.	**MOONGLOW AND THEME FROM "PICNIC"** (ASCAP)—M. Stoloff Theme From "Picnic" (ASCAP)—Dec 29888	15	15
16.	**CANADIAN SUNSET** (BMI)— H. Winterhalter-E. Heywood This Is Real (ASCAP)—Vic 20-6537	17	2
17.	**ON THE STREET WHERE YOU LIVE** (ASCAP)—V. Damone We All Need Love (ASCAP)—Col 40654	14	8
18.	**FOOL** (BMI)—S. Clark Lonesome for a Letter (BMI)—Dot 15481	—	1
19.	**SONG FOR A SUMMER NIGHT (PARTS I & II)** (ASCAP)—M. Miller Col 40730—ASCAP	—	1
19.	**STRANDED IN THE JUNGLE** (BMI)—Cadets I Want You (BMI)—Modern 994	16	2

• Best Selling Sheet Music

Tunes are ranked in order of their current national selling importance at the sheet music jobber level.

This Week		Last Week	Weeks on Chart
1.	**Allegheny Moon** (Oxford)	1	9
2.	**Whatever Will Be, Will Be** (Che Sera, Sera Art)	2	7
3.	**Wayward Wind** (Warman)	3	13
4.	**My Prayer** (Shapiro-Bernstein)	5	6
5.	**Canadian Sunset** (Meridian)	6	3
6.	**On the Street Where You Live** (Chappell)	4	16
7.	**I Want You, I Need You, I Love You** (Presley)	9	5
8.	**Song for a Summer Night** (April)	—	1
9.	**Hound Dog** (E. Presley & Lion Music)	—	1
10.	**I Almost Lost My Mind** (Hill & Range)	8	9
11.	**Ivory Tower** (E. H. Morris)	7	18
12.	**Moonglow** (Mills-Columbia Pictures)	10	15
13.	**Picnic** (Shapiro-Bernstein)	12	15
14.	**Sweet, Old-Fashioned Girl** (Valor)	14	6
15.	**It Only Hurts for a Little While** (Advanced)	12	4

• Most Played by Jockeys

For survey week ending August 15

SIDES are ranked in order of the greatest number of plays on disk jockey radio shows thruout the country. Results are based on The Billboard's weekly survey among the nation's disk jockeys. The reverse side of each record is also listed.

This Week		Last Week	Weeks on Chart
1.	**MY PRAYER** (ASCAP)—Platters Heaven on Earth (ASCAP)—Mercury 70893	1	7
2.	**WHATEVER WILL BE, WILL BE** (ASCAP)—Doris Day I Gotta Sing Away These Blues (BMI)—Col 40704	3	8
3.	**DON'T BE CRUEL** (BMI)—E. Presley Hound Dog (BMI)—Vic 20-6604	7	3
4.	**ALLEGHENY MOON** (ASCAP)— P. Page Strangest Romance (ASCAP)—Mercury 70878	2	9
5.	**WAYWARD WIND** (BMI)—G. Grant No More Than Forever (ASCAP)—Era 1013	4	16
6.	**HOUND DOG** (BMI)—E. Presley Don't Be Cruel (BMI)—Vic 20-6604	6	4
7.	**I ALMOST LOST MY MIND** (BMI)— P. Boone I'm in Love With You (BMI)—Dot 15472	5	11
8.	**CANADIAN SUNSET** (BMI)— H. Winterhaler-E. Heywood This Is Real (ASCAP)—Vic 20-6537	12	5
9.	**BORN TO BE WITH YOU** (ASCAP)— Chordettes Love Never Changes (ASCAP)—Cadence 1291	8	12
10.	**MORE** (ASCAP)—P. Como Glendora (BMI)—Vic 20-6554	11	9
11.	**ON THE STREET WHERE YOU LIVE** (ASCAP)—V. Damone We All Need Love (ASCAP)—Col 40654	9	19
12.	**FLYING SAUCER (PARTS I & II)**— Buchanan & Goodman Luniverse 101	17	3
13.	**I WANT YOU, I NEED YOU, I LOVE YOU** (BMI)—E. Presley My Baby Left Me (BMI)—Vic 20-6540	10	11
14.	**SWEET OLD-FASHIONED GIRL** (ASCAP)—T. Brewer Goodbye, John (BMI)—Coral 61636	13	8
15.	**SONG FOR A SUMMER NIGHT (PARTS I & II)**—M. Miller Col 40730—ASCAP	20	3
16.	**MOONGLOW AND THEME FROM "PICNIC"** (ASCAP)—M. Stoloff Theme From "Picnic" (ASCAP)—Dec 29888	14	19
17.	**CANADIAN SUNSET** (BMI)— A. Williams High Upon a Mountain (ASCAP)—Cadence 1297	15	2
18.	**YOU DON'T KNOW ME** (BMI)— J. Vale Enchanted (ASCAP)—Col 40710	16	3
19.	**FABULOUS CHARACTER** (ASCAP)— S. Vaughan Other Woman (ASCAP)—Mercury 70885	22	3
20.	**SOFT SUMMER BREEZE**— E. Heywood Heywood's Bounce (BMI)—Mercury 70863	21	2
21.	**THAT'S ALL THERE IS TO THAT** (BMI)—Nat (King) Cole My Dream Sonata (ASCAP)—Cap 3456	23	4
22.	**BE-BOP-A-LULA** (BMI)— G. Vincent Woman Love (BMI)—Cap 3450	—	8
23.	**GLENDORA** (BMI)—P. Como More (ASCAP)—Vic 20-6554	24	10
24.	**FROM THE CANDY STORE ON THE CORNER** (ASCAP)—T. Bennett Happiness Street (ASCAP)—Col 40726	19	2
25.	**TONIGHT YOU BELONG TO ME** (ASCAP)—Patience & Prudence A Smile and a Ribbon (ASCAP)—Liberty 55022	—	1

THE TOP 100

For survey week ending August 15

A list of the Top 100 **RECORD SIDES** in the nation according to a **COMBINED TABULATION** of Dealer, Disk Jockey and Juke Box Operator replies to The Billboard's weekly popular record Best Seller and Most Played surveys. Its purpose is to provide Disk Jockeys with additional programming material and to give trade exposure to NEWER records just beginning to show action in the field.

Pos.	Song	Artist	Label	Last Week
1.	MY PRAYER	Platters	Mercury	1
2.	WHATEVER WILL BE, WILL BE	Doris Day	Columbia	2
3.	ALLEGHENY MOON	P. Page	Mercury	2
3.	HOUND DOG	E. Presley	Victor	6
5.	I ALMOST LOST MY MIND	P. Boone	Dot	4
6.	DON'T BE CRUEL	E. Presley	Victor	17
7.	WAYWARD WIND	G. Grant	Era	5
8.	I WANT YOU, I NEED YOU, I LOVE YOU	E. Presley	Victor	7
9.	FLYING SAUCER	Buchanan & Goodman	Luniverse	13
10.	BORN TO BE WITH YOU	Chordettes	Cadence	8
11.	CANADIAN SUNSET	H. Winterhalter-E. Heywood	Victor	12
12.	MORE	P. Como	Victor	10
13.	SWEET OLD-FASHIONED GIRL	T. Brewer	Coral	9
14.	BE-BOP-A-LULA	G. Vincent	Capitol	13
15.	SONG FOR A SUMMER NIGHT	M. Miller	Columbia	24
16.	ON THE STREET WHERE YOU LIVE	V. Damone	Columbia	11
17.	IT ONLY HURTS A LITTLE WHILE	Ames Brothers	Victor	16
18.	MOONGLOW AND THEME FROM "PICNIC"	M. Stoloff	Decca	15
19.	FOOL	S. Clark	Dot	27
20.	SOFT SUMMER BREEZE	E. Heywood	Mercury	18
20.	YOU DON'T KNOW ME	J. Vale	Columbia	20
22.	THAT'S ALL THERE IS TO THAT	Nat (King) Cole	Capitol	18
23.	GLENDORA	P. Como	Victor	22
24.	TONIGHT YOU BELONG TO ME	Patience & Prudence	Liberty	48
25.	I'M IN LOVE AGAIN	F. Domino	Imperial	21
26.	CANADIAN SUNSET	A. Williams	Cadence	34
27.	FABULOUS CHARACTER	S. Vaughan	Mercury	28
28.	APE CALL	N. Norvus	Dot	35
28.	STRANDED IN THE JUNGLE	Cadets	Modern	23
30.	WHEN MY DREAMBOAT COMES HOME	F. Domino	Imperial	32
31.	SOMEBODY UP THERE LIKES ME	P. Como	Victor	42
32.	STANDING ON THE CORNER	Four Lads	Columbia	25
33.	GHOST TOWN	D. Cherry	Columbia	31
34.	RIP IT UP	Little Richard	Specialty	43
35.	AFTER THE LIGHTS GO DOWN LOW	A. Hibbler	Decca	59
35.	FEVER	L. W. John	King	32
37.	WEARY BLUES	McGuire Sisters	Coral	44
38.	TREASURE OF LOVE	C. McPhatter	Atlantic	25
39.	HAPPINESS STREET	G. Gibbs	Mercury	—
39.	I ONLY KNOW I LOVE YOU	Four Aces	Decca	36
39.	PORTUGUESE WASHERWOMAN	J. (Fingers) Carr	Capitol	37
42.	HONKY TONK	B. Doggett	King	54
43.	OLD PHILOSOPHER	E. Lawrence	Coral	55
44.	SO-LONG	F. Domino	Imperial	78
45.	LOVE, LOVE, LOVE	Clovers	Atlantic	41
46.	MOONGLOW AND THEME FROM "PICNIC"	G. Cates	Coral	28
47.	RIP IT UP	B. Haley	Decca	48
48.	TRANSFUSION	N. Norvus	Dot	56
48.	WAYWARD WIND	T. Ritter	Capitol	38
50.	STRANDED IN THE JUNGLE	Jayhawks	Flash	45
51.	MAMA, TEACH ME TO DANCE	E. Gorme	ABC-Paramount	60
52.	LOVE, LOVE, LOVE	Diamonds	Mercury	39
53.	STRANDED IN THE JUNGLE	Gadabouts	Mercury	50
54.	GIVE US THIS DAY	J. James	M-G-M	30
55.	MY BLUE HEAVEN	F. Domino	Imperial	58
56.	VOICES	Fontane Sisters	Dot	47
57.	HEAVEN ON EARTH	Platters	Mercury	69
58.	PICNIC	McGuire Sisters	Coral	46
59.	THEME FROM "THE PROUD ONES"	N. Riddle	Capitol	57
60.	FROM THE CANDY STORE ON THE CORNER	T. Bennett	Columbia	74
61.	EXPERIMENTS WITH MICE	J. Dankworth	Capitol	—
62.	ENGLISH MUFFINS AND IRISH STEW	S. Syms	Decca	72
63.	YOU'RE SENSATIONAL	F. Sinatra	Capitol	52
64.	FOOL	Gallahads	Jubilee	80
64.	IVORY TOWER	C. Carr	Fraternity	64
64.	LET THE GOOD TIMES ROLL	Shirley & Lee	Aladdin	—
67.	WALK HAND IN HAND	T. Martin	Victor	72
68.	I PROMISE TO REMEMBER	Teen-Agers	Gee	86
68.	MIRACLE OF LOVE	E. Rodgers	Columbia	68
68.	ON THE STREET WHERE YOU LIVE	E. Fisher	Victor	40
68.	TEEN-AGER'S MOTHER	B. Haley	Decca	—
72.	CLAY IDOL	B. Johnson	Bally	83
73.	IVORY TOWER	G. Storm	Dot	50
74.	TRUE LOVE	J. Powell	Verve	—
75.	CASUAL LOOK	Six Teens	Flip	84
75.	LOLA'S THEME	S. Allen	Coral	81
77.	AWAY ALL BOATS	A. Hibbler	Decca	99
78.	I'LL BE AROUND	D. Cherry	Columbia	—
79.	HAPPINESS STREET	T. Bennett	Columbia	66
80.	I DON'T WANT NOBODY	W. Herman	Capitol	90
80.	TO LOVE AGAIN	Four Aces	Decca	—
82	HAPPY WHISTLER	D. Robertson	Capitol	63
83.	READY TEDDY	Little Richard	Specialty	67
84.	I COULD HAVE DANCED ALL NIGHT	R. Clooney	Columbia	69
84.	I'M IN LOVE AGAIN	Fontane Sisters	Dot	86
84.	STANDING ON THE CORNER	D. Martin	Capitol	66
84.	TUMBLING TUMBLEWEEDS	R. Williams	Kapp	—
88.	IN A SHANTY IN OLD SHANTY TOWN	S. Smith	Epic	62
88.	LOLA'S THEME	M. Mathieson	Columbia	82
90.	BOPPIN' THE BLUES	C. Perkins	Sun	—
91.	JOHNNY CONCHO THEME	F. Sinatra	Capitol	—
92.	IN THE ALPS	McGuire Sisters-L. Welk	Coral	74
92.	KA DING DONG	G. Clefs	Pilgrim	69
94.	MY DREAM SONATA	Nat (King) Cole	Capitol	—
95.	HEARTBREAK HOTEL	S. Freberg	Capitol	—
96.	HEARTBREAK HOTEL	E. Presley	Victor	92
97.	TE AMO	D. Jacobs	Coral	—
98.	BUS STOP SONG	Four Lads	Columbia	—
99.	HOW LUCKY YOU ARE	J. James	M-G-M	93
100.	AFTER SCHOOL	T. Charles	Decca	—
100.	ST. THERESE OF THE ROSES	B. Ward	Decca	—

CAUTION TO DEALERS AND JUKE BOX OPERATORS

The Billboard's Top 100 is NOT designed to provide tested information for buying purposes. This function is most reliably served by other regular weekly features: Best Sellers in Stores, Most Played in Juke Boxes, Coming Up Strong and Best Buys.

• Best Sellers in Stores

For survey week ending August 22

RECORDS are ranked in order of their current national selling importance at the retail level, as determined by The Billboard's weekly survey of the top volume dealers in every important market area. When significant action is reported on both sides of a record, points are combined to determine position on the chart. In such a case, both sides are listed in bold type, the leading side on top.

This Week		Last Week	Weeks on Chart
1.	**HOUND DOG** (BMI)—E. Presley **DON'T BE CRUFL** (BMI) Vic 20-6604	1	5
2.	**MY PRAYER** (ASCAP)—Platters Heaven on Earth (ASCAP)—Mercury 70893	2	8
3.	**WHATEVER WILL BE, WILL BE** (ASCAP)—Doris Day I Gotta Sing Away These Blues (BMI)—Col 40704	4	9
4.	**FLYING SAUCER**—Buchanan & Goodman Luniverse 101	3	4
5.	**CANADIAN SUNSET** (BMI)—H. Winterhalter This Is Real (ASCAP)—Vic 20-6537	8	6
6.	**ALLEGHENY MOON** (ASCAP)—P. Page Strangest Romance (ASCAP)—Mercury 70878	5	9
7.	**I WANT YOU, I NEED YOU, I LOVE YOU** (BMI)—E. Presley My Baby Left Me (BMI)—Vic 20-6540	5	14
8.	**BE-BOP-A-LULA** (BMI)—G. Vincent Woman Love (BMI)—Cap 3450	7	11
9.	**I ALMOST LOST MY MIND** (BMI)—P. Boone I'm in Love With You (BMI)—Dot 15472	9	12
10.	**TONIGHT YOU BELONG TO ME** (ASCAP)—Patience & Prudence A Smile and a Ribbon (ASCAP)—Liberty 55022	15	2
11.	**HONKY TONK (PARTS I & II)** B. Doggett King 4950	18	2
12.	**WAYWARD WIND** (BMI)—G. Grant No More Than Forever (ASCAP)—Era 1013	10	18
13.	**SONG FOR A SUMMER NIGHT (PARTS I & II)**—(ASCAP)—M. Miller Col 40730	12	4
14.	**FOOL** (BMI)—S. Clark Lonesome for a Letter (BMI)—Dot 15481	13	4
15.	**SWEET OLD-FASHIONED GIRL** (ASCAP)—T. Brewer Goodbye, John (BMI)—Coral 61636	16	11
16.	**MORE** (ASCAP)—P. Como **GLENDORA** (BMI)—Vic 20-6554	11	12
17.	**THAT'S ALL THERE IS TO THAT** (BMI)—Nat (King) Cole My Dream Sonata (ASCAP)—Cap 3456	23	7
18.	**IT ONLY HURTS FOR A LITTLE WHILE** (ASCAP)—Ames Brothers If You Want to See Mamie Tonight (ASCAP)—Vic 20-6481	17	14
19.	**BORN TO BE WITH YOU** (ASCAP) Chordettes Love Never Changes (ASCAP)—Cadence 1291	14	11
20.	**YOU DON'T KNOW ME** (BMI)—J. Vale Enchanted (ASCAP)—Col 40710	19	5
21.	**CANADIAN SUNSET** (BMI)—A. Williams High Upon a Mountain (ASCAP)—Cadence 1297	—	1
22.	**SOFT SUMMER BREEZE** (BMI)—E. Heywood Heywood's Bounce (BMI)—Mercury 70863	21	7
23.	**WHEN MY DREAMBOAT COMES HOME** (ASCAP)—F. Domino **SO LONG** (BMI)—Imperial 5396	21	5
24.	**FEVER** (BMI)—L. W. John Letter From My Darling (BMI)—King 4935	—	2
25.	**CASUAL LOOK** (BMI)—Six Teens Teen-Age Promises (BMI)—Flip 315	—	1

• Most Played in Juke Boxes

For survey week ending August 22

RECORDS are ranked in order of the greatest number of plays in juke boxes thruout the country, as determined by The Billboard's weekly survey of the nation's juke box operators. When significant play is reported on both sides of a record, points are combined to determine position on the chart. In such a case, both sides are listed in bold type, the leading side on top.

This Week		Last Week	Weeks on Chart
1.	**HOUND DOG** (BMI)—E. Presley **DON'T BE CRUEL** (BMI)—Vic 20-6604	4	4
2.	**MY PRAYER** (ASCAP)—Platters Heaven on Earth (ASCAP)—Mercury 70893	1	7
3.	**WHATEVER WILL BE, WILL BE** (ASCAP)—Doris Day I Gotta Sing Away These Blues (BMI)—Col 40704	3	6
4.	**ALLEGHENY MOON** (ASCAP)—P. Page Strangest Romance (ASCAP)—Mercury 70878	5	9
5.	**I ALMOST LOST MY MIND** (BMI)—P. Boone I'm In Love With You (BMI)—Dot 15472	2	12
6.	**WAYWARD WIND** (BMI)—G. Grant No More Than Forever (ASCAP)—Era 1013	6	14
7.	**I WANT YOU, I NEED YOU, I LOVE YOU** (BMI)—E. Presley My Baby Left Me (BMI)—Vic 20-6540	7	13
8.	**MORE** (ASCAP)—P. Como **GLENDORA** (BMI)—Vic 20-6554	8	9
9.	**SWEET OLD-FASHIONED GIRL** (ASCAP)—T. Brewer Goodbye, John (BMI)—Coral 61636	8	8
10.	**CANADIAN SUNSET** (BMI)—H. Winterhalter-E. Heywood This Is Real (ASCAP)—Vic 20-6537	16	3
11.	**BORN TO BE WITH YOU** (ASCAP)—Chordettes Love Never Changes (ASCAP)—Cadence 1291	10	10
12.	**IT ONLY HURTS FOR A LITTLE WHILE** (ASCAP)—Ames Brothers If You Want to See Mamie Tonight (ASCAP)—Vic 20-6481	11	11
12.	**FLYING SAUCER** (Parts I & II) Buchanan & Goodman Luniverse 101	12	2
14.	**BE-BOP-A-LULA** (BMI)—G. Vincent Woman Love (BMI)—Cap 3450	12	8
15.	**SONG FOR A SUMMER NIGHT** (Parts I & II)—M. Miller Columbia 40730	19	2
16.	**I'M IN LOVE AGAIN** (BMI)—F. Domino My Blue Heaven (ASCAP)—Imperial 5386	14	16
16.	**WHEN MY DREAMBOAT COMES HOME** (ASCAP)—F. Domino **SO-LONG** (BMI)—Imperial 5316	—	1
18.	**MOONGLOW AND THEME FROM "PICNIC"** (ASCAP)—M. Stoloff Theme From "Picnic" (ASCAP)—Dec 29888	15	16
18.	**FOOL** (BMI)—S. Clark Lonesome for a Letter (BMI)—Dot 15481	18	2
18.	**SOMEBODY UP THERE LIKES ME** (ASCAP)—P. Como Dream Along With Me (ASCAP)—Vic 20-6590	—	1

• Best Selling Sheet Music

Tunes are ranked in order of their current national selling importance at the sheet music jobber level.

This Week		Last Week	Weeks on Chart
1.	**Allegheny Moon** (Oxford)	1	10
1.	**Whatever Will Be, Will Be** (Que Sera, Sera Artists)	2	8
3.	**My Prayer** (Shapiro-Bernstein)	4	7
4.	**Canadian Sunset** (Meridian)	5	4
5.	**Wayward Wind** (Warman)	3	14
6.	**On the Street Where You Live** (Chappell)	6	7
7.	**Song for a Summer Night** (April)	8	2
8.	**Hound Dog** (E. Presley)	9	2
9.	**I Want You, I Need You, I Love You** (E. Presley)	7	6
10.	**I Almost Lost My Mind** (Hill & Range)	10	10
11.	**Soft Summer Breeze** (Regent)	—	1
12.	**Sweet Old-Fashioned Girl** (Valor)	14	7
13.	**Picnic** (Shapiro-Bernstein)	13	16
13.	**Moonglow** (Mills-Columbia Pictures)	12	16
15.	**Walk Hand in Hand** (Republic)	—	16

• Most Played by Jockeys

For survey week ending August 22

SIDES are ranked in order of the greatest number of plays on disk jockey radio shows thruout the country. Results are based on The Billboard's weekly survey among the nation's disk jockeys. The reverse side of each record is also listed.

This Week		Last Week	Weeks on Chart
1.	**MY PRAYER** (ASCAP)—Platters Heaven on Earth (ASCAP)—Mercury 70893	1	8
2.	**DON'T BE CRUEL** (BMI)—E. Presley Hound Dog (BMI)—Vic 20-6604	3	4
3.	**WHATEVER WILL BE, WILL BE** (ASCAP)—Doris Day I Gotta Sing Away These Blues (BMI)—Col 40704	2	9
4.	**HOUND DOG** (BMI)—E. Presley Don't Be Cruel (BMI)—Vic 20-6604	6	5
5.	**ALLEGHENY MOON** (ASCAP)—P. Page Strangest Romance (ASCAP)—Mercury 70878	4	10
6.	**I ALMOST LOST MY MIND** (BMI)—P. Boone I'm in Love With You (BMI)—Dot 15472	7	12
7.	**CANADIAN SUNSET** (BMI)—H. Winterhalter-E. Heywood This Is Real (ASCAP)—Vic 20-6537	8	6
8.	**WAYWARD WIND** (BMI)—G. Grant No More Than Forever (ASCAP)—Era 1013	5	17
9.	**FLYING SAUCER** (Parts I & II) Buchanan & Goodman Luniverse 101	12	4
10.	**CANADIAN SUNSET** (BMI)—A. Williams High Upon a Mountain (ASCAP)—Cadence 1297	17	3
11.	**SWEET OLD-FASHIONED GIRL** (ASCAP)—T. Brewer Goodbye, John (BMI)—Coral 61636	14	9
12.	**SONG FOR A SUMMER NIGHT** (Parts I & II)—M. Miller Col 40730—ASCAP	15	4
13.	**MORE** (ASCAP)—P. Como Glendora (BMI)—Vic 20-6554	10	10
14.	**BORN TO BE WITH YOU** (ASCAP)—Chordettes Love Never Changes (ASCAP)—Cadence 1291	9	13
15.	**ON THE STREET WHERE YOU LIVE** (ASCAP)—V. Damone We All Need Love (ASCAP)—Col 40654	11	20
16.	**FROM THE CANDY STORE ON THE CORNER** (ASCAP)—T. Bennett Happiness Street (ASCAP)—Col 40726	24	3
17.	**FOOL** (BMI)—S. Clark Lonesome for a Letter (BMI)—Dot 15481	—	1
18.	**I WANT YOU, I NEED YOU, I LOVE YOU** (BMI)—E. Presley My Baby Left Me (BMI)—Vic 20-6540	13	12
19.	**FABULOUS CHARACTER** (ASCAP)—S. Vaughan Other Woman (ASCAP)—Mercury 70885	19	4
20.	**TONIGHT YOU BELONG TO ME** (ASCAP)—Patience & Prudence A Smile and a Ribbon (ASCAP)—Liberty 55022	25	2
21.	**HAPPINESS STREET** (ASCAP)—G. Gibbs Happiness Is a Thing Called Joe (ASCAP) Mercury 70920	—	1
22.	**SOMEBODY UP THERE LIKES ME** (ASCAP)—P. Como Dream Along With Me (ASCAP)—Vic 20-6590	—	1
23.	**AFTER THE LIGHTS GO DOWN LOW** (BMI)—A. Hibbler I Was Telling Her About You (ASCAP)—Dec 29982	—	1
24.	**ENGLISH MUFFINS AND IRISH STEW** (ASCAP)—S. Syms Walk Sweet (ASCAP)—Dec 29969	—	1
25.	**SOFT SUMMER BREEZE** (BMI)—E. Heywood Heywood's Bounce (BMI)—Mercury 70863	20	3

THE TOP 100

For survey week ending August 22

A list of the Top 100 RECORD SIDES in the nation according to a COMBINED TABULATION of Dealer, Disk Jockey and Juke Box Operator replies to The Billboard's weekly popular record Best Seller and Most Played surveys. Its purpose is to provide Disk Jockeys with additional programming material and to give trade exposure to NEWER records just beginning to show action in the field.

Pos.	Song, Artist, Label	Last Week
1.	**MY PRAYER**—Platters, Mercury	1
2.	**HOUND DOG**—E. Presley, Victor	3
2.	**WHATEVER WILL BE, WILL BE**—Doris Day, Columbia	2
4.	**DON'T BE CRUEL**—E. Presley, Victor	6
5.	**ALLEGHENY MOON**—P. Page, Mercury	3
6.	**I ALMOST LOST MY MIND**—P. Boone, Dot	5
7.	**CANADIAN SUNSET**—H. Winterhalter-E. Heywood, Victor	11
8.	**FLYING SAUCER**—Buchanan & Goodman, Luniverse	9
9.	**WAYWARD WIND**—G. Grant, Era	7
10.	**I WANT YOU, I NEED YOU, I LOVE YOU**—E. Presley, Victor	8
11.	**SWEET OLD-FASHIONED GIRL**—T. Brewer, Coral	13
12.	**SONG FOR A SUMMER NIGHT**—M. Miller, Columbia	15
13.	**BORN TO BE WITH YOU**—Chordettes, Cadence	10
14.	**MORE**—P. Como, Victor	12
15.	**FOOL**—S. Clark, Dot	19
16.	**BE-BOP-A-LULA**—G. Vincent, Capitol	14
16.	**TONIGHT YOU BELONG TO ME**—Patience & Prudence, Liberty	24
18.	**IT ONLY HURTS FOR A LITTLE WHILE**—Ames Brothers, Victor	17
19.	**ON THE STREET WHERE YOU LIVE**—V. Damone, Columbia	16
20	**CANADIAN SUNSET**—A. Williams, Cadence	26
20.	**YOU DON'T KNOW ME**—J. Vale, Columbia	20
22.	**THAT'S ALL THERE IS TO THAT**—N. (King) Cole, Capitol	22
23.	**MOONGLOW AND THEME FROM "PICNIC"**—M. Stoloff, Decca	18
23.	**SOFT SUMMER BREEZE**—E. Heywood, Mercury	20
25.	**WHEN MY DREAMBOAT COMES HOME**—F. Domino, Imperial	30
26.	**SOMEBODY UP THERE LIKES ME**—P. Como, Victor	31
27.	**AFTER THE LIGHTS GO DOWN LOW**—A. Hibbler, Decca	35
28.	**FABULOUS CHARACTER**—S. Vaughan, Mercury	27
29.	**HONKY TONK**—B. Doggett, King	42
30.	**GLENDORA**—P. Como, Victor	23
31.	**I'M IN LOVE AGAIN**—F. Domino, Imperial	25
32.	**RIP IT UP**—B. Haley, Decca	47
33.	**APE CALL**—N. Norvus, Dot	28
34.	**OLD PHILOSPHER**—E. Lawrence, Coral	43
35.	**STRANDED IN THE JUNGLE**—Cadets, Modern	28
36.	**GHOST TOWN**—D. Cherry, Columbia	33
37.	**RIP IT UP**—Little Richard, Specialty	34
38.	**WEARY BLUES**—McGuire Sisters, Coral	47
39.	**MAMA, TEACH ME TO DANCE**—E. Gorme, ABC-Paramount	51
40.	**FEVER**—L. W. John, King	35
40.	**I ONLY KNOW I LOVE YOU**—Four Aces, Decca	39
40.	**MOONGLOW AND THEME FROM "PICNIC"**—G. Cates, Coral	46
43.	**HAPPINESS STREET**—G. Gibbs, Mercury	39
44.	**LOVE, LOVE, LOVE**—Clovers, Atlantic	45
45.	**WHEN THE WHITE LILACS BLOOM AGAIN**—H. Zacharaias, Decca	—
46.	**SO-LONG**—F. Domino, Imperial	44
46.	**WITH A LITTLE BIT OF LUCK**—Fontane Sisters, Dot	—
48.	**THEME FROM "THE PROUD ONES"**—N. Riddle, Capitol	59
49.	**STANDING ON THE CORNER**—Four Lads, Columbia	32
50.	**GIVE US THIS DAY**—J. James, M-G-M	54
51.	**ENGLISH MUFFINS AND IRISH STEW**—S. Syms, Decca	62
51.	**TREASURE OF LOVE**—C. McPhatter, Atlantic	38
53.	**WAYWARD WIND**—T. Ritter, Capitol	48
54.	**LOVE, LOVE, LOVE**—Diamonds, Mercury	52
55.	**LET THE GOOD TIMES ROLL**—Shirley & Lee, Aladdin	64
56.	**PORTUGUESE WASHERWOMAN**—J. (Fingers) Carr, Capitol	39
57.	**ST. THERESE OF THE ROSES**—B. Ward, Decca	100
57.	**TRUE LOVE**—J. Powell, Verve	74
59.	**BUS STOP SONG**—Four Lads, Columbia	98
59.	**TRUE LOVE**—Four Aces, Decca	80
61.	**HAPPINESS STREET**—T. Bennett, Columbia	79
61.	**YOU'RE SENSATIONAL**—F. Sinatra, Capitol	63
63.	**STRANDED IN THE JUNGLE**—Jay Hawks, Flash	50
64.	**CASUAL LOOK**—Six Teens, Flip	75
65.	**HOUSE WITH LOVE IN IT**—Four Lads, Columbia	—
66.	**ITALIAN THEME**—C. Stapleton, London	—
67.	**FOOL**—Gallahads, Jubilee	64
68,	**TEEN-AGERS MOTHER**—B. Haley, Decca	68
69.	**IN THE MIDDLE OF THE HOUSE**—V. Monroe, Victor	—
70.	**KA DING DONG**—G. Clefs, Pilgrim	92
71.	**MIRACLE OF LOVE**—E. Rodgers, Columbia	68
72.	**CLAY IDOL**—D. Johnson, Bally	72
72.	**FROM THE CANDY STORE ON THE CORNER**—T. Bennett, Columbia	60
74.	**WALK HAND IN HAND**—T. Martin, Victor	67
75.	**I DON'T WANT NOBODY**—W. Herman, Capitol	80
76.	**IT'S BETTER IN THE DARK**—T. Martin, Victor	—
77.	**MY DREAM SONATA**—N. (King) Cole, Capitol	94
78.	**ON THE STREET WHERE YOU LIVE**—E. Fisher, Victor	68
79.	**STRANDED IN THE JUNGLE**—Gadabouts, Mercury	53
80.	**IN A SHANTY IN OLD SHANTY TOWN**—S. Smith, Epic	88
80.	**IN THE MIDDLE OF THE HOUSE**—R. Draper, Mercury	—
82.	**EXPERIMENTS WITH MICE**—J. Dankworth, Capitol	61
83.	**TRANSFUSION**—N. Norvus, Dot	48
84.	**LOLA'S THEME**—M. Mathieson, Columbia	88
85.	**SEE SAW**—Moonglows, Chess	—
86.	**BEAUTIFUL FRIENDSHIP**—E. Fitzgerald, Decca	—
87.	**TUMBLING TUMBLEWEEDS**—R. Williams, Kapp	84
88.	**JOHNNY CONCHO THEME**—F. Sinatra, Capitol	91
89.	**HOW LUCKY YOU ARE**—J. James, M-G-M	99
90.	**HEAVEN ON EARTH**—Platters, Mercury	57
91.	**DREAM ALONG WITH ME**—P. Como, Victor	—
92.	**PICNIC**—McGuire Sisters, Coral	58
93.	**HAPPY WHISTLER**—D. Robertson, Capitol	82
94.	**HEARTBREAK HOTEL**—E. Presley, Victor	96
94.	**IVORY TOWER**—C. Carr, Fraternity	64
94.	**I'M JUST WALKING IN THE RAIN**—J. Ray, Columbia	—
97.	**I PROMISE TO REMEMBER**—Teen-Agers, Gee	68
98.	**IN THE ALPS**—McGuire Sisters & L. Welk, Coral	92
99.	**HEART HIDE AWAY**—C. Carr, Fraternity	—
100.	**BOPPIN' THE BLUES**—C. Perkins, Sun	90
100.	**WHEN THE WHITE LILACS BLOOM**—F. ZaBach, Mercury	—

CAUTION TO DEALERS AND JUKE BOX OPERATORS

The Billboard's Top 100 is NOT designed to provide tested information for buying purposes. This function is most reliably served by other regular weekly features: Best Sellers in Stores, Most Played in Juke Boxes, Coming Up Strong and Best Buys.

• Best Sellers in Stores

For survey week ending August 29

RECORDS are ranked in order of their current national selling importance at the retail level, as determined by The Billboard's weekly survey of the top volume dealers in every important market area. When significant action is reported on both sides of a record, points are combined to determine position on the chart. In such a case, both sides are listed in bold type, the leading side on top.

This Week	Record	Last Week	Weeks on Chart
1.	**HOUND DOG** (BMI)—E. Presley **DON'T BE CRUEL** (BMI)—Vic 20-6604	1	6
2.	**MY PRAYER** (ASCAP)—Platters Heaven on Earth (ASCAP)—Mercury 70893	2	9
3.	**WHATEVER WILL BE, WILL BE** (ASCAP)—Doris Day I Gotta Sing Away These Blues (BMI)—Col 40704	3	10
4.	**FLYING SAUCER**—Buchannan & Goodman Luniverse 101	4	5
5.	**CANADIAN SUNSET** (BMI)—H. Winterhalter-E. Heywood This Is Real (ASCAP)—Vic 20-6537	5	7
6.	**ALLEGHENY MOON** (ASCAP)—P. Page Strangest Romance (ASCAP)—Mercury 70878	6	10
7.	**TONIGHT YOU BELONG TO ME** (ASCAP)—Patience & Prudence A Smile and a Ribbon (ASCAP)—Liberty 55022	10	3
8.	**BE-BOP-A-LULA** (BMI)—G. Vincent Woman Love (BMI)—Cap 3450	8	12
9.	**SONG FOR A SUMMER NIGHT (PARTS I & II)** (ASCAP)—M. Miller Col 40730—ASCAP	13	5
10.	**HONKY TONK (PARTS I & II)**—B. Doggett King 4950—BMI	11	3
11.	**FOOL** (BMI)—S. Clark Lonesome for a Letter (BMI)—Dot 15481	14	5
12.	**I ALMOST LOST MY MIND** (BMI)—P. Boone I'm in Love With You (BMI)—Dot 15472	9	13
13.	**I WANT YOU, I NEED YOU, I LOVE YOU** (BMI)—E. Presley My Baby Left Me (BMI)—Vic 20-6540	7	15
14.	**CANADIAN SUNSET** (BMI)—A. Williams High Up on a Mountain (ASCAP)—Cadence 1297	21	2
15.	**WAYWARD WIND** (BMI)—G. Grant No More Than Forever (ASCAP)—Era 1013	12	19
16.	**YOU DON'T KNOW ME** (BMI)—J. Vale Enchanted (ASCAP)—Col 40710	20	6
17.	**SOFT SUMMER BREEZE** (BMI)—E. Heywood Heywood's Bounce (BMI)—Mercury 70863	22	8
18.	**MORE** (ASCAP)—P. Como **GLENDORA** (BMI)—Vic 20-6554	16	13
19.	**BORN TO BE WITH YOU** (ASCAP)—Chordettes Love Never Changes (ASCAP)—Cadence 1291	19	12
20.	**SWEET OLD-FASHIONED GIRL** (ASCAP)—T. Brewer Goodbye, John (BMI)—Coral 61636	15	12
21.	**IT ONLY HURTS FOR A LITTLE WHILE** (ASCAP)—Ames Brothers If You Want to See Mamie Tonight (ASCAP)—Vic 20-6481	18	15
22.	**THAT'S ALL THERE IS TO THAT** (BMI)—Nat (King) Cole My Dream Sonata (ASCAP)—Cap 3456	17	8
23.	**WHEN MY DREAMBOAT COMES HOME** (ASCAP)—F. Domino So-Long (BMI)—Imperial 5396	23	6
24.	**MOONGLOW AND THEME FROM "PICNIC"** (ASCAP)—M. Stoloff Theme From "Picnic" (ASCAP)—Dec 29888	—	20
25.	**JUST WALKING IN THE RAIN** (BMI)—J. Ray In the Candlelight (ASCAP)—Col 40729	—	1

• Most Played in Juke Boxes

For survey week ending August 29

RECORDS are ranked in order of the greatest number of plays in juke boxes thruout the country, as determined by The Billboard's weekly survey of the nation's juke box operators. When significant play is reported on both sides of a record, points are combined to determine position on the chart. In such a case, both sides are listed in bold type, the leading side on top.

This Week	Record	Last Week	Weeks on Chart
1.	**HOUND DOG** (BMI)—E. Presley **DON'T BE CRUEL** (BMI)—Vic 20-6604	1	5
2.	**MY PRAYER** (ASCAP)—Platters Heaven on Earth (ASCAP)—Mercury 70893	2	8
3.	**WHATEVER WILL BE, WILL BE** Doris Day I Gotta Sing Away These Blues (BMI)—Col 40704	3	7
4.	**ALLEGHENY MOON** (ASCAP)—P. Page Strangest Romance (ASCAP)—Mercury 70878	4	10
5.	**I ALMOST LOST MY MIND** (BMI)—P. Boone I'm in Love With You (BMI)—Dot 15472	5	13
6.	**I WANT YOU, I NEED YOU, I LOVE YOU** (BMI)—E. Presley My Baby Left Me (BMI)—Vic 20-6540	7	14
7.	**WAYWARD WIND** (BMI)—G. Grant No More Than Forever (ASCAP)—Era 1013	6	15
8.	**CANADIAN SUNSET** (BMI)—H. Winterhalter-E. Heywood This Is Real (ASCAP)—Vic 20-6537	10	4
9.	**SWEET OLD-FASHIONED GIRL** (ASCAP)—T. Brewer Goodbye, John (BMI)—Coral 61636	9	9
10.	**FLYING SAUCER (PARTS I & II)**—Buchanan & Goodman Luniverse 101	12	3
11.	**MORE** (ASCAP)—P. Como **GLENDORA** (BMI)—Vic 20-6554	8	10
12.	**IT ONLY HURTS FOR A LITTLE WHILE** (ASCAP)—Ames Brothers If You Want to See Mamie Tonight (ASCAP)—Vic 20-6481	12	12
13.	**BE-BOP-A-LULA** (BMI)—G. Vincent Woman Love (BMI)—Cap 3450	14	9
14.	**WHEN MY DREAMBOAT COMES HOME** (ASCAP)—F. Domino **SO-LONG** (BMI)—Imperial 5316	16	2
15.	**BORN TO BE WITH YOU** (ASCAP)—Chordettes Love Never Changes (ASCAP)—Cadence 1291	11	11
16.	**SONG FOR A SUMMER NIGHT (PARTS I & II)** (ASCAP)—M. Miller Columbia 40730	15	3
17.	**FOOL** (BMI)—S. Clark Lonesome for a Letter (BMI)—Dot 15481	18	3
18.	**YOU DON'T KNOW ME** (BMI)—J. Vale Enchanted (ASCAP)—Col 40710	—	1
19.	**TONIGHT YOU BELONG TO ME** (ASCAP)—Patience & Prudence A Smile and a Ribbon (ASCAP)—Liberty 55022	—	1
20.	**CANADIAN SUNSET** (BMI)—A. Williams High Upon a Mountain (ASCAP)—Cadence 1297	—	1

• Best Selling Sheet Music

Tunes are ranked in order of their current national selling importance at the sheet music jobber level.

This Week	Title	Last Week	Weeks on Chart
1.	**Whatever Will Be, Will Be** (Que Sera, Sera Art)	1	9
2.	**Allegheny Moon** (Oxford)	1	11
3.	**Canadian Sunset** (Meridian)	4	5
4.	**My Prayer** (Shapiro-Bernstein)	3	8
5.	**Wayward Wind** (Warman)	5	15
6.	**Song for a Summer Night** (April)	7	3
7.	**Soft, Summer Breeze** (Regent)	11	2
8.	**On the Street Where You Live** (Chappell)	6	8
9.	**Hound Dog** (E. Presley)	8	3
10.	**Tonight You Belong to Me** (Mills)	—	1
11.	**I Want You, I Need You, I Love You** (Presley)	9	7
11.	**Walk Hand in Hand** (Republic)	15	17
13.	**I Almost Lost My Mind** (Hill & Range)	10	11
13.	**Picnic** (Shaprio-Bernstein)	13	17
15.	**It Only Hurts for a Little While** (Advanced)	—	5

• Most Played by Jockeys

For survey week ending August 29

SIDES are ranked in order of the greatest number of plays on disk jockey radio shows thruout the country. Results are based on The Billboard's weekly survey among the nation's disk jockeys. The reverse side of each record is also listed.

This Week	Record	Last Week	Weeks on Chart
1.	**DON'T BE CRUEL** (BMI)—E. Presley Hound Dog (BMI)—Vic 20-6604	2	5
2.	**MY PRAYER** (ASCAP)—Platters Heaven on Earth (ASCAP)—Mercury 70893	1	9
3.	**WHATEVER WILL BE, WILL BE** (ASCAP)—Doris Day I Gotta Sing Away These Blues (BMI)—Col 40704	3	10
4.	**HOUND DOG** (BMI)—E. Presley Don't Be Cruel (BMI)—Vic 20-6604	4	6
5.	**CANADIAN SUNSET** (BMI)—H. Winterhalter-E. Heywood This Is Real (ASCAP)—Vic 20-6537	7	7
6.	**ALLEGHENY MOON** (ASCAP)—P. Page Strangest Romance (ASCAP)—Mercury 70878	5	11
7.	**TONIGHT YOU BELONG TO ME** (ASCAP)—Patience & Prudence A Smile and a Ribbon (ASCAP)—Liberty 55022	20	3
8.	**WAYWARD WIND** (BMI)—G. Grant No More Than Forever (ASCAP)—Era 1013	8	18
9.	**FLYING SAUCER (PARTS I & II)**—Buchanan & Goodman Luniverse 101	9	5
10.	**SONG FOR A SUMMER NIGHT (PARTS & II)** (ASCAP) Col 40730—ASCAP	12	5
11.	**I ALMOST LOST MY MIND** (BMI)—P. Boone I'm in Love With You (BMI)—Dot 15472	6	13
12.	**CANADIAN SUNSET** (BMI)—A. Williams High Upon a Mountain (ASCAP)—Cadence 1297	10	4
13.	**BORN TO BE WITH YOU** (ASCAP)—Chordettes Love Never Changes (ASCAP)—Cadence 1291	14	14
14.	**I WANT YOU, I NEED YOU, I LOVE YOU** (BMI)—E. Presley My Baby Left Me (BMI)—Vic 20-6540	18	13
15.	**SWEET OLD-FASHIONED GIRL** (ASCAP)—T. Brewer Goodbye, John (BMI)—Coral 61636	11	10
16.	**SOFT SUMMER BREEZE**—E. Heywood Heywood's Bounce (BMI)—Mercury 70863	25	4
17.	**FOOL** (BMI)—S. Clark Lonesome for a Letter (BMI)—Dot 15481	17	2
18.	**MORE** (ASCAP)—P. Como Glendora (BMI)—Vic 20-6554	13	11
19.	**YOU DON'T KNOW ME** (BMI)—J. Vale Enchanted (ASCAP)—Col 40710	—	4
20.	**THAT'S ALL THERE IS TO THAT** (BMI)—Nat (King) Cole My Dream Sonata (ASCAP)—Cap 3456	—	5
21.	**AFTER THE LIGHTS GO DOWN LOW** (BMI)—A. Hibbler I Was Telling Her About You (ASCAP)—Decca 29982	23	2
22.	**ON THE STREET WHERE YOU LIVE** (ASCAP)—V. Damone We All Need Love (ASCAP)—Col 40654	15	21
23.	**HAPPINESS STREET** (ASCAP)—G. Gibbs Happiness Is a Thing Called Joe (ASCAP)—Mercury 70920	21	2
24.	**BE-BOP-A-LULA** (BMI)—G. Vincent Woman Love (BMI)—Cap 3450	—	9
25.	**WHEN THE WHITE LILACS BLOOM AGAIN** (ASCAP)—H. Zacharias Blue Blues (BMI)—Decca 30039	—	1

THE TOP 100

For survey week ending August 29

A list of the Top 100 RECORD SIDES in the nation according to a COMBINED TABULATION of Dealer, Disk Jockey and Juke Box Operator replies to The Billboard's weekly popular record Best Seller and Most Played surveys. Its purpose is to provide Disk Jockeys with additional programming material and to give trade exposure to NEWER records just beginning to show action in the field.

Pos.	Song, Artist, Label	Last Week
1.	**MY PRAYER**—Platters, Mercury	1
2.	**HOUND DOG**—E. Presley, Victor	2
3.	**DON'T BE CRUEL**—E. Presley, Victor	4
3.	**WHATEVER WILL BE, WILL BE**—Doris Day, Columbia	2
5.	**ALLEGHENY MOON**—P. Page, Mercury	5
6.	**CANADIAN SUNSET**—H. Winterhalter-E. Heywood, Victor	7
7.	**FLYING SAUCER**—Buchanan & Goodman, Luniverse	8
8.	**I ALMOST LOST MY MIND**—P. Boone, Dot	6
9.	**WAYWARD WIND**—G. Grant, Era	9
10.	**TONIGHT YOU BELONG TO ME**—Patience & Prudence, Liberty	16
11.	**I WANT YOU, I NEED YOU, I LOVE YOU**—E. Presley, Victor	10
12.	**SONG FOR A SUMMER NIGHT**—M. Miller, Columbia	12
13.	**FOOL**—S. Clark, Dot	15
13.	**SWEET OLD-FASHIONED GIRL**—T. Brewer, Coral	11
15.	**BE-BOP-A-LULA**—G. Vincent, Capitol	16
15.	**BORN TO BE WITH YOU**—Chordettes, Cadence	13
15.	**CANADIAN SUNSET**—A. Williams, Cadence	20
18.	**MORE**—P. Como, Victor	14
19.	**YOU DON'T KNOW ME**—J. Vale, Columbia	20
20.	**SOFT, SUMMER BREEZE**—E. Heywood, Mercury	23
21.	**IT ONLY HURTS FOR A LITTLE WHILE**—Ames Brothers, Victor	18
22.	**HONKY TONK**—B. Doggett, King	29
22.	**WHEN MY DREAMBOAT COMES HOME**—F. Domino, Imperial	25
24.	**THAT'S ALL THERE IS TO THAT**—Nat (King) Cole, Capitol	22
25.	**ON THE STREET WHERE YOU LIVE**—V. Damone, Columbia	19
26.	**AFTER THE LIGHTS GO DOWN LOW**—A. Hibbler, Decca	27
27.	**RIP IT UP**—Little Richard, Specialty	37
28.	**MOONGLOW AND THEME FROM "PICNIC"**—M. Stoloff, Decca	23
29.	**GLENDORA**—P. Como, Victor	30
30.	**SOMEBODY UP THERE LIKES ME**—P. Como, Victor	26
31.	**RIP IT UP**—B. Haley, Decca	32
32.	**MIRACLE OF LOVE**—E. Rodgers, Columbia	71
33.	**HAPPINESS STREET**—G. Gibbs, Mercury	43
34.	**MAMA, TEACH ME TO DANCE**—E. Gorme, ABC-Paramount	39
35.	**WHEN THE WHITE LILACS BLOOM AGAIN**—B. Vaughn, Dot	—
36.	**FABULOUS CHARACTER**—S. Vaughan, Mercury	28
36.	**LET THE GOOD TIMES ROLL**—Shirley & Lee, Aladdin	55
38.	**I'M IN LOVE AGAIN**—F. Domino, Imperial	31
39.	**FEVER**—L. W. John, King	40
40.	**IN THE MIDDLE OF THE HOUSE**—V. Monroe, Victor	69
41.	**APE CALL**—N. Norvus, Dot	33
41.	**JUST WALKING IN THE RAIN**—J. Ray, Columbia	94
43.	**GHOST TOWN**—D. Cherry, Columbia	36
43.	**OLD PHILOSOPHER**—E. Lawrence, Coral	34
45.	**HOUSE WITH LOVE IN IT**—Four Lads, Columbia	65
46.	**WHEN THE WHITE LILACS BLOOM AGAIN**—H. Zacharaias, Decca	45
47.	**IN THE MIDDLE OF THE HOUSE**—R. Draper, Mercury	80
48.	**CASUAL LOOK**—Six Teens, Flip	64
49.	**LOVE, LOVE, LOVE**—Clovers, Atlantic	44
49.	**WEARY BLUES**—McGuire Sisters, Coral	—
51.	**HEAVEN ON EARTH**—Platters, Mercury	—
51.	**STRANDED IN THE JUNGLE**—Cadets, Modern	35
53.	**GIVE US THIS DAY**—J. James, M-G-M	58
54.	**FROM THE CANDY STORE ON THE CORNER**—T. Bennett, Columbia	72
55.	**KA DING DONG**—G. Clefs, Pilgrim	70
56.	**ON THE STREET WHERE YOU LIVE**—E. Fisher, Victor	78
57.	**BUS STOP SONG**—Four Lads, Columbia	59
57.	**HAPPINESS STREET**—T. Bennett, Columbia	61
57.	**I ONLY KNOW I LOVE YOU**—Four Aces, Decca	40
60.	**IT'S BETTER IN THE DARK**—T. Martin, Victor	76
61.	**YOU'RE SENSATIONAL**—F. Sinatra, Capitol	61
62.	**TUMBLING TUMBLEWEEDS**—R. Williams, Kapp	87
63.	**THEME FROM "THE PROUD ONES"**—N. Riddle, Capitol	48
64.	**LOVE, LOVE, LOVE**—Diamonds, Mercury	54
64.	**ITALIAN THEME**—C. Stapleton, London	66
64.	**ST. THERESE OF THE ROSES**—B. Ward, Decca	57
64.	**TRUE LOVE**—B. Crosby-G. Kelly, Capitol	—
68.	**FOOL**—Gallahads, Jubilee	67
68.	**STRANDED IN THE JUNGLE**—Jay Hawks, Flash	63
70.	**SO-LONG**—F. Domino, Imperial	46
71.	**I PROMISE TO REMEMBER**—Teen-Agers, Gee	97
72.	**TRUE LOVE**—J. Powell, Verve	57
73.	**CLAY IDOL**—B. Johnson, Bally	72
73.	**MOONGLOW AND THEME FROM "PICNIC"**—G. Cates, Coral	40
73.	**WAYWARD WIND**—T. Ritter, Capitol	53
76.	**PICNIC**—McGuire Sisters, Coral	92
77.	**FORTY-NINE SHADES OF GREEN**—Ames Brothers, Victor	—
77.	**STANDING ON THE CORNER**—Four Lads, Columbia	49
79.	**ENGLISH MUFFINS AND IRISH STEW**—S. Syms, Decca	51
80.	**OH, MY MARIA**—E. Fisher, Victor	—
80.	**TREASURE OF LOVE**—C. McPhatter, Atlantic	51
82.	**WHEN THE WHITE LILACS BLOOM AGAIN**—L. Holmes, M-G-M	—
83.	**IN A SHANTY IN OLD SHANTY TOWN**—S. Smith, Epic	80
83.	**EARTHBOUND**—S. Davis Jr., Decca	—
83.	**STRANDED IN THE JUNGLE**—Gadabouts, Mercury	79
83.	**WHEN THE WHITE LILACS BLOOM AGAIN**—F. ZaBach, Mercury	100
87.	**VOICES**—Fontane Sisters, Dot	—
88.	**KA DING DONG**—Diamonds, Mercury	—
89.	**THINGS I NEVER HAD**—K. Starr, Victor	—
90.	**SEE-SAW**—Moonglows, Chess	85
91.	**EXPERIMENTS WITH MICE**—J. Dankworth, Capitol	82
91.	**LOLA'S THEME**—S. Allen, Coral	—
91.	**MY BLUE HEAVEN**—F. Domino, Imperial	—
94.	**DAYDREAMS**—A. Mooney, M-G-M	—
95.	**IN THE STILL OF THE NIGHT**—Satins, Ember	—
96.	**HOW LUCKY YOU ARE**—J. James, M-G-M	89
97.	**GOOD BOOK**—K. Starr, Victor	—
98.	**HEARTACHES**, S. Smith, Epic	—
99.	**AFTER SCHOOL**—T. Charles, Decca	—
100.	**MY BABY LEFT ME**—E. Presley, Victor	—
100.	**SUMMER SWEETHEART**—Ames Brothers, Victor	—

CAUTION TO DEALERS AND JUKE BOX OPERATORS

The Billboard's Top 100 is NOT designed to provide tested information for buying purposes. This function is most reliably served by other regular weekly features: Best Sellers in Stores, Most Played in Juke Boxes, Coming Up Strong and Best Buys.

• Best Sellers in Stores

For survey week ending September 5

RECORDS are ranked in order of their current national selling importance at the retail level, as determined by The Billboard's weekly survey of the top volume dealers in every important market area. When significant action is reported on both sides of a record, points are combined to determine position on the chart. In such a case, both sides are listed in bold type, the leading side on top.

This Week		Last Week	Weeks on Chart
1.	**HOUND DOG** (BMI)—E. Presley / **DON'T BE CRUEL** (BMI)—Vic 20-6604	1	7
2.	**MY PRAYER** (ASCAP)—Platters / Heaven on Earth (ASCAP)—Mercury 70893	2	10
3.	**WHATEVER WILL BE, WILL BE** (ASCAP)—Doris Day / I Gotta Sing Away These Blues (BMI)—Col 40704	3	11
4.	**CANADIAN SUNSET** (BMI)—H. Winterhalter / This Is Real (ASCAP)—Vic 20-6537	5	8
5.	**TONIGHT YOU BELONG TO ME** (ASCAP)—Patience & Prudence / A Smile and a Ribbon (ASCAP)—Liberty 55022	7	4
6.	**FLYING SAUCER**—Buchanan & Goodman / Luniverse 101	4	6
7.	**HONKY TONK (PARTS I & II)**—B. Doggett / King 4950—BMI	10	4
8.	**ALLEGHENY MOON** (ASCAP)—P. Page / Strangest Romance (ASCAP)—Mercury 70878	6	11
9.	**FOOL** (BMI)—S. Clark / Lonesome for a Letter (BMI)—Dot 15481	11	6
10.	**CANADIAN SUNSET** (BMI)—A. Williams / High Up on a Mountain (ASCAP)—Cadence 1297	14	3
11.	**BE-BOP-A-LULA** (BMI)—G. Vincent / Woman Love (BMI)—Cap 3450	8	13
12.	**SONG FOR A SUMMER NIGHT (PARTS I & II)** (ASCAP)—M. Miller / Col 40730	9	6
13.	**SOFT SUMMER BREEZE** (BMI)—E. Heywood / Heywood's Bounce (BMI)—Mercury 70863	17	9
14.	**I ALMOST LOST MY MIND** (BMI)—P. Boone / I'm in Love With You (BMI)—Dot 15472	12	14
15.	**JUST WALKING IN THE RAIN**—(BMI) J. Ray / In the Candlelight (ASCAP)—Col 40729	25	2
16.	**YOU DON'T KNOW ME** (BMI)—J. Vale / Enchanted (ASCAP)—Col 40710	16	7
17.	**WAYWARD WIND** (BMI)—G. Grant / No More Than Forever (ASCAP)—Era 1013	15	20
18.	**I WANT YOU, I NEED YOU, I LOVE YOU** (BMI)—E. Presley / My Baby Left Me (BMI)—Vic 20-6540	13	16
19.	**IT ONLY HURTS FOR A LITTLE WHILE** (ASCAP)—Ames Brothers / If You Want to See Mamie Tonight (ASCAP)—Vic 20-6481	21	16
20.	**THAT'S ALL THERE IS TO THAT** (BMI)—Nat (King) Cole / My Dream Sonata (ASCAP)—Cap 3456	22	9
21.	**AFTER THE LIGHTS GO DOWN LOW** (BMI)—A. Hibbler / I Was Telling Her About You (ASCAP)—Dec 29982	—	1
21.	**WHEN THE WHITE LILACS BLOOM AGAIN** (ASCAP)—H. Zarcharias / Blue Blues (BMI)—Dec 30039	—	1
23.	**WHEN MY DREAMBOAT COMES HOME** (ASCAP)—F. Domino / **SO-LONG** (BMI)—Imperial 5396	23	7
24.	**KA DING DONG** (BMI)—G. Clefs / Darla, My Darlin' (BMI)—Pilgrim 24971	—	1
25.	**RIP IT UP** (BMI)—B. Haley / Teen-Ager's Mother (BMI)—Dec 30028	—	1

• Most Played in Juke Boxes

For survey week ending September 5

RECORDS are ranked in order of the greatest number of plays in juke boxes thruout the country, as determined by The Billboard's weekly survey of the nation's juke box operators. When significant play is reported on both sides of a record, points are combined to determine position on the chart. In such a case, both sides are listed in bold type, the leading side on top.

This Week		Last Week	Weeks on Chart
1.	**HOUND DOG** (BMI)—E. Presley / **DON'T BE CRUEL** (BMI)—Vic 20-6604	1	6
2.	**MY PRAYER** (ASCAP)—Platters / **HEAVEN ON EARTH** (ASCAP)—Mercury 70893	2	9
3.	**WHATEVER WILL BE, WILL BE**—Doris Day / I Gotta Sing Away These Blues (BMI)—Col 40704	3	8
4.	**ALLEGHENY MOON** (ASCAP)—P. Page / Strangest Romance (ASCAP)—Mercury 70878	4	11
5.	**CANADIAN SUNSET** (BMI)—H. Winterhalter-E. Heywood / This Is Real (ASCAP)—Vic 20-6537	8	5
6.	**I ALMOST LOST MY MIND** (BMI)—P. Boone / I'm In Love With You (BMI)—Dot 15472	5	14
7.	**I WANT YOU, I NEED YOU, I LOVE YOU** (BMI)—E. Presley / My Baby Left Me (BMI)—Vic 20-6540	6	15
8.	**WAYWARD WIND** (BMI)—G. Grant / No More Than Forever (ASCAP)—Era 1013	7	16
9.	**FLYING SAUCER (PARTS I & II)**—Buchannan & Goodman / Luniverse 101	10	4
10.	**TONIGHT YOU BELONG TO ME** (ASCAP)—Patience & Prudence / A Smile and a Ribbon (ASCAP)—Liberty 55022	19	2
11.	**IT ONLY HURTS FOR A LITTLE WHILE** (ASCAP)—Ames Brothers / If You Want to See Mamie Tonight (ASCAP)—Vic 20-6481	12	13
12.	**CANADIAN SUNSET** (BMI)—A. Williams / High Upon the Mountain (ASCAP)—Cadence 1297	20	2
13.	**SWEET, OLD-FASHIONED GIRL** (ASCAP)—T. Brewer / Goodbye, John (BMI)—Coral 61636	9	10
14.	**BE-BOP-A-LULA** (BMI)—G. Vincent / Woman Love (BMI)—Cap 3450	13	10
15.	**WHEN MY DREAMBOAT COMES HOME** (ASCAP)—F. Domino / **SO-LONG** (BMI)—Imperial 5316	14	3
15.	**FOOL** (BMI)—S. Clark / Lonesome for a Letter (BMI)—Dot 15481	17	4
17.	**MORE** (ASCAP)—P. Como / Glendora (BMI)—Vic 20-6554	11	11
17.	**HONKY TONK (PARTS I & II)** (BMI)—B. Doggett / King 4950	—	1
19.	**SONG FOR A SUMMER NIGHT (PARTS I & II)** (ASCAP)—M. Miller / Col 40730	16	4
20.	**YOU DON'T KNOW ME** (BMI)—J. Vale / Enchanted (ASCAP)—Col 40710	18	2
20.	**SOFT SUMMER BREEZE** (BMI)—E. Heywood / Heywood Bounce (BMI)—Mercury 70863	—	2

• Best Selling Sheet Music

Tunes are ranked in order of their current national selling importance at the sheet music jobber level.

This Week		Last Week	Weeks on Chart
1.	**Whatever Will Be, Will Be** (Que Sera, Sera Art)	1	10
2.	**Allegheny Moon** (Oxford)	2	12
3.	**Canadian Sunset** (Meridian)	3	6
4.	**My Prayer** (Shapiro-Bernstein)	4	9
5.	**Song for a Summer Night** (April)	6	4
5.	**Soft, Summer Breeze** (Regent)	7	3
7.	**Wayward Wind** (Warman)	5	6
8.	**Hound Dog** (Presley-Lion)	9	4
9.	**On the Street Where You Live** (Chappell)	8	9
9.	**Tonight You Belong to Me** (Mills)	10	2
11.	**Don't Be Cruel** (Presley-Shalimar)	—	1
12.	**Walk Hand in Hand** (Republic)	11	18
13.	**Moonglow** (Mills-Columbia Pictures)	—	17
14.	**Picnic** (Shapiro-Bernstein)	13	18
15.	**I Almost Lost My Mind** (Hill & Range)	13	12

• Most Played by Jockeys

For survey week ending September 5

SIDES are ranked in order of the greatest number of plays on disk jockey radio shows thruout the country. Results are based on The Billboard's weekly survey among the nation's disk jockeys. The reverse side of each record is also listed.

This Week		Last Week	Weeks on Chart
1.	**DON'T BE CRUEL** (BMI)—E. Presley / Hound Dog (BMI)—Vic 20-6604	1	6
2.	**MY PRAYER** (ASCAP)—Platters / Heaven on Earth (ASCAP)—Mercury 70893	2	10
3.	**WHATEVER WILL BE, WILL BE** (ASCAP)—Doris Day / I Gotta Sing Away These Blues (BMI)—Col 40704	3	11
4.	**HOUND DOG** (BMI)—E. Presley / Don't Be Cruel (BMI)—Vic 20-6604	4	7
5.	**CANADIAN SUNSET** (BMI)—H. Winterhalter-E. Heywood / This Is Real (ASCAP)—Vic 20-6537	5	8
6.	**ALLEGHENY MOON** (ASCAP)—P. Page / Strangest Romance (ASCAP)—Mercury 70878	6	12
7.	**TONIGHT YOU BELONG TO ME** (ASCAP)—Patience & Prudence / A Smile and a Ribbon (ASCAP)—Liberty 55022	7	4
8.	**CANADIAN SUNSET** (BMI)—A. Williams / High Upon a Mountain (ASCAP)—Cadence 1297	12	5
9.	**SONG FOR A SUMMER NIGHT (PARTS I & II)** (ASCAP)—M. Miller / Col 40730	10	6
10.	**FLYING SAUCER (PARTS I & II)**—Buchanan & Goodman / Luniverse 101	9	6
11.	**FROM THE CANDY STORE ON THE CORNER** (ASCAP)—T. Bennett / Happiness Street (ASCAP)—Col 40726	—	1
12.	**AFTER THE LIGHTS GO DOWN LOW** (BMI)—A. Hibbler / I Was Telling Her About You (ASCAP)—Decca 29982	21	3
13.	**ST. THERESE OF THE ROSES** (BMI)—B. Ward / Home Is Where You Hang Your Heart (BMI)—Dec 29933	—	1
14.	**SOFT SUMMER BREEZE**—E. Heywood / Heywood's Bounce (BMI)—Mercury 70863	16	5
15.	**WAYWARD WIND** (BMI)—G. Grant / No More Than Forever (ASCAP)—Era 1013	8	19
15.	**YOU DON'T KNOW ME** (BMI)—J. Vale / Enchanted (ASCAP)—Col 40710	19	5
17.	**IN THE MIDDLE OF THE HOUSE** (ASCAP)—V. Monroe / Rollin' Heart (BMI)—Vic 20-6619	—	1
18.	**I ALMOST LOST MY MIND** (BMI)—J. Boone / I'm in Love With You (BMI)—Dot 15472	11	14
19.	**FOOL** (BMI)—S. Clark / Lonesome for a Letter (BMI)—Dot 15481	17	3
20.	**HAPPINESS STREET** (ASCAP)—G. Gibbs / Happiness Is a Thing Called Joe (ASCAP)—Mercury 70920	23	3
21.	**SWEET, OLD-FASHIONED GIRL** (ASCAP)—T. Brewer / Goodbye, John (BMI)—Coral 61636	15	11
21.	**ENGLISH MUFFINS AND IRISH STEW**—S. Syms / Walk Sweet—Decca 29969	—	2
23.	**MORE** (ASCAP)—P. Como / Glendora (BMI)—Vic 20-6554	18	12
24.	**THAT'S ALL THERE IS TO THAT** (BMI)—Nat (King) Cole / My Dream Sonata (ASCAP)—Cap 3456	20	6
24.	**FABULOUS CHARACTER** (ASCAP)—S. Vaughan / Other Woman (ASCAP)—Mercury 70885	—	5

THE TOP 100

For survey week ending September 5

A list of the Top 100 RECORD SIDES in the nation according to a COMBINED TABULATION of Dealer, Disk Jockey and Juke Box Operator replies to The Billboard's weekly popular record Best Seller and Most Played surveys. Its purpose is to provide Disk Jockeys with additional programming material and to give trade exposure to NEWER records just beginning to show action in the field.

Pos.	Song, Artist, Label	Last Week
1.	**DON'T BE CRUEL**—E. Presley, Victor	3
1.	**MY PRAYER**—Platters, Mercury	1
3.	**HOUND DOG**—E. Presley, Victor	2
4.	**WHATEVER WILL BE, WILL BE**—Doris Day, Columbia	3
5.	**CANADIAN SUNSET**—H. Winterhalter-E. Heywood, Victor	6
6.	**ALLEGHENY MOON**—P. Page, Mercury	5
7.	**TONIGHT YOU BELONG TO ME**—Patience & Prudence, Liberty	10
8.	**FLYING SAUCER**—Buchanan & Goodman, Luniverse	7
9.	**CANADIAN SUNSET**—A. Williams, Cadence	15
10.	**I ALMOST LOST MY MIND**—P. Boone, Dot	8
11.	**SONG FOR A SUMMER NIGHT**—M. Miller, Columbia	12
12.	**WAYWARD WIND**—G. Grant, Era	9
13.	**FOOL**—S. Clark, Dot	13
14.	**SOFT, SUMMER BREEZE**—E. Heywood, Mercury	20
15.	**YOU DON'T KNOW ME**—J. Vale, Columbia	19
16.	**HONKY TONK**—B. Doggett, King	22
17.	**AFTER THE LIGHTS GO DOWN LOW**—A. Hibbler, Decca	26
18.	**SWEET, OLD-FASHIONED GIRL**—T. Brewer, Coral	13
19.	**BE-BOP-A-LULA**—G. Vincent, Capitol	15
20.	**I WANT YOU, I NEED YOU, I LOVE YOU**—E. Presley, Victor	11
21.	**MORE**—P. Como, Victor	18
22.	**IT ONLY HURTS FOR A LITTLE WHILE**—Ames Brothers, Victor	21
23.	**THAT'S ALL THERE IS TO THAT**—Nat (King) Cole, Capitol	24
24.	**BORN TO BE WITH YOU**—Chordettes, Cadence	15
25.	**IN THE MIDDLE OF THE HOUSE**—V. Monroe, Victor	40
26.	**HOUSE WITH LOVE IN IT**—Four Lads, Columbia	45
27.	**JUST WALKING IN THE RAIN**—J. Ray, Columbia	41
28.	**WHEN THE WHITE LILACS BLOOM AGAIN**—H. Zacharaias, Decca	46
29.	**BUS STOP SONG**—Four Lads, Columbia	57
30.	**FABULOUS CHARACTER**—S. Vaughan, Mercury	36
30.	**RIP IT UP**—B. Haley, Decca	31
32.	**WHEN THE WHITE LILACS BLOOM AGAIN**—B. Vaughn, Dot	35
33.	**FROM THE CANDY STORE ON THE CORNER**—T. Bennett, Columbia	54
34.	**ON THE STREET WHERE YOU LIVE**—V. Damone, Columbia	25
35.	**HAPPINESS STREET**—G. Gibbs, Mercury	33
35.	**MIRACLE OF LOVE**—E. Rodgers, Columbia	32
37.	**MAMA, TEACH ME TO DANCE**—E. Gorme, ABC-Paramount	34
38.	**LET THE GOOD TIMES ROLL**—Shirley & Lee, Aladdin	36
39.	**MOONGLOW AND THEME FROM "PICNIC"**—M. Stoloff, Decca	28
40.	**RIP IT UP**—Little Richard, Specialty	27
40.	**WHEN MY DREAMBOAT COMES HOME**—F. Domino, Imperial	22
42.	**ST. THERESE OF THE ROSES**—B. Ward, Decca	64
43.	**IN THE MIDDLE OF THE HOUSE**—R. Draper, Mercury	47
44.	**GHOST TOWN**—D. Cherry, Columbia	43
45.	**FEVER**—L. W. John, King	39
46.	**HEAVEN ON EARTH**—Platters, Mercury	51
47.	**SO LONG**—F. Domino, Imperial	70
48.	**OLD PHILOSOPHER**—E. Lawrence, Coral	43
49.	**GIVE US THIS DAY**—J. James, M-G-M	53
50.	**CASUAL LOOK**—Six Teens, Flip	48
51.	**ITALIAN THEME**—C. Stapleton, London	64
52.	**HAPPINESS STREET**—T. Bennett, Columbia	57
53.	**STRANDED IN THE JUNGLE**—Cadets, Modern	51
54.	**TRUE LOVE**—Bing Crosby & Grace Kelly, Capitol	64
55.	**OUT OF SIGHT, OUT OF MIND**—Five Keys, Capitol	—
56.	**CHAINS OF LOVE**—P. Boone, Dot	—
57.	**KA DING DONG**—G. Clefs, Pilgrim	55
58.	**SOMEBODY UP THERE LIKES ME**—P. Como, Victor	30
59.	**ENGLISH MUFFINS AND IRISH STEW**—S. Syms, Decca	79
60.	**IN THE STILL OF THE NIGHT**—Satins, Ember	95
61.	**SEE-SAW**—Moonglows, Chess	90
62.	**FOOL**—Gallahads, Jubilee	68
62.	**TRUE LOVE**—J. Powell, Verve	72
64.	**I WALK THE LINE**—J. Cash, Sun	—
65.	**APE CALL**—N. Norvus, Dot	41
66.	**FORTY-NINE SHADES OF GREEN**—Ames Brothers, Victor	77
67.	**KA DING DONG**—Diamonds, Mercury	88
68.	**NOW IS THE HOUR**—G. Storm, Dot	—
69.	**GLENDORA**—P. Como, Victor	29
69.	**TUMBLING TUMBLEWEED**—R. Williams, Kapp	62
71.	**KA DING DONG**—Hilltoppers, Dot	—
71.	**WEARY BLUES**—McGuire Sisters, Coral	49
73.	**I'M IN LOVE AGAIN**—F. Domino, Imperial	38
74.	**BEAUTIFUL FRIENDSHIP**—E. Fitzgerald, Decca	—
75.	**HEARTACHES**—S. Smith, Epic	98
75.	**WHERE THERE'S LIFE**—G. Cates, Coral	—
77.	**YOU'RE SENSATIONAL**—F. Sinatra, Capitol	61
78.	**VOICES**—Fontane Sisters, Dot	87
79.	**I DON'T WANT NOBODY**—W. Herman, Capitol	—
80.	**TREASURE OF LOVE**—C. McPhatter, Atlantic	80
81.	**EARTHBOUND**—S. Davis Jr., Decca	83
82.	**SUMMER SWEETHEART**—Ames Brothers, Victor	100
83.	**WHEN THE WHITE LILACS BLOOM AGAIN**—L. Holmes, M-G-M	82
84.	**THEME FROM "THE PROUD ONES"**—N. Riddle, Capitol	63
85.	**EXPERIMENTS WITH MICE**—J. Dankworth, Capitol	91
85.	**LOVE, LOVE, LOVE**—Clovers, Atlantic	49
87.	**WHEN THE WHITE LILACS BLOOM AGAIN**—F. ZaBach, Mercury	83
88.	**FRIENDLY PERSUASION**—P. Boone, Dot	—
89.	**MY BLUE HEAVEN**—F. Domino, Imperial	91
90.	**WHEN THE TIDE IS HIGH**—G. Grant, Era	—
90.	**YOU'RE IN LOVE**—G. Grant, Era	—
92.	**GOOD BOOK**—K. Starr, Victor	97
93.	**EARTHBOUND**—M. Lanza, Victor	—
93.	**HOW LUCKY YOU ARE**—J. James, M-G-M	96
93.	**LOLA'S THEME**—S. Allen, Coral	91
93.	**WHEN THE WHITE LILACS BLOOM AGAIN**—L. Welk, Coral	—
97.	**TEEN-AGER'S MOTHER**—B. Haley, Decca	—
98.	**HAPPY WHISTLER**—D. Robertson, Capitol	—
98.	**I ONLY KNOW I LOVE YOU**—Four Aces, Decca	57
100.	**LOVE, LOVE, LOVE**—Diamonds, Mercury	64
100.	**PICNIC**—McGuire Sisters, Coral	76
100.	**THINGS I NEVER HAD**—K. Starr, Victor	89

CAUTION TO DEALERS AND JUKE BOX OPERATORS

The Billboard's Top 100 is NOT designed to provide tested information for buying purposes. This function is most reliably served by other regular weekly features: Best Sellers in Stores, Most Played in Juke Boxes, Coming Up Strong and Best Buys.

• Best Sellers in Stores

For survey week ending September 12

RECORDS are ranked in order of their current national selling importance at the retail level, as determined by The Billboard's weekly survey of the top volume dealers in every important market area. When significant action is reported on both sides of a record, points are combined to determine position on the chart. In such a case, both sides are listed in bold type, the leading side on top.

This Week		Last Week	Weeks on Chart
1.	**DON'T BE CRUEL** (BMI)—E. Presley Hound Dog (BMI)—Vic 20-6604	1	8
2.	**MY PRAYER** (ASCAP)—Platters Heaven on Earth (ASCAP)—Mercury 70893	2	11
3.	**WHATEVER WILL BE, WILL BE** (ASCAP)—Doris Day I Gotta Sing Away These Blues (BMI)—Col 40704	3	12
4.	**CANADIAN SUNSET** (BMI)—H. Winterhalter This Is Real (ASCAP)—Vic 20-6537	4	9
5.	**TONIGHT YOU BELONG TO ME** (ASCAP)—Patience & Prudence A Smile and a Ribbon (ASCAP)—Liberty 55022	5	5
6.	**HONKY TONK (PARTS I & II)**—B. Doggett King 4950—BMI	7	5
7.	**FOOL** (BMI)—S. Clark Lonesome for a Letter (BMI)—Dot 15481	9	7
8.	**ALLEGHENY MOON** (ASCAP)—P. Page Strangest Romance (ASCAP)—Mercury 70878	8	12
9.	**FLYING SAUCER**—Buchanan & Goodman Luniverse 101	6	7
10.	**JUST WALKING IN THE RAIN** (BMI)—J. Ray In the Candlelight (ASCAP)—Col 40729	15	3
11.	**CANADIAN SUNSET** (BMI)—A. Williams High Upon a Mountain (ASCAP)—Cadence 1297	10	4
12.	**SONG FOR A SUMMER NIGHT (PARTS I & II)** (ASCAP)—M. Miller Col 40730—ASCAP	12	7
13.	**SOFT SUMMER BREEZE** (BMI)—E. Heywood Heywood's Bounce (BMI)—Mercury 70863	13	10
14.	**BE-BOP-A-LULA** (BMI)—G. Vincent Woman Love (BMI)—Cap 3450	11	14
15.	**YOU DON'T KNOW ME** (BMI)—J. Vale Enchanted (ASCAP)—Col 40710	16	8
16.	**I WANT YOU, I NEED YOU, I LOVE YOU** (BMI)—E. Presley My Baby Left Me (BMI)—Vic 20-6540	18	17
17.	**HOUSE WITH LOVE IN IT**—Four Lads **BUS STOP SONG** (ASCAP)—Col 40736	—	1
18.	**I ALMOST LOST MY MIND** (BMI)—P. Boone I'm in Love With You (BMI)—Dot 15472	14	15
19.	**WHEN THE WHITE LILACS BLOOM AGAIN** (ASCAP)—H. Zacharaias Blue Blues (BMI)—Dec 30039	21	2
20.	**AFTER THE LIGHTS GO DOWN LOW** (BMI)—A. Hibbler I Was Telling Her About You (ASCAP)—Dec 29982	21	2
21.	**THAT'S ALL THERE IS TO THAT** (BMI)—Nat (King) Cole My Dream Sonata (ASCAP)—Cap 3456	20	10
22.	**FRIENDLY PERSUASION** (ASCAP)—P. Boone **CHAINS OF LOVE** (BMI)—Dot 15490	—	1
23.	**ST. THERESE OF THE ROSES** (BMI)—B. Ward Home Is Where You Hang Your Heart (BMI)—Dec 29933	—	1
24.	**MIRACLE OF LOVE** (ASCAP)—E. Rodgers Unwanted Heart (ASCAP)—Col 40708	—	1
25.	**IT ONLY HURTS FOR A LITTLE WHILE** (ASCAP)—Ames Brothers If You Want to See Mamie Tonight (ASCAP)—Vic 20-6481	19	17

• Most Played in Juke Boxes

For survey week ending September 12

RECORDS are ranked in order of the greatest number of plays in juke boxes thruout the country, as determined by The Billboard's weekly survey of the nation's juke box operators. When significant play is reported on both sides of a record, points are combined to determine position on the chart. In such a case, both sides are listed in bold type, the leading side on top.

This Week		Last Week	Weeks on Chart
1.	**DON'T BE CRUEL** (BMI)—E. Presley **HOUND DOG** (BMI)—Vic 20-6604	1	7
2.	**MY PRAYER** (ASCAP)—Platters Heaven on Earth (ASCAP)—Mercury 70893	2	10
3.	**WHATEVER WILL BE, WILL BE** (ASCAP)—Doris Day I Gotta Sing Away These Blues (BMI)—Col 40704	3	9
4.	**CANADIAN SUNSET** (BMI)—H. Winterhalter-E. Heywood This Is Real (ASCAP)—Vic 20-6537	5	6
5.	**ALLEGHENY MOON** (ASCAP)—P. Page Strangest Romance (ASCAP)—Mercury 70878	4	12
6.	**TONIGHT YOU BELONG TO ME** (ASCAP)—Patience & Prudence A Smile and a Ribbon (ASCAP)—Liberty 55022	10	3
7.	**I ALMOST LOST MY MIND** (BMI)—P. Boone I'm in Love With You (BMI)—Dot 15472	6	15
8.	**I WANT YOU, I NEED YOU, I LOVE YOU** (BMI)—E. Presley My Baby Left Me (BMI)—Vic 20-6540	7	16
8.	**FOOL** (BMI)—S. Clark Lonesome for a Letter (BMI)—Dot 15481	15	5
10.	**CANADIAN SUNSET** (BMI)—A. Williams High Upon the Mountain (ASCAP)—Cadence 1297	12	3
11.	**FLYING SAUCER (PARTS I & II)**—Buchanan & Goodman Luniverse 101	9	5
12.	**HONKY TONK (PARTS I & II)** (BMI)—B. Doggett King 4950	17	2
13.	**SONG FOR A SUMMER NIGHT (PARTS I & II)** (ASCAP)—M. Miller Columbia 40730	19	5
13.	**BE-BOP-A-LULA** (BMI)—G. Vincent Woman Love (BMI)—Cap 3450	14	11
15.	**WAYWARD WIND** (BMI)—G. Grant No More Than Forever (ASCAP)—Era 1013	8	17
15.	**SOFT SUMMER BREEZE** (BMI)—E. Heywood Heywood's Bounce (BMI)—Mercury 70863	20	3
17.	**IT ONLY HURTS FOR A LITTLE WHILE** (ASCAP)—Ames Brothers If You Want to See Mamie Tonight (ASCAP)—Vic 20-6481	11	14
18.	**YOU DON'T KNOW ME** (BMI)—J. Vale Enchanted (ASCAP)—Col 40710	20	3
18.	**JUST WALKING IN THE RAIN** (BMI)—J. Ray In the Candlelight (ASCAP)—Col 40729	—	1
20.	**SWEET, OLD-FASHIONED GIRL** (ASCAP)—T. Brewer Goodbye, John (BMI)—Coral 61636	13	11
20.	**AFTER THE LIGHTS GO DOWN LOW** (BMI)—A. Hibbler I Was Telling Her About You (ASCAP)—Dec 29982	—	1

• Best Selling Sheet Music

Tunes are ranked in order of their current national selling importance at the sheet music jobber level.

This Week		Last Week	Weeks on Chart
1.	**Whatever Will Be, Will Be (Que Sera Sera)** (Artists Music)	1	11
2.	**Allegheny Moon** (Oxford)	2	13
3.	**Canadian Sunset** (Meridian)	3	7
4.	**My Prayer** (Shapiro-Bernstein)	4	10
5.	**Soft Summer Breeze** (Regent)	5	4
6.	**Song for a Summer Night** (April)	5	5
7.	**Wayward Wind** (Warman)	7	7
8.	**Don't Be Cruel** (Presley-Shalimar)	11	2
9.	**Tonight You Belong to Me** (Mills)	9	3
10.	**Hound Dog** (Presley-Lion)	8	5
11.	**On the Street Where You Live** (Chappell)	9	10
12.	**I Almost Lost My Mind** (Hill & Range)	15	13
13.	**I Want You, I Need You, I Love You** (Presley)	—	8
14.	**Walk Hand in Hand** (Republic)	12	19
15.	**Happiness Street** (Planetary)	—	1

• Most Played by Jockeys

For survey week ending September 12

SIDES are ranked in order of the greatest number of plays on disk jockey radio shows thruout the country. Results are based on The Billboard's weekly survey among the nation's disk jockeys. The reverse side of each record is also listed.

This Week		Last Week	Weeks on Chart
1.	**DON'T BE CRUEL** (BMI)—E. Presley Hound Dog (BMI)—Vic 20-6604	1	7
2.	**MY PRAYER** (ASCAP)—Platters Heaven on Earth (ASCAP)—Mercury 70893	2	11
3.	**WHATEVER WILL BE, WILL BE** (ASCAP)—Doris Day I Gotta Sing Away These Blues (BMI)—Col 40704	3	12
4.	**CANADIAN SUNSET** (BMI)—E. Heywood-H. Winterhalter This Is Real (ASCAP)—Vic 20-6537	5	9
5.	**HOUND DOG** (BMI)—E. Presley Don't Be Cruel (BMI)—Vic 20-6604	4	8
6.	**ALLEGHENY MOON** (ASCAP)—P. Page Strangest Romance (ASCAP)—Mercury 70878	6	13
7.	**TONIGHT YOU BELONG TO ME** (ASCAP)—Patience & Prudence A Smile and a Ribbon (ASCAP)—Liberty 55022	7	5
8.	**SONG FOR A SUMMER NIGHT (PARTS I & II)** (ASCAP)—M. Miller Col 40730	9	7
9.	**CANADIAN SUNSET** (BMI)—A. Williams High Upon a Mountain (ASCAP)—Cadence 1297	8	6
10.	**AFTER THE LIGHTS GO DOWN LOW** (BMI)—A. Hibbler I Was Telling Her About You (ASCAP) Decca 29982	12	4
11.	**IN THE MIDDLE OF THE HOUSE** (ASCAP)—V. Monroe Rollin' Heart (BMI)—Vic 20-6619	17	2
12.	**WHEN THE WHITE LILACS BLOOM AGAIN** (ASCAP)—H. Zacharias Blue Blues—Dec 30039	—	2
13.	**HONKY TONK (PARTS I & II)** (BMI)—B. Doggett King 4950	—	1
14.	**SOFT SUMMER BREEZE**—E. Heywood Heywood's Bounce (BMI)—Mercury 70863	14	6
15.	**FROM THE CANDY STORE ON THE CORNER** (ASCAP)—T. Bennett Happiness Street (ASCAP)—Col 40726	11	2
16.	**FOOL** (BMI)—S. Clark Lonesome for a Letter (BMI)—Dot 15481	19	4
17.	**I ALMOST LOST MY MIND** (BMI)—P. Boone I'm in Love With You (BMI)—Dot 15472	18	15
18.	**ST. THERESE OF THE ROSES** (BMI)—B. Ward Home Is Where You Hang Your Heart (BMI)—Dec 29933	13	2
18.	**FRIENDLY PERSUASION** (ASCAP)—P. Boone Chains of Love (ASCAP)—Dot 15490	—	1
20.	**YOU DON'T KNOW ME** (BMI)—J. Vale Enchanted (ASCAP)—Col 40710	15	6
21.	**HAPPINESS STREET** (ASCAP)—G. Gibbs Happiness Is a Thing Called Joe (ASCAP)—Mercury 70920	20	4
22.	**FLYING SAUCER (PARTS I & II)**—Buchanan & Goodman Luniverse 101	10	7
23.	**THAT'S ALL THERE IS TO THAT** (BMI)—Nat (King) Cole My Dream Sonata (ASCAP)—Cap 3456	24	7
24.	**ENGLISH MUFFINS AND IRISH STEW**—S. Syms Walk Sweet—Decca 29969	21	3
25.	**MORE** (ASCAP)—P. Como Glendora (BMI)—Vic 20-6554	23	13

THE TOP 100

For survey week ending September 12

A list of the Top 100 RECORD SIDES in the nation according to a COMBINED TABULATION of Dealer, Disk Jockey and Juke Box Operator replies to The Billboard's weekly popular record Best Seller and Most Played surveys. Its purpose is to provide Disk Jockeys with additional programming material and to give trade exposure to NEWER records just beginning to show action in the field.

Pos.	Song, Artist, Label	Last Week
1.	**DON'T BE CRUEL**—E. Presley, Victor	1
2.	**MY PRAYER**—Platters, Mercury	1
3.	**HOUND DOG**—E. Presley, Victor	3
4.	**WHATEVER WILL BE, WILL BE**—Doris Day, Columbia	4
5.	**CANADIAN SUNSET**—H. Winterhalter-E. Heywood, Victor	5
6.	**TONIGHT YOU BELONG TO ME**—Patience & Prudence, Liberty	7
7.	**ALLEGHENY MOON**—P. Page, Mercury	6
8.	**CANADIAN SUNSET**—A. Williams, Cadence	9
9.	**FOOL**—S. Clark, Dot	13
9.	**HONKY TONK**—B. Doggett, King	16
11.	**SONG FOR A SUMMER NIGHT**—M. Miller, Columbia	11
12.	**I ALMOST LOST MY MIND**—P. Boone, Dot	10
13.	**FLYING SAUCER**—Buchanan & Goodman, Luniverse	8
13.	**SOFT SUMMER BREEZE**—E. Heywood, Mercury	14
15.	**AFTER THE LIGHTS GO DOWN LOW**—A. Hibbler, Decca	17
16.	**YOU DON'T KNOW ME**—J. Vale, Columbia	15
17.	**JUST WALKING IN THE RAIN**—J. Ray, Columbia	27
18.	**WHEN THE WHITE LILACS BLOOM AGAIN**—H. Zacharias, Decca	28
19.	**THAT'S ALL THERE IS TO THAT**—N. (King) Cole, Capitol	23
20.	**IT ONLY HURTS FOR A LITTLE WHILE**—Ames Brothers, Victor	32
21.	**IN THE MIDDLE OF THE HOUSE**—V. Monroe, Victor	25
22.	**I WANT YOU, I NEED YOU, I LOVE YOU**—E. Presley, Victor	20
23.	**MORE**—P. Como, Victor	21
24.	**WAYWARD WIND**—G. Grant, Era	12
25.	**HOUSE WITH LOVE IN IT**—Four Lads, Columbia	26
26.	**BE-BOP-A-LULA**—G. Vincent, Capitol	19
27.	**SWEET, OLD-FASHIONED GIRL**—T. Brewer, Coral	18
28.	**BUS STOP SONG**—Four Lads, Columbia	29
28.	**WAYWARD WIND**—T. Ritter, Capitol	—
30.	**BORN TO BE WITH YOU**—Chordettes, Cadence	24
31.	**IN THE MIDDLE OF THE HOUSE**—R. Draper, Mercury	43
32.	**HAPPINESS STREET**—G. Gibbs, Mercury	35
33.	**MIRACLE OF LOVE**—E. Rodgers, Columbia	35
34.	**WHEN MY DREAMBOAT COMES HOME**—F. Domino, Imperial	40
35.	**FROM THE CANDY STORE ON THE CORNER**—T. Bennett, Columbia	33
35.	**WHEN THE WHITE LILACS BLOOM AGAIN**—B. Vaughn, Dot	35
37.	**LET THE GOOD TIMES ROLL**—Shirley & Lee, Aladdin	38
38.	**GHOST TOWN**—D. Cherry, Columbia	44
38.	**ST. THERESE OF THE ROSES**—B. Ward, Decca	42
40.	**RIP IT UP**—B. Haley, Decca	30
41.	**HAPPINESS STREET**—T. Bennett, Columbia	52
42.	**FEVER**—L. W. John, King	45
43.	**ON THE STREET WHERE YOU LIVE**—V. Damone, Columbia	34
44.	**FRIENDLY PERSUASION**—P. Boone, Dot	88
44.	**ITALIAN THEME**—C. Stapleton, London	51
44.	**RIP IT UP**—Little Richard, Specialty	40
47.	**SOMEBODY UP THERE LIKES ME**—P. Como, Victor	58
48.	**FABULOUS CHARACTER**—S. Vaughan, Mercury	30
49.	**CHANGE OF LOVE**—P. Boone, Dot	56
50.	**KA DING DONG**—Diamonds, Mercury	67
51.	**HEAVEN ON EARTH**—Platters, Mercury	46
52.	**OUT OF SIGHT, OUT OF MIND**—Five Keys, Capitol	55
53.	**IN THE STILL OF THE NIGHT**—Satins, Ember	60
54.	**GREEN DOOR**—J. Lowe, Dot	—
55.	**TRUE LOVE**—Bing Crosby-Grace Kelly, Capitol	54
56.	**KA DING DONG**—G-Clefs, Pilgrim	57
57.	**SEE SAW**—Moonglows, Chess	61
58.	**KA DING DONG**—Hilltoppers, Dot	71
59.	**WHEN THE WHITE LILACS BLOOM AGAIN**—L. Holmes, M-G-M	83
60.	**FRIENDLY PERSUASION**—Four Aces, Decca	—
61.	**TONIGHT YOU BELONG TO ME**—Lennon Sisters-L. Welk, Coral	—
62.	**MOONGLOW AND THEME FROM "PICNIC"**—M. Stoloff, Decca	39
63.	**ENGLISH MUFFINS AND IRISH STEW**—S. Syms, Decca	59
63.	**I'M IN LOVE AGAIN**—F. Domino, Imperial	73
65.	**MAMA, TEACH ME TO DANCE**—E. Gorme, ABC-Paramount	37
66.	**SO-LONG**—F. Domino, Imperial	47
66.	**WHEN THE WHITE LILACS BLOOM AGAIN**—F. ZaBach, Mercury	87
68.	**EVERY DAY OF MY LIFE**—McGuire Sisters, Coral	—
69.	**SADIE'S SHAWL**—B. Sharples, London	—
70.	**TUMBLING TUMBLEWEED**—R. Williams, Kapp	69
71.	**TRUE LOVE**—J. Powell, Verve	52
72.	**OLD PHILOSOPHER**—E. Lawrence, Coral	48
73.	**STRANDED IN THE JUNGLE**—Cadets, Modern	53
73.	**WHEN THE WHITE LILACS BLOOM AGAIN**—L. Welk, Coral	93
73.	**ONE KISS LED TO ANOTHER**—Coasters, Atco	—
76.	**CASUAL LOOK**—Six Teens, Flip	50
77.	**WHERE THERE'S LIFE**—G Cates, Coral	75
78.	**HEARTACHES**—S. Smith, Epic	75
79.	**FROM THE CANDY STORE ON THE CORNER**—Rover Boys, ABC-Paramount	—
80.	**FORTY-NINE SHADES OF GREEN**—Ames Brothers, Victor	66
81.	**FOOL**—Gallahads, Jubilee	62
81.	**I WALK THE LINE**—J. Cash, Sun	64
83.	**DON'T CRY**—F. Laine, Columbia	—
83.	**I ONLY KNOW I LOVE YOU**—Four Aces, Decca	98
83.	**NOW IS THE HOUR**—G. Storm, Dot	68
86.	**WAR AND PEACE**—V. Damone, Columbia	—
87.	**GIVE US THIS DAY**—J. James, M-G-M	49
87.	**DEAR ELVIS**—Audrey Plus	—
89.	**EARTHBOUND**—S. Davis Jr., Decca	81
89.	**I LOVE MICKEY**—T. Brewer, Coral	—
91.	**LOVE, LOVE, LOVE**—Diamonds, Mercury	100
92.	**WELL, DID YOU EVAH?**—Bing Crosby-F. Sinatra, Capitol	—
92.	**SOFT SUMMER BREEZE**—Diamonds, Mercury	—
94.	**I DON'T WANT NOBODY**—W. Herman, Capitol	79
95.	**EARTHBOUND**—M. Lanza, Victor	93
96.	**ENDLESS**—McGuire Sisters, Coral	—
97.	**TEEN-AGER'S MOTHER**—B. Haley, Decca	97
98.	**GLENDORA**—P. Como, Victor	69
99.	**YOU'RE SENSATIONAL**—F. Sinatra, Capitol	77
100.	**APE CALL**—N. Norvus, Dot	65

CAUTION TO DEALERS AND JUKE BOX OPERATORS

The Billboard's Top 100 is NOT designed to provide tested information for buying purposes. This function is most reliably served by other regular weekly features: Best Sellers in Stores, Most Played in Juke Boxes, Coming Up Strong and Best Buys.

• Best Sellers in Stores

For survey week ending September 19

RECORDS are ranked in order of their current national selling importance at the retail level, as determined by The Billboard's weekly survey of the top volume dealers in every important market area. When significant action is reported on both sides of a record, points are combined to determine position on the chart. In such a case, both sides are listed in bold type, the leading side on top.

This Week		Last Week	Weeks on Chart
1.	**DON'T BE CRUEL** (BMI)—E. Presley. **HOUND DOG** (BMI)—Vic 20-6604	1	9
2.	**MY PRAYER** (ASCAP)—Platters. Heaven on Earth (ASCAP)—Mercury 70893	2	12
3.	**CANADIAN SUNSET** (BMI)—H. Winterhalter. This Is Real (ASCAP)—Vic 20-6537	4	10
4.	**WHATEVER WILL BE, WILL BE** (ASCAP)—Doris Day. I Gotta Sing Away These Blues (BMI)—Col 40704	3	13
5.	**HONKY TONK (PARTS I & II)**—B. Doggett. King 4950—BMI	6	6
6.	**TONIGHT YOU BELONG TO ME** (ASCAP)—Patience & Prudence. A Smile and a Ribbon (ASCAP)—Liberty 55022	5	6
7.	**FOOL** (BMI)—S. Clark. Lonesome for a Letter (BMI)—Dot 15481	7	8
8.	**JUST WALKING IN THE RAIN** (BMI)—J. Ray. In the Candlelight (ASCAP)—Col 40729	10	4
9.	**ALLEGHENY MOON** (ASCAP)—P. Page. Strangest Romance (ASCAP)—Mercury 70878	8	13
10.	**CANADIAN SUNSET** (BMI)—A. Williams. High Upon a Mountain (ASCAP)—Cadence 1297	11	5
11.	**SOFT SUMMER BREEZE** (BMI)—E. Heywood. Heywood's Bounce (BMI)—Mercury 70863	13	11
12.	**SONG FOR A SUMMER NIGHT (PARTS I & II)** (ASCAP)—M. Miller. Col 40730—ASCAP	12	8
13.	**FLYING SAUCER**—Buchanan & Goodman. Luniverse 101	9	8
14.	**YOU DON'T KNOW ME** (BMI)—J. Vale. Enchanted (ASCAP)—Col 40710	15	9
15.	**CHAINS OF LOVE** (BMI)—P. Boone. **FRIENDLY PERSUASION** (ASCAP)—Dot 15490	22	2
16.	**GREEN DOOR** (BMI)—J. Lowe. (Story of) The Little Man in Chinatown (BMI)—Dot 15486	—	1
17.	**BE-BOP-A-LULA** (BMI)—G. Vincent. Woman Love (BMI)—Cap 3450	14	15
18.	**I WANT YOU, I NEED YOU, I LOVE YOU** (BMI)—E. Presley. My Baby Left Me (BMI)—Vic 20-6540	16	18
19.	**WHEN THE WHITE LILACS BLOOM AGAIN** (ASCAP)—H. Zacharias. Blue Blues (BMI)—Dec 30039	19	3
20.	**ST. THERESE OF THE ROSES** (BMI)—B. Ward. Home Is Where You Hang Your Heart (BMI)—Dec 29933	23	2
21.	**TONIGHT YOU BELONG TO ME** (ASCAP)—Lennon Sisters-L. Welk. When the White Lilacs Bloom Again (ASCAP) Coral 61701	—	1
22.	**BUS STOP SONG** (ASCAP)—Four Lads. **HOUSE WITH LOVE IN IT** (ASCAP)—Col 40736	17	2
23.	**AFTER THE LIGHTS GO DOWN LOW** (BMI)—A. Hibbler. I Was Telling Her About You (ASCAP)—Dec 29982	20	3
24.	**MIRACLE OF LOVE** (ASCAP)—E. Rodgers. Unwanted Heart (ASCAP)—Col 40708	24	2
25.	**I ALMOST LOST MY MIND** (BMI)—P. Boone. I'm in Love With You (BMI)—Dot 15472	18	16

• Most Played in Juke Boxes

For survey week ending September 19

RECORDS are ranked in order of the greatest number of plays in juke boxes thruout the country, as determined by The Billboard's weekly survey of the nation's juke box operators. When significant play is reported on both sides of a record, points are combined to determine position on the chart. In such a case, both sides are listed in bold type, the leading side on top.

This Week		Last Week	Weeks on Chart
1.	**HOUND DOG** (BMI)—E. Presley. **DON'T BE CRUEL** (BMI)—Vic 20-6604	1	8
2.	**MY PRAYER** (ASCAP)—Platters. Heaven on Earth (ASCAP)—Mercury 70893	2	11
3.	**WHATEVER WILL BE, WILL BE** (ASCAP)—Doris Day. I Gotta Sing Away These Blues (BMI)—Col 40704	3	10
4.	**CANADIAN SUNSET** (MBI)—H. Winterhalter-E. Heywood. This Is Real (ASCAP)—Vic 20-6537	4	7
5.	**ALLEGHENY MOON** (ASCAP)—P. Page. Strangest Romance (ASCAP)—Mercury 70878	5	13
6.	**TONIGHT YOU BELONG TO ME** (ASCAP)—Patience & Prudence. A Smile and a Ribbon (ASCAP)—Liberty 55022	6	4
7.	**FOOL** (BMI)—S. Clark. Lonesome For a Letter (BMI)—Dot 15481	8	6
8.	**HONKY TONK (Parts I & II)** (BMI)—B. Doggett. King 4950	12	3
9.	**CANADIAN SUNSET** (BMI)—A. Williams. The Mountain (ASCAP)—Cadence 1297	10	4
9.	**I ALMOST LOST MY MIND** (BMI)—P. Boone. I'm In Love With You (BMI)—Dot 15472	7	16
11.	**SONG FOR A SUMMER NIGHT (Parts I & II)** (ASCAP)—M. Miller. Columbia 40730	13	6
12.	**FLYING SAUCER (Parts I & II)**—Buchanan & Goodman. Luniverse 101	11	6
13.	**I WANT YOU, I NEED YOU, I LOVE YOU** (BMI)—E. Presley. My Baby Left Me (BMI)—Vic 20-6540	8	17
14.	**YOU DON'T KNOW ME** (BMI)—J. Vale. Enchanted (ASCAP)—Col 40710	18	4
14.	**SOFT SUMMER BREEZE** (BMI)—E. Heywood. Heywood's Bounce (BMI)—Mercury 70863	15	4
14.	**JUST WALKING IN THE RAIN** (BMI)—J. Ray. In the Candlelight (ASCAP)—Col 40729	18	2
17.	**BE-BOP-A-LULA** (BMI)—G. Vincent. Woman Love (BMI)—Cap 3450	13	12
18.	**WHEN THE WHITE LILACS BLOOM AGAIN** (ASCAP)—B. Vaughn. Spanish Diary (ASCAP)—Dot 15491	—	1
19.	**WAYWARD WIND** (BMI)—G. Grant. No More Than Forever (ASCAP)—Era 1013	15	18
19.	**WHEN MY DREAMBOAT COMES HOME** (ASCAP)—F. Domino. So Long (BMI)—Imperial 5316	—	4

• Best Selling Sheet Music

Tunes are ranked in order of their current national selling importance at the sheet music jobber level.

This Week		Last Week	Weeks on Chart
1.	**Allegheny Moon** (Oxford)	2	14
2.	**Whatever Will Be, Will Be (Que Sera Sera)** (Artists Music)	1	12
3.	**Canadian Sunset** (Meridian)	3	8
4.	**Soft Summer Breeze** (Regent)	5	5
5.	**Song for a Summer Night** (April)	6	6
6.	**Tonight You Belong to Me** (Mills)	9	4
7.	**My Prayer** (Shapiro-Bernstein)	4	11
8.	**Don't Be Cruel** (Presley-Shalimar)	8	3
9.	**Wayward Wind** (Warman)	7	8
10.	**Hound Dog** (Presley-Lion)	10	6
11.	**Happiness Street** (Planetary)	15	2
11.	**You Don't Know Me** (Hill & Range)	—	1
13.	**True Love** (Buxton Hill)	—	1
14.	**Walk Hand in Hand** (Republic)	14	20
15.	**When the White Lilacs Bloom Again** (Harms)	—	1

• Most Played by Jockeys

For survey week ending September 19

SIDES are ranked in order of the greatest number of plays on disk jockey radio shows thruout the country. Results are based on The Billboard's weekly survey among the nation's disk jockeys. The reverse side of each record is also listed.

This Week		Last Week	Weeks on Chart
1.	**DON'T BE CRUEL** (BMI)—E. Presley. Hound Dog (BMI)—Vic 20-6604	1	8
2.	**MY PRAYER** (ASCAP)—Platters. Heaven on Earth (ASCAP)—Mercury 70893	2	12
3.	**CANADIAN SUNSET** (BMI)—H. Winterhalter-E. Heywood. This Is Real (ASCAP)—Vic 20-6537	4	10
4.	**WHATEVER WILL BE, WILL BE** (ASCAP)—Doris Day. Away These Blues (BMI)—Col 40704	3	13
5.	**HOUND DOG** (BMI)—E. Presley. Don't Be Cruel (BMI)—Vic 20-6604	5	9
6.	**TONIGHT YOU BELONG TO ME** (ASCAP)—Patience & Prudence. A Smile and a Ribbon (ASCAP)—Liberty 55022	7	6
7.	**CANADIAN SUNSET** (BMI)—A. Williams. High Upon a Mountain (ASCAP)—Cadence 1297	9	7
8.	**SONG FOR A SUMMER NIGHT (Parts I & II)**—M. Miller. Col 40730	8	8
9.	**HONKY TONK (Parts I & II)**—B. Doggett. King 4950	13	2
10.	**ALLEGHENY MOON** (ASCAP)—P. Page. Strangest Romance (ASCAP)—Mercury 70878	6	14
11.	**JUST WALKING IN THE RAIN** (BMI)—J. Ray. In the Candlelight (ASCAP)—Col 40792	—	1
12.	**FRIENDLY PERSUASION** (ASCAP) P. Boone. Chains of Love (ASCAP)—Dot 15490	18	2
13.	**AFTER THE LIGHTS GO DOWN LOW** (BMI)—A. Hibbler. I Was Telling Her About You (ASCAP)—Dec 29982	10	5
14.	**SOFT SUMMER BREEZE** (BMI)—E. Heywood. Heywood's Bounce (BMI)—Mercury 70863	14	7
15.	**YOU DON'T KNOW ME** (BMI) J. Vale. Enchanted (ASCAP)—Col 40710	20	7
16.	**IN THE MIDDLE OF THE HOUSE** (ASCAP)—V. Monroe. Rollin' Heart (BMI)—Vic 20-6619	11	3
17.	**WHEN THE WHITE LILACS BLOOM AGAIN** (ASCAP)—H. Zacharias. Blue Blues (BMI)—Dec 30039	12	3
18.	**FROM THE CANDY STORE OF THE CORNER** (ASCAP)—T. Bennett. Happiness Street (ASCAP)—Col 40726	15	3
19.	**FOOL** (BMI)—S. Clark. Lonesome for a Letter (BMI)—Dot 15481	16	5
20.	**HOUSE WITH LOVE IN IT** (ASCAP) Four Lads. Bus Stop Song (ASCAP)—Col 40736	—	1
21.	**WHEN THE WHITE LILACS BLOOM AGAIN** (ASCAP)—B. Vaughn. Spanish Diary (ASCAP)—Dot 15491	—	1
22.	**ST. THERESE OF THE ROSES** (BMI)—B. Ward. Home Is Where You Hang Your Heart (BMI)—Dec 29933	18	3
23.	**GREEN DOOR** (BMI)—J. Lowe. (The Story of) The Little Man In Chinatown (BMI)—Dot 15486	—	1
24.	**BUS STOP SONG** (ASCAP)—Four Lads. House With Love In It (ASCAP)—Col 40736	—	1
25.	**I ALMOST LOST MY MIND** (BMI)—P. Boone. I'm In Love With You (BMI)—Dot 15472	17	16

THE TOP 100

For survey week ending September 19

A list of the Top 100 RECORD SIDES in the nation according to a COMBINED TABULATION of Dealer, Disk Jockey and Juke Box Operator replies to The Billboard's weekly popular record Best Seller and Most Played surveys. Its purpose is to provide Disk Jockeys with additional programming material and to give trade exposure to NEWER records just beginning to show action in the field.

Pos.	Song, Artist, Label	Last Week
1.	DON'T BE CRUEL—E. Presley, Victor	1
2.	MY PRAYER—Platters, Mercury	2
3.	HOUND DOG—E. Presley, Victor	3
4.	CANADIAN SUNSET—E. Heywood-H. Winterhalter, Victor	5
5.	WHATEVER WILL BE, WILL BE—Doris Day, Columbia	4
6.	TONIGHT YOU BELONG TO ME—Patience & Prudence, Liberty	6
7.	HONKY TONK—B. Doggett, King	9
8.	ALLEGHENY MOON—P. Page, Mercury	7
9.	CANADIAN SUNSET—A. Williams, Cadence	8
10.	SONG FOR A SUMMER NIGHT—M. Miller, Columbia	11
11.	FOOL—S. Clark, Dot	9
11.	JUST WALKING IN THE RAIN—J. Ray, Columbia	17
13.	SOFT SUMMER BREEZE—E. Heywood, Mercury	13
14.	YOU DON'T KNOW ME—J. Vale, Columbia	16
15.	FLYING SAUCER—Buchanan & Goodman, Luniverse	13
16.	WHEN THE WHITE LILACS BLOOM AGAIN—H. Zacharaias, Decca	18
17.	AFTER THE LIGHTS GO DOWN LOW—A. Hibbler, Decca	15
18.	I ALMOST LOST MY MIND—P. Boone, Dot	12
19.	I WANT YOU, I NEED YOU, I LOVE YOU—E. Presley, Victor	22
20.	WAYWARD WIND—G. Grant, Era	24
21.	THAT'S ALL THERE IS TO THAT—N. (King) Cole, Capitol	19
22.	WHEN THE WHITE LILACS BLOOM AGAIN—B. Vaughn, Dot	35
23.	IN THE MIDDLE OF THE HOUSE—V. Monroe, Victor	21
24.	IN THE MIDDLE OF THE HOUSE—R. Draper, Mercury	31
25.	HAPPINESS STREET—G. Gibbs, Mercury	32
26.	CHAINS OF LOVE—P. Boone, Dot	49
26.	FRIENDLY PERSUASION—P. Boone, Dot	44
28.	MIRACLE OF LOVE—E. Rodgers, Columbia	33
29.	ST. THERESE OF THE ROSES—B. Ward, Decca	38
30.	HOUSE WITH LOVE IN IT—Four Lads, Columbia	25
31.	BE-BOP-A-LULA—G. Vincent, Capitol	26
32.	BORN TO BE WITH YOU—Chordettes, Cadence	30
33.	SWEET, OLD FASHIONED GIRL—T. Brewer, Coral	27
34.	IN THE STILL OF THE NIGHT—Satins, Ember	53
36.	KA DING DONG—Diamonds, Mercury	50
35.	WHEN MY DREAMBOAT COMES HOME—F. Domino, Imperial	34
37.	GHOST TOWN—D. Cherry, Columbia	38
37.	IT ONLY HURTS FOR A LITTLE WHILE—Ames Brothers, Victor	30
39.	GREEN DOOR—J. Lowe, Dot	54
39.	ITALIAN THEME—C. Stapleton, London	44
41.	RIP IT UP—B. Haley, Decca	40
42.	TONIGHT YOU BELONG TO ME—Lennon Sisters-L. Welk, Coral	61
43.	ON THE STREET WHERE YOU LIVE—V. Damone, Columbia	43
44.	MORE—P. Como, Victor	23
45.	BUS STOP SONG—Four Lads, Columbia	28
45.	TRUE LOVE—Bing Crosby-Grace Kelly, Capitol	55
47.	HAPPINESS STREET—T. Bennett, Columbia	41
48.	LET THE GOOD TIMES ROLL—Shirley & Lee, Aladdin	37
49.	RIP IT UP—Little Richard, Specialty	44
50.	WHEN THE WHITE LILACS BLOOM AGAIN—F. ZaBach, Mercury	66
51.	TRUE LOVE—J. Powell, Verve	71
52.	OUT OF SIGHT, OUT OF MIND—Five Keys, Capitol	52
53.	KA DING DONG—G-Clefs, Pilgrim	56
54.	YOU'LL NEVER, NEVER KNOW—Platters, Mercury	—
55.	FORTY-NINE SHADES OF GREEN—Ames Brothers, Victor	80
55.	FABULOUS CHARACTER—S. Vaughan, Mercury	48
57.	MAMA, TEACH ME TO DANCE—E. Gorme, ABC-Paramount	65
58.	SOFT SUMMER BREEZE—Diamonds, Mercury	92
59.	NOW IS THE HOUR—G. Storm, Dot	83
60.	TUMBLING TUMBLEWEEDS—R. Williams, Kapp	70
61.	KA DING DONG—Hilltoppers, Dot	58
62.	I WALK THE LINE—J. Cash, Sun	81
63.	SEE SAW—Moonglows, Chess	57
64.	ENDLESS—McGuire Sisters, Coral	57
65.	LAY DOWN YOUR ARMS—A. Sheldon, Columbia	—
66.	I'M IN LOVE AGAIN—F. Domino, Imperial	63
67.	FROM THE CANDY STORE ON THE CORNER—T. Bennett, Columbia	35
68.	IT ISN'T RIGHT—Platters, Mercury	—
69.	EV'RY DAY OF MY LIFE—McGuire Sisters, Coral	68
70	GIVE US THIS DAY—J. James, M-G-M	87
71.	HEARTACHES—S. Smith, Epic	78
71.	HEAVEN ON EARTH—Platters, Mercury	51
71.	WHEN THE WHITE LILACS BLOOM AGAIN—L. Holmes, M-G-M	59
74.	CASUAL LOOK—Six Teens, Flip	76
75.	EARTHBOUND—S. Davis Jr., Decca	89
76.	SADIE'S SHAWL—B. Sharples, London	69
77.	SOMEBODY UP THERE LIKES ME—P. Como, Victor	47
78.	TONIGHT YOU BELONG TO ME—K. Chandler-J. Wakely, Decca	—
79.	FEVER—L. W. John, King	42
80.	MOONGLOW AND THEME FROM "PICNIC"—M. Stoloff, Decca	62
81.	EARTHBOUND—M. Lanza, Victor	95
82.	WHEN THE WHITE LILACS BLOOM AGAIN—L. Welk, Coral	73
83.	YOU'RE SENSATIONAL—F. Sinatra, Capitol	99
84.	LAY DOWN YOUR ARMS—Chordettes, Cadence	—
85.	FRIENDLY PERSUASION—Four Aces, Decca	60
86.	SO-LONG—F. Domino, Imperial	66
87.	BLUE MOON—E. Presley, Victor	—
87.	I LOVE MICKEY—T. Brewer, Coral	89
89.	WAR AND PEACE—V. Damone, Columbia	86
90.	ENGLISH MUFFINS AND IRISH STEW—S. Syms, Decca	63
91.	FROM A SCHOOL RING TO A WEDDING RING Rover Boys, ABC-Paramount	79
91.	TEEN-AGER'S MOTHER—B. Haley, Decca	97
93.	APE CALL—N. Norvus, Dot	100
94.	LOVE, LOVE, LOVE—Diamonds, Mercury	91
94.	OLD PHILOSOPHER—E. Lawrence, Coral	72
94.	WELL, DID YOU EVAH?—Bing Crosby-F. Sinatra, Capitol	92
97.	GLENDORA—P. Como, Victor	98
98.	I ONLY KNOW I LOVE YOU—Four Aces, Decca	83
99.	GOOD BOOK—K. Starr, Victor	—
100.	YOU'RE IN LOVE—G. Grant, Era	—

CAUTION TO DEALERS AND JUKE BOX OPERATORS

The Billboard's Top 100 is NOT designed to provide tested information for buying purposes. This function is most reliably served by other regular weekly features: Best Sellers in Stores, Most Played in Juke Boxes, Coming Up Strong and Best Buys.

• Best Sellers in Stores

For survey week ending September 26

RECORDS are ranked in order of their current national selling importance at the retail level, as determined by The Billboard's weekly survey of the top volume dealers in every important market area. When significant action is reported on both sides of a record, points are combined to determine position on the chart. In such a case, both sides are listed in bold type, the leading side on top.

This Week		Last Week	Weeks on Chart
1.	**DON'T BE CRUEL** (BMI)—E. Presley **HOUND DOG** (BMI)—Vic 20-6604	1	10
2.	**HONKY TONK** (Parts I & II)—B. Doggett King 4950	5	7
3.	**CANADIAN SUNSET** (BMI)—H. Winterhalter This Is Real (ASCAP)—Vic 20-6537	3	11
4.	**TONIGHT YOU BELONG TO ME** (ASCAP)—Patience & Prudence A Smile and a Ribbon (ASCAP)—Liberty 55022	6	7
5.	**WHATEVER WILL BE, WILL BE** (ASCAP)—Doris Day I Gotta Sing Away These Blues (BMI)—Col 40704	4	14
6.	**MY PRAYER** (ASCAP)—Platters Heaven on Earth (ASCAP)—Mercury 70893	2	13
7.	**JUST WALKING IN THE RAIN** (BMI)—J. Ray In the Candlelight (ASCAP)—Col 40729	8	5
8.	**GREEN DOOR** (BMI)—J. Lowe (Story of) The Little Man in Chinatown (BMI)—Dot 15486	16	2
9.	**FOOL** (BMI)—S. Clark Lonesome for a Letter (BMI)—Dot 15481	7	9
10.	**CANADIAN SUNSET** (BMI)—A. Williams High Up on a Mountain (ASCAP)—Cadence 1297	10	6
11.	**FRIENDLY PERSUASION** (ASCAP)—P. Boone **CHAINS OF LOVE** (BMI)—Dot 15490	15	3
12.	**SOFT SUMMER BREEZE** (BMI)—E. Heywood Heywood's Bounce (BMI)—Mercury 70863	11	12
13.	**ALLEGHENY MOON** (ASCAP)—P. Page Strangest Romance (ASCAP)—Mercury 70878	9	14
14.	**SONG FOR A SUMMER NIGHT** (Parts I & II (ASCAP)—M. Miller Col 40730	12	9
14.	**YOU DON'T KNOW ME** (BMI)—J. Vale Enchanted (ASCAP)—Col 40710	14	10
16.	**HOUSE WITH LOVE IN IT**—Four Lads **BUS STOP SONG** (ASCAP)	22	3
17.	**TRUE LOVE** (ASCAP)—B. Crosby & G. Kelly Well, Did You Evah (ASCAP)—Cap 3507	—	1
18.	**TRUE LOVE** (ASCAP)—J. Powell Mind If I Make Love to You? (ASCAP)—Verve 2018	—	1
19.	**WHEN THE WHITE LILACS BLOOM AGAIN** (ASCAP)—H. Zacharaias Blue Blues—Dec 30039	19	4
20.	**ST. THERESE OF THE ROSES** (BMI)—B. Ward Home Is Where You Hang Your Heart (BMI) Dec 29933	20	3
21.	**AFTER THE LIGHTS GO DOWN LOW** (BMI)—A. Hibbler I Was Telling Her About You (ASCAP)—Dec 29982	23	4
22.	**YOU'LL NEVER, NEVER KNOW** (ASCAP)—Platters **IT ISN'T RIGHT** (BMI)—Mercury 70949 (ASCAP)—Mercury 20949	—	1
23.	**OUT OF SIGHT, OUT OF MIND** (BMI)—Five Keys That's Right (BMI)—Cap 3502	—	1
24.	**TONIGHT YOU BELONG TO ME** (ASCAP—Lennon Sisters-L. Welk When the White Lilacs Bloom Again (ASCAP)—Coral 61701	21	2
25.	**MIRACLE OF LOVE** (ASCAP)—E. Rodgers Unwanted Heart (ASCAP)—Col 40708	24	3

• Most Played in Juke Boxes

For survey week ending September 26

RECORDS are ranked in order of the greatest number of plays in juke boxes thruout the country, as determined by The Billboard's weekly survey of the nation's juke box operators. When significant play is reported on both sides of a record, points are combined to determine position on the chart. In such a case, both sides are listed in bold type, the leading side on top.

This Week		Last Week	Weeks on Chart
1.	**DON'T BE CRUEL** (BMI)—E. Presley **HOUND DOG** (BMI)—Vic 20-6604	1	9
2.	**MY PRAYER** (ASCAP)—Platters Heaven on Earth (ASCAP)—Mercury 70893	2	12
3.	**WHATEVER WILL BE, WILL BE** (ASCAP)—Doris Day I Gotta Sing Away These Blues (BMI)—Col 40704	3	11
4.	**TONIGHT YOU BELONG TO ME** (ASCAP)—Patience & Prudence A Smile and a Ribbon (ASCAP)—Liberty 55022	6	5
5.	**CANADIAN SUNSET** (BMI)—H. Winterhalter-E. Heywood This Is Real (ASCAP)—Vic 20-6537	4	8
6.	**HONKY TONK** (Parts I & II) (BMI)—B. Doggett King 4950	8	4
7.	**ALLEGHENY MOON** (ASCAP)—P. Page Strangest Romance (ASCAP)—Mercury 70878	5	14
8.	**FOOL** (BMI)—S. Clark Lonesome for a Letter (BMI)—Dot 15481	7	7
9.	**CANADIAN SUNSET** (BMI)—A. Williams High Upon the Mountain (ASCAP)—Cadence 1297	9	5
10.	**SONG FOR A SUMMER NIGHT** (Parts I & II) (ASCAP)—M. Miller Columbia 40730	11	7
11.	**JUST WALKING IN THE RAIN** (BMI)—J. Ray In the Candlelight (ASCAP)—Col 40729	14	3
12.	**I ALMOST LOST MY MIND** (BMI)—P. Boone I'm in Love With You (BMI)—Dot 15472	9	17
13.	**SOFT SUMMER BREEZE** (BMI)—E. Heywood Heywood's Bounce (BMI)—Mercury 70863	14	5
14.	**FLYING SAUCER** (Parts I & II)—Buchanan & Goodman Luniverse 101	12	7
14.	**AFTER THE LIGHTS GO DOWN LOW** (BMI)—A. Hibbler I Was Telling Her About You (ASCAP)—Dec 29982	—	1
16.	**YOU DON'T KNOW ME** (BMI)—J. Vale Enchanted (ASCAP)—Col 40710	14	5
17.	**I WANT YOU, I NEED YOU, I LOVE YOU** (BMI)—E. Presley My Baby Left Me (BMI)—Vic 20-6540	13	18
18.	**IT ONLY HURTS FOR A LITTLE WHILE** (ASCAP)—Ames Brothers If You Want to See Mamie Tonight (ASCAP)—Vic 20-6481	—	15
18.	**CHAINS OF LOVE** (BMI)—P. Boone **FRIENDLY PERSUASION** (ASCAP)—Dot 15490	—	1
20.	**BE-BOP-A-LULA** (BMI)—G. Vincent Woman Love (BMI)—Cap 3450	17	13

• Best Selling Sheet Music

Tunes are ranked in order of their current national selling importance at the sheet music jobber level.

This Week		Last Week	Weeks on Chart
1.	**Whatever Will Be, Will Be** (Que Sera, Sera)	2	13
2.	**Canadian Sunset** (Meridian)	3	9
3.	**Allegheny Moon** (Oxford)	1	15
4.	**Tonight You Belong to Me** (Bregman, Vocco & Conn)	6	5
5.	**Soft Summer Breeze** (Regent)	4	6
6.	**Don't Be Cruel** (Presley-Shalimar)	8	4
7.	**Song for a Summer Night** (April)	5	7
8.	**True Love** (Buxton Hill)	13	2
9.	**Wayward Wind** (Warman)	9	9
10.	**My Prayer** (Shapiro-Bernstein)	7	12
11.	**Hound Dog** (Presley-Lion)	10	7
12.	**When the White Lilacs Bloom Again** (Harms)	15	2
13.	**Happiness Street** (Planetary)	11	3
14.	**You Don't Know Me** (Hill & Range)	11	2
15.	**Walk Hand in Hand** (Republic)	14	21

• Most Played by Jockeys

For survey week ending September 26

SIDES are ranked in order of the greatest number of plays on disk jockey radio shows thruout the country. Results are based on The Billboard's weekly survey among the nation's disk jockeys. The reverse side of each record is also listed.

This Week		Last Week	Weeks on Chart
1.	**DON'T BE CRUEL** (BMI)—E. Presley Hound Dog (BMI)—Vic 20-6604	1	9
2.	**MY PRAYER** (ASCAP)—Platters Heaven on Earth (ASCAP)—Mercury 70893	2	13
3.	**CANADIAN SUNSET** (BMI)—H. Winterhalter-E. Heywood This Is Real (ASCAP)—Vic 20-6537	3	11
4.	**WHATEVER WILL BE, WILL BE** (ASCAP)—Doris Day I Gotta Sing Away These Blues (BMI)—Col 40704	4	14
5.	**TONIGHT YOU BELONG TO ME** (ASCAP)—Patience & Prudence A Smile and a Ribbon (ASCAP)—Liberty 55022	6	7
6.	**HOUND DOG** (BMI)—E. Presley Don't Be Cruel (BMI)—Vic 20-6604	5	10
7.	**CANADIAN SUNSET** (BMI)—A. Williams High Upon a Mountain (ASCAP)—Cadence 1297	7	8
7.	**JUST WALKING IN THE RAIN** (BMI)—J. Ray In the Candlelight (ASCAP)—Col 40729	11	2
9.	**FRIENDLY PERSUASION** (ASCAP)—P. Boone Chains of Love (ASCAP)—Dot 15490	12	3
10.	**HONKY TONK** (Parts I & II)—B. Doggett King 4950 (BMI)—B. Doggett	9	3
11.	**GREEN DOOR** (BMI)—J. Lowe Little Man in Chinatown (BMI)—Dot 15486	23	2
12.	**SONG FOR A SUMMER NIGHT** (Parts I & II)—M. Miller Col 40730—ASCAP	8	9
13.	**ALLEGHENY MOON** (ASCAP)—P. Page Strangest Romance (ASCAP)—Mercury 70878	10	15
14.	**SOFT SUMMER BREEZE** (BMI)—E. Heywood Heywood's Bounce (BMI)—Mercury 70863	14	8
15.	**AFTER THE LIGHTS GO DOWN LOW** (BMI)—A. Hibbler I Was Telling Her About You (ASCAP)—Decca 29982	13	6
16.	**YOU DON'T KNOW ME** (BMI)—J. Vale Enchanted (ASCAP)—Col 40710	15	8
17.	**WHEN THE WHITE LILACS BLOOM AGAIN** (ASCAP)—H. Zacharias Blue Blues—Dec 30039	17	4
18.	**MIRACLE OF LOVE** (ASCAP)—E. Rodgers Unwanted Heart (ASCAP)—Col 40708	—	1
19.	**IN THE MIDDLE OF THE HOUSE** (ASCAP)—V. Monroe Rollin' Heart (BMI)—Vic 20-6619	16	4
20.	**HAPPINESS STREET** (ASCAP)—G. Gibbs Happiness Is a Thing Called Joe (ASCAP)—Mercury 70920	—	5
21.	**BUS STOP SONG** (ASCAP)—Four Lads House With Love in It (ASCAP)—Col 40736	24	2
22.	**FOOL** (BMI)—S. Clark Lonsome for a Letter (BMI)—Dot 15481	19	6
23.	**TRUE LOVE** (ASCAP)—Bing Crosby & G. Kelly Well Did You Evah (ASCAP)—Cap 3507	—	1
24.	**TONIGHT YOU BELONG TO ME** (ASCAP)—Lennon Sisters-L. Welk When the White Lilacs Bloom Again (ASCAP)—Coral 61701	—	1
25.	**HOUSE WITH LOVE IN IT** (ASCAP)—Four Lads Bus Stop Song (ASCAP)—Col 40736	20	2

THE TOP 100

For survey week ending September 26

A list of the Top 100 **RECORD SIDES** in the nation according to a **COMBINED TABULATION** of Dealer, Disk Jockey and Juke Box Operator replies to The Billboard's weekly popular record Best Seller and Most Played surveys. Its purpose is to provide Disk Jockeys with additional programming material and to give trade exposure to NEWER records just beginning to show action in the field.

Pos.	Song, Artist, Label	Week Last
1.	**DON'T BE CRUEL**—E. Presley, Victor	1
2.	**HOUND DOG**—E. Presley, Victor	3
3.	**MY PRAYER**—Platters, Mercury	2
4.	**CANADIAN SUNSET**—E. Heywood-H. Winterhalter, Victor	4
5.	**WHATEVER WILL BE, WILL BE**—Doris, Day, Columbia	5
6.	**TONIGHT YOU BELONG TO ME**—Patience & Prudence, Liberty	6
7.	**HONKY TONK**—B. Doggett, King	7
8.	**JUST WALKING IN THE RAIN**—J. Ray, Columbia	11
9.	**CANADIAN SUNSET**—A. Williams, Cadence	9
10.	**ALLEGHENY MOON**—P. Page. Mercury	8
11.	**SONG FOR A SUMMER NIGHT**—M. Miller, Columbia	10
12.	**SOFT SUMMER BREEZE**—E. Heywood, Mercury	13
13.	**FOOL**—S. Clark, Dot	11
14.	**GREEN DOOR**—J. Lowe, Dot	39
15.	**YOU DON'T KNOW ME**—J. Vale, Columbia	14
16.	**AFTER THE LIGHTS GO DOWN**—A. Hibbler, Decca	17
16.	**FRIENDLY PERSUASION**—P. Boone, Dot	26
18.	**WHEN THE WHITE LILACS BLOOM AGAIN**—H. Zacharaias, Decca	16
19.	**MIRACLE OF LOVE**—E. Rodgers, Columbia	28
20.	**CHAINS OF LOVE**—P. Boone, Dot	26
21.	**FLYING SAUCER**—Buchanan & Goodman, Luniverse	15
22.	**TONIGHT YOU BELONG TO ME**—Lennon Sisters-L. Welk, Coral	42
23.	**I ALMOST LOST MY MIND**—P. Boone, Dot	18
23.	**HOUSE WITH LOVE IN IT**—Four Lads, Columbia	30
25.	**ITALIAN THEME**—C. Stapleton, London	39
26.	**HAPPINESS STREET**—G. Gibbs, Mercury	25
27.	**OUT OF SIGHT, OUT OF MIND**—Five Keys, Capitol	52
28.	**WHEN THE WHITE LILACS BLOOM AGAIN**—B. Vaughn, Dot	22
29.	**THAT'S ALL THERE IS TO THAT**—N. (King) Cole, Capitol	21
30.	**BE-BOP-A-LULA**—G. Vincent, Capitol	31
30.	**IN THE MIDDLE OF THE HOUSE**—V. Monroe, Victor	23
32.	**I WANT YOU, I NEED YOU, I LOVE YOU**—E.Presley, Victor	19
33.	**IN THE MIDDLE OF THE HOUSE**—R. Draper, Mercury	24
34.	**SOFT SUMMER BREEZE**—Diamonds, Mercury	58
35.	**WAYWARD WIND**—G. Grant, Era	20
36.	**TRUE LOVE**—J. Powell, Verve	51
37.	**TRUE LOVE**—Bing Crosby-G. Kelly, Capitol	45
38.	**KA DING DONG**—Hilltoppers, Dot	61
39.	**HAPPINESS STREET**—T. Bennett, Columbia	47
39.	**KA DING DONG**—Diamonds, Mercury	35
41.	**YOU'LL NEVER, NEVER KNOW**—Platters, Mercury	54
42.	**BUS STOP SONG**—Four Lads, Columbia	45
43.	**I WALK THE LINE**—J. Cash, Sun	62
44.	**LET THE GOOD TIMES ROLL**—Shirley & Lee, Aladdin	48
45.	**IN THE STILL OF THE NIGHT**—Satins, Ember	34
45.	**MORE**—P. Como, Victor	44
47.	**ST. THERESE OF THE ROSES**—B. Ward, Decca	29
48.	**WHEN MY DREAMBOAT COMES HOME**—F. Domino, Imperial	35
49.	**FORTY-NINE SHADES OF GREEN**—Ames Brothers, Victor	55
50.	**IT ISN'T RIGHT**—Platters, Mercury	68
51.	**IT ONLY HURTS FOR A LITTLE WHILE**—Ames Brothers, Victor	37
52.	**ENDLESS**—McGuire Sisters, Coral	64
52.	**FROM THE CANDY STORE ON THE CORNER**—T. Bennett, Columbia	67
52.	**SWEET, OLD-FASHIONED GIRL**—T. Brewer, Coral	33
55.	**SEE-SAW**—Moonglows, Chess	63
56.	**EARTHBOUND**—S. Davis Jr., Decca	75
57.	**GHOST TOWN**—D. Cherry, Columbia	37
57.	**HEART AND SOUL**—J. Maddox, Dot	—
57.	**WHEN THE WHITE LILACS BLOOM AGAIN**—F. ZaBach, Mercury	50
60.	**WAR AND PEACE**—V. Damone, Columbia	89
61.	**BLUE MOON**—E. Presley, Victor	87
61.	**LAY DOWN YOUR ARMS**—Chordettes, Cadence	84
61.	**NOW IS THE HOUR**—G. Storm, Dot	59
64.	**BORN TO BE WITH YOU**—Chordettes, Cadence	32
65.	**RIP IT UP**—B. Haley, Decca	41
66.	**KA DING DONG**—G Clefs, Pilgrim	53
67.	**SUMMER SWEETHEART**—Ames Brothers, Victor	—
68.	**EV'RY DAY OF MY LIFE**—McGuire Sisters, Coral	69
69.	**I CAN'T LOVE YOU ENOUGH**—L. Baker, Atlantic	—
69.	**SADIE'S SHAWL**—B. Sharples, London	76
71.	**RIP IT UP**—Little Richard, Specialty	49
72.	**FRIENDLY PERSUASION**—Four Aces, Decca	85
73.	**BLUEBERRY HILL**—F. Domino, Imperial	—
73.	**EAST OF EDEN**, D. Jacobs, Coral	—
75.	**MOONGLOW AND THEME FROM PICNIC**—M. Stoloff, Decca	80
75.	**WHEN THE TIDE IS HIGH**—G. Grant, Era	—
77.	**FEVER**—L. W. John. King	79
77.	**TUMBLING TUMBLEWEED**—R. Williams, Kapp	60
79.	**OLD PHILOSOPHER**—E. Lawrence, Coral	94
80.	**WHEN THE WHITE LILACS BLOOM AGAIN**—L. Welk, Coral	82
80.	**YOU'RE SENSATIONAL**—F. Sinatra, Capitol	83
82.	**WAYWARD WIND**—T. Ritter, Capitol	—
83.	**I ONLY KNOW I LOVE YOU**—Four Aces, Decca	98
84.	**EARTHBOUND**—M. Lanza, Victor	81
85.	**CASUAL LOOK**—Six Teens, Flip	74
86.	**YOU'RE IN LOVE**—G. Grant, Era	100
87.	**I LOVE MICKEY**—T. Brewer, Coral	87
88.	**HEARTACHES**—S. Smith, Epic	71
89.	**GOOD BOOK**—K. Starr, Victor	99
89.	**ON THE STREET WHERE YOU LIVE**—E. Fisher, Victor	—
91.	**HEAVEN ON EARTH**—Platters, Mercury	71
92.	**IT HAPPENED AGAIN**—S. Vaughan, Mercury	—
93.	**FOOL**—Gallahads, Jubilee	—
94.	**TONIGHT YOU BELONG TO ME**—K. Chandler-J. Wakely, Decca	78
95.	**HEART WITHOUT A SWEETHEART**—G Storm, Dot	—
95.	**WHEN THE WHITE LILACS BLOOM AGAIN**—L. Holmes, M-G-M	71
95.	**NAMELY YOU**—D. Cherry, Columbia	—
95.	**LAY DOWN YOUR ARMS**—A. Sheldon, Columbia	65
99.	**FABULOUS CHARACTER**—S. Vaughan, Mercury	55
100.	**GIVE US THIS DAY**—J. James, M-G-M	70
100.	**THINGS I NEVER HAD**—K. Starr, Victor	—

CAUTION TO DEALERS AND JUKE BOX OPERATORS

The Billboard's Top 100 is NOT designed to provide tested information for buying purposes. This function is most reliably served by other regular weekly features: Best Sellers in Stores, Most Played in Juke Boxes, Coming Up Strong and Best Buys.

• Best Sellers in Stores

For survey week ending October 3

RECORDS are ranked in order of their current national selling importance at the retail level, as determined by The Billboard's weekly survey of the top volume dealers in every important market area. When significant action is reported on both sides of a record, points are combined to determine position on the chart. In such a case, both sides are listed in bold type, the leading side on top.

This Week		Last Week	Weeks on Chart
1.	**DON'T BE CRUEL** (BMI)—E. Presley. **HOUND DOG** (BMI)—Vic 20-6604	1	11
2.	**HONKY TONK (PARTS I & II)**—B. Doggett. King 4950	2	8
3.	**CANADIAN SUNSET** (BMI)—H. Winterhalter. This Is Real (ASCAP)—Vic 20-6537	3	12
4.	**JUST WALKING IN THE RAIN** (BMI)—J. Ray. In the Candlelight (ASCAP)—Col 40729	7	6
5.	**TONIGHT YOU BELONG TO ME** (ASCAP)—Patience & Prudence. A Smile and a Ribbon (ASCAP)—Liberty 55022	4	8
6.	**WHATEVER WILL BE, WILL BE** (ASCAP)—Doris Day. I Gotta Sing Away These Blues (BMI)—Col 40704	5	15
7.	**MY PRAYER** (ASCAP)—Platters. Heaven on Earth (ASCAP)—Mercury 70893	6	14
8.	**GREEN DOOR** (BMI)—J. Lowe. (Story of) The Little Man in Chinatown (BMI)—Dot 15486	8	3
9.	**FOOL** (BMI)—S. Clark. Lonesome for a Letter (BMI)—Dot 15481	9	10
10.	**CANADIAN SUNSET** (BMI)—A. Williams. High Up on a Mountain (ASCAP)—Cadence 1297	10	7
11.	**FRIENDLY PERSUASION** (ASCAP)—P. Boone. **CHAINS OF LOVE** (BMI)—Dot 15490	11	4
12.	**TRUE LOVE** (ASCAP)—B. Crosby-G. Kelly. Well, Did You Evah? (ASCAP)—Cap 3507	17	2
13.	**SOFT SUMMER BREEZE** (BMI)—E. Heywood. Heywood's Bounce (BMI)—Mercury 70863	12	13
14.	**BLUEBERRY HILL** (ASCAP)—F. Domino. Honey Chile (BMI)—Imperial 5407	—	1
15.	**ALLEGHENY MOON** (ASCAP)—P. Page. Strangest Romance (ASCAP)—Mercury 70878	13	15
16.	**IT ISN'T RIGHT** (BMI)—Platters. **YOU'LL NEVER, NEVER KNOW** (BMI)—Mercury 70949	—	1
17.	**TONIGHT YOU BELONG TO ME** (ASCAP)—Lennon Sisters-L. Welk. When the White Lilacs Bloom Again (ASCAP)—Coral 61701	24	3
18.	**YOU DON'T KNOW ME** (BMI)—J. Vale. Enchanted (ASCAP)—Col 40710	14	11
19.	**TRUE LOVE** (ASCAP)—J. Powell. Mind If I Make Love to You? (ASCAP)—Verve 2018	18	2
20.	**CINDY, OH, CINDY** (BMI)—V. Martin. Only If I Praise the Lord (BMI)—Glory 247	—	1
21.	**SONG FOR A SUMMER NIGHT (PARTS I & II)** (ASCAP)—M. Miller. Col 40730	14	10
22.	**AFTER THE LIGHTS GO DOWN LOW** (BMI)—A. Hibbler. I Was Telling Her About You (ASCAP)—Dec 29982	21	5
23.	**BUS STOP SONG** (ASCAP)—Four Lads. **HOUSE WITH LOVE IN IT** (ASCAP)—Col 40736	—	4
24.	**IN THE STILL OF THE NIGHT** (BMI)—Satins. Jones Girl (BMI)—Ember 10005	—	1
25.	**ST. THERESE OF THE ROSES** (BMI)—B. Ward. Home Is Where You Hang Your Heart (BMI)—Dec 29933	20	4
25.	**SEE-SAW** (BMI) (Moonglows). When I'm With You (BMI)—Chess 1629	—	1

• Most Played in Juke Boxes

For survey week ending October 3

RECORDS are ranked in order of the greatest number of plays in juke boxes thruout the country, as determined by The Billboard's weekly survey of the nation's juke box operators. When significant play is reported on both sides of a record, points are combined to determine position on the chart. In such a case, both sides are listed in bold type, the leading side on top.

This Week		Last Week	Weeks on Chart
1.	**DON'T BE CRUEL** (BMI)—E. Presley. **HOUND DOG** (BMI)—Vic 20-6604	1	10
2.	**MY PRAYER** (ASCAP)—Platters. Heaven on Earth (ASCAP)—Mercury 70893	2	13
3.	**HONKY TONK** (Parts I & II) (BMI)—B. Doggett. King 4950	6	5
4.	**WHATEVER WILL BE, WILL BE** (ASCAP)—Doris Day. I Gotta Sing Away These Blues (BMI)—Col 40704	3	12
5.	**TONIGHT YOU BELONG TO ME** (ASCAP)—Patience & Prudence. A Smile and a Ribbon (ASCAP)—Liberty 55022	4	6
6.	**CANADIAN SUNSET** (BMI)—H. Winterhalter-E. Heywood. This Is Real (ASCAP)—Vic 20-6537	5	9
7.	**ALLEGHENY MOON** (ASCAP)—P. Page. Strangest Romance (ASCAP)—Mercury 70878	7	15
8.	**JUST WALKING IN THE RAIN** (BMI)—J. Ray. In the Candlelight (ASCAP)—Col 40729	11	4
9.	**CANADIAN SUNSET** (BMI)—A. Williams. High Upon the Mountain (ASCAP)—Cadence 1297	9	6
10.	**FOOL** (BMI)—S. Clark. Lonesome for a Letter (BMI)—Dot 15481	8	8
11.	**GREEN DOOR** (BMI)—J. Lowe. (The Story of) The Little Man in Chinatown) (BMI)—Dot 15486	—	1
12.	**SONG FOR A SUMMER NIGHT** (Parts I & II) (ASCAP)—M. Miller. Columbia 40730	10	8
12.	**CHAINS OF LOVE** (BMI)—P. Boone. **FRIENDLY PERSUASION** (ASCAP)—Dot 15490	18	2
14.	**AFTER THE LIGHTS GO DOWN LOW** (BMI)—A. Hibbler. I Was Telling Her About You (ASCAP)—Dec 29982	14	2
15.	**SOFT SUMMER BREEZE** (BMI). E. Heywood. Heywood's Bounce (BMI)—Mercury 70863	13	6
16.	**IT ISN'T RIGHT** (BMI)—Platters. **YOU'LL NEVER, NEVER KNOW** (BMI)—Mercury 70949	—	1
17.	**I ALMOST LOST MY MIND** (BMI)—P. Boone. I'm in Love With You (BMI)—Dot 15472	12	18
18.	**IT ONLY HURTS FOR A LITTLE WHILE** (ASCAP)—Ames Brothers. If You Want to See Mamie Tonight (ASCAP)—Vic 20-6481	18	16
19.	**WHEN THE WHITE LILACS BLOOM AGAIN** (ASCAP)—H. Zacharias. Blue Blues (BMI)—Dec 30039	—	1
20.	**FLYING SAUCER** (Parts I & II) Buchanan & Goodman. Luniverse 101	14	8

• Best Selling Sheet Music

Tunes are ranked in order of their current national selling importance at the sheet music jobber level.

This Week		Last Week	Weeks on Chart
1.	**Whatever Will Be, Will Be** (Que Sera Sera)	1	14
2.	**Allegheny Moon** (Oxford)	3	16
3.	**Canadian Sunset** (Meridian)	2	10
4.	**Tonight You Belong to Me** (Mills)	4	6
5.	**Soft Summer Breeze** (Regent)	5	7
6.	**True Love** (Buxton Hill)	8	3
7.	**Don't Be Cruel** (Presley-Shalimar)	6	5
8.	**My Prayer** (Shapiro-Bernstein)	10	13
9.	**Song for a Summer Night** (April)	7	8
10.	**Wayward Wind** (Warman)	9	10
11.	**When the White Lilacs Bloom Again** (Harms)	12	3
12.	**Hound Dog** (Presley-Lion)	11	8
13.	**Just Walking in the Rain** (Golden Wist)	—	1
14.	**Walk Hand in Hand** (Republic)	15	22
15.	**Happiness Street** (Planetary)	13	4

• Most Played by Jockeys

For survey week ending October 3

SIDES are ranked in order of the greatest number of plays on disk jockey radio shows thruout the country. Results are based on The Billboard's weekly survey among the nation's disk jockeys. The reverse side of each record is also listed.

This Week		Last Week	Weeks on Chart
1.	**DON'T BE CRUEL** (BMI)—E. Presley. Hound Dog (BMI)—Vic 20-6604	1	10
2.	**CANADIAN SUNSET** (BMI)—H. Winterhalter-E. Heywood. This Is Real (ASCAP)—Vic 20-6537	3	12
3.	**JUST WALKING IN THE RAIN** (BMI)—J. Ray. In the Candlelight (ASCAP)—Col.-40729	7	3
4.	**MY PRAYER** (ASCAP)—Platters. Heaven on Earth (ASCAP)—Mercury 70893	2	14
5.	**GREEN DOOR** (BMI)—J. Lowe. (Story of) The Little Man in Chinatown (BMI)—Dot 15486	11	3
6.	**HONKY TONK** (Parts I & II) (BMI)—B. Doggett. King 4950 (BMI)	10	4
7.	**FRIENDLY PERSUASION** (ASCAP)—P. Boone. Chains of Love (ASCAP)—Dot 15490	9	4
8.	**TONIGHT YOU BELONG TO ME** (ASCAP)—Patience & Prudence. A Smile and a Ribbon (ASCAP)—Liberty 55022	5	8
9.	**CANADIAN SUNSET** (BMI)—A. Williams. High Upon a Mountain (ASCAP)—Cadence 1297	7	9
10.	**WHATEVER WILL BE, WILL BE** (ASCAP)—Doris Day. I Gotta Sing Away These Blues (BMI)—Col 40704	4	15
11.	**HOUND DOG** (BMI)—E. Presley. Don't Be Cruel (BMI)—Vic 20-6604	6	11
12.	**SONG FOR A SUMMER NIGHT** (Parts I & II) (ASCAP)—M. Miller. ASCAP—Col 40730	12	10
13.	**TRUE LOVE** (ASCAP)—B. Crosby & G. Kelly. Well, Did You Evah (ASCAP)—Cap 3507	23	2
14.	**SOFT SUMMER BREEZE** (BMI)—E. Heywood. Heywood's Bounce (BMI)—Mercury 70863	14	9
15.	**ALLEGHENY MOON** (ASCAP)—P. Page. Strangest Romance (ASCAP)—Mercury 70878	13	16
16.	**AFTER THE LIGHTS GO DOWN LOW** (BMI)—A. Hibbler. I Was Telling Her About You (ASCAP)—Decca 29982	15	7
17.	**YOU DON'T KNOW ME** (BMI)—J. Vale. Enchanted (ASCAP)—Col 40710	16	9
18.	**IN THE MIDDLE OF THE HOUSE** (ASCAP)—V. Monroe. Rollin' Heart (BMI)—Vic 20-6619	19	5
19.	**FOOL** (BMI)—S. Clark. Lonesome for a Letter (BMI—Dot 15481	22	7
20.	**TONIGHT YOU BELONG TO ME** (ASCAP)—Lennon Sisters-L. Welk. When the White Lilacs Bloom Again (ASCAP)—Coral 61701	24	2
21.	**BUS STOP SONG** (ASCAP)—Four Lads. House With Love in It (ASCAP)—Col 40736	21	3
22.	**FROM THE CANDY STORE ON THE CORNER** (ASCAP)—T. Bennett. Happiness Street (ASCAP)—Col 40726	—	4
23.	**WHEN THE WHITE LILACS BLOOM AGAIN** (ASCAP)—H. Zacharias. Blue Blues (BMI)—Dec 30039	17	5
24.	**IN THE MIDDLE OF THE HOUSE** (ASCAP)—R. Draper. Rollin' Heart (BMI)—Mercury 70921	—	1
25.	**HOUSE WITH LOVE IN IT** (ASCAP)—Four Lads. Bus Stop Song (ASCAP)—Col 40736	25	3
25.	**I CAN'T LOVE YOU ENOUGH** (BMI)—L. Baker. Still (BMI)—Atlantic 1004	—	1

THE TOP 100

For survey week ending October 3

A list of the Top 100 RECORD SIDES in the nation according to a COMBINED TABULATION of Dealer, Disk Jockey and Juke Box Operator replies to The Billboard's weekly popular record Best Seller and Most Played surveys. Its purpose is to provide Disk Jockeys with additional programming material and to give trade exposure to NEWER records just beginning to show action in the field.

Pos.	Song, Artist, Label	Last Week
1.	**DON'T BE CRUEL**—E. Presley, Victor	1
2.	**HONKY TONK**—B. Doggett, King	7
3.	**CANADIAN SUNSET**—E. Heywood-H. Winterhalter, Victor	4
4.	**MY PRAYER**—Platters, Mercury	3
5.	**JUST WALKING IN THE RAIN**—J. Ray, Columbia	8
6.	**HOUND DOG**—E. Presley, Victor	2
7.	**TONIGHT YOU BELONG TO ME**—Patience & Prudence, Liberty	6
8.	**WHATEVER WILL BE, WILL BE**—Doris Day, Columbia	5
9.	**GREEN DOOR**—J. Lowe, Dot	14
10.	**CANADIAN SUNSET**—A. Williams, Cadence	9
11.	**FRIENDLY PERSUASION**—P. Boone, Dot	16
12.	**ALLEGHENY MOON**—P. Page, Mercury	10
13.	**FOOL**—S. Clark, Dot	13
14.	**SOFT SUMMER BREEZE**—E. Heywood, Mercury	12
15.	**SONG FOR A SUMMER NIGHT**—M. Miller, Columbia	11
16.	**AFTER THE LIGHTS GO DOWN LOW**—A. Hibbler, Decca	16
17.	**YOU DON'T KNOW ME**—J. Vale, Columbia	15
18.	**I ALMOST LOST MY MIND**—P. Boone, Dot	23
19.	**WHEN THE WHITE LILACS BLOOM AGAIN**—H. Zacharaias, Decca	18
20.	**IN THE MIDDLE OF THE HOUSE**—R. Draper, Mercury	33
21.	**BLUEBERRY HILL**—F. Domino, Imperial	73
22.	**MIRACLE OF LOVE**—E. Rodgers, Columbia	19
22.	**TONIGHT YOU BELONG TO ME**—Lennon Sisters-L. Welk, Coral	22
24.	**CHAINS OF LOVE**—P. Boone, Dot	20
25.	**YOU'LL NEVER, NEVER KNOW**—Platters, Mercury	41
26.	**BUS STOP SONG**—Four Lads, Columbia	42
27.	**ST. THERESE OF THE ROSES**—B. Ward, Decca	47
28.	**SEE-SAW**—Moonglows, Chess	55
29.	**IN THE STILL OF THE NIGHT**—Satins, Ember	45
30.	**IT ISN'T RIGHT**—Platters, Mercury	50
31.	**IN THE MIDDLE OF THE HOUSE**—V. Monroe, Victor	30
32.	**HOUSE WITH LOVE IN IT**—Four Lads, Columbia	23
32.	**LET THE GOOD TIMES ROLL**—Shirley & Lee, Aladdin	44
34.	**HAPPINESS STREET**—G. Gibbs, Mercury	26
35.	**TRUE LOVE**—Bing Crosby-G. Kelly, Capitol	37
36.	**LAY DOWN YOUR ARMS**—Chordettes, Cadence	61
37.	**TRUE LOVE**—J. Powell, Verve	36
38.	**HAPPINESS STREET**—T. Bennett, Columbia	39
39.	**KA DING DONG**—Hilltoppers, Dot	38
40.	**OUT OF SIGHT, OUT OF MIND**—Five Keys, Capitol	27
41.	**FLYING SAUCER**—Buchanan & Goodman, Luniverse	21
42.	**RIP IT UP**—B. Haley, Decca	65
43.	**I WALK THE LINE**—J. Cash, Sun	43
43.	**THAT'S ALL THERE IS TO THAT**—N. (King) Cole, Capitol	29
45.	**BE-BOP-A-LULA**—G. Vincent, Capitol	30
46.	**WHEN THE WHITE LILACS BLOOM AGAIN**—B. Vaughn, Dot	28
47.	**ITALIAN THEME**—C. Stapleton, London	25
48.	**I CAN'T LOVE YOU ENOUGH**—L. Baker, Atlantic	69
49.	**CINDY, OH CINDY**—V. Martin, Glory	—
50.	**WAYWARD WIND**—G. Grant, Era	35
51.	**FROM THE CANDY STORE ON THE CORNER**—T. Bennett, Columbia	52
52.	**KA DING DONG**—Diamonds, Mercury	39
53.	**GHOST TOWN**—D. Cherry, Columbia	57
54.	**EARTHBOUND**—S. Davis Jr., Decca	56
55.	**BLUE MOON**—E. Presley, Victor	61
56.	**EV'RY DAY OF MY LIFE**—McGuire Sisters, Coral	68
57.	**IT ONLY HURTS FOR A LITTLE WHILE**—Ames Brothers, Victor	51
58.	**BORN TO BE WITH YOU**—Chordettes, Cadence	64
59.	**WAR AND P?ACE**—V. Damone, Columbia	60
60.	**FORTY NINE SHADES OF GREEN**—Ames Brothers, Victor	49
60.	**I WANT YOU, I NEED YOU, I LOVE YOU**—E. Presley, Victor	32
62.	**KA DING DONG**—G. Clefs, Pilgrim	66
63.	**SADIE'S SHAWL**—B. Sharples, London	69
64.	**NOW IS THE HOUR**—G. Storm, Dot	61
64.	**WHEN MY DREAMBOAT COMES HOME**—F. Domino, Imperial	48
66.	**HEART AND SOUL**—J. Maddox, Dot	57
67.	**FRIENDLY PERSUASION**—Four Aces, Decca	72
67.	**RIP IT UP**—Little Richard, Specialty	71
69.	**WHEN THE WHITE LILACS BLOOM AGAIN**—F. ZaBach, Mercury	57
70.	**FOOL**—Gallahads, Jubilee	93
71.	**SOFT SUMMER BREEZE**—Diamonds, Mercury	34
72.	**SUMMER SWEETHEART**—Ames Brothers, Victor	67
73.	**ENDLESS**—McGuire Sisters, Coral	52
73.	**FAITHFUL HUSSAR**—T. Heath, London	—
73.	**LAY DOWN YOUR ARMS**—A. Sheldon, Columbia	95
76.	**MOONGLOW AND THEME FROM "PICNIC"**—M. Stoloff, Decca	75
77.	**I DON'T CARE IF THE SUN DON'T SHINE**—E. Presley, Victor	—
78.	**WHEN THE WHITE LILACS BLOOM AGAIN**—L. Welk, Coral	80
79.	**FEVER**—L. W. John, King	77
79.	**MORE**—P. Como, Victor	45
81.	**NAMELY YOU**—D. Cherry, Columbia	95
82.	**TUMBLING TUMBLEWEED**—R. Williams, Kapp	77
83.	**YOU'RE IN LOVE**—G. Grant, Era	86
84.	**MAMA, TEACH ME TO DANCE**—E. Gorme, ABC-Paramount	—
85.	**EARTHBOUND**—M. Lanza, Victor	84
86.	**STILL**—Fontane Sisters, Dot	—
87.	**ON THE STREET WHERE YOU LIVE**—V. Damone, Columbia	—
88.	**PLEASE DON'T LEAVE ME**—Fontane Sisters, Dot	—
89.	**FROM A SCHOOL RING TO A WEDDING RING**—Rover Boys, ABC-Paramount	—
90.	**HEART WITHOUT A SWEETHEART**—G. Storm, Dot	95
90.	**IT HAPPENED AGAIN**—S. Vaughan, Mercury	92
90.	**SWEET, OLD-FASHIONED GIRL**—T. Brewer, Caral	52
93.	**TONIGHT YOU BELONG TO ME**—K. Chandler- J. Wakely, Decca	94
94.	**NOW YOU HAS JAZZ**—B. Crosby-L. Armstrong, Capitol	—
95.	**HEARTACHES**—S. Smith, Epic	88
96.	**FABULOUS CHARACTER**—S. Vaughan, Mercury	—
96.	**YOU'RE SENSATIONAL**—F. Sinatra, Capitol	80
98.	**HEAVEN ON EARTH**—Platters, Mercury	91
99.	**SO-LONG**—F. Domino, Imperial	—
100.	**GIVE US THIS DAY**—J. James, M-G-M	100

CAUTION TO DEALERS AND JUKE BOX OPERATORS

The Billboard's Top 100 is NOT designed to provide tested information for buying purposes. This function is most reliably served by other regular weekly features: Best Sellers in Stores, Most Played in Juke Boxes, Coming Up Strong and Best Buys.

• Best Sellers in Stores

For survey week ending October 10

RECORDS are ranked in order of their current national selling importance at the retail level, as determined by The Billboard's weekly survey of the top volume dealers in every important market area. When significant action is reported on both sides of a record, points are combined to determine position on the chart. In such a case, both sides are listed in bold type, the leading side on top.

This Week		Last Week	Weeks on Chart
1.	**DON'T BE CRUEL** (BMI)—E. Presley. **HOUND DOG** (BMI)—Vic 20-6604	1	12
2.	**LOVE ME TENDER** (BMI)—E. Presley. Any Way You Want Me (BMI)—Vic 20-6643	—	1
3.	**GREEN DOOR** (BMI)—J. Lowe. (Story of) The Little Man in Chinatown (BMI)—Dot 15456	8	4
4.	**HONKY TONK (PARTS I & II)** (BMI)—B. Doggett. King 4950 (BMI)	2	9
5.	**JUST WALKING IN THE RAIN** (BMI)—J. Ray. In the Candlelight (ASCAP)—Col 40729	4	7
6.	**CANADIAN SUNSET** (BMI)—H. Winterhalter. This Is Real (ASCAP)—Vic 20-6537	3	13
7.	**TONIGHT YOU BELONG TO ME** (ASCAP)—Patience & Prudence. A Smile and a Ribbon (ASCAP)—Liberty 55022	5	9
8.	**WHATEVER WILL BE, WILL BE** (ASCAP)—Doris Day. (BMI)—I Gotta Sing Away These Blues (BMI)—Col 40704	6	16
9.	**FRIENDLY PERSUASION** (ASCAP)—P. Boone. **CHAINS OF LOVE** (BMI)—Dot 15490	11	5
10.	**MY PRAYER** (ASCAP)—Platters. Heaven on Earth (ASCAP)—Mercury 70893	7	15
11.	**BLUEBERRY HILL** (ASCAP)—F. Domino. Honey Chile (BMI)—Imperial 5407	14	2
12.	**TRUE LOVE** (ASCAP)—B. Crosby-G. Kelly. Well, Did You Evah (ASCAP)—Cap 3507	12	3
13.	**IT ISN'T RIGHT** (BMI)—Platters. **YOU'LL NEVER, NEVER KNOW** (BMI)—Mercury 70948	16	2
14.	**CANADIAN SUNSET** (BMI)—A. Williams. High Up on a Mountain (ASCAP)—Cadence 1297	10	8
15.	**CINDY, OH CINDY** (BMI)—V. Martin. Only If I Praise the Lord (BMI)—Glory 247	20	2
16.	**FOOL** (BMI)—S. Clark. Lonesome for a Letter (BMI)—Dot 15481	9	11
17.	**TRUE LOVE** (ASCAP)—J. Powell. Mind If I Make Love to You? (ASCAP)—Verve 2018	19	3
18.	**SOFT SUMMER BREEZE** (BMI)—E. Heywood. Heywood's Bounce (BMI)—Mercury 70863	13	14
19.	**TONIGHT YOU BELONG TO ME** (ASCAP)—Lennon Sisters-L. Welk. Lilacs Bloom Again (ASCAP)—Coral 61701	17	4
20.	**LET THE GOOD TIMES ROLL** (BMI)—Shirley & Lee. Do You Mean to Hurt Me So? (BMI)—Aladdin 3325	—	1
21.	**ALLEGHENY MOON** (ASCAP)—P. Page. Strangest Romance (ASCAP)—Mercury 70878	15	16
22.	**AFTER THE LIGHTS GO DOWN LOW** (BMI)—A. Hibbler. I Was Telling Her About You (ASCAP)—Dec 29982	22	6
23.	**YOU DON'T KNOW ME** (BMI)—J. Vale. Enchanted (ASCAP)—Col 40710	18	12
24.	**I WALK THE LINE** (BMI)—J. Cash. Get Rhythm (BMI)—Sun 241	—	1
25.	**OUT OF SIGHT, OUT OF MIND** (BMI)—Five Keys. That's Right (BMI)—Cap 3502	—	2

• Most Played in Juke Boxes

For survey week ending October 10

RECORDS are ranked in order of the greatest number of plays in juke boxes thruout the country, as determined by The Billboard's weekly survey of the nation's juke box operators. When significant play is reported on both sides of a record, points are combined to determine position on the chart. In such a case, both sides are listed in bold type, the leading side on top.

This Week		Last Week	Weeks on Chart
1.	**DON'T BE CRUEL** (BMI)—E. Presley. **HOUND DOG** (BMI)—Vic 20-6604	1	11
2.	**HONKY TONK** (Parts I & II) (BMI)—B. Doggett. King 4950	3	6
3.	**CANADIAN SUNSET** (BMI)—H. Winterhalter-E. Heywood. This Is Real (ASCAP)—Vic 20-6537	6	10
4.	**MY PRAYER** (ASCAP)—Platters. Heaven on Earth (ASCAP)—Mercury 70893	2	14
5.	**TONIGHT YOU BELONG TO ME** (ASCAP)—Patience & Prudence. A Smile and a Ribbon (ASCAP)—Liberty 55022	5	7
6.	**WHATEVER WILL BE, WILL BE** (ASCAP)—Doris Day. I Gotta Sing Away These Blues (BMI)—Col 40704	4	13
7.	**GREEN DOOR** (BMI)—J. Lowe. (The Story of) The Little Man in Chinatown (BMI)—Dot 15486	11	2
8.	**JUST WALKING IN THE RAIN** (BMI)—J. Ray. In the Candlelight (ASCAP)—Col 40729	8	5
9.	**FOOL** (BMI)—S. Clark. Lonesome for a Letter (BMI)—Dot 15481	10	9
10.	**CHAINS OF LOVE** (BMI)—P. Boone. **FRIENDLY PERSUASION** (ASCAP)—Dot 15490	12	3
11.	**CANADIAN SUNSET** (BMI)—A. Williams. High Upon the Mountain (ASCAP)—Cadence 1297	9	7
12.	**ALLEGHENY MOON** (ASCAP)—P. Page. Strangest Romance (ASCAP)—Mercury 70878	7	16
13.	**IT ISN'T RIGHT** (BMI)—Platters. (BMI)—Mercury 70948. **YOU'LL NEVER, NEVER KNOW** (BMI)—Mercury 70948	16	2
14.	**BLUEBERRY HILL** (ASCAP)—F. Domino. Honey Chile (BMI)—Imperial 5407	—	1
15.	**AFTER THE LIGHTS GO DOWN LOW** (BMI)—A. Hibbler. I Was Telling Her About You (ASCAP)—Dec 29982	14	3
16.	**SONG FOR A SUMMER NIGHT** (Parts I & II) (ASCAP)—M. Miller. Columbia 40730	12	9
17.	**SOFT SUMMER BREEZE** (BMI)—E. Heywood. Heywood's Bounce (BMI)—Mercury 70863	15	7
18.	**YOU DON'T KNOW ME** (BMI)—J. Vale. Enchanted (ASCAP)—Col 40710	—	6
19.	**LAY DOWN YOUR ARMS** (BMI)—Chordettes. Teen-Age Goodnight (BMI)—Cadence 1299	—	1
20.	**WHEN THE WHITE LILACS BLOOM AGAIN** (ASCAP)—H. Zacharaias. Blue Blues (BMI)—Dec 30039	19	2

• Best Selling Sheet Music

Tunes are ranked in order of their current national selling importance at the sheet music jobber level.

This Week		Last Week	Weeks on Chart
1.	**Whatever Will Be, Will Be (Que Sera, Sera)** (Artists Music)	1	15
2.	**Allegheny Moon** (Oxford)	2	17
3.	**Canadian Sunset** (Meridian)	3	11
4.	**Tonight You Belong to Me** (Mills)	4	7
5.	**True Love** (Buxton Hill)	6	4
6.	**Don't Be Cruel** (Presley-Shalimar)	7	6
7.	**Soft Summer Breeze** (Regent)	5	8
8.	**My Prayer** (Shapiro-Bernstein)	8	14
9.	**Just Walking in the Rain** (Golden West)	13	2
9.	**Love Me Tender** (Presley)	—	1
11.	**Song for a Summer Night** (April)	8	9
12.	**Lay Down Your Arms** (Ludlow)	—	1
13.	**When the White Lilacs Bloom Again** (Harms)	11	4
14.	**Wayward Wind** (Warman)	10	11
15.	**Happiness Street** (Planetary)	15	5

• Most Played by Jockeys

For survey week ending October 10

SIDES are ranked in order of the greatest number of plays on disk jockey radio shows thruout the country. Results are based on The Billboard's weekly survey among the nation's disk jockeys. The reverse side of each record is also listed.

This Week		Last Week	Weeks on Chart
1.	**DON'T BE CRUEL** (BMI)—E. Presley. Hound Dog (BMI)—Vic 20-6604	1	11
2.	**CANADIAN SUNSET** (BMI)—H. Winterhalter-E. Heywood. This Is Real (ASCAP)—Vic 20-6537	2	13
3.	**GREEN DOOR** (BMI)—J. Lowe. (Story of) The Little Man in Chinatown (BMI)—Dot 15466	5	4
4.	**JUST WALKING IN THE RAIN** (BMI)—J. Ray. In the Candlelight (ASCAP)—Col 40729	3	4
5.	**FRIENDLY PERSUASION** (ASCAP)—P. Boone. Chains of Love (ASCAP)—Dot 15490	7	5
6.	**HONKY TONK (PARTS I & II)** (BMI)—B. Doggett. King 4950—BMI	6	5
7.	**TONIGHT YOU BELONG TO ME** (ASCAP)—Patience & Prudence. A Smile and a Ribbon (ASCAP)—Liberty 55022	8	9
8.	**MY PRAYER** (ASCAP)- Platters. Heaven on Earth (ASCAP)—Mercury 70893	4	15
9.	**CANADIAN SUNSET** (BMI)—A. Williams. High Upon a Mountain (ASCAP)—Cadence 1297	9	10
10.	**WHATEVER WILL BE, WILL BE** (ASCAP)— Doris Day. I Gotta Sing Away These Blues (BMI)—Col 40704	10	16
11.	**LOVE ME TENDER** (BMI)—E. Presley. Any Way You Want Me (ASCAP)—Vic 20-6643	—	1
12.	**TRUE LOVE** (ASCAP)—B. Crosby & G. Kelly. Well Did You Evah? (ASCAP)—Cap 3507	13	3
13.	**HOUND DOG** (BMI)—E. Presley. Don't Be Cruel (BMI)—Vic 20-6604	11	12
14.	**SOFT SUMMER BREEZE** (BMI)—E. Heywood. Heywood's Bounce (BMI)—Mercury 70863	14	10
15.	**BLUEBERRY HILL** (ASCAP)—F. Domino. Honey Chile (BMI)—Imperial 5407	—	1
16.	**SONG FOR A SUMMER NIGHT (PARTS I & II)** (ASCAP)—M. Miller. Col 40730—ASCAP	12	11
17.	**BUS STOP SONG** (ASCAP)—Four Lads. House With Love in It (ASCAP)—Col 40736	21	4
18.	**FOOL** (BMI)—S. Clark. Lonesome for a Letter (BMI)—Dot 15481	19	8
19.	**ALLEGHENY MOON** (ASCAP)—P. Page. Strangest Romance (ASCAP)—Mercury 70878	15	17
20.	**YOU CAN'T RUN AWAY FROM IT** (ASCAP)—Four Aces. Friendly Persuasion (ASCAP)—Dec 30041	—	1
21.	**ST. THERESE OF THE ROSES** (BMI)— B. Ward. Home Is Where You Hang Your Heart (BMI)—Dec 29933	—	4
22.	**TONIGHT YOU BELONG TO ME** (ASCAP)—Lennon Sisters-L. Welk. When the White Lilacs Bloom Again (ASCAP)—Coral 61701	20	3
23.	**MIRACLE OF LOVE** (BMI)—E. Rodgers. Unwanted Heart (ASCAP)—Col 40708	—	2
24.	**YOU DON'T KNOW ME** (BMI)—J. Vale. Enchanted (ASCAP)—Col 40710	17	10
25.	**HOUSE WITH LOVE IN IT** (ASCAP)—Four Lads. Bus Stop Song (ASCAP)—Col 40736	25	4

THE TOP 100

For survey week ending October 10

A list of the Top 100 RECORD SIDES in the nation according to a COMBINED TABULATION of Dealer, Disk Jockey and Juke Box Operator replies to The Billboard's weekly popular record Best Seller and Most Played surveys. Its purpose is to provide Disk Jockeys with additional programming material and to give trade exposure to NEWER records just beginning to show action in the field.

Pos.	Song, Artist, Label	Last Week
1.	**DON'T BE CRUEL**—E. Presley, Victor	1
2.	**CANADIAN SUNSET**—E. Heywood-H. Winterhalter, Victor	3
3.	**HONKY TONK**—B. Doggett, King	2
4.	**GREEN DOOR**—J. Lowe, Dot	9
5.	**JUST WALKING IN THE RAIN**—J. Ray, Columbia	5
6.	**TONIGHT YOU BELONG TO ME**—Patience & Prudence, Liberty	7
7.	**MY PRAYER**—Platters, Mercury	4
8.	**WHATEVER WILL BE, WILL BE**—Doris Day, Columbia	8
9.	**HOUND DOG**—E. Presley, Victor	6
10.	**FRIENDLY PERSUASION**—P. Boone, Dot	11
11.	**CANADIAN SUNSET**—A. Williams, Cadence	10
12.	**LOVE ME TENDER**—E. Presley, Victor	—
13.	**BLUEBERRY HILL**—F. Domino, Imperial	21
14.	**FOOL**—S. Clark, Dot	13
15.	**SOFT SUMMER BREEZE**—E. Heywood, Mercury	14
16.	**ALLEGHENY MOON**—P. Page, Mercury	12
17.	**SONG FOR A SUMMER NIGHT**—M. Miller, Columbia	15
18.	**TRUE LOVE**—Bing Crosby-G. Kelly, Capitol	35
19.	**TONIGHT YOU BELONG TO ME**—Lennon Sisters-L. Welk, Coral	22
20.	**YOU'LL NEVER, NEVER KNOW**—Platters, Mercury	25
21.	**AFTER THE LIGHTS GO DOWN LOW**—A. Hibbler, Decca	16
22.	**YOU DON'T KNOW ME**—J. Vale, Columbia	17
23.	**BUS STOP SONG**—Four Lads, Columbia	26
24.	**MIRACLE OF LOVE**—E. Rodgers, Columbia	22
25.	**CINDY, OH, CINDY**—V. Martin, Glory	49
26.	**CHAINS OF LOVE**—P. Boone, Dot	24
26.	**IN THE MIDDLE OF THE HOUSE**—R. Draper, Mercury	20
26.	**LAY DOWN YOUR ARMS**—Chordettes, Cadence	36
29.	**I WALK THE LINE**—J. Cash, Sun	43
29.	**IT ISN'T RIGHT**—Platters, Mercury	30
31.	**WHEN THE WHITE LILACS BLOOM AGAIN**—H. Zacharaias, Decca	19
32.	**IN THE MIDDLE OF THE HOUSE**—V. Monroe, Victor	31
33.	**LET THE GOOD TIMES ROLL**—Shirley and Lee, Aladdin	32
34.	**ST. THERESE OF THE ROSES**—B. Ward, Decca	27
35.	**TRUE LOVE**—J. Powell, Verve	37
36.	**FLYING SAUCER**—Buchanan & Goodman, Luniverse	41
37.	**HAPPINESS STREET**—G. Gibbs, Mercury	34
37.	**OUT OF SIGHT, OUT OF MIND**—Five Keys, Capitol	40
39.	**WHEN THE WHITE LILACS BLOOM AGAIN**—B. Vaughn, Dot	46
40.	**CINDY, OH, CINDY**—E. Fisher, Victor	—
41.	**HOUSE WITH LOVE IN IT**—Four Lads, Columbia	32
42.	**SEE-SAW**—Moonglows, Chess	28
43.	**EV'RY DAY OF MY LIFE**—McGuire Sisters, Coral	56
44.	**ITALIAN THEME**—C. Stapleton, London	47
45.	**GARDEN OF EDEN**—J. Valino, Vik	—
46.	**I WANT YOU, I NEED YOU, I LOVE YOU**—E. Presley, Victor	60
47.	**HAPPINESS STREET**—T. Bennett, Columbia	38
48.	**EARTHBOUND**—S. Davis Jr., Decca	54
49.	**FRIENDLY PERSUASION**—Four Aces, Decca	67
50.	**I CAN'T LOVE YOU ENOUGH**—L. Baker, Atlantic	48
50.	**TONIGHT YOU BELONG TO ME**—K. Chandler-J. Wakely, Decca	93
52.	**KA DING DONG**—Hilltoppers, Dot	39
53.	**EARTHBOUND**—M. Lanza, Victor	85
53.	**IN THE STILL OF THE NIGHT**—Satins, Ember	29
55.	**ENDLESS**—McGuire Sisters, Coral	73
55.	**PLEASE DON'T LEAVE ME**—Fontane Sisters, Dot	88
57.	**WHEN MY DREAMBOAT COMES HOME**—F. Domino, Imperial	64
58.	**KA DING DONG**—Diamonds, Mercury	52
59.	**RIP IT UP**—Little Richard, Spepcialty	67
60.	**WHEN THE WHITE LILACS BLOOM AGAIN**—F. ZaBach, Mercury	69
61.	**LAY DOWN YOUR ARMS**—A. Sheldon, Columbia	73
62.	**SADIE'S SHAWL**—B. Sharples, London	63
63.	**JAMAICA FAREWELL**—H. Belafonte, Victor	—
64.	**BLUE MOON**—E. Presley, Victor	55
64.	**FAITHFUL HUSSAR**—T. Heath, London	73
64.	**RIP IT UP**—B. Haley, Decca	42
67.	**THAT'S ALL THERE IS TO THAT**—Nat (King) Cole, Capitol	44
68.	**NAMELY YOU**—D. Cherry, Columbia	81
69.	**YOU'RE IN LOVE**—G. Grant, Era	83
70.	**YOU CAN'T RUN AWAY FROM IT**—Four Aces, Decca	—
71.	**CITY OF ANGELS**—Highlights, Bally	—
72.	**FORTY NINE SHADES OF GREEN**—Ames Brothers, Victor	60
73.	**IT HAPPENED AGAIN**—S. Vaughan, Mercury	90
74.	**I DON'T CARE IF THE SUN DON'T SHINE**—E. Presley, Victor	77
75.	**FROM THE CANDY STORE ON THE CORNER**—T. Bennett, Columbia	51
76.	**IT'S YOURS**—DeCastro Sisters, Abbott	—
77.	**ABC'S OF LOVE**—Teen-Agers, Gee	—
77.	**GIANT**—L. Baxter, Capitol	—
79.	**HEART WITHOUT A SWEETHEART**—G. Storm, Dot	90
79.	**LOVE IN A HOME**—Doris Day, Columbia	—
81.	**BE-BOP-A-LULA**—G. Vincent, Capitol	45
82.	**I ALMOST LOST MY MIND**—P. Boone, Dot	18
83.	**CASUAL LOOK**—Six Teens, Flip	—
83.	**WAR AND PEACE**—V. Damone, Columbia	59
83.	**YOU'RE SENSATIONAL**—F. Sinatra, Capitol	96
86.	**HEART AND SOUL**—J. Maddox, Dot	66
87.	**WHEN THE WHITE LILACS BLOOM AGAIN**—L. Welk, Coral	78
88.	**NOW YOU HAS JAZZ**—Bing Crosby-L. Armstrong, Capitol	94
88.	**SUMMER SWEETHEART**—Ames Brothers, Victor	72
90.	**JULIE**—Doris Day, Columbia	—
91.	**NOW IS THE HOUR**—G. Storm, Dot	64
92.	**KA DING DONG**—G-Clefs, Pilgrim	62
93.	**GIANT**—J. Pleis, Decca	—
94.	**TEEN-AGE GOODNIGHT**—Chordettes, Cadence	—
94.	**WHEN THE WHITE LILACS BLOOM AGAIN**—L. Holmes, M-G-M	—
96.	**FOOL**—Gallahads, Jubilee	70
96.	**RACE WITH THE DEVIL**—G. Vincent, Capitol	—
96.	**SWEET, OLD-FASHIONED GIRL**—T. Brewer, Coral	90
99.	**SOFT SUMMER BREEZE**—Diamonds, Mercury	71
99.	**WAYWARD WIND**—G. Grant, Era	50

CAUTION TO DEALERS AND JUKE BOX OPERATORS

The Billboard's Top 100 is NOT designed to provide tested information for buying purposes. This function is most reliably served by other regular weekly features: Best Sellers in Stores, Most Played in Juke Boxes, Coming Up Strong and Best Buys.

• Best Sellers in Stores

For survey week ending October 17

RECORDS are ranked in order of their current national selling importance at the retail level, as determined by The Billboard's weekly survey of the top volume dealers in every important market area. When significant action is reported on both sides of a record, points are combined to determine position on the chart. In such a case, both sides are listed in bold type, the leading side on top.

This Week		Last Week	Weeks on Chart
1.	**DON'T BE CRUEL** (BMI)—E. Presley **HOUND DOG** (BMI)—Vic 20-6604	1	13
2.	**LOVE ME TENDER** (BMI)—E. Presley Any Way You Want Me (BMI)—Vic 20-6643	2	2
3.	**GREEN DOOR** (BMI)—J. Lowe (Story of) The Little Man in Chinatown (BMI)—Dot 15486	3	5
4.	**HONKY TONK** (Parts I & II) (BMI)—B. Doggett King 4950—BMI	4	10
5.	**JUST WALKING IN THE RAIN** (BMI)—J. Ray In The Candlelight (ASCAP)—Col 40729	5	8
6.	**CANADIAN SUNSET** (BMI)—H. Winterhalter This Is Real (ASCAP)—Vic 20-6537	6	14
7.	**TONIGHT YOU BELONG TO ME** (ASCAP)—Patience & Prudence A Smile and a Ribbon (ASCAP)—Liberty 55022	7	10
8.	**WHATEVER WILL BE, WILL BE** (ASCAP)—Doris Day I Gotta Sing Away These Blues (BMI)—Col 40704	8	17
9.	**BLUEBERRY HILL** (ASCAP)—F. Domino Honey Chile (BMI)—Imperial 5407	11	3
10.	**FRIENDLY PERSUASION** (ASCAP)—P. Boone **CHAINS OF LOVE** (BMI)—Dot 15490	9	6
11.	**TRUE LOVE** (ASCAP)—B. Crosby-G. Kelly Well, Did You Evah (ASCAP)—Cap 3507	12	4
12.	**MY PRAYER** (ASCAP)—Platters Heaven on Earth (ASCAP)—Mercury 70893	10	16
13.	**CINDY, OH, CINDY** (BMI)—V. Martin Only If I Praise the Lord (BMI)—Glory 247	15	3
14.	**CANADIAN SUNSET** (BMI)—A. Williams High Up on a Mountain (ASCAP)—Cadence 1297	14	9
15.	**TRUE LOVE** (ASCAP)—J. Powell Mind If I Make Love to You? (ASCAP)—Verve 2018	17	4
16.	**FOOL** (BMI)—S. Clark Lonesome for a Letter (BMI)—Dot 15481	16	12
17.	**YOU'LL NEVER, NEVER KNOW** (BMI)—Platters **IT ISN'T RIGHT** (BMI)—Mercury 70848	13	3
18.	**SOFT SUMMER BREEZE** (BMI)—E. Heywood Heywood's Bounce (BMI)—Mercury 70863	18	15
19.	**YOU DON'T KNOW ME** (BMI)—J. Vale Enchanted (ASCAP)—Col 40710	23	13
20.	**ALLEGHENY MOON** (ASCAP)—P. Page Strangest Romance (ASCAP)—Mercury 70878	21	17
21.	**LET THE GOOD TIMES ROLL** (BMI)—Shirley & Lee Do You Mean to Hurt Me So? (BMI)—Aladdin 3325	20	2
22.	**TONIGHT YOU BELONG TO ME** (ASCAP)—Lennon Sisters-L. Welk When the White Lilacs Bloom Again (ASCAP)—Coral 61701	19	5
23.	**MIRACLE OF LOVE** (ASCAP)—E. Rodgers Unwanted Heart (ASCAP)—Col 40708	—	4
24.	**OUT OF SIGHT, OUT OF MIND** (BMI)—Five Keys That's Right (BMI)—Cap 3502	25	3
24.	**HOUSE WITH LOVE IN IT** (ASCAP)—Four Lads **BUS STOP SONG** (ASCAP)—Col 40736	—	5

• Most Played in Juke Boxes

For survey week ending October 17

RECORDS are ranked in order of the greatest number of plays in juke boxes thruout the country, as determined by The Billboard's weekly survey of the nation's juke box operators. When significant play is reported on both sides of a record, points are combined to determine position on the chart. In such a case, both sides are listed in bold type, the leading side on top.

This Week		Last Week	Weeks on Chart
1.	**DON'T BE CRUEL** (BMI)—E. Presley **HOUND DOG** (BMI)—Vic 20-6643	1	12
2.	**HONKY TONK** (PARTS I & II) (BMI)—B. Doggett King 4950	2	7
3.	**JUST WALKING IN THE RAIN** (BMI)—J. Ray In the Candlelight (ASCAP)—Col 40729	8	6
4.	**WHATEVER WILL BE, WILL BE** (ASCAP)—Doris Day I Gotta Sing Away These Blues (BMI)—Col 40704	6	14
5.	**CANADIAN SUNSET** (BMI) H. Winterhalter-E. Heywood This Is Real (ASCAP)—Vic 20-6537	3	11
6.	**TONIGHT YOU BELONG TO ME** (ASCAP) Patience and Prudence A Smile and a Ribbon (ASCAP)—Liberty 55022	5	8
6.	**GREEN DOOR** (BMI)—J. Lowe (The Story of) The Little Man in Chinatown (BMI)—Dot 15486	7	3
8.	**MY PRAYER** (ASCAP)—Platters Heaven on Earth (ASCAP)—Mercury 70893	4	15
9.	**FOOL** (BMI)—S. Clark Lonesome for a Letter (BMI)—Dot 15481	9	10
9.	**FRIENDLY PERSUASION** (ASCAP)—P. Boone **CHAINS OF LOVE** (BMI)—Dot 15490	10	4
11.	**ALLEGHENY MOON** (ASCAP)—P. Page Strangest Romance (ASCAP)—Mercury 70878	12	17
12.	**BLUEBERRY HILL** (ASCAP)—F. Domino Honey Chile (BMI)—Imperial 5407	14	2
13.	**YOU'LL NEVER, NEVER KNOW** (BMI)—Platters **IT ISN'T RIGHT** (BMI)—Mercury 70948	13	3
14.	**CANADIAN SUNSET** (BMI)—A. Williams High Upon the Mountain (ASCAP)—Cadence 1297	11	8
15.	**YOU DON'T KNOW ME** (BMI)—J. Vale Enchanted (ASCAP)—Col 40710	18	7
15.	**LOVE ME TENDER** (BMI)—E. Presley Any Way You Want Me (ASCAP)—Vic 20-6643	—	1
17.	**TONIGHT YOU BELONG TO ME** (ASCAP)—Lennon Sisters-L. Welk When the White Lilacs Bloom Again (ASCAP)—Coral 61701	—	1
18.	**SOFT SUMMER BREEZE** (BMI)—E. Heywood Heywood's Bounce (BMI)—Mercury 70863	17	8
19.	**AFTER THE LIGHTS GO DOWN LOW** (BMI)—A. Hibbler I Was Telling Her About You (ASCAP)—Dec 29982	15	4
19.	**LAY DOWN YOUR ARMS** (BMI)—Chordettes Teen-Age Goodnight (BMI)—Cadence 1299	19	2

• Best Selling Sheet Music

Tunes are ranked in order of their current national selling importance at the sheet music jobbers level.

This Week		Last Week	Weeks on Chart
1.	**Whatever Will Be, Will Be (Que Sera, Sera)** (Artists Music)	1	16
2.	**Allegheny Moon** (Oxford)	2	18
3.	**Canadian Sunset** (Meridian)	3	12
4.	**Tonight You Belong to Me** (Mills)	4	8
5.	**True Love** (Buxton Hill)	5	6
6.	**Just Walking in the Rain** (Golden West)	9	3
7.	**Love Me Tender** (Presley)	9	2
8.	**Soft Summer Breeze** (Regent)	7	9
8.	**Don't Be Cruel** (Presley-Shalimar)	6	7
10.	**My Prayer** (Shapiro-Bernstein)	8	15
11.	**Song for a Summer Night** (April)	11	10
12.	**Honky Tonk** (Billace)	—	1
13.	**Green Door** (Trinity)	—	1
14.	**Wayward Wind** (Warman)	14	12
14.	**Lay Down Your Arms** (Ludlow)	12	8

• Most Played by Jockeys

For survey week ending October 17

SIDES are ranked in order of the greatest number of plays on disk jockey radio shows thruout the country. Results are based on The Billboard's weekly survey among the nation's disk jockeys. The reverse side of each record is also listed.

This Week		Last Week	Weeks on Chart
1.	**DON'T BE CRUEL** (BMI)—E. Presley Hound Dog (BMI)—Vic 20-6604	1	12
2.	**GREEN DOOR** (BMI)—J. Lowe (Story of) The Little Man in Chinatown (BMI)—Dot 15486	3	5
3.	**JUST WALKING IN THE RAIN** (BMI)—J. Ray In the Candlelight (ASCAP)—Col 40729	4	5
4.	**LOVE ME TENDER** (BMI)—E. Presley Any Way You Want Me (BMI)—Vic 20-6643	11	2
5.	**CANADIAN SUNSET** (BMI)—H. Winterhalter-E. Heywood This Is Real (ASCAP)—Vic 20-6537	2	14
6.	**FRIENDLY PERSUASION** (ASCAP)—P. Boone Chains of Love (ASCAP)—Dot 15490	5	6
7.	**TONIGHT YOU BELONG TO ME** (ASCAP)—Patience & Prudence A Smile and a Ribbon (ASCAP)—Liberty 55022	7	10
8.	**HONKY TONK** (Parts I & II) (BMI)—B. Doggett King 4950—BMI	6	6
9.	**CANADIAN SUNSET** (BMI)—A. Williams High Upon a Mountain (ASCAP)—Cadence 1297	9	11
10.	**WHATEVER WILL BE, WILL BE** (ASCAP)—Doris Day I Gotta Sing Away These Blues (BMI)—Col 40704	10	17
11.	**TRUE LOVE** (ASCAP)—B. Crosby-G. Kelly Well, Did You Evah? (ASCAP)—Cap 3507	12	4
12.	**MY PRAYER** (ASCAP)—Platters Heaven on Earth (ASCAP)—Mercury 70893	8	16
13.	**HOUND DOG** (BMI)—E. Presley Don't Be Cruel (BMI)—Vic 20-6604	13	13
14.	**SOFT SUMMER BREEZE** (BMI)—E. Heywood Heywood's Bounce (BMI)—Mercury 70863	14	11
15.	**BLUEBERRY HILL** (ASCAP)—F. Domino Honey Chile (BMI)—Imperial 5407	15	2
16.	**TONIGHT YOU BELONG TO ME** (ASCAP)—Lennon Sisters-L. Welk When the White Lilacs Bloom Again (ASCAP)—Coral 61701	22	4
17.	**JEALOUS LOVER** (ASCAP)—F. Sinatra You Forgot All the Words (BMI)—Cap 3552	—	1
18.	**SONG FOR A SUMMER NIGHT** (PARTS I & II)—M. Miller Col 40730—ASCAP	16	12
19.	**WHEN THE WHITE LILACS BLOOM AGAIN** (ASCAP)—H. Zacharaias Blue Blues (BMI)—Dec 30039	—	6
20.	**CINDY, OH CINDY** (BMI)—E. Fisher Around the World (ASCAP)—Vic 20-6677	—	1
21.	**ALLEGHENY MOON** (ASCAP)—P. Page Strangest Romance (ASCAP)—Mercury 70878	19	18
22.	**MIRACLE OF LOVE** (ASCAP)—E. Rodgers Unwanted Heart (ASCAP)—Col 40708	23	3
23.	**AFTER THE LIGHTS GO DOWN LOW** (BMI)—A. Hibbler I Was Telling Her About You (ASCAP)—Decca 29982	—	8
23.	**HAPPINESS STREET** (ASCAP)—G. Gibbs Happiness Is a Thing Called Joe (ASCAP)—Mercury 70920	—	6
25.	**YOU CAN'T RUN AWAY FROM IT** (ASCAP)—Four Aces Friendly Persuasion (ASCAP)—Dec 30041	20	2

THE TOP 100

For survey week ending October 17

A list of the Top 100 RECORD SIDES in the nation according to a COMBINED TABULATION of Dealer, Disk Jockey and Juke Box Operator replies to The Billboard's weekly popular record Best Seller and Most Played surveys. Its purpose is to provide Disk Jockeys with additional programming material and to give trade exposure to NEWER records just beginning to show action in the field.

Pos.	Song, Artist, Label	Last Week
1.	**DON'T BE CRUEL**—E. Presley, Victor	1
2.	**JUST WALKING IN THE RAIN**—J. Ray, Columbia	5
3.	**GREEN DOOR**—J. Lowe, Dot	4
4.	**HONKY TONK**—B. Doggett, King	3
5.	**CANADIAN SUNSET**—E. Heywood-H. Winterhalter, Victor	2
6.	**LOVE ME TENDER**—E. Presley, Victor	12
7.	**TONIGHT YOU BELONG TO ME**—Patience & Prudence, Liberty	6
8.	**WHATEVER WILL BE, WILL BE**—Doris Day, Columbia	8
9.	**HOUND DOG**—E. Presley, Victor	9
10.	**FRIENDLY PERSUASION**—P. Boone, Dot	10
11.	**MY PRAYER**—Platters, Mercury	7
12.	**BLUEBERRY HILL**—F. Domino, Imperial	13
13.	**CANADIAN SUNSET**—A Williams, Cadence	11
14.	**SOFT SUMMER BREEZE**—E. Heywood, Mercury	15
15.	**ALLEGHENY MOON**—P Page, Mercury	16
16.	**TONIGHT YOU BELONG TO ME**—Lennon Sisters-L. Welk, Coral	19
17.	**FOOL**—S. Clark, Dot	14
17.	**TRUE LOVE**—Bing Crosby-G. Kelly, Capitol	18
19.	**YOU DON'T KNOW ME**—J. Vale, Columbia	22
20.	**MIRACLE OF LOVE**—E. Rodgers, Columbia	24
21.	**SONG FOR A SUMMER NIGHT**—M. Miller, Columbia	17
22.	**AFTER THE LIGHTS GO DOWN LOW**—A. Hibbler, Decca	21
23.	**YOU'LL NEVER, NEVER KNOW**—Platters, Mercury	20
24.	**CHAINS OF LOVE**—P. Boone, Dot	26
24.	**IT ISN'T RIGHT**—Platters, Mercury	29
26.	**CINDY, OH, CINDY**—V. Martin, Glory	25
27.	**LET THE GOOD TIMES ROLL**—Shirley & Lee, Aladdin	33
28.	**TRUE LOVE**—J. Powell, Verve	35
29.	**WHEN THE WHITE LILACS BLOOM AGAIN**—H. Zacharaias, Decca	31
30.	**LAY DOWN YOUR ARMS**—Chordettes, Cadence	26
31.	**IN THE MIDDLE OF THE HOUSE**—V. Monroe, Victor	32
32.	**IN THE MIDDLE OF THE HOUSE**—R. Draper, Mercury	26
33.	**BUS STOP SONG**—Four Lads. Columbia	23
34.	**CINDY, OH, CINDY**—E. Fisher, Victor	40
35.	**HOUSE WITH LOVE IN IT**—Four Lads, Columbia	41
36.	**GARDEN OF EDEN**—J. Valino, Vik	45
37.	**I WALK THE LINE**—J. Cash, Sun	29
38.	**ST. THERESE OF THE ROSES**—B. Ward, Decca	34
39	**OUT OF SIGHT, OUT OF MIND**—Five Keys, Capitol	37
40.	**EV'RY DAY OF MY LIFE**—McGuire Sisters. Coral	43
41.	**IN THE STILL OF THE NIGHT**—Satins, Ember	53
42.	**SEE-SAW**—Moonglows, Chess	42
43.	**HAPPINESS STREET**—G. Gibbs, Mercury	37
44.	**JEALOUS LOVER**—F. Sinatra, Capitol	—
45.	**PETTICOATS OF PORTUGAL**—D. Jacobs, Coral	—
46.	**EARTHBOUND**—S Davis Jr., Decca	48
47.	**I WANT YOU, I NEED YOU, I LOVE YOU**—E. Presley, Victor	46
48.	**I CAN'T LOVE YOU ENOUGH**—L. Baker, Atlantic	50
49.	**HAPPINESS STREET**.—T. Bennett, Columbia	47
49.	**NIGHT LIGHTS**—N. (King) Cole, Capitol	—
49.	**TWO DIFFERENT WORLDS**—D. Rondo, Jubilee	—
52.	**SADIE'S SHAWL**—B. Sharples, London	62
52.	**TONIGHT YOU BELONG TO ME**—K. Chandler-J. Wakely. Decca	50
54.	**WHEN THE WHITE LILACS BLOOM AGAIN**—B. Vaughn, Dot	39
55.	**MAMA FROM THE TRAIN**—P. Page, Mercury	—
56.	**PLEASE DON'T LEAVE ME**—Fontane Sisters, Dot	55
57.	**FLYING SAUCER**—Buchannan & Goodman, Luniverse	36
57.	**FRIENDLY PERSUASION**—Four Aces, Decca	49
59.	**LAY DOWN YOUR ARMS**—A. Sheldon, Columbia	61
59.	**THAT'S ALL THERE IS TO THAT**—N. (King) Cole, Capitol	67
61.	**BE-BOP-A-LULA**—G. Vincent, Capitol	81
61.	**ITALIAN THEME**—C Stapleton, London	44
63.	**HEART AND SOUL**—J. Maddox, Dot	86
64.	**KA DING DONG**—Diamonds, Mercury	58
65.	**NAMELY YOU**—D. Cherry, Columbia	68
66.	**JAMAICA FAREWELL**—H. Belafonte, Victor	63
67.	**ENDLESS**—McGuire Sisters, Coral	55
67.	**FAITHFUL HUSSAR**—T. Heath, London	64
69.	**WAR AND PEACE**—V. Damone, Columbia	83
70.	**SOFT SUMMER BREEZE**—Diamonds, Mercury	99
71.	**KA DING DONG**—Hilltoppers, Dot	52
72.	**SINGING THE BLUES**—G. Mitchell, Columbia	—
72.	**PRISCILLA**—E. Cooley, Roost	—
74.	**I MISS YOU SO**—C. Connor, Atlantic	—
75.	**WHEN THE WHITE LILACS BLOOM AGAIN**—F. ZaBach, Mercury	60
76.	**FROM THE CANDY STORE ON THE CORNER**—T. Bennett, Columbia	75
77.	**RIP IT UP**—Little Richard, Specialty	59
78.	**YOU CAN'T RUN AWAY FROM IT**—Four Aces, Decca	70
79.	**NOW IS THE HOUR**—G. Storm, Dot	91
80.	**SO LONG**—F. Domino, Imperial	—
81.	**KA DING DONG**—G-Clefs, Pilgram	92
82.	**WHEN THE WHITE LILACS BLOOM AGAIN**—L. Welk, Coral	87
83.	**I ALMOST LOST MY MIND**—P. Boone, Dot	82
84.	**BLUE MOON**—E. Presley. Victor	64
84.	**RIP IT UP**—B. Haley, Decca	64
86.	**YOU'RE IN LOVE**—G. Grant, Era	69
87.	**I DON'T CARE IF THE SUN DON'T SHINE**—E. Presley, Victor	74
87.	**TEEN-AGE GOODNIGHT**—Chordettes, Cadence	94
89.	**NOW YOU HAS JAZZ**—Bing Crosby-L. Armstrong, Capitol	88
90.	**HEART WITHOUT A SWEETHEART**—G. Storm, Dot	79
90.	**LOVE IN A HOME**—Doris Day, Columbia	79
90.	**STILL**—Fontane Sisters, Dot	—
90.	**TO THE ENDS OF THE EARTH**—N. (King) Cole, Capitol	—
94.	**IT HAPPENED AGAIN**—S. Vaughan, Mercury	73
95.	**WHEN MY DREAMBOAT COMES HOME**—F. Domino, Imperial	57
96.	**WAYWARD WIND**—G. Grant, Era	99
97.	**EARTHBOUND**—M. Lanza, Victor	53
97.	**JUST LOVE ME**—J. P. Morgan, Victor	—
99.	**HEAVEN ON EARTH**—Platters, Mercury	—
99.	**IT'S YOURS**—DeCastro Sisters, Abbott	76
99.	**SUMMER SWEETHEART**—Ames Brothers, Victor	88

CAUTION TO DEALERS AND JUKE BOX OPERATORS

The Billboard's Top 100 is NOT designed to provide tested information for buying purposes. This function is most reliably served by other regular weekly features: Best Sellers in Stores, Most Played in Juke Boxes, Coming Up Strong and Best Buys.

• Best Sellers in Stores

For survey week ending October 24

RECORDS are ranked in order of their current national selling importance at the retail level, as determined by The Billboard's weekly survey of the top volume dealers in every important market area. When significant action is reported on both sides of a record, points are combined to determine position on the chart. In such a case, both sides are listed in bold type, the leading side on top.

This Week	Record	Last Week	Weeks on Chart
1.	**LOVE ME TENDER** (BMI)—E. Presley Any Way you Want Me (BMI)—Vic 20-6643	2	3
2.	**DON'T BE CRUEL** (BMI)—E. Presley. **HOUND DOG** (BMI)—Vic 20-6604	1	14
3.	**GREEN DOOR** (BMI)—J. Lowe...... (Story of) The Little Man in Chinatown (BMI)—Dot 15486	3	6
4.	**JUST WALKING IN THE RAIN** (BMI)—J. Ray.................. In the Candlelight (ASCAP)—Col 40729	5	9
5.	**HONKY TONK (Parts I & II)** (BMI)—B. Doggett...................... King 4950—BMI	4	11
6.	**BLUEBERRY HILL** (ASCAP)—F. Domino...................... Honey Chile (BMI)—Imperial 5407	9	4
7.	**CANADIAN SUNSET** (BMI)—H. Winterhalter................ This Is Real (ASCAP)—Vic 20-6537	6	15
8.	**TRUE LOVE** (ASCAP)—B. Crosby-G. Kelly......................... Well, Did You Evah (ASCAP)—Cap 3507	11	5
9.	**TONIGHT YOU BELONG TO ME** (ASCAP)—Patience & Prudence..... A Smile and a Ribbon (ASCAP)—Liberty 55022	7	11
10.	**FRIENDLY PERSUASION** (ASCAP) P. Boone...................... **CHAINS OF LOVE** (BMI)—Dot 15490	10	7
11.	**SINGING THE BLUES** (BMI) G. Mitchell.................... Crazy With Love (ASCAP)—Col 40769	—	1
12.	**WHATEVER WILL BE, WILL BE** (ASCAP)—Doris Day............ I Gotta Sing Away These Blues (BMI)—Col 40704	8	18
13.	**CINDY, OH, CINDY** (BMI)—V. Martin......................... Only If I Praise the Lord (BMI)—Glory 247	13	4
14.	**IT ISN'T RIGHT** (BMI)—Platters.... **YOU'LL NEVER, NEVER KNOW** (BMI)—Mercury 70948	17	4
15.	**TRUE LOVE** (ASCAP)—J. Powell.... Mind If I Make Love to You? (ASCAP)—Verve 2018	15	5
16.	**TONIGHT YOU BELONG TO ME** (ASCAP)—Lennon Sisters-L. Welk........................ When the White Lilacs Bloom Again (ASCAP)—Coral 61701	22	6
17.	**MY PRAYER** (ASCAP)—Platters...... Heaven on Earth (ASCAP)—Mercury 70893	12	17
18.	**CANADIAN SUNSET** (BMI)—A. Williams........................ High Up on a Mountain (ASCAP)—Cadence 1297	14	10
19.	**FOOL** (BMI)—S. Clark............. Lonesome for a Letter (BMI)—Dot 15481	16	13
20.	**SOFT SUMMER BREEZE** (BMI)—E. Heywood................... Heywood's Bounce (BMI)—Mercury 70863	18	16
21.	**CINDY, OH, CINDY** (BMI)—E. Fisher Around the World (ASCAP)—Vic 20-6677	—	1
22.	**I WALK THE LINE** (BMI)—J. Cash.. Get Rhythm (BMI)—Sun 241	—	2
23.	**YOU DON'T KNOW ME** (BMI)—J. Vale......................... Enchanted (ASCAP)—Col 40710	19	14
24.	**JEALOUS LOVER** (ASCAP)—F. Sinatra....................... You Forgot All the Words (BMI)—Cap 3552	—	1
25.	**LET THE GOOD TIMES ROLL** (BMI)—Shirley & Lee............. Do You Mean to Hurt Me So? (BMI)—Aladdin 3325	21	3

• Most Played in Juke Boxes

For survey week ending October 24

RECORDS are ranked in order of the greatest number of plays in juke boxes thruout the country, as determined by The Billboard's weekly survey of the nation's juke box operators. When significant play is reported on both sides of a record, points are combined to determine position on the chart. In such a case, both sides are listed in bold type, the leading side on top.

This Week	Record	Last Week	Weeks on Chart
1.	**DON'T BE CRUEL** (BMI)—E. Presley **HOUND DOG** (BMI)—Vic 20-6643	1	13
2.	**HONKY TONK (PARTS I & II)** (BMI)—B. Doggett................ King 4950	2	8
3.	**GREEN DOOR** (BMI)—J. Lowe...... (The Story of) The Little Man in Chinatown (BMI)—Dot 15486	6	4
4.	**JUST WALKING IN THE RAIN** (BMI)—J. Ray.................. In the Candlelight (ASCAP)—Col 40729	3	7
5.	**CANADIAN SUNSET** (BMI)—H. Winterhalter-E. Heywood....... This Is Real (ASCAP)—Vic 20-6537	5	12
6.	**WHATEVER WILL BE, WILL BE** (ASCAP)—Doris Day............. I Gotta Sing Away These Blues (BMI)—Col 40704	4	15
7.	**TONIGHT YOU BELONG TO ME** (ASCAP)—Patience & Prudence..... A Smile and a Ribbon (ASCAP)—Liberty 55022	6	9
8.	**FRIENDLY PERSUASION** (ASCAP)—P. Boone....................... **CHAINS OF LOVE** (BMI)—Dot 15490	9	5
9.	**MY PRAYER** (ASCAP)—Platters...... Heaven On Earth (ASCAP)—Mercury 70893	8	16
10.	**LOVE ME TENDER** (BMI)—E. Presley......................... Any Way You Want Me (ASCAP)—Vic 20-6643	15	2
11.	**FOOL** (BMI)—S. Clark............. Lonesome for a Letter (BMI)—Dot 15481	9	11
12.	**BLUEBERRY HILL** (ASCAP)—F. Domino...................... Honey Chile (BMI)—Imperial 5407	12	3
13.	**ALLEGHENY MOON** (ASCAP)—P. Page......................... Strangest Romance (ASCAP)—Mercury 70878	11	18
13.	**YOU'LL NEVER, NEVER KNOW** (BMI)—Platters...................... **IT ISN'T RIGHT** (BMI)—Mercury 70948	13	4
15.	**SOFT SUMMER BREEZE** (BMI)—E. Heywood................... Heywood's Bounce (BMI)—Mercury 70863	18	9
16.	**CANADIAN SUNSET** (BMI)—A. Williams..................... High Upon the Mountain (ASCAP)—Cadence 1297	14	9
17.	**LAY DOWN YOUR ARMS** (BMI)—Chordettes .... Teen-Age Goodnight (BMI)—Cadence 1299	19	3
17.	**TRUE LOVE** (ASCAP)—Bing Crosby-G. Kelly............. Well, Did You Evah? (ASCAP)—Cap 3507	—	1
19.	**YOU DON'T KNOW ME** (BMI)—J. Vale......................... Enchanted (ASCAP)—Col 40710	15	8
20.	**TONIGHT YOU BELONG TO ME** (ASCAP)—Lennon Sisters-L. Welk... When the White Lilacs Bloom Again (ASCAP)—Coral 61701	17	2

• Best Selling Sheet Music

Tunes are ranked in order of their current national selling importance at the sheet music jobber level.

This Week	Title	Last Week	Weeks on Chart
1.	**Allegheny Moon** (Oxford)	2	19
2.	**Love Me Tender** (Presley)	7	3
3.	**Whatever Will Be, Will Be (Que Sera, Sera)** (Artists)	1	17
4.	**Tonight You Belong to Me** (Mills)............	4	9
5.	**Canadian Sunset,** (Meridian)	3	13
6.	**True Love** (Buxton Hill)	5	6
7.	**Just Walking in the Rain** (Golden West)	6	4
8.	**Don't Be Cruel** (Presley-Shalimar)	8	8
8.	**Honky Tonk** (Billace)	12	2
10.	**My Prayer** (Shapiro-Bernstein)	10	16
11.	**Friendly Persuasion** (Feist)	—	1
12.	**Green Door** (Trinity)	13	2
13.	**Soft Summer Breeze** (Regent)	8	10
14.	**Lay Down Your Arms** (Ludlow)	14	3
15.	**Italian Theme** (Maurice)	—	1

• Most Played by Jockeys

For survey week ending October 24

SIDES are ranked in order of the greatest number of plays on disk jockey radio shows thruout the country. Results are based on The Billboard's weekly survey among the nation's disk jockeys. The reverse side of each record is also listed.

This Week	Record	Last Week	Weeks on Chart
1.	**LOVE ME TENDER** (BMI)—E. Presley......................... Any Way You Want Me (BMI)—Vic 20-6643	4	3
2.	**GREEN DOOR** (BMI)—J. Lowe...... (Story of) The Little Man in Chinatown (BMI)—Dot 15486	2	6
3.	**DON'T BE CRUEL** (BMI)—E. Presley. Hound Dog (BMI)—Vic 20-6604	1	13
4.	**JUST WALKING IN THE RAIN** (BMI)—J. Ray.................... In the Candlelight (ASCAP)—Col 40729	3	6
5.	**CANADIAN SUNSET** (BMI)—H. Winterhalter-E. Heywood....... This Is Real (ASCAP)—Vic 20-6537	5	15
6.	**FRIENDLY PERSUASION** (ASCAP)—P. Boone .... Chains of Love (ASCAP)—Dot 15490	6	7
7.	**TRUE LOVE** (ASCAP)—B. Crosby-G. Kelly............... Well, Did You Evah? (ASCAP)—Cap 3507	11	5
8.	**TONIGHT YOU BELONG TO ME** (ASCAP)—Patience & Prudence..... A Smile and a Ribbon (ASCAP)—Liberty 55022	7	11
9.	**CANADIAN SUNSET** (BMI)—A. Williams..................... High Upon a Mountain (ASCAP)—Cadence 1297	9	12
10.	**BLUEBERRY HILL** (ASCAP)—F. Domino...................... Honey Chile (BMI)—Imperial 5407	15	3
11.	**HONKY TONK (Parts I & II)** (BMI)—B. Doggett...................... King 4950—BMI	8	7
12.	**WHATEVER WILL BE, WILL BE** (ASCAP)—Doris Day............. I Gotta Sing Away These Blues (BMI)—Col 40704	10	18
13.	**JEALOUS LOVER** (ASCAP)—F. Sinatra...................... You Forget All the Words (BMI)—Cap 3552	17	2
14.	**CINDY, OH CINDY** (BMI)—E. Fisher. Around the World (ASCAP)—Vic 20-6677	20	2
15.	**SINGING THE BLUES** (BMI)—G. Mitchell....................... Crazy With Love (ASCAP)—Col 40769	—	1
16.	**MAMA FROM THE TRAIN** (ASCAP)—P. Page................ Every Time—I Feel His Spirit (BMI)—Mercury 70971	—	1
17.	**NIGHT LIGHTS** (ASCAP)—Nat (King) Cole.................. To the Ends of the Earth (BMI)—Cap 3551	—	1
18.	**TWO DIFFERENT WORLDS** (ASCAP)—D. Rondo............... He Made You Mine (ASCAP)—Jubilee 5256	—	1
19.	**TONIGHT YOU BELONG TO ME** (ASCAP)—Lennon Sisters-L. Welk... When the White Lilacs Bloom Again (ASCAP)—Coral 61701	16	5
20.	**HOUND DOG** (BMI)—E. Presley..... Don't Be Cruel (BMI)—Vic 20-6604	13	14
21.	**AFTER THE LIGHTS GO DOWN LOW** (BMI)—A. Hibbler........... I Was Telling Her About You (ASCAP)—Decca 29982	23	9
22.	**ST. THERESE OF THE ROSES** (BMI)—B. Ward.................. Home Is Where You Hang Your Heart (BMI)—Dec 29933	—	5
23.	**MY PRAYER** (ASCAP)—Platters....... Heaven On Earth (ASCAP)—Mercury 70893	12	17
24.	**IN THE MIDDLE OF THE HOUSE** (ASCAP)—R. Draper Rollin' Heart (BMI)—Mercury 70921	—	2
25.	**SOFT SUMMER BREEZE** (BMI)—E. Heywood......................... Heywood's Bounce (BMI)—Mercury 70863	14	12

THE TOP 100

For survey week ending October 24

A list of the Top 100 RECORD SIDES in the nation according to a COMBINED TABULATION of Dealer, Disk Jockey and Juke Box Operator replies to The Billboard's weekly popular record Best Seller and Most Played surveys. Its purpose is to provide Disk Jockeys with additional programming material and to give trade exposure to NEWER records just beginning to show action in the field.

Pos.	Song, Artist, Label	Last Week
1.	**GREEN DOOR**—J. Lowe, Dot	3
2.	**DON'T BE CRUEL**—E. Presley, Victor	1
3.	**JUST WALKING IN THE RAIN**—J. Ray, Columbia	2
3.	**LOVE ME TENDER**—E. Presley, Victor	6
5.	**CANADIAN SUNSET**—E. Heywood-H. Winterhalter, Victor	5
6.	**HONKY TONK**—B. Doggett, King	4
7.	**TONIGHT YOU BELONG TO ME**—Patience & Prudence, Liberty	7
8.	**BLUEBERRY HILL**—F. Domino, Imperial	12
9.	**FRIENDLY PERSUASION**—P. Boone, Dot	10
9.	**WHATEVER WILL BE, WILL BE**—Doris Day, Columbia	8
11.	**TRUE LOVE**—Bing Crosby-G. Kelly, Capitol	17
12.	**HOUND DOG**—E. Presley, Victor	9
13.	**CANADIAN SUNSET**—A. Williams, Cadence	13
14.	**MY PRAYER**—Platters, Mercury	11
15.	**TONIGHT YOU BELONG TO ME**—Lennon Sisters-L. Welk, Coral	16
16.	**SOFT SUMMER BREEZE**—E. Heywood, Mercury	14
17.	**CINDY, OH, CINDY**—V. Martin, Glory	26
18.	**JEALOUS LOVER**—F. Sinatra, Capitol	44
19.	**SINGING THE BLUES**—G Mitchell, Columbia	72
20.	**YOU'LL NEVER, NEVER KNOW**—Platters, Mercury	23
20.	**CINDY, OH, CINDY**—E. Fisher, Victor	34
22.	**ALLEGHENY MOON**—P. Page, Mercury	15
22.	**FOOL**—S. Clark, Dot	17
24.	**LAY DOWN YOUR ARMS**—Chordettes, Cadence	30
25.	**YOU DON'T KNOW ME**—J. Vale, Columbia	19
25.	**AFTER THE LIGHTS GO DOWN LOW**—A. Hibbler, Decca	22
27.	**IT ISN'T RIGHT**—Platters, Mercury	24
28.	**MIRACLE OF LOVE**—E. Rodgers, Columbia	20
29.	**CHAINS OF LOVE**—P. Boone, Dot	24
30.	**TRUE LOVE**—J. Powell, Verve	28
31.	**SONG FOR A SUMMER NIGHT**—M. Miller, Columbia	21
32.	**MAMA FROM THE TRAIN**—P. Page, Mercury	55
33.	**BUS STOP SONG**—Four Lads, Columbia	33
34.	**IN THE STILL OF THE NIGHT**—Satins, Ember	41
34.	**PETTICOATS OF PORTUGAL**—D. Jacobs, Coral	45
36.	**I WALK THE LINE**—J. Cash, Sun	37
36.	**ST. THERESE OF THE ROSES**—B. Ward, Decca	38
38.	**EV'RYDAY OF MY LIFE**—McGuire Sisters, Coral	40
39.	**LET THE GOOD TIMES ROLL**—Shirley and Lee, Aladdin	27
40.	**IN THE MIDDLE OF THE HOUSE**—R. Draper, Mercury	32
41.	**GARDEN OF EDEN**—J. Valino, Vik	36
42.	**IN THE MIDDLE OF THE HOUSE**—V. Monroe, Victor	31
43.	**OUT OF SIGHT OUT OF MIND**—Five Keys, Capitol	39
44.	**NIGHT LIGHTS**—Nat (King) Cole, Capitol	49
45.	**FRIENDLY PERSUASION**—Four Aces, Decca	57
46.	**SEE-SAW**—Moonglows, Chess	42
46.	**TWO DIFFERENT WORLDS**—D. Rondo, Jubilee	49
48.	**HOUSE WITH LOVE IN IT**—Four Lads, Columbia	35
49.	**TONIGHT YOU BELONG TO ME**—K. Chandler-J. Wakely, Decca	52
50.	**TEEN-AGE GOODNIGHT**—Chordettes, Cadence	87
51.	**WHEN THE WHITE LILACS BLOOM AGAIN**—H. Zacharaias, Decca	29
52.	**FAITHFUL HUSSAR**—T. Heath, London	67
52.	**JAMAICA FAREWELL**—H. Belafonte, Victor	66
54.	**EARTHBOUND**—S. Davis Jr., Decca	46
54.	**I CAN'T LOVE YOU ENOUGH**—L. Baker, Atlantic	48
56.	**ANY WAY YOU WANT ME**—E. Presley, Victor	—
57.	**ENDLESS**—McGuire Sisters, Coral	67
58.	**KA DING DONG**—Hilltoppers, Dot	71
58.	**MOONLIGHT LOVE**—P. Como, Victor	—
60.	**HAPPINESS STREET**—G. Gibbs, Mercury	43
61.	**FIRST BORN**—Tennessee Ernie, Capitol	—
62.	**PLEASE DON'T LEAVE ME**—Fontane Sisters, Dot	56
63.	**ITALIAN THEME**—C. Stapleton, London	61
64.	**WAR AND PEACE**—V. Damone, Columbia	69
65.	**BLUE MOON**—E. Presley, Victor	84
65.	**SADIE'S SHAWL**—B. Sharples, London	52
67.	**PRISCILLA**—E. Cooley, Roost	72
68.	**CITY OF ANGELS**—Highlights, Bally	—
69.	**SINGING THE BLUES**—M. Robbins, Columbia	—
70.	**JULIE**—Doris Day, Columbia	—
71.	**RIP IT UP**—B. Haley, Decca	84
71.	**WHEN MY DREAMBOAT COMES HOME**—F. Domino, Imperial	95
73.	**IT HAPPENED AGAIN**—S. Vaughan, Mercury	94
74.	**ROSE AND A BABY RUTH**—G Hamilton IV, ABC-Paramount	—
75.	**LAY DOWN YOUR ARMS**—A. Sheldon, Columbia	59
75.	**THAT'S ALL THERE IS TO THAT**—Nat (King) Cole, Capitol	59
77.	**I DON'T CARE IF THE SUN DON'T SHINE**—E. Presley, Victor	87
78.	**MIRACLE OF LOVE**—G. Gibson, ABC-Paramount	—
79.	**I MISS YOU SO**—C. Connor, Atlantic	74
79.	**RUDY'S ROCK**—B. Haley, Decca	—
79.	**SOFT SUMMER BREEZE**—Diamonds, Mercury	70
82.	**HAPPINESS STREET**—T. Bennett, Columbia	49
83.	**TO THE ENDS OF THE EARTH**—Nat (King) Cole, Capitol	90
83.	**WHEN THE WHITE LILACS BLOOM AGAIN**—L. Welk, Coral	82
85.	**WHEN THE WHITE LILACS BLOOM AGAIN**—B. Vaughn, Dot	54
86.	**SO LONG**—F. Domino, Imperial	80
87.	**YOU CAN'T RUN AWAY FROM IT**—Four Aces, Decca	78
88.	**WAYWARD WIND**—G. Grant, Era	96
89.	**RIP IT UP**—Little Richard, Specialty	77
90.	**WHEN THE WHITE LILACS BLOOM AGAIN**—L. Holmes, M-G-M	—
91.	**NAMELY YOU**—D. Cherry, Columbia	65
92.	**BLUEBERRY HILL**—L. Armstrong, Decca	—
93.	**WHEN THE WHITE LILACS BLOOM AGAIN**—F. ZaBach, Mercury	75
94.	**KA DING DONG**—G. Clefs, Pilgrim	81
95.	**ABC'S OF LOVE**—Teen-Agers, Gee	—
96.	**I WANT YOU, I NEED YOU, I LOVE YOU**—E. Presley, Victor	47
97.	**GIANT**—A. Mooney, M-G-M	—
97.	**KA DING DONG**—Diamonds, Mercury	64
97.	**NOW YOU HAS JAZZ**—Bing Crosby & L. Armstrong, Capitol	89
100.	**EARTHBOUND**—M. Lanza, Victor	97

CAUTION TO DEALERS AND JUKE BOX OPERATORS

The Billboard's Top 100 is NOT designed to provide tested information for buying purposes. This function is most reliably served by other regular weekly features: Best Sellers in Stores, Most Played in Juke Boxes, Coming Up Strong and Best Buys.

• Best Sellers in Stores

For survey week ending October 31

RECORDS are ranked in order of their current national selling importance at the retail level, as determined by The Billboard's weekly survey of the top volume dealers in every important market area. When significant action is reported on both sides of a record, points are combined to determine position on the chart. In such a case, both sides are listed in bold type, the leading side on top.

This Week		Last Week	Weeks on Chart
1.	**LOVE ME TENDER** (BMI)—E. Presley **ANY WAY YOU WANT ME** (BMI)—Vic 20-6643	1	4
2.	**GREEN DOOR** (BMI)—J. Lowe (Story of) The Little Man in Chinatown (BMI)—Dot 15486	3	7
3.	**DON'T BE CRUEL** (BMI)—E.Presley **HOUND DOG** (BMI)—Vic 20-6604	2	15
4.	**JUST WALKING IN THE RAIN** (BMI)—J. Ray In the Candlelight (ASCAP)—Col 40729	4	10
5.	**SINGING THE BLUES** (BMI)—G. Mitchell Crazy With Love (ASCAP)—Col 40769	11	2
6.	**HONKY TONK** (Parts I & II) (BMI) B. Doggett King 4950	5	12
7.	**BLUEBERRY HILL** (ASCAP)—F. Domino Honey Chile (BMI)—Imperial 5407	6	5
8.	**TRUE LOVE** (ASCAP)—B. Crosby-G. Kelly Well, Did You Evah? (ASCAP)—Cap 3507	8	6
9.	**FRIENDLY PERSUASION** (ASCAP)—P. Boone **CHAINS OF LOVE** (BMI)—Dot 15490	10	8
10.	**TONIGHT YOU BELONG TO ME** Patience & Prudence A Smile and a Ribbon (ASCAP)—Liberty 55022	9	12
11.	**CANADIAN SUNSET** (BMI) H. Winterhalter This Is Real (ASCAP)—Vic 20-6537	7	16
12.	**CINDY, OH, CINDY** (BMI) V. Martin Only If I Praise the Lord (BMI)—Glory 247	13	5
13.	**HEY, JEALOUS LOVER** (ASCAP)—F. Sinatra You Forgot All the Words (BMI)—Cap 3552	24	2
14.	**WHATEVER WILL BE, WILL BE** (ASCAP)—Doris Day I Gotta Sing Away These Blues (BMI)—Col 40704	12	19
15.	**YOU'LL NEVER, NEVER KNOW** (BMI)—Platters **IT ISN'T RIGHT** (BMI)—Mercury 70948	14	5
16.	**TRUE LOVE** (ASCAP)—J. Powell Mind If I Make Love to You (ASCAP)—Verve 2018	15	6
17.	**I WALK THE LINE** (BMI)—J.Cash Get Rhythm (BMI)—Sun 241	22	3
18.	**LAY DOWN YOUR ARMS**—Chordettes **TEEN-AGE GOODNIGHT** (BMI)—Cadence 1299	—	1
19.	**CINDY, OH, CINDY** (BMI)—E. Fisher Around the World (ASCAP)—Vic 20-6677	21	2
20.	**CITY OF ANGELS** (BMI)—Highlights Listen, My Love (BMI)—Bally 1016	—	1
21.	**GARDEN OF EDEN** (BMI)—J. Valino Caravan (ASCAP)—Vik 0226	—	1
22.	**TONIGHT YOU BELONG TO ME** (ASCAP)—Lennon Sisters-L. Welk When the White Lilacs Bloom Again (ASCAP)—Coral 61701	16	7
23.	**MY PRAYER** (ASCAP)—Platters Heaven On Earth (ASCAP)—Mercury 70893	17	18
24.	**CANADIAN SUNSET** (BMI)—A. Williams High Up on a Mountain (ASCAP)—Cadence 1297	18	11
25.	**TO THE END OF THE EARTH** (BMI)—Nat (King) Cole **NIGHT LIGHTS** (ASCAP)—Cap 3551	—	1

• Most Played in Juke Boxes

For survey week ending October 31

RECORDS are ranked in order of the greatest number of plays in juke boxes thruout the country, as determined by The Billboard's weekly survey of the nation's juke box operators. When significant play is reported on both sides of a record, points are combined to determine position on the chart. In such a case, both sides are listed in bold type, the leading side on top.

This Week		Last Week	Weeks on Chart
1.	**DON'T BE CRUEL** (BMI)—E. Presley. **HOUND DOG** (BMI)—Vic 20-6643	1	14
2.	**GREEN DOOR** (BMI)—J. Lowe (The Story of) The Little Man in Chinatown (BMI)—Dot 15486	3	5
3.	**JUST WALKING IN THE RAIN** (BMI)—J. Ray In the Candlelight (ASCAP)—Col 40729	4	8
4.	**LOVE ME TENDER** (BMI)—E. Presley Any Way You Want Me (ASCAP)—Vic 20-6643	10	3
5.	**HONKY TONK (PARTS I & II)** (BMI)—B. Doggett King 4950	2	9
6.	**CANADIAN SUNSET** (BMI)—H. Winterhalter-E. Heywood This Is Real (ASCAP)—Vic 20-6537	5	13
7.	**BLUEBERRY HILL** (ASCAP)—F. Domino Honey Chile (BMI)—Imperial 5407	12	4
8.	**TONIGHT YOU BELONG TO ME** (ASCAP)—Patience & Prudence A Smile and a Ribbon (ASCAP)—Liberty 55022	7	10
9.	**FRIENDLY PERSUASION** (ASCAP)—P. Boone **CHAINS OF LOVE** (BMI)—Dot 15490	8	6
10.	**WHATEVER WILL BE, WILL BE** (ASCAP)—Doris Day I Gotta Sing Away These Blues (BMI)—Col 40704	6	16
11.	**YOU'LL NEVER, NEVER KNOW** (BMI)—Platters **IT ISN'T RIGHT** (BMI)—Mercury 70948	13	5
12.	**TRUE LOVE** (ASCAP)—B. Crosby-G. Kelly Well, Did You Evah? (ASCAP)—Cap 3507	17	2
13.	**MY PRAYER** (ASCAP)—Platters Heaven on Earth (ASCAP)—Mercury 70893	9	17
14.	**SINGING THE BLUES** (BMI)—G. Mitchell Crazy With Love (ASCAP)—Col 40769	—	1
15.	**FOOL** (BMI)—S. Clark Lonesome for a Letter (BMI)—Dot 15481	11	12
16.	**CINDY, OH, CINDY** (BMI)—V. Martin Only If I Praise the Lord (BMI)—Glory 247	—	1
17.	**LAY DOWN YOUR ARMS** (BMI)—Chordettes Teen-Age Goodnight (BMI)—Cadence 1299	17	4
18.	**I WALK THE LINE** (BMI)—J. Cash Get Rhythm (BMI)—Sun 241	—	1
19.	**CANADIAN SUNSET** (BMI)—A. Williams High Upon the Mountain (ASCAP)—Cadence 1297	16	10
20.	**ALLEGHENY MOON** (ASCAP)— Strangest Romance (ASCAP)—Mercury 70878	13	19

• Best Selling Sheet Music

Tunes are ranked in order of their current national selling importance at the sheet music jobber level.

This Week		Last Week	Weeks on Chart
1.	**Whatever Will Be, Will Be (Que Sera, Sera)** (Artists)	3	18
2.	**Love Me Tender** (Presley)	2	4
3.	**True Love** (Buxton Hill)	6	7
4.	**Tonight You Belong to Me** (Mills)	4	10
5.	**Canadian Sunset** (Meridian)	5	14
6.	**Allegheny Moon** (Oxford)	1	20
6.	**Just Walking in the Rain** (Golden West)	7	5
8.	**Honky Tonk** (Billace)	8	3
9.	**Green Door** (Trinity)	12	3
10.	**Friendly Persuasion** (Feist)	11	2
10.	**Don't Be Cruel** (Presley-Shalimar)	8	9
12.	**Lay Down Your Arms** (Ludlow)	14	4
12.	**Cindy, Oh, Cindy** (E. B. Marks-Bryden)	—	1
14.	**My Prayer** (Shapiro-Bernstein)	10	17
15.	**Blueberry Hill** (Chappell)	—	1

• Most Played by Jockeys

For survey week ending October 31

SIDES are ranked in order of the greatest number of plays on disk jockey radio shows thruout the country. Results are based on The Billboard's weekly survey among the nation's disk jockeys. The reverse side of each record is also listed.

This Week		Last Week	Weeks on Chart
1.	**LOVE ME TENDER** (BMI)—E. Presley Any Way You Want Me (BMI)—Vic 20-6643	1	4
2.	**GREEN DOOR** (BMI)—J. Lowe (Story of) The Little Man in Chinatown (BMI)—Dot 15486	2	7
3.	**TRUE LOVE** (ASCAP)—B. Crosby-G. Kelly Well, Did You Evah? (ASCAP)—Cap 3507	7	6
4.	**DON'T BE CRUEL** (BMI)—E. Presley Hound Dog (BMI)—Vic 20-6604	3	14
5.	**JUST WALKING IN THE RAIN** (BMI)—J. Ray In the Candlelight (ASCAP)—Col 40729	4	7
6.	**FRIENDLY PERSUASION** (ASCAP)—P. Boone Chains of Love (ASCAP)—Dot 15490	6	8
7.	**CANADIAN SUNSET** (BMI)—H. Winterhalter-E. Heywood This Is Real (ASCAP)—Vic 20-6537	5	16
8.	**SINGING THE BLUES** (BMI)—G. Mitchell Crazy With Love (ASCAP)—Col 40769	15	2
9.	**BLUEBERRY HILL** (ASCAP)—F. Domino Honey Chile (BMI)—Imperial 5407	10	4
10.	**HONKY TONK (PARTS I & II)**—B. Doggett King 4950—BMI	11	8
11.	**HEY! JEALOUS LOVER** (ASCAP)—F. Sinatra You Forget All the Words (BMI)—Cap 3552	13	3
12.	**TONIGHT YOU BELONG TO ME** (ASCAP)—Patience & Prudence A Smile and a Ribbon (ASCAP)—Liberty 55022	8	12
13.	**CANADIAN SUNSET** (BMI)—A. Williams High Upon a Mountain (ASCAP)—Cadence 1297	9	13
14.	**CINDY, OH, CINDY** (BMI)—E. Fisher Around the World (ASCAP)—Vic 20-6677	14	3
15.	**WHATEVER WILL BE, WILL BE** (ASCAP)—Doris Day I Gotta Sing Away These Blues (BMI)—Col 40704	12	19
16.	**TONIGHT YOU BELONG TO ME** (ASCAP)—Lennon Sisters-L. Welk When the White Lilacs Bloom Again (ASCAP)—Coral 61701	19	6
17.	**PETTICOATS OF PORTUGAL** (BMI)—D. Jacobs Song of the Vagabonds-Only a Rose (ASCAP)—Coral 61724	—	1
18.	**YOU'LL NEVER, NEVER KNOW** (BMI)—Platters It Isn't Right (BMI)—Mercury 70948	—	1
19.	**TWO DIFFERENT WORLDS** (ASCAP)—D. Rondo He Made You Mine (ASCAP)—Jubilee 5256	18	2
20.	**HOUND DOG** (BMI)—E. Presley Don't Be Cruel (BMI)—Vic 20-6604	20	15
21.	**LAY DOWN YOUR ARMS** (BMI)—Chordettes Teen Age Goodnight (BMI)—Cadence 1299	—	1
22.	**MAMA FROM THE TRAIN** (ASCAP)—P. Page Every Time—I Feel His Spirit (BMI)—Mercury 70971	16	2
23.	**NIGHT LIGHTS** (ASCAP)—Nat (King) Cole To the Ends of the Earth (BMI)—Cap 3551	17	2
24.	**CINDY, OH, CINDY** (BMI)—V. Martin Only If I Praise the Lord (BMI)—Glory 247	—	1
25.	**I WALK THE LINE** (BMI)—J. Cash Get Rhythm (BMI)—Sun 241	—	1

THE TOP 100

For survey week ending October 31

A list of the Top 100 RECORD SIDES in the nation according to a COMBINED TABULATION of Dealer, Disk Jockey and Juke Box Operator replies to The Billboard's weekly popular record Best Seller and Most Played surveys. Its purpose is to provide Disk Jockeys with additional programming material and to give trade exposure to NEWER records just beginning to show action in the field.

Pos.	Song, Artist, Label	Last Week
1.	GREEN DOOR—J. Lowe, Dot	1
2.	LOVE ME TENDER—E. Presley, Victor	3
3.	DON'T BE CRUEL—E. Presley, Victor	2
4.	JUST WALKING IN THE RAIN—J. Ray, Columbia	3
5.	HONKY TONK—B. Doggett, King	6
6.	BLUEBERRY HILL—F. Domino, Imperial	8
6.	CANADIAN SUNSET—E. Heywood-H. Winterhalter, Victor	5
6.	TRUE LOVE—Bing Crosby-G. Kelly, Capitol	11
9.	FRIENDLY PERSUASION—P. Boone, Dot	9
10.	SINGING THE BLUES—G. Mitchell, Columbia	19
11.	TONIGHT YOU BELONG TO ME—Patience & Prudence, Liberty	7
12.	WHATEVER WILL BE, WILL BE—Doris Day, Columbia	9
13.	HOUND DOG—E. Presley, Victor	12
14.	YOU'LL NEVER, NEVER KNOW—Platters, Mercury	20
15.	HEY, JEALOUS LOVER—F. Sinatra, Capitol	18
16.	CINDY, OH, CINDY—V. Martin, Glory	17
17.	CINDY, OH, CINDY—E. Fisher, Victor	20
18.	CANADIAN SUNSET—A. Williams, Cadence	13
19.	I WALK THE LINE—J. Cash, Sun	36
19.	TONIGHT YOU BELONG TO ME—Lennon Sisters-L. Welk, Coral	15
21.	LAY DOWN YOUR ARMS—Chordettes, Cadence	24
22.	MY PRAYER—Platters, Mercury	14
23.	IT ISN'T RIGHT—Platters, Mercury	27
24.	TRUE LOVE—J. Powell, Verve	30
25.	GARDEN OF EDEN—J. Valino, Vik	41
25.	TWO DIFFERENT WORLDS—D. Rondo, Jubilee	46
27.	MAMA FROM THE TRAIN—P. Page, Mercury	32
27.	PETTICOATS OF PORTUGAL—D. Jacobs, Coral	34
29.	FOOL—S. Clark, Dot	22
30.	CHAINS OF LOVE—P. Boone, Dot	29
31.	SOFT SUMMER BREEZE—E. Heywood, Mercury	16
32.	IN THE STILL OF THE NIGHT—Satins, Ember	34
32.	OUT OF SIGHT, OUT OF MIND—Five Keys, Capitol	43
34.	MIRACLE OF LOVE—E. Rodgers, Columbia	28
35.	LET THE GOOD TIMES ROLL—Shirley & Lee, Aladdin	39
35.	YOU DON'T KNOW ME—J. Vale, Columbia	25
37.	NIGHT LIGHTS—Nat (King) Cole, Capitol	44
38.	IN THE MIDDLE OF THE HOUSE—R. Draper, Mercury	40
39.	TO THE ENDS OF THE EARTH—Nat (King) Cole, Capitol	83
40.	ANY WAY YOU WANT ME—E. Presley, Victor	56
41.	ALLEGHENY MOON—P. Page, Mercury	22
41.	EV'RYDAY OF MY LIFE—McGuire Sisters, Coral	38
43.	BUS STOP SONG—Four Lads, Columbia	33
44.	AFTER THE LIGHTS GO DOWN LOW—A. Hibbler, Decca	25
45.	ST. THERESE OF THE ROSES—B. Ward, Decca	36
46.	FIRST BORN—T. Ernie, Capitol	61
47.	JAMAICA FAREWELL—H. Belafonte, Victor	52
48.	PRISCILLA—E. Cooley, Roost	67
49.	ROSE AND A BABY RUTH—G. Hamilton IV, ABC-Paramount	74
50.	FRIENDLY PERSUASION—Four Aces, Decca	45
51.	CITY OF ANGELS—Highlights, Bally	68
51.	SONG FOR A SUMMER NIGHT—M. Miller, Columbia	31
53.	SLOW WALK—S. Austin, Mercury	—
54.	TEEN-AGE GOODNIGHT—Chordettes, Cadence	50
55.	I CAN'T LOVE YOU ENOUGH—L. Baker, Atlantic	54
56.	WHEN THE WHITE LILACS BLOOM AGAIN—H. Zacharaias, Decca	51
57.	SEE-SAW—Moonglows, Chess	46
58.	FAITHFUL HUSSAR—T. Heath, London	52
59.	IN THE MIDDLE OF THE HOUSE—V. Monroe, Victor	42
60.	HOUSE WITH LOVE IN IT—Four Lads, Columbia	48
61.	TONIGHT YOU BELONG TO ME—K. Chandler-J. Wakely, Decca	49
62.	LAY DOWN YOUR ARMS—A. Sheldon, Columbia	75
63.	HAPPINESS STREET—G. Gibbs, Mercury	60
63.	KA DING DONG—Hilltoppers, Dot	58
65.	I MISS YOU SO—C. Conner, Atlantic	79
66.	BLUE MOON—E. Presley, Victor	65
67.	EARTHBOUND—S. Davis Jr., Decca	54
67.	MOONLIGHT LOVE—P. Como, Victor	58
69.	SINGING THE BLUES—M. Robbins, Columbia	69
70.	STAR YOU WISHED UPON LAST NIGHT—G. MacKenzie, Vik	—
71.	WHEN THE WHITE LILACS BLOOM AGAIN—B. Vaughn, Dot	85
72.	BLUEBERRY HILL—L. Armstrong, Decca	92
72.	IT HAPPENED AGAIN—S. Vaughan, Mercury	73
72.	TWO DIFFERENT WORLDS—R. Williams-J. P. Morgan, Kapp	—
72.	WAR AND PEACE—V. Damone, Columbia	64
76.	HAPPINESS STREET—T. Bennett, Columbia	82
76	I DON'T CARE IF THE SUN DON'T SHINE—E. Presley, Victor	77
78.	MUTUAL ADMIRATION SOCIETY—T. Brewer, Coral	—
79.	JULIE—Doris Day, Columbia	70
79.	SADIE'S SHAWL—B. Sharples, London	65
81.	MARRIED I CAN ALWAYS GET—T. King, Victor	—
81.	CHINCHERINCHEE—P. Como, Victor	—
81.	JUST IN TIME—T. Bennett, Columbia	—
84.	LOVE IN A HOME—Doris Day, Columbia	—
85.	FROM THE CANDY STORE ON THE CORNER—T. Bennett, Columbia	—
86.	NAMELY YOU—D. Cherry, Columbia	91
87	ENDLESS—McGuire Sisters, Coral	57
87	AUTUMN WALTZ—T. Bennett, Columbia	—
87.	ITALIAN THEME—C. Stapleton, London	63
87.	PLEASE DON'T LEAVE ME—Fontane Sisters, Dot	62
91.	MIRACLE OF LOVE—G. Gibson, ABC-Paramount	78
91.	WHEN MY DREAMBOAT COMES HOME—F. Domino, Imperial	71
93.	WHEN THE WHITE LILACS BLOOM AGAIN—L. Welk, Coral	83
94.	CRAZY WITH LOVE—G. Mitchell, Columbia	—
95.	STILL—Fontane Sisters, Dot	—
96.	I ALMOST LOST MY MIND—P. Boone, Dot	—
97.	SEE-SAW—D. Cornell, Coral	—
98.	RIP IT UP—B. Haley, Decca	71
99.	RUDY'S ROCK—B. Haley, Decca	79
100.	THAT'S ALL THERE IS TO THAT—Nat (King) Cole, Capitol	75

CAUTION TO DEALERS AND JUKE BOX OPERATORS

The Billboard's Top 100 is NOT designed to provide tested information for buying purposes. This function is most reliably served by other regular weekly features: Best Sellers in Stores, Most Played in Juke Boxes, Coming Up Strong and Best Buys.

• Best Sellers in Stores

For survey week ending November 7

RECORDS are ranked in order of their current national selling importance at the retail level, as determined by The Billboard's weekly survey of the top volume dealers in every important market area. When significant action is reported on both sides of a record, points are combined to determine position on the chart. In such a case, both sides are listed in bold type, the leading side on top.

This Week		Last Week	Weeks on Chart
1.	**LOVE ME TENDER** (BMI)—E. Presley **ANY WAY YOU WANT ME** (BMI)—Vic 20-6643	1	5
2.	**GREEN DOOR** (BMI)—J. Lowe (Story of) The Little Man in Chinatown (BMI)—Dot 15486	2	8
3.	**JUST WALKING IN THE RAIN** (BMI)—J. Ray In the Candlelight (ASCAP)—Col. 40729	4	11
4.	**SINGING THE BLUES** (BMI)—G. Mitchell Crazy With Love (ASCAP)—Col 40769	5	3
5.	**DON'T BE CRUEL** (BMI)—E. Presley **HOUND DOG** (BMI)—Vic 20-6604	3	16
6.	**BLUEBERRY HILL** (ASCAP)—F. Domino Honey Chile (BMI)—Imperial 5407	7	6
7.	**TRUE LOVE** (ASCAP)—B. Crosby-G. Kelly Well, Did You Evah? (ASCAP)—Cap 3507	8	7
8.	**HONKY TONK** (Parts I & II) (BMI)—B. Doggett King 4950	6	13
9.	**FRIENDLY PERSUASION** (ASCAP)—P. Boone **CHAINS OF LOVE** (BMI)—Dot 15490	9	9
10.	**CANADIAN SUNSET** (BMI)—H. Winterhalter This is Real (ASCAP)—Vic 20-6537	11	17
11.	**TONIGHT YOU BELONG TO ME** (ASCAP)—Patience & Prudence A Smile and a Ribbon (ASCAP)—Liberty 55022	10	13
12.	**CINDY, OH, CINDY** (BMI)—V. Martin Only If I Praise the Lord (BMI)—Glory 247	12	6
13.	**HEY! JEALOUS LOVER** (ASCAP)—F. Sinatra You Forgot All the Words (BMI)—Cap 3552	13	3
14.	**CINDY, OH, CINDY** (BMI)—E. Fisher Around the World (ASCAP)—Vic 20-6677	19	3
15.	**YOU'LL NEVER, NEVER KNOW** (BMI)—Platters It Isn't Right (BMI)—Mercury 70948	15	6
16.	**TRUE LOVE** (ASCAP)—J. Powell Mind If I Make Love to You? (ASCAP)—Verve 2018	16	7
17.	**WHATEVER WILL BE, WILL BE** (ASCAP)—Doris Day I Gotta Sing Away These Blues (BMI)—Col 40704	14	20
18.	**I WALK THE LINE** (BMI)—J. Cash Get Rhythm (BMI)—Sun 241	17	4
19.	**ROSE AND A BABY RUTH** (BMI)—G. Hamilton IV If You Don't Know (BMI)—ABC-Paramount 9756	—	1
20.	**GARDEN OF EDEN** (BMI)—J. Valino Caravan (ASCAP)—Vik 0226	21	2
21.	**LAY DOWN YOUR ARMS** (BMI)—Chordettes Teen-Age Goodnight (BMI)—Cadence 1299	18	2
22.	**PRISCILLA** (BMI)—E. Cooley Got a Little Woman (BMI)—Roost 621	—	1
23.	**LET THE GOOD TIMES ROLL** (BMI)—Shirley & Lee Do You Mean to Hurt Me So? (BMI)—Aladdin 3325	—	4
23.	**NIGHT LIGHTS** (ASCAP)—Nat (King) Cole To the Ends of the Earth (BMI)—Cap 3551	25	2
25.	**CANADIAN SUNSET** (BMI)—A. Williams High Upon a Mountain (ASCAP)—Cadence 1297	24	12

• Most Played in Juke Boxes

For survey week ending November 7

RECORDS are ranked in order of the greatest number of plays in juke boxes thruout the country, as determined by The Billboard's weekly survey of the nation's juke box operators. When significant play is reported on both sides of a record, points are combined to determine position on the chart. In such a case, both sides are listed in bold type, the leading side on top.

This Week		Last Week	Weeks on Chart
1.	**GREEN DOOR** (BMI)—J. Lowe (The Story of) The Little Man in Chinatown (BMI)—Dot 15486	2	6
2.	**DON'T BE CRUEL** (BMI)—E. Presley **HOUND DOG** (BMI)—Vic 20-6643	1	15
2.	**JUST WALKING IN THE RAIN** (BMI)—J. Ray In the Candlelight (ASCAP)—Col 40729	3	9
4.	**LOVE ME TENDER** (BMI)—E. Presley Any Way You Want Me (ASCAP)—Vic 20-6643	4	4
5.	**HONKY TONK** (Parts I & II) (BMI)—B. Doggett King 4950	5	10
6.	**BLUEBERRY HILL** (ASCAP)—F. Domino Honey Chile (BMI)—Imperial 5407	7	5
7.	**CANADIAN SUNSET** (BMI)—H. Winterhalter-E. Heywood This Is Real (ASCAP)—Vic 20-6537	6	14
8.	**FRIENDLY PERSUASION** (ASCAP)—P. Boone **CHAINS OF LOVE** (BMI)Dot 15490	9	7
9.	**SINGING THE BLUES** (BMI)—G. Mitchell Crazy With Love (ASCAP)—Col 40769	14	2
10.	**TONIGHT YOU BELONG TO ME** (ASCAP)—Patience & Prudence A Smile and a Ribbon (ASCAP)—Liberty 55022	8	11
11.	**YOU'LL NEVER, NEVER KNOW** (BMI)—Platters **IT ISN'T RIGHT** (BMI)—Mercury 70948	11	6
12.	**TRUE LOVE** (ASCAP)—B. Crosby-G. Kelly Well, Did You Evah? (ASCAP)—Cap 3507	12	3
13.	**WHATEVER WILL BE, WILL BE** (ASCAP)—Doris Day I Gotta Sing Away These Blues (BMI)—Col 40704	10	17
14.	**MY PRAYER** (ASCAP)—Platters Heaven on Earth (ASCAP)—Mercury 70893	13	18
15.	**CINDY, OH, CINDY** (BMI)—V. Martin Only If I Praise the Lord (BMI)—Glory 247	16	2
16.	**LAY DOWN YOUR ARMS** (BMI)—Chordettes Teen-Age Goodnight (BMI)—Cadence 1299	17	5
17.	**CINDY, OH, CINDY** (BMI)—E. Fisher Around the World (ASCAP)—Vic 20-6677	—	1
18.	**CANADIAN SUNSET** (BMI)—A. Williams High Upon a Mountain (ASCAP)—Cadence 1297	19	11
19.	**I WALK THE LINE** (BMI)—J. Cash Get Rhythm (BMI)—Sun 241	18	2
19.	**FOOL** (BMI)—S. Clark Lonesome for a Letter (BMI)—Dot 15481	15	13

• Best Selling Sheet Music

Tunes are ranked in order of their current national selling importance at the sheet music jobber level.

This Week		Last Week	Weeks on Chart
1.	**Love Me Tender** (Presley)	2	5
2.	**True Love** (Buxton Hill)	3	8
3.	**Whatever Will Be, Will Be (Que Sera, Sera)** (Artists)	1	19
4.	**Tonight You Belong to Me** (Mills)	4	11
5.	**Allegheny Moon** (Oxford)	6	21
6.	**Canadian Sunset** (Meridian)	5	15
7.	**Just Walking in the Rain** (Golden West)	6	6
8.	**Friendly Persuasion** (Feist)	10	3
9.	**Green Door** (Trinity)	9	4
10.	**Honky Tonk** (Billace)	8	4
11.	**Cindy, Oh, Cindy** (E. B. Marks-Bryden)	12	2
12.	**Lay Down Your Arms** (Ludlow)	12	5
13.	**Don't Be Cruel** (Presley-Shalimar)	10	10
14.	**Hey, Jealous Lover** (Barton)	—	1
15.	**Two Different Worlds** (Spier)	—	1

• Most Played by Jockeys

For survey week ending November 7

SIDES are ranked in order of the greatest number of plays on disk jockey radio shows thruout the country. Results are based on The Billboard's weekly survey among the nation's disk jockeys. The reverse side of each record is also listed.

This Week		Last Week	Weeks on Chart
1.	**LOVE ME TENDER** (BMI)—E. Presley Any Way You Want Me (BMI)—Vic 20-6643	1	5
2.	**GREEN DOOR** (BMI)—J. Lowe (Story of) The Little Man in Chinatown (BMI)—Dot 15486	2	8
3.	**SINGING THE BLUES** (BMI)—G. Mitchell Crazy With Love (ASCAP)—Col 40769	8	3
4.	**TRUE LOVE** (ASCAP)—B. Crosby-G. Kelly Well, Did You Evah? (ASCAP)—Cap 3507	3	7
5.	**DON'T BE CRUEL** (BMI)—E. Presley Hound Dog (BMI)—Vic 20-6604	4	15
6.	**JUST WALKING IN THE RAIN** (BMI)—J. Ray In the Candlelight (ASCAP)—Col 40729	5	8
7.	**FRIENDLY PERSUASION** (ASCAP)—P. Boone Chains of Love (ASCAP)—Dot 15490	6	9
8.	**HEY! JEALOUS LOVER** (ASCAP)—F. Sinatra You Forget All the Words (BMI)—Cap 3552	11	4
9.	**CANADIAN SUNSET** (BMI)—H. Winterhalter-E. Heywood This Is Real (ASCAP)—Vic 20-6537	7	17
10.	**HONKY TONK** (Parts I & II) B. Doggett King 4950—BMI	10	9
11.	**BLUEBERRY HILL** (ASCAP)—F. Domino Honey Chile (BMI)—Imperial 5407	9	5
12.	**CINDY, OH, CINDY** (BMI)—E. Fisher Around the World (ASCAP)—Vic 20-6677	14	4
13.	**NIGHT WINDS** (ASCAP)—Nat (King) Cole To the Ends of the Earth (BMI)—Cap 3551	23	3
14.	**TONIGHT YOU BELONG TO ME** (ASCAP)—Patience & Prudence A Smile and a Ribbon (ASCAP)—Liberty 55022	12	13
15.	**TWO DIFFERENT WORLDS** (ASCAP)—D. Rondo He Made You Mine (ASCAP)—Jubilee 5256	19	3
16.	**WHATEVER WILL BE, WILL BE** (ASCAP)—Doris Day I Gotta Sing Away These Blues (BMI)—Col 40704	15	20
17.	**CINDY, OH, CINDY** (BMI)—V. Martin Only If I Praise the Lord (BMI)—Glory 247	24	2
18.	**CANADIAN SUNSET** (BMI)—A. Williams High Upon a Mountain (ASCAP)—Cadence 1297	13	14
19.	**PETTICOATS OF PORTUGAL** (BMI)—D. Jacobs Song of the Vagabonds/Only a Rose (ASCAP)—Coral 61724	17	2
20.	**LAY DOWN YOUR ARMS** (BMI)—Chordettes Teen-Age Goodnight (BMI)—Cadence 1299	21	2
21.	**TONIGHT YOU BELONG TO ME** (ASCAP)—Lennon Sisters-L. Welk When the White Lilacs Bloom Again (ASCAP)—Coral 61701	16	7
22.	**GARDEN OF EDEN** (BMI)—J. Valino Caravan (ASCAP)—Vik 0226	—	1
23.	**MAMA FROM THE TRAIN** (ASCAP)—P. Page Every Time—I Feel His Spirit (BMI)—Mercury 70971	22	3
24.	**AUTUMN WALTZ** (ASCAP)—T. Bennett Just in Time (ASCAP)—Col 40770	—	1
25.	**ROSE AND A BABY RUTH** (BMI)—G. Hamilton IV If You Don't Know (BMI)—ABC-Paramount 9756	—	1

THE TOP 100

For survey week ending November 7

A list of the Top 100 RECORD SIDES in the nation according to a COMBINED TABULATION of Dealer, Disk Jockey and Juke Box Operator replies to The Billboard's weekly popular record Best Seller and Most Played surveys. Its purpose is to provide Disk Jockeys with additional programming material and to give trade exposure to NEWER records just beginning to show action in the field.

Pos.	Song, Artist, Label	Last Week
1.	**GREEN DOOR**—J. Lowe, Dot	1
1.	**LOVE ME TENDER**—E. Presley, Victor	2
3.	**JUST WALKING IN THE RAIN**—J. Ray, Columbia	4
4.	**DON'T BE CRUEL**—E. Presley, Victor	3
5.	**SINGING THE BLUES**—G. Mitchell, Columbia	10
6.	**TRUE LOVE**—Bing Crosby-G. Kelly, Capitol	6
7.	**BLUEBERRY HILL**—F. Domino, Imperial	6
7.	**HONKY TONK**—B. Doggett, King	5
9.	**CANADIAN SUNSET**—H. Winterhalter-E. Heywood, Victor	6
10.	**FRIENDLY PERSUASION**—P. Boone, Dot	9
11.	**TONIGHT YOU BELONG TO ME**—Patience & Prudence, Liberty	11
12.	**CINDY, OH, CINDY**—E. Fisher, Victor	17
12.	**CINDY, OH, CINDY**—V. Martin, Glory	16
14.	**WHATEVER WILL BE, WILL BE**—Doris Day, Columbia	12
15.	**HEY! JEALOUS LOVER**—F. Sinatra, Capitol	15
16.	**LAY DOWN YOUR ARMS**—Chordettes, Cadence	21
17.	**CANADIAN SUNSET**—A. Williams, Cadence	18
18.	**YOU'LL NEVER, NEVER KNOW**—Platters, Mercury	14
19.	**HOUND DOG**—E. Presley, Victor	13
19.	**I WALK THE LINE**—J. Cash, Sun	19
19.	**TWO DIFFERENT WORLDS**—D. Rondo, Jubilee	25
22.	**GARDEN OF EDEN**—J. Valino, Vik	25
23.	**TONIGHT YOU BELONG TO ME**—Lennon Sisters-L. Welk, Coral	19
24.	**MAMA FROM THE TRAIN**—P. Page, Mercury	27
25.	**IT ISN'T RIGHT**—Platters, Mercury	23
25.	**MY PRAYER**—Platters, Mercury	22
27.	**PETTICOATS OF PORTUGAL**—D. Jacobs, Coral	27
28.	**ROSE AND A BABY RUTH**—G. Hamilton IV, ABC Paramount	49
29.	**NIGHT LIGHTS**—Nat (King) Cole, Capitol	37
30.	**TRUE LOVE**—J. Powell, Verve	24
31.	**IN THE STILL OF THE NIGHT**—Satins, Ember	32
32.	**OUT OF SIGHT OUT OF MIND**—Five Keys, Capitol	32
33.	**ANY WAY YOU WANT ME**—E. Presley, Victor	40
34.	**SOFT SUMMER BREEZE**—E. Heywood, Mercury	31
35.	**YOU DON'T KNOW ME**—J. Vale, Columbia	35
36.	**MUTUAL ADMIRATION SOCIETY**—T. Brewer, Coral	78
37.	**EV'RYDAY OF MY LIFE**—McGuire Sisters, Coral	41
38.	**LET THE GOOD TIMES ROLL**—Shirley & Lee, Aladdin	35
39.	**ALLEGHENY MOON**—P. Page, Mercury	41
40.	**AFTER THE LIGHTS GO DOWN**—A. Hibbler, Decca	44
41.	**MIRACLE OF LOVE**—E. Rodgers, Columbia	34
42.	**JAMAICA FAREWELL**—H. Belafonte, Victor	47
43.	**TO THE ENDS OF THE EARTH**—Nat (King) Cole, Capitol	39
44.	**CITY OF ANGELS**—Highlights, Bally	51
45.	**PRISCILLA**—E. Cooley, Roost	48
46.	**CONFIDENTIAL**—S. Knight, Dot	—
46.	**FOOL**—S. Clark, Dot	29
48.	**SLOW WALK**—S. Austin, Mercury	53
49.	**IN THE MIDDLE OF THE HOUSE**—R. Draper, Mercury	38
50.	**BLUEBERRY HILL**—L. Armstrong, Decca	72
50.	**MOONLIGHT LOVE**—P. Como, Victor	67
50.	**WHEN THE WHITE LILACS BLOOM AGAIN**—H. Zacharaias, Decca	56
53.	**BUS STOP SONG**—Four Lads, Columbia	43
53.	**FIRST BORN**—T. Ernie, Capitol	46
55.	**IN THE MIDDLE OF THE HOUSE**—V. Monroe, Victor	59
56.	**STAR YOU WISHED UPON LAST NIGHT**—G. MacKenzie, Vik	70
57.	**TEEN-AGE GOODNIGHT**—Chordettes, Cadence	54
58.	**I CAN'T LOVE YOU ENOUGH**—L. Baker, Atlantic	55
59.	**CHAINS OF LOVE**—P. Boone, Dot	30
59.	**JUST IN TIME**—T. Bennett, Columbia	81
61.	**FRIENDLY PERSUASION**—Four Aces, Decca	50
62.	**TWO DIFFERENT WORLDS**—R. Williams-J. Morgan, Kapp	72
63.	**HAPPINESS STREET**—T. Bennett, Columbia	76
63.	**RUDY'S ROCK**—B. Haley, Decca	99
65.	**AUTUMN WALTZ**—T. Bennett, Columbia	87
65.	**HAPPINESS STREET**—G. Gibbs, Mercury	63
65.	**LAY DOWN YOUR ARMS**—A. Sheldon, Columbia	62
68.	**MIRACLE OF LOVE**—G. Gibson, ABC Paramount	91
69.	**CHINCHERINCHEE**—P. Como, Victor	81
70.	**WHEN THE WHITE LILACS BLOOM AGAIN**—L. Welk, Coral	93
71.	**HOUSE WITH LOVE IN IT**—Four Lads, Columbia	60
71.	**NEW YORK'S MY HOME**—S. Davis Jr., Decca	—
73.	**ST. THERESE OF THE ROSES**—B. Ward, Decca	45
74.	**SEE-SAW**—D. Cornell, Coral	97
75.	**FAITHFUL HUSSAR**—T. Heath, London	58
75.	**SADIE'S SHAWL**—B. Sharples, London	79
77.	**GIANT**—A. Mooney, MGM	—
77.	**SONG FOR A SUMMER NIGHT**—M. Miller, Columbia	51
77.	**WAR AND PEACE**—V. Damone, Columbia	72
80.	**ON TRIAL**—Buchanan & Goodman, Luniverse	—
81.	**SEE-SAW**—Moonglows, Chess	57
82.	**I DON'T CARE IF THE SUN DON'T SHINE**—E. Presley, Victor	76
83.	**MARRIED I CAN ALWAYS GET**—T. King, Victor	81
84.	**SINCE I MET YOU BABY**—I. J. Hunter, Atlantic	—
84.	**LOVE ME**—E. Presley, Victor	—
86.	**SINGING THE BLUES**—M. Robbins, Columbia	69
87.	**IT HAPPENED AGAIN**—S. Vaughan, Mercury	72
88.	**EARTHBOUND**—S. Davis Jr., Decca	67
89.	**KA DING DONG**—Hilltoppers, Dot	63
90.	**ITALIAN THEME**—C. Stapleton, London	87
91.	**TONIGHT YOU BELONG TO ME**—K. Chandler-J. Wakely, Decca	61
92.	**BLUE MOON**—E. Presley, Victor	66
93.	**SOFT SUMMER BREEZE**—Diamonds, Mercury	—
94.	**IT'S YOURS**—De Castro Sisters, Victor	—
94.	**JULIA**—Doris Day, Columbia	79
96.	**LOVE IN A HOME**—Doris Day, Columbia	84
96.	**LOVE ME GOOD**—J. Stafford, Columbia	—
98.	**YOU'RE IN LOVE**—G. Grant, Era	—
99.	**WHEN THE WHITE LILACS BLOOM AGAIN**—F. Zabach, Mercury	—
100.	**YOU CAN'T RUN AWAY FROM IT**—Four Aces, Decca	—

CAUTION TO DEALERS AND JUKE BOX OPERATORS

The Billboard's Top 100 is NOT designed to provide tested information for buying purposes. This function is most reliably served by other regular weekly features: Best Sellers in Stores, Most Played in Juke Boxes, Coming Up Strong and Best Buys.

• Best Sellers in Stores

For survey week ending November 14

RECORDS are ranked in order of their current national selling importance at the retail level, as determined by The Billboard's weekly survey of the top volume dealers in every important market area. When significant action is reported on both sides of a record, points are combined to determine position on the chart. In such a case, both sides are listed in bold type, the leading side on top.

This Week		Last Week	Weeks on Chart
1.	**LOVE ME TENDER** (BMI)—E. Presley Any Way You Want Me (BMI)—Vic 20-6643	1	6
2.	**GREEN DOOR** (BMI)—J. Lowe (The Story of) the Little Man From Chinatown (BMI)—Dot 15486	2	9
3.	**SINGING THE BLUES** (BMI)—G. Mitchell Crazy With Love (ASCAP)—Col 40769	4	4
4.	**JUST WALKING IN THE RAIN** (BMI)—J. Ray In the Candlelight (ASCAP)—Col 40729	3	12
5.	**DON'T BE CRUEL** (BMI)—E. Presley **HOUND DOG** (BMI)—Vic 20-6604	5	17
6.	**BLUEBERRY HILL** (ASCAP)—F. Domino Honey Chile (BMI)—Imperial 5407	6	7
7.	**TRUE LOVE** (ASCAP)—B. Crosby-G. Kelly Well, Did You Evah? (ASCAP)—Cap 3507	7	8
8.	**HONKY TONK** (Parts I & II) (BMI)—B. Doggett King 4950	8	14
9.	**FRIENDLY PERSUASION** (ASCAP)—P. Boone Chains of Love (BMI)—Dot 15490	9	10
10.	**CINDY, OH, CINDY** (BMI)—E. Fisher Around the World (ASCAP)—Vic 20-6677	14	4
11.	**CANADIAN SUNSET** (BMI)—H. Winterhalter This Is Real (ASCAP)—Vic 20-6537	10	18
12.	**HEY, JEALOUS LOVER** (ASCAP)—F. Sinatra You Forgot All the Words (BMI)—Cap 3552	13	4
13.	**CINDY, OH, CINDY** (BMI)—V. Martin Only If I Praise the Lord (BMI)—Glory 247	12	7
14.	**ROSE AND A BABY RUTH** (BMI)—G. Hamilton IV If You Don't Know (BMI)—ABC-Paramount 9756	19	2
15.	**TONIGHT YOU BELONG TO ME** (ASCAP)—Patience & Prudence A Smile and a Ribbon (ASCAP)—Liberty 55022	11	14
16.	**GARDEN OF EDEN** (BMI)—J. Valino Caravan (ASCAP)—Vik 0226	20	3
17.	**YOU'LL NEVER, NEVER KNOW** (BMI)—Platters It Isn't Right (BMI)—Mercury 70948	15	7
18.	**I WALK THE LINE** (BMI)—J. Cash Get Rhythm (BMI)—Sun 241	18	5
19.	**CITY OF ANGELS**—Highlights Listen, My Love—Bally 1016	—	2
20.	**PRISCILLA** (BMI)—E. Cooley Got a Little Woman (BMI)—Roost 621	22	2
21.	**ROCK-A-BYE YOUR BABY** (ASCAP)—J. Lewis Come Rain Or Come Shine (ASCAP)—Dec 30124	—	1
22.	**NIGHT LIGHTS** (ASCAP)—Nat (King) Cole To the Ends of the Earth (BMI)—Cap 3551	23	3
23.	**MAMA FROM THE TRAIN** (ASCAP)—P. Page Every Time—I Feel His Spirit (BMI)—Mercury 70971	—	1
24.	***LOVE ME** (BMI)—E. Presley Vic EPA 992	—	1
25.	**TRUE LOVE** (ASCAP)—J. Powell Mind If I Make Love to You? (ASCAP)—Verve 2018	16	8

*(Not available as a Pop Single; available on RCA Victor 45 EPA-992 and in RCA Victor 33⅓ "Elvis" LPM 1382)

• Most Played in Juke Boxes

For survey week ending November 14

RECORDS are ranked in order of the greatest number of plays in juke boxes thruout the country, as determined by The Billboard's weekly survey of the nation's juke box operators. When significant play is reported on both sides of a record, points are combined to determine position on the chart. In such a case, both sides are listed in bold type, the leading side on top.

This Week		Last Week	Weeks on Chart
1.	**GREEN DOOR** (BMI)—J. Lowe (The Story of) The Little Man in Chinatown (BMI)—Dot 15486	1	7
2.	**LOVE ME TENDER** (BMI)—E. Presley Any Way You Want Me (ASCAP)—Vic 20-6643	4	5
3.	**JUST WALKING IN THE RAIN** (BMI)—J. Ray In the Candlelight (ASCAP)—Col 40729	2	10
4.	**DON'T BE CRUEL** (BMI)—E. Presley **HOUND DOG** (BMI)—Vic 20-6643	2	16
5.	**HONKY TONK** (Parts I & II) (BMI)—B. Doggett King 4950	5	11
6.	**BLUEBERRY HILL** (ASCAP)—F. Domino Honey Chile (BMI)—Imperial 5407	6	6
7.	**SINGING THE BLUES** (BMI)—G. Mitchell Crazy With Love (ASCAP)—Col 40769	9	3
8.	**CANADIAN SUNSET** (BMI)—H. Winterhalter-E. Heywood This Is Real (ASCAP)—Vic 20-6537	7	15
9.	**FRIENDLY PERSUASION** (ASCAP)—P. Boone Chains of Love (BMI)—Dot 15490	8	8
10.	**TONIGHT YOU BELONG TO ME** (ASCAP)—Patience & Prudence A Smile and a Ribbon (ASCAP)—Liberty 55022	10	12
11.	**TRUE LOVE** (ASCAP)—B. Crosby-G. Kelly Well, Did You Evah? (ASCAP)—Cap 3507	12	4
12.	**CINDY, OH, CINDY** (BMI)—V. Martin Only If I Praise the Lord (BMI)—Glory 247	15	3
13.	**YOU'LL NEVER, NEVER KNOW** (BMI)—Platters **IT ISN'T RIGHT** (BMI)—Mercury 70984	11	7
14.	**WHATEVER WILL BE, WILL BE** (ASCAP)—Doris Day I Gotta Sing Away These Blues (BMI)—Col 40704	13	18
15.	**MY PRAYER** (ASCAP)—Platters Heaven on Earth (ASCAP)—Mercury 70893	14	19
16.	**LAY DOWN YOUR ARMS** (BMI)—Chordettes Teen-Age Goodnight (BMI)—Cadence 1299	16	6
17.	**CONFIDENTIAL** (BMI)—S. Knight Jail Bird (BMI)—Dot 15507	—	1
18.	**HEY, JEALOUS LOVER** (ASCAP)—F. Sinatra You Forgot All the Words (BMI)—Cap 3552	—	1
19.	**CINDY, OH, CINDY** (BMI)—E. Fisher Around the World (ASCAP)—Vic 20-6677	17	2
20.	**PETTICOATS OF PORTUGAL** (BMI)—D. Jacobs Song of the Vagabonds/Only a Rose (ASCAP)—Coral 61724	—	1

• Best Selling Sheet Music

Tunes are ranked in order of their current national selling importance at the sheet music jobber level.

This Week		Last Week	Weeks on Chart
1.	**Love Me Tender** (Presley)	1	6
2.	**True Love** (Buxton Hill)	2	9
3.	**Just Walking in the Rain** (Golden West)	7	7
4.	**Whatever Will Be, Will Be (Que Sera, Sera)** (Artists)	3	20
5.	**Tonight You Belong to Me** (Mills)	4	12
6.	**Allegheny Moon** (Oxford)	5	22
7.	**Green Door** (Trinity)	9	8
8.	**Canadian Sunset** (Meridian)	6	16
9.	**Friendly Persuasion** (Feist)	8	4
10.	**Cindy, Oh, Cindy** (E. B. Marks-Bryden)	11	3
11.	**Honky Tonk** (Billace)	10	5
12.	**Blueberry Hill** (Chappell)	—	2
13.	**Don't Be Cruel** (Presley-Shalimar)	13	11
14.	**Two Different Worlds** (Spier)	15	2
15.	**Singing the Blues** (Acuff-Rose)	—	1

• Most Played by Jockeys

For survey week ending November 14

SIDES are ranked in order of the greatest number of plays on disk jockey radio shows thruout the country. Results are based on The Billboard's weekly survey among the nation's disk jockeys. The reverse side of each record is also listed.

This Week		Last Week	Weeks on Chart
1.	**LOVE ME TENDER** (BMI)—E. Presley Any Way You Want Me (BMI)—Vic 20-6643	1	6
2.	**GREEN DOOR** (BMI)—J. Lowe (The Story of) The Little Man in Chinatown (BMI)—Dot 15486	2	9
3.	**SINGING THE BLUES** (BMI)—G. Mitchell Crazy With Love (ASCAP)—Col 40769	3	4
4.	**TRUE LOVE** (ASCAP)—B. Crosby-G. Kelly Well, Did You Evah? (ASCAP)—Cap 3507	4	8
5.	**JUST WALKING IN THE RAIN** (BMI)—J. Ray In the Candlelight (ASCAP)—Col 40729	6	9
6.	**HEY, JEALOUS LOVER** (ASCAP)—F. Sinatra You Forget All the Words (BMI)—Cap 3552	8	5
7.	**FRIENDLY PERSUASION** (ASCAP)—P. Boone Chains of Love (ASCAP)—Dot 15490	7	10
8.	**DON'T BE CRUEL** (BMI)—E. Presley Hound Dog (BMI)—Vic 20-6604	5	16
9.	**BLUEBERRY HILL** (ASCAP)—F. Domino Honey Chile (BMI)—Imperial 5407	11	6
10.	**CANADIAN SUNSET** (BMI)—H. Winterhalter-E. Heywood This Is Real (ASCAP)—Vic 20-6537	9	18
11.	**TWO DIFFERENT WORLDS** (ASCAP)—D. Rondo He Made You Mine (ASCAP)—Jubilee 5256	15	4
12.	**CINDY, OH, CINDY** (BMI)—V. Martin Only If I Praise the Lord (BMI)—Glory 247	17	3
13.	**NIGHT LIGHTS** (ASCAP)—Nat (King) Cole To the Ends of the Earth (BMI)—Cap 3551	13	4
14.	**ROSE AND A BABY RUTH** (BMI)—G. Hamilton IV If You Don't Know (BMI)—ABC-Paramount 9756	25	2
15.	**HONKY TONK** (Parts I & II)—B. Doggett King 4950—BMI	10	10
16.	**CINDY, OH, CINDY** (BMI)—E. Fisher Around the World (ASCAP)—Vic 20-6677	12	5
17.	**CANADIAN SUNSET** (BMI)—A. Williams High Upon a Mountain (ASCAP)—Cadence 1297	18	15
18.	**AUTUMN WALTZ** (ASCAP)—T. Bennett Just in Time (ASCAP)—Col 40770	24	2
19.	**TONIGHT YOU BELONG TO ME** (ASCAP)—Patience & Prudence A Smile and a Ribbon (ASCAP)—Liberty 55022	14	14
20.	**PETTICOATS OF PORTUGAL** (BMI)—D. Jacobs Song of the Vagabonds/Only a Rose (ASCAP)—Coral 61724	19	3
21.	**MAMA FROM THE TRAIN** (ASCAP)—P. Page Every Time—I Feel His Spirit (BMI)—Mercury 70971	23	4
22.	**I CAN'T LOVE YOU ENOUGH** (BMI)—L. Baker Still (BMI)—Atlantic 1104	—	1
23.	**GARDEN OF EDEN** (BMI)—J. Valino Caravan (ASCAP)—Vik 0226	22	2
24.	**LAY DOWN YOUR ARMS** (BMI)—Chordettes Teen-Age Goodnight (BMI)—Cadence 1299	20	3
25.	**TO THE ENDS OF THE EARTH** (BMI)—Nat (King) Cole Night Lights (ASCAP)—Cap 3551	—	1

THE TOP 100

For survey week ending November 14

A list of the Top 100 RECORD SIDES in the nation according to a COMBINED TABULATION of Dealer, Disk Jockey and Juke Box Operator replies to The Billboard's weekly popular record Best Seller and Most Played surveys. Its purpose is to provide Disk Jockeys with additional programming material and to give trade exposure to NEWER records just beginning to show action in the field.

Pos.	Song, Artist, Label	Last Week
1.	**LOVE ME TENDER**—E. Presley, Victor	1
2.	**GREEN DOOR**—J. Lowe, Dot	1
3.	**JUST WALKING IN THE RAIN**—J. Ray, Columbia	3
4.	**SINGING THE BLUES**—G. Mitchell, Columbia	5
5.	**DON'T BE CRUEL**—E. Presley, Victor	4
6.	**BLUEBERRY HILL**—F. Domino, Imperial	7
7.	**TRUE LOVE**—Bing Crosby-G. Kelly, Capitol	6
8.	**FRIENDLY PERSUASION**—P. Boone, Dot	10
9.	**HONKY TONK**—B. Doggett, King	7
10.	**CANADIAN SUNSET**—E. Heywood-H. Winterhalter, Victor	9
11.	**HEY, JEALOUS LOVER**—F. Sinatra, Capitol	15
12.	**CINDY, OH, CINDY**—V. Martin, Glory	12
13.	**TONIGHT YOU BELONG TO ME**—Patience & Prudence, Liberty	11
14.	**CINDY, OH, CINDY**—E. Fisher, Victor	12
15.	**ROSE AND A BABY RUTH**—G. Hamilton IV, ABC-Paramount	28
16.	**YOU'LL NEVER, NEVER KNOW**—Platters, Mercury	18
17.	**MAMA FROM THE TRAIN**—P. Page, Mercury	24
18.	**GARDEN OF EDEN**—J. Valino, Vik	22
19.	**HOUND DOG**—E. Presley, Victor	19
19.	**LAY DOWN YOUR ARMS**—Chordettes, Cadence	16
21.	**PETTICOATS OF PORTUGAL**—D. Jacobs, Coral	27
22.	**NIGHT LIGHTS**—Nat (King) Cole, Capitol	29
23.	**I WALK THE LINE**—J. Cash, Sun	19
24.	**TWO DIFFERENT WORLDS**—D. Rondo, Jubilee	19
25.	**WHATEVER WILL BE, WILL BE**—Doris Day, Columbia	14
26.	**MUTUAL ADMIRATION SOCIETY**—T. Brewer, Coral	36
27.	**CANADIAN SUNSET**—A. Williams, Cadence	17
28.	**TONIGHT YOU BELONG TO ME**—Lennon Sisters-L. Welk, Coral	23
29.	**JAMAICA FAREWELL**—H. Belafonte, Victor	42
30.	**CITY OF ANGELS**—Highlights, Bally	44
31.	**CONFIDENTIAL**—S. Knight, Dot	46
32.	**FOOL**—S. Clark, Dot	46
32.	**IT ISN'T RIGHT**—Platters, Mercury	25
34.	**RUDY'S ROCK**—B. Haley, Decca	43
35.	**ANY WAY YOU WANT ME**—E. Presley, Victor	33
36.	**SOFT SUMMER BREEZE**—E. Heywood, Mercury	34
37.	**PRISCILLA**—E. Cooley, Roost	45
37.	**SINGING THE BLUES**—M. Robbins, Columbia	86
39.	**SLOW WALK**—S. Austin, Mercury	48
39.	**TO THE ENDS OF THE EARTH**—Nat (King) Cole, Capitol	43
41.	**LOVE ME**—E. Presley, Victor	84
42.	**MIRACLE OF LOVE**—E. Rodgers, Columbia	41
43.	**TRUE LOVE**—J. Powell, Verve	30
44.	**AFTER THE LIGHTS GO DOWN LOW**—A. Hibbler, Decca	40
45.	**TEEN-AGE GOODNIGHT**—Chordettes, Cadence	57
46.	**IN THE MIDDLE OF THE HOUSE**—R. Draper, Mercury	49
46.	**YOU DON'T KNOW ME**—J. Vale, Columbia	35
48.	**MY PRAYER**—Platters, Mercury	25
49.	**SINCE I MET YOU, BABY**—I. J. Hunter, Atlantic	84
50.	**OUT OF SIGHT, OUT OF MIND**—Five Keys, Capitol	32
51.	**MOONLIGHT LOVE**—P. Como, Victor	50
52.	**AUTUMN WALTZ**—T. Bennett, Columbia	65
53.	**STAR YOU WISHED UPON LAST NIGHT**—G. MacKenzie, Vik	56
54.	**IN THE STILL OF THE NIGHT**—Satins, Ember	31
55.	**FRIENDLY PERSUASION**—Four Aces, Decca	61
56.	**LET THE GOOD TIMES ROLL**—Shirley & Lee, Aladdin	58
57.	**CHAINS OF LOVE**—P. Boone, Dot	59
58.	**SLOW WALK**—B. Doggett, King	—
59.	**ALLEGHENY MOON**—P. Page, Mercury	39
60.	**ON LONDON BRIDGE**—J. Stafford, Columbia	—
61.	**EV'RYDAY OF MY LIFE**—McGuire Sisters, Coral	37
62.	**FIRST BORN**—Tennessee Ernie, Capitol	53
63.	**ROCK-A-BYE YOUR BABY**—J. Lewis, Decca	—
64.	**I CAN'T LOVE YOU ENOUGH**—L. Baker, Atlantic	58
64.	**JULIE**—Doris Day, Columbia	94
66.	**I DREAMED**—B. Johnson, Bally	—
66.	**NEW YORK'S MY HOME**—S. Davis Jr., Decca	71
68.	**JUST IN TIME**—T. Bennett, Columbia	59
68.	**I WOULDN'T KNOW WHERE TO BEGIN**—E. Arnold, Victor	—
70.	**ST. THERESE OF THE ROSES**—B. Ward, Decca	73
71.	**SEE-SAW**—Moonglows, Chess	81
72.	**TWO DIFFERENT WORLDS**—R. Williams & J. Morgan, Kapp	62
73.	**CHINCHERINCHEE**—P. Como, Victor	69
74.	**BLUEBERRY HILL**—L. Armstrong, Decca	50
75.	**MARRIED I CAN ALWAYS GET**—T. King, Victor	83
76.	**IT'S YOURS**—De Castro Sisters—Victor	94
76.	**SONG FOR A SUMMER NIGHT**—M. Miller, Columbia	77
76.	**WHEN THE WHITE LILACS BLOOM AGAIN**—H. Zacharaias, Decca	50
79.	**I SAW ESAU**—Ames Brothers, Victor	—
80.	**HAPPINESS STREET**—G. Gibbs, Mercury	65
80.	**CONFESSION OF A SINNER**—Stylers, Jubilee	—
82.	**TONIGHT YOU BELONG TO ME**—K. Chandler & J. Wakely, Decca	91
83.	**AUCTIONEER**—L. Van Dyke, Dot	—
84.	**EARTHBOUND**—S. Davis Jr., Decca	88
84.	**FAITHFUL HUSSAR**—T. Heath, London	75
86.	**HOUSE WITH LOVE IN IT**—Four Lads, Columbia	71
87.	**EVERY TIME—I FEEL HIS SPIRIT**—P. Page, Mercury	—
87.	**IT HAPPENED AGAIN**—S. Vaughan, Mercury	87
87.	**STILL**—Fontane Sisters, Dot	—
87.	**SADIE'S SHAWL**—B. Sharples, London	75
87.	**SEE-SAW**—D. Cornell, Coral	74
92.	**THAT'S ALL THERE IS TO THAT**—Nat (King) Cole, Capitol	—
93.	**BLUE MOON**—E. Presley, Victor	92
93.	**NAMELY YOU**—D. Cherry, Columbia	—
95.	**CRAZY WITH LOVE**—T. Brewer, Coral	—
96.	**IN THE MIDDLE OF THE HOUSE**—V. Monroe, Victor	55
97.	**PLEASE DON'T LEAVE ME**—Fontane Sisters, Dot	—
98.	**I MISS YOU SO**—C. Connor, Atlantic	—
99.	**GIANT**—L. Baxter, Capitol	—
99.	**ITALIAN THEME**—C. Stapleton, London	90

CAUTION TO DEALERS AND JUKE BOX OPERATORS

The Billboard's Top 100 is NOT designed to provide tested information for buying purposes. This function is most reliably served by other regular weekly features: Best Sellers in Stores, Most Played in Juke Boxes, Coming Up Strong and Best Buys.

• Best Sellers in Stores

For survey week ending November 21

RECORDS are ranked in order of their current national selling importance at the retail level, as determined by The Billboard's weekly survey of the top volume dealers in every important market area. When significant action is reported on both sides of a record, points are combined to determine position on the chart. In such a case, both sides are listed in bold type, the leading side on top.

This Week	Title	Last Week	Weeks on Chart
1.	**LOVE ME TENDER** (BMI)—E. Presley Any Way You Want Me (BMI)—Vic 20-6643	1	7
2.	**SINGING THE BLUES** (BMI)—G. Mitchell Crazy With Love (ASCAP)—Col 40769	3	5
3.	**GREEN DOOR** (BMI)—J. Lowe (Story of) The Little Man in Chinatown (BMI)—Dot 15486	2	10
4.	**JUST WALKING IN THE RAIN** (BMI)—J. Ray In the Candlelight (ASCAP)—Col 40729	4	13
5.	**TRUE LOVE** (ASCAP)—B. Crosby-G. Kelly Well, Did You Evah? (ASCAP)—Cap 3507	7	9
6.	**BLUEBERRY HILL** (ASCAP)—F. Domino Honey Chile (BMI)—Imperial 5407	6	8
7.	**DON'T BE CRUEL** (BMI)—E. Presley **HOUND DOG** (BMI)—Vic 20-6604	5	18
8.	**HONKY TONK** (PARTS I & II—B. Doggett King 4950—BMI	8	15
9.	**HEY, JEALOUS LOVER** (ASCAP)—F. Sinatra You Forgot All the Words (BMI)—Cap 3552	12	5
10.	**FRIENDLY PERSUASION** (ASCAP) P. Boone **CHAINS OF LOVE** (BMI)—Dot 15490	9	11
11.	**ROSE AND A BABY RUTH** (BMI)—G. Hamilton IV If You Don't Know (BMI)—ABC-Paramount 9765	14	3
12.	**CINDY, OH, CINDY** (BMI)—V. Martin Only If I Praise the Lord (BMI)—Glory 247	10	5
13.	**CANADIAN SUNSET** (BMI)—H. Winterhalter This Is Real (ASCAP)—Vic 20-6537	11	19
14.	**CINDY, OH, CINDY** (BMI) E. Fisher Around the World (ASCAP)—Vic 20-6677	13	8
15.	**YOU'LL NEVER, NEVER KNOW** (BMI)—Platters **IT ISN'T RIGHT** (BMI)—Mercury 70948	17	8
16.	**GARDEN OF EDEN** (BMI)—J. Valino Caravan (ASCAP)—Vik 0226	16	4
17.	**MAMA FROM THE TRAIN** (ASCAP)—P. Page Every Time I Feel His Spirit (BMI)—Mercury 70971	22	4
18.	**ROCK-A-BYE YOUR BABY** (ASCAP)—J. Lewis Come Rain or Come Shine (ASCAP)—Dec 30124	21	2
18.	**TONIGHT YOU BELONG TO ME** (ASCAP)—Patience & Prudence A Smile and a Ribbon (ASCAP)—Liberty 55022	15	15
20.	**MAMA FROM THE TRAIN** (ASCAP)—P. Page Every Time I Feel His Spirit (BMI)—Mercury 70971	23	2
21.	***LOVE ME** (BMI)—E. Presley Vic EPA 992	24	2
22.	**PRISCILLA** (BMI)—E. Cooley Got a Little Woman (BMI)—Roost 621	20	3
23.	**PETTICOATS OF PORTUGAL** (BMI)—D. Jacobs Song of the Vagabonds—Only a Rose (ASCAP)—Coral 61724	—	1
24.	**MUTUAL ADMIRATION SOCIETY** (ASCAP)—T. Brewer Crazy With Love (ASCAP)—Coral 61737	—	1
25.	**SLOW WALK** (BMI)—S. Austin Wildwood (BMI)—Mercury 70963	—	1

*(Not available as a Pop Single. Available on RCA Victor 45 EPA 992 and in RCA Victor 33⅓ "Elvis" LPM 1382)

• Most Played in Juke Boxes

For survey week ending November 21

RECORDS are ranked in order of the greatest number of plays in juke boxes thruout the country, as determined by The Billboard's weekly survey of the nation's juke box operators. When significant play is reported on both sides of a record, points are combined to determine position on the chart. In such a case, both sides are listed in bold type, the leading side on top.

This Week	Title	Last Week	Weeks on Chart
1.	**GREEN DOOR** (BMI)—J. Lowe (The Story of) The Little Man in Chinatown (BMI)—Dot 15486	1	8
2.	**LOVE ME TENDER** (BMI)—E. Presley **ANY WAY YOU WANT ME** (ASCAP)—Vic 20-6643	2	6
3.	**JUST WALKING IN THE RAIN** (BMI)—J. Ray In the Candlelight (ASCAP)—Col 40729	3	11
4.	**DON'T BE CRUEL** (BMI)—E. Presley **HOUND DOG** (BMI)—Vic 20-6643	4	17
5.	**BLUEBERRY HILL** (ASCAP)—F. Domino Honey Chile (BMI)—Imperial 5407	6	7
6.	**SINGING THE BLUES** (BMI)—G. Mitchell Crazy With Love (ASCAP)—Col 40769	7	4
7.	**HONKY TONK** (PARTS I & II) (BMI)—B. Doggett King 4950—BMI	5	12
8.	**TRUE LOVE** (ASCAP)—B. Crosby-G. Kelly Well, Did You Evah? (ASCAP)—Cap 3507	11	5
9.	**CANADIAN SUNSET** (BMI)—H. Winterhalter-E. Heywood This Is Real (ASCAP)—Vic 20-6537	8	16
10.	**FRIENDLY PERSUASION** (ASCAP)—P. Boone Chains of Love (BMI)—Dot 15490	9	9
11.	**CINDY, OH, CINDY** (BMI)—V. Martin Only If I Praise the Lord (BMI)—Glory 247	12	4
12.	**TONIGHT YOU BELONG TO ME** (ASCAP)—Patience & Prudence A Smile and a Ribbon (ASCAP)—Liberty 55022	10	13
13.	**WHATEVER WILL BE, WILL BE** (ASCAP)—Doris Day I Gotta Sing Away These Blues (BMI)—Col 40704	14	19
14.	**ROSE AND A BABY RUTH** (BMI)—G. Hamilton IV If You Don't Know (BMI)—ABC-Paramount 9765	—	1
15.	**HEY, JEALOUS LOVER** (ASCAP)—F. Sinatra You Forgot All the Words (BMI)—Cap 3552	18	2
16.	**YOU'LL NEVER NEVER KNOW** It Isn't Right (BMI)—Mercury 70948		
17.	**I WALK THE LINE** (BMI)—J. Cash Get Rhythm (BMI)—Sun 241	—	3
18.	**CINDY, OH, CINDY** (BMI)—E. Fisher Around the World (ASCAP)—Vic 20-6677	19	3
19.	**CONFIDENTIAL** (BMI)—S. Knight Jail Bird (BMI)—Dot 15507	17	2
20.	**LAY DOWN YOUR ARMS** (BMI)—Chordettes Teen-Age Goodnight (BMI)—Cadence 1299	16	7

• Best Selling Sheet Music

Tunes are ranked in order of their current national selling importance at the sheet music jobber level.

This Week	Title	Last Week	Weeks on Chart
1.	**Love Me Tender** (Presley)	1	7
2.	**True Love** (Buxton Hill)	2	10
3.	**Just Walking in the Rain** (Golden West)	3	8
4.	**Tonight You Belong to Me** (Mills)	5	3
5.	**Green Door** (Trinity)	7	6
6.	**Singing the Blues** (Acuff-Rose)	15	2
7.	**Cindy, Oh, Cindy** (E. B. Marks-Bryden)	10	4
8.	**Friendly Persuasion** (Feist)	9	8
8.	**Canadian Sunset** (Meridian)	8	17
10.	**Blueberry Hill** (Chappell)	12	3
11.	**Whatever Will Be, Will Be (Que Sera, Sera)** (Artists)	4	21
12.	**Allegheny Moon** (Oxford)	6	23
13.	**Hey, Jealous Lover** (Barton)	—	2
14.	**Two Different Worlds** (Spier)	14	3
15.	**Mama From the Train** (Remick)	—	1

• Most Played by Jockeys

For survey week ending November 21

SIDES are ranked in order of the greatest number of plays on disk jockey radio shows thruout the country. Results are based on The Billboard's weekly survey among the nation's disk jockeys. The reverse side of each record is also listed.

This Week	Title	Last Week	Weeks on Chart
1.	**LOVE ME TENDER** (BMI)—E. Presley Any Way You Want Me (BMI)—Vic 20-6643	1	7
2.	**SINGING THE BLUES** (BMI)—G. Mitchell Crazy With Love (ASCAP)—Col 40769	3	5
3.	**GREEN DOOR** (BMI)—J. Lowe (Story of) The Little Man in Chinatown (BMI)—Dot 15486	2	10
4.	**TRUE LOVE** (ASCAP)—B. Crosby-G. Kelly Well, Did You Evah? (ASCAP)—Cap 3507	4	9
5.	**JUST WALKING IN THE RAIN** (BMI)—J. Ray In the Candlelight (ASCAP)—Col 40729	5	10
6.	**HEY, JEALOUS LOVER** (ASCAP)—F. Sinatra You Forgot All the Words (BMI)—Cap 3552	6	6
7.	**BLUEBERRY HILL** (ASCAP)—F. Domino Honey Chile (BMI)—Imperial 5407	9	7
8.	**FRIENDLY PERSUASION** (ASCAP)—P. Boone Chains of Love (ASCAP)—Dot 15490	7	11
9.	**DON'T BE CRUEL** (BMI)—E. Presley Hound Dog (BMI)—Vic 20-6604	8	17
10.	**ROSE AND A BABY RUTH** (BMI)—G. Hamilton IV If You Don't Know (BMI)—ABC-Paramount 9765	14	3
11.	**CANADIAN SUNSET** (BMI)—H. Winterhalter-E. Heywood This Is Real (ASCAP)—Vic 20-6537	10	19
12.	**CINDY, OH, CINDY** (BMI)—E. Fisher Around the World (ASCAP)—Vic 20 6677	16	6
13.	***LOVE ME** (BMI)—E. Presley Vic EPA 992—BMI	—	1
14.	**HONKY TONK** (PARTS I & II)—B. Doggett King 4950—BMI	15	11
15.	**TWO DIFFERENT WORLDS** (ASCAP)—D. Rondo He Made You Mine (ASCAP)—Jubilee 5256	11	5
16.	**NIGHT LIGHTS** (ASCAP)—Nat (King) Cole To the Ends of the Earth (BMI)—Cap 3551	13	5
17.	**MAMA FROM THE TRAIN** (ASCAP)—P. Page Every Time I Feel His Spirit (BMI)—Mercury 70971	21	5
18.	**CINDY, OH, CINDY** (BMI)—V. Martin Only If I Praise the Lord (BMI)—Glory 247	12	4
19.	**GARDEN OF EDEN** (BMI)—J. Valino Caravan (ASCAP)—Vik 0226	23	3
20.	**ANY WAY YOU WANT ME** (ASCAP)—E. Presley Love Me Tender (BMI)—Vic 20-6643	—	1
21.	**TONIGHT YOU BELONG TO ME** (ASCAP)—Lennon Sisters-L. Welk When the White Lilacs Bloom Again (ASCAP)—Coral 61701	—	8
22.	**I WOULDN'T KNOW WHERE TO BEGIN** (ASCAP)—E. Arnold Ballad of Wes Tancred (ASCAP)—Vic 20-6699	—	1
23.	**AUTUMN WALTZ** (ASCAP)—T. Bennett Just In Time (ASCAP)—Col 40770	18	3
24.	**YOU'LL NEVER, NEVER KNOW** (BMI)—Platters It Isn't Right (BMI)—Mercury 70948	—	2
25.	**I WALK THE LINE** (BMI)—J. Cash Get Rhythm (BMI)—Sun 241	—	2
25.	**TONIGHT YOU BELONG TO ME** (ASCAP)—Patience & Prudence A Smile and a Ribbon (ASCAP)—Liberty 55022	19	15

*(Not available as a Pop Single, available on RCA Victor 45EPA-992 and in RCA Victor 33⅓ "Elvis" LPM 1382)

THE TOP 100

For survey week ending November 21

A list of the Top 100 RECORD SIDES in the nation according to a COMBINED TABULATION of Dealer, Disk Jockey and Juke Box Operator replies to The Billboard's weekly popular record Best Seller and Most Played surveys. Its purpose is to provide Disk Jockeys with additional programming material and to give trade exposure to NEWER records just beginning to show action in the field.

Pos.	Song, Artist, Label	Last Week
1.	**LOVE ME TENDER**—E. Presley, Victor	1
2.	**GREEN DOOR**—J. Lowe, Dot	2
3.	**SINGING THE BLUES**—G. Mitchell, Columbia	4
4.	**JUST WALKING IN THE RAIN**—J. Ray, Columbia	3
5.	**BLUEBERRY HILL**—F. Domino, Imperial	6
5.	**TRUE LOVE**—Bing Crosby-G. Kelly, Capitol	7
7.	**DON'T BE CRUEL**—E. Presley, Victor	5
8.	**FRIENDLY PERSUASION**—P. Boone, Dot	8
9.	**HONKY TONK**—B. Doggett, King	9
9.	**HEY, JEALOUS LOVER**—F. Sinatra, Capitol	11
11.	**CANADIAN SUNSET**—H. Winterhalter-E. Heywood, Victor	10
12.	**ROSE AND A BABY RUTH**—G. Hamilton IV, ABC-Paramount	15
13.	**CINDY, OH, CINDY**—E. Fisher, Victor	14
14.	**CINDY, OH, CINDY**—V. Martin, Glory	12
15.	**TONIGHT YOU BELONG TO ME**—Patience & Prudence, Liberty	13
16.	**YOU'LL NEVER, NEVER KNOW**—Platters, Mercury	16
17.	**MAMA FROM THE TRAIN**—P. Page, Mercury	17
18.	**NIGHT LIGHTS**—Nat (King) Cole, Capitol	22
19.	**I WALK THE LINE**—J. Cash, Sun	23
20.	**GARDEN OF EDEN**—J. Valino, Vik	18
21.	**PETTICOATS OF PORTUGAL**—D. Jacobs, Coral	21
22.	**MUTUAL ADMIRATION SOCIETY**—T. Brewer, Coral	26
23.	**TONIGHT YOU BELONG TO ME**—Lennon Sisters-L. Welk, Coral	28
24.	**LAY DOWN YOUR ARMS**—Chordettes, Cadence	19
24.	**LOVE ME**—E. Presley, Victor	41
26.	**CONFIDENTIAL**—S. Knight, Dot	31
27.	**ANY WAY YOU WANT ME**—E. Presley, Victor	35
28.	**WHATEVER WILL BE, WILL BE**—Doris Day, Columbia	25
29.	**TWO DIFFERENT WORLDS**—D. Rondo, Jubilee	24
30.	**PRISCILLA**—E. Cooley, Roost	37
31.	**HOUND DOG**—E. Presley, Victor	19
32.	**IT ISN'T RIGHT**—Platters, Mercury	32
33.	**CANADIAN SUNSET**—A. Williams, Cadence	27
34.	**ROCK-A-BYE YOUR BABY**—J. Lewis, Decca	63
35.	**IN THE STILL OF THE NIGHT**—Satins, Ember	54
36.	**CHAINS OF LOVE**—P. Boone, Dot	57
37.	**SINCE I MET YOU, BABY**—I. J. Hunter, Atlantic	49
38.	**CITY OF ANGELS**—Highlights, Bally	30
38.	**RUDY'S ROCK**—B. Haley, Decca	34
40.	**GONNA GET ALONG WITHOUT YA NOW**—Patience & Prudence, Liberty	—
41.	**AUTUMN WALTZ**—T. Bennett, Columbia	52
42.	**MOONLIGHT LOVE**—P. Como, Victor	51
43.	**SINGING THE BLUES**—M. Robbins, Columbia	37
43.	**SLOW WALK**—E. Austin, Mercury	39
45.	**OUT OF SIGHT, OUT OF MIND**—Five Keys, Capitol	50
46.	**TRUE LOVE**—J. Powell, Verve	43
47.	**ON LONDON BRIDGE**—J. Stafford, Columbia	60
47.	**SOFT SUMMER BREEZE**—E. Heywood, Mercury	36
49.	**AFTER THE LIGHTS GO DOWN LOW**—A Hibbler, Decca	44
49.	**FOOL**—S. Clark, Dot	32
51.	**MOONLIGHT GAMBLER**—F. Laine, Columbia	—
52.	**SLOW WALK**—B. Doggett, King	58
53.	**CRAZY WITH LOVE**—G. Mitchell, Columbia	—
53.	**JAMAICA FAREWELL**—H. Belafonte, Victor	29
55.	**ALLEGHENY MOON**—P. Page, Mercury	59
55.	**STAR YOU WISHED UPON LAST NIGHT**—G. MacKenzie, Vik	53
57.	**MUTUAL ADMIRATION SOCIETY**—J. P. Morgan-E. Arnold, Victor	—
57.	**SEE-SAW**—D. Cornell, Coral	87
59.	**MY PRAYER**—Platters, Mercury	48
59.	**NEW YORK'S MY HOME**—S. Davis Jr., Decca	66
61.	**FIRST BORN**—Tennessee Ernie, Capitol	62
62.	**I DREAMED**—B. Johnson, Bally	66
63.	**GIANT**—L. Baxter, Capitol	99
64.	**I WOULDN'T KNOW WHERE TO BEGIN**—E. Arnold, Victor	68
65.	**AUCTIONEER**—L. Van Dyke, Dot	83
66.	**LET THE GOOD TIMES ROLL**—Shirley & Lee, Aladdin	56
66.	**TO THE END OF THE EARTH**—Nat (King) Cole, Capitol	39
68.	**BLUEBERRY HILL**—L. Armstrong, Decca	74
68.	**FRIENDLY PERSUASION**—Four Aces, Decca	55
68.	**JUST IN TIME**—T. Bennett, Columbia	68
71.	**SEE-SAW**—Moonglows, Chess	71
72.	**CONFESSION OF A SINNER**—Stylers, Jubilee	80
73.	**I CAN'T LOVE YOU ENOUGH**—L. Baker, Atlantic	64
74.	**IT'S YOURS**—De Castros Sisters, Victor	76
75.	**I SAW ESAU**—Ames Brothers, Victor	79
76.	**SOMEONE TO LOVE**—Four Aces, Decca	—
77.	**JULIE**—Doris Day, Columbia	64
77.	**TWO DIFFERENT WORLDS**—R. Williams & J. Moragn, Kapp	72
79.	**TEEN-AGE GOODNIGHT**—Chordettes, Cadence	45
79.	**TRICKY**—G. Jenkins, Decca	—
81.	**MIRACLE OF LOVE—E. Rodgers, Columbia**	42
82.	**MARRIED I CAN ALWAYS GET**—T. King, Victor	75
82.	**YOU DON'T KNOW ME**—J. Vale, Columbia	87
85.	**I MISS YOU SO**—C. Connor, Atlantic	98
86.	**CHINCHERINCHEE**—P. Como, Victor	73
86.	**MIRACLE OF LOVE**—G. Gibson, ABC Paramount	—
86.	**STILL**—Fontane Sisters, Dot	87
89.	**FADED SUMMER LOVE**—G. Shaw, Decca	—
89.	**SADIE'S SHAWL**—B. Sharples, London	87
91.	**CRAZY WITH LOVE**—T. Brewer, Coral	95
92.	**EV'RYDAY OF MY LIFE**—McGuire Sisters, Coral	61
93.	**FAITHFUL HUSSAR**—T. Heath, London	84
94.	**BLUE MOON**—E. Presley, Victor	93
94.	**EARTHBOUND**—S. Davis Jr., Decca	84
94.	**HAPPINESS STREET**—G. Gibbs, Mercury	80
94.	**SONG OF THE SPARROW**—M. Miller, Columbia	—
94.	**WHEN MY BLUE MOON TURNS TO GOLD AGAIN**—E. Presley, Victor	—
99.	**IN THE MIDDLE OF THE HOUSE**—R. Draper, Mercury	46
99.	**NAMELY YOU**—D. Cherry, Columbia	93
99.	**YOU CAN'T RUN AWAY FROM IT**—Four Aces, Decca	—

CAUTION TO DEALERS AND JUKE BOX OPERATORS

The Billboard's Top 100 is NOT designed to provide tested information for buying purposes. This function is most reliably served by other regular weekly features: Best Sellers in Stores, Most Played in Juke Boxes, Coming Up Strong and Best Buys.

• Best Sellers in Stores

For survey week ending November 28

RECORDS are ranked in order of their current national selling importance at the retail level, as determined by The Billboard's weekly survey of the top volume dealers in every important market area. When significant action is reported on both sides of a record, points are combined to determine position on the chart. In such a case, both sides are listed in bold type, the leading side on top.

This Week		Last Week	Weeks on Chart
1.	**SINGING THE BLUES** (BMI)—G. Mitchell Crazy With Love (ASCAP)—Col 40769	2	6
2.	**LOVE ME TENDER** (BMI)—E. Presley Any Way You Want Me (ASCAP)—Vic 20-6643	1	8
3.	**GREEN DOOR** (BMI)—J. Lowe (Story of) The Little Man in Chinatown (BMI)—Dot 15486	3	11
4.	**BLUEBERRY HILL** (ASCAP)—F. Domino Honey Chile (BMI)—Imperial 5407	6	9
5.	**JUST WALKING IN THE RAIN** (BMI)—J. Ray In the Candlelight (ASCAP)—Col 40729	4	14
6.	**TRUE LOVE** (ASCAP)—B. Crosby-G. Kelly Well, Did You Evah? (ASCAP)—Cap 3507	5	10
7.	**DON'T BE CRUEL** (BMI)—E. Presley. **HOUND DOG** (BMI)—Vic 20-6604	7	19
8.	**HEY, JEALOUS LOVER** (ASCAP)—F. Sinatra You Forgot All the Words (BMI)—Cap 3552	9	6
9.	**ROSE AND A BABY RUTH** (BMI)—G. Hamilton IV If You Don't Know (BMI)—ABC-Paramount 9765	11	4
10.	**HONKY TONK** (PARTS I & II)—B. Doggett King 4950—(BMI)	8	16
11.	**FRIENDLY PERSUASION** (ASCAP)—P. Boone Chains of Love (BMI)—Dot 15490	10	12
12.	**CINDY, OH, CINDY** (BMI)—E. Fisher Around the World (ASCAP)—Vic 20-6677	14	9
13.	***LOVE ME** (BMI)—E. Presley Vic EPA 992	21	3
14.	**CINDY, OH, CINDY** (BMI)—V. Martin Only If I Praise the Lord (BMI)—Glory 247	12	6
15.	**ROCK-A-BYE YOUR BABY** (ASCAP)—J. Lewis Come Rain Or Come Shine (ASCAP)—Dec 30124	18	3
16.	**GARDEN OF EDEN** (BMI)—J. Valino. Caravan (ASCAP)—Vik 0226	16	5
17.	**MAMA FROM THE TRAIN** (ASCAP)—P. Page Every Time—I Feel His Spirit (BMI)—Mercury 70971	20	3
18.	**NIGHT LIGHTS** (ASCAP)—Nat (King) Cole To the Ends of the Earth (BMI)—Cap 3551	17	5
19.	**SINCE I MET YOU, BABY** (BMI)—I. J. Hunter You Can't Stop This Rocking and Rolling (BMI)—Atlantic 1111	—	1
20.	**SLOW WALK** (BMI)—S. Austin Wildwood (BMI)—Mercury 70965	25	2
21.	**AUCTIONEER** (ASCAP)—L. Van Dyke. I Fell In Love With a Pony Tail (ASCAP)—Dot 15503	—	1
22.	**PRISCILLA** (BMI)—E. Cooley Got a Little Woman (BMI)—Roost 621	22	4
23.	**TWO DIFFERENT WORLDS** (ASCAP)—D. Rondo He Made You Mine (BMI) —Jubilee 5256	—	1
24.	**TRUE LOVE** (ASCAP)—J. Powell Mind If I Make Love to You (ASCAP)—Verve 2018	—	1
25.	**GONNA GET ALONG WITHOUT YA, NOW** (ASCAP)—Patience & Prudence Money Tree (ASCAP)—Liberty 55040	—	1

*(Not available as a Pop Single, available on RCA Victor 45 EPA 992 and in RCA Victor 33⅓ "Elvis" LPM 1382)

• Most Played in Juke Boxes

For survey week ending November 28

RECORDS are ranked in order of the greatest number of plays in juke boxes thruout the country, as determined by The Billboard's weekly survey of the nation's juke box operators. When significant play is reported on both sides of a record, points are combined to determine position on the chart. In such a case, both sides are listed in bold type, the leading side on top.

This Week		Last Week	Weeks on Chart
1.	**LOVE ME TENDER** (BMI)—E. Presley **ANY WAY YOU WANT ME** (ASCAP)—Vic 20-6643	2	7
2.	**GREEN DOOR** (BMI)—J. Lowe (The Story of) The Little Man in Chinatown (BMI)—Dot 15486	1	9
3.	**JUST WALKING IN THE RAIN** (BMI)—J. Ray In the Candlelight (ASCAP)—Col 40729	3	12
4.	**SINGING THE BLUES** (BMI)—G. Mitchell Crazy With Love (ASCAP)—Col 40769	6	5
5.	**BLUEBERRY HILL** (ASCAP)—F. Domino Honey Chile (BMI)—Imperial 5407	5	8
6.	**DON'T BE CRUEL** (BMI)—E. Presley. **HOUND DOG** (BMI)—Vic 20-6643	4	18
7.	**TRUE LOVE** (ASCAP)—B. Crosby-G. Kelly Well, Did You Evah? (ASCAP)—Col 3507	8	6
8.	**HONKY TONK** (PARTS I & II) (BMI)—B. Doggett King 4950	7	13
9.	**HEY, JEALOUS LOVER** (ASCAP)—F. Sinatra You Forgot All the Words (BMI)—Cap 3552	15	3
10.	**CINDY, OH, CINDY** (BMI)—V. Martin Only If I Praise the Lord (BMI)—Glory 247	11	5
11.	**FRIENDLY PERSUASION** (ASCAP)—P. Boone Chains of Love (BMI)—Dot 15490	10	10
12.	**ROSE AND A BABY RUTH** (BMI)—G. Hamilton IV If You Don't Know (BMI)—ABC-Paramount 9765	14	2
13.	**CINDY, OH, CINDY** (BMI)—E. Fisher. Around the World (ASCAP)—Vic 20-6677	18	4
14.	**MAMA FROM THE TRAIN** (ASCAP)—P. Page Every Time—I Feel His Spirit (BMI)—Mercury 70971	—	1
15.	**CANADIAN SUNSET** (BMI)—H. Winterhalter-E. Heywood This Is Real (ASCAP)—Vic 20-6537	9	17
16.	**YOU'LL NEVER, NEVER KNOW** (BMI)—Platters It Isn't Right (BMI)—Mercury 70948	16	9
17.	**GARDEN OF EDEN** (BMI)—J. Valino. Caravan (ASCAP)—Vik 0226	—	1
18.	**TONIGHT YOU BELONG TO ME** (ASCAP)—Patience & Prudence A Smile and a Ribbon (ASCAP)—Liberty 55022	12	14
19.	**SINGING THE BLUES** (BMI)—M. Robbins I Can't Quit (BMI)—Col 21545	—	1
20.	**CONFIDENTIAL** (BMI)—S. Knight Jail Bird (BMI)—Dot 15507	19	3

• Best Selling Sheet Music

Tunes are ranked in order of their current national selling importance at the sheet music jobber level.

This Week		Last Week	Weeks on Chart
1.	**True Love** (Buxton Hill)	2	11
2.	**Love Me Tender** (Presley)	1	8
3.	**Just Walking in the Rain** (Golden West)	3	9
4.	**Singing the Blues** (Acuff-Rose)	6	3
5.	**Green Door** (Trinity)	5	7
6.	**Cindy, Oh, Cindy** (E. B. Marks-Bryden)	7	5
7.	**Blueberry Hill** (Chappell)	10	4
8.	**Two Different Worlds** (Spier)	14	4
9.	**Friendly Persuasion** (Feist)	8	6
10.	**Tonight You Belong to Me** (Mills)	4	4
11.	**Canadian Sunset** (Meridian)	8	18
12.	**Allegheny Moon** (Oxford)	12	24
13.	**Hey, Jealous Lover** (Barton)	13	3
14.	**Honky Tonk** (Billace)	—	6
15.	**Whatever Will Be, Will Be (Que Sera, Sera)** (Artists)	11	22

• Most Played by Jockeys

For survey week ending November 28

SIDES are ranked in order of the greatest number of plays on disk jockey radio shows thruout the country. Results are based on The Billboard's weekly survey among the nation's disk jockeys. The reverse side of each record is also listed.

This Week		Last Week	Weeks on Chart
1.	**SINGING THE BLUES** (BMI)—G. Mitchell Crazy With Love (ASCAP)—Col 40769	2	6
2.	**LOVE ME TENDER** (BMI)—E. Presley Any Way You Want Me (BMI)—Vic 20-6643	1	8
3.	**GREEN DOOR** (BMI)—J. Lowe (The Story of) The Little Man in Chinatown (BMI)—Dot 15486	3	11
4.	**TRUE LOVE** (ASCAP)—B. Crosby-G. Kelly Well, Did You Evah? (ASCAP)—Cap 3507	4	10
5.	**JUST WALKING IN THE RAIN** (BMI)—J. Ray In The Candlelight (ASCAP)—Col 40729	5	11
6.	**HEY, JEALOUS LOVER** (ASCAP)—F. Sinatra You Forget All the Words (BMI)—Cap 3552	6	7
7.	***LOVE ME** (BMI)—E. Presley Vic EPA-992	13	2
8.	**FRIENDLY PERSUASION** (ASCAP)—P. Boone Chains of Love (ASCAP)—Dot 15490	8	12
9.	**BLUEBERRY HILL** (ASCAP)—F. Domino Honey Chile (BMI)—Imperial 5407	7	8
10.	**ROSE AND A BABY RUTH** (BMI)—G. Hamilton IV If You Don't Know (BMI)—ABC-Paramount 9765	10	4
11.	**NIGHT LIGHTS** (ASCAP)—Nat (King) Cole To the Ends of the Earth (BMI)—Cap 3551	16	6
12.	**GARDEN OF EDEN** (BMI)—J. Valino. Caravan (ASCAP)—Vik 0226	19	4
13.	**TWO DIFFERENT WORLDS** (ASCAP)—D. Rondo He Made You Mine (ASCAP)—Jubilee 5256	15	6
14.	**MAMA FROM THE TRAIN** (ASCAP)—P. Page Every Time—I Feel His Spirit (BMI)—Mercury 70971	17	6
15.	**DON'T BE CRUEL** (BMI)—E. Presley. Hound Dog (BMI)—Vic 20-6604	9	18
16.	**PETTICOATS OF PORTUGAL** (BMI)—D. Jacobs Song of the Vagabonds/Only a Rose (ASCAP)—Coral 61724	—	4
17.	**CINDY, OH, CINDY** (BMI)—E. Fisher. Around the World (ASCAP)—Vic 20-6677	12	7
18.	**SINCE I MET YOU, BABY** (BMI)—I. J. Hunter You Can't Stop This Rocking and Rolling (BMI)—Atlantic 1111	—	1
19.	**GONNA GET ALONG WITHOUT YA NOW** (ASCAP)—Patience & Prudence Money Tree (ASCAP)—Liberty 55040	—	1
20.	**MONEY TREE** (ASCAP)—M. Whiting. Maybe I Love Him (ASCAP)—Cap 3586	—	1
21.	**CANADIAN SUNSET** (BMI)—H. Winterhalter-E. Heywood This Is Real (ASCAP)—Vic 20-6537	11	20
22.	**CINDY, OH, CINDY** (BMI)—V. Martin Only If I Praise the Lord (BMI)—Glory 247	18	5
23.	**ANY WAY YOU WANT ME** (ASCAP)—E. Presley Love Me Tender (BMI)—Vic 20-6643	20	2
24.	**HONKY TONK** (PARTS I & II)—B. Doggett King 4950—BMI	14	12
25.	**JAMAICA FAREWELL** (ASCAP)—H. Belafonte Once Was (ASCAP)—Vic 20-6663	—	1

*(Not available as a Pop Single, available on RCA Victor 45 EPA-992 and in RCA Victor 33⅓ "Elvis" LPM 1382)

THE TOP 100

For survey week ending November 28

A list of the Top 100 RECORD SIDES in the nation according to a COMBINED TABULATION of Dealer, Disk Jockey and Juke Box Operator replies to The Billboard's weekly popular record Best Seller and Most Played surveys. Its purpose is to provide Disk Jockeys with additional programming material and to give trade exposure to NEWER records just beginning to show action in the field.

Pos.	Song, Artist, Label	Last Week
1.	**SINGING THE BLUES**—G. Mitchell, Columbia	3
2.	**LOVE ME TENDER**—E. Presley, Victor	1
3.	**GREEN DOOR**—J. Lowe, Dot	2
4.	**JUST WALKING IN THE RAIN**—J. Ray, Columbia	4
5.	**TRUE LOVE**—Bing Crosby-G. Kelly, Capitol	5
6.	**BLUEBERRY HILL**—F. Domino, Imperial	5
7.	**HEY, JEALOUS LOVER**—F. Sinatra, Capitol	9
8.	**DON'T BE CRUEL**—E. Presley, Victor	7
9.	**FRIENDLY PERSUASION**—P. Boone, Dot	8
10.	**ROSE AND A BABY RUTH**—G. Hamilton IV, ABC-Paramount	12
11.	**HONKY TONK**—B. Doggett, King	9
12.	**CINDY, OH, CINDY**—E. Fisher, Victor	13
13.	**MAMA FROM THE TRAIN**—P. Page, Mercury	17
14.	**GARDEN OF EDEN**—J. Valino, Vik	20
15.	**CINDY, OH, CINDY**—V. Martin, Glory	14
16.	**NIGHT LIGHTS**—Nat (King) Cole, Capitol	18
17.	**LOVE ME**—E. Presley, Victor	24
18.	**CANADIAN SUNSET**—H. Winterhalter-E. Heywood, Victor	11
19.	**SLOW WALK**—S. Austin, Mercury	43
20.	**PETTICOATS OF PORTUGAL**—D. Jacobs, Coral	21
21.	**MUTUAL ADMIRATION SOCIETY**—T. Brewer, Coral	22
22.	**I WALK THE LINE**—J. Cash, Sun	19
23.	**SINCE I MET YOU, BABY**—I. J. Hunter, Atlantic	37
23.	**TWO DIFFERENT WORLDS**—D. Rondo, Jubilee	29
25.	**YOU'LL NEVER, NEVER KNOW**—Platters, Mercury	16
26.	**SINGING THE BLUES**—M. Robbins, Columbia	43
27.	**CONFIDENTIAL**—S. Knight, Dot	26
27.	**HOUND DOG**—E. Presley, Victor	31
29.	**ROCK-A-BYE YOUR BABY**—J. Lewis, Decca	34
30.	**GONNA GET ALONG WITHOUT YA NOW**—Patience & Prudence, Liberty	40
31.	**MOONLIGHT GAMBLER**—F. Laine, Columbia	51
32.	**LAY DOWN YOUR ARMS**—Chordettes, Cadence	24
33.	**TONIGHT YOU BELONG TO ME**—Patience & Prudence, Liberty	15
34.	**JAMAICA FAREWELL**—H. Belafonte, Victor	52
35.	**PRISCILLA**—E. Cooley, Roost	30
36.	**CANADIAN SUNSET**—A. Williams, Cadence	33
36.	**CITY OF ANGELS**—Highlights, Bally	38
36.	**RUDY'S ROCK**—B. Haley, Decca	38
39.	**TONIGHT YOU BELONG TO ME**—Lennon Sisters-L, Welk, Coral	23
40.	**IT ISN'T RIGHT**—Platters, Mercury	32
41.	**TRUE LOVE**—J. Powell, Verve	46
42.	**ANY WAY YOU WANT ME**—E. Presley, Victor	27
42.	**STAR YOU WISHED UPON LAST NIGHT**—G. MacKenzie, Vik	55
44.	**AUCTIONEER**—L. Van Dyke, Dot	65
45.	**MIRACLE OF LOVE**—E. Rodgers, Columbia	81
46.	**WHATEVER WILL BE, WILL BE**—Doris Day, Columbia	28
47.	**SOMEONE TO LOVE**—Four Aces, Decca	76
48.	**OUT OF SIGHT, OUT OF MIND**—Five Keys, Capitol	45
49.	**I DREAMED**—B. Johnson, Bally	62
49.	**IN THE STILL OF THE NIGHT**—Satins, Ember	35
51.	**BLUEBERRY HILL**—L. Armstrong, Decca	68
51.	**MUTUAL ADMIRATION SOCIETY**—E. Arnold-J. P. Morgan, Victor	57
51.	**ON LONDON BRIDGE**—J. Stafford, Columbia	47
54.	**BABY DOLL**—A. Williams, Cadence	—
55.	**JUST IN TIME**—T. Bennett, Columbia	68
56.	**CRAZY WITH LOVE**—G. Mitchell, Columbia	53
57.	**FADED SUMMER LOVE**—G. Shaw, Decca	89
58.	**AUTUMN WALTZ**—T. Bennett, Columbia	41
58.	**TO THE ENDS OF THE EARTH**—Nat (King) Cole, Capitol	66
60.	**CHINCHERINCHEE**—P. Como, Victor	86
61.	**WHEN MY BLUE MOON TURNS TO GOLD AGAIN**—E. Presley, Victor	94
62.	**LOVE ME GOOD**—J. Stafford, Columbia	—
63.	**MONEY TREE**—M. Whiting, Capitol	—
64.	**LOVE ME TENDER**—H. Rene, Victor	—
65.	**I'LL ALWAYS BE IN LOVE WITH YOU**—J. Pleis, Decca	—
66.	**FIRST BORN**—T. Ernie, Capitol	61
66.	**GOODNIGHT MY LOVE**—McGuire Sisters, Coral	—
68.	**I SAW ESAU**—Ames Brothers, Victor	75
68.	**JULIE**—Doris Day, Columbia	77
70.	**SEE-SAW**—D. Cornell, Coral	57
71.	**NEW YORK'S MY HOME**—S. Davis Jr., Decca	59
72.	**SLOW WALK**—B. Doggett, King	52
73.	**CHAINS OF LOVE**—P. Boone, Dot	36
74.	**FOOL**—S. Clark, Dot	49
75.	**AFTER THE LIGHTS GO DOWN LOW**—A. Hibbler, Decca	49
76.	**GIANT**—L. Baxter, Capitol	63
77.	**I WOULDN'T KNOW WHERE TO BEGIN**—E. Arnold, Victor	64
78.	**EV'RYDAY OF MY LIFE**—McGuire Sisters, Coral	92
78.	**MONEY TREE**—Patience & Prudence, Liberty	—
80.	**ALLEGHENY MOON**—P. Page, Mercury	55
80.	**SOFT SUMMER BREEZE**—E. Heywood, Mercury	—
82.	**TWO DIFFERENT WORLDS**—J. Morgan & R. Williams, Kapp	77
83.	**TRA LA LA**—G. Gibbs, Mercury	—
84.	**MOONLIGHT LOVE**—P. Como, Victor	42
84.	**WHEN THE WHITE LILACS BLOOM AGAIN**—H. Zacharais, Decca	—
86.	**I MISS YOU SO**—C. Connor, Atlantic	85
86.	**MIRACLE OF LOVE**—G. Gibson, ABC-Paramount	86
88.	**CRAZY WITH LOVE**—T. Brewer, Coral	91
88.	**LET THE GOOD TIMES ROLL**—Shirley & Lee, Aladdin	66
88.	**ARMEN'S THEME**—J. Reisman, Victor	—
91.	**SADIE'S SHAWL**—B. Sharples, London	89
92.	**BLUE MOON**—E. Presley, Victor	94
93.	**PLEASE DON'T LEAVE ME**—Fontane Sisters, Dot	—
93.	**TEEN-AGE GOODNIGHT**—Chordettes, Cadence	—
95.	**SINCE I MET YOU, BABY**—M. Carson, Columbia	—
96.	**ITALIAN THEME**—C. Stapleton, London	—
96.	**YOU CAN'T RUN AWAY FROM IT**—Four Aces, Decca	99
98.	**CHEAT**—S. Clark, Dot	—
98.	**CONFESSION OF A SINNER**—Stylers, Jubilee	72
98.	**I CAN'T LOVE YOU ENOUGH**—L. Baker, Atlantic	73

CAUTION TO DEALERS AND JUKE BOX OPERATORS

The Billboard's Top 100 is NOT designed to provide tested information for buying purposes. This function is most reliably served by other regular weekly features: Best Sellers in Stores, Most Played in Juke Boxes, Coming Up Strong and Best Buys.

• Best Sellers in Stores

For survey week ending December 5

RECORDS are ranked in order of their current national selling importance at the retail level, as determined by The Billboard's weekly survey of the top volume dealers in every important market area. When significant action is reported on both sides of a record, points are combined to determine position on the chart. In such a case, both sides are listed in bold type, the leading side on top.

This Week		Last Week	Weeks on Chart
1.	**SINGING THE BLUES** (BMI)—G. Mitchell Crazy With Love (ASCAP)—Col 40769	1	7
2.	**LOVE ME TENDER** (BMI)—E. Presley Any Way You Want Me (ASCAP)—Vic 20-6643	2	9
3.	**GREEN DOOR** (BMI)—J. Lowe (Story of) The Little Man in Chinatown (BMI)—Dot 15486	3	12
4.	**BLUEBERRY HILL** (ASCAP)—F. Domino Honey Chile (BMI)—Imperial 5407	4	10
5.	**JUST WALKING IN THE RAIN** (BMI)—J. Ray In the Candlelight (ASCAP)—Col 40729	5	15
6.	**TRUE LOVE** (ASCAP)—B. Crosby-G. Kelly Well, Did You Evah? (ASCAP)—Cap 3507	6	11
7.	**ROSE AND A BABY RUTH** (BMI)—G. Hamilton IV If You Don't Know—(BMI) ABC-Paramount 9765	9	5
8.	**DON'T BE CRUEL** (BMI)—E. Presley **HOUND DOG** (BMI)—Vic 20-6604	7	20
9.	***LOVE ME** (BMI)—E. Presley Vic EPA 992	13	4
10.	**HEY, JEALOUS LOVER** (ASCAP)—F. Sinatra You Forgot All the Words (BMI)—Cap 3552	8	7
11.	**HONKY TONK (Parts I & II)** (BMI)—B. Doggett King 4950	10	17
12.	**FRIENDLY PERSUASION** (ASCAP)—P. Boone Chains of Love (BMI)—Dot 15490	11	13
13.	**GARDEN OF EDEN** (BMI)—J. Valino Caravan (ASCAP)—Vik 0226	16	6
14.	**ROCK-A-BYE YOUR BABY** (ASCAP)—J. Lewis Come Rain or Come Shine (ASCAP)—Dec 30124	15	4
15.	**CINDY, OH, CINDY** (BMI)—E. Fisher Around the World (ASCAP)—Vic 20-6677	12	10
16.	**CINDY, OH, CINDY** (BMI)—V. Martin Only If I Praise the Lord (BMI)—Glory 247	14	7
17.	**SINCE I MET YOU, BABY** (BMI)—I. J. Hunter You Can't Stop This Rocking and Rolling (BMI)—Atlantic 1111	19	2
18.	**GONNA GET ALONG WITHOUT YA, NOW** (ASCAP)—Patience & Prudence Money Tree (ASCAP)—Liberty 55040	25	2
19.	**CONFIDENTIAL** (BMI)—S. Knight Jail Bird (BMI)—Dot 15507	—	1
20.	**MAMA FROM THE TRAIN** (ASCAP)—P. Page Every Time—I Feel His Spirit (BMI)—Mercury 70971	17	4
21.	**SLOW WALK** (BMI)—S. Austin Wildwood (BMI)—Mercury 70963	20	3
22.	**NIGHT LIGHTS** (ASCAP)—Nat (King) Cole To the Ends of the Earth (BMI)—Cap 3551	18	6
23.	**TWO DIFFERENT WORLDS** (ASCAP)—D. Rondo He Made You Mine (BMI)—Jubilee 5256	23	2
24.	**CITY OF ANGELS** (BMI)—Highlights Listen, My Love (ASCAP)—Bally 1016	—	3
25.	**MOONLIGHT GAMBLER** (ASCAP)—F. Laine Lotus Land (ASCAP)—Col 40780	—	1

*(Not Available as a Pop Single. Available on RCA Victor 45 EPA 992 and in RCA Victor 33⅓ "Elvis" LPM 1382)

• Most Played in Juke Boxes

For survey week ending December 5

RECORDS are ranked in order of the greatest number of plays in juke boxes thruout the country, as determined by The Billboard's weekly survey of the nation's juke box operators. When significant play is reported on both sides of a record, points are combined to determine position on the chart. In such a case, both sides are listed in bold type, the leading side on top.

This Week		Last Week	Weeks on Chart
1.	**SINGING THE BLUES** (BMI)—G. Mitchell Crazy With Love (ASCAP)—Col 40769	4	6
2.	**LOVE ME TENDER** (BMI)—E. Presley **ANY WAY YOU WANT ME** (ASCAP)—Vic 20-6643	1	8
3.	**GREEN DOOR** (BMI)—J. Lowe (The Story of) The Little Man in Chinatown (BMI)—Dot 15486	2	10
4.	**JUST WALKING IN THE RAIN** (BMI)—J. Ray In the Candlelight (ASCAP)—Col 40729	3	13
5.	**BLUEBERRY HILL** (ASCAP)—F. Domino Honey Chile (BMI)—Imperial 5407	5	9
6.	**HONKY TONK (PARTS I & II)** (BMI)—B. Doggett King 4950	8	14
7.	**TRUE LOVE** (ASCAP)—B. Crosby-G. Kelly Well, Did You Evah? (ASCAP)—Cap 3507	7	7
8.	**DON'T BE CRUEL** (BMI)—E. Presley. **HOUND DOG** (BMI)—Vic 20-6643	6	19
9.	**HEY, JEALOUS LOVER** (ASCAP)—F. Sinatra You Forgot All the Words (BMI)—Cap 3552	9	4
10.	**CINDY, OH, CINDY** (BMI)—V. Martin Only If I Praise The Lord (BMI)—Glory 247	10	6
11.	**CINDY, OH, CINDY** (BMI)—E. Fisher. Around the World (ASCAP)—Vic 20-6677	13	5
12.	**MAMA FROM THE TRAIN** (ASCAP)—P. Page Every Time—I Feel His Spirit (BMI)—Mercury 70971	14	2
13.	**GARDEN OF EDEN** (BMI)—J. Valino. Caravan (ASCAP)—Vik 0226	17	2
14.	**YOU'LL NEVER, NEVER KNOW** (BMI)—Platters It Isn't Right (BMI)—Mercury 70948	16	10
15.	**CANADIAN SUNSET** (BMI)—H. Winterhalter-E. Heywood This Is Real (ASCAP)—Vic 20-6537	15	18
16.	**TONIGHT YOU BELONG TO ME** (ASCAP)—Patience & Prudence A Smile and a Ribbon (ASCAP)—Liberty 55022	18	15
17.	**ROSE AND A BABY RUTH** (BMI)—G. Hamilton IV If You Don't Know (BMI)—ABC-Paramount 9765	12	3
17.	**CONFIDENTIAL** (BMI)—S. Knight Jail Bird (BMI)—Dot 15507	20	4
19.	**FRIENDLY PERSUASION** (ASCAP)—P. Boone Chains of Love (BMI)—Dot 15490	11	11
20.	***LOVE ME**—E. Presley Vic EPA-992—BMI	—	1

*Not available as a Pop Single, available on RCA Victor 45 EPA-992 and on RCA Victor 33⅓ "Elvis" LPM 1382

• Best Selling Sheet Music

Tunes are ranked in order of their current national selling importance at the sheet music jobber level.

This Week		Last Week	Weeks on Chart
1.	**True Love** (Buxton Hill)	1	12
2.	**Love Me Tender** (Presley)	2	9
3.	**Singing the Blues** (Acuff-Rose)	4	4
4.	**Just Walking in the Rain** (Golden West)	3	10
5.	**Green Door** (Trinity)	5	8
6.	**Blueberry Hill** (Chappell)	7	5
7.	**Cindy, Oh, Cindy** (E. B. Marks-Bryden)	6	6
8.	**Two Different Worlds** (Spier)	8	5
9.	**Friendly Persuasion** (Feist)	9	7
10.	**Tonight You Belong to Me** (Mills)	10	6
11.	**Canadian Sunset** (Meridian)	11	19
12.	**Allegheny Moon** (Oxford)	12	25
13.	**Whatever Will Be, Will Be (Que Sera, Sera)** (Artists)	15	23
14.	**Mama From the Train** (Remick)	—	2
15.	**Love Me** (Hill & Range)	—	1

• Most Played by Jockeys

For survey week ending December 5

SIDES are ranked in order of the greatest number of plays on disk jockey radio shows thruout the country. Results are based on The Billboard's weekly survey among the nation's disk jockeys. The reverse side of each record is also listed.

This Week		Last Week	Weeks on Chart
1.	**SINGING THE BLUES** (BMI)—G. Mitchell Crazy With Love (ASCAP)—Col 40769	1	7
2.	**LOVE ME TENDER** (BMI)—E. Presley Any Way You Want Me (ASCAP)—Vic 20-6643	2	9
3.	**GREEN DOOR** (BMI)—J. Lowe (Story of) The Little Man in Chinatown (BMI)—Dot 15486	3	12
4.	**TRUE LOVE** (ASCAP)—B. Crosby-G. Kelly Well, Did You Evah? (ASCAP)—Cap 3507	4	11
5.	**HEY, JEALOUS LOVER** (ASCAP)—F. Sinatra You Forgot All the Words (BMI)—Cap 3552	6	8
6.	**JUST WALKING IN THE RAIN** (BMI)—J. Ray In the Candlelight (ASCAP)—Col 40729	5	12
7.	**BLUEBERRY HILL** (ASCAP)—F. Domino Honey Chile (BMI)—Imperial 5407	9	9
8.	***LOVE ME** (BMI)—E. Presley Vic EPA-992	7	3
9.	**FRIENDLY PERSUASION** (ASCAP)—P. Boone Chains of Love (ASCAP)—Dot 15490	8	13
10.	**ROSE AND A BABY RUTH** (BMI)—G. Hamilton IV If You Don't Know (BMI)—ABC-Paramount 9765	10	5
11.	**CINDY, OH, CINDY** (BMI)—E. Fisher. Around the World (ASCAP)—Vic 20-6677	17	8
12.	**MAMA FROM THE TRAIN** (ASCAP)—P. Page Every Time—I Feel His Spirit (BMI)—Mercury 70971	14	7
13.	**GARDEN OF EDEN** (BMI)—J. Valino. Caravan (ASCAP)—Vik 0226	12	5
14.	**NIGHT LIGHTS** (ASCAP)—Nat (King) Cole To the Ends of the Earth (BMI)—Cap 3551	11	7
15.	**TWO DIFFERENT WORLDS** (ASCAP)—D. Rondo He Made You Mine (ASCAP)—Jubilee 5256	13	7
16.	**GONNA GET ALONG WITHOUT YA, NOW** (ASCAP)—Patience & Prudence Money Tree (ASCAP)—Liberty 55040	19	2
17.	**PETTICOATS OF PORTUGAL** (BMI)—D. Jacobs Song of the Vagabonds—Only a Rose (ASCAP)—Coral 61724	16	5
18.	**MOONLIGHT GAMBLER** (ASCAP)—F. Laine Lotus Land (ASCAP)—Col 40780	—	1
19.	**I DREAMED** (BMI)—B. Johnson If It's Wrong to Love You (BMI)—Bally 1020	—	1
20.	**HONKY TONK (PARTS I & II)**—B. Doggett King 4950—BMI	24	13
21.	**SINCE I MET YOU, BABY** (BMI)—I. J. Hunter You Can't Stop This Rocking and Rolling (BMI)—Atlantic 1111	18	2
22.	**CINDY, OH, CINDY** (BMI)—V. Martin Only If I Praise The Lord (BMI)—Glory 247	22	6
23.	**AUTUMN WALTZ** (ASCAP)—T. Bennett Just in Time (ASCAP)—Col 40770	—	4
24.	**MUTUAL ADMIRATION SOCIETY** (ASCAP)—T. Brewer Crazy With Love (ASCAP)—Coral 61737	—	1
25.	**CANADIAN SUNSET** (BMI)—H. Winterhalter-E. Heywood This Is Real (ASCAP)—Vic 20-6537	21	21

*Not available as a Pop Single, available on RCA Victor 45 EPA-992 and on RCA Victor 33⅓ "Elvis" LPM 1382

THE TOP 100

For survey week ending December 5

A list of the Top 100 RECORD SIDES in the nation according to a COMBINED TABULATION of Dealer, Disk Jockey and Juke Box Operator replies to The Billboard's weekly popular record Best Seller and Most Played surveys. Its purpose is to provide Disk Jockeys with additional programming material and to give trade exposure to NEWER records just beginning to show action in the field.

Pos.	Song, Artist, Label	Last Week
1.	SINGING THE BLUES—G. Mitchell, Columbia	1
2.	LOVE ME TENDER—E. Presley, Victor	2
3.	GREEN DOOR—J. Lowe, Dot	3
4.	JUST WALKING IN THE RAIN—J. Ray, Columbia	4
5.	BLUEBERRY HILL—F. Domino, Imperial	6
6.	TRUE LOVE—B. Crosby-G. Kelly, Capitol	5
7.	HEY, JEALOUS LOVER—F. Sinatra, Capitol	7
8.	ROSE AND A BABY RUTH—G. Hamilton IV, ABC Paramount	10
9.	LOVE ME—E. Presley, Victor	17
10.	CINDY, OH, CINDY—E. Fisher, Victor	12
10.	HONKY TONK—B. Doggett, King	11
12.	GARDEN OF EDEN—J. Valino, Vik	14
13.	FRIENDLY PERSUASION—P. Boone, Dot	9
14.	DON'T BE CRUEL—E. Presley, Victor	8
14.	MAMA FROM THE TRAIN—P. Page, Mercury	13
16.	CINDY, OH, CINDY—V. Martin, Glory	15
17.	NIGHT LIGHTS—Nat (King) Cole, Capitol	16
18.	GONNA GET ALONG WITHOUT YA NOW—Patience & Prudence, Liberty	30
19.	TWO DIFFERENT WORLDS—D. Rondo, Jubilee	23
20.	CONFIDENTIAL—S. Knight, Dot	27
20.	MOONLIGHT GAMBLER—F. Laine, Columbia	31
22.	CANADIAN SUNSET—E. Heywood & H. Winterhalter, Victor	18
23.	ROCK-A-BYE YOUR BABY—J. Lewis, Decca	29
23.	SLOW WALK—S. Austin, Mercury	19
25.	MUTUAL ADMIRATION SOCIETY—T. Brewer, Coral	21
26.	SINCE I MET YOU, BABY—I. J. Hunter, Atlantic	23
27.	I WALK THE LINE—J. Cash, Sun	22
28.	YOU'LL NEVER, NEVER KNOW—Platters, Mercury	25
29.	BLUEBERRY HILL—L. Armstrong, Decca	51
30.	PETTICOATS OF PORTUGAL—D. Jacobs, Coral	20
31.	AUCTIONEER—L. Van Dyke—Dot	44
32.	TONIGHT YOU BELONG TO ME—Patience & Prudence, Liberty	33
33.	SINGING THE BLUES—M. Robbins, Columbia	26
34.	PRISCILLA—E. Cooley, Roost	35
35.	HOUND DOG—E. Presley, Victor	27
35.	LAY DOWN YOUR ARMS—Chordettes, Cadence	32
37.	SLOW WALK—B. Doggett, King	72
38.	CITY OF ANGELS—Highlights, Bally	36
39.	I DREAMED—B. Johnson, Bally	49
40.	JAMAICA FAREWELL—H. Belafonte, Victor	34
41.	TWO DIFFERENT WORLDS—R. Williams & J. Morgan, Kapp	52
42.	STAR YOU WISHED UPON LAST NIGHT—G. Mac Kenzie, Vik	42
43.	ANY WAY YOU WANT ME—E. Presley, Victor	42
44.	LOVE ME TENDER—H. Rene, Victor	64
45.	ON LONDON BRIDGE—J. Stafford, Columbia	55
46.	JUST IN TIME—T. Bennett, Columbia	55
47.	IN THE STILL OF THE NIGHT—Satins, Ember	49
47.	MUTUAL ADMIRATION SOCIETY—E. Arnold-J. P. Morgan, Victor	51
49.	WHEN MY BLUE MOON TURNS TO GOLD AGAIN—E. Presley Victor	61
50.	TRUE LOVE—J. Powell, Verve	41
51.	I SAW ESAU—Ames Brothers, Victor	68
52.	TRA LA LA—G. Gibbs, Mercury	83
52.	FIRST BORN—Tennessee Ernie, Capitol	66
54.	TONIGHT YOU BELONG TO ME—Lennon Sisters-L. Welk, Coral	39
55.	RUDY'S ROCK—B. Haley, Decca	36
55.	I MISS YOU SO—C. Connor, Atlantic	86
57.	SINCE I MET YOU, BABY—M. Carson, Columbia	—
57.	MONEY TREE—M. Whiting, Capitol	63
59.	CHINCHERINCHEE—P. Como, Victor	60
60.	OUT OF SIGHT, OUT OF MIND—Five Keys, Capitol	48
60.	IT ISN'T RIGHT—Platters, Mercury	40
62.	GOODNIGHT, MY LOVE—McGuire Sisters, Coral	66
63.	WHATEVER WILL BE, WILL BE—Doris Day, Columbia	46
63.	AUTUMN WALTZ—T. Bennett, Columbia	58
65.	WISDOM OF A FOOL—Five Keys, Capitol	—
66.	FADED SUMMER LOVE—G. Shaw, Decca	57
67.	FOOL—S. Clark, Dot	74
68.	SOMEONE TO LOVE—Four Aces, Decca	47
68.	CANADIAN SUNSET—A. Williams, Cadence	36
70.	WRITTEN ON THE WIND—Four Aces, Decca	—
71.	BABY DOLL—A. Williams, Cadence	54
71.	FRIENDLY PERSUASION—Four Aces, Decca	—
73.	CRAZY WITH LOVE—T. Brewer, Coral	88
74.	ALLEGHENY MOON—P. Page, Mercury	80
74.	CHEAT—S. Clark, Dot	98
76.	MY PRAYER—Platters, Mercury	—
77.	ARMEN'S THEME—J. Reisman, Victor	88
78.	I FEEL GOOD—Shirley & Lee, Aladdin	—
79.	TO THE ENDS OF THE EARTH—Nat (King) Cole, Capitol	58
80.	AIN'T GOT NO HOME—C. Henry, Argo	—
81.	SOFT SUMMER BREEZE—E. Heywood, Mercury	80
82.	ARMEN'S THEME—D. Seville, Liberty	—
83.	PETTICOATS OF PORTUGAL—B. Vaughn, Dot	—
84.	MONEY TREE—Patience & Prudence, Liberty	78
85.	LET THE GOOD TIMES ROLL—Shirley & Lee, Aladdin	88
86.	GIVE ME—E. Rodgers, Columbia	—
87.	I WOULDN'T KNOW WHERE TO BEGIN—E. Arnold, Victor	77
87.	MIRACLE OF LOVE—G. Gibson, ABC-Paramount	86
89.	MOONLIGHT LOVE—P. Como, Victor	84
90.	CRAZY WITH LOVE—G. Mitchell, Columbia	56
90.	IT HAPPENED AGAIN—S. Vaughan, Mercury	—
92.	SEE SAW—D. Cornell, Coral	70
93.	SADIE'S SHAWL—B. Sharples, London	91
94.	TRA LA LA—L. Baker, Atlantic	—
94.	JULIE—Doris Day, Columbia	68
96.	STILL—Fontane Sisters, Dot	—
96.	AFTER THE LIGHTS GO DOWN LOW—A. Hibbler, Decca	75
96.	CHAINS OF LOVE—P. Boone, Dot	73
99.	YOU DON'T KNOW ME—J. Vale, Columbia	—
100.	GIANT—L. Baxter, Capitol	76

CAUTION TO DEALERS AND JUKE BOX OPERATORS

The Billboard's Top 100 is NOT designed to provide tested information for buying purposes. This function is most reliably served by other regular weekly features: Best Sellers in Stores, Most Played in Juke Boxes, Coming Up Strong and Best Buys.

• Best Sellers in Stores

For survey week ending December 12

RECORDS are ranked in order of their current national selling importance at the retail level, as determined by The Billboard's weekly survey of the top volume dealers in every important market area. When significant action is reported on both sides of a record, points are combined to determine position on the chart. In such a case, both sides are listed in bold type, the leading side on top.

This Week		Last Week	Weeks on Chart
1.	**SINGING THE BLUES** (BMI)—G. Mitchell Crazy With Love (ASCAP)—Col 40769	1	8
2.	**LOVE ME TENDER** (BMI)—E. Presley Any Way You Want Me (ASCAP)—Vic 20-6643	2	10
3.	**GREEN DOOR** (BMI)—J. Lowe (Story of) The Little Man in Chinatown (BMI)—Dot 15486	3	13
4.	**BLUEBERRY HILL** (ASCAP)—F. Domino Honey Chile (BMI)—Imperial 5407	4	11
5.	**JUST WALKING IN THE RAIN** (BMI)—J. Ray In the Candlelight (ASCAP)—Col 40729	5	16
6.	**TRUE LOVE** (ASCAP)—B. Crosby-G. Kelly Well, Did You Evah? (ASCAP)—Cap 3507	6	12
7.	**ROSE AND A BABY RUTH** (BMI)—G. Hamilton IV If You Don't Know (BMI)—ABC-Paramount 9765	7	6
8.	***LOVE ME** (BMI)—E. Presley Vic EPA 992	9	5
9.	**HEY, JEALOUS LOVER** (ASCAP)—F. Sinatra You Forgot All the Words (BMI)—Cap 3552	10	8
10.	**DON'T BE CRUEL** (BMI)—E. Presley **HOUND DOG** (BMI)—Vic 20-6604	8	21
11.	**HONKY TONK** (Parts I & II)—B. Doggett King 4950—BMI	11	18
12.	**GONNA GET ALONG WITHOUT YA, NOW** (ASCAP)—Patience & Prudence Money Tree (ASCAP)—Liberty 55040	18	3
13.	**ROCK-A-BYE YOUR BABY** (ASCAP)—J. Lewis Come Rain or Come Shine (ASCAP)—Dec 30124	14	5
14.	**CINDY, OH, CINDY** (BMI)—E. Fisher Around the World (ASCAP)—Vic 20-6677	15	11
15.	**SINCE I MET YOU, BABY** (BMI)—I. J. Hunter You Can't Stop This Rocking and Rolling (BMI)—Atlantic 1111	17	3
16.	**CINDY, OH, CINDY** (BMI)—V. Martin Only If I Praise the Lord (BMI)—Glory 247	16	8
17.	**FRIENDLY PERSUASION** (ASCAP)—P. Boone Chains of Love (BMI)—Dot 15490	12	14
18.	**GARDEN OF EDEN** (BMI)—J. Valino Caravan (ASCAP)—Vik 0226	13	7
19.	**JAMAICA FAREWELL** (ASCAP)—H. Belafonte Once Was (ASCAP)—Vic 20-6663	—	1
20.	**MAMA FROM THE TRAIN** (ASCAP)—P. Page Every Time—I Feel His Spirit (BMI)—Mercury 70971	20	5
21.	**BANANA BOAT SONG** (BMI)—Tarriers No Hidin' Place (BMI)—Glory 249	—	1
22.	**CONFIDENTIAL** (BMI)—S. Knight Jail Bird (BMI)—Dot 15507	19	2
23.	**DON'T FORBID ME** (BMI)—P. Boone Anastasia (ASCAP)—Dot 15521	—	1
24.	**CITY OF ANGELS** (BMI)—Highlights Listen, My Love (ASCAP)—Bally 1016	24	4
25.	**MOONLIGHT GAMBLER** (ASCAP)—F. Laine Lotus Land (ASCAP)—Col 40780	25	2
25.	**NIGHT LIGHTS** (ASCAP)—Nat (King) Cole To the Ends of the Earth (BMI)—Cap 3551	22	7

*(Not Available as a Pop Single. Available on RCA Victor 45 EPA 992 and in RCA Victor 33⅓ "Elvis" LPM 1382)

• Most Played in Juke Boxes

For survey week ending December 12

RECORDS are ranked in order of the greatest number of plays in juke boxes thruout the country, as determined by The Billboard's weekly survey of the nation's juke box operators. When significant play is reported on both sides of a record, points are combined to determine position on the chart. In such a case, both sides are listed in bold type, the leading side on top.

This Week		Last Week	Weeks on Chart
1.	**SINGING THE BLUES** (BMI)—G. Mitchell Crazy With Love (ASCAP)—Col 40769	1	7
2.	**GREEN DOOR** (BMI)—J. Lowe (The Story of) The Little Man in Chinatown (BMI)—Dot 15486	3	11
3.	**LOVE ME TENDER** (BMI)—E. Presley **ANY WAY YOU WANT ME** (ASCAP)—Vic 20-6643	2	9
4.	**JUST WALKING IN THE RAIN** (BMI)—J. Ray In the Candlelight (ASCAP)—Col 40729	4	14
5.	**BLUEBERRY HILL** (ASCAP)—F. Domino Honey Chile (BMI)—Imperial 5407	5	10
6.	**HONKY TONK** (Parts I & II) (BMI)—B. Doggett King 4950	6	15
7.	**TRUE LOVE** (ASCAP)—B. Crosby-G. Kelly Well, Did You Evah? (ASCAP)—Cap 3507	7	8
8.	**DON'T BE CRUEL** (BMI)—E. Presley **HOUND DOG** (BMI)—Vic 20-6643	8	20
9.	**CINDY, OH, CINDY** (BMI)—V. Martin Only If I Praise the Lord (BMI)—Glory 247	10	7
10.	**HEY, JEALOUS LOVER** (ASCAP)—F. Sinatra You Forgot All the Words (BMI)—Cap 3552	9	5
11.	**CINDY, OH, CINDY** (BMI)—E. Fisher Around the World (ASCAP)—Vic 20-6677	11	6
12.	**MAMA FROM THE TRAIN** (ASCAP)—P. Page Every Time—I Feel His Spirit (BMI)—Mercury 70071	12	3
13.	**ROSE AND A BABY RUTH** (BMI)—G. Hamilton IV If You Don't Know (BMI)—ABC-Paramount 9765	17	4
14.	**GARDEN OF EDEN** (BMI)—J. Valino Caravan (ASCAP)—Vik 0226	13	3
15.	**YOU'LL NEVER, NEVER KNOW** (BMI)—Platters It Isn't Right (BMI)—Mercury 70948	14	11
15.	* **LOVE ME**—E. Presley Vic EPA-992—BMI	20	2
17.	**SLOW WALK** (BMI)—S. Austin Wildwood (ASCAP)—Mercury 70963	—	1
17.	**GONNA GET ALONG WITHOUT YA NOW** (ASCAP)—Patience & Prudence Money Tree (ASCAP)—Liberty 55040	—	1
19.	**CONFIDENTIAL** (BMI)—S. Knight Jail Bird (BMI)—Dot 15507	17	5
20.	**I WALK THE LINE** (BMI)—J. Cash Get Rhythm (BMI)—Sun 241	—	4

*(Not Available as a Pop Single. Available on RCA Victor 45 EPA-992 and in RCA Victor 33⅓ "Elvis" LPM 1382)

• Best Selling Sheet Music

Tunes are ranked in order of their current national selling importance at the sheet music jobber level.

This Week		Last Week	Weeks on Chart
1.	**Love Me Tender** (Presley)	2	10
2.	**True Love** (Buxton Hill)	1	13
3.	**Singing the Blues** (Acuff-Rose)	3	5
4.	**Just Walking in the Rain** (Golden West)	4	11
5.	**Green Door** (Trinity)	5	9
6.	**Blueberry Hill** (Chappell)	6	6
7.	**Friendly Persuasion** (Feist)	9	8
8.	**Cindy, Oh, Cindy** (E. B. Marks-Bryden)	7	7
9.	**Two Different Worlds** (Spier)	8	6
10.	**Canadian Sunset** (Meridian)	11	20
11.	**Tonight You Belong to Me** (Mills)	10	6
12.	**Mutual Admiration Society** (Chappell)	—	1
13.	**Mama From the Train** (Remick)	14	3
13.	**Love Me** (Hill & Range)	15	2
15.	**Hey, Jealous Lover** (Barton)	—	4

• Most Played by Jockeys

For survey week ending December 12

SIDES are ranked in order of the greatest number of plays on disk jockey radio shows thruout the country. Results are based on The Billboard's weekly survey among the nation's disk jockeys. The reverse side of each record is also listed.

This Week		Last Week	Weeks on Chart
1.	**SINGING THE BLUES** (BMI)—G. Mitchell Crazy With Love (ASCAP)—Col 40769	1	8
2.	**GREEN DOOR** (BMI)—J. Lowe (Story of) The Little Man in Chinatown (BMI)—Dot 15486	3	13
3.	**LOVE ME TENDER** (BMI)—E. Presley Any Way You Want Me (ASCAP)—Vic 20-6643	2	10
4.	**TRUE LOVE** (ASCAP)—B. Crosby-G. Kelly Well, Did You Evah? (ASCAP)—Cap 3507	4	12
5.	* **LOVE ME** (BMI)—E. Presley Vic EPA-992	8	4
6.	**HEY, JEALOUS LOVER** (ASCAP)—F. Sinatra You Forgot All the Words (BMI)—Cap 3552	5	9
7.	**BLUEBERRY HILL** (ASCAP)—F. Domino Honey Chile (BMI)—Imperial 5407	7	10
8.	**JUST WALKING IN THE RAIN** (BMI)—J. Ray In the Candlelight (ASCAP)—Col 40729	6	13
9.	**ROSE AND A BABY RUTH** (BMI)—G. Hamilton IV If You Don't Know (BMI)—ABC-Paramount 9765	10	6
10.	**CINDY, OH, CINDY** (BMI)—E. Fisher Around the World (ASCAP)—Vic 20-6677	11	9
11.	**GONNA GET ALONG WITHOUT YA NOW**—Patience & Prudence Money Tree (ASCAP)—Liberty 55040	16	3
12.	**FRIENDLY PERSUASION** (ASCAP)—P. Boone Chains of Love (ASCAP)—Dot 15490	9	14
13.	**TWO DIFFERENT WORLDS** (ASCAP)—D. Rondo He Made You Mine (ASCAP)—Jubilee 5256	15	8
14.	**NIGHT LIGHTS** (ASCAP)—Nat (King) Cole To the Ends of the Earth (BMI)—Cap 3551	14	8
15.	**MOONLIGHT GAMBLER** (ASCAP)—F. Laine Lotus Land (ASCAP)—Col 40780	18	2
16.	**SINCE I MET YOU, BABY** (BMI)—I. J. Hunter You Can't Stop This Rocking and Rolling (BMI)—Atlantic 1111	21	3
17.	**GARDEN OF EDEN** (BMI)—J. Valino Caravan (ASCAP)—Vik 0226	13	6
18.	**ROCK-A-BYE YOUR BABY** (ASCAP)—J. Lewis Come Rain or Come Shine (ASCAP)—Dec 30124	—	1
19.	**MAMA FROM THE TRAIN** (ASCAP)—P. Page Every Time—I Feel His Spirit (BMI)—Mercury 70971	12	8
20.	**I DREAMED** (BMI)—B. Johnson If It's Wrong to Love You (BMI)—Bally 1020	19	2
21.	**MONEY TREE** (ASCAP)—M. Whiting Maybe I Love Him (ASCAP)—Cap 3586	—	2
22.	**HONKY TONK** (Parts I & II)—B. Doggett King 4950—BMI	20	14
23.	**CINDY, OH, CINDY** (BMI)—V. Martin Only If I Praise the Lord (BMI)—Glory 247	22	7
24.	**TRA LA LA** (BMI)—G. Gibbs Morning, Noon, and Night (BMI)—Mercury 70998	—	1
25.	**JAMAICA, FAREWELL** (ASCAP)—H. Belafonte Once Was (ASCAP)—Vic 20-6663 (BMI)—Vic 20-6663	—	2

*(Not Available as a Pop Single. Available on RCA Victor 45 EPA-992 and in RCA Victor 33⅓ "Elvis" LPM 1382)

THE TOP 100

For survey week ending December 12

A list of the Top 100 RECORD SIDES in the nation according to a COMBINED TABULATION of Dealer, Disk Jockey and Juke Box Operator replies to The Billboard's weekly popular record Best Seller and Most Played surveys. Its purpose is to provide Disk Jockeys with additional programming material and to give trade exposure to NEWER records just beginning to show action in the field.

Pos.	Song, Artist, Label	Last Week
1.	**SINGING THE BLUES**—G. Mitchell, Columbia	1
1.	**LOVE ME TENDER**—E. Presley, Victor	2
3.	**JUST WALKING IN THE RAIN**—J. Ray, Columbia	4
4.	**BLUEBERRY HILL**—F. Domino, Imperial	5
5.	**TRUE LOVE**—Bing Crosby-G. Kelly, Capitol	6
6.	**HEY, JEALOUS LOVER**—F. Sinatra, Capitol	7
6.	**ROSE AND A BABY RUTH**—G. Hamilton IV, ABC Paramount	8
8.	**LOVE ME**—E. Presley, Victor	9
9.	**GREEN DOOR**—J. Lowe, Dot	3
10.	**HONKY TONK**—B. Doggett, King	10
11.	**CINDY, OH CINDY**—E. Fisher, Victor	10
12.	**CINDY, OH CINDY**—V. Martin, Glory	16
12.	**GONNA GET ALONG WITHOUT YA, NOW**—Patience & Prudence, Liberty	18
14.	**GARDEN OF EDEN**—J. Valino, Vik	12
15.	**DON'T BE CRUEL**—E. Presley, Victor	14
15.	**FRIENDLY PERSUASION**—P. Boone, Dot	13
15.	**MAMA FROM THE TRAIN**—P. Page, Mercury	14
18.	**ROCK-A-BYE YOUR BABY**—J. Lewis, Decca	23
19.	**SINCE I MET YOU, BABY**—I. J. Hunter, Atlantic	26
20.	**CONFIDENTIAL**—S. Knight, Dot	20
20.	**NIGHT LIGHTS**—Nat (King) Cole, Capitol	17
22.	**TWO DIFFERENT WORLDS**—D. Rondo, Jubilee	19
23.	**JAMAICA, FAREWELL**—H. Belafonte, Victor	40
24.	**MOONLIGHT GAMBLER**—F. Laine, Columbia	20
25.	**MUTUAL ADMIRATION SOCIETY**—T. Brewer, Coral	25
26.	**CANADIAN SUNSET**—E. Heywood & H. Winterhalter, Victor	22
27.	**I WALK THE LINE**—J. Cash, Sun	27
28.	**SLOW WALK**—S. Austin, Mercury	23
29.	**AUCTIONEER**—L. Van Dyke, Dot	31
30.	**YOU'LL NEVER NEVER KNOW**—Platters, Mercury	28
31.	**SINGING THE BLUES**—M. Robbins, Columbia	33
32.	**PRISCILLA**—E. Cooley, Roost	34
33.	**SLOW WALK**—B. Doggett, King	37
34.	**BABY DOLL**—A. Williams, Cadence	71
35.	**GOODNIGHT, MY LOVE**—McGuire Sisters, Coral	62
36.	**HOUND DOG**—E. Presley, Victor	35
37.	**PETTICOATS OF PORTUGAL**—D. Jacobs, Coral	30
38.	**ON LONDON BRIDGE**—J. Stafford, Columbia	45
39.	**TRA LA LA**—G. Gibbs, Mercury	52
40.	**I DREAMED**—B. Johnson, Bally	39
41.	**CITY OF ANGELS**—Highlights, Bally	38
42.	**LAY DOWN YOUR ARMS**—Chordettes, Cadence	45
43.	**DON'T FORBID ME**—P. Boone, Dot	—
44.	**WHEN MY BLUE MOON TURNS TO GOLD AGAIN**—E. Presley, Victor	49
45.	**WISDOM OF A FOOL**—Five Keys, Capitol	65
46.	**ARMEN'S THEME**—J. Reisman, Victor	77
46.	**STAR YOU WISHED UPON LAST NIGHT**—G. MacKenzie, Vik	42
48.	**ARMEN'S THEME**—D. Seville, Liberty	82
48.	**MUTUAL ADMIRATION SOCIETY**—J. P. Morgan & E. Arnold, Victor	47
50.	**BANANA BOAT SONG**—Tarriers, Glory	—
50.	**JUST IN TIME**—T. Bennett, Columbia	46
52.	**ANASTASIA**—P. Boone, Dot	—
53.	**MARY'S BOY CHILD**—H. Belafonte, Victor	—
54.	**AIN'T GOT NO HOME**—C. Henry, Argo	80
54	**FADED SUMMER LOVE**—G. Shaw, Decca	66
56.	**SINCE I MET YOU, BABY**—M. Carson, Columbia	57
57.	**MONEY TREE**—M. Whiting, Capitol	57
57.	**SOMEONE TO LOVE**—Four Aces, Decca	68
59.	**ANY WAY YOU WANT ME**—E. Presley, Victor	43
60.	**I FEEL GOOD**—Shirley & Lee, Aladdin	78
61.	**IN THE STILL OF THE NIGHT**—Satins, Ember	47
61	**TRUE LOVE**—J. Powell, Verve	50
63.	**TONIGHT YOU BELONG TO ME**—Patience & Prudence, Liberty	32
64.	**GIVE ME**—E. Rodgers, Columbia	86
64.	**I WOULDN'T KNOW WHERE TO BEGIN**—E. Arnold, Victor	87
66.	**CANADIAN SUNSET**—A. Williams, Cadence	68
67.	**TWO DIFFERENT WORLDS**—J. Morgan & R. Williams, Kapp	41
68.	**AUTUMN WALTZ**—T. Bennett, Columbia	63
69.	**FIRST BORN**—Tennessee Ernie, Capitol	52
70.	**I SAW ESSAU**—Ames Brothers, Victor	51
70.	**WHATEVER WILL BE, WILL BE**—Doris Day, Columbia	63
72.	**LOVE ME TENDER**—H. Rene, Victor	44
72.	**PARTY'S OVER**—Doris Day, Columbia	—
74.	**I LOVE MY BABY**—J. Corey, Columbia	—
75.	**FRIENDLY PERSUASION**—Four Aces, Decca	71
76.	**THOUSAND MILES AWAY**—Heartbeats, Rama	—
76	**ONE IN A MILLION**—Platters, Mercury	—
78.	**DANCING CHANDELIER**—S. Syms, Decca	—
79.	**CHEAT**—S. Clark, Dot	74
79.	**CONFESSION OF A SINNER**—Stylers, Jubilee	—
79.	**MONEY TREE**—Patience & Prudence, Liberty	84
82.	**LEFT ARM OF BUDDA**—L. Baxter, Capitol	—
83.	**TEENAGE GOODNIGHT**—Chordettes, Cadence	—
84.	**MOONLIGHT LOVE**—P. Como, Victor	89
85.	**CRAZY WITH LOVE**—T. Brewer, Coral	73
86.	**WHEN THE WHITE LILACS BLOOM AGAIN**—F. Zabach, Mercury	—
87.	**YOU DON'T KNOW ME**—J. Vale, Columbia	99
88.	**I MISS YOU SO**—C. Connor, Atlantic	55
89.	**BLUE MOON**—E. Presley, Victor	—
89.	**IT ISN'T RIGHT**—Platters, Mercury	60
91.	**AUCTIONEER**—C. Miller, Mercury	—
91.	**RUDY'S ROCK**—B. Haley, Decca	55
91.	**WRITTEN ON THE WIND**—Four Aces, Decca	70
94.	**CRAZY WITH LOVE**—G. Mitchell, Columbia	90
95.	**TO THE ENDS OF THE EARTH**—Nat (King) Cole, Capitol	79
96.	**JULIE**—Doris Day, Columbia	94
97.	**LET THE GOOD TIMES ROLL**—Shirley & Lee, Aladdin	85
97.	**DREAMY EYES**—Four Preps, Capitol	—
99.	**CHINCHERCHEE**—P. Como, Victor	59
99.	**SADIE'S SHAWL**—B. Sharples, London	93
99.	**WAR AND PEACE**—V. Damone, Columbia	—

CAUTION TO DEALERS AND JUKE BOX OPERATORS

The Billboard's Top 100 is NOT designed to provide tested information for buying purposes. This function is most reliably served by other regular weekly features: Best Sellers in Stores, Most Played in Juke Boxes, Coming Up Strong and Best Buys.

• Best Sellers in Stores

For survey week ending December 19

RECORDS are ranked in order of their current national selling importance at the retail level, as determined by The Billboard's weekly survey of the top volume dealers in every important market area. When significant action is reported on both sides of a record, points are combined to determine position on the chart. In such a case, both sides are listed in bold type, the leading side on top.

This Week		Last Week	Weeks on Chart
1.	**SINGING THE BLUES** (BMI)—G. Mitchell Crazy With Love (ASCAP)—Col 40769	1	9
2.	**LOVE ME TENDER** (BMI)—E. Presley Any Way You Want Me (ASCAP)—Vic 20-6643	2	11
3.	**GREEN DOOR** (BMI)—J. Lowe (Story of) The Little Man in Chinatown (BMI)—Dot 15486	3	14
4.	**BLUEBERRY HILL** (ASCAP)—F. Domino Honey Chile (BMI)—Imperial 5407	4	12
5.	**TRUE LOVE** (ASCAP)—B. Crobsy-G. Kelly Well, Did You Evah? (ASCAP)—Cap 3507	6	13
6.	**JUST WALKING IN THE RAIN** (BMI)—J. Ray In the Candlelight (ASCAP)—Col 40729	5	17
7.	***LOVE ME** (BMI)—E. Presley Vic EPA-992	8	6
8.	**ROSE AND A BABY RUTH** (BMI)—G. Hamilton IV If You Don't Know (BMI)—ABC-Paramount 9765	7	7
9.	**BANANA BOAT SONG** (BMI)—Tarriers No Hidin' Place (BMI)—Glory 249	21	2
10.	**ROCK-A-BYE YOUR BABY** (ASCAP)—J. Lewis Come Rain or Come Shine (ASCAP)—Dec 30124	13	6
11.	**HEY, JEALOUS LOVER** (ASCAP)—F. Sinatra You Forgot All the Words (BMI)—Cap 3552	9	9
12.	**SINCE I MET YOU, BABY** (BMI)—I. J. Hunter You Can't Stop This Rocking and Rolling (BMI)—Atlantic 1111	15	4
13.	**MOONLIGHT GAMBLER** (ASCAP)—F. Laine Lotus Land (ASCAP)—Col 40780	25	3
14.	**CINDY, OH, CINDY** (BMI)—E. Fisher Around the World (ASCAP)—Vic 20-6677	14	12
15.	**MARY'S BOY CHILD** (ASCAP)—H. Belafonte Venezuela—Vic 20-6734	—	1
16.	**GONNA GET ALONG WITHOUT YA, NOW** (ASCAP)—Patience & Prudence Money Tree (ASCAP)—Liberty 55040	12	4
17.	**DON'T BE CRUEL** (BMI)—E. Presley **HOUND DOG** (BMI)—Vic 20-6604	10	22
18.	**HONKY TONK** (Parts I & II)—B. Doggett King 4950—BMI	11	19
19.	**MAMA FROM THE TRAIN** (ASCAP)—P. Page Every Time—I Feel His Spirit (BMI)—Mercury 70971	20	6
20.	**DON'T FORBID ME** (BMI)—P. Boone Anastasia (ASCAP)—Dot 15521	23	2
21.	**GARDEN OF EDEN** (BMI)—J. Valino Caravan (ASCAP)—Vik 0226	18	8
22.	**CINDY, OH, CINDY** (BMI)—V. Martin Only If I Praise the Lord (BMI)—Glory 247	16	9
23.	**CONFIDENTIAL** (BMI)—S. Knight Jail Bird (BMI)—Dot 15507	22	3
24.	**JAMAICA FAREWELL** (ASCAP)—H. Belafonte Once Was (ASCAP)—Vic 20-6663	19	2
25.	**SLOW WALK** (BMI)—S. Austin Wildwood (BMI)—Mercury 70963	—	4

(Now Available as a Pop Single. Available on RCA Victor 45 EPA 992 and in RCA Victor 33⅓ "Elvis" LPM 1382)

• Most Played in Juke Boxes

For survey week ending December 19

RECORDS are ranked in order of the greatest number of plays in juke boxes thruout the country, as determined by The Billboard's weekly survey of the nation's juke box operators. When significant play is reported on both sides of a record, points are combined to determine position on the chart. In such a case, both sides are listed in bold type, the leading side on top.

This Week		Last Week	Weeks on Chart
1.	**SINGING THE BLUES** (BMI)—G. Mitchell Crazy With Love (ASCAP)—Col 40769	1	8
2.	**GREEN DOOR** (BMI)—J. Lowe (The Story of) The Little Man in Chinatown (BMI)—Dot 15486	2	12
3.	**LOVE ME TENDER** (BMI)—E. Presley Any Way You Want Me (ASCAP)—Vic 20-6643	3	10
4.	**JUST WALKING IN THE RAIN** (BMI)—J. Ray In the Candlelight (ASCAP)—Col 40729	4	15
5.	**BLUEBERRY HILL** (ASCAP)—F. Domino Honey Chile (BMI)—Imperial 5407	5	11
6.	**TRUE LOVE** (ASCAP)—B. Crosby-G. Kelly Well, Did You Evah? (ASCAP)—Cap 3507	7	9
7.	**DON'T BE CRUEL** (BMI)—E. Presley **HOUND DOG** (BMI)—Vic 20-6643	8	21
8.	**HONKY TONK (PARTS I & II)** (BMI)—B. Doggett King 4950	6	16
9.	**HEY, JEALOUS LOVER** (ASCAP)—Frank Sinatra You Forget All the Words (BMI)—Cap 3552	10	6
10.	**CINDY, OH, CINDY** (BMI)—V. Martin Only If I Praise the Lord (BMI)—Glory 247	9	8
11.	**ROSE AND A BABY RUTH** (BMI)—G. Hamilton IV If You Don't Know (BMI)—ABC-Paramount 9765	13	5
12.	**MAMA FROM THE TRAIN** (ASCAP)—P. Page Every Time—I Feel His Spirit (BMI)—Mercury 70971	12	4
13.	***LOVE ME**—E. Presley Vic EPA-992—BMI	15	3
14.	**CINDY, OH, CINDY** (BMI)—E. Fisher Around the World (ASCAP)—Vic 20-6677	11	7
15.	**GARDEN OF EDEN** (BMI)—J. Valino Caravan (ASCAP)—Vik 0226	14	4
16.	**FRIENDLY PERSUASION** (ASCAP)—P. Boone Chains of Love (BMI)—Dot 15490	—	12
17.	**SINGING THE BLUES** (BMI)—M. Robbins I Can't Quit (BMI)—Col 21545	—	2
18.	**GONNA GET ALONG WITHOUT YA NOW** (ASCAP)—Patience & Prudence Money Tree (ASCAP)—Liberty 55040	17	2
19.	**SLOW WALK** (BMI)—S. Austin Wildwood (ASCAP)—Mercury 70963	17	2
19.	**I WALK THE LINE** (BMI)—J. Cash Get Rhythm (BMI)—Sun 241	20	5

*(Now Available as a Pop Single. Available on RCA Victor 45 EPA-992 and in RCA Victor 33⅓ "Elvis" LPM 1382)

• Best Selling Sheet Music

Tunes are ranked in order of their current national selling importance at the sheet music jobber level.

This Week		Last Week	Weeks on Chart
1.	**Love Me Tender** (Presley)	1	11
2.	**True Love** (Buxton Hill)	2	14
2.	**Singing the Blues** (Acuff-Rose)	3	6
4.	**Just Walking in the Rain** (Golden West)	4	12
5.	**Green Door** (Trinity)	5	10
6.	**Blueberry Hill** (Chappell)	6	7
7.	**Cindy, Oh, Cindy** (E. B. Marks-Bryden)	8	8
8.	**Friendly Persuasion** (Feist)	7	9
9.	**Two Different Worlds** (Spier)	9	7
10.	**Love Me** (Hill & Range)	13	3
11.	**White Christmas** (Berlin)	—	1
12.	**Rudolph, the Red-Nosed Reindeer** (St. Nicholas)	—	1
13.	**Hey, Jealous Lover** (Barton)	15	5
14.	**Rose and a Baby Ruth** (Bentley)	—	1
15.	**Tonight You Belong to Me** (Mills)	11	7

• Most Played by Jockeys

For survey week ending December 19

SIDES are ranked in order of the greatest number of plays on disk jockey radio shows thruout the country. Results are based on The Billboard's weekly survey among the nation's disk jockeys. The reverse side of each record is also listed.

This Week		Last Week	Weeks on Chart
1.	**SINGING THE BLUES** (BMI)—G. Mitchell Crazy With Love (ASCAP)—Col 40769	1	9
2.	**LOVE ME TENDER** (BMI)—E. Presley Any Way You Want Me (ASCAP)—Vic 20-6643	3	11
3.	**GREEN DOOR** (BMI)—J. Lowe (Story of) The Little Man in Chinatown (BMI)—Dot 15486	2	14
4.	***LOVE ME** (BMI)—E. Presley Vic EPA-992	5	5
5.	**HEY, JEALOUS LOVER** (ASCAP)—F. Sinatra You Forgot All the Words (BMI)—Cap 3552	6	10
6.	**TRUE LOVE** (ASCAP)—B. Crosby-G. Kelly Well, Did You Evah? (ASCAP)—Cap 3507	4	13
7.	**BLUEBERRY HILL** (ASCAP)—F. Domino Honey Chile (BMI)—Imperial 5407	7	11
8.	**JUST WALKING IN THE RAIN** (BMI)—J. Ray In the Candlelight (ASCAP)—Col 40729	8	14
9.	**MOONLIGHT GAMBLER** (ASCAP)—F. Laine Lotus Land (ASCAP)—Col 40780	15	3
10.	**ROSE AND A BABY RUTH** (BMI)—G. Hamilton IV If You Don't Know (BMI)—ABC-Paramount 9765	9	7
11.	**CINDY, OH, CINDY** (BMI)—E. Fisher Around the World (ASCAP)—Vic 20-6677	10	10
12.	**FRIENDLY PERSUASION** (ASCAP)—P. Boone Chains of Love (ASCAP)—Dot 15490	12	15
13.	**GONNA GET ALONG WITHOUT YA NOW**—Patience & Prudence Money Tree (ASCAP)—Liberty 55040	11	4
14.	**SINCE I MET YOU, BABY** (BMI)—I. J. Hunter You Can't Stop This Rocking and Rolling (BMI)—Atlantic 1111	16	4
15.	**GARDEN OF EDEN** (BMI)—J. Valino Caravan (ASCAP)—Vik 0226	17	7
16.	**DON'T FORBID ME** (BMI)—P. Boone Anastasia (ASCAP)—Dot 15521	—	1
17.	**MAMA FROM THE TRAIN** (ASCAP)—P. Page Every Time—I Feel His Spirit (BMI)—Mercury 70971	19	9
18.	**BANANA BOAT SONG** (BMI)—Tarriers No Hidin' Place (BMI)—Glory 249	—	1
19.	***WHEN MY BLUE MOON TURNS TO GOLD AGAIN**—E. Presley Vic EPA-992—BMI	—	1
20.	**ROCK-A-BYE YOUR BABY** (ASCAP)—J. Lewis Come Rain or Come Shine (ASCAP)—Dec 30124	18	2
21.	**NIGHT LIGHTS** (ASCAP)—Nat (King) Cole To the Ends of the Earth (BMI)—Cap 3551	14	9
22.	**MONEY TREE** (ASCAP)—M. Whiting Maybe I Love Him (ASCAP)—Cap 3586	21	3
23.	**JAMAICA FAREWELL** (ASCAP)—H. Belafonte Once Was (ASCAP)—Vic 20-6663	25	3
24.	**I DREAMED** (BMI)—B. Johnson If It's Wrong to Love You (BMI)—Bally 1020	20	3
25.	**TWO DIFFERENT WORLDS** (ASCAP)—D. Rondo He Made You Mine (ASCAP)—Jubilee 5256	13	9

*(Now Available as a Pop Single. Available on RCA Victor 45 EPA-992 and in RCA Victor 33⅓ "Elvis" LPM 1382.

THE TOP 100

For survey week ending December 19

A list of the Top 100 RECORD SIDES in the nation according to a COMBINED TABULATION of Dealer, Disk Jockey and Juke Box Operator replies to The Billboard's weekly popular record Best Seller and Most Played surveys. Its purpose is to provide Disk Jockeys with additional programming material and to give trade exposure to NEWER records just beginning to show action in the field.

Pos.	Song, Artist, Label	Last Week
1.	SINGING THE BLUES—G. Mitchell, Columbia	1
2.	LOVE ME TENDER—E. Presley, Victor	2
3.	GREEN DOOR—J. Lowe, Dot	9
4.	BLUEBERRY HILL—F. Domino, Imperial	4
5.	TRUE LOVE—Bing Crosby & G. Kelly, Capitol	5
6.	JUST WALKING IN THE RAIN—J. Ray, Columbia	3
7.	LOVE ME—E. Presley, Victor	8
8.	HEY, JEALOUS LOVER—F. Sinatra, Capitol	6
8.	ROSE AND A BABY RUTH—G. Hamilton IV, ABC-Paramount	6
10.	CINDY, OH, CINDY—E. Fisher, Victor	11
11.	MAMA FROM THE TRAIN—P. Page, Mercury	15
12.	GONNA GET ALONG WITHOUT YA NOW—Patience & Prudence, Liberty	12
12.	SINCE I MET YOU, BABY—I. J. Hunter, Atlantic	19
14.	GARDEN OF EDEN—J. Valino, Vik	14
15.	MOONLIGHT GAMBLER—F. Laine, Columbia	24
15.	ROCK-A-BYE YOUR BABY—J. Lewis, Decca	18
17.	HONKY TONK—B. Doggett, King	10
18.	FRIENDLY PERSUASION—P. Boone, Dot	15
19.	CINDY, OH, CINDY—V. Martin, Glory	12
20.	BANANA BOAT SONG—Tarriers, Glory	50
21.	CONFIDENTIAL—S. Knight, Dot	20
21.	MARY'S BOY CHILD—H. Belafonte, Victor	53
23.	SLOW WALK—S. Austin, Mercury	28
24.	JAMAICA FAREWELL—H. Belafonte, Victor	23
25.	NIGHT LIGHTS—Nat (King) Cole, Capitol	20
26.	DON'T BE CRUEL—E. Presley, Victor	15
27.	MUTUAL ADMIRATION SOCIETY—T. Brewer, Coral	25
28.	TWO DIFFERENT WORLDS—D. Rondo, Jubilee	22
29.	SINGING THE BLUES—M. Robbins, Columbia	31
30.	DON'T FORBID ME—P. Boone, Dot	43
31.	I DREAMED—B. Johnson, Bally	40
31.	AUCTIONEER—L. Van Dyke, Dot	29
33.	BABY DOLL—A. Williams, Cadence	34
34.	CANADIAN SUNSET—E. Heywood & H. Winterhalter, Victor	26
35.	PETTICOATS OF PORTUGAL—D. Jacobs, Coral	37
36.	PRISCILLA—E. Cooley, Roost	32
37.	JIM DANDY—L. Baker, Atlantic	—
38.	WHEN MY BLUE MOON TURNS TO GOLD AGAIN—E. Presley, Victor	44
39.	GOODNIGHT, MY LOVE—McGuire Sisters, Coral	35
40.	SLOW WALK—B. Doggett, King	33
40.	YOU'LL NEVER, NEVER KNOW—Platters, Mercury	30
42.	I FEEL GOOD—Shirley & Lee, Aladdin	60
43.	YOUNG LOVE—S. James, Capitol	—
44.	AIN'T GOT NO HOME—C. Henry, Argo	54
45.	ON LONDON BRIDGE—J. Stafford, Columbia	38
46.	SINCE I MET YOU, BABY—M. Carson, Columbia	56
47.	OLD SHEP—E. Presley, Victor	—
48.	WISDOM OF A FOOL—Five Keys, Capitol	45
49.	ARMEN'S THEME—D. Seville, Liberty	48
50.	CITY OF ANGELS—Highlights, Bally	41
51.	ANASTASIA—P. Boone, Dot	52
52.	ARMEN'S THEME—J. Reisman, Victor	46
53.	TRA LA LA—G. Gibbs, Mercury	39
54.	HOUND DOG—E. Presley, Victor	36
54.	POOR BOY—E. Presley, Victor	—
56.	MUTUAL ADMIRATION SOCIETY—J. P. Morgan-E. Arnold, Victor	48
57.	FADED SUMMER LOVE—G. Shaw, Decca	54
58.	JUST IN TIME—T. Bennett, Columbia	50
59.	AUCTIONEER—C. Miller, Mercury	91
60.	BLUEBERRY HILL—L. Armstrong, Decca	—
61.	FIRST BORN—T. Ernie, Capitol	69
62.	STAR YOU WISHED UPON LAST NIGHT—G. Mac Kenzie, Vik	46
63.	CANADIAN SUNSET—A. Williams, Cadence	66
64.	MONEY TREE—M. Whiting, Capitol	57
65.	WHITE CHRISTMAS—Bing Crosby, Decca	—
66.	I SAW ESAU—Ames Brothers, Victor	70
67.	ONE IN A MILLION—Platters, Mercury	76
68.	TONIGHT YOU BELONG TO ME—Patience & Prudence, Liberty	63
69.	I MISS YOU SO—C. Connor, Atlantic	88
70.	ANY WAY YOU WANT ME—E. Presley, Victor	59
71.	TWO DIFFERENT WORLDS—J. Morgan & R. Williams, Kapp	67
72.	IN THE STILL OF THE NIGHT—Satins, Ember	61
73.	BANANA BOAT SONG—S. Vaughan, Mercury	—
74.	MOONLIGHT LOVE—P. Como, Victor	84
75.	MONEY TREE—Patience & Prudence, Liberty	79
76.	ON MY WORD OF HONOR—Platters, Mercury	—
76.	GIVE ME—E. Rodgers, Columbia	64
78.	PARALYZED—E. Presley, Victor	—
79.	THOUSAND MILES AWAY—Heartbeats, Rama	76
80.	TWO DIFFERENT WORLDS—D. Haymes, Capitol	—
81.	SOMEONE TO LOVE—Four Aces, Decca	57
82.	I LOVE MY BABY—J. Corey, Columbia	74
82.	PARTY'S OVER—Doris Day, Columbia	72
84.	GREENSLEEVES—Beverly Sisters, London	—
85.	TRUE LOVE—J. Powell, Verve	61
86.	TEEN-AGE GOODNIGHT—Chordettes, Cadence	83
86.	LOVE ME TENDER—H. Rene, Victor	—
88.	BANANA BOAT SONG—Fontane Sisters, Dot	—
88.	I WALK THE LINE—J. Cash, Sun	27
90.	PETTICOATS OF PORTUGAL—E. Vaughn, Dot	—
91.	GIANT—J. Pleis, Decca	—
92.	TO THE ENDS OF THE EARTH—Nat (King) Cole, Capitol	95
93.	BLUE MOON—E. Presley, Victor	89
93.	CHINCHERCHEE—P. Como, Victor	99
95.	JULIE—Doris Day, Columbia	96
96.	IT ISN'T RIGHT—Platters, Mercury	89
97.	LAY DOWN YOUR ARMS—Chordettes, Cadence	42
98.	DANCING CHANDELIER—S. Syms, Decca	78
99.	CRAZY WITH LOVE—G. Mitchell, Columbia	94
100.	FRIENDLY PERSUASION—Four Aces, Decca	75
100.	RUDY'S ROCK—B. Haley, Decca	91

CAUTION TO DEALERS AND JUKE BOX OPERATORS

The Billboard's Top 100 is NOT designed to provide tested information for buying purposes. This function is most reliably served by other regular weekly features: Best Sellers in Stores, Most Played in Juke Boxes, Coming Up Strong and Best Buys.

• Best Sellers in Stores

For survey week ending December 26

RECORDS are ranked in order of their current national selling importance at the retail level, as determined by The Billboard's weekly survey of the top volume dealers in every important market area. When significant action is reported on both sides of a record, points are combined to determine position on the chart. In such a case, both sides are listed in bold type, the leading side on top.

This Week		Last Week	Weeks on Chart
1.	**SINGING THE BLUES** (BMI)—G. Mitchell Crazy With Love (ASCAP)—Col 40769	1	10
2.	**GREEN DOOR** (BMI)—J. Lowe (Story of) The Little Man in Chinatown (BMI)—Dot 15486	3	15
3.	**LOVE ME TENDER** (BMI)—E. Presley Any Way You Want Me (ASCAP)—Vic 20-6643	2	12
4.	**BLUEBERRY HILL** (ASCAP)—F. Domino Honey Chile (BMI)—Imperial 5407	4	13
5.	**JUST WALKING IN THE RAIN** (BMI)—J. Ray In The Candlelight (ASCAP)—Col 40729	6	18
6.	**TRUE LOVE** (ASCAP)—B. Crosby-G. Kelly Well, Did You Evah? (ASCAP)—Cap 3507	5	14
7.	***LOVE ME** (BMI)—E. Presley Vic EPA 992	7	7
8.	**BANANA BOAT SONG** (BMI)—Tarriers No Hidin' Place (BMI)—Glory 249	9	3
9.	**ROSE AND A BABY RUTH** (BMI)—G. Hamilton IV If You Don't Know (BMI)—ABC-Paramount 9765	8	8
10.	**ROCK-A-BYE YOUR BABY** (ASCAP)—J. Lewis Come Rain or Come Shine (ASCAP)—Dec 30124	10	7
11.	**DON'T FORBID ME** (BMI)—P. Boone **ANASTASIA** (ASCAP)—Dot 15521	20	3
12.	**MARY'S BOY CHILD** (ASCAP)—H. Belafonte Venezuela—Vic 20-6734	15	2
13.	**MOONLIGHT GAMBLER** (ASCAP)—F. Laine Lotus Land (ASCAP)—Col 40780	13	4
14.	**HEY, JEALOUS LOVER** (ASCAP)—F. Sinatra You Forgot All the Words (BMI)—Cap 3552	11	10
15.	**CINDY, OH, CINDY** (BMI)—E. Fisher Around the World (ASCAP)—Vic 20-6677	14	13
16.	**CINDY, OH, CINDY** (BMI)—V. Martin Only If I Praise the Lord (BMI)—Glory 247	22	10
17.	**GONNA GET ALONG WITHOUT YA NOW** (ASCAP)—**Patience & Prudence** Money Tree (ASCAP)—Liberty 55040	16	5
18.	**DON'T BE CRUEL** (BMI)—E. Presley **HOUND DOG** (BMI)—Vic 20-6604	17	23
19.	**JAMAICA FAREWELL** (ASCAP)—H. Belafonte Once Was (ASCAP)—Vic 20-6663	24	3
20.	**SINCE I MET YOU, BABY** (BMI)—I. J. Hunter You Can't Stop This Rocking and Rolling (BMI)—Atlantic 1111	12	5
21.	**CONFIDENTIAL** (BMI)—S. Knight Jail Bird (BMI)—Dot 15507	23	4
22.	**YOUNG LOVE** (BMI)—S. James You're the Reason I'm in Love (BMI)—Cap 3602	—	1
23.	**HONKY TONK (PARTS I & II)**—B. Doggett King 4950—BMI	18	20
24.	**AUCTIONEER** (ASCAP)—L. Van Dyke I Fell in Love With a Pony Tail (ASCAP)—Dot 15503	—	2
25.	**GARDEN OF EDEN** (BMI)—J. Valino Caravan (ASCAP)—Vik 0226	21	9

*(Not Available as a Pop Single. Available on RCA Victor 45 EPA-992 and in RCA Victor 33⅓ "Elvis" LPM 1382)

• Most Played in Juke Boxes

For survey week ending December 26

RECORDS are ranked in order of the greatest number of plays in juke boxes thruout the country, as determined by The Billboard's weekly survey of the nation's juke box operators. When significant play is reported on both sides of a record, points are combined to determine position on the chart. In such a case, both sides are listed in bold type, the leading side on top.

This Week		Last Week	Weeks on Chart
1.	**SINGING THE BLUES** (BMI)—G. Mitchell Crazy With Love (ASCAP)—Col 40769	1	9
2.	**GREEN DOOR** (BMI)—J. Lowe (The Story of) The Little Man in Chinatown (BMI)—Dot 15486	2	13
3.	**LOVE ME TENDER** (BMI)—E. Presley Any Way You Want Me (ASCAP)—Vic 20-6643	3	11
4.	**BLUEBERRY HILL** (ASCAP)—F. Domino Honey Chile (BMI)—Imperial 5407	5	12
5.	**JUST WALKING IN THE RAIN** (BMI)—J. Ray In the Candlelight (ASCAP)—Col 40729	4	16
6.	**TRUE LOVE** (ASCAP)—B. Crosby-G. Kelly Well, Did You Evah? (ASCAP)—Cap 3507	6	10
7.	**HEY, JEALOUS LOVER** (ASCAP)—F. Sinatra You Forgot All the Words (BMI)—Cap 3552	9	7
8.	**HONKY TONK (Parts I & II)** (BMI)—B. Doggett King 4950	8	17
9.	**DON'T BE CRUEL** (BMI)—E. Presley. **HOUND DOG** (BMI)—Vic 20-6643	7	22
10.	**CINDY, OH, CINDY** (BMI)—V. Martin Only If I Praise the Lord (BMI)—Glory 247	10	9
10.	**CINDY, OH, CINDY** (BMI)—E. Fisher Around the World (ASCAP)—Vic 20-6677	14	8
12.	**ROSE AND A BABY RUTH** (BMI)—G. Hamilton IV If You Don't Know (BMI)—ABC-Paramount 9765	11	6
13.	**MAMA FROM THE TRAIN** (ASCAP)—P. Page Every Time—I Feel His Spirit (BMI)—Mercury 70971	12	5
14.	***LOVE ME**—E. Presley Vic EPA-992—(BMI)	13	4
14.	**SINCE I MET YOU, BABY** (BMI)—I. J. Hunter You Can't Stop This Rocking and Rolling (BMI)—Atlantic 1111	—	1
16.	**GARDEN OF EDEN** (BMI)—J. Valino Caravan (ASCAP)—Vik 0226	15	5
17.	**ROCK-A-BYE YOUR BABY** (ASCAP)—J. Lewis Come Rain or Come Shine (ASCAP)—Dec 30124	—	1
18.	**SINGING THE BLUES** (BMI)—M. Robbins I Can't Quit (BMI)—Col 21545	17	3
19.	**MOONLIGHT GAMBLER** (ASCAP)—F. Laine Lotus Land (ASCAP)—Col 40780	—	1
20.	**GONNA GET ALONG WITHOUT YA NOW** (ASCAP)—Patience & Prudence Money Tree (ASCAP)—Liberty 55040	18	3
20.	**PRISCILLA** (BMI)—E. Cooley Got a Little Woman (BMI)—Roost 621	—	1

*(Not available as a Pop Single. Available on RCA Victor 45 EPA-992 and in RCA Victor 33⅓ "Elvis" LPM 1382)

• Best Selling Sheet Music

Tunes are ranked in order of their current national selling importance at the sheet music jobber level.

This Week		Last Week	Weeks on Chart
1.	**Love Me Tender** (Presley)	1	12
2.	**Singing the Blues** (Acuff-Rose)	2	7
3.	**True Love** (Buxton Hill)	2	15
4.	**Green Door** (Trinity)	5	11
5.	**Just Walking in the Rain** (Golden West)	4	13
6.	**Cindy, Oh, Cindy** (E. B. Marks-Bryden)	7	9
7.	**Blueberry Hill** (Chappell)	6	8
8.	**Friendly Persuasion** (Feist)	8	10
9.	**Hey, Jealous Lover** (Barton)	13	6
10.	**Two Different Worlds** (Spier)	9	8
11.	**Love Me** (Hill & Range)	10	4
12.	**Rose and a Baby Ruth** (Bentley)	14	2
13.	**Canadian Sunset** (Meridian)	—	21
14.	**Mutual Admiration Society** (Chappell)	—	2
15.	**Mama From the Train** (Remick)	—	4

• Most Played by Jockeys

For survey week ending December 26

SIDES are ranked in order of the greatest number of plays on disk jockey radio shows thruout the country. Results are based on The Billboard's weekly survey among the nation's disk jockeys. The reverse side of each record is also listed.

This Week		Last Week	Weeks on Chart
1.	**SINGING THE BLUES** (BMI)—G. Mitchell Crazy With Love (ASCAP)—Col 40769	1	10
2.	***LOVE ME** (BMI)—E. Presley Vic EPA—992	4	6
3.	**GREEN DOOR** (BMI)—J. Lowe (Story of) The Little Man in Chinatown (BMI)—Dot 15486	3	15
4.	**LOVE ME TENDER** (BMI)—E. Presley Any Way You Want Me (ASCAP)—Vic 20-6643	2	12
5.	**TRUE LOVE** (ASCAP)—B. Crosby-G. Kelly Well, Did You Evah? (ASCAP)—Cap 3507	6	14
6.	**HEY, JEALOUS LOVER** (ASCAP)—F. Sinatra You Forget All the Words (BMI)—Cap 3552	5	11
7.	**ROSE AND A BABY RUTH** (BMI)—G. Hamilton IV If You Don't Know (BMI)—ABC-Paramount 9765	10	8
8.	**DON'T FORBID ME** (BMI)—P. Boone Anastasia (ASCAP)—Dot 15521	16	2
9.	**MOONLIGHT GAMBLER** (ASCAP)—F. Laine Lotus Land (ASCAP)—Col 40780	9	4
10.	**JUST WALKING IN THE RAIN** (BMI)—J. Ray In the Candlelight (ASCAP)—Col 40729	8	15
11.	**GONNA GET ALONG WITHOUT YA NOW** (ASCAP)—Patience & Prudence Money Tree (ASCAP)—Liberty 55040	13	5
12.	**MARY'S BOY CHILD** (ASCAP)—H. Belafonte Venezuela—Vic 20-6734	—	1
13.	**TWO DIFFERENT WORLDS** (ASCAP)—D. Rondo He Made You Mine (ASCAP)—Jubilee 5256	25	10
14.	**SINCE I MET YOU, BABY** (BMI)—I. J. Hunter You Can't Stop This Rocking and Rolling (BMI)—Atlantic 1111	14	5
15.	**BLUEBERRY HILL** (ASCAP)—F. Domino Honey Chile (BMI)—Imperial 5407	7	12
16.	**BANANA BOAT SONG** (BMI)—Tarriers No Hidin' Place (BMI)—Glory 249	18	2
17.	**I DREAMED** (BMI)—B. Johnson If It's Wrong to Love You (BMI)—Bally 1020	24	4
18.	**CINDY, OH, CINDY** (BMI)—E. Fisher Around the World (ASCAP)—Vic 20-6677	11	11
18.	**YOUNG LOVE** (BMI)—S. James You're the Reason (BMI)—Cap 3602	—	1
20.	**ROCK-A-BYE YOUR BABY** (ASCAP)—J. Lewis Come Rain or Come Shine (ASCAP)—Dec 30124	20	3
21.	**MONEY TREE** (ASCAP)—M. Whiting Maybe I Love Him (ASCAP)—Cap 3586	22	4
22.	**GARDEN OF EDEN** (BMI)—J. Valino Caravan (ASCAP)—Vik 0226	15	8
23.	**FRIENDLY PERSUASION** (ASCAP)—P. Boone Chains of Love (ASCAP)—Dot 15490	12	16
24.	****POOR BOY**—E. Presley Vic EPA 40006	—	1
25.	**JAMAICA FAREWELL** (ASCAP)—H. Belafonte Once Was (ASCAP)—Vic 20-6663	23	4

*Not available as a Pop Single, available on RCA Victor 45 EPA 992 and in RCA Victor "Elvis" LPM 1382)

**(Not available as a Pop Single, available on RCA Victor 45 EPA 40006 (Sound Track from the Movie "Love Me Tender")

THE TOP 100

For survey week ending December 26

A list of the Top 100 RECORD SIDES in the nation according to a COMBINED TABULATION of Dealer, Disk Jockey and Juke Box Operator replies to The Billboard's weekly popular record Best Seller and Most Played surveys. Its purpose is to provide Disk Jockeys with additional programming material and to give trade exposure to NEWER records just beginning to show action in the field.

Pos.	Song, Artist, Label	Last Week
1.	SINGING THE BLUES—G. Mitchell, Columbia	1
2.	GREEN DOOR—J. Lowe, Dot	3
3.	LOVE ME TENDER—E. Presley, Victor	2
4.	TRUE LOVE—Bing Crosby & G. Kelly, Capitol	5
5.	JUST WALKING IN THE RAIN—J. Ray, Columbia	6
6.	BLUEBERRY HILL—F. Domino, Imperial	4
6.	LOVE ME—E. Presley, Victor	7
8.	HEY, JEALOUS LOVER—F. Sinatra, Capitol	8
8.	ROSE AND A BABY RUTH—G. Hamilton IV, ABC-Paramount	8
10.	MOONLIGHT GAMBLER—F. Laine, Columbia	15
11.	CINDY, OH, CINDY—E. Fisher, Victor	10
12.	ROCK-A-BYE YOUR BABY—J. Lewis, Decca	15
12.	SINCE I MET YOU, BABY—I. J. Hunter, Atlantic	12
14.	GONNA GET ALONG WITHOUT YA NOW—Patience & Prudence, Liberty	12
15.	MARY'S BOY CHILD—H. Belafonte, Victor	21
16.	DON'T FORBID ME—P. Boone, Dot	30
17.	BANANA BOAT SONG—Tarriers, Glory	20
18.	CINDY, OH, CINDY—V. Martin, Glory	19
19.	GARDEN OF EDEN—J. Valino, Vik	14
20.	MAMA FROM THE TRAIN—P. Page, Mercury	11
21.	FRIENDLY PERSUASION—P. Boone, Dot	18
22.	HONKY TONK—B. Doggett, King	17
23.	JAMAICA FAREWELL—H. Belafonte, Victor	24
24.	DON'T BE CRUEL—E. Presley, Victor	26
25.	I DREAMED—B. Johnson, Bally	31
26.	PRISCILLA—E. Cooley, Roost	36
27.	SLOW WALK—B. Doggett, King	40
28.	CONFIDENTIAL—S. Knight, Dot	21
29.	MUTUAL ADMIRATION SOCIETY—T. Brewer, Coral	27
30.	YOUNG LOVE—S. James, Capitol	43
31.	TWO DIFFERENT WORLDS—D. Rondo, Jubilee	28
32.	SINGING THE BLUES—M. Robbins, Columbia	29
33.	AUCTIONEER—L. Van Dyke, Dot	31
34.	BABY DOLL—A. Williams, Cadence	33
34.	NIGHT LIGHTS—Nat (King) Cole, Capitol	25
36.	CITY OF ANGELS—Highlights, Bally	50
37.	I WALK THE LINE— J. Cash, Sun	88
38.	I FEEL SO GOOD—Shirley & Lee, Aladdin	42
39.	SINCE I MET YOU, BABY—M. Carson, Columbia	46
40.	POOR BOY—E. Presley, Victor	54
41.	WHEN MY BLUE MOON TURNS TO GOLD AGAIN— E. Presley, Victor	38
42.	ARMEN'S THEME—D. Seville, Liberty	49
42.	ON LONDON BRIDGE—J. Stafford, Columbia	45
44.	ANASTASIA—P. Boone, Dot	51
44.	BANANA BOAT SONG—Fontane Sisters, Dot	88
46.	GOODNIGHT, MY LOVE—McGuire Sisters, Coral	39
46.	TWO DIFFERENT WORLDS—R. Williams & J. Morgan, Kapp	71
48.	ON MY WORD OF HONOR—Platters, Mercury	76
49.	MONEY TREE, M. Whiting, Capitol	64
50.	GREENSLEEVES—Beverly Sisters, London	84
50.	JIM DANDY—L. Baker, Atlantic	87
52.	TRA LA LA—G. Gibbs, Mercury	53
53.	THOUSAND MILES AWAY—Heartbeats, Rama	79
54.	SLOW WALK—S. Austin, Mercury	23
55.	PETTICOATS OF PORTUGAL—D. Jacobs, Coral	35
56.	AIN'T GOT NO HOME—C. Henry, Argo	44
57.	I MISS YOU SO—C. Connor, Atlantic	69
58.	BLUE MONDAY—F. Domino, Imperial	—
58.	BANANA BOAT SONG—S. Vaughan, Mercury	73
60.	BLUE MOON—E. Presley, Victor	93
61.	ARMEN'S THEME—J. Reismen, Victor	52
62.	HOUND DOG—E. Presley, Victor	54
63.	STAR YOU WISHED UPON LAST NIGHT—G. MacKenzie, Vik	62
64.	MUTUAL ADMIRATION SOCIETY—J. P. Morgan & E. Arnold, Victor	56
65.	RUDY'S ROCK—B. Haley, Decca	100
66.	FADED SUMMER LOVE—G. Shaw, Decca	57
66.	AUCTIONEER—C. Miller, Mercury	59
68.	PARTY'S OVER—Doris Day, Columbia	82
69.	JUST IN TIME—T. Bennett, Columbia	58
70.	TRUE LOVE—J. Powell, Verve	85
71.	DANCING CHANDELIER—S. Syms, Decca	98
72.	I SAW ESAU—Ames Brothers, Victor	66
73.	LOVE IS STRANGE—Mickey & Sylvia, Groove	—
74.	PARALYZED—E. Presley, Victor	78
75.	BY YOU, BY YOU, BY YOU—J. Lowe, Dot	—
75.	ONE IN A MILLION—Platters, Mercury	67
75.	TONIGHT YOU BELONG TO ME—Patience & Prudence, Liberty	68
78.	LOVE ME TENDER—H. Rene, Victor	86
79.	YOU'LL NEVER, NEVER KNOW—Platters, Mercury	40
80.	CRAZY WITH LOVE—G. Mitchell, Columbia	99
81.	BLUEBERRY HILL—L. Armstrong, Decca	60
81.	CANADIAN SUNSET—E. Heywood-H. Winterhalter, Victor	34
83.	IN THE STILL OF THE NIGHT—Satins, Ember	72
84.	CANADIAN SUNSET—A. Williams, Cadence	63
85.	I WOULDN'T KNOW WHERE TO BEGIN—E. Arnold, Victor	—
85.	I LOVE MY BABY—J. Corey, Columbia	82
87.	GIVE ME—E. Rodgers, Columbia	76
87.	TWO DIFFERENT WORLDS—D. Haymes, Capitol	80
87.	WIDSOM OF A FOOL—Five Keys, Capitol	48
90.	IT ISN'T RIGHT—Platters, Mercury	96
91.	PETTICOATS OF PORTUGAL—B. Vaughn, Mercury	90
92.	AUTUMN WALTZ—T. Bennett, Columbia	—
93.	FRIENDLY PERSUASION—Four Aces, Decca	100
93.	OUT OF SIGHT, OUT OF MIND—Five Keys, Capitol	—
93.	SADIE'S SHAWL—B. Sharples, London	—
93.	SOMEONE TO LOVE—Four Aces, Decca	81
97.	STILL—L. Baker, Atlantic	—
98.	DREAMY EYES—Four Preps, Capitol	—
99.	FIRST BORN—T. Ernie, Capitol	61
99.	I CAN'T LOVE YOU ENOUGH—L. Baker, Atlantic	—
99.	LAY DOWN YOUR ARMS—Chordettes, Cadence	97

CAUTION TO DEALERS AND JUKE BOX OPERATORS

The Billboard's Top 100 is NOT designed to provide tested information for buying purposes. This function is most reliably served by other regular weekly features: Best Sellers in Stores, Most Played in Juke Boxes, Coming Up Strong and Best Buys.

• Best Sellers in Stores

For survey week ending January 2

RECORDS are ranked in order of their current national selling importance at the retail level, as determined by The Billboard's weekly survey of the top volume dealers in every important market area. When significant action is reported on both sides of a record, points are combined to determine position on the chart. In such a case, both sides are listed in bold type, the leading side on top.

This Week		Last Week	Weeks on Chart
1.	**SINGING THE BLUES** (BMI)—G. Mitchell Crazy With Love (ASCAP)—Col 40769	1	11
2.	**GREEN DOOR** (BMI)—J. Lowe (Story of) The Little Man in Chinatown (BMI)—Dot 15486	2	16
3.	**LOVE ME TENDER** (BMI)—E. Presley Any Way You Want Me (ASCAP)—Vic 20-6643	3	13
4.	**BLUEBERRY HILL** (ASCAP)—F. Domino Honey Chile (BMI)—Imperial 5407	4	14
5.	**TRUE LOVE** (ASCAP)—B. Crosby-G. Kelly Well, Did You Evah (ASCAP)—Cap 3507	6	15
6.	**JUST WALKING IN THE RAIN** (BMI)—J. Ray In the Candlelight (ASCAP)—Col 40729	5	19
7.	**BANANA BOAT SONG** (BMI)—Tarriers No Hindin' Place (BMI)—Glory 249	8	4
8.	★**LOVE ME** (BMI)—E. Presley Vic EPA-992	7	8
9.	**ROSE AND A BABY RUTH** (BMI)—G. Hamilton IV If You Don't Know (BMI)—ABC-Paramount 9765	9	9
10.	**MOONLIGHT GAMBLER** (ASCAP)—F. Laine Lotus Land (ASCAP)—Col 40780	13	5
11.	**DON'T FORBID ME** (BMI)—P. Boone Anastasia (ASCAP)—Dot 15521	11	4
12.	**YOUNG LOVE** (BMI)—S. James You're the Reason I'm in Love (BMI)—Cap 3602	22	2
13.	**CINDY, OH CINDY** (BMI)—E. Fisher Around the World (ASCAP)—Vic 20-6677	15	14
14.	**GARDEN OF EDEN** (BMI)—J. Valino Caravan (ASCAP)—Vik 0226	25	10
15.	**ROCK-A-BYE YOUR BABY** (ASCAP)—J. Lewis Come Rain or Come Shine (ASCAP)—Dec 30124	10	8
16.	**HEY! JEALOUS LOVER** (ASCAP)—F. Sinatra You Forgot All the Words (BMI)—Cap 3552	14	11
17.	**BLUE MONDAY** (BMI)—F. Domino **WHAT'S THE REASON (I'M NOT PLEASING YOU)** (ASCAP)—Imperial 5417	—	1
18.	**JAMAICA FAREWELL** (ASCAP)—H. Belafonte Once Was (ASCAP)—Vic 20-6663	19	4
19.	**SINCE I MET YOU BABY** (BMI)—I. J. Hunter You Can't Stop This Rocking and Rolling (BMI)—Atlantic 1111	20	6
20	**AIN'T GOT NO HOME** (BMI)—C. Henry Troubles, Troubles (BMI)—Argo 5259	—	1
21.	**GONNA GET ALONG WITHOUT YA NOW** (ASCAP)—Patience & Prudence Money Tree (ASCAP)—Liberty 55040	17	6
22.	**BANANA BOAT SONG** (BMI)—H. Belafonte Star-O (ASCAP)—Vic 20-6771	—	1
23.	**HONKY TONK** (Parts I & II)—B. Doggett King 4950—BMI	23	21
24.	**LOVE IS STRANGE** (BMI)—Mickey & Sylvia I'm Going Home (BMI)—Groove 0175	—	1
25.	**CITY OF ANGELS**—Highlights Listen, My Love—Bally 1016	—	5

★(Not available as a Pop Single. Availble on RCA Victor 45 EPA-992 and in RCA Victor 33⅓ "Elvis" LPM 1382)

• Most Played in Juke Boxes

For survey week ending January 2

RECORDS are ranked in order of the greatest number of plays in juke boxes thruout the country, as determined by The Billboard's weekly survey of the nation's juke box operators. When significant play is reported on both sides of a record, points are combined to determine position on the chart. In such a case, both sides are listed in bold type, the leading side on top.

This Week		Last Week	Weeks on Chart
1.	**SINGING THE BLUES** (BMI)—G. Mitchell Crazy With Love (ASCAP)—Col 40769	1	10
2.	**GREEN DOOR** (BMI)—J. Lowe (The Story of) The Little Man in Chinatown (BMI)—Dot 15486	2	14
3.	**BLUEBERRY HILL** (ASCAP)—F. Domino Honey Chile (BMI)—Imperial 5407	4	13
4.	**LOVE ME TENDER** (BMI)—E. Presley Any Way You Want Me (ASCAP)—Vic 20-6643	3	12
5.	**JUST WALKING IN THE RAIN** (BMI)—J. Ray In the Candlelight (ASCAP)—Col 40729	5	17
6.	**TRUE LOVE** (ASCAP)—B. Crosby-G. Kelly Well, Did You Evah? (ASCAP)—Cap 3507	6	11
7.	**HEY! JEALOUS LOVER** (ASCAP)—F. Sinatra You Forgot All the Words (BMI)—Cap 3552	7	8
8.	**ROSE AND A BABY RUTH** (BMI)—G. Hamilton IV If You Don't Know (BMI)—ABC-Paramount 9765	12	7
8.	**MOONLIGHT GAMBLER** (ASCAP)—F. Laine Lotus Land (ASCAP)—Col 40780	19	2
10.	**HONKY TONK (PARTS I & II)** (BMI)—B. Doggett King 4950	8	18
10.	**CINDY, OH CINDY** (BMI)—E. Fisher Around the World (ASCAP)—Vic 20-6677	10	9
12.	★**LOVE ME**—E. Presley Vic EPA-992 BMI	14	5
13.	**ROCK-A-BYE YOUR BABY** (ASCAP)—J. Lewis Come Rain or Come Shine (ASCAP)—Dec 30124	17	2
14.	**DON'T BE CRUEL** (BMI)—E. Presley **HOUND DOG** (BMI)—Vic 20-6643	9	23
15.	**SINCE I MET YOU BABY** (BMI)—I. J. Hunter You Can't Stop This Rocking and Rolling (BMI)—Atlantic 1111	14	2
16.	**MAMA FROM THE TRAIN** (ASCAP)—P. Page Every Time—I Feel His Spirit (BMI)—Mercury 70971	13	6
16.	**GONNA GET ALONG WITHOUT YA NOW** (ASCAP)—Patience & Prudence Money Tree (ASCAP)—Liberty 55040	20	4
16.	**DON'T FORBID ME** (BMI)—P. Boone Anastasia (ASCAP)—Dot 15521	—	1
19.	**CINDY, OH CINDY** (BMI)—V. Martin Only If I Praise the Lord (BMI)—Glory 247	10	10
19.	**BANANA BOAT SONG** (BMI)—Tarriers No Hidin' Place (BMI)—Glory 249	—	1

★(Not available as a Pop Single. Available on RCA Victor 45 EPA-992 and in RCA Victor 33⅓ "Elvis" LPM 1382)

• Best Selling Sheet Music

Tunes are ranked in order of their current national selling importance at the sheet music jobber level.

This Week		Last Week	Weeks on Chart
1.	**Love Me Tender** (Presley)	1	13
2.	**Singing the Blues** (Acuff-Rose)	2	8
3.	**True Love** (Buxton Hill)	3	16
4.	**Just Walking in the Rain** (Golden West)	5	14
5.	**Green Door** (Trinity)	4	12
6.	**Cindy, Oh Cindy** (E. B. Marks-Bryden)	6	10
7.	**Blueberry Hill** (Chappell)	7	9
8.	**Friendly Persuasion** (Feist)	8	11
9.	**Love Me** (Hill & Range)	12	5
10.	**Hey! Jealous Lover** (Barton)	9	7
11.	**Two Different Worlds** (Spier)	10	9
12.	**Rose and a Baby Ruth** (Bentley)	13	3
13.	**Canadian Sunset** (Meridian)	13	22
13.	**Mama From the Train** (Remick)	15	5
15.	**Gonna Get Along Without Ya Now** (Kellum)	—	1

• Most Played by Jockeys

For survey week ending January 2

SIDES are ranked in order of the greatest number of plays on disk jockey radio shows thruout the country. Results are based on The Billboard's weekly survey among the nation's disk jockeys. The reverse side of each record is also listed.

This Week		Last Week	Weeks on Chart
1.	**SINGING THE BLUES** (BMI)—G. Mitchell Crazy With Love (ASCAP)—Col 40769	1	11
2.	★**LOVE ME**—E. Presley Vic EPA-992	2	7
3.	**HEY! JEALOUS LOVER** (ASCAP)—F. Sinatra You Forgot All the Words (BMI)—Cap 3552	6	12
4.	**MOONLIGHT GAMBLER** (ASCAP)—F. Laine Lotus Land (ASCAP)—Col 40780	9	5
5.	**TRUE LOVE** (ASCAP)—B. Crosby-G. Kelly Well, Did You Evah? (ASCAP)—Cap 3507	5	15
6.	**LOVE ME TENDER** (BMI)—E. Presley Any Way You Want Me (ASCAP)—Vic 20-6643	4	13
7.	**BANANA BOAT SONG** (BMI)—Tarriers No Hindin' Place (BMI)—Glory 249	16	3
8.	**GREEN DOOR** (BMI)—J. Lowe (Story of) The Little Man in Chinatown (BMI)—Dot 15486	3	16
9.	**DON'T FORBID ME** (BMI)—P. Boone Anastasia (ASCAP)—Dot 15521	8	3
10.	**YOUNG LOVE** (BMI)—S. James You're the Reason I'm in Love (BMI)—Cap 3602	18	2
11.	**BLUEBERRY HILL** (ASCAP)—F. Domino Honey Chile (BMI)—Imperial 5407	15	13
12.	**JUST WALKING IN THE RAIN** (BMI)—J. Ray In the Candlelight (ASCAP)—Col 40729	10	16
13.	**GONNA GET ALONG WITHOUT YA NOW**—Patience & Prudence Money Tree (ASCAP)—Liberty 55040	11	6
14.	**JAMAICA FAREWELL** (ASCAP)—H. Belafonte Once Was (ASCAP)—Vic 20-6663	25	5
15.	**ROSE AND A BABY RUTH** (BMI)—G. Hamilton IV If You Don't Know (BMI)—ABC-Paramount 9765	7	9
16.	**SINCE I MET YOU BABY** (BMI)—I. J. Hunter You Can't Stop This Rocking and Rolling (BMI)—Atlantic 1111	14	6
17.	**I DREAMED** (BMI)—B. Johnson If It's Wrong to Love You (BMI)—Bally 1030	17	5
17.	**ROCK-A-BYE YOUR BABY** (ASCAP)—J. Lewis Come Rain or Come Shine (ASCAP)—Dec 30124	20	4
19.	**BANANA BOAT SONG** (BMI)—H. Belafonte Star-O (ASCAP)—Vic 20-6771	—	1
20.	**MARY'S BOY CHILD** (ASCAP)—H. Belafonte Venezuela Vic 20-6734	12	2
21.	**BANANA BOAT SONG** (BMI)—S. Vaughan I've Got a New Heartache (BMI)—Mercury 71020	—	1
22.	**GARDEN OF EDEN** (BMI)—J. Valino Caravan (ASCAP)—Vik 0226	22	9
23.	**TWO DIFFERENT WORLDS** (ASCAP)—D. Rondo He Made You Mine (ASCAP)—Jubilee 5256	13	11
23.	**MONEY TREE** (ASCAP)—M. Whiting Maybe I Love Him (ASCAP)—Cap 3586	21	5
25.	**BANANA BOAT SONG** (BMI)—Fontane Sisters Honolulu Moon Dot 15527	—	1

★(Not available as a Pop Single. Available on RCA Victor 45 EPA-992 and in RCA Victor 33⅓ "Elvis" LPM 1382)

THE TOP 100

For survey week ending January 2

A list of the Top 100 RECORD SIDES in the nation according to a COMBINED TABULATION of Dealer, Disk Jockey and Juke Box Operator replies to The Billboard's weekly popular record Best Seller and Most Played surveys. Its purpose is to provide Disk Jockeys with additional programming material and to give trade exposure to NEWER records just beginning to show action in the field.

Pos.	Song, Artist, Label	Last Week
1.	SINGING THE BLUES—G. Mitchell, Columbia	1
2.	GREEN DOOR—J. Lowe, Dot	2
3.	LOVE ME TENDER—E. Presley, Victor	3
4.	TRUE LOVE—Bing Crosby-G. Kelly, Capitol	4
5.	BLUEBERRY HILL—F. Domino, Imperial	6
6.	LOVE ME—E. Presley, Victor	6
6.	MOONLIGHT GAMBLER—F. Laine, Columbia	10
8.	JUST WALKING IN THE RAIN—J. Ray, Columbia	5
9.	HEY! JEALOUS LOVER—F. Sinatra, Capitol	8
10.	ROSE AND A BABY RUTH—G. Hamilton, ABC-Paramount	8
11.	BANANA BOAT SONG—Tarriers, Glory	17
12.	DON'T FORBID ME—P. Boone, Dot	16
13.	ROCK-A-BYE YOUR BABY—J. Lewis, Decca	12
14.	SINCE I MET YOU BABY—I. J. Hunter, Atlantic	12
15.	GONNA GET ALONG WITHOUT YA NOW—Patience & Prudence, Liberty	14
16.	CINDY, OH CINDY—E. Fisher, Victor	11
17.	GARDEN OF EDEN—J. Valino, Vik	19
18.	JAMAICA FAREWELL—H. Belafonte, Victor	23
19.	YOUNG LOVE—S. James, Capitol	30
20.	MAMA FROM THE TRAIN—P. Page, Mercury	20
21.	HONKY TONK—B. Doggett, King	22
22.	CINDY, OH CINDY—V. Martin, Glory	18
23.	I DREAMED—B. Johnson, Bally	25
24.	FRIENDLY PERSUASION—P. Boone, Dot	21
24.	MARY'S BOY CHILD—H. Belafonte, Victor	15
26.	SLOW WALK—B. Doggett, King	27
27.	BANANA BOAT SONG—H. Belafonte, Victor	—
28.	CONFIDENTIAL—S. Knight, Dot	28
29.	SINGING THE BLUES—M. Robbins, Columbia	32
30.	NIGHT LIGHTS—Nat (King) Cole, Capitol	34
31.	TWO DIFFERENT WORLDS—D. Rondo, Jubilee	31
32.	BLUE MONDAY—F. Domino, Imperial	58
32.	GOODNIGHT MY LOVE—McGuire Sisters, Coral	46
34.	SINCE I MET YOU BABY—M. Carson, Columbia	39
35.	AUCTIONEER—L. Van Dyke, Dot	33
35.	PRISCILLA—E. Cooley, Roost	26
37.	SLOW WALK—S. Austin, Mercury	54
38.	ON MY WORD OF HONOR—Platters, Mercury	48
39.	JIM DANDY—L. Baker, Atlantic	50
40.	WISDOM OF A FOOL—Five Keys, Capitol	87
41.	DON'T BE CRUEL—E. Presley, Victor	24
41.	MUTUAL ADMIRATION SOCIETY—T. Brewer, Coral	29
43.	LOVE IS STRANGE—Mickey & Sylvia, Groove	73
44.	BABY DOLL—A. Williams, Cadence	34
45.	BANANA BOAT SONG—S. Vaughan, Mercury	58
46.	WHEN MY BLUE MOON TURNS TO GOLD AGAIN—E. Presley, Victor	41
47.	ANASTASIA—P. Boone, Dot	44
47.	GREENSLEEVES—Beverly Sisters, London	50
49.	AIN'T GOT NO HOME—C. Henry, Argo	56
50.	BANANA BOAT SONG—Fontane Sisters, Dot	44
50.	BANANA BOAT SONG—S. Lawrence, Coral	—
50.	POOR BOY—E. Presley, Victor	40
53.	HOUND DOG—E. Presley, Victor	62
54.	WHAT'S THE REASON (I'M NOT PLEASING YOU)—F. Domino, Imperial	—
55.	TRA LA LA—G. Gibbs, Mercury	52
56.	ARMEN'S THEME—D. Seville, Liberty	42
57.	CITY OF ANGELS—Highlights, Bally	36
58.	ONE IN A MILLION—Platters, Mercury	75
58.	ON LONDON BRIDGE—J. Stafford, Columbia	42
60.	YOUNG LOVE—T. Hunter, Dot	—
61.	I LOVE MY BABY—J. Corey, Columbia	85
61.	MONEY TREE—M. Whiting, Capitol	49
63.	PARALYZED—E. Presley, Victor	74
64.	CINCO ROBLES—R. Arms, Era	—
65.	THOUSAND MILES AWAY—Heartbeats, Rama	53
66.	I SAW ESAU—Ames Brothers, Victor	72
67.	YOU DON'T OWE ME A THING—J. Ray, Columbia	—
68.	JUST IN TIME—T. Bennett, Columbia	69
69.	BY YOU, BY YOU, BY YOU—J. Lowe, Dot	75
70.	TWO DIFFERENT WORLDS—J. Morgan & R. Williams, Kapp	46
71.	TRUE LOVE—J. Powell, Verve	70
72.	STAR YOU WISHED UPON LAST NIGHT—G. Mac Kenzie, Vik	63
73.	YOUNG LOVE—Crew Cuts, Mercury	—
74.	CANADIAN SUNSET—E. Heywood-H. Winterhalter, Victor	81
75.	DREAMY EYES—Four Preps, Capitol	98
75.	I WALK THE LINE—J. Cash, Sun	37
77.	PETTICOATS OF PORTUGAL—D. Jacobs, Coral	55
78.	BLUEBERRY HILL—L. Armstrong, Decca	81
19.	AUCTIONEER—C. Miller, Mercury	66
80.	ARMEN'S THEME—J. Reisman, Victor	61
80.	I MISS YOU SO—C. Connor, Atlantic	57
82.	I FEEL GOOD—Shirley & Lee, Aladdin	38
82.	RUDY'S ROCK—B. Haley, Decca	65
84.	DANCING CHANDELIER—S. Syms, Decca	71
85.	FIRST BORN—T. Ernie, Capitol	99
86.	PARTY'S OVER—Doris Day, Columbia	68
87.	MONEY TREE—Patience & Prudence, Liberty	—
88.	BLUE MOON—E. Presley, Victor	60
88.	CINCO ROBLES—L. Paul & M. Ford, Capitol	—
88.	I WOULDN'T KNOW WHERE TO BEGIN—E. Arnold, Victor	85
88.	YOU'LL NEVER, NEVER KNOW—Platters, Mercury	79
92.	FADED SUMMER LOVE—G. Shaw, Decca	66
93.	CONFESSION OF A SINNER—Stylers, Jubilee	—
93.	WRITTEN ON THE WIND—Four Aces, Decca	—
95.	MUTUAL ADMIRATION SOCIETY—J. P. Morgan & E. Arnold, Victor	64
96.	CRAZY WITH LOVE—G. Mitchell, Columbia	80
96.	GIVE ME—E. Rodgers, Columbia	87
96.	SOMEONE TO LOVE—Four Aces, Decca	93
99.	TONIGHT YOU BELONG TO ME—Patience & Prudence, Liberty	75
100.	FRIENDLY PERSUASION—Four Aces, Decca	93
100.	LAY DOWN YOUR ARMS—Chordettes, Cadence	99
100.	TO THE ENDS OF THE EARTH—Nat (King) Cole, Capitol	—

CAUTION TO DEALERS AND JUKE BOX OPERATORS

The Billboard's Top 100 is NOT designed to provide tested information for buying purposes. This function is most reliably served by other regular weekly features: Best Sellers in Stores, Most Played in Juke Boxes, Coming Up Strong and Best Buys.

• Best Sellers in Stores

For survey week ending January 9

RECORDS are ranked in order of their current national selling importance at the retail level, as determined by The Billboard's weekly survey of the top volume dealers in every important market area. When significant action is reported on both sides of a record, points are combined to determine position on the chart. In such a case, both sides are listed in bold type, the leading side on top.

This Week	Record	Last Week	Weeks on Chart
1.	**SINGING THE BLUES** (BMI)—G. Mitchell. Crazy With Love (ASCAP)—Col 40769	1	12
2.	**GREEN DOOR** (BMI)—J. Lowe. (Story of) The Little Man in Chinatown (BMI)—Dot 15486	2	17
3.	**BLUEBERRY HILL** (ASCAP)—F. Domino. Honey Chile (BMI)—Imperial 5407	4	15
3.	**YOUNG LOVE** (BMI)—S. James. You're the Reason (I'm in Love) (BMI)—Cap 3602	12	3
5.	**BANANA BOAT SONG** (BMI)—Tarriers. No Hidin' Place (BMI)—Glory 249	7	5
6.	**DON'T FORBID ME** (BMI)—P. Boone. Anastasia (ASCAP)—Dot 15521	11	5
7.	**LOVE ME TENDER** (BMI)—E. Presley. Any Way You Want Me (ASCAP)—Vic 20-6643	3	14
8.	**MOONLIGHT GAMBLER** (ASCAP)—F. Laine. Lotus Land (ASCAP)—Col 40780	10	6
9.	**JUST WALKING IN THE RAIN** (BMI)—J. Ray. In the Candlelight (ASCAP)—Col 40729	6	20
10.	★**LOVE ME** (BMI)—E. Presley. Vic EPA-992	8	9
11.	**TRUE LOVE** (ASCAP)—B. Crosby-G. Kelly. Well, Did You Evah? (ASCAP)—Cap 3507	5	16
12.	**YOUNG LOVE** (BMI)—T. Hunter. Red Sails in the Sunset (ASCAP)—Dot 15533	—	1
13.	**ROSE AND A BABY RUTH** (BMI)—G. Hamilton IV. If You Don't Know (BMI)—ABC-Paramount 9765	9	10
14.	**BANANA BOAT SONG** (BMI)—H. Belafonte. Star-O (ASCAP)—Vic 20-6771	22	2
15.	**BLUE MONDAY** (BMI)—F. Domino. **WHAT'S THE REASON (I'M NOT PLEASING YOU)** (ASCAP)—Imperial 5417	17	2
16.	**SINCE I MET YOU BABY** (BMI)—I. J. Hunter. You Can't Stop This Rocking and Rolling (BMI)—Atlantic 1111	19	7
17.	**JAMAICA FAREWELL** (ASCAP)—H. Belafonte. Once Was (ASCAP)—Vic 20-6663	18	5
18.	**CINDY, OH CINDY** (BMI)—E. Fisher. Around the World (ASCAP)—Vic 20-6677	13	15
19.	**HEY! JEALOUS LOVER** (ASCAP)—F. Sinatra. You Forgot All the Words (BMI)—Cap 3552	16	12
20.	**LOVE IS STRANGE** (BMI)—Mickey & Sylvia. I'm Going Home (BMI)—Groove 0175	24	2
21.	**ROCK-A-BYE YOUR BABY** (ASCAP)—J. Lewis. Come Rain or Come Shine (ASCAP)—Dec 30124	15	9
22.	**GONNA GET ALONG WITHOUT YA NOW** (ASCAP)—Patience & Prudence. Money Tree (ASCAP)—Liberty 55040	21	7
23.	**CINDY, OH CINDY** (BMI)—V. Martin. Only If I Praise the Lord (BMI)—Glory 247	—	10
24.	**I DREAMED** (BMI)—B. Johnson. If It's Wrong to Love You (BMI)—Bally 1020	—	1
25.	**AIN'T GOT NO HOME** (BMI)—C. Henry. Troubles Troubles (BMI)—Argo 5259	20	2
25.	**HONKY TONK** (Parts 1 & II)—B. Doggett. King 4950—BMI	23	22

★(Not Available as a Pop Single. Available on RCA Victor 45 EPA 992 and in RCA Victor 33⅓ "Elvis" LPM 1382)

• Most Played in Juke Boxes

For survey week ending January 9

RECORDS are ranked in order of the greatest number of plays in juke boxes thruout the country, as determined by The Billboard's weekly survey of the nation's juke box operators. When significant play is reported on both sides of a record, points are combined to determine position on the chart. In such a case, both sides are listed in bold type, the leading side on top.

This Week	Record	Last Week	Weeks on Chart
1.	**SINGING THE BLUES** (BMI)—G. Mitchell. Crazy With Love (ASCAP)—Col 40769	1	11
2.	**BLUEBERRY HILL** (ASCAP)—F. Domino. Honey Chile (BMI)—Imperial 5407	3	14
3.	**GREEN DOOR** (BMI)—J. Lowe. (The Story of) The Little Man in Chinatown (BMI)—Dot 15486	2	15
4.	**LOVE ME TENDER** (BMI)—E. Presley. Any Way You Want Me (ASCAP)—Vic 20-6643	4	13
5.	**JUST WALKING IN THE RAIN** (BMI)—J. Ray. In the Candlelight (ASCAP)—Col 40729	5	18
6.	**TRUE LOVE** (ASCAP)—B. Crosby-G. Kelly. Well, Did You Evah? (ASCAP)—Cap 3507	6	12
7.	**MOONLIGHT GAMBLER** (ASCAP)—F. Laine. Lotus Land (ASCAP)—Col 40780	8	3
8.	**ROSE AND A BABY RUTH** (BMI)—G. Hamilton IV. If You Don't Know (BMI)—ABC-Paramount 9765	8	8
9.	★**LOVE ME**—E. Presley. Vic EPA-992—BMI	12	6
10.	**HEY! JEALOUS LOVER** (ASCAP)—F. Sinatra. You Forgot All the Words (BMI)—Cap 3552	7	9
11.	**CINDY, OH CINDY** (BMI)—E. Fisher. Around the World (ASCAP)—Vic 20-6677	10	10
12.	**DON'T FORBID ME** (BMI)—P. Boone. Anastasia (ASCAP)—Dot 15521	16	2
13.	**HONKY TONK** (PARTS I & II) (BMI)—B. Doggett. King 4950	10	19
14.	**BANANA BOAT SONG** (BMI)—Tarriers. No Hidin' Place (BMI)—Glory 249	19	2
15.	**ROCK-A-BYE YOUR BABY** (ASCAP)—J. Lewis. Come Rain or Come Shine (ASCAP)—Dec 30124	13	3
16.	**SINCE I MET YOU BABY** (BMI)—I. J. Hunter. You Can't Stop This Rockin' and Rolling (BMI)—Atlantic 1111	15	3
17.	**GARDEN OF EDEN** (BMI)—J. Valino. Caravan (ASCAP)—Vik 0226	—	6
18.	**GONNA GET ALONG WITHOUT YA NOW** (ASCAP)—Patience & Prudence. Money Tree (ASCAP)—Liberty 55040	16	5
19.	**DON'T BE CRUEL** (BMI)—E. Presley. Hound Dog (BMI)—Vic 20-6643	14	24
20.	**SLOW WALK** (BMI)—S. Austin. Wildwood (ASCAP)—Mercury 70963	—	2

★(Not available as a Pop Single, available on RCA Victor 45 EPA-992 and in RCA Victor 33⅓ "Elvis" LPM 1382)

• Best Selling Sheet Music

Tunes are ranked in order of their current national selling importance at the sheet music jobber level.

This Week	Title	Last Week	Weeks on Chart
1.	**Love Me Tender** (Presley)	1	14
1.	**Singing the Blues** (Acuff-Rose)	2	9
3.	**True Love** (Buxton Hill)	3	17
4.	**Cindy, Oh Cindy** (E. B. Marks-Bryden)	6	11
5.	**Blueberry Hill** (Chappell)	7	10
6.	**Just Walking in the Rain** (Golden West)	4	15
7.	**Green Door** (Trinity)	5	13
8.	**Friendly Persuasion** (Feist)	8	12
9.	**Love Me** (Hill & Range)	9	6
10.	**Banana Boat Song** (E. B. Marks-Bryden)	—	1
11.	**Two Different Worlds** (Spier)	11	10
12.	**Hey! Jealous Lover** (Barton)	10	8
13.	**Gonna Get Along Without Ya Now** (Kellum)	15	2
14.	**Anastasia** (Feist)	—	1
15.	**Canadian Sunset** (Meridian)	13	23

• Most Played by Jockeys

For survey week ending January 9

SIDES are ranked in order of the greatest number of plays on disk jockey radio shows thruout the country. Results are based on The Billboard's weekly survey among the nation's disk jockeys. The reverse side of each record is also listed.

This Week	Record	Last Week	Weeks on Chart
1.	**SINGING THE BLUES** (BMI)—G. Mitchell. Crazy With Love (ASCAP)—Col 40769	1	12
2.	**DON'T FORBID ME** (BMI)—P. Boone. Anastasia (ASCAP)—Dot 15521	9	4
3.	★**LOVE ME** (BMI)—E. Presley. Vic EPA-992	2	8
4.	**YOUNG LOVE** (BMI)—S. James. You're the Reason (I'm in Love) (BMI)—Cap 3602	10	3
5.	**MOONLIGHT GAMBLER** (ASCAP)—F. Laine. Lotus Land (ASCAP)—Col 40780	4	6
6.	**BANANA BOAT SONG** (BMI)—Tarriers. No Hidin' Place (BMI)—Glory 249	7	4
7.	**BANANA BOAT SONG** (BMI)—H. Belafonte. Star-O (ASCAP)—Vic 20-6771	19	2
8.	**GREEN DOOR** (BMI)—J. Lowe. (Story of) The Little Man in Chinatown (BMI)—Dot 15486	8	17
9.	**YOUNG LOVE** (BMI)—T. Hunter. Red Sails in the Sunset (ASCAP)—Dot 15533	—	1
10.	**TRUE LOVE** (ASCAP)—B. Crosby-G. Kelly. Well, Did You Evah? (ASCAP)—Cap 3507	5	16
11.	**LOVE ME TENDER** (BMI)—E. Presley. Any Way You Want Me (ASCAP)—Vic 20-6643	6	14
12.	**GONNA GET ALONG WITHOUT YA NOW**—Patience & Prudence. Money Tree (ASCAP)—Liberty 55040	13	7
13.	**HEY! JEALOUS LOVER** (ASCAP)—F. Sinatra. You Forgot All the Words (BMI)—Cap 3552	3	13
14.	**I DREAMED** (BMI)—B. Johnson. If It's Wrong to Love You (BMI)—Bally 1020	17	6
15.	**SINCE I MET YOU BABY** (BMI)—I. J. Hunter. You Can't Stop This Rockin' and Rolling (BMI)—Atlantic 1111	16	7
16.	**BANANA BOAT SONG** (BMI)—Fontane Sisters. Honolulu Moon (ASCAP)—Dot 15527	25	2
17.	**BLUEBERRY HILL** (ASCAP)—F. Domino. Honey Chile (BMI)—Imperial 5407	11	14
18.	**JUST WALKING IN THE RAIN** (BMI)—J. Ray. In the Candlelight (ASCAP)—Col 40729	12	17
19.	**ROSE AND A BABY RUTH** (BMI)—G. Hamilton IV. If You Don't Know (BMI)—ABC-Paramount 9765	15	10
20.	**ROCK-A-BYE YOUR BABY** (ASCAP)—J. Lewis. Come Rain or Come Shine (ASCAP)—Dec 30124	17	5
21.	**BANANA BOAT SONG** (BMI)—S. Vaughan. I've Got a New Heartache (BMI)—Mercury 71020	21	2
22.	★**WHEN MY BLUE MOON TURNS TO GOLD AGAIN**—E. Presley. Vic EPA-992	—	1
23.	**JAMAICA FAREWELL** (ASCAP)—H. Belafonte. Once Was (ASCAP)—Vic 20-6663	14	6
24.	**YOU DON'T OWE ME A THING** (BMI)—J. Ray. Look Homeward, Angel (BMI)—Col 40803	—	1
25.	★★**POOR BOY**—E. Presley. Vic EPA-40006	—	2

★ Not available as a Pop Single, available on RCA Victor 45 EPA-992 and in RCA Victor 33⅓ "Elvis" LPM 1382.

★★ Not available as a Pop Single, available on RCA Victor 45 EPA 40006 (Sound Track from the Movie, "Love Me Tender").

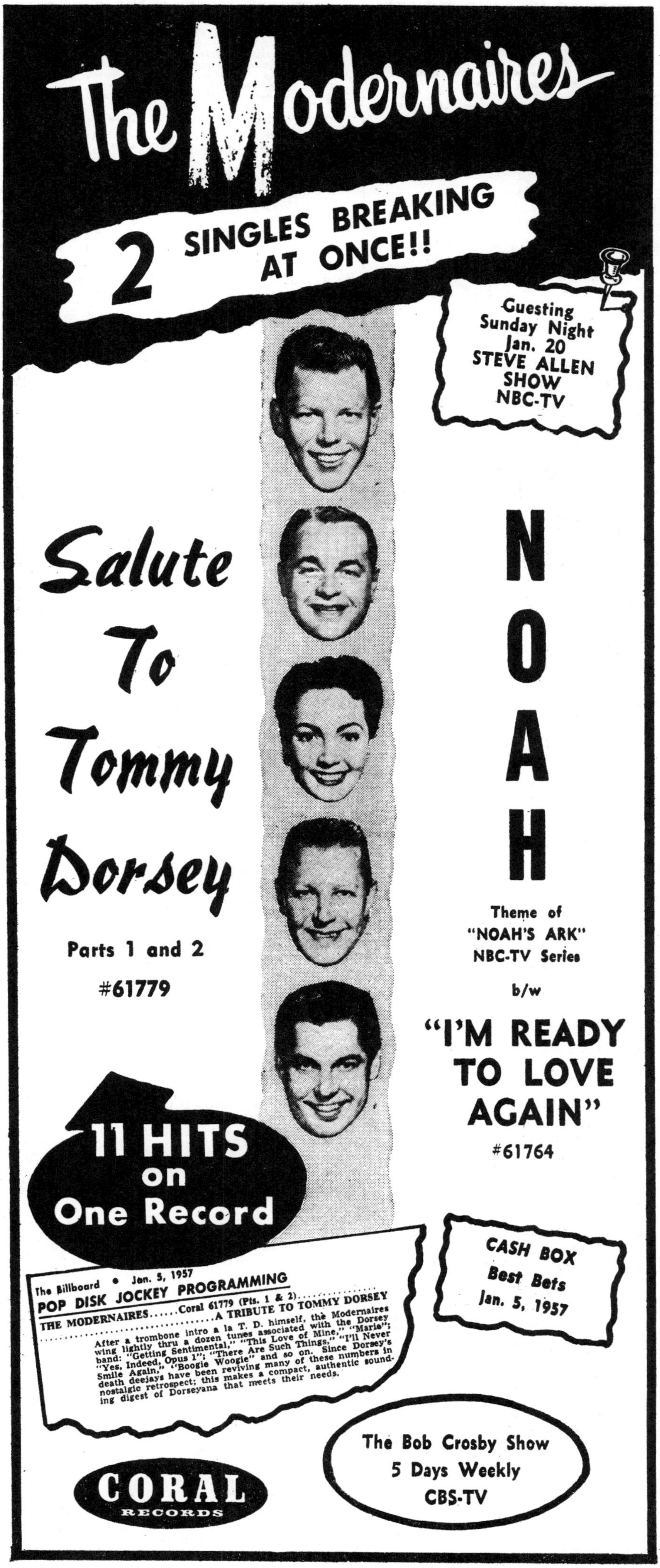

THE TOP 100

For survey week ending January 9

A list of the Top 100 RECORD SIDES in the nation according to a COMBINED TABULATION of Dealer, Disk Jockey and Juke Box Operator replies to The Billboard's weekly popular record Best Seller and Most Played surveys. Its purpose is to provide Disk Jockeys with additional programming material and to give trade exposure to NEWER records just beginning to show action in the field.

Pos.	Song, Artist, Label	Last Week
1.	**SINGING THE BLUES**—G. Mitchell, Columbia	1
2.	**GREEN DOOR**—J. Lowe, Dot	2
3.	**DON'T FORBID ME**—P. Boone, Dot	12
3.	**MOONLIGHT GAMBLER**—F. Laine, Columbia	6
5.	**BLUEBERRY HILL**—F. Domino, Imperial	5
6.	**LOVE ME**—E. Presley, Victor	6
6.	**LOVE ME TENDER**—E. Presley, Victor	3
8.	**BANANA BOAT SONG**—Tarriers, Glory	11
9.	**TRUE LOVE**—B. Crosby-G. Kelly, Capitol	4
10.	**JUST WALKING IN THE RAIN**—J. Ray, Columbia	8
11.	**YOUNG LOVE**—S. James, Capitol	19
12.	**ROSE AND A BABY RUTH**—G. Hamilton IV, ABC-Paramount	9
12.	**BANANA BOAT SONG**—H. Belafonte, Victor	27
14.	**HEY! JEALOUS LOVER**—F. Sinatra, Capitol	9
15.	**YOUNG LOVE**—T. Hunter, Dot	60
16.	**SINCE I MET YOU BABY**—I. J. Hunter, Atlantic	14
16.	**GONNA GET ALONG WITHOUT YA NOW**—Patience & Prudence, Liberty	15
18.	**ROCK-A-BYE YOUR BABY**—J. Lewis, Decca	13
19.	**GARDEN OF EDEN**—J. Valino, Vik	17
20.	**BLUE MONDAY**—F. Domino, Imperial	32
21.	**I DREAMED**—B. Johnson, Bally	23
22.	**JAMAICA FAREWELL**—H. Belafonte, Victor	18
23.	**CINDY, OH CINDY**—E. Fisher, Victor	16
24.	**HONKY TONK**—B. Doggett, King	21
25.	**CINDY, OH CINDY**—V. Martin, Glory	22
26.	**YOU DON'T OWE ME A THING**—J. Ray, Columbia	67
27.	**LOVE IS STRANGE**—Mickey & Sylvia, Groove	43
28.	**ON MY WORD OF HONOR**—Platters, Mercury	38
29.	**FRIENDLY PERSUASION**—P. Boone, Dot	24
30.	**MAMA FROM THE TRAIN**—P. Page, Mercury	20
31.	**WHEN MY BLUE MOON TURNS TO GOLD AGAIN**—E. Presley, Victor	46
32.	**JIM DANDY**—L. Baker, Atlantic	39
33.	**BANANA BOAT SONG**—S. Lawrence, Coral	50
33.	**AUCTIONEER**—L. Van Dyke, Dot	35
35.	**WISDOM OF A FOOL**—Five Keys, Capitol	40
36.	**BANANA BOAT SONG**—Fontane Sisters, Dot	50
37.	**SLOW WALK**—S. Austin, Mercury	37
38.	**TWO DIFFERENT WORLDS**—D. Rondo, Jubilee	31
39.	**CONFIDENTIAL**—S. Knight, Dot	28
40.	**BANANA BOAT SONG**—S. Vaughan, Mercury	45
41.	**CINCO ROBLES**—R. Arms, Era	64
41.	**GREENSLEEVES**—Beverly Sisters, London	47
43.	**AIN'T GOT NO HOME**—C. Henry, Argo	49
44.	**ANASTASIA**—P. Boone, Dot	47
45.	**ONE IN A MILLION**—Platters, Mercury	58
46.	**POOR BOY**—E. Presley, Victor	50
47.	**SINGING THE BLUES**—M. Robbins, Columbia	29
47.	**YOUNG LOVE**—Crew Cuts, Mercury	—
49.	**GOODNIGHT, MY LOVE**—McGuire Sisters, Coral	32
50.	**NIGHT LIGHTS**—Nat (King) Cole, Capitol	30
51.	**MUTUAL ADMIRATION SOCIETY**—T. Brewer, Coral	41
51.	**SLOW WALK**—B. Doggett, King	26
53.	**WHAT'S THE REASON (I'M NOT PLEASING YOU)?**—F. Domino, Imperial	54
54.	**KNEE DEEP IN THE BLUES**—G. Mitchell, Columbia	—
55.	**DON'T BE CRUEL**—E. Presley, Victor	41
56.	**BABY DOLL**—A. Williams, Cadence	44
57.	**BY YOU, BY YOU, BY YOU**—J. Lowe, Dot	69
58.	**JUST IN TIME**—T. Bennett, Columbia	68
59.	**PARALYZED**—E. Presley, Victor	63
60.	**CITY OF ANGELS**—Highlights, Bally	57
61.	**GIVE ME**—E. Rodgers, Columbia	96
62.	**AUCTIONEER**—C. Miller, Mercury	79
63.	**LOVE ME TENDER**—H. Rene, Victor	—
63.	**PARTY'S OVER**—Doris Day, Columbia	86
65.	**MUTUAL ADMIRATION SOCIETY**—J. P. Morgan & E. Arnold, Victor	95
66.	**BLUEBERRY HILL**—L. Armstrong, Decca	78
67.	**TRUE LOVE**—J. Powell, Verve	71
68.	**DANCING CHANDELIER**—S. Syms, Decca	84
69.	**CINCO ROBLES**—L. Paul & M. Ford, Capitol	88
70.	**MARY'S BOY CHILD**—H. Belafonte, Victor	24
71.	**I MISS YOU SO**—C. Connor, Atlantic	80
72.	**ARMEN'S THEME**—D. Seville, Liberty	86
73.	**TONIGHT YOU BELONG TO ME**—Patience & Prudence, Liberty	99
73.	**TRA LA LA**—G. Gibbs, Mercury	55
75.	**YOUR LOVE FOR ME**—F. Sinatra, Capitol	—
76.	**MONEY TREE**—M. Whiting, Capitol	61
77.	**WHY?**—Cues, Capitol	—
78.	**I LOVE MY BABY**—J. Corey, Columbia	61
78.	**PETTICOATS OF PORTUGAL**—D. Jacobs, Coral	77
80.	**LAY DOWN YOUR ARMS**—Chordettes, Cadence	100
80.	**ON LONDON BRIDGE**—J. Stafford, Columbia	58
82.	**THOUSAND MILES AWAY**—Heartbeats, Rama	65
83.	**I WALK THE LINE**—J. Cash, Sun	75
84.	**PRISCILLA**—E. Cooley, Roost	35
84.	**WRITTEN ON THE WIND**—Four Aces, Decca	93
86.	**TO THE ENDS OF THE EARTH**—Nat (King) Cole, Capitol	100
86.	**CAN I STEAL A LITTLE LOVE?**—F. Sinatra, Capitol	—
86.	**DREAMY EYES**—Four Preps, Capitol	75
89.	**ARMEN'S THEME**—J. Reisman, Victor	80
90.	**I FEEL SO GOOD**—Shirley & Lee, Aladdin	82
90.	**SINCE I MET YOU BABY**—M. Carson, Columbia	34
92.	**CANADIAN SUNSET**—E. Heywood-H. Winterhalter, Victor	74
92.	**STAR YOU WISHED UPON LAST NIGHT**—G. MacKenzie, Vik	72
94.	**HOUND DOG**—E. Presley, Victor	53
94.	**I SEE ESAU**—Ames Brothers, Victor	66
96.	**CRAZY WITH LOVE**—G. Mitchell, Columbia	96
97.	**YOU'LL NEVER, NEVER KNOW**—Platters, Mercury	88
98.	**TWO DIFFERENT WORLDS**—J. Morgan & R. Williams, Kapp	70
99.	**LITTLE BY LITTLE**—N. Brown, Savoy	—
100.	**I FEEL THE BEAT**—J. Lowe, Dot	—

CAUTION TO DEALERS AND JUKE BOX OPERATORS

The Billboard's Top 100 is NOT designed to provide tested information for buying purposes. This function is most reliably served by other regular weekly features: Best Sellers in Stores, Most Played in Juke Boxes, Coming Up Strong and Best Buys.

• Best Sellers in Stores

For survey week ending January 16

RECORDS are ranked in order of their current national selling importance at the retail level, as determined by The Billboard's weekly survey of the top volume dealers in every important market area. When significant action is reported on both sides of a record, points are combined to determine position on the chart. In such a case, both sides are listed in bold type, the leading side on top.

This Week		Last Week	Weeks on Chart
1.	SINGING THE BLUES (BMI)—G. Mitchell Crazy With Love (ASCAP)—Col 40769	1	13
2.	YOUNG LOVE (BMI)—S. James You're the Reason (I'm in Love) (BMI)—Cap 3602	3	4
3.	DON'T FORBID ME (BMI)—P. Boone ANASTASIA (ASCAP)—Dot 15521	6	6
4.	YOUNG LOVE (BMI)—T. Hunter Red Sails in the Sunset (ASCAP)—Dot 15533	12	2
5.	MOONLIGHT GAMBLER (ASCAP)—F. Laine Lotus Land (ASCAP)—Col 40780	8	7
6.	BANANA BOAT SONG (BMI)—Tarriers No Hidin' Place (BMI)—Glory 249	5	6
7.	BLUEBERRY HILL (ASCAP)—F. Domino Honey Chile (BMI)—Imperial 5407	3	16
8.	GREEN DOOR (BMI)—J. Lowe (Story of) The Little Man in Chinatown (BMI)—Dot 15486	2	18
9.	BANANA BOAT (DAY-O) (ASCAP)—H. Belafonte Star-O (ASCAP)—Vic 20-6771	14	3
10.	LOVE ME TENDER (BMI)—E. Presley Any Way You Want Me (ASCAP)—Vic 20-6643	7	15
11.	BLUE MONDAY (BMI)—F. Domino What's the Reason (I'm Not Pleasing You (ASCAP)—Imperial 5417	15	3
12.	★LOVE ME (BMI)—E. Presley Vic EPA 992	10	10
13.	JUST WALKING IN THE RAIN (BMI)—J. Ray In the Candlelight (ASCAP)—Col 40729	9	21
14.	TRUE LOVE (ASCAP)—B. Crosby-G Kelly Well, Did You Evah (ASCAP)—Cap 3507	11	17
15.	ROSE AND A BABY RUTH (BMI)—G. Hamilton IV If You Don't Know (BMI)—ABC-Paramount 9765	13	11
16.	TOO MUCH (BMI)—E. Presley Playing for Keeps (BMI)—Vic 20-6800	—	1
17.	ROCK-A-BYE YOUR BABY (ASCAP)—J. Lewis Come Rain or Come Shine (ASCAP)—Dec 30124	21	10
18.	SINCE I MET YOU BABY (BMI)—I. J. Hunter You Can't Stop This Rocking and Rolling (BMI)—Atlantic 1111	16	8
19.	JAMAICA FAREWELL (ASCAP)—H. Belafonte Once Was (ASCAP)—Vic 20-6663	17	6
20.	LOVE IS STRANGE (BMI)—Mickey & Sylvia I'm Going Home (BMI)—Groove 0175	20	3
21.	GONNA GET ALONG WITHOUT YA NOW (ASCAP)—Patience & Prudence Money Tree (ASCAP)—Liberty 55040	22	8
22.	CINDY, OH CINDY (BMI)—E. Fisher Around the World (ASCAP)—Vic 20-6677	18	16
23.	YOU DON'T OWE ME A THING (BMI)—J. Ray Look Homeward, Angel (BMI)—Col 40803	—	1
23.	ON MY WORD OF HONOR (BMI)—Platters ONE IN A MILLION (BMI)—Mercury 71011	—	1
25.	I DREAMED (BMI)—B. Johnson If It's Wrong to Love You (BMI)—Bally 1020	24	2

★(Not available as a Pop Single. Available on RCA Victor 45 EPA 992 and in RCA Victor 33⅓ "Elvis" LPM 1382.)

• Most Played in Juke Boxes

For survey week ending January 16

RECORDS are ranked in order of the greatest number of plays in juke boxes thruout the country, as determined by The Billboard's weekly survey of the nation's juke box operators. When significant play is reported on both sides of a record, points are combined to determine position on the chart. In such a case, both sides are listed in bold type, the leading side on top.

This Week		Last Week	Weeks on Chart
1.	SINGING THE BLUES (BMI)—G. Mitchell Crazy With Love (ASCAP)—Col 40769	1	12
2.	BLUEBERRY HILL (ASCAP)—F. Domino Honey Chile (BMI)—Imperial 5407	2	15
3.	GREEN DOOR (BMI)—J. Lowe (The Story of) The Little Man in Chinatown (BMI)—Dot 15486	3	16
4.	LOVE ME TENDER (BMI)—E. Presley Any Way You Want Me (ASCAP)—Vic 20-6643	4	14
5.	JUST WALKING IN THE RAIN (BMI)—J. Ray In the Candlelight (ASCAP)—Col 40729	5	19
6.	DON'T FORBID ME (BMI)—P. Boone Anastasia (ASCAP)—Dot 15521	12	3
7.	TRUE LOVE (ASCAP)—B. Crosby-G. Kelly Well, Did You Evah? (ASCAP)—Cap 3507	6	13
8.	★LOVE ME—E. Presley Vic EPA-992—BMI	9	7
9.	MOONLIGHT GAMBLER (ASCAP)—F. Laine Lotus Land (ASCAP)—Col 40780	7	4
10.	ROSE AND A BABY RUTH (BMI)—G. Hamilton IV If You Don't Know (BMI)—ABC-Paramount 9765	8	9
11.	HEY! JEALOUS LOVER (ASCAP)—F. Sinatra You Forgot All the Words (BMI)—Cap 3552	10	10
12.	BANANA BOAT SONG (BMI)—Tarriers No Hidin' Place (BMI)—Glory 249	14	3
13.	CINDY, OH CINDY (BMI)—E. Fisher Around the World (ASCAP)—Vic 20-6677	11	11
14.	YOUNG LOVE (BMI)—S. James You're the Reason (I'm in Love) (BMI)—Cap 3602	—	1
15.	YOUNG LOVE (BMI)—T. Hunter Red Sails in the Sunset (ASCAP)—Dot 15533	—	1
16.	ROCK-A-BYE YOUR BABY (ASCAP)—J. Lewis Come Rain or Come Shine (ASCAP)—Dec 30124	15	4
17.	BLUE MONDAY (BMI)—F. Domino What's the Reason (I'm Not Pleasing You) (ASCAP)—Imperial 5417	—	1
18.	HONKY TONK (PARTS I & II) (BMI)—B. Doggett King 4950	13	20
19.	GARDEN OF EDEN (BMI)—J. Valino Caravan (ASCAP)—Vik 0226	17	7
20.	SINCE I MET YOU BABY (BMI)—I. J. Hunter You Can't Stop This Rocking and Rolling (BMI)—Atlantic 1111	16	4
20.	ON MY WORD OF HONOR (BMI)—Platters One in a Million (BMI)—Mercury 71011	—	1

★(Not available as a Pop Single. Available on RCA Victor 45 EPA-992 and in RCA Victor 33⅓ "Elvis" LPM 1382.)

• Best Selling Sheet Music

Tunes are ranked in order of their current national selling importance at the sheet music jobber level.

This Week		Last Week	Weeks on Chart
1.	True Love (Buxton Hill)	3	18
1.	Singing the Blues (Acuff-Rose)	1	10
3.	Love Me Tender (Presley)	1	15
4.	Green Door (Trinity)	7	14
5.	Blueberry Hill (Chappell)	5	11
6.	Banana Boat Song (E. B. Marks-Bryden)	10	2
7.	Just Walking in the Rain (Golden West)	6	16
8.	Cindy, Oh Cindy (E. B. Marks-Bryden)	4	12
9.	Young Love (Lowery)	—	1
10.	Don't Forbid Me (Roosevelt)	—	1
11.	Moonlight Gambler (E. H. Morris)	—	1
12.	Love Me (Hill & Range)	9	7
13.	Friendly Persuasion (Feist)	8	13
14.	Hey! Jealous Lover (Barton)	12	9
15.	Mama From the Train (Remick)	—	6

• Most Played by Jockeys

For survey week ending January 16

SIDES are ranked in order of the greatest number of plays on disk jockey radio shows thruout the country. Results are based on The Billboard's weekly survey among the nation's disk jockeys. The reverse side of each record is also listed.

This Week		Last Week	Weeks on Chart
1.	SINGING THE BLUES (BMI)—G. Mitchell Crazy With Love (ASCAP)—Col 40769	1	13
2.	YOUNG LOVE (BMI)—S. James You're the Reason (I'm in Love) (BMI)—Cap 3602	4	4
3.	YOUNG LOVE (BMI)—T. Hunter Red Sails in the Sunset (ASCAP)—Dot 15533	9	2
4.	DON'T FORBID ME (BMI)—P. Boone Anastasia (ASCAP)—Dot 15521	2	5
5.	★LOVE ME (BMI)—E. Presley Vic EPA-992	3	9
6.	MOONLIGHT GAMBLER (ASCAP)—F. Laine Lotus Land (ASCAP)—Col 40780	5	7
7.	BANANA BOAT SONG (BMI)—Tarriers No Hidin' Place (BMI)—Glory 249	6	5
8.	GREEN DOOR (BMI)—J. Lowe (Story of) The Little Man in Chinatown (BMI)—Dot 15486	8	18
9.	HEY! JEALOUS LOVER (ASCAP)—F. Sinatra You Forget All the Words (BMI)—Cap 3552	13	14
10.	BANANA BOAT (DAY-O) (ASCAP)—H. Belafonte Star-O (ASCAP)—Vic 20-6771	7	3
11.	TRUE LOVE (ASCAP)—B. Crosby-G. Kelly Well, Did You Evah? (ASCAP)—Cap 3507	10	17
12.	BLUEBERRY HILL (ASCAP)—F. Domino Honey Chile (BMI)—Imperial 5407	17	15
13.	I DREAMED (BMI)—B. Johnson If It's Wrong to Love You (BMI)—Bally 1020	14	7
14.	GONNA GET ALONG WITHOUT YA NOW—Patience & Prudence Money Tree (ASCAP)—Liberty 55040	12	8
15.	LOVE ME TENDER (BMI)—E. Presley Any Way You Want Me (ASCAP)—Vic 20-6643	11	15
16.	BANANA BOAT SONG (BMI)—Fontane Sisters Honolulu Moon (ASCAP)—Dot 15527	16	3
17.	ROSE AND A BABY RUTH (BMI)—G. Hamilton IV If You Don't Know (BMI)—ABC-Paramount 9765	19	11
18.	YOUNG LOVE (BMI)—Crew Cuts Little By Little (BMI)—Mercury 71022	—	1
19.	BANANA BOAT SONG (BMI)—S. Vaughan I've Got a New Heartache (BMI)—Mercury 71020	21	3
20.	JUST WALKING IN THE RAIN (BMI)—J. Ray In the Candlelight (ASCAP)—Col 40729	18	18
21.	ROCK-A-BYE YOUR BABY (ASCAP)—J. Lewis Come Rain or Come Shine (ASCAP)—Dec 30124	20	6
22.	SINCE I MET YOU BABY (BMI)—I. J. Hunter You Can't Stop This Rocking and Rolling (BMI)—Atlantic 1111	15	8
23.	YOU DON'T OWE ME A THING (BMI)—J. Ray Look Homeward, Angel (BMI)—Col 40803	24	2
24.	BLUE MONDAY (BMI)—F. Domino What's the Reason (I'm Not Pleasing You) (ASCAP)—Imperial 5417	—	2
25.	JAMAICA FAREWELL (ASCAP)—H. Belafonte Once Was (ASCAP)—Vic 20-6663	23	7

★(Not available as a Pop Single. Available on RCA Victor 45 EPA-992 and in RCA Victor 33⅓ "Elvis" LPM 1382.)

when answering ads . . .

Say You Saw It in The Billboard

THE TOP 100

For survey week ending January 16

A list of the Top 100 RECORD SIDES in the nation according to a COMBINED TABULATION of Dealer, Disk Jockey and Juke Box Operator replies to The Billboard's weekly popular record Best Seller and Most Played surveys. Its purpose is to provide Disk Jockeys with additional programming material and to give trade exposure to NEWER records just beginning to show action in the field.

Pos.	Song, Artist, Label	This Week
1.	**SINGING THE BLUES**—G. Mitchell, Columbia	1
2.	**DON'T FORBID ME**—P. Boone, Dot	3
3.	**YOUNG LOVE**—S. James, Capitol	11
4.	**GREEN DOOR**—J. Lowe, Dot	2
4.	**MOONLIGHT GAMBLER**—F. Laine, Columbia	3
6.	**YOUNG LOVE**—T. Hunter, Dot	15
7.	**BLUEBERRY HILL**—F. Domino, Imperial	5
8.	**BANANA BOAT SONG**—Tarriers, Glory	8
8.	**LOVE ME**—E. Presley, Victor	6
10.	**LOVE ME TENDER**—E. Presley, Victor	6
11.	**TRUE LOVE**—Bing Crosby & G. Kelly, Capitol	9
12.	**JUST WALKING IN THE RAIN**—J. Ray, Columbia	10
13.	**BANANA BOAT (DAY-O)**—H. Belafonte, Victor	12
14.	**ROSE AND A BABY RUTH**—G. Hamilton IV, Epic	12
15.	**HEY! JEALOUS LOVER**—F. Sinatra, Capitol	14
16.	**BLUE MONDAY**—F. Domino, Imperial	20
17.	**ROCK-A-BYE YOUR BABY**—J. Lewis, Decca	18
18.	**GONNA GET ALONG WITHOUT YA NOW**—Patience & Prudence, Liberty	16
18.	**SINCE I MET YOU BABY**—I. J. Hunter, Atlantic	16
20.	**CINDY, OH CINDY**—E. Fisher, Victor	23
21.	**GARDEN OF EDEN**—J. Valino, Vik	19
22.	**I DREAMED**—B. Johnson, Bally	21
22.	**JAMAICA FAREWELL**—H. Belafonte, Victor	22
24.	**YOUNG LOVE**—Crew Cuts, Mercury	47
25.	**LOVE IS STRANGE**—Mickey & Sylvia, Groove	27
26.	**BANANA BOAT SONG**—Fontane Sisters, Dot	36
27.	**WHEN MY BLUE MOON TURNS TO GOLD AGAIN**—E. Presley, Victor	31
28.	**JIM DANDY**—L. Baker, Atlantic	32
28.	**YOU DON'T OWE ME A THING**—J. Ray, Columbia	26
30.	**TOO MUCH**—E. Presley, Victor	—
31.	**BANANA BOAT SONG**—S. Vaughan, Mercury	40
31.	**ONE IN A MILLION**—Platters, Mercury	45
31.	**ON MY WORD OF HONOR**—Platters, Mercury	28
34.	**AUCTIONEER**—L. Van Dyke, Dot	33
35.	**BANANA BOAT SONG**—S. Lawrence, Coral	33
35.	**POOR BOY**—E. Presley, Victor	46
37.	**ANASTASIA**—P. Boone, Dot	44
38.	**CINDY, OH CINDY**—V. Martin, Glory	25
39.	**TWO DIFFERENT WORLDS**—D. Rondo, Jubilee	38
40.	**HONKY TONK**—B. Doggett, King	24
41.	**MAMA FROM THE TRAIN**—P. Page, Mercury	30
42.	**AIN'T GOT NO HOME**—C. Henry, Argo	43
43.	**KNEE DEEP IN THE BLUES**—G. Mitchell, Columbia	54
43.	**BY YOU, BY YOU, BY YOU**—J. Lowe, Dot	57
45.	**I LOVE MY BABY**—J. Corey, Columbia	78
46.	**CINCO ROBLES**—R. Arms, Era	41
47.	**CAN I STEAL A LITTLE LOVE?**—F. Sinatra, Capitol	86
48.	**WISDOM OF A FOOL**—Five Keys, Capitol	35
49.	**FRIENDLY PERSUASION**—P. Boone, Dot	29
50.	**WHAT'S THE REASON (I'M NOT PLEASING YOU)?**—F. Domino, Imperial	53
51.	**DON'T BE CRUEL**—E. Presley, Victor	55
52.	**BABY DOLL**—A. Williams, Cadence	56
53.	**SLOW WALK**—S. Austin, Mercury	37
53.	**WRINGLE WRANGLE**—F. Parker, Disneyland	—
55.	**MUTUAL ADMIRATION SOCIETY**—T. Brewer, Coral	51
56.	**SLOW WALK**—B. Doggett, King	51
57.	**SINCE I MET YOU BABY**—M. Carson, Columbia	90
58.	**WRINGLE WRANGLE**—B. Hayes, Cadence	—
59.	**NIGHT LIGHTS**—Nat (King) Cole, Capitol	50
60.	**MONEY TREE**—M. Whiting, Capitol	76
61.	**LOOK HOMEWARD ANGEL**—J. Ray, Columbia	—
62.	**CONFIDENTIAL**—S. Knight, Dot	39
63.	**GOODNIGHT MY LOVE**—McGuire Sisters, Coral	49
63.	**AUCTIONEER**—C. Miller, Mercury	62
65.	**CITY OF ANGELS**—Highlights, Bally	60
65.	**TO NEED YOU**—Four Lads, Columbia	—
67.	**PARALYZED**—E. Presley, Victor	59
68.	**GIRL CAN'T HELP IT**—Little Richard, Specialty	—
69.	**RUDY'S ROCK**—B. Haley, Decca	—
70.	**I FEEL GOOD**—Shirley & Lee, Aladdin	90
71.	**PARTY'S OVER**—Doris Day, Columbia	63
71.	**YOUR LOVE FOR ME**—F. Sinatra, Capitol	75
73.	**I MISS YOU SO**—C. Connor, Atlantic	71
74.	**CRAZY WITH LOVE**—G. Mitchell, Columbia	96
75.	**CINCO ROBLES**—L. Paul & M. Ford, Capitol	69
76.	**WRITTEN ON THE WIND**—Four Aces, Decca	84
77.	**CANADIAN SUNSET**—E. Heywood & H. Winterhalter, Victor	92
78.	**DANCING CHANDELIER**—S. Syms, Decca	68
79.	**GIVE ME**—E. Rodgers, Columbia	61
79.	**SINGING THE BLUES**—M. Robbins, Columbia	47
79.	**TRUE LOVE**—J. Powell, Verve	67
82.	**LITTLE BY LITTLE**—N. Brown, Savoy	99
83.	**I WOULDN'T KNOW WHERE TO BEGIN**—E. Arnold, Victor	—
84.	**I FEEL THE BEAT**—J. Lowe, Dot	100
85.	**ARMEN'S THEME**—J. Resiman, Victor	89
85.	**YOU'LL NEVER, NEVER KNOW**—Platters, Mercury	97
88.	**ARMEN'S THEME**—D. Seville, Liberty	72
88.	**STAR YOU WISHED UPON LAST NIGHT**—G. MacKenzie, Vik	92
90.	**LOVE ME TENDER**—H. Rene, Victor	—
91.	**JUST IN TIME**—T. Bennett, Columbia	58
91.	**ON LONDON BRIDGE**—J. Stafford, Columbia	80
93.	**LAY DOWN YOUR ARMS**—Chordettes, Cadence	80
94.	**TEENAGE GOODNIGHT**—Chordettes, Cadence	—
94.	**SOME DAY SOON**—E. Fisher, Victor	—
96.	**DREAMY EYES**—Four Preps, Capitol	86
96.	**MONEY TREE**—Patience & Prudence, Liberty	—
98.	**THOUSAND MILES AWAY**—Heartbeats, Rama	82
98.	**TO THE ENDS OF THE EARTH**—Nat (King) Cole, Capitol	86
100.	**IN THE STILL OF THE NIGHT**—Satins, Ember	—

CAUTION TO DEALERS AND JUKE BOX OPERATORS

The Billboard's Top 100 is NOT designed to provide tested information for buying purposes. This function is most reliably served by other regular weekly features: Best Sellers in Stores, Most Played in Juke Boxes, Coming Up Strong and Best Buys.

• Best Sellers in Stores

For survey week ending January 23

RECORDS are ranked in order of their current national selling importance at the retail level, as determined by The Billboard's weekly survey of the top volume dealers in every important market area. When significant action is reported on both sides of a record, points are combined to determine position on the chart. In such a case, both sides are listed in bold type, the leading side on top.

This Week		Last Week	Weeks on Chart
1.	SINGING THE BLUES (BMI)—G. Mitchell Crazy With Love (ASCAP)—Col 40769	1	14
2.	YOUNG LOVE (BMI)—S. James You're the Reason (I'm in Love) (BMI)—Cap 3602	2	5
3.	YOUNG LOVE (BMI)—T. Hunter Red Sails in the Sunset (ASCAP)—Dot 15533	4	3
4.	DON'T FORBID ME (BMI)—P. Boone ANASTASIA (ASCAP)—Dot 15521	3	7
5.	TOO MUCH (BMI)—E. Presley PLAYING FOR KEEPS (BMI)—Vic 20-6800	16	2
6.	BANANA BOAT (DAY-O) (ASCAP)—H. Belafonte Star-O (ASCAP)—Vic 20-6771	9	4
7.	BANANA BOAT SONG (BMI)—Tarriers No Hidin' Place (BMI)—Glory 249	6	7
8.	MOONLIGHT GAMBLER (ASCAP)—F. Laine Lotus Land (ASCAP)—Col 40780	5	8
9.	BLUE MONDAY (BMI)—F. Domino WHAT'S THE REASON (I'M NOT PLEASING YOU)? (ASCAP)—Imperial 5417	11	4
10.	BLUEBERRY HILL (ASCAP)—F. Domino Honey Chile (BMI)—Imperial 5407	7	17
11.	GREEN DOOR (BMI)—J. Lowe (Story of) The Little Man in Chinatown (BMI)—Dot 15486	8	19
12.	LOVE ME TENDER (BMI)—E. Presley Any Way You Want Me (ASCAP)—Vic 20-6643	10	16
13.	★LOVE ME (BMI)—E. Presley Vic EPA 992	12	11
14.	ROSE AND A BABY RUTH (BMI)—G. Hamilton IV If You Don't Know (BMI)—ABC-Paramount 9765	15	12
15.	TRUE LOVE (ASCAP)—B. Crosby-G. Kelly Well, Did You Evah (ASCAP)—Cap 3507	14	18
16.	JUST WALKING IN THE RAIN (BMI)—J. Ray In the Candlelight (ASCAP)—Col 40729	13	22
17.	JAMAICA FAREWELL (ASCAP)—H. Belafonte Once Way (ASCAP)—Vic 20-6663	19	7
18.	LOVE IS STRANGE (BMI)—Mickey & Sylvia I'm Going Home (BMI)—Groove 0175	20	4
19.	ROCK-A-BYE YOUR BABY (ASCAP)—J. Lewis Come Rain or Come Shine (ASCAP)—Dec 30124	17	11
20.	JIM DANDY (BMI)—L. Baker Tra La La (BMI)—Atlantic 1116	—	1
21.	YOU DON'T OWE ME THING (BMI)—J. Ray Look Homeward, Angel (BMI)—Col 40803	23	2
22.	SINCE I MET YOU BABY (BMI)—J. J. Hunter You Can't Stop This Rocking and Rolling (BMI)—Atlantic 1111	18	9
23.	GONNA GET ALONG WITHOUT YA NOW (ASCAP)—Patience & Prudence Money Tree (ASCAP)—Liberty 55040	21	9
23.	HEY! JEALOUS LOVER (ASCAP)—F. Sinatra You Forgot All the Words (BMI)—Cap 3552	—	13
25.	I DREAMED (BMI)—B. Johnson If It's Wrong to Love You (BMI)—Bally 1020	25	3

★(Not available as a Pop Single, available on RCA Victor 45 EPA-992 and in RCA Victor 33⅓ "Elvis" LPM 1382.)

• Most Played in Juke Boxes

For survey week ending January 23

RECORDS are ranked in order of the greatest number of plays in juke boxes thruout the country, as determined by The Billboard's weekly survey of the nation's juke box operators. When significant play is reported on both sides of a record, points are combined to determine position on the chart. In such a case, both sides are listed in bold type, the leading side on top.

This Week		Last Week	Weeks on Chart
1.	SINGING THE BLUES (BMI)—G. Mitchell Crazy With Love (ASCAP)—Col 40769	1	13
2.	BLUEBERRY HILL (ASCAP)—F. Domino Honey Chile (BMI)—Imperial 5407	2	16
3.	DON'T FORBID ME (BMI)—P. Boone Anastasia (ASCAP)—Dot 15521	6	4
4.	GREEN DOOR (BMI)—J. Lowe (The Story of) The Little Man in Chinatown (BMI)—Dot 15486	3	17
5.	LOVE ME TENDER (BMI)—E. Presley Any Way You Want Me (ASCAP)—Vic 20-6643	4	15
6.	MOONLIGHT GAMBLER (ASCAP)—F. Laine Lotus Land (ASCAP)—Col 40780	9	5
7.	BANANA BOAT SONG (BMI)—Tarriers No Hidin' Place (BMI)—Glory 249	12	4
8.	JUST WALKING IN THE RAIN (BMI)—J. Ray In the Candlelight (ASCAP)—Col 40729	5	20
9.	YOUNG LOVE (BMI)—S. James You're the Reason (I'm in Love) (BMI)—Cap 3602	14	2
10.	TRUE LOVE (ASCAP)—B. Crosby-G. Kelly Well, Did You Evah? (ASCAP)—Cap 3507	7	14
11.	★LOVE ME—E. Presley Vic EPA-992—BMI	8	8
12.	YOUNG LOVE (BMI)—T. Hunter Red Sails in the Sunset (ASCAP)—Dot 15533	15	2
13.	BLUE MONDAY (BMI)—F. Domino WHAT'S THE REASON (I'M NOT PLEASING YOU)?—Imperial 5417	17	2
14.	ROCK-A-BYE YOUR BABY (ASCAP)—J. Lewis Come Rain or Come Shine (ASCAP)—Dec 30124	16	5
15.	ROSE AND A BABY RUTH (BMI)—G. Hamilton IV If You Don't Know (BMI)—ABC-Paramount 9765	10	10
16.	HEY! JEALOUS LOVER (ASCAP)—F. Sinatra You Forgot All the Words (BMI)—Cap 3552	11	11
17.	CINDY, OH CINDY (BMI)—E. Fisher Around the World (ASCAP)—Vic 20-6677	13	12
18.	BANANA BOAT SONG (DAY-O) (ASCAP)—H. Belafonte Star-O (ASCAP)—Vic 20-6771	—	1
19.	AUCTIONEER (ASCAP)—L. Van Dyke I Fell in Love With a Pony Tail (ASCAP)—Dot 15503	—	1
20.	SINCE I MET YOU BABY (BMI)—I. J. Hunter You Can't Stop This Rocking and Rolling (BMI)—Atlantic 1111	—	4
20.	SINGING THE BLUES (BMI)—M. Robbins I Can't Quit (BMI)—Col 21545	—	4

★(Not available as a Pop Single. Available on RCA Victor 45 EPA-992 and in RCA Victor 33⅓ "Elvis" LPM 1382.)

• Best Selling Sheet Music

Tunes are ranked in order of their current national selling importance at the sheet music jobber level.

This Week		Last Week	Weeks on Chart
1.	**Singing the Blues** (Acuff-Rose)	1	11
2.	**Love Me Tender** (Presley)	3	16
3.	**True Love** (Buxton Hill)	1	19
4.	**Banana Boat Song** (E. B. Marks-Bryden)	6	3
5.	**Blueberry Hill** (Chappell)	5	12
6.	**Green Door** (Trinity)	4	15
7.	**Young Love** (Lowery)	9	2
8.	**Cindy, Oh Cindy** (E. B. Marks-Bryden)	8	13
9.	**Just Walking in the Rain** (Golden West)	7	17
10.	**Don't Forbid Me** (Roosevelt)	10	2
10.	**Moonlight Gambler** (E. H. Morris)	11	2
12.	**Gonna Get Along Without Ya Now** (Kellum)	—	3
13.	**Anastasia** (Feist)	—	2
14.	**Love Me** (Hill & Range)	12	8
15.	**Friendly Persuasion** (Feist)	13	14

• Most Played by Jockeys

For survey week ending January 23

SIDES are ranked in order of the greatest number of plays on disk jockey radio shows thruout the country. Results are based on The Billboard's weekly survey among the nation's disk jockeys. The reverse side of each record is also listed.

This Week		Last Week	Weeks on Chart
1.	SINGING THE BLUES (BMI)—G. Mitchell Crazy With Love (ASCAP)—Col 40769	1	14
2.	YOUNG LOVE (BMI)—S. James You're the Reason (I'm in Love) (BMI)—Cap 3602	2	5
3.	DON'T FORBID ME (BMI)—P. Boone Anastasia (ASCAP)—Dot 15521	4	6
4.	YOUNG LOVE (BMI)—T. Hunter Red Sails in the Sunset (ASCAP)—Dot 15533	3	3
5.	BANANA BOAT (DAY-O) (ASCAP)—H. Belafonte Star-O (ASCAP)—Vic 20-6771	10	4
6.	MOONLIGHT GAMBLER (ASCAP)—F. Laine Lotus Land (ASCAP)—Col 40780	6	8
7.	BANANA BOAT SONG (BMI)—Tarriers No Hidin' Place (BMI)—Glory 249	7	6
8.	LOVE ME (BMI)—E. Presley Vic EPA-992	—	1
9.	TOO MUCH (BMI)—E. Presley Playing for Keeps (BMI)—Vic 20-6800	—	1
10.	I DREAMED (BMI)—B. Johnson If It's Wrong to Love You (BMI)—Bally 1020	13	8
11.	GREEN DOOR (BMI)—J. Lowe (Story of) The Little Man in Chinatown (BMI)—Dot 15486	8	19
12.	BLUE MONDAY (BMI)—F. Domino What's the Reason (I'm Not Pleasing You)? (ASCAP)—Imperial 5417	24	2
13.	YOU DON'T OWE ME A THING (BMI)—J. Ray Look Homeward, Angel (ASCAP)—Col 40803	23	3
14.	HEY! JEALOUS LOVER (ASCAP)—F. Sinatra You Forgot All the Words (BMI)—Cap 3552	9	15
15.	JAMAICA FAREWELL (ASCAP)—H. Belafonte Once Was (ASCAP)—Vic 20-6663	25	8
16.	TRUE LOVE (ASCAP)—B. Crosby-G. Kelly Well, Did You Evah? (ASCAP)—Cap 3507	11	18
17.	GONNA GET ALONG WITHOUT YA NOW—Patience & Prudence Money Tree (ASCAP)—Liberty 55040	14	9
18.	BANANA BOAT SONG (BMI)—Fontane Sisters Honolulu Moon (ASCAP)—Dot 15527	16	4
19.	BLUEBERRY HILL (ASCAP)—F. Domino Honey Chile (BMI)—Imperial 5407	12	16
20.	LOVE ME TENDER (BMI)—E. Presley Any Way You Want Me (ASCAP)—Vic 20-6643	15	16
21.	I LOVE MY BABY (ASCAP)—J. Corey Egghead (ASCAP)—Col 40794	—	1
22.	BANANA BOAT SONG (BMI)—S. Vaughan I've Got a New Heartache (BMI)—Mercury 71020	19	4
23.	ROCK-A-BYE YOUR BABY (ASCAP)—J. Lewis Come Rain or Come Shine (ASCAP)—Dec 30124	21	7
24.	SINCE I MET YOU BABY (BMI)—I. J. Hunter You Can't Stop This Rocking and Rolling (BMI)—Atlantic 1111	22	9
25.	ROSE AND A BABY RUTH (BMI)—G. Hamilton IV If You Don't Know (BMI)—ABC-Paramount 9765	17	12

★(Not available as a Pop Single. Available on RCA Victor 45 EPA-992 and in RCA Victor 33⅓ "Elvis" LPM 1382.)

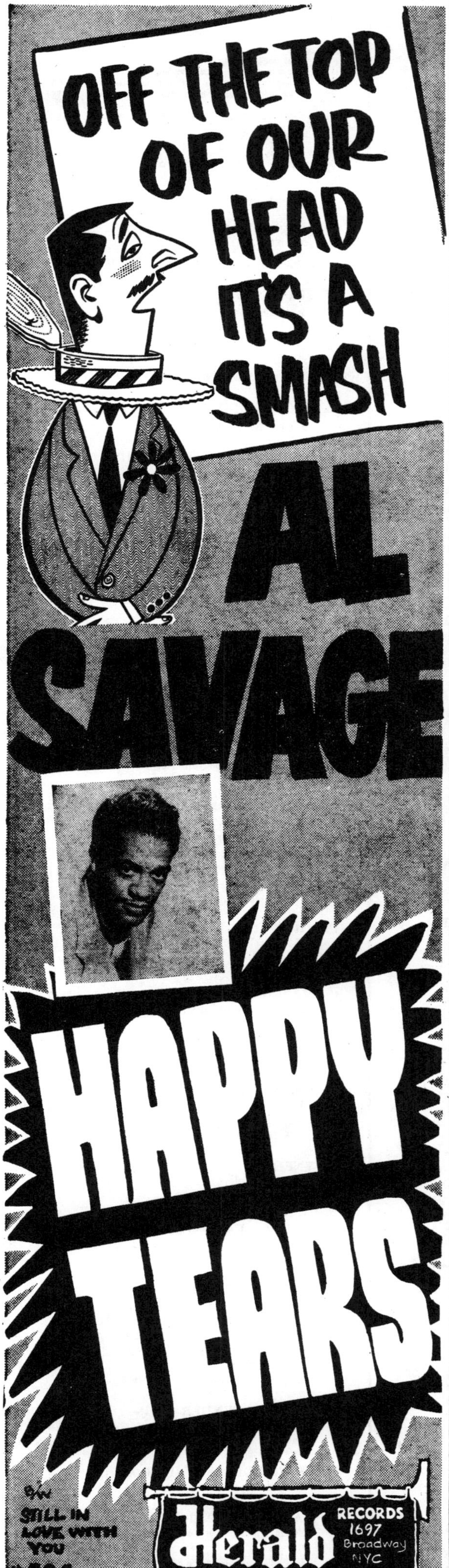

THE TOP 100

For survey week ending January 23

A list of the Top 100 RECORD SIDES in the nation according to a COMBINED TABULATION of Dealer, Disk Jockey and Juke Box Operator replies to The Billboard's weekly popular record Best Seller and Most Played surveys. Its purpose is to provide Disk Jockeys with additional programming material and to give trade exposure to NEWER records just beginning to show action in the field.

Pos.	Song, Artist, Label	This Week
1.	**SINGING THE BLUES**—G. Mitchell, Columbia	1
2.	**DON'T FORBID ME**—P. Boone, Dot	2
3.	**YOUNG LOVE**—S. James, Capitol	3
4.	**YOUNG LOVE**—T. Hunter, Dot	6
5.	**MOONLIGHT GAMBLER**—F. Laine, Columbia	4
6.	**BANANA BOAT SONG**—Tarriers, Glory	8
7.	**GREEN DOOR**—J. Lowe, Dot	4
8.	**BANANA BOAT (DAY-O)**—H. Belafonte, Victor	13
9.	**BLUEBERRY HILL**—F. Domino, Imperial	7
10.	**LOVE ME**—E. Presley, Victor	8
11.	**LOVE ME TENDER**—E. Presley, Victor	10
12.	**BLUE MONDAY**—F. Domino, Imperial	16
13.	**TRUE LOVE**—Bing Crosby-G. Kelly, Capitol	11
14.	**HEY! JEALOUS LOVER**—F, Sinatra, Capitol	15
14.	**ROSE AND A BABY RUTH**—G. Hamilton IV, ABC-Paramount	14
16.	**ROCK-A-BYE YOUR BABY**—J. Lewis, Decca	17
17.	**TOO MUCH**—E. Presley, Victor	30
18.	**JAMAICA FAREWELL**—H. Belafonte, Victor	22
19.	**JUST WALKING IN THE RAIN**—J. Ray, Columbia	12
20.	**GONNA GET ALONG WITHOUT YA NOW**—Patience & Prudence, Liberty	18
21.	**SINCE I MET YOU BABY**—I, J, Hunter, Atlantic	18
22.	**YOU DON'T OWE ME A THING**—J. Ray, Columbia	28
23.	**I DREAMED**—B. Johnson, Bally	22
24.	**JIM DANDY**—L. Baker, Atlantic	28
24.	**LOVE IS STRANGE**—Mickey & Sylvia, Groove	25
26.	**BANANA BOAT SONG**—Fontane Sisters, Dot	26
27.	**ON MY WORD OF HONOR**—Platters, Mercury	31
28.	**CINDY, OH CINDY**—E. Fisher, Victor	20
28.	**CINCO ROBLES**—R. Arms, Era	46
30.	**BANANA BOAT SONG**—S. Lawrence, Coral	35
31.	**WHO NEEDS YOU**—Four Lads, Columbia	65
32.	**GARDEN OF EDEN**—J. Valino, Vik	21
33.	**YOUNG LOVE**—Crew Cuts, Mercury	24
34.	**AIN'T GOT NO HOME**—C. Henry, Argo	42
35.	**POOR BOY**—E. Presley, Victor	35
36.	**KNEE DEEP IN THE BLUES**—G. Mitchell, Columbia	43
37.	**LOOK HOMEWARD ANGEL**—J. Ray, Columbia	61
38.	**I LOVE MY BABY**—J. Corey, Columbia	45
38.	**WHEN MY BLUE MOON TURNS TO GOLD AGAIN**—E. Presley, Victor	27
40.	**ANASTÁSIA**—P. Boone, Dot	37
41.	**PLAYING FOR KEEPS**—E. Presley, Victor	—
42.	**CAN I STEAL A LITTLE LOVE**—F. Sinatra, Capitol	47
43.	**AUCTIONEER**—L. Van Dyke, Dot	34
44.	**CINCO ROBLES**—L. Paul & M. Ford, Capitol	75
45.	**ONE IN A MILLION**—Platters, Mercury	31
46.	**BY YOU, BY YOU, BY YOU**—J. Lowe, Dot	43
47.	**WRINGLE WRANGLE**—F. Parker, Disneyland	53
48.	**SINGING THE BLUES**—M. Robbins, Columbia	79
48.	**GREENSLEEVES**—Beverly Sisters, London	—
50.	**WHAT'S THE REASON (I'M NOT PLEASING YOU)**—F. Domino, Imperial	50
51.	**HONKY TONK**—B. Doggett, King	40
52.	**BANANA BOAT SONG**—S. Vaughan, Mercury	31
53.	**TAKE ME BACK BABY**—G. Mitchell, Columbia	—
54.	**FRIENDLY PERSUASION**—P. Boone, Dot	49
55.	**SINCE I MET YOU BABY**—M. Carson, Columbia	57
56.	**DREAMY EYES**—Four Preps, Capitol	96
57.	**CINDY, OH CINDY**—V. Martin, Glory	38
58.	**DON'T BE CRÛEL**—E. Presley, Victor	50
59.	**SLOW WALK**—S. Austin, Mercury	53
59.	**TWO DIFFERENT WORLDS**—D. Rondo, Jubilee	39
61.	**MAMA FROM THE TRAIN**—P. Page, Mercury	41
61.	**WRITTEN ON THE WIND**—Four Aces, Decca	76
61.	**WISDOM OF A FOOL**—Five Keys, Capitol	48
64.	**BABY DOLL**—A. Williams, Cadence	52
64.	**WRINGLE WRANGLE**—B. Hayes, ABC-Paramount	58
66.	**MONEY TREE**—M. Whiting, Capitol	60
67.	**CONFIDENTIAL**—S. Knight, Dot	62
67.	**NIGHT LIGHTS**—Nat (King) Cole, Capitol	59
69.	**BAD BOY**—Jive Bombers, Savoy	—
70.	**I MISS YOU SO**—C. Connor, Atlantic	73
71.	**SLOW WALK**—B. Doggett, King	56
72.	**REPEAT AFTER ME**—P. Page, Mercury	—
73.	**DANCING CHANDELIER**—S. Syms, Decca	78
73.	**MONEY TREE**—Patience & Prudence, Liberty	96
75.	**RED SAILS IN THE SUNSET**—T. Hunter, Dot	—
76.	**CITY OF ANGELS**—Highlights, Bally	65
77.	**THOUSAND MILES AWAY**—Heartbeats, Rama	98
78.	**PARALYZED**—E. Presley, Victor	67
79.	**LITTLE BY LITTLE**—N. Brown, Savoy	82
79.	**PARTY'S OVER**—Doris Day, Columbia	71
81.	**CRAZY WITH LOVE**—G. Mitchell, Columbia	74
82.	**YOUR LOVE FOR ME**—F. Sinatra, Capitol	71
83.	**GOODNIGHT MY LOVE**—McGuire Sisters, Coral	63
84.	**HOLIDAY FOR TROMBONES**—P. Faith, Columbia	—
85.	**HOUND DOG**—E. Presley, Victor	—
86.	**WITHOUT LOVE**—C. McPhatter, Atlantic	—
87.	**MUTUAL ADMIRATION SOCIETY**—T. Brewer, Coral	55
87.	**WHAT IS A TEEN-AGE GIRL**—T. Edwards, Coral	—
89.	**ARMEN'S THEME**—D. Seville, Liberty	88
90.	**ARMEN'S THEME**—J. Reisman, Victor	85
91.	**I WALK THE LINE**—J. Cash, Sun	—
92.	**MARIANNE**—T. Gilkyson, Columbia	—
92.	**TREES**—A. Hibbler, Decca	—
94.	**TRUE LOVE**—J. Powell, Verve	79
95.	**AUCTIONEER**—C. Miller, Mercury	63
96.	**JUST IN TIME**—T. Bennett, Columbia	91
97.	**BLUE MOON**—E. Presley, Victor	—
97.	**FRIENDLY PERSUASION**—Four Aces, Decca	—
99.	**LOVE ME TENDER**—H. Rene, Victor	90
99.	**ON LONDON BRIDGE**—J. Stafford, Columbia	91

CAUTION TO DEALERS AND JUKE BOX OPERATORS

The Billboard's Top 100 is NOT designed to provide tested information for buying purposes. This function is most reliably served by other regular weekly features: Best Sellers in Stores, Most Played in Juke Boxes, Coming Up Strong and Best Buys.

• Best Sellers in Stores

For survey week ending January 30

RECORDS are ranked in order of their current national selling importance at the retail level, as determined by The Billboard's weekly survey of the top volume dealers in every important market area. When significant action is reported on both sides of a record, points are combined to determine position on the chart. In such a case, both sides are listed in bold type, the leading side on top.

This Week	Record	Last Week	Weeks on Chart
1.	**TOO MUCH** (BMI)—E. Presley / **PLAYING FOR KEEPS** (BMI) / Vic 20-6800	5	3
2.	**YOUNG LOVE** (BMI)—S. James / You're the Reason (I'm in Love) (BMI)—Cap 3602	2	6
3.	**DON'T FORBID ME** (BMI)—P. Boone / **ANASTASIA** (ASCAP)—Dot 15521	4	8
4.	**YOUNG LOVE** (BMI)—T. Hunter / **RED SAILS IN THE SUNSET** (ASCAP)—Dot 15533	3	4
5.	**SINGING THE BLUES** (BMI)—G. Mitchell / Crazy With Love (ASCAP)—Col 40769	1	15
6.	**BANANA BOAT (DAY-O)** (ASCAP)—H. Belafonte / Star-O (ASCAP)—Vic 20-6771	6	5
7.	**MOONLIGHT GAMBLER** (ASCAP)—F. Laine / Lotus Land (ASCAP)—Col 40780	8	9
8.	**BANANA BOAT SONG** (BMI)—Tarriers / No Hidin' Place (BMI)—Glory 249	7	8
9.	**BLUE MONDAY** (BMI)—F. Domino / What's the Reason (I'm Not Pleasing You)? (ASCAP)—Imperial 5417	9	5
10.	**GREEN DOOR** (BMI)—J. Lowe / (Story of) The Little Man in Chinatown (BMI)—Dot 15486	11	20
11.	**BLUEBERRY HILL** (ASCAP)—F. Domino / Honey Chile (BMI)—Imperial 5407	10	18
12.	**LOVE ME TENDER** (BMI)—E. Presley / Any Way You Want Me (ASCAP)—Vic 20-6643	12	17
13.	**★LOVE ME** (BMI)—E. Presley / Vic EPA-992	13	12
14.	**ROCK-A-BYE YOUR BABY** (ASCAP)—J. Lewis / Come Rain or Come Shine (ASCAP)—Dec 30124	19	12
15.	**YOU DON'T OWE ME A THING** (BMI)—J. Ray / **LOOK HOMEWARD, ANGEL** (BMI)—Col 40803	21	3
16.	**ROSE AND A BABY RUTH** (BMI)—G. Hamilton IV / If You Don't Know (BMI)—ABC-Paramount 9765	14	13
17.	**JAMAICA FAREWELL** (ASCAP)—H. Belafonte / Once Was (ASCAP)—Vic 20-6663	17	8
18.	**TRUE LOVE** (ASCAP)—B. Crosby-G. Kelly / Well, Did You Evah? (ASCAP)—Cap 3507	15	19
18.	**LOVE IS STRANGE** (BMI)—Mickey & Sylvia / I'm Going Home (BMI)—Groove 0175	18	5
20.	**ONE IN A MILLION** (BMI)—Platters / **ON MY WORD OF HONOR** (BMI)—Mercury 71011	—	2
21.	**WRINGLE WRANGLE** (ASCAP)—F. Parker / Wringle Wrangle/Camarata (ASCAP)—Disneyland F 39	—	1
22.	**JUST WALKING IN THE RAIN** (BMI)—J. Ray / In the Candlelight (ASCAP)—Col 40729	16	23
23.	**JIM DANDY** (BMI)—L. Baker / Tra La La (BMI)—Atlantic 1116	20	2
24.	**SINCE I MET YOU BABY** (BMI)—I. J. Hunter / You Can't Stop This Rocking and Rolling (BMI)—Atlantic 1111	22	10
25.	**HEY! JEALOUS LOVER** (ASCAP)—F. Sinatra / You Forgot All the Words (BMI)—Cap 3552	23	14

★ (Not available as a Pop Single, Available on RCA Victor 45 EPA-992 and on RCA Victor 33⅓ "Elvis" LPM 1382)

• Most Played in Juke Boxes

For survey week ending January 30

RECORDS are ranked in order of the greatest number of plays in juke boxes thruout the country, as determined by The Billboard's weekly survey of the nation's juke box operators. When significant play is reported on both sides of a record, points are combined to determine position on the chart. In such a case, both sides are listed in bold type, the leading side on top.

This Week	Record	Last Week	Weeks on Chart
1.	**SINGING THE BLUES** (BMI)—G. Mitchell / Crazy With Love (ASCAP)—Col 40769	1	14
2.	**DON'T FORBID ME** (BMI)—P. Boone / Anastasia (ASCAP)—Dot 15521	3	5
3.	**MOONLIGHT GAMBLER** (ASCAP)—F. Laine / Lotus Land (ASCAP)—Col 40780	6	6
4.	**BANANA BOAT SONG** (BMI)—Tarriers / No Hidin' Place (BMI)—Glory 249	7	5
5.	**BLUEBERRY HILL** (ASCAP)—F. Domino / Honey Chile (BMI)—Imperial 5407	2	17
6.	**YOUNG LOVE** (BMI)—S. James / You're the Reason (I'm in Love) (BMI)—Cap 3602	9	3
7.	**YOUNG LOVE** (BMI)—T. Hunter / Red Sails in the Sunset (ASCAP)—Dot 15533	12	3
8.	**GREEN DOOR** (BMI)—J. Lowe / (The Story of) The Little Man in Chinatown (BMI)—Dot 15486	4	18
9.	**LOVE ME TENDER** (BMI)—E. Presley / Any Way You Want Me (ASCAP)—Vic 20-6643	5	16
10.	**BLUE MONDAY** (BMI)—F. Domino / **WHAT'S THE REASON (I'M NOT PLEASING YOU)?** (ASCAP)—Imperial 5417	13	3
11.	**★LOVE ME**—E. Presley / Vic EPA-992—BMI	11	9
12.	**TRUE LOVE** (ASCAP)—B. Crosby-G. Kelly / Well, Did You Evah? (ASCAP)—Cap 3507	10	15
13.	**ROSE AND A BABY RUTH** (BMI)—G. Hamilton IV / If You Don't Know (BMI)—ABC-Paramount 9765	15	11
14.	**BANANA BOAT (DAY-O)** (ASCAP)—H. Belafonte / Star-O (ASCAP)—Vic 20-6771	18	2
15.	**ROCK-A-BYE YOUR BABY** (ASCAP)—J. Lewis / Come Rain or Come Shine (ASCAP)—Dec 30124	14	6
16.	**TOO MUCH** (BMI)—E. Presley / Playing for Keeps (BMI)—Vic 20-6800	—	1
17.	**JUST WALKING IN THE RAIN** (ASCAP)—F. Sinatra / In the Candlelight (ASCAP)—Col 40729	8	21
18.	**HEY! JEALOUS LOVER** (ASCAP)—F. Sinatra / You Forgot All the Words (BMI)—Cap 3552	16	12
18.	**YOUNG LOVE** (BMI)—Crew Cuts / Little by Little (BMI)—Mercury 71022	—	1
20.	**YOU DON'T OWE ME A THING** (BMI)—J. Ray / Look Homeward, Angel (BMI)—Col 40803	—	1

★ (Not available as a Pop Single. Available on RCA Victor 45 EPA-992 and on RCA Victor 33⅓ "Elvis" LPM 1382)

• Best Selling Sheet Music

Tunes are ranked in order of their current national selling importance at the sheet music jobber level.

This Week	Title	Last Week	Weeks on Chart
1.	**Singing the Blues** (Acuff-Rose)	1	12
2.	**Young Love** (Lowery)	7	3
3.	**True Love** (Buxton Hill)	3	20
4.	**Love Me Tender** (Presley)	2	17
5.	**Banana Boat Song** (E. B. Marks-Bryden)	4	4
6.	**Don't Forbid Me** (Roosevelt)	10	3
7.	**Green Door** (Trinity)	6	16
8.	**Blueberry Hill** (Chappell)	5	13
9.	**Moonlight Gambler** (E. H. Morris)	10	3
10.	**Cindy, Oh Cindy** (E. B. Marks-Bryden)	8	14
11.	**Gonna Get Along Without Ya Now** (Kellum)	12	4
12.	**Since I Met You Baby** (Progressive)	—	1
13.	**Anastasia** (Feist)	13	3
14.	**Just Walking in the Rain** (Golden West)	9	18
15.	**Love Me** (Hill & Range)	14	9

• Most Played by Jockeys

For survey week ending January 30

SIDES are ranked in order of the greatest number of plays on disk jockey radio shows thruout the country. Results are based on The Billboard's weekly survey among the nation's disk jockeys. The reverse side of each record is also listed.

This Week	Record	Last Week	Weeks on Chart
1.	**YOUNG LOVE** (BMI)—S. James / You're the Reason (I'm in Love) (BMI)—Cap 3602	2	6
2.	**DON'T FORBID ME** (BMI)—P. Boone / Anastasia (ASCAP)—Dot 15521	3	7
3.	**SINGING THE BLUES** (BMI)—G. Mitchell / Crazy With Love (ASCAP)—Col 40769	1	15
4.	**YOUNG LOVE** (BMI)—T. Hunter / Red Sails in the Sunset (ASCAP)—Dot 15533	4	4
5.	**BANANA BOAT (DAY-O)** (ASCAP)—H. Belafonte / Star-O (ASCAP)—Vic 20-6771	5	5
6.	**TOO MUCH** (BMI)—E. Presley / Playing for Keeps (BMI)—Vic 20-6800	9	2
7.	**BANANA BOAT SONG** (BMI)—Tarriers / No Hidin' Place (BMI)—Glory 249	7	7
8.	**MOONLIGHT GAMBLER** (ASCAP)—F. Laine / Lotus Land (ASCAP)—Col 40780	6	9
9.	**I DREAMED** (BMI)—B. Johnson / If It's Wrong to Love You (BMI)—Bally 1020	10	9
10.	**★LOVE ME** (BMI)—E. Presley / Vic EPA-992	8	11
11.	**YOU DON'T OWE ME A THING** (BMI)—J. Ray / Look Homeward, Angel (BMI)—Col 40803	13	4
12.	**BLUE MONDAY** (BMI)—F. Domino / What's the Reason (I'm Not Pleasing You)? (ASCAP)—Imperial 5417	12	3
13.	**BANANA BOAT SONG** (BMI)—Fontane Sisters / Honolulu Moon (ASCAP)—Dot 15527	18	5
14.	**GREEN DOOR** (BMI)—J. Lowe / (The Story of) The Little Man in Chinatown (BMI)—Dot 15486	11	20
15.	**TRUE LOVE** (ASCAP)—B. Crosby-G. Kelly / Well, Did You Evah? (ASCAP)—Cap 3507	16	19
16.	**MARIANNE** (BMI)—T. Gilkyson / Goodbye, Chiquita (BMI)—Col 40817	—	1
17.	**YOUNG LOVE** (BMI)—Crew Cuts / Little by Little (BMI)—Mercury 71022	—	2
18.	**SINCE I MET YOU BABY** (BMI)—I. J. Hunter / You Can't Stop This Rocking and Rolling (BMI)—Atlantic 1111	24	10
19.	**KNEE DEEP IN THE BLUES** (BMI)—G. Mitchell / Take Me Back (ASCAP)—Col 40820	—	1
20.	**JAMAICA FAREWELL** (ASCAP)—H. Belafonte / Once Was (ASCAP)—Vic 20-6663	15	9
21.	**LOVE IS STRANGE** (BMI)—Mickey & Sylvia / I'm Going Home (BMI)—Groove 0175	—	1
22.	**BLUEBERRY HILL** (ASCAP)—F. Domino / Honey Chile (BMI)—Imperial 5407	19	17
23.	**LOVE ME TENDER** (BMI)—E. Presley / Any Way You Want Me (ASCAP)—Vic 20-6643	20	17
24.	**CINCO ROBLES** (BMI)—R. Arms / World Is Made of Lisa (BMI)—Era 1026	—	1
24.	**MARIANNE** (BMI)—Hilltoppers / You're Wasting Your Time (ASCAP)—Dot 15537	—	1

★ (Not available as a Pop Single. Available on RCA Victor 45 EPA-992 and on RCA Victor 33⅓ "Elvis" LPM 1382)

THE TOP 100

For survey week ending January 30

A list of the Top 100 RECORD SIDES in the nation according to a COMBINED TABULATION of Dealer, Disk Jockey and Juke Box Operator replies to The Billboard's weekly popular record Best Seller and Most Played surveys. Its purpose is to provide Disk Jockeys with additional programming material and to give trade exposure to NEWER records just beginning to show action in the field.

Pos.	Song, Artist, Label	Last Week
1.	DON'T FORBID ME, P. Boone, Dot	2
2.	SINGING THE BLUES, G. Mitchell, Columbia	1
3.	YOUNG LOVE, S. James, Capitol	3
4.	YOUNG LOVE, T. Hunter, Dot	4
5.	MOONLIGHT GAMBLER, F. Laine, Columbia	5
6.	BANANA BOAT SONG, Tarriers, Glory	6
7.	TOO MUCH, E. Presley, Victor	17
8.	BANANA BOAT (DAY-O), H. Belafonte, Victor	8
9.	BLUE MONDAY, F. Domino, Imperial	12
10.	GREEN DOOR, J. Lowe, Dot	7
11.	LOVE ME, E. Presley, Victor	10
12.	BLUEBERRY HILL, F. Domino, Imperial	9
13.	LOVE ME TENDER, E. Presley, Victor	11
13.	TRUE LOVE, Bing Crosby & G. Kelly, Capitol	13
15.	YOU DON'T OWE ME A THING, J. Ray, Columbia	22
16.	ROCK-A-BYE YOUR BABY, J. Lewis, Decca	16
17.	JAMAICA FAREWELL, H. Belafonte, Victor	18
18.	I DREAMED, B. Johnson, Bally	23
18.	SINCE I MET YOU BABY, I. J Hunter, Atlantic	21
20.	LOVE IS STRANGE, Mickey & Sylvia, Groove	24
21.	HEY! JEALOUS LOVER, F. Sinatra, Capitol	14
21.	ROSE AND A BABY RUTH, G. Hamilton IV, ABC-Paramount	14
23.	KNEE DEEP IN THE BLUES, G. Mitchell, Columbia	36
24.	JUST WALKING IN THE RAIN, J. Ray, Columbia	19
25.	BANANA BOAT SONG, Fontane Sisters, Dot	26
25.	CINCO ROBLES, R. Arms, Era	28
27.	WHO NEEDS YOU, Four Lads, Columbia	31
28.	GONNA GET ALONG WITHOUT YA NOW, Patience & Prudence, Liberty	20
29.	JIM DANDY, L. Baker, Atlantic	24
29.	ON MY WORD OF HONOR, Platters, Mercury	27
31.	YOUNG LOVE, Crew Cuts, Mercury	33
32.	CAN I STEAL A LITTLE LOVE? F. Sinatra, Capitol	42
32.	I LOVE MY BABY, J. Corey, Columbia	38
34.	BANANA BOAT SONG, S. Lawrence, Coral	30
35.	AIN'T GOT NO HOME, C. Henry, Argo	34
36.	LOOK HOMEWARD, ANGEL, J. Ray, Columbia	37
37.	BANANA BOAT SONG, S. Vaughan, Mercury	52
38.	CINDY, OH CINDY, E. Fisher, Victor	28
38.	ONE IN A MILLION, Platters, Mercury	45
40.	PLAYING FOR KEEPS, E. Presley, Victor	41
41.	MARIANNE, T. Gilkyson, Columbia	92
42.	GARDEN OF EDEN, J. Valino, Vik	32
43.	MARIANNE, Hilltoppers, Dot	—
44.	WHEN MY BLUE MOON TURNS TO GOLD AGAIN, E. Presley, Victor	38
45.	WRINGLE WRANGLE, F. Parker, Disneyland	47
46.	WRINGLE WRANGLE, B. Hayes, ABC-Paramount	64
47.	AUCTIONEER, L. Van Dyke, Dot	43
48.	POOR BOY, E. Presley, Victor	35
49.	ANASTASIA, P. Boone, Dot	40
50.	MAMA FROM THE TRAIN, P. Page, Mercury	61
51.	FRIENDLY PERSUASION, P. Boone, Dot	54
52.	I MISS YOU SO, C Connor, Atlantic	70
53.	CINCO ROBLES, L. Paul & Mary Ford, Capitol	44
53.	REPEAT AFTER ME, P. Page, Mercury	72
55.	MONEY TREE, M. Whiting, Capitol	66
55.	TAKE ME BACK BABY, G. Mitchell, Columbia	53
57.	GIRL CAN'T HELP IT, Little Richard, Specialty	—
57.	RED SAILS IN THE SUNSET, T. Hunter, Dot	75
57.	WHAT'S THE REASON (I'M NOT PLEASING YOU)? F. Domino, Imperial	50
60.	WHAT IS A TEEN-AGE GIRL? T. Edwards, Coral	87
61.	HONKY TONK, B. Doggett, King	51
62.	GREENSLEEVES, Beverly Sisters, London	48
63.	LITTLE BY LITTLE, N Brown, Savoy	79
63.	SLOW WALK, S. Austin, Mercury	59
65.	BABY DOLL, A. Williams, Cadence	64
66.	SINGING THE BLUES, M. Robbins, Columbia	48
66.	SINCE I MET YOU BABY, M. Carson, Columbia	55
68.	BY YOU, BY YOU, BY YOU, J. Lowe, Dot	46
68.	WITHOUT LOVE, C. McPhatter, Atlantic	86
70.	BALLERINA, Nat (King) Cole, Capitol	—
71.	WONDERFUL WONDERFUL, J. Mathis, Columbia	—
72.	WISDOM OF A FOOL, Five Keys, Capitol	61
73.	WRITTEN ON THE WIND, Four Aces, Decca	61
74.	CHANTEZ CHANTEZ, D Shore, Victor	—
75.	CINDY, OH CINDY, V. Martin, Glory	57
76.	YOUR LOVE FOR ME, F. Sinatra, Capitol	82
76.	BAD BOY, Jive Bombers, Savoy	69
76.	DREAMY EYES, Four Preps, Capitol	56
79.	SLOW WALK, B Doggett, King	71
80.	THOUSAND MILES AWAY, Heartbeats, Rama	77
81.	TWO DIFFERENT WORLDS, D. Rondo, Jubilee	59
82.	CRAZY WITH LOVE, G Mitchell, Columbia	81
83.	DON'T BE CRUEL, E. Presley, Victor	58
83.	RUDY'S ROCK, B. Haley, Decca	—
85.	NIGHT LIGHTS, Nat (King) Cole, Capitol	67
86.	GIVE ME, E. Rodgers, Columbia	—
86.	MUTUAL ADMIRATION SOCIETY, J. P. Morgan & E. Arnold, Victor	—
88.	MONEY TREE, Patience & Prudence, Liberty	73
89.	DANCING CHANDELIER, S. Syms, Decca	73
90.	YOU ARE MY FIRST LOVE, Nat (King) Cole, Capitol	—
91.	TRUE LOVE, J. Powell, Verve	94
92.	PARALYZED, E. Presley, Victor	78
92.	MUTUAL ADMIRATION SOCIETY, T. Brewer, Coral	87
92.	ARMEN'S THEME, J. Reisman, Victor	90
92.	ON LONDON BRIDGE, J. Stafford, Columbia	99
96.	WHAT IS A TEEN-AGE BOY? T. Edwards, Coral	—
97.	CONFIDENTIAL, S. Knight, Dot	67
97.	PARTY'S OVER, Doris Day, Columbia	79
99.	FRIENDLY PERSUASION, Four Aces, Decca	97
99.	I WALK THE LINE, J. Cash, Sun	91
99.	I FEEL THE BEAT, J. Lowe, Dot	—

CAUTION TO DEALERS AND JUKE BOX OPERATORS

The Billboard's Top 100 is NOT designed to provide tested information for buying purposes. This function is most reliably served by other regular weekly features: Best Sellers in Stores, Most Played in Juke Boxes, Coming Up Strong and Best Buys.

• Best Sellers in Stores

For survey week ending February 6

RECORDS are ranked in order of their current national selling importance at the retail level, as determined by The Billboard's weekly survey of the top volume dealers in every important market area. When significant action is reported on both sides of a record, points are combined to determine position on the chart. In such a case, both sides are listed in bold type, the leading side on top.

This Week		Last Week	Weeks on Chart
1.	TOO MUCH (BMI)—E. Presley Playing for Keeps (BMI)—Vic 20-6800	1	4
2.	YOUNG LOVE (BMI)—T. Hunter Red Sails in the Sunset (ASCAP)—Dot 15533	4	5
3.	DON'T FORBID ME (BMI)—P. Boone ANASTASIA (ASCAP)—Dot 15521	3	9
4.	YOUNG LOVE (BMI)—S. James You're the Reason (I'm in Love) (BMI)—Cap 3602	2	7
5.	BANANA BOAT (DAY-O) (ASCAP)—H. Belafonte Star-O (ASCAP)—Vic 20-6771	6	6
6.	SINGING THE BLUES (BMI)—G. Mitchell Crazy With Love (ASCAP)—Col 40769	5	16
7.	BANANA BOAT SONG (BMI)—Tarriers No Hidin' Place (BMI)—Glory 249	8	9
8.	MOONLIGHT GAMBLER (ASCAP)—F. Laine Lotus Land (ASCAP)—Col 40780	7	10
9.	BLUE MONDAY (BMI)—F. Domino What's the Reason (I'm Not Pleasing You)? (ASCAP)—Imperial 5417	9	6
10.	YOU DON'T OWE ME A THING (BMI)—J. Ray LOOK HOMEWARD, ANGEL (BMI)—Col 40803	15	4
11.	MARIANNE (BMI)—T. Gilkyson Goodbye, Chiquita (BMI)—Col 40817	—	1
12.	LOVE IS STRANGE (BMI)—Mickey & Sylvia I'm Going Home (BMI)—Groove 0175	18	6
13.	ROCK-A-BYE YOUR BABY (ASCAP)—J. Lewis Come Rain or Come Shine (ASCAP)—Dec 30124	14	13
13.	SINCE I MET YOU BABY (BMI)—I. J. Hunter You Can't Stop This Rocking and Rolling (BMI)—Atlantic 1111	24	11
15.	BLUEBERRY HILL (ASCAP)—F. Domino Honey Chile (BMI)—Imperial 5407	11	19
16.	WRINGLE WRANGLE (ASCAP)—F. Parker Wringle Wrangle/Camarata (ASCAP)—Disneyland F 39	21	2
17.	JIM DANDY (BMI)—L. Baker Tra La La (BMI)—Atlantic 1116	23	3
18.	LOVE ME TENDER (BMI)—E. Presley Any Way You Want Me (ASCAP)—Vic 20-6643	12	18
18.	JAMAICA FAREWELL (ASCAP)—H. Belafonte Once Was (ASCAP)—Vic 20-6663	17	9
20.	GREEN DOOR (BMI)—J. Lowe (The Story of) The Little Man in Chinatown (BMI)—Dot 15486	10	21
21.	KNEE DEEP IN THE BLUES (BMI)—G. Mitchell TAKE ME BACK (ASCAP)—Col 40820	—	1
22.	★LOVE ME (BMI)—E. Presley Vic EPA-992	13	13
22.	TRUE LOVE (ASCAP)—B. Crosby-G. Kelly Well, Did You Evah? (ASCAP)—Cap 3507	18	20
22.	WHO NEEDS YOU (ASCAP)—Four Lads It's So Easy to Forget (BMI)— Col 40811	—	1
25.	I DREAMED (BMI)—B. Johnson If It's Wrong to Love You (BMI)—Bally 1020	—	4
25.	MARIANNE (BMI)—Hilltoppers You're Wasting Your Time (ASCAP)—Dot 15537	—	1

★ (Not available as a Pop Single. Available on RCA Victor 45 EPA 992 and in RCA Victor 33⅓ "Elvis" LPM 1382)

• Most Played in Juke Boxes

For survey week ending February 6

RECORDS are ranked in order of the greatest number of plays in juke boxes thruout the country, as determined by The Billboard's weekly survey of the nation's juke box operators. When significant play is reported on both sides of a record, points are combined to determine position on the chart. In such a case, both sides are listed in bold type, the leading side on top.

This Week		Last Week	Weeks on Chart
1.	SINGING THE BLUES (BMI)—G. Mitchell Crazy With Love (ASCAP)—Col 40769	1	15
2.	DON'T FORBID ME (BMI)—P. Boone Anastasia (ASCAP)—Dot 15521	2	6
3.	YOUNG LOVE (BMI)—T. Hunter Red Sails in the Sunset (ASCAP)—Dot 15533	7	4
4.	YOUNG LOVE (BMI)—S. James You're the Reason (I'm in Love) (BMI)—Cap 3602	6	4
5.	MOONLIGHT GAMBLER (ASCAP)—F. Laine Lotus Land (ASCAP)—Col 40780	3	7
6.	BANANA BOAT SONG (BMI)—Tarriers No Hidin' Place (BMI)—Glory 249	4	6
7.	TOO MUCH (BMI)—E. Presley Playing for Keeps (BMI)—Vic 20-6800	16	2
8.	BLUEBERRY HILL (ASCAP)—F. Domino Honey Chile (BMI)—Imperial 5407	5	18
9.	BLUE MONDAY (BMI)—F. Domino What's the Reason (I'm Not Pleasing You)? (ASCAP)—Imperial 5417	10	4
10.	GREEN DOOR (BMI)—J. Lowe (The Story of) The Little Man in Chinatown (BMI)—Dot 15486	8	19
11.	BANANA BOAT SONG (DAY-O) (ASCAP)—H. Belafonte Star-O (ASCAP)—Vic 20-6771	14	3
12.	★LOVE ME—E. Presley Vic EPA-992—BMI	11	10
13.	LOVE ME TENDER (BMI)—E. Presley Any Way You Want Me (ASCAP)—Vic 20-6643	9	17
14.	YOU DON'T OWE ME A THING (BMI)—J. Ray Look Homeward, Angel (BMI)—Col 40803	20	2
15.	TRUE LOVE (ASCAP)—B. Crosby G. Kelly Well, Did You Evah? (ASCAP)—Cap 3507	12	16
16.	ROCK-A-BYE YOUR BABY (ASCAP)—J. Lewis Come Rain or Come Shine (ASCAP)—Dec 30124	15	7
17.	YOUNG LOVE (BMI)—Crew Cuts Little by Little (BMI)—Mercury 71022	18	2
18.	KNEE DEEP IN THE BLUES (BMI)—G. Mitchell Take Me Back (ACAP)—Col 40820	—	1
18.	I DREAMED (BMI)—B. Johnson If It's Wrong to Love You (BMI)—Bally 1020	—	1
20.	ROSE AND A BABY RUTH (BMI)—G. Hamilton IV If You Don't Know (BMI)—ABC-Paramount 9765	13	12

★ (Not available as a Pop Single. Available on RCA Victor 45 EPA-992 and on RCA Victor 33⅓ "Elvis" LPM 1382)

• Best Selling Sheet Music

Tunes are ranked in order of their current selling importance at the sheet music jobber level.

This Week		Last Week	Weeks on Chart
1.	Banana Boat Song (E. B. Marks-Bryden)	5	5
2.	Young Love (Lowery)	2	4
3.	True Love (Buxton Hill)	3	21
4.	Singing the Blues (Acuff-Rose)	1	13
5.	Love Me Tender (Presley)	4	18
6.	Don't Forbid Me (Roosevelt)	6	4
7.	Cinco Robles (Warman)	—	1
8.	Cindy, Oh Cindy (E. B. Marks-Bryden)	10	15
9.	Anastasia (Feist)	13	4
10.	Moonlight Gambler (E. H. Morris)	9	4
11.	Green Door (Trinity)	7	17
12.	Blueberry Hill (Chappell)	8	14
13.	Too Much (Southern Belle-Presley)	—	1
14.	Gonna Get Along Without Ya Now (Kellum)	11	8
14.	Since I Met You Baby (Progressive)	12	2

• Most Played by Jockeys

For survey week ending February 6

SIDES are ranked in order of the greatest number of plays on disk jockey radio shows thruout the country. Results are based on The Billboard's weekly survey among the nation's disk jockeys. The reverse side of each record is also listed.

This Week		Last Week	Weeks on Chart
1.	YOUNG LOVE (BMI)—T. Hunter Red Sails in the Sunset (ASCAP)—Dot 15533	4	5
2.	YOUNG LOVE (BMI)—S. James You're the Reason (I'm in Love) (BMI)—Cap 3602	1	7
3.	DON'T FORBID ME (BMI)—P. Boone Anastasia (ASCAP)—Dot 15521	2	8
4.	TOO MUCH (BMI)—E. Presley Playing for Keeps (BMI)—Vic 20-6800	6	3
5.	BANANA BOAT SONG (DAY-O) (ASCAP)—H. Belafonte Star-O (ASCAP)—Vic 20-6771	5	6
6.	SINGING THE BLUES (BMI)—G. Mitchell Crazy With Love (ASCAP)—Col 40769	3	16
7.	MOONLIGHT GAMBLER (ASCAP)—F. Laine Lotus Land (ASCAP)—Col 40780	8	10
8.	BANANA BOAT SONG (BMI)—Tarriers No Hidin' Place (BMI)—Glory 249	7	8
9.	I DREAMED (BMI)—B. Johnson If It's Wrong to Love You (BMI)—Bally 1020	9	10
10.	YOU DON'T OWE ME A THING (BMI)—J. Ray Look Homeward, Angel (BMI)—Col 40803	11	5
11.	BLUE MONDAY (BMI)—F. Domino What's the Reason (I'm Not Pleasing You)? (ASCAP)—Imperial 5417	12	4
12.	MARIANNE (BMI)—Hilltoppers You're Wasting Your Time (ASCAP)—Dot 15537	24	2
13.	MARIANNE (BMI)—T. Gilkyson Goodbye, Chiquita (BMI)—Col 40817	16	2
14.	LOVE IS STRANGE (BMI)—Mickey & Sylvia I'm Going Home (BMI)—Groove 0175	21	2
15.	WHO NEEDS YOU? (ASCAP)—Four Lads It's So Easy to Forget (BMI)—Col 40811	—	1
16.	★LOVE ME (BMI)—E. Presley Vic EPA-992	10	12
17.	BANANA BOAT SONG (BMI)—Fontane Sisters Honolulu Moon (ASCAP)—Dot 15527	13	6
18.	BANANA BOAT SONG (BMI)—S. Lawrence Long Before I Knew You (ASCAP)—Coral 61761	—	1
19.	KNEE DEEP IN THE BLUES (BMI)—G. Mitchell Take Me Back (ASCAP)—Col 40820	19	2
20.	JIM DANDY (BMI)—L. Baker Tra La La (BMI)—Atlantic 1116	—	1
21.	TRUE LOVE (ASCAP)—B. Crosby-G. Kelly Well, Did You Evah? (ASCAP)—Cap 3507	15	20
22.	GREEN DOOR (BMI)—J. Lowe (The Story of) The Little Man in Chinatown (BMI)—Dot 15486	14	21
22.	CAN I STEAL A LITTLE LOVE? (ASCAP)—F. Sinatra Your Love for Me (BMI)—Cap 3608	—	1
24.	PLAYING FOR KEEPS (BMI)—E. Presley Too Much (BMI)—Vic 20-6800	—	1
25.	ROCK-A-BYE YOUR BABY (ASCAP)—J. Lewis Come Rain or Come Shine (ASCAP)—Dec 30124	—	8

★ (Not available as a Pop Single. Available on RCA Victor 45 EPA-992 and on RCA Victor 33⅓ "Elvis" LPM 1382)

THE TOP 100

For survey week ending February 6

A list of the Top 100 RECORD SIDES in the nation according to a COMBINED TABULATION of Dealer, Disk Jockey and Juke Box Operator replies to The Billboard's weekly popular record Best Seller and Most Played surveys. Its purpose is to provide Disk Jockeys with additional programming material and to give trade exposure to NEWER records just beginning to show action in the field.

Pos.	Song, Artist, Label	Last Week
1.	**YOUNG LOVE,** T. Hunter, Dot	4
2.	**DON'T FORBID ME,** P. Boone, Dot	1
2.	**YOUNG LOVE,** S. James, Capitol	3
4.	**TOO MUCH,** E. Presley, Victor	7
5.	**SINGING THE BLUES,** G. Mitchell, Columbia	2
6.	**MOONLIGHT GAMBLER,** F. Laine, Columbia	5
7.	**BANANA BOAT (DAY-O),** H. Belafonte, Victor	8
7.	**BANANA BOAT SONG,** Tarriers, Glory	6
9.	**BLUE MONDAY, F. Domino,** Imperial	9
10.	**YOU DON'T OWE ME A THING,** J. Ray, Columbia	15
11.	**LOVE ME,** E. Presley, Victor	11
12.	**GREEN DOOR,** J. Lowe, Dot	10
12.	**I DREAMED,** B. Johnson, Bally	18
14.	**ROCK-A-BYE YOUR BABY,** J. Lewis, Decca	16
15.	**BLUEBERRY HILL,** F. Domino, Imperial	12
16.	**TRUE LOVE,** Bing Crosby & G. Kelly, Capitol	13
17.	**LOVE IS STRANGE,** Mickey & Sylvia, Groove	20
18.	**MARIANNE,** Hilltoppers, Dot	43
19.	**KNEE DEEP IN THE BLUES,** G. Mitchell, Columbia	23
20.	**JAMAICA FAREWELL,** H. Belafonte, Victor	17
21.	**WHO NEEDS YOU,** Four Lads, Columbia	27
22.	**BANANA BOAT SONG,** Fontane Sisters, Dot	25
22.	**MARIANNE,** T. Gilkyson, Columbia	41
24.	**SINCE I MET YOU BABY,** I. J. Hunter, Atlantic	18
25.	**ROSE AND A BABY RUTH,** G. Hamilton IV, ABC-Paramount	21
26.	**LOVE ME TENDER,** E. Presley, Victor	13
27.	**JIM DANDY,** L. Baker, Atlantic	29
28.	**I LOVE MY BABY,** J. Corey, Columbia	32
29.	**CAN I STEAL A LITTLE LOVE,** F. Sinatra, Capitol	32
30.	**HEY! JEALOUS LOVER,** F. Sinatra, Capitol	21
30.	**YOUR WILD HEART,** J. Layne, Mercury	—
32.	**JUST WALKING IN THE RAIN,** J. Ray, Columbia	24
33.	**GONNA GET ALONG WITHOUT YA NOW,** Patience & Prudence, Liberty	28
34.	**PLAYING FOR KEEPS,** E. Presley, Victor	40
34.	**WRINGLE WRANGLE,** F. Parker, Disneyland	45
36.	**BANANA BOAT SONG,** S. Lawrence, Coral	34
37.	**CINCO ROBLES,** R. Arms, Era	25
37.	**WRINGLE WRANGLE.** B. Hayes, ABC-Paramount	46
39.	**I MISS YOU SO,** C. Connor, Atlantic	52
40.	**ON MY WORD OF HONOR,** Platters, Mercury	29
41.	**AIN'T GOT NO HOME,** C. Henry, Argo	35
42.	**AUCTIONEER,** L. Van Dyke, Dot	47
43.	**CINCO ROBLES,** L. Paul & M. Ford, Capitol	53.
44.	**ANASTASIA,** P. Boone, Dot	49
45.	**CINDY, OH CINDY,** E. Fisher, Victor	38
45.	**GARDEN OF EDEN,** J. Valino, Vik	42
45.	**YOUNG LOVE,** Crew Cuts, Mercury	31
48.	**LOOK HOMEWARD, ANGEL,** J. Ray, Columbia	36
49.	**POOR BOY,** E. Presley, Victor	48
50.	**BANANA BOAT SONG,** S. Vaughan, Mercury	37
51.	**WITHOUT LOVE,** C. McPhatter, Atlantic	68
52.	**BUTTERFLY,** C. Gracie, Cameo	—
53.	**FRIENDLY PERSUASION,** P. Boone, Dot	51
54.	**CHANTEZ CHANTEZ,** D. Shore, Victor	74
55.	**WHAT'S THE REASON (I'M NOT PLEASING YOU)?** F. Domino, Imperial	57
56.	**LITTLE BY LITTLE,** M. Marlo, ABC-Paramount,	—
57.	**LITTLE BY LITTLE,** N. Brown, Savoy	63
58.	**BAD BOY,** Jive Bombers, Savoy	76
59.	**BALLERINA,** Nat (King) Cole, Capitol	70
60.	**YOUR LOVE FOR ME,** F. Sinatra, Capitol	76
61.	**GIRL CAN'T HELP IT,** Little Richard, Specialty	57
61.	**REPEAT AFTER ME,** P. Page, Mercury	53
63.	**RED SAILS IN THE SUNSET,** T. Hunter, Dot	57
64.	**HONKY TONK,** B. Doggett, King	61
65.	**WHAT IS A TEENAGE GIRL?** T. Edwards, Coral	60
66.	**BABY DOLL,** A. Williams, Cadence	65
67.	**ONE IN A MILLION,** Platters, Mercury	38
68.	**WRITTEN ON THE WIND,** Four Aces, Decca	73
69.	**BY YOU, BY YOU, BY YOU,** J. Lowe, Dot	68
70.	**SINGING THE BLUES,** M. Robbins, Columbia	66
71.	**TAKE ME BACK,** G. Mitchell, Columbia	55
72.	**CINDY, OH CINDY,** V. Martin, Glory	75
72.	**DREAMY EYES,** Four Preps, Capitol	76
74.	**BIRTHDAY PARTY,** S. Austin, Mercury	—
74.	**GREENSLEEVES,** Beverly Sisters, London	62
76.	**COME GO WITH ME,** D. Vikings, Dot	—
76.	**MONEY TREE,** M. Whiting, Capitol	55
76.	**SINCE I MET YOU BABY,** M. Carson, Columbia	66
79.	**CITY OF ANGELS,** Highlights, Bally	—
80.	**MONEY TREE,** Patience & Prudence, Liberty	88
81.	**WONDERFUL WONDERFUL,** J. Mathis, Columbia	71
82.	**ONLY ONE LOVE,** G. Hamilton IV, ABC-Paramount	—
83.	**RAM-BUNK-SHUSH,** B. Doggett, King	—
83.	**WHEN MY BLUE MOON TURNS TO GOLD AGAIN,** E. Presley, Victor	44
85.	**AUCTIONEER,** C. Miller, Mercury	—
86.	**MAMA FROM THE TRAIN,** P. Page, Mercury	50
87.	**TWO DIFFERENT WORLDS,** R. Williams & J. Morgan, Kapp	—
88.	**ON LONDON BRIDGE,** J. Stafford, Columbia	92
88.	**TIGER LILY,** R. Draper, Mercury	—
90.	**YOU ARE MY FIRST LOVE,** Nat (King) Cole, Capitol	90
91.	**NIGHT LIGHTS,** Nat (King) Cole, Capitol	85
92.	**SHIRLEY,** Schoolboys, Okeh	—
93.	**JUST IN TIME,** T. Bennett, Columbia	—
94.	**THOUSAND MILES AWAY,** Heartbeats, Rama	80
95.	**PARTY'S OVER,** Doris Day, Columbia	97
95.	**TWO DIFFERENT WORLDS,** D. Rondo, Jubilee	81
97.	**BLUE MOON,** E. Presley, Victor	—
97.	**WISDOM OF A FOOL,** Five Keys, Capitol	72
99.	**OLD SHEP,** E. Presley, Victor	—
100.	**CRAZY WITH LOVE,** G. Mitchell, Columbia	82

CAUTION TO DEALERS AND JUKE BOX OPERATORS

The Billboard's Top 100 is NOT designed to provide tested information for buying purposes. This function is most reliably served by other regular weekly features: Best Sellers in Stores, Most Played in Juke Boxes, Coming Up Strong and Best Buys.

• Best Sellers in Stores

For survey week ending February 13

RECORDS are ranked in order of their current national selling importance at the retail level, as determined by The Billboard's weekly survey of the top volume dealers in every important market area. When significant action is reported on both sides of a record, points are combined to determine position on the chart. In such a case, both sides are listed in bold type, the leading side on top.

This Week		Last Week	Weeks on Chart
1.	**TOO MUCH** (BMI)—E. Presley Playing for Keeps (BMI)—Vic 20-6800	1	5
2.	**YOUNG LOVE** (BMI)—T. Hunter Red Sails in the Sunset (ASCAP)—Dot 15533	2	6
3.	**DON'T FORBID ME** (BMI)—P. Boone Anastasia (ASCAP)—Dot 15521	3	10
4.	**YOUNG LOVE** (BMI)—S. James You're the Reason (I'm in Love) (BMI)—Cap 3602	4	8
5.	**BANANA BOAT (DAY-O)** (ASCAP)—H. Belafonte Star-O (ASCAP)—Vic 20-6771	5	7
6.	**SINGING THE BLUES** (BMI)—G. Mitchell Crazy With Love (ASCAP)—Col 40769	6	17
7.	**BANANA BOAT SONG** (BMI)—Tarriers No Hidin' Place (BMI)—Glory 249	7	10
8.	**MOONLIGHT GAMBLER** (ASCAP)—F. Laine Lotus Land (ASCAP)—Col 40780	8	11
9.	**BLUE MONDAY** (BMI)—F. Domino What's the Reason (I'm Not Pleasing You)? (ASCAP)—Imperial 5417	9	7
10.	**MARIANNE** (BMI)—T. Gilkyson Goodbye, Chiquita (BMI)—Col 40817	11	2
11.	**YOU DON'T OWE ME A THING** (BMI)—J. Ray Look Homeward, Angel (BMI)—Col 40803	10	5
12.	**WRINGLE WRANGLE** (ASCAP)—F. Parker Wringle Wrangle/Camarata (ASCAP)—Disneyland F 43	16	3
13.	**LOVE IS STRANGE** (BMI)—Mickey & Sylvia I'm Going Home (BMI)—Groove 0175	12	7
13.	**WHO NEEDS YOU?** (ASCAP)—Four Lads It's So Easy to Forget (BMI)—Col 40811	22	2
15.	**BUTTERFLY** (BMI)—C. Gracie Ninety-Nine Ways (BMI)—Cameo 105	—	1
16.	**TEEN-AGE CRUSH** (BMI)—T. Sands Hep Dee Hootie (BMI)—Cap 3639	—	1
17.	**MARIANNE** (BMI)—Hilltoppers You're Wasting Your Time (ASCAP)—Dot 15537	25	2
18.	**BLUEBERRY HILL** (ASCAP)—F. Domino Honey Chile (BMI)—Imperial 5407	15	20
19.	**ROCK-A-BYE YOUR BABY** (ASCAP)—J. Lewis Come Rain or Come Shine (ASCAP)—Dec 30124	13	14
20.	**JIM DANDY** (BMI)—L. Baker Tra La La (BMI)—Atlantic 1116	17	4
21.	**JAMAICA FAREWELL** (ASCAP)—H. Belafonte Once Was (ASCAP)—Vic 20-6663	18	10
22.	**CINCO ROBLES** (BMI)—R. Arms World is Made of Liza (BMI)—Era 1026	—	1
23.	**KNEE DEEP IN THE BLUES** (BMI)—G. Mitchell **TAKE ME BACK** (ASCAP)—Col 40820	21	2
24.	**★LOVE ME** (BMI)—E. Presley Vic EPA-992	22	14
25.	**LOVE ME TENDER** (BMI)—E. Presley Any Way You Want Me (ASCAP)—Vic 20-6643	18	10

★ (Not available as a Pop Single. Available on RCA Victor 45 EPA-992 and in RCA Victor 33⅓ "Elvis" LPM 1382)

• Most Played in Juke Boxes

For survey week ending February 13

RECORDS are ranked in order of the greatest number of plays in juke boxes thruout the country, as determined by The Billboard's weekly survey of the nation's juke box operators. When significant play is reported on both sides of a record, points are combined to determine position on the chart. In such a case, both sides are listed in bold type, the leading side on top.

This Week		Last Week	Weeks on Chart
1.	**DON'T FORBID ME** (BMI)—P. Boone Anastasia (ASCAP)—Dot 15521	2	7
2.	**YOUNG LOVE** (BMI)—T. Hunter Red Sails in the Sunset (ASCAP)—Dot 15533	3	5
3.	**SINGING THE BLUES** (BMI)—G. Mitchell Crazy With Love (ASCAP)—Col 40769	1	16
4.	**YOUNG LOVE** (BMI)—S. James You're the Reason (I'm in Love) (BMI)—Cap 3602	4	5
5.	**TOO MUCH** (BMI)—E. Presley Playing for Keeps (BMI)—Vic 20-6800	7	3
6.	**MOONLIGHT GAMBLER** (ASCAP)—F. Laine Lotus Land (ASCAP)—Col 40780	5	8
7.	**BANANA BOAT SONG** (BMI)—Tarriers No Hidin' Place (BMI)—Glory 249	6	7
8.	**BLUE MONDAY** (BMI)—F. Domino What's the Reason (I'm Not Pleasing You) (ASCAP)—Imperial 5417	9	5
9.	**BANANA BOAT SONG (DAY-O)** (ASCAP)—H. Belafonte Star-O (ASCAP)—Vic 20-6771	11	4
10.	**BLUEBERRY HILL** (ASCAP)—F. Domino Honey Chile (BMI)—Imperial 5407	8	19
11.	**GREEN DOOR** (BMI)—J. Lowe (The Story of) The Little Man in Chinatown (BMI)—Dot 15486	10	20
12.	**YOU DON'T OWE ME A THING** (BMI)—J. Ray Look Homeward, Angel (BMI)—Col 40803	14	3
13.	**LOVE ME TENDER** (BMI)—E. Presley **ANY WAY YOU WANT ME** (ASCAP)—Vic 20-6643	13	18
14.	**MARIANNE** (BMI)—Hilltoppers You're Wasting Your Time (ASCAP)—Dot 15537	—	1
15.	**I DREAMED** (BMI)—B. Johnson If It's Wrong to Love You (BMI)—Bally 1020	18	2
16.	**★LOVE ME**—E. Presley Vic EPA-992—BMI	12	11
17.	**JAMAICA FAREWELL** (ASCAP)—H. Belafonte Once Was (ASCAP)—Vic 20-6663	—	1
18.	**BANANA BOAT SONG** (BMI)—Fontane Sisters Honolulu Moon (ASCAP)—Dot 15527	—	1
19.	**MARIANNE** (BMI)—T. Gilkyson Goodbye, Chiquita (BMI)—Col 40817	—	1
20.	**YOUR WILD HEART** (ASCAP)—J. Layne Dum Dum (ASCAP)—Mercury 71038	—	1
20.	**ROCK-A-BYE YOUR BABY** (ASCAP)—J. Lewis Come Rain or Come Shine (ASCAP)—Dec 30124	16	8

★ (Not available as a Pop Single. Available on RCA Victor 45 EPA-992 and in RCA Victor 33⅓ "Elvis" LPM 1382)

• Best Selling Sheet Music

Tunes are ranked in order of their current selling importance at the sheet music jobber level.

This Week		Last Week	Weeks on Chart
1.	**Young Love** (Lowery)	2	5
2.	**Banana Boat Song** (E. B. Marks-Bryden)	1	6
3.	**True Love** (Buxton Hill)	3	22
4.	**Love Me Tender** (Presley)	5	19
5.	**Singing the Blues** (Acuff-Rose)	4	14
6.	**Cinco Robles** (Warman)	7	2
7.	**Don't Forbid Me** (Roosevelt)	6	5
8.	**Anastasia** (Feist)	9	5
9.	**Blueberry Hill** (Chappell	12	15
10.	**Gonna Get Along Without Ya Now** (Kellum)	14	6
11.	**Green Door** (Trinity)	11	18
12.	**Moonlight Gambler** (E. H. Morris)	10	5
13.	**Too Much** (Southern Belle-Presley)	13	2
14.	**Cindy, Oh Cindy** (E. B. Marks-Bryden)	8	16
15.	**Since I Met You Baby** (Progressive)	14	3

• Most Played by Jockeys

For survey week ending February 13

SIDES are ranked in order of the greatest number of plays on disk jockey radio shows thruout the country. Results are based on The Billboard's weekly survey among the nation's disk jockeys. The reverse side of each record is also listed.

This Week		Last Week	Weeks on Chart
1.	**YOUNG LOVE** (BMI)—T. Hunter Red Sails in the Sunset (ASCAP)—Dot 15533	1	6
2.	**YOUNG LOVE** (BMI)—S. James You're the Reason (I'm in Love) (BMI)—Cap 3602	2	8
3.	**DON'T FORBID ME** (BMI)—P. Boone Anastasia (ASCAP)—Dot 15531	3	9
4.	**TOO MUCH** (BMI)—E. Presley Playing for Keeps (BMI)—Vic 20-6800	4	4
5.	**BANANA BOAT SONG (DAY-O)** (ASCAP)—H. Belafonte Star-O (ASCAP)—Vic 20-6771	5	7
6.	**MOONLIGHT GAMBLER** (ASCAP)—F. Laine Lotus Land (ASCAP)—Col 40780	7	11
7.	**SINGING THE BLUES** (BMI)—G. Mitchell Crazy With Love (ASCAP)—Col 40769	6	17
8.	**BANANA BOAT SONG** (BMI)—Tarriers No Hidin' Place (BMI)—Glory 249	8	9
9.	**BLUE MONDAY** (BMI)—F. Domino What's the Reason (I'm Not Pleasing You)? (ASCAP)—Imperial 5417	11	5
10.	**YOU DON'T OWE ME A THING** (BMI)—J. Ray Look Homeward, Angel (BMI)—Col 40803	10	6
11.	**MARIANNE** (BMI)—T. Gilkyson Goodbye, Chiquita (BMI)—Col 40817	13	3
12.	**MARIANNE** (BMI)—Hilltoppers You're Wasting Your Time (ASCAP)—Dot 15537	12	3
13.	**I DREAMED** (BMI)—B. Johnson If It's Wrong to Love You (BMI)—Bally 1020	9	11
14.	**WHO NEEDS YOU?** (ASCAP)—Four Lads It's So Easy to Forget (BMI)—Col 40811	15	2
15.	**LOVE IS STRANGE** (BMI)—Mickey & Sylvia I'm Going Home (BMI)—Groove 0175	14	3
16.	**BANANA BOAT SONG** (BMI)—Fontane Sisters Honolulu Moon—Dot 15527	17	7
17.	**CAN I STEAL A LITTLE LOVE?** (ASCAP)—F. Sinatra Your Love for Me (BMI)—Cap 3608	22	2
18.	**KNEE DEEP IN THE BLUES** (BMI) G. Mitchell Take Me Back (ASCAP)—Col 40820	19	3
19.	**WITHOUT LOVE** (BMI)—C. McPhatter I Make Believe (BMI)—Atlantic 1117	—	1
20.	**BANANA BOAT SONG** (BMI)—S. Vaughan I've Got a New Heartache (BMI)—Mercury 71020	—	5
21.	**PLAYING FOR KEEPS** (BMI)—E. Presley Too Much (BMI)—Vic 20-6800	24	2
22.	**BALLERINA** (ASCAP)—Nat (King) Cole You Are My First Love (ASCAP)—Cap 3619	—	1
23.	**TRUE LOVE** (ASCAP)—B. Crosby-G. Kelly Well, Did You Evah? (ASCAP)—Cap 3507	21	21
23.	**CINCO ROBLES** (BMI)—R. Arms World Is Made of Lisa (BMI)—Era 1026	—	2
25.	**CHANTEZ CHANTEZ** (ASCAP)—D. Shore Honkeytonk Heart (ASCAP)—Vic 20-6792	—	1

THE TOP 100

For survey week ending February 13

A list of the Top 100 RECORD SIDES in the nation according to a COMBINED TABULATION of Dealer, Disk Jockey and Juke Box Operator replies to The Billboard's weekly popular record Best Seller and Most Played surveys. Its purpose is to provide Disk Jockeys with additional programming material and to give trade exposure to NEWER records just beginning to show action in the field.

Pos.	Song, Artist, Label	Last Week
1.	**YOUNG LOVE,** T. Hunter, Dot	1
2.	**DON'T FORBID ME,** P. Boone, Dot	2
3.	**YOUNG LOVE,** S. James, Capitol	2
3.	**TOO MUCH,** E. Presley, Victor	4
5.	**SINGING THE BLUES,** G. Mitchell, Columbia	5
6.	**BANANA BOAT (DAY-O),** H. Belafonte, Victor	7
7.	**MOONLIGHT GAMBLER,** F. Laine, Columbia	6
8.	**BANANA BOAT SONG,** Tarriers, Glory	7
9.	**BLUE MONDAY,** F. Domino, Imperial	9
10.	**YOU DON'T OWE ME A THING,** J. Ray, Columbia	10
11.	**MARIANNE,** T. Gilkyson, Columbia	22
12.	**MARIANNE,** Hilltoppers, Dot	18
13.	**I DREAMED**—B. Johnson, Bally	12
14.	**WHO NEEDS YOU?** Four Lads, Columbia	21
15.	**LOVE IS STRANGE,** Mickey & Sylvia, Groove	17
16.	**BLUEBERRY HILL,** F. Domino, Imperial	15
17.	**LOVE ME,** E. Presley, Victor	11
18.	**JAMAICA FAREWELL,** H. Belafonte, Victor	20
19.	**KNEE DEEP IN THE BLUES,** G. Mitchell, Columbia	19
20.	**GREEN DOOR,** J. Lowe, Dot	12
21.	**WRINGLE WRANGLE,** F. Parker, Disneyland	34
22.	**ROCK-A-BYE YOUR BABY,** J. Lewis, Decca	14
23.	**CINCO ROBLES,** R. Arms, Era	37
24.	**BANANA BOAT SONG,** Fontane Sisters, Dot	22
24.	**TRUE LOVE,** Bing Crosby-G. Kelly, Capitol	16
26.	**SINCE I MET YOU BABY,** I. J. Hunter, Atlantic	24
27.	**CAN I STEAL A LITTLE LOVE?** F. Domino, Capitol	29
27.	**LOVE ME TENDER,** E. Presley, Victor	26
29.	**I LOVE MY BABY,** J Corey, Columbia	28
30.	**JIM DANDY,** L. Baker, Atlantic	27
31.	**BUTTERFLY,** C. Gracie, Cameo	52
32.	**BANANA BOAT SONG,** S. Lawrence, Coral	36
33.	**YOUR WILD HEART,** J. Layne, Mercury	30
34.	**WRINGLE WRANGLE,** B. Hayes, ABC-Paramount	37
35.	**CINCO ROBLES,** L. Paul & M. Ford Capitol	43
36.	**PLAYING FOR KEEPS,** E. Presley, Victor	34
37.	**BALLERINA,** Nat (King) Cole, Capitol	59
38.	**HEY! JEALOUS LOVER,** F. Sinatra, Capitol	30
38.	**WITHOUT LOVE,** C. McPhatter, Atlantic	51
40.	**CHANTEZ CHANTEZ,** D. Shore, Victor	54
41.	**ON MY WORD OF HONOR,** Platters, Mercury	40
42.	**BUTTERFLY,** A Williams, Cadence	—
42.	**TEEN-AGE CRUSH,** T. Sands, Capitol	—
44.	**AIN'T GOT NO HOME,** C. Henry, Argo	41
45.	**ANASTASIA,** P. Boone, Dot	44
46.	**ROSE AND A BABY RUTH,** G. Hamilton IV, ABC-Paramount	25
47.	**TAKE ME BACK BABY,** G. Mitchell, Columbia	71
48.	**JUST WALKING IN THE RAIN,** J. Ray, Columbia	32
49.	**I MISS YOU SO,** C. Connor, Atlantic	39
50.	**GONNA GET ALONG WITHOUT YA NOW,** Patience & Prudence, Liberty	33
51.	**GARDEN OF EDEN,** J. Valino, Vik	45
52.	**LOOK HOMEWARD ANGEL,** J. Ray, Columbia	48
52.	**WALKIN' AFTER MIDNIGHT,** P. Cline, Decca	—
54.	**ROUND AND ROUND,** P. Como, Victor	—
55.	**LITTLE BY LITTLE,** M. Marlo, ABC-Paramount	56
56.	**YOUNG LOVE,** Crew Cuts, Mercury	45
57.	**WHAT IS A TEENAGE GIRL?** T. Edwards, Coral	65
58.	**LUCKY LIPS,** R Brown, Atlantic	—
59.	**BANANA BOAT SONG,** S. Vaughan, Mercury	50
60.	**CINDY, OH CINDY,** E. Fisher, Victor	45
61.	**GIRL CAN'T HELP IT,** Little Richard, Specialty	61
62.	**ONLY ONE LOVE,** G. Hamilton IV, ABC-Paramount	82
62.	**WHEN MY BLUE MOON TURNS TO GOLD AGAIN,** E. Presley, Victor	83
62.	**WONDERFUL WONDERFUL,** J. Mathis, Columbia	81
65.	**YOU ARE MY FIRST LOVE,** Nat (King) Cole, Capitol	90
66.	**AUCTIONEER,** L. Van Dyke, Dot	42
67.	**BAD BOY,** Jive Bombers, Savoy	58
68.	**PARTY DOLL,** B. Knox, Roulette	—
69.	**FRIENDLY PERSUASION,** P. Boone, Dot	53
70.	**LITTLE BY LITTLE,** N. Brown, Savoy	57
70.	**PARTY DOLL,** S. Lawrence, Coral	—
72.	**ONE IN A MILLION,** Platters, Mercury	67
72.	**WRITTEN ON THE WIND,** Four Aces, Decca	68
74.	**CITY OF ANGELS,** Highlights, Bally	79
74.	**YOUR LOVE FOR ME,** F. Sinatra, Capitol	60
76.	**BY YOU, BY YOU, BY YOU,** J. Lowe, Dot	69
76.	**RAM-BUNK-SHUSH,** B. Doggett, King	83
78.	**LET'S GO CALYPSO,** R. Draper, Mercury	—
79.	**GREENSLEEVES,** Beverly Sisters, London	74
80.	**ALMOST PARADISE,** N. Petty, ABC-Paramount	—
81.	**TWO DIFFERENT WORLDS,** D. Rondo, Jubilee	95
82.	**WISDOM OF A FOOL,** Five Keys, Capitol	97
83.	**SINCE I MET YOU BABY,** M. Carson, Columbia	76
84.	**BABY DOLL,** A. Williams, Cadence	66
84.	**CRAZY WITH LOVE,** G. Mitchell, Columbia	100
86.	**SO RARE,** J. Dorsey, Fraternity	—
87.	**PARTY'S OVER,** Doris Day, Columbia	95
88.	**WHAT'S THE REASON (I'M NOT PLEASING YOU)?** F. Domino, Imperial	55
89.	**HONKY TONK,** B. Doggett, King	64
89.	**RED SAILS IN THE SUNSET,** T. Hunter, Dot	63
91.	**SHIRLEY,** Schoolboys, Okeh	92
92.	**ANY WAY YOU WANT ME,** E. Presley, Victor	—
92.	**I FEEL GOOD,** Shirley and Lee, Aladdin	—
94.	**MONEY TREE,** M. Whiting, Capitol	76
94.	**I'M STICKING WITH YOU,** J. Bowen, Roulette	—
96.	**REPEAT AFTER ME,** P. Page, Mercury	61
97.	**HOLIDAY FOR TROMBONES,** D. Rose, M-G-M	—
98.	**POOR BOY,** E. Presley, Victor	49
99.	**AUCTIONEER,** C. Miller, Mercury	85
100.	**COME GO WITH ME,** D. Vikings, Dot	76
100.	**I WALK THE LINE,** J. Cash, Sun	—

CAUTION TO DEALERS AND JUKE BOX OPERATORS

The Billboard's Top 100 is NOT designed to provide tested information for buying purposes. This function is most reliably served by other regular weekly features: Best Sellers in Stores, Most Played in Juke Boxes, Coming Up Strong and Best Buys.

• Best Sellers in Stores

For survey week ending February 20

RECORDS are ranked in order of their current national selling importance at the retail level, as determined by The Billboard's weekly survey of the top volume dealers in every important market area. When significant action is reported on both sides of a record, points are combined to determine position on the chart. In such a case, both sides are listed in bold type, the leading side on top.

This Week	Record	Last Week	Weeks on Chart
1.	YOUNG LOVE (BMI)—T. Hunter Red Sails in the Sunset (ASCAP)—Dot 15533	2	7
2.	TOO MUCH (BMI)—E. Presley Playing for Keeps (BMI)—Vic 20-6800	1	6
3.	DON'T FORBID ME (BMI)—P. Boone Anastasia (ASCAP)—Dot 15521	3	11
4.	YOUNG LOVE (BMI)—S. James You're the Reason (I'm in Love) (BMI)—Cap 3602	4	9
5.	BANANA BOAT (DAY-O) (ASCAP)—H. Belafonte Star-O (ASCAP)—Vic 20-6771	5	8
6.	MARIANNE (BMI)—T. Gilkyson Goodbye, Chiquita (BMI)—Col 40817	10	3
7.	BANANA BOAT SONG (BMI)—Tarriers No Hidin' Place (BMI)—Glory 249	7	11
8.	TEEN-AGE CRUSH (BMI)—T. Sands Hep Dee Hootie (BMI)—Cap 3639	16	2
9.	MOONLIGHT GAMBLER (ASCAP)—F. Laine Lotus Land (ASCAP)—Col 40780	8	12
10.	BUTTERFLY (BMI)—C. Gracie Ninety-Nine Ways (BMI)—Cameo 105	15	2
11.	BLUE MONDAY (BMI)—F. Domino What's the Reason (I'm Not Pleasing You)? (ASCAP)—Imperial 5417	9	8
12.	SINGING THE BLUES (BMI)—G. Mitchell Crazy With Love (ASCAP)—Col 40769	6	18
13.	WHO NEEDS YOU (ASCAP)—Four Lads It's So Easy to Forget (BMI)—Col 40811	13	3
14.	LOVE IS STRANGE (BMI)—Mickey & Sylvia I'm Going Home (BMI)—Groove 0175	13	8
15.	MARIANNE (BMI)—Hilltoppers You're Wasting Your Time (ASCAP)—Dot 15537	17	3
16.	YOU DON'T OWE ME A THING (BMI)—J. Ray Look Homeward, Angel (BMI)—Col 40803	11	6
17.	JIM DANDY (BMI)—L. Baker Tra La La (BMI)—Atlantic 1116	20	5
18.	WRINGLE WRANGLE (ASCAP)—F. Parker Wringle Wrangle/Camarata (ASCAP)—Disneyland F 43	12	4
19.	BUTTERFLY (BMI)—A. Williams It Doesn't Take Very Long (ASCAP)—Cadence 1308	—	1
20.	PARTY DOLL (BMI)—B. Knox My Baby's Gone (BMI)—Roulette 4002	—	1
21.	COME, GO WITH ME (BMI)—D. Vikings How Can I Find True Love? (BMI)—Dot 15538	—	1
22.	I DREAMED (BMI)—B. Johnson If It's Wrong to Love You (BMI)—Bally 1020	—	5
23.	KNEE DEEP IN THE BLUES (BMI)—G. Mitchell Take Me Back (ASCAP)—Col 40820	23	3
23.	WALKIN' AFTER MIDNIGHT (BMI)—P. Cline Poor Man's Roses (ASCAP)—Dec 30221	—	1
25.	LUCKY LIPS (BMI)—R. Brown My Heart Is Breaking Over You (BMI)—Atlantic 1125	—	1

• Most Played in Juke Boxes

For survey week ending February 20

RECORDS are ranked in order of the greatest number of plays in juke boxes thruout the country, as determined by The Billboard's weekly survey of the nation's juke box operators. When significant play is reported on both sides of a record, points are combined to determine position on the chart. In such a case, both sides are listed in bold type, the leading side on top.

This Week	Record	Last Week	Weeks on Chart
1.	YOUNG LOVE (BMI)—T. Hunter Red Sails in the Sunset (ASCAP)—Dot 15533	2	6
2.	DON'T FORBID ME (BMI)—P. Boone Anastasia (ASCAP)—Dot 15521	1	8
3.	TOO MUCH (BMI)—E. Presley PLAYING FOR KEEPS (BMI)—Vic 20-6800	5	4
4.	YOUNG LOVE (BMI)—S. James You're the Reason (I'm in Love) (BMI)—Cap 3602	4	6
5.	SINGING THE BLUES (BMI)—G. Mitchell Crazy With Love (ASCAP)—Col 40769	3	17
6.	BANANA BOAT SONG (BMI) Tarriers No Hidin' Place (BMI)—Glory 249	7	8
7.	MOONLIGHT GAMBLER (ASCAP)—F. Laine Lotus Land (ASCAP)—Col 40780	6	9
8.	BLUE MONDAY (BMI)—F. Domino What's the Reason (I'm Not Pleasing You)? (ASCAP)—Imperial 5417	8	6
9.	BANANA BOAT (DAY-O) (ASCAP)—H. Belafonte Star-O (ASCAP)—Vic 20-6771	9	5
10.	MARIANNE (BMI)—Hilltoppers You're Wasting Your Time (ASCAP)—Dot 15537	14	2
11.	MARIANNE (BMI)—T. Gilkyson Goodbye, Chiquita (BMI)—Col 40817	19	2
12.	BLUEBERRY HILL (ASCAP)—F. Domino Honey Chile (BMI)—Imperial 5407	10	20
13.	YOU DON'T OWE ME A THING—(BMI)—J. Ray Look Homeward, Angel (BMI)—Col 40803	12	4
14.	BANANA BOAT SONG (BMI)—Fontane Sisters Honolulu Moon (ASCAP)—Dot 15527	18	2
15.	GREEN DOOR (BMI)—J. Lowe (The Story of) The Little Man in Chinatown (BMI)—Dot 15486	11	21
16.	KNEE DEEP IN THE BLUES (BMI)—G. Mitchell Take Me Back (ASCAP)—Col 40820	—	2
17.	BUTTERFLY (BMI)—C. Gracie Ninety-Nine Ways (BMI)—Cameo 105	—	1
18.	I DREAMED (BMI)—B. Johnson If It's Wrong to Love You (BMI)—Bally 1020	15	3
19.	ROCK-A-BYE YOUR BABY (ASCAP)—J. Lewis Come Rain or Come Shine (ASCAP)—Dec 30124	20	9
20.	TEEN-AGE CRUSH (BMI)—T. Sands. Hep Dee Hootie (BMI)—Cap 3639	—	1

• Best Selling Sheet Music

Tunes are ranked in order of their current selling importance at the sheet music jobber level.

This Week	Tune	Last Week	Weeks on Chart
1.	**Young Love** (Lowery)	1	6
2.	**Banana Boat Song** (E. B. Marks-Bryden)	2	7
3.	**True Love** (Buxton Hill)	3	23
4.	**Cinco Robles** (Warman)	6	3
5.	**Don't Forbid Me** (Roosevelt)	7	6
6.	**Love Me Tender** (Presley)	4	20
7.	**Singing the Blues**, Acuff-Rose	5	15
8.	**Anastasia** (Feist)	8	6
9.	**Gonna Get Along Without You Now** (Kellum)	10	7
10.	**Marianne** (Montclare)	—	1
11.	**Moonlight Gambler** (E. H. Morris)	12	6
12.	**Blueberry Hill** (Chappell)	9	16
13.	**Too Much** (Southern Belle-Presley)	13	3
14.	**Green Door** (Trinity)	11	19
15.	**Since I Met You Baby** (Progressive)	15	4

• Most Played by Jockeys

For survey week ending February 20

SIDES are ranked in order of the greatest number of plays on disk jockey radio shows thruout the country. Results are based on The Billboard's weekly survey among the nation's disk jockeys. The reverse side of each record is also listed.

This Week	Record	Last Week	Weeks on Chart
1.	YOUNG LOVE (BMI)—T. Hunter Red Sails in the Sunset (ASCAP)—Dot 15533	1	7
2.	YOUNG LOVE (BMI)—S. James You're the Reason (I'm in Love) (BMI)—Cap 3602	2	9
3.	TOO MUCH (BMI)—E. Presley Playing for Keeps (BMI)—Vic 20-6800	4	5
4.	DON'T FORBID ME (BMI)—P. Boone Anastasia (ASCAP)—Dot 15521	3	10
5.	BANANA BOAT (DAY-O) (ASCAP)—H. Belafonte Star-O (ASCAP)—Vic 20-6771	5	8
6.	MARIANNE (BMI)—T. Gilkyson Goodbye, Chiquita (BMI)—Col 40817	11	4
7.	MOONLIGHT GAMBLER (ASCAP)—F. Laine Lotus Land (ASCAP)—Col 40780	6	12
8.	BANANA BOAT SONG (BMI)—Tarriers No Hidin' Place (BMI)—Glory 249	8	10
9.	MARIANNE (BMI)—Hilltoppers You're Wasting Your Time (ASCAP)— Dot 15537	12	4
10.	SINGING THE BLUES (BMI)—G. Mitchell Crazy With Love (ASCAP)—Col 40769	7	18
11.	LOVE IS STRANGE (BMI)—Mickey & Sylvia I'm Going Home (BMI)—Groove 0175	15	4
12.	WHO NEEDS YOU (ASCAP)—Four Lads It's So Easy to Forget (BMI)—Col 40811	14	3
13.	BLUE MONDAY (BMI)—F. Domino What's the Reason (I'm Not Pleasing You) (ASCAP)—Imperial 5417	9	6
14.	YOU DON'T OWE ME A THING (BMI)—J. Ray Look Homeward, Angel (BMI)—Col 40803	10	7
15.	CAN I STEAL A LITTLE LOVE (ASCAP)—F. Sinatra Your Love for Me (BMI)—Cap 3608	17	3
16.	I DREAMED (BMI)—B. Johnson If It's Wrong to Love You (BMI)—Bally 1020	13	12
17.	KNEE DEEP IN THE BLUES (BMI)—G. Mitchell Take Me Back (ASCAP)—Col 40820	18	4
18.	BUTTERFLY (BMI)—C. Gracie Ninety-Nine Ways (BMI)—Cameo 105	—	1
19.	TEEN-AGE CRUSH (BMI)—T. Sands Hep Dee Hootie (BMI)—Cap 3639	—	1
20.	BANANA BOAT SONG (BMI)—Fontane Sisters Honolulu Moon (ASCAP)—Dot 15527	16	8
21.	WITHOUT LOVE (BMI)—C. McPhatter I Make Believe (BMI)—Atlantic 1117	19	2
22.	BALLERINA (ASCAP)—Nat (King) Cole You Are My First Love (ASCAP)—Cap 3619	22	2
23.	TRUE LOVE (ASCAP)—B. Crosby-G. Kelly Well, Did You Evah? (ASCAP)—Cap 3507	23	22
24.	ROUND AND ROUND (BMI)—P. Como Mi Casa, Su Casa (ASCAP)—Vic 20-6815	—	1
25.	PLAYING FOR KEEPS (BMI)—E. Presley Too Much (BMI)—Vic 20-6800	21	3
25.	★LOVE ME (BMI)—E. Presley Vic EPA-992	—	13

★ (Not available as a Pop Single. Available on RCA Victor 45 EPA-992 and in RCA Victor 33⅓ "Elvis" LPM 1382)

THE TOP 100

For survey week ending February 20

A list of the Top 100 RECORD SIDES in the nation according to a COMBINED TABULATION of Dealer, Disk Jockey and Juke Box Operator replies to The Billboard's weekly popular record Best Seller and Most Played surveys. Its purpose is to provide Disk Jockeys with additional programming material and to give trade exposure to NEWER records just beginning to show action in the field.

Pos.	Song, Artist, Label	Last Week
1.	**YOUNG LOVE,** T. Hunter, Dot	1
2.	**TOO MUCH,** E. Presley, Victor	3
3.	**DON'T FORBID ME,** P. Boone, Dot	2
4.	**YOUNG LOVE,** S. James, Capitol	3
5.	**BANANA BOAT SONG (Day-O),** H. Belafonte, Victor	6
6.	**BANANA BOAT SONG,** Tarriers, Glory	8
7.	**MOONLIGHT GAMBLER,** F. Laine, Columbia	7
7.	**MARIANNE,** T. Gilkyson, Columbia	11
9.	**SINGING THE BLUES,** G Mitchell, Columbia	5
10.	**BLUE MONDAY,** F. Domino, Imperial	9
11.	**MARIANNE,** Hilltoppers, Dot	12
12.	**YOU DON'T OWE ME A THING,** J. Ray, Columbia	10
13.	**LOVE IS STRANGE,** Mickey & Sylvia, Groove	15
14.	**TEEN-AGE CRUSH,** T. Sands, Capitol	42
15.	**I DREAMED,** B. Johnson, Bally	13
16.	**KNEE DEEP IN THE BLUES,** G Mitchell, Columbia	19
17.	**BUTTERFLY,** A. Williams, Cadence	42
18.	**WHO NEEDS YOU,** Four Lads, Columbia	14
19.	**BUTTERFLY,** C. Gracie, Cameo	31
20.	**CAN I STEAL A LITTLE LOVE?** F. Sinatra, Capitol	27
21.	**BLUEBERRY HILL,** F. Domino, Imperial	16
22.	**JIM DANDY,** L. Baker, Atlantic	30
23.	**ROCK-A-BYE YOUR BABY,** J. Lewis, Decca	22
24.	**WRINGLE WRANGLE,** F. Parker, Disneyland	21
25.	**JAMAICA FAREWELL,** H. Belafonte, Victor	18
26.	**SINCE I MET YOU BABY,** I. J. Hunter, Atlantic	26
27.	**BANANA BOAT SONG,** Fontane Sisters, Dot	24
28.	**CINCO ROBLES,** R. Arms, Era	23
29.	**TRUE LOVE,** Bing Crosby & Grace Kelly, Capitol	24
30.	**WAKIN' AFTER MIDNIGHT,** P. Cline, Decca	52
31.	**BANANA BOAT SONG.** S. Lawrence, Coral	32
32.	**ROUND AND ROUND,** P. Como, Victor	54
33.	**PARTY DOLL,** B. Knox, Roulette	68
33.	**WRINGLE WRANGLE,** B. Hayes, ABC-Paramount	34
35.	**I LOVE MY BABY,** J. Corey, Columbia	29
36.	**BALLERINA,** Nat (King) Cole, Capitol	37
37.	**PLAYING FOR KEEPS,** E. Presley, Victor	36
37.	**YOUR WILD HEART,** J. Layne, Mercury	33
39.	**LUCKY LIPS,** R. Brown, Atlantic	58
40.	**LOVE ME,** E. Presley, Victor	17
41.	**LOVE ME TENDER,** E. Presley, Victor	27
42.	**I MISS YOU SO,** C. Connor, Atlantic	49
43.	**CHANTEZ CHANTEZ,** D. Shore, Victor	40
44.	**AIN'T GOT NO HOME,** C. Henry, Argo	44
45.	**GREEN DOOR,** J. Lowe, Dot	20
45.	**ONLY ONE LOVE,** G. Hamilton IV, ABC-Paramount	62
45.	**PARTY DOLL,** S. Lawrence, Coral	70
48.	**I'M STICKIN' WITH YOU,** J. Bowen, Roulette	94
49.	**GONE,** F. Huskey, Capitol	—
49.	**GIRL CAN'T HELP IT,** Little Richard, Specialty	61
51.	**WITHOUT LOVE,** C. McPhatter, Atlantic	38
52.	**ONE IN A MILLION,** Platters, Mercury	72
53.	**ON MY WORD OF HONOR,** Platters, Mercury	41
53.	**TAKE ME BACK BABY.** G Mitchell, Columbia	47
55.	**ANASTASIA,** P. Boone, Dot	45
55.	**GONNA GET ALONG WITHOUT YA NOW,** Patience & Prudence, Liberty	50
57.	**LOOK HOMEWARD ANGEL,** J. Ray, Columbia	52
57.	**LET'S GO CALYPSO,** R. Draper, Mercury	78
59.	**CINCO ROBLES,** L. Paul & M. Ford, Capitol	35
60.	**JUST WALKING IN THE RAIN,** J. Ray, Columbia	48
60.	**YOUNG LOVE,** Crew Cuts, Mercury	56
62.	**ROSE AND A BABY RUTH,** G. Hamilton IV, ABC-Paramount	46
63.	**ALMOST PARADISE,** R. Williams, Kapp	—
64.	**WONDERFUL WONDERFUL,** J. Mathis, Columbia	62
65.	**BAD BOY,** Jive Bombers, Savoy	67
66.	**WRITTEN ON THE WIND,** Four Aces, Decca	72
67.	**ALMOST PARADISE,** L. Stein, Unique	—
67.	**HEY! JEALOUS LOVER,** F Sinatra, Capitol	38
69.	**BANANA BOAT SONG,** S. Vaughan, Mercury	59
70.	**YOU ARE MY FIRST LOVE,** Nat (King) Cole, Capitol	65
71.	**COME GO WITH ME,** D. Vikings, Dot	100
72.	**RAM-BUNK-SHUSH,** B. Doggett, King	76
73.	**ALMOST PARADISE,** N. Petty, ABC-Paramount	80
73.	**ONE STEP AT A TIME,** B. Lee, Decca	—
75.	**POOR BOY,** E. Presley, Victor	98
76.	**SO RARE,** J. Dorsey, Fraternity	86
77.	**WHAT'S THE REASON (I'M NOT PLEASING YOU)?** F. Domino, Imperial	88
78.	**WISDOM OF A FOOL,** Five Keys, Capitol	82
79.	**THOUSAND MILES AWAY,** Heartbeats, Rama	—
80.	**LITTLE BY LITTLE,** M. Marlo, ABC-Paramount	55
81.	**LITTLE BY LITTLE,** N. Brown, Savoy	70
82.	**RED SAILS IN THE SUNSET,** T. Hunter, Dot	89
83.	**BY YOU, BY YOU, BY YOU,** J. Lowe Dot	76
83.	**WHAT IS A TEEN-AGE GIRL,** T. Edwards, Coral	57
85.	**MONEY TREE,** M Whiting, Capitol	94
86.	**CITY OF ANGELS,** Highlights, Bally	74
86.	**AUCTIONEER,** L. Van Dyke, Dot	66
88.	**NIGHT LIGHTS,** Nat (King) Cole, Capitol	—
89.	**DREAMY EYES,** Four Preps, Capitol	—
90.	**TIGER LILY,** R. Draper, Mercury	—
91.	**LEAVE IT TO LOVE,** S. Vaughan, Mercury	—
92.	**POOR MAN'S ROSES,** P Page, Mercury	—
92.	**SKYLINER,** C. MacRae, Decca	—
94.	**PARTY'S OVER,** Doris Day, Columbia	87
94.	**VERY SPECIAL LOVE,** M. Miller, Columbia	—
96.	**HONKY TONK,** B. Doggett, King	89
96.	**JUST BECAUSE,** L. Price, ABC-Paramount	—
98.	**MARIANNE,** B. Ives, Decca	—
99.	**BUTTERFLY,** B. Carroll, Bally	—
100.	**BABY DOLL,** A. Williams, Cadence	84
100.	**WHEN MY BLUE MOON TURNS TO GOLD AGAIN,** E. Presley, Victor	62

• Best Sellers in Stores

For survey week ending February 27

RECORDS are ranked in order of their current national selling importance at the retail level, as determined by The Billboard's weekly survey of the top volume dealers in every important market area. When significant action is reported on both sides of a record, points are combined to determine position on the chart. In such a case, both sides are listed in bold type, the leading side on top.

This Week		Last Week	Weeks on Chart
1.	**YOUNG LOVE** (BMI)—T. Hunter Red Sails in the Sunset (ASCAP)—Dot 15533	1	8
2.	**TOO MUCH** (BMI)—E. Presley Playing for Keeps (BMI)—Vic 20-6800	2	7
3.	**DON'T FORBID ME** (BMI)—P. Boone Anastasia (ASCAP)—Dot 15521	3	12
4.	**TEEN-AGE CRUSH** (BMI)—T. Sands Hep Dee Hootie (BMI)—Cap 3639	8	3
5.	**BANANA BOAT (DAY-O)** (ASCAP)—H. Belafonte Star-O (ASCAP)—Vic 20-6771	5	9
6.	**YOUNG LOVE** (BMI)—S. James You're the Reason (I'm in Love) (BMI)—Cap 3602	4	10
7.	**MARIANNE** (BMI)—T. Gilkyson Goodbye, Chiquita (BMI)—Col 40817	6	4
8.	**BUTTERFLY** (BMI)—C. Gracie Ninety-Nine Ways (BMI)—Cameo 105	10	3
9.	**BANANA BOAT SONG** (BMI)—Tarriers No Hidin' Place (BMI)—Glory 249	7	12
10.	**BUTTERFLY** (BMI)—A. Williams It Doesn't Take Very Long (ASCAP)—Cadence 1308	19	2
11.	**MOONLIGHT GAMBLER** (ASCAP)—F. Laine Lotus Land (ASCAP)—Col 40780	9	13
12.	**MARIANNE** (BMI)—Hilltoppers You're Wasting Your Time (ASCAP)—Dot 15537	15	4
13.	**ROUND AND ROUND** (BMI)—P. Como Mi Casa, Su Casa (ASCAP)—Vic 20-6815	—	1
14.	**LOVE IS STRANGE** (BMI)—Mickey & Sylvia I'm Going Home (BMI)—Groove 0175	14	9
15.	**BLUE MONDAY** (BMI)—F. Domino What's the Reason (I'm Not Pleasing You)? (ASCAP)—Imperial 5417	11	9
16.	**PARTY DOLL** (BMI)—B. Knox My Baby's Gone (BMI)—Roulette 4002	20	2
17.	**SINGING THE BLUES** (BMI)—G. Mitchell Crazy With Love (ASCAP)—Col 40769	12	19
18.	**I'M WALKIN'** (BMI)—F. Domino I'm in the Mood for Love (ASCAP)—Imperial 5428	—	1
19.	**I'M STICKIN' WITH YOU** (BMI)—J. Bowen Ever-Lovin' Fingers (BMI)—Roulette 4001	—	1
20.	**WHO NEEDS YOU** (ASCAP)—Four Lads It's So Easy to Forget (BMI)—Col 40811	13	4
21.	**COME GO WITH ME** (BMI)—D. Vikings How Can I Find Love? (BMI)—Dot 15538	21	2
22.	**WALKIN' AFTER MIDNIGHT** (BMI)—P. Cline Poor Man's Roses (ASCAP)—Dec 30221	23	2
23.	**YOU DON'T OWE ME A THING** (BMI)—J. Ray Look Homeward, Angel (BMI)—Col 40803	16	7
24.	**WRINGLE WRANGLE** (ASCAP)—F. Parker Wringle Wrangle/Camarata (ASCAP)—Disneyland F 43	18	5
25.	**JIM DANDY** (BMI)—L. Baker Tra La La (BMI)—Atlantic 1116	17	6

• Most Played in Juke Boxes

For survey week ending February 27

RECORDS are ranked in order of the greatest number of plays in juke boxes thruout the country, as determined by The Billboard's weekly survey of the nation's juke box operators. When significant play is reported on both sides of a record, points are combined to determine position on the chart. In such a case, both sides are listed in bold type, the leading side on top.

This Week		Last Week	Weeks on Chart
1.	**TOO MUCH** (BMI)—E. Presley **PLAYING FOR KEEPS** (BMI)—Vic 20-6800	3	5
2.	**YOUNG LOVE** (BMI)—T. Hunter Red Sails in the Sunset (ASCAP)—Dot 15533	1	7
3.	**DON'T FORBID ME** (BMI)—P. Boone Anastasia (ASCAP)—Dot 15521	2	9
4.	**YOUNG LOVE** (BMI)—S. James You're the Reason (I'm in Love) (BMI)—Cap 3602	4	7
5.	**BLUE MONDAY** (BMI)—F. Domino What's the Reason (I'm Not Pleasing You)? (ASCAP)—Imperial 5417	8	7
6.	**BANANA BOAT (DAY-O)** (ASCAP)—H. Belafonte Star-O (ASCAP)—Vic 20-6771	9	6
7.	**SINGING THE BLUES** (BMI)—G. Mitchell Crazy With Love (ASCAP)—Col 40769	5	18
8.	**BANANA BOAT SONG** (BMI)—Tarriers No Hidin' Place (BMI)—Glory 249	6	9
9.	**MARIANNE** (BMI)—Hilltoppers You're Wasting Your Time (ASCAP)—Dot 15537	10	3
10.	**MOONLIGHT GAMBLER** (ASCAP)—F. Laine Lotus Land (ASCAP)—Col 40780	7	10
11.	**MARIANNE** (BMI)—T. Gilkyson Goodbye, Chiquita (BMI)—Col 40817	11	3
12.	**YOU DON'T OWE ME A THING** (BMI)—J. Ray Look Homeward, Angel (BMI)—Col 40803	13	5
13.	**BUTTERFLY** (BMI)—C. Gracie Ninety-Nine Ways (BMI)—Cameo 105	17	2
14.	**TEEN-CRUSH** (BMI)—T. Sands Hep Dee Hootie (BMI)—Cap 3639	20	2
15.	**BLUEBERRY HILL** (ASCAP)—F. Domino Honey Chile (BMI)—Imperial 5407	12	21
16.	**KNEE DEEP IN THE BLUES** (BMI)—G. Mitchell Take Me Back (ASCAP)—Col 40820	16	3
17.	**LOVE IS STRANGE** (BMI) Mickey & Sylvia I'm Going Home (BMI)—Groove 0175	—	1
18.	**I DREAMED** (BMI)—B. Johnson If It's Wrong to Love You (BMI)—Bally 1020	18	4
19.	**BUTTERFLY** (BMI)—A. Williams It Doesn't Take Very Long (ASCAP)—Cadence 1308	—	1
20.	**PARTY DOLL** (BMI)—B. Knox My Baby's Gone (BMI)—Roulette 4002	—	1

• Best Selling Sheet Music

Tunes are ranked in order of their current national selling importance at the sheet music jobber level.

This Week		Last Week	Weeks on Chart
1.	**Young Love** (Lowery)	1	7
2.	**Banana Boat Song** (E. B. Marks-Bryden)	2	8
3.	**True Love** (Buxton Hill)	3	24
4.	**Don't Forbid Me** (Roosevelt)	5	7
5.	**Cinco Robles** (Warman)	4	4
6.	**Love Me Tender,** (Presley)	6	21
7.	**Singing the Blues** (Acuff-Rose)	7	16
8.	**Anastasia** (Feist)	8	7
9.	**Marianne** (Montclare)	10	2
10.	**Gonna Get Along Without Ya Now** (Kellum)	9	8
11.	**Too Much** (Southern Belle-Presley)	13	4
12.	**Blueberry Hill** (Chappell)	12	17
13.	**Moonlight Gambler** (E. H. Morris)	11	7
14.	**Since I Met You Baby** (Progressive)	15	5
15.	**Wringle Wrangle** (Disney)	—	1

• Most Played by Jockeys

For survey week ending February 27

SIDES are ranked in order of the greatest number of plays on disk jockey radio shows thruout the country. Results are based on The Billboard's weekly survey among the nation's disk jockeys. The reverse side of each record is also listed.

This Week		Last Week	Weeks on Chart
1.	**YOUNG LOVE** (BMI)—T. Hunter Red Sails in the Sunset (ASCAP)—Dot 15533	1	8
2.	**TOO MUCH** (BMI)—E. Presley Playing for Keeps (BMI)—Vic 20-6800	3	6
3.	**YOUNG LOVE** (BMI)—S. James You're the Reason (I'm in Love) (BMI)—Cap 3602	2	10
4.	**DON'T FORBID ME** (BMI)—P. Boone Anastasia (ASCAP)—Dot 15521	4	11
5.	**BANANA BOAT (DAY-O)** (ASCAP)—H. Belafonte Star-O (ASCAP)—Vic 20-6771	5	9
6.	**MARIANNE** (BMI)—T. Gilkyson Goodbye, Chiquita (BMI)—Col 40817	6	5
7.	**MARIANNE** (BMI)—Hilltoppers You're Wasting Your Time (ASCAP)—Dot 15537	9	5
8.	**TEEN-AGE CRUSH** (BMI)—T Sands Hep Dee Hootie (BMI)—Cap 3639	19	2
9.	**WHO NEEDS YOU** (ASCAP)—Four Lads It's So Easy to Forget (BMI)—Col 40811	12	4
10.	**MOONLIGHT GAMBLER** (ASCAP)—F. Laine Lotus Land (ASCAP)—Col 40780	7	13
11.	**I DREAMED** (BMI)—B. Johnson If It's Wrong to Love You (BMI)—Bally 1020	16	13
12.	**ROUND AND ROUND** (BMI)—P. Como Mi Casa, Su Casa (ASCAP)—Vic 20-6815	24	2
13.	**BUTTERFLY** (BMI)—A. Williams It Doesn't Take Very Long (ASCAP)—Cadence 1308	—	1
14.	**LOVE IS STRANGE** (BMI)—Mickey & Sylvia I'm Going Home (BMI)—Groove 0175	11	5
15.	**BLUE MONDAY** (BMI)—F. Domino What's the Reason (I'm Not Pleasing You)? (ASCAP)—Imperial 5417	13	7
16.	**YOU DON'T OWE ME A THING** (BMI)—J. Ray Look Homeward, Angel (BMI)—Col 40803	14	8
17.	**SINGING THE BLUES** (BMI)—G. Mitchell Crazy With Love (ASCAP)—Col 40769	10	19
18.	**BUTTERFLY** (BMI)—C. Gracie Ninety-Nine Ways (BMI)—Cameo 105	18	2
19.	**BANANA BOAT SONG** (BMI)—Tarriers No Hidin' Place (BMI)—Glory 249	8	11
20.	**PARTY DOLL** (BMI)—B. Knox My Baby's Gone (BMI)—Roulette 4002	—	1
21.	**BALLERINA** (ASCAP)—Nat (King) Cole You Are My First Love (ASCAP)—Cap 3619	22	3
22.	**CAN I STEAL A LITTLE LOVE?** (ASCAP)—F. Sinatra Your Love for Me (BMI)—Cap 3608	15	4
23.	**JIM DANDY** (BMI)—L. Baker Tra La La (BMI)—Atlantic 1116	—	2
24.	**BANANA BOAT SONG** (BMI)—Fontane Sisters Honolulu Moon (ASCAP)—Dot 15527	20	9
25.	**LUCKY LIPS** (BMI)—R. Brown My Heart Is Breaking Over You (BMI)—Atlantic 1125	—	1
25.	**PARTY DOLL** (BMI)—S. Lawrence Pum-Pa-Lum (ASCAP)—Coral 61792	—	1

THE TOP 100

For survey week ending February 27

A list of the Top 100 RECORD SIDES in the nation according to a COMBINED TABULATION of Dealer, Disk Jockey and Juke Box Operator replies to The Billboard's weekly popular record Best Seller and Most Played surveys. Its purpose is to provide Disk Jockeys with additional programming material and to give trade exposure to NEWER records just beginning to show action in the field.

Pos.	Song, Artist, Label	Last Week
1.	**YOUNG LOVE,** T. Hunter, Dot	1
2.	**TOO MUCH,** E. Presley, Victor	2
3.	**DON'T FORBID ME,** P. Boone, Dot	3
4.	**YOUNG LOVE,** S. James, Capitol	4
5.	**BANANA BOAT (DAY-O),** H. Belafonte, Victor	5
6.	**MARIANNE,** T. Gilkyson, Columbia	7
7.	**TEEN-AGE CRUSH,** T. Sands, Capitol	14
8.	**MARIANNE,** Hilltoppers, Dot	11
9.	**MOONLIGHT GAMBLER,** F. Laine, Columbia	7
10.	**BLUE MONDAY,** F. Domino, Imperial	10
11.	**BANANA BOAT SONG,** Tarriers, Glory	6
12.	**BUTTERFLY,** C. Gracie, Cameo	19
13.	**SINGING THE BLUES,** G. Mitchell, Columbia	9
14.	**BUTTERFLY,** A. Williams, Cadence	17
15.	**LOVE IS STRANGE,** Mickey & Sylvia, Groove	13
16.	**WHO NEEDS YOU,** Four Lads, Columbia	18
17.	**YOU DON'T OWE ME A THING,** J. Ray, Columbia	12
18.	**PARTY DOLL,** B. Knox, Roulette	33
19.	**I DREAMED,** B. Johnson, Bally	15
19.	**ROUND AND ROUND,** P. Como, Victor	32
21.	**KNEE DEEP IN THE BLUES,** G. Mitchell, Columbia	16
22.	**PARTY DOLL,** S. Lawrence, Coral	45
23.	**JIM DANDY,** L. Baker, Atlantic	22
24.	**CAN I STEAL A LITTLE LOVE?** F. Sinatra, Capitol	20
25.	**WALKIN' AFTER MIDNIGHT,** P. Cline, Decca	30
26.	**LUCKY LIPS,** R. Brown, Atlantic	39
26.	**ROCK-A-BYE YOUR BABY,** J. Lewis, Decca	23
28.	**SINCE I MET YOU BABY,** I. J. Hunter, Atlantic	26
28.	**WRINGLE WRANGLE,** F. Parker, Disneyland	24
30.	**AIN'T GOT NO HOME,** C. Henry, Argo	44
30.	**BANANA BOAT SONG,** Fontane Sisters, Dot	27
32.	**BANANA BOAT SONG,** S. Lawrence, Coral	31
32.	**I'M STICKIN' WITH YOU,** J. Bowen, Roulette	48
34.	**CINCO ROBLES,** R. Arms, Era	28
35.	**CHANTEZ CHANTEZ,** D. Shore, Victor	43
35.	**I'M WALKIN',** F. Domino, Imperial	30
37.	**I MISS YOU SO,** C. Connor, Atlantic	42
37.	**ONLY ONE LOVE,** G. Hamilton IV, ABC-Paramount	45
39.	**JAMAICA FAREWELL,** H. Belafonte, Victor	25
40.	**GONE,** F. Huskey, Capitol	49
40.	**YOUR WILD HEART,** J. Layne, Mercury	37
42.	**I LOVE MY BABY,** J. Corey, Columbia	35
43.	**BLUEBERRY HILL,** F. Domino, Imperial	21
44.	**WRINGLE WRANGLE,** B. Hayes, ABC-Paramount	33
45.	**CINCO ROBLES,** L. Paul & M. Ford, Capitol	59
46.	**ALMOST PARADISE,** R. Williams, Kapp	63
47.	**BALLERINA,** Nat (King) Cole, Capitol	36
48.	**TRUE LOVE,** Bing Crosby-G. Kelly, Capitol	29
49.	**ALMOST PARADISE,** L. Stein, Unique	67
50.	**GREEN DOOR,** J. Lowe, Dot	45
51.	**BAD BOY,** Jive Bombers, Savoy	65
52.	**COME GO WITH ME,** D. Vikings, Dot	71
53.	**LET'S GO CALYPSO,** R. Draper, Mercury	57
54.	**TRICKY,** R. Marterie, Mercury	—
55.	**BANANA BOAT SONG,** S. Vaughan, Mercury	69
56.	**POOR MAN'S ROSES,** P. Page, Mercury	92
57.	**PLAYING FOR KEEPS,** E. Presley, Victor	37
58.	**WONDERFUL, WONDERFUL,** J. Mathis, Columbia	64
59.	**ANASTASIA,** P. Boone, Dot	55
60.	**LOOK HOMEWARD, ANGEL,** J. Ray, Columbia	57
6[illegible].	**GIRL CAN'T HELP IT,** Little Richard, Specialty	49
62.	**LOVE ME,** E. Presley, Victor	40
62.	**SO RARE,** J. Dorsey, Fraternity	76
64.	**MARIANNE,** Lane Brothers, Victor	—
64.	**WITHOUT LOVE,** C. McPhatter, Atlantic	51
66.	**PARTY DOLL,** N. Petty Trio, ABC-Paramount	73
67.	**RAM-BUNK-SHUSH,** B. Doggett, King	72
67.	**WRITTEN ON THE WIND,** Four Aces, Decca	66
69.	**FOOLS FALL IN LOVE,** Drifters, Atlantic	—
70.	**TAKE ME BACK,** G. Mitchell, Columbia,	53
71.	**YOUNG LOVE,** Crew Cuts, Mercury	60
72.	**THOUSAND MILES AWAY,** Heartbeats, Rama	79
73.	**EVER-LOVIN' FINGERS,** J. Bowen, Roulette	—
74.	**LOVE ME TENDER,** E. Presley, Victor	41
75.	**MI CASA, SU CASA,** P. Como, Victor	—
75.	**POOR BOY,** E. Presley, Victor	75
77.	**GARDEN OF EDEN,** J. Valino, Vik	—
78.	**YOU ARE MY FIRST LOVE,** Nat (King) Cole, Capitol	70
79.	**JUST WALKING IN THE RAIN,** J. Ray, Columbia	60
80.	**GONNA GET ALONG WITHOUT YA NOW,** Patience & Prudence, Liberty	55
80.	**ONE STEP AT A TIME,** B. Lee, Decca	73
80.	**ON MY WORD OF HONOR,** Platters, Mercury	53
80.	**WHAT'S THE REASON (I'M NOT PLEASING YOU)?** F. Domino, Imperial	77
84.	**JUST BECAUSE,** L. Price, ABC-Paramount	96
85.	**WHEN MY BLUE MOON TURNS TO GOLD AGAIN,** E. Presley, Victor	100
86.	**MARIANNE,** B. Ives, Decca	98
87.	**ONE IN A MILLION,** Platters, Mercury	52
88.	**WATERMELON SONG,** T. Ernie, Capitol	—
89.	**NOTHING IS TOO GOOD FOR YOU,** Harvey Boys, Cadence	—
90.	**BY YOU, BY YOU, BY YOU,** J. Lowe, Dot	83
90.	**HOLD 'EM JOE,** H. Belafonte, Victor	—
92.	**LITTLE BY LITTLE,** M. Marlo, ABC-Paramount	80
93.	**DREAMY EYES,** Four Preps, Capitol	89
93.	**ONE SUIT,** T. Ernie, Capitol	—
95.	**SINGING THE BLUES,** M. Robbins, Columbia	—
96.	**REPEAT AFTER ME,** P. Page, Mercury	—
96.	**TOWER'S TROT,** D. Jacobs, Coral	—
96.	**YOUR LOVE FOR ME,** F. Sinatra, Capitol	—
99.	**GREENSLEEVES,** Beverly Sisters, London	—
100.	**LITTLE BY LITTLE,** N. Brown, Savoy	81
100.	**RED SAILS IN THE SUNSET,** T. Hunter, Dot	82

CAUTION TO DEALERS AND JUKE BOX OPERATORS

The Billboard's Top 100 is NOT designed to provide tested information for buying purposes. This function is most reliably served by other regular weekly features: Best Sellers in Stores, Most Played in Juke Boxes, Coming Up Strong and Best Buys.

• Best Sellers in Stores

For survey week ending March 6

RECORDS are ranked in order of their current national selling importance at the retail level, as determined by The Billboard's weekly survey of the top volume dealers in every important market area. When significant action is reported on both sides of a record, points are combined to determine position on the chart. In such a case, both sides are listed in bold type, the leading side on top.

This Week	Record	Last Week	Weeks on Chart
1.	**YOUNG LOVE** (BMI)—T. Hunter — Red Sails in the Sunset (ASCAP)—Dot 15533	1	9
2.	**TEEN-AGE CRUSH** (BMI)—T. Sands — Hep Dee Hootie (BMI)—Cap 3639	4	4
3.	**TOO MUCH** (BMI)—E. Presley — Playing for Keeps (BMI)—Vic 20-6800	2	8
4.	**DON'T FORBID ME** (BMI)—P. Boone — Anastasia (ASCAP)—Dot 15521	3	13
5.	**BANANA BOAT (DAY-O)** (ASCAP)—H. Belafonte — Star-O (ASCAP)—Vic 20-6771	5	10
6.	**MARIANNE** (BMI)—T. Gilkyson — Goodbye, Chiquita (BMI)—Col 40817	7	5
7.	**BUTTERFLY** (BMI)—C. Gracie — Ninety-Nine Ways (BMI)—Cameo 105	8	4
8.	**YOUNG LOVE** (BMI)—S. James — You're the Reason (I'm in Love) (BMI)—Cap 3602	6	11
9.	**ROUND AND ROUND** (BMI)—P. Como / **MI CASA, SU CASA** (ASCAP)—Vic 20-6815	13	2
10.	**PARTY DOLL** (BMI)—B. Knox — My Baby's Gone (BMI)—Roulette 4002	16	3
11.	**LOVE IS STRANGE** (BMI)—Mickey & Sylvia — I'm Going Home (BMI)—Groove 0175	14	10
12.	**BUTTERFLY** (BMI)—A. Williams — It Doesn't Take Very Long (ASCAP)—Cadence 1308	10	3
13.	**MARIANNE** (BMI)—Hilltoppers — You're Wasting Your Time (ASCAP)—Dot 15537	12	5
14.	**I'M WALKIN'** (BMI)—F. Domino — I'm in the Mood for Love (ASCAP)—Imperial 5428	18	2
15.	**BLUE MONDAY** (BMI)—F. Domino — What's the Reason (I'm Not Pleasing You)? (ASCAP)—Imperial 5417	15	10
16.	**MOONLIGHT GAMBLER** (ASCAP)—F. Laine — Lotus Land (ASCAP)—Col 40780	11	14
17.	**BANANA BOAT SONG** (BMI)—Tarriers — No Hidin' Place (BMI)—Glory 249	9	13
18.	**I'M STICKIN' WITH YOU** (BMI)—J. Bowen — Ever-Lovin' Fingers (BMI)—Roulette 4001	19	2
19.	**COME GO WITH ME** (BMI)—D. Vikings — How Can I Find Love? (BMI)—Dot 15538	21	3
20.	**WHO NEEDS YOU** (ASCAP)—Four Lads — It's So Easy to Forget (BMI)—Col 40811	20	5
21.	**PARTY DOLL** (BMI)—S. Lawrence — Pum-Pa-Lum (ASCAP)—Coral 61792	—	1
22.	**I DREAMED** (BMI)—B. Johnson — If It's Wrong to Love You (BMI)—Bally 1020	—	6
22.	**LITTLE DARLIN'** (BMI)—Diamonds — Faithful and True (BMI)—Mercury 71060	—	1
24.	**WALKIN' AFTER MIDNIGHT** (BMI)—P. Cline — Poor Man's Roses (ASCAP)—Dec 30221	22	3
25.	**SINGING THE BLUES** (BMI)—G. Mitchell — Crazy With Love (ASCAP)—Col 40769	17	20
25.	**ALMOST PARADISE** (BMI)—R. Williams — For the First Time (ASCAP)—Kapp 175	—	1

• Most Played in Juke Boxes

For survey week ending March 6

RECORDS are ranked in order of the greatest number of plays in juke boxes thruout the country, as determined by The Billboard's weekly survey of the nation's juke box operators. When significant play is reported on both sides of a record, points are combined to determine position on the chart. In such a case, both sides are listed in bold type, the leading side on top.

This Week	Record	Last Week	Weeks on Chart
1.	**YOUNG LOVE** (BMI)—T. Hunter — Red Sails in the Sunset (ASCAP)—Dot 15533	2	8
2.	**TOO MUCH** (BMI)—E. Presley — Playing for Keeps (BMI)—Vic 20-6800	1	6
3.	**DON'T FORBID ME** (BMI)—P. Boone — Anastasia (ASCAP)—Dot 15521	3	10
4.	**YOUNG LOVE** (BMI)—S. James — You're the Reason (I'm in Love) (BMI)—Cap 3602	4	8
5.	**BANANA BOAT (DAY-O)** (ASCAP)—H. Belafonte — Star-O (ASCAP)—Vic 20-6771	6	7
6.	**MARIANNE** (BMI)—Hilltoppers — You're Wasting Your Time (ASCAP)—Dot 15537	9	4
7.	**MOONLIGHT GAMBLER** (ASCAP)—F. Laine — Lotus Land (ASCAP)—Col 40780	10	11
8.	**MARIANNE** (BMI)—T. Gilkyson — Goodbye, Chiquita (BMI)—Col 40817	11	4
9.	**BANANA BOAT SONG** (BMI)—Tarriers — No Hidin' Place (BMI)—Glory 249	8	10
10.	**BLUE MONDAY** (BMI)—F. Domino — What's the Reason (I'm Not Pleasing You) (ASCAP)—Imperial 5417	5	8
11.	**SINGING THE BLUES** (BMI)—G. Mitchell — Crazy With Love (ASCAP)—Col 40769	7	19
12.	**YOU DON'T OWE ME A THING** (BMI)—J. Ray — Look Homeward, Angel (BMI)—Col 40803	12	6
13.	**BUTTERFLY** (BMI)—A. Williams — It Doesn't Take Very Long (ASCAP)—Cadence 1308	19	2
14.	**TEEN-AGE CRUSH** (BMI)—T. Sands — Hep Dee Hootie (BMI)—Cap 3639	14	3
15.	**BUTTERFLY** (BMI)—C. Gracie — Ninety-Nine Ways (BMI)—Cameo 105	13	3
16.	**KNEE DEEP IN THE BLUES** (BMI)—G. Mitchell — Take Me Back (ASCAP)—Col 40820	16	4
17.	**WHO NEEDS YOU** (ASCAP)—Four Lads — It's So Easy to Forget (BMI)—Col 40811	—	1
18.	**PARTY DOLL** (BMI)—B. Knox — My Baby's Gone (BMI)—Roulette 4002	20	2
19.	**PARTY DOLL** (BMI)—S. Lawrence — Pum-Pa-Lum (ASCAP)—Coral 61792	—	1
20.	**WALKIN' AFTER MIDNIGHT** (BMI)—P. Cline — Poor Man's Roses (BMI)—Dec 30221	—	1

• Best Selling Sheet Music

Tunes are ranked in order of their current national selling importance at the sheet music jobber level.

This Week	Title	Last Week	Weeks on Chart
1.	**Young Love** (Lowery)	1	8
2.	**Banana Boat Song** (E. B. Marks-Bryden)	2	9
3.	**Marianne** (Montclare)	9	3
4.	**Don't Forbid Me** (Roosevelt)	4	8
5.	**True Love** (Buxton Hill)	3	25
6.	**Cinco Robles** (Warman)	5	5
7.	**Butterfly** (Mayland-Presley)	—	1
8.	**Love Me Tender** (Presley)	6	22
9.	**Singing the Blues** (Acuff-Rose)	7	17
10.	**Anastasia** (Feist)	8	8
11.	**Who Needs You** (Korwin)	—	1
12.	**Too Much** (Southern Belle-Presley)	11	5
13.	**Round and Round** (Rush)	—	1
14.	**Moonlight Gambler** (E. H. Morris)	13	8
15.	**Blueberry Hill** (Chappell)	12	18

• Most Played by Jockeys

For survey week ending March 6

SIDES are ranked in order of the greatest number of plays on disk jockey radio shows thruout the country. Results are based on The Billboard's weekly survey among the nation's disk jockeys. The reverse side of each record is also listed.

This Week	Record	Last Week	Weeks on Chart
1.	**YOUNG LOVE** (BMI)—T. Hunter — Red Sails in the Sunset (ASCAP)—Dot 15533	1	9
2.	**TOO MUCH** (BMI)—E. Presley — Playing for Keeps (BMI)—Vic 20-6800	2	7
3.	**YOUNG LOVE** (BMI)—S. James — You're the Reason (I'm in Love) (BMI)—Cap 3602	3	11
4.	**DON'T FORBID ME** (BMI)—P. Boone — Anastasia (ASCAP)—Dot 15521	4	12
5.	**MARIANNE** (BMI)—T. Gilkyson — Goodbye, Chiquita (BMI)—Col 40817	6	6
6.	**MARIANNE** (BMI)—Hilltoppers — You're Wasting Your Time (ASCAP)—Dot 15537	7	6
7.	**TEEN-AGE CRUSH** (BMI)—T Sands — Hep Dee Hootie (BMI)—Cap 3639	8	3
8.	**BUTTERFLY** (BMI)—A. Williams — It Doesn't Take Very Long (ASCAP)—Cadence 1308	13	2
9.	**WHO NEEDS YOU** (ASCAP)—Four Lads — It's So Easy to Forget (BMI)—Col 40811	9	5
10.	**ROUND AND ROUND** (BMI)—P. Como — Mi Casa, Su Casa (ASCAP)—Vic 20-6815	12	3
11.	**LOVE IS STRANGE** (BMI)—Mickey & Sylvia — I'm Going Home (BMI)—Groove 0175	14	6
12.	**BANANA BOAT (DAY-O)** (ASCAP)—H. Belafonte — Star-O (ASCAP)—Vic 20-6771	5	10
13.	**PARTY DOLL** (BMI)—B. Knox — My Baby's Gone (BMI)—Roulette 4002	20	2
14.	**I DREAMED** (BMI)—B. Johnson — If It's Wrong to Love You (BMI)—Bally 1020	11	14
15.	**MOONLIGHT GAMBLER** (ASCAP)—F. Laine — Lotus Land (ASCAP)—Col 40780	10	14
16.	**BUTTERFLY** (BMI)—C. Gracie — Ninety-Nine Ways (BMI)—Cameo 105	18	3
17.	**BLUE MONDAY** (BMI)—F. Domino — What's the Reason (I'm Not Pleasing You) (ASCAP)—Imperial 5417	15	8
18.	**BALLERINA** (ASCAP)—Nat (King) Cole — You Are My First Love (ASCAP)—Cap 3619	21	4
19.	**CAN I STEAL A LITTLE LOVE** (ASCAP)—F. Sinatra — Your Love for Me (BMI)—Cap 3608	22	5
20.	**SINGING THE BLUES** (BMI)—G. Mitchell — Crazy With Love (ASCAP)—Col 40769	17	20
21.	**BANANA BOAT SONG** (BMI)—Tarriers — No Hidin' Place (BMI)—Glory 249	19	12
22.	**YOU DON'T OWE ME A THING** (BMI)—J. Ray — Look Homeward, Angel (BMI)—Col 40803	16	9
23.	**GONE** (BMI)—F. Huskey — Missing Persons (BMI)—Cap 3628	—	1
24.	**BANANA BOAT SONG** (BMI)—Fontane Sisters — Honolulu Moon (ASCAP)—Dot 15527	24	10
25.	**WALKIN' AFTER MIDNIGHT** (BMI)—P. Cline — Poor Man's Roses (BMI)—Dec 30221	—	1

THE TOP 100

For survey week ending March 6

A list of the Top 100 **RECORD SIDES** in the nation according to a **COMBINED TABULATION** of Dealer, Disk Jockey and Juke Box Operator replies to The Billboard's weekly popular record Best Seller and Most Played surveys. Its purpose is to provide Disk Jockeys with additional programming material and to give trade exposure to NEWER records just beginning to show action in the field.

Pos.	Song, Artist, Label	Last Week
1.	**YOUNG LOVE,** T. Hunter, Dot	1
2.	**TOO MUCH,** E. Presley, Victor	2
3.	**DON'T FORBID ME,** P. Boone, Dot	3
4.	**YOUNG LOVE,** S. James, Capitol	4
5.	**MARIANNE,** T. Gilkyson, Columbia	6
6.	**BANANA BOAT (DAY-O),** H. Belafonte, Victor	5
7.	**TEEN-AGE CRUSH,** T. Sands, Capitol	7
8.	**MARIANNE,** Hilltoppers, Dot	8
9.	**BUTTERFLY,** A. Williams, Cadence	14
10.	**MOONLIGHT GAMBLER,** F. Laine, Columbia	9
11.	**BUTTERFLY,** C. Gracie, Cameo	12
12.	**ROUND AND ROUND,** P. Como, Victor	19
13.	**PARTY DOLL,** B Knox, Roulette	18
14.	**BLUE MONDAY,** F. Domino, Imperial	10
15.	**LOVE IS STRANGE,** Mickey & Sylvia, Groove	15
16.	**WHO NEEDS YOU,** Four Lads, Columbia	16
17.	**BANANA BOAT SONG,** Tarriers, Glory	11
18.	**SINGING THE BLUES,** G. Mitchell, Columbia	13
19.	**YOU DON'T OWE ME A THING,** J. Ray, Columbia	17
20.	**PARTY DOLL,** S. Lawrence, Coral	22
21.	**WALKIN' AFTER MIDNIGHT,** P. Cline, Decca	25
22.	**I DREAMED,** B. Johnson, Bally	19
23.	**JIM DANDY,** L. Baker, Atlantic	23
24.	**KNEE DEEP IN THE BLUES,** G. Mitchell, Columbia	21
25.	**I'M STICKIN' WITH YOU,** J. Bowen, Roulette	32
26.	**COME GO WITH ME,** D. Vikings, Dot	52
27.	**I'M WALKIN',** F. Domino, Imperial	35
28.	**GONE,** F. Huskey, Capitol	40
29.	**CAN I STEAL A LITTLE LOVE,** F. Sinatra, Capitol	24
30.	**LUCKY LIPS,** R. Brown, Atlantic	26
31.	**CINCO ROBLES,** R. Arms, Era	34
32.	**JAMAICA FAREWELL,** H. Belafonte, Victor	39
33.	**WRINGLE WRANGLE,** F. Parker, Disneyland	28
34.	**I MISS YOU SO,** C. Connor, Atlantic	37
35.	**BANANA BOAT SONG,** Fontane Sisters, Dot	30
36.	**BAD BOY,** Jive Bombers, Savoy	51
36.	**ONLY ONE LOVE,** G. Hamilton IV, ABC-Paramount	37
38.	**BALLERINA,** Nat (King) Cole, Capitol	47
38.	**CHANTEZ CHANTEZ,** D. Shore, Victor	35
40.	**ALMOST PARADISE,** R. Williams, Kapp	46
41.	**I LOVE MY BABY,** J. Corey, Columbia	42
41.	**YOUR WILD HEART,** J. Layne, Mercury	40
43.	**ALMOST PARADISE,** L. Stein, Unique	49
44.	**CINCO ROBLES,** L. Paul & M. Ford, Capitol	45
44.	**ROCK-A-BYE YOUR BABY,** J. Lewis, Decca	46
46.	**SINCE I MET YOU BABY,** I. J. Hunter, Atlantic	28
47.	**TRUE LOVE,** Bing Crosby & G. Kelly, Capitol	48
48.	**BANANA BOAT SONG,** S. Lawrence, Coral	32
49.	**WHY, BABY, WHY,** P. Boone, Dot	—
50.	**MI CASA SU CASA,** P. Como, Victor	75
51.	**TAKE ME BACK,** G. Mitchell, Columbia	70
52.	**WRINGLE WRANGLE,** B. Hayes, ABC-Paramount	44
53.	**ONE STEP AT A TIME,** B. Lee, Decca	80
53.	**TRICKY,** R. Marterie, Mercury	54
55.	**LOOK HOMEWARD, ANGEL,** J. Ray, Columbia	60
56.	**JUST BECAUSE,** L. Price, ABC-Paramount	84
57	**WONDERFUL WONDERFUL,** J. Mathis, Columbia	58
58.	**LOVE ME,** E. Presley, Victor	62
58.	**LOVE ME TENDER,** E Presley, Victor	74
58.	**I'M WAITING JUST FOR YOU,** P. Boone, Dot	—
61.	**ANASTASIA,** P. Boone, Dot	59
61.	**PLAYING FOR KEEPS,** E. Presley, Victor	57
63.	**RED SAILS IN THE SUNSET,** T. Hunter, Dot	100
63.	**WALL,** P. Page. Mercury	—
65.	**GIRL CAN'T HELP IT,** Little Richard, Specialty	61
66.	**BLUEBERRY HILL,** F. Domino, Imperial	43
67.	**LITTLE DARLIN',** Diamonds, Mercury	—
68.	**SILENT LIPS,** G. Gibbs, Mercury	—
69.	**BANANA BOAT SONG,** S. Vaughan, Mercury	55
70.	**EVER-LOVIN' FINGERS,** J. Bowen, Roulette	73
71.	**LET'S GO CALYPSO,** R. Draper, Mercury	53
72.	**GREEN DOOR,** J. Lowe, Dot	50
73.	**MARIANNE,** Lane Brothers, Victor	64
74.	**AIN'T GOT NO HOME,** C. Henry, Argo	30
75.	**RAM-BUNK-SHUSH,** B. Doggett, King	67
76.	**SITTIN' IN THE BALCONY,** J. Dee, Colonial	—
77.	**THOUSAND MILES AWAY,** Heartbeats, Rama	72
78.	**ALMOST PARADISE,** N. Petty Trio, ABC-Paramount	—
79.	**YOUNG LOVE,** Crew Cuts, Mercury	71
80.	**ROSE AND A BABY RUTH,** G. Hamilton IV, ABC-Paramount	—
81.	**SINGING THE BLUES,** M. Robbins, Columbia	95
82.	**ON MY WORD OF HONOR,** Platters, Mercury	80
83.	**GONNA GET ALONG WITHOUT YA NOW,** Patience & Prudence, Liberty	80
84.	**LITTLE BY LITTLE,** N. Brown, Savoy	100
84.	**WITHOUT LOVE,** C. McPhatter, Atlantic	64
86.	**POOR MAN'S ROSES,** P. Page, Mercury	56
87.	**WATERMELON SONG,** T. Ernie, Capitol	88
88.	**WRITTEN ON THE WIND,** Four Aces, Decca	67
89.	**BIG BEAT,** D. Jacobs, Coral	—
89.	**SO RARE,** J. Dorsey, Fraternity	62
91.	**PUM-PA-LUM,** S. Lawrence, Coral	—
92.	**ON TREASURE ISLAND,** G. Storm, Dot	—
93.	**NOTHING IS TOO GOOD FOR YOU,** Harvey Boys, Cadence	89
94.	**WHAT'S THE REASON (I'M NOT PLEASING YOU),** F. Domino, Imperial	80
95.	**HOLD 'EM JOE,** H. Belafonte, Victor	90
96.	**YOUR LOVE FOR ME,** F. Sinatra, Capitol	96
96.	**'S WONDERFUL,** Conniff, Columbia	—
98.	**DREAMY EYES,** Four Preps, Capitol	93
99.	**LUCKY LIPS,** G. Storm, Dot	—
100.	**ONE SUIT,** T. Ernie, Capitol	93
100.	**MANGOS,** R. Clooney, Columbia	—
100.	**TOWER'S TROT,** D. Jacobs, Coral	96
100.	**BUTTERFLY,** B. Carroll, Unique	—

CAUTION TO DEALERS AND JUKE BOX OPERATORS

The Billboard's Top 100 is NOT designed to provide tested information for buying purposes. This function is most reliably served by other regular weekly features: Best Sellers in Stores, Most Played in Juke Boxes, Coming Up Strong and Best Buys.

• Best Sellers in Stores

For survey week ending March 13

RECORDS are ranked in order of their current national selling importance at the retail level, as determined by The Billboard's weekly survey of the top volume dealers in every important market area. When significant action is reported on both sides of a record, points are combined to determine position on the chart. In such a case, both sides are listed in bold type, the leading side on top.

This Week		Last Week	Weeks on Chart
1.	**YOUNG LOVE** (BMI)—T. Hunter Red Sails in the Sunset (ASCAP)—Dot 15533	1	10
2.	**TEEN-AGE CRUSH** (BMI)—T. Sands Hep Dee Hootie (BMI)—Cap 3639	2	5
3.	**PARTY DOLL** (BMI)—B. Knox My Baby's Gone (BMI)—Roulette 4002	10	4
4.	**ROUND AND ROUND** (BMI)—P. Como Mi Casa, Su Casa (ASCAP)—Vic 20-6815	9	3
5.	**BUTTERFLY** (BMI)—C. Gracie Ninety-Nine Ways (BMI)—Cameo 105	7	5
6.	**I'M WALKIN'** (BMI)—F. Domino I'm in the Mood for Love (ASCAP)—Imperial 5428	14	3
7.	**TOO MUCH** (BMI)—E. Presley Playing for Keeps (BMI)—Vic 20-6800	3	9
8.	**BANANA BOAT (DAY-O)** (ASCAP)—H. Belafonte Star-O (ASCAP)—Vic 20-6771	5	11
9.	**MARIANNE** (BMI)—T. Gilkyson Goodbye, Chiquita (BMI)—Col 40817	6	6
10.	**BUTTERFLY** (BMI)—A. Williams It Doesn't Take Very Long (ASCAP)—Cadence 1308	12	4
11.	**DON'T FORBID ME** (BMI)—P. Boone Anastasia (ASCAP)—Dot 15521	4	14
12.	**YOUNG LOVE** (BMI)—S. James You're the Reason (I'm in Love) (BMI)—Cap 3602	8	12
13.	**MARIANNE** (BMI)—Hilltoppers You're Wasting Your Time (ASCAP)—Dot 15537	13	6
14.	**LITTLE DARLIN'** (BMI)—Diamonds Faithful and True (BMI)—Mercury 71060	22	2
15.	**COME GO WITH ME** (BMI)—D. Vikings How Can I Find Love? (BMI)—Dot 15538	19	4
16.	**LOVE IS STRANGE** (BMI)—Mickey & Sylvia I'm Going Home (BMI)—Groove 0175	11	11
17.	**PARTY DOLL** (BMI)—S. Lawrence Pum-Pa-Lum (ASCAP)—Coral 61792	21	2
18.	**WHY, BABY, WHY?** (BMI)—P. Boone **I'M WAITING JUST FOR YOU** (BMI)—Dot 15545	—	1
19.	**GONE** (BMI)—F. Husky Missing Persons (BMI)—Capitol 3628	—	1
20.	**I'M STICKIN' WITH YOU** (BMI)—J. Bowen Ever-Lovin' Fingers (BMI)—Roulette 4001	18	3
21.	**WALKIN' AFTER MIDNIGHT** (BMI)—P. Cline Poor Man's Roses (ASCAP)—Dec 30221	24	4
22.	**WHO NEEDS YOU?** (ASCAP)—Four Lads It's So Easy to Forget (BMI)—Col 40811	20	6
23.	**MOONLIGHT GAMBLER** (ASCAP)—F. Laine Lotus Land (ASCAP)—Col 40780	16	15
24.	**BANANA BOAT SONG** (BMI)—Tarriers No Hidin' Place (BMI)—Glory 249	17	14
25.	**BLUE MONDAY** (BMI)—F. Domino What's the Reason (I'm Not Pleasing You)? (ASCAP)—Imperial 5417	15	11

• Most Played in Juke Boxes

For survey week ending March 13

RECORDS are ranked in order of the greatest number of plays in juke boxes thruout the country, as determined by The Billboard's weekly survey of the nation's juke box operators. When significant play is reported on both sides of a record, points are combined to determine position on the chart. In such a case, both sides are listed in bold type, the leading side on top.

This Week		Last Week	Weeks on Chart
1.	**YOUNG LOVE** (BMI)—T. Hunter Red Sails in the Sunset (ASCAP)—Dot 15533	1	9
2.	**TOO MUCH** (BMI)—E. Presley Playing for Keeps (BMI)—Vic 20-6800	2	7
3.	**DON'T FORBID ME** (BMI)—P. Boone Anastasia (ASCAP)—Dot 15521	3	11
4.	**MARIANNE** (BMI)—Hilltoppers You're Wasting Your Time (ASCAP)—Dot 15537	6	5
5.	**YOUNG LOVE** (BMI)—S. James You're the Reason (I'm in Love) (BMI)—Cap 3602	4	9
6.	**MARIANNE** (BMI)—T. Gilkyson Goodbye, Chiquita (BMI)—Col 40817	8	5
7.	**BUTTERFLY** (BMI)—A. Williams It Doesn't Take Very Long (ASCAP)—Cadence 1308	13	3
8.	**BANANA BOAT (DAY-O)**, (ASCAP)—H. Belafonte Star-O (ASCAP)—Vic 20-6771	5	8
9.	**TEEN-AGE CRUSH** (BMI)—T. Sands Hep Dee Hootie (BMI)—Cap 3639	14	4
10.	**BANANA BOAT SONG** (BMI)—Tarriers No Hidin' Place (BMI)—Glory 249	9	11
11.	**BLUE MONDAY** (BMI)—F. Domino What's the Reason (I'm Not Pleasing You) (ASCAP)—Imperial 5417	10	9
12.	**BUTTERFLY** (BMI)—C. Gracie Ninety-Nine Ways (BMI)—Cameo 105	15	4
13.	**MOONLIGHT GAMBLER** (ASCAP)—F. Laine Lotus Land (ASCAP)—Col 40780	7	12
14.	**PARTY DOLL** (BMI)—B. Knox My Baby's Gone (BMI)—Roulette 4002	18	3
15.	**ROUND AND ROUND** (BMI)—P. Como Mi Casa, Su Casa (ASCAP)—Vic 20-6815	—	1
16.	**WALKIN' AFTER MIDNIGHT** (BMI)—P. Cline Poor Man's Roses (BMI)—Dec 30221	20	2
17.	**YOU DON'T OWE ME A THING** (BMI)—J. Ray Look Homeward, Angel (BMI)—Col 40803	12	7
18.	**SINGING THE BLUES** (BMI)—G. Mitchell Crazy With Love (ASCAP)—Col 40769	11	20
19.	**PARTY DOLL** (BMI)—S. Lawrence Pum-Pa Lum (ASCAP)—Coral 61792	19	2
20.	**KNEE DEEP IN THE BLUES** (BMI)—G. Mitchell Take Me Back (ASCAP)—Col 40820	16	5
20.	**I'M WALKIN'** (BMI)—F. Domino I'm in the Mood for Love (ASCAP)—Imperial 5428	—	1

• Best Selling Sheet Music

Tunes are ranked in order of their current national selling importance at the sheet music jobber level.

This Week		Last Week	Weeks on Chart
1.	**Young Love** (Lowery)	1	9
2.	**Marianne** (Montclare)	3	4
3.	**Banana Boat Song** (E. B. Marks-Bryden)	2	10
4.	**Don't Forbid Me** (Roosevelt)	4	9
5.	**Butterfly** (Mayland-Presley)	7	2
6.	**True Love** (Buxton Hill)	5	26
6.	**Cinco Robles** (Warman)	6	6
8.	**Why, Baby, Why?** (Winneton)	—	1
9.	**Too Much** (Southern Belle-Presley)	12	6
9.	**Round and Round** (Rush)	13	2
11.	**Who Needs You** (Korwin)	11	2
12.	**Almost Paradise** (Peer)	—	1
12.	**Chantez Chantez** (Cromwell)	—	1
14.	**Anastasia** (Feist)	10	9
15.	**Love Me Tender** (Presley)	8	23

• Most Played by Jockeys

For survey week ending March 13

SIDES are ranked in order of the greatest number of plays on disk jockey radio shows thruout the country. Results are based on The Billboard's weekly survey among the nation's disk jockeys. The reverse side of each record is also listed.

This Week		Last Week	Weeks on Chart
1.	**YOUNG LOVE** (BMI)—T. Hunter Red Sails in the Sunset (ASCAP)—Dot 15533	1	10
2.	**BUTTERFLY** (BMI)—A. Williams It Doesn't Take Very Long (ASCAP)—Cadence 1308	8	3
3.	**YOUNG LOVE** (BMI)—S. James You're the Reason (I'm in Love) (BMI)—Cap 3602	3	12
4.	**DON'T FORBID ME** (BMI)—P. Boone Anastasia (ASCAP)—Dot 15521	4	13
5.	**TOO MUCH** (BMI)—E. Presley Playing for Keeps (BMI)—Vic 20-6800	2	8
6.	**TEEN-AGE CRUSH** (BMI)—T. Sands Hep Dee Hootie (BMI)—Cap 3639	7	4
7.	**ROUND AND ROUND** (BMI)—P. Como Mi Casa, Su Casa (ASCAP)—Vic 20-6815	10	4
8.	**MARIANNE** (BMI)—T. Gilkyson Goodbye, Chiquita (BMI)—Col 40817	5	7
9.	**MARIANNE** (BMI)—Hilltoppers You're Wasting Your Time (ASCAP)—Dot 15537	6	7
10.	**BANANA BOAT (DAY-O)** (ASCAP)—H. Belafonte Star-O (ASCAP)—Vic 20-6771	12	11
11.	**PARTY DOLL** (BMI)—B. Knox My Baby's Gone (BMI)—Roulette 4002	13	3
12.	**I'M WALKIN'** (BMI)—F. Domino I'm in the Mood for Love (ASCAP)—Imperial 5428	—	1
13.	**WHO NEEDS YOU** (ASCAP)—Four Lads It's so Easy to Forget (BMI)—Col 40811	9	6
14.	**BUTTERFLY** (BMI)—C. Gracie Ninety-Nine Ways (BMI)—Cameo 105	16	4
15.	**LOVE IS STRANGE** (BMI)—Mickey & Sylvia I'm Going Home (BMI)—Groove 0175	11	7
16.	**GONE** (BMI)—F. Husky Missing Persons (BMI)—Cap 3628	23	2
17.	**PARTY DOLL** (BMI)—S. Lawrence Pum-Pa-Lum (ASCAP)—Coral 61792	—	2
18.	**BANANA BOAT SONG** (BMI)—Tarriers No Hidin' Place (BMI)—Glory 249	21	13
19.	**BALLERINA** (ASCAP)—Nat (King) Cole You Are My First Love (ASCAP)—Cap 3619	18	5
20.	**WHY, BABY, WHY** (BMI)—P. Boone I'm Waiting Just for You (BMI)—Dot 15545	—	1
21.	**MOONLIGHT GAMBLER** (ASCAP)—F. Laine Lotus Land (ASCAP)—Col 40780	15	15
22.	**YOU DON'T OWE ME A THING** (BMI)—J. Ray Look Homeward, Angel (BMI)—Col 40803	22	10
23.	**BLUE MONDAY** (BMI)—F. Domino What's the Reason (I'm Not Pleasing You) (ASCAP)—Imperial 5417	17	9
24.	**WALKIN' AFTER MIDNIGHT** (BMI)—P. Cline Poor Man's Roses (BMI)—Dec 30221	25	2
25.	**POOR MAN'S ROSES** (ASCAP)—P. Page Wall (ASCAP)—Mercury 71059	—	1

THE TOP 100

For survey week ending March 13

A list of the Top **100 RECORD SIDES** in the nation according to a **COMBINED TABULATION** of Dealer, Disk Jockey and Juke Box Operator replies to The Billboard's weekly popular record Best Seller and Most Played surveys. Its purpose is to provide Disk Jockeys with additional programming material and to give trade exposure to NEWER records just beginning to show action in the field.

Pos.	Song, Artist, Label	Last Week
1.	**YOUNG LOVE,** T. Hunter, Dot	1
2.	**TOO MUCH,** E. Presley, Victor	2
3.	**TEEN-AGE CRUSH,** T. Sands, Capitol	7
4.	**DON'T FORBID ME,** P. Boone, Dot	3
5.	**BUTTERFLY,** A. Williams, Cadence	9
6.	**YOUNG LOVE,** S. James, Capitol	4
7.	**MARIANNE,** T. Gilkyson, Columbia	5
8.	**ROUND AND ROUND,** P. Como, Victor	12
9.	**BANANA BOAT (DAY-O),** H. Belafonte, Victor	6
9.	**MARIANNE,** Hilltoppers, Dot	8
11.	**PARTY DOLL,** B. Knox, Roulette	13
12.	**BUTTERFLY,** C. Gracie, Cameo	11
13.	**I'M WALKIN',** F. Domino, Imperial	27
14.	**BANANA BOAT SONG,** Tarriers, Glory	17
15.	**PARTY DOLL,** S. Lawrence, Coral	20
15.	**LOVE IS STRANGE,** Mickey & Sylvia, Groove	15
17.	**MOONLIGHT GAMBLER,** F. Laine, Columbia	10
17.	**WHO NEEDS YOU,** Four Lads, Columbia	16
19.	**BLUE MONDAY,** F. Domino, Imperial	14
20.	**WALKIN' AFTER MIDNIGHT,** P. Cline, Decca	21
21.	**GONE,** F. Husky, Capitol	28
22.	**LITTLE DARLIN',** Diamonds, Mercury	67
23.	**WHY, BABY, WHY?** P. Boone, Dot	49
24.	**COME GO WITH ME,** D. Vikings, Dot	26
25.	**SINGING THE BLUES,** G. Mitchell, Columbia	18
26.	**JIM DANDY,** L. Baker, Atlantic	23
27.	**I DREAMED,** B. Johnson, Bally	22
28.	**KNEE DEEP IN THE BLUES,** G. Mitchell, Columbia	24
29.	**I'M STICKIN' WITH YOU,** J. Bowen, Roulette	25
30.	**LUCKY LIPS,** R. Brown, Atlantic	30
31.	**POOR MAN'S ROSES,** P. Page, Mercury	86
32.	**I'M SORRY,** Platters, Mercury	—
33.	**MAMA LOOK-A BOO-BOO,** H. Belafonte, Victor	—
33.	**ONLY ONE LOVE,** G. Hamilton IV, ABC-Paramount	36
35.	**ALMOST PARADISE,** R. Williams, Kapp	40
36.	**CINCO ROBLES,** L. Paul & M. Ford, Capitol	44
37.	**WRINGLE WRANGLE,** F. Parker, Disneyland	33
38.	**I'M WAITING JUST FOR YOU,** P. Boone, Dot	58
39.	**CINCO ROBLES,** R. Arms, Era	31
40.	**YOUR WILD HEART,** J. Layne, Mercury	41
41.	**BALLERINA,** Nat (King) Cole, Capitol	38
41.	**CHANTEZ CHANTEZ,** D. Shore, Victor	38
43.	**BAD BOY,** Jive Bombers, Savoy	36
43.	**WALL,** P. Page, Mercury	63
45.	**ALMOST PARADISE,** L. Stein, Unique	43
45.	**TRICKY,** R. Marterie, Mercury	53
47.	**WRINGLE WRANGLE,** B. Hayes, ABC-Paramount	52
48.	**CAN I STEAL A LITTLE LOVE?** F. Sinatra, Capitol	29
49.	**JUST BECAUSE,** L. Price, ABC-Paramount	56
50.	**BANANA BOAT SONG,** Fontane Sisters, Dot	35
51.	**I LOVE MY BABY,** J. Corey, Columbia	41
52.	**JAMAICA FAREWELL,** H. Belafonte, Victor	32
52.	**ROCK-A-BYE YOUR BABY,** J. Lewis, Decca	44
54.	**BLUEBERRY HILL,** F. Domino, Imperial	66
55.	**SITTIN' IN THE BALCONY,** B. Cochran, Liberty	—
56.	**ONE STEP AT A TIME,** B. Lee, Decca	53
57.	**I MISS YOU SO,** C. Connor, Atlantic	34
58.	**GIRL CAN'T HELP IT,** Little Richard, Specialty	65
59.	**SITTIN' IN THE BALCONY,** J. Dee, Colonial	76
60.	**THOUSAND MILES AWAY,** Heartbeats, Rama	77
61.	**ON MY WORD OF HONOR,** Platters, Mercury	82
61.	**SINCE I MET YOU BABY,** I. J. Hunter, Atlantic	46
63.	**EVER-LOVIN' FINGERS,** J. Bowen, Roulette	70
63.	**WRITTEN ON THE WIND,** Four Aces, Decca	88
65.	**LET'S GO CALYPSO,** R. Draper, Mercury	71
65.	**PLAYING FOR KEEPS,** E. Presley, Victor	61
65.	**TRUE LOVE,** Bing Crosby & G. Kelly, Capitol	47
68.	**PAMELA THROWS A PARTY,** J. Reisman, Victor	—
69.	**BANANA BOAT SONG,** S. Lawrence, Coral	48
70.	**WONDERFUL WONDERFUL,** J. Mathis, Columbia	57
71.	**ALMOST PARADISE,** N. Petty Trio, ABC-Paramount	78
71.	**YOUNG LOVE,** Crew Cuts, Mercury	79
73.	**TOWER'S TROT,** D. Jacobs, Coral	100
74.	**ON TREASURE ISLAND,** G. Storm, Dot	92
75.	**BANANA BOAT SONG,** S. Vaughan, Mercury	69
76.	**CALYPSO MELODY,** D. Rose, M-G-M	—
76.	**WITHOUT LOVE,** C. McPhatter, Atlantic	84
78.	**MI CASA SU CASA,** P. Como, Victor	50
78.	**RED SAILS IN THE SUNSET,** T. Hunter, Dot	63
80.	**PUM-PA-LUM,** S. Lawrence, Coral	91
81.	**ANASTASIA,** P. Boone, Dot	61
82.	**SILENT LIPS,** G. Gibbs, Mercury	68
83.	**RAM-BUNK-SHUSH,** B. Doggett, King	75
84.	**FOOLS FALL IN LOVE,** Drifters, Atlantic	—
84.	**HOLD 'EM JOE,** H. Belafonte, Victor	95
84.	**NOTHING IS TOO GOOD FOR YOU,** Harvey Boys, Cadence	93
87.	**BIG BEAT,** D. Jacobs, Coral	89
88.	**MANGOS,** R. Clooney, Columbia	100
89.	**YOUR TRUE LOVE,** C. Perkins, Sun	—
90.	**LUCILLE,** Little Richard, Specialty	—
91.	**MARIANNE,** B. Ives, Decca	—
91.	**WIND IN THE WILLOW,** J. Stafford, Columbia	—
93.	**ONE SUIT,** T. Ernie, Capitol	100
94.	**PIED PIPER,** B. Williams, Coral	—
95.	**SO RARE,** J. Dorsey, Fraternity	89
96.	**LUCKY LIPS,** G. Storm, Dot	99
97.	**SHIP THAT NEVER SAILED,** D. Carroll, Mercury	—
98.	**AIN'T GOT NO HOME,** C. Henry, Argo	74
98.	**BABY DOLL,** A. Williams, Cadence	—
100.	**ROSE AND A BABY RUTH,** G. Hamilton IV, ABC-Paramount	80
100.	**NINETY-NINE WAYS,** T. Hunter, Dot	—

CAUTION TO DEALERS AND JUKE BOX OPERATORS

The Billboard's Top 100 is NOT designed to provide tested information for buying purposes. This function is most reliably served by other regular weekly features: Best Sellers in Stores, Most Played in Juke Boxes, Coming Up Strong and Best Buys.

• Best Sellers in Stores

For survey week ending March 20

RECORDS are ranked in order of their current national selling importance at the retail level, as determined by The Billboard's weekly survey of the top volume dealers in every important market area. When significant action is reported on both sides of a record, points are combined to determine position on the chart. In such a case, both sides are listed in bold type, the leading side on top.

This Week		Last Week	Weeks on Chart
1.	PARTY DOLL (BMI)—B. Knox. My Baby's Gone (BMI)—Roulette 4002	3	5
2.	ROUND AND ROUND (BMI)—P. Como. Mi Casa, Su Casa (ASCAP)—Vic 20-6815	4	4
3.	BUTTERFLY (BMI)—C. Gracie. Ninety-Nine Ways (BMI)—Cameo 105	5	6
4.	BUTTERFLY (BMI)—A. Williams. It Doesn't Take Very Long (ASCAP)—Cadence 1308	10	5
5.	TEEN-AGE CRUSH (BMI)—T. Sands. Hep Dee Hootie (BMI)—Cap 3639	2	6
6.	I'M WALKIN' (BMI)—F. Domino. I'm in the Mood for Love (ASCAP)—Imperial 5428	6	4
7.	LITTLE DARLIN' (BMI)—Diamonds. Faithful and True (BMI)—Mercury 71060	14	3
8.	YOUNG LOVE (BMI)—T. Hunter. Red Sails in the Sunset (ASCAP)—Dot 15533	1	11
9.	MARIANNE (BMI)—T. Gilkyson. Goodbye, Chiquita (BMI)—Col 40817	9	7
10.	WHY, BABY, WHY? (BMI)—P. Boone. **I'M WAITING JUST FOR YOU** (BMI)—Dot 15545	18	2
11.	DON'T FORBID ME (BMI)—P. Boone. Anastasia (ASCAP)—Dot 15521	11	15
12.	COME GO WITH ME (BMI)—D. Vikings. How Can I Find Love? (BMI)—Dot 15538	15	5
13.	MARIANNE (BMI)—Hilltoppers. You're Wasting Your Time (ASCAP)—Dot 15537	13	7
14.	PARTY DOLL (BMI)—S. Lawrence. **PUM-PA-LUM** (ASCAP)—Coral 61792	17	3
14.	TOO MUCH (BMI)—E. Presley. Playing for Keeps (BMI)—Vic 20-6800	7	10
16.	BANANA BOAT (DAY-O) (ASCAP)—H. Belafonte. Star-O (ASCAP)—Vic 20-6771	8	12
17.	GONE (BMI)—F. Huskey. Missing Persons (BMI)—Cap 3628	19	2
18.	YOUNG LOVE (BMI)—S. James. You're the Reason (I'm in Love) (BMI)—Cap 3602	12	13
19.	LOVE IS STRANGE (BMI)—Mickey & Sylvia. I'm Going Home (BMI)—Groove 0175	16	12
20.	I'M STICKIN' WITH YOU (BMI)—J. Bowen. Ever-Lovin' Fingers (BMI)—Roulette 4001	20	4
21.	WALKIN' AFTER MIDNIGHT (BMI)—P. Cline. Poor Man's Roses (ASCAP)—Dec 30221	21	5
22.	MAMA LOOK-A BOO-BOO (BMI)—H. Belafonte. Don't Ever Love Me (ASCAP)—Vic 20-6830	—	1
23.	SITTIN' IN THE BALCONY (BMI)—E. Cochran. Dark Lonely Street (BMI)—Liberty 55056	—	1
24.	I'M SORRY (BMI)—Platters. He's Mine (BMI)—Mercury 71032	—	1
25.	BANANA BOAT SONG (BMI)—Tarriers. No Hidin' Place (BMI)—Glory 249	24	13
25.	NINETY-NINE WAYS (BMI)—T. Hunter. Don't Get Around Much Anymore (ASCAP)—Dot 15548	—	1

• Most Played in Juke Boxes

For survey week ending March 20

RECORDS are ranked in order of the greatest number of plays in juke boxes thruout the country, as determined by The Billboard's weekly survey of the nation's juke box operators. When significant play is reported on both sides of a record, points are combined to determine position on the chart. In such a case, both sides are listed in bold type, the leading side on top.

This Week		Last Week	Weeks on Chart
1.	YOUNG LOVE (BMI—T. Hunter. Red Sails in the Sunset (ASCAP)—Dot 15533	1	10
2.	TOO MUCH (BMI)—E. Presley. Playing for Keeps (BMI)—Vic 20-6800	2	8
3.	DON'T FORBID ME (BMI)—P. Boone. Anastasia (ASCAP)—Dot 15521	3	12
4.	MARIANNE (BMI)—Hilltoppers. You're Wasting Your Time (ASCAP)—Dot 15537	4	6
5.	BUTTERFLY (BMI)—R. Williams. It Doesn't Take Very Long (ASCAP)—Cadence 1308	7	4
6.	MARIANNE (BMI)—T. Gilkyson. Goodbye, Chiquita (BMI)—Col 40817	6	6
7.	TEEN-AGE CRUSH (BMI)—T. Sands. Hep Dee Hootie (BMI)—Cap 3639	9	5
8.	BUTTERFLY (BMI)—C. Gracie. Ninety-Nine Ways (BMI)—Cameo 105	12	5
9.	PARTY DOLL (BMI)—B. Knox. My Baby's Gone (BMI)—Roulette 4002	14	5
10.	YOUNG LOVE (BMI)—S. James. You're the Reason (I'm in Love) (BMI)—Cap 3602	5	10
11.	ROUND AND ROUND (BMI)—P. Como. Mi Casa Su Casa (ASCAP)—Vic 20-6815	15	2
12.	BANANA BOAT (DAY-O) (ASCAP)—H. Belafonte. Star-O (ASCAP)—Vic 20-6771	8	9
13.	WALKIN' AFTER MIDNIGHT (BMI)—P. Cline. Poor Man's Roses (BMI)—Dec 30221	16	3
14.	I'M WALKIN' (BMI)—F. Domino. I'm in the Mood for Love (ASCAP)—Imperial 5428	20	2
15.	BANANA BOAT SONG (BMI)—Tarriers. No Hidin' Place (BMI)—Glory 249	10	12
15.	WHY, BABY, BABY? (BMI)—P. Boone. **I'M WAITING JUST FOR YOU** (BMI)—Dot 15545	—	1
17.	BLUE MON[illegible]Y (BMI)—F. Domino. What's the R[illegible]n (I'm Not Pleasing You)? (ASCAP)—[illegible]rial 5417	11	10
18.	MOONLIGHT GAMBLER (ASCAP)—F. Laine. Lotus Land (ASCAP)—Col 40780	13	13
19.	PARTY DOLL (BMI)—S. Lawrence. Pum-Pa-Lum (ASCAP)—Coral 61792	19	3
20.	LITTLE DARLIN' (BMI)—Diamonds. Faithful and True (BMI)—Mercury 71060	—	1

• Best Selling Sheet Music

Tunes are ranked in order of their current national selling importance at the sheet music jobber level.

This Week		Last Week	Weeks on Chart
1.	Marianne (Montclare)	2	5
2.	Butterfly (Mayland-Presley)	5	3
3.	Young Love (Lowery)	1	10
4.	Banana Boat Song (E. B. Marks-Bryden)	3	11
5.	Round and Round (Rush)	9	3
6.	Chantez Chantez (Cromwell)	12	2
7.	Almost Paradise (Peer)	12	2
8.	Don't Forbid Me (Roosevelt)	4	10
9.	Cinco Robles (Warman)	6	7
10.	Party Doll (Jacie)	—	1
11.	Wringle Wrangle (Disney)	—	2
12.	True Love (Buxton Hill)	6	27
12.	Too Much (Southern Belle-Presley)	9	7
14.	Love Me Tender (Presley)	15	24

• Most Played by Jockeys

For survey week ending March 20

SIDES are ranked in order of the greatest number of plays on disk jockey radio shows thruout the country. Results are based on The Billboard's weekly survey among the nation's disk jockeys. The reverse side of each record is also listed.

This Week		Last Week	Weeks on Chart
1.	BUTTERFLY (BMI)—A. Williams. It Doesn't Take Very Long (ASCAP)—Cadence 1308	2	4
2.	ROUND AND ROUND (BMI)—P. Como. Mi Casa, Su Casa (ASCAP)—Vic 20-6815	7	5
3.	YOUNG LOVE (BMI)—T. Hunter. Red Sails in the Sunset (ASCAP)—Dot 15533	1	11
4.	TEEN-AGE CRUSH (BMI)—T. Sands. Hep Dee Hootie (BMI)—Cap 3639	6	5
5.	YOUNG LOVE (BMI)—S. James. You're the Reason (I'm in Love) (BMI)—Cap 3602	3	13
6.	MARIANNE (BMI)—T. Gilkyson. Goodbye, Chiquita (BMI)—Col 40817	8	8
7.	PARTY DOLL (BMI)—B. Knox. My Baby's Gone (BMI)—Roulette 4002	11	4
8.	DON'T FORBID ME (BMI)—P. Boone. Anastasia (ASCAP)—Dot 15521	4	14
9.	TOO MUCH (BMI)—E. Presley. Playing for Keeps (BMI)—Vic 20-6800	5	9
10.	MARIANNE (BMI)—Hilltoppers. You're Wasting Your Time (ASCAP)—Dot 15537	9	8
11.	I'M WALKIN' (BMI)—F. Domino. I'm in the Mood for Love (ASCAP)—Imperial 5428	12	2
12.	BANANA BOAT (DAY-O) (ASCAP)—H. Belafonte. Star-O (ASCAP)—Vic 20-6771	10	12
13.	BUTTERFLY (BMI)—C. Gracie. Ninety-Nine Ways (BMI)—Cameo 105	14	5
14.	PARTY DOLL (BMI)—S. Lawrence. Pum-Pa-Lum (ASCAP)—Coral 61792	17	3
15.	WHO NEEDS YOU? (ASCAP)—Four Lads. It's So Easy to Forget (BMI)—Col 40811	13	7
16.	WHY, BABY, WHY? (BMI)—P. Boone. I'm Waiting Just for You (BMI)—Dot 15545	20	2
17.	LITTLE DARLIN' (BMI)—Diamonds. Faithful and True (BMI)—Mercury 71060	—	1
18.	GONE (BMI)—F. Huskey. Missing Persons (BMI)—Cap 3628	16	3
19.	LOVE IS STRANGE (BMI)—Mickey & Sylvia. I'm Going Home (BMI)—Groove 0175	15	8
20.	NINETY-NINE WAYS (BMI)—T. Hunter. Don't Get Around Much Anymore (ASCAP)—Dot 15548	—	1
21.	I DREAMED (BMI)—B. Johnson. If It's Wrong to Love You (BMI)—Bally 1020	—	15
22.	WALKIN' AFTER MIDNIGHT (BMI)—P. Cline. Poor Man's Roses (BMI)—Dec 30221	24	3
23.	POOR MAN'S ROSES (ASCAP)—P. Page. Wall (ASCAP)—Mercury 71059	25	2
24.	CHANTEZ-CHANTEZ (ASCAP)—D. Shore. Honky Tonk Heart (BMI)—Vic 20-6792	—	2
25.	MOONLIGHT GAMBLER (ASCAP)—F. Laine. Lotus Land (ASCAP)—Col 40780	21	16

THE TOP 100

For survey week ending March 20

A list of the Top 100 **RECORD SIDES** in the nation according to a **COMBINED TABULATION** of Dealer, Disk Jockey and Juke Box Operator replies to The Billboard's weekly popular record Best Seller and Most Played surveys. Its purpose is to provide Disk Jockeys with additional programming material and to give trade exposure to NEWER records just beginning to show action in the field.

Song	Artist & Label	Last Week
1. **BUTTERFLY,**	A. Williams, Cadence	5
2. **YOUNG LOVE,**	T. Hunter, Dot	1
3. **ROUND AND ROUND,**	P. Como, Victor	8
4. **TEEN-AGE CRUSH,**	T. Sands, Capitol	3
5. **PARTY DOLL,**	B. Knox, Roulette	11
6. **DON'T FORBID ME,**	P. Boone, Dot	4
6. **MARIANNE,**	T. Gilkyson, Columbia	7
8. **BUTTERFLY,**	C. Gracie, Cameo	12
8. **TOO MUCH,**	E. Presley, Victor	2
10. **MARIANNE,**	Hilltoppers, Dot	9
11. **I'M WALKIN',**	F. Domino, Imperial	13
12. **YOUNG LOVE,**	S. James, Capitol	6
13. **BANANA BOAT (DAY-O),**	H. Belafonte, Victor	9
14. **LITTLE DARLIN',**	Diamonds, Mercury	22
15. **PARTY DOLL,**	S. Lawrence, Coral	15
16. **WHY, BABY, WHY?**	P. Boone, Dot	23
17. **WALKIN' AFTER MIDNIGHT,**	P. Cline, Decca	20
18. **LOVE IS STRANGE,**	Mickey & Sylvia, Groove	15
19. **GONE,**	F. Husky, Capitol	21
20. **WHO NEEDS YOU,**	Four Lads, Columbia	17
21. **MOONLIGHT GAMBLER,**	F. Laine, Columbia	17
22. **COME GO WITH ME,**	D. Vikings, Dot	24
23. **BANANA BOAT SONG,**	Tarriers, Glory	14
24. **I'M SORRY,**	Platters, Mercury	32
25. **MAMA LOOK A BOO BOO,**	H. Belafonte, Victor	33
26. **I'M STICKIN' WITH YOU,**	J. Bowen, Roulette	29
27. **BLUE MONDAY,**	F. Domino, Imperial	19
27. **POOR MAN'S ROSES,**	P. Page, Mercury	31
29. **SITTIN' IN THE BALCONY,**	E. Cochran, Liberty	55
30. **I'M WAITING JUST FOR YOU,**	P. Boone, Dot	38
31. **I DREAMED,**	B. Johnson, Bally	27
32. **JIM DANDY,**	L. Baker, Atlantic	26
33. **ALMOST PARADISE,**	R. Williams, Kapp	35
34. **CHANTEZ CHANTEZ,**	D. Shore, Victor	41
35. **SINGING THE BLUES,**	G. Mitchell, Columbia	25
36. **YOU DON'T OWE ME A THING,**	J. Ray, Columbia	—
37. **LUCKY LIPS,**	R. Brown, Atlantic	30
38. **ONLY ONE LOVE,**	G. Hamilton IV, ABC-Paramount	33
39. **ALMOST PARADISE,**	L. Stein, Unique	45
39. **TRICKY,**	R. Marterie, Mercury	45
41. **LUCILLE,**	Little Richard, Specialty	90
42. **NINETY-NINE WAYS,**	T. Hunter, Dot	100
43. **CINCO ROBLES,**	L. Paul & M. Ford, Capitol	36
43. **ONE STEP AT A TIME,**	B. Lee, Decca	56
45. **SITTIN' IN THE BALCONY,**	J. Dee, Colonial	59
46. **BLUEBERRY HILL,**	F. Domino, Imperial	54
47. **KNEE DEEP IN THE BLUES,**	G. Mitchell, Columbia	28
48. **CAN I STEAL A LITTLE LOVE?**	F. Sinatra, Capitol	48
49. **BAD BOY,**	Jive Bombers, Savoy	43
50. **PIED PIPER,**	B. Williams, Coral	94
51. **JUST BECAUSE,**	L. Price, ABC-Paramount	49
51. **JAMAICA FAREWELL,**	H. Belafonte, Victor	52
51. **MANGOS,**	R. Clooney, Columbia	88
54. **BANANA BOAT SONG,**	Fontane Sisters, Dot	50
55. **PUM-PA-LUM,**	S. Lawrence, Coral	80
56. **WONDERFUL WONDERFUL,**	J. Mathis, Columbia	70
57. **WALL,**	P. Page, Mercury	43
58. **BALLERINA,**	Nat (King) Cole, Capitol	41
59. **I MISS YOU SO,**	C. Connor, Atlantic	57
59. **THOUSAND MILES AWAY,**	Heartbeats, Rama	60
61. **BANANA BOAT SONG,**	S. Lawrence, Coral	69
61. **SINCE I MET YOU BABY,**	I. J. Hunter, Atlantic	61
63. **PAMELA THROWS A PARTY,**	J. Reisman, Victor	68
64. **ALMOST PARADISE,**	N Petty Trio, ABC-Paramount	7[illegible]
65. **SHIP THAT NEVER SAILED,**	D. Carroll, Mercury	97
66. **I LOVE MY BABY,**	J. Corey, Columbia	51
67. **YOUR WILD HEART,**	J. Layne, Mercury	40
68. **PARTY DOLL,**	W. Manone, Decca	—
69. **CINCO ROBLES,**	R. Arms, Era	39
70. **LOVE IS A GOLDEN RING,**	F. Laine, Columbia	—
71. **CALYPSO MELODY,**	D. Rose, M-G-M	76
71. **FOOLS FALL IN LOVE,**	Drifters, Atlantic	84
73. **WIND IN THE WILLOW,**	J. Stafford, Columbia	91
74. **WRINGLE WRANGLE,**	B. Hayes, ABC-Paramount	47
75. **EVER-LOVIN' FINGERS,**	J. Bowen, Roulette	63
75. **MI CASA SU CASA,**	P Como, Victor	78
77. **ANASTASIA,**	P. Boone, Dot	81
77. **LUCKY LIPS,**	G. Storm, Dot	96
77. **SO RARE,**	J. Dorsey, Fraternity	95
80. **BAHAMA MAMA,**	Four Aces, Decca	—
80. **SILENT LIPS,**	G. Gibbs, Mercury	82
82. **YOUR TRUE LOVE,**	C. Perkins, Sun	89
83. **TOWER'S TROT,**	D. Jacobs, Coral	73
84. **MARIANNE,**	Lane Brothers, Victor	—
85. **AIN'T GOT NO HOME,**	C. Henry, Argo	98
86. **ROCK-A-BYE YOUR BABY,**	J. Lewis, Decca	52
87. **WRINGLE WRANGLE,**	F. Parker, Disneyland	37
88. **FIRST DATE, FIRST KISS, FIRST LOVE,**	S. James, Capitol	—
89. **DON'T GET AROUND MUCH ANYMORE,**	T. Hunter, Dot	—
89. **PRETEND,**	T. Smith, United	—
91. **PLAYING FOR KEEPS,**	E. Presley, Victor	65
92. **DREAMY EYES,**	Four Preps, Capitol	—
93. **HOLD 'EM JOE,**	H. Belafonte, Victor	84
94. **LET THERE BE YOU,**	Five Keys, Capitol	—
95. **BANANA BOAT SONG,**	S. Vaughan, Mercury	75
96. **YOU'RE MINE,**	Four Aces, Decca	—
97. **RED SAILS IN THE SUNSET,**	T. Hunter, Dot	78
98. **ON MY WORD OF HONOR,**	Platters, Mercury	61
99. **LET GO CALYPSO,**	R. Draper, Mercury	65
99. **WITHOUT LOVE,**	C. McPhatter, Atlantic	76

CAUTION TO DEALERS AND JUKE BOX OPERATORS

The Billboard's Top 100 is NOT designed to provide tested information for buying purposes. This function is most reliably served by other regular weekly features: Best Sellers in Stores, Most Played in Juke Boxes, Coming Up Strong and Best Buys.

• Best Sellers in Stores

For survey week ending March 27

RECORDS are ranked in order of their current national selling importance at the retail level, as determined by The Billboard's weekly survey of the top volume dealers in every important market area. When significant action is reported on both sides of a record, points are combined to determine position on the chart. In such a case, both sides are listed in bold type, the leading side on top.

This Week		Last Week	Weeks on Chart
1.	**ROUND AND ROUND** (BMI)—P. Como Mi Casa, Su Casa (ASCAP)—Vic 20-6815	2	5
2.	**LITTLE DARLIN'** (BMI)—Diamonds Faithful and True (BMI)—Mercury 71060	7	4
3.	**PARTY DOLL** (BMI)—B. Knox My Baby's Gone (BMI)—Roulette 4002	1	6
4.	**BUTTERFLY** (BMI)—C. Gracie Ninety-Nine Ways (BMI)—Cameo 105	3	7
5.	**I'M WALKIN'** (BMI)—F. Domino I'm in the Mood for Love (ASCAP)—Imperial 5428	6	5
6.	**COME GO WITH ME** (BMI)—D. Vikings How Can I Find True Love? (BMI)—Dot 15538	12	6
7.	**TEEN-AGE CRUSH** (BMI)—T. Sands Hep Dee Hootie (BMI)—Cap 3639	5	7
8.	**BUTTERFLY** (BMI)—A. Williams It Doesn't Take Very Long (ASCAP)—Cadence 1308	4	6
9.	**ALL SHOOK UP** (BMI)—E. Presley That's When Your Heartaches Begin (ASCAP)—Vic 20-6870	—	1
10.	**GONE** (BMI)—F. Husky Missing Persons (BMI)—Cap 3628	17	3
11.	**WHY, BABY, WHY?** (BMI)—P. Boone **I'M WAITING JUST FOR YOU** (BMI)—Dot 15545	10	3
12.	**MARIANNE** (BMI)—T. Gilkyson Goodbye, Chiquita (BMI)—Col 40817	9	8
12.	**YOUNG LOVE** (BMI)—T. Hunter Red Sails in the Sunset (ASCAP)—Dot 15533	8	12
14.	**MAMA LOOK-A BOOBOO** (BMI)—H. Belafonte Don't Ever Love Me (ASCAP)—Vic 20-6830	22	2
15.	**BANANA BOAT (DAY-O)** (ASCAP)—H. Belafonte Star-O (ASCAP)—Vic 20-6771	16	13
16.	**DON'T FORBID ME** (BMI)—P. Boone Anastasia (ASCAP)—Dot 15521	11	16
17.	**PARTY DOLL** (BMI)—S. Lawrence Pum-Pa-Lum (ASCAP)—Coral 61792	14	4
18.	**I'M STICKIN' WITH YOU** (BMI)—J. Bowen Ever-Lovin' Fingers (BMI)—Roulette 4001	20	5
19.	**MARIANNE** (BMI)—Hilltoppers You're Wasting Your Time (ASCAP)—Dot 15537	13	8
20.	**YOUNG LOVE** (BMI)—S. James You're the Reason (I'm in Love) (BMI)—Cap 3602	18	14
21.	**TOO MUCH** (BMI)—E. Presley Playing for Keeps (BMI)—Vic 20-6800	14	11
22.	**SITTIN' IN THE BALCONY** (BMI)—E. Cochran Dark Lonely Street (BMI)—Liberty 55056	23	2
23.	**NINETY-NINE WAYS** (BMI)—T. Hunter Don't Get Around Much Anymore (ASCAP)—Dot 15548	25	2
24.	**WALKIN' AFTER MIDNIGHT** (BMI)—P. Cline Poor Man's Roses (ASCAP)—Dec 30221	21	6
25.	**WHO NEEDS YOU?** (ASCAP)—Four Lads It's So Easy to Forget (BMI)—Col 40811	—	6

• Most Played in Juke Boxes

For survey week ending March 27

RECORDS are ranked in order of the greatest number of plays in juke boxes thruout the country, as determined by The Billboard's weekly survey of the nation's juke box operators. When significant play is reported on both sides of a record, points are combined to determine position on the chart. In such a case, both sides are listed in bold type, the leading side on top.

This Week		Last Week	Weeks on Chart
1.	**YOUNG LOVE** (BMI)—T. Hunter Red Sails in the Sunset (ASCAP)—Dot 15533	1	11
2.	**BUTTERFLY** (BMI)—A. Williams It Doesn't Take Very Long (ASCAP)—Cadence 1308	5	5
3.	**MARIANNE** (BMI)—Hilltoppers You're Wasting Your Time (ASCAP)—Dot 15537	4	7
4.	**MARIANNE** (BMI)—T. Gilkyson Goodbye, Chiquita (BMI)—Col 40817	6	7
5.	**TOO MUCH** (BMI)—E. Presley Playing for Keeps (BMI)—Vic 20-6800	2	9
6.	**BUTTERFLY** (BMI)—C. Gracie Ninety-Nine Ways (BMI)—Cameo 105	8	6
7.	**DON'T FORBID ME** (BMI)—P. Boone Anastasia (ASCAP)—Dot 15521	3	13
8.	**PARTY DOLL** (BMI)—B. Knox My Baby's Gone (BMI)—Roulette 4002	9	5
9.	**TEEN-AGE CRUSH** (BMI)—T. Sands Hep Dee Hootie (BMI)—Cap 3639	7	6
10.	**ROUND AND ROUND** (BMI)—P. Como Mi Casa, Su Casa (ASCAP)—Vic 20-6815	11	3
11.	**I'M WALKIN'** (BMI)—F. Domino I'm in the Mood for Love (ASCAP)—Imperial 5428	14	3
12.	**WALKIN' AFTER MIDNIGHT** (BMI)—P. Cline Poor Man's Roses (BMI)—Dec 30221	13	4
13.	**YOUNG LOVE** (BMI)—S. James You're the Reason (I'm in Love) (BMI)—Cap 3602	10	11
14.	**WHY, BABY, WHY?** (BMI)—P. Boone **I'M WAITING JUST FOR YOU** (BMI)—Dot 15545	15	2
15.	**BANANA BOAT (DAY-O)** (ASCAP)—H. Belafonte Star-O (ASCAP)—Vic 20-6771	12	10
16.	**PARTY DOLL** (BMI)—S. Lawrence Pum-Pa-Lum (ASCAP)—Coral 61792	19	4
17.	**LITTLE DARLIN'** (BMI)—Diamonds Faithful and True (BMI)—Mercury 71060	20	2
18.	**GONE** (BMI)—F. Husky Missing Persons (BMI)—Cap 3628	—	1
19.	**MOONLIGHT GAMBLER** (ASCAP)—F. Laine Lotus Land (ASCAP)—Col 40780	18	14
20.	**WHO NEEDS YOU?** (ASCAP)—Four Lads It's So Easy to Forget (BMI)—Col 40811	—	2
20.	**SITTIN' IN THE BALCONY** (BMI)—E. Cochran Dark Lonely Street (BMI)—Liberty 55056	—	1

• Best Selling Sheet Music

Tunes are ranked in order of their current national selling importance at the sheet music jobber level.

This Week		Last Week	Weeks on Chart
1.	**Marianne** (Montclare)	1	6
2.	**Young Love** (Lowery)	3	11
3.	**Round and Round** (Rush)	5	4
4.	**Butterfly** (Mayland-Presley)	2	4
5.	**Banana Boat Song** (E. B. Marks-Bryden)	4	12
6.	**Chantez Chantez** (Cromwell)	6	3
7.	**Almost Paradise** (Peer)	7	3
8.	**Who Needs You?** (Korwin)	—	3
9.	**Party Doll** (Jacie)	10	2
10.	**Cinco Robles** (Warman)	9	8
11.	**Too Much** (Southern Belle-Presley)	12	8
12.	**Don't Forbid Me** (Roosevelt)	8	11
13.	**Gone** (Hill & Range)	—	1
14.	**True Love** (Buxton Hill)	12	28
15.	**Wringle Wrangle** (Disney)	11	3

• Most Played by Jockeys

For survey week ending March 27

SIDES are ranked in order of the greatest number of plays on disk jockey radio shows thruout the country. Results are based on The Billboard's weekly survey among the nation's disk jockeys. The reverse side of each record is also listed.

This Week		Last Week	Weeks on Chart
1.	**BUTTERFLY** (BMI)—A. Williams It Doesn't Take Very Long (ASCAP)—Cadence 1308	1	5
2.	**ROUND AND ROUND** (BMI)—P. Como Mi Casa, Su Casa (ASCAP)—Vic 20-6815	2	6
3.	**YOUNG LOVE** (BMI)—T. Hunter Red Sails in the Sunset (ASCAP)—Dot 15533	3	12
4.	**TEEN-AGE CRUSH** (BMI)—T. Sands Hep Dee Hootie (BMI)—Cap 3639	4	6
5.	**PARTY DOLL** (BMI)—B. Knox My Baby's Gone (BMI)—Roulette 4002	7	5
6.	**YOUNG LOVE** (BMI)—S. James You're the Reason (I'm in Love) (BMI)—Cap 3602	5	14
7.	**I'M WALKIN'** (BMI)—F. Domino I'm in the Mood for Love (ASCAP)—Imperial 5428	11	3
8.	**GONE** (BMI)—F. Husky Missing Persons (BMI)—Cap 3628	18	4
9.	**MARIANNE** (BMI)—T. Gilkyson Goodbye, Chiquita (BMI)—Col 40817	6	9
10.	**PARTY DOLL** (BMI)—S. Lawrence Pum-Pa-Lum (ASCAP)—Coral 61792	14	4
11.	**LITTLE DARLIN'** (BMI)—Diamonds Faithful and True (BMI)—Mercury 71060	17	2
12.	**TOO MUCH** (BMI)—E. Presley Playing for Keeps (BMI)—Vic 20-6800	9	10
13.	**DON'T FORBID ME** (BMI)—P. Boone Anastasia (ASCAP)—Dot 15521	8	15
14.	**MARIANNE** (BMI)—Hilltoppers You're Wasting Your Time (ASCAP)—Dot 15537	10	9
15.	**BUTTERFLY** (BMI)—C. Gracie Ninety-Nine Ways (BMI)—Cameo 105	13	6
16.	**WHY, BABY, WHY?** (BMI)—P. Boone I'm Waiting Just for You (BMI)—Dot 15545	16	3
17.	**WHO NEEDS YOU?** (ASCAP)—Four Lads It's So Easy to Forget (BMI)—Col 40811	15	8
18.	**BANANA BOAT (DAY-O)**, (ASCAP)—H. Belafonte Star-O (ASCAP)—Vic 20-6771	12	13
19.	**NINETY-NINE WAYS** (BMI)—T. Hunter Don't Get Around Much Anymore (ASCAP)—Dot 15548	20	2
20.	**POOR MAN'S ROSES** (ASCAP)—P. Page Wall (ASCAP)—Mercury 71059	23	3
21.	**COME GO WITH ME** (BMI)—D. Vikings How Can I Find True Love? (BMI)—Dot 15538	—	1
22.	**WALKIN' AFTER MIDNIGHT** (BMI)—P. Cline Poor Man's Roses (BMI)—Dec 30221	22	4
23.	**I'M STICKIN' WITH YOU** (BMI)—J. Bowen Ever-Lovin' Fingers (BMI)—Roulette 4001	—	1
24.	**MAMA LOOK-A BOOBOO** (BMI)—H. Belafonte Don't Ever Love Me (ASCAP)—Vic 20-6830	—	1
25.	**LOVE IS STRANGE** (BMI)—Mickey & Sylvia I'm Going Home (BMI)—Groove 0175	19	9

THE TOP 100

For survey week ending March 27

A list of the Top 100 RECORD SIDES in the nation according to a COMBINED TABULATION of Dealer, Disk Jockey and Juke Box Operator replies to The Billboard's weekly popular record Best Seller and Most Played surveys. Its purpose is to provide Disk Jockeys with additional programming material and to give trade exposure to NEWER records just beginning to show action in the field.

Song	Artist & Label	Last Week
1.	**BUTTERFLY,** A. Williams, Cadence	1
2.	**ROUND AND ROUND,** P. Como, Victor	3
3.	**YOUNG LOVE,** T. Hunter, Dot	2
4.	**PARTY DOLL,** B. Knox, Roulette	5
5.	**TEEN-AGE CRUSH,** T. Sands, Capitol	4
6.	**I'M WALKIN',** F. Domino, Imperial	11
7.	**MARIANNE,** T. Gilkyson, Columbia	6
8.	**BUTTERFLY,** C. Gracie, Cameo	8
9.	**LITTLE DARLIN',** Diamonds, Mercury	14
10.	**GONE,** F. Husky, Capitol	19
11.	**DON'T FORBID ME,** P. Boone, Dot	6
11.	**MARIANNE,** Hilltoppers, Dot	10
13.	**TOO MUCH,** E. Presley, Victor	8
14.	**YOUNG LOVE,** S. James, Capitol	12
15.	**PARTY DOLL,** S. Lawrence, Coral	15
16.	**WHY, BABY, WHY?** P. Boone, Dot	16
17.	**BANANA BOAT (DAY-O),** H. Belafonte, Victor	13
18.	**WALKIN, AFTER MIDNIGHT,** P. Cline, Decca	17
19.	**WHO NEEDS YOU?** Four Lads, Columbia	20
20.	**COME GO WITH ME,** D. Vikings, Dot	22
21.	**MAMA LOOK-A BOOBOO,** H. Belafonte, Victor	25
22.	**I'M STICKIN' WITH YOU,** J. Bowen, Roulette	26
23.	**NINETY-NINE WAYS,** T. Hunter, Dot	42
24.	**SITTIN' IN THE BALCONY,** E. Cochran, Liberty	29
25.	**LOVE IS STRANGE,** Mickey & Sylvia, Groove	18
26.	**ALL SHOOK UP,** E. Presley, Victor	—
27.	**I'M WAITING JUST FOR YOU,** P. Boone, Dot	30
28.	**ALMOST PARADISE,** R. Williams, Kapp	33
29.	**I'M SORRY,** Platters, Mercury	24
30.	**BANANA BOAT SONG,** Tarriers, Glory	23
31.	**ALMOST PARADISE,** L. Stein, Unique	39
32.	**LUCILLE,** Little Richard, Specialty	41
33.	**MOONLIGHT GAMBLER,** F. Laine, Columbia	21
34.	**I DREAMED,** B. Johnson, Bally	31
35.	**JUST BECAUSE,** L. Price, ABC-Paramount	51
35.	**JIM DANDY,** L. Baker, Atlantic	32
37.	**TRICKY,** R. Marterie, Mercury	39
38.	**SITTIN' IN THE BALCONY,** J. Dee, Colonial	45
39.	**POOR MAN'S ROSES,** P. Page, Mercury	27
40.	**CHANTEZ CHANTEZ,** D. Shore, Victor	34
41.	**ONLY ONE LOVE,** G. Hamilton IV, ABC-Paramount	38
42.	**SO RARE,** J. Dorsey, Fraternity	77
43.	**BLUE MONDAY,** F. Domino, Imperial	27
44.	**ONE STEP AT A TIME,** B. Lee, Decca	43
45.	**PUM-PA-LUM,** S. Lawrence, Coral	55
46.	**CALYPSO MELODY,** D. Rose, M-G-M	71
47.	**LUCKY LIPS,** R. Brown, Atlantic	37
48.	**SINGING THE BLUES,** G. Mitchell, Columbia	35
48.	**YOU DON'T OWE ME A THING,** J. Ray, Columbia	36
50.	**LOVE IS A GOLDEN RING,** F. Laine, Columbia	70
50.	**MANGOS,** R. Clooney, Columbia	51
52.	**AFTER SCHOOL,** R. Starr, Dale	—
53.	**FIRST DATE, FIRST KISS, FIRST LOVE,** S. James, Capitol	88
54.	**BAD BOY,** Jive Bombers, Savoy	49
55.	**BAHAMA MAMA,** Four Aces, Decca	80
55.	**PAMELA THROWS A PARTY,** J. Reisman, Victor	63
57.	**ALMOST PARADISE,** N. Petty Trio, ABC-Paramount	64
57.	**WALL,** P. Page, Mercury	57
59.	**BALLERINA,** N. (King) Cole, Capitol	58
60.	**WONDERFUL WONDERFUL,** J. Mathis, Columbia	56
61.	**BUTTERFLY,** B. Carroll, Bally	—
62.	**WALL,** E. Rodgers, Columbia	—
63.	**WRINGLE WRANGLE,** B. Hayes, ABC-Paramount	74
64.	**ANASTASIA,** P. Boone, Dot	77
65.	**EMPTY ARMS,** T. Brewer, Coral	—
66.	**KNEE DEEP IN THE BLUES,** G. Mitchell, Columbia	47
67.	**CINCO ROBLES,** R. Arms, Era	69
67.	**SEND ME SOME LOVIN',** Little Richard, Specialty	—
67.	**YOUR TRUE LOVE,** C. Perkins, Sun	82
70.	**PARTY DOLL,** W. Manone, Decca	68
71.	**ROCK-A-BILLY,** G. Mitchell, Columbia	—
72.	**THOUSAND MILES AWAY,** Heartbeats, Rama	59
73.	**'S WONDERFUL,** R. Conniff, Columbia	—
74.	**BANANA BOAT SONG,** S. Lawrence, Coral	61
75.	**MI CASA, SU CASA,** P. Como, Victor	75
76.	**YOU'RE MINE,** Four Aces, Decca	96
77.	**JAMAICA FAREWELL,** H. Belafonte, Victor	51
78.	**SCHOOL DAY,** C. Berry, Chess	—
79.	**I MISS YOU SO,** C. Connor, Atlantic	59
80.	**LITTLE DARLIN',** Gladiolas, Excello	—
81.	**LOOK HOMEWARD ANGEL,** J. Ray, Columbia	—
82.	**ON TREASURE ISLAND,** G. Storm, Dot	—
83.	**LET THERE BE YOU,** Five Keys, Capitol	94
84.	**BLUEBERRY HILL,** F. Domino, Imperial	46
84.	**MARIANNE,** B. Ives, Decca	—
86.	**PLEDGE OF LOVE,** K. Copeland, Imperial	—
86.	**SINCE I MET YOU BABY,** I. J. Hunter, Atlantic	61
88.	**CINCO ROBLES,** L. Paul & M. Ford, Capitol	43
89.	**FOOLS FALL IN LOVE,** Drifters, Atlantic	71
90.	**PIED PIPER,** B. Williams, Coral	50
91.	**HE'S MINE,** Platters, Mercury	—
92.	**CAN I STEAL A LITTLE LOVE?** F. Sinatra, Capitol	48
93.	**LOVE ME,** E. Presley, Victor	—
94.	**BANANA BOAT SONG,** Fontane Sisters, Dot	54
94.	**MARIANNE,** Lane Brothers, Victor	84
96.	**BIG BEAT,** D. Jacobs, Coral	—
97.	**I LOVE MY BABY,** J. Corey, Columbia	66
98.	**DON'T GET AROUND MUCH ANYMORE,** T. Hunter, Dot	89
99.	**TRUE LOVE,** Bing Crosby & G. Kelly, Capitol	—
100.	**FORTY CUPS OF COFFEE,** B. Haley, Decca	—
100.	**PRETEND,** T. Smith, United	89
100.	**WITHOUT LOVE,** C. McPhatter, Atlantic	—

CAUTION TO DEALERS AND JUKE BOX OPERATORS

The Billboard's Top 100 is NOT designed to provide tested information for buying purposes. This function is most reliably served by other regular weekly features: Best Sellers in Stores, Most Played in Juke Boxes, Coming Up Strong and Best Buys.

• Best Sellers in Stores

For survey week ending April 3

RECORDS are ranked in order of their current national selling importance at the retail level, as determined by The Billboard's weekly survey of the top volume dealers in every important market area. When significant action is reported on both sides of a record, points are combined to determine position on the chart. In such a case, both sides are listed in bold type, the leading side on top.

This Week	Record	Last Week	Weeks on Chart
1.	**ALL SHOOK UP** (BMI)—E. Presley That's When Your Heartaches Begin (ASCAP)—Vic 20-6870	9	2
2.	**LITTLE DARLIN'** (BMI)—Diamonds Faithful and True (BMI)—Mercury 71060	2	5
3.	**PARTY DOLL** (BMI)—B. Knox My Baby's Gone (BMI)—Roulette 4002	3	7
4.	**ROUND AND ROUND** (BMI)—P. Como Mi Casa, Su Casa (ASCAP)—Vic 20-6815	1	6
5.	**BUTTERFLY** (BMI)—A. Williams It Doesn't Take Very Long (ASCAP)—Cadence 1308	8	7
5.	**WHY, BABY, WHY?** (BMI)—P. Boone **I'M WAITING JUST FOR YOU** (BMI)—Dot 15545	11	4
7.	**COME GO WITH ME** (BMI)—D. Vikings How Can I Find Love? (BMI)—Dot 15538	6	7
8.	**I'M WALKIN'** (BMI)—F. Domino I'm in the Mood for Love (ASCAP)—Imperial 5428	5	6
9.	**GONE** (BMI)—F. Husky Missing Persons (BMI)—Cap 3628	10	4
10.	**BUTTERFLY** (BMI)—C. Gracie Ninety-Nine Ways (BMI)—Cameo 105	4	8
11.	**TEEN-AGE CRUSH** (BMI)—T. Sands Hep Dee Hootie (BMI)—Cap 3639	7	8
12.	**MAMA LOOK-A BOOBOO** (BMI)—H. Belafonte Don't Ever Love Me (ASCAP)—Vic 20-6830	14	3
13.	**MARIANNE** (BMI)—T. Gilkyson Goodbye, Chiquita (BMI)—Col 40817	12	9
14.	**PARTY DOLL** (BMI)—S. Lawrence Pum-Pa-Lum (ASCAP)—Coral 61792	17	5
15.	**MARIANNE** (BMI)—Hilltoppers You're Wasting Your Time (ASCAP)—Dot 15537	19	9
16.	**YOUNG LOVE** (BMI)—T. Hunter Red Sails in the Sunset (ASCAP)—Dot 15533	12	13
17.	**NINETY-NINE WAYS** (BMI)—T. Hunter Don't Get Around Much Anymore (ASCAP)—Dot 15548	23	3
18.	**I'M STICKIN' WITH YOU** (BMI)—J. Bowen Ever-Lovin' Fingers (BMI)—Roulette 4001	18	6
19.	**TOO MUCH** (BMI)—E. Presley Playing for Keeps (BMI)—Vic 20-6800	21	12
20.	**DON'T FORBID ME** (BMI)—P. Boone Anastasia (ASCAP)—Dot 15521	16	17
21.	**LUCILLE** (BMI)—Little Richard **SEND ME SOME LOVIN'** (BMI)—Specialty 598	—	1
22.	**BANANA BOAT (DAY-O)** (ASCAP)—H. Belafonte Star-O (ASCAP)—Vic 20-6771	15	14
22.	**SITTIN' IN THE BALCONY** (BMI)—E. Cochran Dark Lonely Street (BMI)—Liberty 55056	22	3
24.	**HE'S MINE** (BMI)—Platters I'm Sorry (BMI)—Mercury 71032	—	1
25.	**WALKIN' AFTER MIDNIGHT** (BMI)—P. Cline Poor Man's Roses (ASCAP)—Dec 30221	24	7

• Most Played in Juke Boxes

For survey week ending April 3

RECORDS are ranked in order of the greatest number of plays in juke boxes thruout the country, as determined by The Billboard's weekly survey of the nation's juke box operators. When significant play is reported on both sides of a record, points are combined to determine position on the chart. In such a case, both sides are listed in bold type, the leading side on top.

This Week	Record	Last Week	Weeks on Chart
1.	**BUTTERFLY** (BMI)—C. Gracie Ninety-Nine Ways (BMI)—Cameo 105	6	7
2.	**PARTY DOLL** (BMI)—B. Knox My Baby's Gone (BMI)—Roulette 4002	8	6
3.	**YOUNG LOVE** (BMI)—T. Hunter Red Sails in the Sunset (ASCAP)—Dot 15533	1	12
3.	**BUTTERFLY** (BMI)—A. Williams It Doesn't Take Very Long (ASCAP)—Cadence 1308	2	6
5.	**MARIANNE** (BMI)—T. Gilkyson Goodbye, Chiquita (BMI)—Col 40817	4	8
6.	**I'M WALKIN'** (BMI)—F. Domino I'm in the Mood for Love (ASCAP)—Imperial 5428	11	4
7.	**ROUND AND ROUND** (BMI)—P. Como Mi Casa, Su Casa (ASCAP)—Vic 20-6815	10	4
8.	**MARIANNE** (BMI)—Hilltoppers Your Wasting Your Time (ASCAP)—Dot 15537	3	8
9.	**TEEN-AGE CRUSH** (BMI)—T. Sands Hep Dee Hootie (BMI)—Cap 3639	9	7
10.	**WHY, BABY, WHY?** (BMI)—P. Boone **I'M WAITING JUST FOR YOU** (BMI)—Dot 15545	14	3
10.	**LITTLE DARLIN'** (BMI)—Diamonds Faithful and True (BMI)—Mercury 71060	17	3
12.	**YOUNG LOVE** (BMI)—S. James You're the Reason (I'm in Love) (BMI)—Cap 3602	13	12
13.	**DON'T FORBID ME** (BMI)—P. Boone Anastasia (ASCAP)—Dot 15521	7	14
14.	**TOO MUCH** (BMI)—E. Presley Playing for Keeps (BMI)—Vic 20-6800	5	10
15.	**WALKIN' AFTER MIDNIGHT** (BMI)—P. Cline Poor Man's Roses (BMI)—Dec 30221	12	5
16.	**GONE** (BMI)—F. Husky Missing Persons (BMI)—Cap 3628	18	2
17.	**PARTY DOLL** (BMI) S. Lawrence Pum-Pa-Lum (ASCAP)—Coral 61792	16	5
18.	**BANANA BOAT (DAY-O)** (ASCAP)—H. Belafonte Star-O (ASCAP)—Vic 20-6771	15	11
19.	**ALL SHOOK UP** (BMI)—E. Presley That's When Your Heartaches Begin (ASCAP)—Vic 20-6870	—	1
19.	**MAMA LOOK-A BOOBOO** (BMI)—H. Belafonte Don't Ever Love Me (ASCAP)—Vic 20-6830	—	1
19.	**NINETY-NINE WAYS** (BMI)—T. Hunter Don't Get Around Much Anymore (ASCAP)—Dot 15548	—	1

• Best Selling Sheet Music

Tunes are ranked in order of their current national selling importance at the sheet music jobber level.

This Week	Title	Last Week	Weeks on Chart
1.	**Marianne** (Montclare)	1	7
2.	**Round and Round** (Rush)	3	5
3.	**Butterfly** (Mayland-Presley)	4	5
4.	**Young Love** (Lowery)	2	12
5.	**Chantez-Chantez** (Cromwell)	6	4
6.	**Almost Paradise** (Peer)	7	4
6.	**Party Doll** (Jacie)	9	3
8.	**Banana Boat Song** (E. B. Marks-Bryden)	5	13
9.	**Who Needs You?** (Korwin)	8	4
10.	**Cinco Robles** (Warman)	10	9
11.	**Why Baby, Why?** (Winneton)	—	1
12.	**Don't Forbid Me** (Roosevelt)	12	12
13.	**Too Much** (Southern-Belle-Presley)	11	9
14.	**Teen-Age Crush** (Central Songs)	—	1
15.	**Gone** (Hill & Range)	13	2

• Most Played by Jockeys

For survey week ending April 3

SIDES are ranked in order of the greatest number of plays on disk jockey radio shows thruout the country. Results are based on The Billboard's weekly survey among the nation's disk jockeys. The reverse side of each record is also listed.

This Week	Record	Last Week	Weeks on Chart
1.	**ROUND AND ROUND** (BMI)—P. Como Mi Casa, Su Casa (ASCAP)—Vic 20-6815	2	7
2.	**BUTTERFLY** (BMI)—A. Williams It Doesn't Take Very Long (ASCAP)—Cadence 1308	1	6
3.	**LITTLE DARLIN'** (BMI)—Diamonds Faithful and True (BMI)—Mercury 71060	11	3
4.	**I'M WALKIN'** (BMI)—F. Domino I'm in the Mood for Love (ASCAP)—Imperial 5428	7	4
5.	**PARTY DOLL** (BMI)—S. Lawrence Pum-Pa-Lum (ASCAP)—Coral 61792	10	5
6.	**PARTY DOLL** (BMI)—B. Knox My Baby's Gone (BMI)—Roulette 4002	5	6
7.	**ALL SHOOK UP** (BMI)—E. Presley That's When Your Heartaches Begin (ASCAP)—Vic 20-6870	—	1
8.	**GONE** (BMI)—F. Husky Missing Persons (BMI)—Cap 3628	8	5
9.	**WHY, BABY, WHY?** (BMI)—P. Boone I'm Waiting Just for You (BMI)—Dot 15545	16	4
10.	**YOUNG LOVE** (BMI)—T. Hunter Red Sails in the Sunset (ASCAP)—Dot 15533	3	13
11.	**TEEN-AGE CRUSH** (BMI)—T. Sands Hep Dee Hootie (BMI)—Cap 3639	4	7
12.	**MARIANNE** (BMI)—T. Gilkyson Goodbye, Chiquita (BMI)—Col 40817	9	10
13.	**MARIANNE** (BMI)—Hiltoppers You're Wasting Your Time (ASCAP)—Dot 15537	14	10
14.	**POOR MAN'S ROSES** (ASCAP)—P. Page Wall (ASCAP)—Mercury 71059	20	4
15.	**NINETY-NINE WAYS** (BMI)—T. Hunter Don't Get Around Much Anymore (ASCAP)—Dot 15548	19	3
16.	**COME GO WITH ME** (BMI)—D. Vikings How Can I Find True Love? (BMI)—Dot 15538	21	2
17.	**DON'T FORBID ME** (BMI)—P. Boone Anastasia (ASCAP)—Dot 15521	13	16
18.	**YOUNG LOVE** (BMI)—S. James You're the Reason (I'm in Love) (BMI)—Cap 3602	6	15
19.	**WHO NEEDS YOU?** (ASCAP)—Four Lads It's So Easy to Forget (BMI)—Col 40811	17	9
20.	**BUTTERFLY** (BMI)—C. Gracie Ninety-Nine Ways (BMI)—Cameo 105	15	7
21.	**TOO MUCH** (BMI)—E. Presley Playing for Keeps (BMI)—Vic 20-6800	12	11
22.	**CHANTEZ-CHANTEZ** (ASCAP)—D. Shore Honky Tonk Heart (BMI)—Vic 20-6792	—	3
23.	**BANANA BOAT (DAY-O)** (ASCAP)—H. Belafonte Star-O (ASCAP)—Vic 20-6771	18	14
24.	**I'M STICKIN' WITH YOU** (BMI)—J. Bowen Ever-Lovin' Fingers (BMI)—Roulette 4001	23	2
25.	**TRICKY** (BMI)—R. Marterie Travel at Your Own Risk (ASCAP)—Mercury 71050	—	1

THE TOP 100

For survey week ending April 3

A list of the Top 100 RECORD SIDES in the nation according to a COMBINED TABULATION of Dealer, Disk Jockey and Juke Box Operator replies to The Billboard's weekly popular record Best Seller and Most Played surveys. Its purpose is to provide Disk Jockeys with additional programming material and to give trade exposure to NEWER records just beginning to show action in the field.

Pos.	Song, Artist, Label	Last Week
1.	**BUTTERFLY,** A. Williams, Cadence	1
2.	**PARTY DOLL,** B. Knox, Roulette	4
3.	**ROUND AND ROUND,** P. Como, Victor	2
4.	**LITTLE DARLIN',** Diamonds, Mercury	9
5.	**I'M WALKIN',** F. Domino, Imperial	6
6.	**ALL SHOOK UP,** E. Presley, Victor	26
6.	**YOUNG LOVE,** T. Hunter, Dot	3
8.	**MARIANNE,** T. Gilkyson, Columbia	7
9.	**BUTTERFLY,** C. Gracie, Cameo	8
9.	**TEEN-AGE CRUSH,** T. Sands, Capitol	5
11.	**GONE,** F. Husky, Capitol	10
11.	**WHY, BABY, WHY?** P. Boone, Dot	16
13.	**PARTY DOLL,** S. Lawrence, Coral	15
14.	**MARIANNE,** Hilltoppers, Dot	11
15.	**DON'T FORBID ME,** P. Boone, Dot	11
16.	**NINETY NINE WAYS,** T. Hunter, Dot	23
17.	**COME GO WITH ME,** D. Vikings, Dot	20
18.	**TOO MUCH,** E. Presley, Victor	13
19.	**MAMA LOOK-A BOOBOO,** H. Belafonte, Victor	21
20.	**YOUNG LOVE,** S. James, Capitol	14
21.	**BANANA BOAT (DAY-O),** H. Belafonte, Victor	17
22.	**I'M STICKIN' WITH YOU,** J. Bowen, Roulette	22
22.	**WALKIN' AFTER MIDNIGHT,** P. Cline, Decca	18
24.	**SITTIN' IN THE BALCONY,** E. Cochran, Liberty	24
25.	**WHO NEEDS YOU,** Four Lads, Columbia	19
26.	**LOVE IS STRANGE,** Mickey & Sylvia, Groove	25
27.	**LUCILLE,** Little Richard, Specialty	32
28.	**I'M SORRY,** Platters, Mercury	29
29.	**JUST BECAUSE,** L. Price, ABC-Paramount	35
30.	**BANANA BOAT SONG,** Tarriers, Glory	30
31.	**ALMOST PARADISE,** R. Williams, Kapp	28
31.	**CHANTEZ-CHANTEZ,** D. Shore, Victor	40
33.	**I'M WAITING JUST FOR YOU,** P. Boone, Dot	27
34.	**ROCK-A-BILLY,** G. Mitchell, Columbia	71
35.	**POOR MAN'S ROSES,** P. Page, Mercury	39
36.	**SO RARE,** J. Dorsey, Fraternity	42
37.	**I DREAMED,** B. Johnson, Bally	34
38.	**TRICKY,** R Marterie, Mercury	37
39.	**ALMOST PARADISE,** L. Stein, Unique	31
40.	**MANGOS,** R. Clooney, Columbia	50
41.	**PLEDGE OF LOVE,** K. Copeland, Imperial	86
42.	**CALYPSO MELODY,** D Rose, M-G-M	46
43.	**ONLY ONE LOVE,** G. Hamilton IV, ABC-Paramount	41
44.	**SITTIN' IN THE BALCONY.** J. Dee, Colonial	38
45.	**JIM DANDY,** L. Baker, Atlantic	35
46.	**SCHOOL DAY,** C. Berry Chess	78
47.	**LITTLE DARLIN',** Gladiolas, Excello	80
48.	**HE'S MINE,** Platters, Mercury	91
49.	**FIRST DATE, FIRST KISS, FIRST LOVE,** S. James, Capitol	53
49.	**LUCKY LIPS,** Ruth Brown, Atlantic	47
51.	**LOVE IS A GOLDEN RING,** F. Laine, Columbia	50
52.	**ONE STEP AT A TIME,** B. Lee, Decca	44
53.	**BAHAMA MAMA,** Four Aces, Decca	55
54.	**SEND ME SOME LOVIN',** Little Richard, Specialty	67
55.	**AFTER SCHOOL,** R. Starr, Dale	52
56.	**MOONLIGHT GAMBLER,** F. Laine, Columbia	33
57	**PAMELA THROWS A PARTY,** J. Reisman, Victor	55
58.	**PEACE IN THE VALLEY,** E. Presley, Victor	—
59.	**WHITE SPORT COAT,** M. Robbins, Columbia	—
59.	**WONDERFUL WONDERFUL,** J. Mathis, Columbia	60
59.	**THAT'S WHEN YOUR HEARTACHES BEGIN,** E. Presley, Victor	—
62.	**BALLERINA,** Nat King Cole, Capitol	59
63.	**BANANA BOAT (DAY-O),** S. Freberg, Capitol	—
64.	**PARTY DOLL,** W. Manone, Decca	70
65.	**ALMOST PARADISE,** N. Petty Trio, ABC-Paramount	57
65.	**CAN I STEAL A LITTLE LOVE,** F. Sinatra, Capitol	92
67.	**YOUNG LOVE,** Crew Cuts, Mercury	—
68.	**BUTTERFLY,** B. Carroll, Bally	61
68.	**DARK MOON,** B. Guitar, Dot	—
70.	**FORTY CUPS OF COFFEE,** B. Haley, Decca	100
71.	**BLUE MONDAY,** F. Domino, Imperial	43
72.	**PLEDGE OF LOVE,** M. Torok, Decca	—
73.	**THOUSAND MILES AWAY,** Heartbeats, Rama	72
74.	**BANANA BOAT SONG,** Fontane Sisters, Dot	94
75.	**WALL,** P. Page, Mercury	57
76.	**MI CASA SU CASA,** P. Como, Victor	75
76	**SINGING THE BLUES,** G. Mitchell, Columbia	48
76.	**WRINGLE WRANGLE,** B. Hayes, ABC-Paramount	63
79.	**EMPTY ARMS,** T Brewer, Coral	65
80.	**BAD BOY,** Jive Bombers, Savoy	54
81.	**LUCKY LIPS,** G. Storm, Dot	—
82.	**SINCE I MET YOU BABY,** I J. Hunter, Atlantic	86
83.	**CINCO ROBLES,** L. Paul & M Ford, Capitol	88
84.	**YOU'RE MINE,** Four Aces, Decca	76
85.	**PUM-PA-LUM,** S. Lawrence, Coral	46
86.	**I MISS YOU SO,** C. Connor, Atlantic	79
86.	**I'LL TAKE ROMANCE,** E. Gorme, ABC-Paramount	—
86.	**SHIP THAT NEVER SAILED,** D. Carroll, Mercury	—
86.	**TRUE LOVE,** Bing Crosby & G. Kelly, Capitol	99
90.	**CINCO ROBLES,** R. Arms, Era	67
90.	**TILL,** P. Faith, Columbia	—
92.	**EMPTY ARMS,** I. J. Hunter, Atlantic	—
93.	**DO I LOVE YOU,** V. Damone, Columbia	—
94	**YOUR TRUE LOVE,** C. Perkins, Sun	67
95.	**'S WONDERFUL,** R. Conniff, Columbia	73
95.	**SHIP THAT NEVER SAILED,** B. Vaughn, Dot	—
97.	**ANASTASIA,** P. Boone, Dot	64
97.	**LET THERE BE YOU,** Five Keys, Capitol	83
99.	**BANANA BOAT SONG,** S. Lawrence, Coral	74
99.	**EVER LOVIN' FINGERS,** J. Bowen, Roulette	—

CAUTION TO DEALERS AND JUKE BOX OPERATORS

The Billboard's Top 100 is NOT designed to provide tested information for buying purposes. This function is most reliably served by other regular weekly features: Best Sellers in Stores, Most Played in Juke Boxes, Coming Up Strong and Best Buys.

• Best Sellers in Stores

For survey week ending April 10

RECORDS are ranked in order of their current national selling importance at the retail level, as determined by The Billboard's weekly survey of the top volume dealers in every important market area. When significant action is reported on both sides of a record, points are combined to determine position on the chart. In such a case, both sides are listed in bold type, the leading side on top.

This Week		Last Week	Weeks on Chart
1.	**ALL SHOOK UP** (BMI)—E. Presley That's When Your Heartaches Begin (ASCAP)—Vic 20-6870	1	3
2.	**LITTLE DARLIN'** (BMI)—Diamonds Faithful and True (BMI)—Mercury 71060	2	6
3.	**ROUND AND ROUND** (BMI)—P. Como Mi Casa, Su Casa (ASCAP)—Vic 20-6815	4	7
4.	**PARTY DOLL** (BMI)—B. Knox My Baby's Gone (BMI)—Roulette 4002	3	8
5.	**COME GO WITH ME** (BMI)—D. Vikings How Can I Find True Love? (BMI)—Dot 15538	7	8
6.	**GONE** (BMI)—F. Husky Missing Persons (BMI)—Cap 3628	9	5
7.	**WHY, BABY, WHY?** (BMI)—P. Boone **I'M WAITING JUST FOR YOU** (BMI)—Dot 15545	5	5
8.	**BUTTERFLY** (BMI)—A. Williams It Doesn't Take Very Long (ASCAP)—Cadence 1308	5	8
9.	**I'M WALKIN'** (BMI)—F. Domino I'm in the Mood for Love (ASCAP)—Imperial 5428	8	7
10.	**BUTTERFLY** (BMI)—C. Gracie Ninety-Nine Ways (BMI)—Cameo 105	10	9
11.	**MAMA LOOK-A BOOBOO** (BMI)—H. Belafonte Don't Ever Love Me (ASCAP)—Vic 20-6830	12	4
12.	**PARTY DOLL** (BMI)—S. Lawrence Pum-Pa-Lum (ASCAP)—Coral 61792	14	6
13.	**TEEN-AGE CRUSH** (BMI)—T. Sands Hep Dee Hootie (BMI)—Cap 3639	11	9
14.	**I'M SORRY** (BMI)—Platters **HE'S MINE** (BMI)—Mercury 71032	24	2
15.	**NINETY-NINE WAYS** (BMI)—T. Hunter Don't Get Around Much Anymore (ASCAP)—Dot 15548	17	4
16.	**I'M STICKIN' WITH YOU** (BMI)—J. Bowen Ever-Lovin Fingers (BMI)—Roulette 1001	18	7
17.	**SCHOOL DAY** (BMI)—C. Berry Deep Feeling (BMI)—Chess 1653	—	1
18.	**MARIANNE** (BMI)—T. Gilkyson Goodbye, Chiquita (BMI)—Col 40817	13	10
19.	**ROCK-A-BILLY** (ASCAP)—G. Mitchell Hoot Owl (ASCAP)—Col 40877	—	1
20.	**SO RARE** (ASCAP)—J. Dorsey Sophisticated Swing (ASCAP)—Fraternity 755	—	1
21.	**YOUNG LOVE** (BMI)—T. Hunter Red Sails in the Sunset (ASCAP)—Dot 15533	16	14
22.	**BANANA BOAT (DAY-O)** (ASCAP)—H. Belafonte Star-O (ASCAP)—Vic 20-6771	22	15
23.	**ALMOST PARADISE** (BMI)—R. Williams For the First Time (ASCAP)—Kapp 175	—	2
24.	**SITTIN' IN THE BALCONY** (BMI)—E. Cochran Dark Lonely Street (BMI)—Liberty 55056	22	4
25.	**MARIANNE** (BMI)—Hilltoppers You're Wasting Your Time (ASCAP)—Dot 15537	15	10

• Most Played in Juke Boxes

For survey week ending April 10

RECORDS are ranked in order of the greatest number of plays in juke boxes thruout the country, as determined by The Billboard's weekly survey of the nation's juke box operators. When significant play is reported on both sides of a record, points are combined to determine position on the chart. In such a case, both sides are listed in bold type, the leading side on top.

This Week		Last Week	Weeks on Chart
1.	**BUTTERFLY** (BMI)—C. Gracie Ninety-Nine Ways (BMI)—Cameo 105	1	8
2.	**PARTY DOLL** (BMI)—B. Knox My Baby's Gone (BMI)—Roulette 4002	2	7
3.	**ROUND AND ROUND** (BMI)—P. Como Mi Casa Su Casa (ASCAP)—Vic 20-6815	7	5
4.	**ALL SHOOK UP** (BMI)—E. Presley That's When Your Heartaches Begin (ASCAP)—Vic 20-6870	19	2
5.	**I'M WALKIN'** (BMI)—F. Domino I'm in the Mood for Love (ASCAP)—Imperial 5428	6	5
6.	**LITTLE DARLIN'** (BMI)—Diamonds Faithful and True (BMI)—Mercury 71060	10	4
7.	**BUTTERFLY** (BMI)—A. Williams It Doesn't Take Very Long (ASCAP)—Cadence 1308	3	7
8.	**WHY, BABY, WHY?** (BMI)—P. Boone I'm Waiting Just for You (BMI)—Dot 15545	10	4
9.	**YOUNG LOVE** (BMI)—T. Hunter Red Sails in the Sunset (ASCAP)—Dot 15533	3	13
10.	**MARIANNE** (BMI)—Hilltoppers You're Wasting Your Time (ASCAP)—Dot 15537	8	9
11.	**TEEN-AGE CRUSH** (BMI)—T. Sands Hep Dee Hootie (BMI)—Cap 3639	9	8
12.	**MARIANNE** (BMI)—T. Gilkyson Goodbye, Chiquita (BMI)—Col 40817	5	9
13.	**GONE** (BMI)—F. Husky Missing Persons (BMI)—Cap 3628	16	3
14.	**PARTY DOLL** (BMI)—S. Lawrence Pum-Pa-Lum (ASCAP)—Coral 61792	17	6
15.	**WALKIN' AFTER MIDNIGHT** (BMI)—P. Cline Poor Man's Roses (BMI)—Dec 30221	15	6
16.	**YOUNG LOVE** (BMI)—S. James You're the Reason I'm in Love (BMI)—Cap 3602	12	13
17.	**DON'T FORBID ME** (BMI)—P. Boone Anastasia (ASCAP)—Dot 15521	13	15
18.	**MAMA LOOK-A BOOBOO** (BMI)—H. Belafonte Don't Ever Love Me (ASCAP)—Vic 20-6830	19	2
19.	**TOO MUCH** (BMI)—E. Presley Playing for Keeps (BMI)—Vic 20-6800	14	11
20.	**NINETY-NINE WAYS** (BMI)—T. Hunter Don't Get Around Much Anymore (ASCAP)—Dot 15548	19	2

• Best Selling Sheet Music

Tunes are ranked in order of their current national selling importance at the sheet music jobber level.

This Week		Last Week	Weeks on Chart
1.	**Marianne** (Montclare)	1	8
2.	**Round and Round** (Rush)	2	6
3.	**Butterfly** (Mayland-Presley)	3	6
4.	**Chantez Chantez** (Cromwell)	5	5
5.	**Almost Paradise** (Peer)	6	5
6.	**Young Love** (Lowery)	4	13
7.	**Why, Baby, Why?** (Winneton)	11	2
8.	**Banana Boat Song** (E. B. Marks-Bryden)	8	14
9.	**All Shook Up** (Shalimar-Presley)	—	1
10.	**Who Needs You** (Korwin)	9	5
11.	**Ninety-Nine Ways** (Mayland)	—	1
12.	**Do I Love You?** (Williamson)	—	1
13.	**Cinco Robles** (Warman)	10	10
13.	**Party Doll** (Jacie)	6	4
15.	**Teen-Age Crush** (Central Songs)	14	2
15.	**Wind in the Willow** (Broadcast)	—	1

• Most Played by Jockeys

For survey week ending April 10

SIDES are ranked in order of the greatest number of plays on disk jockey radio shows thruout the country. Results are based on The Billboard's weekly survey among the nation's disk jockeys. The reverse side of each record is also listed.

This Week		Last Week	Weeks on Chart
1.	**ROUND AND ROUND** (BMI)—P. Como Mi Casa, Su Casa (ASCAP)—Vic 20-6815	1	8
2.	**ALL SHOOK UP** (BMI)—E. Presley That's When Your Heartaches Begin (ASCAP)—Vic 20-6870	7	2
3.	**BUTTERFLY** (BMI)—A. Williams It Doesn't Take Very Long (ASCAP)—Cadence 1308	2	7
4.	**LITTLE DARLIN'** (BMI)—Diamonds Faithful and True (BMI)—Mercury 71060	3	4
5.	**PARTY DOLL** (BMI)—B. Knox My Baby's Gone (BMI)—Roulette 4002	6	7
6.	**GONE** (BMI)—F. Husky Missing Persons (BMI)—Cap 3628	8	6
7.	**PARTY DOLL** (BMI)—S. Lawrence Pum-Pa-Lum (ASCAP)—Coral 61792	5	6
8.	**I'M WALKIN'** (BMI)—F. Domino I'm in the Mood for Love (ASCAP)—Imperial 5428	4	5
9.	**WHY, BABY, WHY?** (BMI)—P. Boone I'm Waiting Just for You (BMI)—Dot 15545	9	5
10.	**TEEN-AGE CRUSH** (BMI)—T. Sands Hep Dee Hootie (BMI)—Cap 3639	11	8
11.	**COME GO WITH ME** (BMI)—D. Vikings How Can I Find True Love (BMI)—Dot 15538	16	3
12.	**YOUNG LOVE** (BMI)—T. Hunter Red Sails in the Sunset (ASCAP)—Dot 15533	10	14
13.	**BUTTERFLY** (BMI)—C. Gracie Ninety-Nine Ways (BMI)—Cameo 105	20	8
14.	**MARIANNE** (BMI)—T. Gilkyson Goodbye, Chiquita (BMI)—Col 40817	12	11
15.	**NINETY-NINE WAYS** (BMI)—T. Hunter Don't Get Around Much Anymore (ASCAP)—Dot 15548	15	4
16.	**MAMA LOOK-A BOOBOO** (BMI)—H. Belafonte Don't Ever Love Me (ASCAP)—Vic 20-6830	—	2
17.	**MARIANNE** (BMI)—Hilltoppers You're Wasting Your Time (ASCAP)—Dot 15537	13	11
18.	**YOUNG LOVE** (BMI)—S. James You're the Reason I'm in Love (BMI)—Cap 3602	18	16
19.	**CHANTEZ-CHANTEZ** (ASCAP)—D. Shore Honkytonk Heart (BMI)—Vic 20-6792	22	4
20.	**I'M STICKING WITH YOU** (BMI)—J. Bowen Ever-Lovin' Fingers (BMI)—Roulette 4001	24	3
21.	**LOVE IS A GOLDEN RING** (BMI)—F. Laine There's Not a Moment to Spare (ASCAP)—Col 40856	—	1
22.	**SITTIN' IN THE BALCONY** (BMI)—E. Cochran Dark Lonely Street (BMI)—Liberty 55056	—	1
23.	**MANGOS** (ASCAP)—R. Clooney Independent (ASCAP)—Col 40835	—	1
23.	**WHO NEEDS YOU?** (ASCAP)—Four Lads It's So Easy to Forget (BMI)—Col 40811	19	10
25.	**FIRST DATE, FIRST KISS, FIRST LOVE** (BMI)—S. James Speak to Me (BMI)—Cap 3674	—	1

THE TOP 100

For survey week ending April 10

A list of the Top **100 RECORD SIDES** in the nation according to a **COMBINED TABULATION** of Dealer, Disk Jockey and Juke Box Operator replies to The Billboard's weekly popular record Best Seller and Most Played surveys. Its purpose is to provide Disk Jockeys with additional programming material and to give trade exposure to NEWER records just beginning to show action in the field.

Pos.	Song, Artist, Label	Last Week
1.	**ALL SHOOK UP,** E. Presley, Victor	6
1.	**ROUND AND ROUND,** P. Como, Victor	3
3.	**LITTLE DARLIN',** Diamonds, Mercury	4
4.	**PARTY DOLL,** B. Knox, Roulette	2
5.	**BUTTERFLY,** A. Williams, Cadence	1
6.	**I'M WALKIN',** F. Domino, Imperial	5
7.	**BUTTERFLY,** C. Gracie, Cameo	9
8.	**GONE,** F. Husky, Capitol	11
8.	**WHY, BABY, WHY?** P. Boone, Dot	11
10.	**PARTY DOLL,** S. Lawrence, Coral	13
11.	**TEEN-AGE CRUSH,** T. Sands, Capitol	9
12.	**COME GO WITH ME,** D. Vikings, Dot	17
13.	**YOUNG LOVE,** T. Hunter, Dot	6
14.	**MARIANNE,** T. Gilkyson, Columbia	8
15.	**MAMA LOOK-A BOOBOO,** H. Belafonte, Victor	19
16.	**NINETY-NINE WAYS,** T. Hunter, Dot	16
17.	**MARIANNE,** Hilltoppers, Dot	14
18.	**I'M STICKIN' WITH YOU,** J Bowen, Roulette	22
19.	**SITTIN' IN THE BALCONY,** E. Cochran, Liberty	24
20.	**BANANA BOAT (DAY-O),** H. Belafonte, Victor	21
21.	**YOUNG LOVE,** S. James, Capitol	20
22.	**ROCK-A-BILLY,** G. Mitchell, Columbia	34
22.	**WALKIN' AFTER MIDNIGHT,** P. Cline, Decca	22
24.	**DON'T FORBID ME,** P Boone, Dot	15
25.	**I'M SORRY,** Platters, Mercury	28
26.	**WHO NEEDS YOU,** Four Lads, Columbia	25
27.	**CHANTEZ CHANTEZ,** Dinah Shore, Victor	31
28.	**TOO MUCH,** E. Presley, Victor	18
29.	**POOR MAN'S ROSES,** P. Page, Mercury	35
30.	**ALMOST PARADISE,** R Williams, Kapp	31
31.	**LUCILLE,** Little Richard, Specialty	31
32.	**PLEDGE OF LOVE,** K. Copeland, Imperial	41
33.	**LOVE IS A GOLDEN RING,** F. Laine, Columbia	51
33.	**SCHOOL DAY,** C. Berry, Chess	46
35.	**LOVE IS STRANGE,** Mickey & Sylvia, Groove	26
36.	**JUST BECAUSE,** L. Price, ABC-Paramount	29
36.	**SO RARE,** J. Dorsey, Fraternity	36
38.	**I'M WAITING JUST FOR YOU,** P. Boone, Dot	33
39.	**FIRST DATE, FIRST KISS, FIRST LOVE,** S. James, Capitol	49
40.	**MANGOS,** R. Clooney, Columbia	40
41.	**LITTLE DARLIN',** Gladiolas, Excello	47
42.	**ALMOST PARADISE,** L. Stein, Unique	39
43.	**EMPTY ARMS,** T. Brewer, Coral	79
44.	**HE'S MINE,** Platters, Mercury	48
45.	**BANANA BOAT (DAY-O),** S. Freberg, Capitol	63
46.	**TRICKY,** R. Marterie, Mercury	38
46.	**WONDERFUL WONDERFUL,** J. Mathis, Columbia	59
48.	**WHITE SPORT COAT,** M. Robbins, Columbia	59
49.	**PEACE IN THE VALLEY,** E. Presley, Victor	58
50.	**PLEDGE OF LOVE,** D. Contino, Mercury	—
51.	**EMPTY ARMS,** I. J Hunter, Atlantic	92
52.	**BANANA BOAT SONG,** Tarriers, Glory	30
53.	**DARK MOON,** G. Storm, Dot	—
54.	**AFTER SCHOOL,** R. Starr, Dale	55
55.	**BALLERINA,** N. (King) Cole, Capitol	62
55.	**SITTIN' IN THE BALCONY,** J. Dee, Colonial	44
57.	**ONLY ONE LOVE,** G. Hamilton IV, ABC-Paramount	43
58.	**BAHAMA MAMA,** Four Aces, Decca	53
58.	**DARK MOON,** B. Guitar, Dot	68
60.	**BAD BOY,** Jive Bombers, Savoy	80
61.	**CALYPSO MELODY,** D Rose, M-G-M	42
62.	**MOONLIGHT GAMBLER,** F. Laine, Columbia	56
62.	**PUM-PA-LUM,** S. Lawrence, Coral	85
64.	**THERE OUGHTA BE A LAW,** Mickey & Sylvia, Groove	—
65.	**SEND ME SOME LOVIN',** Little Richard, Specialty	54
66.	**WALL,** E. Rodgers, Columbia	—
67.	**JIM DANDY,** L. Baker, Atlantic	45
68.	**JAMIE BOY,** K. Starr, Victor	—
69.	**LET THERE BE YOU,** Five Keys, Capitol	97
70.	**CAN I STEAL A LITTLE LOVE?** F. Sinatra, Capitol	65
71.	**FORTY CUPS OF COFFEE,** B. Haley, Decca	70
72.	**LUCKY LIPS,** Ruth Brown, Atlantic	49
73.	**THAT'S WHEN YOUR HEARTACHES BEGIN,** E. Presley, Victor	59
74.	**ONE STEP AT A TIME,** B. Lee, Decca	52
75.	**WALL,** P Page, Mercury	75
76.	**PARTY DOLL,** W. Manone, Decca	64
77.	**ALMOST PARADISE,** N. Petty Trio, ABC-Paramount	65
78.	**PLEDGE OF LOVE,** M. Torok, Decca	72
78.	**TRUE LOVE GONE,** B Madigan, M-G-M	—
80.	**BUTTERFLY,** B. Carroll, Bally	68
81.	**YES, TONIGHT JOSEPHINE,** J. Ray, Columbia	—
82.	**MI CASA SU CASA,** P. Como, Victor	76
83.	**TWELVE O'CLOCK TONIGHT,** Doris Day, Columbia	—
84.	**TO BE WITH YOU,** Highlights, Bally	—
85.	**TILL,** P. Faith, Columbia	90
85.	**WRITTEN ON THE WIND,** Four Aces, Decca	—
87.	**LET IT BE ME,** J. Corey, Columbia	—
88.	**I MISS YOU SO,** C. Connor, Atlantic	86
89.	**MARIANNE,** B. Ives, Decca	—
90.	**EVER-LOVIN' FINGERS,** J. Bowen, Roulette	99
91.	**DO I LOVE YOU?** V. Damone, Columbia	93
91.	**RING-A-DING-A-DING,** T. Sands, Capitol	—
91.	**DON'T EVER LOVE ME,** H. Belafonte, Victor	—
94.	**RAM-BUNK-SHUSH,** B. Doggett, King	—
94.	**WIND IN THE WILLOW,** J. Stafford, Columbia	—
96.	**TONIGHT MY HEART WILL BE CRYING,** E. Fisher, Victor	—
97.	**DO I LOVE YOU?** T. Martin, Victor	—
98.	**C. C. RIDER,** C. Willis, Atlantic	—
98.	**PRETEND,** T Smith, United	—
100.	**BANANA BOAT SONG,** Fontane Sisters, Dot	74
100.	**TOWER'S TROT,** D Jacobs, Coral	—
100.	**YOU ARE MY FIRST LOVE,** N. (King) Cole, Capitol	—

CAUTION TO DEALERS AND JUKE BOX OPERATORS

The Billboard's Top 100 is NOT designed to provide tested information for buying purposes. This function is most reliably served by other regular weekly features: Best Sellers in Stores, Most Played in Juke Boxes, Coming Up Strong and Best Buys.

• Best Sellers in Stores

For survey week ending April 17

RECORDS are ranked in order of their current national selling importance at the retail level, as determined by The Billboard's weekly survey of the top volume dealers in every important market area. When significant action is reported on both sides of a record, points are combined to determine position on the chart. In such a case, both sides are listed in bold type, the leading side on top.

This Week		Last Week	Weeks on Chart
1.	ALL SHOOK UP (BMI)—E. Presley That's When Your Heartaches Begin (ASCAP)—Vic 20-6870	1	4
2.	LITTLE DARLIN' (BMI)—Diamonds Faithful and True (BMI)—Mercury 71060	2	7
3.	ROUND AND ROUND (BMI)—P. Como Mi Casa, Su Casa (ASCAP)—Vic 20-6815	3	8
4.	PARTY DOLL (BMI)—B. Knox My Baby's Gone (BMI)—Roulette 4002	4	9
5.	COME GO WITH ME (BMI)—D. Vikings How Can I Find True Love? (BMI)—Dot 15538	5	9
6.	GONE (BMI)—F. Husky Missing Persons (BMI)—Cap 3628	6	6
7.	I'M WALKIN' (BMI)—F. Domino I'm in the Mood for Love (ASCAP)—Imperial 5428	9	8
8.	SCHOOL DAY (BMI)—C. Berry Deep Feeling (BMI)—Chess 1653	17	2
9.	WHY, BABY, WHY? (BMI)—P. Boone I'm Waiting Just for You (BMI)—Dot 15545	7	6
10.	BUTTERFLY (BMI)—A. Williams It Doesn't Take Very Long (ASCAP)—Cadence 1308	8	9
11.	BUTTERFLY (BMI)—C. Gracie Ninety-Nine Ways (BMI)—Cameo 105	10	10
12.	NINETY-NINE WAYS (BMI)—T. Hunter Don't Get Around Much Anymore (ASCAP)—Dot 15548	15	5
13.	MAMA LOOK-A BOOBOO (BMI)—H. Belafonte Don't Ever Love Me (ASCAP)—Vic 20-6830	11	5
14.	SO RARE (ASCAP)—J. Dorsey Sophisticated Swing (ASCAP)—Fraternity 755	20	2
15.	TEEN-AGE CRUSH (BMI)—T. Sands Hep Dee Hootie (BMI)—Cap 3639	13	10
16.	ROCK-A-BILLY (ASCAP)—G. Mitchell Hoot Owl (ASCAP)—Col 40877	19	2
17.	PARTY DOLL (BMI)—S. Lawrence Pum-Pa-Lum (ASCAP)—Coral 61792	12	7
18.	I'M SORRY (BMI)—Platters HE'S MINE (BMI)—Mercury 71032	14	3
18.	I'M STICKIN' WITH YOU (BMI) J. Bowen Ever-Lovin' Fingers (BMI)—Roulette 4001	16	8
20.	MARIANNE (BMI)—T. Gilkyson Goodbye, Chiquita (BMI)—Col 40817	18	11
21.	DARK MOON (BMI)—B. Guitar Big Mike (BMI)—Dot 15550	—	1
22.	ALMOST PARADISE (BMI)—R. Williams For the First Time (ASCAP)—Kapp 175	23	3
23.	LUCILLE (BMI)—Little Richard Send Me Some Lovin' (BMI)—Specialty 598	—	2
24.	SITTIN' IN THE BALCONY (BMI)—E. Cochran Dark Lonely Street (BMI)—Liberty 55056	24	5
25.	YOUNG LOVE (BMI)—T. Hunter Red Sails in the Sunset (ASCAP)—Dot 15533	21	15
25.	DAY'O BANANA BOAT SONG (ASCAP)—S. Freeberg Tele-Vee-Shun (ASCAP)—Cap 3687	—	1

• Most Played in Juke Boxes

For survey week ending April 17

RECORDS are ranked in order of the greatest number of plays in juke boxes thruout the country, as determined by The Billboard's weekly survey of the nation's juke box operators. When significant play is reported on both sides of a record, points are combined to determine position on the chart. In such a case, both sides are listed in bold type, the leading side on top

This Week		Last Week	Weeks on Chart
1.	ALL SHOOK UP (BMI)—E. Presley That's When Your Heartaches Begin (ASCAP)—Vic 20-6870	4	3
2.	LITTLE DARLIN' (BMI)—Diamonds Faithful and True (BMI)—Mercury 71060	6	5
3.	PARTY DOLL (BMI)—B. Knox My Baby's Gone (BMI)—Roulette 4002	2	8
4.	ROUND AND ROUND (BMI)—P. Como Mi Casa Su Casa (ASCAP)—Vic 20-6815	3	6
5.	GONE (BMI)—F. Husky Missing Persons (BMI)—Cap 3628	13	4
6.	BUTTERFLY (BMI)—A. Williams It Doesn't Take Very Long (ASCAP)—Cadence 1308	7	8
7.	I'M WALKIN' (BMI)—F. Domino I'm in the Mood for Love (ASCAP)—Imperial 5428	5	6
8.	WHY, BABY, WHY? (BMI)—P. Boone I'm Waiting Just for You (BMI)—Dot 15545	8	5
9.	BUTTERFLY (BMI)—C. Gracie Ninety-Nine Ways (BMI)—Cameo 105	1	9
10.	MARIANNE (BMI)—Hilltoppers You're Wasting Your Time (ASCAP)—Dot 15537	10	10
11.	TEEN-AGE CRUSH (BMI)—T. Sands Hep Dee Hootie (BMI)—Cap 3639	11	9
11.	I'M SORRY (BMI)—Platters HE'S MINE (BMI)—Mercury 71032	—	1
13.	WALKIN' AFTER MIDNIGHT (BMI)—P. Cline Poor Man's Roses (BMI)—Dec 30221	15	7
14.	YOUNG LOVE (BMI)—S. James You're the Reason (I'm in Love) (BMI)—Cap 3602	16	14
15.	I'M STICKIN' WITH YOU (BMI)—J. Bowen Ever-Lovin' Fingers (BMI)—Roulette 4001	—	1
16.	PARTY DOLL (BMI)—S. Lawrence Pum-Pa-Lum (ASCAP)—Coral 61792	14	7
17.	TOO MUCH (BMI)—E. Presley Playing for Keeps (BMI)—Vic 20-6800	19	12
18.	NINETY-NINE WAYS (BMI)—T. Hunter Don't Get Around Much Anymore (ASCAP)—Dot 15548	20	3
19.	DON'T FORBID ME (BMI)—P. Boone Anastasia (ASCAP)—Dot 15521	17	16
20.	SO RARE (ASCAP)—J. Dorsey Sophisticated Swing (ASCAP)—Fraternity 755	—	1

• Best Selling Sheet Music

Tunes are ranked in order of their current national selling importance at the sheet music jobber level.

This Week		Last Week	Weeks on Chart
1.	**Round and Round** (Rush)	2	7
2.	**Marianne** (Montclare)	1	9
3.	**Butterfly** (Mayland-Presley)	3	7
4.	**Chantez-Chantez** (Cromwell)	4	6
5.	**So Rare** (Robbins)	—	1
6.	**All Shook Up** (Shalimar-Presley)	9	2
7.	**Why, Baby, Why?** (Winneton)	7	3
8.	**Almost Paradise** (Peer)	5	6
9.	**Young Love** (Lowery)	6	14
10.	**Banana Boat Song** (E. B. Marks-Bryden)	8	15
11.	**Ninety-Nine Ways** (Mayland)	11	2
12.	**Who Needs You** (Korwin)	10	6
13.	**Cinco Robles** (Warman)	13	11
13.	**Do I Love You?** (Williamson)	12	2
15.	**Party Doll** (Jacie)	13	5

• Most Played by Jockeys

For survey week ending April 17

SIDES are ranked in order of the greatest number of plays on disk jockey radio shows thruout the country. Results are based on The Billboard's weekly survey among the nation's disk jockeys The reverse side of each record is also listed

This Week		Last Week	Weeks on Chart
1.	ALL SHOOK UP (BMI)—E. Presley That's When Your Heartaches Begin (ASCAP)—Vic 20-6870	2	3
2.	ROUND AND ROUND (BMI)—P. Como Mi Casa, Su Casa (ASCAP)—Vic 20-6815	1	9
3.	LITTLE DARLIN' (BMI)—Diamonds Faithful and True (BMI)—Mercury 71060	4	5
4.	BUTTERFLY (BMI)—A. Williams It Doesn't Take Very Long (ASCAP)—Cadence 1308	3	8
5.	PARTY DOLL (BMI)—B. Knox My Baby's Gone (BMI)—Roulette 4002	5	8
6.	GONE (BMI)—F. Husky Missing Persons (BMI)—Cap 3628	6	7
7.	COME GO WITH ME (BMI)—D. Vikings How Can I Find True Love? (BMI)—Dot 15538	11	4
8.	WHY, BABY, WHY? (BMI)—P. Boone I'm Waiting Just for You (BMI)—Dot 15545	9	6
9.	I'M WALKIN' (BMI)—F. Domino I'm in the Mood for Love (ASCAP)—Imperial 5428	8	6
10.	PARTY DOLL (BMI)—S. Lawrence Pum-Pa-Lum (ASCAP)—Coral 61792	7	7
11.	NINETY-NINE WAYS (BMI)—T. Hunter Don't Get Around Much Anymore (ASCAP)—Dot 15548	15	5
12.	SCHOOL DAY (BMI)—C. Berry Deep Feeling (BMI)—Chess 1653	—	1
13.	WHO NEEDS YOU? (ASCAP)—Four Lads It's So Easy To Forget (BMI)—Col 40811	23	11
14.	BUTTERFLY (BMI)—C. Gracie Ninety-Nine Ways (BMI)—Cameo 105	13	9
15.	TEEN-AGE CRUSH (BMI)—T. Sands Hep Dee Hootie (BMI)—Cap 3639	10	9
15.	ALMOST PARADISE (BMI)—R. Williams For the First Time (ASCAP)—Kapp 175	—	1
17.	ROCK-A-BILLY (ASCAP)—G. Mitchell Hoot Owl (ASCAP)—Col 40877	—	1
18.	SITTIN' IN THE BALCONY (BMI)—E. Cochran Dark Lonely Street (BMI)—Liberty 55056	22	2
19.	MAMA LOOK-A BOOBOO (BMI)—H. Belafonte Don't Ever Love Me (ASCAP)—Vic 20-6830	16	3
20.	LOVE IS A GOLDEN RING (BMI)—F. Laine There's Not a Moment to Spare (ASCAP)—Col 40856	21	2
20.	MARIANNE (BMI)—Hilltoppers You're Wasting Your Time (ASCAP)—Dot 15537	17	12
22.	CHANTEZ-CHANTEZ (ASCAP)—D. Shore Honkytonk Heart (BMI)—Vic 20-6792	19	5
23.	YOUNG LOVE (BMI)—T. Hunter Red Sails in the Sunset (ASCAP)—Dot 15533	12	15
24.	I'M STICKIN' WITH YOU (BMI)—J. Bowen Ever-Lovin' Fingers (BMI)—Roulette 4001	20	4
24.	MANGOS (ASCAP)—R. Clooney Independent (ASCAP)—Col 40835	23	2

FOLK TALENT AND TUNES

Around the Horn

Abbie Neal and Her Ranch Girls inaugurate a new weekly radio show from the Royal Ballroom, Wilkinsburg, Pa., by remote thru the facilities of WWVA, Wheeling, W. Va., Friday night, April 26, 11:15-11.45. Abbie will bring in a guest artist each week. . . . Cuzzin Bill Hamby and His Country Cuzzins have just launched their second tour for USO Camp Shows, Inc., playing isolated military bases in Japan, Korea, Okinawa and Formosa. Current tour is for 10 weeks. His show, "Cuzzin Bill's Corral," on WAVI, Dayton, O., is being handled during his absence by Al Morris, of the WAVI staff. Hamby and his group are tenatively set to tour Europe for USO in the fall to play three weeks in Greenland and Iceland over the Christmas holidays.

Johnny Cash, Sonny James, Carl Perkins and **Jerry Lee Lewis** began a tour arranged by **Ed Watt,** of "Big D Jamboree," Dallas, at Minneapolis, last Saturday (20). Package worked Saulte St. Marie, Ont., Sunday (21); Sudbury, Ont., Monday (22); Pembroke, Ont., Tuesday (23), and Ottawa, Ont., Wednesday (24). On April 26, Cash headlines a unit with **Carl Perkins, Jerry Lee Lewis** and **Wanda Jackson** in Fort Frances, Ont., following with Duluth, Minn., April 27; Des Moines, Ia., 28; Aberdeen, S. D., 29; Moorhead, Minn., 30; Winnipeg, Man., May 1; Saskatoon, Man., 2; Calgary, Alta., 3; Camrose, Alta., 5; Trail, B. C., 6; Cranbrook, B. C., 7; Lethbridge, Alta., 8; LaCombe, Alta., 9; Edmonton, Alta., 10; Regina, Sask., 11, and Billings, Mont., 12. Latter dates were set by **Bob Neal,** of Stars, Inc., Memphis, thru an arrangement with promoter **A. V. Bamford.**

With the Jockeys

Eddie Bond (Mercury-Starday), who recently left KWEM, West Memphis, Ark., is now spinning a three-hour show each Saturday night over WHHM, Memphis. Bond recently formed Eddie Bond Enterprises, with offices in Memphis. . . . **Randy Blake,** whose "Suppertime Frolic" has been a long-time favorite over Chicago's WJJD, has moved the show, via tape, to WLW, Cincinnati, where it is heard 8:05-9:30, p.m. Tuesday thru Sunday. Blake will continue to make his home at 831 South Wabash Avenue, Chicago.

John Stephenson, Stephenson Music Publications, Fort Worth, is prepping plans for a tape-recorded deejay show. Artists are asked to send releases to Stephenson at Avery, Tex. . . . Deejays who have recently changed jobs include Ed Hamilton, from KCIJ, Shreveport, La., to XERF, Del Rio, Tex., and Neal Merritt, from KONO, San Antonio, to KCIJ, Shreveport. . . . John Galley, of KATR, a 50,000-watter in Corpus Christi, Tex., says he's is in need of wax.

Georgie Riddle, formerly of Knoxville, recently joined WARU, Peru, Ind., where he is helming a one-hour morning show five days a week. **Betty Lee and Walter Riddle,** who are also heard over WARU, are appearing at the Rainbow, Peru, six nights a week. . . . **Myrna Lorrie,** CFPA, Port Arthur, Ont., who was recently pacted by RCA Victor, has as her first release "That's What Sweethearts Do," written by her personal manager, **Don Grashey,** and her brother, **David.** Flip side is "Die, I Thought I Would," penned by **Shorty Long.** . . . **Jack Kingston,** CHML, Hamilton, Ont., has a new one on the Quality label, "Snug As a Bug (in a Rug)," which he penned himself, b.w. "Letter Edged in Black."

Mike Michael, KDMS, El Dorado, Ark., types: "The Philip Morris Country Music Show played here recently to a turnaway crowd. KDMS handled promotion. Carl Smith, Red Sovine, Goldie Hill, Biff Collie, Mimi Roman, Ronnie Self and Bun Wilson guested on my program. After the show, KDMS hosted the cast to a dinner of Mexican food at the Velvetex Grill here. Several PM execs also attended and had a big time."

Pete Burrows, heard 1-3 p.m. over KDNT, Denton, Tex., recently had **Bill Boyd** (Starday) as a guest. . . . **Abbie Neal,** heard over WAMO, Homestead, Pa., from 7-10 a.m., Monday thru Friday, with her "Abbie Neal Show," is also working personal appearances with her band, the **Ranch Girls.** She and her aggregation have a new Admiral release out, "If Again" b.w. "Until I Dream." . . . **Ken Parsons,** KLRA, Little Rock, Ark., who helms an all-night stanza, the "Country - Fried Show," recently had as guests **Bonnie Brown,** of the Brown Trio, and **Dave Rich.**

Capt. Ozzie Waters, veteran c.&w. entertainer, is now helming a 30-minute daily show over KLAK, Lakewood, Colo. He also works the Max Mosco Western TV stanza over KBTV, Denver, Friday and Saturday afternoons. Besides his broadcasting chores, Waters vocals and plays guitar three shows a night at a local nitery. . . . Ed Scott, after two and a half years at KLZ-TV, Denver CBS outlet, has moved his Western tele film show to KBTV, Denver. Scott also operates a c.&w. talent agency.

Bill Mack, KWFT, Wichita Falls, Tex., types: "I have incorporated a new feature, 'Country Music Star of the Month,' on all of my shows. In this new seg I feature several recordings by the spotlighted artist on my three daily shows and on my four-hour Saturday stanza. Also, during each month I do a special one-hour show where I play a taped interview that has been made with the chosen artist. The artist for April was Hank Snow."

Ken Parsons, of Connie B. Gay's Little Rock station, KLRA, reports that Billy Riley and His Little Green Men (Sun) were recent visitors on his all-night "Country-Fried Show" following their appearance on a Bob Neal bill at Little Rock's Robinson Auditorium. Show was headlined by Johnny Cash, with Carl Perkins; Jerry Lee Lewis, Onie Wheeler and Glenn Douglas. . . . Jay Thompson, with KSTB, Breckenridge, Tex., for seven years, is now deejaying the wax over KMLW, Marlin, Tex.

George Popkins, who helms "Pop's Country Store" over WXGI, Richmond, Va., writes: "As a tie-in with trade's **Hank Snow** 20-year testimonial, I recently featured a two-hour salute to the singer on my show. A new album was introduced, Snow "finds" were played, catalog numbers were featured and biographical data was used. It was one of the most successful programs of this type that we've ever done." . . . **Tommy Farr** (Coin), formerly with WQOK, Greenville, S. C., is now spinning the platters over WJHB, Talladega, Ala. Farr, who is a vocalist with **Peck Powell's Covered Wagon Boys,** has a new Coin recording, "Take Care of Her," due out soon.

More Folk Talent and Tunes on Page 59

STRAIGHT FROM THE SHOULDER

NEW YORK—These days one is likely to find a great talent anywhere. We are reminded of this by a communication from Urban Fuerst, of Delphos, O., who says: ". . . Altho I have never acted or sung with music . . . I can truthfully say I can sing just about as good as Como, Crosby and Boone. . . . I think also that I could make another John Wayne altho I am not as big as he and don't look like him, but I can play it calm and cool. . . . My shoulders and arm muscles are quite prominent and if handled right I think a big thing could be built up. . . . As I said before any suggestions would be appreciated."

ANOTHER 3-WAY PRESLEY CROWN

NEW YORK—Elvis Presley walked off with another Triple Crown Award this week, with his new disk, "All Shook Up," No. 1 in all three pop chart categories—retail, jockey and juke.

The platter also took the No. 1 slot on the "Top 100" list, and the tune is No. 1 on "The Honor Roll of Hits." At the same time, the Presley record is No. 3 on the rhythm and blues retail chart and No. 2 on the r.&b. jockey chart. It is No. 5 on the country and western retail list and No. 4 on the c.&w. jockey chart.

Herzstam and Wegner New Allied Veeps

HOLLYWOOD — Daken K. Broadhead, president of Allied Record Manufacturing Company, last week named John F. Wegner vice-president for administration and finance, and Ned R. Herzstam, vice-president in charge of sales and public relations.

Both Wegner and Herzstam are veteran employees of the company, Wegner joining Allied in 1945, and Herzstam in 1951. A former Eastern representative for Allied, Wegner has assisted Broadhead in administrative matters since his return to the Coast in 1952.

Herzstam formerly was sales promotion manager of Capitol Records and, in addition to his new post, continues as a vice-president of Allied Record Sales Company and Western repertoire and sales manager for Urania Records Distributing Company.

New appointments, including the existing vice-president in charge of manufacturing, Samuel Salzman, are in line with Allied's expansion program.

THE TOP 100

For survey week ending April 17

A list of the Top 100 RECORD SIDES in the nation according to a COMBINED TABULATION of Dealer, Disk Jockey and Juke Box Operator replies to The Billboard's weekly popular record Best Seller and Most Played surveys. Its purpose is to provide Disk Jockeys with additional programming material and to give trade exposure to NEWER records just beginning to show action in the field.

Pos.	Song, Artist, Label	Last Week
1.	**ALL SHOOK UP,** E. Presley, Victor	1
2.	**LITTLE DARLIN',** Diamonds, Mercury	3
3.	**ROUND AND ROUND,** P. Como, Victor	2
4.	**PARTY DOLL,** B. Knox, Roulette	4
5.	**GONE,** F. Husky, Capitol	8
6.	**BUTTERFLY,** A. Williams, Cadence	5
7.	**I'M WALKIN',** F. Domino, Imperial	6
8.	**WHY, BABY, WHY?** P. Boone, Dot	8
9.	**BUTTERFLY,** C. Gracie, Cameo	7
10.	**COME GO WITH ME,** D. Vikings, Dot	12
11.	**NINETY-NINE WAYS,** T. Hunter, Dot	16
12.	**PARTY DOLL,** S. Lawrence, Coral	10
12.	**TEEN-AGE CRUSH,** T. Sands, Capitol	11
14.	**I'M STICKIN' WITH YOU,** J. Bowen, Roulette	18
14.	**MAMA LOOK-A BOOBOO,** H. Belafonte, Victor	15
16.	**MARIANNE,** Hilltoppers, Dot	17
17.	**ROCK-A-BILLY,** G. Mitchell, Columbia	22
18.	**SITTIN' IN THE BALCONY,** E. Cochran, Liberty	19
19.	**I'M SORRY,** Platters, Mercury	25
20.	**SO RARE,** J. Dorsey, Fraternity	36
21.	**SCHOOL DAY,** C. Berry, Chess	33
21.	**YOUNG LOVE,** T. Hunter, Dot	13
23.	**MARIANNE,** T. Gilkyson, Columbia	14
24.	**DARK MOON,** B. Guitar, Dot	58
25.	**WHO NEEDS YOU?** Four Lads, Columbia	26
26.	**ALMOST PARADISE,** R. Williams, Kapp	30
27.	**YOUNG LOVE,** S. James, Capitol	21
28.	**LOVE IS A GOLDEN RING,** F. Laine, Columbia	33
29.	**WHITE SPORT COAT,** M. Robbins, Columbia	48
30.	**DON'T FORBID ME,** P. Boone, Dot	24
31.	**CHANTEZ CHANTEZ,** D. Shore, Victor	27
32.	**PLEDGE OF LOVE,** K. Copeland, Imperial	32
32.	**WALKIN' AFTER MIDNIGHT,** P. Cline, Decca	22
34.	**BANANA BOAT (DAY-O),** H. Belafonte, Victor	20
35.	**TOO MUCH,** E. Presley, Victor	28
36.	**POOR MAN'S ROSES,** P. Page, Mercury	29
37.	**HE'S MINE,** Platters, Mercury	44
38.	**EMPTY ARMS,** T. Brewer, Coral	43
39.	**LUCILLE,** Little Richard, Specialty	31
40.	**MANGOS,** R. Clooney, Columbia	40
41.	**JUST BECAUSE,** L. Price, ABC-Paramount	36
42.	**PLEDGE OF LOVE,** D. Contino, Mercury	50
43.	**DAY'O BANANA BOAT,** S. Freberg, Capitol	45
43.	**FIRST DATE, FIRST KISS, FIRST LOVE,** S. James, Capitol	39
45.	**SITTIN' IN THE BALCONY,** J. Dee, Colonial	55
46.	**PLEDGE OF LOVE,** M. Torok, Decca	78
47.	**THERE OUGHTA BE A LAW,** Mickey & Sylvia, Vik	64
48.	**LOVE IS STRANGE,** Mickey & Sylvia, Grove	35
48.	**WONDERFUL, WONDERFUL,** J. Mathis, Columbia	46
50.	**AFTER SCHOOL,** R. Starr, Dale	54
50.	**I'M WAITING JUST FOR YOU,** P. Boone, Dot	38
52.	**TRICKY,** R. Marterie, Mercury	46
53.	**ALMOST PARADISE,** L. Stein, Unique	42
53.	**WIND IN THE WILLOW,** J. Stafford, Columbia	94
55.	**EMPTY ARMS,** I. J. Hunter, Atlantic	51
56.	**PARTY DOLL,** W. Manone, Decca	76
57.	**LET IT BE ME,** J. Corey, Columbia	57
58.	**PEACE IN THE VALLEY,** E. Presley, Victor	49
58.	**THAT'S WHEN YOUR HEARTACHES BEGIN,** E. Presley, Victor	73
60.	**CRAZY LOVE,** F. Sinatra, Capitol	—
60.	**YES, TONIGHT, JOSEPHINE,** J. Ray, Columbia	81
62.	**DO I LOVE YOU?** V. Damone, Columbia	91
62.	**JAMIE BOY,** K. Starr, Victor	68
64.	**TILL,** P. Faith, Columbia	85
65.	**CALYPSO MELODY,** D. Rose, M-G-M	61
66.	**I'LL TAKE ROMANCE,** E. Gorme, ABC-Paramount	—
67.	**BALLERINA,** N. K. Cole, Capitol	55
68.	**IT ALL DEPENDS ON YOU,** J. Lewis, Decca	—
69.	**ONE STEP AT A TIME,** B. Lee, Decca	74
70.	**WITHOUT LOVE,** C. McPhatter, Atlantic	—
70.	**YOUR TRUE LOVE,** C. Perkins, Sun	—
70.	**MY LOVE SONG,** T. Sands, Capitol	—
73.	**LITTLE LONELINESS,** K. Starr, Victor	—
74.	**DON'T GET AROUND MUCH ANYMORE,** T. Hunter, Dot	—
75.	**ALMOST PARADISE,** N. Petty Trio, ABC-Paramount	77
76.	**SEND ME SOME LOVIN',** Little Richard, Specialty	65
77.	**BUTTERFLY,** B. Carroll, Bally	80
77.	**I LOVE MY GIRL,** Hilltoppers, Dot	—
79.	**BANANA BOAT SONG,** Tarriers, Glory	52
79.	**SO LONG MY LOVE,** F. Sinatra, Capitol	—
81.	**PUM-PA-LUM,** S. Lawrence, Coral	62
81.	**TOWER'S TROT,** D. Jacobs, Coral	100
83.	**BAD BOY,** Jive Bombers, Savoy	60
84.	**'S WONDERFUL,** R. Conniff, Columbia	—
84.	**CAN I STEAL A LITTLE LOVE?** F. Sinatra, Capitol	70
84.	**DARK MOON,** G. Storm, Dot	53
87.	**BAHAMA MAMA,** Four Aces, Decca	58
87.	**SINGING THE BLUES,** G. Mitchell, Columbia	—
89.	**CINCO ROBLES,** R. Arms, Era	—
89.	**I DREAMED,** B. Johnson, Bally	—
91.	**PAMELA THROWS A PARTY,** J. Reismen, Victor	—
92.	**I MISS YOU SO,** C. Connor, Atlantic	88
92.	**LET THERE BE YOU,** Five Keys, Capitol	69
92.	**WRITTEN ON THE WIND,** Four Aces, Decca	85
96.	**BANANA BOAT SONG,** Fontane Sisters, Dot	100
96.	**MOONLIGHT GAMBLER,** F. Laine, Columbia	62
98.	**MAMA GUITAR,** D. Cornell, Coral	—
98.	**MAMA GUITAR,** J. La Rosa, Victor	—
98.	**PIED PIPER,** B. Williams, Coral	—
98.	**TWELVE O'CLOCK TONIGHT,** Doris Day, Columbia	83

CAUTION TO DEALERS AND JUKE BOX OPERATORS

The Billboard's Top 100 is NOT designed to provide tested information for buying purposes. This function is most reliably served by other regular weekly features: Best Sellers in Stores, Most Played in Juke Boxes, Coming Up Strong and Best Buys.

• Best Sellers in Stores

For survey week ending April 24

RECORDS are ranked in order of their current national selling importance at the retail level, as determined by The Billboard's weekly survey of the top volume dealers in every important market area. When significant action is reported on both sides of a record, points are combined to determine position on the chart. In such a case, both sides are listed in bold type, the leading side on top.

This Week		Last Week	Weeks on Chart
1.	**ALL SHOOK UP** (BMI)—E. Presley That's When Your Heartaches Begin (ASCAP)—Vic 20-6870	1	5
2.	**LITTLE DARLIN'** (BMI)—Diamonds Faithful and True (BMI)—Mercury 71060	2	8
3.	**ROUND AND ROUND** (BMI)—P. Como Mi Casa, Su Casa (ASCAP)—Vic 20-6815	3	9
4.	**PARTY DOLL** (BMI)—B. Knox My Baby's Gone (BMI)—Roulette 4002	4	10
5.	**GONE** (BMI)—F. Husky Missing Persons (BMI)—Cap 3628	6	7
6.	**SCHOOL DAY** (BMI)—C. Berry Deep Feeling (BMI)—Chess 1653	8	3
7.	**COME GO WITH ME** (BMI)—D. Vikings How Can I Find Love? (BMI)—Dot 15538	5	10
8.	**I'M WALKIN'** (BMI)—F. Domino I'm in the Mood for Love (ASCAP)—Imperial 5428	7	9
9.	**WHY, BABY, WHY?** (BMI)—P. Boone I'm Waiting Just for You (BMI)—Dot 15545	9	7
10.	**SO RARE** (ASCAP)—J. Dorsey Sophisticated Swing (ASCAP)—Fraternity 755	14	3
11.	**MAMA LOOK-A BOOBOO** (BMI) H. Belafonte Don't Ever Love Me (ASCAP)—Vic 20-6830	13	6
12.	**BUTTERFLY** (BMI)—A. Williams It Doesn't Take Very Long (ASCAP)—Cadence 1308	10	10
13.	**BUTTERFLY** (BMI)—C. Gracie Ninety-Nine Ways (BMI)—Cameo 105	11	11
14.	**PARTY DOLL** (BMI)—S. Lawrence Pum-Pa-Lum (ASCAP)—Coral 61792	17	8
15.	**ROCK-A-BILLY** (ASCAP)—G. Mitchell Hoot Owl (ASCAP)—Col 40877	16	3
16.	**TEEN-AGE CRUSH** (BMI)—T. Sands Hep Dee Hootie (ASCAP)—Cap 3639	15	11
17.	**WHITE SPORT COAT** (BMI)—M. Robbins Grown-Up Tears (BMI)—Col 40864	—	1
18.	**HE'S MINE** (BMI)—Platters I'm Sorry (BMI)—Mercury 71032	—	3
19.	**I'M STICKIN' WITH YOU** (BMI)—J. Bowen Ever-Lovin' Fingers (BMI)—Roulette 4001	18	9
20.	**NINETY-NINE WAYS** (BMI)—T. Hunter Don't Get Around Much Anymore (ASCAP)—Dot 15548	12	6
21.	**DARK MOON**—B. Guitar Big Mike (BMI)—Dot 15550	21	2
22.	**LUCILLE** (BMI)—Little Richard Send Me Some Lovin' (BMI)—Specialty 598	23	3
23.	**EMPTY ARMS**—T. Brewer Ricky Tick Song—Coral 61805	—	1
23.	**SITTIN' IN THE BALCONY** (BMI)—E. Cochran Dark Lonely Street (BMI)—Liberty 55056	24	6
25.	**ALMOST PARADISE** (BMI)—R. Williams For the First Time (ASCAP)—Kapp 175	22	4
25.	**PLEDGE OF LOVE**—M. Torok What's Behind That Strange Door Dec 30230	—	1

• Most Played in Juke Boxes

For survey week ending April 24

RECORDS are ranked in order of the greatest number of plays in juke boxes thruout the country, as determined by The Billboard's weekly survey of the nation's juke box operators. When significant play is reported on both sides of a record, points are combined to determine position on the chart. In such a case, both sides are listed in bold type, the leading side on top.

This Week		Last Week	Weeks on Chart
1.	**ALL SHOOK UP** (BMI)—E. Presley That's When Your Heartaches Begin (ASCAP)—Vic 20-6870	1	4
2.	**LITTLE DARLIN'** (BMI)—Diamonds Faithful and True (BMI)—Mercury 71060	2	6
3.	**ROUND AND ROUND** (BMI)—P. Como Mi Casa, Su Casa (ASCAP)—Vic 20-6815	4	7
4.	**PARTY DOLL** (BMI)—B. Knox My Baby's Gone (BMI)—Roulette 4002	3	9
5.	**I'M WALKIN'** (BMI)—F. Domino I'm in the Mood for Love (ASCAP)—Imperial 5428	6	7
6.	**BUTTERFLY** (BMI)—A. Williams It Doesn't Take Very Long (ASCAP)—Cadence 1308	5	9
7.	**WHY, BABY, WHY?** (BMI)—P. Boone **I'M WAITING JUST FOR YOU** (BMI)—Dot 15545	7	6
8.	**BUTTERFLY** (BMI)—C. Gracie Ninety-Nine Ways (BMI)—Cameo 105	8	10
9.	**TEEN-AGE CRUSH** (BMI)—T. Sands Hep Dee Hootie (BMI)—Cap 3639	10	10
10.	**GONE** (BMI)—F. Husky Missing Persons (BMI)—Cap 3628	5	4
11.	**PARTY DOLL** (BMI)—S. Lawrence Pum-Pa-Lum (ASCAP)—Coral 61792	15	8
12.	**MARIANNE** (BMI)—Hilltoppers You're Wasting Your Time (ASCAP)—Dot 15537	9	11
12.	**COME GO WITH ME** (BMI)—D. Vikings How Can I Find True Love? (BMI)—Dot 15538	—	1
14.	**MARIANNE** (BMI)—T. Gilkyson Goodbye, Chiquita (BMI)—Col 40817	20	11
15.	**I'M SORRY** (BMI)—Platters **HE'S MINE** (BMI)—Mercury 71032	10	2
16.	**WALKIN' AFTER MIDNIGHT** (BMI)—P. Cline Poor Man's Roses (BMI)—Dec 30221	12	8
17.	**I'M STICKIN' WITH YOU** (BMI)—J. Bowen Ever-Lovin' Fingers (BMI)—Roulette 4001	14	2
18.	**NINETY-NINE WAYS** (BMI)—T. Hunter Don't Get Around Much Anymore (ASCAP)—Dot 15548	17	4
19.	**YOUNG LOVE** (BMI)—S. James You're the Reason (I'm in Love) (BMI)—Cap 3602	13	15
20.	**YOUNG LOVE** (BMI)—T. Hunter Red Sails in the Sunset (ASCAP)—Dot 15533	—	14

• Best Selling Sheet Music

Tunes are ranked in order of their current national selling importance at the sheet music jobber level.

This Week		Last Week	Weeks on Chart
1.	**Round and Round** (Rush)	1	8
1.	**Marianne** (Montclare)	2	10
3.	**Butterfly**, (Mayland-Presley)	3	8
4.	**All Shook Up** (Shalimar-Presley)	6	3
5.	**Almost Paradise** (Peer)	8	7
6.	**Why, Baby, Why?** (Winneton)	7	4
7.	**Chantez-Chantez** (Cromwell)	4	7
8.	**Ninety-Nine Ways**, (Mayland)	11	3
9.	**Young Love** (Lowery)	9	15
10.	**Do I Love You?** (Williamson)	13	3
11.	**Banana Boat Song** (E. B. Marks-Bryden)	10	16
12.	**Come Go With Me** (Gil-Feebee)	—	1
12.	**Who Needs You?** (Korwin)	12	8
14.	**Party Doll** (Jacie)	15	6
15.	**So Rare** (Robbins)	5	2

• Most Played by Jockeys

For survey week ending April 24

SIDES are ranked in order of the greatest number of plays on disk jockey radio shows thruout the country. Results are based on The Billboard's weekly survey among the nation's disk jockeys. The reverse side of each record is also listed.

This Week		Last Week	Weeks on Chart
1.	**ALL SHOOOK UP** (BMI)—E. Presley That's When Your Heartaches Begin (ASCAP)—Vic 20-6870	1	4
2.	**ROUND AND ROUND** (BMI)—P. Como Mi Casa, Sn Casa (ASCAP)—Vic 20-6815	2	10
3.	**LITTLE DARLIN'** (BMI)—Diamonds Faithful and True (BMI)—Mercury 71060	3	6
4.	**GONE** (BMI)—F. Husky Missing Persons (BMI)—Cap 3628	6	8
5.	**BUTTERFLY** (BMI)—A. Williams It Doesn't Take Very Long (ASCAP)—Cadence 1308	4	9
6.	**PARTY DOLL** (BMI)—B. Knox My Baby's Gone (BMI)—Roulette 4002	5	9
7.	**WHY, BABY, WHY?** (BMI)—P. Boone I'm Waiting Just for You (BMI)—Dot 15545	8	7
8.	**COME GO WITH ME** (BMI)—D. Vikings How Can I Find True Love? (BMI)—Dot 15538	7	5
9.	**PARTY DOLL** (BMI)—S. Lawrence Pum-Pa-Lum (ASCAP)—Coral 61792	10	8
10.	**LOVE IS A GOLDEN RING** (BMI)—F. Laine There's Not a Moment to Spare (ASCAP)—Col 40856	20	3
11.	**SCHOOL DAY** (BMI)—C. Berry Deep Feeling (BMI)—Chess 1653	12	2
12.	**I'M WALKIN'** (BMI)—F. Domino I'm in the Mood for Love (ASCAP)—Imperial 5428	9	7
13.	**WHITE SPORT COAT** (BMI)—M. Robbins Grown-Up Tears (BMI)—Col 40864	—	1
14.	**MAMA LOOK-A BOOBOO** (BMI)—H. Belafonte Don't Ever Love Me (ASCAP)—Vic 20-6830	19	4
14.	**PLEDGE OF LOVE** (BMI)—K. Copeland Night Air (BMI)—Imperial 5432	—	1
16.	**SO RARE** (ASCAP)—J. Dorsey Sophisticated Swing (ASCAP)—Fraternity 755	—	1
17.	**NINETY-NINE WAYS** (BMI)—T. Hunter Don't Get Around Much Anymore (ASCAP)—Dot 15548	11	6
18.	**ROCK-A-BILLY** (ASCAP)—G. Mitchell Hoot Owl (ASCAP)—Col 40877	17	2
19.	**ALMOST PARADISE** (BMI)—R. Williams For the First Time (ASCAP)—Kapp 175	15	2
20.	**MANGOS** (ASCAP)—R. Clooney Independent (ASCAP)—Col 40835	24	3
21.	**TEEN-AGE CRUSH** (BMI)—T. Sands Hep Dee Hootie (BMI)—Cap 3639	15	10
22.	**WHO NEEDS YOU** (ASCAP)—Four Lads It's So Easy to Forget (BMI)—Col 40811	13	12
23.	**BUTTERFLY** (BMI)—C. Gracie Ninety-Nine Ways (BMI)—Cameo 105	14	10
24.	**CHANTEZ-CHANTEZ** (ASCAP)—D. Shore Honkytonk Heart (BMI)—Vic 20-6792	22	6
25.	**SITTIN' IN THE BALCONY** (BMI)—E. Cochran Dark Lonely Street (BMI)—Liberty 55056	18	3

THE TOP 100

For survey week ending April 24

A list of the Top 100 **RECORD SIDES** in the nation according to a **COMBINED TABULATION** of Dealer, Disk Jockey and Juke Box Operator replies to The Billboard's weekly popular record Best Seller and Most Played surveys. Its purpose is to provide Disk Jockeys with additional programming material and to give trade exposure to NEWER records just beginning to show action in the field.

Pos.	Song, Artist, Label	Last Week
1.	**ALL SHOOK UP,** E. Presley, Victor	1
2.	**LITTLE DARLIN',** Diamonds, Mercury	2
3.	**ROUND AND ROUND,** P. Como, Victor	3
4.	**PARTY DOLL,** B. Knox, Roulette	4
5.	**GONE,** F. Husky, Capitol	5
6.	**BUTTERFLY,** A. Williams, Cadence	6
6.	**WHY, BABY, WHY?** P. Boone, Dot	8
8.	**I'M WALKIN',** F. Domino, Imperial	7
9.	**COME GO WITH ME,** D. Vikings, Dot	10
10.	**PARTY DOLL,** S. Lawrence, Coral	12
11.	**SCHOOL DAY,** C. Berry. Chess	21
12.	**BUTTERFLY,** C. Gracie, Cameo	9
13.	**MAMA LOOK-A BOOBOO,** H. Belafonte, Victor	14
13.	**SO RARE,** J. Dorsey. Fraternity	20
13.	**TEEN-AGE CRUSH,** T. Sands, Capitol	12
16.	**NINETY-NINE WAYS,** T. Hunter, Dot	11
17.	**WHITE SPORT COAT,** M. Robbins, Columbia	29
18.	**I'M STICKIN' WITH YOU,** J. Bowen, Roulette	14
18.	**ROCK-A-BILLY,** G. Mitchell, Columbia	17
20.	**MARIANNE,** T. Gilkyson, Columbia	23
21.	**SITTIN' IN THE BALCONY,** E. Cochran, Liberty	18
22.	**MARIANNE,** Hilltoppers, Dot	16
23.	**LOVE IS A GOLDEN RING,** F. Laine, Columbia	28
24.	**EMPTY ARMS,** T. Brewer, Coral	38
25.	**PLEDGE OF LOVE,** K. Copelend, Imperial	32
26.	**ALMOST PARADISE,** R. Williams, Kapp	26
27.	**DARK MOON,** B. Guitar. Dot	24
28.	**LUCILLE,** Little Richard, Specialty	39
29.	**I'M SORRY,** Platters, Mercury	25
30.	**WHO NEEDS YOU?** Four Lads, Columbia	26
31.	**MANGOS,** R. Clooney, Columbia	40
32.	**YOUNG LOVE,** T. Hunter, Dot	13
33.	**CHANTEZ CHANTEZ,** D. Shore, Victor	27
34.	**WALKIN' AFTER MIDNIGHT,** P. Cline, Decca	22
35.	**PLEDGE OF LOVE,** K. Copeland, Imperial	32
36.	**HE'S MINE,** Platters, Mercury	44
37.	**JUST BECAUSE,** L. Price, ABC-Paramount	36
38.	**DARK MOON,** G. Storm, Dot	53
39.	**PEACE IN THE VALLEY,** E. Presley, Victor	49
40.	**DON'T FORBID ME,** P. Boone, Dot	24
41.	**FIRST DATE, FIRST KISS, FIRST LOVE,** S. James, Capitol	49
42.	**YOUNG LOVE,** S. James, Capitol	21
43.	**BANANA BOAT (DAY-O),** H. Belafonte, Victor	20
44.	**AFTER SCHOOL,** R. Starr, Dale	54
45.	**PLEDGE OF LOVE,** D. Contino, Mercury	50
46.	**POOR MAN'S ROSES,** P. Page, Mercury,	29
47.	**WONDERFUL, WONDERFUL,** J. Mathis, Dot	38
48.	**THERE OUGHT TO BE A LAW,** Mickey & Sylvia, Vik	64
49.	**SITTIN' IN THE BALCONY,** J. Dee, Colonial	45
50.	**'DAY-O-BANANA BOAT SONG,** S. Freberg, Capitol	43
51.	**EMPTY ARMS,** I. J. Hunter, Atlantic	55
51.	**LITTLE DARLIN',** Gladiolas,	60
51.	**YES, TONIGHT, JOSEPHINE,** J. Ray, Columbia	60
54.	**JAMIE BOY** K. Starr, Victor	62
54.	**RING A DING,** T. Sands, Capitol	—
56.	**TOO MUCH,** E. Presley, Victor	35
57.	**TRICKY,** R. Marterie, Mercury	52
58.	**IT'S NOT FOR ME TO SAY,** J. Mathis, Columbia	—
59.	**WIND IN THE WILLOW,** J. Stafford, Columbia	53
60.	**ONE STEP AT A TIME,** B. Lee, Decca	69
60.	**THAT'S WHEN YOUR HEARTACHES BEGIN,** E. Presley, Victor	58
62.	**CALYPSO MELODY,** D. Rose, M-G-M	65
63.	**C. C. RIDER,** C. Willis, Atlantic	—
63.	**TILL,** P. Faith, Columbia	64
65.	**LOVE IS STRANGE,** Mickey & Sylvia, Groove	48
66.	**I'M WAITIN' JUST FOR YOU,** P. Boone, Dot	50
66.	**I'LL TAKE ROMANCE,** E. Gorme, ABC-Paramount	66
68.	**ALMOST PARADISE,** N. Petty Trio, ABC-Paramount	75
68.	**MAMA GUITAR,** D Cornell, Coral	98
68.	**SEND ME SOME LOVIN',** Little Richard, Specialty	76
71.	**MY LOVE SONG,** T. Sands, Capitol	70
72.	**PLEDGE OF LOVE,** J. Janis, ABC-Paramount	—
73.	**LET IT BE ME,** J Corey, Columbia	57
74.	**PARTY DOLL,** W. Manone, Decca	56
74.	**I'M SERIOUS,** Hilltoppers, Dot	—
76.	**FOUR WALLS,** J. Reeves, Victor	—
77.	**CAN I STEAL A LITTLE LOVE?** F. Sinatra, Capitol	84
78.	**DO I LOVE YOU?** V. Damone, Columbia	62
79.	**ALMOST PARADISE,** L. Stein, Unique	53
80.	**LITTLE WHITE LIES,** B. Johnson, Bally	—
81	**LITTLE LONELINESS,** K. Starr, Victor	73
82.	**BAHAMA MAMA,** Four Aces, Decca	87
82.	**WHEN ROCK 'N' ROLL COMES TO TRINIDAD,** N. K. Cole, Capitol	—
84.	**TWELVE O'CLOCK TONIGHT,** Doris Day, Columbia	98
85.	**JIM' DANDY,** L. Baker, Atlantic	—
86.	**SHISH KEBAH,** R. Marterie, Mercury	—
87.	**I MISS YOU SO,** C. Connor. Atlantic	92
87.	**I LOVE MY GIRL,** Hilltoppers, Dot	77
89.	**HAREM DANCE,** Armenian Jazz Sextet, Kapp	—
89.	**PARTY DOLL,** R. Brown, Imperial	—
89.	**ON TREASURE ISLAND,** G. Storm, Dot	—
92.	**LEAP FROG,** C. Alaimo, M-G-M	—
93.	**JAMAICA FAREWELL,** H. Belafonte, Victor	—
94.	**DO I LOVE YOU?** T Martin, Victor	—
95.	**BALLERINA,** N. K. Cole, Capitol	67
95.	**SO LONG MY LOVE,** F. Sinatra. Capitol	79
95.	**MAKE LIKE A BUNNY, HONEY,** J. Corey, Columbia	—
98.	**YOU'RE MINE,** Four Aces, Decca	—
99.	**ANASTASIA,** P. Boone, Dot	—
100.	**YOUR TRUE LOVE,** C. Perkins, Sun	70

CAUTION TO DEALERS AND JUKE BOX OPERATORS

The Billboard's Top 100 is NOT designed to provide tested information for buying purposes. This function is most reliably served by other regular weekly features: Best Sellers in Stores, Most Played in Juke Boxes, Coming Up Strong and Best Buys.

• Best Sellers in Stores

For survey week ending May 1

RECORDS are ranked in order of their current national selling importance at the retail level, as determined by The Billboard's weekly survey of the top volume dealers in every important market area. When significant action is reported on both sides of a record, points are combined to determine position on the chart. In such a case, both sides are listed in bold type, the leading side on top.

This Week		Last Week	Weeks on Chart
1.	**ALL SHOOK UP** (BMI)—E. Presley... That's When Your Heartaches Begin (ASCAP)—Vic 20-6870	1	6
2.	**LITTLE DARLIN'** (BMI)—Diamonds.. Faithful and True (BMI)—Mercury 71060	2	9
3.	**ROUND AND ROUND** (BMI)—P. Como.... Mi Casa, Su Casa (ASCAP)—Vic 20-6815	3	10
4.	**COME GO WITH ME** (BMI)—D. Vikings.... How Can I Find Love? (BMI)—Dot 15538	7	11
5.	**SCHOOL DAY** (BMI)—C. Berry...... Deep Feeling (BMI)—Chess 1653	6	4
6.	**GONE** (BMI)—F. Husky.... Missing Persons (BMI)—Cap 3628	5	8
7.	**PARTY DOLL** (BMI)—B. Knox....... My Baby's Gone (BMI)—Roulette 4002	4	11
8.	**WHY, BABY, WHY?** (BMI)—P. Boone. I'm Waiting Just for You (BMI)—Dot 15545	9	8
9.	**SO RARE** (ASCAP)—J. Dorsey........ Sophisticated Swing (ASCAP)—Fraternity 755	10	4
10.	**ROCK-A-BILLY** (ASCAP)—G. Mitchell. Hoot Owl (ASCAP)—Col 40877	15	4
11.	**I'M WALKIN'** (BMI)—F. Domino.... I'm in the Mood for Love (ASCAP)—Imperial 5428	8	10
12.	**DARK MOON** (BMI)—B. Guitar..... Big Mike (BMI)—Dot 15550	21	3
13.	**WHITE SPORT COAT** (BMI)—M. Robbins.... Grown Up Tears (BMI)—Col 40864	17	2
14.	**MAMA LOOK-A BOOBOO** (BMI)—H. Belafonte.... Don't Ever Love Me (ASCAP)—Vic 20-6830	11	7
15.	**BUTTERFLY** (BMI)—A. Williams..... It Doesn't Take Very Long (ASCAP)—Cadence 1308	12	11
16.	**BUTTERFLY** (BMI)—C. Gracie...... Ninety-Nine Ways (BMI)—Cameo 105	13	12
17.	**I'M SORRY** (BMI)—Platters.......... **HE'S MINE** (BMI)—Mercury 71032	18	4
18.	**I'M WALKIN'** (BMI)—R. Nelson...... A Teenager's Romance (ASCAP)—Verve 10047	—	1
19.	**PARTY DOLL** (BMI)—S. Lawrence... Pum-Pa-Lum (ASCAP)—Coral 61792	14	9
20.	**DARK MOON** (BMI)—G. Storm...... Little Too Late (BMI)—Dot 15550	—	1
21.	**I'M STICKIN' WITH YOU** (BMI)—J. Bowen.... Ever-Lovin' Fingers (BMI)—Roulette 4001	19	10
22.	**LOVE IS A GOLDEN RING** (BMI)—F. Laine.... There's Not a Moment to Spare (ASCAP)—Col 40856	—	1
23.	**PLEDGE OF LOVE** (BMI)—K. Copeland.... Night Air (BMI)—Imperial 5432	—	1
24.	**NINETY-NINE WAYS** (BMI)—T. Hunter.... Don't Get Around Much Anymore (ASCAP)—Dot 15548	20	7
25.	**PEACE IN THE VALLEY**—E. Presley. Vic EPA-4054	—	1

• Most Played in Juke Boxes

For survey week ending May 1

RECORDS are ranked in order of the greatest number of plays in juke boxes thruout the country, as determined by The Billboard's weekly survey of the nation's juke box operators. When significant play is reported on both sides of a record, points are combined to determine position on the chart. In such a case, both sides are listed in bold type, the leading side on top.

This Week		Last Week	Weeks on Chart
1.	**ALL SHOOK UP** (BMI)—E. Presley... That's When Your Heartaches Begin (ASCAP)—Vic 20-6870	1	5
2.	**LITTLE DARLIN'** (BMI)—Diamonds.. Faithful and True (BMI)—Mercury 71060	2	7
3.	**ROUND AND ROUND** (BMI)—P. Como.... Mi Casa Su Casa (ASCAP)—Vic 20-6815	3	8
4.	**PARTY DOLL** (BMI)—B. Knox....... My Baby's Gone (BMI)—Roulette 4002	4	10
5.	**GONE** (BMI)—F. Husky.... Missing Persons (BMI)—Cap 3628	10	5
6.	**I'M WALKIN'** (BMI)—F. Domino.... I'm in the Mood for Love (ASCAP)—Imperial 5428	5	8
7.	**BUTTERFLY** (BMI)—A. Williams.... It Doesn't Take Very Long (ASCAP)—Cadence 1308	6	10
8.	**WHY, BABY, WHY?** (BMI)—P. Boone. I'm Waiting Just for You (BMI)—Dot 15545	7	7
9.	**COME GO WITH ME** (BMI)—D. Vikings.... How Can I Find True Love? (BMI)—Dot 15538	12	2
10.	**BUTTERFLY** (BMI)—C. Gracie....... Ninety-Nine Ways (BMI)—Cameo 105	8	11
11.	**PARTY DOLL** (BMI)—S. Lawrence... Pum-Pa-Lum (ASCAP)—Coral 61792	11	9
12.	**MARIANNE** (BMI)—Hilltoppers...... You're Wasting Your Time (ASCAP)—Dot 15537	12	12
12.	**SO RARE** (ASCAP)—J. Dorsey....... Sophisticated Swing (ASCAP)—Fraternity 755	—	2
14.	**SCHOOL DAY** (BMI)—C. Berry...... Deep Feeling (BMI)—Chess 1653	—	1
15.	**TEEN-AGE CRUSH** (BMI)—T. Sands. Hep Dee Hootie (BMI)—Cap 3639	9	11
15.	**EMPTY ARMS** (BMI)—T. Brewer.... Ricky-Tick Song (BMI)—Coral 61085	—	1
17.	**NINETY-NINE WAYS** (BMI)—T. Hunter.... Don't Get Around Much Anymore (ASCAP)—Dot 15548	18	5
18.	**WHITE SPORT COAT** (BMI)—M. Robbins.... Grown Up Tears (BMI)—Columbia 40864	—	1
19.	**I'M STICKIN' WITH YOU** (BMI)—J. Bowen.... Ever-Lovin' Fingers (BMI)—Roulette 4001	17	3
19.	**DARK MOON** (BMI)—B. Guitar...... Big Mike (BMI)—Fabor 5018	—	1

• Best Selling Sheet Music

Tunes are ranked in order of their current national selling importance at the sheet music jobber level.

This Week		Last Week	Weeks on Chart
1.	**Round and Round** (Rush)	1	9
2.	**All Shook Up** (Shalimar-Presley)	4	4
3.	**Marianne** (Montclare)	2	11
4.	**Why, Baby, Why?** (Winneton)	6	5
5.	**Butterfly** (Mayland-Presley)	3	9
6.	**Almost Paradise** (Peer)	5	8
7.	**Chantez-Chantez** (Cromwell)	7	8
8.	**Little Darlin'** (Excelloree)	—	1
9.	**White Sport Coat** (Acuff-Rose)	—	1
10.	**Gone** (Hill & Range)	—	3
10.	**Do I Love You?** (Williamson)	10	4
12.	**Ninety-Nine Ways** (Mayland)	8	4
13.	**Come Go With Me** (Gil-Feebee)	13	2
14.	**Dark Moon** (Dandelion)	—	1
15.	**Young Love** (Lowery)	9	16

• Most Played by Jockeys

For survey week ending May 1

SIDES are ranked in order of the greatest number of plays on disk jockey radio shows thruout the country. Results are based on The Billboard's weekly survey among the nation's disk jockeys. The reverse side of each record is also listed.

This Week		Last Week	Weeks on Chart
1.	**ALL SHOOK UP** (BMI)—E. Presley... That's When Your Heartaches Begin (ASCAP)—Vic 20-6870	1	5
2.	**LITTLE DARLIN'** (BMI)—Diamonds.. Faithful and True (BMI)—Mercury 71060	3	7
3.	**ROUND AND ROUND** (BMI)—P. Como.... Mi Casa, Su Casa (ASCAP)—Vic 20-6815	2	11
4.	**GONE** (BMI)—F. Husky.... Missing Persons (BMI)—Cap 3628	4	9
5.	**BUTTERFLY** (BMI)—A. Williams.... It Doesn't Take Very Long (ASCAP)—Cadence 1308	5	10
6.	**COME GO WITH ME** (BMI)—D. Vikings.... How Can I Find True Love? (BMI)—Dot 15538	8	6
7.	**PARTY DOLL** (BMI)—B. Knox....... My Baby's Gone (BMI)—Roulette 4002	6	10
8.	**WHITE SPORT COAT** (BMI)—M. Robbins.... Grown Up Tears (BMI)—Col 40864	13	2
9.	**SCHOOL DAY** (BMI)—C. Berry...... Deep Feeling (BMI)—Chess 1653	11	3
10.	**SO RARE** (ASCAP)—J. Dorsey....... Sophisticated Swing (ASCAP)—Fraternity 755	16	2
11.	**WHY, BABY, WHY?** (BMI)—P. Boone. I'm Waiting Just for You (BMI)—Dot 15545	7	8
12.	**PLEDGE OF LOVE** (BMI)—P. Copeland.... Night Air (BMI)—Imperial 5432	14	2
13.	**DARK MOON** (BMI)—B. Guitar...... Big Mike (BMI)—Dot 15550	—	1
14.	**MAMA LOOK-A BOOBOO** (BMI)—H. Belafonte.... Don't Ever Love Me (ASCAP)—Vic 20-6830	14	5
15.	**ROCK-A-BILLY** (ASCAP)—G. Mitchell.... Hoot Owl (ASCAP)—Col 40877	18	3
16.	**LOVE IS A GOLDEN RING** (BMI)—F. Laine.... There's Not a Moment to Spare (ASCAP)—Col 40856	10	4
16.	**I'M WALKIN'** (BMI)—F. Domino..... I'm in the Mood for Love (ASCAP)—Imperial 5428	12	8
18.	**PARTY DOLL** (BMI)—S. Lawrence... Pum-Pa-Lum (ASCAP)—Coral 61792	9	9
19.	**MANGOS** (ASCAP)—R. Clooney..... Independent (ASCAP)—Col 40835	20	4
19.	**EMPTY ARMS** (BMI)—T. Brewer..... Ricky Tick Song (BMI)—Coral 61805	—	1
21.	**CHANTEZ-CHANTEZ** (ASCAP)—D. Shore.... Honkytonk Heart (BMI)—Vic 20-6792	24	7
22.	**ALMOST PARADISE** (BMI)—R. Williams.... For the First Time (ASCAP)—Kapp 175	19	3
23.	**SITTIN' IN THE BALCONY** (BMI)—E. Cochran.... Dark, Lonely Street (BMI)—Liberty 55056	25	4
23.	**YES, TONIGHT, JOSEPHINE** (BMI)—J. Ray.... No Wedding Today (ASCAP)—Col 40893	—	1
25.	**BUTTERFLY** (BMI)—C. Gracie....... Ninety-Nine Ways (BMI)—Cameo 105	23	11

THE TOP 100

For survey week ending May 1

A list of the Top 100 RECORD SIDES in the nation according to a COMBINED TABULATION of Dealer, Disk Jockey and Juke Box Operator replies to The Billboard's weekly popular record Best Seller and Most Played surveys. Its purpose is to provide Disk Jockeys with additional programming material and to give trade exposure to NEWER records just beginning to show action in the field.

Pos.	Song, Artist, Label	Last Week
1.	**ALL SHOOK-UP,** E. Presley, Victor	1
2.	**LITTLE DARLIN',** Diamonds, Mercury	2
3.	**ROUND AND ROUND,** P. Como, Victor	3
4.	**GONE,** F. Husky, Capitol	5
5.	**PARTY DOLL,** B. Knox, Roulette	4
6.	**COME GO WITH ME,** D. Vikings, Dot	9
7.	**BUTTERFLY,** A. Williams, Cadence	6
7.	**WHY, BABY, WHY?** P. Boone, Dot	7
9.	**SCHOOL DAY,** C. Berry. Chess	11
10.	**SO RARE,** J. Dorsey, Fraternity	13
11.	**I'M WALKIN',** F. Domino, Imperial	8
12.	**WHITE SPORT COAT,** M. Robbins, Columbia	17
13.	**DARK MOON,** B. Guitar, Dot	27
14.	**PARTY DOLL,** S. Lawrence, Coral	10
15.	**MAMA LOOK-A BOOBOO,** H. Belafonte, Victor	13
15.	**ROCK-A-BILLY,** G. Mitchell, Columbia	18
17.	**BUTTERFLY,** C. Gracie, Cameo	12
18.	**EMPTY ARMS,** T. Brewer, Coral	24
19.	**TEEN-AGE CRUSH,** T. Sands, Capitol	13
20.	**NINETY-NINE WAYS,** T. Hunter, Dot	16
21.	**PLEDGE OF LOVE,** K. Copeland, Imperial	25
22.	**DARK MOON,** G. Storm. Dot	38
23.	**LOVE IS A GOLDEN RING,** F. Laine, Columbia	23
24.	**I'M STICKIN' WITH YOU,** J. Bowen, Roulette	18
25.	**I'M SORRY,** Platters, Mercury	29
26.	**MARIANNE,** T. Gilkyson, Columbia	20
27.	**SITTIN' IN THE BALCONY,** E. Cochran, Liberty	21
28.	**ALMOST PARADISE,** R Williams, Kapp	26
29.	**CHANTEZ-CHANTEZ,** D. Shore, Victor	33
30.	**MANGOS,** R. Clooney. Columbia	31
31.	**HE'S MINE,** Platters, Mercury	36
32.	**WALKIN' AFTER MIDNIGHT,** P. Cline, Decca	34
33.	**JUST BECAUSE,** L. Price, ABC-Paramount	37
34.	**LUCILLE,** Little Richard, Specialty	28
35.	**MARIANNE,** Hilltoppers, Dot	22
36.	**WONDERFUL, WONDERFUL,** J. Mathis, Columbia	47
37.	**AFTER SCHOOL,** R. Starr, Dale	44
38.	**YOUNG LOVE,** T Hunter, Dot	32
39.	**FOUR WALLS,** J. Reeves, Victor	76
40.	**BANANA BOAT (DAY-O),** H. Belafonte, Victor	43
41.	**PLEDGE OF LOVE,** M. Torok, Decca	35
41.	**WHO NEEDS YOU,** Four Lads, Columbia	30
43.	**SHISH KEBAB,** R. Marterie, Mercury	86
44.	**PLEDGE OF LOVE,** D. Contino, Mercury	45
45.	**YES, TONIGHT, JOSEPHINE,** J. Ray, Columbia	51
46.	**PEACE IN THE VALLEY,** E. Presley, Victor	39
46.	**YOUNG LOVE,** S. James, Capitol	42
48.	**DAY-O BANANA BOAT SONG,** S. Freberg. Capitol	50
48.	**FIRST DATE, FIRST KISS, FIRST LOVE,** S. James, Capitol	41
50.	**RING-A-DING,** T. Sands, Capitol	54
51.	**IT'S NOT FOR ME TO SAY,** J. Mathis, Columbia	58
52.	**EMPTY ARMS,** I. J. Hunter, Atlantic	51
52.	**I'M WALKIN',** R. Nelson, Verve	—
54.	**LITTLE DARLIN',** Gladiolas, Excello	51
54.	**POOR MAN'S ROSES,** P Page, Mercury	46
56.	**MAMA GUITAR,** D. Cornell, Coral	68
56.	**WIND IN THE WILLOW,** J. Stafford, Columbia	59
58.	**ALMOST PARADISE,** L. Stein. Unique	79
59.	**C. C. RIDER,** C. Willis, Atlantic	63
59.	**TRICKY,** R. Marterie, Mercury	57
61.	**I'M WAITING JUST FOR YOU,** P. Boone, Dot	66
62.	**MY LOVE SONG,** T. Sands, Capitol	71
63.	**PLEDGE OF LOVE,** J. Janis, ABC-Paramount	72
64.	**LET IT BE ME,** J. Corey. Columbia	73
65.	**SITTIN' IN THE BALCONY,** J. Dee, Colonial	49
65.	**TALKIN' TO THE BLUES,** J. Lowe, Dot	—
67.	**WHEN ROCK AND ROLL COMES TO TRINIDAD,** N. (King) Cole, Capitol	82
68.	**TWELVE O'CLOCK TONIGHT,** Doris Day, Columbia	84
69.	**YOUNG BLOOD.** Coasters, Atco	—
70.	**1492,** B. Johnson, Bally	—
71.	**JAMIE BOY,** K. Starr, Victor	54
72.	**I'M STICKIN' WITH YOU,** Fontane Sisters, Dot	—
72.	**LOVE LETTERS IN THE SAND,** P. Boone, Dot	—
72.	**I'LL TAKE ROMANCE,** E. Gorme, ABC-Paramount	66
75.	**DON'T FORBID ME,** P. Boone, Dot	40
75.	**I MISS YOU SO,** C. Connor, Atlantic	87
77.	**THERE OUGHTA BE A LAW,** Mickey and Sylvia, Vik	48
77.	**TILL,** P. Faith, Columbia	63
79.	**SO LONG MY LOVE,** F. Sinatra, Capitol	95
80.	**FOUR WALLS,** J Lowe, Dot	—
81.	**CALYPSO MELODY,** D Rose, M-G-M	62
81.	**JIM DANDY,** L. Baker, Atlantic	85
83.	**THAT'S WHEN YOUR HEARTACHES BEGIN,** E. Presley, Victor	60
84.	**I JUST DON'T KNOW** Four Lads, Columbia	—
85.	**CAN I STEAL A LITTLE LOVE,** F. Sinatra, Capitol	77
85.	**PARTY DOLL,** W. Manone, Decca	74
87.	**BAD BOY,** Jive Bombers, Savoy	—
88.	**LITTLE WHITE LIES,** B. Johnson, Bally	80
89.	**I LOVE MY GIRL,** C. Morley, ABC-Paramount	—
90.	**STARDUST,** N. (King) Cole, Capitol	—
91.	**DON'T CRY MY LOVE,** V. Lynn, London	—
91.	**ONE STEP AT A TIME,** B. Lee, Decca	60
91.	**TRUE LOVE GONE,** B. Madigan, M-G-M	—
94.	**LITTLE LONLINESS,** K. Starr, Victor	81
94.	**YOUR TRUE LOVE,** C. Perkins, Sun	100
96.	**ALMOST PARADISE,** N. Petty Trio, ABC-Paramount	68
97.	**FABULOUS,** C. Gracie, Cameo	—
98.	**BERNADINE,** P. Boone, Dot	—
98.	**SAY IT ISN'T SO,** T. King, Victor	—
100.	**DO I LOVE YOU,** V. Damone, Columbia	78
100.	**HAREM DANCE,** Armenian Jazz Sextet, Kapp	89

CAUTION TO DEALERS AND JUKE BOX OPERATORS

The Billboard's Top 100 is NOT designed to provide tested information for buying purposes. This function is most reliably served by other regular weekly features: Best Sellers in Stores, Most Played in Juke Boxes, Coming Up Strong and Best Buys.

• Best Sellers in Stores

For survey week ending May 8

RECORDS are ranked in order of their current national selling importance at the retail level, as determined by The Billboard's weekly survey of the top volume dealers in every important market area. When significant action is reported on both sides of a record, points are combined to determine position on the chart. In such a case, both sides are listed in bold type, the leading side on top.

This Week		Last Week	Weeks on Chart
1.	ALL SHOOK UP (BMI)—E. Presley; That's When Your Heartaches Begin (ASCAP)—Vic 20-6870	1	7
2.	LITTLE DARLIN' (BMI)—Diamonds; Faithful and True (BMI)—Mercury 71060	2	10
3.	SCHOOL DAY (BMI)—C. Berry; Deep Feeling (BMI)—Chess 1613	5	5
4.	ROUND AND ROUND (BMI)—P. Como; Mi Casa, Su Casa (ASCAP)—Vic 20-6815	3	11
5.	COME GO WITH ME (BMI)—D. Vikings; How Can I Find Love? (BMI)—Dot 16538	4	12
6.	GONE (BMI)—F. Husky; Missing Persons (BMI)—Cap 3628	6	9
7.	SO RARE (ASCAP)—J. Dorsey; Sophisticated Swing (ASCAP)—Fraternity 755	9	5
8.	PARTY DOLL (BMI)—B. Knox; My Baby's Gone (BMI)—Roulette 4002	7	12
9.	I'M WALKIN' (BMI)—R. Nelson; A TEENAGER'S ROMANCE (ASCAP)—Verve 10047	18	2
10.	WHITE SPORT COAT (BMI)—M. Robbins; Grown Up Tears (BMI)—Col 40864	13	3
11.	DARK MOON (BMI)—B. Guitar; Big Mike (BMI)—Dot 15550	12	4
12.	ROCK-A-BILLY (ASCAP)—G. Mitchell; Hoot Owl (ASCAP)—Col 40877	10	5
13.	LOVE LETTERS IN THE SAND (ASCAP)—P. Boone; BERNARDINE (ASCAP)—Dot 15570	—	1
14.	WHY, BABY, WHY (BMI)—P. Boone; I'm Waiting Just for You (BMI)—Dot 15545	8	9
15.	DARK MOON (BMI)—G. Storm; Little Too Late (BMI)—Dot 15550	20	2
16.	HE'S MINE (BMI)—Platters; I'M SORRY (BMI)—Mercury 71032	—	5
17.	MAMA LOOK-A BOOBOO (BMI)—H. Belafonte; Don't Ever Love Me (ASCAP)—Vic 20-6830	14	8
18.	FOUR WALLS (BMI)—J. Reeves; I Know and You Know (BMI)—Vic 20-6874	—	1
19.	BUTTERFLY (BMI)—C. Gracie; Ninety-Nine Ways (BMI)—Cameo 105	16	13
20.	BUTTERFLY (BMI)—A. Williams; It Doesn't Take Very Long (ASCAP)—Cadence 1308	15	12
21.	I'M WALKIN' (BMI)—F. Domino; I'm in the Mood for Love (ASCAP)—Imperial 5428	11	11
22.	WONDERFUL, WONDERFUL (BMI)—J. Mathis; Since You Went Away (BMI)—Glory 256	—	1
23.	MANGOS (ASCAP)—R. Clooney; Independent (ASCAP)—Col 40835	—	1
24.	ROSIE-LEE (BMI)—Melo Tones; I'll Never Fall in Love Again (BMI)—Gee 1037	—	1
25.	C. C. RIDER (BMI)—C. Willis; Ease the Pain (BMI)—Atlantic 1130	—	1

• Most Played in Juke Boxes

For survey week ending May 8

RECORDS are ranked in order of the greatest number of plays in juke boxes thruout the country, as determined by The Billboard's weekly survey of the nation's juke box operators. When significant play is reported on both sides of a record, points are combined to determine position on the chart. In such a case, both sides are listed in bold type, the leading side on top.

This Week		Last Week	Weeks on Chart
1.	ALL SHOOK UP (BMI)—E. Presley; That's When Your Heartaches Begin (ASCAP)—Vic 20-6870	1	6
2.	LITTLE DARLIN' (BMI)—Diamonds; Faithful and True (BMI)—Mercury 71060	2	8
3.	ROUND AND ROUND (BMI)—P. Como; Mi Casa, Su Casa (ASCAP)—Vic 20-6815	3	9
4.	GONE (BMI)—F. Husky; Missing Persons (BMI)—Cap 3628	5	6
5.	PARTY DOLL (BMI)—B. Knox; My Baby's Gone (BMI)—Roulette 4002	4	11
6.	COME GO WITH ME (BMI)—D. Vikings; How Can I Find True Love (BMI)—Dot 15538	9	3
7.	I'M WALKIN' (BMI)—F. Domino; I'm in the Mood for Love (ASCAP)—Imperial 5428	6	9
8.	WHY, BABY, WHY? (BMI)—P. Boone; I'm Waitin' Just for You (BMI)—Dot 15545	8	8
9.	BUTTERFLY (BMI)—A. Williams; It Doesn't Take Very Long (ASCAP)—Cadence 1308	7	11
10.	SO RARE (ASCAP)—J. Dorsey; Sophisticated Swing (ASCAP)—Fraternity 755	12	3
11.	WHITE SPORT COAT (BMI) M. Robbins; Grown-Up Tears (BMI)—Columbia 40864	18	2
11.	DARK MOON (BMI)—B. Guitar; Big Mike (BMI)—Fabor 5018	19	2
13.	EMPTY ARMS (BMI)—T. Brewer; Ricky-Tick Song (BMI)—Coral 61085	15	2
14.	ROCK-A-BILLY—G. Mitchell; Hoot Owl (ASCAP)—Columbia 40877	—	1
15.	SCHOOL DAY (BMI)—C. Berry; Deep Feeling (BMI)—Chess 1653	14	2
16.	BUTTERFLY (BMI)—C. Gracie; Ninety-Nine Ways (BMI)—Cameo 105	10	12
17.	NINETY-NINE WAYS (BMI)—T. Hunter; Don't Get Around Much Anymore (ASCAP)—Dot 15548	17	6
18.	PARTY DOLL (BMI)—S. Lawrence; Pum-Pa-Lum (ASCAP)—Coral 61792	11	10
19.	DARK MOON (BMI)—G. Storm; Little Too Late (BMI)—Dot 15558	—	1
20.	MARIANNE (BMI)—Hilltoppers; You're Wasting Your Time (ASCAP)—Dot 15537	12	13

• Best Selling Sheet Music

Tunes are ranked in order of their current national selling importance at the sheet music jobber level.

This Week		Last Week	Weeks on Chart
1.	**Round and Round** (Rush)	1	10
2.	**All Shook Up** (Shalimar-Presley)	2	5
3.	**Why Baby Why** (Winneton)	4	6
4.	**Little Darlin** (Excelloree)	8	2
5.	**Marianne** (Montclare)	3	12
6.	**Butterfly** (Mayland-Presley)	5	10
7.	**White Sport Coat** (Acuff-Rose)	9	2
8.	**Chantez-Chantez** (Cromwell)	7	9
9.	**Almost Paradise** (Peer)	6	9
10.	**Gone** (Hill & Range)	10	4
11.	**Dark Moon** (Dandelion)	14	2
12.	**Ninety-Nine Ways** (Mayland)	12	5
13.	**Come Go With Me** (Gil-Feebee)	13	3
14.	**Four Walls** (Springfield)	—	1
15.	**Do I Love You?** (Williamson)	10	5

• Most Played by Jockeys

For survey week ending May 8

SIDES are ranked in order of the greatest number of plays on disk jockey radio shows thruout the country. Results are based on The Billboard's weekly survey among the nation's disk jockeys. The reverse side of each record is also listed.

This Week		Last Week	Weeks on Chart
1.	ALL SHOOK UP (BMI)—E. Presley; That's When Your Heartaches Begin (ASCAP)—Vic 20-6870	1	6
2.	ROUND AND ROUND (BMI)—P. Como; Mi Casa, Su Casa (ASCAP)—Vic 20-6815	3	12
3.	LITTLE DARLIN' (BMI)—Diamonds; Faithful and True (BMI)—Mercury 71060	2	8
4.	GONE (BMI)—F. Husky; Missing Persons (BMI)—Cap 3628	4	10
5.	SO RARE (ASCAP)—J. Dorsey; Sophisticated Swing (ASCAP)—Fraternity 755	10	3
6.	PARTY DOLL (BMI)—B. Knox; My Baby's Gone (BMI)—Roulette 4002	7	11
7.	COME GO WITH ME (BMI)—D. Vikings; How Can I Find True Love (BMI)—Dot 15538	6	7
8.	BUTTERFLY (BMI)—A. Williams; It Doesn't Take Very Long (ASCAP)—Cadence 1308	5	11
9.	SCHOOL DAY (BMI)—C. Berry; Deep Feeling (BMI)—Chess 1653	9	4
10.	LOVE LETTERS IN THE SAND (ASCAP)—P. Boone; Bernadine (ASCAP)—Dot 15570	—	1
11.	SHISH KEBAB (BMI)—R. Marterie; Bop a Boo-Bop a Doo (ASCAP)—Mercury 71092	—	1
12.	I'M WALKIN' (BMI)—F. Domino; I'm in the Mood for Love (ASCAP)—Imperial 5428	16	9
13.	WHY, BABY, WHY? (BMI)—P. Boone; I'm Waiting Just for You (BMI)—Dot 15545	11	9
13.	DARK MOON (BMI)—G. Storm; Little Too Late (BMI)—Dot 15550	—	1
15.	PARTY DOLL (BMI)—S. Lawrence; Pum--Pa-Lum (ASCAP)—Cadence 61792	18	10
16.	WHITE SPORT COAT (BMI)—M. Robbins; Grown-Up Tears (BMI)—Col 40864	8	3
17.	MANGOS (ASCAP)—R. Clooney; Independent (ASCAP)—Col 40835	19	5
18.	ROCK-A-BILLY (ASCAP)—G. Mitchell; Hoot Owl (ASCAP)—Col 40877	15	4
19.	PLEDGE OF LOVE (BMI)—K. Copeland; Night Air (BMI)—Imperial 5432	12	3
20.	TALKIN' TO THE BLUES (BMI)—J. Lowe; Four Walls (BMI)—Dot 15569	—	1
21.	YES, TONIGHT, JOSEPHINE (BMI)—J. Ray; No Wedding Today (ASCAP)—Col 40893	23	2
22.	DARK MOON (BMI)—B. Guitar; Big Mike (BMI)—Dot 15550	13	2
23.	ALMOST PARADISE (BMI)—R. Williams; For the First Time (ASCAP)—Kapp 175	22	4
24.	CHANTEZ-CHANTEZ (ASCAP)—D. Shore; Honkytonk Heart (BMI)—Vic 20-6792	21	8
25.	LOVE IS A GOLDEN RING (BMI)—F. Laine; There's Not a Moment to Spare (ASCAP)—Col 40856	16	5

THE TOP 100

For survey week ending May 8

A list of the Top 100 RECORD SIDES in the nation according to a COMBINED TABULATION of Dealer, Disk Jockey and Juke Box Operator replies to The Billboard's weekly popular record Best Seller and Most Played surveys. Its purpose is to provide Disk Jockeys with additional programming material and to give trade exposure to NEWER records just beginning to show action in the field.

Pos.	Song, Artist, Label	Last Week
1.	**ALL SHOOK UP**, E. Presley, Victor	1
2.	**LITTLE DARLIN'**, Diamonds, Mercury	2
3.	**ROUND AND ROUND**, P. Como, Victor	3
4.	**GONE**, F. Husky, Capitol	4
5.	**COME GO WITH ME**, D. Vikings, Dot	6
6.	**PARTY DOLL**, B. Knox, Roulette	5
7.	**SO RARE**, J. Dorsey, Fraternity	10
8.	**SCHOOL DAY**, C. Berry, Chess	9
9.	**WHY, BABY, WHY?** P. Boone, Dot	7
10.	**WHITE SPORT COAT**, M. Robbins, Columbia	12
11.	**BUTTERFLY**, A. Williams, Cadence	7
12.	**I'M WALKIN'**, F. Domino, Imperial	11
13.	**DARK MOON**, B. Guitar, Dot	13
13.	**ROCK-A-BILLY**, G. Mitchell, Columbia	15
15.	**DARK MOON**, G. Storm, Dot	22
16.	**BUTTERFLY**, C. Gracie, Cameo	17
17.	**PARTY DOLL**, S. Lawrence, Coral	14
18.	**EMPTY ARMS**, T. Brewer, Coral	18
19.	**MAMA LOOK-A BOOBOO**, H. Belafonte, Victor	15
20.	**I'M SORRY**, Platters, Mercury	25
21.	**LOVE LETTERS IN THE SAND**, P. Boone, Dot	72
22.	**YES, TONIGHT, JOSEPHINE**, J. Ray, Columbia	45
23.	**LOVE IS A GOLDEN THING**, F. Laine, Columbia	23
24.	**PLEDGE OF LOVE**, K. Copeland, Imperial	21
25.	**MANGOS**, R. Clooney, Columbia	30
26.	**PLEDGE OF LOVE**, M. Torok, Decca	41
27.	**ALMOST PARADISE**, R. Williams, Kapp	28
28.	**NINETY-NINE WAYS**, T. Hunter, Dot	20
29.	**WHO NEEDS YOU**, Four Lads, Columbia	41
30.	**SHISH KEBAB**, R. Marterie, Mercury	43
31.	**HE'S MINE**, Platters, Mercury	31
32.	**AFTER SCHOOL**, R. Starr, Dale	37
33.	**I'M WALKIN'**, R. Nelson, Verve	52
34.	**TEEN-AGE CRUSH**, T. Sands, Capitol	19
34.	**WONDERFUL, WONDERFUL**, J. Mathis, Columbia	36
36.	**FOUR WALLS**, J. Reeves, Victor	39
37.	**SITTIN' IN THE BALCONY**, E. Cochran, Liberty	27
38.	**I'M STICKIN' WITH YOU**, J. Bowen, Roulette	24
39.	**MARIANNE**, T. Gilkyson, Columbia	26
40.	**LUCILLE**, Little Richard, Specialty	34
41.	**MARIANNE**, Hilltoppers, Dot	35
42.	**BERNADINE**, P. Boone, Dot	98
43.	**TALKIN' TO THE BLUES**, J. Lowe, Dot	65
44.	**FOUR WALLS**, J. Lowe, Dot	80
45.	**JUST BECAUSE**, L. Price, ABC-Paramount	33
45.	**WALKIN' AFTER MIDNIGHT**, P. Cline, Decca	32
47.	**MAMA GUITAR**, D. Cornell, Coral	56
48.	**DAY-O BANANA BOAT SONG**, S. Freeberg, Capitol	48
48.	**CHANTEZ-CHANTEZ**, D. Shore, Victor	29
50.	**YOUNG BLOOD**, Coasters, Atco	69
51.	**FABULOUS**, C. Gracie, Cameo	97
52.	**LITTLE WHITE LIES**, B. Johnson, Bally	88
53.	**I JUST DON'T KNOW**, Four Lads, Columbia	84
54.	**RING-A-DING**, T. Sands, Capitol	50
55.	**ALMOST PARADISE**, L. Stein, Unique	58
56.	**ALMOST PARADISE**, N. Petty Trio, ABC-Paramount	96
57.	**BANANA BOAT (DAY-O)**, H. Belafonte, Victor	40
58.	**CALYPSO MELODY**, D. Rose, M-G-M	81
59.	**LITTLE DARLIN'**, Gladiolas, Excello	54
60.	**THERE OUGHTA BE A LAW**, Mickey and Sylvia, Vik	77
61.	**PLEDGE OF LOVE**, D. Contino, Mercury	44
62.	**I LOVE MY GIRL**, C. Morley, ABC-Paramount	89
62.	**YOUNG LOVE**, T. Hunter, Dot	38
65.	**IT'S NOT FOR ME TO SAY**, J. Mathis, Columbia	51
66.	**ROCK YOUR BABY TO SLEEP**, B. Knox, Roulette	—
67.	**EMPTY ARMS**, I. J. Hunter, Atlantic	52
67.	**HAREM DANCE**, Armenian Jazz Sextet, Kapp	100
67.	**WIND IN THE WILLOW**, J. Stafford, Columbia	56
70.	**PEACE IN THE VALLEY**, E. Presley, Victor	46
71.	**C. C. RIDER**, C. Willis, Atlantic	59
72.	**I'LL TAKE ROMANCE**, E. Gorme, ABC-Paramount	72
72.	**TRICKY**, R. Marterie, Mercury	59
74.	**SO LONG, MY LOVE**, F. Sinatra, Capitol	79
75.	**I LOVE MY GIRL**, Hilltoppers, Dot	—
76.	**MY LOVE SONG**, T. Sands, Capitol	62
76.	**SEARCHING**, Coasters, Atco	—
78.	**I'M STICKIN' WITH YOU**, Fontane Sisters, Dot	72
79.	**CAN I STEAL A LITTLE LOVE**, F. Sinatra, Capitol	85
79.	**POOR MAN'S ROSES**, P. Page, Mercury	54
81.	**WHEN ROCK AND ROLL COMES TO TRINIDAD**, Nat (King) Cole, Capitol	67
82.	**DO I LOVE YOU**, V. Damone, Columbia	100
82.	**DO I LOVE YOU**, T. Martin, Victor	—
84.	**FORTY CUPS OF COFFEE**, B. Haley, Decca	—
84.	**TWELVE O'CLOCK TONIGHT**, Doris Day, Columbia	68
86.	**BUTTERFLY**, B. Carroll, Bally	—
86.	**1492**, B. Johnson, Bally	70
88.	**TILL**, P. Faith, Columbia	77
89.	**SEND ME SOME LOVIN'**, Little Richard, Specialty	—
90.	**DON'T EVER LOVE ME**, H. Belafonte, Victor	—
91.	**ROSIE LEE**, Mello Tones, Gee	—
92.	**I'M WAITING JUST FOR YOU**, P. Boone, Dot	61
93.	**TRUE LOVE GONE**, B. Madigan, M-G-M	91
94.	**PLEDGE OF LOVE**, J. Janis, ABC-Paramount	63
95.	**VALLEY OF TEARS**, F. Domino, Imperial	—
96.	**LUCKY LIPS**, G. Storm, Dot	—
97.	**YOUNG LOVE**, S. James, Capitol	46
98.	**DON'T FORBID ME**, P. Boone, Dot	75
98.	**JAMIE BOY**, K. Starr, Victor	71
100.	**OVER THE MOUNTAIN**, Johnnie and Joe, J & S	—

CAUTION TO DEALERS AND JUKE BOX OPERATORS

The Billboard's Top 100 is NOT designed to provide tested information for buying purposes. This function is most reliably served by other regular weekly features: Best Sellers in Stores, Most Played in Juke Boxes, Coming Up Strong and Best Buys.

• Best Sellers in Stores

For survey week ending May 15

RECORDS are ranked in order of their current national selling importance at the retail level, as determined by The Billboard's weekly survey of the top volume dealers in every important market area. When significant action is reported on both sides of a record, points are combined to determine position on the chart. In such a case, both sides are listed in bold type, the leading side on top.

This Week		Last Week	Weeks on Chart
1.	**ALL SHOOK UP** (BMI)—E. Presley That's When Your Heartaches Begin (ASCAP)—Vic 20-6870	1	8
2.	**LITTLE DARLIN'** (BMI)—Diamonds Faithful and True (BMI)—Mercury 71060	2	11
3.	**SCHOOL DAY** (BMI)—C. Berry Deep Feeling (BMI)—Chess 1653	3	6
4.	**LOVE LETTERS IN THE SAND** (ASCAP)—P. Boone Bernardine (ASCAP)—Dot 15570	13	2
5.	**WHITE SPORT COAT** (BMI)—M. Robbins Grown Up Tears (BMI)—Col 40864	10	4
6.	**GONE** (BMI)—F. Husky Missing Persons (BMI)—Cap 3628	6	10
7.	**I'M WALKIN'** (BMI)—R. Nelson **A TEENAGER'S ROMANCE** (ASCAP)—Verve 10047	9	3
8.	**ROUND AND ROUND** (BMI)—P. Como Mi Casa, Su Casa (ASCAP)—Vic 20-6815	4	12
8.	**SO RARE** (ASCAP)—J. Dorsey Sophisticated Swing (ASCAP)—Fraternity 755	7	6
10.	**COME GO WITH ME** (BMI)—Dell-Vikings How Can I Find Love? (BMI)—Dot 15538	5	13
11.	**DARK MOON** (BMI)—G. Storm Little too Late (BMI)—Dot 1550	15	3
12.	**DARK MOON**—B. Guitar Big Mike—Dot 15550	11	5
13.	**ROCK-A-BILLY** (ASCAP)—G. Mitchell Hoot Owl (ASCAP)—Col 40877	12	8
14.	**PARTY DOLL** (BMI)—B. Knox My Baby's Gone (BMI)—Roulette 4002	8	13
15.	**WHY, BABY, WHY?** (BMI)—P. Boone I'm Waiting Just for You (BMI)—Dot 15545	14	10
16.	**YOUNG BLOOD** (BMI)—Coasters **SEARCHIN'** (BMI)—Atco 6087	—	1
17.	**I'M SORRY** (BMI)—Platters **HE'S MINE** (BMI)—Mercury 71032	—	5
18.	**FABULOUS** (BMI)—C. Gracie Just Lookin' (ASCAP)—Cameo 107	—	1
19.	**BUTTERFLY** (BMI)—C. Gracie Ninety-Nine Ways (BMI)—Cameo 105	19	14
20.	**FOUR WALLS** (BMI)—J. Reeves I Know and You Know (BMI)—Vic 20-6874	18	2
21.	**I'M WALKIN'** (BMI)—F. Domino I'm in the Mood for Love (ASCAP)—Imperial 5428	21	12
22.	**MAMA LOOK-A BOOBOO** (BMI)—H. Belafonte Don't Ever Love Me (ASCAP)—Vic 20-6830	17	9
23.	**C. C. RIDER** (BMI)—C. Willis Ease the Pain (BMI)—Atlantic 1130	25	2
24.	**START MOVIN'** (BMI)—S. Mineo Love Affair (BMI)—Epic 9216	—	1
25.	**PARTY DOLL** (BMI)—S. Lawrence Pum-Pa-Lum (ASCAP)—Coral 61792	—	10

• Most Played in Juke Boxes

For survey week ending May 15

RECORDS are ranked in order of the greatest number of plays in juke boxes throughout the country, as determined by The Billboard's weekly survey of the nation's juke box operators. When significant play is reported on both sides of a record, points are combined to determine position on the chart. In such a case, both sides are listed in bold type, the leading side on top.

This Week		Last Week	Weeks on Chart
1.	**ALL SHOOK UP** (BMI)—E. Presley That's When Your Heartaches Begin (ASCAP)—Vic 20-6870	1	7
2.	**LITTLE DARLIN'** (BMI)—Diamonds Faithful and True (BMI)—Mercury 71060	2	9
3.	**ROUND AND ROUND** (BMI)—P. Como Mi Casa Su Casa (ASCAP)—Vic 20-6815	3	10
4.	**GONE** (BMI)—F. Husky Missing Persons (BMI)—Cap 3628	4	7
5.	**PARTY DOLL** (BMI)—B. Knox My Baby's Gone (BMI)—Roulette 4002	5	12
6.	**COME GO WITH ME** (BMI)—Dell-Vikings How Can I Find True Love? (BMI)—Dot 15538	6	4
7.	**WHITE SPORT COAT** (BMI)—M. Robbins Grown-Up Tears (BMI)—Columbia 40864	11	3
8.	**SCHOOL DAY** (BMI)—C. Berry Deep Feeling (BMI)—Chess 1653	15	3
9.	**I'M WALKIN'** (BMI)—F. Domino I'm in the Mood for Love (ASCAP)—Imperial 5428	7	10
10.	**SO RARE** (ASCAP)—J. Dorsey Sophisticated Swing (ASCAP)—Fraternity 755	10	4
11.	**DARK MOON** (BMI)—G. Storm Little Too Late (BMI)—Dot 15558	19	2
12.	**WHY, BABY, WHY?** (BMI)—P. Boone I'm Waiting Just for You (BMI)—Dot 15545	8	9
13.	**LOVE LETTER IN THE SAND** (ASCAP)—P. Boone Bernardine (ASCAP)—Dot 15570	—	1
14.	**BUTTERFLY** (BMI)—A. Williams It Doesn't Take Very Long (ASCAP)—Cadence 1308	9	12
15.	**ROCK-A-BILLY** (ASCAP)—G. Mitchell Hoot Owl (ASCAP)—Col 40877	14	2
16.	**DARK MOON** (BMI)—B. Guitar Big Mike (BMI)—Fabor 5018	11	3
17.	**NINETY-NINE WAYS** (BMI)—T. Hunter Don't Get Around Much Anymore (ASCAP)—Dot 15548	17	7
18.	**I'M WALKIN'** (BMI)—R. Nelson **TEEN-AGER'S ROMANCE** (ASCAP)—Verve 10047	—	1
19.	**YOUNG BLOOD** (BMI)—Coasters **SEARCHIN'** (BMI)—Atco 6087	—	1
20.	**EMPTY ARMS** (BMI)—T. Brewer Ricky-Tick Song (BMI)—Coral 61085	13	3

• Best Selling Sheet Music

Tunes are ranked in order of their current national selling importance at the sheet music jobber level.

This Week		Last Week	Weeks on Chart
1.	**Round and Round** (Rush)	1	11
2.	**All Shook Up** (Shalimar-Presley)	2	6
3.	**Dark Moon** (Dandelion)	11	3
4.	**Little Darlin'** (Excelloree)	4	3
5.	**White Sport Coat** (Acuff-Rose)	7	3
6.	**Why Baby Why** (Winneton)	3	7
7.	**Come Go With Me** (Gil-Feebee)	13	4
8.	**Chantez-Chantez** (Cromwell)	8	10
9.	**Marianne** (Montclare)	5	13
10.	**Almost Paradise** (Peer)	9	10
11.	**Butterfly** (Mayland-Presley)	6	11
12.	**Empty Arms** (Ivory)	—	1
13.	**Four Walls** (Springfield)	14	2
14.	**Gone** (Hill & Range)	10	5
15.	**Calypso Melody** (Cromwell)	—	1

• Most Played by Jockeys

For survey week ending May 15

SIDES are ranked in order of the greatest number of plays on disk jockey radio shows throughout the country. Results are based on The Billboard's weekly survey among the nation's disk jockeys. The reverse side of each record is also listed.

This Week		Last Week	Weeks on Chart
1.	**ALL SHOOK UP** (BMI)—E. Presley That's When Your Heartaches Begin (ASCAP)—Vic 20-6870	1	7
2.	**LITTLE DARLIN'** (BMI)—Diamonds Faithful and True (BMI)—Mercury 71060	3	9
3.	**ROUND AND ROUND** (BMI)—P. Como Mi Casa Su Casa (ASCAP)—Vic 20-6815	2	13
4.	**GONE** (BMI)—F. Husky Missing Persons (BMI)—Cap 3628	4	11
5.	**SO RARE** (ASCAP)—J. Dorsey Sophisticated Swing (ASCAP)—Fraternity 755	5	4
6.	**WHITE SPORT COAT** (BMI)—M. Robbins Grown-Up Tears (BMI)—Col 40864	16	4
7.	**SCHOOL DAY** (BMI)—C. Berry Deep Feeling (BMI)—Chess 1653	9	5
8.	**COME GO WITH ME** (BMI)—Dell-Vikings How Can I Find True Love? (BMI)—Dot 15538	7	8
9.	**LOVE LETTERS IN THE SAND** (ASCAP)—P. Boone Bernardine (ASCAP)—Dot 15570	10	2
10.	**MANGOS** (ASCAP)—R. Clooney Independent (ASCAP)—Col 40835	17	6
11.	**DARK MOON** (BMI)—G. Storm Little Too Late (BMI)—Dot 15550	13	2
12.	**DARK MOON** (BMI)—B. Guitar Big Mike (BMI)—Dot 15550	22	3
13.	**WHY, BABY, WHY?** (BMI)—P. Boone I'm Waiting Just for You (BMI)—Dot 15545	13	10
14.	**BUTTERFLY** (BMI)—A. Williams It Doesn't Take Very Long (ASCAP)—Cadence 1308	8	12
15.	**PARTY DOLL** (BMI)—B. Knox My Baby's Gone (BMI)—Roulette 4002	6	12
15.	**I'M WALKIN'** (BMI)—F. Domino I'm in the Mood for Love (ASCAP)—Imperial 5428	12	10
17.	**PLEDGE OF LOVE** (BMI)—K. Copeland Night Air (BMI)—Imperial 5432	19	4
17.	**SHISH KEBAB** (BMI)—R. Marterie Bop a Boo-Bop a Doo (ASCAP)—Mercury 71092	11	2
19.	**EMPTY ARMS** (BMI)—T. Brewer Ricky Tick Song (BMI)—Coral 61805	—	2
20.	**FOUR WALLS** (BMI)—J. Reeves I Know and You Know (BMI)—Vic 20-6874	—	1
21.	**ROCK-A-BILLY** (ASCAP)—G. Mitchell Hoot Owl (ASCAP)—Col 40877	18	5
21.	**IT'S NOT FOR ME TO SAY** (ASCAP)—J. Mathis Warm and Tender (ASCAP)—Col 40851	—	1
23.	**I JUST DON'T KNOW** (ASCAP)—Four Lads Golly (ASCAP)—Col 40914	—	1
24.	**BERNARDINE** (ASCAP)—P. Boone Love Letters in the Sand (ASCAP)—Dot 15570	—	1
24.	**YES, TONIGHT, JOSEPHINE** (BMI)—J. Ray No Wedding Today (ASCAP)—Col 40893	21	3

THE TOP 100

For survey week ending May 15

A list of the Top 100 RECORD SIDES in the nation according to a COMBINED TABULATION of Dealer, Disk Jockey and Juke Box Operator replies to The Billboard's weekly popular record Best Seller and Most Played surveys. Its purpose is to provide Disk Jockeys with additional programming material and to give trade exposure to NEWER records just beginning to show action in the field.

Pos.	Song, Artist, Label	Pos. Last Wk.
1.	**ALL SHOOK UP,** E. Presley, Victor	1
2.	**LITTLE DARLIN',** Diamonds, Mercury	2
3.	**ROUND AND ROUND,** P. Como, Victor	3
4.	**GONE,** F. Husky, Capitol	4
5.	**WHITE SPORT COAT,** M. Robbins, Columbia	10
6.	**SCHOOL DAY,** C. Berry, Chess	8
7.	**SO RARE,** J. Dorsey, Fraternity	7
8.	**COME GO WITH ME,** D. Vikings, Dot	5
9.	**LOVE LETTERS IN THE SAND,** P. Boone, Dot	21
10.	**DARK MOON,** G. Storm, Dot	15
11.	**PARTY DOLL,** B. Knox, Roulette	6
12.	**WHY BABY WHY,** P. Boone, Dot	9
13.	**DARK MOON,** B. Guitar, Dot	13
14.	**I'M WALKIN',** F. Domino, Imperial	12
15.	**ROCK-A-BILLY,** G. Mitchell, Columbia	13
16.	**FOUR WALLS,** J. Reeves, Victor	36
17.	**PLEDGE OF LOVE,** K. Copeland, Imperial	24
18.	**EMPTY ARMS,** T. Brewer, Coral	18
19.	**PARTY DOLL,** S. Lawrence, Coral	17
20.	**BUTTERFLY,** A. Williams, Cadence	11
21.	**I'M SORRY,** Platters, Mercury	20
22.	**YES TONIGHT, JOSEPHINE,** J. Ray, Columbia	22
23.	**LOVE IS A GOLDEN RING,** F. Laine, Columbia	23
24.	**MAMA LOOK-A BOOBOO,** H. Belafonte, Victor	19
25.	**WONDERFUL, WONDERFUL,** J. Mathis, Columbia	34
26.	**BUTTERFLY,** C. Gracie, Cameo	16
27.	**I'M WALKIN',** R. Nelson, Verve	33
27.	**PLEDGE OF LOVE,** M. Torok, Decca	26
29.	**NINETY-NINE WAYS,** T. Hunter, Dot	28
29.	**TALKIN' TO THE BLUES,** J. Lowe, Dot	43
31.	**SHISH KEBAB,** R. Marterie, Mercury	30
32.	**I'M STICKIN' WITH YOU,** J. Bowen, Roulette	38
33.	**I JUST DON'T KNOW,** Four Lads, Columbia	53
34.	**MANGOS,** R. Clooney, Columbia	25
35.	**HE'S MINE,** Platters, Mercury	34
36.	**FABULOUS,** C. Gracie, Cameo	51
37.	**FOUR WALLS,** J Lowe, Dot	44
38.	**SEARCHIN',** Coasters, Atco	76
39.	**BERNARDINE,** P. Boone, Dot	42
40.	**JUST BECAUSE,** L. Price, ABC-Paramount	45
41.	**LUCILLE,** Little Richard, Specialty	40
42.	**TEEN-AGER'S ROMANCE,** R. Nelson, Verve	—
43.	**GOIN' STEADY,** T. Sands, Capitol	—
44.	**IT'S NOT FOR ME TO SAY,** J. Mathis, Columbia	65
45.	**YOUNG BLOOD,** Coasters, Atco	50
46.	**C. C. RIDER,** C. Willis, Atlantic	71
47.	**AFTER SCHOOL,** R. Starr, Dale	32
48.	**WHEN ROCK 'N' ROLL COMES TO TRINIDAD,** Nat (King) Cole, Capitol	81
50.	**ALMOST PARADISE,** R. Williams, Kapp	27
50.	**MARIANNE,** T. Gilkyson, Columbia	39
52.	**PLEDGE OF LOVE,** D. Contino, Mercury	61
53.	**CHANTEZ-CHANTEZ,** D. Shore, Victor	48
53.	**FREIGHT TRAIN,** R. Draper, Mercury	—
55.	**TEEN-AGE CRUSH,** T. Sands, Capitol	34
56.	**MAMA GUITAR,** D. Cornell, Coral	47
57.	**LITTLE WHITE LIES,** B. Johnson, Bally	52
57.	***PEACE IN THE VALLEY,** E. Presley, Victor	70
59.	**SITTIN' IN THE BALCONY,** E. Cochran, Liberty	37
60.	**GONNA FIND ME A BLUEBIRD,** M. Rainwater, M-G-M	—
61.	**I LIKE YOUR KIND OF LOVE,** A. Williams, Cadence	—
62.	**EMPTY ARMS,** I. J. Hunter, Atlantic	67
63.	**GIRL WITH THE GOLDEN BRAIDS,** P. Como, Victor	—
64.	**BYE, BYE LOVE,** Everly Brothers, Cadence	—
64.	**START MOVIN',** S. Mineo, Epic	—
66.	**I'LL TAKE ROMANCE,** E. Gorme, ABC-Paramount	72
67.	**OVER THE MOUNTAIN,** Johnnie and Joe, J & S	100
68.	**OLD CAPE COD,** P. Page, Mercury	—
69.	**LET IT BE ME,** J. Corey, Columbia	—
70.	**CAN I STEAL A LITTLE LOVE,** F. Sinatra, Capitol	79
71.	**MY LOVE SONG,** T. Sands, Capitol	76
72.	**FIRST DATE, FIRST KISS, FIRST LOVE,** S. James, Capitol	—
73.	**JUST TO HOLD MY HAND,** C. McPhatter, Atlantic	—
74.	**WALKIN' AFTER MIDNIGHT,** P. Cline, Decca	45
75.	**LITTLE DARLIN',** Gladiolas, Excello	59
76.	**WITH ALL MY HEART,** J. Scott, Decca	—
77.	**WHO NEEDS YOU,** Four Lads, Columbia	29
78.	**WONDERING,** P. Page, Mercury	—
78.	**YES TONIGHT, JOSEPHINE,** J. Ray, Columbia	—
79.	**HAREM DANCE,** Armenian Jazz Sextet, Kapp	67
80.	**ONE FOR MY BABY,** T. Bennett, Columbia	—
80.	**SITTIN' IN THE BALCONY,** J. Dee, Colonial	—
80.	**TILL,** P. Faith, Columbia	88
83.	**DAY-O BANANA BOAT,** S. Freberg, Capitol	48
84.	**CALYPSO MELODY,** D. Rose, M-G-M	58
85.	**ROSIE LEE,** Mello Tones, Gee	91
86.	**BANANA BOAT (DAY-O),** H. Belafonte, Victor	57
86.	**SO LONG MY LOVE,** F. Sinatra, Capitol	74
88.	**DO I LOVE YOU,** V. Damone, Columbia	82
88.	**MARIANNE,** Hilltoppers, Dot	41
90.	**AROUND THE WORLD,** Bing-Crosby-V. Young, Decca	—
91.	**ALMOST PARADISE,** L. Stein, Unique	55
92.	**1492,** B. Johnson, Bally	86
93.	**I NEED YOUR LOVIN',** C. Twitty, Mercury	—
94.	**WARM UP TO ME BABY,** J. Bowen, Roulette	—
95.	**SEND ME SOME LOVIN',** Little Richard, Specialty	89
96.	**WIND IN THE WILLOW,** J. Stafford, Columbia	67
97.	**THAT'S WHEN YOUR HEARTACHES BEGIN,** E. Presley, Victor	—
98.	**I LOVE MY GIRL,** Hilltoppers, Dot	75
99.	**YOUNG LOVE,** T. Hunter, Dot	62
100.	**TWELVE O'CLOCK TONIGHT,** Doris Day, Columbia	84

* (Not available as a Pop Single. Available on RCA Victor EPA-40545)

CAUTION TO DEALERS AND JUKE BOX OPERATORS

The Billboard's Top 100 is NOT designed to provide tested information for buying purposes. This function is most reliably served by other regular weekly features: Best Sellers in Stores, Most Played in Juke Boxes, Coming Up Strong and Best Buys.

• Best Sellers in Stores

For survey week ending May 22

RECORDS are ranked in order of their current national selling importance at the retail level, as determined by The Billboard's weekly survey of the top volume dealers in every important market area. When significant action is reported on both sides of a record, points are combined to determine position on the chart. In such a case, both sides are listed in bold type, the leading side on top.

This Week	Title	Last Week	Weeks on Chart
1.	**ALL SHOOK UP** (BMI)—E. Presley That's When Your Heartaches Begin (ASCAP)—Vic 20-6870	1	9
2.	**LOVE LETTERS IN THE SAND** (ASCAP)—Pat Boone **BERNARDINE** (ASCAP)—Dot 15570	4	3
3.	**SCHOOL DAY** (BMI)—C. Berry Deep Feeling (BMI)—Chess 1653	3	7
4.	**LITTLE DARLIN'** (BMI)—Diamonds Faithful and True (BMI)—Mercury 71060	2	12
5.	**WHITE SPORT COAT** (BMI)—M. Robbins Grown Up Tears (BMI)—Col 40864	5	5
6.	**SO RARE** (ASCAP)—J. Dorsey Sophisticated Swing (ASCAP)—Fraternity 755	8	7
7.	**I'M WALKIN'** (BMI)—R. Nelson **A TEENAGER'S ROMANCE** (ASCAP)—Verve 10047	7	4
8.	**COME GO WITH ME** (BMI)—Del Vikings How Can I Find Love? (BMI)—Dot 15538	10	14
9.	**GONE** (BMI)—F. Husky Missing Persons (BMI)—Cap 3628	6	11
10.	**ROUND AND ROUND** (BMI)—P. Como Mi Casa, Su Casa (ASCAP)—Vic 20-6815	8	13
11.	**DARK MOON** (BMI)—G. Storm Little Too Late (BMI)—Dot 15558	11	4
12.	**DARK MOON** (BMI)—B. Guitar Big Mike (BMI)—Dot 15550	12	6
13.	**ROCK-A-BILLY** (ASCAP)—G. Mitchell Hoot Owl (ASCAP)—Col 40877	13	7
14.	**FOUR WALLS** (BMI)—J. Reeves I Know and You Know (BMI)—Vic 20-6874	20	3
15.	**START MOVIN'** (BMI)—S. Mineo Love Affair (BMI)—Epic 9216	24	2
16.	**YOUNG BLOOD** (BMI)—Coasters **SEARCHIN'** (BMI)—Atco 6087	16	2
17.	**BYE BYE LOVE** (BMI)—Everly Brothers I Wonder If I Care as Much? (BMI)—Cadence 1315	—	1
18.	**IT'S NOT FOR ME TO SAY** (BMI) J. Mathis Warm and Tender (BMI)—Col 40851	—	1
19.	**FABULOUS** (BMI)—C. Gracie Just Lookin' (ASCAP)—Cameo 107	18	2
20.	**PARTY DOLL** (BMI)—B. Knox My Baby's Gone (BMI)—Roulette 4002	14	14
21.	**VALLEY OF TEARS** (BMI)—F. Domino It's You I Love (BMI)—Imperial 5442	—	1
22.	**OVER THE MOUNTAIN** (BMI)—Johnnie & Joe My Baby's Gone On, On (BMI)—J & S 1664	—	1
22.	**HE'S MINE** (BMI)—Platters **I'M SORRY** (BMI)—Mercury 71032	—	7
24.	**WONDERFUL WONDERFUL** (BMI)—J. Mathis When Sunny Gets Blue—Col 40784	—	2
25.	**WHY, BABY, WHY?** (BMI)—P. Boone I'm Waiting Just for You (BMI)—Dot 15545	15	11

• Most Played in Juke Boxes

For survey week ending May 22

RECORDS are ranked in order of the greatest number of plays in juke boxes thruout the country, as determined by The Billboard's weekly survey of the nation's juke box operators. When significant play is reported on both sides of a record, points are combined to determine position on the chart. In such a case, both sides are listed in bold type, the leading side on top.

This Week	Title	Last Week	Weeks on Chart
1.	**ALL SHOOK UP** (BMI)—E. Presley That's When Your Heartaches Begin (ASCAP)—Vic 20-6870	1	8
2.	**LITTLE DARLIN'** (BMI)—Diamonds Faithful and True (BMI)—Mercury 71060	2	10
3.	**ROUND AND ROUND** (BMI)—P. Como Mi Casa, Su Casa (ASCAP)—Vic 20-6815	3	11
4.	**GONE** (BMI)—F. Husky Missing Persons (BMI)—Cap 3628	4	8
5.	**DARK MOON** (BMI)—G. Storm Little Too Late (BMI)—Dot 15558	11	3
6.	**WHITE SPORT COAT** (BMI)—M. Robbins Grown Up Tears (BMI)—Columbia 40864	7	4
7.	**COME GO WITH ME** (BMI)—Del Vikings How Can I Find True Love? (BMI)—Dot 15538	6	5
7.	**SCHOOL DAY** (BMI)—C. Berry Deep Feeling (BMI)—Chess 1653	8	4
9.	**SO RARE** (ASCAP)—J. Dorsey Sophisticated Swing (ASCAP)—Fraternity 755	10	5
10.	**PARTY DOLL** (BMI)—B. Knox My Baby's Gone (BMI)—Roulette 4002	5	13
10.	**LOVE LETTERS IN THE SAND** (ASCAP)—P. Boone Bernardine (ASCAP)—Dot 15570	13	2
12.	**YOUNG BLOOD** (BMI)—Coasters **SEARCHIN'** (BMI)—Atco 6087	19	2
13.	**I'M WALKIN'** (BMI)—F. Domino I'm in the Mood for Love (ASCAP)—Imperial 5428	9	11
14.	**DARK MOON** (BMI)—B. Guitar Big Mike (BMI)—Fabor 5018	16	4
15.	**WHY, BABY, WHY?** (BMI)—P. Boone I'm Waiting Just for You (BMI)—Dot 15545	12	10
16.	**I'M WALKIN'** (BMI)—R. Nelson **TEENAGER'S ROMANCE** (ASCAP)—Verve 10047	18	2
17.	**ROCK-A-BILLY** (ASCAP)—G. Mitchell Hoot Owl (ASCAP)—Col 40877	15	3
18.	**I'M SORRY** (BMI)—Platters **HE'S MINE** (BMI)—Mercury 71032	—	3
19.	**BUTTERFLY** (BMI)—A. Williams It Doesn't Take Very Long (ASCAP)—Cadence 1308	14	13
20.	**FOUR WALLS** (BMI)—J. Reeves I Know and You Know (BMI)—Vic 20-6874	—	1

• Best Selling Sheet Music

Tunes are ranked in order of their current national selling importance at the sheet music jobber level.

This Week	Title	Last Week	Weeks on Chart
1.	**All Shook Up** (Shalimar-Presley	2	7
1.	**Dark Moon** (Dandelion)	3	4
3.	**Round and Round** (Rush)	1	12
4.	**White Sport Coat** (Acuff-Rose)	5	4
5.	**Little Darlin'** (Excelloree)	4	4
6.	**Come Go With Me** (Gil-Feebee)	7	5
7.	**Why, Baby, Why** (Winneton)	6	8
8.	**Marianne** (Montclare)	9	14
9.	**Chantez-Chantez** (Cromwell)	8	11
10.	**Love Letters in the Sand** (Bourne)	—	1
11.	**Butterfly** (Mayland-Presley)	11	12
12.	**Almost Paradise** (Peer)	10	11
13.	**Four Walls** (Springfield)	13	3
14.	**Empty Arms** (Ivory)	12	2
15.	**Rock-A-Billy** (Oxford)	—	1

• Most Played by Jockeys

For survey week ending May 22

SIDES are ranked in order of the greatest number of plays on disk jockey radio shows thruout the country. Results are based on The Billboard's weekly survey among the nation's disk jockeys. The reverse side of each record is also listed.

This Week	Title	Last Week	Weeks on Chart
1.	**ALL SHOOK UP** (BMI)—E. Presley That's When Your Heartaches Begin (ASCAP)—Vic 20-6870	1	8
2.	**LOVE LETTERS IN THE SAND** (ASCAP)—P. Boone Bernardine (ASCAP)—Dot 15570	9	3
3.	**ROUND AND ROUND** (BMI)—P. Como Mi Casa, Su Casa (ASCAP)—Vic 20-6815	3	14
4.	**LITTLE DARLIN'** (BMI)—Diamonds Faithful and True (BMI)—Mercury 71060	2	10
5.	**SO RARE** (ASCAP)—J. Dorsey Sophisticated Swing (ASCAP)—Fraternity 755	5	5
6.	**WHITE SPORT COAT** (BMI)—M. Robbins Grown Up Tears (BMI)—Col 40864	6	5
7.	**SCHOOL DAY** (BMI)—C. Berry Deep Feeling (BMI)—Chess 1653	7	6
8.	**GONE** (BMI)—F. Husky Missing Persons (BMI)—Cap 3628	4	12
9.	**DARK MOON** (BMI)—G. Storm Little Too Late (BMI)—Dot 15550	11	3
10.	**COME GO WITH ME** (BMI)—Del Vikings How Can I Find True Love (BMI)—Dot 15538	8	9
11.	**DARK MOON** (BMI)—B. Guitar Big Mike (BMI)—Dot 15550	12	4
12.	**YES, TONIGHT, JOSEPHINE** (BMI)—J. Ray No Wedding Today (ASCAP)—Col 40893	24	4
13.	**MANGOS** (ASCAP)—R. Clooney Independent (ASCAP)—Col 40835	10	7
14.	**BERNARDINE** (ASCAP)—P. Boone Love Letters in the Sand (ASCAP)—Dot 15570	24	2
15.	**FOUR WALLS** (BMI)—J. Reeves I Know and You Know (BMI)—Vic 20-6874	20	2
16.	**FOUR WALLS** (BMI)—J. Lowe Talking to the Blues (BMI)—Dot 15569	—	1
17.	**I JUST DON'T KNOW** (ASCAP)—Four Lads Golly (ASCAP)—Col 40914	23	2
18.	**BUTTERFLY** (BMI)—A. Williams It Doesn't Take Very Long (ASCAP)—Cadence 1308	14	13
19.	**GIRL WITH THE GOLDEN BRAIDS** (ASCAP)—P. Como My Little Baby (BMI)—Vic 20-6904	—	1
20.	**WHY, BABY, WHY** (BMI)—P. Boone I'm Waiting Just for You (BMI)—Dot 15545	13	11
21.	**IT'S NOT FOR ME TO SAY** (ASCAP)—J. Mathis Warm and Tender (ASCAP)—Col 40851	21	2
22.	**PARTY DOLL** (BMI)—B. Knox My Baby's Gone (BMI)—Roulette 4002	15	13
23.	**WONDERFUL, WONDERFUL** (BMI)—J. Mathis When Sunny Gets Blue (BMI)—Col 40784	—	1
24.	**HE'S MINE** (BMI)—Platters I'm Sorry (BMI)—Mercury 71032	—	1
24.	**SHISH KEBAB** (BMI)—R. Marterie Bop a Boo-Bop a Doo (ASCAP)—Mercury 71092	17	3

THE TOP 100

For survey week ending May 22

A list of the Top 100 RECORD SIDES in the nation according to a COMBINED TABULATION of Dealer, Disk Jockey and Juke Box Operator replies to The Billboard's weekly popular record Best Seller and Most Played surveys. Its purpose is to provide Disk Jockeys with additional programming material and to give trade exposure to NEWER records just beginning to show action in the field.

Pos.	Song, Artist, Label	Pos. Last Wk.
1.	**ALL SHOOK UP,** E. Presley, Victor	1
2.	**LITTLE DARLIN',** Diamonds, Mercury	1
3.	**ROUND AND ROUND,** P. Como, Victor	3
3.	**LOVE LETTERS IN THE SAND,** P. Boone, Dot	9
5.	**SCHOOL DAY,** C. Berry, Chess	6
6.	**WHITE SPORT COAT,** M. Robbins, Columbia	5
7.	**SO RARE,** J. Dorsey, Fraternity	7
7.	**GONE,** F. Husky, Capitol	4
9.	**COME GO WITH ME,** Del Vikings, Dot	8
9.	**DARK MOON,** G. Storm, Dot	10
11.	**DARK MOON—**B. Guitar, Dot	13
12.	**FOUR WALLS,** J. Reeves, Victor	16
13.	**PARTY DOLL,** B. Knox, Roulette	11
14.	**WHY BABY WHY,** P. Boone, Dot	12
15.	**ROCK-A-BILLY,** G. Mitchell, Columbia	15
16.	**I'M WALKIN',** F. Domino, Imperial	14
17.	**TEENAGER'S ROMANCE,** R. Nelson, Verve	42
18.	**YES TONIGHT, JOSEPHINE,** J. Ray, Columbia	22
19.	**YOUNG BLOOD,** Coasters, Atco	45
20.	**SEARCHIN',** Coasters, Atco	38
21.	**WONDERFUL, WONDERFUL,** J. Mathis, Columbia	25
22.	**I JUST DON'T KNOW,** Four Lads, Columbia	33
23.	**HE'S MINE,** Platters, Mercury	35
24.	**BERNARDINE,** P. Boone, Dot	39
24.	**BUTTERFLY,** A. Williams, Cadence	20
26.	**START MOVIN',** S. Mineo, Epic	—
26.	**GOIN' STEADY,** T. Sands, Capitol	43
28.	**PLEDGE OF LOVE,** K. Copeland, Im erial	17
28.	**I'M WALKIN',** R. Nelson, Verve	27
30.	**EMPTY ARMS,** T. Brewer, Coral	18
30.	**TALKIN' TO THE BLUES,** J. Lowe, Dot	29
32.	**FREIGHT TRAIN,** R. Draper, Mercury	53
32.	**VALLEY OF TEARS,** F. Domino, Imperial	—
34.	**FOUR WALLS,** J. Lowe, Dot	37
35.	**IT'S NOT FOR ME TO SAY,** J. Mathis, Columbia	44
36.	**SHISH KEBAB,** R. Marterie, Mercury	31
37.	**MANGOS,** R. Clooney, Columbia	34
38.	**I'M SORRY,** Platters, Mercury	21
39.	**LOVE IS A COLDEN RING,** F. Laine, Columbia	23
40.	**BYE, BYE, BYE,** Everly Brothers, Cadence	64
41.	**GIRL WITH THE GOLDEN BRAIDS,** P. Como, Victor	63
42.	**PARTY DOLL,** S. Lawrence, Coral	19
43.	**EMPTY ARMS,** I. J. Hunter, Atlantic	62
44.	**GONNA FIND ME A BLUEBIRD,** M. Rainwater, M-G-M	60
45.	**FREIGHT TRAIN,** C. McDevitt-N. Whiskey, Chic	—
46.	**PLEDGE OF LOVE,** M. Torok, Decca	27
47.	**C. C. RIDER,** C. Willis, Atlantic	46
48.	**I'M STICKING WITH YOU,** J. Bowen, Roulette	32
48.	**NINETY-NINE WAYS,** T. Hunter, Dot	29
50.	**FABULOUS,** C. Gracie, Cameo	36
50.	**MAMA LOOK-A BOOBOO,** H. Belafonte, Victor	24
50.	**OVER THE MOUNTAIN,** Johnnie & Joe, J & S	67
53.	**LITTLE WHITE LIES,** B. Johnson, Bally	57
54.	**ROCK YOUR BABY TO SLEEP,** B. Knox, Roulette	—
54.	**I LIKE YOUR KIND OF LOVE,** A. Williams, Cadence	61
56.	**OLD CAPE COD,** P. Page, Mercury	68
57.	**ALMOST PARADISE,** R. Williams, Kapp	50
58.	**AFTER SCHOOL,** R. Starr, Dale	47
59.	**AROUND THE WORLD,** Bing Crosby-V. Young, Decca	90
60.	**CHANTEZ CHANTEZ,** D. Shore, Victor	53
61.	**MAMA GUITAR,** D. Cornell, Coral	56
62.	**WHEN ROCK 'N' ROLL COMES TO TRINIDAD,** Nat (King) Cole, Capitol	48
63.	**PLEDGE OF LOVE,** D. Contino, Mercury	52
64.	***PEACE IN THE VALLEY,** E. Presley, Victor	57
65.	**WITH ALL MY HEART,** J. Sands, Columbia	—
66.	**DON'T CRY MY LOVE,** V. Lynn, London	—
67.	**IT'S YOU I LOVE,** F. Domino, Imperial	—
68.	**CAN'T WAIT FOR SUMMER,** S. Lawrence, Coral	—
69.	**ONE FOR MY BABY,** T. Bennett, Columbia	80
70.	**QUEEN OF THE SENIOR PROM,** Mills Brothers, Decca	—
71.	**I'LL TAKE ROMANCE,** E. Gorme, ABC-Paramount	66
72.	**WONDERING,** P. Page, Mercury	78
73.	**LUCILLE,** Little Richard, Specialty	41
74.	**ROSIE LEE,** Mello Tones, Gee	85
75.	**DO I LOVE YOU?** V. Damone, Columbia	88
76.	**MY LITTLE BABY,** P. Como, Victor	—
77.	**JUST BECAUSE,** L. Price, ABC-Paramount	40
78.	**HAREM DANCE,** Armenian Jazz Sextet, Kapp	79
79.	**TOO LATE,** G. Austin, Victor	—
80.	**BUTTERFLY,** C. Gracie, Cameo	26
81.	**LITTLE DARLIN',** Gladiolas, Excello	75
81.	**WARM UP TO ME BABY,** J. Bowen, Roulette	94
83.	**MY DREAM,** Platters, Mercury	—
83.	**TEEN-AGE CRUSH,** T. Sands, Capitol	55
85.	**WIND IN THE WILLOW,** J. Stafford, Columbia	96
86.	**RANG TANG DING DONG,** Cellos	—
87.	**SITTIN' IN THE BALCONY,** E. Cochran, Liberty	59
88.	**ALMOST PARADISE,** L. Stein, Unique	91
88.	**TILL, P. Faith, Columbia**	80
90.	**WHITE SPORT COAT,** J. Desmond, Coral	—
91.	**PARTY DOLL,** Roy Brown, Imperial	—
91.	**DO I LOVE YOU,** T. Martin, Victor	—
93.	**SITTIN' IN THE BALCONY,** J. Dee, Colonial	80
94.	**FABULOUS,** S. Lawrence, Coral	—
94.	**1492,** B. Johnson, Bally	92
96.	**SHANGRI-LA,** Four Coins	—
96.	**TINA,** Easy Riders, Columbia	—
96.	**WALKIN' AFTER MIDNIGHT,** P. Cline, Decca	74
99.	**CALYPSO MELODY,** D. Rose, M-G-M	84
99.	**MARIANNE,** T. Gilkyson, Columbia	50

*(Not available as a Pop Single. Available on RCA Victor EPA-4054.)

CAUTION TO DEALERS AND JUKE BOX OPERATORS

The Billboard's Top 100 is NOT designed to provide tested information for buying purposes. This function is most reliably served by other regular weekly features: Best Sellers in Stores, Most Played in Juke Boxes, Coming Up Strong and Best Buys.

• Best Sellers in Stores

For survey week ending May 29

RECORDS are ranked in order of their current national selling importance at the retail level, as determined by The Billboard's weekly survey of the top volume dealers in every important market area. When significant action is reported on both sides of a record, points are combined to determine position on the chart. In such a case, both sides are listed in bold type, the leading side on top.

This Week		Last Week	Weeks on Chart
1.	**LOVE LETTERS IN THE SAND** (ASCAP)—Pat Boone **BERNARDINE** (ASCAP)—Dot 15570	2	4
2.	**WHITE SPORT COAT** (BMI)—Marty Robbins Grown-Up Tears (BMI)—Col 40864	5	6
3.	**ALL SHOOK UP** (BMI)—Elvis Presley That's When Your Heartaches Begin (ASCAP)—Vic 20-6870	1	10
4.	**I'M WALKIN'** (BMI)—Ricky Nelson **A TEENAGER'S ROMANCE** (ASCAP—Verve 10047	7	5
5.	**SO RARE** (ASCAP)—Jimmy Dorsey Sophisticated Swing (ASCAP)—Fraternity 755	6	8
6.	**SCHOOL DAY** (BMI)—Chuck Berry Deep Feeling (BMI)—Chess 1653	3	8
7.	**LITTLE DARLIN'** (BMI)—Diamonds Faithful and True (BMI)—Mercury 71060	4	13
8.	**DARK MOON** (BMI)—Gale Storm Little Too Late (BMI)—Dot 15550	11	5
9.	**START MOVIN'** (BMI)—Sal Mineo Love Affair (BMI)—Epic 9216	15	3
10.	**DARK MOON** (BMI)—Bonnie Guitar Big Mike (BMI)—Dot 15550	12	7
11.	**COME GO WITH ME** (BMI)—Del Vikings How Can I Find Love? (BMI)—Dot 15538	8	15
12.	**BYE BYE LOVE** (BMI)—Everly Brothers I Wonder If I Care as Much (BMI)—Cadence 1315	17	2
13.	**GONE** (BMI)—Ferlin Husky Missing Persons (BMI)—Cap 3628	9	12
14.	**YOUNG BLOOD** (BMI)—Coasters **SEARCHIN'** (BMI)—Atco 6087	16	3
15.	**ROUND AND ROUND** (BMI)—Perry Como Mi Casa, Su Casa (ASCAP)—Vic 20-6815	10	14
16.	**FOUR WALLS** (BMI)—Jim Reeves I Know and You Know (BMI)—Vic 20-6874	14	4
17.	**FABULOUS** (BMI)—Charlie Gracie Just Lookin' (ASCAP)—Cameo 107	19	3
18.	**IT'S NOT FOR ME TO SAY** (ASCAP)—Johnny Mathis Warm and Tender (ASCAP)—Col 40851	18	2
19.	**FOUR WALLS** (BMI)—Jim Lowe **TALKING TO THE BLUES** (BMI)—Dot 15569	—	1
20.	**ROCK-A-BILLY** (ASCAP)—Guy Mitchell Hoot Owl (ASCAP)—Coly 40877	13	8
21.	**WONDERFUL WONDERFUL** (BMI)—Johnny Mathis When Sunny Gets Blue (BMI)—Col 40784	24	3
21.	**FREIGHT TRAIN** (ASCAP)—Rusty Draper Seven Come Eleven (BMI)—Mercury 71102	—	1
23.	**OVER THE MOUNTAIN** (BMI)—Johnnie & Joe My Baby's Gone On, On (BMI)—Chess 1654	22	2
24.	**COIN' STEADY** (BMI)—Tommy Sands Ring My Phone (BMI)—Cap 3723	—	1
25.	**VALLEY OF TEARS** (BMI)—Fats Domino It's You I Love (BMI)—Imperial 5442	21	2

• Most Played in Juke Boxes

For survey week ending May 29

RECORDS are ranked in order of the greatest number of plays in juke boxes thruout the country, as determined by The Billboard's weekly survey of the nation's juke box operators. When significant play is reported on both sides of a record, points are combined to determine position on the chart. In such a case, both sides are listed in bold type, the leading side on top.

This Week		Last Week	Weeks on Chart
1.	**ALL SHOOK UP** (BMI)—E. Presley That's When Your Heartaches Begin (ASCAP)—Vic 20-6870	1	9
2.	**LITTLE DARLIN'** (BMI)—Diamonds Faithful and True (BMI)—Mercury 71060	2	11
3.	**LOVE LETTERS IN THE SAND** (ASCAP)—P. Boone **BERNARDINE** (ASCAP)—Dot 15570	10	3
4.	**GONE** (BMI)—F. Husky Missing Persons (BMI)—Cap 3628	4	9
5.	**DARK MOON** (BMI)—G. Storm Little Too Late (BMI)—Dot 15558	5	4
5.	**WHITE SPORT COAT** (BMI)—M. Robbins Grown Up Tears (BMI)—Columbia 40864	6	5
7.	**ROUND AND ROUND** (BMI)—P. Como Mi Casa, Su Casa (ASCAP)—Vic 20-6815	3	12
7.	**SO RARE** (ASCAP)—J. Dorsey Sophisticated Swing (ASCAP)—Fraternity 755	9	6
9.	**SCHOOL DAY** (BMI)—C. Berry Deep Feeling (BMI)—Chess 1653	7	5
10.	**COME GO WITH ME** (BMI)—Del Vikings How Can I Find True Love? (BMI)—Dot 15538	7	6
11.	**PARTY DOLL** (BMI)—B. Knox My Baby's Gone (BMI)—Roulette 4002	10	14
12.	**DARK MOON** (BMI)—B. Guitar Big Mike (BMI)—Fabor 5018	14	5
12.	**TEENAGER'S ROMANCE** (ASCAP)—R. Nelson **I'M WALKIN'** (BMI)—Verve 10047	—	2
14.	**FOUR WALLS** (BMI)—J. Reeves I Know and You Know (BMI)—Vic 20-6874	20	2
15.	**TALKIN' TO THE BLUES** (BMI)—J. Lowe **FOUR WALLS** (BMI)—Dot 15569	—	1
16.	**WHY, BABY, WHY?** (BMI)—P. Boone I'm Waiting Just for You (BMI)—Dot 15545	15	11
16.	**SEARCHIN'** (BMI)—Coasters Young Blood (BMI)—Atco 6987	—	2
18.	**I'M WALKIN'** (BMI)—F. Domino I'm in the Mood for Love (ASCAP)—Imperial 5428	13	12
18.	**HE'S MINE** (BMI)—Platters **I'M SORRY** (BMI)—Mercury 71032	18	4
18.	**BYE BYE LOVE** (BMI)—Everly Brothers I Wonder If I Care as Much (BMI)—Cadence 1315	—	1

• Best Selling Sheet Music

Tunes are ranked in order of their current national selling importance at the sheet music jobber level

This Week		Last Week	Weeks on Chart
1.	**Dark Moon** (Dandelion)	1	5
2.	**Round and Round** (Rush)	3	13
3.	**All Shook Up** (Shalimar-Presley)	1	8
4.	**Little Darlin'** (Excellorec)	5	5
5.	**White Sport Coat** (Acuff-Rose)	4	5
6.	**Come Go With Me** (Gil-Fecbee)	6	6
7.	**Marianne** (Montclare)	8	15
8.	**Chantez-Chantez** (Cromwell)	9	12
9.	**Love Letters in the Sand** (Bourne)	10	2
10.	**Why, Baby, Why?** (Winneton)	7	9
11.	**Butterfly** (Mayland-Presley)	11	13
12.	**Four Walls** (Springfield)	13	4
13.	**Almost Paradise** (Peer)	12	12
14.	**Empty Arms** (Ivory)	14	3
15.	**Rock-a-Billy** (Oxford)	15	2

• Most Played by Jockeys

For survey week ending May 29

SIDES are ranked in order of the greatest number of plays on disk jockey radio shows thruout the country. Results are based on The Billboard's weekly survey among the nation's disk jockeys. The reverse side of each record is also listed.

This Week		Last Week	Weeks on Chart
1.	**ALL SHOOK UP** (BMI)—E. Presley That's When Your Heartaches Begin (ASCAP)—Vic 20-6870	1	9
2.	**LOVE LETTERS IN THE SAND** (ASCAP)—P. Boone Bernardine (ASCAP)—Dot 15570	2	4
3.	**LITTLE DARLIN'** (BMI)—Diamonds Faithful and True (BMI)—Mercury 71060	4	11
4.	**WHITE SPORT COAT** (BMI)—M. Robbins Grown Up Tears (BMI)—Col 40864	6	6
5.	**SO RARE** (ASCAP)—J. Dorsey Sophisticated Swing (ASCAP)—Fraternity 755	5	6
6.	**SCHOOL DAY** (BMI)—C. Berry Deep-Feeling (BMI)—Chess 1653	7	7
7.	**GONE** (BMI)—F. Husky Missing Persons (BMI)—Cap 3628	8	13
8.	**ROUND AND ROUND** (BMI)—P. Como Mi Casa, Su Casa (ASCAP)—Vic 20-6815	3	15
9.	**DARK MOON** (BMI)—G. Storm Little Too Late (BMI)—Dot 15550	9	4
10.	**COME GO WITH ME** (BMI)—Del Vikings How Can I Find True Love? (BMI)—Dot 15538	10	10
11.	**FOUR WALLS** (BMI)—J. Reeves I Know and You Know (BMI)—Vic 20-6874	15	3
12.	**SEARCHIN'** (BMI)—Coasters Young Blood (BMI)—Atco 6987	—	1
13.	**DARK MOON** (BMI)—B. Guitar Big Mike (BMI)—Dot 15550	11	5
14.	**SHISH KEBAB** (BMI)—R. Marterie Bop a Boo-Bop a Doo (ASCAP)—Mercury 71092	24	4
15.	**GIRL WITH THE GOLDEN BRAIDS** (BMI)—P. Como My Little Baby (BMI)—Vic 20-6004	19	2
15.	**FREIGHT TRAIN** (ASCAP)—R. Draper Seven Come Eleven (BMI)—Mercury 71102	—	1
17.	**MANGOS** (ASCAP)—R. Clooney Independent (ASCAP)—Col 40835	13	8
17.	**OLD CAPE COD** (ASCAP)—P. Page Wondering (BMI)—Mercury 71101	—	1
19.	**TEENAGER'S ROMANCE** (ASCAP)—R. Nelson I'm Walkin' (BMI)—Verve 10047	—	1
20.	**YES, TONIGHT, JOSEPHINE** (BMI)—J. Ray No Wedding Today (ASCAP)—Col 40893	12	5
21.	**BYE BYE LOVE** (BMI)—Everly Brothers I Wonder If I Care as Much (BMI)—Cadence 1315	—	1
22.	**WONDERING** (BMI)—P. Page Old Cape Cod (ASCAP)—Mercury 71101	—	1
23.	**ROCK YOUR LITTLE BABY TO SLEEP** (BMI)—B. Knox Don't Make Me Cry (BMI)—Roulette 4009	—	1
23.	**FOUR WALLS** (BMI)—J. Lowe Talkin' to the Blues (BMI)—Dot 15569	16	2
25.	**START MOVIN'** (BMI)—S. Mineo Love Affair (BMI)—Epic 9216	—	1

MAY 27, 1957

THE BILLBOARD'S

• Review Spotlight on . . .

POP DISK JOCKEY PROGRAMMING

MANTOVANI ORK....London 1746..................AROUND THE WORLD (Young, ASCAP)

Other versions of the movie theme have already grabbed extensive jockey play, but this one rates spins on basis of quality performance and excellent trumpet solo. Lush, richly orchestrated instrumental programming material. Flip is "The Road to Ballingarry" (ASCAP).

THE TOP 100

For survey week ending May 29

A list of the Top 100 RECORD SIDES in the nation according to a COMBINED TABULATION of Dealer, Disk Jockey and Juke Box Operator replies to The Billboard's weekly popular record Best Seller and Most Played surveys. Its purpose is to provide Disk Jockeys with additional programming material and to give trade exposure to NEWER records just beginning to show action in the field.

Pos.	Song, Artist, Label	Pos. Last Wk.
1.	**ALL SHOOK UP,** Elvis Presley, Victor	1
2.	**LOVE LETTERS IN THE SAND,** Pat Boone, Dot	3
3.	**LITTLE DARLIN',** Diamonds, Mercury	2
3.	**WHITE SPORT COAT,** Marty Robbins, Columbia	6
5.	**SO RARE,** Jimmy Dorsey, Fraternity	7
6.	**SCHOOL DAY,** Chuck Berry, Chess	5
7.	**DARK MOON,** Gale Storm, Dot	9
8.	**GONE,** Ferlin Husky, Capitol	7
9.	**ROUND AND ROUND,** Perry Como, Victor	3
10.	**COME GO WITH ME,** Del Vikings, Dot	9
11.	**DARK MOON,** Bonnie Guitar, Dot	11
12.	**FOUR WALLS,** Jim Reeves, Victor	12
13.	**SEARCHING,** Coasters, Atco	20
13.	**TEENAGER'S ROMANCE,** Ricky Nelson, Verve	17
15.	**BYE BYE LOVE,** Everly Brothers, Cadence	40
16.	**START MOVIN',** Sal Mineo, Epic	26
17.	**FREIGHT TRAIN,** Rusty Draper, Mercury	32
18.	**ROCK-A-BILLY,** Guy Mitchell, Columbia	15
19.	**I'M WALKIN',** Ricky Nelson, Verve	28
20.	**EMPTY ARMS,** Teresa Brewer, Coral	30
21.	**FOUR WALLS,** Jim Lowe, Dot	34
21.	**GOIN' STEADY,** Tommy Sands, Capitol	26
23.	**IT'S NOT FOR ME TO SAY,** Johnny Mathis, Columbia	35
24.	**VALLEY OF TEARS,** Fats Domino, Imperial	32
25.	**PARTY DOLL,** Buddy Knox, Roulette	13
26.	**WONDERFUL WONDERFUL,** Johnny Mathis, Columbia	21
27.	**GIRL WITH THE GOLDEN BRAIDS,** Perry Como, Victor	41
28.	**WHY, BABY, WHY?** Pat Boone, Dot	14
29.	**SHISH KEBAB,** Ralph Marterie, Mercury	36
30.	**BERNARDINE,** Pat Boone, Dot	24
31.	**FABULOUS,** Charlie Gracie, Cameo	50
31.	**TALKIN' TO THE BLUES,** Jim Lowe, Dot	30
33.	**I'M WALKIN',** Fats Domino, Imperial	16
34.	**I LIKE YOUR KIND OF LOVE,** Andy Williams, Cadence	54
34.	**OLD CAPE COD,** Patti Page, Mercury	56
36.	**LOVE IS A GOLDEN RING,** Frankie Laine, Columbia	39
36.	**ROCK YOUR LITTLE BABY TO SLEEP,** Buddy Knox, Roulette	54
38.	**PLEDGE OF LOVE,** Ken Copeland, Imperial	28
39.	**HE'S MINE,** Platters, Mercury	23
40.	**OVER THE MOUNTAIN,** Johnnie & Joe, Chess	50
41.	**FREIGHT TRAIN,** Charles McDevitt & Nancy Whiskey, Chic	45
42.	**MANGOS,** Rosemary Clooney, Columbia	37
43.	**BUTTERFLY,** Andy Williams, Cadence	24
43.	**LITTLE WHITE LIES,** Betty Johnson, Bally	53
45.	**CAN'T WAIT FOR SUMMER,** Steve Lawrence, Coral	68
46.	**YOUNG BLOOD,** Coasters, Atco	19
47.	**ALMOST PARADISE,** Roger Williams, Kapp	57
48.	**MY LITTLE BABY,** Perry Como, Victor	76
49.	**ONE FOR MY BABY,** Tony Bennett, Columbia	69
50.	**I JUST DON'T KNOW,** Four Lads, Columbia	22
51.	**I'M SORRY,** Platters, Mercury	38
52.	**IT'S YOU I LOVE,** Fats Domino, Imperial	67
53.	**PLEDGE OF LOVE,** Mitchell Torok, Decca	46
53.	**QUEEN OF THE SENIOR PROM,** Mills Brothers, Decca	71
55.	**DON'T CRY MY LOVE,** Vera Lynn, London	66
56.	**AROUND THE WORLD,** Victor Young, Decca	59
57.	**C. C. RIDER,** Chuck Willis, Atlantic	47
58.	**EMPTY ARMS,** Ivory Joe Hunter, Atlantic	43
59.	**MY DREAM,** Platters, Mercury	83
60.	**ROSIE LEE,** Mello Tones, Gee	74
61.	**GONNA FIND ME A BLUEBIRD,** Eddy Arnold, Victor	—
62.	**WHITE SPORT COAT,** Johnny Desmond, Coral	90
63.	**I'M STICKIN' WITH YOU,** Jim Bowen, Roulette	48
64.	**COCOANUT WOMAN,** Harry Belafonte, Victor	—
65.	**I'LL TAKE ROMANCE,** Eydie Gorme, ABC-Paramount	71
66.	**AFTER SCHOOL,** Randy Starr, Dale	58
66.	**WARM UP TO ME BABY,** Jim Bowen, Roulette	81
68.	**MAMA LOOK-A BOOBOO,** Harry Belafonte, Victor	50
69.	**BUTTERFLY,** Charlie Gracie, Cameo	80
69.	**MAMA GUITAR,** Don Cornell, Coral	61
69.	**NINETY-NINE WAYS,** Tab Hunter, Dot	48
72.	**LITTLE DARLIN',** Gladiolas, Excello	81
73.	**PLEDGE OF LOVE,** Dick Contino, Mercury	63
74.	**BYE BYE LOVE,** Webb Pierce, Decca	—
75.	**TOO LATE,** Gene Austin, Victor	79
76.	**DO I LOVE YOU?** Vic Damone, Columbia	75
77.	**FABULOUS,** Steve Lawrence, Coral	94
78.	**SITTIN' IN THE BALCONY,** Eddie Cochran, Liberty	87
79.	**ISLAND IN THE SUN,** Harry Belafonte, Victor	—
80.	**WHO NEEDS YOU,** Four Lads, Columbia	—
80.	**I'M GONNA SIT RIGHT DOWN AND WRITE MYSELF A LETTER** Billy Williams, Coral	—
80.	**PARTY DOLL,** Steve Lawrence, Coral	42
83.	**DON'T CALL ME SWEETIE,** Eileen Rodgers, Columbia	—
84.	**GONNA FIND ME A BLUEBIRD,** Joyce Hahn, Cadence	—
85.	**MARIANNE,** Terry Gilkyson, Columbia	99
86.	**CRAZY LOVE,** Frank Sinatra, Capitol	—
86.	**LUCILLE,** Little Richard, Specialty	73
88.	**WHEN ROCK 'N' ROLL COMES TO TRINIDAD,** Nat (King) Cole, Capitol	62
89.	**CHANTEZ-CHANTEZ,** Dinah Shore, Victor	60
90.	***PEACE IN THE VALLEY,** Elvis Presley, Victor	64
90.	**RANG TANG DING DING,** Cellos, Apollo	86
92.	**WALKIN' THE FLOOR OVER YOU,** Georgia Gibbs, Mercury	—
92.	**SHANGRI-LA,** Four Coins, Epic	96
94.	**MY LOVE SONG,** Tommy Sands, Capitol	—
95.	**I LOVE MY GIRL,** Cozy Morley, ABC-Paramount	—
96.	**JUST TO HOLD MY HAND,** Clyde McPhatter, Atlantic	—
96.	**SHRINE OF ST. CECELIA,** Faron Young, Capitol	—
98.	**1492,** Betty Johnson, Bally	94
99.	**HAREM DANCE,** Armenian Jazz Sextet, Kapp	78
100.	**WALKIN' AFTER MIDNIGHT,** Patsy Cline, Decca	96

* (Not available as a Pop Single. Available on RCA Victor EPA-4054.)

CAUTION TO DEALERS AND JUKE BOX OPERATORS

The Billboard's Top 100 is NOT designed to provide tested information for buying purposes. This function is most reliably served by other regular weekly features: Best Sellers in Stores, Most Played in Juke Boxes, Coming Up Strong and Best Buys.

• Best Sellers in Stores

For survey week ending June 5

RECORDS are ranked in order of their current national selling importance at the retail level, as determined by The Billboard's weekly survey of the top volume dealers in every important market area. When significant action is reported on both sides of a record, points are combined to determine position on the chart. In such a case, both sides are listed in bold type, the leading side on top.

This Week		Last Week	Weeks on Chart
1.	**LOVE LETTERS IN THE SAND** (ASCAP)—Pat Boone **BERNARDINE** (ASCAP)—Dot 15570	1	5
2.	**TEENAGER'S ROMANCE** (ASCAP)—Ricky Nelson **I'M WALKIN'** (BMI)—Verve 10047	4	6
3.	**WHITE SPORT COAT** (BMI)—Marty Robbins Grown Up Tears (BMI)—Col 40864	2	7
4.	**SO RARE** (ASCAP)—Jimmy Dorsey Sophisticated Swing (ASCAP)—Fraternity 755	5	9
5.	**BYE BYE LOVE** (BMI)—Everly Brothers I Wonder If I Care as Much (BMI)—Cadence 1315	12	1
6.	**ALL SHOOK UP** (BMI)—Elvis Presley That's When Your Heartaches Begin (ASCAP)—Vic 20-6870	3	4
7.	**DARK MOON** (BMI)—Gale Storm Little Too Late (BMI)—Dot 15558	8	6
8.	**SCHOOL DAY** (BMI)—Chuck Berry Deep Feeling (BMI)—Chess 1653	6	9
9.	**LITTLE DARLIN'** (BMI)—Diamonds Faithful and True (BMI)—Mercury 71060	7	14
10.	**START MOVIN'** (BMI)—Sal Mineo Love Affair (BMI)—Epic 9216	9	4
11.	**SEARCHIN'** (BMI)—Coasters **YOUNG BLOOD** (BMI)—Atco 6087	14	4
12.	**DARK MOON**—Bonnie Guitar Big Mike (BMI)—Dot 15550	10	8
13.	**COME GO WITH ME** (BMI)—Del Vikings How Can I Find Love? (BMI)—Dot 15538	11	16
14.	**FOUR WALLS** (BMI)—Jim Reeves I Know and You Know (BMI)—Vic 20-6874	16	5
15.	**IT'S NOT FOR ME TO SAY** (ASCAP)—Johnny Mathis Warm and Tender (ASCAP)—Col 40851	18	3
16.	**GONE** (BMI)—Ferlin Husky Missing Persons (BMI)—Cap 3628	13	13
17.	**FREIGHT TRAIN** (ASCAP)—Dusty Draper Seven Come Eleven (BMI)—Mercury 71102	22	2
18.	**GOIN' STEADY** (BMI)—Tommy Sands Ring My Phone (BMI)—Cap 3723	24	2
19.	**I LIKE YOUR KIND OF LOVE** (BMI)—Andy Williams Stop Teasin' Me (ASCAP)—Cadence 1323	—	1
20.	**ROUND AND ROUND** (BMI)—Perry Como Mi Casa, Su Casa (ASCAP)—Vic 20-6815	15	15
21.	**FABULOUS** (BMI)—Charlie Gracie Just Lookin' (ASCAP)—Cameo 107	17	4
21.	**FOUR WALLS** (BMI)—Jim Lowe **TALKING TO THE BLUES** (BMI)—Dot 15569	19	2
21.	**OVER THE MOUNTAIN** (BMI)—Johnnie & Joe My Baby's Gone On, On (BMI)—Chess 1664	23	3
24.	**WITH ALL MY HEART** (ASCAP)—Jodie Sands More Than Only Friends (ASCAP)—Chancellor 1003	—	1
25.	**OLD CAPE COD** (ASCAP)—Patti Page Wondering (BMI)—Mercury 71101	—	1

• Most Played in Juke Boxes

For survey week ending June 5

RECORDS are ranked in order of the greatest number of plays in juke boxes thruout the country, as determined by The Billboard's weekly survey of the nation's juke box operators. When significant play is reported on both sides of a record, points are combined to determine position on the chart. In such a case, both sides are listed in bold type, the leading side on top.

This Week		Last Week	Weeks on Chart
1.	**ALL SHOOK UP** (BMI)—Elvis Presley That's When Your Heartaches Begin (ASCAP)—Vic 20-6870	1	10
2.	**LOVE LETTERS IN THE SAND** (ASCAP)—Pat Boone **BERNARDINE** (ASCAP)—Dot 15570	3	4
3.	**LITTLE DARLIN'** (BMI)—Diamonds Faithful and True (BMI)—Mercury 71060	2	12
4.	**WHITE SPORT COAT** (BMI)—Marty Robbins Grown-Up Tears (BMI)—Columbia 40864	6	6
5.	**DARK MOON** (BMI)—Gale Storm Little Too Late (BMI)—Dot 15558	5	5
6.	**GONE** (BMI)—Ferlin Husky Missing Persons (BMI)—Cap 3628	4	10
7.	**SO RARE** (ASCAP)—Jimmy Dorsey Sophisticated Swing (ASCAP)—Fraternity 755	8	7
8.	**SCHOOL DAY** (BMI)—Chuck Berry Deep Feeling (BMI)—Chess 1653	9	6
9.	**ROUND AND ROUND** (BMI)—Perry Como Mi Casa Su Casa (ASCAP)—Vic 20-6815	7	13
10.	**SEARCHIN'** (BMI)—Coasters Young Blood (BMI)—Atco 6987	18	13
11.	**COME GO WITH ME** (BMI)—Del Vikings How Can I Find True Love? (BMI)—Dot 15538	10	7
12.	**DARK MOON** (BMI)—Bonnie Guitar Big Mike (BMI)—Fabor 5018	12	6
13.	**FOUR WALLS** (BMI)—Jim Reeves I Know and You Know (BMI)—Vic 20-6874	14	3
14.	**BYE BYE LOVE** (BMI)—Everly Brothers I Wonder If I Care as Much (BMI)—Cadence 1315	18	2
15.	**FOUR WALLS** (BMI)—Jim Lowe **TALKIN' TO THE BLUES** (BMI)—Dot 15569	15	2
16.	**TEENAGER'S ROMANCE** (ASCAP)—Ricky Nelson **I'M WALKIN'** (BMI)—Verve 10047	12	3
17.	**PARTY DOLL** (BMI)—Buddy Knox My Baby's Gone (BMI)—Roulette 4002	11	15
18.	**GONNA FIND ME A BLUEBIRD** (BMI)—Marvin Rainwater So You Think You've Got Troubles (BMI)—M-G-M 12412	—	1
19.	**EMPTY ARMS** (BMI)—Teresa Brewer Ricky-Tick Song (BMI)—Coral 61085	—	4
20.	**WHY, BABY, WHY?** (BMI)—Pat Boone I'm Waiting Just for You (BMI)—Dot 15545	16	12

• Best Selling Sheet Music

Tunes are ranked in order of their current national selling importance at the sheet music jobber level.

This Week		Last Week	Weeks on Chart
1.	**Dark Moon** (Dandelion)	1	6
2.	**Love Letters in the Sand** (Bourne)	8	3
3.	**All Shook Up** (Shalimar-Presley)	3	9
4.	**White Sport Coat** (Acuff-Rose)	5	6
5.	**Little Darlin'** (Excelloree)	4	6
6.	**Round and Round** (Rush)	2	14
7.	**Four Walls** (Springfield)	12	5
8.	**Come Go With Me** (Gil-Feebee)	6	7
9.	**So Rare** (Robbins)	—	2
9.	**Marianne** (Montclare)	7	16
11.	**Why, Baby, Why?** (Winneton)	10	10
12.	**Chantez-Chantez** (Cromwell)	8	13
13.	**Empty Arms** (Ivory)	14	4
14.	**Rock-a-Billy** (Oxford)	15	3
15.	**School Day** (Arc)	—	1

• Most Played by Jockeys

For survey week ending June 5

SIDES are ranked in order of the greatest number of plays on disk jockey radio shows thruout the country. Results are based on The Billboard's weekly survey among the nation's disk jockeys. The reverse side of each record is also listed.

This Week		Last Week	Weeks on Chart
1.	**LOVE LETTERS IN THE SAND** (ASCAP)—Pat Boone Bernardine (ASCAP)—Dot 15570	2	5
2.	**ALL SHOOK UP** (BMI)—Elvis Presley That's When Your Heartaches Begin (ASCAP)—Vic 20-6870	1	10
3.	**SO RARE** (ASCAP)—Jimmy Dorsey Sophisticated Swing (ASCAP)—Fraternity 755	5	6
4.	**LITTLE DARLIN'** (BMI)—Diamonds Faithful and True (BMI)—Mercury 71060	3	12
5.	**WHITE SPORT COAT** (BMI)—Marty Robbins Grown-Up Tears (BMI)—Col 40864	4	7
6.	**DARK MOON** (BMI)—Bonnie Guitar Big Mike (BMI)—Dot 15550	13	6
6.	**FREIGHT TRAIN** (ASCAP)—Rusty Draper Seven Come Eleven (BMI)—Mercury 71102	15	2
8.	**ROUND AND ROUND** (BMI)—Perry Como Mi Casa, Su Casa (ASCAP)—Vic 20-6815	8	16
9.	**SCHOOL DAY** (BMI)—Chuck Berry Deep Feeling (BMI)—Chess 1653	6	8
10.	**SHISH KEBAB** (BMI)—Ralph Marterie Bop a Boo-Bop a Doo (ASCAP)—Mercury 71092	14	5
11.	**DARK MOON** (BMI)—Gale Storm Little Too Late (BMI)—Dot 15550	9	5
12.	**WONDERING** (BMI)—Patti Page Old Cape Cod (ASCAP)—Mercury 71101	22	2
13.	**OLD CAPE COD** (ASCAP)—Patti Page Wondering (BMI)—Mercury 71101	17	2
14.	**FOUR WALLS** (BMI)—Jim Reeves I Know and You Know (BMI)—Vic 20-6874	11	4
15.	**COME GO WITH ME** (BMI)—Del Vikings How Can I Find True Love? (BMI)—Dot 15538	10	11
16.	**GONE** (BMI)—Ferlin Husky Missing Persons (BMI)—Cap 3628	7	14
17.	**GIRL WITH THE GOLDEN BRAIDS** (BMI)—Perry Como My Little Baby (BMI)—Vic 20-6904	15	3
18.	**TEENAGER'S ROMANCE** (ASCAP)—Ricky Nelson I'm Walkin' (BMI)—Verve 10047	19	2
19.	**SEARCHIN'** (BMI)—Coasters Young Blood (BMI)—Atco 6987	12	2
20.	**I JUST DON'T KNOW** (ASCAP)—Four Lads Golly (ASCAP)—Col 40914	—	3
21.	**IT'S NOT FOR ME TO SAY** (ASCAP)—Johnny Mathis Warm and Tender (ASCAP)—Col 40851	—	3
21.	**VALLEY OF TEARS** (BMI)—Fats Domino It's You I Love (BMI)—Imperial 5442	—	1
23.	**MANGOS** (ASCAP)—Rosemary Clooney Independent (ASCAP)—Col 40835	17	9
24.	**EMPTY ARMS** (BMI)—Teresa Brewer Ricky-Tick Song (BMI)—Coral 61805	—	3
25.	**BYE BYE LOVE** (BMI)—Everly Brothers I Wonder If I Care as Much (BMI)—Cadence 1315	21	2
25.	**WONDERFUL, WONDERFUL** (BMI)—Johnny Mathis When Sunny Gets Blue (BMI)—Col 40784	—	2

THE TOP 100

For survey week ending June 5

A list of the Top 100 RECORD SIDES in the nation according to a COMBINED TABULATION of Dealer, Disk Jockey and Juke Box Operator replies to The Billboard's weekly popular record Best Seller and Most Played surveys. Its purpose is to provide Disk Jockeys with additional programming material and to give trade exposure to NEWER records just beginning to show action in the field.

Pos.	Song, Artist, Label	Pos. Last Wk.
1.	**LOVE LETTERS IN THE SAND,** Pat Boone, Dot	2
2.	**ALL SHOOK UP,** Elvis Presley, Victor	1
3.	**WHITE SPORT COAT,** Marty Robbins, Columbia	3
4.	**SO RARE,** Jimmy Dorsey, Fraternity	5
5.	**LITTLE DARLIN',** Diamonds, Mercury	3
6.	**DARK MOON,** Gale Storm, Dot	8
7.	**SCHOOL DAY,** Chuck Berry, Chess	6
8.	**DARK MOON,** Bonnie Guitar, Dot	11
9.	**ROUND AND ROUND,** Perry Como, Victor	9
10.	**COME GO WITH ME,** Del Vikings, Dot	10
10.	**GONE,** Ferlin Husky, Capitol	8
12.	**FOUR WALLS,** Jim Reeves, Victor	12
13.	**TEENAGER'S ROMANCE,** Ricky Nelson, Verve	13
14.	**BYE BYE LOVE,** Everly Brothers, Cadence	15
15.	**SEARCHIN',** Coasters, Atco	13
16.	**FREIGHT TRAIN,** Rusty Draper, Mercury	17
17.	**I'M WALKIN',** Ricky Nelson, Verve	19
18.	**YOUNG BLOOD,** Coasters, Atco	46
19.	**OLD CAPE COD,** Patti Page, Mercury	34
20.	**IT'S NOT FOR ME TO SAY,** Johnny Mathis, Columbia	23
21.	**TALKIN' TO THE BLUES,** Jim Lowe, Dot	31
22.	**VALLEY OF TEARS,** Fats Domino, Imperial	24
23.	**BERNARDINE,** Pat Boone, Dot	30
23.	**FOUR WALLS,** Jim Lowe, Dot	21
25.	**I LIKE YOUR KIND OF LOVE,** Andy Williams, Cadence	34
26.	**GOIN' STEADY,** Tommy Sands, Capitol	21
27.	**START MOVIN',** Sal Mineo, Epic	16
28.	**I JUST DON'T KNOW,** Four Lads, Columbia	50
29.	**EMPTY ARMS,** Teresa Brewer, Coral	20
30.	**WONDERFUL, WONDERFUL,** Johnny Mathis, Columbia	26
31.	**OVER THE MOUNTAIN,** Johnnie & Joe, Chess	40
32.	**SHISH KEBAB,** Ralph Marterie, Mercury	29
33.	**YES, TONIGHT, JOSEPHINE,** Johnnie Ray, Columbia	—
34.	**ROCK A BILLY,** Guy Mitchell, Columbia	18
35.	**GIRL WITH THE GOLDEN BRAIDS,** Perry Como, Victor	27
36.	**ROCK YOUR LITTLE BABY TO SLEEP,** Buddy Knox, Roulette	36
37.	**GONNA FIND ME A BLUEBIRD,** Marvin Rainwater, M-G-M	—
38.	**MY DREAM,** Platters, Mercury	59
39.	**MANGOS,** Rosemary Clooney, Columbia	42
40.	**FREIGHT TRAIN,** Charles McDevitt-Nancy Whiskey, Chic	41
40.	**WHY, BABY, WHY?** Pat Boone, Dot	28
42.	**CAN'T WAIT FOR SUMMER,** Steve Lawrence, Coral	45
43.	**C. C. RIDER,** Chuck Willis, Atlantic	57
44.	**QUEEN OF THE SENIOR PROM,** Mills Brothers, Decca	53
45.	**WITH ALL MY HEART,** Jodie Sands, Chancellor	—
46.	**HE'S MINE,** Platters, Mercury	39
47.	**FABULOUS,** Charlie Gracie, Cameo	31
47.	**PARTY DOLL,** Buddy Knox, Roulette	25
49.	**I'M SORRY,** Platters, Mercury	51
50.	**AROUND THE WORLD,** Victor Young, Decca	56
51.	**WONDERING,** Patti Page, Mercury	—
52.	**IT'S YOU I LOVE,** Fats Domino, Imperial	52
53.	**PLEDGE OF LOVE,** Ken Copeland, Imperial	38
54.	**LITTLE WHITE LIES,** B Johnson, Bally	43
55.	**I'M WALKIN',** Fats Domino, Imperial	33
56.	**ONE FOR MY BABY,** Tony Bennett, Columbia	49
57.	**DON'T CRY MY LOVE,** Vera Lynn, London	55
58.	**MY LITTLE BABY,** Perry Como, Victor	48
59.	**SUSIE Q,** Dale Hawkins, Checker	—
60.	**BILLY GOAT,** Bill Haley, Decca	—
61.	**BUTTERFLY,** Andy Williams, Cadence	43
62.	**COCOANUT WOMAN,** Harry Belafonte, Victor	64
63.	**LOVE IS A GOLDEN RING,** Frankie Laine, Columbia	36
64.	**ALMOST PARADISE,** Roger Williams, Kapp	47
65.	**ROSIE-LEE,** Mello Tones, Gee	60
66.	**I'LL TAKE ROMANCE,** Eydie Gorme, ABC-Paramount	65
67.	**PLEDGE OF LOVE,** Mitchell Torok, Decca	53
68.	**SHANGRI-LA,** Four Coins, Epic	92
69.	**MAMA GUITAR,** Don Cornell, Coral	69
70.	**PARTY DOLL,** Steve Lawrence, Coral	80
71.	**CHANTEZ CHANTEZ,** Dinah Shore, Victor	89
71.	**FABULOUS,** Steve Lawrence, Coral	77
73.	**BYE BYE LOVE,** Webb Pierce, Decca	74
73.	**WARM UP TO ME BABY,** Jim Bowen, Roulette	66
75.	**GONNA FIND ME A BLUEBIRD,** Eddy Arnold, Victor	61
76.	**TILL,** Percy Faith, Columbia	—
77.	**AFTER SCHOOL,** Randy Starr, Dale	—
77.	**LITTLE DARLIN',** Gladiolas, Excello	72
79.	****STARDUST,** Nat (King) Cole, Capitol	—
79.	**LUCILLE,** Little Richard, Specialty	86
81.	**I'M GOONA SIT RIGHT DOWN AND WRITE MYSELF A LETTER.** Billy Williams, Coral	80
82.	**FALLEN STAR,** Jimmy Newman, Dot	—
83.	**DO I LOVE YOU?** Tony Martin, Victor	—
84.	**DO I LOVE YOU?** Vic Damone, Columbia	76
84.	**MAMA LOOK-A BOOBOO,** Harry Belafonte, Victor	68
86.	***PEACE IN THE VALLEY,** Elivs Presley, Victor	90
86.	**I'M STICKIN' WITH YOU,** Jim Bowen, Roulette	63
88.	**TEENAGE CRUSH,** Tommy Sands, Capitol	—
89.	**SITTIN' IN THE BALCONY,** Eddie Cochran, Liberty	78
90.	**SO LONG MY LOVE,** Warren Smith, Sun	—
91.	**GONNA FIND ME A BLUEBIRD,** Joyce Hahn, Cadence	84
92.	**NINETY-NINE WAYS,** Tab Hunter, Dot	69
92.	**WHEN ROCK 'N' ROLL COME TO TRINDAD,** Nat (King) Cole, Capitol	88
94.	**SUNSHINE GIRL,** Eddie Fisher, Victor	—
95	**TRUST IN ME,** Chris Connor, Atlantic	—
96.	**CRAZY LOVE,** Frank Sinatra, Capitol	86
96.	**AROUND THE WORLD,** Mantovani, London	—
98.	**TINA,** Easy Riders, Columbia	—
98.	**1492,** Betty Johnson, Bally	98
100.	**ROCKIN' SHOES,** Ames Brothers, Victor	—

*(Not available as a Pop Single, Available on RCA Victor EPA 4054)

**(Not available as a Pop Single. Available on Capitol EAP-2-824)

CAUTION TO DEALERS AND JUKE BOX OPERATORS

The Billboard's Top 100 is NOT designed to provide tested information for buying purposes. This function is most reliably served by other regular weekly features: Best Sellers in Stores, Most Played in Juke Boxes, Coming Up Strong and Best Buys.

• Best Sellers in Stores

For survey week ending June 12

RECORDS are ranked in order of their current national selling importance at the retail level, as determined by The Billboard's weekly survey of the top volume dealers in every important market area. When significant action is reported on both sides of a record, points are combined to determine position on the chart. In such a case, both sides are listed in bold type, the leading side on top.

This Week		Last Week	Weeks on Chart
1.	**LOVE LETTERS IN THE SAND** (ASCAP)—Pat Boone Bernardine (ASCAP)—Dot 15570	1	6
2.	**BYE BYE LOVE** (BMI)—Everly Brothers I Wonder If I Care as Much (BMI)—Cadence 1315	5	4
3.	**WHITE SPORT COAT** (BMI)—Marty Robbins Grown-Up Tears (BMI)—Col 40864	3	8
4.	**SO RARE** (ASCAP)—Jimmy Dorsey Sophisticated Swing (ASCAP)—Fraternity 755	4	10
5.	**TEENAGER'S ROMANCE** (ASCAP)—Ricky Nelson **I'M WALKIN'** (BMI)—Verve 10047	2	7
6.	**DARK MOON** (BMI)—Gale Storm Little Too Late (BMI)—Dot 15558	7	7
7.	**SEARCHIN'** (BMI)—Coasters **YOUNG BLOOD** (BMI)—Atco 6087	11	5
8.	**ALL SHOOK UP** (BMI)—Elvis Presley That's When Your Heartaches Begin (ASCAP)—Vic 20-6870	6	5
9.	**LITTLE DARLIN'** (BMI)—Diamonds Faithful and True (BMI)—Mercury 71060	9	15
10.	**SCHOOL DAY** (BMI)—Chuck Berry Deep Feeling (BMI)—Chess 1653	8	10
11.	**START MOVIN'** (BMI)—Sal Mineo Love Affair (BMI)—Epic 9216	10	5
12.	**IT'S NOT FOR ME TO SAY** (ASCAP)—Johnny Mathis Warm and Tender (ASCAP)—Col 40851	15	4
13.	**I LIKE YOUR KIND OF LOVE** (BMI)—Andy Williams Stop Teasin' Me (ASCAP)—Cadence 1323	19	2
14.	**COME GO WITH ME** (BMI)—Del Vikings How Can I Find True Love? (BMI)—Dot 15538	13	17
14.	**FOUR WALLS** (BMI)—Jim Reeves I Know and You Know (BMI)—Vic 20-6874	14	6
16.	**DARK MOON** (BMI)—Bonnie Guitar Big Mike (BMI)—Dot 15550	12	9
17.	**GONE** (BMI)—Ferlin Husky Missing Persons (BMI)—Cap 3628	16	14
17.	**OLD CAPE COD** (ASCAP)—Patti Page Wondering (BMI)—Mercury 71101	25	2
19.	**OVER THE MOUNTAIN** (BMI)—Johnnie & Joe My Baby's Gone On, On (BMI)—Chess 1664	21	4
20.	**I'M GONNA SIT RIGHT DOWN AND WRITE MYSELF A LETTER** (ASCAP)—Billy Williams Date With the Blues (ASCAP)—Coral 61830	—	1
21.	**WITH ALL MY HEART** (ASCAP)—Jodie Sands More Than Only Friends (ASCAP)—Chancellor 1003	24	2
22.	**VALLEY OF TEARS** (BMI)—Fats Domino It's You I Love (BMI)—Imperial 5442	—	3
23.	**ROCK YOUR LITTLE BABY TO SLEEP** (BMI)—Buddy Knox Don't Make Me Cry (BMI)—Roulette 4009	—	1
24.	**FABULOUS** (BMI)—Charlie Gracie Just Lookin' (ASCAP)—Cameo 107	21	5
25.	**FREIGHT TRAIN** (ASCAP)—Rusty Draper Seven Come Eleven (BMI)—Mercury 71102	17	3

• Most Played in Juke Boxes

For survey week ending June 12

RECORDS are ranked in order of the greatest number of plays in juke boxes thruout the country, as determined by The Billboard's weekly survey of the nation's juke box operators. When significant play is reported on both sides of a record, points are combined to determine position on the chart. In such a case, both sides are listed in bold type, the leading side on top.

This Week		Last Week	Weeks on Chart
1.	**ALL SHOOK UP** (BMI)—Elvis Presley That's When Your Heatraches Begin (ASCAP)—Vic 20-6870	1	11
2.	**LOVE LETTERS IN THE SAND** (ASCAP)—Pat Boone Bernardine (ASCAP)—Dot 15570	2	5
3.	**LITTLE DARLIN'** (BMI)—Diamonds Faithful and True (BMI)—Mercury 71060	3	13
4.	**DARK MOON** (BMI)—Gale Storm Little Too Late (BMI)—Dot 15558	5	6
5.	**WHITE SPORT COAT** (BMI)—Marty Robbins Grown Up Tears (BMI)—Col 40864	4	7
6.	**SO RARE** (ASCAP)—Jimmy Dorsey Sophisticated Swing (ASCAP)—Fraternity 755	7	8
7.	**SCHOOL DAY** (BMI)—Chuck Berry Deep Feeling (BMI)—Chess 1653	8	7
8.	**GONE** (BMI)—Ferlin Husky Missing Persons (BMI)—Cap 3628	6	11
9.	**BYE BYE LOVE** (BMI)—Everly Brothers I Wonder If I Care as Much (BMI)—Cadence 1315	14	3
10.	**SEARCHIN'** (BMI)—Coasters **YOUNG BLOOD** (BMI)—Atco 6987	10	14
11.	**DARK MOON** (BMI)—Bonnie Guitar Big Mike (BMI)—Dot 15550	12	7
12.	**ROUND AND ROUND** (BMI)—Perry Como Mi Casa Su Casa (ASCAP)—Vic 20-6815	9	14
13.	**FOUR WALLS** (BMI)—Jim Reeves I Know and You Know (BMI)—Vic 20-6874	13	4
14.	**COME GO WITH ME** (BMI)—Del Vikings How Can I Find True Love? (BMI)—Dot 15538	11	8
15.	**FOUR WALLS** (BMI)—Jim Lowe **TALKIN' TO THE BLUES** (BMI)—Dot 15569	15	3
16.	**TEENAGER'S ROMANCE** (ASCAP)—Ricky Nelson **I'M WALKIN'** (BMI)—Verve 10047	16	4
17.	**OVER THE MOUNTAIN** (BMI)—Johnnie & Joe My Baby's Gone On, On (BMI)—Chess 1664	—	1
18.	**START MOVIN'** (BMI)—Sal Mineo Love Affair (BMI)—Epic 9216	—	1
19.	**I LIKE YOUR KIND OF LOVE**—Andy Williams Stop Teasin' Me (ASCAP)—Cadence 1323	—	1
20.	**GONNA FIND ME A BLUEBIRD** (BMI)—Marvin Rainwater So You Think You Got Troubles (BMI)—M-G-M 12412	18	2

• Best Selling Sheet Music

Tunes are ranked in order of their current national selling importance at the sheet music jobber level.

This Week		Last Week	Weeks on Chart
1.	**Love Letters in the Sand** (Bourne)	2	4
2.	**Dark Moon** (Dandelion)	1	7
3.	**White Sport Coat** (Acuff-Rose)	4	7
4.	**All Shook Up** (Shalimar-Presley)	3	10
5.	**Round and Round** (Rush)	6	15
6.	**Four Walls** (Springfield)	2	6
7.	**Little Darlin'**, (Excellorec)	5	7
8.	**So Rare** (Robbins)	9	3
9.	**Come Go With Me** (Gil-Feebee)	8	8
10.	**Marianne** (Montclare)	9	17
10.	**Empty Arms** (Ivory)	13	6
12.	**Why Baby Why** (Winneton)	11	11
13.	**Rock-A-Billy** (Oxford)	14	4
14.	**School Day** (Arc)	15	2
14.	**Chantez-Chantez** (Cromwell)	12	14

• Most Played by Jockeys

For survey week ending June 12

SIDES are ranked in order of the greatest number of plays on disk jockey radio shows thruout the country. Results are based on The Billboard's weekly survey among the nation's disk jockeys. The reverse side of each record is also listed.

This Week		Last Week	Weeks on Chart
1.	**LOVE LETTERS IN THE SAND** (ASCAP)—Pat Boone Bernardine (ASCAP)—Dot 15570	1	6
2.	**SO RARE** (ASCAP)—Jimmy Dorsey Sophisticated Swing (ASCAP)—Fraternity 755	3	7
3.	**ALL SHOOK UP** (BMI)—Elvis Presley That's When Your Heartaches Begin (ASCAP)—Vic 20-6870	2	11
4.	**WHITE SPORT COAT** (BMI)—Marty Robbins Grown Up Tears (BMI)—Col 40864	5	8
5.	**IT'S NOT FOR ME TO SAY** (ASCAP)—Johnny Mathis Warm and Tender (ASCAP)—Col 40851	21	4
6.	**DARK MOON** (BMI)—Gale Storm Little Too Late (BMI)—Dot 15558	11	6
7.	**OLD CAPE COD** (ASCAP)—Patti Page Wondering (BMI)—Mercury 71101	13	3
8.	**BYE BYE LOVE** (BMI)—Everly Brothers I Wonder If I Care as Much (BMI)—Cadence 1315	25	3
9.	**LITTLE DARLIN'** (BMI)—Diamonds Faithful and True (BMI)—Mercury 71060	4	13
10.	**YOUNG BLOOD** (BMI)—Coasters Searchin' (BMI)—Atco 6087	—	2
11.	**SCHOOL DAY** (BMI)—Chuck Berry Deep Feeling (BMI)—Chess 1653	9	9
12.	**TEENAGER'S ROMANCE** (ASCAP)—Ricky Nelson I'm Walkin' (BMI)—Verve 10047	18	3
13.	**SEARCHIN'** (BMI)—Coasters Young Blood (BMI)—Atco 5987	19	3
14.	**DARK MOON** (BMI)—Bonnie Guitar Big Mike (BMI)—Dot 15550	6	7
15.	**ROUND AND ROUND** (BMI)—Perry Como Mi Casa, Su Casa (ASCAP)—Vic 20-6815	8	17
16.	**FREIGHT TRAIN** (ASCAP)—Rusty Draper Seven Come Eleven (BMI)—Mercury 71102	6	3
17.	**START MOVIN'** (BMI)—Sal Mineo Love Affair (BMI)—Epic 9261	—	2
18.	**GIRL WITH THE GOLDEN BRAIDS** (BMI)—Perry Como My Little Baby (BMI)—Vic 20-6004	17	4
19.	**FOUR WALLS** (BMI)—Jim Reeves I Know and You Know (BMI)—Vic 20-6874	14	5
20.	**I LIKE YOUR KIND OF LOVE** (BMI)—Andy Williams Stop Teasin' Me (ASCAP)—Cadence 1323	—	1
21.	**VALLEY OF TEARS** (BMI)—Fats Domino It's You I Love (BMI)—Imperial 5442	21	2
22.	**GONE** (BMI)—Ferlin Husky Missing Persons (BMI)—Cap 3628	16	15
23.	**WITH ALL MY HEART** (ASCAP)—Jodie Sands More Than Only Friends (ASCAP)—Chancellor 1003	—	1
24.	**WONDERFUL, WONDERFUL** (BMI)—Johnny Mathis When Sunny Gets Blue (BMI)—Col 40784	25	3
25.	**I JUST DON'T KNOW** (ASCAP)—Four Lads Golly (ASCAP)—Col 40914	20	4

THE TOP 100

For survey week ending June 12

A list of the Top 100 RECORD SIDES in the nation according to a COMBINED TABULATION of Dealer, Disk Jockey and Juke Box Operator replies to The Billboard's weekly popular record Best Seller and Most Played surveys. Its purpose is to provide Disk Jockeys with additional programming material and to give trade exposure to NEWER records just beginning to show action in the field.

Pos.	Song, Artist, Label	Pos. Last Wk.
1.	**LOVE LETTERS IN THE SAND,** Pat Boone, Dot	1
2.	**ALL SHOOK UP,** Elvis Presley, Victor	2
3.	**SO RARE,** Jimmy Dorsey, Fraternity	4
3.	**WHITE SPORT COAT,** Marty Robbins, Columbia	3
5.	**DARK MOON,** Gale Storm, Dot	6
6.	**BYE BYE LOVE,** Everly Brothers, Cadence	14
7.	**LITTLE DARLIN',** Diamonds, Mercury	5
8.	**YOUNG BLOOD,** Coasters, Atco	18
9.	**SCHOOL DAY,** Chuck Berry, Chess	7
10.	**SEARCHIN',** Coasters, Atco	15
10.	**TEENAGER'S ROMANCE,** Ricky Nelson, Verve	13
12.	**DARK MOON,** Bonnie Guitar, Dot	8
13.	**START MOVIN',** Sal Mineo, Epic	27
14.	**IT'S NOT FOR ME TO SAY,** Johnny Mathis, Columbia	20
15.	**GONE,** Ferlin Husky, Capitol	10
16.	**OLD CAPE COD,** Patti Page, Mercury	19
17.	**I LIKE YOUR KIND OF LOVE,** Andy Williams, Cadence	25
18.	**FOUR WALLS,** Jim Reeves, Victor	23
19.	**ROUND AND ROUND,** Perry Como, Victor	9
20.	**COME GO WITH ME,** Del Vikings, Dot	10
20.	**FOUR WALLS,** Jim Lowe, Dot	12
22.	**VALLEY OF TEARS,** Fats Domino, Imperial	22
23.	**ROCK YOUR LITTLE BABY TO SLEEP,** Buddy Knox, Roulette	36
24.	**FREIGHT TRAIN,** Rusty Draper, Mercury	16
25.	**OVER THE MOUNTAIN,** Johnnie and Joe, Chess	31
25.	**WITH ALL MY HEART,** Jodie Sands, Chancellor	45
27.	**I'M WALKIN',** Ricky Nelson, Verve	17
28.	**I JUST DON'T KNOW,** Four Lads, Columbia	28
29.	**TALKIN' TO THE BLUES,** Jim Lowe, Dot	21
30.	**WONDERFUL, WONDERFUL,** Johnny Mathis, Columbia	30
30.	**GOIN' STEADY,** Tommy Sands, Capitol	26
30.	**GONNA SIT RIGHT DOWN (AND WRITE MYSELF A LETTER),** Billy Williams, Coral	81
30.	**MY DREAM,** Platters, Mercury	38
34.	**ROCK-A-BILLY,** Guy Mitchell, Columbia	34
34.	**EMPTY ARMS,** Teresa Brewer, Coral	29
34.	**GIRL WITH THE GOLDEN BRAIDS,** Perry Como, Victor	35
37.	**FABULOUS,** Charlie Gracie, Cameo	47
38.	**YES TONIGHT, JOSEPHINE,** Johnnie Ray, Columbia	33
39.	**QUEEN OF THE SENIOR PROM,** Mills Brothers, Decca	44
40.	**SHANGRI-LA,** Four Coins, Epic	68
41.	**SHISH KEBAB,** Ralph Marterie, Mercury	32
42.	**SUSIE Q,** Dale Hawkins, Checker	59
43.	**MANGOS,** Rosie Clooney, Columbia	39
44.	**FREIGHT TRAIN,** Charlie McDevitt-Nancy Whiskey, Chic	40
45.	**BERNARDINE,** Pat Boone, Dot	23
46.	**AROUND THE WORLD,** Victor Young, Decca	50
47.	**CAN'T WAIT FOR SUMMER,** Steve Lawrence, Coral	42
48.	**GONNA FIND ME A BLUEBIRD,** Marvin Rainwater, M-G-M	37
49.	**SEND FOR ME,** Nat (King) Cole, Capitol	—
50.	**I'M WALKIN',** Fats Domino, Imperial	55
51.	**GONNA FIND ME A BLUEBIRD,** Eddy Arnold, Victor	75
52.	**WONDERING,** Patti Page, Mercury	51
53.	**WHY BABY WHY,** Pat Boone, Dot	40
54.	**JENNY JENNY,** Little Richard, Specialty	—
55.	**MY LITTLE BABY,** Perry Como, Victor	58
56.	**PARTY DOLL,** Buddy Knox, Roulette	47
57.	**WARM UP TO ME BABY,** Jim Bowen, Roulette	73
58.	**AROUND THE WORLD,** Mantovani, London	96
59.	**COCONUT WOMAN,** Harry Belafonte, Victor	62
60.	**ISLAND IN THE SUN,** Harry Belafonte, Victor	—
60.	**LITTLE DARLIN',** Gladiolas, Excello	77
62.	**ROSIE-LEE,** Mello-Tones, Gee	65
62.	**C. C. RIDER,** Chuck Willis, Atlantic	43
64.	**HE'S MINE,** Platters, Mercury	46
65.	**LITTLE WHITE LIES,** Betty Johnson, Bally	54
66.	**ONE FOR MY BABY,** Tony Bennett, Columbia	56
67.	**IT'S YOU I LOVE,** Fats Domino, Imperial	52
68.	**SO YOUNG,** Clyde Stacy, Candlelight	—
69.	**THAT'S LIFE,** Jack Pleis, Decca	—
70.	**FALLEN STAR,** Jimmy Newman, Dot	82
70.	**MY PERSONAL POSSESSION,** Nat (King) Cole, Capitol	—
72.	**SO LONG MY LOVE,** Warren Smith, Sun	90
72.	**AROUND THE WORLD,** Bing Crosby, Decca	—
74.	**PLEDGE OF LOVE,** Ken Copeland, Imperial	53
75.	**BILLY GOAT,** Bill Haley, Decca	60
76.	**TOO LATE,** Gene Austin, Victor	—
77.	**I'M SORRY,** Platters, Mercury	49
78.	**I'LL TAKE ROMANCE,** Eydie Gorme, ABC-Paramount	66
79.	**RANG TANG DING DING,** Cellos, Apollo	—
80.	**CHANTEZ-CHANTEZ,** Dinah Shore, Victor	71
80.	**DON'T CRY, MY LOVE,** Vera Lynn, London	57
82.	**BYE BYE LOVE,** Webb Pierce, Decca	73
83.	**RAINBOW,** Russ Hamilton, Kapp	—
83.	**SWEET STUFF,** Guy Mitchell, Columbia	—
85.	**TEARDROPS FROM MY HEART,** Teresa Brewer, Coral	—
86.	**RING-A-DING,** Tommy Sands, Capitol	—
87.	**THAT'S WHEN YOUR HEARTACHES BEGIN,** Elvis Presley, Victor	—
88.	**JUST TO HOLD MY HAND,** Clyde McPhatter, Atlantic	—
89.	**YOUR KISSES KILL ME,** Eydie Gorme, ABC-Paramount	—
90.	***STARDUST,** Nat (King) Cole, Capitol	79
91.	**STARDUST,** Billy Ward, Liberty	—
92.	**CATTLE CALL,** Dinah Shore, Victor	—
93.	**MY LOVE SONG,** Tommy Sands, Capitol	—
94.	**LET IT BE ME,** Jill Corey, Columbia	—
95.	**TILL,** Percy Faith, Columbia	76
96.	**BUTTERFLY,** Andy Williams, Cadence	61
97.	**WHO NEEDS YOU?** Four Lads, Columbia	—
98.	**CALYPSO MELODY,** David Rose, M-G-M	—
98.	**FABULOUS,** Steve Lawrence, Coral	71
100.	**ALMOST PARADISE,** Roger Williams, Kapp	64

*(Not available as a Pop Single. Available on Capitol EAP-2-824)

CAUTION TO DEALERS AND JUKE BOX OPERATORS

The Billboard's Top 100 is NOT designed to provide tested information for buying purposes. This function is most reliably served by other regular weekly features: Best Sellers in Stores, Most Played in Juke Boxes, Coming Up Strong and Best Buys.

STORE RECORDED SALES — NEW YORK UNIVERSITY SCHOOL OF RETAILING — THE BILLBOARD

Best Sellers in Stores

FOR SURVEY WEEK ENDING JUNE 19, 1957

The information given in this chart is based on actual sales to customers in a scientific sample of the nation's retail record outlets during the week ending on the date shown above. Sample design, sample size, and all methods used in this continuing study of retail record sales are under the direct and continuing supervision and control of the School of Retailing of New York University.

This Week		Last Week	Weeks on Chart
1.	LOVE LETTERS IN THE SAND BERNARDINE (ASCAP)—Dot 15570 (ASCAP)—Pat Boone	1	7
2.	BYE BYE LOVE (BMI)—Everly Brothers I Wonder If I Care as Much (BMI)—Cadence 1315	2	5
3.	SO RARE (ASCAP)—Jimmy Dorsey Sophisticated Swing (ASCAP)—Fraternity 755	3	11
4.	TENNAGER'S ROMANCE (ASCAP)—Ricky Nelson I'M WALKIN'—Verve 10047	4	8
5.	ALL SHOOK UP (BMI)—Elvis Presley That's When Your Heartaches Begin (ASCAP)—Vic 20-6870	5	6
6.	SEARCHIN' (BMI)—Coasters YOUNG BLOOD (BMI)—Atco 6087	6	6
7.	DARK MOON (BMI)—Gale Storm Little Too Late (BMI)—Dot 15558	7	8
8.	WHITE SPORT COAT (BMI)—Marty Robbins Grown Up Tears (BMI)—Col 40864	8	9
9.	START MOVIN' (BMI)—Sal Mineo LOVE AFFAIR (BMI)—Epic 9216	9	6
10.	LITTLE DARLIN' (BMI)—Diamonds Faithful and True (BMI)—Mercury 71060	10	16
11.	I LIKE YOUR KIND OF LOVE (BMI)—Andy Williams Stop Teasin' Me (ASCAP)—Cadence 1323	11	3
12.	VALLEY OF TEARS (BMI)—Fats Domino IT'S YOU I LOVE (BMI)—Imperial 5442	12	4
13.	OLD CAPE COD (ASCAP)—Patti Page WONDERING (BMI)—Mercury 71101	13	3
13.	C. C. RIDER (BMI)—Chuck Willis Ease the Pain (BMI)—Atlantic 1130	13	3
15.	FOUR WALLS (BMI)—Jim Reeves I Know and You Know (BMI)—Vic 20-6874	15	4
16.	FABULOUS (BMI)—Charlie Gracie Just Lookin' (ASCAP)—Cameo 107	16	6
17.	COME GO WITH ME (BMI)—Del Vikings How Can I Find True Love? (BMI)—Dot 15538	17	18
18.	SCHOOL DAY (BMI)—Chuck Berry Deep Feeling (BMI)—Chess 1653	18	11
19.	OVER THE MOUNTAIN (BMI)—Johnnie & Joe My Baby's Gone On, On (BMI)—Chess 1664	19	5
20.	JENNY, JENNY (BMI)—Little Richard MISS ANN (BMI)—Specialty 606	20	1
21.	FREIGHT TRAIN (ASCAP)—Rusty Draper Seven Come Eleven (BMI)—Mercury 71102	21	4
21.	GOIN' STEADY (BMI)—Tommy Sands RING MY PHONE (BMI)—Cap 3723	21	3
23.	TEDDY BEAR (ASCAP)—Elvis Presley LOVING YOU (BMI)—Vic 20-7000	23	1
24.	GONE (BMI)—Ferlin Husky Missing Persons (BMI)—Cap 3628	24	15
24.	GONNA FIND ME A BLUEBIRD (BMI)—Marvin Rainwater So You Think You Got Troubles (BMI)—M-G-M 1241?	24	2
26.	IT'S NOT FOR ME TO SAY (ASCAP)—Johnny Mathis Warm and Tender (ASCAP)—Col 40851	26	5
26.	HE'S MINE (BMI)—Platters I'm Sorry (BMI)—Mercury 71032	26	8
26.	GIRL WITH GOLDEN BRAIDS (ASCAP)—Perry Como MY LITTLE BABY (BMI)—RCA Vic 20-6904	26	1
29.	MY DREAM (ASCAP)—Platters I Wanna (BMI)—Mercury 71093	29	1
29.	I'M WALKIN' (BMI)—Fats Domino I'm in the Mood for Love (ASCAP)—Imperial 5428	29	13

IMPORTANT: A few wide fluctuations between positions this week and last week will be noted. These are due in part to faster sales information being secured direct from record dealers thru the research methods supervised by NYU's School of Retailing.

Most Played by Jockeys

FOR SURVEY WEEK ENDING JUNE 19, 1957

SIDES are ranked in order of the greatest number of plays on disk jockey radio shows thruout the country. Results are based on The Billboard's weekly survey among the nation's disk jockeys. The reverse side of each record is also listed.

This Week		Last Week	Weeks on Chart
1.	LOVE LETTERS IN THE SAND (ASCAP)—Pat Boone Bernardine (ASCAP)—Dot 15570	1	7
2.	SO RARE (ASCAP)—Jimmy Dorsey Sophisticated Swing (ASCAP)—Fraternity 755	2	8
3.	BYE BYE LOVE (BMI)—Everly Brothers I Wonder If I Care as Much (BMI)—Cadence 1315	8	4
4.	WHITE SPORT COAT (BMI)—Marty Robbins Grown Up Tears (BMI)—Col 40864	4	9
5.	ALL SHOOK UP (BMI)—Elvis Presley That's When Your Heartaches Begin (ASCAP)—Vic 20-6870	3	12
6.	IT'S NOT FOR ME TO SAY (ASCAP)—Johnny Mathis Warm and Tender (ASCAP)—Col 40851	5	5
7.	OLD CAPE COD (ASCAP)—Patti Page Wondering (BMI)—Mercury 71101	7	4
8.	DARK MOON (BMI)—Gale Storm Little Too Late (BMI)—Dot 15558	6	7
9.	FREIGHT TRAIN (ASCAP)—Rusty Draper Seven Come Eleven (BMI)—Mercury 71102	16	4
10.	SEARCHIN' (BMI)—Coasters Young Blood (BMI)—Atco 6987	13	4
11.	TEENAGER'S ROMANCE (ASCAP)—Ricky Nelson I'm Walkin' (BMI)—Verve 10047	12	4
12.	LITTLE DARLIN' (BMI)—Diamonds Faithful and True (BMI)— Mercury 71060	9	14
13.	GIRL WITH THE GOLDEN BRAIDS (BMI)—Perry Como My Little Baby (BMI)—Vic 20-6904	18	5
14.	FOUR WALLS (BMI)—Jimmy Reeves I Know and You Know (BMI)—Vic 20-6874	19	6
15.	WITH ALL MY HEART (ASCAP)-Jodie Sands More Than Only Friends (ASCAP)—Chancellor 1003	23	2
16.	START MOVIN' (BMI)—Sal Mineo Love Affair (BMI)—Epic 9216	17	3
16.	GOIN' STEADY (BMI)—Tommy Sands Ring My Phone (BMI)—Cap 3723	—	1
18.	SCHOOL DAY (BMI)—Chuck Berry Deep Feeling (BMI)—Chess 1653	11	10
19.	VALLEY OF TEARS (BMI)—Fats Domino It's You I Love (BMI)—Imperial 5442	21	3
20.	DARK MOON (BMI)—Bonnie Guitar Big Mike (BMI)—Dot 15550	14	8
21.	SHISH KEBAB (BMI)—Ralph Marterie Bop A Doo-Bop A Doo (ASCAP)—Mercury 71092	—	1
22.	I LIKE YOUR KIND OF LOVE (BMI)—Andy Williams Stop Teasin' Me (ASCAP)—Cadence 1323	20	2
23.	I'M GONNA SIT RIGHT DOWN (ASCAP)—Billy Williams Date With the Blues (ASCAP)—Coral 61830	—	1
24.	WONDERING (BMI)—Patti Page Old Cape Cod (ASCAP)—Mercury 71101	—	2
25.	LITTLE WHITE LIES (BMI)—Betty Johnson I Dreamed (ASCAP)—Bally 1033	—	1

THE TOP 100

FOR SURVEY WEEK ENDING JUNE 19

A list of the **Top 100 RECORD SIDES** in the nation according to a Combined **TABULATION** of Dealer unit sales and Disk Jockey replies to The Billboard's weekly popular record Most Played survey. Its purpose is to provide Disk Jockeys with additional programming material and to give trade exposure to NEWER records just beginning to show action in the field.

Pos.	Song, Artist, Label	Pos. Last Wk.
1.	**LOVE LETTERS IN THE SAND,** Pat Boone, Dot	1
2	**SO RARE,** Jimmy Dorsey, Fraternity	3
3.	**BYE BYE LOVE,** Everly Brothers, Cadence	6
4.	**ALL SHOOK UP,** Elvis Presley, Victor	2
5.	**WHITE SPORT COAT,** Marty Robbins, Coulmbia	3
6.	**DARK MOON,** Gale Storm, Dot	5
7.	**OLD CAPE COD,** Patti Page, Mercury	16
8.	**TEENAGER'S ROMANCE,** Ricky Nelson, Verve	10
9.	**SEARCHIN',** Coasters, Atco	10
10.	**LITTLE DARLIN',** Diamonds, Mercury	7
11.	**FREIGHT TRAIN,** Rusty Draper, Mercury	24
12.	**START MOVIN',** Sal Minco, Epic	13
13.	**FOUR WALLS,** Jim Reeves, Victor	20
14.	**I LIKE YOUR KIND OF LOVE,** Andy Williams, Cadence	17
15.	**GIRL WITH THE GOLDEN BRAIDS,** Perry Como, Victor	34
16.	**VALLEY OF TEARS,** Fats Domino, Imperial	22
17.	**IT'S NOT FOR ME TO SAY,** Johnny Mathis, Columbia	14
18.	**SCHOOL DAY,** Chuck Berry, Chess	9
19.	**GOIN' STEADY,** Tommy Sands, Capitol	30
20.	**WITH ALL MY HEART,** Jòdie Sands, Chancellor	25
21.	**DARK MOON,** Bonnie Guitar, Dot	12
22.	**YOUNG BLOOD,** Coasters, Atco	8
23.	**COME GO WITH ME,** Del Vikings, Dot	20
24.	**GONE,** Ferlin Husky, Capitol	15
25.	**ROCK YOUR LITTLE BABY TO SLEEP,** Buddy Knox, Roulette	23
26.	**I'M GONNA SIT RIGHT DOWN (AND WRITE MYSELF A LETTER)** Billy Williams, Coral	30
27.	**OVER THE MOUNTAIN,** Johnnie & Joe, Chess	25
27.	**ROUND AND ROUND,** Perry Como, Victor	19
29	**C. C. RIDER,** Chuck Willis, Atlantic	62
29.	**MY DREAM,** Platters, Mercury	30
31.	**FABULOUS,** Charlie Gracie, Cameo	37
32.	**SHISH KEBAB,** Ralph Marterie, Mercury	41
33.	**WONDERFUL, WONDERFUL,** Johnny Mathis, Columbia	30
34.	**GONNA FIND ME A BLUEBIRD,** Marvin Rainwater, M-G-M	48
35.	**WONDERING,** Patti Page, Mercury	52
36.	**JENNY, JENNY,** Little Richard, Speciaty	54
37.	**BERNARDINE,** Pat Boone, Dot	45
37	**I'M WALKIN',** Ricky Nelson, Verve	27
39.	**FOUR WALLS,** Jim Lowe, Dot	20
40.	**LITTLE WHITE LIES,** Betty Johnson, Bally	65
41.	**ALMOST PARADISE,** Roger Williams, Kapp	100
42.	**FALLEN STAR,** Jimmy Newman, Dot	70
42.	**SUSIE Q,** Dale Hawkins, Checker	42
44.	**AROUND THE WORLD,** Victor Young, Decca	—
45.	**ROCK-A-BILLY,** Guy Mitchell, Columbia	34
46.	**CAN'T WAIT FOR SUMMER,** Steve Lawrence, Coral	47
47.	**TEDDY BEAR,** Elvis Presley, Victor	—
48.	**HE'S MINE,** Platters, Mercury	64
48.	**I JUST DON'T KNOW,** Four Lads, Columbia	28
48.	**I'M WALKIN',** Fats Domino, Imperial	50
48.	**QUEEN OF THE SENIOR PROM,** Mills Brothers, Decca	49
52.	**WHO NEEDS YOU,** Four Lads, Columbia	97
53.	**SHANGRI-LA,** Four Coins, Epic	40
53.	**YOUR KISSES KILL ME,** Eydie Gorme, ABC-Paramount	89
55.	**EMPTY ARMS,** Teresa Brewer, Coral	34
55.	**TALKIN' TO THE BLUES,** Jim Lowe, Dot	29
57.	**JUST TO HOLD MY HAND,** Clyde McPhatter, Atlantic	88
57.	**MY LITTLE BABY,** Perry Como, Victor	55
59.	**AROUND THE WORLD,** Mantovani, London	58
59.	**PLEDGE OF LOVE,** Ken Copland, Imperial	74
61.	**AROUND THE WORLD,** Bing Crosby, Decca	72
61.	**COCOANUT WOMAN,** Harry Belafonte, Victor	59
63.	**FREIGHT TRAIN,** Charles McDevitt & Nancy Whiskey, Chic	44
63.	**ONE FOR MY BABY,** Tony Bennett, Columbia	66
65.	**EMPTY ARMS,** Ivory Joe Hunter, Atlantic	—
66.	**PARTY DOLL,** Buddy Knox, Roulette	56
67.	**LUCILLE,** Little Richard, Specialty	—
67.	**SEND FOR ME,** Nat (King) Cole, Capitol	49
69.	**WIND IN THE WILLOW,** Jo Stafford, Columbia	—
70.	**PARTY DOLL,** Steve Lawrence, Coral	—
70.	**WHOLE LOTTA SHAKIN' GOIN' ON,** Jerry Lee Lewis, Sun	—
72.	**MANGOS,** Rosemary Clooney, Columbia	43
72.	**GONNA FIND ME A BLUEBIRD,** Eddy Arnold, Victor	51
72.	**WHY, BABY, WHY?** Pat Boone, Dot	53
72.	**MY PERSONAL POSSESSION,** Nat (King) Cole, Capitol	70
76.	**LOVE IS A GOLDEN RING,** Frankie Laine, Columbia	—
76.	**WARM UP TO ME BABY,** Johnny Bowman, Roulette	57
76.	**WORDS OF LOVE,** Diamonds, Mercury	—
79.	**ISLAND IN THE SUN,** Harry Belafonte, Victor	60
80.	**MAMA LOOK-A BOOBOO,** Harry Belafonte, Victor	—
81.	**BILLY GOAT,** Bill Haley, Decca	75
81.	**FABULOUS,** Steve Lawrence, Coral	98
81.	**JUST BECAUSE,** Loyde Price, ABC-Paramount	—
81.	**LET IT BE ME,** Jill Corey, Columbia	94
81.	**YES, TONIGHT, JOSEPHINE,** Johnnie Ray, Columbia	38
81.	**LOVING YOU,** Elvis Presley, Victor	—
87.	**CHANTEZ, CHANTEZ,** Dinah Shore, Victor	80
87.	**DON'T CRY MY LOVE,** Vera Lynn, London	80
87.	**DON'T CALL ME SWEETIE,** Eileen Rodgers, Columbia	—
87.	**SHORT FAT FANNIE,** Larry Williams, Specialty	—
91.	**BYE BYE LOVE,** Webb Pierce, Decca	82
91.	**GONNA FIND ME A BLUEBIRD,** Joyce Hahn, Cadence	—
91.	**IT'S YOU I LOVE,** Fats Domino, Imperial	67
91.	**I'LL TAKE ROMANCE,** Eydie Gorme, ABC-Paramount	78
91.	**ROSIE-LEE,** Mello Tones, Gee	62
91.	***STARDUST,** Nat (King) Cole, Capitol	90
97.	**CRAZY LOVE,** Frank Sinatra, Capitol	—
97.	**FIRST DATE, FIRST KISS, FIRST LOVE,** Sonny James, Capitol	—
97.	**TILL,** Percy Faith, Columbia	95
100.	**BLUE MONDAY,** Fats Domino, Imperial	—

*** (Not available as a Pop Single. Available on Capitol EAP-2-824.)**

CAUTION TO DEALERS AND JUKE BOX OPERATORS

The Billboard's Top 100 is NOT designed to provide tested information for buying purposes. This function is most reliably served by other regular weekly features: Best Sellers in Stores, Most Played in Juke Boxes, Coming Up Strong and Best Buys.

STORE RECORDED SALES — NEW YORK UNIVERSITY SCHOOL OF RETAILING • THE BILLBOARD

Best Sellers in Stores

FOR SURVEY WEEK ENDING JUNE 22, 1957

The information given in this chart is based on actual sales to customers in a scientific sample of the nation's retail record outlets during the week ending on the date shown above. Sample design, sample size, and all methods used in this continuing study of retail record sales are under the direct and continuing supervision and control of the School of Retailing of New York University.

This Week		Last Week	Weeks on Chart
1.	**LOVE LETTERS IN THE SAND** (ASCAP) Pat Boone; **BERNARDINE** (ASCAP)—Dot 15570	1	8
2.	**BYE BYE LOVE** (BMI)—Everly Brothers; I Wonder if I Care as Much? (BMI)—Cadence 1315	2	6
3.	**SO RARE** (ASCAP)—Jimmy Dorsey; Sophisticated Swing (ASCAP)—Fraternity 755	3	12
4.	**TEDDY BEAR** (ASCAP)—Elvis Presley; **LOVING YOU** (BMI)—Vic 20-7000	23	2
5.	**SEARCHIN'** (BMI)—Coasters; **YOUNG BLOOD** (BMI)—Atco 6087	6	7
6.	**TEENAGER'S ROMANCE** (ASCAP)—Ricky Nelson; **I'M WALKIN'** (BMI)—Verve 10047	4	9
7.	**DARK MOON** (BMI)—Gale Storm; Little Too Late (BMI)—Dot 15558	7	9
8.	**ALL SHOOK UP** (BMI)—Elvis Presley; That's When Your Heartaches Begin (ASCAP)—Vic 20-6870	5	7
9.	**WHITE SPORT COAT** (BMI)—Marty Robbins; Grown-Up Tears (BMI)—Col 40864	8	10
10.	**VALLEY OF TEARS** (BMI)—Fats Domino; **IT'S YOU I LOVE** (BMI)—Imperial 5442	12	5
11.	**JENNY, JENNY** (BMI)—Little Richard; **MISS ANN** (BMI)—Specialty 606	20	2
12.	**START MOVIN'** (BMI)—Sal Mineo; **LOVE AFFAIR** (BMI)—Epic 9216	9	7
13.	**C. C. RIDER** (BMI)—Chuck Willis; Ease the Pain (BMI)—Atlantic 1130	13	4
13.	**I LIKE YOUR KIND OF LOVE** (BMI)—Andy Williams; Stop Teasin' Me (ASCAP)—Cadence 1323	11	4
15.	**LITTLE DARLIN'** (BMI)—Diamonds; Faithful and True (BMI)—Mercury 71060	10	17
16.	**IT'S NOT FOR ME TO SAY** (ASCAP)—Johnny Mathis; Warm and Tender (ASCAP)—Col 40851	26	6
17.	**OVER THE MOUNTAIN** (BMI)—Johnnie & Joe; My Baby's Gone On, On (BMI)—Chess 1664	19	6
18.	**FOUR WALLS** (BMI)—Jim Reeves; I Know and You Know (BMI)—Vic 20-6874	15	5
19.	**COME GO WITH ME** (BMI)—Del Vikings; How Can I Find True Love? (BMI)—Dot 15538	17	19
20.	**OLD CAPE COD** (ASCAP)—Patti Page; **WONDERING** (BMI)—Mercury 71101	13	4
21.	**SCHOOL DAY** (BMI)—Chuck Berry; Deep Feeling (BMI)—Chess 1653	18	12
21.	**I'M GONNA SIT RIGHT DOWN** (ASCAP)—Billy Williams; Date With the Blues (ASCAP)—Coral 61830	—	2
23.	**FREIGHT TRAIN** (ASCAP)—Rusty Draper; Seven Come Eleven (BMI)—Mercury 71102	21	5
24.	**MY DREAM** (ASCAP)—Platters; I Wanna (BMI)—Mercury 71093	29	2
24.	**SEND FOR ME** (BMI)—Nat (King) Cole; **MY PERSONAL POSSESSION** (BMI)—Cap 3737	—	1
26.	**GOIN' STEADY** (BMI)—Tommy Sands; **RING MY PHONE** (BMI)—Cap 3723	21	4
27.	**SUSIE Q** (BMI)—Dale Hawkins; Don't Treat Me This Way (BMI)—Checker 863	—	1
28.	**GIRL WITH THE GOLDEN BRAIDS** (ASCAP)—Perry Como; **MY LITTLE BABY** (BMI)—Vic 20-6904	26	2
29.	**LET THE FOUR WINDS BLOW** (BMI)—Roy Brown; Diddy-Y-Diddy-O (BMI)—Imperial 5439	—	1
30.	**ROCK YOUR LITTLE BABY TO SLEEP** (BMI)—Buddy Knox; Don't Make Me Cry (BMI)—Roulette 4009	—	2

Most Played by Jockeys

FOR SURVEY WEEK ENDING JUNE 22, 1957

SIDES are ranked in order of the greatest number of plays on disk jockey radio shows thruout the country. Results are based on The Billboard's weekly survey among the nation's disk jockeys. The reverse side of each record is also listed.

This Week		Last Week	Weeks on Chart
1.	**LOVE LETTERS IN THE SAND** (ASCAP)—Pat Boone; Bernardine (ASCAP)—Dot 15570	1	8
2.	**SO RARE** (ASCAP)—Jimmy Dorsey; Sophisticated Swing (ASCAP)—Fraternity 755	2	9
3.	**BYE BYE LOVE**—Everly Brothers; Cadence 1315 (BMI)	3	5
4.	**OLD CAPE COD** (ASCAP)—Patti Page; Wondering (BMI)—Mercury 71101	7	5
5.	**WHITE SPORT COAT** (BMI)—Marty Robbins; Grown Up Tears (BMI)—Col 40964	4	10
6.	**SEARCHIN'** (BMI)—Coasters; Young Blood (BMI)—Atco 6987	10	5
7.	**DARK MOON** (BMI)—Gale Storm; Little Too Late (BMI)—Dot 15558	8	8
8.	**ALL SHOOK UP** (BMI)—Elvis Presley; That's When Your Heartaches Begin (ASCAP)—Vic 20-6870	5	13
9.	**TEENAGER'S ROMANCE** (ASCAP)—Ricky Nelson; I'm Walkin' (BMI)—Verve 10047	11	5
10.	**I LIKE YOUR KIND OF LOVE** (BMI)—Andy Williams; Stop Teasin' Me (ASCAP)—Cadence 1323	22	3
11.	**IT'S NOT FOR ME TO SAY** (ASCAP)—Johnny Mathis; Warm and Tender (ASCAP)—Col 40851	6	6
12.	**I'M GONNA SIT RIGHT DOWN** (ASCAP)—Billy Williams; Dates With the Blues (ASCAP)—Coral 61830	23	3
13.	**FREIGHT TRAIN** (ASCAP)—Rusty Draper; Seven Come Eleven (BMI)—Mercury 71102	9	5
14.	**TEDDY BEAR** (BMI)—Elvis Presley; Loving You (BMI)—Victor 7000	—	1
15.	**DARK MOON** (BMI)—Bonnie Guitar; Big Mike (BMI)—Dot 15550	20	9
15.	**YOUNG BLOOD** (BMI)—Coasters; Searchin' (BMI)—Atco 6087	—	1
17.	**FOUR WALLS** (BMI)—Jim Reeves; I Know and You Know (BMI)—Vic 20-6874	14	7
18.	**WITH ALL MY HEART** (ASCAP)—Jodie Sands; More Than Only Friends (ASCAP)—Chancellor 1003	15	3
19.	**VALLEY OF TEARS** (BMI)—Fats Domino; It's You I Love (BMI)—Imperial 5442	19	4
20.	**LITTLE DARLIN'** (BMI)—Diamonds; Faithful and True (BMI)—Mercury 71060	12	15
21.	**ROCK YOUR BABY TO SLEEP** (BMI)—Buddy Knox; Don't Make Me Cry (BMI)—Roulette 4009	—	2
22.	**COME GO WITH ME** (BMI)—Del Vikings; How Can I Find True Love (BMI)—Dot 15538	—	11
23.	**GIRL WITH THE GOLDEN BRAIDS** (BMI)—Perry Como; My Little Baby (BMI)—Vic 20-6904	13	6
23.	**WONDERING** (BMI)—Patti Page; Old Cape Cod (ASCAP)—Mercury 71101	24	3
25.	**SCHOOL DAY** (BMI)—Chuck Berry; Deep Feeling (BMI)—Chess 1653	18	11

NEW YORK UNIVERSITY SCHOOL OF RETAILING · THE BILLBOARD · STORE RECORDED SALES

The Top 100 Sides

FOR SURVEY WEEK ENDING JUNE 22

A list of the top 100 record sides in the nation according to a tabulation of dealer unit sales. Its purpose primarily is to provide disk jockeys with additional programming material and to give trade exposure to newer sides just beginning to show action in the field. IT IS NOT A RECORD SALES CHART.

Pos.	Song, Artist and Label	Position Last Wk.
1.	**LOVE LETTERS IN THE SAND,** Pat Boone, Dot	1
2.	**BYE BYE LOVE,** Everly Brothers, Cadence	3
3.	**SO RARE,** Jimmy Dorsey, Fraternity	2
4.	**TEDDY BEAR,** Elvis Presley, Victor	47
5.	**WHITE SPORT COAT,** Marty Robbins, Columbia	5
6.	**ALL SHOOK UP,** Elvis Presley, Victor	4
7.	**DARK MOON,** Gale Storm, Dot	6
8.	**SEARCHIN',** Coasters, Atco	9
9.	**TEENAGER'S ROMANCE,** Ricky Nelson, Verve	8
10.	**START MOVIN',** Sal Mineo, Epic	12
11.	**I LIKE YOUR KIND OF LOVE,** Andy Williams, Cadence	14
12.	**LITTLE DARLIN',** Diamonds, Mercury	10
13.	**VALLEY OF TEARS,** Fats Domino, Imperial	16
14.	**C. C. RIDER,** Chuck Willis, Atlantic	29
15.	**FOUR WALLS,** Jim Reeves, Victor	13
16.	**OVER THE MOUNTAIN,** Johnnie & Joe, Chess	27
17.	**JENNY JENNY,** Little Richard, Specialty	36
17.	**OLD CAPE COD,** Patti Page, Mercury	7
19.	**SCHOOL DAY,** Chuck Berry, Chess	18
20.	**COME GO WITH ME,** Del Vikings, Dot	23
20.	**IT'S NOT FOR ME TO SAY,** Johnny Mathis, Columbia	17
22.	**YOUNG BLOOD,** Coasters, Atco	22
23.	**FREIGHT TRAIN,** Rusty Draper, Mercury	11
24.	**I'M WALKIN',** Ricky Nelson, Verve	37
25.	**GONE,** Ferlin Husky, Capitol	24
26.	**FABULOUS,** Charlie Gracie, Cameo	31
27.	**I'M GONNA SIT RIGHT DOWN (AND WRITE MYSELF A LETTER),** Billy Williams, Coral	26
28.	**MY DREAM,** Platters, Mercury	29
29.	**GOIN' STEADY,** Tommy Sands, Capitol	19
30.	**SUSIE Q,** Dale Hawkins, Checker	42
31.	**GONNA FIND ME A BLUEBIRD,** Marvin Rainwater, M-G-M	34
32.	**ROCK-A-BILLY,** Guy Mitchell, Columbia	45
33.	**ROCK YOUR LITTLE BABY TO SLEEP,** Buddy Knox, Roulette	25
34.	**ROUND AND ROUND,** Perry Como, Victor	27
34.	**WONDERFUL, WONDERFUL,** Johnny Mathis, Columbia	33
36.	**SHANGRI-LA,** Four Coins, Epic	53
36.	**WITH ALL MY HEART,** Jodie Sands, Chancellor	20
38.	**LET THE FOUR WINDS BLOW,** Roy Brown, Imperial	—
39.	**HE'S MINE,** Platters, Mercury	48
40.	**GIRL WITH THE GOLDEN BRAIDS,** Perry Como, Victor	15
41.	**I'M WALKIN',** Fats Domino, Imperial	48
42.	**DARK MOON,** Bonnie Guitar, Dot	21
43.	**JUST TO HOLD MY HAND,** Clyde McPhatter, Atlantic	57
44.	**BERNARDINE,** Pat Boone, Dot	37
45.	**FALLEN STAR,** Jimmy Newman, Dot	42
45.	**SEND FOR ME,** Nat (King) Cole, Capitol	67
47.	**LUCILLE,** Little Richard, Specialty	67
48.	**FOUR WALLS,** Jim Lowe, Dot	39
49.	**EMPTY ARMS,** Ivory Joe Hunter, Atlantic	65
49.	**SHORT FAT FANNIE,** Larry Williams, Specialty	87
51.	**LOVIN' YOU,** Elvis Presley, Victor	81
52.	**EMPTY ARMS,** Teresa Brewer, Coral	55
53.	**STARDUST,** Billy Ward, Liberty	—
53.	**WHOLE LOTTA SHAKIN' GOIN' ON,** Jerry Lee Lewis, Sun	70
55.	**CAN'T WAIT FOR SUMMER,** Steve Lawrence, Coral	46
56.	**WHY, BABY, WHY?** Pat Boone, Dot	72
56.	**MISS ANN,** Little Richard, Specialty	—
56.	**PARTY DOLL,** Buddy Knox, Roulette	66
59.	**I JUST DON'T KNOW,** Four Lads, Columbia	48
59.	**MAMA LOOK-A BOOBOO,** Harry Belafonte, Victor	80
61.	**COCOANUT WOMAN,** Harry Belafonte, Victor	61
61.	**IT'S YOU I LOVE,** Fats Domino, Imperial	91
61.	**WIND IN THE WILLOW,** Jo Stafford, Columbia	69
64.	**BILLY GOAT,** Bill Haley, Decca	81
65.	**JUST BECAUSE,** Loyde Price, ABC-Paramount	81
65.	**QUEEN OF THE SENIOR PROM,** Mills Brothers, Decca	48
67.	**AROUND THE WORLD,** Bing Crosby, Decca	61
67.	**YES, TONIGHT, JOSEPHINE,** Johnnie Ray, Columbia	81
69.	**EVERYONE'S LAUGHING,** Spaniels, Vee Jay	—
69.	**ISLAND IN THE SUN,** Harry Belafonte, Victor	79
71.	**BUTTERFLY,** Andy Williams, Cadence	—
71.	**FABULOUS,** Steve Lawrence, Coral	81
71.	**FIRST DATE, FIRST KISS, FIRST LOVE,** Sonny James, Capitol	97
71.	**TAMMY,** Ames Brothers, Victor	—
71.	**TOO MUCH,** Elvis Presley, Victor	—
76.	**AROUND THE WORLD,** Victor Young, Decca	44
76.	**ALMOST PARADISE,** Roger Williams, Kapp	41
76.	**JIM DANDY GOT MARRIED,** Laverne Baker, Atlantic	—
76.	**MY PERSONAL POSSESSION,** Nat (King) Cole, Capitol	72
76.	**SHISH KEBAB,** Ralph Marterie, Mercury	32
81.	**BYE BYE LOVE,** Webb Pierce, Decca	91
81.	**NINETY-NINE WAYS,** Tab Hunter, Dot	—
81.	**HYPNOTIZED,** Drifters, Atlantic	—
81.	**PLEDGE OF LOVE,** Ken Copeland, Imperial	59
85.	**AROUND THE WORLD,** Mantovani, London	59
85.	**BLUE MONDAY,** Fats Domino, Imperial	100
85.	**DEAREST,** Mickey & Sylvia, Vik	—
85.	**HOUND DOG,** Elvis Presley, Victor	—
85.	**LOVE IS A GOLDEN RING,** Frankie Laine, Columbia	76
85.	**MY LITTLE BABY,** Perry Como, Victor	57
85.	**PARTY DOLL,** Steve Lawrence, Coral	70
85.	**TEEN-AGE CRUSH,** Tommy Sands, Capitol	—
85.	**WARM UP TO ME BABY,** Jimmy Bowen, Roulette	76
85.	**YOUNG LOVE,** Tab Hunter, Dot	—
85.	**DON'T CRY MY LOVE,** Vera Lynn, London	87
95.	**LOVE ME TENDER,** Elvis Presley, Victor	—
95.	**SEND ME SOME LOVIN',** Little Richard, Specialty	—
95.	**WONDERING,** Patti Page, Mercury	35
99.	**GONNA FIND ME A BLUEBIRD,** Joyce Hahn, Cadence	91
99.	**NEXT IN LINE,** Johnny Cash, Sun	—

STORE RECORDED SALES — NEW YORK UNIVERSITY SCHOOL OF RETAILING · THE BILLBOARD

Best Sellers in Stores

The information given in this chart is based on actual sales to customers in a scientific sample of the nation's retail record outlets during the week ending on the date shown above. Sample design, sample size, and all methods used in this continuing study of retail record sales are under the direct and continuing supervision and control of the School of Retailing of New York University.

FOR SURVEY WEEK ENDING JUNE 29, 1957

This Week		Last Week	Weeks on Chart
1.	TEDDY BEAR (ASCAP)—Elvis Presley LOVING YOU (BMI)—Vic 20-7000	4	3
2.	BYE BYE LOVE (BMI)—Everly Brothers I WONDER IF I CARE AS MUCH (BMI)—Cadence 1315	2	7
3.	LOVE LETTERS IN THE SAND (ASCAP)—Pat Boone BERNARDINE (ASCAP)—Dot 15570	1	9
4.	SO RARE (ASCAP)—Jimmy Dorsey Sophisticated Swing (ASCAP)—Fraternity 755	3	13
5.	SEARCHIN' (BMI)—Coasters YOUNG BLOOD (BMI)—Atco 6087	5	8
6.	IT'S NOT FOR ME TO SAY (ASCAP) Johnny Mathis Warm and Tender (ASCAP)—Col 40851	16	7
7.	WHITE SPORT COAT (BMI)—Marty Robbins Grown Up Tears (BMI)—Col 40864	9	11
8.	VALLEY OF TEARS (BMI)—Fats Domino IT'S YOU I LOVE (BMI)—Imperial 5442	10	6
9.	I'M GONNA SIT RIGHT DOWN (ASCAP)—Billy Williams Date With the Blues (ASCAP)—Coral 61830	21	3
10.	JENNY, JENNY (BMI)—Little Richard MISS ANN (BMI)—Specialty 606	11	3
10.	OVER THE MOUNTAIN (BMI)—Johnnie & Joe My Baby's Gone On, On (BMI)—Chess 1664	17	7
10.	I LIKE YOUR KIND OF LOVE (BMI)—Andy Williams Stop Teasin' Me (ASCAP)—Cadence 1323	13	5
13.	OLD CAPE COD (ASCAP)—Patti Page WONDERING (BMI)—Mercury 71101	20	5
14.	ALL SHOOK UP (BMI)—Elvis Presley That's When Your Heartaches Begin (ASCAP)—Vic 20-6870	8	8
15.	DARK MOON (BMI)—Gale Storm Little Too Late (BMI)—Dot 15558	7	10
16.	TEENAGER'S ROMANCE (ASCAP)—Ricky Nelson I'M WALKIN (BMI)—Verve 10047	6	10
17.	C. C. RIDER (BMI)—Chuck Willis Ease the Pain (BMI)—Atlantic 1130	13	5
18.	SHORT FAT FANNIE (BMI)—Larry Williams High School Dance (BMI)—Specialty 608	—	1
19.	SEND FOR ME (BMI)—Nat (King) Cole MY PERSONAL POSSESSION (BMI)—Cap 3737	24	2
20.	START MOVIN' (BMI)—Sal Mineo LOVE AFFAIR (BMI)—Epic 9216	12	8
21.	LITTLE DARLIN' (BMI)—Diamonds Faithful and True (BMI)—Mercury 71060	15	18
22.	SHANGRI-LA (ASCAP)—Four Coins First In Line (ASCAP)—Epic 9213	—	1
23.	WONDERFUL, WONDERFUL (BMI)—Johnny Mathis When Sunny Gets Blue—Col 40784	—	4
24.	COME GO WITH ME (BMI)—Del Vikings How Can I Find True Love? (BMI)—Dot 15538	19	20
25.	FOUR WALLS (BMI)—Jim Reeves I Know and You Know (BMI)—Vic 20-6874	18	6
26.	SCHOOL DAY (BMI)—Chuck Berry Deep Feeling (BMI)—Chess 1653	21	13
27.	SUSIE Q (BMI)—Dale Hawkins Don't Treat Me This Way (BMI)—Checker 663	27	2
27.	JUST TO HOLD MY HAND (BMI)—Clyde McPhatter No Matter What (ASCAP)—Atlantic 1133	—	1
29.	WITH ALL MY HEART (ASCAP)—Jodie Sands More Than Only Friends (ASCAP)—Chancellor 1003	—	3
29.	COCOANUT WOMAN (ASCAP) Harry Belafonte ISLAND IN THE SUN (ASCAP)—Vic 20-6885	—	1

Most Played by Jockeys

SIDES are ranked in order of the greatest number of plays on disk jockey radio shows thruout the country. Results are based on The Billboard's weekly survey among the nation's disk jockeys. The reverse side of each record is also listed.

FOR SURVEY WEEK ENDING JUNE 29, 1957

This Week		Last Week	Weeks on Chart
1.	LOVE LETTERS IN THE SAND (ASCAP)—Pat Boone Bernardine (ASCAP)—Dot 15570	1	9
2.	SO RARE (ASCAP)—Jimmy Dorsey Sophisticated Swing (ASCAP)—Fraternity 755	2	10
3.	BYE BYE LOVE (BMI)—Everly Brothers I Wonder If I Care as Much? (BMI)—Cadence 1315	3	6
4.	OLD CAPE COD (ASCAP)—Patti Page Wondering (BMI)—Mercury 71101	4	6
5.	WHITE SPORT COAT (BMI)—Marty Robbins Grown Up Tears (BMI)—Col 40864	5	11
6.	TEDDY BEAR (ASCAP)—Elvis Presley Loving You (BMI)—Vic 7000	15	10
7.	SEARCHIN' (BMI)—Coasters Young Blood (BMI)—Atco 6987	6	6
8.	TEENAGER'S ROMANCE (ASCAP)—Ricky Nelson I'm Walkin' (BMI)—Verve 10047	9	6
9.	DARK MOON (BMI)— Little Too Late (BMI)—Dot 15558	7	9
10.	IT'S NOT FOR ME TO SAY (ASCAP)—Johnny Mathis Warm and Tender (ASCAP)—Col 40851	11	7
11.	I'M GONNA SIT RIGHT DOWN (ASCAP)—Billy Williams Date With the Blues (ASCAP)—Coral 61830	12	4
12.	I LIKE YOUR KIND OF LOVE (BMI)—Andy Williams Stop Teasin' Me (ASCAP)—Cadence 1323	10	4
13.	ALL SHOOK UP (BMI)—Elvis Presley That's When Your Heartaches Begin (ASCAP)—Vic 20-6870	8	14
14.	FREIGHT TRAIN (ASCAP)—Rusty Draper Seven Come Eleven (BMI)—Mercury 71102	13	6
15.	VALLEY OF TEARS (BMI)—Fats Domino It's You I Love (BMI)—Imperial 5442	19	5
16.	WITH ALL MY HEART (ASCAP) Jodie Sands More Than Only Friends (ASCAP)—Chancellor 1003	18	4
17.	ROCK YOUR BABY TO SLEEP (BMI)—Buddy Knox Don't Make Me Cry (BMI)—Roulette 4009	21	8
18.	YOUNG BLOOD (BMI)—Coasters Searchin' (BMI)—Atco 6087	15	2
19.	GIRL WITH THE GOLDEN BRAIDS (BMI)—Perry Como My Little Baby (BMI)—Vic 20-6904	23	7
20.	WONDERFUL, WONDERFUL (BMI) Johnny Mathis When Sunny Gets Blue (BMI)—Col 40784	—	3
20.	FOUR WALLS (BMI)—Jim Lowe Talking to the Blues (BMI)—Dot 15569	—	3
22.	GOIN' STEADY (BMI)—Tommy Sands Ring My Phone (BMI)—Cap 5723	—	2
23.	AROUND THE WORLD (ASCAP)—Victor Young Around the World (Vocal) (ASCAP)—Decca 30262	—	1
24.	START MOVIN' (BMI)—Sal Mineo Love Affair (BMI)—Epic 9216	26	5
25.	DARK MOON (BMI)—Bonnie Guitar Big Mike (BMI)—Dot 15550	15	10

STORE RECORDED SALES — NEW YORK UNIVERSITY SCHOOL OF RETAILING — THE BILLBOARD

TOP 100 SIDES

FOR SURVEY WEEK ENDING JUNE 29

This is a tabulation of dealer unit sales listed according to the specific side requested by customers. No attempt is made to add sides together to reflect actual record sales. It is therefore a tabulation of sides or songs, and not records. This fact, together with longer four-week survey periods, explains variation between the top 30 sides as reflected in this chart, and top 30 record sellers as reflected in "Best Sellers in Stores."

1.	**LOVE LETTERS IN THE SAND,** Pat Boone, Dot	1
2.	**BYE BYE LOVE,** Everly Brothers, Cadence	2
3.	**SO RARE,** Jimmy Dorsey, Fraternity	3
4.	**TEDDY BEAR,** Elvis Presley, Victor	4
5.	**WHITE SPORT COAT,** Marty Robbins, Columbia	5
6.	**ALL SHOOK UP,** Elvis Presley, Victor	6
7.	**SEARCHIN',** Coasters, Atco	8
8.	**DARK MOON,** Gale Storm, Dot	7
9.	**I LIKE YOUR KIND OF LOVE,** Andy Williams, Cadence	11
10.	**IT'S NOT FOR ME TO SAY,** Johnny Mathis, Columbia	20
11.	**OVER THE MOUNTAIN,** Johnnie & Joe, Chess	16
12.	**LITTLE DARLIN',** Diamonds, Mercury	12
12.	**TEENAGER'S ROMANCE,** Ricky Nelson, Verve	9
14.	**C. C. RIDER,** Chuck Willis, Atlantic	14
14.	**OLD CAPE COD,** Patti Page, Mercury	17
16.	**START MOVIN',** Sal Mineo, Epic	10
17.	**VALLEY OF TEARS,** Fats Domino, Imperial	13
18.	**I'M GONNA SIT RIGHT DOWN (AND WRITE MYSELF A LETTER),** Billy Williams, Coral	27
19.	**JENNY JENNY,** Little Richard, Specialty	17
20.	**COME GO WITH ME,** Del Vikings, Dot	20
21.	**FOUR WALLS,** Jim Reeves, Victor	15
22.	**SCHOOL DAY,** Chuck Berry, Chess	19
23.	**YOUNG BLOOD.** Coasters, Atco	22
24.	**FREIGHT TRAIN,** Rusty Draper, Mercury	23
24.	**SEND FOR ME,** Nat (King) Cole, Capitol	45
26.	**SHORT FAT FANNIE,** Larry Williams, Specialty	49
27.	**SHANGRI-LA,** Four Coins, Epic	36
28.	**WONDERFUL, WONDERFUL,** Johnny Mathis, Columbia	24
29.	**SUSIE-Q,** Dale Hawkins, Checker	30
30.	**JUST TO HOLD MY HAND,** Clyde McPhatter, Atlantic	43
31.	**FABULOUS,** Charlie Gracie, Cameo	26
31.	**WITH ALL MY HEART,** Jodie Sands, Chancellor	36
33.	**MY DREAM,** Platters, Mercury	28
34.	**GONNA FIND ME A BLUEBIRD,** Marvin Rainwater, M-G-M	31
35.	**GONE,** Ferlin Husky, Capitol	25
36.	**GOIN' STEADY,** Tommy Sands, Capitol	29
36.	**I'M WALKIN',** Ricky Nelson, Verve	24
38.	**ROCK YOUR LITTLE BABY TO SLEEP,** Buddy Knox, Roulette	33
39.	**LOVIN' YOU,** Elvis Presley, Victor	51
40.	**HE'S MINE,** Platters, Mercury	39
41.	**GIRL WITH THE GOLDEN BRAIDS,** Perry Como, Victor	40
42.	**BERNARDINE,** Pat Boone, Dot	44
42.	**FOUR WALLS,** Jim Lowe, Dot	48
44.	**ROCK-A-BILLY,** Guy Mitchell, Columbia	32
45.	**EMPTY ARMS,** Ivory Joe Hunter, Atlantic	49
46.	**WHOLE LOTTA SHAKIN' GOIN' ON,** Jerry Lee Lewis, Sun	53
47.	**FALLEN STAR,** Jimmy Newman, Dot	45
47.	**JUST BECAUSE,** Loyde Price, ABC-Paramount	65
47.	**LET THE FOUR WINDS BLOW,** Roy Brown, Imperial	38
47.	**ROUND AND ROUND,** Perry Como, Victor	34
51.	**STARDUST,** Billy Ward, Liberty	53
52.	**DARK MOON,** Bonnie Guitar, Dot	42
53.	**COCOANUT WOMAN,** Harry Belafonte, Victor	61
53.	**I'M WALKIN',** Fats Domino, Imperial	41
55.	**IT'S YOU I LOVE,** Fats Domino, Imperial	61
56.	**LUCILLE,** Little Richard, Specialty	47
57.	**AROUND THE WORLD,** Mantovani, London,	85
58.	**WHY, BABY, WHY?** Pat Boone, Dot	56
59.	**CAN'T WAIT FOR SUMMER,** Steve Lawrence, Coral	55
60.	**PARTY DOLL,** Buddy Knox, Roulette	56
60.	**EMPTY ARMS,** Teresa Brewer, Coral	52
62.	**ISLAND IN THE SUN,** Harry Belafonte, Victor	69
62.	**MAMA LOOK-A BOOBOO,** Harry Belafonte, Victor	59
64.	**I JUST DON'T KNOW.** Four Lads, Columbia	59
64.	**MISS ANN,** Little Richard, Specialty	56
66.	**WHISPERING BELLS,** Del Vikings, Dot	—
67.	**AROUND THE WORLD,** Bing Crosby, Decca	67
67.	**SUN IS SHINING,** Jim Reed, Vee Jay	—
69.	**BILLY GOAT,** Bill Haley, Decca	64
69.	**SHISH KEBAB,** Ralph Marterie, Mercury	76
71.	**QUEEN OF THE SENIOR PROM,** Mills Brothers, Decca	65
72.	**TAMMY,** Ames Brothers, Victor	71
72.	**WIND IN THE WILLOW,** Jo Stafford, Columbia	61
74.	**AROUND THE WORLD,** Victor Young, Decca	76
74.	**WHAT CAN I DO,** Donnie Elbert, Deluxe	—
74.	**YES, TONIGHT, JOSEPHINE,** Johnnie Ray, Columbia	67
77.	**IT HURTS TO BE IN LOVE,** Annie Laurie, Deluxe	—
77.	**SEND ME SOME LOVIN',** Little Richard, Specialty	95
79.	**EVERYONE'S LAUGHING,** Spaniels, Vee Jay	69
79.	**JIM DANDY GOT MARRIED,** Laverne Baker, Atlantic	76
79.	**HYPNOTIZED,** Drifters, Atlantic	81
79.	**PLEASE SEND ME SOMEONE TO LOVE,** Moonglows, Chess	—
83.	**CAN I COME OVER,** Velours, Omyx	—
83.	**MY LITTLE BABY,** Perry Como, Victor	85
83.	**NEXT TIME YOU SEE ME,** Little Jr. Parker, Duke	—
83.	**TOO MUCH,** Elvis Presley, Victor	71
87.	**BUTTERFLY,** Andy Williams, Cadence,	71
87.	**ALMOST PARADISE,** Roger Williams, Kapp	76
87.	**DEAREST,** Mickey & Sylvia, Vik	85
87.	**FALLEN STAR,** Ferlin Husky, Capitol	—
87.	**PLEDGE OF LOVE,** Ken Copeland, Imperial	81
92.	**BLUE MONDAY,** Fats Domino, Imperial	85
92.	**FABULOUS,** Steve Lawrence, Coral	71
92.	**FIRST DATE, FIRST KISS, FIRST LOVE,** Sonny James, Capitol	71
92.	**HOUND DOG,** Elvis Presley, Victor	85
92.	**MY PERSONAL POSSESSION,** Nat (King) Cole, Capitol	76
92.	**ONE FOR MY BABY,** Tony Bennett, Columbia	—
92.	**PARTY DOLL,** Steve Lawrence, Coral	85
92.	**TALKIN' TO THE BLUES,** Jim Lowe, Dot	—
100.	**DON'T CRY MY LOVE,** Vera Lynn, London	85

NEW YORK UNIVERSITY SCHOOL OF RETAILING — STORE RECORDED SALES — THE BILLBOARD

Best Sellers in Stores

FOR SURVEY WEEK ENDING JULY 6, 1957

The information given in this chart is based on actual sales to customers in a scientific sample of the nation's retail record outlets during the week ending on the date shown above. Sample design, sample size, and all methods used in this continuing study of retail record sales are under the direct and continuing supervision and control of the School of Retailing of New York University.

This Week		Last Week	Weeks on Chart
1.	TEDDY BEAR (ASCAP) / LOVING YOU (BMI) — Elvis Presley—Vic 20-7000	1	4
2.	LOVE LETTERS IN THE SAND (ASCAP) / BERNARDINE (ASCAP) — Pat Boone—Dot 15570	3	10
3.	SO RARE (ASCAP)—Jimmy Dorsey — Sophisticated Swing (ASCAP)—Fraternity 755	4	14
4.	BYE BYE LOVE (BMI)—Everly Brothers — I Wonder If I Care as Much (BMI)—Cadence 1315	2	8
5.	SEARCHIN' (BMI) / YOUNG BLOOD (BMI) — Coasters—Atco 6087	5	9
6.	IT'S NOT FOR ME TO SAY (ASCAP)—Johnny Mathis — Warm and Tender (ASCAP)—Col 40851	6	8
7.	I'M GONNA SIT RIGHT DOWN (ASCAP)—Billy Williams — Date With the Blues (ASCAP)—Coral 61830	9	4
8.	SEND FOR ME (BMI) / MY PERSONAL POSSESSION (BMI) — Nat (King) Cole—Cap 3737	19	3
9.	OVER THE MOUNTAIN (BMI)—Johnnie & Joe — My Baby's Gone On, On (BMI)—Chess 1664	10	8
10.	SHORT FAT FANNIE (BMI)—Larry Williams — High School Dance (BMI)—Specialty 608	18	2
11.	OLD CAPE COD (ASCAP) / WONDERING (BMI) — Patti Page—Mercury 71101	13	6
12.	WHITE SPORT COAT (BMI)—Marty Robbins — Grown-Up Tears (BMI)—Col 40864	7	12
13.	VALLEY OF TEARS (BMI) / IT'S YOU I LOVE (BMI) — Fats Domino—Imperial 5442	8	7
14.	DARK MOON (BMI)—Gale Storm — Little Too Late (BMI)—Dot 15559	15	11
15.	JENNY, JENNY (BMI) / MISS ANN (BMI) — Little Richard—Specialty 606	10	4
16.	C. C. RIDER (BMI)—Chuck Willis — Ease the Pain (BMI)—Atlantic 1130	17	6
17.	I LIKE YOUR KIND OF LOVE (BMI)—Andy Williams — Stop Teasin' Me (ASCAP)—Cadence 1323	10	6
17.	ALL SHOOK UP (BMI)—Elvis Presley — That's When Your Heartaches Begin (ASCAP) Vic 20-6870	14	9
19.	WONDERFUL, WONDERFUL (BMI)—Johnny Mathis — When Sunny Gets Blue (BMI)—Col 40784	23	5
20.	COME GO WITH ME (BMI)—Del Vikings — How Can I Find True Love? (BMI)—Dot 15538	24	21
21.	LITTLE DARLIN' (BMI)—Diamonds — Faithful and True (BMI)—Mercury 71060	21	19
22.	WHISPERING BELLS (BMI)—Del Vikings — Don't Be a Fool (BMI)—Dot 15592	—	1
23.	TEENAGER'S ROMANCE (ASCAP) / I'M WALKIN' (BMI) — Ricky Nelson—Verve 10047	16	11
24.	START MOVIN' (BMI) / LOVE AFFAIR (BMI) — Sal Mineo—Epic 9216	20	9
25.	COCOANUT WOMAN (ASCAP) / ISLAND IN THE SUN (ASCAP) — Harry Belafonte—Vic 20-6885	29	2
26.	JUST TO HOLD MY HAND (BMI)—Clyde McPhatter — No Matter What (ASCAP)—Atlantic 1133	27	2
27.	MY DREAM (ASCAP) / I WANNA (BMI) — Platters—Mer 71093	—	2
28.	WITH ALL MY HEART (ASCAP)—Jodie Sands — More Than Only Friends (ASCAP)—Chancellor 1003	29	4
29.	SHANGRI-LA (ASCAP)—Four Coins — First in Line (ASCAP)—Epic 9213	22	2
30.	WHOLE LOTTA SHAKIN' GOIN' ON (BMI)—Jerry Lee Lewis — It'll Be Me (BMI)—Sun 267	—	1

Most Played by Jockeys

FOR SURVEY WEEK ENDING JULY 6, 1957

SIDES are ranked in order of the greatest number of plays on disk jockey radio shows thruout the country. Results are based on The Billboard's weekly survey among the nation's disk jockeys. The reverse side of each record is also listed.

This Week		Last Week	Weeks on Chart
1.	LOVE LETTERS IN THE SAND (ASCAP)—Pat Boone — Bernardine (ASCAP)—Dot 15570	1	10
2.	BYE BYE LOVE (BMI)—Everly Brothers — I Wonder If I Care as Much (BMI)—Cadence 1315	3	7
3.	SO RARE (ASCAP)—Jimmy Dorsey — Sophisticated Swing (ASCAP)—Fraternity 755	2	11
4.	TEDDY BEAR (ASCAP)—Elvis Presley — Loving You (BMI)—Vic 7000	6	11
5.	OLD CAPE COD (ASCAP)—Patti Page — Wondering (BMI)—Mercury 71101	4	7
6.	I'M GONNA SIT RIGHT DOWN (ASCAP)—Billy Williams — Date With the Blues (ASCAP)—Coral 61830	11	5
7.	FREIGHT TRAIN (ASCAP)—Rusty Draper — Seven Come Eleven (BMI)—Mercury 71102	14	7
8.	I LIKE YOUR KIND OF LOVE (BMI)—Andy Williams — Stop Teasin' Me (ASCAP)—Cadence 1323	12	5
9.	IT'S NOT FOR ME TO SAY (ASCAP)—Johnny Mathis — Warm and Tender (ASCAP)—Col 40851	10	8
10.	SEARCHIN' (BMI)—Coasters — Young Blood (BMI)—Atco 6987	7	7
11.	TEENAGER'S ROMANCE (ASCAP)—Ricky Nelson — I'm Walkin' (BMI)—Verve 10047	8	7
12.	COOL SHAKE (ASCAP) / JITTERBUG MARY (BMI) — Del Vikings—Mercury 71132	—	1
13.	VALLEY OF TEARS (BMI)—Fats Domino — It's You I Love (BMI)—Imperial 5442	15	6
13.	WHITE SPORT COAT (BMI)—Marty Robbins — Grown-Up Tears (BMI)—Col 40864	5	12
15.	WORDS OF LOVE (BMI) / DON'T SAY GOODBYE (BMI) — Diamonds—Mercury 71128	—	1
16.	DARK MOON (BMI)—Gale Storm — Little Too Late (BMI)—Dot 15558	9	10
17.	WONDERFUL, WONDERFUL (BMI)—Johnny Mathis — When Sunny Gets Blue (BMI)—Col 40784	20	4
18.	WONDERING (BMI)—Patti Page — Old Cape Cod (ASCAP)—Mercury 71101	—	4
18.	SHANGRI-LA (ASCAP) / FIRST IN LINE (ASCAP) — Four Coins—Epic 9213	—	1
20.	SEND FOR ME (BMI) / MY PERSONAL POSSESSION (BMI) — Nat (King) Cole—Cap 3737	—	1
20.	FALLEN STAR (BMI) / LET ME HOLD YOU IN MY ARMS (BMI) — Nick Noble—Mercury 71124	—	1
22.	YOUNG BLOOD (BMI)—Coasters — Searchin' (BMI)—Atco 6087	18	3
23.	ROCK YOUR BABY TO SLEEP (BMI) / DON'T MAKE ME CRY (BMI) — Buddy Knox—Roulette 4009	17	4
23.	ALL SHOOK UP (BMI)—Elvis Presley — That's When Your Heartaches Begin (ASCAP)—Vic 20-6870	13	15
25.	WITH ALL MY HEART (ASCAP)—Jodie Sands — More Than Only Friends (ASCAP)—Chancellor 1003	16	5

NEW YORK UNIVERSITY SCHOOL OF RETAILING — STORE RECORDED SALES — THE BILLBOARD

Top 100 Sides

FOR SURVEY WEEK ENDING JULY 6

This is a tabulation of dealer unit sales listed according to the specific side requested by customers. No attempt is made to add sides together to reflect actual record sales. It is therefore a tabulation of sides or songs, and not records. This fact, together with longer four-week survey periods, explains variation between the top 30 sides as reflected in this chart, and top 30 record sellers as reflected in "Best Sellers in Stores."

Pos.	Song, Artist and Label	Pos. Last Wk.
1.	**TEDDY BEAR,** Elvis Presley, Victor	4
2.	**LOVE LETTERS IN THE SAND,** Pat Boone, Dot	1
3.	**SO RARE,** Jimmy Dorsey, Fraternity	3
4.	**BYE BYE LOVE,** Everly Brothers, Cadence	2
5.	**IT'S NOT FOR ME TO SAY,** Johnny Mathis, Columbia	10
6.	**SEARCHIN',** Coasters, Atco	7
7.	**DARK MOON,** Gale Storm, Dot	8
8.	**WHITE SPORT COAT,** Marty Robbins, Columbia	5
9.	**I'M GONNA SIT RIGHT DOWN (AND WRITE MYSELF A LETTER,** Billy Williams, Coral	18
10.	**ALL SHOOK UP,** Elvis Presley, Victor	6
11.	**OVER THE MOUNTAIN,** Johnnie & Joe, Chess	11
12.	**C. C. RIDER,** Chuck Willis, Atlantic	14
13.	**I LIKE YOUR KIND OF LOVE,** Andy Williams, Cadence	9
14.	**SEND FOR ME,** Nat (King) Cole, Capitol	24
15.	**OLD CAPE COD,** Patti Page, Mercury	14
16.	**LITTLE DARLIN',** Diamonds, Mercury	12
17.	**SHORT FAT FANNY,** Larry Williams, Specialty	26
18.	**JENNY JENNY,** Little Richard, Specialty	19
19.	**COME GO WITH ME,** Del Vikings, Dot	20
20.	**START MOVIN',** Sal Mineo, Epic	16
21.	**TEENAGER'S ROMANCE,** Ricky Nelson, Verve	12
21.	**VALLEY OF TEARS,** Fats Domino, Imperial	17
23.	**WONDERFUL, WONDERFUL,** Johnny Mathis, Columbia	28
24.	**YOUNG BLOOD,** Coasters, Atco	23
25.	**FOUR WALLS,** Jim Reeves, Victor	21
26.	**MY DREAM,** Platters, Mercury	33
27.	**SCHOOL DAY,** Chuck Berry, Chess	22
28.	**SHANGRI-LA,** Four Coins, Epic	27
29.	**SUSIE-Q,** Dale Hawkins, Checker	29
29.	**WITH ALL MY HEART,** Jodie Sands, Chancellor	31
31.	**JUST TO HOLD MY HAND,** Clyde McPhatter, Atlantic	30
31.	**WHISPERING BELLS,** Del Vikings, Dot	66
33.	**FREIGHT TRAIN,** Dusty Draper, Mercury	24
34.	**WHOLE LOTTA SHAKIN' GOIN' ON,** Jerry Lee Lewis, Sun	46
35.	**GONNA FIND ME A BLUEBIRD,** Marvin Rainwater, M-G-M	34
35.	**LOVING YOU,** Elvis Presley, Victor	39
37.	**STARDUST,** Billy Ward, Liberty	51
38.	**BERNARDINE,** Pat Boone, Dot	42
39.	**ROCK YOUR LITTLE BABY TO SLEEP,** Buddy Knox, Roulette	38
40.	**GOIN' STEADY,** Tommy Sands, Capitol	36
40.	**GIRL WITH THE GOLDEN BRAIDS,** Perry Como, Victor	41
42.	**FOUR WALLS,** Jim Lowe, Dot	42
43.	**FALLEN STAR,** Jim Newman, Dot	47
43.	**IT'S YOU I LOVE,** Fats Domino, Imperial	55
45.	**GONE,** Ferlin Husky, Capitol	35
46.	**FABULOUS,** Charlie Gracie, Cameo	31
47.	**LET THE FOUR WINDS BLOW,** Roy Brown, Imperial	47
48.	**COCOANUT WOMAN,** Harry Belafonte, Victor	53
48.	**I'M WALKIN',** Ricky Nelson, Verve	36
50.	**AROUND THE WORLD,** Mantovani, London	57
51.	**DARK MOON,** Bonnie Guitar, Dot	52
52.	**HE'S MINE,** Platters, Mercury	40
53.	**ROUND AND ROUND,** Perry Como, Victor	47
54.	**EMPTY ARMS,** Ivory Joe Hunter, Atlantic	45
55.	**JUST BECAUSE,** Lloyd Price, ABC-Paramount	47
55.	**ROCK-A-BILLY,** Guy Mitchell, Columbia	44
57.	**AROUND THE WORLD,** Bing Crosby, Decca	67
57.	**WHITE SILVER SANDS,** Dave Gardner, OJ	—
59.	**TAMMY,** Ames Brothers, Victor	72
60.	**MISS ANN,** Little Richard, Specialty	64
61.	**I'M WALKIN',** Fats Domino, Imperial	53
61.	**LUCILLE,** Little Richard, Specialty	56
63.	**WHY, BABY, WHY?** Pat Boone, Dot	58
63.	**ISLAND IN THE SUN,** Harry Belafonte, Victor	62
65.	**MAMA LOOK-A-BOOBOO,** Harry Belafonte, Victor	62
65.	**SUN IS SHINING,** Jim Reed, Vee Jay	67
67.	**AROUND THE WORLD,** Victor Young, Decca	74
67.	**WHAT CAN I DO?** Donnie Elbert, Deluxe	74
69.	**CAN'T WAIT FOR SUMMER,** Steve Lawrence, Coral	59
70.	**I JUST DON'T KNOW,** Four Lads, Columbia	64
71.	**PARTY DOLL,** Buddy Knox, Roulette	60
71.	**SEND ME SOME LOVIN',** Little Richard, Specialty	77
73.	**EMPTY ARMS,** Teresa Brewer, Coral	60
73.	**IT HUPTS TO BE IN LOVE,** Annie Laurie, Deluxe	77
75.	**DON'T ASK ME,** Duvs, Gone	—
76.	**BILLY GOAT,** Bill Haley Decca	69
77.	**SHISH KEBAB,** Ralph Marterie, Mercury	69
78.	**DIANA,** Paul Anka, ABC-Paramount	—
78.	**EVERYBODY'S SOMEBODY'S FOOL,** Heartbeats, Hall	—
78.	**PLEASE SEND ME SOMEONE TO LOVE,** Moonglows, Chess	79
81.	**EVERYONE'S LAUGHING,** Spaniels, Vee Jay	79
81.	**MY PERSONAL POSSESSION,** Nat (King) Cole, Capitol	92
81.	**QUEEN OF THE SENIOR PROM,** Mills Brothers, Decca	71
84.	**ONE FOR MY BABY,** Tony Bennett, Columbia	92
85.	**FALLEN STAR,** Ferlin Husky, Capitol	87
86.	**CAN I COME OVER?** Velours, Omyx	83
86.	**DYNAMITE,** Brenda Lee, Decca	—
86.	**SWEETEST ONE,** Crests, Joyce	—
89.	**DESIRE,** Charts, Everlast	—
89.	**FRAULEIN,** Bobby Helms, Decca	—
89.	**TEARDROPS FROM MY HEART,** Teresa Brewer, Coral	—
89.	**TALKIN' TO THE BLUES,** Jim Lowe, Dot	92
93.	**FALLEN STAR,** Hilltoppers, Dot	—
93.	**RANG TANG DING DONG,** Cellos, Apollo	—
93.	**YES, TONIGHT, JOSEPHINE,** Johnnie Ray, Columbia	74
96.	**ROCKIN' SHOES,** Ames Brothers, Victor	—
97.	**NEXT TIME YOU SEE ME,** Little Jr. Parker, Duke	83
97.	**SUMMER LOVE,** Joni James, Vocal	—
97.	**WHITE SILVER SANDS,** Don Rondo, Jubilee	—
100.	**NEXT IN LINE,** Johnny Cash, Sun	—
100.	**SO STRANGE,** Jesters, Winley	—

NEW YORK UNIVERSITY SCHOOL OF RETAILING · STORE RECORDED SALES · THE BILLBOARD

Best Sellers in Stores

FOR SURVEY WEEK ENDING JULY 13, 1957

The information given in this chart is based on actual sales to customers in a scientific sample of the nation's retail record outlets during the week ending on the date shown above. Sample design, sample size, and all methods used in this continuing study of retail record sales are under the direct and continuing supervision and control of the School of Retailing of New York University.

This Week	Title	Last Week	Weeks on Chart
1.	TEDDY BEAR (ASCAP) / LOVING YOU (BMI) — Elvis Presley—Vic 20-7000	1	5
2.	LOVE LETTERS IN THE SAND (ASCAP) / BERNARDINE (ASCAP) — Pat Boone—Dot 15570	2	11
3.	BYE BYE LOVE (BMI)—Everly Brothers — I Wonder If I Care as Much (BMI)—Cadence 1315	4	9
4.	SO RARE (ASCAP)—Jimmy Dorsey — Sophisticated Swing (ASCAP)—Fraternity 755	3	15
5.	SEARCHIN' (BMI) / YOUNG BLOOD (BMI) — Coasters—Atco 6187	5	10
6.	IT'S YOU I LOVE (BMI) / VALLEY OF TEARS (BMI) — Fats Domino—Imperial 5442	—	8
7.	SEND FOR ME (BMI) / MY PERSONAL POSSESSION (BMI) — Nat (King) Cole—Cap 3737	8	4
8.	OLD CAPE COD (ASCAP) / WONDERING (BMI) — Patti Page—Mercury 71101	11	7
9.	OVER THE MOUNTAIN (BMI)—Johnnie & Joe — My Baby's Gone On, On (BMI)—Chess 1654	9	9
10.	DARK MOON (BMI)—Gale Storm — Little Too Late (BMI)—Dot 15558	14	12
11.	SHORT FAT FANNIE (BMI)—Larry Williams — High School Dance (BMI)—Specialty 608	10	3
12.	IT'S NOT FOR ME TO SAY (ASCAP)—Johnny Mathis — Warm and Tender (ASCAP)—Col 40851	6	9
13.	JENNY, JENNY (BMI) / MISS ANN (BMI) — Little Richard—Specialty 606	15	5
14.	TEENAGER'S ROMANCE (ASCAP) / I'M WALKIN' (BMI) — Ricky Nelson—Verve 10047	23	12
15.	WHITE SPORT COAT (BMI)—Marty Robbins — Grown Up Tears (BMI)—Col 40864	12	13
16.	C. C. RIDER (BMI)—Chuck Willis — Ease the Pain (BMI)—Atlantic 1130	16	7
17.	I'M GONNA SIT RIGHT DOWN (ASCAP)—Billy Williams — Date With the Blues (ASCAP)—Coral 61830	7	5
18.	WONDERFUL, WONDERFUL (BMI)—Johnny Mathis — When Sunny Gets Blue—Col 40784	19	5
19.	WHISPERING BELLS (BMI)—Del Vikings — Don't Be a Fool (BMI)—Dot 15592	22	2
20.	ALL SHOOK UP (BMI)—Elvis Presley — That's When Your Heartaches Begin (ASCAP)—Vic 20-6870	17	10
21.	AROUND THE WORLD (ASCAP) / (VOCAL) (ASCAP) — Victor Young—Decca 30262	—	1
22.	COME GO WITH ME (BMI)—Del Vikings — How Can I Find True Love? (BMI)—Dot 15538	20	22
23.	LITTLE DARLIN' (BMI)—Diamonds — Faithful and True (BMI)—Mercury 71060	21	20
24.	STARDUST (ASCAP)—Billy Ward — Lucinda (BMI)—Liberty 55071	—	1
25.	START MOVIN' (BMI)—Sal Mineo — Love Affair (BMI)—Epic 9216	24	10
26.	MY DREAM (ASCAP) / I WANNA (BMI) — Platters—Mer 71093	27	3
27.	GONNA FIND ME A BLUEBIRD (BMI)—Marvin Rainwater — So You Think You've Got Trouble (BMI)—M-G-M 12412	—	1
28.	FREIGHT TRAIN (ASCAP)—Rusty Draper — Seven Come Eleven (BMI)—Mercury 71102	—	4
29.	WHITE SILVER SANDS (BMI)—Dave Gardner — Fat Charlie—OJ 1002	—	1
30.	FOUR WALLS (BMI)—Jim Reeves — I Know and You Know (BMI)—Vic 20-6874	—	7
30.	AROUND THE WORLD (ASCAP)—Mantovani — The Road to Ballingarry (ASCAP)—London 1746	—	1
30.	ISLAND IN THE SUN (ASCAP) / COCOANUT WOMAN (ASCAP) — Harry Belafonte—Vic 6885	—	3

Most Played by Jockeys

FOR SURVEY WEEK ENDING JULY 13, 1957

SIDES are ranked in order of the greatest number of plays on disk jockey radio shows thruout the country. Results are based on The Billboard's weekly survey among the nation's disk jockeys. The reverse side of each record is also listed.

This Week	Title	Last Week	Weeks on Chart
1.	LOVE LETTERS IN THE SAND (ASCAP)—Pat Boone — Bernardine (ASCAP)—Dot 15570	1	11
2.	TEDDY BEAR (ASCAP)—Elvis Presley — Loving You (BMI)—Vic 7000	4	12
3.	BYE BYE LOVE (BMI)—Everly Brothers — I Wonder If I Care as Much (BMI)—Cadence 1315	2	8
4.	SO RARE (ASCAP)—Jimmy Dorsey — Sophisticated Swing (ASCAP)—Fraternity 755	3	12
5.	OLD CAPE COD (ASCAP)—Patti Page — Wondering (BMI)—Mercury 71101	5	8
6.	I'M GONNA SIT RIGHT DOWN (ASCAP)—Billy Williams — Date With the Blues (ASCAP)—Coral 61830	6	5
7.	IT'S NOT FOR ME TO SAY (ASCAP)—Johnny Mathis — Warm and Tender (ASCAP)—Col 40851	9	9
8.	SEARCHIN' (BMI)—Coasters — Young Blood (BMI)—Atco 6987	10	8
9.	SEND FOR ME (BMI)—Nat (King) Cole — My Personal Possession (BMI)—Cap 3737	20	2
10.	I LIKE YOUR KIND OF LOVE (BMI)—Andy Williams — Stop Teasin' Me (ASCAP)—Cadence 1323	8	6
11.	SHANGRI-LA (ASCAP)—Four Coins — First in Line (ASCAP)—Epic 9213	18	2
12.	TAMMY (ASCAP)—Debbie Reynolds — French Heels (ASCAP)—Coral 61851	—	1
13.	AROUND THE WORLD (ASCAP)—Victor Young — Around the World (Vocal) (ASCAP)—Dec 30262	—	2
14.	DARK MOON (BMI)—Gale Storm — Little Too Late (BMI)—Dot 15558	16	11
14.	WONDERFUL, WONDERFUL (BMI)—Johnny Mathis — When Sunny Gets Blue (BMI)—Col 40784	17	15
16.	TEENAGER'S ROMANCE (ASCAP)—Ricky Nelson — I'm Walkin' (BMI)—Verve 10047	11	8
17.	WITH ALL MY HEART (ASCAP)—Jodie Sands — More Than Only Friends (ASCAP)—Chancellor 1003	25	6
18.	TAMMY (ASCAP)—Ames Brothers — Rockin' Shoes (BMI)—Vic 6930	—	1
19.	FREIGHT TRAIN (ASCAP)—Rusty Draper — Seven Come Eleven (BMI)—Mercury 71102	7	8
20.	LOVING YOU (BMI)—Elvis Presley — Teddy Bear (ASCAP)—Vic 7000	—	1
21.	SHORT FAT FANNIE (BMI)—Larry Williams — High School Dance (BMI)—Specialty 608	—	1
22.	AROUND THE WORLD (ASCAP)—Mantovani — The Road to Ballinganny (ASCAP)—London 1746	—	1
23.	FALLEN STAR (BMI)—Jimmy Newman — I Can't Go On This Way (ASCAP)—Dot 15574	—	1
24.	BERNARDINE (ASCAP)—Pat Boone — Love Letters in the Sand (ASCAP)—Dot 15570	—	3
25.	YOU'RE CHEATIN' YOURSELF (ASCAP)—Frank Sinatra — Something Wonderful Happens (ASCAP)—Cap 3744	—	1

STORE RECORDED SALES — NEW YORK UNIVERSITY SCHOOL OF RETAILING — THE BILLBOARD

Top 100 Sides

FOR SURVEY WEEK ENDING JULY 13

This is a tabulation of dealer unit sales listed according to the specific side requested by customers. No attempt is made to add sides together to reflect actual record sales. It is therefore a tabulation of sides or songs, and not records. This fact, together with longer four-week survey periods, explains variation between the top 30 sides as reflected in this chart, and top 30 record sellers as reflected in "Best Sellers in Stores."

Pos.	Song, Artist and Label	Pos. Last Wk.
1.	**TEDDY BEAR,** Elvis Presley, Victor	1
2.	**LOVE LETTERS IN THE SAND,** Pat Boone, Dot	2
3.	**BYE BYE LOVE,** Everly Brothers, Cadence	4
4.	**SO RARE,** Jimmy Dorsey, Fraternity	3
5.	**SEARCHIN',** Coasters, Atco	6
6.	**IT'S NOT FOR ME TO SAY,** Johnny Mathis, Columbia	5
7.	**SEND FOR ME,** Nat (King) Cole, Capitol	14
8.	**OVER THE MOUNTAIN,** Johnnie & Joe, Chess	11
9.	**OLD CAPE COD,** Patti Page, Mercury	15
10.	**DARK MOON,** Gale Storm, Dot	7
11.	**SHORT FAT FANNIE,** Larry Williams, Specialty	17
12.	**WHITE SPORT COAT,** Marty Robbins, Columbia	8
13.	**I'M GONNA SIT RIGHT DOWN,** Billy Williams, Coral	9
14.	**C. C. RIDER,** Chuck Willis, Atlantic	12
15.	**ALL SHOOK UP,** Elvis Presley, Victor	10
16.	**JENNY JENNY,** Little Richard, Specialty	18
17.	**WONDERFUL, WONDERFUL,** Johnny Mathis, Columbia	23
18.	**VALLEY OF TEARS,** Fats Domino, Imperial	21
19.	**YOUNG BLOOD,** Coasters, Atco	24
20.	**I LIKE YOUR KIND OF LOVE,** Andy Williams, Cadence	13
21.	**LITTLE DARLIN',** Diamonds, Mercury	16
22.	**IT'S YOU I LOVE,** Fats Domino, Imperial	43
23.	**COME GO WITH ME,** Del Vikings, Dot	19
24.	**TEENAGER'S ROMANCE,** Ricky Nelson, Verve	21
25.	**START MOVIN',** Sal Mineo, Epic	20
26.	**WHISPERING BELLS,** Del Vikings, Dot	31
27.	**SHANGRI-LA,** Four Coins, Epic	28
28.	**STARDUST,** Billy Ward, Liberty	37
29.	**MY DREAM,** Platters, Mercury	26
30.	**FOUR WALLS,** Jim Reeves, Victor	25
31.	**LOVING YOU,** Elvis Presley, Victor	35
32.	**FREIGHT TRAIN,** Rusty Draper, Mercury	33
33.	**GONNA FIND ME A BLUEBIRD,** Marvin Rainwater, M-G-M	35
34.	**SCHOOL DAY,** Chuck Berry, Chess	27
35.	**SUSIE-Q,** Dale Hawkins, Checkers	29
36.	**WITH ALL MY HEART,** Jodie Sands, Chancellor	29
37.	**AROUND THE WORLD IN 80 DAYS,** Mantovani, London	50
38.	**BERNARDINE,** Pat Boone, Dot	38
39.	**WHOLE LOTTA SHAKIN' GOIN' ON,** Jerry Lee Lewis, Sun	34
40.	**JUST TO HOLD MY HAND,** Clyde McPhatter, Atlantic	31
41.	**LET THE FOUR WINDS BLOW,** Roy Brown, Imperial	47
42.	**AROUND THE WORLD IN 80 DAYS,** Victor Young, Decca	67
43.	**WHITE SILVER SANDS,** Dave Gardner, OJ	57
44.	**ROCK YOUR LITTLE BABY TO SLEEP,** Buddy Knox, Roulette	39
45.	**GIRL WITH THE GOLDEN BRAIDS,** Perry Como, Victor	40
46.	**DIANA,** Paul Anka, ABC-Paramount	78
46.	**I'M WALKIN',** Ricky Nelson, Verve	48
48.	**TAMMY,** Ames Brothers, Victor	59
49.	**FOUR WALLS,** Jim Lowe, Dot	43
50.	**WHITE SILVER SANDS,** Don Rondo, Jubilee	97
51.	**COCOANUT WOMAN,** Harry Belafonte, Victor	48
51.	**FALLEN STAR,** Jim Newman, Dot	43
53.	**ISLAND IN THE SUN,** Harry Belafonte, Victor	63
54.	**GONE,** Ferlin Husky, Capitol	45
55.	**GOIN' STEADY,** Tommy Sands, Capitol	49
56.	**TO THE AISLE,** The Five Satins, Ember	—
57.	**EMPTY ARMS,** Ivory Joe Hunter, Atlantic	54
57.	**FLYING SAUCER,** Buchanan & Goodman, Luniverse	—
59.	**DARK MOON,** Bonnie Guitar, Dot	51
59.	**MISS ANN,** Little Richard, Specialty	60
61.	**FALLEN STAR,** Ferlin Husky, Capitol	85
61.	**ROUND AND ROUND,** Perry Como, Victor	53
63.	**FABULOUS,** Charlie Gracie, Cameo	46
64.	**AROUND THE WORLD IN 80 DAYS,** Bing Crosby, Decca	57
65.	**WHAT CAN I DO,** Donnie Elbert, Deluxe	67
66.	**HE'S MINE,** Platters, Mercury	40
67.	**IT HURTS TO BE IN LOVE,** Annie Laurie, Deluxe	73
68.	**JUST BECAUSE,** Lloyd Price, ABC-Paramount	55
68.	**SUN IS SHINING,** Jim Reed, Vee Jay	65
68.	**TAMMY,** Debbie Reynolds, Coral	—
71.	**MAMA LOOK-A BOO-BOO,** Harry Belafonte, Victor	65
71.	**ROCK-A-BILLY,** Guy Mitchell, Columbia	55
73.	**PLEASE SEND ME SOMEONE TO LOVE,** Moonglows, Chess	78
74.	**CAN'T WAIT FOR SUMMER,** Steve Lawrence, Coral	69
74.	**DON'T ASK ME,** Dubs, Gone	75
74.	**NEXT TIME YOU SEE ME,** Little Jr. Parker, Duke	97
77.	**FALLEN STAR,** Hilltoppers, Dot	93
78.	**WHY, BABY, WHY?** Pat Boone, Dot	63
78.	**LUCILLE,** Little Richard, Specialty	61
78.	**TEARDROPS FROM MY HEART,** Teresa Brewer, Coral	89
81.	**SEND ME SOME LOVIN',** Little Richard, Specialty	71
82.	**BUILD YOUR LOVE,** Johnnie Ray, Columbia	—
82.	**EVERYBODY'S SOMEBODY'S FOOL,** Heartbeats, Hull	78
82.	**I'M WALKIN',** Fats Domino, Imperial	61
85.	**GOODY, GOODY,** Teenagers, Gee	—
86.	**BILLY GOAT,** Bill Haley, Decca	76
86.	**PARTY DOLL,** Buddy Knox, Roulette	71
86.	**SHISH KEBAB,** Ralph Marterie, Mercury	77
89.	**TALKIN' TO THE BLUES,** Jim Lowe, Dot	89
90.	**RANG TANG DING DONG,** Cellos, Apollo	93
91.	**DYNAMITE,** Brenda Lee, Decca	86
91.	**GONNA FIND ME A BLUEBIRD,** Eddie Arnold, Victor	—
91.	**I JUST DON'T KNOW,** Four Lads, Columbia	70
91.	**ROCKIN' SHOES,** Ames Brothers, Victor	96
95.	**BE CAREFUL WITH A FOOL,** B. B. King, RPM	—
95.	**EMPTY ARMS,** Teresa Brewer, Coral	73
97.	**CAN I COME OVER,** Velours, Onyx	86
97.	**DESIRIE,** Charts, Everlast	89
97.	**MY PERSONAL POSSESSION,** Nat (King) Cole, Capitol	81
100.	**ONE FOR MY BABY,** Tony Bennett, Columbia	84
100.	**SWEETEST ONE,** Crests, Joyce	86

NEW YORK UNIVERSITY SCHOOL OF RETAILING — STORE RECORDED SALES — THE BILLBOARD

Best Sellers in Stores

FOR SURVEY WEEK ENDING JULY 20, 1957

The information given in this chart is based on actual sales to customers in a scientific sample of the nation's retail record outlets during the week ending on the date shown above. Sample design, sample size, and all methods used in this continuing study of retail record sales are under the direct and continuing supervision and control of the School of Retailing of New York University.

This Week		Last Week	Weeks on Chart
1.	TEDDY BEAR (ASCAP) / LOVING YOU (BMI) — Elvis Presley—Vic 20-7000	1	6
2.	LOVE LETTERS IN THE SAND (ASCAP) / BERNARDINE (ASCAP) — Pat Boone—Dot 15570	2	12
3.	SEARCHIN' (BMI) / YOUNG BLOOD (BMI) — Coasters—Atco 6187	5	11
4.	BYE BYE LOVE (BMI)—Everly Brothers — I Wonder If I Care as Much (BMI)—Cadence 1315	3	10
5.	SO RARE (ASCAP)—Jimmy Dorsey — Sophisticated Swing (ASCAP)—Fraternity 755	4	16
6.	SEND FOR ME (BMI) / MY PERSONAL POSSESSION (BMI) — Nat (King) Cole—Cap 3737	7	5
7.	IT'S YOU I LOVE (BMI) / VALLEY OF TEARS (BMI) — Fats Domino—Imperial 5442	6	9
8.	SHORT FAT FANNIE (BMI)—Larry Williams — High School Dance (BMI)—Specialty 608	11	4
9.	OLD CAPE COD (ASCAP)—Patti Page — Wondering (BMI)—Mercury 71101	8	8
10.	WHISPERING BELLS (BMI)—Del Vikings — Don't Be a Fool (BMI)—Dot 15592	19	3
10.	TAMMY (ASCAP)—Debbie Reynolds — French Heels (ASCAP)—Coral 61851	—	1
12.	JENNY, JENNY (BMI) / MISS ANN (BMI) — Little Richard	13	6
13.	TEENAGER'S ROMANCE (ASCAP) / I'M WALKIN' (BMI) — Ricky Nelson	14	13
14.	DARK MOON (BMI)—Gale Storm — Little Too Late (BMI)—Dot 15558	10	13
15.	OVER THE MOUNTAIN (BMI)—Johnnie & Joe — My Baby's Gone On, On (BMI)—Chess 1664	9	10
16.	STARDUST (ASCAP)—Billy Ward — Lucinda (BMI)—Liberty 55071	24	2
17.	WHITE SILVER SANDS (BMI)—Don Rondo — Stars Fell on Alabama (ASCAP)—Jubilee 5288	—	1
18.	I'M GONNA SIT RIGHT DOWN (ASCAP)—Billy Williams — Date With the Blues (ASCAP)—Coral 61830	17	6
19.	IT'S NOT FOR ME TO SAY (ASCAP)—Johnny Mathis — Warm and Tender (ASCAP)—Col 40851	12	10
20.	AROUND THE WORLD (ASCAP)—Victor Young — (Vocal) (ASCAP)—Decca 30262	21	2
21.	DIANA (BMI)—Paul Anka — Don't Gamble With Love (BMI)—ABC-Paramount 9831	—	1
22.	WHITE SILVER SANDS (BMI)—Dave Gardner — Fat Charlie—OJ 1002	29	2
23.	WHITE SPORT COAT (BMI)—Marty Robbins — Grown-Up Tears (BMI)—Col 40864	15	14
23.	AROUND THE WORLD (ASCAP)—Mantovani — The Road to Ballingarry (ASCAP)—London 1746	30	2
23.	FLYING SAUCER—Buchanan & Goodman — Martian Melody (BMI)—Luniverse 105	—	1
26.	C. C. RIDER (BMI)—Chuck Willis — Ease the Pain (BMI)—Atlantic 1130	16	8
26.	START MOVIN' (BMI)—Sal Mineo — Love Affair (BMI)—Epic 9216	25	11
28.	WONDERFUL, WONDERFUL (BMI)—Johnny Mathis — When Sunny Gets Blue (BMI)—Col 40784	18	6
29.	ALL SHOOK UP (BMI)—Elvis Presley — That's When Your Heartaches Begin (ASCAP)—Vic 20-6870	20	11
29.	GONNA FIND ME A BLUEBIRD (BMI)—Marvin Rainwater — So You Think You've Got Trouble (BMI)—M-G-M 12412	27	2

Most Played by Jockeys

FOR SURVEY WEEK ENDING JULY 20, 1957

SIDES are ranked in order of the greatest number of plays on disk jockey radio shows thruout the country. Results are based on The Billboard's weekly survey among the nation's disk jockeys. The reverse side of each record is also listed.

This Week		Last Week	Weeks on Chart
1.	TEDDY BEAR (ASCAP)—Elvis Presley — Loving You (ASCAP)—Vic 7000	2	13
2.	LOVE LETTERS IN THE SAND (ASCAP)—Pat Boone — Bernardine (ASCAP)—Dot 15570	1	12
3.	OLD CAPE COD (ASCAP)—Patti Page — Wondering (BMI)—Mercury 71101	5	9
4.	BYE BYE LOVE (BMI)—Everly Brothers — I Wonder If I Care as Much (BMI)—Cadence 1315	3	9
5.	I'M GONNA SIT RIGHT DOWN (ASCAP)—Billy Williams — Date With the Blues (ASCAP)—Coral 61830	6	6
6.	SO RARE (ASCAP)—Jimmy Dorsey — Sophisticated Swing (ASCAP)—Fraternity 755	4	13
7.	IT'S NOT FOR ME TO SAY (ASCAP)—Johnny Mathis — Warm and Tender (ASCAP)—Col 40851	7	10
8.	TAMMY (ASCAP)—Debbie Reynolds — French Heels (ASCAP)—Coral 61851	12	2
9.	SEARCHIN' (BMI)—Coasters — Young Blood (BMI)—Atco 6987	8	9
10.	I LIKE YOUR KIND OF LOVE (BMI)—Andy Williams — Stop Teasin' Me (ASCAP)—Cadence 1323	10	7
11.	TAMMY (ASCAP)—Ames Brothers — Rockin' Shoes (BMI)—Vic 6930	18	2
12.	SHANGRI-LA (ASCAP)—Four Coins — First in Line (ASCAP)—Epic 9213	11	3
13.	WORDS OF LOVE (BMI)—Diamonds — Don't Say Goodbye (BMI)—Mer 71128	—	2
14.	SEND FOR ME (BMI)—Nat (King) Cole — My Personal Possession (BMI)—Cap 3737	9	3
15.	WHITE SILVER SANDS (BMI)—Don Rondo — Stars Fell On Alabama (ASCAP)—Jubilee 5288	—	1
16.	SHORT FAT FANNIE (BMI)—Larry Williams — High School Dance (BMI)—Specialty 608	21	2
17.	WONDERFUL, WONDERFUL (BMI)—Johnny Mathis — When Sunny Gets Blue (BMI)—Col 40784	14	16
18.	AROUND THE WORLD (ASCAP)—Mantovani — The Road to Ballingarry (ASCAP)—London 1746	22	2
19.	AROUND THE WORLD (ASCAP)—Victor Young — Around the World (Vocal) (ASCAP)—Dec 30262	13	3
19.	WITH ALL MY HEART (ASCAP)—Jodie Sands — More Than Only Friends (ASCAP)—Chancellor 1003	17	7
21.	LOVING YOU (BMI)—Elvis Presley — Teddy Bear (BMI)—Vic 7000	20	2
22.	DARK MOON (BMI)—Gale Storm — Little Too Late (BMI)—Dot 15558	14	12
23.	BERNARDINE (ASCAP)—Pat Boone — Love Letters in the Sand (ASCAP)—Dot 15570	—	4
23.	WHITE SILVER SANDS (BMI)—Owen Bradley Quintet — Midnight Blues (BMI)—Dec 30363	—	1
23.	STARDUST (ASCAP)—Billy Ward — Lucinda (BMI)—Liberty 55071	—	1

STORE RECORDED SALES — NEW YORK UNIVERSITY SCHOOL OF RETAILING • THE BILLBOARD

Top 100 Sides

FOR SURVEY WEEK ENDING JULY 20

This is a tabulation of dealer unit sales listed according to the specific side requested by customers. No attempt is made to add sides together to reflect actual record sales. It is therefore a tabulation of sides or songs, and not records. This fact, together with longer four-week survey periods, explains variation between the top 30 sides as reflected in this chart, and top 30 record sellers as reflected in "Best Sellers in Stores."

Pos.	Song, Artist, Label	Pos. Last Wk.
1.	**TEDDY BEAR,** Elvis Presley, Victor	1
2.	**LOVE LETTERS IN THE SAND,** Pat Boone, Dot	2
3.	**BYE BYE LOVE,** Everly Brothers, Cadence	3
4.	**SO RARE,** Jimmy Dorsey, Fraternity	4
5.	**SEARCHIN',** Coasters, Atco	5
6.	**SHORT FAT FANNIE,** Larry Williams, Specialty	11
7.	**SEND FOR ME,** Nat (King) Cole, Capitol	7
8.	**IT'S NOT FOR ME TO SAY,** Johnny Mathis, Columbia	6
9.	**OLD CAPE COD,** Patti Page, Mercury	9
10.	**I'M GONNA SIT RIGHT DOWN,** Billy Williams, Coral	13
11.	**OVER THE MOUNTAIN,** Johnnie & Joe, Chess	8
12.	**WHISPERING BELLS,** Del Vikings, Dot	26
13.	**DARK MOON,** Gale Storm, Dot	10
14.	**JENNY JENNY,** Little Richard, Specialty	16
15.	**WHITE SPORT COAT,** Marty Robbins, Columbia	12
16.	**C. C. RIDER,** Chuck Willis, Atlantic	14
17.	**WONDERFUL WONDERFUL,** Johnny Mathis, Columbia	17
18.	**ALL SHOOK UP,** Elvis Presley, Victor	15
19.	**STARDUST,** Billy Ward, Liberty	28
20.	**I LIKE YOUR KIND OF LOVE,** Andy Willams, Cadence	13
21.	**TEENAGERS ROMANCE,** Ricky Nelson, Verve	24
22.	**TAMMY,** Debbie Reynolds, Coral	68
23.	**VALLEY OF TEARS,** Fats Domino, Imperial	18
23.	**YOUNG BLOOD,** Coasters, Atco	19
25.	**LITTLE DARLIN',** Diamonds, Mercury	21
26.	**IT'S YOU I LOVE,** Fats Domino, Imperial	22
27.	**START MOVIN',** Sal Mineo, Epic	25
28.	**COME GO WITH ME,** Del Vikings, Dot	23
29.	**WHITE SILVER SANDS,** Don Rondo, Jubilee	50
30.	**SHANGRI-LA,** Four Coins, Epic	27
31.	**LOVING YOU,** Elvis Presley, Victor	31
32.	**BERNARDINE,** Pat Boone, Dot	38
32.	**WHITE SILVER SANDS,** Dave Gardner, OJ	43
34.	**AROUND THE WORLD,** Mantovani, London	37
35.	**AROUND THE WORLD,** Victor Young, Decca	42
36.	**GONNA FIND ME A BLUEBIRD,** Marvin Rainwater, M-G-M	33
37.	**SUSIE Q,** Dale Hawkins, Checker	35
38.	**WHOLE LOTTA SHAKIN' GOIN' ON,** Jerry Lee Lewis, Sun	39
39.	**FREIGHT TRAIN,** Rusty Draper, Mercury	32
39.	**FOUR WALLS,** Jim Reeves, Victor	30
41.	**WITH ALL MY HEART,** Jodie Sands, Chancellor	36
42.	**MY DREAM,** Platters, Mercury	29
43.	**FLYING SAUCER,** Buchanan & Goodman, Luniverse	57
43.	**SCHOOL DAY,** Chuck Berry, Chess	34
45.	**JUST TO HOLD MY HAND,** Clyde McPhatter, Atlantic	40
46.	**TAMMY,** Ames Brothers, Victor	48
47.	**ISLAND IN THE SUN,** Harry Belafonte, Victor	53
48.	**TO THE AISLE,** Five Satins, Ember	56
48.	**LET THE FOUR WINDS BLOW,** Roy Brown, Imperial	41
50.	**DIANA,** Paul Anka, ABC-Paramount	46
50.	**FALLEN STAR,** Ferlin Husky, Capitol	61
52.	**GIRL WITH THE GOLDEN BRAIDS,** Perry Como, Victor	45
53.	**ROCK YOUR LITTLE BABY TO SLEEP,** Buddy Knox, Roulette	44
54.	**COCOANUT WOMAN,** Harry Belafonte, Victor	51
55.	**FALLEN STAR,** Jim Newman, Dot	51
56.	**FOUR WALLS,** Jim Lowe, Dot	49
57.	**I'M WALKIN',** Ricky Nelson, Verve	46
58.	**BUILD YOUR LOVE,** Johnny Ray, Columbia	82
58.	**GOODY GOODY,** Teenagers, Gee	85
60.	**RAINBOW,** Russ Hamilton, Kapp	—
61.	**FABULOUS,** Charlie Gracie, Cameo	63
61.	**IT HURTS TO BE IN LOVE,** Annie Laurie, Deluxe	67
61.	**WHAT CAN I DO?** Donnie Elbert, Deluxe	65
64.	**IS IT WRONG?** Warner Mack, Decca	—
64.	**TEARDROPS FROM MY HEART,** Terese Brewer, Coral	78
66.	**HE'S MINE,** Platters, Mercury	66
66.	**MISS ANN,** Little Richard, Specialty	59
68.	**AROUND THE WORLD,** Bing Crosby, Decca	64
68.	**RANG TANG DING DONG,** The Cellos, Apollo	90
70.	**DARK MOON,** Bonnie Guitar, Dot	59
70.	**SUN IS SHINING,** Jim Reed, Vee Jay	68
72.	**EMPTY ARMS,** Ivory Joe Hunter, Atlantic	57
72.	**GOING STEADY,** Tommy Sands, Capitol	55
74.	**GONE,** Ferlin Husky, Capitol	54
74.	**FALLEN STAR,** Hilltoppers, Dot	77
76.	**PLEASE SEND ME SOMEONE TO LOVE,** Moonglows, Chess	73
77.	**NEXT TIME YOU SEE ME,** Little Jr. Parker, Duke	74
78.	**BYE BYE LOVE,** Webb Pierce, Decca	—
78.	**JUST BECAUSE,** Lloyd Price, ABC-Paramount	68
80.	**ARROW OF LOVE,** Six Teens, Flip	—
80.	**DON'T ASK ME,** Dubs, Gone	74
80.	**MAMA LOOK AT BOO BOO,** Harry Belafonte, Victor	71
85.	**COOL SHAKE,** Del Vikings, Dot	—
85.	**EVERYBODY'S SOMEBODY'S FOOL,** Heartaches, Hull	82
87.	**CAN'T WAIT FOR SUMMER,** Steve Lawrence, Coral	74
87.	**I'M WALKIN',** Fats Domino, Imperial	82
87.	**ROUND AND ROUND,** Perry Como, Victor	—
91.	**SEND ME SOME LOVIN',** Little Richard, Specialty	81
92.	**MISS YOU SO,** Lillian Offitt, Excello	—
93.	**LUCILLE,** Little Richard, Specialty	78
93.	**ROCKIN' SHOES,** Ames Brothers, Victor	91
95.	**OH BABY DOLL,** Chuck Berry, Chess	—
96.	**SHISH KEBAB,** Ralph Marterie, Mercury	86
97.	**DESIRIE,** Charts, Everlast	97
97.	**WHITE SILVER SANDS,** Owen Bradley Quintet, Decca	—
99.	**CAN I COME OVER?** Velours, Onyx	97
99.	**FRAULEIN,** Bobby Helms, Decca	—
99.	**WHY, BABY, WHY?** Pat Boone, Dot	78
99.	**PASSING STRANGERS,** Sarah Vaughn & Billy Eckstein, Mercury	—
99.	**TALKIN' TO THE BLUES,** Jim Lowe, Dot	89

NEW YORK UNIVERSITY SCHOOL OF RETAILING — STORE RECORDED SALES — THE BILLBOARD

Best Sellers in Stores

FOR SURVEY WEEK ENDING JULY 27, 1957

The information given in this chart is based on actual sales to customers in a scientific sample of the nation's retail record outlets during the week ending on the date shown above. Sample design, sample size, and all methods used in this continuing study of retail record sales are under the direct and continuing supervision and control of the School of Retailing of New York University.

This Week		Last Week	Weeks on Chart
1.	TEDDY BEAR (ASCAP) / LOVING YOU (BMI) / Elvis Presley—Vic 20-7000	1	7
2.	LOVE LETTERS IN THE SAND (ASCAP) / BERNARDINE (ASCAP) / Pat Boone—Dot 15570	2	13
3.	BYE BYE LOVE (BMI)—Everly Brothers / I Wonder If I Care as Much (BMI)—Cadence 1315	4	11
4.	SEARCHIN' (BMI) / YOUNG BLOOD (BMI) / Coasters—Atco 6187	3	12
5.	SHORT FAT FANNIE (BMI)—Larry Williams / High School Dance (BMI)—Specialty 608	8	5
6.	TAMMY (ASCAP)—Debbie Reynolds / French Heels (ASCAP)—Coral 61851	10	2
7.	SO RARE (ASCAP)—Jimmy Dorsey / Sophisticated Swing (ASCAP)—Fraternity 755	5	17
8.	SEND FOR ME (BMI) / MY PERSONAL POSSESSION (BMI) / Nat (King) Cole—Cap 3737	6	6
9.	I'M GONNA SIT RIGHT DOWN (ASCAP)—Billy Williams / Date With the Blues (ASCAP)—Coral 61830	18	7
10.	WHISPERING BELLS (BMI)—Del Vikings / Don't Be a Fool (BMI)—Dot 15592	10	4
11.	IT'S NOT FOR ME TO SAY (ASCAP)—Johnny Mathis / Warm and Tender (ASCAP)—Col 40851	19	11
12.	WHITE SILVER SANDS (BMI)—Don Rondo / Stars Fell on Alabama (ASCAP)—Jubilee 5288	17	2
13.	OLD CAPE COD (ASCAP) / WONDERING (BMI) / Patti Page—Mercury 71101	9	9
14.	STARDUST (ASCAP)—Billy Ward / Lucinda (BMI)—Liberty 55071	16	3
15.	JENNY, JENNY (BMI)—Little Richard / Miss Ann (BMI)—Specialty 606	12	7
16.	TEENAGER'S ROMANCE (ASCAP) / I'M WALKIN' (BMI) / Ricky Nelson—Verve 10074	13	14
17.	DARK MOON (BMI)—Gale Storm / Little Too Late (BMI)—Dot 15558	14	14
18.	DIANA (BMI)—Paul Anka / Don't Gamble With Love (BMI)—ABC-Paramount 9831	21	2
19.	OVER THE MOUNTAIN (BMI)—Johnnie & Joe / My Baby's Gone On, On (BMI)—Chess 1654	15	11
20.	AROUND THE WORLD (ASCAP) (VOCAL) (ASCAP) / Victor Young—Decca 30262	20	3
21.	FLYING SAUCER—Buchanan & Goodman / Martian Melody (BMI)—Luniverse 105	23	2
22.	I LIKE YOUR KIND OF LOVE (BMI) / Stop Teasin' Me (ASCAP)—Cadence 1323	—	7
23.	WHITE SILVER SANDS (BMI)—Dave Gardner / Fat Charlie—OJ 1002	22	3
23.	ALL SHOOK UP (BMI)—Elvis Presley / That's When Your Heartaches Begin (ASCAP)—Vic 20-6870	29	12
25.	AROUND THE WORLD—Mantovani / The Road to Ballingarry (ASCAP)—London 1746	23	3
25.	WHOLE LOTTA SHAKIN' GOIN' ON (BMI)—Jerry Lee Lewis / It'll Be Me (BMI)—Sun 267	—	2
27.	VALLEY OF TEARS (BMI)—Fats Domino / It's You I Love (BMI)—Imperial 5442	7	10
28.	RAINBOW (ASCAP)—Russ Hamilton / We Will Make Love (ASCAP)—Kapp 184	—	1
29.	START MOVIN' (BMI) / LOVE AFFAIR (BMI) / Sal Mineo—Epic 9216	26	12
30.	WONDERFUL, WONDERFUL (BMI)—Johnny Mathis / When Sunny Gets Blue (BMI)—Col 40784	28	7
30.	SHANGRI-LA (ASCAP)—Four Coins / First in Line (ASCAP)—Epic 9213	—	3

Most Played by Jockeys

FOR SURVEY WEEK ENDING JULY 27, 1957

SIDES are ranked in order of the greatest number of plays on disk jockey radio shows thruout the country. Results are based on The Billboard's weekly survey among the nation's disk jockeys. The reverse side of each record is also listed.

This Week		Last Week	Weeks on Chart
1.	TEDDY BEAR (ASCAP)—Elvis Presley / Loving You (BMI)—Vic 7000	1	14
2.	LOVE LETTERS IN THE SAND (ASCAP)—Pat Boone / Bernardine (ASCAP)—Dot 15570	2	13
3.	I'M GONNA SIT RIGHT DOWN (ASCAP)—Billy Williams / Date With the Blues (ASCAP)—Coral 61830	5	7
4.	OLD CAPE COD (ASCAP)—Patti Page / Wondering (BMI)—Mercury 71101	3	10
5.	BYE BYE LOVE (BMI)—Everly Brothers / I Wonder If I Care as Much (BMI)—Cadence 1315	4	10
6.	IT'S NOT FOR ME TO SAY (ASCAP)—Johnny Mathis / Warm and Tender (ASCAP)—Col 40851	7	11
6.	TAMMY (ASCAP)—Debbie Reynolds / French Heels (ASCAP)—Coral 61851	8	3
8.	SO RARE (ASCAP)—Jimmy Dorsey / Sophisticated Swing (ASCAP)—Fraternity 755	6	14
9.	WHITE SILVER SANDS (BMI)—Don Rondo / Stars Fell on Alabama (ASCAP)—Jubilee 5288	15	2
10.	TAMMY (ASCAP)—Ames Brothers / Rockin' Shoes (BMI)—Vic 6930	11	3
11.	SEARCHIN' (BMI)—Coasters / Young Blood (BMI)—Atco 6987	9	10
12.	SEND FOR ME (BMI)—Nat (King) Cole / My Personal Possession (BMI)—Cap 3737	14	4
13.	AROUND THE WORLD (ASCAP)—Mantovani / The Road to Ballingarry (ASCAP)—London 1746	18	3
14.	SHANGRI-LA (ASCAP)—Four Coins / First in Line (ASCAP)—Epic 9213	12	4
15.	SHORT FAT FANNIE (BMI)—Larry Williams / High School Dance (BMI)—Specialty 608	16	3
16.	AROUND THE WORLD (ASCAP)—Victor Young / Around the World (Vocal) (ASCAP)—Dec 30262	19	4
17.	WITH ALL MY HEART (ASCAP)—Jodie Sands / More Than Only Friends (ASCAP)—Chancellor 1003	19	8
18.	I LIKE YOUR KIND OF LOVE (BMI)—Andy Williams / Stop Teasin' Me (ASCAP)—Cadence 1323	10	8
18.	WHITE SILVER SANDS—Owen Bradley Quintet / Midnight Blues (BMI)—Dec 30363	23	2
20.	RAINBOW (ASCAP)—Russ Hamilton / We Will Make Love (ASCAP)—Kapp 184	—	1
21.	MY PERSONAL POSSESSION (BMI)—Nat (King) Cole / Send for Me (BMI)—Cap 3737	—	1
22.	STARDUST (ASCAP)—Billy Ward / Lucinda (BMI)—Liberty 55071	25	2
23.	WONDERFUL, WONDERFUL (BMI)—Johnny Mathis / When Sunny Gets Blue (BMI)—Col 40784	17	17
24.	LOVE ME TO PIECES (BMI)—Jill Corey / Love (BMI)—Col 40955	—	1
25.	LOVING YOU (BMI)—Elvis Presley / Teddy Bear (ASCAP)—Vic 7000	21	3

Top 100 Sides

FOR SURVEY WEEK ENDING JULY 27

This is a tabulation of dealer unit sales listed according to the specific side requested by customers. No attempt is made to add sides together to reflect actual record sales. It is therefore a tabulation of sides or songs, and not records. This fact, together with longer four-week survey periods, explains variation between the top 30 sides as reflected in this chart, and top 30 record sellers as reflected in "Best Sellers in Stores."

Pos.	Song, Artist, Label	Pos. Last Wk.
1.	**TEDDY BEAR,** Elvis Presley, Victor	1
2.	**LOVE LETTERS IN THE SAND,** Pat Boone, Dot	2
3.	**BYE BYE LOVE,** Everly Brothers, Cadence	3
4.	**SO RARE,** Jimmy Dorsey, Fraternity	4
5.	**SEARCHIN',** Coasters, Atco	5
6.	**SHORT FAT FANNIE,** Larry Williams, Specialty	6
7.	**SEND FOR ME,** Nat (King) Cole, Capitol	7
8.	**I'M GONNA SIT RIGHT DOWN,** Billy Williams, Coral	10
9.	**WHISPERING BELLS,** Del Vikings, Dot	12
10.	**OLD CAPE COD,** Patti Page, Mercury	9
11.	**IT'S NOT FOR ME TO SAY,** Johnny Mathis, Columbia	8
12.	**DARK MOON,** Gale Storm, Dot	13
12.	**TAMMY,** Debbie Reynolds, Coral	22
14.	**OVER THE MOUNTAIN,** Johnnie & Joe, Chess	11
15.	**JENNY JENNY,** Little Richard, Specialty	14
16.	**STARDUST,** Billy Ward, Liberty	19
17.	**WHITE SILVER SANDS,** Don Rondo, Jubilee	29
18.	**WHITE SPORT COAT,** Marty Robbins, Columbia	15
19.	**WONDERFUL WONDERFUL,** Johnny Mathis, Columbia	17
20.	**C. C. RIDER,** Chuck Willis, Atlantic	16
20.	**TEENAGERS ROMANCE,** Ricky Nelson, Verve	21
22.	**ALL SHOOK UP,** Elvis Presley, Victor	18
23.	**YOUNG BLOOD,** Coasters, Atco	23
24.	**VALLEY OF TEARS,** Fats Domino, Imperial	23
25.	**START MOVIN',** Sal Mineo, Epic	27
26.	**FLYING SAUCER,** Buchanan & Goodman, Luniverse	43
27.	**IT'S YOU I LOVE,** Fats Domino, Imperial	26
28.	**I LIKE YOUR KIND OF LOVE,** Andy Williams, Cadence	20
28.	**WHITE SILVER SANDS,** Dave Gardner, OJ	32
30.	**AROUND THE WORLD,** Mantovani, London	34
30.	**GONNA FIND ME A BLUEBIRD,** Marvin Rainwater, M-G-M	36
32.	**BERNARDINE,** Pat Boone, Dot	32
33.	**DIANA,** Paul Anka, ABC-Paramount	50
34.	**AROUND THE WORLD,** Victor Young, Decca	35
35.	**LITTLE DARLIN',** Diamonds, Mercury	25
36.	**WHOLE LOTTA SHAKIN' GOING ON,** Jerry Lee Lewis, Sun	38
37.	**LOVING YOU,** Elvis Presley, Victor	31
38.	**SHANGRI-LA,** Four Coins, Epic	30
39.	**COME GO WITH ME,** Del Vikings, Dot	28
40.	**FREIGHT TRAIN,** Rusty Draper, Mercury	39
41.	**FOUR WALLS,** Jim Reeves, Victor	39
42.	**SUSIE Q,** Dale Hawkins, Checker	37
43.	**MY DREAM,** Platters, Mercury	42
44.	**LET THE FOUR WINDS BLOW,** Roy Brown, Imperial	48
45.	**WITH ALL MY HEART,** Jodie Sands, Chancellor	41
46.	**TO THE AISLE,** Five Satins, Ember	48
46.	**RAINBOW,** Russ Hamilton, Kapp	60
48.	**SCHOOL DAYS,** Chuck Berry, Chess	43
49.	**ISLAND IN THE SUN,** Harry Belafonte, Victor	47
50.	**FALLEN STAR,** Ferlin Husky, Capitol	50
51.	**TAMMY,** Ames Brothers, Victor	46
52.	**GOODY GOODY,** Teenagers, Gee	58
53.	**GIRL WITH THE GOLDEN BRAIDS,** Perry Como, Victor	52
54.	**FALLEN STAR,** Jim Newman, Dot	55
55.	**COOL SHAKE,** Del Vikings, Mercury	85
56.	**I'M WALKIN',** Ricky Nelson, Verve	57
57.	**AROUND THE WORLD,** Bing Crosby, Decca	68
58.	**JUST TO HOLD MY HAND,** Clyde McPhatter, Atlantic	45
58.	**MISS ANN,** Little Richard, Specialty	66
58.	**ROCK YOUR LITTLE BABY TO SLEEP,** Buddy Knox, Roulette	53
61.	**IS IT WRONG?** Warner Mack, Decca	64
62.	**OH BABY DOLL,** Chuck Berry, Chess	95
62.	**RANG TANG DING DONG,** The Cellos, Apollo	68
64.	**TEARDROPS FROM MY HEART,** Teresa Brewer, Coral	64
65.	**BUILD YOUR LOVE,** Johnny Ray, Columbia	58
66.	**MY PERSONAL POSSESSION,** Nat (King) Cole, Capitol	—
66.	**MISS YOU SO,** Lillian Offitt, Excello	92
68.	**FOUR WALLS,** Jim Lowe, Dot	56
69.	**COCOANUT WOMAN,** Harry Belafonte, Victor	54
69.	**DARK MOON,** Bonnie Guitar, Dot	70
69.	**MR. LEE,** Bobbettes, Atlantic	—
72.	**DON'T ASK ME,** Dubs, Gone	80
72.	**FALLEN STAR,** Hilltoppers, Dot	74
74.	**HE'S MINE,** Platters, Mercury	66
74.	**LOVE ME TO PIECES,** Jill Corey, Columbia	—
76.	**BYE BYE LOVE,** Webb Pierce, Decca	78
76.	**DYNAMITE,** Brenda Lee, Decca	—
78.	**GOIN' STEADY,** Tommy Sands, Capitol	72
78.	**GONE,** Ferlin Husky, Capitol	74
78.	**IN THE MIDDLE OF AN ISLAND,** Tony Bennett, Columbia	—
81.	**I'M WALKIN',** Fats Domino, Imperial	87
81	**WHAT CAN I DO?** Donnie Elbert, De Luxe	61
81.	**WHITE SILVER SANDS,** Owen Bradley, Decca	97
84.	**FABULOUS,** Charlie Gracie, Cameo	61
84.	**IT HURTS TO BE IN LOVE,** Annie Laurie, De Luxe	61
84.	**ROUND AND ROUND,** Perry Como, Victor	87
87.	**ARROW OF LOVE,** Six Teens, Flip	80
88.	**PLEASE SEND ME SOMEONE TO LOVE,** Moonglows, Chess	76
89.	**FRAULEIN,** Bobby Helms, Decca	99
89.	**LUCILLE,** Little Richard, Specialty	93
89.	**SUN IS SHINING,** Jim Reed, Vee Jay	70
92.	**CAN'T WAIT FOR SUMMER,** Steve Lawrence, Coral	87
92	**MAMA LOOK-A BOO-BOO,** Harry Belafonte, Victor	80
92.	**THINK,** Five Royals, King	—
95.	**EMPTY ARMS,** Ivory Joe Hunter, Atlantic	72
96.	**ROCKIN' SHOES,** Ames Brothers, Victor	93
96.	**SHISH KEBAB,** Ralph Marterie, Mercury	96
98.	**FARTHER UP THE ROAD,** Bobby Blue Bland, Duke	—
98.	**NEXT TIME YOU SEE ME,** Little Jr. Parker, Duke	77
98.	**PASSING STRANGERS,** Sarah Vaughan & Billy Eckstein, Mercury	99

NEW YORK UNIVERSITY SCHOOL OF RETAILING · STORE RECORDED SALES · THE BILLBOARD

Best Sellers in Stores

FOR SURVEY WEEK ENDING AUGUST 3, 1957

The information given in this chart is based on actual sales to customers in a scientific sample of the nation's retail record outlets during the week ending on the date shown above. Sample design, sample size, and all methods used in this continuing study of retail record sales are under the direct and continuing supervision and control of the School of Retailing of New York University.

This Week		Last Week	Weeks on Chart
1.	TEDDY BEAR (ASCAP)—Elvis Presley / LOVING YOU (BMI)—Vic 20-7000	1	8
2.	LOVE LETTERS IN THE SAND (ASCAP)—Pat Boone / BERNARDINE (ASCAP)—Dot 15570	2	14
3.	BYE BYE LOVE (BMI)—Everly Brothers / I Wonder If I Care as Much (BMI)—Cadence 1315	3	12
4.	SEARCHIN' (BMI)—Coasters / YOUNG BLOOD (BMI)—Atco 6187	4	13
5.	TAMMY (ASCAP)—Debbie Reynolds / French Heels (ASCAP)—Coral 61851	6	3
6.	SEND FOR ME (BMI)—Nat (King) Cole / MY PERSONAL POSSESSION (BMI)—Cap 3737	8	7
7.	I'M GONNA SIT RIGHT DOWN (ASCAP)—Billy Williams / Date With the Blues (ASCAP)—Coral 61830	9	8
8.	SHORT FAT FANNIE (BMI)—Larry Williams / HIGH SCHOOL DANCE (BMI)—Specialty 608	5	6
9.	SO RARE (ASCAP)—Jimmy Dorsey / Sophisticated Swing (ASCAP)—Fraternity 755	7	18
10.	WHISPERING BELLS (BMI)—Del Vikings / Don't Be a Fool (BMI)—Dot 15592	10	5
11.	WHITE SILVER SANDS (BMI)—Don Rondo / Stars Fell on Alabama (ASCAP)—Jubilee 5288	12	3
12.	IT'S NOT FOR ME TO SAY (ASCAP)—Johnny Mathis / Warm and Tender (ASCAP)—Col 40851	11	12
13.	RAINBOW (ASCAP)—Russ Hamilton / We Will Make Love (ASCAP)—Kapp 184	28	2
14.	OLD CAPE COD (ASCAP)—Patti Page / WONDERING (BMI)—Mercury 71101	13	10
15.	STARDUST (ASCAP)—Billy Ward / Lucinda (BMI)—Liberty 55071	14	4
15.	DIANA (BMI)—Paul Anka / Don't Gamble With Love (BMI)—ABC-Paramount 9831	18	3
17.	WHOLE LOTTA SHAKIN' GOIN' ON (BMI)—Jerry Lee Lewis / It'll Be Me (BMI)—Sun 267	25	3
18.	FLYING SAUCER—Buchanan & Goodman / Martian Melody—Luniverse 105	21	3
19.	GONNA FIND ME A BLUEBIRD (BMI)—Marvin Rainwater / So You Think You've Got Trouble (BMI)—M-G-M 12412	—	3
20.	DARK MOON (BMI)—Gale Storm / Little Too Late (BMI)—Dot 15558	17	15
21.	TEENAGER'S ROMANCE (ASCAP)—Ricky Nelson / I'M WALKIN' (BMI)—Verve 10074	16	15
21.	LOVE ME TO PIECES (BMI)—Jill Corey / Love (BMI)—Col 40955	—	1
23.	JENNY, JENNY (BMI)—Little Richard / MISS ANN (BMI)—Specialty 606	15	8
23.	AROUND THE WORLD (VOCAL) (ASCAP)—Decca 30262 Victor Young	20	4
25.	IN THE MIDDLE OF AN ISLAND (ASCAP)—Tony Bennett / I Am (ASCAP)—Col 40965	—	1
26.	TAMMY (BMI)—Ames Brothers / ROCKIN' SHOES (ASCAP)—Vic 6930	—	1
27.	MR. LEE (BMI)—Bobbettes / Look at the Stars (BMI)—Atlantic 1144	—	1
28.	REMEMBER YOU'RE MINE (ASCAP)—Pat Boone / There's a Gold Mine in the Sky (ASCAP)—Dot 15602	—	1
29.	SHANGRI-LA (ASCAP)—Four Coins / First in Line (ASCAP)—Epic 9213	30	4
30.	AROUND THE WORLD—Mantovani / The Road to Ballingarry (ASCAP)—London 1746	25	4

Most Played by Jockeys

FOR SURVEY WEEK ENDING AUGUST 3, 1957

SIDES are ranked in order of the greatest number of plays on disk jockey radio shows thruout the country. Results are based on The Billboard's weekly survey among the nation's disk jockeys. The reverse side of each record is also listed.

This Week		Last Week	Weeks on Chart
1.	TEDDY BEAR (ASCAP)—Elvis Presley / Loving You (BMI)—Vic 7000	1	15
2.	LOVE LETTERS IN THE SAND (ASCAP)—Pat Boone / Bernardine (ASCAP)—Dot 15570	2	14
3.	TAMMY (ASCAP)—Debbie Reynolds / French Heels (ASCAP)—Coral 61851	6	4
4.	I'M GONNA SIT RIGHT DOWN (ASCAP)—Billy Williams / Date With the Blues (ASCAP)—Coral 61830	3	8
5.	OLD CAPE COD (ASCAP)—Patti Page / Wondering (BMI)—Mercury 71101	4	11
6.	BYE BYE LOVE (BMI)—Everly Brothers / I Wonder If I Care as Much (BMI)—Cadence 1315	5	11
7.	WHITE SILVER SANDS (BMI)—Don Rondo / Stars Fell on Alabama (ASCAP)—Jubilee 5288	9	3
8.	IT'S NOT FOR ME TO SAY (ASCAP)—Johnny Mathis / Warm and Tender (ASCAP)—Col 40851	6	12
9.	SO RARE (ASCAP)—Jimmy Dorsey / Sophisticated Swing (ASCAP)—Fraternity 755	8	15
10.	DIANA (BMI)—Paul Anka / Don't Gamble With Love (BMI)—ABC-Paramount 9831	—	1
11.	TAMMY (ASCAP)—Ames Brothers / Rockin' Shoes (BMI)—Vic 6930	10	4
12.	RAINBOW (ASCAP)—Russ Hamilton / We Will Make Love (ASCAP)—Kapp 184	20	2
13.	SEARCHIN' (BMI) — Coasters / Young Blood (BMI)—Atco 6987	11	11
14.	SHANGRI-LA (ASCAP)—Four Coins / First in Line (ASCAP)—Epic 9213	14	5
14.	LOVE ME TO PIECES (BMI)—Jill Corey / Love (BMI)—Col 40955	24	2
16.	WHOLE LOTTA SHAKIN' GOIN' ON (BMI)—Jerry Lee Lewis / It'll Be Me (BMI)—Sun 267	—	1
17.	SEND FOR ME (BMI)—Nat (King) Cole / My Personal Possession (BMI)—Cap 3737	12	5
18.	AROUND THE WORLD (ASCAP)—Mantovani / The Road to Ballingarry (ASCAP)—London 1746	13	4
19.	WITH ALL MY HEART (ASCAP)—Jodie Sands / More Than Only Friends (ASCAP)—Chancellor 1003	17	9
20.	SHORT FAT FANNIE (BMI)—Larry Williams / High School Dance (BMI)—Specialty 608	15	4
20.	AROUND THE WORLD (ASCAP)—Victor Young / Around the World (Vocal) (ASCAP)—Dec 30262	16	5
20.	WHISPERING BELLS (BMI)—Del Vikings / Don't Be a Fool (BMI)—Dot 15592	—	1
23.	WONDERFUL, WONDERFUL (BMI)—Johnny Mathis / When Johnny Gets Blue (BMI)—Col 40784	23	18
24.	MY PERSONAL POSSESSION (BMI)—Nat (King) Cole / Send for Me (BMI)—Cap 3737	21	2
25.	WHITE SILVER SANDS—Owen Bradley Quintet / Midnight Blues (BMI)—Dec 30363	18	3

Top 100 Sides

FOR SURVEY WEEK ENDING AUGUST 3

This is a tabulation of dealer unit sales listed according to the specific side requested by customers. No attempt is made to add sides together to reflect actual record sales. It is therefore a tabulation of sides or songs, and not records. This fact, together with longer four-week survey periods, explains variation between the top 30 sides as reflected in this chart, and top 30 record sellers as reflected in "Best Sellers in Stores."

Pos.	Song, Artist and Label	Pos. Last Wk.
1.	**TEDDY BEAR,** Elvis Presley, Victor	1
2.	**BYE BYE LOVE,** Everly Brothers, Cadence	3
3.	**LOVE LETTERS IN THE SAND,** Pat Boone, Dot	2
4.	**SO RARE,** Jimmy Dorsey, Fraternity	4
5.	**SEARCHIN',** Coasters, Atco	5
6.	**SHORT FAT FANNY,** Larry Williams, Specialty	6
7.	**TAMMY,** Debbie Reynolds, Coral	12
8.	**SEND FOR ME,** Nat (King) Cole, Capitol	7
9.	**WHISPERING BELLS,** Del Vikings, Dot	9
10.	**I'M GONNA SIT RIGHT DOWN,** Billy Williams, Coral	8
11.	**OLD CAPE COD,** Patti Page, Mercury	10
12.	**WHITE SILVER SANDS,** Don Rondo, Jubilee	17
13.	**STARDUST,** Billy Ward, Liberty	16
14.	**IT'S NOT FOR ME TO SAY,** Johnny Mathis, Columbia	11
15.	**DARK MOON,** Gale Storm, Dot	12
16.	**JENNY JENNY,** Little Richard, Specialty	15
17.	**DIANA,** Paul Anka, ABC-Paramount	33
18.	**OVER THE MOUNTAIN,** Johnnie & Joe, Chess	14
19.	**FLYING SAUCER,** Buchanan & Goodman, Luniverse	26
20.	**TEENAGERS ROMANCE,** Ricky Nelson, Verve	20
21.	**RAINBOW,** Russ Hamilton, Kapp	46
22.	**GONNA FIND ME A BLUEBIRD,** Marvin Rainwater, M-G-M	30
23.	**WHOLE LOTTA SHAKIN' GOING ON,** Jerry Lee Lewis, Sun	36
24.	**YOUNG BLOOD,** Coasters, Atco	23
25.	**AROUND THE WORLD,** Mantovani, London	30
26.	**AROUND THE WORLD,** Victor Young, Decca	34
27.	**WHITE SPORT COAT,** Marty Robbins, Columbia	18
28.	**BERNARDINE,** Pat Boone, Dot	32
29.	**SHANGRI-LA,** Four Coins, Epic	38
30.	**START MOVIN',** Sal Mineo, Epic	25
31.	**VALLEY OF TEARS,** Fats Domino, Imperial	24
32.	**ALL SHOOK UP,** Elvis Presley, Victor	22
32.	**LOVING YOU,** Elvis Presley, Victor	37
32.	**WHITE SILVER SANDS,** Dave Gardner, OJ	28
35.	**C. C. RIDER,** Chuck Willis, Atlantic	20
36.	**WONDERFUL WONDERFUL,** Johnny Mathis, Columbia	19
37.	**FREIGHT TRAIN,** Rusty Draper, Mercury	40
38.	**IT'S YOU I LOVE,** Fats Domino, Imperial	27
39.	**TO THE AISLE,** Five Satins, Ember	46
40.	**FOUR WALLS,** Jim Reeves, Victor	41
41.	**TAMMY,** Ames Brothers, Victor	51
42.	**I LIKE YOUR KIND OF LOVE,** Andy Williams, Cadence	28
43.	**SUSIE Q,** Dale Hawkins, Checker	42
44.	**LET THE FOUR WINDS BLOW,** Roy Brown, Imperial	44
45.	**LOVE ME TO PIECES,** Jill Corey, Columbia	74
46.	**ISLAND IN THE SUN,** Harry Belafonte, Victor	49
47.	**FALLEN STAR,** Ferlin Husky, Capitol	50
48.	**GOODY GOODY,** Teenagers, Gee	52
49.	**MR. LEE,** Bobbettes, Atlantic	69
50.	**LITTLE DARLIN',** Diamonds, Mercury	35
51.	**IN THE MIDDLE OF AN ISLAND,** Tony Bennett, Columbia	78
52.	**SCHOOL DAY,** Chuck Berry, Chess	48
53.	**MY DREAM,** Platters, Mercury	43
54.	**COOL SHAKE,** Del Vikings, Mercury	53
54.	**WITH ALL MY HEART,** Jodie Sands, Chancellor	45
56.	**COME GO WITH ME,** Del Vikings, Dot	39
57.	**OH BABY DOLL,** Chuck Berry, Chess	62
58.	**ROCK YOUR LITTLE BABY TO SLEEP,** Buddy Knox, Roulette	58
59.	**BUILD YOUR LOVE,** Johnnie Ray, Columbia	65
60.	**AROUND THE WORLD,** Bing Crosby, Decca	57
60.	**I'M WALKIN',** Ricky Nelson, Verve	56
62.	**HE'S MINE,** Platters, Mercury	74
62.	**FALLEN STAR,** Hilltoppers, Dot	72
62.	**IS IT WRONG?** Warner Mack, Decca	62
65.	**THAT'LL BE THE DAY,** Crickets, Brunswick	—
66.	**FALLEN STAR,** Jim Newman, Dot	54
67.	**MY PERSONAL POSSESSION,** Nat (King) Cole, Capitol	66
68.	**GIRL WITH THE GOLDEN BRAIDS,** Perry Como, Victor	53
68.	**REMEMBER YOU'RE MINE,** Pat Boone, Dot	—
68.	**RANG TANG DING DONG,** The Cellos, Apollo	62
71.	**TEARDROPS FROM MY HEART,** Teresa Brewer, Coral	64
71.	**WHITE SILVER SANDS,** Owen Bradley, Decca	81
73.	**DARK MOON,** Bonnie Guitar, Dot	69
73.	**LONG LONELY NIGHTS,** Clyde McPhatter, Atlantic	—
75.	**MISS ANN,** Little Richard, Specialty	58
76.	**BYE BYE LOVE,** Webb Pierce, Decca	76
77.	**DYNAMITE,** Brenda Lee, Decca	76
77.	**GONE,** Ferlin Husky, Capitol	78
79.	**FRAULEIN,** Bobby Helms, Decca	89
80.	**FOUR WALLS,** Jim Lowe, Dot	68
80.	**MISS YOU SO,** Lillian Offitt, Excello	66
82.	**FARTHER UP THE ROAD,** Bobby Blue Bland, Duke	98
82.	**THINK,** Five Royals, King	92
84.	**WHAT WILL I TELL MY HEART?** Fats Domino, Imperial	—
85.	**I LOVE YOU SO MUCH IT HURTS,** Charlie Gracie, Cameo	—
85.	**LONG LONELY NIGHTS,** Lee Andrews, Chess	—
87.	**GOIN' STEADY,** Tommy Sands, Capitol	78
87.	**I'M WALKIN',** Fats Domino, Imperial	81
87.	**PASSING STRANGERS,** Sarah Vaughan & Billy Eckstine, Mercury	98
87.	**PLEASE SEND ME SOMEONE TO LOVE,** Moonglows, Chess	88
91.	**ARROW OF LOVE,** Six Teens, Flip	87
91.	**FABULOUS,** Charlie Gracie, Cameo	84
91.	**HONEYCOMB,** Jimmie Rodgers, Roulette	—
94.	**FIRST KISS,** Norman Petty Trio, Columbia	—
94.	**IT HURTS TO BE IN LOVE,** Annie Laurie, De Luxe	84
94.	**NEXT TIME YOU SEE ME,** Little Jr. Parker, Duke	98
94.	**WHAT CAN I DO?** Donnie Elbert, De Luxe	81
94.	**WHEN I SEE YOU,** Fats Domino, Imperial	—
99.	**GONNA FIND ME A BLUEBIRD,** Eddy Arnold, Victor	—
99.	**JUST TO HOLD MY HAND,** Clyde McPhatter, Atlantic	58
99.	**LUCILLE,** Little Richard, Specialty	89
99.	**ROCKING PNEUMONIA,** Huey Smith, Ace	—
99.	**SHISH KEBAB,** Ralph Marterie, Mercury	96

NEW YORK UNIVERSITY SCHOOL OF RETAILING — STORE RECORDED SALES — THE BILLBOARD

Best Sellers in Stores

FOR SURVEY WEEK ENDING AUGUST 10, 1957

The information given in this chart is based on actual sales to customers in a scientific sample of the nation's retail record outlets during the week ending on the date shown above. Sample design, sample size, and all methods used in this continuing study of retail record sales are under the direct and continuing supervision and control of the School of Retailing of New York University.

This Week		Last Week	Weeks on Chart
1.	TEDDY BEAR (ASCAP)—Elvis Presley / LOVING YOU (BMI)—Vic 20-7000	1	9
2.	LOVE LETTERS IN THE SAND (ASCAP)—Pat Boone / BERNARDINE (ASCAP)—Dot 15570	2	15
3.	TAMMY (ASCAP)—Debbie Reynolds / French Heels (ASCAP)—Coral 61851	5	4
4.	BYE BYE LOVE (BMI)—Everly Brothers / I Wonder If I Care as Much (BMI)—Cadence 1315	3	13
5.	SEARCHIN' (BMI)—Coasters / YOUNG BLOOD (BMI)—Atco 6187	4	14
6.	DIANA (BMI)—Paul Anka / Don't Gamble With Love (BMI)—ABC-Paramount 9831	15	4
7.	RAINBOW (ASCAP)—Russ Hamilton / We Will Make Love (ASCAP)—Kapp 184	13	3
8.	I'M GONNA SIT RIGHT DOWN (ASCAP)—Billy Williams / Date With the Blues (ASCAP)—Coral 61830	7	9
9.	WHITE SILVER SANDS (BMI)—Don Rondo / Stars Fell on Alabama (ASCAP)—Jubilee 5288	11	4
10.	SO RARE (ASCAP)—Jimmy Dorsey / Sophisticated Swing (ASCAP)—Fraternity 755	9	19
11.	LOVE ME TO PIECES (BMI)—Jill Corey / Love (BMI)—Col 40955	21	2
12.	WHISPERING BELLS (BMI)—Del Vikings / Don't Be a Fool (BMI)—Dot 15592	10	6
13.	SEND FOR ME (BMI)—Nat (King) Cole / MY PERSONAL POSSESSION (BMI)—Cap 3737	6	8
13.	REMEMBER YOU'RE MINE (ASCAP)—Pat Boone / There's a Gold Mine in the Sky (ASCAP)—Dot 15602	28	2
15.	WHOLE LOTTA' SHAKIN' GOIN' ON (BMI)—Jerry Lee Lewis / It'll Be Mine (BMI)—Sun 267	17	4
16.	IT'S NOT FOR ME TO SAY (ASCAP)—Johnny Mathis / Warm and Tender (ASCAP)—Col 40851	12	13
17.	STARDUST (ASCAP)—Billy Ward / Lucinda (BMI)—Liberty 55071	15	5
18.	SHORT FAT FANNIE (BMI)—Larry Williams / High School Dance (BMI)—Specialty 608	8	7
19.	IN THE MIDDLE OF AN ISLAND (ASCAP)—Tony Bennett / I AM (ASCAP)—Col 40965	25	2
20.	FLYING SAUCER—Buchanan & Goodman / Martian Melody (BMI)—Luniverse 105	18	4
21.	THAT'LL BE THE DAY (BMI)—Crickets / I'm Lookin' for Someone to Love (BMI)—Brunswick 55009	—	1
22.	JENNY, JENNY (BMI)—Little Richard / MISS ANN (BMI)—Specialty 606	23	9
23.	OLD CAPE COD (ASCAP)—Patti Page / WONDERING (BMI)—Mercury 71101	14	11
24	SHANGRI-LA (ASCAP)—Four Coins / First in Line (ASCAP)—Epic 9213	29	5
25.	TO THE AISLE (BMI)—Five Satins / Wish I Had My Baby (BMI)—Ember 1019	—	1
26.	GONNA FIND ME A BLUEBIRD (BMI)—Marvin Rainwater / So You Think You've Got Trouble (BMI)—M-G-M 12412	19	4
27.	TAMMY (BMI)—Ames Brothers / ROCKIN' SHOES (ASCAP)—Vic 6930	26	2
28.	WHITE SPORT COAT (BMI)—Marty Robbins / Grown-Up Tears (BMI)—Col 40864	—	15
28.	HONEY COMB (ASCAP)—Jimmie Rodgers / Their Hearts Were Full of Spring (ASCAP)—Roulette 4015	—	1
30.	MR. LEE (BMI)—Bobbettes / Look at the Stars (BMI)—Atlantic 1144	27	2

Most Played by Jockeys

FOR SURVEY WEEK ENDING AUGUST 10, 1957

SIDES are ranked in order of the greatest number of plays on disk jockey radio shows thruout the country. Results are based on The Billboard's weekly survey among the nation's disk jockeys. The reverse side of each record is also listed.

This Week		Last Week	Weeks on Chart
1.	TAMMY (ASCAP)—Debbie Reynolds / French Heels (ASCAP)—Coral 61851	3	5
2.	TEDDY BEAR (ASCAP)—Elvis Presley / Loving You (BMI)—Vic 7000	1	16
3.	I'M GONNA SIT RIGHT DOWN (ASCAP)—Billy Williams / Date With the Blues (ASCAP)—Coral 61830	4	9
4.	OLD CAPE COD (ASCAP)—Patti Page / Wondering (BMI)—Mer 71101	5	12
5.	BYE BYE LOVE (BMI)—Everly Brothers / I Wonder If I Care as Much (BMI)—Cadence 1315	6	12
6.	LOVE LETTERS IN THE SAND (ASCAP)—Pat Boone / Bernardine (ASCAP)—Dot 15570	2	15
7.	TAMMY (ASCAP)—Ames Brothers / Rockin' Shoes (BMI)—Vic 6930	11	5
8.	WHITE SILVER SANDS (BMI)—Don Rondo / Stars Fell on Alabama (ASCAP)—Jubilee 5288	7	4
9.	IT'S NOT FOR ME TO SAY (ASCAP) Johnny Mathis / Warm and Tender (ASCAP)—Col 40851	8	13
10.	SO RARE (ASCAP)—Jimmy Dorsey / Sophisticated Swing (ASCAP)—Fraternity 755	9	16
11.	SEND FOR ME (BMI)—Nat (King) Cole / My Personal Possession (BMI)—Cap 3737	17	6
12.	STARDUST (ASCAP)—Billy Ward / Lucinda (BMI)—Liberty 55071	—	3
13.	WHOLE LOTTA SHAKIN' GOIN' ON (BMI)—Jerry Lee Lewis / I'll Be Me (BMI)—Sun 267	16	2
14.	RAINBOW (ASCAP)—Russ Hamilton / We Will Make Love (ASCAP)—Kapp 184	12	3
15.	SHORT FAT FANNIE (BMI)—Larry Williams / High School Dance (BMI)—Specialty 608	20	5
16.	DIANA (BMI)—Paul Anka / Don't Gamble With Love (BMI)—ABC-Paramount 9831	10	2
17.	AROUND THE WORLD (ASCAP)—Mantovani / The Road to Ballingarry (ASCAP)—London 1746	18	5
18.	SEARCHIN' (BMI)—Coasters / Young Blood (BMI)—Atco 6987	13	12
19.	WHISPERING BELLS (BMI—Del Vikings / Don't Be a Fool (BMI)—Dot 15592	20	2
20.	LOVING YOU (BMI)—Elvis Presley / Teddy Bear (ASCAP)—Vic 7000	—	4
20.	THERE'S A GOLD MINE IN THE SKY (ASCAP)—Pat Boone / Remember You're Mine (ASCAP)—Dot 16602	—	1
22.	LOVE ME TO PIECES (BMI)—Jill Corey / Love (BMI)—Col 40955	15	3
23.	SHANGRI-LA (ASCAP)—Four Coins / First in Line (ASCAP)—Epic 9213	14	6
24.	BERNARDINE (ASCAP)—Pat Boone / Love Letters in the Sand (ASCAP)—Dot 15570	—	5
25.	IN THE MIDDLE OF AN ISLAND (ASCAP)—Tony Bennett / I Am (ASCAP)—Col 40965	—	1

Top 100 Sides

STORE RECORDED SALES — NEW YORK UNIVERSITY SCHOOL OF RETAILING — THE BILLBOARD

FOR SURVEY WEEK ENDING AUGUST 10

This is a tabulation of dealer unit sales listed according to the specific side requested by customers. No attempt is made to add sides together to reflect actual record sales. It is therefore a tabulation of sides or songs, and not records. This fact, together with longer four-week survey periods, explains variation between the top 30 sides as reflected in this chart, and top 30 record sellers as reflected in "Best Sellers in Stores."

1.	**TEDDY BEAR,** Elvis Presley, Victor	1
2.	**BYE BYE LOVE,** Everly Brothers, Cadence	2
3.	**LOVE LETTERS IN THE SAND,** Pat Boone, Dot	3
4.	**TAMMY,** Debbie Reynolds, Coral	7
5.	**SEARCHIN',** Coasters, Atco	5
6.	**I'M GONNA SIT RIGHT DOWN,** Billy Williams, Coral	10
7.	**SO RARE,** Jimmy Dorsey, Fraternity	4
8.	**SHORT FAT FANNIE,** Larry Williams, Specialty	6
9.	**WHISPERING BELLS,** Del Vikings, Dot	9
10.	**WHITE SILVER SANDS,** Don Rondo, Jubilee	12
11.	**SEND FOR ME,** Nat (King) Cole, Capitol	8
12.	**IT'S NOT FOR ME TO SAY,** Johnny Mathis, Columbia	14
13.	**DIANA,** Paul Anka, ABC-Paramount	17
14.	**RAINBOW,** Russ Hamilton, Kapp	21
15.	**STARDUST,** Billy Ward, Liberty	13
16.	**OLD CAPE COD,** Patti Page, Mercury	11
17.	**WHOLE LOTTA SHAKIN' GOIN' ON,** Jerry Lee Lewis, Sun	23
18.	**JENNY JENNY,** Little Richard, Specialty	16
19.	**FLYING SAUCER,** Buchanan & Goodman, Luniverse	19
20.	**LOVE ME TO PIECES,** Jill Corey, Columbia	45
21.	**DARK MOON,** Gale Storm, Dot	15
22.	**OVER THE MOUNTAIN,** Johnnie & Joe, Chess	18
23.	**SHANGRI-LA,** Four Coins, Epic	29
24.	**I LIKE YOUR KIND OF LOVE,** Andy Williams, Cadence	42
25.	**GONNA FIND ME A BLUEBIRD,** Marvin Rainwater, M-G-M	22
26.	**TEENAGER'S ROMANCE,** Ricky Nelson, Verve	20
27.	**WHITE SPORT COAT,** Marty Robbins, Columbia	27
28.	**BERNARDINE,** Pat Boone, Dot	28
29.	**LOVING YOU,** Elvis Presley, Victor	32
30.	**TO THE AISLE,** Five Satins, Ember	39
30.	**IN THE MIDDLE OF AN ISLAND,** Tony Bennett, Columbia	51
32.	**AROUND THE WORLD IN 80 DAYS,** Mantovani, London	25
33.	**START MOVIN',** Sal Mineo, Epic	30
34.	**AROUND THE WORLD IN 80 DAYS,** Victor Young, Decca	26
35.	**WHITE SILVER SANDS,** Dave Gardner, OJ	33
36.	**VALLEY OF TEARS,** Fats Domino, Imperial	31
36.	**WONDERFUL WONDERFUL,** Johnny Mathis, Columbia	36
38.	**ALL SHOOK UP,** Elvis Presley, Victor	32
39.	**THAT'LL BE THE DAY,** Crickets, Brunswick	65
40.	**TAMMY,** Ames Brothers, Victor	41
41.	**MR. LEE,** Bobbettes, Atlantic	49
41.	**YOUNG BLOOD,** Coasters, Atco	24
43.	**FOUR WALLS,** Jim Reeves, Victor	40
44.	**FREIGHT TRAIN,** Rusty Draper, Mercury	37
45.	**ISLAND IN THE SUN,** Harry Belafonte, Victor	46
46.	**GOODY GOODY,** Teenagers, Gee	48
46.	**SUSIE-Q,** Dale Hawkins, Checker	43
48.	**C. C. RIDER,** Chuck Willis, Atlantic	35
49.	**COOL SHAKE,** Del Vikings, Mercury	54
50.	**LET THE FOUR WINDS BLOW,** Roy Brown, Imperial	44
51.	**FALLEN STAR,** Ferlin Husky, Capitol	47
52.	**HONEYCOMB,** Jimmie Rodgers, Roulette	91
52.	**REMEMBER YOU'RE MINE,** Pat Boone, Dot	68
54.	**LONG LONELY NIGHTS,** Lee Andrews, Chess	85
55.	**LITTLE DARLIN',** Diamonds, Mercury	50
56.	**LONG LONELY NIGHTS,** Clyde McPhatter, Atlantic	73
57.	**FALLEN STAR,** Jim Newman, Dot	66
57.	**GOLD MINE IN THE SKY,** Pat Boone, Dot	—
59.	**WITH ALL MY HEART,** Jodie Sands, Chancellor	54
60.	**FALLEN STAR,** Hilltoppers, Dot	62
61.	**OH BABY DOLL,** Chuck Berry, Chess	57
62.	**WHEN I SEE YOU,** Fats Domino, Imperial	94
63.	**IS IT WRONG,** Warner Mack, Decca	63
63.	**MY PERSONAL POSSESSION,** Nat (King) Cole, Capitol	67
65.	**BUILD YOUR LOVE,** Johnnie Ray, Columbia	59
65.	**COME GO WITH ME,** Del Vikings, Dot	56
65.	**FRAULEIN,** Bobby Helms, Decca	79
68.	**HE'S MINE,** Platters, Mercury	62
68.	**RANG TANG DING DONG,** Cellos, Apollo	68
68.	**SCHOOL DAY,** Chuck Berry, Chess	52
68.	**WHITE SILVER SANDS,** Owen Bradley, Decca	71
72.	**DYNAMITE,** Brenda Lee, Decca	77
73.	**AROUND THE WORLD IN 80 DAYS,** Bing Crosby, Decca	60
73.	**MY DREAM,** Platters, Mercury	53
73.	**MISS ANN,** Little Richard, Specialty	75
73.	**ROCK YOUR LITTLE BABY TO SLEEP,** Buddy Knox, Roulette	58
77.	**I LOVE YOU SO MUCH IT HURTS,** Charlie Gracie, Cameo	85
77.	**I'M WALKIN',** Ricky Nelson, Verve	60
77.	**ROCKIN' PNEUMONIA,** Huey Smith, Ace	99
80.	**FARTHER UP THE ROAD,** Bobby Blue Bland, Duke	82
80.	**WHAT WILL I TELL MY HEART,** Fats Domino, Imperial	—
82.	**BYE BYE LOVE,** Webb Pierce, Decca	76
82.	**DARK MOON,** Bonnie Guitar, Dot	73
82.	**PASSING STRANGERS,** Sarah Vaughan & Billy Eckstine, Mercury	87
85.	**DARLING IT'S WONDERFUL,** Lovers, Lamp	—
85.	**GONE,** Ferlin Husky, Capitol	77
85.	**GIRL WITH THE GOLDEN BRAIDS,** Perry Como, Victor	68
88.	**FIRST KISS,** Norman Petty Trio, Columbia	94
88.	**FOUR WALLS,** Jim Lowe, Dot	80
88.	**MISS YOU SO,** Lillian Offitt, Excello	80
88.	**TEARDROPS FROM MY HEART,** Teresa Brewer, Coral	71
88.	**THINK,** Five Royals, King	82
93.	**I AM,** Tony Bennett, Columbia	—
94.	**JUNE NIGHT,** Jimmy Dorsey, Fraternity	—
96.	**ROCKIN' SHOES,** Ames Brothers, Victor	—
97.	**I'M WALKIN',** Fats Domino, Imperial	87
98.	**AROUND THE WORLD,** McGuire Sisters, Coral	—
98.	**LOTTA LOVIN',** Gene Vincent, Capitol	—
98.	**ROUND AND ROUND,** Perry Como, Victor	—
98.	**TONIGHT TONIGHT,** Mello-Kings, Herald	—

STORE RECORDED SALES — NEW YORK UNIVERSITY SCHOOL OF RETAILING — THE BILLBOARD

Best Sellers in Stores

FOR SURVEY WEEK ENDING AUGUST 17, 1957

The information given in this chart is based on actual sales to customers in a scientific sample of the nation's retail record outlets during the week ending on the date shown above. Sample design, sample size, and all methods used in this continuing study of retail record sales are under the direct and continuing supervision and control of the School of Retailing of New York University.

This Week		Last Week	Weeks on Chart
1.	TAMMY (ASCAP)—Debbie Reynolds... French Heels (ASCAP)—Coral 61851	3	5
2.	TEDDY BEAR (ASCAP)—Elvis Presley. LOVING YOU (BMI)—Vic 20-7000	1	10
3.	DIANA (BMI)—Paul Anka............ Don't Gamble With Love (BMI)—ABC-Paramount 9831	6	5
4.	SEARCHIN' (BMI)—Coasters......... YOUNG BLOOD (BMI)—Atco 6087	5	13
5.	LOVE LETTERS IN THE SAND (ASCAP)—Pat Boone............... BERNARDINE (ASCAP)—Dot 15570	2	16
6.	BYE BYE LOVE (BMI)—Everly Brothers.................... I Wonder If I Care as Much (BMI)—Cadence 1315	4	14
7.	THAT'LL BE THE DAY (BMI)—Crickets .... I'm Lookin' for Someone to Love (BMI)—Brunswick 55009	21	2
8.	RAINBOW (ASCAP)—Russ Hamilton... We Will Make Love (ASCAP)—Kapp 184	7	4
9.	SEND FOR ME (BMI)—Nat (King) Cole................... MY PERSONAL POSSESSION (BMI)—Cap 3737	13	9
10.	SO RARE (ASCAP)—Jimmy Dorsey.... Sophisticated Swing (ASCAP)—Fraternity 755	10	20
11.	WHITE SILVER SANDS (BMI)—Don Rondo........................ Stars Fell on Alabama (ASCAP)—Jubilee 5288	9	5
12.	WHISPERING BELLS (BMI)—Del Vikings...................... Don't Be a Fool (BMI)—Dot 15592	12	7
13.	SHORT FAT FANNIE (BMI)—Larry Williams................... High School Dance (BMI)—Specialty 608	18	8
13.	REMEMBER YOU'RE MINE (ASCAP)—Pat Boone............... THERE'S A GOLD MINE IN THE SKY (ASCAP)—Dot 15602	13	3
15.	I'M GONNA SIT RIGHT DOWN AND WRITE MYSELF A LETTER (ASCAP)—Billy Williams............ DATE WITH THE BLUES (ASCAP)—Coral 61830	8	10
16.	WHOLE LOTTA SHAKIN' GOIN' ON (BMI)—Jerry Lee Lewis............ It'll Be Mine (BMI)—Sun 267	15	5
17.	LOVE ME TO PIECES (BMI)—Jill Corey Love (BMI)—Col 40955	11	3
18.	HONEYCOMB (ASCAP)—Jimmie Rodgers.................. Their Hearts Were Full of Spring (ASCAP)—Roulette 4015	28	2
19.	JENNY, JENNY (BMI)—Little Richard. MISS ANN (BMI)—Specialty 606	22	10
20.	STARDUST (ASCAP)—Billy Ward..... Lucinda (BMI)—Liberty 55071	17	6
21.	IN THE MIDDLE OF AN ISLAND (ASCAP)—Tony Bennett............ I AM (ASCAP)—Col 40965	19	3
21.	OLD CAPE COD (ASCAP)—Patti Page. WONDERING (BMI)—Mercury 71101	23	12
23.	FLYING SAUCER—Buchanan & Goodman .... Martian Melody (BMI)—Luniverse 105	20	5
24.	MR. LEE (BMI)—Bobbettes .... Look at the Stars (BMI)—Atlantic 1144	30	3
25.	IT'S NOT FOR ME TO SAY (ASCAP)—Johnny Mathis..................... Warm and Tender (ASCAP)—Col 40851	16	14
26.	TO THE AISLE (BMI)—Five Satins... Wish I Had My Baby (BMI)—Ember 1019	25	2
27.	TAMMY (BMI)—Ames Brothers....... ROCKIN' SHOES (ASCAP)—Vic 6930	27	3
27.	SHANGRI-LA (ASCAP)—Four Coins... First in Line (ASCAP)—Epic 9213	24	6
29.	GOODY GOODY (ASCAP)—Teenagers .... Creation of Love (BMI)—Gee 1039	—	1
30.	WHEN I SEE YOU (BMI)—Fats Domino...................... WHAT WILL I TELL MY HEART? (ASCAP)—Imperial 5454	—	1

Most Played by Jockeys

FOR SURVEY WEEK ENDING AUGUST 17, 1957

SIDES are ranked in order of the greatest number of plays on disk jockey radio shows thruout the country. Results are based on The Billboard's weekly survey among the nation's disk jockeys. The reverse side of each record is also listed.

This Week		Last Week	Weeks on Chart
1.	TAMMY (ASCAP)—Debbie Reynolds.. French Heels (ASCAP)—Coral 61851	1	6
2.	TEDDY BEAR (ASCAP)—Elvis Presley.. Loving You (BMI)—Vic 7000	2	17
3.	I'M GONNA SIT RIGHT DOWN AND WRITE MYSELF A LETTER (ASCAP)—Billy Williams............ Date With the Blues (ASCAP)—Coral 61830	3	10
4.	LOVE LETTERS IN THE SAND (ASCAP)—Pat Boone............... Bernardine (ASCAP)—Dot 15570	6	16
5.	TAMMY (ASCAP)—Ames Brothers..... Rockin' Shoes (BMI)—Vic 6930	7	6
6.	OLD CAPE COD (ASCAP)—Patti Page Wondering (BMI)—Mercury 71101	4	13
7.	BYE BYE LOVE (BMI)—Everly Brothers.................... I Wonder If I Care as Much (BMI)—Cadence 1315	5	13
8.	WHITE SILVER SANDS (BMI)—Don Rondo.......................... Stars Fell on Alabama (ASCAP)—Jubilee 5288	8	5
9.	HONEYCOMB (ASCAP)—Jimmy Rodgers Their Hearts Were Full of Spring (ASCAP)—Roulette 4015	—	1
10.	IT'S NOT FOR ME TO SAY (ASCAP)—Johnny Mathis.................... Warm and Tender (ASCAP)—Col 40851	9	14
11.	RAINBOW (ASCAP)—Russ Hamilton... We Will Make Love—Kapp 184	14	4
12.	REMEMBER YOU'RE MINE (ASCAP)—Pat Boone....................... There's a Gold Mine in the Sky (ASCAP)—Dot 15602	—	1
13.	AROUND THE WORLD (ASCAP)—Mantovani .... The Road to Ballingarry (ASCAP)—London 1746	17	6
14.	SEND FOR ME (BMI)—Nat (King) Cole.................... My Personal Possession (BMI)—Cap 3737	11	7
14.	IN THE MIDDLE OF THE ISLAND (ASCAP)—Tony Bennett............ I Am (ASCAP)—Col 40965	25	2
16.	DIANA (BMI)—Paul Anka............ Don't Gamble With Love (BMI)—ABC-Paramount 9831	16	3
17.	WHOLE LOTTA SHAKIN' GOIN' ON (BMI)—Jerry Lee Lewis............ It'll Be Mine (BMI)—Sun 267	13	3
18.	AROUND THE WORLD (ASCAP)—Victor Young....................... Around the World (Vocal) (ASCAP)—Dec 30262	—	6
19.	STARDUST (ASCAP)—Billy Ward..... Lucinda (BMI)—Liberty 55071	12	4
19.	WHISPERING BELLS (BMI)—Del Vikings...................... Don't Be a Fool (BMI)—Dot 15592	19	3
21.	SO RARE (ASCAP)—Jimmy Dorsey.... Sophisticated Swing (ASCAP)—Fraternity 755	10	17
22.	LOVE ME TO PIECES (BMI)—Jill Corey Love (BMI)—Col 40955	22	4
23.	SHANGRI-LA (ASCAP)—Four Coins... First in Line (ASCAP)—Epic 9213	23	7
24.	LOVING YOU (BMI)—Elvis Presley.... Teddy Bear (ASCAP)—Vic 7000	20	5
25.	THAT'LL BE THE DAY (BMI)—Crickets I'm Lookin' for Someone to Love (BMI)—Brunswick 55009	—	

STORE RECORDED SALES — NEW YORK UNIVERSITY SCHOOL OF RETAILING — THE BILLBOARD

Top 100 Sides

FOR SURVEY WEEK ENDING AUGUST 17

This is a tabulation of dealer unit sales listed according to the specific side requested by customers. No attempt is made to add sides together to reflect actual record sales. It is therefore a tabulation of sides or songs, and not records. This fact, together with longer four-week survey periods, explains variation between the top 30 sides as reflected in this chart, and top 30 record sellers as reflected in "Best Sellers in Stores."

Position	Song, Artist, Label	Position Last Week
1.	**TEDDY BEAR,** Elvis Presley, Victor	1
2.	**TAMMY,** Debbie Reynolds, Coral	4
3.	**BYE BYE LOVE,** Everly Brothers, Cadence	2
4.	**LOVE LETTERS IN THE SAND,** Pat Boone, Dot	3
5.	**SEARCHIN',** Coasters, Atco	5
6.	**DIANA,** Paul Anka, ABC-Paramount	13
7.	**SO RARE,** Jimmy Dorsey, Fraternity	7
8.	**I'M GONNA SIT RIGHT DOWN AND WRITE MYSELF A LETTER,** Billy Williams, Coral	6
9.	**SHORT FAT FANNIE,** Larry Williams, Specialty	8
10.	**WHISPERING BELLS,** Del Vikings, Dot	9
11.	**SEND FOR ME,** Nat (King) Cole, Capitol	11
12.	**RAINBOW,** Russ Hamilton, Kapp	14
13.	**WHITE SILVER SANDS,** Don Rondo, Jubilee	10
14.	**WHOLE LOTTA SHAKIN' GOIN' ON,** Jerry Lee Lewis, Sun	17
15.	**THAT'LL BE THE DAY,** Crickets, Brunswick	39
16.	**STARDUST,** Billy Ward, Liberty	15
17.	**IT'S NOT FOR ME TO SAY,** Johnny Mathis, Columbia	12
18.	**OLD CAPE COD,** Patti Page, Mercury	16
19.	**LOVE ME TO PIECES,** Jill Corey, Columbia	20
20.	**FLYING SAUCER,** Buchanan & Goodman, Luniverse	19
21.	**JENNY JENNY,** Little Richard, Specialty	18
22.	**IN THE MIDDLE OF AN ISLAND,** Tony Bennett, Columbia	30
23.	**MR. LEE,** Bobbettes, Atlantic	41
24.	**HONEYCOMB,** Jimmie Rodgers, Roulette	52
25.	**SHANGRI-LA,** Four Coins, Epic	23
26.	**GONNA FIND ME A BLUEBIRD,** Marvin Rainwater, M-G-M	25
27.	**TO THE AISLE,** Five Satins, Ember	30
28.	**REMEMBER YOU'RE MINE,** Pat Boone, Dot	52
29.	**AROUND THE WORLD,** Mantovani, London	32
30.	**GOODY GOODY,** Teenagers, Gee	46
31.	**I LIKE YOUR KIND OF LOVE,** Andy Williams, Cadence	24
32.	**WHITE SPORT COAT,** Marty Robbins, Columbia	27
33.	**LOVING YOU,** Elvis Presley, Victor	28
34.	**TAMMY,** Ames Brothers, Victor	40
35.	**DARK MOON,** Gale Storm, Dot	21
36.	**OVER THE MOUNTAIN,** Johnnie & Joe, Chess	22
37.	**WONDERFUL WONDERFUL,** Johnny Mathis, Columbia	36
38.	**TEENAGERS ROMANCE,** Ricky Nelson, Verve	26
39.	**ALL SHOOK UP,** Elvis Presley, Victor	38
39.	**BERNARDINE,** Pat Boone, Dot	28
41.	**FOUR WALLS,** Jim Reeves, Victor	43
42.	**ISLAND IN THE SUN,** Harry Belafonte, Victor	45
43.	**WHEN I SEE YOU,** Fats Domino, Imperial	62
44.	**YOUNG BLOOD,** Coasters, Atco	41
45.	**LONG LONELY NIGHTS,** Lee Andrews, Chess	54
46.	**COOL SHAKE,** Del Vikings, Mercury	49
46.	**LET THE FOUR WINDS BLOW,** Roy Brown, Imperial	50
48.	**THERE'S A GOLD MINE IN THE SKY,** Pat Boone, Dot	57
48.	**VALLEY OF TEARS,** Fats Domino, Imperial	36
50.	**START MOVIN',** Sal Mineo, Epic	33
51.	**SUSIE Q,** Dale Hawkins, Checker	46
52.	**AROUND THE WORLD,** Victor Young, Decca	34
52.	**FREIGHT TRAIN,** Rusty Draper, Mercury	44
54.	**C. C. RIDER,** Chuck Willis, Atlantic	48
55.	**FALLEN STAR,** Ferlin Husky, Capitol	51
56.	**WHITE SILVER SANDS,** Dave Gardner, OJ	35
57.	**LONG LONELY NIGHTS,** Clyde McPhatter, Atlantic	56
58.	**FALLEN STAR,** Hilltoppers, Dot	60
59.	**OH BABY DOLL,** Chuck Berry, Chess	61
60.	**FALLEN STAR,** Jimmy Newman, Dot	57
61.	**AROUND THE WORLD,** Bing Crosby, Decca	73
61.	**WITH ALL MY HEART,** Jodi Sands, Chancellor	59
63.	**FRAULEIN,** Bobby Helms, Decca	65
64.	**WHAT WILL I TELL MY HEART?** Fats Domino, Imperial	80
64.	**MY PERSONAL POSSESSION,** Nat (King) Cole, Capitol	63
66.	**DARLING IT'S WONDERFUL,** Lovers, Lamp	85
66.	**IN THE MIDDLE OF AN ISLAND,** Tennessee Ernie Ford, Capitol	—
68.	**JUNE NIGHT,** Jimmy Dorsey, Fraternity	94
68.	**SCHOOL DAYS,** Chuck Berry, Chess	63
70.	**ROCKIN' PNEUMONIA AND THE BOOGIE WOOGIE FLU** Huey Smith, Chess	77
71.	**COME GO WITH ME,** Del Vikings, Dot	65
71.	**I LOVE YOU SO MUCH IT HURTS,** Charlie Gracie, Cameo	77
73.	**AROUND THE WORLD,** McGuire Sisters, Coral	98
73.	**LITTLE DARLIN',** Diamonds, Mercury	55
75.	**YOU'RE MY ONE AND ONLY LOVE,** Ricky Nelson, Verve	—
76.	**ROCKIN' SHOES,** Ames Brothers, Victor	96
77.	**LOTTA LOVIN',** Gene Vincent, Capitol	98
78.	**BUILD YOUR LOVE,** Johnnie Ray, Columbia	65
78.	**FARTHER UP THE ROAD,** Bobby (Blue) Bland, Duke	80
80.	**DARK MOON,** Bonnie Guitar, Dot	82
80.	**HIGH SCHOOL ROMANCE,** George Hamilton IV, ABC-Paramount	94
80.	**ROCK YOUR BABY TO SLEEP,** Buddy Knox, Roulette	73
83.	**HE'S MINE,** Platters, Mercury	68
83.	**MY DREAM,** Platters, Mercury	73
85.	**DYNAMITE,** Brenda Lee, Decca	72
85.	**MISS ANN,** Little Richard, Specialty	73
87.	**AND THAT REMINDS ME,** Della Reese, Jubilee	—
87.	**FASCINATION,** Jane Morgan, Kapp	—
89.	**FOUR WALLS,** Jim Lowe, Dot	88
89.	**PASSING STRANGERS,** Sarah Vaughan & Billy Eckstine, Mercury	82
89.	**TONIGHT TONIGHT,** Mello-Kings, Herald	98
92.	**FIRST KISS,** Norman Petty Trio, Columbia	88
92.	**I'M WALKIN',** Ricky Nelson, Verve	77
92.	**JAY-DEE'S BOOGIE WOOGIE,** Jimmy Dorsey, Fraternity	—
95.	**BLACK SLACKS,** Joe Bennett & Sparkletones, ABC-Paramount	—
95.	**GONE,** Ferlin Husky, Capitol	85
97.	**ZIP ZIP,** Diamonds, Mercury	—
98.	**IS IT WRONG?** Warner Mack, Decca	63
98.	**MISS YOU SO,** Lillian Offitt, Excello	88
98.	**ROUND AND ROUND,** Perry Como, Victor	98
98.	**RANG TANG DING DONG,** Cellos, Apollo	68
98.	**WHITE SILVER SANDS,** Owen Bradley, Decca	68

NEW YORK UNIVERSITY SCHOOL OF RETAILING · THE BILLBOARD · STORE RECORDED SALES

Best Sellers in Stores

FOR SURVEY WEEK ENDING AUGUST 24, 1957

The information given in this chart is based on actual sales to customers in a scientific sample of the nation's retail record outlets during the week ending on the date shown above. Sample design, sample size, and all methods used in this continuing study of retail record sales are under the direct and continuing supervision and control of the School of Retailing of New York University.

This Week		Last Week	Weeks on Chart
1.	TAMMY (ASCAP)—Debbie Reynolds. French Heels (ASCAP)—Coral 61851	1	6
2.	DIANA (BMI)—Paul Anka. Don't Gamble With Love (BMI)—ABC-Paramount 9831	3	6
3.	TEDDY BEAR (ASCAP)—Elvis Presley. LOVING YOU (BMI)—Vic 20-7000	2	11
4.	THAT'LL BE THE DAY (BMI)—Crickets. I'm Lookin' for Someone to Love (BMI)—Brunswick 55009	7	3
5.	BYE BYE LOVE (BMI)—Everly Brothers. I Wonder If I Care as Much (BMI)—Cadence 1315	6	15
6.	WHOLE LOTTA SHAKIN' GOIN' ON (BMI)—Jerry Lee Lewis. It'll Be Mine (BMI)—Sun 267	16	6
7.	SEND FOR ME (BMI)—Nat (King) Cole. MY PERSONAL POSSESSION (BMI)—Cap 3737	9	10
8.	HONEYCOMB (ASCAP)—Jimmie Rodgers. Their Hearts Were Full of Spring (ASCAP)—Roulette 4015	18	3
9.	LOVE LETTERS IN THE SAND (ASCAP)—Pat Boone. BERNARDINE (ASCAP)—Dot 15570	5	17
10.	SEARCHIN' (BMI)—Coasters. Young Blood (BMI)—Atco 6087	4	16
11.	SHORT FAT FANNIE (BMI)—Larry Williams. HIGH SCHOOL DANCE (BMI)—Specialty 608	13	9
12.	WHISPERING BELLS (BMI)—Del Vikings. Don't Be a Fool (BMI)—Dot 15592	12	8
13.	REMEMBER YOU'RE MINE (ASCAP)—Pat Boone. THERE'S A GOLD MINE IN THE SKY (ASCAP)—Dot 15602	13	4
14.	RAINBOW (ASCAP)—Russ Hamilton. We Will Make Love (ASCAP)—Kapp 184	8	5
15.	STARDUST (ASCAP)—Billy Ward. Lucinda (BMI)—Liberty 55071	20	7
16.	MR. LEE (BMI)—Bobbettes. Look at the Stars (BMI)—Atlantic 1144	24	4
17.	WHITE SILVER SANDS (BMI)—Don Rondo. Stars Fell on Alabama (ASCAP)—Jubilee 5288	11	6
18.	I'M GONNA SIT RIGHT DOWN AND WRITE MYSELF A LETTER (ASCAP)—Billy Williams. DATE WITH THE BLUES (ASCAP)—Coral 61830	15	11
19.	SO RARE (ASCAP)—Jimmy Dorsey. Sophisticated Swing (ASCAP)—Fraternity 755	10	21
20.	GOODY GOODY (ASCAP)—Teenagers. Creation of Love (BMI)—Gee 1039	29	2
21.	IN THE MIDDLE OF AN ISLAND (ASCAP)—Tony Bennett. I AM (ASCAP)—Col 40965	21	4
22.	OLD CAPE COD (ASCAP)—Patti Page. WONDERING (BMI)—Mercury 71101	21	13
23.	FLYING SAUCER—Buchanan & Goodman. Martian Melody, Luniverse 105	23	6
23.	JENNY, JENNY (BMI)—Little Richard. MISS ANN (BMI)—Specialty 606	19	11
25.	IT'S NOT FOR ME TO SAY (ASCAP)—Johnny Mathis. Warm and Tender (ASCAP)—Col 40851	25	15
26.	LOVE ME TO PIECES (BMI)—Jill Corey. Love (BMI)—Col 40955	17	4
26.	TAMMY (BMI)—Ames Brothers. ROCKIN' SHOES (ASCAP)—Vic 6930	27	4
28.	TO THE AISLE (BMI)—Five Satins. Wish I Had My Baby (BMI)—Ember 1019	26	3
29.	WHEN I SEE YOU (BMI)—Fats Domino. WHAT WILL I TELL MY HEART? (ASCAP)—Imperial 5454	30	2
30.	AROUND THE WORLD (ASCAP)—Mantovani. The Road to Ballingarry (ASCAP)—London 1746	—	5

Most Played by Jockeys

FOR SURVEY WEEK ENDING AUGUST 24, 1957

SIDES are ranked in order of the greatest number of plays on disk jockey radio shows thruout the country. Results are based on The Billboard's weekly survey among the nation's disk jockeys. The reverse side of each record is also listed.

This Week		Last Week	Weeks on Chart
1.	TAMMY (ASCAP)—Debbie Reynolds. French Heels (ASCAP)—Coral 61851	1	7
2.	TEDDY BEAR (ASCAP)—Elvis Presley. Loving You (BMI)—Vic 7000	2	18
3.	I'M GONNA SIT RIGHT DOWN AND WRITE MYSELF A LETTER (ASCAP)—Billy Williams. Date With the Blues (ASCAP)—Coral 61830	3	11
4.	HONEYCOMB (ASCAP)—Jimmy Rodgers. Their Hearts Were Full of Spring (ASCAP)—Roulette 4015	9	2
5.	TAMMY (ASCAP)—Ames Brothers. Rockin' Shoes (BMI)—Vic 6930	5	7
6.	LOVE LETTERS IN THE SAND (ASCAP)—Pat Boone. Bernardine (ASCAP)—Dot 15570	4	17
7.	RAINBOW (ASCAP)—Russ Hamilton. We Will Make Love — Kapp 184	11	5
8.	IT'S NOT FOR ME TO SAY (ASCAP)—Johnny Mathis. Warm and Tender (ASCAP)—Col 40851	10	15
9.	WHITE SILVER SANDS (BMI)—Don Rondo. Stars Fell on Alabama (ASCAP)—Jubilee 5288	8	6
10.	OLD CAPE COD (ASCAP)—Patti Page. Wondering (BMI)—Mercury 71101	6	13
11.	REMEMBER YOU'RE MINE (ASCAP)—Pat Boone. There's a Gold Mine in the Sky (ASCAP)—Dot 15602	12	2
12.	SEND FOR ME (BMI)—Nat (King) Cole. My Personal Possesion (BMI)—Cap 3737	14	8
12.	AROUND THE WORLD (ASCAP)—Mantovani. The Road to Ballingarry (ASCAP)—London 1746	13	7
14.	DIANA (BMI)—Paul Anka. Don't Gamble With Love (BMI)—ABC-Paramount 9831	16	4
15.	WHOLE LOTTA SHAKIN' GOIN' ON (BMI)—Jerry Lee Lewis. It'll Be Mine (BMI)—Sun 267	17	4
16.	THAT'LL BE THE DAY (BMI)—Crickets. I'm Lookin' for Someone to Love (BMI)—Brunswick 55009	25	2
17.	IN THE MIDDLE OF AN ISLAND (ASCAP)—Tony Bennett. I Am (ASCAP)—Col 40965	14	3
18.	BYE BYE LOVE (BMI)—Everly Brothers. I Wonder If I Care as Much (BMI)—Cadence 1315	7	14
19.	LOVE ME TO PIECES (BMI)—Jill Corey. Love (BMI)—Col 40955	22	5
20.	STARDUST (ASCAP)—Billy Ward. Lucinda (BMI)—Liberty 55071	19	5
21.	GOODY GOODY (ASCAP)—Teenagers. Creation of Love (BMI)—Gee 1039	—	1
22.	SHANGRI-LA (ASCAP)—Four Coins. First in Line (ASCAP)—Epic 9213	23	8
23.	WHISPERING BELLS (BMI)—Del Vikings. Don't Be a Fool (BMI)—Dot 15592	19	4
24.	WHITE SILVER SANDS—Owen Bradley Quintet. Midnight Blues (BMI)—Dec 30363	—	4
25.	SHORT FAT FANNIE (BMI)—Larry Williams. High School Dance (BMI)—Specialty 608	—	6

STORE RECORDED SALES — NEW YORK UNIVERSITY SCHOOL OF RETAILING — THE BILLBOARD

Top 100 Sides

FOR SURVEY WEEK ENDING AUGUST 24

This is a tabulation of dealer unit sales listed according to the specific side requested by customers. No attempt is made to add sides together to reflect actual record sales. It is therefore a tabulation of sides or songs, and not records. This fact, together with longer four-week survey periods, explains variation between the top 30 sides as reflected in this chart, and top 30 record sellers as reflected in "Best Sellers in Stores."

Position	Song, Artist, Label	Position Last Week
1.	**TAMMY,** Debbie Reynolds, Coral	2
2.	**DIANA,** Paul Anka, ABC-Paramount	6
3.	**TEDDY BEAR,** Elvis Presley, Victor	1
4.	**BYE BYE LOVE,** Everly Brothers, Cadence	3
5.	**LOVE LETTERS IN THE SAND,** Pat Boone, Dot	4
6.	**THAT'LL BE THE DAY,** Crickets, Brunswick	15
7.	**SEARCHIN',** Coasters, Atco	5
8.	**WHOLE LOTTA SHAKIN' GOIN' ON,** Jerry Lee Lewis, Sun	14
9.	**RAINBOW,** Russ Hamilton, Kapp	12
10.	**WHISPERING BELLS,** Del Vikings, Dot	10
11.	**SEND FOR ME,** Nat (King) Cole, Capitol	11
12.	**WHITE SILVER SANDS,** Don Rondo, Jubilee	13
13.	**SHORT FAT FANNIE,** Larry Williams, Specialty	9
14.	**I'M GONNA SIT RIGHT DOWN AND WRITE MYSELF A LETTER** Billy Williams, Coral	8
15.	**SO RARE,** Jimmy Dorsey, Fraternity	7
16.	**HONEYCOMB,** Jimmie Rodgers, Roulette	24
17.	**STARDUST,** Billy Ward, Liberty	16
18.	**LOVE ME TO PIECES,** Jill Corey, Columbia	19
19.	**IT'S NOT FOR ME TO SAY,** Johnny Mathis, Columbia	17
20.	**MR. LEE,** Bobbettes, Atlantic	23
21.	**IN THE MIDDLE OF AN ISLAND,** Tony Bennett, Columbia	22
22.	**FLYING SAUCER,** Buchanan & Goodman, Luniverse	20
23.	**OLD CAPE COD,** Patti Page, Mercury	18
24.	**REMEMBER YOU'RE MINE,** Pat Boone, Dot	28
25.	**GOODY GOODY,** Teenagers, Gee	30
26.	**TO THE AISLE,** Five Satins, Ember	27
27.	**JENNY, JENNY,** Little Richard, Specialty	21
28.	**SHANGRI-LA,** Four Coins, Epic	25
29.	**THERE'S A GOLD MINE IN THE SKY,** Pat Boone, Dot	48
29.	**TAMMY,** Ames Brothers, Victor	34
31.	**GONNA FIND ME A BLUEBIRD,** Marvin Rainwater, M-G-M	26
32.	**AROUND THE WORLD,** Mantovani, London	29
32.	**OVER THE MOUNTAIN,** Johnnie & Joe, Chess	36
34.	**LOVING YOU,** Elvis Presley, Victor	33
35.	**WONDERFUL WONDERFUL,** Johnny Mathis, Columbia	37
36.	**I LIKE YOUR KIND OF LOVE,** Andy Williams, Cadence	31
37.	**WHITE SPORT COAT,** Marty Robbins, Columbia	32
38.	**BERNARDINE,** Pat Boone, Dot	39
39.	**WHEN I SEE YOU,** Fats Domino, Imperial	43
40.	**TEENAGER'S ROMANCE,** Ricky Nelson, Verve	38
41.	**AROUND THE WORLD,** Victor Young, Decca	52
42.	**DARK MOON,** Gale Storm, Dot	35
43.	**FOUR WALLS,** Jim Reeves, Victor	41
44.	**ISLAND IN THE SUN,** Harry Belafonte, Victor	42
45.	**LONG LONELY NIGHTS,** Lee Andrews, Chess	45
46.	**ALL SHOOK UP,** Elvis Presley, Victor	39
47.	**SUSIE Q,** Dale Hawkins, Checker	51
48.	**DARLING IT'S WONDERFUL,** Lovers, Lamp	66
48.	**VALLEY OF TEARS,** Fats Domino, Imperial	48
50.	**START MOVIN',** Sal Mineo, Epic	50
51.	**LET THE FOUR WINDS BLOW,** Roy Brown, Imperial	46
52.	**AND THAT REMINDS ME,** Della Reese, Jubilee	87
53.	**COOL SHAKE,** Del Vikings, Mercury	46
53.	**YOUNG BLOOD,** Coasters, Atco	44
55.	**LOTTA LOVIN',** Gene Vincent, Capitol	77
56.	**FALLEN STAR,** Jimmy Newman, Dot	60
57.	**JUNE NIGHT,** Jimmy Dorsey, Fraternity	68
57.	**LONG LONELY NIGHTS,** Clyde McPhatter, Atlantic	57
59.	**IN THE MIDDLE OF AN ISLAND,** Tennessee Ernie Ford, Capitol	66
60.	**FALLEN STAR,** Ferlin Husky, Capitol	55
60.	**WHITE SILVER SANDS,** Dave Gardner, OJ	56
62.	**FREIGHT TRAIN,** Rusty Draper, Mercury	52
63.	**FASCINATION,** Jane Morgan, Kapp	87
63.	**WITH ALL MY HEART,** Jodie Sands, Chancellor	61
65.	**C. C. RIDER,** Chuck Willis, Atlantic	54
65.	**FALLEN STAR,** Hilltoppers, Dot	58
67.	**FRAULEIN,** Bobby Helms, Decca	63
68.	**ROCKIN' PNEUMONIA AND THE BOOGIE WOOGIE FLU,** Huey Smith, Ace	70
69.	**HULA LOVE,** Buddy Knox, Roulette	—
70.	**SCHOOL DAY,** Chuck Berry, Chess	68
71.	**AROUND THE WORLD,** Bing Crosby, Decca	61
71.	**BON VOYAGE,** Janice Harper, Prep	—
73.	**BLACK SLACKS,** Joe Bennett & Sparkletones, ABC-Paramount	95
74.	**MY HEART REMINDS ME,** Kay Starr, Victor	—
74.	**OH, BABY DOLL,** Chuck Berry, Chess	59
74.	**YOU'RE MY ONE AND ONLY LOVE,** Ricky Nelson, Verve	75
77.	**JAY-DEE'S BOOGIE WOOGIE,** Jimmy Dorsey, Fraternity	92
78.	**DANCIN',** Perry Como, Victor	—
78.	**WHAT WILL I TELL MY HEART,** Fats Domino, Imperial	64
78.	**ROCKIN' SHOES,** Ames Brothers, Victor	76
81.	**FARTHER UP THE ROAD,** Bobby (Blue) Bland, Duke	78
81.	**FIRST KISS,** Norman Petty Trio, Columbia	92
81.	**ZIP ZIP,** Diamonds, Mercury	97
84.	**BUILD YOUR LOVE,** Johnnie Ray, Columbia	78
84.	**COME GO WITH ME,** Del Vikings, Dot	71
84.	**MY PERSONAL POSSESSION,** Nat (King) Cole, Capitol	64
84.	**ROCK YOUR LITTLE BABY TO SLEEP,** Buddy Knox, Roulette	80
88.	**PASSING STRANGERS,** Sarah Vaughan & Billy Eckstine, Mercury	89
89.	**AROUND THE WORLD,** McGuire Sisters, Coral	73
89.	**FASCINATION,** Dick Jacobs, Coral	—
89.	**LITTLE DARLIN',** Diamonds, Mercury	73
92.	**CHICKEN BABY CHICKEN,** Tony Harris, Ebb	—
92.	**HIGH SCHOOL ROMANCE,** George Hamilton IV, ABC-Paramount	80
92.	**REBEL,** Carol Jarvis, Dot	—
95.	**DARK MOON,** Bonnie Guitar, Dot	80
95.	**HE'S MINE,** Platters, Mercury	83
97.	**FASCINATION,** David Carroll, Mercury	—
97.	**MISS ANN,** Little Richard, Specialty	85
97.	**ROUND AND ROUND,** Perry Como, Victor	98
100.	**DYNAMITE,** Brenda Lee, Decca	85
100.	**FOUR WALLS,** Jim Lowe, Dot	89

STORE RECORDED SALES — NEW YORK UNIVERSITY SCHOOL OF RETAILING • THE BILLBOARD

Best Sellers in Stores

FOR SURVEY WEEK ENDING AUGUST 31, 1957

The information given in this chart is based on actual sales to customers in a scientific sample of the nation's retail record outlets during the week ending on the date shown above. Sample design, sample size, and all methods used in this continuing study of retail record sales are under the direct and continuing supervision and control of the School of Retailing of New York University.

This Week	Title	Last Week	Weeks on Chart
1.	DIANA (BMI)—Paul Anka; Don't Gamble With Love (BMI)—ABC-Paramount 9831	2	7
2.	TAMMY (ASCAP)—Debbie Reynolds; French Heels (ASCAP)—Coral 61851	1	7
3.	WHOLE LOTTA SHAKIN' GOIN' ON (BMI)—Jerry Lee Lewis; It'll Be Mine (BMI)—Sun 267	6	7
4.	TEDDY BEAR (ASCAP)—Elvis Presley; LOVING YOU (BMI)—Vic 20-7000	3	12
5.	THAT'LL BE THE DAY (BMI)—Crickets; I'm Lookn' for Someone to Love (BMI)—Brunswick 55009	4	4
6.	HONEYCOMB (ASCAP)—Jimmie Rodgers; Their Hearts Were Full of Spring (ASCAP)—Roulette 4015	8	4
7.	SEND FOR ME (BMI)—Nat (King) Cole; MY PERSONAL POSSESSION (BMI)—Cap 3737	7	11
7.	RAINBOW (ASCAP)—Russ Hamilton; We Will Make Love (ASCAP)—Kapp 184	14	6
9.	MR. LEE (BMI)—Bobbettes; Look at the Stars (BMI)—Atlantic 1144	16	5
10.	SEARCHIN' (BMI)—Coasters; YOUNG BLOOD (BMI)—Atco 6087	10	17
10.	IN THE MIDDLE OF AN ISLAND (ASCAP)—Tony Bennett; I AM (ASCAP)—Col 40965	21	5
12.	LOVE LETTERS IN THE SAND (ASCAP)—Pat Boone; BERNARDINE (ASCAP)—Dot 15570	9	18
13.	BYE BYE LOVE (BMI)—Everly Brothers; I Wonder If I Care as Much (BMI)—Cadence 1315	5	16
14.	THERE'S A GOLD MINE IN THE SKY (ASCAP)—Pat Boone; REMEMBER YOU'RE MINE (ASCAP)—Dot 15602	13	5
15.	WHISPERING BELLS (BMI)—Del Vikings; Don't Be a Fool (BMI)—Dot 15592	12	9
15.	STARDUST (ASCAP)—Billy Ward; Lucinda (BMI)—Liberty 55071	15	8
17.	WHITE SILVER SANDS (BMI)—; Stars Fell on Alabama (ASCAP)—Jubilee 5288	17	7
18.	IT'S NOT FOR ME TO SAY (ASCAP)—Johnny Mathis; Warm and Tender (ASCAP)—Col 40851	25	16
19.	SHORT FAT FANNIE (BMI)—Larry Williams; HIGH SCHOOL DANCE (BMI)—Specialty 608	11	10
19.	I'M GONNA SIT RIGHT DOWN AND WRITE MYSELF A LETTER (ASCAP)—Billy Williams; DATE WITH THE BLUES (ASCAP)—Coral 61830	18	12
21.	LOVE ME TO PIECES (BMI)—Jill Corey; Love (BMI)—Col 40955	26	5
22.	FASCINATION (ASCAP)—Jane Morgan; Midnight in Athens (ASCAP)—Kapp 191	—	1
23.	AND THAT REMINDS ME (ASCAP)—Della Reese; I Cried for You (ASCAP)—Jubilee 5292	—	1
24.	AROUND THE WORLD (ASCAP)—Victor Young; (VOCAL) (ASCAP)—Decca 30262	—	5
25.	GOODY GOODY (ASCAP)—Teenagers; Creation of Love (BMI)—Gee 1039	20	3
26.	HULA LOVE (BMI)—Buddy Knox; Devil Woman (BMI)—Roulette 4018	—	1
27.	SO RARE (ASCAP)—Jimmy Dorsey; Sophisticated Swing (ASCAP)—Fraternity 755	19	22
28.	TAMMY (BMI)—Ames Brothers; ROCKIN' SHOES (ASCAP)—Vic 6930	26	5
28.	WONDERFUL, WONDERFUL (BMI)—Johnny Mathis; When Sunny Gets Blue (BMI)—Col 40784	—	7
30.	JUNE NIGHT (ASCAP)—Jimmy Dorsey; JAY-DEE'S BOOGIE WOOGIE (BMI) Fraternity 777	—	1

Most Played by Jockeys

FOR SURVEY WEEK ENDING AUGUST 31, 1957

SIDES are ranked in order of the greatest number of plays on disk jockey radio shows thruout the country. Results are based on The Billboard's weekly survey among the nation's disk jockeys. The reverse side of each record is also listed.

This Week	Title	Last Week	Weeks on Chart
1.	TAMMY (ASCAP)—Debbie Reynolds; French Heels (ASCAP)—Coral 61851	1	8
2.	HONEYCOMB (ASCAP)—Jimmie Rodgers; Their Hearts Were Full of Spring (ASCAP)—Roulette 4015	4	3
3.	DIANA (BMI)—Paul Anka; Don't Gamble With Love (BMI)—ABC-Paramount 9831	14	5
3.	THAT'LL BE THE DAY (BMI)—Crickets; I'm Lookin' for Someone to Love (BMI)—Brunswick 55009	16	3
5.	TEDDY BEAR (ASCAP)—Elvis Presley; Loving You (BMI)—Vic 7000	2	19
6.	REMEMBER YOU'RE MINE (ASCAP)—Pat Boone; There's a Gold Mine in the Sky (ASCAP)—Dot 15602	11	3
7.	WHITE SILVER SANDS (BMI)—Don Rondo; Stars Fell on Alabama (ASCAP)—Jubilee 5288	9	7
8.	RAINBOW (ASCAP)—Russ Hamilton; We Will Make Love (ASCAP)—Kapp 184	7	6
9.	I'M GONNA SIT RIGHT DOWN AND WRITE MYSELF A LETTER (ASCAP)—Billy Williams; Date With the Blues (ASCAP)—Coral 61830	3	12
10.	TAMMY (ASCAP)—Ames Brothers; Rockin' Shoes (BMI)—Vic 6930	5	8
11.	LOVE ME TO PIECES (BMI)—Jill Corey; Love (BMI)—Col 40955	19	6
12.	LOVE LETTERS IN THE SAND (ASCAP)—Pat Boone; Bernardine (ASCAP)—Dot 15570	6	18
12.	WHOLE LOTTA SHAKIN' GOIN' ON (BMI)—Jerry Lee Lewis; It'll Be Mine (BMI)—Sun 267	15	5
14.	IN THE MIDDLE OF AN ISLAND (ASCAP)—Tony Bennett; I Am (ASCAP)—Col 40965	17	4
15.	IT'S NOT FOR ME TO SAY (ASCAP)—Johnny Mathis; Warm and Tender (ASCAP)—Col 40851	8	16
15.	AROUND THE WORLD (ASCAP)—Mantovani; The Road to Ballingarry (ASCAP)—London 1746	12	8
17.	OLD CAPE COD (ASCAP)—Patti Page; Wondering (BMI)—Mercury 71101	10	14
18.	BYE BYE LOVE (BMI)—Everly Brothers; I Wonder If I Care as Much (BMI)—Cadence 1315	18	15
19.	SEND FOR ME (BMI)—Nat (King) Cole; My Personal Possession (BMI)—Cap 3737	12	9
20.	FASCINATION (ASCAP)—Jane Morgan; Midnight in Athens (ASCAP)—Kapp 191	—	1
21.	JUNE NIGHT (ASCAP)—Jimmy Dorsey; Jay-Dee's Boogie Woogie (BMI)—Fraternity 777	—	1
22.	LOVING YOU (BMI)—Elvis Presley; Teddy Bear (ASCAP)—Vic 7000	—	6
23.	SO RARE (ASCAP)—Jimmy Dorsey; Sophisticated Swing (ASCAP)—Fraternity 755	—	18
24.	FASCINATION (ASCAP)—Dinah Shore; Till (ASCAP)—Vic 6980	—	1
25.	STARDUST (ASCAP)—Billy Ward; Lucinda (BMI)—Liberty 55071	20	6

STORE RECORDED SALES — NEW YORK UNIVERSITY SCHOOL OF RETAILING — THE BILLBOARD

Top 100 Sides

FOR SURVEY WEEK ENDING AUGUST 31

This is a tabulation of dealer unit sales listed according to the specific side requested by customers. No attempt is made to add sides together to reflect actual record sales. It is therefore a tabulation of sides or songs, and not records. This fact, together with longer four-week survey periods, explains variation between the top 30 sides as reflected in this chart, and top 30 record sellers as reflected in "Best Sellers in Stores."

Position	Song, Artist, Label	Position Last Week
1.	**TAMMY,** Debbie Reynolds, Coral	1
2.	**DIANA,** Paul Anka, ABC-PARAMOUNT	2
3.	**TEDDY BEAR,** Elvis Presley, Victor	3
4.	**WHOLE LOTTA SHAKIN' GOIN' ON,** Jerry Lee Lewis, Sun	8
5.	**THAT'LL BE THE DAY,** Crickets, Brunswick	6
6.	**BYE BYE LOVE,** Everly Brothers, Cadence	4
7.	**SEARCHIN',** Coasters, Atco	7
8.	**RAINBOW,** Russ Hamilton, Kapp	9
9.	**HONEYCOMB,** Jimmie Rodgers, Roulette	16
10.	**SEND FOR ME,** Nat (King) Cole	11
11.	**LOVE LETTERS IN THE SAND,** Pat Boone, Dot	5
12.	**WHITE SILVER SANDS,** Don Rondo, Jubilee	12
13.	**WHISPERING BELLS,** Del Vikings, Dot	10
14.	**SHORT FAN FANNIE,** Larry Williams, Specialty	13
15.	**MR. LEE,** Bobbettes, Atlantic	20
16.	**I'M GONNA SIT RIGHT DOWN AND WRITE MYSELF A LETTER,** Billy Williams, Coral	14
16.	**STARDUST,** Billy Ward, Liberty	17
18.	**IN THE MIDDLE OF AN ISLAND,** Tony Bennett, Columbia	21
19.	**SO RARE,** Jimmy Dorsey, Fraternity	15
20.	**LOVE ME TO PIECES,** Jill Corey, Columbia	18
21.	**IT'S NOT FOR ME TO SAY,** Johnny Mathis, Columbia	19
22.	**OLD CAPE COD,** Patti Page, Mercury	23
23.	**FLYING SAUCER,** Buchanan & Goodman, Luniverse	22
24.	**GOODY GOODY,** Teenagers, Gee	25
25.	**TO THE AISLE,** Five Satins, Ember	26
26.	**REMEMBER YOU'RE MINE,** Pat Boone, Dot	24
27.	**JENNY, JENNY,** Little Richard, Specialty	27
28.	**SHANGRI-LA,** Four Coins, Epic	28
29.	**THERE'S A GOLD MINE IN THE SKY,** Pat Boone, Dot	29
30.	**WONDERFUL, WONDERFUL,** Johnny Mathis, Columbia	35
31.	**AROUND THE WORLD,** Mantovani, London	32
32.	**FASCINATION,** Jane Morgan, Kapp	63
33.	**AND THAT REMINDS ME,** Della Reese, Jubilee	52
34.	**LOVING YOU,** Elvis Presley, Victor	34
34.	**TAMMY,** Ames Brothers, Victor	29
36.	**WHEN I SEE YOU,** Fats Domino, Imperial	39
37.	**OVER THE MOUNTAIN,** Johnnie & Joe, Chess	32
38.	**I LIKE YOUR KIND OF LOVE,** Andy Williams, Cadence	36
39.	**AROUND THE WORLD,** Victor Young, Decca	41
40.	**WHITE SPORT COAT,** Marty Robbins, Columbia	37
41.	**GONNA FIND ME A BLUEBIRD,** Marvin Rainwater, M-G-M	31
41.	**YOU'RE MY ONE AND ONLY LOVE,** Ricky Nelson, Verve	—
43.	**LOTTA LOVIN',** Gene Vincent, Capitol	55
44.	**BERNARDINE,** Pat Boone, Dot	38
44.	**SUSIE Q,** Dale Hawkins, Checker	47
46.	**LONG, LONELY NIGHTS,** Lee Andrews, Chess	44
47.	**JUNE NIGHT,** Jimmy Dorsey, Fraternity	57
48.	**ALL SHOOK UP,** Elvis Presley, Victor	46
49.	**HULA LOVE,** Buddy Knox, Roulette	69
50.	**COOL SHAKE,** Del Vikings, Mercury	53
51.	**TEENAGER'S ROMANCE,** Ricky Nelson, Verve	40
52.	**ISLAND IN THE SUN,** Harry Belafonte, Victor	44
53.	**FOUR WALLS,** Jim Reeves, Victor	43
54.	**DARLING IT'S WONDERFUL,** Lovers, Lamp	48
55.	**VALLEY OF TEARS,** Fats Domino, Imperial	48
56.	**IN THE MIDDLE OF AN ISLAND,** Tennessee Ernie Ford, Capitol	—
56.	**LET THE FOUR WINDS BLOW,** Roy Brown, Imperial	51
56.	**WITH ALL MY HEART,** Jodie Sands, Chancellor	63
59.	**ROCKIN' PNEUMONIA AND THE BOOGIE WOOGIE FLU** Huey Smith, Ace	68
60.	**FALLEN STAR,** Jimmy Newman, Dot	56
60.	**YOUNG BLOOD,** Coasters, Atco	53
62.	**FALLEN STAR,** Ferlin Husky, Capitol	60
62.	**LONG LONELY NIGHTS,** Clyde McPhatter, Atlantic	57
64.	**DARK MOON,** Gale Storm, Dot	42
65.	**BLACK SLACKS,** Joe Bennett & The Sparkletones, ABC-Paramount	73
65.	**FRAULEIN,** Bobby Helms, Decca	67
67.	**FALLEN STAR,** Hilltoppers, Dot	65
67.	**MY HEART REMINDS ME,** Kay Starr, Victor	74
67.	**START MOVIN',** Sal Mineo, Epic	50
70.	**FREIGHT TRAIN,** Rusty Draper, Mercury	62
70.	**ZIP, ZIP,** Diamonds, Mercury	81
72.	**SCHOOL DAYS,** Chuck Berry, Chess	76
73.	**C. C. RIDER,** Chuck Willis, Atlantic	65
73.	**FASCINATION,** David Carroll, Mercury	97
75.	**BON VOYAGE,** Janice Harper, Prep	71
75.	**LASTING LOVE,** Sal Mineo, Epic	—
77.	**AROUND THE WORLD,** Bing Crosby, Decca	71
77.	**FASCINATION,** Dick Jacobs, Coral	89
77.	**FARTHER UP THE ROAD,** Bobby (Blue) Bland, Duke	81
77.	**WHITE SILVER SANDS,** Dave Gardner, OJ	60
81.	**AN AFFAIR TO REMEMBER,** Vic Damone, Columbia	—
81.	**DANCIN',** Perry Como, Victor	78
83.	**JUST BETWEEN YOU AND ME,** Chordettes, Cadence	—
83.	**REBEL,** Carol Jarvis, Dot	92
85.	**MOONLIGHT SWIM,** Nick Nobel, Mercury	—
85.	**ROCKIN' SHOES,** Ames Brothers, Victor	78
87.	**BUILD YOUR LOVE,** Johnnie Ray, Columbia	84
87.	**JAY-DEE'S BOOGIE WOOGIE,** Jimmy Dorsey, Fraternity	77
89.	**CHICKEN BABY CHICKEN,** Tony Harris, Ebb	92
89.	**GOTTA GET TO YOUR HOUSE,** David Seville, Liberty	—
89.	**HIGH SCHOOL ROMANCE,** George Hamilton IV, AB-Paramount	92
92.	**AROUND THE WORLD,** McGuire Sisters, Coral	89
92.	**MISS YOU SO,** Lillian Offit, Entre	—
92.	**SWINGIN' SWEETHEARTS,** Ron Goodwin, Capitol	—
95.	**OH BABY DOLL,** Chuck Berry, Chess	74
96.	**FIRST KISS,** Norman Petty Trio, Columbia	81
96.	**PASSING STRANGERS,** Sarah Vaughan & Billy Eckstine, Mercury	88
98.	**COME GO WITH ME,** Del Vikings, Dot	84
98.	**ROUND AND ROUND,** Perry Como, Victor	97
100.	**WHAT WILL I TELL MY HEART?** Fats Domino, Imperial	78

Best Sellers in Stores

FOR SURVEY WEEK ENDING SEPTEMBER 7, 1957

The information given in this chart is based on actual sales to customers in a scientific sample of the nation's retail record outlets during the week ending on the date shown above. Sample design, sample size, and all methods used in this continuing study of retail record sales are under the direct and continuing supervision and control of the School of Retailing of New York University.

This Week		Last Week	Weeks on Chart
1.	TAMMY (ASCAP)—Debbie Reynolds / French Heels (ASCAP)—Coral 61851	2	8
2.	DIANA (BMI)—Paul Anka / Don't Gamble With Love (BMI)—ABC-Paramount 9831	1	8
3.	WHOLE LOTTA' SHAKIN' GOIN' ON (BMI)—Jerry Lee Lewis / It'll Be Mine (BMI)—Sun 267	3	8
4.	THAT'LL BE THE DAY (BMI)—Crickets / I'm Lookin' for Someone to Love (BMI)—Brunswick 55009	5	5
5.	TEDDY BEAR (ASCAP)—Elvis Presley / LOVING YOU (BMI)—Vic 20-7000	4	13
6.	HONEYCOMB (ASCAP)—Jimmie Rodgers / Their Hearts Were Full of Spring (ASCAP)—Roulette 4015	6	5
7.	RAINBOW (ASCAP)—Russ Hamilton / We Will Make Love (ASCAP)—Kapp 184	7	7
8.	MR. LEE (BMI)—Bobbettes / Look at the Stars (BMI)—Atlantic 1144	9	6
9.	SEARCHIN' (BMI)—Coasters / YOUNG BLOOD (BMI)—Atco 6087	10	18
10.	IN THE MIDDLE OF AN ISLAND (ASCAP)—Tony Bennett / I AM (ASCAP)—Col 40965	10	6
11.	IT'S NOT FOR ME TO SAY (ASCAP)—Johnny Mathis / Warm and Tender (ASCAP)—Col 40851	18	17
12.	SEND FOR ME (BMI)—Nat (King) Cole / MY PERSONAL POSSESSION (BMI)—Cap 3737	7	12
13.	LOVE LETTERS IN THE SAND (ASCAP)—Pat Boone / BERNARDINE (ASCAP)—Dot 15570	12	19
14.	THERE'S A GOLD MINE IN THE SKY (ASCAP)—Pat Boone / REMEMBER YOU'RE MINE (ASCAP)—Dot 15602	14	6
15.	WHITE SILVER SANDS (BMI)—Don Rondo / Stars Fell on Alabama (ASCAP)—Jubilee 5288	17	8
16.	STARDUST (ASCAP)—Billy Ward / Lucinda (BMI)—Liberty 55071	15	9
17.	WHISPERING BELLS (BMI)—Del Vikings / Don't Be a Fool (BMI)—Dot 15592	15	10
18.	I'M GONNA SIT RIGHT DOWN AND WRITE MYSELF A LETTER (ASCAP)—Billy Williams / DATE WITH THE BLUES (ASCAP)—Coral 61830	19	13
19.	SHORT FAT FANNIE (BMI)—Larry Williams / High School Dance (BMI) Specialty 608	19	11
20.	BYE BYE LOVE (BMI)—Everly Brothers / I Wonder If I Care As Much (BMI)—Cadence 1315	13	17
21.	FASCINATION (ASCAP)—Jane Morgan / Midnight in Athens (ASCAP)—Kapp 191	22	2
22.	LOVE ME TO PIECES (BMI)—Jill Corey / Love (BMI)—Col 40955	21	6
23.	AROUND THE WORLD (ASCAP)—Victor Young / (VOCAL) (ASCAP)—Decca 30262	24	6
24.	TAMMY (BMI) Ames Brothers / ROCKIN' SHOES (ASCAP)—Vic 6930	28	6
25.	SO RARE (ASCAP)—Jimmy Dorsey / Sophisticated Swing (ASCAP)—Fraternity 755	27	23
26.	YOU'RE MY ONE AND ONLY LOVE (ASCAP)—Ricky Nelson / HONEY ROCK (ASCAP)—Verve 10070	—	1
27.	JUNE NIGHT (ASCAP)—Jimmy Dorsey / JAY-DEE'S BOOGIE WOOGIE (BMI)—Fraternity 777	30	2
28.	HULA LOVE (BMI)—Buddy Knox / Devil Woman (BMI)—Roulette 4018	26	2
28.	JUST BETWEEN YOU AND ME (BMI)—Chordettes / SOFT SANDS (BMI)—Cadence 1330	—	1
30.	WONDERFUL WONDERFUL (BMI)—Johnny Mathis / When Sunny Gets Blue—Col 40784	28	8

Most Played by Jockeys

FOR SURVEY WEEK ENDING SEPTEMBER 7, 1957

SIDES are ranked in order of the greatest number of plays on disk jockey radio shows thruout the country. Results are based on The Billboard's weekly survey among the nation's disk jockeys. The reverse side of each record is also listed.

This Week		Last Week	Weeks on Chart
1.	TAMMY (ASCAP)—Debbie Reynolds / French Heels (ASCAP)—Coral 61851	1	9
2.	HONEYCOMB (ASCAP)—Jimmie Rodgers / Their Hearts Were Full of Spring (ASCAP)—Roulette 4015	2	4
3.	DIANA (BMI)—Paul Anka / Don't Gamble With Love (BMI)—ABC-Paramount 9831	3	6
4.	RAINBOW (ASCAP)—Russ Hamilton / We Will Make Love—Kapp 184	8	7
5.	TAMMY (ASCAP)—Ames Brothers / Rockin' Shoes (BMI)—Vic 6930	10	9
6.	THAT'LL BE THE DAY (BMI)—Crickets / I'm Lookin' for Someone to Love (BMI)—Brunswick 55009	3	4
7.	REMEMBER YOU'RE MINE (ASCAP)—Pat Boone / There's a Gold Mine in the Sky (ASCAP)—Dot 15602	6	4
8.	TEDDY BEAR (ASCAP)—Elvis Presley / Loving You (BMI)—Vic 7000	5	20
9.	WHITE SILVER SANDS (BMI)—Don Rondo / Stars Fell on Alabama (ASCAP)—Jubilee 5288	7	8
10.	WHOLE LOTTA SHAKIN' GOIN' ON (BMI)—Jerry Lee Lewis / It'll Be Mine (BMI)—Sun 267	12	6
11.	I'M GONNA SIT RIGHT DOWN AND WRITE MYSELF A LETTER (ASCAP)—Billy Williams / Date With the Blues (ASCAP)—Coral 61830	9	13
12.	FASCINATION (ASCAP)—Jane Morgan / Midnight in Athens (ASCAP)—Kapp 191	20	2
13.	BYE BYE LOVE (BMI)—Everly Brothers / I Wonder If I Care As Much (BMI)—Cadence 1315	18	16
14.	OLD CAPE COD (ASCAP)—Patti Page / Wondering (BMI)—Mercury 71101	17	15
15.	LOVE ME TO PIECES (BMI)—Jill Corey / Love (BMI)—Col 40955	11	7
16.	LOVE LETTERS IN THE SAND (ASCAP)—Pat Boone / Bernardine (ASCAP)—Dot 15570	12	19
17.	IN THE MIDDLE OF AN ISLAND (ASCAP)—Tony Bennett / I Am (ASCAP)—Col 40965	14	5
18.	JUST BETWEEN YOU AND ME (BMI)—Chordettes / Soft Sands (BMI)—Cadence 1330	—	1
19.	AROUND THE WORLD (ASCAP)—Victor Young / Around the World (Vocal) (ASCAP)—Dec 30262	—	7
20.	CHANCES ARE (ASCAP)—Johnny Mathis / The Twelfth of Never (ASCAP)—Col 40993	—	1
21.	AROUND THE WORLD (ASCAP)—Mantovani / The Road to Ballingarry (ASCAP)—London 1746	15	9
22.	FASCINATION (ASCAP)—Dick Jacobs / Summertime in Venice (ASCAP)—Coral 61864	—	1
23.	MY HEART REMINDS ME (ASCAP)—Kay Starr / Flim Flam Floo (BMI)—Vic 6981	—	1
24.	THERE'S A GOLD MINE IN THE SKY (ASCAP)—Pat Boone / Remember You're Mine (ASCAP)—Dot 15602	—	2
25.	HULA LOVE (BMI)—Buddy Knox / Devil Woman (BMI)—Roulette 4018	—	1

NEW YORK UNIVERSITY SCHOOL OF RETAILING — STORE RECORDED SALES — THE BILLBOARD

Top 100 Sides

FOR SURVEY WEEK ENDING SEPTEMBER 7

This is a tabulation of dealer unit sales listed according to the specific side requested by customers. No attempt is made to add sides together to reflect actual record sales. It is therefore a tabulation of sides or songs, and not records. This fact, together with longer four-week survey periods, explains variation between the top 30 sides as reflected in this chart, and top 30 record sellers as reflected in "Best Sellers in Stores."

Position, Song, Artist, Label	Position Last Week
1. **TAMMY,** Debbie Reynolds, Coral	1
2. **DIANA,** Paul Anka, ABC-Paramount	2
3. **THAT'LL BE THE DAY,** Crickets, Brunswick	5
3. **WHOLE LOTTA SHAKIN' GOIN' ON,** Jerry Lee Lewis, Sun	4
5. **TEDDY BEAR,** Elvis Presley, Victor	3
6. **HONEYCOMB,** Jimmie Rodgers, Roulette	9
7. **RAINBOW,** Russ Hamilton, Kapp	8
8. **MR. LEE,** Bobbettes, Atlantic	15
9. **BYE BYE LOVE,** Everly Brothers, Cadence	6
10. **SEARCHIN',** Coasters, Atco	7
11. **SEND FOR ME,** Nat (King) Cole, Capitol	10
12. **WHISPERING BELLS,** Del Vikings, Dot	13
13. **SHORT FAT FANNIE,** Larry Williams, Specialty	14
14. **IN THE MIDDLE OF AN ISLAND,** Tony Bennett, Columbia	18
15. **STARDUST,** Billy Ward, Liberty	16
16. **IT'S NOT FOR ME TO SAY,** Johnny Mathis, Columbia	21
17. **WHITE SILVER SANDS,** Don Rondo, Jubilee	12
18. **LOVE LETTERS IN THE SAND,** Pat Boone, Dot	11
19. **I'M GONNA SIT RIGHT DOWN AND WRITE MYSELF A LETTER,** Billy Williams, Coral	16
20. **SO RARE,** Jimmy Dorsey, Fraternity	19
21. **LOVE ME TO PIECES,** Jill Corey, Columbia	20
22. **GOODY GOODY,** Frankie Lymon, Gee	24
23. **REMEMBER YOU'RE MINE,** Pat Boone, Dot	26
24. **OLD CAPE COD,** Patti Page, Mercury	22
25. **FASCINATION,** Jane Morgan, Kapp	32
26. **AROUND THE WORLD,** Mantovani, London	31
27. **FLYING SAUCER,** Buchanan & Goodman, Luniverse	23
28. **TO THE AISLE,** Five Satins, Ember	25
28. **YOU'RE MY ONE AND ONLY LOVE,** Ricky Nelson, Verve	41
30. **HULA LOVE,** Buddy Knox, Roulette	49
31. **WONDERFUL WONDERFUL,** Johnny Mathis, Columbia	30
32. **JENNY JENNY,** Little Richard, Specialty	27
33. **THERE'S A GOLD MINE IN THE SKY,** Pat Boone, Dot	29
34. **TAMMY,** Ames Brothers, Victor	35
35. **AND THAT REMINDS ME,** Della Reese, Jubilee	33
36. **SHANGRI-LA,** Four Coins, Epic	28
37. **AROUND THE WORLD,** Victor Young, Decca	39
38. **LOTTA LOVIN',** Gene Vincent, Capitol	43
39. **LOVING YOU,** Elvis Presley, Victor	34
40. **JUNE NIGHT,** Jimmy Dorsey, Fraternity	47
41. **WHEN I SEE YOU,** Fats Domino, Imperial	36
42. **BLACK SLACKS,** Joe Bennett & the Sparkletones, ABC-Paramount	65
43. **FARTHER UP THE ROAD,** Bobby (Blue) Bland, Duke	77
43. **SUSIE Q,** Dale Hawkins, Checker	44
45. **ZIP ZIP,** Diamonds, Mercury	70
46. **ALL SHOOK UP,** Elvis Presley, Victor	48
47. **JUST BETWEEN YOU AND ME,** Chordettes, Cadence	83
47. **OVER THE MOUNTAIN,** Johnnie & Joe, Chess	37
49. **LASTING LOVE,** Sal Mineo, Epic	75
50. **I LIKE YOUR KIND OF LOVE,** Andy Williams, Cadence	38
50. **MOONLIGHT SWIM,** Nick Noble, Mercury	85
52. **ISLAND IN THE SUN,** Harry Belafonte, Victor	52
52. **ROCKIN' PNEUMONIA AND THE BOOGIE WOOGIE FLU,** Huey Smith, Ace	59
54. **BERNARDINE,** Pat Boone, Dot	44
54. **GONNA FIND ME A BLUEBIRD,** Marvin Rainwater, M-G-M	41
56. **FASCINATION,** David Carroll, Mercury	73
56. **REBEL,** Carol Jarvis, Dot	83
58. **TEENAGERS' ROMANCE,** Ricky Nelson, Verve	51
59. **MY HEART REMINDS ME,** Kay Starr, Victor	67
59. **WHITE SPORT COAT,** Marty Robbins, Columbia	40
61. **LONG LONELY NIGHTS,** Lee Andrews, Chess	46
62. **BON VOYAGE,** Janice Harper, Prep	75
62. **COOL SHAKE,** Del Vikings, Mercury	50
64. **FRAULEIN,** Bobby Helms, Decca	65
64. **HAPPY, HAPPY BIRTHDAY BABY,** Tune Weavers, Checker	—
64. **LONG LONELY NIGHTS,** Clyde McPhatter, Atlantic	62
64. **LET THE FOUR WINDS BLOW,** Roy Brown, Imperial	56
64. **ROCKIN' SHOES,** Ames Brothers, Victor	85
69. **FASCINATION**—Dick Jacobs, Coral	77
69. **FOUR WALLS,** Jim Reeves, Victor	53
69. **IN THE MIDDLE OF AN ISLAND,** Tennessee Ernie Ford, Capitol	56
69. **WITH ALL MY HEART,** Jodie Sands, Chancellor	56
73. **DARLING IT'S WONDERFUL,** Lovers, Lamp	54
74. **AN AFFAIR TO REMEMBER,** Vic Damone, Columbia	81
75. **SWINGING SWEETHEARTS,** Ron Goodwin, Capitol	92
76. **DANCIN',** Perry Como, Victor	81
77. **FALLEN STAR,** Ferlin Husky, Capitol	62
77. **YOUNG BLOOD,** Coasters, Atco	60
79. **AROUND THE WORLD,** Bing Crosby, Decca	77
79. **CHANCES ARE,** Johnny Mathis, Columbia	—
81. **FALLEN STAR,** Jimmy Newman, Dot	60
81. **SCHOOL DAYS,** Chuck Berry, Chess	72
83. **C. C. RIDER,** Chuck Willis, Atlantic	73
84. **JAY DEE'S BOOGIE WOOGIE,** Jimmy Dorsey, Fraternity	87
85. **HUMPTY DUMPTY HEART,** Lavern Baker, Atlantic	—
86. **DARK MOON,** Gale Storm, Dot	84
86. **START MOVIN',** Sal Mineo, Epic	67
86. **VALLEY OF TEARS,** Fats Domino, Imperial	55
89. **FALLEN STAR,** Hilltoppers, Dot	67
90. **GOTTA GET TO YOUR HOUSE,** David Seville, Liberty	89
90. **MISS YOU SO,** Lillian Offitt, Entre	92
92. **MY PERSONAL POSSESSION,** Nat (King) Cole, Capitol	—
92. **WHITE SILVER SANDS,** Dave Gardner, OJ	77
94. **THIRD FINGER LEFT HAND,** Eileen Rodgers, Columbia	—
95. **BUILD YOUR LOVE,** Johnnie Ray, Columbia	87
95. **ANGRY,** Frank Pizani, Bally	—
97. **CHICKEN BABY CHICKEN,** Tony Harris, Ebb	89
97. **DRIVE IN SHOW,** Eddie Cochran, Liberty	—
99. **I'LL TAKE YOU HOME AGAIN KATHLEEN,** Slim Whitman, Imperial	—
100. **FREIGHT TRAIN,** Rusty Draper, Mercury	70
100. **WHAT WILL I TELL MY HEART,** Fats Domino, Imperial	100
100. **SONG OF THE BAREFOOT MAILMAN,** Billy Leach, Bally	—

NEW YORK UNIVERSITY SCHOOL OF RETAILING — STORE RECORDED SALES — THE BILLBOARD

Best Sellers in Stores

FOR SURVEY WEEK ENDING SEPTEMBER 14, 1957

The information given in this chart is based on actual sales to customers in a scientific sample of the nation's retail record outlets during the week ending on the date shown above. Sample design, sample size, and all methods used in this continuing study of retail record sales are under the direct and continuing supervision and control of the School of Retailing of New York University.

This Week		Last Week	Weeks on Chart
1.	THAT'LL BE THE DAY (BMI)—Crickets I'm Lookin' for Someone to Love (BMI)—Brunswick 55009	4	6
2.	TAMMY (ASCAP)—Debbie Reynolds French Heels (ASCAP)—Coral 61851	1	9
3.	DIANA (BMI)—Paul Anka Don't Gamble With Love (BMI)—ABC-Paramount 9831	2	9
4.	HONEYCOMB (ASCAP)—Jimmie Rodgers Their Hearts Were Full of Spring (ASCAP)—Roulette 4015	6	6
5.	WHOLE LOTTA' SHAKIN' GOIN' ON (BMI)—Jerry Lee Lewis It'll Be Mine (BMI)—Sun 267	3	9
6.	TEDDY BEAR (ASCAP)—Elvis Presley LOVING YOU (BMI)—Vic 20-7000	5	14
7.	MR. LEE (BMI)—Bobbettes Look at the Stars (BMI)—Atlantic 1144	8	7
8.	RAINBOW (ASCAP)—Russ Hamilton We Will Make Love (ASCAP)—Kapp 184	7	8
9.	IN THE MIDDLE OF AN ISLAND (ASCAP)—Tony Bennett I AM (ASCAP)—Col 40965	10	7
10.	REMEMBER YOU'RE MINE (ASCAP)—Pat Boone THERE'S A GOLD MINE IN THE SKY (ASCAP)—Dot 15602	14	7
11.	CHANCES ARE (ASCAP)—Johnny Mathis The Twelfth of Never (ASCAP)—Col 40993	—	1
12.	SEARCHIN' (BMI)—Coasters YOUNG BLOOD (BMI)—Atco 6087	9	19
13.	BYE BYE LOVE (BMI)—Everly Brothers I Wonder If I Care as Much (BMI)—Cadence 1315	20	18
14.	YOU'RE MY ONE AND ONLY LOVE (ASCAP)—Ricky Nelson HONEY ROCK (ASCAP)—Verve 10070	26	2
15.	IT'S NOT FOR ME TO SAY (ASCAP)—Johnny Mathis Warm and Tender (ASCAP)—Col 40851	11	18
16.	LOVE LETTERS IN THE SAND (ASCAP)—Pat Boone BERNARDINE (ASCAP)—Dot 15570	13	20
17.	HAPPY HAPPY BIRTHDAY BABY (BMI)—Tune Weavers Ol' Man River (ASCAP)—Checker 872	—	1
18.	SHORT FAT FANNIE (BMI)—Larry Williams High School Dance (BMI)—Specialty 608	19	12
19.	STARDUST (ASCAP)—Billy Ward Lucinda (BMI)—Liberty 55071	16	10
20.	HULA LOVE (BMI)—Buddy Knox Devil Woman (BMI)—Roulette 4018	28	3
21.	SEND FOR ME (BMI)—Nat King Cole MY PERSONAL POSSESSION (BMI)—Cap 3737	12	13
22.	JUST BETWEEN YOU AND ME (BMI)—Chordettes SOFT SANDS (BMI)—Cadence 1330	28	2
23.	FASCINATION (ASCAP)—Jane Morgan Fascination (Instrumental) (ASCAP)—Kapp 191	21	3
23.	LOTTA LOVIN' (BMI)—Gene Vincent WEAR MY RING (BMI)—Cap 3763	—	1
25.	BLACK SLACKS (BMI)—Joe Bennett and the Sparkletones Boppin Rock Boogie (BMI)—ABC-Paramount 9837	—	1
26.	WHITE SILVER SANDS (BMI)—Don Rondo Stars Fell on Alabama (ASCAP)—Jubilee 5288	15	9
27.	GOODY GOODY (ASCAP)—Frankie Lymon and the Teenagers Creation of Love (BMI)—Gee 1039	—	4
28.	I'M GONNA SIT RIGHT DOWN AND WRITE MYSELF A LETTER (ASCAP)—Billy Williams DATE WITH THE BLUES (ASCAP)—Coral 61830	18	14
29.	WHISPERING BELLS (BMI)—Del Vikings Don't Be a Fool (BMI)—Dot 15592	17	11
30.	LOVE ME TO PIECES (BMI)—Jill Corey Love (BMI)—Col 40955	22	7
30.	AROUND THE WORLD (ASCAP)—Victor Young (VOCAL) (ASCAP)—Decca 30262	23	7

Most Played by Jockeys

FOR SURVEY WEEK ENDING SEPTEMBER 14, 1957

SIDES are ranked in order of the greatest number of plays on disk jockey radio shows thruout the country. Results are based on The Billboard's weekly survey among the nation's disk jockeys. The reverse side of each record is also listed.

This Week		Last Week	Weeks on Chart
1.	HONEYCOMB (ASCAP)—Jimmie Rodgers Their Hearts Were Full of Spring (ASCAP)—	2	5
2.	TAMMY (ASCAP)—Debbie Reynolds French Heels—ASCAP)—Coral 61851	1	10
3.	DIANA (BMI)—Paul Anka Don't Gamble With Love (BMI)—ABC-Paramount 9831	3	7
4.	THAT'LL BE THE DAY (BMI)—Crickets I'm Lookin' for Someone to Love (BMI)—Brunswick 55009	6	5
5.	CHANCES ARE (ASCAP)—Johnny Mathis The Twelfth of Never (ASCAP)—Col 40993	20	2
6.	RAINBOW (ASCAP)—Russ Hamilton We Will Make Love—Kapp 184	4	8
6.	MR. LEE (BMI)—Bobbettes Look at the Stars (BMI)—Atlantic 1144	—	1
8.	REMEMBER YOU'RE MINE (ASCAP)—Pat Boone There's a Gold Mine in the Sky (ASCAP)—Dot 15602	7	5
9.	TAMMY (ASCAP)—Ames Brothers Rockin' Shoes (BMI)—Vic 6930	5	10
9.	WHOLE LOTTA SHAKIN' GOIN' ON (BMI)—Jerry Lee Lewis It'll Be Mine (BMI)—Sun 267	10	7
11.	FASCINATION (ASCAP)—Jane Morgan Fascination (ASCAP)—Kapp 191	12	3
12.	I'M GONNA SIT RIGHT DOWN AND WRITE MYSELF A LETTER (ASCAP)—Billy Williams Date With the Blues (ASCAP)—Coral 61830	11	14
13.	IN THE MIDDLE OF AN ISLAND (ASCAP)—Tony Bennett I Am (ASCAP)—Col 40965	17	6
14.	MY HEART REMINDS ME (ASCAP)—Kay Starr Flim Flam Floo (BMI)—Vic 6981	23	2
15.	WHITE SILVER SANDS (BMI)—Don Rondo Stars Fell on Alabama (ASCAP)—Jubilee 5288	9	9
16.	FASCINATION (ASCAP)—Dinah Shore Till (ASCAP)—Vic 6980	—	1
17.	TEDDY BEAR (ASCAP)—Elvis Presley Loving You (BMI)—Vic 7000	8	21
18.	JUST BETWEEN YOU AND ME (BMI)—Chordettes Soft Sands (BMI)—Cadence 1330	18	2
19.	AROUND THE WORLD (ASCAP)—Mantovani The Road to Ballingarry (ASCAP)—London 1746	21	10
19.	LOVE ME TO PIECES (BMI)—Jill Corey Love (BMI)—Col 40955	15	8
21.	SEND FOR ME (BMI)—Nat King Cole My Personal Possession (BMI)—Cap 3737	—	10
22.	IT'S NOT FOR ME TO SAY (ASCAP)—Johnny Mathis Warm and Tender (ASCAP)—Col 40851	—	17
23.	IN THE MIDDLE OF AN ISLAND (ASCAP)—Tennessee Ernie Ford Ivy League (ASCAP)—Cap 3762	—	1
23.	BYE BYE LOVE (BMI)—Everly Brothers I Wonder If I Care as Much (BMI)—Cadence 1315	13	17
25.	HULA LOVE (BMI)—Buddy Knox Devil Woman (BMI)—Roulette 4018	25	2

Top 100 Sides

FOR SURVEY WEEK ENDING SEPTEMBER 14

This is a tabulation of dealer unit sales listed according to the specific side requested by customers. No attempt is made to add sides together to reflect actual record sales. It is therefore a tabulation of sides or songs, and not records. This fact, together with longer four-week survey periods, explains variation between the top 30 sides as reflected in this chart, and top 30 record sellers as reflected in "Best Sellers in Stores."

Position, Song, Artist, Label	Position Last Week
1. **TAMMY,** Debbie Reynolds, Coral	1
2. **DIANA,** Paul Anka, ABC-Paramount	2
3. **THAT'LL BE THE DAY,** Crickets, Brunswick	3
4. **WHOLE LOTTA SHAKIN' GOIN' ON,** Jerry Lee Lewis, Sun	3
5. **HONEYCOMB,** Jimmie Rodgers, Roulette	6
6. **TEDDY BEAR,** Elvis Presley, Victor	5
7. **MR. LEE,** Bobbettes, Atlantic	8
8. **RAINBOW,** Russ Hamilton, Kapp	7
9. **IN THE MIDDLE OF AN ISLAND,** Tony Bennett, Columbia	14
10. **BYE BYE LOVE,** Everly Brothers, Cadence	9
11. **IT'S NOT FOR ME TO SAY,** Johnny Mathis, Columbia	16
12. **SEARCHIN',** Coasters, Atco	10
13. **STARDUST,** Billy Ward, Liberty	15
14. **SEND FOR ME,** Nat King Cole, Capitol	11
15. **SHORT FAT FANNIE,** Larry Williams, Specialty	13
16. **WHITE SILVER SANDS,** Don Rondo, Jubilee	17
17. **WHISPERING BELLS,** Del Vikings, Dot	12
18. **LOVE LETTERS IN THE SAND,** Pat Boone, Dot	18
19. **I'M GONNA SIT RIGHT DOWN AND WRITE MYSELF A LETTER,** Billy Williams, Coral	19
20. **FASCINATION,** Jane Morgan, Kapp	25
21. **HULA LOVE,** Buddy Knox, Roulette	30
22. **YOU'RE MY ONE AND ONLY LOVE,** Ricky Nelson, Verve	28
23. **LOVE ME TO PIECES,** Jill Corey, Columbia	21
24. **GOODY GOODY,** Frankie Lyman and the Teenagers, Gee	22
25. **REMEMBER YOU'RE MINE,** Pat Boone, Dot	23
26. **CHANCES ARE,** Johnny Mathis, Columbia	79
27. **LOTTA LOVIN',** Gene Vincent, Capitol	38
28. **THERE'S A GOLD MINE IN THE SKY,** Pat Boone, Dot	33
29. **AND THAT REMINDS ME,** Della Reese, Jubilee	35
30. **HAPPY HAPPY BIRTHDAY,** Tune Weavers, Checker	64
30. **BLACK SLACKS,** Joe Bennett & The Sparkletones, ABC-Paramount	42
32. **SO RARE,** Jimmy Dorsey, Fraternity	20
33. **AROUND THE WORLD,** Victor Young, Decca	37
34. **TO THE AISLE,** Five Satins, Ember	28
35. **AROUND THE WORLD,** Mantovani, London	26
36. **JUST BETWEEN YOU AND ME,** Chordettes, Cadence	47
37. **FLYING SAUCER,** Buchanan & Goodman, Luniverse	27
37. **LASTING LOVE,** Sal Mineo, Epic	49
39. **JUNE NIGHT,** Jimmy Dorsey, Fraternity	40
40. **OLD CAPE COD,** Patti Page, Mercury	24
41. **MOONLIGHT SWIM,** Nick Noble, Mercury	50
42. **WONDERFUL, WONDERFUL,** Johnny Mathis, Columbia	31
43. **JENNY, JENNY,** Little Richard, Specialty	32
43. **TAMMY,** Ames Brothers, Victor	34
45. **SHANGRI-LA,** Four Coins, Epic	36
46. **LOVING YOU,** Elvis Presley, Victor	39
47. **FARTHER UP THE ROAD,** Bobby (Blue) Bland, Duke	43
48. **WHEN I SEE YOU,** Fats Domino, Imperial	41
48. **AN AFFAIR TO REMEMBER,** Vic Damone, Columbia	74
50. **REBEL,** Carol Jarvis, Dot	56
51. **BON VOYAGE,** Janice Harper, Prep	62
52. **LONG LOVELY NIGHTS,** Clyde McPhatter, Atlantic	64
53. **SUSIE Q,** Dale Hawkins, Checker	43
54. **FASCINATION,** Dick Jacobs, Coral	69
54. **LONG LONELY NIGHTS,** Lee Andrews, Chess	61
54. **ZIP ZIP,** Diamonds, Mercury	45
57. **COOL SHAKE,** Del Vikings, Mercury	62
57. **ROCKIN' PNEUMONIA AND THE BOOGIE WOOGIE FLU,** Huey Smith, Ace	52
59. **BERNARDINE,** Pat Boone, Dot	54
60. **FRAULEIN,** Bobby Helms, Decca	64
61. **MY HEART REMINDS ME,** Kay Starr, Victor	59
62. **SWINGIN' SWEETHEARTS,** Ron Goodwin, Capitol	75
63. **ISLAND IN THE SUN,** Harry Belafonte, Victor	52
63. **ALL SHOOK UP,** Elvis Presley, Victor	46
65. **OVER THE MOUNTAIN,** Johnnie & Joe, Chess	47
66. **FASCINATION,** David Carroll, Mercury	56
67. **GONNA FIND ME A BLUEBIRD,** Marvin Rainwater, M-G-M	54
67. **ROCKIN' SHOES,** Ames Brothers, Victor	64
69. **IN THE MIDDLE OF AN ISLAND,** Tennessee Ernie Ford, Capitol	69
70. **ANGRY,** Frankie Pizani, Bally	95
71. **DARLING IT'S WONDERFUL,** Lovers, Lamp	73
71. **HUMPTY DUMPTY HEART,** La Vern Baker, Atlantic	85
71. **FALLEN STAR,** Ferlin Husky, Capitol	77
71. **TEENAGER'S ROMANCE,** Ricky Nelson, Verve	58
71. **WITH ALL MY HEART,** Jodie Sands, Chancellor	69
76. **WHITE SPORT COAT,** Marty Robbins, Columbia	59
77. **GOTTA GET TO YOUR HOUSE,** David Seville, Liberty	90
78. **JAY DEE'S BOOGIE WOOGIE,** Jimmy Dorsey, Fraternity	84
79. **LET THE FOUR WINDS BLOW,** Roy Brown, Imperial	64
79. **C. C. RIDER,** Chuck Willis, Atlantic	83
81. **FOUR WALLS,** Jim Reeves, Victor	69
82. **DRIVE-IN SHOW,** Eddie Cochran, Liberty	97
82. **I LIKE YOUR KIND OF LOVE,** Andy Williams, Cadence	50
82. **SOFT SANDS,** Chordettes, Cadence	—
82. **THIRD FINGER, LEFT HAND,** Eileen Rodgers, Columbia	97
82. **YOUNG BLOOD,** Coasters, Atco	77
87. **LIPS OF WINE,** Andy Williams, Cadence	—
87. **MY PERSONAL POSSESSION,** Nat King Cole, Capitol	92
87. **SONG OF THE BAREFOOT MAILMAN,** Billy Leach, Bally	100
87. **START MOVIN',** Sal Mineo, Epic	86
87. **WITH YOU ON MY MIND,** King Cole Trio, Capitol	—
87. **AROUND THE WORLD,** Bing Crosby, Decca	79
93. **MY ONE SIN,** Four Coins, Epic	—
94. **FALLEN STAR,** Jimmy Newman, Dot	81
95. **DANCIN',** Perry Como, Victor	76
95. **I'LL TAKE YOU HOME AGAIN KATHLEEN,** Slim Whitman, Imperial	—
95. **MISS YOU SO,** Lillian Offitt, Entre	90
98. **DUMPLINS,** Ernie Freeman, Imperial	—
98. **SCHOOL DAYS,** Chuck Berry, Chess	81
100. **HIGH SCHOOL ROMANCE,** George Hamilton IV, ABC-Paramount	—
100. **AROUND THE WORLD,** McGuire Sisters, Coral	—

Best Sellers in Stores

FOR SURVEY WEEK ENDING SEPTEMBER 21, 1957

The information given in this chart is based on actual sales to customers in a scientific sample of the nation's retail record outlets during the week ending on the date shown above. Sample design, sample size, and all methods used in this continuing study of retail record sales are under the direct and continuing supervision and control of the School of Retailing of New York University.

This Week	Title	Last Week	Weeks on Chart
1.	HONEYCOMB (ASCAP)—Jimmie Rodgers Their Hearts Were Full of Spring (ASCAP)—Roulette 4015	4	7
2.	TAMMY (ASCAP)—Debbie Reynolds French Heels (ASCAP)—Coral 61851	2	10
3.	THAT'LL BE THE DAY (BMI)—Crickets I'm Lookin' for Someone to Love (BMI)—Brunswick 55009	1	7
4.	DIANA (BMI)—Paul Anka Don't Gamble With Love (BMI)—ABC-Paramount 9831	3	10
5.	WHOLE LOTTA SHAKIN' GOIN' ON (BMI)—Jerry Lee Lewis It'll Be Mine (BMI)—Sun 267	5	10
6.	CHANCES ARE (ASCAP)—Johnny Mathis The Twelfth of Never (ASCAP)—Col 40993	11	2
7.	MR. LEE (BMI)—Bobbettes Look at the Stars—Atlantic 1144	7	8
8.	TEDDY BEAR (ASCAP)—Elvis Presley LOVING YOU (BMI)—Vic 7000	6	15
8.	RAINBOW (ASCAP)—Russ Hamilton We Will Make Love (ASCAP)—Kapp 184	8	9
8.	HAPPY, HAPPY BIRTHDAY, BABY (BMI)—Tune Weavers Ol' Man River (ASCAP)—Checker 872	17	2
11.	IN THE MIDDLE OF AN ISLAND (ASCAP)—Tony Bennett I AM (ASCAP)—Vol 40965	9	8
12.	REMEMBER YOU'RE MINE (ASCAP)—Pat Boone THERE'S A GOLD MINE IN THE SKY (ASCAP)—Dot 15602	10	8
13.	LOTTA LOVIN' (BMI)—Gene Vincent Wear My Ring (BMI)—Cap 3763	23	2
14.	YOU'RE MY ONE AND ONLY LOVE (ASCAP)—Ricky Nelson HONEY ROCK (ASCAP)—Verve 10070	14	3
15.	JUST BETWEEN YOU AND ME (BMI)—Chordettes SOFT SANDS (BMI)—Cadence 1330	22	3
16.	HULA LOVE (BMI)—Buddy Knox Devil Woman (BMI)—Roulette 4018	20	4
17.	FASCINATION (ASCAP)—Jane Morgan Fascination (Instrumental) (ASCAP)—Kapp 191	23	4
18.	BYE BYE LOVE (BMI)—Everly Brothers I Wonder If I Care as Much (BMI)—Cadence 1315	13	19
19.	STARDUST (ASCAP)—Billy Ward Lucinda (BMI)—Liberty 55071	19	11
20.	SEND FOR ME (BMI)—Nat King Cole MY PERSONAL POSSESSION (BMI)—Cap 3737	21	14
21.	LOVE LETTERS IN THE SAND (ASCAP)—Pat Boone BERNARDINE (ASCAP)—Dot 15570	16	21
22.	IT'S NOT FOR ME TO SAY (ASCAP)—Johnny Mathis Warm and Tender (ASCAP)—Col 40851	15	19
23.	SHORT FAT FANNIE (BMI)—Larry Williams HIGH SCHOOL DANCE (BMI)—Specialty 608	18	13
24.	SEARCHIN' (BMI)—Coasters YOUNG BLOOD (BMI)—Atco 6087	12	20
25.	WAKE UP LITTLE SUSIE (BMI)—Everly Brothers Maybe Tomorrow (BMI)—Cadence 1337	—	1
26.	BLACK SLACKS (BMI)—Joe Bennett & The Sparkletones Boppin' Rock Boogie (BMI)—ABC-Paramount 9837	25	2
27.	LASTING LOVE (BMI)—Sal Mineo YOU SHOULDN'T DO THAT (BMI)—Epic 9227	—	1
28.	AROUND THE WORLD (ASCAP)—Victor Young (VOCAL) (ASCAP)—Decca 30262	30	8
28.	WHITE SILVER SANDS (BMI)—Don Rondo Stars Fell on Alabama (ASCAP)—Jubilee 5288	26	10
30.	GOODY GOODY (ASCAP)—Frankie Lymon and the Teenagers Creation of Love (BMI)—Gee 1039	27	5

Most Played by Jockeys

FOR SURVEY WEEK ENDING SEPTEMBER 21, 1957

SIDES are ranked in order of the greatest number of plays on disk jockey radio shows thruout the country. Results are based on The Billboard's weekly survey among the nation's disk jockeys. The reverse side of each record is also listed.

This Week	Title	Last Week	Weeks on Chart
1.	HONEYCOMB (ASCAP)—Jimmie Rodgers Their Hearts Were Full of Spring (ASCAP)—Roulette 4015	1	6
2.	DIANA (BMI)—Paul Anka Don't Gamble With Love (BMI)—ABC-Paramount 9831	3	8
3.	TAMMY (ASCAP)—Debbie Reynolds French Heels (ASCAP)—Coral 61851	2	11
4.	THAT'LL BE THE DAY (BMI)—Crickets I'm Lookin' for Someone to Love (BMI)—Brunswick 55009	4	6
5.	CHANCES ARE (ASCAP)—Johnny Mathis The Twelfth of Never (ASCAP)—Col 40993	5	3
6.	RAINBOW (ASCAP)—Russ Hamilton We Will Make Love—Kapp 184	6	9
7.	TAMMY (ASCAP)—Ames Brothers Rockin' Shoes (BMI)—Vic 6930	9	11
8.	JUST BETWEEN YOU AND ME (BMI)—Chordettes Soft Sands (BMI)—Cadence 1330	18	3
9.	REMEMBER YOU'RE MINE (ASCAP)—Pat Boone There's a Gold Mine in the Sky (ASCAP)—Dot 15602	8	6
10.	MR. LEE (BMI)—Bobbettes Look at the Stars (BMI)—Atlantic 1144	6	2
11.	MY HEART REMINDS ME (ASCAP)—Kay Starr Flim Flam Floo (BMI)—Vic 6981	14	3
12.	WHOLE LOTTA SHAKIN' GOIN' ON (BMI)—Jerry Lee Lewis It'll Be Mine (BMI)—Sun 267	9	8
13.	FASCINATION (ASCAP)—Jane Morgan Fascination (Instrumental) (ASCAP)—Kapp 191	11	4
14.	HULA LOVE (BMI)—Buddy Knox Devil Woman (BMI)—Roulette 4018	25	3
15.	FASCINATION (ASCAP)—Dinah Shore Till (ASCAP)—Vic 6980	16	2
16.	ZIP ZIP (BMI)—Diamonds Oh! How I Wish (BMI)—Mercury 71165	—	1
17.	FASCINATION (ASCAP)—Dick Jacobs Summertime in Venice (ASCAP)—Coral 61864	—	2
18.	LOTTA LOVIN' (BMI)—Gene Vincent Wear My Ring (BMI)—Cap 3763	—	1
19.	AND THAT REMINDS ME (ASCAP)—Della Reese I Cried for You (ASCAP)—Jubilee 5292	—	1
20.	IN THE MIDDLE OF AN ISLAND (ASCAP)—Tony Bennett I Am (ASCAP)—Col 40965	13	7
21.	BLACK SLACKS (BMI)—Joe Bennett & Sparkletones Boppin' Rock Boogie (BMI)—ABC-Paramount 9837	—	1
22.	WAKE UP LITTLE SUSIE (BMI)—Everly Brothers Maybe Tomorrow (BMI)—Cadence 1337	—	1
23.	LOVE ME TO PIECES (BMI)—Jill Corey Love (BMI)—Col 40955	19	9
24.	WHITE SILVER SANDS (BMI)—Don Rondo Stars Fell on Alabama (ASCAP)—Jubilee 5288	15	10
25.	IT'S NOT FOR ME TO SAY (ASCAP)—Johnny Mathis Warm and Tender (ASCAP)—Col 40851	22	18

NEW YORK UNIVERSITY SCHOOL OF RETAILING · STORE RECORDED SALES · THE BILLBOARD

Top 100 Sides

FOR SURVEY WEEK ENDING SEPTEMBER 21

This is a tabulation of dealer unit sales listed according to the specific side requested by customers. No attempt is made to add sides together to reflect actual record sales. It is therefore a tabulation of sides or songs, and not records. This fact, together with longer four-week survey periods, explains variation between the top 30 sides as reflected in this chart, and top 30 record sellers as reflected in "Best Sellers in Stores."

Position, Song, Artist, Label	Position Last Week
1. **TAMMY,** Debbie Reynolds, Coral	1
2. **DIANA,** Paul Anka, ABC-Paramount	2
3. **HONEYCOMB,** Jimmie Rodgers, Roulette	5
4. **WHOLE LOTTA SHAKIN' GOIN' ON,** Jerry Lee Lewis, Sun	4
5. **THAT'LL BE THE DAY,** Crickets, Brunswick	3
6. **MR. LEE,** Bobbettes, Atlantic	7
7. **RAINBOW,** Russ Hamilton, Kapp	8
8. **TEDDY BEAR,** Elvis Presley, Victor	6
9. **IN THE MIDDLE OF AN ISLAND,** Tony Bennett, Columbia	9
10. **CHANCES ARE,** Johnny Mathis, Columbia	26
11. **IT'S NOT FOR ME TO SAY,** Johnny Mathis, Columbia	11
12. **SEARCHIN',** Coasters, Atco	12
13. **HAPPY, HAPPY BIRTHDAY, BABY,** Tune Weavers, Checker	36
14. **STARDUST,** Billy Ward, Liberty	13
15. **BYE BYE LOVE,** Everly Brothers, Cadence	10
16. **FASCINATION,** Jane Morgan, Kapp	20
17. **SEND FOR ME,** Nat King Cole, Capitol	14
18. **YOU'RE MY ONE AND ONLY LOVE,** Ricky Nelson, Verve	22
19. **SHORT FAT FANNIE,** Larry Williams, Specialty	15
20. **HULA LOVE,** Buddy Knox, Roulette	21
21. **LOTTA LOVIN',** Gene Vincent, Capitol	27
21. **WHITE SILVER SANDS,** Don Rondo, Jubilee	16
23. **LOVE LETTERS IN THE SAND,** Pat Boone, Dot	18
24. **WHISPERING BELLS,** Del Vikings, Dot	17
25. **LOVE ME TO PIECES,** Jill Corey, Columbia	23
26. **I'M GONNA SIT RIGHT DOWN AND WRITE MYSELF A LETTER.** Billy Williams, Coral	19
27. **REMEMBER YOU'RE MINE,** Pat Boone, Dot	25
28. **BLACK SLACKS,** Joe Bennett & The Sparkletones, ABC-Paramount	30
29. **JUST BETWEEN YOU AND ME,** Chordettes, Cadence	36
30. **GOODY GOODY,** Frankie Lymon and the Teenagers, Gee	24
31. **THERE'S A GOLD MINE IN THE SKY,** Pat Boone, Dot	28
32. **AND THAT REMINDS ME,** Della Reese, Jubilee	29
33. **AROUND THE WORLD,** Mantovani, London	35
34. **AROUND THE WORLD,** Victor Young, Decca	33
35. **LASTING LOVE,** Sal Mineo, Epic	37
36. **SO RARE,** Jimmy Dorsey, Fraternity	32
37. **MOONLIGHT SWIM,** Nick Noble, Mercury	41
38. **TO THE AISLE,** Five Satins, Ember	34
38. **LOVING YOU,** Elvis Presley, Victor	46
40. **AN AFFAIR TO REMEMBER,** Vic Damone, Columbia	48
41. **JUNE NIGHT,** Jimmy Dorsey, Fraternity	39
42. **OLD CAPE COD,** Patti Page, Mercury	40
43. **WAKE UP LITTLE SUSIE,** Everly Brothers, Cadence	—
44. **WONDERFUL WONDERFUL,** Johnny Mathis, Columbia	42
45. **FARTHER UP THE ROAD,** Bobby (Blue) Bland, Duke	47
46. **TAMMY,** Ames Brothers, Victor	43
47. **FRAULEIN,** Bobby Helms, Decca	60
47. **ZIP ZIP,** Diamonds, Mercury	54
49. **LONG LONELY NIGHTS,** Clyde McPhatter, Atlantic	52
50. **FLYING SAUCER,** Buchanan & Goodman, Luniverse	37
50. **JENNY JENNY,** Little Richard, Specialty	43
52. **FASCINATION,** Dick Jacobs, Coral	54
52. **SWINGIN' SWEETHEARTS,** Ron Goodwin, Capitol	62
54. **REBEL,** Carol Jarvis, Dot	50
55. **LONG LONELY NIGHTS,** Lee Andrews, Chess	54
56. **LIPS OF WINE,** Andy Williams, Cadence	87
56. **SHANGRI LA,** Four Coins, Epic	45
58. **WHEN I SEE YOU,** Fats Domino, Imperial	48
59. **BON VOYAGE,** Janice Harper, Prep	51
59. **COOL SHAKE,** Del Vikings, Mercury	57
59. **IN THE MIDDLE OF AN ISLAND,** Tennessee Ernie Ford, Capitol	69
62. **DEEP PURPLE,** Billy Ward and His Dominoes, Liberty	—
63. **ROCKIN' PNEUMONIA AND THE BOOGIE WOOGIE FLU,** Huey Smith, Ace	87
64. **WITH YOU ON MY MIND,** Nat King Cole, Capitol	87
65. **KEEP A-KNOCKIN',** Little Richard, Specialty	—
65. **SUSIE Q,** Dale Hawkins, Checker	83
67. **BERNARDINE,** Pat Boone, Dot	59
67. **FASCINATION,** David Carroll, Mercury	66
69. **MY HEART REMINDS ME,** Kay Starr, Victor	61
69. **PEANUTS,** Little Joe and the Thrillers, Okeh	45
71. **ANGRY,** Frank Pizani, Bally	70
72. **GONNA FIND ME A BLUEBIRD,** Marvin Rainwater, M-G-M	67
72. **FALLEN STAR,** Ferlin Husky, Capitol	71
72. **ISLAND IN THE SUN,** Harry Belafonte, Victor	63
75. **MY ONE SIN,** Four Coins, Epic	93
75. **ROCKIN' SHOES,** Ames Brothers, Victor	67
77. **PLAYTHING,** Ted Newman, Rev	—
77. **SOFT SANDS,** Chordettes, Cadence	82
79. **AROUND THE WORLD,** Bing Crosby, Decca	87
79. **JAY DEE'S BOOGIE WOOGIE,** Jimmy Dorsey, Fraternity	78
79. **MY PERSONAL POSSESSION,** Nat King Cole, Capitol	87
82. **ALL SHOOK UP,** Elvis Presley, Victor	63
82. **HUMPTY DUMPTY HEART,** LaVern Baker, Atlantic	71
82. **WHITE SPORT COAT,** Marty Robbins, Columbia	76
85. **GOTTA GET TO YOUR HOUSE,** David Seville, Liberty	77
86. **DRIVE IN SHOW,** Eddie Cochran, Liberty	82
86. **SONG OF THE BAREFOOT MAILMAN,** Billy Leach, Bally	87
88. **LONELY CHAIR,** Lloyd Price, Krc	—
89. **ALONE,** Sheperd Sisters, Lance	—
89. **C. C. RIDER,** Chuck Willis, Atlantic	79
89. **WITH ALL MY HEART,** Jodie Sands, Chancellor	71
89. **YOUNG BLOOD,** Coasters, Atco	82
93. **AROUND THE WORLD,** McGuire Sisters, Coral	100
93. **DUMPLINS,** Doc Bagby, Okeh	—
93. **I'LL TAKE YOU HOME AGAIN, KATHLEEN,** Slim Whitman, Imperial	95
93. **I LIKE YOUR KIND OF LOVE,** Andy Williams, Cadence	82
97. **DUMPLINS,** Ernie Freeman, Imperial	98
97. **HE'S GONE,** Chantels, End	—
99. **HONEST I DO,** Jimmy Reed, Vee Jay	—
99. **LET THE FOUR WINDS BLOW,** [illegible] Brown, Imperial	79
99. **OVER THE MOUNTAIN,** Johnnie & Joe, Chess	65

STORE RECORDED SALES — NEW YORK UNIVERSITY SCHOOL OF RETAILING — THE BILLBOARD

Best Sellers in Stores

FOR SURVEY WEEK ENDING SEPTEMBER 28, 1957

The information given in this chart is based on actual sales to customers in a scientific sample of the nation's retail record outlets during the week ending on the date shown above. Sample design, sample size, and all methods used in this continuing study of retail record sales are under the direct and continuing supervision and control of the School of Retailing of New York University.

This Week		Last Week	Weeks on Chart
1.	HONEYCOMB (ASCAP)—Jimmie Rodgers Their Hearts Were Full of Spring (ASCAP)—Roulette 4015	1	8
2.	WAKE UP LITTLE SUSIE (BMI)—Everly Brothers Maybe Tomorrow (BMI)—Cadence 1337	25	2
3.	TAMMY (ASCAP)—Debbie Reynolds French Heels (ASCAP)—Coral 61851	2	11
4.	DIANA (BMI)—Paul Anka Don't Gamble With Love (BMI)—ABC-Paramount 9831	4	11
4.	WHOLE LOTTA SHAKIN' GOIN' ON (BMI)—Jerry Lee Lewis It'll Be Mine (BMI)—Sun 267	5	11
6.	THAT'LL BE THE DAY (BMI)—Crickets I'm Lookin' for Someone to Love (BMI)—Brunswick 55009	3	8
7.	CHANCES ARE (ASCAP)—Johnny Mathis The Twelfth of Never (ASCAP)—Col 40993	6	3
8.	HAPPY, HAPPY BIRTHDAY, BABY (BMI)—Tune Weavers Ol' Man River (ASCAP)—Checker 872	8	3
9.	MR. LEE (BMI)—Bobbettes Look at the Stars—Atlantic 1144	7	9
10.	REMEMBER YOU'RE MINE (ASCAP)—Pat Boone THERE'S A GOLD MINE IN THE SKY (ASCAP)—Dot 15602	12	9
11.	RAINBOW (ASCAP)—Russ Hamilton We Will Make Love (ASCAP)—Kapp 184	8	10
12.	FASCINATION (ASCAP)—Jane Morgan Fascination (Instrumental) (ASCAP)—Kapp 191	17	5
13.	TEDDY BEAR (ASCAP)—Elvis Presley LOVING YOU (BMI)—Vic 7000	8	16
14.	HULA LOVE (BMI)—Buddy Knox Devil Woman (BMI)—Roulette 4018	16	5
15.	LOTTA LOVIN' (BMI)—Gene Vincent WEAR MY RING (BMI)—Cap 3763	13	3
16.	KEEP A' KNOCKIN' (BMI)—Little Richard Can't Believe You Wanna Leave (BMI)—Specialty 661	—	1
17.	IN THE MIDDLE OF AN ISLAND (ASCAP)—Tony Bennett I AM (ASCAP)—Col 40965	11	9
18.	JUST BETWEEN YOU AND ME (BMI)—Chordettes SOFT SANDS (BMI)—Cadence 1330	15	4
19.	BE-BOP BABY (BMI)—Ricky Nelson HAVE I TOLD YOU LATELY THAT I LOVE YOU (BMI)—Imperial 5463	—	1
20.	BLACK SLACKS (BMI)—Joe Bennett & Sparkletones Boppin' Rock Boogie (BMI)—ABC-Paramount 9837	26	3
21.	STARDUST (ASCAP)—Billy Ward Lucinda (BMI)—Liberty 55071	19	12
22.	YOU'RE MY ONE AND ONLY LOVE (ASCAP)—Ricky Nelson HONEY ROCK (ASCAP)—Verve 10070	15	4
23.	IT'S NOT FOR ME TO SAY (ASCAP)—Johnny Mathis Warm and Tender (ASCAP)—Col 40851	22	20
24.	SEND FOR ME (BMI)—Nat King Cole MY PERSONAL POSSESSION (BMI)—Cap 3737	20	15
25.	SEARCHIN' (BMI)—Coasters YOUNG BLOOD (BMI)—Atco 6087	24	21
26.	BYE BYE LOVE (BMI)—Everly Brothers I Wonder If I Care as Much (BMI)—Cadence 1315	18	20
27.	LOVE LETTERS IN THE SAND Pat Boone BERNARDINE (ASCAP)—Dot 15570	21	22
28.	SHORT FAT FANNIE (BMI)—Larry Williams HIGH SCHOOL DANCE (BMI)—Specialty 608	23	14
28.	DEEP PURPLE (ASCAP)—Billy Ward & His Dominoes Do It Again (BMI)—Liberty 5599	—	1
30.	WHITE SILVER SANDS (BMI)—Don Rondo Stars Fell on Alabama (ASCAP)—Jubilee 5288	28	11
30.	PEANUTS (BMI)—Little Joe & the Thrillers Lilly Lou (BMI)—Okeh 7088	—	1

Most Played by Jockeys

FOR SURVEY WEEK ENDING SEPTEMBER 28, 1957

SIDES are ranked in order of the greatest number of plays on disk jockey radio shows thruout the country. Results are based on The Billboard's weekly survey among the nation's disk jockeys. The reverse side of each record is also listed.

This Week		Last Week	Weeks on Chart
1.	HONEYCOMB (ASCAP)—Jimmie Rodgers Their Hearts Were Full of Spring (ASCAP) —Roulette 4015	1	7
2.	TAMMY (ASCAP)—Debbie Reynolds French Heels (ASCAP)—Coral 61851	3	12
3.	DIANA (BMI)—Paul Anka Don't Gamble With Love (BMI)—ABC-Paramount 9831	2	9
4.	THAT'LL BE THE DAY (BMI)—Crickets I'm Lookin' for Someone to Love (BMI)—Brunswick 55009	4	7
5.	CHANCES ARE (ASCAP)—Johnny Mathis The Twelfth of Never (ASCAP)—Col 40993	5	4
6.	WAKE UP LITTLE SUSIE (BMI)—Everly Brothers Maybe Tomorrow (BMI)—Cadence 1337	22	2
7.	TAMMY (ASCAP)—Ames Brothers Rockin' Shoes (BMI)—Vic 6930	7	12
8.	RAINBOW (ASCAP)—Russ Hamilton We Will Make Love—Kapp 184	6	10
9.	HULA LOVE (BMI)—Buddy Knox Devil Woman (BMI)—Roulette 4018	14	4
10.	MY HEART REMINDS ME (ASCAP)—Kay Starr Flim Flam Floo (BMI)—Vic 6981	11	4
10.	WHOLE LOTTA SHAKIN' GOIN' ON (BMI)—Jerry Lee Lewis It'll Be Mine (BMI)—Sun 267	12	9
12.	JUST BETWEEN YOU AND ME (BMI)—Chordettes Soft Sands (BMI)—Cadence 1330	8	4
13.	MR. LEE (BMI)—Bobbettes Look at the Stars (BMI)—Atlantic 1144	10	3
14.	FASCINATION (ASCAP)—Jane Morgan Fascination (Instrumental) (ASCAP)—Kapp 191	13	5
15.	MELODIE D'AMOUR (BMI)—Ames Brothers So Little Time (BMI)—Vic 7046	—	1
16.	REMEMBER YOU'RE MINE (ASCAP)—Pat Boone There's a Gold Mine in the Sky (ASCAP)—Dot 15602	9	7
17.	FASCINATION (ASCAP)—Dinah Shore Till (ASCAP)—Vic 6980	15	3
18.	AN AFFAIR TO REMEMBER (ASCAP)—Vic Damone In the Eyes of the World (ASCAP)—Col 40945	—	1
19.	LOTTA LOVIN' (BMI)—Gene Vincent Wear My Ring (BMI)—Cap 3763	18	2
20.	FASCINATION (ASCAP)—Dick Jacobs Summertime in Venice (ASCAP)—Coral 61864	17	3
20.	IN THE MIDDLE OF AN ISLAND (ASCAP)—Tony Bennett I Am (ASCAP)—Col 40965	20	3
22.	AND THAT REMINDS ME (ASCAP)—Della Reese I Cried for You (ASCAP)—Jubilee 5292	19	2
23.	HAPPY, HAPPY BIRTHDAY, BABY (BMI)—Tune Weavers Ol' Man River (ASCAP)—Checker 872	—	1
24.	MOONLIGHT SWIM (BMI)—Tony Perkins First Romance (BMI)—Vic 7020	—	1
25.	BLACK SLACKS (BMI)—Joe Bennett & Sparkletones Boppin' Rock Boogie (BMI)—ABC-Paramount 9837	21	2

Top 100 Sides

STORE RECORDED SALES — NEW YORK UNIVERSITY SCHOOL OF RETAILING — THE BILLBOARD

FOR SURVEY WEEK ENDING SEPTEMBER 28

This is a tabulation of dealer unit sales listed according to the specific side requested by customers. No attempt is made to add sides together to reflect actual record sales. It is therefore a tabulation of sides or songs, and not records. This fact, together with longer four-week survey periods, explains variation between the top 30 sides as reflected in this chart, and top 30 record sellers as reflected in "Best Sellers in Stores."

Position, Song, Artist, Label	Position Last Week
1. **HONEYCOMB,** Jimmie Rodgers, Roulette	3
2. **TAMMY,** Debbie Reynolds, Coral	1
3. **THAT'LL BE THE DAY,** Crickets, Brunswick	5
4. **DIANA,** Paul Anka, ABC-Paramount	2
5. **WHOLE LOTTA SHAKIN' GOIN' ON,** Jerry Lee Lewis, Sun	4
6. **MR. LEE,** Bobbettes, Atlantic	6
7. **CHANCES ARE,** Johnny Mathis, Columbia	10
8. **RAINBOW,** Russ Hamilton, Kapp	7
9. **WAKE UP LITTLE SUSIE,** Everly Brothers, Cadence	43
10. **HAPPY. HAPPY BIRTHDAY, BABY,** Tune Weavers, Checker	13
11. **IN THE MIDDLE OF AN ISLAND,** Tony Bennett, Columbia	9
12. **TEDDY BEAR,** Elvis Presley, Victor	8
13. **FASCINATION,** Jane Morgan, Kapp	16
13. **HULA LOVE,** Buddy Knox, Roulette	20
15. **LOTTA LOVIN',** Gene Vincent, Capitol	21
16. **YOU'RE MY ONE AND ONLY LOVE,** Ricky Nelson, Verve	18
17. **IT'S NOT FOR ME TO SAY,** Johnny Mathis, Columbia	11
18. **STARDUST,** Billy Ward, Liberty	14
19. **BYE BYE LOVE,** Everly Brothers, Cadence	15
20. **BLACK SLACKS,** Joe Bennett & the Sparkletones, ABC-Paramount	28
21. **SHORT FAT FANNIE,** Larry Williams, Specialty	19
22. **JUST BETWEEN YOU AND ME,** Chordettes, Cadence	29
23. **REMEMBER YOU'RE MINE,** Pat Boone, Dot	27
24. **SEARCHIN',** Coasters, Atco	12
25. **WHITE SILVER SANDS,** Don Rondo, Jubilee	21
26. **SEND FOR ME,** Nat King Cole, Capitol	17
27. **LOVE LETTERS IN THE SAND,** Pat Boone, Dot	23
28. **KEEP A' KNOCKIN',** Little Richard, Specialty	65
29. **THERE'S A GOLD MINE IN THE SKY,** Pat Boone, Dot	31
30. **LOVE ME TO PIECES,** Jill Corey, Columbia	25
31. **GOODY GOODY,** Frankie Lymon and Teenagers, Gee	30
32. **AROUND THE WORLD,** Mantovani, London	33
32. **WHISPERING BELLS,** Del Vikings, Dot	24
34. **I'M GONNA SIT RIGHT DOWN AND WRITE MYSELF A LETTER** Billy Williams, Coral	26
35. **AND THAT REMINDS ME,** Della Reese, Jubilee	32
36. **AN AFFAIR TO REMEMBER,** Vic Damone, Columbia	40
37. **LASTING LOVE,** Sal Mineo, Epic	35
38. **LOVING YOU,** Elvis Presley, Victor	38
39. **AROUND THE WORLD,** Victor Young, Decca	34
40. **DEEP PURPLE,** Billy Ward and His Dominoes, Liberty	62
41. **FRAULEIN,** Bobby Helms, Decca	47
41. **PEANUTS,** Little Joe and the Thrillers, Okeh	69
43. **TO THE AISLE,** Five Satins, Ember	38
44. **FARTHER UP THE ROAD,** Bobby (Blue) Bland, Duke	45
45. **ZIP ZIP,** Diamonds, Mercury	47
46. **BON VOYAGE,** Janice Harper, Prep	59
47. **LIPS OF WINE,** Andy Williams, Cadence	56
47. **WITH YOU ON MY MIND,** Nat King Cole, Capitol	64
49. **MY ONE SIN,** Four Coins, Epic	75
50. **SO RARE,** Jimmy Dorsey, Fraternity	36
51. **LONG LONELY NIGHTS,** Clyde McPhatter, Atlantic	49
51. **JUNE NIGHT,** Jimmy Dorsey, Fraternity	41
51. **BE BOP,** Ricky Nelson, Imperial	—
54. **FASCINATION,** Dick Jacobs, Coral	52
54. **MOONLIGHT SWIM,** Nick Noble, Mercury	37
54. **REBEL,** Carol Jarvis, Dot	54
57. **TAMMY,** Ames Brothers, Victor	46
58. **PLAYTHING,** Ted Newman, Rev	77
59. **IN THE MIDDLE OF AN ISLAND,** Tennessee Ernie Ford, Capitol	59
60. **LONG LONELY NIGHTS,** Lee Andrews, Chess	55
61. **MY HEART REMINDS ME,** Kay Starr, Victor	69
62. **ALONE,** Sheperd Sisters, Lance	89
62. **WHEN I SEE YOU,** Fats Domino, Imperial	58
64. **OLD CAPE COD,** Patti Page, Mercury	42
65. **ROCKIN' PNEUMONIA AND THE BOOGIE WOOGIE FLU** Huey Smith, Ace	63
65. **BERNARDINE,** Pat Boone, Dot	67
67. **FLYING SAUCER,** Buchanan & Goodman, Luniverse	50
67. **JENNY JENNY,** Little Richard, Specialty	50
69. **DUMPLINS,** Doc Bagby, Okeh	93
69. **SWINGIN' SWEETHEARTS,** Ron Goodwin, Capitol	52
71. **COOL SHAKE,** Del Vikings, Mercury	59
72. **WONDERFUL WONDERFUL,** Johnny Mathis, Columbia	44
73. **HUMPTY DUMPTY HEART,** Lavern Baker, Atlantic	82
74. **MELODIE D'AMOUR.** Ames Brothers, Victor	—
74. **ALL SHOOK UP,** Elvis Presley, Victor	82
76. **FASCINATION,** David Carroll, Mercury	67
77. **THINK,** Five Royals, King	—
78. **SHANGRI LA,** Four Coins, Epic	56
78. **SOFT SANDS,** Chordettes, Cadence	77
80. **GONNA FIND ME A BLUEBIRD,** Marvin Rainwater. M-G-M	72
80. **SUSIE Q,** Dale Hawkins, Checker	65
80. **ISLAND IN THE SUN,** Harry Belafonte, Victor	72
83. **MY PERSONAL POSSESSION,** Nat King Cole, Capitol	79
83. **FALLEN STAR,** Ferlin Husky, Capitol	72
85. **JAY DEE'S BOOGIE WOOGIE,** Jimmy Dorsey, Fraternity	79
86. **DUMPLINS,** Ernie Freeman, Imperial	97
86. **HONEST I DO,** Jimmy Reed, Vee Jay	99
88. **DESIREE,** Charts, Everlast	—
89. **BACK TO SCHOOL,** Jimmie Rodgers, Roulette	—
89. **YOUNG BLOOD,** Coasters, Atco	89
89. **HAVE I TOLD YOU LATELY THAT I LOVE YOU** Ricky Nelson, Imperial	—
92. **C. C. RIDER,** Chuck Willis, Atlantic	89
92. **TONIGHT, TONIGHT,** Mello-Kings, Herald	—
92. **AROUND THE WORLD,** Bing Crosby, Decca	79
95. **DRIVE-IN SHOW,** Eddie Cochran, Liberty	86
96. **DARLING IT'S WONDERFUL,** Lovers, Lamp	—
96. **ROCKIN' SHOES,** Ames Brothers, Victor	75
98. **FASCINATION,** Dinah Shore, Victor	—
99. **LET THE FOUR WINDS BLOW,** Roy Brown, Imperial	99
99. **OVER THE MOUNTAIN,** Johnnie & Joe, Chess	99

Best Sellers in Stores

FOR SURVEY WEEK ENDING OCTOBER 5, 1957

The information given in this chart is based on actual sales to customers in a scientific sample of the nation's retail record outlets during the week ending on the date shown above. Sample design, sample size, and all methods used in this continuing study of retail record sales are under the direct and continuing supervision and control of the School of Retailing of New York University.

This Week		Last Week	Weeks on Chart
1.	WAKE UP LITTLE SUSIE (BMI)—Everly Brothers Maybe Tomorrow (BMI)—Cadence 1337	2	3
2.	HONEYCOMB (ASCAP)—Jimmie Rodgers Their Hearts Were Full of Spring (ASCAP)—Roulette 4015	1	9
3.	TAMMY (ASCAP)—Debbie Reynolds French Heels (ASCAP)—Coral 61851	3	12
4.	JAILHOUSE ROCK (BMI)—Elvis Presley TREAT ME NICE (BMI)—Vic 7035	—	1
5.	DIANA (BMI)—Paul Anka Don't Gamble With Love (BMI)—ABC-Paramount 9831	4	12
6.	THAT'LL BE THE DAY (BMI)—Crickets I'm Lookin' for Someone to Love (BMI)—Brunswick 55009	6	9
7.	CHANCES ARE (ASCAP)—Johnny Mathis The Twelfth of Never (ASCAP)—Col 40993	7	4
8.	HAPPY, HAPPY BIRTHDAY, BABY (BMI)—Tune Weavers Ol' Man River (ASCAP)—Checker 872	8	4
9.	MR. LEE (BMI)—Bobbettes Look at the Stars—Atlantic 1144	9	10
10.	KEEP A' KNOCKIN' (BMI)—Little Richard Can't Believe You Wanna Leave (BMI)—Specialty 661	16	2
11.	WHOLE LOTTA SHAKIN' GOIN' ON (BMI)—Jerry Lee Lewis It'll Be Mine (BMI)—Sun 267	4	12
12.	FASCINATION (ASCAP)—Jane Morgan Fascination (Instrumental) (ASCAP)—Kapp 191	12	6
13.	BE-BOP BABY (BMI)—Ricky Nelson HAVE I TOLD YOU LATELY THAT I LOVE YOU (BMI)—Imperial 546	19	2
14.	HULA LOVE (BMI)—Buddy Knox Devil Woman (BMI)—Roulette 4018	14	6
15.	REMEMBER YOU'RE MINE (ASCAP)—Pat Boone THERE'S A GOLD MINE IN THE SKY (ASCAP)—Dot 15602	10	10
16.	LOTTA LOVIN' (BMI)—Gene Vincent WEAR MY RING (BMI)—Cap 3763	15	4
17.	RAINBOW (ASCAP)—Russ Hamilton We Will Make Love (ASCAP)—Kapp 184	11	11
18.	BLACK SLACKS (BMI)—Joe Bennett & Sparkletones Boppin' Rock Boogie (BMI)—ABC-Paramount 9837	20	4
19.	JUST BETWEEN YOU AND ME (BMI)—Chordettes SOFT SANDS (BMI)—Cadence 1330	18	5
20.	TEDDY BEAR (ASCAP)—Elvis Presley LOVING YOU (BMI)—Vic 7000	13	17
21.	MELODIE D'AMOUR (BMI)—Ames Brothers So Little Time (BMI)—Vic 7046	—	1
22.	PEANUTS (BMI)—Little Joe & The Thrillers Lilly Lou (BMI)—Okeh 4-7088	30	2
23.	IN THE MIDDLE OF AN ISLAND (ASCAP)—Tony Bennett I Am (ASCAP)—Col 40965	17	10
24.	LOVE LETTERS IN THE SAND (ASCAP)—Pat Boone BERNARDINE (ASCAP)—Dot 15570	27	23
25.	YOU'RE MY ONE AND ONLY LOVE (ASCAP)—Ricky Nelson HONEY ROCK (ASCAP)—Verve 10070	22	5
26.	SEND FOR ME (BMI)—Nat King Cole. MY PERSONAL POSSESSION (BMI)—Cap 3737	—	15
27.	BYE BYE LOVE (BMI)—Everly Brothers I Wonder If I Care as Much (BMI)—Cadence 1315	26	21
28.	MY ONE SIN (BMI)—Four Coins This Life (ASCAP)—Epic 9229	—	1
29.	DEEP PURPLE (ASCAP)—Billy Ward & His Dominoes Do It Again (BMI)—Liberty 5599	28	2
30.	AROUND THE WORLD (ASCAP)—Victor Young Decca 30262 (Vocal) (ASCAP)	—	9

Most Played by Jockeys

FOR SURVEY WEEK ENDING OCTOBER 5, 1957

SIDES are ranked in order of the greatest number of plays on disk jockey radio shows thruout the country. Results are based on The Billboard's weekly survey among the nation's disk jockeys. The reverse side of each record is also listed.

This Week		Last Week	Weeks on Chart
1.	HONEYCOMB (ASCAP)—Jimmie Rodgers Their Hearts Were Full of Spring (ASCAP)—Roulette 4015	1	8
2.	CHANCES ARE (ASCAP)—Johnny Mathis The Twelfth of Never (ASCAP)—Col 40993	5	5
3.	WAKE UP LITTLE SUSIE (BMI)—Everly Brothers Maybe Tomorrow (BMI)—Cadence 1337	6	3
3.	TAMMY (ASCAP)—Debbie Reynolds French Heels (ASCAP)—Coral 61851	2	13
5.	DIANA (BMI)—Paul Anka Don't Gamble With Love (BMI)—ABC-Paramount 9831	3	10
6.	THAT'LL BE THE DAY (BMI)—Crickets I'm Lookin' for Someone to Love (BMI)—Brunswick 55009	4	8
7.	FASCINATION (ASCAP)—Jane Morgan Fascination (Instrumental) (ASCAP)—Kapp 191	14	6
8.	JAILHOUSE ROCK (BMI)—Elvis Presley Treat Me Nice (BMI)—Vic 7035	—	1
9.	MY HEART REMINDS ME (ASCAP)—Kay Starr Flim Flam Floo (BMI)—Vic 6981	10	5
10.	TAMMY (ASCAP)—Ames Brothers Rockin' Shoes (BMI)—Vic 6930	7	13
11.	REMEMBER YOU'RE MINE (ASCAP)—Pat Boone There's a Gold Mine in the Sky (ASCAP)—Dot 15602	16	8
12.	HAPPY, HAPPY BIRTHDAY, BABY (BMI)—Tune Weavers Ol' Man River (ASCAP)—Checker 872	23	2
13.	RAINBOW (ASCAP)—Russ Hamilton We Will Make Love—Kapp 184	8	11
14.	JUST BETWEEN YOU AND ME (BMI)—Chordettes Soft Sands (BMI)—Cadence 1330	12	5
15.	MR. LEE (BMI)—Bobbettes Look at the Stars (BMI)—Atlantic 1144	13	4
15.	MELODIE D'AMOUR (BMI)—Ames Brothers So Little Time (BMI)—Vic 7046	15	2
17.	AND THAT REMINDS ME (ASCAP)—Della Reese I Cried for You (ASCAP)—Jubliee 5292	22	3
18.	LOTTA LOVIN' (BMI)—Gene Vincent Wear My Ring (BMI)—Cap 3763	19	3
19.	THE TWELFTH OF NEVER (ASCAP)—Johnny Mathis Chances Are (ASCAP)—Col 40993	—	1
20.	AN AFFAIR TO REMEMBER (ASCAP)—Vic Damone In the Eyes of the World (ASCAP)—Col 40945	18	2
21.	JUST BORN (BMI)—Perry Como Ivy Rose (ASCAP)—Vic 7050	—	1
22.	HULA LOVE (BMI)—Buddy Knox Devil Woman (BMI)—Roulette 4018	9	5
22.	WHOLE LOTTA SHAKIN' GOIN' ON (BMI)—Jerry Lee Lewis It'll Be Mine (BMI)—Sun 267	10	10
24.	MY SPECIAL ANGEL (BMI)— Standing at the End of My World (BMI)—Dec 30423	—	1
25.	FASCINATION (ASCAP)—Dinah Shore Till (ASCAP)—Vic 6980	17	4

NEW YORK UNIVERSITY SCHOOL OF RETAILING · STORE RECORDED SALES · THE BILLBOARD

Top 100 Sides

FOR SURVEY WEEK ENDING OCTOBER 5

This is a tabulation of dealer unit sales listed according to the specific side requested by customers. No attempt is made to add sides together to reflect actual record sales. It is therefore a tabulation of sides or songs, and not records. This fact, together with longer four-week survey periods, explains variation between the top 30 sides as reflected in this chart, and top 30 record sellers as reflected in "Best Sellers in Stores."

Position	Song, Artist, Label	Last Week
1.	**HONEYCOMB,** Jimmie Rodgers, Roulette	1
2.	**TAMMY,** Debbie Reynolds, Coral	2
3.	**WAKE UP LITTLE SUSIE,** Everly Brothers, Cadence	9
4.	**THAT'LL BE THE DAY,** Crickets, Brunswick	3
5.	**DIANA,** Paul Anka, ABC-Paramount	4
6.	**WHOLE LOTTA SHAKIN' GOIN' ON,** Jerry Lee Lewis, Sun	5
7.	**CHANCES ARE,** Johnny Mathis, Columbia	7
8.	**HAPPY, HAPPY BIRTHDAY, BABY,** Tune Weavers, Checker	10
9.	**MR. LEE,** Bobbettes, Atlantic	6
10.	**RAINBOW,** Russ Hamilton, Kapp	8
11.	**FASCINATION,** Jane Morgan, Kapp	13
12.	**HULA LOVE,** Buddy Knox, Roulette	13
13.	**IN MIDDLE OF AN ISLAND,** Tony Bennett, Columbia	11
14.	**LOTTA LOVIN',** Gene Vincent, Capitol	15
15.	**JAILHOUSE ROCK,** Elvis Presley, Victor	—
16.	**KEEP A' KNOCKIN',** Little Richard, Specialty	28
17.	**BLACK SLACKS,** Joe Bennett & the Sparkletones, ABC-Paramount	20
18.	**YOU'RE MY ONE AND ONLY LOVE,** Ricky Nelson, Verve	16
19.	**BYE BYE LOVE,** Everly Brothers, Cadence	19
20.	**TEDDY BEAR,** Elvis Presley, Victor	12
21.	**JUST BETWEEN YOU AND ME,** Chordettes, Cadence	22
22.	**STARDUST,** Bily Ward, Liberty	18
23.	**REMEMBER YOU'RE MINE,** Pat Boone, Dot	23
24.	**WHITE SILVER SANDS,** Don Rondo, Jubilee	25
25.	**IT'S NOT FOR ME TO SAY,** Johnny Mathis, Columbia	17
26.	**SEND FOR ME,** Nat King Cole, Capitol	26
27.	**SHORT FAT FANNIE,** Larry Williams, Specialty	21
28.	**BE BOP BABY,** Ricky Nelson, Imperial	51
29.	**THERE'S A GOLD MINE IN THE SKY,** Pat Boone, Dot	29
30.	**LOVE LETTERS IN THE SAND,** Pat Boone, Dot	27
30.	**PEANUTS,** Little Joe and the Thrillers, Okeh	41
32.	**DEEP PURPLE,** Billy Ward and His Dominoes, Liberty	40
33.	**AND THAT REMINDS ME,** Della Reese, Jubilee	35
34.	**SEARCHIN',** Coasters, Atco	24
35.	**AN AFFAIR TO REMEMBER,** Vic Damone, Columbia	36
36.	**AROUND THE WORLD,** Mantovani, London	32
36.	**I'M GONNA SIT RIGHT DOWN AND WRITE MYSELF A LETTER** Billy Williams, Coral	34
38.	**LOVE ME TO PIECES,** Jill Corey, Columbia	30
39.	**LIPS OF WINE,** Andy Williams, Cadence	47
40.	**FRAULEIN,** Bobby Helms, Decca	41
41.	**GOODY GOODY,** Frankie Lymon and Teenagers, Gee	31
41.	**MY ONE SIN,** Four Coins, Epic	49
43.	**WITH YOU ON MY MIND,** Nat King Cole, Capitol	47
44.	**WHISPERING BELLS,** Dell Vikings, Dot	32
45.	**MELODIE D'AMOUR,** Ames Brothers, Victor	74
46.	**LASTING LOVE,** Sal Mineo, Epic	37
47.	**ZIP ZIP,** Diamonds, Mercury	45
48.	**LOVING YOU,** Elvis Presley, Victor	38
49.	**BON VOYAGE,** Janice Harper, Prep	46
50.	**AROUND THE WORLD,** Victor Young, Decca	39
50.	**PLAYTHING,** Ted Newman, Rev	58
52.	**ALONE,** Sheperd Sisters, Lance	62
53.	**REBEL,** Carol Jarvis, Dot	54
54.	**LONG LONELY NIGHTS,** Clyde McPhatter, Atlantic	51
55.	**TO THE AISLE,** Five Satins, Ember	43
55.	**MY SPECIAL ANGEL,** Bobby Helms, Decca	—
57.	**BACK TO SCHOOL,** Timmie Rodgers, Cameo	89
57.	**HAVE I TOLD YOU LATELY THAT I LOVE YOU,** Ricky Nelson, Imperial	89
59.	**FASCINATION,** Dick Jacobs, Coral	54
60.	**MY HEART REMINDS ME,** Kay Starr, Victor	61
61.	**FARTHER UP THE ROAD,** Bobby (Blue) Bland, Duke	44
61.	**IN THE MIDDLE OF AN ISLAND,** Tennessee Ernie Ford, Capitol	59
63.	**AROUND THE WORLD,** Bing Crosby, Decca	92
63.	**JUNE NIGHT,** Jimmy Dorsey, Fraternity	51
63.	**MOONLIGHT SWIM,** Nick Noble, Mercury	54
66.	**HONEST I DO,** Jimmy Reed, Vee-Jay	86
67.	**BERNARDINE,** Pat Boone, Dot	65
68.	**COOL SHAKE,** Dell Vikings, Mercury	71
68.	**TAMMY,** Ames Brothers, Victor	57
70.	**DUMPLINS,** Doc Bagby, Okeh	69
71.	**SO RARE,** Jimmy Dorsey, Fraternity	50
72.	**LONG LONELY NIGHTS,** Lee Andrews, Chess	60
73.	**SOFT SANDS,** Chordettes, Cadence	78
73.	**SWINGIN' SWEETHEARTS,** Ron Goodwin, Capitol	69
75.	**ROCKIN' PNEUMONIA AND THE BOOGIE WOOGIE FLU,** Huey Smith, Ace	65
75.	**THINK,** Five Royals, King	77
77.	**JENNY JENNY,** Little Richard, Specialty	67
77.	**HUMPTY DUMPTY HEART,** La Vern Baker, Atlantic	73
79.	**WHEN I SEE YOU,** Fats Domino, Imperial	62
80.	**DUMPLINS,** Ernie Freeman, Imperial	86
80.	**JAY DEE'S BOOGIE WOOGIE,** Jimmy Dorsey, Fraternity	85
82.	**FLYING SAUCER,** Buchanan & Goodman, Luniverse	67
83.	**DEEP BLUE SEA,** Jimmy Dean, Columbia	—
83.	**GONNA FIND ME A BLUEBIRD,** Marvin Rainwater, M-G-M	80
85.	**MOONLIGHT SWIM,** Tony Perkins, Victor	—
85.	**OLD CAPE COD,** Patti Page, Mercury	64
85.	**TONIGHT, TONIGHT,** Mello-Kings, Herald	92
88.	**ALL SHOOK UP,** Elvis Presley, Victor	74
88.	**DARLING, IT'S WONDERFUL,** Lovers, Lamp	96
88.	**SUSIE Q,** Dale Hawkins, Checker	80
91.	**SHANGRI LA,** Four Coins, Epic	78
92.	**DRIVE-IN SHOW,** Eddie Cochran, Liberty	95
92.	**HE'S GONE,** Chantels, End	—
92.	**MY SHOES KEEP WALKIN' BACK TO YOU,** Ray Price, Columbia	—
95.	**SILHOUETTES,** Rays, Cameo	—
95.	**YOUNG BLOOD,** Coasters, Atco	89
97.	**HOME OF THE BLUES,** Johnny Cash, Sun	—
97.	**FALLEN STAR,** Ferlin Husky, Capitol	83
97.	**WONDERFUL, WONDERFUL,** Jihnny Mathis, Columbia	72
100.	**C C RIDER,** Chuck Willis, Atlantic	92

Best Sellers in Stores

FOR SURVEY WEEK ENDING OCTOBER 12, 1957

The information given in this chart is based on actual sales to customers in a scientific sample of the nation's retail record outlets during the week ending on the date shown above. Sample design, sample size, and all methods used in this continuing study of retail record sales are under the direct and continuing supervision and control of the School of Retailing of New York University.

This Week		Last Week	Weeks on Chart
1.	JAILHOUSE ROCK (BMI)—Elvis Presley TREAT ME NICE (BMI)—Vic 7035	4	2
2.	WAKE UP LITTLE SUSIE (BMI)—Everly Brothers Maybe Tomorrow (BMI)—Cadence 1337	1	4
3.	HONEYCOMB (ASCAP)—Jimmie Rodgers Their Hearts Were Full of Spring (ASCAP)—Roulette 4015	2	10
4.	TAMMY (ASCAP)—Debbie Reynolds French Heels (ASCAP)—Coral 61851	3	13
5.	CHANCES ARE (ASCAP)—Johnnie Mathis The Twelfth of Never (ASCAP)—Col 40993	7	5
6.	BE-BOP BABY (BMI)—Ricky Nelson HAVE I TOLD YOU LATELY THAT I LOVE YOU? (BMI)—Imperial 546	13	3
7.	DIANA (BMI)—Paul Anka Don't Gamble With Love (BMI)—ABC-Paramount 9831	5	13
8.	HAPPY, HAPPY BIRTHDAY, BABY (BMI)—Tune Weavers Ol' Man River (ASCAP)—Checker 872	8	5
9.	KEEP A' KNOCKIN' (BMI)—Little Richard Can't Believe You Wanna Leave (BMI)—Specialty 611	10	3
10.	THAT'LL BE THE DAY (BMI)—Crickets I'm Lookin' for Someone to Love (BMI)—Brunswick 55009	6	10
11.	MR. LEE (BMI)—Bobbettes Look at the Stars—Atlantic 1144	9	11
12.	WHOLE LOTTA SHAKIN' GOIN' ON (BMI)—Jerry Lee Lewis It'll Be Mine (BMI)—Sun 267	11	13
13.	HULA LOVE (BMI)—Buddy Knox Devil Woman (BMI)—Roulette 4018	14	7
14.	FASCINATION (ASCAP)—Jane Morgan Fascination (Instrumental) (ASCAP)—Kapp 191	12	7
14.	LOTTA LOVIN' (BMI)—Gene Vincent Wear My Ring (BMI)—Cap 3763	16	5
16.	SILHOUETTES (BMI)—The Rays Daddy Cool (BMI)—Cameo 117	—	1
17.	REMEMBER YOU'RE MINE (ASCAP)—Pat Boone THERE'S A GOLD MINE IN THE SKY (ASCAP)—Dot 15602	15	11
18.	RAINBOW (ASCAP)—Russ Hamilton We Will Make Love (ASCAP)—Kapp 184	17	12
19.	MY SPECIAL ANGEL (BMI)—Bobby Helms Standing at the End of My World (BMI)—Dec 30423	—	1
20.	JUST BETWEEN YOU AND ME (BMI)—Chordettes SOFT SANDS (BMI)—Cadence 1330	19	6
21.	IN THE MIDDLE OF AN ISLAND (ASCAP)—Tony Bennett I Am (ASCAP)—Col 40965	23	11
22.	MELODIE D'AMOUR (BMI)—Ames Brothers So Little Time (BMI)—Vic 7046	21	2
23.	BLACK SLACKS (BMI)—Joe Bennett & Sparkletones Boppin' Rock Boogie (BMI)—ABC-Paramount 9837	18	5
24.	PEANUTS (BMI)—Little Joe & The Thrillers Lilly Lou (BMI)—Okeh 4-7088	22	3
25.	AROUND THE WORLD (ASCAP)—Bing Crosby (INSTRUMENTAL WALTZ)—Dec 30262	30	10
26.	DEEP PURPLE (ASCAP)—Billy Ward & His Dominoes Do It Again (BMI)—Liberty 5599	29	3
27.	SEND FOR ME (BMI)—Nat King Cole MY PERSONAL POSSESSION (BMI)—Cap 3737	26	16
28.	TEDDY BEAR (ASCAP)—Elvis Presley LOVING YOU (BMI)—Vic 7000	20	18
29.	WAIT AND SEE (BMI)—Fats Domino I STILL LOVE YOU (BMI)—Imperial 5467	—	1
30.	WHITE SILVER SANDS (BMI)—Don Rondo Stars Fell on Alabama (ASCAP)—Jubilee 5288	—	12

Most Played by Jockeys

FOR SURVEY WEEK ENDING OCTOBER 12, 1957

SIDES are ranked in order of the greatest number of plays on disk jockey radio shows thruout the country. Results are based on The Billboard's weekly survey among the nation's disk jockeys. The reverse side of each record is also listed.

This Week		Last Week	Weeks on Chart
1.	CHANCES ARE (ASCAP)—Johnny Mathis The Twelfth of Never (ASCAP)—Col 40993	2	6
2.	HONEYCOMB (ASCAP)—Jimmie Rodgers Their Hearts Were Full of Spring (ASCAP)—Roulette 4015	1	9
3.	WAKE UP LITTLE SUSIE (BMI)—Everly Brothers Maybe Tomorrow (BMI)—Cadence 1337	8	4
4.	TAMMY (ASCAP)—Debbie Reynolds French Heels (ASCAP)—Coral 61851	3	14
5.	DIANA (BMI)—Paul Anka Don't Gamble With Love (BMI)—ABC-Paramount 9831	5	11
6.	JAILHOUSE ROCK (BMI)—Elvis Presley Treat Me Nice (BMI)—Vic 7035	8	2
7.	FASCINATION (ASCAP)—Jane Morgan Fascination (Instrumentals) (ASCAP)—Kapp 191	7	7
8.	THAT'LL BE THE DAY (BMI)—Crickets I'm Lookin' for Someone to Love (BMI)—Brunswick 55009	6	9
9.	MELODIE D'AMOUR (BMI)—Ames Brothers So Little Time (BMI)—Vic 7046	15	3
10.	RAINBOW (ASCAP)—Russ Hamilton We Will Make Love—Kapp 184	13	12
11.	MY HEART REMINDS ME (ASCAP)—Kay Starr Flim Flam Floo (BMI)—Vic 6981	9	6
12.	AND THAT REMINDS ME (ASCAP)—Della Reese I Cried for You (ASCAP)—Jubilee 5292	17	4
13.	HULA LOVE (BMI)—Buddy Knox Devil Woman (BMI)—Roulette 4018	22	6
14.	THE TWELFTH OF NEVER (ASCAP)—Johnny Mathis Chances Are (ASCAP)—Col 40993	19	2
15.	JUST BETWEEN YOU AND ME (BMI)—Chordettes Soft Sands (BMI)—Cadence 1330	14	6
16.	AN AFFAIR TO REMEMBER (ASCAP)—Vic Damone In the Eyes of the World (ASCAP)—Col 40945	20	3
17.	LIPS OF WINE (BMI)—Andy Williams Straight From My Heart (ASCAP)—Cadence 1336	—	1
18.	JUST BORN (BMI)—Perry Como Ivy Rose (ASCAP)—Vic 7050	21	2
18.	WHOLE LOTTA SHAKIN' GOIN' ON Jerry Lee Lewis (BMI)— It'll Be Mine (BMI)—Sun 267	22	11
20.	TREAT ME NICE (BMI)—Elvis Presley Jailhouse Rock (BMI)—Vic 7035	—	1
21.	REMEMBER YOU'RE MINE (ASCAP)—Pat Boone There's a Gold Mine in the Sky (ASCAP)—Dot 15602	11	9
21.	BLACK SLACKS (BMI)—Joe Bennett & Sparkletones Boppin' Rock Boogie (BMI)—ABC-Paramount 9837	—	3
23.	TAMMY (ASCAP)—Ames Brothers Rockin' Shoes (BMI)—Vic 6930	10	14
23.	FASCINATION (ASCAP)—Dick Jacobs Summertime in Venice (ASCAP)—Coral 61864	—	4
25.	FASCINATION (ASCAP)—Dinah Shore Till (ASCAP)—Vic 6980	25	5
25.	IVY ROSE (ASCAP)—Perry Como Just Born (BMI)—Vic 7050	—	1

Top 100 Sides

NEW YORK UNIVERSITY SCHOOL OF RETAILING · STORE RECORDED SALES · THE BILLBOARD

FOR SURVEY WEEK ENDING OCTOBER 12

This is a tabulation of dealer unit sales listed according to the specific side requested by customers. No attempt is made to add sides together to reflect actual record sales. It is therefore a tabulation of sides or songs, and not records. This fact, together with longer four-week survey periods, explains variation between the top 30 sides as reflected in this chart, and top 30 record sellers as reflected in "Best Sellers in Stores."

Position, Song, Artist, Label	Last Week
1. **WAKE UP LITTLE SUSIE,** Everly Brothers, Cadence	3
2. **HONEYCOMB,** Jimmie Rodgers, Roulette	1
3. **JAILHOUSE ROCK,** Elvis Presley, Victor	15
4. **TAMMY,** Debbie Reynolds, Coral	2
5. **DIANA,** Paul Anka, ABC-Paramount	5
6. **CHANCES ARE,** Johnny Mathis, Columbia	7
7. **THAT'LL BE THE DAY,** Crickets, Brunswick	4
7. **WHOLE LOTTA SHAKIN' GOIN' ON,** Jerry Lee Lewis, Sun	6
9. **HAPPY, HAPPY BIRTHDAY, BABY,** Tune Weavers, Checker	8
10. **MR. LEE,** Bobbettes, Atlantic	9
11. **KEEP A' KNOCKIN',** Little Richard, Specialty	16
12. **HULA LOVE,** Buddy Knox, Roulette	12
13. **FASCINATION,** Jane Morgan, Kapp	11
14. **RAINBOW,** Russ Hamilton, Kapp	10
15. **LOTTA LOVIN',** Gene Vincent, Capitol	14
16. **BE BOP BABY,** Ricky Nelson, Imperial	28
17. **IN THE MIDDLE OF AN ISLAND,** Tony Bennett, Columbia	13
18. **BLACK SLACKS,** Joe Bennett & the Sparkletones, ABC-Paramount	17
19. **JUST BETWEEN YOU AND ME,** Chordettes, Cadence	21
20. **REMEMBER YOU'RE MINE,** Pat Boone, Dot	23
21. **STARDUST,** Billy Ward, Liberty	22
22. **YOU'RE MY ONE AND ONLY LOVE,** Ricky Nelson, Verve	18
23. **IT'S NOT FOR ME TO SAY,** Johnny Mathis, Columbia	25
23. **PEANUTS,** Little Joe and the Thrillers, Okeh	30
25. **DEEP PURPLE,** Billy Ward and His Dominoes, Liberty	32
26. **SEND FOR ME,** Nat King Cole, Capitol	26
26. **TEDDY BEAR,** Elvis Presley, Victor	20
28. **BYE BYE LOVE,** Everly Brothers, Cadence	19
29. **THERE'S A GOLD MINE IN THE SKY,** Pat Boone, Dot	29
30. **WHITE SILVER SANDS,** Don Rondo, Jubilee	24
31. **MELODIE D'AMOUR,** Ames Brothers, Victor	45
32. **AND THAT REMINDS ME,** Della Reese, Jubilee	33
33. **SHORT FAT FANNIE,** Larry Williams, Specialty	27
33. **SILHOUETTES,** Rays, Cameo	95
35. **MY SPECIAL ANGEL,** Bobby Helms, Decca	55
36. **FRAULEIN,** Bobby Helms, Decca	40
37. **AROUND THE WORLD,** Mantovani, London	36
37. **AN AFFAIR TO REMEMBER,** Vic Damone, Columbia	35
39. **WITH YOU ON MY MIND,** Nat King Cole, Capitol	43
40. **LIPS OF WINE,** Andy Williams, Cadence	39
41. **MY ONE SIN,** Four Coins, Epic	41
42. **LOVE LETTERS IN THE SAND,** Pat Boone, Dot	30
43. **HAVE I TOLD YOU LATELY THAT I LOVE YOU,** Ricky Nelson, Imperial	57
44. **SEARCHIN',** Coasters, Atco	34
45. **LOVE ME TO PIECES,** Jill Corey, Columbia	38
45. **PLAYTHING,** Ted Newman, Rev	50
45. **WHISPERING BELLS,** Dell Vikings, Dot	44
45. **ZIP ZIP,** Diamonds, Mercury	47
49. **ALONE,** Sheperd Sisters, Lance	52
49. **I'M GONNA SIT RIGHT DOWN AND WRITE MYSELF A LETTER** Billy Williams, Coral	36
51. **LOVING YOU,** Elvis Presley, Victor	48
52. **GOODY GOODY,** Frankie Lymon and Teenagers, Gee	41
53. **BON VOYAGE,** Janice Harper, Prep	49
53. **BACK TO SCHOOL,** Timmie Rodgers, Cameo	57
55. **REBEL,** Carol Jarvis, Dot	53
56. **TO THE AISLE,** Five Satins, Ember	55
57. **AROUND THE WORLD,** Victor Young, Decca	50
57. **HONEST I DO,** Jimmy Reed, Vee Jay	66
59. **MY HEART REMINDS ME,** Kay Starr, Victor	60
60. **AROUND THE WORLD,** Bing Crosby, Decca	63
61. **TREAT ME NICE,** Elvis Presley, Victor	—
62. **FASCINATION,** Dick Jacobs, Coral	59
62. **LONG LONELY NIGHTS,** Clyde McPhatter, Atlantic	54
64. **IN THE MIDDLE OF AN ISLAND,** Tennessee Ernie Ford, Capitol	61
65. **FARTHER UP THE ROAD,** Bobbie (Blue) Bland, Duke	61
65. **MOONLIGHT SWIM,** Nick Noble, Mercury	63
65. **TAMMY,** Ames Brothers, Victor	68
68. **LITTLE BITTY PRETTY ONE,** Thurston Harris, Aladdin	—
69. **LASTING LOVE,** Sal Mineo, Epic	46
70. **MY SHOES KEEP WALKIN' BACK TO YOU,** Ray Price, Columbia	92
70. **THINK,** Five Royals, King	75
72. **DUMPLIN'S,** Doc Bagby, Okeh	70
72. **PLAYTHING,** Nick Todd, Dot	—
74. **BERNARDINE,** Pat Boone, Dot	67
75. **JUNE NIGHT,** Jimmy Dorsey, Fraternity	63
75. **SO RARE,** Jimmy Dorsey, Fraternity	71
77. **DUMPLIN'S,** Ernie Freeman, Imperial	80
78. **HE'S GONE,** Chantels, End	92
79. **JUST BORN,** Perry Como, Victor	—
79. **OLD CAPE COD,** Patti Page, Mercury	85
79. **SWINGIN' SWEETHEARTS,** Ron Goodwin, Capitol	73
79. **WONDERFUL, WONDERFUL,** Johnny Mathis, Columbia	97
79. **WAIT AND SEE,** Fats Domino, Imperial	—
84. **COOL SHAKE,** Del Vikings, Mercury	68
84. **DARLING IT'S WONDERFUL,** Lovers, Lamp	88
84. **MOONLIGHT SWIM,** Tony Perkins, Victor	85
84. **ROCKIN' PNEUMONIA AND THE BOOGIE WOOGIE FLU,** Huey Smith, Ace	75
88. **HOME OF THE BLUES,** Johnny Cash, Sun	97
88. **HUMPTY DUMPTY HEART,** La Vern Baker, Atlantic	77
88. **IDOL WITH THE GOLDEN HEAD,** Coasters, Atco	—
88. **JAY DEE'S BOOGIE WOOGIE,** Jimmy Dorsey, Fraternity	80
88. **SOFT SANDS,** Chordettes, Cadence	73
88. **TILL,** Percy Faith, Columbia	—
94. **GONNA FIND ME A BLUEBIRD,** Marvin Rainwater, M-G-M	83
94. **JENNY JENNY,** Little Richard, Specialty	77
94. **YOU SEND ME,** Sam Cooke, Keene	—
97. **ALL SHOOK UP,** Elvis Presley, Victor	88
97. **SILHOUETTES,** Steve Gibson & the Red Caps, ABC-Paramount	—
97. **TONIGHT, TONIGHT,** Mello-Kings, Herald	85
100. **DRIVE IN SHOW,** Eddie Cochran, Liberty	92

Best Sellers in Stores

FOR SURVEY WEEK ENDING, OCTOBER 19, 1957

The information given in this chart is based on actual sales to customers in a scientific sample of the nation's retail record outlets during the week ending on the date shown above. Sample design, sample size, and all methods used in this continuing study of retail record sales are under the direct and continuing supervision and control of the School of Retailing of New York University.

This Week	Title	Last Week	Weeks on Chart
1.	JAILHOUSE ROCK (BMI)—Elvis Presley / TREAT ME NICE (BMI)—Vic 7035	1	3
2.	WAKE UP LITTLE SUSIE (BMI)—Everly Brothers / Maybe Tomorrow (BMI)—Cadence 1337	2	5
3.	BE-BOP BABY (BMI)—Ricky Nelson / HAVE I TOLD YOU LATELY THAT I LOVE YOU? (BMI)—Imperial 5463	6	4
4.	CHANCES ARE (ASCAP)—Johnny Mathis / THE TWELFTH OF NEVER (ASCAP) Col 40993	5	6
5.	SILHOUETTES (BMI)—The Rays / Daddy Cool (BMI)—Cameo 117	16	2
6.	YOU SEND ME (BMI)—Sam Cooke / Summertime (ASCAP)—Keen 34013	—	1
7.	TAMMY (ASCAP)—Debbie Reynolds / French Heels (ASCAP)—Coral 61851	4	14
8.	HONEYCOMB (ASCAP)—Jimmie Rodgers / Their Hearts Were Full of Spring (ASCAP)—Roulette 4015	3	11
9.	DIANA (BMI)—Paul Anka / Don't Gamble With Love (BMI)—ABC-Paramount 9831	7	14
10.	KEEP A' KNOCKIN' (BMI)—Little Richard / Can't Believe You Wanna Leave (BMI)—Specialty 611	9	4
11.	HAPPY, HAPPY BIRTHDAY, BABY (BMI)—Tune Weavers / Ol' Man River (ASCAP)—Checker 872	8	6
12.	WHOLE LOTTA' SHAKIN' GOIN' ON (BMI)—Jerry Lee Lewis / It'll Be Mine (BMI)—Sun 267	12	14
13.	LOTTA LOVIN' (BMI)—Gene Vincent / WEAR MY RING (BMI)—Cap 3763	14	6
14.	HULA LOVE (BMI)—Buddy Knox / Devil Woman (BMI)—Roulette 4018	13	8
15.	LITTLE BITTY PRETTY ONE (BMI)—Thurston Harris / I Hope You Won't Hold It Against Me (BMI)—Aladdin 3398	—	1
16.	MR. LEE (BMI)—Bobbettes / Look at the Stars—Atlantic 1144	11	12
17.	THAT'LL BE THE DAY (BMI)—Crickets / I'm Lookin' for Someone to Love (BMI)—Brunswick 55009	10	11
18.	REMEMBER YOU'RE MINE (ASCAP)—Pat Boone / There's a Gold Mine in the Sky (ASCAP)—Dot 15602	17	12
19.	MY SPECIAL ANGEL (BMI)—Bobby Helms / Standing at the End of My World (BMI)—Dec 30423	19	2
20.	FASCINATION (ASCAP)—Jane Morgan / Fascination (Instrumental) (ASCAP)—Kapp 191	14	8
21.	RAINBOW (ASCAP)—Russ Hamilton / We Will Make Love (ASCAP)—Kapp 184	18	13
22.	MELODIE D'AMOUR (BMI)—Ames Brothers / So Little Time (BMI)—Vic 7046	22	3
23.	WAIT AND SEE (BMI)—Fats Domino / I STILL LOVE YOU (BMI)—Imperial 5467	29	2
24.	IN THE MIDDLE OF AN ISLAND (ASCAP)—Tony Bennett / I AM (ASCAP)—Col 40965	21	12
25.	JUST BETWEEN YOU AND ME (BMI)—Chordettes / SOFT SANDS (BMI)—Cadence 1330	20	7
26.	BLACK SLACKS (BMI)—Joe Bennett & Sparkletones / Boppin' Rock Boogie (BMI)—ABC-Paramount 9837	23	6
27.	DEEP PURPLE (ASCAP)—Billy Ward & His Dominoes / Do It Again (BMI)—Liberty 55099	26	4
28.	JUST BORN (BMI)—Perry Como / IVY ROSE (ASCAP)—Vic 7050	—	1
29.	SEND FOR ME (BMI)—Nat King Cole / MY PERSONAL POSSESSION (BMI)—Cap 3737	27	17
30.	PEANUTS (BMI)—Little Joe & The Thrillers / Lilly Lou (BMI)—Okeh 7088	24	4

Most Played by Jockeys

FOR SURVEY WEEK ENDING OCTOBER 19, 1957

SIDES are ranked in order of the greatest number of plays on disk jockey radio shows thruout the country. Results are based on The Billboard's weekly survey among the nation's disk jockeys. The reverse side of each record is also listed.

This Week	Title	Last Week	Weeks on Chart
1.	WAKE UP LITTLE SUSIE (BMI)—Everly Brothers / Maybe Tomorrow (BMI)—Cadence 1337	3	5
2.	CHANCES ARE (ASCAP)—Johnny Mathis / The Twelfth of Never (ASCAP)—Col 40993	1	7
3.	JAILHOUSE ROCK (BMI)—Elvis Presley / Treat Me Nice (BMI)—Vic 7035	6	3
4.	HONEYCOMB (ASCAP)—Jimmie Rodgers / Their Hearts Were Full of Spring (ASCAP)—Roulette 4015	2	10
5.	MELODIE D'AMOUR (BMI)—Ames Brothers / So Little Time (BMI)—Vic 7046	9	4
6.	TAMMY (ASCAP)—Debbie Reynolds / French Heels (ASCAP)—Coral 61851	4	15
7.	FASCINATION (ASCAP)—Jane Morgan / Fascination (Instrumental) (ASCAP)—Kapp 191	7	8
8.	MY SPECIAL ANGEL (BMI)—Bobby Helms / Standing at the End of My World (BMI)—Dec 30423	—	1
9.	DIANA (BMI)—Paul Anka / Don't Gamble With Love (BMI)—ABC-Paramount 9831	5	12
10.	BE-BOP BABY (BMI)—Ricky Nelson / Have I Told You Lately That I Love You? (BMI)—Imperial 5463	—	1
11.	SILHOUETTES (BMI)—The Rays / Daddy Cool (BMI)—Cameo 117	—	1
12.	APRIL LOVE (ASCAP)—Pat Boone / When the Swallows Come Back to Capistrano (ASCAP)—Dot 15660	—	1
13.	MY HEART REMINDS ME (ASCAP)—Kay Starr / Flim Flam Floo (BMI)—Vic 6981	11	7
14.	AND THAT REMINDS ME (ASCAP)—Della Reese / I Cried for You (ASCAP)—Jubilee 5292	12	5
15.	JUST BORN (BMI)—Perry Como / Ivy Rose (ASCAP)—Vic 7050	18	3
16.	THE TWELFTH OF NEVER (ASCAP)—Johnny Mathis / Chances Are (ASCAP)—Col 40993	14	3
17.	JUST BETWEEN YOU AND ME (BMI)—Chordettes / Soft Sands (BMI)—Cadence 1330	15	7
18.	TREAT ME NICE (BMI)—Elvis Presley / Jailhouse Rock (BMI)—Vic 7035	20	2
19.	TAMMY (ASCAP)—Ames Brothers / Rockin' Shoes (BMI)—Vic 6930	23	15
20.	THAT'LL BE THE DAY (BMI)—Crickets / I'm Lookin' for Someone to Love (BMI)—Brunswick 55009	8	10
20.	IVY ROSE (ASCAP)—Perry Como / Just Born (BMI)—Vic 7050	25	2
22.	HULA LOVE (BMI)—Buddy Knox / Devil Women (BMI)—Roulette 4018	13	7
23.	ALL THE WAY (ASCAP)—Frank Sinatra / Chicago (ASCAP)—Cap 3793	—	1
24.	FASCINATION (ASCAP)—Dinah Shore / Till (ASCAP)—Vic 6980	25	6
25.	HAPPY, HAPPY BIRTHDAY, BABY (BMI)—Tune Weavers / Ol' Man River (ASCAP)—Checker 872	—	3

NEW YORK UNIVERSITY SCHOOL OF RETAILING · STORE RECORDED SALES · THE BILLBOARD

Top 100 Sides

FOR SURVEY WEEK ENDING OCTOBER 19

This is a tabulation of dealer unit sales listed according to the specific side requested by customers. No attempt is made to add sides together to reflect actual record sales. It is therefore a tabulation of sides or songs, and not records. This fact, together with longer four-week survey periods, explains variation between the top 30 sides as reflected in this chart, and top 30 record sellers as reflected in "Best Sellers in Stores."

Position, Song, Artist Label	Last Week
1. **WAKE UP LITTLE SUSIE,** Everly Brothers, Cadence	1
2. **JAILHOUSE ROCK,** Elvis Presley, Victor	3
3. **TAMMY,** Debbie Reynolds, Coral	4
4. **HONEYCOMB,** Jimmie Rodgers, Roulette	2
5. **HAPPY, HAPPY BIRTHDAY, BABY,** Tune Weavers, Checker	9
6. **THAT'LL BE THE DAY,** Crickets, Brunswick	7
7. **CHANCES ARE,** Johnny Mathis, Columbia	6
8. **KEEP A' KNOCKIN',** Little Richard, Specialty	11
9. **WHOLE LOTTA SHAKIN' GOIN' ON,** Jerry Lee Lewis, Sun	7
10. **BE-BOP BABY,** Ricky Nelson, Imperial	16
11. **MR. LEE,** Bobbettes, Atlantic	10
12. **DIANA,** Paul Anka, ABC-Paramount	5
12. **HULA LOVE,** Buddy Knox, Roulette	12
14. **SILHOUETTES,** Rays, Cameo	33
15. **LOTTA LOVIN',** Gene Vincent, Capitol	15
16. **YOU SEND ME,** Sam Cooke, Keen	94
17. **RAINBOW,** Russ Hamilton, Kapp	14
18. **FASCINATION,** Jane Morgan, Kapp	13
19. **MELODIE D'AMOUR,** Ames Brothers, Victor	31
20. **IN THE MIDDLE OF AN ISLAND,** Tony Bennett, Columbia	17
21. **MY SPECIAL ANGEL,** Bobby Helms, Decca	35
22. **REMEMBER YOU'RE MINE,** Pat Boone, Dot	20
23. **JUST BETWEEN YOU AND ME,** Chordettes, Cadence	19
24. **PEANUTS,** Little Joe and the Thrillers, Okeh	23
25. **LITTLE BITTY PRETTY ONE,** Thurston Harris, Aladdin	68
26. **WHITE SILVER SANDS,** Don Rondo, Jubilee	30
27. **SEND FOR ME,** Nat King Cole, Capitol	26
27. **STARDUST,** Billy Ward, Liberty	21
29. **MY ONE SIN,** Four Coins, Epic	41
30. **BLACK SLACKS,** Joe Bennett & the Sparkletones, ABC-Paramount	18
30. **YOU'RE MY ONE AND ONLY LOVE,** Ricky Nelson, Verve	22
32. **TEDDY BEAR,** Elvis Presley, Victor	26
33. **IT'S NOT FOR ME TO SAY,** Johnny Mathis, Columbia	23
34. **AND THAT REMINDS ME,** Della Reese, Jubilee	32
34. **WITH YOU ON MY MIND,** Nat King Cole, Capitol	39
36. **TREAT ME NICE,** Elvis Presley, Victor	61
37. **HAVE I TOLD YOU LATELY THAT I LOVE YOU?** Ricky Nelson, Imperial	43
38. **DEEP PURPLE,** Billy Ward and His Dominoes, Liberty	25
39. **SHORT FAT FANNIE,** Larry Williams, Specialty	33
40. **LOVE LETTERS IN THE SAND,** Pat Boone, Dot	42
40. **LIPS OF WINE,** Andy Williams, Cadence	40
42. **I'M GONNA SIT RIGHT DOWN AND WRITE MYSELF A LETTER,** Billy Williams, Coral	49
43. **PLAYTHING,** Nick Todd, Dot	72
43. **BACK TO SCHOOL,** Timmie Rodgers, Cameo	53
45. **ZIP ZIP,** Diamonds, Mercury	45
46. **MOONLIGHT SWIM,** Tony Perkins, Victor	84
47. **JUST BORN,** Perry Como, Victor	79
48. **REBEL,** Carol Jarvis, Dot	55
49. **FRAULEIN,** Bobby Helms, Decca	36
50. **BYE BYE LOVE,** Everly Brothers, Cadence	28
50. **THERE'S A GOLD MINE IN THE SKY,** Pat Boone, Dot	29
50. **PLAYTHING,** Ted Newman, Rev	45
53. **HONEST I DO,** Jimmy Reed, Vee Jay	57
53. **MY HEART REMINDS ME,** Kay Starr, Victor	59
53. **WAIT AND SEE,** Fats Domino, Imperial	79
53. **WHISPERING BELLS,** Del Vikings, Dot	45
57. **AROUND THE WORLD,** Bing Crosby, Decca	60
57. **AN AFFAIR TO REMEMBER,** Vic Damone, Columbia	37
57. **SEARCHIN',** Coasters, Atco	44
60. **AROUND THE WORLD,** Mantovani, London	37
61. **IN THE MIDDLE OF AN ISLAND,** Tennessee Ernie Ford, Capitol	64
61. **LOVE ME TO PIECES,** Jill Corey, Columbia	45
63. **MY SHOES KEEP WALKIN' BACK TO YOU,** Ray Price, Columbia	70
64. **ALONE,** Sheperd Sisters, Lance	49
65. **TAMMY,** Ames Brothers, Victor	65
66. **I'M AVAILABLE,** Margie Rayburn, Liberty	—
66. **THINK,** Five Royals, King	70
66. **LONG LONELY NIGHTS,** Clyde McPhatter, Atlantic	62
66. **LOVING YOU,** Elvis Presley, Victor	51
70. **SWANEE RIVER ROCK,** Ray Charles, Atlantic	—
71. **HE'S GONE,** Chantels, End	78
71. **MR. FIRE EYES,** Bonnie Guitar, Dot	—
71. **SILHOUETTES,** Steve Gibson and the Red Caps, ABC-Paramount	97
74. **TO THE AISLE,** Five Satins, Ember	56
74. **GOODY GOODY,** Frankie Lymon and the Teenagers, Gee	52
74. **SO RARE,** Jimmy Dorsey, Fraternity	75
77. **JUNE NIGHT,** Jimmy Dorsey, Fraternity	75
77. **THERE'S ONLY YOU,** Don Rondo, Jubilee	—
79. **DUMPLIN'S,** Ernie Freeman, Imperial	77
79. **FRAULEIN,** Steve Lawrence, Coral	—
79. **IDOL WITH THE GOLDEN HEAD,** Coasters, Atco	88
79. **I STILL LOVE YOU,** Fats Domino, Imperial	—
79. **LASTING LOVE,** Sal Mineo, Epic	69
84. **AROUND THE WORLD,** Victor Young, Decca	57
84. **CHICAGO,** Frank Sinatra, Capitol	—
84. **FARTHER UP THE ROAD** Bobby (Blue) Bland, Duke	65
84. **I'LL REMEMBER TODAY,** Patti Page, Mercury	—
84. **ROCKIN' PNEUMONIA AND THE BOOGIE WOOGIE FLU** Huey Smith, Ace	84
84. **TILL,** Percy Faith, Columbia	88
90. **HUMPTY DUMPTY HEART,** Lavern Baker, Atlantic	88
90. **TONIGHT TONIGHT,** Mello-Kings, Herald	97
90. **TILL,** Roger Williams, Kapp	—
93. **BON VOYAGE,** Janice Harper, Prep	53
93. **HOME OF THE BLUES,** Johnny Cash, Sun	88
93. **SOFT SANDS,** Chordettes, Cadence	88
96. **JENNY JENNY,** Little Richard, Specialty	94
96. **MOONLIGHT SWIM,** Nick Noble, Mercury	65
96. **ONLY BECAUSE,** Platters, Mercury	—
96. **SWINGIN' SWEETHEARTS,** Ron Goodwin, Capitol	79
96. **WONDERFUL, WONDERFUL,** Johnny Mathis, Columbia	79

Best Sellers in Stores

FOR SURVEY WEEK ENDING OCTOBER 26, 1957

The information given in this chart is based on actual sales to customers in a scientific sample of the nation's retail record outlets during the week ending on the date shown above. Sample design, sample size, and all methods used in this continuing study of retail record sales are under the direct and continuing supervision and control of the School of Retailing of New York University.

This Week	Title	Last Week	Weeks on Chart
1.	JAILHOUSE ROCK (BMI)—Elvis Presley / TREAT ME NICE (BMI)—Vic 7035	1	4
2.	WAKE UP LITTLE SUSIE (BMI)—Everly Brothers / Maybe Tomorrow (BMI)—Cadence 1337	2	6
3.	YOU SEND ME (BMI)—Sam Cooke / SUMMERTIME (ASCAP)—Keen 34013	6	2
4.	SILHOUETTES (BMI)—The Rays / Daddy Cool (BMI)—Cameo 117	5	3
5.	BE-BOP BABY (BMI)—Ricky Nelson / HAVE I TOLD YOU LATELY THAT I LOVE YOU? (BMI)—Imperial 5463	3	5
6.	CHANCES ARE (ASCAP)—Johnny Mathis / THE TWELFTH OF NEVER (ASCAP)—Col 40993	4	7
7.	HONEYCOMB (ASCAP)—Jimmie Rodgers / Their Hearts Were Full of Spring (ASCAP)—Roulette 4015	8	12
8.	TAMMY (ASCAP)—Debbie Reynolds / French Heels (ASCAP)—Coral 61851	7	15
9.	LITTLE BITTY PRETTY ONE (BMI)—Thurston Harris / I Hope You Won't Hold It Against Me (ASCAP)—Aladdin 3398	15	2
10.	DIANA (BMI)—Paul Anka / Don't Gamble With Love (BMI)—ABC-Paramount 9831	9	15
11.	MY SPECIAL ANGEL (BMI)—Bobby Helms / Standing at the End of My World (BMI)—Dec 30423	19	3
12.	KEEP A' KNOCKIN' (BMI)—Little Richard / Can't Believe You Wanna Leave (BMI)—Specialty 611	10	5
13.	MELODIE D'AMOUR (BMI)—Ames Brothers / So Little Time (BMI)—Vic 7046	22	4
14.	HAPPY, HAPPY BIRTHDAY, BABY (BMI)—Tune Weavers / Ol' Man River (ASCAP)—Checker 872	11	7
15.	LOTTA LOVIN' (BMI)—Gene Vincent / WEAR MY RING (BMI)—Cap 3763	13	7
16.	FASCINATION (ASCAP)—Jane Morgan / Fascination (Instrumental) (ASCAP)—Kapp 191	20	9
17.	HULA LOVE (BMI)—Buddy Knox / Devil Woman (BMI)—Roulette 4018	14	9
18.	WHOLE LOTTA SHAKIN' GOIN' ON (BMI)—Jerry Lee Lewis / It'll Be Mine (BMI)—Sun 267	12	15
19.	JUST BORN (BMI)—Perry Como / IVY ROSE (ASCAP)—Vic 7050	28	2
20.	APRIL LOVE (ASCAP)—Pat Boone / WHEN THE SWALLOWS COME BACK TO CAPISTRANO (ASCAP)—Dot 15660	—	1
21.	MR. LEE (BMI)—Bobbettes / Look at the Stars—Atlantic 1144	16	13
22.	THAT'LL BE THE DAY (BMI)—Crickets / I'm Lookin' for Someone to Love (BMI)—Brunswick 55009	17	12
23.	RAINBOW (ASCAP)—Russ Hamilton / We Will Make Love (ASCAP)—Kapp 184	21	14
23.	DEEP PURPLE (ASCAP)—Billy Ward & His Dominoes / Do It Again (BMI)—Liberty 55099	27	5
25.	PEANUTS Little Joe & The Thrillers / Lilly Lou (BMI)—Okeh 7088	30	5
26.	WAIT AND SEE (BMI)—Fats Domino / I STILL LOVE YOU (BMI)—Imperial 5467	23	3
27.	ALONE (BMI)—Shepherd Sisters / Congratulations to Someone (ASCAP)—Lance 125	—	1
28.	REMEMBER YOU'RE MINE (ASCAP)—Pat Boone / THERE'S A GOLD MINE IN THE SKY (ASCAP)—Dot 15602	18	13
29.	BLACK SLACKS (BMI)—Joe Bennett & Sparkletones / Boppin' Rock Boogie (BMI)—ABC-Paramount 9837	26	7
30.	WITH YOU ON MY MIND (ASCAP)—Nat King Cole / Raintree County (ASCAP)—Cap 3782	—	1

Most Played by Jockeys

FOR SURVEY WEEK ENDING OCTOBER 26, 1957

SIDES are ranked in order of the greatest number of plays on disk jockey radio shows throughout the country. Results are based on The Billboard's weekly survey among the nation's disk jockeys. The reverse side of each record is also listed.

This Week	Title	Last Week	Weeks on Chart
1.	WAKE UP LITTLE SUSIE (BMI)—Everly Brothers / Maybe Tomorrow (BMI)—Cadence 1337	1	6
2.	JAILHOUSE ROCK (BMI)—Elvis Presley / Treat Me Nice (BMI)—Vic 7035	3	4
3.	CHANCES ARE (ASCAP)—Johnny Mathis / The Twelfth of Never (ASCAP)—Col 40993	2	8
4.	HONEYCOMB (ASCAP)—Jimmie Rodgers / Their Hearts Were Full of Spring (ASCAP)—Roulette 4015	4	11
5.	MELODIE D'AMOUR (BMI)—Ames Brothers / So Little Time (BMI)—Vic 7046	5	5
6.	TAMMY (ASCAP)—Debbie Reynolds / French Heels (ASCAP)—Coral 61851	6	16
7.	FASCINATION (ASCAP)—Jane Morgan / Fascination (Instrumental) (ASCAP)—Kapp 191	7	9
8.	APRIL LOVE (ASCAP)—Pat Boone / When the Swallows Come Back to Capistrano (ASCAP)—Dot 15660	12	2
9.	SILHOUETTES (BMI)—The Rays / Daddy Cool (BMI)—Cameo 117	11	2
9.	THAT'LL BE THE DAY (BMI)—Crickets / I'm Lookin' for Someone to Love (BMI)—Brunswick 55009	20	11
11.	BE-BOP BABY (BMI)—Ricky Nelson / Have I Told You Lately That I Love You (BMI)—Imperial 5463	10	2
12.	THE TWELFTH OF NEVER (ASCAP)—Johnny Mathis / Chances Are (ASCAP)—Col 40993	16	4
13.	MY HEART REMINDS ME (ASCAP)—Kay Starr / Flim Flam Floo (BMI)—Vic 6981	13	8
14.	MY SPECIAL ANGEL (BMI)—Bobby Helms / Standing at the End of My World (BMI)—Dec 30423	8	2
15.	DIANA (BMI)—Paul Anka / Don't Gamble With Love (BMI)—ABC-Paramount 9831	9	13
16.	JUST BORN (BMI)—Perry Como / Ivy Rose (ASCAP)—Vic 7050	15	4
17.	ALL THE WAY (ASCAP)—Frank Sinatra / Chicago (ASCAP)—Cap 3793	23	2
18.	IVY ROSE (ASCAP)—Perry Como / Just Born (BMI)—Vic 7050	20	3
19.	TREAT ME NICE (BMI)—Elvis Presley / Jailhouse Rock (BMI)—Vic 7035	18	3
20.	HAPPY, HAPPY BIRTHDAY, BABY (BMI)—Tune Weavers / Ol' Man River (ASCAP)—Checker 872	25	4
21.	SILHOUETTES (BMI)—Diamonds / Daddy Cool (BMI)—Mercury 71197	—	1
22.	AND THAT REMINDS ME (ASCAP)—Della Reese / I Cried for You (ASCAP)—Jubilee 5292	14	6
23.	TAMMY (ASCAP)—Ames Brothers / Rockin' Shoes (BMI)—Vic 6930	19	16
24.	KEEP A' KNOCKIN' (BMI)—Little Richard / Can't Believe You Wanna Leave (BMI)—Specialty 611	—	1
25.	YOU SEND ME (BMI)—Sam Cooke / Summertime (ASCAP)—Keen 34013	—	1

Top 100 Sides

STORE RECORDED SALES — NEW YORK UNIVERSITY SCHOOL OF RETAILING — THE BILLBOARD

FOR SURVEY WEEK ENDING OCTOBER 26

This is a tabulation of dealer unit sales listed according to the specific side requested by customers. No attempt is made to add sides together to reflect actual record sales. It is therefore a tabulation of sides or songs, and not records. This fact, together with longer four-week survey periods, explains variation between the top 30 sides as reflected in this chart, and top 30 record sellers as reflected in "Best Sellers in Stores."

Position, Song, Artist, Label	Last Week
1. **JAILHOUSE ROCK,** Elvis Presley, Victor	2
2. **WAKE UP LITTLE SUSIE,** Everly Brothers, Cadence	1
3. **SILHOUETTES,** Rays, Cameo	14
4. **HONEYCOMB,** Jimmie Rodgers, Roulette	4
5. **CHANCES ARE,** Johnny Mathis, Columbia	7
6. **YOU SEND ME,** Sam Cooke, Keen	16
7. **BE-BOP BABY,** Ricky Nelson, Imperial	10
8. **TAMMY,** Debbie Reynolds, Coral	3
9. **DIANA,** Paul Anka, ABC-Para.	12
10. **KEEP A' KNOCKIN',** Little Richard, Specialty	8
11. **HAPPY, HAPPY BIRTHDAY, BABY,** Tune Weavers, Checker	5
12. **THAT'LL BE THE DAY,** Crickets, Brunswick	6
13. **LITTLE BITTY PRETTY ONE,** Thurston Harris, Aladdin	25
14. **MR. LEE,** Bobbettes, Atlantic	11
15. **WHOLE LOTTA SHAKIN' GOIN' ON,** Jerry Lee Lewis, Sun	9
15. **MY SPECIAL ANGEL,** Bobby Helms, Decca	21
17. **HULA LOVE,** Buddy Knox, Roulette	12
18. **FASCINATION,** Jane Morgan, Kapp	18
18. **LOTTA LOVIN',** Gene Vincent, Capitol	15
20. **MELODIE D'AMOUR,** Ames Brothers, Victor	19
21. **RAINBOW,** Russ Hamilton, Kapp	17
22. **DEEP PURPLE,** Billy Ward and His Dominoes, Liberty	38
23. **PEANUTS,** Little Joe and the Thrillers, Okeh	24
24. **IN THE MIDDLE OF AN ISLAND,** Tony Bennett, Columbia	20
25. **BLACK SLACKS,** Joe Bennett & the Sparkletones, ABC-Paramount	30
26. **REMEMBER YOU'RE MINE,** Pat Boone, Dot	22
27. **TREAT ME NICE,** Elvjs Presley, Victor	36
28. **JUST BETWEEN YOU AND ME,** Chordettes, Cadence	23
29. **HAVE I TOLD YOU LATELY THAT I LOVE YOU,** Ricky Nelson, Imperial	37
30. **JUST BORN,** Perry Como, Victor	47
31. **ALONE,** Shepherd Sisters, Lance	64
32. **HONEST I DO,** Jimmy Reed, Vee Jay	53
33. **WITH YOU ON MY MIND,** Nat King Cole, Capitol	34
34. **WAIT AND SEE,** Fats Domino, Imperial	53
35. **SEND FOR ME,** Nat King Cole, Capitol	27
36. **STARDUST,** Billy Ward, Liberty	27
37. **BACK TO SCHOOL AGAIN,** Timmie Rodgers, Cameo	43
38. **MY ONE SIN,** Four Coins, Epic	29
38. **AND THAT REMINDS ME,** Della Reese, Jubilee	34
38. **WHITE SILVER SANDS, Don Rondo, Jubilee**	26
41. **PLAYTHING,** Nick Todd, Dot	43
42. **FRAULEIN,** Bobby Helms, Decca	49
43. **IT'S NOT FOR ME TO SAY,** Johnny Mathis, Columbia	33
43. **MOONLIGHT SWIM,** Tony Perkins, Victor	46
43. **TEDDY BEAR,** Elvis Presley, Victor	32
46. **APRIL LOVE,** Pat Boone, Dot	—
46. **AN AFFAIR TO REMEMBER,** Vic Damone, Columbia	57
48. **AROUND THE WORLD,** Mantovani, London	60
48. **THERE'S A GOLD MINE IN THE SKY,** Pat Boone, Dot	50
50. **BYE BYE LOVE,** Everly Brothers, Cadence	50
51. **LOVE LETTERS IN THE SAND,** Pat Boone, Dot	40
51. **LIPS OF WINE,** Andy Williams, Cadence	40
53. **SHORT FAT FANNIE,** Larry Williams, Specialty	39
54. **AROUND THE WORLD,** Bing Crosby, Decca	57
54. **YOU'RE MY ONE AND ONLY LOVE,** Ricky Nelson, Verve	30
56. **FARTHER UP THE ROAD,** Bobby (Blue) Bland, Duke	84
57. **TILL,** Roger Williams, Kapp	90
58. **I'M AVAILABLE,** Margie Rayburn, Liberty	66
59. **IN THE MIDDLE OF AN ISLAND,** Tennessee Ernie Ford, Capitol	61
59. **SWANEE RIVER ROCK,** Ray Charles, Atlantic	70
61. **FRAULEIN,** Steve Lawrence, Coral	79
61. **REBEL,** Carol Jarvis, Dot	48
63. **SILHOUETTES,** Steve Gibson and the Red Caps, ABC-Paramount	71
64. **IDOL WITH THE GOLDEN HEAD,** Coasters, Atco	79
64. **MY HEART REMINDS ME,** Kay Starr, Victor	53
64. **ZIP ZIP,** Diamonds, Mercury	45
67. **I'M GONNA SIT RIGHT DOWN AND WRITE MYSELF A LETTER,** Billy Williams, Coral	42
68. **SOFT,** Bill Doggett, King	—
69. **AROUND THE WORLD,** Victor Young, Decca	—
69. **IVY ROSE,** Perry Como, Victor	—
71. **TO THE AISLE,** Five Satins, Ember	74
71. **BON VOYAGE,** Janice Harper, Prep	93
71. **GOODY GOODY,** Frankie Lymon and the Teenagers, Gee	74
71. **MY SHOES KEEP WALKIN' BACK TO YOU,** Ray Price, Columbia	63
75. **DUMPLINS,** Ernie Freeman, Imperial	79
75. **MR. FIRE EYES,** Bonnie Guitar, Dot	71
75. **TAMMY,** Ames Brothers, Victor	65
78. **ALL THE WAY,** Frank Sinatra, Capitol	—
78. **I'LL REMEMBER TODAY,** Patti Page, Mercury	84
78. **WHISPERING BELLS,** Del Vikings, Dot	53
81. **I STILL LOVE YOU,** Fats Domino, Imperial	79
81. **ONLY BECAUSE,** Platters, Mercury	96
81. **THERE'S ONLY YOU,** Don Rondo, Jubilee	77
84. **PLAYTHING,** Ted Newman, Rev	50
85. **CHICAGO,** Frank Sinatra, Capitol	84
85. **LOVING YOU,** Elvis Presley, Victor	66
85. **SUMMERTIME,** Sam Cooke, Keen	—
88. **HOME OF THE BLUES,** Johnny Cash, Sun	93
88. **LONG LONELY NIGHTS,** Clyde McPhatter, Atlantic	66
88. **LASTING LOVE,** Sal Mineo, Epic	79
88. **MISS YOU SO,** Lillian Offitt, Excello	—
88. **SO RARE,** Jimmy Dorsey, Fraternity	74
93. **FASCINATION,** Dick Jacobs, Coral	—
93. **HE'S GONE,** Chantels, End	71
93. **REET PETITE,** Jackie Wilson, Brunswick	—
96. **COULD THIS BE MAGIC,** Dubs, Gone	—
96. **SEARCHIN',** Coasters, Atco	—
96. **ROCKIN' PNEUMONIA AND THE BOOGIE WOOGIE FLU,** Huey Smith, Ace	—
96. **THE TWELFTH OF NEVER,** Johnny Mathis, Columbia	—
96. **THINK,** Five Royals, King	—

Best Sellers in Stores

FOR SURVEY WEEK ENDING NOVEMBER 2, 1957

The information given in this chart is based on actual sales to customers in a scientific sample of the nation's retail record outlets during the week ending on the date shown above. Sample design, sample size, and all methods used in this continuing study of retail record sales are under the direct and continuing supervision and control of the School of Retailing of New York University.

This Week	Title	Last Week	Weeks on Chart
1.	JAILHOUSE ROCK (BMI)—Elvis Presley / TREAT ME NICE (BMI)—Vic 7035	1	5
2.	YOU SEND ME (BMI)—Sam Cooke / SUMMERTIME (ASCAP)—Keen 34013	3	3
3.	WAKE UP LITTLE SUSIE (BMI)—Everly Brothers / Maybe Tomorrow (BMI)—Cadence 1337	2	7
4.	SILHOUETTES (BMI)—The Rays / Daddy Cool (BMI)—Cameo 117	4	4
5.	BE-BOP BABY (BMI)—Ricky Nelson / HAVE I TOLD YOU LATELY THAT I LOVE YOU (BMI)—Imperial 5463	5	6
6.	LITTLE BITTY PRETTY ONE (BMI)—Thurston Harris / I Hope You Won't Hold It Against Me (ASCAP)—Aladdin 3398	9	3
7.	CHANCES ARE (ASCAP)—Johnny Mathis / THE TWELFTH OF NEVER (ASCAP)—Col 40993	6	8
8.	MY SPECIAL ANGEL (BMI)—Bobby Helms / Standing at the End of My World (BMI)—Dec 30423	11	4
9.	HONEYCOMB (ASCAP)—Jimmie Rodgers / Their Hearts Were Full of Spring (ASCAP)—Roulette 4015	7	13
10.	TAMMY (ASCAP)—Debbie Reynolds / French Heels (ASCAP)—Coral 61851	8	16
11.	APRIL LOVE (ASCAP)—Pat Boone / WHEN THE SWALLOWS COME BACK TO CAPISTRANO (ASCAP)—Dot 15660	20	2
12.	MELODIE D'AMOUR (BMI)—Ames Brothers / So Little Time (BMI)—Vic 7046	13	5
13.	FASCINATION (ASCAP)—Jane Morgan / Fascination (Instrumental) (ASCAP)—Kapp 191	16	10
14.	KEEP A' KNOCKIN' (BMI)—Little Richard / Can't Believe You Wanna Leave—Specialty 611	12	6
15.	JUST BORN (BMI)—Perry Como / IVY ROSE (ASCAP)—Vic 7050	19	3
16.	DIANA (BMI)—Paul Anka / Don't Gamble With Love (BMI)—ABC-Paramount 9831	10	16
17.	HAPPY, HAPPY BIRTHDAY, BABY (BMI)—Tune Weavers / Ol' Man River (ASCAP)—Checker 872	14	8
18.	ALONE (BMI)—Shepherd Sisters / Congratulations to Someone (ASCAP)—Lance 125	27	2
19.	LOTTA LOVIN' (BMI)—Gene Vincent / WEAR MY RING (BMI)—Cap 3763	15	8
20.	DEEP PURPLE (ASCAP)—Billy Ward & His Dominoes / Do It Again (BMI)—Liberty 55099	23	6
21.	HULA LOVE (BMI)—Buddy Knox / Devil Woman (BMI)—Roulette 4018	17	10
21.	ALL THE WAY (ASCAP)—Frank Sinatra / CHICAGO (ASCAP)—Cap 3793	—	1
23.	WHOLE LOTTA SHAKIN' GOIN' ON (BMI)—Jerry Lee Lewis / It'll Be Mine (BMI)—Sun 267	18	16
24.	MR. LEE (BMI)—Bobbettes / Look at the Stars—Atlantic 1144	21	14
25.	RAINBOW (ASCAP)—Russ Hamilton / We Will Make Love (ASCAP)—Kapp 184	23	15
26.	COULD THIS BE MAGIC (BMI)—Dubs / Such Lovin' (BMI)—Gone 5011	—	1
27.	PEANUTS (BMI)—Little Joe & The Thrillers / Lilly Lou (BMI)—Okeh 7088	25	6
28.	WAIT AND SEE (BMI)—Fats Domino / I STILL LOVE YOU (BMI)—Imperial 5467	26	3
29.	I'M AVAILABLE (BMI)—Margie Rayburn / If You Were (ASCAP)—Liberty 55102	—	1
30.	BONY MARONIE (BMI)—Larry Williams / YOU BUG ME, BABY (BMI)—Specialty 615	—	1
31.	THAT'LL BE THE DAY (BMI)—Crickets / I'm Lookin' for Someone to Love (BMI)—Brunswick 55009	22	13
32.	TILL (ASCAP)—Roger Williams / Big Town (ASCAP)—Kapp 197	—	1
33.	BLACK SLACKS (BMI)—Joe Bennett & Sparkletones / Boppin' Rock Boogie (BMI)—ABC-Paramount 9837	29	8
34.	MY ONE SIN (BMI)—Four Coins / This Life (ASCAP)—Epic 9229	—	2
35.	WITH YOU ON MY MIND (ASCAP)—Nat King Cole / RAINTREE COUNTY (ASCAP)—Cap 3782	30	2
36.	HONEST I DO (BMI)—Jimmy Reed / Signals of Love (BMI)—Vee-Jay 253	—	1
37.	BACK TO SCHOOL AGAIN (BMI)—Timmie Rodgers / I've Got a Dog Who Loves Me (BMI)—Cameo 116	—	1
38.	REMEMBER YOU'RE MINE (ASCAP)—Pat Boone / THERE'S A GOLD MINE IN THE SKY (ASCAP)—Dot 15602	28	14
39.	AND THAT REMINDS ME (ASCAP)—Della Reese / I Cried for You (ASCAP)—Jubilee 5292	—	2
40.	ROCK AND ROLL MUSIC (BMI)—Chuck Berry / Blue Feeling (BMI)—Chess 1671	—	1
41.	WUN'ERFUL, WUN'ERFUL (PARTS 1 & 2) (ASCAP)—Stan Freeberg	—	8
42.	JUST BETWEEN YOU AND ME (BMI)—Chordettes / SOFT SANDS (BMI)—Cadence 1330	—	8
43.	I'LL REMEMBER TODAY (BMI)—Patti Page / My. How the Time Goes By (ASCAP)—Mercury 71189	—	1
43.	PEGGY SUE (BMI)—Buddy Holly / Everyday (BMI)—Coral 61885	—	1
45.	PARTY TIME (BMI)—Sal Mineo / The Words That I Whisper (BMI)—Epic 9246	—	1
46.	FRAULEIN (BMI)—Bobby Helms / Heartsick Feeling (BMI)—Dec 30194	—	1
47.	TEDDY BEAR (ASCAP)—Elvis Presley / LOVING YOU (BMI)—Vic 7000	—	19
48.	IN THE MIDDLE OF AN ISLAND (ASCAP)—Tony Bennett / I Am (ASCAP)—Col 40965	21	14
49.	SEND FOR ME (BMI)—Nat King Cole / MY PERSONAL POSSESSION (BMI)—Cap 3737	—	18
50.	SWANEE RIVER ROCK (TALKIN' 'BOUT THAT RIVER) (BMI)—Ray Charles / I Want a Little Girl (ASCAP)—Atlantic 1154	—	

THIS WEEK'S BEST BUYS

Special telephone reports indicate these recent releases have broken out in one or more key areas and have excellent potential for placing on The Billboard's best seller charts.

KISSES SWEETER THAN WINE (Favorite, ASCAP) — Jimmie Rodgers—Roulette 4031—The side is jumping in all markets and appears a strong bet to repeat the success of "Honeycomb." Flip is "Better Loved You'll Never Be," (Planetary, ASCAP). A previous Billboard "Spotlight" pick.

RAUNCHY (Hi Lo, BMI)—Ernie Freeman—Imperial 5474—Bill Justis—Phillips International 3519—Both versions are competing heavily for top coin on this tune. Either is a good bet to collect a lot of loot. Flip of Freeman's platter is "Puddin'," (Travis, MI). The Justis flip is "The Midnite Man," (Knox, BMI). Both are previous Billboard "Spotlight" picks

REET PETITE (Souchie, BMI)—Jackie Wilson—Brunswick 55024—Platter is going well in both pop and r.&b. markets. It has all the signs of becoming a big one. Flip is "By the Light of the Silvery Moon," (Remick, ASCAP).

RECENT POP RELEASES COMING UP STRONG

FOR SURVEY WEEK ENDING NOVEMBER 2

The information given in this chart is based on actual sales to customers in a scientific sample of the nation's retail record outlets during the week ending on the date shown above. Sample design, sample size and all methods used in this continuing study of retail record sales are under the direct and continuing supervision and control of the School of Retailing of New York University.

Liechtensteiner Polka .... ***Will Glahe*** (ASCAP) London 1755

Reet Petite .... ***Jackie Wilson*** (BMI) Brunswick 55024

Raunchy .... ***Ernie Freeman*** (BMI) Imperial 5474

Raunchy .... ***Bill Justis*** (BMI) Phillips International 3519

Soft .... ***Bill Doggett*** (BMI) King 5080

Most Played by Jockeys

FOR SURVEY WEEK ENDING NOVEMBER 2

SIDES are ranked in order of the greatest number of plays on disk jockey radio shows thruout the country. Results are based on The Billboard's weekly survey among the nation's disk jockeys. The reverse side of each record is also listed.

Week This		Last Week	Weeks on Chart
1.	WAKE UP LITTLE SUSIE (BMI)—Everly Brothers Maybe Tomorrow (BMI)—Cadence 1337	1	7
2.	JAILHOUSE ROCK (BMI)—Elvis Presley Treat Me Nice (BMI)—Vic 7035	2	5
3.	CHANCES ARE (ASCAP)—Johnny Mathis The Twelfth of Never (ASCAP)—Col 40993	3	9
4.	APRIL LOVE (ASCAP)—Pat Boone When the Swallows Come Back to Capistrano (ASCAP)—Dot 15660	8	3
5.	MELODIE D'AMOUR (BMI)—Ames Brothers So Little Time (BMI)—Vic 7046	5	6
6.	HONEYCOMB (ASCAP)—Jimmie Rodgers Their Hearts Were Full of Spring (ASCAP)—Roulette 4015	4	12
7.	SILHOUETTES (BMI)—The Rays Daddy Cool (BMI)—Cameo 117	9	3
8.	YOU SEND ME (BMI)—Sam Cooke Summertime (ASCAP)—Keen 34013	25	2
9.	FASCINATION (ASCAP)—Jane Morgan Fascination (Instrumental) (ASCAP)—Kapp 191	7	10
10.	SILHOUETTES (BMI)—Diamonds Daddy Cool (BMI)—Mercury 71197	21	2
11.	MY HEART REMINDS ME (ASCAP)—Kay Starr Flim Flam Floo (BMI)—Vic 6981	13	9
12.	THE TWELFTH OF NEVER (ASCAP)—Johnny Mathis Chances Are (ASCAP)—Col 40993	12	5
13.	TAMMY (ASCAP)—Debbie Reynolds French Heels (ASCAP)—Coral 61851	6	17
14.	BE-BOP BABY (BMI)—Ricky Nelson Have I Told You Lately That I Love You (BMI)—Imperial 5463	11	3
14.	JUST BORN (BMI)—Perry Como Ivy Rose (ASCAP)—Vic 7050	16	5
16.	ALL THE WAY (ASCAP)—Frank Sinatra Chicago (ASCAP)—Cap 3793	17	3
16.	YOU SEND ME (BMI)—Teresa Brewer Would I Were (ASCAP)—Coral 61898	—	1
18.	MY SPECIAL ANGEL (BMI)—Bobby Helms Standing at the End of My World (BMI)—Dec 30423	14	3
19.	IVY ROSE (ASCAP)—Perry Como Just Born (BMI)—Vic 7050	18	4
20.	TREAT ME NICE (BMI)—Elvis Presley Jailhouse Rock (BMI)—Vic 7035	19	4
21.	I'M AVAILABLE (BMI)—Margie Rayburn If You Were (ASCAP)—Liberty 55102	—	1
22.	HAPPY, HAPPY BIRTHDAY, BABY (BMI)—Tune Weavers Ol' Man River (ASCAP)—Checker 872	20	5
22.	PEGGY SUE (BMI)—Buddy Holly Everyday (BMI)—Coral 61885	—	1
22.	ALONE (BMI)—Shepherd Sisters Congratulations to Someone (ASCAP)—Lance 125	—	1
25.	THAT'LL BE THE DAY (BMI)—Crickets I'm Lookin' for Someone to Love (BMI)—Brunswick 55009	9	12

NEW YORK UNIVERSITY SCHOOL OF RETAILING · STORE RECORDED SALES · THE BILLBOARD

Top 100 Sides

FOR SURVEY WEEK ENDING NOVEMBER 2

This is a tabulation of dealer unit sales listed according to the specific side requested by customers. No attempt is made to add sides together to reflect actual record sales. It is therefore a tabulation of sides or songs, and not records. This fact, together with longer four-week survey periods, explains variation between the top 30 sides as reflected in this chart, and top 30 record sellers as reflected in "Best Sellers in Stores."

Position, Song Artist, Label	Last Week
1. **JAILHOUSE ROCK,** Elvis Presley, Vic	1
2. **WAKE UP LITTLE SUSIE,** Everly Brothers, Cadence	2
3. **SILHOUETTES,** Rays, Cameo	3
4. **YOU SEND ME,** Sam Cooke, Keen	6
5. **BE-BOP BABY,** Ricky Nelson, Imperial	7
6. **CHANCES ARE,** Johnny Mathis, Columbia	5
7. **LITTLE BITTY PRETTY ONE,** Thurston Harris, Aladdin	13
8. **HONEYCOMB,** Jimmie Rodgers, Roulette	4
9. **TAMMY,** Debbie Reynolds, Coral	8
10. **MY SPECIAL ANGEL,** Bobby Helms, Decca	15
11. **DIANA,** Paul Anka, ABC-Paramount	9
12. **KEEP A' KNOCKIN',** Little Richard, Specialty	10
13. **HAPPY, HAPPY BIRTHDAY, BABY,** Tune Weavers, Checker	11
14. **MELODIE D'AMOUR,** Ames Brothers, Victor	20
15. **FASCINATION,** Jane Morgan Kapp	18
16. **LOTTA LOVIN',** Gene Vincent, Capitol	18
17. **WHOLE LOTTA LOVIN' GOIN' ON,** Jerry Lee Lewis, Sun	15
18. **HULA LOVE,** Buddy Knox, Roulette	17
19. **MR. LEE,** Bobbettes, Atlantic	14
20. **APRIL LOVE,** Pat Boone, Dot	46
21. **THAT'LL BE THE DAY,** Crickets, Brunswick	12
22. **RAINBOW,** Russ Hamilton, Kapp	21
23. **DEEP PURPLE,** Billly Ward and His Dominoes, Liberty	22
24. **JUST BORN,** Perry Como, Victor	30
25. **ALONE,** Shepherd Sisters, Lance	31
26. **PEANUTS,** Little Joe and the Thrillers, Okeh	23
27. **WAIT AND SEE,** Fats Domino, Imperial	34
28. **BLACK SLACKS,** Joe Bennett & the Sparkletones, ABC-Paramount	25
29. **I'M AVAILABLE,** Margie Rayburn, Liberty	58
30. **REMEMBER YOU'RE MINE,** Pat Boone, Dot	26
30. **TREAT ME NICE,** Elvis Presley, Victor	27
32. **IN THE MIDDLE OF AN ISLAND,** Tony Bennett, Columbia	24
33. **ALL THE WAY,** Frank Sinatra, Capitol	78
34. **AND THAT REMINDS ME,** Della Reese, Jubilee	38
35. **HAVE I TOLD YOU LATELY THAT I LOVE YOU,** Ricky Nelson, Imperial	29
35. **MY ONE SIN,** Four Coins, Epic	38
37. **BACK TO SCHOOL,** Timmie Rodgers, Cameo	37
37. **HONEST I DO,** Jimmy Reed, Vee Jay	32
37. **JUST BETWEEN YOU AND ME,** Chordettes, Cadence	28
40. **TILL,** Roger Williams, Kapp	57
41. **COULD THIS BE MAGIC,** Dubs, Gone	96
42. **WITH YOU ON MY MIND,** Nat King Cole, Capitol	33
43. **STARDUST,** Billy Ward, Liberty	36
44. **MOONLIGHT SWIM,** Tony Perkins, Victor	43
44. **PLAYTHING,** Nick Todd, Dot	41
46. **SEND FOR ME,** Nat King Cole, Capitol	35
47. **FRAULEIN,** Bobby Helms, Decca	42
48. **AN AFFAIR TO REMEMBER,** Vic Damone, Columbia	46
49. **AROUND THE WORLD,** Mantovani, London	48
49. **SWANEE RIVER ROCK (Talkin' 'Bout That River),** Ray Charles, Atlantic	59
51. **IT'S NOT FOR ME TO SAY,** Johnny Mathis, Columbia	43
52. **IVY ROSE,** Perry Como, Victor	69
53. **I'LL REMEMBER TODAY,** Patti Page, Mercury	78
54. **FRAULEIN,** Steve Lawrence, Coral	61
54. **ROCK AND ROLL MUSIC,** Chuck Berry, Chess	—
54. **TEDDY BEAR,** Elvis Presley, Victor	43
54. **WUNDERFUL, WUNDERFUL,** Stan Freberg, Capitol	—
58. **BONY MORONIE,** Larry Williams, Specialty	—
59. **THERE'S A GOLD MINE IN THE SKY,** Pat Boone, Dot	48
59. **SOFT,** Bill Doggett, King	68
61. **PEGGY SUE,** Buddy Holly, Coral	—
61. **REBEL,** Carol Jarvis, Dot	61
63. **FARTHER UP THE ROAD,** Bobby (Blue) Bland, Duke	56
64. **LIPS OF WINE,** Andy Williams, Cadence	51
64. **PARTY TIME,** Sal Mineo, Epic	—
64. **REET PETITE,** Jackie Wilson, Brunswick	93
67. **IDOL WITH THE GOLDEN HEAD,** Coasters, Atco	64
67. **WHITE SILVER SANDS,** Don Rondo, Jubilee	38
69. **AROUND THE WORLD,** Victor Young, Decca	69
69. **IN THE MIDDLE OF AN ISLAND,** Tennessee Ernie Ford, Capitol	59
71. **BON VOYAGE,** Janice Harper, Prep	71
72. **SHORT FAT FANNIE,** Larry Williams, Specialty	53
73. **MISTER FIRE EYES,** Bonnie Guitar, Dot	75
73. **ONLY BECAUSE,** Platters, Mercury	81
75. **GOODY GOODY,** Frankie Lymon and the Teenagers, Gee	71
75. **YOU'RE MY ONE AND ONLY LOVE,** Ricky Nelson, Verve	54
77. **FASCINATION,** Dick Jacobs, Coral	93
77. **MY HEART REMINDS ME,** Kay Starr, Victor	64
77. **THE STORY OF MY LIFE,** Marty Robbins, Columbia	—
77. **TONIGHT, TONIGHT,** Mello-Kings, Herald	—
81. **TO THE AISLE,** Five Satins, Ember	71
81. **HE'S GONE,** Chantels, End	93
81. **LOVE LETTERS IN THE SAND,** Pat Boone, Dot	51
81. **MY SHOES KEEP WALKING BACK TO YOU,** Ray Price, Columbia	71
81. **TAMMY,** Ames Brothers, Victor	75
81. **THE TWELFTH OF NEVER,** Johnny Mathis, Columbia	96
81. **WHEN THE SWALLOWS COME BACK TO CAPISTRANO,** Pat Boone, Dot	—
88. **DEEP BLUE SEA,** Jimmie Dean, Columbia	—
88 **I STILL LOVE YOU,** Fats Domino, Imperial	81
88. **SUMMERTIME,** Sam Cooke, Keen	85
88. **SILHOUETTES,** Diamonds, Mercury	—
88. **THINK,** Five Royals, King	96
88. **YOU BUG ME, BABY,** Larry Williams, Specialty	—
94. **AROUND THE WORLD,** Bing Crosby, Decca	54
94. **GOT A DATE WITH AN ANGEL,** Billy Williams, Coral	—
94. **MISS YOU SO,** Lillian Offitt, Excello	88
94. **SILHOUETTES,** Steve Gibson and the Red Caps, ABC-Paramount	63
98. **FASCINATION,** David Carroll, Mercury	—
98. **LASTING LOVE,** Sal Mineo, Epic	88
100. **BYE BYE LOVE,** Everly Brothers, Cadence	50

Best Sellers in Stores

The information given in this chart is based on actual sales to customers in a scientific sample of the nation's retail record outlets during the week ending on the date shown above. Sample design, sample size, and all methods used in this continuing study of retail record sales are under the direct and continuing supervision and control of the School of Retailing of New York University.

FOR SURVEY WEEK ENDING NOVEMBER 9, 1957

This Week		Last Week	Weeks on Chart
1.	JAILHOUSE ROCK (BMI)—Elvis Presley TREAT ME NICE (BMI)—Vic 7035	1	6
2.	WAKE UP LITTLE SUSIE (BMI)— Everly Brothers Maybe Tomorrow (BMI)—Cadence 1337	3	8
3.	YOU SEND ME (BMI)—Sam Cooke SUMMERTIME (ASCAP)—Keen 34013	2	4
4.	SILHOUETTES (BMI)—The Rays Daddy Cool (BMI)—Cameo 117	4	5
5	BE-BOP BABY (BMI)—Ricky Nelson HAVE I TOLD YOU LATELY THAT I LOVE YOU (BMI)—Imperial 5463	5	7
6.	LITTLE BITTY PRETTY ONE (BMI)— Thurston Harris I Hope You Won't Hold It Against Me (ASCAP)—Aladdin 3398	6	4
7.	MY SPECIAL ANGEL (BMI)— Bobby Helms Standing at the End of My World (BMI)—Dec 30423	8	5
8.	APRIL LOVE (ASCAP)—Pat Boone WHEN THE SWALLOWS COME BACK TO CAPISTRANO (ASCAP)—Dot 15660	11	3
9.	CHANCES ARE (ASCAP)— Johnny Mathis THE TWELFTH OF NEVER (ASCAP)—Col 40993	7	9
10.	HONEYCOMB (ASCAP)— Jimmie Rodgers Their Hearts Were Full of Spring (ASCAP)—Roulette 4015	9	14
11.	TAMMY (ASCAP)—Debbie Reynolds French Heels (ASCAP)—Coral 61851	10	17
12.	JUST BORN (BMI)—Perry Como IVY ROSE (ASCAP)—Vic 7050	15	4
13.	FASCINATION (ASCAP)—Jane Morgan Fascination (Instrumental) (ASCAP)—Kapp 191	13	11
14.	MELODIE D'AMOUR (BMI)— Ames Brothers So Little Time (BMI)—Vic 7046	12	6
15.	KEEP A' KNOCKIN' (BMI)— Little Richard Can't Believe You Wanna Leave—Specialty 611	14	7
16.	HAPPY, HAPPY BIRTHDAY, BABY (BMI)—Tune Weavers Ol' Man River (ASCAP)—Checker 872	17	9
17.	ALL THE WAY (ASCAP)— Frank Sinatra CHICAGO (ASCAP)—Cap 3793	21	2
17.	I'M AVAILABLE (BMI)— Margie Rayburn If You Were (ASCAP)—Liberty 55102	29	2
19.	ROCK AND ROLL MUSIC (BMI)— Chuck Berry Blue Feeling (BMI)—Chess 1671	40	2
20.	BONY MORONIE (BMI)— Larry Williams YOU BUG ME, BABY (BMI)—Specialty 615	30	2
21.	RAUNCHY (BMI)—Bill Justis The Midnite Man (BMI)—Phillips International 3519	—	1
22.	HULA LOVE (BMI)—Buddy Knox Devil Woman (BMI)—Roulette 4018	21	11
23.	DIANA (BMI)—Paul Anka Don't Gamble With Love (BMI)—ABC-Paramount 9831	16	17
24.	ALONE (BMI)—Shepherd Sisters Congratulations to Someone (ASCAP)—Lance 125	18	3
25.	PEGGY SUE (BMI)—Buddy Holly Everyday (BMI)—Coral 61885	43	2
26.	RAUNCHY (BMI)—Ernie Freeman Puddin' (BMI)—Imperial 5474	—	1
27.	COULD THIS BE MAGIC (BMI)—Dubs Such Lovin' (BMI)—Gone 5011	26	2
28.	LOTTA LOVIN' (BMI)—Gene Vincent WEAR MY RING (BMI)—Cap 3763	19	9
28.	TILL (ASCAP)—Roger Williams Big Town (ASCAP)—Kapp 197	32	2
30.	WAIT AND SEE (BMI)—Fats Domino I STILL LOVE YOU (BMI)—Imperial 5467	28	4
31.	I'LL REMEMBER TODAY (BMI)— Patti Page My, How Time Goes By (ASCAP)—Mercury 71189	43	2
32.	WUN'ERFUL, WUN'ERFUL (PARTS I & 2) (ASCAP)— Stan Freberg Cap 3815	41	2
33.	AND THAT REMINDS ME (ASCAP)— Della Reese I Cried for You (ASCAP)—Jubilee 5292	39	3
34.	YOU SEND ME (BMI)—Teresa Brewer Would I Were (ASCAP)—Coral 61898	—	1
35.	RAINBOW (ASCAP)—Russ Hamilton We Will Make Love (ASCAP)—Kapp 184	25	16
36.	DEEP PURPLE (ASCAP)— Billy Ward & His Dominoes Do It Again (BMI)—Liberty 55099	20	7
37.	MY ONE SIN (BMI)—Four Coins This Life (ASCAP)—Epic 9229	34	3
38.	BACK TO SCHOOL AGAIN (BMI)— Timmie Rodgers I've Got a Dog Who Loves Me (BMI)—Cameo 116	37	2
39.	WHOLE LOTTA SHAKIN' GOIN' ON (BMI)—Jerry Lee Lewis It'll Be Mine (BMI)—Sun 267	23	17
40.	THAT'LL BE THE DAY (BMI)— Crickets I'm Lookin' for Someone to Love (BMI)—Brunswick 55009	31	14
41.	MR. LEE (BMI)—Bobbettes Look at the Stars—Atlantic 1144	24	15
42.	SWANEE RIVER ROCK (TALKIN' 'BOUT THAT RIVER) Ray Charles I Want a Little Girl (ASCAP)—Atlantic 1154	50	2
43.	PEANUTS (BMI)— Little Joe & The Thrillers Lilly Lou (BMI)—Okeh 7088	27	7
44.	BLACK SLACKS (BMI)— Joe Bennett & Sparkletones Boppin' Rock Boogie (BMI)—ABC-Paramount 9837	33	9
45.	REMEMBER YOU'RE MINE (ASCAP)— Pat Boone THERE'S A GOLD MINE IN THE SKY (ASCAP)—Dot 15602	38	15
46.	IN THE MIDDLE OF AN ISLAND (ASCAP)—Tonny Bennett I Am (ASCAP)—Col 40965	48	15
47.	LIECHTENSTEINER POLKA (ASCAP)— Will Glahe Schweitzer Polka (BMI)—London 1755	—	1
48.	FRAULEIN (BMI)—Bobby Helms Heartsick Feeling (BMI)—Dec 30194	46	2
49.	PARTY TIME (BMI)—Sal Mineo The Words That I Whisper (BMI)—Epic 9246	45	2
50.	HONEST I DO (BMI)—Jimmy Reed Signals of Love (BMI)—Vee-Jay 253	36	2
50.	THE STORY OF MY LIFE (ASCAP)— Marty Robbins Once-A-Week Date (BMI)—Col 41013	—	1

THIS WEEK'S BEST BUYS

Special telephone reports indicate these recent releases have broken out in one or more key areas and have excellent potential for placing on The Billboard's best seller charts.

GREAT BALLS OF FIRE (BRS, BMI)—Jerry Lee Lewis—Sun 281—Side is hot in all markets. Flip is "You Win Again" (Acuff-Rose, BMI). A previous Billboard "Spotlight" pick.

LOVE ME FOREVER (Greta, BMI)—Four Esquires—Paris 509—Disk has begun to click in most of the top marts, and present indications are that it's going to be a loot platter. Flip is "I Ain't Been Right Since You Left" (Gold, ASCAP).

Week in and week out you'll find more news, more record reviews, more advertising on the fast-moving record business in The Billboard, the communications center of the music industry.

RECENT POP RELEASES COMING UP STRONG

FOR SURVEY WEEK ENDING NOVEMBER 9

The information given in this chart is based on actual sales to customers in a scientific sample of the nation's retail record outlets during the week ending on the date shown above. Sample design, sample size and all methods used in this continuing study of retail record sales are under the direct and continuing supervision and control of the School of Retailing of New York University.

Hey! Little Girl .... *Techniques* (BMI) Roulette 4030

The Joker .... *Billy Myles* (BMI) Ember 1026

Kisses Sweeter Than Wine .... *Jimmy Rodgers* (ASCAP) Roulette 4031

Little Bitty Pretty One .... *Bobby Day* (BMI) Class 211

Love Me Forever .... *Four Esquires* (BMI) Paris 509

Reet Petite .... *Jackie Wilson* (BMI) Brunswick 55024

Most Played by Jockeys

FOR SURVEY WEEK ENDING NOVEMBER 9

SIDES are ranked in order of the greatest number of plays on disk jockey radio shows thruout the country. Results are based on The Billboard's weekly survey among the nation's disk jockeys. The reverse side of each record is also listed.

Week This		Last Week	Weeks on Chart
1.	WAKE UP LITTLE SUSIE (BMI)—Everly Brothers Maybe Tomorrow (BMI)—Cadence 1337	1	8
2.	JAILHOUSE ROCK (BMI)—Elvis Presley Treat Me Nice (BMI)—Vic 7035	2	6
3.	CHANCES ARE (ASCAP)—Johnny Mathis The Twelfth of Never (ASCAP)—Col 40993	3	10
4.	APRIL LOVE (ASCAP)—Pat Boone When the Swallows Come Back to Capistrano (ASCAP)—Dot 15660	4	4
5.	SILHOUETTES (BMI)—The Rays Daddy Cool (BMI)—Cameo 117	7	4
6.	YOU SEND ME (BMI)—Sam Cooke Summertime (ASCAP)—Keen 34013	8	3
7.	HONEYCOMB (ASCAP)—Jimmie Rodgers Their Hearts Were Full of Spring (ASCAP)—Roulette 4015	6	13
8.	MELODIE D'AMOUR (BMI)—Ames Brothers So Little Time (BMI)—Vic 7046	5	7
9.	THE TWELFTH OF NEVER (ASCAP)—Johnny Mathis Chance Are (ASCAP)—Col 40993	12	6
10.	BE-BOP BABY (BMI)—Ricky Nelson Have I Told You Lately That I Love You (BMI)—Imperial 5463	14	4
10.	MY SPECIAL ANGEL (BMI)—Bobby Helms Standing at the End of My World (BMI)—Dec 30423	18	4
12.	SILHOUETTES (BMI)—Diamonds Daddy Cool (BMI)—Mercury 71197	10	3
12.	ALL THE WAY (ASCAP)—Frank Sinatra Chicago (ASCAP)—Cap 3793	16	4
14.	FASCINATION (ASCAP)—Jane Morgan Fascination (Instrumentals) (ASCAP)—Kapp 191	9	11
15.	JUST BORN (BMI)—Perry Como Ivy Rose (ASCAP)—Vic 7050	14	6
16.	TAMMY (ASCAP)—Debbie Reynolds French Heels (ASCAP)—Coral 61851	13	18
17.	KISSES SWEETER THAN WINE (ASCAP)—Jimmie Rodgers Better Loved You'll Never Be (ASCAP)—Roulette 4031	—	1
18.	LITTLE BITTY PRETTY ONE (BMI)—Thurston Harris I Hope You Won't Hold It Against Me (BMI)—Aladdin 3398	—	1
19.	MY HEART REMINDS ME (ASCAP)—Kay Starr Flim Flam Floo (BMI)—Vic 6981	11	10
20.	IVY ROSE (ASCAP)—Perry Como Just Born (BMI)—Vic 7050	19	5
21.	TREAT ME NICE (BMI)—Elvis Presley Jailhouse Rock (BMI)—Vic 7035	20	5
22.	YOU SEND ME (BMI)—Teresa Brewer Would I Were (ASCAP)—Coral 61898	16	2
22.	HULA LOVE (BMI)—Buddy Knox Devil Woman (BMI)—Roulette 4018	—	8
22.	CA C'CEST L'AMOUR (ASCAP)—Tony Bennett I Never Felt More Like Falling in Love (ASCAP)—Col 41032	—	1
25.	I'M AVAILABLE (BMI)—Margie Rayburn If You Were (ASCAP)—Liberty 55102	21	2

STORE RECORDED SALES — NEW YORK UNIVERSITY SCHOOL OF RETAILING — THE BILLBOARD

Top 100 Sides

FOR SURVEY WEEK ENDING NOVEMBER 9

This is a tabulation of dealer unit sales listed according to the specific side requested by customers. No attempt is made to add sides together to reflect actual record sales. It is therefore a tabulation of sides or songs, and not records. This fact, together with longer four-week survey periods, explains variation between the top 30 sides as reflected in this chart, and top 30 record sellers as reflected in "Best Sellers in Stores."

Position, Song Artist, Label	Last Week
1. **JAILHOUSE ROCK,** Elvis Presley, Victor	1
2. **WAKE UP LITTLE SUSIE,** Everly Brothers, Cadence	2
3. **YOU SEND ME,** Sam Cooke, Keen	4
4. **SILHOUETTES,** Rays, Cameo	3
5. **BE-BOP BABY,** Ricky Nelson, Imperial	5
6. **LITTLE BITTY PRETTY ONE,** Thurston Harris, Aladdin	7
7. **CHANCES ARE,** Johnny Mathis, Columbia	6
8. **MY SPECIAL ANGEL,** Bobby Helms, Decca	10
9. **HONEYCOMB,** Jimmie Rodgers, Roulette	8
10. **TAMMY,** Debbie Reynolds, Coral	9
11. **APRIL LOVE,** Pat Boone, Dot	20
12. **MELODIE D'AMOUR,** Ames Brothers, Victor	14
13. **KEEP A' KNOCKIN',** Little Richard, Specialty	12
14. **DIANA,** Paul Anka, ABC-Paramount	11
15. **FASCINATION,** Jane Morgan, Kapp	15
16. **HAPPY, HAPPY BIRTHDAY, BABY,** Tune Weavers, Checker	13
17. **HULA LOVE,** Buddy Knox, Roulette	18
18. **LOTTA LOVIN',** Gene Vincent, Capitol	16
19 **JUST BORN,** Perry Como, Victor	24
20. **ALONE,** Shepherd Sisters, Lance	25
21. **I'M AVAILABLE,** Margie Rayburn, Liberty	29
22. **WHOLE LOTTA SHAKIN' GOIN' ON,** Jerry Lee Lewis, Sun	17
23. **RAINBOW,** Russ Hamilton, Kapp	22
24. **DEEP PURPLE,** Billy Ward and His Dominos, Liberty	23
25. **MR. LEE,** Bobbettes, Atlantic,	19
25. **THAT'LL BE THE DAY,** Crickets, Brunswick	21
27. **ROCK AND ROLL MUSIC,** Chuck Berry, Chess	54
28. **ALL THE WAY,** Frank Sinatra, Capitol	33
29. **PEANUTS,** Little Joe and the Thrillers, Okeh	26
30. **COULD THIS BE MAGIC,** Dubs, Gone	41
31. **RAUNCHY,** Bill Justis, Phillips International	—
31. **WAIT AND SEE,** Fats Domino, Imperial	27
33. **TILL,** Roger Williams, Kapp	40
34. **BLACK SLACKS,** Joe Bennett & the Sparkletones, ABC-Paramount	28
35. **PEGGY SUE,** Buddy Holly, Coral	61
36. **BACK TO SCHOOL AGAIN,** Timmie Rodgers, Cameo	37
37. **MY ONE SIN,** Four Coins, Epic	35
38. **IN THE MIDDLE OF AN ISLAND,** Tony Bennett, Columbia	32
39. **AND THAT REMINDS ME,** Della Reese, Jubilee	34
39. **RAUNCHY,** Ernie Freeman, Imperial	—
41. **HONEST I DO,** Jimmy Reed, Vee Jay	37
41. **I'LL REMEMBER TODAY,** Patti Page, Mercury	53
43. **BONY MORONIE,** Larry Williams, Specialty	58
44. **SWANEE RIVER ROCK (TALKIN' 'BOUT THAT RIVER)** Ray Charles, Atlantic	49
45. **WUN'ERFUL, WUN'ERFUL,** Stan Freberg, Capitol	54
46. **REMEMBER YOU'RE MINE,** Pat Boone, Dot	30
46. **TREAT ME NICE,** Elvis Presley, Victor	30
48. **WITH YOU ON MY MIND,** Nat King Cole, Capitol	42
49. **HAVE I TOLD YOU LATELY THAT I LOVE YOU,** Ricky Nelson, Imperial	35
49. **IVY ROSE,** Perry Como, Victor	52
49. **MOONLIGHT SWIM,** Tony Perkins, Victor	44
52. **FRAULEIN,** Bobby Helms, Decca	47
53. **PLAYTHING,** Nick Todd, Dot	44
54. **SEND FOR ME,** Nat King Cole, Capitol	46
55. **FRAULEIN,** Steve Lawrence, Coral	54
55. **SEND FOR ME,** Teresa Brewer, Coral	—
57. **JUST BETWEEN YOU AND ME,** Chordettes, Cadence	37
58. **FARTHER UP THE ROAD,** Bobby (Blue) Bland, Duke	63
58. **STARDUST,** Billy Ward, Liberty	43
60. **AN AFFAIR TO REMEMBER,** Vic Damone, Columbia	48
61. **IT'S NOT FOR ME TO SAY,** Johnny Mathis, Columbia	51
62. **REBEL,** Carol Jarvis, Dot	61
62. **REET PETITE,** Jackie Wilson, Brunswick	64
62. **SOFT,** Bill Doggett, King	59
65. **AROUND THE WORLD,** Mantovani, London	49
65. **ONLY BECAUSE,** Platters, Mercury	73
65. **THE STORY OF MY LIFE,** Marty Robbins, Columbia	77
68. **LIECHTENSTEINER POLKA,** Will Glahe, London	—
69. **AROUND THE WORLD,** Victor Young, Decca	69
69. **PARTY TIME,** Sal Mineo, Epic	64
71. **BON VOYAGE,** Janice Harper, Prep	71
71. **DEEP BLUE SEA,** Jimmy Dean, Columbia	88
71. **LIPS OF WINE,** Andy Williams, Cadence	64
71. **SILHOUETTES,** Diamonds, Mercury	88
75. **MISTER FIRE EYES,** Bonnie Guitar, Dot	73
75. **TEDDY BEAR,** Elvis Presley, Victor	54
77. **JOKER,** Billy Myles, Ember	—
78. **GOT A DATE WITH AN ANGEL,** Billy Williams, Coral	94
78. **WHITE SILVER SANDS,** Don Rondo, Jubilee	67
80. **IDOL WITH THE GOLDEN HEAD,** Coasters, Atco	67
80. **I STILL LOVE YOU,** Fats Domino, Imperial	88
80. **LITTLE BITTY PRETTY ONE,** Bobby Day, Class	—
80. **WHEN THE SWALLOWS COME BACK TO CAPISTRANO,** Pat Boone, Dot	81
84. **CHICAGO,** Frank Sinatra, Capitol	—
85. **AROUND THE WORLD,** Bing Crosby, Decca	94
85. **THERE'S A GOLD MINE IN THE SKY,** Pat Boone, Dot	59
85. **I NEED YOU SO,** B. B. King, RPM	—
85. **KISSES SWEETER THAN WINE,** Jimmie Rodgers, Roulette	—
85. **LOVE ME FOREVER,** Four Esquires, Paris	—
85. **SUMMERTIME,** Sam Cooke, Keen	88
85. **THE TWELFTH OF NEVER,** Johnny Mathis, Columbia	81
85. **YOU BUG ME, BABY,** Larry Williams, Specialty	88
93. **HEY, LITTLE GIRL,** Techniques, Roulette	—
93. **FASCINATION,** Dick Jacobs, Coral	77
93. **LOVE LETTERS IN THE SAND,** Pat Boone, Dot	81
93. **PLAYTHING,** Ted Newman, Rev	—
93. **TONIGHT, TONIGHT,** Mello-Kings, Herald	77
98. **BYE BYE LOVE,** Everly Brothers, Cadence	100
98. **MY HEART REMINDS ME,** Kay Starr, Victor	77
98. **TAMMY,** Ames Brothers, Victor	81

Best Sellers in Stores

FOR SURVEY WEEK ENDING NOVEMBER 16, 1957

The information given in this chart is based on actual sales to customers in a scientific sample of the nation's retail record outlets during the week ending on the date shown above. Sample design, sample size, and all methods used in this continuing study of retail record sales are under the direct and continuing supervision and control of the School of Retailing of New York University.

This Week		Last Week	Weeks on Chart
1.	**JAILHOUSE ROCK** (BMI)—Elvis Presley **TREAT ME NICE** (BMI)—Vic 7035	1	7
2.	**WAKE UP LITTLE SUSIE** (BMI)—Everly Brothers Maybe Tomorrow (BMI)—Cadence 1337	2	9
3.	**YOU SEND ME** (BMI)—Sam Cooke **SUMMERTIME** (ASCAP)—Keen 34013	3	5
4.	**SILHOUETTES** (BMI)—The Rays Daddy Cool (BMI)—Cameo 117	4	6
5.	**BE-BOP BABY** (BMI)—Ricky Nelson **HAVE I TOLD YOU LATELY THAT I LOVE YOU** (BMI)—Imperial 5463	5	8
6.	**APRIL LOVE** (ASCAP)—Pat Boone **WHEN THE SWALLOWS COME BACK TO CAPISTRANO** (ASCAP)—Dot 15660	8	4
7.	**CHANCES ARE** (ASCAP)—Johnny Mathis **THE TWELFTH OF NEVER** (ASCAP)—Col 40993	9	10
8.	**MY SPECIAL ANGEL** (BMI)—Bobby Helms Standing at the End of My World (BMI)—Dec 30423	7	6
9.	**RAUNCHY** (BMI)—Bill Justis The Midnite Man (BMI)—Phillips International 3519	21	2
10.	**LITTLE BITTY PRETTY ONE** (BMI)—Thurston Harris I Hope You Won't Hold It Against Me (ASCAP)—Aladdin 3398	6	5
11.	**RAUNCHY** (BMI)—Ernie Freeman Puddin' (BMI)—Imperial 5474	26	2
12.	**ROCK AND ROLL MUSIC** (BMI)—Chuck Berry Blue Feeling (BMI)—Chess 1671	19	3
13.	**FASCINATION** (ASCAP)—Jane Morgan Fascination (Instrumental) (ASCAP)—Kapp 191	13	12
14.	**HONEYCOMB** (ASCAP)—Jimmie Rodgers Their Hearts Were Full of Spring (ASCAP)—Roulette 4015	10	15
15.	**I'M AVAILABLE** (BMI)—Margie Rayburn If You Were (ASCAP)—Liberty 55102	17	3
16.	**MELODIE D'AMOUR** (BMI)—Ames Brothers So Little Time (BMI)—Vic 7046	14	7
17.	**TAMMY** (ASCAP)—Debbie Reynolds French Heels (ASCAP)—Coral 61851	11	18
17.	**JUST BORN** (BMI)—Perry Como **IVY ROSE** (ASCAP)—Vic 7050	12	5
19.	**PEGGY SUE** (BMI)—Buddy Holly Everyday (BMI)—Coral 61885	25	3
20.	**ALL THE WAY** (ASCAP)—Frank Sinatra **CHICAGO** (ASCAP)—Cap 3793	17	3
21.	**BONY MORONIE** (BMI)—Larry Williams **YOU BUG ME, BABY** (BMI)—Specialty 615	20	3
22.	**KISSES SWEETER THAN WINE** (ASCAP)—Jimmie Rodgers Better Loved You'll Never Be (ASCAP)—Roulette 4031	—	1
23.	**HAPPY, HAPPY BIRTHDAY, BABY** (BMI)—Tune Weavers Ol' Man River (ASCAP)—Checker 872	16	10
24.	**KEEP A' KNOCKIN'** (BMI)—Little Richard Can't Believe You Wanna Leave—Specialty 611	15	8
25.	**COULD THIS BE MAGIC?** (BMI)—Dubs Such Lovin' (BMI)—Gone 5011	27	3
26.	**HULA LOVE** (BMI)—Buddy Knox Devil Woman (BMI)—Roulette 4018	22	12
27.	**YOU SEND ME** (BMI)—Teresa Brewer Would I Were (ASCAP)—Coral 61898	34	2
28.	**TILL** (ASCAP)—Roger Williams Big Town (ASCAP)—Kapp 197	28	3
29.	**ALONE** (BMI)—Shepherd Sisters Congratulations to Someone (ASCAP)—Lance 125	24	4
30.	**LIECHTENSTEINER POLKA** (ASCAP)—Will Glahe Schweitzer Polka (BMI)—London 1755	47	2
31.	**LOTTA LOVIN'** (BMI)—Gene Vincent Wear My Ring (BMI)—Cap 3763	28	10
32.	**WAIT AND SEE** (BMI)—Fats Domino I Still Love You (BMI)—Imperial 5467	30	5
33.	**I'LL REMEMBER TODAY** (BMI)—Patti Page My, How the Time Goes By (ASCAP)—Mercury 71189	31	3
34.	**SWANEE RIVER ROCK** (Talkin' 'Bout That River) Ray Charles I Want a Little Girl (ASCAP)—Atlanta 1154	42	3
35.	**THE JOKER** (BMI)—Billy Myles Honey Bee (BMI)—Ember 1026	—	1
36.	**HONEST I DO** (BMI)—Jimmy Reed Signals of Love (BMI)—Vee Jay 253	50	3
37.	**DIANA** (BMI)—Paul Anka Don't Gamble With Love (BMI)—ABC-Paramount 9831	23	18
38.	**HEY, LITTLE GIRL** (BMI)—Techniques In a Roundabout Way (BMI)—Roulette 4030	—	1
39.	**AND THAT REMINDS ME** (ASCAP)—Della Reese I Cried for You (ASCAP)—Jubilee 5292	33	4
40.	**WUN'ERFUL, WUN'ERFUL** (PARTS 1 & 2)—Stan Freberg Cap 3815	32	3
41.	**PEANUTS** (BMI)—Little Joe & the Thrillers Lilly Lou (BMI)—Okeh 7088	43	8
42.	**WHOLE LOTTA' SHAKIN' GOIN' ON** Jerry Lee Lewis It'll Be Mine (BMI)—Sun 267	39	18
43.	**BACK TO SCHOOL AGAIN** (BMI)—Timmie Rogers I've Got a Dog Who Loves Me (BMI)—Cameo 116	38	3
44.	**THAT'LL BE THE DAY** (BMI)—Crickets I'm Lookin' for Someone to Love (BMI)—Brunswick 55009	40	15
45.	**PLAYTHING** (BMI)—Nick Todd The Honey Song (ASCAP)—Dot 15643	—	2
46.	**TEARDROPS** (BMI)—Lee Andrews & The Hearts Girl Around the Corner (BMI)—Chess 1675	—	1
47.	**WITH YOU ON MY MIND** (ASCAP)—Nat King Cole Raintree County (ASCAP)—Cap 3782	—	3
48.	**SOFT** (BMI)—Bill Doggett Hot Ginger (BMI)—King 5080	—	1
49.	**AROUND THE WORLD** (ASCAP)—Victor Young (Vocal) (ASCAP)—Decca 30262	—	12
50.	**REMEMBER YOU'RE MINE** (ASCAP)—Pat Boone There's a Gold Mine in the Sky (ASCAP)—Dot 15602	45	16

THIS WEEK'S BEST BUYS

Special telephone reports indicate these recent releases have broken out in one or more key areas and have excellent potential for placing on The Billboard's best seller charts.

WILD IS THE WIND (Ross-Jungnickel, ASCAP)
NO LOVE (BUT YOUR LOVE) (Weiss & Barry, BMI) — **Johnny Mathis**—Columbia 41060—Platter is rocketing off in similar fashion to the artist's previous disk. It appears a two-sided hit. A previous Billboard "Spotlight" pick.

WHY DON'T THEY UNDERSTAND (Hollis, BMI)—**George Hamilton, IV**—ABC-Paramount 9862—All markets register very strong reports. This looks like Hamilton's biggest yet! Flip is "Even Tho," (Acuff-Rose, BMI). A previous Billboard "Spotlight" pick.

OH, BOY! (Nor-Va-Jak, BMI)—**The Crickets**—Brunswick 55035—Action on this release isn't as strong comparatively as on their previous click, but the side is beginning to move well in most of the top markets. Flip is "Not Fade Away," (Nor-Va-Jak, BMI). A previous Billboard "Spotlight" pick.

ROCK-A-CHICKA (Old Charter, BMI)—**Warner Mack**—Decca 30471—See comments in This Week's C&W Best Buys.

AT THE HOP (Singular, BMI) — **Danny & The Juniors** — ABC-Paramount 9871—Strong sales are reported in most of the major (Singular, BMI). A previous Billboard "Spotlight" pick.

RECENT POP RELEASES COMING UP STRONG

FOR SURVEY WEEK ENDING NOVEMBER 16

The information given in this chart is based on actual sales to customers in a scientific sample of the nation's retail record outlets during the week ending on the date shown above. Sample design, sample size and all methods used in this continuing study of retail record sales are under the direct and continuing supervision and control of the School of Retailing of New York University.

Great Balls of Fire . . . . ***Jerry Lee Lewis***
(BMI) Sun 281

Love Me Forever . . . . ***Four Esquires***
(BMI) Paris 509

Oh Boy! . . . . ***The Crickets***
(BMI) Brunswick 55035

Most Played by Jockeys

FOR SURVEY WEEK ENDING NOVEMBER 16

SIDES are ranked in order of the greatest number of plays on disk jockey radio shows thruout the country. Results are based on The Billboard's weekly survey among the nation's disk jockeys. The reverse side of each record is also listed.

Week This		Last Week	Weeks on Chart
1.	JAILHOUSE ROCK (BMI)—Elvis Presley Treat Me Nice (BMI)—Vic 7035	2	7
2.	WAKE UP LITTLE SUSIE (BMI)—Everly Brothers Maybe Tomorrow (BMI)—Cadence 1337	1	9
3.	YOU SEND ME (BMI)—Sam Cooke Summertime (ASCAP)—Keen 34013	6	4
4.	APRIL LOVE (ASCAP)—Pat Boone When the Swallows Come Back to Capistrano (ASCAP)—Dot 15660	4	5
5.	CHANCES ARE (ASCAP)—Johnny Mathis The Twelfth of Never (ASCAP)—Col 40993	3	11
6.	SILHOUETTES (BMI)—The Rays Daddy Cool (BMI)—Cameo 117	5	5
7.	MELODIE D'AMOUR (BMI)—Ames Brothers So Little Time (BMI)—Vic 7046	8	8
8.	YOU SEND ME (BMI)—Teresa Brewer Would I Were (ASCAP)—Coral 61898	22	3
9.	ALL THE WAY (ASCAP)—Frank Sinatra Chicago (ASCAP)—Cap 3793	12	5
10.	THE TWELFTH OF NEVER (ASCAP)—Johnny Mathis Chances Are (ASCAP)—Col 40993	9	7
11.	RAUNCHY (BMI)—Bill Justis The Midnite Man (BMI)—Phillips International 3519	—	1
12.	SILHOUETTES (BMI)—Diamonds Daddy Cool (BMI)—Mercury 71197	12	4
13.	BE-BOP BABY (BMI)—Ricky Nelson Have I Told You Lately That I Love You (BMI)—Imperial 5463	10	5
14.	I'M AVAILABLE (BMI)—Margie Rayburn If You Were (ASCAP)—Liberty 55102	25	3
15.	HONEYCOMB (ASCAP)—Jimmie Rodgers Their Hearts Were Full of Spring (ASCAP)—Roulette 4015	7	14
16.	JUST BORN (BMI)—Perry Como Ivy Rose (ASCAP)—Vic 7050	15	7
17.	MY SPECIAL ANGEL (BMI)—Bobby Helms Standing at the End of My World (BMI)—Dec 30423	10	5
18.	KISSES SWEETER THAN WINE (ASCAP)—Jimmie Rodgers Better Loved You'll Never Be (ASCAP)—Roulette 4031	17	2
19.	LITTLE BITTY PRETTY ONE (BMI)—Thurston Harris I Hope You Won't Hold It Against Me (BMI)—Aladdin 3398	18	2
20.	FASCINATION (ASCAP)—Jane Morgan Fascination (Instrumentals) (ASCAP)—Kapp 191	14	12
21.	PEGGY SUE (BMI)—Buddy Holly Everyday (BMI)—Coral 61885	—	2
22.	THE JOKER—Hilltoppers Chicken, Chicken—Dot 15662	—	1
23.	TREAT ME NICE (BMI)—Elvis Presley Jailhouse Rock (BMI)—Vic 7035	21	6
24.	TILL (ASCAP)—Roger Williams Big Town (ASCAP)—Kapp 197	—	1
25.	IVY ROSE (ASCAP)—Perry Como Just Born (BMI)—Vic 7050	20	6

NEW YORK UNIVERSITY SCHOOL OF RETAILING · STORE RECORDED SALES · THE BILLBOARD

Top 100 Sides

FOR SURVEY WEEK ENDING NOVEMBER 16

This is a tabulation of dealer unit sales listed according to the specific side requested by customers. No attempt is made to add sides together to reflect actual record sales. It is therefore a tabulation of sides or songs, and not records. This fact, together with longer four-week survey periods, explains variation between the top 30 sides as reflected in this chart, and top 30 record sellers as reflected in "Best Sellers in Stores."

Position, Song, Artist, Label	Last Week
1. **JAILHOUSE ROCK,** Elvis Presley, Victor	1
2. **WAKE UP LITTLE SUSIE,** Everly Brothers, Cadence	2
3. **YOU SEND ME,** Sam Cooke, Keen	3
4. **SILHOUETTES,** Rays, Cameo	4
5. **BE-BOP BABY,** Ricky Nelson, Imperial	5
6. **LITTLE BITTY PRETTY ONE,** Thurston Harris, Aladdin	6
7. **MY SPECIAL ANGEL,** Bobby Helms, Decca	8
8. **CHANCES ARE,** Johnny Mathis, Columbia	7
9. **APRIL LOVE,** Pat Boone, Dot	11
10. **HONEYCOMB,** Jimmie Rodgers, Roulette	9
11. **TAMMY,** Debbie Reynolds, Coral	10
12. **MELODIE D'AMOUR,** Ames Brothers, Victor	12
13. **FASCINATION,** Jane Morgan, Kapp	15
14. **RAUNCHY,** Bill Justis, Phillips International	31
15. **KEEP A' KNOCKIN',** Little Richard, Specialty	13
16. **HAPPY, HAPPY BIRTHDAY, BABY,** Tune Weavers, Checker	16
17. **I'M AVAILABLE,** Margie Rayburn, Liberty	21
17. **RAUNCHY,** Ernie Freeman, Imperial	39
19. **ROCK AND ROLL MUSIC,** Chuck Berry, Chess	27
20. **DIANA,** Paul Anka, ABC-Paramount	14
21. **JUST BORN,** Perry Como, Victor	19
22. **ALL THE WAY,** Frank Sinatra Capitol	28
22. **ALONE,** Shepherd Sisters, Lance	20
24. **HULA LOVE,** Buddy Knox, Roulette	17
25. **COULD THIS BE MAGIC,** Dubs, Gone	30
26. **LOTTA LOVIN',** Gene Vincent, Capitol	18
27. **PEGGY SUE,** Buddy Holly, Coral	35
28. **TILL,** Roger Williams, Kapp	33
29. **WHOLE LOTTA SHAKIN' GOIN' ON,** Jerry Lee Lewis, Sun	22
30. **PEANUTS,** Little Joe and the Thrillers, Okeh	29
31. **DEEP PURPLE,** Billy Ward and His Dominoes, Liberty	24
32. **THAT'LL BE THE DAY,** Crickets Burnswick	25
33. **RAINBOW,** Russ Hamilton, Kapp	23
34. **MR. LEE,** Bobbettes, Atlantic	25
34. **WAIT AND SEE,** Fats Domino, Imperial	31
36. **BONY MORONIE,** Larry Williams, Specialty	43
37. **HONEST I DO,** Jimmy Reed, Vee Jay	41
38. **KISSES SWEETER THAN WINE,** Jimmie Rodgers, Roulette	85
38. **AND THAT REMINDS ME,** Della Reese, Jubilee	39
38. **WUN'ERFUL, WUN'ERFUL,** Stan Freberg, Capitol	45
41. **BACK TO SCHOOL AGAIN,** Timmie Rodgers, Cameo	36
42. **I'LL REMEMBER TODAY,** Patti Page, Mercury	41
43. **YOU SEND ME,** Teresa Brewer, Coral	55
44. **BLACK SLACKS,** Joe Bennett & The Sparkletones, ABC-Paramount	34
45. **IVY ROSE,** Perry Como, Victor	49
45. **SWANEE RIVER ROCK (TALKIN' 'BOUT THAT RIVER),** Ray Charles, Atlantic	44
47. **MY ONE SIN,** Four Coins, Epic	37
47. **PARTY TIME,** Sal Mineo, Epic	69
49. **LIECHTENSTEINER POLKA,** Will Glahe, London	68
50. **IN THE MIDDLE OF THE AN ISLAND,** Tony Bennett, Columbia	38
51. **PLAYTHING,** Nick Todd, Dot	53
52. **SOFT,** Bill Doggett, King	62
53. **REMEMBER YOU'RE MINE,** Pat Boone, Dot	46
53. **YOU BUG ME, BABY,** Larry Williams, Specialty	85
55. **FRAULEIN,** Bobby Helms, Decca	52
56. **FRAULEIN,** Steve Lawrence, Coral	55
57. **JOKER,** Billy Myles, Ember	77
57. **STORY OF MY LIFE,** Marty Robbins, Columbia	65
59. **WITH YOU ON MY MIND,** Nat King Cole, Capitol	48
60. **MOONLIGHT SWIM,** Tony Perkins, Victor	49
60. **SEND FOR ME,** Nat King Cole, Capitol	54
62. **REET PETITE,** Jackie Wilson, Brunswick	62
63. **TREAT ME NICE,** Elvis Presley, Victor	46
64. **FARTHER UP THE ROAD,** Bobby (Blue) Bland, Duke	58
65. **AN AFFAIR TO REMEMBER,** Vic Damone, Columbia	60
66. **REBEL,** Carol Jarvis, Dot	62
67. **JUST BETWEEN YOU AND ME,** Chordettes, Cadence	57
67. **LOVE ME FOREVER,** Four Esquires, Paris	85
69. **HEY, LITTLE GIRL,** Techniques, Roulette	93
69. **LITTLE BITTY PRETTY ONE,** Bobby Day, Class	80
71. **AROUND THE WORLD,** Victor Young, Decca	69
71. **DEEP BLUE SEA,** Jimmy Dean, Columbia	71
73. **AROUND THE WORLD,** Mantovani, London	65
73. **HAVE I TOLD YOU LATELY THAT I LOVE YOU,** Ricky Nelson, Imperial	49
75. **IT'S NOT FOR ME TO SAY,** Johnny Mathis, Columbia	61
75. **STARDUST,** Billy Ward, Liberty	58
77. **ONLY BECAUSE,** Platters, Mercury	65
77. **SILHOUETTES,** Diamonds, Mercury	71
79. **MISTER FIRE EYES,** Bonnie Guitar, Dot	75
79. **TEARDROPS,** Lee Andrews and The Hearts, Chess	—
81. **SUMMERTIME,** Sam Cooke, Keen	85
82. **BUZZ, BUZZ, BUZZ,** Hollywood Flames, Ebb	—
82. **BON VOYAGE,** Janice Harper, Prep	71
82. **PLAYTHING,** Ted Newman, Rev	93
82. **TEDDY BEAR,** Elvis Presley, Victor	75
86. **PRETEND YOU DON'T SEE HER,** Jerry Vale, Columbia	—
86. **THE TWELFTH OF NEVER,** Johnny Mathis, Columbia	85
88. **TONIGHT, TONIGHT,** Mello-Kings, Herald	93
89. **GREAT BALLS OF FIRE,** Jerry Lee Lewis, Sun	—
89. **LIPS OF WINE,** Andy Williams, Cadence	71
89. **OH BOY,** Crickets, Brunswick	—
92. **CHICAGO,** Frank Sinatra, Capitol	84
92. **IDOL WITH THE GOLDEN HEAD,** Coasters, Atco	80
94. **TAMMY,** Ames Brothers, Victor	98
94. **WHEN THE SWALLOWS COME BACK TO CAPISTRANO,** Pat Boone, Dot	80
96. **AROUND THE WORLD,** Bing Crosby, Decca	85
96. **GOT A DATE WITH AN ANGEL,** Billy Williams, Coral	78
96. **JOKER,** Hilltoppers, Dot	—
99. **SILHOUETTES,** Steve Gibson & The Red Caps, ABC-Paramount	—
99. **THINK,** Five Royals, King	—

NEW YORK UNIVERSITY SCHOOL OF RETAILING • STORE RECORDED SALES • THE BILLBOARD

Best Sellers in Stores

The information given in this chart is based on actual sales to customers in a scientific sample of the nation's retail record outlets during the week ending on the date shown above. Sample design, sample size, and all methods used in this continuing study of retail record sales are under the direct and continuing supervision and control of the School of Retailing of New York University.

FOR SURVEY WEEK ENDING NOVEMBER 23, 1957

This Week	Record	Last Week	Weeks on Chart
1.	YOU SEND ME (BMI)—Sam Cooke SUMMERTIME (ASCAP)—Keen 34013	3	6
2.	JAILHOUSE ROCK (BMI)—Elvis Presley TREAT ME NICE (BMI)—Vic 7035	1	8
3.	WAKE UP LITTLE SUSIE (BMI)—Everly Brothers Maybe Tomorrow (BMI)—Cadence 1337	2	10
4.	SILHOUETTES (BMI)—The Rays Daddy Cool (BMI)—Cameo 117	4	7
5.	RAUNCHY (BMI)—Bill Justis The Midnite Man (BMI)—Phillips International 3519	9	3
6.	BE-BOP BABY (BMI)—Ricky Nelson HAVE I TOLD YOU LATELY THAT I LOVE YOU (BMI)—Imperial 5463	5	9
7.	APRIL LOVE (ASCAP)—Pat Boone WHEN THE SWALLOWS COME BACK TO CAPISTRANO (ASCAP)—Dot 15660	6	5
8.	CHANCES ARE (ASCAP)—Johnny Mathis THE TWELFTH OF NEVER (ASCAP)—Col 40993	7	11
9.	LITTLE BITTY PRETTY ONE (BMI)—Thurston Harris I Hope You Won't Hold It Against Me (ASCAP)—Aladdin 3398	10	6
10.	MY SPECIAL ANGEL (BMI)—Bobby Helms Standing at the End of My World (BMI)—Dec 30423	8	7
11.	RAUNCHY (BMI)—Ernie Freeman Puddin' (BMI)—Imperial 5474	11	3
12.	ROCK AND ROLL MUSIC (BMI)—Chuck Berry Blue Feeling (BMI)—Chess 1671	12	4
13.	PEGGY SUE (BMI)—Buddy Holly Everday (BMI)—Coral 61885	19	4
14.	KISSES SWEETER THAN WINE (ASCAP)—Jimmie Rodgers Better Loved You'll Never Be (ASCAP)—Roulette 4031	22	2
15.	I'M AVAILABLE (BMI)—Margie Rayburn If You Were (ASCAP)—Liberty 55102	15	4
16.	ALL THE WAY (ASCAP)—Frank Sinatra Chicago (ASCAP)—Cap 3793	20	4
17.	FASCINATION (ASCAP)—Jane Morgan Fascination (Instrumental) (ASCAP)—Kapp 191	13	13
18.	MELODIE D'AMOUR (BMI)—Ames Brothers So Little Time (BMI)—Vic 7046	16	8
19.	JUST BORN (BMI)—Perry Como IVY ROSE (ASCAP)—Vic 7050	17	6
20.	TAMMY (ASCAP)—Debbie Reynolds French Heels (ASCAP)—Coral 61851	17	19
21.	HONEYCOMB (ASCAP)—Jimmie Rodgers Their Hearts Were Full of Spring (ASCAP)—Roulette 4015	14	16
22.	LIECHTENSTEINER POLKA (ASCAP)—Will Glahe Schweitzer Polka (BMI)—London 1755	30	3
23.	COULD THIS BE MAGIC? (BMI)—Dubs Such Lovin' (BMI)—Gone 5011	25	4
24.	BONY MORONIE (BMI) Larry Williams YOU BUG ME, BABY (BMI)—Specialty 615	21	4
25.	THE JOKER (BMI)—Billy Myles Honey Bee (BMI)—Ember 1026	35	2
26.	KEEP A' KNOCKIN' (BMI)—Little Richard Can't Believe You Wanna Leave—Specialty 611	24	9
26.	HULA LOVE (BMI)—Buddy Knox Devil Woman (BMI)—Roulette 4018	26	13
28.	GREAT BALLS OF FIRE (BMI)—Jerry Lee Lewis You Win Again (BMI)—Sun 281	—	1
29.	HAPPY, HAPPY BIRTHDAY, BABY (BMI)—Tune Weavers Ol' Man River (ASCAP)—Checker 872	23	11
30.	ALONE (BMI)—Shepherd Sisters Congratulations to Someone (ASCAP)—Lance 125	29	5
31.	YOU SEND ME (BMI)—Teresa Brewer Would I Were (ASCAP)—Coral 61898	27	3
32.	OH, BOY (BMI)—Crickets Not Fade Away (BMI)—Brunswick 55035	—	1
33.	TILL (ASCAP)—Roger Williams Big Town (ASCAP)—Kapp 197	28	4
34.	LOTTA LOVIN' (BMI)—Gene Vincent Wear My Ring (BMI)—Cap 3763	31	11
35.	SOFT (BMI)—Bill Doggett Hot Ginger (BMI)—King 5080	48	2
36.	THAT'LL BE THE DAY (BMI)—Crickets I'm Lookin' for Someone to Love (BMI)—Brunswick 55009	44	16
37.	WITH YOU ON MY MIND (ASCAP)—Nat King Cole RAINTREE COUNTY (ASCAP)—Cap 3782	47	4
38.	BUZZ, BUZZ, BUZZ (BMI)—Hollywood Flames Crazy (BMI)—Ebb 119	—	1
39.	PEANUTS (BMI)—Little Joe & The Thrillers Lilly Lou (BMI)—Okeh 7088	41	9
40.	BACK TO SCHOOL AGAIN (BMI)—Timmie Rodgers I've Got a Dog Who Loves Me (BMI)—Cameo 116	43	4
41.	THE STORY OF MY LIFE (ASCAP)—Marty Robbins Once-a-Week Date (BMI)—Col 41013	—	1
41.	WHY DON'T THEY UNDERSTAND (BMI)—George Hamilton IV Even Tho (BMI)—ABC-Paramount 9862	—	1
43.	HEY, LITTLE GIRL (BMI)—Techniques In a Round About Way (BMI)—Roulette 4030	38	2
44.	LOVE ME FOREVER (BMI)—Four Esquires I Ain't Been Right Since You Left (ASCAP)—Paris 509	—	1
45.	WAIT AND SEE (BMI)—Fats Domino I Still Love You (BMI)—Imperial 5467	32	6
46.	HONEST I DO (BMI)—Jimmy Reed Signals of Love (BMI)—Vee Jay 253	36	4
47.	WHOLE LOTTA SHAKIN' GOIN' ON (BMI)—Jerry Lee Lewis It'll Be Mine (BMI)—Sun 267	42	19
48.	PLAYTHING (BMI)—Nick Todd The Honey Song (ASCAP)—Dot 15643	45	3
49.	SWANEE RIVER ROCK (Talkin' 'Bout That River) Ray Charles I Want a Little Girl (ASCAP)—Atlantic 1154	34	4
50.	AND THAT REMINDS ME (ASCAP)—Della Reese I Cried for You (ASCAP)—Jubilee 5292	39	4

THIS WEEK'S BEST BUYS

Special telephone reports indicate these recent releases have broken out in one or more key areas and have excellent potential for placing on The Billboard's best seller charts.

CHRISTMAS RECORDS

LET'S LIGHT THE CHRISTMAS TREE (Broadcast, BMI) — Ruby Wright—Fraternity 787—The side is a big territorial favorite in the Southern Ohio area. Action in all the major marts in that locale is strong. Flip is "Merry, Merry, Merry, Merry Christmas" (Buckeye, ASCAP).

NEW YORK UNIVERSITY SCHOOL OF RETAILING • STORE RECORDED SALES • THE BILLBOARD

RECENT POP RELEASES COMING UP STRONG

FOR SURVEY WEEK ENDING NOVEMBER 23

The information given in this chart is based on actual sales to customers in a scientific sample of the nation's retail record outlets during the week ending on the date shown above. Sample design, sample size and all methods used in this continuing study of retail record sales are under the direct and continuing supervision and control of the School of Retailing of New York University.

At the Hop . . . . ***Danny and the Junior***
(BMI) ABC-Paramount 9871

Wild Is the Wind
No Love (But Your Love) . . . . ***Johnny Mathis***
(ASCAP); (BMI) Columbia 41060

Most Played by Jockeys

FOR SURVEY WEEK ENDING NOVEMBER 23

SIDES are ranked in order of the greatest number of plays on disk jockey radio shows thruout the country. Results are based on The Billboard's weekly survey among the nation's disk jockeys. The reverse side of each record is also listed.

Week This		Last Week	Weeks on Chart
1.	**JAILHOUSE ROCK** (BMI)—Elvis Presley Treat Me Nice (BMI)—Vic 7035	1	8
2.	**YOU SEND ME** (BMI)—Sam Cooke Summertime (ASCAP)—Keen 34013	3	5
3.	**APRIL LOVE** (ASCAP)—Pat Boone When the Swallows Come Back to Capistrano (ASCAP)—Dot 15660	4	6
4.	**WAKE UP LITTLE SUSIE** (BMI)—Everly Brothers Maybe Tomorrow (BMI)—Cadence 1337	2	10
5.	**CHANCES ARE** (ASCAP)—Johnny Mathis The Twelfth of Never (ASCAP)—Col 40993	5	12
6.	**ALL THE WAY** (ASCAP)—Frank Sinatra Chicago (ASCAP)—Cap 3793	9	6
7.	**SILHOUETTES** (BMI)—The Rays Daddy Cool (BMI)—Cameo 117	6	6
8.	**MELODIE D'AMOUR** (BMI)—Ames Brothers So Little Time (BMI)—Vic 7046	7	9
9.	**YOU SEND ME** (BMI)—Teresa Brewer Would I Were (ASCAP)—Coral 61898	8	4
10.	**KISSES SWEETER THAN WINE** (ASCAP)—Jimmie Rodgers Better Loved You'll Never Be (ASCAP)—Roulette 4031	18	3
11.	**RAUNCHY** (BMI)—Bill Justis The Midnite Man (BMI)—Phillips International 3519	11	2
12.	**LITTLE BITTY PRETTY ONE** (BMI)—Thurston Harris I Hope You Won't Hold It Against Me (BMI)—Aladdin 3398	19	3
13.	**JUST BORN** (BMI)—Perry Como Ivy Rose (ASCAP)—Vic 7050	16	8
14.	**THE TWELFTH OF NEVER** (ASCAP)—Johnny Mathis Chances Are (ASCAP)—Col 40993	10	8
15.	**SILHOUETTES** (BMI)—Diamonds Daddy Cool (BMI)—Mercury 71197	12	5
15.	**PEGGY SUE** (BMI)—Buddy Holly Everyday (BMI)—Coral 61885	21	3
17.	**MY SPECIAL ANGEL** (BMI)—Bobby Helms Standing at the End of My World (BMI)—Dec 30423	17	6
18.	**RAUNCHY** (BMI)—Ernie Freeman Puddin' (BMI)—Imperial 5474	—	1
19.	**BE-BOP BABY** (BMI)—Ricky Nelson Have I Told You Lately That I Love You (BMI)—Imperial 5463	13	6
19.	**HONEYCOMB** (ASCAP)—Jimmie Rodgers Their Hearts Were Full of Spring (ASCAP)—Roulette 4015	15	15
21.	**I'M AVAILABLE** (BMI)—Margie Rayburn If You Were (ASCAP)—Liberty 55102	14	4
22.	**IVY ROSE** (ASCAP)—Perry Como Just Born (BMI)—Vic 7050	25	7
23.	**I'LL REMEMBER TODAY** (BMI)—Patti Page My, How the Time Goes By (ASCAP)—Mercury 71189	—	1
24.	**I'LL NEVER SAY, NEVER AGAIN, AGAIN** (ASCAP)—Dinah Shore The Kiss That Rocked the World (BMI)—Vic 7056	—	1
25.	**LIECHTENSTEINER POLKA** (ASCAP)—Will Glahe Schweitzer Polka (BMI)—London 1755	—	1
25.	**TILL** (ASCAP)—Roger Williams Big Town (ASCAP)—Kapp 197	24	2

Top 100 Sides

FOR SURVEY WEEK ENDING NOVEMBER 23

This is a tabulation of dealer unit sales listed according to the specific side requested by customers. No attempt is made to add sides together to reflect actual record sales. It is therefore a tabulation of sides or songs, and not records. This fact, together with longer four-week survey periods, explains variation between the top 30 sides as reflected in this chart, and top 30 record sellers as reflected in "Best Sellers in Stores."

Position, Song, Artist, Label	Last Week
1. **JAILHOUSE ROCK,** Elvis Presley, Victor	1
2. **YOU SEND ME,** Sam Cooke, Keen	3
3. **WAKE UP LITTLE SUSIE,** Everly Brothers, Cadence	2
4. **SILHOUETTES,** Rays, Cameo	4
5. **BE-BOP BABY,** Ricky Nelson, Imperial	5
6. **LITTLE BITTY PRETTY ONE,** Thurston Harris, Aladdin	6
7. **APRIL LOVE,** Pat Boone, Dot	9
8. **MY SPECIAL ANGEL,** Bobby Helms, Decca	7
9. **CHANCES ARE,** Johnny Mathis, Columbia	8
10. **RAUNCHY,** Bill Justis, Phillips International	14
11. **HONEYCOMB,** Jimmie Rodgers, Roulette	10
12. **FASCINATION,** Jane Morgan, Kapp	13
13. **ROCK AND ROLL MUSIC,** Chuck Berry, Chess	19
14. **MELODIE D'AMOUR,** Ames Brothers, Victor	12
15. **RAUNCHY,** Ernie Freeman, Imperial	17
16. **TAMMY,** Debbie Reynolds, Coral	11
17. **I'M AVAILABLE,** Margie Rayburn, Liberty	17
18. **PEGGY SUE,** Buddy Holly, Coral	27
19. **ALL THE WAY,** Frank Sinatra, Capitol	22
20. **JUST BORN,** Perry Como, Victor	21
20. **KEEP A' KNOCKIN',** Little Richard, Specialty	15
22. **HAPPY, HAPPY BIRTHDAY, BABY,** Tune Weavers, Checker	16
23. **HULA LOVE,** Buddy Knox, Roulette	24
24. **COULD THIS BE MAGIC,** Dubs, Gone	25
25. **KISSES SWEETER THAN WINE,** Jimmie Rodgers, Roulette	38
26. **ALONE,** Shepherd Sisters, Lance	22
27. **TILL,** Roger Williams,, Kapp	28
28. **LOTTA LOVIN',** Gene Vincent, Capitol	26
29. **DIANA,** Paul Anka, ABC-Paramount	20
30. **LIECHTENSTEINER POLKA,** Will Glahe, London	49
31. **YOU SEND ME,** Teresa Brewer, Coral	43
32. **I'LL REMEMBER TODAY,** Patti Page, Mercury	42
33. **WAIT AND SEE,** Fats Domino, Imperial	34
34. **JOKER,** Billy Myles, Ember	57
34. **AND THAT REMINDS ME,** Della Reese, Jubilee	38
36. **THAT'LL BE THE DAY,** Crickets, Brunswick	32
36. **WUN'ERFUL, WUN'ERFUL,** Stan Freberg, Capitol	38
38. **BACK TO SCHOOL AGAIN,** Timmie Rodgers, Cameo	41
39. **PEANUTS,** Little Joe and the Thrillers, Okeh	30
39. **RAINBOW,** Russ Hamilton, Kapp	33
41. **WHOLE LOTTA SHAKIN' GOIN' ON,** Jerry Lee Lewis, Sun	29
42. **BONY MORONIE,** Larry Williams, Specialty	36
43. **SWANEE RIVER ROCK (TALKIN' 'BOUT THAT RIVER),** Ray Charles, Atlantic	45
44. **STORY OF MY LIFE,** Marty Robbins, Columbia	57
45. **HONEST I DO,** Jimmy Reed, Vee Jay	37
45. **IVY ROSE,** Perry Como, Victor	45
47. **DEEP PURPLE,** Billy Ward and His Dominoes, Liberty	31
48. **WITH YOU ON MY MIND,** Nat King Cole, Capitol	59
49. **BLACK SLACKS,** Joe Bennett and the Sparkletones, ABC-Paramount	44
49. **MY ONE SIN,** Four Coins, Epic	47
51. **HEY, LITTLE GIRL,** Techniques, Roulette	69
51. **LOVE ME FOREVER,** Four Esquires, Paris	67
51. **PLAYTHING,** Nick Todd, Dot	51
51. **SOFT,** Bill Doggett, King	52
55. **MR. LEE,** Bobbettes, Atlantic	34
56. **IN THE MIDDLE OF AN ISLAND,** Tony Bennett, Columbia	50
57. **FRAULEIN,** Bobby Helms, Decca	55
57. **GREAT BALLS OF FIRE,** Jerry Lee Lewis, Sun	89
57. **LITTLE BITTY PRETTY ONE,** Bobby Day, Class	69
57. **OH BOY,** Crickets, Brunswick	89
61. **REMEMBER YOU'RE MINE,** Pat Boone, Dot	53
62. **BUZZ, BUZZ, BUZZ,** Hollywood Flames, Ebb	82
62. **FRAULEIN,** Steve Lawrence, Coral	56
64. **TEARDROPS,** Lee Andrews and the Hearts, Chess	79
65. **AN AFFAIR TO REMEMBER,** Vic Damone, Columbia	65
65. **SEND FOR ME,** Nat King Cole, Capitol	60
67. **DEEP BLUE SEA,** Jimmy Dean Columbia	71
67. **REET PETITE,** Jackie Wilson, Brunswick	62
69. **MOONLIGHT SWIM,** Tony Perkins, Victor	60
69. **PRETEND YOU DON'T SEE HER,** Jerry Vale, Columbia	86
71. **AROUND THE WORLD,** Victor Young, Decca	71
71. **REBEL,** Carol Jarvis, Dot	66
71. **YOU BUG ME, BABY,** Larry Williams, Specialty	53
74. **WHY DON'T THEY UNDERSTAND,** George Hamilton IV, ABC-Paramount	—
75. **PARTY TIME,** Sal Mineo Epic	47
75. **JOKER,** Hilltoppers, Dot	—
77. **JUST BETWEEN YOU AND ME,** Chordettes, Cadence	67
77. **HAVE I TOLD YOU LATELY THAT I LOVE YOU,** Ricky Nelson, Imperial	73
77. **MISTER FIRE EYES,** Bonnie Guitar, Dot	79
80. **AROUND THE WORLD,** Mantovani, London	73
81. **SILHOUETTES,** Diamonds, Mercury	77
82. **TREAT ME NICE,** Elvis Presley, Victor	63
83. **IT'S NOT FOR ME TO SAY,** Johnny Mathis, Columbia	75
84. **LET'S LIGHT THE CHRISTMAS TREE,** Ruby Wright, Fraternity	—
85. **FARTHER UP THE ROAD,** Bobby (Blue) Bland, Duke	64
85. **LIECHTENSTEINER POLKA,** Lawrence Welk, Coral	—
85. **RAUNCHY,** Billy Vaughn, Dot	—
88. **ONLY BECAUSE,** Platters, Mercury	77
88. **STARDUST,** Billy Ward, Liberty	75
88. **THE TWELFTH OF NEVER,** Johnny Mathis, Columbia	86
91. **AROUND THE WORLD,** Bing Crosby, Decca	96
91. **CHICAGO,** Frank Sinatra, Capitol	92
93. **MAJESTY OF LOVE,** Marvin Rainwater-Connie Francis, M-G-M	—
93. **NERVOUS BOOGIE,** Paul Gayten, Argo	—
93. **PLAYTHING,** Ted Newman, Rev	82
93. **ROCK AND CRY,** Clyde McPhatter, Atlantic	—
93. **TAMMY,** Ames Brothers, Victor	94
98. **BON VOYAGE,** Janice Harper, Prep	82
98. **LIPS OF WINE,** Andy Williams, Cadence	89
98. **TONIGHT, TONIGHT,** Mello-Kings, Herald	88
98. **THINK,** Five Royals, King	99

Best Sellers in Stores

The information given in this chart is based on actual sales to customers in a scientific sample of the nation's retail record outlets during the week ending on the date shown above. Sample design, sample size, and all methods used in this continuing study of retail record sales are under the direct and continuing supervision and control of the School of Retailing of New York University.

FOR SURVEY WEEK ENDING NOVEMBER 30, 1957

This Week		Last Week	Weeks on Chart
1.	YOU SEND ME (BMI)—Sam Cooke / SUMMERTIME (ASCAP)—Keen 34013	1	7
2.	JAILHOUSE ROCK (BMI)—Elvis Presley / TREAT ME NICE (BMI)—Vic 7035	2	9
3.	RAUNCHY (BMI)—Bill Justis / The Midnite Man (BMI)—Phillips International 3519	5	4
4.	APRIL LOVE (ASCAP)—Pat Boone / WHEN THE SWALLOWS COME BACK TO CAPISTRANO (ASCAP)—Dot 15660	7	6
5.	CHANCES ARE (ASCAP)—Johnny Mathis / THE TWELFTH OF NEVER (ASCAP)—Col 40993	8	12
6.	WAKE UP LITTLE SUSIE (BMI)—Everly Brothers / Maybe Tomorrow (BMI)—Cadence 1337	3	11
7.	SILHOUETTES (BMI)—The Rays / Daddy Cool (BMI)—Cameo 117	4	8
8.	PEGGY SUE (BMI)—Buddy Holly / Everyday (BMI)—Coral 61885	13	5
9.	ROCK AND ROLL MUSIC (BMI)—Chuck Berry / Blue Feeling (BMI)—Chess 1671	12	5
10.	BE-BOP BABY (BMI)—Ricky Nelson / HAVE I TOLD YOU LATELY THAT I LOVE YOU (BMI)—Imperial 5463	6	10
11.	LITTLE BITTY PRETTY ONE (BMI)—Thurston Harris / I Hope You Won't Hold It Against Me (ASCAP)—Aladdin 3398	9	7
12.	GREAT BALLS OF FIRE (BMI)—Jerry Lee Lewis / You Win Again (BMI)—Sun 281	28	2
13.	KISSES SWEETER THAN WINE (ASCAP)—Jimmie Rodgers / Better Loved You'll Never Be (ASCAP)—Roulette 4031	14	3
14.	AT THE HOP (BMI)—Danny and the Juniors / Sometimes (BMI)—ABC-Paramount 9871	—	1
15.	MY SPECIAL ANGEL (BMI)—Bobby Helms / Standing at the End of My World (BMI)—Dec 30423	10	8
16.	LIECHTENSTEINER POLKA (ASCAP) Will Glahe / Schweitzer Polka (BMI)—London 1755	22	4
17.	JUST BORN (BMI)—Perry Como / IVY ROSE (ASCAP)—Vic 7050	19	7
18.	ALL THE WAY (ASCAP)—Frank Sinatra / CHICAGO (ASCAP)—Cap 3793	16	5
19.	I'M AVAILABLE (BMI)—Margie Rayburn / If You Were (ASCAP)—Liberty 55102	15	5
20.	MELODIE D'AMOUR (BMI)—Ames Brothers / So Little Time (BMI)—Vic 7046	18	9
21.	RAUNCHY (BMI)—Ernie Freeman / Puddin' (BMI)—Imperial 5474	11	4
22	FASCINATION (ASCAP)—Jane Morgan / Fascination (Instrumental) (ASCAP)—Kapp 191	17	14
23.	HONEYCOMB (ASCAP)—Jimmie Rodgers / Their Hearts Were Full of Spring (ASCAP)—Roulette 4015	21	17
24.	BONY MORONIE (BMI)—Larry Williams / YOU BUG ME (BMI)—Specialty 615	24	5
25.	WHY DON'T THEY UNDERSTAND? (BMI)—George Hamilton IV / Even Tho' (BMI)—ABC-Paramount 9862	41	2
26.	OH, BOY (BMI)—Crickets / Not Fade Away (BMI)—Brunswick 55035	32	2
27.	TAMMY (ASCAP)—Debbie Reynolds / French Heels (ASCAP)—Coral 61851	20	20
28.	THE JOKER (BMI)—Billy Myles / Honey Bee (BMI)—Ember 1026	25	3
29.	HEY, LITTLE GIRL (BMI)—Techniques / In a Round About Way (BMI)—Roulette 4030	43	3
30.	TEARDROPS (BMI)—Lee Andrews and the Hearts / Girl Around the Corner (BMI)—Chess 1675	—	2
31.	KEEP A' KNOCKIN' (BMI)—Little Richard / Can't Believe You Wanna Leave—Specialty 611	26	10
32.	HULA LOVE (BMI)—Buddy Knox / Devil Woman (BMI)—Roulette 4018	26	14
33.	COULD THIS BE MAGIC? (BMI)—Dubs / Such Lovin' (BMI)—Gone 5011	23	5
34.	TILL (ASCAP)—Roger Williams / Big Town (ASCAP)—Kapp 197	33	5
35.	HAPPY, HAPPY BIRTHDAY, BABY (BMI)—Tune Weavers / Ol' Man River (ASCAP)—Checker 872	29	12
36.	BUZZ, BUZZ, BUZZ (BMI)—Hollywood Flames / Crazy (BMI)—Ebb 119	38	2
37.	WITH YOU ON MY MIND (ASCAP)—Nat King Cole / RAINTREE COUNTY (ASCAP)—Cap 3782	37	5
38.	THE STORY OF MY LIFE (ASCAP)—Marty Robbins / Once-a-Week Date (BMI)—Col 41013	41	2
39.	YOU SEND ME (BMI)—Teresa Brewer / Would I Were (ASCAP)—Coral 61898	31	4
40.	WUN'ERFUL, WUN'ERFUL (Parts 1 & 2) (ASCAP)—Stan Freberg / Cap 3815	—	4
41.	LET'S LIGHT THE CHRISTMAS TREE (BMI)—Ruby Wright / Merry, Merry, Merry, Merry Christmas (ASCAP)—Fraternity 787	—	1
42.	I'LL REMEMBER TODAY (BMI)—Patti Page / My, How the Time Goes By (ASCAP)—Mercury 71189	—	1
43.	THAT'LL BE THE DAY (BMI)—Crickets / I'm Lookin' for Someone to Love (BMI)—Brunswick 55009	36	17
44.	AND THAT REMINDS ME (ASCAP)—Della Reese / I Cried for You (ASCAP)—Jubilee 5292	50	5
45.	DANCE TO THE BOP (BMI)—Gene Vincent / I Got It (BMI)—Cap 3839	—	1
46.	ALONE (BMI)—Shepherd Sisters / Congratulations to Someone (ASCAP)—Lance 125	30	6
47.	WAIT AND SEE (BMI)—Fats Domino / I Still Love You (BMI)—Imperial 5467	45	7
48.	LIECHTENSTEINER POLKA (ASCAP)—Lawrence Welk / You Know Too Much (ASCAP)—Coral 61900	—	1
49.	PEANUTS (BMI)—Little Joe & The Thrillers / Lilly Lou (BMI)—Okeh 7088	39	10
50.	BACK TO SCHOOL AGAIN (BMI)—Timmie Rodgers / I've Got a Dog Who Loves Me (BMI)—Cameo 116	40	5

THIS WEEK'S BEST BUYS

Special telephone reports indicate these recent releases have broken out in one or more key areas and have excellent potential for placing on The Billboard's best seller charts.

I'LL COME RUNNING BACK TO YOU (Venice, BMI)—Sam Cooke—Specialty 619—All of the top markets are hot for this one. It looks like a winner. Flip is "Forever" (Venice, BMI). A previous Billboard "Spotlight" pick.

PUT A LIGHT IN THE WINDOW (Planetary, ASCAP)—The Four Lads—Columbia 41058—The side is beginning to move well in all of the major marts. This appears their biggest recently. Flip is "The Things We Did Last Summer" (Styne & Cahn, ASCAP). Previous Billboard "Spotlight" pick.

LOVE BUG CRAWL (Mayflower, BMI)—Jimmy Edwards—Mercury 71209—Platter has been out for several weeks and is now starting to register strongly. Good sales in all marts. Flip is "Honey Lovin'" (Mayflower, BMI). A previously Billboard "Spotlight" pick.

CHRISTMAS RECORDS

JINGLE BELL ROCK (Cornell, ASCAP)—Bobby Helms—Decca 30513—This looks like the biggest Christmas record of the season. Strong sales are reported in both pop and c.&w.; markets. Flip is "Captain Santa Claus" (Amber, ASCAP). A previous Billboard "Spotlight" pick.

RECENT POP RELEASES COMING UP STRONG

FOR SURVEY WEEK ENDING NOVEMBER 30

The information given in this chart is based on actual sales to customers in a scientific sample of the nation's retail record outlets during the week ending on the date shown above. Sample design, sample size and all methods used in this continuing study of retail record sales are under the direct and continuing supervision and control of the School of Retailing of New York University.

No Love (But Your Love) . . . . *Johnny Mathis*
(BMI) Columbia 41060

Put a Light in the Window . . . . *Four Lads*
(ASCAP) Columbia 41058

Most Played by Jockeys

FOR SURVEY WEEK ENDING NOVEMBER 30

SIDES are ranked in order of the greatest number of plays on disk jockey radio shows thruout the country. Results are based on The Billboard's weekly survey among the nation's disk jockeys. The reverse side of each record is also listed.

Week This		Last Week	Weeks on Chart
1.	YOU SEND ME (BMI)—Sam Cooke Summertime (ASCAP)—Keen 34013	2	6
2.	JAILHOUSE ROCK (BMI)—Elvis Presley Treat Me Nice (BMI)—Vic 7035	1	9
3.	APRIL LOVE (ASCAP)—Pat Boone When the Swallows Come Back to Capistrano (ASCAP)—Dot 15660	3	7
4.	ALL THE WAY (ASCAP)—Frank Sinatra Chicago (ASCAP)—Cap 3793	6	7
5.	RAUNCHY (BMI)—Bill Justis The Midnite Man (BMI)—Phillips International 3519	11	3
6.	KISSES SWEETER THAN WINE (ASCAP)—Jimmie Rodgers Better Loved You'll Never Be (ASCAP)—Roulette 4031	10	4
7.	CHANCES ARE (ASCAP)—Johnny Mathis The Twelfth of Never (ASCAP)—Col 40993	5	13
8.	WAKE UP LITTLE SUSIE (BMI)—Everly Brothers Maybe Tomorrow (BMI)—Cadence 1337	4	11
9.	SILHOUETTES (BMI)—The Rays Daddy Cool (BMI)—Cameo 117	7	7
10.	MELODIE D'AMOUR (BMI)—Ames Brothers So Little Time (BMI)—Vic 7046	8	10
11.	YOU SEND ME (BMI)—Teresa Brewer Would I Were (ASCAP)—Coral 61898	9	5
12.	THE TWELFTH OF NEVER (ASCAP)—Johnny Mathis Chances Are (ASCAP)—Col 40993	14	9
13.	RAUNCHY (BMI)—Ernie Freeman Puddin' (BMI)—Imperial 5474	18	2
14.	PEGGY SUE (BMI)—Buddy Holly Everyday (BMI)—Coral 61885	15	4
15.	PUT A LIGHT IN THE WINDOW (ASCAP)—Four Lads The Things We Did Last Summer (ASCAP)—Col 41085	—	1
16.	I'M AVAILABLE (BMI)—Margie Rayburn If You Were (ASCAP)—Liberty 55102	21	5
17.	JUST BORN (BMI)—Perry Como Ivy Rose (ASCAP)—Vic 7050	13	9
18.	MY SPECIAL ANGEL (BMI)—Bobby Helms Standing at the End of My World (BMI)—Dec 30423	17	7
19.	LITTLE BITTY PRETTY ONE (BMI)—Thurston Harris I Hope You Won't Hold It Against Me (BMI)—Aladdin 3398	12	4
20.	GREAT BALLS OF FIRE (BMI)—Jerry Lee Lewis You Win Again (BMI)—Sun 281	—	1
21.	FASCINATION (ASCAP)—Jane Morgan Fascination (Instrumental) (ASCAP)—Kapp 191	—	13
22.	TILL (ASCAP)—Roger Williams Big Town (ASCAP)—Kapp 197	25	3
23.	SILHOUETTES (BMI)—Diamonds Daddy Cool (BMI)—Mercury 71197	15	6
24.	IVY ROSE (ASCAP)—Perry Como Just Born (BMI)—Vic 7050	22	8
25.	BE-BOP BABY (BMI)—Ricky Nelson Have I Told You Lately That I Love You? (BMI)—Imperial 5463	19	7

Top 100 Sides

FOR SURVEY WEEK ENDING NOVEMBER 30

This is a tabulation of dealer unit sales listed according to the specific side requested by customers. No attempt is made to add sides together to reflect actual record sales. It is therefore a tabulation of sides or songs, and not records. This fact, together with longer four-week survey periods, explains variation between the top 30 sides as reflected in this chart, and top 30 record sellers as reflected in "Best Sellers in Stores."

Pos.	Song, Artist Label	Last Week
1.	**JAILHOUSE ROCK,** Elvis Presley, Victor	1
1.	**YOU SEND ME,** Sam Cooke, Keen	2
3.	**WAKE UP LITTLE SUSIE,** Everly Brothers, Cadence	3
4.	**SILHOUETTES,** Rays, Cameo	4
5.	**RAUNCHY,** Bill Justis, Phillips International	10
6.	**APRIL LOVE,** Pat Boone, Dot	7
7.	**BE-BOP BABY,** Ricky Nelson, Imperial	5
8.	**CHANCES ARE,** Johnny Mathis, Columbia	9
9.	**LITTLE BITTY PRETTY ONE,** Thurston Harris, Aladdin	6
10.	**MY SPECIAL ANGEL,** Bobby Helms, Decca	8
11.	**ROCK AND ROLL MUSIC,** Chuck Berry, Chess	13
12.	**PEGGY SUE,** Buddy Holly, Coral	18
13.	**RAUNCHY,** Ernie Freeman, Imperial	15
14.	**KISSES SWEETER THAN WINE,** Jimmie Rodgers, Roulette	25
15.	**FASCINATION,** Jane Morgan, Kapp	12
16.	**I'M AVAILABLE,** Margie Rayburn, Liberty	17
17.	**HONEYCOMB,** Jimmie Rodgers, Roulette	11
18.	**MELODIE D'AMOUR,** Ames Brothers, Victor	14
19.	**ALL THE WAY,** Frank Sinatra, Capitol	19
19.	**GREAT BALLS OF FIRE,** Jerry Lee Lewis, Sun	57
21.	**TAMMY,** Debbie Reynolds, Coral	16
22.	**LIECHTENSTEINER POLKA,** Will Glahe, London	30
23.	**AT THE HOP,** Danny and the Juniors, ABC-Paramount	—
24.	**JUST BORN,** Perry Como, Victor	20
25.	**HAPPY, HAPPY BIRTHDAY, BABY,** Tune Weavers, Checker	22
26.	**KEEP A' KNOCKIN',** Little Richard, Specialty	20
27.	**BONY MORONIE,** Larry Williams, Specialty	42
27.	**COULD THIS BE MAGIC,** Dubs, Gone	24
27.	**HULA LOVE,** Buddy Knox, Roulette	23
30.	**THE JOKER,** Billy Myles, Ember	34
31.	**TILL,** Roger Williams, Kapp	27
31.	**YOU SEND ME,** Teresa Brewer, Coral	31
33.	**HEY, LITTLE GIRL,** Techniques, Roulette	51
34.	**OH BOY,** Crickets, Brunswick	57
35.	**ALONE,** Shepherd Sisters, Lance	26
36.	**WHY DON'T THEY UNDERSTAND,** George Hamilton IV, ABC-Paramount	74
37.	**IVY ROSE,** Perry Como, Victor	45
37.	**TEARDROPS,** Lee Andrews and the Hearts, Chess	64
39.	**I'LL REMEMBER TODAY,** Patti Page, Mercury	32
40.	**WUN'ERFUL, WUN'ERFUL,** Stan Freberg, Capitol	36
41.	**AND THAT REMINDS ME,** Della Reese, Jubilee	34
42.	**LOTTA LOVIN',** Gene Vincent, Capitol	28
42.	**PEANUTS,** Little Joe and the Thrillers, Okeh	39
42.	**SWANEE RIVER ROCK (TALKIN' 'BOUT THAT RIVER),** Ray Charles, Atlantic	43
42.	**THAT'LL BE THE DAY,** Crickets, Brunswick	36
46.	**BUZZ, BUZZ, BUZZ,** Hollywood Flames, Ebb	62
47.	**BACK TO SCHOOL AGAIN,** Timmie Rodgers, Cameo	38
47.	**WITH YOU ON MY MIND,** Nat King Cole, Capitol	48
49.	**STORY OF MY LIFE,** Marty Robbins, Columbia	44
50.	**WAIT AND SEE,** Fats Domino, Imperial	33
51.	**DIANA,** Paul Anka, ABC-Paramount	29
51.	**WHOLE LOTTA SHAKIN' GOIN' ON,** Jerry Lee Lewis, Sun	41
53.	**SOFT,** Bill Doggett, King	51
54.	**YOU BUG ME, BABY,** Larry Williams, Specialty	71
55.	**HONEST I DO,** Jimmy Reed, Vee Jay	45
55.	**LOVE ME FOREVER,** Four Esquires, Paris	51
55.	**PLAYTHING,** Nick Todd, Dot	51
58.	**BLACK SLACKS,** Joe Bennett and the Sparkletones, ABC-Paramount	49
58.	**RAINBOW,** Russ Hamilton, Kapp	39
60.	**FRAULEIN,** Bobby Helms, Decca	57
61.	**LITTLE BITTY PRETTY ONE,** Bobby Day, Class	57
62.	**AN AFFAIR TO REMEMBER,** Viç Damone, Columbia	65
62.	**THE TWELFTH OF NEVER,** Johnny Mathis, Columbia	88
64.	**IN THE MIDDLE OF AN ISLAND,** Tony Bennett Columbia	56
64.	**REET PETITE,** Jackie Wilson, Brunswick	67
66.	**FRAULEIN,** Steve Lawrence, Coral	62
66.	**THE JOKER,** Hilltoppers, Dot	75
66.	**PARTY TIME,** Sal Mineo, Epic	75
69.	**MY ONE SIN,** Four Coins, Epic	49
69.	**NERVOUS BOOGIE,** Paul Gayten, Argo	93
69.	**PRETEND YOU DON'T SEE HER,** Jerry Vale, Columbia	69
69.	**REMEMBER YOU'RE MINE,** Pat Boone, Dot	61
69.	**RAUNCHY,** Billy Vaughn, Dot	85
74.	**MR. LEE,** Bobbettes, Atlantic	55
74.	**SEND FOR ME,** Nat King Cole, Capitol	65
76.	**ARDOUND THE WORLD,** Mantovani, London	80
76.	**MOONLIGHT SWIM,** Tony Perkins, Victor	69
78.	**AROUND THE WORLD,** Victor Young, Decca	71
78.	**LET'S LIGHT THE CHRISTMAS TREE,** Ruby Wright, Fraternity	84
80.	**LIECHTENSTEINER POLKA,** Lawrence Welk, Coral	85
80.	**ONLY BECAUSE,** Platters, Mercury	88
82.	**REBEL,** Carol Jarvis, Dot	71
83.	**DANCE OF THE BOP,** Gene Vincent, Capitol	—
84.	**DEEP PURPLE,** Billy Ward, Liberty	47
84.	**TREAT ME NICE,** Elvis Presley, Victor	82
86.	**FARTHER UP THE ROAD,** Bobby (Blue) Bland, Duke	85
86.	**SILHOUETTES,** Diamonds, Mercury	81
88.	**DEEP BLUE SEA,** Jimmy Dean, Columbia	67
89.	**THE CREATURE,** Buchanan & Ancell, Flying Saucer	—
90.	**AROUND THE WORLD,** Bing Crosby, Decca	91
91.	**HA! HA! HA!** Kay Armen, Decca	—
91.	**LIPS OF WINE,** Andy Williams, Cadence	98
91.	**MISTER FIRE EYES,** Bonnie Guitar, Dot	77
91.	**PUT A LIGHT IN THE WINDOW,** Four Lads, Columbia	—
95.	**TAMMY,** Ames Brothers, Victor	93
96.	**CA C'EST L'AMOUR,** Tony Bennett, Columbia	—
96.	**GOT A DATE WITH AN ANGEL,** Billy Williams, Coral	—
96.	**IT'S NOT FOR ME TO SAY,** Johnny Mathis, Columbia	83
96.	**LOVE LETTERS IN THE SAND,** Pat Boone, Dot	—
100.	**JUST BETWEEN YOU AND ME,** Chordettes, Cadence	77

Best Sellers in Stores

FOR SURVEY WEEK ENDING DECEMBER 7, 1957

The information given in this chart is based on actual sales to customers in a scientific sample of the nation's retail record outlets during the week ending on the date shown above. Sample design, sample size, and all methods used in this continuing study of retail record sales are under the direct and continuing supervision and control of the School of Retailing of New York University.

This Week		Last Week	Weeks on Chart
1.	JAILHOUSE ROCK (BMI)—Elvis Presley TREAT ME NICE (BMI)—Vic 7035	2	10
2.	RAUNCHY (BMI)—Bill Justis The Midnite Man (BMI)—Philips International 3519	3	5
3.	YOU SEND ME (BMI)—Sam Cooke SUMMERTIME (ASCAP)—Keen 34013	1	8
4.	APRIL LOVE (ASCAP)—Pat Boone WHEN THE SWALLOWS COME BACK TO CAPISTRANO (ASCAP)—Dot 15660	4	7
5.	AT THE HOP (BMI)—Danny and the Juniors Sometimes (BMI)—ABC-Paramount 9871	14	2
6.	GREAT BALLS OF FIRE (BMI)—Jerry Lee Lewis You Win Again (BMI)—Sun 281	12	3
7.	PEGGY SUE (BMI)—Buddy Holly Everyday (BMI)—Coral 61885	8	6
8.	CHANCES ARE (ASCAP)—Johnny Mathis THE TWELFTH OF NEVER (ASCAP)—Col 40993	5	13
9.	ROCK AND ROLL MUSIC (BMI)—Chuck Berry Blue Feeling (BMI)—Chess 1671	9	6
10.	WAKE UP LITTLE SUSIE (BMI)—Everly Brothers Maybe Tomorrow (BMI)—Cadence 1337	6	12
11.	SILHOUETTES (BMI)—The Rays Daddy Cool (BMI)—Cameo 117	7	9
12.	KISSES SWEETER THAN WINE (BMI)—Jimmie Rodgers Better Loved You'll Never Be (ASCAP)—Roulette 4031	13	4
13.	BE-BOP BABY (BMI)—Ricky Nelson HAVE I TOLD YOU LATELY THAT I LOVE YOU? (BMI)—Imperial 5468	10	11
14.	MY SPECIAL ANGEL (BMI)—Bobby Helms Standing at the End of My World (BMI)—Dec 30423	15	9
15.	LITTLE BITTY PRETTY ONE (BMI)—Thurston Harris I Hope You Won't Hold It Against Me (ASCAP)—Aladdin 3398	11	8
16.	LIECHTENSTEINER POLKA (ASCAP)—Will Glahe Schweitzer Polka (BMI)—London 1755	16	5
17.	RAUNCHY (BMI)—Ernie Freeman Puddin' (BMI)—Imperial 5474	21	5
18.	JUST BORN (BMI)—Perry Como IVY ROSE (ASCAP)—Vic 7050	17	8
19.	ALL THE WAY (ASCAP)—Frank Sinatra CHICAGO (ASCAP)—Cap 3793	18	6
20.	MELODIE D'AMOUR (BMI)—Ames Brothers So Little Time (BMI)—Vic 7046	20	10
21.	BONY MORONIE (BMI)—Larry Williams YOU BUG ME, BABY (BMI)—Specialty 615	24	6
22.	WHY DON'T THEY UNDERSTAND? (BMI)—George Hamilton IV Even Tho (BMI)—ABC-Paramount 9862	25	3
23.	HONEYCOMB (ASCAP)—Jimmie Rodgers Their Hearts Were Full of Spring (ASCAP)—Roluette 4015	23	18
24.	FASCINATION (ASCAP)—Jane Morgan Fascination (Instrumental) (ASCAP)—Kapp 191	22	15
25.	I'M AVAILABLE (BMI)—Margie Rayburn If You Were (ASCAP)—Liberty 55102	19	6
26.	OH, BOY (BMI)—Crickets Not Fade Away (BMI)—Brunswick 55035	26	3
27.	TAMMY (ASCAP)—Debbie Reynolds French Heels (ASCAP)—Coral 61851	27	21
28.	TEARDROPS (BMI)—Lee Andrews and the Hearts Girl Around the Corner (BMI)—Chess 1675	30	3
29.	BUZZ, BUZZ, BUZZ (BMI)—Hollywood Flames CRAZY (BMI)—Ebb 119	36	3
30.	WILD IS THE WIND (ASCAP)—Johnny Mathis NO LOVE (BUT YOUR LOVE) (BMI)—Col 41060	—	1
31.	KEEP A' KNOCKIN' (BMI)—Little Richard Can't Believe You Wanna Leave—Specialty 611	31	11
32.	BLACK SLACKS (BMI)—Joe Bennett & Sparkletones Boppin' Rock Boogie (BMI)—ABC-Paramount 9837	—	10
33.	TILL (ASCAP)—Roger Williams Big Town (ASCAP)—Kapp 197	34	6
34.	THE JOKER (BMI)—Billy Myles Honey Bee (BMI)—Ember 1026	28	4
35.	HAPPY, HAPPY BIRTHDAY, BABY (BMI)—Tune Weavers Ol' Man River (ASCAP)—Checker 872	35	13
36.	PEANUTS (BMI)—Little Joe & the Thrillers Lilly Lou (BMI)—Okeh 7088	49	11
37.	HULA LOVE (BMI)—Buddy Knox Devil Woman (BMI)—Roulette 4018	32	15
38.	I'LL REMEMBER TODAY (BMI)—Patti Page My, How the Time Goes By (ASCAP)—Mercury 71189	42	5
39.	PUT A LIGHT IN THE WINDOW (ASCAP)—Four Lads The Things We Did Last Summer (ASCAP)—Col 41058	—	1
40.	COULD THIS BE MAGIC? (BMI)—Dubs Such Lovin' (BMI)—Gone 5011	33	6
41.	THE STORY OF MY LIFE (ASCAP)—Marty Robbins Once-a-Week Date (BMI)—Col 41013	38	3
42.	YOU SEND ME (BMI)—Teresa Brewer Would I Were (ASCAP)—Coral 61898	39	5
43.	THAT'LL BE THE DAY (BMI)—Crickets I'm Lookin' for Someone to Love (BMI)—Brunswick 55009	43	18
44.	DANCE TO THE BOP (BMI)—Gene Vincent I Got It (BMI)—Cap 3839	45	2
45.	PRETEND YOU DON'T SEE HER (ASCAP)—Jerry Vale The Spreading Chestnut (BMI)—Col 41010	—	1
46.	WITH YOU ON MY MIND (ASCAP)—Nat King Cole RAINTREE COUNTY (ASCAP)—Cap 3782	37	6
47.	WUN'ERFUL, WUN'ERFUL (Parts 1 & 2) (ASCAP)—Stan Freberg Cap 3815	40	5
48.	AND THAT REMINDS ME (ASCAP)—Della Reese I Cried for You (ASCAP)—Jubilee 5292	44	6
49.	FRAULEIN (BMI)—Bobby Helms Heartsick Feeling (BMI)—Dec 30194	—	3
50.	WHITE CHRISTMAS (ASCAP)—Bing Crosby God Rest Ye Merry, Gentlemen (ASCAP)—Dec 23778	—	1

THIS WEEK'S BEST BUYS

Special telephone reports indicate these recent releases have broken out in one or more key areas and have excellent potential for placing on The Billboard's best seller charts.

WAITIN' IN SCHOOL (Reeve, BMI)

STOOD UP (Commodore, BMI)—Ricky Nelson—Imperial 5483—The platter is taking off in all markets. The young artist appears to have another two-sided hit. Requests on each side are about equal at this point. A previous Billboard "Spotlight" pick.

(I LOVE YOU) FOR SENTIMENTAL REASONS (Duchess, BMI)—Sam Cooke—Keen 4002—This looks like a big one. It's registering solidly in all markets. Flip is "Desire Me," (Guild, BMI). A previous Billboard "Spotlight" pick.

THE BIG BEAT (Travis, BMI)

I WANT YOU TO KNOW (Commodore, BMI)—Fats Domino—Imperial 5477—This is the artist's strongest recently. It seems a two-sided winner. Both sides are much in demand. Good sales strength in all markets. A previous Billboard "Spotlight" pick.

RECENT POP RELEASES COMING UP STRONG

FOR SURVEY WEEK ENDING DECEMBER 7

The information given in this chart is based on actual sales to customers in a scientific sample of the nation's retail record outlets during the week ending on the date shown above. Sample design, sample size and all methods used in this continuing study of retail record sales are under the direct and continuing supervision and control of the School of Retailing of New York University.

You Can Make It, If You Try . . . . *Gene Allison*
(BMI) Vee Jay 713

Week in and week out you'll find more news, more record reviews, more advertising on the fast-moving record business in The Billboard, the communications center of the music industry.

Most Played by Jockeys

FOR SURVEY WEEK ENDING DECEMBER 7

SIDES are ranked in order of the greatest number of plays on disk jockey radio shows thruout the country. Results are based on The Billboard's weekly survey among the nation's disk jockeys. The reverse side of each record is also listed.

This Week		Last Week	Weeks on Chart
1.	**APRIL LOVE** (ASCAP)—Pat Boone When the Swallows Come Back to Capistrano (ASCAP)—Dot 15660	3	8
2.	**YOU SEND ME** (BMI)—Sam Cooke Summertime (ASCAP)—Keen 34013	1	7
3.	**KISSES SWEETER THAN WINE** (ASCAP)—Jimmie Rodgers Better Loved You'll Never Be (ASCAP)—Roulette 4031	6	5
4.	**ALL THE WAY** (ASCAP)—Frank Sinatra Chicago (ASCAP)—Cap 3793	4	8
5.	**JAILHOUSE ROCK** (BMI)—Elvis Presley Treat Me Nice (BMI)—Vic 7035	2	10
6.	**RAUNCHY** (BMI)—Bill Justis The Midnite Man (BMI)—Phillips International 3519	5	4
7.	**RAUNCHY** (BMI)—Ernie Freeman Puddin' (BMI)—Imperial 5474	13	3
8.	**PEGGY SUE** (BMI)—Buddy Holly Everyday (BMI)—Coral 61885	14	5
9.	**I'M AVAILABLE** (BMI)—Margie Rayburn If You Were (ASCAP)—Liberty 55102	16	6
10.	**SILHOUETTES** (BMI)—The Rays Daddy Cool (BMI)—Cameo 117	9	8
11.	**YOU SEND ME** (BMI)—Teresa Brewer Would I Were (ASCAP)—Coral 61898	11	6
12.	**MY SPECIAL ANGEL** (BMI)—Bobby Helms Standing at the End of My World (BMI)—Dec 30423	18	8
13.	**CHANCES ARE** (ASCAP)—Johnny Mathis The Twelfth of Never (ASCAP)—Col 40993	7	14
14.	**WAKE UP LITTLE SUSIE** (BMI)—Everly Brothers Maybe Tomorrow (BMI)—Cadence 1337	8	12
15.	**MELODIE D'AMOUR** (BMI)—Ames Brothers So Little Time (BMI)—Vic 7046	10	11
16.	**JUST BORN** (BMI)—Perry Como Ivy Rose (ASCAP)—Vic 7050	17	10
17.	**PUT A LIGHT IN THE WINDOW** (ASCAP)—Four Lads The Things We Did Last Summer (ASCAP)—Col 41058	15	2
18.	**LIECHTENSTEINER POLKA** (ASCAP)—Will Glahe Schweitzer Polka (BMI)—London 1755	—	1
19.	**RAUNCHY** (BMI)—Billy Vaughn Sail Along Silvery Moon (ASCAP)—Dot 15661	—	1
20.	**LITTLE BITTY PRETTY ONE** (BMI)—Thurston Harris I Hope You Won't Hold It Against Me (BMI)—Aladdin 3398	19	5
21.	**GREAT BALLS OF FIRE** (BMI)—Jerry Lee Lewis You Win Again (BMI)—Sun 281	20	2
22.	**WILD IS THE WIND** (ASCAP)—Johnny Mathis No Love (But Your Love) (BMI)—Col 41060	—	1
23.	**THE JOKER** (BMI)—Hilltoppers Chicken, Chicken (ASCAP)—Dot 15662	—	1
24.	**THE TWELFTH OF NEVER** (ASCAP)—Johnny Mathis Chances Are (ASCAP)—Col 40993	12	10
25.	**THE STORY OF MY LIFE** (ASCAP)—Marty Robbins Once-a-Week Date (BMI)—Col 41013	—	1
25.	**LOVE ME FOREVER** (BMI)—Four Esquires I Ain't Been Right Since You Left (ASCAP)—Paris 509	—	1

Top 100 Sides

NEW YORK UNIVERSITY SCHOOL OF RETAILING · THE BILLBOARD · STORE RECORDED SALES

FOR SURVEY WEEK ENDING DECEMBER 7

This is a tabulation of dealer unit sales listed according to the specific side requested by customers. No attempt is made to add sides together to reflect actual record sales. It is therefore a tabulation of sides or songs, and not records. This fact, together with longer four-week survey periods, explains variation between the top 30 sides as reflected in this chart, and top 30 record sellers as reflected in "Best Sellers in Stores."

Pos.	Song, Artist, Label	Last Week
1.	**YOU SEND ME,** Sam Cooke, Keen	1
2.	**JAILHOUSE ROCK,** Elvis Presley, Victor	1
3.	**RAUNCHY,** Bill Justis, Phillips International	5
4.	**WAKE UP LITTLE SUSIE,** Everly Brothers, Cadence	3
5.	**SILHOUETTES,** Rays, Cameo	4
6.	**APRIL LOVE**—Pat Boone, Dot	6
7.	**CHANCES ARE,** Johnny Mathis, Columbia	8
8.	**BE-BOP BABY,** Ricky Nelson, Imperial	7
9.	**ROCK AND ROLL MUSIC,** Chuck Berry, Chess	11
10.	**PEGGY SUE,** Buddy Holly, Coral	12
11.	**LITTLE BITTY PRETTY ONE,** Thurston Harris, Aladdin	9
12.	**MY SPECIAL ANGEL,** Bobby Helms, Decca	10
13.	**KISSES SWEETER THAN WINE,** Jimmie Rodgers, Roulette	14
14.	**GREAT BALLS OF FIRE,** Jerry Lee Lewis, Sun	19
15.	**RAUNCHY,** Ernie Freeman, Imperial	13
16.	**AT THE HOP,** Danny and the Juniors, ABC-Paramount	23
17.	**ALL THE WAY,** Frank Sinatra, Capitol	19
18.	**MELODIE D'AMOUR,** Ames Brothers, Victor	18
19.	**I'M AVAILABLE,** Margie Rayburn, Liberty	16
20.	**LIECHTENSTEINER POLKA,** Will Glahe, London	22
21.	**FASCINATION,** Jane Morgan, Kapp	15
22.	**HONEYCOMB,** Jimmie Rodgers, Roulette	17
23.	**TAMMY,** Debbie Reynolds, Coral	21
24.	**JUST BORN,** Perry Como, Victor	24
25.	**WHY DON'T THEY UNDERSTAND,** George Hamilton IV, ABC-Paramount	36
26.	**OH BOY,** Crickets, Brunswick	34
27.	**BONY MORONIE,** Larry Williams, Specialty	27
28.	**COULD THIS BE MAGIC,** Dubs, Gone	27
29.	**KEEP A' KNOCKIN',** Little Richard, Specialty	26
30.	**THE JOKER,** Billy Myles, Ember	30
31.	**HULA LOVE,** Buddy Knox, Roulette	27
32.	**HAPPY, HAPPY BIRTHDAY, BABY,** Tune Weavers, Checker	25
33.	**TILL,** Roger Williams, Kapp	31
34.	**BUZZ, BUZZ, BUZZ,** Hollywood Flames, Ebb	46
34.	**TEARDROPS,** Lee Andrews and the Hearts, Chess	37
36.	**YOU SEND ME,** Teresa Brewer, Coral	31
37.	**IVY ROSE,** Perry Como, Victor	37
38.	**PEANUTS,** Little Joe and the Thrillers, Okeh	42
39.	**ALONE,** Shepherd Sisters, Lance	35
40.	**THE STORY OF MY LIFE,** Marty Robbins, Columbia	49
41.	**THAT'LL BE THE DAY,** Crickets, Brunswick	42
42.	**BLACK SLACKS,** Joe Bennett and the Sparkletones, ABC-Paramount	58
42.	**I'LL REMEMBER TODAY,** Patti Page, Mercury	39
44.	**WITH YOU ON MY MIND,** Nat King Cole, Capitol	47
45.	**BACK TO SCHOOL AGAIN,** Timmy Rodgers, Cameo	47
46.	**LOTTA LOVIN',** Gene Vincent, Capitol	42
46.	**AND THAT REMINDS ME,** Della Reese, Jubilee	41
46.	**WHOLE LOTTA SHAKIN' GOIN' ON,** Jerry Lee Lewis, Sun	51
49.	**WUN'ERFUL, WUN'ERFUL,** Stan Freberg, Capitol	40
50.	**SWANEE RIVER ROCK (TALKIN' 'BOUT THAT RIVER),** Ray Charles, Atlantic	42
51.	**WAIT AND SEE,** Fats Domino, Imperial	50
52.	**YOU BUG ME, BABY,** Larry Williams, Specialty	54
53.	**SOFT,** Bill Doggett, King	53
54.	**LOVE ME FOREVER,** Four Esquires, Paris	55
55.	**PLAYTHING,** Nick Todd, Dot	55
55.	**RAUNCHY,** Billy Vaughn, Dot	69
57.	**DIANA,** Paul Anka, ABC-Paramount	51
57.	**THE JOKER,** Hilltoppers, Dot	66
59.	**PRETEND YOU DON'T SEE HER,** Jerry Vale, Columbia	69
60.	**RAINBOW,** Russ Hamilton, Kapp	58
61.	**DANCE TO THE BOP,** Gene Vincent, Capitol	83
61.	**LITTLE BITTY PRETTY ONE,** Bobby Day, Class	61
63.	**FRAULEIN,** Bobby Helms, Decca	60
64.	**HONEST I DO,** Jimmy Reed, Vee Jay	55
64.	**MR. LEE,** Bobbettes, Atlantic	74
66.	**THE TWELFTH OF NEVER,** Johnny Mathis, Columbia	62
67.	**AROUND THE WORLD,** Mantovani, London	76
68.	**AN AFFAIR TO REMEMBER,** Vic Damone, Columbia	62
68.	**LIECHTENSTEINER POLKA,** Lawrence Welk, Coral	80
68.	**NERVOUS BOOGIE,** Paul Gayten, Argo	69
68.	**PUT A LIGHT IN THE WINDOW,** Four Lads, Columbia	91
68.	**REET PETITE,** Jackie Wilson, Brunswick	64
73.	**PARTY TIME,** Sal Mineo, Epic	66
74.	**MY ONE SIN,** Four Coins, Epic	69
74.	**SEND FOR ME,** Nat King Cole, Capitol	74
76.	**AROUND THE WORLD,** Victor Young, Decca	78
76.	**REMEMBER YOU'RE MINE,** Pat Boone, Dot	69
78.	**WHITE CHRISTMAS,** Bing Crosby, Decca	—
79.	**DEEP PURPLE,** Billy Ward, Liberty	84
79.	**FRAULEIN,** Steve Lawrence, Coral	66
79.	**SILHOUETTES,** Diamonds, Mercury	86
79.	**WILD IS THE WIND,** Johnny Mathis, Columbia	—
83.	**MOONLIGHT SWIM,** Tony Perkins, Victor	76
83.	**YOU CAN MAKE IT IF YOU TRY,** Gene Allison, Vee Jay	—
85.	**THE CREATURE,** Buchanan & Ancell, Flying Saucer	89
86.	**AROUND THE WORLD,** Bing Crosby, Decca	90
86.	**LOVE ME FOREVER,** Eydie Gorme, ABC-Paramount	—
86.	**REBEL,** Carol Jarvis, Dot	82
86.	**TREAT ME NICE,** Elvis Presley, Victor	84
86.	**THAT'S ALL I WANT FROM YOU,** Silva-Tones, Argo	—
91.	**IN THE MIDDLE OF AN ISLAND,** Tony Bennett, Columbia	64
91.	**IT'S NOT FOR ME TO SAY,** Johnny Mathis, Columbia	96
91.	**THAT'S WHY I WAS BORN,** Janice Harper, Prep	—
94.	**DEEP BLUE SEA,** Jimmy Dean, Columbia	88
94.	**LOVE LETTERS IN THE SAND,** Pat Boone, Dot	96
94.	**ONLY BECAUSE,** Platters, Mercury	80
97.	**CA C'EST L'AMOUR,** Tony Bennett, Columbia	96
97.	**JUST BETWEEN YOU AND ME,** Chordettes, Cadence	100
97.	**I LOVE YOU BABY,** Paul Anka, ABC-Paramount	—
97.	**THINK,** Five Royals, King	—

Best Sellers in Stores

The information given in this chart is based on actual sales to customers in a scientific sample of the nation's retail record outlets during the week ending on the date shown above. Sample design, sample size, and all methods used in this continuing study of retail record sales are under the direct and continuing supervision and control of the School of Retailing of New York University.

FOR SURVEY WEEK ENDING DECEMBER 14, 1957

This Week	Record	Last Week	Weeks on Chart
1.	APRIL LOVE (ASCAP)—Pat Boone; WHEN THE SWALLOWS COME BACK TO CAPISTRANO (ASCAP)—Dot 15660	4	8
2.	AT THE HOP (BMI)—Danny and the Juniors; Sometimes (BMI)—ABC-Paramount 9871	5	3
3.	JAILHOUSE ROCK (BMI)—Elvis Presley; TREAT ME NICE (BMI)—Vic 7035	1	11
4.	RAUNCHY (BMI)—Bill Justis; The Midnite Man (BMI)—Phillips International 3519	2	6
5.	YOU SEND ME (BMI)—Sam Cooke; SUMMERTIME (ASCAP)—Keen 34013	3	9
6.	PEGGY SUE (BMI)—Buddy Holly; Everyday (BMI)—Coral 61885	7	7
7.	GREAT BALLS OF FIRE (BMI)—Jerry Lee Lewis; You Win Again (BMI)—Sun 281	6	4
8.	KISSES SWEETER THAN WINE (BMI)—Jimmie Rodgers; Better Loved You'll Never Be (ASCAP)—Roulette 4031	12	5
9.	CHANCES ARE (ASCAP)—Johnny Mathis; THE TWELFTH OF NEVER (ASCAP)—Col 40993	8	14
10.	ROCK AND ROLL MUSIC (BMI)—Chuck Berry; Blue Feeling (BMI)—Chess 1671	9	7
11.	SILHOUETTES (BMI)—The Rays; Daddy Cool (BMI)—Cameo 117	11	10
12.	RAUNCHY (BMI)—Ernie Freeman; Puddin' (BMI)—Imperial 5474	17	6
13.	MY SPECIAL ANGEL (BMI)—Bobby Helms; Standing at the End of My World (BMI)—Dec 30423	14	10
14.	WAKE UP LITTLE SUSIE (BMI)—Everly Brothers; Maybe Tomorrow (BMI)—Cadence 1337	10	13
15.	BONY MORONIE (BMI)—Larry Williams; YOU BUG ME, BABY (BMI)—Specialty 615	21	7
16.	BE-BOP BABY (BMI)—Ricky Nelson; HAVE I TOLD YOU LATELY THAT I LOVE YOU (BMI)—Imperial 5468	13	12
17.	ALL THE WAY (ASCAP)—Frank Sinatra; CHICAGO (ASCAP)—Capitol 3793	19	7
18.	JUST BORN (BMI)—Perry Como; IVY ROSE (ASCAP)—Vic 7050	18	9
19.	MELODIE D'AMOUR (BMI)—Ames Brothers; So Little Time (BMI)—Vic 7046	20	11
20.	WHY DON'T THEY UNDERSTAND? (BMI)—George Hamilton IV; Even Tho' (BMI)—ABC-Paramount 9862	22	4
21.	OH, BOY (BMI)—Crickets; Not Fade Away (BMI)—Brunswick 55035	26	4
22.	LIECHTENSTEINER POLKA (ASCAP)—Will Glahe; Schweitzer Polka (BMI)—London 1755	16	6
23.	I'M AVAILABLE (BMI)—Margie Rayburn; If You Were (ASCAP)—Liberty 55102	25	7
24.	BUZZ, BUZZ, BUZZ (BMI)—Hollywood Flames; Crazy (BMI)—Ebb 119	29	4
25.	I'LL COME RUNNING BACK TO YOU (BMI)—Sam Cooke; FOREVER (BMI)—Specialty 619	—	1
26.	LITTLE BITTY PRETTY ONE (BMI)—Thurston Harris; I Hope You Won't Hold It Against Me (ASCAP)—Aladdin 3308	15	9
27.	HONEYCOMB (ASCAP)—Jimmie Rodgers; Their Hearts Were Full of Spring (ASCAP)—Roulette 4015	23	19
28.	TEARDROPS (BMI)—Lee Andrews and the Hearts; Girl Around the Corner (BMI)—Chess 1675	28	4
29.	FASCINATION (ASCAP)—Jane Morgan; Fascination (Instrumental) (ASCAP)—Kapp 191	24	16
30.	TAMMY (ASCAP)—Debbie Reynolds; French Heels (ASCAP)—Coral 61851	27	22
31.	WILD IS THE WIND (ASCAP)—Johnny Mathis; NO LOVE (BUT YOUR LOVE) (BMI)—Col 41060	30	2
32.	THE JOKER (BMI)—Billy Myles; Honey Bee (BMI)—Ember 1026	34	5
33.	RAUNCHY (BMI)—Billy Vaughn; SAIL ALONG SILVERY MOON (ASCAP)—Dot 15661	—	1
34.	THE JOKER (BMI)—Hilltoppers; Chicken, Chicken (ASCAP)—Dot 15662	—	1
35.	THE BIG BEAT (BMI)—Fats Domino; I Want You to Know (BMI)—Imperial 5477	—	1
36.	WHITE CHRISTMAS (ASCAP)—Bing Crosby; God Rest Ye Merry, Gentlemen (ASCAP)—Dec 23778	50	2
37.	THE STORY OF MY LIFE (ASCAP)—Marty Robbins; Once-a-Week Date (BMI)—Col 41013	41	4
38.	KEEP A' KNOCKIN' (BMI)—Little Richard; Can't Believe You Wanna Leave—Specialty 611	31	12
39.	PUT A LIGHT IN THE WINDOW (ASCAP)—Four Lads; The Things We Did Last Summer (ASCAP)—Col 41058	39	2
40.	COULD THIS BE MAGIC? (BMI)—Dubs; Such Lovin' (BMI)—Gone 5011	40	7
41.	JINGLE BELL ROCK (ASCAP)—Bobby Helms; Captain Santa Claus (ASCAP)—Dec 30513	—	1
41.	SANTA AND THE SATELLITE (BMI)—Buchanan and Goodman; Part 2 (BMI)—Luniverse 107	—	1
43.	TILL (ASCAP)—Roger Williams; Big Town (ASCAP)—Kapp 197	33	7
44.	HARD TIMES (THE SLOP) (BMI)—Noble (Thin Man) Watts; I'm Walkin' the Floor Over You (BMI)—Baton 249	—	1
45.	BLACK SLACKS (BMI)—Joe Bennett & Sparkletones; Boppin' Rock Boogie (BMI)—ABC-Paramount 9837	32	11
46.	YOU SEND ME (BMI)—Teresa Brewer; Would I Were (ASCAP)—Coral 61898	42	6
47.	HAPPY, HAPPY BIRTHDAY, BABY (BMI)—Tune Weavers; Ol' Man River (ASCAP)—Checker 872	35	14
48.	PEANUTS (BMI)—Little Joe & the Thrillers; Lilly Lou (BMI)—Okeh 7088	36	12
49.	DANCE TO THE BOP (BMI)—Gene Vincent; I Got It (BMI)—Cap 3839	44	3
50.	AROUND THE WORLD (ASCAP)—Bing Crosby; (INSTRUMENTAL) (ASCAP)—	—	13

THIS WEEK'S BEST BUYS

Special telephone reports indicate these recent releases have broken out in one or more key areas and have excellent potential for placing on The Billboard's best seller charts.

PENNY LOAFERS AND BOBBY SOCKS (Pamco, BMI)—Joe Bennett & the Sparkeltones—(ABC-Paramount 9867)—Sales are leaping in all marts. It looks like a loot platter. Flip is "Rocket" (Pamco, BMI). A previous Billboard "Spotlight" pick.

THE STROLL (Meridian, BMI)—The Diamonds—Mercury 71242—This is the biggest by the crew in several tries. Sales are strong in all markets. Flip is "Land of Beauty" (Pure, BMI). A previous Billboard "Spotlight" pick.

SUGARTIME (Nor-Va-Jak, BMI)—The McGuire Sisters—Coral 61924—Signs are that this will be a big one. Action is heavy in all markets. Flip is "Banana Split" (Rosemeadow, BMI). A previous Billboard "Spotlight" pick.

RECENT POP RELEASES COMING UP STRONG

FOR SURVEY WEEK ENDING DECEMBER 14

The information given in this chart is based on actual sales to customers in a scientific sample of the nation's retail record outlets during the week ending on the date shown above. Sample design, sample size and all methods used in this continuing study of retail record sales are under the direct and continuing supervision and control of the School of Retailing of New York University.

Penny Loafers and Bobby Socks . . . . *Joe Bennett and the Sparkletones*
(BMI) ABC-Paramount 9867

You Can Make It, If You Try . . . . *Gene Allison*
(BMI) Vee Jay 713

Most Played by Jockeys

FOR SURVEY WEEK ENDING DECEMBER 14

SIDES are ranked in order of the greatest number of plays on disk jockey radio shows thruout the country. Results are based on The Billboard's weekly survey among the nation's disk jockeys. The reverse side of each record is also listed.

This Week		Last Week	Weeks on Chart
1.	APRIL LOVE (ASCAP)—Pat Boone When the Swallows Come Back to Capistrano (ASCAP)—Dot 15660	1	9
2.	YOU SEND ME (BMI)—Sam Cooke Summertime (ASCAP)—Keen 34013	2	8
3.	ALL THE WAY (ASCAP)—Frank Sinatra Chicago (ASCAP)—Cap 3793	4	9
4.	KISSES SWEETER THAN WINE (BMI)—Jimmie Rodgers Better Loved You'll Never Be (ASCAP)—Roulette 4031	3	6
5.	JAILHOUSE ROCK (BMI)—Elvis Presley Treat Me Nice (BMI)—Vic 7035	5	11
6.	RAUNCHY (BMI)—Bill Justis The Midnite Man (BMI)—Phillips International 3519	6	5
7.	RAUNCHY (BMI)—Ernie Freeman Puddin' (BMI)—Imperial 5474	7	4
8.	PEGGY SUE (BMI)—Buddy Holly Everyday (BMI)—Coral 61885	8	6
9.	YOU SEND ME (BMI)—Teresa Brewer Would I Were (ASCAP)—Coral 61898	11	7
10.	RAUNCHY (BMI)—Billy Vaughn Sail Along Silvery Moon (ASCAP)—Dot 15661	19	2
11.	CHANCES ARE (ASCAP)—Johnny Mathis The Twelfth of Never (ASCAP)—Col 40993	13	15
12.	PUT A LIGHT IN THE WINDOW (ASCAP)—Four Lads The Things We Did Last Summer (ASCAP)—Col 41058	17	3
13.	I'M AVAILABLE (BMI)—Margie Rayburn If You Were (ASCAP)—Liberty 55102	9	7
14.	GREAT BALLS OF FIRE (BMI)—Jerry Lee Lewis You Win Again (BMI)—Sun 281	21	3
15.	SILHOUETTES (BMI)—Diamonds Daddy Cool (BMI)—Mercury 71197	—	7
16.	AT THE HOP (BMI)—Danny and the Juniors Sometimes (BMI)—ABC-Paramount 9871	—	1
17.	MY SPECIAL ANGEL (BMI)—Bobby Helms Standing at the End of My World (BMI)—Dec 30423	12	9
18.	SILHOUETTES (BMI)—The Rays Daddy Cool (BMI)—Cameo 117	10	9
19.	THE TWELFTH OF NEVER (ASCAP)— Chances Are (ASCAP)—Col 40993	24	11
20.	MELODIE D'AMOUR (BMI)—Ames Brothers So Little Time (BMI)—Vic 7046	15	12
21.	OH, BOY! (BMI)—Crickets Not Fade Away (BMI)—Brunswick 55035	—	1
22.	THE STORY OF MY LIFE (ASCAP)—Marty Robbins Once-A-Week Date (BMI)—Col 41013	25	2
23.	JUST BORN (BMI)—Perry Como Ivy Rose (ASCAP)—Vic 7050	16	11
24.	JINGLE BELL ROCK (ASCAP)—Bobby Helms Captain Santa Claus (ASCAP)—Dec 30513	—	1
25.	THE JOKER (BMI)—Hilltoppers Chicken, Chicken (ASCAP)—Dot 15662	23	2

Top 100 Sides

FOR SURVEY WEEK ENDING DECEMBER 14

This is a tabulation of dealer unit sales listed according to the specific side requested by customers. No attempt is made to add sides together to reflect actual record sales. It is therefore a tabulation of sides or songs, and not records. This fact, together with longer four-week survey periods, explains variation between the top 30 sides as reflected in this chart, and top 30 record sellers as reflected in "Best Sellers in Stores."

Pos.	Song, Artist, Label	Last Week
1.	**YOU SEND ME,** Sam Cooke. Keen	1
2.	**JAILHOUSE ROCK,** Elvis Presley, Victor	2
3.	**RAUNCHY,** Bill Justis, Phillips International	3
4.	**APRIL LOVE,** Pat Boone, Dot	6
5.	**PEGGY SUE,** Buddy Holly, Coral	10
6.	**AT THE HOP,** Danny and the Juniors, ABC-Paramount	16
7.	**SILHOUETTES,** Rays, Cameo	5
8.	**ROCK AND ROLL MUSIC,** Chuck Berry, Chess	9
9.	**GREAT BALLS OF FIRE,** Jerry Lee Lewis, Sun	14
10.	**WAKE UP LITTLE SUSIE,** Everly Brothers, Cadence	4
11.	**CHANCES ARE,** Johnny Mathis, Columbia	7
12.	**KISSES SWEETER THAN WINE,** Jimmie Rodgers, Roulette	13
13.	**BE-BOP BABY,** Ricky Nelson, Imperial	8
14.	**MY SPECIAL ANGEL,** Bobby Helms, Decca	12
15.	**RAUNCHY,** Ernie Freeman, Imperial	15
16.	**LITTLE BITTY PRETTY ONE,** Thurston Harris, Aladdin	11
17.	**ALL THE WAY,** Frank Sinatra, Capitol	17
18.	**MELODIE D'AMOUR,** Ames Brothers, Victor	18
19.	**LIECHTENSTEINER POLKA,** Will Glahe, London	20
20.	**I'M AVAILABLE,** Margie Rayburn, Liberty	19
21.	**WHY DON'T THEY UNDERSTAND?** George Hamilton IV, ABC-Paramount	25
22.	**HONEYCOMB,** Jimmie Rodgers, Roulette	22
23.	**BONY MORONIE,** Larry Williams, Specialty	27
23.	**OH BOY,** Crickets, Brunswick	26
25.	**FASCINATION,** Jane Morgan, Kapp	21
26.	**JUST BORN,** Perry Como, Victor	24
27.	**TAMMY,** Debbie Reynolds, Coral	23
28.	**BUZZ, BUZZ, BUZZ,** Hollywood Flames, Ebb	34
29.	**TEARDROPS,** Lee Andrews and the Hearts, Chess	34
30.	**THE JOKER,** Billy Myles, Ember	30
31.	**KEEP A' KNOCKIN',** Little Richard, Specialty	29
32.	**IVY ROSE,** Perry Como, Victor	37
33.	**THE STORY OF MY LIFE,** Marty Robbins, Columbia	40
34.	**COULD THIS BE MAGIC?** Dubs, Gone	28
35.	**TILL,** Roger Williams, Kapp	33
36.	**HULA LOVE,** Buddy Knox, Roulette	31
37.	**THE JOKER,** Hilltoppers, Dot	57
38.	**HAPPY, HAPPY BIRTHDAY, BABY,** Tune Weavers, Checker	32
38.	**I'LL COME RUNNING BACK TO YOU,** Sam Cooke, Specialty	—
38.	**YOU SEND ME,** Teresa Brewer, Coral	36
41.	**PUT A LIGHT IN THE WINDOW,** Four Lads, Columbia	68
42.	**WHITE CHRISTMAS,** Bing Crosby, Decca	78
43.	**DANCE TO THE BOP,** Gene Vincent, Capitol	61
43.	**I'LL REMEMBER TODAY,** Patti Page, Mercury	42
45.	**ALONE,** Shepherd Sisters, Lance	39
45.	**PEANUTS,** Little Joe and the Thrillers, Okeh	38
45.	**YOU BUG ME, BABY,** Larry Williams, Specialty	52
48.	**BLACK SOCKS,** Joe Bennett and the Sparkletones, ABC-Paramount	42
48.	**RAUNCHY,** Billy Vaughn, Dot	55
50.	**WUN'ERFUL, WUN'ERFUL,** Stan Freberg, Capitol	49
51.	**WILD IS THE WIND,** Johnny Mathis, Columbia	79
51.	**TWELFTH OF NEVER,** Johnny Mathis, Columbia	66
53.	**THE BIG BEAT,** Fats Domino, Imperial	—
53.	**WITH YOU ON MY MIND,** Nat King Cole, Capitol	44
55.	**PRETEND YOU DON'T SEE HER,** Jerry Vale, Columbia	59
55.	**THAT'LL BE THE DAY,** Crickets, Brunswick	41
55.	**WAIT AND SEE,** Fats Domino, Imperial	51
58.	**FRAULEIN,** Bobby Helms, Decca	63
58.	**LOVE ME FOREVER,** Four Esquires, Paris	54
58.	**AND THAT REMINDS ME,** Della Reese, Jubilee	46
61.	**BACK TO SCHOOL AGAIN,** Timmy Rodgers, Cameo	45
62.	**LIECHTENSTEINER POLKA,** Lawrence Welk, Coral	68
62.	**NO LOVE (BUT YOUR LOVE),** Johnny Mathis, Columbia	—
64.	**LITTLE BITTY PRETTY ONE,** Bobby Day, Class	61
64.	**SOFT,** Billy Doggett, King	53
66.	**SWANEE RIVER ROCK (TALKIN' 'BOUT THAT RIVER),** Ray Charles, Atlantic	50
67.	**JINGLE BELL ROCK,** Bobby Helms, Decca	—
67.	**MR. LEE,** Bobbettes, Atlantic	64
67.	**REET PETITE,** Jackie Wilson, Brunswick	68
67.	**SANTA AND THE SATELLITE,** Buchanan and Goodman, Luniverse	—
71.	**HARD TIMES (THE SLOP),** Noble (Thin Man) Watts, Baton	—
71.	**WHOLE LOTTA SHAKIN' GOIN' ON,** Jerry Lee Lewis, Sun	46
73.	**AROUND THE WORLD,** Mantovani, London	67
73.	**DIANA,** Paul Anka, ABC-Paramount	57
75.	**LOTTA LOVIN',** Gene Vincent, Capitol	46
75.	**RAINBOW,** Russ Hamilton, Kapp	60
77.	**YOU CAN MAKE IT IF YOU TRY,** Gene Allison, Vee Jay	83
77.	**HONEST I DO,** Jimmy Reed, Vee Jay	64
79.	**HEY SCHOOLGIRL,** Tom and Jerry, Big	—
79.	**SILHOUETTES,** Diamonds, Mercury	79
81.	**PLAYTHING,** Nick Todd, Dot	55
82.	**AN AFFAIR TO REMEMBER,** Vic Damone, Columbia	68
83.	**SAIL ALONG SILVERY MOON,** Billy Vaughn, Dot	—
84.	**AROUND THE WORLD,** Bing Crosby, Decca	86
84.	**NERVOUS BOOGIE,** Paul Gayten, Argo	68
84.	**PARTY TIME,** Sal Mineo, Epic	73
84.	**THAT'S WHY I WAS BORN,** Janice Harper, Prep	91
88.	**AROUND THE WORLD,** Victor Young, Decca	76
89.	**PENNY LOAFERS AND BOBBY SOCKS,** Joe Bennett and the Sparkletones, ABC-Paramount	—
90.	**THE CREATURE,** Buchanan and Ancell, Flying Saucer	85
90.	**MY ONE SIN,** Four Coins, Epic	74
90.	**FOREVER,** Sam Cooke, Keen	—
93.	**LOVE ME FOREVER,** Eydie Gorme, ABC-Paramount	86
93.	**LIPS OF WINE,** Andy Williams, Cadence	—
93.	**THAT'S ALL I WANT FROM YOU,** Silva-Tones, Argo	86
96.	**IN THE MIDDLE OF AN ISLAND,** Tony Bennett, Columbia	91
96.	**MOONLIGHT SWIM,** Tony Perkins, Victor	83
96.	**REMEMBER YOU'RE MINE,** Pat Boone, Dot	76
99.	**LITTLE SANDY SLEIGHFOOT,** Jimmy Dean, Columbia	—
99.	**LOVE LETTERS IN THE SAND,** Pat Boone, Dot	94

Best Sellers in Stores

STORE RECORDED SALES — NEW YORK UNIVERSITY SCHOOL OF RETAILING — THE BILLBOARD

The information given in this chart is based on actual sales to customers in a scientific sample of the nation's retail record outlets during the week ending on the date shown above. Sample design, sample size, and all methods used in this continuing study of retail record sales are under the direct and continuing supervision and control of the School of Retailing of New York University

FOR SURVEY WEEK ENDING DECEMBER 21, 1957

This Week		Last Week	Weeks on Chart
1.	APRIL LOVE (ASCAP)—Pat Boone When the Swallows Come Back to Capistrano (ASCAP)—Dot 15660	1	9
2.	AT THE HOP (BMI)—Danny and the Juniors Sometimes (BMI)—ABC-Paramount 9871	2	4
3.	PEGGY SUE (BMI)—Buddy Holly Everyday (BMI)—Coral 61885	6	8
4.	GREAT BALLS OF FIRE (BMI)—Jerry Lee Lewis You Win Again (BMI)—Sun 281	7	5
5.	RAUNCHY (BMI)—Bill Justis The Midnite Man (BMI)—Phillips International 3519	4	7
6.	JAILHOUSE ROCK (BMI)—Elvis Presley TREAT ME NICE (BMI)—Vic 7035	3	12
7.	YOU SEND ME (BMI)—Sam Cooke SUMMERTIME (ASCAP)—Keen 34013	5	10
8.	KISSES SWEETER THAN WINE (BMI)—Jimmie Rodgers Better Loved You'll Never Be (ASCAP)—Roulette 4031	8	6
9.	SILHOUETTES (BMI)—The Rays Daddy Cool (BMI)—Cameo 117	11	11
10.	ROCK AND ROLL MUSIC (BMI)—Chuck Berry Blue Feeling (BMI)—Chess 1671	10	8
11.	CHANCES ARE (ASCAP)—Johnny Mathis THE TWELFTH OF NEVER (ASCAP)—Col 40993	9	15
12.	WAKE UP LITTLE SUSIE (BMI)—Everly Brothers Maybe Tomorrow (BMI)—Cadence 1337	14	14
13.	RAUNCHY (BMI)—Ernie Freeman Puddin' (BMI)—Imperial 5474	12	7
14.	BONY MORONIE (BMI)—Larry Williams YOU BUG ME, BABY (BMI)—Specialty 615	15	8
15.	ALL THE WAY (ASCAP)—Frank Sinatra CHICAGO (ASCAP)—Cap 3793	17	8
16.	OH, BOY! (BMI)—Crickets Not Fade Away (BMI)—Brunswick 55035	21	5
17.	BE-BOP BABY (BMI)—Ricky Nelson HAVE I TOLD YOU LATELY THAT I LOVE YOU? (BMI)—Imperial 5463	16	13
18.	MY SPECIAL ANGEL (BMI)—Bobby Helms Standing at the End of My World (BMI)—Dec 30423	13	11
19.	MELODIE D'AMOUR (BMI)—Ames Brothers So Little Time (BMI)—Vic 7046	19	12
20.	TEARDROPS (BMI)—Lee Andrews and the Hearts Girl Around the Corner (BMI)—Chess 1675	28	5
21.	BUZZ, BUZZ, BUZZ (BMI)—Hollywood Flames Crazy (BMI)—Ebb 119	24	5
22.	STOOD UP (BMI)—Ricky Nelson WAITIN' IN SCHOOL (BMI)—Imperial 5483	—	1
23.	WHY DON'T THEY UNDERSTAND? (BMI)—George Hamilton IV Even Tho' (BMI)—ABC-Paramount 9862	20	5
24.	JUST BORN (BMI)—Perry Como IVY ROSE (ASCAP)—Vic 7050	18	10
25.	JINGLE BELL ROCK (ASCAP)—Bobby Helms Captain Santa Claus (ASCAP)—Dec 30513	41	2
26.	HONEYCOMB (ASCAP)—Jimmie Rodgers Their Hearts Were Full of Spring (ASCAP)—Roulette 4015	27	20
27.	LIECHTENSTEINER POLKA (ASCAP)—Will Glahe Schweitzer Polka (BMI)—London 1755	22	7
28.	I'M AVAILABLE (BMI)—Margie Rayburn If You Were (ASCAP)—Liberty 55102	23	8
29.	THE BIG BEAT (BMI)—Fats Domino I WANT YOU TO KNOW (BMI)—Imperial 5477	35	2
30.	I'LL COME RUNNING BACK TO YOU (BMI)—Sam Cooke FOREVER (BMI)—Specialty 619	25	2
31.	WILD IS THE WIND (ASCAP)—Johnny Mathis NO LOVE (BUT YOUR LOVE) (BMI)—Col 41060	31	3
32.	LITTLE BITTY PRETTY ONE Thurston Harris I Hope You Won't Hold It Against Me (ASCAP)—Aladdin 3398	26	10
33.	RAUNCHY (BMI)—Billy Vaughn SAIL ALONG SILVERY MOON (ASCAP)—Dot 15661	33	2
34.	FASCINATION (ASCAP)—Jane Morgan Fascination (Instrumental) (ASCAP)—Kapp 191	29	17
35.	THE JOKER (BMI)—Billy Myles Honey Bee (BMI)—Ember 1026	32	6
36.	SANTA AND THE SATELLITE (BMI)—Buchanan and Goodman Part 2 (BMI)—Luniverse 107	41	2
37.	TAMMY (ASCAP)—Debbie Reynolds French Heels (ASCAP)—Coral 61851	30	23
38.	THE STORY OF MY LIFE (ASCAP)—Marty Robbins Once-a-Week Date (BMI)—Col 41013	37	5
39.	PUT A LIGHT IN THE WINDOW (ASCAP)—Four Lads The Things We Did Last Summer (ASCAP)—Col 41058	39	3
40.	COULD THIS BE MAGIC? (BMI)—Dubs Such Lovin' (BMI)—Gone 5011	40	8
41.	WHITE CHRISTMAS (ASCAP)—Bing Crosby God Rest Ye Merry, Gentlemen (ASCAP)—Dec 23778	36	3
42.	PENNY LOAFERS AND BOBBY SOCKS (BMI)—Joe Bennett and Sparkletones Rocket (BMI)—ABC-Paramount 9867	—	1
43.	THE JOKER (BMI)—Hilltoppers Chicken, Chicken (ASCAP)—Dot 15662	34	2
44.	LITTLE SANDY SLEIGHFOOT—Jimmy Dean When They Ring the Golden Bells—Col 41025	—	1
45.	TILL (ASCAP)—Roger Williams Big Town (ASCAP)—Kapp 197	43	8
46.	HARD TIMES (THE SLOP) (BMI)—Noble (Thin Man) Watts I'm Walkin' the Floor Over You (BMI)—Baton 249	44	2
47.	DANCE TO THE BOP (BMI)—Gene Vincent I Got It (BMI)—Cap 3839	49	4
48.	HEY! LITTLE GIRL (BMI)—Techniques In a Round About Way (BMI)—Roulette 4030	—	1
49.	YOU SEND ME (BMI)—Teresa Brewer Would I Were (ASCAP)—Coral 61898	46	7
50.	(I LOVE YOU) FOR SENTIMENTAL REASONS (BMI)—Sam Cooke DESIRE ME (BMI)—Keen 4002	—	1

THIS WEEK'S BEST BUYS

Special telephone reports indicate these recent releases have broken out in one or more key areas and have excellent potential for placing on The Billboard's best seller charts.

LA DEE DAH (Conley, BMI)—Billy & Lillie—(Swan 4002)—This is a big one. Sales are jumping in all of the major marts. Flip is "The Monster" (Conley, BMI). A previous Billboard "Spotlight" pick.

A VERY SPECIAL LOVE (Korwin, ASCAP)—Johnny Nash—(ABC-Paramount 9874). The platter has been out for a while, but sales have been building gradually. Action at this point in most of the top markets is strong. Flip is "Won't You Let Me Share My Love" (Rayven, BMI). A previous Billboard "Spotlight" pick.

RECENT POP RELEASES COMING UP STRONG

STORE RECORDED SALES — NEW YORK UNIVERSITY SCHOOL OF RETAILING — THE BILLBOARD

FOR SURVEY WEEK ENDING DECEMBER 21

The information given in this chart is based on actual sales to customers in a scientific sample of the nation's retail record outlets during the week ending on the date shown above. Sample design, sample size and all methods used in this continuing study of retail record sales are under the direct and continuing supervision and control of the School of Retailing of New York University.

A Very Special Love . . . . *Johnny Nash*
(ASCAP) ABC-Paramount 9874

You Can Make It, If You Try . . . . *Gene Allison*
(BMI) Vee Jay 713

Most Played by Jockeys

FOR SURVEY WEEK ENDING DECEMBER 21

SIDES are ranked in order of the greatest number of plays on disk jockey radio shows thruout the country. Results are based on The Billboard's weekly survey among the nation's disk jockeys. The reverse side of each record is also listed.

This Week		Last Week	Weeks on Chart
1.	APRIL LOVE (ASCAP)—Pat Boone When the Swallows Come Back to Capistrano (ASCAP)—Dot 15660	1	10
2.	YOU SEND ME (BMI)—Sam Cooke Summertime (ASCAP)—Keen 34013	2	9
3.	ALL THE WAY (ASCAP)—Frank Sinatra Chicago (ASCAP)—Cap 3793	3	10
4.	KISSES SWEETER THAN WINE (BMI)—Jimmie Rodgers Better Loved You'll Never Be (ASCAP)—Roulette 4031	4	7
5.	RAUNCHY (BMI)—Bill Justis The Midnite Man (BMI)—Phillips International 3519	6	6
6.	JAILHOUSE ROCK (BMI)—Elvis Presley Treat Me Nice (BMI)—Vic 7035	5	12
7.	RAUNCHY (BMI)—Ernie Freeman Puddin' (BMI)—Imperial 5474	7	5
8.	PEGGY SUE (BMI)—Buddy Holly Everyday (BMI)—Coral 61885	8	7
9.	YOU SEND ME (BMI)—Teresa Brewer Would I Were (ASCAP)—Coral 61898	9	8
10.	CHANCES ARE (ASCAP)—Johnny Mathis The Twelfth of Never (ASCAP)—Col 40993	11	16
11.	RAUNCHY (BMI)—Billy Vaughn Sail Along Silvery Moon (ASCAP)—Dot 15661	10	3
12.	PUT A LIGHT IN THE WINDOW (ASCAP)—Four Lads The Things We Did Last Summer (ASCAP)—Col 41058	12	4
13.	I'M AVAILABLE (BMI)—Margie Rayburn If You Were (ASCAP)—Liberty 55102	13	8
14.	GREAT BALLS OF FIRE (BMI)—Jerry Lee Lewis You Win Again (BMI)—Sun 281	14	4
15.	AT THE HOP (BMI)—Danny and the Juniors Sometimes (BMI)—ABC-Paramount 9871	16	2
16.	SILHOUETTES (BMI)—The Rays Daddy Cool (BMI)—Cameo 117	18	10
17.	THE TWELFTH OF NEVER (ASCAP)—Johnny Mathis Chances Are (ASCAP)—Col 40993	19	12
18.	SILHOUETTES (BMI)—Diamonds Daddy Cool (BMI)—Mercury 71197	15	8
19.	MY SPECIAL ANGEL (BMI)—Bobby Helms Standing at the End of My World (BMI)—Dec 30423	17	10
20.	OH, BOY! (BMI)—Crickets Not Fade Away (BMI)—Brunswick 55035	21	2
21.	MELODIE D'AMOUR (BMI)—Ames Brothers So Little Time (BMI)—Vic 7046	20	13
22.	THE STORY OF MY LIFE (ASCAP)—Marty Robbins Once-a-Week Date (BMI)—Col 41013	22	3
23.	THE JOKER (BMI)—Hilltoppers Chicken, Chicken (ASCAP)—Dot 15662	25	3
24.	LOVE ME FOREVER (BMI)—Eydie Gorme Let Me Be Loved (ASCAP)—ABC-Paramount 9863	—	1
25.	JUST BORN (BMI)—Perry Como Ivy Rose (ASCAP)—Vic 7050	23	12

Top 100 Sides

FOR SURVEY WEEK ENDING DECEMBER 21

This is a tabulation of dealer unit sales listed according to the specific side requested by customers. No attempt is made to add sides together to reflect actual record sales. It is therefore a tabulation of sides or songs, and not records. This fact, together with longer four-week survey periods, explains variation between the top 30 sides as reflected in this chart, and top 30 record sellers as reflected in "Best Sellers in Stores."

Pos.	Song, Artist, Label	Last Week
1.	**APRIL LOVE,** Pat Boone, Dot	4
2.	**AT THE HOP,** Danny and the Juniors, ABC-Paramount	6
3.	**PEGGY SUE,** Buddy Holly, Coral	5
4.	**GREAT BALLS OF FIRE,** Jerry Lee Lewis, Sun	9
5.	**RAUNCHY,** Bill Justis, Phillips International	3
6.	**JAILHOUSE ROCK,** Elvis Presley, Victor	2
6.	**YOU SEND ME,** Sam Cooke, Keen	1
8.	**KISSES SWEETER THAN WINE,** Jimmie Rodgers, Roulette	12
9.	**SILHOUETTES,** Rays, Cameo	7
10.	**ROCK AND ROLL MUSIC,** Chuck Berry, Chess	8
11.	**WAKE UP LITTLE SUSIE,** Everly Brothers, Cadence	10
12.	**RAUNCHY,** Ernie Freeman, Imperial	15
13.	**CHANCES ARE,** Johnny Mathis, Columbia	11
14.	**OH, BOY!** Crickets, Brunswick	23
15.	**ALL THE WAY,** Frank Sinatra, Capitol	17
15.	**MY SPECIAL ANGEL,** Bobby Helms, Decca	14
17.	**BE-BOP BABY,** Ricky Nelson, Imperial	13
18.	**BONY MORONIE,** Larry Williams, Specialty	23
19.	**MELODIE D'AMOUR,** Ames Brothers, Victor	18
20.	**TEARDROPS,** Lee Andrews and the Hearts, Chess	29
21.	**BUZZ, BUZZ, BUZZ,** Hollywood Flames, Ebb	28
22.	**WHY DON'T THEY UNDERSTAND?** George Hamilton IV, ABC-Paramount	21
23.	**JINGLE BELL ROCK,** Bobby Helms, Decca	67
24.	**HONEYCOMB,** Jimmie Rodgers, Roulette	22
25.	**I'M AVAILABLE,** Margie Rayburn, Liberty	20
26.	**LIECHTENSTEINER POLKA,** Will Glahe, London	19
27.	**LITTLE BITTY PRETTY ONE,** Thurston Harris, Aladdin	16
28.	**JUST BORN,** Perry Como, Victor	26
29.	**FASCINATION,** Jane Morgan, Kapp	25
30.	**I'LL COME RUNNING BACK TO YOU,** Sam Cooke, Specialty	38
31.	**THE JOKER,** Billy Myles, Ember	30
32.	**SANTA AND THE SATELLITE,** Buchanan & Goodman, Luniverse	67
33.	**STOOD UP,** Ricky Nelson, Imperial	—
34.	**THE STORY OF MY LIFE,** Marty Robbins, Columbia	33
34.	**TAMMY,** Debbie Reynolds, Coral	27
36.	**THE BIG BEAT,** Fats Domino, Imperial	53
37.	**PUT A LIGHT IN THE WINDOW,** Four Lads, Columbia	41
37.	**WILD IS THE WIND,** Johnny Mathis, Columbia	51
39.	**WAITIN' IN SCHOOL,** Ricky Nelson, Imperial	—
40.	**COULD THIS BE MAGIC?** Dubs, Gone	34
41.	**WHITE CHRISTMAS,** Bing Crosby, Decca	42
42.	**RAUNCHY,** Billy Vaughn, Dot	48
43.	**THE JOKER,** Hilltoppers, Dot	37
43.	**PENNY LOAFERS AND BOBBY SOCKS,** Joe Bennett and the Sparkletones, ABC-Paramount	89
45.	**LITTLE SANDY SLEIGHFOOT,** Jimmy Dean, Columbia	99
45.	**TILL,** Roger Williams, Kapp	35
47.	**IVY ROSE,** Perry Como, Victor	32
48.	**HARD TIMES (THE SLOP),** Noble (Thin Man) Watts, Baton	71
49.	**DANCE TO THE BOP,** Gene Vincent, Capitol	43

Starting with this issue, The Top 100 Sides chart will be a compilation of dealer unit sales for two-week survey periods. This faster service will give a more accurate and up-to-date picture of record sides as requested thruout the nation.

Pos.	Song, Artist, Label	Last Week
50.	**I WANT YOU TO KNOW,** Fats Domino, Imperial	—
51.	**HEY! LITTLE GIRL,** Techniques, Roulette	—
51.	**NO LOVE (BUT YOUR LOVE),** Johnny Mathis, Columbia	62
53.	**YOU SEND ME,** Teresa Brewer, Coral	38
54.	**ALONE,** Shepherd Sisters, Lance	45
54.	**LET'S LIGHT THE CHRISTMAS TREE,** Ruby Wright, Fraternity	—
54.	**SILENT NIGHT,** Bing Crosby, Decca	—
57.	**KEEP A' KNOCKIN',** Little Richard, Specialty	31
57.	**YOU BUG ME, BABY,** Larry Williams, Specialty	45
59.	**HAPPY, HAPPY BIRTHDAY, BABY,** Tune Weavers, Checker	38
60.	**FOREVER,** Sam Cooke, Specialty	90
60.	**FRAULEIN,** Bobby Helms, Decca	58
60.	**SAIL ALONG SILVERY MOON,** Billy Vaughn, Dot	83
60.	**SILHOUETTES,** Diamonds, Mercury	79
64.	**LITTLE BITTY PRETTY ONE,** Bobby Day, Class	64
64.	**LOVE ME FOREVER,** Four Esquires, Paris	58
66.	**HONEST I DO,** Jimmy Reed, Vee Jay	77
66.	**REET PETITE,** Jackie Wilson, Brunswick	67
66.	**THE TWELFTH OF NEVER,** Johnny Mathis, Columbia	51
66.	**WUN'ERFUL, WUN'ERFUL,** Stan Freberg, Capitol	50
70.	**RUDOLPH, THE RED-NOSED REINDEER,** Gene Autry, Challenge	—
71.	**I'LL REMEMBER TODAY,** Patti Page, Mercury	43
71.	**LIECHTENSTEINER POLKA,** Lawrence Welk, Coral	62
73.	**THIS IS THE NIGHT,** Valiants, Keen	—
74.	**A VERY SPECIAL LOVE,** Johnny Nash, ABC-Paramount	—
74.	**GEISHA GIRL,** Hank Locklin, Victor	—
74.	**JINGLE BELLS,** Perry Como, Victor	—
74.	**PRETEND YOU DON'T SEE HER,** Jerry Vale, Columbia	55
78.	**AROUND THE WORLD,** Mantovani, London	73
78.	**(I LOVE YOU) FOR SENTIMENTAL REASONS,** Sam Cooke, Specialty	—
78.	**HULA LOVE,** Buddy Knox, Roulette	36
78.	**PEANUTS,** Little Joe and the Thrillers, Okeh	45
78.	**SUGARTIME,** McGuire Sisters, Coral	—
78.	**SILVER BELLS,** Bing Crosby, Decca	—
78.	**WAIT AND SEE,** Fats Domino, Imperial	55
85.	**DIANA,** Paul Anka, ABC-Paramount	73
85.	**THAT'S WHY I WAS BORN,** Janice Harper, Prep	84
87.	**BLACK SLACKS,** Joe Bennett and the Sparkletones, ABC-Paramount	48
87.	**SOFT,** Bill Doggett, King	64
87.	**THE STROLL,** Diamonds, Mercury	—
87.	**SWANEE RIVER ROCK (TALKIN' 'BOUT THAT RIVER),** Ray Charles, Atlantic	66
87.	**YOU CAN MAKE IT IF YOU TRY,** Gene Allison, Vee Jay	77
92.	**AROUND THE WORLD,** Bing Crosby, Decca	84
92.	**AT THE HOP,** Nick Todd, Dot	—
92.	**THE CREATURE,** Buchanan & Goodman, Luniverse	90
92.	**DESIRE ME,** Sam Cooke, Keen	—
92.	**UH HUH,** Sonny James, Capitol	—
97.	**BACK TO SCHOOL AGAIN,** Timmy Rodgers, Cameo	61
97.	**LOVING YOU,** Elvis Presley, Victor	-
97.	**HOW LOVELY IS CHRISTMAS,** Bing Crosby, Decca	—
97.	**LOVE LETTERS IN THE SAND,** Pat Boone, Dot	99

Best Sellers in Stores

FOR SURVEY WEEK ENDING DECEMBER 28, 1957

The information given in this chart is based on actual sales to customers in a scientific sample of the nation's retail record outlets during the week ending on the date shown above. Sample design, sample size, and all methods used in this continuing study of retail record sales are under the direct and continuing supervision and control of the School of Retailing of New York University.

This Week	Record	Last Week	Weeks on Chart
1.	AT THE HOP (BMI)—Danny and the Juniors — Sometimes (BMI)—ABC-Paramount 9871	2	5
2.	GREAT BALLS OF FIRE (BMI)—Jerry Lee Lewis — You Win Again (BMI)—Sun 281	4	6
3.	APRIL LOVE (ASCAP)—Pat Boone — When the Swallows Come Back to Capistrano (ASCAP)—Dot 15660	1	10
4.	STOOD UP (BMI)—Ricky Nelson — WAITIN' IN SCHOOL (BMI)—Imperial 5483	22	2
5.	PEGGY SUE (BMI)—Buddy Holly — Everyday (BMI)—Coral 61885	3	9
6.	RAUNCHY (BMI)—Bill Justis — The Midnite Man (BMI)—Phillips International 3519	5	8
7.	JAILHOUSE ROCK (BMI)—Elvis Presley — TREAT ME NICE (BMI)—Vic 7035	6	13
8.	KISSES SWEETER THAN WINE (BMI)—Jimmie Rodgers — Better Loved You'll Never Be (ASCAP)—Roulette 4031	8	7
9.	JINGLE BELL ROCK (ASCAP)—Bobby Helms — Captain Santa Claus (ASCAP)—Dec 30513	25	3
10.	YOU SEND ME (BMI)—Sam Cooke — SUMMERTIME (ASCAP)—Keen 34013	7	11
11.	SILHOUETTES (BMI)—The Rays — Daddy Cool (BMI)—Cameo 117	9	12
12.	WAKE UP LITTLE SUSIE (BMI)—Everly Brothers — Maybe Tomorrow (BMI)—Cadence 1337	12	15
13.	ROCK AND ROLL MUSIC (BMI)—Chuck Berry — Blue Feeling (BMI)—Chess 1671	10	9
14.	OH, BOY! (BMI)—Crickets — Not Fade Away (BMI)—Brunswick 55035	16	6
15.	BE-BOP BABY (BMI)—Ricky Nelson — HAVE I TOLD YOU LATELY THAT L LOVE YOU (BMI)—Imperial 5463	17	14
16.	MY SPECIAL ANGEL (BMI)—Bobby Helms — Standing at the End of My World BMI)—Dec 30423	18	12
17.	RAUNCHY (BMI)—Ernie Freeman — Puddin' (BMI)—Imperial 5474	13	8
18.	BONY MORONIE (BMI)—Larry Williams — YOU BUG ME, BABY (BMI)—Specialty 615	14	9
19.	CHANCES ARE (ASCAP)—Johnny Mathis — THE TWELFTH OF NEVER (ASCAP)—Col 40993	11	16
20.	ALL THE WAY (ASCAP)—Frank Sinatra — CHICAGO (ASCAP)—Cap 3793	15	9
21.	TEARDROPS (BMI)—Lee Andrews and the Hearts — Girl Around the Corner (BMI)—Chess 1675	20	6
22.	WHY DON'T THEY UNDERSTAND? (BMI)—George Hamilton IV — Even Tho' (BMI)—ABC-Paramount 9862	23	6
23.	BUZZ, BUZZ, BUZZ (BMI)—Hollywood Flames — Crazy (BMI)—Ebb 119	21	6
24.	MELODIE D'AMOUR (BMI)—Ames Brothers — So Little Time (BMI)—Vic 7046	19	13
25.	RAUNCHY (BMI)—Billy Vaughn — SAIL ALONG SILVERY MOON (ASCAP)—Dot 15661	33	3
26.	HONEYCOMB (ASCAP)—Jimmie Rodgers — Their Hearts Were Full of Spring (ASCAP)—Roulette 4015	26	21
27.	LIECHTENSTEINER POLKA (ASCAP)—Will Glahe — Schweitzer Polka (BMI)—London 1755	27	8
28.	JUST BORN (BMI)—Perry Como — IVY ROSE (ASCAP)—Vic 7050	24	11
29.	THE BIG BEAT (BMI)—Fats Domino — I WANT YOU TO KNOW (BMI)—Imperial 5477	29	3
30.	I'M AVAILABLE (BMI)—Margie Rayburn — If You Were (ASCAP)—Liberty 55102	28	9
31.	LITTLE BITTY PRETTY ONE (BMI)—Thurston Harris — I Hope You Won't Hold It Against Me (ASCAP)—Aladdin 3398	32	11
32.	(I LOVE YOU) FOR SENTIMENTAL REASONS (BMI)—Sam Cooke — DESIRE ME (BMI)—Keen 4002	50	2
33.	WILD IS THE WIND (ASCAP)—Johnny Mathis — NO LOVE (BUT YOUR LOVE) (BMI)—Col 41060	31	4
34.	THE STORY OF MY LIFE (ASCAP)—Marty Robbins — Once-a-Week Date (BMI)—Col 41013	38	6
35.	I'LL COME RUNNING BACK TO YOU (BMI)—Sam Cooke — FOREVER (BMI)—Specialty 619	30	3
36.	FASCINATION (ASCAP)—Jane Morgan — Fascination (Instrumental) (ASCAP)—Kapp 191	34	18
37.	LITTLE SANDY SLEIGHFOOT (ASCAP)—Jimmy Dean — When They Ring the Golden Bells—Col 41025	44	2
38.	WHITE CHRISTMAS (ASCAP)—Bing Crosby — God Rest Ye Merry, Gentlemen (ASCAP)—Dec 23778	41	4
39.	PUT A LIGHT IN THE WINDOW (ASCAP)—Four Lads — The Things We Did Last Summer (ASCAP)—Col 41058	39	4
40.	THE STROLL (BMI)—Diamonds — Land of Beauty (BMI)—Mercury 71242	—	1
41.	SANTA AND THE SATELLITE (BMI)—Buchanan and Goodman — Part 2 (BMI)—Luniverse 107	36	3
42.	SUGARTIME (BMI)—McGuire Sisters — Banana Split (BMI)—Coral 61924	—	1
43.	TAMMY (ASCAP)—Debbie Reynolds — French Heels (ASCAP)—Coral 61851	37	24
44.	COULD THIS BE MAGIC? (BMI)—Dubs — Such Lovin' (BMI)—Gone 5011	40	9
45.	THE JOKER (BMI)—Billy Myles — Honey Bee (BMI)—Ember 1026	35	7
46.	THE JOKER (BMI)—Hilltoppers — Chicken, Chicken (ASCAP)—Dot 15662	43	3
47.	TILL (ASCAP)—Roger Williams — Big Town (ASCAP)—Kapp 197	45	9
48.	HEY! LITTLE GIRL (BMI)—Techniques — In a Round About Way (BMI)—Roulette 4030	48	2
49.	HEY, SCHOOLGIRL (BMI)—Tom and Jerry — Dancin' Wild (BMI)—Big 613	—	1
50.	DANCE TO THE BOP (BMI)—Gene Vincent — I Got It (BMI)—Cap 3839	47	5

THIS WEEK'S BEST BUYS

Special telephone reports indicate these recent releases have broken out in one or more key areas and have excellent potential for placing on The Billboard's best seller charts.

DON'T LET GO (Roosevelt, BMI)—Roy Hamilton—(Epic 9257)—This is the strongest by the artist in recent tries. It's registering well in all markets. Flip is "The Right to Love" (Sheldon, BMI). A previous Billboard "Spotlight" pick.

Week in and week out you'll find more news, more record reviews, more advertising on the fast-moving record business in The Billboard, the communications center of the music industry.

RECENT POP RELEASES COMING UP STRONG

FOR SURVEY WEEK ENDING DECEMBER 28

The information given in this chart is based on actual sales to customers in a scientific sample of the nation's retail record outlets during the week ending on the date shown above. Sample design, sample size and all methods used in this continuing study of retail record sales are under the direct and continuing supervision and control of the School of Retailing of New York University.

La De Dah . . . . . *Billy & Lille* (BMI) Swan 4002

Oh, Julie . . . . . *Crescendos* (BMI) Nasco 6005

A Very Special Love . . . . . *Johnny Nash* (ASCAP) ABC-Paramount 9874

Get a Job . . . . . *Silhouettes* (BMI) Ember 1029

Most Played by Jockeys

FOR SURVEY WEEK ENDING DECEMBER 28

SIDES are ranked in order of the greatest number of plays on disk jockey radio shows thruout the country Results are based on The Billboard's weekly survey among the nation's disk jockeys. The reverse side of each record is also listed.

This Week		Last Week	Weeks on Chart
1.	APRIL LOVE (ASCAP)—Pat Boone When the Swallows Come Back to Capistrano (ASCAP)—Dot 15660	1	11
2.	ALL THE WAY (ASCAP)—Frank Sinatra Chicago (ASCAP)—Cap 3793	3	11
3.	YOU SEND ME (BMI)—Sam Cooke Summertime (ASCAP)—Keen 34013	2	10
4.	KISSES SWEETER THAN WINE (BMI)—Jimmie Rodgers Better Loved You'll Never Be (ASCAP)—Roulette 4031	4	8
5.	AT THE HOP (BMI)—Danny and the Juniors Sometimes (BMI)—ABC-Paramount 9871	15	3
6.	RAUNCHY (BMI)—Ernie Freeman Puddin' (BMI)—Imperial 5474	7	6
7.	PEGGY SUE (BMI)—Buddy Holly Everyday (BMI)—Coral 61885	8	8
8.	PUT A LIGHT IN THE WINDOW (ASCAP)—Four Lads The Things We Did Last Summer (ASCAP)—Col 41058	12	5
9.	RAUNCHY (BMI)—Bill Justis The Midnite Man (BMI)—Phillips International 3519	5	7
10.	YOU SEND ME (BMI)—Teresa Brewer Would I Were (ASCAP)—Coral 61898	9	9
11.	JINGLE BELL ROCK (ASCAP)—Bobby Helms Captain Santa Claus (ASCAP)—Dec 30513	—	1
12.	GREAT BALLS OF FIRE (BMI)—Jerry Lee Lewis You Win Again (BMI)—Sun 281	14	5
13.	CHANCES ARE (ASCAP)—Johnny Mathis The Twelfth of Never (ASCAP)—Col 40993	10	17
14.	SUGARTIME (BMI)—McGuire Sisters Banana Split (BMI)—Coral 61924	—	1
15.	JAILHOUSE ROCK (BMI)—Elvis Presley Treat Me Nice (BMI)—Vic 7035	6	13
16.	RAUNCHY (BMI)—Billy Vaughn Sail Along Silvery Moon (ASCAP)—Dot 15661	11	4
17.	I'M AVAILABLE (BMI)—Margie Rayburn If You Were (ASCAP)—Liberty 55102	13	9
18.	WHY DON'T THEY UNDERSTAND? (BMI)—George Hamilton IV Even Tho' (BMI)—ABC-Paramount 9862	—	1
19.	MY SPECIAL ANGEL (BMI)—Bobby Helms Standing at the End of My World (BMI)—Dec 30423	19	11
20.	THE STORY OF MY LIFE (ASCAP)—Marty Robbins Once-a-Week Date (BMI)—Col 41013	22	4
21.	NO LOVE (BUT YOUR LOVE (BMI)—Johnny Mathis Wild Is the Wind (ASCAP)—Col 41060	—	1
22.	THE TWELFTH OF NEVER (ASCAP)—Johnny Mathis Chances Are (ASCAP)—Col 40993	17	13
23.	MELODIE D'AMOUR (BMI)—Ames Brothers So Little Time (BMI)—Vic 7046	21	14
24.	LIECHTENSTEINER POLKA (ASCAP)—Will Glahe Schweitzer Polka (BMI)—London 1755	—	2
25.	OH, BOY! (BMI)—Crickets Not Fade Away (BMI)—Brunswick 55035	20	3

Top 100 Sides

FOR SURVEY WEEK ENDING DECEMBER 28

This is a tabulation of dealer individual record sales listed according to the specific side requested by customers. No attempt is made to add sides together to reflect actual record sales. This is, therefore, a tabulation of sides or songs, and not records. This is the reason for any possible variation that occurs between the top 50 sides as reflected in this chart, and the top 50 record sellers as reflected in the "Best Sellers in Stores" chart.

Pos.	Song, Artist, Label	Last Week
1.	AT THE HOP, Danny and the Juniors, ABC-Paramount	2
2.	GREAT BALLS OF FIRE, Jerry Lee Lewis, Sun	4
3.	APRIL LOVE, Pat Boone, Dot	1
4.	PEGGY SUE, Buddy Holly, Coral	3
5.	RAUNCHY, Bill Justis, Phillips International	5
6.	JAILHOUSE ROCK, Elvis Presley, Victor	6
7.	KISSES SWEETER THAN WINE, Jimmie Rodgers, Roulette	8
8.	JINGLE BELL ROCK, Bobby Helms, Decca	23
9.	YOU SEND ME, Sam Cooke, Keen	6
10.	STOOD UP, Ricky Nelson, Imperial	33
11.	SILHOUETTES, Rays, Cameo	9
12.	WAKE UP LITTLE SUSIE, Everly Brothers, Cadence	11
13.	ROCK AND ROLL MUSIC, Chuck Berry, Chess	10
14.	OH, BOY! Crickets, Brunswick	14
15.	MY SPECIAL ANGEL, Bobby Helms, Decca	15
16.	BE-BOP BABY, Ricky Nelson, Imperial	17
17.	RAUNCHY, Ernie Freeman, Imperial	12
18.	ALL THE WAY, Frank Sinatra, Capitol	15
19.	CHANCES ARE, Johnny Mathis, Columbia	13
20.	BONY MORONIE, Larry Williams, Specialty	18
21.	TEARDROPS, Lee Andrews and the Hearts, Chess	20
22.	WAITIN' IN SCHOOL, Ricky Nelson, Imperial	39
23.	WHY DON'T THEY UNDERSTAND? George Hamilton IV, ABC-Paramount	22
24.	BUZZ, BUZZ, BUZZ, Hollywood Flames, Ebb	21
25.	MELODIE D'AMOUR, Ames Brothers, Victor	19
26.	HONEYCOMB, Jimmie Rodgers, Roulette	24
26.	LIECHTENSTEINER POLKA, Will Glahe, London	26
28.	I'M AVAILABLE, Margie Rayburn, Liberty	25
29.	LITTLE BITTY PRETTY ONE, Thurston Harris, Aladdin	27
30.	THE STORY OF MY LIFE, Marty Robbins, Columbia	34
31.	FASCINATION, Jane Morgan, Kapp	29
32.	LITTLE SANDY SLEIGHFOOT, Jimmy Dean, Columbia	45
33.	RAUNCHY, Billy Vaughn, Dot	42
34.	WHITE CHRISTMAS, Bing Crosby, Decca	41
35.	PUT A LIGHT IN THE WINDOW, Four Lads, Columbia	37
36.	I'LL COME RUNNING BACK TO YOU, Sam Cooke, Specialty	30
36.	JUST BORN, Perry Como, Victor	28
36.	SANTA AND THE SATELLITE, Buchanan and Goodman, Luniverse	32
36.	THE STROLL, Diamonds, Mercury	87
40.	THE BIG BEAT, Fats Domino, Imperial	36
41.	SUGARTIME, McGuire Sisters, Coral	78
42.	TAMMY, Debbie Reynolds, Coral	34
42.	WILD IS THE WIND, Johnny Mathis, Columbia	37
44.	COULD THIS BE MAGIC? Dubs, Gone	40
45.	SAIL ALONG SILVERY MOON, Billy Vaughn, Dot	60
46.	IVY ROSE, Perry Como, Victor	47
46.	THE JOKER, Billy Myles, Ember	31
48.	I WANT YOU TO KNOW, Fats Domino, Imperial	50
49.	(I LOVE YOU) FOR SENTIMENTAL REASONS, Sam Cooke, Keen	78
50.	DESIRE ME Sam Cooke, Keen	92

This chart is now a compilation of dealer unit sales by record sides for the same survey period that is reflected in the Best Sellers in Stores chart. This chart, therefore, is now reflecting each week the Top 100 sides not records as sold in stores thruout the nation.

Pos.	Song, Artist, Label	Last Week
51.	THE JOKER, Hilltoppers, Dot	43
52.	TILL, Roger Williams, Kapp	45
53.	HEY! LITTLE GIRL, Techniques, Roulette	51
54.	DANCE TO THE BOP, Gene Vincent, Capitol	49
54.	HEY, SCHOOLGIRL, Tom and Jerry, Big	—
56.	HAPPY, HAPPY BIRTHDAY, BABY, Tune Weavers, Checker	59
56.	YOU BUG ME, BABY, Larry Williams, Specialty	57
58.	OH JULIE, Crescendos, Nasco	—
58.	PENNY LOAFERS AND BOBBY SOCKS, Joe Bennett and the Sparkletones, ABC-Paramount	43
60.	HULA LOVE, Buddy Knox, Roulette	78
60.	KEEP A' KNOCKIN', Little Richard, Specialty	57
60.	NO LOVE (BUT YOUR LOVE), Johnny Mathis, Columbia	51
60.	YOU SEND ME, Teresa Brewer, Coral	53
64.	A VERY SPECIAL LOVE, Johnny Nash, ABC-Paramount	74
64.	HENRIETTA, Jimmie Dee, Dot	—
64.	YOU CAN MAKE IT IF YOU TRY, Gene Allison, Vee Jay	87
67.	LET'S LIGHT THE CHRISTMAS TREE, Ruby Wright, Fraternity	54
67.	SILENT NIGHT, Bing Crosby, Decca	54
69.	THIS IS THE NIGHT, Valiants, Keen	73
70.	PRETEND YOU DON'T SEE HER, Jerry Vale, Columbia	74
71.	FRAULEIN, Bobby Helms, Decca	60
71.	RUDOLPH, THE RED-NOSED REINDEER, Gene Autry, Challenge	70
73.	ALONE, Shepherd Sisters, Lance	54
73.	DIANA, Paul Anka, ABC-Paramount	85
75.	LA DEE DAH, Billy and Lillie, Swan	—
75.	PEANUTS, Little Joe and the Thrillers, Okeh	78
77.	SILHOUETTES, Diamonds, Mercury	60
77.	THE TWELFTH OF NEVER, Johnny Mathis, Columbia	66
79.	AROUND THE WORLD, Mantovani, London	78
79.	BACK TO SCHOOL AGAIN, Timmy Rodgers, Cameo	97
79.	SILVER BELLS, Bing Crosby, Decca	78
82.	LOVE LETTERS IN THE SAND, Pat Boone, Dot	97
82.	SWANEE RIVER ROCK (TALKIN' 'BOUT THAT RIVER), Ray Charles, Atlantic	87
82.	THAT'LL BE THE DAY, Crickets, Brunswick	—
82.	WAIT AND SEE, Fats Domino, Imperial	78
82.	WUN'ERFUL, WUN'ERFUL, Stan Freberg, Capitol	66
87.	FOREVER, Sam Cooke, Specialty	60
87.	GEISHA GIRL, Hank Locklin, Victor	74
87.	JINGLE BELLS, Perry Como, Victor	74
87.	LIECHTENSTEINER POLKA, Lawrence Welk, Coral	71
87.	THAT'S WHY I WAS BORN, Janice Harper, Prep	85
87.	TEDDY BEAR. Elvis Presley, Victor	—
93.	AT THE HOP, Nick Todd, Dot	92
93.	I'LL REMEMBER TODAY, Patti Page, Mercury	71
93.	REET PETITE, Jackie Wilson, Brunswick	66
93.	LOVING YOU, Elvis Presley, Victor	97
93.	TREAT ME NICE, Elvis Presley, Victor	—
98.	LOVE ME FOREVER, Four Esquires, Paris	64
99.	LITTLE BITTY PRETTY ONE, Bobby Day, Class	64
99.	THE CREATURE, Buchanan and Goodman, Luniverse	92

Best Sellers in Stores

The information given in this chart is based on actual sales to customers in a scientific sample of the nation's retail record outlets during the week ending on the date shown above. Sample design, sample size, and all methods used in this continuing study of retail record sales are under the direct and continuing supervision and control of the School of Retailing of New York University.

FOR SURVEY WEEK ENDING JANUARY 4, 1958

This Week		Last Week	Weeks on Chart
1.	AT THE HOP (BMI)—Danny and the Juniors Sometimes (BMI)—ABC-Paramount 9871	1	6
2.	STOOD UP (BMI)—Ricky Nelson WAITIN' IN SCHOOL (BMI)—Imperial 5483	4	3
3.	GREAT BALLS OF FIRE (BMI)—Jerry Lee Lewis You Win Again (BMI)—Sun 281	2	7
4.	APRIL LOVE (ASCAP)—Pat Boone When the Swallows Come Back to Capistrano (ASCAP)—Dot 15660	3	11
5.	PEGGY SUE (BMI)—Buddy Holly Everyday (BMI)—Coral 61885	5	10
6.	JAILHOUSE ROCK (BMI)—Elvis Presley TREAT ME NICE (BMI)—Vic 7035	7	14
7.	JINGLE BELL ROCK (ASCAP)—Bobby Helms Captain Santa Claus (ASCAP)—Dec 30513	9	4
8.	YOU SEND ME (BMI)—Sam Cooke SUMMERTIME (ASCAP)—Keen 34013	10	12
9.	KISSES SWEETER THAN WINE (BMI)—Jimmie Rodgers Better Loved You'll Never Be (ASCAP)—Roulette 4031	8	8
10.	RAUNCHY (BMI)—Bill Justis The Midnite Man (BMI)—Phillips International 3519	6	9
11.	SILHOUETTES (BMI)—The Rays Daddy Cool (BMI)—Cameo 117	11	13
12.	OH, BOY! (BMI)—Crickets Not Fade Away (BMI)—Brunswick 55035	14	7
13.	MY SPECIAL ANGEL (BMI)—Bobby Helms Standing at the End of My World (BMI)—Dec 30423	16	13
14.	WAKE UP LITTLE SUSIE (BMI)—Everly Brothers Maybe Tomorrow (BMI)—Cadence 1337	12	16
15.	ROCK AND ROLL MUSIC (BMI)—Chuck Berry Blue Feeling (BMI)—Chess 1671	13	10
16.	CHANCES ARE (ASCAP)—Johnny Mathis THE TWELFTH OF NEVER (ASCAP)—Col 40993	19	17
17.	BONY MORONIE (BMI)—Larry Williams YOU BUG ME, BABY (BMI)—Specialty 615	18	10
18.	RAUNCHY (BMI)—Ernie Freeman Puddin' (BMI)—Imperial 5474	17	9
19.	BE-BOP BABY (BMI)—Ricky Nelson HAVE I TOLD YOU LATELY THAT I LOVE YOU (BMI)—Imperial 5463	15	15
20.	ALL THE WAY (ASCAP)—Frank Sinatra CHICAGO (ASCAP)—Cap 3793	20	10
21.	SAIL ALONG SILVERY MOON (ASCAP)—Billy Vaughn RAUNCHY (BMI)—Dot 15661	25	4
22.	THE STROLL (BMI)—Diamonds Land of Beauty (BMI)—Mercury 71242	40	2
23.	BUZZ, BUZZ, BUZZ (BMI)—Hollywood Flames Crazy (BMI)—Ebb 119	23	7
24.	WHY DON'T THEY UNDERSTAND? (BMI)—George Hamilton IV Even Tho' (BMI)—ABC-Paramount 9862	22	7
25.	JUST BORN (BMI)—Perry Como IVY ROSE (ASCAP)—Vic 7050	28	12
26.	THE BIG BEAT (BMI)—Fats Domino I WANT YOU TO KNOW (BMI)—Imperial 5477	29	4
27.	TEARDROPS (BMI)—Lee Andrews and the Hearts Girl Around the Corner (BMI)—Chess 1675	21	7
28.	FASCINATION (ASCAP)—Jane Morgan Fascination (Instrumental) (ASCAP)—Kapp 191	36	19
29.	MELODIE D'AMOUR (BMI)—Ames Brothers So Little Time (BMI)—Vic 7046	24	14
30.	SUGARTIME (BMI)—McGuire Sisters Banana Split (BMI)—Coral 61924	42	2
31.	I'M AVAILABLE (BMI)—Margie Rayburn If You Were (ASCAP)—Liberty 55102	30	10
32.	(I LOVE YOU) FOR SENTIMENTAL REASONS (BMI)—Sam Cooke DESIRE ME (BMI)—Keen 4002	32	3
33.	LIECHTENSTEINER POLKA (ASCAP)—Will Glahe Schweitzer Polka (BMI)—London 1755	27	9
34.	I'LL COME RUNNING BACK TO YOU (BMI)—Sam Cooke FOREVER (BMI)—Specialty 619	35	4
35.	THE STORY OF MY LIFE (ASCAP)—Marty Robbins Once-a-Week Date (BMI)—Col 41013	34	7
36.	LA DEE DAH (BMI)—Billy and Lillie The Monster (BMI)—Swan 4002	—	1
37.	NO LOVE (BUT YOUR LOVE) (BMI)—Johnny Mathis WILD IS THE WIND (ASCAP)—Col 41060	33	5
38.	LITTLE BITTY PRETTY ONE (BMI)—Thurston Harris I Hope You Won't Hold It Against Me (ASCAP)—Aladdin 3398	31	12
39.	HONEYCOMB (ASCAP)—Jimmie Rodgers Their Hearts Were Full of Spring (ASCAP)—Roulette 4015	26	22
40.	PUT A LIGHT IN THE WINDOW (ASCAP)—Four Lads The Things We Did Last Summer (ASCAP)—Col 41058	39	5
41.	OH, JULIE (BMI)—Crescendos My Little Girl (BMI)—Nasco 6005	—	1
42.	LITTLE SANDY SLEIGHFOOT (ASCAP)—Jimmy Dean When They Ring the Golden Bells—Col 41025	37	3
43.	WHITE CHRISTMAS (ASCAP)—Bing Crosby God Rest Ye Merry, Gentlemen (ASCAP)—Dec 23778	38	5
44.	THE JOKER (BMI)—Hilltoppers Chicken, Chicken (ASCAP)—Dot 15662	46	4
45.	TAMMY (ASCAP)—Debbie Reynolds French Heels (ASCAP)—Coral 61851	43	25
46.	SANTA AND THE SATELLITE (BMI)—Buchanan and Goodman Part 2 (BMI)—Luniverse 107	41	4
47.	HENRIETTA (BMI)—Jimmy Dee Don't Cry No More (BMI)—Dot 15664	—	1
48.	THE JOKER (BMI)—Billy Myles Honey Bee (BMI)—Ember 1026	45	8
49.	TILL (ASCAP)—Roger Williams Big Town (ASCAP)—Kapp 197	47	10
50.	KEEP A' KNOCKIN' (BMI)—Little Richard Can't Believe You Want to Leave—Specialty 611	—	13

THIS WEEK'S BEST BUYS

Special telephone reports indicate these recent releases have broken out in one or more key areas and have excellent potential for placing on The Billboard's best seller charts.

GET A JOB (Ulysses & Bagby, BMI)—**The Silhouettes—Ember 29**—This is a hot one. It's moving strongly in all markets. Flip is "I Am Lonely" (Ulysses & Bagby, BMI). A previous Billboard Spotlight pick.

DEDE DINAH (Debmar, ASCAP)—**Frankie Avalon—Chancellor 1011**—Sales are jumping in all marts. This appears to be a big one. Flip is "Ooh La La" (Debmar, ASCAP). A previous Billboard Spotlight pick.

JO-ANN (Figure, BMI)—**The Playmates—Roulette 4037**—Action on the side is heavy in most of the major marts. Elsewhere, sales are starting to build. Flip is "You Can't Stop Me From Dreaming" (Figure, BMI).

RECENT POP RELEASES COMING UP STRONG

FOR SURVEY WEEK ENDING JANUARY 4

The information given in this chart is based on actual sales to customers in a scientific sample of the nation's retail record outlets during the week ending on the date shown above. Sample design, sample size and all methods used in this continuing study of retail record sales are under the direct and continuing supervision and control of the School of Retailing of New York University.

Don't Let Go . . . *Roy Hamilton* (BMI) Epic 9257

Get a Job . . . *Silhouettes* (BMI) Ember 1029

A Very Special Love . . . *Johnny Nash* (ASCAP) ABC-Paramount 9874

You Can Make It, If You Try . . . *Gene Allison* (BMI) Vee Jay 256

Most Played by Jockeys

FOR SURVEY WEEK ENDING JANUARY 4

SIDES are ranked in order of the greatest number of plays on disk jockey radio shows thruout the country. Results are based on The Billboard's weekly survey among the nation's disk jockeys. The reverse side of each record is also listed.

This Week		Last Week	Weeks on Chart
1.	**APRIL LOVE** (ASCAP)—Pat Boone When the Swallows Come Back to Capistrano (ASCAP)—Dot 15660	1	12
2.	**AT THE HOP** (BMI)—Danny and the Juniors Sometimes (BMI)—ABC-Paramount 9871	5	4
3.	**KISSES SWEETER THAN WINE** (BMI)—Jimmie Rodgers Better Loved You'll Never Be (ASCAP)—Roulette 4031	4	9
4.	**RAUNCHY** (BMI)—Ernie Freeman Puddin' (BMI)—Imperial 5474	6	7
5.	**ALL THE WAY** (ASCAP)—Frank Sinatra Chicago (ASCAP)—Cap 3793	2	12
6.	**YOU SEND ME** (BMI)—Sam Cooke Summertime (ASCAP)—Keen 34013	3	11
7.	**PEGGY SUE** (BMI)—Buddy Holly Everyday (BMI)—Coral 61885	7	9
8.	**RAUNCHY** (BMI)—Bill Justis The Midnite Man (BMI)—Phillips International 3519	9	8
9.	**GREAT BALLS OF FIRE** (BMI)—Jerry Lee Lewis You Win Again (BMI)—Sun 281	12	6
10.	**WHY DON'T THEY UNDERSTAND?** (BMI)—George Hamilton IV Even Tho' (BMI)—ABC-Paramount 9862	18	2
11.	**PUT A LIGHT IN THE WINDOW** (ASCAP)—Four Lads The Things We Did Last Summer (ASCAP)—Col 41058	8	6
12.	**JINGLE BELL ROCK** (ASCAP)—Bobby Helms Captain Santa Claus (ASCAP)—Dec 30513	11	2
13.	**SUGARTIME** (BMI)—McGuire Sisters Banana Split (BMI)—Coral 61924	14	2
14.	**CHANCES ARE** (ASCAP)—Johnny Mathis The Twelfth of Never (ASCAP)—Col 40993	13	18
15.	**THE STORY OF MY LIFE** (ASCAP)—Marty Robbins Once-a-Week Date (BMI)—Col 41013	20	5
16.	**THE STROLL** (BMI)—Diamonds Land of Beauty (BMI)—Mercury 71242	—	1
17.	**I'M AVAILABLE** (BMI)—Margie Rayburn If You Were (ASCAP)—Liberty 55102	17	10
18.	**THE TWELFTH OF NEVER** (ASCAP)—Johnny Mathis Chances Are (ASCAP)—Col 40993	22	14
19.	**YOU SEND ME** (BMI)—Teresa Brewer Would I Were (ASCAP)—Coral 61898	10	10
20.	**OH, BOY!** (BMI)—Crickets Not Fade Away (BMI)—Brunswick 55035	25	4
21.	**CATCH A FALLING STAR** (ASCAP)—Perry Como Magic Moments (ASCAP)—Vic 7128	—	1
22.	**RAUNCHY** (BMI)—Billy Vaughn Sail Along Silvery Moon (ASCAP)—Dot 15661	16	5
23.	**DANCE TO THE BOP** (BMI)—Gene Vincent I Got It (BMI)—Cap 3839	—	1
24.	**WILD IS THE WIND** (ASCAP)—Johnny Mathis No Love (But Your Love) (BMI)—Col 41060	—	2
25.	**JAILHOUSE ROCK** (BMI)—Elvis Presley Treat Me Nice (BMI)—Vic 7035	15	14

Top 100 Sides

FOR SURVEY WEEK ENDING JANUARY 4

This is a tabulation of dealer individual record sales listed according to the specific side requested by customers. No attempt is made to add sides together to reflect actual record sales. This is, therefore, a tabulation of sides or songs, and not records. This is the reason for any possible variation that occurs between the top 50 sides as reflected in this chart, and the top 50 record sellers as reflected in the "Best Sellers in Stores" chart.

Pos.	Song, Artist, Label	Last Week
1.	**AT THE HOP,** Danny and the Juniors, ABC-Paramount	1
2.	**GREAT BALLS OF FIRE,** Jerry Lee Lewis, Sun	2
3.	**APRIL LOVE,** Pat Boone, Dot	3
4.	**PEGGY SUE,** Buddy Holly, Coral	4
5.	**STOOD UP,** Ricky Nelson, Imperial	10
6.	**JINGLE BELL ROCK,** Bobby Helms, Decca	8
7.	**JAILHOUSE ROCK,** Elvis Presley, Victor	6
8.	**YOU SEND ME,** Sam Cooke, Keen	9
9.	**KISSES SWEETER THAN WINE,** Jimmie Rodgers, Roulette	7
10.	**RAUNCHY,** Bill Justis, Phillips International	5
11.	**SILHOUETTES,** Rays, Cameo	11
12.	**OH, BOY!** Crickets, Brunswick	14
13.	**MY SPECIAL ANGEL,** Bobby Helms, Decca	15
14.	**WAKE UP LITTLE SUSIE,** Everly Brothers, Cadence	12
15.	**ROCK AND ROLL MUSIC,** Chuck Berry, Chess	13
16.	**RAUNCHY,** Ernie Freeman, Imperial	17
17.	**BE-BOP BABY,** Ricky Nelson, Imperial	16
18.	**CHANCES ARE,** Johnny Mathis, Columbia	19
19.	**ALL THE WAY,** Frank Sinatra, Capitol	18
20.	**BONY MORONIE,** Larry Williams, Specialty	20
21.	**WAITIN' IN SCHOOL,** Ricky Nelson, Imperial	22
22.	**THE STROLL,** Diamonds, Mercury	36
23.	**BUZZ, BUZZ, BUZZ,** Hollywood Flames, Ebb	24
24.	**WHY DON'T THEY UNDERSTAND?** George Hamilton IV, ABC-Paramount	23
25.	**TEARDROPS,** Lee Andrews and the Hearts, Chess	21
26.	**FASCINATION,** Jane Morgan, Kapp	31
27.	**MELODIE D'AMOUR,** Ames Brothers, Victor	25
28.	**SUGARTIME,** McGuire Sisters, Coral	41
29.	**I'M AVAILABLE,** Margie Rayburn, Liberty	28
30.	**LIECHTENSTEINER POLKA,** Will Glahe, London	26
31.	**THE STORY OF MY LIFE,** Marty Robbins, Columbia	30
32.	**LA DEE DAH,** Billy and Lillie, Swan	75
33.	**SAIL ALONG SILVERY MOON,** Billy Vaughn, Dot	45
33.	**LITTLE BITTY PRETTY ONE,** Thurston Harris, Aladdin	29
35.	**HONEYCOMB,** Jimmie Rodgers, Roulette	26
36.	**I'LL COME RUNNING BACK TO YOU,** Sam Cooke, Specialty	36
37.	**PUT A LIGHT IN THE WINDOW,** Four Lads, Columbia	35
38.	**THE BIG BEAT,** Fats Domino, Imperial	40
39.	**RAUNCHY,** Billy Vaughn, Dot	33
40.	**JUST BORN,** Perry Como, Victor	36
41.	**OH JULIE,** Crescendos, Nasco	58
42.	**LITTLE SANDY SLEIGHFOOT,** Jimmy Dean, Columbia	32
43.	**IVY ROSE,** Perry Como, Victor	46
44.	**WHITE CHRISTMAS,** Bing Crosby, Decca	34
44.	**THE JOKER,** Hilltoppers, Dot	51
46.	**(I LOVE YOU) FOR SENTIMENTAL REASONS,** Sam Cooke, Keen	49
47.	**DESIRE ME,** Sam Cooke, Keen	50
48.	**NO LOVE (BUT YOUR LOVE),** Johnny Mathis, Columbia	60
49.	**TAMMY,** Debbie Reynolds, Coral	42
49.	**I WANT YOU TO KNOW,** Fats Domino, Imperial	48

This chart is now a compilation of dealer unit sales by record sides for the same survey period that is reflected in the Best Sellers in Stores chart. This chart, therefore, is now reflecting each week the Top 100 sides not records as sold in stores thruout the nation.

Pos.	Song, Artist, Label	Last Week
51.	**SANTA AND THE SATELLITE,** Buchanan & Goodman, Luniverse	36
52.	**WILD IS THE WIND,** Johnny Mathis, Columbia	42
53.	**HENRIETTA,** Jimmie Dee, Dot	64
53.	**THE JOKER,** Billy Myles, Ember	46
53.	**TILL,** Roger Williams, Kapp	52
53.	**KEEP A' KNOCKIN',** Little Richard, Specialty	60
57.	**PENNY LOAFERS AND BOBBY SOCKS,** Joe Bennett and the Sparkletones, ABC-Paramount	58
58.	**COULD THIS BE MAGIC?** Dubs, Gone	44
59.	**YOU BUG ME, BABY,** Larry Williams, Specialty	56
60.	**DANCE TO THE BOP,** Gene Vincent, Capitol	54
60.	**HULA LOVE,** Buddy Knox, Roulette	60
60.	**MARCH FROM RIVER KWAI, AND COLONEL BOGEY,** Mitch Miller, Columbia	—
63.	**HAPPY, HAPPY BIRTHDAY, BABY,** Tune Weavers, Checker	56
63.	**PRETEND YOU DON'T SEE HER,** Jerry Vale, Columbia	70
65.	**YOU CAN MAKE IT IF YOU TRY,** Gene Allison, Vee Jay	64
66.	**A VERY SPECIAL LOVE,** Johnny Nash, ABC-Paramount	64
67.	**YOU SEND ME,** Teresa Brewer, Coral	60
67.	**HEY, LITTLE GIRL,** Techniques, Roulette	53
67.	**THE TWELFTH OF NEVER,** Johnny Mathis, Columbia	77
70.	**AT THE HOP,** Nick Todd, Dot	93
70.	**SHE'S NEAT,** Dale Wright, Fraternity	—
72.	**BACK TO SCHOOL AGAIN,** Timmy Rodgers, Cameo	79
73.	**DON'T LET GO,** Roy Hamilton, Epic	—
73.	**HEY, SCHOOLGIRL,** Tom and Jerry, Big	54
73.	**LOVE ME FOREVER,** Four Esquires, Paris	98
76.	**ALONE,** Shepherd Sisters, Lance	73
77.	**AROUND THE WORLD,** Victor Young, Decca	—
77.	**HARD TIMES (THE SLOP),** Noble (Thin Man) Watts, Baton	—
77.	**WALKIN' WITH MR. LEE,** Lee Allen, Ember	—
77.	**YOU'RE THE GREATEST,** Billy Scott, Cameo	—
81.	**DO WHAT YOU DID,** Thurston Harris, Aladdin	—
81.	**SWANEE RIVER ROCK (TALKIN' 'BOUT THAT RIVER),** Ray Charles, Atlantic	82
81.	**WHOLE LOTTA SHAKIN' GOIN' ON,** Jerry Lee Lewis, Sun	—
84.	**DIANA,** Paul Anka, ABC-Paramount	73
84.	**FOREVER,** Sam Cooke, Specialty	87
84.	**THIS IS THE NIGHT,** Valiants, Keen	69
84.	**THAT'LL BE THE DAY,** Crickets, Brunswick	82
84.	**WAIT AND SEE,** Fats Domino, Imperial	82
89.	**SILENT NIGHT,** Bing Crosby, Decca	67
90.	**GEISHA GIRL,** Hank Locklin, Victor	87
91.	**DEEP BLUE SEA,** Jimmy Dean, Columbia	—
91.	**I'LL REMEMBER TODAY,** Patti Page, Mercury	93
91.	**TEDDY BEAR,** Elvis Presley, Victor	87
94.	**HONEST I DO,** Jimmy Reed, Vee Jay	—
94.	**SOFT,** Bill Doggett, King	—
96.	**MY ONE SIN,** Four Coins, Epic	—
96.	**MR. LEE,** Bobbettes, Atlantic	—
96.	**REMEMBER YOU'RE MINE,** Pat Boone, Dot	—
96.	**SILHOUETTES,** Diamonds, Mercury	77
100.	**AROUND THE WORLD,** Mantovani, London	79
100.	**RUDOLPH, THE RED-NOSED REINDEER,** Gene Autry, Challenge	71

STORE RECORDED SALES — NEW YORK UNIVERSITY SCHOOL OF RETAILING — THE BILLBOARD

Best Sellers in Stores

The information given in this chart is based on actual sales to customers in a scientific sample of the nation's retail record outlets during the week ending on the date shown above. Sample design, sample size, and all methods used in this continuing study of retail record sales are under the direct and continuing supervision and control of the School of Retailing of New York University.

FOR SURVEY WEEK ENDING JANUARY 11, 1958

This Week	Title	Last Week	Weeks on Chart
1.	AT THE HOP (BMI)—Danny and the Juniors Sometimes (BMI)—ABC-Paramount 9871	1	7
2.	STOOD UP (BMI)—Ricky Nelson WAITIN' IN SCHOOL (BMI)—Imperial 5483	2	4
3.	GREAT BALLS OF FIRE (BMI)—Jerry Lee Lewis YOU WIN AGAIN (BMI)—Sun 281	3	8
4.	APRIL LOVE (ASCAP)—Pat Boone WHEN THE SWALLOWS COME BACK TO CAPISTRANO (ASCAP)—Dot 15660	4	12
5.	PEGGY SUE (BMI)—Buddy Holly Everyday (BMI)—Coral 61885	5	11
6.	JAILHOUSE ROCK (BMI)—Elvis Presley Treat Me Nice (BMI)—Vic 7035	6	15
7.	RAUNCHY (BMI)—Bill Justis The Nidnite Man (BMI)—Phillips International 3519	10	10
8.	KISSES SWEETER THAN WINE (BMI)—Jimmie Rodgers Better Loved You'll Never Be (ASCAP)—Roulette 4031	9	9
9.	YOU SEND ME (BMI)—Sam Cooke SUMMERTIME (ASCAP)—Keen 34013	8	13
10.	SILHOUETTES (BMI)—The Rays DADDY COOL (BMI)—Cameo 117	11	14
11.	OH, BOY! (BMI)—Crickets Not Fade Away (BMI)—Brunswick 55035	12	8
12.	THE STROLL (BMI)—Diamonds Land of Beauty (BMI)—Mercury 71242	22	3
13.	LA DEE DAH (BMI)—Billy and Lillie The Monster (BMI)—Swan 4002	36	2
14.	BUZZ, BUZZ, BUZZ (BMI)—Hollywood Flames Crazy (BMI)—Ebb 119	23	8
15.	SUGARTIME (BMI)—McGuire Sisters Banana Split (BMI)—Coral 61924	30	3
16.	SAIL ALONG SILVERY MOON (ASCAP)—Billy Vaughn RAUNCHY (BMI)—Dot 15661	21	5
17.	CHANCES ARE (ASCAP)—Johnny Mathis THE TWELFTH OF NEVER (ASCAP)—Col 40993	16	18
18.	ROCK AND ROLL MUSIC (BMI)—Chuck Berry Blue Feeling (BMI)—Chess 1671	15	11
19.	JINGLE BELL ROCK—Bobby Helms Captain Santa Claus—Decca 30513	7	5
20.	BONY MORONIE (BMI)—Larry Williams YOU BUG ME, BABY (BMI)—Specialty 615	17	11
21.	MY SPECIAL ANGEL (BMI)—Bobby Helms Standing at the End of My World (BMI)—Dec 30423	13	14
22.	WAKE UP LITTLE SUSIE (BMI)—Everly Brothers Maybe Tomorrow (BMI)—Cadence 1337	14	17
23.	RAUNCHY (BMI)—Ernie Freeman Puddin' (BMI)—Imperial 5474	18	10
24.	BE-BOP BABY (BMI)—Ricky Nelson HAVE I TOLD YOU LATELY THAT I LOVE YOU? (BMI)—Imperial 5463	19	16
25.	ALL THE WAY (ASCAP)—Frank Sinatra CHICAGO (ASCAP)—Cap 3793	20	21
26.	WHY DON'T THEY UNDERSTAND? (BMI)—George Hamilton IV Even Tho' (BMI)—ABC-Paramount 9862	24	8
27.	JUST BORN (BMI)—Perry Como IVY ROSE (ASCAP)—Vic 7050	25	13
28.	FASCINATION (ASCAP)—Jane Morgan Fascination (Instrumental) (ASCAP)—Kapp 191	28	20
29.	LIECHTENSTEINER POLKA (ASCAP)—Will Glahe Schweitzer Polka (BMI)—London 1755	33	10
30.	(I LOVE YOU) FOR SENTIMENTAL REASONS (BMI)—Sam Cooke DESIRE ME (BMI)—Keen 4002	32	4
31.	THE BIG BEAT (BMI)—Fats Domino I WANT YOU TO KNOW (BMI)—Imperial 5477	26	5
32.	TEARDROPS (BMI)—Lee Andrews and the Hearts Girl Around the Corner (BMI)—Chess 1675	27	8
33.	OH, JULIE (BMI)—Crescendos My Little Girl (BMI)—Nasco 6005	41	2
34.	GET A JOB (BMI)—Silhouettes I Am Lonely (BMI)—Ember 1029	—	1
35.	WILD IS THE WIND (ASCAP)—Johnny Mathis NO LOVE (BUT YOUR LOVE) (BMI)—Col 41060	37	6
36.	I'LL COME RUNNING BACK TO YOU (BMI)—Sam Cooke FOREVER (BMI)—Specialty 619	34	5
37.	THE STORY OF MY LIFE (ASCAP)—Marty Robbins Once-a-Week Date (BMI)—Col 41013	35	8
38.	I'M AVAILABLE (BMI)—Margie Rayburn If You Were (ASCAP)—Liberty 55102	31	11
39.	HONEYCOMB (ASCAP)—Jimmie Rodgers Their Hearts Were Full of Spring (ASCAP)—Roulette 4015	39	23
40.	PUT A LIGHT IN THE WINDOW (ASCAP)—Four Lads The Things We Did Last Summer (ASCAP)—Col 41058	40	6
41.	MELODIE D'AMOUR (BMI)—Ames Brothers So Little Time (BMI)—Vic 7046	29	15
42.	LITTLE BITTY PRETTY ONE (BMI)—Thurston Harris I Hope You Won't Hold It Against Me (ASCAP)—Aladdin 3398	38	13
43.	DON'T LET GO (BMI)—Roy Hamilton The Right to Love (BMI)—Epic 9257	—	1
44.	JO-ANN (BMI)—Playmates You Can't Stop Me From Dreaming (BMI)—Roulette 4037	—	1
45.	A VERY SPECIAL LOVE (ASCAP)—Johnny Nash Won't You Let Me Share My Love? (BMI)—ABC-Paramount 9874	—	1
46.	MARCH FROM THE RIVER KWAI AND COLONEL BOGEY (ASCAP)—Mitch Miller Hey! Little Baby (BMI)—Col 41066	—	1
47.	THE JOKER (BMI)—Hilltoppers Chicken, Chicken (ASCAP)—Dot 15662	44	5
48.	MAYBE (BMI)—Chantels Come My Little Baby (BMI)—End 1005	—	1
49.	THE JOKER (BMI)—Billy Myles Honey Bee (BMI)—Ember 1026	48	9
50.	HEY, SCHOOLGIRL (BMI)—Tom and Jerry Dancin' Wild (BMI)—Big 613	—	2

THIS WEEK'S BEST BUYS

Special telephone reports indicate these recent releases have broken out in one or more key areas and have excellent potential for placing on The Billboard's best seller charts.

DON'T (Presley, BMI)
I BEG OF YOU (Presley, BMI)—Elvis Presley—RCA Victor 7150—Both sides are big in all markets. "Don't" has edge.

COME TO ME (Korwin, ASCAP)—Johnny Mathis—Columbia 41082—This side is also hot in r.&b. marts. Flip is "When I Am With You" (Mathis, ASCAP).

MAGIC MOMENTS (Famous, ASCAP)
CATCH A FALLING STAR (Marvin, ASCAP)—Perry Como—RCA Victor 7128—"Magic Moments" is currently the stronger side. Flip, "Catch a Falling Star," is also hot.

WITCHCRAFT (Morris, ASCAP)
TELL HER YOU LOVE HER (Mr. Music, BMI)—Frank Sinatra—Capitol 3859—"Witchcraft" is getting more action now, but "Tell Her You Love Her" is also scoring.

ANGEL SMILE (Winneton, BMI)—Nat King Cole—Capitol 3860—The side is doing well in both pop and r.&b. markets. Flip is "Back in My Arms" (Weiss & Barry, BMI).

YOU ARE MY DESTINY (Pamco, BMI)—Paul Anka—ABC-Paramount 9880—The side is strong in all markets. Flip is "When I Stop Loving You" (Figure, BMI).

All are previous Billboard Spotlight picks.

STORE RECORDED SALES — NEW YORK UNIVERSITY SCHOOL OF RETAILING — THE BILLBOARD

RECENT POP RELEASES COMING UP STRONG

FOR SURVEY WEEK ENDING JANUARY 11

The information given in this chart is based on actual sales to customers in a scientific sample of the nation's retail record outlets during the week ending on the date shown above. Sample design, sample size and all methods used in this continuing study of retail record sales are under the direct and continuing supervision and control of the School of Retailing of New York University.

Catch a Falling Star
Magic Moments . . . . *Perry Como*
(ASCAP); (ASCAP) RCA Victor 7128

Dede Dinah . . . . *Frankie Avalon*
(ASCAP) Chancellor 1011

You Are My Destiny . . . . *Paul Anka*
(BMI) ABC-Paramount 9880

Most Played by Jockeys

FOR SURVEY WEEK ENDING JANUARY 11

SIDES are ranked in order of the greatest number of plays on disk jockey radio shows thruout the country. Results are based on The Billboard's weekly survey among the nation's disk jockeys. The reverse side of each record is also listed.

This Week		Last Week	Weeks on Chart
1.	APRIL LOVE (ASCAP)—Pat Boone When the Swallows Come Back to Capistrano (ASCAP)—Dot 15660	1	13
2.	AT THE HOP (BMI)—Danny and the Juniors Sometimes (BMI)—ABC-Paramount 9871	2	5
3.	KISSES SWEETER THAN WINE (BMI)—Jimmie Rodgers Better Loved You'll Never Be (ASCAP)—Roulette 4031	3	10
4.	PEGGY SUE (BMI)—Buddy Holly Everyday (BMI)—Coral 61885	7	10
5.	RAUNCHY (BMI)—Ernie Freeman Puddin' (BMI)—Imperial 5474	4	8
6.	ALL THE WAY (ASCAP)—Frank Sinatra Chicago (ASCAP)—Cap 3793	5	13
7.	YOU SEND ME (BMI)—Sam Cooke Summertime (ASCAP)—Keen 34013	6	12
8.	RAUNCHY (BMI)—Bill Justis The Midnite Man (BMI)—Phillips International 3519	8	9
9.	GREAT BALLS OF FIRE (BMI)—Jerry Lee Lewis You Win Again (BMI)—Sun 281	9	7
10.	SUGARTIME (BMI)—McGuire Sisters Banana Split (BMI)—Coral 61924	13	3
11.	WHY DON'T THEY UNDERSTAND? (BMI)—George Hamilton IV Even Tho' (BMI)—ABC-Paramount 9862	10	3
12.	PUT A LIGHT IN THE WINDOW (ASCAP)—Four Lads The Things We Did Last Summer (ASCAP)—Col 41058	11	7
13.	THE STROLL (BMI)—Diamonds Land of Beauty (BMI)—Mercury 71242	16	2
14.	MAGIC MOMENTS (ASCAP)—Perry Como Catch a Falling Star (ASCAP)—Vic 7128	—	1
15.	YOU SEND ME (BMI)—Teresa Brewer Would I Were (ASCAP)—Coral 61898	19	11
16.	RAUNCHY (BMI)—Billy Vaughn Sail Along Silvery Moon (ASCAP)—Dot 15661	22	6
17.	CATCH A FALLING STAR (ASCAP)—Perry Como Magic Moments (ASCAP)—Vic 7128	21	2
18.	JAILHOUSE ROCK (BMI)—Elvis Presley Treat Me Nice (BMI)—Vic 7035	25	15
19.	WITCHCRAFT (ASCAP)—Frank Sinatra Tell Her You Love Her (BMI)—Cap 3859	—	1
20.	A VERY SPECIAL LOVE (ASCAP)—Debbie Reynolds I Saw a Country Boy (ASCAP)—Coral 61897	—	1
21.	TEARDROPS (BMI)—Lee Andrews and the Hearts Girl Around the Corner (BMI)—Chess 1675	—	1
22.	26 MILES (BMI)—Four Preps It's You (ASCAP)—Cap 3845	—	1
23.	OH, BOY! (BMI)—Crickets Not Fade Away (BMI)—Brunswick 55035	20	5
24.	WAITIN' IN SCHOOL (BMI)—Ricky Nelson Stood Up (BMI)—Imperial 5483	—	1
25.	I'M AVAILABLE (BMI)—Margie Rayburn If You Were (ASCAP)—Liberty 55102	17	11

Top 100 Sides

FOR SURVEY WEEK ENDING JANUARY 11

This is a tabulation of dealer individual record sales listed according to the specific side requested by customers. No attempt is made to add sides together to reflect actual record sales. This is, therefore, a tabulation of sides or songs, and not records. This is the reason for any possible variation that occurs between the top 50 sides as reflected in this chart, and the top 50 record sellers as reflected in the "Best Sellers in Stores" chart.

Pos.	Song, Artist, Label	Last Week
1.	**AT THE HOP,** Danny and the Juniors, ABC-Paramount	1
2.	**GREAT BALLS OF FIRE,** Jerry Lee Lewis, Sun	2
3.	**APRIL LOVE,** Pat Boone, Dot	3
4.	**PEGGY SUE,** Buddy Holly, Coral	4
5.	**STOOD UP,** Ricky Nelson, Imperial	5
6.	**JAILHOUSE ROCK,** Elvis Presley, Victor	7
7.	**RAUNCHY,** Bill Justis, Phillips International	10
8.	**KISSES SWEETER THAN WINE,** Jimmie Rodgers, Roulette	9
9.	**YOU SEND ME,** Sam Cooke, Keen	8
10.	**OH, BOY!** Crickets, Brunswick	12
11.	**SILHOUETTES,** Rays, Cameo	11
12.	**THE STROLL,** Diamonds, Mercury	22
13.	**LA DEE DAH,** Billy and Lillie, Swan	32
14.	**BUZZ, BUZZ, BUZZ,** Hollywood Flames, Ebb	23
15.	**SUGARTIME,** McGuire Sisters, Coral	28
16.	**ROCK AND ROLL MUSIC,** Chuck Berry, Chess	15
17.	**JINGLE BELL ROCK,** Bobby Helms, Decca	6
18.	**MY SPECIAL ANGEL,** Bobby Helms, Decca	13
19.	**WAKE UP LITTLE SUSIE,** Everly Brothers, Cadence	14
20.	**CHANCES ARE,** Johnny Mathis, Columbia	18
21.	**RAUNCHY,** Ernie Freeman, Imperial	16
22.	**BE-BOP BABY,** Ricky Nelson, Imperial	17
23.	**WHY DON'T THEY UNDERSTAND?** George Hamilton IV, ABC-Paramount	24
24.	**WAITIN' IN SCHOOL,** Ricky Nelson, Imperial	21
25.	**BONY MORONIE,** Larry Williams, Specialty	20
26.	**ALL THE WAY,** Frank Sinatra, Capitol	19
27.	**FASCINATION,** Jane Morgan, Kapp	26
28.	**SAIL ALONG SILVERY MOON,** Billy Vaughn, Dot	33
29.	**LIECHTENSTEINER POLKA,** Will Glahe, London	30
30.	**TEARDROPS,** Lee Andrews and the Hearts, Chess	25
31.	**OH JULIE,** Crescendos, Nasco	41
32.	**GET A JOB,** Silhouettes, Ember	—
33.	**THE STORY OF MY LIFE,** Marty Robbins, Columbia	31
34.	**I'M AVAILABLE,** Margie Rayburn, Liberty	29
35.	**HONEYCOMB,** Jimmie Rodgers, Roulette	35
36.	**PUT A LIGHT IN THE WINDOW,** Four Lads, Columbia	37
37.	**I'LL COME RUNNING BACK TO YOU,** Sam Cooke, Specialty	36
38.	**JUST BORN,** Perry Como, Victor	40
39.	**MELODIE D'AMOUR,** Ames Brothers, Victor	27
40.	**LITTLE BITTY PRETTY ONE,** Thurston Harris, Aladdin	33
41.	**RAUNCHY,** Billy Vaughn, Dot	39
42.	**THE BIG BEAT,** Fats Domino, Imperial	38
43.	**DON'T LET GO,** Roy Hamilton, Epic	73
44.	**(I LOVE YOU) FOR SENTIMENTAL REASONS,** Sam Cooke, Keen	46
45.	**JO ANN,** Playmates, Roulette	—
46.	**A VERY SPECIAL LOVE,** Johnny Nash, ABC-Paramount	66
47.	**MARCH FROM "THE RIVER KWAI," AND "COLONEL BOGEY,"** Mitch Miller, Columbia	60
48.	**DESIRE ME,** Sam Cooke, Keen	47
49.	**THE JOKER,** Hilltoppers, Dot	44
50.	**IVY ROSE,** Perry Como, Victor	43

This chart is now a compilation of dealer unit sales by record sides for the same survey period that is reflected in the Best Sellers in Stores chart. This chart, therefore, is now reflecting each week the Top 100 sides not records as sold in stores thruout the nation.

Pos.	Song, Artist, Label	Last Week
51.	**WILD IS THE WIND,** Johnny Mathis, Columbia	52
52.	**I WANT YOU TO KNOW,** Fats Domino, Imperial	49
53.	**THE JOKER,** Billy Myles, Ember	53
53.	**MAYBE,** Chantels, End	—
55.	**NO LOVE (BUT YOUR LOVE),** Johnny Mathis, Columbia	48
56.	**HEY! SCHOOLGIRL,** Tom and Jerry, Big	73
57.	**DO WHAT YOU DID,** Thurston Harris, Aladdin	81
58.	**TAMMY,** Debbie Reynolds, Coral	49
59.	**COULD THIS BE MAGIC?** Dubs, Gone	58
59.	**PRETEND YOU DON'T SEE HER,** Jerry Vale, Columbia	63
59.	**WALKIN' WITH MR. LEE,** Lee Allen, Ember	77
62.	**HENRIETTA,** Jimmie Dee, Dot	53
62.	**YOU ARE MY DESTINY,** Paul Anka, ABC-Paramount	—
62.	**PENNY LOAFERS AND BOBBY SOCKS,** Joe Bennett and the Sparkletones, ABC-Paramount	57
65.	**SHE'S NEAT,** Dale Wright, Fraternity	70
65.	**DEDE DINAH,** Frankie Avalon, Chancellor	—
67.	**DANCE TO THE BOP,** Gene Vincent, Capitol	60
68.	**TILL,** Roger Williams, Kapp	53
68.	**KEEP A' KNOCKIN',** Little Richard, Specialty	53
70.	**HEY! LITTLE SCHOOL GIRL,** Techniques, Roulette	67
70.	**HARD TIMES (THE SLOP),** Noble (Thin Man) Watts, Baton	77
72.	**LOVE ME FOREVER,** Four Esquires, Paris	73
73.	**THIS IS THE NIGHT,** Valiants, Keen	84
73.	**YOU'RE THE GREATEST,** Billy Scott, Cameo	77
75.	**YOU BUG ME, BABY,** Larry Williams, Specialty	59
76.	**SANTA AND THE SATELLITE,** Buckanan & Goodman, Luniverse	36
76.	**THE TWELFTH OF NEVER,** Johnny Mathis, Columbia	67
78.	**MAGIC MOMENTS,** Perry Como, Victor	—
78.	**ROCK-A-CHICKA,** Warner Mack, Decca	—
78.	**YOU SEND ME,** Teresa Brewer, Coral	67
81.	**AT THE HOP,** Nick Todd, Dot	70
81.	**SOFT,** Bill Doggett, King	94
83.	**I'LL REMEMBER TODAY,** Patti Page, Mercury	91
83.	**SWANEE RIVER ROCK (TALKIN' 'BOUT THAT RIVER),** Ray Charles, Atlantic	81
85.	**AROUND THE WORLD,** Victor Young, Decca	77
85.	**FARTHER UP THE ROAD,** Bobby (Blue) Bland, Duke	—
85.	**HAPPY, HAPPY BIRTHDAY, BABY,** Tune Weavers, Checker	63
85.	**TWENTY-SIX MILES,** Four Preps, Capitol	—
89.	**ALONE,** Shepherd Sisters, Lance	76
89.	**MR. LEE,** Bobbettes, Atlantic	96
89.	**WHOLE LOTTA SHAKIN' GOIN' ON,** Jerry Lee Lewis, Sun	81
92.	**DIANA,** Paul Anka, ABC-Paramount	84
92.	**HULA LOVE,** Buddy Knox, Roulette	60
92.	**WHITE CHRISTMAS,** Bing Crosby, Decca	44
96.	**YOU CAN MAKE IT IF YOU TRY,** Gene Allison, Vee Jay	65
96.	**LOVE BUG CRAWL,** Jimmy Edwards, Mercury	—
96.	**LITTLE SANDY SLEIGHFOOT,** Jimmy Dean, Columbia	42
98.	**GEISHA GIRL,** Hank Locklin, Victor	90
99.	**CATCH A FALLING STAR,** Perry Como, Victor	—
99.	**MR. FIRE EYES,** Bonnie Guitar, Dot	—

STORE RECORDED SALES — NEW YORK UNIVERSITY SCHOOL OF RETAILING — THE BILLBOARD

Best Sellers in Stores

FOR SURVEY WEEK ENDING JANUARY 18, 1958

The information given in this chart is based on actual sales to customers in a scientific sample of the nation's retail record outlets during the week ending on the date shown above. Sample design, sample size, and all methods used in this continuing study of retail record sales are under the direct and continuing supervision and control of the School of Retailing of New York University.

This Week		Last Week	Weeks on Chart
1.	AT THE HOP (BMI)—Danny and the Juniors. Sometimes (BMI)—ABC-Paramount 9871	1	8
2.	STOOD UP (BMI)—Ricky Nelson. WAITIN' IN SCHOOL (BMI)—Imperial 5483	2	5
3.	GREAT BALLS OF FIRE (BMI)—Jerry Lee Lewis. YOU WIN AGAIN (BMI)—Sun 281	3	9
4.	PEGGY SUE (BMI)—Buddy Holly. Fveryday (BMI)—Coral 61885	5	12
5.	APRIL LOVE (ASCAP)—Pat Boone. WHEN THE SWALLOWS COME BACK TO CAPISTRANO (ASCAP)—Dot 15660	4	13
6.	GET A JOB (BMI)—Silhouettes. I Am Lonely (BMI)—Ember 1029	34	2
7.	SAIL ALONG SILVERY MOON (ASCAP)—Billy Vaughn. RAUNCHY (BMI)—Dot 15661	16	6
8.	THE STROLL (BMI)—Diamonds. Land of Beauty (BMI)—Mercury 71242	12	4
9.	SUGARTIME (BMI)—McGuire Sisters. Banana Split (BMI)—Coral 61924	15	4
10.	LA DEE DAH (BMI)—Billy and Lillie. The Monster (BMI)—Swan 4002	13	3
11.	RAUNCHY (BMI)—Bill Justis. The Midnite Man (BMI)—Phillips International 3519	7	11
12.	BUZZ, BUZZ, BUZZ (BMI)—Hollywood Flames. Crazy (BMI)—Ebb 119	14	9
13.	KISSES SWEETER THAN WINE (BMI)—Jimmie Rodgers. Better Loved You'll Never Be (ASCAP)—Roulette 4031	8	10
14.	OH, BOY! (BMI)—Crickets. Not Fade Away (BMI)—Brunswick 55035	11	9
15.	JAILHOUSE ROCK (BMI)—Elvis Presley. TREAT ME NICE (BMI)—Vic 7035	6	16
16.	YOU SEND ME (BMI)—Sam Cooke. SUMMERTIME (ASCAP)—Keen 34013	9	14
17.	SILHOUETTES (BMI)—The Rays. DADDY COOL (BMI)—Cameo 117	10	15
18.	BONY MORONIE (BMI)—Larry Williams. YOU BUG ME, BABY (BMI)—Specialty 615	20	12
19.	WHY DON'T THEY UNDERSTAND? (BMI)—George Hamilton IV. Even Tho' (BMI)—ABC-Paramount 9862	26	9
20.	CHANCES ARE (ASCAP)—Johnny Mathis. THE TWELFTH OF NEVER (ASCAP)—Col 40993	17	19
21.	RAUNCHY (BMI)—Ernie Freeman. Puddin' (BMI)—Imperial 5474	23	11
22.	LIECHTENSTEINER POLKA (ASCAP)—Will Glahe. Schweitzer Polka (BMI)—London 1755	29	11
23.	BE-BOP BABY (BMI)—Ricky Nelson. HAVE I TOLD YOU LATELY THAT I LOVE YOU (BMI)—Imperial 5463	24	17
24.	DON'T LET GO (BMI)—Roy Hamilton. The Right to Love (BMI)—Epic 9257	43	2
25.	DON'T (BMI)—Elvis Presley. I BEG OF YOU (BMI)—Victor 7150	—	1
26.	ALL THE WAY (ASCAP)—Frank Sinatra. CHICAGO (ASCAP)—Cap 3793	25	12
27.	WAKE UP LITTLE SUSIE (BMI)—Everly Brothers. Maybe Tomorrow (BMI)—Cadence 1337	22	18
28.	OH, JULIE (BMI)—Crescendos. My Little Girl (BMI)—Nasco 6005	33	3
29.	ROCK AND ROLL MUSIC (BMI)—Chuck Berry. Blue Feeling (BMI)—Chess 1671	18	12
30.	MY SPECIAL ANGEL (BMI)—Bobby Helms. Standing at the End of My World (BMI)—Dec 30423	21	15
31.	(I LOVE YOU) FOR SENTIMENTAL REASONS (BMI)—Sam Cooke. DESIRE ME (BMI)—Keen 4002	30	5
32.	I WANT YOU TO KNOW (BMI)—Fats Domino. THE BIG BEAT (BMI)—Imperial 5477	31	6
33.	TEARDROPS (BMI)—Lee Andrews and the Hearts. Girl Around the Corner (BMI)—Chess 1675	32	9
34.	JUST BORN (BMI)—Perry Como. IVY ROSE (ASCAP)—Vic 7050	27	14
35.	FASCINATION (ASCAP)—Jane Morgan. Fascination (Instrumental) (ASCAP)—Kapp 191	28	21
36.	MAYBE (BMI)—Chantels. Come My Little Baby (BMI)—End 1005	48	2
37.	JO-ANN (BMI)—Playmates. You Can't Stop Me From Dreaming (BMI)—Roulette 4037	44	2
38.	DEDE DINAH (ASCAP)—Frankie Avalon. Ooh La La (ASCAP)—Chancellor 1011	—	1
39.	I'LL COME RUNNING BACK TO YOU (BMI)—Sam Cooke. FOREVER (BMI)—Specialty 619	36	6
40.	THE STORY OF MY LIFE (ASCAP)—Marty Robbins. Once-a-Week Date (BMI)—Col 41013	37	9
41.	I'M AVAILABLE (BMI)—Margie Rayburn. If You Were (ASCAP)—Liberty 55102	38	12
42.	MAGIC MOMENTS (ASCAP)—Perry Como. CATCH A FALLING STAR (ASCAP)—Victor 7128	—	1
43.	HONEYCOMB (ASCAP)—Jimmie Rodgers. Their Hearts Were Full of Spring (ASCAP)—Roulette 4015	39	24
44.	WILD IS THE WIND (ASCAP)—Johnny Mathis. NO LOVE (BUT YOUR LOVE) (BMI)—Col 41060	35	7
45.	YOU ARE MY DESTINY (BMI)—Paul Anka. When I Stop Loving You (BMI)—ABC-Paramount 9880	—	1
46.	PUT A LIGHT IN YOUR WINDOW (ASCAP)—Four Lads. The Things We Did Last Summer (ASCAP)—Col 41058	40	7
47.	MARCH FROM THE RIVER KWAI, AND "COLONEL BOGEY" (ASCAP)—Mitch Miller. Hey, Little Baby (BMI)—Col 41066	46	2
48.	A VERY SPECIAL LOVE (ASCAP)—Johnny Nash. Won't You Let Me Share My Love (BMI)—ABC-Paramount 9874	45	2
49.	MELODIE D'AMOUR (BMI) Ames Brothers. So Little Time (BMI)—Vic 7046	41	10
50.	LITTLE BITTY PRETTY ONE (BMI)—Thurston Harris. I Hope You Won't Hold It Against Me (ASCAP)—Aladdin 3398	42	14

THIS WEEK'S BEST BUYS

Special telephone reports indicate these recent releases have broken out in one or more key areas and have excellent potential for placing on The Billboard's best seller charts.

THIS LITTLE GIRL OF MINE (Progressive, BMI)

SHOULD WE TELL HIM (Acuff-Rose, BMI)—Everly Brothers—Cadence 1342—Looks like another two-sided hit for the duo. Both sides are strong in all marts. A previous Billboard Spotlight pick.

SHORT SHORTS (Admiration, BMI)—The Royal Teens—ABC-Paramount 9882—This is a big one. All markets report that sales are heavy. Flip is "Planet Rock" (Brunswick, BMI). A previous Billboard Spotlight pick.

TWENTY-SIX MILES (Beechwood, BMI)—The Four Preps—Capitol 3826—Heaviest action for the side is on the West Coast, but it's also beginning to register strongly elsewhere. Flip is "It's You" Frank, ASCAP).

STORE RECORDED SALES — NEW YORK UNIVERSITY SCHOOL OF RETAILING — THE BILLBOARD

RECENT POP RELEASES COMING UP STRONG

FOR SURVEY WEEK ENDING JANUARY 18

The information given in this chart is based on actual sales to customers in a scientific sample of the nation's retail record outlets during the week ending on the date shown above. Sample design, sample size and all methods used in this continuing study of retail record sales are under the direct and continuing supervision and control of the School of Retailing of New York University.

Short Shorts . . . . ***The Royal Teens***
(BMI) ABC-Paramount 9882

Twenty-Six Miles . . . . ***Four Preps***
(BMI) Capitol 3845

Most Played by Jockeys

FOR SURVEY WEEK ENDING JANUARY 18

SIDES are ranked in order of the greatest number of plays on disk jockey radio shows thruout the country. Results are based on The Billboard's weekly survey among the nation's disk jockeys. The reverse side of each record is also listed.

This Week		Last Week	Weeks on Chart
1.	**AT THE HOP** (BMI)—Danny and the Juniors Sometimes (BMI)—ABC-Paramount 9871	2	6
2.	**APRIL LOVE** (ASCAP)—Pat Boone When the Swallows Come Back to Capistrano (ASCAP)—Dot 15660	1	14
3.	**SUGARTIME** (BMI)—McGuire Sisters Banana Split (BMI)—Coral 61924	10	4
4.	**PEGGY SUE** (BMI)—Buddy Holly Everyday (BMI)—Coral 61885	4	11
5.	**KISSES SWEETER THAN WINE** (BMI)—Jimmie Rodgers Better Loved You'll Never Be (ASCAP)—Roulette 4031	3	11
6.	**ALL THE WAY** (ASCAP)—Frank Sinatra Chicago (ASCAP)—Cap 3793	6	14
7.	**RAUNCHY** (BMI)—Ernie Freeman Puddin' (BMI)—Imperial 5474	5	9
8.	**THE STROLL** (BMI)—Diamonds Land of Beauty (BMI)—Mercury 71242	13	3
9.	**WITCHCRAFT** (ASCAP)—Frank Sinatra Tell Her You Love Her (BMI)—Cap 3859	19	2
10.	**MAGIC MOMENTS** (ASCAP)—Perry Como Catch a Falling Star (ASCAP)—Vic 7128	14	2
11.	**WHY DON'T THEY UNDERSTAND?** (BMI)—George Hamilton IV Even Tho' (BMI)—ABC-Paramount 9862	11	4
12.	**RAUNCHY** (BMI)—Bill Justis The Midnite Man (BMI)—Phillips International 3519	8	10
13.	**GREAT BALLS OF FIRE** (BMI)—Jerry Lee Lewis You Win Again (BMI)—Sun 281	9	8
14.	**YOU SEND ME** (BMI)—Sam Cooke Summertime (ASCAP)—Keen 34013	7	13
15.	**STOOD UP** (BMI)—Ricky Nelson Waitin' in School (BMI)—Imperial 5483	—	1
16.	**DON'T LET GO** (BMI)—Roy Hamilton The Right to Love (BMI)—Epic 9257	—	1
17.	**GET A JOB** (BMI)—Silhouettes I Am Lonely (BMI)—Ember 1029	—	1
18.	**RAUNCHY** (BMI)—Billy Vaughn Sail Along Silvery Moon (ASCAP)—Dot 15661	16	7
19.	**CATCH A FALLING STAR** (ASCAP)—Perry Como Magic Moments (ASCAP)—Vic 7128	17	3
20.	**PUT A LIGHT IN THE WINDOW** (ASCAP)—Four Lads The Things We Did Last Summer (ASCAP)—Col 41058	12	8
21.	**SAIL ALONG SILVERY MOON** (ASCAP)—Billy Vaughn Raunchy (BMI)—Dot 15661	—	1
22.	**OH, BOY!** (BMI)—Crickets Not Fade Away (BMI) Brunswick 55035	23	6
23.	**MARCH FROM THE RIVER KWAI, AND "COLONEL BOGEY"**—Mitch Miller Hey Little Baby (BMI)—Col 41066	—	1
24.	**LA DEE DAH** (BMI)—Billy and Lillie The Monster (BMI)—Swan 4002	—	1
25.	**THE STORY OF MY LIFE** (ASCAP)—Marty Robbins Once-a-Week Date (BMI)—Col 41013	—	6

Top 100 Sides

FOR SURVEY WEEK ENDING JANUARY 18

This is a tabulation of dealer individual record sales listed according to the specific side requested by customers. No attempt is made to add sides together to reflect actual record sales. This is, therefore, a tabulation of sides or songs, and not records. This is the reason for any possible variation that occurs between the top 50 sides as reflected in this chart, and the top 50 record sellers as reflected in the "Best Sellers in Stores" chart.

Pos.	Song, Artist, Label	Last Week
1.	**AT THE HOP,** Danny and the Juniors, ABC-Paramount	1
2.	**GREAT BALLS OF FIRE,** Jerry Lee Lewis, Sun	2
3.	**PEGGY SUE,** Buddy Holly, Coral	4
4.	**APRIL LOVE,** Pat Boone, Dot	3
5.	**STOOD UP,** Ricky Nelson, Imperial	5
6.	**GET A JOB,** Silhouettes, Ember	32
7.	**THE STROLL,** Diamonds, Mercury	12
8.	**SUGARTIME,** McGuire Sisters, Coral	15
9.	**LA DEE DAH,** Billy and Lillie, Swan	13
10.	**RAUNCHY,** Bill Justis, Phillips International	7
11.	**BUZZ, BUZZ, BUZZ,** Hollywood Flames, Ebb	14
12.	**KISSES SWEETER THAN WINE,** Jimmie Rodgers, Roulette	8
13.	**OH, BOY!** Crickets, Brunswick	10
14.	**JAILHOUSE ROCK,** Elvis Presley, Victor	6
15.	**YOU SEND ME,** Sam Cooke, Keen	9
16.	**SAIL ALONG SILVERY MOON,** Billy Vaughn, Dot	28
17.	**SILHOUETTES,** Rays, Cameo	11
17.	**WHY DON'T THEY UNDERSTAND?** George Hamilton IV, ABC-Paramount	23
19.	**BONY MORONIE,** Larry Williams, Specialty	25
20.	**RAUNCHY,** Ernie Freeman, Imperial	21
21.	**WAITIN' IN SCHOOL,** Ricky Nelson, Imperial	24
22.	**LIECHTENSTEINER POLKA,** Will Glahe, London	29
23.	**BE-BOP BABY,** Ricky Nelson, Imperial	22
23.	**DON'T LET GO,** Roy Hamilton, Epic	43
25.	**CHANCES ARE,** Johnny Mathis, Columbia	20
26.	**WAKE UP LITTLE SUSIE,** Everly Brothers, Cadence	19
26.	**OH, JULIE,** Crescendos, Nasco	31
28.	**ROCK AND ROLL MUSIC,** Chuck Berry, Chess	16
28.	**MY SPECIAL ANGEL,** Bobby Helms, Decca	18
30.	**ALL THE WAY,** Frank Sinatra, Capitol	26
31.	**TEARDROPS,** Lee Andrews and the Hearts, Chess	30
32.	**FASCINATION,** Jane Morgan, Kapp	27
32.	**MAYBE,** Chantels, End	53
34.	**JO ANN,** Playmates, Roulette	45
35.	**DEDE DINAH,** Frankie Avalon, Chancellor	65
36.	**THE STORY OF MY LIFE,** Marty Robbins, Columbia	33
37.	**I'M AVAILABLE,** Margie Rayburn, Liberty	34
38.	**HONEYCOMB,** Jimmie Rodgers, Roulette	35
39.	**I'LL COME RUNNING BACK TO YOU,** Sam Cooke, Specialty	37
40.	**DON'T,** Elvis Presley, Victor	—
41.	**YOU ARE MY DESTINY,** Paul Anka, ABC-Paramount	62
42.	**RAUNCHY,** Billy Vaughn, Dot	41
43.	**PUT A LIGHT IN THE WINDOW,** Four Lads, Columbia	36
44.	**(I LOVE YOU) FOR SENTIMENTAL REASONS,** Sam Cooke, Keen	44
45.	**JUST BORN,** Perry Como, Victor	38
46.	**MARCH FROM "THE RIVER KWAI," AND "COLONEL BOGEY,"** Mitch Miller, Columbia	47
47.	**A VERY SPECIAL LOVE,** Johnny Nash, ABC-Paramount	46
48.	**I WANT YOU TO KNOW,** Fats Domino, Imperial	52
48.	**MELODIE D'AMOUR,** Ames Brothers, Victor	39

This chart is now a compilation of dealer unit sales by record sides for the same survey period that is reflected in the Best Sellers in Stores chart. This chart, therefore, is now reflecting each week the Top 100 sides not records as sold in stores thruout the nation.

Pos.	Song, Artist, Label	Last Week
50.	**LITTLE BITTY PRETTY ONE,** Thurston Harris, Aladdin	40
51.	**THE BIG BEAT,** Fats Domino, Imperial	42
52.	**PRETEND YOU DON'T SEE HER,** Jerry Vale, Columbia	59
53.	**DESIRE ME,** Sam Cooke, Keen	48
54.	**HEY! LITTLE GIRL,** Techniques, Roulette	70
55.	**WILD IS THE WIND,** Johnny Mathis, Columbia	51
56.	**I BEG OF YOU,** Elvis Presley, Victor	—
57.	**MAGIC MOMENTS,** Perry Como, Victor	78
58.	**THE JOKER,** Billy Myles, Ember	53
58.	**HEY! SCHOOLGIRL,** Tom and Jerry, Big	56
60.	**CATCH A FALLING STAR,** Perry Como, Victor	99
61.	**WALKIN' WITH MR. LEE,** Lee Allen, Ember	59
62.	**THE JOKER,** Hilltoppers, Dot	49
62.	**COULD THIS BE MAGIC?** Dubs, Gone	59
64.	**DO WHAT YOU DID,** Thurston Harris, Aladdin	57
64.	**TWENTY-SIX MILES,** Four Preps, Capitol	85
66.	**HENRIETTA,** Jimmie Dee, Dot	62
66.	**SHORT SHORTS,** Royal Teens, ABC-Paramount	—
68.	**DANCE TO THE BOP,** Gene Vincent, Capitol	67
69.	**TAMMY,** Debbie Reynolds, Coral	58
70.	**TILL,** Roger Williams, Kapp	68
70.	**YOU CAN MAKE IT IF YOU TRY,** Gene Allison, Vee Jay	96
72.	**IVY ROSE,** Perry Como, Victor	50
73.	**HARD TIMES (THE SLOP),** Noble (Thin Man) Watts, Baton	70
74.	**NO LOVE (BUT YOUR LOVE),** Johnny Mathis, Columbia	55
74.	**ROCK-A-CHICKA,** Warner Mack, Decca	78
76.	**GEISHA GIRL,** Hank Locklin, Victor	95
76.	**YOU'RE THE GREATEST,** Billy Scott, Cameo	73
78.	**JINGLE BELL ROCK,** Bobby Helms, Decca	17
78.	**THIS IS THE NIGHT,** Valiants, Keen	73
78.	**LOVE BUG CRAWL,** Jimmy Edwards, Mercury	96
81.	**THE TWELFTH OF NEVER,** Johnny Mathis, Columbia	76
81.	**SWINGING SHEPHERD BLUES,** Johnny Page Quintet, Federal	—
81.	**YOU SEND ME,** Teresa Brewer, Coral	78
84.	**KEEP A' KNOCKIN',** Little Richard, Specialty	68
84.	**SHE'S NEAT,** Dale Wright, Fraternity	65
86.	**PENNY LOAFERS AND BOBBY SOCKS,** Joe Bennett and the Sparkletones, ABC-Paramount	62
86.	**SOFT,** Bill Doggett, King	81
88.	**BERTHA LOU,** Clint Miller, ABC-Paramount	—
89.	**YELLOW DOG BLUES,** Joe Darensbourg and the Dixie Flyers, Lark	—
89.	**FARTHER UP THE ROAD,** Bobby (Blue) Bland, Duke	85
91.	**ANGEL SMILE,** Nat King Cole, Capitol	—
91.	**SWANEE RIVER ROCK (TALKIN' 'BOUT THAT RIVER),** Ray Charles, Atlantic	83
93.	**YELLOW DOG BLUES,** Johnny Maddox, Dot	—
93.	**MR. LEE,** Bobbettes, Atlantic	89
95.	**A VERY SPECIAL LOVE,** Debbie Reynolds, Coral	—
95.	**I'LL REMEMBER TODAY,** Patti Page, Mercury	83
97.	**LITTLE PIGEON,** Sal Mineo, Epic	—
97.	**DIANA,** Paul Anka, ABC-Paramount	92
97.	**HULA LOVE,** Buddy Knox, Roulette	92
97.	**THAT'S ALL RIGHT,** Little Jr. Parker, Duke	—

Best Sellers in Stores

FOR SURVEY WEEK ENDING JANUARY 25, 1958

The information given in this chart is based on actual sales to customers in a scientific sample of the nation's retail record outlets during the week ending on the date shown above. Sample design, sample size, and all methods used in this continuing study of retail record sales are under the direct and continuing supervision and control of the School of Retailing of New York University.

This Week		Last Week	Weeks on Chart
1.	AT THE HOP (BMI)—Danny and the Juniors; Sometimes (BMI)—ABC-Paramount 9871	1	9
2.	GET A JOB (BMI)—Silhouettes; I Am Lonely (BMI)—Ember 1029	6	3
3.	DON'T (BMI)—Elvis Presley; I BEG OF YOU (BMI)—Victor 7150	25	2
4.	STOOD UP (BMI)—Ricky Nelson; WAITIN' IN SCHOOL (BMI)—Imperial 5483	2	6
5.	SAIL ALONG SILVERY MOON (ASCAP)—Billy Vaughn; RAUNCHY (BMI)—Dot 15661	7	7
6.	PEGGY SUE (BMI)—Buddy Holly; Everyday (BMI)—Coral 61885	4	13
7.	GREAT BALLS OF FIRE (BMI)—Jerry Lee Lewis; YOU WIN AGAIN (BMI)—Sun 281	3	10
8.	APRIL LOVE (ASCAP)—Pat Boone; When the Swallows Come Back to Capistrano (ASCAP)—Dot 15660	5	14
9.	SUGARTIME (BMI)—McGuire Sisters; Banana Split (BMI)—Coral 61924	9	5
10.	THE STROLL (BMI)—Diamonds; Land of Beauty (BMI)—Mercury 71242	8	5
11.	LA DEE DAH (BMI)—Billy and Lillie; The Monster (BMI)—Swan 4002	10	4
12.	KISSES SWEETER THAN WINE (BMI)—Jimmie Rodgers; Better Loved You'll Never Be (ASCAP)—Roulette 4031	13	11
13.	OH, BOY (BMI)—Crickets; Not Fade Away (BMI)—Brunswick 55035	14	10
14.	YOU SEND ME (BMI)—Sam Cooke; Summertime (ASCAP)—Keen 34013	16	15
15.	SHORT SHORTS (BMI)—Royal Teens; Planet Rock (BMI)—ABC-Paramount 9882	—	1
16.	SILHOUETTES (BMI)—The Rays; DADDY COOL (BMI)—Cameo 117	17	16
17.	CATCH A FALLING STAR (ASCAP)—Perry Como; MAGIC MOMENTS (ASCAP)—Victor 7128	42	2
18.	JAILHOUSE ROCK (BMI)—Elvis Presley; TREAT ME NICE (BMI)—Vic 7035	15	17
19.	RAUNCHY (BMI)—Bill Justis; The Midnite Man (BMI)—Phillips International 3519	11	12
20.	BUZZ, BUZZ, BUZZ (BMI)—Hollywood Flames; Crazy (BMI)—Ebb 119	12	10
21.	BONY MORONIE (BMI)—Larry Williams; YOU BUG ME, BABY (BMI)—Specialty 615	18	13
22.	WHY DON'T THEY UNDERSTAND? (BMI)—George Hamilton IV; Even Tho' (BMI)—ABC-Paramount 9862	19	10
23.	DON'T LET GO (BMI)—Roy Hamilton; The Right to Love (BMI)—Epic 9257	24	3
24.	DEDE DINAH (ASCAP)—Frankie Avalon; Ooh La La (ASCAP)—Chancellor 1011	38	2
25.	CHANCES ARE (ASCAP)—Johnny Mathis; THE TWELFTH OF NEVER (ASCAP)—Col 40993	20	20
26.	RAUNCHY (BMI)—Ernie Freeman; Puddin' (BMI)—Imperial 5474	21	12
27.	MAYBE (BMI)—Chantels; Come My Little Baby (BMI)—End 1005	36	3
28.	LIECHTENSTEINER POLKA (ASCAP)—Will Glahe; Schweitzer Polka (BMI)—London 1755	22	12
29.	WAKE UP LITTLE SUSIE (BMI)—Everly Brothers; Maybe Tomorrow (BMI)—Cadence 1337	27	19
30.	OH, JULIE (BMI)—Crescendos; My Little Girl (BMI)—Nasco 6005	28	4
31.	THE STORY OF MY LIFE (ASCAP)—Marty Robbins; Once-a-Week Date (BMI)—Col 41013	40	10
32.	(I LOVE YOU) FOR SENTIMENTAL REASONS (BMI)—Sam Cooke; DESIRE ME (BMI)—Keen 4002	31	6
33.	I'LL COME RUNNING BACK TO YOU (BMI)—Sam Cooke; FOREVER (BMI)—Specialty 619	39	7
34.	BE-BOP BABY (BMI)—Ricky Nelson; Have I Told You Lately That I Love You (BMI)—Imperial 5463	23	18
35.	YOU ARE MY DESTINY (BMI)—Paul Anka; When I Stop Loving You (BMI)—ABC-Paramount 9880	45	2
36.	ROCK AND ROLL MUSIC (BMI)—Chuck Berry; Blue Feeling (BMI)—Chess 1671	29	13
37.	TEARDROPS (BMI)—Lee Andrews and the Hearts; Girl Around the Corner (BMI)—Chess 1675	33	10
38.	I WANT YOU TO KNOW (BMI)—Fats Domino; THE BIG BEAT (BMI)—Imperial 5477	32	7
39.	I'M AVAILABLE (BMI)—Margie Rayburn; If You Were (ASCAP)—Liberty 55102	41	13
40.	ALL THE WAY (ASCAP)—Frank Sinatra; CHICAGO (ASCAP)—Cap 3793	26	13
41.	MY SPECIAL ANGEL (BMI)—Bobby Helms; Standing at the End of My World (BMI)—Dec 30423	30	16
42.	JO-ANN (BMI)—Playmates; You Can't Stop Me From Dreaming (BMI)—Roulette 4037	37	3
43.	MARCH FROM THE RIVER KWAI, AND "COLONEL BOGEY" (ASCAP)—Mitch Miller; Hey, Little Baby (BMI)—Col 41066	47	3
44.	FASCINATION (ASCAP)—Jane Morgan; Fascination (Instrumental) (ASCAP)—Kapp 191	35	22
45.	LITTLE PIGEON (BMI)—Sal Mineo; Cuttin' In (BMI)—Epic 9260	—	1
46.	HONEYCOMB (ASCAP)—Jimmie Rodgers; Their Hearts Were Full of Spring (ASCAP)—Roulette 4015	43	25
47.	LITTLE BITTY PRETTY ONE (BMI)—Thurston Harris; I Hope You Won't Hold It Against Me (ASCAP)—Aladdin 3398	50	15
48.	WILD IS THE WIND (ASCAP)—Johnny Mathis; NO LOVE (BUT YOUR LOVE) (BMI)—Col 41060	44	8
49.	WITCHCRAFT (ASCAP)—Frank Sinatra; Tell Her You Love Her (BMI)—Capitol 3859	—	1
50.	JUST BORN (BMI)—Perry Como; IVY ROSE (ASCAP)—Vic 7050	34	15

THIS WEEK'S BEST BUYS

Special telephone reports indicate these recent releases have broken out in one or more key areas and have excellent potential for placing on The Billboard's best seller charts.

IT'S TOO SOON TO KNOW (Morris, ASCAP)—Pat Boone—Dot 15690—The side is stepping out in all markets. This looks like another hit for the artist. Flip is "A Wonderful Time Up There" (Fowler, BMI). A previous Billboard Spotlight pick.

GOOD GOLLY, MISS MOLLY (Venice, BMI)—Little Richard—Specialty 624—This is a hot one. It's collecting heaps of coin in both pop and r.&b. markets. Flip is "Hey-Hey-Hey-Hey!" (Venice, BMI). A previous Billboard Spotlight pick.

RECENT POP RELEASES COMING UP STRONG

FOR SURVEY WEEK ENDING JANUARY 25

The information given in this chart is based on actual sales to customers in a scientific sample of the nation's retail record outlets during the week ending on the date shown above. Sample design, sample size and all methods used in this continuing study of retail record sales are under the direct and continuing supervision and control of the School of Retailing of New York University.

Angel Smile . . . *Nat King Cole* (BMI) Capitol 3860

Ballad of a Teenage Queen . . . *Johnny Cash* (BMI) Sun 283

Swingin' Shepherd Blues . . . *Moe Koffman* (BMI) Jubilee 5311

Twenty-Six Miles . . . *Four Preps* (BMI) Capitol 3845

Most Played by Jockeys

FOR SURVEY WEEK ENDING JANUARY 25

SIDES are ranked in order of the greatest number of plays on disk jockey radio shows thruout the country. Results are based on The Billboard's weekly survey among the nation's disk jockeys. The reverse side of each record is also listed.

This Week		Last Week	Weeks on Chart
1.	**AT THE HOP** (BMI)—Danny and the Juniors Sometimes (BMI)—ABC-Paramount 9871	1	7
2.	**SUGARTIME** (BMI)—McGuire Sisters Banana Split (BMI)—Coral 61924	3	5
3.	**APRIL LOVE** (ASCAP)—Pat Boone When the Swallows Come Back to Capistrano (ASCAP)—Dot 15660	2	15
4.	**THE STROLL** (BMI)—Diamonds Land of Beauty (BMI)—Mercury 71242	8	4
5.	**PEGGY SUE** (BMI)—Buddy Holly Everyday (BMI)—Coral 61885	4	12
6.	**CATCH A FALLING STAR** (ASCAP)—Perry Como Magic Moments (ASCAP)—Vic 7128	19	4
7.	**ALL THE WAY** (ASCAP)—Frank Sinatra Chicago (ASCAP)—Cap 3793	6	15
8.	**MAGIC MOMENTS** (ASCAP)—Perry Como Catch a Falling Star (ASCAP)—Vic 7128	10	3
9.	**GET A JOB** (BMI)—Silhouettes I Am Lonely (BMI)—Ember 1029	17	2
10.	**KISSES SWEETER THAN WINE** (BMI)—Jimmie Rodgers Better Loved You'll Never Be (ASCAP)—Roulette 4031	5	12
11.	**WITCHCRAFT** (ASCAP)—Frank Sinatra Tell Her You Love Her (BMI)—Cap 3859	9	3
12.	**STOOD UP** (BMI)—Ricky Nelson Waitin' in School (BMI)—Imperial 5483	15	2
13.	**SAIL ALONG SILVERY MOON** (ASCAP)—Billy Vaughn Raunchy (BMI)—Dot 15661	21	2
14.	**GREAT BALLS OF FIRE** (BMI)—Jerry Lee Lewis You Win Again (BMI)—Sun 281	13	9
15.	**DON'T** (BMI)—Elvis Presley I Beg of You (BMI)—Vic 7150	—	1
16.	**WHY DON'T THEY UNDERSTAND?** (BMI)—George Hamilton IV Even Tho' (BMI)—ABC-Paramount 9862	11	5
17.	**RAUNCHY** (BMI)—Ernie Freeman Puddin' (BMI)—Imperial 5474	7	10
18.	**I BEG OF YOU** (BMI)—Elvis Presley Don't (BMI)—Vic 7150	—	1
19.	**PUT A LIGHT IN THE WINDOW** (ASCAP)—Four Lads The Things We Did Last Summer (ASCAP)—Col 41058	20	9
20.	**MARCH FROM THE RIVER KWAI, AND "COLONEL BOGEY"** (ASCAP)—Mitch Miller Hey, Little Baby (BMI)—Col 41066	23	2
21.	**OH, JULIE** (BMI)—Crescendos My Little Girl (BMI)—Nasco 6005	—	1
22.	**YOU SEND ME** (BMI)—Sam Cooke Summertime (ASCAP)—Keen 34013	14	14
23.	**A VERY SPECIAL LOVE** (ASCAP)—Johnny Nash Won't You Let Me Share My Love (BMI)—ABC-Paramount 9874	—	1
24.	**LA DEE DAH** (BMI)—Billy and Lillie The Monster (BMI)—Swan 4002	24	2
25.	**26 MILES** (BMI)—Four Preps It's You (ASCAP)—Cap 3845	—	2

Top 100 Sides

FOR SURVEY WEEK ENDING JANUARY 25

This is a tabulation of dealer individual record sales listed according to the specific side requested by customers. No attempt is made to add sides together to reflect actual record sales. This is, therefore, a tabulation of sides or songs, and not records. This is the reason for any possible variation that occurs between the top 50 sides as reflected in this chart, and the top 50 record sellers as reflected in the "Best Sellers in Stores" chart.

Pos.	Song, Artist, Label	Last Week
1.	**AT THE HOP,** Danny and the Juniors, ABC-Paramount	1
2.	**GET A JOB,** Silhouettes, Ember	6
3.	**PEGGY SUE,** Buddy Holly, Coral	3
4.	**GREAT BALLS OF FIRE,** Jerry Lee Lewis, Sun	2
5.	**SAIL ALONG SILVERY MOON,** Billy Vaughn, Dot	16
6.	**APRIL LOVE.** Pat Boone, Dot	4
7.	**SUGARTIME,** McGuire Sisters, Coral	8
8.	**THE STROLL,** Diamonds, Mercury	7
9.	**STOOD UP,** Ricky Nelson, Imperial	2
10.	**DON'T,** Elvis Presley, Victor	40
11.	**LA DEE DAH,** Billy and Lillie, Swan	9
12.	**KISSES SWEETER THAN WINE,** Jimmie Rodgers, Roulette	12
13.	**I BEG OF YOU,** Elvis Presley, Victor	56
14.	**OH, BOY!** Crickets, Brunswick	13
15.	**YOU SEND ME,** Sam Cooke, Keen	15
16.	**SHORT SHORTS,** Royal Teens, ABC-Paramount	66
17.	**SILHOUETTES,** Rays, Cameo	17
18.	**RAUNCHY,** Bill Justis, Phillips International	10
18.	**BUZZ, BUZZ, BUZZ,** Hollywood Flames, Ebb	11
20.	**WHY DON'T THEY UNDERSTAND?** George Hamilton IV, ABC-Paramount	17
21.	**JAILHOUSE ROCK,** Elvis Presley, Victor	14
21.	**BONY MORONIE,** Larry Williams, Specialty	19
23.	**DON'T LET GO,** Roy Hamilton, Epic	23
24.	**DEDE DINAH,** Frankie Avalon, Chancellor	35
25.	**RAUNCHY,** Ernie Freeman, Imperial	20
25.	**WAITIN' IN SCHOOL,** Ricky Nelson, Imperial	21
27.	**MAYBE,** Chantels, End	32
28.	**LIECHTENSTEINER POLKA,** Will Glahe, London	22
29.	**WAKE UP LITTLE SUSIE,** Everly Brothers, Cadence	26
30.	**OH, JULIE,** Crescendos, Nasco	26
30.	**THE STORY OF MY LIFE.** Marty Robbins, Columbia	36
32.	**CHANCES ARE,** Johnny Mathis, Columbia	25
33.	**BE-BOP BABY,** Ricky Nelson, Imperial	23
33.	**YOU ARE MY DESTINY,** Paul Anka, ABC-Paramount	41
35.	**ROCK AND ROLL MUSIC,** Chuck Berry, Chess	28
36.	**CATCH A FALLING STAR,** Perry Como, Victor	60
37.	**TEARDROPS,** Lee Andrews and the Hearts, Chess	31
38.	**ALL THE WAY,** Frank Sinatra, Capitol	30
39.	**I'LL COME RUNNING BACK TO YOU,** Sam Cooke, Specialty	39
40.	**I'M AVAILABLE,** Margie Rayburn, Liberty	37
41.	**MY SPECIAL ANGEL,** Bobby Helms, Decca	28
42.	**JO ANN,** Playmates, Roulette	34
43.	**RAUNCHY,** Billy Vaughn, Dot	42
44.	**MARCH FROM THE RIVER KWAI, AND COLONEL BOGEY** Mitch Miller, Columbia	46
45.	**FASCINATION,** Jane Morgan, Kapp	32
45.	**(I LOVE YOU) FOR SENTIMENTAL REASONS,** Sam Cooke, Keen	44
47.	**LITTLE PIGEON,** Sal Mineo, Epic	97
48.	**MAGIC MOMENTS,** Perry Como, Victor	57
49.	**HONEYCOMB,** Jimmie Rodgers, Roulette	38
49.	**LITTLE BITTY PRETTY ONE,** Thurston Harris, Aladdin	50
51.	**WITCHCRAFT,** Frank Sinatra, Capitol	—
52.	**PRETEND YOU DON'T SEE HER,** Jerry Vale, Columbia	52
52.	**YOU CAN MAKE IT IF YOU TRY,** Gene Allison, Vee Jay	70
54.	**I WANT YOU TO KNOW,** Fats Domino, Imperial	48
54.	**MELODIE D'AMOUR,** Ames Brothers, Victor	48
56.	**DESIRE ME.** Sam Cooke, Keen	53
56.	**TILL,** Roger Williams, Kapp	70
58.	**A VERY SPECIAL LOVE,** Johnny Nash, ABC-Paramount	47
58.	**TWENTY-SIX MILES,** Four Preps, Capitol	64
60.	**HEY! LITTLE GIRL,** Techniques, Roulette	54
61.	**PUT A LIGHT IN THE WINDOW,** Four Lads, Columbia	43
61.	**THE BIG BEAT,** Fats Domino, Imperial	51
63.	**BALLAD OF A TEEN-AGE QUEEN,** Johnny Cash, Sun	—
64.	**SWINGING SHEPHERD BLUES,** Moe Koffman Quartet, Jubilee	—
65.	**WILD IS THE WIND,** Johnny Mathis, Columbia	55
66.	**GEISHA GIRL,** Hank Locklin, Victor	76
67.	**DANCE TO THE BOP,** Gene Vincent, Capitol	68
68.	**THE JOKER,** Billy Myles, Ember	58
68.	**HEY! SCHOOLGIRL,** Tom and Jerry, Big	58
68.	**THE JOKER,** Hilltoppers, Dot	62
68.	**COULD THIS BE MAGIC?** Dubs, Gone	62
72.	**HENRIETTA,** Jimmie Dee, Dot	66
73.	**HARD TIMES (THE SLOP),** Noble (Thin Man) Watts, Baton	73
73.	**SWINGING SHEPHERD BLUES,** Johnny Pate Quintet, Federal	81
73.	**SHE'S NEAT,** Dale Wright, Fraternity	84
73.	**THE TWELFTH OF NEVER,** Johnny Mathis, Columbia	81
73.	**WALKIN' WITH MR. LEE,** Lee Allen, Ember	61
73.	**YELLOW DOG BLUES,** Joe Darensbourg and the Dixie Flyers, Lark	89
79.	**JUST BORN,** Perry Como, Victor	45
79.	**IVY ROSE,** Perry Como, Victor	72
81.	**ANGEL SMILE,** Nat King Cole, Capitol	91
81.	**DO WHAT YOU DID,** Thurston Harris, Aladdin	64
83.	**YOU SEND ME,** Teresa Brewer, Coral	81
83.	**YOU'RE THE GREATEST,** Billy Scott, Cameo	76
85.	**A VERY SPECIAL LOVE,** Debbie Reynolds, Coral	95
85.	**TAMMY,** Debbie Reynolds, Coral	69
87.	**BERTHA LOU,** Clint Miller, ABC-Paramount	88
87.	**YELLOW DOG BLUES,** Johnny Maddox, Dot	93
89.	**BETTY AND DUPREE,** Chuck Willis, Atlantic	—
89.	**NO LOVE (BUT YOUR LOVE),** Johnny Mathis, Columbia	74
89.	**PENNY LOAFERS AND BOBBY SOCKS** Joe Bennett and the Sparkletones, ABC-Paramount	86
89.	**THIS IS THE NIGHT,** Valiants, Keen	78
93.	**ANNA MARIE,** Jim Reeves, Victor	—
93.	**FRAULEIN,** Bobby Helms, Decca	—
93.	**HULA LOVE,** Buddy Knox, Roulette	97
93.	**SWANEE RIVER ROCK (TALKIN' 'BOUT THAT RIVER)** Ray Charles, Atlantic	91
97.	**FOREVER,** Sam Cooke, Specialty	—
97.	**HELPLESS,** Platters, Mercury	—
97.	**ROCK-A-CHICKA,** Warner Mack, Decca	74
100.	**LOVE BUG CRAWL,** Jimmy Edwards, Mercury	78
100.	**BELONGING TO SOMEONE,** Patti Page, Mercury	—

Best Sellers in Stores

FOR SURVEY WEEK ENDING FEBRUARY 1, 1958

The information given in this chart is based on actual sales to customers in a scientific sample of the nation's retail record outlets during the week ending on the date shown above. Sample design, sample size, and all methods used in this continuing study of retail record sales are under the direct and continuing supervision and control of the School of Retailing of New York University.

This Week	Title	Last Week	Weeks on Chart
1.	**DON'T** (BMI)—Elvis Presley **I BEG OF YOU** (BMI)—Victor 7150	3	3
2.	**AT THE HOP** (BMI)—Danny and the Juniors Sometimes (BMI)—ABC-Paramount 9871	1	10
3.	**GET A JOB** (BMI)—Silhouettes I Am Lonely (BMI)—Ember 1029	2	4
4.	**STOOD UP** (BMI)—Ricky Nelson **WAITIN' IN SCHOOL** (BMI)—Imperial 5483	4	7
5.	**SAIL ALONG SILVERY MOON** (ASCAP)—Billy Vaughn **RAUNCHY** (BMI)—Dot 15661	5	8
6.	**SHORT SHORTS** (BMI)—Royal Teens Planet Rock (BMI)—ABC-Paramount 9882	15	2
7.	**THE STROLL** (BMI)—Diamonds Land of Beauty (BMI)—Mercury 71242	10	6
8.	**SUGARTIME** (BMI)—McGuire Sisters Banana Split (BMI)—Coral 61924	9	6
9.	**CATCH A FALLING STAR** (ASCAP)—Perry Como **MAGIC MOMENTS** (ASCAP)—Vic 7128	17	3
10.	**GREAT BALLS OF FIRE** (BMI)—Jerry Lee Lewis **YOU WIN AGAIN** (BMI)—Sun 281	7	11
11.	**PEGGY SUE** (BMI)—Buddy Holly Everyday (BMI)—Coral 61885	6	14
12.	**DEDE DINAH** (ASCAP)—Frankie Avalon Ooh La La (ASCAP)—Chancellor 1011	24	3
13.	**LA DEE DAH** (BMI)—Billy and Lillie The Monster (BMI)—Swan 4002	11	5
14.	**YOU ARE MY DESTINY** (BMI)—Paul Anka When I Stop Loving You (BMI)—ABC-Paramount 9880	35	3
15.	**APRIL LOVE** (ASCAP)—Pat Boone When the Swallows Come Back to Capistrano (ASCAP)—Dot 15660	8	15
16.	**MAYBE** (BMI)—Chantels Come My Little Baby (BMI)—End 1005	27	4
17.	**(I LOVE YOU) FOR SENTIMENTAL REASONS** (BMI)—Sam Cooke **DESIRE ME** (BMI)—Keen 4002	32	7
18.	**I'LL COME RUNNING BACK TO YOU** (BMI)—Sam Cooke **FOREVER** (BMI)—Specialty 619	33	8
19.	**DON'T LET GO** (BMI)—Roy Hamilton The Right to Love (BMI)—Epic 9257	23	4
20.	**KISSES SWEETER THAN WINE** (BMI)—Jimmie Rodgers Better Loved You'll Never Be (ASCAP)—Roulette 4031	12	12
21.	**OH, JULIE** (BMI)—Crescendos My Little Girl (BMI)—Nasco 6005	30	5
22.	**YOU SEND ME** (BMI)—Sam Cooke **SUMMERTIME** (ASCAP)—Keen 34013	14	16
23.	**LIECHTENSTEINER POLKA** (ASCAP)—Will Glahe Schweitzer Polka (BMI)—London 1755	28	13
24.	**OH, BOY!** (BMI)—Crickets Not Fade Away (BMI)—Brunswick 55035	13	11
25.	**BUZZ, BUZZ, BUZZ** (BMI)—Hollywood Flames Crazy (BMI)—Ebb 119	20	11
26.	**JO-ANN** (BMI)—Playmates You Can't Stop Me From Dreaming (BMI)—Roulette 4037	42	4
27.	**CHANCES ARE** (ASCAP)—Johnny Mathis **THE TWELFTH OF NEVER** (ASCAP)—Col 40993	25	21
28.	**JAILHOUSE ROCK** (BMI)—Elvis Presley **TREAT ME NICE** (BMI)—Vic 7035	18	18
29.	**BONY MORONIE** (BMI)—Larry Williams **YOU BUG ME, BABY** (BMI)—Specialty 615	21	14
30.	**RAUNCHY** (BMI)—Bill Justis The Midnite Man (BMI)—Phillips International 3519	19	13
31.	**WHY DON'T THEY UNDERSTAND?** (BMI)—George Hamilton IV Even Tho' (BMI)—ABC-Paramount 9862	22	11
32.	**BALLAD OF A TEEN-AGE QUEEN** (BMI)—Johnny Cash Big River (BMI)—Sun 283	—	1
33.	**ALL THE WAY** (ASCAP)—Frank Sinatra **CHICAGO** (ASCAP)—Cap 3793	40	14
34.	**SILHOUETTES** (BMI)—The Rays **DADDY COOL** (BMI)—Cameo 117	16	17
35.	**WAKE UP LITTLE SUSIE** (BMI)—Everly Brothers Maybe Tomorrow (BMI)—Cadence 1337	29	20
36.	**I WANT YOU TO KNOW** (BMI)—Fats Domino **THE BIG BEAT** (BMI)—Imperial 5477	38	8
37.	**TEARDROPS** (BMI)—Lee Andrews and the Hearts Girl Around the Corner (BMI)—Chess 1675	37	11
38.	**MARCH FROM THE RIVER KWAI, AND "COLONEL BOGEY"** (ASCAP)—Mitch Miller Hey, Little Baby (BMI)—Col 41066	43	4
39.	**SWINGING SHEPHERD BLUES** (BMI)—Moe Koffman Quartet Hambourg Bound (BMI)—Jubilee 5311	—	1
40.	**THE STORY OF MY LIFE** (ASCAP)—Marty Robbins Once-a-Week Date (BMI)—Col 41013	31	11
41.	**WITCHCRAFT** (ASCAP)—Frank Sinatra Tell Her You Love Her (BMI)—Capitol 3859	49	2
42.	**TWENTY-SIX MILES** (BMI)—Four Preps It's You (ASCAP)—Cap 3826	—	1
43.	**RAUNCHY** (BMI)—Ernie Freeman Puddin' (BMI)—Imperial 5474	26	13
44.	**ROCK AND ROLL MUSIC** (BMI)—Chuck Berry Blue Feeling (BMI)—Chess 1671	36	14
45.	**WILD IS THE WIND** (ASCAP)—Johnny Mathis **NO LOVE (BUT YOUR LOVE)** (BMI)—Col 41060	48	9
46.	**YOU CAN MAKE IT IF YOU TRY** (BMI)—Gene Allison Hey, Hey, I Love You (BMI)—Vee Jay 713	—	1
47.	**A VERY SPECIAL LOVE** (ASCAP)—Johnny Nash Won't You Let Me Share My Love (BMI)—ABC-Paramount 9874	—	3
48.	**SWINGING SHEPHERD BLUES** (BMI)—Johnny Pate Quintet The Elder (BMI)—Federal 12312	—	1
49.	**I'M AVAILABLE** (BMI)—Margie Rayburn If You Were (ASCAP)—Liberty 55102	39	14
50.	**LITTLE PIGEON** (BMI)—Sal Mineo Cuttin' In (BMI)—Epic 9260	45	2

THIS WEEK'S BEST BUYS

Special telephone reports indicate these recent releases have broken out in one or more key areas and have excellent potential for placing on The Billboard's best seller charts.

SWEET LITTLE SIXTEEN (Arc, BMI)—**Chuck Berry**—Chess 1683—This appears to be the hottest disk around. Sales are big in all marts. Flip is "Reelin' and Rocking (Arc, BMI). A previous Billboard Spotlight pick.

CLICK CLACK (Grant & Doo, BMI)—**Dickey Doo & the Don'ts**—Swan 4001—All markets report heavy action on the side. It looks like a winner. Flip is "Did You Cry" (Grant & Doo, BMI).

OH-OH, I'M FALLING IN LOVE AGAIN (Planetary, ASCAP)—**Jimmie Rodgers**—Roulette 4045—This looks like the third big one in a row for the artist. It's strong in all marts. Flip is "The Long Hot Summer (Feist, ASCAP). A previous Billboard Spotlight pick.

BE MINE TONIGHT (Cedarwood, BMI)

ARE YOU SINCERE? (Peer, BMI)—**Andy Williams**—Cadence 1340—Both sides are getting action. "Be Mine Tonight" holds a slight edge. The platter is moving well in all marts.

RECENT POP RELEASES COMING UP STRONG

FOR SURVEY WEEK ENDING FEBRUARY 1

The information given in this chart is based on actual sales to customers in a scientific sample of the nation's retail record outlets during the week ending on the date shown above. Sample design, sample size and all methods used in this continuing study of retail record sales are under the direct and continuing supervision and control of the School of Retailing of New York University.

Angel Smile . . . . *Nat King Cole* (BMI) Capitol 3860

Click Clack . . . . *Dickey Doo & The Don'ts* (BMI) Swan 4001

Come to Me . . . . *Johnny Mathis* (ASCAP) Columbia 41082

She's Neat . . . . *Dale Wright* (ASCAP) Fraternity 761

Most Played by Jockeys

FOR SURVEY WEEK ENDING FEBRUARY 1

SIDES are ranked in order of the greatest number of plays on disk jockey radio shows thruout the country. Results are based on The Billboard's weekly survey among the nation's disk jockeys. The reverse side of each record is also listed.

This Week		Last Week	Weeks on Chart
1.	AT THE HOP (BMI)—Danny and the Juniors Sometimes (BMI)—ABC-Paramount 9871	1	8
2.	SUGARTIME (BMI)—McGuire Sisters Banana Split (BMI)—Coral 61924	2	6
3.	PEGGY SUE (BMI)—Buddy Holly Everyday (BMI)—Coral 61885	5	13
4.	CATCH A FALLING STAR (ASCAP)—Perry Como Magic Moments (ASCAP)—Vic 7128	6	5
5.	STOOD UP (BMI)—Ricky Nelson Waitin' in School (BMI)—Imperial 5483	12	3
6.	THE STROLL (BMI)—Diamonds Land of Beauty (BMI)—Mercury 71242	4	5
7.	DON'T (BMI)—Elvis Presley I Beg of You (BMI)—Vic 7150	15	2
8.	Magic Moments (ASCAP) Perry Como Catch a Falling Star (ASCAP)—Vic 7128	8	4
9.	GET A JOB (BMI)—Silhouettes I Am Lonely (BMI)—Ember 1029	9	3
10.	OH, JULIE (BMI)—Crescendos My Little Girl (BMI)—Nasco 6005	21	2
11.	APRIL LOVE (ASCAP)—Pat Boone When the Swallows Come Back to Capistrano (ASCAP)—Dot 15660	3	16
12.	WITCHCRAFT (ASCAP)—Frank Sinatra Tell Her You Love Her (BMI)—Cap 3859	11	4
13.	26 MILES (BMI)—Four Preps It's You (ASCAP)—Cap 3845	25	3
14.	SAIL ALONG SILVERY MOON (ASCAP)—Billy Vaughn Raunchy (BMI)—Dot 15661	13	3
15.	I BEG OF YOU (BMI)—Elvis Presley Don't (BMI)—Vic 7150	18	2
16.	YOU ARE MY DESTINY (BMI)—Paul Anka When I Stop Loving You (BMI)—ABC-Paramount 9880	—	1
17.	DON'T LET GO (BMI)—Roy Hamilton The Right to Love (BMI)—Epic 9257	—	2
18.	ALL THE WAY (ASCAP)—Frank Sinatra Chicago (ASCAP)—Cap 3793	7	16
19.	WHY DON'T THEY UNDERSTAND? (BMI)—George Hamilton IV Even Tho' (BMI)—ABC-Paramount 9862	16	6
20.	SHORT SHORTS (BMI)—Royal Teens Planet Rock (BMI)—ABC-Paramount 9882	—	1
20.	BELONGING TO SOMEONE (ASCAP)—Patti Page Bring Us Together (ASCAP)—Mercury 71247	—	1
22.	COME TO ME (ASCAP)—Johnny Mathis When I Am With You (ASCAP)—Col 41082	—	1
23.	LA DEE DAH (BMI)—Billy and Lillie The Monster (BMI)—Swan 4002	24	3
24.	AT THE HOP (BMI)—Nick Todd I Do (BMI)—Dot 15675	—	1
25.	KISSES SWEETER THAN WINE (BMI)—Jimmie Rodgers Better Loved You'll Never Be (ASCAP)—Roulette 4031	10	13

Top 100 Sides

FOR SURVEY WEEK ENDING FEBRUARY 1

This is a tabulation of dealer individual record sales listed according to the specific side requested by customers. No attempt is made to add sides together to reflect actual record sales. This is, therefore, a tabulation of sides or songs, and not records. This is the reason for any possible variation that occurs between the top 50 sides as reflected in this chart, and the top 50 record sellers as reflected in the "Best Sellers in Stores" chart.

Pos.	Song, Artist, Label	Last Week
1.	**AT THE HOP,** Danny and the Juniors, ABC-Paramount	1
2.	**GET A JOB,** Silhouettes, Ember	2
3.	**SHORT SHORTS,** Royal Teens, ABC-Paramount	16
4.	**DON'T,** Elvis Presley, Victor	10
5.	**SAIL ALONG SILVERY MOON,** Billy Vaughn, Dot	5
6.	**THE STROLL,** Diamonds, Mercury	8
7.	**SUGARTIME,** McGuire Sisters, Coral	7
8.	**I BEG OF YOU,** Elvis Presley, Victor	13
9.	**GREAT BALLS OF FIRE,** Jerry Lee Lewis, Sun	4
10.	**PEGGY SUE,** Buddy Holly, Coral	3
11.	**STOOD UP,** Ricky Nelson, Imperial	9
12.	**DEDE DINAH,** Frankie Avalon, Chancellor	24
13.	**LA DEE DAH,** Billy and Lillie, Swan	11
14.	**YOU ARE MY DESTINY,** Paul Anka, ABC-Paramount	33
15.	**APRIL LOVE,** Pat Boone, Dot	6
16.	**MAYBE,** Chantels, End	27
17.	**CATCH A FALLING STAR,** Perry Como, Victor	36
18.	**WAITIN' IN SCHOOL,** Fats Domino, Imperial	25
19.	**DON'T LET GO,** Roy Hamilton, Epic	23
20.	**KISSES SWEETER THAN WINE,** Jimmie Rodgers, Roulette	12
20.	**OH, JULIE,** Crescendos, Nasco	30
22.	**I'LL COME RUNNING BACK TO YOU,** Sam Cooke, Specialty	39
22.	**LIECHTENSTEINER POLKA,** Will Glahe, London	28
22.	**YOU SEND ME,** Sam Cooke, Keen	15
25.	**OH, BOY,** Crickets, Brunswick	14
26.	**BUZZ, BUZZ, BUZZ,** Hollywood Flames, Ebb	18
26.	**JO ANN,** Playmates, Roulette	42
28.	**JAILHOUSE ROCK,** Elvis Presley, Victor	21
29.	**RAUNCHY,** Bill Justis, Phillips International	18
30.	**BONY MORONIE,** Larry Williams, Specialty	21
31.	**WHY DON'T THEY UNDERSTAND?** George Hamilton IV, ABC-Paramount	20
32.	**BALLAD OF A TEEN-AGE QUEEN,** Johnny Cash, Sun	63
33.	**ALL THE WAY,** Frank Sinatra, Capitol	38
33.	**CHANCES ARE,** Johnny Mathis, Columbia	32
35.	**WAKE UP LITTLE SUSIE,** Everly Brothers, Cadence	29
36.	**MARCH FROM THE RIVER KWAI, AND COLONEL BOGEY,** Mitch Miller, Columbia	44
37.	**SILHOUETTES,** Rays, Cameo	17
37.	**TEARDROPS,** Lee Andrews and the Hearts, Chess	37
39.	**MAGIC MOMENTS,** Perry Como, Victor	48
39.	**THE STORY OF MY LIFE,** Marty Robbins, Columbia	30
39.	**SWINGING SHEPHERD BLUES,** Moe Koffman Quartet, Jubilee	64
39.	**WITCHCRAFT,** Frank Sinatra, Capitol	51
43.	**TWENTY-SIX MILES,** Four Preps, Capitol	58
44.	**(I LOVE YOU) FOR SENTIMENTAL REASONS,** Sam Cooke, Keen	45
44.	**ROCK AND ROLL MUSIC,** Chuck Berry, Chess	35
44.	**RAUNCHY,** Ernie Freeman, Imperial	25
47.	**A VERY SPECIAL LOVE,** Johnny Nash, ABC-Paramount	58
47.	**DESIRE ME,** Sam Cooke, Keen	56
47.	**YOU CAN MAKE IT IF YOU TRY,** Gene Allison, Vee Jay	52
50.	**SWINGING SHEPHERD BLUES,** Johnny Pate Quintet, Federal	73
51.	**I WANT YOU TO KNOW,** Fats Domino, Imperial	54
51.	**I'M AVAILABLE,** Margie Rayburn, Liberty	40
51.	**LITTLE PIGEON,** Sal Mineo, Epic	47
54.	**SHE'S NEAT,** Dale Wright, Fraternity	73
55.	**MY SPECIAL ANGEL,** Bobby Helms, Decca	41
56.	**WILD IS THE WIND,** Johnny Mathis, Columbia	65
57.	**RAUNCHY,** Billy Vaughn, Dot	43
58.	**CLICK CLICK,** Dickie Doo and the Don'ts, Swan	—
59.	**BE-BOP BABY,** Ricky Nelson, Imperial	33
59.	**YELLOW DOG BLUES,** Joe Darensbourg and the Dixie Flyers, Lark	73
61.	**WALKIN' WITH MR. LEE,** Lee Allen, Ember	73
62.	**BELONGING TO SOMEONE,** Patti Page, Mercury	100
62.	**HEY! SCHOOLGIRL,** Tom and Jerry, Big	68
62.	**PUT A LIGHT IN THE WINDOW,** Four Lads, Columbia	61
65.	**LITTLE BITTY PRETTY ONE,** Thurston Harris, Aladdin	49
66.	**COULD THIS BE MAGIC?** Dubs, Gone	68
66.	**TILL,** Roger Williams, Kapp	56
68.	**THE BIG BEAT,** Fats Domino, Imperial	61
68.	**FASCINATION,** Jane Morgan, Kapp	45
68.	**THIS LITTLE GIRL OF MINE,** Everly Brothers, Cadence	—
71.	**PRETEND YOU DON'T SEE HER,** Jerry Vale, Columbia	52
72.	**ANGEL SMILE,** Nat King Cole, Capitol	81
72.	**COME TO ME,** Johnny Mathis, Columbia	—
74.	**NO LOVE (BUT YOUR LOVE),** Johnny Mathis, Columbia	89
75.	**HONEYCOMB,** Jimmie Rodgers, Roulette	49
75.	**MELODIE D'AMOUR,** Ames Brothers, Victor	54
77.	**HEY! LITTLE GIRL,** Techniques, Roulette	60
77.	**DO WHAT YOU DID,** Thurston Harris, Aladdin	81
77.	**THE JOKER,** Hilltoppers, Dot	68
77.	**THE TWELFTH OF NEVER,** Johnny Mathis, Columbia	73
81.	**GEISHA GIRL,** Hank Locklin, Victor	66
81.	**SHAKE A HAND,** Mike Pedicin Quintet, Cameo	—
83.	**AT THE HOP,** Nick Todd, Dot	—
83.	**A VERY SPECIAL LOVE,** Debbie Reynolds, Coral	85
83.	**HARD TIMES (THE SLOP),** Nobel (Thin Man) Watts, Baton	73
83.	**SOFT,** Bill Doggett, King	—
87.	**BERTHA LOU,** Clint Miller, ABC-Paramount	87
87.	**BETTY AND DUPREE,** Chuck Willis, Atlantic	89
87.	**TAMMY.** Debbie Reynolds, Coral	85
90.	**IVY ROSE,** Perry Como, Victor	79
90.	**PENNY LOAFERS AND BOBBY SOCKS,** Joe Bennett and the Sparkletones, ABC-Paramount	89
92.	**JULIE,** Sammy Salvo, Victor	—
92.	**MARCH FORM THE RIVER KWAI, AND COLONEL BOGEY,** Edmundo Ros, London	—
92.	**YOU'RE THE GREATEST,** Billy Scott, Cameo	83
95.	**HENRIETTA,** Jimmie Dee, Dot	72
95.	**HELPLESS,** Platters, Mercury	97
95.	**THE JOKER,** Billy Myles, Ember	68
95.	**SWINGIN' DADDY,** Buddy Knox, Roulette	—
99.	**JUST BORN,** Perry Como, Victor	79
99.	**SILHOUETTES,** Diamonds, Mercury	—

Best Sellers in Stores

FOR SURVEY WEEK ENDING FEBRUARY 8, 1958

The information given in this chart is based on actual sales to customers in a scientific sample of the nation's retail record outlets during the week ending on the date shown above. Sample design, sample size, and all methods used in this continuing study of retail record sales are under the direct and continuing supervision and control of the School of Retailing of New York University.

This Week		Last Week	Weeks on Chart
1.	DON'T (BMI)—Elvis Presley I BEG OF YOU (BMI)—Victor 7150	1	4
2.	AT THE HOP (BMI)—Danny and the Juniors Sometimes (BMI)—ABC-Paramount 9871	2	11
3.	GET A JOB (BMI)—Silhouettes I Am Lonely (BMI)—Ember 1029	3	5
4.	SHORT SHORTS (BMI)—Royal Teens Planet Rock (BMI)—ABC-Paramount 9882	6	3
5.	STOOD UP (BMI)—Ricky Nelson WAITIN' IN SCHOOL (BMI)—Imperial 5483	4	8
6.	SAIL ALONG SILVERY MOON (ASCAP)—Billy Vaughn RAUNCHY (BMI)—Dot 15661	5	9
7.	CATCH A FALLING STAR (ASCAP)—Perry Como MAGIC MOMENTS (ASCAP)—Vic 7128	9	4
8.	THE STROLL (BMI)—Diamonds Land of Beauty (BMI)—Mercury 71242	7	7
9.	DEDE DINAH (ASCAP)—Frankie Avalon Ooh La La (ASCAP)—Chancellor 1011	12	4
10.	SUGARTIME (BMI)—McGuire Sisters Banana Split (BMI)—Coral 61924	8	7
11.	YOU ARE MY DESTINY (BMI)—Paul Anka When I Stop Loving You (BMI)—ABC-Paramount 9880	14	4
12.	OH, JULIE (BMI)—Crescendos My Little Girl (BMI)—Nasco 6005	21	6
13.	GREAT BALLS OF FIRE (BMI)—Jerry Lee Lewis YOU WIN AGAIN (BMI)—Sun 281	10	12
14.	PEGGY SUE (BMI)—Buddy Holly Everyday (BMI)—Coral 61885	11	15
15.	APRIL LOVE (ASCAP)—Pat Boone When the Swallows Come Back to Capistrano (ASCAP)—Dot 15660	15	16
16.	LA DEE DAH (BMI)—Billy and Lillie The Monster (BMI)—Swan 4002	13	6
17.	MAYBE (BMI)—Chantels Come My Little Baby (BMI)—End 1005	16	5
18.	DON'T LET GO (BMI)—Roy Hamilton The Right to Love (BMI)—Epic 9257	19	5
19.	JO-ANN (BMI)—Playmates You Can't Stop Me From Dreaming (BMI)—Roulette 4037	26	5
20.	TWENTY-SIX MILES (BMI)—Four Preps It's You (ASCAP)—Cap 3826	42	2
21.	LIECHTENSTEINER POLKA (ASCAP)—Will Glahe Schweitzer Polka (BMI)—London 1755	23	14
22.	I'LL COME RUNNING BACK TO YOU (BMI)—Sam Cooke FOREVER (BMI)—Specialty 619	18	9
23.	MARCH FROM THE RIVER KWAI, AND "COLONEL BOGEY" (ASCAP)—Mitch Miller Hey, Little Baby (BMI)—Col 41066	38	5
24.	WITCHCRAFT (ASCAP)—Frank Sinatra Tell Her You Love Her (BMI)—Capitol 3859	41	3
25.	IT'S TOO SOON TO KNOW (ASCAP)—Pat Boone A WONDERFUL TIME UP THERE (BMI)—Dot 15690	—	1
26.	(I LOVE YOU) FOR SENTIMENTAL REASONS (BMI)—Sam Cooke DESIRE ME (BMI)—Keen 4002	17	8
27.	BUZZ, BUZZ, BUZZ (BMI)—Hollywood Flames Crazy (BMI)—Ebb 119	25	12
28.	WHY DON'T THEY UNDERSTAND? (BMI)—George Hamilton IV Even Tho' (BMI)—ABC-Paramount 9862	31	12
29.	CLICK CLACK (BMI)—Dickey Doo and the Don'ts Did You Cry? (BMI)—Swan 4001	—	1
30.	YOU SEND ME (BMI)—Sam Cooke SUMMERTIME (ASCAP)—Keen 34013	22	17
31.	OH, BOY (BMI)—Crickets Not Fade Away (BMI)—Brunswick 55035	24	12
32.	KISSES SWEETER THAN WINE (BMI)—Jimmie Rodgers Better Loved You'll Never Be (ASCAP)—Roulette 4031	20	13
33.	BALLAD OF A TEEN-AGE QUEEN (BMI)—Johnny Cash Big River (BMI)—Sun 283	32	2
34.	ALL THE WAY (ASCAP)—Frank Sinatra CHICAGO (ASCAP)—Cap 3793	33	15
35.	RAUNCHY (BMI)—Bill Justis The Midnite Man (BMI)—Phillips International 3519	30	14
36.	SWINGING SHEPHERD BLUES (BMI)—Moe Koffman Quartet Hambourg Bound (BMI)—Jubilee 5311	39	2
37.	WILD IS THE WIND (ASCAP)—Johnny Mathis NO LOVE (BUT YOUR LOVE) (BMI)—Col 41060	45	10
38.	THIS LITTLE GIRL OF MINE (BMI)—Everly Brothers Should We Tell Him? (BMI)—Cadence 1342	—	1
39.	CHANCES ARE (ASCAP)—Johnny Mathis THE TWELFTH OF NEVER (ASCAP)—Col 40993	27	22
40.	I WANT YOU TO KNOW (BMI)—Fats Domino THE BIG BEAT (BMI)—Imperial 5477	36	9
41.	JAILHOUSE ROCK (BMI)—Elvis Presley Treat Me Nice (BMI)—Vic 7035	28	19
42.	BONY MORONIE (BMI)—Larry Williams YOU BUG ME, BABY (BMI)—Specialty 615	29	15
43.	TEARDROPS (BMI)—Lee Andrews and the Hearts Girl Around the Corner (BMI)—Chess 1675	37	12
44.	OH-OH, I'M FALLING IN LOVE AGAIN (ASCAP)—Jimmie Rodgers The Long Hot Summer (ASCAP)—Roulette 4045	—	1
45.	THE STORY OF MY LIFE (ASCAP)—Marty Robbins Once-a-Week Date (BMI)—Col 41013	40	12
46.	SWEET LITTLE SIXTEEN (BMI)—Chuck Berry Reelin' and Rocking (BMI)—Chess 1683	—	1
47.	SHE'S NEAT (ASCAP)—Dale Wright Say That You Care (ASCAP)—Fraternity 792	—	1
48.	SWINGING SHEPHERD BLUES BMI)—Johnny Pate Quintet The Elder (BMI)—Federal 12312	48	2
49.	ARE YOU SINCERE? (BMI)—Andy Williams Be Mine Tonight (BMI)—Cadence 1340	—	1
50.	COME TO ME (ASCAP)—Johnny Mathis When I Am With You (ASCAP)—Col 41082	—	1

THIS WEEK'S BEST BUYS

Special telephone reports indicate these recent releases have broken out in one or more key areas and have excellent potential for placing on The Billboard's best seller charts.

TEQUILA (Jat, BMI)—The Champs—Challenge 1016—This is a big one. All markets report strong sales. Flip is "Train to Nowhere" (Golden West, BMI). A previous Billboard Spotlight pick.

WHO'S SORRY NOW (Mills, ASCAP)—Connie Francis—M-G-M 12588—A real sleeper. It's erupted in all marts. Flip is "You Were Only Fooling" (Shapiro-Bernstein, ASCAP).

THE LITTLE BLUE MAN (Trinity, BMI)—Betty Johnson—Atlantic 1169—The tune is attracting coin in all marts. It looks like a winner. Flip is "Winter in Miami" (Town, ASCAP). A previous Billboard Spotlight pick.

RECENT POP RELEASES COMING UP STRONG

FOR SURVEY WEEK ENDING FEBRUARY 8

The information given in this chart is based on actual sales to customers in a scientific sample of the nation's retail record outlets during the week ending on the date shown above. Sample design, sample size and all methods used in this continuing study of retail record sales are under the direct and continuing supervision and control of the School of Retailing of New York University.

Angel Smile .... *Nat King Cole*
(BMI) Capitol 3860

Good Golly, Miss Molly .... *Little Richard*
(BMI) Specialty 624

Little Pigeon .... *Sal Mineo*
(BMI) Epic 9260

Most Played by Jockeys

FOR SURVEY WEEK ENDING FEBRUARY 8

SIDES are ranked in order of the greatest number of plays on disk jockey radio shows thruout the country. Results are based on The Billboard's weekly survey among the nation's disk jockeys. The reverse side of each record is also listed.

This Week		Last Week	Weeks on Chart
1.	**SUGARTIME** (BMI)—McGuire Sisters Banana Split (BMI)—Coral 61924	2	7
2.	**DON'T** (BMI)—Elvis Presley I Beg of You (BMI)—Vic 7150	7	3
3.	**CATCH A FALLING STAR** (ASCAP)—Perry Como Magic Moments (ASCAP)—Vic 7128	4	6
4.	**AT THE HOP** (BMI)—Danny and the Juniors Sometimes (BMI)—ABC-Paramount 9871	1	9
5.	**GET A JOB** (BMI)—Silhouettes I Am Lonely (BMI)—Ember 1029	9	4
6.	**WITCHCRAFT** (ASCAP)—Frank Sinatra Tell Her You Love Her (BMI)—Cap 3859	12	5
7.	**MAGIC MOMENTS** (ASCAP)—Perry Como Catch a Falling Star (ASCAP)—Vic 7128	8	5
8.	**SAIL ALONG SILVERY MOON** (ASCAP)—Billy Vaughn Raunchy (BMI)—Dot 15661	14	4
9.	**THE STROLL** (BMI)—Diamonds Land of Beauty (BMI)—Mercury 71242	6	6
10.	**26 MILES** (BMI)—Four Preps It's You (ASCAP)—Cap 3845	13	4
11.	**I BEG OF YOU** (BMI)—Elvis Presley Don't (BMI)—Vic 7150	15	3
12.	**OH, JULIE** (BMI)—Crescendos My Little Girl (BMI)—Nasco 6005	10	3
13.	**SHORT SHORTS** (BMI)—Royal Teens Planet Rock (BMI)—ABC-Paramount 9882	20	2
14.	**APRIL LOVE** (ASCAP)—Pat Boone When the Swallows Come Back to Capistrano (ASCAP)—Dot 15660	11	17
15.	**STOOD UP** (BMI)—Ricky Nelson Waitin' in School (BMI)—Imperial 5483	5	4
16.	**WHY DON'T THEY UNDERSTAND?** (BMI)—George Hamilton IV Even Tho' (BMI)—ABC-Paramount 9862	19	7
17.	**YOU ARE MY DESTINY** (BMI)—Paul Anka When I Stop Loving You (BMI)—ABC-Paramount 9880	16	2
18.	**DON'T LET GO** (BMI)—Roy Hamilton The Right to Love (BMI)—Epic 9257	17	3
19.	**ALL THE WAY** (ASCAP)—Frank Sinatra Chicago (ASCAP)—Cap 3793	18	17
20.	**BELONGING TO SOMEONE** (ASCAP)—Patti Page Bring Us Together (ASCAP)—Mercury 71247	20	2
21.	**AT THE HOP** (BMI)—Nick Todd I Do (BMI)—Dot 15675	24	2
22.	**BALLAD OF A TEENAGE QUEEN** (BMI)—Johnny Cash Big River (BMI)—Sun 283	—	1
23.	**KISSES SWEETER THAN WINE** (BMI)—Jimmie Rodgers Better Loved You'll Never Be (ASCAP)—Roulette 4031	25	14
24.	**GREAT BALLS OF FIRE** (BMI)—Jerry Lee Lewis You Win Again (BMI)—Sun 281	—	10
25.	**SWINGING SHEPHERD BLUES** (BMI)—Moe Koffman Quartet Hambourg Bound (BMI)—Jubilee 5311	—	1

Top 100 Sides

FOR SURVEY WEEK ENDING FEBRUARY 8

This is a tabulation of dealer individual record sales listed according to the specific side requested by customers. No attempt is made to add sides together to reflect actual record sales. This is, therefore, a tabulation of sides or songs, and not records. This is the reason for any possible variation that occurs between the top 50 sides as reflected in this chart, and the top 50 record sellers as reflected in the "Best Sellers in Stores" chart.

Pos.	Song, Artist, Label	Last Week
1.	**AT THE HOP,** Danny and the Juniors, AB-Paramount	1
2.	**GET A JOB,** Silhouettes, Ember	2
3.	**DON'T,** Elvis Presley, Victor	4
4.	**SHORT SHORTS,** Royal Teens, ABC-Paramount	3
5.	**THE STROLL,** Diamonds, Mercury	6
6.	**SAIL ALONG SILVERY MOON,** Billy Vaughn, Dot	5
7.	**DEDE DINAH,** Frankie Avalon, Chancellor	12
8.	**SUGARTIME,** McGuire Sisters, Coral	7
9.	**YOU ARE MY DESTINY,** Paul Anka, ABC-Paramount	14
10.	**OH, JULIE, Crescendos, Nasco**	20
11.	**CATCH A FALLING STAR,** Perry Como, Victor	17
12.	**STOOD UP,** Ricky Nelson, Imperial	11
13.	**GREAT BALLS OF FIRE,** Jerry Lee Lewis, Sun	9
14.	**I BEG OF YOU,** Elvis Presley, Victor	8
15.	**PEGGY SUE.** Buddy Holly, Coral	10
15.	**APRIL LOVE,** Pat Boone, Dot	15
17.	**LA DEE DAH,** Billy and Lillie, Swan	13
18.	**MAYBE,** Chantels, End	16
19.	**DON'T LET GO,** Roy Hamilton, Epic	19
20.	**JO ANN,** Playmates, Roulette	26
21.	**WAITIN' IN SCHOOL,** Fats Domino, Imperial	18
22.	**TWENTY-SIX MILES,** Four Preps, Capitol	43
23.	**LIECHTENSTEINER POLKA,** Will Glahe, London	22
24.	**MARCH FROM THE RIVER KWAI, AND COLONEL BOGEY,** Mitch Miller, Columbia	36
25.	**I'LL COME RUNNING BACK TO YOU,** Sam Cooke, Specialty	22
25.	**WITCHCRAFT,** Frank Sinatra, Capitol	39
27.	**BUZZ, BUZZ, BUZZ,** Hollywood Flames, Ebb	26
28.	**WHY DON'T THEY UNDERSTAND,** George Hamilton IV, ABC-Paramount	31
29.	**CLICK CLACK,** Dickey Doo and the Don'ts, Swan	58
30.	**OH, BOY,** Crickets, Brunswick	25
30.	**YOU SEND ME,** Sam Cooke, Keen	22
32.	**BALLAD OF A TEENAGE QUEEN,** Johnny Cash, Sun	32
32.	**KISSES SWEETER THAN WINE,** Jimmie Rodgers, Roulette	20
34.	**IT'S TOO SOON TO KNOW,** Pat Boone, Dot	—
35.	**MAGIC MOMENTS,** Perry Como, Victor	39
36.	**RAUNCHY,** Bill Justis, Phillips International	29
36.	**SWINGING SHEPHERD BLUES,** Moe Koffman Quartet, Jubilee	39
36.	**ALL THE WAY,** Frank Sinatra, Capitol	33
39.	**THIS LITTLE GIRL OF MINE,** Everly Brothers, Cadence	68
40.	**JAILHOUSE ROCK,** Elvis Presley, Victor	28
41.	**BONY MORONIE,** Larry Williams, Specialty	30
42.	**TEARDROPS,** Lee Andrews and the Hearts, Chess	37
43.	**(I LOVE YOU) FOR SENTIMENTAL REASONS,** Sam Cooke, Keen	44
43.	**OH-OH I'M FALLING IN LOVE AGAIN,** Jimmie Rodgers, Roulette	—
45.	**THE STORY OF MY LIFE,** Marty Robbins, Columbia	39
46.	**SWEET LITTLE SIXTEEN,** Chuck Berry, Chess	—
46.	**CHANCES ARE,** Johnny Mathis, Columbia	33
48.	**I WANT YOU TO KNOW,** Fats Domino, Imperial	51
49.	**SHE'S NEAT,** Dale Wright, Fraternity	54
49.	**SWINGING SHEPHERD BLUES,** Johnny Pate Quintet, Federal	50
51.	**ARE YOU SINCERE,** Andy Williams, Cadence	—
52.	**WILD IS THE WIND,** Johnny Mathis, Columbia	56
52.	**COME TO ME,** Johnny Mathis, Columbia	72
54.	**WAKE UP LITTLE SUSIE,** Everly Brothers, Cadence	35
54.	**YELLOW DOG BLUES,** Joe Darensbourg and the Dixie Flyers, Lark	59
54.	**WALKIN' WITH MR. LEE,** Lee Allen, Ember	61
57.	**GOOD GOLLY MISS MOLLY,** Little Richard, Specialty	—
57.	**SILHOUETTES,** Rays, Cameo	37
57.	**RAUNCHY,** Ernie Freeman, Imperial	44
57.	**A VERY SPECIA.L LOVE,** Johnny Nash, ABC-Paramount	47
57.	**YOU CAN MAKE IT IF YOU TRY,** Gene Allison, Vee Jay	47
82.	**BELONGING TO SOMEONE,** Patti Page, Merceury	62
63.	**DESIRE ME,** Sam Cooke, Keen	47
63.	**MY SPECIAL ANGEL,** Bobby Helms, Decca	55
65.	**ROCK AND ROLL MUSIC,** Chuck Berry, Chess	44
66.	**ANGEL SMILE,** Nat King Cole, Capitol	72
66.	**HENRIETTA,** Jimmie Dee, Dot	95
68.	**RAUNCHY,** Billy Vaughn, Dot	57
69.	**LITTLE PIGEON,** Sal Mineo, Epic	51
69.	**FASCINATION,** Jane Morgan, Kapp	68
71.	**HEY! SCHOOLGIRL,** Tom and Jerry, Big	62
71.	**PUT A LIGHT IN THE WINDOW,** Four Lads, Columbia	62
71.	**NO LOVE (BUT YOUR LOVE),** Johnny Mathis, Columbia	74
71.	**SHAKE A HAND,** Mike Pedicin Quintet, Cameo	81
75.	**DO WHAT YOU DID,** Thurston Harris, Aladdin	77
75.	**MARCH FROM THE RIVER KWAI, AND COLONEL BOGEY,** Edmundo Ros, London	92
77.	**A WONDERFUL TIME UP THERE,** Pat Boone, Dot	—
77.	**I'M AVAILABLE,** Margie Rayburn, Liberty	—
77.	**BIG BEAT,** Fats Domino, Imperial	68
77.	**HEY, LITTLE GIRL,** Techniques, Roulette	77
81.	**SING, BOY, SING,** Tommy Sands, Capitol	—
81.	**COULD THIS BE MAGIC,** Dubs, Gone	66
81.	**THE TWELFTH OF NEVER,** Johnny Mathis, Columbia	77
81.	**GEISHA GIRL,** Hank Locklin, Victor	81
85.	**PRETEND YOU DON'T SEE HER,** Jerry Vale, Columbia	71
85.	**BETTY AND DUPREE,** Chuck Willis, Atlantic	87
85.	**TAMMY,** Debbie Reynolds, Coral	87
88.	**MELODIE D'AMOUR,** Ames Brothers, Victor	75
88.	**SOFT,** Bill Doggett, King	83
88.	**HELPLESS,** Platters, Mercury	95
91.	**BERTHA LOU,** Clint Miller, ABC-Paramount	87
91.	**SWINGIN' DADDY,** Buddy Knox, Roulette	95
93.	**AT THE HOP,** Nick Todd, Dot	83
93.	**HARD TIMES (THE SLOP),** Nobel (Thin Man) Watts, Baton	83
95.	**YOU WIN AGAIN,** Jerry Lee Lewis, Sun	—
95.	**BE-BOP BABY,** Ricky Nelson, Imperial	59
95.	**HONEYCOMB,** Jimmie Rodgers, Roulette	75
95.	**THE JOKER,** Billy Myles, Ember	95
99.	**TILL,** Roger Williams, Kapp	66
100.	**JULIE,** Sammy Salvo, Victor	92

STORE RECORDED SALES — NEW YORK UNIVERSITY SCHOOL OF RETAILING • THE BILLBOARD •

Best Sellers in Stores

FOR SURVEY WEEK ENDING FEBRUARY 15, 1958

The information given in this chart is based on actual sales to customers in a scientific sample of the nation's retail record outlets during the week ending on the date shown above. Sample design, sample size, and all methods used in this continuing study of retail record sales are under the direct and continuing supervision and control of the School of Retailing of New York University.

This Week		Last Week	Weeks on Chart
1.	DON'T (BMI)—Elvis Presley / I BEG OF YOU (BMI)—Victor 7150	1	5
2.	GET A JOB (BMI)—Silhouettes / I Am Lonely (BMI)—Ember 1029	3	6
3.	CATCH A FALLING STAR (ASCAP)—Perry Como / MAGIC MOMENTS (ASCAP)—Victor 7128	7	5
4.	AT THE HOP (BMI)—Danny and the Juniors / Sometimes (BMI)—ABC-Paramount 9871	2	12
5.	SAIL ALONG SILVERY MOON (ASCAP)—Billy Vaughn / RAUNCHY (BMI)—Dot 15661	6	10
6.	SHORT SHORTS (BMI)—Royal Teens / Planet Rock (BMI)—ABC-Paramount 9882	4	4
7.	SUGARTIME (BMI)—McGuire Sisters / Banana Split (BMI)—Coral 61924	10	8
8.	STOOD UP (BMI)—Ricky Nelson / WAITIN' IN SCHOOL (BMI)—Imperial 5483	5	9
9.	YOU ARE MY DESTINY (BMI)—Paul Anka / When I Stop Loving You (BMI)—ABC-Paramount 9880	11	5
10.	OH, JULIE (BMI)—Crescendos / My Little Girl (BMI)—Nasco 6005	12	7
11.	THE STROLL (BMI)—Diamonds / Land of Beauty (BMI)—Mercury 71242	8	8
12.	IT'S TOO SOON TO KNOW (ASCAP)—Pat Boone / A WONDERFUL TIME UP THERE (BMI)—Dot 15690	25	2
13.	DEDE DINAH (ASCAP)—Frankie Avalon / Ooh La La (ASCAP)—Chancellor 1011	9	5
14.	TWENTY-SIX MILES (BMI)—Four Preps / It's You (ASCAP)—Cap 3845	20	3
15.	DON'T LET GO (BMI)—Roy Hamilton / The Right to Love (BMI)—Epic 9257	18	6
16.	LA DEE DAH (BMI)—Billy and Lillie / The Monster (BMI)—Swan 4002	16	7
17.	PEGGY SUE (BMI)—Buddy Holly / Everyday (BMI)—Coral 61885	14	16
18.	APRIL LOVE (ASCAP)—Pat Boone / When the Swallows Come Back to Capistrano (ASCAP)—Dot 15660	15	17
19.	SWEET LITTLE SIXTEEN (BMI)—Chuck Berry / Reelin' and Rocking (BMI)—Chess 1683	46	2
20.	WITCHCRAFT (ASCAP)—Frank Sinatra / Tell Her You Love Her (BMI)—Cap 3859	24	4
21.	MARCH FROM THE RIVER KWAI AND "COLONEL BOGEY" (ASCAP)—Mitch Miller / Hey, Little Baby (BMI)—Col 41066	23	6
22.	JO-ANN (BMI)—Playmates / You Can't Stop Me From Dreaming (BMI)—Roulette 4037	19	6
23.	ARE YOU SINCERE? (BMI)—Andy Williams / Be Mine Tonight (BMI)—Cadence 1340	49	2
24.	GREAT BALLS OF FIRE (BMI)—Jerry Lee Lewis / You Win Again (BMI)—Sun 281	13	13
25.	OH-OH, I'M FALLING IN LOVE AGAIN (ASCAP)—Jimmie Rodgers / The Long Hot Summer (ASCAP)—Roulette 4045	44	2
26.	THIS LITTLE GIRL OF MINE (BMI)—Everly Brothers / Should We Tell Him (BMI)—Cadence 1342	38	2
27.	MAYBE (BMI)—Chantels / Come My Little Baby (BMI)—End 1005	17	6
28.	LIECHTENSTEINER POLKA (ASCAP)—Will Glahe / Schweitzer Polka (BMI)—London 1755	21	15
29.	GOOD GOLLY, MISS MOLLY (BMI)—Little Richard / Hey-Hey-Hey-Hey! (BMI)—Specialty 624	—	1
30.	CLICK CLACK (BMI)—Dickey Doo and the Don'ts / Did You Cry (BMI)—Swan 4001	29	2
31.	OH, BOY! (BMI)—Crickets / Not Fade Away (BMI)—Brunswick 55035	31	13
32.	BELONGING TO SOMEONE (ASCAP)—Patti Page / Bring Us Together (ASCAP)—Mercury 71247	—	1
33.	WHY DON'T THEY UNDERSTAND? (BMI)—George Hamilton IV / Even Tho' (BMI)—ABC-Paramount 9862	28	13
34.	BALLAD OF A TEENAGE QUEEN (BMI)—Johnny Cash / Big River (BMI)—Sun 283	33	3
35.	I'LL COME RUNNING BACK TO YOU (BMI)—Sam Cooke / FOREVER (BMI)—Specialty 619	22	10
36.	SWINGING SHEPHERD BLUES (BMI)—Moe Koffman Quartet / Hambourg Bound (BMI)—Jubilee 5311	36	3
37.	ALL THE WAY (ASCAP)—Frank Sinatra / CHICAGO (ASCAP)—Capitol 3793	34	16
38.	SHE'S NEAT (ASCAP)—Dale Wright / Say That You Care (ASCAP)—Fraternity 792	47	2
39.	ANGEL SMILE (BMI)—Nat King Cole / Back in My Arms (BMI)—Cap 3860	—	1
40.	COME TO ME (ASCAP)—Johnny Mathis / When I Am With You (ASCAP)—Col 41082	50	2
41.	WILD IS THE WIND (ASCAP)—Johnny Mathis / NO LOVE (BUT YOUR LOVE) (BMI)—Columbia 41060	37	11
42.	BONY MORONIE (BMI)—Larry Williams / YOU BUG ME, BABY (BMI)—Specialty 615	42	16
43.	YELLOW DOG BLUES—(ASCAP) Joe Darensbourg and the Dixie Flyers / Martinique (BMI)—Lark 452	—	1
44.	CHANCES ARE (ASCAP)—Johnny Mathis / THE TWELFTH OF NEVER (ASCAP) Columbia 40993	39	23
45.	YOU SEND ME (BMI)—Sam Cooke / SUMMERTIME (ASCAP)—Keen 34013	30	18
46.	BUZZ, BUZZ, BUZZ (BMI)—Hollywood Flames / Crazy (BMI)—Ebb 119	27	13
47.	SING, BOY, SING (ASCAP)—Tommy Sands / Crazy 'Cause I Love You (BMI)—Cap 3867	—	1
48.	DESIRE ME (BMI)—Sam Cooke / (I LOVE YOU) FOR SENTIMENTAL REASONS (BMI)—Keen 4002	26	9
49.	KISSES SWEETER THAN WINE (BMI)—Jimmie Rodgers / Better Loved You'll Never Be (ASCAP)—Roulette 4031	32	14
50.	THE STORY OF MY LIFE (ASCAP)—Marty Robbins / Once-a-Week Date (BMI)—Col 41013	45	13

THIS WEEK'S BEST BUYS

Special telephone reports indicate these recent releases have broken out in one or more key areas and have excellent potential for placing on The Billboard's best seller charts.

BREATHLESS (Homefolks-Obie, BMI)—Jerry Lee Lewis—Sun 288—The side appears to be another smash for the artist. It's big in all markets. Flip is "Down the Line" (Hi-Lo, BMI). A previous Billboard Spotlight pick.

ROCK AND ROLL IS HERE TO STAY (Singular, BMI)—Danny & the Juniors—ABC-Paramount 9888—Action is heavy in all markets. Flip is "School Boy Romance" (Singular, BMI). A previous Billboard Spotlight pick.

BAD MOTORCYCLE (Thornett, BMI)—The Storey Sisters—Cameo 126—All marts report strong sales for the side. It looks like a winner. Flip is "Sweet Daddy" (Thornett, BMI). A previous Billboard Spotlight pick.

RECENT POP RELEASES COMING UP STRONG

STORE RECORDED SALES — NEW YORK UNIVERSITY SCHOOL OF RETAILING • THE BILLBOARD •

FOR SURVEY WEEK ENDING FEBRUARY 15

The information given in this chart is based on actual sales to customers in a scientific sample of the nation's retail record outlets during the week ending on the date shown above. Sample design, sample size and all methods used in this continuing study of retail record sales are under the direct and continuing supervision and control of the School of Retailing of New York University.

The Little Blue Man . . . . *Betty Johnson* (BMI) Atlantic 1169

Tequila . . . . *The Champs* (BMI) Challenge 1016

The Walk . . . . *Jimmie McCracklin* (BMI) Checker 885

Who's Sorry Now . . . . *Connie Francis* (ASCAP) M-G-M 12588

Most Played by Jockeys

FOR SURVEY WEEK ENDING FEBRUARY 15

SIDES are ranked in order of the greatest number of plays on disk jockey radio shows thruout the country. Results are based on The Billboard's weekly survey among the nation's disk jockeys. The reverse side of each record is also listed.

This Week		Last Week	Weeks on Chart
1.	SUGARTIME (BMI)—McGuire Sisters Banana Split (BMI)—Coral 61924	1	8
2.	DON'T (BMI)—Elvis Presley I Beg of You (BMI)—Vic 7150	2	4
3.	GET A JOB (BMI)—Silhouettes I Am Lonely (BMI)—Ember 1029	5	5
4.	MAGIC MOMENTS (ASCAP)—Perry Como Catch a Falling Star ASCAP)—Vic 7128	7	6
5.	CATCH A FALLING STAR (ASCAP)—Perry Como Magic Moments (ASCAP)—Vic 7128	3	7
6.	AT THE HOP (BMI)—Danny and the Juniors Sometimes (BMI)—ABC-Paramount 9871	4	10
7.	OH, JULIE (BMI)—Crescendos My Little Girl (BMI)—Nasco 6005	12	4
8	SHORT SHORTS (BMI)—Royal Teens Planet Rock (BMI)—ABC-Paramount 9882	13	3
9.	TWENTY-SIX MILES (BMI)—Four Preps It's You (ASCAP)—Cap 3845	10	5
10.	SAIL ALONG SILVERY MOON (ASCAP)—Billy Vaughn Raunchy (BMI)—Dot 15661	8	5
11.	WITCHCRAFT (ASCAP)—Frank Sinatra Tell Her You Love Her (BMI)—Cap 3859	6	6
12.	OH-OH, I'M FALLING IN LOVE AGAIN (ASCAP)—Jimmie Rodgers The Long Hot Summer (ASCAP)—Roulette 4045	—	1
13.	BELONGING TO SOMEONE (ASCAP)—Patti Page Bring Us Together (ASCAP)—Mercury 71247	20	3
14.	IT'S TOO SOON TO KNOW (ASCAP)—Pat Boone A Wonderful Time Up There (BMI)—Dot 15690	—	1
15.	I BEG OF YOU (BMI)—Elvis Presley Don't (BMI)—Vic 7150	11	4
16.	YOU ARE MY DESTINY (BMI)—Paul Anka When I Stop Loving You (BMI)—ABC-Paramount 9880	17	3
17.	THE LITTLE BLUE MAN (BMI)—Betty Johnson Winter in Miami (ASCAP)—Atlantic 1169	—	1
18.	THE STROLL (BMI)—Diamonds Land of Beauty (BMI)—Mercury 71242	9	7
19.	ARE YOU SINCERE (BMI)—Andy Williams Be Mine Tonight (BMI)—Cadence 1340	—	1
20.	DON'T LET GO (BMI)—Roy Hamilton The Right to Love (BMI)—Epic 9257	18	4
21.	PEGGY SUE (BMI)—Buddy Holly Everyday (BMI)—Coral 61885	—	14
22.	APRIL LOVE (ASCAP)—Pat Boone When the Swallows Come Back to Capistrano (ASCAP)—Dot 15660	14	18
23.	SWINGING SHEPHERD BLUES (BMI)—Moe Koffman Quartet Hambourg Bound (BMI)—Jubilee 5311	25	2
24.	DEDE DINAH (ASCAP)—Frankie Avalon Ooh La La (ASCAP)—Chancellor 1011	—	1
25.	SING, BOY, SING (ASCAP)—Tommy Sands Crazy 'Cause I Love You (BMI)—Cap 3867	—	1

Top 100 Sides

FOR SURVEY WEEK ENDING FEBRUARY 15

This is a tabulation of dealer individual record sales listed according to the specific side requested by customers. No attempt is made to add sides together to reflect actual record sales. This is, therefore, a tabulation of sides or songs, and not records. This is the reason for any possible variation that occurs between the top 50 sides as reflected in this chart, and the top 50 record sellers as reflected in the "Best Sellers in Stores" chart.

Pos.	Song, Artist, Label	Last Week
1.	GET A JOB, Silhouettes, Ember	2
2.	AT THE HOP, Danny and the Juniors, ABC-Paramount	1
3.	DON'T, Elvis Presley, Victor	3
4.	SHORT SHORTS, Royal Teens, ABC-Paramount	4
5.	SUGARTIME, McGuire Sisters, Coral	8
6.	SAIL ALONG SILVERY MOON, Billy Vaughn, Dot	6
7.	YOU ARE MY DESTINY, Paul Anka, ABC-Paramount	9
8.	OH, JULIE, Crescendos, Nasco	10
9.	CATCH A FALLING STAR, Perry Como, Victor	11
10.	THE STROLL, Diamonds, Mercury	5
11.	DEDE DINAH, Frankie Avalon, Chancellor	7
12.	TWENTY-SIX MILES, Four Preps, Capitol	22
13.	STOOD UP, Ricky Nelson, Imperial	12
14.	IT'S TOO SOON TO KNOW, Pat Boone, Dot	34
15.	DON'T LET GO, Roy Hamilton, Epic	19
16.	LA DEE DAH, Billy and Lillie, Swan	17
17.	PEGGY SUE, Buddy Holly, Coral	15
17.	APRIL LOVE, Pat Boone, Dot	15
19.	SWEET LITTLE SIXTEEN, Chuck Berry, Chess	46
20.	WITCHCRAFT, Frank Sinatra, Capitol	26
21.	MARCH FROM THE RIVER KWAI AND "COLONEL BOGEY," Mitch Miller, Columbia	24
22.	I BEG OF YOU, Elvis Presley, Victor	14
23.	JO-ANN, Playmates, Roulette	20
24.	ARE YOU SINCERE, Andy Williams, Cadence	51
25.	OH-OH, I'M FALLING IN LOVE AGAIN, Jimmie Rodgers, Roulette	43
26.	GREAT BALLS OF FIRE, Jerry Lee Lewis, Sun	13
27.	MAGIC MOMENTS, Perry Como, Victor	35
28.	THIS LITTLE GIRL OF MINE, Everly Brothers, Cadence	39
29.	MAYBE, Chantels, End	18
30.	LIECHTENSTEINER POLKA, Will Glahe, London	23
31.	GOOD GOLLY, MISS MOLLY, Little Richard, Specialty	57
32.	CLICK CLACK, Dickey Doo and the Don'ts, Swan	29
33.	OH, BOY! Crickets, Brunswick	30
34.	WHY DON'T THEY UNDERSTAND? George Hamilton IV, ABC-Paramount	28
34.	BELONGING TO SOMEONE, Patti Page, Mercury	62
36.	BALLAD OF A TEENAGE QUEEN, Johnny Cash, Sun	32
37.	WAITIN' IN SCHOOL, Ricky Nelson, Imperial	21
37.	SWINGING SHEPHEHD BLUES, Moe Koffman Quartet, Jubilee	36
39.	I'LL COME RUNNING BACK TO YOU, Sam Cooke, Keen	25
39.	SHE'S NEAT, Dale Wright, Fraternity	49
41.	ALL THE WAY, Frank Sinatra, Capitol	36
42.	WONDERFUL TIME UP THERE, Pat Boone, Dot	77
43.	COME TO ME, Johnny Mathis, Columbia	52
43.	ANGEL SMILE, Nat King Cole, Capitol	66
45.	YELLOW DOG BLUES, Joe Darensbourg and the Dixie Flyers, Lark	54
46.	BUZZ, BUZZ, BUZZ, Hollywood Flames, Ebb	27
46.	YOU SEND ME, Sam Cooke, Keen	30
46.	BONY MORONIE, Larry Williams, Specialty	41
49.	SING, BOY, SING, Tommy Sands, Capitol	81
50.	KISSES SWEETER THAN WINE, Jimmie Rodgers, Roulette	32
50.	THE STORY OF MY LIFE, Marty Robbins, Columbia	45
52.	TEARDROPS, Lee Andrews and the Hearts, Chess	42
52.	A VERY SPECIAL LOVE, Johnny Nash, ABC-Paramount	57
54.	LITTLE BLUE MAN, Betty Johnson, Atlantic	—
54.	RAUNCHY, Bill Justis, Phillips International	36
54.	WILD IS THE WIND, Johnny Mathis, Columbia	52
57.	WHO'S SORRY NOW, Connie Francis, M-G-M	—
58.	WALKIN' WITH MR. LEE, Lee Allen, Ember	54
59.	RAUNCHY, Ernie Freeman, Imperial	57
60.	SWINGING SEPHERD BLUES, David Rose, M-G-M	—
60.	CHANCES ARE, Johnny Mathis, Columbia	46
60.	MY SPECIAL ANGEL, Bobby Helms, Decca	63
60.	HENRIETTA, Jimmie Dee, Dot	66
64.	JAILHOUSE ROCK, Elvis Presley, Victor	40
65.	HELPLESS, Platters, Mercury	88
66.	"7-11," Gone All Stars, Gone	—
67.	TEQUILA, Champs, Challenge	—
67.	YOU CAN MAKE IT IF YOU TRY, Gene Allison, Vee Jay	57
67.	RAUNCHY, Billy Vaughn, Dot	68
67.	LITTLE PIGEON, Sal Mineo, Epic	69
71.	THE WALK, Jimmie McCracklin, Checker	—
71.	WE BELONG TOGETHER, Robert and Johnny, Old Town	—
71.	SWINGING SHEPHERD BLUES, Johnny Pate Quintet, Federal	49
74.	LITTLE GYPSY, Ames Brothers, Victor	—
74.	DESIRE ME, Sam Cooke, Keen	63
76.	SO TOUGH, Casuals, Backbeat	—
76.	ROCK AND ROLL MUSIC, Chuck Berry, Chess	65
78.	JULIE, Sammy Salvo, Victor	100
79.	I'M AVAILABLE, Margie Rayburn, Liberty	77
79.	GEISHA GIRL, Hank Locklin, Victor	81
79.	BERTHA LOU, Clint Miller, ABC-Paramount	91
79.	HARD TIMES (THE SLOP), Nobel (Thin Man) Watts, Eaton	93
83.	I CAN'T STOP LOVING YOU, Don Gibson, Victor	—
83.	WAKE UP LITTLE SUSIE, Everly Brothers, Cadence	54
83.	SILHOUETTES, Rays, Cameo	57
83.	FASCINATION, Jane Morgan, Kapp	69
83.	PUT A LIGHT IN THE WINDOW, Four Lads, Columbia	71
83.	DO WHAT YOU DID, Thurston Harris, Aladdin	75
83.	BETTY AND DUPREE, Chuck Willis, Atlantic	85
90.	(I LOVE YOU) FOR SENTIMENTAL REASONS, Sam Cooke, Keen	43
90.	THE JOKER, Hilltoppers, Dot	—
92.	MARCH FROM THE RIVER KWAI AND "COLONEL BOGEY," Art Mooney, M-G-M	—
92.	HEY! SCHOOLGIRL, Tom and Jerry, Big	71
92.	MARCH FROM THE RIVER KWAI AND "COLONEL BOGEY," Edmundo Ros, London	75
92.	SWINGIN' DADDY, Buddy Knox, Roulette	91
96.	THIS IS THE NIGHT, Valiants, Keen	—
96.	I WANT YOU TO KNOW, Fats Domino, Imperial	48
98.	THE TWELFTH OF NEVER, Johnny Mathis, Columbia	81
99.	NO LOVE (BUT YOUR LOVE), Johnny Mathis, Columbia	71
99.	HEY LITTLE GIRL, Techniques, Roulette	77

NEW YORK UNIVERSITY SCHOOL OF RETAILING · STORE RECORDED SALES · THE BILLBOARD

BEST SELLING POP SINGLES IN STORES

The information given in this chart is based on actual sales to customers in a scientific sample of the nation's retail record outlets during the week ending on the date shown above. Sample design, sample size, and all methods used in this continuing study of retail record sales are under the direct and continuing supervision and control of the School of Retailing of New York University.

FOR SURVEY WEEK ENDING FEBRUARY 22, 1958

This Week	Title	Last Week	Weeks on Chart
1.	**DON'T** (BMI)—Elvis Presley; **I BEG OF YOU** (BMI)—Victor 7150	1	6
2.	**GET A JOB** (BMI)—Silhouettes; I Am Lonely (BMI)—Ember 1029	2	7
3.	**CATCH A FALLING STAR** (ASCAP)—Perry Como; **MAGIC MOMENTS** (ASCAP)—Victor 7128	3	6
4.	**SHORT SHORTS** (BMI)—Royal Teens; Planet Rock (BMI)—ABC-Paramount 9882	6	5
5.	**TWENTY-SIX MILES** (BMI)—Four Preps; It's You (ASCAP)—Cap 3845	14	4
6.	**OH, JULIE** (BMI)—Crescendos; My Little Girl (BMI)—Nasco 6005	10	8
7.	**SWEET LITTLE SIXTEEN** (BMI)—Chuck Berry; Reelin' and Rocking (BMI)—Chess 1683	19	3
8.	**SAIL ALONG SILVERY MOON** (ASCAP)—Billy Vaughn; **RAUNCHY** (BMI)—Dot 15661	5	11
9.	**AT THE HOP** (BMI)—Danny and the Juniors; Sometimes (BMI)—ABC-Paramount 9871	4	13
10.	**IT'S TOO SOON TO KNOW** (ASCAP)—Pat Boone; **A WONDERFUL TIME UP THERE** (BMI)—Dot 15690	12	3
11.	**THE STROLL** (BMI)—Diamonds; Land of Beauty (BMI)—Mercury 71242	11	9
12.	**YOU ARE MY DESTINY** (BMI)—Paul Anka; When I Stop Loving You (BMI)—ABC-Paramount 9880	9	6
13.	**SUGARTIME** (BMI)—McGuire Sisters; Banana Split (BMI)—Coral 61924	7	9
14.	**DON'T LET GO** (BMI)—Roy Hamilton; The Right to Love (BMI)—Epic 9257	15	7
15.	**STOOD UP** (BMI)—Ricky Nelson; **WAITIN' IN SCHOOL** (BMI)—Imperial 5483	8	10
16.	**LA DEE DAH** (BMI)—Billy and Lilly; The Monster (BMI)—Swan 4002	16	8
17.	**MAYBE** (BMI)—Chantels; Come My Little Baby (BMI)—End 1005	27	7
18.	**DEDE DINAH** (ASCAP)—Frankie Avalon; Ooh La La (ASCAP)—Chancellor 1011	13	6
19.	**ARE YOU SINCERE?** (BMI)—Andy Williams; Be Mine Tonight (BMI)—Cadence 1340	23	3
20.	**WHO'S SORRY NOW** (ASCAP)—Connie Francis; You Were Only Fooling (ASCAP)—M-G-M 12588	—	1
21.	**BALLAD OF A TEENAGE QUEEN** (BMI)—Johnny Cash; Big River (BMI)—Sun 283	34	4
22.	**THE WALK** (BMI)—Jimmie McCracklin; I'm to Blame (BMI)—Checker 885	—	1
23.	**TEQUILA** (BMI)—The Champs; Train Is Nowhere (BMI)—Challenge 1016	—	1
24.	**APRIL LOVE** (ASCAP)—Pat Boone; When the Swallows Come Back to Capistrano (ASCAP)—Dot 15660	18	18
25.	**OH-OH, I'M FALLING IN LOVE AGAIN** (ASCAP)—Jimmie Rodgers; The Long ot Summer (ASCAP)—Roulette 4045	25	3
26.	**GOOD GOLLY, MISS MOLLY** (BMI)—Little Richard; Hey-Hey-Hey-Hey (BMI)—Specialty 624	29	2
27.	**MARCH FROM THE RIVER KWAI AND "COLONEL BOGEY"** (ASCAP)—Mitch Miller; Hey Little Baby (BMI)—Col 41066	21	7
28.	**WITCHCRAFT** (ASCAP)—Frank Sinatra; Tell Her You Love Her (BMI)—Cap 3859	20	5
29.	**JO-ANN** (BMI)—Playmates; You Can't Stop Me From Dreaming (BMI)—Roulette 4037	22	7
30.	**"7-11"** (BMI)—Gone All Stars; Down Yonder Rock (BMI)—Gone 5016	—	1
31.	**PEGGY SUE** (BMI)—Buddy Holly; Everyday (BMI)—Coral 61885	17	17
32.	**WE BELONG TOGETHER**—Robert and Johnny; Walking in the Rain — Old Town 1047	—	1
33.	**ANGEL SMILE** (BMI)—Nat King Cole; Back in My Arms (BMI)—Cap 3860	39	2
34.	**LIECHTENSTEINER POLKA** (ASCAP)—Will Glahe; Schweitzer Polka (BMI)—London 1755	28	16
35.	**BELONGING TO SOMEONE** (ASCAP)—Patti Page; Bring Us Together (ASCAP)—Mercury 71247	32	2
36.	**THE LITTLE BLUE MAN** (BMI)—Betty Johnson; Winter in Miami (ASCAP)—Atlantic 1169	—	1
37.	**THIS LITTLE GIRL OF MINE** (BMI)—Everly Brothers; Should We Tell Him (BMI)—Cadence 1342	26	3
38.	**CLICK CLACK** (BMI)—Dickey Doo and the Dont's; Did You Cry (BMI)—Swan 4001	30	3
39.	**BEEN SO LONG** (BMI)—Pastels; My One and Only Dream (BMI)—Argo 5287	—	1
40.	**SHE'S NEAT** (ASCAP)—Dale Wright; Say That You Care (ASCAP)—Fraternity 792	38	3
41.	**GREAT BALLS OF FIRE** (BMI)—Jerry Lee Lewis; **YOU WIN AGAIN** (BMI)—Sun 281	24	14
42.	**SO TOUGH** (BMI)—Casuals; I Love My Darling (BMI)—Back Beat 503	—	1
43.	**SWINGING SHEPHERD BLUES** (BMI)—Johnny Pate Quintet; The Elder (BMI)—Federal 12312	—	2
44.	**ALL THE WAY** (ASCAP)—Frank Sinatra; **CHICAGO** (ASCAP)—Cap 3793	37	17
45.	**OH, BOY!** (BMI)—Crickets; Not Fade Away (BMI)—Brunswick 55035	31	14
46.	**WHY DON'T THEY UNDERSTAND?** (BMI)—George Hamilton IV; Even Tho' (BMI)—ABC-Paramount 9862	33	14
47.	**SWINGING SHEPHERD BLUES** (BMI)—David Rose; Rock Fiddle (ASCAP)—M-G-M 12608	—	1
47.	**ROCK AND ROLL IS HERE TO STAY** (BMI)—Danny and the Juniors; School Boy Romance (BMI)—ABC-Paramount 9888	—	1
49.	**COME TO ME** (ASCAP)—Johnny Mathis; When I Am With You (ASCAP)—Col 41082	40	3
50.	**DESIRE ME** (BMI)—Sam Cooke; **(I LOVE YOU) FOR SENTIMENTAL REASONS** (BMI)—Keen 4002	48	10

THIS WEEK'S BEST BUYS

Special telephone reports indicate these recent releases have broken out in one or more key areas and have excellent potential for placing on The Billboard's best seller charts.

MAYBE BABY (Nor-Va-Jak-Melody Lane, BMI)—The Crickets—Brunswick 55053—The side is strong in all markets. It looks like another big one for the artists. Flip is "Tell Me How" (Stardust, BMI). A previous Billboard Spotlight pick.

LOLLIPOP (Marks, BMI)—The Chordettes—Cadence 1345—The platter has taken off strongly in all marts. It appears a winner. Flip is "Baby, Come-a Back-a" (Budd, ASCAP). A previous Billboard Spotlight pick.

NEW YORK UNIVERSITY SCHOOL OF RETAILING · STORE RECORDED SALES · THE BILLBOARD

RECENT POP RELEASES COMING UP STRONG

FOR SURVEY WEEK ENDING FEBRUARY 22

The information given in this chart is based on actual sales to customers in a scientific sample of the nation's retail record outlets during the week ending on the date shown above. Sample design, sample size and all methods used in this continuing study of retail record sales are under the direct and continuing supervision and control of the School of Retailing of New York University.

Bad Motorcycle . . . . *The Storey Sisters*
(BMI) Cameo 126

Oh, Lonesome Me . . . . *Don Gibson*
(BMI) RCA Victor 7133

Most Played by Jockeys

FOR SURVEY WEEK ENDING FEBRUARY 22

SIDES are ranked in order of the greatest number of plays on disk jockey radio shows thruout the country. Results are based on The Billboard's weekly survey among the nation's disk jockeys. The reverse side of each record is also listed.

This Week		Last Week	Weeks on Chart
1.	SUGARTIME (BMI)—McGuire Sisters Banana Split (BMI)—Coral 61924	1	9
2.	DON'T (BMI)—Elvis Presley I Beg of You (BMI)—Vic 7150	2	5
3.	CATCH A FALLING STAR (ASCAP)—Perry Como Magic Moments (ASCAP)—Vic 7128	5	8
4.	TWENTY-SIX MILES (BMI)—Four Preps It's You (ASCAP)—Cap 3845	9	6
5.	MAGIC MOMENTS (ASCAP)—Perry Como Catch a Falling Star (ASCAP)—Vic 7128	4	7
6.	SAIL ALONG SILVERY MOON (ASCAP)—Billy Vaughn Raunchy (BMI)—Dot 15661	10	6
7.	OH-OH, I'M FALLING IN LOVE AGAIN (ASCAP)—Jimmie Rodgers The Long Hot Summer (ASCAP)—Roulette 4045	12	2
8.	WITCHCRAFT (ASCAP)—Frank Sinatra Tell Her You Love Her (BMI)—Cap 3859	11	7
9.	YOU ARE MY DESTINY (BMI)—Paul Anka When I Stop Loving You (BMI)—ABC-Paramount 9880	16	4
10.	OH JULIE (BMI)—Crescendos My Little Girl (BMI)—Nasco 6005	7	5
11.	SHORT SHORTS (BMI)—Royal Teens Planet Rock (BMI)—ABC-Paramount 9882	8	4
12.	AT THE HOP (BMI)—Danny and the Juniors Sometimes (BMI)—ABC-Paramount 9871	6	11
13.	GET A JOB (BMI)—Silhouettes I Am Lonely (BMI)—Ember 1029	3	6
14.	I BEG OF YOU (BMI)—Elvis Presley Don't (BMI)—Vic 7150	15	5
15.	SWEET LITTLE SIXTEEN (BMI)—Chuck Berry Reelin' and Rocking (BMI)—Chess 1683	—	1
16.	A WONDERFUL TIME UP THERE (BMI)—Pat Boone It's Too Soon to Know (ASCAP)—Dot 15690	—	1
17.	BELONGING TO SOMEONE (ASCAP)—Patti Page Bring Us Together (ASCAP)—Mercury 71247	13	4
18.	APRIL LOVE (ASCAP)—Pat Boone When the Swallows Come Back to Capistrano (ASCAP)—Dot 15660	22	19
19.	ARE YOU SINCERE? (BMI)—Andy Williams Be Mine Tonight (BMI)—Cadence 1340	19	2
20.	DON'T LET GO (BMI)—Roy Hamilton The Right to Love (BMI)—Epic 9257	20	5
21.	GET A JOB (BMI)—Mills Brothers I Found a Million Dollar Baby (ASCAP)—Dot 15695	—	1
22.	IT'S TOO SOON TO KNOW (ASCAP)—Pat Boone A Wonderful Time Up There (BMI)—Dot 15690	14	2
23.	OH, JULIE (BMI)—Sammy Salvo Say Yeah (BMI)—Vic 7097	—	1
24.	THE STROLL (BMI)—Diamonds The Stroll (BMI)—Mercury 71242	18	8
25.	SWINGING SHEPHERD BLUES (BMI)—Moe Koffman Quartet Hambourg Bound (BMI)—Jubilee 5311	23	3

NEW YORK UNIVERSITY SCHOOL OF RETAILING · STORE RECORDED SALES · THE BILLBOARD

Top 100 Sides

FOR SURVEY WEEK ENDING FEBRUARY 22

This is a tabulation of dealer individual record sales listed according to the specific side requested by customers. No attempt is made to add sides together to reflect actual record sales. This is, therefore, a tabulation of sides or songs, and not records. This is the reason for any possible variation that occurs between the top 50 sides as reflected in this chart, and the top 50 record sellers as reflected in the "Best Sellers in Stores" chart.

Pos.	Song, Artist, Label	Last Week
1.	**GET A JOB,** Silhouettes, Ember	1
2.	**DON'T,** Elvis Presley, Victor	3
3.	**SHORT SHORTS,** Royal Teens, ABC-Paramount	4
4.	**TWENTY-SIX MILES,** Four Preps, Capitol	12
5.	**OH, JULIE,** Crescendos, Nasco	8
6.	**SWEET LITTLE SIXTEEN,** Chuck Berry, Chess	19
7.	**AT THE HOP,** Danny and the Juniors, ABC-Paramount	2
8.	**THE STROLL,** Diamonds, Mercury	10
9.	**SAIL ALONG SILVERY MOON,** Billy Vaughn, Dot	6
10.	**YOU ARE MY DESTINY,** Paul Anka, ABC-Paramount	7
11.	**SUGARTIME,** McGuire Sisters, Coral	5
12.	**CATCH A FALLING STAR,** Perry Como, Victor	9
13.	**DON'T LET GO,** Roy Hamilton, Epic	15
14.	**LA DEE DAH,** Billy and Lillie, Swan	16
15.	**MAYBE,** Chantels, End	29
16.	**DEDE DINAH,** Frankie Avalon, Chancellor	11
17.	**ARE YOU SINCERE?** Andy Williams, Cadence	24
18.	**IT'S TOO SOON TO KNOW,** Pat Boone, Dot	14
19.	**WHO'S SORRY NOW,** Connie Francis, M-G-M	57
20.	**BALLAD OF A TEENAGE QUEEN,** Johnny Cash, Sun	36
21.	**THE WALK,** Jimmie McCracklin, Checker	71
22.	**STOOD UP,** Ricky Nelson, Imperial	12
23.	**TEQUILA,** Champs, Challenge	67
24.	**APRIL LOVE,** Pat Boone, Dot	17
25.	**OH-OH, I'M FALLING IN LOVE AGAIN,** Jimmie Rodgers, Roulette	25
26.	**GOOD GOLLY, MISS MOLLY,** Little Richard, Specialty	31
27.	**MARCH FROM THE RIVER KWAI AND "COLONEL BOGEY"** Mitch Miller, Columbia	21
28.	**WITCHCRAFT,** Frank Sinatra, Capitol	20
29.	**JO-ANN,** Playmates, Roulette	23
30.	**I BEG OF YOU,** Elvis Presley, Victor	22
31.	**"7-11,"** Gone All Stars, Gone	66
32.	**PEGGY SUE,** Buddy Holly, Coral	17
32.	**WONDERFUL TIME UP THERE,** Pat Boone, Dot	42
34.	**MAGIC MOMENTS,** Perry Como, Victor	27
35.	**ANGEL SMILE,** Nat King Cole, Capitol	43
35.	**WE BELONG TOGETHER,** Robert and Johnny, Old Town	71
37.	**LIECHTENSTEINER POLKA,** Will Glahe, London	30
38.	**BELONGING TO SOMEONE,** Patti Page, Mercury	34
39.	**THIS LITTLE GIRL OF MINE,** Everly Brothers, Cadence	28
39.	**CLICK CLACK,** Dickey Doo and The Don'ts, Swan	32
39.	**LITTLE BLUE MAN,** Betty Johnson, Atlantic	54
42.	**BEEN SO LONG,** Pastels, Argo	—
43.	**SHE'S NEAT,** Dale Wright, Fraternity	39
44.	**GREAT BALLS OF FIRE,** Jerry Lee Lewis, Sun	26
44.	**SWINGING SHEPHERD BLUES,** Johnny Pate Quintet, Federal	71
44.	**SO TOUGH,** Casuals, Backbeat	76
47.	**OH, BOY!** Crickets, Brunswick	33
47.	**ALL THE WAY,** Frank Sinatra, Capitol	41
49.	**WHY DON'T THEY UNDERSTAND?** George Hamilton IV, ABC-Paramount	34
50.	**ROCK AND ROLL IS HERE TO STAY** Danny and the Juniors, ABC-Paramount	—
50.	**COME TO ME,** Johnny Mathis, Columbia	43
50.	**SWINGING SHEPHERD BLUES,** David Rose, M-G-M	60
53.	**YOU CAN MAKE IT IF YOU TRY,** Gene Allison, Vee Jay	67
54.	**WAITIN' IN SCHOOL,** Ricky Nelson, Imperial	37
55.	**WALKIN' WITH MR. LEE,** Lee Allen, Ember	58
56.	**YELLOW DOG BLUES,** Joe Darensbourg and The Dixie Flyers, Lark	45
56.	**A VERY SPECIAL LOVE,** Johnny Nash, ABC-Paramount	52
56.	**HELPLESS,** Platters, Mercury	65
56.	**BETTY AND DUPREE,** Chuck Willis, Atlantic	83
60.	**BONY MORONIE,** Larry Williams, Specialty	46
61.	**SWINGING SEPHERD BLUES,** Moe Koffman Quartet, Jubilee	37
61.	**I'LL COME RUNNING BACK TO YOU,** Sam Cooke, Keen	39
63.	**SING, BOY, SING,** Tommy Sands, Capitol	49
63.	**KISSES SWEETER THAN WINE,** Jimmie Rodgers, Roulette	50
65.	**THE STORY OF MY LIFE,** Marty Robbins, Columbia	50
65.	**CHANCES ARE,** Johnny Mathis, Columbia	60
67.	**BAD MOTORCYCLE,** Storey Sisters, Cameo	—
67.	**TEARDROPS,** Lee Andrews and The Hearts, Chess	52
67.	**RAUNCHY,** Bill Justis, Phillips International	54
67.	**WILD IS THE WIND,** Johnny Mathis, Columbia	54
67.	**LITTLE GYPSY,** Ames Brothers, Victor	74
72.	**RAUNCHY,** Ernie Freeman, Imperial	59
72.	**DESIRE ME,** Sam Cooke, Keen	74
72.	**I'M AVAILABLE,** Margie Rayburn, Liberty	79
75.	**RAUNCHY,** Billy Vaughn, Dot	67
76.	**MAYBE, BABY,** Crickets, Brunswick	—
76.	**HENRIETTA,** Jimmie Dee, Dot	60
76.	**JAILHOUSE ROCK,** Elvis Presley, Victor	64
76.	**TEQUILA,** Eddie Platt, ABC-Paramount	—
76.	**ROCK AND ROLL MUSIC,** Chuck Berry, Chess	76
81.	**OH, JULIE,** Sammy Salvo, Victor	78
81.	**BERTHA LOU,** Clint Miller, ABC-Paramount	79
81.	**YOU SEND ME,** Sam Cooke, Keen	46
84.	**BUZZ, BUZZ, BUZZ,** Hollywood Flames, Ebb	46
85.	**THE PLEA,** Jesters, Winley	—
85.	**I CAN'T STOP LOVING YOU,** Don Gibson, Victor	83
85.	**SWINGIN' DADDY,** Buddy Knox, Roulette	92
88.	**MARCH FROM THE RIVER KWAI AND "COLONEL BOGEY"** Art Mooney, M-G-M	92
89.	**BREATHLESS,** Jeery Lee Lewis, Sun	—
90.	**SO TOUGH,** Kuff Linx, Challenge	—
90.	**MY SPECIAL ANGEL,** Bobby Helms, Decca	60
90.	**LITTLE PIGEON,** Sal Mineo, Epic	67
90.	**WAKE UP LITTLE SUSIE,** Everly Brothers, Cadence	83
90.	**(I LOVE YOU) FOR SENTIMENTAL REASONS,** Sam Cooke, Keen	90
95.	**YELLOW DOG BLUES,** Charles Magnante, Dot	—
95.	**PUT A LIGHT IN THE WINDOW,** Four Lads, Columbia	83
97.	**BIG GUITAR,** Owen Bradley Quintet, Decca	—
97.	**GEISHA GIRL,** Hank Locklin, Victor	79
97.	**DO WHAT YOU DID,** Thurston Harris, Aladdin	83
97.	**MARCH FROM THE RIVER KWAI AND "COLONEL BOGEY"** Edmundo Ros, London	92

BEST SELLING POP SINGLES IN STORES

STORE RECORDED SALES — NEW YORK UNIVERSITY SCHOOL OF RETAILING — THE BILLBOARD

The information given in this chart is based on actual sales to customers in a scientific sample of the nation's retail record outlets during the week ending on the date shown above. Sample design, sample size, and all methods used in this continuing study of retail record sales are under the direct and continuing supervision and control of the School of Retailing of New York University.

FOR SURVEY WEEK ENDING MARCH 1, 1958

This Week	Title	Last Week	Weeks on Chart
1.	DON'T (BMI)—Elvis Presley / I BEG OF YOU (BMI)—Victor 7150	1	7
2.	GET A JOB (BMI)—Silhouettes / I Am Lonely (BMI)—Ember 1029	2	8
3.	SWEET LITTLE SIXTEEN (BMI)—Chuck Berry / Reelin' and Rocking (BMI)—Chess 1683	7	4
4.	A WONDERFUL TIME UP THERE (BMI)—Pat Boone / IT'S TOO SOON TO KNOW (ASCAP)—Dot 15690	10	4
5.	SHORT SHORTS (BMI)—Royal Teens / Planet Rock (BMI)—ABC-Paramount 9882	4	6
6.	OH, JULIE (BMI)—Crescendos / My Little Girl (BMI)—Nasco 6005	6	9
7.	TWENTY-SIX MILES (BMI)—Four Preps / It's You (ASCAP)—Cap 3845	5	5
8.	CATCH A FALLING STAR (ASCAP)—Perry Como / MAGIC MOMENTS (ASCAP)—Vic 7128	3	7
9.	SAIL ALONG SILVERY MOON (ASCAP)—Billy Vaughn / RAUNCHY (BMI)—Dot 15661	8	12
10.	WHO'S SORRY NOW (ASCAP)—Connie Francis / You Were Only Fooling (ASCAP)—M-G-M 12588	20	2
11.	THE WALK (BMI)—Jimmy McCracklin / I'm to Blame (BMI)—Checker 885	22	2
12.	TEQUILA (BMI)—The Champs / Train to Nowhere (BMI)—Challenge 1016	23	2
13.	THE STROLL (BMI)—Diamonds / Land of Beauty (BMI)—Mercury 71242	11	10
14.	AT THE HOP (BMI)—Danny and the Juniors / Sometimes (BMI)—ABC-Paramount 9871	9	14
15.	SUGARTIME (BMI)—McGuire Sisters / Banana Split (BMI)—Coral 61924	13	10
16.	YOU ARE MY DESTINY (BMI)—Paul Anka / When I Stop Loving You (BMI)—ABC-Paramount 9880	12	7
17.	GOOD GOLLY, MISS MOLLY (BMI)—Little Richard / Hey-Hey-Hey-Hey (BMI)—Specialty 624	26	3
18.	BALLAD OF A TEENAGE QUEEN (BMI)—Johnny Cash / Big River (BMI)—Sun 283	21	5
19.	DEDE DINAH (ASCAP)—Frankie Avalon / Ooh La La (ASCAP)—Chancellor 1011	18	7
20.	MAYBE (BMI)—Chantels / Come My Little Baby (BMI)—End 1005	17	8
21.	DON'T LET GO (BMI)—Roy Hamilton / The Right to Love (BMI)—Epic 9257	14	8
22.	STOOD UP (BMI)—Ricky Nelson / WAITIN' IN SCHOOL (BMI)—Imperial 5483	15	11
23.	ARE YOU SINCERE? (BMI)—Andy Williams / Be Mine Tonight (BMI)—Cadence 1340	19	4
24.	OH-OH, I'M FALLING IN LOVE AGAIN (ASCAP)—Jimmie Rodgers / The Long Hot Summer (ASCAP)—Roulette 4045	25	4
25.	BEEN SO LONG (BMI)—Pastels / My One and Only Dream (BMI)—Argo 5287	39	2
26.	BREATHLESS (BMI)—Jerry Lee Lewis / Down the Line (BMI)—Sun 288	—	1
27.	MAYBE BABY (BMI)—Crickets / Tell Me How (BMI)—Brunswick 55053	—	1
28.	LA DEE DAH (BMI)—Billy and Lillie / The Monster (BMI)—Swan 4002	16	9
29.	CLICK CLACK (BMI)—Dickey Doo and the Don'ts / Did You Cry (BMI)—Swan 4001	38	4
30.	ROCK AND ROLL IS HERE TO STAY (BMI)—Danny and the Juniors / School Boy Romance (BMI)—ABC-Paramount 9888	47	2
31.	WITCHCRAFT (ASCAP)—Frank Sinatra / Tell Her You Love Her (BMI)—Capitol 3859	28	6
32.	WE BELONG TOGETHER Robert and Johnny / Walking in the Rain—Old Town 1047	32	2
33.	BETTY AND DUPREE (BMI)—Chuck Willis / My Crying Eyes (BMI)—Atlantic 1168	—	1
34.	THE LITTLE BLUE MAN (BMI)—Betty Johnson / Winter in Miami (ASCAP)—Atlantic 1169	36	2
35.	TEQUILA (BMI)—Eddie Platt / Popcorn (BMI)—ABC-Paramount 9899	—	1
36.	YOU CAN MAKE IT IF YOU TRY (BMI)—Gene Allison / Hey, Hey, I Love You (BMI)—Vee Jay 713	—	2
37.	JO-ANN (BMI)—Playmates / You Can't Stop Me From Dreaming (BMI)—Roulette 4037	29	8
38.	"7-11" (BMI)—Gone All Stars / Down Yonder Rock (BMI)—Gone 5016	30	2
39.	ANGEL SMILE (BMI)—Nat King Cole / Back in My Arms (BMI)—Cap 3860	33	3
40.	SWINGING SHEPHERD BLUES (BMI)—Moe Koffman Quartet / Hambourg Bound (BMI)—Jubilee 5311	—	4
41.	APRIL LOVE (ASCAP)—Pat Boone / WHEN THE SWALLOWS COME BACK TO CAPISTRANO (ASCAP)—Dot 15660	24	19
42.	LIECHTENSTEINER POLKA (ASCAP)—Will Glahe / Schweitzer Polka (BMI)—London 1755	34	17
43.	MARCH FROM THE RIVER KWAI AND "COLONEL BOGEY" (ASCAP)—Mitch Miller / Hey, Little Baby (BMI)—Col 41066	27	8
44.	SWINGING SHEPHERD BLUES (BMI)—Johnny Pate Quintet / The Elder (BMI)—Federal 12312	43	3
45.	BAD MOTORCYCLE (BMI)—Storey Sisters / Sweet Daddy (BMI)—Cameo 126	—	1
46.	COME TO ME (ASCAP)—Johnny Mathis / When I Am With You (ASCAP)—Col 41082	49	4
47.	SO TOUGH (BMI)—Casuals / I Love My Darling (BMI)—Back Beat 503	42	2
48.	GREAT BALLS OF FIRE (BMI)—Jerry Lee Lewis / You Win Again (BMI)—Sun 281	41	15
49.	THIS LITTLE GIRL OF MINE (BMI)—Everly Brothers / Should We Tell Him (BMI)—Cadence 1342	37	4
50.	SHE'S NEAT (ASCAP)—Dale Wright / Say That You Care (ASCAP)—Fraternity 792	40	4

THIS WEEK'S BEST BUYS

Special telephone reports indicate these recent releases have broken out in one or more key areas and have excellent potential for placing on The Billboard's best seller charts.

DINNER WITH DRAC (Parts I & 2) (Mayland, BMI)—**John Zacherle**—Cameo 130—This is a strong disk in all marts. A previous Billboard "Spotlight" pick.

THE COLLEGE MAN (Knox, BMI)—**Bill Justis**—Phillips International 3522—This looks like a smash successor to "Raunchy." It's doing well in all major markets. Flip is "The Stranger" (Knox, BMI). A previous Billboard "Spotlight" pick.

YOU WERE MADE FOR ME (Andrea, BMI)—**Sam Cooke**—Keen 4009—All markets report strong sales for the platter. Flip is "Lonely Island" (Happy House, ASCAP). A previous Billboard "Spotlight" pick.

LAZY MARY (Shapiro-Bernstein, ASCAP)—**Lou Monte**—RCA Victor 7160—The disk is strongest in the Middle Atlantic and New England areas. It's also climbing in other major markets. Flip is "Angelique" (Clara, ASCAP).

BIG GUITAR (Time, BMI)—**Owen Bradley**—Decca 30564—The side has been out for several weeks. It's now started to perk in most of the top marts. Flip is "Sentimental Dream" (Forrest, BMI). A previous Billboard "Spotlight" pick.

RECENT POP RELEASES COMING UP STRONG

STORE RECORDED SALES — NEW YORK UNIVERSITY SCHOOL OF RETAILING — THE BILLBOARD

FOR SURVEY WEEK ENDING MARCH 1

The information given in this chart is based on actual sales to customers in a scientific sample of the nation's retail record outlets during the week ending on the date shown above. Sample design, sample size and all methods used in this continuing study of retail record sales are under the direct and continuing supervision and control of the School of Retailing of New York University.

Lollipop . . . . *Chordettes*
(BMI) Cadence 1345

Oh, Lonesome Me . . . . *Don Gibson*
(BMI) RCA Victor 7133

Big Guitar . . . . *Owen Bradley*
(BMI) Decca 30564

Most Played by Jockeys

FOR SURVEY WEEK ENDING MARCH 1

SIDES are ranked in order of the greatest number of plays on disk jockey radio shows thruout the country. Results are based on The Billboard's weekly survey among the nation's disk jockeys. The reverse side of each record is also listed.

This Week		Last Week	Weeks on Chart
1.	SUGARTIME (BMI)—McGuire Sisters Banana Split (BMI)—Coral 61924	1	10
2.	TWENTY-SIX MILES (BMI)—Four Preps It's You (ASCAP)—Cap 3845	4	7
3.	DON'T (BMI)—Elvis Presley I Beg of You (BMI)—Vic 7150	2	6
4.	CATCH A FALLING STAR (ASCAP)—Perry Como Magic Moments (ASCAP)—Vic 7128	3	9
5.	MAGIC MOMENTS (ASCAP)—Perry Como Catch a Falling Star (ASCAP)—Vic 7128	5	8
6.	SHORT SHORTS (BMI)—Royal Teens Planet Rock (BMI)—ABC-Paramount 9882	11	5
7.	WITCHCRAFT (ASCAP)—Frank Sinatra Tell Her You Love Her (BMI)—Cap 3859	8	8
8.	GET A JOB (BMI)—Silhouettes I Am Lonely (BMI)—Ember 1029	13	7
9.	OH-OH, I'M FALLING IN LOVE AGAIN (ASCAP)—Jimmie Rodgers The Long Hot Summer (ASCAP)—Roulette 4045	7	3
10.	YOU ARE MY DESTINY (BMI)—Paul Anka When I Stop Loving You (BMI)—ABC-Paramount 9880	9	5
11.	SWEET LITTLE SIXTEEN (BMI)—Chuck Berry Reelin' and Rocking (BMI)—Chess 1683	15	2
12.	SAIL ALONG SILVERY MOON (ASCAP)—Billy Vaughn Raunchy (BMI)—Dot 15661	6	7
13.	OH, JULIE (BMI)—Crescendos My Little Girl (BMI)—Nasco 6005	10	6
14.	BELONGING TO SOMEONE (ASCAP)—Patti Page Bring Us Together (ASCAP)—Mercury 71247	17	5
15.	IT'S TOO SOON TO KNOW (ASCAP)—Pat Boone A Wonderful Time Up There (BMI)—Dot 15690	22	3
16.	A WONDERFUL TIME UP THERE (BMI)—Pat Boone It's Too Soon to Know (ASCAP)—Dot 15690	16	2
17.	AT THE HOP (BMI)—Danny and the Juniors Sometimes (BMI)—ABC-Paramount 9871	12	12
18.	ARE YOU SINCERE (BMI)—Andy Williams Be Mine Tonight (BMI)—Cadence 1340	19	3
19.	THE STROLL (BMI)—Diamonds Land of Beauty (BMI)—Mercury 71242	24	9
20.	TEQUILA (BMI)—The Champs Train Is Nowhere (BMI)—Challenge 1016	—	1
21.	I BEG OF YOU (BMI)—Elvis Presley Don't (BMI)—Vic 7150	14	6
22.	WHO'S SORRY NOW (ASCAP)—Connie Francis You Were Only Fooling (ASCAP)—M-G-M 12588	—	1
23.	LOLLIPOP (BMI)—Chordettes Baby, Come-A-Back-A (ASCAP)—Cadence 1345	—	1
24.	SING, BOY, SING (ASCAP)—Tommy Sands Crazy 'Cause I Love You (BMI)—Cap 3867	—	2
25.	GET A JOB (BMI)—Mills Brothers I Found a Million Dollar Baby (ASCAP)—Dot 15695	21	2

Top 100 Sides

FOR SURVEY WEEK ENDING MARCH 1

This is a tabulation of dealer individual record sales listed according to the specific side requested by customers. No attempt is made to add sides together to reflect actual record sales. This is, therefore, a tabulation of sides or songs, and not records. This is the reason for any possible variation that occurs between the top 50 sides as reflected in this chart, and the top 50 record sellers as reflected in the "Best Sellers in Stores" chart.

Pos.	Song, Artist, Label	Last Week
1.	**DON'T,** Elvis Presley, Victor	2
2.	**GET A JOB,** Silhouettes, Ember	1
3.	**SWEET LITTLE SIXTEEN,** Chuck Berry, Chess	6
4.	**SHORT SHORTS,** Royal Teens, ABC-Paramount	3
5.	**OH, JULIE,** Crescendos, Nasco	5
6.	**TWENTY-SIX MILES,** Four Preps, Capitol	4
7.	**WHO'S SORRY NOW,** Connie Francis, M-G-M	19
7.	**THE WALK,** Jimmy McCracklin, Checker	21
9.	**TEQUILA,** Champs, Challenge	23
10.	**THE STROLL,** Diamonds, Mercury	8
11.	**AT THE HOP,** Danny and the Juniors, ABC-Paramount	7
11.	**SAIL ALONG SILVERY MOON,** Billy Vaughn, Dot	9
13.	**SUGARTIME,** McGuire Sisters, Coral	11
14.	**YOU ARE MY DESTINY,** Paul Anka, ABC-Paramount	10
14.	**CATCH A FALLING STAR,** Perry Como, Victor	12
16.	**GOOD GOLLY, MISS MOLLY,** Little Richard, Specialty	26
17.	**A WONDERFUL TIME UP THERE,** Pat Boone, Dot	32
18.	**BALLAD OF A TEENAGE QUEEN,** Johnny Cash, Sun	20
19.	**DEDE DINAH,** Frankie Avalon, Chancellor	16
20.	**MAYBE,** Chantels, End	15
21.	**DON'T LET GO,** Roy Hamilton, Epic	13
22.	**ARE YOU SINCERE?** Andy Williams, Cadence	17
22.	**OH-OH, I'M FALLING IN LOVE AGAIN,** Jimmie Rodgers, Roulette	25
24.	**IT'S TOO SOON TO KNOW,** Pat Boone, Dot	18
24.	**BEEN SO LONG,** Pastels, Argo	42
26.	**BREATHLESS,** Jerry Lee Lewis, Sun	89
27.	**MAYBE, BABY,** Crickets, Brunswick	76
28.	**LA DEE DAH,** Billy and Lillie, Swan	14
28.	**CLICK CLACK,** Dickey Doo and the Don'ts, Swan	39
28.	**ROCK AND ROLL IS HERE TO STAY,** Danny and the Juniors, ABC-Paramount	50
31.	**STOOD UP,** Ricky Nelson, Imperial	22
32.	**WITCHCRAFT,** Frank Sinatra, Capitol	28
33.	**WE BELONG TOGETHER,** Robert and Johnny, Old Town	35
34.	**THE LITTLE BLUE MAN,** Betty Johnson, Atlantic	39
34.	**BETTY AND DUPREE,** Chuck Willis, Atlantic	56
36.	**TEQUILA,** Eddie Platt, ABC-Paramount	76
37.	**YOU CAN MAKE IT IF YOU TRY,** Gene Allison, Vee Jay	53
38.	**JO-ANN,** Playmates, Roulette	29
38.	**"7-11,"** Gone All Stars, Gone	31
40.	**I BEG OF YOU,** Elvis Presley, Victor	30
41.	**ANGEL SMILE,** Nat King Cole, Capitol	35
41.	**SWINGING SHEPHERD BLUES,** Moe Koffman Quartet, Jubilee	61
43.	**MAGIC MOMENTS,** Perry Como, Victor	34
43.	**LIECHTENSTEINER POLKA,** Will Glahe, London	37
45.	**APRIL LOVE,** Pat Boone, Dot	24
46.	**MARCH FROM THE RIVER KWAI AND "COLONEL BOGEY,"** Mitch Miller, Columbia	27
46.	**SWINGING SHEPHERD BLUES,** Johnny Pate Quintet, Federal	44
48.	**COME TO ME,** Johnny Mathis, Columbia	50
48.	**BAD MOTORCYCLE,** Storey Sisters, Cameo	67
50.	**SO TOUGH,** Casuals, Back Beat	44
51.	**SHE'S NEAT,** Dale Wright, Fraternity	43
52.	**THIS LITTLE GIRL OF MINE,** Everly Brothers, Cadence	39
52.	**GREAT BALLS OF FIRE,** Jerry Lee Lewis, Sun	44
54.	**ALL THE WAY,** Frank Sinatra, Capitol	47
55.	**PEGGY SUE,** Buddy Holly, Coral	32
56.	**LOLLIPOP,** Chordettes, Cadence	—
56.	**OH, LONESOME ME,** Don Gibson, Victor	—
58.	**BELONGING TO SOMEONE,** Patti Page, Merucry	38
58.	**OH, BOY!** Crickets, Brunswick	47
60.	**SING, BOY, SING,** Tommy Sands, Capitol	63
60.	**KISSES SWEETER THAN WINE,** Jimmie Rodgers, Roulette	63
62.	**WHY DON'T THEY UNDERSTAND?** George Hamilton IV, ABC-Paramount	49
63.	**WAITIN' IN SCHOOL,** Ricky Nelson, Imperial	54
63.	**WALKIN' WITH MR. LEE,** Lee Allen, Ember	55
63.	**HELPLESS,** Platters, Mercury	56
66.	**SWINGING SHEPHERD BLUES,** David Rose, M-G-M	50
66.	**THE STORY OF MY LIFE,** Marty Robbins, Columbia	65
66.	**DESIRE ME,** Sam Cooke, Keen	72
66.	**JAILHOUSE ROCK,** Elvis Presley, Victor	76
66.	**BUZZ, BUZZ, BUZZ,** Hollywood Flames, Ebb	84
66.	**BIG GUITAR,** Owen Bradley Quintet, Decca	97
72.	**CHANCES ARE,** Johnny Mathis, Columbia	65
72.	**RAUNCHY,** Billy Vaughn, Dot	75
74.	**I CAN'T HELP IT,** Margaret Whiting, Dot	—
74.	**I'LL COME RUNNING BACK TO YOU,** Sam Cooke, Keen	61
74.	**HENRIETTA,** Jimmie Dee, Dot	76
74.	**THE PLEA,** Jesters, Winley	85
78.	**RAUNCHY,** Bill Justis, Phillips International	67
78.	**SO TOUGH,** Kuft Linx, Challenge	90
80.	**DINNER WITH DRAC,** John Zacherle, Cameo	—
80.	**WILD IS THE WIND,** Johnny Mathis, Columbia	67
80.	**RAUNCHY,** Ernie Freeman, Imperial	72
80.	**SWINGIN' DADDY,** Buddy Knox, Roulette	85
84.	**COLLEGE MAN,** Bill Justis, Phillips International	—
84.	**LAZY MARY,** Lou Monte, Victor	—
86.	**YELLOW DOG BLUES,** Joe Darensbourg and the Dixie Flyers, Lark	56
87.	**BONY MORONIE,** Larry Williams, Specialty	60
87.	**MY SPECIAL ANGEL,** Bobby Helms, Decca	90
89.	**MILLION MILES FROM NOWHERE,** Brook Benton, Vik	—
89.	**SUGAH WOOGA,** Playmates, Savoy	—
89.	**YOU SEND ME,** Sam Cooke, Keen	81
89.	**WAKE UP LITTLE SUSIE,** Everly Brothers, Cadence	90
89.	**(I LOVE YOU) FOR SENTIMENTAL REASONS,** Sam Cooke, Keen	90
94.	**BOP-A-LENA,** Ronnie Self, Columbia	—
94.	**JEANNIE, JEANNIE, JEANNIE,** Eddie Cochran, Liberty	—
94.	**ROCK AND ROLL MUSIC,** Chuck Berry, Chess	76
94.	**BERTHA LOU,** Clint Miller, ABC-Paramount	81
94.	**YELLOW DOG BLUES,** Charles Magnante, Dot	95
94.	**PUT A LIGHT IN THE WINDOW,** Four Lads, Columbia	95
94.	**MARCH FROM THE RIVER KWAI AND "COLONEL BOGEY,"** Edmundo Ros, London	97
94.	**I WANT YOU TO KNOW,** Fats Domino, Imperial	—

BEST SELLING POP SINGLES IN STORES

The information given in this chart is based on actual sales to customers in a scientific sample of the nation's retail record outlets during the week ending on the date shown above. Sample design, sample size, and all methods used in this continuing study of retail record sales are under the direct and continuing supervision and control of the School of Retailing of New York University.

FOR SURVEY WEEK ENDING MARCH 8, 1958

This Week		Last Week	Weeks on Chart
1.	TEQUILA (BMI)—The Champs Train to Nowhere (BMI)—Challenge 1016	12	3
2.	SWEET LITTLE SIXTEEN (BMI)—Chuck Berry Reelin' and Rocking (BMI)—Chess 1683	3	5
3.	DON'T (BMI)—Elvis Presley I BEG OF YOU (BMI)—Victor 7150	1	8
4.	A WONDERFUL TIME UP THERE (BMI)—Pat Boone IT'S TOO SOON TO KNOW (ASCAP)—Dot 15690	4	5
5.	TWENTY-SIX MILES (BMI)—Four Preps It's You (ASCAP)—Cap 3845	7	6
6.	CATCH A FALLING STAR (ASCAP)—Perry Como MAGIC MOMENTS (ASCAP)—Vic 7128	8	8
7.	OH, JULIE (BMI)—Crescendos My Little Girl (BMI)—Nasco 6005	6	10
8.	WHO'S SORRY NOW (ASCAP)—Connie Francis You Were Only Fooling (ASCAP)—M-G-M 12588	10	3
9.	SAIL ALONG SILVERY MOON (ASCAP)—Billy Vaughn RAUNCHY (BMI)—Dot 15661	9	13
10.	GET A JOB (BMI)—Silhouettes I Am Lonely (BMI)—Ember 1029	2	9
11.	THE WALK (BMI)—Jimmy McCracklin I'm to Blame (BMI)—Checker 885	11	3
12.	SUGARTIME (BMI)—McGuire Sisters Banana Split (BMI)—Coral 61924	15	11
13.	GOOD GOLLY, MISS MOLLY (BMI)—Little Richard Hey-Hey-Hey-Hey! (BMI)—Specialty 624	17	4
14.	SHORT SHORTS (BMI)—Royal Teens Planet Rock (BMI)—ABC-Paramount 9882	5	7
15.	LOLLIPOP (BMI)—Chordettes Baby, Com-A Back-A (ASCAP)—Cadence 1345	—	1
16.	BREATHLESS (BMI)—Jerry Lee Lewis Down the Line (BMI)—Sun 288	26	2
17.	THE STROLL (BMI)—Diamonds Land of Beauty (BMI)—Mercury 71242	13	11
18.	AT THE HOP (BMI)—Danny and the Juniors Sometimes (BMI)—ABC-Paramount 9871	14	15
19.	ROCK AND ROLL IS HERE TO STAY Danny and the Juniors (BMI) School Boy Romance (BMI)—ABC-Paramount 9888	30	3
20.	YOU ARE MY DESTINY (BMI)—Paul Anka When I Stop Loving You (BMI)—ABC-Paramount 9880	16	8
21.	MAYBE, BABY (BMI)—Crickets Tell Me How (BMI)—Brunswick 55053	27	2
22.	DEDE DINAH (ASCAP)—Frankie Avalon Ooh La La (ASCAP)—Chancellor 1011	19	8
23.	OH-OH, I'M FALLING IN LOVE AGAIN (ASCAP)—Jimmy Rodgers The Long Hot Summer (ASCAP)—Roulette 4045	24	5
24.	STOOD UP (BMI)—Ricky Nelson WAITIN' IN SCHOOL (BMI)—Imperial 5483	22	12
25.	DINNER WITH DRAC (BMI)—John Zacherle Parts 1 & 2—Cameo 130	—	1
26.	ARE YOU SINCERE? (BMI)—Andy Williams Be Mine Tonight (BMI)—Cadence 1340	23	5
27.	BALLAD OF A TEENAGE QUEEN (BMI)—Johnny Cash BIG RIVER (BMI)—Sun 283	18	6
28.	MAYBE (BMI)—Chantels Come My Little Baby (BMI)—End 1005	20	9
29.	WITCHCRAFT (ASCAP)—Frank Sinatra Tell Her You Love Her (BMI)—Capitol 3859	31	7
30.	DON'T LET GO (BMI)—Roy Hamilton The Right to Love (BMI)—Epic 9257	21	9
31.	LAZY MARY (ASCAP)—Lou Monte Angelique (ASCAP)—Vic 7160	—	1
32.	CLICK CLACK (BMI)—Dickey Doo and the Don'ts Did You Cry (BMI)—Swan 4001	29	5
33.	BETTY AND DUPREE (BMI)—Chuck Willis My Crying Eyes (BMI)—Atlantic 1168	33	2
34.	THE LITTLE BLUE MAN (BMI)—Betty Johnson Winter in Miami (ASCAP)—Atlantic 1169	34	3
35.	LA DEE DAH (BMI)—Billy and Lillie The Monster (BMI)—Swan 4002	28	10
36.	SWINGING SHEPHERD BLUES (BMI)—Moe Koffman Quartet Hambourg Bound (BMI)—Jubilee 5311	40	5
37.	BEEN SO LONG (BMI)—Pastels My One and Only Dream (BMI)—Argo 5287	25	3
38.	TEQUILA (BMI)—Eddie Platt Popcorn (BMI)—ABC-Paramount 9899	35	2
39.	JO-ANN (BMI)—Playmates You Can't Stop Me From Dreaming (BMI)—Roulette 4037	37	9
40.	"7-11" (BMI)—Gone All Stars Down Yonder Rock (BMI)—Gone 5016	38	3
41.	COME TO ME (ASCAP)—Johnny Mathis When I Am With You (ASCAP)—Col 41082	46	5
42.	OH, LONESOME ME (BMI)—Don Gibson I CAN'T STOP LOVING YOU (BMI)—Vic 7133	—	1
43.	MARCH FROM THE RIVER KWAI AND "COLONEL BOGEY" (ASCAP)—Mitch Miller Hey, Little Baby (BMI)—Col 41066	43	9
44.	GREAT BALLS OF FIRE (BMI)—Jerry Lee Lewis YOU WIN AGAIN (BMI)—Sun 281	48	16
45.	SHE'S NEAT (ASCAP)—Dale Wright Say That You Care (ASCAP)—Fraternity 792	50	5
46.	SING, BOY, SING (ASCAP)—Tommy Sands Crazy 'Cause I Love You (BMI)—Cap 3867	—	2
47.	YOU CAN MAKE IT IF YOU TRY (BMI)—Gene Allison Hey, Hey, I Love You (BMI)—Vee Jay 713	36	3
48.	THIS LITTLE GIRL OF MINE (BMI)—Everly Brothers SHOULD WE TELL HIM (BMI)—Cadence 1342	49	5
49.	WE BELONG TOGETHER (BMI)—Robert and Johnny In the Rain—Old Town 1047	32	3
50.	BAD MOTORCYCLE (BMI)—Storey Sisters Sweet Daddy (BMI)—Cameo 126	45	2

THIS WEEK'S BEST BUYS

Special telephone reports indicate these recent releases have broken out in one or more key areas and have excellent potential for placing on The Billboard's best seller charts.

YES, MY DARLING (Travis, BMI)—**Fats Domino**—Imperial 5492—The side is doing well in all marts. It's also a strong r.&b. item. Flip is "Don't You Know I Love You," (Reeve, BMI). A previous Billboard "Spotlight" pick.

BILLY (Mills, ASCAP)—**Kathy Linden**—Felsted 8410—The side has caught on in a big way in all of the top centers. Flip is "If I Could Hold You in My Arms," (Knollwood, ASCAP).

ARRIVEDERCI, ROMA (Connelly, ASCAP) — **Roger Williams** — Kapp 210—This appears to be another click for the artist. It's moving well in all marts. Flip is "The Sentimental Touch," (Oxford, ASCAP). A previous Billboard "Spotlight" pick.

HE'S GOT THE WHOLE WORLD IN HIS HANDS (Chappell, ASCAP)—**Laurie London**—Capitol 3891—This is a hot platter in most of the top marts. Elsewhere, it's building. Flip is "Handed Down" (Chappell, ASCAP).

RECENT POP RELEASES COMING UP STRONG

FOR SURVEY WEEK ENDING MARCH 8

The information given in this chart is based on actual sales to customers in a scientific sample of the nation's retail record outlets during the week ending on the date shown above. Sample design, sample size and all methods used in this continuing study of retail record sales are under the direct and continuing supervision and control of the School of Retailing of New York University.

Big Guitar . . . . *Owen Bradley*
(BMI) Decca 30564

College Man . . . . *Bill Justin*
(BMI) Phillips International 3522

Lonely Island . . . . *Sam Cooke*
(BMI) Keen 4009

Most Played by Jockeys

FOR SURVEY WEEK ENDING MARCH 8

SIDES are ranked in order of the greatest number of plays on disk jockey radio shows thruout the country. Results are based on The Billboard's weekly survey among the nation's disk jockeys. The reverse side of each record is also listed.

This Week		Last Week	Weeks on Chart
1.	DON'T (BMI)—Elvis Presley I Beg of You (BMI)—Vic 7150	3	7
2.	TWENTY-SIX MILES (BMI)—Four Preps It's You (ASCAP)—Cap 3845	2	8
3.	CATCH A FALLING STAR (ASCAP) Perry Como Magic Moments (ASCAP)—Vic 7128	4	10
4.	SUGARTIME (BMI)—McGuire Sisters Banana Split (BMI)—Coral 61924	1	11
5.	SWEET LITTLE SIXTEEN (BMI)—Chuck Berry Reelin' and Rocking (BMI)—Chess 1683	11	3
6.	ARE YOU SINCERE (BMI)—Andy Williams Be Mine Tonight (BMI)—Cadence 1340	18	4
7.	SAIL ALONG SILVERY MOON (ASCAP)—Billy Vaughn Raunchy (BMI)—Dot 15661	12	8
8.	TEQUILA (BMI)—The Champs Train to Nowhere (BMI)—Challenge 1016	20	2
9.	WHO'S SORRY NOW (ASCAP)—Connie Francis You Were Only Fooling (ASCAP)—M-G-M 12588	22	2
10.	WITCHCRAFT (ASCAP)—Frank Sinatra Tell Her You Love Her (BMI)—Cap 3859	7	9
11.	OH, JULIE (BMI) Crescendos My Little Girl (BMI)—Nasco 6005	13	7
12.	OH-OH, I'M FALLING IN LOVE AGAIN (ASCAP)—Jimmie Rodgers The Long Hot Summer (ASCAP)—Roulette 4045	9	4
13.	GET A JOB (BMI)—Silhouettes I Am Lonely (BMI)—Ember 1029	8	8
14.	LOLLIPOP (BMI)—Chordettes Baby, Come-A Back-A (ASCAP)—Cadence 1345	23	2
15.	SHORT SHORTS (BMI)—Royal Teens Planet Rock (BMI)—ABC-Paramount 9882	6	6
16.	MAGIC MOMENTS (ASCAP)—Perry Como Catch a Falling Star (ASCAP)—Vic 7128	5	9
17.	IT'S TOO SOON TO KNOW (ASCAP)—Pat Boone A Wonderful Time Up There (BMI)—Dot 15690	15	4
18.	YOU ARE MY DESTINY (BMI)—Paul Anka When I Stop Loving You (BMI)—ABC-Paramount 9880	10	6
19.	A WONDERFUL TIME UP THERE (BMI)—Pat Boone It's Too Soon to Know (ASCAP)—Dot 15690	16	3
20.	BELONGING TO SOMEONE (ASCAP)—Patti Page Bring Us Together (ASCAP)—Mercury 71247	14	6
21.	MAYBE, BABY (BMI)—Crickets Tell Me How (BMI)—Brunswick 55053	—	1
22.	AT THE HOP (BMI)—Danny and the Juniors Sometimes (BMI)—ABC-Paramount 9871	17	13
23.	I BEG OF YOU (BMI)—Elvis Presley Don't (BMI)—Vic 7150	21	7
24.	BALLAD OF A TEENAGE QUEEN B(MI)—Johnny Cash Big River (BMI)—Sun 283	—	2
25.	BREATHLESS (BMI)—Jerry Lee Lewis Down the Line (BMI)—Sun 288	—	1
25.	THE LITTLE BLUE MAN (BMI)—Betty Johnson Winter in Miami (BMI)—Atlantic 1169	—	1

NEW YORK UNIVERSITY SCHOOL OF RETAILING · THE BILLBOARD · STORE RECORDED SALES

Top 100 Sides

FOR SURVEY WEEK ENDING MARCH 8

This is a tabulation of dealer individual record sales listed according to the specific side requested by customers. No attempt is made to add sides together to reflect actual record sales. This is, therefore, a tabulation of sides or songs, and not records. This is the reason for any possible variation that occurs between the top 50 sides as reflected in this chart, and the top 50 record sellers as reflected in the "Best Sellers in Stores" chart.

Pos.	Song, Artist, Label	Last Week
1.	**TEQUILA,** Champs, Challenge	9
2.	**SWEET LITTLE SIXTEEN,** Chuck Berry, Chess	3
3.	**DON'T,** Elvis Presley, Victor	1
4.	**TWENTY-SIX MILES,** Four Preps, Capitol	6
5.	**OH, JULIE,** Crescendos, Nasco	5
6.	**WHO'S SORRY NOW?** Connie Francis, M-G-M	7
7.	**GET A JOB,** Silhouettes, Ember	2
8.	**THE WALK,** Jimmy McCracklin, Checker	7
8.	**SUGARTIME,** McGuire Sisters, Coral	13
10.	**GOOD GOLLY, MISS MOLLY,** Little Richard, Specialty	16
11.	**SHORT SHORTS,** Royal Teens, ABC-Paramount	4
12.	**SAIL ALONG SILVERY MOON,** Billy Vaughn, Dot	11
13.	**CATCH A FALLING STAR,** Perry Como, Victor	14
13.	**LOLLIPOP,** Chordettes, Cadence	56
15.	**BREATHLESS,** Jerry Lee Lewis, Sun	26
16.	**A WONDERFUL TIME UP THERE,** Pat Boone, Dot	17
17.	**THE STROLL,** Diamonds, Mercury	10
18.	**IT'S TOO SOON TO KNOW,** Pat Boone, Dot	24
19.	**AT THE HOP,** Danny and the Juniors, ABC-Paramount	11
20.	**ROCK AND ROLL IS HERE TO STAY,** Danny and the Juniors, ABC-Paramount	28
21.	**YOU ARE MY DESTINY,** Paul Anka, ABC-Paramount	14
22.	**MAYBE, BABY,** Crickets, Brunswick	27
23.	**DEDE DINAH,** Frankie Avalon, Chancellor	19
24.	**OH-OH, I'M FALLING IN LOVE AGAIN,** Jimmie Rodgers, Roulette	22
25.	**DINNER WITH DRAC,** John Zacherle, Cameo	80
26.	**ARE YOU SINCERE?** Andy Williams, Cadence	22
27.	**MAYBE,** Chantels, End	20
28.	**BALLAD OF A TEENAGE QUEEN,** Johnny Cash, Sun	18
29.	**WITCHCRAFT,** Frank Sinatra, Capitol	32
30.	**DON'T LET GO,** Roy Hamilton, Epic	21
31.	**CLICK CLACK,** Dickey Doo and the Don'ts, Swan	28
31.	**STOOD UP,** Ricky Nelson, Imperial	31
31.	**LAZY MARY,** Lou Monte, Victor	84
34.	**BETTY AND DUPREE,** Chuck Willis, Atlantic	34
35.	**THE LITTLE BLUE MAN,** Betty Johnson, Atlantic	34
36.	**LA DEE DAH,** Billy and Lillie, Swan	28
37.	**SWINGING SHEPHERD BLUES,** Moe Koffman Quartet, Jubilee	41
38.	**MAGIC MOMENTS,** Perry Como, Victor	43
39.	**BEEN SO LONG,** Pastels, Argo	24
39.	**TEQUILA,** Eddie Platt, ABC-Paramount	36
41.	**JO-ANN,** Playmates, Roulette	38
42.	**"7-11,"** Gone All Stars, Gone	38
43.	**COME TO ME,** Johnny Mathis, Columbia	48
44.	**MARCH FROM THE RIVER KWAI AND "COLONEL BOGEY,"** Mitch Miller, Columbia	46
44.	**SHE'S NEAT,** Dale Wright, Fraternity	51
46.	**SING, BOY, SING,** Tommy Sands, Capitol	60
47.	**YOU CAN MAKE IT IF YOU TRY,** Gene Allison, Vee Jay	37
47.	**GREAT BALLS OF FIRE,** Jerry Lee Lewis, Sun	52
49.	**OH, LONESOME ME,** Don Gibson, Victor	56
50.	**WE BELONG TOGETHER,** Robert and Johnny, Old Town	33
50.	**I BEG OF YOU,** Elvis Presley, Victor	40
50.	**BAD MOTORCYCLE,** Storey Sisters, Cameo	48
53.	**LIECHTENSTEINER POLKA,** Will Glahe, London	43
53.	**COLLEGE MAN,** Bill Justis, Phillips International	84
55.	**ANGEL SMILE,** Nat King Cole, Capitol	41
55.	**THIS LITTLE GIRL OF MINE,** Everly Brothers, Cadence	52
55.	**BELONGING TO SOMEONE,** Patti Page, Mercury	58
58.	**APRIL LOVE,** Pat Boone, Dot	45
58.	**SO TOUGH,** Casuals, Back Beat	50
58.	**ALL THE WAY,** Frank Sinatra, Capitol	54
58.	**BIG GUITAR,** Owen Bradley Quintet, Decca	66
62.	**SWINGING SHEPHERD BLUES,** Johnny Pate Quintet, Federal	46
63.	**KISSES SWEETER THAN WINE,** Jimmie Rodgers, Roulette	60
63.	**SWINGING SHEPHERD BLUES,** David Rose, M-G-M	66
65.	**PEGGY SUE,** Buddy Holly, Coral	55
66.	**WAITIN' IN SCHOOL,** Ricky Nelson, Imperial	63
66.	**I'LL COME RUNNING BACK TO YOU,** Sam Cooke, Keen	74
68.	**WHY DON'T THEY UNDERSTAND?** George Hamilton IV, ABC-Paramount	62
68.	**HELPLESS,** Platters, Mercury	63
70.	**OH, BOY!** Crickets, Brunswick	58
70.	**THE STORY OF MY LIFE,** Marty Robbins, Columbia	66
72.	**LOLLIPOP,** Ronald and Ruby, Victor	—
72.	**CHANCES ARE,** Johnny Mathis, Columbia	72
72.	**YOU SEND ME,** Sam Cooke, Keen	89
72.	**BOP-A-LENA,** Ronnie Self, Columbia	94
76.	**LONELY ISLAND,** Sam Cooke, Keen	—
76.	**YES, MY DARLING,** Fats Domino, Imperial	—
76.	**JAILHOUSE ROCK,** Elvis Presley, Victor	66
76.	**RAUNCHY,** Billy Vaughn, Dot	72
76.	**SO TOUGH,** Kuft Linx, Challenge	78
76.	**YELLOW DOG BLUES,** Joe Darensbourg and the Dixie Flyers, Lark	86
82.	**BUZZ, BUZZ, BUZZ.** Hollywood Flames, Ebb	66
82.	**I CAN'T HELP IT,** Margaret Whiting, Dot	74
82.	**MILLION MILES FROM NOWHERE,** Brook Benton, Vik	89
85.	**UH-HUH, OH YEAH,** Steve Lawrence, Coral	—
85.	**RAUNCHY,** Ernie Freeman, Imperial	80
85.	**SWINGIN' DADDY,** Buddy Knox, Roulette	80
85.	**I WANT YOU TO KNOW,** Fats Domino, Imperial	94
89.	**BILLY,** Kathy Linden, Felsted	—
89.	**DESIRE ME,** Sam Cooke, Keen	66
91.	**BABY BABY,** Billy Williams, Coral	—
91.	**MOVIN' 'N' GROOVIN',** Duane Eddy, Jamie	—
91.	**RAUNCHY,** Bill Justis, Phillips International	78
94.	**WALKIN' WITH MR. LEE,** Lee Allen, Ember	63
94.	**WILD IS THE WIND,** Johnny Mathis, Columbia	80
94.	**MY SPECIAL ANGEL,** Bobby Helms, Decca	87
94.	**MARCH FROM THE RIVER KWAI AND "COLONEL BOGEY,"** Edmundo Ros, London	94
94.	**LITTLE PIGEON,** Sal Mineo, Epic	—
94.	**FASCINATION,** Jane Morgan, Kapp	—
100.	**REMEMBER,** Velours, Onyx	—
100.	**WAKE UP LITTLE SUSIE,** Everly Brothers, Cadence	89

BEST SELLING POP SINGLES IN STORES

The information given in this chart is based on actual sales to customers in a scientific sample of the nation's retail record outlets during the week ending on the date shown above. Sample design, sample size, and all methods used in this continuing study of retail record sales are under the direct and continuing supervision and control of the School of Retailing of New York University.

FOR SURVEY WEEK ENDING MARCH 15, 1958

This Week	Record	Last Week	Weeks on Chart
1.	TEQUILA (BMI)—The Champs Train to Nowhere (BMI)—Challenge 1016	1	4
2.	SWEET LITTLE SIXTEEN (BMI)—Chuck Berry Reelin' and Rocking (BMI)—Chess 1683	2	6
3.	LOLLIPOP (BMI)—Chordettes Baby, Come-A, Back-A (ASCAP)—Cadence 1345	15	2
4.	IT'S TOO SOON TO KNOW (ASCAP)—Pat Boone A WONDERFUL TIME UP THERE (BMI)—Dot 15690	4	6
5.	WHO'S SORRY NOW (ASCAP)—Connie Francis You Were Only Fooling (ASCAP)—M-G-M 12588	8	4
6.	DON'T (BMI)—Elvis Presley I BEG OF YOU (BMI)—Victor 7150	3	9
7.	CATCH A FALLING STAR (ASCAP)—Perry Como MAGIC MOMENTS (ASCAP)—Vic 7128	6	9
8.	TWENTY-SIX MILES (BMI)—Four Preps It's You (ASCAP)—Cap 3845	5	7
9.	OH, JULIE (BMI)—Crescendos My Little Girl (BMI)—Nasco 6005	7	11
10.	SAIL ALONG SILVERY MOON (ASCAP)—Billy Vaughn RAUNCHY (BMI)—Dot 15661	9	14
11.	DINNER WITH DRAC (BMI)—John Zacherle Parts 1 and 2—Cameo 130	25	2
12.	BREATHLESS (BMI)—Jerry Lee Lewis Down the Line (BMI)—Sun 288	16	3
13.	SUGARTIME (BMI)—McGuire Sisters Banana Split (BMI)—Coral 61924	12	12
14.	THE WALK (BMI)—Jimmy McCracklin I'm to Blame (BMI)—Checker 885	11	4
15.	SHORT SHORTS (BMI)—Royal Teens Planet Rock (BMI)—ABC-Paramount 9882	14	8
16.	GOOD GOLLY, MISS MOLLY (BMI)—Little Richard Hey-Hey-Hey-Hey! (BMI)—Specialty 624	13	5
17.	GET A JOB (BMI)—Silhouettes I Am Lonely (BMI)—Ember 1029	10	10
18.	LAZY MARY (ASCAP)—Lou Monte Angelique (ASCAP)—Vic 7160	31	2
19.	ROCK AND ROLL IS HERE TO STAY (BMI)—Danny and the Juniors School Boy Romance (BMI)—ABC-Paramount 9888	19	4
20.	ARE YOU SINCERE? (BMI)—Andy Williams Be Mine Tonight (BMI)—Cadence 1340	26	6
21.	MAYBE BABY (BMI)—Crickets Tell Me How (BMI)—Brunswick 55053	21	3
22.	THE STROLL (BMI)—Diamonds Land of Beauty (BMI)—Mercury 71242	17	12
23.	BALLAD OF A TEENAGE QUEEN (BMI)—Johnny Cash Big River (BMI)—Sun 283	27	7
24.	OH-OH, I'M FALLING IN LOVE AGAIN (ASCAP)—Jimmie Rodgers The Long Hot Summer (ASCAP)—Roulette 4045	23	6
25.	MAYBE (BMI)—Chantels Come My Little Baby (BMI)—End 1005	28	10
26.	DEDE DINAH (ASCAP)—Frankie Avalon Ooh La La (ASCAP)—Chancellor 1011	22	9
27.	WITCHCRAFT (ASCAP)—Frank Sinatra Tell Her You Love Her (BMI)—Capitol 3859	29	8
28.	AT THE HOP (BMI)—Danny and the Juniors Sometimes (BMI)—ABC-Paramount 9871	18	16
29.	YOU ARE MY DESTINY (BMI)—Paul Anka When I Stop Loving You (BMI)—ABC-Paramount 9880	20	9
30.	STOOD UP (BMI)—Ricky Nelson WAITIN' IN SCHOOL (BMI)—Imperial 5483	24	13
31.	THE LITTLE BLUE MAN (BMI)—Betty Johnson Winter in Miami (ASCAP)—Atlantic 1169	34	4
32.	DON'T LET GO (BMI)—Roy Hamilton The Right to Love (BMI)—Epic 9257	30	10
33.	BETTY AND DUPREE (BMI)—Chuck Willis My Crying Eyes (BMI)—Atlantic 1168	33	3
34.	"7-11" (BMI)—Gene All Stars Down Yonder Rock (BMI)—Gone 5016	40	4
35.	LONELY ISLAND (BMI)—Sam Cooke YOU WERE MADE FOR ME (BMI)—Keen 4009	—	1
36.	CLICK CLACK (BMI)—Dickey Doo and the Don'ts Did You Cry (BMI)—Swan 4001	32	6
37.	TEQUILA (BMI)—Eddie Platt Popcorn (BMI)—ABC-Paramount 9899	38	3
38.	APRIL LOVE (ASCAP)—Pat Boone When the Swallows Come Back to Capistrano (ASCAP)—Dot 15660	—	20
39.	BELONGING TO SOMEONE (ASCAP)—Patti Page Bring Us Together (ASCAP)—Mercury 71247	—	3
40.	LOLLIPOP (BMI)—Ronald and Ruby Fickle Baby (BMI)—Vic 7174	—	1
41.	MARCH FROM THE RIVER KWAI AND "COLONEL BOGEY" (ASCAP)—Mitch Miller Hey, Little Baby (BMI)—Col 41066	43	10
42.	COLLEGE MAN (BMI)—Bill Justis The Stranger (BMI)—Phillips International 3522	—	1
42.	BILLY (ASCAP)—Kathy Linden If I Could Hold You in My Arms (ASCAP)—Felsted 8410	—	1
44.	SWINGING SHEPHERD BLUES (BMI)—Moe Koffman Quartet Hambourg Bound (BMI)—Jubilee 5311	36	6
45.	OH, LONESOME ME (BMI)—Don Gibson I CAN'T STOP LOVING YOU (BMI)—Vic 7133	42	2
46.	ALL THE WAY (ASCAP)—Frank Sinatra CHICAGO (ASCAP)—Cap 3793	—	18
46.	SO TOUGH (BMI)—Casuals I Love My Darling (BMI)—Back Beat 503	—	3
48.	BIG GUITAR (BMI)—Owen Bradley Quintet Sentimental Dream (BMI)—Dec 30564	—	1
49.	LA DEE DAH (BMI)—Billy and Lillie The Monster (BMI)—Swan 4002	35	11
50.	ANGEL SMILE (BMI)—Nat King Cole Back in My Arms (BMI)—Cap 3860	—	4

THIS WEEK'S BEST BUYS

Special telephone reports indicate these recent releases have broken out in one or more key areas and have excellent potential for placing on The Billboard's best seller charts.

DIZZY, MISS LIZZIE (Venice, BMI)—Larry Williams—Specialty 626—Looks like another dual market smash for the artist. It's strong in pop and r.&b. marts. Flip is "Slow Down," (Venice, BMI). A previous Billboard "Spotlight" pick.

EVERY NIGHT (BMI)—The Chantels—End 1015—The chicks appear to have another winner. All the top marts report strong sales for the disk. Flip is "Whoever You Are," (BMI). A previous Billboard "Spotlight" pick.

WISHING FOR YOUR LOVE (Rayven, BMI) — The Voxpoppers—Mercury 71282—The side is collecting coin in all of the major markets. It looks like a sure chart platter. Flip is "The Last Drag," (Addit, BMI). A previous Billboard "Spotlight" pick.

TO BE LOVED (Pearl, BMI)—Jackie Wilson—Brunswick 55052—Sales are jumping for the record. It's been out for a while, but now appears a strong bet to score. Flip is "Come Back to Me," (Pearl, BMI). A previous Billboard "Spotlight" pick.

RECENT POP RELEASES COMING UP STRONG

FOR SURVEY WEEK ENDING MARCH 15

The information given in this chart is based on actual sales to customers in a scientific sample of the nation's retail record outlets during the week ending on the date shown above. Sample design, sample size and all methods used in this continuing study of retail record sales are under the direct and continuing supervision and control of the School of Retailing of New York University.

Bop-A-Lena . . . . . . *Ronnie Self*
(BMI) Columbia 41102

He's Got the Whole World in His Hands . *Laurie London*
(ASCAP) Capitol 3891

Yes, My Darling . . . . . . *Fats Domino*
(BMI) Imperial 5492

Most Played by Jockeys

FOR SURVEY WEEK ENDING MARCH 18

SIDES are ranked in order of the greatest number of plays on disk jockey radio shows thruout the country. Results are based on The Billboard's weekly survey among the nation's disk jockeys. The reverse side of each record is also listed.

This Week		Last Week	Weeks on Chart
1.	CATCH A FALLING STAR (ASCAP)—Perry Como Magic Moments (ASCAP)—Vic 7128	3	11
2.	TWENTY-SIX MILES (BMI)—Four Preps It's You (ASCAP)—Cap 3845	2	9
3.	ARE YOU SINCERE (BMI)—Andy Williams Be Mine Tonight (BMI)—Cadence 1340	6	5
4.	TEQUILA (BMI)—The Champs Train to Nowhere (BMI)—Challenge 1016	8	3
5.	SWEET LITTLE SIXTEEN (BMI)—Chuck Berry Reelin' and Rocking (BMI)—Chess 1683	5	4
6.	LOLLIPOP (BMI)—Chordettes Baby, Come-A Back-A (ASCAP)—Cadence 1345	14	3
7.	SUGARTIME (BMI)—McGuire Sisters Banana Split (BMI)—Coral 61924	4	12
8.	WHO'S SORRY NOW (ASCAP)—Connie Francis You Were Only Fooling (ASCAP)—M-G-M 12588	9	3
9.	DON'T (BMI)—Elvis Presley I Beg of You (BMI)—Vic 7150	1	8
10.	MAGIC MOMENTS (ASCAP)—Perry Como Catch a Falling Star (ASCAP)—Vic 7128	16	10
11.	A WONDERFUL TIME UP THERE (BMI)—Pat Boone It's Too Soon to Know (ASCAP)—Dot 15690	19	4
12.	WITCHCRAFT (ASCAP)— Tell Her You Love Her (BMI)—Cap 3859	10	10
13.	OH, JULIE (BMI)—Crescendos My Little Girl (BMI)—Nasco 6005	11	8
14.	YOU ARE MY DESTINY (BMI)—Paul Anka When I Stop Loving You (BMI)—ABC-Paramount 9880	18	7
15.	HE'S GOT THE WHOLE WORLD IN HIS HANDS (ASCAP)—Laurie London Handed Down (ASCAP)—Cap 3891	—	1
16.	OH-OH, I'M FALLING IN LOVE AGAIN (ASCAP)—Jimmie Rodgers The Long Hot Summer (ASCAP)—Roulette 4045	12	5
17.	IT'S TOO SOON TO KNOW (ASCAP)—Pat Boone A Wonderful Time Up There (BMI)—Dot 15690	17	5
18.	SHORT SHORTS (BMI)—Royal Teens Planet Rock (BMI)—ABC-Paramount 9882	15	7
19.	BELONGING TO SOMEONE (ASCAP)—Patti Page Bring Us Together (ASCAP)—Mercury 71247	20	7
20.	MAYBE BABY (BMI)—Crickets Tell Me How (BMI)—Brunswick 55053	21	2
21.	SAIL ALONG SILVERY MOON (ASCAP)—Billy Vaughn Raunchy (BMI)—Dot 15661	7	9
22.	GET A JOB (BMI)—Silhouettes I Am Lonely (BMI)—Ember 1029	13	9
23.	THE LITTLE BLUE MAN (BMI)—Betty Johnson Winter in Miami (ASCAP)—Atlantic 1169	25	3
24.	BALLAD OF A TEENAGE QUEEN (BMI)—Johnny Cash Big River (BMI)—Sun 283	24	3
25.	SWINGING SHEPHERD BLUES (BMI)—Moe Koffman Quartet Hambourg Bound (BMI)—Jubilee 5311	—	4

NEW YORK UNIVERSITY SCHOOL OF RETAILING — STORE RECORDED SALES — THE BILLBOARD

Top 100 Sides

FOR SURVEY WEEK ENDING MARCH 15

This is a tabulation of dealer individual record sales listed according to the specific side requested by customers. No attempt is made to add sides together to reflect actual record sales. This is, therefore, a tabulation of sides or songs, and not records. This is the reason for any possible variation that occurs between the top 50 sides as reflected in this chart, and the top 50 record sellers as reflected in the "Best Sellers in Stores" chart.

Pos.	Song, Artist, Label	Last Week
1.	**TEQUILA,** Champs, Challenge	1
2.	**SWEET LITTLE SIXTEEN,** Chuck Berry, Chess	2
3.	**LOLLIPOP,** Chordettes, Cadence	13
4.	**WHO'S SORRY NOW?** Connie Francis, M-G-M	6
5.	**TWENTY-SIX MILES,** Four Preps, Capitol	4
6.	**OH, JULIE,** Crescendos, Nasco	5
7.	**DINNER WITH DRAC,** John Zacherle, Cameo	25
8.	**DON'T,** Elvis Presley, Victor	3
9.	**SAIL ALONG SILVERY MOON,** Billy Vaughn, Dot	12
10.	**SUGARTIME,** McGuire Sisters, Coral	8
10.	**CATCH A FALLING STAR,** Perry Como, Victor	13
12.	**BREATHLESS,** Jerry Lee Lewis, Sun	15
13.	**IT'S TOO SOON TO KNOW,** Pat Boone, Dot	18
14.	**THE WALK,** Jimmy McCracklin, Checker	8
15.	**SHORT SHORTS,** Royal Teens, ABC-Paramount	11
16.	**GOOD GOLLY, MISS MOLLY,** Little Richard, Specialty	10
17.	**GET A JOB,** Silhouettes, Ember	7
18.	**LAZY MARY,** Lou Monte, Victor	31
19.	**ROCK AND ROLL IS HERE TO STAY,** Danny and the Juniors, ABC-Paramount	20
20.	**ARE YOU SINCERE?** Andy Williams, Cadence	26
21.	**MAYBE BABY,** Crickets, Brunswick	22
22.	**THE STROLL,** Diamonds, Mercury	17
22.	**BALLAD OF A TEENAGE QUEEN,** Johnny Cash, Sun	28
24.	**OH-OH. I'M FALLING IN LOVE AGAIN,** Jimmie Rodgers, Roulette	24
25.	**MAYBE,** Chantels, End	27
26.	**A WONDERFUL TIME UP THERE,** Pat Boone, Dot	16
27.	**DEDE DINAH,** Frankie Avalon, Chancellor	23
27.	**WITCHCRAFT,** Frank Sinatra, Capitol	29
29.	**AT THE HOP,** Danny and the Juniors, ABC-Paramount	19
30.	**YOU ARE MY DESTINY,** Paul Anka, ABC-Paramount	21
31.	**THE LITTLE BLUE MAN,** Betty Johnson, Atlantic	35
32.	**DON'T LET GO,** Roy Hamilton, Epic	30
33.	**STOOD UP,** Ricky Nelson, Imperial	31
33.	**BETTY AND DUPREE,** Chuck Willis, Atlantic	34
33.	**"7-11,"** Gone All-Stars, Gone	42
36.	**CLICK CLACK,** Dickey Doo and the Don'ts, Swan	31
37.	**TEQUILA,** Eddie Platt, ABC-Paramount	39
38.	**APRIL LOVE,** Pat Boone, Dot	58
39.	**BELONGING TO SOMEONE,** Patti Page, Mercury	55
40.	**MARCH FROM THE RIVER KWAI AND "COLONEL BOGEY,"** Mitch Miller, Columbia	44
40.	**LOLLIPOP,** Ronald and Ruby, Victor	72
42.	**SWINGING SHEPHERD BLUES,** Moe Koffman Quartet, Jubilee	37
42.	**COLLEGE MAN,** Bill Justis, Phillips International	53
42.	**SO TOUGH,** Casuals, Back Beat	58
42.	**BILLY,** Kathy Linden, Felsted	89
46.	**LA DEE DAH,** Billy and Lilly, Swan	36
46.	**ANGEL SMILE,** Nat King Cole, Capitol	55
46.	**ALL THE WAY,** Frank Sinatra, Capitol	58
46.	**BIG GUITAR,** Owen Bradley Quintet, Decca	58
50.	**MAGIC MOMENTS,** Perry Como, Victor	38
51.	**COME TO ME,** Johnny Mathis, Columbia	43
52.	**GREAT BALLS OF FIRE,** Jerry Lee Lewis, Sun	47
52.	**OH, LONESOME ME,** Don Gibson, Victor	49
54.	**SHE'S NEAT,** Dale Wright, Fraternity	44
55.	**JO-ANN,** Playmates, Roulette	41
55.	**SING, BOY, SING,** Tommy Sands, Capitol	46
55.	**WE BELONG TOGETHER,** Robert and Johnny, Old Town	50
55.	**LONELY ISLAND,** Sam Cooke, Keen	76
59.	**I BEG OF YOU,** Elvis Presley, Victor	50
59.	**SWINGING SHEPHERD BLUES,** Johnny Pate Quintet, Federal	62
61.	**HE'S GOT THE WHOLE WORLD IN HIS HANDS,** Laurie London, Capitol	—
61.	**THIS LITTLE GIRL OF MINE,** Everly Brothers, Cadence	55
63.	**DANCING WITH MY SHADOW,** Four Voices, Columbia	—
63.	**BOP-A-LENA,** Ronnie Self, Columbia	72
65.	**YOU WERE MADE FOR ME,** Sam Cooke, Keen	—
65.	**BAD MOTORCYCLE,** Storey Sisters, Cameo	50
65.	**YES, MY DARLING,** Fats Domino, Imperial	76
68.	**LIECHTENSTEINER POLKA,** Will Glahe, London	53
68.	**WAITIN' IN SCHOOL,** Ricky Nelson, Imperial	66
68.	**YOU SEND ME,** Sam Cooke, Keen	72
71.	**BEEN SO LONG,** Pastels, Argo	39
72.	**MOOVIN' 'N' GROOVIN',** Duane Eddy, Jamie	91
73.	**KISSES SWEETER THAN WINE,** Jimmie Rodgers, Roulette	63
73.	**SWINGING SHEPHERD BLUES,** David Rose, M-G-M	63
73.	**UH-HUH, OH, YEAH,** Steve Lawrence, Coral	85
76.	**DON'T YOU JUST KNOW IT,** Huey Smith, Ace	—
76.	**I'LL COME RUNNING BACK TO YOU,** Sam Cooke, Keen	66
78.	**PEGGY SUE,** Buddy Holly, Coral	65
78.	**BABY BABY,** Billy Williams, Coral	91
80.	**BOOK OF LOVE,** Monatones, Argo	—
80.	**WHY DON'T THEY UNDERSTAND?** George Hamilton IV, ABC-Paramount	68
80.	**RAUNCHY,** Billy Vaughn, Dot	76
83.	**ROCK AND ROLL RHAPSODY,** Four Aces, Decca	—
83.	**YEA, YEA,** Kendall Sisters, Argo	—
83.	**YOU CAN MAKE IT IF YOU TRY,** Gene Allison, Vee Jay	47
83.	**THE STORY OF MY LIFE,** Marty Robbins, Columbia	70
83.	**CHANCES ARE,** Johnny Mathis, Columbia	72
83.	**REMEMBER,** Velours, Onyx	100
89.	**THE SHAKE,** Mark IV, Cosmic	—
89.	**SO TOUGH,** Kuff Linx, Challenge	76
89.	**YELLOW DOG BLUES,** Joe Darensbourg and the Dixie Flyers, Lark	76
89.	**WALKIN' WITH MR. LEE,** Lee Allen, Ember	94
89.	**LITTLE PIGEON,** Sal Mineo, Epic	94
94.	**YOUR NAME IS BEAUTIFUL,** Carl Smith, Columbia	—
94.	**HELPLESS,** Platters, Mercury	68
94.	**JAILHOUSE ROCK,** Elvis Presley, Victor	76
94.	**MILLION MILES FROM NOWHERE,** Brook Benton, Vik	82
94.	**RAUNCHY,** Bill Justis, Phillips International	91
94.	**FASCINATION,** Jane Morgan, Kapp	94
100.	**OH, BOY!** Crickets, Brunswick	70

BEST SELLING POP SINGLES IN STORES

The information given in this chart is based on actual sales to customers in a scientific sample of the nation's retail record outlets during the week ending on the date shown above. Sample design, sample size, and all methods used in this continuing study of retail record sales are under the direct and continuing supervision and control of the School of Retailing of New York University.

FOR SURVEY WEEK ENDING MARCH 22, 1958

This Week		Last Week	Weeks on Chart
1.	**TEQUILA** (BMI)—The Champs Train to Nowhere (BMI)—Challenge 1016	1	5
2.	**LOLLIPOP** (BMI)—Chordettes Baby, Come-A Back-A (ASCAP)—Cadence 1345	3	3
3.	**SWEET LITTLE SIXTEEN** (BMI)—Chuck Berry Reelin' and Rocking (BMI)—Chess 1683	2	7
4.	**A WONDERFUL TIME UP THERE** (BMI)—Pat Boone **IT'S TOO SOON TO KNOW** (ASCAP)—Dot 15690	4	7
5.	**WHO'S SORRY NOW** (ASCAP)—Connie Francis You Were Only Fooling (ASCAP)—M-G-M 12588	5	5
6.	**DON'T** (BMI)—Elvis Presley **I BEG OF YOU** (BMI)—Victor 7150	6	10
7.	**SAIL ALONG SILVERY MOON** (ASCAP)—Billy Vaughn **RAUNCHY** (BMI)—Dot 15661	10	15
8.	**DINNER WITH DRAC** (BMI)—John Zacherle Parts 1 and 2—Cameo 130	11	3
9.	**CATCH A FALLING STAR** (ASCAP)—Perry Como **MAGIC MOMENTS** (ASCAP)	7	10
10.	**SUGARTIME** (BMI)—McGuire Sisters Banana Split (BMI)—Coral 61924	13	13
11.	**ARE YOU SINCERE** (BMI)—Andy Williams Be Mine Tonight (BMI)—Cadence 1340	20	7
12.	**BREATHLESS** (BMI)—Jerry Lee Lewis Down the Line (BMI)—Sun 288	12	4
13.	**HE'S GOT THE WHOLE WORLD IN HIS HANDS** (ASCAP)—Laurie London Handed Down (ASCAP)—Cap 3891	—	1
14.	**TWENTY-SIX MILES** (BMI)—Four Preps It's You (ASCAP)—Cap 3845	8	8
15.	**OH, JULIE** (BMI)—Crescendos My Little Girl (BMI)—Nasco 6005	9	12
16.	**BALLAD OF A TEENAGE QUEEN** (BMI)—Johnny Cash **BIG RIVER** (BMI)—Sun 283	23	8
17.	**THE WALK** (BMI)—Jimmy McCracklin I'm to Blame (BMI)—Checker 885	14	5
18.	**MAYBE BABY** (BMI)—Crickets Tell Me How (BMI)—Brunswick 55053	21	4
19.	**LAZY MARY** (ASCAP)—Lou Monte Angelique (ASCAP)—Vic 7160	18	3
20.	**THE LITTLE BLUE MAN** (BMI)—Betty Johnson Winter in Miami (ASCAP)—Atlantic 1169	31	5
21.	**GET A JOB** (BMI)—Silhouettes I Am Lonely (BMI)—Ember 1029	17	11
22.	**SHORT SHORTS** (BMI)—Royal Teens Planet Rock (BMI)—ABC-Paramount 9882	15	9
23.	**GOOD GOLLY, MISS MOLLY** (BMI)—Little Richard Hey-Hey-Hey-Hey! (BMI)—Specialty 624	16	6
24.	**THE STROLL** (BMI)—Diamonds Land of Beauty (BMI)—Mercury 71242	22	13
25.	**MAYBE** (BMI)—Chantels Come My Little Baby (BMI)—End 1005	25	11
26.	**DON'T YOU JUST KNOW IT?** (BMI)—Huey Smith High Blood Pressure (BMI)—Ace 545	—	1
27.	**ROCK AND ROLL IS HERE TO STAY** (BMI)—Danny and the Juniors School Boy Romance (BMI)—ABC-Paramount 9888		
28.	**YOU WERE MADE FOR ME** (BMI)—Sam Cooke **LONELY ISLAND** (ASCAP)—Keen 4009	35	2
29.	**OH-OH, I'M FALLING IN LOVE AGAIN** (ASCAP)—Jimmie Rodgers The Long Hot Summer (ASCAP)—Roulette 4045	24	7
30.	**DEDE DINAH** (ASCAP)—Frankie Avalon Ooh La La (ASCAP)—Chancellor 1011	26	10
31.	**WITCHCRAFT** (ASCAP)—Frank Sinatra Tell Her You Love Her (BMI)—Capitol 3859	27	9
32.	**BILLY** (ASCAP)—Kathy Linden If I Could Hold You In My Arms (ASCAP)—Felsted 8410	42	2
33.	**YOU ARE MY DESTINY** (BMI)—Paul Anka When I Stop Loving You (BMI)—ABC-Paramount 9880	29	10
34.	**AT THE HOP** (BMI)—Danny and the Juniors Sometimes (BMI)—ABC-Paramount 9871	28	17
35.	**TEQUILA** (BMI)—Eddie Platt Popcorn (BMI)—ABC-Paramount 9899	37	4
36.	**OH LONESOME ME** (BMI)—Don Gibson I Can't Stop Loving You (BMI)—Vic 7133	45	3
37.	**STOOD UP** (BMI)—Ricky Nelson **WAITIN' IN SCHOOL** (BMI)—Imperial 5483	30	14
38.	**DON'T LET GO** (BMI)—Roy Hamilton The Right to Love (BMI)—Epic 9257	32	11
39.	**MARCH FROM THE RIVER KWAI AND "COLONEL BOGEY"** (ASCAP)—Mitch Miller Hey, Little Baby (BMI)—Col 41066	41	11
40.	**LOLLIPOP** (BMI)—Ronald and Ruby Fickle Baby (BMI)—Vic 7174	40	2
41.	**NOW AND FOR ALWAYS** (ASCAP)—George Hamilton IV One Heart (ASCAP)—ABC-Paramount 9898	—	1
42.	**SWINGING SHEPHERD BLUES** (BMI)—Moe Koffman Quartet Hambourg Bound (BMI)—Jubilee 5311	44	7
43.	**CLICK CLACK** (BMI)—Dickey Doo and the Don'ts Did You Cry (BMI)—Swan 4001	36	7
44.	**BELONGING TO SOMEONE** (ASCAP)—Patti Page Bring Us Together (ASCAP)—Mercury 71247	39	4
45.	**COLLEGE MAN** (BMI)—Bill Justis The Stranger (BMI)—Phillips International 3522	42	2
46.	**SO TOUGH** (BMI)—Casuals I Love My Darling (BMI)—Back Beat 503	46	4
47.	**BOOK OF LOVE** (BMI)—Monatones You Never Loved Me (BMI)—Argo 5290	—	1
48.	**BEEN SO LONG** (BMI)—Pastels My One and Only Dream (BMI)—Argo 5287	—	4
49.	**SING, BOY, SING** (ASCAP)—Tommy Sands Crazy 'Cause I Love You (BMI)—Cap 3867	—	3
50.	**DANCING WITH MY SHADOW** (ASCAP)—Four Voices Bon Bon (ASCAP)—Col 41078	—	1

THIS WEEK'S BEST BUYS

Special telephone reports indicate these recent releases have broken out in one or more key areas and have excellent potential for placing on The Billboard's best seller charts.

BELIEVE WHAT YOU SAY (Reeve, BMI)

MY BUCKET'S GOT A HOLE IN IT (Pickwick, ASCAP)—**Ricky Nelson** — Imperial 5503 — Both sides are much in demand. The platter appears a two-sided hit. All markets report good action. A previous Billboard "Spotlight" pick.

TWILIGHT TIME (Porgie, BMI)—The Platters—Mercury 71289—This is the hottest by the group in a while. It's leaping in all marts. Flip is "Out of My Mind," (Figure, BMI).

Week in and week out you'll find more news, more record reviews, more advertising on the fast-moving record business in The Billboard, the communications center of the music industry.

RECENT POP RELEASES COMING UP STRONG

FOR SURVEY WEEK ENDING MARCH 22

The information given in this chart is based on actual sales to customers in a scientific sample of the nation's retail record outlets during the week ending on the date shown above. Sample design, sample size and all methods used in this continuing study of retail record sales are under the direct and continuing supervision and control of the School of Retailing of New York University.

Believe What You Say
My Bucket's Got a Hole in It . . . . ***Ricky Nelson***
(BMI); (ASCAP) Imperial 5503

Every Night . . . . ***Chantels***
(BMI) End 1015

Return to Me . . . . ***Dean Martin***
(ASCAP) Capitol 3984

Yes, My Darling . . . . ***Fats Domino***
(BMI) Imperial 5492

Most Played by Jockeys

FOR SURVEY WEEK ENDING MARCH 22

SIDES are ranked in order of the greatest number of plays on disk jockey radio shows thruout the country. Results are based on The Billboard's weekly survey among the nation's disk jockeys. The reverse side of each record is also listed.

This Week		Last Week	Weeks on Chart
1.	TEQUILA (BMI)—The Champs Train to Nowhere (BMI)—Challenge 1016	4	4
2.	LOLLIPOP (BMI)—Chordettes Baby, Come-A Back-A (ASCAP)—Cadence 1345	6	4
3.	CATCH A FALLING STAR (ASCAP)—Perry Como Magic Moments (ASCAP)—Vic 7128	1	12
4.	TWENTY-SIX MILES (BMI)—Four Preps It's You (ASCAP)—Cap 3845	2	10
5.	SUGARTIME (BMI)—McGuire Sisters Banana Split (BMI)—Coral 61924	7	13
6.	ARE YOU SINCERE (BMI)—Andy Williams Be Mine Tonight (BMI)—Cadence 1340	3	6
7.	SWEET LITTLE SIXTEEN (BMI)—Chuck Berry Reelin' and Rocking (BMI)—Chess 1683	5	5
8.	WHO'S SORRY NOW (ASCAP)—Connie Francis You Were Only Fooling (ASCAP)—M-G-M 12588	8	4
9.	DON'T (BMI)—Elvis Presley I Beg of You (BMI)—Vic 7150	9	9
10.	A WONDERFUL TIME UP THERE (BMI)—Pat Boone It's Too Soon to Know (ASCAP)—Dot 15690	11	5
11.	HE'S GOT THE WHOLE WORLD IN HIS HANDS (ASCAP)—Laurie London Handed Down (ASCAP)—Cap 3891	15	2
12.	WITCHCRAFT (ASCAP)—Frank Sinatra Tell Her You Love Her (BMI)—Cap 3859	12	11
13.	MAGIC MOMENTS (ASCAP)—Perry Como Catch a Falling Star (ASCAP)—Vic 7128	10	11
14.	BALLAD OF A TEENAGE QUEEN (BMI)—Johnny Cash Big River (BMI)—Sun 283	24	4
15.	SAIL ALONG SILVERY MOON (ASCAP)—Billy Vaughn Raunchy (BMI)—Dot 15661	21	10
16.	YOU ARE MY DESTINY (BMI)—Paul Anka When I Stop Loving You (BMI)—ABC-Paramount 9880	14	8
17.	IT'S TOO SOON TO KNOW (ASCAP)—Pat Boone A Wonderful Time Up There (BMI)—Dot 15690	17	6
18.	OH, JULIE (BMI)—Crescendos My Little Girl (BMI)—Nasco 6005	13	9
19.	OH-OH, I'M FALLING IN LOVE AGAIN (ASCAP)—Jimmie Rodgers The Long Hot Summer (ASCAP)—Roulette 4045	16	6
20.	TEQUILA (BMI)—Eddie Platt Popcorn (BMI)—ABC-Paramount 9899	—	1
21.	BELONGING TO SOMEONE (ASCAP)—Patti Page Bring Us Together (ASCAP)—Mercury 71247	19	8
22.	THE LITTLE BLUE MAN (BMI)—Betty Johnson Winter in Miami (ASCAP)—Atlantic 1169	23	4
23.	A VERY PRECIOUS LOVE (ASCAP)—Ames Brothers Don't Leave Me Now (BMI)—Vic 7167	—	1
24.	SHORT SHORTS (BMI)—Royal Teens Planet Rock (BMI)—ABC-Paramount 9882	18	8
25.	SWINGING SHEPHERD BLUES (BMI)—Moe Koffman Quartet Hambourg Bound (BMI)—Jubilee 5311	25	5

Top 100 Sides

FOR SURVEY WEEK ENDING MARCH 22

This is a tabulation of dealer individual record sales listed according to the specific side requested by customers. No attempt is made to add sides together to reflect actual record sales. This is, therefore, a tabulation of sides or songs, and not records. This is the reason for any possible variation that occurs between the top 50 sides as reflected in this chart, and the top 50 record sellers as reflected in the "Best Sellers in Stores" chart.

Pos.	Song, Artist, Label	Last Week
1.	TEQUILA, Champs, Challenge	1
2.	LOLLIPOP, Chordettes, Cadence	3
3.	SWEET LITTLE SIXTEEN, Chuck Berry, Chess	2
4.	WHO'S SORRY NOW, Connie Francis, M-G-M	4
5.	DON'T, Elvis Presley, Victor	9
6.	DINNER WITH DRAC, John Zacherle, Cameo	8
7.	SAIL ALONG SILVERY MOON, Billy Vaughn, Dot	10
8.	SUGARTIME, McGuire Sisters, Coral	11
9.	CATCH A FALLING STAR, Perry Como, Victor	11
10.	ARE YOU SINCERE? Andy Williams, Cadence	20
11.	BREATHLESS, Jerry Lee Lewis, Sun	5
12.	HE'S GOT THE WHOLE WORLD IN HIS HANDS, Laurie London, Capitol	61
13.	TWENTY-SIX MILES, Four Preps, Capitol	6
14.	A WONDERFUL TIME UP THERE, Pat Boone, Dot	26
15.	OH, JULIE, Crescendos, Nasco	7
16.	THE WALK, Jimmy McCracklin, Checker	14
16.	BALLAD OF A TEENAGE QUEEN, Johnny Cash, Sun	22
18.	MAYBE BABY, Crickets, Brunswick	21
19.	IT'S TOO SOON TO KNOW, Pat Boone, Dot	13
20.	LAZY MARY, Lou Monte, Victor	18
20.	LITTLE BLUE MAN, Betty Johnson, Atlantic	31
22.	GET A JOB, Silhouettes, Ember	17
23.	SHORT SHORTS, Royal Teens, ABC-Paramount	15
24.	GOOD GOLLY, MISS MOLLY, Little Richard, Specialty	16
25.	THE STROLL, Diamonds. Mercury	22
25.	MAYBE, Chantels, End	25
27.	ROCK AND ROLL IS HERE TO STAY, Danny and the Juniors, ABC-Paramount	19
27.	DON'T YOU JUST KNOW IT, Huey Smith, Ace	76
29.	OH-OH, I'M FALLING IN LOVE AGAIN, Jimmie Rodgers, Roulette	24
29.	DEDE DINAH, Frankie Avalon, Chancellor	27
31.	WITCHCRAFT, Frank Sinatra, Capitol	27
31.	BILLY, Kathy Linden, Felsted	42
33.	YOU ARE MY DESTINY, Paul Anka, ABC-Paramount	30
34.	AT THE HOP, Danny and the Juniors, ABC-Paramount	29
35.	TEQUILA, Eddie Platt, ABC-Paramount	37
36.	OH LONESOME ME, Don Gibson, Victor	52
37.	DON'T LET GO, Roy Hamilton, Epic	32
38.	MARCH FROM THE RIVER KWAI AND "COLONEL BOGEY," Mitch Miller, Columbia	40
39.	YOU WERE MADE FOR ME, Sam Cooke, Keen	65
39.	LOLLIPOP, Ronald and Ruby, Victor	40
41.	NOW AND FOR ALWAYS, George Hamilton IV, ABC-Paramount	—
42.	THE SWINGING SHEPHERD BLUES, Moe Koffman Quartet, Jubilee	42
43.	STOOD UP, Ricky Nelson, Imperial	33
43.	CLICK CLACK, Dickey Doo and the Don'ts, Swan	36
43.	BELONGING TO SOMEONE, Patti Page, Mercury	39
46.	COLLEGE MAN, Bill Justis, Phillips International	42
46.	SO TOUGH, Casuals, Back Beat	42
48.	BOOK OF LOVE, Monatones, Argo	80
49.	BEEN SO LONG, Pastels, Argo	71
50.	SING, BOY, SING, Tommy Sands, Capitol	55
51.	LONELY ISLAND, Sam Cooke, Keen	55
51.	DANCING WITH MY SHADOW, Four Voices, Columbia	63
53.	APRIL LOVE, Pat Boone, Dot	38
53.	MAGIC MOMENTS, Perry Como, Victor	50
55.	ANGEL SMILE, Nat King Cole, Capitol	46
55.	YES, MY DARLING, Fats Domino, Imperial	65
57.	COME TO ME, Johnny Mathis, Columbia	51
57.	GREAT BALLS OF FIRE, Jerry Lee Lewis, Sun	52
59.	MY BUCKET'S GOT A HOLE IN IT, Ricky Nelson, Imperial	—
59.	BIG GUITAR, Owen Bradley Quintet, Decca	46
59.	WE BELONG TOGETHER, Robert and Johnny, Old Town	55
62.	BETTY AND DUPREE, Chuck Willis, Atlantic	33
62.	ALL THE WAY, Frank Sinatra, Capitol	46
64.	WHOLE LOTTA WOMAN, Marvin Rainwater, M-G-M	—
64.	BOP-A-LENA, Ronnie Self, Columbia	63
66.	ROCK AND ROLL RHAPSODY, Four Aces, Decca	83
67.	EVERY NIGHT, Chantels, End	—
67.	"7-11," Gone All Stars, Gone	33
69.	LA DEE DAH, Billy and Lillie, Swan	46
69.	THIS LITTLE GIRL OF MINE, Everly Brothers, Cadence	61
69.	YOU CAN MAKE IT IF YOU TRY, Gene Allison, Vee Jay	83
69.	THE SHAKE, Mark IV, Cosmic	89
73.	JO-ANN, Playmates, Roulette	55
73.	YEA, YEA, Kendall Sisters, Argo	83
75.	SHE'S NEAT, Dale Wright, Fraternity	54
75.	BAD MOTORCYCLE, Storey Sisters, Cameo	65
75.	PEGGY SUE, Buddy Holly, Coral	78
78.	THAT'S ALRIGHT, Little Jr. Parker, Duke	—
78.	SO TOUGH, Kuff Link, Challenge	89
80.	I CAN'T HELP IT, Margaret Whiting, Dot	—
80.	THE SWINGING SHEPHERD BLUES, Johnny Pate, Federal	59
80.	LIECHTENSTEINER POLKA, Will Glahe, London	68
80.	WAITIN' IN SCHOOL, Ricky Nelson, Imperial	68
80.	YOU SEND ME, Sam Cooke, Keen	68
80.	YOUR NAME IS BEAUTIFUL, Carl Smith, Columbia	99
86.	MOOVIN' 'N' GROOVIN', Duane Eddy, Jamie	72
86.	KISSES SWEETER THAN WINE, Jimmie Rodgers, Roulette	73
86.	THE SWINGING SHEPHERD BLUES, David Rose, M-G-M	73
86.	RAUNCHY, Bill Justis, Phillips International	94
90.	I BEG OF YOU, Elvis Presley, Victor	59
90.	THE STORY OF MY LIFE, Marty Robbins, Columbia	83
90.	JAILHOUSE ROCK, Elvis Presley, Victor	94
93.	WHY DON'T THEY UNDERSTAND? George Hamilton IV, ABC-Paramount	80
93.	RAUNCHY, Billy Vaughn, Dot	80
93.	REMEMBER, Velours, Onyx	83
93.	MILLION MILES FROM NOWHERE, Brook Benton, Vik	94
93.	OH, BOY! Crickets, Brunswick	100
93.	GEISHA GIRL, Hank Locklin, Victor	—
93.	WAKE UP LITTLE SUSIE, Everly Brothers, Cadence	—
93.	WILD IS THE WIND, Johnny Mathis, Columbia	—

BEST SELLING POP SINGLES IN STORES

The information given in this chart is based on actual sales to customers in a scientific sample of the nation's retail record outlets during the week ending on the date shown above. Sample design, sample size, and all methods used in this continuing study of retail record sales are under the direct and continuing supervision and control of the School of Retailing of New York University.

FOR SURVEY WEEK ENDING MARCH 29, 1958

This Week		Last Week	Weeks on Chart
1.	**TEQUILA** (BMI)—The Champs Train to Nowhere (BMI)—Challenge 1016	1	6
2.	**SWEET LITTLE SIXTEEN** (BMI)—Chuck Berry Reelin' and Rocking (BMI)—Chess 1683	3	8
3.	**LOLLIPOP** (BMI)—Chordettes Baby, Come-A Back-A (ASCAP)—Cadence 1345	2	4
4.	**A WONDERFUL TIME UP THERE** (BMI)—Pat Boone **IT'S TOO SOON TO KNOW** (ASCAP)—Dot 15690	4	8
5.	**HE'S GOT THE WHOLE WORLD IN HIS HANDS** (ASCAP)—Laurie London Handed Down (ASCAP)—Cap 3891	13	2
6.	**WHO'S SORRY NOW** (ASCAP)—Connie Francis You Were Only Fooling (ASCAP)—M-G-M 12588	5	6
7.	**SUGARTIME** (BMI)—McGuire Sisters Banana Split (BMI)—Coral 61924	10	14
8.	**DON'T** (BMI)—Elvis Presley **I BEG OF YOU** (BMI)—Victor 7150	6	11
9.	**BREATHLESS** (BMI)—Jerry Lee Lewis Down the Line (BMI)—Sun 288	12	5
10.	**CATCH A FALLING STAR** (ASCAP)—Perry Como **MAGIC MOMENTS** (ASCAP)—Vic 7128	9	11
11.	**SAIL ALONG SILVERY MOON** (ASCAP)—Billy Vaughn Raunchy (BMI)—Dot 15661	7	16
12.	**ARE YOU SINCERE?** (BMI)—Andy Williams Be Mine Tonight (BMI)—Cadence 1340	11	8
13.	**DON'T YOU JUST KNOW IT** (BMI)—Huey Smith High Blood Pressure (BMI)—Ace 545	26	2
14.	**DINNER WITH DRAC** (BMI)—John Zacherle Parts 1 and 2—Cameo 130	8	4
15.	**TWENTY-SIX MILES** (BMI)—Four Preps It's You (ASCAP)—Cap 3845	14	9
16.	**BALLAD OF A TEENAGE QUEEN** (BMI)—Johnny Cash **BIG RIVER** (BMI)—Sun 283	16	9
17.	**MY BUCKET'S GOT A HOLE IN IT** (ASCAP)—Ricky Nelson **BELIEVE WHAT YOU SAY** (BMI)—Imperial 5503	—	1
18.	**THE WALK** (BMI)—Jimmie McCracklin I'm to Blame (BMI)—Checker 885	17	6
19.	**OH, JULIE** (BMI)—Crescendos My Little Girl (BMI)—Nasco 6005	15	13
20.	**THE LITTLE BLUE MAN** (BMI)—Betty Johnson Winter in Miami (ASCAP)—Atlantic 1169	20	6
21.	**MAYBE BABY** (BMI)—Crickets Tell Me How (BMI)—Brunswick 55053	18	5
22.	**BILLY** (ASCAP)—Kathy Linden If I Could Hold You in My Arms (ASCAP)—Felsted 8410	32	3
23.	**SHORT SHORTS** (BMI)—Royal Teens Planet Rock (BMI)—ABC-Paramount 9882	22	10
24.	**GOOD GOLLY, MISS MOLLY** (BMI)—Little Richard Hey-Hey-Hey-Hey! (BMI)—Specialty 624	23	7
25.	**MAYBE** (BMI)—Chantels Come My Little Baby (BMI)—End 1005	25	12
26.	**OH-OH, I'M FALLING IN LOVE AGAIN** (ASCAP)—Jimmie Rodgers The Long Hot Summer (ASCAP)—Roulette 4045	29	8
27.	**YOU WERE MADE FOR ME** (BMI)—Sam Cooke **LONELY ISLAND** (ASCAP)—Keen 4009	28	3
28.	**GET A JOB** (BMI)—Silhouettes I Am Lonely (BMI)—Ember 1029	21	12
29.	**BOOK OF LOVE** (BMI)—Monatones You Never Loved Me (BMI)—Argo 5290	47	2
30.	**THE STROLL** (BMI)—Diamonds Land of Beauty (BMI)—Mercury 71242	24	14
31.	**LAZY MARY** (ASCAP)—Lou Monte Angelique (ASCAP)—Vic 7160	19	4
32.	**OH! LONESOME ME** (BMI)—Don Gibson **I CAN'T STOP LOVING YOU** (BMI)—Vic 7133	36	4
33.	**ROCK AND ROLL IS HERE TO STAY** (BMI)—Danny and the Juniors School Boy Romance (BMI)—ABC-Paramount 9888	27	6
34.	**MARCH FROM THE RIVER KWAI AND "COLONEL BOGEY"** (ASCAP)—Mitch Miller Hey Little Baby (BMI)—Col 41066	39	12
35.	**YOU ARE MY DESTINY** (BMI)—Paul Anka When I Stop Loving You (BMI)—ABC-Paramount 9880	33	11
36.	**DEDE DINAH** (ASCAP)—Frankie Avalon Ooh La La (ASCAP)—Chancellor 1011	30	11
37.	**NOW AND FOR ALWAYS** (ASCAP)—George Hamilton IV One Heart (ASCAP)—ABC-Paramount 9898	41	2
38.	**AT THE HOP** (BMI)—Danny and the Juniors Sometimes (BMI)—ABC-Paramount 9871	34	18
39.	**DON'T LET GO** (BMI)—Roy Hamilton The Right to Love (BMI)—Epic 9257	38	12
40.	**EVERY NIGHT** (BMI)—Chantels Whoever You Are (BMI)—End 1050	—	1
41.	**BEEN SO LONG** (BMI)—Pastels My One and Only Dream (BMI)—Argo 5287	48	5
42.	**WITCHCRAFT** (ASCAP)—Frank Sinatra Tell Her You Love Her (BMI)—Capitol 3859	31	10
43.	**LOLLIPOP** (BMI)—Ronald and Ruby Fickle Baby (BMI)—Vic 7174	40	3
44.	**TEQUILA** (BMI)—Eddie Platt Popcorn (BMI)—ABC-Paramount 9899	35	5
45.	**COLLEGE MAN** (BMI)—Bill Justis The Stranger (BMI)—Phillips International 3522	45	3
46.	**SO TOUGH** (BMI)—Casuals I Love My Darling (BMI)—Back Beat 503	46	5
47.	**WAITIN' IN SCHOOL** (BMI)— **STOOD UP** (BMI)—Ricky Nelson Imperial 5483	37	15
48.	**SWINGING SHEPHERD BLUES** (BMI)—Moe Koffman Quartet Hambourg Bound (BMI)—Jubilee 5311	42	8
49.	**TUMBLING TUMBLEWEEDS** (ASCAP)—Billy Vaughn Trying (ASCAP)—Dot 15710	—	1
50.	**RETURN TO ME** (ASCAP)—Dean Martin Forgetting You (ASCAP)—Cap 3894	—	1
50.	**SING, BOY, SING** (ASCAP)—Tommy Sands Crazy 'Cause I Love You (BMI)—Cap 3867	49	4

THIS WEEK'S BEST BUYS

Special telephone reports indicate these recent releases have broken out in one or more key areas and have excellent potential for placing on The Billboard's best seller charts.

TUMBLING TUMBLEWEEDS (Williamson, ASCAP)—**Billy Vaughn**—Dot 15710—A strong item. It popped onto the charts this week in 49th position. Flip is "Trying" (Randy-Smith, ASCAP). A previous Billboard "Spotlight" pick.

RETURN TO ME (Southern, ASCAP)—**Dean Martin**—Capitol 3984—A comer! It's number 50 this week. Flip is "Forgetting You," (Barton, ASCAP).

WITCH DOCTOR (Monarch, ASCAP)—**David Seville**—Liberty 551328 It's big in all markets. Flip is "Don't Whistle at Me, Baby" Monarch, ASCAP). A previous Billboard "Spotlight" pick.

STAIRWAY OF LOVE (Planetary, ASCAP)—**Marty Robbins**—Columbia 41143—The side appears a pop and c.&w. hit. It's big in all marts. Flip is "Just Married," (De Vorzon, BMI). A previous Billboard "Spotlight" pick.

KEWPIE DOLL (Leeds, ASCAP)—**Dance Only With Me** (Stratford, ASCAP)—**Perry Como**—RCA Victor 7202—Both sides are much in demand. "Kewpie Doll" has the edge at present. A previous Billboard "Spotlight" pick.

I MET HIM ON A SUNDAY (BMI)—**The Shirelles**—Decca 30588—The platter is doing well in all marts. It looks like a big one. Flip is "I Want You to Be My Boyfriend," (Scepter-G&H, BMI).

RECENT POP RELEASES COMING UP STRONG

FOR SURVEY WEEK ENDING MARCH 29

The information given in this chart is based on actual sales to customers in a scientific sample of the nation's retail record outlets during the week ending on the date shown above. Sample design, sample size and all methods used in this continuing study of retail record sales are under the direct and continuing supervision and control of the School of Retailing of New York University.

Twilight Time ....*The Platters*
(BMI) Mercury 71289

Most Played by Jockeys

FOR SURVEY WEEK ENDING MARCH 29

SIDES are ranked in order of the greatest number of plays on disk jockey radio shows thruout the country. Results are based on The Billboard's weekly survey among the nation's disk jockeys. The reverse side of each record is also listed.

This Week		Last Week	Weeks on Chart
1.	TEQUILA (BMI)—The Champs Train to Nowhere (BMI)—Challenege 1016	1	5
2.	LOLLIPOP (BMI)—Chordettes Baby, Come-A Back-A (ASCAP)—Cadence 1345	2	5
3.	CATCH A FALLING STAR (ASCAP)—Perry Como Magic Moments (ASCAP)—Vic 7128	3	13
4.	HE'S GOT THE WHOLE WORLD IN HIS HANDS (ASCAP)—Laurie London Handed Down (ASCAP)—Cap 3891	11	3
5.	TWENTY-SIX MILES (BMI)—Four Preps It's You (ASCAP)—Cap 3845	4	11
6.	ARE YOU SINCERE (BMI)—Andy Williams Be Mine Tonight (BMI)—Cadence 1340	6	7
7.	WHO'S SORRY NOW (ASCAP)—Connie Francis You Were Only Fooling (ASCAP)—M-G-M 12588	8	5
8.	SUGARTIME (BMI)—McGuire Sisters Banana Split (BMI)—Coral 61924	5	14
9.	SWEET LITTLE SIXTEEN (BMI)—Chuck Berry Reelin' and Rocking (BMI)—Chess 1683	7	6
10.	A WONDERFUL TIME UP THERE (BMI)—Pat Boone It's Too Soon to Know (ASCAP)—Dot 15690	10	6
11.	IT'S TOO SOON TO KNOW (ASCAP)—Pat Boone A Wonderful Time Up There (BMI)—Dot 15690	17	7
12.	DON'T (BMI)—Elvis Presley I Beg of You (BMI)—Vic 7150	9	10
13.	WITCHCRAFT (ASCAP)—Frank Sinatra Tell Her You Love Her	12	12
14.	BILLY (ASCAP)—Kathy Linden If I Could Hold You in My Arms (ASCAP)—Felsted 8410	—	1
15.	OH-OH, I'M FALLING IN LOVE AGAIN (ASCAP)—Jimmie Rodgers The Long Hot Summer (ASCAP)—Roulette 4045	19	7
16.	SAIL ALONG SILVERY MOON (ASCAP)—Billy Vaughn Raunchy (BMI)—Dot 15661	15	11
17.	MAYBE BABY (BMI)—Crickets Tell Me How (BMI)—Brunswick 55053	—	3
18.	MAGIC MOMENTS (ASCAP)—Perry Como Catch a Falling Star (ASCAP)—Vic 7128	13	12
19.	THERE'S ONLY ONE OF YOU (ASCAP)—Four Lads Blue Tattoo (ASCAP)—Col 41136	—	1
20.	RETURN TO ME (ASCAP)—Dean Martin Forgetting You (ASCAP)—Cap 3894	—	1
21.	LOLLIPOP (BMI)—Ronald and Ruby Fickle Baby (BMI)—Vic 7174	—	1
22.	TWILIGHT TIME (BMI)—Platters Out of My Mind (BMI)—Mer 71289	—	1
23.	THE WALK (BMI)—Jimmy McCracklin I'm to Blame (BMI)—Checker 885	—	1
24.	THE LITTLE BLUE MAN (BMI)—Betty Johnson Winter in Miami (ASCAP)—Atlantic 1169	22	5
25.	OH! LONESOME ME (BMI)—Don Gibson I Can't Stop Loving You (BMI)—Vic 7133	—	1
25.	BREATHLESS (BMI)—Jerry Lee Lewis Down the Line (BMI)—Sun 288	—	2

Top 100 Sides

FOR SURVEY WEEK ENDING MARCH 29

This is a tabulation of dealer individual record sales listed according to the specific side requested by customers. No attempt is made to add sides together to reflect actual record sales. This is, therefore, a tabulation of sides or songs, and not records. This is the reason for any possible variation that occurs between the top 50 sides as reflected in this chart, and the top 50 record sellers as reflected in the "Best Sellers in Stores" chart.

Pos.	Song, Artist, Label	Last Week
1.	**TEQUILA,** Champs, Challenge	1
2.	**SWEET LITTLE SIXTEEN,** Chuck Berry, Chess	3
3.	**LOLLIPOPS,** Chordettes, Cadence	2
4.	**HE'S GOT THE WHOLE WORLD IN HIS HANDS,** Laurie London, Capitol	12
5.	**WHO'S SORRY NOW?** Connie Francis, M-G-M	4
6.	**SUGARTIME,** McGuire Sisters, Coral	8
7.	**DON'T,** Elvis Presley, Victor	5
7.	**BREATHLESS,** Jerry Lee Lewis. Sun	11
9.	**SAIL ALONG SILVERY MOON,** Billy Vaughn, Dot	7
10.	**ARE YOU SINCERE?** Andy Williams, Cadence	10
11.	**A WONDERFUL TIME UP THERE,** Pat Boone, Dot	14
12.	**DON'T YOU JUST KNOW IT,** Huey Smith, Ace	27
13.	**CATCH A FALLING STAR,** Perry Como, Victor	9
14.	**DINNER WITH DRAC,** John Zacherle, Cameo	6
15.	**TWENTY-SIX MILES,** Four Preps, Capitol	13
16.	**BALLAD OF A TEENAGE QUEEN,** Johnny Cash, Sun	16
17.	**THE WALK,** Jimmy McCracklin, Checker	16
18.	**OH, JULIE,** Crescendos, Nasco	15
19.	**LITTLE BLUE MAN,** Betty Johnson, Atlantic	20
20.	**MAYBE BABY,** Crickets, Brunswick	18
21.	**BILLY,** Kathy Linden, Felsted	31
22.	**IT'S TOO SOON TO KNOW,** Pat Boone, Dot	19
23.	**SHORT SHORTS,** Royal Teens, ABC-Paramount	23
23.	**GOOD GOLLY, MISS MOLLY,** Little Richard, Specialty	24
23.	**MAYBE,** Chantels, End	25
23.	**OH-OH, I'M FALLING IN LOVE AGAIN,** Jimmie Rodgers, Roulette	29
27.	**GET A JOB,** Silhouettes, Ember	22
27.	**BOOK OF LOVE,** Monatones, Argo	48
29.	**THE STROLL,** Diamonds, Mercury	25
29.	**MY BUCKET'S GOT A HOLE IN IT,** Ricky Nelson, Imperial	59
31.	**LAZY MARY,** Lou Monte, Victor	20
32.	**OH LONESOME ME,** Don Gibson, Victor	36
33.	**ROCK AND ROLL IS HERE TO STAY,** Danny and the Juniors, ABC-Paramount	27
34.	**MARCH FROM THE RIVER KWAI AND "COLONEL BOGEY,"** Mitch Miller, Columbia	38
35.	**YOU ARE MY DESTINY,** Paul Anka, ABC-Paramount	33
36.	**DEDE DINAH,** Frankie Avalon, Chancellor	29
37.	**NOW AND FOR ALWAYS,** George Hamilton IV, ABC-Paramount	41
38.	**AT THE HOP,** Danny and the Juniors, ABC-Paramount	34
38.	**DON'T LET GO,** Roy Hamilton, Epic	37
40.	**EVERY NIGHT,** Chantels, End	67
41.	**BEEN SO LONG,** Pastels, Argo	49
42.	**WITCHCRAFT,** Frank Sinatra, Capitol	31
42.	**YOU WERE MADE FOR ME,** Sam Cooke, Keen	39
44.	**LOLLIPOP,** Ronald and Ruby, Victor	39
45.	**TEQUILA,** Eddie Platt, ABC-Paramount	35
45.	**COLLEGE MAN,** Bill Justis, Phillips International	46
45.	**SO TOUGH,** Casuals, Back Beat	46
45.	**MAGIC MOMENTS,** Perry Como, Victor	53
49.	**BELIEVE WHAT YOU SAY,** Ricky Nelson, Imperial	—
49.	**LONELY ISLAND,** Sam Cooke, Keen	51
51.	**THE SWINGING SHEPHERD BLUES,** Moe Koffman Quartet, Jubilee	42
52.	**TUMBLING TUMBLEWEED,** Billy Vaughn, Dot	—
53.	**RETURN TO ME,** Dean Martin, Capitol	—
53.	**BELONGING TO SOMEONE,** Patti Page, Mercury	43
53.	**SING, BOY, SING,** Tommy Sands, Capitol	50
56.	**TWILIGHT TIME,** Platters, Mercury	—
57.	**STOOD UP,** Ricky Nelson, Imperial	43
57.	**THE SWINGING SHEPHERD BLUES,** Johnny Pate, Federal	80
59.	**CLICK CLACK,** Dickey Doo and the Don'ts, Swan	43
60.	**WE BELONG TOGETHER,** Robert and Johnny, Old Town	59
60.	**WHOLE LOTTA WOMAN,** Marvin Rainwater, M-G-M	64
62.	**APRIL LOVE,** Pat Boone, Dot	53
62.	**YES, MY DARLING,** Fats Domino, Imperial	55
64.	**JO-ANN,** Playmates, Roulette	73
65.	**DANCING WITH MY SHADOW,** Four Voices, Columbia	51
65.	**ANGEL SMILE,** Nat King Cole, Capitol	55
65.	**COME TO ME,** Johnny Mathis, Columbia	57
65.	**GREAT BALLS OF FIRE,** Jerry Lee Lewis, Sun	57
65.	**LIECHTENSTEINER POLKA,** Will Glahe, London	80
70.	**ALL THE WAY,** Frank Sinatra, Capitol	62
70.	**THE SWINGING SHEPHERD BLUES,** David Rose, M-G-M	86
72.	**BIG GUITAR,** Owen Bradley Quintet, Decca	59
72.	**BETTY AND DUPREE,** Chuck Willis, Atlantic	69
72.	**YOU SEND ME,** Sam Cooke, Keen	86
76.	**THERE'E ONLY ONE OF YOU,** Four Lads, Columbia	—
76.	**JAILHOUSE ROCK,** Elvis Presley, Victor	90
78.	**TALK TO ME, TALK TO ME,** Little Willie John, King	—
78.	**ROCK AND ROLL RHAPSODY,** Four Aces, Decca	66
78.	**"7-11,"** Gone All Stars, Gone	67
78.	**YOU CAN MAKE IT IF YOU TRY,** Gene Allison, Vee Jay	69
82.	**SHE'S NEAT,** Dale Wright, Faternity	75
82.	**I CAN'T HELP IT,** Margaret Whiting, Dot	80
82.	**KISSES SWEETER THAN WINE,** Jimmie Rodgers, Roulette	86
82.	**WILD IS THE WIND,** Johnny Mathis, Columbia	93
86.	**BAD MOTORCYCLE,** Storey Sisters, Cameo	75
86.	**PEGGY SUE,** Buddy Holly, Coral	75
86.	**THAT'S ALRIGHT,** Little Jr. Parker, Duke	78
86.	**SO TOUGH,** Kuff Linx, Challenge	78
90.	**THE SHAKE,** Mark IV, Cosmic	69
91.	**SWEET ELIZABETH,** Will Glahe, London	—
91.	**BOP-A-LENA,** Ronnie Self, Columbia	64
91.	**THE STORY OF MY LIFE,** Marty Robbins, Columbia	90
91.	**WHY DON'T THEY UNDERSTAND?** George Hamilton IV, ABC-Paramount	93
91.	**RAUNCHY,** Billy Vaughn, Dot	93
91.	**OH, BOY,** Crickets, Brunswick	93
91.	**FRAULEIN,** Bobby Helms, Decca	—
91.	**ROCK AND ROLL MUSIC,** Chuck Berry, Chess	—
91.	**TEARDROPS,** Lee Andrews and the Hearts, Chess	—
91.	**YELLOW DOG BLUES,** Johnny Maddox, Dot	—

BEST SELLING POP SINGLES IN STORES

The information given in this chart is based on actual sales to customers in a scientific sample of the nation's retail record outlets during the week ending on the date shown above. Sample design, sample size, and all methods used in this continuing study of retail record sales are under the direct and continuing supervision and control of the School of Retailing of New York University.

FOR SURVEY WEEK ENDING APRIL 5, 1958

This Week		Last Week	Weeks on Chart
1.	TEQUILA (BMI)—The Champs Train to Nowhere (BMI)—Challenge 1016	1	7
2.	HE'S GOT THE WHOLE WORLD IN HIS HANDS (ASCAP)—Laurie London Handed Down (ASCAP)—Cap 3891	5	3
3.	SWEET LITTLE SIXTEEN (BMI)—Chuck Berry Reelin' and Rocking (BMI)—Chess 1683	2	9
4.	A WONDERFUL TIME UP THERE (BMI)—Pat Boone IT'S TOO SOON TO KNOW (ASCAP)—Dot 15690	4	9
5.	BELIEVE WHAT YOU SAY (BMI)—Ricky Nelson MY BUCKET'S GOT A HOLE IN IT (ASCAP)—Imperial 5503	17	2
6.	LOLLIPOP (BMI)—Chordettes Baby, Come-A Back-A (ASCAP)—Cadence 1345	3	5
7.	TWILIGHT TIME (BMI)—Platters Out of My Mind (BMI)—Mercury 71289	—	1
8.	CATCH A FALLING STAR (ASCAP)—Perry Como MAGIC MOMENTS (ASCAP)—Vic 7128	10	12
9.	WHO'S SORRY NOW (ASCAP)—Connie Francis You Were Only Fooling (ASCAP)—M-G-M 12588	6	7
10.	BOOK OF LOVE (BMI)— Monatones You Never Loved Me (BMI)—Argo 5290	29	3
11.	SAIL ALONG SILVERY MOON (ASCAP)—Billy Vaughn RAUNCHY (BMI)—Dot 15661	11	17
12.	BREATHLESS (BMI)—Jerry Lee Lewis Down the Line (BMI)—Sun 288	9	6
13.	SUGARTIME (BMI)—McGuire Sisters Banana Split (BMI)—Coral 61924	7	15
14.	DON'T YOU JUST KNOW IT (BMI)—Huey Smith High Blood Pressure (BMI)—Ace 545	13	3
15.	TWENTY-SIX MILES (BMI)—Four Preps It's You (ASCAP)—Cap 3845	15	10
16.	ARE YOU SINCERE? (BMI)—Andy Williams Be Mine Tonight (BMI)—Cadence 1340	12	9
17.	DON'T (BMI)—Elvis Presley I BEG OF YOU (BMI)—Vic 7150	8	12
18.	OH, LONESOME ME (BMI)—Don Gibson I CAN'T STOP LOVING YOU (BMI)—Vic 7133	32	5
19.	LAZY MARY (ASCAP)—Lou Monte Angelique (ASCAP)—Vic 7160	31	5
20.	BILLY (ASCAP)—Kathy Linden If I Could Hold You in My Arms (ASCAP) Felsted 8410	22	4
21.	THE WALK (BMI)—Jimmy McCracklin I'm to Blame (BMI)—Checker 885	18	7
22.	MAYBE BABY (BMI)—Crickets Tell Me How (BMI)—Brunswick 55053	21	6
23.	OH, JULIE (BMI)—Crescendos My Little Girl (BMI)—Nasco 6005	19	14
24.	OH-OH, I'M FALLING IN LOVE AGAIN (ASCAP)—Jimmie Rodgers The Long Hot Summer (ASCAP)—Roulette 4045	26	9
25.	THE LITTLE BLUE MAN (BMI)—Betty Johnson Winter in Miami (ASCAP)—Atlantic 1169	20	7
26.	LONELY ISLAND (ASCAP)—Sam Cooke YOU WERE MADE FOR ME (BMI)—Keen 4009	27	4
27.	ROCK AND ROLL IS HERE TO STAY (BMI)—Danny and the Juniors School Boy Romance (BMI)—ABC-Paramount 9888	33	7
28.	BALLAD OF A TEENAGE QUEEN (BMI)—Johnny Cash BIG RIVER (BMI)—Sun 283	16	10
29.	GOOD GOLLY, MISS MOLLY (BMI)—Little Richard Hey-Hey-Hey-Hey! (BMI)—Specialty 624	24	8
30	TUMBLING TUMBLEWEEDS (ASCAP)—Billy Vaughn TRYING (ASCAP)—Dot 15710	49	2
31.	MARCH FROM THE RIVER KWAI AND "COLONEL BOGEY" (ASCAP)—Mitch Miller Hey Little Baby (BMI)—Col 41066	34	13
32.	SHORT SHORTS (BMI)—Royal Teens Planet Rock (BMI)—ABC-Paramount 9882	23	11
33.	GET A JOB (BMI)—Silhouettes I Am Lonely (BMI)—Ember 1029	28	13
34.	DINNER WITH DRAC (BMI)—John Zacherle Parts 1 & 2—Cameo 130	14	5
35.	WITCH DOCTOR (ASCAP)—David Seville Don't Whistle at Me, Baby (ASCAP)—Liberty 55132	—	1
36.	WITCHCRAFT (ASCAP)—Frank Sinatra Tell Her You Love Her (BMI)—Cap 3859	42	11
37.	MAYBE (BMI)—Chantels Come My Little Baby (BMI)—End 1005	25	13
38.	LOOKING BACK (BMI)—Nat King Cole DO I LIKE IT (BMI)—Cap 3939	—	1
39.	YOU ARE MY DESTINY (BMI)—Paul Anka When I Stop Loving You (BMI)—ABC-Paramount 9880	35	12
40.	EVERY NIGHT (BMI)—Chantels Whoever You Are (BMI)—End 1050	40	2
41.	THE STROLL (BMI)—Diamonds Land of Beauty (BMI)—Mercury 71242	30	15
42.	DEDE DINAH (ASCAP)—Frankie Avalon Ooh La La (ASCAP)—Chancellor 1011	36	12
43.	WE BELONG TOGETHER Robert and Johnny In the Rain — Old Town 1047	—	4
44.	ALL THE WAY (ASCAP)—Frank Sinatra CHICAGO (ASCAP)—Cap 3793	—	19
45.	TALK TO ME, TALK TO ME (BMI)—Little Willie John Spasms (BMI)—King 5108	—	1
46.	SO TOUGH (BMI)—Casuals I Love My Darling (BMI)—Back Beat 503	46	6
47.	DON'T LET GO (BMI)—Roy Hamilton The Right to Love (BMI)—Epic 9257	39	13
48.	THERE'S ONLY ONE OF YOU (ASCAP)—Four Lads Blue Tattoo (ASCAP)—Col 41136	—	1
49.	BEEN SO LONG (BMI)—Pastels My One and Only Dream (BMI)—Argo 5287	41	6
50.	AT THE HOP (BMI)—Danny and the Juniors Sometimes (BMI)—ABC-Paramount 9871	38	19

THIS WEEK'S BEST BUYS

Special telephone reports and/or chart action indicate these recent releases have either broken out in one or more key areas or have leaped onto the charts and have excellent potential for placing among the Top 30 of The Billboard's Best Selling Pop Singles in Stores chart. Action sides are listed in capitol letters.

ALL I HAVE TO DO IS DREAM (Acuff-Rose, BMI)—The Everly Brothers—Cadence 1348
Claudette (Acuff-Rose, BMI)

WEAR MY RING AROUND YOUR NECK (Rush-Presley, BMI)
Doncha! Think It's Time (Presley, BMI)—Elvis Presley—RCA Victor 7240

CHANSON D'AMOUR (Meadowlark, ASCAP)—Art and Dotty Todd—Era 1064
Along the Trail With You (Music Productions, ASCAP)
The above records were Billboard Spotlight picks.

SKINNY MINNIE (Valley Brook, ASCAP—Bill Haley and His Comets—Decca 30592
Sway With Me (Valley Brook, ASCAP)

BEST BUYS ON THE CHARTS THIS WEEK

LOOKING BACK (Eden-Sweco, BMI)—Nat King Cole—Capitol 3939
Do I Like It (Sweco, BMI)

THERE'S ONLY ONE OF YOU (Korwin, ASCAP)—The Four Lads—Columbia 41136
Blue Tattoo (Planetary, ASCAP)

Both are previous Billboard Spotlight picks.

RECENT POP RELEASES COMING UP STRONG

FOR SURVEY WEEK ENDING APRIL 5

The information given in this chart is based on actual sales to customers in a scientific sample of the nation's retail record outlets during the week ending on the date shown above. Sample design, sample size and all methods used in this continuing study of retail record sales are under the direct and continuing supervision and control of the School of Retailing of New York University.

Rock and Roll Rhapsody . . . . *Four Aces*
(BMI) Decca 30575

Skinny Minnie . . . . *Bill Haley & His Comets*
(ASCAP) Decca 30592

To Be Loved . . . . *Jackie Wilson*
(BMI) Brunswick 55052

You Excite Me . . . . *Frankie Avalon*
(ASCAP) Chancellor 1016

Most Played by Jockeys

FOR SURVEY WEEK ENDING APRIL 5

SIDES are ranked in order of the greatest number of plays on disk jockey radio shows thruout the country. Results are based on The Billboard's weekly survey among the nation's disk jockeys. The reverse side of each record is also listed.

This Week		Last Week	Weeks on Chart
1.	HE'S GOT THE WHOLE WORLD IN HIS HANDS (ASCAP)—Laurie London Handed Down (ASCAP)—Cap 3891	4	4
2.	TEQUILA (BMI)—The Champs Train to Nowhere (BMI)—Challenge 1016	1	6
3.	LOLLIPOP (BMI)—Chordettes Baby, Come-A Back-A (ASCAP)—Cadence 1345	2	6
4.	ARE YOU SINCERE? (BMI)—Andy Williams Be Mine Tonight (BMI)—Cadence 1340	6	8
5.	TWILIGHT TIME (BMI)—Platters Out of My Mind (BMI)—Mercury 71289	22	2
6.	WHO'S SORRY NOW (ASCAP)—Connie Francis You Were Only Fooling (ASCAP)—M-G-M 12588	7	6
7.	BILLY (ASCAP)—Kathy Linden If I Could Hold You in My Arms (ASCAP)—Felsted 8410	14	2
8.	WITCH DOCTOR (ASCAP)—David Seville Don't Whistle at Me, Baby (ASCAP)—Liberty 55132	—	1
9.	CATCH A FALLING STAR (ASCAP)—Perry Como Magic Moments (ASCAP)—Vic 7128	3	14
10.	A WONDERFUL TIME UP THERE (BMI)—Pat Boone It's Too Soon to Know (ASCAP)—Dot 15690	10	7
11.	SWEET LITTLE SIXTEEN (BMI)—Chuck Berry Reelin' and Rocking (BMI)—Chess 1683	9	7
12.	TWENTY-SIX MILES (BMI)—Four Preps It's You (ASCAP)—Cap 3845	5	12
13.	IT'S TOO SOON TO KNOW (ASCAP)—Pat Boone A Wonderful Time Up There (BMI)—Dot 15690	11	8
14.	SUGARTIME (BMI)—McGuire Sisters Banana Split (BMI)—Coral 61924	8	15
15.	BOOK OF LOVE (BMI)—Monatones You Never Loved Me (BMI)—Argo 5290	—	1
16.	THERE'S ONLY ONE OF YOU (ASCAP)—Four Lads Blue Tattoo (ASCAP)—Col 41136	19	2
17.	RETURN TO ME (ASCAP)—Dean Martin Forgetting You (ASCAP)—Cap 3894	20	2
18.	OH, LONESOME ME (BMI)—Don Gibson I Can't Stop Loving You (BMI)—Vic 7133	25	2
19.	DON'T (BMI)—Elvis Presley I Beg of You (BMI)—Vic 7150	12	11
20.	LOLLIPOP (BMI)—Ronald and Ruby Fickle Baby (BMI)—Vic 7174	21	2
21.	MAYBE BABY (BMI)—Crickets Tell Me How (BMI)—Brunswick 55053	17	4
22.	LAZY MARY (ASCAP)—Lou Monte Angelique (ASCAP)—Vic 7160	—	1
23.	BREATHLESS (BMI)—Jerry Lee Lewis Down the Line (BMI)—Sun 288	25	3
24.	WITCHCRAFT (ASCAP)—Frank Sinatra Tell Her You Love Her (BMI)—Cap 3859	13	13
25.	SAIL ALONG SILVERY MOON (ASCAP)—Billy Vaughn Raunchy (BMI)—Dot 15661	16	12
25.	TEQUILA (BMI)—Eddie Platt Popcorn (BMI)—ABC-Paramount 9899	—	2

Top 100 Sides

NEW YORK UNIVERSITY SCHOOL OF RETAILING · STORE RECORDED SALES · THE BILLBOARD

FOR SURVEY WEEK ENDING APRIL 5

This is a tabulation of dealer individual record sales listed according to the specific side requested by customers. No attempt is made to add sides together to reflect actual record sales. This is, therefore, a tabulation of sides or songs, and not records. This is the reason for any possible variation that occurs between the top 50 sides as reflected in this chart, and the top 50 record sellers as reflected in the "Best Sellers in Stores" chart.

Pos.	Song, Artist, Label	Last Week
1.	**TEQUILA,** Champs, Challenge	1
2.	**HE'S GOT THE WHOLE WORLD IN HIS HANDS** Laurie London, Capitol	4
3.	**SWEET LITTLE SIXTEEN,** Chuck Berry, Chess	2
4.	**LOLLIPOP,** Chordettes, Cadence	3
5.	**TWILIGHT TIME,** Platters, Mercury	56
6.	**WHO'S SORRY NOW,** Connie Francis, M-G-M	5
7.	**BOOK OF LOVE,** Monatones, Argo	27
8.	**BREATHLESS,** Jerry Lee Lewis, Sun	7
9.	**SUGARTIME;** McGuire Sisters, Coral	6
9.	**DON'T YOU JUST KNOW IT,** Huey Smith, Ace	12
11.	**A WONDERFUL TIME UP THERE,** Pat Boone, Dot	11
12.	**CATCH A FALLING STAR,** Perry Como, Victor	13
13.	**SAIL ALONG SILVERY MOON,** Billy Vaughn, Dot	9
14.	**TWENTY-SIX MILES,** Four Preps, Capitol	15
15.	**BELIEVE WHAT YOU SAY,** Ricky Nelson, Imperial	49
15.	**ARE YOU SINCERE?** Andy Williams, Cadence	10
17.	**DON'T,** Elvis Presley, Victor	7
18.	**MY BUCKET'S GOT A HOLE IN IT,** Ricky Nelson, Imperial	29
19.	**LAZY MARY,** Lou Monte, Victor	31
20.	**OH, LONESOME ME,** Don Gibson, Victor	32
20.	**BILLY,** Kathy Linden, Felsted	21
22.	**IT'S TOO SOON TO KNOW,** Pat Boone, Dot	22
23.	**THE WALK,** Jimmy McCracklin, Checker	17
23.	**MAYBE BABY,** Crickets, Brunswick	20
25.	**OH, JULIE,** Crescendos, Nasco	18
26.	**OH-OH, I'M FALLING IN LOVE AGAIN,** Jimmie Rodgers, Roulette	23
27.	**THE LITTLE BLUE MAN,** Betty Johnson, Atlantic	19
28.	**ROCK AND ROLL IS HERE TO STAY** Danny and the Juniors, ABC-Paramount	33
29.	**BALLAD OF A TEENAGE QUEEN,** Johnny Cash, Sun	16
30.	**GOOD GOLLY, MISS MOLLY,** Little Richard, Specialty	23
31.	**MARCH FROM THE RIVER KWAI AND "COLONEL BOGEY"** Mitch Miller, Columbia	34
32.	**SHORT SHORTS,** Royal Teens, ABC-Paramount	23
33.	**GET A JOB,** Silhouettes, Ember	27
34.	**DINNER WITH DRAC,** John Zacherle, Cameo	14
35.	**TUMBLING TUMBLEWEEDS,** Billy Vaughn, Dot	52
36.	**WITCH DOCTOR,** David Seville, Liberty	—
37.	**WITCHCRAFT,** Frank Sinatra, Capitol	42
38.	**MAYBE,** Chantels, End	23
39.	**LONELY ISLAND,** Sam Cooke, Keen	49
40.	**YOU ARE MY DESTINY,** Paul Anka, ABC-Paramount	35
40.	**EVERY NIGHT,** Chantels, End	40
42.	**THE STROLL,** Diamonds, Mercury	29
43.	**DEDE DINAH,** Frankie Avalon, Chancellor	36
44.	**WE BELONG TOGETHER,** Robert and Johnny, Old Town	60
45.	**ALL THE WAY,** Frank Sinatra, Capitol	70
46.	**TALK TO ME, TALK TO ME,** Little Willie John, King	78
47.	**SO TOUGH,** Casuals, Back Beat	45
48.	**DON'T LET GO,** Roy Hamilton, Epic	38
48.	**YOU WERE MADE FOR ME,** Sam Cooke, Keen	42
50.	**BEEN SO LONG,** Pastels, Argo	41
50.	**MAGIC MOMENTS,** Perry Como, Victor	45
50.	**THERE'S ONLY ONE OF YOU,** Four Lads, Columbia	76
53.	**AT THE HOP,** Danny and the Juniors, ABC-Paramount	38
54.	**RETURN TO ME,** Dean Martin, Capitol	53
54.	**TO BE LOVED,** Jackie Wilson, Brunswick	—
56.	**CLICK CLACK,** Dickey Doo and the Don'ts, Swan	59
56.	**LOOKING BACK,** Nat King Cole, Capitol	—
58.	**THE SWINGING SHEPHERD BLUES** Moe Koffman Quartet, Jubilee	51
58.	**SING, BOY, SING,** Tommy Sands, Capitol	53
58.	**YES, MY DARLING,** Fats Domino, Imperial	62
61.	**COLLEGE MAN,** Bill Justis, Phillips International	45
62.	**NOW AND FOR ALWAYS,** George Hamilton IV, ABC-Paramount	37
62.	**LOLLIPOP,** Ronald and Ruby, Victor	44
62.	**THE SWINGING SHEPHERD BLUES,** Johnny Pate Quintet, Federal	57
65.	**TEQUILA,** Eddie Platt, ABC-Paramount	45
65.	**BELONGING TO SOMEONE,** Patti Page, Mercury	53
67.	**APRIL LOVE,** Pat Boone, Dot	62
67.	**DO I LIKE IT?** Nat King Cole, Capitol	—
67.	**SKINNY MINNIE,** Bill Haley and His Comets, Decca	—
70.	**LIECHTENSTEINER POLKA,** Will Glahe, London	65
70.	**ROCK AND ROLL RHAPSODY,** Four Aces, Decca	78
70.	**RAUNCHY,** Billy Vaughn, Dot	91
70.	**YOU EXCITE ME,** Frankie Avalon, Chancellor	—
74.	**STOOD UP,** Ricky Nelson, Imperial	57
75.	**THE SWINGING SHEPHERD BLUES,** David Rose, M-G-M	70
75.	**ANGEL SMILE,** Nat King Cole, Capitol	65
75.	**THIS LITTLE GIRL OF MINE,** Everly Brothers, Cadence	72
75.	**"7-11,"** Gone All Stars, Gone	78
75.	**DIZZY MISS LIZZY,** Larry Williams, Specialty	—
80.	**DANCING WITH MY SHADOW,** Four Voices, Columbia	65
80.	**COME TO ME,** Johnny Mathis, Columbia	65
80.	**BIG GUITAR,** Owen Bradley Quintet, Decca	72
80.	**YOU SEND ME,** Sam Cooke, Keen	72
80.	**JUST MARRIED,** Marty Robbins, Columbia	—
80.	**WISHING FOR YOUR LOVE,** Voxpoppers, Mercury	—
86.	**JO-ANN,** Playmates, Roulette	64
86.	**BETTY AND DUPREE,** Chuck Willis, Atlantic	72
86.	**JAILHOUSE ROCK,** Elvis Presley, Victor	76
86.	**BOP-A-LENA,** Ronnie Self, Columbia	91
86.	**HIGH SIGN,** Diamonds, Mercury	—
86.	**I CAN'T STOP LOVING YOU,** Don Gibson, Victor	—
86.	**TRYING,** Billy Vaughn, Dot	—
93.	**GREAT BALLS OF FIRE,** Jerry Lee Lewis, Sun	65
93.	**WILD IS THE WIND,** Johnny Mathis, Columbia	82
95.	**TEARDROPS,** Lee Andrews and the Hearts, Chess	91
95.	**ARRIVEDERCI ROMA,** Roger Williams, Kapp	—
95.	**CHANSON D'AMOUR,** Art and Dotty Todd, Era	—
95.	**KEWPIE DOLL,** Perry Como. Victor	—
95.	**YELLOW DOG BLUES,** Johnny Maddox, Dot	—
100.	**I BEG OF YOU,** Elvis Presley, Victor	—

STORE RECORDED SALES — NEW YORK UNIVERSITY SCHOOL OF RETAILING — THE BILLBOARD

BEST SELLING POP SINGLES IN STORES

The information given in this chart is based on actual sales to customers in a scientific sample of the nation's retail record outlets during the week ending on the date shown above. Sample design, sample size, and all methods used in this continuing study of retail record sales are under the direct and continuing supervision and control of the School of Retailing of New York University.

FOR SURVEY WEEK ENDING APRIL 12, 1958

This Week	Title	Last Week	Weeks on Chart
1.	**TWILIGHT TIME** (BMI)—Platters Out of My Mind (BMI)—Mer 71289	7	2
2.	**HE'S GOT THE WHOLE WORLD IN HIS HANDS** (ASCAP)—Laurie London Handed Down (ASCAP)—Cap 3891	2	4
3.	**TEQUILA** (BMI)—The Champs Train to Nowhere (BMI)—Challenge 1016	1	8
4.	**BELIEVE WHAT YOU SAY** (BMI)—Ricky Nelson **MY BUCKET'S GOT A HOLE IN IT** (ASCAP)—Imperial 5503	5	3
5.	**WITCH DOCTOR** (ASCAP)—David Seville Don't Whistle at Me, Baby (ASCAP)—Liberty 55132	35	2
6.	**A WONDERFUL TIME UP THERE** (BMI)—Pat Boone **IT'S TOO SOON TO KNOW** (ASCAP)—Dot 15690	4	10
7.	**BOOK OF LOVE** (BMI)—Monatones You Never Loved Me (BMI)—Argo 5290	10	4
8.	**LOLLIPOP** (BMI)—Chordettes Baby, Come-A Back-A (ASCAP)—Cadence 1345	6	6
9.	**WEAR MY RING AROUND YOUR NECK** (BMI)—Elvis Presley Doncha' Think It's Time (BMI)—Vic 7240	—	1
10.	**CATCH A FALLING STAR** (ASCAP)—Perry Como **MAGIC MOMENTS** (ASCAP)—Vic 7128	8	13
11.	**WHO'S SORRY NOW** (ASCAP)—Connie Francis You Were Only Fooling (ASCAP)—M-G-M 12588	9	8
12.	**LAZY MARY** (ASCAP)—Lou Monte Angelique (ASCAP)—Vic 7160	19	6
13.	**OH, LONESOME ME** (BMI)—Don Gibson **I CAN'T STOP LOVING YOU** (BMI)—Vic 7133	18	6
14.	**DON'T YOU JUST KNOW IT** (BMI)—Huey Smith High Blood Pressure (BMI)—Ace 545	14	4
15.	**SWEET LITTLE SIXTEEN** (BMI)—Chuck Berry Reelin' and Rocking (BMI)—Chess 1683	3	10
16.	**BILLY** (ASCAP)—Kathy Linden If I Could Hold You in My Arms (ASCAP)—Felsted 8510	20	5
17.	**SAIL ALONG SILVERY MOON** (ASCAP)—Billy Vaughn **RAUNCHY** (BMI)—Dot 15661	11	18
18.	**SUGARTIME** (BMI)—McGuire Sisters Banana-Split (BMI)—Coral 61924	13	16
19.	**TWENTY-SIX MILES** (BMI)—Four Preps It's You (ASCAP)—Cap 3845	15	11
20.	**BREATHLESS** (BMI)—Jerry Lee Lewis Down the Line (BMI)—Sun 288	12	7
21.	**MARCH FROM THE RIVER KWAI AND "COLONEL BOGEY"** (ASCAP)—Mitch Miller Hey Little Baby (BMI)—Col 41066	31	14
22.	**DON'T** (BMI)—Elvis Presley **I BEG OF YOU** (BMI)—Vic 7150	17	13
23.	**ARE YOU SINCERE** (BMI)—Andy Williams Be Mine Tonight (BMI)—Cadence 1340	16	10
24.	**ROCK AND ROLL IS HERE TO STAY** (BMI)—Danny and the Juniors School Boy Romance (BMI)—ABC-Paramount 9888	27	8
25.	**MAYBE BABY** (BMI)—Crickets Tell Me How (BMI)—Brunswick 55053	22	7
26.	**THE WALK** (BMI)—Jimmy McCracklin I'm to Blame (BMI)—Checker 885	21	8
27.	**THE LITTLE BLUE MAN** (BMI)—Betty Johnson Winter in Miami (ASCAP)—Atlantic 1169	25	8
28.	**RETURN TO ME** (ASCAP)—Dean Martin Forgetting You (ASCAP)—Cap 3984	—	2
29.	**LOOKING BACK** (BMI)—Nat King Cole **DO I LIKE IT** (BMI)—Cap 3939	38	2
30.	**LONELY ISLAND** (ASCAP)—Sam Cooke **YOU WERE MADE FOR ME** (BMI)—Keen 4009	26	5
31.	**GOOD GOLLY, MISS MOLLY** (BMI)—Little Richard Hey-Hey-Hey-Hey! (BMI)—Specialty 624	29	9
32.	**TO BE LOVED** (BMI)—Jackie Wilson Come Back to Me (BMI)—Brunswick 55052	—	1
33.	**OH, JULIE** (BMI)—Crescendos My Little Girl (BMI)—Nasco 6005	23	15
34.	**BALLAD OF A TEENAGE QUEEN** (BMI)—Johnny Cash **BIG RIVER** (BMI)—Sun 283	28	11
35.	**KEWPIE DOLL** (ASCAP)—Perry Como Dance Only With Me (ASCAP)—Vic 7202	—	1
36.	**TUMBLING TUMBLEWEEDS** (ASCAP)—Billy Vaughn **TRYING** (ASCAP)—Dot 15710	30	3
37.	**TALK TO ME, TALK TO ME** (BMI)—Little Willie John Spasms (BMI)—King 5108	45	2
38.	**OH-OH, I'M FALLING IN LOVE AGAIN** (ASCAP)—Jimmie Rodgers The Long Hot Summer (ASCAP)—Roulette 4045	24	10
39.	**WE BELONG TOGETHER**—Robert and Johnny In the Rain—Old Town 1047	43	5
40.	**SKINNY MINNIE** (ASCAP)—Bill Haley and His Comets Sway With Me (ASCAP)—Dec 30592	—	1
40.	**CHANSON D'AMOUR** (ASCAP)—Art and Dotty Todd Along the Trail With You (ASCAP)—Era 1064	—	1
42.	**LET THE BELLS KEEP RINGING** (BMI)—Paul Anka **CRAZY LOVE** (BMI)—ABC-Paramount 9907	—	1
43.	**GET A JOB** (BMI)—Silhouettes I Am Lonely (BMI)—Ember 1029	33	14
44.	**DINNER WITH DRAC** (BMI)—John Zacherle Parts 1 & 2—Cameo 130	34	6
45.	**THERE'S ONLY ONE OF YOU** (ASCAP)—Four Lads Blue Tattoo (ASCAP)—Col 41136	48	2
46.	**EVERY NIGHT** (BMI)—Chantels Whoever You Are (BMI)—End 1050	40	3
47.	**WISHING FOR YOUR LOVE** (BMI)—Voxpoppers The Last Drag (BMI)—Mercury 71282	—	1
48.	**FOR YOUR LOVE** (BMI)—Ed Townsend Over and Over Again (BMI)—Cap 3926	—	1
49.	**WITCHCRAFT** (ASCAP)—Frank Sinatra Tell Her You Love Her (BMI)—Cap 3859	36	12
50.	**SHORT SHORTS** (BMI)—Royal Teens Planet Rock (BMI)—ABC-Paramount 9882	32	12

THIS WEEK'S BEST BUYS

Special telephone reports and/or chart action indicate these recent releases have either broken out in one or more key areas or have leaped onto the charts and have excellent potential for placing among the Top 30 of The Billboard's Best Selling Pop Singles in Stores chart. Action sides are listed in capitol letters.

JOHNNY B. GOODE (Arc, BMI)—Chuck Berry—Chess 1691
Around and Around (Arc, BMI)

YOU EXCITE ME (Debmar, ASCAP)—Frankie Avalon—Chancellor 1016
Darlin' (Debmar, ASCAP)
Both are previous Billboard Spotlight picks.

The following records not previously selected as Best Buys, are on the chart for the first time this week.

LET THE BELLS KEEP RINGING (Spanka, BMI)—Paul Anka—ABC-Paramount 9907
Crazy Love (Spanka, BMI)
A previous Billboard Spotlight pick.

FOR YOUR LOVE (Beechwood, BMI)—Ed Townsend—Capitol 3926
Over and Over Again (Beechwood, BMI)

STORE RECORDED SALES — NEW YORK UNIVERSITY SCHOOL OF RETAILING — THE BILLBOARD

RECENT POP RELEASES COMING UP STRONG

FOR SURVEY WEEK ENDING APRIL 12

The information given in this chart is based on actual sales to customers in a scientific sample of the nation's retail record outlets during the week ending on the date shown above. Sample design, sample size and all methods used in this continuing study of retail record sales are under the direct and continuing supervision and control of the School of Retailing of New York University.

All I Have to Do Is Dream . . . . . ***The Everly Brothers***
(BMI) Cadence 1348

Arrivederci, Roma . . . . . ***Roger Williams***
(ASCAP) Kapp 210

The High Sign . . . . . ***The Diamonds***
(BMI) Mercury 71291

I Met Him on a Sunday . . . . . ***The Shirelles***
(BMI) Decca 30588

Rock and Roll Rhapsody . . . . . ***The Four Aces***
(BMI) Decca 30575

You Excite Me . . . . . ***Frankie Avalon***
(ASCAP) Chancellor 1016

Most Played by Jockeys

FOR SURVEY WEEK ENDING APRIL 12

SIDES are ranked in order of the greatest number of plays on disk jockey radio shows thruout the country. Results are based on The Billboard's weekly survey among the nation's disk jockeys. The reverse side of each record is also listed.

This Week		Last Week	Weeks on Chart
1.	HE'S GOT THE WHOLE WORLD IN HIS HANDS (ASCAP)—Laurie London Handed Down (ASCAP)—Cap 3891	1	5
2.	TEQUILA (BMI)—The Champs Train to Nowhere (BMI)—Challenge 1016	2	7
3.	TWILIGHT TIME (BMI)—Platters Out of My Mind (BMI)—Mer 71289	5	3
4.	LOLLIPOP (BMI)—Chordettes Baby, Come-A Back-A (ASCAP)—Cadence 1345	3	7
5.	ARE YOU SINCERE? (BMI)—Andy Williams Be Mine Tonight (BMI)—Cadence 1340	4	9
6.	WHO'S SORRY NOW (ASCAP)—Connie Francis You Were Only Fooling (ASCAP)—M-G-M 12588	6	7
7.	A WONDERFUL TIME UP THERE (BMI)—Pat Boone It's Too Soon to Know (ASCAP)—Dot 15690	10	8
8.	BILLY (ASCAP)—Kathy Linden If I Could Hold You in My Arms (ASCAP)—Felsted 8510	7	3
9.	CATCH A FALLING STAR (ASCAP)—Perry Como Magic Moments (ASCAP)—Vic 7128	9	15
10.	WITCH DOCTOR (ASCAP)—David Seville Don't Whistle at Me, Baby (ASCAP)—Liberty 55132	8	2
11.	SUGARTIME (BMI)—McGuire Sisters Banana Split (BMI)—Coral 61924	14	16
12.	TWENTY-SIX MILES (BMI)—Four Preps It's You (ASCAP)—Cap 3845	12	13
13.	RETURN TO ME (ASCAP)—Dean Martin Forgetting You (ASCAP)—Cap 3894	17	3
14.	OH, LONESOME ME (BMI)—Don Gibson I Can't Stop Loving You (BMI)—Vic 7133	18	3
15.	KEWPIE DOLL (ASCAP)—Perry Como Dance Only With Me (ASCAP)—Vic 7202	—	1
16.	IT'S TOO SOON TO KNOW (ASCAP)—Pat Boone A Wonderful Time Up There (BMI)—Dot 15690	13	9
17.	THERE'S ONLY ONE OF YOU (ASCAP)Four Lads Blue Tattoo (ASCAP)—Col 41136	16	3
18.	WITCHCRAFT (ASCAP)—Frank Sinatra Tell Her You Love Her (BMI)—Cap 3859	24	14
19.	DON'T (BMI)—Elvis Presley I Beg of You (BMI)—Vic 7150	19	12
20.	CHANSON D'AMOUR (ASCAP)—Art and Dotty Todd Along the Trail With You (ASCAP)—Era 1064	—	1
21.	LOLLIPOP (BMI)—Ronald and Ruby Fickle Baby (BMI)—Vic 7174	20	3
22.	THE LITTLE BLUE MAN (BMI)—Betty Johnson Winter in Miami (ASCAP)—Atlantic 1169	—	6
23.	SWEET LITTLE SIXTEEN (BMI)—Chuck Berry Reelin' and Rocking (BMI)—Chess 1683	11	8
24.	SAIL ALONG SILVERY MOON (ASCAP)—Billy Vaughn Raunchy (BMI)—Dot 15661	25	13
25.	NOW AND FOR ALWAYS (ASCAP)—George Hamilton IV One Heart (ASCAP)—ABC-Paramount 9898	—	1
25.	LAZY MARY (ASCAP)—Lou Monte Angelique (ASCAP)—Vic 7160	22	2

Top 100 Sides

FOR SURVEY WEEK ENDING APRIL 12

This is a tabulation of dealer individual record sales listed according to the specific side requested by customers. No attempt is made to add sides together to reflect actual record sales. This is, therefore, a tabulation of sides or songs, and not records. This is the reason for any possible variation that occurs between the top 50 sides as reflected in this chart, and the top 50 record sellers as reflected in the "Best Sellers in Stores" chart.

Pos.	Song, Artist, Label	Last Week
1.	**TWILIGHT TIME,** Platters, Mercury	5
2.	**HE'S GOT THE WHOLE WORLD IN HIS HANDS,** Laurie London, Capitol	2
3.	**TEQUILA,** Champs, Challenge	1
4.	**WITCH DOCTOR,** David Seville, Liberty	37
5.	**BOOK OF LOVE,** Monatones, Argo	7
6.	**LOLLIPOP,** Chordettes, Cadence	4
7.	**WEAR MY RING AROUND YOUR NECK,** Elvis Presley, Victor	—
8.	**BELIEVE WHAT YOU SAY,** Ricky Nelson, Imperial	15
9.	**CATCH A FALLING STAR,** Perry Como, Victor	12
10.	**A WONDERFUL TIME UP THERE,** Pat Boone, Dot	11
11.	**WHO'S SORRY NOW,** Connie Francis, M-G-M	6
12.	**LAZY MARY,** Lou Monte, Victor	19
13.	**DON'T YOU JUST KNOW IT,** Huey Smith, Ace	9
14.	**SWEET LITTLE SIXTEEN,** Chuck Berry, Chess	3
15.	**OH, LONESOME ME,** Don Gibson, Victor	20
16.	**BILLY,** Kathy Linden, Felsted	20
17.	**SUGARTIME,** McGuire Sisters, Coral	9
18.	**TWENTY-SIX MILES,** Four Preps, Capitol	14
19.	**BREATHLESS,** Jerry Lee Lewis, Sun	8
20.	**SAIL ALONG SILVERY MOON,** Billy Vaughn, Dot	13
21.	**MY BUCKET'S GOT A HOLE IN IT,** Ricky Nelson, Imperial	18
22.	**MARCH FROM THE RIVER KWAI AND "COLONEL BOGEY"** Mitch Miller, Columbia	31
23.	**ARE YOU SINCERE?** Andy Williams, Cadence	15
24.	**IT'S TOO SOON TO KNOW,** Pat Boone, Dot	22
25.	**DON'T,** Elvis Presley, Victor	17
25.	**ROCK AND ROLL IS HERE TO STAY,** Danny and the Juniors, ABC-Paramount	28
27.	**MAYBE, BABY,** Crickets, Brunswick	23
28.	**THE WALK,** Jimmy McCracklin, Checker	23
28.	**THE LITTLE BLUE MAN,** Betty Johnson, Atlantic	27
30.	**RETURN TO ME,** Dean Martin, Capitol	54
31.	**GOOD GOLLY, MISS MOLLY,** Little Richard, Specialty	30
32.	**OH, JULIE,** Crescendos, Nasco	25
32.	**TO BE LOVED,** Jackie Wilson, Brunswick	54
34.	**KEWPIE DOLL,** Perry Como, Victor	95
35.	**BALLAD OF A TEENAGE QUEEN,** Johnny Cash, Sun	29
36.	**TALK TO ME, TALK TO ME,** Little Willie John, King	46
37.	**OH-OH, I'M FALLING IN LOVE AGAIN,** Jimmie Rodgers, Roulettes	26
38.	**WE BELONG TOGETHER,** Robert and Johnny, Old Town	44
39.	**SKINNY MINNIE,** Bill Haley and His Comets, Decca	67
39.	**CHANSON D'AMOUR,** Art and Dotty Todd, Era	95
41.	**GET A JOB,** Silhouetes, Ember	33
41.	**DINNER WITH DRAC,** John Zacherle, Cameo	34
41.	**THERE'S ONLY ONE OF YOU,** Four Lads, Columbia	50
44.	**EVERY NIGHT,** Chantels, End	40
45.	**WISHING FOR YOUR LOVE,** Voxpoppers, Mercury	80
46.	**FOR YOUR LOVE,** Ed Townsend, Capitol	—
46.	**LOOKING BACK,** Nat King Cole, Capitol	56
46.	**WITCHCRAFT,** Frank Sinatra, Capitol	37
49.	**LONELY ISLAND,** Sam Cooke, Keen	39
50.	**SHORT SHORTS,** Royal Teens, ABC-Paramount	32
51.	**TUMBLING TUMBLEWEEDS,** Billy Vaughn, Dot	35
51.	**DEDE DINAH,** Frankie Avalon, Chancellor	43
51.	**YOU EXCITE ME,** Frankie Avalon, Chancellor	70
54.	**JUST MARRIED,** Marty Robbins, Columbia	80
55.	**LET THE BELLS KEEP RINGING,** Paul Anka, ABC-Paramount	—
55.	**YOU ARE MY DESTINY,** Paul Anka, ABC-Paramount	40
57.	**ALL THE WAY,** Frank Sinatra, Capitol	45
58.	**MAYBE,** Chantels, End	38
59.	**CLICK CLACK,** Dickey Doo and the Dont's, Swan	56
60.	**YOU WERE MADE FOR ME,** Sam Cooke, Keen	48
60.	**BEEN SO LONG,** Pastels, Argo	50
60.	**HIGH SIGN,** Diamonds, Mercury	86
63.	**THE STROLL,** Diamonds, Mercury	42
63.	**SO TOUGH,** Casuals, Back Beat	47
63.	**YES, MY DARLING,** Fats Domino, Imperial	58
66.	**SING, BOY, SING,** Tommy Sands, Capitol	58
67.	**I MET HIM ON A SUNDAY,** Shirelles, Decca	—
67.	**DO I LIKE IT?** Nat King Cole, Capitol	67
69.	**ALL I HAVE TO DO IS DREAM,** Everly Brothers, Cadence	—
69.	**DON'T LET GO,** Roy Hamilton, Epic	48
69.	**THE SWINGING SHEPHERD BLUES,** Moe Koffman Quartet, Jubilee	58
69.	**MAGIC MOMENTS,** Perry Como, Victor	50
69.	**ROCK AND ROLL RHAPSODY,** Four Aces, Decca	70
74.	**DONCHA' THINK IT'S TIME,** Elvis Presley, Victor	—
74.	**NOW AND FOR ALWAYS,** George Hamilton IV, ABC-Paramount	62
74.	**ARRIVEDERCI ROMA,** Roger Williams, Kapp	95
77.	**CRAZY LOVE,** Paul Anka, ABC-Paramount	—
77.	**TRYING,** Billy Vaughn, Dot	—
77.	**TEQUILA,** Eddie Platt, ABC-Paramount	65
77.	**STOOD UP,** Ricky Nelson, Imperial	74
81.	**TEACHER'S PET,** Doris Day, Columbia	—
81.	**DANCING WITH MY SHADOW,** Four Voices, Columbia	80
81.	**BIG GUITAR,** Owen Bradley Quintet, Decca	80
84.	**ALL THE TIME,** Johnny Mathis, Columbia	—
84.	**AT THE HOP,** Danny and the Juniors, ABC-Paramount	53
86.	**COME TO ME,** Johnny Mathis, Columbia	80
87.	**BELONGING TO SOMEONE,** Patti Page, Mercury	65
87.	**APRIL LOVE,** Pat Boone, Dot	67
87.	**DIZZY MISS LIZZY,** Larry Williams, Specialty	75
90.	**LOLLIPOP,** Ronald and Ruby, Victor	62
90.	**RAUNCHY,** Billy Vaughn, Dot	70
90.	**ANGEL SMILE,** Nat King Cole, Capitol	75
90.	**THE SWINGING SHEPHERD BLUES,** David Rose, M-G-M	75
90.	**BOP-A-LENA,** Ronnie Self, Columbia	86
90.	**THE STORY OF MY LIFE,** Marty Robbins, Columbia	—
90.	**WILD IS THE WIND,** Johnny Mathis, Columbia	—
97.	**LET'S BE LOVERS,** Playmates, Roulette	—
97.	**"7-11,"** Gone All Stars, Gone	75
97.	**LIECHTENSTEINER POLKA,** Will Glahe, London	70
100.	**BAD MOTORCYCLE,** Storey Sisters, Cameo	—

BEST SELLING POP SINGLES IN STORES

The information given in this chart is based on actual sales to customers in a scientific sample of the nation's retail record outlets during the week ending on the date shown above. Sample design, sample size, and all methods used in this continuing study of retail record sales are under the direct and continuing supervision and control of the School of Retailing of New York University.

FOR SURVEY WEEK ENDING APRIL 19, 1958

This Week		Last Week	Weeks on Chart
1.	WITCH DOCTOR (ASCAP)—David Seville Don't Whistle at Me, Baby (ASCAP)—Liberty 55132	5	3
2.	WEAR MY RING AROUND YOUR NECK (BMI)—Elvis Presley DONCHA' THINK IT'S TIME (BMI)—Vic 7240	9	2
3.	TWILIGHT TIME (BMI)—Platters Out of My Mind (BMI)—Mer 71289	1	3
4.	HE'S GOT THE WHOLE WORLD IN HIS HANDS (ASCAP)—Laurie London Handed Down (ASCAP)—Cap 3891	2	5
5.	TEQUILA (BMI)—Champs Train to Nowhere (BMI)—Challenge 1016	3	9
6.	BOOK OF LOVE (BMI)—Monotones You Never Loved Me (BMI)—Argo 5290	7	5
7.	BELIEVE WHAT YOU SAY (BMI)—Ricky Nelson MY BUCKET'S GOT A HOLE IN IT Imperial 5503	4	4
8.	A WONDERFUL TIME UP THERE (BMI)—Pat Boone IT'S TOO SOON TO KNOW (ASCAP)—Dot 15690	6	11
9.	ALL I HAVE TO DO IS DREAM (BMI)—Everly Brothers Claudette (BMI)—Cadence 1348	—	1
10.	LOLLIPOP (BMI)—Chordettes Baby Come-A Back-A (ASCAP)—Cadence 1345	8	7
11.	OH, LONESOME ME (BMI)—Don Gibson I CAN'T STOP LOVING YOU (BMI)—Vic 7133	13	7
12.	CATCH A FALLING STAR (ASCAP)—Perry Como MAGIC MOMENTS (ASCAP)—Vic 7128	10	14
13.	WHO'S SORRY NOW (ASCAP)—Connie Francis You Were Only Fooling (ASCAP)—M-G-M 12588	11	9
14.	BILLY (ASCAP)—Kathy Linden If I Could Hold You in My Arms (ASCAP)—Felsted 8510	16	6
15.	DON'T YOU JUST KNOW IT (BMI)—Huey Smith High Blood Pressure (BMI)—Ace 545	14	5
16.	LET THE BELLS KEEP RINGING (BMI)—Paul Anka CRAZY LOVE (BMI)—ABC-Paramount 9907	42	2
17.	RETURN TO ME (ASCAP)—Dean Martin Forgetting You (ASCAP)—Cap 3984	28	3
18.	KEWPIE DOLL (ASCAP)—Perry Como Dance Only With Me (ASCAP)—Vic 7202	35	2
19.	SUGARTIME (BMI)—McGuire Sisters Banana Split (BMI)—Coral 61924	18	17
20.	LAZY MARY (ASCAP)—Lou Monte Angelique (ASCAP)—Vic 7160	12	7
21.	BREATHLESS (BMI)—Jerry Lee Lewis Down the Line (BMI)—Sun 288	20	8
22.	SWEET LITTLE SIXTEEN (BMI)—Chuck Berry Reelin' and Rocking (BMI)—Chess 1683	15	11
23.	CHANSON D'AMOUR (ASCAP)—Art and Dotty Todd Along the Trail With You (ASCAP)—Era 1064	40	2
24.	MARCH FROM THE RIVER KWAI AND "COLONEL BOGEY" (ASCAP)—Mitch Miller Hey, Little Baby (BMI)—Col 41066	21	15
25.	SAIL ALONG SILVERY MOON (ASCAP)—Billy Vaughn RAUNCHY (BMI)—Dot 15661	17	19
26.	TWENTY-SIX MILES (BMI)—Four Preps It's You (ASCAP)—Cap 3845	19	12
27.	DON'T (BMI)—Elvis Presley I BEG OF YOU (BMI)—Victor 7150	22	14
28.	LOOKING BACK (BMI)—Nat King Cole DO I LIKE IT (BMI)—Cap 3939	29	3
29.	ARE YOU SINCERE? (BMI)—Andy Williams Be Mine Tonight (BMI)—Cadence 1340	23	11
30.	THE LITTLE BLUE MAN (BMI)—Betty Johnson Winter in Miami (ASCAP)—Atlantic 1169	27	9
31.	FOR YOUR LOVE (BMI)—Ed Townsend Over and Over Again (BMI)—Cap 3926	48	2
32.	THE WALK (BMI)—Jimmy McCracklin I'm to Blame (BMI)—Checker 885	26	9
33.	BALLAD OF A TEENAGE QUEEN (BMI)—Johnny Cash BIG RIVER (BMI)—Sun 283	34	12
34.	DINNER WITH DRAC (BMI)—John Zacherle Parts 1 and 2—Cameo 130	44	7
35.	TO BE LOVED (BMI)—Jackie Wilson Come Back to Me (BMI)—Brunswick 55052	32	2
36.	GOOD GOLLY, MISS MOLLY (BMI)—Little Richard Hey-Hey-Hey-Hey! (BMI)—Specialty 624	31	2
37.	MAYBE BABY (BMI)—Crickets Tell Me How (BMI)—Brunswick 55053	25	8
38.	SKINNY MINNIE (ASCAP)—Bill Haley & His Comets Sway With Me (ASCAP)—Dec 30592	40	2
39.	EVERY NIGHT (BMI)—Chantels Whoever You Are (BMI)—End 1050	46	4
40.	WE BELONG TOGETHER—Robert and Johnny In the Rain—Old Town 1047	39	6
41.	WISHING FOR YOUR LOVE (BMI)—Voxpoppers The Last Drag (BMI)—Mer 71282	47	2
42.	TALK TO ME, TALK TO ME (BMI)—Little Willie John Spasms (BMI)—King 5108	37	3
43.	ROCK AND ROLL IS HERE TO STAY (BMI)—Danny & the Juniors School Boy Romance (BMI)—ABC-Paramount 9888	24	9
44.	OH, JULIE (BMI)—Crescendos My Little Girl (BMI)—Nasco 6005	33	16
45.	THERE'S ONLY ONE OF YOU (ASCAP)—Four Lads Blue Tatoo (ASCAP)—Col 41136	45	3
46.	JUST MARRIED (BMI)—Marty Robbins STAIRWAY OF LOVE (ASCAP)—Col 41143	—	1
47.	TUMBLING TUMBLEWEEDS (ASCAP)—Billy Vaughn TRYING (ASCAP)—Dot 15710	36	4
48.	LONELY ISLAND (ASCAP)—Sam Cooke YOU WERE MADE FOR ME (BMI)—Keen 4009	30	6
49.	I MET HIM ON A SUNDAY (BMI)—Shirellos I Want You to Be My Boy Friend (BMI)—Dec 30588	—	1
50.	YOU EXCITE ME (ASCAP)—Frankie Avalon Darlin' (ASCAP)—Channcellor 1016	—	1
50.	NOW AND FOR ALWAYS (ASCAP)—George Hamilton IV One Heart (ASCAP)—ABC-Paramount 9898	—	3

THIS WEEK'S BEST BUYS

Special telephone reports and/or chart action indicate these recent releases have either broken out in one or more key areas or have leaped onto the charts and have excellent potential for placing among the Top 30 of The Billboard's Best Selling Pop Singles in Stores chart. Action sides are listed in capitol letters.

YOU (Instant, BMI)—The Aquatones—Fargo 1001
She's the One for Me (Instant, BMI)
A previous Billboard Spotlight pick.

SICK AND TIRED (Travis, BMI)
NO, NO (Travis, BMI)—Fats Domino—Imperial 5515
A previous Billboard Spotlight pick.

THE HIGH SIGN (Vivo, BMI)—The Diamonds—Mercury 71291
Chick-Lets (Vivo, BMI)
A previous Billboard Spotlight pick.

SUGAR MOON (Gallatin, BMI)
CHERIE, I LOVE YOU (Harms, ASCAP)—Pat Boone—Dot 15750
A previous Billboard Spotlight pick.

RECENT POP RELEASES COMING UP STRONG

FOR SURVEY WEEK ENDING APRIL 19

The information given in this chart is based on actual sales to customers in a scientific sample of the nation's retail record outlets during the week ending on the date shown above. Sample design, sample size and all methods used in this continuing study of retail record sales are under the direct and continuing supervision and control of the School of Retailing of New York University.

All the Time . . . . . *Johnny Mathis* (ASCAP) Columbia 41152

Arrivederci, Roma . . . . . *Roger Williams* (ASCAP) Kapp 210

Dizzy Miss Lizzie . . . . . *Larry Williams* (BMI) Specialty 626

The High Sign . . . . . *The Diamonds* (BMI) Mercury 71291

Johnny B. Goode . . . . . *Chuck Berry* (BMI) Chess 1691

Most Played by Jockeys

FOR SURVEY WEEK ENDING APRIL 19

SIDES are ranked in order of the greatest number of plays on disk jockey radio shows thruout the country. Results are based on The Billboard's weekly survey among the nation's disk jockeys. The reverse side of each record is also listed.

This Week		Last Week	Weeks on Chart
1.	HE'S GOT THE WHOLE WORLD IN HIS HANDS (ASCAP)—Laurie London Handed Down (ASCAP)—Cap 3891	1	6
2.	TWILIGHT TIME (BMI)—Platters Out of My Mind (BMI)—Mer 71289	3	4
3.	WEAR MY RING AROUND YOUR NECK (BMI)—Elvis Presley Doncha' Think It's Time (BMI)—Vic 7240	—	1
4.	WITCH DOCTOR (ASCAP)—David Seville Don't Whistle at Me, Baby (ASCAP)—Liberty 55132	10	3
5.	ARE YOU SINCERE? (BMI)—Andy Williams Be Mine Tonight (BMI)—Cadence 1340	5	10
6.	WHO'S SORRY NOW (ASCAP)—Connie Francis You Were Only Fooling (ASCAP)—M-G-M 12588	6	8
7.	LOLLIPOP (BMI)—Chordettes Baby, Come-A Back-A (ASCAP)—Cadence 1345	4	8
8.	TEQUILA (BMI)—The Champs Train to Nowhere (BMI)—Challenge 1016	2	8
9.	ALL I HAVE TO DO IS DREAM (BMI)—Everly Brothers Claudette (BMI)—Cadence 1348	—	1
10.	A WONDERFUL TIME UP THERE (BMI)—Pat Boone It's Too Soon to Know (ASCAP)—Dot 15690	7	9
11.	CATCH A FALLING STAR (ASCAP)—Perry Como Magic Moments (ASCAP)—Vic 7128	9	16
12.	KEWPIE DOLL (ASCAP)—Perry Como Dance Only With Me (ASCAP)—Vic 7202	15	2
13.	BILLY (ASCAP)—Kathy Linden If I Could Hold You in My Arms (ASCAP)—Felsted 8510	8	4
14.	OH, LONESOME ME (BMI)—Don Gibson I Can't Stop Loving You (BMI)—Vic 7133	14	4
15.	RETURN TO ME (ASCAP)—Dean Martin Forgetting You (ASCAP)—Cap 3894	13	4
16.	CHANSON D'AMOUR (ASCAP)—Art and Dotty Todd Along the Trail With You (ASCAP)—Era 1064	20	2
17.	BOOK OF LOVE (BMI)—Monotones You Never Loved Me (BMI)—Argo 5290	—	2
18.	SWEET LITTLE SIXTEEN (BMI)—Chuck Berry Reelin' and Rocking (BMI)—Chess 1683	23	9
19.	THERE'S ONLY ONE OF YOU (ASCAP)—Four Lads Blue Tatoo (ASCAP)—Col 41136	17	4
20.	BELIEVE WHAT YOU SAY (BMI)—Ricky Nelson My Bucket's Got a Hole in It (ASCAP)—Imperial 5503	—	1
21.	SUGARTIME (BMI)—McGuire Sisters Banana Split (BMI)—Coral 61924	11	17
22.	IT'S TOO SOON TO KNOW (ASCAP)—Pat Boone A Wonderful Time Up There (BMI)—Dot 15690	16	10
23.	SAIL ALONG SILVERY MOON (ASCAP)—Billy Vaughn Raunchy (BMI)—Dot 15661	24	14
24.	TWENTY-SIX MILES (BMI)—Four Preps It's You (ASCAP)—Cap 3845	12	14
25.	CHANSON D'AMOUR (ASCAP)—Fontane Sisters Cocoanut Grove (ASCAP)—Dot 15736	—	1

Top 100 Sides

FOR SURVEY WEEK ENDING APRIL 19

This is a tabulation of dealer individual record sales listed according to the specific side requested by customers. No attempt is made to add sides together to reflect actual record sales. This is, therefore, a tabulation of sides or songs, and not records. This is the reason for any possible variation that occurs between the top 50 sides as reflected in this chart, and the top 50 record sellers as reflected in the "Best Sellers in Stores" chart.

Pos.	Song, Artist, Label	Last Week
1.	WITCH DOCTOR, David Seville, Liberty	4
2.	TWILIGHT TIME, Platters, Mercury	1
3.	HE'S GOT THE WHOLE WORLD IN HIS HANDS, Laurie London, Capitol	2
4.	WEAR MY RING AROUND YOUR NECK, Elvis Presley, Victor	7
5.	TEQUILA, Champs, Challenge	3
6.	BOOK OF LOVE, Monotones, Argo	5
7.	ALL I HAVE TO DO IS DREAM, Everly Brothers, Cadence	69
8.	LOLLIPOP, Chordettes, Cadence	6
9.	OH, LONESOME ME, Don Gibson, Victor	15
10.	WHO'S SORRY NOW, Connie Francis, M-G-M	11
11.	A WONDERFUL TIME UP THERE, Pat Boone, Dot	10
12.	BILLY, Kathy Linden, Felsted	16
13.	BELIEVE WHAT YOU SAY, Ricky Nelson, Imperial	8
14.	DON'T YOU JUST KNOW IT, Huey Smith, Ace	13
15.	CATCH A FALLING STAR, Perry Como, Victor	9
16.	RETURN TO ME, Dean Martin, Capitol	30
17.	KEWPIE DOLL, Perry Como, Victor	34
18.	SUGARTIME, McGuire Sisters, Coral	17
19.	LAZY MARY, Lou Monte, Victor	12
20.	MY BUCKET'S GOT A HOLE IN IT, Ricky Nelson, Imperial	21
21.	BREATHLESS, Jerry Lee Lewis, Sun	19
22.	SWEET LITTLE SIXTEEN, Chuck Berry, Chess	14
23.	CHANSON D'AMOUR, Art and Dotty Todd, Era	39
24.	MARCH FROM THE RIVER KWAI AND "COLONEL BOGEY," Mitch Miller, Columbia	22
25.	TWENTY-SIX MILES, Four Preps, Capitol	18
26.	SAIL ALONG SILVERY MOON, Billy Vaughn, Dot	20
27.	ARE YOU SINCERE? Andy Williams, Cadence	23
28.	LOOKING BACK, Nat King Cole, Capitol	46
29.	THE LITTLE BLUE MAN, Betty Johnson, Atlantic	28
29.	FOR YOUR LOVE, Ed Townsend, Capitol	46
31.	IT'S TOO SOON TO KNOW, Pat Boone, Dot	24
32.	DON'T, Perry Como, Victor	25
33.	SHORT SHORTS, Royal Teens, ABC-Paramount	50
34.	THE WALK, Jimmy McCracklin, Checker	28
35.	DINNER WITH DRAC, John Zacherle, Cameo	41
36.	TO BE LOVED, Jacklie Wilson, Brunswick	32
36.	LET THE BELLS KEEP RINGING, Paul Anka, ABC-Paramount	55
38.	BALLAD OF A TEENAGE QUEEN, Johnny Cash, Sun	35
38.	CRAZY LOVE, Paul Anka, ABC-Paramount	77
40.	GOOD GOLLY, MISS MOLLY, Little Richard, Specialty	31
41.	MAYBE, BABY, Crickets, Brunswick	27
42.	SKINNY MINNIE, Bill Haley and His Comets, Decca	39
42.	EVERY NIGHT, Chantels, End	44
44.	WE BELONG TOGETHER, Robert and Johnny, Old Town	38
44.	WISHING FOR YOUR LOVE, Voxpoppers, Mercury	45
46.	TALK TO ME, TALK TO ME, Little Willie John, King	36
47.	ROCK AND ROLL IS HERE TO STAY, Danny and the Juniors, ABC-Paramount	25
48.	OH, JULIE, Crescendos, Nasco	32
49.	THERE'S ONLY ONE OF YOU, Four Lads, Columbia	41
50.	I MET HIM ON SUNDAY, Shirelles, Decca	67
51.	YOU EXCITE ME, Frankie Avalon, Chancellor	51
51.	NOW AND FOR ALWAYS, George Hamilton IV, ABC-Paramount	74
53.	MAGIC MOMENTS, Perry Como, Victor	69
53.	DONCHA' THINK IT'S TIME, Elvis Presley, Victor	74
55.	ARRIVEDERCCI ROMA, Roger Williams, Kapp	74
56.	OH-OH, I'M FALLING IN LOVE AGAIN, Jimmie Rodgers, Roulette	37
56.	TUMBLING TUMBLEWEEDS, Billy Vaughn, Dot	51
56.	JUST MARRIED, Marty Robbins, Columbia	54
59.	BEEN SO LONG, Pastels, Argo	60
60.	HIGH SIGN, Diamonds, Mercury	60
61.	WITCHCRAFT, Frank Sinatra, Capitol	46
62.	GET A JOB, Silhouettes, Ember	41
62.	SO TOUGH, Casuals, Back Seat	63
64.	LONELY ISLAND, Sam Cooke, Keen	49
65.	CLICK CLACK, Dickey Doo and the Don'ts, Swan	59
65.	THE STROLL, Diamonds, Mercury	63
67.	JOHNNY B. GOODE, Chuck Berry, Chess	—
67.	ALL THE TIME, Johnny Mathis, Columbia	84
69.	HE'S GOT THE WHOLE WORLD IN HIS HANDS, Mahalia Jackson, Columbia	—
69.	YOU ARE MY DESTINY, Paul Anka, ABC-Paramount	55
69.	TEACHER'S PET, Doris Day, Columbia	81
69.	DIZZY MISS LIZZIE, Larry Williams, Specialty	87
73.	DEDE DINAH, Frankie Avalon, Chancellor	51
73.	ALL THE WAY, Frank Sinatra, Capitol	57
75.	SING, BOY, SING, Tommy Sands, Capitol	66
75.	DON'T LET GO, Roy Hamilton, Epic	69
77.	ROCK AND ROLL RHAPSODY, Four Aces, Decca	69
77.	THE SWINGING SHEPHERD BLUES, Moe Koffman Quartet, Jubilee	69
77.	STOOD UP, Ricky Nelson, Imperial	77
77.	TEQUILA, Eddie Platt, ABC-Paramount	77
81.	RUMBLE, Link Wray, Cadence	—
81.	A VERY PRECIOUS LOVE, Ames Brothers, Victor	—
81.	YOU WERE MADE FOR ME—Sam Cooke, Keen	60
81.	I CAN'T STOP LOVING YOU, Don Gibson, Victor	—
85.	HANG UP MY ROCK AND ROLL SHOES, Chick Willis, Okeh	—
85.	COME TO ME, Johnny Mathis, Columbia	86
87.	FLIP, FLOP AND BOP, Floyd Cramer, Victor	—
87.	YOU, Aquatones, Fargo	—
87.	MAYBE, Chantels, End	58
87.	DANCING WITH MY SHADOW, Four Voices, Columbia	81
87.	BELONGING TO SOMEONE, Patti Page, Mercury	87
87.	LET'S BE LOVERS, Playmates, Roulette.	97
87.	I BEG OF YOU, Elvis Presley, Victor	—
94.	BLUEBIRD'S OVER THE MOUNTAIN, Erzel Hickey, Epic	—
94.	SMOKE GETS IN YOUR EYES, Richard Barrett, M-G-M	—
94.	YES, MY DARLING, Fats Domino, Imperial	63
94.	APRIL LOVE, Pat Boone, Dot	83
94.	LOLLIPOP, Ronald and Ruby, Victor	90
94.	THE STORY OF MY LIFE, Marty Robbins, Columbia	60
94.	COLLEGE MAN, Bill Justis, Phillips International	—

STORE RECORDED SALES — NEW YORK UNIVERSITY SCHOOL OF RETAILING — THE BILLBOARD

BEST SELLING POP SINGLES IN STORES

The information given in this chart is based on actual sales to customers in a scientific sample of the nation's retail record outlets during the week ending on the date shown above. Sample design, sample size, and all methods used in this continuing study of retail record sales are under the direct and continuing supervision and control of the School of Retailing of New York University.

FOR SURVEY WEEK ENDING APRIL 26, 1958

This Week	Title	Last Week	Weeks on Chart
1.	WITCH DOCTOR (ASCAP)—David Seville — Don't Whistle at Me, Baby (ASCAP)—Liberty 55132	1	4
2.	ALL I HAVE TO DO IS DREAM (BMI)—Everly Brothers; CLAUDETTE (BMI)—Cadence 1348	9	2
3.	WEAR MY RING AROUND YOUR NECK (BMI)—Elvis Presley; DONCHA THINK IT'S TIME (BMI)—Vic 7240	2	3
4.	TWILIGHT TIME (BMI)—Platters — Out of My Mind (BMI)—Mer 71289	3	4
5.	HE'S GOT THE WHOLE WORLD IN HIS HANDS (ASCAP)—Laurie London — Handed Down (ASCAP)—Cap 3891	4	6
6.	BOOK OF LOVE (BMI)—Monotones — You Never Loved Me (BMI)—Argo 5290	6	6
7.	OH, LONESOME ME (BMI)—Don Gibson; I CAN'T STOP LOVING YOU (BMI)—Vic 7133	11	8
8.	TEQUILA (BMI)—The Champs — Train to Nowhere (BMI)—Challenge 1016	5	10
9.	RETURN TO ME (ASCAP)—Dean Martin — Forgetting You (ASCAP)—Cap 3894	17	4
10.	A WONDERFUL TIME UP THERE (BMI)—Pat Boone; IT'S TOO SOON TO KNOW (ASCAP)—Dot 15690	8	12
11.	LOLLIPOP (BMI)—Chordettes — Baby, Come-A Back-A (ASCAP)—Cadence 1345	10	8
12.	MY BUCKET'S GOT A HOLE IN IT (ASCAP)—Ricky Nelson; BELIEVE WHAT YOU SAY (BMI)—Imperial 5503	7	5
13.	WHO'S SORRY NOW? (ASCAP)—Connie Francis — You Were Only Fooling (ASCAP)—M-G-M 12588	13	10
14.	LOOKING BACK (BMI)—Nat King Cole; DO I LIKE IT? (BMI)—Cap 3939	28	4
15.	CRAZY LOVE (BMI)—Paul Anka; LET THE BELLS KEEP RINGING (BMI)—ABC-Paramount 9907	16	3
16.	KEWPIE DOLL (ASCAP)—Perry Como — Dance Only With Me (ASCAP)—Vic 7202	18	3
17.	BILLY (ASCAP)—Kathy Linden — If I Could Hold You in My Arms (ASCAP)—Felsted 8510	14	7
18.	CHANSON D'AMOUR (ASCAP)—Art and Dotty Todd — Along the Trail With You (ASCAP)—Era 1064	23	3
19.	CATCH A FALLING STAR (ASCAP)—Perry Como; MAGIC MOMENTS (ASCAP)—Vic 7128	12	15
20.	DON'T YOU JUST KNOW IT? (BMI)—Huey Smith — High Blood Pressure (BMI)—Ace 545	15	6
21.	ARE YOU SINCERE? (BMI)—Andy Williams — Be Mine Tonight (BMI)—Cadence 1340	29	12
22.	JOHNNY B. GOODE (BMI)—Chuck Berry — Around and Around (BMI)—Chess 1691	—	1
23.	SUGARTIME (BMI)—McGuire Sisters — Banana Split (BMI)—Coral 61924	19	18
24.	SAIL ALONG SILVERY MOON (ASCAP)—Billy Vaughn; RAUNCHY (BMI)—Dot 15661	25	20
25.	SKINNY MINNIE (ASCAP)—Bill Haley and His Comets — Sway With Me (ASCAP)—Dec 30592	38	3
26.	LAZY MARY (ASCAP)—Lou Monte — Angelique (ASCAP)—Vic 7160	20	8
27.	BREATHLESS (BMI)—Jerry Lee Lewis — Down the Line (BMI)—Sun 288	21	9
28.	FOR YOUR LOVE (BMI)—Ed Townsend — Over and Over Again (BMI)—Cap 3826	31	3
29.	TO BE LOVED (BMI)—Jackie Wilson — Come Back to Me (BMI)—Brunswick 55052	35	3
30.	JUST MARRIED (BMI)—Marty Robbins; STAIRWAY OF LOVE (ASCAP)—Col 41143	46	2
31.	TWENTY-SIX MILES (BMI)—Four Preps — It's You (ASCAP)—Cap 3845	26	13
32.	SWEET LITTLE SIXTEEN (BMI)—Chuck Berry — Reelin' and Rocking (BMI)—Chess 1683	22	12
33.	DON'T (BMI)—Elvis Presley; I BEG OF YOU (BMI)—Vic 7150	27	15
34.	THE LITTLE BLUE MAN (BMI)—Betty Johnson — Winter in Miami (ASCAP)—Atlantic 1169	30	10
35.	TUMBLING TUMBLEWEEDS (ASCAP)—Billy Vaughn; TRYING (ASCAP)—Dot 15710	47	5
36.	YOU (BMI)—Aquatones — She's the One for Me (BMI)—Fargo 1001	—	1
37.	WE BELONG TOGETHER—Robert and Johnny — In the Rain—Old Town 1047	40	7
38.	SICK AND TIRED (BMI)—Fats Domino; NO, NO (BMI)—Imperial 5515	—	1
39.	BALLAD OF A TEENAGE QUEEN (BMI)—Johnny Cash; BIG RIVER (BMI)—Sun 283	33	13
40.	DINNER WITH DRAC (BMI)—John Zacherle — Parts 1 and 2—Cameo 130	34	8
41.	MARCH FROM THE RIVER KWAI AND "COLONEL BOGEY" (ASCAP)—Mitch Miller — Hey Little Baby (BMI)—Col 41066	24	16
42.	MAYBE BABY (BMI)—Crickets — Tell Me How (BMI)—Brunswick 55053	37	9
43.	TALK TO ME, TALK TO ME (BMI)—Little Willie John — Spasms (BMI)—King 5108	42	4
44.	NOW AND FOR ALWAYS (ASCAP)—George Hamilton IV — One Heart (ASCAP)—ABC-PARAMOUNT 9898	50	4
45.	NEE NEE NA NA NA NA NU NU (ASCAP)—Dickey Doo and the Don'ts — Flip Top Box (BMI)—Swan 4006	—	1
46.	LITTLE TRAIN (BMI)—Marianne Vasel and Erich Storz — Sunny Lane Walk (BMI)—Mercury 71286	—	1
46.	RUMBLE (BMI)—Link Wray and His Ray Men — The Swag (BMI)—Cadence 1347	—	1
48.	THE WALK (BMI)—Jimmy McCracklin — I'm to Blame (BMI)—Checker 885	32	10
49.	EVERY NIGHT (BMI)—Chantels — Whoever You Are (BMI)—End 1050	39	5
50.	THERE'S ONLY ONE OF YOU (ASCAP)—Four Lads — Blue Tatto (ASCAP)—Col 41136	45	4
50.	YOU EXCITE ME (ASCAP)—Frankie Avalon — Darlin' (ASCAP)—Chancellor 1016	50	2

THIS WEEK'S BEST BUYS

Special telephone reports and/or chart action indicate these recent releases have either broken out in one or more key areas or have leaped onto the charts and have excellent potential for placing among the Top 30 of The Billboard's Best Selling Pop Singles in Stores chart. Action sides are listed in capital letters

I'M SORRY I MADE YOU CRY Feist, ASCAP)—Connie Francis—M-G-M 12647 Lock Up Your Heart (Wildcat, BMI)

ZORRO (Disney, BMI)
LOVE'S A TWO WAY STREET (Shelton, BMI)—The Chordettes—Cadence 1349.

SECRETLY (Planetary ASCAP—Jimmie Rodgers—Roulette 4070 Make Me a Miracle (Planetary, ASCAP)

HANG UP MY ROCK AND ROLL SHOES (Rush, BMI)

WHAT AM I LIVING FOR? (Progressive, BMI)—Chuck Willis—Atlantic 1179.

ALL THE TIME (Livingston & Evans, ASCAP)

TEACHER, TEACHER (Korwin, ASCAP)—Johnny Mathis—Columbia 41152.

The above records are previous Billboard Spotlight picks.
The following record, not previously selected as a "Best Buy," is on the charts for the first time this week.

RUMBLE (Valand)—Link Wray—Cadence 1347.

THE SWAG (Valand, BMI)

STORE RECORDED SALES — NEW YORK UNIVERSITY SCHOOL OF RETAILING — THE BILLBOARD

RECENT POP RELEASES COMING UP STRONG

FOR SURVEY WEEK ENDING APRIL 26

The information given in this chart is based on actual sales to customers in a scientific sample of the nation's retail record outlets during the week ending on the date shown above. Sample design, sample size and all methods used in this continuing study of retail record sales are under the direct and continuing supervision and control of the School of Retailing of New York University.

All the Time . . . . . *Johnny Mathis*
(ASCAP) Columbia 41152

Hang Up My Rock and Roll Shoes . . . . *Chuck Willis*
(BMI) Atlantic 1179

The High Sign . . . . . *The Diamonds*
(BMI) Mercury 71291

Most Played by Jockeys

FOR SURVEY WEEK ENDING APRIL 23

SIDES are ranked in order of the greatest number of plays on disk jockey radio shows thruout the country. Results are based on The Billboard's weekly survey among the nation's disk jockeys. The reverse side of each record is also listed.

This Week	Song	Last Week	Weeks on Chart
1.	HE'S GOT THE WHOLE WORLD IN HIS HANDS (ASCAP)—Laurie London Handed Down (ASCAP)—Cap 3891	1	7
2.	TWILIGHT TIME (BMI)—Platters Out of My Mind (BMI)—Mer 71289	2	5
3.	WITCH DOCTOR (ASCAP)—David Seville Don't Whistle at Me, Baby (ASCAP)—Liberty 55132	4	4
4.	ALL I HAVE TO DO IS DREAM (BMI)—Everly Brothers Claudette (BMI)—Cadence 1348	9	2
5.	WEAR MY RING AROUND YOUR NECK (BMI)—Elvis Presley Doncha' Think It's Time (BMI)—Vic 7240	3	2
6.	CHANSON D'AMOUR (ASCAP)—Art and Dotty Todd Along the Trail With You (ASCAP)—Era 1964	16	3
7.	TEQUILA (BMI)—The Champs Train to Nowhere (BMI)—Challenge 1016	8	9
8.	RETURN TO ME (ASCAP)—Dean Martin Forgetting You (ASCAP)—Cap 3894	15	5
9.	KEWPIE DOLL (ASCAP)—Perry Como Dance Only With Me (ASCAP)—Vic 7202	12	3
10.	THERE'S ONLY ONE OF YOU (ASCAP)—Four Lads Blue Tatto (ASCAP)—Col 41136	19	5
11.	BILLY (ASCAP)—Kathy Linden If I Could Hold You in My Arms (ASCAP)—Felsted 8510	13	5
12.	LOLLIPOP (BMI)—Chordettes Baby, Come-A Back-A (ASCAP)—Cadence 1345	7	9
13.	BOOK OF LOVE (BMI)—Monotones You Never Loved Me (BMI)—Argo 5290	17	3
14.	OH, LONESOME ME (BMI)—Don Gibson I Can't Stop Loving You (BMI)—Vic 7133	14	5
15.	A WONDERFUL TIME UP THERE (BMI)—Pat Boone It's Too Soon to Know (ASCAP)—Dot 15690	10	10
16.	ARE YOU SINCERE? (BMI)—Andy Williams Be Mine Tonight (BMI)—Cadence 1340	5	11
17.	WHO'S SORRY NOW? (ASCAP)—Connie Francis You Were Only Fooling (ASCAP)—M-G-M 12588	6	9
18.	WISHING FOR YOUR LOVE (BMI)—Voxpoppers The Last Drag (BMI)—Mercury 71282	—	1
19.	DANCE ONLY WITH ME (ASCAP)—Perry Como Kewpie Doll (ASCAP)—Vic 7202	—	1
20.	ANOTHER TIME, ANOTHER PLACE (ASCAP)—Patti Page These Worldly Wonders (BMI)—Mercury 71294	—	1
21.	ALL THE TIME (ASCAP)—Johnny Mathis Teacher, Teacher (ASCAP)—Col 41152	—	1
22.	SUGARTIME (BMI)—McGuire Sisters Banana Split (BMI)—Coral 61924	21	18
23.	CHANSON D'AMOUR (ASCAP)—Fontane Sisters Cocoanut Grove (ASCAP)—Dot 15736	23	2
24.	BELIEVE WHAT YOU SAY (BMI)—Ricky Nelson My Bucket's Got a Hole in It (ASCAP)—Imperial 5503	20	2
25.	MY BUCKET'S GOT A HOLE IN IT (ASCAP)—Ricky Nelson Believe What You Say (BMI)—Imperial 5503	—	1
25.	BIG MAN (BMI)—Four Preps Stop, Baby (ASCAP)—Cap 3960	—	1

Top 100 Sides

FOR SURVEY WEEK ENDING APRIL 23

This is a tabulation of dealer individual record sales listed according to the specific side requested by customers. No attempt is made to add sides together to reflect actual record sales. This is, therefore, a tabulation of sides or songs, and not records. This is the reason for any possible variation that occurs between the top 50 sides as reflected in this chart, and the top 50 record sellers as reflected in the "Best Sellers in Stores" chart.

Pos.	Song, Artist, Label	Last Week
1.	**WITCH DOCTOR,** David Seville, Liberty	1
2.	**ALL IHAVE TO DO IS DREAM,** Everly Brothers, Cadence	7
3.	**TWILIGHT TIME,** Platters, Mercury	2
4.	**HE'S GOT THE WHOLE WORLD IN HIS HANDS,** Laurie London, Capitol	3
5.	**WEAR MY RING AROUND YOUR NECK,** Elvis Presley, Victor	4
6.	**BOOK OF LOVE,** Monotones, Argo	6
7.	**TEQUILA,** Champs, Challenge	5
8.	**OH, LONESOME ME,** Don Gibson, Victor	9
9.	**RETURN TO ME,** Dean Martin, Capitol	16
10.	**LOLLIPOP,** Chordettes, Cadence	8
11.	**WHO'S SORRY NOW,** Connie Francis, M-G-M	10
12.	**LOOKING BACK,** Nat King Cole, Capitol	28
13.	**KEWPIE DOLL,** Perry Como, Victor	17
14.	**BILLY,** Kathy Linden, Felsted	12
15.	**A WONDERFUL TIME UP THERE,** Pat Boone, Dot	11
16.	**CHANSON D'AMOUR,** Art and Dotty Todd, Era	23
17.	**DON'T YOU JUST KNOW IT,** Huey Smith, Ace	14
18.	**ARE YOU SINCERE?** Andy Williams, Cadence	27
19.	**CRAZY LOVE,** Paul Anka, ABC-Paramount	38
20.	**JOHNNY B. GOODE,** Chuck Berry, Chess	67
21.	**DONCHA' THINK IT'S TIME,** Elvis Presley, Victor	53
22.	**MY BUCKET'S GOT A HOLE IN IT,** Ricky Nelson, Imperial	20
23.	**SUGARTIME,** McGuire Sisters, Coral	18
24.	**BELIEVE WHAT YOU SAY,** Ricky Nelson, Imperial	13
25.	**CATCH A FALLING STAR,** Perry Como, Victor	15
26.	**SAIL ALONG SILVERY MOON,** Billy Vaughn, Dot	26
26.	**SKINNY MINNIE,** Bill Haley and His Comets, Decca	42
28.	**LAZY MARY,** Lou Monte, Victor	19
29.	**BREATHLESS,** Jerry Lee Lewis, Sun	21
29.	**FOR YOUR LOVE,** Ed Townsend, Capitol	29
29.	**TO BE LOVED,** Jackie Wilson, Brunswick	36
32.	**IT'S TOO SOON TO KNOW,** Pat Boone, Dot	31
33.	**TWENTY-SIX MILES,** Four Preps, Capitol	25
34.	**SWEET LITTLE SIXTEEN,** Chuck Berry, Chess	22
35.	**THE LITTLE BLUE MAN,** Betty Johnson, Atlantic	29
36.	**YOU,** Aquatones, Fargo	87
37.	**WE BELONG TOGETHER,** Robert and Johnny, Old Town	44
38.	**DINNER WITH DRAC,** John Zacherle, Cameo	35
39.	**MARCH FROM THE RIVER KWAI AND "COLONEL BOGEY,"** Mitch Miller, Columbia	24
39.	**DON'T,** Elvis Presley, Victor	32
41.	**LET THE BELLS KEEP RINGING,** Paul Anka, ABC-Paramount	36
42.	**MAYBE, BABY,** Crickets, Brunswick	41
42.	**TALK TO ME, TALK TO ME,** Little Willie John, King	46
42.	**TUMBLING TUMBLEWEEDS,** Billy Vaughn, Dot	56
45.	**BALLAD OF A TEENAGE QUEEN,** Johnny Cash, Sun	38
46.	**NOW AND FOR ALWAYS,** George Hamilton IV, ABC-Paramount	51
46.	**JUST MARRIED,** Marty Robbins, Columbia	56
48.	**NEE NEE NA NA NA NA NU NU,** Dickey Doo and the Don'ts, Swan	—
49.	**LITTLE TRAIN,** Marianne Vasel and Erich Storz, Mercury	—
49.	**THE WALK,** Jimmy McCracklin, Checker	34
49.	**EVERY NIGHT,** Chantels, End	42
49.	**THERE'S ONLY ONE OF YOU,** Four Lads, Columbia	49
49.	**YOU EXCITE ME,** Frankie Avalon, Chancellor	51
49.	**RUMBLE,** Link Wray, Cadence	21
55.	**WISHING FOR YOUR LOVE,** Voxpoppers, Mercury	44
56.	**CLAUDETTE,** Everly Brothers, Cadence	—
56.	**HAPPINESS,** Billy and Lillie, Swan	—
56.	**GOOD GOLLY, MISS MOLLY,** Little Richard, Specialty	40
56.	**OH, JULIE,** Crescendos, Nasco	48
56.	**I MET HIM ON A SUNDAY,** Shirelles, Decca	50
56.	**HIGH SIGN,** Diamonds, Mercury	60
62.	**ARRIVEDERCI ROMA,** Roger Williams, Kapp	55
62.	**THE STROLL,** Diamonds, Mercury	65
64.	**MAGIC MOMENTS,** Perry Como, Victor	53
64.	**BEEN SO LONG,** Pastels, Argo	59
64.	**HANG UP MY ROCK AND ROLL SHOES,** Chuck Willis, Atlantic	85
67.	**SICK AND TIRED,** Fats Domino, Imperial	—
68.	**STAIRWAY OF LOVE,** Marty Robbins, Columbia	—
68.	**SHORT SHORTS,** Royal Teens, ABC-Paramount	33
70.	**ROCK AND ROLL IS HERE TO STAY,** Danny and the Juniors, ABC-Paramount	47
70.	**LONELY ISLAND,** Sam Cooke Keen	64
70.	**ALL THE TIME,** Johnny Mathis, Columbia	67
70.	**TEACHER'S PET,** Doris Day, Columbia	69
74.	**NO NO,** Fats Domino Imperial	—
74.	**ALL THE WAY,** Frank Sinatra, Capitol	73
76.	**HAVE FAITH,** Gene Allison, Vee Jay	—
76.	**WITCHCRAFT,** Frank Sinatra, Capitol	61
76.	**SO TOUGH,** Casuals, Back Beat	62
76.	**CLICK CLACK,** Dickey Doo and the Don't, Swan	65
76.	**YOU ARE MY DESTINY,** Paul Anka, ABC-Paramount	69
81.	**SUGAR MOON,** Pat Boone, Dot	—
81.	**TORERO,** Renato Carosone, Capitol	—
83.	**BIG MAN,** Four Preps, Capitol	—
83.	**OH-OH, I'M FALLING IN LOVE AGAIN,** Jimmie Rodgers, Roulette	56
83.	**I CAN'T STOP LOVING YOU,** Don Gibson, Victor	81
86.	**HE'S GOT THE WHOLE WORLD IN HIS HANDS** Mahalia Jackson, Columbia	69
86.	**A VERY PRECIOUS LOVE,** Ames Brothers, Victor	81
88.	**GI GI,** Vic Damone, Columbia	—
88.	**MAYBE,** Chantels, End	87
90.	**SECRETLY,** Jimmie Rodgers, Roulette	—
90.	**ROCK AND ROLL RHAPSODY,** Four Aces, Decca	77
90.	**TEQUILA,** Eddie Platt, ABC-Paramount	77
90.	**COLLEGE MAN,** Bill Justis, Phillips International	94
94.	**TRYING,** Billy Vaughn, Dot	—
94.	**DO I LIKE IT,** Nat King Cole, Capitol	—
96.	**DIZZY, MISS LIZZIE,** Larry Williams, Specialty	69
96.	**COME TO ME,** Johnny Mathis, Columbia	85
96.	**FILP, FLOP AND BOP,** Floyd Cramer, Victor	87
99.	**THE LONG HOT SUMMER,** Jimmie Rodgers, Roulette	—
99.	**TEACHER, TEACHER,** Johnny Mathis, Columbia	—

BEST SELLING POP SINGLES IN STORES

The information given in this chart is based on actual sales to customers in a scientific sample of the nation's retail record outlets during the week ending on the date shown above. Sample design, sample size, and all methods used in this continuing study of retail record sales are under the direct and continuing supervision and control of the School of Retailing of New York University.

FOR SURVEY WEEK ENDING MAY 3, 1958

This Week	Title	Last Week	Weeks on Chart
1.	ALL I HAVE TO DO IS DREAM (BMI)—Everly Brothers CLAUDETTE (BMI)—Cadence 1348	2	3
2.	WITCH DOCTOR (ASCAP)—David Seville Don't Whistle at Me, Baby (ASCAP)—Liberty 55132	1	5
3.	TWILIGHT TIME (BMI)—Platters Out of My Mind (BMI)—Mer 71289	4	5
4.	WEAR MY RING AROUND YOUR NECK (BMI)—Elvis Presley DONCHA' THINK IT'S TIME (BMI)—Vic 7240	3	4
5.	HE'S GOT THE WHOLE WORLD IN HIS HANDS (ASCAP)—Laurie London Handed Down (ASCAP)—Cap 3891	5	7
6.	RETURN TO ME (ASCAP)—Dean Martin Forgetting You (ASCAP)—Cap 3894	9	5
7.	BOOK OF LOVE (BMI)—Monotones You Never Loved Me (BMI)—Argo 5290	6	7
8.	TEQUILA (BMI)—The Champs Train to Nowhere (BMI)—Challenge 1016	8	11
9.	OH, LONESOME ME (BMI)—Don Gibson I CAN'T STOP LOVING YOU (BMI)—Vic 7133	7	9
10.	LOOKING BACK (BMI)—Nat King Cole DO I LIKE IT? (BMI)—Cap 3939	14	5
11.	BELIEVE WHAT YOU SAY (BMI)—Ricky Nelson MY BUCKET'S GOT A HOLE IN IT—Imperial 5503	12	6
12.	JOHNNY B. GOODE (BMI)—Chuck Berry Around and Around (BMI)—Chess 1691	22	2
13.	LOLLIPOP (BMI)—Chordettes Baby, Come-A Back-A (ASCAP)—Cadence 1345	11	9
14.	KEWPIE DOLL (ASCAP)—Perry Como Dance Only With Me (ASCAP)—Vic 7202	16	4
15.	A WONDERFUL TIME UP THERE (BMI)—Pat Boone IT'S TOO SOON TO KNOW (ASCAP)—Dot 15690	10	13
16.	CHANSON D'AMOUR (ASCAP)—Art and Dotty Todd Along the Trail With You (ASCAP)—Era 1064	18	4
17.	BILLY (ASCAP)—Kathy Linden If I Could Hold You in My Arms (ASCAP)—Felsted 8510	17	8
18.	CRAZY LOVE (BMI)—Paul Anka LET THE BELLS KEEP RINGING (BMI)—ABC-Paramount 9907	15	4
19.	WHO'S SORRY NOW? (ASCAP)—Connie Francis You Were Only Fooling (ASCAP)—M-G-M 12588	13	11
20.	DON'T YOU JUST KNOW IT? (BMI)—Huey Smith High Blood Pressure (BMI)—Ace 545	20	7
21.	FOR YOUR LOVE (BMI)—Ed Townsend Over and Over Again (BMI)—Cap 3926	28	4
22.	SICK AND TIRED (BMI)—Fats Domino NO, NO (BMI)—Imperial 5515	38	2
23.	LAZY MARY (ASCAP)—Lou Monte Angelique (ASCAP)—Vic 7160	26	9
24.	SKINNY MINNIE (ASCAP)—Bill Haley and His Comets Sway With Me (ASCAP)—Dec 30592	25	4
25.	BIG MAN (BMI)—Four Preps Stop, Baby (ASCAP)—Cap 3960	—	1
26.	JUST MARRIED (BMI)—Marty Robbins STAIRWAY OF LOVE (ASCAP)—Col 41143	30	3
27.	YOU (BMI)—Aquatones She's the One for Me (BMI)—Fargo 1001	36	2
28.	CATCH A FALLING STAR (ASCAP)—Perry Como MAGIC MOMENTS (ASCAP)—Vic 7128	19	16
29.	ARE YOU SINCERE? (BMI)—Andy Williams Be Mine Tonight (BMI)—Cadence 1340	21	13
30.	SUGAR MOON (BMI)—Pat Boone Cherie, I Love You (ASCAP)—Dot 15750	—	1
31.	SUGARTIME (BMI)—McGuire Sisters Banana Split (BMI)—Coral 61924	23	19
32.	TWENTY-SIX MILES (BMI)—Four Preps It's You (ASCAP)—Cap 3845	31	14
33.	TO BE LOVED (BMI)—Jackie Wilson Come Back to Me (BMI)—Brunswick 55052	29	4
34.	TUMBLING TUMBLEWEEDS (ASCAP)—Billy Vaughn TRYING (ASCAP)—Dot 15710	35	6
35.	WHAT AM I LIVING FOR? (BMI)—Chuck Willis HANG UP MY ROCK AND ROLL SHOES (BMI)—Atlantic 1179	—	1
36.	TORERO (ASCAP)—Renato Carosone Chella lla (ASCAP)—Cap 71080	—	1
37.	DON'T (BMI)—Elvis Presley I BEG OF YOU (BMI)—Vic 7150	33	16
38.	TALK TO ME, TALK TO ME (BMI)—Little Willie John Spasms (BMI)—King 5108	43	5
39.	SAIL ALONG SILVERY MOON (ASCAP)—Billy Vaughn RAUNCHY (BMI)—Dot 15661	24	21
40.	THE LITTLE BLUE MAN (BMI)—Betty Johnson Winter in Miami (ASCAP)—Atlantic 1169	34	11
41.	RUMBLE (BMI)—Link Wray and His Ray Men The Swag (BMI)—Cadence 1347	46	2
42.	ALL THE TIME (ASCAP)—Johnny Mathis TEACHER, TEACHER (ASCAP)—Col 41152	—	1
43.	WE BELONG TOGETHER (BMI)—Robert and Johnny In the Rain (BMI)—Old Town 1047	37	8
44.	NEE NEE NA NA NA NA NU NU (ASCAP)—Dickey Doo and the Don'ts Flip Top Box (BMI)—Swan 4006	45	2
45.	SECRETLY (ASCAP)—Jimmie Rodgers Make Me a Miracle (ASCAP)—Roulette 4070	—	1
46.	BREATHLESS (BMI)—Jerry Lee Lewis Down the Line (BMI)—Sun 288	27	10
47.	SWEET LITTLE SIXTEEN (BMI)—Chuck Berry Reelin' and Rocking (BMI)—Chess 1683	32	13
48.	LITTLE TRAIN (BMI)—Marianne Vasel and Erich Storz Sunny Lane Walk (BMI)—Mercury 71286	46	2
49.	MAYBE BABY (BMI)—Crickets Tell Me How (BMI)—Brunswick 55053	42	10
50.	THERE'S ONLY ONE OF YOU (ASCAP)—Four Lads Blue Tattoo (ASCAP)—Col 41136	50	5

THIS WEEK'S BEST BUYS

Special telephone reports and/or chart action indicate these recent releases have either broken out in one or more key areas or have leaped onto the charts and have excellent potential for placing among the Top 30 of The Billboard's Best Selling Pop Singles in Stores chart. Action sides are listed in capitol letters

A VERY PRECIOUS LOVE (Witmark, ASCAP)—The Ames Brothers—RCA Victor 7167. **Don't Leave Me Now** (Winneton, BMI).

A previous Billboard Spotlight pick.

The following records, not previously selected as "Best Buys," are on the charts for the first time this week.

BIG MAN (Beechwood, BMI)—The Four Preps—Capitol 3960. **Stop, Baby** (Bourne, ASCAP). A previous Billboard Spotlight pick.

TORERO (Leeds, ASCAP)—Renate Carosone—Capitol 71080. **Chella Lla** (Leeds, ASCAP)

RECENT POP RELEASES COMING UP STRONG

FOR SURVEY WEEK ENDING MAY 3

The information given in this chart is based on actual sales to customers in a scientific sample of the nation's retail record outlets, during the week ending on the date shown above. Sample design, sample size and all methods used in this continuing study of retail record sales are under the direct and continuing supervision and control of the School of Retailing of New York University.

The High Sign . . . . ***The Diamonds***
(BMI) Mercury 71291

A Very Precious Love . . . . ***The Ames Brothers***
(ASCAP) RCA Victor 7167

Most Played by Jockeys

FOR SURVEY WEEK ENDING MAY 3

SIDES are ranked in order of the greatest number of plays on disk jockey radio shows thruout the country. Results are based on The Billboard's weekly survey among the nation's disk jockeys. The reverse side of each record is also listed.

This Week		Last Week	Weeks on Chart
1.	**TWILIGHT TIME** (BMI)—Platters Out of My Mind (BMI)—Mer 71289	2	6
2.	**WITCH DOCTOR** (ASCAP)—David Seville Don't Whistle at Me, Baby (ASCAP)—Liberty 55132	3	5
3.	**ALL I HAVE TO DO IS DREAM** (BMI)—Everly Brothers Claudette (BMI)—Cadence 1348	4	3
4.	**HE'S GOT THE WHOLE WORLD IN HIS HANDS** (ASCAP)—Laurie London Handed Down (ASCAP)—Cap 3891	1	8
5.	**WEAR MY RING AROUND YOUR NECK** (BMI)—Elvis Presley Doncha' Think It's Time (BMI)—Vic 7240	5	3
6.	**KEWPIE DOLL** (ASCAP)—Perry Como Dance Only With Me (ASCAP)—Vic 7202	9	4
7.	**CHANSON D'AMOUR** (ASCAP)—Art and Dotty Todd Along the Trail With You (ASCAP)—Era 1964	6	4
8.	**RETURN TO ME** (ASCAP)—Dean Martin Forgetting You (ASCAP)—Cap 3894	8	6
9.	**BOOK OF LOVE** (BMI)—Monotones You Never Loved Me (BMI)—Argo 5290	13	4
10.	**OH, LONESOME ME** (BMI)—Don Gibson I Can't Stop Loving You (BMI)—Vic 7133	14	6
11.	**THERE'S ONLY ONE OF YOU** (ASCAP)—Four Lads Blue Tattoo (ASCAP)—Col 41136	10	6
12.	**TEQUILA** (BMI)—The Champs Train to Nowhere (BMI)—Challenge 1016	7	10
13.	**BIG MAN** (BMI)—Four Preps Stop, Baby (ASCAP)—Cap 3960	25	2
14.	**LOOKING BACK** (BMI)—Nat King Cole Do I Like It (BMI)—Cap 3939	—	1
15.	**WHO'S SORRY NOW?** (ASCAP)—Connie Francis You Were Only Fooling (ASCAP)—M-G-M 12588	17	10
16.	**LOLLIPOP** (BMI)—Chordettes Baby, Come-A Back-A (ASCAP)—Cadence 1345	12	10
17.	**BILLY** (ASCAP)—Kathy Linden If I Could Hold You in My Arms (ASCAP)—Felsted 8510	11	6
18.	**A WONDERFUL TIME UP THERE** (BMI)—Pat Boone It's Too Soon to Know (ASCAP)—Dot 15690	15	11
19.	**LET THE BELLS KEEP RINGING** (BMI)—Paul Anka Crazy Love (BMI)—ABC-Paramount 9907	—	1
20.	**SUGAR MOON** (BMI)—Pat Boone Cherie, I Love You (ASCAP)—Dot 15750	—	1
21.	**CHANSON D'AMOUR** (ASCAP)—Fontane Sisters Cocoanut Grove (ASCAP)—Dot 15736	23	3
22.	**HOW ARE YA' FIXED FOR LOVE?** (ASCAP)—Frank Sinatra and Keely Smith Nothing in Common (ASCAP)—Cap 3952	—	1
23.	**ALL THE TIME** (ASCAP)—Johnny Mathis Teacher, Teacher (ASCAP)—Col 41152	21	2
24.	**ARE YOU SINCERE?** (BMI)—Andy Williams Be Mine Tonight (BMI)- Cadence 1340	16	12
25.	**JOHNNY B. GOODE** (BMI)—Chuck Berry Around and Around (BMI)—Chess 1691	—	1

NEW YORK UNIVERSITY SCHOOL OF RETAILING · STORE RECORDED SALES · THE BILLBOARD

Top 100 Sides

FOR SURVEY WEEK ENDING MAY 3

This is a tabulation of dealer individual record sales listed according to the specific side requested by customers. No attempt is made to add sides together to reflect actual record sales. This is, therefore, a tabulation of sides or songs, and not records. This is the reason for any possible variation that occurs between the top 50 sides as reflected in this chart, and the top 50 record sellers as reflected in the "Best Sellers in Stores" chart.

Pos.	Song, Artist, Label	Last Week
1.	**WITCH DOCTOR,** David Seville, Liberty	1
2.	**ALL I HAVE TO DO IS DREAM,** Everly Brothers, Cadence	2
3.	**TWILIGHT TIME,** Platters, Mercury	3
4.	**HE'S GOT THE WHOLE WORLD IN HIS HANDS,** Laurie London, Capitol	4
5.	**WEAR MY RING AROUND YOUR NECK,** Elvis Presley, Victor	5
6.	**RETURN TO ME,** Dean Martin, Capitol	9
7.	**BOOK OF LOVE,** Monotones, Argo	6
8.	**TEQUILA,** Champs, Challenge	7
9.	**OH, LONESOME ME,** Don Gibson, Victor	8
10.	**LOOKING BACK,** Nat King Cole, Capitol	12
11.	**JOHNNY B. GOODE,** Chuck Berry, Chess	20
12.	**LOLLIPOP,** Chordettes, Cadence	10
13.	**KEWPIE DOLL,** Perry Como, Victor	13
14.	**CHANSON D'AMOUR,** Art and Dotty Todd, Era	16
15.	**BILLY,** Kathy Linden, Felsted	14
16.	**WHO'S SORRY NOW,** Connie Francis, M-G-M	11
17.	**DON'T YOU JUST KNOW IT,** Huey Smith, Ace	17
18.	**FOR YOUR LOVE,** Ed Townsend, Capitol	29
19.	**A WONDERFUL TIME UP THERE,** Pat Boone, Dot	15
20.	**LAZY MARY,** Lou Monte, Victor	28
21.	**BELIEVE WHAT YOU SAY,** Ricky Nelson, Imperial	24
22.	**SKINNY MINNIE,** Bill Haley and His Comets, Decca	26
23.	**CRAZY LOVE,** Paul Anka, ABC-Paramount	19
23.	**BIG MAN,** Four Preps, Capitol	83
25.	**YOU,** Aquatones, Fargo	36
26.	**ARE YOU SINCERE?** Andy Williams, Cadence	18
27.	**MY BUCKET'S GOT A HOLE IN IT,** Ricky Nelson, Imperial	22
27.	**SUGAR MOON,** Pat Boone, Dot	81
29.	**SUGARTIME,** McGuire Sisters, Coral	23
30.	**CATCH A FALLING STAR,** Perry Como, Victor	25
30.	**CLAUDETTE,** Everly Brothers, Cadence	56
32.	**TWENTY-SIX MILES,** Four Preps, Capitol	33
32.	**SICK AND TIRED,** Fats Domino, Imperial	67
34.	**TO BE LOVED,** Jackie Wilson, Brunswick	29
35.	**JUST MARRIED,** Marty Robbins, Columbia	46
36.	**TALK TO ME, TALK TO ME,** Little Willie John, King	42
36.	**TORERO,** Renato Carosone, Capitol	81
38.	**THE LITTLE BLUE MAN,** Betty Johnson, Atlantic	35
38.	**RUMBLE,** Link Wray, Cadence	49
40.	**SAIL ALONG SILVERY MOON**—Billy Vaughn, Dot	26
40.	**WE BELONG TOGETHER,** Robert and Johnny, Old Town	37
40.	**NEE NEE NA NA NA NA NU NU,** Dickey Doo and the Don'ts, Swan	48
43.	**DON'T,** Elvis Presley, Victor	39
44.	**DONCHA' THINK IT'S TIME,** Elvis Presley, Victor	21
45.	**IT'S TOO SOON TO KNOW,** Pat Boone, Dot	32
45.	**TUMBLING TUMBLEWEEDS,** Billy Vaughn, Dot	42
47.	**LET THE BELLS KEEP RINGING,** Paul Anka, ABC-Paramount	41
48.	**SECRETLY,** Jimmie Rodgers, Roulette	90
49.	**BREATHLESS,** Jerry Lee Lewis, Sun	29
50.	**SWEET LITTLE SIXTEEN,** Chuck Berry, Chess	34
50.	**LITTLE TRAIN,** Marianne Vasel and Erich Storz, Mercury	49
52.	**MAYBE, BABY,** Crickets, Brunswick	42
52.	**THERE'S ONLY ONE OF YOU,** Four Lads, Columbia	49
54.	**YOU EXCITE ME,** Frankie Avalon, Chancellor	49
55.	**WHAT AM I LIVING FOR?** Chuck Willis, Atlantic	—
55.	**NOW AND FOR ALWAYS,** George Hamilton IV, ABC-Paramount	46
55.	**HIGH SIGN,** Diamonds, Mercury	56
55.	**NO, NO,** Fats Domino, Imperial	74
59.	**MARCH FROM THE RIVER KWAI, AND "COLONEL BOGEY,"** Mitch Miller, Columbia	39
59.	**BALLAD OF A TEENAGE QUEEN,** Johnny Cash, Sun	45
59.	**TEACHERS'S PET,** Doris Day, Columbia	70
62.	**THE WALK,** Jimmy McCracklin, Checker	49
62.	**WISHING FOR YOUR LOVE,** Voxpoppers, Mercury	55
64.	**MET HIM ON A SUNDAY,** Shirelles, Decca	56
65.	**EVERY NIGHT,** Chantels, End	49
65.	**ALL THE TIME,** Johnny Mathis, Columbia	70
67.	**TEACHER, TEACHER,** Johnny Mathis, Columbia	99
68.	**HAPPINESS,** Billy and Lillie, Swan	56
69.	**THE STROLL,** Diamonds, Mercury	62
69.	**HANG UP MY ROCK AND ROLL SHOES,** Chuck Willis, Atlantic	64
69.	**STAIRWAY OF LOVE,** Marty Robbins, Columbia	68
72.	**DINNER WITH DRAC,** John Zacherle, Cameo	38
73.	**CHANSON D'AMOUR,** Fontane Sisters, Dot	—
73.	**GOOD GOLLY, MISS MOLLY,** Little Richard, Specialty	56
73.	**BEEN SO LONG,** Pastels, Argo	64
73.	**ALL THE WAY,** Frank Sinatra, Capitol	74
73.	**YOU ARE MY DESTINY,** Paul Anka, ABC-Paramount	76
73.	**OH-OH, I'M FALLING IN LOVE AGAIN,** Jimmie Rodgers, Roulette	83
73.	**A VERY PRECIOUS LOVE,** Ames Brothers, Victor	86
73.	**HAVE FAITH,** Gene Allison, Vee Jay	96
81.	**DO YOU WANT TO DANCE?** Bobby Freeman, Josie	—
82.	**JACQUELINE,** Bobby Helms, Decca	—
82.	**HE'S GOT THE WHOLE WORLD IN HIS HANDS,** Mahalia Jackson, Columbia	86
82.	**MAYBE,** Chantels, End	88
85.	**LONELY ISLAND,** Sam Cooke Keen	70
85.	**WITCHCRAFT,** Frank Sinatra, Capitol	76
87.	**ANOTHER TIME, ANOTHER PLACE,** Patti Page, Mercury	—
87.	**BLUEBIRDS OVER THE MOUNTAIN,** Ersel Hickey, Epic	—
87.	**I'M HAPPY,** Four Dates, Chancellor	—
87.	**I'M SORRY I MADE YOU CRY,** Connie Francis, M-G-M	—
87.	**ROCK AND ROLL IS HERE TO STAY,** Danny and the Juniors, ABC-Paramount	70
87.	**THE LONG HOT SUMMER,** Jimmie Rodgers, Roulette	99
93.	**YOU WERE MADE FOR ME,** Sam Cooke, Keen	—
93.	**CLICK CLACK,** Dickey Doo and the Don'ts, Swan	76
93.	**SO TOUGH,** Casuals, Back Beat	76
93.	**TRYING,** Billy Vaughn, Dot	94
93.	**DO I LIKE IT,** Nat King Cole, Capitol	94
98.	**COME WHAT MAY,** Clyde McPhatter, Atlantic	—
98.	**ARRIVEDERCI ROMA,** Roger Williams, Kapp	62
98.	**SHORT SHORTS,** Royal Teens, ABC-Paramount	68

BEST SELLING POP SINGLES IN STORES

STORE RECORDED SALES — New York University School of Retailing — The Billboard

The information given in this chart is based on actual sales to customers in a scientific sample of the nation's retail record outlets during the week ending on the date shown above. Sample design, sample size, and all methods used in this continuing study of retail record sales are under the direct and continuing supervision and control of the School of Retailing of New York University.

FOR SURVEY WEEK ENDING MAY 10, 1958

This Week	Title	Last Week	Weeks on Chart
1.	ALL I HAVE TO DO IS DREAM (BMI)—Everly Brothers / CLAUDETTE (BMI)—Cadence 1348	1	4
2.	WITCH DOCTOR (ASCAP)—David Seville / Don't Whistle at Me, Baby (ASCAP)—Liberty 55132	2	6
3.	WEAR MY RING AROUND YOUR NECK (BMI)—Elvis Presley / DONCHA THINK IT'S TIME? (BMI)—Vic 7240	4	5
4.	TWILIGHT TIME (BMI)—Platters / Out of My Mind (BMI)—Mer 71289	3	6
5.	HE'S GOT THE WHOLE WORLD IN HIS HANDS (ASCAP)—Laurie London / Handed Down (ASCAP)—Cap 3891	5	8
6.	RETURN TO ME (ASCAP)—Dean Martin / Forgetting You (ASCAP)—Cap 3894	6	6
7.	LOOKING BACK (BMI)—Nat King Cole / DO I LIKE IT? (BMI)—Cap 3939	10	6
8.	BOOK OF LOVE (BMI)—Monotones / You Never Loved Me (BMI)—Argo 5290	7	8
9.	TEQUILA (BMI)—The Champs / Train to Nowhere (BMI)—Challenge 1016	8	12
10.	JOHNNY B. GOODE (BMI)—Chuck Berry / Around and Around (BMI)—Chess 1691	12	3
11.	OH, LONESOME ME (BMI)—Don Gibson / I CAN'T STOP LOVING YOU (BMI)—Vic 7133	9	10
12.	KEWPIE DOLL (ASCAP)—Perry Como / Dance Only With Me (ASCAP)—Vic 7202	14	5
13.	CHANSON D'AMOUR (ASCAP)—Art and Dotty Todd / Along the Trail With You (ASCAP)—Era 1064	16	5
14.	BIG MAN (BMI)—Four Preps / Stop, Baby (ASCAP)—Cap 3960	25	2
15.	SUGAR MOON (BMI)—Pat Boone / CHERIE, I LOVE YOU (ASCAP)—Dot 15750	30	2
16.	BELIEVE WHAT YOU SAY (BMI)—Ricky Nelson / MY BUCKET'S GOT A HOLE IN IT (ASCAP)—Imperial 5503	11	7
17.	FOR YOUR LOVE (BMI)—Ed Townsend / Over and Over Again (BMI)—Cap 3926	21	5
18.	SECRETLY (ASCAP)—Jimmie Rodgers / MAKE ME A MIRACLE (ASCAP)—Roulette 4070	45	2
19.	CRAZY LOVE (BMI)—Paul Anka / LET THE BELLS KEEP RINGING (BMI)—ABC-Paramount 9907	18	5
20.	WHAT AM I LIVING FOR? (BMI)—Chuck Willis / HANG UP MY ROCK AND ROLL SHOES (BMI)—Atlantic 1179	35	2
21.	LOLLIPOP (BMI)—Chordettes / Baby, Come-A, Back-A (ASCAP)—Cadence 1345	13	10
22.	A WONDERFUL TIME UP THERE (BMI)—Pat Boone / IT'S TOO SOON TO KNOW (ASCAP)—Dot 15690	15	14
23.	DON'T YOU JUST KNOW IT? (BMI)—Huey Smith / High Blood Pressure (BMI)—Ace 545	20	8
24.	LAZY MARY (ASCAP)—Lou Monte / Angelique (ASCAP)—Vic 7160	23	10
25.	RUMBLE (BMI)—Link Wray and His Ray Men / The Swag (BMI)—Cadence 1347	41	3
26.	SICK AND TIRED (BMI)—Fats Domino / NO, NO (BMI)—Imperial 5515	22	3
27.	YOU (BMI)—Aquatones / She's the One for Me (BMI)—Fargo 1001	27	3
28.	WHO'S SORRY NOW? (ASCAP)—Connie Francis / You Were Only Fooling (ASCAP)—M-G-M 12588	19	12
29.	BILLY (ASCAP)—Kathy Linden / If I Could Hold You in My Arms (ASCAP)—Felsted 8510	17	9
30.	TORERO (ASCAP)—Renato Carosone / Chella Lla (ASCAP)—Cap 71080	36	2
31.	SKINNY MINNIE (ASCAP)—Bill Haley and His Comets / Sway With Me (ASCAP)—Dec 30592	24	5
32.	TEACHER, TEACHER (ASCAP)—Johnny Mathis / ALL THE TIME (ASCAP)—Col 41152	42	2
33.	JUST MARRIED (BMI)—Marty Robbins / STAIRWAY OF LOVE (ASCAP)—Col 41143	26	4
34.	TALK TO ME, TALK TO ME (BMI)—Little Willie John / Spasms (BMI)—King 5108	38	6
35.	SUGARTIME (BMI)—McGuire Sisters / Banana Split (BMI)—Coral 61924	31	20
36.	WE BELONG TOGETHER (BMI)—Robert and Johnny / In the Rain (BMI)—Old Town 1047	43	9
37.	THE HIGH SIGN (BMI)—Diamonds / Chick-Lets (BMI)—Mermury 71291	—	1
38.	CATCH A FALLING STAR (ASCAP)—Perry Como / MAGIC MOMENTS (ASCAP)—Vic 7128	28	17
39.	TO BE LOVED (BMI)—Jackie Wilson / Come Back to Me (BMI)—Brunswick 55052	33	5
40.	TWENTY-SIX MILES (BMI)—Four Preps / It's You (ASCAP)—Cap 3845	32	15
41.	THE LITTLE BLUE MAN (BMI)—Betty Johnson / Winter in Miami (ASCAP)—Atlantic 1169	40	12
42.	NEE NEE NA NA NA NA NU NU (ASCAP)—Dickey Doo and the Don'ts / Flip Top Box (BMI)—Swan 4006	44	3
43.	TUMBLING TUMBLEWEEDS (ASCAP)—Billy Vaughn / TRYING (ASCAP)—Dot 15710	34	7
44.	SAIL ALONG SILVERY MOON (ASCAP)—Billy Vaughn / RAUNCHY (BMI)—Dot 15661	39	22
45.	NOW AND FOR ALWAYS (ASCAP)—George Hamilton IV / One Heart (ASCAP)—ABC-Paramount 9898	—	5
46.	DON'T (BMI)—Elvis Presley / I Beg of You (BMI)—Vic 7150	37	17
47.	ARE YOU SINCERE (BMI)—Andy Williams / Be Mine Tonight (BMI)—Cadence 1340	29	14
48.	I'M SORRY I MADE YOU CRY (ASCAP)—Connie Francis / Lock Up Your Heart (BMI)—M-G-M 12647	—	1
48.	DO YOU WANT TO DANCE? (BMI)—Bobby Freeman / Big Fat Woman (BMI)—Josie 835	—	1
50.	LITTLE TRAIN (BMI)—Marianne Vasel and Erich Storz / Sunny Lane Walk (BMI)—Mercury 71286	48	3

THIS WEEK'S BEST BUYS

Special telephone reports and/or chart action indicate these recent releases have either broken out in one or more key areas or have leaped onto the charts and have excellent potential for placing among the Top 30 of The Billboard's Best Selling Pop Singles in Stores chart. Action sides are listed in capitol letters.

EL RANCHO ROCK (Marks, BMI)

MIDNIGHTER (Golden West, BMI)—The Champs—Challenge 59007

I WONDER WHY (Schwartz, ASCAP)—Dion & The Belmonts—Laurie 3013. Teen Angel (Schwartz, ASCAP)

JENNIE LEE (Daywin, BMI)—Jan & Arnie—Arwin 108—Gotta Getta Date (Daywin, BMI)

All are previous Billboard Spotlight picks.

RECENT POP RELEASES COMING UP STRONG

STORE RECORDED SALES — New York University School of Retailing — The Billboard

FOR SURVEY WEEK ENDING MAY 10

The information given in this chart is based on actual sales to customers in a scientific sample of the nation's retail record outlets during the week ending on the date shown above. Sample design, sample size and all methods used in this continuing study of retail record sales are under the direct and continuing supervision and control of the School of Retailing of New York University.

A Very Precious Love .... *The Ames Brothers*
(ASCAP) RCA Victor 7167

Zorro .... *The Chordettes*
(BMI) Cadence 1349

Most Played by Jockeys

FOR SURVEY WEEK ENDING MAY 10

SIDES are ranked in order of the greatest number of plays on disk jockey radio shows thruout the country. Results are based on The Billboard's weekly survey among the nation's disk jockeys. The reverse side of each record is also listed.

This Week		Last Week	Weeks on Chart
1.	ALL I HAVE TO DO IS DREAM (BMI)—Everly Brothers Claudette (BMI)—Cadence 1348	3	4
2.	WITCH DOCTOR (ASCAP)—David Seville Don't Whistle at Me, Baby (ASCAP)—Liberty 55132	2	6
3.	TWILIGHT TIME (BMI)—Platters Out of My Mind (BMI)—Mer 71289	1	7
4.	WEAR MY RING AROUND YOUR NECK (BMI)—Elvis Presley Doncha' Think It's Time (BMI)—Vic 7240	5	4
5.	HE'S GOT THE WHOLE WORLD IN HIS HANDS (ASCAP)—Laurie London Handed Down (ASCAP)—Cap 3891	4	9
6.	KEWPIE DOLL (ASCAP)—Perry Como Dance Only With Me (ASCAP)—Vic 7202	6	5
7.	CHANSON D'AMOUR (ASCAP)—Art and Dotty Todd Along the Trail With You (ASCAP)—Era 1964	7	5
8.	RETURN TO ME (ASCAP)—Dean Martin Forgetting You (ASCAP)—Cap 3894	8	7
9.	LOOKING BACK (BMI)—Nat King Cole Do I Like It (BMI)—Cap 3939	14	2
10.	BIG MAN (BMI)—Four Preps Stop, Baby (ASCAP)—Cap 3960	13	3
11.	BOOK OF LOVE (BMI)—Monotones You Never Loved Me (BMI)—Argo 5290	9	5
12.	CHANSON D'AMOUR (ASCAP)—Fontane Sisters Cocoanut Grove (ASCAP)—Dot 15736	21	4
13.	SUGAR MOON (BMI)—Pat Boone Cherie, I Love You (ASCAP)—Dot 15750	20	2
14.	SECRETLY (ASCAP)—Jimmie Rodgers Make Me a Miracle (ASCAP)—Roulette 4070	—	1
15.	OH, LONESOME ME (BMI)—Don Gibson I Can't Stop Loving You (BMI)—Vic 7133	10	7
16.	TEQUILA (BMI)—The Champs Train to Nowhere (BMI)—Challenge 1016	12	11
17.	WHO'S SORRY NOW? (ASCAP)—Connie Francis You Were Only Fooling (ASCAP)—M-G-M 12588	15	11
18.	LET THE BELLS KEEP RINGING (BMI)—Paul Anka Crazy Love (BMI)—ABC-Paramount 9907	19	2
19.	JOHNNY B. GOODE (BMI)—Chuck Berry Around and Around (BMI)—Chess 1691	25	2
20.	THERE'S ONLY ONE OF YOU (ASCAP)—Four Lads Blue Tattoo (ASCAP)—Col 41136	11	7
21.	BELIEVE WHAT YOU SAY (BMI)—Ricky Nelson My Bucket's Got a Hole in It (ASCAP)—Imperial 5503	—	3
22.	WHAT AM I LIVING FOR? (BMI)—Chuck Willis Hang Up My Rock and Roll Shoes (BMI)—Atlantic 1179	—	1
23.	DONCHA THINK IT'S TIME? (BMI)—Elvis Presley Wear My Ring Around Your Neck (BMI)—Vic 7240	—	1
24.	TEACHER, TEACHER (ASCAP)—Johnny Mathis All the Time (ASCAP)—Col 41152	—	1
25.	BILLY (ASCAP)—Kathy Linden If I Could Hold You in My Arms (ASCAP)—Felsted 8510	17	7

Top 100 Sides

FOR SURVEY WEEK ENDING MAY 10

This is a tabulation of dealer individual record sales listed according to the specific side requested by customers. No attempt is made to add sides together to reflect actual record sales. This is, therefore, a tabulation of sides or songs, and not records. This is the reason for any possible variation that occurs between the top 50 sides as reflected in this chart, and the top 50 record sellers as reflected in the "Best Sellers in Stores" chart.

Pos.	Song, Artist, Label	Last Week
1.	**ALL I HAVE TO DO IS DREAM,** Everly Brothers, Cadence	2
2.	**WITCH DOCTOR,** David Seville, Liberty	1
3.	**WEAR MY RING AROUND YOUR NECK,** Elvis Presley, Victor	5
4.	**TWILIGHT TIME,** Platters, Mercury	3
5.	**HE'S GOT THE WHOLE WORLD IN HIS HANDS,** Laurie London, Capitol	4
6.	**RETURN TO ME,** Dean Martin, Capitol	6
7.	**BOOK OF LOVE,** Monotones, Argo	7
8.	**LOOKING BACK,** Nat King Cole, Capitol	10
9.	**TEQUILA,** Champs, Challenge	8
10.	**JOHNNY B. GOODE,** Chuck Berry, Chess	11
11.	**OH, LONESOME ME,** Don Gibson, Victor	9
12.	**KEWPIE DOLL,** Perry Como, Victor	13
13.	**CHANSON D'AMOUR,** Art and Dotty Todd, Era	14
14.	**BIG MAN,** Four Preps, Capitol	23
15.	**SUGAR MOON,** Pat Boone, Dot	27
16.	**FOR YOUR LOVE,** Ed Townsend, Capitol	18
17.	**LOLLIPOP,** Chordettes, Cadence	12
18.	**DON'T YOU JUST KNOW IT,** Huey Smith, Ace	17
19.	**LAZY MARY,** Lou Monte, Victor	20
20.	**RUMBLE,** Link Wray, Cadence	38
21.	**SECRETLY,** Jimmie Rodgers, Roulette	48
22.	**YOU,** Aquatones, Fargo	25
23.	**WHO'S SORRY NOW?** Connie Francis, M-G-M	16
24.	**BILLY,** Kathy Linden, Felsted	15
25.	**BELIEVE WHAT YOU SAY,** Ricky Nelson, Imperial	21
26.	**TORERO,** Renato Carosone, Capitol	36
27.	**WHAT AM I LIVING FOR?** Chuck Willis, Atlantic	55
28.	**A WONDERFUL TIME UP THERE,** Pat Boone, Dot	19
29.	**MY BUCKET'S GOT A HOLE IN IT,** Ricky Nelson, Imperial	27
30.	**SICK AND TIRED,** Fats Domino, Imperial	32
31.	**SKINNY MINNIE,** Bill Haley & His Comets, Decca	22
32.	**CRAZY LOVE,** Paul Anka, ABC-Paramount	23
33.	**CLAUDETTE,** Everly Brothers, Cadence	30
34.	**TALK TO ME, TALK TO ME,** Little Willie John, King	36
34.	**LET THE BELLS KEEP RINGING,** Paul Anka, ABC-Paramount	47
36.	**SUGARTIME,** McGuire Sisters, Coral	29
37.	**WE BELONG TOGETHER,** Robert & Johnny, Old Town	40
38.	**HIGH SIGN,** Diamonds, Mercury	55
39.	**CATCH A FALLING STAR,** Perry Como, Victor	30
39.	**TO BE LOVED,** Jackie Wilson, Brunswick	34
41.	**TWENTY-SIX MILES,** Four Preps, Capitol	32
41.	**THE LITTLE BLUE MAN,** Betty Johnson, Atlantic	38
41.	**NEE NEE NA NA NA NA NU NU,** Dickey Doo & the Don'ts, Swan	40
44.	**DON'T,** Elvis Presley, Victor	43
44.	**NOW AND FOR ALWAYS,** George Hamilton IV, ABC-Paramount	55
46.	**JUST MARRIED,** Marty Robbins, Columbia	35
46.	**TUMBLING TUMBLEWEEDS,** Billy Vaughn, Dot	45
48.	**ARE YOU SINCERE?** Andy Williams, Cadence	26
48.	**SAIL ALONG SILVERY MOON,** Billy Vaughn, Dot	40
50.	**HANG UP MY ROCK AND ROLL SHOES,** Chuck Willis, Atlantic	69
50.	**DO YOU WANT TO DANCE?** Bobby Freeman, Josie	81
50.	**I'M SORRY I MADE YOU CRY,** Connie Francis, M-G-M	87
53.	**LITTLE TRAIN,** Marianne Vasel & Erich Storz, Mercury	50
53.	**MARCH FROM THE RIVER KWAI AND "COLONEL BOGEY,"** Mitch Miller, Columbia	59
55.	**TEACHER, TEACHER,** Johnny Mathis, Columbia	67
56.	**IT'S TOO SOON TO KNOW,** Pat Boone, Dot	45
56.	**BREATHLESS,** Jerry Lee Lewis, Sun	49
56.	**YOU EXCITE ME,** Frankie Avalon, Chancellor	54
56.	**TEACHER'S PET,** Doris Day, Columbia	59
56.	**WISHING FOR YOUR LOVE,** Voxpoppers, Mercury	62
56.	**I MET HIM ON A SUNDAY,** Shirelles, Decca	64
62.	**SWEET LITTLE SIXTEEN,** Chuck Berry, Chess	50
62.	**THERE'S ONLY ONE OF YOU,** Four Lads, Columbia	52
62.	**THE WALK,** Jimmy McCracklin, Checker	62
65.	**NO, NO,** Fats Domino, Imperial	55
65.	**A VERY PRECIOUS LOVE,** Ames Brothers, Victor	73
67.	**MAYBE, BABY,** Crickets, Brunswick	52
67.	**BALLAD OF A TEENAGE QUEEN,** Johnny Cash, Sun	59
67.	**EVERY NIGHT,** Chantels, End	65
70.	**CHANSON D'AMOUR,** Fontane Sisters, Dot	73
70.	**JACQUELINE,** Bobby Helms, Decca	82
72.	**I WONDER WHY** Dion & the Belmonts, Laurie	—
72.	**ALL THE TIME,** Johnny Mathis, Columbia	65
74.	**HE'S GOT THE WHOLE WORLD IN HIS HANDS,** Mahalia Jackson, Columbia	82
75.	**OH-OH, I'M FALLING IN LOVE AGAIN,** Jimmie Rodgers, Roulette	73
75.	**BLUEBIRDS OVER THE MOUNTAIN,** Ersel Hickey, Epic	87
77.	**MAKE ME A MIRACLE,** Jimmie Rodgers, Roulette	—
77.	**PRETTY BABY,** Gino & Gina, Mercury	—
77.	**ZORRO,** Chordettes, Cadence	—
77.	**GOOD GOLLY, MISS MOLLY,** Little Richard, Specialty	73
81.	**TEENAGE DOLL,** Tommy Sands, Capitol	—
81.	**ANOTHER TIME, ANOTHER PLACE,** Patti Page, Mercury	87
83.	**ENDLESS SLEEP,** Jody Reynolds, Demon	—
83.	**STAIRWAY OF LOVE,** Marty Robbins, Columbia	69
83.	**COME WHAT MAY,** Clyde McPhatter, Atlantic	98
86.	**DONCHA' THINK IT'S TIME,** Elvis Presley, Victor	44
86.	**DINNER WITH DRAC,** John Zacherle, Cameo	72
86.	**ALL THE WAY,** Frank Sinatra, Capitol	73
86.	**LONELY ISLAND,** Sam Cooke, Keen	85
90.	**HAPPINESS,** Billy & Lillie, Swan	68
90.	**ARRIVEDERCI ROMA,** Roger Williams, Kapp	98
92.	**JENNIE LEE,** Jan & Arnie, Arwin	—
92.	**BEEN SO LONG,** Pastels, Argo	73
92.	**LONG, HOT SUMMER,** Jimmie Rodgers, Roulette	87
92.	**AT THE HOP,** Danny & the Juniors, ABC-Paramount	—
96.	**CHERIE, I LOVE YOU,** Pat Boone, Dot	—
96.	**THE STROLL,** Diamonds, Mercury	69
96.	**HAVE FAITH,** Gene Allison, Vee Jay	73
96.	**MAYBE,** Chantels, End	82
96.	**WITCHCRAFT,** Frank Sinatra, Capitol	85

BEST SELLING POP SINGLES IN STORES

The information given in this chart is based on actual sales to customers in a scientific sample of the nation's retail record outlets during the week ending on the date shown above. Sample design, sample size, and all methods used in this continuing study of retail record sales are under the direct and continuing supervision and control of the School of Retailing of New York University.

FOR SURVEY WEEK ENDING MAY 17, 1958

This Week		Last Week	Weeks on Chart
1.	ALL I HAVE TO DO IS DREAM (BMI)—Everly Brothers / CLAUDETTE (BMI)—Cadence 1348	1	5
2.	WITCH DOCTOR (ASCAP)—David Seville / Don't Whistle at Me, Baby (ASCAP)—Liberty 55132	2	7
3.	WEAR MY RING AROUND YOUR NECK (BMI)—Elvis Presley / DONCHA THINK IT'S TIME? (BMI)—Vic 7240	3	6
4.	TWILIGHT TIME (BMI)—Platters / Out of My Mind (BMI)—Mercury 71289	4	7
5.	LOOKING BACK (BMI)—Nat King Cole / DO I LIKE IT? (BMI)—Cap 3939	7	7
6.	HE'S GOT THE WHOLE WORLD IN HIS HANDS (ASCAP)—Laurie London / Handed Down (ASCAP)—Cap 3891	5	9
7.	RETURN TO ME (ASCAP)—Dean Martin / Forgetting You (ASCAP)—Cap 3894	6	7
8.	BOOK OF LOVE (BMI)—Monotones / You Never Loved Me (BMI)—Argo 5290	8	9
9.	JOHNNY B. GOODE (BMI)—Chuck Berry / Around and Around (BMI)—Chess 1691	10	4
10.	SUGAR MOON (BMI)—Pat Boone / CHERIE, I LOVE YOU (ASCAP)—Dot 15750	15	3
11.	SECRETLY (ASCAP)—Jimmie Rodgers / MAKE ME A MIRACLE (ASCAP)—Roulette 4070	18	3
12.	BIG MAN (BMI)—Four Preps / Stop, Baby (ASCAP)—Cap 3960	14	3
13.	TEQUILA (BMI)—The Champs / Train to Nowhere (BMI)—Challenge 1016	9	13
14.	KEWPIE DOLL (ASCAP)—Perry Como / Dance Only With Me (ASCAP)—Vic 7202	12	6
15.	FOR YOUR LOVE (BMI)—Ed Townsend / Over and Over Again (BMI)—Cap 3926	17	6
16.	WHAT AM I LIVING FOR? (BMI)—Chuck Willis / HANG UP MY ROCK AND ROLL SHOES (BMI)—Atlantic 1179	20	3
17.	CHANSON D'AMOUR (ASCAP)—Art and Dotty Todd / Along the Trail With You (ASCAP)—Era 1064	13	6
18.	OH, LONESOME ME (BMI)—Don Gibson / I CAN'T STOP LOVING YOU (BMI)—Vic 7133	11	11
19.	RUMBLE (BMI)—Link Wray and His Ray Men / The Swag (BMI)—Cadence 1347	25	4
20.	BELIEVE WHAT YOU SAY (BMI)—Ricky Nelson / MY BUCKET'S GOT A HOLE IN IT (ASCAP)—Imperial 5503	16	8
21.	DO YOU WANT TO DANCE? (BMI)—Bobby Freeman / Big Fat Woman (BMI)—Josie 835	48	2
22.	TALK TO ME, TALK TO ME (BMI)—Little Willie John / Spasms (BMI)—King 5108	34	7
23.	CRAZY LOVE (BMI)—Paul Anka / LET THE BELLS KEEP RINGING (BMI)—ABC-Paramount 9907	19	6
24.	YOU (BMI)—Aquatones / She's the Only One for Me (BMI)—Fargo 1001	27	4
25.	DON'T YOU JUST KNOW IT? (BMI)—Huey Smith / High Blood Pressure (BMI)—Ace 545	23	9
26.	TO BE LOVED (BMI)—Jackie Wilson / Come Back to Me (BMI)—Brunswick 55052	39	6
27.	A WONDERFUL TIME UP THERE (BMI)—Pat Boone / IT'S TOO SOON TO KNOW (ASCAP)—Dot 15690	22	15
28.	SICK AND TIRED (BMI)—Fats Domino / NO, NO (BMI)—Imperial 5515	26	4
29.	LOLLIPOP (BMI)—Chordettes / Baby, Come-A Back-A (ASCAP)—Cadence 1345	21	11
30.	TEACHER, TEACHER (ASCAP)—Johnny Mathis / ALL THE TIME (ASCAP)—Col 41152	32	3
31.	JENNIE LEE (BMI)—Jan and Arnie / Gotta Getta Date (BMI)—Arwin 108	—	1
32.	TORERO (ASCAP)—Renato Carosone / Chella Lla (ASCAP)—Cap 71080	30	3
33.	WHO'S SORRY NOW? (ASCAP)—Connie Francis / You Were Only Fooling (ASCAP)—M-G-M 12588	28	13
34.	LAZY MARY (ASCAP)—Lou Monte / Angelique (ASCAP)—Vic 7160	24	11
35.	BILLY (ASCAP)—Kathy Linden / If I Could Hold You in My Arms (ASCAP)—Felsted 8510	29	10
36.	I WONDER WHY? (ASCAP)—Dion and the Belmonts / Teen Angel (ASCAP)—Laurie 3013	—	1
37.	JUST MARRIED (BMI)—Marty Robbins / STAIRWAY OF LOVE (ASCAP)—Col 41143	33	5
38.	ARE YOU SINCERE? (BMI)—Andy Williams / Be Mine Tonight (BMI)—Cadence 1340	47	15
39.	SKINNY MINNIE (ASCAP)—Bill Haley and His Comets / Sway With Me (ASCAP)—Dec 30592	31	6
40.	ENDLESS SLEEP (BMI)—Jody Reynolds / Tight Capris (BMI)—Demon 1507	—	1
41.	ZORRO (BMI)—Chordettes / Love's a Two-Way Street (BMI)—Cadence 1349	—	1
42.	NEE NEE NA NA NA NA NU NU (ASCAP)—Dickey Doo and the Don'ts / Flip-Top Box (BMI)—Swan 4006	42	4
43.	THERE'S ONLY ONE OF YOU (ASCAP)—Four Lads / Blue Tattoo (ASCAP)—Col 41136	—	6
44.	PADRE (ASCAP)—Toni Arden / All at Once (ASCAP)—Dec 30628	—	1
45.	THE HIGH SIGN (BMI)—Diamonds / Chick-Lets (BMI)—Mercury 71291	37	2
46.	SAIL ALONG SILVERY MOON (ASCAP)—Billy Vaughn / RAUNCHY (BMI)—Dot 15661	44	23
47.	WE BELONG TOGETHER (BMI)—Robert and Johnny / In the Rain (BMI)—Old Town 1047	36	10
48.	SUGARTIME (BMI)—McGuire Sisters / Banana Split (BMI)—Coral 61924	35	21
49.	THE WALK (BMI)—Jimmy McCracklin / I'm to Blame (BMI)—Checker 885	—	11
50.	MARCH FROM THE RIVER KWAI AND "COLONEL BOGEY" (ASCAP)—Mitch Miller / Hey! Little Baby (BMI)—Col 41066	—	17

THIS WEEK'S BEST BUYS

Special telephone reports and/or chart action indicate these recent releases have either broken out in one or more key areas or have leaped onto the charts and have excellent potential for placing among the Top 30 of The Billboard's Best Selling Pop Singles in Stores chart. Action sides are listed in capitol letters.

THE PURPLE PEOPLE EATER (Cordial, BMI)—**Sheb Wooley**—M-G-M 12651.
I Can't Believe You're Mine (Robertson, ASCAP).
A previous Billboard Spotlight pick.
The following records, not previously selected as "Best Buys," are on the charts for the first time this week.

ENDLESS SLEEP (Johnston-Montei-Elizabeth, BMI)—**Jody Reynolds** Demon 1507.
Tight Capris (Johnston-Montei-Elizabeth, BMI)
A previous Billboard Spotlight pick.

PADRE (Ross-Jungnickel, ASCAP)—**Toni Arden**—Decca 30628
All at Once (Rosemeadow, ASCAP).

RECENT POP RELEASES COMING UP STRONG

FOR SURVEY WEEK ENDING MAY 17

The information given in this chart is based on actual sales to customers in a scientific sample of the nation's retail record outlets during the week ending on the date shown above. Sample design, sample size and all methods used in this continuing study of retail record sales are under the direct and continuing supervision and control of the School of Retailing of New York University.

El Rancho Rock . . . . ***The Champs***
(BMI) Challenge 59007

A Very Precious Love . . . . ***The Ames Brothers***
(ASCAP) RCA Victor 7167

Most Played by Jockeys

FOR SURVEY WEEK ENDING MAY 17

SIDES are ranked in order of the greatest number of plays on disk jockey radio shows thruout the country. Results are based on The Billboard's weekly survey among the nation's disk jockeys. The reverse side of each record is also listed.

This Week		Last Week	Weeks on Chart
1.	ALL I HAVE TO DO IS DREAM (BMI)—Everly Brothers Claudette (BMI)—Cadence 1348	1	5
2.	WITCH DOCTOR (ASCAP)—David Seville Don't Whistle at Me, Baby (ASCAP)—Liberty 55132	2	7
3.	TWILIGHT TIME (BMI)—Platters Out of My Mind (BMI)—Mer 71289	3	8
4.	WEAR MY RING AROUND YOUR NECK (BMI)—Elvis Presley Doncha' Think It's Time (BMI)—Vic 7240	4	5
5.	HE'S GOT THE WHOLE WORLD IN HIS HANDS (ASCAP)—Laurie London Handed Down (ASCAP)—Cap 3891	5	10
6.	RETURN TO ME (ASCAP)—Dean Martin Forgetting You (ASCAP)—Cap 3894	8	8
7.	BIG MAN (BMI)—Four Preps Stop, Baby (ASCAP)—Cap 3960	10	4
8.	KEWPIE DOLL (ASCAP)—Perry Como Dance Only With Me (ASCAP)—Vic 7202	6	6
9.	CHANSON D'AMOUR (ASCAP)—Art and Dotty Todd Along the Trail With You (ASCAP)—Era 1964	7	6
10.	SUGAR MOON (BMI)—Pat Boone Cherie, I Love You (ASCAP)—Dot 15750	13	3
11.	SECRETLY (ASCAP)—Jimmie Rodgers Make Me a Miracle (ASCAP)—Roulette 4070	14	2
12.	CHANSON D'AMOUR (ASCAP)—Fontane Sisters Cocoanut Grove (ASCAP)—Dot 15736	12	5
13.	OH, LONESOME ME (BMI)—Don Gibson I Can't Stop Loving You (BMI)—Vic 7133	15	8
14.	LOOKING BACK (BMI)—Nat King Cole Do I Like It (BMI)—Cap 3939	9	3
15.	DONCHA THINK IT'S TIME? (BMI)—Elvis Presley Wear My Ring Around Your Neck (BMI)—Vic 7240	23	2
16.	MAKE ME A MIRACLE (ASCAP)—Jimmie Rodgers Secretly (ASCAP)—Roulette 4070	—	1
17.	JOHNNY B. GOODE (BMI)—Chuck Berry Around and Around (BMI)—Chess 1691	19	3
18.	BOOK OF LOVE (BMI)—Monotones You Never Loved Me (BMI)—Argo 5290	11	6
19.	WHAT AM I LIVING FOR? (BMI)—Chuck Willis Hang Up My Rock and Roll Shoes (BMI)—Atlantic 1179	22	2
20.	TORERO (ASCAP)—Renato Carosone Chell Lla (ASCAP)—Cap 71080	—	1
21.	FOR YOUR LOVE (BMI)—Ed Townsend Over and Over Again (BMI)—Cap 3926	—	1
22.	YOU NEED HANDS (ASCAP)—Eydie Gorme Dormi Dormi Dormi (ASCAP)—ABC-Paramount 9925	—	1
23.	BILLY (ASCAP)—Kathy Linden If I Could Hold You in My Arms (ASCAP)—Felsted 8510	25	8
24.	ALL THE TIME (ASCAP)—Johnny Mathis Teacher, Teacher (ASCAP)—Col 41152	—	3
25.	ZORRO (BMI)—Chordettes Love's a Two-Way Street (BMI)—Cadence 1349	—	1

Top 100 Sides

NEW YORK UNIVERSITY SCHOOL OF RETAILING · STORE RECORDED SALES · THE BILLBOARD

FOR SURVEY WEEK ENDING MAY 17

This is a tabulation of dealer individual record sales listed according to the specific side requested by customers. No attempt is made to add sides together to reflect actual record sales. This is, therefore, a tabulation of sides or songs, and not records. This is the reason for any possible variation that occurs between the top 50 sides as reflected in this chart, and the top 50 record sellers as reflected in the "Best Sellers in Stores" chart.

Pos.	Song, Artist, Label	Last Week
1.	**ALL I HAVE TO DO IS DREAM,** Everly Brothers, Cadence	1
2.	**WITCH DOCTOR,** David Seville, Liberty	2
3.	**WEAR MY RING AROUND YOUR NECK,** Elvis Presley, Victor	3
4.	**TWILIGHT TIME,** Platters, Mercury	4
5.	**HE'S GOT THE WHOLE WORLD IN HIS HANDS—** Laurie London, Capitol	1
6.	**LOOKING BACK,** Nat King Cole, Capitol	8
7.	**RETURN TO ME,** Dean Martin, Capitol	6
8.	**BOOK OF LOVE,** Monotones, Argo	7
9.	**JOHNNY B. GOODE,** Chuck Berry, Chess	10
10.	**BIG MAN,** Four Preps, Capitol	14
11.	**TEQUILA,** Champs, Challenge	9
12.	**SUGAR MOON,** Pat Boone, Dot	15
13.	**SECRETLY,** Jimmie Rodgers, Roulette	21
14.	**KEWPIE DOLL,** Perry Como, Victor	12
15.	**FOR YOUR LOVE,** Ed Townsend Capitol	16
16.	**CHANSON D'AMOUR,** Art and Dotty Todd, Era	13
17.	**OH, LONESOME ME,** Don Gibson, Victor	11
18.	**RUMBLE,** Link Wray, Cadence	20
19.	**DO YOU WANT TO DANCE?** Bobby Freeman, Josie	50
20.	**TALK TO ME, TALK TO ME,** Little Willie John, King	34
21.	**YOU,** Aquatones, Fargo	22
22.	**DON'T YOU JUST KNOW IT,** Huey Smith, Ace	18
23.	**TO BE LOVED,** Jackie Wilson, Brunswick	39
24.	**HANG UP MY ROCK AND ROLL SHOES,** Chuck Berry, Chess	50
25.	**LOLLIPOP,** Chordettes, Cadence	17
26.	**WHAT AM I LIVING FOR?** Chuck Willis, Atlantic	27
27.	**TORERO,** Renate Carosone, Capitol	26
27.	**JENNIE LEE,** Jan and Arnie, Arwin	92
29.	**LAZY MARY,** Lou Monte, Victor	19
29.	**WHO'S SORRY NOW,** Connie Francis, M-G-M	23
31.	**BELIEVE WHAT YOU SAY,** Ricky Nelson, Imperial	21
31.	**MY BUCKET'S GOT A HOLE IN IT,** Ricky Nelson, Imperial	29
33.	**BILLY,** Kathy Linden, Felsted	24
34.	**SICK AND TIRED,** Fats Domino, Imperial	30
35.	**ARE YOU SINCERE?** Andy Williams, Cadence	48
35.	**I WONDER WHY,** Dion and the Belmonts, Laurie	72
37.	**SKINNY MINNIE,** Bill Haley and His Comets, Decca	31
37.	**CRAZY LOVE,** Paul Anka, ABC-Paramount	32
39.	**A WONDERFUL TIME UP THERE,** Pat Boone, Dot	28
39.	**LET THE BELLS KEEP RINGING,** Paul Anka, ABC-Paramount	34
39.	**ENDLESS SLEEP,** Jody Reynolds, Demon	83
42.	**NEE NEE NA NA NA NA NU NU,** Dickey Doo and the Don'ts, Swan	41
42.	**ZORRO,** Chordettes, Cadence	77
44.	**THERE'S ONLY ONE OF YOU,** Four Lads, Columbia	62
45.	**PADRE,** Toni Arden, Decca	—
45.	**HIGH SIGN,** Diamonds, Mercury	38
45.	**JUST MARRIED,** Marty Robbins, Columbia	46
48.	**WE BELONG TOGETHER,** Robert and Johnny, Old Town	37
49.	**SUGARTIME,** McGuire Sisters, Coral	36
50.	**MARCH FORM THE RIVER KWAI AND "COLONEL BOGEY,"** Mitch Miller, Columbia	53
50.	**THE WALK,** Jimmy McCracklin, Checker	62
52.	**I'M SORRY I MADE YOU CRY,** Connie Francis, M-G-M	50
53.	**TEACHER, TEACHER,** Johnny Mathis, Columbia	55
54.	**LITTLE TRAIN,** Marianne Vasel and Erich Storz, Mercury	53
54.	**MAKE ME A MIRACLE,** Jimmie Rodgers, Roulette	77
56.	**CATCH A FALLING STAR,** Perry Como, Victor	39
56.	**SAIL ALONG SILVERY MOON,** Billy Vaughn, Dot	48
56.	**IT'S TOO SOON TO KNOW,** Pat Boone, Dot	56
56.	**ALL THE TIME,** Johnny Mathis, Columbia	72
56.	**PRETTY BABY,** Gino and Gina, Mercury	77
61.	**BREATHLESS,** Jerry Lee Lewis, Sun	56
61.	**YOU EXCITE ME,** Frankie Avalon, Chancellor	56
63.	**TUMBLING TUMBLEWEEDS,** Billy Vaughn, Dot	46
63.	**EVERY NIGHT,** Chantels End	67
65.	**I MET HIM ON A SUNDAY,** Shirelles, Decca	56
65.	**A VERY PRECIOUS LOVE,** Ames Brothers, Victor	65
65.	**MAYBE, BABY,** Crickets, Brunswick	67
68.	**EL RANCHO ROCK,** Champs, Challenge	—
68.	**TWENTY-SIX MILES,** Four Preps, Capitol	41
68.	**NOW AND FOR ALWAYS,** George Hamilton IV, ABC-Paramount	44
68.	**SWEET LITTLE SIXTEEN,** Chuck Berry, Chess	62
68.	**CHANSON D'AMOUR,** Fontane Sisters, Dot	70
73.	**CLAUDETTE,** Everly Brothers Cadence	33
73.	**TEACHER'S PET,** Doris Day, Columbia	56
73.	**BALLAD OF A TEENAGE QUEEN,** Johnny Cash, Sun	67
73.	**LONELY ISLAND,** Sam Cooke, Keen	86
77.	**NO, NO,** Fats Domino, Imperial	65
77.	**JACQUELINE,** Bobby Helms, Decca	70
79.	**BEEN SO LONG,** Pastels, Argo	92
80.	**WISHING FOR YOUR LOVE,** Voxpoppers, Mercury	56
81.	**THE LITTLE BLUE MAN,** Betty Johnson, Atlantic	41
81.	**DON'T,** Elvis Presley, Victor	44
81.	**GOOD GOLLY, MISS MOLLY,** Little Richard, Specialty	77
84.	**HE'S GOT THE WHOLE WORLD IN HIS HANDS,** Laurie London, Capitol	74
84.	**BLUEBIRDS OVER THE MOUNTAIN,** Ersel Hickey, Epic	75
84.	**ANOTHER TIME, ANOTHER PLACE,** Patti Page, Mercury	81
84.	**LONG HOT SUMMER,** Jimmie Rodgers, Roulette	92
84.	**CHERIE, I LOVE YOU,** Pat Boone, Dot	96
89.	**TEENAGE DOLL,** Tommy Sands, Capitol	81
90.	**OH-OH, I'M FALLING IN LOVE AGAIN,** Jimmie Rodgers, Roulette	75
91.	**PINK PEDAL PUSHERS,** Carl Perkins, Columbia	—
91.	**COME WHAT MAY,** Clyde McPhatter. Atlantic	83
91.	**STAIRWAY OF LOVE,** Marty Robbins, Columbia	83
91.	**ALL THE WAY,** Frank Sinatra, Capitol	86
91.	**DINNER WITH DRAC,** John Zacherle, Cameo	86
91.	**ARRIVEDERCI ROMA,** Roger Williams, Kapp	90
97.	**ARRIVEDERCI ROMA,** Mario Lanza, Victor	—
97.	**HOW ARE YOU FIXED FOR LOVE,** Frank Sinatra and Keely Smith Capitol	—
97.	**RAVE ON,** Buddy Holly, Coral	—
97.	**HAPPINESS,** Billy and Lillie, Swan	90

BEST SELLING POP SINGLES IN STORES

The information given in this chart is based on actual sales to customers in a scientific sample of the nation's retail record outlets during the week ending on the date shown above. Sample design, sample size, and all methods used in this continuing study of retail record sales are under the direct and continuing supervision and control of the School of Retailing of New York University.

FOR SURVEY WEEK ENDING MAY 24, 1958

This Week		Last Week	Weeks on Chart
1.	**ALL I HAVE TO DO IS DREAM** (BMI)—Everly Brothers; **CLAUDETTE** (BMI)—Cadence 1348	1	6
2.	**WITCH DOCTOR** (ASCAP)—David Seville; Don't Whistle at Me, Baby (ASCAP)—Liberty 55132	2	8
3.	**WEAR MY RING AROUND YOUR NECK** (BMI)—Elvis Presley; **DONCHA' THINK IT'S TIME** (BMI)—Vic 7240	3	7
4.	**TWILIGHT TIME** (BMI)—Platters; Out of My Mind (BMI)—Mer 71289	4	8
5.	**LOOKING BACK** (BMI)—Nat King Cole; **DO I LIKE IT** (BMI)—Cap 3939	5	8
6.	**BIG MAN** (BMI)—Four Preps; Stop, Baby (ASCAP)—Cap 3960	12	4
7.	**PURPLE PEOPLE EATER** (BMI)—Sheb Wooley; I Can't Believe You're Mine (ASCAP)—M-G-M 12651	—	1
8.	**SECRETLY** (ASCAP)—Jimmie Rodgers; **MAKE ME A MIRACLE** (ASCAP)—Roulette 4070	11	4
9.	**HE'S GOT THE WHOLE WORLD IN HIS HANDS** (ASCAP)—Laurie London; Handed Down (ASCAP)—Cap 3891	6	10
10.	**DO YOU WANT TO DANCE?** (BMI)—Bobby Freeman; Big Fat Woman (BMI)—Josie 835	21	3
11.	**JOHNNY B. GOODE** (BMI)—Chuck Berry; Around and Around (BMI)—Chess 1691	9	5
12.	**RETURN TO ME** (ASCAP)—Dean Martin; Forgetting You (ASCAP)—Cap 3894	7	8
13.	**SUGAR MOON** (BMI)—Pat Boone; **CHERIE, I LOVE YOU** (ASCAP)—Dot 15750	10	4
14.	**BOOK OF LOVE** (BMI)—Monotones; You Never Loved Me (BMI)—Argo 5290	8	10
15.	**CHANSON D'AMOUR** (ASCAP)—Art and Dotty Todd; Along the Trail With You (ASCAP)—Era 1064	17	7
16.	**JENNIE LEE** (BMI)—Jan and Arnie; Gotta Getta Date (BMI)—Arwin 108	31	2
17.	**WHAT AM I LIVING FOR?** (BMI)—Chuck Willis; **HANG UP MY ROCK AND ROLL SHOES** (BMI)—Atlantic 1179	16	4
18.	**FOR YOUR LOVE** (BMI)—Ed Townsend; Over and Over Again (BMI)—Cap 3926	15	7
19.	**KEWPIE DOLL** (ASCAP)—Perry Como; Dance Only With Me (ASCAP)—Vic 7202	14	7
20.	**OH, LONESOME ME** (BMI)—Don Gibson; **I CAN'T STOP LOVING YOU** (BMI)—Vic 7133	18	12
21.	**RUMBLE** (BMI)—Link Wray and His Ray Men; The Swag (BMI)—Cadence 1347	19	5
22.	**TALK TO ME, TALK TO ME** (BMI)—Little Willie John; Spasms (BMI)—King 5108	22	8
23.	**TO BE LOVED** (BMI)—Jackie Wilson; Come Back to Me (BMI)—Brunswick 55052	26	7
24.	**LET THE BELLS KEEP RINGING** (BMI)—Paula Anka; **CRAZY LOVE** (BMI)—ABC Paramount 9907	23	7
25.	**TEQUILA** (BMI)—The Champs; Train to Nowhere (BMI)—Challenge 1016	13	14
26.	**YOU** (BMI)—Aquatones; She's the One for Me (BMI)—Fargo 1001	24	5
27.	**BELIEVE WHAT YOU SAY** (BMI)—Ricky Nelson; **MY BUCKET'S GOT A HOLE IN IT** (ASCAP)—Imperial 5503	20	9
28.	**ENDLESS SLEEP** (BMI)—Jody Reynolds; Tight Capris (BMI)—Demon 1507	40	2
29.	**PADRE** (ASCAP)—Toni Arden; All at Once (ASCAP)—Dec 30628	44	2
30.	**TORERO** (ASCAP)—Renato Carosone; Chella Lla (ASCAP)—Cap 71080	32	4
31.	**ZORRO** (BMI)—Chordettes; Love's a Two-Way Street (BMI)—Cadence 1349	41	2
32.	**I WONDER WHY** (ASCAP)—Don and the Belmonts; Teen Angel (ASCAP)—Laurie 3013	36	2
33.	**SICK AND TIRED** (BMI)—Fats Domino; **NO, NO** (BMI)—Imperial 5515	28	5
34.	**TEACHER, TEACHER** (ASCAP)—Johnny Mathis; **ALL THE TIME** (ASCAP)—Col 41152	30	4
35.	**ARE YOU SINCERE?** (BMI)—Andy Williams; Be Mine Tonight (BMI)—Cadence 1340	38	16
36.	**JUST MARRIED** (BMI)—Marty Robbins; **STAIRWAY OF LOVE** (ASCAP)—Col 41143	37	6
37.	**HIGH SCHOOL CONFIDENTIAL** (BMI)—Jerry Lee Lewis; Fools Like Me (BMI)—Sun 296	—	1
38.	**THE WALK** (BMI)—Jimmy McCracklin; I'm to Blame (BMI)—Checker 885	49	12
39.	**EL RANCHO ROCK** (BMI)—Champs; Midnighter (BMI)—Challenge 59007	—	1
40.	**BILLY** (ASCAP)—Kathy Linden; If I Could Hold You in My Arms (ASCAP)—Felsted 8510	35	11
41.	**LOLLIPOP** (BMI)—Chordettes; Baby, Come-A Back-A (ASCAP)—Cadence 1345	29	12
42.	**WHO'S SORRY NOW** (ASCAP)—Connie Francis; You Were Only Fooling (ASCAP)—M-G-M 12588	33	14
43.	**DON'T YOU JUST KNOW IT** (BMI)—Huey Smith; High Blood Pressure (BMI)—Ace 545	25	10
44.	**I'M SORRY I MADE YOU CRY** (ASCAP)—Connie Francis; Lock Up Your Heart (BMI)—M-G-M 12647	—	2
45.	**PRETTY BABY** (BMI)—Gino and Gina; Love's a Carousel (BMI)—Mercury 71233	—	1
45.	**RAVE ON** (BMI)—Buddy Holly; Take Your Time (BMI)—Coral 61985	—	1
47.	**A WONDERFUL TIME UP THERE** (BMI)—Pat Boone; **IT'S TOO SOON TO KNOW** (ASCAP)—Dot 15690	27	16
48.	**THERE'S ONLY ONE OF YOU** (ASCAP)—Four Lads; Blue Tattoo (ASCAP)—Col 41136	43	7
49.	**GUESS THINGS HAPPEN THAT WAY** (BMI)—Johnny Cash; **COME IN, STRANGER** (BMI)—Sun 295	—	1
50.	**LAZY MARY** (ASCAP)—Lou Monte; Angelique (ASCAP)—Vic 7160	34	12

THIS WEEK'S BEST BUYS

Special telephone reports and/or chart action indicate these recent releases have either broken out in one or more key areas or have leaped onto the charts and have excellent potential for placing among the Top 30 of The Billboard's Best Selling Pop Singles in Stores chart. Action sides are listed in capitol letters.

YOU NEED HANDS (Leeds, ASCAP)—Edye Gorme—ABC-Paramount 9925. **Dormi, Dormi, Dormi** (Paramount, ASCAP)

I KNOW WHERE I'M GOIN' (Gil, BMI)—George Hamilton IV—ABC-Paramount 9924

WHO'S TAKING YOU TO THE PROM? (Kahl, BMI)
Both are previous Billboard Spotlight picks.

The following records, not previously selected as Best Buys, are on the charts for the first time this week.

HIGH SCHOOL CONFIDENTIAL (Penron, BMI)—Jerry Lee Lewis—Sun 296. Fools Like Me (Knox, BMI)

GUESS THINGS HAPPEN THAT WAY (Knox, BMI)—Johnny Cash—Sun 295. **Come In, Stranger** (Johnny Cash, BMI)

RAVE ON (Nor-Va-Jak, BMI)—Buddy Holly—Coral 61985. **Take Your Time** (Nor-Va-Jak, BMI)
All are previous Billboard Spotlight picks.

PRETTY BABY (Figure, BMI)—Gino and Gina—Mercury 71283. **Love's a Carousel** (Figure, BMI)

RECENT POP RELEASES COMING UP STRONG

FOR SURVEY WEEK ENDING MAY 24

The information given in this chart is based on actual sales to customers in a scientific sample of the nation's retail record outlets during the week ending on the date shown above. Sample design, sample size and all methods used in this continuing study of retail record sales are under the direct and continuing supervision and control of the School of Retailing of New York University.

Cha Cha Cha . . . . . *The Pets*
(BMI) Arwin 109

Yakety Yak . . . . . *The Coasters*
(BMI) Atco 6116

You Need Hands . . . . . *Eydie Gorme*
(ASCAP) ABC-Paramount 9925

Most Played by Jockeys

FOR SURVEY WEEK ENDING MAY 24

SIDES are ranked in order of the greatest number of plays on disk jockey radio shows thruout the country. Results are based on The Billboard's weekly survey among the nation's disk jockeys. The reverse side of each record is also listed.

This Week		Last Week	Weeks on Chart
1.	ALL I HAVE TO DO IS DREAM (BMI)—Everly Brothers Claudette (BMI)—Cadence 1348	1	6
2.	TWILIGHT TIME (BMI)—Platters Out of My Mind (BMI)—Mer 71289	3	9
3.	WITCH DOCTOR (ASCAP)—David Seville Don't Whistle at Me, Baby (ASCAP)—Liberty 55132	2	8
4.	RETURN TO ME (ASCAP)—Dean Martin Forgetting You (ASCAP)—Cap 3894	6	9
5.	WEAR MY RING AROUND YOUR NECK (BMI)—Elvis Presley Doncha' Think It's Time (BMI)—Vic 7240	4	6
6.	KEWPIE DOLL (ASCAP)—Perry Como Dance Only With Me (ASCAP)—Vic 7202	8	7
7.	BIG MAN (BMI)—Four Preps Stop, Baby (ASCAP)—Cap 3960	7	5
8.	SUGAR MOON (BMI)—Pat Boone Cherie, I Love You (ASCAP)—Dot 15750	10	4
9.	HE'S GOT THE WHOLE WORLD IN HIS HANDS—(ASCAP)—Laurie London Handed Down (ASCAP)—Cap 3891	5	11
10.	PURPLE PEOPLE EATER (BMI)—Sheb Wooley I Can't Believe You're Mine (ASCAP)—M-G-M 12651	—	1
11.	CHANSON D'AMOUR (ASCAP)—Art and Dotty Todd Along the Trail With You (ASCAP)—Era 1064	9	7
12.	SECRETLY (ASCAP)—Jimmie Rodgers Make Me a Miracle (ASCAP)—Roulette 4070	11	3
13.	LOOKING BACK (BMI)—Nat King Cole Do I Like It (BMI)—Cap 3939	14	4
14.	WHAT AM I LIVING FOR? (BMI)—Chuck Willis Hang Up My Rock and Roll Shoes (BMI)—Atlantic 1179	19	3
15.	CHANSON D'AMOUR (ASCAP)—Fontane Sisters Cocoanut Grove (ASCAP)—Dot 15736	12	6
16.	JOHNNY B. GOODE (BMI)—Chuck Berry Around and Around (BMI)—Chess 1691	17	4
17.	YOU NEED HANDS (ASCAP)—Eydie Gorme Dormi, Dormi, Dormi (ASCAP)—ABC-Paramount 9925	22	2
18.	TORERO (ASCAP)—Renato Carosone Chell Lla (ASCAP)—Cap 71080	20	2
19.	OH, LONESOME ME (BMI)—Don Gibson I Can't Stop Loving You (BMI)—Vic 7133	13	9
20.	FOR YOUR LOVE (BMI)—Ed Townsend Over and Over Again (BMI)—Cap 3926	21	2
21.	TEACHER, TEACHER (ASCAP)—Johnny Mathis All the Time (ASCAP)—Col 41152	—	2
22.	ZORRO (BMI)—Chordettes Love's a Two-Way Street (BMI)—Cadence 1349	25	2
23.	A VERY PRECIOUS LOVE (ASCAP)—Ames Brothers Don't Leave Me Now (BMI)—Vic 7167	—	2
24.	BOOK OF LOVE (BMI)—Monotones You Never Loved Me (BMI)—Argo 5290	18	7
25.	JENNIE LEE (BMI)—Jan and Arnie Gotta Getta Date (BMI)—Arwin 108	—	1
25.	LET THE BELLS KEEP RINGING (BMI)—Paul Anka Crazy Love (BMI)—ABC-Paramount 9907	—	3

Top 100 Sides

FOR SURVEY WEEK ENDING MAY 24

This is a tabulation of dealer individual record sales listed according to the specific side requested by customers. No attempt is made to add sides together to reflect actual record sales. This is, therefore, a tabulation of sides or songs, and not records. This is the reason for any possible variation that occurs between the top 50 sides as reflected in this chart, and the top 50 record sellers as reflected in the "Best Sellers in Stores" chart.

Pos.	Song, Artist, Label,	Last Week
1.	**ALL I HAVE TO DO IS DREAM,** Everly Brothers, Cadence	1
2.	**WITCH DOCTOR,** David Seville, Liberty	2
3.	**WEAR MY RING AROUND YOUR NECK,** Elvis Presley, Victor	3
4.	**TWILIGHT TIME,** Platters, Mercury	4
5.	**BIG MAN,** Four Preps, Capitol	10
6.	**LOOKING BACK,** Nat King Cole, Capitol	5
7.	**THE PURPLE PEOPLE EATER,** Sheb Wooley, M-G-M	—
8.	**HE'S GOT THE WHOLE WORLD IN HIS HANDS,** Laurie London, Capitol	5
9.	**DO YOU WANT TO DANCE?** Bobby Freeman, Josie	19
10.	**JOHNNY B. GOODE,** Chuck Berry, Chess	9
11.	**SECRETLY,** Jimmie Rodgers, Roulette	13
12.	**RETURN TO ME,** Dean Martin, Capitol	7
13.	**BOOK OF LOVE,** Monotones, Argo	8
14.	**SUGAR MOON,** Pat Boone, Dot	12
14.	**CHANSON D'AMOUR,** Art and Dotty Todd, Era	16
16.	**JENNIE LEE,** Jan and Arnie, Arwin	27
17.	**FOR YOUR LOVE,** Ed Townsend, Capitol	15
18.	**KEWPIE DOLL,** Perry Como, Victor	14
19.	**OH, LONESOME ME,** Don Gibson, Victor	17
20.	**RUMBLE,** Link Wray, Cadence	18
20.	**TALK TO ME, TALK TO ME,** Little Willie John, King	20
22.	**TO BE LOVED,** Jackie Wilson, Brunswick	23
23.	**TEQUILA,** Champs, Challenge	11
24.	**WHAT AM I LIVING FOR?** Chuck Willis, Atlantic	26
25.	**YOU,** Aquatones, Fargo	21
26.	**ENDLESS SLEEP,** Jody Reynolds, Demon	39
27.	**PADRE,** Toni Arden, Decca	45
28.	**TORERO,** Renate Carosone, Capitol	27
29.	**ZORRO,** Chordettes, Cadence	42
30.	**I WONDER WHY,** Dion and the Belmonts, Laurie	35
31.	**ARE YOU SINCERE?** Andy Williams, Cadence	35
32.	**HANG UP MY ROCK AND ROLL SHOES,** Chuck Willis, Atlantic	24
33.	**SICK AND TIRED,** Fats Domino, Imperial	34
34.	**HIGH SCHOOL CONFIDENTIAL,** Jerry Lee Lewis, Sun	—
34.	**LET THE BELLS KEEP RINGING,** Paul Anka, ABC-Paramount	39
34.	**THE WALK,** Jimmy McCracklin, Checker	50
37.	**BELIEVE WHAT YOU SAY,** Ricky Nelson, Imperial	31
37.	**BILLY,** Kathy Linden, Felsted	33
37.	**EL RONCHO ROCK,** Champs, Challenge	68
40.	**LOLLIPOP,** Chordettes, Cadence	25
41.	**WHO'S SORRY NOW,** Connie Francis, M-G-M	29
41.	**JUST MARRIED,** Marty Robbins, Columbia	45
43.	**DON'T YOU JUST KNOW IT,** Huey Smith, Ace	22
44.	**CRAZY LOVE,** Paul Anka, ABC-Paramount	37
45.	**I'M SORRY I MADE YOU CRY,** Connie Francis, M-G-M	52
46.	**THERE'S ONLY ONE OF YOU,** Four Lads, Columbia	44
46.	**PRETTY BABY,** Gino and Gina, Mercury	56
46.	**RAVE ON,** Buddy Holly, Coral	97
49.	**LAZY MARY,** Lou Monte, Victor	29
50.	**SKINNY MINNIE,** Bill Haley and His Comets, Decca	37
51.	**CHA HUA HUA,** Pets, Arwin	—
52.	**YAKETY YAK,** Coasters, Atco	—
52.	**MY BUCKET'S GOT A HOLE IN IT,** Ricky Nelson, Imperial	—
54.	**TEACHER, TEACHER,** Johnny Mathis, Columbia	53
54.	**ALL THE TIME,** Johnny Mathis, Columbia	56
56.	**GUESS THINGS HAPPEN THAT WAY,** Johnny Cash, Sun	—
56.	**YOU NEED HANDS,** Eydie Gorme, ABC-Paramount	—
56.	**A WONDERFUL TIME UP THERE,** Pat Boone, Dot	39
56.	**MARCH FROM THE RIVER KWAI AND "COLONEL BOGEY,"** Mitch Miller, Columbia	50
60.	**I MET HIM ON A SUNDAY,** Shirelles, Decca	65
61.	**CATCH A FALLING STAR,** Perry Como, Victor	56
61.	**YOU EXCITE ME,** Frankie Avalon, Chancellor	61
63.	**SAIL ALONG SILVERY MOON,** Billy Vaughn, Dot	56
64.	**WOODCHOPPERS' BALL,** Hutch Davie, Atco	—
64.	**NEE NEE NA NA NA NA NU NU,** Dickey Doo and the Don'ts, Swan	42
64.	**LITTLE TRAIN,** Marianne Vasel and Erich Storz, Mercury	54
67.	**HIGH SIGN,** Diamonds, Mercury	45
67.	**WE BELONG TOGETHER,** Robert and Johnny, Old Town	48
67.	**BALLAD OF A TEENAGE QUEEN,** Johnny Cash, Sun	73
67.	**LONELY ISLAND,** Sam Cooke, Keen	73
71.	**JENNIE LEE,** Billy Ward, Liberty	—
72.	**A VERY PRECIOUS LOVE,** Ames Brothers, Victor	65
73.	**MAKE ME A MIRACLE,** Jimmie Rodgers, Roulette	54
73.	**EVERY NIGHT,** Chantels, End	63
73.	**CHANSON D'AMOUR,** Fontane Sisters, Dot	68
73.	**TEACHER'S PET,** Doris Day, Columbia	73
77.	**CHERIE, I LOVE YOU,** Pat Boone, Dot	—
77.	**SEND ME THE PILLOW YOU DREAM ON,** Hank Locklin, Victor	—
77.	**TUMBLING TUMBLEWEEDS,** Billy Vaughn, Dot	63
77.	**NOW AND FOR ALWAYS,** George Hamilton IV, ABC-Paramount	68
77.	**JACQUELINE,** Bobby Helms, Decca	77
77.	**LONG HOT SUMMER,** Jimmie Rodgers, Roulette	84
83.	**SWEET LITTLE SIXTEEN,** Chuck Berry, Chess	68
83.	**TWENTY-SIX MILES,** Four Preps, Capitol	68
83.	**CLAUDETTE,** Everlyn Brothers, Cadence	73
83.	**BEEN SO LONG,** Pastels, Argo	79
83.	**COME WHAT MAY,** Clyde McPhatter, Atlantic	91
88.	**BREATHLESS,** Jerry Lee Lewis, Sun	61
88.	**MAYBE, BABY,** Crickets, Brunswick	65
88.	**DON'T,** Elvis Presley, Victor	81
91.	**SUGARTIME,** McGuire Sisters, Coral	49
91.	**NO. NO,** Fats Domino, Imperial	77
91.	**HE'S GOT THE WHOLE WORLD IN HIS HANDS,** Mahalia Jackson, Columbia	84
94.	**TRY THE IMPOSSIBLE,** Lee Andrews & The Hearts, United Artist	—
94.	**IT'S TOO SOON TO KNOW,** Pat Boone, Dot	56
94.	**DINNER WITH DRAC,** John Zacherle, Cameo	91
94.	**DO I LIKE IT,** Nat King Cole, Capitol	—
94.	**HAVE FAITH,** Gene Allison, Vee Jay	—
94.	**I CAN'T STOP LOVING YOU,** Don Gibson, Victor	—
100.	**ARRIVEDERCI ROMA,** Roger Williams, Kapp	91

BEST SELLING POP SINGLES IN STORES

The information given in this chart is based on actual sales to customers in a scientific sample of the nation's retail record outlets during the week ending on the date shown above. Sample design, sample size, and all methods used in this continuing study of retail record sales are under the direct and continuing supervision and control of the School of Retailing of New York University.

FOR SURVEY WEEK ENDING MAY 31, 1958

This Week	Title	Last Week	Weeks on Chart
1.	**PURPLE PEOPLE EATER** (BMI)—Sheb Wooley I Can't Believe You're Mine (ASCAP)—M-G-M 12651	7	2
2.	**ALL I HAVE TO DO IS DREAM** (BMI)—Everly Brothers **CLAUDETTE** (BMI)—Cadence 1348	1	7
3.	**WITCH DOCTOR** (ASCAP)—David Seville Don't Whistle at Me, Baby (ASCAP)—Liberty 55132	2	9
4.	**RETURN TO ME** (ASCAP)—Dean Martin Forgetting You (ASCAP)—Cap 3894	12	9
5.	**SECRETLY** (ASCAP)—Jimmie Rodgers **MAKE ME A MIRACLE** (ASCAP)—Roulette 4070	8	5
6.	**DO YOU WANT TO DANCE?** (BMI)—Bobby Freeman Big Fat Woman (BMI)—Josie 835	10	4
7.	**BIG MAN** (BMI)—Four Preps Stop, Baby (ASCAP)—Cap 3960	6	5
8.	**LOOKING BACK** (BMI)—Nat King Cole **DO I LIKE IT?** (BMI)—Cap 3939	5	9
9.	**WEAR MY RING AROUND YOUR NECK** (BMI)—Elvis Presley **DONCHA' THINK IT'S TIME?** (BMI)—Vic 7240	3	8
10.	**JOHNNY B. GOODE** (BMI)—Chuck Berry Around and Around (BMI)—Chess 1691	11	6
11.	**TWILIGHT TIME** (BMI)—Platters Out of My Mind (BMI)—Mer 71289	4	9
12.	**JENNIE LEE** (BMI)—Jan and Arnie Gotta Getta Date (BMI)—Arwin 108	16	3
13.	**CHANSON D'AMOUR** (ASCAP)—Art and Dotty Todd Along the Trail With You (ASCAP)—Era 1064	15	8
14.	**SUGAR MOON** (BMI)—Pat Boone **CHERIE, I LOVE YOU** (ASCAP)—Dot 15750	13	5
15.	**HE'S GOT THE WHOLE WORLD IN HIS HANDS** (ASCAP)—Laurie London Handed Down (ASCAP)—Cap 3891	9	11
16.	**BOOK OF LOVE** (BMI)—Monotones You Never Loved Me (BMI)—Argo 5290	14	11
17.	**WHAT AM I LIVING FOR?** (BMI)—Chuck Willis **HANG UP MY ROCK AND ROLL SHOES** (BMI)—Atlantic 1179	17	5
18.	**OH, LONESOME ME** (BMI)—Don Gibson **I CAN'T STOP LOVING YOU** (BMI)—Vic 7133	20	13
19.	**KEWPIE DOLL** (ASCAP)—Perry Como Dance Only With Me (ASCAP)—Vic 7202	19	8
20.	**TORERO** (ASCAP)—Renato Carosone Chella Lla (ASCAP)—Cap 71080	30	5
21.	**FOR YOUR LOVE** (BMI)—Ed Townsend Over and Over Again (BMI)—Cap 3926	18	8
22.	**RUMBLE** (BMI)—Link Wray and His Ray Men The Swag (BMI)—Cadence 1347	21	6
23.	**ENDLESS SLEEP** (BMI)—Jody Reynolds Tight Capris (BMI)—Demon 1507	28	3
24.	**YAKETY YAK** (BMI)—Coasters Zing! Went the Strings of My Heart (ASCAP)—Atco 6116	—	1
25.	**ZORRO** (BMI)—Chordettes Love's a Two-Way Street (BMI)—Cadence 1349	31	3
26.	**LET THE BELLS KEEP RINGING** (BMI)—Paul Anka **CRAZY LOVE** (BMI)—ABC-Paramount 9907	24	8
27.	**HIGH SCHOOL CONFIDENTIAL** (BMI)—Jerry Lee Lewis Fools Like Me (BMI)—Sun 296	37	2
28.	**TO BE LOVED** (BMI)—Jackie Wilson Come Back to Me (BMI)—Brunswick 55052	23	8
29.	**TALK TO ME, TALK TO ME** (BMI)—Little Willie John Spasms (BMI)—King 5108	22	9
30.	**YOU** (BMI)—Aquatones She's the One for Me (BMI)—Fargo 1001	26	6
31.	**EL RANCHO ROCK** (BMI)—Champs Midnighter (BMI)—Challenge 59007	39	2
32.	**GUESS THINGS HAPPEN THAT WAY** (BMI)—Johnny Cash **COME IN, STRANGER** (BMI)—Sun 295	49	2
33.	**BELIEVE WHAT YOU SAY** (BMI)—Ricky Nelson **MY BUCKET'S GOT A HOLE IN IT** (ASCAP)—Imperial 5503	27	10
34.	**PADRE** (ASCAP)—Toni Arden All at Once (ASCAP)—Dec 30628	29	3
35.	**SICK AND TIRED** (BMI)—Fats Domino **NO, NO** (BMI)—Imperial 5515	33	6
36.	**I WONDER WHY?** (ASCAP)—Dion and the Belmonts Teen Angel (ASCAP)—Laurie 3013	32	3
37.	**ALL THE TIME** (ASCAP)—Johnny Mathis **TEACHER, TEACHER** (ASCAP)—Col 41152	34	5
38.	**CHA HUA HUA** (BMI)—Pets Cha-Kow-Ski (BMI)—Arwin 109	—	1
39.	**IT'S BEEN A LONG TIME PRETTY BABY** (BMI)—Gino and Gina Love's a Carousel (BMI)—Mer 71233	45	2
40.	**I'M SORRY I MADE YOU CRY** (ASCAP)—Connie Francis Lock Up Your Heart (BMI)—M-G-M 12647	44	3
41.	**RAVE ON** (BMI)—Buddy Holly Take Your Time (BMI)—Coral 61985	45	2
42.	**YOU NEED HANDS** (ASCAP)—Eydie Gorme Dormi, Dormi, Dormi (ASCAP)—ABC-Paramount 9925	—	1
43.	**BILLY** (ASCAP)—Kathy Linden If I Could Hold You in My Arms (ASCAP)—Felsted 8510	40	12
44.	**JUST MARRIED** (BMI)—Marty Robbins **STAIRWAY OF LOVE** (ASCAP)—Col 41143	36	7
45.	**WHO'S SORRY NOW?** (ASCAP)—Connie Francis You Were Only Fooling (ASCAP)—M-G-M 12588	42	15
46.	**TEQUILA** (BMI)—The Champs Train to Nowhere (BMI)—Challenge 1016	25	15
47.	**TRY THE IMPOSSIBLE** (BMI)—Lee Andrews and the Hearts Nobody's Home (BMI)—United Artist 123	—	1
48.	**THE WALK** (BMI)—Jimmy McCracklin I'm to Blame (BMI)—Checker 885	38	13
49.	**LAZY MARY** (ASCAP)—Lou Monte Angelique (ASCAP)—Vic 7160	50	13
50.	**MARCH FROM THE RIVER KWAI AND "COLONEL BOGEY"** (ASCAP)—Mitch Miller Hey, Little Baby (BMI)—Col 41066	—	18

THIS WEEK'S BEST BUYS

Special telephone reports and/or chart action indicate these recent releases have either broken out in one or more key areas or have leaped onto the charts and have excellent potential for placing among the Top 30 of The Billboard's Best Selling Pop Singles in Stores chart. Action sides are listed in capitol letters

OOH! MY SOUL (Venice, BMI)—**Little Richard—Specialty 633. True, Fine Mama** (Venice, BMI)

A previous Billboard Spotlight pick.

The following records, not previously selected as Best Buys, are on the charts for the first time this week.

YAKETY YAK (Tiger, BMI)—**The Coasters—Atco 6116. Zing! Went the Strings of My Heart** (Harms, ASCAP)

A previous Billboard Spotlight pick.

TRY THE IMPOSSIBLE (Spinmill & G&H, BMI)—**Lee Andrews and the Hearts—United Artists 123. Nobody's Home** (Spinmill & G&H, BMI)

RECENT POP RELEASES COMING UP STRONG

FOR SURVEY WEEK ENDING MAY 31

The information given in this chart is based on actual sales to customers in a scientific sample of the nation's retail record outlets during the week ending on the date shown above. Sample design, sample size and all methods used in this continuing study of retail record sales are under the direct and continuing supervision and control of the School of Retailing of New York University.

Leroy . . . . *Jack Scott*
(BMI) Carlton 462

No Chemise, Please . . . . *Gerry Granahan*
(BMI) Sunbeam 102

The Things I Love . . . . *The Fidelities*
(ASCAP) Baton 252

Woodchopper's Ball . . . . *Hutch Davie*
(ASCAP) Atco 6110

Most Played by Jockeys

FOR SURVEY WEEK ENDING MAY 31

SIDES are ranked in order of the greatest number of plays on disk jockey radio shows thruout the country. Results are based on The Billboard's weekly survey among the nation's disk jockeys. The reverse side of each record is also listed.

This Week		Last Week	Weeks on Chart
1.	**ALL I HAVE TO DO IS DREAM** (BMI)—Everly Brothers Claudette (BMI)—Cadence 1348	1	7
2.	**PURPLE PEOPLE EATER** (BMI)—Sheb Wooley I Can't Believe You're Mine (ASCAP)—M-G-M 12651	10	2
3.	**BIG MAN** (BMI)—Four Preps Stop, Baby (ASCAP)—Cap 3960	7	6
4.	**WITCH DOCTOR** (ASCAP)—David Seville Don't Whistle at Me, Baby (ASCAP)—Liberty 55132	3	9
5.	**TWILIGHT TIME** (BMI)—Platters Out of My Mind (BMI)—Mer 71289	2	10
6.	**SECRETLY** (ASCAP)—Jimmie Rodgers Make Me a Miracle (ASCAP)—Roulette 4070	12	4
7.	**RETURN TO ME** (ASCAP)—Dean Martin Forgetting You (ASCAP)—Cap 3894	4	10
8.	**CHANSON D'AMOUR** (ASCAP)—Art and Dotty Todd Along the Trail With You (ASCAP)—Era 1964	11	8
9.	**WEAR MY RING AROUND YOUR NECK** (BMI)—Elvis Presley Doncha' Think It's Time (BMI)—Vic 7240	5	7
10.	**SUGAR MOON** (BMI)—Pat Boone Cherie, I Love You (ASCAP)—Dot 15750	8	5
11.	**KEWPIE DOLL** (ASCAP)—Perry Como Dance Only With Me (ASCAP)—Vic 7202	6	8
12.	**WHAT AM I LIVING FOR?** (BMI)—Chuck Willis Hang Up My Rock and Roll Shoes (BMI)—Atlantic 1179	14	4
13.	**FOR YOUR LOVE** (BMI)—Ed Townsend Over and Over Again (BMI)—Cap 3926	20	3
14.	**YOU NEED HANDS** (ASCAP)—Eydie Gorme Dormi, Dormi, Dormi (ASCAP)—ABC-Paramount 9925	17	3
15.	**DO YOU WANT TO DANCE?** (BMI)—Bobby Freeman Big Fat Woman (BMI)—Josie 835	—	1
16.	**CHANSON D'AMOUR** (ASCAP)—Fontane Sisters Cocoanut Grove (ASCAP)—Dot 15736	15	7
17.	**LOOKING BACK** (BMI)—Nat King Cole Do I Like It (BMI)—Cap 3939	13	5
18.	**TORERO** (ASCAP)—Renato Carosone Chell Lia (ASCAP)—Cap 71080	18	3
19.	**WHEN THE BOYS TALK ABOUT THE GIRLS** (ASCAP)—Valerie Carr Padre (ASCAP)—Roulette 4066	—	1
20.	**JENNIE LEE** (BMI)—Jan and Arnie Gotta Getta Date (BMI)—Arwin 108	25	2
21.	**HE'S GOT THE WHOLE WORLD IN HIS HANDS** (ASCAP)—Laurie London Handed Down (ASCAP)—Cap 3891	9	12
22.	**ENDLESS SLEEP** (BMI)—Jody Reynolds Tight Capris (BMI)—Demon 1507	—	1
22.	**DON'T GO HOME** (BMI)—Playmates Can't You Get It Through Your Head (BMI)—Roulette 4072	—	1
24.	**JOHNNY B. GOODE** (BMI)—Chuck Berry Around and Around (BMI)—Chess 1691	16	5
25.	**DING DONG** (ASCAP)—McGuire Sisters Since You Went Away to School (BMI)—Coral 61991	—	1
25.	**BOOK OF LOVE** (BMI)—Monotones You Never Loved Me (BMI)—Argo 5290	24	8

NEW YORK UNIVERSITY SCHOOL OF RETAILING · STORE RECORDED SALES · THE BILLBOARD

Top 100 Sides

FOR SURVEY WEEK ENDING MAY 31

This is a tabulation of dealer individual record sales listed according to the specific side requested by customers. No attempt is made to add sides together to reflect actual record sales. This is, therefore, a tabulation of sides or songs, and not records. This is the reason for any possible variation that occurs between the top 50 sides as reflected in this chart, and the top 50 record sellers as reflected in the "Best Sellers in Stores" chart.

Pos.	Song, Artist, Label	Last Week
1.	**THE PURPLE PEOPLE EATER,** Sheb Wooley, M-G-M	7
2.	**ALL I HAVE TO DO IS DREAM,** Everly Brothers, Cadence	1
3.	**WITCH DOCTOR,** David Seville, Liberty	2
4.	**RETURN TO ME,** Dean Martin, Capitol	12
5.	**DO YOU WANT TO DANCE?** Bobby Freeman, Josie	8
6.	**SECRETLY,** Jimmie Rodgers, Roulette	11
7.	**BIG MAN,** Four Preps Capitol	5
8.	**JOHNNY B. GOODE,** Chuck Berry, Chess	10
9.	**LOOKING BACK,** Nat King Cole, Capitol	6
10.	**WEAR MY RING AROUND YOUR NECK,** Elvis Presley Victor	3
11.	**TWILIGHT TIME,** Platters, Mercury	4
12.	**JENNIE LEE,** Jan & Arnie, Arwin	16
13.	**CHANSON D'AMOUR,** Art & Dotty Todd, Era	14
14.	**HE'S GOT THE WHOLE WORLD IN HIS HANDS** Laurie London, Capitol	8
15.	**BOOK OF LOVE,** Monotones, Argo	13
16.	**SUGAR MOON,** Pat Boone, Dot	14
17.	**OH, LONESOME ME,** Don Gibson, Victor	19
18.	**KEWPIE DOLL,** Perry Como, Victor	18
19.	**TORERO,** Renate Carosone, Capitol	28
20.	**FOR YOUR LOVE,** Ed Townsend, Capitol	17
21.	**RUMBLE,** Link Wray, Cadence	20
22.	**WHAT AM I LIVING FOR?** Chuck Willis, Atlantic	24
23.	**ENDLESS SLEEP,** Jody Reynolds, Demon	26
24.	**YAKETY YAK,** Coasters, Atco	52
25.	**ZORRO,** Chordettes, Cadence	29
26.	**HIGH SCHOOL CONFIDENTIAL,** Jerry Lee Lewis, Sun	34
27.	**TO BE LOVED,** Jackie Wilson, Brunswick	22
28.	**TALK TO ME, TALK TO ME,** Little Willie John, King	20
28.	**YOU,** Aquatones, Fargo	25
30.	**EL RANCHO ROCK,** Champs, Challenge	37
31.	**LET THE BELLS KEEP RINGING,** Paul Anka, ABC-Paramount	34
32.	**PADRE,** Toni Arden, Decca	27
33.	**I WONDER WHY,** Dion & the Belmonts, Laurie	30
34.	**IT'S BEEN A LONG TIME PRETTY BABY,** Gino & Gina, Mercury	46
34.	**CHA HUA HUA,** Pets, Arwin	51
36.	**I'M SORRY I MADE YOU CRY,** Connie Francis, M-G-M	45
37.	**RAVE ON,** Buddy Holly, Coral	46
38.	**GUESS THINGS HAPPEN THAT WAY,** Johnny Cash, Sun	56
38.	**YOU NEED HANDS,** Eydie Gorme, ABC-Paramount	56
40.	**SICK AND TIRED,** Fats Domino, Imperial	33
40.	**BILLY,** Kathy Linden, Felsted	37
42.	**WHO'S SORRY NOW?** Connie Francis M-G-M	41
43.	**CRAZY LOVE,** Paul Anka, ABC-Paramount	44
44.	**TEQUILA,** Champs, Challenge	23
44.	**BELIEVE WHAT YOU SAY,** Ricky Nelson, Imperial	37
46.	**THE WALK,** Jimmy McCracklin, Checker	34
46.	**TRY THE IMPOSSIBLE,** Lee Andrews and the Hearts, United Artist	94
48.	**JUST MARRIED,** Marty Robbins, Columbia	41
48.	**LAZY MARY,** Lou Monte, Victor	49
48.	**MARCH FROM THE RIVER KWAI AND "COLONEL BOGEY"** Mitch Miller, Columbia	56
51.	**ARE YOU SINCERE?** Andy Williams, Cadence	31
51.	**LOLLIPOP,** Chordettes, Cadence	40
51.	**I MET HIM ON A SUNDAY,** Shirelles, Decca	60
51.	**WOODCHOPPER'S BALL,** Hutch Davie, Atco	64
55.	**JENNIE LEE,** Billy Ward, Liberty	71
56.	**HANG UP MY ROCK AND ROLL SHOES,** Chuck Willis, Atlantic	32
56.	**SKINNY MINNIE,** Bill Haley & His Comets, Decca	50
58.	**ALL THE TIME,** Johnny Mathis, Columbia	54
59.	**TEACHER, TEACHER,** Johnny Mathis, Columbia	54
60.	**CATCH A FALLING STAR,** Perry Como, Victor	61
61.	**DON'T YOU JUST KNOW IT,** Huey Smith, Ace	43
61.	**SAIL ALONG SILVERY MOON,** Billy Vaughn, Dot	63
63.	**LEROY,** Jack Scott, Carlton	—
63.	**CHERIE, I LOVE YOU,** Pat Boone, Dot	77
63.	**JACQUELINE,** Bobby Helms, Decca	77
67.	**NEE NEE NA NA NA NA NU NU,** Dickey Doo & the Don'ts, Swan	64
67.	**WE BELONG TOGETHER,** Robert and Johnny, Old Town	67
67.	**TEACHER'S PET,** Doris Day, Columbia	73
70.	**MY BUCKET'S GOT A HOLE IN IT,** Ricky Nelson, Imperial	52
70.	**A WONDERFUL TIME UP THERE,** Pat Boone, Dot	56
70.	**MAKE ME A MIRACLE,** Jimmie Rodgers, Roulette	73
73.	**COME IN, STRANGER,** Johnny Cash Sun	—
73.	**NO CHEMISE, PLEASE,** Gerry Granahan, Sunbeam	—
73.	**THINGS I LOVE,** Fidelities, Baton	—
76.	**THERE'S ONLY ONE OF YOU,** Four Lads, Columbia	46
76.	**HIGH SIGN,** Diamonds, Mercury	67
78.	**YOU EXCITE ME,** Frankie Avalon Chancellor	61
78.	**A VERY PRECIOUS LOVE,** Ames Brothers, Victor	72
78.	**LONG, HOT SUMMER,** Jimmie Rodgers, Roulette	77
78.	**SEND ME THE PILLOW YOU DREAM ON,** Hank Locklin, Victor	77
78.	**NO, NO.** Fats Domino, Imperial	91
83.	**YOU'D BE SURPRISED,** Kathy Linden, Felsted	—
83.	**BALLAD OF A TEENAGE QUEEN,** Johnny Cash, Sun	67
83.	**NOW AND FOR ALWAYS,** George Hamilton IV, ABC-Paramount	77
83.	**DON'T,** Elvis Presley, Victor	88
87.	**DONCHA' THINK IT'S TIME,** Elvis Presley, Victor	—
87.	**I KNOW WHERE I'M GOING,** George Hamilton IV, ABC-Paramount	—
87.	**WISHING FOR YOUR LOVE,** Voxpopers, Mercury	—
87.	**CHA HUA HUA,** Eddie Platt, Gone	—
87.	**PRETTY BABY,** Little Richard, Specialty	46
87.	**EVERY NIGHT,** Chantels, End	73
87.	**CLAUDETTE,** Everly Brothers, Cadence	83
87.	**DO I LIKE IT,** Nat King Cole, Capitol	94
87.	**BLUEBIRDS OVER THE MOUNTAINS,** Ersel Hickey, Epic	—
87.	**THE LITTLE BLUE MAN,** Betty Johnson, Atlantic	—
97.	**FLIP TOP BOX,** Dickey Doo & the Don'ts, Swan	—
97.	**LONELY ISLAND,** Sam Cooke, Keen	67
97.	**TUMBLING TUMBLEWEEDS,** Billy Vaughn, Dot	77
97.	**COME WHAT MAY,** Clyde McPhatter, Atlantic	83

STORE RECORDED SALES — New York University School of Retailing — The Billboard

BEST SELLING POP SINGLES IN STORES

The information given in this chart is based on actual sales to customers in a scientific sample of the nation's retail record outlets during the week ending on the date shown above. Sample design, sample size, and all methods used in this continuing study of retail record sales are under the direct and continuing supervision and control of the School of Retailing of New York University.

FOR SURVEY WEEK ENDING JUNE 7, 1958

This Week		Last Week	Weeks on Chart
1.	PURPLE PEOPLE EATER (BMI)—Sheb Wooley I Can't Believe You're Mine (ASCAP)—M-G-M 12651	1	3
2.	ALL I HAVE TO DO IS DREAM (BMI)—Everly Brothers CLAUDETTE (BMI)—Cadence 1348	2	8
3.	WITCH DOCTOR (ASCAP)—David Seville Don't Whistle at Me, Baby (ASCAP)—Liberty 55132	3	10
4.	SECRETLY (ASCAP)—Jimmie Rodgers MAKE ME A MIRACLE (ASCAP)—Roulette 4070	5	6
5.	RETURN TO ME (ASCAP)—Dean Martin Forgetting You (ASCAP)—Cap 3894	4	10
6.	LOOKING BACK (BMI)—Nat King Cole DO I LIKE IT? (BMI)—Cap 3939	8	10
7.	DO YOU WANT TO DANCE? (BMI)—Bobby Freeman Big Fat Woman (BMI)—Josie 835	6	5
8.	YAKETY YAK (BMI)—Coasters Zing! Went the Strings of My Heart (ASCAP)—Atco 6116	24	2
9.	TWILIGHT TIME (BMI)—Platters Out of My Mind (BMI)—Mer 71289	11	10
10.	WEAR MY RING AROUND YOUR NECK (BMI)—Elvis Presley DONCHA' THINK IT'S TIME? (BMI)—Vic 7240	9	9
11.	JOHNNY B. GOODE (BMI)—Chuck Berry Around and Around (BMI)—Chess 1691	10	7
12.	JENNIE LEE (BMI)—Jan and Arnie Gotta Getta Date (BMI)—Arwin 108	12	4
13.	BIG MAN (BMI)—Four Preps Stop, Baby (ASCAP)—Cap 3960	7	6
14.	SUGAR MOON (BMI)—Pat Boone CHERIE, I LOVE YOU (ASCAP)—Dot 15750	14	6
15.	HE'S GOT THE WHOLE WORLD IN HIS HANDS (ASCAP)—Laurie London Handed Down (ASCAP)—Cap 3891	15	12
16.	CHANSON D'AMOUR (ASCAP)—Art and Dotty Todd Along the Trail With You (ASCAP)—Era 1064	13	9
17.	WHAT AM I LIVING FOR? (BMI)—Chuck Willis HANG UP MY ROCK AND ROLL SHOES (BMI)—Atlantic 1179	17	6
18.	ZORRO (BMI)—Chordettes Love's a Two-Way Street (BMI)—Cadence 1349	25	4
19.	FOR YOUR LOVE (BMI)—Ed Townsend Over and Over Again (BMI)—Cap 3926	21	9
20.	ENDLESS SLEEP (BMI)—Jody Reynolds Tight Capris (BMI)—Demon 1507	23	4
21.	TORERO (ASCAP)—Renato Carosone Chella Lla (ASCAP)—Cap 71080	20	6
22.	OH, LONESOME ME (BMI)—Don Gibson I CAN'T STOP LOVING YOU (BMI)—Vic 7133	18	14
23.	KEWPIE DOLL (ASCAP)—Perry Como Dance Only With Me (ASCAP)—Vic 7202	19	9
24.	BOOK OF LOVE (BMI)—Monotones You Never Loved Me (BMI)—Argo 5290	16	12
25.	RUMBLE (BMI)—Link Wray and His Ray Men The Swag (BMI)—Cadence 1347	22	7
26.	HIGH SCHOOL CONFIDENTIAL (BMI)—Jerry Lee Lewis Fools Like Me (BMI)—Sun 296	27	3
27.	LET THE BELLS KEEP RINGING (BMI)—Paul Anka CRAZY LOVE (BMI)—ABC-Paramount 9907	26	9
28.	GUESS THINGS HAPPEN THAT WAY (BMI)—Johnny Cash COME IN, STRANGER (BMI)—Sun 295	32	3
29.	LEROY (BMI)—Jack Scott My True Love (BMI)—Carlton 462	—	1
30.	YOU (BMI)—Aquatones She's the One for Me (BMI)—Fargo 1001	30	7
31.	EL RANCHO ROCK (BMI)—Champs Midnighter (BMI)—Challenge 59007	31	3
32.	TEQUILA (BMI)—The Champs Train to Nowhere (BMI)—Challenge 1016	46	16
33.	TRY THE IMPOSSIBLE (BMI)—Lee Andrews and the Hearts Nobody's Home (BMI)—United Artists 123	47	2
34.	TALK TO ME, TALK TO ME (BMI)—Little Willie John Spasms (BMI)—King 5108	29	10
35.	TO BE LOVED (BMI)—Jackie Wilson Come Back to Me (BMI)—Brunswick 55052	28	9
36.	NO CHEMISE, PLEASE (BMI)—Gerry Granahan Girl of My Dreams (ASCAP)—Sunbeam 102	—	1
37.	SICK AND TIRED (BMI)—Fats Domino NO, NO (BMI)—Imperial 5515	35	7
38.	TEACHER, TEACHER (ASCAP)—Johnny Mathis ALL THE TIME (ASCAP)—Col 41152	37	6
39.	I'M SORRY I MADE YOU CRY (ASCAP)—Connie Francis Lock Up Your Heart (BMI)—M-G-M 12647	40	4
40.	PADRE (ASCAP)—Toni Arden All at Once (ASCAP)—Dec 30628	34	4
41.	RAVE ON (BMI)—Buddy Holly Take Your Time (BMI)—Coral 61985	41	3
42.	FOR YOUR PRECIOUS LOVE (ASCAP)—Jerry Butler and Impressions Sweet Was the Wine (ASCAP)—Falcon 1013; Abner 1013	—	1
43.	BILLY (ASCAP)—Kathy Linden If I Could Hold You in My Arms (ASCAP)—Felsted 8510	43	13
44.	I WONDER WHY? (ASCAP)—Dion and the Belmonts Teen Angel (ASCAP)—Laurie 3013	36	4
45.	I KNOW WHERE I'M GOIN' (BMI)—George Hamilton IV Who's Taking You to the Prom? (BMI)—ABC-Paramount 9924	—	1
46.	PRETTY BABY (BMI)—Gino and Gina Love's a Carousel (BMI)—Mer 71283	—	2
46.	FLIP TOP BOX (BMI)—Dickey Doo and the Don'ts NEE NEE NA NA NA NA NU NU (ASCAP)—Swan 4006	—	5
48.	YOU NEED HANDS (ASCAP)—Eydie Gorme Dormi, Dormi, Dormi (ASCAP)—ABC-Paramount 9925	42	2
49.	MARCH FROM THE RIVER KWAI AND "COLONEL BOGEY" (ASCAP)—Mitch Miller Hey, Little Baby (BMI)—Col 41066	50	19
50.	BELIEVE WHAT YOU SAY (BMI)—Ricky Nelson MY BUCKET'S GOT A HOLE IN IT (ASCAP)—Imperial 5503	33	11
50.	JUST MARRIED (BMI)—Marty Robbins STAIRWAY OF LOVE (ASCAP)—Col 41143	44	8

THIS WEEK'S BEST BUYS

Special telephone reports and/or chart action indicate these recent releases have either broken out in one or more key areas or have leaped onto the charts and have excellent potential for placing among the Top 30 of The Billboard's Best Selling Pop Singles in Stores chart. Action sides are listed in capitol letters.

SPLISH SPLASH (Portrait, BMI)—**Bobby Darin**—Atco 6117. **Judy, Don't Be Moody** (Reis—Progressive, BMI)

DREAM (Golden, ASCAP)—**Betty Johnson**, Atlantic 1186. **How Much** (Trinity, BMI)

Both are previous Billboard Spotlight picks.

PATRICIA (Southern, ASCAP)—**Perez Prado**—RCA Victor 7245. **Why Wait** (Peer Intl., BMI)

WHEN (Sounds & Michele, ASCAP)—**Kalin Twins**—Decca 30642. **Three O'Clock Thrill** (Jason & Lark, BMI)

The following records, not previously selected as Best Buys, are on the chart for the first time this week.

LEROY (Peer Intl., BMI)—**Jack Scott**—Carlton 462. **My True Love** (Starfire—Peer Intl., BMI)

NO CHEMISE, PLEASE (Sunbeam, BMI)—**Gerry Granahan**—Sunbeam 102. **Girl of My Dreams** (Mills, ASCAP)

FOR YOUR PRECIOUS LOVE (Gladstone, ASCAP)—**Jerry Butler and the Impressions**—Abner 1013. **Sweet Was the Wine** (Gladstone, ASCAP)

STORE RECORDED SALES — New York University School of Retailing — The Billboard

RECENT POP RELEASES COMING UP STRONG

FOR SURVEY WEEK ENDING JUNE 7

The information given in this chart is based on actual sales to customers in a scientific sample of the nation's retail record outlets during the week ending on the date shown above. Sample design, sample size and all methods used in this continuing study of retail record sales are under the direct and continuing supervision and control of the School of Retailing of New York University.

Ooh! My Soul . . . . ***Little Richard***

(BMI) Specialty 633

Patricia . . . . ***Perez Prado***

(ASCAP) RCA Victor 7245

Most Played by Jockeys

FOR SURVEY WEEK ENDING JUNE 7

SIDES are ranked in order of the greatest number of plays on disk jockey radio shows thruout the country. Results are based on The Billboard's weekly survey among the nation's disk jockeys. The reverse side of each record is also listed.

This Week		Last Week	Weeks on Chart
1.	**ALL I HAVE TO DO IS DREAM** (BMI)—Everly Brothers Claudette (BMI)—Cadence 1348	1	8
2.	**PURPLE PEOPLE EATER** (BMI)—Sheb Wooley I Can't Believe You're Mine (ASCAP)—M-G-M 12651	2	3
3.	**SECRETLY** (ASCAP)—Jimmie Rodgers Make Me a Miracle (ASCAP)—Roulette 4070	6	5
4.	**RETURN TO ME** (ASCAP)—Dean Martin Forgetting You (ASCAP)—Cap 3894	7	11
5.	**SUGAR MOON** (BMI)—Pat Boone Cherie, I Love You (ASCAP)—Dot 15750	10	6
6.	**TWILIGHT TIME** (BMI)—Platters Out of My Mind (BMI)—Mer 71289	5	11
7.	**BIG MAN** (BMI)—Four Preps Stop, Baby (ASCAP)—Cap 3960	3	7
8.	**WEAR MY RING AROUND YOUR NECK** (BMI)—Elvis Presley Doncha' Think It's Time (BMI)—Vic 7240	9	8
9.	**CHANSON D'AMOUR** (ASCAP)—Art and Dotty Todd Along the Trail With You (ASCAP)—Era 1964	8	9
10.	**WHAT AM I LIVING FOR?** (BMI)—Chuck Willis Hang Up My Rock and Roll Shoes (BMI)—Atlantic 1179	12	5
11.	**KEWPIE DOLL** (ASCAP)—Perry Como Dance Only With Me (ASCAP)—Vic 7202	11	9
12.	**WITCH DOCTOR** (ASCAP)—David Seville Dont' Whistle at Me, Baby (ASCAP)—Liberty 55132	4	10
13.	**PADRE** (ASCAP)—Toni Arden All at Once (ASCAP)—Dec 30628	—	1
14.	**CHANSON D'AMOUR** (ASCAP)—Fontane Sisters Coconut Grove (ASCAP)—Dot 15736	16	8
15.	**ENDLESS SLEEP** (BMI)—Jody Reynolds Tight Capris (BMI)—Demon 1507	22	2
16.	**YOU NEED HANDS** (ASCAP)—Eydie Gorme Dormi, Dormi, Dormi (ASCAP)—ABC-Paramount 9925	14	4
17.	**JENNIE LEE** (BMI)—Jan and Arnie Gotta Getta Date (BMI)—Arwin 108	20	3
18.	**LOOKING BACK** (BMI)—Nat King Cole Do I Like It (BMI)—Cap 3939	17	6
19.	**DO YOU WANT TO DANCE?** (BMI)—Bobby Freeman Big Fat Woman (BMI)—Josie 835	15	2
20.	**HE'S GOT THE WHOLE WORLD IN HIS HANDS** (ASCAP)—Laurie London Handed Down (ASCAP)—Cap 3891	21	13
21.	**TORERO** (ASCAP)—Julius La Rosa Milano (BMI)—Vic 7227	—	1
22.	**FOR YOUR LOVE** (BMI)—Ed Townsend Over and Over Again (BMI)—Cap 3926	13	4
23.	**TORERO** (ASCAP)—Renato Carosone Chella Lla (ASCAP)—Cap 71080	18	4
24.	**ALL THE TIME** (ASCAP)—Johnny Mathis Teacher, Teacher (ASCAP)—Col 41152	—	5
25.	**YAKETY YAK** (BMI)—Coasters Zing! Went the Strings of My Heart (ASCAP)—Atco 6116	—	1

NEW YORK UNIVERSITY SCHOOL OF RETAILING · STORE RECORDED SALES · THE BILLBOARD

Top 100 Sides

FOR SURVEY WEEK ENDING JUNE 7

This is a tabulation of dealer individual record sales listed according to the specific side requested by customers. No attempt is made to add sides together to reflect actual record sales. This is, therefore, a tabulation of sides or songs, and not records. This is the reason for any possible variation that occurs between the top 50 sides as reflected in this chart, and the top 50 record sellers as reflected in the "Best Sellers in Stores" chart.

Pos.	Song, Artist, Label	Last Week
1.	**THE PURPLE PEOPLE EATER,** Sheb Wooley, M-G-M	1
2.	**ALL I HAVE TO DO IS DREAM,** Everly Brothers, Cadence	2
3.	**WITCH DOCTOR,** David Seville, Liberty	3
4.	**SECRETLY,** Jimmie Rodgers, Roulette	6
5.	**RETURN TO ME,** Dean Martin, Capitol	4
6.	**LOOKING BACK,** Nat King Cole, Capitol	9
7.	**DO YOU WANT TO DANCE?** Bobby Freeman, Josie	5
8.	**YAKETY YAK,** Coasters Atco	24
9.	**TWILIGHT TIME,** Platters, Mercury	11
10.	**JOHNNY B. GOODE,** Chuck Berry, Chess	8
10.	**JENNIE LEE,** Jan & Arnie, Arwin	12
12.	**WEAR MY RING AROUND YOUR NECK,** Elvis Presley, Victor	10
13.	**BIG MAN,** Four Preps, Capitol	7
14.	**SUGAR MOON,** Pat Boone, Dot	16
15.	**HE'S GOT THE WHOLE WORLD IN HIS HANDS,** Laurie London, Capitol	14
16.	**CHANSON D'AMOUR,** Art & Dotty Todd, Era	13
17.	**ZORRO,** Chordettes, Cadence	25
18.	**FOR YOUR LOVE,** Ed Townsend, Capitol	20
19.	**ENDLESS SLEEP,** Jody Reynolds, Demon	23
20.	**TORERO,** Renate Carosone, Capitol	19
21.	**OH, LONESOME ME,** Don Gibson, Victor	17
21.	**KEWPIE DOLL,** Perry Como, Victor	18
23.	**BOOK OF LOVE,** Monotones, Argo	15
24.	**RUMBLE,** Link Wray, Cadence	21
25.	**WHAT AM I LIVING FOR?** Chuck Willis, Atlantic	22
26.	**HIGH SCHOOL CONFIDENTIAL,** Jerry Lee Lewis, Sun	26
27.	**LEROY,** Jack Scott, Carlton	63
28.	**YOU,** Aquatones, Frago	28
28.	**GUESS THINGS HAPPEN THAT WAY,** Johnny Cash, Sun	38
30.	**EL RANCHO ROCK,** Champs, Challenge	30
30.	**LET THE BELLS KEEP RINGING,** Paul Anka, ABC-Paramount	31
30.	**TEQUILA,** Champs, Challenge	44
33.	**TRY THE IMPOSSIBLE,** Lee Andrews & the Hearts, United Artists	46
34.	**FOR YOUR PRECIOUS LOVE,** Jerry Butler & the Impressions, Abner	46
34.	**TALK TO ME, TALK TO ME,** Little Willie John, King	28
36.	**TO BE LOVED,** Jackie Wilson, Brunswick	27
37.	**I'M SORRY I MADE YOU CRY,** Connie Francis, M-G-M	36
37.	**NO CHEMISE, PLEASE,** Gerry Granahan, Sunbeam	73
39.	**PADRE,** Toni Arden, Decca	32
39.	**RAVE ON,** Buddy Holly, Coral	37
41.	**BILLY,** Kathy Linden, Felsted	40
42.	**I WONDER WHY,** Dion & the Belmonts, Laurie	33
43.	**HANG UP MY ROCK AND ROLL SHOES,** Chuck Willis, Atlantic	56
43.	**I KNOW WHERE I'M GOIN',** George Hamilton IV, ABC-Paramount	87
45.	**PRETTY BABY,** Gino and Gina, Mercury	34
45.	**SICK AND TIRED,** Fats Domino, Imperial	40
47.	**YOU NEED HANDS,** Eydie Gorme, ABC-Paramount	38
47.	**MARCH FROM THE RIVER KWAI AND "COLONEL BOGEY."** Mitch Miller, Columbia	48
47.	**TEACHER, TEACHER,** Johnny Mathis, Columbia	59
50.	**SKINNY MINNIE,** Bill Haley and His Comets, Decca	56
51.	**LAZY MARY,** Lou Monte, Victor	48
51.	**WE BELONG TOGETHER,** Robert and Johnny, Old Town	67
53.	**DON'T GO HOME,** Playmates, Roulette	—
53.	**CHA HUA HUA,** Pets, Arwin	34
53.	**WHO'S SORRY NOW?** Connie Francis, M-G-M	42
53.	**JUST MARRIED,** Marty Robbins, Columbia	48
53.	**I MET HIM ON A SUNDAY,** Shirelles, Decca	51
53.	**CATCH A FALLING STAR,** Perry Como, Victor	60
53.	**OOH, MY SOUL,** Little Richard, Specialty	87
60.	**GOT A MATCH,** Daddy-O's, Brunswick	—
60.	**BELIEVE WHAT YOU SAY,** Ricky Nelson, Imperial	44
60.	**THINGS I LOVE,** Fidelities, Baton	73
63.	**JACQUELINE,** Bobby Helms, Decca	63
63.	**MAKE ME A MIRACLE,** Jimmie Rodgers, Roulette	70
63.	**YOU'D BE SURPRISED,** Kathy Linden, Felsted	83
66.	**DING DONG,** McGuire Sisters, Coral	—
66.	**PATRICIA,** Perez Prado, Victor	—
66.	**FLIP TOP BOX,** Dickey Doo and the Don'ts, Swan	97
66.	**BEEN SO LONG,** Pastels, Argo	—
70.	**BEWILDERED,** Mickey and Sylvia, Vik	—
70.	**CRAZY LOVE,** Paul Anka, ABC-Paramount	43
70.	**LOLLIPOP,** Chordettes, Cadence	51
70.	**NEE NEE NA NA NA NA NU NU,** Dickey Doo and the Don'ts, Swan	67
74.	**INDIAN LOVE CALL,** Ernie Freeman, Imperial	—
74.	**SAIL ALONG SILVERY MOON,** Billy Vaughn, Dot	61
74.	**TEACHER'S PET,** Doris Day, Columbia	67
74.	**A WONDERFUL TIME UP THERE,** Pat Boone, Dot	70
74.	**COME IN, STRANGER,** Johnny Cash, Sun	73
74.	**CHA HUA HUA,** Eddie Platt, Gone	87
80.	**I LOVE YOU SO,** Chantels, End	—
80.	**CHERIE, I LOVE YOU,** Pat Boone, Dot	63
80.	**LITTLE TRAIN,** Marianne Vasel and Erich Storz, Mercury	63
80.	**CLAUDETTE,** Everly Brothers, Cadence	87
80.	**EVERY NIGHT,** Chantels, End	87
80.	**LITTLE BLUE MAN,** Betty Johnson, Atlantic	—
86.	**WOODCHOPPER'S BALL,** Hutch Davie, Atco	51
86.	**JENNIE LEE,** Billie Ward and His Dominoes, Liberty	55
86.	**ALL THE TIME,** Johnny Mathis, Columbia	58
86.	**DON'T YOU JUST KNOW IT,** Huey Smith, Ace	61
86.	**HIGH NOON,** Diamonds, Mercury	76
86.	**THERE'S ONLY ONE OF YOU,** Four Lads, Columbia	76
86.	**A VERY PRECIOUS LOVE,** Ames Brothers, Victor	78
86.	**BLUEBIRDS OVER THE MOUNTAIN,** Erzel Hickey, Epic	87
86.	**COME WHAT MAY,** Clyde McPhatter, Atlantic	97
95.	**DREAM,** Betty Johnson, Atlantic	—
95.	**MY BUCKETS GOT A HOLE IN IT,** Ricky Nelson, Imperial	70
95.	**NO, NO,** Fats Domino, Imperial	78
95.	**THE LONG HOT SUMMER,** Jimmie Rodgers, Roulette	78
95.	**BREATHLESS,** Jerry Lee Lewis, Sun	—
95.	**HAVE FAITH,** Gene Allison, Vee Jay	—

BEST SELLING POP SINGLES IN STORES

The information given in this chart is based on actual sales to customers in a scientific sample of the nation's retail record outlets during the week ending on the date shown above. Sample design, sample size, and all methods used in this continuing study of retail record sales are under the direct and continuing supervision and control of the School of Retailing of New York University.

FOR SURVEY WEEK ENDING JUNE 14, 1958

This Week	Title / Artist / Label	Last Week	Weeks on Chart
1.	PURPLE PEOPLE EATER (BMI)—Sheb Wooley; I Can't Believe You're Mine (ASCAP)—M-G-M 12651	1	4
2.	ALL I HAVE TO DO IS DREAM (BMI)—Everly Brothers; CLAUDETTE (BMI)—Cadence 1348	2	9
3.	SECRETLY (ASCAP)—Jimmie Rodgers; MAKE ME A MIRACLE (ASCAP)—Roulette 4070	4	7
4.	YAKETY YAK (BMI)—Coasters; Zing! Went the Strings of My Heart (ASCAP)—Atco 6116	8	3
5.	WITCH DOCTOR (ASCAP)—David Seville; Don't Whistle at Me, Baby (ASCAP)—Liberty 55132	3	11
6.	RETURN TO ME (ASCAP)—Dean Martin; Forgetting You (ASCAP)—Cap 3894	5	11
7.	DO YOU WANT TO DANCE? (BMI)—Bobby Freeman; Big Fat Woman (BMI)—Josie 835	7	6
8.	LOOKING BACK (BMI)—Nat King Cole; DO I LIKE IT? (BMI)—Cap 3939	6	11
9.	JENNIE LEE (BMI)—Jan and Arnie; Gotta Getta Date (BMI)—Arwin 108	12	5
10.	ENDLESS SLEEP (BMI)—Jody Reynolds; Tight Capris (BMI)—Demon 1507	20	5
11.	SUGAR MOON (BMI)—Pat Boone; CHERIE, I LOVE YOU (ASCAP)—Dot 15750	14	7
12.	BIG MAN (BMI)—Four Preps; Stop, Baby (ASCAP)—Cap 3960	13	7
13.	TWILIGHT TIME (BMI)—Platters; Out of My Mind (BMI)—Mer 71289	9	11
14.	WEAR MY RING AROUND YOUR NECK (BMI)—Elvis Presley; DONCHA' THINK IT'S TIME (BMI)—Vic 7240	10	10
15.	HE'S GOT THE WHOLE WORLD IN HIS HANDS (ASCAP)—Laurie London; Handed Down (ASCAP)—Cap 3891	15	13
16.	CHANSON D'AMOUR (ASCAP)—Art and Dotty Todd; Along the Trail With You (ASCAP)—Era 1064	16	10
17.	OH, LONESOME ME (BMI)—Don Gibson; I CAN'T STOP LOVING YOU (BMI)—Vic 7133	22	15
18.	JOHNNY B. GOODE (BMI)—Chuck Berry; Around and Around (BMI)—Chess 1691	11	8
19.	WHAT AM I LIVING FOR? (BMI)—Chuck Willis; HANG UP MY ROCK AND ROLL SHOES (BMI)—Atlantic 1179	17	7
20.	ZORRO (BMI)—Chordettes; Love's a Two-Way Street (BMI)—Cadence 1349	18	5
21.	RUMBLE (BMI)—Link Wray and His Ray Men; The Swag (BMI)—Cadence 1347	25	8
22.	FOR YOUR LOVE (BMI)—Ed Townsend; Over and Over Again (BMI)—Cap 3926	19	10
23.	GUESS THINGS HAPPEN THAT WAY (BMI)—Johnny Cash; COME IN, STRANGER (BMI)—Sun 295	28	4
24.	KEWPIE DOLL (ASCAP)—Perry Como; Dance Only With Me (ASCAP)—Vic 7202	23	10
25.	HIGH SCHOOL CONFIDENTIAL (BMI)—Jerry Lee Lewis; Fools Like Me (BMI)—Sun 296	26	4
26.	LET THE BELLS KEEP RINGING (BMI)—Paul Anka; CRAZY LOVE (BMI)—ABC-Paramount 9907	27	10
27.	NO CHEMISE, PLEASE (BMI)—Gerry Granahan; Girl of My Dreams (ASCAP)—Sunbeam 102	36	2
28.	LEROY (BMI)—Jack Scott; My True Love (BMI)—Carlton 462	29	2
29.	PADRE (ASCAP)—Toni Arden; All at Once (ASCAP)—Dec 30628	40	5
30.	TORERO (ASCAP)—Renato Carosone; Chella Lla (ASCAP)—Cap 71080	21	7
31.	TEACHER, TEACHER (ASCAP)—Johnny Mathis; ALL THE TIME (ASCAP)—Col 41152	38	7
32.	FOR YOUR PRECIOUS LOVE (ASCAP)—Jerry Butler and Impressions; Sweet Was the Wine (ASCAP)—Abner 1013	42	2
33.	YOU (BMI)—Aquatones; She's the One for Me (BMI)—Fargo 1001	30	8
34.	I WONDER WHY (ASCAP)—Dion and the Belmonts; Teen Angel (ASCAP)—Laurie 3013	44	5
35.	BOOK OF LOVE (BMI)—Monotones; You Never Loved Me (BMI)—Argo 5290	24	13
36.	PATRICIA (ASCAP)—Perez Prado; Why Wait (BMI)—Vic 7245	—	1
37.	TEQUILA (BMI)—The Champs; Train to Nowhere (BMI)—Challenge 1016	32	17
38.	DON'T GO HOME (BMI)—Playmates; Can't You Get It Through Your Head (BMI)—Roulette 4072	—	1
39.	EL RANCHO ROCK (BMI)—Champs; Midnighter (BMI)—Challenge 59007	31	4
40.	YOU NEED HANDS (ASCAP)—Eydie Gorme; Dormi, Dormi, Dormi (ASCAP)—ABC-Paramount 9925	48	3
41.	OOH! MY SOUL (BMI)—Little Richard; True, Fine Mama (BMI)—Specialty 633	—	1
41.	GOT A MATCH (BMI)—Dady O's; Have a Cigar (BMI)—Cabot 122	—	1
43.	TO BE LOVED (BMI)—Jackie Wilson; Come Back to Me (BMI)—Brunswick 55052	35	10
44.	DING DONG (ASCAP)—McGuire Sisters; Since You Went Away to School (BMI)—Coral 61991	—	1
45.	RAVE ON (BMI)—Buddy Holly; Take Your Time (BMI)—Coral 61985	41	4
46.	TALK TO ME, TALK TO ME (BMI)—Little Willie John; Spasms (BMI)—King 5108	34	11
47.	I'M SORRY I MADE YOU CRY (ASCAP)—Connie Francis; Lock Up Your Heart (BMI)—M-G-M 12647	39	5
48.	I LOVE YOU SO (BMI)—Chantels; How Could You Call It Off? (BMI)—End 1020	—	1
49.	I KNOW WHERE I'M GOIN' (BMI)—George Hamilton IV; Who's Taking You to the Prom? (BMI)—ABC-Paramount 9924	45	2
50.	SPLISH SPLASH (BMI)—Bobby Darin; Judy, Don't Be Moody (BMI)—Atco 6117	—	1

THIS WEEK'S BEST BUYS

Special telephone reports and/or chart action indicate these recent releases have either broken out in one or more key areas or have leaped onto the charts and have excellent potential for placing among the Top 30 of The Billboard's Best Selling Pop Singles in Stores chart. Action sides are listed in capitol letters.

HARD HEADED WOMAN (Gladys, ASCAP)—Elvis Presley—RCA Victor 7280—DON'T ASK ME WHY (Gladys, ASCAP)

A CERTAIN SMILE (Miller, ASCAP)—Johnny Mathis—Columbia 41193—LET IT RAIN (Mathis, ASCAP)

LEFT RIGHT OUT OF YOUR HEART (Shapiro-Bernstein, ASCAP)—Patti Page—Mercury 71331—Longing to Hold You Again (Lear, ASCAP)

YOU'D BE SURPRISED (Berlin, ASCAP)—Kathy Linden—Felsted 8521—Why, Oh Why? (Sudbury, BMI)

The above are previous Billboard Spotlight picks.

WILLIE AND THE HAND JIVE (Dorado, BMI)—The Johnny Otis Show—Capitol 3966—Ring-A-Ling (Dorado, BMI)

RECENT POP RELEASES COMING UP STRONG

FOR SURVEY WEEK ENDING JUNE 14

The information given in this chart is based on actual sales to customers in a scientific sample of the nation's retail record outlets during the week ending on the date shown above. Sample design, sample size and all methods used in this continuing study of retail record sales are under the direct and continuing supervision and control of the School of Retailing of New York University.

Dream . . . . *Betty Johnson* (ASCAP) Atlantic 1186

When . . . . *The Kalin Twins* (ASCAP) Decca 30642

Willie and the Hand Jive . . . . . *The Johnny Otis Show* (BMI) Capitol 3966

Woodchopper's Ball . . . . *Hutch Davis* (ASCAP) Atco 6110

You'd Be Surprised . . . . *Kathy Linden* (ASCAP) Felsted 8521

Most Played by Jockeys

FOR SURVEY WEEK ENDING JUNE 14

SIDES are ranked in order of the greatest number of plays on disk jockey radio shows thruout the country. Results are based on The Billboard's weekly survey among the nation's disk jockeys. The reverse side of each record is also listed.

This Week		Last Week	Weeks on Chart
1.	PURPLE PEOPLE EATER (BMI)—Sheb Wooley I Can't Believe You're Mine (ASCAP)—M-G-M 12651	2	4
2.	ALL I HAVE TO DO IS DREAM (BMI)—Everly Brothers Claudette (BMI)—Cadence 1348	1	9
3.	SECRETLY (ASCAP)—Jimmie Rodgers Make Me a Miracle (ASCAP)—Roulette 4070	3	6
4.	RETURN TO ME (ASCAP)—Dean Martin Forgetting You (ASCAP)—Cap 3894	4	12
5.	BIG MAN (BMI)—Four Preps Stop, Baby (ASCAP)—Cap 3960	7	8
6.	SUGAR MOON (BMI)—Pat Boone Cherie, I Love You (ASCAP)—Dot 15750	5	7
7.	YAKETY YAK (BMI)—Coasters Zing! Went the Strings of My Heart (ASCAP)—Atco 6116	25	2
8.	WITCH DOCTOR (ASCAP)—David Seville Don't Whistle at Me, Baby (ASCAP)—Liberty 55132	12	11
9.	TWILIGHT TIME (BMI)—Platters Out of My Mind (BMI)—Mer 71289	6	12
10.	WHAT AM I LIVING FOR? (BMI)—Chuck Willis Hang Up My Rock and Roll Shoes (BMI)—Atlantic 1179	10	6
11.	YOU NEED HANDS (ASCAP)—Eydie Gorme Dormi, Dormi, Dormi (ASCAP)—ABC-Paramount 9925	16	5
12.	DO YOU WANT TO DANCE? (BMI)—Bobby Freeman Big Fat Woman (BMI)—Josie 835	19	3
13.	PADRE (ASCAP)—Toni Arden All at Once (ASCAP)—Dec 30628	13	2
14.	KEWPIE DOLL (ASCAP)—Perry Como Dance Only With Me (ASCAP)—Vic 7202	11	10
15.	WEAR MY RING AROUND YOUR NECK (BMI)—Elvis Presley Doncha' Think It's Time (BMI)—Vic 7240	8	9
16.	ENDLESS SLEEP (BMI)—Jody Reynolds Tight Capris (BMI)—Demon 1507	15	3
17.	LOOKING BACK (BMI)—Nat King Cole Do I Like It (BMI)—Cap 3939	18	7
18.	CHANSON D'AMOUR (ASCAP)—Art and Dotty Todd Along the Trail With You (ASCAP)—Era 1964	9	10
19.	GUESS THINGS HAPPEN THAT WAY (BMI)—Johnny Cash Come In, Stranger (BMI)—Sun 295	—	1
20.	PRETTY BABY (BMI)—Gino and Gina Love's a Carousel (BMI)—Mer 71283	—	1
21.	CHANSON D'AMOUR (ASCAP)—Fontane Sisters Cocoanut Grove (ASCAP)—Dot 15736	14	9
22.	WHEN THE BOYS TALK ABOUT THE GIRLS (ASCAP)—Valerie Carr Padre (ASCAP)—Roulette 4066	—	2
23.	JENNIE LEE (BMI)—Jan and Arnie Gotta Getta Date (BMI)—Arwin 108	17	4
24.	TORERO (ASCAP)—Renato Carosone Chella Lla (ASCAP)—Cap 71080	23	5
25.	OH, LONESOME ME (BMI)—Don Gibson I Can't Stop Loving You (BMI)—Vic 7133	—	10

Top 100 Sides

FOR SURVEY WEEK ENDING JUNE 14

This is a tabulation of dealer individual record sales listed according to the specific side requested by customers. No attempt is made to add sides together to reflect actual record sales. This is, therefore, a tabulation of sides or songs, and not records. This is the reason for any possible variation that occurs between the top 50 sides as reflected in this chart, and the top 50 record sellers as reflected in the "Best Sellers in Stores" chart.

Pos.	Song, Artist, Label	Last Week
1.	**THE PURPLE PEOPLE EATER,** Sheb Wooley, M-G-M	1
2.	**ALL I HAVE TO DO IS DREAM,** Everly Brothers, Cadence	2
3.	**YAKETY YAK,** Coasters, Atco	8
4.	**WITCH DOCTOR,** David Seville, Liberty	3
5.	**SECRETLY,** Jimmie Rodgers, Roulette	4
6.	**RETURN TO ME,** Dean Martin, Capitol	5
7.	**DO YOU WANT TO DANCE?** Bobby Freeman, Josie	7
8.	**LOOKING BACK,** Nat King Cole, Capitol	6
9.	**JENNIE LEE,** Jan & Arnie, Arwin	10
10.	**ENDLESS SLEEP,** Jody Reynolds, Demon	19
11.	**BIG MAN,** Four Preps, Capitol	13
11.	**SUGAR MOON,** Pat Boone, Dot	14
13.	**TWILIGHT TIME,** Platters, Mercury	9
14.	**HE'S GOT THE WHOLE WORLD IN HIS HANDS** Laurie London, Capitol	15
15.	**WEAR MY RING AROUND YOUR NECK,** Elvis Presley, Victor	12
16.	**CHANSON D'AMOUR,** Art and Dotty Todd, Era	16
17.	**OH, LONESOME ME,** Don Gibson, Victor	21
18.	**JOHNNY B. GOODE,** Chuck Berry, Chess	10
19.	**ZORRO,** Chordettes, Cadence	17
20.	**RUMBLE,** Link Wray and His Ray Men, Cadence	24
21.	**FOR YOUR LOVE,** Ed Townsend, Capitol	18
22.	**KEWPIE DOLL,** Perry Como, Victor	21
22.	**WHAT AM I LIVING FOR?** Chuck Willis, Atlantic	25
24.	**HIGH SCHOOL CONFIDENTIAL,** Jerry Lee Lewis, Sun	26
24.	**GUESS THINGS HAPPEN THAT WAY,** Johnny Cash, Sun	28
26.	**NO CHEMISE, PLEASE,** Gerry Granahan, Sunbeam	37
27.	**LEROY,** Jack Scott, Carlton	27
28.	**PADRE,** Toni Arden, Decca	39
29.	**TORREO,** Renate Carosone, Capitol	20
30.	**FOR YOUR PRECIOUS LOVE,** Jerry Butler and the Impressions, Abner	34
31.	**YOU,** Aquatones, Fargo	28
31.	**I WONDER WHY,** Dion and the Belmonts, Laurie	42
33.	**BOOK OF LOVE,** Monotones, Argo	23
34.	**PATRICIA,** Perez Prado, Victor	66
35.	**TEQUILA,** Champs, Challenge	30
36.	**EL RANCHO ROCK,** Champs, Challenge	30
36.	**LET THE BELLS KEEP RINGING,** Paul Anka, ABC-Paramount	30
36.	**YOU NEED HANDS,** Eydie Gorme, ABC-Paramount	47
36.	**DON'T GO HOME,** Playmates, Roulette	53
40.	**TO BE LOVED,** Jackie Wilson, Brunswick	36
40.	**OOH! MY SOUL,** Little Richard, Specialty	53
40.	**GOT A MATCH,** Daddy-O's, Cabot	60
43.	**RAVE ON,** Buddy Holly, Coral	39
43.	**TEACHER, TEACHER,** Johnny Mathis, Columbia	47
43.	**DING DONG,** McGuire Sisters, Coral	66
46.	**TALK TO ME, TALK TO ME,** Little Willie John, King	34
46.	**I'M SORRY I MADE YOU CRY,** Connie Francis, M-G-M	37
48.	**I LOVE YOU SO,** Chantels, End	80
49.	**I KNOW WHERE I'M GOIN',** George Hamilton IV, ABC-Paramount	43
49.	**CRAZY LOVE,** Paul Anka, ABC-Paramount	70
51.	**SPLISH SPLASH,** Bobby Darin, Atco	—
52.	**SKINNY MINNIE,** Bill Haley and His Comets, Decca	50
52.	**WOODCHOPPER'S BALL,** Hutch Davie, Atco	86
54.	**TRY THE IMPOSSIBLE,** Lee Andrews and the Hearts, United Artist	33
54.	**BILLY,** Kathy Linden, Felsted	41
56.	**(IT'S BEEN A LONG TIME) PRETTY BABY,** Gino and Gina, Mercury	45
57.	**MARCH FROM THE RIVER KWAI AND "COLONEL BOGEY,"** Mitch Miller, Columbia	47
57.	**BEWILDERED,** Mickey and Sylvia, Vik	70
59.	**INDIAN LOVE CALL,** Ernie Freeman, Imperial	74
60.	**WILLIE AND THE HAND JIVE,** Johnny Otis, Capitol	—
60.	**JUST MARRIED,** Marty Robbins, Columbia	53
60.	**CHA HUA HUA,** Pets, Arwin	53
60.	**ALL THE TIME,** Johnny Mathis, Columbia	86
60.	**DREAM,** Betty Johnson, Atlantic	95
65.	**WHEN,** Kalin Twins, Decca	—
65.	**SICK AND TIRED,** Fats Domino, Imperial	45
65.	**YOU'D BE SURPRISED,** Kathy Linden, Felsted	63
68.	**HANG UP MY ROCK AND ROLL SHOES,** Chuck Willis, Atlantic	43
68.	**LAZY MARY,** Lou Monte, Victor	51
68.	**FLIP TOP BOX,** Dickey Doo and the Don'ts, Swan	66
71.	**A VERY PRECIOUS LOVE,** Ames Brothers, Victor	86
72.	**DOTTIE,** Danny and the Juniors, ABC-Paramount	—
72.	**YOUNG, WARM, AND WONDERFUL,** Tony Bennett, Columbia	—
72.	**WE BELONG TOGETHER,** Robert and Johnny, Old Town	51
72.	**WHO'S SORRY NOW,** Connie Francis M-G-M	53
72.	**THINGS I LOVE,** Fidelities, Baton	60
72.	**JACQUELINE,** Bobby Helms, Decca	63
72.	**BEEN SO LONG,** Pastels, Argo	66
72.	**COME IN, STRANGER,** Johnny Cash, Sun	74
80.	**CLAUDETTE,** Everly Brothers, Cadence	80
80.	**THERE'S ONLY ONE OF YOU,** Four Lads, Columbia	86
82.	**GOT A MATCH,** Frank Gallup, ABC-Paramount	—
82.	**COME WHAT MAY,** Clyde McPhatter, Atlantic	86
84.	**WHEN THE BOYS TALK ABOUT THE GIRLS,** Valarie Carr, Roulette	—
84.	**CATCH A FALLING STAR,** Perry Como, Victor	53
84.	**MAKE ME A MIRACLE,** Jimmie Rodgers, Roulette	63
84.	**NEE NEE NA NA NA NA NU NU,** Dickey Doo and the Don'ts, Swan	70
84.	**HAVE FAITH,** Gene Allison, Vee Jay	95
84.	**TUMBLING TUMBLEWEEDS,** Billy Vaughn, Dot	—
90.	**LITTLE PIXIE,** Moe Koffman Quartet, Jubilee	—
90.	**TEACHER'S PET,** Doris Day, Columbia	74
90.	**EVERY NIGHT,** Chantels, End	80
90.	**HIGH SIGN,** Diamonds, Mercury	86
94.	**MOONLIGHT BAY,** Drifters, Atlantic	—
94.	**I MET HIM ON SUNDAY,** Shireiles, Decca	53
94.	**BELIEVE WHAT YOU SAY,** Ricky Nelson, Imperial	60
94.	**CHA HUA HUA,** Eddie Platt, Gone	74
94.	**A WONDERFUL TIME UP THERE,** Pat Boone, Dot	74
94.	**THE LONG HOT SUMMER,** Jimmie Rodgers, Roulette	95
94.	**CHANSON D'AMOUR,** Fontane Sisters, Dot	—

BEST SELLING POP SINGLES IN STORES

The information given in this chart is based on actual sales to customers in a scientific sample of the nation's retail record outlets during the week ending on the date shown above. Sample design, sample size, and all methods used in this continuing study of retail record sales are under the direct and continuing supervision and control of the School of Retailing of New York University.

FOR SURVEY WEEK ENDING JUNE 21, 1958

This Week		Last Week	Weeks on Chart
1.	PURPLE PEOPLE EATER (BMI)—Sheb Wooley I Can't Believe You're Mine (ASCAP)—M-G-M 12651	1	5
2.	YAKETY YAK (BMI)—Coasters Zing! Went the Strings of My Heart (ASCAP)—Atco 6116	4	4
3.	ALL I HAVE TO DO IS DREAM (BMI)—Everly Brothers CLAUDETTE (BMI)—Cadence 1348	2	10
4.	WITCH DOCTOR (ASCAP)—David Seville Don't Whistle at Me Baby (ASCAP)—Liberty 55132	5	12
5.	SECRETLY (ASCAP)—Jimmie Rodgers MAKE ME A MIRACLE (ASCAP)—Roulette 4070	3	8
6.	ENDLESS SLEEP (BMI)—Jody Reynolds Tight Capris (BMI)—Demon 1507	10	6
7.	RETURN TO ME (ASCAP)—Dean Martin Forgetting You (ASCAP)—Cap 3894	6	12
8.	JENNIE LEE (BMI)—Jan and Arnie Gotta Getta Date (BMI)—Arwin 108	9	6
9.	DO YOU WANT TO DANCE? (BMI)—Bobby Freeman Big Fat Woman (BMI)—Josie 835	7	7
10.	BIG MAN (BMI)—Four Preps Stop, Baby (ASCAP)—Cap 3960	12	8
11.	SUGAR MOON (BMI)—Pat Boone Cherie, I Love You (ASCAP)—Dot 15750	11	8
12.	PATRICIA (ASCAP)—Perez Prado Why Wait (BMI)—Vic 7245	36	2
13.	SPLISH SPLASH (BMI)—Bobby Darin Judy, Don't Be Moody (BMI)—Atco 6117	50	2
14.	TWILIGHT TIME (BMI)—Platters Out of My Mind (BMI)—Mer 71289	13	12
15.	HARD HEADED WOMAN (ASCAP)—Elvis Presley Don't Ask Me Why (ASCAP)—Vic 7280	—	1
16.	RUMBLE (BMI)—Link Wray and His Ray Men The Swag (BMI)—Cadence 1347	21	9
17.	JOHNNY B. GOODE (BMI)—Chuck Berry Around and Around (BMI)—Chess 1691	18	9
18.	LOOKING BACK (BMI)—Nat King Cole Do I Like It (BMI)—Cap 3939	8	12
19.	PADRE (ASCAP)—Toni Arden All at Once (ASCAP)—Dec 30628	29	6
20.	OH, LONESOME ME (BMI)—Don Gibson I Can't Stop Loving You (BMI)—Vic 7133	17	16
21.	GUESS THINGS HAPPEN THAT WAY (BMI)—Johnny Cash COME IN, STRANGER (BMI)—Sun 295	23	5
22.	HIGH SCHOOL CONFIDENTIAL (BMI)—Jerry Lee Lewis Fools Like Me (BMI)—Sun 296	25	5
23.	WHAT AM I LIVING FOR? (BMI)—Chuck Willis HANG UP MY ROCK AND ROLL SHOES (BMI)—Atlantic 1179	19	8
24.	I WONDER WHY? (ASCAP)—Dion and the Belmonts Teen Angel (ASCAP)—Laurie 3013	34	6
25.	NO CHEMISE, PLEASE (BMI)—Gerry Granahan Girl of My Dreams (ASCAP)—Sunbeam 102	27	3
26.	LEROY (BMI)—Jack Scott MY TRUE LOVE (BMI)—Carlton 462	28	3
27.	WEAR MY RING AROUND YOUR NECK (BMI)—Elvis Presley Doncha' Think It's Time (BMI)—Vic 7240	14	11
28.	HE'S GOT THE WHOLE WORLD IN HIS HANDS (ASCAP)—Laurie London Handed Down (ASCAP)—Cap 3891	15	14
29.	WHEN (ASCAP)—Kalin Twins Three o'Clock Thrill (BMI)—Dec 30642	—	1
30.	ALL THE TIME (ASCAP)—Johnny Mathis TEACHER, TEACHER (ASCAP)—Col 41152	31	8
31.	OOH! MY SOUL (BMI)—Little Richard TRUE, FINE MAMA (BMI)—Specialty 633	41	2
32.	CHANSON D'AMOUR (ASCAP)—Art and Dotty Todd Along the Trail With You (ASCAP)—Era 1064	16	11
33.	FOR YOUR LOVE (BMI)—Ed Townsend Over and Over Again (BMI)—Cap 3926	22	11
34.	TORERO (ASCAP)—Renato Carosone Chella Lla (ASCAP)—Cap 71080	30	8
35.	LET THE BELLS KEEP RINGING (BMI)—Paul Anka CRAZY LOVE (BMI)—ABC-Paramount 9907	26	11
36.	WILLIE AND THE HAND JIVE (BMI)—Johnny Otis Show Ring-a-Ling (BMI)—Cap 3966	—	1
37.	ZORRO (BMI)—Chordettes Love's a Two-Way Street (BMI)—Cadence 1349	20	6
38.	KEWPIE DOLL (ASCAP)—Perry Como Dance Only With Me (ASCAP)—Vic 7202	24	11
39.	DON'T GO HOME (BMI)—Playmates Can't You Get It Through Your Head (BMI)—Roulette 4072	38	2
40.	YOU NEED HANDS (ASCAP)—Eydie Gorme Dormi, Dormi, Dormi (ASCAP)—ABC-Paramount 9925	40	4
41.	EL RANCHO ROCK (BMI)—Champs Midnighter (BMI)—Challenge 59007	39	5
42.	GOT A MATCH (BMI)—Daddy-O's Have a Cigar (BMI)—Cabot 122	41	2
43.	FOR YOUR PRECIOUS LOVE (ASCAP)—Jerry Butler and Impressions Sweet Was the Wine (ASCAP)—Abner 1013	32	3
44.	I LOVE YOU SO (BMI)—Chantels How Could You Call It Off? (BMI)—End 1020	48	2
45.	YOU (BMI)—Aquatones She's the One for Me (BMI)—Fargo 1001	33	9
46.	BOOK OF LOVE (BMI)—Monotones You Never Loved Me (BMI)—Argo 5290	35	14
47.	(IT'S BEEN A LONG TIME) PRETTY BABY (BMI)—Gino and Gina Love's a Carousel (BMI)—Mer 71283	—	4
48.	CHA HUA HUA (BMI)—Pets Cha-Kow-Ski (BMI)—Arwin 109	—	2
49.	DOTTIE (BMI)—Danny and the Juniors In the Meantime (BMI)—ABC-Parmount 9926	—	1
50.	DING DONG (ASCAP)—McGuire Sisters Since You Went Away to School (BMI)—Coral 61991	44	2

THIS WEEK'S BEST BUYS

Special telephone reports and/or chart action indicate these recent releases have either broken out in one or more key areas or have leaped onto the charts and have excellent potential for placing among the Top 30 of The Billboard's Best Selling Pop Singles in Stores chart. Action sides are listed in capitol letters

POOR LITTLE FOOL (Eric, BMI)—Ricky Nelson—Imperial 5528—Don't Leave Me This Way (Eric, BMI)

IF DREAMS CAME TRUE (Korwin, ASCAP)—Pat Boone—Dot 15785
THAT'S HOW MUCH I LOVE YOU (Fowler, BMI)
The above are previous Billboard Spotlight picks.

REBEL ROUSER (Gregmark, BMI)—Duane Eddy—Jamie 1104—Stalkin' (Gregmark, BMI)

ENCHANTED ISLAND (Korwin, ASCAP)—The Four Lads—Columbia 41194—Guess What the Neighbors'll Say (Dominion, BMI)

RECENT POP RELEASES COMING UP STRONG

FOR SURVEY WEEK ENDING JUNE 21

The information given in this chart is based on actual sales to customers in a scientific sample of the nation's retail record outlets during the week ending on the date shown above. Sample design, sample size and all methods used in this continuing study of retail record sales are under the direct and continuing supervision and control of the School of Retailing of New York University.

Dream . . . . . . *Betty Johnson*
(ASCAP) Atlantic 1186

Left Right Out of Your Heart . . . . . . *Patti Page*
(ASCAP) Mercury 71331

One Summer Night . . . . . . *Danleers*
(BMI) Mercury 71332

Rebel Rouser . . . . . . *Duane Eddy*
(BMI) Jamie 1104

Most Played by Jockeys

FOR SURVEY WEEK ENDING JUNE 21

SIDES are ranked in order of the greatest number of plays on disk jockey radio shows thruout the country. Results are based on The Billboard's weekly survey among the nation's disk jockeys. The reverse side of each record is also listed.

This Week		Last Week	Weeks on Chart
1.	PURPLE PEOPLE EATER (BMI)—Sheb Wooley I Can't Believe You're Mine (ASCAP)—M-G-M 12651	1	5
2.	ALL I HAVE TO DO IS DREAM (BMI)—Everly Brothers Claudette (BMI)—Cadence 1348	2	10
3.	BIG MAN (BMI)—Four Preps Stop, Baby (ASCAP)—Cap 3960	5	9
4.	SECRETLY (ASCAP)—Jimmie Rodgers Make Me a Miracle (ASCAP)—Roulette 4070	3	7
5.	YAKETY YAK (BMI)—Coasters Zing! Went the Strings of My Heart (ASCAP)—Atco 6116	7	3
6.	RETURN TO ME (ASCAP)—Dean Martin Forgetting You (ASCAP)—Cap 3894	4	13
7.	ENDLESS SLEEP (BMI)—Jody Reynolds Tight Capris (BMI)—Demon 1507	16	4
8.	SUGAR MOON (BMI)—Pat Boone Cherie, I Love You (ASCAP)—Dot 15750	6	8
9.	WHAT AM I LIVING FOR? (BMI)—Chuck Willis Hang Up My Rock and Roll Shoes (BMI)—Atlantic 1179	10	7
10.	TWILIGHT TIME (BMI)—Platters Out of My Mind (BMI)—Mer 71289	9	13
11.	WITCH DOCTOR (ASCAP)—David Seville Don't Whistle at Me, Baby (ASCAP)—Liberty 55132	8	12
12.	DO YOU WANT TO DANCE? (BMI)—Bobby Freeman Big Fat Woman (BMI)—Josie 835	12	4
13.	PATRICIA (ASCAP)—Perez Prado Why Wait (BMI)—Vic 7245	—	1
14.	YOU NEED HANDS (ASCAP)—Eydie Gorme Dormi, Dormi, Dormi (ASCAP)—ABC-Paramount 9925	11	6
15.	WHEN (ASCAP)—Kalin Twins Three o'Clock Thrill (BMI)—Dec 30642	—	1
15.	LEFT RIGHT OUT OF YOUR HEART (ASCAP)—Patti Page Longing to Hold You Again (ASCAP)—Mer 71331	—	1
17.	JENNIE LEE (BMI)—Jan and Arnie Gotta Getta Date (BMI)—Arwin 108	23	5
18.	PADRE (ASCAP)—Toni Arden All at Once (ASCAP)—Dec 30628	13	3
19.	DREAM (ASCAP)—Betty Johnson How Much? (BMI)—Atlantic 1186	—	1
20.	ONE SUMMER NIGHT (BMI)—Dandeleers Wheelin' and A-Dealin' (BMI)—Mer 71322	—	1
21.	LOOKING BACK (BMI)—Nat King Cole Do I Like It (BMI)—Cap 3939	17	8
22.	WILLIE AND THE HAND JIVE (BMI)—Johnny Otis Show Ring-a-Ling (BMI)—Cap 3966	—	1
23.	YOUNG AND WARM AND WONDERFUL (ASCAP)—Tony Bennett Now I Lay Me Down to Sleep (ASCAP)—Col 41172	—	1
23.	HARD HEADED WOMAN (ASCAP)—Elvis Presley Don't Ask Me Why (ASCAP)—Vic 7280	—	1
25.	WEAR MY RING AROUND YOUR NECK (BMI)—Elvis Presley Doncha' Think It's Time (BMI)—Vic 7240	15	10

Top 100 Sides

STORE RECORDED SALES — NEW YORK UNIVERSITY SCHOOL OF RETAILING — THE BILLBOARD

FOR SURVEY WEEK ENDING JUNE 21

This is a tabulation of dealer individual record sales listed according to the specific side requested by customers. No attempt is made to add sides together to reflect actual record sales. This is, therefore, a tabulation of sides or songs, and not records. This is the reason for any possible variation that occurs between the top 50 sides as reflected in this chart, and the top 50 record sellers as reflected in the "Best Sellers in Stores" chart.

Pos.	Song, Artist, Label	Last Week
1.	**THE PURPLE PEOPLE EATER,** Sheb Wooley, M-G-M	1
2.	**YAKETY YAK,** Coasters, Atco	3
3.	**ALL I HAVE TO DO IS DREAM,** Everly Brothers, Cadence	2
4.	**WITCH DOCTOR,** David Seville, Liberty	4
5.	**ENDLESS SLEEP,** Jody Reynolds, Demon	10
6.	**RETURN TO ME,** Dean Martin, Capitol	6
7.	**SECRETLY,** Jimmie Rodgers, Roulette	5
8.	**JENNIE LEE,** Jan & Arnie, Arwin	9
9.	**DO YOU WANT TO DANCE?** Bobby Freeman, Josie	7
10.	**BIG MAN,** Four Preps, Capitol	11
11.	**SUGAR MOON,** Pat Boone, Dot	11
12.	**PATRICIA,** Perez Prado, Victor	34
13.	**SPLISH SPLASH,** Bobby Darin, Atco	51
14.	**TWILIGHT TIME,** Platters, Mercury	13
15.	**HARD HEADED WOMAN,** Elvis Presley, Victor	—
16.	**RUMBLE,** Link Wray & His Ray Men, Cadence	20
17.	**JOHNNY B. GOODE,** Chuck Berry, Chess	18
18.	**LOOKING BACK,** Nat King Cole, Capitol	8
19.	**PADRE,** Toni Arden, Decca	28
20.	**OH, LONESOME ME,** Don Gibson, Victor	17
21.	**HIGH SCHOOL CONFIDENTIAL,** Jerry Lee Lewis, Sun	24
22.	**I WONDER WHY,** Dion & the Belmonts, Laurie	31
23.	**NO CHEMISE, PLEASE,** Gerry Granahan, Sunbeam	26
24.	**WEAR MY RING AROUND YOUR NECK,** Elvis Presley, Victor	15
25.	**HE'S GOT THE WHOLE WORLD IN HIS HANDS** Laurie London, Capitol	14
26.	**WHEN,** Kalin Twins, Decca	65
27.	**GUESS THINGS HAPPEN THAT WAY,** Johnny Cash, Sun	24
28.	**CHANSON D'AMOUR,** Art & Dotty Todd, Era	16
29.	**FOR YOUR LOVE,** Ed Townsend, Capitol	21
29.	**WHAT AM I LIVING FOR?** Chuck Willis, Atlantic	22
31.	**TORERO,** Renate Carosone, Capitol	29
32.	**LEROY,** Jack Scott, Carlton	27
33.	**ZORRO,** Chordettes, Cadence	19
33.	**WILLIE AND THE HAND JIVE,** Johnny Otis,, Capitol	60
35.	**OOH! MY SOUL,** Little Richard, Specialty	40
36.	**KEWPIE DOLL,** Perry Como, Victor	22
36.	**DON'T GO HOME,** Playmates, Roulette	36
38.	**YOU NEED HANDS,** Eydie Gorme, ABC-Paramount	36
39.	**EL RANCHO ROCK,** Champs, Challenge	36
40.	**GOT A MATCH,** Daddy-O's, Cabot	40
41.	**FOR YOUR PRECIOUS LOVE,** Jerry Butler & the Impressions, Abner	30
42.	**I LOVE YOU SO,** Chantels, End	48
42.	**ALL THE TIME,** Johnny Mathis, Columbia	60
44.	**YOU,** Aquatones, Fargo	31
45.	**BOOK OF LOVE,** Monotones, Argo	33
46.	**(IT'S BEEN A LONG TIME) PRETTY BABY,** Gino & Gina, Mercury	56
47.	**CHA HUA HUA,** Pets, Arwin	60
48.	**DING DONG,** McGuire Sisters, Coral	43
48.	**DOTTIE,** Danny & the Juniors, ABC-Paramount	72
50.	**REBEL ROUSER,** Duane Eddy, Jamie	—
50.	**TO BE LOVED,** Jackie Wilson, Brunswick	40
50.	**YOU'D BE SURPRISED,** Kathy Linden, Felsted	65
53.	**WOODCHOPPER'S BALL,** Hutch Davie, Atco	52
54.	**ONE SUMMER NIGHT,** Danleers, Mercury	—
54.	**LET THE BELLS KEEP RINGING,** Paul Anka, ABC-Paramount	36
56.	**CRAZY LOVE,** Paul Anka, ABC-Paramount	49
57.	**RAVE ON,** Buddy Holly, Coral	43
58.	**TEACHER, TEACHER,** Johnny Mathis, Columbia,	43
58.	**I'M SORRY I MADE YOU CRY,** Connie Francis, M-G-M	46
58.	**DREAM,** Betty Johnson, Atlantic	60
61.	**MY TRUE LOVE,** Jack Scott, Carlton	—
61.	**I KNOW WHERE I'M GOING,** George Hamilton IV, ABC-Paramount	49
61.	**FLIP TOP BOX,** Dickey Doo & the Don'ts, Swan	68
61.	**YOUNG AND WARM AND WONDERFUL,** Tony Bennett, Columbia	72
61.	**GOT A MATCH,** Frank Gallup, ABC-Paramount	82
66.	**LEFT RIGHT OUT OF YOUR HEART,** Patti Page,, Mercury	—
66.	**YOU'RE MAKING A MISTAKE,** Platters, Mercury	—
66.	**MARCH FROM THE RIVER KWAI AND "COLONEL BOGEY"** Mitch Miller, Columbia	57
66.	**JUST MARRIED,** Marty Robbins, Columbia	60
66.	**HANG UP MY ROCK AND ROLL SHOES,** Chuck Willis, Atlantic	68
66.	**COME IN, STRANGER,** Johnny Cash, Sun	72
72.	**SKINNY MINNIE,** Bill Haley & His Comets, Decca	52
72.	**TRY THE IMPOSSIBLE,** Lee Andrews & the Hearts, United Artists	54
72.	**LITTLE PIXIE,** Moe Koffman, Jubilee	90
72.	**MOONLIGHT BAY,** Drifters, Atlantic	94
76.	**BEWITCHED,** Betty Smith, London	—
76.	**A CERTAIN SMILE,** Johnny Mathis, Columbia	—
76.	**BEWILDERED,** Mickey & Sylvia, Vik	57
76.	**INDIAN LOVE CALL,** Ernie Freeman, Imperial	59
76.	**A VERY PRECIOUS LOVE,** Ames Brothers, Victor	71
76.	**COME WHAT MAY,** Clyde McPhatter, Atlantic	82
82.	**SHIEK OF ARABY,** Lou Monte, Victor	—
82.	**SINGING HILLS,** Billy Vaughn, Dot	—
82.	**LAZY MARY,** Lou Monte, Victor	68
85.	**BLUE BLUE DAY,** Don Gibson,, Victor	—
85.	**TALK TO ME, TALK TO ME,** Little Willie John, King	46
85.	**MAKE ME A MIRACLE,** Jimmie Rodgers, Roulette	84
88.	**TRUE, FINE MAMA,** Little Richard, Specialty	—
88.	**JACQUELINE,** Bobby Helms, Decca	72
88.	**CLAUDETTE,** Everly Brothers, Cadence	80
91.	**ENCHANTED ISLAND,** Four Lads, Columbia	—
91.	**BILLY,** Kathy Linden, Felsted	54
91.	**WE BELONG TOGETHER,** Robert and Johnny, Old Town	72
94.	**TEQUILA,** Champs, Challenge	35
94.	**WHO'S SORRY NOW?** Connie Francis, M-G-M	72
96.	**WHEN THE BOYS TALK ABOUT THE GIRLS,** Valerie Carr, Roulette	84
96.	**HIGH SIGN,** Diamonds, Mercury	90
96.	**TEACHER'S PET,** Doris Day, Columbia	90
96.	**CHANSON D'AMOUR,** Fontane Sisters, Dot	94
96.	**CHA HUA HUA,** Eddie Platt, Gone	94
96.	**THE LONG HOT SUMMER,** Jimime Rodgers, Roulette	94

BEST SELLING POP SINGLES IN STORES

The information given in this chart is based on actual sales to customers in a scientific sample of the nation's retail record outlets during the week ending on the date shown above. Sample design, sample size, and all methods used in this continuing study of retail record sales are under the direct and continuing supervision and control of the School of Retailing of New York University.

FOR SURVEY WEEK ENDING JUNE 28, 1958

This Week		Last Week	Weeks on Chart
1.	PURPLE PEOPLE EATER (BMI)—Sheb Wooley I Can't Believe You're Mine (ASCAP)—M-G-M 12651	1	6
2.	YAKETY YAK (BMI)—Coasters Zing! Went the Strings of My Heart (ASCAP)—Atco 6116	2	5
3.	HARD HEADED WOMAN (ASCAP)—Elvis Presley Don't Ask Me Why? (ASCAP)—Vic 7280	15	2
4.	ALL I HAVE TO DO IS DREAM (BMI)—Everly Brothers Claudette (BMI)—Cadence 1348	3	11
5.	ENDLESS SLEEP (BMI)—Jody Reynolds Tight Capris (BMI)—Demon 1507	6	7
6.	PATRICIA (ASCAP)—Perez Prado Why Wait (BMI)—Vic 7245	12	3
7.	SECRETLY (ASCAP)—Jimmie Rodgers.. MAKE ME A MIRACLE (ASCAP)—Roulette 4070	5	9
8.	SPLISH SPLASH (BMI)—Bobby Darin Judy, Don't Be Moody (BMI)—Atco 6117	13	3
9.	RETURN TO ME (ASCAP)—Dean Martin Forgetting You (ASCAP)—Cap 3894	7	13
10.	WITCH DOCTOR (ASCAP)—David Seville Don't Whistle at Me, Baby (ASCAP)—Liberty 55132	4	13
11.	DO YOU WANT TO DANCE? (BMI)—Bobby Freeman Big Fat Woman (BMI)—Josie 835	9	8
12.	JENNIE LEE (BMI)—Jan and Arnie Gotta Getta Date (BMI)—Arwin 108	8	7
13.	LOOKING BACK (BMI)—Nat King Cole Do I Like It (BMI)—Cap 3939	18	13
14.	TWILIGHT TIME (BMI)—Platters Out of My Mind (BMI)—Mer 71289	14	13
15.	BIG MAN (BMI)—Four Preps Stop, Baby (ASCAP)—Cap 3960	10	9
16.	SUGAR MOON (BMI)—Pat Boone Cherie, I Love You (ASCAP)—Dot 115750	11	9
17.	FOR YOUR PRECIOUS LOVE (ASCAP)—Jerry Butler and Impressions Sweet Was the Wine (ASCAP)—Abner 1013	43	4
18.	POOR LITTLE FOOL (BMI)—Ricky Nelson Don't Leave Me This Way (BMI)—Imperial 5528	—	1
19.	WHEN (ASCAP)—Kalin Twins Three o-Clock Thrill (BMI)—Dec 30642	29	2
20.	GUESS THINGS HAPPEN THAT WAY (BMI)—Johnny Cash COME IN, STRANGER (BMI)—Sun 295	21	6
21.	LEROY (BMI)—Jack Scott MY TRUE LOVE (BMI) Carlton 462	26	4
22.	REBEL-'ROUSER (BMI)—Duane Eddy Stalkin' (BMI)—Jamie 1104	—	1
23.	WHAT AM I LIVING FOR? (BMI)—Chuck Willis HANG UP MY ROCK AND ROLL SHOES (BMI)—Atlantic 1179	23	9
24.	JOHNNY B. GOODE (BMI)—Chuck Berry Around and Around (BMI)—Chess 1691	17	10
25.	PADRE (ASCAP)—Toni Arden All at Once (ASCAP)—Dec 30628	19	7
26.	HIGH SCHOOL CONFIDENTIAL (BMI)—Jerry Lee Lewis Fools Like Me (BMI—Sun 296	22	6
27.	WEAR MY RING AROUND YOUR NECK (BMI)—Elvis Presley Doncha' Think It's Time (BMI)—Vic 7240	27	12
28.	I WONDER WHY (ASCAP)—Dion and the Belmonts Teen Angel (ASCAP)—Laurie 3013	24	7
29.	WILLIE AND THE HAND JIVE (BMI)—Johnny Otis Show Ring-A-Ling (BMI)—Cap 3966	36	2
30.	NO CHEMISE, PLEASE (BMI)—Gerry Granahan Girl of My Dreams (ASCAP)—Sunbeam 102	25	4
31.	OOH! MY SOUL (BMI)—Little Richard TRUE, FINE MAMA (BMI)—Specialty 633	31	3
32.	OH, LONESOME ME (BMI)—Don Gibson I Can't Stop Loving You (BMI)—Vic 7133	20	17
33.	RUMBLE (BMI)—Link Wray and His Ray Men The Swag (BMI)—Cadence 1347	16	10
34.	FOR YOUR LOVE (BMI)—Ed Townsend Over and Over Again (BMI)—Cap 3926	33	12
35.	LEFT RIGHT OUT OF YOUR HEART (ASCAP)— Patti Page Longing to Hold You Again (ASCAP)—Mercury 71331	—	1
36.	ZORRO (BMI)—Chordettes Love's a Two Way Street (BMI)—Cadence 1349	37	7
37.	TORERO (ASCAP)—Renato Carosone Chella Lla (ASCAP)—Cap 71080	34	9
38.	YOU NEED HANDS (ASCAP)—Eydie Gorme Dormi, Dormi, Dormi (ASCAP)—ABC-Paramount 9925	40	5
39.	GOT A MATCH (BMI)—Daddy O's Have a Cigar (BMI)—Cabot 122	42	3
40.	EL RANCHO ROCK (BMI)—Champs Midnighter (BMI)—Challenge 59007	41	6
41.	ONE SUMMER NIGHT (BMI)—Danleers Weelin' and a Dealin' (BMI)—Mercury 71322	—	1
42.	CHANSON D'AMOUR (ASCAP)—Art and Dotty Todd Along the Trail With You (ASCAP)—Era 1064	32	12
43.	DON'T GO HOME (BMI)— Playmates.. Can't You Get It Through Your Head (BMI)—Roulette 4072	39	3
44.	HE'S GOT THE WHOLE WORLD IN HIS HANDS (ASCAP)—Laurie London Handed Down (ASCAP)—Cap 3891	28	15
45.	A CERTAIN SMILE (ASCAP)—Johnny Mathis Let It Rain (ASCAP)—Col 41193	—	1
46.	KEWPIE DOLL (ASCAP)—Perry Como Dance Only With Me (ASCAP)—Vic 7202	38	12
47.	BOOK OF LOVE (BMI)—Monotones You Never Loved Me (BMI)—Argo 5290	46	15
48.	DOTTIE (BMI)—Danny and the Juniors In the Meantime (BMI)—ABC-Paramount 9926	49	2
49.	DING DONG (ASCAP)—McGuire Sisters Since You Went Away to School (BMI)—Coral 61991	50	3
50.	YOU'RE MAKING A MISTAKE (BMI)—Platters My Old Flame (ASCAP)—Mercury 71320	—	1
50.	COME WHAT MAY (BMI)—Clyde McPhatter Let Me Know (BMI)—Atlantic 1185	—	1
50.	BEWITCHED (ASCAP)—Betty Smith Group Hand Jive (BMI)—London 1787	—	1

THIS WEEK'S BEST BUYS

Special telephone reports and/or chart action indicate these recent releases have either broken out in one or more key areas or have leaped onto the charts and have excellent potential for placing among the Top 30 of The Billboard's Best Selling Pop Singles in Stores chart. Action sides are listed in capitol letters

GINGER BREAD (Jimskip-Rambed, BMI)—Frankie Avalon—Chancellor 1021—BLUE BETTY (Criterion-Debmar, ASCAP)

EARLY IN THE MORNING (Royalty, ASCAP)—The Rinky-Dinks—Atco 6121—Now We're One (Portrait, BMI)

Both are previous Billboard Spotlight picks.

The following record, not previously selected as a Best Buy, is on the chart for the first time this week.

ONE SUMMER NIGHT (Addone, BMI)—The Danleers—Mercury 71322—Wheelin' and Dealin' (Addone, BMI)

RECENT POP RELEASES COMING UP STRONG

FOR SURVEY WEEK ENDING JUNE 28

The information given in this chart is based on actual sales to customers in a scientific sample of the nation's retail record outlets during the week ending on the date shown above. Sample design, sample size and all methods used in this continuing study of retail record sales are under the direct and continuing supervision and control of the School of Retailing of New York University.

Blue, Blue Day . . . . *Don Gibson*
(BMI) RCA Victor 7010

Enchanted Island . . . . *The Four Lads*
(ASCAP) Columbia 41194

The Singing Hills . . . . *Billy Vaughn*
(ASCAP) Dot 15771

Most Played by Jockeys

FOR SURVEY WEEK ENDING JUNE 28

SIDES are ranked in order of the greatest number of plays on disk jockey radio shows thruout the country. Results are based on The Billboard's weekly survey among the nation's disk jockeys. The reverse side of each record is also listed.

This Week		Last Week	Weeks on Chart
1.	PURPLE PEOPLE EATER (BMI)—Sheb Wooley... I Can't Believe You're Mine (ASCAP)—M-G-M 12651	1	6
2.	ALL I HAVE TO DO IS DREAM (BMI)—Everly Brothers... Claudette (BMI)—Cadence 1348	2	11
3.	YAKETY YAK (BMI)—Coasters... Zing! Went the Strings of My Heart (ASCAP)—Atco 6116	5	4
4.	SECRETLY (ASCAP)—Jimmie Rodgers... Make Me a Miracle (ASCAP)—Roulette 4070	4	8
5.	RETURN TO ME (ASCAP)—Dean Martin... Forgetting You (ASCAP)—Cap 3894	6	14
6.	SUGAR MOON (BMI)—Pat Boone... Cherie, I Love You (ASCAP)—Dot 15750	8	9
7.	BIG MAN (BMI)—Four Preps... Stop! Baby (ASCAP)—Cap 3960	3	10
8.	ENDLESS SLEEP (BMI)—Jody Reynolds... Tight Capris (BMI)—Demon 1507	7	5
9.	WHAT AM I LIVING FOR? (BMI)—Chuck Willis... Hang Up My Rock and Roll Shoes (BMI)—Atlantic 1179	9	8
10.	HARD HEADED WOMAN (ASCAP)—Elvis Presley.. Don't Ask Me Why (ASCAP)—Vic 7280	23	2
11.	DO YOU WANT TO DANCE? (BMI)—Bobby Freeman... Big Fat Woman (BMI)—Josie 835	12	5
12.	TWILIGHT TIME (BMI)—Platters... Out of My Mind (BMI)—Mercury 71289	10	14
13.	PATRICIA (ASCAP)—Perez Prado... Why Wait? (BMI)—Vic 7245	13	2
14.	SPLISH SPLASH (BMI)—Bobby Darin... Judy, Don't Be Moody (BMI)—Atco 6117	—	1
15.	PADRE (ASCAP)—Toni Arden... All at Once (ASCAP)—Dec 30628	18	4
16.	LOOKING BACK (BMI)—Nat King Cole... Do I Like It? (BMI)—Cap 3939	21	9
17.	WITCH DOCTOR (ASCAP)—David Seville... Don't Whistle at Me, Baby (ASCAP)—Liberty 55132	11	13
18.	GUESS THINGS HAPPEN THAT WAY (BMI)—Johnny Cash... Come In, Stranger (BMI)—Sun 295	—	2
19.	YOU NEED HANDS (ASCAP)—Eydie Gorme... Dormi, Dormi, Dormi (ASCAP)—ABC-Paramount 9925	14	7
20.	WHEN (ASCAP)—Kalin Twins... Three o'Clock Thrill (BMI)—Dec 30642	15	2
21.	LEFT RIGHT OUT OF YOUR HEART (ASCAP)—Patti Page... Longing to Hold You Again (ASCAP)—Mercury 71331	15	2
22.	OH, LONESOME ME (BMI)—Don Gibson... I Can't Stop Loving You (BMI)—Vic 7133	—	11
23.	FOR YOUR LOVE (BMI)—Ed Townsend... Over and Over Again (BMI)—Cap 3926	—	5
24.	JENNIE LEE (BMI)—Jan and Arnie... Gotta Getta Date (BMI)—Arwin 108	17	6
25.	FOR YOUR PRECIOUS LOVE (ASCAP)—Jerry Butler and the Impressions... Sweet Was the Wine (ASCAP)—Abner 1013	—	1
25.	DON'T ASK ME WHY (ASCAP)—Elvis Presley... Hard Headed Woman (ASCAP)—Vic 7280	—	1

Top 100 Sides

FOR SURVEY WEEK ENDING JUNE 28

This is a tabulation of dealer individual record sales listed according to the specific side requested by customers. No attempt is made to add sides together to reflect actual record sales. This is, therefore, a tabulation of sides or songs, and not records. This is the reason for any possible variation that occurs between the top 50 sides as reflected in this chart, and the top 50 record sellers as reflected in the "Best Sellers in Stores" chart.

Pos.	Song, Artist Label	Last Week
1.	**THE PURPLE PEOPLE EATER,** Sheb Wooley, M-G-M	1
2.	**YAKETY YAK,** Coasters, Atco	2
3.	**HARD HEADED WOMAN,** Elvis Presley, Victor	15
4.	**ALL I HAVE TO DO IS DREAM,** Everly Brothers, Cadence	3
5.	**ENDLESS SLEEP,** Jody Reynolds, Demon	5
6.	**PATRICIA,** Perez Prado, Victor	12
7.	**SPLISH SPLASH,** Bobby Darin, Atco	13
8.	**RETURN TO ME,** Dean Martin, Capitol	6
8.	**SECRETLY,** Jimmie Rodgers, Roulette	7
10.	**WITCH DOCTOR,** David Seville, Liberty	4
11.	**DO YOU WANT TO DANCE?** Bobby Freeman, Josie	9
12.	**JENNIE LEE,** Jan and Arnie, Arwin	8
13.	**LOOKING BACK,** Nat King Cole, Capitol	18
14.	**TWILIGHT TIME,** Platters, Mercury	14
15.	**BIG MAN,** Four Preps, Capitol	10
16.	**SUGAR MOON,** Pat Boone, Dot	11
17.	**FOR YOUR PRECIOUS LOVE,** Jerry Butler and the Impressions, Abner	41
18.	**POOR LITTLE FOOL,** Ricky Nelson, Imperial	—
18.	**WHEN,** Kalin Twins, Decca	26
20.	**REBEL-'ROUSER,** Duane Eddy, Jamie	50
21.	**JOHNNY B. GOODE,** Chuck Berry, Chess	17
22.	**PADRE,** Toni Arden, Decca	19
23.	**HIGH SCHOOL CONFIDENTIAL,** Jerry Lee Lewis, Sun	21
24.	**WEAR MY RING AROUND YOUR NECK,** Elvis Presley, Victor	24
25.	**I WONDER WHY,** Dion and the Belmonts, Laurie	22
25.	**GUESS THINGS HAPPEN THAT WAY,** Johnny Cash, Sun	27
27.	**WILLIE AND THE HAND JIVE,** Johnny Otis Show, Capitol	33
28.	**NO CHEMISE, PLEASE,** Gerry Granahan, Sunbeam	23
28.	**WHAT AM I LIVING FOR?** Chuck Willis, Atlantic	29
30.	**OH, LONESOME ME,** Don Gibson, Victor	20
31.	**RUMBLE,** Link Wray and His Ray Men, Cadence	16
31.	**FOR YOUR LOVE,** Ed Townsend, Capitol	29
33.	**LEFT RIGHT OUT OF YOUR HEART,** Patti Page, Mercury	66
34.	**ZORRO,** Chordettes, Cadence	33
35.	**TORERO,** Renate Carosone, Capitol	31
35.	**YOU NEED HANDS,** Eydie Gorme, ABC-Paramount	38
37.	**LEROY,** Jack Scott, Carlton	32
37.	**MY TRUE LOVE,** Jack Scott, Carlton	61
39.	**OOH! MY SOUL,** Little Richard, Specialty	35
40.	**GOT A MATCH,** Daddy-O's, Cabot	40
41.	**EL RANCHO ROCK,** Champs, Challenge	39
42.	**CHANSON D'AMOUR,** Art and Dotty Todd, Era	28
42.	**ONE SUMMER NIGHT,** Danleers, Mercury	54
44.	**DON'T GO HOME,** Playmates, Roulette	36
45.	**HE'S GOT THE WHOLE WORLD IN HIS HANDS,** Laurie London, Capitol	25
46.	**A CERTAIN SMILE,** Johnny Mathis, Columbia	76
47.	**KEWPIE DOLL,** Perry Como, Victor	36
47.	**BOOK OF LOVE,** Monotones, Argo	45
47.	**DING DONG,** McGuire Sisters, Coral	48
47.	**DOTTIE,** Danny and the Juniors, ABC-Paramount	48
51.	**YOU'RE MAKING A MISTAKE,** Platters, Mercury	66
51.	**BEWITCHED,** Betty Smith, London	76
51.	**COME WHAT MAY,** Clyde McPhatter, Atlantic	76
54.	**YOU,** Aquatones, Fargo	44
54.	**(IT'S BEEN A LONG TIME) PRETTY BABY,** Gino and Gina, Mercury	46
54.	**BLUE BLUE DAY,** Don Gibson, Victor	85
54.	**TALK TO ME, TALK TO ME,** Little Willie John, King	85
58.	**DON'T ASK ME WHY,** Elvis Presley, Victor	—
58.	**I LOVE YOU SO,** Chantels, End	42
58.	**CHA HUA HUA,** Pets, Arwin	47
58.	**TO BE LOVED,** Jackie Wilson, Brunswick	50
62.	**SHIEK OF ARABY,** Lou Monte, Victor	82
63.	**THE BIRD ON MY HEAD,** David Seville, Liberty	—
63.	**Flip Top Box,** Dickey Doo and the Don'ts, Swan	61
65.	**YOU'D BE SURPRISED,** Kathy Linden, Felsted	50
65.	**RAVE ON,** Buddy Holly, Coral	57
65.	**ENCHANTED ISLAND,** Four Lads, Columbia	91
68.	**TRUE, FINE MAMA,** Little Richard, Specialty	88
69.	**ALL THE TIME,** Johnny Mathis, Columbia	42
69.	**HANG UP MY ROCK AND ROLL SHOES,** Chuck Willis, Atlantic	66
69.	**SINGING HILLS,** Billy Vaughn, Dot	82
72.	**LET THE BELLS KEEP RINGING,** Paul Anka, ABC-Paramount	54
72.	**I'M SORRY I MADE YOU CRY,** Connie Francis, M-G-M	58
72.	**MARCH FROM THE RIVER KWAI AND "COLONEL BOGEY,"** Mitch Miller, Columbia	66
75.	**GOT A MATCH,** Frank Gallup, ABC-Paramount	61
75.	**COME IN, STRANGER,** Johnny Cash, Sun	66
75.	**MOONLIGHT BAY,** Drifters, Atlantic	72
75.	**BEWILDERED,** Mickey and Sylvia, Vik	76
79.	**LITTLE MARY,** Fats Domino, Imperial	—
79.	**YOUNG AND WARM AND WONDERFUL,** Tony Bennett, Columbia	61
79.	**JUST MARRIED,** Marty Robbins, Columbia	66
79.	**TRY THE IMPOSSIBLE,** Lee Andrews and the Hearts, United Artists	72
79.	**JENNIE LEE,** Billy Ward, Liberty	—
84.	**INDIAN LOVE CALL,** Ernie Freeman, Imperial	76
85.	**DREAM,** Betty Johnson, Atlantic	58
85.	**I KNOW WHERE I'M GOIN',** George Hamilton IV, ABC-Paramount	61
85.	**LITTLE PIXIE,** Moe Koffman Quartet, Jubilee	72
88.	**MAKE ME A MIRACLE,** Jimmie Rodgers, Roulette	85
88.	**WE BELONG TOGETHER,** Robert and Johnny, Old Town	91
90.	**SKINNY MINNIE,** Bill Haley and His Comets, Decca	72
91.	**LAZY MARY,** Lou Monte, Victor	82
91.	**BILLY,** Kathy Linden, Felsted	91
91.	**TEACHER'S PET,** Doris Day, Columbia	96
94.	**CRAZY LOVE,** Paul Anka, ABC-Paramount	56
94.	**TEACHER, TEACHER,** Johnny Mathis, Columbia	58
94.	**SICK AND TIRED,** Fats Domino, Imperial	—
97.	**A VERY PRECIOUS LOVE,** Ames Brothers, Victor	76
97.	**WHO'S SORRY NOW?** Connie Francis, M-G-M	94
99.	**CLAUDETTE,** Everly Brothers, Cadence	88
99.	**CHA HUA HUA,** Eddie Platt, Gone	96

BEST SELLING POP SINGLES IN STORES

The information given in this chart is based on actual sales to customers in a scientific sample of the nation's retail record outlets during the week ending on the date shown above. Sample design, sample size, and all methods used in this continuing study of retail record sales are under the direct and continuing supervision and control of the School of Retailing of New York University.

FOR SURVEY WEEK ENDING JULY 5, 1958

This Week		Last Week	Weeks on Chart
1.	PURPLE PEOPLE EATER (BMI)—Sheb Wooley I Can't Believe You're Mine (ASCAP)—M-G-M 12651	1	7
2.	HARD HEADED WOMAN (ASCAP)—Elvis Presley DON'T ASK ME WHY (ASCAP—Vic 7280	3	3
3.	YAKETY YAK (BMI)—Coasters Zing! Went the Strings of My Heart (ASCAP)—Atco 6116	2	6
4.	POOR LITTLE FOOL (BMI)—Ricky Nelson Don't Leave Me This Way (BMI)—Imperial 5528	18	2
5.	SPLISH SPLASH (BMI)—Bobby Darin Judy, Don't Be Moody (BMI)—Atco 6117	8	4
6.	PATRICIA (ASCAP)—Perez Prado Why Wait? (BMI)—Vic 7245	6	4
7.	ALL I HAVE TO DO IS DREAM (BMI) Everly Brothers CLAUDETTE (BMI)—Cadence 1348	4	12
8.	ENDLESS SLEEP (ASCAP)—Jody Reynolds Tight Capris (BMI)—Demon 1507	5	8
9.	SECRETLY (ASCAP)—Jimmie Rodgers MAKE ME A MIRACLE (ASCAP)—Roulette 4070	7	10
10.	REBEL-'ROUSER (BMI)—Duane Eddy Stalkin' (BMI)—Jamie 1104	22	2
11.	DO YOU WANT TO DANCE? (BMI)—Bobby Freeman Big Pat Woman (BMI)—Josie 835	11	9
12.	FOR YOUR PRECIOUS LOVE (ASCAP)—Jerry Butler and Impressions Sweet Was the Wine (ASCAP)—Abner 1013	17	5
13.	WHEN (ASCAP)—Kalin Twins Three o'Clock Thrill (BMI)—Dec 30642	19	3
14.	RETURN TO ME (ASCAP)—Dean Martin Forgetting You (ASCAP)—Cap 3894	9	14
15.	WHAT AM I LIVING FOR? (BMI)—Chuck Willis HANG UP MY ROCK AND ROLL SHOES (BMI)—Atlantic 1179	23	10
16.	GUESS THINGS HAPPEN THAT WAY (BMI)—Johnny Cash COME IN, STRANGER (BMI)—Sun 295	20	7
17.	WITCH DOCTOR (ASCAP)—David Seville Don't Whistle at Me, Baby (ASCAP)—Liberty 55132	10	14
18.	LEROY (BMI)—Jack Scott MY TRUE LOVE (BMI)—Carlton 462	21	5
19.	LOOKING BACK (BMI)—Nat King Cole Do I Like It (BMI)—Cap 3939	13	14
20.	BIG MAN (BMI)—Four Preps Stop, Baby (ASCAP)—Cap 3960	15	10
21.	JENNIE LEE (BMI)—Jan and Arnie Gotta Getta Date (BMI)—Arwin 108	12	8
22.	TWILIGHT TIME (BMI)—Platters Out of My Mind (BMI)—Mer 71289	14	14
23.	WILLIE AND THE HAND JIVE (BMI) —Johnny Otis Show Ring-a-Ling (BMI)—Cap 3966	29	3
24.	SUGAR MOON (BMI)—Pat Boone Cherie, I Love You (ASCAP)—Dot 15750	16	10
25.	PADRE (ASCAP)—Toni Arden All at Once (ASCAP)—Dec 30628	25	8
26.	HIGH SCHOOL CONFIDENTIAL (BMI)—Jerry Lee Lewis Fools Like Me (BMI)—Sun 296	26	7
27.	OH, LONESOME ME (BMI)—Don Gibson I Can't Stop Loving You (BMI)—Vic 7133	32	18
28.	JOHNNY B. GOODE (BMI)—Chuck Berry Around and Around (BMI)—Chess 1691	24	11
29.	WEAR MY RING AROUND YOUR NECK (BMI)—Elvis Presley Doncha' Think It's Time (BMI)—Vic 7240	27	13
30.	LEFT RIGHT OUT OF YOUR HEART (ASCAP)—Patti Page Longing to Hold You Again (ASCAP)—Mercury 71331	35	2
31.	NO CHEMISE, PLEASE (BMI)—Gerry Granahan Girl of My Dreams (ASCAP)—Sunbeam 102	30	5
32.	I WONDER WHY (ASCAP)—Dion and the Belmonts Teen Angel (ASCAP)—Laurie 3013	28	8
33.	FOR YOUR LOVE (BMI)—Ed Townsend Over and Over Again (BMI)—Cap 3926	34	13
34.	YOU NEED HANDS (ASCAP)—Eydie Gorme Dormi, Dormi, Dormi (ASCAP)—ABC-Paramount 9925	38	6
35.	A CERTAIN SMILE (ASCAP)—Johnny Mathis Let It Rain (ASCAP)—Col 41193	45	2
36.	OOH? MY SOUL (BMI)—Little Richard TRUE, FINE MAMA (BMI)—Specialty 633	31	4
37.	IF DREAMS CAME TRUE (ASCAP) —Pat Boone THAT'S HOW MUCH I LOVE YOU—(BMI)—Dot 15785	—	1
38.	ZORRO (BMI)—Chordettes Love's a Two-Way Street (BMI)—Cadence 1349	36	8
39.	ONE SUMMER NIGHT (BMI)—Danleers Wheelin' and A-Dealin' (BMI)—Mercury 71322	41	2
40.	BLUE BLUE DAY (BMI)—Don Gibson Too Soon to Know (BMI)—Vic 7010	—	1
40.	THE BIRD ON MY HEAD (ASCAP)—David Seville Hey There, Moon (ASCAP)—Liberty 55140	—	1
42.	RUMBLE (BMI)—Link Wray and His Ray Men The Swag (BMI)—Cadence 1347	33	11
43.	TALK TO ME, TALK TO ME (BMI) —Little Willie John Spasms (BMI)—King 5108	—	12
44.	EL RANCHO ROCK (BMI)—Champs Midnighter (BMI)—Challenge 59007	40	7
45.	ENCHANTED ISLAND (ASCAP)—Four Lads Guess What the Neighbors'll Say (BMI)—Col 41194	—	1
46.	DON'T GO HOME? (BMI)—Playmates Can't You Get It Through Your Head (BMI)—Roulette 4072	43	4
47.	COME WHAT MAY (BMI)—Clyde McPhatter Let Me Know (BMI)—Atlantic 1185	50	2
48.	LITTLE MARY (BMI)—Fats Domino Prisoner's Song (ASCAP)—Imperial 5526	—	1
49.	DOTTIE (BMI)—Danny and the Juniors In the Meantime (BMI)—ABC-Paramount 9926	48	3
50.	JUST A DREAM (BMI)—Jimmy Clanton You Aim to Please (BMI)—Ace 546	—	1

THIS WEEK'S BEST BUYS

Special telephone reports and/or chart action indicate these recent releases have either broken out in one or more key areas or have leaped onto the charts and have excellent potential for placing among the Top 30 of The Billboard's Best Selling Pop Singles in Stores chart. Action sides are listed in capitol letters

THE FREEZE (Warman, BMI)—Tony and Joe—Era 1075—Gonna Get a Little Kissin' Tonight (Hilliary, BMI)

A previous Billboard Spotlight pick.

The following records, not previously selected as Best Buys, are on the charts for the first time this week.

LITTLE MARY (Travis, BMI)—Fats Domino—Imperial 5526—Prisoner's Song (Shapiro-Bernstein, ASCAP)

A previous Billboard Spotlight pick.

JUST A DREAM (Ace, BMI)—Jimmy Clanton—Ace 546—You Aim to Please (ACE, BMI)

RECENT POP RELEASES COMING UP STRONG

FOR SURVEY WEEK ENDING JULY 5

The information given in this chart is based on actual sales to customers in a scientific sample of the nation's retail record outlets during the week ending on the date shown above. Sample design, sample size and all methods used in this continuing study of retail record sales are under the direct and continuing supervision and control of the School of Retailing of New York University.

Fever . . . . *Peggy Lee*
(BMI) Capitol 3998

Most Played by Jockeys

FOR SURVEY WEEK ENDING JULY 5

SIDES are ranked in order of the greatest number of plays on disk jockey radio shows thruout the country. Results are based on The Billboard's weekly survey among the nation's disk jockeys. The reverse side of each record is also listed.

This Week		Last Week	Weeks on Chart
1.	PURPLE PEOPLE EATER (BMI)—Sheb Wooley I Can't Believe You're Mine (ASCAP)—M-G-M 12651	1	7
2.	YAKETY YAK (BMI)—Coasters Zing! Went the Strings of My Heart (ASCAP)—Atco 6116	3	5
3.	SECRETLY (ASCAP)—Jimmie Rodgers Make Me a Miracle (ASCAP)—Roulette 4070	4	9
4.	HARD HEADED WOMAN (ASCAP)—Elvis Presley Don't Ask Me Why (ASCAP)—Vic 7280	10	3
5.	PATRICIA (ASCAP)—Perez Prado Why Wait? (BMI)—Vic 7245	13	3
6.	ALL I HAVE TO DO IS DREAM (BMI)—Everly Brothers Claudette (BMI)—Cadence 1348	2	12
7.	SPLISH SPLASH (BMI)—Bobby Darin Judy, Don't Be Moody (BMI)—Atco 6117	14	2
8.	POOR LITTLE FOOL (BMI)—Ricky Nelson Don't Leave Me This Way (BMI)—Imperial 5528	—	1
9.	RETURN TO ME (ASCAP)—Dean Martin Forgetting You (ASCAP)—Cap 3894	5	15
10.	BIG MAN (BMI)—Four Preps Stop, Baby (ASCAP)—Cap 3960	7	11
11.	ENDLESS SLEEP (BMI)—Jody Reynolds Tight Capris (BMI)—Demon 1507	8	6
12.	WHAT AM I LIVING FOR? (BMI)—Chuck Willis Hang Up My Rock and Roll Shoes (BMI)—Atlantic 1179	9	9
13.	MY TRUE LOVE (BMI)—Jack Scott Leroy (BMI)—Carlton 462	—	1
14.	SUGAR MOON (BMI)—Pat Boone Cherie, I Love You (ASCAP)—Dot 15750	6	10
15.	LEFT RIGHT OUT OF YOUR HEART (ASCAP)—Patti Page Longing to Hold You Again (ASCAP)—Mercury 71331	21	3
16.	WHEN (ASCAP)—Kalin Twins Three o'Clock Thrill (BMI)—Dec 30642	20	3
17.	WILLIE AND THE HAND JIVE (BMI) Johnny Otis Show Ring-a-Ling (BMI)—Cap 3966	—	2
18.	DO YOU WANT TO DANCE? (BMI)—Bobby Freeman Big Fat Woman (BMI)—Josie 835	11	6
19.	ENCHANTED ISLAND (ASCAP—Four Lads Guess What the Neighbors'll Say (BMI)—Col 41194	—	1
20.	PADRE (ASCAP)—Toni Arden All at Once (ASCAP)—Dec 30628	15	5
21.	CERTAIN SMILE (ASCAP)—Johnny Mathis Let It Rain (ASCAP)—Col 41193	—	1
22.	KEWPIE DOLL (ASCAP)—Perry Como Dance Only With Me (ASCAP)—Vic 7202	—	11
23.	ONE SUMMER NIGHT (BMI)—Danleers Wheelin' and a-Dealin' (BMI)—Mercury 71322	—	2
24.	YOU NEED HANDS (ASCAP)—Eydie Gorme Dormi, Dormi, Dormi (ASCAP)—ABC-Paramount 9925	19	8
25.	DON'T ASK ME WHY (ASCAP)—Elvis Presley Hard Headed Woman (ASCAP)—Vic 7280	25	2

Top 100 Sides

FOR SURVEY WEEK ENDING JULY 5

This is a tabulation of dealer individual record sales listed according to the specific side requested by customers. No attempt is made to add sides together to reflect actual record sales. This is, therefore, a tabulation of sides or songs, and not records. This is the reason for any possible variation that occurs between the top 50 sides as reflected in this chart, and the top 50 record sellers as reflected in the "Best Sellers in Stores" chart.

Pos.	Song, Artist Label	Last Week
1.	THE PURPLE PEOPLE EATER, Sheb Wooley, M-G-M	1
2.	YAKETY YAK, Coasters, Atco	2
3.	HARD HEADED WOMAN, Elvis Presley, Victor	3
4.	POOR LITTLE FOOL, Ricky Nelson, Imperial	18
5.	SPLISH SPLASH, Bobby Darin, Atco	7
6.	PATRICIA, Perez Prado, Victor	6
7.	ALL I HAVE TO DO IS DREAM, Everly Brothers, Cadence	4
7.	ENDLESS SLEEP, Jody Reynolds, Demon	5
9.	SECRETLY, Jimmie Rodgers, Roulette	8
10.	REBEL-'ROUSER, Duane Eddq, Jamie	20
11.	DO YOU WANT TO DANCE? Bobby Freeman, Josie	11
12.	FOR YOUR PRECIOUS LOVE, Jerry Butler & the Impressions, Abner	17
13.	WHEN, Kalin Twins, Decca	18
14.	RETURN TO ME, Dean Martin, Capitol	8
15.	WHAT AM I LIVING FOR? Chuck Willis, Atlantic	28
16.	WITCH DOCTOR, David Seville, Liberty	10
17.	GUESS THINGS HAPPEN THAT WAY, Johnny Cash, Sun	25
18.	LOOKING BACK, Nat King Cole, Capitol	13
18.	BIG MAN, Four Preps, Capitol	15
20.	JENNIE LEE, Jan & Arnie, Arwin	12
21.	TWILIGHT TIME, Platters, Mercury	14
21.	WILLIE AND THE HAND JIVE, Johnny Otis Show, Capitol	27
23.	SUGAR MOON, Pat Boone, Dot	16
24.	PADRE, Toni Arden, Decca	22
25.	HIGH SCHOOL CONFIDENTIAL, Jerry Lee Lewis, Sun	23
26.	OH, LONESOME ME, Don Gibson, Victor	30
27.	JOHNNY B. GOODE, Chuck Berry, Chess	21
27.	WEAR MY RING AROUND YOUR NECK, Elvis Presley, Victor	24
29.	LEFT RIGHT OUT OF YOUR HEART, Patti Page, Mercury	33
30.	NO CHEMISE, PLEASE, Gerry Granahan, Sunbeam	28
31.	FOR YOUR LOVE, Ed Townsend, Capitol	31
32.	I WONDER WHY, Dion & the Belmonts, Laurie	25
32.	YOU NEED HANDS, Eydie Gorme, ABC-Paramount	35
32.	A CERTAIN SMILE, Johnny Mathis, Columbia	46
35.	LEROY, Jock Scott, Carlton	37
35.	MY TRUE LOVE, Jack Scott, Carlton	37
37.	DON'T ASK ME WHY, Elvis Presley, Victor	58
38.	ZORRO, Chordettes, Cadence	34
39.	ONE SUMMER NIGHT, Danleers, Mercury	42
40.	RUMBLE, Link Wray & His Ray Men, Cadence	31
40.	BLUE BLUE DAY, Don Gibson, Victor	54
40.	THE BIRD ON MY HEAD, David Seville, Liberty	63
43.	OOH! MY SOUL, Little Richard, Specialty	39
43.	EL RANCHO ROCK, Champs, Challenge	41
43.	TALK TO ME, TALK TO ME, Little Willie John, King	54
46.	DON'T GO HOME, Playmates, Roulette	44
46.	ENCHANTED ISLAND, Four Lads, Columbia	65
48.	COME WHAT MAY, Clyde McPhatter, Atlantic	51
49.	DOTTIE, Danny & the Juniors, ABC-Paramount	47
49.	LITTLE MARY, Fats Domino, Imperial	79
51.	JUST A DREAM, Jimmy Clanton, Ace	—
52.	GOT A MATCH, Daddy-O's, Cabot	40
53.	CHANSON D'AMOUR, Art & Dotty Todd, Era	42
53.	HE'S GOT THE WHOLE WORLD IN HIS HANDS Laurie London, Capitol	45
53.	YOU'RE MAKING A MISTAKE, Platters, Mercury	51
56.	BOOK OF LOVE, Monotones, Argo	47
57.	TORERO, Renate Carosone, Capitol	35
57.	RAVE ON, Buddy Holly, Coral	65
57.	GOT A MATCH, Frank Gallup, ABC-Paramount	75
57.	YOUNG AND WARM AND WONDERFUL, Tony Bennett, Columbia	79
61.	DING DONG, McGuire Sisters, Coral	47
61.	BEWITCHED, Betty Smith, London	51
61.	TO BE LOVED, Jackie Wilson, Brunswick	58
61.	FLIP TOP BOX, Dickey Doo & the Don'ts, Swan	63
65.	IF DREAMS CAME TRUE, Pat Boone, Dot	—
65.	THAT'S HOW MUCH I LOVE YOU, Pat Boone, Dot	—
65.	KEWPIE DOLL, Perry Como, Victor	47
65.	THE SINGING HILLS, Billy Vaughn, Dot	69
69.	(IT'S BEEN A LONG TIME) PRETTY BABY, Gino & Gina, Mercury	54
69.	I LOVE YOU SO, Chantels, End	58
69.	JENNIE LEE, Billy Ward, Liberty	79
72.	CHA HUA HUA, Pets, Arwin	58
72.	JUST MARRIED, Marty Robbins, Columbia	79
74.	FEVER, Peggy Lee, Capitol	—
74.	SHIEK OF ARABY, Lou Monte, Victor	62
74.	MARCH FROM THE RIVER KWAI AND "COLONEL BOGEY" Mitch Miller, Columbia	72
77.	ANGEL BABY, Dean Martin, Capitol	—
77.	TRY THE IMPOSSIBLE, Lee Andrews & the Hearts, United Artists	79
79.	DELICIOUS! Jim Backus, Jubilee	—
79.	YOU'D BE SURPRISED, Kathy Linden, Felsted	65
79.	TRUE, FINE MAMA, Little Richard, Specialty	68
79.	I'M SORRY I MADE YOU CRY, Connie Francis, M-G-M	72
79.	BEWILDERED, Mickey & Sylvia, Vik	75
79.	INDIAN LOVE CALL, Ernie Freeman, Imperial	84
85.	LET THE BELLS KEEP RINGING, Paul Anka, ABC-Paramount	72
85.	COME IN, STRANGER, Johnny Cash, Sun	75
85.	I KNOW WHERE I'M GOIN', George Hamilton IV, ABC-Paramount	85
85.	WHO'S SORRY NOW? Connie Francis, M-G-M	97
89.	JEALOUSY, Kitty Wells, Decca	—
89.	YOU, Aquatones, Fargo	54
89.	CRAZY LOVE, Paul Anka, ABC-Paramount	94
92.	MOONLIGHT BAY, Drifters, Atlantic	75
92.	DREAM, Betty Johnson, Atlantic	85
92.	SICK AND TIRED, Fats Domino, Imperial	94
95.	WOODCHOPPER'S BALL, Hutch Davie, Atco	—
95.	HANG UP MY ROCK AND ROLL SHOES, Chuck Willis, Atlantic	69
95.	WE BELONG TOGETHER, Robert & Johnny, Old Town	88
95.	SKINNY MINNIE, Bill Haley & His Comets, Decca	90
99.	ALL THE TIME, Johnny Mathis, Columbia	69
99.	MAKE ME A MIRACLE, Jimmie Rodgers, Roulette	88

BEST SELLING POP SINGLES IN STORES

FOR SURVEY WEEK ENDING JULY 12, 1958

The information given in this chart is based on actual sales to customers in a scientific sample of the nation's retail record outlets during the week ending on the date shown above. Sample design, sample size, and all methods used in this continuing study of retail record sales are under the direct and continuing supervision and control of the School of Retailing of New York University.

This Week	Title	Last Week	Weeks on Chart
1.	HARD HEADED WOMAN (ASCAP)—Elvis Presley; DON'T ASK ME WHY (ASCAP)—Vic 7280	2	4
2.	YAKETY YAK (BMI)—Coasters; Zing, Went the Strings of My Heart (ASCAP)—Atco 6116	3	7
3.	PURPLE PEOPLE EATER (BMI)—Sheb Wooley; I Can't Believe You're Mine (ASCAP)—M-G-M 12651	1	8
4.	SPLISH SPLASH (BMI)—Bobby Darin; Judy, Don't Be Moody (BMI)—Atco 6117	5	5
5.	POOR LITTLE FOOL (BMI)—Ricky Nelson; Don't Leave Me This Way (BMI)—Imperial 5528	4	3
6.	PATRICIA (ASCAP)—Perez Prado; Why Wait? (BMI)—Vic 7245	6	5
7.	REBEL-ROUSER (BMI)—Duane Eddy; Stalkin' (BMI)—Jamie 1104	10	3
8.	WHEN (ASCAP)—Kalin Twins; Three o'Clock Thrill (BMI)—Dec 30642	13	4
9.	ENDLESS SLEEP (BMI)—Jody Reynolds; Tight Capris (BMI)—Demon 1507	8	9
10.	SECRETLY (ASCAP)—Jimmie Rodgers; MAKE ME A MIRACLE (ASCAP)—Roulette 4070	9	11
11.	FOR YOUR PRECIOUS LOVE (ASCAP)—Jerry Butler and Impressions; Sweet Was the Wine (ASCAP)—Abner 1013	12	6
12.	GUESS THINGS HAPPEN THAT WAY (BMI)—Johnny Cash; COME IN, STRANGER (BMI)—Sun 295	16	8
13.	LEROY (BMI)—Jack Scott; MY TRUE LOVE (BMI)—Carlton 462	18	6
14.	ALL I HAVE TO DO IS DREAM (BMI)—Everly Brothers; CLAUDETTE (BMI)—Cadence 1348	7	13
15.	DO YOU WANT TO DANCE? (BMI)—Bobby Freeman; Big Fat Woman (BMI)—Josie 835	11	10
16.	WHAT AM I LIVING FOR? (BMI)—Chuck Willis; HANG UP MY ROCK AND ROLL SHOES (BMI)—Atlantic 1179	15	11
17.	WILLIE AND THE HAND JIVE (BMI)—Johnny Otis Show; Ring-A-Ling (BMI)—Cap 3966	23	4
18.	RETURN TO ME (ASCAP)—Dean Martin; Forgetting You (ASCAP)—Cap 3894	14	15
19.	PADRE (ASCAP)—Toni Arden; All at Once (ASCAP)—Dec 30628	25	9
20.	IF DREAMS CAME TRUE (ASCAP)—Pat Boone; THAT'S HOW MUCH I LOVE YOU (BMI)—Dot 15785	37	2
21.	A CERTAIN SMILE (ASCAP)—Johnny Mathis; Let It Rain (ASCAP)—Col 41193	35	3
22.	WITCH DOCTOR (ASCAP)—David Seville; Don't Whistle at Me, Baby (ASCAP)—Liberty 55132	17	15
23.	BIG MAN (BMI)—Four Preps; Stop, Baby (ASCAP)—Cap 3960	20	11
24.	JUST A DREAM (BMI)—Jimmy Clanton; You Aim to Please (BMI)—Ace 546	50	2
25.	FEVER (BMI)—Peggy Lee; You Don't Know (BMI)—Cap 3998	—	1
26.	LEFT RIGHT OUT OF YOUR HEART (ASCAP)—Patti Page; Longing to Hold You Again (ASCAP)—Mercury 71331	30	3
27.	NO CHEMISE, PLEASE (BMI)—Gerry Granahan; Girl of My Dreams (ASCAP)—Sunbeam 102	31	6
28.	JENNIE LEE (BMI)—Jan and Arnie; Gotta Getta Date (BMI)—Arwin 108	21	9
29.	OH, LONESOME ME (BMI)—Don Gibson; I Can't Stop Loving You (BMI)—Vic 7133	27	19
30.	ONE SUMMER NIGHT (BMI)—Danleers; Wheelin' and A-Dealin' (BMI)—Mercury 71322	39	3
31.	SUGAR MOON (BMI)—Pat Boone; Cherie, I Love You (ASCAP)—Dot 15750	24	11
32.	YOU NEED HANDS (ASCAP)—Eydie Gorme; Dormi, Dormi, Dormi (ASCAP)—ABC-Paramount 9925	34	7
33.	BLUE BLUE DAY (BMI)—Don Gibson; Too Soon to Know (BMI)—Vic 7010	40	2
34.	LOOKING BACK (BMI)—Nat King Cole; Do I Like It (BMI)—Cap 3939	19	15
35.	FOR YOUR LOVE (BMI)—Ed Townsend; Over and Over Again (BMI)—Cap 3926	33	14
36.	I WONDER WHY? (ASCAP)—Dion and the Belmonts; Teen Angel (ASCAP)—Laurie 3013	32	9
37.	ENCHANTED ISLAND (ASCAP)—Four Lads; Guess What the Neighbor'll Say (BMI)—Col 41194	45	2
38.	HIGH SCHOOL CONFIDENTIAL (BMI)—Jerry Lee Lewis; Fools Like Me (BMI)—Sun 296	26	8
39.	DOTTIE (BMI)—Danny and the Juniors; In the Meantime (BMI)—ABC-Paramount 9926	49	4
40.	DELICIOUS! (ASCAP)—Jim Backus; I Need a Vacation (ASCAP)—Jubilee 5330	—	1
41.	TWILIGHT TIME (BMI)—Platters; Out of My Mind (BMI)—Mer 71289	22	15
42.	THE BIRD ON MY HEAD (ASCAP)—David Seville; Hey There, Moon (ASCAP)—Liberty 55140	40	2
43.	ANGEL BABY (BMI)—Dean Martin; I'll Gladly Make the Same Mistake Again (ASCAP)—Cap 3988	—	1
44.	OOH! MY SOUL (BMI)—Little Richard; TRUE, FINE MAMA (BMI)—Specialty 633	36	5
45.	TORERO (ASCAP)—Renato Carosone; Chella Lla (ASCAP)—Cap 71080	—	9
46.	JOHNNY B. GOODE (BMI)—Chuck Berry; Around and Around (BMI)—Chess 1691	28	12
47.	RUMBLE (BMI)—Link Wray and His Ray Men; The Swag (BMI)—Cadence 1347	42	12
48.	DON'T GO HOME (BMI)—Playmates; Can't You Get It Through Your Head (BMI)—Roulette 4072	46	5
49.	GINGER BREAD (BMI)—Frankie Avalon; Blue Betty (ASCAP)—Chancellor 1021	—	1
50.	LITTLE MARY (BMI)—Fats Domino; Prisoner's Song (ASCAP)—Imperial 5526	48	2

THIS WEEK'S BEST BUYS

Special telephone reports and/or chart action indicate these recent releases have either broken out in one or more key areas or have leaped onto the charts and have excellent potential for placing among the Top 30 of The Billboard's Best Selling Pop Singles in Stores chart. Action sides are listed in capitol letters.

COME CLOSER TO ME (Peer Intl., BMI)—Nat King Cole—Capitol 4004—Nothing in the World (Eden-Sweco, BMI)

MOON TALK (Roncom, ASCAP)—Perry Como—RCA Victor 7274—Beats There a Heart So True (Kahl, BMI)

BORN TOO LATE (Mansion, ASCAP)—The Poni Tails—ABC-Paramount 9934—Come On, Joey, Dance With Me (Sheldon, BMI)

The above are previous Billboard Spotlight picks.

EVERYBODY LOVES A LOVER (Korwin, ASCAP)—Doris Day—Columbia 41195—Instant Love (Artists, ASCAP)

LITTLE STAR (Koel, BMI)—The Elegants—APT 25005—Getting Dizzy (Keel, BMI)

The following record, not previously selected as a Best Buy, is on the chart for the first time this week.

FEVER (Lois, BMI)—Peggy Lee—Capitol 3998—You Don't Know (Roosevelt, BMI)

RECENT POP RELEASES COMING UP STRONG

FOR SURVEY WEEK ENDING JULY 12

The information given in this chart is based on actual sales to customers in a scientific sample of the nation's retail record outlets during the week ending on the date shown above. Sample design, sample size and all methods used in this continuing study of retail record sales are under the direct and continuing supervision and control of the School of Retailing of New York University.

Born Too Late . . . . . *Poni Tails* (BMI) ABC-Paramount 9934

Come Close to Me . . . . . *Nat King Cole* (BMI) Capitol 4004

Everybody Loves a Lover . . . . . *Doris Day* (ASCAP) Columbia 41195

The Freeze . . . . . *Tony & Joe* (BMI) Era 1075

Little Star . . . . . *The Elegants* (BMI) APT 25005

Most Played by Jockeys

FOR SURVEY WEEK ENDING JULY 12

SIDES are ranked in order of the greatest number of plays on disk jockey radio shows thruout the country. Results are based on The Billboard's weekly survey among the nation's disk jockeys. The reverse side of each record is also listed.

This Week		Last Week	Weeks on Chart
1.	HARD HEADED WOMAN (ASCAP)—Elvis Presley Don't Ask Me Why? (ASCAP)—Vic 7280	4	4
2.	YAKETY YAK (BMI)—Coasters Zing. Went the Strings of My Heart (ASCAP)—Atco 6116	2	6
3.	PATRICIA (ASCAP)—Perez Prado Why Wait? (BMI)—Vic 7245	5	4
4.	PURPLE PEOPLE EATER (BMI)—Sheb Wooley I Can't Believe You're Mine (ASCAP)—M-G-M 12651	1	8
5.	SPLISH SPLASH (BMI)—Bobby Darin Judy, Don't Be Moody (BMI)—Atco 6117	7	3
6.	POOR LITTLE FOOL (BMI)—Ricky Nelson Don't Leave Me This Way (BMI)—Imperial 5528	8	2
7.	IF DREAMS CAME TRUE (ASCAP)—Pat Boone That's How Much I Love You (BMI)—Dot 15785	—	1
8.	WHEN (ASCAP)—Kalin Twins Three o'Clock Thrill (BMI)—Dec 30642	16	4
9.	LEFT RIGHT OUT OF YOUR HEART (ASCAP)—Patti Page Longing to Hold You Again (ASCAP)—Mercury 71331	15	4
10.	SECRETLY (ASCAP)—Jimmie Rodgers Make Me a Miracle (ASCAP)—Roulette 4070	3	10
11.	ALL I HAVE TO DO IS DREAM (BMI)—Everly Brothers Claudette (BMI)—Cadence 1348	6	13
12.	ENCHANTED ISLAND (ASCAP)—Four Lads Guess What the Neighbor'll Say (BMI)—Col 41194	19	2
13.	RETURN TO ME (ASCAP)—Dean Martin Forgetting You (ASCAP)—Cap 3894	9	16
14.	A CERTAIN SMILE (ASCAP)—Johnny Mathis Let It Rain (ASCAP)—Col 41193	21	2
15.	FEVER (BMI)—Peggy Lee You Don't Know (BMI)—Cap 3998	—	1
16.	ENDLESS SLEEP (BMI)—Jody Reynolds Tight Capris (BMI)—Demon 1507	11	7
17.	BIG MAN (BMI)—Four Preps Stop, Baby (ASCAP)—Cap 3960	10	12
18.	REBEL-'ROUSER (BMI)—Duane Eddy Stalkin' (BMI)—Jamie 1104	—	1
19.	EVERYBODY LOVES A LOVER (ASCAP)—Doris Day Instant Love (ASCAP)—Col 41195	—	1
20.	ONE SUMMER NIGHT (BMI)—Danleers Wheelin' and A-Dealin' (BMI)—Mercury 71322	23	3
21.	WHAT AM I LIVING FOR? (BMI)—Chuck Willis Hang Up My Rock and Roll Shoes (BMI)—Atlantic 1179	12	10
22.	YOU NEED HANDS (ASCAP)—Eydie Gorme Dormi, Dormi, Dormi (ASCAP)—ABC-Paramount 9925	24	9
23.	DO YOU WANT TO DANCE? (BMI)—Bobby Freeman Big Fat Woman (BMI)—Josie 835	18	7
24.	MY TRUE LOVE (BMI)—Jack Scott Leroy (BMI)—Carlton 462	13	2
25.	PADRE (ASCAP)—Toni Arden All at Once (ASCAP)—Dec 30628	20	6

Top 100 Sides

STORE RECORDED SALES — NEW YORK UNIVERSITY SCHOOL OF RETAILING — THE BILLBOARD

FOR SURVEY WEEK ENDING JULY 12

This is a tabulation of dealer individual record sales listed according to the specific side requested by customers. No attempt is made to add sides together to reflect actual record sales. This is, therefore, a tabulation of sides or songs, and not records. This is the reason for any possible variation that occurs between the top 50 sides as reflected in this chart, and the top 50 record sellers as reflected in the "Best Sellers in Stores" chart.

Pos.	Song, Artist, Label	Last Week
1.	**YAKETY YAK,** Coasters, Atco	2
2.	**HARD HEADED WOMAN,** Elvis Presley, Victor	3
3.	**PURPLE PEOPLE EATER,** Sheb Wooley, M-G-M	1
4.	**SPLISH SPLASH,** Bobby Darin, Atco	5
5.	**POOR LITTLE FOOL,** Ricky Nelson, Imperial	4
6.	**PATRICIA,** Perez Prado, Victor	6
7.	**REBEL-'ROUSER,** Duane Eddy, Jamie	10
8.	**WHEN,** Kalin Twins, Decca	13
9.	**ENDLESS SLEEP,** Jody Reynolds, Demon	7
10.	**SECRETLY,** Jimmie Rodgers, Roulette	9
11.	**FOR YOUR PRECIOUS LOVE,** Jerry Butler & the Impressions, Abner	12
12.	**GUESS THINGS HAPPEN THAT WAY,** Johnny Cash, Sun	17
13.	**ALL I HAVE TO DO IS DREAM,** Everly Brothers, Cadence	7
14.	**DO YOU WANT TO DANCE?** Bobby Freeman, Josie	11
15.	**WHAT AM I LIVING FOR?** Chuck Willis, Atlantic	15
16.	**WILLIE AND THE HAND JIVE,** Johnny Otis Show, Capitol	21
17.	**RETURN TO ME,** Dean Martin, Capitol	14
18.	**PADRE,** Toni Arden, Decca	24
19.	**A CERTAIN SMILE,** Johnny Mathis, Columbia	32
20.	**WITCH DOCTOR,** David Seville, Liberty	16
21.	**BIG MAN,** Four Preps, Capitol	18
22.	**JUST A DREAM,** Jimmy Clanton, Ace	51
23.	**IF DREAMS CAME TRUE,** Pat Boone, Dot	65
23.	**FEVER,** Peggy Lee, Capitol	74
25.	**LEFT RIGHT OUT OF YOUR HEART,** Patti Page, Mercury	29
25.	**NO CHEMISE, PLEASE,** Gerry Granahan, Sunbeam	30
25.	**LEROY,** Jack Scott, Carlton	35
28.	**DON'T ASK ME WHY,** Elvis Presley, Victor	37
29.	**JENNIE LEE,** Jan and Arnie, Arwin	20
30.	**OH, LONESOME ME,** Don Gibson, Victor	26
30.	**ONE SUMMER NIGHT,** Danleers, Mercury	39
32.	**SUGAR MOON,** Pat Boone, Dot	23
32.	**MY TRUE LOVE,** Jack Scott, Carlton	35
34.	**YOU NEED HANDS,** Eydie Gorme, ABC-Paramount	32
35.	**BLUE BLUE DAY,** Don Gibson, Victor	40
36.	**LOOKING BACK,** Nat King Cole, Capitol	18
36.	**FOR YOUR LOVE,** Ed Townsend, Capitol	31
38.	**I WONDER WHY?** Dion and the Belmonts, Laurie	32
39.	**ENCHANTED ISLAND,** Four Lads, Columbia	46
40.	**HIGH SCHOOL CONFIDENTIAL,** Jerry Lee Lewis, Sun	25
41.	**DOTTIE,** Danny and the Juniors, ABC-Paramount	49
42.	**TWILIGHT TIME,** Platters, Mercury	21
42.	**DELICIOUS!** Jim Backus, Jubilee	79
44.	**THE BIRD ON MY HEAD,** David Seville, Liberty	40
45.	**ANGEL BABY,** Dean Martin, Capitol	77
46.	**TORERO,** Renato Carosone, Capitol	57
47.	**JOHNNY B. GOODE,** Chuck Berry, Chess	27
47.	**RUMBLE,** Link Wray and His Ray Men, Cadence	40
47.	**DON'T GO HOME,** Playmates, Roulette	46
50.	**GINGERBREAD,** Frankie Avalon, Chancellor	—
51.	**OOH! MY SOUL,** Little Richard, Specialty	43
51.	**LITTLE MARY,** Fats Domino, Imperial	49
53.	**COME CLOSE TO ME,** Nat King Cole, Capitol	—
53.	**EL RANCHO ROCK,** Champs, Challenge	43
53.	**YOU'RE MAKING A MISTAKE,** Platters, Mercury	53
53.	**THAT'S HOW MUCH I LOVE YOU,** Pat Boone, Dot	65
57.	**WEAR MY RING AROUND YOUR NECK,** Elvis Presley, Victor	27
57.	**SHIEK OF ARABY,** Lou Monte, Victor	74
59.	**TALK TO ME, TALK TO ME,** Little Willie John, King	43
59.	**YOUNG AND WARM AND WONDERFUL,** Tony Bennett, Columbia	57
59.	**SINGING HILLS,** Billy Vaughn, Dot	65
62.	**ZORRO,** Chordettes, Cadence	38
62.	**I LOVE YOU SO,** Chantels, End	69
64.	**LITTLE STAR,** Elegants, Apt	—
65.	**COME WHAT MAY,** Clyde McPhatter, Atlantic	48
65.	**HE'S GOT THE WHOLE WORLD IN HIS HANDS** Laurie London, Capitol	53
65.	**(IT'S BEEN A LONG TIME) PRETTY BABY,** Gino and Gina, Mercury	69
68.	**GOT A MATCH?** Daddy-O's, Cabot	52
68.	**RAVE ON,** Buddy Holly, Coral	57
68.	**BEWITCHED,** Betty Smith, London	61
68.	**I KNOW WHERE I'M GOIN',** George Hamilton IV, ABC-Paramount	85
72.	**CHANSON D'AMOUR,** Art and Dotty Todd, Era	53
72.	**GOT A MATCH?** Frank Gallup, ABC-Paramount	57
74.	**EVERYBODY LOVES A LOVER,** Doris Day, Columbia	—
75.	**LITTLE SERENADE,** Teddy Randazzo, Vik	—
75.	**KEWPIE DOLL,** Perry Como, Victor	65
75.	**TRY THE IMPOSSIBLE,** Lee Andrews and the Hearts, United Artists	77
78.	**BORN TOO LATE,** Poni Tails, ABC-Paramount	—
78.	**THE FREEZE,** Tony and Joe, Era	—
78.	**WESTERN MOVIES,** Olympics, Demon	—
78.	**JEALOUSY,** Kitty Wells, Decca	89
82.	**TO BE LOVED,** Jackie Wilson, Brunswick	61
82.	**CHA HUA HUA,** Pets, Arwin	72
84.	**BOOK OF LOVE,** Monotones, Argo	56
84.	**FLIP-TOP BOX,** Dickey Doo and the Don'ts, Swan	61
84.	**YOU'D BE SURPRISED,** Kathy Linden, Felsted	79
87.	**DING DONG,** McGuire Sisters, Coral	61
87.	**JUST MARRIED,** Marty Robbins, Columbia	72
87.	**I'M SORRY I MADE YOU CRY,** Connie Francis, M-G-M	79
87.	**WHO'S SORRY NOW?** Connie Francis, M-G-M	85
87.	**DREAM,** Betty Johnson, Atlantic	92
92.	**THINK IT OVER,** Crickets, Brunswick	—
92.	**WINDY,** Paul Gayten, Argo	—
92.	**WOODCHOPPER'S BALL,** Hutch Davie, Atco	95
92.	**ALL THE TIME,** Johnny Mathis, Columbia	99
96.	**MARCH FROM THE RIVER KWAI AND "COLONEL BOGEY"** Mitch Miller, Columbia	74
96.	**COME IN, STRANGER,** Johnny Cash, Sun	85
96.	**CRAZY LOVE,** Paul Anka, ABC-Paramount	89
99.	**SICK AND TIRED,** Fats Domino, Imperial	92
99.	**SKINNY MINNIE,** Bill Haley and His Comets, Decca	95
99.	**WE BELONG TOGETHER,** Robert and Johnny, Old Town	95

BEST SELLING POP SINGLES IN STORES

The information given in this chart is based on actual sales to customers in a scientific sample of the nation's retail outlets during the week ending on the date shown above. Sample design, sample size, and all methods used in this continuing study of retail record sales are under the direct and continuing supervision and control of the School of Retailing of New York University.

FOR SURVEY WEEK ENDING JULY 19, 1958

This Week		Last Week	Weeks on Chart
1.	HARD-HEADED WOMAN (ASCAP)—Elvis Presley / DON'T ASK ME WHY (ASCAP)—Vic 7280	1	5
2.	PATRICIA (ASCAP)—Perez Prado / Why Wait? (BMI)—Vic 7245	6	6
3.	POOR LITTLE FOOL (BMI)—Ricky Nelson / Don't Leave Me This Way (BMI)—Imperial 5528	5	4
4.	SPLISH SPLASH (BMI)—Bobby Darin / Judy, Don't Be Moody (BMI)—Atco 6117	4	6
5.	YAKETY YAK (BMI)—Coasters / Zing! Went the Strings of My Heart (ASCAP)—Atco 6116	2	8
6.	REBEL-'ROUSER (BMI)—Duane Eddy / Stalkin' (BMI)—Jamie 1104	7	4
7.	WHEN (ASCAP)—Kalin Twins / Three o'Clock Thrill (BMI)—Dec 30642	8	5
8.	PURPLE PEOPLE EATER (BMI)—Sheb Wooley / I Can't Believe You're Mine (ASCAP)—M-G-M 12651	3	9
9.	MY TRUE LOVE (BMI)—Jack Scott / LEROY (BMI)—Carlton 462	13	7
10.	ENDLESS SLEEP (BMI)—Jody Reynolds / Tight Capris (BMI)—Demon 1507	9	10
11.	GUESS THINGS HAPPEN THAT WAY (BMI)—Johnny Cash / COME IN, STRANGER (BMI)—Sun 295	12	9
12.	LITTLE STAR (BMI)—Elegants / Getting Dizzy (BMI)—APT 25005	—	1
13.	IF DREAMS CAME TRUE (ASCAP)—Pat Boone / THAT'S HOW MUCH I LOVE YOU (BMI)—Dot 15785	20	3
14.	WILLIE AND THE HAND JIVE (BMI)—Johnny Otis Show / Ring-a-Ling (BMI)—Cap 3966	17	5
15.	SECRETLY (ASCAP)—Jimmie Rodgers / MAKE ME A MIRACLE (ASCAP)—Roulette 4070	10	12
16.	FOR YOUR PRECIOUS LOVE (ASCAP)—Jerry Butler and Impressions / Sweet Was the Wine (ASCAP)—Abner 1013	11	7
17.	ONE SUMMER NIGHT (BMI)—Danleers / Wheelin' and a-Dealin' (BMI)—Mercury 71322	30	4
18.	DO YOU WANT TO DANCE? (BMI)—Bobby Freeman / Big, Fat Woman (BMI)—Josie 835	15	11
19.	WHAT AM I LIVING FOR? (BMI)—Chuck Willis / HANG UP MY ROCK AND ROLL SHOES (BMI)—Atlantic 1179	16	12
20.	FEVER (BMI)—Peggy Lee / You Don't Know (BMI)—Cap 3998	25	2
21.	GINGER BREAD (BMI)—Frankie Avalon / Blue Betty (ASCAP)—Chancellor 1021	49	2
22.	A CERTAIN SMILE (ASCAP)—Johnny Mathis / Let it Rain (ASCAP)—Col 41193	21	4
23.	RETURN TO ME (ASCAP)—Dean Martin / Forgetting You (ASCAP)—Cap 3894	18	16
24.	LEFT RIGHT OUT OF YOUR HEART (ASCAP)—Patti Page / Longing to Hold You Again (ASCAP)—Mercury 71331	26	4
25.	JUST A DREAM (BMI)—Jimmy Clanton / You Aim to Please (BMI)—Ace 546	24	3
26.	PADRE (ASCAP)—Toni Arden / All at Once (ASCAP)—Dec 30628	19	10
27.	NO CHEMISE, PLEASE (BMI)—Gerry Granahan / Girl of My Dreams (ASCAP)—Sunbeam 102	27	7
28.	WITCH DOCTOR (ASCAP)—David Seville / Don't Whistle at Me, Baby (ASCAP)—Liberty 55132	22	16
29.	ALL I HAVE TO DO IS DREAM (BMI)—Everly Brothers / CLAUDETTE (BMI)—Cadence 1348	14	14
30.	BIG MAN (BMI)—Four Preps / Stop, Baby (ASCAP)—Cap 3960	23	12
31.	JENNIE LEE (BMI)—Jan and Arnie / Gotta Getta Date (BMI)—Arwin 108	28	10
32.	EVERYBODY LOVES A LOVER (ASCAP)—Doris Day / Instant Love (ASCAP)—Col 41195	—	1
33.	BLUE BLUE DAY (BMI)—Don Gibson / Too Soon to Know (BMI)—Vic 7010	33	3
34.	THE BIRD ON MY HEAD (ASCAP)—David Seville / Hey There, Moon (ASCAP)—Liberty 55140	42	3
35.	BORN TOO LATE (ASCAP)—Poni Tails / Come on, Joey, Dance With Me (BMI)—ABC-Paramount 9934	—	1
36.	I WONDER WHY (ASCAP)—Dion and the Belmonts / Teen Angel (ASCAP)—Laurie 3013	36	10
37.	YOU NEED HANDS (ASCAP)—Eydie Gorme / Dormi, Dormi, Dormi (ASCAP)—ABC-Paramount 9925	32	8
38.	ENCHANTED ISLAND (ASCAP)—Four Lads / Guess What the Neighbors'll Say (BMI)—Col 41194	37	3
39.	COME CLOSER TO ME (BMI)—Nat King Cole / Nothing in the World—Cap 4004	—	1
40.	DELICIOUS (ASCAP)—Jim Backus / I Need a Vacation (ASCAP)—Jubilee 5330	40	2
41.	DON'T GO HOME (BMI)—Playmates / Can't You Get it Through Your Head? (BMI)—Roulette 4072	48	6
42.	DOTTIE (BMI)—Danny and the Juniors / In the Meantime (BMI)—ABC-Paramount 9926	39	5
43.	TORERO (ASCAP)—Ronato Carosone / Chella Lla (ASCAP)—Cap 71080	45	10
44.	ANGEL BABY (BMI)—Dean Martin / I'll Gladly Make the Same Mistake Again (ASCAP)—Cap 3988	43	2
45.	SUGAR MOON (BMI)—Pat Boone / Cherie, I Love You (ASCAP)—Dot 15750	31	12
46.	LOOKING BACK (BMI)—Nat King Cole / Do I Like It? (BMI)—Cap 3939	34	16
47.	THE FREEZE (BMI)—Tony and Joe / Gonna Get a Little Kissin' Tonight (BMI)—Era 1075	—	1
47.	STUPID CUPID (BMI)—Connie Francis / Carolina Moon (ASCAP)—M-G-M 12683	—	1
49.	OOH! MY SOUL (BMI)—Little Richard / TRUE, FINE MAMA (BMI)—Specialty 633	44	6
50.	WESTERN MOVIES (BMI)—Olympics / Well! (BMI)—Demon 1508	—	1

THIS WEEK'S BEST BUYS

Special telephone reports and/or chart action indicate these recent releases have either broken out in one or more key areas or have leaped onto the charts and have excellent potential for placing among the Top 30 of The Billboard's Best Selling Pop Singles in Stores chart. Action sides are listed in capital letters.

VACATION TIME (Arc, BMI)—Chuck Berry—Chess 1697 BEAUTIFUL DELILAH (Arc, BMI)

EARLY IN THE MORNING (Royalty, ASCAP)—Buddy Holly—Coral 62066—NOW WE'RE ONE (Portrait, BMI)

YOU'RE A SWEETHEART (Robbins, ASCAP)—Little Willie John—King 5142—LET'S ROCK WHILE THE ROCKIN'S GOOD (Jay & Cee, BMI)

The above are previous Billboard Spotlight picks.

LA PALOMA (Randy-Smith, ASCAP)—Billy Vaughn—Dot 15795—HERE IS MY LOVE (Randy-Smith, ASCAP)

NEL BLU DIPINTO DI BLU (Robbins, ASCAP)—Domenico Modugno—Decca 30677—MARTITA IN CITTA (BIEM)

JUST LIKE IN THE MOVIES (Bae, ASCAP)—The Upbeats—Swan 4010—MY FOOLISH HEART (Joy, ASCAP)

The following records, not previously selected as Best Buys, are on the charts for the first time this week.

STUPID CUPID (Alden, BMI)—Connie Francis—M-G-M 12683—CAROLINA MOON (Cromwell, ASCAP)

WESTERN MOVIES (Elizabeth-Aries, BMI)—The Olympics—Demon 1508—WELL! (Elizabeth-Aries, BMI)

RECENT POP RELEASES COMING UP STRONG

FOR SURVEY WEEK ENDING JULY 19

The information given in this chart is based on actual sales to customers in a scientific sample of the nation's retail record outlets during the week ending on the date shown above. Sample design, sample size and all methods used in this continuing study of retail record sales are under the direct and continuing supervision and control of the School of Retailing of New York University.

Beautiful Delilah . . . . *Chuck Berry*
(BMI) Chess 1697

Early in the Morning . . *Bobby Darin and Rinky Dinks*
(ASCAP) Atco 6121

Early in the Morning . . . . *Buddy Holly*
(ASCAP) Coral 62066

Moon Talk . . . . *Perry Como*
(ASCAP) RCA Victor 7274

Most Played by Jockeys

FOR SURVEY WEEK ENDING JULY 19

SIDES are ranked in order of the greatest number of plays on disk jockey radio shows thruout the country. Results are based on The Billboard's weekly survey among the nation's disk jockeys. The reverse side of each record is also listed.

This Week		Last Week	Weeks on Chart
1.	PATRICIA (ASCAP)—Perez Prado Why Wait? (BMI)—Vic 7245	3	5
2.	POOR LITTLE FOOL (BMI)—Ricky Nelson Don't Leave Me This Way (BMI)—Imperial 5528	6	3
3.	HARD HEADED WOMAN (ASCAP)—Elvis Presley Don't Ask Me Why? (ASCAP)—Vic 7280	1	5
4.	YAKETY YAK (BMI)—Coasters Zing, Went the Strings of My Heart (ASCAP)—Atco 6116	2	7
5.	SPLISH SPLASH (BMI)—Bobby Darin Judy, Don't Be Moody (BMI)—Atco 6117	5	4
6.	EVERYBODY LOVES A LOVER (ASCAP)—Doris Day Instant Love (ASCAP)—Col 41195	19	2
7.	ONE SUMMER NIGHT (BMI)—Danleers Wheelin' and A-Dealin' (BMI)—Mercury 71322	20	4
8.	PURPLE PEOPLE EATER (BMI)—Sheb Wooley I Can't Believe You're Mine (ASCAP)—M-G-M 12651	4	9
9.	WHEN (ASCAP)—Kalin Twins Three o'Clock Thrill (BMI)—Dec 30642	8	5
10.	FEVER (BMI)—Peggy Lee You Don't Know (BMI)—Cap 3998	15	2
11.	IF DREAMS CAME TRUE (ASCAP)—Pat Boone That's How Much I Love You (BMI)—Dot 15785	7	2
12.	LEFT RIGHT OUT OF YOUR HEART (ASCAP)—Patti Page Longing to Hold You Again (ASCAP)—Mercury 71331	9	5
13.	SECRETLY (ASCAP)—Jimmie Rodgers Make Me a Miracle (ASCAP)—Roulette 4070	10	11
14.	REBEL-'ROUSER (BMI)—Duane Eddy Stalkin' (BMI)—Jamie 1104	18	2
15.	ALL I HAVE TO DO IS DREAM (BMI)—Everly Brothers Claudette (BMI)—Cadence 1348	11	14
16.	KATHY-O (ASCAP)—Diamonds Happy Years (ASCAP)—Mercury 71330	—	1
17.	ENCHANTED ISLAND (ASCAP)—Four Lads Guess What the Neighbors'll Say (BMI)—Col 41194	12	3
18.	RETURN TO ME (ASCAP)—Dean Martin Forgetting You (ASCAP)—Cap 3894	13	17
19.	MY TRUE LOVE (BMI)—Jack Scott Leroy (BMI)—Carlton 462	24	3
20.	BLUE BLUE DAY (BMI)—Don Gibson Too Soon to Know (BMI)—Vic 7010	—	1
21.	ENDLESS SLEEP (BMI)—Jody Reynolds Tight Capris (BMI)—Demon 1507	16	8
22.	JUDY (BMI)—Frankie Vaughan Am I Wasting My Time On You? (BMI)—Epic 9273	—	1
23.	PADRE (ASCAP)—Tony Arden All at Once (ASCAP)—Dec 30628	25	7
24.	A CERTAIN SMILE (ASCAP)—Johnny Mathis Let It Rain (ASCAP)—Col 41193	14	3
25.	BAUBLES, BANGLES AND BEADS (ASCAP)—Kirby Stone Four In the Good Old Summertime/Take the Lady (ASCAP)—Col 41183	—	1

Top 100 Sides

FOR SURVEY WEEK ENDING JULY 19

This is a tabulation of dealer individual record sales listed according to the specific side requested by customers. No attempt is made to add sides together to reflect actual record sales. This is, therefore, a tabulation of sides or songs, and not records. This is the reason for any possible variation that occurs between the top 50 sides as reflected in this chart, and the top 50 record sellers as reflected in the "Best Sellers in Stores" chart.

Pos.	Song, Artist, Label	Last Week
1.	**PATRICIA,** Perez Prado, Victor	6
2.	**POOR LITTLE FOOL,** Ricky Nelson, Imperial	5
3.	**HARD HEADED WOMAN,** Elvis Presley, Victor	2
4.	**SPLISH SPLASH,** Bobby Darin, Atco	4
5.	**YAKETY YAK,** Coasters, Atco	1
6.	**REBEL-'ROUSER,** Duane Eddy, Jamie	7
7.	**WHEN,** Kalin Twins, Decca	8
8.	**THE PURPLE PEOPLE EATER,** Sheb Wooley, M-G-M	3
9.	**ENDLESS SLEEP,** Jody Reynolds, Demon	9
10.	**LITTLE STAR,** Elegants, APT	64
11.	**GUESS THINGS HAPPEN THAT WAY,** Johnny Cash, Sun	12
12.	**WILLIE AND THE HAND JIVE,** Johnny Otis Show, Capitol	16
13.	**FOR YOUR PRECIOUS LOVE,** Jerry Butler & the Impressions, Abner	11
14.	**SECRETLY,** Jimmie Rodgers, Roulette	10
15.	**MY TRUE LOVE,** Jack Scott, Carlton	32
16.	**ONE SUMMER NIGHT,** Danleers, Mercury	30
17.	**DO YOU WANT TO DANCE?** Bobby Freeman, Josie	14
17.	**IF DREAMS CAME TRUE,** Pat Boone, Dot	23
17.	**FEVER,** Peggy Lee, Capitol	23
17.	**GINGER BREAD,** Frankie Avalon, Chancellor	50
21.	**WHAT AM I LIVING FOR?** Chuck Willis, Atlantic	15
21.	**A CERTAIN SMILE,** Johnny Mathis, Columbia	19
23.	**RETURN TO ME,** Dean Martin, Capitol	17
23.	**LEFT RIGHT OUT OF YOUR HEART,** Patti Page, Mercury	25
25.	**JUST A DREAM,** Jimmy Clanton, Ace	22
26.	**PADRE,** Toni Arden, Decca	18
27.	**NO CHEMISE, PLEASE,** Gerry Granahan, Sunbeam	25
28.	**WITCH DOCTOR,** David Seville, Liberty	20
29.	**ALL I HAVE TO DO IS DREAM,** Everly Brothers, Cadence	13
30.	**LEROY,** Jack Scott, Carlton	25
31.	**BIG MAN,** Four Preps, Capitol	21
32.	**JENNIE LEE,** Jan & Arnie, Arwin	29
33.	**DON'T ASK ME WHY,** Elvis Presley, Victor	28
34.	**BLUE BLUE DAY,** Don Gibson, Victor	35
34.	**EVERYBODY LOVES A LOVER,** Doris Day, Columbia	74
36.	**THE BIRD ON MY HEAD,** David Seville, Liberty	44
37.	**BORN TOO LATE,** Poni Tails, ABC-Paramount	78
38.	**I WONDER WHY,** Dion & the Belmonts, Laurie	38
39.	**YOU NEED HANDS,** Eydie Gorme, ABC-Paramount	34
40.	**ENCHANTED ISLAND,** Four Lads, Columbia	39
41.	**COME CLOSER TO ME,** Nat King Cole, Capitol	53
42.	**DELICIOUS!** Jim Backus, Jubilee	42
42.	**DON'T GO HOME,** Playmates, Roulette	47
44.	**DOTTIE,** Danny & the Juniors, ABC-Paramount	41
44.	**TORERO,** Renato Carosone, Capitol	46
46.	**ANGEL BABY,** Dean Martin, Capitol	45
47.	**SUGAR MOON,** Pat Boone, Dot	32
48.	**LOOKING BACK,** Nat King Cole, Capitol	36
49.	**STUPID CUPID,** Connie Francis, M-G-M	—
49.	**THE FREEZE,** Tony and Joe, Era	78
51.	**OH, LONESOME,** Don Gibson, Victor	30
51.	**YOU'RE MAKING A MISTAKE,** Platters, Mercury	53
51.	**WESTERN MOVIES,** Olympics, Demon	78
54.	**TWILIGHT TIME,** Platters, Mercury	42
54.	**SHIEK OF ARABY,** Lou Monte, Victor	87
56.	**FOR YOUR LOVE,** Ed Townsend, Capitol	36
56.	**OOH! MY SOUL,** Little Richard, Specialty	81
56.	**LITTLE MARY,** Fats Domino, Imperial	81
56.	**THAT'S HOW MUCH I LOVE YOU,** Pat Boone, Dot	53
56.	**SINGING HILLS,** Billy Vaughn, Dot	59
56.	**BEWITCHED,** Betty Smith, London	68
62.	**TALK TO ME, TALK TO ME,** Little Willie John, King	59
62.	**ZORRO,** Chordettes, Cadence	62
62.	**(IT'S BEEN A LONG TIME) PRETTY BABY,** Gino & Gina, Mercury	65
62.	**THINK IT OVER,** Crickets, Brunswick	92
66.	**HIGH SCHOOL CONFIDENTIAL,** Jerry Lee Lewis, Sun	40
66.	**LITTLE SERENADE,** Teddy Randazzo, Vik	75
68.	**JOHNNY B. GOODE,** Chuck Berry, Chess	47
68.	**RUMBLE,** Link Wray & His Ray Men, Cadence	47
68.	**YOUNG AND WARM AND WONDERFUL,** Tony Bennett, Columbia	59
71.	**THE PURPLE PEOPLE EATER MEETS THE WITCH DOCTOR** Joe South, NRC	—
71.	**I KNOW WHERE I'M GOIN',** George Hamilton IV, ABC-Paramount	68
73.	**MIDNIGHT,** Paul Anka, ABC-Paramount	—
73.	**WEAR MY RING AROUND YOUR NECK,** Elvis Presley, Victor	57
73.	**I LOVE YOU SO,** Chantels, End	62
73.	**HE'S GOT THE WHOLE WORLD IN HIS HANDS,** Laurie London, Capitol	65
77.	**COME IN, STRANGER,** Johnny Cash, Sun	96
78.	**BY THE LIGHT OF THE SILVERY MOON,** Jim Bowen, Roulette	—
78.	**EL RANCHO ROCK,** Champs, Challenge	53
78.	**WINDY,** Paul Gayten, Argo	92
81.	**GOT A MATCH,** Daddy-O's, Cabot	68
81.	**MARCH FROM THE RIVER KWAI AND "COLONEL BOGEY"** Mitch Miller, Columbia	96
83.	**BEAUTIFUL DELILAH,** Chuck Berry, Chess	—
83.	**EARLY IN THE MORNING,** Bobby Darin & the Rinky Dinks.., Atco	—
83.	**CHANSON D'AMOUR,** Art & Dotty Todd, Era	72
83.	**KEWPIE DOLL,** Perry Como, Victor	75
87.	**I'LL GET BY,** Billy Williams, Coral	—
87.	**KATHY-O,** Diamonds, Mercury	—
87.	**MOON TALK,** Perry Como, Victor	—
90.	**OP,** Honeycones, Ember	—
90.	**TRY THE IMPOSSIBLE,** Lee Andrews & the Hearts, United Artists	75
90.	**JEALOUSY,** Kitty Wells, Decca	78
90.	**FLIP TOP BOX,** Dickey Doo & the Don'ts, Swan	84
90.	**DREAM,** Betty Johnson, Atlantic	87
95.	**COME WHAT MAY,** Clyde McPhatter, Atlantic	65
95.	**RAVE ON,** Buddy Holly, Coral	68
95.	**GOT A MATCH,** Frank Gallup, ABC-Paramount	72
95.	**YOU'D BE SURPRISED,** Kathy Linden, Felsted	84
95.	**I'M SORRY I MADE YOU CRY,** Connie Francis, M-G-M	87
95.	**TEACHER, TEACHER,** Johnny Mathis, Columbia	—

The Billboard HOT 100

FOR THE WEEK ENDING AUGUST 10

★ THE STAR PERFORMER designation shows the outstanding upward changes of position in The Hot 100 since last week's chart. Its purpose merely is to provide quick visual identification of the sides which moved up most dramatically or to new entries which first entered the chart at an unusually high position.

Three Weeks Ago	Two Weeks Ago	One Week Ago	This Week	★ Star Performer This Week	TITLE — Artist, Company, Record Number	Weeks on Chart
—	—	—	1		POOR LITTLE FOOL — Ricky Nelson, Imperial 5528	1
—	—	—	2		PATRICIA — Perez Prado, RCA Victor 7245	1
—	—	—	3		SPLISH SPLASH — Bobby Darin, Atco 6117	1
—	—	—	4		HARD HEADED WOMAN — Elvis Presley, RCA Victor 7280	1
—	—	—	5		WHEN — Kalin Twins, Decca 30642	1
—	—	—	6		REBEL-'ROUSER — Duane Eddy, Jamie 1104	1
—	—	—	7		YAKETY YAK — Coasters, Atco 6116	1
—	—	—	8		MY TRUE LOVE — Jack Scott, Carlton 462	1
—	—	—	9		WILLIE AND THE HAND JIVE — Johnny Otis Show, Capitol 3966	1
—	—	—	10		FEVER — Peggy Lee, Capitol 3998	1
—	—	—	11		GINGER BREAD — Frankie Avalon, Chancellor 1021	1
—	—	—	12		JUST A DREAM — Jimmy Clanton, Ace 546	1
—	—	—	13		LEFT RIGHT OUT OF YOUR HEART — Patti Page, Mercury 71331	1
—	—	—	14		IF DREAMS CAME TRUE — Pat Boone, Dot 15785	1
—	—	—	15		FOR YOUR PRECIOUS LOVE — Jerry Butler and the Impressions, Abner 1013	1
—	—	—	16		ONE SUMMER NIGHT — Danleers, Mercury 71322	1
—	—	—	17		ENDLESS SLEEP — Jody Reynolds, Demon 1507	1
—	—	—	18		LITTLE STAR — Elegants, Apt 25005	1
—	—	—	19		EVERYBODY LOVES A LOVER — Doris Day, Columbia 41195	1
—	—	—	20		DO YOU WANT TO DANCE! — Bobby Freeman, Josie 835	1
—	—	—	21		GUESS THINGS HAPPEN THAT WAY — Johnny Cash, Sun 295	1
—	—	—	22		A CERTAIN SMILE — Johnny Mathis, Columbia 41193	1
—	—	—	23		WESTERN MOVIES — Olympics, Demon 1508	1
—	—	—	24		PURPLE PEOPLE EATER — Sheb Wooley, M-G-M 12651	1
—	—	—	25		WHAT AM I LIVING FOR! — Chuck Willis, Atlantic 1179	1
—	—	—	26		BORN TOO LATE — Poni Tails, ABC-Paramount 9934	1
—	—	—	27		THINK IT OVER — Crickets, Brunswick 55072	1
—	—	—	28		SECRETLY — Jimmie Rodgers, Roulette 4070	1
—	—	—	29		ENCHANTED ISLAND — Four Lads, Columbia 41194	1
—	—	—	30		ANGEL BABY — Dean Martin, Capitol 3988	1
—	—	—	31		CHANTILLY LACE — Big Bopper, Mercury 71343	1
—	—	—	32		BLUE BLUE DAY — Don Gibson, RCA Victor 7010	1
—	—	—	33		THE FREEZE — Tony and Joe, Era 1075	1
—	—	—	34		DON'T ASK ME WHY — Elvis Presley, RCA Victor 7280	1
—	—	—	35		ROCK-IN' ROBIN — Bobby Day, Class 229	1
—	—	—	36		NO CHEMISE, PLEASE — Gerry Granahan, Sunbeam 102	1
—	—	—	37		MOON TALK — Perry Como, RCA Victor 7274	1
—	—	—	38		SOMEBODY TOUCHED ME — Buddy Knox, Roulette 4082	1
—	—	—	39		THAT'S HOW MUCH I LOVE YOU — Pat Boone, Dot 15785	1
—	—	—	40		CRAZY EYES FOR YOU — Bobby Hamilton, Apt 25001	1
—	—	—	41		EARLY IN THE MORNING — Buddy Holly, Coral 62006	1
—	—	—	42		YOU CHEATED — Slades, Domino 500	1
—	—	—	43		COME WHAT MAY — Clyde McPhatter, Atlantic 1185	1
—	—	—	44		JENNIE LEE — Jan and Arnie, Arwin 108	1
—	—	—	45		KATHY-O — Diamonds, Mercury 71330	1
—	—	—	46		(It's Been a Long Time) PRETTY BABY — Gino and Gina, Mercury 71283	1
—	—	—	47		I WONDER WHY! — Dion and the Belmonts, Laurie 3013	1
—	—	—	48		RETURN TO ME — Dean Martin, Capitol 3894	1
—	—	—	49		ALL I HAVE TO DO IS DREAM — Everly Brothers, Cadence 1348	1
—	—	—	50		BAUBLES, BANGLES AND BEADS — Kirby Stone Four, Columbia 41183	1
—	—	—	50		BY THE LIGHT OF THE SILVERY MOON — Jimmy Bowen, Roulette 4083	1
—	—	—	52		EARLY IN THE MORNING — Bobby Darin and the Rinky Dinks, Atco 6121	1
—	—	—	53		COME CLOSER TO ME — Nat King Cole, Capitol 4004	1
—	—	—	54		VOLARE (Nel Blu Dipinto Di Blu) — Domenico Modugno, Decca 30677	1
—	—	—	55		LET'S GO STEADY FOR THE SUMMER — Three G's, Columbia 41175	1
—	—	—	56		LEROY — Jack Scott, Carlton 462	1
—	—	—	57		YOU NEED HANDS — Edyie Gorme, ABC-Paramount 9925	1
—	—	—	58		FOOL'S PARADISE — Crickets, Brunswick 55072	1
—	—	—	59		YOUNG AND WARM AND WONDERFUL — Tony Bennett, Columbia 41172	1
—	—	—	60		OVER AND OVER — Bobby Day, Class 229	1

THE INDUSTRY'S FASTEST AND MOST COMPLETE PROGRAMMING AND BUYING GUIDE

These 100 sides are listed in order of their national popularity, as determined by weekly local studies prepared for The Billboard in markets representing a cross-section of the United States. These studies take into consideration such factors as disk jockey plays, juke box activity and record sales.

★ THE STAR PERFORMER designation shows the outstanding upward changes of position in The Hot 100 since last week's chart. Its purpose merely is to provide quick visual identification of the sides which moved up most dramatically or to new entries which first entered the chart at an unusually high position.

THREE WEEKS AGO	TWO WEEKS AGO	ONE WEEK AGO	THIS WEEK	★ STAR PERFORMER THIS WEEK	TITLE Artist, Company, Record Number	WEEKS ON CHART
—	—	—	61		ITCHY TWITCHY FEELING — Bobby Hendricks, Sue 706	1
—	—	—	62		FOR YOUR LOVE — Ed Townsend, Capitol 3926	1
—	—	—	63		HIGH SCHOOL CONFIDENTIAL — Jerry Lee Lewis, Sun 296	1
—	—	—	63		PADRE — Toni Arden, Decca 30628	1
—	—	—	65		YOU'RE MAKING A MISTAKE — Platters, Mercury 71320	1
—	—	—	66		DELICIOUS! — Jim Backus, Jubilee 5330	1
—	—	—	67		BIG MAN — Four Preps, Capitol 3960	1
—	—	—	68		VOLARE (Nel Blu Dipinto Di Blu) — Dean Martin, Capitol 4028	1
—	—	—	69		OP — Honeycones, Ember 1036	1
—	—	—	70		DON'T GO HOME — Playmates, Roulette 4072	1
—	—	—	71		GOT A MATCH — Frank Gallup, ABC-Paramount 9931	1
—	—	—	72		STUPID CUPID — Connie Francis, M-G-M 12683	1
—	—	—	73		HEY, GIRL—HEY, BOY — Oscar McLollie & Jeanette, Class 228	1
—	—	—	74		GOTTA HAVE RAIN — Edyie Gorme, ABC-Paramount 9944	1
—	—	—	74		WIN YOUR LOVE FOR ME — Sam Cooke, Keen 2006	1
—	—	—	76		MIDNIGHT — Paul Anka, ABC-Paramount 9937	1
—	—	—	77		HAPPY YEARS — Diamonds, Mercury 71330	1
—	—	—	78		BETTY LOU GOT A NEW PAIR OF SHOES — Bobby Freeman, Josie 841	1
—	—	—	79		THE BIRD ON MY HEAD — David Seville, Liberty 55140	1
—	—	—	80		JOHNNY B. GOODE — Chuck Berry, Chess 1691	1
—	—	—	81		BEAUTIFUL DELILAH — Chuck Berry, Chess 1697	1
—	—	—	82		BLIP BLOP — Bill Doggett, King 5138	1
—	—	—	83		TRY THE IMPOSSIBLE — Lee Andrews and the Hearts, United Artists 123	1
—	—	—	84		SUMMERTIME BLUES — Eddie Cochran, Liberty 55144	1
—	—	—	85		GOT A MATCH — Daddy-O's, Cabot 122	1
—	—	—	86		TO BE LOVED — Jackie Wilson, Brunswick 55052	1
—	—	—	87		JEALOUSY — Kitty Wells, Decca 30662	1
—	—	—	88		JUST LIKE IN THE MOVIES — Upbeats, Swan 4010	1
—	—	—	89		BLUE BOY — Jim Reeves, RCA Victor 7266	1
—	—	—	90		STAY — Ames Brothers, RCA Victor 7268	1

From The Hot 100:

THE BILLBOARD'S BEST BUYS

These records, of all those listed on The Billboard Hot 100, have shown sales break-out potential for the first time this week. Action sides are listed in capital letters.

BIRD DOG/DEVOTED TO YOU . . . . **The Everly Brothers**
(Acuff-Rose, BMI/Acuff-Rose, BMI) Cadence 1350

VOLARE (NEL BLU DIPINTO DI BLU) . . . . **Dean Martin**
(Robbins, ASCAP) Outta My Mind (Sands, ASCAP) Capitol 4028

SOMEBODY TOUCHED ME . . . . **Buddy Knox**
(Progressive, BMI) C'Mon, Baby (Patricia, BMI) Roulette 4082

ARE YOU REALLY MINE!/THE WIZARD . . . . **Jimmie Rodgers**
(Planetary, ASCAP)/Planetary, ASCAP) Roulette 4090

THE PURPLE PEOPLE EATER MEETS THE WITCH DOCTOR . . . . **Joe Smith**
(Ken-Rick, BMI) My Fondest Memories (Lowery, BMI) NRC 5000

SHE WAS ONLY SEVENTEEN . . . . **Marty Robbins**
(Acuff-Rose, BMI) Sittin' in a Tree House (Famous, ASCAP) Columbia 41208

THINK IT OVER . . . . **The Crickets**
(Cedarwood, BMI) Fool's Paradise (Nor-Va-Jak, BMI) Brunswick 55072

★ THE STAR PERFORMER designation shows the outstanding upward changes of position in The Hot 100 since last week's chart. Its purpose merely is to provide quick visual identification of the sides which moved up most dramatically or to new entries which first entered the chart at an unusually high position.

THREE WEEKS AGO	TWO WEEKS AGO	ONE WEEK AGO	THIS WEEK	★ STAR PERFORMER THIS WEEK	TITLE Artist, Company, Record Number	WEEKS ON CHART
—	—	—	91		THE PURPLE PEOPLE EATER MEETS THE WITCH DOCTOR — Joe South, NRC 5000	1
—	—	—	92		BIRD DOG — Everly Brothers, Cadence 1350	1
—	—	—	93		ARE YOU REALLY MINE! — Jimmie Rodgers, Roulette 4090	1
—	—	—	94		SHE WAS ONLY SEVENTEEN — Marty Robbins, Columbia 41208	1
—	—	—	95		LITTLE MARY — Fats Domino, Imperial 5526	1
—	—	—	96		OVER AND OVER — Thurston Harris, Aladdin 3430	1
—	—	—	97		I BELIEVE IN YOU — Robert and Johnny, Old Town 1021	1
—	—	—	98		LITTLE SERENADE — Ames Brothers, RCA Victor 7268	1
—	—	—	99		I'LL GET BY — Billy Williams, Coral 61999	1
—	—	—	100		JUDY — Frankie Vaughan, Epic 9273	1

BEST SELLING POP SINGLES IN STORES

The information given in this chart is based on actual sales to customers in a scientific sample of the nation's retail outlets during the week ending on the date shown above. Sample design, sample size, and all methods used in this continuing study of retail record sales are under the direct and continuing supervision and control of the School of Retailing of New York University.

FOR SURVEY WEEK ENDING JULY 26, 1958

This Week		Last Week	Weeks on Chart
1.	**POOR LITTLE FOOL** (BMI)—Ricky Nelson Don't Leave Me This Way (BMI)—Imperial 5528	3	5
2.	**PATRICIA** (ASCAP)—Perez Prado Why Wait? (BMI)—Vic 7245	2	7
3.	**HARD HEADED WOMAN** (ASCAP)—Elvis Presley **DON'T ASK ME WHY** (ASCAP)—Vic 7280	1	6
4.	**YAKETY YAK** (BMI)—Coasters Zing! Went the Strings of My Heart (ASCAP)—Atco 6116	5	9
5.	**SPLISH SPLASH** (BMI)—Bobby Darin Judy, Don't Be Moody (BMI)—Atco 6117	4	7
6.	**LITTLE STAR** (BMI)—Elegants Getting Dizzy (BMI)—APT 25005	12	2
7.	**REBEL-'ROUSER** (BMI)—Duane Eddy Stalkin' (BMI)—Jamie 1104	6	5
8.	**WHEN** (ASCAP)—Kalin Twins Three o'Clock Thrill (BMI)—Dec 30642	7	6
9.	**MY TRUE LOVE** (BMI)—Jack Scott **LEROY** (BMI)—Carlton 462	9	8
10.	**PURPLE PEOPLE EATER** (BMI)—Sheb Wooly I Can't Believe You're Mine (ASCAP)—M-G-M 12651	8	10
11.	**IF DREAMS CAME TRUE** (ASCAP)—Pat Boone That's How Much I Love You (BMI)—Dot 15785	13	4
12.	**JUST A DREAM** (BMI)—Jimmy Clanton You Aim to Please (BMI)—Ace 546	25	4
13.	**ENDLESS SLEEP** (BMI)—Jody Reynolds Tight Capris (BMI)—Demon 1507	10	11
14.	**ONE SUMMER NIGHT** (BMI)—Danleers Wheelin' and A-Dealin' (BMI)—Mercury 71322	17	5
15.	**FEVER** (BMI)—Peggy Lee You Don't Know (BMI)—Cap 3998	20	3
16.	**WILLIE AND THE HAND JIVE** (BMI)—Johnny Otis Show Ring-A-Ling (BMI)—Cap 3966	14	6
16.	**FOR YOUR PRECIOUS LOVE** (ASCAP)—Jerry Butler and Impressions Sweet Was the Wine (ASCAP)—Abner 1013	16	8
18.	**GUESS THINGS HAPPEN THAT WAY** (BMI)—Johnny Cash **COME IN, STRANGER** (BMI)—Sun 295	11	10
19.	**LEFT RIGHT OUT OF YOUR HEART** (ASCAP)—Patti Page Longing to Hold You Again (ASCAP)—Mercury 71331	24	5
20.	**GINGER BREAD** (BMI)—Frankie Avalon Blue Betty (ASCAP)—Chancellor 1021	21	3
21.	**A CERTAIN SMILE** (ASCAP)—Johnny Mathis Let It Rain (ASCAP)—Col 41193	22	5
22.	**SECRETLY** (ASCAP)—Jimmie Rodgers Make Me a Miracle (ASCAP)—Roulette 4070	15	13
23.	**BORN TOO LATE** (ASCAP)—Poni Tails Come On, Joey, Dance With Me (BMI)—ABC-Paramount 9934	35	2
23.	**RETURN TO ME** (ASCAP)—Dean Martin Forgetting You (ASCAP)—Cap 3894	23	17
25.	**EVERYBODY LOVES A LOVER** (ASCAP)—Doris Day Instant Love (ASCAP)—Col 41195	32	2
26.	**WHAT AM I LIVING FOR?** (BMI)—Chuck Willis **HANG UP MY ROCK AND ROLL SHOES** (BMI)—Atlantic 1179	19	13
27.	**DO YOU WANT TO DANCE?** (BMI)—Bobby Freeman Big Fat Woman (BMI)—Josie 835	18	12
28.	**NO CHEMISE, PLEASE** (BMI)—Gerry Granahan Girl of My Dreams (ASCAP)—Sunbeam 102	27	8
29.	**PADRE** (ASCAP)—Toni Arden All at Once (ASCAP)—Dec 30628	26	11
30.	**VOLARE (Nel Blu Dipinto Di Blu)** (ASCAP)—Domenico Modugno Marti in Citta (BIEM)—Dec 30677	—	1
31.	**WITCH DOCTOR** (ASCAP)—David Seville Don't Whistle at Me, Baby (ASCAP)—Liberty 55132	28	17
32.	**BLUE, BLUE DAY** (BMI)—Don Gibson Too Soon to Know (BMI)—Vic 7010	33	4
33.	**STUPID CUPID** (BMI)—Connie Francis Carolina Moon (ASCAP)—M-G-M 12683	47	2
34.	**WESTERN MOVIES** (BMI)—Olympics Well! (BMI)—Demon 1508	50	2
35.	**ENCHANTED ISLAND** (ASCAP)—Four Lads Guess What the Neighbors'll Say (BMI)—Col 41194	38	4
36.	**MOON TALK** (ASCAP)—Perry Como Beats There a Heart So True (BMI)—Vic 7242	—	1
37.	**ALL I HAVE TO DO IS DREAM** (BMI)—Everly Brothers Claudette (BMI)—Cadence 1348	29	15
38.	**I WONDER WHY** (ASCAP)—Dion and the Belmonts Teen Angel (ASCAP)—Laurie 3013	36	11
39.	**SUGAR MOON** (BMI)—Pat Boone Cherie, I Love You (ASCAP)—Dot 15750	45	13
40.	**JENNIE LEE** (BMI)—Jan and Arnie Gotta Getta Date (BMI)—Arwin 108	31	11
41.	**YOU NEED HANDS** (ASCAP)—Eydie Gorme Dormi, Dormi, Dormi (ASCAP)—ABC-Paramount 9925	37	9
42.	**DON'T GO HOME** (BMI)—Playmates Can't You Get it Through Your Head (BMI)—Roulette 4072	41	7
43.	**LOOKING BACK** (BMI)—Nat King Cole Do I Like It (BMI)—Cap 3939	46	17
44.	**THINK IT OVER** (BMI)—Crickets Fool's Paradise (BMI)—Brunswick 55072	—	1
45.	**ANGEL BABY** (BMI)—Dean Martin I'll Gladly Make the Same Mistake Again (ASCAP)—Cap 3988	44	3
46.	**HIGH SCHOOL CONFIDENTIAL** (BMI)—Jerry Lee Lewis Fools Like Me (BMI)—Sun 296	—	9
47.	**THE PURPLE PEOPLE EATER MEETS THE WITCH DOCTOR** (BMI)—Joe South My Fondest Memories—NRC 5000	—	1
48.	**THE BIRD ON MY HEAD** (ASCAP)—David Seville Hey There, Moon (ASCAP)—Liberty 55140	34	4
49.	**THE FREEZE** (BMI)—Tony and Joe Gonna Get a Little Kissin' Tonight (BMI)—Era 1075	47	2
50.	**DELICIOUS!** (ASCAP)—Jim Backus I Need a Vacation (ASCAP)—Jubilee 5330	40	3
50.	**FOR YOUR LOVE** (BMI)—Ed Townsend Over and Over Again (BMI)—Cap 3926	—	15

Poni Tails Flying With 'Born Too Late'

Group consists of three 18-year-old girls from Cleveland, O. Toni Cistone, singing lead, La Verne Novak, with the high harmony, and Pattie McCabe, low harmony. They began singing at high school engagements in Lynn, O. and collaborated on writing a song, "Que La." While singing this tune at a benefit, they interested John R. Jewitt, noted Cleveland attorney, who, in turn, introduced them to Tom Illius, a music publisher of the same city.

This started their professional career with Illius as their personal manager. They sold their song to a New York record firm and then appeared in night clubs and other stints where they attracted the attention of Don Costa of ABC-Paramount and a recording contract resulted. First disk was "Just My Luck to Be 15" but currently are on the charts with "Born Too Late" and still going up.

Frankie Avalon Hot With 'Ginger Bread'

This 18-year-old teen-age idol began his singing career just about two years ago in a teen-age night-club opened by his father to curb juvenile delinquency. He plays the trumpet and, in fact, did so for Ray Anthony's ork. His interests, besides music, are golf, football, baseball and driving. He loves rock and roll but also digs jazz the most. He stands 5' 7", weighs 132 pounds.

His first three records "Cupid," "Teacher's Pet" and "De De Dinah" have solidly established him as a teen-age idol. Appearances on the Patti Page shows have hyped his popularity. He has put out one album "Frankie Avalon" and is currently selecting the tunes for his second LP outing. His current smash is "Ginger Bread" which is steadily rising on the charts and gives all indications of being bigger than "De De Dinah."

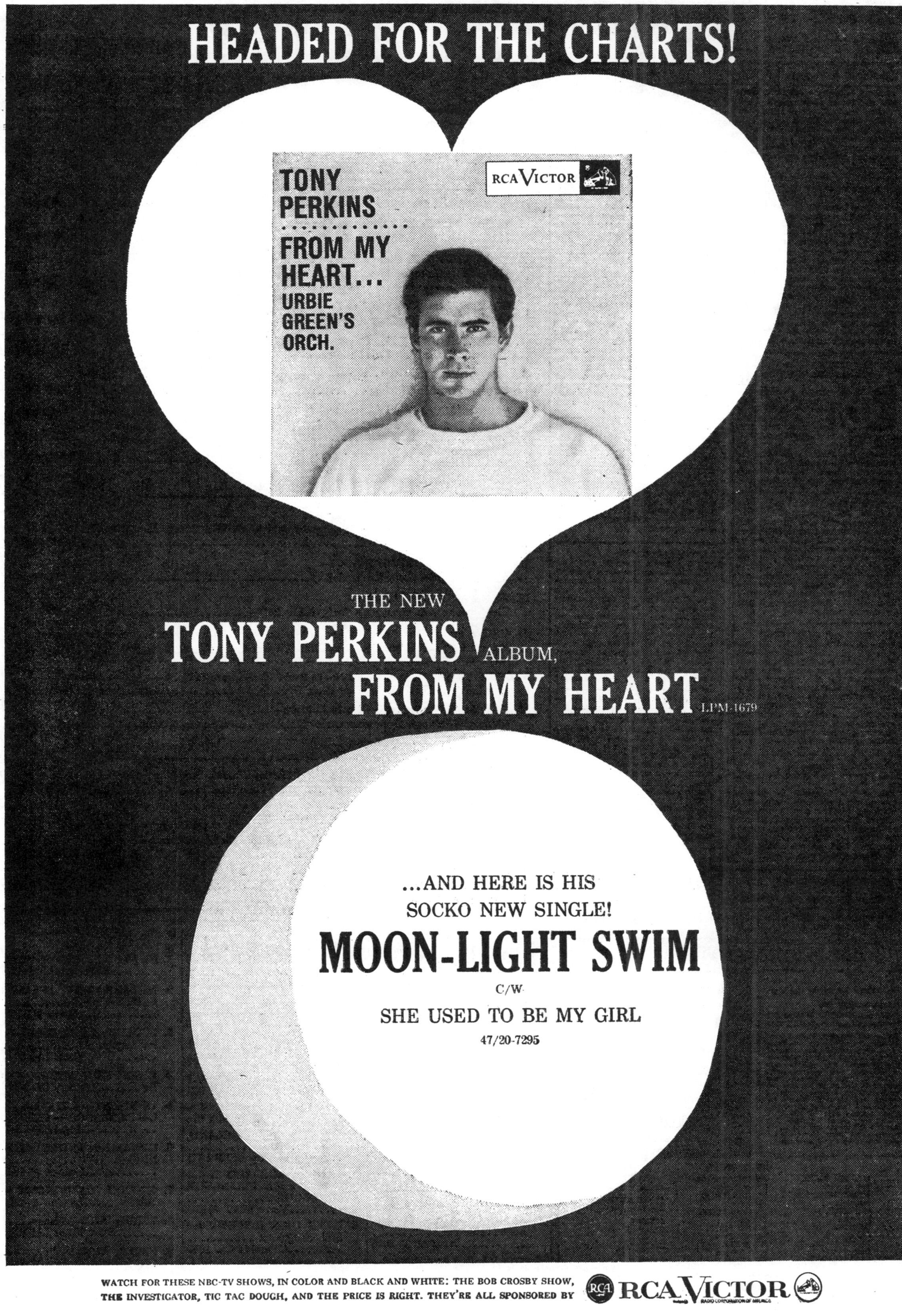
HEADED FOR THE CHARTS!
TONY PERKINS
FROM MY HEART...
URBIE GREEN'S ORCH.
RCA VICTOR
THE NEW
TONY PERKINS ALBUM,
FROM MY HEART LPM-1679
...AND HERE IS HIS
SOCKO NEW SINGLE!
MOON-LIGHT SWIM
C/W
SHE USED TO BE MY GIRL
47/20-7295

The Billboard HOT 100

FOR THE WEEK ENDING AUGUST 17

★ THE STAR PERFORMER designation shows the outstanding upward changes of position in The Hot 100 since last week's chart. Its purpose merely is to provide quick visual identification of the sides which moved up most dramatically or to new entries which first entered the chart at an unusually high position.

Three Weeks Ago	Two Weeks Ago	One Week Ago	This Week	★ Star Performer This Week	Title	Artist, Company, Record Number	Weeks on Chart
—	—	1	1		POOR LITTLE FOOL	Ricky Nelson, Imperial 5528	2
—	—	54	2	★	VOLARE (Nel Blu Dipinto Di Blu))	Domenico Modugno, Decca 30677	2
—	—	2	3		PATRICIA	Perez Prado, RCA Victor 7245	2
—	—	3	4		SPLISH SPLASH	Bobby Darin, Atco 6117	2
—	—	5	5		WHEN	Kalin Twins, Decca 30642	2
—	—	8	6		MY TRUE LOVE	Jack Scott, Carlton 462	2
—	—	4	7		HARD HEADED WOMAN	Elvis Presley, RCA Victor 7280	2
—	—	6	8		REBEL-'ROUSER	Duane Eddy, Jamie 1104	2
—	—	9	9		WILLIE AND THE HAND JIVE	Johnny Otis Show, Capitol 3966	2
—	—	12	9		JUST A DREAM	Jimmy Clanton, Ace 546	2
—	—	7	11		YAKETY YAK	Coasters, Atco 6116	2
—	—	14	12		IF DREAMS CAME TRUE	Pat Boone, Dot 15785	2
—	—	10	13		FEVER	Peggy Lee, Capitol 3998	2
—	—	18	14		LITTLE STAR	Elegants, Apt 25005	2
—	—	11	15		GINGER BREAD	Frankie Avalon, Chancellor 1021	2
—	—	19	16		EVERYBODY LOVES A LOVER	Doris Day, Columbia 41195	2
—	—	16	17		ONE SUMMER NIGHT	Danleers, Mercury 71322	2
—	—	26	18		BORN TOO LATE	Poni Tails, ABC-Paramount 9934	2
—	—	13	19		LEFT RIGHT OUT OF YOUR HEART	Patti Page, Mercury 71331	2
—	—	17	20		ENDLESS SLEEP	Jody Reynolds, Demon 1507	2
—	—	23	21		WESTERN MOVIES	Olympics, Demon 1508	2
—	—	21	22		GUESS THINGS HAPPEN THAT WAY	Johnny Cash, Sun 295	2
—	—	15	23		FOR YOUR PRECIOUS LOVE	Jerry Butler and the Impressions, Abner 1013	2
—	—	52	24	★	EARLY IN THE MORNING	Bobby Darin and the Rinky Dinks, Atco 6121	2
—	—	38	25	★	SOMEBODY TOUCHED ME	Buddy Knox, Roulette 4082	2
—	—	93	26	★	ARE YOU REALLY MINE?	Jimmie Rodgers, Roulette 4090	2
—	—	20	27		DO YOU WANT TO DANCE?	Bobby Freeman, Josie 835	2
—	—	22	28		A CERTAIN SMILE	Johnny Mathis, Columbia 41193	2
—	—	29	29		ENCHANTED ISLAND	Four Lads, Columbia 41194	2
—	—	37	30		MOON TALK	Ferry Como, RCA Victor 7274	2
—	—	25	31		WHAT AM I LIVING FOR?	Chuck Willis, Atlantic 1179	2
—	—	27	32		THINK IT OVER	Crickets, Brunswick 55072	2
—	—	35	33		ROCK-IN' ROBIN	Bobby Day, Class 229	2
—	—	92	34	★	BIRD DOG	Everly Brothers, Cadence 1350	2
—	—	72	35	★	STUPID CUPID	Connie Francis, M-G-M 12683	2
—	—	32	36		BLUE BLUE DAY	Don Gibson, RCA Victor 7010	2
—	—	68	37	★	VOLARE (Nel Blu Dipinto Di Blu)	Dean Martin, Capitol 4028	2
—	—	31	38		CHANTILLY LACE	Big Bopper, Mercury 71343	2
—	—	30	39		ANGEL BABY	Dean Martin, Capitol 3988	2
—	—	41	40		EARLY IN THE MORNING	Buddy Holly, Coral 62006	2
—	—	28	41		SECRETLY	Jimmie Rodgers, Roulette 4070	2
—	—	—	42	★	SUSIE DARLIN'	Robin Luke, Dot 15781	1
—	—	—	43	★	DEVOTED TO YOU	Everly Brothers, Cadence 1350	1
—	—	78	44	★	BETTY LOU GOT A NEW PAIR OF SHOES	Bobby Freeman, Josie 841	2
—	—	89	45	★	BLUE BOY	Jim Reeves, RCA Victor 7266	2
—	—	53	46		COME CLOSER TO ME	Nat King Cole, Capitol 4004	2
—	—	24	47		PURPLE PEOPLE EATER	Sheb Wooley, M-G-M 12651	2
—	—	42	48		YOU CHEATED	Slades, Domino 500	2
—	—	43	49		COME WHAT MAY	Clyde McPhatter, Atlantic 1185	2
—	—	61	50	★	ITCHY TWITCHY FEELING	Bobby Hendricks, Sue 706	2
—	—	—	51	★	ALONE WITH YOU	Faron Young, Capitol 3982	1
—	—	84	52	★	SUMMERTIME BLUES	Eddie Cochran, Liberty 55144	2
—	—	60	53		OVER AND OVER	Bobby Day, Class 229	2
—	—	34	54		DON'T ASK ME WHY	Elvis Presley, RCA Victor 7280	2
—	—	33	55		THE FREEZE	Tony and Joe, Era 1075	2
—	—	56	56		LEROY	Jack Scott, Carlton 462	2
—	—	39	57		THAT'S HOW MUCH I LOVE YOU	Pat Boone, Dot 15785	2
—	—	—	58	★	DRIP DROP	Drifters, Atlantic 1187	1
—	—	36	59		NO CHEMISE, PLEASE	Gerry Granahan, Sunbeam 102	2
—	—	47	60		I WONDER WHY	Dion and the Belmonts, Laurie 3013	2

THE INDUSTRY'S FASTEST AND MOST COMPLETE PROGRAMMING AND BUYING GUIDE

These 100 sides are listed in order of their national popularity, as determined by weekly local studies prepared for The Billboard in markets representing a cross-section of the United States. These studies take into consideration such factors as disk jockey plays, juke box activity and record sales.

★ THE STAR PERFORMER designation shows the outstanding upward changes of position in The Hot 100 since last week's chart. Its purpose merely is to provide quick visual identification of the sides which moved up most dramatically or to new entries which first entered the chart at an unusually high position.

THREE WEEKS AGO	TWO WEEKS AGO	ONE WEEK AGO	THIS WEEK	★ STAR PERFORMER THIS WEEK	TITLE	Artist, Company, Record Number	WEEKS ON CHART
—	—	74	61	★	WIN YOUR LOVE FOR ME	Sam Cooke, Keen 2006	2
—	—	40	62		CRAZY EYES FOR YOU	Bobby Hamilton, Apt 25001	2
—	—	48	63		RETURN TO ME	Dean Martin, Capitol 3894	2
—	—	57	64		YOU NEED HANDS	Edyie Gorme, ABC-Paramount 9925	2
—	—	63	65		PADRE	Toni Arden, Decca 30628	2
—	—	63	66		HIGH SCHOOL CONFIDENTIAL	Jerry Lee Lewis, Sun 296	2
—	—	—	67	★	LEAN JEAN	Bill Haley and His Comets, Decca 30681	1
—	—	65	68		YOU'RE MAKING A MISTAKE	Platters, Mercury 71320	2
—	—	50	69		BY THE LIGHT OF THE SILVERY MOON	Jimmy Bowen, Roulette 4083	2
—	—	83	70		TRY THE IMPOSSIBLE	Lee Andrews and the Hearts, United Artists 123	2
—	—	76	71		MIDNIGHT	Paul Anka, ABC-Paramount 9937	2
—	—	95	72	★	LITTLE MARY	Fats Domino, Imperial 5526	2
—	—	—	73	★	TEARS ON MY PILLOW	The Imperials, End 1027	1
—	—	45	74		KATHY-O	Diamonds, Mercury 71330	2
—	—	55	75		LET'S GO STEADY FOR THE SUMMER	Three G's, Columbia 41175	2
—	—	—	76		JUST MARRIED	Marty Robbins, Columbia 41143	1
—	—	44	77		JENNIE LEE	Jan and Arnie, Arwin 108	2
—	—	—	78		HARVEY'S GOT A GIRLFRIEND	Royal Teens, ABC-Paramount 9945	1
—	—	94	79		SHE WAS ONLY SEVENTEEN	Marty Robbins, Columia 41208	2
—	—	77	80		HAPPY YEARS	Diamonds, Mercury 71330	2
—	—	59	81		YOUNG AND WARM AND WONDERFUL	Tony Bennett, Columbia 41172	2
—	—	—	81		LOOKING BACK	Nat King Cole, Capitol 3939	1
—	—	87	83		JEALOUSY	Kitty Wells, Decca 30662	2
—	—	—	84		YOU'RE A SWEETHEART	Little Willie John, King 5142	1
—	—	—	85		THE WIZARD	Jimmie Rodgers, Roulette 4090	1
—	—	—	86		MOONLIGHT BAY	Drifters, Atlantic 1187	1
—	—	—	87		COME IN, STRANGER	Johnny Cash, Sun 295	1
—	—	—	88		CERVEZA	Boots Brown, RCA Victor 7269	1
—	—	91	89		THE PURPLE PEOPLE EATER MEETS THE WITCH DOCTOR	Joe South, NRC 5000	2
—	—	70	90		DON'T GO HOME	Playmates, Roulette 4072	2

From The Hot 100: THE BILLBOARD'S BEST BUYS

These records, of all those listed on The Billboard Hot 100, have shown sales break-out potential for the first time this week. Action sides are listed in capital letters.

ROCK-IN' ROBIN/OVER AND OVER .... **Bobby Day**
(Recordo, BMI/Recordo, BMI) Class 229

TEARS ON MY PILLOW .... **The Imperials**
(Vanderbuilt-Boonie, ASCAP) Two People in the World (Real Gone, BMI) End 1027

BETTY LOU GOT A NEW PAIR OF SHOES .... **Bobby Freeman**
(Benell-Clockus, BMI) Starlight (Benell-Clockus) Josie 841

ITCHY TWITCHY FEELING .... **Bobby Hendricks**
(Sue, BMI) A Thousand Dreams (Sue, BMI) Sue 706

EARLY IN THE MORNING .... **Buddy Holly**
(Royalty, ASCAP) Now We're One (Portrait, BMI) Coral 62006

★ THE STAR PERFORMER designation shows the outstanding upward changes of position in The Hot 100 since last week's chart. Its purpose merely is to provide quick visual identification of the sides which moved up most dramatically or to new entries which first entered the chart at an unusually high position.

THREE WEEKS AGO	TWO WEEKS AGO	ONE WEEK AGO	THIS WEEK	★ STAR PERFORMER THIS WEEK	TITLE	Artist, Company, Record Number	WEEKS ON CHART
—	—	49	91		ALL I HAVE TO DO IS DREAM	Everly Brothers, Cadence 1348	2
—	—	—	92		LA PALOMA	Billy Vaughn, Dot 15795	1
—	—	97	93		I BELIEVE IN YOU	Robert and Johnny, Old Town 1021	2
—	—	—	94		MIDNIGHTER	Champs, Challenge 59007	1
—	—	—	95		CHARIOT ROCK	Champs, Challenge 59018	1
—	—	—	96		DOWN IN VIRGINIA	Jimmie Reed, Vee Jay 287	1
—	—	—	97		SUNDAY BARBECUE	Tennessee Ernie Ford, Capitol 3997	1
—	—	74	98		GOTTA HAVE RAIN	Edyie Gorme, ABC-Paramount 9944	2
—	—	—	99		NOTHING IN THE WORLD	Nat King Cole, Capitol 4004	1
—	—	50	100		BAUBLES, BANGLES AND BEADS	Kirby Stone Four, Columbia 41183	2

NEW YORK UNIVERSITY SCHOOL OF RETAILING · STORE RECORDED SALES · THE BILLBOARD

BEST SELLING POP SINGLES IN STORES

The information given in this chart is based on actual sales to customers in a scientific sample of the nation's retail outlets during the week ending on the date shown above. Sample design, sample size, and all methods used in this continuing study of retail record sales are under the direct and continuing supervision and control of the School of Retailing of New York University.

FOR SURVEY WEEK ENDING AUGUST 4, 1958

This Week	Title—Artist—Flip Side—Label	Week Last	Chart Weeks on
1.	POOR LITTLE FOOL (BMI)—Ricky Nelson Don't Leave Me This Way (BMI)—Imperial 5528	1	6
2.	VOLARE (Nel Blu Dipinto Di Blu) (ASCAP)—Domonico Modugno Marti in Citta (BIEM)—Dec 30677	30	2
3.	PATRICIA (ASCAP)—Perez Prado Why Wait? (BMI)—Vic 7245	2	8
4.	LITTLE STAR (BMI)—Elegants Getting Dizzy (BMI)—APT 25005	6	3
5.	YAKETY YAK (BMI)—Coasters Zing! Went the Strings of My Heart (ASCAP)—Atco 6116	4	10
6.	HARD HEADED WOMAN (ASCAP)—Elvis Presley DON'T ASK ME WHY? (ASCAP)—Vic 7280	3	7
7.	REBEL-'ROUSER (BMI)—Duane Eddy Stalkin' (BMI)—Jamie 1104	7	6
8.	WHEN (ASCAP)—Kalin Twins Three o'Clock Thrill (BMI)—Dec 30642	8	7
9.	SPLISH SPLASH (BMI)—Bobby Darin Judy, Don't Be Moody (BMI)—Atco 6117	5	8
10.	JUST A DREAM (BMI)—Jimmy Clanton You Aim to Please (BMI)—Ace 546	12	5
11.	LEROY (BMI)—Jack Scott MY TRUE LOVE (BMI)—Carlton 462	9	9
12.	FEVER (BMI)—Peggy Lee You Don't Know (BMI)—Cap 3998	15	4
13.	PURPLE PEOPLE EATER (BMI)—Sheb Wooley I Can't Believe You're Mine (ASCAP)—M-G-M 12651	10	11
14.	LEFT RIGHT OUT OF YOUR HEART (ASCAP)—Patti Page Longing to Hold You Again (ASCAP)—Mercury 71331	19	6
15.	IF DREAMS CAME TRUE (ASCAP)—Pat Boone THAT'S HOW MUCH I LOVE YOU (BMI)—Dot 15785	11	5
16.	WILLIE AND THE HAND JIVE (BMI)—Johnny Otis Show Ring-A-Ling (BMI)—Cap 3966	16	7
17.	BIRD DOG (BMI)—Everly Brothers DEVOTED TO YOU (BMI)—Cadence 1350	—	1
18.	ONE SUMMER NIGHT (BMI)—Danleers Wheelin' and A-Dealin' (BMI)—Mercury 71322	14	6
19.	FOR YOUR PRECIOUS LOVE (ASCAP)—Jerry Butler and Impressions Sweet Was the Wine (ASCAP)—Abner 1013	16	9
20.	BORN TOO LATE (ASCAP)—Poni Tails Come On, Joey Dance With Me (BMI)—ABC-Paramount 9934	23	3
21.	WESTERN MOVIES (BMI)—Olympics Well? (BMI)—Demon 1508	34	3
22.	GINGER BREAD (BMI)—Frankie Avalon Blue Betty (ASCAP)—Chancellor 1021	20	4
23.	A CERTAIN SMILE (ASCAP)—Johnny Mathis Let It Rain (ASCAP)—Col 41193	21	6
24.	RETURN TO ME (ASCAP)—Dean Martin Forgetting You (ASCAP)—Cap 3894	23	18
25.	ENDLESS SLEEP (BMI)—Jody Reynolds Tight Capris (BMI)—Demon 1507	13	12
26.	EVERYBODY LOVES A LOVER (ASCAP)—Doris Day Instant Love (ASCAP)—Col 41195	25	3
27.	GUESS THINGS HAPPEN THAT WAY (BMI)—Johnny Cash COME IN, STRANGER (BMI)—Sun 295	18	11
28.	SECRETLY (ASCAP)—Jimmie Rodgers Make Me a Miracle (ASCAP)—Roulette 4070	22	14
29.	MOON TALK (ASCAP)—Perry Como Beats There a Heart So True (BMI)—Vic 7242	36	2
30.	WHAT AM I LIVING FOR? (BMI)—Chuck Willis HANG UP MY ROCK AND ROLL SHOES (BMI)—Atlantic 1179	26	14
31.	STUPID CUPID (BMI)—Connie Francis Carolina Moon (ASCAP)—M-G-M 12683	33	3
32.	ENCHANTED ISLAND (ASCAP)—Four Lads Guess What the Neighbor'll Say (BMI)—Col 41194	35	5
33.	BLUE, BLUE DAY (BMI)—Don Gibson Too Soon to Know (BMI)—Vic 7010	32	5
34.	EARLY IN THE MORNING (ASCAP)—Bobby Darin and the Rinky Dinks Now We're One (BMI)—Atco 6121	—	1
35.	ALL I HAVE TO DO IS DREAM (BMI)—Everly Brothers Claudette (BMI)—Cadence 1348	37	16
36.	ARE YOU REALLY MINE? (ASCAP)—Jimmie Rodgers The Wizard (ASCAP)—Roulette 4090	—	1
37.	VOLARE (Nel Blu Dipinto Di Blu) (ASCAP)—Dean Martin Outta My Mind (ASCAP)—Cap 4028	—	1
38.	PADRE (ASCAP)—Toni Arden All At Once (ASCAP)—Dec 30628	29	12
39.	WITCH DOCTOR (ASCAP)—David Seville Don't Whistle at Me, Baby (ASCAP)—Liberty 55132	31	18
40.	LOOKING BACK (BMI)—Nat King Cole Do I Like It (BMI)—Cap 3939	43	18
41.	DO YOU WANT TO DANCE? (BMI)—Bobby Freeman Big Fat Woman (BMI)—Josie 835	27	13
42.	YOUNG AND WARM AND WONDERFUL (ASCAP)—Tony Bennett Now I Lay Me Down to Sleep (ASCAP)—Col 41172	—	1
43.	THE FREEZE (BMI)—Tony and Joe Gonna Get a Little Kissin' Tonight (BMI)—Era 1075	49	3
44.	ROCK-IN' ROBIN (BMI)—Bobby Day OVER AND OVER (BMI)—Class 229	—	1
45.	NO CHEMISE, PLEASE (BMI)—Gerry Granahan Girl of My Dreams (ASCAP)—Sunbeam 102	28	9
46.	ANGEL BABY (BMI)—Dean Martin I'll Gladly Make the Same Mistake Again (ASCAP)—Cap 3988	45	4
47.	THE BIRD ON MY HEAD (ASCAP)—David Seville Hey There, Moon (ASCAP)—Liberty 55140	48	5
48.	COME CLOSER TO ME (BMI)—Nat King Cole Nothing in the World—Cap 4004	—	2
49.	SUGAR MOON (BMI)—Pat Boone Cherie, I Love You (ASCAP)—Dot 15750	39	14
50.	I WONDER WHY (ASCAP)—Dion And the Belmonts Teen Angel (ASCAP)—Laurie 3013	38	12

artists' biographies

Domenico Modugno Has Hit of Two Countries

In 1954, Erberto Landi, Modugno's personal manager, was in Milan and caught a show which featured the famous Italian comedian Walter Chiari. On the same bill was a singer of Sicilian songs who played the guitar and went over big with the audience. Landi signed him and arranged for a tour of the United States and Canada. This is how Domenico Modugno was introduced to Americans. He appeared in this country in 1955 and was a success in clubs like the Blue Angel in New York and others.

He returned to Italy and continued writing and singing. His song, "Lazzarella," won second prize in the Festival of Naples. Then his current smash, "Nel Blu Dipinto Di Blu," won him first prize in the San Remo Festival and was a big hit in Italy. He is now returning to our country to appear on the Ed Sullivan Show on both August 17 and September 14.

artists' biographies

Bobby Darin a Real Triple Threat Artist

This young 21-year-old Atco artist is a singer, writer, arranger, performer and musician. That's quite a list of accomplishments and he has been most successful at all of them.

Taking them one at a time—as a singer, Darin has proved to be a teen-age smash plus a polished warbler of other type material for adult audiences. As a writer, he has written his current hit disk, "Splish Splash," plus other tunes which have been recorded by Eddy Arnold, LaVerne Baker, Gene Vincent and others. "Early in the Morning," as recorded by Darin and the Rinky Dinks, was also Darin-written, arranged and directed.

He has performed on television, radio and in night clubs and plays six instruments. He is five feet nine and one-half inches tall, weighs 155 pounds and was born and raised in New York.

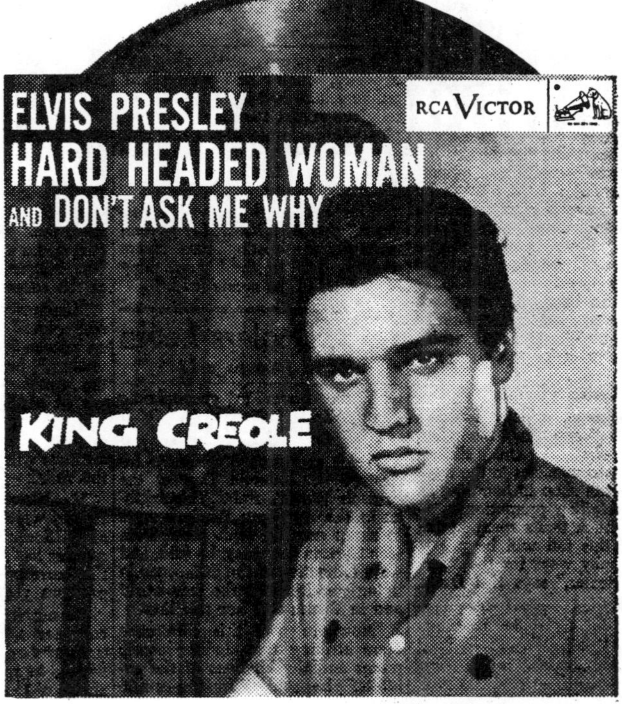

SINGLE RECORD 47/20-7280

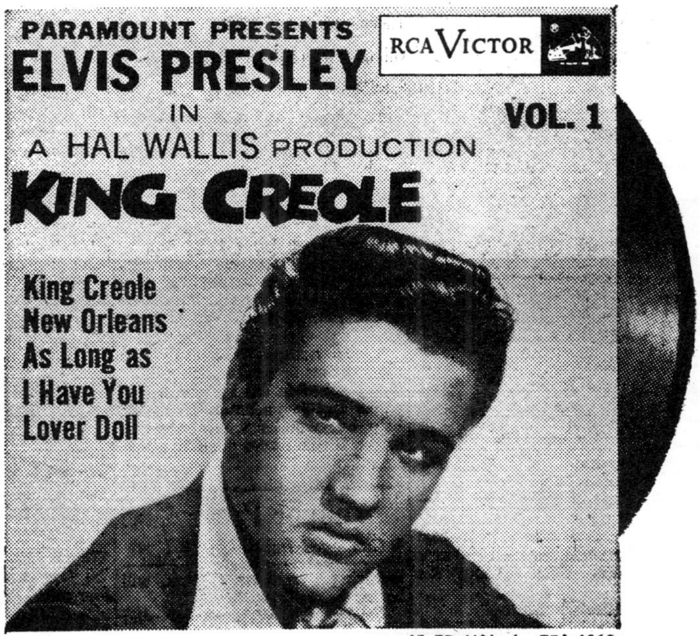

45 EP, VOL. I—EPA-4319

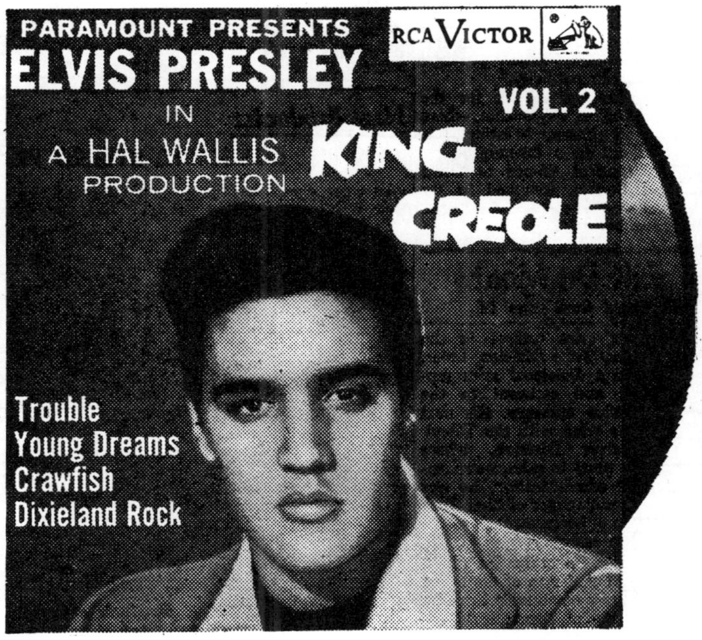

45 EP, VOL. 2—EPA-4321

ELVIS' GREATEST YET!

SENSATIONAL SELLERS

FROM HIS NEW MOVIE, NOW

PLAYING IN OVER 500 THEATRES

KING CREOLE

STOCK NOW FOR THE RUSH!

A HAL WALLIS PARAMOUNT PICTURES PRODUCTION

RCA VICTOR

RADIO CORPORATION OF AMERICA

The Billboard HOT 100

FOR THE WEEK ENDING AUGUST 24

★ THE STAR PERFORMER designation shows the outstanding upward changes of position in The Hot 100 since last week's chart. Its purpose merely is to provide quick visual identification of the sides which moved up most dramatically or to new entries which first entered the chart at an unusually high position.

Three Weeks Ago	Two Weeks Ago	One Week Ago	This Week	★ Star Performer This Week	Title — Artist, Company, Record Number	Weeks on Chart
—	54	2	1		VOLARE (Nel Blu Dipinto Di Blu) — Domenico Modugno, Decca 30677	3
—	18	14	2	★	LITTLE STAR — Elegants, Apt 25005	3
—	8	6	3		MY TRUE LOVE — Jack Scott, Carlton 462	3
—	1	1	4		POOR LITTLE FOOL — Ricky Nelson, Imperial 5528	3
—	2	3	5		PATRICIA — Perez Prado, RCA Victor 7245	3
—	12	9	5		JUST A DREAM — Jimmy Clanton, Ace 546	3
—	5	5	7		WHEN — Kalin Twins, Decca 30642	3
—	6	8	8		REBEL-'ROUSER — Duane Eddy, Jamie 1104	3
—	10	13	9		FEVER — Peggy Lee, Capitol 3998	3
—	3	4	10		SPLISH SPLASH — Bobby Darin, Atco 6117	3
—	11	15	11		GINGER BREAD — Frankie Avalon, Chancellor 1021	3
—	9	9	12		WILLIE AND THE HAND JIVE — Johnny Otis Show, Capitol 3966	3
—	4	7	13		HARD HEADED WOMAN — Elvis Presley, RCA Victor 7280	3
—	19	16	14		EVERYBODY LOVES A LOVER — Doris Day, Columbia 41195	3
—	14	12	15		IF DREAMS CAME TRUE — Pat Boone, Dot 15785	3
—	26	18	16		BORN TOO LATE — Poni Tails, ABC-Paramount 9934	3
—	92	34	17	★	BIRD DOG — Everly Brothers, Cadence 1350	3
—	7	11	18		YAKETY YAK — Coasters, Atco 6116	3
—	23	21	19		WESTERN MOVIES — Olympics, Demon 1508	3
—	68	37	20	★	VOLARE (Nel Blu Dipinto Di Blu) — Dean Martin, Capitol 4028	3
—	16	17	21		ONE SUMMER NIGHT — Danleers, Mercury 71322	3
—	38	25	22		SOMEBODY TOUCHED ME — Buddy Knox, Roulette 4082	3
—	13	19	23		LEFT RIGHT OUT OF YOUR HEART — Patti Page, Mercury 71331	3
—	93	26	24		ARE YOU REALLY MINE! — Jimmie Rodgers, Roulette 4090	3
—	—	43	25	★	DEVOTED TO YOU — Everly Brothers, Cadence 1350	2
—	52	24	26		EARLY IN THE MORNING — Bobby Darin and the Rinky Dinks, Atco 6121	3
—	—	42	27	★	SUSIE DARLIN' — Robin Luke, Dot 15781	2
—	27	32	28		THINK IT OVER — Crickets, Brunswick 55072	3
—	31	38	29		CHANTILLY LACE — Big Bopper, Mercury 71343	3
—	22	28	30		A CERTAIN SMILE — Johnny Mathis, Columbia 41193	3
—	72	35	31		STUPID CUPID — Connie Francis, M-G-M 12683	3
—	17	20	32		ENDLESS SLEEP — Jody Reynolds, Demon 1507	3
—	15	23	33		FOR YOUR PRECIOUS LOVE — Jerry Butler and the Impressions, Abner 1013	3
—	37	30	34		MOON TALK — Perry Como, RCA Victor 7274	3
—	32	36	35		BLUE, BLUE DAY — Don Gibson, RCA Victor 7010	3
—	29	29	36		ENCHANTED ISLAND — Four Lads, Columbia 41194	3
—	41	40	37		EARLY IN THE MORNING — Buddy Holly, Coral 62006	3
—	35	33	38		ROCK-IN' ROBIN — Bobby Day, Class 229	3
—	21	22	39		GUESS THINGS HAPPEN THAT WAY — Johnny Cash, Sun 295	3
—	30	39	40		ANGEL BABY — Dean Martin, Capitol 3988	3
—	61	50	41		ITCHY TWITCHY FEELING — Bobby Hendricks, Sue 706	3
—	25	31	42		WHAT AM I LIVING FOR! — Chuck Willis, Atlantic 1179	3
—	20	27	43		DO YOU WANT TO DANCE! — Bobby Freeman, Josie 835	3
—	84	52	44		SUMMERTIME BLUES — Eddie Cochran, Liberty 55144	3
—	39	57	45	★	THAT'S HOW MUCH I LOVE YOU — Pat Boone, Dot 15785	3
—	78	44	46		BETTY LOU GOT A NEW PAIR OF SHOES — Bobby Freeman, Josie 841	3
—	—	92	47	★	LA PALOMA — Billy Vaughn, Dot 15795	2
—	53	46	48		COME CLOSER TO ME — Nat King Cole, Capitol 4004	3
—	42	48	49		YOU CHEATED — Slades, Domino 500	3
—	33	55	50		THE FREEZE — Tony and Joe, Era 1075	3
—	94	79	51	★	SHE WAS ONLY SEVENTEEN — Marty Robbins, Columbia 41208	3
—	—	—	52	★	HOW THE TIME FLIES — Jerry Wallace, Challenge 59013	1
—	43	49	53		COME WHAT MAY — Clyde McPhatter, Atlantic 1185	3
—	74	61	54		WIN YOUR LOVE FOR ME — Sam Cooke, Keen 2006	3
—	34	54	55		DON'T ASK ME WHY — Elvis Presley, RCA Victor 7280	3
—	45	74	56	★	KATHY-O — Diamonds, Mercury 71330	3
—	60	53	57		OVER AND OVER — Bobby Day, Class 229	3
—	50	69	58	★	BY THE LIGHT OF THE SILVERY MOON — Jimmy Bowen, Roulette 4083	3
—	50	100	59	★	BAUBLES, BANGLES AND BEADS — Kirby Stone Four, Columbia 41183	3
—	—	—	60	★	BORROWED DREAMS — Bobby Helms, Decca 30682	1

THE INDUSTRY'S FASTEST AND MOST COMPLETE PROGRAMMING AND BUYING GUIDE

These 100 sides are listed in order of their national popularity, as determined by weekly local studies prepared for The Billboard in markets representing a cross-section of the United States. These studies take into consideration such factors as disk jockey plays, juke box activity and record sales.

★ THE STAR PERFORMER designation shows the outstanding upward changes of position in The Hot 100 since last week's chart. Its purpose merely is to provide quick visual identification of the sides which moved up most dramatically or to new entries which first entered the chart at an unusually high position.

THREE WEEKS AGO	TWO WEEKS AGO	ONE WEEK AGO	THIS WEEK	★ STAR PERFORMER THIS WEEK	TITLE Artist, Company, Record Number	WEEKS ON CHART
—	73	—	61	★	HEY-BOY, HEY-GIRL — Oscar McLollie & Jeanette, Class 228	2
—	40	62	62		CRAZY EYES FOR YOU — Bobby Hamilton, Apt 25001	3
—	—	73	63		TEARS ON MY PILLOW — Little Anthony and the Imperials, End 1027	2
—	—	85	64	★	THE WIZARD — Jimmie Rodgers, Roulette 4090	2
—	89	45	65		BLUE BOY — Jim Reeves, RCA Victor 7266	3
—	—	84	66	★	YOU'RE A SWEETHEART — Little Willie John, King 5142	2
—	—	—	67	★	NEAR YOU — Roger Williams, Kapp 233	1
—	—	51	68		ALONE WITH YOU — Faron Young, Capitol 3982	2
—	76	71	69		MIDNIGHT — Paul Anka, ABC-Paramount 9937	3
—	36	59	70		NO CHEMISE, PLEASE — Gerry Granahan, Sunbeam 102	3
—	63	65	71		PADRE — Toni Arden, Decca 30628	3
—	—	—	71	★	LAZY SUMMER NIGHT — Four Preps, Capitol 4023	1
—	77	80	73		HAPPY YEARS — Diamonds, Mercury 71330	3
—	—	—	74	★	SUMMERTIME, SUMMERTIME — Jamies, Epic 9281	1
—	88	—	75		JUST LIKE IN THE MOVIES — Upbeats, Swan 4010	2
—	—	—	76	★	STRAIGHTEN UP AND FLY RIGHT — DeJohn Sisters, Sunbeam 106	1
—	28	41	77		SECRETLY — Jimmie Rodgers, Roulette 4070	3
—	—	95	78		CHARIOT ROCK — Champs, Challenge 59018	2
—	66	—	79		DELICIOUS! — Jim Backus, Jubilee 5330	2
—	55	75	80		LET'S GO STEADY FOR THE SUMMER — Three G's, Columbia 41175	3
—	24	47	81		PURPLE PEOPLE EATER — Sheb Wooley, M-G-M 12651	3
—	—	—	81	★	GAS MONEY — Jan & Arnie, Arwin 111	1
—	—	88	83		CERVEZA — Boots Brown, RCA Victor 7269	2
—	82	—	84		BLIP BLOP — Bill Doggett, King 5138	2
—	65	68	85		YOU'RE MAKING A MISTAKE — Platters, Mercury 71320	3
—	—	78	86		HARVEY'S GOT A GIRLFRIEND — Royal Teens, ABC-Paramount 9945	2
—	74	98	87		GOTTA HAVE RAIN — Eydie Gorme, ABC-Paramount 9944	3
—	—	—	88	★	DANCE, EVERYONE, DANCE — Betty Madigan, Coral 62007	1
—	—	—	89		DEVOTION — Janice Harper, Capitol 3984	1
—	—	—	90	★	MY LIFE — Chuck Willis, Atlantic 1192	1

From The Hot 100: THE BILLBOARD'S BEST BUYS

These records, of all those listed on The Billboard Hot 100, have shown sales break-out potential for the first time this week. Action sides are listed in capital letters.

DANCE, EVERYONE, DANCE .... Betty Madigan
(Bourne, ASCAP) My Symphony of Love (Rhyme & Rhythm, ASCAP) Coral 62007

DOWN THE AISLE OF LOVE .... The Quin-Tones
(Myra, BMI) Please, Dear (Myra, BMI) Hunt 321

MY LIFE .... Chuck Willis
(Rush, BMI) Thunder and Lightning (Rush, BMI) Atlantic 1192

NEAR YOU .... Roger Williams
(Supreme, ASCAP) Merry Widow Waltz (Garland, ASCAP) Kapp 233

The above are previous Billboard Spotlight picks.

SUSIE DARLIN' .... Robin Luke
(Congressional, ASCAP) Living's Loving You (Congressional, ASCAP) Dot 15781

★ THE STAR PERFORMER designation shows the outstanding upward changes of position in The Hot 100 since last week's chart. Its purpose merely is to provide quick visual identification of the sides which moved up most dramatically or to new entries which first entered the chart at an unusually high position.

THREE WEEKS AGO	TWO WEEKS AGO	ONE WEEK AGO	THIS WEEK	★ STAR PERFORMER THIS WEEK	TITLE Artist, Company, Record Number	WEEKS ON CHART
—	—	—	91	★	DOWN THE AISLE OF LOVE — The Quin-Tones, Hunt 321	1
—	48	63	92		RETURN TO ME — Dean Martin, Capitol 3894	3
—	—	96	93		DOWN IN VIRGINIA — Jimmie Reed, Vee Jay 287	2
—	—	—	94		FIRE OF LOVE — Jody Reynolds, Demon 1509	1
—	—	—	95		PUT A RING ON MY FINGER — Les Paul & Mary Ford, Columbia 41222	1
—	—	—	96		IT'S ALL IN THE GAME — Tommy Edwards, M-G-M 12688	1
—	—	—	97		MA-MA-MA MARIE — Gaylords, Mercury 71337	1
—	—	—	98		WHERE THE BLUE OF THE NIGHT — Tommy Mara, Felsted 8532	1
—	—	—	99		WHO ARE THEY TO SAY! — DeCastro Sisters, ABC-Paramount 9932	1
—	—	—	100		GOING TO CHICAGO BLUES — Count Basie, Roulette 4088	1

BEST SELLING POP SINGLES IN STORES

STORE RECORDED SALES — NEW YORK UNIVERSITY SCHOOL OF RETAILING — THE BILLBOARD

The information given in this chart is based on actual sales to customers in a scientific sample of the nation's retail outlets during the week ending on the date shown above. Sample design, sample size, and all methods used in this continuing study of retail record sales are under the direct and continuing supervision and control of the School of Retailing of New York University.

FOR SURVEY WEEK ENDING AUGUST 9, 1958

This Week		Week Last	Chart Weeks on
1.	VOLARE (Nel Blu Dipinto Di Blu) (ASCAP)—Domenico Modugno Marti in Citta (BIEM)—Dec 30677	2	3
2.	LITTLE STAR (BMI)—Elegants Getting Dizzy (BMI)—APT 25005	4	4
3.	BIRD DOG (BMI)—Everly Brothers DEVOTED TO YOU (BMI)—Cadence 1350	17	2
4.	POOR LITTLE FOOL (BMI)—Ricky Nelson Don't Leave Me This Way (BMI)—Imperial 5528	1	7
5.	JUST A DREAM (BMI)—Jimmy Clanton You Aim to Please (BMI)—Ace 546	10	6
6.	PATRICIA (ASCAP)—Perez Prado Why Wait? (BMI)—Vic 7245	3	9
7.	MY TRUE LOVE (BMI)—Jack Scott LEROY (BMI)—Carlton 462	11	10
8.	REBEL-'ROUSER (BMI)—Duane Eddy Stalkin' (BMI)—Jamie 1104	7	7
9.	FEVER (BMI)—Peggy Lee You Don't Know (BMI)—Cap 3998	12	5
10.	WHEN (ASCAP)—Kalin Twins Three o'Clock Thrill (BMI)—Dec 30642	8	8
11.	HARD HEADED WOMAN (ASCAP)—Elvis Presley DON'T ASK ME WHY (ASCAP)—Vic 7280	6	8
12.	SPLISH SPLASH (BMI)—Bobby Darin Judy, Don't Be Moody (BMI)—Atco 6117	9	9
13.	YAKETY YAK (BMI)—Coasters Zing! Went the Strings of My Heart (ASCAP)—Atco 6116	5	11
14.	WESTERN MOVIES (BMI)—Olympics Well! (BMI)—Demon 1508	21	4
15.	GIN[illegible]R BREAD (BMI)—F[illegible]e Avalon B[illegible]etty (ASCAP)—Chancellor 1021	22	5
16.	BORN TOO LATE (ASCAP)—Poni Tails Come On, Joey, Dance With Me (BMI)—ABC-Paramount 9934	20	4
17.	WILLIE AND THE HAND JIVE (BMI)—Johnny Otis Show Ring-a-Ling (BMI)—Cap 3966	16	8
18.	IF DREAMS CAME TRUE (ASCAP)—Pat Boone THAT'S HOW MUCH I LOVE YOU (BMI)—Dot 15785	15	6
19.	ONE SUMMER NIGHT (BMI)—Danleers Wheelin' and A-Dealin' (BMI)—Mercury 71322	18	7
20.	VOLARE (Nel Blu Dipinto Di Blu) (ASCAP)—Dean Martin Outta My Mind (ASCAP)—Cap 4028	37	2
21.	LEFT RIGHT OUT OF YOUR HEART (ASCAP)—Patti Page Longing to Hold You Again (ASCAP)—Mercury 71331	14	7
22.	STUPID CUPID (BMI)—Connie Francis Carolina Moon (ASCAP)—M-G-M 12683	31	4
23.	EVERYBODY LOVES A LOVER (ASCAP)—Doris Day Instant Love (ASCAP)—Col 41195	26	4
24.	EARLY IN THE MORNING (ASCAP)—Bobby Darin & the Rinky Dinks Now We're One (BMI)—Atco 6121	34	2
25.	ARE YOU REALLY MINE? (ASCAP)—Jimmie Rodgers The Wizard (ASCAP)—Roulette 4090	36	2
26.	A CERTAIN SMILE (ASCAP)—Johnny Mathis Let It Rain (ASCAP)—Col 41193	23	7
27.	ENDLESS SLEEP (BMI)—Jody Reynolds Tight Capris (BMI)—Demon 1507	25	13
28.	PURPLE PEOPLE EATER (BMI)—Sheb Wooley I Can't Believe You're Mine (ASCAP)—M-G-M 12651	13	12
29.	WHAT AM I LIVING FOR? (BMI)—Chuck Willis HANG UP MY ROCK AND ROLL SHOES (BMI)—Atlantic 1179	30	15
30.	GUESS THINGS HAPPEN THAT WAY (BMI)—Johnny Cash COME IN, STRANGER (BMI)—Sun 295	27	12
31.	FOR YOUR PRECIOUS LOVE (ASCAP)—Jerry Butler & Impressions Sweet Was the Wine (ASCAP)—Abner 1013	19	10
32.	MOON TALK (ASCAP)—Perry Como Beats There a Heart So True (BMI)—Vic 7242	29	3
33.	BLUE BLUE DAY (BMI)—Don Gibson Too Soon to Know (BMI)—Vic 7010	33	6
34.	ROCK-IN' ROBIN (BMI)—Bobby Day OVER AND OVER (BMI)—Class 229	44	2
35.	TEARS ON MY PILLOW (ASCAP)—Little Anthony & the Imperials Two People in the World (BMI)—End 1027	—	1
36.	ENCHANTED ISLAND (ASCAP)—Four Lads Guess What the Neighbors'll Say (BMI)—Col 41194	32	6
37.	RETURN TO ME (ASCAP)—Dean Martin Forgetting You (ASCAP)—Cap 3894	24	19
38.	SECRETLY (ASCAP)—Jimmie Rodgers Make Me a Miracle (ASCAP)—Roulette 4070	28	15
39.	THE FREEZE (BMI)—Tony & Joe Gonna Get a Little Kissin' Tonight (BMI)—Era 1075	43	4
40.	BETTY LOU GOT A NEW PAIR OF SHOES (BMI)—Bobby Freeman Starlight (BMI)—Josie 841	—	1
41.	SUSIE DARLIN' (ASCAP)—Robin Luke Living's Loving You (ASCAP)—Dot 15781	—	1
42.	WITCH DOCTOR (ASCAP)—David Seville Don't Whistle at Me, Baby (ASCAP)—Liberty 55132	39	19
43.	ALL I HAVE TO DO IS DREAM (BMI)—Everly Brothers Claudette (BMI)—Cadence 1348	35	17
44.	ANGEL BABY (BMI)—Dean Martin I'll Gladly Make the Same Mistake Again (ASCAP)—Cap 3988	46	5
45.	EARLY IN THE MORNING (ASCAP)—Buddy Holly Now We're One (BMI)—Coral 62066	—	1
46.	KATHY-O (ASCAP)—Diamonds HAPPY YEARS (ASCAP)—Mercury 71330	—	1
47.	LA PALOMA (ASCAP)—Billy Vaughn Here Is My Love (ASCAP)—Dot 15795	—	1
47.	THINK IT OVER (BMI)—Crickets Fool's Paradise (BMI)—Brunswick 55072	—	1
49.	LOOKING BACK (BMI)—Nat King Cole Do I Like It? (BMI)—Cap 3939	40	19
50.	DO YOU WANT TO DANCE? (BMI)—Bobby Freeman Big Fat Woman (BMI)—Josie 835	41	14
50.	YOUNG AND WARM AND WONDERFUL (ASCAP)—Tony Bennett Now I Lay Me Down to Sleep (ASCAP)—Col 41172	42	2

artists' biographies

Jack Scott on Charts With First Release

This Canadian born Carlton Records artist has been riding the Best Selling Records chart for 10 weeks with his two-sided hit, "Leroy" and "My True Love."

Born in Windsor, Ont., 22 years ago, Jack Scott took to the guitar as soon as he could hold one. His father, a great guitarist in his own right, gave his son his own instrument when he was eight years old. From that point to the present, he has played and composed whenever the opportunity presented itself.

Scott's real monicker is Jack Scafone Jr. and his family left Canada when he was 10 to settle in Hazel Park, Mich., a Detroit suburb. It was here that he first got into show business, starting first as a singer on a local radio show. He is one of seven children and his 13-year-old sister, Linda, has appeared with him many times. He wrote "Leroy" and his favorite sports are baseball, football, swimming and weight lifting.

artists' biographies

Bobby Freeman Hits With Initial Offering

Born in San Francisco, Calif., on June 13, 1940, Bobby Freeman resides there with his mother and grandmother and attends Mission High School. He will graduate in February, 1959. While in school, he has been making money as a newspaper boy, porter, file clerk and delivery boy. He has also been writing songs.

When he was 14 years old, he formed a vocal group called "The Romancers," and sang with them for two years. At that point, he decided to become a single act and sing the songs that came from his own pen.

Morty Palitz, while honeymooning in Frisco, discovered Bobby Freeman and recorded "Do You Want to Dance" and released it on the Josie label. This Freeman-written tune became an overnight smash and has been riding the charts for more than three months.

The Billboard HOT 100

FOR THE WEEK ENDING AUGUST 31

★ THE STAR PERFORMER designation shows the outstanding upward changes of position in The Hot 100 since last week's chart. Its purpose merely is to provide quick visual identification of the sides which moved up most dramatically or to new entries which first entered the chart at an unusually high position.

★ THE STAR PERFORMER designation shows the outstanding upward changes of position in The Hot 100 since last week's chart. Its purpose merely is to provide quick visual identification of the sides which moved up most dramatically or to new entries which first entered the chart at an unusually high position.

Three Weeks Ago	Two Weeks Ago	One Week Ago	This Week	★ Star Performer This Week	Title	Artist, Company, Record Number	Weeks on Chart
18	14	2	1		LITTLE STAR	Elegants, Apt 25005	4
54	2	1	2		VOLARE (Nel Blu Dipinto Di Blu)	Domenico Modugno, Decca 30677	4
92	34	17	3	★	BIRD DOG	Everly Brothers, Cadence 1350	4
12	9	5	4		JUST A DREAM	Jimmy Clanton, Ace 546	4
8	6	3	5		MY TRUE LOVE	Jack Scott, Carlton 462	4
1	1	4	6		POOR LITTLE FOOL	Ricky Nelson, Imperial 5528	4
2	3	5	7		PATRICIA	Perez Prado, RCA Victor 7245	4
10	13	9	8		FEVER	Peggy Lee, Capitol 3998	4
26	18	16	8		BORN TOO LATE	Poni Tails, ABC-Paramount 9934	4
5	5	7	10		WHEN	Kalin Twins, Decca 30642	4
6	8	8	11		REBEL-'ROUSER	Duane Eddy, Jamie 1104	4
9	9	12	12		WILLIE AND THE HAND JIVE	Johnny Otis Show, Capitol 3966	4
23	21	19	13		WESTERN MOVIES	Olympics, Demon 1508	4
19	16	14	14		EVERYBODY LOVES A LOVER	Doris Day, Columbia 41195	4
—	43	25	15	★	DEVOTED TO YOU	Everly Brothers, Cadence 1350	3
3	4	10	16		SPLISH SPLASH	Bobby Darin, Atco 6117	4
11	15	11	17		GINGER BREAD	Frankie Avalon, Chancellor 1021	4
14	12	15	18		IF DREAMS CAME TRUE	Pat Boone, Dot 15785	4
68	37	20	19		VOLARE (Nel Blu Dipinto Di Blu)	Dean Martin, Capitol 4028	4
93	26	24	20		ARE YOU REALLY MINE?	Jimmie Rodgers, Roulette 4090	4
4	7	13	21		HARD HEADED WOMAN	Elvis Presley, RCA Victor 7280	4
72	35	31	22		STUPID CUPID	Connie Francis, M-G-M 12683	4
—	42	27	23		SUSIE DARLIN'	Robin Luke, Dot 15781	3
84	52	44	24	★	SUMMERTIME BLUES	Eddie Cochran, Liberty 55144	4
35	33	38	25	★	ROCK-IN' ROBIN	Bobby Day, Class 229	4
—	73	63	26	★	TEARS ON MY PILLOW	Little Anthony and the Imperials, End 1027	3
16	17	21	27		ONE SUMMER NIGHT	Danleers, Mercury 71322	4
38	25	22	28		SOMEBODY TOUCHED ME	Buddy Knox, Roulette 4082	4
52	24	26	29		EARLY IN THE MORNING	Bobby Darin and the Rinky Dinks, Atco 6121	4
31	38	29	30		CHANTILLY LACE	Big Bopper, Mercury 71343	4
27	32	28	31		THINK IT OVER	Crickets, Brunswick 55072	4
41	40	37	32		EARLY IN THE MORNING	Buddy Holly, Coral 62006	4
13	19	23	33		LEFT RIGHT OUT OF YOUR HEART	Patti Page, Mercury 71331	4
22	28	30	34		A CERTAIN SMILE	Johnny Mathis, Columbia 41193	4
7	11	18	35		YAKETY YAK	Coasters, Atco 6116	4
37	30	34	36		MOON TALK	Perry Como, RCA Victor 7274	4
78	44	46	37		BETTY LOU GOT A NEW PAIR OF SHOES	Bobby Freeman, Josie 841	4
94	79	51	38	★	SHE WAS ONLY SEVENTEEN	Marty Robbins, Columbia 41208	4
—	92	47	39		LA PALOMA	Billy Vaughn, Dot 15795	3
—	—	—	40	★	IT'S ALL IN THE GAME	Tommy Edwards, M-G-M 12688	1
60	53	57	41	★	OVER AND OVER	Bobby Day, Class 229	4
61	50	41	42		ITCHY TWITCHY FEELING	Bobby Hendricks, Sue 706	4
32	36	35	43		BLUE, BLUE DAY	Don Gibson, RCA Victor 7010	4
—	—	71	44	★	LAZY SUMMER NIGHT	Four Preps, Capitol 4023	2
74	61	54	45		WIN YOUR LOVE FOR ME	Sam Cooke, Keen 2006	4
15	23	33	46		FOR YOUR PRECIOUS LOVE	Jerry Butler and the Impressions, Abner 1013	4
20	27	43	47		DO YOU WANT TO DANCE?	Bobby Freeman, Josie 835	4
29	29	36	48		ENCHANTED ISLAND	Four Lads, Columbia 41194	4
—	—	52	49		HOW THE TIME FLIES	Jerry Wallace, Challenge 59013	2
25	31	42	50		WHAT AM I LIVING FOR?	Chuck Willis, Atlantic 1179	4
—	85	64	51	★	WIZARD	Jimmie Rodgers, Roulette 4090	3
50	69	58	52		BY THE LIGHT OF THE SILVERY MOON	Jimmy Bowen, Roulette 4083	4
45	74	56	53		KATHY-O	Diamonds, Mercury 71330	4
34	54	55	54		DON'T ASK ME WHY	Elvis Presley, RCA Victor 7280	4
21	22	39	55		GUESS THINGS HAPPEN THAT WAY	Johnny Cash, Sun 295	4
53	46	48	56		COME CLOSER TO ME	Nat King Cole, Capitol 4004	4
—	—	—	57	★	CAROL	Chuck Berry, Chess 1700	1
33	55	50	58		THE FREEZE	Tony and Joe, Era 1075	4
—	—	95	59	★	PUT A RING ON MY FINGER	Les Paul & Mary Ford, Columbia 41222	2
30	39	40	60		ANGEL BABY	Dean Martin, Capitol 3988	4

THE INDUSTRY'S FASTEST AND MOST COMPLETE PROGRAMMING AND BUYING GUIDE

These 100 sides are listed in order of their national popularity, as determined by weekly local studies prepared for The Billboard in markets representing a cross-section of the United States. These studies take into consideration such factors as disk jockey plays, juke box activity and record sales.

★ THE STAR PERFORMER designation shows the outstanding upward changes of position in The Hot 100 since last week's chart. Its purpose merely is to provide quick visual identification of the sides which moved up most dramatically or to new entries which first entered the chart at an unusually high position.

THREE WEEKS AGO	TWO WEEKS AGO	ONE WEEK AGO	THIS WEEK	★ STAR PERFORMER THIS WEEK	TITLE — Artist, Company, Record Number	WEEKS ON CHART
—	—	74	61		SUMMERTIME, SUMMERTIME — Jamies, Epic 9281	2
—	—	—	62		THE WAYS OF A WOMAN IN LOVE — Johnny Cash, Sun 302	1
63	65	71	63		PADRE — Toni Arden, Decca 30628	4
39	57	45	64		THAT'S HOW MUCH I LOVE YOU — Pat Boone, Dot 15785	4
—	—	—	65	★	WHEN WILL I KNOW — George Hamilton IV, ABC-Paramount 9946	1
74	98	87	66	★	GOTTA HAVE RAIN — Eydie Gorme, ABC-Paramount 9944	4
—	88	83	67	★	CERVEZA — Boots Brown, RCA Victor 7269	3
—	—	88	68	★	DANCE, EVERYONE, DANCE — Betty Madigan, Coral 62007	2
—	95	78	69		CHARIOT ROCK — Champs, Challenge 59018	3
—	51	68	70		ALONE WITH YOU — Faron Young, Capitol 3982	3
17	20	32	71		ENDLESS SLEEP — Jody Reynolds, Demon 1507	4
—	—	—	72	★	CITY LIGHTS — Ray Price, Columbia 41191	1
—	—	76	73		STRAIGHTEN UP AND FLY RIGHT — DeJohn Sisters, Sunbeam 106	2
—	—	—	74	★	COUNT EVERY STAR — Rivieras, Coed 503	1
89	45	65	75		BLUE BOY — Jim Reeves, RCA Victor 7266	4
73	—	61	76		HEY-BOY, HEY-GIRL — Oscar McLollie & Jeanette, Class 228	3
77	80	73	77		HAPPY YEARS — Diamonds, Mercury 71330	4
—	—	—	78	★	THE GREEN MOSQUITO — The Tune Rockers, United Artists 139	1
76	71	69	79		MIDNIGHT — Paul Anka, ABC-Paramount 9937	4
—	—	—	80	★	STRANGE ARE THE WAYS OF LOVE — Gogi Grant, RCA Victor 7294	1
—	—	—	81	★	PRISONER SONG — Warren Storm, Nasco 6015	1
—	—	—	82	★	TOPSY II — Cozy Cole, Love 5003-4	1
56	56	—	83	★	LEROY — Jack Scott, Carlton 462	3
—	—	60	84		BORROWED DREAMS — Bobby Helms, Decca 30682	2
—	58	—	85	★	DRIP DROP — Drifters, Atlantic 1187	2
—	—	89	86		DEVOTION — Janice Harper, Capitol 3984	2
—	—	91	87		DOWN THE AISLE OF LOVE — The Quin-Tones, Hunt 321	2
—	—	—	88	★	NEAR YOU — Roger Williams, Kapp 233	1
—	—	—	89	★	MY LIFE — Chuck Willis, Atlantic 1192	1
—	—	94	90		FIRE OF LOVE — Jody Reynolds, Demon 1509	2

From The Hot 100:

THE BILLBOARD'S BEST BUYS

These records, of all those listed on The Billboard Hot 100, have shown sales break-out potential for the first time this week. Action sides are listed in capital letters.

CAROL .... Chuck Berry
(Chuck Berry—ARC, BMI) Hey, Pedro (Chuck Berry—ARC, BMI) Chess 1700

PUT A RING ON MY FINGER .... Les Paul and Mary Ford
(Hollins, BMI) Fantasy (Jimskip, BMI) Columbia 41222

THE WAYS OF A WOMAN IN LOVE .... Johnny Cash
(Hi Lo, BMI) You're the Nearest Thing to Heaven (E&M—Hi Lo, BMI) Sun 302

LAZY SUMMER NIGHT .... The Four Preps
(Rooney—Spina, ASCAP) Summertime Lies (Morris, ASCAP) Capitol 4023

The above are previous Billboard Spotlight Picks

WIN YOUR LOVE FOR ME .... Sam Cooke
(Hermosa, BMI) Almost in Your Arms (Love Song from "Houseboat") (Famous, ASCAP) Keen 2006

The following records, not previously selected as Best Buys, are on the chart for the first time this week.

SUMMERTIME BLUES .... Eddie Cochran
(American, BMI) Love Again (American, BMI) Liberty 55144

IT'S ALL IN THE GAME .... Tommy Edwards
(Remick, ASCAP) Please Love Me Forever (Ricky, BMI) M-G-M 12688

★ THE STAR PERFORMER designation shows the outstanding upward changes of position in The Hot 100 since last week's chart. Its purpose merely is to provide quick visual identification of the sides which moved up most dramatically or to new entries which first entered the chart at an unusually high position.

THREE WEEKS AGO	TWO WEEKS AGO	ONE WEEK AGO	THIS WEEK	★ STAR PERFORMER THIS WEEK	TITLE — Artist, Company, Record Number	WEEKS ON CHART
—	—	—	91		RAMROD — Duane Eddy, Jamie 1109	1
88	—	75	92		JUST LIKE IN THE MOVIES — Upbeats, Swan 4010	3
24	47	81	93		PURPLE PEOPLE EATER — Sheb Wooley, M-G-M 12651	4
—	—	—	94		YOU CHEATED — The Shields, Dot 15805	1
—	—	—	95		NO ONE KNOWS — Dion and the Belmonts, Laurie 3015	1
48	63	92	96		RETURN TO ME — Dean Martin, Capitol 3894	4
—	—	—	97		THE LITTLE BRASS BAND — David Seville, Liberty 55153	1
—	84	66	98		YOU'RE A SWEETHEART — Little Willie John, King 5142	3
42	48	49	99		YOU CHEATED — Slades, Domino 500	4
—	—	—	100		TREASURE OF LOVE — Eileen Rodgers, Columbia 41214	1

BEST SELLING POP SINGLES IN STORES

STORE RECORDED SALES — NEW YORK UNIVERSITY SCHOOL OF RETAILING — THE BILLBOARD — INC.

The information given in this chart is based on actual sales to customers in a scientific sample of the nation's retail outlets during the week ending on the date shown above. Sample design, sample size, and all methods used in this continuing study of retail record sales are under the direct and continuing supervision and control of the School of Retailing of New York University.

FOR SURVEY WEEK ENDING AUGUST 16, 1958

This Week		Last Week	Weeks on Chart
1.	BIRD DOG (BMI)—Everly Brothers.... DEVOTED TO YOU (BMI)—Cadence 1350	3	3
2.	LITTLE STAR (BMI)—Elegants....... Getting Dizzy (BMI)—APT 25005	2	5
3.	VOLARE (Nel Blu Dipinto Di Blu) (ASCAP)—Domenico Modugno ...... Marti in Citta (BIEM)—Dec 30677	1	4
4.	JUST A DREAM (BMI)—Jimmy Clanton You Aim to Please (BMI)—Ace 546	5	7
5.	POOR LITTLE FOOL—Ricky Nelson.. Don't Leave Me This Way (BMI)—Imperial 5528	4	8
6.	PATRICIA (ASCAP)—Perez Prado .... Why Wait? (BMI)—Vic 7245	6	10
7.	MY TRUE LOVE (BMI)—Jack Scott.... LEROY (BMI)—Carlton 462	7	11
8.	SPLISH SPLASH (BMI)—Bobby Darin Judy, Don't Be Moody (BMI)—Atco 6117	12	10
9.	REBEL-'ROUSER (BMI)—Duane Eddy Stalkin' (BMI)—Jamie 1104	8	8
10.	WHEN (ASCAP)—Kalin Twins........ Three o'Clock Thrill (BMI)—Dec 30642	10	9
11.	FEVER (BMI)—Peggy Lee........... You Don't Know (BMI)—Cap 3998	9	6
12.	BORN TOO LATE (ASCAP)—Poni Tails Come On, Joey, Dance With Me (BMI)—ABC-Paramount 9934	16	5
13.	WESTERN MOVIES (BMI)—Olympics. Well! (BMI)—Demon 1508	14	5
14.	GINGER BREAD (BMI)—Frankie Avalon Blue Betty (ASCAP)—Chancellor 1021	15	6
15.	ARE YOU REALLY MINE? (ASCAP)—Jimmie Rodgers .... THE WIZARD (ASCAP)—Roulette 4090	25	3
16.	HARD HEADED WOMAN (ASCAP)—Elvis Presley .... DON'T ASK ME WHY (ASCAP)—Vic 7280	11	9
17.	YAKETY YAK (BMI)—Coasters........ Zing! Went the Strings of My Heart (ASCAP)—Atco 6116	13	12
18.	WILLIE AND THE HAND JIVE (BMI)—Johnny Otis Show........... Ring-a-Ling (BMI)—Cap 3966	17	9
19.	VOLARE (Nel Blu Dipinto Di Blu) (ASCAP)—Dean Martin .... Outta My Mind (ASCAP)—Cap 4028	20	3
20.	STUPID CUPID (BMI)—Connie Francis Carolina Moon (ASCAP)—M-G-M 12683	22	5
21.	IF DREAMS CAME TRUE (ASCAP)—Pat Boone .... THAT'S HOW MUCH I LOVE YOU (BMI)—Dot 15785	18	7
22.	ROCK-IN' ROBIN—Bobby Day .... OVER AND OVER—Class 229	34	3
23.	EVERYBODY LOVES A LOVER (ASCAP)—Doris Day .... Instant Love (ASCAP)—Col 41195	23	5
24.	TEARS ON MY PILLOW (ASCAP)—Little Anthony and the Imperials.... Two People in the World (BMI)—End 1027	35	2
25.	EARLY IN THE MORNING (ASCAP)—Bobby Darin and the Rinky-Dinks .... Now We're One (BMI)—Atco 6121	24	3
26.	A CERTAIN SMILE (ASCAP)—Johnny Mathis .... Let It Rain (ASCAP)—Col 41193	26	8
27.	ONE SUMMER NIGHT (BMI)—Danleers .... Wheelin' and A-Dealin' (BMI)—Mercury 71322	19	8
28.	GUESS THINGS HAPPEN THAT WAY (BMI)—Johnny Cash .... COME IN, STRANGER (BMI)—Sun 295	30	13
29.	WHAT AM I LIVING FOR? (BMI)—Chuck Willis .... Hang Up My Rock and Roll Shoes (BMI)—Atlantic 1179	29	16
30.	LEFT RIGHT OUT OF YOUR HEART (ASCAP)—Patti Page .... Longing to Hold You Again (ASCAP)—Mercury 71331	21	8
31.	ENDLESS SLEEP (BMI)—Jody Reynolds Tight Capris (BMI)—Demon 1507	27	14
32.	MOON TALK (ASCAP)—Perry Como.. Beats There a Heart So True (BMI)—Vic 7242	32	4
33.	BLUE BLUE DAY (BMI)—Don Gibson Too Soon to Know (BMI)—Vic 7010	33	7
34.	SUMMERTIME BLUES (BMI)—Eddie Cochran .... Love Again (BMI)—Liberty 55144	—	1
35.	PURPLE PEOPLE EATER (BMI)—Sheb Wooley .... I Can't Believe You're Mine (ASCAP)—M-G-M 12651	28	13
36.	SECRETLY (ASCAP)—Jimmie Rodgers. Make Me a Miracle (ASCAP)—Roulette 4070	38	16
37.	SUSIE DARLIN' (ASCAP)—Robin Luke Living's Loving You (ASCAP)—Dot 15781	41	2
38.	THINK IT OVER (BMI)—Crickets.... Fool's Paradise (BMI)—Brunswick 55072	47	2
39.	ENCHANTED ISLAND (ASCAP)—Four Lads .... Guess What the Neighbors'll Say (BMI)—Col 41194	36	7
40.	LA PALOMA (ASCAP)—Billy Vaughn.. Here Is My Love (ASCAP)—Dot 15795	47	2
41.	KATHY-O (ASCAP)—Diamonds .... HAPPY YEARS (ASCAP)—Mercury 71330	46	2
42.	IT'S ALL IN THE GAME (ASCAP)—Tommy Edwards .... Please Love Me Forever (BMI)—M-G-M 12688	—	1
43.	BETTY LOU GOT A NEW PAIR OF SHOES (BMI)—Bobby Freeman...... Starlight (BMI)—Josie 841	40	2
44.	FOR YOUR PRECIOUS LOVE (ASCAP)—Jerry Butler and Impressions Sweet Was the Wine (ASCAP)—Abner 1013	31	11
45.	RETURN TO ME (ASCAP)—Dean Martin Forgetting You (ASCAP)—Cap 3894	37	20
46.	SOMEBODY TOUCHED ME (BMI)—Buddy Knox .... C'Mon, Baby (BMI)—Roulette 4082	—	1
47.	THE FREEZE (BMI)—Tony and Joe.. Gonna Get a Little Kissin' Tonight (BMI)—Era 1075	39	5
48.	EARLY IN THE MORNING (ASCAP)—Buddy Holly .... Now We're One (BMI)—Coral 62066	45	2
49.	HIGH SCHOOL CONFIDENTIAL (BMI)—Jerry Lee Lewis............. Fools Like Me (BMI)—Sun 296	—	10
50.	ANGEL BABY (BMI)—Dean Martin .... I'll Gladly Make the Same Mistake Again (ASCAP)—Cap 3988	44	6

artists' biographies

Buddy Knox Comes Up With Another Hot Disk

Buddy Knox, who's now 25, began his life in Happy, Tex., and his musical career as an undergraduate at West Texas State College. There he met three fellows who were to become his closest friends and with whom he formed a singing and instrumental group called the "Rhythm Orchids." Buddy played the guitar; Jimmy Bowen, the bass; Don Lanier, guitar, and Dave Alldred, drums. After graduation, the boys formed their own record company in Dumas, Tex. When they put out "Party Doll," which Buddy himself had written, New York beckoned and Roulette Records signed the group.

"Party Doll" was followed by another hit, "Rock Your Baby to Sleep," and in "Hula Love" he came up with his third success. Currently, "Somebody Touched Me" is on Billboard's charts and climbing.

T. Edwards Returns And Climbs on Charts

Singing was not a full time occupation for Tommy. While appearing occasionally at East and Midwest clubs and holding down a regular 15-minute radio show in Virginia, his time was mostly devoted to writing and selling songs. In 1946 he sold "That Chick's Too Young to Fry" which Louis Jordan made into a hit.

But then Tommy began to do the singing on the demos himself, and when M-G-M heard him they were greatly enthused, not only over the tune, but especially his appealing voice. Tommy's first three platters for M-G-M sold very well but with the advent of rock and roll he, like many other successful singers, had to alter his style somewhat. He just re-cently re-recorded his former hit "It's All in the Game" which currently is on the way up on Billboard's charts.

Best Wishes from Mercury for a Successful Fall Season

SURE FIRE NEW RELEASE

I Wish

THE PLATTERS

MERCURY 71353

The Billboard HOT 100

FOR THE WEEK ENDING AUGUST 31

★ THE STAR PERFORMER designation shows the outstanding upward changes of position in The Hot 100 since last week's chart. Its purpose merely is to provide quick visual identification of the sides which moved up most dramatically or to new entries which first entered the chart at an unusually high position.

THREE WEEKS AGO	TWO WEEKS AGO	ONE WEEK AGO	THIS WEEK	★ STAR PERFORMER THIS WEEK	TITLE	Artist, Company, Record Number	WEEKS ON CHART
2	1	2	1		VOLARE (Nel Blu Dipinto Di Blu)	Domenico Modugno, Decca 30677	5
14	2	1	2		LITTLE STAR	Elegants, Apt 25005	5
34	17	3	3		BIRD DOG	Everly Brothers, Cadence 1350	5
9	5	4	4		JUST A DREAM	Jimmy Clanton, Ace 546	5
1	4	6	5		POOR LITTLE FOOL	Ricky Nelson, Imperial 5528	5
3	5	7	6		PATRICIA	Perez Prado, RCA Victor 7245	5
6	3	5	7		MY TRUE LOVE	Jack Scott, Carlton 462	5
5	7	10	8		WHEN	Kalin Twins, Decca 30642	5
15	11	17	9		GINGER BREAD	Frankie Avalon, Chancellor 1021	5
26	24	20	10	★	ARE YOU REALLY MINE!	Jimmie Rodgers, Roulette 4090	5
18	16	8	11		BORN TOO LATE	Poni Tails, ABC-Paramount 9934	5
13	9	8	12		FEVER	Peggy Lee, Capitol 3998	5
8	8	11	13		REBEL-'ROUSER	Duane Eddy, Jamie 1104	5
21	19	13	14		WESTERN MOVIES	Olympics, Demon 1508	5
37	20	19	15		VOLARE (Nel Blu Dipinto Di Blu)	Dean Martin, Capitol 4028	5
9	12	12	16		WILLIE AND THE HAND JIVE	Johnny Otis Show, Capitol 3966	5
33	38	25	17		ROCK-IN' ROBIN	Bobby Day, Class 229	5
4	10	16	18		SPLISH SPLASH	Bobby Darin, Atco 6117	5
16	14	14	19		EVERYBODY LOVES A LOVER	Doris Day, Columbia 41195	5
52	44	24	20		SUMMERTIME BLUES	Eddie Cochran, Liberty 55144	5
43	25	15	21		DEVOTED TO YOU	Everly Brothers, Cadence 1350	4
—	—	40	22	★	IT'S ALL IN THE GAME	Tommy Edwards, M-G-M 12688	2
12	15	18	23		IF DREAMS CAME TRUE	Pat Boone, Dot 15785	5
73	63	26	24		TEARS ON MY PILLOW	Little Anthony and the Imperials, End 1027	4
35	31	22	25		STUPID CUPID	Connie Francis, M-G-M 12683	5
7	13	21	26		HARD HEADED WOMAN	Elvis Presley, RCA Victor 7280	5
19	23	33	27		LEFT RIGHT OUT OF YOUR HEART	Patti Page, Mercury 71331	5
25	22	28	28		SOMEBODY TOUCHED ME	Buddy Knox, Roulette 4082	5
42	27	23	29		SUSIE DARLIN'	Robin Luke, Dot 15781	4
30	34	36	30		MOON TALK	Perry Como, RCA Victor 7274	5
92	47	39	31		LA PALOMA	Billy Vaughn, Dot 15795	4
50	41	42	32	★	ITCHY TWITCHY FEELING	Bobby Hendricks, Sue 706	5
24	26	29	33		EARLY IN THE MORNING	Bobby Darin and the Rinky Dinks, Atco 6121	5
38	30	34	34		A CERTAIN SMILE	Johnny Mathis, Columbia 41193	5
17	21	27	35		ONE SUMMER NIGHT	Danleers, Mercury 71322	5
40	37	32	36		EARLY IN THE MORNING	Buddy Holly, Coral 62006	5
11	18	35	37		YAKETY YAK	Coasters, Atco 6116	5
—	71	44	38		LAZY SUMMER NIGHT	Four Preps, Capitol 4023	3
79	51	38	39		SHE WAS ONLY SEVENTEEN	Marty Robbins, Columbia 41208	5
38	29	30	40		CHANTILLY LACE	Big Bopper, Mercury 71343	5
61	54	45	41		WIN YOUR LOVE FOR ME	Sam Cooke, Keen 2006	5
32	28	31	42		THINK IT OVER	Crickets, Brunswick 55072	5
—	91	87	43	★	DOWN THE AISLE OF LOVE	The Quin-Tones, Hunt 321	3
44	46	37	44		BETTY LOU GOT A NEW PAIR OF SHOES	Bobby Freeman, Josie 841	5
85	64	51	45		WIZARD	Jimmie Rodgers, Roulette 4090	4
46	48	56	46	★	COME CLOSER TO ME	Nat King Cole, Capitol 4004	5
53	57	41	47		OVER AND OVER	Bobby Day, Class 229	5
23	33	46	48		FOR YOUR PRECIOUS LOVE	Jerry Butler and the Impressions, Abner 1013	5
—	95	59	49	★	PUT A RING ON MY FINGER	Les Paul & Mary Ford, Columbia 41222	3
—	52	49	50		HOW THE TIME FLIES	Jerry Wallace, Challenge 59013	3
31	42	50	51		WHAT AM I LIVING FOR!	Chuck Willis, Atlantic 1179	5
36	35	43	52		BLUE, BLUE DAY	Don Gibson, RCA Victor 7010	5
—	—	91	53	★	RAMROD	Duane Eddy, Jamie 1109	2
22	39	55	54		GUESS THINGS HAPPEN THAT WAY	Johnny Cash, Sun 295	5
—	67	88	55	★	NEAR YOU	Roger Williams, Kapp 233	3
—	—	57	56		CAROL	Chuck Berry, Chess 1700	2
—	74	61	57		SUMMERTIME, SUMMERTIME	Jamies, Epic 9281	3
—	—	62	58		THE WAYS OF A WOMAN IN LOVE	Johnny Cash, Sun 302	2
69	58	52	59		BY THE LIGHT OF THE SILVERY MOON	Jimmy Bowen, Roulette 4083	2
—	—	78	60	★	THE GREEN MOSQUITO	Tune-Rockers, United Artists 139	2

THE INDUSTRY'S FASTEST AND MOST COMPLETE PROGRAMMING AND BUYING GUIDE

These 100 sides are listed in order of their national popularity, as determined by weekly local studies prepared for The Billboard in markets representing a cross-section of the United States. These studies take into consideration such factors as disk jockey plays, juke box activity and record sales.

★ THE STAR PERFORMER designation shows the outstanding upward changes of position in The Hot 100 since last week's chart. Its purpose merely is to provide quick visual identification of the sides which moved up most dramatically or to new entries which first entered the chart at an unusually high position.

Three Weeks Ago	Two Weeks Ago	One Week Ago	This Week	★ Star Performer This Week	Title — Artist, Company, Record Number	Weeks on Chart
74	56	53	61		KATHY-O — Diamonds, Mercury 71330	5
—	88	68	62		DANCE, EVERYONE, DANCE — Betty Madigan, Coral 62007	3
88	83	67	63		CERVEZA — Boots Brown, RCA Victor 7269	4
98	87	66	64		GOTTA HAVE RAIN — Eydie Gorme, ABC-Paramount 9944	5
—	90	89	65	★	MY LIFE — Chuck Willis, Atlantic 1192	3
—	94	90	66	★	FIRE OF LOVE — Jody Reynolds, Demon 1509	3
95	78	69	67		CHARIOT ROCK — Champs, Challenge 59018	4
—	—	65	68		WHEN WILL I KNOW — George Hamilton IV, ABC-Paramount 9946	2
—	—	94	69	★	YOU CHEATED — The Shields, Dot 15805	2
54	55	54	70		DON'T ASK ME WHY — Elvis Presley, RCA Victor 7280	5
29	36	48	71		ENCHANTED ISLAND — Four Lads, Columbia 41194	5
—	—	72	72		CITY LIGHTS — Ray Price, Columbia 41191	2
—	—	74	73		COUNT EVERY STAR — The Rivieras, Coed 503	2
—	—	—	74	★	TEA FOR TWO CHA CHA — Tommy Dorsey Ork, Decca 30704	1
27	43	47	75		DO YOU WANT TO DANCE? — Bobby Freeman, Josie 835	5
55	50	58	76		THE FREEZE — Tony and Joe, Era 1075	5
—	—	—	77	★	WHEN THE BLUE OF THE NIGHT — Tommy Mara, Felsted 8532	1
—	—	97	78	★	THE LITTLE BRASS BAND — David Seville, Liberty 55153	2
—	—	—	79	★	PROMISE ME, LOVE — Andy Williams, Cadence 1351	1
—	—	—	80	★	VOLARE (Nel Blu Dipinto Di Blu) — McGuire Sisters, Coral 62021	1
—	—	82	81		TOPSY II — Cozy Cole, Love 50034	2
—	89	86	82		DEVOTION — Janice Harper, Capitol 3984	3
—	—	80	83		STRANGE ARE THE WAYS OF LOVE — Gogi Grant, RCA Victor 7294	2
—	—	95	84		NO ONE KNOWS — Dion and the Belmonts, Laurie 3015	2
—	—	—	85	★	PLEASE DON'T DO IT — Dale Wright, Fraternity 818	1
—	—	100	86		TREASURE OF LOVE — Eileen Rodgers, Columbia 41214	2
57	45	64	87		THAT'S HOW MUCH I LOVE YOU — Pat Boone, Dot 15785	5
39	40	60	88		ANGEL BABY — Dean Martin, Capitol 3988	5
56	—	83	89	★	LEROY — Jack Scott, Carlton 462	4
—	—	81	90		PRISONER SONG — Warren Storm, Nasco 6015	2

From The Hot 100:

THE BILLBOARD'S BEST BUYS

These records, of all those listed on The Billboard Hot 100, have shown sales break-out potential for the first time this week. Action sides are listed in capital letters.

PROMISE ME, LOVE . . . . **Andy Williams**
(Thompson, ASCAP) Your Hand, Your Heart, Your Love (Alamo, ASCAP) Cadence 1351
A previous Billboard Spotlight Pick

TEA FOR TWO CHA CHA . . . . **Tommy Dorsey Ork**
(Harms, ASCAP) My Baby Just Cares for Me
(Bregman, Vocco & Conn, ASCAP) Decca 30704

WHEN THE BLUE OF THE NIGHT . . . . **Tommy Mara**
(Chappell, ASCAP) What Makes You So Lovely? (Sudbury, BMI) Felsted 8532

RAMROD . . . . **Duane Eddy**
(Gregmark, BMI) The Walker (Gregmark, BMI) Jamie 1109
A previous Billboard Spotlight Pick

CERVEZA . . . . **Boots Brown**
(Michele, BMI) Juicy (Michele, BMI) RCA Victor 7269

★ THE STAR PERFORMER designation shows the outstanding upward changes of position in The Hot 100 since last week's chart. Its purpose merely is to provide quick visual identification of the sides which moved up most dramatically or to new entries which first entered the chart at an unusually high position.

Three Weeks Ago	Two Weeks Ago	One Week Ago	This Week	★ Star Performer This Week	Title — Artist, Company, Record Number	Weeks on Chart
—	61	76	91		HEY-BOY, HEY-GIRL — Oscar McLollie & Jeanette, Class 228	4
20	32	71	92		ENDLESS SLEEP — Jody Reynolds, Demon 1507	5
—	—	—	93		OVER THE WEEKEND — Playboys, Cameo 142	1
—	—	—	94		BLUE RIBBON BABY — Tommy Sands, Capitol 4036	1
—	—	—	95		OLD MACDONALD — Chargers, RCA Victor 7301	1
—	—	—	96		WEEK END — Kingsmen, East West 115	1
—	—	—	97		UP UNTIL NOW — Johnnie Ray, Columbia 41213	1
—	—	—	98		LA-DO-DADA — Dale Hawkins, Checker 900	1
—	—	—	99		PICKLE UP A DOODLE — Teresa Brewer, Coral 62013	1
—	—	—	100		BIG DADDY — Jill Corey, Columbia 41202	1

BEST SELLING POP SINGLES IN STORES

The information given in this chart is based on actual sales to customers in a scientific sample of the nation's retail outlets during the week ending on the date shown above. Sample design, sample size, and all methods used in this continuing study of retail record sales are under the direct and continuing supervision and control of the School of Retailing of New York University.

FOR SURVEY WEEK ENDING AUGUST 23, 1958

This Week		Last Week	Weeks on Chart
1.	VOLARE (Nel Blu Dipinto Di Blu) (ASCAP)—Domenico Modugno Marti in Citta (BMI)—Dec 30677	3	5
2.	LITTLE STAR (BMI)—Elegants Getting Dizzy (BMI)—Apt 25005	2	6
3.	BIRD DOG (BMI)—Everly Brothers DEVOTED TO YOU (BMI)—Cadence 1350	1	4
4.	JUST A DREAM (BMI)—Jimmy Clanton You Aim to Please (BMI)—Ace 546	4	8
5.	POOR LITTLE FOOL—Ricky Nelson Don't Leave Me This Way (BMI)—Imperial 5528	5	9
6.	PATRICIA (ASCAP)—Perez Prado Why Wait? (BMI)—Vic 7245	6	11
7.	MY TRUE LOVE (BMI)—Jack Scott LEROY (BMI)—Carlton 462	7	12
8.	SPLISH SPLASH (BMI)—Bobby Darin Judy, Don't Be Moody (BMI)—Atco 6117	8	11
9.	WHEN (ASCAP)—Kalin Twins Three o'Clock Thrill (BMI)—Dec 30642	10	10
10.	ARE YOU REALLY MINE? (ASCAP)—Jimmie Rodgers THE WIZARD (ASCAP)—Roulette 4090	15	4
11.	GINGER BREAD (BMI)—Frankie Avalon Blue Betty (ASCAP)—Chancellor 1021	14	7
12.	REBEL-'ROUSER (BMI)—Duane Eddy Stalkin' (BMI)—Jamie 1104	9	9
13.	FEVER (BMI)—Peggy Lee You Don't Know (BMI)—Cap 3998	11	7
14.	BORN TOO LATE (ASCAP)—Poni Tails Come On, Joey, Dance With Me (BMI)—ABC-Paramount 9934	12	6
15.	WESTERN MOVIES (BMI)—Olympics Well! (BMI)—Demon 1508	13	6
16.	VOLARE (Nel Blu Dipinto Di Blu) Dean Martin (ASCAP) Outta My Mind (ASCAP)—Cap 4028	19	4
17.	ROCK-IN' ROBIN—Bobby Day OVER AND OVER—Class 229	22	4
18.	HARD-HEADED WOMAN (ASCAP)—Elvis Presley DON'T ASK ME WHY? (ASCAP)—Vic 7280	16	10
19.	WILLIE AND THE HAND JIVE (BMI)—Johnny Otis Show Ring-a-Ling (BMI)—Cap 3966	18	10
20.	YAKETY YAK (BMI)—Coasters Zing! Went the Strings of My Heart (ASCAP)—Atco 6116	17	13
21.	TEARS ON MY PILLOW (ASCAP)—Little Anthony and the Imperials Two People in the World (BMI)—End 1027	24	3
22.	STUPID CUPID (BMI)—Connie Farncis Carolina Moon (ASCAP)—M-G-M 12683	20	6
23.	IT'S ALL IN THE GAME (ASCAP)—Tommy Edwards Please Love Me Forever (BMI)—M-G-M 12688	42	2
24.	IF DREAMS CAME TRUE (ASCAP)—Pat Boone THAT'S HOW MUCH I LOVE YOU (BMI)—Dot 15785	21	8
25.	EARLY IN THE MORNING (ASCAP)—Bobby Darin and the Rinky-Dinks Now We're One (BMI)—Atco 6121	25	4
26.	A CERTAIN SMILE (ASCAP)—Johnny Mathis Let It Rain (ASCAP)—Col 41193	26	9
27.	LEFT RIGHT OUT OF YOUR HEART (ASCAP)—Patti Page Longing to Hold You Again (ASCAP)—Mercury 71331	30	9
28.	EVERYBODY LOVES A LOVER (ASCAP)—Doris Day Instant Love (ASCAP)—Col 41195	23	6
29.	MOON TALK (ASCAP)—Perry Como Beats There a Heart So True (BMI)—Vic 7242	32	5
30.	SUMMERTIME BLUES (BMI)—Eddie Cochran Love Again (BMI)—Liberty 55144	34	2
31.	GUESS THINGS HAPPEN THAT WAY (BMI)—Johnny Cash COME IN, STRANGER (BMI)—Sun 295	28	14
32.	WHAT AM I LIVING FOR? (BMI)—Chuck Willis Hang Up My Rock and Roll Shoes (BMI)—Atlantic 1179	29	17
33.	LA PALOMA (ASCAP)—Billy Vaughn Here Is My Love (ASCAP)—Dot 15795	40	3
34.	ONE SUMMER NIGHT (BMI)—Danleers Wheelin' and A-Dealin' (BMI)—Mercury 71322	27	9
35.	ITCHY TWITCHY FEELING (BMI)—Bobby Hendricks A Thousand Dreams (BMI)—Sue 706	—	1
36.	BLUE BLUE DAY (BMI)—Don Gibson Too Soon to Know (BMI)—Vic 7010	33	8
37.	PURPLE PEOPLE EATER (BMI)—Sheb Wooley I Can't Believe You're Mine (ASCAP)—M-G-M 12651	35	14
38.	COME CLOSER TO ME (BMI)—Nat King Cole Nothing in the World—Cap 4004	—	3
39.	THE WAYS OF A WOMAN IN LOVE (BMI)—Johnny Cash You're the Nearest Thing to Heaven (BMI)—Sun 302	—	1
40.	SOMEBODY TOUCHED ME (BMI)—Buddy Knox C'mon, Baby (BMI)—Roulette 4082	46	2
41.	THINK IT OVER (BMI)—Crickets Fool's Paradise (BMI)—Brunswick 55072	38	3
42.	SECRETLY (ASCAP)—Jimmie Rodgers Make Me a Miracle (ASCAP)—Roulette 4070	36	17
43.	LAZY SUMMER NIGHT (ASCAP)—Four Preps SUMMERTIME LIES (ASCAP)—Cap 4023	—	1
43.	CERVEZA—Boots Brown (BMI) Juicy (BMI)—Vic 7269	—	1
45.	EARLY IN THE MORNING (ASCAP)—Buddy Holly Now We're One (BMI)—Coral 62066	48	3
46.	ENDLESS SLEEP (BMI)—Jody Reynolds Tight Capris (BMI)—Demon 1507	31	15
47.	RAMROD (BMI)—Duane Eddy The Walker (BMI)—Jamie 1109	—	1
48.	SUSIE DARLIN' (ASCAP)—Robin Luke Living's Loving You (ASCAP)—Dot 15781	37	3
49.	ENCHANTED ISLAND (ASCAP)—Four Lads Guess What the Neighbors'll Say (BMI)—Col 41194	39	8
50.	KATHY-O (ASCAP)—Diamonds HAPPY YEARS (ASCAP)—Mercury 71330	41	3

artists' biographies

Tommy Mara Soars With Crosby Theme

This young 23-year-old Felsted artist is another of the many new singers on the rise. Taking the old Bing Crosby theme, "Where the Blue of the Night," he has, as the saying goes, made it. Currently on the Hot 100 chart and ready to pop onto others, he has been flooded with personal appearance offers.

He made his professional debut at the age of 10 at a New Haven firemen's benefit. At the age of 15, he was acclaimed "Connecticut's King of the Baritones" in a State-wide competition among more than two thousand singers. This led to three-year stint on station WELI, New Haven. He has since been on telethons, in night clubs, on TV and radio programs thruout the country.

He is managed by Sidney H. Ascher who did the press build-up for such as Tony Bennett, Vic Damone, Lisa Kirk and others.

artists' biographies

Bobby Hendricks Has Twitchy Hit Feeling

This Sue recording artist is currently riding the charts with his "Itchy Twitchy Feeling" but is not new to the hit record category. While this is his first for the Sue label and his first hit as a single artist, Bobby Hendricks was the lead singer for the Drifters on their "Moonlight Bay" and "Drip Drop" recordings.

The vital statistics read: Born February 22, 1938 in Columbus, Ohio where he attended Durfee Junior and Central High Schools. He stands 5' 7" tall and weighs 160 pounds.

He started in his home town with a vocal group called the Five Crowns and later joined a group from Baltimore called the Swallows. It was in Baltimore that the Drifters approached him to replace their lead singer who was Army bound. During his eight months with them, he became friendly with their guitar player, Jimmy Oliver, who was both a writer and arranger. It was this combo that produced his current hit disk.

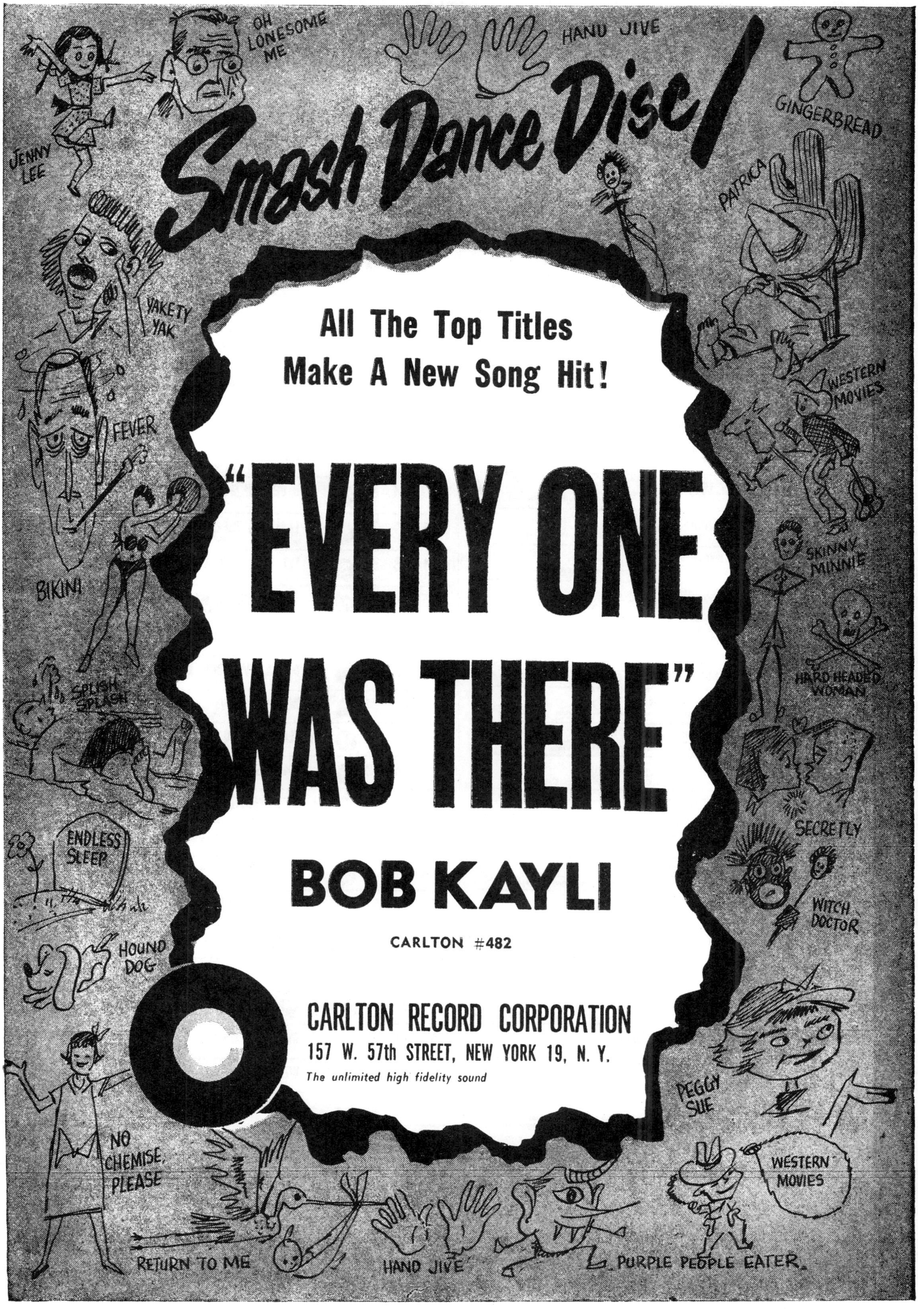
Smash Dance Disc!
All The Top Titles
Make A New Song Hit!
"EVERY ONE WAS THERE"
BOB KAYLI
CARLTON #482
CARLTON RECORD CORPORATION
157 W. 57th STREET, NEW YORK 19, N. Y.
The unlimited high fidelity sound
OH LONESOME ME
HAND JIVE
GINGERBREAD
JENNY LEE
PATRICIA
YAKETY YAK
WESTERN MOVIES
FEVER
SKINNY MINNIE
BIKINI
HARD HEADED WOMAN
SPLISH SPLASH
SECRETLY
ENDLESS SLEEP
WITCH DOCTOR
HOUND DOG
PEGGY SUE
NO CHEMISE, PLEASE
WESTERN MOVIES
RETURN TO ME
HAND JIVE
PURPLE PEOPLE EATER

The Billboard HOT 100

FOR THE WEEK ENDING SEPTEMBER 14

★ THE STAR PERFORMER designation shows the outstanding upward changes of position in The Hot 100 since last week's chart. Its purpose merely is to provide quick visual identification of the sides which moved up most dramatically or to new entries which first entered the chart at an unusually high position.

THREE WEEKS AGO	TWO WEEKS AGO	ONE WEEK AGO	THIS WEEK	★ STAR PERFORMER THIS WEEK	TITLE Artist, Company, Record Number	WEEKS ON CHART
1	2	1	1		VOLARE (Nel Blu Dipinto Di Blu), Domenico Modugno, Decca 30677	6
2	1	2	2		LITTLE STAR, Elegants, Apt 25005	6
17	3	3	3		BIRD DOG, Everly Brothers, Cadence 1350	6
5	4	4	4		JUST A DREAM, Jimmy Clanton, Ace 546	6
5	7	6	5		PATRICIA, Perez Prado, RCA Victor 7245	6
4	6	5	6		POOR LITTLE FOOL, Ricky Nelson, Imperial 5528	6
3	5	7	7		MY TRUE LOVE, Jack Scott, Carlton 462	6
38	25	17	8	★	ROCK-IN' ROBIN, Bobby Day, Class 229	6
11	17	9	9		GINGER BREAD, Frankie Avalon, Chancellor 1021	6
19	13	14	10		WESTERN MOVIES, Olympics, Demon 1508	6
—	40	22	11	★	IT'S ALL IN THE GAME, Tommy Edwards, M-G-M 12688	3
9	8	12	12		FEVER, Peggy Lee, Capitol 3998	6
63	26	24	13	★	TEARS ON MY PILLOW, Little Anthony and the Imperials, End 1027	5
16	8	11	14		BORN TOO LATE, Poni Tails, ABC-Paramount 9934	6
20	19	15	15		VOLARE (Nel Blu Dipinto Di Blu), Dean Martin, Capitol 4028	6
24	20	10	16		ARE YOU REALLY MINE!, Jimmie Rodgers, Roulette 4090	6
12	12	16	17		WILLIE AND THE HAND JIVE, Johnny Otis Show, Capitol 3966	6
14	14	19	18		EVERYBODY LOVES A LOVER, Doris Day, Columbia 41195	6
8	11	13	19		REBEL-'ROUSER, Duane Eddy, Jamie 1104	6
31	22	25	20		STUPID CUPID, Connie Francis, M-G-M 12683	6
7	10	8	21		WHEN, Kalin Twins, Decca 30642	6
25	15	21	22		DEVOTED TO YOU, Everly Brothers, Cadence 1350	5
91	87	43	23	★	DOWN THE AISLE OF LOVE, The Quin-Tones, Hunt 321	4
15	18	23	24		IF DREAMS CAME TRUE, Pat Boone, Dot 15785	6
67	88	55	25	★	NEAR YOU, Roger Williams, Kapp 233	4
47	39	31	26		LA PALOMA, Billy Vaughn, Dot 15795	5
71	44	38	27		LAZY SUMMER NIGHT, Four Preps, Capitol 4023	4
27	23	29	28		SUSIE DARLIN', Robin Luke, Dot 15781	5
34	36	30	29		MOON TALK, Perry Como, RCA Victor 7274	6
—	62	58	30	★	THE WAYS OF A WOMAN IN LOVE, Johnny Cash, Sun 302	3
44	24	20	31		SUMMERTIME BLUES, Eddie Cochran, Liberty 55144	6
21	27	35	32		ONE SUMMER NIGHT, Danleers, Mercury 71322	6
22	28	28	33		SOMEBODY TOUCHED ME, Buddy Knox, Roulette 4082	6
29	30	40	34		CHANTILLY LACE, Big Bopper, Mercury 71343	6
54	45	41	35		WIN YOUR LOVE FOR ME, Sam Cooke, Keen 2006	6
41	42	32	36		ITCHY TWITCHY FEELING, Bobby Hendricks, Sue 706	6
30	34	34	37		A CERTAIN SMILE, Johnny Mathis, Columbia 41193	6
26	29	33	38		EARLY IN THE MORNING, Bobby Darin and the Rinky Dinks, Atco 6121	6
51	38	39	39		SHE WAS ONLY SEVENTEEN, Marty Robbins, Columbia 41208	6
95	59	49	40		PUT A RING OK MY FINGER, Les Paul & Mary Ford, Columbia 41222	4
48	56	46	41		COME CLOSER TO ME, Nat King Cole, Capitol 4004	6
88	68	62	42	★	DANCE, EVERYONE, DANCE, Betty Madigan, Coral 62007	4
—	95	84	43	★	NO ONE KNOWS, Dion and the Belmonts, Laurie 3015	3
—	—	74	44	★	TEA FOR TWO CHA CHA, Tommy Dorsey Ork, Decca 30704	2
10	16	18	45		SPLISH SPLASH, Bobby Darin, Atco 6117	6
—	94	69	46	★	YOU CHEATED, The Shields, Dot 15805	3
37	32	36	47		EARLY IN THE MORNING, Buddy Holly, Coral 62006	6
74	61	57	48	★	SUMMERTIME, SUMMERTIME, Jamies, Epic 9281	4
35	43	52	49		BLUE, BLUE DAY, Don Gibson, RCA Victor 7010	6
46	37	44	50		BETTY LOU GOT A NEW PAIR OF SHOES, Bobby Freeman, Josie 841	6
—	91	53	51		RAMROD, Duane Eddy, Jamie 1109	3
—	57	56	52		CAROL, Chuck Berry, Chess 1700	3
57	41	47	53		OVER AND OVER, Bobby Day, Class 229	6
64	51	45	54		WIZARD, Jimmie Rodgers, Roulette 4090	5
23	33	27	55		LEFT RIGHT OUT OF YOUR HEART, Patti Page, Mercury 71331	6
13	21	26	56		HARD HEADED WOMAN, Elvis Presley, RCA Victor 7280	6
39	55	54	57		GUESS THINGS HAPPEN THAT WAY, Johnny Cash, Sun 295	6
52	49	50	58		HOW THE TIME FLIES, Jerry Wallace, Challenge 59013	4
—	78	60	59		THE GREEN MOSQUITO, Tune-Rockers, United Artists 139	3
28	31	42	60		THINK IT OVER, Crickets, Brunswick 55072	6

THE INDUSTRY'S FASTEST AND MOST COMPLETE PROGRAMMING AND BUYING GUIDE

These 100 sides are listed in order of their national POPULARITY, as determined by weekly local studies prepared for The Billboard in markets representing a cross-section of the United States. These studies take into consideration such factors as disk jockey plays, juke box activity and record sales.

From The Hot 100:

THE BILLBOARD'S BEST BUYS

These records, of all those listed on The Billboard Hot 100, have shown the greatest national SALES BREAK-OUT potential this week for the first time. Action sides are listed in capital letters.

CHANTILLY LACE .... **Big Booper**
(Glad, BMI) Purple People Eater Meets the Witch Doctor (Ken-Rick, BMI) Mercury 71343

YOU CHEATED .... **The Shields**
(Balcones, BMI) That's the Way It's Gonna Be (House of Fortune, BMI) Dot 15805

NO ONE KNOWS .... **Dion & The Belmonts**
(Schwartz, ASCAP) I Can't Go On (Rosalie) (Commodore, BMI) Laurie 3015

A previous Billboard Spotlight Pick

THE GREEN MOSQUITO .... **The Tune Rockers**
(Dimas, BMI) Warm Up (Dimas, BMI) United Artists 139

TOPSY II .... **Cozy Cole**
(Cosmopolitan, BMI) Topsy I (Cosmopolitan, BMI) Love 50034

★ THE STAR PERFORMER designation shows the outstanding upward changes of position in The Hot 100 since last week's chart. Its purpose merely is to provide quick visual identification of the sides which moved up most dramatically or to new entries which first entered the chart at an unusually high position.

THREE WEEKS AGO	TWO WEEKS AGO	ONE WEEK AGO	THIS WEEK	★ STAR PERFORMER THIS WEEK	TITLE — Artist, Company, Record Number	WEEKS ON CHART
90	89	65	61		MY LIFE — Chuck Willis, Atlantic 1192	4
83	67	63	62		CERVEZA — Boots Brown, RCA Victor 7269	5
87	66	64	63		GOTTA HAVE RAIN — Eydie Gorme, ABC-Paramount 9944	6
36	48	71	64		ENCHANTED ISLAND — Four Lads, Columbia 41194	6
58	52	59	65		BY THE LIGHT OF THE SILVERY MOON — Jimmy Bowen, Roulette 4083	3
—	82	81	66	★	TOPSY II — Cozy Cole, Love 50034	3
78	69	67	67		CHARIOT ROCK — Champs, Challenge 59018	5
—	—	79	68		PROMISE ME LOVE — Andy Williams, Cadence 1351	2
—	100	86	69	★	TREASURE OF YOUR LOVE — Eileen Rodgers, Columbia 41214	3
—	—	98	70	★	LA-DO-DADA — Dale Hawkins, Checker 900	2
—	72	72	71		CITY LIGHTS — Ray Price, Columbia 41191	3
—	—	—	72	★	YOUR CHEATIN' HEART — George Hamilton IV, ABC-Paramount 9946	1
42	50	51	73		WHAT AM I LIVING FOR? — Chuck Willis, Atlantic 1179	6
18	35	37	74	★	YAKETY YAK — Coasters, Atco 6116	6
—	65	68	75		WHEN WILL I KNOW — George Hamilton IV, ABC-Paramount 9946	3
—	—	77	76		WHERE THE BLUE OF THE NIGHT — Tommy Mara, Felsted 8532	2
—	—	85	77		PLEASE DON'T DO IT — Dale Wright, Fraternity 818	2
65	75	—	78		BLUE BOY — Jim Reeves, RCA Victor 7266	5
68	70	—	79		ALONE WITH YOU — Faron Young, Capitol 3982	4
56	53	61	80	★	KATHY-O — Diamonds, Mercury 71330	6
—	—	97	81	★	UP UNTIL NOW — Johnnie Ray, Columbia 41213	2
—	74	73	82		COUNT EVERY STAR — The Rivieras, Coed 503	3
—	80	83	83		STRANGE ARE THE WAYS OF LOVE — Gogi Grant, RCA Victor 7294	3
—	—	96	84		WEEK END — Kingsmen, East West 115	2
—	—	—	85		I'LL MAKE IT ALL UP TO YOU — Jerry Lee Lewis, Sun 303	1
45	64	87	86		THAT'S HOW MUCH I LOVE YOU — Pat Boone, Dot 15785	6
—	—	93	87		OVER THE WEEKEND — Playboys, Cameo 142	2
—	—	—	88	★	FIREFLY — Tony Bennett, Columbia 41237	1
—	—	94	89		BLUE-RIBBON BABY — Tommy Sands, Capitol 4036	2
61	76	91	90		HEY-BOY, HEY-GIRL — Oscar McLollie & Jeanette, Class 228	5
66	98	—	91		YOU'RE A SWEETHEART — Little Willie John, King 5142	4
—	—	—	92		INVITATION TO THE BLUES — Ray Price, Columbia 41191	1
—	—	—	93		GUESS I'VE BEEN AROUND TOO LONG — Carl Smith, Columbia 41170	1
—	—	—	94		YES, I WANT YOU — Ivory Joe Hunter, Atlantic 1191	1
—	—	—	95		THUNDER ROAD — Robert Mitchum, Capitol 3986	1
—	—	—	96		MY LUCKY LOVE — Doug Franklin, Colonial 7777	1
32	71	92	97		ENDLESS SLEEP — Jody Reynolds, Demon 1507	6
—	83	89	98	★	LEROY — Jack Scott, Carlton 462	5
40	60	88	99		ANGEL BABY — Dean Martin, Capitol 3988	6
50	58	76	100	★	THE FREEZE — Tony and Joe, Era 1075	6

STORE RECORDED SALES — NEW YORK UNIVERSITY SCHOOL OF RETAILING — THE BILLBOARD

BEST SELLING POP SINGLES IN STORES

The information given in this chart is based on actual sales to customers in a scientific sample of the nation's retail outlets during the week ending on the date shown above. Sample design, sample size, and all methods used in this continuing study of retail record sales are under the direct and continuing supervision and control of the School of Retailing of New York University.

FOR SURVEY WEEK ENDING AUGUST 30, 1958

This Week		Last Week	Weeks on Chart
1.	VOLARE (Nel Blu Dipinto Di Blu) (ASCAP)—Domenico Modugno Marti in Citta (BMI)—Dec 30677	1	6
2.	BIRD DOG (BMI)—Everly Brothers DEVOTED TO YOU (BMI)—Cadence 1350	3	5
3.	LITTLE STAR (BMI)—Elegants Getting Dizzy (BMI)—Apt 25005	2	7
4.	JUST A DREAM (BMI)—Jimmy Clanton You Aim to Please (BMI)—Ace 546	4	9
5.	PATRICIA (ASCAP)—Perez Prado Why Wait? (BMI)—Vic 7245	6	12
6.	POOR LITTLE FOOL (BMI)—Ricky Nelson Don't Leave Me This Way (BMI)—Imperial 5528	5	10
7.	MY TRUE LOVE (BMI)—Jack Scott LEROY (BMI)—Carlton 462	7	13
8.	ROCK-IN' ROBIN (BMI)—Bobby Day OVER AND OVER (BMI)—Class 229	17	5
9.	IT'S ALL IN THE GAME (ASCAP)—Tommy Edwards Please Love Me Forever (BMI)—M-G-M 12688	23	3
10.	TEARS ON MY PILLOW (ASCAP)—Little Anthony and the Imperials Two People in the World (BMI)—End 1027	21	4
11.	GINGER BREAD (BMI)—Frankie Avalon Blue Betty (ASCAP)—Chancellor 1021	11	8
12.	VOLARE (Nel Blu Dipinto Di Blu) (ASCAP)—Dean Martin Outta My Mind (ASCAP)—Cap 4028	16	5
13.	WESTERN MOVIES (BMI)—Olympics Well! (BMI)—Demon 1508	15	7
14.	FEVER (BMI)—Peggy Lee You Don't Know (BMI)—Cap 3998	13	8
15.	BORN TOO LATE (ASCAP)—Poni Tails Come on, Joey, Dance With Me (BMI)—ABC-Paramount 9934	14	7
16.	ARE YOU REALLY MINE? (ASCAP)—Jimmie Rodgers THE WIZARD (ASCAP)—Roulette 4090	10	5
17.	REBEL-'ROUSER (BMI)—Duane Eddy Stalkin' (BMI)—Jamie 1104	12	10
18.	WILLIE AND THE HAND JIVE (BMI)—Johnny Otis Show Ring-a-Ling (BMI)—Cap 3966	19	11
19.	SPLISH SPLASH (BMI)—Bobby Darin Judy, Don't Be Moody (BMI)—Atco 6117	8	12
20.	STUPID CUPID (BMI)—Connie Francis Carolina Moon (ASCAP)—M-G-M 12683	22	7
21.	HARD HEADED WOMAN (ASCAP)—Elvis Presley DON'T ASK ME WHY (ASCAP)—Vic 7280	18	11
22.	EVERYBODY LOVES A LOVER (ASCAP)—Doris Day Instant Love (ASCAP)—Col 41195	28	7
23.	WHEN (ASCAP)—Kalin Twins Three o'Clock Thrill (BMI)—Dec 30642	9	11
24.	IF DREAMS CAME TRUE (ASCAP)—Pat Boone THAT'S HOW MUCH I LOVE YOU (BMI)—Dot 15785	24	9
25.	DOWN THE AISLE OF LOVE (BMI)—Quin-Tones Please, Dear (BMI)—Hunt 321	—	1
26.	NEAR YOU (ASCAP)—Roger Williams Merry Widow Waltz (ASCAP)—Kapp 233	—	1
27.	LA PALOMA (ASCAP)—Billy Vaughn Here Is My Love (ASCAP)—Dot 15795	33	4
28.	MOON TALK (ASCAP)—Perry Como Beats There a Heart So True (BMI)—Vic 7242	29	6
29.	YAKETY YAK (BMI)—Coasters Zing! Went the Strings of My Heart (ASCAP)—Atco 6116	20	14
30.	A CERTAIN SMILE (ASCAP) Johnny Mathis Let It Rain (ASCAP)—Col 41193	26	10
31.	THE WAYS OF A WOMAN IN LOVE (BMI)—Johnny Cash YOU'RE THE NEAREST THING TO HEAVEN (BMI)—Sun 302	39	2
32.	ONE SUMMER NIGHT (BMI)—Danleers Wheelin' and A-Dealin' (BMI)—Mercury 71322	34	10
33.	DANCE, EVERYONE, DANCE (ASCAP)—Betty Madigan My Symphony of Love (ASCAP)—Coral 62007	—	1
34.	LAZY SUMMER NIGHT (ASCAP)—Four Preps SUMMERTIME LIES (ASCAP)—Cap 4023	43	2
35.	WIN YOUR LOVE FOR ME (BMI) Sam Cooke Love Song From "Houseboat" (ASCAP)—Keen 32006	—	1
36.	EARLY IN THE MORNING (ASCAP)—Bobby Darin and the Rinky-Dinks Now We're One (BMI)—Atco 6121	25	5
37.	LEFT RIGHT OUT OF YOUR HEART (ASCAP)—Patti Page Longing to Hold You Again (ASCAP)—Mercury 71331	27	10
38.	ITCHY TWITCHY FEELING (BMI)—Bobby Hendricks A Thousand Dreams (BMI)—Sue 706	35	2
39.	SUSIE DARLIN' (ASCAP)—Robin Luke Living's Loving You (ASCAP)—Dot 15781	48	4
40.	SUMMERTIME BLUES (BMI)—Eddie Cochran Love Again (BMI)—Liberty 55144	30	3
41.	RAMROD (BMI)—Duane Eddy The Walker (BMI)—Jamie 1109	47	2
42.	CERVEZA (BMI)—Boots Brown Juicy (BMI)—Vic 7269	43	2
43.	BETTY LOU GOT A NEW PAIR OF SHOES (BMI)—Bobby Freeman Starlight (BMI)—Josie 841	—	3
44.	COME CLOSER TO ME (BMI)—Nat King Cole Nothing in the World (BMI)—Cap 4004	38	4
45.	SOMEBODY TOUCHED ME (BMI)—Buddy Knox C'mon Baby (BMI)—Roulette 4082	40	3
46.	BLUE BLUE DAY (BMI)—Don Gibson Too Soon to Know (BMI)—Vic 7010	36	9
47.	SUMMERTIME, SUMMERTIME (ASCAP)—Jamies Searching for You (ASCAP)—Epic 9281	—	1
48.	EARLY IN THE MORNING (ASCAP)—Buddy Holly Now We're One (BMI)—Coral 62066	45	4
49.	FOR YOUR PRECIOUS LOVE (ASCAP)—Jerry Butler and Impressions Sweet Was the Wine (ASCAP)—Abner 1013	—	12
50.	NO ONE KNOWS (ASCAP)—Dion and the Belmonts I Can't Go On (Rosalie) (BMI)—Laurie 3015	—	1
50.	WHAT AM I LIVING FOR? (BMI)—Chuck Willis Hang Up My Rock and Roll Shoes (BMI)—Atlantic 1179	32	18

artists' biographies

Eddie Cochran Has Another Big Hit

"Summertime Blues," Eddie Cochran's current chart record, must be certainly providing just

the opposite feeling for the young chanter. Actually, hits are nothing new for Cochran. His debut disk, "Sittin' in the Balcony," was also a best-seller.

Cochran was born October 3, 1938. He is the youngest of five children. He began his career by playing guitar in a country and western band. He met his manager, Jerry Capehart, at a record session. Soon afterward he began to sing and was signed to an exclusive recording contract by Liberty Records.

He has appeared in several motion pictures and on television. His future plans include a serious dramatic career as well as singing.

artists' biographies

'Devotion' Rings Bell For Janice Harper

Petite, pretty Janice Harper, a favorite of the jockeys, is a graduate of Newton High School in Flushing, N. Y. Her first ambition as a child was to become an interior decorator. But, at 15, at the encouragement of friends, she entered an amateur contest as a vocalist and won, winding up with a singing coach.

The coach grew so enthusiastic over her that he sent a dub to a diskery which immediately signed Janice. On the heels of the successful "Bon Voyage," she was signed by Capitol.

Her present hit, "Devotion," climbing steadily on The Billboard's charts, was made with Arnold Goland directing the orchestra and chorus. Via Dick Clark's show, Janice was voted the "Best New Female Vocalist" this past year.

The Billboard HOT 100

FOR THE WEEK ENDING SEPTEMBER 21

★ THE STAR PERFORMER designation shows the outstanding upward changes of position in The Hot 100 since last week's chart. Its purpose merely is to provide quick visual identification of the sides which moved up most dramatically or to new entries which first entered the chart at an unusually high position.

Three Weeks Ago	Two Weeks Ago	One Week Ago	This Week	★ Star Performer This Week	TITLE Artist, Company, Record Number	Weeks on Chart
2	1	1	1		VOLARE (Nel Blu Dipinto Di Blu) — Domenico Modugno, Decca 30677	7
3	3	3	2		BIRD DOG — Everly Brothers, Cadence 1350	7
1	2	2	3		LITTLE STAR — Elegants, Apt 25005	7
40	22	11	4		IT'S ALL IN THE GAME — Tommy Edwards, M-G-M 12688	4
4	4	4	5		JUST A DREAM — Jimmy Clanton, Ace 546	7
25	17	8	6		ROCK-IN' ROBIN — Bobby Day, Class 229	7
8	11	14	7		BORN TOO LATE — Poni Tails, ABC-Paramount 9934	7
13	14	10	8		WESTERN MOVIES — Olympics, Demon 1508	7
26	24	13	9		TEARS ON MY PILLOW — Little Anthony and the Imperials, End 1027	6
23	29	28	10	★	SUSIE DARLIN' — Robin Luke, Dot 15781	6
7	6	5	11		PATRICIA — Perez Prado, RCA Victor 7245	7
5	7	7	12		MY TRUE LOVE — Jack Scott, Carlton 462	7
6	5	6	13		POOR LITTLE FOOL — Ricky Nelson, Imperial 5528	7
15	21	22	14		DEVOTED TO YOU — Everly Brothers, Cadence 1350	6
20	10	16	15		ARE YOU REALLY MINE! — Jimmie Rodgers, Roulette 4090	7
24	20	31	16	★	SUMMERTIME BLUES — Eddie Cochran, Liberty 55144	7
17	9	9	17		GINGER BREAD — Frankie Avalon, Chancellor 1021	7
22	25	20	18		STUPID CUPID — Connie Francis, M-G-M 12683	7
14	19	18	19		EVERYBODY LOVES A LOVER — Doris Day, Columbia 41195	7
87	43	23	20		DOWN THE AISLE OF LOVE — Quin-Tones, Hunt 321	5
19	15	15	21		VOLARE (Nel Blu Dipinto Di Blu) — Dean Martin, Capitol 4028	7
8	12	12	22		FEVER — Peggy Lee, Capitol 3998	7
44	38	27	23		LAZY SUMMER NIGHT — Four Preps, Capitol 4023	5
62	58	30	24		THE WAYS OF A WOMAN IN LOVE — Johnny Cash, Sun 302	4
49	50	58	25	★	HOW THE TIME FLIES — Jerry Wallace, Challenge 59013	5
88	55	25	26		NEAR YOU — Roger Williams, Kapp 233	5
38	39	39	27		SHE WAS ONLY SEVENTEEN — Marty Robbins, Columbia 41208	7
91	53	51	28	★	RAMROD — Duane Eddy, Jamie 1109	4
57	56	52	29	★	CAROL — Chuck Berry, Chess 1700	4
61	57	48	30	★	SUMMERTIME, SUMMERTIME — Jamies, Epic 9281	5
—	74	44	31	★	TEA FOR TWO CHA CHA — Tommy Dorsey Ork, Decca 30704	3
12	16	17	32		WILLIE AND THE HAND JIVE — Johnny Otis Show, Capitol 3966	7
94	69	46	33		YOU CHEATED — Shields, Dot 15805	4
68	62	42	34		DANCE, EVERYONE, DANCE — Betty Madigan, Coral 62007	5
30	40	34	35		CHANTILLY LACE — Big Bopper, Mercury 71343	7
28	28	33	36		SOMEBODY TOUCHED ME — Buddy Knox, Roulette 4082	7
95	84	43	37		NO ONE KNOWS — Dion and the Belmonts, Laurie 3015	4
59	49	40	38		PUT A RING ON MY FINGER — Les Paul & Mary Ford, Columbia 41222	5
45	41	35	39		WIN YOUR LOVE FOR ME — Sam Cooke, Keen 2006	7
10	8	21	40		WHEN — Kalin Twins, Decca 30642	7
11	13	19	41		REBEL-ROUSER — Duane Eddy, Jamie 1104	7
39	31	26	42		LA PALOMA — Billy Vaughn, Dot 15795	6
27	35	32	43		ONE SUMMER NIGHT — Danleers, Mercury 71322	7
—	—	88	44	★	FIREFLY — Tony Bennett, Columbia 41237	2
51	45	54	45		WIZARD — Jimmie Rodgers, Roulette 4090	6
36	30	29	46		MOON TALK — Perry Como, RCA Victor 7274	7
42	32	36	47		ITCHY TWITCHY FEELING — Bobby Hendricks, Sue 706	7
78	60	59	48		THE GREEN MOSQUITO — Tune-Rockers, United Artists 139	4
—	79	68	49	★	PROMISE ME, LOVE — Andy Williams, Cadence 1351	3
82	81	66	50	★	TOPSY II — Cozy Cole, Love 5004	4
56	46	41	51		COME CLOSER TO ME — Nat King Cole, Capitol 4004	7
32	36	47	52		EARLY IN THE MORNING — Buddy Holly, Coral 62006	7
34	34	37	53		A CERTAIN SMILE — Johnny Mathis, Columbia 41193	7
100	86	69	54		TREASURE OF YOUR LOVE — Eileen Rodgers, Columbia 41214	4
18	23	24	55		IF DREAMS CAME TRUE — Pat Boone, Dot 15785	7
89	65	61	56		MY LIFE — Chuck Willis, Atlantic 1192	5
37	44	50	57		BETTY LOU GOT A NEW PAIR OF SHOES — Bobby Freeman, Josie 841	7
16	18	45	58		SPLISH SPLASH — Bobby Darin, Atco 6117	7
—	—	—	59	★	THE TEN COMMANDMENTS OF LOVE — Moonglows, Chess 1705	1
41	47	53	60		OVER AND OVER — Bobby Day, Class 229	7

THE INDUSTRY'S FASTEST AND MOST COMPLETE PROGRAMMING AND BUYING GUIDE

These 100 sides are listed in order of their national POPULARITY, as determined by weekly local studies prepared for The Billboard in markets representing a cross-section of the United States. These studies take into consideration such factors as disk jockey plays, juke box activity and record sales.

★ THE STAR PERFORMER designation shows the outstanding upward changes of position in The Hot 100 since last week's chart. Its purpose merely is to provide quick visual identification of the sides which moved up most dramatically or to new entries which first entered the chart at an unusually high position.

THREE WEEKS AGO	TWO WEEKS AGO	ONE WEEK AGO	THIS WEEK	★ STAR PERFORMER THIS WEEK	TITLE Artist, Company, Record Number	WEEKS ON CHART
—	—	—	61	★	THERE GOES MY HEART — Joni James, M-G-M 12706	1
—	93	87	62	★	OVER THE WEEKEND — Playboys, Cameo 142	3
—	98	70	63		LA-DO-DADA — Dale Hawkins, Checker 900	3
43	52	49	64		BLUE BLUE DAY — Don Gibson, RCA Victor 7010	7
—	—	—	65	★	IT'S ONLY MAKE BELIEVE — Conway Twitty, M-G-M 12677	1
67	63	62	66		CERVEZA — Boots Brown, RCA Victor 7269	6
52	59	65	67		BY THE LIGHT OF THE SILVERY MOON — Jimmy Bowen, Roulette 4083	4
31	42	60	68		THINK IT OVER — Crickets, Brunswick 55072	7
29	33	38	69		EARLY IN THE MORNING — Bobby Darin and the Rinky Dinks, Atco 6121	7
—	—	—	70	★	THE SECRET — Gordon MacRae, Capitol 4033	1
33	27	55	71		LEFT RIGHT OUT OF YOUR HEART — Patti Page, Mercury 71331	7
—	—	—	72	★	BABY FACE — Little Richard, Specialty 645	1
—	—	—	73	★	BREAKUP — Jerry Lee Lewis, Sun 303	1
—	94	89	74	★	BLUE-RIBBON BABY — Tommy Sands, Capitol 4036	3
—	—	96	75	★	MY LUCKY LOVE — Doug Franklin, Colonial 7777	2
—	—	—	76	★	MEXICAN HAT ROCK — Applejacks, Cameo 149	1
74	73	82	77		COUNT EVERY STAR — Rivieras, Coed 503	4
21	26	56	78		HARD HEADED WOMAN — Elvis Presley, RCA Victor 7280	7
—	77	76	79		WHERE THE BLUE OF THE NIGHT — Tommy Mara, Felsted 8532	3
69	67	67	80	★	CHARIOT ROCK — Champs, Challenge 59018	6
99	—	—	81	★	YOU CHEATED — Slades, Domino 500	5
90	66	—	82		FIRE OF LOVE — Jody Reynolds, Demon 1509	4
70	—	79	83		ALONE WITH YOU — Faron Young, Capitol 3982	5
—	—	—	84	★	BIG BROWN EYES — Redjacks, Apt 25006	1
81	—	—	85	★	GAS MONEY — Jan and Arnie, Arwin 111	2
—	96	84	86		WEEK END — Kingsmen, East West 115	3
—	—	—	87	★	THE END — Earl Grant, Decca 30719	1
—	—	95	88		THUNDER ROAD — Robert Mitchum, Capitol 3986	2
75	—	78	89		BLUE BOY — Jim Reeves, RCA Victor 7266	6
35	37	74	90		YAKETY YAK — Coasters, Atco 6116	7

From The Hot 100:

THE BILLBOARD'S BEST BUYS

These records, of all those listed on The Billboard Hot 100, have shown the greatest national SALES BREAK-OUT potential this week for the first time. Action sides are listed in capital letters.

FIREFLY .... Tony Bennett
(Marks, BMI) The Night That Heaven Fell
(Shapiro-Bernstein, ASCAP) Columbia 41237

BABY FACE .... Little Richard
(Remick, ASCAP) I'll Never Let You Go (Venice, BMI) Specialty 645

THE END .... Earl Grant
(Criterion, ASCAP) Hunky Dunky Doo (Criterion, ASCAP) Decca 30719

The above are The Billboard Spotlight picks

HOW THE TIME FLIES .... Jerry Wallace
(Music Productions, ASCAP) With This Ring (Sun-Crest & Jat, BMI)
Challenge 59013

★ THE STAR PERFORMER designation shows the outstanding upward changes of position in The Hot 100 since last week's chart. Its purpose merely is to provide quick visual identification of the sides which moved up most dramatically or to new entries which first entered the chart at an unusually high position.

THREE WEEKS AGO	TWO WEEKS AGO	ONE WEEK AGO	THIS WEEK	★ STAR PERFORMER THIS WEEK	TITLE Artist, Company, Record Number	WEEKS ON CHART
55	54	57	91		GUESS THINGS HAPPEN THAT WAY — Johnny Cash, Sun 295	7
—	—	—	92		TOPSY I — Cozy Cole, Love 50034	1
—	85	77	93		PLEASE DON'T DO IT — Dale Wright, Fraternity 818	3
50	51	73	94		WHAT AM I LIVING FOR? — Chuck Willis, Atlantic 1179	7
53	61	80	95		KATHY-O — Diamonds, Mercury 71330	7
—	97	81	96		UP UNTIL NOW — Johnnie Ray, Columbia 41213	3
66	64	63	97		GOTTA HAVE RAIN — Eydie Gorme, ABC-Paramount 9944	7
—	—	—	98		I WISH — Platters, Mercury 71353	1
—	—	72	99		YOUR CHEATIN' HEART — George Hamilton IV, ABC-Paramount 9946	2
48	71	64	100		ENCHANTED ISLAND — Four Lads, Columbia 41194	7

NEW YORK UNIVERSITY SCHOOL OF RETAILING · STORE RECORDED SALES · THE BILLBOARD

BEST SELLING POP SINGLES IN STORES

The information given in this chart is based on actual sales to customers in a scientific sample of the nation's retail outlets during the week ending on the date shown above. Sample design, sample size, and all methods used in this continuing study of retail record sales are under the direct and continuing supervision and control of the School of Retailing of New York University.

FOR SURVEY WEEK ENDING SEPTEMBER 6, 1958

This Week		Last Week	Weeks on Chart
1.	VOLARE (Nel Blu Dipinto Di Blu) (ASCAP)—Domenico Modugno Marti In Citta (BMI)—Dec 30677	1	7
2.	BIRD DOG (BMI)—Everly Brothers DEVOTED TO YOU (BMI)—Cadence 1350	2	6
3.	LITTLE STAR (BMI)—Elegants Getting Dizzy (BMI)—Apt 25005	3	8
4.	IT'S ALL IN THE GAME (ASCAP)—Tommy Edwards Please Love Me Forever (BMI)—M-G-M 12688	9	4
5.	JUST A DREAM (BMI)—Jimmy Clanton You Aim to Please (BMI)—Ace 546	4	10
6.	ROCK-IN' ROBIN (BMI)—Bobby Day OVER AND OVER (BMI)—Class 229	8	6
7.	PATRICIA (ASCAP)—Perez Prado Why Wait? (BMI)—Vic 7245	5	13
8.	TEARS ON MY PILLOW (ASCAP)—Little Anthony and the Imperials Two People in the World (BMI)—End 1027	10	5
9.	MY TRUE LOVE (BMI)—Jack Scott LEROY (BMI)—Carlton 462	7	14
10.	POOR LITTLE FOOL (BMI)—Ricky Nelson Don't Leave Me This Way (BMI)—Imperial 5528	6	11
11.	WESTERN MOVIES (BMI)—Olympics Well! (BMI)—Demon 1508	13	8
12.	BORN TOO LATE (ASCAP)—Poni Tails Come On, Joey, Dance With Me (BMI)—ABC-Paramount 9934	15	8
13.	VOLARE (Nel Blu Dipinto Di Blu) (ASCAP)—Dean Martin Outta My Mind (ASCAP)—Cap 4028	12	6
14.	GINGER BREAD (BMI)—Frankie Avalon Blue Betty (ASCAP)—Chancellor 1021	11	9
15.	ARE YOU REALLY MINE? (ASCAP)—Jimmie Rodgers THE WIZARD (ASCAP)—Roulette 4090	16	6
16.	SUSIE DARLIN' (ASCAP)—Robin Luke Living's Loving You (ASCAP)—Dot 15781	39	5
17.	EVERYBODY LOVES A LOVER (ASCAP)—Doris Day Instant Love (ASCAP)—Col 41195	22	8
18.	DOWN THE AISLE OF LOVE (BMI)—The Quin-Tones Please, Dear (BMI)—Hunt 321	25	2
19.	WILLIE AND THE HAND JIVE Johnny Otis Show Ring-a-Ling (BMI)—Cap 3966	18	12
20.	FEVER (BMI)—Peggy Lee You Don't Know (BMI)—Cap 3998	14	9
21.	LA PALOMA (ASCAP)—Billy Vaughn Here Is My Love (ASCAP)—Dot 15795	27	5
22.	WIN YOUR LOVE FOR ME (BMI)—Sam Cooke Love Song From "Houseboat" (ASCAP)—Keen 32006	35	2
23.	STUPID CUPID (BMI)—Connie Francis Carolina Moon (ASCAP)—M-G-M 12683	20	8
24.	SUMMERTIME BLUES (BMI)—Eddie Cochran Love Again (BMI)—Liberty 55144	40	4
25.	NEAR YOU (ASCAP)—Roger Williams Merry Widow Waltz (ASCAP)—Kapp 233	26	2
26.	HARD HEADED WOMAN (ASCAP)—Elvis Presley DON'T ASK ME WHY (ASCAP)—Vic 7280	21	12
27.	RAMROD (BMI)—Duane Eddy The Walker (BMI)—Jamie 1109	41	3
28.	THE WAYS OF A WOMAN IN LOVE (BMI)—Johnny Cash YOU'RE THE NEAREST THING TO HEAVEN (BMI)—Sun 302	31	3
29.	REBEL-'ROUSER (BMI)—Duane Eddy Stalkin' (BMI)—Jamie 1104	17	11
30.	WHEN (ASCAP)—Kalin Twins Three o'Clock Thrill (BMI)—Dec 30642	23	12
31.	DANCE, EVERYONE, DANCE (ASCAP)—Betty Madigan My Symphony of Love (ASCAP)—Coral 62007	33	2
32.	NO ONE KNOWS (ASCAP)—Dion and the Belmonts I Can't Go On (Rosalie) (BMI)—Laurie 3015	50	2
13.	SPLISH SPLASH (BMI)—Bobby Darin Judy, Don't Be Moody (BMI)—Atco 6117	19	13
34.	IF DREAMS CAME TRUE (ASCAP)—Pat Boone	24	10
	THAT'S HOW MUCH I LOVE YOU (BMI)—Dot 15785	24	10
35.	YOU CHEATED (BMI)—Shields That's the Way It's Gonna Be (BMI)—Dot 15805	—	1
36.	YAKETY YAK (BMI)—Coasters Zing! Went the Strings of My Heart (ASCAP)—Atco 6116	29	13
37.	A CERTAIN SMILE (ASCAP)—Johnny Mathis Let It Rain (ASCAP)—Col 41193	30	11
38.	CERVEZA (BMI)—Boots Brown Juicy (BMI)—Vic 7269	42	3
39.	ONE SUMMER NIGHT (BMI)—Danleers Wheelin' and A-Dealin (BMI)—Mercury 71322	32	11
40.	ITCHY TWITCHY FEELING (BMI)—Bobby Hendricks A Thousand Dreams (BMI)—Sue 706	38	3
41.	BETTY LOU GOT A NEW PAIR OF SHOES (BMI)—Bobby Freeman Starlight (BMI)—Josie 841	43	4
42.	SUMMERTIME, SUMMERTIME (ASCAP)—The Jamies Searching for You (ASCAP)—Epic 9281	47	2
43.	HOW THE TIME FLIES (ASCAP)—Jerry Wallace With This Ring (BMI)—Challenge 59013	—	1
44.	LAZY SUMMER NIGHT (ASCAP)—Four Props SUMMERTIME LIES (ASCAP)—Cap 4023	34	3
45.	TOPSY I (BMI)—Cozy Cole Topsy II (BMI)—Love 50034	—	1
46.	MY LIFE (BMI)—Chuck Willis Thunder and Lightning (BMI)—Atlantic 1192	—	1
46.	TEA FOR TWO CHA CHA (ASCAP)—Tommy Dorsey Ork. My Baby Just Cares for Me (ASCAP)—Decca 30704	—	1
48.	MOON TALK (ASCAP)—Perry Como Heart So True (BMI)—Vic 7242	28	7
49.	BLUE BLUE DAY (BMI)—Don Gibson Too Soon to Know (BMI)—Vic 7010	46	10
50.	PUT A RING ON MY FINGER (BMI)—Les Paul and Mary Ford Fantasy (BMI)—Col 41222	—	1

artists' biographies

Two in a Row for Dion & Belmonts

Dion & the Belmonts who with their latest, "No One Knows," are batting one thousand with two hits in two tries, are all old friends from Roosevelt High School in the Bronx. The group came to life when a friend of Dion Sussel brought one of Dion's demos to Laurie Records. The company went for it and signed Dion.

Dion told Laurie about three of his friends who sang with him at school functions and parties. They auditioned for Laurie who liked them and were signed as the Belmonts.

The group's first hit, "I Wonder Why," was also the first triumph for the young record company. Three months later Laurie released "No One Knows" which is making spectacular upward jumps on Billboard's Hot 100. Dion sings the lead in the group; Carlo Mastrangelo, bass; Angelo D'Aleo, first tenor, and Fred Milano, second tenor.

artists' biographies

Robin Luke Scores With First Record

Sixteen - year - old Robin Luke lives in Honolulu with his parents and his 5-year-old sister, Susie, who's the "darlin'" for whom he composed his hit tune. The blond, grey-eyed Luke has been singing, writing music and playing the guitar since he was eight, but for only the past year professionally. "Susie Darlin'," his first record, was originally recorded in Hawaii by International Records. It made a great stir, and the master was snapped up by Dot.

Luke's real ambition is to be a doctor, and he wants to study at the University of Southern California. His plans are to combine a singing career with his schooling, just as his favorite, Pat Boone, has done. Besides co-starring on a Honolulu TV program, the lad has been seen and heard stateside on the Dick Clark and Al Jarvis Shows.

we are
rolling
out the
red
carpet
for...
Pat Boone
Singing
"GEE BUT IT'S LONELY"
15825
b/w
"FOR MY GOOD FORTUNE"
Dot RECORDS, Inc. • Sunset and Vine • Hollywood, Calif. • Phone HO 2-3141
THE NATION'S BEST SELLING RECORDS

The Billboard HOT 100

FOR THE WEEK ENDING SEPTEMBER 28

★ THE STAR PERFORMER designation shows the outstanding upward changes of position in The Hot 100 since last week's chart. Its purpose merely is to provide quick visual identification of the sides which moved up most dramatically or to new entries which first entered the chart at an unusually high position.

Three Weeks Ago	Two Weeks Ago	One Week Ago	This Week	★ Star Performer This Week	Title	Artist, Company, Record Number	Weeks on Chart
1	1	1	1		VOLARE (Nel Blu Dipinto Di Blu)	Domenico Modugno, Decca 30677	8
3	3	2	2		BIRD DOG	Everly Brothers, Cadence 1350	8
22	11	4	3		IT'S ALL IN THE GAME	Tommy Edwards, M-G-M 12688	5
2	2	3	4		LITTLE STAR	Elegants, Apt 25005	8
17	8	6	5		ROCK-IN' ROBIN	Bobby Day, Class 229	8
4	4	5	6		JUST A DREAM	Jimmy Clanton, Ace 546	8
24	13	9	7		TEARS ON MY PILLOW	Little Anthony and the Imperials, End 1027	7
29	28	10	8		SUSIE DARLIN'	Robin Luke, Dot 15781	7
11	14	7	9		BORN TOO LATE	Poni Tails, ABC-Paramount 9934	8
21	22	14	10		DEVOTED TO YOU	Everly Brothers, Cadence 1350	7
20	31	16	11		SUMMERTIME BLUES	Eddie Cochran, Liberty 55144	8
55	25	26	12	★	NEAR YOU	Roger Williams, Kapp 233	6
7	7	12	13		MY TRUE LOVE	Jack Scott, Carlton 462	8
50	58	25	14	★	HOW THE TIME FLIES	Jerry Wallace, Challenge 59013	6
6	5	11	15		PATRICIA	Perez Prado, RCA Victor 7245	8
14	10	8	16		WESTERN MOVIES	Olympics, Demon 1508	8
25	20	18	17		STUPID CUPID	Connie Francis, M-G-M 12683	8
19	18	19	18		EVERYBODY LOVES A LOVER	Doris Day, Columbia 41195	8
5	6	13	19		POOR LITTLE FOOL	Ricky Nelson, Imperial 5528	8
74	44	31	20	★	TEA FOR TWO CHA CHA	Tommy Dorsey Ork, Decca 30704	4
38	27	23	21		LAZY SUMMER NIGHT	Four Preps, Capitol 4023	6
43	23	20	22		DOWN THE AISLE OF LOVE	Quin-Tones, Hunt 321	6
56	52	29	23		CAROL	Chuck Berry, Chess 1700	5
10	16	15	24		ARE YOU REALLY MINE!	Jimmie Rodgers, Roulette 4090	8
58	30	24	25		THE WAYS OF A WOMAN IN LOVE	Johnny Cash, Sun 302	5
57	48	30	26		SUMMERTIME, SUMMERTIME	Jamies, Epic 9281	6
9	9	17	27		GINGER BREAD	Frankie Avalon, Chancellor 1021	8
84	43	37	28		NO ONE KNOWS	Dion and the Belmonts, Laurie 3015	5
15	15	21	29		VOLARE (Nel Blu Dipinto Di Blu)	Dean Martin, Capitol 4028	8
—	88	44	30	★	FIREFLY	Tony Bennett, Columbia 41237	3
69	46	33	31		YOU CHEATED	Shields, Dot 15805	5
49	40	38	32		PUT A RING ON MY FINGER	Les Paul & Mary Ford, Columbia 41222	6
12	12	22	33		FEVER	Peggy Lee, Capitol 3998	8
40	34	35	34		CHANTILLY LACE	Big Bopper, Mercury 71343	8
79	68	49	35	★	PROMISE ME, LOVE	Andy Williams, Cadence 1351	4
28	33	36	36		SOMEBODY TOUCHED ME	Buddy Knox, Roulette 4082	8
53	51	28	37		RAMROD	Duane Eddy, Jamie 1109	5
39	39	27	38		SHE WAS ONLY SEVENTEEN	Marty Robbins, Columbia 41208	8
41	35	39	39		WIN YOUR LOVE FOR ME	Sam Cooke, Keen 2006	8
62	42	34	40		DANCE, EVERYONE, DANCE	Betty Madigan, Coral 62007	6
—	—	65	41	★	IT'S ONLY MAKE BELIEVE	Conway Twitty, M-G-M 12677	2
16	17	32	42		WILLIE AND THE HAND JIVE	Johnny Otis Show, Capitol 3966	8
81	66	50	43		TOPSY II	Cozy Cole, Love 5003	5
60	59	48	44		THE GREEN MOSQUITO	Tune-Rockers, United Artists 139	5
86	69	54	45		TREASURE OF YOUR LOVE	Eileen Rodgers, Columbia 41214	5
—	—	59	46	★	THE TEN COMMANDMENTS OF LOVE	Harvey and the Moonglows, Chess 1705	2
—	—	70	47	★	THE SECRET	Gordon MacRae, Capitol 4033	2
47	53	60	48	★	OVER AND OVER	Bobby Day, Class 229	8
—	—	87	49	★	THE END	Earl Grant, Decca 30719	2
94	89	74	50	★	BLUE-RIBBON BABY	Tommy Sands, Capitol 4036	4
—	—	61	51	★	THERE GOES MY HEART	Joni James, M-G-M 12706	2
13	19	41	52		REBEL-'ROUSER	Duane Eddy, Jamie 1104	8
46	41	51	53		COME CLOSER TO ME	Nat King Cole, Capitol 4004	8
—	—	—	54	★	FOR MY GOOD FORTUNE	Pat Boone, Dot 15825	1
45	54	45	55		THE WIZARD	Jimmie Rodgers, Roulette 4090	7
—	—	—	56	★	FIBBIN'	Patti Page, Mercury 71355	1
32	36	47	57		ITCHY TWITCHY FEELING	Bobby Hendricks, Sue 706	8
35	32	43	58		ONE SUMMER NIGHT	Danleers, Mercury 71322	8
67	67	80	59	★	CHARIOT ROCK	Champs, Challenge 59018	7
—	—	—	60	★	THE DAY THE RAINS CAME	Jane Morgan, Kapp 235	1

THE INDUSTRY'S FASTEST AND MOST COMPLETE PROGRAMMING AND BUYING GUIDE

These 100 sides are listed in order of their national POPULARITY, as determined by weekly local studies prepared for The Billboard in markets representing a cross-section of the United States. These studies take into consideration such factors as disk jockey plays, juke box activity and record sales.

★ THE STAR PERFORMER designation shows the outstanding upward changes of position in The Hot 100 since last week's chart. Its purpose merely is to provide quick visual identification of the sides which moved up most dramatically or to new entries which first entered the chart at an unusually high position.

THREE WEEKS AGO	TWO WEEKS AGO	ONE WEEK AGO	THIS WEEK	★ STAR PERFORMER THIS WEEK	TITLE Artist, Company, Record Number	WEEKS ON CHART
31	26	42	61		LA PALOMA — Billy Vaughn, Dot 15795	7
98	70	63	62		LA-DO-DADA — Dale Hawkins, Checker 900	4
—	—	72	63		BABY FACE — Little Richard, Specialty 645	2
8	21	40	64		WHEN — Kalin Twins, Decca 30642	8
—	—	76	65		MEXICAN HAT ROCK — Applejacks, Cameo 149	2
34	37	53	66		A CERTAIN SMILE — Johnny Mathis, Columbia 41193	8
93	87	62	67		OVER THE WEEKEND — Playboys, Cameo 142	4
30	29	46	68		MOON TALK — Perry Como, RCA Victor 7274	8
—	—	—	69	★	GEE, BUT IT'S LONELY — Pat Boone, Dot 15825	1
—	—	73	70		BREAKUP — Jerry Lee Lewis, Sun 303	2
—	—	92	71	★	TOPSY I — Cozy Cole, Love 50034	2
18	45	58	72		SPLISH SPASH — Bobby Darin, Atco 6117	8
33	38	69	73		EARLY IN THE MORNING — Bobby Darin and the Rinky Dinks, Atco 6121	8
—	—	—	74	★	THIS LITTLE GIRL'S GONE ROCKIN' — Ruth Brown, Atlantic 1197	1
44	50	57	75		BETTY LOU GOT A NEW PAIR OF SHOES — Bobby Freeman, Josie 841	8
—	—	—	76	★	NINE MORE MILES — Georgie Young, Cameo 150	1
—	—	—	77	★	COME ON, LET'S GO — Ritchie Valens, Del Fi 4106	1
85	77	93	78	★	PLEASE DON'T DO IT — Dale Wright, Fraternity 818	4
63	62	66	79		CERVEZA — Boots Brown, RCA Victor 7269	7
—	96	75	80		MY LUCKY LOVE — Doug Franklin, Colonial 7777	3
—	—	—	81	★	HIDEAWAY — Four Esquires, Paris 520	1
23	24	55	82		IF DREAMS CAME TRUE — Pat Boone, Dot 15785	8
—	72	99	83	★	YOUR CHEATIN' HEART — George Hamilton IV, ABC-Paramount 9946	3
—	—	—	84	★	WENDY WENDY — Four Coins, Epic 9286	1
—	—	—	85	★	REAL WILD CHILD — Ivan, Coral 62017	1
—	—	81	86		YOU CHEATED — Slades, Domino 500	6
52	49	64	87		BLUE, BLUE DAY — Don Gibson, RCA Victor 7010	8
—	—	—	88		TO KNOW HIM IS TO LOVE HIM — Teddy Bears, Dore 503	1
—	—	84	89		BIG BROWN EYES — Redjacks, Apt 25006	2
66	—	82	90		FIRE OF LOVE — Jody Reynolds, Demon 1509	5

From The Hot 100: THE BILLBOARD'S BEST BUYS

These records, of all those listed on The Billboard Hot 100, have shown the greatest national SALES BREAK-OUT potential this week for the first time. Action sides are listed in capital letters.

FOR MY GOOD FORTUNE .... **PAT BOONE**
GEE, BUT IT'S LONELY
(Roosevelt, BMI) (Acuff-Rose, BMI) Dot 15825

MEXICAN HAT ROCK .... **APPLEJACKS**
(Mayland, BMI) Sophisticated Swing (Mills, ASCAP) Cameo 149

THE DAY THE RAINS CAME .... **JANE MORGAN**
(Garland, ASCAP) Le Jour Ou La Pluie Viendra (Garland, ASCAP) Kapp 235

FIBBIN' .... **PATTI PAGE**
(Igrish-Trojan, BMI) You Will Find Your Love (In Paris) Mercury 71355

The above are previous Billboard Spotlight picks.

THERE GOES MY HEART .... **JONI JAMES**
(Feist, ASCAP) Funny (Parliament, ASCAP) M-G-M 12706

IT'S ONLY MAKE BELIEVE .... **CONWAY TWITTY**
(Marielle, BMI) I'll Try (Marielle, BMI) M-G-M 12677

The correct publisher for "Firefly," one of last week's Best Buy selections, is E. H. Morris, ASCAP.

★ THE STAR PERFORMER designation shows the outstanding upward changes of position in The Hot 100 since last week's chart. Its purpose merely is to provide quick visual identification of the sides which moved up most dramatically or to new entries which first entered the chart at an unusually high position.

THREE WEEKS AGO	TWO WEEKS AGO	ONE WEEK AGO	THIS WEEK	★ STAR PERFORMER THIS WEEK	TITLE Artist, Company, Record Number	WEEKS ON CHART
—	—	98	91		I WISH — Platters, Mercury 71353	2
—	—	—	92		YOUNG SCHOOL GIRL — Fats Domino, Imperial 5537	1
—	—	—	93		NOTHIN' SHAKIN' — Eddie Fontaine, Argo 5309	1
26	56	78	94		HARD HEADED WOMAN — Elvis Presley, RCA Victor 7280	8
59	65	67	95		BY THE LIGHT OF THE SILVERY MOON — Jimmy Bowen, Roulette 4083	5
—	—	—	96		WE HAVE LOVE — Jackie Wilson, Brunswick 55086	1
—	—	—	97		YOU GOT THAT TOUCH — Sonny James, Capitol 4020	1
—	—	—	98		MANY A TIME — Steve Lawrence, Coral 62025	1
—	—	—	99		WHEN WILL I KNOW? — George Hamilton IV, ABC-Paramount 9946	1
—	—	—	100		ITCHY TWITCHY FEELING — Swallows, Federal 12333	1

STORE RECORDED SALES — NEW YORK UNIVERSITY SCHOOL OF RETAILING — THE BILLBOARD

BEST SELLING POP SINGLES IN STORES

The information given in this chart is based on actual sales to customers in a scientific sample of the nation's retail outlets during the week ending on the date shown above. Sample design, sample size, and all methods used in this continuing study of retail record sales are under the direct and continuing supervision and control of the School of Retailing of New York University.

FOR SURVEY WEEK ENDING SEPTEMBER 13, 1958

This Week		Last Week	Weeks on Chart
1.	**VOLARE (Nel Blu Dipinto Di Blu)** (ASCAP)—Domenico Modugno; Marti In Citta (BMI)—Dec 30677	1	8
2.	**BIRD DOG** (BMI)—Everly Brothers; **DEVOTED TO YOU** (BMI)—Cadence 1350	2	7
3.	**IT'S ALL IN THE GAME** (ASCAP)—Tommy Edwards; Please Love Me Forever (BMI)—M-G-M 12688	4	5
4.	**LITTLE STAR** (BMI)—Elegants; Getting Dizzy (BMI)—Apt 25005	3	9
5.	**ROCK-IN' ROBIN** (BMI)—Bobby Day; **OVER AND OVER** (BMI)—Class 229	6	7
6.	**PATRICIA** (ASCAP)—Perez Prado; Why Wait? (BMI)—Vic 7245	7	14
7.	**JUST A DREAM** (BMI)—Jimmy Clanton; You Aim to Please (BMI)—Ace 546	5	11
8.	**TEARS ON MY PILLOW** (ASCAP)—Little Anthony and the Imperials; Two Peoule in the World (BMI)—End 1027	8	6
9.	**POOR LITTLE FOOL** (BMI)—Ricky Nelson; Don't Leave Me This Way (BMI)—Imperial 5528	10	12
10.	**MY TRUE LOVE** (BMI)—Jack Scott; **LEROY** (BMI)—Carlton 462	9	15
11.	**BORN TOO LATE** (ASCAP)—Poni Tails; Come On, Joey, Dance With Me (BMI)—ABC-Paramount 9934	12	9
12.	**WESTERN MOVIES** (BMI)—Olympics; Well! (BMI)—Demon 1508	11	9
13.	**SUSIE DARLIN'** (ASCAP)—Robin Luke; Living's Loving You (ASCAP)—Dot 15781	16	6
14.	**ARE YOU REALLY MINE?** (ASCAP)—Jimmie Rodgers; **THE WIZARD** (ASCAP)—Roulette 4090	15	7
15.	**VOLARE (Nel Blu Dipinto Di Blu)** (ASCAP)—Dean Martin; Outta My Mind (ASCAP)—Cap 4028	13	7
16.	**GINGER BREAD** (BMI)—Frankie Avalon; Blue Betty (ASCAP)—Chancellor 1021	14	10
17.	**SUMMERTIME BLUES** (BMI)—Eddie Cochran; Love Again (BMI)—Liberty 55144	24	5
18.	**DOWN THE AISLE OF LOVE** (BMI)—The Quin-Tones; Please, Dear (BMI)—Hunt 321	18	3
19.	**WILLIE AND THE HAND JIVE** (BMI)—Johnny Otis Show; Ring-a-Ling (BMI)—Cap 3966	19	13
20.	**LA PALOMA** (ASCAP)—Billy Vaughn; Here Is My Love (ASCAP)—Dot 15795	21	6
21.	**EVERYBODY LOVES A LOVER** (ASCAP)—Doris Day; Instant Love (ASCAP)—Col 41195	17	9
22.	**TEA FOR TWO CHA CHA** (ASCAP)—Tommy Dorsey Ork; My Baby Just Cares for Me (ASCAP)—Decca 30704	46	2
23.	**NEAR YOU** (ASCAP)—Roger Williams; Merry Widow Waltz (ASCAP)—Kapp 233	25	3
24.	**STUPID CUPID** (BMI)—Connie Francis; Carolina Moon (ASCAP)—M-G-M 12683	23	9
25.	**FEVER** (BMI)—Peggy Lee; You Don't Know (BMI)—Cap 3998	20	10
26.	**YOU CHEATED** (BMI)—Shields; That's the Way It's Gonna Be (BMI)—Dot 15805	35	2
27.	**RAMROD** (BMI)—Duane Eddy; The Walker (BMI)—Jamie 1109	27	4
28.	**CERVEZA** (BMI)—Boots Brown; Juicy (BMI)—Vic 7269	38	4
29.	**WIN YOUR LOVE FOR ME** (BMI)—Sam Cooke; Love Song From "Houseboat" (ASCAP)—Keen 32006	22	3
30.	**WHEN** (ASCAP)—Kalin Twins; Three o'Clock Thrill (BMI)—Dec 30642	30	13
31.	**THE WAYS OF A WOMAN IN LOVE** (BMI)—Johnny Cash; **YOU'RE THE NEAREST THING TO HEAVEN** (BMI)—Sun 302	28	4
32.	**HARD HEADED WOMAN** (ASCAP)—Elvis Presley; **DON'T ASK ME WHY** (ASCAP)—Vic 7280	26	13
33.	**NO ONE KNOWS** (ASCAP)—Dion and the Belmonts; I Can't Go On (Rosalie) (BMI)—Laurie 3015	32	3
34.	**DANCE, EVERYONE, DANCE** (ASCAP)—Betty Madigan; My Symphony of Love (ASCAP)—Coral 62007	31	3
35.	**WEEK END** (BMI)—Kingsmen; Better Believe It (BMI)—East West 115	—	1
36.	**ITCHY TWITCHY FEELING** (BMI)—Bobby Hendricks; A Thousand Dreams (BMI)—Sue 706	40	4
37.	**LAZY SUMMER NIGHT** (ASCAP)—Four Preps; **SUMMERTIME LIES** (ASCAP)—Cap 4023	44	4
38.	**SPLISH SPLASH** (BMI)—Bobby Darin; Judy, Don't Be Moody (BMI)—Atco 6117	33	14
39.	**SUMMERTIME, SUMMERTIME** (ASCAP)—The Jamies; Searching for You (ASCAP)—Epic 9281	42	3
40.	**HOW THE TIME FLIES** (ASCAP)—Jerry Wallace; With This Ring (BMI)—Challenge 59013	43	2
41.	**REBEL-'ROUSER** (BMI)—Duane Eddy; Stalkin' (BMI)—Jamie 1104	29	12
42.	**YAKETY YAK** (BMI)—Coasters; Zing! Went the Strings of My Heart (ASCAP)—Atco 6116	36	14
43.	**IF DREAMS CAME TRUE** (ASCAP)—Pat Boone; **THAT'S HOW MUCH I LOVE YOU** (BMI)—Dot 15785	34	11
44.	**TOPSY II** (BMI)—Cozy Cole; **TOPSY I** (BMI)—Love 50034	45	2
45.	**A CERTAIN SMILE** (ASCAP)—Johnny Mathis; Let It Rain (ASCAP)—Col 41193	37	12
46.	**ONE SUMMER NIGHT** (BMI)—Danleers; Wheelin' and A-Dealin' (BMI)—Mercury 71322	39	12
47.	**THE END** (ASCAP)—Earl Grant; Dunky Doo (ASCAP)—Decca 30719	—	1
47.	**LA-DO-DADA** (BMI)—Dale Hawkins; Cross-Ties (BMI)—Chess 900	—	1
49.	**MY LIFE** (BMI)—Chuck Willis; Thunder and Lightning (BMI)—Atlantic 1192	46	2
50.	**PUT A RING ON MY FINGER** (BMI)—Les Paul and Mary Ford; Put a Ring On My Finger (BMI)—Col 41222	50	2

artists' biographies

'Near You' Is Big Hit for R. Williams

One of the largest selling pianists in the history of the recording industry was born in Omaha, Neb., the son of a music teacher. At the age of 12, he had already mastered many instruments, but his first love was and has remained the piano. In 1950, Williams received his BA from Idaho State, and the next year won an MA in music from Drake.

In New York, he continued his musical studies at Juilliard and also absorbed contemporary techniques from Teddy Wilson and Lennie Tristano. His big break came after he won the "Arthur Godfrey Talent Scout Show." David Kapp heard and signed him to a contract.

His first disk, "Autumn Leaves," which sold a million and a half, has been a consistent winner ever since. His current smash "Near You," is climbing high on The Billboard's charts and his album "Till" has long been a familiar face on The Billboard's album listings.

artists' biographies

Latest Disk Clicks For Betty Madigan

Songstress Betty Madigan, one of the real beauties in the recording field, has hit it real big with her latest Coral waxing of "Dance, Everyone, Dance," based on "Hava Negilla," the Israeli harvest song.

The thrush, who hails from Washington, D. C., was a local TV and radio and nightclub favorite, when she was discovered by publicist, Arthur Pine, who has been her personal manager for the past five years. Her third record, "Joey," zoomed her into national prominence, and her career has climbed steadily upward ever since.

As a result of the success of "Dance, Everyone, Dance," now scrambling up The Billboard's charts, she is well booked for many of the name spots in the Northeast.

America's Singing Sweetheart
Scores Again!
CONNIE
FRANCIS
SINGS
FALLIN'
HAPPY DAYS
AND
LONELY NIGHTS
K12713
M-G-M Records

The Billboard HOT 100

FOR THE WEEK ENDING OCTOBER 5

★ THE STAR PERFORMER designation shows the outstanding upward changes of position in The Hot 100 since last week's chart. Its purpose merely is to provide quick visual identification of the sides which moved up most dramatically or to new entries which first entered the chart at an unusually high position.

★ THE STAR PERFORMER designation shows the outstanding upward changes of position in The Hot 100 since last week's chart. Its purpose merely is to provide quick visual identification of the sides which moved up most dramatically or to new entries which first entered the chart at an unusually high position.

Three Weeks Ago	Two Weeks Ago	One Week Ago	This Week	★ Star Performer This Week	TITLE Artist, Company, Record Number	Weeks on Chart
11	4	3	1		IT'S ALL IN THE GAME — Tommy Edwards, M-G-M 12688	6
1	1	1	2		VOLARE (Nel Blu Dipinto Di Blu) — Domenico Modugno, Decca 30677	9
3	2	2	3		BIRD DOG — Everly Brothers, Cadence 1350	9
8	6	5	4		ROCK-IN' ROBIN — Bobby Day, Class 229	9
2	3	4	5		LITTLE STAR — Elegants, Apt 25005	9
13	9	7	6		TEARS ON MY PILLOW — Little Anthony and the Imperials, End 1027	8
28	10	8	7		SUSIE DARLIN' — Robin Luke, Dot 15781	8
31	16	11	8		SUMMERTIME BLUES — Eddie Cochran, Liberty 55144	9
4	5	6	9		JUST A DREAM — Jimmy Clanton, Ace 546	9
25	26	12	10		NEAR YOU — Roger Williams, Kapp 233	7
14	7	9	11		BORN TOO LATE — Poni Tails, ABC-Paramount 9934	9
22	14	10	12		DEVOTED TO YOU — Everly Brothers, Cadence 1350	8
58	25	14	13		HOW THE TIME FLIES — Jerry Wallace, Challenge 59013	7
44	31	20	14		TEA FOR TWO CHA CHA — Tommy Dorsey Ork, Decca 30704	5
—	87	49	15	★	THE END — Earl Grant, Decca 30719	3
34	35	34	16	★	CHANTILLY LACE — Big Bopper, Mercury 71343	9
20	18	17	17		STUPID CUPID — Connie Francis, M-G-M 12683	9
52	29	23	18		CAROL — Chuck Berry, Chess 1700	6
7	12	13	19		MY TRUE LOVE — Jack Scott, Carlton 462	9
5	11	15	20		PATRICIA — Perez Prado, RCA Victor 7245	9
46	33	31	21	★	YOU CHEATED — Shields, Dot 15805	6
18	19	18	22		EVERYBODY LOVES A LOVER — Doris Day, Columbia 41195	9
88	44	30	23		FIREFLY — Tony Bennett, Columbia 41237	4
27	23	21	24		LAZY SUMMER NIGHT — Four Preps, Capitol 4023	7
68	49	35	25	★	PROMISE ME, LOVE — Andy Williams, Cadence 1351	5
10	8	16	26		WESTERN MOVIES — Olympics, Demon 1508	9
23	20	22	27		DOWN THE AISLE OF LOVE — Quin-Tones, Hunt 321	7
48	30	26	28		SUMMERTIME, SUMMERTIME — Jamies, Epic 9281	7
16	15	24	29		ARE YOU REALLY MINE! — Jimmie Rodgers, Roulette 4090	9
43	37	28	30		NO ONE KNOWS — Dion and the Belmonts, Laurie 3015	6
15	21	29	31		VOLARE (Nel Blu Dipinto Di Blu) — Dean Martin, Capitol 4028	9
69	54	45	32		TREASURE OF YOUR LOVE — Eileen Rodgers, Columbia 41214	6
—	65	41	33		IT'S ONLY MAKE BELIEVE — Conway Twitty, M-G-M 12677	3
40	38	32	34		PUT A RING ON MY FINGER — Les Paul & Mary Ford, Columbia 41222	7
33	36	36	35		SOMEBODY TOUCHED ME — Buddy Knox, Roulette 4082	9
6	13	19	36		POOR LITTLE FOOL — Ricky Nelson, Imperial 5528	9
35	39	39	37		WIN YOUR LOVE FOR ME — Sam Cooke, Keen 2006	9
51	28	37	38		RAMROD — Duane Eddy, Jamie 1109	6
66	50	43	39		TOPSY II — Cozy Cole, Love 5004	6
12	22	33	40		FEVER — Peggy Lee, Capitol 3998	9
39	27	38	41		SHE WAS ONLY SEVENTEEN — Marty Robbins, Columbia 41208	9
36	47	57	42		ITCHY TWITCHY FEELING — Bobby Hendricks, Sue 706	9
—	70	47	43		THE SECRET — Gordon MacRae, Capitol 4033	3
26	42	61	44	★	LA PALOMA — Billy Vaughn, Dot 15795	8
70	63	62	45	★	LA-DO-DADA — Dale Hawkins, Checker 900	5
—	—	69	46	★	GEE, BUT IT'S LONELY — Pat Boone, Dot 15825	2
17	32	42	47		WILLIE AND THE HAND JIVE — Johnny Otis Show, Capitol 3966	9
—	—	56	48		FIBBIN' — Patti Page, Mercury 71355	2
—	59	46	49		THE TEN COMMANDMENTS OF LOVE — Harvey and the Moonglows, Chess 1705	3
59	48	44	50		THE GREEN MOSQUITO — Tune-Rockers, United Artists 139	6
—	76	65	51		MEXICAN HAT ROCK — Applejacks, Cameo 149	3
—	73	70	52	★	BREAKUP — Jerry Lee Lewis, Sun 303	3
—	—	60	53		THE DAY THE RAINS CAME — Jane Morgan, Kapp 235	2
—	—	81	54	★	HIDEAWAY — Four Esquires, Paris 520	2
—	—	54	55		FOR MY GOOD FORTUNE — Pat Boone, Dot 15825	2
—	72	63	56		BABY FACE — Little Richard, Specialty 645	3
—	100	74	57	★	THIS LITTLE GIRL'S GONE ROCKIN' — Ruth Brown, Atlantic 1197	3
53	60	48	58		OVER AND OVER — Bobby Day, Class 229	9
—	—	—	59	★	NO ONE BUT YOU — Ames Brothers, RCA Victor 7315	1
—	—	—	60	★	PUSSY CAT — Ames Brothers, RCA Victor 7315	1

THE INDUSTRY'S FASTEST AND MOST COMPLETE PROGRAMMING AND BUYING GUIDE

These 100 sides are listed in order of their national POPULARITY, as determined by weekly local studies prepared for The Billboard in markets representing a cross-section of the United States. These studies take into consideration such factors as disk jockey plays, juke box activity and record sales.

★ THE STAR PERFORMER designation shows the outstanding upward changes of position in The Hot 100 since last week's chart. Its purpose merely is to provide quick visual identification of the sides which moved up most dramatically or to new entries which first entered the chart at an unusually high position.

THREE WEEKS AGO	TWO WEEKS AGO	ONE WEEK AGO	THIS WEEK	★ STAR PERFORMER THIS WEEK	TITLE	Artist, Company, Record Number	WEEKS ON CHART
42	34	40	61		DANCE, EVERYONE, DANCE	Betty Madigan, Coral 62007	7
—	61	51	62		THERE GOES MY HEART	Joni James, M-G-M 12706	3
—	98	91	63		I WISH	Platters, Mercury 71353	3
9	17	27	64		GINGER BREAD	Frankie Avalon, Chancellor 1021	9
30	24	25	65		THE WAYS OF A WOMAN IN LOVE	Johnny Cash, Sun 302	6
—	—	—	66	★	LOOK WHO'S BLUE	Don Gibson, RCA Victor 7330	1
—	81	86	67	★	YOU CHEATED	Slades, Domino 500	7
89	74	50	68		BLUE-RIBBON BABY	Tommy Sands, Capitol 4036	5
—	—	76	69		NINE MORE MILES	Georgi Young, Cameo 150	2
62	66	79	70		CERVEZA	Boots Brown, RCA Victor 7269	8
41	51	53	71		COME CLOSER TO ME	Nat King Cole, Capitol 4004	9
—	—	—	72	★	WHEN I GROW TOO OLD TO DREAM	Ed Townsend, Capitol 4048	1
—	—	93	73	★	NOTHIN' SHAKIN'	Eddie Fontaine, Argo 5309	2
—	—	—	74	★	CALL ME	Johnny Mathis, Columbia 41253	1
—	—	84	75		WENDY WENDY	Four Coins, Epic 9286	2
—	—	77	76		COME ON, LET'S GO	Ritchie Valens, Del Fi 4106	2
77	94	78	77		PLEASE DON'T DO IT	Dale Wright, Fraternity 818	5
50	57	75	78		BETTY LOU GOT A NEW PAIR OF SHOES	Bobby Freeman, Josie 841	9
—	—	—	79	★	GIVE MYSELF A PARTY	Don Gibson, RCA Victor 7330	1
—	—	88	80		TO KNOW HIM IS TO LOVE HIM	Teddy Bears, Dore 503	2
24	55	82	81		IF DREAMS CAME TRUE	Pat Boone, Dot 15785	9
37	53	66	82		A CERTAIN SMILE	Johnny Mathis, Columbia 41193	9
—	—	—	83	★	TOM DOOLEY	Kingston Trio, Capitol 4049	1
87	62	67	84		OVER THE WEEKEND	Playboys, Cameo 142	5
—	—	85	85		REAL WILD CHILD	Ivan, Coral 62017	2
21	40	64	86		WHEN	Kalin Twins, Decca 30642	9
—	—	—	87	★	THE DAY I DIED	Playmates, Roulette 4100	1
—	92	71	88		TOPSY I	Cozy Cole, Love 5003	3
—	—	—	89	★	WITH YOUR LOVE	Jack Scott, Carlton 483	1
29	46	68	90		MOON TALK	Perry Como, RCA Victor 7274	9

From The Hot 100:

THE BILLBOARD'S BEST BUYS

These records, of all those listed on The Billboard Hot 100, have shown the greatest national SALES BREAK-OUT potential this week for the first time. Action sides are listed in capital letters.

GIVE MYSELF A PARTY .... **DON GIBSON**
LOOK WHO'S BLUE
(Acuff-Rose, BMI) (Acuff-Rose, BMI) RCA Victor 7330

WHEN I GROW TOO OLD TO DREAM .... **ED TOWNSEND**
(Robbins, ASCAP) You Are Everything (Beechwood, BMI) Capitol 4080

THIS LITTLE GIRL'S GONE ROCKIN' .... **RUTH BROWN**
(Leeds, ASCAP) Why Me (Eden-Progressive, BMI) Atlantic 1197

The above are previous Billboard Spotlight picks.

THE SECRET .... **GORDON MacRAE**
(Daywin, BMI) A Man Once Said (Morris, ASCAP) Capitol 4033

TREASURE OF YOUR LOVE .... **EILEEN RODGERS**
(DeVorzon, BMI) A Little Bit Bluer (Westside, BMI) Columbia 41214

HIDEAWAY .... **THE FOUR ESQUIRES**
(Gold, ASCAP) Repeat After Me (Greta, BMI) Paris 520

NO ONE BUT YOU .... **THE AMES BROTHERS**
PUSSY CAT
(Mellin, BMI) (Paxton, ASCAP) RCA Victor 7315

The correct publisher for "Fibbin'," one of last week's Best Buy selections, is Irish-Trojan, BMI.

★ THE STAR PERFORMER designation shows the outstanding upward changes of position in The Hot 100 since last week's chart. Its purpose merely is to provide quick visual identification of the sides which moved up most dramatically or to new entries which first entered the chart at an unusually high position.

THREE WEEKS AGO	TWO WEEKS AGO	ONE WEEK AGO	THIS WEEK	★ STAR PERFORMER THIS WEEK	TITLE	Artist, Company, Record Number	WEEKS ON CHART
—	—	—	91		BULLWHIP ROCK	Cyclones, Trophy 500	1
—	—	—	92		TIC TOC	Lee Allen, Ember 1039	1
—	—	96	93		WE HAVE LOVE	Jackie Wilson, Brunswick 55086	2
—	—	97	94		YOU GOT THAT TOUCH	Sonny James, Capitol 4020	2
72	99	83	95		YOUR CHEATIN' HEART	George Hamilton IV, ABC-Paramount 9946	4
—	—	—	96		LEAVE ME ALONE	Dickey Doo & the Don'ts, Swan 4014	1
—	—	98	97		MANY A TIME	Steve Lawrence, Coral 62025	2
38	69	73	98		EARLY IN THE MORNING	Bobby Darin and the Rinky Dinks, Atco 6121	9
95	88	—	99		THUNDER ROAD	Robert Mitchum, Capitol 3986	3
—	—	—	100		FORGET ME NOT	Kalin Twins, Decca 30745	1

BEST SELLING POP SINGLES IN STORES

NEW YORK UNIVERSITY SCHOOL OF RETAILING — STORE RECORDED SALES — THE BILLBOARD

The information given in this chart is based on actual sales to customers in a scientific sample of the nation's retail outlets during the week ending on the date shown above. Sample design, sample size, and all methods used in this continuing study of retail record sales are under the direct and continuing supervision and control of the School of Retailing of New York University.

FOR SURVEY WEEK ENDING SEPTEMBER 20, 1958

This Week		Last Week	Weeks on Chart
1.	IT'S ALL IN THE GAME (ASCAP)—Tommy Edwards Please Love Me Forever (BMI)—MGM 12688	3	6
2.	VOLARE (Nel Blu Dipinto Di Blu) (ASCAP)—Domenico Modugno Narti In Citta (BMI)—Dec 30677	1	9
3.	BIRD DOG (BMI)—Everly Brothers DEVOTED TO YOU (BMI)—Cadence 1350	2	8
4.	ROCK-IN' ROBIN (BMI)—Bobby Day OVER AND OVER (BMI)—Class 229	5	8
5.	LITTLE STAR (BMI)—Elegants Getting Dizzy (BMI)—Apt 25005	4	10
6.	PATRICIA (ASCAP)—Perez Prado Why Wait? (BMI)—Vic 7245	6	15
7.	TEARS ON MY PILLOW (ASCAP)—Little Anthony and the Imperials Two People in the World (BMI)—End 1027	8	7
8.	SUSIE DARLIN' (ASCAP)—Robin Luke Living's Loving You (ASCAP)—Dot 15781	13	7
9.	TEA FOR TWO CHA CHA (ASCAP)—Tommy Dorsey Ork My Baby Just Cares for Me (ASCAP)—Decca 30704	22	3
10.	JUST A DREAM (BMI)—Jimmy Clanton You Aim to Please (BMI)—Ace 546	7	12
11.	MY TRUE LOVE (BMI)—Jack Scott LEROY (BMI)—Carlton 462	10	16
12.	POOR LITTLE FOOL (BMI)—Ricky Nelson Don't Leave Me This Way (BMI)—Imperial 5528	9	13
13.	SUMMERTIME BLUES (BMI)—Eddie Cochran Love Again (BMI)—Liberty 55144	17	6
14.	STUPID CUPID (BMI)—Connie Francis Carolina Moon (ASCAP)—MGM 12683	24	10
15.	BORN TOO LATE (ASCAP)—Poni Tails Come On, Joey, Dance With Me (BMI)—ABC-Paramount 9934	11	10
16.	NEAR YOU (ASCAP)—Roger Williams Merry Widow Waltz (ASCAP)—Kapp 233	23	4
17.	ARE YOU REALLY MINE? (ASCAP)—Jimmie Rodgers THE WIZARD (ASCAP)—Roulette 4090	14	8
18.	GINGER BREAD (BMI)—Frankie Avalon Blue Betty (ASCAP)—Chancellor 1021	16	11
19.	FEVER (BMI)—Peggy Lee You Don't Know (BMI)—Cap 3998	25	11
20.	LA PALOMA (ASCAP)—Billy Vaughn Here Is My Love (ASCAP)—Dot 15795	20	7
21.	WESTERN MOVIES (BMI)—Olympics Well! (BMI)—Demon 1508	12	10
22.	YOU CHEATED (BMI)—Shields That's the Way It's Gonna Be (BMI)—Dot 15805	26	3
23.	CERVEZA (BMI)—Boots Brown Juicy (BMI)—Vic 7269	28	5
24.	VOLARE (Nel Blu Dipinto Di Blu) (ASCAP)—Dean Martin Outta My Mind (ASCAP)—Cap 4028	15	8
25.	NO ONE KNOWS (ASCAP)—Dion and the Belmonts I Can't Go On (Rosalie) (BMI)—Laurie 3015	33	4
26.	THE END (ASCAP)—Earl Grant Dunky Doo (ASCAP)—Decca 30719	47	2
27.	CHANTILLY LACE (BMI)—Big Bopper Purple People Eater Meets the Witch Doctor (BMI)—Mercury 71343	—	1
28.	EVERYBODY LOVES A LOVER (ASCAP)—Doris Day Instant Love (ASCAP)—Col 41195	21	10
29.	WILLIE AND THE HAND JIVE (BMI)—Johnny Otis Show Ring-A-Ling (BMI)—Cap 3966	19	14
30.	TOPSY II (BMI)—Cozy Cole Topsy I (BMI)—Love 50034	44	3
31.	SUMMERTIME, SUMMERTIME (ASCAP)—The Jamies Searching for You (ASCAP)—Epic 9281	39	4
32.	REBEL-'ROUSER (BMI)—Duane Eddy Stalkin' (BMI)—Jamie 1104	41	13
33.	DOWN THE AISLE OF LOVE (BMI)—The Quin-Tones Please, Dear (BMI)—Hunt 321	18	4
34.	WIN YOUR LOVE FOR ME (BMI)—Sam Cooke Love Song From "Houseboat" (ASCAP)—Keen 32006	29	4
35.	LAZY SUMMER NIGHT (ASCAP)—Four Preps SUMMERTIME LIES (ASCAP)—Cap 4023	37	5
36.	PUSSY CAT (ASCAP)—Ames Brothers No One But You (BMI)—Vic 7315	—	1
37.	RAMROD (BMI)—Duane Eddy The Walker (BMI)—Jamie 1109	27	5
38.	WEEK END (BMI)—Kingsmen Better Believe It (BMI)—East West 115	35	2
39.	HARD HEADED WOMAN (ASCAP)—Elvis Presley DON'T ASK ME WHY (ASCAP)—Vic 7280	32	14
40.	SOMEBODY TOUCHED ME (BMI)—Buddy Knox C'mon, Baby (BMI)—Roulette 4082	—	4
41.	TEN COMMANDMENTS OF LOVE (BMI)—Harvey and the Moonglows Mean Old Blues (BMI)—Chess 1705	—	1
42.	HOW THE TIME FLIES (ASCAP)—Jerry Wallace With This Ring (BMI)—Challenge 59013	40	3
43.	WHEN (ASCAP)—Kalin Twins Three o'Clock Thrill (BMI)—Dec 30642	30	14
44.	PUT A RING ON MY FINGER (BMI)—Les Paul and Mary Ford Fantasy (BMI)—Col 41222	50	3
45.	ITCHY TWITCHY FEELING (BMI)—Bobby Hendricks A Thousand Dreams (BMI)—Sue 706	36	5
46.	IF DREAMS CAME TRUE (ASCAP)—Pat Boone THAT'S HOW MUCH I LOVE YOU (BMI)—Dot 15785	43	12
47.	THE WAYS OF A WOMAN IN LOVE (BMI)—Johnny Cash YOU'RE THE NEAREST THING TO HEAVEN (BMI)—Sun 302	31	5
48.	SPLISH SPLASH (BMI)—Bobby Darin Judy, Don't Be Moody (BMI)—Atco 6117	38	15
49.	LA-DO-DADA (BMI)—Dale Hawkins Cross-Ties (BMI)—Chess 900	47	2
50.	WHAT AM I LIVING FOR? (BMI)—Chuck Willis Hang Up My Rock and Roll Shoes (BMI)—Atlantic 1179	—	19

artists' biographies

Grant Begins to Soar Via 'The End'

Twenty-six-year-old Earl Grant is a triple threat. Pianist, organist and vocalist, the slim, Kansas City native originally planned to teach music. He studied at the University of Southern California, the Kansas City Conservatory of Music, the New Rochelle Conservatory in New York and De Paul University in Chicago.

Grant's teaching plans were interrupted by a stint in the Army, after which he returned to USC as a graduate student. While working on his thesis, he started to play in small clubs in the Los Angeles area. He was soon spotted by people in the music business, and as a result his career plans were changed once again.

Local club and TV appearances and a Decca recording pact have put Grant in the public eye. His latest release, "The End," is climbing Billboard's charts by leaps and bounds.

artists' biographies

The Jamies Blossom In 'Summertime'

The Jamies started singing together in the choir of the First Baptist Church in Dorchester, Mass. Tom Jameson, a student at Boston University's School of Music, does all the arranging for the group and wrote both "Summertime, Summertime" and "Searching for You."

Serena Jameson, his sister, petite, big-voiced Jeannie Roy and bass Arthur Blair, are the other members of the quartet. Sherm Feller of Boston's Radio Station WEZE listened to the four voices on a dub Tom Jameson brought to his office. He liked what he heard, and afterwards things started happening.

The kids signed with Epic, waxed "Summertime" and spent their summer vacation making personal appearances. They've been on radio, TV and record hops and on Dick Clark's Bandstand.

THE HOTTEST ARTIST IN THE BUSINESS!
5 In A Row...Over A Million!!
RICKY
NELSON
I GOT A FEELING
LONESOME TOWN
RICKY
NELSON
SINGS
#5545
IMPERIAL RECORDS
6425 Hollywood Blvd., Hollywood, Calif.
IN CANADA • LONDON RECORDS, Ltd.

The Billboard HOT 100

FOR THE WEEK ENDING OCTOBER 12

★ THE STAR PERFORMER designation shows the outstanding upward changes of position in The Hot 100 since last week's chart. Its purpose merely is to provide quick visual identification of the sides which moved up most dramatically or to new entries which first entered the chart at an unusually high position.

THREE WEEKS AGO	TWO WEEKS AGO	ONE WEEK AGO	THIS WEEK	★ STAR PERFORMER THIS WEEK	TITLE Artist, Company, Record Number	WEEKS ON CHART
4	3	1	1		IT'S ALL IN THE GAME — Tommy Edwards, M-G-M 12688	7
2	2	3	2		BIRD DOG — Everly Brothers, Cadence 1350	10
6	5	4	3		ROCK-IN' ROBIN — Bobby Day, Class 229	10
1	1	2	4		VOLARE (Nel Blu Dipinto Di Blu) — Domenico Modugno, Decca 30677	10
3	4	5	5		LITTLE STAR — Elegants, Apt 25005	10
9	7	6	6		TEARS ON MY PILLOW — Little Anthony and the Imperials, End 1027	9
10	8	7	7		SUSIE DARLIN' — Robin Luke, Dot 15781	9
31	20	14	8		TEA FOR TWO CHA CHA — Tommy Dorsey Ork, Decca 30704	6
16	11	8	9		SUMMERTIME BLUES — Eddie Cochran, Liberty 55144	10
26	12	10	10		NEAR YOU — Roger Williams, Kapp 233	8
25	14	13	11		HOW THE TIME FLIES — Jerry Wallace, Challenge 59013	8
5	6	9	12		JUST A DREAM — Jimmy Clanton, Ace 546	10
87	49	15	13		THE END — Earl Grant, Decca 30719	4
7	9	11	14		BORN TOO LATE — Poni Tails, ABC-Paramount 9934	10
35	34	16	15		CHANTILLY LACE — Big Bopper, Mercury 71343	10
33	31	21	16		YOU CHEATED — Shields, Dot 15805	7
49	35	25	17		PROMISE ME, LOVE — Andy Williams, Cadence 1351	6
11	15	20	18		PATRICIA — Perez Prado, RCA Victor 7245	10
29	23	18	19		CAROL — Chuck Berry, Chess 1700	7
65	41	33	20	★	IT'S ONLY MAKE BELIEVE — Conway Twitty, M-G-M 12677	4
14	10	12	21		DEVOTED TO YOU — Everly Brothers, Cadence 1350	9
50	43	39	22	★	TOPSY II — Cozy Cole, Love 50034	7
44	30	23	23		FIREFLY — Tony Bennett, Columbia 41237	5
12	13	19	24		MY TRUE LOVE — Jack Scott, Carlton 462	10
47	57	42	25	★	ITCHY TWITCHY FEELING — Bobby Hendricks, Sue 706	10
54	45	32	26		TREASURE OF YOUR LOVE — Eileen Rodgers, Columbia 41214	7
37	28	30	27		NO ONE KNOWS — Dion and the Belmonts, Laurie 3015	7
18	17	17	28		STUPID CUPID — Connie Francis, M-G-M 12683	10
36	36	35	29		SOMEBODY TOUCHED ME — Buddy Knox, Roulette 4082	10
15	24	29	30		ARE YOU REALLY MINE! — Jimmie Rodgers, Roulette 4090	10
20	22	27	31		DOWN THE AISLE OF LOVE — Quin-Tones, Hunt 321	8
8	16	26	32		WESTERN MOVIES — Olympics, Demon 1508	10
23	21	24	33		LAZY SUMMER NIGHT — Four Preps, Capitol 4023	8
—	—	60	34	★	PUSSY CAT — Ames Brothers, RCA Victor 7315	2
—	69	46	35	★	GEE, BUT IT'S LONELY — Pat Boone, Dot 15825	3
30	26	28	36		SUMMERTIME, SUMMERTIME — Jamies, Epic 9281	8
—	—	83	37	★	TOM DOOLEY — Kingston Trio, Capitol 4049	2
22	33	40	38		FEVER — Peggy Lee, Capitol 3998	10
70	47	43	39		THE SECRET — Gordon MacRae, Capitol 4033	4
76	65	51	40	★	MEXICAN HAT ROCK — Applejacks, Cameo 149	4
39	39	37	41		WIN YOUR LOVE FOR ME — Sam Cooke, Keen 2006	10
98	91	63	42	★	I WISH — Platters, Mercury 71353	4
21	29	31	43		VOLARE (Nel Blu Dipinto Di Blu) — Dean Martin, Capitol 4028	10
63	62	45	44		LA-DO-DADA — Dale Hawkins, Checker 900	6
19	18	22	45		EVERYBODY LOVES A LOVER — Doris Day, Columbia 41195	10
—	56	48	46		FIBBIN' — Patti Page, Mercury 71355	3
13	19	36	47		POOR LITTLE FOOL — Ricky Nelson, Imperial 5528	10
—	60	53	48		THE DAY THE RAINS CAME — Jane Morgan, Kapp 235	3
28	37	38	49		RAMROD — Duane Eddy, Jamie 1109	7
100	74	57	50		THIS LITTLE GIRL'S GONE ROCKIN' — Ruth Brown, Atlantic 1197	4
61	51	62	51		THERE GOES MY HEART — Joni James, M-G-M 12706	4
38	32	34	52		PUT A RING ON MY FINGER — Les Paul & Mary Ford, Columbia 41222	8
42	61	44	53		LA PALOMA — Billy Vaughn, Dot 15795	9
—	54	55	54		FOR MY GOOD FORTUNE — Pat Boone, Dot 15825	3
72	63	56	55		BABY FACE — Little Richard, Specialty 645	4
—	88	80	56	★	TO KNOW HIM IS TO LOVE HIM — Teddy Bears, Dore 503	3
—	81	54	57		HIDEAWAY — Four Esquires, Paris 520	3
27	38	41	58		SHE WAS ONLY SEVENTEEN — Marty Robbins, Columbia 41208	10
—	—	72	59	★	WHEN I GROW TOO OLD TO DREAM — Ed Townsend, Capitol 4048	2
—	—	74	60		CALL ME — Johnny Mathis, Columbia 41253	2

★ THE STAR PERFORMER designation shows the outstanding upward changes of position in The Hot 100 since last week's chart. Its purpose merely is to provide quick visual identification of the sides which moved up most dramatically or to new entries which first entered the chart at an unusually high position.

THE INDUSTRY'S FASTEST AND MOST COMPLETE PROGRAMMING AND BUYING GUIDE

These 100 sides are listed in order of their national POPULARITY, as determined by weekly local studies prepared for The Billboard in markets representing a cross-section of the United States. These studies take into consideration such factors as disk jockey plays, juke box activity and record sales.

★ THE STAR PERFORMER designation shows the outstanding upward changes of position in The Hot 100 since last week's chart. Its purpose merely is to provide quick visual identification of the sides which moved up most dramatically or to new entries which first entered the chart at an unusually high position.

Three Weeks Ago	Two Weeks Ago	One Week Ago	This Week	★ Star Performer This Week	Title — Artist, Company, Record Number	Weeks on Chart
48	44	50	61		THE GREEN MOSQUITO — Tune-Rockers, United Artists 139	7
—	—	66	62		LOOK WHO'S BLUE — Don Gibson, RCA Victor 7330	2
—	76	69	63		NINE MORE MILES — Georgie Young, Cameo 150	3
—	93	73	64		NOTHIN' SHAKIN' — Eddie Fontaine, Argo 5309	3
—	—	59	65		NO ONE BUT YOU — Ames Brothers, RCA Victor 7315	2
17	27	64	66		GINGER BREAD — Frankie Avalon, Chancellor 1021	10
32	42	47	67		WILLIE AND THE HAND JIVE — Johnny Otis Show, Capitol 3966	10
59	46	49	68		THE TEN COMMANDMENTS OF LOVE — Harvey and the Moonglows, Chess 1705	4
—	—	—	69	★	HOOPA HOOLA — Betty Johnson, Atlantic 2202	1
24	25	65	70		THE WAYS OF A WOMAN IN LOVE — Johnny Cash, Sun 302	7
—	—	79	71		GIVE MYSELF A PARTY — Don Gibson, RCA Victor 7330	2
—	84	75	72		WENDY WENDY — Four Coins, Epic 9286	3
—	—	—	73	★	HOOLA HOOP SONG — Georgia Gibbs, Roulette 4106	1
—	—	89	74	★	WITH YOUR LOVE — Jack Scott, Carlton 483	2
—	—	100	75	★	FORGET ME NOT — Kalin Twins, Decca 30745	2
81	86	67	76		YOU CHEATED — Slades, Domino 500	8
62	67	84	77		OVER THE WEEKEND — Playboys, Cameo 142	6
92	71	88	78		TOPSY I — Cozy Cole, Love 50034	4
88	—	99	79	★	THUNDER ROAD — Robert Mitchum, Capitol 3986	4
73	70	52	80		BREAKUP — Jerry Lee Lewis, Sun 303	4
—	—	87	81		THE DAY I DIED — Playmates, Roulette 4100	2
55	82	81	82		IF DREAMS CAME TRUE — Pat Boone, Dot 15785	10
—	—	91	83		BULLWHIP ROCK — Cyclones, Trophy 500	2
—	77	76	84		COME ON, LET'S GO — Ritchie Valens, Del Fi 4106	3
74	50	68	85		BLUE-RIBBON BABY — Tommy Sands, Capitol 4036	6
—	—	96	86		LEAVE ME ALONE — Dickey Doo & the Don'ts, Swan 4014	2
—	—	—	87	★	WELL, I'M YOUR MAN — Johnny Tillotson, Cadence 1353	1
—	—	—	88	★	ALL OVER AGAIN — Johnny Cash, Columbia 41251	1
—	85	85	89		REAL WILD CHILD — Ivan, Coral 62017	3
—	—	—	90		A LOVER'S QUESTION — Clyde McPhatter, Atlantic 1199	1
60	48	58	91		OVER AND OVER — Bobby Day, Class 229	10
—	—	—	92		NEED YOU — Donnie Owens, Guyden 2001	1
—	—	—	93		IT'S RAINING OUTSIDE — The Platters, Mercury 71353	1
34	40	61	94		DANCE, EVERYONE, DANCE — Betty Madigan, Coral 62007	8
—	—	—	95		QUEEN OF THE HOP — Bobby Darin, Atco 6127	1
—	—	—	96		FRIED ONIONS — Lord Rockingham's XI, London 1810	1
—	—	—	97		THE BLOB — The Five Blobs, Columbia 41250	1
—	—	—	98		JUST YOUNG — Paul Anka, ABC-Paramount 9956	1
—	—	—	99		THE HULA HOOP SONG — Teresa Brewer, Coral 62003	1
—	—	—	100		JUST YOUNG — Andy Rose, Aamco 100	1

From The Hot 100:

THE BILLBOARD'S BEST BUYS

These records, of all those listed on The Billboard Hot 100, have shown the greatest national SALES BREAK-OUT potential this week for the first time. Action sides are listed in capital letters.

TOM DOOLEY .... **The Kingston Trio**
(Beechwood, BMI) Ruby Red (Shapiro-Bernstein, ASCAP) Capitol 4049

CALL ME .... **Johnny Mathis**
(Meridian, BMI) Stairway to the Sea (Leeds, ASCAP) Columbia 41253

ALL OVER AGAIN .... **Johnny Cash**
(Cash, BMI) What Do I Care (Cash, BMI) Columbia 41251

FORGET ME NOT .... **The Kalin Twins**
(Aldon, BMI) Dream of Me (Ample, BMI) Decca 30745

NINE MORE MILES .... **Georgie Young**
(Lowe, ASCAP) The Sneak (Mayland, BMI) Cameo 150

WITH YOUR LOVE .... **Jack Scott**
(Starfire, BMI) Geraldine (Starfire, BMI) Carlton 483

The above are previous Billboard Spotlight picks.

I WISH
IT'S RAINING OUTSIDE .... **The Platters**
(A.M.C., ASCAP) (A.M.C., ASCAP) Mercury 71353

NEW YORK UNIVERSITY SCHOOL OF RETAILING · STORE RECORDED SALES · THE BILLBOARD

BEST SELLING POP SINGLES IN STORES

The information given in this chart is based on actual sales to customers in a scientific sample of the nation's retail outlets during the week ending on the date shown above. Sample design, sample size, and all methods used in this continuing study of retail record sales are under the direct and continuing supervision and control of the School of Retailing of New York University.

FOR SURVEY WEEK ENDING SEPTEMBER 27, 1958

This Week	Title	Last Week	Weeks on Chart
1.	IT'S ALL IN THE GAME (ASCAP)—Tommy Edwards Please Love Me Forever (BMI)—MGM 12688	1	7
2.	VOLARE (Nel Blu Dipinto Di Blu) (ASCAP)—Domenico Modugno Mariti In Citta (BMI)—Dec 30677	2	10
3.	BIRD DOG (BMI)—Everly Brothers DEVOTED TO YOU (BMI)—Cadence 1350	3	9
4.	ROCK-IN' ROBIN (BMI)—Bobby Day OVER AND OVER (BMI)—Class 229	4	9
5.	LITTLE STAR (BMI)—Elegants Getting Dizzy (BMI)—Apt 25005	5	11
6.	SUSIE DARLIN' (ASCAP)—Robin Luke Living's Loving You (ASCAP)—Dot 15781	8	8
7.	TEARS ON MY PILLOW (ASCAP)—Little Anthony and the Imperials Two People in the World (BMI)—End 1027	7	8
8.	PATRICIA (ASCAP)—Perez Prado Why Wait? (BMI)—Vic 7245	6	16
9.	TEA FOR TWO CHA CHA (ASCAP)—Tommy Dorsey Ork My Baby Just Cares for Me (ASCAP)—Decca 30704	9	4
10.	JUST A DREAM (BMI)—Jimmy Clanton You Aim to Please (BMI)—Ace 546	10	13
11.	MY TRUE LOVE (BMI)—Jack Scott LEROY (BMI)—Carlton 462	11	17
12.	YOU CHEATED (BMI)—Shields That's the Way It's Gonna Be (BMI)—Dot 15805	22	4
13.	SUMMERTIME BLUES (BMI)—Eddie Cochran Love Again (BMI)—Liberty 55144	13	7
14.	FEVER (BMI)—Peggy Lee You Don't Know (BMI)—Cap 3998	19	12
15.	TOPSY II (BMI)—Cozy Cole TOPSY I (BMI)—Love 50034	30	4
16.	CHANTILLY LACE (BMI)—Big Bopper Purple People Eater Meets the Witch Doctor (BMI)—Mercury 71343	27	2
17.	NEAR YOU (ASCAP)—Roger Williams Merry Widow Waltz (ASCAP)—Kapp 233	16	5
18.	VOLARE (Nel Blu Dipinto Di Blu) (ASCAP)—Dean Martin Outta My Mind (ASCAP)—Cap 4028	24	9
19.	STUPID CUPID (BMI)—Connie Francis Carolina Moon (ASCAP)—MGM 12683	14	11
20.	NO ONE KNOWS (ASCAP)—Dion and the Belmonts I Can't Go On (Rosalie) (BMI)—Laurie 3015	25	5
21.	POOR LITTLE FOOL (BMI)—Ricky Nelson Don't Leave Me This Way (BMI)—Imperial 5528	12	14
22.	ARE YOU REALLY MINE? (ASCAP)—Jimmie Rodgers THE WIZARD (ASCAP)—Roulette 4090	17	8
23.	LA PALOMA (ASCAP)—Billy Vaughn Here Is My Love (ASCAP)—Dot 15795	20	8
24.	BORN TOO LATE (ASCAP)—Poni Tails Come On, Joey, Dance With Me (BMI)—ABC-Paramount 9934	15	11
25.	WESTERN MOVIES (BMI)—Olympics Well! (BMI)—Demon 1508	21	11
26.	DOWN THE AISLE OF LOVE (BMI)—Quin-Tones Please, Dear (BMI)—Hunt 321	33	5
18.	GINGER BREAD (BMI)—Frankie Avalon Blue Betty (ASCAP)—Chancellor 1021	18	12
28.	SUMMERTIME, SUMMERTIME (ASCAP)—Jamies Searching for You (ASCAP)—Epic 9281	31	5
29.	CAROL (BMI)—Chuck Berry Hey, Pedro (BMI)—Chess 1700	—	1
29.	FOR MY GOOD FORTUNE (BMI)—Pat Boone GEE, BUT IT'S LONELY (BMI)—Dot 15825	—	1
31.	THE END (ASCAP)—Earl Grant Hunky Dunky Doo (ASCAP)—Decca 30719	26	3
32.	SOMEBODY TOUCHED ME (BMI)—Buddy Knox C'mon, Baby (BMI)—Roulette 4082	40	5
33.	HOW THE TIME FLIES (ASCAP)—Jerry Wallace With This Ring (BMI)—Challenge 59013	42	4
34.	MEXICAN HAT ROCK (BMI)—Applejacks Sophisticated Swing (ASCAP)—Cameo 149	—	1
35.	PUSSY CAT (ASCAP)—Ames Brothers No One But You (BMI)—Vic 7315	36	2
36.	THE WAYS OF A WOMAN IN LOVE (BMI)—Johnny Cash YOU'RE THE NEAREST THING TO HEAVEN (BMI)—Sun 302	47	6
37.	WIN YOUR LOVE FOR ME (BMI)—Sam Cooke Love Song From "Houseboat" (ASCAP)—Keen 32006	34	5
38.	RAMROD (BMI)—Duane Eddy The Walker (BMI)—Jamie 1109	37	6
39.	EVERYBODY LOVES A LOVER (ASCAP)—Doris Day Instant Love (ASCAP)—Col 41195	28	11
40.	WILLIE AND THE HAND JIVE (BMI)—Johnny Otis Show Ring-a-Ling (BMI)—Cap 3966	29	15
41.	REBEL-'ROUSER (BMI)—Duane Eddy Stalkin' (BMI)—Jamie 1104	32	14
42.	HARD HEADED WOMAN (ASCAP)—Elvis Presley DON'T ASK ME WHY (ASCAP)—Vic 7280	39	15
43.	ITCHY TWITCHY FEELING (BMI)—Bobby Hendricks A Thousand Dreams (BMI)—Sue 706	45	6
44.	TEN COMMANDMENTS OF LOVE (BMI)—Harvey and the Moonglows Mean Old Blues (BMI)—Chess 1705	41	2
45.	LA-DO-DADA (BMI)—Dale Hawkins Cross-Ties (BMI)—Chess 900	49	3
46.	I WISH (ASCAP)—Platters It's Raining Outside (ASCAP)—Mercury 71353	—	1
46.	IT'S ONLY MAKE BELIEVE (BMI)—Conway Twitty I'll Try (BMI)—MGM 12677	—	1
48.	A CERTAIN SMILE (ASCAP)—Johnny Mathis Let It Rain (ASCAP)—Col 41193	—	13
49.	WHEN (ASCAP)—Kalin Twins Three o'Clock Thrill (BMI)—Dec 30642	43	15
50.	COME CLOSER TO ME (BMI)—Nat King Cole Nothing in the World—Cap 4004	—	5

artists' biographies

E. Rodgers Scores Hit With 'Treasure'

Eileen Rodgers, Columbia thrush whose "Treasure of Your Love" is attracting wide interest, hails from Pittsburgh. The 5' 8" brunette was overheard by night club owner Lenny Litman and pacted to a 12-week singing engagement. Next followed a tour of local clubs and an appearance on the Chicago TV show, "Courtesy Hours." During a subsequent booking at the Windy City's Town Casino, orchestra leader Charlie Spivak dropped by and heard Miss Rodgers. She was signed and was his featured vocalist for two years.

The the lass soloed in numerous Midwestern clubs. Coming East on the advice of her manager, George Claire, she auditioned for Mitch Miller. Her first waxing was made a week later. The brown-eyed warbler collects records as a hobby. Kay Starr and Frank Sinatra are her special favorites.

artists' biographies

Wallace Clicks With 'How the Time Flies'

Ex-Navy man Jerry Wallace is Missouri-born and California bred. The youth comes by his singing talent naturally. His mother had dabbled in show business for a while and achieved local fame as a torch singer. Wallace's dad was in the grocery business. One day the elder Mr. Wallace traded a crate of eggs for a guitar for his son's 14th birthday, and the gift stimulated the boy's interest in singing.

In high school, the singer excelled in baseball and track and became a pole-vault champion. Next came Navy duty, and the resolve to try his luck in the entertainment world. Wallace's night club debut was at Las Vegas' Golden Nugget. He has since been featured in other U. S. and Canadian clubs. Now free-lancing on TV and recording for Challenge Records, he's vaulting the charts with "How the Time Flies."

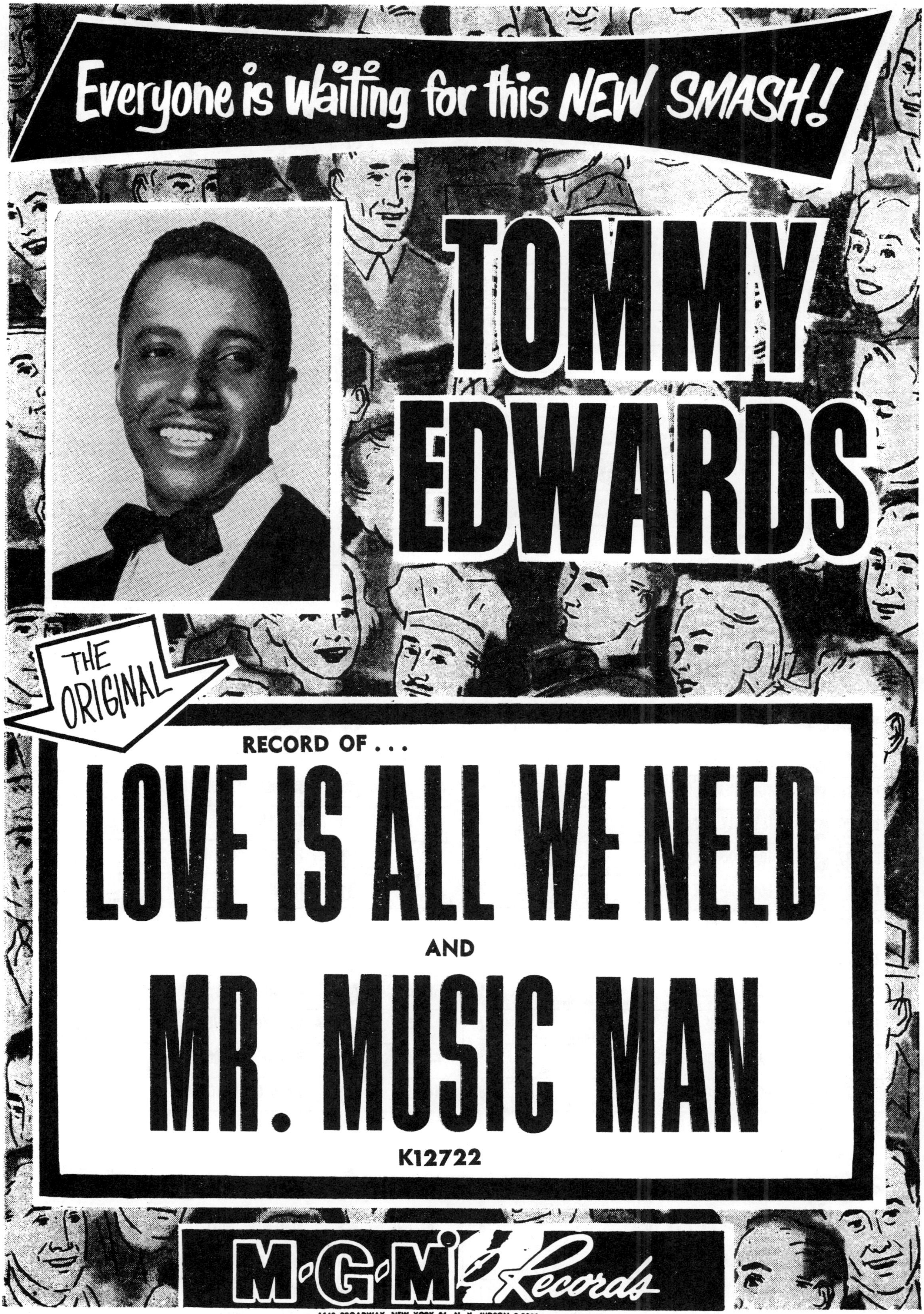
Everyone is Waiting for this NEW SMASH!
TOMMY EDWARDS
THE ORIGINAL
RECORD OF . . .
LOVE IS ALL WE NEED
AND
MR. MUSIC MAN
K12722
M-G-M Records
1540 BROADWAY, NEW YORK 36, N. Y. JUDSON 2-2000

The Billboard HOT 100

FOR THE WEEK ENDING OCTOBER 19

★ THE STAR PERFORMER designation shows the outstanding upward changes of position in The Hot 100 since last week's chart. Its purpose merely is to provide quick visual identification of the sides which moved up most dramatically or to new entries which first entered the chart at an unusually high position.

THREE WEEKS AGO	TWO WEEKS AGO	ONE WEEK AGO	THIS WEEK	★ STAR PERFORMER THIS WEEK	TITLE Artist, Company, Record Number	WEEKS ON CHART
3	1	1	1		IT'S ALL IN THE GAME — Tommy Edwards, M-G-M 12688	8
5	4	3	2		ROCK-IN' ROBIN — Bobby Day, Class 229	11
2	3	2	3		BIRD DOG — Everly Brothers, Cadence 1350	11
7	6	6	4		TEARS ON MY PILLOW — Little Anthony and the Imperials, End 1027	10
8	7	7	5		SUSIE DARLIN' — Robin Luke, Dot 15781	10
1	2	4	6		VOLARE (Nel Blu Dipinto Di Blu) — Domenico Modugno, Decca 30677	11
49	15	13	7		THE END — Earl Grant, Decca 30719	5
4	5	5	8		LITTLE STAR — Elegants, Apt 25005	11
20	14	8	9		TEA FOR TWO CHA CHA — Tommy Dorsey Ork, Decca 30704	7
12	10	10	10		NEAR YOU — Roger Williams, Kapp 233	9
34	16	15	11		CHANTILLY LACE — Big Bopper, Mercury 71343	11
11	8	9	12		SUMMERTIME BLUES — Eddie Cochran, Liberty 55144	11
43	39	22	13		TOPSY II — Cozy Cole, Love 50034	8
6	9	12	14		JUST A DREAM — Jimmy Clanton, Ace 546	11
31	21	16	15		YOU CHEATED — Shields, Dot 15805	8
41	33	20	16		IT'S ONLY MAKE BELIEVE — Conway Twitty, M-G-M 12677	5
—	83	37	17	★	TOM DOOLEY — Kingston Trio, Capitol 4049	3
14	13	11	18		HOW THE TIME FLIES — Jerry Wallace, Challenge 59013	9
10	12	21	19		DEVOTED TO YOU — Everly Brothers, Cadence 1350	10
30	23	23	20		FIREFLY — Tony Bennett, Columbia 41237	6
9	11	14	21		BORN TOO LATE — Poni Tails, ABC-Paramount 9934	11
35	25	17	22		PROMISE ME, LOVE — Andy Williams, Cadence 1351	7
54	55	54	23	★	FOR MY GOOD FORTUNE — Pat Boone, Dot 15825	4
28	30	27	24		NO ONE KNOWS — Dion and the Belmonts, Laurie 3015	8
60	53	48	25	★	THE DAY THE RAINS CAME — Jane Morgan, Kapp 235	4
24	29	30	26		ARE YOU REALLY MINE? — Jimmie Rodgers, Roulette 4090	11
65	51	40	27	★	MEXICAN HAT ROCK — Applejacks, Cameo 149	5
45	32	26	28		TREASURE OF YOUR LOVE — Eileen Rodgers, Columbia 41214	8
—	60	34	29		PUSSY CAT — Ames Brothers, RCA Victor 7315	3
15	20	18	30		PATRICIA — Perez Prado, RCA Victor 7245	11

★ THE STAR PERFORMER designation shows the outstanding upward changes of position in The Hot 100 since last week's chart. Its purpose merely is to provide quick visual identification of the sides which moved up most dramatically or to new entries which first entered the chart at an unusually high position.

THREE WEEKS AGO	TWO WEEKS AGO	ONE WEEK AGO	THIS WEEK	★ STAR PERFORMER THIS WEEK	TITLE Artist, Company, Record Number	WEEKS ON CHART
13	19	24	31		MY TRUE LOVE — Jack Scott, Carlton 462	11
62	45	44	32	★	LA-DO-DADA — Dale Hawkins, Checker 900	7
39	37	41	33		WIN YOUR LOVE FOR ME — Sam Cooke, Keen 2006	11
23	18	19	34		CAROL — Chuck Berry, Chess 1700	8
22	27	31	35		DOWN THE AISLE OF LOVE — Quin-Tones, Hunt 321	9
57	42	25	36		ITCHY TWITCHY FEELING — Bobby Hendricks, Sue 706	11
36	35	29	37		SOMEBODY TOUCHED ME — Buddy Knox, Roulette 4082	11
74	57	50	38	★	THIS LITTLE GIRL'S GONE ROCKIN' — Ruth Brown, Atlantic 1197	5
47	43	39	39		THE SECRET — Gordon MacRae, Capitol 4033	5
88	80	56	40	★	TO KNOW HIM IS TO LOVE HIM — Teddy Bears, Dore 503	4
46	49	68	41	★	THE TEN COMMANDMENTS OF LOVE — Harvey and the Moon Glows, Chess 1705	5
16	26	32	42		WESTERN MOVIES — Olympics, Demon 1508	11
17	17	28	43		STUPID CUPID — Connie Francis, M-G-M 12683	11
69	46	35	44		GEE, BUT IT'S LONELY — Pat Boone, Dot 15825	4
26	28	36	45		SUMMERTIME, SUMMERTIME — Jamies, Epic 9281	9
—	74	60	46		CALL ME — Johnny Mathis, Columbia 41253	3
—	—	73	47	★	THE HULA HOOP SONG — Georgia Gibbs, Roulette 4106	2
56	48	46	48		FIBBIN' — Patti Page, Mercury 71355	4
32	34	52	49		PUT A RING ON MY FINGER — Les Paul & Mary Ford, Columbia 41222	9
63	56	55	50		BABY FACE — Little Richard, Specialty 645	5
91	63	42	51		I WISH — Platters, Mercury 71353	5
—	89	74	52	★	WITH YOUR LOVE — Jack Scott, Carlton 483	3
—	59	65	53		NO ONE BUT YOU — Ames Brothers, RCA Victor 7315	3
44	50	61	54		THE GREEN MOSQUITO — Tune-Rockers, United Artists 139	8
71	88	78	55	★	TOPSY I — Cozy Cole, Love 50034	5
33	40	38	56		FEVER — Peggy Lee, Capitol 3998	11
18	22	45	57		EVERYBODY LOVES A LOVER — Doris Day, Columbia 41198	11
76	69	63	58		NINE MORE MILES — Georgie Young, Cameo 150	4
—	72	59	59		WHEN I GROW TOO OLD TO DREAM — Ed Townsend, Capitol 4048	3
86	67	76	60	★	YOU CHEATED — Slades, Domino 800	9

THE INDUSTRY'S FASTEST AND MOST COMPLETE PROGRAMMING AND BUYING GUIDE

These 100 sides are listed in order of their national POPULARITY, as determined by weekly local studies prepared for The Billboard in markets representing a cross-section of the United States. These studies take into consideration such factors as disk jockey plays, juke box activity and record sales.

★ THE STAR PERFORMER designation shows the outstanding upward changes of position in The Hot 100 since last week's chart. Its purpose merely is to provide quick visual identification of the sides which moved up most dramatically or to new entries which first entered the chart at an unusually high position.

THREE WEEKS AGO	TWO WEEKS AGO	ONE WEEK AGO	THIS WEEK	★ STAR PERFORMER THIS WEEK	TITLE Artist, Company, Record Number	WEEKS ON CHART
51	62	51	61		THERE GOES MY HEART — Joni James, M-G-M 12706	5
—	100	75	62		FORGET ME NOT — Kalin Twins, Decca 30745	3
—	96	86	63	★	LEAVE ME ALONE — Dickey Doo & the Don'ts, Swan 4014	3
37	38	49	64		RAMROD — Duane Eddy, Jamie 1109	8
38	41	58	65		SHE WAS ONLY SEVENTEEN — Marty Robbins, Columbia 41208	11
29	31	43	66		VOLARE (Nel Blu Dipinto Di Blu) — Dean Martin, Capitol 4028	11
—	66	62	67		LOOK WHO'S BLUE — Don Gibson, RCA Victor 7330	3
85	85	89	68	★	REAL WILD CHILD — Ivan, Coral 62017	4
—	79	71	69		GIVE MYSELF A PARTY — Don Gibson, RCA Victor 7330	3
—	—	—	70	★	I GOT A FEELING — Ricky Nelson, Imperial 5545	1
19	36	47	71		POOR LITTLE FOOL — Ricky Nelson, Imperial 5528	11
21	24	33	72		LAZY SUMMER NIGHT — Four Preps, Capitol 4023	9
—	—	69	73		HOOPA HOOLA — Betty Johnson, Atlantic 2202	2
—	—	99	74	★	THE HULA HOOP SONG — Teresa Brewer, Coral 62003	2
25	65	70	75		THE WAYS OF A WOMAN IN LOVE — Johnny Cash, Sun 302	8
—	—	92	76	★	NEED YOU — Doonie Owens, Guyden 2001	2
—	99	79	77		THUNDER ROAD — Robert Mitchum, Capitol 3986	5
—	—	95	78	★	QUEEN OF THE HOP — Bobby Darin, Atco 6127	2
81	54	57	79		HIDEAWAY — Four Esquires, Paris 520	4
77	76	84	80		COME ON, LET'S GO — Ritchie Valens, Del Fi 4106	4
—	—	—	81		JUST YOUNG — Paul Anka, ABC-Paramount 9956	1
—	—	—	82	★	WHAT LITTLE GIRL — Frankie Avalon, Chancellor 1026	1
—	—	97	83		THE BLOB — The Five Blobs, Columbia 41250	2
50	68	85	84		BLUE-RIBBON BABY — Tommy Sands, Capitol 4036	7
—	—	—	85	★	GUAGLIONE — Perez Prado, RCA Victor 7337	1
—	—	—	86	★	FALLIN' — Connie Francis, M-G-M 13713	1
—	—	—	87	★	LOVE MAKES THE WORLD GO 'ROUND — Perry Como, RCA Victor 7353	1
—	—	88	88		ALL OVER AGAIN — Johnny Cash, Columbia 41251	2
—	—	—	89	★	GO CHASE A MOONBEAM — Jerry Vale, Columbia 41238	1
40	61	94	90		DANCE, EVERYONE, DANCE — Betty Madigan, Coral 62007	9

From The Hot 100: THE BILLBOARD'S BEST BUYS

These records, of all those listed on The Billboard Hot 100, have shown the greatest national SALES BREAK-OUT potential this week for the first time. Action sides are listed in capital letters.

I GOT A FEELING . . . . **Ricky Nelson**
(Eric, BMI) Lonesome Town (Eric, BMI) Imperial 5545

FALLIN' . . . . **Connie Francis**
(Aldon, BMI) Happy Days and Lonely Nights (Fisher-Advance, ASCAP) M-G-M 13713

LOVE MAKES THE WORLD GO 'ROUND . . . . **Perry Como**
(Winneton, BMI) Mandolins in the Moonlight (Roncom, ASCAP) RCA Victor 7353

QUEEN OF THE HOP . . . . **Bobby Darin**
(Walden-Tweed, ASCAP) Lost Love (Progressive-Fern, BMI) Atco 6127

TO KNOW HIM IS TO LOVE HIM . . . . **Teddy Bears**
(Warman, BMI) Don't You Worry My Little Pet (Poplar, BMI) Dore 503

WHAT LITTLE GIRL
I'LL WAIT FOR YOU . . . . **Frankie Avalon**
(Rambed, BMI) (Debmar, BMI) Chancellor 1026

GUAGLIONE . . . . **Perez Prado**
(Raphael, ASCAP) Paris (Peer, Intl., BMI) RCA Victor 7337

JUST YOUNG . . . . **Paul Anka**
(Peer Intl., BMI) So It's Goodbye (Spanka, BMI) ABC-Paramount 9956

The above are previous Billboard Spotlight picks.

NEED YOU . . . . **Doonie Owens**
(Malapi, BMI) If I'm Wrong (Malapi, BMI) Guyden 2001

JUST YOUNG . . . . **Andy Rose**
(Peer Intl., BMI) Love-a, Love-a, Love (Allison, ASCAP) Aamco 100

★ THE STAR PERFORMER designation shows the outstanding upward changes of position in The Hot 100 since last week's chart. Its purpose merely is to provide quick visual identification of the sides which moved up most dramatically or to new entries which first entered the chart at an unusually high position.

THREE WEEKS AGO	TWO WEEKS AGO	ONE WEEK AGO	THIS WEEK	★ STAR PERFORMER THIS WEEK	TITLE Artist, Company, Record Number	WEEKS ON CHART
48	58	91	91		OVER AND OVER — Bobby Day, Class 229	10
—	—	100	92		JUST YOUNG — Andy Rose, Aamco 100	2
70	52	80	93		BREAKUP — Jerry Lee Lewis, Sun 303	5
—	—	—	94		BLUE BELL — Mitch Miller, Columbia 41235	1
27	64	66	95		GINGER BREAD — Frankie Avalon, Chancellor 1021	11
—	—	—	96		GERALDINE — Jack Scott, Carlton 483	1
—	—	—	97		NON DIMENTICAR — Nat King Cole, Capitol 4056	1
61	44	53	98		LA PALOMA — Billy Vaughn, Dot 15795	10
—	—	87	99		WELL, I'M YOUR MAN — Johnny Tillotson, Cadence 1353	2
—	—	—	100		I'LL WAIT FOR YOU — Frankie Avalon, Chancellor 1026	1

STORE RECORDED SALES — NEW YORK UNIVERSITY SCHOOL OF RETAILING — THE BILLBOARD

BEST SELLING POP SINGLES IN STORES

The information given in this chart is based on actual sales to customers in a scientific sample of the nation's retail outlets during the week ending on the date shown above. Sample design, sample size, and all methods used in this continuing study of retail record sales are under the direct and continuing supervision and control of the School of Retailing of New York University.

FOR SURVEY WEEK ENDING OCTOBER 4, 1958

This Week		Last Week	Weeks on Chart
1.	IT'S ALL IN THE GAME (ASCAP)—Tommy Edwards. Please Love Me Forever (BMI)—M-G-M 12688	1	8
2.	BIRD DOG (BMI)—Everly Brothers. DEVOTED TO YOU (BMI)—Cadence 1350	3	10
3.	VOLARE (Nel Blu Dipinto Di Blu) (ASCAP)—Domenico Modugno. Mariti in Citta (BMI)—Dec 30677	2	11
4.	ROCK-IN' ROBIN (BMI)—Bobby Day. OVER AND OVER (BMI)—Class 229	4	10
5.	TEARS ON MY PILLOW (ASCAP)—Little Anthony and the Imperials. Two People in the World (BMI)—End 1027	7	9
6.	SUSIE DARLIN' (ASCAP)—Robin Luke. Living's Loving You (ASCAP)—Dot 15781	6	9
7.	LITTLE STAR (BMI)—Elegants. Getting Dizzy (BMI)—Apt 25005	5	12
8.	TEA FOR TWO CHA CHA (ASCAP)—Tommy Dorsey Ork. My Baby Just Cares for Me (ASCAP)—Dec 30704	9	5
9.	PATRICIA (ASCAP)—Perez Prado. Why Wait? (BMI)—Vic 7245	8	17
10.	TOPSY II (BMI)—Cozy Cole. TOPSY I (BMI)—Love 50034	15	5
11.	JUST A DREAM (BMI)—Jimmy Clanton. You Aim to Please (BMI)—Ace 546	10	14
12.	YOU CHEATED (BMI)—Shields. That's the Way It's Gonna Be (BMI)—Dot 15805	12	5
13.	CHANTILLY LACE (BMI)—Big Bopper. Purple People Eater Meets the Witch Doctor (BMI)—Mercury 71343	16	3
14.	VOLARE (Nel Blu Dipinto Di Blu) (ASCAP)—Dean Martin. Outta My Mind (ASCAP)—Cap 4028	18	10
15.	MY TRUE LOVE (BMI)—Jack Scott. LEROY (BMI)—Carlton 462	11	18
16.	NEAR YOU (ASCAP)—Roger Williams. Merry Widow Waltz (ASCAP)—Kapp 233	17	6
17.	SUMMERTIME BLUES (BMI)—Eddie Cochran. Love Again (BMI)—Liberty 55144	13	8
18.	BORN TOO LATE (ASCAP)—Poni Tails. Come On, Joey, Dance With Me (BMI)—ABC-Paramount 9934	24	12
19.	NO ONE KNOWS (ASCAP)—Dion and the Belmonts. I Can't Go On (Rosalie) (BMI)—Laurie 3015	20	6
20.	PUSSY CAT (ASCAP)—Ames Brothers. NO ONE BUT YOU (BMI)—Vic 7315	35	3
21.	GEE, BUT ITS LONELY (BMI)—Pat Boone. FOR MY GOOD FORTUNE (BMI)—Dot 15825	29	2
22.	TOM DOOLEY (BMI)—Kingston Trio. Ruby Red (ASCAP)—Cap 4049	—	1
23.	FEVER (BMI)—Peggy Lee. You Don't Know (BMI)—Cap 3998	14	13
24.	DOWN THE AISLE OF LOVE (BMI)—Quin-Tones. Please, Dear (BMI)—Hunt 321	26	6
25.	ARE YOU REALLY MINE? (ASCAP)—Jimmie Rodgers. THE WIZARD (ASCAP)—Roulette 4090	22	10
26.	THE WAYS OF A WOMAN IN LOVE (BMI)—Johnny Cash. YOU'RE THE NEAREST THING TO HEAVEN (BMI)—Sun 302	36	7
27.	STUPID CUPID (BMI)—Connie Francis. Carolina Moon (ASCAP)—M-G-M 12683	19	12
28.	POOR LITTLE FOOL (BMI)—Ricky Nelson. Don't Leave Me This Way (BMI)—Imperial 5528	21	15
29.	MEXICAN HAT ROCK (BMI)—Applejacks. Sophisticated Swing (ASCAP)—Cameo 149	34	2
30.	IT'S ONLY MAKE BELIEVE (BMI)—Conway Twitty. I'll Try (BMI)—M-G-M 12677	46	2
31.	GINGER BREAD (BMI)—Frankie Avalon. Blue Betty (ASCAP)—Chancellor 1021	27	13
32.	SUMMERTIME, SUMMERTIME (ASCAP)—Jamies. Searching for You (ASCAP)—Epic 9281	28	6
33.	A CERTAIN SMILE (ASCAP)—Johnny Mathis. Let It Rain (ASCAP)—Col 41193	48	14
34.	CAROL (BMI)—Chuck Berry. Hey, Pedro (BMI)—Chess 1700	29	2
35.	LA PALOMA (ASCAP)—Billy Vaughn. Here Is My Love (ASCAP)—Dot 15795	23	9
36.	WESTERN MOVIES (BMI)—Olympics. Well! (BMI)—Demon 1508	25	12
37.	THE END (ASCAP)—Earl Grant. Hunky Dunky Doo (ASCAP)—Dec 30719	31	4
38.	RAMROD (BMI)—Duane Eddy. The Walker (BMI)—Jamie 1109	38	7
39.	TEN COMMANDMENTS OF LOVE (BMI)—Harvey and the Moon Glows. Mean Old Blues (BMI)—Chess 1705	44	3
40.	EVERYBODY LOVES A LOVER (ASCAP)—Doris Day. Instant Love (ASCAP)—Col 41195	39	12
41.	ITCHY TWITCHY FEELING (BMI)—Bobby Hendricks. A Thousand Dreams (BMI)—Sue 706	43	7
42.	THE HULA HOOP SONG (BMI)—Georgia Gibbs. Keep in Touch (BMI)—Roulette 4106	—	1
43.	WIN YOUR LOVE FOR ME (BMI)—Sam Cooke. Love Song From "Houseboat" (ASCAP)—Keen 32006	37	6
44.	LA-DO-DADA (BMI)—Dale Hawkins. Cross-Ties (BMI)—Chess 900	45	4
45.	FIREFLY (ASCAP)—Tony Bennett. The Night That Heaven Fell (BMI)—Col 241237	—	1
45.	THERE GOES MY HEART (ASCAP)—Joni James. Funny (ASCAP)—M-G-M 12706	—	1
47.	HOW THE TIME FLIES (ASCAP)—Jerry Wallace. With This Ring (BMI)—Challenge 59013	33	5
48.	SOMEBODY TOUCHED ME (BMI)—Buddy Knox. C'mon, Baby (BMI)—Roulette 4082	32	6
49.	HARD HEADED WOMAN (ASCAP)—Elvis Presley. DON'T ASK ME WHY (ASCAP)—Vic 7280	42	16
50.	BABY FACE (ASCAP)—Little Richard. I'll Never Let You Go (BMI)—Specialty 645	—	1

artists' biographies

Jockey Richardson Rides a Winner

Jape Richardson, a disk jockey from Southeast Texas, has hit pay dirt in the recording field as Big Bopper. "Chantilly Lace," his first record as Big Bopper, landed a slot on The Billboard's Hot 100 chart back on August 4 and has been climbing steadily since then.

Richardson has been in radio for eight years as a disk jockey and is a writer of numerous compositions which have been recorded by other artists. He also penned his hit tune, "Chantilly Lace" and has recorded two of his own compositions for his next release as Big Bopper on the Mercury label. Recently, Richardson has been making personal appearances and was seen nationally on Dick Clark's Saturday night TV stanza this past September 20.

artists' biographies

Ruth Brown Rocks Upward on Charts

"This Little Gal's Gone Rockin'" is Ruth Brown's most recent success. The 30-year-old, Virginia-born vocalist started singing in church under her father's direction. She got her first professional job with the Lucky Millinder band in Washington in 1948.

Not long afterward Blanche Calloway (Cab's sister) became Miss Brown's manager, and she was scheduled for her first "big break" at New York's Apollo Theater. Then just before her opening came tragedy—a serious auto accident that left her bedridden in a hospital for months.

When she got back on her feet, altho they were in braces she resumed her upward climb. The blues singer fractured her audiences at Manhattan's Cafe Society Downtown, was pacted by Atlantic Records and started on her long list of hits of which "Little Gal" is the latest.

BOOM! 1ST REBEL ROUSER
BOOM! then RAMROD
BOOM! AND NOW...
DUANE EDDY'S
Newest.....
CANNON BALL
JAMIE # 1111
DeeJays! Write us for your sample copy of this great new single
B/W "MASON DIXON LION"
Distributed Nationally by: GONE RECORDING CORP. 1650 Broadway, New York, N. Y.

The Billboard HOT 100

FOR THE WEEK ENDING OCTOBER 26

★ THE STAR PERFORMER designation shows the outstanding upward changes of position in The Hot 100 since last week's chart. Its purpose merely is to provide quick visual identification of the sides which moved up most dramatically or to new entries which first entered the chart at an unusually high position.

THREE WEEKS AGO	TWO WEEKS AGO	ONE WEEK AGO	THIS WEEK	★ STAR PERFORMER THIS WEEK	TITLE Artist, Company, Record Number	WEEKS ON CHART
1	1	1	1		IT'S ALL IN THE GAME — Tommy Edwards, M-G-M 12688	9
4	3	2	2		ROCK-IN' ROBIN — Bobby Day, Class 229	12
39	22	13	3	★	TOPSY II — Cozy Cole, Love 50034	9
3	2	3	4		BIRD DOG — Everly Brothers, Cadence 1350	12
33	20	16	5	★	IT'S ONLY MAKE BELIEVE — Conway Twitty, M-G-M 12677	6
7	7	5	6		SUSIE DARLIN' — Robin Luke, Dot 15781	11
6	6	4	7		TEARS ON MY PILLOW — Little Anthony & the Imperials, End 1027	11
83	37	17	8		TOM DOOLEY — Kingston Trio, Capitol 4049	4
14	8	9	9		TEA FOR TWO CHA CHA — Tommy Dorsey Ork-Warern Covington, Decca 30704	8
16	15	11	10		CHANTILLY LACE — Big Bopper, Mercury 71343	12
15	13	7	11		THE END — Earl Grant, Decca 30719	6
2	4	6	12		VOLARE (Nel Blu Dipinto Di Blu) — Domenico Modugno, Decca 30677	12
5	5	8	13		LITTLE STAR — Elegants, Apt 25005	12
10	10	10	14		NEAR YOU — Roger Williams, Kapp 233	10
21	16	15	15		YOU CHEATED — Shields, Dot 15805	9
80	56	40	16	★	TO KNOW HIM IS TO LOVE HIM — Teddy Bears, Dore 503	5
51	40	27	17	★	MEXICAN HAT ROCK — Applejacks, Cameo 149	6
43	39	39	18	★	THE SECRET — Gordon MacRae, Capitol 4033	6
9	12	14	19		JUST A DREAM — Jimmy Clanton, Ace 546	12
25	17	22	20		PROMISE ME, LOVE — Andy Williams, Cadence 1351	8
—	—	70	21	★	I GOT A FEELING — Ricky Nelson, Imperial 5545	2
60	34	29	22		PUSSY CAT — Ames Brothers, RCA Victor 7315	4
8	9	12	23		SUMMERTIME BLUES — Eddie Cochran, Liberty 55144	12
13	11	18	24		HOW THE TIME FLIES — Jerry Wallace, Challenge 59013	10
12	21	19	25		DEVOTED TO YOU — Everly Brothers, Cadence 1350	11
55	54	23	26		FOR MY GOOD FORTUNE — Pat Boone, Dot 15825	5
53	48	25	27		THE DAY THE RAINS CAME — Jane Morgan, Kapp 235	5
74	60	46	28	★	CALL ME — Johnny Mathis, Columbia 41253	4
23	23	20	29		FIREFLY — Tony Bennett, Columbia 41237	7
30	27	24	30		NO ONE KNOWS — Dion & the Belmonts, Laurie 3015	9
46	35	44	31	★	GEE, BUT IT'S LONELY — Pat Boone, Dot 15825	5
—	73	47	32	★	THE HULA HOOP SONG — Georgia Gibbs, Roulette 4106	3
62	51	61	33	★	THERE GOES MY HEART — Joni James, M-G-M 12706	6
89	74	52	34	★	WITH YOUR LOVE — Jack Scott, Carlton 483	4
100	75	62	35	★	FORGET ME NOT — Kalin Twins, Decca 30745	4
49	68	41	36		THE TEN COMMANDMENTS OF LOVE — Harvey & the Moon Glows, Chess 1705	6
32	26	28	37		TREASURE OF YOUR LOVE — Eileen Rodgers, Columbia 41214	9
—	99	74	38	★	THE HULA HOOP SONG — Teresa Brewer, Coral 62003	3
48	46	48	39		FIBBIN' — Patti Page, Mercury 71355	5
45	44	32	40		LA-DO-DADA — Dale Hawkins, Checker 900	8
27	31	35	41		DOWN THE AISLE OF LOVE — Quin-Tones, Hunt 321	10
11	14	21	42		BORN TOO LATE — Poni Tails, ABC-Paramount 9934	12
56	55	50	43		BABY FACE — Little Richard, Specialty 645	6
—	95	78	44	★	QUEEN OF THE HOP — Bobby Darin, Atco 6127	3
59	65	53	45		NO ONE BUT YOU — Ames Brothers, RCA Victor 7315	4
88	78	55	46		TOPSY I — Cozy Cole, Love 50034	6
—	92	76	47	★	NEED YOU — Donnie Owens, Guyden 2001	3
96	86	63	48	★	LEAVE ME ALONE — Dickey Doo & the Don'ts, Swan 4014	4
17	28	43	49		STUPID CUPID — Connie Francis, M-G-M 12683	12
37	41	33	50		WIN YOUR LOVE FOR ME — Sam Cooke, Keen 2006	12
—	—	—	51	★	POOR BOY — Royal Tones, Jubilee 5338	1
63	42	51	52		I WISH — Platters, Mercury 71353	6
54	57	79	53	★	HIDEAWAY — Four Esquires, Paris 520	5
18	19	34	54		CAROL — Chuck Berry, Chess 1700	9
35	29	37	55		SOMEBODY TOUCHED ME — Buddy Knox, Roulette 4082	12
—	69	73	56	★	HOOPA HOOLA — Betty Johnson, Atlantic 2202	3
57	50	38	57		THIS LITTLE GIRL'S GONE ROCKIN' — Ruth Brown, Atlantic 1197	6
69	63	58	58		NINE MORE MILES — Georgi Young, Cameo 150	5
—	—	97	59	★	NON DIMENTICAR — Nat King Cole, Capitol 4056	2
29	30	26	60		ARE YOU REALLY MINE? — Jimmie Rodgers, Roulette 4090	12

THE INDUSTRY'S FASTEST AND MOST COMPLETE PROGRAMMING AND BUYING GUIDE

These 100 sides are listed in order of their national POPULARITY, as determined by weekly local studies prepared for The Billboard in markets representing a cross-section of the United States. These studies reflect sales registered for each disk up to press time.

★ THE STAR PERFORMER designation shows the outstanding upward changes of position in The Hot 100 since last week's chart. Its purpose merely is to provide quick visual identification of the sides which moved up most dramatically or to new entries which first entered the chart at an unusually high position.

THREE WEEKS AGO	TWO WEEKS AGO	ONE WEEK AGO	THIS WEEK	★ STAR PERFORMER THIS WEEK	TITLE Artist, Company, Record Number	WEEKS ON CHART
42	25	36	61		ITCHY TWITCHY FEELING — Bobby Hendricks, Sue 706	12
99	79	77	62	★	THUNDER ROAD — Robert Mitchum, Capitol 3986	6
19	24	31	63		MY TRUE LOVE — Jack Scott, Carlton 462	12
—	88	88	64	★	ALL OVER AGAIN — Johnny Cash, Columbia 41251	3
—	97	83	65	★	THE BLOB — Five Blobs, Columbia 41250	4
—	—	87	66	★	LOVE MAKES THE WORLD GO 'ROUND — Perry Como, RCA Victor 7353	2
41	58	65	67		SHE WAS ONLY SEVENTEEN — Marty Robbins, Columbia 41208	12
66	62	67	68		LOOK WHO'S BLUE — Don Gibson, RCA Victor 7330	4
—	—	85	69	★	GUAGLIONE — Perez Prado, RCA Victor 7337	2
79	71	69	70		GIVE MYSELF A PARTY — Don Gibson, RCA Victor 7330	4
—	100	92	71	★	JUST YOUNG — Andy Rose, Aamco 100	3
—	—	—	72	★	A LOVER'S QUESTION — Clyde McPhatter, Atlantic 1199	1
—	—	—	73	★	MY LUCKY LOVE — Doug Franklin, Colonial 7777	4
—	—	—	74	★	PLEASE LOVE ME FOREVER — Tommy Edwards, M-G-M 12688	1
65	70	75	75		THE WAYS OF A WOMAN IN LOVE — Johnny Cash, Sun 302	9
—	—	—	76	★	LETTER TO AN ANGEL — Jimmy Clanton, Ace 551	1
—	—	86	77		FALLIN' — Connie Francis, M-G-M 13713	2
20	18	30	78		PATRICIA — Perez Prado, RCA Victor 7245	12
—	—	82	79		WHAT LITTLE GIRL — Frankie Avalon, Chancellor 1026	2
—	—	81	80		JUST YOUNG — Paul Anka, ABC-Paramount 9956	2
28	36	45	81		SUMMERTIME, SUMMERTIME — Jamies, Epic 9281	10
24	33	72	82		LAZY SUMMER NIGHT — Four Preps, Capitol 4023	10
40	38	56	83		FEVER — Peggy Lee, Capitol 3998	12
34	52	49	84		PUT A RING ON MY FINGER — Les Paul & Mary Ford, Columbia 41222	10
68	85	84	85		BLUE-RIBBON BABY — Tommy Sands, Capitol 4036	8
—	—	—	86	★	LONESOME TOWN — Ricky Nelson, Imperial 5545	1
72	59	59	87		WHEN I GROW TOO OLD TO DREAM — Ed Townsend, Capitol 4048	4
22	45	57	88		EVERYBODY LOVES A LOVER — Doris Day, Columbia 41198	12
26	32	42	89		WESTERN MOVIES — Olympics, Demon 1508	12
—	—	—	90	★	WHAT DO I CARE — Johnny Cash, Columbia 41251	1

THE BILLBOARD'S BEST BUYS

These records have shown the greatest national SALES BREAKOUT potential this week for the first time. Action sides are listed in capital letters.

POP

NON DIMENTICAR . . . . Nat King Cole
(Hollis, BMI) Bend a Little My Way (Sweco, BMI) Capitol 4056

A LETTER TO AN ANGEL . . . . Jimmy Clanton
(Ace, BMI) A Part of Me (Ace, BMI) Ace 551

I'LL REMEMBER TONIGHT . . . . Pat Boone
(Feist, ASCAP) The Mardi Gras March (Feist, ASCAP) Dot 1584

LEAVE ME ALONE . . . . Dickey Doo & the Don'ts
(Dee Dee, BMI) Wild Party (Dee Dee, BMI) Swan 4014

CIMARRON . . . . Billy Vaughn
(Peer Intl., BMI) You're My Baby Doll (Randy-Smith, ASCAP) Dot 15836

THE BLOB . . . . The Five Blobs
(Famous, ASCAP) Saturday Night in Tiajuana (Famous, ASCAP) Columbia 41250

The above are previous Billboard Spotlight picks.

POOR BOY . . . . The Royal Tones
(Meridian-Parkwood, BMI) Wail! (Parkwood, BMI) Jubilee 5338

C&W

A WOMAN CAPTURED ME
MY LUCKY FRIEND . . . . Hank Snow
(Silver Star, BMI) (Snow, BMI) RCA Victor 7325

A previous Spotlight pick.

PICK ME UP ON YOUR WAY DOWN . . . . Charlie Walker
(By-Nash of Nashville, BMI) Two Empty Arms (T.N.T., BMI) Columbia 41221

R&B

NO SELECTIONS THIS WEEK

★ THE STAR PERFORMER designation shows the outstanding upward changes of position in The Hot 100 since last week's chart. Its purpose merely is to provide quick visual identification of the sides which moved up most dramatically or to new entries which first entered the chart at an unusually high position.

THREE WEEKS AGO	TWO WEEKS AGO	ONE WEEK AGO	THIS WEEK	★ STAR PERFORMER THIS WEEK	TITLE Artist, Company, Record Number	WEEKS ON CHART
67	76	60	91		YOU CHEATED — Slades, Domino 500	10
31	43	66	92		VOLARE (Nel Blu Dipinto Di Blu) — Dean Martin, Capitol 4028	12
85	89	68	93		REAL WILD CHILD — Ivan, Coral 62017	5
—	—	89	94		GO CHASE A MOONBEAM — Jerry Vale, Columbia 41238	2
—	—	—	95		PARIS — Perez Prado, RCA Victor 7337	1
—	—	—	96		CIMARRON — Billy Vaughn, Dot 15836	1
50	61	54	97		THE GREEN MOSQUITO — Tune-Rockers, United Artists 139	9
—	—	—	98		JEALOUS HEART — Tab Hunter, Warner Bros. 5008	1
76	84	80	99		COME ON, LET'S GO — Ritchie Valens, Del Fi 4106	5
—	87	99	100		WELL, I'M YOUR MAN — Johnny Tillotson, Cadence 1353	3

The Billboard HOT 100

FOR THE WEEK ENDING NOVEMBER 2

★ THE STAR PERFORMER designation shows the outstanding upward changes of position in The Hot 100 since last week's chart. Its purpose merely is to provide quick visual identification of the sides which moved up most dramatically or to new entries which first entered the chart at an unusually high position.

Three Weeks Ago	Two Weeks Ago	One Week Ago	This Week	★ Star Performer This Week	TITLE Artist, Company, Record Number	Weeks on Chart
1	1	1	1		IT'S ALL IN THE GAME — Tommy Edwards, M-G-M 12688	10
20	16	5	2		IT'S ONLY MAKE BELIEVE — Conway Twitty, M-G-M 12677	7
37	17	8	3		TOM DOOLEY — Kingston Trio, Capitol 4049	5
22	13	3	4		TOPSY II — Cozy Cole, Love 5004	10
3	2	2	5		ROCK-IN' ROBIN — Bobby Day, Class 229	13
6	4	7	6		TEARS ON MY PILLOW — Little Anthony & the Imperials, End 1027	12
2	3	4	7		BIRD DOG — Everly Brothers, Cadence 1350	13
8	9	9	8		TEA FOR TWO CHA CHA — Tommy Dorsey Ork-Warren Covington, Decca 30704	9
7	5	6	9		SUSIE DARLIN' — Robin Luke, Dot 15781	12
15	11	10	10		CHANTILLY LACE — Big Bopper, Mercury 71343	13
13	7	11	11		THE END — Earl Grant, Decca 30719	7
75	62	35	12	★	FORGET ME NOT — Kalin Twins, Decca 30745	5
5	8	13	13		LITTLE STAR — Elegants, Apt 25005	13
4	6	12	14		VOLARE (Nel Blu Dipinto Di Blu) — Domenico Modugno, Decca 30677	13
56	40	16	15		TO KNOW HIM IS TO LOVE HIM — Teddy Bears, Dore 503	6
10	10	14	16		NEAR YOU — Roger Williams, Kapp 233	11
16	15	15	17		YOU CHEATED — Shields, Dot 15805	10
—	—	86	18	★	LONESOME TOWN — Ricky Nelson, Imperial 5545	2
34	29	22	19		PUSSY CAT — Ames Brothers, RCA Victor 7315	5
9	12	23	20		SUMMERTIME BLUES — Eddie Cochran, Liberty 55144	13
40	27	17	21		MEXICAN HAT ROCK — Applejacks, Cameo 149	7
68	41	36	22	★	THE TEN COMMANDMENTS OF LOVE — Harvey & the Moon Glows, Chess 1705	7
—	70	21	23		I GOT A FEELING — Ricky Nelson, Imperial 5545	3
50	38	57	24	★	THIS LITTLE GIRL'S GONE ROCKIN' — Ruth Brown, Atlantic 1197	7
11	18	24	25		HOW THE TIME FLIES — Jerry Wallace, Challenge 59013	11
48	25	27	26		THE DAY THE RAINS CAME — Jane Morgan, Kapp 235	6
78	55	46	27	★	TOPSY I — Cozy Cole, Love 50034	7
54	23	26	28		FOR MY GOOD FORTUNE — Pat Boone, Dot 15825	6
12	14	19	29		JUST A DREAM — Jimmy Clanton, Ace 546	13
23	20	29	30		FIREFLY — Tony Bennett, Columbia 41237	8
95	78	44	31	★	QUEEN OF THE HOP — Bobby Darin, Atco 6127	4
39	39	18	32		THE SECRET — Gordon MacRae, Capitol 4033	7
60	46	28	33		CALL ME — Johnny Mathis, Columbia 41253	5
74	52	34	34		WITH YOUR LOVE — Jack Scott, Carlton 483	5
27	24	30	35		NO ONE KNOWS — Dion & the Belmonts, Laurie 3015	10
51	61	33	36		THERE GOES MY HEART — Joni James, M-G-M 12706	7
17	22	20	37		PROMISE ME, LOVE — Andy Williams, Cadence 1351	9
—	—	72	38	★	A LOVER'S QUESTION — Clyde McPhatter, Atlantic 1199	2
44	32	40	39		LA-DO-DADA — Dale Hawkins, Checker 900	9
41	33	50	40	★	WIN YOUR LOVE FOR ME — Sam Cooke, Keen 2006	13
55	50	43	41		BABY FACE — Little Richard, Specialty 645	7
21	19	25	42		DEVOTED TO YOU — Everly Brothers, Cadence 1350	12
92	76	47	43		NEED YOU — Donnie Owens, Guyden 2001	4
86	63	48	44		LEAVE ME ALONE — Dickey Doo & the Don'ts, Swan 4014	5
88	88	64	45	★	ALL OVER AGAIN — Johnny Cash, Columbia 41251	4
71	69	70	46	★	GIVE MYSELF A PARTY — Don Gibson, RCA Victor 7330	5
57	79	53	47		HIDEAWAY — Four Esquires, Paris 520	6
46	48	39	48		FIBBIN' — Patti Page, Mercury 71355	6
97	83	65	49	★	THE BLOB — Five Blobs, Columbia 41250	5
—	—	51	50		POOR BOY — Royal Tones, Jubilee 5338	2
25	36	61	51	★	ITCHY TWITCHY FEELING — Bobby Hendricks, Sue 706	13
73	47	32	52		THE HULA HOOP SONG — Georgia Gibbs, Roulette 4106	4
26	28	37	53		TREASURE OF YOUR LOVE — Eileen Rodgers, Columbia 41214	10
14	21	42	54		BORN TOO LATE — Poni Tails, ABC-Paramount 9934	13
99	74	38	55		THE HULA HOOP SONG — Teresa Brewer, Coral 62003	4
84	80	99	56	★	COME ON, LET'S GO — Ritchie Valens, Del Fi 4106	6
—	97	59	57		NON DIMENTICAR — Nat King Cole, Capitol 4056	3
19	34	54	58		CAROL — Chuck Berry, Chess 1700	10
35	44	31	59		GEE, BUT IT'S LONELY — Pat Boone, Dot 15825	6
—	87	66	60		LOVE MAKES THE WORLD GO 'ROUND — Perry Como, RCA Victor 7353	3

THE INDUSTRY'S FASTEST AND MOST COMPLETE PROGRAMMING AND BUYING GUIDE

These 100 sides are listed in order of their national POPULARITY, as determined by weekly local studies prepared for The Billboard in markets representing a cross-section of the United States. These studies reflect sales registered for each disk up to press time.

★ THE STAR PERFORMER designation shows the outstanding upward changes of position in The Hot 100 since last week's chart. Its purpose merely is to provide quick visual identification of the sides which moved up most dramatically or to new entries which first entered the chart at an unusually high position.

THREE WEEKS AGO	TWO WEEKS AGO	ONE WEEK AGO	THIS WEEK	★ STAR PERFORMER THIS WEEK	TITLE Artist, Company, Record Number	WEEKS ON CHART
—	—	74	61		PLEASE LOVE ME FOREVER — Tommy Edwards, M-G-M 12688	2
24	31	63	62		MY TRUE LOVE — Jack Scott, Carlton 462	13
—	85	69	63		GUAGLIONE — Perez Prado, RCA Victor 7337	3
31	35	41	64		DOWN THE AISLE OF LOVE — Quin-Tones, Hunt 321	11
63	58	58	65		NINE MORE MILES — Georgi Young, Cameo 150	6
62	67	68	66		LOOK WHO'S BLUE — Don Gibson, RCA Victor 7330	5
—	—	—	67	★	THE DAY THE RAINS CAME — Raymond LeFevre, Kapp 231	1
—	—	76	68		LETTER TO AN ANGEL — Jimmy Clanton, Ace 551	2
—	—	—	69	★	I'LL WAIT FOR YOU — Frankie Avalon, Chancellor 1026	1
—	86	77	70		FALLIN' — Connie Francis, M-G-M 13713	3
65	53	45	71		NO ONE BUT YOU — Ames Brothers, RCA Victor 7315	5
—	—	—	72	★	I'LL REMEMBER TONIGHT — Pat Boone, Dot 15840	1
18	30	78	73		PATRICIA — Perez Prado, RCA Victor 7245	13
79	77	62	74		THUNDER ROAD — Robert Mitchum, Capitol 3986	7
58	65	67	75		SHE WAS ONLY SEVENTEEN — Marty Robbins, Columbia 41208	13
29	37	55	76		SOMEBODY TOUCHED ME — Buddy Knox, Roulette 4082	13
70	75	75	77		THE WAYS OF A WOMAN IN LOVE — Johnny Cash, Sun 302	10
69	73	56	78		HOOPA HOOLA — Betty Johnson, Atlantic 2202	4
30	26	60	79		ARE YOU REALLY MINE! — Jimmie Rodgers, Roulette 4090	13
42	51	52	80		I WISH — Platters, Mercury 71353	7
100	92	71	81		JUST YOUNG — Andy Rose, Aamco 100	4
—	—	—	82	★	WALKING ALONG — Diamonds, Mercury 71366	1
—	—	90	83		WHAT DO I CARE — Johnny Cash, Columbia 41251	2
59	59	87	84		WHEN I GROW TOO OLD TO DREAM — Ed Townsend, Capitol 4048	5
—	89	94	85		GO CHASE A MOONBEAM — Jerry Vale, Columbia 41238	3
—	—	96	86		CIMARRON — Billy Vaughn, Dot 15836	2
85	84	85	87		BLUE-RIBBON BABY — Tommy Sands, Capitol 4036	9
—	—	—	88	★	LOVE IS ALL WE NEED — Tommy Edwards, M-G-M 12722	1
—	—	—	89	★	MR. SUCCESS — Frank Sinatra, Capitol 4070	1
—	—	98	90		JEALOUS HEART — Tab Hunter, Warner Bros. 5008	2
28	43	49	91		STUPID CUPID — Connie Francis, M-G-M 12683	13
76	60	91	92		YOU CHEATED — Slades, Domino 500	11
43	66	92	93		VOLARE (Nel Blu Dipinto Di Blu) — Dean Martin, Capitol 4028	13
—	—	—	94		MANDOLINS IN THE MOONLIGHT — Perry Como, RCA Victor 7353	1
—	—	—	95		SOMEDAY — Jodie Sands, Chancellor 1023	1
—	—	—	96		BIG DADDY — Jill Corey, Columbia 41202	2
—	—	—	97		TUNNEL OF LOVE — Doris Day, Columbia 41252	1
—	81	80	98		JUST YOUNG — Paul Anka, ABC-Paramount 9956	3
36	45	81	99		SUMMERTIME, SUMMERTIME — Jamies, Epic 9281	11
61	54	97	100		THE GREEN MOSQUITO — Tune-Rockers, United Artists 139	10

THE BILLBOARD'S BEST BUYS

These records have shown the greatest national SALES BREAKOUT potential this week for the first time. Action sides are listed in capital letters.

POP

COME ON, LET'S GO . . . . Ritchie Valens
(Marna, BMI) Framed (Quintet, BMI) Del Fi 4106

LOVE IS ALL WE NEED . . . . Tommy Edwards
(Sheldon, BMI) Mr. Music Man (Yukon, ASCAP) M-G-M 12722

The above are previous Billboard Spotlight picks.

A LOVER'S QUESTION . . . . Clyde McPhatter
(Eden-Progressive, BMI) I Can't Stand Up Alone (Marpat, BMI) Atlantic 1199

THE DAY THE RAINS CAME . . . . Raymond LeFevre
(Maurice, ASCAP) Butter Fingers (Maurice, ASCAP) Kapp 231

WALKING ALONG . . . . The Diamonds
(Maureen, BMI) Eternal Lovers (Marks, BMI) Mercury 71366

GO CHASE A MOONBEAM . . . . Jerry Vale
(Witmark, ASCAP) Around the Clock (Reis, ASCAP) Columbia 41238

MR. SUCCESS . . . . Frank Sinatra
(Barton ASCAP) Sleep Warm (Sands, ASCAP) Capitol 4070

C&W

NO SELECTIONS THIS WEEK

R&B

NO SELECTIONS THIS WEEK

The Billboard HOT 100

FOR THE WEEK ENDING NOVEMBER 9

★ THE STAR PERFORMER designation shows the outstanding upward changes of position in The Hot 100 since last week's chart. Its purpose merely is to provide quick visual identification of the sides which moved up most dramatically or to new entries which first entered the chart at an unusually high position.

Three Weeks Ago	Two Weeks Ago	One Week Ago	This Week	★ Star Performer This Week	Title — Artist, Company, Record Number	Weeks on Chart
1	1	1	1		IT'S ALL IN THE GAME — Tommy Edwards, M-G-M 12688	11
16	5	2	2		IT'S ONLY MAKE BELIEVE — Conway Twitty, M-G-M 12677	8
13	3	4	3		TOPSY II — Cozy Cole, Love 5034	11
17	8	3	4		TOM DOOLEY — Kingston Trio, Capitol 4049	6
2	2	5	5		ROCK-IN' ROBIN — Bobby Day, Class 229	14
11	10	10	6		CHANTILLY LACE — Big Bopper, Mercury 71343	14
9	9	8	7		TEA FOR TWO CHA CHA — Tommy Dorsey Ork-Warren Covington, Dec 30704	10
7	11	11	8		THE END — Earl Grant, Decca 30719	8
4	7	6	9		TEARS ON MY PILLOW — Little Anthony & the Imperials, End 1027	13
3	4	7	10		BIRD DOG — Everly Brothers, Cadence 1350	14
40	16	15	11		TO KNOW HIM IS TO LOVE HIM — Teddy Bears, Dore 503	7
5	6	9	12		SUSIE DARLIN' — Robin Luke, Dot 15781	13
70	21	23	13	★	I GOT A FEELING — Ricky Nelson, Imperial 5545	4
—	86	18	14		LONESOME TOWN — Ricky Nelson, Imperial 5545	3
78	44	31	15	★	QUEEN OF THE HOP — Bobby Darin, Atco 6127	5
27	17	21	16		MEXICAN HAT ROCK — Applejacks, Cameo 149	8
29	22	19	17		PUSSY CAT — Ames Brothers, RCA Victor 7315	6
6	12	14	18		VOLARE (Nel Blu Dipinto Di Blu) — Domenico Modugno, Decca 30677	14
62	35	12	19		FORGET ME NOT — Kalin Twins, Decca 30745	6
10	14	16	20		NEAR YOU — Roger Williams, Kapp 233	12
8	13	13	21		LITTLE STAR — Elegants, Apt 25005	14
46	28	33	22	★	CALL ME — Johnny Mathis, Columbia 41253	6
15	15	17	23		YOU CHEATED — Shields, Dot 15805	11
25	27	26	24		THE DAY THE RAINS CAME — Jane Morgan, Kapp 235	7
61	33	36	25	★	THERE GOES MY HEART — Joni James, M-G-M 12706	8
79	53	47	26	★	HIDEAWAY — Four Esquires, Paris 520	7
18	24	25	27		HOW THE TIME FLIES — Jerry Wallace, Challenge 59013	12
20	29	30	28		FIREFLY — Tony Bennett, Columbia 41237	9
41	36	22	29		THE TEN COMMANDMENTS OF LOVE — Harvey & the Moon Glows, Chess 1705	8
—	—	67	30	★	THE DAY THE RAINS CAME — Raymond Le Fevre, Kapp 231	2
23	26	28	31		FOR MY GOOD FORTUNE — Pat Boone, Dot 15825	7
—	72	38	32		A LOVER'S QUESTION — Clyde McPhatter, Atlantic 1199	3
83	65	49	33	★	THE BLOB — Five Blobs, Columbia 41250	6
12	23	20	34		SUMMERTIME BLUES — Eddie Cochran, Liberty 55144	14
76	47	43	35		NEED YOU — Donnie Owens, Guyden 2001	5
52	34	34	36		WITH YOUR LOVE — Jack Scott, Carlton 483	6
55	46	27	37		TOPSY I — Cozy Cole, Love 5034	8
19	25	42	38		DEVOTED TO YOU — Everly Brothers, Cadence 1350	13
39	18	32	39		THE SECRET — Gordon MacRae, Capitol 4033	8
24	30	35	40		NO ONE KNOWS — Dion & the Belmonts, Laurie 3015	11
—	—	69	41	★	I'LL WAIT FOR YOU — Frankie Avalon, Chancellor 1026	2
88	64	45	42		ALL OVER AGAIN — Johnny Cash, Columbia 41251	5
—	51	50	43		POOR BOY — Royal Tones, Jubilee 5338	3
86	77	70	44	★	FALLIN' — Connie Francis, M-G-M 13713	4
63	48	44	45		LEAVE ME ALONE — Dickey Doo & the Don'ts, Swan 4014	6
28	37	53	46		TREASURE OF YOUR LOVE — Eileen Rodgers, Columbia 41214	11
—	76	68	47	★	LETTER TO AN ANGEL — Jimmy Clanton, Ace 551	3
32	40	39	48		LA-DO-DADA — Dale Hawkins, Checker 900	10
87	66	60	49	★	LOVE MAKES THE WORLD GO 'ROUND — Perry Como, RCA Victor 7353	4
—	—	72	50	★	I'LL REMEMBER TONIGHT — Pat Boone, Dot 15840	2
50	43	41	51		BABY FACE — Little Richard, Specialty 645	8
97	59	57	52		NON DIMENTICAR — Nat King Cole, Capitol 4056	4
86	69	63	53	★	GUAGLIONE — Perez Prado, RCA Victor 7337	4
—	—	—	54	★	BEEP BEEP — Playmates, Roulette 4115	1
38	57	24	55		THIS LITTLE GIRL'S GONE ROCKIN' — Ruth Brown, Atlantic 1197	8
69	70	46	56		GIVE MYSELF A PARTY — Don Gibson, RCA Victor 7330	6
22	20	37	57		PROMISE ME, LOVE — Andy Williams, Cadence 1351	10
80	99	56	58		COME ON, LET'S GO — Ritchie Valens, Del Fi 4106	7
14	19	29	59		JUST A DREAM — Jimmy Clanton, Ace 546	14
—	—	94	60	★	MANDOLINS IN THE MOONLIGHT — Perry Como, RCA Victor 7353	2

THE INDUSTRY'S FASTEST AND MOST COMPLETE PROGRAMMING AND BUYING GUIDE

These 100 sides are listed in order of their national POPULARITY, as determined by weekly local studies prepared for The Billboard in markets representing a cross-section of the United States. These studies reflect sales registered for each disk up to press time.

★ THE STAR PERFORMER designation shows the outstanding upward changes of position in The Hot 100 since last week's chart. Its purpose merely is to provide quick visual identification of the sides which moved up most dramatically or to new entries which first entered the chart at an unusually high position.

THREE WEEKS AGO	TWO WEEKS AGO	ONE WEEK AGO	THIS WEEK	★ STAR PERFORMER THIS WEEK	TITLE — Artist, Company, Record Number	WEEKS ON CHART
44	31	59	61		GEE, BUT IT'S LONELY — Pat Boone, Dot 15825	7
58	58	65	62		NINE MORE MILES — Georgie Young, Cameo 150	7
—	—	88	63	★	LOVE IS ALL WE NEED — Tommy Edwards, M-G-M 12722	2
48	39	48	64		FIBBIN' — Patti Page, Mercury 71355	7
—	—	—	65	★	I GOT STUNG — Elvis Presley, RCA Victor 7210	1
67	68	66	66		LOOK WHO'S BLUE — Don Gibson, RCA Victor 7330	6
—	—	97	67	★	TUNNEL OF LOVE — Doris Day, Columbia 41252	2
47	32	52	68		THE HULA HOOP SONG — Georgia Gibbs, Roulette 4106	5
92	71	81	69		JUST YOUNG — Andy Rose, Aamco 100	5
—	90	83	70		WHAT DO I CARE — Johnny Cash, Columbia 41251	3
53	45	71	71		NO ONE BUT YOU — Ames Brothers, RCA Victor 7315	6
89	94	85	72		GO CHASE A MOONBEAM — Jerry Vale, Columbia 41238	4
35	41	64	73		DOWN THE AISLE OF LOVE — Quin-Tones, Hunt 321	12
59	87	84	74		WHEN I GROW TOO OLD TO DREAM — Ed Townsend, Capitol 4048	6
—	—	82	75		WALKING ALONG — Diamonds, Mercury 71366	2
—	—	89	76		MR. SUCCESS — Frank Sinatra, Capitol 4070	2
—	—	—	77	★	LIGHT OF LOVE — Peggy Lee, Capitol 4071	1
51	52	80	78		I WISH — Platters, Mercury 71353	8
33	50	40	79		WIN YOUR LOVE FOR ME — Sam Cooke, Keen 2006	14
77	62	74	80		THUNDER ROAD — Robert Mitchum, Capitol 3986	8
84	85	87	81		BLUE-RIBBON BABY — Tommy Sands, Capitol 4036	10
73	56	78	82		HOOPA HOOLA — Betty Johnson, Atlantic 2202	5
—	96	86	83		CIMARRON — Billy Vaughn, Dot 15836	3
81	80	98	84		JUST YOUNG — Paul Anka, ABC-Paramount 9956	4
30	78	73	85		PATRICIA — Perez Prado, RCA Victor 7245	14
—	—	—	86	★	THE MOCKING BIRD — Four Lads, Columbia 41266	1
—	98	90	87		JEALOUS HEART — Tab Hunter, Warner Bros. 5008	3
—	—	—	88	★	CANNON BALL — Duane Eddy, Jamie 1111	1
75	75	77	89		THE WAYS OF A WOMAN IN LOVE — Johnny Cash, Sun 302	11
37	55	76	90		SOMEBODY TOUCHED ME — Buddy Knox, Roulette 4082	14

THE BILLBOARD'S BEST BUYS

These records have shown the greatest national SALES BREAKOUT potential this week for the first time. Action sides are listed in capital letters.

POP

I GOT STUNG . . . . Elvis Presley
(Gladys, ASCAP) One Night (Travis-Presley, BMI) RCA Victor 7210

BEEP BEEP . . . . The Playmates
(H&L, BMI) Your Love (H&L, BMI) Roulette 4115

LIGHT OF LOVE . . . . Peggy Lee
(Singleton, BMI) Sweetheart (Portrait, BMI) Capitol 4071

CANNON BALL . . . . Duane Eddy
(Gregmark, BMI) Mason Dixon Lion (Gregmark, BMI) Jamie 1111

THE MOCKING BIRD . . . . Four Lads
(Beaver, ASCAP) Won't Cha Give Me Something in Return (Dominion, BMI) Columbia 41266

The above are previous Billboard Spotlight picks.

C&W

COUNTRY MUSIC IS HERE TO STAY . . . . Simon Crum
(Bee Gee, BMI) Stand Up, Sit Down, Shut Your Mouth (Cedarwood, BMI) Capitol 4073

R&B

I'M GONNA GET MY BABY . . . . Jimmy Reed
(Conrad, BMI) Odds and Ends (Conrad, BMI) Vee Jay 298

IT DON'T HURT NO MORE . . . . Nappy Brown
(Planemar-Miller-Songcraft, BMI) My Baby (Planemar, BMI) Savoy 1551

The above are previous Billboard Spotlight picks.

★ THE STAR PERFORMER designation shows the outstanding upward changes of position in The Hot 100 since last week's chart. Its purpose merely is to provide quick visual identification of the sides which moved up most dramatically or to new entries which first entered the chart at an unusually high position.

THREE WEEKS AGO	TWO WEEKS AGO	ONE WEEK AGO	THIS WEEK	★ STAR PERFORMER THIS WEEK	TITLE — Artist, Company, Record Number	WEEKS ON CHART
74	38	55	91		THE HULA HOOP SONG — Teresa Brewer, Coral 62003	5
—	—	—	92		DREAMY EYES — Johnny Tillotson, Cadence 1353	1
—	74	61	93		PLEASE LOVE ME FOREVER — Tommy Edwards, M-G-M 12688	3
31	63	62	94		MY TRUE LOVE — Jack Scott, Carlton 462	14
60	91	92	95		YOU CHEATED — Slades, Domino 500	12
—	—	—	96		IT'S RAINING OUTSIDE — Platters, Mercury 71353	1
36	61	51	97		ITCHY TWITCHY FEELING — Bobby Hendricks, Sue 706	14
—	—	—	98		A PART OF ME — Jimmy Clanton, Ace 551	1
21	42	54	99		BORN TOO LATE — Poni Tails, ABC-Paramount 9934	14
—	—	—	100		THAT OLD BLACK MAGIC — Keely Smith & Louis Prima, Capitol 4063	1

The Billboard HOT 100

FOR THE WEEK ENDING NOVEMBER 16

★ THE STAR PERFORMER designation shows the outstanding upward changes of position in The Hot 100 since last week's chart. Its purpose merely is to provide quick visual identification of the sides which moved up most dramatically or to new entries which first entered the chart at an unusually high position.

Three Weeks Ago	Two Weeks Ago	One Week Ago	This Week	★ Star Performer This Week	Title	Artist, Company, Record Number	Weeks on Chart
5	2	2	1		IT'S ONLY MAKE BELIEVE	Conway Twitty, M-G-M 12677	9
8	3	4	2		TOM DOOLEY	Kingston Trio, Capitol 4049	7
1	1	1	3		IT'S ALL IN THE GAME	Tommy Edwards, M-G-M 12688	12
3	4	3	4		TOPSY II	Cozy Cole, Love 50034	12
16	15	11	5		TO KNOW HIM IS TO LOVE HIM	Teddy Bears, Dore 503	8
10	10	6	6		CHANTILLY LACE	Big Bopper, Mercury 71343	15
9	8	7	7		TEA FOR TWO CHA CHA	Tommy Dorsey Ork-Warren Covington, Dec 30704	11
11	11	8	8		THE END	Earl Grant, Decca 30719	9
2	5	5	9		ROCK-IN' ROBIN	Bobby Day, Class 229	15
21	23	13	10		I GOT A FEELING	Ricky Nelson, Imperial 5545	5
86	18	14	11		LONESOME TOWN	Ricky Nelson, Imperial 5545	4
6	9	12	12		SUSIE DARLIN'	Robin Luke, Dot 15781	14
44	31	15	13		QUEEN OF THE HOP	Bobby Darin, Atco 6127	6
7	6	9	14		TEARS ON MY PILLOW	Little Anthony & the Imperials, End 1027	14
4	7	10	15		BIRD DOG	Everly Brothers, Cadence 1350	15
17	21	16	16		MEXICAN HAT ROCK	Applejacks, Cameo 149	9
35	12	19	17		FORGET ME NOT	Kalin Twins, Decca 30745	7
—	—	65	18	★	I GOT STUNG	Elvis Presley, RCA Victor 7210	2
—	—	54	19	★	BEEP BEEP	Playmates, Roulette 4115	2
72	38	32	20	★	A LOVER'S QUESTION	Clyde McPhatter, Atlantic 1199	4
28	33	22	21		CALL ME	Johnny Mathis, Columbia 41253	7
27	26	24	22		THE DAY THE RAINS CAME	Jane Morgan, Kapp 235	8
22	19	17	23		PUSSY CAT	Ames Brothers, RCA Victor 7315	7
14	16	20	24		NEAR YOU	Roger Williams, Kapp 233	13
33	36	25	25		THERE GOES MY HEART	Joni James, M-G-M 12706	9
53	47	26	26		HIDEAWAY	Four Esquires, Paris 520	8
15	17	23	27		YOU CHEATED	Shields, Dot 15805	12
34	34	36	28		WITH YOUR LOVE	Jack Scott, Carlton 483	7
47	43	35	29		NEED YOU	Donnie Owens, Guyden 2001	6
—	—	—	30	★	ONE NIGHT	Elvis Presley, RCA Victor 7210	1
51	50	43	31	★	POOR BOY	Royal Tones, Jubilee 5338	4
36	22	29	32		THE TEN COMMANDMENTS OF LOVE	Harvey & the Moon Glows, Chess 1705	9
18	32	39	33		THE SECRET	Gordon MacRae, Capitol 4033	9
29	30	28	34		FIREFLY	Tony Bennett, Columbia 41237	10
65	49	33	35		THE BLOB	Five Blobs, Columbia 41250	7
23	20	34	36		SUMMERTIME BLUES	Eddie Cochran, Liberty 55144	15
—	67	30	37		THE DAY THE RAINS CAME	Raymond Le Fevre, Kapp 231	3
64	45	42	38		ALL OVER AGAIN	Johnny Cash, Columbia 41251	6
24	25	27	39		HOW THE TIME FLIES	Jerry Wallace, Challenge 59013	13
13	13	21	40		LITTLE STAR	Elegants, Apt 25005	15
76	68	47	11		LETTER TO AN ANGEL	Jimmy Clanton, Ace 551	4
26	28	31	42		FOR MY GOOD FORTUNE	Pat Boone, Dot 15825	8
—	88	63	43	★	LOVE IS ALL WE NEED	Tommy Edwards, M-G-M 12722	3
77	70	44	44		FALLIN'	Connie Francis, M-G-M 13713	5
30	35	40	45		NO ONE KNOWS	Dion & the Belmonts, Laurie 3015	12
59	57	52	46		NON DIMENTICAR	Nat King Cole, Capitol 4056	5
—	69	41	47		I'LL WAIT FOR YOU	Frankie Avalon, Chancellor 1026	3
—	72	50	48		I'LL REMEMBER TONIGHT	Pat Boone, Dot 15840	3
66	60	49	49		LOVE MAKES THE WORLD GO 'ROUND	Perry Como, RCA Victor 7353	5
—	89	76	50	★	MR. SUCCESS	Frank Sinatra, Capitol 4070	3
—	—	—	51	★	PROBLEMS	Everly Brothers, Cadence 1355	1
48	44	45	52		LEAVE ME ALONE	Dickey Doo & the Don'ts, Swan 4014	7
—	82	75	53	★	WALKING ALONG	Diamonds, Mercury 71366	3
70	46	56	54		GIVE MYSELF A PARTY	Don Gibson, RCA Victor 7330	7
69	63	53	55		GUAGLIONE	Perez Prado, RCA Victor 7337	5
37	53	46	56		TREASURE OF YOUR LOVE	Eileen Rodgers, Columbia 41214	12
12	14	18	57		VOLARE (Nel Blu Dipinto Di Blu)	Domenico Modugno, Decca 30677	15
57	24	55	58		THIS LITTLE GIRL'S GONE ROCKIN'	Ruth Brown, Atlantic 1197	9
31	59	61	59		GEE, BUT IT'S LONELY	Pat Boone, Dot 15825	8
94	85	72	60	★	GO CHASE A MOONBEAM	Jerry Vale, Columbia 41238	5

THE INDUSTRY'S FASTEST AND MOST COMPLETE PROGRAMMING AND BUYING GUIDE

These 100 sides are listed in order of their national POPULARITY, as determined by weekly local studies prepared for The Billboard in markets representing a cross-section of the United States. These studies reflect sales registered for each disk up to press time.

★ THE STAR PERFORMER designation shows the outstanding upward changes of position in The Hot 100 since last week's chart. Its purpose merely is to provide quick visual identification of the sides which moved up most dramatically or to new entries which first entered the chart at an unusually high position.

THREE WEEKS AGO	TWO WEEKS AGO	ONE WEEK AGO	THIS WEEK	★ STAR PERFORMER THIS WEEK	TITLE	Artist, Company, Record Number	WEEKS ON CHART
68	66	66	61		LOOK WHO'S BLUE	Don Gibson, RCA Victor 7330	7
—	94	60	62		MANDOLINS IN THE MOONLIGHT	Perry Como, RCA Victor 7353	3
20	37	57	63		PROMISE ME, LOVE	Andy Williams, Cadence 1351	11
—	—	98	64	★	A PART OF ME	Jimmy Clanton, Ace 551	2
—	97	67	65		TUNNEL OF LOVE	Doris Day, Columbia 41252	3
45	71	71	66		NO ONE BUT YOU	Ames Brothers, RCA Victor 7315	7
—	—	—	67	★	BIMBOMBEY	Jimmie Rodgers, Roulette 4116	1
25	42	38	68		DEVOTED TO YOU	Everly Brothers, Cadence 1350	14
90	83	70	69		WHAT DO I CARE	Johnny Cash, Columbia 41251	4
96	86	83	70		CIMARRON	Billy Vaughn, Dot 15836	4
—	—	88	71	★	CANNON BALL	Duane Eddy, Jamie 1111	2
99	56	58	72		COME ON, LET'S GO	Ritchie Valens, Del Fi 4106	8
—	—	77	73		LIGHT OF LOVE	Peggy Lee, Capitol 4017	2
39	48	64	74		FIBBIN'	Patti Page, Mercury 71355	8
98	92	87	75		JEALOUS HEART	Tab Hunter, Warner Bros. 5008	4
—	—	86	76		THE MOCKING BIRD	Four Lads, Columbia 41266	2
46	27	37	77		TOPSY I	Cozy Cole, Love 50034	9
43	41	51	78		BABY FACE	Little Richard, Specialty 645	9
—	—	—	79	★	I WANT TO BE HAPPY CHA CHA	Enoch Light & the Light Brigade, Grand Award 1020	1
—	—	—	80	★	SWEET LITTLE ROCK AND ROLL	Chuck Berry, Chess 1709	1
—	—	—	81	★	THE WORLD'S OUTSIDE	Four Coins, Epic 9295	1
52	80	78	82		I WISH	Platters, Mercury 71353	9
—	—	100	83	★	THAT OLD BLACK MAGIC	Keely Smith & Louis Prima, Capitol 4063	2
58	65	62	84		NINE MORE MILES	Georgie Young, Cameo 150	8
87	84	74	85		WHEN I GROW TOO OLD TO DREAM	Ed Townsend, Capitol 4048	7
19	29	59	86		JUST A DREAM	Jimmy Clanton, Ace 546	15
40	39	48	87		LA-DO-DADA	Dale Hawkins, Checker 900	11
62	74	80	88		THUNDER ROAD	Robert Mitchum, Capitol 3986	9
50	40	79	89		WIN YOUR LOVE FOR ME	Sam Cooke, Keen 2006	15
—	—	92	90		DREAMY EYES	Johnny Tillotson, Cadence 1353	2

THE BILLBOARD'S BEST BUYS

These records have shown the greatest national SALES BREAKOUT potential this week for the first time. Action sides are listed in capital letters.

POP

BIMBOMBEY . . . . Jimmie Rodgers
(Planetary, ASCAP) You Understand Me (Planetary, ASCAP) Roulette 4116

PROBLEMS . . . . The Everly Brothers
(Acuff-Rose, BMI) Love of My Life (Acuff-Rose, BMI) Cadence 1355

**SWEET LITTLE ROCK AND ROLL
JOE JOE GUN** . . . . Chuck Berry
(Arc, BMI) (Arc, BMI) Chess 1709

THE WORLD OUTSIDE . . . . The Four Coins
(Chappell, ASCAP) Roselle (Peer Intl., BMI) Epic 9295

JEALOUS HEART . . . . Tab Hunter
(Acuff-Rose, BMI) Lonesome Road (Paramount, ASCAP) Warner Brothers 5008

I WANT TO BE HAPPY CHA CHA . . . Enoch Light & The Light Brigade
(Harms, ASCAP) Cara Mia Cha Cha (Record Songs, ASCAP) Grand Award 1020

The above are previous Billboard Spotlight picks.

TUNNEL OF LOVE . . . . Doris Day
(Daywin, BMI) Run Away, Skidaddle, Skidoo (Artists, ASCAP) Columbia 41252

C&W

LIFE TO GO . . . . Stonewall Jackson
(Starrite, BMI) Misery Known as Heartache (Cedarwood, BMI) Columbia 41257

R&B

No selections this week.

★ THE STAR PERFORMER designation shows the outstanding upward changes of position in The Hot 100 since last week's chart. Its purpose merely is to provide quick visual identification of the sides which moved up most dramatically or to new entries which first entered the chart at an unusually high position.

THREE WEEKS AGO	TWO WEEKS AGO	ONE WEEK AGO	THIS WEEK	★ STAR PERFORMER THIS WEEK	TITLE	Artist, Company, Record Number	WEEKS ON CHART
71	81	69	91		JUST YOUNG	Andy Rose, Aamco 100	6
—	—	—	92		HOLD IT	Bill Doggett, King 5149	1
—	—	—	93		CRAZY COUNTRY HOP	Johnny Otis, Capitol 4060	1
—	—	—	94		JEALOUS HEART	Fontane Sisters, Dot 15853	1
—	—	—	95		IT DON'T HURT NO MORE	Nappy Brown, Savoy 1551	1
85	87	81	96		BLUE-RIBBON BABY	Tommy Sands, Capitol 4036	11
—	—	—	97		A HOUSE, A CAR AND A WEDDING RING	Dale Hawkins, Checker 906	1
—	—	—	98		FLAMINGO L'AMORE	Gaylords, Mercury 71369	1
—	—	—	99		ALMOST IN YOUR ARMS	Johnny Nash, ABC-Paramount 9960	3
—	—	—	100		WHITE BUCKS AND SADDLE SHOES	Bobby Pedrick Jr., Big Top 3004	1

The Billboard HOT 100

FOR THE WEEK ENDING NOVEMBER 23

★ THE STAR PERFORMER designation shows the outstanding upward changes of position in The Hot 100 since last week's chart. Its purpose merely is to provide quick visual identification of the sides which moved up most dramatically or to new entries which first entered the chart at an unusually high position.

THREE WEEKS AGO	TWO WEEKS AGO	ONE WEEK AGO	THIS WEEK	★ STAR PERFORMER THIS WEEK	TITLE	Artist, Company, Record Number	WEEKS ON CHART
3	4	2	1		TOM DOOLEY	Kingston Trio, Capitol 4049	8
2	2	1	2		IT'S ONLY MAKE BELIEVE	Conway Twitty, M-G-M 12677	10
4	3	4	3		TOPSY II	Cozy Cole, Love 50034	13
1	1	3	4		IT'S ALL IN THE GAME	Tommy Edwards, M-G-M 12688	13
15	11	5	5		TO KNOW HIM IS TO LOVE HIM	Teddy Bears, Dore 503	9
—	54	19	6	★	BEEP BEEP	Playmates, Roulette 4115	3
10	6	6	7		CHANTILLY LACE	Big Bopper, Mercury 71343	16
18	14	11	8		LONESOME TOWN	Ricky Nelson, Imperial 5545	5
31	15	13	9		QUEEN OF THE HOP	Bobby Darin, Atco 6127	7
23	13	10	10		I GOT A FEELING	Ricky Nelson, Imperial 5545	6
—	65	18	11		I GOT STUNG	Elvis Presley, RCA Victor 7410	3
11	8	8	12		THE END	Earl Grant, Decca 30719	10
8	7	7	13		TEA FOR TWO CHA CHA	Tommy Dorsey Ork-Warren Covington, Decca 30704	12
—	—	30	14	★	ONE NIGHT	Elvis Presley, RCA Victor 7410	2
5	5	9	15		ROCK-IN' ROBIN	Bobby Day, Class 229	16
12	19	17	16		FORGET ME NOT	Kalin Twins, Decca 30745	8
19	17	23	17		PUSSY CAT	Ames Brothers, RCA Victor 7315	8
21	16	16	18		MEXICAN HAT ROCK	Applejacks, Cameo 149	10
36	25	25	19		THERE GOES MY HEART	Joni James, M-G-M 12706	10
69	41	47	20	★	I'LL WAIT FOR YOU	Frankie Avalon, Chancellor 1026	4
47	26	26	21		HIDEAWAY	Four Esquires, Paris 520	9
38	32	20	22		A LOVER'S QUESTION	Clyde McPhatter, Atlantic 1199	5
33	22	21	23		CALL ME	Johnny Mathis, Columbia 41253	8
50	43	31	24		POOR BOY	Royal Tones, Jubilee 5338	5
—	88	71	25	★	CANNON BALL	Duane Eddy, Jamie 1111	3
6	9	14	26		TEARS ON MY PILLOW	Little Anthony & the Imperials, End 1027	15
9	12	12	27		SUSIE DARLIN'	Robin Luke, Dot 15781	15
43	35	29	28		NEED YOU	Donnie Owens, Guyden 2001	7
68	47	41	29	★	LETTER TO AN ANGEL	Jimmy Clanton, Ace 551	5
70	44	44	30	★	FALLIN'	Connie Francis, M-G-M 13713	6
26	24	22	31		THE DAY THE RAINS CAME	Jane Morgan, Kapp 235	9
16	20	24	32		NEAR YOU	Roger Williams, Kapp 233	14
60	49	49	33	★	LOVE MAKES THE WORLD GO 'ROUND	Perry Como, RCA Victor 7353	6
7	10	15	34		BIRD DOG	Everly Brothers, Cadence 1350	16
72	50	48	35	★	I'LL REMEMBER TONIGHT	Pat Boone, Dot 15840	4
—	—	81	36	★	THE WORLD OUTSIDE	Four Coins, Epic 9295	2
88	63	43	37		LOVE IS ALL WE NEED	Tommy Edwards, M-G-M 12722	4
27	37	77	38	★	TOPSY I	Cozy Cole, Love 50034	10
82	75	53	39	★	WALKING ALONG	Diamonds, Mercury 71366	4
67	30	37	40		THE DAY THE RAINS CAME	Raymond Le Fevre, Kapp 231	4
—	86	76	41	★	THE MOCKING BIRD	Four Lads, Columbia 41266	3
—	—	51	42		PROBLEMS	Everly Brothers, Cadence 1355	2
30	28	34	43		FIREFLY	Tony Bennett, Columbia 41237	11
89	76	50	44		MR SUCCESS	Frank Sinatra, Capitol 4070	4
35	40	45	45		NO ONE KNOWS	Dion & the Belmonts, Laurie 3015	13
34	36	28	46		WITH YOUR LOVE	Jack Scott, Carlton 483	8
94	60	62	47	★	MANDOLINS IN THE MOONLIGHT	Perry Como, RCA Victor 7353	4
17	23	27	48		YOU CHEATED	Shields, Dot 15805	13
45	42	38	49		ALL OVER AGAIN	Johnny Cash, Columbia 41251	7
49	33	35	50		THE BLOB	Five Blobs, Columbia 41250	8
—	—	67	51	★	BIMBOMBEY	Jimmie Rodgers, Roulette 4116	2
57	52	46	52		NON DIMENTICAR	Nat King Cole, Capitol 4056	6
83	70	69	53	★	WHAT DO I CARE	Johnny Cash, Columbia 41251	5
20	34	36	54		SUMMERTIME BLUES	Eddie Cochran, Liberty 55144	16
71	71	66	55	★	NO ONE BUT YOU	Ames Brothers, RCA Victor 7315	8
56	58	72	56	★	COME ON, LET'S GO	Ritchie Valens, Del Fi 4106	9
97	67	65	57		TUNNEL OF LOVE	Doris Day, Columbia 41252	4
66	66	61	58		LOOK WHO'S BLUE	Don Gibson, RCA Victor 7330	8
63	53	55	59		GUAGLIONE	Perez Prado, RCA Victor 7337	6
—	98	64	60		A PART OF ME	Jimmy Clanton, Ace 551	3

THE INDUSTRY'S FASTEST AND MOST COMPLETE PROGRAMMING AND BUYING GUIDE

These 100 sides are listed in order of their national POPULARITY, as determined by weekly local studies prepared for The Billboard in markets representing a cross-section of the United States. These studies reflect sales registered for each disk up to press time.

★ THE STAR PERFORMER designation shows the outstanding upward changes of position in The Hot 100 since last week's chart. Its purpose merely is to provide quick visual identification of the sides which moved up most dramatically or to new entries which first entered the chart at an unusually high position.

THREE WEEKS AGO	TWO WEEKS AGO	ONE WEEK AGO	THIS WEEK	★ STAR PERFORMER THIS WEEK	TITLE	Artist, Company, Record Number	WEEKS ON CHART
28	31	42	61		FOR MY GOOD FORTUNE	Pat Boone, Dot 15825	9
—	100	83	62	★	THAT OLD BLACK MAGIC	Keely Smith & Louis Prima, Capitol 4063	3
—	77	73	63		LIGHT OF LOVE	Peggy Lee, Capitol 4017	3
22	29	32	64		THE TEN COMMANDMENTS OF LOVE	Harvey & the Moon Glows, Chess 1705	10
86	83	70	65		CIMARRON	Billy Vaughn, Dot 15836	5
—	—	79	66		I WANT TO BE HAPPY CHA CHA	Enoch Light & the Light Brigade, Grand Award 1020	2
—	—	80	67		SWEET LITTLE ROCK AND ROLL	Chuck Berry, Chess 1709	2
90	87	75	68		JEALOUS HEART	Tab Hunter, Warner Bros. 5008	5
32	39	33	69		THE SECRET	Gordon MacRae, Capitol 4033	10
53	46	56	70		TREASURE OF YOUR LOVE	Eileen Rodgers, Columbia 41214	13
—	—	—	71	★	PLEDGING MY LOVE	Roy Hamilton, Epic 9294	1
44	45	52	72		LEAVE ME ALONE	Dickey Doo & the Don'ts, Swan 4014	8
48	64	74	73		FIBBIN'	Patti Page, Mercury 71355	9
—	—	—	74		LOVE YOU MOST OF ALL	Sam Cooke, Keen 2008	1
37	57	63	75		PROMISE ME, LOVE	Andy Williams, Cadence 1351	12
85	72	60	76		GO CHASE A MOONBEAM	Jerry Vale, Columbia 41238	6
46	56	54	77		GIVE MYSELF A PARTY	Don Gibson, RCA Victor 7330	8
—	—	99	78	★	ALMOST IN YOUR ARMS	Johnny Nash, ABC-Paramount 9960	4
—	—	—	79	★	PHILADELPHIA, U.S.A.	Nu Tornados, Carlton 492	1
40	79	89	80		WIN YOUR LOVE FOR ME	Sam Cooke, Keen 2006	16
—	—	—	81	★	WHOLE LOTTA LOVING	Fats Domino, Imperial 5553	1
13	21	40	82		LITTLE STAR	Elegants, Apt 25005	16
25	27	39	83		HOW THE TIME FLIES	Jerry Wallace, Challenge 59013	14
24	55	58	84		THIS LITTLE GIRL'S GONE ROCKIN'	Ruth Brown, Atlantic 1197	10
80	78	82	85		I WISH	Platters, Mercury 71353	10
—	—	—	86	★	SMOKE GETS IN YOUR EYES	Platters, Mercury 71383	1
—	—	93	87		CRAZY COUNTRY HOP	Johnny Otis, Capitol 4060	2
14	18	57	88		VOLARE (Nel Blu Dipinto Di Blu)	Domenico Modugno, Decca 30677	16
—	—	—	89	★	JOE JOE GUN	Chuck Berry, Chess 1709	1
—	—	100	90		WHITE BUCKS AND SADDLE SHOES	Bobby Pedrick Jr., Big Top 3004	2

THE BILLBOARD'S BEST BUYS

These records have shown the greatest national SALES BREAKOUT potential this week for the first time. Action sides are listed in capital letters.

POP

SMOKE GETS IN YOUR EYES . . . . The Platters
(Harms, ASCAP) No Matter What You Are (A.M.C., ASCAP) Mercury 71383

WHOLE LOTTA LOVING
COQUETTE . . . . Fats Domino
(Marquis, BMI) (Feist, ASCAP) Imperial 5553

The above are previous Billboard Spotlight picks

PHILADELPHIA, U. S. A. . . . . Nu Tornados
(Southern, ASCAP) Magic Record (Music Maestro, BMI) Carlton 492

LOVE YOU MOST OF ALL . . . . Sam Cooke
(Hermosa, BMI) Blue Moon (Robbins, ASCAP) Keen 2008

PLEDGING MY LOVE
MY ONE AND ONLY LOVE . . . . Roy Hamilton
(Lion-Weber, BMI) (Sherwin, ASCAP) Epic 9294

C&W

WHAT AM I LIVING FOR . . . . Ernest Tubb
(Progressive, BMI) Goodbye Sunshine (Tubb, BMI) Decca 30759

A previous Billboard Spotlight pick

R&B

ROCKHOUSE (PARTS I & II) . . . . Ray Charles Ork
(Progressive, BMI) Atlantic 2006

A previous Billboard Spotlight pick

★ THE STAR PERFORMER designation shows the outstanding upward changes of position in The Hot 100 since last week's chart. Its purpose merely is to provide quick visual identification of the sides which moved up most dramatically or to new entries which first entered the chart at an unusually high position.

THREE WEEKS AGO	TWO WEEKS AGO	ONE WEEK AGO	THIS WEEK	★ STAR PERFORMER THIS WEEK	TITLE	Artist, Company, Record Number	WEEKS ON CHART
—	—	—	91		CINDERELLA	Four Preps, Capitol 4078	1
—	—	—	92		COQUETTE	Fats Domino, Imperial 5553	1
65	62	84	93		NINE MORE MILES	Georgie Young, Cameo 150	9
41	51	78	94		BABY FACE	Little Richard, Specialty 645	10
74	80	88	95		THUNDER ROAD	Robert Mitchum, Capitol 3986	10
—	—	—	96		EVERYONE WAS THERE	Bob Kayli	1
81	69	91	97		JUST YOUNG	Andy Rose, Aamco 100	7
39	48	87	98		LA-DO-DADA	Dale Hawkins, Checker 900	12
—	—	97	99		A HOUSE, A CAR AND A WEDDING RING	Dale Hawkins, Checker 906	3
59	61	59	100		GEE, BUT IT'S LONELY	Pat Boone, Dot 15825	9

The Billboard HOT 100

FOR THE WEEK ENDING NOVEMBER 30

★ THE STAR PERFORMER designation shows the outstanding upward changes of position in The Hot 100 since last week's chart. Its purpose merely is to provide quick visual identification of the sides which moved up most dramatically or to new entries which first entered the chart at an unusually high position.

Three Weeks Ago	Two Weeks Ago	One Week Ago	This Week	★ Star Performer This Week	TITLE	Artist, Company, Record Number	Weeks on Chart
2	1	2	1		IT'S ONLY MAKE BELIEVE	Conway Twitty, M-G-M 12677	11
4	2	1	2		TOM DOOLEY	Kingston Trio, Capitol 4049	9
11	5	5	3		TO KNOW HIM IS TO LOVE HIM	Teddy Bears, Dore 503	10
3	4	3	4		TOPSY II	Cozy Cole, Love 50034	14
1	3	4	5		IT'S ALL IN THE GAME	Tommy Edwards, M-G-M 12688	14
54	19	6	6		BEEP BEEP	Playmates, Roulette 4115	4
—	30	14	7		ONE NIGHT	Elvis Presley, RCA Victor 7210	3
65	18	11	8		I GOT STUNG	Elvis Presley, RCA Victor 7210	4
14	11	8	9		LONESOME TOWN	Ricky Nelson, Imperial 5545	6
15	13	9	10		QUEEN OF THE HOP	Bobby Darin, Atco 6127	8
13	10	10	11		I GOT A FEELING	Ricky Nelson, Imperial 5545	7
8	8	12	12		THE END	Earl Grant, Decca 30719	11
6	6	7	13		CHANTILLY LACE	Big Bopper, Mercury 71343	17
7	7	13	14		TEA FOR TWO CHA CHA	Tommy Dorsey Ork-Warren Covington, Decca 30704	13
88	71	25	15	★	CANNON BALL	Duane Eddy, Jamie 1111	4
19	17	16	16		FORGET ME NOT	Kalin Twins, Decca 30745	9
—	51	42	17	★	PROBLEMS	Everly Brothers, Cadence 1355	3
5	9	15	18		ROCK-IN' ROBIN	Bobby Day, Class 229	17
32	20	22	19		A LOVER'S QUESTION	Clyde McPhatter, Atlantic 1199	6
16	16	18	20		MEXICAN HAT ROCK	Applejacks, Cameo 149	11
24	22	31	21	★	THE DAY THE RAINS CAME	Jane Morgan, Kapp 235	10
17	23	17	22		PUSSY CAT	Ames Brothers, RCA Victor 7315	9
63	43	37	23	★	LOVE IS ALL WE NEED	Tommy Edwards, M-G-M 12722	5
22	21	23	24		CALL ME	Johnny Mathis, Columbia 41253	9
47	41	29	25		LETTER TO AN ANGEL	Jimmy Clanton, Ace 551	6
25	25	19	26		THERE GOES MY HEART	Joni James, M-G-M 12706	11
41	47	20	27		I'LL WAIT FOR YOU	Frankie Avalon, Chancellor 1026	5
43	31	24	28		POOR BOY	Royal Tones, Jubilee 5338	6
75	53	39	29	★	WALKING ALONG	Diamonds, Mercury 71366	5
35	29	28	30		NEED YOU	Donnie Owens, Guyden 2001	8
—	81	36	31		THE WORLD OUTSIDE	Four Coins, Epic 9295	3
26	26	21	32		HIDEAWAY	Four Esquires, Paris 520	10
9	14	26	33		TEARS ON MY PILLOW	Little Anthony & the Imperials, End 1027	16
86	76	41	34		THE MOCKING BIRD	Four Lads, Columbia 41266	4
50	48	35	35		I'LL REMEMBER TONIGHT	Pat Boone, Dot 15840	5
100	83	62	36	★	THAT OLD BLACK MAGIC	Keely Smith & Louis Prima, Capitol 4063	4
30	37	40	37		THE DAY THE RAINS CAME	Raymond Le Fevre, Kapp 231	10
12	12	27	38		SUSIE DARLIN'	Robin Luke, Dot 15781	16
33	35	50	39	★	THE BLOB	Five Blobs, Columbia 41250	9
49	49	33	40		LOVE MAKES THE WORLD GO 'ROUND	Perry Como, RCA Victor 7353	7
44	44	30	41		FALLIN'	Connie Francis, M-G-M 13713	7
58	72	56	42	★	COME ON, LET'S GO	Ritchie Valens, Del Fi 4106	10
67	65	57	43	★	TUNNEL OF LOVE	Doris Day, Columbia 41252	5
—	67	51	44		BIMBOMBEY	Jimmie Rodgers, Roulette 4116	3
52	46	52	45		NON DIMENTICAR	Nat King Cole, Capitol 4056	7
10	15	34	46		BIRD DOG	Everly Brothers, Cadence 1350	17
20	24	32	47		NEAR YOU	Roger Williams, Kapp 233	15
29	32	64	48	★	THE TEN COMMANDMENTS OF LOVE	Harvey & the Moonglows, Chess 1705	11
—	—	81	49	★	WHOLE LOTTA LOVING	Fats Domino, Imperial 5553	2
—	—	86	50	★	SMOKE GETS IN YOUR EYES	Platters, Mercury 71353	2
76	50	44	51		MR. SUCCESS	Frank Sinatra, Capitol 4070	5
70	69	53	52		WHAT DO I CARE	Johnny Cash, Columbia 41251	6
98	64	60	53		A PART OF ME	Jimmy Clanton, Ace 551	4
37	77	38	54		TOPSY I	Cozy Cole, Love 50034	11
—	—	79	55	★	PHILADELPHIA, U.S.A.	Nu Tornados, Carlton 492	2
36	28	46	56		WITH YOUR LOVE	Jack Scott, Carlton 483	9
—	79	66	57		I WANT TO BE HAPPY CHA CHA	Enoch Light & the Light Brigade, Grand Award 1020	3
42	38	49	58		ALL OVER AGAIN	Johnny Cash, Columbia 41251	8
31	42	61	59		FOR MY GOOD FORTUNE	Pat Boone, Dot 15825	10
83	70	65	60		CIMARRON	Billy Vaughn, Dot 15836	6

THE INDUSTRY'S FASTEST AND MOST COMPLETE PROGRAMMING AND BUYING GUIDE

These 100 sides are listed in order of their national POP-ULARITY, as determined by weekly local studies prepared for The Billboard in markets representing a cross-section of the United States. These studies reflect sales registered for each disk up to press time.

★ THE STAR PERFORMER designation shows the outstanding upward changes of position in The Hot 100 since last week's chart. Its purpose merely is to provide quick visual identification of the sides which moved up most dramatically or to new entries which first entered the chart at an unusually high position.

THREE WEEKS AGO	TWO WEEKS AGO	ONE WEEK AGO	THIS WEEK	★ STAR PERFORMER THIS WEEK	TITLE Artist, Company, Record Number	WEEKS ON CHART
46	56	70	61		TREASURE OF YOUR LOVE — Eileen Rodgers, Columbia 41214	14
40	45	45	62		NO ONE KNOWS — Dion & the Belmonts, Laurie 3015	14
39	33	69	63		THE SECRET — Gordon MacRae, Capitol 4033	11
77	73	63	64		LIGHT OF LOVE — Peggy Lee, Capitol 4017	4
—	—	71	65		PLEDGING MY LOVE — Roy Hamilton, Epic 9294	2
23	27	48	66		YOU CHEATED — Shields, Dot 15805	14
66	61	58	67		LOOK WHO'S BLUE — Don Gibson, RCA Victor 7330	9
—	80	67	68		SWEET LITTLE ROCK AND ROLLER — Chuck Berry, Chess 1709	3
60	62	47	69		MANDOLINS IN THE MOONLIGHT — Perry Como, RCA Victor 7353	5
87	75	68	70		JEALOUS HEART — Tab Hunter, Warner Bros. 5008	6
28	34	43	71		FIREFLY — Tony Bennett, Columbia 41237	12
—	—	—	72	★	NEED YOUR LOVE — Bobby Freeman, Josie 844	1
56	54	77	73		GIVE MYSELF A PARTY — Don Gibson, RCA Victor 7330	9
—	—	74	74		LOVE YOU MOST OF ALL — Sam Cooke, Keen 2008	2
53	55	59	75		GUAGLIONE — Perez Prado, RCA Victor 7337	7
—	—	—	76	★	SING, SING, SING — Bernie Lowe Ork, Cameo 153	1
27	39	83	77		HOW THE TIME FLIES — Jerry Wallace, Challenge 59013	15
21	40	82	78		LITTLE STAR — Elegants, Apt 25005	17
55	58	84	79		THIS LITTLE GIRL'S GONE ROCKIN' — Ruth Brown, Atlantic 1197	11
—	100	90	80		WHITE BUCKS AND SADDLE SHOES — Bobby Pedrick Jr., Big Top 3004	3
—	—	—	81	★	INTERMISSION RIFF — Bernie Lowe Ork, Cameo 153	1
79	89	80	82		WIN YOUR LOVE FOR ME — Sam Cooke, Keen 2006	17
—	—	89	83		JO JO GUNNE — Chuck Berry, Chess 1709	2
71	66	55	84		NO ONE BUT YOU — Ames Brothers, RCA Victor 7315	9
—	—	—	85	★	LOVE OF MY LIFE — Everly Brothers, Cadence 1355	1
—	—	—	86	★	GOTTA TRAVEL ON — Billy Grammer, Monument 400	1
—	99	78	87		ALMOST IN YOUR ARMS — Johnny Nash, ABC-Paramount 9960	5
—	—	—	88	★	LONELY TEARDROPS — Jackie Wilson, Brunswick 55105	1
—	95	—	89		IT DON'T HURT NO MORE — Nappy Brown, Savoy 1551	2
80	88	95	90		THUNDER ROAD — Robert Mitchum, Capitol 3986	11

THE BILLBOARD'S BEST BUYS

These records have shown the greatest national SALES BREAKOUT potential this week for the first time. Action sides are listed in capital letters.

POP

SING, SING, SING / INTERMISSION RIFF .... Bernie Lowe Ork
(Robbins, ASCAP) (Golden, ASCAP) Cameo 153

GOTTA TRAVEL ON .... Billy Grammer
(Saga, BMI) Chasing a Dream (Combine, BMI) Monument 400

NEED YOUR LOVE .... Bobby Freeman
(Clockus-Bennell, BMI) Shame on You, Miss Johnson (Clockus-Bennell, BMI) Josie 844

The above are previous Billboard Spotlight picks

THAT OLD BLACK MAGIC .... Louis Prima and Keely Smith
(Famous, ASCAP) You Are My Love (Weiss & Berry, BMI) Capitol 4063

LONELY TEARDROPS .... Jackie Wilson
(Pearl, BMI) In the Blue of Evening (Shapiro-Bernstein, ASCAP) Brunswick 55105

C&W

YOU'RE GOING BACK TO YOUR OLD WAYS AGAIN ... Hank Thompson
(Brazos, BMI) I've Run Out of Tomorrows (Brazos, BMI) Capitol 4085

R&B

NO SELECTIONS THIS WEEK.

★ THE STAR PERFORMER designation shows the outstanding upward changes of position in The Hot 100 since last week's chart. Its purpose merely is to provide quick visual identification of the sides which moved up most dramatically or to new entries which first entered the chart at an unusually high position.

THREE WEEKS AGO	TWO WEEKS AGO	ONE WEEK AGO	THIS WEEK	★ STAR PERFORMER THIS WEEK	TITLE Artist, Company, Record Number	WEEKS ON CHART
—	—	—	91		16 CANDLES — The Crests, Coed 506	1
—	—	—	92		THE WORLD OUTSIDE — Four Aces, Decca 30764	1
—	—	—	93		DONNA — Ritchie Valens, Del-Fi 4110	1
—	—	—	94		C'MON EVERYBODY — Eddie Cochran, Liberty 55166	1
45	52	72	95		LEAVE ME ALONE — Dickey Doo & the Don'ts, Swan 4014	9
—	—	96	96		EVERYONE WAS THERE — Bob Kayli, Carlton 482	2
—	93	87	97		CRAZY COUNTRY HOP — Johnny Otis Show, Capitol 4060	3
72	60	76	98		GO CHASE A MOONBEAM — Jerry Vale, Columbia 41238	7
—	—	—	99		THE WEDDING — June Valli, Mercury 71383	1
—	—	—	100		SWEETHEART — Peggy Lee, Capitol 4107	1

The Billboard HOT 100

FOR THE WEEK ENDING DECEMBER 7

★ THE STAR PERFORMER designation shows the outstanding upward changes of position in The Hot 100 since last week's chart. Its purpose merely is to provide quick visual identification of the sides which moved up most dramatically or to new entries which first entered the chart at an unusually high position.

Three Weeks Ago	Two Weeks Ago	One Week Ago	This Week	★ Star Performer This Week	TITLE Artist, Company, Record Number	Weeks on Chart
5	5	3	1		TO KNOW HIM IS TO LOVE HIM — Teddy Bears, Dore 503	11
2	1	2	2		TOM DOOLEY — Kingston Trio, Capitol 4049	10
1	2	1	3		IT'S ONLY MAKE BELIEVE — Conway Twitty, M-G-M 12677	12
19	6	6	4		BEEP BEEP — Playmates, Roulette 4115	5
30	14	7	5		ONE NIGHT — Elvis Presley, RCA Victor 7210	4
4	3	4	6		TOPSY II — Cozy Cole, Love 50034	15
11	8	9	7		LONESOME TOWN — Ricky Nelson, Imperial 5545	6
51	42	17	8		PROBLEMS — Everly Brothers, Cadence 1355	4
18	11	8	9		I GOT STUNG — Elvis Presley, RCA Victor 7210	5
3	4	5	10		IT'S ALL IN THE GAME — Tommy Edwards, M-G-M 12688	15
13	9	10	11		QUEEN OF THE HOP — Bobby Darin, Atco 6127	9
10	10	11	12		I GOT A FEELING — Ricky Nelson, Imperial 5545	8
8	12	12	13		THE END — Earl Grant, Decca 30719	12
20	22	19	14		A LOVER'S QUESTION — Clyde McPhatter, Atlantic 1199	7
47	20	27	15	★	I'LL WAIT FOR YOU — Frankie Avalon, Chancellor 1026	6
6	7	13	16		CHANTILLY LACE — Big Bopper, Mercury 71343	18
31	24	28	17	★	POOR BOY — Royal Tones, Jubilee 5338	7
43	37	23	18		LOVE IS ALL WE NEED — Tommy Edwards, M-G-M 12722	6
71	25	15	19		CANNON BALL — Duane Eddy, Jamie 1111	5
17	16	16	20		FORGET ME NOT — Kalin Twins, Decca 30748	10
81	36	31	21	★	THE WORLD OUTSIDE — Four Coins, Epic 9295	4
—	86	50	22	★	SMOKE GETS IN YOUR EYES — Platters, Mercury 71353	3
67	51	44	23	★	BIMBOMBEY — Jimmie Rodgers, Roulette 4116	4
7	13	14	24		TEA FOR TWO CHA CHA — Tommy Dorsey Ork-Warren Covington, Decca 30704	14
26	21	32	25		HIDEAWAY — Four Esquires, Paris 520	11
—	81	49	26	★	WHOLE LOTTA LOVING — Fats Domino, Imperial 5553	3
22	31	21	27		THE DAY THE RAINS CAME — Jane Morgan, Kapp 235	11
29	28	30	28		NEED YOU — Donnie Owens, Guyden 2001	9
21	23	24	29		CALL ME — Johnny Mathis, Columbia 41253	10
53	39	29	30		WALKING ALONG — Diamonds, Mercury 71366	6
41	29	25	31		LETTER TO AN ANGEL — Jimmy Clanton, Ace 551	7
16	18	20	32		MEXICAN HAT ROCK — Applejacks, Cameo 149	12
23	17	22	33		PUSSY CAT — Ames Brothers, RCA Victor 7315	10
48	35	35	34		I'LL REMEMBER TONIGHT — Pat Boone, Dot 15840	6
83	62	36	35		THAT OLD BLACK MAGIC — Keely Smith & Louis Prima, Capitol 4063	5
9	15	18	36		ROCK-IN' ROBIN — Bobby Day, Class 229	18
25	19	26	37		THERE GOES MY HEART — Joni James, M-G-M 12706	12
64	60	53	38	★	A PART OF ME — Jimmy Clanton, Ace 551	5
76	41	34	39		THE MOCKING BIRD — Four Lads, Columbia 41266	5
37	40	37	40		THE DAY THE RAINS CAME — Raymond Le Fevre, Kapp 231	11
50	44	51	41	★	MR. SUCCESS — Frank Sinatra, Capitol 4070	6
—	—	88	42	★	LONELY TEARDROPS — Jackie Wilson, Brunswick 55105	2
—	—	86	43	★	GOTTA TRAVEL ON — Billy Grammer, Monument 400	2
65	57	43	44		TUNNEL OF LOVE — Doris Day, Columbia 41252	6
46	52	45	45		NON DIMENTICAR — Nat King Cole, Capitol 4056	8
77	38	54	46		TOPSY I — Cozy Cole, Love 50034	12
80	67	68	47	★	SWEET LITTLE ROCK AND ROLLER — Chuck Berry, Chess 1709	4
—	—	85	48	★	LOVE OF MY LIFE — Everly Brothers, Cadence 1355	2
79	66	57	49		I WANT TO BE HAPPY CHA CHA — Enoch Light & the Light Brigade, Grand Award 1020	4
14	26	33	50		TEARS ON MY PILLOW — Little Anthony & the Imperials, End 1027	17
—	79	55	51		PHILADELPHIA, U.S.A. — Nu Tornados, Carlton 492	3
—	71	65	52	★	PLEDGING MY LOVE — Roy Hamilton, Epic 9294	3
70	65	60	53		CIMARRON — Billy Vaughn, Dot 15836	7
32	64	48	54		THE TEN COMMANDMENTS OF LOVE — Harvey & the Moonglows, Chess 1705	12
49	33	40	55		LOVE MAKES THE WORLD GO 'ROUND — Perry Como, RCA Victor 7353	8
44	30	41	56		FALLIN' — Connie Francis, M-G-M 13713	8
—	—	76	57	★	SING, SING, SING — Bernie Lowe Ork, Cameo 153	2
—	—	72	58	★	NEED YOUR LOVE — Bobby Freeman, Josie 844	2
—	74	74	59	★	LOVE YOU MOST OF ALL — Sam Cooke, Keen 2008	3
69	53	52	60		WHAT DO I CARE — Johnny Cash, Columbia 41251	7

THE INDUSTRY'S FASTEST AND MOST COMPLETE PROGRAMMING AND BUYING GUIDE

These 100 sides are listed in order of their national POPULARITY, as determined by weekly local studies prepared for The Billboard in markets representing a cross-section of the United States. These studies reflect sales registered for each disk up to press time.

★ THE STAR PERFORMER designation shows the outstanding upward changes of position in The Hot 100 since last week's chart. Its purpose merely is to provide quick visual identification of the sides which moved up most dramatically or to new entries which first entered the chart at an unusually high position.

THREE WEEKS AGO	TWO WEEKS AGO	ONE WEEK AGO	THIS WEEK	★ STAR PERFORMER THIS WEEK	TITLE Artist, Company, Record Number	WEEKS ON CHART
—	—	81	61	★	INTERMISSION RIFF — Bernie Lowe Ork, Cameo 153	2
—	—	—	62	★	THE CHIPMUNK SONG — David Seville & the Chipmunks, Liberty 55168	1
35	50	39	63		THE BLOB — Five Blobs, Columbia 41250	10
75	68	70	64		JEALOUS HEART — Tab Hunter, Warner Bros. 5008	7
45	45	62	65		NO ONE KNOWS — Dion & the Belmonts, Laurie 3015	15
—	—	—	66	★	TURVY II — Cozy Cole, Love 5014	1
62	47	69	67		MANDOLINS IN THE MOONLIGHT — Perry Como, RCA Victor 7353	6
42	61	59	68		FOR MY GOOD FORTUNE — Pat Boone, Dot 15825	11
33	69	63	69		THE SECRET — Gordon MacRae, Capitol 4033	12
—	—	—	70	★	NOBODY BUT YOU — Dee Clark, Abner 1019	1
24	32	47	71		NEAR YOU — Roger Williams, Kapp 233	16
12	27	38	72		SUSIE DARLIN' — Robin Luke, Dot 15781	17
55	59	75	73		GUAGLIONE — Perez Prado, RCA Victor 7337	8
100	90	80	74		WHITE BUCKS AND SADDLE SHOES — Bobby Pedrick Jr., Big Top 3004	4
—	—	93	75	★	DONNA — Ritchie Valens, Del-Fi 4110	2
34	43	71	76		FIREFLY — Tony Bennett, Columbia 41237	13
38	49	58	77		ALL OVER AGAIN — Johnny Cash, Columbia 41251	9
15	34	46	78		BIRD DOG — Everly Brothers, Cadence 1350	18
61	58	67	79		LOOK WHO'S BLUE — Don Gibson, RCA Victor 7330	10
73	63	64	80		LIGHT OF LOVE — Peggy Lee, Capitol 4017	5
—	—	91	81		16 CANDLES — The Crests, Coed 506	2
—	—	94	82		C'MON EVERYBODY — Eddie Cochran, Liberty 55166	2
—	—	92	83		THE WORLD OUTSIDE — Four Aces, Decca 30764	2
—	—	99	84	★	THE WEDDING — June Valli, Mercury 71383	2
72	56	42	85		COME ON, LET'S GO — Ritchie Valens, Del-Fi 4106	11
39	83	77	86		HOW THE TIME FLIES — Jerry Wallace, Challenge 59013	16
—	—	—	87	★	TEEN COMMANDMENTS — P. Anka, J. Nash, G. Hamilton IV, ABC-Paramount 9974	1
97	99	—	88	★	A HOUSE, A CAR AND A WEDDING RING — Dale Hawkins, Checker 906	3
28	46	56	89		WITH YOUR LOVE — Jack Scott, Carlton 483	10
—	—	—	90	★	LITTLE RED RIDING HOOD — Big Bopper, Mercury 71375	1
56	70	61	91		TREASURE OF YOUR LOVE — Eileen Rodgers, Columbia 41214	15
—	—	—	92		I WANT TO BE HAPPY CHA CHA — Tommy Dorsey Ork-Warren Covington, Decca 30790	1
—	—	—	93		A HOUSE, A CAR AND A WEDDING RING — Mike Preston, London 1834	1
27	48	66	94		YOU CHEATED — Shields, Dot 15805	15
54	77	73	95		GIVE MYSELF A PARTY — Don Gibson, RCA Victor 7330	10
99	78	87	96		ALMOST IN YOUR ARMS — Johnny Nash, ABC-Paramount 9960	6
—	91	—	97		CINDERELLA — Four Preps, Capitol 4078	2
—	—	100	98		SWEETHEART — Peggy Lee, Capitol 4107	2
—	—	—	99		SEVEN MINUTES IN HEAVEN — Poni Tails, ABC-Paramount 9969	1
—	89	83	100		JO JO GUNNE — Chuck Berry, Chess 1709	3

THE BILLBOARD'S BEST BUYS

These records have shown the greatest national SALES BREAKOUT potential this week for the first time. Action sides are listed in capital letters.

POP

THE CHIPMUNK SONG .... David Seville and the Chipmunks
(Monarch, ASCAP) Almost Good (Monarch, ASCAP) Liberty 55168

TURVY II .... Cozy Cole
(Love, ASCAP) Turvy 1 (Love, ASCAP) Love 5014

NOBODY BUT YOU .... Dee Clark
(Gladstone, ASCAP) When I Call on You (Tollie, BMI) Abner 1019

C&W

BILLY BAYOU .... Jim Reeves
(Tree, BMI) I'd Like to Be (Barton, BMI) RCA Victor 7380

MR. MOON .... Carl Smith

THE BEST YEARS OF MY LIFE
(Peer International, BMI) (Cedarwood, BMI) Columbia 41290

The above are previous Billboard Spotlight picks

R&B

NO SELECTIONS THIS WEEK.

The Billboard HOT 100

FOR THE WEEK ENDING DECEMBER 14

★ THE STAR PERFORMER designation shows the outstanding upward changes of position in The Hot 100 since last week's chart. Its purpose merely is to provide quick visual identification of the sides which moved up most dramatically or to new entries which first entered the chart at an unusually high position.

★ THE STAR PERFORMER designation shows the outstanding upward changes of position in The Hot 100 since last week's chart. Its purpose merely is to provide quick visual identification of the sides which moved up most dramatically or to new entries which first entered the chart at an unusually high position.

THREE WEEKS AGO	TWO WEEKS AGO	ONE WEEK AGO	THIS WEEK	★ STAR PERFORMER THIS WEEK	TITLE	Artist, Company, Record Number	WEEKS ON CHART
5	3	1	1		TO KNOW HIM IS TO LOVE HIM	Teddy Bears, Dore 503	12
1	2	2	2		TOM DOOLEY	Kingston Trio, Capitol 4049	11
2	1	3	3		IT'S ONLY MAKE BELIEVE	Conway Twitty, M-G-M 12677	13
6	6	4	4		BEEP BEEP	Playmates, Roulette 4115	6
14	7	5	5		ONE NIGHT	Elvis Presley, RCA Victor 7210	5
42	17	8	6		PROBLEMS	Everly Brothers, Cadence 1355	5
8	9	7	7		LONESOME TOWN	Ricky Nelson, Imperial 5545	7
3	4	6	8		TOPSY II	Cozy Cole, Love 50034	16
11	8	9	9		I GOT STUNG	Elvis Presley, RCA Victor 7210	6
9	10	11	10		QUEEN OF THE HOP	Bobby Darin, Atco 6127	10
86	50	22	11	★	SMOKE GETS IN YOUR EYES	Platters, Mercury 71353	4
4	5	10	12		IT'S ALL IN THE GAME	Tommy Edwards, M-G-M 12688	16
10	11	12	13		I GOT A FEELING	Ricky Nelson, Imperial 5545	9
22	19	14	14		A LOVER'S QUESTION	Clyde McPhatter, Atlantic 1199	8
7	13	16	15		CHANTILLY LACE	Big Bopper, Mercury 71343	19
81	49	26	16	★	WHOLE LOTTA LOVIN'	Fats Domino, Imperial 5553	4
25	15	19	17		CANNON BALL	Duane Eddy, Jamie 1111	6
51	44	23	18		BIMBOMBEY	Jimmie Rodgers, Roulette 4116	5
37	23	18	19		LOVE IS ALL WE NEED	Tommy Edwards, M-G-M 12722	7
12	12	13	20		THE END	Earl Grant, Decca 30719	13
20	27	15	21		I'LL WAIT FOR YOU	Frankie Avalon, Chancellor 1026	7
62	36	35	22	★	THAT OLD BLACK MAGIC	Keely Smith & Louis Prima, Capitol 4063	6
13	14	24	23		TEA FOR TWO CHA CHA	Tommy Dorsey Ork-Warren Covington, Decca 30704	15
24	28	17	24		POOR BOY	Royal Tones, Jubilee 9338	8
28	30	28	25		NEED YOU	Donnie Owens, Guyden 2001	10
36	31	21	26		THE WORLD OUTSIDE	Four Coins, Epic 9295	5
16	16	20	27		FORGET ME NOT	Kalin Twins, Decca 30745	11
31	21	27	28		THE DAY THE RAINS CAME	Jane Morgan, Kapp 235	12
29	25	31	29		LETTER TO AN ANGEL	Jimmy Clanton, Ace 551	8
—	86	43	30	★	GOTTA TRAVEL ON	Billy Grammer, Monument 400	3
21	32	25	31		HIDEAWAY	Four Esquires, Paris 520	12
41	34	39	32		THE MOCKING BIRD	Four Lads, Columbia 41266	6
—	88	42	33		LONELY TEARDROPS	Jackie Wilson, Brunswick 55105	3
39	29	30	34		WALKING ALONG	Diamonds, Mercury 71366	7
23	24	29	35		CALL ME	Johnny Mathis, Columbia 41253	11
19	26	37	36		THERE GOES MY HEART	Joni James, M-G-M 12706	13
—	—	62	37	★	THE CHIPMUNK SONG	David Seville & the Chipmunks, Liberty 55168	2
15	18	36	38		ROCK-IN' ROBIN	Bobby Day, Class 229	19
60	53	38	39		A PART OF ME	Jimmy Clanton, Ace 551	6
35	35	34	40		I'LL REMEMBER TONIGHT	Pat Boone, Dot 15840	7
17	22	33	41		PUSSY CAT	Ames Brothers, RCA Victor 7315	11
—	—	87	42	★	TEEN COMMANDMENTS	P. Anka, J. Nash, G. Hamilton IV, ABC-Paramount 9974	2
18	20	32	43		MEXICAN HAT ROCK	Applejacks, Cameo 149	13
65	60	53	44		CIMARRON	Billy Vaughn, Dot 15836	8
79	55	51	45		PHILADELPHIA, U.S.A.	Nu Tornados, Carlton 492	4
38	54	46	46		TOPSY I	Cozy Cole, Love 50034	13
44	51	41	47		MR. SUCCESS	Frank Sinatra, Capitol 4070	7
66	57	49	48		I WANT TO BE HAPPY CHA CHA	Enocn Light & the Light Brigade, Grand Award 1020	5
57	43	44	49		NON DIMENTICAR	Nat King Cole, Capitol 4056	9
71	65	52	50		PLEDGING MY LOVE	Roy Hamilton, Epic 9294	4
33	40	55	51		LOVE MAKES THE WORLD GO 'ROUND	Perry Como, RCA Victor 7353	9
—	76	57	52		SING, SING, SING	Bernie Lowe Ork, Cameo 153	3
52	45	45	53		TUNNEL OF LOVE	Doris Day, Columbia 41252	7
—	72	58	54		NEED YOUR LOVE	Bobby Freeman, Josie 844	3
—	93	75	55	★	DONNA	Ritchie Valens, Del-Fi 4110	3
64	48	54	56		THE TEN COMMANDMENTS OF LOVE	Harvey & the Moonglows, Chess 1705	13
—	—	—	57	★	MY HAPPINESS	Connie Francis, M-G-M 12738	1
—	—	66	58		TURVY II	Cozy Cole, Love 5014	2
67	68	47	59		SWEET LITTLE ROCK AND ROLLER	Chuck Berry, Chess 1709	5
30	41	56	60		FALLIN'	Connie Francis, M-G-M 13713	9

THE INDUSTRY'S FASTEST AND MOST COMPLETE PROGRAMMING AND BUYING GUIDE

These 100 sides are listed in order of their national POPULARITY, as determined by weekly local studies prepared for The Billboard in markets representing a cross-section of the United States. These studies reflect sales registered for each disk up to press time.

★ THE STAR PERFORMER designation shows the outstanding upward changes of position in The Hot 100 since last week's chart. Its purpose merely is to provide quick visual identification of the sides which moved up most dramatically or to new entries which first entered the chart at an unusually high position.

THREE WEEKS AGO	TWO WEEKS AGO	ONE WEEK AGO	THIS WEEK	★ STAR PERFORMER THIS WEEK	TITLE	Artist, Company, Record Number	WEEKS ON CHART
—	—	—	61	★	PEEK-A-BOO	Cadillacs, Josie 846	1
47	69	67	62		MANDOLINS IN THE MOONLIGHT	Perry Como, RCA Victor 7353	7
—	—	70	63		NOBODY BUT YOU	Dee Clark, Abner 1019	2
—	—	—	64	★	BIG BOPPER'S WEDDING	Big Bopper, Mercury 71375	1
74	74	59	65		LOVE YOU MOST OF ALL	Sam Cooke, Keen 2008	4
—	81	61	66		INTERMISSION RIFF	Bernie Lowe Ork, Cameo 153	3
68	70	64	67		JEALOUS HEART	Tab Hunter, Warner Bros. 5008	8
—	91	81	68		16 CANDLES	The Crests, Coed 506	3
—	—	—	69	★	MANHATTAN SPIRITUAL	Reg Owen, Palette 5005	1
50	39	63	70		THE BLOB	Five Blobs, Columbia 41250	11
—	99	84	71		THE WEDDING	June Valli, Mercury 71383	3
—	—	90	72	★	LITTLE RED RIDING HOOD	Big Bopper, Mercury 71375	2
—	85	48	73		LOVE OF MY LIFE	Everly Brothers, Cadence 1355	3
26	33	50	74		TEARS ON MY PILLOW	Little Anthony & the Imperials, End 1027	18
40	37	40	75		THE DAY THE RAINS CAME	Raymond Le Fevre, Kapp 231	12
49	58	77	76		ALL OVER AGAIN	Johnny Cash, Columbia 41251	10
—	94	82	77		C'MON EVERYBODY	Eddie Cochran, Liberty 55166	3
53	52	60	78		WHAT DO I CARE	Johnny Cash, Columbia 41251	8
—	92	83	79		THE WORLD OUTSIDE	Four Aces, Decca 30764	3
—	—	—	80	★	COME PRIMA	Tony Dalardo, Mercury 71327	1
—	—	92	81		I WANT TO BE HAPPY CHA CHA	Tommy Dorsey Ork-Warren Covington, Decca 30790	2
69	63	69	82		THE SECRET	Gordon MacRae, Capitol 4033	13
—	—	—	83	★	THE DIARY	Neil Sedaka, RCA Victor 7408	1
45	62	65	84		NO ONE KNOWS	Dion & the Belmonts, Laurie 3015	16
32	47	71	85		NEAR YOU	Roger Williams, Kapp 233	17
—	—	—	86	★	THE WORLD OUTSIDE	Roger Williams, Kapp 246	1
91	—	97	87		CINDERELLA	Four Preps, Capitol 4078	3
63	64	80	88		LIGHT OF LOVE	Peggy Lee, Capitol 4017	6
99	—	88	89		A HOUSE, A CAR AND A WEDDING RING	Dale Hawkins, Checker 906	4
—	—	—	90	★	DIAMOND RING	Jerry Wallace, Challenge 59027	1

THE BILLBOARD'S BEST BUYS

These records have shown the greatest national SALES BREAKOUT potential this week for the first time. Action sides are listed in capital letters.

POP

MY HAPPINESS . . . . . Connie Francis
(Happiness, ASCAP) Never Before (Saunders, ASCAP) M-G-M 12738

PEEK-A-BOO . . . . . The Cadillacs
(Tri-Park, BMI) Oh, Oh, Lolita (Wemar, ASCAP) Josie 846

THE TEEN COMMANDMENTS . . . . . Paul Anka, George Hamilton IV and Johnny Nash
(Pamco, BMI) If You Learn to Pray (Ampco, ASCAP) ABC-Paramount 9974

BIG BOPPER'S WEDDING . . . . . Big Bopper
LITTLE RED RIDING HOOD
(Starrite, BMI) (Starrite, BMI) Mercury 71375

DONNA . . . . . Ritchie Valens
(Kemo, BMI) La Bamba (Kemo, BMI) Del Fi 4110

C&W

I GOTTA TALK TO YOUR HEART . . . . . Hank Locklin
(Starday, BMI) The Other Side of the Door (Tray, ASCAP) RCA Victor 7393

The above are previous Billboard Spotlight picks

R&B

NO SELECTIONS THIS WEEK.

★ THE STAR PERFORMER designation shows the outstanding upward changes of position in The Hot 100 since last week's chart. Its purpose merely is to provide quick visual identification of the sides which moved up most dramatically or to new entries which first entered the chart at an unusually high position.

THREE WEEKS AGO	TWO WEEKS AGO	ONE WEEK AGO	THIS WEEK	★ STAR PERFORMER THIS WEEK	TITLE	Artist, Company, Record Number	WEEKS ON CHART
—	—	—	91		THE FOOL & THE ANGEL	Bobby Helms, Decca 30749	1
56	42	85	92		COME ON, LET'S GO	Ritchie Valens, Del-Fi 4106	12
—	—	—	93		I CRIED A TEAR	La Vern Baker, Atlantic 2007	1
—	—	—	94		STAGGER LEE	Lloyd Price, ABC-Paramount 9927	1
—	—	—	95		BILLY BAYOU	Jim Reeves, RCA Victor 7380	1
87	97	—	96		CRAZY COUNTRY HOP	Johnny Otis Show, Capitol 4060	4
48	66	94	97		YOU CHEATED	Shields, Dot 15805	16
—	—	—	98		DANCE WITH THE TEACHER	Olympics, Demon 1512	1
—	—	—	99		DON'T YOU KNOW YOCKOMO	Huey (Piano) Smith, Ace 553	1
59	75	73	100		GUAGLIONE	Perez Prado, RCA Victor 7337	9

The Billboard HOT 100

FOR THE WEEK ENDING DECEMBER 21

★ THE STAR PERFORMER designation shows the outstanding upward changes of position in The Hot 100 since last week's chart. Its purpose merely is to provide quick visual identification of the sides which moved up most dramatically or to new entries which first entered the chart at an unusually high position.

Three Weeks Ago	Two Weeks Ago	One Week Ago	This Week	★ Star Performer This Week	TITLE Artist, Company, Record Number	Weeks on Chart
3	1	1	1		TO KNOW HIM IS TO LOVE HIM, Teddy Bears, Dore 503	13
17	8	6	2		PROBLEMS, Everly Brothers, Cadence 1355	6
2	2	2	3		TOM DOOLEY, Kingston Trio, Capitol 4049	12
7	5	5	4		ONE NIGHT, Elvis Presley, RCA Victor 7210	6
6	4	4	5		BEEP BEEP, Playmates, Roulette 4115	7
50	22	11	6		SMOKE GETS IN YOUR EYES, Platters, Mercury 71353	5
9	7	7	7		LONESOME TOWN, Ricky Nelson, Imperial 5545	8
1	3	3	8		IT'S ONLY MAKE BELIEVE, Conway Twitty, M-G-M 12677	14
8	9	9	9		I GOT STUNG, Elvis Presley, RCA Victor 7210	7
—	62	37	10	★	THE CHIPMUNK SONG, David Seville & the Chipmunks, Liberty 55168	3
44	23	18	11		BIMBOMBEY, Jimmie Rodgers, Roulette 4116	6
4	6	8	12		TOPSY II, Cozy Cole, Love 5004	17
19	14	14	13		A LOVER'S QUESTION, Clyde McPhatter, Atlantic 1199	9
10	11	10	14		QUEEN OF THE HOP, Bobby Darin, Atco 6127	11
49	26	16	15		WHOLE LOTTA LOVING, Fats Domino, Imperial 5553	5
23	18	19	16		LOVE IS ALL WE NEED, Tommy Edwards, M-G-M 12722	8
11	12	13	17		I GOT A FEELING, Ricky Nelson, Imperial 5545	10
36	35	22	18		THAT OLD BLACK MAGIC, Keely Smith & Louis Prima, Capitol 4063	7
15	19	17	19		CANNON BALL, Duane Eddy, Jamie 1111	7
86	43	30	20	★	GOTTA TRAVEL ON, Billy Grammer, Monument 400	4
12	13	20	21		THE END, Earl Grant, Decca 30719	14
28	17	24	22		POOR BOY, Royal Tones, Jubilee 9338	9
27	15	21	23		I'LL WAIT FOR YOU, Frankie Avalon, Chancellor 1026	8
88	42	33	24		LONELY TEARDROPS, Jackie Wilson, Brunswick 55105	4
5	10	12	25		IT'S ALL IN THE GAME, Tommy Edwards, M-G-M 12688	17
13	16	15	26		CHANTILLY LACE, Big Bopper, Mercury 71343	19
30	28	25	27		NEED YOU, Donnie Owens, Guyden 2001	11
25	31	29	28		LETTER TO AN ANGEL, Jimmy Clanton, Ace 551	9
21	27	28	29		THE DAY THE RAINS CAME, Jane Morgan, Kapp 235	13
31	21	26	30		THE WORLD OUTSIDE, Four Coins, Epic 9295	6
14	24	23	31		TEA FOR TWO CHA CHA, Tommy Dorsey Ork-Warren Covington, Decca 30704	16
29	30	34	32		WALKING ALONG, Diamonds, Mercury 71366	8
93	75	55	33	★	DONNA, Ritchie Valens, Del-Fi 4110	4
—	87	42	34		TEEN COMMANDMENTS, P. Anka, G. Hamilton IV, J. Nash, ABC-Paramount 9974	3
16	20	27	35		FORGET ME NOT, Kalin Twins, Decca 30745	12
74	59	65	36	★	LOVE YOU MOST OF ALL, Sam Cooke, Keen 2008	5
55	51	45	37		PHILADELPHIA, U.S.A., Nu Tornados, Carlton 492	5
—	—	57	38	★	MY HAPPINESS, Connie Francis, M-G-M 12738	2
22	33	41	39		PUSSY CAT, Ames Brothers, RCA Victor 7315	12
85	48	73	40	★	LOVE OF MY LIFE, Everly Brothers, Cadence 1355	4
—	66	58	41	★	TURVY II, Cozy Cole, Love 5014	3
—	—	61	42	★	PEEK-A-BOO, Cadillacs, Josie 846	2
24	29	35	43		CALL ME, Johnny Mathis, Columbia 41253	12
—	—	64	44	★	BIG BOPPER'S WEDDING, Big Bopper, Mercury 71375	2
34	39	32	45		THE MOCKING BIRD, Four Lads, Columbia 41266	7
76	57	52	46		SING, SING, SING, Bernie Lowe Ork, Cameo 153	4
51	41	47	47		MR. SUCCESS, Frank Sinatra, Capitol 4070	8
91	81	68	48	★	16 CANDLES, The Crests, Coed 506	4
60	53	44	49		CIMARRON, Billy Vaughn, Dot 15836	9
32	25	31	50		HIDEAWAY, Four Esquires, Paris 520	13
—	—	83	51	★	THE DIARY, Neil Sedaka, RCA Victor 7408	2
99	84	71	52		THE WEDDING, June Valli, Mercury 71383	4
65	52	50	53		PLEDGING MY LOVE, Roy Hamilton, Epic 9294	5
35	34	40	54		I'LL REMEMBER TONIGHT, Pat Boone, Dot 15840	8
—	—	69	55	★	MANHATTAN SPIRITUAL, Reg Owen, Palette 5005	2
68	47	59	56		SWEET LITTLE ROCK AND ROLLER, Chuck Berry, Chess 1709	6
26	37	36	57		THERE GOES MY HEART, Joni James, M-G-M 12706	14
69	67	62	58		MANDOLINS IN THE MOONLIGHT, Perry Como, RCA Victor 7353	8
—	70	63	59		NOBODY BUT YOU, Dee Clark, Abner 1019	3
57	49	48	60		I WANT TO BE HAPPY CHA CHA, Enoch Light & the Light Brigade, Grand Award 1020	6

THE INDUSTRY'S FASTEST AND MOST COMPLETE PROGRAMMING AND BUYING GUIDE

These 100 sides are listed in order of their national POPULARITY, as determined by weekly local studies prepared for The Billboard in markets representing a cross-section of the United States. These studies reflect sales registered for each disk up to press time.

★ THE STAR PERFORMER designation shows the outstanding upward changes of position in The Hot 100 since last week's chart. Its purpose merely is to provide quick visual identification of the sides which moved up most dramatically or to new entries which first entered the chart at an unusually high position.

THREE WEEKS AGO	TWO WEEKS AGO	ONE WEEK AGO	THIS WEEK	★ STAR PERFORMER THIS WEEK	TITLE Artist, Company, Record Number	WEEKS ON CHART
72	58	54	61		NEED YOUR LOVE — Bobby Freeman, Josie 844	4
70	64	67	62		JEALOUS HEART — Tab Hunter, Warner Bros. 5008	9
92	83	79	63	★	THE WORLD OUTSIDE — Four Aces, Decca 30764	4
53	38	39	64		A PART OF ME — Jimmy Clanton, Ace 551	7
94	82	77	65		C'MON EVERYBODY — Eddie Cochran, Liberty 55166	4
—	—	—	66	★	DONDE ESTA SANTA CLAUS! — Augie Rios, Metro 20010	1
20	32	43	67		MEXICAN HAT ROCK — Applejacks, Cameo 149	14
43	44	49	68		NON DIMENTICAR — Nat King Cole, Capitol 4056	10
18	36	38	69		ROCK-IN' ROBIN — Bobby Day, Class 229	20
—	92	81	70		I WANT TO BE HAPPY CHA CHA — Tommy Dorsey Ork-Warren Covington, Decca 30790	3
—	—	86	71	★	THE WORLD OUTSIDE — Roger Williams, Kapp 246	2
—	—	80	72		COME PRIMA — Tony Dalardo, Mercury 71327	2
48	54	56	73		THE TEN COMMANDMENTS OF LOVE — Harvey & the Moonglows, Chess 1705	14
37	40	75	74		THE DAY THE RAINS CAME — Raymond Le Fevre, Kapp 231	13
—	—	93	75	★	I CRIED A TEAR — LaVern Baker, Atlantic 2007	2
—	97	87	76		CINDERELLA — Four Preps, Capitol 4078	4
—	—	94	77	★	STAGGER LEE — Lloyd Price, ABC-Paramount 9927	2
—	—	—	78	★	IT'S JUST ABOUT TIME — Johnny Cash, Sun 309	1
45	45	53	79		TUNNEL OF LOVE — Doris Day, Columbia 41252	8
—	—	—	80	★	TRY ME — James Brown, Federal 12337	1
—	—	—	81	★	GOODBYE BABY — Jack Scott, Carlton 493	1
58	77	76	82		ALL OVER AGAIN — Johnny Cash, Columbia 41251	11
—	—	—	83	★	RUN, RUDOLPH, RUN — Chuck Berry, Chess 1714	1
81	61	66	84		INTERMISSION RIFF — Bernie Lowe Ork, Cameo 153	4
—	—	—	85	★	I JUST THOUGHT YOU'D LIKE TO KNOW — Johnny Cash, Sun 309	1
33	50	74	86		TEARS ON MY PILLOW — Little Anthony & the Imperials, End 1027	19
40	55	51	87		LOVE MAKES THE WORLD GO 'ROUND — Perry Como, RCA Victor 7353	10
—	—	90	88		DIAMOND RING — Jerry Wallace, Challenge 59027	2
83	100	—	89		JO JO GUNNE — Chuck Berry, Chess 1709	4
—	—	—	90	★	MERRY CHRISTMAS BABY — Chuck Berry, Chess 1714	1

THE BILLBOARD'S BEST BUYS

These records have shown the greatest national SALES BREAKOUT potential this week for the first time. Action sides are listed in capital letters.

POP

IT'S JUST ABOUT TIME .... Johnny Cash
I JUST THOUGHT YOU'D LIKE TO KNOW
(Clement, BMI) (Hi-Lo, BMI) Sun 309

STAGGER LEE .... Lloyd Price
(Sheldon, BMI) You Need Love (Pamco, BMI) ABC-Paramount 9927

GOODBYE BABY .... Jack Scott
(Starfire, BMI) Save My Soul (Starfire, BMI) Carlton 493

I CRIED A TEAR .... La Vern Baker
(Progressive, BMI) Dix-A-Billy (Sounds, ASCAP) Atlantic 2007

MANHATTAN SPIRITUAL .... Reg Owen Ork
(Zodiac, BMI) Ritual Blues (Zodiac, BMI) Palette 5005

The above are previous Billboard Spotlight picks

16 CANDLES .... The Crests
(Coronation, BMI) Beside You (Winneton, BMI) Coed 506

CHRISTMAS

DONDE ESTA SANTA CLAUS! .... Augie Rios
(Ragtime, ASCAP) Ol' Fatso (Shapiro-Bernstein, ASCAP) Metro 20010

RUN, RUDOLPH, RUN .... Chuck Berry
MERRY CHRISTMAS, BABY
(Arc, BMI) (St. Louis, ASCAP) Chess 1714

C&W

WHICH OF US IS TO BLAME! .... The Wilburn Brothers
(Ridgeway, ASCAP) Knoxville Girl (Sure-Fire, BMI) Decca 30787

SITTIN' ALONE .... Webb Pierce
I'M LETTING YOU GO
(Cedarwood, BMI) (Cedarwood, BMI) Decca 30789

The above are previous Billboard Spotlight picks

R&B

NO SELECTIONS THIS WEEK.

★ THE STAR PERFORMER designation shows the outstanding upward changes of position in The Hot 100 since last week's chart. Its purpose merely is to provide quick visual identification of the sides which moved up most dramatically or to new entries which first entered the chart at an unusually high position.

THREE WEEKS AGO	TWO WEEKS AGO	ONE WEEK AGO	THIS WEEK	★ STAR PERFORMER THIS WEEK	TITLE Artist, Company, Record Number	WEEKS ON CHART
—	—	91	91		THE FOOL & THE ANGEL — Bobby Helms, Decca 30749	2
—	—	—	92		PHILADELPHIA, U.S.A. — Art Lund, Coral 62054	1
—	90	72	93		LITTLE RED RIDING HOOD — Big Bopper, Mercury 71375	3
—	88	89	94		A HOUSE, A CAR AND A WEDDING RING — Dale Hawkins, Checker 906	5
42	85	92	95		COME ON, LET'S GO — Ritchie Valens, Del-Fi 4106	13
—	—	—	96		PRETTY GIRLS EVERYWHERE — Eugene Church, Class 235	1
—	—	—	97		DREAMY EYES — Johnny Tillotson, Cadence 1353	3
—	—	—	98		SEVEN MINUTES IN HEAVEN — Poni Tails, ABC-Paramount 9969	1
41	56	60	99		FALLIN' — Connie Francis, M-G-M 13713	10
—	—	—	100		COME PRIMA — Polly Bergen, Columbia 41275	1

The Billboard HOT 100

FOR THE WEEK ENDING DECEMBER 28

★ THE STAR PERFORMER designation shows the outstanding upward changes of position in The Hot 100 since last week's chart. Its purpose merely is to provide quick visual identification of the sides which moved up most dramatically or to new entries which first entered the chart at an unusually high position.

★ THE STAR PERFORMER designation shows the outstanding upward changes of position in The Hot 100 since last week's chart. Its purpose merely is to provide quick visual identification of the sides which moved up most dramatically or to new entries which first entered the chart at an unusually high position.

Three Weeks Ago	Two Weeks Ago	One Week Ago	This Week	★ Star Performer This Week	Title	Artist, Company, Record Number	Weeks on Chart
62	37	10	1	★	THE CHIPMUNK SONG	David Seville & the Chipmunks, Liberty 55168	4
22	11	6	2		SMOKE GETS IN YOUR EYES	Platters, Mercury 71353	6
1	1	1	3		TO KNOW HIM IS TO LOVE HIM	Teddy Bears, Dore 503	14
8	6	2	4		PROBLEMS	Everly Brothers, Cadence 1355	7
2	2	3	5		TOM DOOLEY	Kingston Trio, Capitol 4049	13
5	5	4	6		ONE NIGHT	Elvis Presley, RCA Victor 7210	7
4	4	5	7		BEEP BEEP	Playmates, Roulette 4115	8
7	7	7	8		LONESOME TOWN	Ricky Nelson, Imperial 5345	9
3	3	8	9		IT'S ONLY MAKE BELIEVE	Conway Twitty, M-G-M 12677	15
14	14	13	10		A LOVER'S QUESTION	Clyde McPhatter, Atlantic 1199	10
9	9	9	11		I GOT STUNG	Elvis Presley, RCA Victor 7210	8
26	16	15	12		WHOLE LOTTA LOVING	Fats Domino, Imperial 5553	6
23	18	11	13		BIMBOMBEY	Jimmie Rodgers, Roulette 4116	7
43	30	20	14		GOTTA TRAVEL ON	Billy Grammer, Monument 400	5
18	19	16	15		LOVE IS ALL WE NEED	Tommy Edwards, M-G-M 12722	9
11	10	14	16		QUEEN OF THE HOP	Bobby Darin, Atco 6127	12
—	57	38	17	★	MY HAPPINESS	Connie Francis, M-G-M 12738	3
19	17	19	18		CANNON BALL	Duane Eddy, Jamie 1111	8
42	33	24	19		LONELY TEARDROPS	Jackie Wilson, Brunswick 55105	5
6	8	12	20		TOPSY II	Cozy Cole, Love 50034	18
15	21	23	21		I'LL WAIT FOR YOU	Frankie Avalon, Chancellor 1026	9
12	13	17	22		I GOT A FEELING	Ricky Nelson, Imperial 5545	11
17	24	22	23		POOR BOY	Royal Tones, Jubilee 9338	10
35	22	18	24		THAT OLD BLACK MAGIC	Keely Smith & Louis Prima, Capitol 4063	8
16	15	26	25		CHANTILLY LACE	Big Bopper, Mercury 71343	20
51	45	37	26	★	PHILADELPHIA, U.S.A.	Nu Tornados, Carlton 492	6
75	55	33	27		DONNA	Ritchie Valens, Del-Fi 4110	5
28	25	27	28		NEED YOU	Donnie Owens, Guyden 2001	12
10	12	25	29		IT'S ALL IN THE GAME	Tommy Edwards, M-G-M 12688	18
21	26	30	30		THE WORLD OUTSIDE	Four Coins, Epic 9295	7
—	69	55	31	★	MANHATTAN SPIRITUAL	Reg Owen, Palette 5005	3
81	68	48	32	★	16 CANDLES	The Crests, Coed 506	5
30	34	32	33		WALKING ALONG	Diamonds, Mercury 71366	9
13	20	21	34		THE END	Earl Grant, Decca 30719	15
—	61	42	35		PEEK-A-BOO	Cadillacs, Josie 846	3
59	65	36	36		LOVE YOU MOST OF ALL	Sam Cooke, Keen 2008	6
87	42	34	37		TEEN COMMANDMENTS	P. Anka, G. Hamilton IV, J. Nash, ABC-Paramount 9974	4
—	64	44	38		BIG BOPPER'S WEDDING	Big Bopper, Mercury 71375	3
—	—	—	39	★	(ALL OF A SUDDEN) MY HEART SINGS	Paul Anka, ABC-Paramount 9987	1
34	40	54	40	★	I'LL REMEMBER TONIGHT	Pat Boone, Dot 15840	9
—	83	51	41	★	THE DIARY	Neil Sedaka, RCA Victor 7408	3
31	29	28	42		LETTER TO AN ANGEL	Jimmy Clanton, Ace 551	10
82	77	65	43	★	C'MON EVERYBODY	Eddie Cochran, Liberty 55166	5
66	58	41	44		TURVY II	Cozy Cole, Love 5014	4
—	93	75	45	★	I CRIED A TEAR	LaVern Baker, Atlantic 2007	3
39	32	45	46		THE MOCKING BIRD	Four Lads, Columbia 41266	8
27	28	29	47		THE DAY THE RAINS CAME	Jane Morgan, Kapp 235	14
29	35	43	48		CALL ME	Johnny Mathis, Columbia 41253	13
33	41	39	49		PUSSY CAT	Ames Brothers, RCA Victor 7315	13
20	27	35	50		FORGET ME NOT	Kalin Twins, Decca 30745	13
24	23	31	51		TEA FOR TWO CHA CHA	Tommy Dorsey Ork-Warren Covington, Decca 30704	17
70	63	59	52		NOBODY BUT YOU	Dee Clark, Abner 1019	4
—	—	66	53	★	DONDE ESTA SANTA CLAUS?	Augie Rios, Metro 20010	2
47	59	56	54		SWEET LITTLE ROCK AND ROLLER	Chuck Berry, Chess 1709	7
84	71	52	55		THE WEDDING	June Valli, Mercury 71383	5
—	—	—	56	★	ALL AMERICAN BOY	Billy Parson, Fraternity 835	1
—	—	—	57	★	JINGLE BELL ROCK	Bobby Helms, Decca 30513	1
57	52	46	58		SING, SING, SING	Bernie Lowe Ork, Cameo 153	5
52	50	53	59		PLEDGING MY LOVE	Roy Hamilton, Epic 9294	6
53	44	49	60		CIMARRON	Billy Vaughn, Dot 15836	10

THE INDUSTRY'S FASTEST AND MOST COMPLETE PROGRAMMING AND BUYING GUIDE

These 100 sides are listed in order of their national POPULARITY, as determined by weekly local studies prepared for The Billboard in markets representing a cross-section of the United States. These studies reflect sales registered for each disk up to press time.

★ THE STAR PERFORMER designation shows the outstanding upward changes of position in The Hot 100 since last week's chart. Its purpose merely is to provide quick visual identification of the sides which moved up most dramatically or to new entries which first entered the chart at an unusually high position.

THREE WEEKS AGO	TWO WEEKS AGO	ONE WEEK AGO	THIS WEEK	★ STAR PERFORMER THIS WEEK	TITLE Artist, Company, Record Number	WEEKS ON CHART
25	31	50	61		HIDEAWAY — Four Esquires, Paris 520	14
—	—	78	62	★	IT'S JUST ABOUT TIME — Johnny Cash, Sun 309	2
—	—	—	63	★	DON'T PITY ME — Dion & the Belmonts, Laurie 3021	1
—	—	—	64	★	ROCK-A-CONGA — Applejacks, Cameo 155	1
37	36	57	65		THERE GOES MY HEART — Joni James, M-G-M 12706	15
—	94	77	66		STAGGER LEE — Lloyd Price, ABC-Paramount 9927	3
—	—	80	67		TRY ME — James Brown, Federal 12337	2
—	—	81	68		GOODBYE BABY — Jack Scott, Carlton 493	2
97	87	76	69		CINDERELLA — Four Preps, Capitol 4078	5
—	80	72	70		COME PRIMA — Tony Dalardo, Mercury 71327	3
40	75	74	71		THE DAY THE RAINS CAME — Raymond Le Fevre, Kapp 231	14
54	56	73	72		THE TEN COMMANDMENTS OF LOVE — Harvey & the Moonglows, Chess 1705	15
—	—	83	73		RUN, RUDOLPH, RUN — Chuck Berry, Chess 1714	2
64	67	62	74		JEALOUS HEART — Tab Hunter, Warner Bros. 5008	10
—	—	100	75	★	COME PRIMA — Polly Bergen, Columbia 41275	2
41	47	47	76		MR. SUCCESS — Frank Sinatra, Capitol 4070	9
—	—	—	77	★	LUCKY LADYBUG — Billy & Lillie, Swan 4020	1
48	73	40	78		LOVE OF MY LIFE — Everly Brothers, Cadence 1355	5
—	—	90	79		MERRY CHRISTMAS BABY — Chuck Berry, Chess 1714	2
32	43	67	80		MEXICAN HAT ROCK — Applejacks, Cameo 149	15
—	—	—	81	★	TEASIN' — The Quaker City Boys, Swan 4023	1
67	62	58	82		MANDOLINS IN THE MOONLIGHT — Perry Como, RCA Victor 7353	9
—	90	88	83		DIAMOND RING — Jerry Wallace, Challenge 59027	3
—	91	91	84		THE FOOL AND THE ANGEL — Bobby Helms, Decca 30749	3
—	—	98	85		SEVEN MINUTES IN HEAVEN — Poni Tails, ABC-Paramount 9969	2
—	—	—	86	★	WHITE CHRISTMAS — Bing Crosby, Decca 23778	1
44	49	68	87		NON DIMENTICAR — Nat King Cole, Capitol 4056	11
—	—	—	88	★	THE LITTLE DRUMMER BOY — Harry Simeon Chorale, 20th Fox 121	1
49	48	60	89		I WANT TO BE HAPPY CHA CHA — Enoch Light & the Light Brigade, Grand Award 1020	7
58	54	61	90		NEED YOUR LOVE — Bobby Freeman, Josie 844	5

THE BILLBOARD'S BEST BUYS

These records have shown the greatest national SALES BREAKOUT potential this week for the first time. Action sides are listed in capital letters.

POP

ROCK-A-CONGA . . . . The Applejacks
(Mayland, BMI) Am I Blue (Witmark, ASCAP) Cameo 155

DON'T PITY ME . . . . Dion & The Belmonts
(We Three, BMI) Just You (Schwartz, ASCAP) Laurie 3021

THE DIARY . . . . Neil Sedaka
(Aldon, BMI) No Vacancy (Aldon, BMI) RCA Victor 7408

(ALL OF A SUDDEN) MY HEART SINGS . . . . Paul Anka
(Leeds, ASCAP) That's Love (Spanka, BMI) ABC-Paramount 9987

The above are previous Billboard Spotlight picks

LUCKY LADYBUG . . . . Billy & Lillie
(Conley, BMI) I Promise You (Conley, BMI) Swan 4020

TEASIN' . . . . The Quaker City Boys
(Kellem, ASCAP) Won't 'Y' Come Out, Mary Ann? (Mayland, BMI) Swan 4023

ALL-AMERICAN BOY . . . . Bill Parsons
(Buckeye, ASCAP) Rubber Dolly (Buckeye, ASCAP) Fraternity 835

C'MON EVERYBODY . . . . Eddie Cochran
(Metric, BMI) Dont Ever Let Me Go (American, BMI) Liberty 55166

CHRISTMAS

THE LITTLE DRUMMER BOY . . . . Harry Simeon Chorale
(Delaware, ASCAP) Die Lorelei (Robbins, ASCAP) 20th Fox 121

A previous Billboard Spotlight pick

C&W

NO SELECTIONS THIS WEEK.

R&B

NO SELECTIONS THIS WEEK.

★ THE STAR PERFORMER designation shows the outstanding upward changes of position in The Hot 100 since last week's chart. Its purpose merely is to provide quick visual identification of the sides which moved up most dramatically or to new entries which first entered the chart at an unusually high position.

THREE WEEKS AGO	TWO WEEKS AGO	ONE WEEK AGO	THIS WEEK	★ STAR PERFORMER THIS WEEK	TITLE Artist, Company, Record Number	WEEKS ON CHART
36	38	69	91		ROCK-IN' ROBIN — Bobby Day, Class 229	21
—	—	97	92		DREAMY EYES — Johnny Tilotson, Cadence 1353	4
—	—	92	93		PHILADELPHIA, U.S.A. — Art Lund, Coral 62054	2
100	—	89	94		JO JO GUNNE — Chuck Berry, Chess 1709	5
—	—	—	95		ROCKHOUSE II — Ray Charles, Atlantic 2006	1
—	—	—	96		WIGGLE WIGGLE — Accents, Brunswick 55100	1
—	—	—	97		SO MUCH — Little Anthony & the Imperials, End 1036	1
—	—	—	98		THE REASON — Chanels, Deb 500	1
—	—	—	99		HERE I STAND — Wade Flemons, Vee Jay 295	1
—	—	—	100		DANCE WITH THE TEACHER — Olympics, Demon 1512	1

The Billboard HOT 100

FOR THE WEEK ENDING JANUARY 4

★ THE STAR PERFORMER designation shows the outstanding upward changes of position in The Hot 100 since last week's chart. Its purpose merely is to provide quick visual identification of the sides which moved up most dramatically or to new entries which first entered the chart at an unusually high position.

THREE WEEKS AGO	TWO WEEKS AGO	ONE WEEK AGO	THIS WEEK	★ STAR PERFORMER THIS WEEK	TITLE Artist, Company, Record Number	WEEKS ON CHART
37	10	1	1		THE CHIPMUNK SONG — David Seville & the Chipmunks, Liberty 55168	4
11	6	2	2		SMOKE GETS IN YOUR EYES — Platters, Mercury 71353	7
1	1	3	3		TO KNOW HIM IS TO LOVE HIM — Teddy Bears, Dore 503	15
5	4	6	4		ONE NIGHT — Elvis Presley, RCA Victor 7210	8
6	2	4	5		PROBLEMS — Everly Brothers, Cadence 1355	8
2	3	5	6		TOM DOOLEY — Kingston Trio, Capitol 4049	14
7	7	8	7		LONESOME TOWN — Ricky Nelson, Imperial 5345	10
4	5	7	8		BEEP BEEP — Playmates, Roulette 4115	9
14	13	10	9		A LOVER'S QUESTION — Clyde McPhatter, Atlantic 1199	11
16	15	12	10		WHOLE LOTTA LOVING — Fats Domino, Imperial 5553	7
30	20	14	11		GOTTA TRAVEL ON — Billy Grammer, Monument 400	6
3	8	9	12		IT'S ONLY MAKE BELIEVE — Conway Twitty, M-G-M 12677	16
57	38	17	13		MY HAPPINESS — Connie Francis, M-G-M 12738	4
9	9	11	14		I GOT STUNG — Elvis Presley, RCA Victor 7210	9
18	11	13	15		BIMBOMBEY — Jimmie Rodgers, Roulette 4116	8
33	24	19	16		LONELY TEARDROPS — Jackie Wilson, Brunswick 55105	6
10	14	16	17		QUEEN OF THE HOP — Bobby Darin, Atco 6127	13
55	33	27	18		DONNA — Ritchie Valens, Del-Fi 4110	6
19	16	15	19		LOVE IS ALL WE NEED — Tommy Edwards, M-G-M 12722	10
13	17	22	20		I GOT A FEELING — Ricky Nelson, Imperial 5545	12
24	22	23	21		POOR BOY — Royal Tones, Jubilee 9338	11
69	55	31	22		MANHATTAN SPIRITUAL — Reg Owen, Palette 5005	4
21	23	21	23		I'LL WAIT FOR YOU — Frankie Avalon, Chancellor 1026	10
22	18	24	24		THAT OLD BLACK MAGIC — Keely Smith & Louis Prima, Capitol 4063	9
68	48	32	25		16 CANDLES — Crests, Coed 506	6
65	36	36	26	★	LOVE YOU MOST OF ALL — Sam Cooke, Keen 2008	7
45	37	26	27		PHILADELPHIA, U.S.A. — Nu Tornados, Carlton 492	7
8	12	20	28		TOPSY II — Cozy Cole, Love 50034	19
—	—	88	29	★	THE LITTLE DRUMMER BOY — Harry Simeon Chorale, 20th Fox 121	2
—	81	68	30	★	GOODBYE BABY — Jack Scott, Carlton 493	3
17	19	18	31		CANNON BALL — Duane Eddy, Jamie 1111	9
83	51	41	32		THE DIARY — Neil Sedaka, RCA Victor 7408	4
42	34	37	33		TEEN COMMANDMENTS — P. Anka, G. Hamilton IV, J. Nash, ABC-Paramount 9974	5
93	75	45	34	★	I CRIED A TEAR — LaVern Baker, Atlantic 2007	4
—	—	57	35	★	JINGLE BELL ROCK — Bobby Helms, Decca 30513	2
58	41	44	36		TURVY II — Cozy Cole, Love 5014	5
15	26	25	37		CHANTILLY LACE — Big Bopper, Mercury 71343	21
12	25	29	38		IT'S ALL IN THE GAME — Tommy Edwards, M-G-M 12688	19
—	—	56	39	★	ALL AMERICAN BOY — Billy Parson, Fraternity 835	2
26	30	30	40		THE WORLD OUTSIDE — Four Coins, Epic 9295	8
20	21	34	41		THE END — Earl Grant, Decca 30719	16
64	44	38	42		BIG BOPPER'S WEDDING — Big Bopper, Mercury 71375	4
—	—	39	43		(ALL OF A SUDDEN) MY HEART SINGS — Paul Anka, ABC-Paramount 9987	2
—	—	—	44	★	GREEN CHRISTMAS — Stan Freberg, Capitol 4097	1
50	53	59	45	★	PLEDGING MY LOVE — Roy Hamilton, Epic 9294	7
63	59	52	46		NOBODY BUT YOU — Dee Clark, Abner 1019	5
—	66	53	47		DONDE ESTA SANTA CLAUS! — Augie Rios, Metro 20010	3
77	65	43	48		C'MON EVERYBODY — Eddie Cochran, Liberty 55166	6
35	43	48	49		CALL ME — Johnny Mathis, Columbia 41253	14
61	42	35	50		PEEK-A-BOO — Cadillacs, Josie 846	4
71	52	55	51		THE WEDDING — June Valli, Mercury 71383	6
59	56	54	52		SWEET LITTLE ROCK AND ROLLER — Chuck Berry, Chess 1709	8
94	77	66	53	★	STAGGER LEE — Lloyd Price, ABC-Paramount 9927	4
—	78	62	54		IT'S JUST ABOUT TIME — Johnny Cash, Sun 309	3
—	—	63	55		DON'T PITY ME — Dion & the Belmonts, Laurie 3021	2
—	—	77	56	★	LUCKY LADYBUG — Billy & Lillie, Swan 4020	2
52	46	58	57		SING, SING, SING — Bernie Lowe Ork, Cameo 153	6
—	—	64	58		ROCK-A-CONGA — Applejacks, Cameo 155	2
29	28	42	59		LETTER TO AN ANGEL — Jimmy Clanton, Ace 551	11
23	31	51	60		TEA FOR TWO CHA CHA — Tommy Dorsey Ork-Warren Covington, Decca 30704	18

THE INDUSTRY'S FASTEST AND MOST COMPLETE PROGRAMMING AND BUYING GUIDE

These 100 sides are listed in order of their national POPULARITY, as determined by weekly local studies prepared for The Billboard in markets representing a cross-section of the United States. These studies reflect sales registered for each disk up to press time.

★ THE STAR PERFORMER designation shows the outstanding upward changes of position in The Hot 100 since last week's chart. Its purpose merely is to provide quick visual identification of the sides which moved up most dramatically or to new entries which first entered the chart at an unusually high position.

Three Weeks Ago	Two Weeks Ago	One Week Ago	This Week	★ Star Performer This Week	Title	Artist, Company, Record Number	Weeks on Chart
—	80	67	61		TRY ME	James Brown, Federal 12337	3
25	27	28	62		NEED YOU	Donnie Owens, Guyden 2001	13
31	50	61	63		HIDEAWAY	Four Esquires, Paris 520	15
47	47	76	64		MR. SUCCESS	Frank Sinatra, Capitol 4070	10
40	54	40	65		I'LL REMEMBER TONIGHT	Pat Boone, Dot 15840	10
—	—	86	66	★	WHITE CHRISTMAS	Bing Crosby, Decca 23778	2
—	100	75	67		COME PRIMA	Polly Bergen, Columbia 41275	3
—	—	81	68		TEASIN'	The Quaker City Boys, Swan 4023	2
—	83	73	69		RUN, RUDOLPH, RUN	Chuck Berry, Chess 1714	3
32	45	46	70		THE MOCKING BIRD	Four Lads, Columbia 41266	9
—	90	79	71		MERRY CHRISTMAS, BABY	Chuck Berry, Chess 1714	3
—	—	—	72	★	HAWAIIAN WEDDING SONG	Andy Williams, Cadence 1358	1
—	—	—	73	★	BLUE HAWAII	Billy Vaughn, Dot 15879	1
87	76	69	74		CINDERELLA	Four Preps, Capitol 4078	6
34	32	33	75		WALKING ALONG	Diamonds, Mercury 71366	10
—	—	—	76	★	THE WORRYING KIND	Tommy Sands, Capitol 4082	1
91	91	84	77		THE FOOL AND THE ANGEL	Bobby Helms, Decca 30749	4
90	88	83	78		DIAMOND RING	Jerry Wallace, Challenge 59027	4
—	—	95	79	★	ROCKHOUSE II	Ray Charles, Atlantic 2006	2
73	40	78	80		LOVE OF MY LIFE	Everly Brothers, Cadence 1355	6
—	—	—	81	★	LA BAMBA	Ritchie Valens, Del-Fi 4110	1
41	39	49	82		PUSSY CAT	Ames Brothers, RCA Victor 7315	14
—	97	92	83		DREAMY EYES	Johnny Tillotson, Cadence 1353	5
72	93	—	84		LITTLE RED RIDING HOOD	Big Bopper, Mercury 71375	4
—	—	96	85		WIGGLE WIGGLE	Accents, Brunswick 55100	2
27	35	50	86		FORGET ME NOT	Kalin Twins, Decca 30745	14
—	—	97	87		SO MUCH	Little Anthony & the Imperials, End 1036	2
—	—	—	88	★	VOICE IN MY HEART	Eydie Gorme, ABC-Paramount 9971	1
—	92	93	89		PHILADELPHIA, U.S.A.	Art Lund, Coral 62054	3
28	29	47	90		THE DAY THE RAINS CAME	Jane Morgan, Kapp 235	15

THE BILLBOARD'S BEST BUYS

These records have shown the greatest national SALES BREAKOUT potential this week for the first time. Action sides are listed in capital letters.

POP

THE HAWAIIAN WEDDING SONG .... **Andy Williams**
(Criterion, ASCAP) The House of Bamboo (Pickwick, ASCAP) Cadence 1358

BLUE HAWAII .... **Billy Vaughn**
(Famous, ASCAP) Tico Tico (Peer Int'l, BMI) Dot 15879

TRY ME .... **James Brown**
(Witso, BMI) Tell Me What I Did Wrong (Wisto, BMI) Federal 12337

RED RIVER ROSE .... **Ames Brothers**
(Duchess, BMI) When the Summer Comes Again (Winneton, BMI) RCA Victor 7413

The above are previous Billboard Spotlight picks

C&W

THAT'S WHAT IT'S LIKE TO BE LONESOME .... **Ray Price**
KISSING YOUR PICTURE
(Tree, BMI) (Cedarwood, BMI) Columbia 41309

A previous Billboard Spotlight pick

R&B

ENDS AND ODDS .... **Jimmy Reed**
(Conrad, BMI) I Told You Baby (Conrad, BMI) Vee Jay 304

★ THE STAR PERFORMER designation shows the outstanding upward changes of position in The Hot 100 since last week's chart. Its purpose merely is to provide quick visual identification of the sides which moved up most dramatically or to new entries which first entered the chart at an unusually high position.

Three Weeks Ago	Two Weeks Ago	One Week Ago	This Week	★ Star Performer This Week	Title	Artist, Company, Record Number	Weeks on Chart
36	57	65	91		THERE GOES MY HEART	Joni James, M-G-M 12706	16
—	—	—	92		THE BLUEBIRD, THE BUZZARD, AND THE ORIOLE	Bobby Day, Class 241	1
—	—	—	93		FUNNY	Jessie Blevins, RCA Victor 7387	1
80	72	70	94		COME PRIMA	Tony Dalardo, Mercury 71327	4
62	58	82	95		MANDOLINS IN THE MOONLIGHT	Perry Como, RCA Victor 7353	10
—	—	—	96		THE WORLD OUTSIDE	Roger Williams, Kapp 246	2
56	73	72	97		THE TEN COMMANDMENTS OF LOVE	Harvey & the Moonglows, Chess 1705	16
—	—	—	98		SAVE MY SOUL	Jack Scott, Carlton 493	1
—	—	—	99		HEARTBEAT	Buddy Holly, Coral 62051	1
—	—	—	100		RED RIVER ROSE	Ames Brothers, RCA Victor 7413	1

The Billboard HOT 100

FOR THE WEEK ENDING JANUARY 11

★ THE STAR PERFORMER designation shows the outstanding upward changes of position in The Hot 100 since last week's chart. Its purpose merely is to provide quick visual identification of the sides which moved up most dramatically or to new entries which first entered the chart at an unusually high position.

★ THE STAR PERFORMER designation shows the outstanding upward changes of position in The Hot 100 since last week's chart. Its purpose merely is to provide quick visual identification of the sides which moved up most dramatically or to new entries which first entered the chart at an unusually high position.

THREE WEEKS AGO	TWO WEEKS AGO	ONE WEEK AGO	THIS WEEK	★ STAR PERFORMER THIS WEEK	TITLE — Artist, Company, Record Number	WEEKS ON CHART
10	1	1	1		THE CHIPMUNK SONG — David Seville & the Chipmunks, Liberty 55168	5
6	2	2	2		SMOKE GETS IN YOUR EYES — Platters, Mercury 71353	8
1	3	3	3		TO KNOW HIM IS TO LOVE HIM — Teddy Bears, Dore 503	16
2	4	5	4		PROBLEMS — Everly Brothers, Cadence 1355	9
4	6	4	5		ONE NIGHT — Elvis Presley, RCA Victor 7210	9
38	17	13	6		MY HAPPINESS — Connie Francis, M-G-M 12738	5
3	5	6	7		TOM DOOLEY — Kingston Trio, Capitol 4049	15
13	10	9	8		A LOVER'S QUESTION — Clyde McPhatter, Atlantic 1199	12
20	14	11	9		GOTTA TRAVEL ON — Billy Grammer, Monument 400	7
15	12	10	10		WHOLE LOTTA LOVING — Fats Domino, Imperial 5553	8
7	8	7	11		LONESOME TOWN — Ricky Nelson, Imperial 5345	11
5	7	8	12		BEEP BEEP — Playmates, Roulette 4115	10
11	13	15	13		BIMBOMBEY — Jimmie Rodgers, Roulette, 4116	9
9	11	14	14		I GOT STUNG — Elvis Presley, RCA Victor 7210	10
33	27	18	15		DONNA — Ritchie Valens, Del-Fi 4110	7
—	88	29	16	★	THE LITTLE DRUMMER BOY — Harry Simeon Chorale, 20th Fox 121	3
14	16	17	17		QUEEN OF THE HOP — Bobby Darin, Atco 6127	14
48	32	25	18		16 CANDLES — Crests, Coed 506	7
8	9	12	19		IT'S ONLY MAKE BELIEVE — Conway Twitty, M-G-M 12677	17
24	19	16	20		LONELY TEARDROPS — Jackie Wilson, Brunswick 55105	7
51	41	32	21	★	THE DIARY — Neil Sedaka, RCA Victor 7408	5
55	31	22	22		MANHATTAN SPIRITUAL — Reg Owen Ork, Palette 5005	5
81	68	30	23		GOODBYE BABY — Jack Scott, Carlton 493	4
16	15	19	24		LOVE IS ALL WE NEED — Tommy Edwards, M-G-M 12722	11
23	21	23	25		I'LL WAIT FOR YOU — Frankie Avalon, Chancellor 1026	11
19	18	31	26		CANNON BALL — Duane Eddy, Jamie 1111	10
—	77	56	27	★	LUCKY LADYBUG — Billy & Lillie, Swan 4020	3
37	26	27	28		PHILADELPHIA, U.S.A. — Nu Tornados, Carlton 492	8
34	37	33	29		TEEN COMMANDMENTS — P. Anka, G. Hamilton IV, J. Nash, ABC-Paramount 9974	6
18	24	24	30		THAT OLD BLACK MAGIC — Keely Smith & Louis Prima, Capitol 4063	10
36	36	26	31		LOVE YOU MOST OF ALL — Sam Cooke, Keen 2008	8
22	23	21	32		POOR BOY — Royal Tones, Jubilee 9338	12
—	56	39	33		ALL AMERICAN BOY — Billy Parson, Fraternity 835	3
17	22	20	34		I GOT A FEELING — Ricky Nelson, Imperial 5545	13
65	43	48	35	★	C'MON EVERYBODY — Eddie Cochran, Liberty 55166	7
77	66	53	36	★	STAGGER LEE — Lloyd Price, ABC-Paramount 9927	5
—	39	43	37		(ALL OF A SUDDEN) MY HEART SINGS — Paul Anka, ABC-Paramount 9987	3
75	45	34	38		I CRIED A TEAR — LaVern Baker, Atlantic 2007	5
30	30	40	39		THE WORLD OUTSIDE — Four Coins, Epic 9295	9
—	63	55	40	★	DON'T PITY ME — Dion & the Belmonts, Laurie 3021	3
42	35	50	41		PEEK-A-BOO — Cadillacs, Josie 846	5
12	20	28	42		TOPSY II — Cozy Cole, Love 50034	20
25	29	38	43		IT'S ALL IN THE GAME — Tommy Edwards, M-G-M 12688	20
41	44	36	44		TURVY II — Cozy Cole, Love 5014	6
—	57	35	45		JINGLE BELL ROCK — Bobby Helms, Decca 30513	3
52	55	51	46		THE WEDDING — June Valli, Mercury 71383	7
66	53	47	47		DONDE ESTA SANTA CLAUS! — Augie Rios, Metro 20010	4
—	—	72	48	★	HAWAIIAN WEDDING SONG — Andy Williams, Cadence 1358	2
21	34	41	49		THE END — Earl Grant, Decca 30719	17
—	64	58	50		ROCK-A-CONGA — Applejacks, Cameo 155	3
78	62	54	51		IT'S JUST ABOUT TIME — Johnny Cash, Sun 309	4
44	38	42	52		BIG BOPPER'S WEDDING — Big Bopper, Mercury 71375	5
—	—	44	53		GREEN CHRISTMAS — Stan Freberg, Capitol 4097	2
59	52	46	54		NOBODY BUT YOU — Dee Clark, Abner 1019	6
26	25	37	55		CHANTILLY LACE — Big Bopper, Mercury 71343	22
53	59	45	56		PLEDGING MY LOVE — Roy Hamilton, Epic 9294	8
80	67	61	57		TRY ME — James Brown, Federal 12337	4
—	81	68	58		TEASIN' — Quaker City Boys, Swan 4023	3
—	—	73	59	★	BLUE HAWAII — Billy Vaughn, Dot 15879	2
—	—	100	60	★	RED RIVER ROSE — Ames Brothers, RCA Victor 7413	2

THE INDUSTRY'S FASTEST AND MOST COMPLETE PROGRAMMING AND BUYING GUIDE

These 100 sides are listed in order of their national POPULARITY, as determined by weekly local studies prepared for The Billboard in markets representing a cross-section of the United States. These studies reflect sales registered for each disk up to press time.

★ THE STAR PERFORMER designation shows the outstanding upward changes of position in The Hot 100 since last week's chart. Its purpose merely is to provide quick visual identification of the sides which moved up most dramatically or to new entries which first entered the chart at an unusually high position.

THREE WEEKS AGO	TWO WEEKS AGO	ONE WEEK AGO	THIS WEEK	★ STAR PERFORMER THIS WEEK	TITLE Artist, Company, Record Number	WEEKS ON CHART
—	96	85	61	★	WIGGLE, WIGGLE — Accents, Brunswick 55100	3
50	61	63	62		HIDEAWAY — Four Esquires, Paris 520	16
32	33	75	63		WALKING ALONG — Diamonds, Mercury 71366	11
27	28	62	64		NEED YOU — Donnie Owens, Guyden 2001	14
28	42	59	65		LETTER TO AN ANGEL — Jimmy Clanton, Ace 551	12
45	46	70	66		THE MOCKING BIRD — Four Lads, Columbia 41266	10
97	92	83	67	★	DREAMY EYES — Johnny Tillotson, Cadence 1353	6
31	51	60	68		TEA FOR TWO CHA CHA — Tommy Dorsey Ork-Warren Covington, Decca 30704	19
—	—	92	69	★	THE BLUEBIRD, THE BUZZARD AND THE ORIOLE — Bobby Day, Class 241	2
72	70	94	70	★	COME PRIMA — Tony Dalardo, Mercury 71327	5
—	—	—	71	★	DON'T YOU KNOW YOCKOMO — Huey (Piano) Smith, Ace 553	2
56	54	52	72		SWEET LITTLE ROCK AND ROLLER — Chuck Berry, Chess 1709	9
—	—	—	73	★	YOU ARE BEAUTIFUL — Johnny Mathis, Columbia 41304	1
46	58	57	74		SING, SING, SING — Bernie Lowe Ork, Cameo 153	7
91	84	77	75		THE FOOL AND THE ANGEL — Bobby Helms, Decca 30749	5
100	75	67	76		COME PRIMA — Polly Bergen, Columbia 41275	4
—	—	—	77	★	DANCE WITH THE TEACHER — Olympics, Demon 1512	2
—	—	—	78	★	PETER GUNN THEME — Ray Anthony, Capitol 4041	1
—	—	—	79	★	I TALK TO THE TREES CHA CHA — Edmondo Ros, London 1834	1
—	—	81	80		LA BAMBA — Ritchie Valens, Del-Fi 4110	2
—	—	—	81	★	YELLOW BIRD — Mills Brothers, Dot 15858	1
—	—	—	82		LET'S LOVE — Johnny Mathis, Columbia 41304	1
—	—	—	83	★	THE GIRL ON PAGE 44 — The Four Lads, Columbia 41310	1
—	—	—	84	★	MAY YOU ALWAYS — The McGuire Sisters, Coral 62059	1
96	—	—	85	★	PRETTY GIRLS EVERYWHERE — Eugene Church, Class 235	2
—	—	—	86	★	LITTLE SPACE GIRL — Jessie Lee Turner, Carlton 496	1
39	49	82	87		PUSSY CAT — Ames Brothers, RCA Victor 7315	15
—	—	—	88	★	ONE ROSE — Teresa Brewer, Coral 62057	1
—	—	—	89	★	TEACH ME TONIGHT CHA CHA — De Castro Sisters, ABC-Paramount 9988	1
47	76	64	90		MR. SUCCESS — Frank Sinatra, Capitol 4070	11

THE BILLBOARD'S BEST BUYS

These records have shown the greatest national SALES BREAKOUT potential this week for the first time. Action sides are listed in capital letters.

POP

THE BLUEBIRD, THE BUZZARD AND THE ORIOLE .... **Bobby Day**
(Recordo, BMI) Alone Too Long (Recordo, BMI) Class 241

LET'S LOVE .... **Johnny Mathis**
YOU ARE BEAUTIFUL
(Cathryl, ASCAP) (Williamson, ASCAP) Columbia 41304

DON'T YOU KNOW, YOCKOMO .... **Huey (Piano) Smith**
(Ace, BMI) Well, I'll Be John Brown (Ace, BMI) Ace 553

The above are previous Billboard Spotlight picks

WIGGLE, WIGGLE .... **The Accents**
(Kingsway, ASCAP) Dreamin' and Schemin' (Playersville, ASCAP) Brunswick 55100

C&W

NO SELECTIONS THIS WEEK.

R&B

NO SELECTIONS THIS WEEK.

★ THE STAR PERFORMER designation shows the outstanding upward changes of position in The Hot 100 since last week's chart. Its purpose merely is to provide quick visual identification of the sides which moved up most dramatically or to new entries which first entered the chart at an unusually high position.

THREE WEEKS AGO	TWO WEEKS AGO	ONE WEEK AGO	THIS WEEK	★ STAR PERFORMER THIS WEEK	TITLE Artist, Company, Record Number	WEEKS ON CHART
54	40	65	91		I'LL REMEMBER TONIGHT — Pat Boone, Dot 15840	11
76	69	74	92		CINDERELLA — Four Preps, Capitol 4078	7
—	—	93	93		FUNNY — Jessie Blevins, RCA Victor 7387	2
35	50	86	94		FORGET ME NOT — Kalin Twins, Decca 30745	15
—	—	—	95		THAT'S WHY I CRY — Buddy Knox, Roulette 4120	1
—	—	99	96		HEARTBEAT — Buddy Holly, Coral 62051	2
43	48	49	97		CALL ME — Johnny Mathis, Columbia 41253	15
—	—	—	98		TALL PAUL — Annette, Disneyland 118	1
—	—	—	99		SERMONETTE — Della Reese, Jubilee 5345	1
—	—	—	100		GAZACHSTAHAGEN — Wild Cats, United Artists 154	1

The Billboard HOT 100

FOR THE WEEK ENDING JANUARY 18

★ THE STAR PERFORMER designation shows the outstanding upward changes of position in The Hot 100 since last week's chart. Its purpose merely is to provide quick visual identification of the sides which moved up most dramatically or to new entries which first entered the chart at an unusually high position.

Three Weeks Ago	Two Weeks Ago	One Week Ago	This Week	★ Star Performer This Week	Title	Artist, Company, Record Number	Weeks on Chart
1	1	1	1		THE CHIPMUNK SONG	David Seville & the Chipmunks, Liberty 55168	6
2	2	2	2		SMOKE GETS IN YOUR EYES	Platters, Mercury 71353	9
17	13	6	3		MY HAPPINESS	Connie Francis, M-G-M 12738	6
14	11	9	4		GOTTA TRAVEL ON	Billy Grammer, Monument 400	8
3	3	3	5		TO KNOW HIM IS TO LOVE HIM	Teddy Bears, Dore 503	17
12	10	10	6		WHOLE LOTTA LOVING	Fats Domino, Imperial 5553	9
10	9	8	7		A LOVER'S QUESTION	Clyde McPhatter, Atlantic 1199	13
6	4	5	8		ONE NIGHT	Elvis Presley, RCA Victor 7210	10
4	5	4	9		PROBLEMS	Everly Brothers, Cadence 1355	10
8	7	11	10		LONESOME TOWN	Ricky Nelson, Imperial 5345	11
5	6	7	11		TOM DOOLEY	Kingston Trio, Capitol 4049	16
32	25	18	12		16 CANDLES	Crests, Coed 506	8
88	29	16	13		THE LITTLE DRUMMER BOY	Harry Simeone Chorale, 20th Fox 121	4
13	15	13	14		BIMBOMBEY	Jimmie Rodgers, Roulette 4116	10
27	18	15	15		DONNA	Ritchie Valens, Del-Fi 4110	8
7	8	12	16		BEEP BEEP	Playmates, Roulette 4115	11
19	16	20	17		LONELY TEARDROPS	Jackie Wilson, Brunswick 55105	8
11	14	14	18		I GOT STUNG	Elvis Presley, RCA Victor 7210	11
68	30	23	19		GOODBYE BABY	Jack Scott, Carlton 493	5
31	22	22	20		MANHATTAN SPIRITUAL	Reg Owen Ork, Palette 5005	6
66	53	36	21	★	STAGGER LEE	Lloyd Price, ABC-Paramount 9927	6
9	12	19	22		IT'S ONLY MAKE BELIEVE	Conway Twitty, M-G-M 12677	18
41	32	21	23		THE DIARY	Neil Sedaka, RCA Victor 7408	6
77	56	27	24		LUCKY LADYBUG	Billy and Lillie, Swan 4020	4
39	43	37	25	★	(ALL OF A SUDDEN) MY HEART SINGS	Paul Anka, ABC-Paramount 9987	4
56	39	33	26		ALL AMERICAN BOY	Billy Parson, Fraternity 835	4
36	26	31	27		LOVE YOU MOST OF ALL	Sam Cooke, Keen 2008	9
45	34	38	28	★	I CRIED A TEAR	LaVern Baker, Atlantic 2007	6
16	17	17	29		QUEEN OF THE HOP	Bobby Darin, Atco 6127	15
15	19	24	30		LOVE IS ALL WE NEED	Tommy Edwards, M-G-M 12722	12
26	27	28	31		PHILADELPHIA, U.S.A.	Nu Tornados, Carlton 492	9
21	23	25	32		I'LL WAIT FOR YOU	Frankie Avalon, Chancellor 1026	12
52	46	54	33	★	NOBODY BUT YOU	Dee Clark, Abner 1019	7
—	72	48	34	★	HAWAIIAN WEDDING SONG	Andy Williams, Cadence 1358	3
18	31	26	35		CANNON BALL	Duane Eddy, Jamie 1111	11
35	50	41	36		PEEK-A-BOO	Cadillacs, Josie 846	6
23	21	32	37		POOR BOY	Royal Tones, Jubilee 9338	13
22	20	34	38		I GOT A FEELING	Ricky Nelson, Imperial 5545	14
37	33	29	39		TEEN COMMANDMENTS	P. Anka, G. Hamilton IV, J. Nash, ABC-Paramount 9974	7
64	58	50	40	★	ROCK-A-CONGA	Applejacks, Cameo 155	4
—	100	60	41	★	RED RIVER ROSE	Ames Brothers, RCA Victor 7413	3
43	48	35	42		C'MON EVERYBODY	Eddie Cochran, Liberty 55166	8
55	51	46	43		THE WEDDING	June Valli, Mercury 71383	8
—	—	78	44	★	PETER GUNN THEME	Ray Anthony, Capitol 4041	2
24	24	30	45		THAT OLD BLACK MAGIC	Keely Smith and Louis Prima, Capitol 4063	11
—	—	84	46	★	MAY YOU ALWAYS	McGuire Sisters, Coral 62059	2
62	54	51	47		IT'S JUST ABOUT TIME	Johnny Cash, Sun 309	5
67	61	57	48		TRY ME	James Brown, Federal 12337	5
—	73	59	49	★	BLUE HAWAII	Billy Vaughn, Dot 15879	3
81	68	58	50		TEASIN'	Quaker City Boys, Swan 4023	4
63	55	40	51		DON'T PITY ME	Dion and the Belmonts, Laurie 3021	4
—	—	82	52	★	LET'S LOVE	Johnny Mathis, Columbia 41304	2
59	45	56	53		PLEDGING MY LOVE	Roy Hamilton, Epic 9294	9
—	81	80	54	★	LA BAMBA	Ritchie Valens, Del-Fi 4110	3
96	85	61	55		WIGGLE, WIGGLE	Accents, Brunswick 55100	4
44	36	44	56		TURVY II	Cozy Cole, Love 5014	7
38	42	52	57		BIG BOPPER'S WEDDING	Big Bopper, Mercury 71375	6
29	38	43	58		IT'S ALL IN THE GAME	Tommy Edwards, M-G-M 12688	21
20	28	42	59		TOPSY II	Cozy Cole, Love 50034	21
70	94	70	60	★	COME PRIMA	Tony Dalardo, Mercury 71327	6

THE INDUSTRY'S FASTEST AND MOST COMPLETE PROGRAMMING AND BUYING GUIDE

These 100 sides are listed in order of their national POPULARITY, as determined by weekly local studies prepared for The Billboard in markets representing a cross-section of the United States. These studies reflect sales registered for each disk up to press time.

★ THE STAR PERFORMER designation shows the outstanding upward changes of position in The Hot 100 since last week's chart. Its purpose merely is to provide quick visual identification of the sides which moved up most dramatically or to new entries which first entered the chart at an unusually high position.

THREE WEEKS AGO	TWO WEEKS AGO	ONE WEEK AGO	THIS WEEK	★ STAR PERFORMER THIS WEEK	TITLE Artist, Company, Record Number	WEEKS ON CHART
—	—	86	61	★	LITTLE SPACE GIRL — Jesse Lee Turner, Carlton 496	2
—	—	73	62		YOU ARE BEAUTIFUL — Johnny Mathis, Columbia 41304	2
—	—	71	63		DON'T YOU KNOW YOCKOMO — Huey (Piano) Smith, Ace 553	3
—	92	69	64		THE BLUEBIRD, THE BUZZARD AND THE ORIOLE — Bobby Day, Class 241	3
30	40	39	65		THE WORLD OUTSIDE — Four Coins, Epic 9295	10
—	—	83	66	★	THE GIRL ON PAGE 44 — The Four Lads, Columbia 41310	2
25	37	55	67		CHANTILLY LACE — Big Bopper, Mercury 71343	23
34	41	49	68		THE END — Earl Grant, Decca 30719	18
—	—	—	69	★	THE CHILDREN'S MARCHING SONG — Cyril Stapleton, London 1851	1
57	35	45	70		JINGLE BELL ROCK — Bobby Helms, Decca 30513	4
—	—	77	71		DANCE WITH THE TEACHER — Olympics, Demon 1512	3
—	—	98	72	★	TALL PAUL — Annette, Disneyland 118	2
—	—	—	73	★	THE CHILDREN'S MARCHING SONG — Mitch Miller, Columbia 41317	1
—	—	81	74		YELLOW BIRD — Mills Brothers, Dot 15858	2
—	—	88	75		ONE ROSE — Teresa Brewer, Coral 62057	2
—	—	89	76		TEACH ME TONIGHT CHA CHA — De Castro Sisters, ABC-Paramount 9988	2
33	75	63	77		WALKING ALONG — Diamonds, Mercury 71366	12
—	—	79	78		I TALKED TO THE TREES CHA CHA — Edmundo Ros, London 1834	2
—	—	—	79	★	I'M A MAN — Fabian, Chancellor 1029	1
75	67	76	80		COME PRIMA — Polly Bergen, Columbia 41275	5
—	93	93	81		FUNNY — Jesse Belvin, RCA Victor 7387	3
—	—	85	82		PRETTY GIRLS EVERYWHERE — Eugene Church, Class 235	3
—	—	—	83	★	TRUST IN ME — Patti Page, Mercury 71400	1
84	77	75	84		THE FOOL AND THE ANGEL — Bobby Helms, Decca 30749	6
92	83	67	85		DREAMY EYES — Johnny Tillotson, Cadence 1353	7
51	60	68	86		TEA FOR TWO CHA CHA — Tommy Dorsey Ork-Warren Covington, Decca 30704	20
—	99	96	87		HEARTBEAT — Buddy Holly, Coral 62051	3
—	—	95	88		THAT'S WHY I CRY — Buddy Knox, Roulette 4120	2
—	—	100	89		GAZACHSTAHAGEN — Wild Cats, United Artists 154	2
—	—	—	90	★	PETITE FLEUR — Chris Barber's Jazz Band, Laurie 3022	1

THE BILLBOARD'S BEST BUYS

These records have shown the greatest national SALES BREAKOUT potential this week for the first time. Action sides are listed in capital letters.

POP

THE CHILDREN'S MARCHING SONG .... Cyril Stapleton
(Miller, ASCAP) The Inn of the Sixth Happiness (Miller, ASCAP) London 1851

THE CHILDREN'S MARCHING SONG .... Mitch Miller
(Miller, ASCAP) Carolina in the Morning (Harms, ASCAP) Columbia 41317

THE LITTLE SPACE GIRL .... Jesse Lee Turner
(Longhorn, BMI) Shake, Baby, Shake (Longhorn, BMI) Carlton 496

The above are previous Billboard Spotlight picks

PETER GUNN THEME .... Ray Anthony
(Northridge, ASCAP) Tango for Two (Moonlight, BMI) Capitol 4041

MAY YOU ALWAYS .... The McGuire Sisters
(Hecht-Lancaster & Buzzell, ASCAP) Achoo-Cha Cha (Iris-Trojan, BMI) Coral 62059

C&W

MOMMY FOR A DAY .... Kitty Wells
ALL THE TIME
(Fairway, BMI) (Cedarwood, BMI) Decca 30804

R&B

NO SELECTIONS THIS WEEK.

★ THE STAR PERFORMER designation shows the outstanding upward changes of position in The Hot 100 since last week's chart. Its purpose merely is to provide quick visual identification of the sides which moved up most dramatically or to new entries which first entered the chart at an unusually high position.

THREE WEEKS AGO	TWO WEEKS AGO	ONE WEEK AGO	THIS WEEK	★ STAR PERFORMER THIS WEEK	TITLE Artist, Company, Record Number	WEEKS ON CHART
—	76	—	91		THE WORRYIN' KIND — Tommy Sands, Capitol 4082	2
—	—	—	92		THERE'S GOOD ROCKING TONIGHT — Pat Boone, Dot 15888	1
61	63	62	93		HIDEAWAY — Four Esquires, Paris 520	17
28	62	64	94		NEED YOU — Donnie Owens, Guyden, 2001	15
—	—	—	95		O FALLING STAR — The Four Knights, Coral 62045	1
—	—	—	96		NOLA — Billy Williams, Coral 62069	1
—	—	—	97		WITH THE WIND AND THE RAIN IN YOUR HAIR — Pat Boone, Dot 15888	1
—	—	—	98		RASPBERRIES, STRAWBERRIES — Kingston Trio, Capitol 4114	1
—	—	—	99		YOU CAN'T GET TO HEAVEN ON ROLLER SKATES — Betty Johnson, Atlantic 2009	1
—	—	—	100		IT'S ONLY THE BEGINNING — The Kalin Twins, Decca 30807	1

The Billboard HOT 100

FOR THE WEEK ENDING JANUARY 25

★ THE STAR PERFORMER designation shows the outstanding upward changes of position in The Hot 100 since last week's chart. Its purpose merely is to provide quick visual identification of the sides which moved up most dramatically or to new entries which first entered the chart at an unusually high position.

★ THE STAR PERFORMER designation shows the outstanding upward changes of position in The Hot 100 since last week's chart. Its purpose merely is to provide quick visual identification of the sides which moved up most dramatically or to new entries which first entered the chart at an unusually high position.

THREE WEEKS AGO	TWO WEEKS AGO	ONE WEEK AGO	THIS WEEK	★ STAR PERFORMER THIS WEEK	TITLE — Artist, Company, Record Number	WEEKS ON CHART
2	2	2	1		SMOKE GETS IN YOUR EYES — Platters, Mercury 71383	10
13	6	3	2		MY HAPPINESS — Connie Francis, M-G-M 12738	7
1	1	1	3		THE CHIPMUNK SONG — David Seville & the Chipmunks, Liberty 55168	7
18	15	15	4	★	DONNA — Ritchie Valens, Del-Fi 4110	9
25	18	12	5		16 CANDLES — Crests, Coed 506	9
9	8	7	6		A LOVER'S QUESTION — Clyde McPhatter, Atlantic 1199	14
11	9	4	7		GOTTA TRAVEL ON — Billy Grammer, Monument 400	9
10	10	6	8		WHOLE LOTTA LOVING — Fats Domino, Imperial 5553	10
53	36	21	9	★	STAGGER LEE — Lloyd Price, ABC-Paramount 9972	7
3	3	5	10		TO KNOW HIM IS TO LOVE HIM — Teddy Bears, Dore 503	18
5	4	9	11		PROBLEMS — Everly Brothers, Cadence 1355	11
16	20	17	12		LONELY TEARDROPS — Jackie Wilson, Brunswick 55105	9
4	5	8	13		ONE NIGHT — Elvis Presley, RCA Victor 7410	11
7	11	10	14		LONESOME TOWN — Ricky Nelson, Imperial 5545	12
30	23	19	15		GOODBYE BABY — Jack Scott, Carlton 493	6
22	22	20	16		MANHATTAN SPIRITUAL — Reg Owen Ork, Palette 5005	7
39	33	26	17		ALL AMERICAN BOY — Bill Parsons, Fraternity 835	5
6	7	11	18		TOM DOOLEY — Kingston Trio, Capitol 4049	17
15	13	14	19		BIMBOMBEY — Jimmie Rodgers, Roulette 4116	11
8	12	16	20		BEEP BEEP — Playmates, Roulette 4115	12
32	21	23	21		THE DIARY — Neil Sedaka, RCA Victor 7408	7
14	14	18	22		I GOT STUNG — Elvis Presley, RCA Victor 7410	11
29	16	13	23		THE LITTLE DRUMMER BOY — Harry Simeone Chorale, 20th Fox 121	5
43	37	25	24		(ALL OF A SUDDEN) MY HEART SINGS — Paul Anka, ABC-Paramount 9987	5
56	27	24	25		LUCKY LADYBUG — Billy and Lillie, Swan 4020	5
46	54	33	26		NOBODY BUT YOU — Dee Clark, Abner 1019	8
—	84	46	27	★	MAY YOU ALWAYS — McGuire Sisters, Coral 62059	3
50	41	36	28		PEEK-A-BOO — Cadillacs, Josie 846	7
17	17	29	29		QUEEN OF THE HOP — Bobby Darin, Atco 6127	16
72	48	34	30		HAWAIIAN WEDDING SONG — Andy Williams, Cadence 1358	4
26	31	27	31		LOVE YOU MOST OF ALL — Sam Cooke, Keen 2008	10
27	28	31	32		PHILADELPHIA, U.S.A. — Nu Tornados, Carlton 492	10
81	80	54	33	★	LA BAMBA — Ritchie Valens, Del-Fi 4110	4
—	78	44	34	★	PETER GUNN THEME — Ray Anthony, Capitol 4041	3
34	38	28	35		I CRIED A TEAR — LaVern Baker, Atlantic 2007	7
12	19	22	36		IT'S ONLY MAKE BELIEVE — Conway Twitty, M-G-M 12677	19
100	60	41	37		RED RIVER ROSE — Ames Brothers, RCA Victor 7413	4
23	25	32	38		I'LL WAIT FOR YOU — Frankie Avalon, Chancellor 1026	13
58	50	40	39		ROCK-A-CONGA — Applejacks, Cameo 155	5
—	—	69	40	★	THE CHILDREN'S MARCHING SONG — Cyril Stapleton, London 1851	2
48	35	42	41		C'MON EVERYBODY — Eddie Cochran, Liberty 55166	9
19	24	30	42		LOVE IS ALL WE NEED — Tommy Edwards, M-G-M 12722	13
—	98	72	43	★	TALL PAUL — Annette, Disneyland 118	3
51	46	43	44		THE WEDDING — June Valli, Mercury 71382	9
68	58	50	45		TEASIN' — Quaker City Boys, Swan 4023	5
—	86	61	46	★	LITTLE SPACE GIRL — Jesse Lee Turner, Carlton 496	3
21	32	37	47		POOR BOY — Royal Tones, Jubilee 5338	14
20	34	38	48		I GOT A FEELING — Ricky Nelson, Imperial 5545	15
—	82	52	49		LET'S LOVE — Johnny Mathis, Columbia 41304	3
—	—	97	50	★	WITH THE WIND AND THE RAIN IN YOUR HAIR — Pat Boone, Dot 15888	2
85	61	55	51		WIGGLE, WIGGLE — Accents, Brunswick 55100	5
73	59	49	52		BLUE HAWAII — Billy Vaughn, Dot 15879	4
55	40	51	53		DON'T PITY ME — Dion and the Belmonts, Laurie 3021	5
—	—	73	54	★	THE CHILDREN'S MARCHING SONG — Mitch Miller, Columbia 41317	2
24	30	45	55		THAT OLD BLACK MAGIC — Keely Smith and Louis Prima, Capitol 4063	12
—	—	79	56	★	I'M A MAN — Fabian, Chancellor 1029	2
54	51	47	57		IT'S JUST ABOUT TIME — Johnny Cash, Sun 309	6
—	71	63	58		DON'T YOU KNOW YOCKOMO — Huey (Piano) Smith, Ace 553	4
92	69	64	59		THE BLUEBIRD, THE BUZZARD AND THE ORIOLE — Bobby Day, Class 241	4
—	73	62	60		YOU ARE BEAUTIFUL — Johnny Mathis, Columbia 41304	3

THE INDUSTRY'S FASTEST AND MOST COMPLETE PROGRAMMING AND BUYING GUIDE

These 100 sides are listed in order of their national POPULARITY, as determined by weekly local studies prepared for The Billboard in markets representing a cross-section of the United States. These studies reflect sales registered for each disk up to press time.

★ THE STAR PERFORMER designation shows the outstanding upward changes of position in The Hot 100 since last week's chart. Its purpose merely is to provide quick visual identification of the sides which moved up most dramatically or to new entries which first entered the chart at an unusually high position.

THREE WEEKS AGO	TWO WEEKS AGO	ONE WEEK AGO	THIS WEEK	★ STAR PERFORMER THIS WEEK	TITLE	Artist, Company, Record Number	WEEKS ON CHART
61	57	48	61		TRY ME	James Brown, Federal 12337	6
—	—	83	62	★	TRUST IN ME	Patti Page, Mercury 71400	2
33	29	39	63		TEEN COMMANDMENTS	P. Anka, G. Hamilton IV, J. Nash, ABC-Paramount 9974	8
—	85	82	64	★	PRETTY GIRLS EVERYWHERE	Eugene Church, Class 235	4
—	83	66	65		THE GIRL ON PAGE 44	The Four Lads, Columbia 41310	3
42	52	57	66		BIG BOPPER'S WEDDING	Big Bopper, Mercury 71375	7
31	26	35	67		CANNON BALL	Duane Eddy, Jamie 1111	12
—	—	90	68	★	PETITE FLEUR	Chris Barber's Jazz Band, Laurie 3022	2
—	—	100	69	★	IT'S ONLY THE BEGINNING	The Kalin Twins, Decca 30807	2
—	81	74	70		YELLOW BIRD	Mills Brothers, Dot 15858	3
—	—	—	71	★	DON'T TAKE YOUR GUNS TO TOWN	Johnny Cash, Columbia 41313	1
76	—	91	72	★	THE WORRYIN' KIND	Tommy Sands, Capitol 4082	3
98	—	—	73	★	SAVE MY SOUL	Jack Scott, Carlton 493	2
83	67	85	74		DREAMY EYES	Johnny Tillotson, Cadence 1353	8
45	56	53	75		PLEDGING MY LOVE	Roy Hamilton, Epic 9294	10
—	89	76	76		TEACH ME TONIGHT CHA CHA	DeCastro Sisters, ABC-Paramount 9988	3
41	49	68	77		THE END	Earl Grant, Decca 30719	19
—	100	89	78		GAZACHSTAHAGEN	Wild Cats, United Artists 154	3
36	44	56	79		TURVY II	Cozy Cole, Love 5013	8
—	—	92	80		THERE'S GOOD ROCKING TONIGHT	Pat Boone, Dot 15888	2
—	88	75	81		ONE ROSE	Teresa Brewer, Coral 62057	3
99	96	87	82		HEARTBEAT	Buddy Holly, Coral 62051	4
—	—	95	83		O' FALLING STAR	Four Knights, Coral 62045	2
—	—	98	84		RASPBERRIES, STRAWBERRIES	Kingston Trio, Capitol 4114	2
—	—	—	85	★	TEASABLE PLEASABLE YOU	Buddy Knox, Roulette 76397	1
—	—	—	86	★	LOVERS NEVER SAY GOODBYE	Flamingos, End 1035	1
—	79	78	87		I TALK TO THE TREES CHA CHA	Edmundo Ros, London 1834	3
40	39	65	88		THE WORLD OUTSIDE	Four Coins, Epic 9295	11
—	—	—	89	★	THE LONELY ONE	Duane Eddy, Jamie 1117	1
37	55	67	90		CHANTILLY LACE	Big Bopper, Mercury 71343	24

THE BILLBOARD'S BEST BUYS

These records have shown the greatest national SALES BREAKOUT potential this week for the first time. Action sides are listed in capital letters.

POP

DON'T TAKE YOUR GUNS TO TOWN .... **Johnny Cash**
(Cash, BMI) I Still Miss Someone (Cash BMI) Columbia 41313

WITH THE WIND AND THE RAIN IN YOUR HAIR .... **Pat Boone**
GOOD ROCKIN' TONIGHT
(Paramount, ASCAP) (Blue Ridge, BMI) Dot 15888

TRUST IN ME .... **Patti Page**
(Advanced, ASCAP) Under the Sun Valley Moon (Lear, ASCAP) Mercury 71400

IT'S ONLY THE BEGINNING .... **Kalin Twins**
(Daniels, ASCAP) Oh! My Goodness (Jason, BMI) Decca 30807

The above are previous Billboard Spotlight picks

I'M A MAN .... **Fabian**
(Rio Grande, BMI) Hypnotized (January, BMI) Chancellor 1029

TALL PAUL .... **Annette**
(Wonderland, BMI) Ma, He's Making Eyes at Me (Mills, ASCAP) Disneyland 118

PETITE FLEUR .... **Chris Barber's Jazz Band**
(Hill & Range, BMI) Wild Cat Blues (Pickwick, ASCAP) Laurie 3022

C&W

WHEN IT'S SPRINGTIME IN ALASKA .... **Johnny Horton**
(Cajun, BMI) Whispering Pines (Buna, BMI) Columbia 41308

A previous Billboard Spotlight pick

R&B

THE RIGHT TIME .... **Ray Charles**
(Crossroads, BMI) Tell All the World About You (Progressive, BMI) Atlantic 2010

A previous Billboard Spotlight pick

★ THE STAR PERFORMER designation shows the outstanding upward changes of position in The Hot 100 since last week's chart. Its purpose merely is to provide quick visual identification of the sides which moved up most dramatically or to new entries which first entered the chart at an unusually high position.

THREE WEEKS AGO	TWO WEEKS AGO	ONE WEEK AGO	THIS WEEK	★ STAR PERFORMER THIS WEEK	TITLE	Artist, Company, Record Number	WEEKS ON CHART
—	77	71	91		DANCE WITH THE TEACHER	Olympics, Demon 1512	4
67	76	80	92		COME PRIMA	Polly Bergen, Columbia 41275	6
—	—	—	93		I'LL SAIL MY SHIP ALONE	Jerry Lee Lewis, Sun 312	1
—	—	—	94		MATILDA	Cookie & His Cupcakes, Judd 1002	1
—	—	—	95		HERE I STAND	Wade Flemons, Vee Jay 295	2
—	—	—	96		MY MAN	Peggy Lee, Capitol 4115	1
—	—	—	97		THERE MUST BE A WAY	Joni James, M-G-M 12746	1
93	93	81	98		FUNNY	Jesse Belvin, RCA Victor 7387	4
94	70	60	99		COME PRIMA	Tony Dalardo, Mercury 71327	7
—	—	—	100		WHO CARES	Don Gibson, RCA Victor 7437	1

The Billboard HOT 100

FOR THE WEEK ENDING FEBRUARY 1

★ THE STAR PERFORMER designation shows the outstanding upward changes of position in The Hot 100 since last week's chart. Its purpose merely is to provide quick visual identification of the sides which moved up most dramatically or to new entries which first entered the chart at an unusually high position.

THREE WEEKS AGO	TWO WEEKS AGO	ONE WEEK AGO	THIS WEEK	★ STAR PERFORMER THIS WEEK	TITLE	Artist, Company, Record Number	WEEKS ON CHART
2	2	1	1		SMOKE GETS IN YOUR EYES	Platters, Mercury 71383	11
6	3	2	2		MY HAPPINESS	Connie Francis, M-G-M 12738	8
15	15	4	3		DONNA	Ritchie Valens, Del-Fi 4110	10
18	12	5	4		16 CANDLES	Crests, Coed 506	10
36	21	9	5		STAGGER LEE	Lloyd Price, ABC-Paramount 9972	8
9	4	7	6		GOTTA TRAVEL ON	Billy Grammer, Monument 400	10
8	7	6	7		A LOVER'S QUESTION	Clyde McPhatter, Atlantic 1199	15
20	17	12	8		LONELY TEARDROPS	Jackie Wilson, Brunswick 55105	10
23	19	15	9		GOODBYE BABY	Jack Scott, Carlton 493	7
10	6	8	10		WHOLE LOTTA LOVING	Fats Domino, Imperial 5553	11
84	46	27	11	★	MAY YOU ALWAYS	McGuire Sisters, Coral 62059	4
33	26	17	12		ALL AMERICAN BOY	Bill Parsons, Fraternity 835	6
22	20	16	13		MANHATTAN SPIRITUAL	Reg Owen Ork, Palette 5005	8
27	24	25	14	★	LUCKY LADYBUG	Billy and Lillie, Swan 4020	6
1	1	3	15		THE CHIPMUNK SONG	David Seville and the Chipmunks, Liberty 55168	8
11	10	14	16		LONESOME TOWN	Ricky Nelson, Imperial 5545	13
5	8	13	17		ONE NIGHT	Elvis Presley, RCA Victor 7410	12
3	5	10	18		TO KNOW HIM IS TO LOVE HIM	Teddy Bears, Dore 503	19
21	23	21	19		THE DIARY	Neil Sedaka, RCA Victor 7408	8
37	25	24	20		(ALL OF A SUDDEN) MY HEART SINGS	Paul Anka, ABC-Paramount 9987	6
4	9	11	21		PROBLEMS	Everly Brothers, Cadence 1355	12
78	44	34	22	★	PETER GUNN THEME	Ray Anthony, Capitol 4041	4
48	34	30	23		HAWAIIAN WEDDING SONG	Andy Williams, Cadence 1358	5
7	11	18	24		TOM DOOLEY	Kingston Trio, Capitol 4049	18
13	14	19	25		BIMBOMBEY	Jimmy Rodgers, Roulette 4116	12
16	13	23	26		THE LITTLE DRUMMER BOY	Harry Simeone Chorale, 20th Fox 121	6
38	28	35	27		I CRIED A TEAR	LaVern Baker, Atlantic 2007	8
54	33	26	28		NOBODY BUT YOU	Dee Clark, Abner 1019	9
12	16	20	29		BEEP BEEP	Playmates, Roulette 4115	13
—	69	40	30	★	THE CHILDREN'S MARCHING SONG	Cyril Stapleton, London 1851	3
14	18	22	31		I GOT STUNG	Elvis Presley, RCA Victor 7410	12
31	27	31	32		LOVE YOU MOST OF ALL	Sam Cooke, Keen 2008	11
80	54	33	33		LA BAMBA	Ritchie Valens, Del-Fi 4110	5
—	97	50	34	★	WITH THE WIND AND THE RAIN IN YOUR HAIR	Pat Boone, Dot 15888	3
—	73	54	35	★	THE CHILDREN'S MARCHING SONG	Mitch Miller, Columbia 41317	3
86	61	46	36	★	LITTLE SPACE GIRL	Jesse Lee Turner, Carlton 496	4
60	41	37	37		RED RIVER ROSE	Ames Brothers, RCA Victor 7413	5
50	40	39	38		ROCK-A-CONGA	Applejacks, Cameo 155	6
58	50	45	39		TEASIN'	Quaker City Boys, Swan 4023	6
17	29	29	40		QUEEN OF THE HOP	Bobby Darin, Atco 6127	17
98	72	43	41		TALL PAUL	Annette, Disneyland 118	4
25	32	38	42		I'LL WAIT FOR YOU	Frankie Avalon, Chancellor 1026	14
59	49	52	43		BLUE HAWAII	Billy Vaughn, Dot 15879	5
41	36	28	44		PEEK-A-BOO	Cadillacs, Josie 846	8
—	79	56	45	★	I'M A MAN	Fabian, Chancellor 1029	3
24	30	42	46		LOVE IS ALL WE NEED	Tommy Edwards, M-G-M 12722	14
40	51	53	47		DON'T PITY ME	Dion and the Belmonts, Laurie 3021	6
82	52	49	48		LET'S LOVE	Johnny Mathis, Columbia 41304	4
—	—	71	49	★	DON'T TAKE YOUR GUNS TO TOWN	Johnny Cash, Columbia 41313	2
—	90	68	50	★	PETITE FLEUR	Chris Barber's Jazz Band, Laurie 3022	3
35	42	41	51		C'MON EVERYBODY	Eddie Cochran, Liberty 55166	10
83	66	65	52	★	THE GIRL ON PAGE 44	The Four Lads, Columbia 41310	4
—	83	62	53		TRUST IN ME	Patti Page, Mercury 71400	3
69	64	59	54		THE BLUEBIRD, THE BUZZARD AND THE ORIOLE	Bobby Day, Class 241	5
57	48	61	55		TRY ME	James Brown, Federal 12337	7
71	63	58	56		DON'T YOU KNOW YOCKOMO	Huey (Piano) Smith, Ace 553	5
—	100	69	57	★	IT'S ONLY THE BEGINNING	The Kalin Twins, Decca 30807	3
85	82	64	58		PRETTY GIRLS EVERYWHERE	Eugene Church, Class 235	5
32	37	47	59		POOR BOY	Royal Tones, Jubilee 5338	15
73	62	60	60		YOU ARE BEAUTIFUL	Johnny Mathis, Columbia 41304	3

THE INDUSTRY'S FASTEST AND MOST COMPLETE PROGRAMMING AND BUYING GUIDE

These 100 sides are listed in order of their national POPULARITY, as determined by weekly local studies prepared for The Billboard in markets representing a cross-section of the United States. These studies reflect sales registered for each disk up to press time.

★ THE STAR PERFORMER designation shows the outstanding upward changes of position in The Hot 100 since last week's chart. Its purpose merely is to provide quick visual identification of the sides which moved up most dramatically or to new entries which first entered the chart at an unusually high position.

Three Weeks Ago	Two Weeks Ago	One Week Ago	This Week	★ Star Performer This Week	TITLE — Artist, Company, Record Number	Weeks on Chart
—	—	86	61	★	LOVERS NEVER SAY GOODBYE — Flamingos, End 1035	2
—	—	89	62	★	THE LONELY ONE — Duane Eddy, Jamie 1117	2
67	85	74	63		DREAMY EYES — Johnny Tillotson, Cadence 1353	9
—	—	—	64	★	AMBROSE (PART 5) — Linda Laurie, Glory 290	1
19	22	36	65		IT'S ONLY MAKE BELIEVE — Conway Twitty, M-G-M 12677	20
28	31	32	66		PHILADELPHIA, U.S.A. — Nu Tornados, Carlton 492	11
61	55	51	67		WIGGLE, WIGGLE — Accents, Brunswick 55100	6
30	45	55	68		THAT OLD BLACK MAGIC — Keely Smith and Louis Prima, Capitol 4063	13
—	91	72	69		THE WORRYIN' KIND — Tommy Sands, Capitol 4082	4
46	43	44	70		THE WEDDING — June Valli, Mercury 71382	10
34	38	48	71		I GOT A FEELING — Ricky Nelson, Imperial 5545	16
—	—	—	72	★	THE SHAG — Billy Graves, Monument 401	1
100	89	78	73		GAZACHSTAHAGEN — Wild Cats, United Artists 154	4
81	74	70	74		YELLOW BIRD — Mills Brothers, Dot 15858	4
56	53	75	75		PLEDGING MY LOVE — Roy Hamilton, Epic 9294	11
—	98	84	76		RASPBERRIES, STRAWBERRIES — Kingston Trio, Capitol 4114	3
79	78	87	77		I TALK TO THE TREES CHA CHA — Edmundo Ros, London 1834	4
—	—	73	78		SAVE MY SOUL — Jack Scott, Carlton 493	3
—	92	80	79		THERE'S GOOD ROCKING TONIGHT — Pat Boone, Dot 15888	3
—	—	95	80	★	HERE I STAND — Wade Flemons, Vee Jay 295	3
88	75	81	81		ONE ROSE — Teresa Brewer, Coral 62057	4
—	—	—	82	★	FIRST ANNIVERSARY — Cathy Carr, Roulette 4125	1
54	47	57	83		IT'S JUST ABOUT TIME — Johnny Cash, Sun 309	7
—	—	—	84	★	I GOT A WIFE — Mark IV, Mercury 71403	1
—	95	83	85		O' FALLING STAR — Four Knights, Coral 62045	3
89	76	76	86		TEACH ME TONIGHT CHA CHA — DeCastro Sisters, ABC-Paramount 9988	4
—	—	97	87		THERE MUST BE A WAY — Joni James, M-G-M 12746	2
—	—	—	88	★	I'VE HAD IT — Bell Notes, Time 1004	2
—	—	—	89	★	SHE SAY (OOM DOOBY DOOM) — The Diamonds, Mercury 71404	1
—	—	100	90		WHO CARES — Don Gibson, RCA Victor 7437	2

THE BILLBOARD'S BEST BUYS

These records have shown the greatest national SALES BREAKOUT potential this week for the first time. Action sides are listed in capital letters.

POP

THE LONELY ONE ..... Duane Eddy
(Gregmark, BMI) Detour (Hill & Range, BMI) Jamie 1117

THE GIRL ON PAGE 44 ..... The Four Lads
(Korwin, ASCAP) Sunday (Williamson, ASCAP) Columbia 41310

GAZACHSTAHAGEN ..... The Wild Cats
(Sea Lark Enterprises, BMI) Billy's Cha Cha (Conquest, ASCAP) United Artists 154

The above are previous Billboard Spotlight picks

PRETTY GIRLS EVERYWHERE ..... Eugene Church
(Recordo, BMI) For the Rest of My Life (Recordo, BMI) Class 235

LOVERS NEVER SAY GOODBYE ..... The Flamingos
(Ivy-Gee, BMI) That Love Is You (Regent, BMI) End 1035

AMBROSE (Part 5) ..... Linda Laurie
(Bryden, BMI) Ooh, What a Lover (Bryden, BMI) Glory 290

C&W

NO SELECTIONS THIS WEEK

R&B

NO SELECTIONS THIS WEEK

★ THE STAR PERFORMER designation shows the outstanding upward changes of position in The Hot 100 since last week's chart. Its purpose merely is to provide quick visual identification of the sides which moved up most dramatically or to new entries which first entered the chart at an unusually high position.

Three Weeks Ago	Two Weeks Ago	One Week Ago	This Week	★ Star Performer This Week	TITLE — Artist, Company, Record Number	Weeks on Chart
—	—	85	91		TEASABLE, PLEASABLE YOU — Buddy Knox, Roulette 4120	2
—	—	—	92		IT'S JUST A MATTER OF TIME — Brook Benton, Mercury 71394	1
—	—	94	93		MATILDA — Cookie and His Cupcakes, Judd 1002	2
—	—	—	94		ALRIGHT, OKAY, YOU WIN — Peggy Lee, Capitol 4115	1
—	—	—	95		WICKED RUBY — Danny Zella, Fox 10057	1
—	—	—	96		EVENING RAIN — Earl Grant, Decca 30819	1
—	—	—	97		PLAIN JANE — Bobby Darin, Atco 6133	1
—	—	—	98		RAWHIDE — Link Wray, Epic 9300	1
—	—	—	99		THE STORY OF MY LOVE — Conway Twitty, M-G-M 12748	1
—	—	—	100		TRAGEDY — Thomas Wayne, Fernwood 109	11

The Billboard HOT 100

FOR THE WEEK ENDING FEBRUARY 8

★ THE STAR PERFORMER designation shows the outstanding upward changes of position in The Hot 100 since last week's chart. Its purpose merely is to provide quick visual identification of the sides which moved up most dramatically or to new entries which first entered the chart at an unusually high position.

Three Weeks Ago	Two Weeks Ago	One Week Ago	This Week	★ Star Performer This Week	TITLE Artist, Company, Record Number	Weeks on Chart
2	1	1	1		SMOKE GETS IN YOUR EYES — Platters, Mercury 71383	12
26	17	12	2	★	ALL AMERICAN BOY — Bill Parsons, Fraternity 835	7
15	4	3	3		DONNA — Ritchie Valens, Del-Fi 4110	11
12	5	4	4		16 CANDLES — Crests, Coed 506	11
21	9	5	5		STAGGER LEE — Lloyd Price, ABC-Paramount 9972	9
3	2	2	6		MY HAPPINESS — Connie Francis, M-G-M 12738	9
4	7	6	7		GOTTA TRAVEL ON — Billy Grammer, Monument 400	11
17	12	8	8		LONELY TEARDROPS — Jackie Wilson, Brunswick 55105	11
7	6	7	9		A LOVER'S QUESTION — Clyde McPhatter, Atlantic 1199	16
19	15	9	10		GOODBYE BABY — Jack Scott, Carlton 493	8
20	16	13	11		MANHATTAN SPIRITUAL — Reg Owen Ork, Palette 5005	9
6	8	10	12		WHOLE LOTTA LOVING — Fats Domino, Imperial 5553	12
72	43	41	13	★	TALL PAUL — Annette, Disneyland 118	5
23	21	19	14		THE DIARY — Neil Sedaka, RCA Victor 7408	9
25	24	20	15		(ALL OF A SUDDEN) MY HEART SINGS — Paul Anka, ABC-Paramount 9987	7
34	30	23	16		HAWAIIAN WEDDING SONG — Andy Williams, Cadence 1358	6
46	27	11	17		MAY YOU ALWAYS — McGuire Sisters, Coral 62059	5
44	34	22	18		PETER GUNN THEME — Ray Anthony, Capitol 4041	5
28	35	27	19		I CRIED A TEAR — LaVern Baker, Atlantic 2007	9
69	40	30	20	★	THE CHILDREN'S MARCHING SONG — Cyril Stapleton, London 1851	4
33	26	28	21		NOBODY BUT YOU — Dee Clark, Abner 1019	10
54	33	33	22	★	LA BAMBA — Ritchie Valens, Del-Fi 4110	6
1	3	15	23		THE CHIPMUNK SONG — David Seville and the Chipmunks, Liberty 55168	9
5	10	18	24		TO KNOW HIM IS TO LOVE HIM — Teddy Bears, Dore 503	20
24	25	14	25		LUCKY LADYBUG — Billy and Lillie, Swan 4020	7
61	46	36	26	★	LITTLE SPACE GIRL — Jesse Lee Turner, Carlton 496	5
14	19	25	27		BIMBOMBEY — Jimmie Rodgers, Roulette 4116	13
8	13	17	28		ONE NIGHT — Elvis Presley, RCA Victor 7410	13
73	54	35	29		THE CHILDREN'S MARCHING SONG — Mitch Miller, Columbia 41317	4
10	14	16	30		LONESOME TOWN — Ricky Nelson, Imperial 5545	14
97	50	34	31		WITH THE WIND AND THE RAIN IN YOUR HAIR — Pat Boone, Dot 15888	4
9	11	21	32		PROBLEMS — Everly Brothers, Cadence 1355	13
11	18	24	33		TOM DOOLEY — Kingston Trio, Capitol 4049	19
—	89	62	34	★	THE LONELY ONE — Duane Eddy, Jamie 1117	3
90	68	50	35	★	PETITE FLEUR — Chris Barber's Jazz Band, Laurie 3022	4
13	24	26	36		THE LITTLE DRUMMER BOY — Harry Simeone Chorale, 20th Fox 121	7
49	52	43	37		BLUE HAWAII — Billy Vaughn, Dot 15879	6
79	56	45	38		I'M A MAN — Fabian, Chancellor 1029	4
—	71	49	39	★	DON'T TAKE YOUR GUNS TO TOWN — Johnny Cash, Columbia 41313	3
41	37	37	40		RED RIVER ROSE — Ames Brothers, RCA Victor 7413	6
27	31	32	41		LOVE YOU MOST OF ALL — Sam Cooke, Keen 2008	12
50	45	39	42		TEASIN' — Quaker City Boys, Swan 4023	7
83	62	53	43	★	TRUST IN ME — Patti Page, Mercury 71400	4
52	49	48	44		LET'S LOVE — Johnny Mathis, Columbia 41304	5
—	—	84	45	★	I GOT A WIFE — Mark IV, Mercury 71403	2
18	22	31	46		I GOT STUNG — Elvis Presley, RCA Victor 7410	13
40	39	38	47		ROCK-A-CONGA — Applejacks, Cameo 155	7
16	20	29	48		BEEP BEEP — Playmates, Roulette 4115	14
51	53	47	49		DON'T PITY ME — Dion and the Belmonts, Laurie 3021	7
48	61	55	50		TRY ME — James Brown, Federal 12337	8
42	41	51	51		C'MON EVERYBODY — Eddie Cochran, Liberty 55166	11
—	—	89	52	★	SHE SAY (OOM DOOBY DOOM) — The Diamonds, Mercury 71404	2
82	64	58	53		PRETTY GIRLS EVERYWHERE — Eugene Church, Class 235	6
—	86	61	54		LOVERS NEVER SAY GOODBYE — Flamingos, End 1035	3
36	28	44	55		PEEK-A-BOO — Cadillacs, Josie 846	9
100	69	57	56		IT'S ONLY THE BEGINNING — The Kalin Twins, Decca 30807	4
92	80	79	57	★	GOOD ROCKIN' TONIGHT — Pat Boone, Dot 15888	4
—	—	64	58		AMBROSE (PART 5) — Linda Laurie, Glory 290	2
30	42	46	59		LOVE IS ALL WE NEED — Tommy Edwards, M-G-M 12722	15
66	65	52	60		THE GIRL ON PAGE 44 — The Four Lads, Columbia 41310	5

THE INDUSTRY'S FASTEST AND MOST COMPLETE PROGRAMMING AND BUYING GUIDE

These 100 sides are listed in order of their national POPULARITY, as determined by weekly local studies prepared for The Billboard in markets representing a cross-section of the United States. These studies reflect sales registered for each disk up to press time.

★ THE STAR PERFORMER designation shows the outstanding upward changes of position in The Hot 100 since last week's chart. Its purpose merely is to provide quick visual identification of the sides which moved up most dramatically or to new entries which first entered the chart at an unusually high position.

THREE WEEKS AGO	TWO WEEKS AGO	ONE WEEK AGO	THIS WEEK	★ STAR PERFORMER THIS WEEK	TITLE Artist, Company, Record Number	WEEKS ON CHART
32	38	42	61		I'LL WAIT FOR YOU — Frankie Avalon, Chancellor 1026	15
—	97	87	62	★	THERE MUST BE A WAY — Joni James, M-G-M 12746	3
89	78	73	63		GAZACHSTAHAGEN — Wild Cats, United Artists 154	5
29	29	40	64		QUEEN OF THE HOP — Bobby Darin, Atco 6127	18
—	—	72	65		THE SHAG — Billy Graves, Monument 401	2
43	44	70	66		THE WEDDING — June Valli, Mercury 71382	11
—	—	88	67	★	I'VE HAD IT — Bell Notes, Time 1004	3
37	47	59	68		POOR BOY — Royal Tones, Jubilee 5338	16
—	—	—	69	★	CHARLIE BROWN — Coasters, Atco 6132	1
98	84	76	70		RASPBERRIES, STRAWBERRIES — Kingston Trio, Capitol 4114	4
—	—	94	71	★	ALRIGHT, OKAY, YOU WIN — Peggy Lee, Capitol 4115	2
—	—	97	72	★	PLAIN JANE — Bobby Darin, Atco 6133	2
—	—	92	73	★	IT'S JUST A MATTER OF TIME — Brook Benton, Mercury 71394	2
—	—	100	74	★	TRAGEDY — Thomas Wayne, Fernwood 109	12
62	60	60	75		YOU ARE BEAUTIFUL — Johnny Mathis, Columbia 41304	4
—	—	—	76	★	APPLE BLOSSOM TIME — Tab Hunter, Warner Bros. 5032	1
74	70	74	77		YELLOW BIRD — Mills Brothers, Dot 15858	5
75	81	81	78		ONE ROSE — Teresa Brewer, Coral 62057	5
—	—	82	79		FIRST ANNIVERSARY — Cathy Carr, Roulette 4125	2
—	95	80	80		HERE I STAND — Wade Flemons, Vee Jay 295	4
—	100	90	81		WHO CARES — Don Gibson, RCA Victor 7437	3
63	58	56	82		DON'T YOU KNOW YOCKOMO — Huey (Piano) Smith, Ace 553	6
—	—	96	83		EVENING RAIN — Earl Grant, Decca 30819	2
—	94	93	84		MATILDA — Cookie and His Cupcakes, Judd 1002	3
—	—	—	85	★	MY MAN — Peggy Lee, Capitol 4115	1
—	—	95	86		WICKED RUBY — Danny Zella, Fox 10057	2
91	72	69	87		THE WORRYIN' KIND — Tommy Sands, Capitol 4082	5
53	75	75	88		PLEDGING MY LOVE — Roy Hamilton, Epic 9294	12
55	51	67	89		WIGGLE, WIGGLE — Accents, Brunswick 55100	7
38	48	71	90		I GOT A FEELING — Ricky Nelson, Imperial 5545	17

THE BILLBOARD'S BEST BUYS

These records have shown the greatest national SALES BREAKOUT potential this week for the first time. Action sides are listed in capital letters.

POP

SHE SAY (OOM DOOBY DOOM) .... The Diamonds
(Stratton, BMI) From the Bottom of My Heart (Rush, BMI) Mercury 71404

MY MAN .... Peggy Lee
ALRIGHT, OKAY, YOU WIN
(Feist, ASCAP) (Munson, ASCAP) Capitol 4115

PLAIN JANE .... Bobby Darin
(Rumbalero-Fern-Progressive, BMI) While I'M Gone (Fern-Progressive, BMI) Atco 6133

THERE MUST BE A WAY .... Joni James
(Valando, ASCAP) Sorry for Myself (Saunders, ASCAP) M-G-M 12746

APPLE BLOSSOM TIME .... Tab Hunter
(Broadway-Vogel, ASCAP) My Only Love (Witmark, ASCAP) Warner Bros. 5032

The above are previous Billboard Spotlight picks

I GOT A WIFE .... Mark IV
(Pure, BMI) Ah-Oo-Gah (Pure, BMI) Mercury 71403

CHARLIE BROWN .... The Coasters
(Tiger, BMI) Three Cool Cats (Tiger, BMI) Atco 6132

I'VE HAD IT .... The Bell Notes
(Brent, BMI) Be Mine (Brent, BMI) Time 1004

IT'S JUST A MATTER OF TIME .... Brook Benton
(Eden, BMI) Hurtin' Inside (Eden, BMI) Mercury 71394

TRAGEDY .... Thomas Wayne
(Bluff City, BMI) Saturday Date (Dacapo, BMI) Fernwood 109

C&W

NO SELECTIONS THIS WEEK

R&B

NO SELECTIONS THIS WEEK

★ THE STAR PERFORMER designation shows the outstanding upward changes of position in The Hot 100 since last week's chart. Its purpose merely is to provide quick visual identification of the sides which moved up most dramatically or to new entries which first entered the chart at an unusually high position.

THREE WEEKS AGO	TWO WEEKS AGO	ONE WEEK AGO	THIS WEEK	★ STAR PERFORMER THIS WEEK	TITLE Artist, Company, Record Number	WEEKS ON CHART
—	—	99	91		THE STORY OF MY LOVE — Conway Twitty, M-G-M 12748	2
31	32	66	92		PHILADELPHIA, U.S.A. — Nu Tornados, Carlton 492	12
22	36	65	93		IT'S ONLY MAKE BELIEVE — Conway Twitty, M-G-M 12677	21
—	—	98	94		RAWHIDE — Link Wray, Epic 9300	2
—	—	—	95		NOLA — Billy Williams, Coral 62069	3
—	—	—	96		GIVE ME YOUR LOVE — Nat King Cole, Capitol 4125	1
—	—	—	97		TEARDROPS WILL FALL — Dicky Doo and the Don'ts, Swan 4025	1
64	59	54	98		THE BLUEBIRD, THE BUZZARD AND THE ORIOLE — Bobby Day, Class 241	6
—	—	—	99		THE HANGING TREE — Marty Robbins, Columbia 41235	1
—	—	—	100		MADRID — Nat King Cole, Capitol 4125	1

The Billboard HOT 100

FOR THE WEEK ENDING FEBRUARY 15

★ THE STAR PERFORMER designation shows the outstanding upward changes of position in The Hot 100 since last week's chart. Its purpose merely is to provide quick visual identification of the sides which moved up most dramatically or to new entries which first entered the chart at an unusually high position.

Three Weeks Ago	Two Weeks Ago	One Week Ago	This Week	★ Star Performer This Week	Title	Artist, Company, Record Number	Weeks on Chart
9	5	5	1		STAGGER LEE	Lloyd Price, ABC-Paramount 9972	10
5	4	4	2		16 CANDLES	Crests, Coed 506	12
4	3	3	3		DONNA	Ritchie Valens, Del-Fi 4110	12
1	1	1	4		SMOKE GETS IN YOUR EYES	Platters, Mercury 71383	13
17	12	2	5		ALL AMERICAN BOY	Bill Parsons, Fraternity 835	8
2	2	6	6		MY HAPPINESS	Connie Francis, M-G-M 12738	10
12	8	8	7		LONELY TEARDROPS	Jackie Wilson, Brunswick 55105	12
7	6	7	8		GOTTA TRAVEL ON	Billy Grammer, Monument 400	12
15	9	10	9		GOODBYE BABY	Jack Scott, Carlton 493	9
16	13	11	10		MANHATTAN SPIRITUAL	Reg Owen Ork, Palette 5005	10
6	7	9	11		A LOVER'S QUESTION	Clyde McPhatter, Atlantic 1199	17
35	27	19	12		I CRIED A TEAR	LaVern Baker, Atlantic 2007	10
40	30	20	13		THE CHILDREN'S MARCHING SONG	Cyril Stapleton, London 1851	5
30	23	16	14		HAWAIIAN WEDDING SONG	Andy Williams, Cadence 1358	7
24	20	15	15		(ALL OF A SUDDEN) MY HEART SINGS	Paul Anka, ABC-Paramount 9987	8
54	35	29	16	★	THE CHILDREN'S MARCHING SONG	Mitch Miller, Columbia 41317	5
34	22	18	17		PETER GUNN THEME	Ray Anthony, Capitol 4041	6
43	41	13	18		TALL PAUL	Annette, Disneyland 118	6
21	19	14	19		THE DIARY	Neil Sedaka, RCA Victor 7408	10
46	36	26	20		LITTLE SPACE GIRL	Jesse Lee Turner, Carlton 496	6
50	34	31	21	★	WITH THE WIND AND THE RAIN IN YOUR HAIR	Pat Boone, Dot 15888	5
68	50	35	22	★	PETITE FLEUR	Chris Barber's Jazz Band, Laurie 3022	5
27	11	17	23		MAY YOU ALWAYS	McGuire Sisters, Coral 62059	6
25	14	25	24		LUCKY LADYBUG	Billy and Lilie, Swan 4020	8
8	10	12	25		WHOLE LOTTA LOVING	Fats Domino, Imperial 5553	13
89	62	34	26		THE LONELY ONE	Duane Eddy, Jamie 1117	4
26	28	21	27		NOBODY BUT YOU	Dee Clark, Abner 1019	11
3	15	23	28		THE CHIPMUNK SONG	David Seville and the Chipmunks, Liberty 55168	10
—	—	69	29	★	CHARLIE BROWN	Coasters, Atco 6132	2
33	33	22	30		LA BAMBA	Ritchie Valens, Del-Fi 4110	7
56	45	38	31		I'M A MAN	Fabian, Chancellor 1029	5
10	18	24	32		TO KNOW HIM IS TO LOVE HIM	Teddy Bears, Dore 503	21
71	49	39	33		DON'T TAKE YOUR GUNS TO TOWN	Johnny Cash, Columbia 41313	4
—	84	45	34	★	I GOT A WIFE	Mark IV, Mercury 71403	3
13	17	28	35		ONE NIGHT	Elvis Presley, RCA Victor 7410	14
—	88	67	36	★	I'VE HAD IT	Bell Notes, Time 1004	4
14	16	30	37		LONESOME TOWN	Ricky Nelson, Imperial 5545	17
—	92	73	38	★	IT'S JUST A MATTER OF TIME	Brook Benton, Mercury 71394	3
37	37	40	39		RED RIVER ROSE	Ames Brothers, RCA Victor 7413	7
—	89	52	40	★	SHE SAY (OOM DOOBY DOOM)	The Diamonds, Mercury 71404	3
31	32	41	41		LOVE YOU MOST OF ALL	Sam Cooke, Keen 2008	13
45	39	42	42		TEASIN'	Quaker City Boys, Swan 4023	8
19	25	27	43		BIMBOMBEY	Jimmie Rodgers, Roulette 4116	14
64	58	53	44		PRETTY GIRLS EVERYWHERE	Eugene Church, Class 235	7
69	57	56	45	★	IT'S ONLY THE BEGINNING	The Kalin Twins, Decca 30807	5
53	47	49	46		DON'T PITY ME	Dion and the Belmonts, Laurie 3021	8
—	100	74	47	★	TRAGEDY	Thomas Wayne, Fernwood 109	13
62	53	43	48		TRUST IN ME	Patti Page, Mercury 71400	5
80	79	57	49		GOOD ROCKIN' TONIGHT	Pat Boone, Dot 15888	5
61	55	50	50		TRY ME	James Brown, Federal 12337	9
49	48	44	51		LET'S LOVE	Johnny Mathis, Columbia 41304	6
97	87	62	52	★	THERE MUST BE A WAY	Joni James, M-G-M 12746	4
18	24	33	53		TOM DOOLEY	Kingston Trio, Capitol 4049	20
86	61	54	54		LOVERS NEVER SAY GOODBYE	Flamingos, End 1035	4
52	43	37	55		BLUE HAWAII	Billy Vaughn, Dot 15879	7
—	97	72	56	★	PLAIN JANE	Bobby Darin, Atco 6133	3
78	73	63	57		GAZACHSTAHAGEN	Wild Cats, United Artists 154	6
11	21	32	58		PROBLEMS	Everly Brothers, Cadence 1355	14
—	—	76	59	★	APPLE BLOSSOM TIME	Tab Hunter, Warner Bros. 5032	2
—	99	91	60	★	THE STORY OF MY LOVE	Conway Twitty, M-G-M 12748	3

THE INDUSTRY'S FASTEST AND MOST COMPLETE PROGRAMMING AND BUYING GUIDE

These 100 sides are listed in order of their national POPULARITY, as determined by weekly local studies prepared for The Billboard in markets representing a cross-section of the United States. These studies reflect sales registered for each disk up to press time.

★ THE STAR PERFORMER designation shows the outstanding upward changes of position in The Hot 100 since last week's chart. Its purpose merely is to provide quick visual identification of the sides which moved up most dramatically or to new entries which first entered the chart at an unusually high position.

THREE WEEKS AGO	TWO WEEKS AGO	ONE WEEK AGO	THIS WEEK	★ STAR PERFORMER THIS WEEK	TITLE	Artist, Company, Record Number	WEEKS ON CHART
—	—	95	61	★	NOLA	Billy Williams, Coral 62069	3
39	38	47	62		ROCK-A-CONGA	Applejacks, Cameo 155	8
100	90	81	63	★	WHO CARES	Don Gibson, RCA Victor 7437	4
—	82	79	64	★	FIRST ANNIVERSARY	Cathy Carr, Roulette 4125	3
24	26	36	65		THE LITTLE DRUMMER BOY	Harry Simeone Chorale, 20th Fox 121	8
22	31	46	66		I GOT STUNG	Elvis Presley, RCA Victor 7410	14
44	70	66	67		THE WEDDING	June Valli, Mercury 71382	12
65	52	60	68		THE GIRL ON PAGE 44	The Four Lads, Columbia 41310	6
—	94	71	69		ALRIGHT, OKAY, YOU WIN	Peggy Lee, Capitol 4115	3
94	93	84	70		MATILDA	Cookie and His Cupcakes, Judd 1002	4
28	44	55	71		PEEK-A-BOO	Cadillacs, Josie 846	10
—	98	94	72	★	RAWHIDE	Link Wray, Epic 9300	3
84	76	70	73		RASPBERRIES, STRAWBERRIES	Kingston Trio, Capitol 4114	5
—	96	83	74		EVENING RAIN	Earl Grant, Decca 30819	3
—	64	58	75		AMBROSE (PART 5)	Linda Laurie, Glory 290	3
42	46	59	76		LOVE IS ALL WE NEED	Tommy Edwards, M-G-M 12722	16
—	95	86	77		WICKED RUBY	Danny Zella, Fox 10057	3
20	29	48	78		BEEP BEEP	Playmates, Roulette 4115	15
41	51	51	79		C'MON EVERYBODY	Eddie Cochran, Liberty 55166	12
—	72	65	80		THE SHAG	Billy Graves, Monument 401	3
—	—	85	81		MY MAN	Peggy Lee, Capitol 4115	2
—	—	96	82		GIVE ME YOUR LOVE	Nat King Cole, Capitol 4125	2
47	59	68	83		POOR BOY	Royal Tones, Jubilee 5338	17
95	80	80	84		HERE I STAND	Wade Flemons, Vee Jay 295	5
—	—	100	85	★	MADRID	Nat King Cole, Capitol 4125	2
—	—	97	86		TEARDROPS WILL FALL	Dicky Doo and the Don'ts, Swan 4025	2
72	69	87	87		THE WORRYIN' KIND	Tommy Sands, Capitol 4082	6
—	—	—	88	★	NOLA	Morgan Brothers, M-G-M 12747	1
—	—	—	89	★	SEA CRUISE	Frankie Ford, Ace 554	1
—	—	99	90		THE HANGING TREE	Marty Robbins, Columbia 41325	2

THE BILLBOARD'S BEST BUYS

These records have shown the greatest national SALES BREAKOUT potential this week for the first time. Action sides are listed in capital letters.

POP

THE STORY OF MY LOVE ... Conway Twitty
(Marielle, BMI) Make Me Know You're Mine (Ross-Jungnickel, ASCAP) M-G-M 12748

WHO CARES ... Don Gibson
(Acuff-Rose, BMI) A Stranger to Me (Acuff-Rose, BMI) RCA Victor 7437

NOLA ... Billy Williams
(Fox, ASCAP) Tied to the Strings of Your Heart (Drake, BMI) Coral 62069

The above are previous Billboard Spotlight picks

FIRST ANNIVERSARY ... Cathy Carr
(Planetary, ASCAP) With Love (Favorite, ASCAP) Roulette 4125

RAWHIDE ... Link Wray
(Andval, BMI) Dixie-Doodle (Andval, BMI) Epic 9300

C&W

NO SELECTIONS THIS WEEK

R&B

NO SELECTIONS THIS WEEK

★ THE STAR PERFORMER designation shows the outstanding upward changes of position in The Hot 100 since last week's chart. Its purpose merely is to provide quick visual identification of the sides which moved up most dramatically or to new entries which first entered the chart at an unusually high position.

THREE WEEKS AGO	TWO WEEKS AGO	ONE WEEK AGO	THIS WEEK	★ STAR PERFORMER THIS WEEK	TITLE	Artist, Company, Record Number	WEEKS ON CHART
38	42	61	91		I'LL WAIT FOR YOU	Frankie Avalon, Chancellor 1026	16
60	60	75	92		YOU ARE BEAUTIFUL	Johnny Mathis, Columbia 41304	5
29	40	64	93		QUEEN OF THE HOP	Bobby Darin, Atco 6127	19
—	—	—	94		JUPITER-C	Pat and the Satellite, Atco 6131	1
—	—	—	95		THE RIGHT TIME	Ray Charles, Atlantic 2010	1
—	—	—	96		BLAH, BLAH, BLAH	Nicola Paone, ABC-Paramount 9993	1
—	—	—	97		MIDNIGHT OIL	Charlie Blackwell, Warner Bros. 5031	1
—	—	—	98		ARE YOU LONESOME TONIGHT	Jaye P. Morgan, M-G-M 12757	1
—	—	—	99		VENUS	Frankie Avalon, Chancellor 1031	1
—	—	—	100		MOONLIGHT SERENADE	The Rivieras, Coed 508	1

The Billboard HOT 100

FOR THE WEEK ENDING FEBRUARY 22

★ THE STAR PERFORMER designation shows the outstanding upward changes of position in The Hot 100 since last week's chart. Its purpose merely is to provide quick visual identification of the sides which moved up most dramatically or to new entries which first entered the chart at an unusually high position.

★ THE STAR PERFORMER designation shows the outstanding upward changes of position in The Hot 100 since last week's chart. Its purpose merely is to provide quick visual identification of the sides which moved up most dramatically or to new entries which first entered the chart at an unusually high position.

THREE WEEKS AGO	TWO WEEKS AGO	ONE WEEK AGO	THIS WEEK	★ STAR PERFORMER THIS WEEK	TITLE	Artist, Company, Record Number	WEEKS ON CHART
5	5	1	1		STAGGER LEE	Lloyd Price, ABC-Paramount 9972	11
4	4	2	2		16 CANDLES	Crests, Coed 506	13
3	3	3	3		DONNA	Ritchie Valens, Del-Fi 4110	13
1	1	4	4		SMOKE GETS IN YOUR EYES	Platters, Mercury 71383	14
12	2	5	5		ALL AMERICAN BOY	Bill Parsons, Fraternity 835	9
2	6	6	6		MY HAPPINESS	Connie Francis, M-G-M 12738	11
8	8	7	7		LONELY TEARDROPS	Jackie Wilson, Brunswick 55105	13
9	10	9	8		GOODBYE BABY	Jack Scott, Carlton 493	10
6	7	8	9		GOTTA TRAVEL ON	Billy Grammer, Monument 400	13
13	11	10	10		MANHATTAN SPIRITUAL	Reg Owen Ork, Palette 5005	11
23	16	14	11		HAWAIIAN WEDDING SONG	Andy Williams, Cadence 1358	8
41	13	18	12		TALL PAUL	Annette, Disneyland 118	7
50	35	22	13		PETITE FLEUR	Chris Barber's Jazz Band, Laurie 3022	6
27	19	12	14		I CRIED A TEAR	LaVern Baker, Atlantic 2007	11
30	20	13	15		THE CHILDREN'S MARCHING SONG	Cyril Stapleton, London 1851	6
22	18	17	16		PETER GUNN THEME	Ray Anthony, Capitol 4041	7
7	9	11	17		A LOVER'S QUESTION	Clyde McPhatter, Atlantic 1199	18
35	29	16	18		THE CHILDREN'S MARCHING SONG	Mitch Miller, Columbia 41317	6
20	15	15	19		(ALL OF A SUDDEN) MY HEART SINGS	Paul Anka, ABC-Paramount 9987	9
—	69	29	20		CHARLIE BROWN	Coasters, Atco 6132	3
11	17	23	21		MAY YOU ALWAYS	McGuire Sisters, Coral 62059	7
34	31	21	22		WITH THE WIND AND THE RAIN IN YOUR HAIR	Pat Boone, Dot 15888	6
62	34	26	23		THE LONELY ONE	Duane Eddy, Jamie 1117	5
36	26	20	24		LITTLE SPACE GIRL	Jesse Lee Turner, Carlton 496	7
88	67	36	25	★	I'VE HAD IT	Bell Notes, Time 1004	5
14	25	24	26		LUCKY LADYBUG	Billy and Lillie, Swan 4020	9
19	14	19	27		THE DIARY	Neil Sedaka, RCA Victor 7408	11
84	45	34	28		I GOT A WIFE	Mark IV, Mercury 71403	4
89	52	40	29	★	SHE SAY (OOM DOOBY DOOM)	The Diamonds, Mercury 71404	4
28	21	27	30		NOBODY BUT YOU	Dee Clark, Abner 1019	12
45	38	31	31		I'M A MAN	Fabian, Chancellor 1029	6
49	39	33	32		DON'T TAKE YOUR GUNS TO TOWN	Johnny Cash, Columbia 41313	5
87	62	52	33	★	THERE MUST BE A WAY	Joni James, M-G-M 12746	5
33	22	30	34		LA BAMBA	Ritchie Valens, Del-Fi 4110	8
99	91	60	35	★	THE STORY OF MY LOVE	Conway Twitty, M-G-M 12748	4
92	73	38	36		IT'S JUST A MATTER OF TIME	Brook Benton, Mercury 71394	4
10	12	25	37		WHOLE LOTTA LOVING	Fats Domino, Imperial 5553	14
100	74	47	38		TRAGEDY	Thomas Wayne, Fernwood 109	14
—	95	61	39	★	NOLA	Billy Williams, Coral 62069	4
15	23	28	40		THE CHIPMUNK SONG	David Seville and the Chipmunks, Liberty 55168	11
37	40	39	41		RED RIVER ROSE	Ames Brothers, RCA Victor 7413	8
58	53	44	42		PRETTY GIRLS EVERYWHERE	Eugene Church, Class 235	8
18	24	32	43		TO KNOW HIM IS TO LOVE HIM	Teddy Bears, Dore 503	22
32	41	41	44		LOVE YOU MOST OF ALL	Sam Cooke, Keen 2008	14
97	72	56	45	★	PLAIN JANE	Bobby Darin, Atco 6133	4
47	49	46	46		DON'T PITY ME	Dion and the Belmonts, Laurie 3021	9
57	56	45	47		IT'S ONLY THE BEGINNING	The Kalin Twins, Decca 30807	6
53	43	48	48		TRUST IN ME	Patti Page, Mercury 71400	6
—	76	59	49	★	APPLE BLOSSOM TIME	Tab Hunter, Warner Bros. 5032	3
43	37	55	50		BLUE HAWAII	Billy Vaughn, Dot 15879	8
25	27	43	51		BIMBOMBEY	Jimmie Rodgers, Roulette 4116	15
61	54	54	52		LOVERS NEVER SAY GOODBYE	Flamingos, End 1035	5
—	—	99	53	★	VENUS	Frankie Avalon, Chancellor 1031	2
82	79	64	54	★	FIRST ANNIVERSARY	Cathy Carr, Roulette 4125	4
79	57	49	55		GOOD ROCKIN' TONIGHT	Pat Boone, Dot 15888	6
39	42	42	56		TEASIN'	Quaker City Boys, Swan 4023	9
90	81	63	57		WHO CARES	Don Gibson, RCA Victor 7437	5
52	60	68	58	★	THE GIRL ON PAGE 44	The Four Lads, Columbia 41310	7
55	50	50	59		TRY ME	James Brown, Federal 12337	10
16	30	37	60		LONESOME TOWN	Ricky Nelson, Imperial 5545	18

THE INDUSTRY'S FASTEST AND MOST COMPLETE PROGRAMMING AND BUYING GUIDE

These 100 sides are listed in order of their national POPULARITY, as determined by weekly local studies prepared for The Billboard in markets representing a cross-section of the United States. These studies reflect sales registered for each disk up to press time.

★ THE STAR PERFORMER designation shows the outstanding upward changes of position in The Hot 100 since last week's chart. Its purpose merely is to provide quick visual identification of the sides which moved up most dramatically or to new entries which first entered the chart at an unusually high position.

Three Weeks Ago	Two Weeks Ago	One Week Ago	This Week	★ Star Performer This Week	Title	Artist, Company, Record Number	Weeks on Chart
17	28	35	61		ONE NIGHT	Elvis Presley, RCA Victor 7410	15
64	58	75	62		AMBROSE (PART 5)	Linda Laurie, Glory 290	4
48	44	51	63		LET'S LOVE	Johnny Mathis, Columbia 41304	7
98	94	72	64		RAWHIDE	Link Wray, Epic 9300	4
—	—	—	65	★	ANTHONY BOY	Chuck Berry, Chess 1716	1
96	83	74	66		EVENING RAIN	Earl Grant, Decca 30819	4
93	84	70	67		MATILDA	Cookie and His Cupcakes, Judd 1002	5
94	71	69	68		ALRIGHT, OKAY, YOU WIN	Peggy Lee, Capitol 4115	4
73	63	57	69		GAZACHSTAHAGEN	Wild Cats, United Artists 154	7
—	—	—	70	★	ALVIN'S HARMONICA	David Seville and the Chipmunks, Liberty 55179	1
95	86	77	71		WICKED RUBY	Danny Zella, Fox 10057	4
67	89	—	72	★	WIGGLE WIGGLE	Accents, Brunswick 55100	8
—	—	—	73	★	PLEASE MR. SUN	Tommy Edwards, M-G-M 12757	1
—	97	86	74		TEARDROPS WILL FALL	Dicky Doo and the Don'ts, Swan 4025	3
—	—	98	75	★	ARE YOU LONESOME TONIGHT?	Jaye P. Morgan, M-G-M 12752	2
—	—	—	76	★	WHEN THE SAINTS GO MARCHING IN	Fats Domino, Imperial 5569	1
21	32	58	77		PROBLEMS	Everly Brothers, Cadence 1355	15
38	47	62	78		ROCK-A-CONGA	Applejacks, Cameo 155	9
72	65	80	79		THE SHAG	Billy Graves, Monument 401	4
70	66	67	80		THE WEDDING	June Valli, Mercury 71382	13
—	—	—	81	★	TELLING LIES	Fats Domino, Imperial 5569	1
—	96	82	82		GIVE ME YOUR LOVE	Nat King Cole, Capitol 4125	3
26	36	65	83		THE LITTLE DRUMMER BOY	Harry Simeone Chorale, 20th Fox 121	9
76	70	73	84		RASPBERRIES, STRAWBERRIES	Kingston Trio, Capitol 4114	6
—	—	94	85		JUPITER-C	Pat and the Satellite, Atco 6131	2
24	33	53	86		TOM DOOLEY	Kingston Trio, Capitol 4049	21
—	—	—	87	★	MISS YOU	Jaye P. Morgan, M-G-M 12752	1
—	—	88	88		NOLA	Morgan Brothers, M-G-M 12747	2
69	87	87	89		THE WORRYIN' KIND	Tommy Sands, Capitol 4082	7
—	85	81	90		MY MAN	Peggy Lee, Capitol 4115	3
—	—	96	91		BLAH, BLAH, BLAH	Nicola Paone, ABC-Paramount 9993	2
—	—	89	92		SEA CRUISE	Frankie Ford, Ace 554	2
—	99	90	93		THE HANGING TREE	Marty Robbins, Columbia 41325	3
—	—	—	94		SINCE I DON'T HAVE YOU	The Skyliners, Calico 103	1
—	—	97	95		MIDNIGHT OIL	Charlie Blackwell, Warner Bros. 5031	2
—	—	—	96		PINK SHOELACES	Dodie Stevens, Crystalette 724	1
—	—	100	97		MOONLIGHT SERENADE	The Rivieras, Coed 508	2
—	—	—	98		I DON'T NEED YOU ANYMORE	Teddy Bears, Imperial 5562	1
—	100	85	99		MADRID	Nat King Cole, Capitol 4125	3
31	46	66	100		I GOT STUNG	Elvis Presley, RCA Victor 7410	15

★ THE STAR PERFORMER designation shows the outstanding upward changes of position in The Hot 100 since last week's chart. Its purpose merely is to provide quick visual identification of the sides which moved up most dramatically or to new entries which first entered the chart at an unusually high position.

THE BILLBOARD'S BEST BUYS

These records have shown the greatest national SALES BREAKOUT potential this week for the first time. Action sides are listed in capital letters.

POP

VENUS .... Frankie Avalon
(Rambed-Jimskip, BMI) I'm Broke (Rambed-Jimskip, BMI) Chancellor 1031

ANTHONY BOY .... Chuck Berry
(Arc, BMI) That's My Desire (Mills, ASCAP) Chess 1716

ALVIN'S HARMONICA .... David Seville and the Chipmunks
(Monarch, ASCAP) Mediocre (Monarch, ASCAP) Liberty 55179

PLEASE MR. SUN .... Tommy Edwards
(Weiss & Barry, BMI) The Morning Side of the Mountain (Remick, ASCAP) M-G-M 12757

WHEN THE SAINTS GO MARCHING IN .... Fats Domino
TELLING LIES
(Marquis, BMI) (Reeve, BMI) Imperial 5569

The above are previous Billboard Spotlight picks

ARE YOU LONESOME TONIGHT? .... Jaye P. Morgan
MISS YOU
(Bourne, ASCAP) (Santly-Joy, ASCAP) M-G-M 12752

C&W

NO SELECTIONS THIS WEEK

R&B

NO SELECTIONS THIS WEEK

The Billboard HOT 100

FOR THE WEEK ENDING MARCH 1

★ THE STAR PERFORMER designation shows the outstanding upward changes of position in The Hot 100 since last week's chart. Its purpose merely is to provide quick visual identification of the sides which moved up most dramatically or to new entries which first entered the chart at an unusually high position.

THREE WEEKS AGO	TWO WEEKS AGO	ONE WEEK AGO	THIS WEEK	★ STAR PERFORMER THIS WEEK	TITLE	Artist, Company, Record Number	WEEKS ON CHART
5	1	1	1		STAGGER LEE	Lloyd Price, ABC-Paramount 9972	12
3	3	3	2		DONNA	Ritchie Valens, Del-Fi 4110	14
4	2	2	3		16 CANDLES	Crests, Coed 506	14
2	5	5	4		ALL AMERICAN BOY	Bill Parsons, Fraternity 835	10
69	29	20	5	★	CHARLIE BROWN	Coasters, Atco 6132	4
19	12	14	6		I CRIED A TEAR	LaVern Baker, Atlantic 2007	12
13	18	12	7		TALL PAUL	Annette, Disneyland 118	8
35	22	13	8		PETITE FLEUR	Chris Barber's Jazz Band, Laurie 3022	7
8	7	7	9		LONELY TEARDROPS	Jackie Wilson, Brunswick 55105	14
18	17	16	10		PETER GUNN THEME	Ray Anthony, Capitol 4041	8
6	6	6	11		MY HAPPINESS	Connie Francis, M-G-M 12738	12
1	4	4	12		SMOKE GETS IN YOUR EYES	Platters, Mercury 71383	15
16	14	11	13		HAWAIIAN WEDDING SONG	Andy Williams, Cadence 1358	9
11	10	10	14		MANHATTAN SPIRITUAL	Reg Owen Ork, Palette 5005	12
7	8	9	15		GOTTA TRAVEL ON	Billy Grammer, Monument 400	14
10	9	8	16		GOODBYE BABY	Jack Scott, Carlton 493	11
29	16	18	17		THE CHILDREN'S MARCHING SONG	Mitch Miller, Columbia 41317	7
67	36	25	18		I'VE HAD IT	Bell Notes, Time 1004	6
20	13	15	19		THE CHILDREN'S MARCHING SONG	Cyril Stapleton, London 1851	7
15	15	19	20		(ALL OF A SUDDEN) MY HEART SINGS	Paul Anka, ABC-Paramount 9987	10
31	21	22	21		WITH THE WIND AND THE RAIN IN YOUR HAIR	Pat Boone, Dot 15888	7
52	40	29	22		SHE SAY (OOM DOOBY DOOM)	The Diamonds, Mercury 71404	5
17	23	21	23		MAY YOU ALWAYS	McGuire Sisters, Coral 62059	8
73	38	36	24	★	IT'S JUST A MATTER OF TIME	Brook Benton, Mercury 71394	5
9	11	17	25		A LOVER'S QUESTION	Clyde McPhatter, Atlantic 1199	19
34	26	23	26		THE LONELY ONE	Duane Eddy, Jamie 1117	6
45	34	28	27		I GOT A WIFE	Mark IV, Mercury 71403	5
—	99	53	28	★	VENUS	Frankie Avalon, Chancellor 1031	3
91	60	35	29		THE STORY OF MY LOVE	Conway Twitty, M-G-M 12748	5
—	—	70	30	★	ALVIN'S HARMONICA	David Seville and the Chipmunks, Liberty 55179	2
26	20	24	31		LITTLE SPACE GIRL	Jesse Lee Turner, Carlton 496	8
74	47	38	32		TRAGEDY	Thomas Wayne, Fernwood 109	15
76	59	49	33	★	APPLE BLOSSOM TIME	Tab Hunter, Warner Bros. 5032	4
39	33	32	34		DON'T TAKE YOUR GUNS TO TOWN	Johnny Cash, Columbia 41313	6
25	24	26	35		LUCKY LADYBUG	Billy and Lillie, Swan 4020	10
14	19	27	36		THE DIARY	Neil Sedaka, RCA Victor 7408	12
53	44	42	37		PRETTY GIRLS EVERYWHERE	Eugene Church, Class 235	9
72	56	45	38		PLAIN JANE	Bobby Darin, Atco 6133	5
95	61	39	39		NOLA	Billy Williams, Coral 62069	5
62	52	33	40		THERE MUST BE A WAY	Joni James, M-G-M 12746	6
38	31	31	41		I'M A MAN	Fabian, Chancellor 1029	7
56	45	47	42		IT'S ONLY THE BEGINNING	The Kalin Twins, Decca 30807	7
81	63	57	43	★	WHO CARES	Don Gibson, RCA Victor 7437	6
22	30	34	44		LA BAMBA	Ritchie Valens, Del-Fi 4110	9
21	27	30	45		NOBODY BUT YOU	Dee Clark, Abner 1019	13
79	64	54	46		FIRST ANNIVERSARY	Cathy Carr, Roulette 4125	5
94	72	64	47	★	RAWHIDE	Link Wray, Epic 9300	5
49	46	46	48		DON'T PITY ME	Dion and the Belmonts, Laurie 3021	10
40	39	41	49		RED RIVER ROSE	Ames Brothers, RCA Victor 7413	9
50	50	59	50		TRY ME	James Brown, Federal 12337	11
37	55	50	51		BLUE HAWAII	Billy Vaughn, Dot 15879	8
89	—	72	52	★	WIGGLE WIGGLE	Accents, Brunswick 55100	9
—	—	73	53	★	PLEASE MR. SUN	Tommy Edwards, M-G-M 12757	2
54	54	52	54		LOVERS NEVER SAY GOODBYE	Flamingos, End 1035	6
—	88	88	55	★	NOLA	Morgan Brothers, M-G-M 12747	3
65	80	79	56	★	THE SHAG	Billy Graves, Monument 401	5
12	25	37	57		WHOLE LOTTA LOVING	Fats Domino, Imperial 5553	15
—	89	92	58	★	SEA CRUISE	Frankie Ford, Ace 554	3
—	96	91	59	★	BLAH, BLAH, BLAH	Nicola Paone, ABC-Paramount 9993	3
—	—	65	60		ANTHONY BOY	Chuck Berry, Chess 1716	2

THE INDUSTRY'S FASTEST AND MOST COMPLETE PROGRAMMING AND BUYING GUIDE

These 100 sides are listed in order of their national POPULARITY, as determined by weekly local studies prepared for The Billboard in markets representing a cross-section of the United States. These studies reflect sales registered for each disk up to press time.

★ THE STAR PERFORMER designation shows the outstanding upward changes of position in The Hot 100 since last week's chart. Its purpose merely is to provide quick visual identification of the sides which moved up most dramatically, or to new entries which first entered the chart at an unusually high position.

Three Weeks Ago	Two Weeks Ago	One Week Ago	This Week	★ Star Performer This Week	Title — Artist, Company, Record Number	Weeks on Chart
97	86	74	61		TEARDROPS WILL FALL — Dickey Doo and the Don'ts, Swan 4025	4
84	70	67	62		MATILDA — Cookie and His Cupcakes, Judd 1002	6
83	74	66	63		EVENING RAIN — Earl Grant, Decca 30819	5
58	75	62	64		AMBROSE (PART 5) — Linda Laurie, Glory 290	5
—	—	—	65	★	NEVER BE ANYONE ELSE BUT YOU — Ricky Nelson, Imperial 5565	1
—	98	75	66		ARE YOU LONESOME TONIGHT? — Jaye P. Morgan, M-G-M 12752	3
—	—	—	67	★	TOMBOY — Perry Como, RCA Victor 7464	1
—	—	76	68		WHEN THE SAINTS GO MARCHING IN — Fats Domino, Imperial 5569	2
43	48	48	69		TRUST IN ME — Patti Page, Mercury 71400	7
71	69	68	70		ALRIGHT, OKAY, YOU WIN — Peggy Lee, Capitol 4115	5
23	28	40	71		THE CHIPMUNK SONG — David Seville and the Chipmunks, Liberty 55168	12
60	68	58	72		THE GIRL ON PAGE 44 — The Four Lads, Columbia 41310	8
87	87	89	73	★	THE WORRYIN' KIND — Tommy Sands, Capitol 4082	8
44	51	63	74		LET'S LOVE — Johnny Mathis, Columbia 41304	8
63	57	69	75		GAZACHSTAHAGEN — Wild Cats, United Artists 154	8
—	—	96	76	★	PINK SHOELACES — Dodie Stevens, Crystalette 724	2
—	—	81	77		TELLING LIES — Fats Domino, Imperial 5569	2
—	—	—	78	★	HURTIN' INSIDE — Brook Benton, Mercury 71394	1
28	35	61	79		ONE NIGHT — Elvis Presley, RCA Victor 7410	16
41	41	44	80		LOVE YOU MOST OF ALL — Sam Cooke, Keen 2008	15
—	94	85	81		JUPITER-C — Pat and the Satellite, Atco 6131	3
—	—	—	82	★	IT DOESN'T MATTER ANYMORE — Buddy Holly, Coral 62074	1
99	90	93	83		THE HANGING TREE — Marty Robbins, Columbia 41325	4
24	32	43	84		TO KNOW HIM IS TO LOVE HIM — Teddy Bears, Dore 503	23
—	—	94	85		SINCE I DON'T HAVE YOU — The Skyliners, Calico 103	2
27	43	51	86		BIMBOMBEY — Jimmie Rodgers, Roulette 4116	16
—	—	87	87		MISS YOU — Jaye P. Morgan, M-G-M 12752	2
70	73	84	88		RASPBERRIES, STRAWBERRIES — Kingston Trio, Capitol 4114	7
57	49	55	89		GOOD ROCKIN' TONIGHT — Pat Boone, Dot 15888	7
—	100	97	90		MOONLIGHT SERENADE — The Rivieras, Coed 508	3
—	97	95	91		MIDNIGHT OIL — Charlie Blackwell, Warner Bros. 5031	3
47	62	78	92		ROCK-A-CONGA — Applejacks, Cameo 155	10
—	—	—	93		I'M NEVER GONNA TELL — Jimmie Rodgers, Roulette 4129	1
—	—	—	94		BUNNY HOP — The Applejacks, Cameo 158	1
—	—	—	95		I'VE GOT YOU UNDER MY SKIN — Louis Prima and Keely Smith, Capitol 4140	1
96	82	82	96		GIVE ME YOUR LOVE — Nat King Cole, Capitol 4125	4
86	77	71	97		WICKED RUBY — Danny Zella, Fox 10057	5
—	—	—	98		SHIRLEY — John Fred, Montel 1002	1
85	81	90	99		MY MAN — Peggy Lee, Capitol 4115	4
—	—	—	100		GLAD RAGS — Tennessee Ernie Ford, Capitol 4107	1

THE BILLBOARD'S BEST BUYS

These records have shown the greatest national SALES BREAKOUT potential this week for the first time. Action sides are listed in capital letters.

POP

NEVER BE ANYONE ELSE BUT YOU .... Ricky Nelson
(Eric, BMI) It's Late (Eric, BMI) Imperial 5565

TOMBOY .... Perry Como
(Rancom, ASCAP) Kiss Me and Kiss Me and Kiss Me (Leeds, ASCAP) RCA Victor 7464

SEA CRUISE .... Frankie Ford
(Ace, BMI) Roberta (Ace, BMI) Ace 554

THE SHAG .... Billy Graves
(Combine, BMI) Uncertain (Combine, BMI) Monument 401

The above are previous Billboard Spotlight picks

BLAH, BLAH, BLAH .... Nicola Paone
(Dominion, BMI) Cia, Bellezza (Dominion, BMI) ABC-Paramount 9993

C&W

DOGGONE THAT TRAIN .... Hank Snow
FATHER TIME AND MOTHER LOVE
(Southern, ASCAP) (Cedarwood, BMI) RCA Victor 7448

A previous Billboard Spotlight pick

R&B

NO SELECTIONS THIS WEEK

The Billboard HOT 100

FOR THE WEEK ENDING MARCH 8

★ THE STAR PERFORMER designation shows the outstanding upward changes of position in The Hot 100 since last week's chart. Its purpose merely is to provide quick visual identification of the sides which moved up most dramatically or to new entries which first entered the chart at an unusually high position.

THREE WEEKS AGO	TWO WEEKS AGO	ONE WEEK AGO	THIS WEEK	★ STAR PERFORMER THIS WEEK	TITLE Artist, Company, Record Number	WEEKS ON CHART
1	1	1	1		STAGGER LEE — Lloyd Price, ABC-Paramount 9972	13
3	3	2	2		DONNA — Ritchie Valens, Del-Fi 4110	15
29	20	5	3		CHARLIE BROWN — Coasters, Atco 6132	5
2	2	3	4		16 CANDLES — Crests, Coed 506	15
22	13	8	5		PETITE FLEUR — Chris Barber's Jazz Band, Laurie 3022	8
12	14	6	6		I CRIED A TEAR — LaVern Baker, Atlantic 2007	13
99	53	28	7	★	VENUS — Frankie Avalon, Chancellor 1031	4
17	16	10	8		PETER GUNN THEME — Ray Anthony, Capitol 4041	9
5	5	4	9		ALL AMERICAN BOY — Bill Parsons, Fraternity 835	11
—	70	30	10	★	ALVIN'S HARMONICA — David Seville and the Chipmunks, Liberty 55179	3
14	11	13	11		HAWAIIAN WEDDING SONG — Andy Williams, Cadence 1358	10
18	12	7	12		TALL PAUL — Annette, Disneyland 118	9
36	25	18	13		I'VE HAD IT — Bell Notes, Time 1004	7
7	7	9	14		LONELY TEARDROPS — Jackie Wilson, Brunswick 55105	15
38	36	24	15		IT'S JUST A MATTER OF TIME — Brook Benton, Mercury 71394	6
4	4	12	16		SMOKE GETS IN YOUR EYES — Platters, Mercury 71383	16
6	6	11	17		MY HAPPINESS — Connie Francis, M-G-M 12738	13
8	9	15	18		GOTTA TRAVEL ON — Billy Grammer, Monument 400	15
23	21	23	19		MAY YOU ALWAYS — McGuire Sisters, Coral 62059	9
16	18	17	20		THE CHILDREN'S MARCHING SONG — Mitch Miller, Columbia 41317	8
40	29	22	21		SHE SAY (OOM DOOBY DOOM) — The Diamonds, Mercury 71404	6
47	38	32	22	★	TRAGEDY — Thomas Wayne, Fernwood 109	16
13	15	19	23		THE CHILDREN'S MARCHING SONG — Cyril Stapleton, London 1851	8
9	8	16	24		GOODBYE BABY — Jack Scott, Carlton 493	12
34	28	27	25		I GOT A WIFE — Mark IV, Mercury 71403	6
21	22	21	26		WITH THE WIND AND THE RAIN IN YOUR HAIR — Pat Boone, Dot 15888	8
10	10	14	27		MANHATTAN SPIRITUAL — Reg Owen Ork, Palette 5005	13
60	35	29	28		THE STORY OF MY LIFE — Conway Twitty, M-G-M 12748	6
15	19	20	29		(ALL OF A SUDDEN) MY HEART SINGS — Paul Anka, ABC-Paramount 9987	11
26	23	26	30		THE LONELY ONE — Duane Eddy, Jamie 1117	7
59	49	33	31		APPLE BLOSSOM TIME — Tab Hunter, Warner Bros. 5032	5
11	17	25	32		A LOVER'S QUESTION — Clyde McPhatter, Atlantic 1199	20
33	32	34	33		DON'T TAKE YOUR GUNS TO TOWN — Johnny Cash, Columbia 41313	7
52	33	40	34		THERE MUST BE A WAY — Joni James, M-G-M 12746	7
20	24	31	35		LITTLE SPACE GIRL — Jesse Lee Turner, Carlton 496	9
44	42	37	36		PRETTY GIRLS EVERYWHERE — Eugene Church, Class 235	10
30	34	44	37		LA BAMBA — Ritchie Valens, Del-Fi 4110	10
56	45	38	38		PLAIN JANE — Bobby Darin, Atco 6133	6
—	73	53	39	★	PLEASE MR. SUN — Tommy Edwards, M-G-M 12757	3
61	39	39	40		NOLA — Billy Williams, Coral 62069	6
—	—	65	41	★	NEVER BE ANYONE ELSE BUT YOU — Ricky Nelson, Imperial 5565	2
64	54	46	42		FIRST ANNIVERSARY — Cathy Carr, Roulette 4125	6
89	92	58	43	★	SEA CRUISE — Frankie Ford, Ace 554	4
24	26	35	44		LUCKY LADYBUG — Billy and Lillie, Swan 4020	11
—	—	82	45	★	IT DOESN'T MATTER ANYMORE — Buddy Holly, Coral 62074	2
27	30	45	46		NOBODY BUT YOU — Dee Clark, Abner 1019	14
19	27	36	47		THE DIARY — Neil Sedaka, RCA Victor 7408	13
31	31	41	48		I'M A MAN — Fabian, Chancellor 1029	8
—	96	76	49	★	PINK SHOELACES — Dodie Stevens, Crystalette 724	3
88	88	55	50		NOLA — Morgan Brothers, M-G-M 12747	4
45	47	42	51		IT'S ONLY THE BEGINNING — The Kalin Twins, Decca 30807	8
70	67	62	52	★	MATILDA — Cookie and His Cupcakes, Judd 1002	7
80	79	56	53		THE SHAG — Billy Graves, Monument 401	6
—	72	52	54		WIGGLE WIGGLE — Accents, Brunswick 55100	10
72	64	47	55		RAWHIDE — Link Wray, Epic 9300	6
—	76	68	56	★	WHEN THE SAINTS GO MARCHING IN — Fats Domino, Imperial 5569	3
96	91	59	57		BLAH, BLAH, BLAH — Nicola Paone, ABC-Paramount 9993	4
63	57	43	58		WHO CARES! — Don Gibson, RCA Victor 7437	7
54	52	54	59		LOVERS NEVER SAY GOODBYE — Flamingos, End 1035	7
46	46	48	60		DON'T PITY ME — Dion and the Belmonts, Laurie 3021	11

THE INDUSTRY'S FASTEST AND MOST COMPLETE PROGRAMMING AND BUYING GUIDE

These 100 sides are listed in order of their national POPULARITY, as determined by weekly local studies prepared for The Billboard in markets representing a cross-section of the United States. These studies reflect sales registered for each disk up to press time.

★ THE STAR PERFORMER designation shows the outstanding upward changes of position in The Hot 100 since last week's chart. Its purpose merely is to provide quick visual identification of the sides which moved up most dramatically or to new entries which first entered the chart at an unusually high position.

THREE WEEKS AGO	TWO WEEKS AGO	ONE WEEK AGO	THIS WEEK	★ STAR PERFORMER THIS WEEK	TITLE	Artist, Company, Record Number	WEEKS ON CHART
86	74	61	61		TEARDROPS WILL FALL	Dickey Doo and the Don'ts, Swan 4025	5
—	—	67	62		TOMBOY	Perry Como, RCA Victor 7464	2
74	66	63	63		EVENING RAIN	Earl Grant, Decca 30819	6
75	62	64	64		AMBROSE (PART 5)	Linda Laurie, Glory 290	6
98	75	66	65		ARE YOU LONESOME TONIGHT?	Jaye P. Morgan, M-G-M 12752	4
39	41	49	66		RED RIVER ROSE	Ames Brothers, RCA Victor 7413	10
—	81	77	67		TELLING LIES	Fats Domino, Imperial 5569	3
97	95	91	68	★	MIDNIGHT OIL	Charlie Blackwell, Warner Bros. 5031	4
68	58	72	69		THE GIRL ON PAGE 44	The Four Lads, Columbia 41310	9
—	—	—	70	★	NO OTHER ARMS, NO OTHER LIPS	Chordettes, Cadence 1361	1
90	93	83	71		THE HANGING TREE	Marty Robbins, Columbia 41325	5
—	—	—	72	★	WHERE WERE YOU (ON OUR WEDDING DAY)?	Lloyd Price, ABC-Paramount 9997	1
50	59	50	73		TRY ME	James Brown, Federal 12337	12
—	65	60	74		ANTHONY BOY	Chuck Berry, Chess 1716	3
—	—	—	75	★	IF I DIDN'T CARE	Connie Francis, M-G-M 12769	1
—	—	93	76	★	I'M NEVER GONNA TELL	Jimmie Rodgers, Roulette 4129	2
55	50	51	77		BLUE HAWAII	Billy Vaughn, Dot 15879	9
—	—	94	78	★	BUNNY HOP	The Applejacks, Cameo 158	2
87	89	73	79		THE WORRYIN' KIND	Tommy Sands, Capitol 4082	9
73	84	88	80		RASPBERRIES, STRAWBERRIES	Kingson Trio, Capitol 4114	8
—	—	78	81		HURTIN' INSIDE	Brook Benton, Mercury 71394	2
48	48	69	82		TRUST IN ME	Patti Page, Mercury 71400	8
—	94	85	83		SINCE I DON'T HAVE YOU	The Skyliners, Calico 103	3
—	—	98	84		SHIRLEY	John Fred, Montel 1002	2
51	63	74	85		LET'S LOVE	Johnny Mathis, Columbia 41304	9
69	68	70	86		ALRIGHT, OKAY, YOU WIN	Peggy Lee, Capitol 4115	6
—	—	—	87	★	NO OTHER ARMS, NO OTHER LOVE	Four Aces, Decca 30822	1
41	44	80	88		LOVE YOU MOST OF ALL	Sam Cooke, Keen 2008	16
100	97	90	89		MOONLIGHT SERENADE	The Rivieras, Coed 508	4
49	55	89	90		GOOD ROCKIN' TONIGHT	Pat Boone, Dot 15888	8

THE BILLBOARD'S BEST BUYS

These records have shown the greatest national SALES BREAKOUT potential this week for the first time. Action sides are listed in capital letters.

POP

IT DOESN'T MATTER ANYMORE .... **Buddy Holly**
(Spanka, BMI) Raining in My Heart (Acuff-Rose, BMI) Coral 62074

NO OTHER ARMS, NO OTHER LIPS .... **The Chordettes**
(Whitney-Kramer-Zaret, ASCAP) We Should Be Together (Cedarwood, BMI) Cadence 1361

WHERE WERE YOU (ON OUR WEDDING DAY)? .... **Lloyd Price**
(Pamco, BMI) Is It Really Love? (Mellin, BMI) ABC-Paramount 9997

BUNNY HOP .... **The Applejacks**
(Moonlight, BMI) Night Train Stroll (Frederick, BMI) Cameo 158

I'M NEVER GONNA TELL .... **Jimmie Rodgers**
(Planetary, ASCAP) Because You're Young (Planetary, ASCAP) Roulette 4129

IF I DIDN'T CARE .... **Connie Francis**
(Chappell, ASCAP) Toward the End of the Day (Francon, ASCAP) M-G-M 12769

The above are previous Billboard Spotlight picks

PINK SHOE LACES .... **Dodie Stevens**
(Pioneer, BMI) Coming of Age (Virgo, BMI) Crystalette 724

C&W

WHITE LIGHTNING .... **George Jones**
(Starrite, BMI) Long Time to Forget (Starday, BMI) Mercury 71406

R&B

NO SELECTIONS THIS WEEK

★ THE STAR PERFORMER designation shows the outstanding upward changes of position in The Hot 100 since last week's chart. Its purpose merely is to provide quick visual identification of the sides which moved up most dramatically or to new entries which first entered the chart at an unusually high position.

THREE WEEKS AGO	TWO WEEKS AGO	ONE WEEK AGO	THIS WEEK	★ STAR PERFORMER THIS WEEK	TITLE	Artist, Company, Record Number	WEEKS ON CHART
—	—	—	91		IT'S LATE	Ricky Nelson, Imperial 9061	1
35	61	79	92		ONE NIGHT	Elvis Presley, RCA Victor 7410	17
—	—	—	93		THE MORNING SIDE OF THE MOUNTAIN	Tommy Edwards, M-G-M 12757	1
81	90	99	94		MY MAN	Peggy Lee, Capitol 4115	5
—	87	87	95		MISS YOU	Jaye P. Morgan, M-G-M 12752	3
—	—	—	96		THE SEARCH	Dean Reed, Capitol 4121	1
—	—	95	97		I'VE GOT YOU UNDER MY SKIN	Louis Prima and Keely Smith, Capitol 4140	2
—	—	—	98		CITY LIGHTS	Ivory Joe Hunter, Dot 15860	1
94	85	81	99		JUPITER-C	Pat and the Satellites, Atco 6131	4
—	—	—	100		THE ANSWER TO A MAIDEN'S PRAYER	June Valli, Mercury 71422	1

The Billboard HOT 100

FOR THE WEEK ENDING MARCH 15

★ THE STAR PERFORMER designation shows the outstanding upward changes of position in The Hot 100 since last week's chart. Its purpose merely is to provide quick visual identification of the sides which moved up most dramatically or to new entries which first entered the chart at an unusually high position.

Three Weeks Ago	Two Weeks Ago	One Week Ago	This Week	★ Star Performer This Week	Title	Artist, Company, Record Number	Weeks on Chart
53	28	7	1		VENUS	Frankie Avalon, Chancellor 1031	5
20	5	3	2		CHARLIE BROWN	Coasters, Atco 6132	6
1	1	1	3		STAGGER LEE	Lloyd Price, ABC-Paramount 9972	14
3	2	2	4		DONNA	Ritchie Valens, Del-Fi 4110	16
70	30	10	5		ALVIN'S HARMONICA	David Seville and the Chipmunks, Liberty 55179	4
25	18	13	6		I'VE HAD IT	Bell Notes, Time 1004	8
36	24	15	7		IT'S JUST A MATTER OF TIME	Brook Benton, Mercury 71394	7
13	8	5	8		PETITE FLEUR	Chris Barber's Jazz Band, Laurie 3022	9
14	6	6	9		I CRIED A TEAR	LaVern Baker, Atlantic 2007	14
2	3	4	10		16 CANDLES	Crests, Coed 506	16
11	13	11	11		HAWAIIAN WEDDING SONG	Andy Williams, Cadence 1358	11
16	10	8	12		PETER GUNN THEME	Ray Anthony, Capitol 4041	10
12	7	12	13		TALL PAUL	Annette, Disneyland 118	10
5	4	9	14		ALL AMERICAN BOY	Bill Parsons, Fraternity 835	12
38	32	22	15		TRAGEDY	Thomas Wayne, Fernwood 109	17
21	23	19	16		MAY YOU ALWAYS	McGuire Sisters, Coral 62059	10
7	9	14	17		LONELY TEARDROPS	Jackie Wilson, Brunswick 55105	16
18	17	20	18		THE CHILDREN'S MARCHING SONG	Mitch Miller, Columbia 41317	9
—	65	41	19	★	NEVER BE ANYONE ELSE BUT YOU	Ricky Nelson, Imperial 5565	3
29	22	21	20		SHE SAY (OOM DOOBY DOOM)	The Diamonds, Mercury 71404	7
6	11	17	21		MY HAPPINESS	Connie Francis, M-G-M 12738	14
9	15	18	22		GOTTA TRAVEL ON	Billy Grammer, Monument 400	16
15	19	23	23		THE CHILDREN'S MARCHING SONG	Cyril Stapleton, London 1851	9
10	14	27	24		MANHATTAN SPIRITUAL	Reg Owen Ork, Palette 5005	14
4	12	16	25		SMOKE GETS IN YOUR EYES	Platters, Mercury 71383	17
8	16	24	26		GOODBYE BABY	Jack Scott, Carlton 493	13
28	27	25	27		I GOT A WIFE	Mark IV, Mercury 71403	7
34	44	37	28		LA BAMBA	Ritchie Valens, Del-Fi 4110	11
19	20	29	29		(ALL OF A SUDDEN) MY HEART SINGS	Paul Anka, ABC-Paramount 9987	12
35	29	28	30		THE STORY OF MY LOVE	Conway Twitty, M-G-M 12748	7
22	21	26	31		WITH THE WIND AND THE RAIN IN YOUR HAIR	Pat Boone, Dot 15888	9
23	26	30	32		THE LONELY ONE	Duane Eddy, Jamie 1117	8
96	76	49	33	★	PINK SHOELACES	Dodie Stevens, Crystalette 724	4
49	33	31	34		APPLE BLOSSOM TIME	Tab Hunter, Warner Bros. 5032	6
92	58	43	35		SEA CRUISE	Frankie Ford, Ace 554	5
—	82	45	36		IT DOESN'T MATTER ANYMORE	Buddy Holly, Coral 62074	3
73	53	39	37		PLEASE, MR. SUN	Tommy Edwards, M-G-M 12757	4
32	34	33	38		DON'T TAKE YOUR GUNS TO TOWN	Johnny Cash, Columbia 41313	8
33	40	34	39		THERE MUST BE A WAY	Joni James, M-G-M 12746	8
17	25	32	40		A LOVER'S QUESTION	Clyde McPhatter, Atlantic 1199	21
42	37	36	41		PRETTY GIRLS EVERYWHERE	Eugene Church, Class 235	11
54	46	42	42		FIRST ANNIVERSARY	Cathy Carr, Roulette 4125	7
64	47	55	43	★	RAWHIDE	Link Wray, Epic 9300	7
—	—	91	44	★	IT'S LATE	Ricky Nelson, Imperial 5565	2
94	85	83	45	★	SINCE I DON'T HAVE YOU	The Skyliners, Calico 103	4
24	31	35	46		LITTLE SPACE GIRL	Jesse Lee Turner, Carlton 496	10
39	39	40	47		NOLA	Billy Williams, Coral 62069	7
—	67	62	48	★	TOMBOY	Perry Como, RCA Victor 7464	3
67	62	52	49		MATILDA	Cookie and His Cupcakes, Judd 1002	8
81	77	67	50	★	TELLING LIES	Fats Domino, Imperial 5569	4
45	38	38	51		PLAIN JANE	Bobby Darin, Atco 6133	7
62	64	64	52	★	AMBROSE (PART 5)	Linda Laurie, Glory 290	7
72	52	54	53		WIGGLE, WIGGLE	Accents, Brunswick 55100	11
—	—	70	54	★	NO OTHER ARMS, NO OTHER LIPS	Chordettes, Cadence 1361	2
—	—	—	55	★	COME SOFTLY TO ME	Fleetwoods, Dolphin 1	1
76	68	56	56		WHEN THE SAINTS GO MARCHING IN	Fats Domino, Imperial 5569	4
88	55	50	57		NOLA	Morgan Brothers, M-G-M 12747	5
95	91	68	58	★	MIDNIGHT OIL	Charlie Blackwell, Warner Bros. 5031	5
57	43	58	59		WHO CARES?	Don Gibson, RCA Victor 7437	8
93	83	71	60		THE HANGING TREE	Marty Robbins, Columbia 41325	6

THE INDUSTRY'S FASTEST AND MOST COMPLETE PROGRAMMING AND BUYING GUIDE

These 100 sides are listed in order of their national POPULARITY, as determined by weekly local studies prepared for The Billboard in markets representing a cross-section of the United States. These studies reflect sales registered for each disk up to press time.

★ THE STAR PERFORMER designation shows the outstanding upward changes of position in The Hot 100 since last week's chart. Its purpose merely is to provide quick visual identification of the sides which moved up most dramatically or to new entries which first entered the chart at an unusually high position.

Three Weeks Ago	Two Weeks Ago	One Week Ago	This Week	★ Star Performer This Week	Title — Artist, Company, Record Number	Weeks on Chart
52	54	59	61		LOVERS NEVER SAY GOODBYE — Flamingos, End 1035	8
31	41	48	62		I'M A MAN — Fabian, Chancellor 1029	9
30	45	46	63		NOBODY BUT YOU — Dee Clark, Abner 1019	15
—	—	75	64		IF I DIDN'T CARE — Connie Francis, M-G-M 12769	2
—	—	72	65		WHERE WERE YOU (ON OUR WEDDING DAY)? — Lloyd Price, ABC-Paramount 9997	2
—	—	—	66	★	EVERYBODY LIKES TO CHA CHA — Sam Cooke, Keen 2018	1
—	—	—	67		I'M NEVER GONNA TELL ON YOU — Jimmie Rodgers, Roulette 4129	1
91	59	57	68		BLAH, BLAH, BLAH — Nicola Paone, ABC-Paramount 9993	5
79	56	53	69		THE SHAG — Billy Graves, Monument 401	7
—	94	78	70		BUNNY HOP — The Applejacks, Cameo 158	3
27	36	47	71		THE DIARY — Neil Sedaka, RCA Victor 7408	14
26	35	44	72		LUCKY LADYBUG — Billy and Lillie, Swan 4020	12
75	66	65	73		ARE YOU LONESOME TONIGHT? — Jaye P. Morgan, M-G-M 12752	5
—	—	87	74		NO OTHER ARMS, NO OTHER LIPS — Four Aces, Decca 30822	2
74	61	61	75		TEARDROPS WILL FALL — Dickey Doo and the Don'ts, Swan 4025	6
65	60	74	76		ANTHONY BOY — Chuck Berry, Chess 1716	4
47	42	51	77		IT'S ONLY THE BEGINNING — The Kalin Twins, Decca 30807	9
87	87	95	78	★	MISS YOU — Jaye P. Morgan, M-G-M 12752	4
—	—	93	79		THE MORNING SIDE OF THE MOUNTAIN — Tommy Edwards, M-G-M 12757	2
97	90	89	80		MOONLIGHT SERENADE — The Rivieras, Coed 508	5
—	—	—	81	★	GUITAR BOOGIE SHUFFLE — The Virtues, Hunt 324	1
—	98	84	82		SHIRLEY — John Fred, Montel 1002	3
66	63	63	83		EVENING RAIN — Earl Grant, Decca 30819	7
46	48	60	84		DON'T PITY ME — Dion and the Belmonts, Laurie 3021	12
—	—	—	85	★	BALLAD OF A GIRL AND BOY — Graduates, Shan-Todd 0055	1
—	—	—	86	★	THIS SHOULD GO ON FOREVER — Rod Bernard, Argo 5327	1
—	—	100	87		THE ANSWER TO A MAIDEN'S PRAYER — June Valli, Mercury 71422	2
59	50	73	88		TRY ME — James Brown, Federal 12337	13
48	69	82	89		TRUST IN ME — Patti Page, Mercury 71400	3
—	—	—	90	★	I GO APE — Neil Sedaka, RCA Victor 7473	1

THE BILLBOARD'S BEST BUYS

These records have shown the greatest national SALES BREAKOUT potential this week for the first time. Action sides are listed in capital letters.

POP

COME SOFTLY TO ME .... The Fleetwoods
(Cornerstone, BMI) I Care So Much (Cornerstone, BMI) Dolphin 1

EVERYBODY LIKES TO CHA CHA .... Sam Cooke
(Kags-Hermosa, BMI) Little Things You Do (Kags-Hermosa, BMI) Keen 2018

GUITAR BOOGIE SHUFFLE .... The Virtues
(Shapiro-Bernstein, ASCAP) Guitar in Orbit (Tone-Craft, BMI) Hunt 324

The above are previous Billboard Spotlight picks

SINCE I DON'T HAVE YOU .... The Skyliners
(Calico, ASCAP) One Night, One Night (Calico, ASCAP) Calico 104

C&W

NO SELECTIONS THIS WEEK

R&B

NO SELECTIONS THIS WEEK

★ THE STAR PERFORMER designation shows the outstanding upward changes of position in The Hot 100 since last week's chart. Its purpose merely is to provide quick visual identification of the sides which moved up most dramatically or to new entries which first entered the chart at an unusually high position.

Three Weeks Ago	Two Weeks Ago	One Week Ago	This Week	★ Star Performer This Week	Title — Artist, Company, Record Number	Weeks on Chart
—	—	—	91		NO REGRETS — Jim Barnes, Gibraltar 101	1
—	—	98	92		CITY LIGHTS — Ivory Joe Hunter, Dot 15860	2
—	—	—	93		I KNEEL AT YOUR THRONE — Joe Medlin, Mercury 71415	1
—	—	—	94		BECAUSE YOU'RE YOUNG — Jimmie Rodgers, Roulette 4129	1
—	—	—	95		TEARDROPS ON YOUR LETTER — Hank Ballard and the Midnighters, King 5171	1
—	—	—	96		I CAN'T SIT DOWN — Marie and Rex, Carlton 502	1
—	—	—	97		CIAO, CIAO BAMBINA — Domenico Modugno, Decca 30845	1
58	72	69	98		THE GIRL ON PAGE 44 — The Four Lads, Columbia 41310	10
—	—	—	99		CHIP OFF THE OLD BLOCK — Eddy Arnold, RCA Victor 7435	1
—	—	—	100		OH WHY — Teddy Bears, Imperial 5562	1

The Billboard HOT 100

FOR THE WEEK ENDING MARCH 22

★ THE STAR PERFORMER designation shows the outstanding upward changes of position in The Hot 100 since last week's chart. Its purpose merely is to provide quick visual identification of the sides which moved up most dramatically or to new entries which first entered the chart at an unusually high position.

THREE WEEKS AGO	TWO WEEKS AGO	ONE WEEK AGO	THIS WEEK	★ STAR PERFORMER THIS WEEK	TITLE	Artist, Company, Record Number	WEEKS ON CHART
28	7	1	1		VENUS	Frankie Avalon, Chancellor 1031	6
5	3	2	2		CHARLIE BROWN	Coasters, Atco 6132	7
30	10	5	3		ALVIN'S HARMONICA	David Seville and the Chipmunks, Liberty 55179	5
24	15	7	4		IT'S JUST A MATTER OF TIME	Brook Benton, Mercury 71394	8
1	1	3	5		STAGGER LEE	Lloyd Price, ABC-Paramount 9972	15
18	13	6	6		I'VE HAD IT	Bell Notes, Time 1004	9
2	2	4	7		DONNA	Ritchie Valens, Del-Fi 4110	17
32	22	15	8		TRAGEDY	Thomas Wayne, Fernwood 109	18
65	41	19	9	★	NEVER BE ANYONE ELSE BUT YOU	Ricky Nelson, Imperial 5565	4
10	8	12	10		PETER GUNN THEME	Ray Anthony, Capitol 4041	11
8	5	8	11		PETITE FLEUR	Chris Barber's Jazz Band, Laurie 3022	10
6	6	9	12		I CRIED A TEAR	LaVern Baker, Atlantic 2007	15
13	11	11	13		HAWAIIAN WEDDING SONG	Andy Williams, Cadence 1358	12
7	12	13	14		TALL PAUL	Annette, Disneyland 118	11
3	4	10	15		16 CANDLES	Crests, Coed 506	17
—	—	55	16	★	COME SOFTLY TO ME	Fleetwoods, Dolphin 1	2
76	49	33	17	★	PINK SHOELACES	Dodie Stevens, Crystalette 724	5
22	21	20	18		SHE SAY (OOM DOOBY DOOM)	The Diamonds, Mercury 71404	8
4	9	14	19		ALL AMERICAN BOY	Bill Parsons, Fraternity 835	13
82	45	36	20	★	IT DOESN'T MATTER ANYMORE	Buddy Holly, Coral 62074	4
—	91	44	21	★	IT'S LATE	Ricky Nelson, Imperial 5565	3
23	19	16	22		MAY YOU ALWAYS	McGuire Sisters, Coral 62059	11
17	20	18	23		THE CHILDREN'S MARCHING SONG	Mitch Miller, Columbia 41317	10
27	25	27	24		I GOT A WIFE	Mark IV, Mercury 71403	8
53	39	37	25	★	PLEASE, MR. SUN	Tommy Edwards, M-G-M 12757	5
9	14	17	26		LONELY TEARDROPS	Jackie Wilson, Brunswick 55105	17
47	55	43	27	★	RAWHIDE	Link Wray, Epic 9300	8
16	24	26	28		GOODBYE BABY	Jack Scott, Carlton 493	14
21	26	31	29		WITH THE WIND AND THE RAIN IN YOUR HAIR	Pat Boone, Dot 15888	10
19	23	23	30		THE CHILDREN'S MARCHING SONG	Cyril Stapleton, London 1851	10
20	29	29	31		(ALL OF A SUDDEN) MY HEART SINGS	Paul Anka, ABC-Paramount 9987	13
29	28	30	32		THE STORY OF MY LOVE	Conway Twitty, M-G-M 12748	8
58	43	35	33		SEA CRUISE	Frankie Ford, Ace 554	6
33	31	34	34		APPLE BLOSSOM TIME	Tab Hunter, Warner Bros. 5032	7
26	30	32	35		THE LONELY ONE	Duane Eddy, Jamie 1117	9
15	18	22	36		GOTTA TRAVEL ON	Billy Grammer, Monument 400	17
11	17	21	37		MY HAPPINESS	Connie Francis, M-G-M 12738	15
83	71	60	38	★	THE HANGING TREE	Marty Robbins, Columbia 41325	7
14	27	24	39		MANHATTAN SPIRITUAL	Reg Owen Ork, Palette 5005	15
12	16	25	40		SMOKE GETS IN YOUR EYES	Platters, Mercury 71383	18
44	37	28	41		LA BAMBA	Ritchie Valens, Del-Fi 4110	12
39	40	47	42		NOLA	Billy Williams, Coral 62069	8
85	83	45	43		SINCE I DON'T HAVE YOU	The Skyliners, Calico 103	5
67	62	48	44		TOMBOY	Perry Como, RCA Victor 7464	4
46	42	42	45		FIRST ANNIVERSARY	Cathy Carr, Roulette 4125	8
—	70	54	46		NO OTHER ARMS, NO OTHER LIPS	Chordettes, Cadence 1361	3
—	93	79	47	★	THE MORNING SIDE OF THE MOUNTAIN	Tommy Edwards, M-G-M 12757	3
37	36	41	48		PRETTY GIRLS EVERYWHERE	Eugene Church, Class 235	12
34	33	38	49		DON'T TAKE YOUR GUNS TO TOWN	Johnny Cash, Columbia 41313	9
68	56	56	50		WHEN THE SAINTS GO MARCHING IN	Fats Domino, Imperial 5569	5
62	52	49	51		MATILDA	Cookie and His Cupcakes, Judd 1002	9
—	—	81	52	★	GUITAR BOOGIE SHUFFLE	The Virtues, Hunt 324	2
25	32	40	53		A LOVER'S QUESTION	Clyde McPhatter, Atlantic 1199	22
40	34	39	54		THERE MUST BE A WAY	Joni James, M-G-M 12746	9
—	75	64	55		IF I DIDN'T CARE	Connie Francis, M-G-M 12769	3
91	68	58	56		MIDNIGHT OIL	Charlie Blackwell, Warner Bros. 5031	6
—	72	65	57		WHERE WERE YOU (ON OUR WEDDING DAY)?	Lloyd Price, ABC-Paramount 9997	3
—	—	90	58	★	I GO APE	Neil Sedaka, RCA Victor 7473	2
43	58	59	59		TELLING LIES	Fats Domino, Imperial 5569	5
—	—	86	60	★	THIS SHOULD GO ON FOREVER	Rod Bernard, Argo 5327	2

THE INDUSTRY'S FASTEST AND MOST COMPLETE PROGRAMMING AND BUYING GUIDE

These 100 sides are listed in order of their national POPULARITY, as determined by weekly local studies prepared for The Billboard in markets representing a cross-section of the United States. These studies reflect sales registered for each disk up to press time.

★ THE STAR PERFORMER designation shows the outstanding upward changes of position in The Hot 100 since last week's chart. Its purpose merely is to provide quick visual identification of the sides which moved up most dramatically or to new entries which first entered the chart at an unusually high position.

Three Weeks Ago	Two Weeks Ago	One Week Ago	This Week	★ Star Performer This Week	Title	Artist, Company, Record Number	Weeks on Chart
—	—	66	61		EVERYBODY LIKES TO CHA CHA	Sam Cooke, Keen 2018	2
92	76	67	62		I'M NEVER GONNA TELL ON YOU	Jimmie Rodgers, Roulette 4129	4
38	38	51	63		PLAIN JANE	Bobby Darin, Atco 6133	8
31	35	46	64		LITTLE SPACE GIRL	Jesse Lee Turner, Carlton 496	11
55	50	57	65		NOLA	Morgan Brothers, M-G-M 12747	6
52	54	53	66		WIGGLE, WIGGLE	Accents, Brunswick 55100	12
59	57	68	67		BLAH, BLAH, BLAH	Nicola Paone, ABC-Paramount 9993	6
—	—	—	68	★	HAPPY ORGAN	Baby Cortez, Clock 1009	1
56	53	69	69		THE SHAG	Billy Graves, Monument 401	8
54	59	61	70		LOVERS NEVER SAY GOODBYE	Flamingos, End 1035	9
45	46	63	71		NOBODY BUT YOU	Dee Clark, Abner 1019	16
41	48	62	72		I'M A MAN	Fabian, Chancellor 1029	10
36	47	71	73		THE DIARY	Neil Sedaka, RCA Victor 7408	15
64	64	52	74		AMBROSE (PART 5)	Linda Laurie, Glory 290	8
35	44	72	75		LUCKY LADYBUG	Billy and Lillie, Swan 4020	13
90	89	80	76		MOONLIGHT SERENADE	The Rivieras, Coed 508	6
42	51	77	77		IT'S ONLY THE BEGINNING	The Kalin Twins, Decca 30807	10
94	78	70	78		BUNNY HOP	The Applejacks, Cameo 158	4
—	100	87	79		THE ANSWER TO A MAIDEN'S PRAYER	June Valli, Mercury 71422	3
66	65	73	80		ARE YOU LONESOME TONIGHT?	Jaye P. Morgan, M-G-M 12752	6
—	—	85	81		BALLAD OF A GIRL AND BOY	Graduates, Shan-Todd 0055	2
—	87	74	82		NO OTHER ARMS, NO OTHER LIPS	Four Aces, Decca 30822	3
87	95	78	83		MISS YOU	Jaye P Morgan, M-G-M 12752	5
—	—	—	84	★	SORRY, I RAN ALL THE WAY HOME	The Impalas, Cub 9022	1
—	—	93	85		I KNEEL AT YOUR THRONE	Joe Medlin, Mercury 71415	2
60	74	76	86		ANTHONY BOY	Chuck Berry, Chess 1716	5
—	—	—	87	★	AS TIME GOES BY	Johnny Nash, ABC-Paramount 9996	1
—	—	94	88		BECAUSE YOU'RE YOUNG	Jimmie Rodgers, Roulette 4129	2
78	81	—	89		HURTIN' INSIDE	Brook Benton, Mercury 71394	3
—	—	91	90		NO REGRETS	Jimmy Barnes, Gibraltar 101	2
—	—	100	91		OH WHY	Teddy Bears, Imperial 5562	2
43	58	59	92		WHO CARES?	Don Gibson, RCA Victor 7437	9
—	—	95	93		TEARDROPS ON YOUR LETTER	Hank Ballard and the Midnighters, King 5171	2
—	—	96	94		I CAN'T SIT DOWN	Marie and Rex, Carlton 502	2
98	84	82	95		SHIRLEY	John Fred, Montel 1002	4
—	—	—	96		HEAVENLY LOVER	Teresa Brewer, Coral 62084	1
—	—	99	97		CHIP OFF THE OLD BLOCK	Eddy Arnold, RCA Victor 7435	2
—	—	—	98		COME TO ME	Marv Johnson, United Artists 160	1
—	—	—	99		TEENAGE HEAVEN	Eddie Cochran, Liberty 55177	1
—	—	—	100		YEAH YEAH	Dale Hawkins, Checker 916	1

THE BILLBOARD'S BEST BUYS

These records have shown the greatest national SALES BREAKOUT potential this week for the first time. Action sides are listed in capital letters.

POP

THE HAPPY ORGAN .... Dave (Baby) Cortez
(Lowell, BMI) Love Me As I Love You (Lowell, BMI) Clock 1009

I GO APE .... Neil Sedaka
(Aldon, BMI) Moon of Gold (Aldon, BMI) RCA Victor 7473

THE HANGING TREE .... Marty Robbins
(Witmark, ASCAP) The Blues Country Style (Advanced, ASCAP) Columbia 41325

MOONLIGHT SERENADE .... The Rivieras
(Robbins, ASCAP) Neither Rain Nor Snow (Winneton, BMI) Coed 508

The above are previous Billboard Spotlight picks

THIS SHOULD GO ON FOREVER .... Rod Bernard
(Jamil, BMI) Pardon, Mr. Gordon (Jamil, BMI) Argo 5327

C&W

FOREIGN CAR .... Hank Locklin
WHEN THE BAND PLAYS THE BLUES
(Western Hills, BMI) (Cedarwood, BMI) RCA Victor 7472

A previous Billboard Spotlight pick

R&B

NO SELECTIONS THIS WEEK

The Billboard HOT 100

FOR THE WEEK ENDING MARCH 29

★ THE STAR PERFORMER designation shows the outstanding upward changes of position in The Hot 100 since last week's chart. Its purpose merely is to provide quick visual identification of the sides which moved up most dramatically or to new entries which first entered the chart at an unusually high position.

THREE WEEKS AGO	TWO WEEKS AGO	ONE WEEK AGO	THIS WEEK	★ STAR PERFORMER THIS WEEK	TITLE Artist, Company, Record Number	WEEKS ON CHART
7	1	1	1		VENUS — Frankie Avalon, Chancellor 1031	7
3	2	2	2		CHARLIE BROWN — Coasters, Atco 6132	8
10	5	3	3		ALVIN'S HARMONICA — David Seville and the Chipmunks, Liberty 55179	6
15	7	4	4		IT'S JUST A MATTER OF TIME — Brook Benton, Mercury 71394	9
22	15	8	5		TRAGEDY — Thomas Wayne, Fernwood 109	19
—	55	16	6	★	COME SOFTLY TO ME — Fleetwoods, Dolphin 1	3
13	6	6	7		I'VE HAD IT — Bell Notes, Time 1004	10
1	3	5	8		STAGGER LEE — Lloyd Price, ABC-Paramount 9972	16
41	19	9	9		NEVER BE ANYONE ELSE BUT YOU — Ricky Nelson, Imperial 5565	5
2	4	7	10		DONNA — Ritchie Valens, Del-Fi 4110	18
49	33	17	11		PINK SHOELACES — Dodie Stevens, Crystalette 724	6
8	12	10	12		PETER GUNN THEME — Ray Anthony, Capitol 4041	12
5	8	11	13		PETITE FLEUR — Chris Barber's Jazz Band, Laurie 3022	11
6	9	12	14		I CRIED A TEAR — LaVern Baker, Atlantic 2007	16
12	13	14	15		TALL PAUL — Annette, Disneyland 118	12
11	11	13	16		HAWAIIAN WEDDING SONG — Andy Williams, Cadence 1358	13
91	44	21	17		IT'S LATE — Ricky Nelson, Imperial 5565	4
39	37	25	18		PLEASE, MR. SUN — Tommy Edwards, M-G-M 12757	6
21	20	18	19		SHE SAY (OOM DOOBY DOOM) — The Diamonds, Mercury 71404	9
45	36	20	20		IT DOESN'T MATTER ANYMORE — Buddy Holly, Coral 62074	5
4	10	15	21		16 CANDLES — Crests, Coed 506	18
19	16	22	22		MAY YOU ALWAYS — McGuire Sisters, Coral 62059	12
55	43	27	23		RAWHIDE — Link Wray, Epic 9300	9
43	35	33	24		SEA CRUISE — Frankie Ford, Ace 554	7
9	14	19	25		ALL AMERICAN BOY — Bill Parsons, Fraternity 835	14
20	18	23	26		THE CHILDREN'S MARCHING SONG — Mitch Miller, Columbia 41317	11
83	45	43	27	★	SINCE I DON'T HAVE YOU — The Skyliners, Calico 103	6
25	27	24	28		I GOT A WIFE — Mark IV, Mercury 71403	9
14	17	26	29		LONELY TEARDROPS — Jackie Wilson, Brunswick 55105	18
37	28	41	30	★	LA BAMBA — Ritchie Valens, Del-Fi 4110	13
28	30	32	31		THE STORY OF MY LOVE — Conway Twitty, M-G-M 12748	9
93	79	47	32	★	THE MORNING SIDE OF THE MOUNTAIN — Tommy Edwards, M-G-M 12757	4
—	81	52	33	★	GUITAR BOOGIE SHUFFLE — The Virtues, Hunt 324	3
29	29	31	34		(ALL OF A SUDDEN) MY HEART SINGS — Paul Anka, ABC-Paramount 9987	14
30	32	35	35		THE LONELY ONE — Duane Eddy, Jamie 1117	10
62	48	44	36		TOMBOY — Perry Como, RCA Victor 7464	5
23	23	30	37		THE CHILDREN'S MARCHING SONG — Cyril Stapleton, London 1851	11
—	86	60	38	★	THIS SHOULD GO ON FOREVER — Rod Bernard, Argo 5327	3
71	60	38	39		THE HANGING TREE — Marty Robbins, Columbia 41325	8
24	26	28	40		GOODBYE BABY — Jack Scott, Carlton 493	15
72	65	57	41	★	WHERE WERE YOU (ON OUR WEDDING DAY)! — Lloyd Price, ABC-Paramount 9997	4
75	64	55	42	★	IF I DIDN'T CARE — Connie Francis, M-G-M 12769	4
42	42	45	43		FIRST ANNIVERSARY — Cathy Carr, Roulette 4125	9
40	47	42	44		NOLA — Billy Williams, Coral 62069	9
16	25	40	45		SMOKE GETS IN YOUR EYES — Platters, Mercury 71383	19
70	54	46	46		NO OTHER ARMS, NO OTHER LIPS — Chordettes, Cadence 1361	4
52	49	51	47		MATILDA — Cookie and His Cupcakes, Judd 1002	10
26	31	29	48		WITH THE WIND AND THE RAIN IN YOUR HAIR — Pat Boone, Dot 15888	11
—	90	58	49		I GO APE — Neil Sedaka, RCA Victor 7473	3
17	21	37	50		MY HAPPINESS — Connie Francis, M-G-M 12738	16
36	41	48	51		PRETTY GIRLS EVERYWHERE — Eugene Church, Class 235	13
31	34	34	52		APPLE BLOSSOM TIME — Tab Hunter, Warner Bros. 5032	8
56	56	50	53		WHEN THE SAINTS GO MARCHING IN — Fats Domino, Imperial 5569	6
18	22	36	54		GOTTA TRAVEL ON — Billy Grammer, Monument 400	18
68	58	56	55		MIDNIGHT OIL — Charlie Blackwell, Warner Bros. 5031	7
—	66	61	56		EVERYBODY LIKES TO CHA CHA — Sam Cooke, Keen 2018	3
—	—	68	57	★	HAPPY ORGAN — Baby Cortez, Clock 1009	2
76	67	62	58		I'M NEVER GONNA TELL ON YOU — Jimmie Rodgers, Roulette 4129	5
58	59	59	59		TELLING LIES — Fats Domino, Imperial 5569	6
—	—	96	60	★	HEAVENLY LOVER — Teresa Brewer, Coral 62084	2

★ THE STAR PERFORMER designation shows the outstanding upward changes of position in The Hot 100 since last week's chart. Its purpose merely is to provide quick visual identification of the sides which moved up most dramatically or to new entries which first entered the chart at an unusually high position.

THE INDUSTRY'S FASTEST AND MOST COMPLETE PROGRAMMING AND BUYING GUIDE

These 100 sides are listed in order of their national POPULARITY, as determined by weekly local studies prepared for The Billboard in markets representing a cross-section of the United States. These studies reflect sales registered for each disk up to press time.

★ THE STAR PERFORMER designation shows the outstanding upward changes of position in The Hot 100 since last week's chart. Its purpose merely is to provide quick visual identification of the sides which moved up most dramatically or to new entries which first entered the chart at an unusually high position.

THREE WEEKS AGO	TWO WEEKS AGO	ONE WEEK AGO	THIS WEEK	★ STAR PERFORMER THIS WEEK	TITLE	Artist, Company, Record Number	WEEKS ON CHART
34	39	54	61		THERE MUST BE A WAY	Joni James, M-G-M 12746	10
38	51	63	62		PLAIN JANE	Bobby Darin, Atco 6133	9
50	57	65	63		NOLA	Morgan Brothers, M-G-M 12747	7
—	—	—	64	★	A FOOL SUCH AS I	Elvis Presley, RCA Victor 7506	1
—	—	100	65	★	YEAH YEAH	Dale Hawkins, Checker 916	2
—	—	84	66	★	SORRY, I RAN ALL THE WAY HOME	The Impalas, Cub 9022	2
89	80	76	67		MOONLIGHT SERENADE	The Rivieras, Coed 508	7
33	38	49	68		DON'T TAKE YOUR GUNS TO TOWN	Johnny Cash, Columbia 41313	10
27	24	39	69		MANHATTAN SPIRITUAL	Reg Owen Ork, Palette 5005	16
57	68	67	70		BLAH, BLAH, BLAH	Nicola Paone, ABC-Paramount 9993	7
100	87	79	71		THE ANSWER TO A MAIDEN'S PRAYER	June Valli, Mercury 71422	4
—	—	—	72	★	TIAJUANA JAIL	Kingston Trio, Capitol 4167	1
—	—	—	73	★	FRIED EGGS	Intruders, Fame 101	1
—	85	81	74		BALLAD OF A GIRL AND BOY	Graduates, Shan-Todd 0055	3
35	46	64	75		LITTLE SPACE GIRL	Jesse Lee Turner, Carlton 496	12
—	—	87	76		AS TIME GOES BY	Johnny Nash, ABC-Paramount 9996	2
32	40	53	77		A LOVER'S QUESTION	Clyde McPhatter, Atlantic 1199	23
—	—	98	78	★	COME TO ME	Marv Johnson, United Artists 160	2
—	—	—	79	★	WISHFUL THINKING	Little Anthony and the Imperials, End 1039	1
—	—	—	80	★	COME SOFTLY TO ME	Ronnie Height, Dore 516	1
—	—	—	81	★	THE BEAT	Rockin' R's, Tempus 7541	1
—	—	—	82	★	RECORD HOP BLUES	The Quarter Notes, Wizz 715	1
81	—	89	83		HURTIN' INSIDE	Brook Benton, Mercury 71394	4
84	82	95	84		SHIRLEY	John Fred, Montel 1002	5
—	—	—	85	★	TELL HIM NO	Travis and Bob, Sandy 1017	1
46	63	71	86		NOBODY BUT YOU	Dee Clark, Abner 1019	17
—	95	93	87		TEARDROPS ON YOUR LETTER	Hank Ballard and the Midnighters, King 5171	3
64	52	74	88		AMBROSE (PART 5)	Linda Laurie, Glory 290	9
—	93	85	89		I KNEEL AT YOUR THRONE	Joe Medlin, Mercury 71415	3
—	94	88	90		BECAUSE YOU'RE YOUNG	Jimmie Rodgers, Roulette 4129	3

THE BILLBOARD'S BEST BUYS

These records have shown the greatest national SALES BREAKOUT potential this week for the first time. Action sides are listed in capital letters.

POP

A FOOL SUCH AS I .... **Elvis Presley**
I NEED YOUR LOVE TONIGHT
(Leeds, ASCAP) (Gladys, ASCAP) RCA Victor 7506

YEAH YEAH .... **Dale Hawkins**
(Bon Bob-Bel Aire, BMI) Lonely Nights (Ace, BMI) Checker 916

TIAJUANA JAIL .... **The Kingston Trio**
(Falstaff, BMI) Oh Cindy (Beechwood, BMI) Capitol 4167

FRIED EGGS .... **The Intruders**
(Aurelio, BMI) Jefferie's Rock (Aurelio, BMI) Fame 101

COME TO ME .... **Marv Johnson**
(Jobete, BMI) Whisper (Gordy-Jobete, BMI) United Artists 160

AS TIME GOES BY .... **Johnny Nash**
(Harms, ASCAP) The Voice of Love (Gold, ASCAP) ABC-Paramount 9996

The above are previous Billboard Spotlight picks

HEAVENLY LOVER .... **Teresa Brewer**
(Skidmore, ASCAP) Fair Weather Sweetheart (Willow, ASCAP) Coral 62084

SORRY, I RAN ALL THE WAY HOME .... **The Impalas**
(Figure, BMI) Fool, Fool, Fool (Figure, BMI) Cub 9022

C&W

WHAT GOES ON IN YOUR HEART .... **Webb Pierce**
(Cedarwood, BMI) A Thousand Miles to Go (Cedarwood, BMI) Decca 30858

A previous Billboard Spotlight pick

R&B

NO SELECTIONS THIS WEEK

★ THE STAR PERFORMER designation shows the outstanding upward changes of position in The Hot 100 since last week's chart. Its purpose merely is to provide quick visual identification of the sides which moved up most dramatically or to new entries which first entered the chart at an unusually high position.

THREE WEEKS AGO	TWO WEEKS AGO	ONE WEEK AGO	THIS WEEK	★ STAR PERFORMER THIS WEEK	TITLE	Artist, Company, Record Number	WEEKS ON CHART
—	—	—	91		FOR A PENNY	Pat Boone, Dot 15914	1
53	69	69	92		THE SHAG	Billy Graves, Monument 401	9
—	—	—	93		ENCHANTED	The Platters, Mercury 71247	1
59	61	70	94		LOVERS NEVER SAY GOODBYE	Flamingos, End 1035	10
—	—	—	95		JIMMY KISS AND RUN	Diane Maxwell, Challenge 59039	1
—	—	—	96		SIX NIGHTS A WEEK	The Crests, Coed 509	1
—	—	—	97		THAT'S WHY	Jackie Wilson, Brunswick 55121	1
—	—	—	98		SOMEONE	Johnny Mathis, Columbia 41355	1
—	—	—	99		TELL HIM NO	Dean and Marc, Bullseye 1025	1
—	—	—	100		SWEET ANNIE LAURIE	Sammy Turner and the Twisters, Big Top 3007	1

The Billboard HOT 100

FOR THE WEEK ENDING APRIL 5

★ THE STAR PERFORMER designation shows the outstanding upward changes of position in The Hot 100 since last week's chart. Its purpose merely is to provide quick visual identification of the sides which moved up most dramatically or to new entries which first entered the chart at an unusually high position.

THREE WEEKS AGO	TWO WEEKS AGO	ONE WEEK AGO	THIS WEEK	★ STAR PERFORMER THIS WEEK	TITLE	Artist, Company, Record Number	WEEKS ON CHART
1	1	1	1		VENUS	Frankie Avalon, Chancellor 1031	8
55	16	6	2		COME SOFTLY TO ME	Fleetwoods, Dolphin 1	4
2	2	2	3		CHARLIE BROWN	Coasters, Atco 6132	9
7	4	4	4		IT'S JUST A MATTER OF TIME	Brook Benton, Mercury 71394	10
15	8	5	5		TRAGEDY	Thomas Wayne, Fernwood 109	20
5	3	3	6		ALVIN'S HARMONICA	David Seville and the Chipmunks, Liberty 55179	7
19	9	9	7		NEVER BE ANYONE ELSE BUT YOU	Ricky Nelson, Imperial 5565	6
33	17	11	8		PINK SHOELACES	Dodie Stevens, Crystalette 724	7
6	6	7	9		I'VE HAD IT	Bell Notes, Time 1004	11
44	21	17	10		IT'S LATE	Ricky Nelson, Imperial 5565	5
37	25	18	11		PLEASE, MR. SUN	Tommy Edwards, M-G-M 12757	7
4	7	10	12		DONNA	Ritchie Valens, Del-Fi 4110	19
36	20	20	13		IT DOESN'T MATTER ANYMORE	Buddy Holly, Coral 62074	6
81	52	33	14	★	GUITAR BOOGIE SHUFFLE	The Virtues, Hunt 324	4
11	13	16	15		HAWAIIAN WEDDING SONG	Andy Williams, Cadence 1358	14
3	5	8	16		STAGGER LEE	Lloyd Price, ABC-Paramount 9972	17
45	43	27	17	★	SINCE I DON'T HAVE YOU	The Skyliners, Calico 103	7
35	33	24	18		SEA CRUISE	Frankie Ford, Ace 554	8
12	10	12	19		PETER GUNN THEME	Ray Anthony, Capitol 4041	13
9	12	14	20		I CRIED A TEAR	LaVern Baker, Atlantic 2007	17
8	11	13	21		PETITE FLEUR	Chris Barber's Jazz Band, Laurie 3022	12
20	18	19	22		SHE SAY (OOM DOOBY DOOM)	The Diamonds, Mercury 71404	10
65	57	41	23	★	WHERE WERE YOU (ON OUR WEDDING DAY)?	Lloyd Price, ABC-Paramount 9997	5
13	14	15	24		TALL PAUL	Annette, Disneyland 118	13
64	55	42	25	★	IF I DIDN'T CARE	Connie Francis, M-G-M 12769	5
—	—	64	26	★	A FOOL SUCH AS I	Elvis Presley, RCA Victor 7506	2
54	46	46	27	★	NO OTHER ARMS, NO OTHER LIPS	Chordettes, Cadence 1361	5
86	60	38	28	★	THIS SHOULD GO ON FOREVER	Rod Bernard, Argo 5327	4
48	44	36	29		TOMBOY	Perry Como, RCA Victor 7464	6
79	47	32	30		THE MORNING SIDE OF THE MOUNTAIN	Tommy Edwards, M-G-M 12757	5
16	22	22	31		MAY YOU ALWAYS	McGuire Sisters, Coral 62059	13
—	—	72	32	★	TIAJUANA JAIL	Kingston Trio, Capitol 4167	2
—	—	—	33	★	I NEED YOUR LOVE TONIGHT	Elvis Presley, RCA Victor 7506	1
66	61	56	34	★	EVERYBODY LIKES TO CHA CHA	Sam Cooke, Keen 2018	4
—	68	57	35	★	HAPPY ORGAN	Dave (Baby) Cortez, Clock 1009	3
67	62	58	36	★	I'M NEVER GONNA TELL	Jimmie Rodgers, Roulette 4129	6
43	27	23	37		RAWHIDE	Link Wray, Epic 9300	10
18	23	26	38		THE CHILDREN'S MARCHING SONG	Mitch Miller, Columbia 41317	12
30	32	31	39		THE STORY OF MY LOVE	Conway Twitty, M-G-M 12748	10
60	38	39	40		THE HANGING TREE	Marty Robbins, Columbia 41325	9
27	24	28	41		I GOT A WIFE	Mark IV, Mercury 71403	10
90	58	49	42		I GO APE	Neil Sedaka, RCA Victor 7473	4
47	42	44	43		NOLA	Billy Williams, Coral 62069	10
10	15	21	44		16 CANDLES	Crests, Coed 506	19
42	45	43	45		FIRST ANNIVERSARY	Cathy Carr, Roulette 4125	10
34	34	52	46		APPLE BLOSSOM TIME	Tab Hunter, Warner Bros. 5032	9
—	—	85	47	★	TELL HIM NO	Travis and Bob, Sandy 1017	2
80	76	67	48	★	MOONLIGHT SERENADE	The Rivieras, Coed 508	8
23	30	37	49		THE CHILDREN'S MARCHING SONG	Cyril Stapleton, London 1851	12
59	59	59	50		TELLING LIES	Fats Domino, Imperial 5569	7
—	—	80	51	★	COME SOFTLY TO ME	Ronnie Height, Dore 516	2
32	35	35	52		THE LONELY ONE	Duane Eddy, Jamie 1117	11
—	—	91	53	★	FOR A PENNY	Pat Boone, Dot 15914	2
—	84	66	54	★	SORRY, I RAN ALL THE WAY HOME	The Impalas, Cub 9022	3
56	50	53	55		WHEN THE SAINTS GO MARCHING IN	Fats Domino, Imperial 5569	7
14	19	25	56		ALL AMERICAN BOY	Bill Parsons, Fraternity 835	15
—	100	65	57		YEAH YEAH	Dale Hawkins, Checker 916	3
—	96	60	58		HEAVENLY LOVER	Teresa Brewer, Coral 62084	3
28	41	30	59		LA BAMBA	Ritchie Valens, Del-Fi 4110	14
29	31	34	60		(ALL OF A SUDDEN) MY HEART SINGS	Paul Anka, ABC-Paramount 9987	15

THE INDUSTRY'S FASTEST AND MOST COMPLETE PROGRAMMING AND BUYING GUIDE

These 100 sides are listed in order of their national POPULARITY, as determined by weekly local studies prepared for The Billboard in markets representing a cross-section of the United States. These studies reflect sales registered for each disk up to press time.

★ THE STAR PERFORMER designation shows the outstanding upward changes of position in The Hot 100 since last week's chart. Its purpose merely is to provide quick visual identification of the sides which moved up most dramatically or to new entries which first entered the chart at an unusually high position.

Three Weeks Ago	Two Weeks Ago	One Week Ago	This Week	★ Star Performer This Week	Title — Artist, Company, Record Number	Weeks on Chart
—	—	—	61	★	TAKE A MESSAGE TO MARY — Everly Brothers, Cadence 1364	1
94	88	90	62	★	BECAUSE YOU'RE YOUNG — Jimmie Rodgers, Roulette 4129	4
17	26	29	63		LONELY TEARDROPS — Jackie Wilson, Brunswick 55105	19
31	29	48	64		WITH THE WIND AND THE RAIN IN YOUR HAIR — Pat Boone, Dot 15888	12
—	87	76	65		AS TIME GOES BY — Johnny Nash, ABC-Paramount 9996	3
41	48	51	66		PRETTY GIRLS EVERYWHERE — Eugene Church, Class 235	14
49	51	47	67		MATILDA — Cookie and His Cupcakes, Judd 1002	11
—	—	81	68		THE BEAT — Rockin' R's, Tempus 7541	2
—	—	—	69	★	POOR JENNY — Everly Brothers, Cadence 1364	1
—	—	—	70	★	GUESS WHO — Jesse Belvin, RCA Victor 7469	1
87	79	71	71		THE ANSWER TO A MAIDEN'S PRAYER — June Valli, Mercury 71422	5
26	28	40	72		GOODBYE BABY — Jack Scott, Carlton 493	16
38	49	68	73		DON'T TAKE YOUR GUNS TO TOWN — Johnny Cash, Columbia 41313	11
—	98	78	74		COME TO ME — Marv Johnson, United Artists 160	3
—	—	73	75		FRIED EGGS — Intruders, Fame 101	2
—	—	96	76	★	SIX NIGHTS A WEEK — The Crests, Coed 509	2
22	36	54	77		GOTTA TRAVEL ON — Billy Grammer, Monument 400	19
39	54	61	78		THERE MUST BE A WAY — Joni James, M-G-M 12746	11
—	—	—	79	★	TURN ME LOOSE — Fabian, Chancellor 1033	1
—	—	97	80	★	THAT'S WHY — Jackie Wilson, Brunswick 55121	2
74	—	—	81	★	NO OTHER ARMS, NO OTHER LIPS — Four Aces, Decca 30822	3
—	—	—	82	★	THREE STARS — Tommy Dee, Crest 1057	1
—	—	98	83	★	SOMEONE — Johnny Mathis, Columbia 41355	2
—	—	93	84		ENCHANTED — The Platters, Mercury 71427	2
21	37	50	85		MY HAPPINESS — Connie Francis, M-G-M 12738	17
58	56	55	86		MIDNIGHT OIL — Charlie Blackwell, Warner Bros. 5031	8
—	—	—	87	★	ROCKIN' CRICKETS — Hot Toddys, Shan-Todd 0056	1
—	—	—	88	★	WHO'S THAT KNOCKIN' — Genies, Shad 5002	1
—	—	—	89	★	HAWAIIAN WAR CHANT — Billy Vaughn, Dot 15900	1
—	—	—	90	★	FRENCH FOREIGN LEGION — Frank Sinatra, Capitol 4155	1

THE BILLBOARD'S BEST BUYS

These records have shown the greatest national SALES BREAKOUT potential this week for the first time. Action sides are listed in capital letters.

POP

FOR A PENNY .... **Pat Boone**
(Roosevelt, BMI) The Wang Dang Taffy Apple Tango (Spoone, ASCAP) Dot 15914

TAKE A MESSAGE TO MARY .... **Everly Brothers**
POOR JENNY
(Acuff-Rose, BMI) (Acuff-Rose, BMI) Cadence 1364

TELL HIM NO .... **Travis and Bob**
(Burnt, Oak, BMI) We're Too Young (Singing River, BMI) Sandy 1017

SIX NIGHTS A WEEK .... **The Crests**
(Winneton, BMI) I Do (Winneon, BMI) Coed 509

SOMEONE .... **Johnny Mathis**
(Cathryl, ASCAP) Very Much in Love (Mathis, ASCAP) Columbia 41355

ALMOST GROWN .... **Chuck Berry**
(Arc, BMI) Little Queenie (Arc, BMI) Chess 1722

TURN ME LOOSE .... **Fabian**
(Avalon, BMI) Stop Thief! (Rambed, BMI) Chancellor 1033

THAT'S WHY .... **Jackie Wilson**
(Pearl, BMI) Love Is All (Figure, BMI) Brunswick 55121

ENCHANTED .... **The Platters**
(Choice, ASCAP) The Sound and the Fury (Feist, ASCAP) Mercury 71427

The above are previous Billboard Spotlight picks

C&W

NO SELECTIONS THIS WEEK

R&B

NO SELECTIONS THIS WEEK

★ THE STAR PERFORMER designation shows the outstanding upward changes of position in The Hot 100 since last week's chart. Its purpose merely is to provide quick visual identification of the sides which moved up most dramatically or to new entries which first entered the chart at an unusually high position.

Three Weeks Ago	Two Weeks Ago	One Week Ago	This Week	★ Star Performer This Week	Title — Artist, Company, Record Number	Weeks on Chart
57	65	63	91		NOLA — Morgan Brothers, M-G-M 12747	8
—	—	—	92		HOUSE OF LOVE — Scott Garrett, Laurie 3032	1
—	—	—	93		STAR LOVE — Playmates, Roulette 4136	1
—	—	79	94		WISHFUL THINKING — Little Anthony and the Imperials, End 1039	2
—	—	—	95		RAINING IN MY HEART — Buddy Holly, Coral 62074	1
—	—	—	96		ALMOST GROWN — Chuck Berry, Chess 1722	1
—	—	—	97		I MISS YOU SO — Paul Anka, ABC-Paramount 10011	1
—	—	—	98		BOOM-A-DIP-DIP — Stan Robinson, Monument 402	1
—	—	—	99		YEP! — Duane Eddy, Jamie 1122	1
—	—	—	100		THE CHICK — Lee and Paul, Columbia 41337	1

The Billboard HOT 100

FOR THE WEEK ENDING APRIL 12

★ THE STAR PERFORMER designation shows the outstanding upward changes of position in The Hot 100 since last week's chart. Its purpose merely is to provide quick visual identification of the sides which moved up most dramatically or to new entries which first entered the chart at an unusually high position.

★ THE STAR PERFORMER designation shows the outstanding upward changes of position in The Hot 100 since last week's chart. Its purpose merely is to provide quick visual identification of the sides which moved up most dramatically or to new entries which first entered the chart at an unusually high position.

THREE WEEKS AGO	TWO WEEKS AGO	ONE WEEK AGO	THIS WEEK	STAR PERFORMER THIS WEEK	TITLE	Artist, Company, Record Number	WEEKS ON CHART
1	1	1	1		VENUS	Frankie Avalon, Chancellor 1031	9
16	6	2	2		COME SOFTLY TO ME	Fleetwoods, Dolphin 1	5
4	4	4	3		IT'S JUST A MATTER OF TIME	Brook Benton, Mercury 71394	11
17	11	8	4		PINK SHOELACES	Dodie Stevens, Crystalette 724	8
8	5	5	5		TRAGEDY	Thomas Wayne, Fernwood 109	21
9	9	7	6		NEVER BE ANYONE ELSE BUT YOU	Ricky Nelson, Imperial 5565	7
2	2	3	7		CHARLIE BROWN	Coasters, Atco 6132	10
3	3	6	8		ALVIN'S HARMONICA	David Seville and the Chipmunks, Liberty 55179	8
21	17	10	9		IT'S LATE	Ricky Nelson, Imperial 5565	6
52	33	14	10		GUITAR BOOGIE SHUFFLE	The Virtues, Hunt 324	5
6	7	9	11		I'VE HAD IT	Bell Notes, Time 1004	12
—	—	33	12	★	I NEED YOUR LOVE TONIGHT	Elvis Presley, RCA Victor 7506	2
—	64	26	13	★	A FOOL SUCH AS I	Elvis Presley, RCA Victor 7506	3
33	24	18	14		SEA CRUISE	Frankie Ford, Ace 554	9
43	27	17	15		SINCE I DON'T HAVE YOU	The Skyliners, Calico 103	8
13	16	15	16		HAWAIIAN WEDDING SONG	Andy Williams, Cadence 1358	15
25	18	11	17		PLEASE, MR. SUN	Tommy Edwards, M-G-M 12757	8
20	20	13	18		IT DOESN'T MATTER ANYMORE	Buddy Holly, Coral 62074	7
5	8	16	19		STAGGER LEE	Lloyd Price, ABC-Paramount 9972	18
—	72	32	20	★	TIAJUANA JAIL	Kingston Trio, Capitol 4167	3
60	38	28	21		THIS SHOULD GO ON FOREVER	Rod Bernard, Argo 5327	5
55	42	25	22		IF I DIDN'T CARE	Connie Francis, M-G-M 12769	6
—	85	47	23	★	TELL HIM NO	Travis and Bob, Sandy 1017	3
57	41	23	24		WHERE WERE YOU (ON OUR WEDDING DAY)?	Lloyd Price, ABC-Paramount 9997	6
68	57	35	25	★	THE HAPPY ORGAN	Dave (Baby) Cortez, Clock 1009	4
11	13	21	26		PETITE FLEUR	Chris Barber's Jazz Band, Laurie 3022	13
47	32	30	27		THE MORNING SIDE OF THE MOUNTAIN	Tommy Edwards, M-G-M 12757	6
10	12	19	28		PETER GUNN THEME	Ray Anthony, Capitol 4041	14
46	46	27	29		NO OTHER ARMS, NO OTHER LIPS	Chordettes, Cadence 1361	6
12	14	20	30		I CRIED A TEAR	LaVern Baker, Atlantic 2007	18
7	10	12	31		DONNA	Ritchie Valens, Del-Fi 4110	20
18	19	22	32		SHE SAY (OOM DOOBY DOOM)	The Diamonds, Mercury 71404	11
44	36	29	33		TOMBOY	Perry Como, RCA Victor 7464	7
61	56	34	34		EVERYBODY LIKES TO CHA CHA	Sam Cooke, Keen 2018	5
—	93	84	35	★	ENCHANTED	The Platters, Mercury 71427	3
—	91	53	36	★	FOR A PENNY	Pat Boone, Dot 15914	3
62	58	36	37		I'M NEVER GONNA TELL	Jimmie Rodgers, Roulette 4129	7
22	22	31	38		MAY YOU ALWAYS	McGuire Sisters, Coral 62059	14
—	—	79	39	★	TURN ME LOOSE	Fabian, Chancellor 1033	2
96	60	58	40	★	HEAVENLY LOVER	Teresa Brewer, Coral 62084	4
14	15	24	41		TALL PAUL	Annette, Disneyland 118	14
58	49	42	42		I GO APE	Neil Sedaka, RCA Victor 7473	5
—	—	70	43	★	GUESS WHO	Jesse Belvin, RCA Victor 7469	2
84	66	54	44	★	SORRY, I RAN ALL THE WAY HOME	The Impalas, Cub 9022	4
—	80	51	45		COME SOFTLY TO ME	Ronnie Height, Dore 516	3
38	39	40	46		THE HANGING TREE	Marty Robbins, Columbia 41325	10
27	23	37	47		RAWHIDE	Link Wray, Epic 9300	11
76	67	48	48		MOONLIGHT SERENADE	The Rivieras, Coed 508	9
24	28	41	49		I GOT A WIFE	Mark IV, Mercury 71403	11
—	—	82	50	★	THREE STARS	Tommy Dee, Crest 1057	2
15	21	44	51		16 CANDLES	Crests, Coed 506	20
59	59	50	52		TELLING LIES	Fats Domino, Imperial 5569	8
100	65	57	53		YEAH YEAH	Dale Hawkins, Checker 916	4
—	—	61	54		TAKE A MESSAGE TO MARY	Everly Brothers, Cadence 1364	2
32	31	39	55		THE STORY OF MY LOVE	Conway Twitty, M-G-M 12748	11
42	44	43	56		NOLA	Billy Williams, Coral 62069	11
35	35	52	57		THE LONELY ONE	Duane Eddy, Jamie 1117	12
34	52	46	58		APPLE BLOSSOM TIME	Tab Hunter, Warner Bros. 5032	10
87	76	65	59		AS TIME GOES BY	Johnny Nash, ABC-Paramount 9996	4
23	26	38	60		THE CHILDREN'S MARCHING SONG	Mitch Miller, Columbia 41317	13

THE INDUSTRY'S FASTEST AND MOST COMPLETE PROGRAMMING AND BUYING GUIDE

These 100 sides are listed in order of their national POPULARITY, as determined by weekly local studies prepared for The Billboard in markets representing a cross-section of the United States. These studies reflect sales registered for each disk up to press time.

★ THE STAR PERFORMER designation shows the outstanding upward changes of position in The Hot 100 since last week's chart. Its purpose merely is to provide quick visual identification of the sides which moved up most dramatically or to new entries which first entered the chart at an unusually high position.

THREE WEEKS AGO	TWO WEEKS AGO	ONE WEEK AGO	THIS WEEK	★ STAR PERFORMER THIS WEEK	TITLE Artist, Company, Record Number	WEEKS ON CHART
—	—	99	61	★	YEP! Duane Eddy, Jamie 1122	2
41	30	59	62		LA BAMBA Ritchie Valens, Del-Fi 4110	15
98	78	74	63		COME TO ME Marv Johnson, United Artists 160	4
—	81	68	64		THE BEAT Rockin' R's, Tempus 7541	3
31	34	60	65		(ALL OF A SUDDEN) MY HEART SINGS Paul Anka, ABC-Paramount 9987	16
—	98	83	66	★	SOMEONE Johnny Mathis, Columbia 41355	3
30	37	49	67		THE CHILDREN'S MARCHING SONG Cyril Stapleton, London 1851	13
45	43	45	68		FIRST ANNIVERSARY Cathy Carr, Roulette 4125	11
—	—	69	69		POOR JENNY Everly Brothers, Cadence 1364	2
—	96	76	70		SIX NIGHTS A WEEK The Crests, Coed 509	3
26	29	63	71		LONELY TEARDROPS Jackie Wilson, Brunswick 55105	20
—	—	96	72	★	ALMOST GROWN Chuck Berry, Chess 1722	2
—	97	80	73		THAT'S WHY Jackie Wilson, Brunswick 55121	3
88	90	62	74		BECAUSE YOU'RE YOUNG Jimmie Rodgers, Roulette 4129	5
19	25	56	75		ALL AMERICAN BOY Bill Parsons, Fraternity 835	16
51	47	67	76		MATILDA Cookie and His Cupcakes, Judd 1002	12
—	—	—	77	★	SO FINE Fiestas, Old Town 1062	1
—	—	97	78	★	I MISS YOU SO Paul Anka, ABC-Paramount 10011	2
—	73	75	79		FRIED EGGS Intruders, Fame 101	3
—	—	81	80		NO OTHER ARMS, NO OTHER LIPS Four Aces, Decca 30822	4
48	51	66	81		PRETTY GIRLS EVERYWHERE Eugene Church, Class 235	15
—	99	—	82	★	TELL HIM NO Dean and Mark, Bullseye 1025	2
—	—	—	83	★	LOVEY DOVEY Clyde McPhatter, Atlantic 2018	1
29	48	64	84		WITH THE WIND AND THE RAIN IN YOUR HAIR Pat Boone, Dot 15888	13
—	—	87	85		ROCKIN' CRICKETS Hot Toddys, Shan-Todd 0056	2
49	68	73	86		DON'T TAKE YOUR GUNS TO TOWN Johnny Cash, Columbia 41313	12
—	—	90	87		FRENCH FOREIGN LEGION Frank Sinatra, Capitol 4155	2
—	—	95	88		RAINING IN MY HEART Buddy Holly, Coral 62074	2
—	—	98	89		BOOM-A-DIP-DIP Stan Robinson, Monument 402	2
36	54	77	90		GOTTA TRAVEL ON Billy Grammer, Monument 400	20

THE BILLBOARD'S BEST BUYS

These records have shown the greatest national SALES BREAKOUT potential this week for the first time. Action sides are listed in capital letters.

POP

I MISS YOU SO .... Paul Anka
(Leeds, ASCAP) Late Last Night (Spanka, BMI) ABC Paramount 10011

YEP! .... Duane Eddy
(Gregmark, BMI) 3:30 Blues (Gregmark, BMI) Jamie 1122

The above are previous Billboard Spotlight picks

GUESS WHO .... Jesse Belvin
(Michele, BMI) My Girl Is Just Enough Woman for Me (Chappell, ASCAP) RCA Victor 7469

THREE STARS .... Tommy Dee
(American, BMI) I'll Never Change (American, BMI) Crest 1057

C&W

WHAT DO YOU KNOW ABOUT HEARTACHES ...... Johnnie & Jack
(Starday, BMI) I Wonder If You Know (C & I, BMI) RCA Victor 7478

A previous Billboard Spotlight pick

R&B

NO SELECTIONS THIS WEEK

★ THE STAR PERFORMER designation shows the outstanding upward changes of position in The Hot 100 since last week's chart. Its purpose merely is to provide quick visual identification of the sides which moved up most dramatically or to new entries which first entered the chart at an unusually high position.

THREE WEEKS AGO	TWO WEEKS AGO	ONE WEEK AGO	THIS WEEK	★ STAR PERFORMER THIS WEEK	TITLE Artist, Company, Record Number	WEEKS ON CHART
—	—	88	91		WHO'S THAT KNOCKIN' Genies, Shad 5002	2
—	—	93	92		STAR LOVE Playmates, Roulette 4136	2
56	55	86	93		MIDNIGHT OIL Charlie Blackwell, Warner Bros. 5031	9
37	50	85	94		MY HAPPINESS Connie Francis, M-G-M 12738	18
—	—	—	95		ONLY YOU Frank Pourcel, Capitol 4165	1
—	—	—	96		77 SUNSET STRIP Don Ralke, Warner Bros. 5025	1
50	53	55	97		WHEN THE SAINTS GO MARCHING IN Fats Domino, Imperial 5569	8
—	—	—	98		THAT'S MY LITTLE SUZIE Ritchie Valens, Del-Fi 4114	1
—	—	—	99		I NEVER FELT LIKE THIS Jack Scott, Carlton 504	1
54	61	78	100		THERE MUST BE A WAY Joni James, M-G-M 12746	12

The Billboard HOT 100

FOR THE WEEK ENDING APRIL 19

★ THE STAR PERFORMER designation shows the outstanding upward changes of position in The Hot 100 since last week's chart. Its purpose merely is to provide quick visual identification of the sides which moved up most dramatically or to new entries which first entered the chart at an unusually high position.

Three Weeks Ago	Two Weeks Ago	One Week Ago	This Week	★ Star Performer This Week	Title	Artist, Company, Record Number	Weeks on Chart
6	2	2	1		COME SOFTLY TO ME	Fleetwoods, Dolphin 1	6
1	1	1	2		VENUS	Frankie Avalon, Chancellor 1031	10
11	8	4	3		PINK SHOELACES	Dodie Stevens, Crystalette 724	9
4	4	3	4		IT'S JUST A MATTER OF TIME	Brook Benton, Mercury 71394	12
5	5	5	5		TRAGEDY	Thomas Wayne, Fernwood 109	22
9	7	6	6		NEVER BE ANYONE ELSE BUT YOU	Ricky Nelson, Imperial 5565	8
2	3	7	7		CHARLIE BROWN	Coasters, Atco 6132	11
64	26	13	8		A FOOL SUCH AS I	Elvis Presley, RCA Victor 7506	4
33	14	10	9		GUITAR BOOGIE SHUFFLE	The Virtues, Hunt 324	6
—	33	12	10		I NEED YOUR LOVE TONIGHT	Elvis Presley, RCA Victor 7506	3
17	10	9	11		IT'S LATE	Ricky Nelson, Imperial 5565	7
27	17	15	12		SINCE I DON'T HAVE YOU	The Skyliners, Calico 103	9
57	35	25	13	★	THE HAPPY ORGAN	Dave (Baby) Cortez, Clock 1009	5
72	32	20	14		TIAJUANA JAIL	Kingston Trio, Capitol 4167	4
24	18	14	15		SEA CRUISE	Frankie Ford, Ace 554	10
85	47	23	16		TELL HIM NO	Travis and Bob, Sandy 1017	4
—	79	39	17	★	TURN ME LOOSE	Fabian, Chancellor 1033	3
3	6	8	18		ALVIN'S HARMONICA	David Seville and the Chipmunks, Liberty 55179	9
7	9	11	19		I'VE HAD IT	Bell Notes, Time 1004	13
38	28	21	20		THIS SHOULD GO ON FOREVER	Rod Bernard, Argo 5327	6
—	82	50	21	★	THREE STARS	Tommy Dee, Crest 1057	3
93	84	35	22	★	ENCHANTED	The Platters, Mercury 71427	4
18	11	17	23		PLEASE, MR. SUN	Tommy Edwards, M-G-M 12757	9
20	13	18	24		IT DOESN'T MATTER ANYMORE	Buddy Holly, Coral 62074	8
66	54	44	25	★	SORRY, I RAN ALL THE WAY HOME	The Impalas, Cub 9022	5
16	15	16	26		HAWAIIAN WEDDING SONG	Andy Williams, Cadence 1358	16
91	53	36	27		FOR A PENNY	Pat Boone, Dot 15914	4
41	23	24	28		WHERE WERE YOU (ON OUR WEDDING DAY)?	Lloyd Price, ABC-Paramount 9997	7
42	25	22	29		IF I DIDN'T CARE	Connie Francis, M-G-M 12769	7
97	80	73	30	★	THAT'S WHY	Jackie Wilson, Brunswick 55121	4
32	30	27	31		THE MORNING SIDE OF THE MOUNTAIN	Tommy Edwards, M-G-M 12757	7
46	27	29	32		NO OTHER ARMS, NO OTHER LIPS	Chordettes, Cadence 1361	7
56	34	34	33		EVERYBODY LIKES TO CHA CHA	Sam Cooke, Keen 2018	6
10	12	31	34		DONNA	Ritchie Valens, Del-Fi 4110	21
—	70	43	35		GUESS WHO	Jesse Belvin, RCA Victor 7469	3
8	16	19	36		STAGGER LEE	Lloyd Price, ABC-Paramount 9972	19
19	22	32	37		SHE SAY (OOM DOOBY DOOM)	The Diamonds, Mercury 71404	12
12	19	28	38		PETER GUNN THEME	Ray Anthony, Capitol 4041	15
96	76	70	39	★	SIX NIGHTS A WEEK	The Crests, Coed 509	4
58	36	37	40		I'M NEVER GONNA TELL	Jimmie Rodgers, Roulette 4129	8
39	40	46	41		THE HANGING TREE	Marty Robbins, Columbia 41325	11
14	20	30	42		I CRIED A TEAR	LaVern Baker, Atlantic 2007	19
49	42	42	43		I GO APE	Neil Sedaka, RCA Victor 7473	6
—	97	78	44	★	I MISS YOU SO	Paul Anka, ABC-Paramount 10011	3
60	58	40	45		HEAVENLY LOVER	Teresa Brewer, Coral 62084	5
—	99	61	46	★	YEP!	Duane Eddy, Jamie 1122	3
67	48	48	47		MOONLIGHT SERENADE	The Rivieras, Coed 508	10
—	96	72	48	★	ALMOST GROWN	Chuck Berry, Chess 1722	3
78	74	63	49	★	COME TO ME	Marv Johnson, United Artists 160	5
—	61	54	50		TAKE A MESSAGE TO MARY	Everly Brothers, Cadence 1364	3
36	29	33	51		TOMBOY	Perry Como, RCA Victor 7464	12
65	57	53	52		YEAH YEAH	Dale Hawkins, Checker 916	5
99	—	82	53	★	TELL HIM NO	Dean and Marc, Bullseye 1025	3
76	65	59	54		AS TIME GOES BY	Johnny Nash, ABC-Paramount 9996	5
13	21	26	55		PETITE FLEUR	Chris Barber's Jazz Band, Laurie 3022	14
22	31	38	56		MAY YOU ALWAYS	McGuire Sisters, Coral 62059	15
81	68	64	57		THE BEAT	Rockin' R's, Tempus 7541	4
98	83	66	58		SOMEONE	Johnny Mathis, Columbia 41355	4
23	37	47	59		RAWHIDE	Link Wray, Epic 9300	12
—	—	77	60	★	SO FINE	Fiestas, Old Town 1062	2

THE INDUSTRY'S FASTEST AND MOST COMPLETE PROGRAMMING AND BUYING GUIDE

These 100 sides are listed in order of their national POPULARITY, as determined by weekly local studies prepared for The Billboard in markets representing a cross-section of the United States. These studies reflect sales registered for each disk up to press time.

★ THE STAR PERFORMER designation shows the outstanding upward changes of position in The Hot 100 since last week's chart. Its purpose merely is to provide quick visual identification of the sides which moved up most dramatically or to new entries which first entered the chart at an unusually high position.

THREE WEEKS AGO	TWO WEEKS AGO	ONE WEEK AGO	THIS WEEK	★ STAR PERFORMER THIS WEEK	TITLE Artist, Company, Record Number	WEEKS ON CHART
—	—	83	61	★	LOVEY DOVEY — Clyde McPhatter, Atlantic 2018	2
80	51	45	62		COME SOFTLY TO ME — Ronnie Height, Dore 516	4
28	41	49	63		I GOT A WIFE — Mark IV, Mercury 71403	12
21	44	51	64		16 CANDLES — Crests, Coed 506	21
15	24	41	65		TALL PAUL — Annette, Disneyland 118	15
52	46	58	66		APPLE BLOSSOM TIME — Tab Hunter, Warner Bros. 5032	11
—	69	69	67		POOR JENNY — Everly Brothers, Cadence 1364	3
44	43	56	68		NOLA — Billy Williams, Coral 62069	12
—	90	87	69	★	FRENCH FOREIGN LEGION — Frank Sinatra, Capitol 4155	3
—	—	—	70	★	GOODBYE, JIMMY, GOODBYE — Kathy Linden, Felsted 8571	1
35	52	57	71		THE LONELY ONE — Duane Eddy, Jamie 1117	13
29	63	71	72		LONELY TEARDROPS — Jackie Wilson, Brunswick 55105	21
47	67	76	73		MATILDA — Cookie and His Cupcakes, Judd 1002	13
34	60	65	74		(ALL OF A SUDDEN) MY HEART SINGS — Paul Anka, ABC-Paramount 9987	17
—	93	92	75	★	STAR LOVE — Playmates, Roulette 4136	3
—	—	—	76	★	THE KISSING TREE — Billy Grammer, Monument 403	1
—	—	98	77	★	THAT'S MY LITTLE SUZIE — Ritchie Valens, Del-Fi 4114	2
—	—	—	78	★	THE WALLS HAVE EARS — Patti Page, Mercury 71428	1
—	—	95	79	★	ONLY YOU — Frank Pourcel, Capitol 4165	2
59	50	52	80		TELLING LIES — Fats Domino, Imperial 5569	9
—	—	—	81	★	I STILL GET A THRILL — Joni James, M-G-M 12779	1
43	45	68	82		FIRST ANNIVERSARY — Cathy Carr, Roulette 4125	12
—	98	89	83		BOOM-A-DIP-DIP — Stan Robinson, Monument 402	3
26	38	60	84		THE CHILDREN'S MARCHING SONG — Mitch Miller, Columbia 41317	14
—	88	91	85		WHO'S THAT KNOCKIN' — Genies, Shad 5002	3
31	39	55	86		THE STORY OF MY LOVE — Conway Twitty, M-G-M 12748	12
—	—	—	87	★	BONAPARTE'S RETREAT — Billy Grammer, Monument 403	1
—	—	—	88	★	I THINK I'M GONNA KILL MYSELF — Buddy Knox, Roulette 4140	1
—	—	96	89		77 SUNSET STRIP — Don Ralke, Warner Bros. 5025	2
—	—	—	90	★	JO-JO THE DOG-FACED BOY — Annette, Vista 336	1

THE BILLBOARD'S BEST BUYS

These records have shown the greatest national SALES BREAKOUT potential this week for the first time. Action sides are listed in capital letters.

POP

LOVEY DOVEY . . . . . Clyde McPhatter
(Progressive, BMI) My Island of Dreams (Progressive, BMI) Atlantic 2018

THAT'S MY LITTLE SUZIE . . . . . Ritchie Valens
(Kemo, BMI) In a Turkish Town (Kemo, BMI) Del Fi 4114

I STILL GET A THRILL . . . . . Joni James
(Words & Music, ASCAP) Perhaps (Parliament, ASCAP) M-G-M 12779

THE KISSING TREE . . . . . Billy Grammer
BONAPARTE'S RETREAT
(Carlfred, ASCAP) (Acuff-Rose, BMI) Monument 403

THE WALLS HAVE EARS . . . . . Patti Page
(Shapiro-Bernstein, ASCAP) My Promise (Egap, BMI) Mercury 71428

The above are previous Billboard Spotlight picks

GOODBYE, JIMMY, GOODBYE . . . . . Kathy Linden
(Knollwood, ASCAP) Heartaches at Sweet Sixteen (Irish-Trojan, BMI) Felsted 8571

ONLY YOU . . . . . Frank Pourcel
(Wildwood, ASCAP) Rainy Night in Paris (Beechwood, BMI) Capitol 4165

FRENCH FOREIGN LEGION . . . . . Frank Sinatra
(Barton, ASCAP) Time After Time (Sands, ASCAP) Capitol 4155

C&W

NO SELECTIONS THIS WEEK

R&B

NO SELECTIONS THIS WEEK

★ THE STAR PERFORMER designation shows the outstanding upward changes of position in The Hot 100 since last week's chart. Its purpose merely is to provide quick visual identification of the sides which moved up most dramatically or to new entries which first entered the chart at an unusually high position.

THREE WEEKS AGO	TWO WEEKS AGO	ONE WEEK AGO	THIS WEEK	★ STAR PERFORMER THIS WEEK	TITLE Artist, Company, Record Number	WEEKS ON CHART
—	—	—	91		I'VE COME OF AGE — Billy Storm, Columbia 41356	1
37	49	67	92		THE CHILDREN'S MARCHING SONG — Cyril Stapleton, London 1851	14
—	—	99	93		I NEVER FELT LIKE THIS — Jack Scott, Carlton 504	2
—	—	—	94		LONELY FOR YOU — Gary Stites, Carlton 508	1
—	—	—	95		QUIET VILLAGE — Martin Denny, Liberty 55162	1
—	—	—	96		MY HEART IS AN OPEN BOOK — Carl Dobkins Jr., Decca 30803	1
48	64	84	97		WITH THE WIND AND THE RAIN IN YOUR HAIR — Pat Boone, Dot 15888	14
—	—	—	98		LITTLE QUEENIE — Chuck Berry, Chess 1722	1
—	—	—	99		YOU CAN'T BE TRUE DEAR — Mary Kaye Trio, Warner Bros. 5050	1
—	—	—	100		KANSAS CITY — Wilbert Harrison, Fury 1023	1

The Billboard HOT 100

FOR THE WEEK ENDING APRIL 26

★ THE STAR PERFORMER designation shows the outstanding upward changes of position in The Hot 100 since last week's chart. Its purpose merely is to provide quick visual identification of the sides which moved up most dramatically or to new entries which first entered the chart at an unusually high position.

Three Weeks Ago	Two Weeks Ago	One Week Ago	This Week	★ Star Performer This Week	Title	Artist, Company, Record Number	Weeks on Chart
2	2	1	1		COME SOFTLY TO ME	Fleetwoods, Dolphin 1	7
1	1	2	2		VENUS	Frankie Avalon, Chancellor 1031	11
8	4	3	3		PINK SHOELACES	Dodie Stevens, Crystalette 724	10
33	12	10	4		I NEED YOUR LOVE TONIGHT	Elvis Presley, RCA Victor 7506	4
26	13	8	5		A FOOL SUCH AS I	Elvis Presley, RCA Victor 7506	5
7	6	6	6		NEVER BE ANYONE ELSE BUT YOU	Ricky Nelson, Imperial 5565	9
14	10	9	7		GUITAR BOOGIE SHUFFLE	The Virtues, Hunt 324	7
4	3	4	8		IT'S JUST A MATTER OF TIME	Brook Benton, Mercury 71394	13
5	5	5	9		TRAGEDY	Thomas Wayne, Fernwood 109	23
10	9	11	10		IT'S LATE	Ricky Nelson, Imperial 5565	8
47	23	16	11		TELL HIM NO	Travis and Bob, Sandy 1017	5
32	20	14	12		TIAJUANA JAIL	Kingston Trio, Capitol 4167	5
35	25	13	13		THE HAPPY ORGAN	Dave (Baby) Cortez, Clock 1009	6
18	14	15	14		SEA CRUISE	Frankie Ford, Ace 554	11
17	15	12	15		SINCE I DON'T HAVE YOU	The Skyliners, Calico 103	10
3	7	7	16		CHARLIE BROWN	Coasters, Atco 6132	12
79	39	17	17		TURN ME LOOSE	Fabian, Chancellor 1033	4
82	50	21	18		THREE STARS	Tommy Dee, Crest 1057	4
84	35	22	19		ENCHANTED	The Platters, Mercury 71427	5
54	44	25	20		SORRY, I RAN ALL THE WAY HOME	The Impalas, Cub 9022	6
80	73	30	21		THAT'S WHY	Jackie Wilson, Brunswick 55121	5
28	21	20	22		THIS SHOULD GO ON FOREVER	Rod Bernard, Argo 5327	7
53	36	27	23		FOR A PENNY	Pat Boone, Dot 15914	5
11	17	23	24		PLEASE, MR. SUN	Tommy Edwards, M-G-M 12757	10
23	24	28	25		WHERE WERE YOU (ON OUR WEDDING DAY)?	Lloyd Price, ABC-Paramount 9997	8
13	18	24	26		IT DOESN'T MATTER ANYMORE	Buddy Holly, Coral 62074	9
6	8	18	27		ALVIN'S HARMONICA	David Seville and the Chipmunks, Liberty 55179	10
25	22	29	28		IF I DIDN'T CARE	Connie Francis, M-G-M 12769	8
9	11	19	29		I'VE HAD IT	Bell Notes, Time 1004	14
99	61	46	30	★	YEP!	Duane Eddy, Jamie 1122	4
34	34	33	31		EVERYBODY LIKES TO CHA CHA	Sam Cooke, Keen 2018	7
61	54	50	32	★	TAKE A MESSAGE TO MARY	Everly Brothers, Cadence 1364	4
70	43	35	33		GUESS WHO	Jesse Belvin, RCA Victor 7469	4
27	29	32	34		NO OTHER ARMS, NO OTHER LIPS	Chordettes, Cadence 1361	8
15	16	26	35		HAWAIIAN WEDDING SONG	Andy Williams, Cadence 1358	17
69	69	67	36	★	POOR JENNY	Everly Brothers, Cadence 1364	4
74	63	49	37	★	COME TO ME	Marv Johnson, United Artists 160	6
76	70	39	38		SIX NIGHTS A WEEK	The Crests, Coed 509	5
96	72	48	39		ALMOST GROWN	Chuck Berry, Chess 1722	4
97	78	44	40		I MISS YOU SO	Paul Anka, ABC-Paramount 10011	4
30	27	31	41		THE MORNING SIDE OF THE MOUNTAIN	Tommy Edwards, M-G-M 12757	8
—	82	53	42	★	TELL HIM NO	Dean and Marc, Bullseye 1025	4
—	95	79	43	★	ONLY YOU	Frank Pourcel, Capitol 4165	3
65	59	54	44	★	AS TIME GOES BY	Johnny Nash, ABC-Paramount 9996	6
83	66	58	45	★	SOMEONE	Johnny Mathis, Columbia 41355	5
36	37	40	46		I'M NEVER GONNA TELL	Jimmie Rodgers, Roulette 4129	9
—	—	70	47	★	GOODBYE, JIMMY, GOODBYE	Kathy Linden, Felsted 8571	2
42	42	43	48		I GO APE	Neil Sedaka, RCA Victor 7473	7
12	31	34	49		DONNA	Ritchie Valens, Del-Fi 4110	22
51	45	62	50	★	COME SOFTLY TO ME	Ronnie Height, Dore 516	5
58	40	45	51		HEAVENLY LOVER	Teresa Brewer, Coral 62084	6
—	83	61	52		LOVEY DOVEY	Clyde McPhatter, Atlantic 2018	3
57	53	52	53		YEAH YEAH	Dale Hawkins, Checker 916	6
19	28	38	54		PETER GUNN THEME	Ray Anthony, Capitol 4041	16
—	77	60	55		SO FINE	Fiestas, Old Town 1062	3
37	47	59	56		RAWHIDE	Link Wray, Epic 9300	13
22	32	37	57		SHE SAY (OOM DOOBY DOOM)	The Diamonds, Mercury 71404	13
20	30	42	58		I CRIED A TEAR	LaVern Baker, Atlantic 2007	20
40	46	41	59		THE HANGING TREE	Marty Robbins, Columbia 41325	12
—	98	77	60	★	THAT'S MY LITTLE SUZIE	Ritchie Valens, Del-Fi 4114	3

THE INDUSTRY'S FASTEST AND MOST COMPLETE PROGRAMMING AND BUYING GUIDE

These 100 sides are listed in order of their national POPULARITY, as determined by weekly local studies prepared for The Billboard in markets representing a cross-section of the United States. These studies reflect sales registered for each disk up to press time.

★ THE STAR PERFORMER designation shows the outstanding upward changes of position in The Hot 100 since last week's chart. Its purpose merely is to provide quick visual identification of the sides which moved up most dramatically or to new entries which first entered the chart at an unusually high position.

Three Weeks Ago	Two Weeks Ago	One Week Ago	This Week	Star Performer This Week	TITLE — Artist, Company, Record Number	Weeks on Chart
90	87	69	61		FRENCH FOREIGN LEGION — Frank Sinatra, Capitol 4155	4
—	—	—	62	★	WANG DANG TAFFY APPLE TANGO — Pat Boone, Dot 15914	1
48	48	47	63		MOONLIGHT SERENADE — The Rivieras, Coed 508	11
16	19	36	64		STAGGER LEE — Lloyd Price, ABC-Paramount 9972	20
29	33	51	65		TOMBOY — Perry Como, RCA Victor 7464	13
—	—	—	66	★	ENDLESSLY — Brook Benton, Mercury 71443	1
68	64	57	67		THE BEAT — Rockin' R's, Tempus 7541	5
21	26	55	68		PETITE FLEUR — Chris Barber's Jazz Band, Laurie 3022	15
—	—	—	69	★	TEENAGER IN LOVE — Dion and the Belmonts, Laurie 3027	1
—	—	81	70		I STILL GET A THRILL — Joni James, M-G-M 12779	2
—	—	100	71	★	KANSAS CITY — Wilbert Harrison, Fury 1023	2
—	—	—	72	★	KOOKIE, KOOKIE (LEND ME YOUR COMB) — Edward Byrnes with Connie Stevens, Warner Bros. 5047	1
—	—	76	73		THE KISSING TREE — Billy Grammer, Monument 403	2
88	91	85	74		WHO'S THAT KNOCKIN' — Genies, Shad 5002	4
—	—	—	75	★	GOONIGHT, IRENE — Billy Williams, Coral 62101	1
—	96	89	76		77 SUNSET STRIP — Don Ralke, Warner Bros. 5025	3
—	—	78	77		THE WALLS HAVE EARS — Patti Page, Mercury 71248	2
—	—	—	78	★	I NEED YOUR LOVIN' — Roy Hamilton, Epic 9307	1
—	—	95	79	★	QUIET VILLAGE — Martin Denny, Liberty 55162	2
—	—	90	80		JO-JO THE DOG-FACED BOY — Annette, Vista 336	2
—	—	87	81		BONAPARTE'S RETREAT — Billy Grammer, Monument 403	2
67	76	73	82		MATILDA — Cookie and His Cupcakes, Judd 1002	14
—	—	88	83		I THINK I'M GONNA KILL MYSELF — Buddy Knox, Roulette 4140	2
93	92	75	84		STAR LOVE — Playmates, Roulette 4136	4
—	—	91	85		I'VE COME OF AGE — Billy Storm, Columbia 41356	2
31	38	56	86		MAY YOU ALWAYS — McGuire Sisters, Coral 62059	16
—	—	94	87		LONELY FOR YOU — Gary Stites, Carlton 508	2
—	—	—	88	★	YOU'RE SO FINE — The Falcons, Unart 2016	1
—	99	93	89		I NEVER FELT LIKE THIS — Jack Scott, Carlton 504	3
—	—	—	90	★	DREAM LOVER — Bobby Darin, Atco 6140	1

THE BILLBOARD'S BEST BUYS

These records have shown the greatest national SALES BREAKOUT potential this week for the first time. Action sides are listed in capital letters.

POP

ENDLESSLY . . . . Brook Benton
(Meridian, BMI) So Close (Eden, BMI) Mercury 71443

KANSAS CITY . . . . Wilbert Harrison
(Fire, BMI) Listen, My Darling (Fire, BMI) Fury 1023

A TEENAGER IN LOVE . . . . Dion & the Belmonts
(Rumbalero, BMI) I've Cried Before (Rumbalero, BMI) Laurie 3027

The above are previous Billboard Spotlight picks

KOOKIE, KOOKIE (LEND ME YOUR COMB) . . . . Edward Byrnes with Connie Stevens
(Witmark, ASCAP) You're the Top (Harmes, ASCAP) Warner Bros. 5047

77 SUNSET STRIP . . . . Don Ralke
(Witmark, ASCAP) Sebastian (Witmark, ASCAP) Warner Bros. 5025

QUIET VILLAGE . . . . Martin Denny
(Baxter-Wright, BMI) Llama Serenade (Disney, ASCAP) Liberty 55162

C&W

NO SELECTIONS THIS WEEK

R&B

NO SELECTIONS THIS WEEK

★ THE STAR PERFORMER designation shows the outstanding upward changes of position in The Hot 100 since last week's chart. Its purpose merely is to provide quick visual identification of the sides which moved up most dramatically or to new entries which first entered the chart at an unusually high position.

Three Weeks Ago	Two Weeks Ago	One Week Ago	This Week	Star Performer This Week	TITLE — Artist, Company, Record Number	Weeks on Chart
98	89	83	91		BOOM-A-DIP-DIP — Stan Robinson, Monument 402	4
—	—	99	92		YOU CAN'T BE TRUE DEAR — Mary Kaye Trio, Warner Bros. 5050	2
—	—	—	93		A TOUCH OF PINK — Jerry Wallace, Challenge 59040	1
—	—	—	94		I KNEEL AT YOUR THRONE — Joe Medlin, Mercury 71415	4
—	—	—	95		I WAITED TOO LONG — LaVern Baker, Atlantic 2021	1
—	—	—	96		WALKIN' TO MOTHER'S — Ray Anthony, Capitol 4176	1
—	—	—	97		I TOLD MYSELF A LIE — Clyde McPhatter, M-G-M 12780	1
—	—	—	98		THAT'S ALL I WANT — Bobby Day, Class 245	1
—	—	—	99		TWO BROTHERS — David Hill, Kapp 266	1
—	—	—	100		PIPE DREAMS — Jimmy Beck, Champion 1002	1

The Billboard HOT 100

FOR THE WEEK ENDING MAY 3

★ THE STAR PERFORMER designation shows the outstanding upward changes of position in The Hot 100 since last week's chart. Its purpose merely is to provide quick visual identification of the sides which moved up most dramatically or to new entries which first entered the chart at an unusually high position.

THREE WEEKS AGO	TWO WEEKS AGO	ONE WEEK AGO	THIS WEEK	★ STAR PERFORMER THIS WEEK	TITLE	Artist, Company, Record Number	WEEKS ON CHART
2	1	1	1		COME SOFTLY TO ME	Fleetwoods, Dolphin 1	8
13	8	5	2		A FOOL SUCH AS I	Elvis Presley, RCA Victor 7506	6
1	2	2	3		VENUS	Frankie Avalon, Chancellor 1031	12
4	3	3	4		PINK SHOE LACES	Dodie Stevens, Crystalette 724	11
10	9	7	5		GUITAR BOOGIE SHUFFLE	The Virtues, Hunt 324	8
25	13	13	6		THE HAPPY ORGAN	Dave (Baby) Cortez, Clock 1009	7
12	10	4	7		I NEED YOUR LOVE TONIGHT	Elvis Presley, RCA Victor 7506	5
23	16	11	8		TELL HIM NO	Travis and Bob, Sandy 1017	6
44	25	20	9	★	SORRY, I RAN ALL THE WAY HOME	The Impalas, Cub 9022	7
39	17	17	10		TURN ME LOOSE	Fabian, Chancellor 1033	5
6	6	6	11		NEVER BE ANYONE ELSE BUT YOU	Ricky Nelson, Imperial 5565	10
15	12	15	12		SINCE I DON'T HAVE YOU	The Skyliners, Calico 103	11
35	22	19	13		ENCHANTED	The Platters, Mercury 71427	6
50	21	18	14		THREE STARS	Tommy Dee, Crest 1057	5
20	14	12	15		TIJUANA JAIL	Kingston Trio, Capitol 4167	6
5	5	9	16		TRAGEDY	Thomas Wayne, Fernwood 109	24
73	30	21	17		THAT'S WHY	Jackie Wilson, Brunswick 55121	6
14	15	14	18		SEA CRUISE	Frankie Ford, Ace 554	12
3	4	8	19		IT'S JUST A MATTER OF TIME	Brook Benton, Mercury 71394	14
9	11	10	20		IT'S LATE	Ricky Nelson, Imperial 5565	9
21	20	22	21		THIS SHOULD GO ON FOREVER	Rod Bernard, Argo 5327	8
54	50	32	22	★	TAKE A MESSAGE TO MARY	Everly Brothers, Cadence 1364	5
36	27	23	23		FOR A PENNY	Pat Boone, Dot 15914	6
—	100	71	24	★	KANSAS CITY	Wilbert Harrison, Fury 1023	3
—	—	72	25	★	KOOKIE, KOOKIE (LEND ME YOUR COMB)	Edward Byrnes with Connie Stevens, Warner Bros. 5047	2
7	7	16	26		CHARLIE BROWN	Coasters, Atco 6132	13
69	67	36	27		POOR JENNY	Everly Brothers, Cadence 1364	5
70	39	38	28	★	SIX NIGHTS A WEEK	The Crests, Coed 509	6
18	24	26	29		IT DOESN'T MATTER ANYMORE	Buddy Holly, Coral 62074	10
95	79	43	30	★	ONLY YOU	Frank Pourcel, Capitol 4165	4
63	49	37	31		COME TO ME	Marv Johnson, United Artists 160	7
—	70	47	32	★	GOODBYE, JIMMY, GOODBYE	Kathy Linden, Felsted 8571	3
78	44	40	33		I MISS YOU SO	Paul Anka, ABC-Paramount 10011	5
—	—	69	34	★	A TEENAGER IN LOVE	Dion and the Belmonts, Laurie 3027	2
43	35	33	35		GUESS WHO	Jesse Belvin, RCA Victor 7469	5
—	95	79	36	★	QUIET VILLAGE	Martin Denny, Liberty 55162	3
34	33	31	37		EVERYBODY LIKES TO CHA CHA	Sam Cooke, Keen 2018	8
77	60	55	38	★	SO FINE	Fiestas, Old Town 1062	4
72	48	39	39		ALMOST GROWN	Chuck Berry, Chess 1722	5
61	46	30	40		YEP!	Duane Eddy, Jamie 1122	5
24	28	25	41		WHERE WERE YOU (ON OUR WEDDING DAY)?	Lloyd Price, ABC-Paramount 9997	9
82	53	42	42		TELL HIM NO	Dean and Marc, Bullseye 1025	5
11	19	29	43		I'VE HAD IT	Bell Notes, Time 1004	15
66	58	45	44		SOMEONE	Johnny Mathis, Columbia 41355	6
22	29	28	45		IF I DIDN'T CARE	Connie Francis, M-G-M 12769	9
27	31	41	46		THE MORNING SIDE OF THE MOUNTAIN	Tommy Edwards, M-G-M 12757	9
17	23	24	47		PLEASE, MR. SUN	Tommy Edwards, M-G-M 12757	11
29	32	34	48		NO OTHER ARMS, NO OTHER LIPS	Chordettes, Cadence 1361	9
16	26	35	49		HAWAIIAN WEDDING SONG	Andy Williams, Cadence 1358	18
8	18	27	50		ALVIN'S HARMONICA	David Seville and the Chipmunks, Liberty 55179	11
83	61	52	51		LOVEY DOVEY	Clyde McPhatter, Atlantic 2018	4
59	54	44	52		AS TIME GOES BY	Johnny Nash, ABC-Paramount 9996	7
—	—	90	53	★	DREAM LOVER	Bobby Darin, Atco 6140	2
—	—	66	54	★	ENDLESSLY	Brook Benton, Mercury 71443	2
98	77	60	55		THAT'S MY LITTLE SUZIE	Ritchie Valens, Del-Fi 4114	4
—	88	83	56	★	I THINK I'M GONNA KILL MYSELF	Buddy Knox, Roulette 4140	3
—	87	81	57	★	BONAPARTE'S RETREAT	Billy Grammer, Monument 403	3
—	81	70	58	★	I STILL GET A THRILL	Joni James, M-G-M 12779	3
37	40	46	59		I'M NEVER GONNA TELL	Jimmie Rodgers, Roulette 4129	10
—	94	87	60	★	LONELY FOR YOU	Gary Stites, Carlton 508	3

THE INDUSTRY'S FASTEST AND MOST COMPLETE PROGRAMMING AND BUYING GUIDE

These 100 sides are listed in order of their national POPULARITY, as determined by weekly local studies prepared for The Billboard in markets representing a cross-section of the United States. These studies reflect sales registered for each disk up to press time.

★ THE STAR PERFORMER designation shows the outstanding upward changes of position in The Hot 100 since last week's chart. Its purpose merely is to provide quick visual identification of the sides which moved up most dramatically or to new entries which first entered the chart at an unusually high position.

THREE WEEKS AGO	TWO WEEKS AGO	ONE WEEK AGO	THIS WEEK	★ STAR PERFORMER THIS WEEK	TITLE Artist, Company, Record Number	WEEKS ON CHART
—	91	85	61	★	I'VE COME OF AGE — Billy Storm, Columbia 41356	3
32	37	57	62		SHE SAY (OOM DOOBY DOOM) — The Diamonds, Mercury 71404	14
—	—	78	63	★	I NEED YOUR LOVIN' — Roy Hamilton, Epic 9307	2
—	—	62	64		WANG DANG TAFFY APPLE TANGO — Pat Boone, Dot 15914	2
—	—	—	65	★	PERSONALITY — Lloyd Price, ABC-Paramount 10018	1
—	76	73	66		THE KISSING TREE — Billy Grammer, Monument 403	3
45	62	50	67		COME SOFTLY TO ME — Ronnie Height, Dore 516	6
40	45	51	68		HEAVENLY LOVER — Teresa Brewer, Coral 62084	7
96	89	76	69		77 SUNSET STRIP — Don Ralke, Warner Bros. 5025	4
30	42	58	70		I CRIED A TEAR — LaVern Baker, Atlantic 2007	21
91	85	74	71		WHO'S THAT KNOCKIN' — Genies, Shad 5002	5
—	—	88	72	★	YOU'RE SO FINE — The Falcons, Unart 2013	2
—	90	80	73		JO-JO THE DOG-FACED BOY — Annette, Vista 336	3
28	38	54	74		PETER GUNN THEME — Ray Anthony, Capitol 4041	17
—	99	92	75	★	YOU CAN'T BE TRUE DEAR — Mary Kaye Trio, Warner Bros. 5050	3
—	—	—	76	★	THERE'S NO FOOL LIKE A YOUNG FOOL — Tab Hunter, Warner Bros. 5051	1
—	—	—	77	★	FRANKIE'S MAN JOHNNY — Johnny Cash, Columbia 41317	1
99	93	89	78		I NEVER FELT LIKE THIS — Jack Scott, Carlton 504	4
76	73	82	79		MATILDA — Cookie and His Cupcakes, Judd 1002	15
—	—	—	80	★	CASTIN' MY SPELL — Johnny Otis Show, Capitol 4168	1
—	98	—	81	★	LITTLE QUEENIE — Chuck Berry, Chess 1722	2
—	—	100	82	★	PIPE DREAMS — Jimmy Beck, Champion 1002	2
—	96	—	83	★	MY HEART IS AN OPEN BOOK — Carl Dobkins Jr., Decca 30803	2
42	43	48	84		I GO APE — Neil Sedaka, RCA Victor 7473	8
64	57	67	85		THE BEAT — Rockin' R's, Tempus 7541	6
19	36	64	86		STAGGER LEE — Lloyd Price, ABC-Paramount 9972	21
—	—	—	87	★	ROBBIN' THE CRADLE — Tony Bellus, NRC 023	1
—	—	—	88	★	CROSSFIRE — Johnny and the Hurricanes, Warwick 502	2
—	—	—	89	★	GIDGET — Jimmy Darren, Colpix 113	1
—	—	99	90		TWO BROTHERS — David Hill, Kapp 266	2

THE BILLBOARD'S BEST BUYS

These records have shown the greatest national SALES BREAKOUT potential this week for the first time. Action sides are listed in capital letters.

POP

DREAM LOVER .... **Bobby Darin**
(Fern-Progressive, BMI) Bullmoose (Fern-Progressive BMI) Atco 6140

I THINK I'M GONNA KILL MYSELF .... **Buddy Knox**
(January, BMI) To Be With You (Patricia, BMI) Roulette 4140

THERE'S NO FOOL LIKE A YOUNG FOOL .... **Tab Hunter**
(Spartan-E.D.M., ASCAP) I'll Never Smile Again (Pickwick, ASCAP) Warner 5051

FRANKIE'S MAN JOHNNY .... **Johnny Cash**
(Cash, BMI) You Dreamer, You (Cash, BMI) Columbia 41371

I'VE COME OF AGE .... **Billy Storm**
(We Three, BMI) This Is Always (Bregman, Vocco & Conn, ASCAP) Columbia 41356

PERSONALITY .... **Lloyd Price**
(Lloyd-Logan, BMI) Have You Ever Had the Blues? (Lloyd-Logan, BMI) ABC-Paramount 10018

The above are previous Billboard Spotlight picks

I NEED YOUR LOVIN' .... **Roy Hamilton**
(Peer Intl.-Walnut, BMI) Blue Prelude (World, ASCAP) Epic 9307

C&W

ANYBODY'S GIRL .... **Hank Thompson**
(Brazos Valley, BMI) Total Strangers (Texoma, ASCAP) Capitol 4182

HEARTACHES BY THE NUMBER .... **Ray Price**
(Pamper, BMI) Wall of Tears (Cedarwood, BMI) Columbia 41374

The above are previous Billboard Spotlight picks

R&B

THAT'S ENOUGH .... **Ray Charles**
(Progressive, BMI) Tell Me How Do You Feel (Progressive, BMI) Atlantic 2022

A previous Billboard Spotlight pick

★ THE STAR PERFORMER designation shows the outstanding upward changes of position in The Hot 100 since last week's chart. Its purpose merely is to provide quick visual identification of the sides which moved up most dramatically or to new entries which first entered the chart at an unusually high position.

THREE WEEKS AGO	TWO WEEKS AGO	ONE WEEK AGO	THIS WEEK	★ STAR PERFORMER THIS WEEK	TITLE Artist, Company, Record Number	WEEKS ON CHART
87	69	61	91		FRENCH FOREIGN LEGION — Frank Sinatra, Capitol 4155	5
—	—	93	92		A TOUCH OF PINK — Jerry Wallace, Challenge 59040	2
—	—	—	93		THE BATTLE OF NEW ORLEANS — Johnny Horton, Columbia 41339	1
—	—	95	94		I WAITED TOO LONG — LaVern Baker, Atlantic 2021	2
—	—	—	95		YOUR CHEATIN' HEART — Billy Vaughn, Dot 15936	1
—	—	—	96		A STRING OF TRUMPETS — The Trumpeteers, Splash 800	1
—	—	97	97		I TOLD MYSELF A LIE — Clyde McPhatter, M-G-M 12780	2
31	34	49	98		DONNA — Ritchie Valens, Del-Fi 4110	23
—	—	—	99		SUMMER DREAMS — McGuire Sisters, Coral 62106	1
46	41	59	100		THE HANGING TREE — Marty Robbins, Columbia 41325	13

The Billboard HOT 100

FOR THE WEEK ENDING MAY 10

★ THE STAR PERFORMER designation shows the outstanding upward changes of position in The Hot 100 since last week's chart. Its purpose merely is to provide quick visual identification of the sides which moved up most dramatically or to new entries which first entered the chart at an unusually high position.

Three Weeks Ago	Two Weeks Ago	One Week Ago	This Week	★ Star Performer This Week	Title	Artist, Company, Record Number	Weeks on Chart
1	1	1	1		COME SOFTLY TO ME	Fleetwoods, Dolphin 1	9
13	13	6	2		THE HAPPY ORGAN	Dave (Baby) Cortez, Clock 1009	8
25	20	9	3		SORRY, I RAN ALL THE WAY HOME	The Impalas, Cub 9022	8
3	3	4	4		PINK SHOE LACES	Dodie Stevens, Crystalette 724	12
9	7	5	5		GUITAR BOOGIE SHUFFLE	The Virtues, Hunt 324	9
8	5	2	6		A FOOL SUCH AS I	Elvis Presley, RCA Victor 7506	7
10	4	7	7		I NEED YOUR LOVE TONIGHT	Elvis Presley, RCA Victor 7506	6
16	11	8	8		TELL HIM NO	Travis and Bob, Sandy 1017	7
2	2	3	9		VENUS	Frankie Avalon, Chancellor 1031	13
17	17	10	10		TURN ME LOOSE	Fabian, Chancellor 1033	6
21	18	14	11		THREE STARS	Tommy Dee, Crest 1057	6
22	19	13	12		ENCHANTED	The Platters, Mercury 71427	7
30	21	17	13		THAT'S WHY	Jackie Wilson, Brunswick 55121	7
12	15	12	14		SINCE I DON'T HAVE YOU	The Skyliners, Calico 103	12
14	12	15	15		TIJUANA JAIL	Kingston Trio, Capitol 4167	7
100	71	24	16		KANSAS CITY	Wilbert Harrison, Fury 1023	4
50	32	22	17		TAKE A MESSAGE TO MARY	Everly Brothers, Cadence 1364	6
6	6	11	18		NEVER BE ANYONE ELSE BUT YOU	Ricky Nelson, Imperial 5565	11
—	72	25	19		KOOKIE, KOOKIE (LEND ME YOUR COMB)	Edward Byrnes with Connie Stevens, Warner Bros. 5047	3
—	69	34	20	★	A TEENAGER IN LOVE	Dion and the Belmonts, Laurie 3027	3
5	9	16	21		TRAGEDY	Thomas Wayne, Fernwood 109	25
67	36	27	22		POOR JENNY	Everly Brothers, Cadence 1364	6
15	14	18	23		SEA CRUISE	Frankie Ford, Ace 554	13
79	43	30	24		ONLY YOU	Frank Pourcel, Capitol 4165	5
20	22	21	25		THIS SHOULD GO ON FOREVER	Rod Bernard, Argo 5327	9
27	23	23	26		FOR A PENNY	Pat Boone, Dot 15914	7
95	79	36	27		QUIET VILLAGE	Martin Denny, Liberty 55162	4
39	38	28	28		SIX NIGHTS A WEEK	The Crests, Coed 509	7
—	90	53	29	★	DREAM LOVER	Bobby Darin, Atco 6140	3
4	8	19	30		IT'S JUST A MATTER OF TIME	Brook Benton, Mercury 71394	15
49	37	31	31		COME TO ME	Marv Johnson, United Artists 160	8
48	39	39	32		ALMOST GROWN	Chuck Berry, Chess 1722	6
60	55	38	33		SO FINE	Fiestas, Old Town 1062	5
70	47	32	34		GOODBYE, JIMMY, GOODBYE	Kathy Linden, Felsted 8571	4
11	10	20	35		IT'S LATE	Ricky Nelson, Imperial 5565	10
—	—	93	36	★	THE BATTLE OF NEW ORLEANS	Johnny Horton, Columbia 41339	2
35	33	35	37		GUESS WHO	Jesse Belvin, RCA Victor 7469	6
—	66	54	38	★	ENDLESSLY	Brook Benton, Mercury 71443	3
24	26	29	39		IT DOESN'T MATTER ANYMORE	Buddy Holly, Coral 62074	11
58	45	44	40		SOMEONE	Johnny Mathis, Columbia 41355	7
44	40	33	41		I MISS YOU SO	Paul Anka, ABC-Paramount 10011	6
33	31	37	42		EVERYBODY LIKES TO CHA CHA	Sam Cooke, Keen 2018	9
7	16	26	43		CHARLIE BROWN	Coasters, Atco 6132	14
23	24	47	44		PLEASE, MR. SUN	Tommy Edwards, M-G-M 12757	12
53	42	42	45		TELL HIM NO	Dean and Marc, Bullseye 1025	6
46	30	40	46		YEP!	Duane Eddy, Jamie 1122	6
31	41	46	47		THE MORNING SIDE OF THE MOUNTAIN	Tommy Edwards, M-G-M 12757	10
—	—	65	48	★	PERSONALITY	Lloyd Price, ABC-Paramount 10018	2
61	52	51	49		LOVEY DOVEY	Clyde McPhatter, Atlantic 2018	5
19	29	43	50		I'VE HAD IT	Bell Notes, Time 1004	16
81	70	58	51		I STILL GET A THRILL	Joni James, M-G-M 12779	4
54	44	52	52		AS TIME GOES BY	Johnny Nash, ABC-Paramount 9996	8
26	35	49	53		HAWAIIAN WEDDING SONG	Andy Williams, Cadence 1358	19
32	34	48	54		NO OTHER ARMS, NO OTHER LIPS	Chordettes, Cadence 1361	10
88	83	56	55		I THINK I'M GONNA KILL MYSELF	Buddy Knox, Roulette 4140	4
91	85	61	56		I'VE COME OF AGE	Billy Storm, Columbia 41356	4
29	28	45	57		IF I DIDN'T CARE	Connie Francis, M-G-M 12769	10
28	25	41	58		WHERE WERE YOU (ON OUR WEDDING DAY)?	Lloyd Price, ABC-Paramount 9997	10
—	88	72	59	★	YOU'RE SO FINE	The Falcons, Unart 2013	3
87	81	57	60		BONAPARTE'S RETREAT	Billy Grammer, Monument 403	4

THE INDUSTRY'S FASTEST AND MOST COMPLETE PROGRAMMING AND BUYING GUIDE

These 100 sides are listed in order of their national POPULARITY, as determined by weekly local studies prepared for The Billboard in markets representing a cross-section of the United States. These studies reflect sales registered for each disk up to press time.

★ THE STAR PERFORMER designation shows the outstanding upward changes of position in The Hot 100 since last week's chart. Its purpose merely is to provide quick visual identification of the sides which moved up most dramatically or to new entries which first entered the chart at an unusually high position.

THREE WEEKS AGO	TWO WEEKS AGO	ONE WEEK AGO	THIS WEEK	★ STAR PERFORMER THIS WEEK	TITLE Artist, Company, Record Number	WEEKS ON CHART
94	87	60	61		LONELY FOR YOU — Gary Stites, Carlton 508	4
—	78	63	62		I NEED YOUR LOVIN' — Roy Hamilton, Epic 9307	3
—	—	80	63	★	CASTIN' MY SPELL — Johnny Otis Show, Capitol 4168	2
77	60	55	64		THAT'S MY LITTLE SUZIE — Ritchie Valens, Del-Fi 4114	5
—	62	64	65		WANG DANG TAFFY APPLE TANGO — Pat Boone, Dot 15914	3
—	—	88	66	★	CROSSFIRE — Johnny and the Hurricanes, Warwick 502	3
40	46	59	67		I'M NEVER GONNA TELL — Jimmie Rodgers, Roulette 4129	11
—	—	76	68		THERE'S NO FOOL LIKE A YOUNG FOOL — Tab Hunter, Warner Bros. 5051	2
—	95	94	69	★	I WAITED TOO LONG — LaVern Baker, Atlantic 2021	3
—	—	89	70	★	GIDGET — Jimmy Darren, Colpix 113	2
—	—	77	71		FRANKIE'S MAN JOHNNY — Johnny Cash, Columbia 41317	2
57	67	85	72		THE BEAT — Rockin' R's, Tempus 7541	7
—	—	—	73	★	KANSAS CITY — Hank Ballard and the Midnighters, King 5195	1
45	51	68	74		HEAVENLY LOVER — Teresa Brewer, Coral 62084	8
90	80	73	75		JO-JO THE DOG-FACED BOY — Annette, Vista 336	4
—	97	97	76	★	I TOLD MYSELF A LIE — Clyde McPhatter, M-G-M 12780	3
—	—	—	77	★	LONESOME OLD HOUSE — Don Gibson, RCA Victor 7505	1
76	73	66	78		THE KISSING TREE — Billy Grammer, Monument 403	4
85	74	71	79		WHO'S THAT KNOCKIN' — Genies, Shad 5002	6
—	—	96	80	★	STRING OF TRUMPETS — The Trumpeteers, Splash 800	2
—	—	—	81	★	JUST KEEP IT UP — Dee Clark, Abner 1026	1
—	—	95	82		YOUR CHEATIN' HEART — Billy Vaughn, Dot 15936	2
—	—	87	83		ROBBIN' THE CRADLE — Tony Bellus, NRC 023	2
78	77	—	84	★	THE WALLS HAVE EARS — Patti Page, Mercury 71428	3
—	—	—	85	★	PEACE — McGuire Sisters, Coral 62106	1
89	76	69	86		77 SUNSET STRIP — Don Ralke, Warner Bros. 5025	5
—	—	—	87	★	YOU MADE ME LOVE YOU — Nat King Cole, Capitol 4184	1
—	—	99	88		SUMMER DREAMS — McGuire Sisters, Coral 62106	2
—	—	—	89	★	YOUNG IDEAS — Chico Holiday, RCA Victor 7499	1
—	—	—	90	★	WHITE LIGHTNING — George Jones, Mercury 71406	1
96	—	83	91		MY HEART IS AN OPEN BOOK — Carl Dobkins Jr., Decca 30803	3
—	—	—	92		FOUNTAIN OF YOUTH — Four Lads, Columbia 41365	1
98	—	81	93		LITTLE QUEENIE — Chuck Berry, Chess 1722	3
18	27	50	94		ALVIN'S HARMONICA — David Seville and the Chipmunks, Liberty 55179	12
—	—	—	95		OLD SPANISH TOWN — Bell Notes, Time 1010	1
—	—	—	96		SEPARATE WAYS — Sarah Vaughan, Mercury 71433	1
69	61	91	97		FRENCH FOREIGN LEGION — Frank Sinatra, Capitol 4155	6
—	—	—	98		KANSAS CITY — Rocky Olson, Chess 1723	1
—	—	—	99		THREE STARS — Ruby Wright, King 5192	1
—	—	—	100		TALK OF THE SCHOOL — Sonny James, Capitol 4178	1

THE BILLBOARD'S BEST BUYS

These records have shown the greatest national SALES BREAKOUT potential this week for the first time. Action sides are listed in capital letters.

POP

THE BATTLE OF NEW ORLEANS ... Johnny Horton
(Warden, BMI) All for the Love of a Girl (American, BMI) Columbia 41339

I WAITED TOO LONG ... LaVern Baker
(Aldon, BMI) You're Teasin' Me (Progressive, BMI) Atlantic 2021

I TOLD MYSELF A LIE ... Clyde McPhatter
(Wemar, BMI) The Masquerade Is Over (DeSylvia, Brown & Henderson, ASCAP) M-G-M 12780

LONESOME OLD HOUSE ... Don Gibson
(Acuff-Rose, BMI) I Couldn't Care Less (Acuff-Rose, BMI) RCA Victor 7505

YOU MADE ME LOVE YOU ... Nat King Cole
(Broadway, ASCAP) I Must Be Dreaming (Sweco, BMI) Capitol 4184

The above are previous Billboard Spotlight picks

GIDGET ... Jimmy Darren
(Columbia Pictures, ASCAP) You (Camarillo, BMI) Colpix 113

YOU'RE SO FINE ... The Falcons
(Alhika, BMI) Goddess of Angels (Alhika, BMI) Unart 2016

C&W

NO SELECTIONS THIS WEEK.

R&B

NO SELECTIONS THIS WEEK.

The Billboard HOT 100

FOR THE WEEK ENDING MAY 17

★ THE STAR PERFORMER designation shows the outstanding upward changes of position in The Hot 100 since last week's chart. Its purpose merely is to provide quick visual identification of the sides which moved up most dramatically or to new entries which first entered the chart at an unusually high position.

THREE WEEKS AGO	TWO WEEKS AGO	ONE WEEK AGO	THIS WEEK	★ STAR PERFORMER THIS WEEK	TITLE	Artist, Company, Record Number	WEEKS ON CHART
13	6	2	1		THE HAPPY ORGAN	Dave (Baby) Cortez, Clock 1009	9
20	9	3	2		SORRY, I RAN ALL THE WAY HOME	The Impalas, Cub 9022	9
1	1	1	3		COME SOFTLY TO ME	Fleetwoods, Dolphin 1	10
72	25	19	4	★	KOOKIE, KOOKIE (LEND ME YOUR COMB)	Edward Byrnes with Connie Stevens, Warner Bros. 5047	4
5	2	6	5		A FOOL SUCH AS I	Elvis Presley, RCA Victor 7506	8
71	24	16	6	★	KANSAS CITY	Wilbert Harrison, Fury 1023	5
7	5	5	7		GUITAR BOOGIE SHUFFLE	The Virtues, Hunt 324	10
3	4	4	8		PINK SHOE LACES	Dodie Stevens, Crystalette 724	13
17	10	10	9		TURN ME LOOSE	Fabian, Chancellor 1033	7
4	7	7	10		I NEED YOUR LOVE TONIGHT	Elvis Presley, RCA Victor 7506	7
11	8	8	11		TELL HIM NO	Travis and Bob, Sandy 1017	8
69	34	20	12		A TEENAGER IN LOVE	Dion and the Belmonts, Laurie 3027	4
18	14	11	13		THREE STARS	Tommy Dee, Crest 1057	7
2	3	9	14		VENUS	Frankie Avalon, Chancellor 1031	14
19	13	12	15		ENCHANTED	The Platters, Mercury 71427	8
90	53	29	16	★	DREAM LOVER	Bobby Darin, Atco 6140	4
21	17	13	17		THAT'S WHY	Jackie Wilson, Brunswick 55121	8
32	22	17	18		TAKE A MESSAGE TO MARY	Everly Brothers, Cadence 1364	7
79	36	27	19		QUIET VILLAGE	Martin Denny, Liberty 55162	5
43	30	24	20		ONLY YOU	Frank Pourcel, Capitol 4165	6
12	15	15	21		TIJUANA JAIL	Kingston Trio, Capitol 4167	8
15	12	14	22		SINCE I DON'T HAVE YOU	The Skyliners, Calico 103	13
—	93	36	23	★	THE BATTLE OF NEW ORLEANS	Johnny Horton, Columbia 41339	3
47	32	34	24	★	GOODBYE, JIMMY, GOODBYE	Kathy Linden, Felsted 8571	5
55	38	33	25		SO FINE	Fiestas, Old Town 1062	6
6	11	18	26		NEVER BE ANYONE ELSE BUT YOU	Ricky Nelson, Imperial 5565	12
36	27	22	27		POOR JENNY	Everly Brothers, Cadence 1364	7
66	54	38	28	★	ENDLESSLY	Brook Benton, Mercury 71443	4
10	20	35	29		IT'S LATE	Ricky Nelson, Imperial 5565	11
23	23	26	30		FOR A PENNY	Pat Boone, Dot 15914	8
22	21	25	31		THIS SHOULD GO ON FOREVER	Rod Bernard, Argo 5327	10
9	16	21	32		TRAGEDY	Thomas Wayne, Fernwood 109	16
14	18	23	33		SEA CRUISE	Frankie Ford, Ace 554	14
38	28	28	34		SIX NIGHTS A WEEK	The Crests, Coed 509	8
33	35	37	35		GUESS WHO	Jesse Belvin, RCA Victor 7469	7
39	39	32	36		ALMOST GROWN	Chuck Berry, Chess 1722	7
37	31	31	37		COME TO ME	Marv Johnson, United Artists 160	9
—	65	48	38	★	PERSONALITY	Lloyd Price, ABC-Paramount 10018	3
8	19	30	39		IT'S JUST A MATTER OF TIME	Brook Benton, Mercury 71394	16
40	33	41	40		I MISS YOU SO	Paul Anka, ABC-Paramount 10011	7
45	44	40	41		SOMEONE	Johnny Mathis, Columbia 41355	8
42	42	45	42		TELL HIM NO	Dean and Marc, Bullseye 1025	7
85	61	56	43	★	I'VE COME OF AGE	Billy Storm, Columbia 41356	5
26	29	39	44		IT DOESN'T MATTER ANYMORE	Buddy Holly, Coral 62074	12
—	89	70	45	★	GIDGET	Jimmy Darren, Colpix 113	3
31	37	42	46		EVERYBODY LIKES TO CHA CHA	Sam Cooke, Keen 2018	10
—	88	66	47	★	CROSSFIRE	Johnny and the Hurricanes, Warwick 502	4
—	—	81	48	★	JUST KEEP IT UP	Dee Clark, Abner 1026	2
87	60	61	49	★	LONELY FOR YOU	Gary Stites, Carlton 508	5
81	57	60	50	★	BONAPARTE'S RETREAT	Billy Grammer, Monument 403	5
44	52	52	51		AS TIME GOES BY	Johnny Nash, ABC-Paramount 9996	9
30	40	46	52		YEP!	Duane Eddy, Jamie 1122	7
70	58	51	53		I STILL GET A THRILL	Joni James, M-G-M 12779	5
95	94	69	54	★	I WAITED TOO LONG	LaVern Baker, Atlantic 2021	4
60	55	64	55		THAT'S MY LITTLE SUZIE	Ritchie Valens, Del-Fi 4114	6
83	56	55	56		I THINK I'M GONNA KILL MYSELF	Buddy Knox, Roulette 4140	5
—	80	63	57		CASTIN' MY SPELL	Johnny Otis Show, Capitol 4163	3
41	46	47	58		THE MORNING SIDE OF THE MOUNTAIN	Tommy Edwards, M-G-M 12757	11
52	51	49	59		LOVEY DOVEY	Clyde McPhatter, Atlantic 2018	6
—	—	98	60	★	KANSAS CITY	Rocky Olson, Chess 1723	2

THE INDUSTRY'S FASTEST AND MOST COMPLETE PROGRAMMING AND BUYING GUIDE

These 100 sides are listed in order of their national POPULARITY, as determined by weekly local studies prepared for The Billboard in markets representing a cross-section of the United States. These studies reflect sales registered for each disk up to press time.

★ THE STAR PERFORMER designation shows the outstanding upward changes of position in The Hot 100 since last week's chart. Its purpose merely is to provide quick visual identification of the sides which moved up most dramatically or to new entries which first entered the chart at an unusually high position.

Three Weeks Ago	Two Weeks Ago	One Week Ago	This Week	★ Star Performer This Week	Title — Artist, Company, Record Number	Weeks on Chart
34	48	54	61		NO OTHER ARMS, NO OTHER LIPS — Chordettes, Cadence 1361	11
—	99	88	62	★	SUMMER DREAMS — McGuire Sisters, Coral 62106	3
24	47	44	63		PLEASE, MR. SUN — Tommy Edwards, M-G-M 12757	13
88	72	59	64		YOU'RE SO FINE — The Falcons, Unart 2013	4
73	66	78	65		THE KISSING TREE — Billy Grammer, Monument 403	5
16	26	43	66		CHARLIE BROWN — Coasters, Atco 6132	15
78	63	62	67		I NEED YOUR LOVIN' — Roy Hamilton, Epic 9307	4
—	76	68	68		THERE'S NO FOOL LIKE A YOUNG FOOL — Tab Hunter, Warner Bros. 5051	3
—	87	83	69		ROBBIN' THE CRADLE — Tony Bellus, NRC 023	3
97	97	76	70		I TOLD MYSELF A LIE — Clyde McPhatter, M-G-M 12780	4
—	—	77	71		LONESOME OLD HOUSE — Don Gibson, RCA Victor 7505	2
—	—	73	72		KANSAS CITY — Hank Ballard and the Midnighters, King 5195	2
—	—	90	73	★	WHITE LIGHTNING — George Jones, Mercury 71406	2
—	77	71	74		FRANKIE'S MAN JOHNNY — Johnny Cash, Columbia 41317	3
—	—	—	75	★	I'M READY — Fats Domino, Imperial 5585	1
35	49	53	76		HAWAIIAN WEDDING SONG — Andy Williams, Cadence 1358	20
—	96	80	77		A STRING OF TRUMPETS — Trumpeteers, Splash 800	3
—	—	89	78		YOUNG IDEAS — Chico Holiday, RCA Victor 7499	2
25	41	58	79		WHERE WERE YOU (ON OUR WEDDING DAY)? — Lloyd Price, ABC-Paramount 9997	11
—	81	93	80		LITTLE QUEENIE — Chuck Berry, Chess 1722	4
—	—	87	81		YOU MADE ME LOVE YOU — Nat King Cole, Capitol 4184	2
29	43	50	82		I'VE HAD IT — Bell Notes, Time 1004	17
61	91	97	83		FRENCH FOREIGN LEGION — Frank Sinatra, Capitol 4155	7
28	45	57	84		IF I DIDN'T CARE — Connie Francis, M-G-M 12769	11
—	—	85	85		PEACE — McGuire Sisters, Coral 62106	2
—	—	—	86	★	ROCKIN' CRICKETS — Hot Toddys, Shan-Todd 0056	3
—	—	—	87	★	MARGIE — Fats Domino, Imperial 5585	1
—	—	100	88		TALK OF THE SCHOOL — Sonny James, Capitol 4178	2
—	95	82	89		YOUR CHEATIN' HEART — Billy Vaughn, Dot 15936	3
—	—	92	90		FOUNTAIN OF YOUTH — Four Lads, Columbia 41365	2
—	83	91	91		MY HEART IS AN OPEN BOOK — Carl Dobkins Jr., Decca 30803	4
—	—	—	92		ETERNALLY — Thomas Wayne, Fernwood 111	1
—	—	—	93		LITTLE DIPPER — Mickey Mozart, Quintet, Roulette 4148	1
62	64	65	94		WANG DANG TAFFY APPLE TANGO — Pat Boone, Dot 15914	4
—	—	95	95		OLD SPANISH TOWN — Bell Notes, Time 1010	2
—	—	—	96		TALLAHASSEE LASSIE — Freddy Cannon, Swan 4031	1
—	—	—	97		KANSAS CITY — Little Richard, Specialty 664	1
77	—	84	98		THE WALLS HAVE EARS — Patti Page, Mercury 71428	4
67	85	72	99		THE BEAT — Rockin' R's, Tempus 7541	8
—	—	—	100		LOVE ME IN THE DAYTIME — Doris Day, Columbia 41354	1

THE BILLBOARD'S BEST BUYS

These records have shown the greatest national SALES BREAKOUT potential this week for the first time. Action sides are listed in capital letters.

POP

JUST KEEP IT UP .... Dee Clark
(Shalimar & Tollie, BMI) Whispering Grass (Mills, ASCAP) Abner 1026

CROSSFIRE .... Johnny & the Hurricanes
(Vicki, BMI) Lazy (Vicki, BMI) Warwick 502

SUMMER DREAMS .... McGuire Sisters
PEACE
(Rio Grande, BMI) (Southern-Loop, ASCAP) Coral 62106

I'M READY .... Fats Domino
MARGIE
(Post-Vanderbuilt, BMI) (Mills-Fisher, ASCAP) Imperial 5585

The above are previous Billboard Spotlight picks

LONELY FOR YOU .... Gary Stites
(Jones, BMI) Shine That Ring (Jones, BMI) Carlton 508

C&W

I LOVE EVERYBODY .... The Wilburn Brothers
(Sure Fire, BMI) Somebody's Back in Town (Sure-Fire, BMI) Decca 30871

A previous Billboard Spotlight pick.

R&B

TAKE OUT SOME INSURANCE .... Jimmy Reed
(Roosevelt & Tollie, BMI) You Know I Love You (Conrad, BMI) Vee Jay 314

A previous Billboard Spotlight pick.

The Billboard HOT 100

FOR THE WEEK ENDING MAY 24

★ STAR PERFORMERS showed the greatest upward progress on the Hot 100 this week.

■ Indicates that STEREO SINGLE version is available.

Three Weeks Ago	Two Weeks Ago	One Week Ago	This Week	★ Star Performer	TITLE, Artist, Company, Record Number	Weeks on Chart
24	16	6	1		KANSAS CITY, Wilbert Harrison, Fury 1023	6
9	3	2	2		SORRY, I RAN ALL THE WAY HOME, The Impalas, Cub 9022	10
6	2	1	3		THE HAPPY ORGAN, Dave (Baby) Cortez, Clock 1009	10
25	19	4	4		■ KOOKIE, KOOKIE (LEND ME YOUR COMB), Edward Byrnes with Connie Stevens, Warner Bros. 5047	5
34	20	12	5		A TEENAGER IN LOVE, Dion and the Belmonts, Laurie 3027	5
53	29	16	6	★	DREAM LOVER, Bobby Darin, Atco 6140	5
93	36	23	7	★	THE BATTLE OF NEW ORLEANS, Johnny Horton, Columbia 41339	4
36	27	19	8	★	■ QUIET VILLAGE, Martin Denny, Liberty 55162	6
10	10	9	9		■ TURN ME LOOSE, Fabian, Chancellor 1033	8
4	4	8	10		PINK SHOE LACES, Dodie Stevens, Crystalette 724	14
2	6	5	11		A FOOL SUCH AS I, Elvis Presley, RCA Victor 7506	9
5	5	7	12		■ GUITAR BOOGIE SHUFFLE, The Virtues, Hunt 324	11
13	12	15	13		ENCHANTED, The Platters, Mercury 71427	9
30	24	20	14		ONLY YOU, Frank Pourcel, Capitol 4165	7
1	1	3	15		■ COME SOFTLY TO ME, Fleetwoods, Dolphin 1	11
22	17	18	16		TAKE A MESSAGE TO MARY, Everly Brothers, Cadence 1364	8
7	7	10	17		I NEED YOUR LOVE TONIGHT, Elvis Presley, RCA Victor 7506	8
54	38	28	18	★	ENDLESSLY, Brook Benton, Mercury 71443	5
8	8	11	19		TELL HIM NO, Travis and Bob, Sandy 1017	9
17	13	17	20		THAT'S WHY, Jackie Wilson, Brunswick 55121	9
38	33	25	21		SO FINE, Fiestas, Old Town 1062	7
65	48	38	22	★	■ PERSONALITY, Lloyd Price, ABC-Paramount 10018	4
32	34	24	23		■ GOODBYE, JIMMY, GOODBYE, Kathy Linden, Felsted 8571	6
14	11	13	24		■ THREE STARS, Tommy Dee, Crest 1057	8
15	15	21	25		■ TIJUANA ʼAIL, Kingston Trio, Capitol 4167	9
3	9	14	26		■ VENUS, Frankie Avalon, Chancellor 1031	15
12	14	22	27		SINCE I DON'T HAVE YOU, The Skyliners, Calico 103	14
27	22	27	28		POOR JENNY, Everly Brothers, Cadence 1364	8
28	28	34	29		SIX NIGHTS A WEEK, The Crests, Coed 509	9
31	31	37	30		COME TO ME, Marv Johnson, United Artists 160	10
35	37	35	31		■ GUESS WHO, Jesse Belvin, RCA Victor 7469	8
39	32	36	32		ALMOST GROWN, Chuck Berry, Chess 1722	8
11	18	26	33		NEVER BE ANYONE ELSE BUT YOU, Ricky Nelson, Imperial 5565	13
61	56	43	34		I'VE COME OF AGE, Billy Storm, Columbia 41356	6
20	35	29	35		IT'S LATE, Ricky Nelson, Imperial 5565	12
44	40	41	36		SOMEONE, Johnny Mathis, Columbia 41355	9
23	26	30	37		■ FOR A PENNY, Pat Boone, Dot 15914	9
21	25	31	38		THIS SHOULD GO ON FOREVER, Rod Bernard, Argo 5327	11
18	23	33	39		SEA CRUISE, Frankie Ford, Ace 554	15
60	61	49	40		LONELY FOR YOU, Gary Stites, Carlton 508	6
37	42	46	41		■ EVERYBODY LIKES TO CHA CHA, Sam Cooke, Keen 2018	11
89	70	45	42		GIDGET, Jimmy Darren, Colpix 113	4
52	52	51	43		■ AS TIME GOES BY, Johnny Nash, ABC-Paramount 9996	10
16	21	32	44		TRAGEDY, Thomas Wayne, Fernwood 109	17
—	81	48	45		JUST KEEP IT UP, Dee Clark, Abner 1026	3
—	—	75	46	★	I'M READY, Fats Domino, Imperial 5585	2
33	41	40	47		■ I MISS YOU SO, Paul Anka, ABC-Paramount 10011	8
94	69	54	48		I WAITED TOO LONG, LaVern Baker, Atlantic 2021	5
19	30	39	49		IT'S JUST A MATTER OF TIME, Brook Benton, Mercury 71394	17
72	59	64	50	★	YOU'RE SO FINE, The Falcons, Unart 2013	5
57	60	50	51		■ BONAPARTE'S RETREAT, Billy Grammer, Monument 403	6
80	63	57	52		CASTIN' MY SPELL, Johnny Otis Show, Capitol 4168	4
—	—	96	53	★	TALLAHASSEE LASSIE, Freddy Cannon, Swan 4031	2
88	66	47	54		CROSSFIRE, Johnny and the Hurricanes, Warwick 502	5
40	46	52	55		YEP!, Duane Eddy, Jamie 1122	8
—	87	81	56	★	YOU MADE ME LOVE YOU, Nat King Cole, Capitol 4184	3
—	—	—	57	★	■ LIPSTICK ON YOUR COLLAR, Connie Francis, M-G-M 12793	1
58	51	53	58		■ I STILL GET A THRILL, Joni James, M-G-M 12779	6
99	88	62	59		SUMMER DREAMS, McGuire Sisters, Coral 62106	4
66	78	65	60		■ THE KISSING TREE, Billy Grammer, Monument 403	6
83	91	91	61	★	MY HEART IS AN OPEN BOOK, Carl Dobkins Jr., Decca 30803	5
—	—	87	62	★	MARGIE, Fats Domino, Imperial 5585	2
—	—	—	63	★	SO CLOSE, Brook Benton, Mercury 71443	1
—	—	—	64	★	■ MY MELANCHOLY BABY, Tommy Edwards, M-G-M 12794	1
29	39	44	65		IT DOESN'T MATTER ANYMORE, Buddy Holly, Coral 62074	13
—	—	—	66	★	■ FRANKIE, Connie Francis, M-G-M 12793	1
—	—	86	67	★	ROCKIN' CRICKETS, Hot Toddys, Shan-Todd 0056	4
87	83	69	68		ROBBIN' THE CRADLE, Tony Bellus, NRC 023	4
76	68	68	69		THERE'S NO FOOL LIKE A YOUNG FOOL, Tab Hunter, Warner Bros. 5051	4
55	64	55	70		THAT'S MY LITTLE SUZIE, Ritchie Valens, Del-Fi 4114	7
90	80	77	71		A STRING OF TRUMPETS, Trumpeteers, Splash 800	4
46	47	58	72		■ THE MORNING SIDE OF THE MOUNTAIN, Tommy Edwards, M-G-M 12757	12
63	62	67	73		I NEED YOUR LOVIN', Roy Hamilton, Epic 9307	5
—	—	—	74	★	TALL COOL ONE, Wailers, Golden Crest 518	1
—	98	60	75		KANSAS CITY, Rocky Olson, Chess 1723	3
—	73	72	76		■ KANSAS CITY, Hank Ballard and the Midnighters, King 5195	3
—	—	—	77	★	HALLELUJAH, I LOVE HIM SO, Peggy Lee, Capitol 4189	1
—	89	78	78		■ YOUNG IDEAS, Chico Holiday, RCA Victor 7499	3
77	71	74	79		FRANKIE'S MAN, JOHNNY, Johnny Cash, Columbia 41317	4
—	—	—	80	★	BONGO ROCK, Preston Epps, Original 4	1
—	77	71	81		LONESOME OLD HOUSE, Don Gibson, RCA Victor 7505	3
95	82	89	82		YOUR CHEATIN' HEART, Billy Vaughn, Dot 15936	4
—	95	95	83		OLD SPANISH TOWN, Bell Notes, Time 1010	3
42	45	42	84		TELL HIM NO, Dean and Marc, Bullseye 1025	8
—	—	—	85	★	GRADUATION'S HERE, Fleetwoods, Dolton 3	1
—	—	—	86	★	JUDY, David Seville, Liberty 55193	1
—	—	—	87	★	HEY, LITTLE LUCY, Conway Twitty, M-G-M 12785	1
51	49	59	88	★	ALONG CAME JONES, Coasters, Atco 6141	1
—	—	—	89		LOVEY DOVEY, Clyde McPhatter, Atlantic 2018	7
—	—	—	90	★	THE CLASS, Chubby Checker, Parkway 804	1
—	—	—	91		RUSSIAN BANDSTAND, Spencer and Spencer, Argo 5331	1
—	—	—	92		ONLY ONE LOVE, Steve Lawrence, ABC-Paramount 10005	1
97	76	70	93		I TOLD MYSELF A LIE, Clyde McPhatter, M-G-M 12780	5
—	—	—	94		THE WONDER OF YOU, Ray Peterson, RCA Victor 7513	1
—	—	97	95		KANSAS CITY, Little Richard, Specialty 664	2
56	55	56	96		I THINK I'M GONNA KILL MYSELF, Buddy Knox, Roulette 4140	6
—	85	85	97		PEACE, McGuire Sisters, Coral 62106	3
—	—	—	98		SOMEONE TO COME HOME TO, Ames Brothers, RCA Victor 7526	1
—	100	88	99		TALK OF THE SCHOOL, Sonny James, Capitol 4178	3
—	—	—	100		I CAN'T GET YOU OUT OF MY HEART, Al Martino, 20th Fox 132	1

THE BILLBOARD'S BEST BUYS

These records have shown the greatest national SALES BREAKOUT potential this week.

POP

- ● **LIPSTICK ON YOUR COLLAR** — **FRANKIE**, Connie Francis (Joy, ASCAP) (Aldon, BMI) M-G-M 12793
- ● **MY MELANCHOLY BABY**, Tommy Edwards (Shapiro-Bernstein, ASCAP) M-G-M 12794
- **MY HEART IS AN OPEN BOOK**, Carl Dobkins Jr. (Sequence, BMI) Decca 30803
- ● **TALLAHASSEE LASSIE**, Freddy Cannon (Conley, BMI) Swan 4031
- **A STRING OF TRUMPETS**, The Trumpeteers (Portrait, BMI) Splash 900
- **CASTIN' MY SPELL**, The Johnny Otis Show (Moonbeam, ASCAP) Capitol 4168

C&W

No selections this week.

R&B

- ● **FIVE LONG YEARS** — **I'M HOLDING ON**, Little Jr. Parker (Frederick, BMI) (Lion, BMI) Duke 306

● Previous Billboard Spotlight picks.

THE HOT 100: A TO Z

TITLE	POSITION
A Fool Such as I	11
A String of Trumpets	71
A Teenager in Love	5
Almost Grown	32
Along Came Jones	88
As Time Goes By	43
Battle of New Orleans, The	7
Bonaparte's Retreat	51
Bongo Rock	80
Castin' My Spell	52
Class, The	90
Come Softly to Me	15
Come to Me	30
Crossfire	54
Dream Lover	6
Enchanted	13
Endlessly	18
Everybody Likes to Cha Cha	41
Fc a Penny	37
Frankie	66
Frankie's Man Johnny	79
Gidget	42
Goodbye, Jimmy, Goodbye	23
Graduation's Here	85
Guess Who	31
Guitar Boogie Shuffle	12
Halleltjah, I Love Him So	77
Happy Organ, The	3
Hey Little Lucy	87
I Can't Get You Out of My Heart	100
I Miss You So	47
I Need Your Love Tonight	17
I Need Your Lovin'	73
I Still Get a Thrill	58
I Think I'm Gonna Kill Myself	96
I Told Myself a Lie	93
I Waited Too Long	48
I'm Ready	46
It Doesn't Matter Anymore	65
It's Just a Matter of Time	49
It's Late	35
I've Come of Age	34
Judy	86
Just Keep It Up	45
Kansas City (Ballard)	76
Kansas City (Harrison)	1
Kansas City (Olson)	75
Kansas City (Little Richard)	95
Kissing Tree, The	60
Kookie, Kookie (Lend Me Your Comb)	4
L pstick on Your Collar	57
Lonely for You	40
Lonesome Old House	81
Lovey Dovey	89
Margie	62
Morning Side of the Mountain, The	72
My Heart Is an Open Book	61
My Melancholy Baby	64
Never Be Anyone Else But You	33
Old Spanish Town	83
Only Love Me	92
Only You	14
Peace	97
Personality	22
Pink Shoelaces	10
Poor Jenny	28
Quiet Village	8
Robbin' the Cradle	68
Rockin' Crickets	67
Russian Bandstand	91
Sea Cruise	39
Since I Don't Have You	27
Sˈx Nights a Week	29
So Close	63
So Fine	21
Someone	36
Someone to Come Home To	98
Sorry, I Ran All the Way Home	2
Summer Dreams	59
Take a Message to Mary	16
Talk of the School	99
Tall Cool One	74
Tallahassee Lassie	53
Tell Him No (Dean & Marc)	84
Tell Him No (Travis & Bob)	19
That's My Little Susie	70
That's Why	20
There's No Fool Like a Young Fool	69
This Should Go on Forever	38
Three Stars	24
Tijuana Jail	25
Tragedy	44
Turn Me Loose	9
Venus	26
Wonder of You, The	94
Yep!	55
You Made Me Love You	56
Young Ideas	78
Your Cheatin' Heart	82
You're So Fine	50

The Billboard HOT 100

FOR THE WEEK ENDING MAY 31

★ STAR PERFORMERS showed the greatest upward progress on the Hot 100 this week.

■ Indicates that STEREO SINGLE version is available.

THREE WEEKS AGO	TWO WEEKS AGO	ONE WEEK AGO	THIS WEEK	★ STAR PERFORMER	TITLE, Artist, Company, Record Number.	WEEKS ON CHART
16	6	1	1		KANSAS CITY, Wilbert Harrison, Fury 1023	7
36	23	7	2		THE BATTLE OF NEW ORLEANS, Johnny Horton, Columbia 41339	5
29	16	6	3		DREAM LOVER, Bobby Darin, Atco 6140	6
3	2	2	4		SORRY, I RAN ALL THE WAY HOME, The Impalas, Cub 9022	11
19	4	4	5		■ KOOKIE, KOOKIE (LEND ME YOUR COMB), Edward Byrnes with Connie Stevens, Warner Bros. 5047	6
2	1	3	6		THE HAPPY ORGAN, Dave (Baby) Cortez, Clock 1009	11
20	12	5	7		A TEENAGER IN LOVE, Dion and the Belmonts, Laurie 3027	6
27	19	8	8		■ QUIET VILLAGE, Martin Denny, Liberty 55162	7
48	38	22	9	★	■ PERSONALITY, Lloyd Price, ABC-Paramount 10018	5
24	20	14	10		ONLY YOU, Frank Pourcel, Capitol 4165	8
6	5	11	11		A FOOL SUCH AS I, Elvis Presley, RCA Victor 7506	10
10	9	9	12		■ TURN ME LOOSE, Fabian, Chancellor 1033	9
38	28	18	13		ENDLESSLY, Brook Benton, Mercury 71443	6
33	25	21	14		SO FINE, Fiestas, Old Town 1062	8
5	7	12	15		■ GUITAR BOOGIE SHUFFLE, The Virtues, Hunt 324	12
12	15	13	16		ENCHANTED, The Platters, Mercury 71427	10
4	8	10	17		PINK SHOE LACES, Dodie Stevens, Crystalette 724	15
24	24	23	18		■ GOODBYE, JIMMY, GOODBYE, Kathy Linden, Felsted 8571	7
17	18	16	19		TAKE A MESSAGE TO MARY, Everly Brothers, Cadence 1364	9
7	10	17	20		I NEED YOUR LOVE TONIGHT, Elvis Presley, RCA Victor 7506	9
1	3	15	21		■ COME SOFTLY TO ME, Fleetwoods, Dolphin 1	12
8	11	19	22		TELL HIM NO, Travis and Bob, Sandy 1017	10
13	17	20	23		THAT'S WHY, Jackie Wilson, Brunswick 55121	10
11	13	24	24		■ THREE STARS, Tommy Dee, Crest 1057	9
14	22	27	25		SINCE I DON'T HAVE YOU, The Skyliners, Calico 103	15
22	27	28	26		POOR JENNY, Everly Brothers, Cadence 1364	9
15	21	25	27		■ TIJUANA JAIL, Kingston Trio, Capitol 4167	10
61	49	40	28	★	LONELY FOR YOU, Gary Stites, Carlton 508	7
—	75	46	29	★	I'M READY, Fats Domino, Imperial 5585	3
—	96	53	30	★	TALLAHASSE LASSIE, Freddy Cannon, Swan 4031	3
9	14	26	31		■ VENUS, Frankie Avalon, Chancellor 1031	16
28	34	29	32		SIX NIGHTS A WEEK, The Crests, Coed 509	10
37	35	31	33		■ GUESS WHO, Jesse Belvin, RCA Victor 7469	9
81	48	45	34	★	■ JUST KEEP IT UP, Dee Clark, Abner 1026	4
40	41	36	35		SOMEONE, Johnny Mathis, Columbia 41355	10
56	43	34	36		I'VE COME OF AGE, Billy Storm, Columbia 41356	7
31	37	30	37		COME TO ME, Marv Johnson, United Artists 160	11
32	36	32	38		ALMOST GROWN, Chuck Berry, Chess 1722	9
23	33	39	39		SEA CRUISE, Frankie Ford, Ace, 554	16
18	26	33	40		NEVER BE ANYONE ELSE BUT YOU, Ricky Nelson, Imperial 5565	14
—	—	57	41	★	■ LIPSTICK ON YOUR COLLAR, Connie Francis, M-G-M 12793	2
26	30	37	42		■ FOR A PENNY, Pat Boone, Dot 15914	10
—	—	66	43	★	■ FRANKIE, Connie Francis, M-G-M 12793	2
69	54	48	44		I WAITED TOO LONG, LaVern Baker, Atlantic 2021	6
70	45	42	45		GIDGET, Jimmy Darren, Colpix 113	5
87	81	56	46	★	■ YOU MADE ME LOVE YOU, Nat King Cole, Capitol 4184	4
91	91	61	47	★	MY HEART IS AN OPEN BOOK, Carl Dobkins Jr., Decca 30803	6
—	—	80	48	★	BONGO ROCK, Preston Epps, Original 4	2
42	46	41	49		■ EVERYBODY LIKES TO CHA CHA, Sam Cooke, Keen 2018	12
25	31	38	50		THIS SHOULD GO ON FOREVER, Rod Bernard, Argo 5327	12

THE BILLBOARD'S BEST BUYS

These records have shown the greatest national SALES BREAKOUT potential this week.

POP

- ● BOBBY SOX TO STOCKINGS
  A BOY WITHOUT A GIRL, Frankie Avalon (Debmar, ASCAP) (Arch, ASCAP) Chancellor 1036
- ● ALONG CAME JONES, The Coasters, (Tiger, BMI) Atco 6141
- ● BONGO ROCK, Preston Epps (Drive-In, BMI) Original 4
- ● THE CLASS, Chubby Checker (Lowe, ASCAP) Parkway 804
- THE WONDER OF YOU, Ray Peterson (Random, BMI) RCA Victor 7513
- WHAT A DIFF'RENCE A DAY MAKES, Dinah Washington (Marks, BMI) Mercury 71435
- TALL COOL ONE, The Wailers (C.F.G., BMI) Golden Crest 518

C&W

- ● YOUR WILD LIFE'S GONNA GET YOU DOWN
  YOU'LL NEVER BE MINE AGAIN, Kitty Wells (Acuff-Rose, BMI) (Tree, BMI) Decca 30890

R&B

No selections this week.

● Previous Billboard Spotlight picks.

THE HOT 100: A TO Z

★ STAR PERFORMERS showed the greatest upward progress on the Hot 100 this week.

■ Indicates that STEREO SINGLE version is available.

THREE WEEKS AGO	TWO WEEKS AGO	ONE WEEK AGO	THIS WEEK	★ STAR PERFORMER	TITLE, Artist, Company, Record Number.	WEEKS ON CHART
—	—	74	51	★	TALL COOL ONE, Wailers, Golden Crest 518	2
52	51	43	52		AS TIME GOES BY, Johnny Nash, ABC-Paramount 9996	11
59	64	50	53		■ YOU'RE SO FINE, The Falcons, Unart 2013	6
63	57	52	54		CASTIN' MY SPELL, Johnny Otis Show, Capitol 4168	5
—	—	64	55		■ MY MELANCHOLY BABY, Tommy Edwards, M-G-M 12794	2
66	47	54	56		CROSSFIRE, Johnny and the Hurricanes, Warwick 502	6
—	86	67	57	★	ROCKIN' CRICKETS, Hot Toddy, Shan-Todd 0056	5
60	50	51	58		■ BONAPARTE'S RETREAT, Billy Grammer, Monument 403	7
—	—	63	59		SO CLOSE, Brook Benton, Mercury 71443	2
—	—	—	60	★	■ BOBBY SOX TO STOCKINGS, Frankie Avalon, Chancellor 1036	1
—	—	88	61	★	ALONG CAME JONES, Coasters, Atco 6141	2
88	62	59	62		SUMMER DREAMS, McGuire Sisters, Coral 62106	5
—	—	—	63	★	■ A BOY WITHOUT A GIRL, Frankie Avalon, Chancellor 1036	1
35	29	35	64		IT'S LATE, Ricky Nelson, Imperial 5565	13
30	39	49	65		IT'S JUST A MATTER OF TIME, Brook Benton, Mercury 71394	18
98	60	75	66		KANSAS CITY, Rocky Olson, Chess 1723	4
—	—	94	67	★	THE WONDER OF YOU, Ray Peterson, RCA Victor 7513	2
21	32	44	68		TRAGEDY, Thomas Wayne, Fernwood 109	18
—	87	62	69		MARGIE, Fats Domino, Imperial 5585	3
71	74	79	70		FRANKIE'S MAN, JOHNNY, Johnny Cash, Columbia 41317	5
80	77	71	71		A STRING OF TRUMPETS, Trumpeteers, Splash 800	5
—	—	85	72		GRADUATION'S HERE, Fleetwoods, Dolton 3	2
68	68	69	73		■ THERE'S NO FOOL LIKE A YOUNG FOOL, Tab Hunter, Warner Bros. 5051	5
89	78	78	74		■ YOUNG IDEAS, Chico Holiday, RCA Victor 7499	4
—	—	—	75	★	I MUST BE DREAMING, Nat King Cole, Capitol 4184	1
—	—	90	76		THE CLASS, Chubby Checker, Parkway 804	2
—	—	—	77	★	WHAT A DIFF'RENCE A DAY MAKES, Dinah Washington, Mercury 71435	1
46	52	55	78		YEP! Duane Eddy, Jamie 1122	9
83	69	68	79		ROBBIN' THE CRADLE, Tony Bellus, NRC 023	5
39	44	65	80		IT DOESN'T MATTER ANYMORE, Buddy Holly, Coral 62074	14
—	—	—	81	★	HUSHABY, Mystics, Laurie 3028	1
64	55	70	82		THAT'S MY LITTLE SUZIE, Ritchie Valens, Del fi 4114	8
—	—	92	83		ONLY LOVE ME, Steve Lawrence, ABC-Paramount 10005	2
—	—	89	84		LOVEY DOVEY, Clyde McPhatter, Atlantic 2018	8
—	—	77	85		HALLELUJAH, I LOVE HIM SO, Peggy Lee, Capitol 4189	2
41	40	47	86		■ I MISS YOU SO, Paul Anka, ABC-Paramount 10011	9
—	—	—	87	★	THE BATTLE OF NEW ORLEANS, Vaughn Monroe, RCA Victor 7495	1
90	73	—	88		WHITE LIGHTNING, George Jones, Mercury 71406	2
—	—	—	89	★	THERE IS SOMETHING ON YOUR MIND, Big Jay McNeely, Swingin' 614	1
73	72	76	90		■ KANSAS CITY, Hank Ballard and the Midnighters, King 5195	3
78	65	60	91		■ THE KISSING TREE, Billy Grammer, Monument 403	7
—	—	—	92		LONELY SATURDAY NIGHT, Don French, Lancer 104	1
—	—	98	93		SOMEONE TO COME HOME TO, Ames Brothers, RCA Victor 7526	2
—	—	100	94		I CAN'T GET YOU OUT OF MY HEART, Al Martino, 20th Fox 132	2
82	89	82	95		YOUR CHEATIN' HEART, Billy Vaughn, Dot 15936	5
—	—	—	96		STRAIGHT FLUSH, Frantics, Dolton 2	1
—	—	91	97		RUSSIAN BANDSTAND, Spencer and Spencer, Argo 5331	2
—	—	—	98		WATERLOO, Stonewall Jackson, Columbia 41393	1
51	53	58	99		■ I STILL GET A THRILL, Joni James, M-G-M 12779	7
100	88	99	100		TALK OF THE SCHOOL, Sonny James, Capitol 4178	4

FOR THE WEEK ENDING JUNE 7

The Billboard HOT 100

★ STAR PERFORMERS showed the greatest upward progress on the Hot 100 this week.

S Indicates that STEREO SINGLE version is available.

Three Weeks Ago	Two Weeks Ago	One Week Ago	This Week	Stereo	TITLE, Artist, Company, Record No.	Weeks on Chart
23	7	2	1		THE BATTLE OF NEW ORLEANS — Johnny Horton, Columbia 41339	6
6	1	1	2		KANSAS CITY — Wilbert Harrison, Fury	8
16	6	3	3		DREAM LOVER — Bobby Darin, Atco 6140	7
19	8	8	4	S	QUIET VILLAGE — Martin Denny, Liberty 55162	8
38	22	9	5	S	PERSONALITY — Lloyd Price, ABC-Paramount 10018	6
12	5	7	6		A TEENAGER IN LOVE — Dion and the Belmonts, Laurie	7
4	4	5	7	S	KOOKIE, KOOKIE (LEND ME YOUR COMB) — Ed Byrnes/Connie Stevens, Warner Bros. 5047	7
2	2	4	8		SORRY, I RAN ALL THE WAY HOME — The Impalas, Cub	12
20	14	10	9		ONLY YOU — Frank Pourcel, Capitol 4165	9
1	3	6	10		THE HAPPY ORGAN — Dave (Baby) Cortez, Clock 1009	12
24	23	18	11	S	GOODBYE, JIMMY, GOODBYE — Kathy Linden, Felsted 8571	8
25	21	14	12		SO FINE — Fiestas, Old Town 1062	9
28	18	13	13	S	ENDLESSLY — Brook Benton, Mercury 71443	7
9	9	12	14	S	TURN ME LOOSE — Fabian, Chancellor 1033	10
96	53	30	★15		TALLAHASSEE LASSIE — Freddy Cannon, Swan 4031	4
15	13	16	16		ENCHANTED — The Platters, Mercury 71427	11
75	46	29	★17		I'M READY — Fats Domino, Imperial 5585	4
18	16	19	18		TAKE A MESSAGE TO MARY — Everly Brothers, Cadence 1364	10
5	11	11	19		A FOOL SUCH AS I — Elvis Presley, RCA Victor 7506	11
8	10	17	20		PINK SHOE LACES — Dodie Stevens, Crystalette 724	16
7	12	15	21	S	GUITAR BOOGIE SHUFFLE — The Virtues, Hunt 324	13
—	66	43	★22	S	FRANKIE — Connie Francis, M-G-M 12793	3
—	57	41	★23	S	LIPSTICK ON YOUR COLLAR — Connie Francis, M-G-M 12793	3
49	40	28	24		LONELY FOR YOU — Gary Stites, Carlton 508	8
17	20	23	25		THAT'S WHY — Jackie Wilson, Brunswick 55121	11
11	19	22	26		TELL HIM NO — Travis and Bob, Sandy 1017	11
13	24	24	27	S	THREE STARS — Tommy Dee, Crest 1057	10
43	34	36	28		I'VE COME OF AGE — Billy Storm, Columbia 41356	8
10	17	20	29		I NEED YOUR LOVE TONIGHT — Elvis Presley, RCA Victor 7506	10
—	88	61	★30		ALONG CAME JONES — Coasters, Atco 6141	3
91	61	47	★31		MY HEART IS AN OPEN BOOK — Carl Dobkins Jr., Decca 30803	7
48	45	34	32	S	JUST KEEP IT UP — Dee Clark, Abner 1026	5
54	48	44	★33		I WAITED TOO LONG — LaVern Baker, Atlantic 2021	7
3	15	21	34	S	COME SOFTLY TO ME — Fleetwoods, Dolphin 1	13
—	—	60	★35	S	BOBBY SOX TO STOCKINGS — Frankie Avalon, Chancellor 1036	2
47	54	56	★36		CROSSFIRE — Johnny and the Hurricanes, Warwick 502	7
—	74	51	★37		TALL COOL ONE — Wailers, Golden Crest 518	3
—	80	48	★38	S	BONGO ROCK — Preston Epps, Original 4	3
35	31	33	39	S	GUESS WHO — Jesse Belvin, RCA Victor 7469	10
36	32	38	40		ALMOST GROWN — Chuck Berry, Chess 1722	10
27	28	26	41		POOR JENNY — Everly Brothers, Cadence 1364	10
34	29	32	42		SIX NIGHTS A WEEK — The Crests, Coed 509	11
21	25	27	43	S	TIJUANA JAIL — Kingston Trio, Capitol 4167	11
64	50	53	44	S	YOU'RE SO FINE — The Falcons, Unart 2013	7
81	56	46	45	S	YOU MADE ME LOVE YOU — Nat King Cole, Capitol 4184	5
22	27	25	46		SINCE I DON'T HAVE YOU — The Skyliners, Calico 103	16
—	94	67	★47		THE WONDER OF YOU — Ray Peterson, RCA Victor 7513	3
41	36	35	48		SOMEONE — Johnny Mathis, Columbia 41355	11
—	64	55	49	S	MY MELANCHOLY BABY — Tommy Edwards, M-G-M 12794	3
37	30	37	50		COME TO ME — Marv Johnson, United Artists 160	12
45	42	45	51		GIDGET — Jimmy Darren, Colpix 113	6
—	—	—	★52	S	LONELY BOY — Paul Anka, ABC-Paramount 10022	1
—	—	63	★53	S	A BOY WITHOUT A GIRL — Frankie Avalon, Chancellor 1036	2
—	63	59	54		SO CLOSE — Brook Benton, Mercury 71443	3
62	59	62	55		SUMMER DREAMS — McGuire Sisters, Coral 62106	6
87	62	69	★56		MARGIE — Fats Domino, Imperial 5585	4
74	79	70	★57		FRANKIE'S MAN, JOHNNY — Johnny Cash, Columbia 41317	6
—	—	77	★58		WHAT A DIFF'RENCE A DAY MAKES — Dinah Washington, Mercury 71435	2
—	—	81	★59		HUSHABY — Mystics, Laurie 3028	3
—	—	—	★60		I ONLY HAVE EYES FOR YOU — Flamingos, End 1046	1
86	67	57	61		ROCKIN' CRICKETS — Hot Toddys, Shan-Todd 0056	6
—	92	83	★62		ONLY LOVE ME — Steve Lawrence, ABC-Paramount 10005	3
30	37	42	63	S	FOR A PENNY — Pat Boone, Dot 15914	11
—	85	72	64	S	GRADUATION'S HERE — Fleetwoods, Dolphin 3	3
—	90	76	65		THE CLASS — Chubby Checker, Parkway 804	3
—	—	98	★66		WATERLOO — Stonewall Jackson, Columbia 41393	2
77	71	71	67		A STRING OF TRUMPETS — Trumpeteers, Splash 800	6
—	—	—	★68	S	RING-A-LING-A-LARIO — Jimmie Rodgers, Roulette 4158	1
—	—	75	69		I MUST BE DREAMING — Nat King Cole, Capitol 4184	2
69	68	79	70		ROBBIN' THE CRADLE — Tony Bellus, NRC 023	6
93	—	—	★71		LITTLE DIPPER — Mickey Mozart, Roulette 4148	2
—	—	92	★72		LONELY SATURDAY NIGHT — Don French, Lancer 104	2
—	—	—	★73		DANNY BOY — Sil Austin, Mercury 71442	1
—	—	—	★74		VELVET WATERS — Megatrons, Acousticon 101	1
73	—	88	75		WHITE LIGHTNING — George Jones, Mercury 71406	3
95	83	—	★76		OLD SPANISH TOWN — Bell Notes, Time 1010	4
—	100	94	★77		I CAN'T GET YOU OUT OF MY HEART — Al Martino, 20th Fox 132	3
—	98	93	★78		SOMEONE TO COME HOME TO — Ames Brothers, RCA Victor 7526	3
50	51	58	79	S	BONAPARTE'S RETREAT — Billy Grammer, Monument 403	8
26	33	40	80		NEVER BE ANYONE ELSE BUT YOU — Ricky Nelson, Imperial 5565	15
32	44	68	81		TRAGEDY — Thomas Wayne, Fernwood 109	19
—	—	—	★82		MONA LISA — Carl Mann, Phillips International 3539	1
46	41	49	83	S	EVERYBODY LIKES TO CHA CHA — Sam Cooke, Keen 2018	13
—	—	89	84		THERE IS SOMETHING ON YOUR MIND — Big Jay McNeely, Swingin' 614	2
88	99	100	★85		TALK OF THE SCHOOL — Sonny James, Capitol 4178	5
—	—	—	★86	S	IT'S ONLY THE GOOD TIMES — Tommy Edwards, M-G-M 12794	1
—	—	—	★87		THIS I SWEAR — Skyliners, Calico 106	1
78	78	74	88	S	YOUNG IDEAS — Chico Holiday, RCA Victor 7499	5
14	26	31	89		VENUS — Frankie Avalon, Chancellor 1031	17
—	—	—	★90		SWEET CHILE — Sheb Wooley, M-G-M 12781	1
33	39	39	91		SEA CRUISE — Frankie Ford, Ace 554	17
—	—	96	92		STRAIGHT FLUSH — Frantics, Dolton 2	2
—	—	—	93		MARY ANN THOMAS — Bobby Freeman, Josie 863	1
—	87	—	94		HEY, LITTLE LUCY — Conway Twitty, M-G-M 12785	2
—	—	—	95		YES-SIR-EE — Dodie Stevens, Crystalette 728	1
—	—	—	96	S	LIKE YOUNG — Andre Previn and David Rose, M-G-M 12792	1
—	—	—	97		POINTED TOE SHOES — Carl Perkins, Columbia 41379	1
—	—	—	98		THERE GOES MY BABY — The Drifters, Atlantic 2025	1
—	—	—	99		CHERRYSTONE — Addrisi Brothers, Del-Fi 4116	1
—	—	—	100		JACK O' DIAMONDS — Ruth Brown, Atlantic 2026	1

FOR THE WEEK ENDING JUNE 14

The Billboard HOT 100

★ STAR PERFORMERS showed the greatest upward progress on the Hot 100 this week.

S Indicates that STEREO SINGLE version is available.

Three Weeks Ago	Two Weeks Ago	One Week Ago	This Week	Stereo	Title, Artist, Company, Record No.	Weeks on Chart
7	2	1	1		THE BATTLE OF NEW ORLEANS — Johnny Horton, Columbia 41339	7
6	3	3	2		DREAM LOVER — Bobby Darin, Atco 6140	8
22	9	5	3	S	PERSONALITY — Lloyd Price, ABC-Paramount 10018	7
1	1	2	4		KANSAS CITY — Wilbert Harrison, Fury 1023	9
8	8	4	5	S	QUIET VILLAGE — Martin Denny, Liberty 55162	9
5	7	6	6		A TEENAGER IN LOVE — Dion and the Belmonts, Laurie 3027	8
4	5	7	7	S	KOOKIE, KOOKIE (LEND ME YOUR COMB) — Ed Byrnes/Connie Stevens, Warner Bros. 5047	8
2	4	8	8		SORRY, I RAN ALL THE WAY HOME — The Impalas, Cub 9022	13
14	10	9	9		ONLY YOU — Frank Pourcel, Capitol 4165	10
3	6	10	10		THE HAPPY ORGAN — Dave (Baby) Cortez, Clock 1009	13
53	30	15	11		TALLAHASSEE LASSIE — Freddy Cannon, Swan 4031	5
18	13	13	12	S	ENDLESSLY — Brook Benton, Mercury 71443	8
21	14	12	13		SO FINE — Fiestas, Old Town 1062	10
23	18	11	14	S	GOODBYE, JIMMY, GOODBYE — Kathy Linden, Felsted 8571	9
88	61	30	★15		ALONG CAME JONES — Coasters, Atco 6141	4
46	29	17	16		I'M READY — Fats Domino, Imperial 5585	5
57	41	23	17	S	LIPSTICK ON YOUR COLLAR — Connie Francis, M-G-M 12793	4
—	—	52	★18	S	LONELY BOY — Paul Anka, ABC-Paramount 10022	2
66	43	22	19	S	FRANKIE — Connie Francis, M-G-M 12793	4
45	34	32	★20	S	JUST KEEP IT UP — Dee Clark, Abner 1026	6
13	16	16	21		ENCHANTED — The Platters, Mercury 71427	12
9	12	14	22	S	TURN ME LOOSE — Fabian, Chancellor 1033	11
54	56	36	★23		CROSSFIRE — Johnny and the Hurricanes, Warwick 502	8
80	48	38	★24	S	BONGO ROCK — Preston Epps, Original 4	4
—	60	35	★25	S	BOBBY SOX TO STOCKINGS — Frankie Avalon, Chancellor 1036	3
64	55	49	★26	S	MY MELANCHOLY BABY — Tommy Edwards, M-G-M 12794	4
11	11	19	27		A FOOL SUCH AS I — Elvis Presley, RCA Victor 7506	12
40	28	24	28	S	LONELY FOR YOU — Gary Stites, Carlton 508	9
12	15	21	29	S	GUITAR BOOGIE SHUFFLE — The Virtues, Hunt 324	14
10	17	20	30		PINK SHOE LACES — Dodie Stevens, Crystalette 724	17
61	47	31	31		MY HEART IS AN OPEN BOOK — Carl Dopkins Jr., Decca 30803	8
50	53	44	★32	S	YOU'RE SO FINE — The Falcons, Unart 2013	8
16	19	18	33		TAKE A MESSAGE TO MARY — Everly Brothers, Cadence 1364	11
34	36	28	34		I'VE COME OF AGE — Billy Storm, Columbia 41356	9
—	—	60	★35		I ONLY HAVE EYES FOR YOU — Flamingos, End 1046	2
20	23	25	36		THAT'S WHY — Jackie Wilson, Brunswick 55121	12
—	—	71	★37		LITTLE DIPPER — Mickey Mozart, Roulette 4148	3
63	59	54	★38		SO CLOSE — Brook Benton, Mercury 71443	4
—	98	66	★39		WATERLOO — Stonewall Jackson, Columbia 41393	3
31	33	39	40	S	GUESS WHO — Jesse Belvin, RCA Victor 7469	11
74	51	37	41		TALL COOL ONE — Wailers, Golden Crest 518	4
32	38	40	42		ALMOST GROWN — Chuck Berry, Chess 1722	11
94	67	47	43		THE WONDER OF YOU — Ray Peterson, RCA Victor 7513	4
28	26	41	44		POOR JENNY — Everly Brothers, Cadence 1364	11
90	76	65	★45		THE CLASS — Chubby Checker, Parkway 804	4
17	20	29	46		I NEED YOUR LOVE TONIGHT — Elvis Presley, RCA Victor 7506	11
—	81	59	★47		HUSHABYE — Mystics, Laurie 3028	4
85	72	64	★48	S	GRADUATION'S HERE — Fleetwoods, Dolton 3	4
—	77	58	49		WHAT A DIFF'RENCE A DAY MAKES — Dinah Washington, Mercury 71435	3
48	44	33	50		I WAITED TOO LONG — LaVern Baker, Atlantic 2021	8
62	69	56	51		MARGIE — Fats Domino, Imperial 5585	5
30	37	50	52		COME TO ME — Marv Johnson, United Artists 160	13
56	46	45	53	S	YOU MADE ME LOVE YOU — Nat King Cole, Capitol 4184	6
42	45	51	54		GIDGET — Jimmy Darren, Colpix 113	7
27	25	46	55		SINCE I DON'T HAVE YOU — The Skyliners, Calico 103	17
—	—	68	★56	S	RING-A-LING-A-LARIO — Jimmie Rodgers, Roulette 4158	2
24	24	27	57	S	THREE STARS — Tommy Dee, Crest 1057	11
19	22	26	58		TELL HIM NO — Travis and Bob, Sandy 1017	12
68	79	70	★59		ROBBIN' THE CRADLE — Tony Bellus, NRC 023	7
15	21	34	60	S	COME SOFTLY TO ME — Fleetwoods, Dolphin 1	14
25	27	43	61	S	TIJUANA JAIL — Kingston Trio, Capitol 4167	12
—	—	87	★62		THIS I SWEAR — Skyliners, Calico 106	2
36	35	48	63		SOMEONE — Johnny Mathis, Columbia 41355	12
71	71	67	64		A STRING OF TRUMPETS — Trumpeteers, Splash 800	7
29	32	42	65		SIX NIGHTS A WEEK — The Crests, Coed 509	12
67	57	61	66		ROCKIN' CRICKETS — Hot Toddys, Shan-Todd 0056	7
—	—	—	★67	S	I'M GONNA CHANGE HIM — Cathy Carr, Roulette 4152	1
—	89	84	★68		THERE IS SOMETHING ON YOUR MIND — Big Jay McNeely, Swingin' 614	3
—	63	53	69	S	A BOY WITHOUT A GIRL — Frankie Avalon, Chancellor 1036	3
—	—	82	70		MONA LISA — Carl Mann, Phillips International 3539	2
—	—	—	★71	S	ONLY SIXTEEN — Sam Cooke, Keen 2022	1
79	70	57	72		FRANKIE'S MAN, JOHNNY — Johnny Cash, Columbia 41317	7
—	88	75	73		WHITE LIGHTNING — George Jone, Mercury 71406	4
—	75	69	74		I MUST BE DREAMING — Nat King Cole, Capitol 4184	3
59	62	55	75		SUMMER DREAMS — McGuire Sisters, Coral 62106	7
100	94	77	76		I CAN'T GET YOU OUT OF MY HEART — Al Martino, 20th Fox 132	4
—	—	98	★77		THERE GOES MY BABY — The Drifters, Atlantic 2025	2
—	—	73	78		DANNY BOY — Sil Austin, Mercury 71442	2
—	—	74	79		VELVET WATERS — Megatrons, Acousticon 101	2
—	92	72	80		LONELY SATURDAY NIGHT — Don French, Lancer 104	3
—	—	90	81		SWEET CHILE — Sheb Wooley, M-G-M 12781	2
92	83	62	82		ONLY LOVE ME — Steve Lawrence, ABC-Paramount 10005	4
78	74	88	83	S	YOUNG IDEAS — Chico Holiday, RCA Victor 7499	6
—	—	—	★84	S	FORTY DAYS — Ronnie Hawkins, Roulette 4154	1
76	90	—	★85		KANSAS CITY — Kaye Ballard and the Midnighters, King 5195	5
98	93	78	86		SOMEONE TO COME HOME TO — Ames Brothers, RCA Victor 7526	4
33	40	80	87		NEVER BE ANYONE ELSE BUT YOU — Ricky Nelson, Imperial 5565	16
83	—	76	88		OLD SPANISH TOWN — Bell Notes, Time 1010	5
51	58	79	89	S	BONAPARTE'S RETREAT — Billy Grammer, Monument 403	9
—	—	93	90		MARY ANN THOMAS — Bobby Freeman, Josie 863	2
—	96	92	91		STRAIGHT FLUSH — Frantics, Dolton 2	3
—	—	—	92	S	I KNOW — Perry Como, RCA Victor 7541	1
—	—	97	93		POINTED TOE SHOES — Carl Perkins, Columbia 41379	2
—	—	99	94		CHERRYSTONE — Addrisi Brothers, Del Fi 4116	2
—	—	—	95	S	LA PLUME DE MA TANTE — Hugo and Luigi, RCA Victor 7518	1
—	—	100	96		JACK O' DIAMONDS — Ruth Brown, Atlantic 2026	2
—	—	86	97	S	IT'S ONLY THE GOOD TIMES — Tommy Edwards, M-G-M 12794	2
—	—	—	98		ONE LOVE, ONE HEART — Four Coins, Epic 9314	1
—	—	—	99		FLOWER OF LOVE — The Crests, Coed 511	1
—	—	—	100		THE WHISTLING ORGAN — Dave (Baby) Cortez, Clock 1009	1

The Billboard HOT 100

FOR THE WEEK ENDING JUNE 21

★ STAR PERFORMERS showed the greatest upward progress on the Hot 100 this week.

S Indicates that STEREO SINGLE version is available.

Three Weeks Ago	Two Weeks Ago	One Week Ago	This Week	Stereo	Title, Artist, Company, Record No.	Weeks on Chart
2	1	1	1		THE BATTLE OF NEW ORLEANS — Johnny Horton, Columbia 41339	8
9	5	3	2	S	PERSONALITY — Lloyd Price, ABC-Paramount 10018	8
3	3	2	3		DREAM LOVER — Bobby Darin, Atco 6140	9
8	4	5	4	S	QUIET VILLAGE — Martin Denny, Liberty 55162	10
1	2	4	5		KANSAS CITY — Wilbert Harrison, Fury 1023	10
7	6	6	6		A TEENAGER IN LOVE — Dion and the Belmonts, Laurie 3027	9
30	15	11	7		TALLAHASSEE LASSIE — Freddy Cannon, Swan 4031	6
—	52	18	★8	S	LONELY BOY — Paul Anka, ABC-Paramount 10022	3
5	7	7	9	S	KOOKIE, KOOKIE (LEND ME YOUR COMB) — Ed Byrnes/Connie Stevens, Warner Bros. 5047	9
10	9	9	10		ONLY YOU — Frank Pourcel, Capitol 4165	11
14	12	13	11		SO FINE — Fiestas, Old Town 1062	11
4	8	8	12		SORRY, I RAN ALL THE WAY HOME — The Impalas, Cub 9022	14
61	30	15	13		ALONG CAME JONES — Coasters, Atco 6141	5
6	10	10	14		THE HAPPY ORGAN — Dave (Baby) Cortez, Clock 1009	14
41	23	17	15	S	LIPSTICK ON YOUR COLLAR — Connie Francis, M-G-M 12793	5
43	22	19	16	S	FRANKIE — Connie Francis, M-G-M 12793	5
13	13	12	17	S	ENDLESSLY — Brook Benton, Mercury 71443	9
18	11	14	18	S	GOODBYE, JIMMY, GOODBYE — Kathy Linden, Felsted 8571	10
29	17	16	19		I'M READY — Fats Domino, Imperial 5585	6
60	35	25	20	S	BOBBY SOX TO STOCKINGS — Frankie Avalon, Chancellor 1036	4
48	38	24	21	S	BONGO ROCK — Preston Epps, Original 4	5
34	32	20	22	S	JUST KEEP IT UP — Dee Clark, Abner 1026	7
56	36	23	23		CROSSFIRE — Johnny and the Hurricanes, Warwick 502	9
98	66	39	★24		WATERLOO — Stonewall Jackson, Columbia 41393	4
53	44	32	25	S	YOU'RE SO FINE — The Falcons, Unart 2013	9
55	49	26	26	S	MY MELANCHOLY BABY — Tommy Edwards, M-G-M 12794	5
47	31	31	27		MY HEART IS AN OPEN BOOK — Carl Dopkins Jr., Decca 30803	9
63	53	69	★28	S	A BOY WITHOUT A GIRL — Frankie Avalon, Chancellor 1036	4
—	60	35	29		I ONLY HAVE EYES FOR YOU — Flamingos, End 1046	3
12	14	22	30	S	TURN ME LOOSE — Fabian, Chancellor 1033	12
81	59	47	★31		HUSHABYE — Mystics, Laurie 3028	5
16	16	21	32		ENCHANTED — The Platters, Mercury 71427	13
28	24	28	33	S	LONELY FOR YOU — Gary Stites, Carlton 508	10
36	28	34	34		I'VE COME OF AGE — Billy Storm, Columbia 41356	10
—	71	37	35		LITTLE DIPPER — Mickey Mozart, Roulette 4148	4
—	87	62	★36		THIS I SWEAR — Skyliners, Calico 106	3
—	68	56	★37	S	RING-A-LING-A-LARIO — Jimmie Rodgers, Roulette 4158	3
67	47	43	38		THE WONDER OF YOU — Ray Peterson, RCA Victor 7513	5
76	65	45	39		THE CLASS — Chubby Checker, Parkway 804	5
44	33	50	★40		I WAITED TOO LONG — LaVern Baker, Atlantic 2021	9
45	51	54	★41		GIDGET — Jimmy Darren, Colpix 113	8
17	20	30	42		PINK SHOE LACES — Dodie Stevens, Crystalette 724	18
11	19	27	43		A FOOL SUCH AS I — Elvis Presley, RCA Victor 7506	13
72	64	48	44	S	GRADUATION'S HERE — Fleetwoods, Dolton 3	5
15	21	29	45	S	GUITAR BOOGIE SHUFFLE — The Virtues, Hunt 324	15
51	37	41	46		TALL COOL ONE — Wailers, Golden Crest 518	5
79	70	59	★47		ROBBIN' THE CRADLE — Tony Bellus, NRC 023	8
—	98	77	★48		THERE GOES MY BABY — The Drifters, Atlantic 2025	3
77	58	49	49	S	WHAT A DIFF'RENCE A DAY MAKES — Dinah Washington, Mercury 71435	4
19	18	33	50		TAKE A MESSAGE TO MARY — Everly Brothers, Cadence 1364	12
—	82	70	★51		MONA LISA — Carl Mann, Phillips International 3539	3
33	39	40	52	S	GUESS WHO — Jesse Belvin, RCA Victor 7469	12
46	45	53	53	S	YOU MADE ME LOVE YOU — Nat King Cole, Capitol 4184	7
69	56	51	54		MARGIE — Fats Domino, Imperial 5585	6
—	—	—	★55	S	TIGER — Fabian, Chancellor 1037	1
37	50	52	56		COME TO ME — Marv Johnson, United Artists 160	14
—	—	71	★57	S	ONLY SIXTEEN — Sam Cooke, Keen 2022	2
59	54	38	58		SO CLOSE — Brook Benton, Mercury 71443	5
20	29	46	59		I NEED YOUR LOVE TONIGHT — Elvis Presley, RCA Victor 7506	12
57	61	66	60		ROCKIN' CRICKETS — Hot Toddys, Shan-Todd 0056	8
—	—	—	★61		TWIXT TWELVE AND TWENTY — Pat Boone, Dot 15995	1
—	—	—	★62		SINCE YOU'VE BEEN GONE — Clyde McPhatter, Atlantic 2028	1
—	—	67	63	S	I'M GONNA CHANGE HIM — Cathy Carr, Roulette 4152	2
—	73	78	64	S	DANNY BOY — Sil Austin, Mercury 71442	3
—	74	79	65		VELVET WATERS — Megatrons, Acousticon 101	3
21	34	60	66	S	COME SOFTLY TO ME — Fleetwoods, Dolphin 1	15
26	41	44	67		POOR JENNY — Everly Brothers, Cadence 1364	12
71	67	64	68		A STRING OF TRUMPETS — Trumpeteers, Splash 800	8
23	25	36	69		THAT'S WHY — Jackie Wilson, Brunswick 55121	13
—	90	81	70		SWEET CHILE — Sheb Wooley, M-G-M 12781	3
89	84	68	71		THERE IS SOMETHING ON YOUR MIND — Big Jay McNeely, Swingin' 614	4
22	26	58	72		TELL HIM NO — Travis and Bob, Sandy 1017	13
35	48	63	73		SOMEONE — Johnny Mathis, Columbia 41355	13
—	—	—	★74		M.T.A. — Kingston Trio, Capitol 4221	1
94	77	76	75		I CAN'T GET YOU OUT OF MY HEART — Al Martino, 20th Fox 132	5
38	40	42	76		ALMOST GROWN — Chuck Berry, Chess 1722	12
27	43	61	77	S	TIJUANA JAIL — Kingston Trio, Capitol 4167	13
24	27	57	78	S	THREE STARS — Tommy Dee, Crest 1057	12
—	—	84	79	S	FORTY DAYS — Ronnie Hawkins, Roulette 4154	2
—	—	—	★80	S	WONDERFUL YOU — Jimmie Rodgers, Roulette 4158	1
—	—	—	★81		WITH MY EYES WIDE OPEN I'M DREAMING — Patti Page, Mercury 71469	1
—	—	98	★82		ONE LOVE, ONE HEART — Four Coins, Epic 9314	2
—	76	88	83		OLD SPANISH TOWN — Bell Notes, Time 1010	6
90	—	85	84		KANSAS CITY — Hank Ballard and the Midnighters, King 5195	6
25	46	55	85		SINCE I DON'T HAVE YOU — The Skyliners, Calico 103	18
—	—	92	86	S	I KNOW — Perry Como, RCA Victor 7541	2
—	—	99	87		FLOWER OF LOVE — The Crests, Coed 511	2
—	—	—	★88		LITTLE BOY BLUE — Huelyn Duvall, Challenge 59014	1
—	—	100	89		THE WHISTLING ORGAN — Dave (Baby) Cortez, Clock 1009	2
32	42	65	90		SIX NIGHTS A WEEK — The Crests, Coed 509	13
—	—	95	91	S	LA PLUME DE MA TANTE — Hugo and Luigi, RCA Victor 7518	2
—	—	—	92		TABOO — Arthur Lyman, Hi-Fi 550	1
—	—	—	93	S	A PRAYER AND A JUKE BOX — Little Anthony, End 1047	1
—	86	97	94	S	IT'S ONLY THE GOOD TIMES — Tommy Edwards, M-G-M 12794	3
87	—	—	95		THE BATTLE OF NEW ORLEANS — Vaughn Monroe, RCA Victor 7495	2
—	—	—	96		FORTY MILES OF BAD ROAD — Duane Eddy, Jamie 11260	1
—	—	—	97		SMALL WORLD — Johnny Mathis, Columbia 41410	1
—	—	—	98		HIGH HOPES — Frank Sinatra, Capitol 4214	1
—	—	—	99		WITH MY EYES WIDE OPEN, I'M DREAMING — Enoch Light, Grand Award 1032	1
—	—	—	100		CAP AND GOWN — Marty Robbins, Columbia 41408	1

The Billboard HOT 100

FOR THE WEEK ENDING JUNE 28

★ STAR PERFORMERS showed the greatest upward progress on the Hot 100 this week.

S Indicates that STEREO SINGLE version is available.

Three Weeks Ago	Two Weeks Ago	One Week Ago	This Week	Stereo	Title, Artist, Company, Record No.	Weeks on Chart
1	1	1	1		THE BATTLE OF NEW ORLEANS — Johnny Horton, Columbia 41339	9
5	3	2	2	S	PERSONALITY — Lloyd Price, ABC-Paramount 10018	9
3	2	3	3		DREAM LOVER — Bobby Darin, Atco 6140	10
52	18	8	4	S	LONELY BOY — Paul Anka, ABC-Paramount 10022	4
2	4	5	5		KANSAS CITY — Wilbert Harrison, Fury 1023	11
4	5	4	6	S	QUIET VILLAGE — Martin Denny, Liberty 55162	11
15	11	7	7		TALLAHASSEE LASSIE — Freddy Cannon, Swan 4031	7
6	6	6	8		A TEENAGER IN LOVE — Dion and the Belmonts, Laurie 3027	10
30	15	13	9		ALONG CAME JONES — Coasters, Atco 6141	6
23	17	15	10	S	LIPSTICK ON YOUR COLLAR — Connie Francis, M-G-M 12793	6
22	19	16	11	S	FRANKIE — Connie Francis, M-G-M 12793	6
9	9	10	12		ONLY YOU — Frank Pourcel, Capitol 4165	12
35	25	20	13	S	BOBBY SOX TO STOCKINGS — Frankie Avalon, Chancellor 1036	5
7	7	9	14	S	KOOKIE, KOOKIE (LEND ME YOUR COMB) — Ed Byrnes/Connei Stevens, Warner Bros. 5047	10
12	13	11	15		SO FINE — Fiestas, Old Town 1062	12
38	24	21	16	S	BONGO ROCK — Preston Epps, Original 4	6
66	39	24	17		WATERLOO — Stonewall Jackson, Columbia 41393	5
17	16	19	18		I'M READY — Fats Domino, Imperial 5585	7
60	35	29	★19	S	I ONLY HAVE EYES FOR YOU — Flamingos, End 1046	4
8	8	12	20		SORRY, I RAN ALL THE WAY HOME — The Impalas, Cub 9022	15
53	69	28	21	S	A BOY WITHOUT A GIRL — Frankie Avalon, Chancellor 1036	5
32	20	22	22	S	JUST KEEP IT UP — Dee Clark, Abner 1026	8
13	12	17	23	S	ENDLESSLY — Brook Benton, Mercury 71443	10
36	23	23	24		CROSSFIRE — Johnny and the Hurricanes, Warwick 502	10
10	10	14	25		THE HAPPY ORGAN — Dave (Baby) Cortez, Clock 1009	15
31	31	27	26		MY HEART IS AN OPEN BOOK — Carl Dopkins Jr., Decca 30803	10
11	14	18	27	S	GOODBYE, JIMMY, GOODBYE — Kathy Linden, Felsted 8571	11
47	43	38	★28		THE WONDER OF YOU — Ray Peterson, RCA Victor 7513	6
49	26	26	29	S	MY MELANCHOLY BABY — Tommy Edwards, M-G-M 12794	6
87	62	36	30		THIS I SWEAR — Skyliners, Calico 106	4
44	32	25	31	S	YOU'RE SO FINE — The Falcons, Unart 2013	10
71	37	35	32		LITTLE DIPPER — Mickey Mozart, Roulette 4148	5
59	47	31	33		HUSHABYE — Mystics, Laurie 3028	6
—	—	55	★34	S	TIGER — Fabian, Chancellor 1037	2
68	56	37	35	S	RING-A-LING-A-LARIO — Jimmie Rodgers, Roulette 4158	4
37	41	46	★36		TALL COOL ONE — Wailers, Golden Crest 518	6
28	34	34	37		I'VE COME OF AGE — Billy Storm, Columbia 41356	11
65	45	39	38		THE CLASS — Chubby Checker, Parkway 804	6
64	48	44	39	S	GRADUATION'S HERE — Fleetwoods, Dolton 3	6
58	49	49	40	S	WHAT A DIFF'RENCE A DAY MAKES — Dinah Washington, Mercury 71435	5
98	77	48	41		THERE GOES MY BABY — The Drifters, Atlantic 2025	4
33	50	40	42		I WAITED TOO LONG — LaVern Baker, Atlantic 2021	10
70	59	47	43		ROBBIN' THE CRADLE — Tony Bellus, NRC 023	9
24	28	33	44	S	LONELY FOR YOU — Gary Stites, Carlton 508	11
16	21	32	45		ENCHANTED — The Platters, Mercury 71427	14
82	70	51	46		MONA LISA — Carl Mann, Phillips International 3539	4
14	22	30	47	S	TURN ME LOOSE — Fabian, Chancellor 1033	13
51	54	41	48		GIDGET — Jimmy Darren, Colpix 113	9
—	—	74	★49		M.T.A. — Kingston Trio, Capitol 4221	2
—	—	96	★50		FORTY MILES OF BAD ROAD — Duane Eddy, Jamie 11260	2
—	71	57	51	S	ONLY SIXTEEN — Sam Cooke, Keen 2022	3
56	51	54	52		MARGIE — Fats Domino, Imperial 5585	7
77	76	75	★53		I CAN'T GET YOU OUT OF MY HEART — Al Martino, 20th Fox 132	6
—	—	61	54	S	TWIXT TWELVE AND TWENTY — Pat Boone, Dot 15995	2
—	—	62	55		SINCE YOU'VE BEEN GONE — Clyde McPhatter, Atlantic 2028	2
—	—	—	★56		BACK IN THE U.S.A. — Chuck Berry, Chess 1729	1
74	79	65	57		VELVET WATERS — Megatrons, Acousticon 101	4
45	53	53	58	S	YOU MADE ME LOVE YOU — Nat King Cole, Capitol 4184	8
73	78	64	59	S	DANNY BOY — Sil Austin, Mercury 71442	4
—	—	—	★60		LAVENDER BLUE — Sammy Turner, Big Top 3016	1
61	66	60	61		ROCKIN' CRICKETS — Hot Toddys, Shan-Todd 0056	9
—	—	80	★62	S	WONDERFUL YOU — Jimmie Rodgers, Roulette 4158	2
—	—	—	★63		I'LL BE SATISFIED — Jackie Wilson, Brunswick 55136	1
—	84	79	★64	S	FORTY DAYS — Ronnie Hawkins, Roulette 4154	3
—	67	63	65	S	I'M GONNA CHANGE HIM — Cathy Carr, Roulette 4152	3
21	29	45	66	S	GUITAR BOOGIE SHUFFLE — The Virtues, Hunt 324	16
—	—	92	★67		TABOO — Arthur Lymon, Hi-Fi 550	2
—	—	—	★68		REMEMBER WHEN — Platters, Mercury 71467	1
39	40	52	69	S	GUESS WHO — Jesse Belvin, RCA Victor 7469	13
—	—	81	70		WITH MY EYES WIDE OPEN I'M DREAMING — Patti Page, Mercury 71469	2
19	27	43	71		A FOOL SUCH AS I — Elvis Presley, RCA Victor 7506	14
67	44	68	72		A STRING OF TRUMPETS — Trumpeteers, Splash 800	9
54	38	58	73		SO CLOSE — Brook Benton, Mercury 71443	6
—	92	86	74	S	I KNOW — Perry Como, RCA Victor 7541	3
90	81	70	75		SWEET CHILE — Sheb Wooley, M-G-M 12781	4
29	46	59	76		I NEED YOUR LOVE TONIGHT — Elvis Presley, RCA Victor 7506	13
—	100	89	77		THE WHISTLING ORGAN — Dave (Baby) Cortez, Clock 1009	3
—	—	100	★78		CAP AND GOWN — Marty Robbins, Columbia 41408	1
84	68	71	79		THERE IS SOMETHING ON YOUR MIND — Big Jay McNeely, Swingin' 614	5
50	52	56	80		COME TO ME — Marv Johnson, United Artists 160	15
—	99	87	81		FLOWER OF LOVE — The Crests, Coed 511	3
—	—	—	★82		GOTTA NEW GIRL — Bobby Day, Class 252	1
96	—	—	★83		LIKE YOUNG — Andre Previn & David Rose, M-G-M 12793	2
—	—	—	★84		I LOVE AN ANGEL — Little Bill & the Bluenotes, Dolton 4	1
99	94	—	★85		CHERRYSTONE — Addrisi Brothers, Del Fi 4116	3
69	74	—	86		I MUST BE DREAMING — Nat King Cole, Capitol 4184	4
40	42	76	87		ALMOST GROWN — Chuck Berry, Chess 1722	13
—	—	97	88		SMALL WORLD — Johnny Mathis, Columbia 41410	2
—	85	84	89		KANSAS CITY — Hank Ballard and the Midnighters, King 5195	7
—	—	93	90	S	A PRAYER AND A JUKE BOX — Little Anthony and the Imperials, End 1047	2
18	33	50	91		TAKE A MESSAGE TO MARY — Everly Brothers, Cadence 1364	13
—	—	98	92		HIGH HOPES — Frank Sinatra, Capitol 4214	2
—	—	88	93		LITTLE BOY BLUE — Huelyn Duvall, Challenge 59014	2
20	30	42	94		PINK SHOE LACES — Dodie Stevens, Crystalette 724	19
—	95	91	95	S	LA PLUME DE MA TANTE — Hugo and Luigi, RCA Victor 7518	3
34	60	66	96	S	COME SOFTLY TO ME — Fleetwoods, Dolphin 1	16
—	—	—	97		CIAO CIAO BAMBINA — Jackie Noguez, Jamie 1127	1
—	—	—	98		IT WAS I — Skip & Flip, Brent 7002	1
46	55	85	99		SINCE I DON'T HAVE YOU — The Skyliners, Calico 103	19
—	—	—	100		OH WHAT A FOOL — The Impalas, Cub 9033	1

FOR THE WEEK ENDING JULY 5

The Billboard HOT 100

★ STAR PERFORMERS showed the greatest upward progress on the Hot 100 this week.

S Indicates that STEREO SINGLE version is available.

Three Weeks Ago	Two Weeks Ago	One Week Ago	This Week	Stereo	Title, Artist, Company, Record No.	Weeks on Chart
1	1	1	1		THE BATTLE OF NEW ORLEANS — Johnny Horton, Columbia 41339	10
3	2	2	2	S	PERSONALITY — Lloyd Price, ABC-Paramount 10018	10
18	8	4	3	S	LONELY BOY — Paul Anka, ABC-Paramount 10022	5
2	3	3	4		DREAM LOVER — Bobby Darin, Atco 6140	11
17	15	10	5	S	LIPSTICK ON YOUR COLLAR — Connie Francis, M-G-M 12793	7
11	7	7	6		TALLAHASSEE LASSIE — Freddy Cannon, Swan 4031	8
4	5	5	7		KANSAS CITY — Wilbert Harrison, Fury 1023	12
5	4	6	8	S	QUIET VILLAGE — Martin Denny, Liberty 55162	12
15	13	9	9		ALONG CAME JONES — Coasters, Atco 6141	7
6	6	8	10		A TEENAGER IN LOVE — Dion and the Belmonts, Laurie 3027	11
19	16	11	11	S	FRANKIE — Connie Francis, M-G-M 12793	7
39	24	17	12		WATERLOO — Stonewall Jackson, Columbia 41393	6
25	20	13	13	S	BOBBY SOX TO STOCKINGS — Frankie Avalon, Chancellor 1036	6
24	21	16	14	S	BONGO ROCK — Preston Epps, Original 4	7
35	29	19	15	S	I ONLY HAVE EYES FOR YOU — Flamingos, End 1046	5
69	28	21	16	S	A BOY WITHOUT A GIRL — Frankie Avalon, Chancellor 1036	6
31	27	26	17		MY HEART IS AN OPEN BOOK — Carl Dopkins Jr., Decca 30803	11
20	22	22	18	S	JUST KEEP IT UP — Dee Clark, Abner 1026	9
—	55	34	19 ★	S	TIGER — Fabian, Chancellor 1037	3
47	31	33	20 ★	S	HUSHABYE — Mystics, Laurie 3028	7
32	25	31	21 ★	S	YOU'RE SO FINE — The Falcons, Unart 2013	11
13	11	15	22		SO FINE — Fiestas, Old Town 1062	13
9	10	12	23		ONLY YOU — Frank Pourcel, Capitol 4165	13
7	9	14	24	S	KOOKIE, KOOKIE (LEND ME YOUR COMB) — Ed Byrnes/Connie Stevens, Warner Bros. 5047	11
43	38	28	25		THE WONDER OF YOU — Ray Peterson, RCA Victor 7513	7
49	49	40	26 ★	S	WHAT A DIFF'RENCE A DAY MAKES — Dinah Washington, Mercury 71435	6
62	36	30	27		THIS I SWEAR — Skyliners, Calico 106	5
—	74	49	28 ★		M.T.A. — Kingston Trio, Capitol 4221	3
16	19	18	29		I'M READY — Fats Domino, Imperial 5585	8
23	23	24	30		CROSSFIRE — Johnny and the Hurricanes, Warwick 502	11
—	96	50	31 ★		FORTY MILES OF BAD ROAD — Duane Eddy, Jamie 11260	3
56	37	35	32	S	RING-A-LING-A-LARIO — Jimmie Rodgers, Roulette 4158	5
37	35	32	33		LITTLE DIPPER — Mickey Mozart, Roulette 4148	6
77	48	41	34		THERE GOES MY BABY — The Drifters, Atlantic 2025	5
—	61	54	35 ★	S	TWIXT TWELVE AND TWENTY — Pat Boone, Dot 15995	3
14	18	27	36	S	GOODBYE, JIMMY, GOODBYE — Kathy Linden, Felsted 8571	12
26	26	29	37	S	MY MELANCHOLY BABY — Tommy Edwards, M-G-M 12794	7
10	14	25	38		THE HAPPY ORGAN — Dave (Baby) Cortez, Clock 1009	16
59	47	43	39		ROBBIN' THE CRADLE — Tony Bellus, NRC 023	10
12	17	23	40	S	ENDLESSLY — Brook Benton, Mercury 71443	11
8	12	20	41		SORRY, I RAN ALL THE WAY HOME — The Impalas, Cub 9022	16
71	57	51	42	S	ONLY SIXTEEN — Sam Cooke, Keen 2022	4
34	34	37	43		I'VE COME OF AGE — Billy Storm, Columbia 41356	12
76	75	53	44	S	I CAN'T GET YOU OUT OF MY HEART — Al Martino, 20th Fox 132	7
84	79	64	45 ★	S	FORTY DAYS — Ronnie Hawkins, Roulette 4154	4
—	80	62	46	S	WONDERFUL YOU — Jimmie Rodgers, Roulette 4158	3
28	33	44	47	S	LONELY FOR YOU — Gary Stites, Carlton 508	12
—	—	63	48		I'LL BE SATISFIED — Jackie Wilson, Brunswick 55136	2
—	—	60	49 ★		LAVENDER BLUE — Sammy Turner, Big Top 3016	2
70	51	46	50		MONA LISA — Carl Mann, Phillips International 3539	5
79	65	57	51		VELVET WATERS — Megatrons, Acousticon 101	5
—	—	56	52		BACK IN THE U.S.A. — Chuck Berry, Chess 1729	2
—	62	55	53		SINCE YOU'VE BEEN GONE — Clyde McPhatter, Atlantic 2028	3
54	41	48	54		GIDGET — Jimmy Darren, Colpix 113	10
—	—	83	55 ★		LIKE YOUNG — Andre Previn & David Rose, M-G-M 12793	3
41	46	36	56		TALL COOL ONE — Wailers, Golden Crest 518	7
48	44	39	57	S	GRADUATION'S HERE — Fleetwoods, Dolton 3	7
—	—	68	58 ★		REMEMBER WHEN — Platters, Mercury 71467	2
—	92	67	59		TABOO — Arthur Lymon, Hi-Fi 550	3
92	86	74	60 ★	S	I KNOW — Perry Como, RCA Victor 7541	4
45	39	38	61		THE CLASS — Chubby Checker, Parkway 804	7
100	89	77	62 ★		THE WHISTLING ORGAN — Dave (Baby) Cortez, Clock 1009	4
—	—	—	63 ★		JUST A LITTLE TOO MUCH — Ricky Nelson, Imperial 5595	1
—	81	70	64		WITH MY EYES WIDE OPEN I'M DREAMING — Patti Page, Mercury 71469	3
50	40	42	65		I WAITED TOO LONG — LaVern Baker, Atlantic 2021	11
—	97	88	66 ★		SMALL WORLD — Johnny Mathis, Columbia 41410	3
—	—	—	67 ★		QUIET THREE — Duane Eddy, Jamie 1126	1
—	98	92	68 ★		HIGH HOPES — Frank Sinatra, Capitol 4214	3
66	60	61	69		ROCKIN' CRICKETS — Hot Toddys, Shan-Todd 0056	10
—	—	98	70 ★		IT WAS I — Skip & Flip, Brent 7002	2
—	—	84	71		I LOVE AN ANGEL — Little Bill & the Bluenotes, Dolton 4	2
68	71	79	72		THERE IS SOMETHING ON YOUR MIND — Big Jay McNeely, Swingin' 614	6
38	58	73	73		SO CLOSE — Brook Benton, Mercury 71443	7
—	100	78	74		CAP AND GOWN — Marty Robbins, Columbia 41408	3
51	54	52	75		MARGIE — Fats Domino, Imperial 5585	8
—	—	97	76 ★		CIAO CIAO BAMBINA — Jacky Noguez, Jamie 1127	2
67	63	65	77	S	I'M GONNA CHANGE HIM — Cathy Carr, Roulette 4152	4
94	—	85	78		CHERRYSTONE — Addrisi Brothers, Del Fi 4116	4
—	—	—	79 ★		YES-SIR-EE — Dodie Stevens, Crystalette 728	2
99	87	81	80		FLOWER OF LOVE — The Crests, Coed 511	4
—	93	90	81	S	A PRAYER AND A JUKE BOX — Little Anthony and the Imperials, End 1047	3
21	32	45	82		ENCHANTED — The Platters, Mercury 71427	15
78	64	59	83	S	DANNY BOY — Sil Austin, Mercury 71442	5
81	70	75	84		SWEET CHILE — Sheb Wooley, M-G-M 12781	5
—	—	—	85 ★	S	TILL THERE WAS YOU — Anita Bryant, Carlton 512	1
98	82	—	86		ONE LOVE, ONE HEART — Four Coins, Epic 9314	3
—	—	—	87 ★		SWEET SOMEONE — Eddie & Betty Cole, Warner Bros. 5054	1
95	91	95	88	S	LA PLUME DE MA TANTE — Hugo and Luigi, RCA Victor 7518	4
—	—	—	89 ★		FIVE PENNIES — Dodie Stevens, Crystalette 728	1
—	—	—	90 ★		SEE YOU IN SEPTEMBER — The Tempos, Climax 102	1
—	88	93	91		LITTLE BOY BLUE — Huelyn Duvall, Challenge 59014	3
88	83	—	92		OLD SPANISH TOWN — Bell Notes, Time 1010	7
—	—	—	93		KISSIN' TIME — Bobby Rydell, Cameo 160	1
—	—	—	94		BEACH TIME — Roger Smith, Warner Bros 5068	1
27	43	71	95		A FOOL SUCH AS I — Elvis Presley, RCA Victor 7506	15
—	—	100	96		OH WHAT A FOOL — The Impalas, Cub 9033	2
53	53	58	97	S	YOU MADE ME LOVE YOU — Nat King Cole, Capitol 4184	9
—	—	—	98		HERE COMES SUMMER — Jerry Keller, Kapp 277	1
—	—	—	99		HAPPY VACATION — Jackie Lee, Swan 4034	1
—	—	—	100	S	THE WAY I WALK — Jack Scott, Carlton 514	1

FOR THE WEEK ENDING JULY 12 — The Billboard HOT 100

★ STAR PERFORMERS showed the greatest upward progress on the Hot 100 this week.

S Indicates that STEREO SINGLE version is available.

Three Weeks Ago	Two Weeks Ago	One Week Ago	This Week	Stereo	Title, Artist, Company, Record No.	Weeks on Chart
1	1	1	1		THE BATTLE OF NEW ORLEANS — Johnny Horton, Columbia 41339	11
8	4	3	2	S	LONELY BOY — Paul Anka, ABC-Paramount 10022	6
2	2	2	3	S	PERSONALITY — Lloyd Price, ABC-Paramount 10018	11
3	3	4	4		DREAM LOVER — Bobby Darin, Atco 6140	12
15	10	5	5	S	LIPSTICK ON YOUR COLLAR — Connie Francis, M-G-M 12793	8
24	17	12	6		WATERLOO — Stonewall Jackson, Columbia 41393	7
7	7	6	7		TALLAHASSE LASSIE — Freddy Cannon, Swan 4031	9
20	13	13	8	S	BOBBY SOX TO STOCKINGS — Frankie Avalon, Chancellor 1036	7
16	11	11	9	S	FRANKIE — Connie Francis, M-G-M 12793	8
55	34	19	10	S	TIGER — Fabian, Chancellor 1037	4
13	9	9	11		ALONG CAME JONES — Coasters, Atco 6141	8
28	21	16	12	S	A BOY WITHOUT A GIRL — Frankie Avalon, Chancellor 1036	7
27	26	17	13		MY HEART IS AN OPEN BOOK — Carl Dobkins Jr., Decca 30803	11
4	6	8	14	S	QUIET VILLAGE — Martin Denny, Liberty 55162	13
21	16	14	15	S	BONGO ROCK — Preston Epps, Original 4	8
29	19	15	16	S	I ONLY HAVE EYES FOR YOU — Flamingos, End 1046	6
5	5	7	17		KANSAS CITY — Wilbert Harrison, Fury 1023	13
74	49	28	18		M.T.A. — Kingston Trio, Capitol 4221	4
6	8	10	19		A TEENAGER IN LOVE — Dion and the Belmonts, Laurie 3027	12
25	31	21	20	S	YOU'RE SO FINE — The Falcons, Unart 2013	12
22	22	18	21	S	JUST KEEP IT UP — Dee Clark, Abner 1026	10
31	33	20	22	S	HUSHABYE — Mystics, Laurie 3028	8
96	50	31	23		FORTY MILES OF BAD ROAD — Duane Eddy, Jamie 11260	4
1	54	35	★ 24	S	TWIXT TWELVE AND TWENTY — Pat Boone, Dot 15995	4
9	40	26	25	S	WHAT A DIFF'RENCE A DAY MAKES — Dinah Washington, Mercury 71435	7
6	30	27	26		THIS I SWEAR — Skyliners, Calico 106	6
8	28	25	27		THE WONDER OF YOU — Ray Peterson, RCA Victor 7513	8
8	41	34	28		THERE GOES MY BABY — The Drifters, Atlantic 2025	6
1	15	22	29		SO FINE — Fiestas, Old Town 1062	14
5	32	33	30		LITTLE DIPPER — Mickey Mozart, Roulette 4148	7
-	60	49	★ 31	S	LAVENDER BLUE — Sammy Turner, Big Top 3016	3
7	51	42	★ 32	S	ONLY SIXTEEN — Sam Cooke, Keen 2022	5
-	63	48	★ 33		I'LL BE SATISFIED — Jackie Wilson, Brunswick 55136	3
47	43	39	34		ROBBIN' THE CRADLE — Tony Bellus, NRC 023	11
10	12	23	35		ONLY YOU — Frank Pourcel, Capitol 4165	14
23	24	30	36		CROSSFIRE — Johnny and the Hurricanes, Warwick 502	12
37	35	32	37	S	RING-A-LING-A-LARIO — Jimmie Rodgers, Roulette 4158	6
9	14	24	38	S	KOOKIE, KOOKIE (LEND ME YOUR COMB) — Ed Byrnes/Connie Stevens, Warner Bros. 5047	12
19	18	29	39		I'M READY — Fats Domino, Imperial 5585	9
80	62	46	40	S	WONDERFUL YOU — Jimmie Rodgers, Roulette 4158	4
—	56	52	★ 41		BACK IN THE U.S.A. — Chuck Berry, Chess 1729	3
—	—	63	★ 42		JUST A LITTLE TOO MUCH — Ricky Nelson, Imperial 5595	2
—	—	—	★ 43		A BIG HUNK O' LOVE — Elvis Presley, RCA Victor 7600	1
34	37	43	44		I'VE COME OF AGE — Billy Storm, Columbia 41356	13
100	78	74	★ 45		CAP AND GOWN — Marty Robbins, Columbia 41408	4
75	53	44	46	S	I CAN'T GET YOU OUT OF MY HEART — Al Martino, 20th Fox 132	8
—	—	67	★ 47		QUIET THREE — Duane Eddy, Jamie 1126	4
46	36	56	48		TALL COOL ONE — Wailers, Golden Crest 518	8
—	68	58	49	S	REMEMBER WHEN — Platters, Mercury 71467	3
51	46	50	50		MONA LISA — Carl Mann, Phillips International 3539	6
—	83	55	51	S	LIKE YOUNG — Andre Previn & David Rose, M-G-M 12793	4
17	23	40	52	S	ENDLESSLY — Brook Benton, Mercury 71443	12
—	—	—	53		SWEETER THAN YOU — Ricky Nelson, Imperial 5595	1
33	44	47	54	S	LONELY FOR YOU — Gary Stites, Carlton 508	13
92	67	59	55		TABOO — Arthur Lymon, Hi-Fi 550	4
79	64	45	56	S	FORTY DAYS — Ronnie Hawkins, Roulette 4154	5
86	74	60	57	S	I KNOW — Perry Como, RCA Victor 7541	5
97	88	66	58		SMALL WORLD — Johnny Mathis, Columbia 41410	4
62	55	53	59		SINCE YOU'VE BEEN GONE — Clyde McPhatter, Atlantic 2028	4
81	70	64	60		WITH MY EYES WIDE OPEN I'M DREAMING — Patti Page, Mercury 71469	4
89	77	62	61		THE WHISTLING ORGAN — Dave (Baby) Cortez, Clock 1009	5
—	85	78	★ 62		CHERRYSTONE — Addrisi Brothers, Del Fi 4116	5
65	57	51	63		VELVET WATERS — Megatrons, Acousticon 101	6
71	79	72	64		THERE IS SOMETHING ON YOUR MIND — Big Jay McNeely, Swingin' 614	7
—	—	—	★ 65		RAGTIME COWBOY JOE — David Seville and the Chipmunks, Liberty 55200	1
—	84	71	66		I LOVE AN ANGEL — Little Bill & the Bluenotes, Dolton 4	3
26	29	37	67	S	MY MELANCHOLY BABY — Tommy Edwards, M-G-M 12794	8
98	92	68	68		HIGH HOPES — Frank Sinatra, Capitol 4214	4
—	—	98	★ 69		HERE COMES SUMMER — Jerry Keller, Kapp 277	2
14	25	38	70		THE HAPPY ORGAN — Dave (Baby) Cortez, Clock 1009	17
12	20	41	71		SORRY, I RAN ALL THE WAY HOME — The Impalas, Cub 9022	17
—	97	76	72		CIAO CIAO BAMBINA — Jacky Noguez, Jamie 1127	3
18	27	36	73	S	GOODBYE, JIMMY, GOODBYE — Kathy Linden, Felsted 8571	13
—	98	70	74		IT WAS I — Skip & Flip, Brent 7002	3
—	—	85	75	S	TILL THERE WAS YOU — Anita Bryant, Carlton 512	2
70	75	84	76	S	SWEET CHILE — Sheb Wooley, M-G-M 12781	6
—	—	100	★ 77	S	THE WAY I WALK — Jack Scott, Carlton 514	2
—	—	—	★ 78		BEI MIR BIST DU SCHOEN — Louis Prima and Keely Smith, Dot 15956	1
87	81	80	79		FLOWER OF LOVE — The Crests, Coed 511	5
64	59	83	80	S	DANNY BOY — Sil Austin, Mercury 71442	6
41	48	54	81		GIDGET — Jimmy Darren, Colpix 113	11
—	—	—	★ 82		WHAT'D I SAY — Ray Charles, Atlantic 2031	1
82	—	86	83		ONE LOVE, ONE HEART — Four Coins, Epic 9314	4
—	—	—	★ 84		TEN THOUSAND DRUMS — Carl Smith, Columbia 41417	1
—	—	—	★ 85		SEA OF LOVE — Phil Phillips, Mercury 71465	1
91	95	88	86	S	LA PLUME DE MA TANTE — Hugo and Luigi, RCA Victor 7518	5
—	—	87	87		SWEET SOMEONE — Eddie & Betty Cole, Warner Bros. 5054	2
—	—	79	88		YES-SIR-EE — Dodie Stevens, Crystalette 728	2
—	—	—	★ 89	S	WHAT IS LOVE — Playmates, Roulette 4160	1
—	—	90	90		SEE YOU IN SEPTEMBER — The Tempos, Climax 102	2
—	—	93	91		KISSIN' TIME — Bobby Rydell, Cameo 160	2
—	100	96	92		OH WHAT A FOOL — The Impalas, Cub 9033	3
—	—	94	93		BEACH TIME — Roger Smith, Warner Bros. 5068	2
44	39	57	94	S	GRADUATION'S HERE — Fleetwoods, Dolton 3	8
—	—	99	95		HAPPY VACATION — Jackie Lee, Swan 4034	2
—	—	—	96		LONELY GUITAR — Annette, Vista 339	1
—	—	—	97		SWEET SUGAR LIPS — Kalin Twins, Decca 30911	1
—	—	—	98		CRACKIN' UP — Bo Diddley, Checker 924	1
93	90	81	99	S	A PRAYER AND A JUKE BOX — Little Anthony and the Imperials, End 1047	4
60	61	69	100		ROCKIN' CRICKETS — Hot Toddys, Shan-Todd 0056	11

FOR THE WEEK ENDING JULY 19

The Billboard HOT 100

★ STAR PERFORMERS showed the greatest upward progress on the Hot 100 this week.

S Indicates that STEREO SINGLE version is available.

THREE WEEKS AGO	TWO WEEKS AGO	ONE WEEK AGO	THIS WEEK	STEREO	TITLE	Artist, Company, Record No.	WEEKS ON CHART
4	3	2	1	S	LONELY BOY	Paul Anka, ABC-Paramount 10022	7
1	1	1	2		THE BATTLE OF NEW ORLEANS	Johnny Horton, Columbia 41339	12
2	2	3	3	S	PERSONALITY	Lloyd Price, ABC-Paramount 10018	12
17	12	6	4		WATERLOO	Stonewall Jackson, Columbia 41393	8
10	5	5	5	S	LIPSTICK ON YOUR COLLAR	Connie Francis, M-G-M 12793	9
34	19	10	6	S	TIGER	Fabian, Chancellor 1037	5
3	4	4	7		DREAM LOVER	Bobby Darin, Atco 6140	13
7	6	7	8		TALLAHASSEE LASSIE	Freddy Cannon, Swan 4031	10
26	17	13	9		MY HEART IS AN OPEN BOOK	Carl Dobkins Jr., Decca 30803	12
21	16	12	10	S	A BOY WITHOUT A GIRL	Frankie Avalon, Chancellor 1036	8
19	15	16	11	S	I ONLY HAVE EYES FOR YOU	Flamingos, End 1046	7
13	13	8	12	S	BOBBY SOX TO STOCKINGS	Frankie Avalon, Chancellor 1036	8
50	31	23	★13		FORTY MILES OF BAD ROAD	Duane Eddy, Jamie 1126	5
11	11	9	14	S	FRANKIE	Connie Francis, M-G-M 12793	9
49	28	18	15		M.T.A.	Kingston Trio, Capitol 4221	5
9	9	11	16		ALONG CAME JONES	Coasters, Atco 6141	9
31	21	20	17	S	YOU'RE SO FINE	The Falcons, Unart 2013	13
54	35	24	18	S	TWIXT TWELVE AND TWENTY	Pat Boone, Dot 15995	5
16	14	15	19	S	BONGO ROCK	Preston Epps, Original 4	9
41	34	28	20		THERE GOES MY BABY	The Drifters, Atlantic 2025	7
6	8	14	21	S	QUIET VILLAGE	Martin Denny, Liberty 55162	14
22	18	21	22	S	JUST KEEP IT UP	Dee Clark, Abner 1026	11
40	26	25	23	S	WHAT A DIFF'RENCE A DAY MAKES	Dinah Washington, Mercury 71435	8
—	—	53	★24		SWEETER THAN YOU	Ricky Nelson, Imperial 5595	2
—	—	43	★25		A BIG HUNK O' LOVE	Elvis Presley, RCA Victor 7600	2
60	49	31	26	S	LAVENDER BLUE	Sammy Turner, Big Top 3016	4
33	20	22	27	S	HUSHABYE	Mystics, Laurie 3028	9
51	42	32	28	S	ONLY SIXTEEN	Sam Cooke, Keen 2022	6
5	7	17	29		KANSAS CITY	Wilbert Harrison, Fury 1023	14
30	27	26	30		THIS I SWEAR	Skyliners, Calico 106	7
28	25	27	31		THE WONDER OF YOU	Ray Peterson, RCA Victor 7513	9
—	63	42	★32		JUST A LITTLE TOO MUCH	Ricky Nelson, Imperial 5595	3
8	10	19	33		A TEENAGER IN LOVE	Dion and the Belmonts, Laurie 3027	13
43	39	34	34		ROBBIN' THE CRADLE	Tony Bellus, NRC 023	12
63	48	33	35		I'LL BE SATISFIED	Jackie Wilson, Brunswick 55136	4
—	—	65	★36		RAGTIME COWBOY JOE	David Seville and the Chipmunks, Liberty 55200	2
56	52	41	37		BACK IN THE U.S.A.	Chuck Berry, Chess 1729	4
32	33	30	38		LITTLE DIPPER	Mickey Mozart, Roulette 4148	8
—	—	—	★39		MY WISH CAME TRUE	Elvis Presley, RCA Victor 7600	1
55	53	59	★40		SINCE YOU'VE BEEN GONE	Clyde McPhatter, Atlantic 2028	5
46	50	50	41		MONA LISA	Carl Mann, Phillips International 3539	7
68	58	49	42	S	REMEMBER WHEN	Platters, Mercury 71467	4
—	—	82	★43		WHAT'D I SAY	Ray Charles, Atlantic 2031	2
79	72	64	★44		THERE IS SOMETHING ON YOUR MIND	Big Jay McNeely, Swingin' 614	8
15	22	29	45		SO FINE	Fiestas, Old Town 1062	15
—	98	69	★46		HERE COMES SUMMER	Jerry Keller, Kapp 277	3
74	60	57	★47	S	I KNOW	Perry Como, RCA Victor 7541	6
—	—	85	★48		SEA OF LOVE	Phil Phillips, Mercury 71465	2
97	76	72	★49		CIAO CIAO BAMBINA	Jacky Noguez, Jamie 1127	4
12	23	35	50		ONLY YOU	Frank Pourcel, Capitol 4165	15
83	55	51	51	S	LIKE YOUNG	Andre Previn & David Rose, M-G-M 12792	5
35	32	37	52	S	RING-A-LING-A-LARIO	Jimmie Rodgers, Roulette 4158	7
64	45	56	53	S	FORTY DAYS	Ronnie Hawkins, Roulette 4154	6
88	66	58	54		SMALL WORLD	Johnny Mathis, Columbia 41410	5
—	67	47	55		QUIET THREE	Duane Eddy, Jamie 1126	5
92	68	68	★56		HIGH HOPES	Frank Sinatra, Capitol 4214	5
24	30	36	57		CROSSFIRE	Johnny and the Hurricanes, Warwick 502	13
62	46	40	58	S	WONDERFUL YOU	Jimmie Rodgers, Roulette 4158	5
70	64	60	59		WITH MY EYES WIDE OPEN I'M DREAMING	Patti Page, Mercury 71469	5
53	44	46	60	S	I CAN'T GET YOU OUT OF MY HEART	Al Martino, 20th Fox 132	9
18	29	39	61		I'M READY	Fats Domino, Imperial 5585	10
—	100	77	★62	S	THE WAY I WALK	Jack Scott, Carlton 514	3
36	56	48	63		TALL COOL ONE	Wailers, Golden Crest 518	9
67	59	55	64		TABOO	Arthur Lyman, Hi-Fi 550	5
—	85	75	65	S	TILL THERE WAS YOU	Anita Bryant, Carlton 512	3
78	74	45	66		CAP AND GOWN	Marty Robbins, Columbia 41408	5
—	—	89	★67	S	WHAT IS LOVE	Playmates, Roulette 4160	2
57	51	63	68		VELVET WATERS	Megatrons, Acousticon 101	7
98	70	74	69		IT WAS I	Skip & Flip, Brent 7002	4
84	71	66	70		I LOVE AN ANGEL	Little Bill & the Bluenotes, Dolton 4	4
—	—	78	71		BEI MIR BIST DU SCHOEN	Louis Prima and Keely Smith, Dot 15956	2
77	62	61	72		THE WHISTLING ORGAN	Dave (Baby) Cortez, Clock 1012	6
85	78	62	73		CHERRYSTONE	Addrisi Brothers, Del Fi 4116	6
37	43	44	74		I'VE COME OF AGE	Billy Storm, Columbia 41356	14
48	54	81	75		GIDGET	Jimmy Darren, Colpix 113	12
—	—	—	★76		THANK YOU PRETTY BABY	Brook Benton, Mercury 71478	1
44	47	54	77	S	LONELY FOR YOU	Gary Stites, Carlton 508	14
59	83	80	78	S	DANNY BOY	Sil Austin, Mercury 71442	7
—	—	84	79		TEN THOUSAND DRUMS	Carl Smith, Columbia 41417	2
14	24	38	80	S	KOOKIE, KOOKIE (LEND ME YOUR COMB)	Ed Byrnes/Connie Stevens, Warner Bros. 5047	13
23	40	52	81	S	ENDLESSLY	Brook Benton, Mercury 71443	13
27	36	73	82	S	GOODBYE, JIMMY, GOODBYE	Kathy Linden, Felsted 8571	14
81	80	79	83		FLOWER OF LOVE	The Crests, Coed 511	6
—	—	96	84		LONELY GUITAR	Annette, Vista 339	2
—	90	90	85		SEE YOU IN SEPTEMBER	The Tempos, Climax 102	3
—	93	91	86		KISSIN' TIME	Bobby Rydell, Cameo 160	3
—	—	—	★87		KATY TOO	Johny Cash, Sun 321	1
—	—	—	★88		TENNESSEE STUD	Eddy Arnold, RCA Victor 7542	1
—	94	93	89		BEACH TIME	Roger Smith, Warner Bros. 5068	3
100	96	92	90		OH WHAT A FOOL	The Impalas, Cub 9033	4
20	41	71	91		SORRY, I RAN ALL THE WAY HOME	The Impalas, Cub 9022	18
—	—	98	92		CRACKIN' UP	Bo Diddley, Checker 924	2
—	—	—	93		TO A SOLDIER BOY	The Tassels, Madison 117	1
—	—	—	94		I'M COMIN' HOME	Marv Johnson, United Artists 175	1
—	—	—	95		ROCKIN' IN THE JUNGLE	The Eternals, Hollywood 68	1
—	—	—	96		DEDICATED TO THE ONE I LOVE	Shirells, Sceptor 1203	1
—	—	—	97		LITTLE GIRL	Ritchie Valens, Del Fi 4117	1
—	—	—	98		BELLS, BELLS, BELLS	Billy and Lilly, Swan 4036	[illegible]
—	—	—	99		I STILL GET JEALOUS	Joni James, M-G-M 12779	[illegible]
—	—	—	100		ON AN EVENING IN ROMA	Dean Martin, Capitol 4222	[illegible]

FOR THE WEEK ENDING JULY 26

The Billboard HOT 100

★ STAR PERFORMERS showed the greatest upward progress on the Hot 100 this week.

S Indicates that STEREO SINGLE version is available.

TITLE, Artist, Company, Record No.

Three Weeks Ago	Two Weeks Ago	One Week Ago	This Week	Stereo	Title, Artist, Company, Record No.	Weeks on Chart
3	2	1	1	S	LONELY BOY — Paul Anka, ABC-Paramount 10022	8
1	1	2	2		THE BATTLE OF NEW ORLEANS — Johnny Horton, Columbia 41339	13
19	10	6	3	S	TIGER — Fabian, Chancellor 1037	6
12	6	4	4		WATERLOO — Stonewall Jackson, Columbia 41393	9
2	3	3	5	S	PERSONALITY — Lloyd Price, ABC-Paramount 10018	13
17	13	9	6		MY HEART IS AN OPEN BOOK — Carl Dobkins Jr., Decca 30803	13
6	7	8	7		TALLAHASSEE LASSIE — Freddy Cannon, Swan 4031	11
5	5	5	8	S	LIPSTICK ON YOUR COLLAR — Connie Francis, M-G-M 12793	10
—	43	25	9		A BIG HUNK O' LOVE — Elvis Presley, RCA Victor 7600	3
4	4	7	10		DREAM LOVER — Bobby Darin, Atco 6140	14
13	8	12	11	S	BOBBY SOX TO STOCKINGS — Frankie Avalon, Chancellor 1036	9
31	23	13	12	S	FORTY MILES OF BAD ROAD — Duane Eddy, Jamie 1126	6
15	16	11	★ 13	S	I ONLY HAVE EYES FOR YOU — Flamingos, End 1046	8
16	12	10	14	S	A BOY WITHOUT A GIRL — Frankie Avalon, Chancellor 1036	9
11	9	14	15	S	FRANKIE — Connie Francis, M-G-M 12793	10
34	28	20	16		THERE GOES MY BABY — The Drifters, Atlantic 2025	8
35	24	18	17	S	TWIXT TWELVE AND TWENTY — Pat Boone, Dot 15995	6
—	53	24	18		SWEETER THAN YOU — Ricky Nelson, Imperial 5595	3
28	18	15	19		M.T.A. — Kingston Trio, Capitol 4221	6
21	20	17	20	S	YOU'RE SO FINE — The Falcons, Unart 2013	14
20	22	27	21	S	HUSHABYE — Mystics, Laurie 3028	10
26	25	23	22	S	WHAT A DIFF'RENCE A DAY MAKES — Dinah Washington, Mercury 71435	9
63	42	32	23		JUST A LITTLE TOO MUCH — Ricky Nelson, Imperial 5595	4
49	31	26	★ 24	S	LAVENDER BLUE — Sammy Turner, Big Top 3016	5
—	65	36	★ 25	S	RAGTIME COWBOY JOE — David Seville and the Chipmunks, Liberty 55200	3
14	15	19	26	S	BONGO ROCK — Preston Epps, Original 4	10
—	—	39	27		MY WISH CAME TRUE — Elvis Presley, RCA Victor 7600	2
48	33	35	28		I'LL BE SATISFIED — Jackie Wilson, Brunswick 55136	5
25	27	31	29		THE WONDER OF YOU — Ray Peterson, RCA Victor 7513	10
27	26	30	30		THIS I SWEAR — Skyliners, Calico 106	8
39	34	34	31		ROBBIN' THE CRADLE — Tony Bellus, NRC 023	13
18	21	22	★ 32	S	JUST KEEP IT UP — Dee Clark, Abner 1026	12
—	82	43	33		WHAT'D I SAY — Ray Charles, Atlantic 2031	3
10	19	33	34		A TEENAGER IN LOVE — Dion and the Belmonts, Laurie 3027	14
98	69	46	35	S	HERE COMES SUMMER — Jerry Keller, Kapp 277	4
9	11	16	★ 36		ALONG CAME JONES — Coasters, Atco 6141	10
8	14	21	37	S	QUIET VILLAGE — Martin Denny, Liberty 55162	15
—	85	48	38		SEA OF LOVE — Phil Phillips, Mercury 71465	3
42	32	28	★ 39	S	ONLY SIXTEEN — Sam Cooke, Keen 2022	7
66	58	54	★ 40		SMALL WORLD — Johnny Mathis, Columbia 41410	6
58	49	42	41	S	REMEMBER WHEN — Platters, Mercury 71467	5
33	30	38	42		LITTLE DIPPER — Mickey Mozart, Roulette 4148	9
53	59	40	★ 43		SINCE YOU'VE BEEN GONE — Clyde McPhatter, Atlantic 2028	6
7	17	29	★ 44		KANSAS CITY — Wilbert Harrison, Fury 1023	15
72	64	44	45		THERE IS SOMETHING ON YOUR MIND — Big Jay McNeely, Swingin' 614	9
55	51	51	★ 46	S	LIKE YOUNG — Andre Previn & David Rose, M-G-M 12792	6
67	47	55	★ 47	S	QUIET THREE — Duane Eddy, Jamie 1126	6
76	72	49	★ 48	S	CIAO CIAO BAMBINA — Jacky Noguez, Jamie 1127	5
50	50	41	★ 49		MONA LISA — Carl Mann, Phillips International 3539	8
70	74	69	50		IT WAS I — Skip & Flip, Brent 7002	5
68	68	56	51		HIGH HOPES — Frank Sinatra, Capitol 4214	6
85	75	65	52	S	TILL THERE WAS YOU — Anita Bryant, Carlton 512	4
100	77	62	53	S	THE WAY I WALK — Jack Scott, Carlton 514	4
—	84	79	54		TEN THOUSAND DRUMS — Carl Smith, Columbia 41417	3
—	89	67	55	S	WHAT IS LOVE — Playmates, Roulette 4160	3
22	29	45	★ 56		SO FINE — Fiestas, Old Town 1062	16
—	96	84	57		LONELY GUITAR — Annette, Vista 339	3
52	41	37	58		BACK IN THE U.S.A. — Chuck Berry, Chess 1729	5
51	63	68	59		VELVET WATERS — Megatrons, Acousticon 101	8
—	—	76	60		THANK YOU PRETTY BABY — Brook Benton, Mercury 71478	2
60	57	47	61	S	I KNOW — Perry Como, RCA Victor 7541	7
62	61	72	★ 62		THE WHISTLING ORGAN — Dave (Baby) Cortez, Clock 1012	7
46	40	58	63	S	WONDERFUL YOU — Jimmie Rodgers, Roulette 4158	6
64	60	59	64	S	WITH MY EYES WIDE OPEN I'M DREAMING — Patti Page, Mercury 71469	6
32	37	52	65	S	RING-A-LING-A-LARIO — Jimmie Rodgers, Roulette 4158	8
56	48	63	66		TALL COOL ONE — Wailers, Golden Crest 518	10
74	45	66	★ 67		CAP AND GOWN — Marty Robbins, Columbia 41408	6
30	36	57	68		CROSSFIRE — Johnny and the Hurricanes, Warwick 502	14
—	78	71	69	S	BEI MIR BIST DU SCHOEN — Louis Prima and Keely Smith, Dot 15956	3
45	56	53	70	S	FORTY DAYS — Ronnie Hawkins, Roulette 4154	7
83	80	78	71	S	DANNY BOY — Sil Austin, Mercury 71442	8
23	35	50	72		ONLY YOU — Frank Pourcel, Capitol 4165	16
71	66	70	73		I LOVE AN ANGEL — Little Bill & the Bluenotes, Dolton 4	5
93	91	86	74		KISSIN' TIME — Bobby Rydell, Cameo 160	4
—	98	92	75		CRACKIN' UP — Bo Diddley, Checker 924	3
—	—	93	★ 76		TO A SOLDIER BOY — The Tassels, Madison 117	2
—	—	99	77		I STILL GET JEALOUS — Joni James, M-G-M 12807	2
—	—	95	78		ROCKIN' IN THE JUNGLE — The Eternals, Hollywood 68	2
—	—	—	79		SUGAREE — Rusty York, Chess 1730	1
—	—	88	80	S	TENNESSEE STUD — Eddy Arnold, RCA Victor 7542	2
90	90	85	81		SEE YOU IN SEPTEMBER — The Tempos, Climax 102	4
—	—	—	82		WITH ALL OF MY HEART — Brook Benton, Mercury 71478	1
29	39	61	83		I'M READY — Fats Domino, Imperial 5585	11
—	—	96	84		DEDICATED TO THE ONE I LOVE — Shirells, Sceptor 1203	2
—	—	87	85		KATY TOO — Johny Cash, Sun 321	2
96	92	90	86		OH WHAT A FOOL — The Impalas, Cub 9033	5
—	—	94	★ 87		I'M COMIN' HOME — Marv Johnson, United Artists 175	2
59	55	64	★ 88	S	TABOO — Arthur Lymon, Hi-Fi 550	6
—	—	—	89		MONA LISA — Conway Twitty, M-G-M 12804	1
—	—	—	90		CRY — The Knightsbridge Strings, Top Rank 2006	1
—	—	100	91		ON AN EVENING IN ROMA — Dean Martin, Capitol 4222	2
—	—	97	92		LITTLE GIRL — Ritchie Valens, Del Fi 4117	2
—	—	—	93		MARTINIQUE — Martin Denny, Liberty 55199	1
—	—	98	94		BELLS, BELLS, BELLS — Billy and Lilly, Swan 4036	2
—	—	—	95		LINDA LU — Ray Sharpe, Jamie 1128	1
94	93	89	96		BEACH TIME — Roger Smith, Warner Bros. 5068	4
—	—	—	97	S	A GIRL LIKE YOU — Gary Stites, Carlton 516	1
—	—	—	98		MAKIN' LOVE — Floyd Robinson, RCA Victor 7529	1
—	—	—	99		BROKEN-HEARTED MELODY — Sarah Vaughan, Mercury 71477	1
—	—	—	100		SUMMER'S LOVE — Richard Barrett and the Chantels, Gone 5060	1

FOR THE WEEK ENDING AUGUST 2

The Billboard HOT 100

★ STAR PERFORMERS showed the greatest upward progress on the Hot 100 this week.

S Indicates that STEREO SINGLE version is available.

This Week	One Week Ago	Two Weeks Ago	Three Weeks Ago	TITLE, Artist, Company, Record No.	Stereo	Weeks on Chart
1	1	1	2	LONELY BOY — Paul Anka, ABC-Paramount 10022	S	9
2	2	2	1	THE BATTLE OF NEW ORLEANS — Johnny Horton, Columbia 41339		14
3	3	6	10	TIGER — Fabian, Chancellor 1037	S	7
4	4	4	6	WATERLOO — Stonewall Jackson, Columbia 41393		10
5	9	25	43	A BIG HUNK O' LOVE — Elvis Presley, RCA Victor 7600		4
6	6	9	13	MY HEART IS AN OPEN BOOK — Carl Dobkins Jr., Decca 30803		14
7	16	20	28	THERE GOES MY BABY — The Drifters, Atlantic 2025		9
8	8	5	5	LIPSTICK ON YOUR COLLAR — Connie Francis, M-G-M 12793	S	11
9	12	13	23	FORTY MILES OF BAD ROAD — Duane Eddy, Jamie 1126	S	7
10	5	3	3	PERSONALITY — Lloyd Price, ABC-Paramount 10018	S	14
★11	23	32	42	JUST A LITTLE TOO MUCH — Ricky Nelson, Imperial 5595		5
★12	24	26	31	LAVENDER BLUE — Sammy Turner, Big Top 3016	S	6
13	13	11	16	I ONLY HAVE EYES FOR YOU — Flamingos, End 1146	S	9
14	22	23	25	WHAT A DIFF'RENCE A DAY MAKES — Dinah Washington, Mercury 71435	S	10
15	18	24	53	SWEETER THAN YOU — Ricky Nelson, Imperial 5595		4
16	11	12	8	BOBBY SOX TO STOCKINGS — Frankie Avalon, Chancellor 1036	S	10
17	14	10	12	A BOY WITHOUT A GIRL — Frankie Avalon, Chancellor 1036	S	10
18	25	36	65	RAGTIME COWBOY JOE — David Seville and the Chipmunks, Liberty 55200	S	4
19	19	15	18	M.T.A. — Kingston Trio, Capitol 4221		7
20	17	18	24	TWIXT TWELVE AND TWENTY — Pat Boone, Dot 15955	S	7
21	20	17	20	YOU'RE SO FINE — The Falcons, Unart 2013	S	15
22	27	39	—	MY WISH CAME TRUE — Elvis Presley, RCA Victor 7600		3
23	21	27	22	HUSHABYE — Mystics, Laurie 3028	S	11
24	15	14	9	FRANKIE — Connie Francis, M-G-M 12793	S	11
25	28	35	33	I'LL BE SATISFIED — Jackie Wilson, Brunswick 55136		6
26	33	43	82	WHAT'D I SAY — Ray Charles, Atlantic 2031		4
27	7	8	7	TALLAHASSEE LASSIE — Freddy Cannon, Swan 4031		12
28	35	46	69	HERE COMES SUMMER — Jerry Keller, Kapp 277	S	5
29	10	7	4	DREAM LOVER — Bobby Darin, Atco 6140		15
★30	40	54	58	SMALL WORLD — Johnny Mathis, Columbia 41410		7
★31	55	67	89	WHAT IS LOVE — Playmates, Roulette 4160	S	4
★32	48	49	72	CIAO CIAO BAMBINA — Jacky Noguez, Jamie 1127	S	6
★33	50	69	74	IT WAS I — Skip & Flip, Brent 7002		6
34	31	34	34	ROBBIN' THE CRADLE — Tony Bellus, NRC 023		14
35	38	48	85	SEA OF LOVE — Phil Phillips, Mercury 71465		4
★36	52	65	75	TILL THERE WAS YOU — Anita Bryant, Carlton 512	S	5
37	26	19	15	BONGO ROCK — Preston Epps, Original 4	S	11
38	29	31	27	THE WONDER OF YOU — Ray Peterson, RCA Victor 7513		11
★39	49	41	50	MONA LISA — Carl Mann, Phillips International 3539		9
40	39	28	32	ONLY SIXTEEN — Sam Cooke, Keen 2022	S	8
41	30	30	26	THIS I SWEAR — Skyliners, Calico 106		9
42	43	40	59	SINCE YOU'VE BEEN GONE — Clyde McPhatter, Atlantic 2028		7
43	32	22	21	JUST KEEP IT UP — Dee Clark, Abner 1026	S	13
44	41	42	49	REMEMBER WHEN — Platters, Mercury 71467	S	6
45	53	62	77	THE WAY I WALK — Jack Scott, Carlton 514	S	5
46	47	55	47	QUIET THREE — Duane Eddy, Jamie 1126	S	7
★47	60	76	—	THANK YOU PRETTY BABY — Brook Benton, Mercury 71478		3
48	51	56	68	HIGH HOPES — Frank Sinatra, Capitol 4214		7
49	54	79	84	TEN THOUSAND DRUMS — Carl Smith, Columbia 41417		4
50	57	84	96	LONELY GUITAR — Annette, Vista 339		4
51	36	16	11	ALONG CAME JONES — Coasters, Atco 6141		11
52	45	44	64	THERE IS SOMETHING ON YOUR MIND — Big Jay McNeely, Swingin' 614		10
53	58	37	41	BACK IN THE U.S.A. — Chuck Berry, Chess 1729		6
54	46	51	51	LIKE YOUNG — Andre Previn & David Rose, M-G-M 12792	S	7
55	37	21	14	QUIET VILLAGE — Martin Denny, Liberty 55162	S	16
56	61	47	57	I KNOW — Perry Como, RCA Victor 7541	S	8
★57	81	85	90	SEE YOU IN SEPTEMBER — The Tempos, Climax 102		5
58	66	63	48	TALL COOL ONE — Wailers, Golden Crest 518		11
★59	74	86	91	KISSIN' TIME — Bobby Rydell, Cameo 167		5
★60	76	93	—	TO A SOLDIER BOY — The Tassels, Madison 117		3
61	34	33	19	A TEENAGER IN LOVE — Dion and the Belmonts, Laurie 3027		15
62	75	92	98	CRACKIN' UP — Bo Diddley, Checker 924		4
★63	—	—	—	THE THREE BELLS — Browns, RCA Victor 7555	S	1
64	68	57	36	CROSSFIRE — Johnny and the Hurricanes, Warwick 502		15
65	77	99	—	I STILL GET JEALOUS — Joni James, M-G-M 12807		3
★66	98	—	—	MAKIN' LOVE — Floyd Robinson, RCA Victor 7529		2
★67	—	—	—	I'M GONNA BE A WHEEL SOMEDAY — Fats Domino, Imperial 5606		1
68	63	58	40	WONDERFUL YOU — Jimmie Rodgers, Roulette 4158	S	7
69	71	78	80	DANNY BOY — Sil Austin, Mercury 71442	S	9
★70	99	—	—	BROKEN-HEARTED MELODY — Sarah Vaughan, Mercury 71477		2
71	64	59	60	WITH MY EYES WIDE OPEN I'M DREAMING — Patti Page, Mercury 71469	S	7
72	42	38	30	LITTLE DIPPER — Mickey Mozart, Roulette 4148		10
73	80	88	—	TENNESSEE STUD — Eddy Arnold, RCA Victor 7542	S	3
★74	91	100	—	ON AN EVENING IN ROMA — Dean Martin, Capitol 4222		3
★75	96	89	93	BEACH TIME — Roger Smith, Warner Bros. 5068		5
76	90	—	—	CRY — The Knightsbridge Strings, Top Rank 2006		2
77	79	—	—	SUGAREE — Rusty York, Chess 1730		2
78	69	71	78	BEI MIR BIST DU SCHOEN — Louis Prima and Keely Smith, Dot 15956	S	4
79	89	—	—	MONA LISA — Conway Twitty, M-G-M 12804		2
80	73	70	66	I LOVE AN ANGEL — Little Bill & the Bluenotes, Dolton 4		6
81	85	87	—	KATY TOO — Johnny Cash, Sun 321		3
82	70	53	56	FORTY DAYS — Ronnie Hawkins, Roulette 4154	S	8
83	62	72	61	THE WHISTLING ORGAN — Dave (Baby) Cortez, Clock 1012		8
84	41	29	17	KANSAS CITY — Wilbert Harrison, Fury 1023		16
85	87	94	—	I'M COMIN' HOME — Marv Johnson, United Artists 175		3
86	97	—	—	A GIRL LIKE YOU — Gary Stites, Carlton 516	S	2
87	84	96	—	DEDICATED TO THE ONE I LOVE — Shirells, Sceptor 1203		3
88	93	—	—	MARTINIQUE — Martin Denny, Liberty 55199	S	2
89	—	—	87	SWEET SOMEONE — Eddie & Betty Cole, Warner Bros. 5054		3
90	95	—	—	LINDA LU — Ray Sharpe, Jamie 1128		2
91	94	98	—	BELLS, BELLS, BELLS — Billy and Lilly, Swan 4036		3
92	59	68	63	VELVET WATERS — Megatrons, Acousticon 101		9
93	100	—	—	SUMMER'S LOVE — Richard Barrett and the Chantels, Gone 5060		2
94	78	95	—	ROCKIN' IN THE JUNGLE — The Eternals, Hollywood 68		3
95	—	—	—	SLEEP WALK — Santo and Johnny, Canadian-American 103		[illegible]
96	—	—	—	SO HIGH, SO LOW — LaVern Baker, Atlantic 2033		[illegible]
97	—	—	—	WITH OPEN ARMS — Jane Morgan, Kapp 284		[illegible]
98	—	—	—	HALF-BREED — Marvin Rainwater, M-G-M 12803		[illegible]
99	—	—	—	YOU DON'T KNOW GIRLS — Kathy Linden, Felsted 8587		[illegible]
100	—	—	—	WHO SHOT SAM — George Jones, Mercury 71464		[illegible]

FOR THE WEEK ENDING AUGUST 9

The Billboard HOT 100

★ STAR PERFORMERS showed the greatest upward progress on the Hot 100 this week.

S Indicates that STEREO SINGLE version is available.

TITLE, Artist, Company, Record No.

This Week	One Week Ago	Two Weeks Ago	Three Weeks Ago	Title, Artist, Company, Record No.	Stereo	Weeks on Chart
1	1	1	1	LONELY BOY — Paul Anka, ABC-Paramount 10022	S	10
2	5	9	25	A BIG HUNK O' LOVE — Elvis Presley, RCA Victor 7600		5
3	6	6	9	MY HEART IS AN OPEN BOOK — Carl Dobkins Jr., Decca 30803		15
4	2	2	2	THE BATTLE OF NEW ORLEANS — Johnny Horton, Columbia 41339		15
5	3	3	6	TIGER — Fabian, Chancellor 1037	S	8
6	7	16	20	THERE GOES MY BABY — The Drifters, Atlantic 2025		10
7	4	4	4	WATERLOO — Stonewall Jackson, Columbia 41393		11
8	12	24	26	LAVENDER BLUE — Sammy Turner, Big Top 3016	S	7
9	15	18	24	SWEETER THAN YOU — Ricky Nelson, Imperial 5595		5
10	9	12	13	FORTY MILES OF BAD ROAD — Duane Eddy, Jamie 1126	S	8
11	8	8	5	LIPSTICK ON YOUR COLLAR — Connie Francis, M-G-M 12793	S	12
12	11	23	32	JUST A LITTLE TOO MUCH — Ricky Nelson, Imperial 5595		6
13	14	22	23	WHAT A DIFF'RENCE A DAY MAKES — Dinah Washington, Mercury 71435	S	11
14	22	27	39	MY WISH CAME TRUE — Elvis Presley, RCA Victor 7600		4
★15	26	33	43	WHAT'D I SAY — Ray Charles, Atlantic 2031		5
16	18	25	36	RAGTIME COWBOY JOE — David Seville and the Chipmunks, Liberty 55200	S	5
17	13	13	11	I ONLY HAVE EYES FOR YOU — Flamingos, End 1146	S	10
	28	35	46	HERE COMES SUMMER — Jerry Keller, Kapp 277	S	6
19	10	5	3	PERSONALITY — Lloyd Price, ABC-Paramount 10018	S	15
20	25	28	35	I'LL BE SATISFIED — Jackie Wilson, Brunswick 55136		7
★	35	38	48	SEA OF LOVE — Phil Phillips, Mercury 71465		5
	33	50	69	IT WAS I — Skip & Flip, Brent 7002		7
23	16	11	12	BOBBY SOX TO STOCKINGS — Frankie Avalon, Chancellor 1036	S	11
24	17	14	10	A BOY WITHOUT A GIRL — Frankie Avalon, Chancellor 1036	S	11
25	31	55	67	WHAT IS LOVE — Playmates, Roulette 4160	S	5
26	30	40	54	SMALL WORLD — Johnny Mathis, Columbia 41410		8
27	24	15	14	FRANKIE — Connie Francis, M-G-M 12793	S	12
★	47	60	76	THANK YOU PRETTY BABY — Brook Benton, Mercury 71478	S	12
	21	20	17	YOU'RE SO FINE — The Falcons, Unart 2013	S	16
	19	19	15	M.T.A. — Kingston Trio, Capitol 4221		8
	34	31	34	ROBBIN' THE CRADLE — Tony Bellus, NRC 023		15
	63	—	—	THE THREE BELLS — Browns, RCA Victor 7555	S	2
	36	52	65	TILL THERE WAS YOU — Anita Bryant, Carlton 512	S	6
34	32	48	49	CIAO CIAO BAMBINA — Jacky Noguez, Jamie 1127	S	7
35	20	17	18	TWIXT TWELVE AND TWENTY — Pat Boone, Dot 15955	S	8
36	23	21	27	HUSHABYE — Mystics, Laurie 3028	S	12
37	45	53	62	THE WAY I WALK — Jack Scott, Carlton 514	S	6
38	42	43	40	SINCE YOU'VE BEEN GONE — Clyde McPhatter, Atlantic 2028		8
★39	66	98	—	MAKIN' LOVE — Floyd Robinson, RCA Victor 7529		3
40	41	30	30	THIS I SWEAR — Skyliners, Calico 106		10
41	27	7	8	TALLAHASSEE LASSIE — Freddy Cannon, Swan 4031		13
★42	57	81	85	SEE YOU IN SEPTEMBER — The Tempos, Climax 102		6
43	49	54	79	TEN THOUSAND DRUMS — Carl Smith, Columbia 41417		5
44	38	29	31	THE WONDER OF YOU — Ray Peterson, RCA Victor 7513		12
45	44	41	42	REMEMBER WHEN — Platters, Mercury 71467	S	7
46	29	10	7	DREAM LOVER — Bobby Darin, Atco 6140		16
47	39	49	41	MONA LISA — Carl Mann, Phillips International 3539		10
48	40	39	28	ONLY SIXTEEN — Sam Cooke, Keen 2022	S	9
★49	59	74	86	KISSIN' TIME — Bobby Rydell, Cameo 167		6
50	37	26	19	BONGO ROCK — Preston Epps, Original 4	S	12
51	46	47	55	QUIET THREE — Duane Eddy, Jamie 1126	S	8
★52	67	—	—	I'M GONNA BE A WHEEL SOMEDAY — Fats Domino, Imperial 5606		2
53	43	32	22	JUST KEEP IT UP — Dee Clark, Abner 1026	S	14
★54	70	99	—	BROKEN-HEARTED MELODY — Sarah Vaughan, Mercury 71477		3
55	60	76	93	TO A SOLDIER BOY — The Tassels, Madison 117	S	4
56	52	45	44	THERE IS SOMETHING ON YOUR MIND — Big Jay McNeely, Swingin' 614		11
57	50	57	84	LONELY GUITAR — Annette, Vista 339		5
58	48	51	56	HIGH HOPES — Frank Sinatra, Capitol 4214		8
★59	74	91	100	ON AN EVENING IN ROMA — Dean Martin, Capitol 4022		4
★60	76	90	—	CRY — The Knightsbridge Strings, Top Rank 2006	S	3
61	54	46	51	LIKE YOUNG — Andre Previn & David Rose, M-G-M 12792	S	8
62	53	58	37	BACK IN THE U.S.A. — Chuck Berry, Chess 1729		7
63	65	77	99	I STILL GET JEALOUS — Joni James, M-G-M 12807	S	4
64	75	96	89	BEACH TIME — Roger Smith, Warner Bros. 5068		6
★65	—	—	—	BABY TALK — Jan and Dean, Dore 522		1
★66	—	—	—	RED RIVER ROCK — Johnny and the Hurricanes, Warwick 509		1
67	73	80	88	TENNESSEE STUD — Eddy Arnold, RCA Victor 7542	S	4
★68	97	—	—	WITH OPEN ARMS — Jane Morgan, Kapp 284		2
69	81	85	87	KATY TOO — Johnny Cash, Sun 321		4
★70	—	—	—	LEAVE MY KITTEN ALONE — Little Willie John, King 5219		1
71	79	89	—	MONA LISA — Conway Twitty, M-G-M 12804		3
★72	96	—	—	SO HIGH, SO LOW — LaVern Baker, Atlantic 2033		2
★73	—	—	—	CARIBBEAN — Mitchell Torok, Guyden 2018		1
74	58	66	63	TALL COOL ONE — Wailers, Golden Crest 518		12
★75	—	—	—	ANGEL FACE — Jimmy Darren, Colpix 119		1
★76	—	—	—	MY OWN TRUE LOVE — Jimmy Clanton, Ace 567		1
★77	95	—	—	SLEEP WALK — Santo and Johnny, Canadian-American 103		2
78	78	69	71	BEI MIR BIST DU SCHOEN — Louis Prima and Keely Smith, Dot 15956	S	5
79	51	36	16	ALONG CAME JONES — Coasters, Atco 6141		12
80	86	97	—	A GIRL LIKE YOU — Gary Stites, Carlton 516	S	3
81	69	71	78	DANNY BOY — Sil Austin, Mercury 71442	S	10
82	85	87	94	I'M COMIN' HOME — Marv Johnson, United Artists 175		4
83	87	84	96	DEDICATED TO THE ONE I LOVE — Shirells, Scepter 1203		4
84	56	61	47	I KNOW — Perry Como, RCA Victor 7541	S	9
85	98	—	—	HALF-BREED — Marvin Rainwater, M-G-M 12803		2
86	90	95	—	LINDA LU — Ray Sharpe, Jamie 1128		3
87	89	—	—	SWEET SOMEONE — Eddie & Betty Cole, Warner Bros. 5054		4
88	91	94	98	BELLS, BELLS, BELLS — Billie and Lilly, Swan 4036		4
★89	—	—	—	TIME MARCHES ON — Roy Hamilton, Epic 9323		1
90	62	75	92	CRACKIN' UP — Bo Diddley, Checker 924		5
91	—	—	—	PORGY — Nina Simone, Bethlehem 11021		1
92	—	—	—	SOLDIER'S JOY — Hawkshaw Hawkins, Columbia 41419		1
93	99	—	—	YOU DON'T KNOW GIRLS — Kathy Linden, Felsted 8587		2
94	—	—	—	MIDNIGHT FLYER — Nat King Cole, Capitol 4248		1
95	—	—	—	I GOT STRIPES — Johnny Cash, Columbia 30427		1
96	—	—	—	MIAMI — Eugene Church, Class 254		1
97	77	79	—	SUGAREE — Rusty York, Chess 1730		3
98	100	—	—	WHO SHOT SAM — George Jones, Mercury 71464	S	2
99	—	—	—	GEE — George Hamilton IV, ABC-Paramount 10028		1
100	—	—	—	ALIMONY — Frankie Ford, Ace 566		1

FOR THE WEEK ENDING AUGUST 16

The Billboard HOT 100

★ STAR PERFORMERS showed the greatest upward progress on the Hot 100 this week.

S Indicates that STEREO SINGLE version is available.

This Week	One Week Ago	Two Weeks Ago	Three Weeks Ago	TITLE, Artist, Company, Record No.	Stereo	Weeks on Chart
1	2	5	9	A BIG HUNK O' LOVE — Elvis Presley RCA Victor 7600		6
2	1	1	1	LONELY BOY — Paul Anka, ABC-Paramount 10022	S	11
3	3	6	6	MY HEART IS AN OPEN BOOK — Carl Dobkins Jr., Decca 30803		16
4	6	7	16	THERE GOES MY BABY — The Drifters, Atlantic 2025		11
5	8	12	24	LAVENDER BLUE — Sammy Turner, Big Top 3016	S	8
6	5	3	3	TIGER — Fabian, Chancellor 1037	S	9
7	4	2	2	THE BATTLE OF NEW ORLEANS — Johnny Horton, Columbia 41339		16
8	13	14	22	WHAT A DIFF'RENCE A DAY MAKES — Dinah Washington, Mercury 71435	S	12
9	15	26	33	WHAT'D I SAY — Ray Charles, Atlantic 2031		6
10	7	4	4	WATERLOO — Stonewall Jackson, Columbia 41393		12
11	10	9	12	FORTY MILES OF BAD ROAD — Duane Eddy, Jamie 1126	S	9
12	9	15	18	SWEETER THAN YOU — Ricky Nelson, Imperial 5595		6
13	12	11	23	JUST A LITTLE TOO MUCH — Ricky Nelson, Imperial 5595		7
14	14	22	27	MY WISH CAME TRUE — Elvis Presley, RCA Victor 7600		5
15	21	35	38	SEA OF LOVE — Phil Phillips, Mercury 71465		6
★ 16	32	63	—	THE THREE BELLS — Browns, RCA Victor 7555	S	3
17	22	33	50	IT WAS I — Skip & Flip, Brent 7002		8
18	18	28	35	HERE COMES SUMMER — Jerry Keller, Kapp 277	S	7
19	16	18	25	RAGTIME COWBOY JOE — David Seville and the Chipmunks, Liberty 55200	S	6
20	26	30	40	SMALL WORLD — Johnny Mathis, Columbia 41410		9
21	25	31	55	WHAT IS LOVE — Playmates, Roulette 4160	S	6
22	17	13	13	I ONLY HAVE EYES FOR YOU — Flamingos, End 1146	S	11
23	28	47	60	THANK YOU PRETTY BABY — Brook Benton, Mercury 71478	S	13
★ 24	34	32	48	CIAO CIAO BAMBINA — Jacky Noguez, Jamie 1127	S	8
★ 25	47	39	49	MONA LISA — Carl Mann, Phillips International 3539		11
26	11	8	8	LIPSTICK ON YOUR COLLAR — Connie Francis, M-G-M 12793	S	13
27	19	10	5	PERSONALITY — Lloyd Price, ABC-Paramount 10018	S	16
28	31	34	31	ROBBIN' THE CRADLE — Tony Bellus, NRC 023		16
29	29	21	20	YOU'RE SO FINE — The Falcons, Unart 2013	S	17
30	20	25	28	I'LL BE SATISFIED — Jackie Wilson, Brunswick 55136		8
31	33	36	52	TILL THERE WAS YOU — Anita Bryant, Carlton 512	S	7
32	36	23	21	HUSHABYE — Mystics, Laurie 3028	S	13
33	24	17	14	A BOY WITHOUT A GIRL — Frankie Avalon, Chancellor 1036	S	12
34	27	24	15	FRANKIE — Connie Francis, M-G-M 12793	S	13
35	42	57	81	SEE YOU IN SEPTEMBER — The Tempos, Climax 102		7
36	37	45	53	THE WAY I WALK — Jack Scott, Carlton 514	S	7
★ 37	49	59	74	KISSIN' TIME — Bobby Rydell, Cameo 167		7
★ 38	52	67	—	I'M GONNA BE A WHEEL SOMEDAY — Fats Domino, Imperial 5606		3
39	39	66	98	MAKIN' LOVE — Floyd Robinson, RCA Victor 7529		4
★ 40	65	—	—	BABY TALK — Jan and Dean, Dore 522		2
41	30	19	19	M.T.A. — Kingston Trio, Capitol 4221		9
★ 42	76	—	—	MY OWN TRUE LOVE — Jimmy Clanton, Ace 567		2
43	35	20	17	TWIXT TWELVE AND TWENTY — Pat Boone, Dot 15955	S	9
44	23	16	11	BOBBY SOX TO STOCKINGS — Frankie Avalon, Chancellor 1036	S	12
45	54	70	99	BROKEN-HEARTED MELODY — Sarah Vaughan, Mercury 71477		4
★ 46	—	—	—	I WANT TO WALK YOU HOME — Fats Domino, Imperial 5606		1
47	38	42	43	SINCE YOU'VE BEEN GONE — Clyde McPhatter, Atlantic 2028		9
★ 48	58	48	51	HIGH HOPES — Frank Sinatra, Capitol 4214		9
★ 49	75	—	—	ANGEL FACE — Jimmy Darren, Colpix 119		2
★ 50	66	—	—	RED RIVER ROCK — Johnny and the Hurricanes, Warwick 509		2
51	44	38	29	THE WONDER OF YOU — Ray Peterson, RCA Victor 7513		13
52	43	49	54	TEN THOUSAND DRUMS — Carl Smith, Columbia 41417		6
53	67	73	80	TENNESSEE STUD — Eddy Arnold, RCA Victor 7542	S	5
★ 54	60	76	90	CRY — The Knightsbridge Strings, Top Rank 2006	S	4
★ 55	77	95	—	SLEEP WALK — Santo and Johnny, Canadian-American 103		3
56	46	29	10	DREAM LOVER — Bobby Darin, Atco 6140		17
★ 57	71	79	89	MONA LISA — Conway Twitty, M-G-M 12804		4
58	61	54	46	LIKE YOUNG — Andre Previn & David Rose, M-G-M 12792	S	9
59	40	41	30	THIS I SWEAR — Skyliners, Calico 106		11
60	56	52	45	THERE IS SOMETHING ON YOUR MIND — Big Jay McNeely, Swingin' 614		12
61	59	74	91	ON AN EVENING IN ROMA — Dean Martin, Capitol 4022		5
62	68	97	—	WITH OPEN ARMS — Jane Morgan, Kapp 284		3
63	50	37	26	BONGO ROCK — Preston Epps, Original 4	S	13
64	55	60	76	TO A SOLDIER BOY — The Tassels, Madison 117	S	5
★ 65	—	—	—	I'M GONNA GET MARRIED — Lloyd Price, ABC-Paramount 10032	S	1
66	69	81	85	KATY TOO — Johnny Cash, Sun 321		5
67	72	96	—	SO HIGH, SO LOW — LaVern Baker, Atlantic 2033		3
68	73	—	—	CARIBBEAN — Mitchell Torok, Guyden 2018		2
69	70	—	—	LEAVE MY KITTEN ALONE — Little Willie John, King 5219		2
★ 70	85	98	—	HALF-BREED — Marvin Rainwater, M-G-M 12803		3
71	63	65	77	I STILL GET JEALOUS — Joni James, M-G-M 12807	S	5
72	53	43	32	JUST KEEP IT UP — Dee Clark, Abner 1026	S	15
73	51	46	47	QUIET THREE — Duane Eddy, Jamie 1126	S	9
74	45	44	41	REMEMBER WHEN — Platters, Mercury 71467	S	8
75	57	50	57	LONELY GUITAR — Annette, Vista 339		6
76	64	75	96	BEACH TIME — Roger Smith, Warner Bros. 5068		7
77	41	27	7	TALLAHASSEE LASSIE — Freddy Cannon, Swan 4031		14
78	91	—	—	PORGY — Nina Simone, Bethlehem 11021		2
79	48	40	39	ONLY SIXTEEN — Sam Cooke, Keen 2022	S	10
★ 80	99	—	—	GEE — George Hamilton IV, ABC-Paramount 10028		2
81	86	90	95	LINDA LU — Ray Sharpe, Jamie 1128		4
★ 82	—	—	—	LIKE I LOVE YOU — Edd Byrnes & Friend, Warner Bros 5087		1
83	80	86	97	A GIRL LIKE YOU — Gary Stites, Carlton 516	S	4
84	81	69	71	DANNY BOY — Sil Austin, Mercury 71442	S	11
85	96	—	—	MIAMI — Eugene Church, Class 254		2
★ 86	—	—	—	I'VE BEEN THERE — Tommy Edwards, M-G-M 12814	S	1
87	92	—	—	SOLDIER'S JOY — Hawkshaw Hawkins, Columbia 41419		2
88	89	—	—	TIME MARCHES ON — Roy Hamilton, Epic 9323		2
89	95	—	—	I GOT STRIPES — Johnny Cash, Columbia 30427		2
90	94	—	—	MIDNIGHT FLYER — Nat King Cole, Capitol 4248		2
91	78	78	69	BEI MIR BIST DU SCHOEN — Louis Prima and Keely Smith, Dot 15956	S	6
92	93	99	—	YOU DON'T KNOW GIRLS — Kathy Linden, Felsted 8587		3
93	98	100	—	WHO SHOT SAM — George Jones, Mercury 71464	S	3
94	74	58	66	TALL COOL ONE — Wailers, Golden Crest 518		13
95	—	—	—	DON'T TELL ME YOUR TROUBLES — Don Gibson, RCA Victor 7566		1
96	—	—	—	FURRY MURRAY — The Tradewinds, RCA Victor 7553		1
97	100	—	—	ALIMONY — Frankie Ford, Ace 566		2
98	—	—	—	JUST AS MUCH AS EVER — Bob Beckham, Decca 30861		1
99	62	53	58	BACK IN THE U.S.A. — Chuck Berry, Chess 1729		8
100	—	—	—	I AIN'T NEVER — Webb Pierce, Decca 30923		1

FOR THE WEEK ENDING AUGUST 23

The Billboard HOT 100

★ STAR PERFORMERS showed the greatest upward progress on the Hot 100 this week.

S Indicates that STEREO SINGLE version is available.

This Week	One Week Ago	Two Weeks Ago	Three Weeks Ago	TITLE, Artist, Company, Record No.	Stereo	Weeks on Chart
1	1	2	5	A BIG HUNK O' LOVE — Elvis Presley, RCA Victor 7600		7
2	4	6	7	THERE GOES MY BABY — The Drifters, Atlantic 2025		12
3	3	3	6	MY HEART IS AN OPEN BOOK — Carl Dobkins Jr., Decca 30803		17
4	5	8	12	LAVENDER BLUE — Sammy Turner, Big Top 3016	S	9
5	2	1	1	LONELY BOY — Paul Anka, ABC-Paramount 10022	S	12
6	9	15	26	WHAT'D I SAY — Ray Charles, Atlantic 2031		7
7	16	32	63	THE THREE BELLS — Browns, RCA Victor 7555	S	4
8	8	13	14	WHAT A DIFF'RENCE A DAY MAKES — Dinah Washington, Mercury 71435	S	13
9	13	12	11	JUST A LITTLE TOO MUCH — Ricky Nelson, Imperial 5595		8
10	11	10	9	FORTY MILES OF BAD ROAD — Duane Eddy, Jamie 1126	S	10
11	6	5	3	TIGER — Fabian, Chancellor 1037	S	10
12	14	14	22	MY WISH CAME TRUE — Elvis Presley, RCA Victor 7600		6
13	7	4	2	THE BATTLE OF NEW ORLEANS — Johnny Horton, Columbia 41339		17
14	18	18	28	HERE COMES SUMMER — Jerry Keller, Kapp 277	S	8
15	17	22	33	IT WAS I — Skip & Flip, Brent 7002		9
16	21	25	31	WHAT IS LOVE — Playmates, Roulette 4160	S	7
17	10	7	4	WATERLOO — Stonewall Jackson, Columbia 41393		13
18	12	9	15	SWEETER THAN YOU — Ricky Nelson, Imperial 5595		7
19	23	28	47	THANK YOU PRETTY BABY — Brook Benton, Mercury 71478	S	14
20	26	11	8	LIPSTICK ON YOUR COLLAR — Connie Francis, M-G-M 12793	S	14
21	20	26	30	SMALL WORLD — Johnny Mathis, Columbia 41410		10
22	15	21	35	SEA OF LOVE — Phil Phillips, Mercury 71465		7
★23	37	49	59	KISSIN' TIME — Bobby Rydell, Cameo 167		8
★24	46	—	—	I WANT TO WALK YOU HOME — Fats Domino, Imperial 5606		2
25	28	31	34	ROBBIN' THE CRADLE — Tony Bellus, NRC 023		17
★26	38	52	67	I'M GONNA BE A WHEEL SOMEDAY — Fats Domino, Imperial 5606		4
★27	40	65	—	BABY TALK — Jan and Dean, Dore 522		3
28	19	16	18	RAGTIME COWBOY JOE — David Seville and the Chipmunks, Liberty 55200	S	7
29	35	42	57	SEE YOU IN SEPTEMBER — The Tempos, Climax 102		8
30	31	33	36	TILL THERE WAS YOU — Anita Bryant, Carlton 512	S	8
31	25	47	39	MONA LISA — Carl Mann, Phillips International 3539		12
32	24	34	32	CIAO CIAO BAMBINA — Jacky Noguez, Jamie 1127	S	9
★33	55	77	95	SLEEP WALK — Santo and Johnny, Canadian-American 103		4
★34	45	54	70	BROKEN-HEARTED MELODY — Sarah Vaughan, Mercury 71477		5
★35	65	—	—	I'M GONNA GET MARRIED — Lloyd Price, ABC-Paramount 10032	S	2
★36	50	66	—	RED RIVER ROCK — Johnny and the Hurricanes, Warwick 509		3
37	39	39	66	MAKIN' LOVE — Floyd Robinson, RCA Victor 7529		5
38	36	37	45	THE WAY I WALK — Jack Scott, Carlton 514	S	8
39	22	17	13	I ONLY HAVE EYES FOR YOU — Flamingos, End 1146	S	12
40	42	76	—	MY OWN TRUE LOVE — Jimmy Clanton, Ace 567		3
41	27	19	10	PERSONALITY — Lloyd Price, ABC-Paramount 10018	S	17
★42	57	71	79	MONA LISA — Conway Twitty, M-G-M 12804		5
43	30	20	25	I'LL BE SATISFIED — Jackie Wilson, Brunswick 55136		9
44	32	36	23	HUSHABYE — Mystics, Laurie 3028	S	14
45	48	53	48	HIGH HOPES — Frank Sinatra, Capitol 4214		10
46	34	27	24	FRANKIE — Connie Francis, M-G-M 12793	S	14
47	49	75	—	ANGEL FACE — Jimmy Darren, Colpix 119		3
48	53	67	73	TENNESSEE STUD — Eddy Arnold, RCA Victor 7542	S	6
★49	68	73	—	CARIBBEAN — Mitchell Torok, Guyden 2018		3
50	29	29	21	YOU'RE SO FINE — The Falcons, Unart 2013	S	18
★51	78	91	—	PORGY — Nina Simone, Bethlehem 11021		3
52	41	30	19	M.T.A. — Kingston Trio, Capitol 4221		10
53	54	60	76	CRY — The Knightsbridge Strings, Top Rank 2006	S	5
54	62	68	97	WITH OPEN ARMS — Jane Morgan, Kapp 284		4
55	47	38	42	SINCE YOU'VE BEEN GONE — Clyde McPhatter, Atlantic 2028		10
★56	—	—	—	(TILL) I KISSED YOU — Everly Brothers, Cadence 1369		1
57	52	43	49	TEN THOUSAND DRUMS — Carl Smith, Columbia 41417		7
★58	81	86	90	LINDA LU — Ray Sharpe, Jamie 1128		5
59	43	35	20	TWIXT TWELVE AND TWENTY — Pat Boone, Dot 15955	S	10
60	69	70	—	LEAVE MY KITTEN ALONE — Little Willie John, King 5219		3
61	67	72	96	SO HIGH, SO LOW — LaVern Baker, Atlantic 2033		4
62	44	23	16	BOBBY SOX TO STOCKINGS — Frankie Avalon, Chancellor 1036	S	13
63	61	59	74	ON AN EVENING IN ROMA — Dean Martin, Capitol 4022		6
64	75	57	50	LONELY GUITAR — Annette, Vista 339		7
65	60	56	52	THERE IS SOMETHING ON YOUR MIND — Big Jay McNeely, Swingin' 614		13
66	70	85	98	HALF-BREED — Marvin Rainwater, M-G-M 12803		4
★67	85	96	—	MIAMI — Eugene Church, Class 254		3
68	58	61	54	LIKE YOUNG — Andre Previn & David Rose, M-G-M 12793	S	10
69	51	44	38	THE WONDER OF YOU — Ray Peterson, RCA Victor 7513		14
70	33	24	17	A BOY WITHOUT A GIRL — Frankie Avalon, Chancellor 1036	S	13
71	59	40	41	THIS I SWEAR — Skyliners, Calico 106		12
72	71	63	65	I STILL GET JEALOUS — Joni James, M-G-M 12807	S	6
73	82	—	—	LIKE I LOVE YOU — Edd Byrnes & Friend, Warner Bros 5087		2
74	86	—	—	I'VE BEEN THERE — Tommy Edwards, M-G-M 12814	S	2
★75	100	—	—	I AIN'T NEVER — Webb Pierce, Decca 30923		2
76	89	95	—	I GOT STRIPES — Johnny Cash, Columbia 30427		3
77	66	69	81	KATY TOO — Johnny Cash, Sun 321		6
★78	—	—	—	MARY LOU — Ronnie Hawkins, Roulette 4178		1
79	80	99	—	GEE — George Hamilton IV, ABC-Paramount 10028		3
80	90	94	—	MIDNIGHT FLYER — Nat King Cole, Capitol 4248		3
81	73	51	46	QUIET THREE — Duane Eddy, Jamie 1126	S	10
★82	—	—	—	MORGEN — Ivo Robic, Laurie 3033		1
83	77	41	27	TALLAHASSEE LASSIE — Freddy Cannon, Swan 4031		15
84	88	89	—	TIME MARCHES ON — Roy Hamilton, Epic 9323		3
85	95	—	—	DON'T TELL ME YOUR TROUBLES — Don Gibson, RCA Victor 7566		2
★86	—	—	—	PRIMROSE LANE — Jerry Wallace, Challenge 59047		1
87	83	80	86	A GIRL LIKE YOU — Gary Stites, Carlton 516	S	5
88	74	45	44	REMEMBER WHEN — Platters, Mercury 71467	S	9
89	64	55	60	TO A SOLDIER BOY — The Tassels, Madison 117	S	6
★90	—	—	—	MAU-MAU — Wailers, Golden Crest 526		1
91	96	—	—	FURRY MURRAY — The Tradewinds, RCA Victor 7555		2
92	84	81	69	DANNY BOY — Sil Austin, Mercury 71442	S	12
93	98	—	—	JUST AS MUCH AS EVER — Bob Beckham, Decca 30861		2
94	76	64	75	BEACH TIME — Roger Smith, Warner Bros. 5068		8
95	—	—	—	THE ANGELS LISTENED IN — The Crests, Coed 515		1
96	—	88	91	BELLS, BELLS, BELLS — Billy & Lillie, Swan 4036		5
97	—	—	—	SMILE — Tony Bennett, Columbia 41434		1
98	—	—	—	IF YOU LOVE ME — LaVern Baker, Atlantic 2033		1
99	—	—	—	A GIRL'S WORK IS NEVER DONE — Chordettes, Cadence 1366		1
100	—	—	—	SAL'S GOT A SUGAR LIP — Johnny Horton, Columbia 41437		1

FOR THE WEEK ENDING AUGUST 30

The Billboard HOT 100

★ STAR PERFORMERS showed the greatest upward progress on the Hot 100 this week.

S Indicates that STEREO SINGLE version is available.

This Week	One Week Ago	Two Weeks Ago	Three Weeks Ago	TITLE, Artist, Company, Record No.	Stereo	Weeks on Chart
1	7	16	32	THE THREE BELLS — Browns, RCA Victor 7555	S	5
★ 2	22	15	21	SEA OF LOVE — Phil Phillips, Mercury 71465		8
3	4	5	8	LAVENDER BLUE — Sammy Turner, Big Top 3016	S	10
4	1	1	2	A BIG HUNK O' LOVE — Elvis Presley, RCA Victor 7600		8
5	3	3	3	MY HEART IS AN OPEN BOOK — Carl Dobkins Jr., Decca 30803		18
6	6	9	15	WHAT'D I SAY — Ray Charles, Atlantic 2031		8
7	2	4	6	THERE GOES MY BABY — The Drifters, Atlantic 2025		13
★ 8	33	55	77	SLEEP WALK — Santo and Johnny, Canadian-American 103		5
9	8	8	13	WHAT A DIFF'RENCE A DAY MAKES — Dinah Washington, Mercury 71435	S	14
★ 10	24	46	—	I WANT TO WALK YOU HOME — Fats Domino, Imperial 5606		3
★ 11	35	65	—	I'M GONNA GET MARRIED — Lloyd Price, ABC-Paramount 10032	S	3
12	15	17	22	IT WAS I — Skip & Flip, Brent 7002		10
13	5	2	1	LONELY BOY — Paul Anka, ABC-Paramount 10022	S	13
14	10	11	10	FORTY MILES OF BAD ROAD — Duane Eddy, Jamie 1126	S	11
15	16	21	25	WHAT IS LOVE — Playmates, Roulette 4160	S	8
16	12	14	14	MY WISH CAME TRUE — Elvis Presley, RCA Victor 7600		6
★ 17	27	40	65	BABY TALK — Jan and Dean, Dore 522		4
18	19	23	28	THANK YOU PRETTY BABY — Brook Benton, Mercury 71478	S	15
19	23	37	49	KISSIN' TIME — Bobby Rydell, Cameo 167		9
★ 20	36	50	66	RED RIVER ROCK — Johnny and the Hurricanes, Warwick 509	S	4
★ 21	34	45	54	BROKEN-HEARTED MELODY — Sarah Vaughan, Mercury 71477		6
22	9	13	12	JUST A LITTLE TOO MUCH — Ricky Nelson, Imperial 5595		9
23	18	12	9	SWEETER THAN YOU — Ricky Nelson, Imperial 5595		8
24	14	18	18	HERE COMES SUMMER — Jerry Keller, Kapp 277	S	9
25	13	7	4	THE BATTLE OF NEW ORLEANS — Johnny Horton, Columbia 41339		18
26	29	35	42	SEE YOU IN SEPTEMBER — The Tempos, Climax 102		9
27	11	6	5	TIGER — Fabian, Chancellor 1037	S	11
28	26	38	52	I'M GONNA BE A WHEEL SOMEDAY — Fats Domino, Imperial 5606		5
29	17	10	7	WATERLOO — Stonewall Jackson, Columbia 41393		14
★ 30	42	57	71	MONA LISA — Conway Twitty, M-G-M 12804		6
31	37	39	39	MAKIN' LOVE — Floyd Robinson, RCA Victor 7529		5
32	25	28	31	ROBBIN' THE CRADLE — Tony Bellus, NRC 023		18
★ 33	56	—	—	('TIL) I KISSED YOU — Everly Brothers, Cadence 1369		2
34	40	42	76	MY OWN TRUE LOVE — Jimmy Clanton, Ace 567	S	4
35	38	36	37	THE WAY I WALK — Jack Scott, Carlton 514	S	9
36	31	25	47	MONA LISA — Carl Mann, Phillips International 3539		13
37	21	20	26	SMALL WORLD — Johnny Mathis, Columbia 41410		11
38	30	31	33	TILL THERE WAS YOU — Anita Bryant, Carlton 512	S	9
★ 39	51	78	91	PORGY — Nina Simone, Bethlehem 11021	S	4
40	32	24	34	CIAO CIAO BAMBINA — Jacky Noguez, Jamie 1127	S	10
41	20	26	11	LIPSTICK ON YOUR COLLAR — Connie Francis, M-G-M 12793	S	15
★ 42	75	100	—	I AIN'T NEVER — Webb Pierce, Decca 30923		3
★ 43	54	62	68	WITH OPEN ARMS — Jane Morgan, Kapp 284	S	5
44	28	19	16	RAGTIME COWBOY JOE — David Seville and the Chipmunks, Liberty 55200	S	8
45	49	68	73	CARIBBEAN — Mitchell Torok, Guyden 2018		4
★ 46	58	81	86	LINDA LU — Ray Sharpe, Jamie 1128		6
47	47	49	75	ANGEL FACE — Jimmy Darren, Colpix 119	S	4
★ 48	73	82	—	LIKE I LOVE YOU — Edd Byrnes & Friend, Warner Bros. 5087		3
49	48	53	67	TENNESSEE STUD — Eddy Arnold, RCA Victor 7542	S	7
50	45	48	53	HIGH HOPES — Frank Sinatra, Capitol 4214		11
★ 51	86	—	—	PRIMROSE LANE — Jerry Wallace, Challenge 59047		2
★ 52	64	75	57	LONELY GUITAR — Annettee, Vista 339		8
53	41	27	19	PERSONALITY — Lloyd Price, ABC-Paramount 10018	S	18
54	61	67	72	SO HIGH, SO LOW — LaVern Baker, Atlantic 2033		5
★ 55	76	89	95	I GOT STRIPES — Johnny Cash, Columbia 41427		4
56	44	32	36	HUSHABYE — Mystics, Laurie 3028	S	15
57	43	30	20	I'LL BE SATISFIED — Jackie Wilson, Brunswick 55136		10
★ 58	69	51	44	THE WONDER OF YOU — Ray Peterson, RCA Victor 7513		15
★ 59	—	—	—	MACK THE KNIFE — Bobby Darin, Atco 6147		1
★ 60	82	—	—	MORGEN — Ivo Robic, Laurie 3033		2
61	53	54	60	CRY — The Knightsbridge Strings, Top Rank 2006	S	6
62	55	47	38	SINCE YOU'VE BEEN GONE — Clyde McPhatter, Atlantic 2028		11
★ 63	78	—	—	MARY LOU — Ronnie Hawkins, Roulette 4178		2
64	50	29	29	YOU'RE SO FINE — The Falcons, Unart 2013	S	19
65	39	22	17	I ONLY HAVE EYES FOR YOU — Flamingos, End 1146	S	13
66	80	90	94	MIDNIGHT FLYER — Nat King Cole, Capitol 4248		4
67	46	34	27	FRANKIE — Connie Francis, M-G-M 12793	S	15
68	66	70	85	HALF-BREED — Marvin Rainwater, M-G-M 12803		5
69	74	86	—	I'VE BEEN THERE — Tommy Edwards, M-G-M 12814	S	3
★ 70	—	—	—	JOHNNY REB — Johnny Horton, Columbia 41437		1
71	63	61	59	ON AN EVENING IN ROMA — Dean Martin, Capitol 4222		7
72	67	85	96	MIAMI — Eugene Church, Class 254		4
★ 73	—	—	—	POISON IVY — Coasters, Atco 6146		1
74	77	66	69	KATY TOO — Johnny Cash, Sun 321		7
75	60	69	70	LEAVE MY KITTEN ALONE — Little Willie John, King 5219		4
76	65	60	56	THERE IS SOMETHING ON YOUR MIND — Big Jay McNeely, Swingin' 614		14
77	52	41	30	M.T.A. — Kingston Trio, Capitol 4221		11
78	90	—	—	MAU-MAU — Wailers, Golden Crest 526		2
★ 79	98	—	—	IF YOU LOVE ME — LaVern Baker, Atlantic 2033		2
★ 80	95	—	—	THE ANGELS LISTENED IN — The Crests, Coed 515		2
★ 81	—	—	—	THE MUMMY — Bob McFadden & Dor, Brunswick 55140		1
82	57	52	43	TEN THOUSAND DRUMS — Carl Smith, Columbia 41417		8
83	68	58	61	LIKE YOUNG — Andre Previn & David Rose, M-G-M 12792	S	11
84	89	64	55	TO A SOLDIER BOY — The Tassels, Madison 117	S	7
85	97	—	—	SMILE — Tony Bennett, Columbia 41434		2
★ 86	—	—	—	HEY LITTLE GIRL — Dee Clark, Abner 1029		1
★ 87	—	—	—	TRUE, TRUE HAPPINESS — Johnny Tillotson, Cadence 1364		1
★ 88	—	—	—	FIVE FEET HIGH AND RISING — Johnny Cash, Columbia 41427		1
★ 89	—	—	—	CHAPEL OF DREAMS — Dubs, Gone 5046		1
★ 90	—	—	—	OKEFENOKEE — Freddie Cannon, Swan 4038		1
91	79	80	99	GEE — George Hamilton IV, ABC-Paramount 10028		4
92	93	98	—	JUST AS MUCH AS EVER — Bob Beckham, Decca 30861		3
93	99	—	—	A GIRL'S WORK IS NEVER DONE — Chordettes, Cadence 1366		2
94	—	—	—	TWICE AS NICE — Clyde McPhatter, M-G-M 12816	S	1
95	59	43	35	TWIXT TWELVE AND TWENTY — Pat Boone, Dot 15955	S	11
96	100	—	—	SAL'S GOT A SUGAR LIP — Johnny Horton, Columbia 41437		2
97	70	33	24	A BOY WITHOUT A GIRL — Frankie Avalon, Chancellor 1036	S	14
98	—	—	—	POCO, LOCO — Gene and Eunice, Case 101		1
99	96	—	88	BELLS, BELLS, BELLS — Billy & Lillie, Swan 4036		6
100	—	—	—	I LOOKED AT HEAVEN — Tommy Edwards, M-G-M 12814	S	1

FOR THE WEEK ENDING SEPTEMBER 6 — The Billboard HOT 100

★ STAR PERFORMERS showed the greatest upward progress on the Hot 100 this week.

S Indicates that STEREO SINGLE version is available.

THIS WEEK	ONE WEEK AGO	TWO WEEKS AGO	THREE WEEKS AGO	TITLE, Artist, Company, Record No.	STEREO	WEEKS ON CHART
1	1	7	16	THE THREE BELLS — Browns, RCA Victor 7555	S	6
2	2	22	15	SEA OF LOVE — Phil Phillips, Mercury 71465		9
3	8	33	55	SLEEP WALK — Santo and Johnny, Canadian-American 103		6
4	3	4	5	LAVENDER BLUE — Sammy Turner, Big Top 3016	S	11
5	11	35	65	I'M GONNA GET MARRIED — Lloyd Price, ABC-Paramount 10032	S	4
6	6	6	9	WHAT'D I SAY — Ray Charles, Atlantic 2031		9
7	4	1	1	A BIG HUNK O' LOVE — Elvis Presley, RCA Victor 7600		9
8	7	2	4	THERE GOES MY BABY — The Drifters, Atlantic 2025		14
★9	20	36	50	RED RIVER ROCK — Johnny and the Hurricanes, Warwick 509	S	5
10	10	24	46	I WANT TO WALK YOU HOME — Fats Domino, Imperial 5606		4
11	12	15	17	IT WAS I — Skip & Flip, Brent 7002		11
12	5	3	3	MY HEART IS AN OPEN BOOK — Carl Dobkins Jr., Decca 30803		19
★13	33	56	—	('TIL) I KISSED YOU — Everly Brothers, Cadence 1369		3
14	21	34	45	BROKEN-HEARTED MELODY — Sarah Vaughan, Mercury 71477		7
15	19	23	37	KISSIN' TIME — Bobby Rydell, Cameo 167		10
16	18	19	23	THANK YOU PRETTY BABY — Brook Benton, Mercury 71478	S	16
17	17	27	40	BABY TALK — Jan and Dean, Dore 522		5
18	9	8	8	WHAT A DIFF'RENCE A DAY MAKES — Dinah Washington, Mercury 71435	S	15
19	15	16	21	WHAT IS LOVE — Playmates, Roulette 4160	S	9
20	22	9	13	JUST A LITTLE TOO MUCH — Ricky Nelson, Imperial 5595		10
21	16	12	14	MY WISH CAME TRUE — Elvis Presley, RCA Victor 7600		7
22	28	26	38	I'M GONNA BE A WHEEL SOMEDAY — Fats Domino, Imperial 5606		6
23	14	10	11	FORTY MILES OF BAD ROAD — Duane Eddy, Jamie 1126	S	12
24	13	5	2	LONELY BOY — Paul Anka, ABC-Paramount 10022	S	14
25	24	14	18	HERE COMES SUMMER — Jerry Keller, Kapp 277	S	10
26	23	18	12	SWEETER THAN YOU — Ricky Nelson, Imperial 5595		9
27	31	37	39	MAKIN' LOVE — Floyd Robinson, RCA Victor 7529		6
★28	39	51	78	PORGY — Nina Simone, Bethlehem 11021	S	5
29	30	42	57	MONA LISA — Conway Twitty, M-G-M 12804		7
30	26	29	35	SEE YOU IN SEPTEMBER — The Tempos, Climax 102		10
★31	45	49	68	CARIBBEAN — Mitchell Torok, Guyden 2018		5
32	32	25	28	ROBBIN' THE CRADLE — Tony Bellus, NRC 023		19
33	37	21	20	SMALL WORLD — Johnny Mathis, Columbia 41410		12
34	25	13	7	THE BATTLE OF NEW ORLEANS — Johnny Horton, Columbia 41339		19
35	38	30	31	TILL THERE WAS YOU — Anita Bryant, Carlton 512	S	10
36	34	40	42	MY OWN TRUE LOVE — Jimmy Clanton, Ace 567	S	5
37	36	31	25	MONA LISA — Carl Mann, Phillips International 3539		14
38	42	75	100	I AIN'T NEVER — Webb Pierce, Decca 30923		4
39	43	54	62	WITH OPEN ARMS — Jane Morgan, Kapp 284	S	6
★40	60	82	—	MORGEN — Ivo Robic, Laurie 3033		3
41	50	45	48	HIGH HOPES — Frank Sinatra, Capitol 4214		12
42	48	73	82	LIKE I LOVE YOU — Edd Byrnes & Friend, Warner Bros. 5087	S	4
★43	59	—	—	MACK THE KNIFE — Bobby Darin, Atco 6147		2
44	27	11	6	TIGER — Fabian, Chancellor 1037	S	12
45	51	86	—	PRIMROSE LANE — Jerry Wallace, Challenge 59047		3
46	35	38	36	THE WAY I WALK — Jack Scott, Carlton 514	S	10
47	55	76	89	I GOT STRIPES — Johnny Cash, Columbia 41427		5
48	29	17	10	WATERLOO — Stonewall Jackson, Columbia 41393		15
49	46	58	81	LINDA LU — Ray Sharpe, Jamie 1128		7
50	40	32	24	CIAO CIAO BAMBINA — Jacky Noguez, Jamie 1127	S	11
★51	81	—	—	THE MUMMY — Bob McFadden & Dor, Brunswick 55140		2
52	54	61	67	SO HIGH, SO LOW — LaVern Baker, Atlantic 2033		6
53	49	48	53	TENNESSEE STUD — Eddy Arnold, RCA Victor 7542	S	8
★54	73	—	—	POISON IVY — Coasters, Atco 6146		2
55	41	20	26	LIPSTICK ON YOUR COLLAR — Connie Francis, M-G-M 12793	S	16
56	63	78	—	MARY LOU — Ronnie Hawkins, Roulette 4177		3
57	47	47	49	ANGEL FACE — Jimmy Darren, Colpix 119	S	5
58	66	80	90	MIDNIGHT FLYER — Nat King Cole, Capitol 4248		5
59	52	64	75	LONELY GUITAR — Annettee, Vista 339		9
★60	70	—	—	JOHNNY REB — Johnny Horton, Columbia 41437		2
★61	86	—	—	HEY LITTLE GIRL — Dee Clark, Abner 1029		2
★62	80	95	—	THE ANGELS LISTENED IN — The Crests, Coed 515		3
63	69	74	86	I'VE BEEN THERE — Tommy Edwards, M-G-M 12814	S	4
64	61	53	54	CRY — The Knightsbridge Strings, Top Rank 2006	S	7
★65	—	—	—	JUST ASK YOUR HEART — Frankie Avalon, Chancellor 1040	S	1
66	62	55	47	SINCE YOU'VE BEEN GONE — Clyde McPhatter, Atlantic 2028		12
★67	—	—	—	PUT YOUR HEAD ON MY SHOULDER — Paul Anka, ABC-Paramount 10040	S	1
★68	—	—	—	SOMETHIN' ELSE — Eddie Cochran, Liberty 55203		1
★69	—	—	—	YOU'RE GONNA MISS ME — Connie Francis, M-G-M 12824	S	1
70	71	63	61	ON AN EVENING IN ROMA — Dean Martin, Capitol 4222		8
71	78	90	—	MAU-MAU — Wailers, Golden Crest 526		3
★72	87	—	—	TRUE, TRUE HAPPINESS — Johnny Tillotson, Cadence 1365		2
73	82	57	52	TEN THOUSAND DRUMS — Carl Smith, Columbia 41417		9
★74	89	—	—	CHAPEL OF DREAMS — Dubs, Gone 5046		2
75	68	66	70	HALF-BREED — Marvin Rainwater, M-G-M 12803		6
76	85	97	—	SMILE — Tony Bennett, Columbia 41434		3
77	57	43	30	I'LL BE SATISFIED — Jackie Wilson, Brunswick 55136		11
78	75	60	69	LEAVE MY KITTEN ALONE — Little Willie John, King 5219		5
79	74	77	66	KATY TOO — Johnny Cash, Sun 321		8
80	44	28	19	RAGTIME COWBOY JOE — David Seville and the Chipmunks, Liberty 55200	S	9
81	91	79	80	GEE — George Hamilton IV, ABC-Paramount 10028		5
82	76	65	60	THERE IS SOMETHING ON YOUR MIND — Big Jay McNeely, Swingin' 614		15
83	90	—	—	OKEFENOKEE — Freddie Cannon, Swan 4038		2
★84	—	—	—	THE THREE BELLS — Dick Flood, Monument 408		1
85	72	67	85	MIAMI — Eugene Church, Class 254		5
86	83	68	58	LIKE YOUNG — Andre Previn & David Rose, M-G-M 12792	S	12
★87	—	—	—	SUZY BABY — Bobby Vee & the Shadows, Liberty 55208		1
88	92	93	98	JUST AS MUCH AS EVER — Bob Beckham, Decca 30861		4
89	93	99	—	A GIRL'S WORK IS NEVER DONE — Chordettes, Cadence 1366		3
★90	—	—	—	BETTY, MY ANGEL — Jerry Fuller, Challenge 59052		1
91	94	—	—	TWICE AS NICE — Clyde McPhatter, M-G-M 12816	S	2
92	—	—	—	I CRIED — Joe Damiano, Chancellor 1039		1
93	64	50	29	YOU'RE SO FINE — The Falcons, Unart 2013	S	20
94	98	—	—	POCO, LOCO — Gene and Eunice, Case 101		2
95	96	100	—	SAL'S GOT A SUGAR LIP — Johnny Horton, Columbia 41437		3
96	—	—	—	SWEET BIRD OF YOUTH — Nat King Cole, Capitol 4248		1
97	53	41	27	PERSONALITY — Lloyd Price, ABC-Paramount 10018	S	19
98	56	44	32	HUSHABYE — Mystics, Laurie 3028	S	16
99	58	69	51	THE WONDER OF YOU — Ray Peterson, RCA Victor 7513		16
100	—	—	—	CATERPILLAR CRAWL — The Strangers, Titan 1701		1

The Billboard HOT 100

FOR THE WEEK ENDING SEPTEMBER 13

★ STAR PERFORMERS showed the greatest upward progress on the Hot 100 this week.

S Indicates that STEREO SINGLE version is available.

This Week	One Week Ago	Two Weeks Ago	Three Weeks Ago	TITLE, Artist, Company, Record No.	Stereo	Weeks on Chart
1	1	1	7	THE THREE BELLS — Browns, RCA Victor 7555	S	7
2	3	8	33	SLEEP WALK — Santo and Johnny, Canadian-American 103		7
3	2	2	22	SEA OF LOVE — Phil Phillips, Mercury 71465		10
4	5	11	35	I'M GONNA GET MARRIED — Lloyd Price, ABC-Paramount 10032	S	5
5	9	20	36	RED RIVER ROCK — Johnny and the Hurricanes, Warwick 509	S	6
6	13	33	56	('TIL) I KISSED YOU — Everly Brothers, Cadence 1369		4
7	14	21	34	BROKEN-HEARTED MELODY — Sarah Vaughan, Mercury 71477		8
8	4	3	4	LAVENDER BLUE — Sammy Turner, Big Top 3016	S	12
9	6	6	6	WHAT'D I SAY — Ray Charles, Atlantic 2031		10
10	10	10	24	I WANT TO WALK YOU HOME — Fats Domino, Imperial 5606		5
11	17	17	27	BABY TALK — Jan and Dean, Dore 522		6
12	8	7	2	THERE GOES MY BABY — The Drifters, Atlantic 2025		15
13	7	4	1	A BIG HUNK O' LOVE — Elvis Presley, RCA Victor 7600		10
14	15	19	23	KISSIN' TIME — Bobby Rydell, Cameo 167		11
15	11	12	15	IT WAS I — Skip & Flip, Brent 7002		12
16	12	5	3	MY HEART IS AN OPEN BOOK — Carl Dobkins Jr., Decca 30803		20
17	18	9	8	WHAT A DIFF'RENCE A DAY MAKES — Dinah Washington, Mercury 71435	S	16
18	16	18	19	THANK YOU PRETTY BABY — Brook Benton, Mercury 71478	S	17
19	19	15	16	WHAT IS LOVE — Playmates, Roulette 4160	S	10
20	22	28	26	I'M GONNA BE A WHEEL SOMEDAY — Fats Domino, Imperial 5606		7
21	27	31	37	MAKIN' LOVE — Floyd Robinson, RCA Victor 7529		7
22	21	16	12	MY WISH CAME TRUE — Elvis Presley, RCA Victor 7600		8
23	30	26	29	SEE YOU IN SEPTEMBER — The Tempos, Climax 102		11
★24	43	59	—	MACK THE KNIFE — Bobby Darin, Atco 6147		3
25	25	24	14	HERE COMES SUMMER — Jerry Keller, Kapp 277	S	11
26	32	32	25	ROBBIN' THE CRADLE — Tony Bellus, NRC 023		20
27	28	39	51	I LOVES YOU PORGY — Nina Simone, Bethlehem 11021	S	6
★28	45	51	86	PRIMROSE LANE — Jerry Wallace, Challenge 59047		4
★29	40	60	82	MORGEN — Ivo Robic, Laurie 3033		4
30	41	50	45	HIGH HOPES — Frank Sinatra, Capitol 4214		13
31	20	22	9	JUST A LITTLE TOO MUCH — Ricky Nelson, Imperial 5595		11
32	23	14	10	FORTY MILES OF BAD ROAD — Duane Eddy, Jamie 1126	S	13
33	36	34	40	MY OWN TRUE LOVE — Jimmy Clanton, Ace 567	S	6
★34	54	73	—	POISON IVY — Coasters, Atco 6146		3
35	31	45	49	CARIBBEAN — Mitchell Torok, Guyden 2018		6
36	33	37	21	SMALL WORLD — Johnny Mathis, Columbia 41410		13
37	24	13	5	LONELY BOY — Paul Anka, ABC-Paramount 10022	S	15
38	35	38	30	TILL THERE WAS YOU — Anita Bryant, Carlton 512	S	11
39	37	36	31	MONA LISA — Carl Mann, Phillips International 3539		15
40	29	30	42	MONA LISA — Conway Twitty, M-G-M 12804		8
★41	67	—	—	PUT YOUR HEAD ON MY SHOULDER — Paul Anka, ABC-Paramount 10040	S	2
42	34	25	13	THE BATTLE OF NEW ORLEANS — Johnny Horton, Columbia 41339		20
43	26	23	18	SWEETER THAN YOU — Ricky Nelson, Imperial 5595		10
44	38	42	75	I AIN'T NEVER — Webb Pierce, Decca 30923		5
45	47	55	76	I GOT STRIPES — Johnny Cash, Columbia 41427	S	6
46	51	81	—	THE MUMMY — Bob McFadden & Dor, Brunswick 55140		3
47	39	43	54	WITH OPEN ARMS — Jane Morgan, Kapp 284	S	7
★48	61	86	—	HEY LITTLE GIRL — Dee Clark, Abner 1029		3
49	42	48	73	LIKE I LOVE YOU — Edd Byrnes & Friend, Warner Bros. 5087	S	5
★50	62	80	95	THE ANGELS LISTENED IN — The Crests, Coed 515		4
51	56	63	78	MARY LOU — Ronnie Hawkins, Roulette 4177		4
★52	65	—	—	JUST ASK YOUR HEART — Frankie Avalon, Chancellor 1040	S	2
★53	69	—	—	YOU'RE GONNA MISS ME — Connie Francis, M-G-M 12814	S	2
54	60	70	—	JOHNNY REB — Johnny Horton, Columbia 41437		3
55	58	66	80	MIDNIGHT FLYER — Nat King Cole, Capitol 4248		6
56	63	69	74	I'VE BEEN THERE — Tommy Edwards, M-G-M 12814	S	5
57	57	47	47	ANGEL FACE — Jimmy Darren, Colpix 119	S	6
★58	68	—	—	SOMETHIN' ELSE — Eddie Cochran, Liberty 55203		2
★59	84	—	—	THE THREE BELLS — Dick Flood, Monument 408		2
60	46	35	38	THE WAY I WALK — Jack Scott, Carlton 514	S	11
61	44	27	11	TIGER — Fabian, Chancellor 1037	S	13
62	52	54	61	SO HIGH, SO LOW — LaVern Baker, Atlantic 2033		7
63	59	52	64	LONELY GUITAR — Annette, Vista 339		10
64	72	87	—	TRUE, TRUE HAPPINESS — Johnny Tillotson, Cadence 1365		3
65	78	75	60	LEAVE MY KITTEN ALONE — Little Willie John, King 5219		6
★66	83	90	—	OKEFENOKEE — Freddie Cannon, Swan 4038		3
67	49	46	58	LINDA LU — Ray Sharpe, Jamie 1128		8
68	71	78	90	MAU-MAU — Wailers, Golden Crest 526		4
69	53	49	48	TENNESSEE STUD — Eddy Arnold, RCA Victor 7542	S	9
70	48	29	17	WATERLOO — Stonewall Jackson, Columbia 41393		16
★71	—	—	—	I'M A HOG FOR YOU — Coasters, Atco 6146		1
★72	—	—	—	LONELY STREET — Andy Williams, Cadence 1370		1
73	81	91	79	GEE — George Hamilton IV, ABC-Paramount 10028		6
★74	100	—	—	CATERPILLAR CRAWL — The Strangers, Titan 1701		2
★75	—	—	—	MR. BLUE — Fleetwoods, Dolton 5		1
★76	—	—	—	BATTLE OF KOOKAMONGA — Homer & Jethro, RCA Victor 7585	S	1
★77	—	—	—	COME ON AND GET ME — Fabian, Chancellor 1041	S	1
★78	—	—	—	BATTLE HYMN OF THE REPUBLIC — The Mormon Tabernacle Choir, Columbia 41459		1
79	70	71	63	ON AN EVENING IN ROMA — Dean Martin, Capitol 4222		9
80	76	85	97	SMILE — Tony Bennett, Columbia 41434		4
81	95	96	100	SAL'S GOT A SUGAR LIP — Johnny Horton, Columbia 41437		4
★82	—	—	—	WHERE — Platters, Mercury 71502	S	1
★83	—	—	—	BREAKING UP IS HARD TO DO — Jivin' Gene, Mercury 71485		1
★84	—	—	—	TEEN BEAT — Sandy Nelson, Original 5		1
85	88	92	93	JUST AS MUCH AS EVER — Bob Beckham, Decca 30861		5
86	87	—	—	SUZY BABY — Bobby Vee & the Shadows, Liberty 55208		2
★87	—	—	—	THE SHAPE I'M IN — Johnny Restivo, RCA Victor 7559		1
88	82	76	65	THERE IS SOMETHING ON YOUR MIND — Big Jay McNeely, Swingin' 614		16
89	55	41	20	LIPSTICK ON YOUR COLLAR — Connie Francis, M-G-M 12793	S	17
90	94	98	—	POCO, LOCO — Gene and Eunice, Case 101		3
91	92	—	—	I CRIED — Joe Damiano, Chancellor 1039		2
92	77	57	43	I'LL BE SATISFIED — Jackie Wilson, Brunswick 55136		12
93	75	68	66	HALF-BREED — Marvin Rainwater, M-G-M 12803		7
94	66	62	55	SINCE YOU'VE BEEN GONE — Clyde McPhatter, Atlantic 2028		13
95	50	40	32	CIAO CIAO BAMBINA — Jacky Noguez, Jamie 1127	S	12
96	96	—	—	SWEET BIRD OF YOUTH — Nat King Cole, Capitol 4248		2
97	—	—	—	YOU WERE MINE — Fireflies, Ribbon 6901		1
98	74	89	—	CHAPEL OF DREAMS — Dubs, Gone 5046		3
99	90	—	—	BETTY, MY ANGEL — Jerry Fuller, Challenge 59052		2
100	—	—	—	YOU BETTER KNOW IT — Jackie Wilson, Brunswick 55149		1

FOR THE WEEK ENDING SEPTEMBER 20

The Billboard HOT 100

★ STAR PERFORMERS showed the greatest upward progress on the Hot 100 this week.

S Indicates that STEREO SINGLE version is available.

This Week	One Week Ago	Two Weeks Ago	Three Weeks Ago	TITLE, Artist, Company, Record No.	Stereo	Weeks on Chart
1	1	1	1	THE THREE BELLS — Browns, RCA Victor 7555	S	8
2	2	3	8	SLEEP WALK — Santo and Johnny, Canadian-American 103		8
3	4	5	11	I'M GONNA GET MARRIED — Lloyd Price, ABC-Paramount 10032	S	6
4	3	2	2	SEA OF LOVE — Phil Phillips, Mercury 71465		11
5	6	13	33	('TIL) I KISSED YOU — Everly Brothers, Cadence 1369		5
6	5	9	20	RED RIVER ROCK — Johnny and the Hurricanes, Warwick 509	S	7
7	7	14	21	BROKEN-HEARTED MELODY — Sarah Vaughan, Mercury 71477		9
8	10	10	10	I WANT TO WALK YOU HOME — Fats Domino, Imperial 5606		6
★9	24	43	59	MACK THE KNIFE — Bobby Darin, Atco 6147		4
10	11	17	17	BABY TALK — Jan and Dean, Dore 522		7
11	8	4	3	LAVENDER BLUE — Sammy Turner, Big Top 3016	S	13
12	14	15	19	KISSIN' TIME — Bobby Rydell, Cameo 167		12
13	9	6	6	WHAT'D I SAY — Ray Charles, Atlantic 2031		11
14	12	8	7	THERE GOES MY BABY — The Drifters, Atlantic 2025		16
★15	34	54	73	POISON IVY — Coasters, Atco 6146		4
16	18	16	18	THANK YOU PRETTY BABY — Brook Benton, Mercury 71478	S	20
17	20	22	28	I'M GONNA BE A WHEEL SOMEDAY — Fats Domino, Imperial 5606		8
18	17	18	9	WHAT A DIFF'RENCE A DAY MAKES — Dinah Washington, Mercury 71435	S	17
19	15	11	12	IT WAS I — Skip & Flip, Brent 7002		13
20	13	7	4	A BIG HUNK O' LOVE — Elvis Presley, RCA Victor 7600		11
21	29	40	60	MORGEN — Ivo Robic, Laurie 3033		5
22	21	27	31	MAKIN' LOVE — Floyd Robinson, RCA Victor 7529		8
★23	59	84	—	THE THREE BELLS — Dick Flood, Monument 408		3
★24	44	38	42	I AIN'T NEVER — Webb Pierce, Decca 30923		6
25	16	12	5	MY HEART IS AN OPEN BOOK — Carl Dobkins Jr., Decca 30803		21
26	27	28	39	I LOVES YOU PORGY — Nina Simone, Bethlehem 11021	S	7
★27	48	61	86	HEY LITTLE GIRL — Dee Clark, Abner 1029		4
★28	84	—	—	TEEN BEAT — Sandy Nelson, Original 5		2
★29	41	67	—	PUT YOUR HEAD ON MY SHOULDER — Paul Anka, ABC-Paramount 10040	S	3
30	19	19	15	WHAT IS LOVE — Playmates, Roulette 4160	S	11
31	28	45	51	PRIMROSE LANE — Jerry Wallace, Challenge 59047		5
32	23	30	26	SEE YOU IN SEPTEMBER — The Tempos, Climax 102		12
33	33	36	34	MY OWN TRUE LOVE — Jimmy Clanton, Ace 567	S	7
★34	75	—	—	MR. BLUE — Fleetwoods, Dolton 5		2
★35	52	65	—	JUST ASK YOUR HEART — Frankie Avalon, Chancellor 1040	S	3
36	22	21	16	MY WISH CAME TRUE — Elvis Presley, RCA Victor 7600		9
★37	76	—	—	BATTLE OF KOOKAMONGA — Homer & Jethro, RCA Victor 7585	S	2
★38	50	62	80	THE ANGELS LISTENED IN — The Crests, Coed 515		5
39	46	51	81	THE MUMMY — Bob McFadden & Dor, Brunswick 55140		4
40	35	31	45	CARIBBEAN — Mitchell Torok, Guyden 2018		7
41	25	25	24	HERE COMES SUMMER — Jerry Keller, Kapp 277	S	12
42	26	32	32	ROBBIN' THE CRADLE — Tony Bellus, NRC 023		21
★43	53	69	—	YOU'RE GONNA MISS ME — Connie Francis, M-G-M 12814	S	3
44	36	33	37	SMALL WORLD — Johnny Mathis, Columbia 41410		14
45	30	41	50	HIGH HOPES — Frank Sinatra, Capitol 4214		14
46	32	23	14	FORTY MILES OF BAD ROAD — Duane Eddy, Jamie 1126	S	14
47	49	42	48	LIKE I LOVE YOU — Edd Byrnes & Friend, Warner Bros. 5087	S	6
48	40	29	30	MONA LISA — Conway Twitty, M-G-M 12804		9
★49	74	100	—	CATERPILLAR CRAWL — The Strangers, Titan 1701		3
50	31	20	22	JUST A LITTLE TOO MUCH — Ricky Nelson, Imperial 5595		12
51	55	58	66	MIDNIGHT FLYER — Nat King Cole, Capitol 4248		7
★52	71	—	—	I'M A HOG FOR YOU — Coasters, Atco 6146		2
53	45	47	55	I GOT STRIPES — Johnny Cash, Columbia 41427	S	7
★54	64	72	87	TRUE, TRUE HAPPINESS — Johnny Tillotson, Cadence 1365		4
55	38	35	38	TILL THERE WAS YOU — Anita Bryant, Carlton 512	S	12
★56	66	83	90	OKEFENOKEE — Freddie Cannon, Swan 4038		4
57	62	52	54	SO HIGH, SO LOW — LaVern Baker, Atlantic 2033		8
★58	78	—	—	BATTLE HYMN OF THE REPUBLIC — The Mormon Tabernacle Choir, Columbia 41459		2
59	51	56	63	MARY LOU — Ronnie Hawkins, Roulette 4177		5
60	43	26	23	SWEETER THAN YOU — Ricky Nelson, Imperial 5595		11
61	54	60	70	JOHNNY REB — Johnny Horton, Columbia 41437		4
62	58	68	—	SOMETHIN' ELSE — Eddie Cochran, Liberty 55203		3
63	67	49	46	LINDA LU — Ray Sharpe, Jamie 1128		9
64	72	—	—	LONELY STREET — Andy Williams, Cadence 1370		2
65	65	78	75	LEAVE MY KITTEN ALONE — Little Willie John, King 5219		7
66	47	39	43	WITH OPEN ARMS — Jane Morgan, Kapp 284	S	8
67	56	63	69	I'VE BEEN THERE — Tommy Edwards, M-G-M 12814	S	6
★68	—	—	—	FOOL'S HALL OF FAME — Pat Boone, Dot 15982		1
69	77	—	—	COME ON AND GET ME — Fabian, Chancellor 1041	S	2
70	39	37	36	MONA LISA — Carl Mann, Phillips International 3539		16
71	57	57	47	ANGEL FACE — Jimmy Darren, Colpix 119	S	7
★72	97	—	—	YOU WERE MINE — Fireflies, Ribbon 6901		2
73	80	76	85	SMILE — Tony Bennett, Columbia 41434		5
★74	—	—	—	DECK OF CARDS — Wink Martindale, Dot 15968		1
★75	100	—	—	YOU BETTER KNOW IT — Jackie Wilson, Brunswick 55149		2
76	60	46	35	THE WAY I WALK — Jack Scott, Carlton 514	S	12
77	86	87	—	SUZY BABY — Bobby Vee & the Shadows, Liberty 55208		3
78	69	53	49	TENNESSEE STUD — Eddy Arnold, RCA Victor 7542	S	10
79	82	—	—	WHERE — Platters, Mercury 71502	S	2
80	87	—	—	THE SHAPE I'M IN — Johnny Restivo, RCA Victor 7559		2
81	79	70	71	ON AN EVENING IN ROMA — Dean Martin, Capitol 4222		10
82	83	—	—	BREAKING UP IS HARD TO DO — Jivin' Gene, Mercury 71485		2
★83	—	—	—	LOVE POTION #9 — Clovers, United Artists 180		1
84	73	81	91	GEE — George Hamilton IV, ABC-Paramount 10028		7
★85	—	—	88	FIVE FEET HIGH AND RISING — Johnny Cash, Columbia 41427		2
86	—	—	—	DON'T TELL ME YOUR TROUBLES — Don Gibson, RCA Victor 7566		3
87	98	74	89	CHAPEL OF DREAMS — Dubs, Gone 5046		4
★88	—	—	—	EVERY LITTLE THING I DO — Dion & the Belmonts, Laurie 3035		1
★89	—	—	—	(7 LITTLE GIRLS) SITTIN' IN THE BACK SEAT — Paul Evans & the Curls, Guaranteed 200		1
★90	—	—	—	WORRIED MAN — Kingston Trio, Capitol 4271		1
91	42	34	25	THE BATTLE OF NEW ORLEANS — Johnny Horton, Columbia 41339		21
92	68	71	78	MAU-MAU — Wailers, Golden Crest 526		5
93	—	—	—	FOG CUTTER — Frantics, Dolton 6		1
94	63	59	52	LONELY GUITAR — Annette, Vista 339		11
95	—	—	—	PRIVATE EYE — Olympics, Arvee 562		1
96	81	95	96	SAL'S GOT A SUGAR LIP — Johnny Horton, Columbia 41437		5
97	—	—	—	WISH IT WERE ME — Platters, Mercury 71502	S	1
98	—	—	—	ONE MORE SUNRISE — Leslie Uggams, Columbia 41451		1
99	—	—	—	I'LL NEVER FALL IN LOVE AGAIN — Johnny Fay, Columbia 41438		1
100	—	—	—	I AIN'T NEVER — Four Preps, Capitol 4256		1

FOR THE WEEK ENDING SEPTEMBER 27

The Billboard HOT 100

★ STAR PERFORMERS showed the greatest upward progress on the Hot 100 this week.

S Indicates that STEREO SINGLE version is available.

This Week	One Week Ago	Two Weeks Ago	Three Weeks Ago	Star	TITLE	Artist, Company, Record No.	Stereo	Weeks on Chart
1	2	2	3		SLEEP WALK	Santo and Johnny, Canadian-American 103		9
2	1	1	1		THE THREE BELLS	Browns, RCA Victor 7555	S	9
3	3	4	5		I'M GONNA GET MARRIED	Loyd Price, ABC-Paramount 10032	S	7
4	5	6	13		('TIL) I KISSED YOU	Everly Brothers, Cadence 1369		6
5	4	3	2		SEA OF LOVE	Phil Phillips, Mercury 71465		12
6	6	5	9		RED RIVER ROCK	Johnny and the Hurricanes, Warwick 509	S	8
7	9	24	43		MACK THE KNIFE	Bobby Darin, Dore 522		5
8	7	7	14		BROKEN-HEARTED MELODY	Sarah Vaughan, Mercury 71477		10
9	8	10	10		I WANT TO WALK YOU HOME	Fats Domino, Imperial 5606		7
10	29	41	67	★	PUT YOUR HEAD ON MY SHOULDER	Paul Anka, ABC-Paramount 10040	S	4
11	12	14	15		KISSIN' TIME	Bobby Rydell, Cameo 167		13
12	15	34	54		POISON IVY	Coasters, Atco 6146		5
13	21	29	40		MORGEN	Ivo Robic, Laurie 3033		6
14	35	52	65	★	JUST ASK YOUR HEART	Frankie Avalon, Chancellor 1040	S	4
15	28	84	—	★	TEEN BEAT	Sandy Nelson, Original Sound 5		3
16	34	75	—	★	MR. BLUE	Fleetwoods, Dolton 5		3
17	31	28	45	★	PRIMROSE LANE	Jerry Wallace, Challenge 59047		6
18	10	11	17		BABY TALK	Jan and Dean, Dore 522		8
19	37	76	—	★	BATTLE OF KOOKAMONGA	Homer & Jethro, RCA Victor 7585	S	3
20	27	48	61		HEY LITTLE GIRL	Dee Clark, Abner 1029	S	5
21	13	9	6		WHAT'D I SAY	Ray Charles, Atlantic 2031		12
22	11	8	4		LAVENDER BLUE	Sammy Turner, Big Top 3016	S	14
23	22	21	27		MAKIN' LOVE	Floyd Robinson, RCA Victor 5729		9
24	23	59	84		THE THREE BELLS	Dick Flood, Monument 408		4
25	26	27	28		I LOVES YOU PORGY	Nina Simone, Bethlehem 11021	S	8
26	24	44	38		I AIN'T NEVER	Webb Pierce, Decca 30923		7
27	16	18	16		THANK YOU PRETTY BABY	Brook Benton, Mercury 71478	S	21
28	59	51	56	★	MARY LOU	Ronnie Hawkins, Roulette 4177	S	6
29	58	78	—	★	BATTLE HYMN OF THE REPUBLIC	The Mormon Tabernacle Choir, Columbia 41459		3
30	19	15	11		IT WAS I	Skip & Flip, Brent 7002		14
31	40	35	31		CARIBBEAN	Mitchell Torok, Guyden 2018		8
32	18	17	18		WHAT A DIFF'RENCE A DAY MAKES	Dinah Washington, Mercury 71435	S	18
33	33	33	36		MY OWN TRUE LOVE	Jimmy Clanton, Ace 567	S	8
34	14	12	8		THERE GOES MY BABY	The Drifters, Atlantic 2025		17
35	38	50	62		THE ANGELS LISTENED IN	The Crests, Coed 515		6
36	17	20	22		I'M GONNA BE A WHEEL SOMEDAY	Fats Domino, Imperial 5606		9
37	43	53	69		YOU'RE GONNA MISS ME	Connie Francis, M-G-M 12814	S	4
38	52	71	—	★	I'M A HOG FOR YOU	Coasters, Atco 6146		3
39	30	19	19		WHAT IS LOVE	Playmates, Roulette 4160	S	12
40	90	—	—	★	WORRIED MAN	Kingston Trio, Capitol 4271		2
41	64	72	—	★	LONELY STREET	Andy Williams, Cadence 1370		3
42	20	13	7		A BIG HUNK O' LOVE	Elvis Presley, RCA Victor 7600		12
43	53	45	47	★	I GOT STRIPES	Johnny Cash, Columbia 41427	S	8
44	42	26	32		ROBBIN' THE CRADLE	Tony Bellus, NRC 023		22
45	25	16	12		MY HEART IS AN OPEN BOOK	Carl Dobkins Jr., Decca 30803		22
46	56	66	83	★	OKEFENOKEE	Freddie Cannon, Swan 4038		5
47	39	46	51		THE MUMMY	Bob McFadden & Dor, Brunswick 55140		5
48	68	—	—	★	FOOL'S HALL OF FAME	Pat Boone, Dot 15982	S	2
49	36	22	21		MY WISH CAME TRUE	Elvis Presley, RCA Victor 7600		10
50	69	77	—	★	COME ON AND GET ME	Fabian, Chancellor 1041	S	3
51	48	40	29		MONA LISA	Conway Twitty, M-G-M 12804		10
52	32	23	30		SEE YOU IN SEPTEMBER	The Tempos, Climax 102		13
53	67	56	63	★	I'VE BEEN THERE	Tommy Edwards, M-G-M 12814	S	7
54	61	54	60		JOHNNY REB	Johnny Horton, Columbia 41437		5
55	57	62	52		SO HIGH, SO LOW	LaVern Baker, Atlantic 2033		9
56	49	74	100		CATERPILLAR CRAWL	The Strangers, Titan 1701		4
57	72	97	—	★	YOU WERE MINE	Fireflies, Ribbon 6901		3
58	74	—	—	★	DECK OF CARDS	Wink Martindale, Dot 15968		2
59	75	100	—	★	YOU BETTER KNOW IT	Jackie Wilson, Brunswick 55149	S	3
60	51	55	58		MIDNIGHT FLYER	Nat King Cole, Capitol 4248		8
61	47	49	42		LIKE I LOVE YOU	Edd Byrnes & Friend, Warner Bros. 5087	S	7
62	—	—	—	★	GOT THE FEELING	Fabian, Chancellor 1041	S	1
63	62	58	68		SOMETHIN' ELSE	Eddie Cochran, Liberty 55203		4
64	45	30	41		HIGH HOPES	Frank Sinatra, Capitol 4214		15
65	54	64	72		TRUE, TRUE HAPPINESS	Johnny Tillotson, Cadence 1365		5
66	46	32	23		FORTY MILES OF BAD ROAD	Duane Eddy, Jamie 1126	S	15
67	81	79	70		ON AN EVENING IN ROMA	Dean Martin, Capitol 4222		11
68	41	25	25		HERE COMES SUMMER	Jerry Keller, Kapp 277	S	13
69	79	82	—		WHERE	Platters, Mercury 71502	S	3
70	—	—	—	★	SKI KING	E. C. Beatty, Colonial 7003		1
71	—	—	—	★	SAY MAN	Bo Diddley, Checker 931		1
72	63	67	49		LINDA LU	Ray Sharpe, Jamie 1128		10
73	88	—	—	★	EVERY LITTLE THING I DO	Dion & the Belmonts, Laurie 3035		2
74	—	—	—	★	DON'T YOU KNOW	Della Reese, RCA Victor 7591	S	1
75	89	—	—		(7 LITTLE GIRLS) SITTIN' IN THE BACK SEAT	Paul Evans & the Curls, Guaranteed 200		2
76	85	—	—		FIVE FEET HIGH AND RISING	Johnny Cash, Columbia 41427		3
77	97	—	—	★	WISH IT WERE ME	Platters, Mercury 71502	S	2
78	60	43	26		SWEETER THAN YOU	Ricky Nelson, Imperial 5595		12
79	—	—	—	★	BOOGIE BEAR	Boyd Bennett, Mercury 71479		1
80	83	—	—		LOVE POTION #9	Clovers, United Artists 180		2
81	99	—	—	★	I'LL NEVER FALL IN LOVE AGAIN	Johnnie Ray, Columbia 41438	S	2
82	—	—	—	★	SHOUT	The Isley Brothers, RCA Victor 7588	S	1
83	73	80	76		SMILE	Tony Bennett, Columbia 41434		6
84	66	47	39		WITH OPEN ARMS	Jane Morgan, Kapp 284	S	9
85	55	38	35		TILL THERE WAS YOU	Anita Bryant, Carlton 512	S	13
86	85	—	88		JUST AS MUCH AS EVER	Bob Beckham, Decca 30861		7
87	65	65	78		LEAVE MY KITTEN ALONE	Little Willie John, King 5219		8
88	—	—	—	★	TUCUMCARI	Jimmie Rodgers, Roulette 4191		1
89	80	87	—		THE SHAPE I'M IN	Johnny Restivo, RCA Victor 7559		3
90	—	—	—	★	TWO FOOLS	Frankie Avalon, Chancellor 1040		1
91	96	81	95		SAL'S GOT A SUGAR LIP	Johnny Horton, Columbia 41437		6
92	50	31	20		JUST A LITTLE TOO MUCH	Ricky Nelson, Imperial 5595		13
93	77	86	87		SUZY BABY	Bobby Vee & the Shadows, Liberty 55208		4
94	—	—	—		SIX BOYS AND SEVEN GIRLS	Anita Bryant, Carlton 518		1
95	76	60	46		THE WAY I WALK	Jack Scott, Carlton 514	S	13
96	71	57	57		ANGEL FACE	Jimmy Darren, Colpix 119	S	8
97	44	36	33		SMALL WORLD	Johnny Mathis, Columbia 41410		15
98	—	—	—		PLENTY GOOD LOVIN'	Connie Francis, M-G-M 12824	S	1
99	—	—	—		IN THE MOOD	Ernie Fields, Rendezvous 110		1
100	87	98	74		CHAPEL OF DREAMS	Dubs, Gone 5046		[illegible]

FOR THE WEEK ENDING OCTOBER 4

The Billboard HOT 100

★ STAR PERFORMERS showed the greatest upward progress on the Hot 100 this week.

S Indicates that STEREO SINGLE version is available.

This Week	One Week Ago	Two Weeks Ago	Three Weeks Ago	Title	Artist, Company, Record No.	Stereo	Weeks on Chart
1	1	2	2	SLEEP WALK	Santo and Johnny, Canadian-American 103		10
2	7	9	24	MACK THE KNIFE	Bobby Darin, Atco 6147		6
3	2	1	1	THE THREE BELLS	Browns, RCA Victor 7555	S	10
4	4	5	6	('TIL) I KISSED YOU	Everly Brothers, Cadence 1369		7
5	3	3	4	I'M GONNA GET MARRIED	Lloyd Price, ABC-Paramount 10032	S	8
6	5	4	3	SEA OF LOVE	Phil Phillips, Mercury 71465		13
7	10	29	41	PUT YOUR HEAD ON MY SHOULDER	Paul Anka, ABC-Paramount 10040	S	5
8	6	6	5	RED RIVER ROCK	Johnny and the Hurricanes, Warwick 509	S	9
9	15	28	84	TEEN BEAT	Sandy Nelson, Original Sound 5		4
10	8	7	7	BROKEN-HEARTED MELODY	Sarah Vaughan, Mercury 71477		11
11	12	15	34	POISON IVY	Coasters, Atco 6146		6
12	16	34	75	MR. BLUE	Fleetwoods, Dolton 5		4
13	14	35	52	JUST ASK YOUR HEART	Frankie Avalon, Chancellor 1040	S	5
14	9	8	10	I WANT TO WALK YOU HOME	Fats Domino, Imperial 5606		8
15	17	31	28	PRIMROSE LANE	Jerry Wallace, Challenge 59047		7
16	13	21	29	MORGEN	Ivo Robic, Laurie 3033		7
17	19	37	76	BATTLE OF KOOKAMONGA	Homer & Jethro, RCA Victor 7585	S	4
18	18	10	11	BABY TALK	Jan and Dean, Dore 522		9
★ 19	41	64	72	LONELY STREET	Andy Williams, Cadence 1370		4
20	23	22	21	MAKIN' LOVE	Floyd Robinson, RCA Victor 7529		10
21	25	26	27	I LOVES YOU PORGY	Nina Simone, Bethlehem 11021	S	9
22	11	12	14	KISSIN' TIME	Bobby Rydell, Cameo 167		14
23	29	58	78	BATTLE HYMN OF THE REPUBLIC	The Mormon Tabernacle Choir, Columbia 41459		4
24	20	27	48	HEY LITTLE GIRL	Dee Clark, Abner 1029	S	6
25	22	11	8	LAVENDER BLUE	Sammy Turner, Big Top 3016	S	15
26	28	59	51	MARY LOU	Ronnie Hawkins, Roulette 4177	S	7
27	31	40	35	CARIBBEAN	Mitchell Torok, Guyden 2018		9
28	24	23	59	THE THREE BELLS	Dick Flood, Monument 408		5
29	26	24	44	I AIN'T NEVER	Webb Pierce, Decca 30923		8
★ 30	48	68	—	FOOL'S HALL OF FAME	Pat Boone, Dot 15982	S	3
31	40	90	—	WORRIED MAN	Kingston Trio, Capitol 4271		3
32	36	17	20	I'M GONNA BE A WHEEL SOMEDAY	Fats Domino, Imperial 5606		10
★ 33	57	72	97	YOU WERE MINE	Fireflies, Ribbon 6901		4
34	37	43	53	YOU'RE GONNA MISS ME	Connie Francis, M-G-M 12824	S	5
35	35	38	50	THE ANGELS LISTENED IN	The Crests, Coed 515		7
36	27	16	18	THANK YOU PRETTY BABY	Brook Benton, Mercury 71478	S	22
★ 37	50	69	77	COME ON AND GET ME	Fabian, Chancellor 1041	S	4
38	34	14	12	THERE GOES MY BABY	The Drifters, Atlantic 2025		18
39	21	13	9	WHAT'D I SAY	Ray Charles, Atlantic 2031		13
★ 40	58	74	—	DECK OF CARDS	Wink Martindale, Dot 15968		3
41	33	33	33	MY OWN TRUE LOVE	Jimmy Clanton, Ace 567	S	9
★ 42	71	—	—	SAY MAN	Bo Diddley, Checker 931		2
43	46	56	66	OKEFENOKEE	Freddie Cannon, Swan 4038		6
44	30	19	15	IT WAS I	Skip & Flip, Brent 7002		15
45	38	52	71	I'M A HOG FOR YOU	Coasters, Atco 6146		4
★ 46	75	89	—	(7 LITTLE GIRLS) SITTIN' IN THE BACK SEAT	Paul Evans & the Curls, Guaranteed 200		3
47	32	18	17	WHAT A DIFF'RENCE A DAY MAKES	Dinah Washington, Mercury 71435	S	19
★ 48	59	75	100	YOU BETTER KNOW IT	Jackie Wilson, Brunswick 55149	S	4
49	43	53	45	I GOT STRIPES	Johnny Cash, Columbia 41427	S	9
★ 50	74	—	—	DON'T YOU KNOW	Della Reese, RCA Victor 7591	S	2
51	51	48	40	MONA LISA	Conway Twitty, M-G-M 12804		11
52	61	47	49	LIKE I LOVE YOU	Edd Byrnes & Friend, Warner Bros. 5087	S	8
53	47	39	46	THE MUMMY	Bob McFadden & Dor, Brunswick 55140		6
54	62	—	—	GOT THE FEELING	Fabian, Chancellor 1041	S	2
55	44	42	26	ROBBIN' THE CRADLE	Tony Bellus, NRC 023		23
56	64	45	30	HIGH HOPES	Frank Sinatra, Capitol 4214		16
★ 57	70	—	—	SKI KING	E. C. Beatty, Colonial 7003		2
★ 58	86	85	—	JUST AS MUCH AS EVER	Bob Beckham, Decca 30861		8
★ 59	69	79	82	WHERE	Platters, Mercury 71502	S	4
★ 60	73	88	—	EVERY LITTLE THING I DO	Dion & the Belmonts, Laurie 3035		3
61	53	67	56	I'VE BEEN THERE	Tommy Edwards, M-G-M 12814	S	8
62	39	30	19	WHAT IS LOVE	Playmates, Roulette 4160	S	13
63	42	20	13	A BIG HUNK O' LOVE	Elvis Presley, RCA Victor 7600		13
★ 64	90	—	—	TWO FOOLS	Frankie Avalon, Chancellor 1040		2
65	55	57	62	SO HIGH, SO LOW	LaVern Baker, Atlantic 2033		10
66	80	83	—	LOVE POTION #9	Clovers, United Artists 180		3
★ 67	88	—	—	TUCUMCARI	Jimmie Rodgers, Roulette 4191		2
68	45	25	16	MY HEART IS AN OPEN BOOK	Carl Dobkins Jr., Decca 30803		23
★ 69	84	66	47	WITH OPEN ARMS	Jane Morgan, Kapp 284	S	10
★ 70	—	—	—	DARLING I LOVE YOU	Al Martino, 20th Fox 153		1
71	67	81	79	ON AN EVENING IN ROMA	Dean Martin, Capitol 4222		12
72	82	—	—	SHOUT	The Isley Brothers, RCA Victor 7588	S	2
73	63	62	58	SOMETHIN' ELSE	Eddie Cochran, Liberty 55203		5
74	65	54	64	TRUE, TRUE HAPPINESS	Johnny Tillotson, Cadence 1365		6
★ 75	—	—	—	DANNY BOY	Conway Twitty, M-G-M 12826	S	1
76	60	51	55	MIDNIGHT FLYER	Nat King Cole, Capitol 4248		9
77	81	99	—	I'LL NEVER FALL IN LOVE AGAIN	Johnnie Ray, Columbia 41438	S	3
★ 78	—	—	—	I'LL BE SEEING YOU	Tommy Sands, Capitol 4259		1
★ 79	—	100	—	I AIN'T NEVER	Four Preps, Capitol 4256		2
★ 80	—	—	—	LIVING DOLL	Cliff Richard & the Drifters, ABC-Paramount 10042		1
81	54	61	54	JOHNNY REB	Johnny Horton, Columbia 41437		6
82	79	—	—	BOOGIE BEAR	Boyd Bennett, Mercury 71479		2
★ 83	—	—	—	IT HAPPENED TODAY	The Skyliners, Calico 109		1
84	52	32	23	SEE YOU IN SEPTEMBER	The Tempos, Climax 102		14
85	94	—	—	SIX BOYS AND SEVEN GIRLS	Anita Bryant, Carlton 518		2
86	—	—	—	BOO BOO STICK BEAT	Chet Atkins, RCA Victor 7589		1
87	—	—	—	TORQUAY	Fireballs, Top Rank 2008		1
88	72	63	67	LINDA LU	Ray Sharpe, Jamie 1128		11
89	56	49	74	CATERPILLAR CRAWL	The Strangers, Titan 1701		5
90	98	—	—	PLENTY GOOD LOVIN'	Connie Francis, M-G-M 12824	S	2
91	95	76	60	THE WAY I WALK	Jack Scott, Carlton 514	S	14
92	77	97	—	WISH IT WERE ME	Platters, Mercury 71502	S	3
93	87	65	65	LEAVE MY KITTEN ALONE	Little Willie John, King 5219		9
94	91	96	81	SAL'S GOT A SUGAR LIP	Johnny Horton, Columbia 41437		7
95	99	—	—	IN THE MOOD	Ernie Fields, Rendezvous 110		2
96	—	—	—	FIRST LOVE, FIRST TEARS	Duane Eddy, Jamie 1130	S	1
97	—	—	—	THE ENCHANTED SEA	The Islanders, May Flower 16		1
98	—	—	90	POCO LOCO	Gene & Eunice, Case 101		4
99	100	87	98	CHAPEL OF DREAMS	Dubs, Gone 5069		6
100	—	—	91	I CRIED	Joe Damiano, Chancellor 1039		3

FOR THE WEEK ENDING OCTOBER 11

The Billboard HOT 100

★ STAR PERFORMERS showed the greatest upward progress on the Hot 100 this week.

S Indicates that STEREO SINGLE version is available.

THIS WEEK	ONE WEEK AGO	TWO WEEKS AGO	THREE WEEKS AGO	TITLE, Artist, Company, Record No.	STEREO	WEEKS ON CHART
1	2	7	9	MACK THE KNIFE — Bobby Darin, Atco 6147		7
2	7	10	29	PUT YOUR HEAD ON MY SHOULDER — Paul Anka, ABC-Paramount 10040	S	6
3	1	1	2	SLEEP WALK — Santo and Johnny, Canadian-American 103		11
4	4	4	5	('TIL) I KISSED YOU — Everly Brothers, Cadence 1369		8
5	3	2	1	THE THREE BELLS — Browns, RCA Victor 7555	S	11
6	9	15	28	TEEN BEAT — Sandy Nelson, Original Sound 5		5
7	5	3	3	I'M GONNA GET MARRIED — Lloyd Price, ABC-Paramount 10032	S	9
8	12	16	34	MR. BLUE — Fleetwoods, Dolton 5		5
9	8	6	6	RED RIVER ROCK — Johnny and the Hurricanes, Warwick 509	S	10
10	11	12	15	POISON IVY — Coasters, Atco 6146		7
11	6	5	4	SEA OF LOVE — Phil Phillips, Mercury 71465		14
12	13	14	35	JUST ASK YOUR HEART — Frankie Avalon, Chancellor 1040	S	6
13	10	8	7	BROKEN-HEARTED MELODY — Sarah Vaughan, Mercury 71477		12
14	19	41	64	LONELY STREET — Andy Williams, Cadence 1370		5
15	15	17	31	PRIMROSE LANE — Jerry Wallace, Challenge 59047		8
16	16	13	21	MORGEN — Ivo Robic, Laurie 3033		8
17	17	19	37	BATTLE OF KOOKAMONGA — Homer & Jethro, RCA Victor 7585	S	5
18	21	25	26	I LOVES YOU PORGY — Nina Simone, Bethlehem 11021	S	10
19	23	29	58	BATTLE HYMN OF THE REPUBLIC — The Mormon Tabernacle Choir, Columbia 41459		5
20	14	9	8	I WANT TO WALK YOU HOME — Fats Domino, Imperial 5606		9
21	24	20	27	HEY LITTLE GIRL — Dee Clark, Abner 1029		7
★22	40	58	74	DECK OF CARDS — Wink Martindale, Dot 15968		4
★23	50	74	—	DON'T YOU KNOW — Della Reese, RCA Victor 7591	S	3
24	31	40	90	WORRIED MAN — Kingston Trio, Capitol 4271		4
25	20	23	22	MAKIN' LOVE — Floyd Robinson, RCA Victor 7529		11
26	18	18	10	BABY TALK — Jan and Dean, Dore 522		10
27	26	28	59	MARY LOU — Ronnie Hawkins, Roulette 4177	S	8
★28	42	71	—	SAY MAN — Bo Diddley, Checker 931		3
29	30	48	68	FOOL'S HALL OF FAME — Pat Boone, Dot 15982	S	4
30	29	26	24	I AIN'T NEVER — Webb Pierce, Decca 30923		9
31	35	35	38	THE ANGELS LISTENED IN — The Crests, Coed 515		8
32	37	50	69	COME ON AND GET ME — Fabian, Chancellor 1041	S	5
33	33	57	72	YOU WERE MINE — Fireflies, Ribbon 6901		5
★34	46	75	89	(7 LITTLE GIRLS) SITTIN' IN THE BACK SEAT — Paul Evans & the Curls, Guaranteed 200		4
35	34	37	43	YOU'RE GONNA MISS ME — Connie Francis, M-G-M 12814	S	6
36	27	31	40	CARIBBEAN — Mitchell Torok, Guyden 2018		10
37	32	36	17	IM GONNA BE A WHEEL SOMEDAY — Fats Domino, Imperial 5606		11
38	28	24	23	THE THREE BELLS — Dick Flood, Monument 408		6
39	22	11	12	KISSIN' TIME — Bobby Rydell, Cameo 167		15
40	25	22	11	LAVENDER BLUE — Sammy Turner, Big Top 3016	S	16
41	48	59	75	YOU BETTER KNOW IT — Jackie Wilson, Brunswick 55149	S	5
42	36	27	16	THANK YOU PRETTY BABY — Brook Benton, Mercury 71478	S	23
★43	75	—	—	DANNY BOY — Conway Twitty, M-G-M 12826	S	2
44	45	38	52	I'M A HOG FOR YOU — Coasters, Atco 6146		5
★45	—	—	—	WOO-HOO — Rock-A-Teens, Roulette 4192		1
★46	95	99	—	IN THE MOOD — Ernie Fields, Rendezvous 110		3
★47	58	86	85	JUST AS MUCH AS EVER — Bob Beckham, Decca 30861		9
★48	60	73	88	EVERY LITTLE THING I DO — Dion & the Belmonts, Laurie 3035		4
★49	87	—	—	TORQUAY — Fireballs, Top Rank 2008		2
50	39	21	13	WHAT'D I SAY — Ray Charles, Atlantic 2031		14
51	57	70	—	SKI KING — E. C. Beatty, Colonial 7003		3
★52	67	88	—	TUCUMCARI — Jimmie Rodgers, Roulette 4191		3
53	59	69	79	WHERE — Platters, Mercury 71502	S	5
★54	64	90	—	TWO FOOLS — Frankie Avalon, Chancellor 1040		3
★55	66	80	83	LOVE POTION #9 — Clovers, United Artists 180		4
56	43	46	56	OKEFENOKEE — Freddie Cannon, Swan 4038		7
57	41	33	33	MY OWN TRUE LOVE — Jimmy Clanton, Ace 567	S	10
★58	—	—	—	MISTY — Johnny Mathis, Columbia 41483		1
59	61	53	67	I'VE BEEN THERE — Tommy Edwards, M-G-M 12814	S	9
60	54	62	—	GOT THE FEELING — Fabian, Chancellor 1041	S	3
61	49	43	53	I GOT STRIPES — Johnny Cash, Columbia 41427	S	10
62	76	60	51	MIDNIGHT FLYER — Nat King Cole, Capitol 4248		10
63	44	30	19	IT WAS I — Skip & Flip, Brent 7002		16
64	38	34	14	THERE GOES MY BABY — The Drifters, Atlantic 2025		19
65	72	82	—	SHOUT — The Isley Brothers, RCA Victor 7588	S	3
66	78	—	—	I'LL BE SEEING YOU — Tommy Sands, Capitol 4259		2
67	80	—	—	LIVIN' DOLL — Cliff Richard & the Drifters, ABC-Paramount 10042		2
68	70	—	—	DARLING, I LOVE YOU — Al Martino, 20th Fox 153		2
★69	90	98	—	PLENTY GOOD LOVIN' — Connie Francis, M-G-M 12824	S	3
★70	85	94	—	SIX BOYS AND SEVEN GIRLS — Anita Bryant, Carlton 518		3
★71	86	—	—	BOO BOO STICK BEAT — Chet Atkins, RCA Victor 7589		2
72	56	64	45	HIGH HOPES — Frank Sinatra, Capitol 4214		17
73	82	79	—	BOOGIE BEAR — Boyd Bennett, Mercury 71479		3
74	53	47	39	THE MUMMY — Bob McFadden & Dor, Brunswick 55140		7
75	77	81	99	I'LL NEVER FALL IN LOVE AGAIN — Johnnie Ray, Columbia 41438	S	4
76	52	61	47	LIKE I LOVE YOU — Edd Byrnes & Friend, Warner Bros. 5087	S	9
★77	—	—	—	SOME KIND-A EARTHQUAKE — Duane Eddy, Jamie 1130	S	1
78	—	83	—	IT HAPPENED TODAY — The Skyliners, Calico 109		2
79	47	32	18	WHAT A DIFF'RENCE A DAY MAKES — Dinah Washington, Mercury 71435	S	20
★80	98	—	—	POCO LOCO — Gene & Eunice, Case 101		5
★81	97	—	—	THE ENCHANTED SEA — The Islanders, May Flower 16		2
82	88	72	63	LINDA LU — Ray Sharpe, Jamie 1128		12
83	69	84	66	WITH OPEN ARMS — Jane Morgan, Kapp 284	S	11
84	73	63	62	SOMETHIN' ELSE — Eddie Cochran, Liberty 55203		6
85	74	65	54	TRUE, TRUE HAPPINESS — Johnny Tillotson, Cadence 1365		7
86	—	—	—	IF I GIVE MY HEART TO YOU — Kitty Kallen, Columbia 41473		1
87	51	51	48	MONA LISA — Conway Twitty, M-G-M 12804		12
★88	—	—	—	HEARTACHES BY THE NUMBER — Guy Mitchell, Columbia 41476		1
89	92	77	97	WISH IT WERE ME — Platters, Mercury 71502	S	4
90	81	54	61	JOHNNY REB — Johnny Horton, Columbia 41437		7
91	71	67	81	ON AN EVENING IN ROMA — Dean Martin, Capitol 4222		13
92	89	56	49	CATERPILLAR CRAWL — The Strangers, Titan 1701		6
93	—	—	—	JOEY'S SONG — Bill Haley and His Comets, Decca 30956		1
94	—	—	—	UNFORGETTABLE — Dinah Washington, Mercury 71508		1
95	—	—	—	JUST TO BE WITH YOU — The Passions, Audicon 102		1
96	63	42	20	A BIG HUNK O' LOVE — Elvis Presley, RCA Victor 7600		14
97	55	44	42	ROBBIN' THE CRADLE — Tony Bellus, NRC 023		24
98	—	—	—	BAD GIRL — The Miracles, Chess 1734		1
99	96	—	—	FIRST LOVE, FIRST TEARS — Duane Eddy, Jamie 1130	S	2
100	—	—	—	LOVE WALKED IN — The Flamingos, End 1055		1

FOR THE WEEK ENDING OCTOBER 18

The Billboard HOT 100

★ STAR PERFORMERS showed the greatest upward progress on the Hot 100 this week.

S Indicates that STEREO SINGLE version is available.

This Week	One Week Ago	Two Weeks Ago	Three Weeks Ago	TITLE, Artist, Company, Record No.	Stereo	Weeks on Chart
1	1	2	7	MACK THE KNIFE — Bobby Darin, Atco 6147		8
2	2	7	10	PUT YOUR HEAD ON MY SHOULDER — Paul Anka, ABC-Paramount 10040	S	7
3	8	12	16	MR. BLUE — Fleetwoods, Dolton 5		6
4	3	1	1	SLEEP WALK — Santo and Johnny, Canadian-American 103		12
5	4	4	4	('TIL) I KISSED YOU — Everly Brothers, Cadence 1369		9
6	6	9	15	TEEN BEAT — Sandy Nelson, Original Sound 5		6
7	10	11	12	POISON IVY — Coasters, Atco 6146		8
8	5	3	2	THE THREE BELLS — Browns, RCA Victor 7555	S	12
9	12	13	14	JUST ASK YOUR HEART — Frankie Avalon, Chancellor 1040	S	7
10	14	19	41	LONELY STREET — Andy Williams, Cadence 1370		6
11	9	8	6	RED RIVER ROCK — Johnny and the Hurricanes, Warwick 509	S	11
12	7	5	3	I'M GONNA GET MARRIED — Lloyd Price, ABC-Paramount 10032	S	10
13	15	15	17	PRIMROSE LANE — Jerry Wallace, Challenge 59047		9
14	17	17	19	BATTLE OF KOOKAMONGA — Homer & Jethro, RCA Victor 7585	S	6
15	11	6	5	SEA OF LOVE — Phil Phillips, Mercury 71465		15
16	13	10	8	BROKEN-HEARTED MELODY — Sarah Vaughan, Mercury 71477		13
17	22	40	58	DECK OF CARDS — Wink Martindale, Dot 15968		5
18	16	16	13	MORGEN — Ivo Robic, Laurie 3033		9
19	19	23	29	BATTLE HYMN OF THE REPUBLIC — The Mormon Tabernacle Choir, Columbia 41459		6
20	18	21	25	I LOVES YOU PORGY — Nina Simone, Bethlehem 11021	S	11
21	21	24	20	HEY LITTLE GIRL — Dee Clark, Abner 1029	S	8
22	24	31	40	WORRIED MAN — Kingston Trio, Capitol 4271		5
23	23	50	74	DON'T YOU KNOW — Della Reese, RCA Victor 7591	S	4
24	28	42	71	SAY MAN — Bo Diddley, Checker 931		4
25	20	14	9	I WANT TO WALK YOU HOME — Fats Domino, Imperial 5606		10
26	31	35	35	THE ANGELS LISTENED IN — The Crests, Coed 515		9
27	25	20	23	MAKIN' LOVE — Floyd Robinson, RCA Victor 7529		12
28	34	46	75	7 LITTLE GIRLS (SITTIN' IN THE BACK SEAT) — Paul Evans & the Curls, Guaranteed 200		5
29	32	37	50	COME ON AND GET ME — Fabian, Chancellor 1041	S	6
30	33	33	57	YOU WERE MINE — Fireflies, Ribbon 6901		6
31	29	30	48	FOOL'S HALL OF FAME — Pat Boone, Dot 15982	S	5
★32	52	67	88	TUCUMCARI — Jimmie Rodgers, Roulette 4191		4
33	27	26	28	MARY LOU — Ronnie Hawkins, Roulette 4177	S	9
34	30	29	26	I AIN'T NEVER — Webb Pierce, Decca 30923		10
★35	46	95	99	IN THE MOOD — Ernie Fields, Rendezvous 110		4
36	43	75	—	DANNY BOY — Conway Twitty, M-G-M 12826	S	3
37	41	48	59	YOU BETTER KNOW IT — Jackie Wilson, Brunswick 55149	S	6
38	47	58	86	JUST AS MUCH AS EVER — Bob Beckham, Decca 30861		10
39	35	34	37	YOU'RE GONNA MISS ME — Connie Francis, M-G-M 12824	S	7
40	45	—	—	WOO-HOO — Rock-A-Teens, Roulette 4192		2
41	26	18	18	BABY TALK — Jan and Dean, Dore 522		11
42	36	27	31	CARIBBEAN — Mitchell Torok, Guyden 2018		11
43	38	28	24	THE THREE BELLS — Dick Flood, Monument 408		7
44	53	59	69	WHERE — Platters, Mercury 71502	S	6
★45	81	97	—	THE ENCHANTED SEA — The Islanders, May Flower 16		3
★46	67	80	—	LIVIN' DOLL — Cliff Richard & the Drifters, ABC-Paramount 10042		3
★47	58	—	—	MISTY — Johnny Mathis, Columbia 41483		2
48	48	60	73	EVERY LITTLE THING I DO — Dion & the Belmonts, Laurie 3035		5
★49	71	86	—	BOO BOO STICK BEAT — Chet Atkins, RCA Victor 7589		3
50	51	57	70	SKI KING — E. C. Beatty, Colonial 7003		4
51	49	87	—	TORQUAY — Fireballs, Top Rank 2008		3
★52	66	78	—	I'LL BE SEEING YOU — Tommy Sands, Capitol 4259		3
★53	88	—	—	HEARTACHES BY THE NUMBER — Guy Mitchell, Columbia 41476		2
54	39	22	11	KISSIN' TIME — Bobby Rydell, Cameo 167		16
55	37	32	36	I'M GONNA BE A WHEEL SOMEDAY — Fats Domino, Imperial 5606		12
56	44	45	38	I'M A HOG FOR YOU — Coasters, Atco 6146		6
★57	77	—	—	SOME KIND-A EARTHQUAKE — Duane Eddy, Jamie 1130	S	2
58	54	64	90	TWO FOOLS — Frankie Avalon, Chancellor 1040		4
★59	86	—	—	IF I GIVE MY HEART TO YOU — Kitty Kallen, Columbia 41473		2
60	55	66	80	LOVE POTION #9 — Clovers, United Artists 180		5
★61	89	92	77	WISH IT WERE ME — Platters, Mercury 71502	S	5
62	70	85	94	SIX BOYS AND SEVEN GIRLS — Anita Bryant, Carlton 518		4
63	68	70	—	DARLING, I LOVE YOU — Al Martino, 20th Fox 153		3
★64	94	—	—	UNFORGETTABLE — Dinah Washington, Mercury 71508		2
65	65	72	82	SHOUT — The Isley Brothers, RCA Victor 7588	S	4
66	61	49	43	I GOT STRIPES — Johnny Cash, Columbia 41427	S	11
★67	—	—	—	WE GOT LOVE — Bobby Rydell, Cameo 169		1
68	42	36	27	THANK YOU PRETTY BABY — Brook Benton, Mercury 71478	S	24
69	60	54	62	GOT THE FEELING — Fabian, Chancellor 1041	S	4
★70	—	—	—	I DIG GIRLS — Bobby Rydell, Cameo 169		1
71	56	43	46	OKEFENOKEE — Freddie Cannon, Swan 4038		8
72	62	76	60	MIDNIGHT FLYER — Nat King Cole, Capitol 4248		11
★73	—	—	—	OH, CAROL — Neil Sedaka, RCA Victor 7595		1
74	59	61	53	I'VE BEEN THERE — Tommy Edwards, M-G-M 12814	S	10
75	69	90	98	PLENTY GOOD LOVIN' — Connie Francis, M-G-M 12824	S	4
★76	99	96	—	FIRST LOVE, FIRST TEARS — Duane Eddy, Jamie 1130	S	3
77	50	39	21	WHAT'D I SAY — Ray Charles, Atlantic 2031		15
78	75	77	81	I'LL NEVER FALL IN LOVE AGAIN — Johnnie Ray, Columbia 41438	S	5
79	74	53	47	THE MUMMY — Bob McFadden & Dor, Brunswick 55140		8
80	92	89	56	CATERPILLAR CRAWL — The Strangers, Titan 1701		7
81	57	41	33	MY OWN TRUE LOVE — Jimmy Clanton, Ace 567	S	11
82	78	—	83	IT HAPPENED TODAY — The Skyliners, Calico 109		3
★83	—	—	—	RUNNING BEAR — Johnny Preston, Mercury 71474		1
84	97	55	44	ROBBIN' THE CRADLE — Tony Bellus, NRC 023		25
85	85	74	65	TRUE, TRUE HAPPINESS — Johnny Tillotson, Cadence 1365		8
86	90	81	54	JOHNNY REB — Johnny Horton, Columbia 41437		8
★87	—	—	—	IF YOU DON'T WANT MY LOVIN' — Carl Dobkins Jr., Decca 30656		1
88	80	98	—	POCO LOCO — Gene & Eunice, Case 101		6
89	82	88	72	LINDA LU — Ray Sharpe, Jamie 1128		13
90	93	—	—	JOEY'S SONG — Bill Haley & His Comets, Decca 30956		2
91	40	25	22	LAVENDER BLUE — Sammy Turner, Big Top 3016	S	17
92	—	—	—	I DON'T KNOW — Ruth Brown, Atlantic 2035		1
93	98	—	—	BAD GIRL — The Miracles, Chess 1734		2
94	—	—	—	GOODBYE CHARLIE — Patti Page, Mercury 71510		1
95	84	73	63	SOMETHIN' ELSE — Eddie Cochran, Liberty 55203		7
96	73	82	79	BOOGIE BEAR — Boyd Bennett, Mercury 71479		4
97	—	—	—	DANCE WITH ME — The Drifters, Atlantic 2040		1
98	—	—	—	STORY OF OUR LOVE — Johnny Mathis, Columbia 41483		1
99	100	—	—	LOVE WALKED IN — The Flamingos, End 1055		2
100	—	—	—	THERE COMES A TIME — Jack Scott, Carlton 519	S	1

FOR THE WEEK ENDING OCTOBER 25

The Billboard HOT 100

★ STAR PERFORMERS showed the greatest upward progress on the Hot 100 this week.

S Indicates that STEREO SINGLE version is available.

This Week	One Week Ago	Two Weeks Ago	Three Weeks Ago	Title, Artist, Company, Record No.	Stereo	Weeks on Chart
1	1	1	2	MACK THE KNIFE — Bobby Darin, Atco 6147		9
2	2	2	7	PUT YOUR HEAD ON MY SHOULDER — Paul Anka, ABC-Paramount 10040	S	8
3	3	8	12	MR. BLUE — Fleetwoods, Dolton 5		7
4	6	6	9	TEEN BEAT — Sandy Nelson, Original Sound 5		7
5	5	4	4	('TIL) I KISSED YOU — Everly Brothers, Cadence 1369		10
6	4	3	1	SLEEP WALK — Santo and Johnny, Canadian-American 103		13
7	10	14	19	LONELY STREET — Andy Williams, Cadence 1370		7
8	7	10	11	POISON IVY — Coasters, Atco 6146		9
9	9	12	13	JUST ASK YOUR HEART — Frankie Avalon, Chancellor 1040	S	8
10	8	5	3	THE THREE BELLS — Browns, RCA Victor 7555	S	13
11	13	15	15	PRIMROSE LANE — Jerry Wallace, Challenge 59047		10
12	12	7	5	I'M GONNA GET MARRIED — Lloyd Price, ABC-Paramount 10032	S	11
★13	23	23	50	DON'T YOU KNOW — Della Reese, RCA Victor 7591	S	5
14	11	9	8	RED RIVER ROCK — Johnny and the Hurricanes, Warwick 509	S	12
15	17	22	40	DECK OF CARDS — Wink Martindale, Dot 15968		6
16	19	19	23	BATTLE HYMN OF THE REPUBLIC — The Mormon Tabernacle Choir, Columbia 41459		7
17	18	16	16	MORGEN — Ivo Robic, Laurie 3033		10
18	14	17	17	BATTLE OF KOOKAMONGA — Homer & Jethro, RCA Victor 7585	S	7
19	16	13	10	BROKEN-HEARTED MELODY — Sarah Vaughan, Mercury 71477		14
20	22	24	31	WORRIED MAN — Kingston Trio, Capitol 4271		6
21	20	18	21	I LOVES YOU PORGY — Nina Simone, Bethlehem 11021	S	12
22	26	31	35	THE ANGELS LISTENED IN — The Crests, Coed 515		10
23	28	34	46	7 LITTLE GIRLS (SITTIN' IN THE BACK SEAT) — Paul Evans & the Curls, Guaranteed 200		6
24	24	28	42	SAY MAN — Bo Diddley, Checker 931		5
25	21	21	24	HEY LITTLE GIRL — Dee Clark, Abner 1029	S	9
★26	36	43	75	DANNY BOY — Conway Twitty, M-G-M 12826	S	4
27	15	11	6	SEA OF LOVE — Phil Phillips, Mercury 71465		16
28	35	46	95	IN THE MOOD — Ernie Fields, Rendezvous 110		5
★29	53	88	—	HEARTACHES BY THE NUMBER — Guy Mitchell, Columbia 41476		3
30	27	25	20	MAKIN' LOVE — Floyd Robinson, RCA Victor 7529		13
31	30	33	33	YOU WERE MINE — Fireflies, Ribbon 6901		7
32	38	47	58	JUST AS MUCH AS EVER — Bob Beckham, Decca 30861		11
33	25	20	14	I WANT TO WALK YOU HOME — Fats Domino, Imperial 5606		11
34	33	27	26	MARY LOU — Ronnie Hawkins, Roulette 4177	S	10
35	40	45	—	WOO-HOO — Rock-A-Teens, Roulette 4192		3
36	31	29	30	FOOL'S HALL OF FAME — Pat Boone, Dot 15982	S	6
37	45	81	97	THE ENCHANTED SEA — The Islanders, May Flower 16		4
38	32	52	67	TUCUMCARI — Jimmie Rodgers, Roulette 4191		5
39	47	58	—	MISTY — Johnny Mathis, Columbia 41483		3
40	34	30	29	I AIN'T NEVER — Webb Pierce, Decca 30923		11
★41	73	—	—	OH, CAROL — Neil Sedaka, RCA Victor 7595		2
42	51	49	87	TORQUAY — Fireballs, Top Rank 2008		4
★43	60	55	56	LOVE POTION #9 — Clovers, United Artists 180		6
44	37	41	48	YOU BETTER KNOW IT — Jackie Wilson, Brunswick 55149	S	7
45	46	67	80	LIVING DOLL — Cliff Richard & the Drifters, ABC-Paramount 10042		4
★46	57	77	—	SOME KIND-A EARTHQUAKE — Duane Eddy, Jamie 1130	S	3
★47	59	86	—	IF I GIVE MY HEART TO YOU — Kitty Kallen, Columbia 41473		3
★48	67	—	—	WE GOT LOVE — Bobby Rydell, Cameo 169		2
★49	64	94	—	UNFORGETTABLE — Dinah Washington, Mercury 71508		3
★50	65	65	72	SHOUT (I) — Isley Brothers, RCA Victor 7588	S	5
51	52	66	78	I'LL BE SEEING YOU — Tommy Sands, Capitol 4259		4
52	42	36	27	CARIBBEAN — Mitchell Torok, Guyden 2018		12
53	49	71	86	BOO BOO STICK BEAT — Chet Atkins, RCA Victor 7589		4
54	39	35	34	YOU'RE GONNA MISS ME — Connie Francis, M-G-M 12824	S	8
55	29	32	37	COME ON AND GET ME — Fabian, Chancellor 1041	S	7
56	50	51	57	SKI KING — E. C. Beatty, Colonial 7003		5
57	48	48	60	EVERY LITTLE THING I DO — Dion & the Belmonts, Laurie 3035		6
58	41	26	18	BABY TALK — Jan and Dean, Dore 522		12
★59	76	99	96	FIRST LOVE, FIRST TEARS — Duane Eddy, Jamie 1130	S	4
★60	—	—	—	SO MANY WAYS — Brook Benton, Mercury 71512	S	1
61	44	53	59	WHERE — Platters, Mercury 71502	S	7
62	62	70	85	SIX BOYS AND SEVEN GIRLS — Anita Bryant, Carlton 518		5
63	63	68	70	DARLING, I LOVE YOU — Al Martino, 20th Fox 153		4
★64	90	93	—	JOEY'S SONG — Bill Haley & His Comets, Decca 30956		3
65	55	37	32	I'M GONNA BE A WHEEL SOMEDAY — Fats Domino, Imperial 5606		13
★66	—	—	—	TALK TO ME — Frank Sinatra, Capitol 4284		1
67	43	38	28	THE THREE BELLS — Dick Flood, Monument 408		8
68	70	—	—	I DIG GIRLS — Bobby Rydell, Cameo 169		2
69	56	44	45	I'M A HOG FOR YOU — Coasters, Atco 6146		7
70	69	60	54	GOT THE FEELING — Fabian, Chancellor 1041	S	5
71	61	89	92	WISH IT WERE ME — Platters, Mercury 71502	S	6
★72	87	—	—	IF YOU DON'T WANT MY LOVIN' — Carl Dobkins Jr., Decca 30656		2
★73	—	—	—	LOVER'S PRAYER — Dion and the Belmonts, Laurie 3035		1
74	75	69	90	PLENTY GOOD LOVIN' — Connie Francis, M-G-M 12824	S	5
75	71	56	43	OKEFENOKEE — Freddie Cannon, Swan 4038		9
★76	92	—	—	I DON'T KNOW — Ruth Brown, Atlantic 2035		2
★77	97	—	—	DANCE WITH ME — The Drifters, Atlantic 2040		2
78	88	80	98	POCO LOCO — Gene & Eunice, Case 101		7
79	78	75	77	I'LL NEVER FALL IN LOVE AGAIN — Johnnie Ray, Columbia 41438	S	6
80	58	54	64	TWO FOOLS — Frankie Avalon, Chancellor 1040		5
81	91	40	25	LAVENDER BLUE — Sammy Turner, Big Top 3016	S	18
82	95	84	73	SOMETHIN' ELSE — Eddie Cochran, Liberty 55203		8
★83	100	—	—	THERE COMES A TIME — Jack Scott, Carlton 519	S	2
84	54	39	22	KISSIN' TIME — Bobby Rydell, Cameo 167		17
85	84	97	55	ROBBIN' THE CRADLE — Tony Bellus, NRC 023		26
86	83	—	—	RUNNING BEAR — Johnny Preston, Mercury 71474		2
★87	—	—	—	TENNESSEE WALTZ — Jerry Fuller, Challenge 59057		1
88	99	100	—	LOVE WALKED IN — The Flamingos, End 1055		3
89	72	62	76	MIDNIGHT FLYER — Nat King Cole, Capitol 4248		12
90	94	—	—	GOODBYE CHARLIE — Patti Page, Mercury 71510		2
91	82	78	—	IT HAPPENED TODAY — The Skyliners, Calico 109		4
92	—	—	—	LIVING DOLL — David Hill, Kapp 293		1
93	85	85	74	TRUE, TRUE HAPPINESS — Johnny Tillotson, Cadence 1365		9
94	81	57	41	MY OWN TRUE LOVE — Jimmy Clanton, Ace 567	S	12
95	—	95	—	JUST TO BE WITH YOU — The Passions, Audicon 102		2
96	—	—	—	IGMOO — Stonewall Jackson, Columbia 41488		1
97	—	—	—	HIGH SCHOOL U.S.A. — Tommy Facenda, Atlantic 2051 to 2078		1
98	—	—	—	CLOUDS — The Spacemen, Alton 254		1
99	—	—	—	MIDNIGHT STROLL — Revels, Norgolde 103		1
100	—	—	—	DON'T TAKE THE STARS — The Mystics, Laurie 3038		1

FOR THE WEEK ENDING NOVEMBER 1

The Billboard HOT 100

★ STAR PERFORMERS showed the greatest upward progress on the Hot 100 this week.

S Indicates that STEREO SINGLE version is available.

This Week	One Week Ago	Two Weeks Ago	Three Weeks Ago	TITLE, Artist, Company, Record No.	Stereo	Weeks on Chart
1	1	1	1	MACK THE KNIFE — Bobby Darin, Atco 6147		10
2	3	3	8	MR. BLUE — Fleetwoods, Dolton 5		8
3	2	2	2	PUT YOUR HEAD ON MY SHOULDER — Paul Anka, ABC-Paramount 10040	S	9
4	4	6	6	TEEN BEAT — Sandy Nelson, Original Sound 5		8
5	13	23	23	DON'T YOU KNOW — Della Reese, RCA Victor 7591	S	6
6	7	10	14	LONELY STREET — Andy Williams, Cadence 1370		8
7	9	9	12	JUST ASK YOUR HEART — Frankie Avalon, Chancellor 1040	S	9
8	11	13	15	PRIMROSE LANE — Jerry Wallace, Challenge 59047		11
9	8	7	10	POISON IVY — Coasters, Atco 6146		10
10	15	17	22	DECK OF CARDS — Wink Martindale, Dot 15968		7
11	5	5	4	('TIL) I KISSED YOU — Everly Brothers, Cadence 1369		11
12	6	4	3	SLEEP WALK — Santo and Johnny, Canadian-American 103		14
13	16	19	19	BATTLE HYMN OF THE REPUBLIC — The Mormon Tabernacle Choir, Columbia 41459		8
14	14	11	9	RED RIVER ROCK — Johnny and the Hurricanes, Warwick 509	S	13
★15	28	35	46	IN THE MOOD — Ernie Fields, Rendezvous 110		6
16	10	8	5	THE THREE BELLS — Browns, RCA Victor 7555	S	14
17	23	28	34	7 LITTLE GIRLS (SITTIN' IN THE BACK SEAT) — Paul Evans & the Curls, Guaranteed 200		7
18	17	18	16	MORGEN — Ivo Robic, Laurie 3033		11
19	12	12	7	I'M GONNA GET MARRIED — Lloyd Price, ABC-Paramount 10032	S	12
20	24	24	28	SAY MAN — Bo Diddley, Checker 931		6
★21	31	30	33	YOU WERE MINE — Fireflies, Ribbon 6901		8
22	20	22	24	WORRIED MAN — Kingston Trio, Capitol 4271		7
23	25	21	21	HEY LITTLE GIRL — Dee Clark, Abner 1029	S	10
24	29	53	88	HEARTACHES BY THE NUMBER — Guy Mitchell, Columbia 41476		4
★25	41	73	—	OH, CAROL — Neil Sedaka, RCA Victor 7595		3
26	26	36	43	DANNY BOY — Conway Twitty, M-G-M 12826	S	5
27	22	26	31	THE ANGELS LISTENED IN — The Crests, Coed 515		11
28	60	—	—	SO MANY WAYS — Brook Benton, Mercury 71512	S	2
29	18	14	17	BATTLE OF KOOKAMONGA — Homer & Jethro, RCA Victor 7585	S	8
30	39	47	58	MISTY — Johnny Mathis, Columbia 41483		4
31	21	20	18	I LOVES YOU PORGY — Nina Simone, Bethlehem 11021	S	13
32	19	16	13	BROKEN-HEARTED MELODY — Sarah Vaughan, Mercury 71477		15
33	37	45	81	THE ENCHANTED SEA — The Islanders, May Flower 16		5
★34	49	64	94	UNFORGETTABLE — Dinah Washington, Mercury 71508	S	4
35	35	40	45	WOO-HOO — Rock-A-Teens, Roulette 4192		4
36	34	33	27	MARY LOU — Ronnie Hawkins, Roulette 4177	S	11
37	46	57	77	SOME KIND-A EARTHQUAKE — Duane Eddy, Jamie 1130	S	4
★38	48	67	—	WE GOT LOVE — Bobby Rydell, Cameo 169		3
39	42	51	49	TORQUAY — Fireballs, Top Rank 2008		5
40	32	38	47	JUST AS MUCH AS EVER — Bob Beckham, Decca 30861		12
41	30	27	25	MAKIN' LOVE — Floyd Robinson, RCA Victor 7529		14
42	43	60	55	LOVE POTION #9 — Clovers, United Artists 180		7
43	45	46	67	LIVING DOLL — Cliff Richard & the Drifters, ABC-Paramount 10042		5
44	47	59	86	IF I GIVE MY HEART TO YOU — Kitty Kallen, Columbia 41473		4
45	38	32	52	TUCUMCARI — Jimmie Rodgers, Roulette 4191	S	6
★46	77	97	—	DANCE WITH ME — The Drifters, Atlantic 2035		3
47	50	65	65	SHOUT (I) — Isley Brothers, RCA Victor 7588	S	6
48	36	31	29	FOOL'S HALL OF FAME — Pat Boone, Dot 15982	S	7
49	57	48	48	EVERY LITTLE THING I DO — Dion & the Belmonts, Laurie 3035		7
50	27	15	11	SEA OF LOVE — Phil Phillips, Mercury 71465		17
★51	97	—	—	HIGH SCHOOL U.S.A. — Tommy Facenda, Atlantic 51 to 78		2
★52	—	—	—	BELIEVE ME — Royal Teens, Capitol 4261		1
53	44	37	41	YOU BETTER KNOW IT — Jackie Wilson, Brunswick 55149	S	8
54	61	44	53	WHERE — Platters, Mercury 71502	S	8
55	40	34	30	I AIN'T NEVER — Webb Pierce, Decca 30923		12
56	64	90	93	JOEY'S SONG — Bill Haley & His Comets, Decca 30956		4
57	33	25	20	I WANT TO WALK YOU HOME — Fats Domino, Imperial 5606		12
58	53	49	71	BOO BOO STICK BEAT — Chet Atkins, RCA Victor 7589		5
59	54	39	35	YOU'RE GONNA MISS ME — Connie Francis, M-G-M 12824	S	9
60	66	—	—	TALK TO ME — Frank Sinatra, Capitol 4284		2
61	51	52	66	I'LL BE SEEING YOU — Tommy Sands, Capitol 4259		5
★62	91	82	78	IT HAPPENED TODAY — The Skyliners, Calico 109		5
63	56	50	51	SKI KING — E. C. Beatty, Colonial 7003		6
64	62	62	70	SIX BOYS AND SEVEN GIRLS — Anita Bryant, Carlton 518	S	6
65	78	88	80	POCO LOCO — Gene & Eunice, Case 101		8
66	59	76	99	FIRST LOVE, FIRST TEARS — Duane Eddy, Jamie 1130	S	5
67	72	87	—	IF YOU DON'T WANT MY LOVIN' — Carl Dobkins Jr., Decca 30656		3
★68	87	—	—	TENNESSEE WALTZ — Bobby Comstock, Blaze 349		2
69	74	75	69	PLENTY GOOD LOVIN' — Connie Francis, M-G-M 12824	S	6
70	63	63	68	DARLING, I LOVE YOU — Al Martino, 20th Fox 153		5
71	83	100	—	THERE COMES A TIME — Jack Scott, Carlton 519	S	3
★72	—	—	—	PRETEND — Carl Mann, Phillips International 3546		1
73	76	92	—	I DON'T KNOW — Ruth Brown, Atlantic 2035		3
★74	98	—	—	CLOUDS — The Spacemen, Alton 254		2
75	52	42	36	CARIBBEAN — Mitchell Torok, Guyden 2018		13
76	86	83	—	RUNNING BEAR — Johnny Preston, Mercury 71474		3
77	73	—	—	LOVER'S PRAYER — Dion and the Belmonts, Laurie 3035		2
78	82	95	84	SOMETHIN' ELSE — Eddie Cochran, Liberty 55203		9
★79	—	—	—	TENNESSEE WALTZ — Jerry Fuller, Challenge 59057		1
★80	—	—	—	BE MY GUEST — Fats Domino, Imperial 5629		1
★81	—	—	—	THE ENCHANTED SEA — Martin Denny, Liberty 55212	S	1
★82	—	—	—	BREAKING UP IS HARD TO DO — Jivin' Gene, Mercury 71485		3
83	55	29	32	COME ON AND GET ME — Fabian, Chancellor 1041	S	8
★84	—	—	—	YOU MEAN EVERYTHING TO ME — Fleetwoods, Dolton 5		1
85	69	56	44	I'M A HOG FOR YOU — Coasters, Ateo 6146		8
86	71	61	89	WISH IT WERE ME — Platters, Mercury 71502	S	7
★87	—	—	—	THE HUNCH — Bobby Peterson, V-Tone 205		1
★88	—	—	—	COME INTO MY HEART — Lloyd Price, ABC-Paramount 10062	S	1
★89	—	—	—	I'LL BE SEEING YOU — Poni Tails, ABC-Paramount 10047		1
90	90	94	—	GOODBYE CHARLIE — Patti Page, Mercury 71510	S	3
91	—	—	—	FIRST NAME INITIAL — Annette, Vista 349		1
92	95	—	—	JUST TO BE WITH YOU — The Passions, Audicon 102		2
93	92	—	—	LIVING DOLL — David Hill, Kapp 293		2
94	—	—	—	I'VE BEEN AROUND — Fats Domino, Imperial 5629		1
95	96	—	—	IGMOO — Stonewall Jackson, Columbia 41488		2
96	99	—	—	MIDNIGHT STROLL — Revels, Norgolde 103		2
97	—	—	—	THE HUNCH — Paul Gayten, Anna 1006		1
98	100	—	—	DON'T TAKE THE STARS — The Mystics, Laurie 3038		2
99	—	—	—	MY HEART BECAME OF AGE — Annette, Vista 349		1
100	—	—	—	THERE'S A GIRL — Jan and Dean, Dore 531		1

FOR THE WEEK ENDING NOVEMBER 8

The Billboard HOT 100

★ STAR PERFORMERS showed the greatest upward progress on the Hot 100 this week.

S Indicates that STEREO SINGLE version is available.

This Week	One Week Ago	Two Weeks Ago	Three Weeks Ago	Title, Artist, Company, Record No.	Stereo	Weeks on Chart
1	1	1	1	MACK THE KNIFE — Bobby Darin, Atco 6147		11
2	2	3	3	MR. BLUE — Fleetwoods, Dolton 5		9
3	3	2	2	PUT YOUR HEAD ON MY SHOULDER — Paul Anka, ABC-Paramount 10040	S	10
4	5	13	23	DON'T YOU KNOW — Della Reese, RCA Victor 7591	S	7
5	4	4	6	TEEN BEAT — Sandy Nelson, Original Sound 5		9
6	6	7	10	LONELY STREET — Andy Williams, Cadence 1370		9
7	10	15	17	DECK OF CARDS — Wink Martindale, Dot 15968		8
8	8	11	13	PRIMROSE LANE — Jerry Wallace, Challenge 59047		12
9	7	9	9	JUST ASK YOUR HEART — Frankie Avalon, Chancellor 1040	S	10
10	9	8	7	POISON IVY — Coasters, Atco 6146		11
11	11	5	5	('TIL) I KISSED YOU — Everly Brothers, Cadence 1369		12
★12	24	29	53	HEARTACHES BY THE NUMBER — Guy Mitchell, Columbia 41476		5
★13	28	60	—	SO MANY WAYS — Brook Benton, Mercury 71512	S	3
14	15	28	35	IN THE MOOD — Ernie Fields, Rendezvous 110		7
15	17	23	28	7 LITTLE GIRLS (SITTIN' IN THE BACK SEAT) — Paul Evans & the Curls, Guaranteed 200		8
16	13	16	19	BATTLE HYMN OF THE REPUBLIC — The Mormon Tabernacle Choir, Columbia 41459		9
17	25	41	73	OH, CAROL — Neil Sedaka, RCA Victor 7595		4
★18	30	39	47	MISTY — Johnny Mathis, Columbia 41483		5
19	26	26	36	DANNY BOY — Conway Twitty, M-G-M 12826	S	6
20	12	6	4	SLEEP WALK — Santo and Johnny, Canadian-American 103		15
21	21	31	30	YOU WERE MINE — Fireflies, Ribbon 6901		9
★22	38	48	67	WE GOT LOVE — Bobby Rydell, Cameo 169		4
23	14	14	11	RED RIVER ROCK — Johnny and the Hurricanes, Warwick 509	S	14
★24	35	35	40	WOO-HOO — Rock-A-Teens, Roulette 4192		5
25	22	20	22	WORRIED MAN — Kingston Trio, Capitol 4271		8
26	20	24	24	SAY MAN — Bo Diddley, Checker 931		7
27	27	22	26	THE ANGELS LISTENED IN — The Crests, Coed 515		12
28	19	12	12	I'M GONNA GET MARRIED — Lloyd Price, ABC-Paramount 10032	S	13
29	34	49	64	UNFORGETTABLE — Dinah Washington, Mercury 71508	S	5
30	33	37	45	THE ENCHANTED SEA — The Islanders, May Flower 16		6
31	23	25	21	HEY LITTLE GIRL — Dee Clark, Abner 1029	S	11
32	16	10	8	THE THREE BELLS — Browns, RCA Victor 7555	S	15
33	18	17	18	MORGEN — Ivo Robic, Laurie 3033		12
★34	46	77	97	DANCE WITH ME — The Drifters, Atlantic 2040		4
35	42	43	60	LOVE POTION #9 — Clovers, United Artists 180		8
36	43	45	46	LIVING DOLL — Cliff Richard & the Drifters, ABC-Paramount 10042		6
37	37	46	57	SOME KIND-A EARTHQUAKE — Duane Eddy, Jamie 1130	S	5
38	45	38	32	TUCUMCARI — Jimmie Rodgers, Roulette 4191	S	7
39	31	21	20	I LOVES YOU PORGY — Nina Simone, Bethlehem 11021	S	14
40	36	34	33	MARY LOU — Ronnie Hawkins, Roulette 4177	S	12
41	40	32	38	JUST AS MUCH AS EVER — Bob Beckham, Decca 30861		13
42	39	42	51	TORQUAY — Fireballs, Top Rank 2008		6
43	29	18	14	BATTLE OF KOOKAMONGA — Homer & Jethro, RCA Victor 7585	S	9
44	44	47	59	IF I GIVE MY HEART TO YOU — Kitty Kallen, Columbia 41473		5
45	32	19	16	BROKEN-HEARTED MELODY — Sarah Vaughan, Mercury 71477		16
46	52	—	—	BELIEVE ME — Royal Teens, Capitol 4261		2
47	41	30	27	MAKIN' LOVE — Floyd Robinson, RCA Victor 7529		15
48	56	64	90	JOEY'S SONG — Bill Haley & His Comets, Decca 30956		5
49	51	97	—	HIGH SCHOOL U.S.A. — Tommy Facenda, Atlantic 51 to 78		3
50	47	50	65	SHOUT (I) — Isley Brothers, RCA Victor 7588	S	7
★51	80	—	—	BE MY GUEST — Fats Domino, Imperial 5629		2
★52	65	78	88	POCO LOCO — Gene & Eunice, Case 101		9
53	60	66	—	TALK TO ME — Frank Sinatra, Capitol 4284		3
54	48	36	31	FOOL'S HALL OF FAME — Pat Boone, Dot 15982	S	8
★55	88	—	—	COME INTO MY HEART — Lloyd Price, ABC-Paramount 10062	S	2
56	53	44	37	YOU BETTER KNOW IT — Jackie Wilson, Brunswick 55149	S	9
★57	68	87	—	TENNESSEE WALTZ — Bobby Comstock, Blaze 349		3
★58	74	98	—	CLOUDS — The Spacemen, Alton 254		3
59	62	91	82	IT HAPPENED TODAY — The Skyliners, Calico 109		6
60	66	59	76	FIRST LOVE, FIRST TEARS — Duane Eddy, Jamie 1130	S	6
61	49	57	48	EVERY LITTLE THING I DO — Dion & the Belmonts, Laurie 3035		8
62	58	53	49	BOO BOO STICK BEAT — Chet Atkins, RCA Victor 7589		6
★63	91	—	—	FIRST NAME INITIAL — Annette, Vista 349		2
64	73	76	92	I DON'T KNOW — Ruth Brown, Atlantic 2035		4
★65	81	—	—	THE ENCHANTED SEA — Martin Denny, Liberty 55212	S	2
66	72	—	—	PRETEND — Carl Mann, Phillips International 3546		2
67	55	40	34	I AIN'T NEVER — Webb Pierce, Decca 30923		13
68	57	33	25	I WANT TO WALK YOU HOME — Fats Domino, Imperial 5606		13
69	82	—	—	BREAKING UP IS HARD TO DO — Jivin' Gene, Mercury 71485		4
70	54	61	44	WHERE — Platters, Mercury 71502	S	9
71	50	27	15	SEA OF LOVE — Phil Phillips, Mercury 71465		18
★72	—	—	70	I DIG GIRLS — Bobby Rydell, Cameo 169		3
73	79	—	—	TENNESSEE WALTZ — Jerry Fuller, Challenge 59057		2
★74	99	—	—	MY HEART BECAME OF AGE — Annette, Vista 349		2
★75	—	—	—	ALWAYS — Sammy Turner, Big Top 3029		1
76	76	86	83	RUNNING BEAR — Johnny Preston, Mercury 71474		4
★77	—	—	—	(IF YOU CRY) TRUE LOVE, TRUE LOVE — Drifters, Atlantic 2040		1
★78	94	—	—	I'VE BEEN AROUND — Fats Domino, Imperial 5629		2
79	77	73	—	LOVER'S PRAYER — Dion and the Belmonts, Laurie 3035		3
80	59	54	39	YOU'RE GONNA MISS ME — Connie Francis, M-G-M 12824	S	10
★81	—	—	—	YOU WENT BACK ON YOUR WORD — Clyde McPhatter, Atlantic 2038		1
82	71	83	100	THERE COMES A TIME — Jack Scott, Carlton 519	S	4
83	87	—	—	THE HUNCH — Bobby Peterson, V-Tone 205		2
84	75	52	42	CARIBBEAN — Mitchell Torok, Guyden 2018		14
★85	—	—	—	STARRY EYED — Gary Stites, Carlton 521	S	1
86	70	63	63	DARLING, I LOVE YOU — Al Martino, 20th Fox 153		6
87	92	95	—	JUST TO BE WITH YOU — The Passions, Audiocon 102		3
88	97	—	—	THE HUNCH — Paul Gayten, Anna 1006		2
★89	—	—	—	SCARLET RIBBONS — Browns, RCA Victor 7614	S	1
90	96	99	—	MIDNIGHT STROLL — Revels, Norgolde 103		3
91	69	74	75	PLENTY GOOD LOVIN' — Connie Francis, M-G-M 12824	S	7
92	84	—	—	YOU MEAN EVERYTHING TO ME — Fleetwoods, Dolton 5		2
93	—	—	—	TINY TIM — LaVern Baker, Atlantic 2041		1
94	—	—	—	YOU'VE GOT WHAT IT TAKES — Marv Johnson, United Artists 185		1
95	—	—	—	REVILLE ROCK — Johnny and the Hurricanes, Warwick 513	S	1
96	—	—	—	FANCY NANCY — Skip and Flip, Brent 7005		1
97	100	—	—	THERE'S A GIRL — Jan and Dean, Dore 531		2
98	—	—	—	HONESTLY AND TRULY — Tommy Edwards, M-G-M 12837	S	1
99	—	—	—	SMOOTH OPERATOR — Sarah Vaughan, Mercury 71519		1
100	—	—	—	WHEEL OF FORTUNE — The Knightsbridge Strings, Top Rank 2014		1

FOR THE WEEK ENDING NOVEMBER 15

The Billboard HOT 100

★ STAR PERFORMERS showed the greatest upward progress on the Hot 100 this week.

S Indicates that STEREO SINGLE version is available.

This Week	One Week Ago	Two Weeks Ago	Three Weeks Ago	TITLE, Artist, Company, Record No.	Stereo	Weeks on Chart
1	1	1	1	MACK THE KNIFE — Bobby Darin, Atco 6147		12
2	2	2	3	MR. BLUE — Fleetwoods, Dolton 5		10
3	3	3	2	PUT YOUR HEAD ON MY SHOULDER — Paul Anka, ABC-Paramount 10040	S	11
4	4	5	13	DON'T YOU KNOW — Della Reese, RCA Victor 7591	S	8
5	6	6	7	LONELY STREET — Andy Williams, Cadence 1370		10
6	5	4	4	TEEN BEAT — Sandy Nelson, Original Sound 5		10
7	7	10	15	DECK OF CARDS — Wink Martindale, Dot 15968		9
8	8	8	11	PRIMROSE LANE — Jerry Wallace, Challenge 59047		13
9	15	17	23	7 LITTLE GIRLS (SITTIN' IN THE BACK SEAT) — Paul Evans & the Curls, Guaranteed 200		9
10	12	24	29	HEARTACHES BY THE NUMBER — Guy Mitchell, Columbia 41476		6
11	19	26	26	DANNY BOY — Conway Twitty, M-G-M 12826	S	7
12	13	28	60	SO MANY WAYS — Brook Benton, Mercury 71512	S	4
13	14	15	28	IN THE MOOD — Ernie Fields, Rendezvous 110		8
14	10	9	8	POISON IVY — Coasters, Atco 6146		12
15	9	7	9	JUST ASK YOUR HEART — Frankie Avalon, Chancellor 1040	S	11
16	17	25	41	OH, CAROL — Neil Sedaka, RCA Victor 7595		5
★17	29	34	49	UNFORGETTABLE — Dinah Washington, Mercury 71508	S	6
★18	30	33	37	THE ENCHANTED SEA — The Islanders, May Flower 16		7
19	11	11	5	('TIL) I KISSED YOU — Everly Brothers, Cadence 1369		13
20	18	30	39	MISTY — Johnny Mathis, Columbia 41483		6
21	22	38	48	WE GOT LOVE — Bobby Rydell, Cameo 169		5
★22	51	80	—	BE MY GUEST — Fats Domino, Imperial 5629		3
★23	34	46	77	DANCE WITH ME — The Drifters, Atlantic 2040		5
24	16	13	16	BATTLE HYMN OF THE REPUBLIC — The Mormon Tabernacle Choir, Columbia 41459		10
25	24	35	35	WOO-HOO — Rock-A-Teens, Roulette 4192		6
26	21	21	31	YOU WERE MINE — Fireflies, Ribbon 6901		10
27	31	23	25	HEY LITTLE GIRL — Dee Clark, Abner 1029	S	12
28	23	14	14	RED RIVER ROCK — Johnny and the Hurricanes, Warwick 509	S	15
29	20	12	6	SLEEP WALK — Santo and Johnny, Canadian-American 103		16
30	25	22	20	WORRIED MAN — Kingston Trio, Capitol 4271		9
31	36	43	45	LIVING DOLL — Cliff Richard & the Drifters, ABC-Paramount 10042		7
32	26	20	24	SAY MAN — Bo Diddley, Checker 931		8
33	35	42	43	LOVE POTION #9 — Clovers, United Artists 180		9
34	33	18	17	MORGEN — Ivo Robic, Laurie 3033		13
35	27	27	22	THE ANGELS LISTENED IN — The Crests, Coed 515		13
★36	78	94	—	I'VE BEEN AROUND — Fats Domino, Imperial 5629		3
37	41	40	32	JUST AS MUCH AS EVER — Bob Beckham, Decca 30861		14
★38	49	51	97	HIGH SCHOOL U.S.A. — Tommy Facenda, Atlantic 51 to 78		4
39	44	44	47	IF I GIVE MY HEART TO YOU — Kitty Kallen, Columbia 41473		6
40	37	37	46	SOME KIND-A EARTHQUAKE — Duane Eddy, Jamie 1130	S	6
★41	65	81	—	THE ENCHANTED SEA — Martin Denny, Liberty 55212	S	3
42	42	39	42	TORQUAY — Fireballs, Top Rank 2008		7
43	46	52	—	BELIEVE ME — Royal Teens, Capitol 4261		3
★44	55	88	—	COME INTO MY HEART — Lloyd Price, ABC-Paramount 10062	S	3
★45	95	—	—	REVEILLE ROCK — Johnny and the Hurricanes, Warwick 513	S	2
46	48	56	64	JOEY'S SONG — Bill Haley & His Comets, Decca 30956		6
47	38	45	38	TUCUMCARI — Jimmie Rodgers, Roulette 4191	S	8
48	53	60	66	TALK TO ME — Frank Sinatra, Capitol 4284		4
49	58	74	98	CLOUDS — The Spacemen, Alton 254		4
50	47	41	30	MAKIN' LOVE — Floyd Robinson, RCA Victor 7529		16
51	52	65	78	POCO LOCO — Gene & Eunice, Case 101		10
52	32	16	10	THE THREE BELLS — Browns, RCA Victor 7555	S	16
53	40	36	34	MARY LOU — Ronnie Hawkins, Roulette 4177	S	13
54	56	53	44	YOU BETTER KNOW IT — Jackie Wilson, Brunswick 55149	S	10
55	50	47	50	SHOUT (I) — Isley Brothers, RCA Victor 7588	S	8
★56	75	—	—	ALWAYS — Sammy Turner, Big Top 3029		2
★57	77	—	—	(IF YOU CRY) TRUE LOVE, TRUE LOVE — Drifters, Atlantic 2040		2
58	63	91	—	FIRST NAME INITIAL — Annette, Vista 349		3
59	28	19	12	I'M GONNA GET MARRIED — Lloyd Price, ABC-Paramount 10032	S	14
60	54	48	36	FOOL'S HALL OF FAME — Pat Boone, Dot 15982	S	9
61	45	32	19	BROKEN-HEARTED MELODY — Sarah Vaughan, Mercury 71477		17
62	62	58	53	BOO BOO STICK BEAT — Chet Atkins, RCA Victor 7589		7
63	39	31	21	I LOVES YOU PORGY — Nina Simone, Bethlehem 11021	S	15
64	64	73	76	I DON'T KNOW — Ruth Brown, Atlantic 2035		5
65	60	66	69	FIRST LOVE, FIRST TEARS — Duane Eddy, Jamie 1130	S	7
66	66	72	—	PRETEND — Carl Mann, Phillips International 3546		3
67	59	62	91	IT HAPPENED TODAY — The Skyliners, Calico 109		7
★68	90	96	99	MIDNIGHT STROLL — Revels, Norgolde 103		4
69	43	29	18	BATTLE OF KOOKAMONGA — Homer & Jethro, RCA Victor 7585	S	10
70	67	55	40	I AIN'T NEVER — Webb Pierce, Decca 30923		14
71	76	76	86	RUNNING BEAR — Johnny Preston, Mercury 71474		5
★72	94	—	—	YOU'VE GOT WHAT IT TAKES — Marv Johnson, United Artists 185		2
73	81	—	—	YOU WENT BACK ON YOUR WORD — Clyde McPhatter, Atlantic 2038		2
74	74	99	—	MY HEART BECAME OF AGE — Annette, Vista 349		3
75	89	—	—	SCARLET RIBBONS — Browns, RCA Victor 7614	S	2
76	57	68	87	TENNESSEE WALTZ — Bobby Comstock, Blaze 349		4
77	85	—	—	STARRY EYED — Gary Stites, Carlton 521	S	2
78	83	87	—	THE HUNCH — Bobby Peterson, V-Tone 205		3
79	82	71	83	THERE COMES A TIME — Jack Scott, Carlton 519	S	5
★80	—	—	—	MARINA — Rocco Granata, Laurie 3041		1
81	73	79	—	TENNESSEE WALTZ — Jerry Fuller, Challenge 59057		3
82	93	—	—	TINY TIM — LaVern Baker, Atlantic 2041		2
83	88	97	—	THE HUNCH — Paul Gayten, Anna 1106		3
84	87	92	95	JUST TO BE WITH YOU — The Passions, Audicon 102		4
85	96	—	—	FANCY NANCY — Skip and Flip, Brent 7005		2
★86	—	—	—	UH! OH! — The Nutty Squirrels, Hanover 4540		1
★87	—	—	—	HAPPY ANNIVERSARY — Jane Morgan, Kapp 305		1
★88	—	—	—	EL PASO — Marty Robbins, Columbia 41511		1
89	99	—	—	SMOOTH OPERATOR — Sarah Vaughan, Mercury 71519		2
★90	—	—	—	HAPPY ANNIVERSARY — Four Lads, Columbia 41497		1
91	100	—	—	WHEEL OF FORTUNE — The Knightsbridge Strings, Top Rank 2014		2
92	—	89	—	I'LL BE SEEING YOU — Poni Tails, ABC-Paramount 10047		2
93	—	—	—	ONE MORE CHANCE — Rod Bernard, Mercury 71507		1
94	—	—	—	DONT DESTROY ME — Crash Craddock, Columbia 41470		1
95	98	—	—	HONESTLY AND TRULY — Tommy Edwards, M-G-M 12837	S	2
96	—	—	—	I'M MOVIN' ON — Ray Charles, Atlantic 2043		1
97	97	100	—	THERE'S A GIRL — Jan and Dean, Dore 531		3
98	—	—	—	OLD SHEP — Ralph De Marco, Guaranteed 202		1
99	—	—	—	THERE I'VE SAID IT AGAIN — Sam Cooke, Keen 82105		1
100	—	—	—	WONT'CHA COME HOME — Lloyd Price, ABC-Paramount 10062	S	1

FOR THE WEEK ENDING NOVEMBER 22

The Billboard HOT 100

★ STAR PERFORMERS showed the greatest upward progress on the Hot 100 this week.

S Indicates that STEREO SINGLE version is available.

This Week	One Week Ago	Two Weeks Ago	Three Weeks Ago	Title, Artist, Company, Record No.	Stereo	Weeks on Chart
1	2	2	2	MR. BLUE — Fleetwoods, Dolton 5		11
2	1	1	1	MACK THE KNIFE — Bobby Darin, Atco 6147		13
3	4	4	5	DON'T YOU KNOW — Della Reese, RCA Victor 7591	S	9
4	3	3	3	PUT YOUR HEAD ON MY SHOULDER — Paul Anka, ABC-Paramount 10040	S	12
★5	10	12	24	HEARTACHES BY THE NUMBER — Guy Mitchell, Columbia 41476		7
6	5	6	6	LONELY STREET — Andy Williams, Cadence 1370		11
7	6	5	4	TEEN BEAT — Sandy Nelson, Original Sound 5		11
8	7	7	10	DECK OF CARDS — Wink Martindale, Dot 15968		10
9	12	13	28	SO MANY WAYS — Brook Benton, Mercury 71512	S	5
10	8	8	8	PRIMROSE LANE — Jerry Wallace, Challenge 59047		14
11	13	14	15	IN THE MOOD — Ernie Fields, Rendezvous 110		9
★12	21	22	38	WE GOT LOVE — Bobby Rydell, Cameo 169		6
13	9	15	17	7 LITTLE GIRLS (SITTIN' IN THE BACK SEAT) — Paul Evans & the Curls, Guaranteed 200		10
14	11	19	26	DANNY BOY — Conway Twitty, M-G-M 12826	S	8
15	18	30	33	THE ENCHANTED SEA — Islanders, May Flower 16		8
★16	23	34	46	DANCE WITH ME — The Drifters, Atlantic 2040		6
★17	22	51	80	BE MY GUEST — Fats Domino, Imperial 5629		4
18	17	29	34	UNFORGETTABLE — Dinah Washington, Mercury 71508	S	7
19	16	17	25	OH, CAROL — Neil Sedaka, RCA Victor 7595		6
20	20	18	30	MISTY — Johnny Mathis, Columbia 41483		7
21	25	24	35	WOO-HOO — Rock-A-Teens, Roulette 4192		7
22	26	21	21	YOU WERE MINE — Fireflies, Ribbon 6901		11
★23	33	35	42	LOVE POTION #9 — Clovers, United Artists 180		10
24	15	9	7	JUST ASK YOUR HEART — Frankie Avalon, Chancellor 1040	S	12
25	24	16	13	BATTLE HYMN OF THE REPUBLIC — Mormon Tabernacle Choir, Columbia 41459		11
26	14	10	9	POISON IVY — Coasters, Atco 6146		13
27	19	11	11	('TIL) I KISSED YOU — Everly Brothers, Cadence 1369		14
★28	38	49	51	HIGH SCHOOL U.S.A. — Tommy Facenda, Atlantic 51 to 78		5
★29	45	95	—	REVEILLE ROCK — Johnny and the Hurricanes, Warwick 513	S	3
30	32	26	20	SAY MAN — Bo Diddley, Checker 931		9
★31	41	65	81	THE ENCHANTED SEA — Martin Denny, Liberty 55212	S	4
32	31	36	43	LIVING DOLL — Richard & the Drifters, ABC-Paramount 10042		8
33	36	78	94	I'VE BEEN AROUND — Fats Domino, Imperial 5629		4
34	39	44	44	IF I GIVE MY HEART TO YOU — Kitty Kallen, Columbia 41473		7
★35	56	75	—	ALWAYS — Sammy Turner, Big Top 3029		3
36	37	41	40	JUST AS MUCH AS EVER — Bob Beckham, Decca 30861		15
37	43	46	52	BELIEVE ME — Royal Teens, Capitol 4261		4
★38	72	94	—	YOU'VE GOT WHAT IT TAKES — Marv Johnson, United Artists 185		3
39	42	42	39	TORQUAY — Fireballs, Top Rank 2008		8
40	48	53	60	TALK TO ME — Frank Sinatra, Capitol 4284		5
41	49	58	74	CLOUDS — The Spacemen, Alton 254		5
★42	57	77	—	(IF YOU CRY) TRUE LOVE, TRUE LOVE — Drifters, Atlantic 2040		3
★43	100	—	—	WONT'CHA COME HOME — Lloyd Price, ABC-Paramount 10062	S	2
44	35	27	27	THE ANGELS LISTENED IN — The Crests, Coed 515		14
★45	68	90	96	MIDNIGHT STROLL — Revels, Norgolde 103		5
★46	—	72	—	I DIG GIRLS — Bobby Rydell, Cameo 169		4
47	44	55	88	COME INTO MY HEART — Lloyd Price, ABC-Paramount 10062	S	4
48	51	52	65	POCO LOCO — Gene & Eunice, Case 101		11
49	46	48	56	JOEY'S SONG — Bill Haley & His Comets, Decca 30956		7
★50	75	89	—	SCARLET RIBBONS — Browns, RCA Victor 7614	S	3
★51	80	—	—	MARINA — Rocco Granata, Laurie 3041		2
★52	76	57	68	TENNESSEE WALTZ — Bobby Comstock, Blaze 349		5
53	27	31	23	HEY LITTLE GIRL — Dee Clark, Abner 1029	S	13
54	30	25	22	WORRIED MAN — Kingston Trio, Capitol 4271		10
★55	—	—	—	THE BIG HURT — Toni Fisher, Signet 275		1
56	28	23	14	RED RIVER ROCK — Johnny and the Hurricanes, Warwick 509	S	16
57	29	20	12	SLEEP WALK — Santo and Johnny, Canadian-American 103		17
58	40	37	37	SOME KIND-A EARTHQUAKE — Duane Eddy, Jamie 1130	S	7
59	34	33	18	MORGEN — Ivo Robic, Laurie 3033		14
60	65	60	66	FIRST LOVE, FIRST TEARS — Duane Eddy, Jamie 1130	S	8
61	55	50	47	SHOUT (I) — Isley Brothers, RCA Victor 7588	S	9
62	50	47	41	MAKIN' LOVE — Floyd Robinson, RCA Victor 7529		17
★63	81	73	79	TENNESSEE WALTZ — Jerry Fuller, Challenge 59057		4
64	66	66	72	PRETEND — Carl Mann, Philips International 3546		4
★65	82	93	—	TINY TIM — LaVern Baker, Atlantic 2041		3
★66	89	99	—	SMOOTH OPERATOR — Sarah Vaughan, Mercury 71519		3
★67	—	—	—	THE BEST OF EVERYTHING — Johnny Mathis, Columbia 41491		1
★68	96	—	—	I'M MOVIN' ON — Ray Charles, Atlantic 2043		2
69	58	63	91	FIRST NAME INITIAL — Annette, Vista 349		4
70	86	—	—	UH! OH! — The Nutty Squirrels, Hanover 4540		2
71	85	96	—	FANCY NANCY — Skip and Flip, Brent 7005		3
72	73	81	—	YOU WENT BACK ON YOUR WORD — Clyde McPhatter, Atlantic 2038		3
★73	88	—	—	EL PASO — Marty Robbins, Columbia 41511		2
★74	93	—	—	ONE MORE CHANCE — Rod Bernard, Mercury 71507		2
75	53	40	36	MARY LOU — Ronnie Hawkins, Roulette 4177	S	14
76	61	45	32	BROKEN-HEARTED MELODY — Sarah Vaughan, Mercury 71477		18
77	90	—	—	HAPPY ANNIVERSARY — Four Lads, Columbia 41497		2
78	62	62	58	BOO BOO STICK BEAT — Chet Atkins, RCA Victor 7589		8
79	77	85	—	STARRY EYED — Gary Stites, Carlton 521	S	3
80	52	32	16	THE THREE BELLS — Browns, RCA Victor 7555	S	17
★81	—	—	—	HOUND DOG MAN — Fabian, Chancellor 1044	S	1
82	78	83	87	THE HUNCH — Bobby Peterson, V-Tone 205		4
83	87	—	—	HAPPY ANNIVERSARY — Jane Morgan, Kapp 305		2
84	47	38	45	TUCUMCARI — Jimmie Rodgers, Roulette 4191	S	9
85	83	88	97	THE HUNCH — Paul Gayten, Anna 1106		4
86	67	59	62	IT HAPPENED TODAY — The Skyliners, Calico 109		8
87	92	—	89	I'LL BE SEEING YOU — Poni Tails, ABC-Paramount 10047		3
88	91	100	—	WHEEL OF FORTUNE — The Knightsbridge Strings, Top Rank 2014		3
89	84	87	92	JUST TO BE WITH YOU — The Passions, Audicon 102		5
90	99	—	—	THERE I'VE SAID IT AGAIN — Sam Cooke, Keen 82105		2
91	98	—	—	OLD SHEP — Ralph De Marco, Guaranteed 202		2
92	—	—	—	GOODNIGHT MY LOVE — Ray Peterson, RCA Victor 7635		1
93	—	—	—	GILEE — Sonny Spencer, Memo 17984		1
94	95	98	—	HONESTLY AND TRULY — Tommy Edwards, M-G-M 12837	S	3
95	—	—	—	MARINA — Jacky Noguez, Jamie 1137		1
96	—	—	—	GOD BLESS AMERICA — Connie Francis, M-G-M 12841	S	1
97	—	—	—	(NEW IN) THE WAYS OF LOVE — Tommy Edwards, M-G-M 12837	S	1
98	—	—	—	I WALK THE LINE — Don Costa, United Artists 190		1
99	64	64	73	I DON'T KNOW — Ruth Brown, Atlantic 2035		6
100	—	—	—	SO YOUNG — Clyde Stacey, Argyle 1001		1

FOR THE WEEK ENDING NOVEMBER 29

The Billboard HOT 100

★ STAR PERFORMERS showed the greatest upward progress on the Hot 100 this week.

S Indicates that STEREO SINGLE version is available.

This Week	One Week Ago	Two Weeks Ago	Three Weeks Ago	TITLE, Artist, Company, Record No.	Stereo	Weeks on Chart
1	2	1	1	MACK THE KNIFE — Bobby Darin, Atco 6147		14
2	1	2	2	MR. BLUE — Fleetwoods, Dolton 5		12
3	3	4	4	DON'T YOU KNOW — Della Reese, RCA Victor 7591	S	10
4	5	10	12	HEARTACHES BY THE NUMBER — Guy Mitchell, Columbia 41476		8
5	4	3	3	PUT YOUR HEAD ON MY SHOULDER — Paul Anka, ABC-Paramount 10040	S	13
6	9	12	13	SO MANY WAYS — Brook Benton, Mercury 71512	S	6
7	8	7	7	DECK OF CARDS — Wink Martindale, Dot 15968		11
8	11	13	14	IN THE MOOD — Ernie Fields, Rendezvous 110		10
9	10	8	8	PRIMROSE LANE — Jerry Wallace, Challenge 59047		15
10	12	21	22	WE GOT LOVE — Bobby Rydell, Cameo 169		7
11	6	5	6	LONELY STREET — Andy Williams, Cadence 1370		12
12	13	9	15	7 LITTLE GIRLS (SITTIN' IN THE BACK SEAT) — Paul Evans & the Curls, Guaranteed 200		11
13	7	6	5	TEEN BEAT — Sandy Nelson, Original Sound 5		12
14	17	22	51	BE MY GUEST — Fats Domino, Imperial 5629		5
★15	20	20	18	MISTY — Johnny Mathis, Columbia 41483		8
★16	21	25	24	WOO-HOO — Rock-A-Teens, Roulette 4192		8
17	15	18	30	THE ENCHANTED SEA — Islanders, Mayflower 16		9
18	14	11	19	DANNY BOY — Conway Twitty, M-G-M 12826	S	9
19	19	16	17	OH, CAROL — Neil Sedaka, RCA Victor 7595		7
20	16	23	34	DANCE WITH ME — The Drifters, Atlantic 2040		7
21	18	17	29	UNFORGETTABLE — Dinah Washington, Mercury 71508	S	8
22	22	26	21	YOU WERE MINE — Fireflies, Ribbon 6901		12
23	25	24	16	BATTLE HYMN OF THE REPUBLIC — Mormon Tabernacle Choir, Columbia 41459		12
★24	35	56	75	ALWAYS — Sammy Turner, Big Top 3029		4
25	29	45	95	REVEILLE ROCK — Johnny and the Hurricanes, Warwick 513	S	4
★26	37	43	46	BELIEVE ME — Royal Teens, Capitol 4261		5
27	23	33	35	LOVE POTION #9 — Clovers, United Artists 180		11
28	31	41	65	THE ENCHANTED SEA — Martin Denny, Liberty 55212	S	5
29	28	39	49	HIGH SCHOOL U.S.A. — Tommy Facenda, Atlantic 51 to 78		6
30	32	31	36	LIVING DOLL — Richard & the Drifters, ABC-Paramount 10042		9
31	24	15	9	JUST ASK YOUR HEART — Frankie Avalon, Chancellor 1040	S	13
32	38	72	94	YOU GOT WHAT IT TAKES — Marv Johnson, United Artists 185		4
★33	50	75	89	SCARLET RIBBONS — Browns, RCA Victor 7614	S	4
34	42	57	77	(IF YOU CRY) TRUE LOVE, TRUE LOVE — Drifters, Atlantic 2040		4
★35	47	44	55	COME INTO MY HEART — Lloyd Price, ABC-Paramount 10062	S	5
★36	55	—	—	THE BIG HURT — Toni Fisher, Signet 275		2
37	34	39	44	IF I GIVE MY HEART TO YOU — Kitty Kallen, Columbia 41473		8
38	45	68	90	MIDNIGHT STROLL — Revels, Norgolde 103		6
★39	51	80	—	MARINA — Rocco Granata, Laurie 3041		3
40	40	48	53	TALK TO ME — Frank Sinatra, Capitol 4284		6
41	36	37	41	JUST AS MUCH AS EVER — Bob Beckham, Decca 30861		16
★42	81	—	—	HOUND DOG MAN — Fabian, Chancellor 1044	S	2
43	26	14	10	POISON IVY — Coasters, Atco 6146		14
44	33	36	78	I'VE BEEN AROUND — Fats Domino, Imperial 5629		5
45	27	19	11	('TIL) I KISSED YOU — Everly Brothers, Cadence 1369		15
46	30	32	26	SAY MAN — Bo Diddley, Checker 931		10
47	39	42	42	TORQUAY — Fireballs, Top Rank 2008		9
48	49	46	48	JOEY'S SONG — Bill Haley & His Comets, Decca 30956		8
49	48	51	52	POCO LOCO — Gene & Eunice, Case 101		12
★50	70	86	—	UH! OH! — The Nutty Squirrels, Hanover 4540		3
★51	73	88	—	EL PASO — Marty Robbins, Columbia 41511		3
52	52	76	57	TENNESSEE WALTZ — Bobby Comstock, Blaze 349		6
53	41	49	58	CLOUDS — The Spacemen, Alton 254		6
54	43	100	—	WON'TCHA COME HOME — Lloyd Price, ABC-Paramount 10062	S	3
★55	68	96	—	I'M MOVIN' ON — Ray Charles, Atlantic 2043		3
56	46	—	72	I DIG GIRLS — Bobby Rydell, Cameo 169		5
57	64	66	66	PRETEND — Carl Mann, Philips International 3546		5
★58	96	—	—	GOD BLESS AMERICA — Connie Francis, M-G-M 12841	S	2
59	58	40	37	SOME KIND-A EARTHQUAKE — Duane Eddy, Jamie 1130	S	8
60	54	30	25	WORRIED MAN — Kingston Trio, Capitol 4271		11
★61	—	—	—	FRIENDLY WORLD — Fabian, Chancellor 1044	S	1
62	66	89	99	SMOOTH OPERATOR — Sarah Vaughan, Mercury 71519		4
63	59	34	33	MORGEN — Ivo Robic, Laurie 3033		15
64	56	28	23	RED RIVER ROCK — Johnny and the Hurricanes, Warwick 509	S	17
★65	94	95	98	HONESTLY AND TRULY — Tommy Edwards, M-G-M 12837	S	4
66	67	—	—	THE BEST OF EVERYTHING — Johnny Mathis, Columbia 41491		2
67	53	27	31	HEY LITTLE GIRL — Dee Clark, Abner 1029	S	14
★68	85	83	88	THE HUNCH — Paul Gayten, Anna 1106		5
69	75	53	40	MARY LOU — Ronnie Hawkins, Roulette 4177	S	15
★70	97	—	—	(NEW IN) THE WAYS OF LOVE — Tommy Edwards, M-G-M 12837	S	2
71	82	78	83	THE HUNCH — Bobby Peterson, V-Tone 205		5
★72	—	—	—	WAY DOWN YONDER IN NEW ORLEANS — Freddie Cannon, Swan 4043		1
73	65	82	93	TINY TIM — LaVern Baker, Atlantic 2041		4
★74	—	—	—	IT'S TIME TO CRY — Paul Anka, ABC-Paramount 10064	S	1
75	69	58	63	FIRST NAME INITIAL — Annette, Vista 349		5
★76	—	—	—	AMONG MY SOUVENIRS — Connie Francis, M-G-M 12841	S	1
77	44	35	27	THE ANGELS LISTENED IN — The Crests, Coed 515		15
78	92	—	—	GOODNIGHT MY LOVE — Ray Peterson, RCA Victor 7635		2
79	74	93	—	ONE MORE CHANCE — Rod Bernard, Mercury 71507		3
★80	—	—	—	PRETTY BLUE EYES — Steve Lawrence, ABC-Paramount 10058	S	1
81	90	—	—	THERE I'VE SAID IT AGAIN — Sam Cooke, Keen 82105		2
82	77	90	—	HAPPY ANNIVERSARY — Four Lads, Columbia 41497		3
★83	98	—	—	I'LL WALK THE LINE — Don Costa, United Artists 190		2
84	93	—	—	GILEE — Sonny Spencer, Memo 17984		2
85	71	85	96	FANCY NANCY — Skip and Flip, Brent 7005		4
86	—	71	76	RUNNING BEAR — Johnny Preston, Mercury 71474		6
★87	—	—	—	TALK THAT TALK — Jackie Wilson, Brunswick 55165		1
88	60	65	60	FIRST LOVE, FIRST TEARS — Duane Eddy, Jamie 1130	S	9
★89	—	—	—	SANDY — Larry Hall, Strand 25007		1
90	57	29	20	SLEEP WALK — Santo and Johnny, Canadian-American 103		18
91	79	77	85	STARRY EYED — Gary Stites, Carlton 521	S	4
92	76	61	45	BROKEN-HEARTED MELODY — Sarah Vaughan, Mercury 71477		19
93	—	—	—	STORY OF OUR LOVE — Johnny Mathis, Columbia 41483		1
94	95	—	—	MARINA — Jacky Noguez, Jamie 1137		2
95	—	—	—	WHY — Frankie Avalon, Chancellor 1045	S	1
96	83	87	—	HAPPY ANNIVERSARY — Jane Morgan, Kapp 305		3
97	89	84	87	JUST TO BE WITH YOU — The Passions, Audicon 102		6
98	63	81	73	TENNESSEE WALTZ — Jerry Fuller, Challenge 59057		5
99	100	—	—	SO YOUNG — Clyde Stacey, Argyle 1001		2
100	—	—	—	WE TOLD YOU NOT TO MARRY — Titus Turner, Glover 201		1

The Billboard HOT 100

FOR THE WEEK ENDING DECEMBER 6

★ STAR PERFORMERS showed the greatest upward progress on the Hot 100 this week.

S Indicates that STEREO SINGLE version is available.

TITLE, Artist, Company, Record No.

This Week	One Week Ago	Two Weeks Ago	Three Weeks Ago	Title, Artist, Company, Record No.	Stereo	Weeks on Chart
1	1	2	1	MACK THE KNIFE — Bobby Darin, Atco 6147		15
2	3	3	4	DON'T YOU KNOW — Della Reese, RCA Victor 7591	S	11
3	2	1	2	MR. BLUE — Fleetwoods, Dolton 5		13
4	4	5	10	HEARTACHES BY THE NUMBER — Guy Mitchell, Columbia 41476		9
5	8	11	13	IN THE MOOD — Ernie Fields, Rendezvous 110		11
6	6	9	12	SO MANY WAYS — Brook Benton, Mercury 71512	S	7
7	5	4	3	PUT YOUR HEAD ON MY SHOULDER — Paul Anka, ABC-Paramount 10040	S	14
8	10	12	21	WE GOT LOVE — Bobby Rydell, Cameo 169		8
★9	14	17	22	BE MY GUEST — Fats Domino, Imperial 5629		6
10	12	13	9	7 LITTLE GIRLS (SITTIN' IN THE BACK SEAT) — Paul Evans & the Curls, Guaranteed 200		12
11	7	8	7	DECK OF CARDS — Wink Martindale, Dot 15968		12
12	15	20	20	MISTY — Johnny Mathis, Columbia 41483		9
★13	19	19	16	OH, CAROL — Neil Sedaka, RCA Victor 7595		8
14	18	14	11	DANNY BOY — Conway Twitty, M-G-M 12826	S	10
★15	20	16	23	DANCE WITH ME — The Drifters, Atlantic 2040		8
16	11	6	5	LONELY STREET — Andy Williams, Cadence 1370		13
17	9	10	8	PRIMROSE LANE — Jerry Wallace, Challenge 59047		16
★18	36	55	—	THE BIG HURT — Toni Fisher, Signet 275		3
★19	24	35	56	ALWAYS — Sammy Turner, Big Top 3029		5
20	21	18	17	UNFORGETTABLE — Dinah Washington, Mercury 71508	S	9
★21	33	50	75	SCARLET RIBBONS — Browns, RCA Victor 7614	S	5
22	17	15	18	THE ENCHANTED SEA — Islanders, Mayflower 16		10
23	16	21	25	WOO-HOO — Rock-A-Teens, Roulette 4192		9
24	22	22	26	YOU WERE MINE — Fireflies, Ribbon 6901		13
★25	50	70	86	UH! OH! — The Nutty Squirrels, Hanover 4540		4
26	13	7	6	TEEN BEAT — Sandy Nelson, Original Sound 5		13
★27	51	73	88	EL PASO — Marty Robbins, Columbia 41511		4
28	25	29	45	REVEILLE ROCK — Johnny and the Hurricanes, Warwick 513	S	5
29	26	37	43	BELIEVE ME — Royal Teens, Capitol 4261		6
30	35	47	44	COME INTO MY HEART — Lloyd Price, ABC-Paramount 10062	S	6
31	27	23	33	LOVE POTION #9 — Clovers, United Artists 180		12
★32	42	81	—	HOUND DOG MAN — Fabian, Chancellor 1044	S	3
33	34	42	57	(IF YOU CRY) TRUE LOVE, TRUE LOVE — Drifters, Atlantic 2040		5
34	32	38	72	YOU GOT WHAT IT TAKES — Marv Johnson, United Artists 185		5
35	38	45	68	MIDNIGHT STROLL — Revels, Norgolde 103		7
36	39	51	80	MARINA — Rocco Granata, Laurie 3041		4
37	23	25	24	BATTLE HYMN OF THE REPUBLIC — Mormon Tabernacle Choir, Columbia 41459		13
38	40	40	48	TALK TO ME — Frank Sinatra, Capitol 4284		7
39	41	36	37	JUST AS MUCH AS EVER — Bob Beckham, Decca 30861		17
★40	74	—	—	IT'S TIME TO CRY — Paul Anka, ABC-Paramount 10064	S	2
★41	61	—	—	FRIENDLY WORLD — Fabian, Chancellor 1044	S	2
42	37	34	39	IF I GIVE MY HEART TO YOU — Kitty Kallen, Columbia 41473		9
43	28	31	41	THE ENCHANTED SEA — Martin Denny, Liberty 55212	S	6
44	29	28	39	HIGH SCHOOL U.S.A. — Tommy Facenda, Atlantic 51 to 78		7
45	44	33	36	I'VE BEEN AROUND — Fats Domino, Imperial 5629		6
★46	58	96	—	GOD BLESS AMERICA — Connie Francis, M-G-M 12841	S	3
47	48	49	46	JOEY'S SONG — Bill Haley & His Comets, Decca 30956		9
★48	75	69	58	FIRST NAME INITIAL — Annette, Vista 349		6
49	55	68	96	I'M MOVIN' ON — Ray Charles, Atlantic 2043		4
★50	—	—	—	I WANNA BE LOVED — Ricky Nelson, Imperial 5614		1
51	30	32	31	LIVING DOLL — Richard & the Drifters, ABC-Paramount 10042		10
52	54	43	100	WON'TCHA COME HOME — Lloyd Price, ABC-Paramount 10062	S	4
★53	95	—	—	WHY — Frankie Avalon, Chancellor 1045	S	2
★54	80	—	—	PRETTY BLUE EYES — Steve Lawrence, ABC-Paramount 10058	S	2
55	47	39	42	TORQUAY — Fireballs, Top Rank 2008		10
★56	76	—	—	AMONG MY SOUVENIRS — Connie Francis, M-G-M 12841	S	2
57	62	66	89	SMOOTH OPERATOR — Sarah Vaughan, Mercury 71519		5
58	53	41	49	CLOUDS — The Spacemen, Alton 254		7
★59	86	—	71	RUNNING BEAR — Johnny Preston, Mercury 71474		7
★60	72	—	—	WAY DOWN YONDER IN NEW ORLEANS — Freddie Cannon, Swan 4043		2
61	46	30	32	SAY MAN — Bo Diddley, Checker 931		11
62	66	67	—	THE BEST OF EVERYTHING — Johnny Mathis, Columbia 41491		3
63	73	65	82	TINY TIM — LaVern Baker, Atlantic 2041		5
★64	89	—	—	SANDY — Larry Hall, Strand 25007		2
65	31	24	15	JUST ASK YOUR HEART — Frankie Avalon, Chancellor 1040	S	14
66	65	94	95	HONESTLY AND TRULY — Tommy Edwards, M-G-M 12837	S	5
67	70	97	—	(NEW IN) THE WAYS OF LOVE — Tommy Edwards, M-G-M 12837	S	3
68	63	59	34	MORGEN — Ivo Robic, Laurie 3033		16
69	56	46	—	I DIG GIRLS — Bobby Rydell, Cameo 169		6
70	43	26	14	POISON IVY — Coasters, Atco 6146		15
71	57	64	66	PRETEND — Carl Mann, Phillips International 3546		6
72	83	98	—	I'LL WALK THE LINE — Don Costa, United Artists 190		3
73	78	92	—	GOODNIGHT MY LOVE — Ray Peterson, RCA Victor 7635		4
74	79	74	93	ONE MORE CHANCE — Rod Bernard, Mercury 71507		4
75	49	48	51	POCO LOCO — Gene & Eunice, Case 101		13
★76	—	—	—	TEARDROP — Santo and Johnny, Canadian-American 107		1
77	68	85	83	THE HUNCH — Paul Gayten, Anna 1106		6
78	71	82	78	THE HUNCH — Bobby Peterson, V-Tone 205		6
79	52	52	76	TENNESSEE WALTZ — Bobby Comstock, Blaze 349		7
80	45	27	19	('TIL) I KISSED YOU — Everly Brothers, Cadence 1369		16
★81	—	—	—	MARINA — Willy Alberti, London 1888		1
82	84	93	—	GILEE — Sonny Spencer, Memo 17984		3
83	87	—	—	TALK THAT TALK — Jackie Wilson, Brunswick 55165		2
84	81	90	—	THERE I'VE SAID IT AGAIN — Sam Cooke, Keen 82105		3
85	91	79	77	STARRY EYED — Gary Stites, Carlton 521	S	5
★86	—	—	—	MIGHTY GOOD — Ricky Nelson, Imperial 5614		1
87	94	95	—	MARINA — Jacky Noguez, Jamie 1137		3
88	97	89	84	JUST TO BE WITH YOU — The Passions, Audicon 102		7
89	96	83	87	HAPPY ANNIVERSARY — Jane Morgan, Kapp 305		4
★90	—	—	—	SYMPHONY — Sammy Turner, Big Top 3029		1
91	85	71	85	FANCY NANCY — Skip and Flip, Brent 7005		5
92	67	53	27	HEY LITTLE GIRL — Dee Clark, Abner 1029	S	15
93	100	—	—	WE TOLD YOU NOT TO MARRY — Titus Turner, Clover 201		2
94	69	75	53	MARY LOU — Ronnie Hawkins, Roulette 4177	S	16
95	—	—	—	SHADOWS — The Five Suns, Ember 1056		1
96	—	—	—	BEYOND THE SUNSET — Pat Boone, Dot 16006		1
97	77	44	35	THE ANGELS LISTENED IN — The Crests, Coed 515		16
98	—	—	—	SMOKIE (PART II) — Bill Black's Combo, Hi 2018		1
99	—	—	—	TEACH ME TIGER — April Stevens, Imperial 5626		1
100	82	77	90	HAPPY ANNIVERSARY — Four Lads, Columbia 41497		4

FOR THE WEEK ENDING DECEMBER 13

The Billboard HOT 100

★ STAR PERFORMERS showed the greatest upward progress on the Hot 100 this week.

[S] Indicates that STEREO SINGLE version is available.

This Week	One Week Ago	Two Weeks Ago	Three Weeks Ago	TITLE, Artist, Company, Record No.	Stereo	Weeks on Chart
1	1	1	2	MACK THE KNIFE — Bobby Darin, Atco 6147		16
2	4	4	5	HEARTACHES BY THE NUMBER — Guy Mitchell, Columbia 41476		10
3	3	2	1	MR. BLUE — Fleetwoods, Dolton 5		14
4	2	3	3	DON'T YOU KNOW — Della Reese, RCA Victor 7591	S	12
5	5	8	11	IN THE MOOD — Ernie Fields, Rendezvous 110		12
6	8	10	12	WE GOT LOVE — Bobby Rydell, Cameo 169		9
7	6	6	9	SO MANY WAYS — Brook Benton, Mercury 71512	S	8
8	9	14	17	BE MY GUEST — Fats Domino, Imperial 5629		7
9	13	19	19	OH, CAROL — Neil Sedaka, RCA Victor 7595		9
10	14	18	14	DANNY BOY — Conway Twitty, M-G-M 12826	S	11
11	7	5	4	PUT YOUR HEAD ON MY SHOULDER — Paul Anka, ABC-Paramount 10040	S	15
12	11	7	8	DECK OF CARDS — Wink Martindale, Dot 15968		13
13	12	15	20	MISTY — Johnny Mathis, Columbia 41483		10
14	10	12	13	7 LITTLE GIRLS (SITTIN' IN THE BACK SEAT) — Paul Evans & the Curls, Guaranteed 200		13
★15	27	51	73	EL PASO — Marty Robbins, Columbia 41511		5
★16	21	33	50	SCARLET RIBBONS — Browns, RCA Victor 7614	S	6
17	18	36	55	THE BIG HURT — Toni Fisher, Signet 275		4
★18	40	74	—	IT'S TIME TO CRY — Paul Anka, ABC-Paramount 10064	S	3
★19	25	50	70	UH! OH! (Part II) — The Nutty Squirrels, Hanover 4540		5
★20	30	35	47	COME INTO MY HEART — Lloyd Price, ABC-Paramount 10062	S	7
★21	32	42	81	HOUND DOG MAN — Fabian, Chancellor 1044	S	4
22	19	24	35	ALWAYS — Sammy Turner, Big Top 3029		6
23	15	20	16	DANCE WITH ME — The Drifters, Atlantic 2040		9
★24	53	95	—	WHY — Frankie Avalon, Chancellor 1045	S	3
★25	41	61	—	FRIENDLY WORLD — Fabian, Chancellor 1044	S	3
26	16	11	6	LONELY STREET — Andy Williams, Cadence 1370		14
27	23	16	21	WOO-HOO — Rock-A-Teens, Roulette 4192		10
28	28	25	29	REVEILLE ROCK — Johnny and the Hurricanes, Warwick 513	S	6
29	17	9	10	PRIMROSE LANE — Jerry Wallace, Challenge 59047		17
30	20	21	18	UNFORGETTABLE — Dinah Washington, Mercury 71508	S	10
★31	60	72	—	WAY DOWN YONDER IN NEW ORLEANS — Freddie Cannon, Swan 4043		3
32	36	39	51	MARINA — Rocco Granata, Laurie 3041		5
33	39	41	36	JUST AS MUCH AS EVER — Bob Beckham, Decca 30861		18
34	33	34	42	(IF YOU CRY) TRUE LOVE, TRUE LOVE — Drifters, Atlantic 2040		6
35	22	17	15	THE ENCHANTED SEA — Islanders, Mayflower 16		11
36	29	26	37	BELIEVE ME — Royal Teens, Capitol 4261		7
★37	64	89	—	SANDY — Larry Hall, Strand 25007		3
★38	56	76	—	AMONG MY SOUVENIRS — Connie Francis, M-G-M 12841	S	3
39	34	32	38	YOU GOT WHAT IT TAKES — Marv Johnson, United Artists 185		6
★40	50	—	—	I WANNA BE LOVED — Ricky Nelson, Imperial 5614		2
41	26	13	7	TEEN BEAT — Sandy Nelson, Original Sound 5		14
42	48	75	69	FIRST NAME INITIAL — Annette, Vista 349		7
43	38	40	40	TALK TO ME — Frank Sinatra, Capitol 4284		8
★44	54	80	—	PRETTY BLUE EYES — Steve Lawrence, ABC-Paramount 10058	S	3
45	49	55	68	I'M MOVIN' ON — Ray Charles, Atlantic 2043		5
46	35	38	45	MIDNIGHT STROLL — Revels, Norgolde 103		8
47	31	27	23	LOVE POTION #9 — Clovers, United Artists 180		13
48	24	22	22	YOU WERE MINE — Fireflies, Ribbon 6901		14
49	47	48	49	JOEY'S SONG — Bill Haley & His Comets, Decca 30956		10
50	57	62	66	SMOOTH OPERATOR — Sarah Vaughan, Mercury 71519		6
51	59	86	—	RUNNING BEAR — Johnny Preston, Mercury 71474		8
★52	76	—	—	TEARDROP — Santo and Johnny, Canadian-American 107		2
53	42	37	34	IF I GIVE MY HEART TO YOU — Kitty Kallen, Columbia 41473		10
54	44	29	28	HIGH SCHOOL U.S.A. — Tommy Facenda, Atlantic 51 to 78		8
55	37	23	25	BATTLE HYMN OF THE REPUBLIC — Mormon Tabernacle Choir, Columbia 41459		14
56	52	54	43	WON'TCHA COME HOME — Lloyd Price, ABC-Paramount 10062	S	5
57	51	30	32	LIVING DOLL — Richard & the Drifters, ABC-Paramount 10042		11
58	45	44	33	I'VE BEEN AROUND — Fats Domino, Imperial 5629		7
59	46	58	96	GOD BLESS AMERICA — Connie Francis, M-G-M 12841	S	4
★60	81	—	—	MARINA — Willy Alberti, London 1888		2
★61	86	—	—	MIGHTY GOOD — Ricky Nelson, Imperial 5614		2
62	58	53	41	CLOUDS — The Spacemen, Alton 254		8
63	62	66	67	THE BEST OF EVERYTHING — Johnny Mathis, Columbia 41491		4
64	43	28	31	THE ENCHANTED SEA — Martin Denny, Liberty 55212	S	7
★65	98	—	—	SMOKIE (PART II) — Bill Black's Combo, Hi 2018		2
66	67	70	97	(NEW IN) THE WAYS OF LOVE — Tommy Edwards, M-G-M 12837	S	4
67	72	83	98	I'LL WALK THE LINE — Don Costa, United Artists 190		4
68	66	65	94	HONESTLY AND TRULY — Tommy Edwards, M-G-M 12837	S	6
69	73	78	92	GOODNIGHT MY LOVE — Ray Peterson, RCA Victor 7635		5
70	55	47	39	TORQUAY — Fireballs, Top Rank 2008		11
★71	—	—	—	A YEAR AGO TONIGHT — The Crests, Coed 521		1
72	83	87	—	TALK THAT TALK — Jackie Wilson, Brunswick 55165		3
★73	88	97	89	JUST TO BE WITH YOU — The Passions, Audicon 102		8
74	70	43	26	POISON IVY — Coasters, Atco 6146		16
75	63	73	65	TINY TIM — LaVern Baker, Atlantic 2041		6
76	61	46	30	SAY MAN — Bo Diddley, Checker 931		12
★77	—	—	—	WHAT ABOUT US — The Coasters, Atco 6153		1
78	65	31	24	JUST ASK YOUR HEART — Frankie Avalon, Chancellor 1040	S	15
79	85	91	79	STARRY EYED — Gary Stites, Carlton 521	S	6
80	77	68	85	THE HUNCH — Paul Gayten, Anna 1106		7
81	71	57	64	PRETEND — Carl Mann, Phillips International 3546		7
82	68	63	59	MORGEN — Ivo Robic, Laurie 3033		17
★83	—	—	—	THE HAPPY REINDEER — Dancer, Prancer & Nervous, Capitol 4300		1
84	74	79	74	ONE MORE CHANCE — Rod Bernard, Mercury 71507		5
85	89	96	83	HAPPY ANNIVERSARY — Jane Morgan, Kapp 305		5
86	84	81	90	THERE I'VE SAID IT AGAIN — Sam Cooke, Keen 82105		4
87	93	100	—	WE TOLD YOU NOT TO MARRY — Titus Turner, Clover 201		3
88	96	—	—	BEYOND THE SUNSET — Pat Boone, Dot 16006		2
89	90	—	—	SYMPHONY — Sammy Turner, Big Top 3029		2
90	78	71	82	THE HUNCH — Bobby Peterson, V-Tone 205		7
91	82	84	93	GILEE — Sonny Spencer, Memo 17984		4
92	79	52	52	TENNESSEE WALTZ — Bobby Comstock, Blaze 349		8
93	—	—	—	LUCKY DEVIL — Carl Dobkins Jr., Decca 31020		1
94	95	—	—	SHADOWS — The Five Suns, Ember 1056		2
95	99	—	—	TEACH ME TIGER — April Stevens, Imperial 5626		2
96	—	—	—	SHIMMY SHIMMY KO KO BOP — Little Anthony & The Imperials, End 1060		1
97	100	82	77	HAPPY ANNIVERSARY — Four Lads, Columbia 41497		5
98	—	—	—	GO, JIMMY, GO — Jimmy Clanton, Ace 575		1
99	—	—	—	HOW ABOUT THAT — Dee Clark, Abner 1032		1
100	—	—	—	UH! OH! (Part I) — The Nutty Squirrels, Hanover 4540		1

FOR THE WEEK ENDING DECEMBER 20

The Billboard HOT 100

★ STAR PERFORMERS showed the greatest upward progress on the Hot 100 this week.

S Indicates that STEREO SINGLE version is available.

This Week	One Week Ago	Two Weeks Ago	Three Weeks Ago	Title, Artist, Company, Record No.	Stereo	Weeks on Chart
1	2	4	4	HEARTACHES BY THE NUMBER — Guy Mitchell, Columbia 41476		11
2	3	3	2	MR. BLUE — Fleetwoods, Dolton 5		15
3	1	1	1	MACK THE KNIFE — Bobby Darin, Atco 6147		17
4	5	5	8	IN THE MOOD — Ernie Fields, Rendezvous 110		13
★5	24	53	95	WHY — Frankie Avalon, Chancellor 1045	S	4
6	6	8	10	WE GOT LOVE — Bobby Rydell, Cameo 169		10
7	4	2	3	DON'T YOU KNOW — Della Reese, RCA Victor 7591	S	13
8	7	6	6	SO MANY WAYS — Brooks Benton, Mercury 71512	S	9
★9	18	40	74	IT'S TIME TO CRY — Paul Anka, ABC-Paramount 10064	S	4
★10	17	18	36	THE BIG HURT — Toni Fisher, Signet 275		5
11	15	27	51	EL PASO — Marty Robbins, Columbia 41511		6
12	8	9	14	BE MY GUEST — Fats Domino, Imperial 5629		8
★13	31	60	72	WAY DOWN YONDER IN NEW ORLEANS — Freddie Cannon, Swan 4043		4
14	9	13	19	OH, CAROL — Neil Sedaka, RCA Victor 7595		10
15	19	25	50	UH! OH! (Part II) — The Nutty Squirrels, Hanover 4540		6
★16	21	32	42	HOUND DOG MAN — Fabian, Chancellor 1044	S	5
17	13	12	15	MISTY — Johnny Mathis, Columbia 41483		11
18	16	21	33	SCARLET RIBBONS — Browns, RCA Victor 7614	S	7
19	10	14	18	DANNY BOY — Conway Twitty, M-G-M 12826	S	12
★20	44	54	80	PRETTY BLUE EYES — Steve Lawrence, ABC-Paramount 10058	S	4
★21	38	56	76	AMONG MY SOUVENIRS — Connie Francis, M-G-M 12841	S	4
22	22	19	24	ALWAYS — Sammy Turner, Big Top 3029		7
★23	40	50	—	I WANNA BE LOVED — Ricky Nelson, Imperial 5614		3
24	23	15	20	DANCE WITH ME — The Drifters, Atlantic 2040		10
25	20	30	35	COME INTO MY HEART — Lloyd Price, ABC-Paramount 10062	S	8
26	14	10	12	7 LITTLE GIRLS (SITTIN' IN THE BACK SEAT) — Paul Evans & the Curls, Guaranteed 200		14
27	25	41	61	FRIENDLY WORLD — Fabian, Chancellor 1044	S	4
28	28	28	25	REVEILLE ROCK — Johnny and the Hurricanes, Warwick 513	S	7
29	30	20	21	UNFORGETTABLE — Dinah Washington, Mercury 71508	S	11
★30	52	76	—	TEARDROP — Santo and Johnny, Canadian-American 107		3
31	37	64	89	SANDY — Larry Hall, Strand 25007		4
★32	42	48	75	FIRST NAME INITIAL — Annette, Vista 349		8
33	34	33	34	(IF YOU CRY) TRUE LOVE, TRUE LOVE — Drifters, Atlantic 2040		7
34	32	36	39	MARINA — Rocco Granata, Laurie 3041		6
35	36	29	26	BELIEVE ME — Royal Teens, Capitol 4261		8
36	11	7	5	PUT YOUR HEAD ON MY SHOULDER — Paul Anka, ABC-Paramount 10040	S	16
37	33	39	41	JUST AS MUCH AS EVER — Bob Beckham, Decca 30861		19
38	12	11	7	DECK OF CARDS — Wink Martindale, Dot 15968		14
39	29	17	9	PRIMROSE LANE — Jerry Wallace, Challenge 59047		18
40	45	49	55	I'M MOVIN' ON — Ray Charles, Atlantic 2043		6
★41	51	59	86	RUNNING BEAR — Johnny Preston, Mercury 71474		9
42	26	16	11	LONELY STREET — Andy Williams, Cadence 1370		15
43	39	34	32	YOU GOT WHAT IT TAKES — Marv Johnson, United Artists 185		7
44	50	57	62	SMOOTH OPERATOR — Sarah Vaughan, Mercury 71519		7
45	27	23	16	WOO-HOO — Rock-A-Teens, Roulette 4192		11
★46	60	81	—	MARINA — Willy Alberti, London 1888		3
47	54	44	29	HIGH SCHOOL U.S.A. — Tommy Facenda, Atlantic 51 to 78		9
★48	65	98	—	SMOKIE (PART II) — Bill Black's Combo, Hi 2081		3
49	43	38	40	TALK TO ME — Frank Sinatra, Capitol 4284		9
50	48	24	22	YOU WERE MINE — Fireflies, Ribbon 6901		15
51	58	45	44	I'VE BEEN AROUND — Fats Domino, Imperial 5629		8
52	47	31	27	LOVE POTION #9 — Clovers, United Artists 180		14
53	35	22	17	THE ENCHANTED SEA — Islanders, Mayflower 16		12
★54	100	—	—	UH! OH! (Part I) — The Nutty Squirrels, Hanover 4540		2
55	61	86	—	MIGHTY GOOD — Ricky Nelson, Imperial 5614		3
★56	72	83	87	TALK THAT TALK — Jackie Wilson, Brunswick 55165		4
57	46	35	38	MIDNIGHT STROLL — Revels, Norgolde 103		9
58	53	42	37	IF I GIVE MY HEART TO YOU — Kitty Kallen, Columbia 41473		11
59	67	72	83	I'LL WALK THE LINE — Don Costa, United Artists 190		5
60	59	46	58	GOD BLESS AMERICA — Connie Francis, M-G-M 12841	S	5
61	57	51	30	LIVING DOLL — Richard & the Drifters, ABC-Paramount 10042		12
62	41	26	13	TEEN BEAT — Sandy Nelson, Original Sound 5		15
63	62	58	53	CLOUDS — The Spacemen, Alton 254		9
64	69	73	78	GOODNIGHT MY LOVE — Ray Peterson, RCA Victor 7635		6
65	71	—	—	A YEAR AGO TONIGHT — The Crests, Coed 521		2
66	55	37	23	BATTLE HYMN OF THE REPUBLIC — Mormon Tabernacle Choir, Columbia 41459		15
67	77	—	—	WHAT ABOUT US — The Coasters, Atco 6153		2
68	70	55	47	TORQUAY — Fireballs, Top Rank 2008		
69	73	88	97	JUST TO BE WITH YOU — The Passions, Audicon 102		
★70	—	—	—	VILLAGE OF ST. BERNADETTE — Andy Williams, Cadence 1374		
71	56	52	54	WON'TCHA COME HOME — Lloyd Price, ABC-Paramount 10062	S	
72	68	66	65	HONESTLY AND TRULY — Tommy Edwards, M-G-M 12837	S	
73	49	47	48	JOEY'S SONG — Bill Haley & His Comets, Decca 30956		
★74	98	—	—	GO, JIMMY, GO — Jimmy Clanton, Ace 575		
75	63	62	66	THE BEST OF EVERYTHING — Johnny Mathis, Columbia 41491		
76	64	43	28	THE ENCHANTED SEA — Martin Denny, Liberty 55212	S	
77	66	67	70	(NEW IN) THE WAYS OF LOVE — Tommy Edwards, M-G-M 12837	S	
78	88	96	—	BEYOND THE SUNSET — Pat Boone, Dot 16006		
79	75	63	73	TINY TIM — LaVern Baker, Atlantic 2041		
80	83	—	—	THE HAPPY REINDEER — Dancer, Prancer & Nervous, Capitol 4300		
★81	—	—	—	NOT ONE MINUTE MORE — Della Reese, RCA Victor 7644	S	
82	89	90	—	SYMPHONY — Sammy Turner, Big Top 3029		
83	87	93	100	WE TOLD YOU NOT TO MARRY — Titus Turner, Clover 201		
84	84	74	79	ONE MORE CHANCE — Rod Bernard, Mercury 71507		
85	93	—	—	LUCKY DEVIL — Carl Dobkins Jr., Decca 31020		
86	95	99	—	TEACH ME TIGER — April Stevens, Imperial 5626		
87	94	95	—	SHADOWS — The Five Satins, Ember 1056		
88	99	—	—	HOW ABOUT THAT — Dee Clark, Abner 1032		
★89	—	—	—	CHIPMUNK SONG — David Seville and the Chipmunks, Liberty 55250	S	
90	96	—	—	SHIMMY SHIMMY KO KO BOP — Little Anthony & The Imperials, End 1060		
91	78	65	31	JUST ASK YOUR HEART — Frankie Avalon, Chancellor 1040	S	
92	—	—	—	DO-RE-MI — Mitch Miller and the Kids, Columbia 41499		
93	—	—	—	EBB TIDE — Bobby Freeman, Josie 872		
94	85	89	96	HAPPY ANNIVERSARY — Jane Morgan, Kapp 305		
95	79	85	91	STARRY EYED — Gary Stites, Carlton 521	S	
96	—	—	—	I DON'T KNOW WHAT IT IS — The Blue Notes, Brooke 111		
97	—	—	—	CANDY APPLE RED — Bonnie Guitar, Dolton 10		
98	—	—	—	COO COO-U — The Kingston Trio, Capitol 4303		
99	—	—	—	THE LITTLE DRUMMER BOY — Harry Simeone Chorale, 20th Fox 121	[illegible]	
100	—	—	—	JUST COME HOME — Hugo and Luigi, RCA Victor 7639	[illegible]	

FOR THE WEEK ENDING DECEMBER 27

The Billboard HOT 100

★ STAR PERFORMERS showed the greatest upward progress on the Hot 100 this week.

S Indicates that STEREO SINGLE version is available.

One Week Ago	Two Weeks Ago	Three Weeks Ago	Title, Artist, Company, Record No.	Stereo	Weeks on Chart
1	2	4	HEARTACHES BY THE NUMBER — Guy Mitchell, Columbia 41476		12
5	24	53	WHY — Frankie Avalon, Chancellor 1045	S	5
11	15	27	EL PASO — Marty Robbins, Columbia 41511		7
10	17	18	THE BIG HURT — Toni Fisher, Signet 275		6
13	31	60	WAY DOWN YONDER IN NEW ORLEANS — Freddie Cannon, Swan 4043		5
9	18	40	IT'S TIME TO CRY — Paul Anka, ABC-Paramount 10064	S	5
3	1	1	MACK THE KNIFE — Bobby Darin, Atco 6147		18
6	6	8	WE GOT LOVE — Bobby Rydell, Cameo 169		11
21	38	56	AMONG MY SOUVENIRS — Connie Francis, M-G-M 12841	S	5
16	21	32	HOUND DOG MAN — Fabian, Chancellor 1044	S	6
4	5	5	IN THE MOOD — Ernie Fields, Rendezvous 110		14
27	25	41	FRIENDLY WORLD — Fabian, Chancellor 1044	S	5
7	4	2	DON'T YOU KNOW — Della Reese, RCA Victor 7591	S	14
18	16	21	SCARLET RIBBONS — Browns, RCA Victor 7614	S	8
8	7	6	SO MANY WAYS — Brooks Benton, Mercury 71512	S	10
4	9	13	OH, CAROL — Neil Sedaka, RCA Victor 7595		11
2	3	3	MR. BLUE — Fleetwoods, Dolton 5		16
5	19	25	UH! OH! (Part II) — The Nutty Squirrels, Hanover 4540		7
0	44	54	PRETTY BLUE EYES — Steve Lawrence, ABC-Paramount 10058	S	5
3	40	50	I WANNA BE LOVED — Ricky Nelson, Imperial 5614		4
2	8	9	BE MY GUEST — Fats Domino, Imperial 5629		9
7	13	12	MISTY — Johnny Mathis, Columbia 41483		12
0	52	76	TEARDROP — Santo and Johnny, Canadian-American 107		4
1	51	59	RUNNING BEAR — Johnny Preston, Mercury 71474		10
3	39	34	YOU GOT WHAT IT TAKES — Marv Johnson, United Artists 185		8
5	20	30	COME INTO MY HEART — Lloyd Price, ABC-Paramount 10062	S	9
9	10	14	DANNY BOY — Conway Twitty, M-G-M 12826	S	13
8	65	98	SMOKIE (PART II) — Bill Black's Combo, Hi 2081		4
	37	64	SANDY — Larry Hall, Strand 25007		5
8	28	28	REVEILLE ROCK — Johnny and the Hurricanes, Warwick 513	S	8
4	32	36	MARINA — Rocco Granata, Laurie 3041		7
2	42	48	FIRST NAME INITIAL — Annette, Vista 349		9
4	23	15	DANCE WITH ME — The Drifters, Atlantic 2040		11

This Week	One Week Ago	Two Weeks Ago	Three Weeks Ago	Title, Artist, Company, Record No.	Stereo	Weeks on Chart
34	22	22	19	ALWAYS — Sammy Turner, Big Top 3029		8
★35	74	98	—	GO, JIMMY, GO — Jimmy Clanton, Ace 575		3
★36	60	59	46	GOD BLESS AMERICA — Connie Francis, M-G-M 12841	S	6
37	37	33	39	JUST AS MUCH AS EVER — Bob Beckham, Decca 30861		20
★38	55	61	86	MIGHTY GOOD — Ricky Nelson, Imperial 5614		4
39	33	34	33	(IF YOU CRY) TRUE LOVE, TRUE LOVE — Drifters, Atlantic 2040		8
40	35	36	29	BELIEVE ME — Royal Teens, Capitol 4261		9
41	26	14	10	7 LITTLE GIRLS (SITTIN' IN THE BACK SEAT) — Paul Evans & the Curls, Guaranteed 200		15
42	29	30	20	UNFORGETTABLE — Dinah Washington, Mercury 71508	S	12
43	36	11	7	PUT YOUR HEAD ON MY SHOULDER — Paul Anka, ABC-Paramount 10040	S	17
★44	56	72	83	TALK THAT TALK — Jackie Wilson, Brunswick 55165		5
45	54	100	—	UH! OH! (Part I) — The Nutty Squirrels, Hanover 4540		3
46	46	60	81	MARINA — Willy Alberti, London 1888		4
47	99	—	—	THE LITTLE DRUMMER BOY — Harry Simeone Chorale, 20th Fox 121	S	2
48	38	12	11	DECK OF CARDS — Wink Martindale, Dot 15968		15
49	47	54	44	HIGH SCHOOL U.S.A. — Tommy Facenda, Atlantic 51 to 78		10
50	39	29	17	PRIMROSE LANE — Jerry Wallace, Challenge 59047		19
★51	63	62	58	CLOUDS — The Spacemen, Alton 254		10
★52	81	—	—	NOT ONE MINUTE MORE — Della Reese, RCA Victor 7644	S	2
53	52	47	31	LOVE POTION #9 — Clovers, United Artists 180		15
54	44	50	57	SMOOTH OPERATOR — Sarah Vaughan, Mercury 71519		8
55	40	45	49	I'M MOVIN' ON — Ray Charles, Atlantic 2043		7
★56	70	—	—	VILLAGE OF ST. BERNADETTE — Andy Williams, Cadence 1374		2
57	65	71	—	A YEAR AGO TONIGHT — The Crests, Coed 521		3
58	49	43	38	TALK TO ME — Frank Sinatra, Capitol 4284		10
59	42	26	16	LONELY STREET — Andy Williams, Cadence 1370		16
60	71	56	52	WON'TCHA COME HOME — Lloyd Price, ABC-Paramount 10062	S	7
★61	88	99	—	HOW ABOUT THAT — Dee Clark, Abner 1032		3
62	50	48	24	YOU WERE MINE — Fireflies, Ribbon 6901		16
63	51	58	45	I'VE BEEN AROUND — Fats Domino, Imperial 5629		9
64	64	69	73	GOODNIGHT MY LOVE — Ray Peterson, RCA Victor 7635		7
65	67	77	—	WHAT ABOUT US — The Coasters, Atco 6153		3
66	59	67	72	I'LL WALK THE LINE — Don Costa, United Artists 190		6
67	45	27	23	WOO-HOO — Rock-A-Teens, Roulette 4192		12
★68	89	—	—	CHIPMUNK SONG — David Seville and the Chipmunks, Liberty 55250	S	2
69	61	57	51	LIVING DOLL — Richard & the Drifters, ABC-Paramount 10042		13
70	58	53	42	IF I GIVE MY HEART TO YOU — Kitty Kallen, Columbia 41473		12
71	78	88	96	BEYOND THE SUNSET — Pat Boone, Dot 16006		4
72	68	70	55	TORQUAY — Fireballs, Top Rank 2008		13
★73	100	—	—	JUST COME HOME — Hugo and Luigi, RCA Victor 7639	S	2
74	79	75	63	TINY TIM — LaVern Baker, Atlantic 2041		8
★75	92	—	—	DO-RE-MI — Mitch Miller and the Kids, Columbia 41499		2
76	80	83	—	THE HAPPY REINDEER — Dancer, Prancer & Nervous, Capitol 4300		3
77	57	46	35	MIDNIGHT STROLL — Revels, Norgolde 103		10
78	77	66	67	(NEW IN) THE WAYS OF LOVE — Tommy Edwards, M-G-M 12837	S	6
79	53	35	22	THE ENCHANTED SEA — Islanders, Mayflower 16		13
80	72	68	66	HONESTLY AND TRULY — Tommy Edwards, M-G-M 12837	S	8
81	84	84	74	ONE MORE CHANCE — Rod Bernard, Mercury 71507		7
★82	—	—	—	CLIMB EVERY MOUNTAIN — Tony Bennett, Columbia 41520		1
83	83	87	93	WE TOLD YOU NOT TO MARRY — Titus Turner, Clover 201		5
84	85	93	—	LUCKY DEVIL — Carl Dobkins Jr., Decca 31020		3
★85	—	—	—	BACIARE, BACIARE — Dorothy Collins, Top Rank 2024		1
86	94	85	89	HAPPY ANNIVERSARY — Jane Morgan, Kapp 305		7
87	66	55	37	BATTLE HYMN OF THE REPUBLIC — Mormon Tabernacle Choir, Columbia 41459		16
★88	—	—	—	RUN, RED, RUN — Coasters, Atco 6153		1
89	96	—	—	I DON'T KNOW WHAT IT IS — The Blue Notes, Brooke 111		2
90	90	96	—	SHIMMY, SHIMMY, KO-KO BOP — Little Anthony & The Imperials, End 1060		3
91	—	—	—	THE LITTLE DRUMMER BOY — Johnny Cash, Columbia 41481		1
92	62	41	26	TEEN BEAT — Sandy Nelson, Original Sound 5		16
93	—	—	—	SWINGIN' ON A RAINBOW — Frankie Avalon, Chancellor 1045	S	1
94	—	—	—	LET'S TRY IT AGAIN — Clyde McPhatter, M-G-M 12843		1
95	73	49	47	JOEY'S SONG — Bill Haley & His Comets, Decca 30956		12
96	—	—	—	THIS TIME OF THE YEAR — Brook Benton, Mercury 71554	S	1
97	97	—	—	CANDY APPLE RED — Bonnie Guitar, Dolton 10		2
98	—	—	—	IF I HAD A GIRL — Rod Lauren, RCA Victor 7645	S	1
99	—	—	—	SWEET NUTHIN'S — Brenda Lee, Decca 30967		1
100	—	—	—	TEEN ANGEL — Mark Dinning, M-G-M 12845		1

FOR WEEK ENDING JANUARY 3

The Billboard HOT 100

★ STAR PERFORMERS showed the greatest upward progress on the Hot 100 this week.

S Indicates that STEREO SINGLE version is available.

This Week	One Week Ago	Two Weeks Ago	Three Weeks Ago	Title, Artist, Company, Record No.	Stereo	Weeks on Chart
1	2	5	24	WHY — Frankie Avalon, Chancellor 1045	S	6
2	3	11	15	EL PASO — Marty Robbins, Columbia 41511		8
3	4	10	17	THE BIG HURT — Toni Fisher, Signet 275		7
4	6	9	18	IT'S TIME TO CRY — Paul Anka, ABC-Paramount 10064	S	6
5	5	13	31	WAY DOWN YONDER IN NEW ORLEANS — Freddie Cannon, Swan 4043		6
6	1	1	2	HEARTACHES BY THE NUMBER — Guy Mitchell, Columbia 41476		13
7	9	21	38	AMONG MY SOUVENIRS — Connie Francis, M-G-M 12841	S	6
8	7	3	1	MACK THE KNIFE — Bobby Darin, Atco 6147		19
9	10	16	21	HOUND DOG MAN — Fabian, Chancellor 1044	S	7
★10	19	20	44	PRETTY BLUE EYES — Steve Lawrence, ABC-Paramount 10058	S	6
★11	24	41	51	RUNNING BEAR — Johnny Preston, Mercury 71474		11
12	8	6	6	WE GOT LOVE — Bobby Rydell, Cameo 169		12
13	14	18	16	SCARLET RIBBONS — Browns, RCA Victor 7614	S	9
14	18	15	19	UH! OH! (Part II) — The Nutty Squirrels, Hanover 4540		8
★15	47	99	—	THE LITTLE DRUMMER BOY — Harry Simeone Chorale, 20th Fox 121	S	3
★16	29	31	37	SANDY — Larry Hall, Strand 25007		6
17	15	8	7	SO MANY WAYS — Brooks Benton, Mercury 71512	S	11
18	11	4	5	IN THE MOOD — Ernie Fields, Rendezvous 110		15
★19	35	74	98	GO, JIMMY, GO — Jimmy Clanton, Ace 575		4
20	12	27	25	FRIENDLY WORLD — Fabian, Chancellor 1044	S	6
21	13	7	4	DON'T YOU KNOW — Della Reese, RCA Victor 7591	S	14
22	17	2	3	MR. BLUE — Fleetwoods, Dolton 5		16
23	28	48	65	SMOKIE (Part II) — Bill Black's Combo, Hi 2081		5
24	21	12	8	BE MY GUEST — Fats Domino, Imperial 5629		10
25	16	14	9	OH, CAROL — Neil Sedaka, RCA Victor 7595		12
26	20	23	40	I WANNA BE LOVED — Ricky Nelson, Imperial 5614		5
27	25	43	39	YOU GOT WHAT IT TAKES — Marv Johnson, United Artists 185		9
★28	56	70	—	THE VILLAGE OF ST. BERNADETTE — Andy Williams, Cadence 1374		3
29	32	32	42	FIRST NAME INITIAL — Annette, Vista 349		10
30	23	30	52	TEARDROP — Santo and Johnny, Canadian-American 107		5
31	26	25	20	COME INTO MY HEART — Lloyd Price, ABC-Paramount 10062	S	10
★32	52	81	—	NOT ONE MINUTE MORE — Della Reese, RCA Victor 7644	S	3
33	27	19	10	DANNY BOY — Conway Twitty, M-G-M 12826	S	14
★34	76	80	83	THE HAPPY REINDEER — Dancer, Prancer & Nervous, Capitol 4300		4
35	31	34	32	MARINA — Rocco Granata, Laurie 3041		8
36	22	17	13	MISTY — Johnny Mathis, Columbia 41483		13
37	33	24	23	DANCE WITH ME — The Drifters, Atlantic 2040		12
38	37	37	33	JUST AS MUCH AS EVER — Bob Beckham, Decca 30861		21
39	36	60	59	GOD BLESS AMERICA — Connie Francis, M-G-M 12841	S	7
40	34	22	22	ALWAYS — Sammy Turner, Big Top 3029		9
★41	68	89	—	CHIPMUNK SONG — David Seville and the Chipmunks, Liberty 55250	S	3
42	46	46	60	MARINA — Willy Alberti, London 1888		5
43	44	56	72	TALK THAT TALK — Jackie Wilson, Brunswick 55165		6
44	30	28	28	REVEILLE ROCK — Johnny and the Hurricanes, Warwick 513	S	9
45	38	55	61	MIGHTY GOOD — Ricky Nelson, Imperial 5614		5
46	51	63	62	CLOUDS — The Spacemen, Alton 254		11
47	40	35	36	BELIEVE ME — Royal Teens, Capitol 4261		10
★48	93	—	—	SWINGIN' ON A RAINBOW — Frankie Avalon, Chanacellor 1045	S	2
★49	61	88	99	HOW ABOUT THAT — Dee Clark, Abner 1032		4
★50	100	—	—	TEEN ANGEL — Mark Dinning, M-G-M 12845		2
★51	65	67	77	WHAT ABOUT US — The Coasters, Atco 6153		4
52	57	65	71	A YEAR AGO TONIGHT — The Crests, Coed 521		4
★53	78	77	66	(NEW IN) THE WAYS OF LOVE — Tommy Edwards, M-G-M 12837	S	7
54	49	47	54	HIGH SCHOOL U.S.A. — Tommy Facenda, Atlantic 51 to 78		11
★55	73	100	—	JUST COME HOME — Hugo and Luigi, RCA Victor 7639	S	3
56	39	33	34	(IF YOU CRY) TRUE LOVE, TRUE LOVE — Drifters, Atlantic 2040		9
★57	86	94	85	HAPPY ANNIVERSARY — Jane Morgan, Kapp 305		8
★58	—	—	—	HE'LL HAVE TO GO — Jim Reeves, RCA Victor 7643		1
★59	—	—	—	WHITE CHRISTMAS — Bing Crosby, Decca 23778		1
60	50	39	29	PRIMROSE LANE — Jerry Wallace, Challenge 59047		20
★61	—	—	—	MARY, DON'T YOU WEEP — Stonewall Jackson, Columbia 41533		1
★62	98	—	—	IF I HAD A GIRL — Rod Lauren, RCA Victor 7645	S	2
★63	91	—	—	THE LITTLE DRUMMER BOY — Johnny Cash, Columbia 41481		2
64	55	40	45	I'M MOVING ON — Ray Charles, Atlantic 2043		8
65	45	54	100	UH! OH! (Part I) — The Nutty Squirrels, Hanover 4540		4
66	41	26	14	7 LITTLE GIRLS (SITTIN' IN THE BACK SEAT) — Paul Evans & the Curls, Guaranteed 200		16
★67	—	—	—	NO LOVE HAVE I — Webb Pierce, Decca 31021		1
68	48	38	12	DECK OF CARDS — Wink Martindale, Dot 15968		
69	60	71	56	WON'TCHA COME HOME — Lloyd Price, ABC-Paramount 10062	S	
70	75	92	—	DO-RE-MI — Mitch Miller and the Kids, Columbia 41499		
71	53	52	47	LOVE POTION #9 — Clovers, United Artists 180		
★72	—	—	—	WHERE OR WHEN — Dion & the Belmonts, Laurie 3044		
73	85	—	—	BACIARE, BACIARE — Dorothy Collins, Top Rank 2024		
★74	94	—	—	LET'S TRY AGAIN — Clyde McPhatter, M-G-M 12843	S	
75	81	84	84	ONE MORE CHANCE — Rod Bernard, Mercury 71507		
76	90	90	96	SHIMMY, SHIMMY, KO-KO BOP — Little Anthony & the Imperials, End 1060		
★77	96	—	—	THIS TIME OF THE YEAR — Brook Benton, Mercury 71554	S	
★78	—	—	—	DOWN BY THE STATION — Four Preps, Capitol 4312		
79	42	29	30	UNFORGETTABLE — Dinah Washington, Mercury 71508	S	
80	89	96	—	I DON'T KNOW WHAT IT IS — The Blue Notes, Brooke 111		
81	82	—	—	CLIMB EV'RY MOUNTAIN — Tony Bennett, Columbia 41520		
82	84	85	93	LUCKY DEVIL — Carl Dobkins Jr., Decca 31020		
★83	—	—	—	BONNIE CAME BACK — Duane Eddy, Jamie 1144		
84	88	—	—	RUN, RED, RUN — Coasters, Atco 6153		
85	71	78	88	BEYOND THE SUNSET — Pat Boone, Dot 16006		
86	43	36	11	PUT YOUR HEAD ON MY SHOULDER — Paul Anka, ABC-Paramount 10040		
★87	—	—	—	HANDY MAN — Jimmy Jones, Cub 9049		
★88	—	—	—	PROMISE ME A ROSE — Anita Bryant, Carlton 523		
★89	—	—	—	LONELY BLUE BOY — Conway Twitty, M-G-M 12857		
90	99	—	—	SWEET NUTHIN'S — Brenda Lee, Decca 30967		
91	—	—	—	HONEY HUSH — Joe Turner, Atlantic 1001		
92	54	44	50	SMOOTH OPERATOR — Sarah Vaughan, Mercury 71519		
93	—	—	—	LITTLE THINGS MEAN A LOT — Joni James, M-G-M 12849		
94	—	—	—	DO-RE-MI — Anita Bryant, Carlton 523		
95	74	79	75	TINY TIM — LaVern Baker, Atlantic 2041		
96	83	83	87	WE TOLD YOU NOT TO MARRY — Titus Turner, Clover 201		
97	58	49	43	TALK TO ME — Frank Sinatra, Capitol 4284		
98	—	—	—	HARLEM NOCTURNE — Viscounts, Madison 123		
99	—	—	—	THE SOUND OF MUSIC — Patti Page, Mercury 71555		
100	—	—	—	DARLING LORRAINE — Knockouts, Shad 5013		

THE SONG TITLES

This alphabetical listing of all charted titles shows each title's artist, plus its debut date from the chart on which it first appeared and its peak position from the chart on which it achieved its highest ranking.

A song with more than one charted version is listed once, with the artists' names listed below. The artist with the earliest charted version is shown first. Songs that have the same title, but are different tunes, are listed separately, with the song that charted earliest shown first.

All titles shown on each chart during the initial weeks of 1955 are included in this section, even though many debuted prior to January 1, 1955. For those that debuted earlier, an asterisk follows the date (ex.: 1/1/55*).

It should be pointed out that the titles in this section are listed exactly as they appear on the actual records. Unfortunately, the charts were not always as precise; and, therefore, you will occasionally notice a difference in the way a title is listed in this section versus the charts.

Cross-references are used throughout this section to aid in finding a title. If you have trouble, please keep the following rules in mind: titles in which an apostrophe is used within a word come before titles using the complete spelling (Goin' comes before Going); titles beginning with a contraction follow titles that begin with a similar non-contracted word (Can't follows Can); titles such as "C.C. Rider" and "M.T.A." are found at the beginning of their respective letters, however, initialed titles which actually spell out a word like "R-O-C-K" are sorted with the normal spelling of the word.

Two-word titles which have the exact same spelling as one-word titles are listed together alphabetically (ex.: "Teen-Age" and "Teenage"). Titles which are identical, except for an apostrophized word in one of the titles, are also listed together alphabetically (ex.: "Breakin' Away" and "Breaking Away").

During the '50s a handful of records hit the charts, fell off, and then re-charted within a short period of time. In a few instances, months went by before a record re-charted. To aid in following each record's chart history, a list was compiled of records which re-charted after an eight week or longer absence, but less than one year, from their last chart appearance. That list appears below and includes the date each record re-charted. Please note that records which re-charted after more than a one-year absence are listed, with a new debut date, in the main song title section.

RE-ENTRIES

Records which re-charted after an eight week or longer absence, but less than one year, from their last chart appearance. These re-entry dates are not shown in the title section.

Pop Chart	Date Re-Charted	Weeks Off Chart	
Top 100	7/8/57	21	**Hound Dog** *Elvis Presley*
Top 100	10/21/57	16	**Till** *Percy Faith*
Top 100	7/1/57	15	**Love Me Tender** *Elvis Presley*
Top 100	2/4/56	11	**Magic Melody** *Les Paul and Mary Ford*
Top 100	9/22/56	10	**Don't Cry** *Frankie Laine with Paul Weston*
Top 100	12/29/56	9	**Giant** *Jack Pleis*
Top 100	10/7/57	9	**Deserie** *Charts*
Top 100	6/30/56	8	**We All Need Love** *Percy Faith*
Top 100	9/8/56	8	**Daydreams** Art Mooney
Top 100	7/1/57	8	**Too Much** *Elvis Presley*
Best Sellers	11/11/57	8	**And That Reminds Me** *Della Reese*
Top 100	3/31/58	8	**That's Alright** *Little Junior Parker*

A

10/20/56 **ABC's Of Love** *Frankie Lymon & The Teenagers*
11/19/55 **Adorable** *Fontane Sisters*
9/9/57 **Affair To Remember (Our Love Affair)** *Vic Damone*
7/21/56 **After School** *Tommy Charles*
4/6/57 **After School** *Randy Starr*
8/4/56 **After The Lights Go Down Low** *Al Hibbler*
12/15/56 **Ain't Got No Home** *Clarence "Frog man" Henry*
Ain't That A Shame
7/9/55 *Pat Boone*
7/16/55 *Fats Domino*
6/18/55 **Alabama Jubilee** *Ferko String Band*
8/3/59 **Alimony** *Frankie Ford*
12/22/58 **All American Boy** *Bill Parsons (Bobby Bare)*
11/12/55 **All At Once You Love Her** *Perry Como*
4/21/58 **All I Have To Do Is Dream** *Everly Brothers*
3/10/56 **All Night Long** *Jo Stafford*
12/22/58 **(All of a Sudden) My Heart Sings** *Paul Anka*
10/6/58 **All Over Again** *Johnny Cash*
4/6/57 **All Shook Up** *Elvis Presley*
4/21/58 **All The Time** *Johnny Mathis*
10/28/57 **All The Way** *Frank Sinatra*
1/28/56 **All The Way 'Round The World** *Mills Brothers*
6/16/56 **Allegheny Moon** *Patti Page*
3/30/59 **Almost Grown** *Chuck Berry*
11/10/58 **Almost In Your Arms** *Johnny Nash*
Almost Paradise
2/23/57 *Norman Petty Trio*
3/2/57 *Lou Stein*
3/2/57 *Roger Williams*
9/30/57 **Alone (Why Must I Be Alone)** *Shepherd Sisters*
8/11/58 **Alone With You** *Faron Young*
5/18/59 **Along Came Jones** *Coasters*
1/26/59 **Alright, Okay, You Win** *Peggy Lee*
2/16/59 **Alvin's Harmonica** *Chipmunks*
11/2/59 **Always** *Sammy Turner*
1/26/59 **Ambrose (Part Five)** *Linda Laurie*
11/23/59 **Among My Souvenirs** *Connie Francis*
11/12/55 **Amukiriki (The Lord Willing)** *Les Paul & Mary Ford*
12/22/56 **Anastasia** *Pat Boone*
And That Reminds Me
8/26/57 *Della Reese*
9/2/57 *Kay Starr*
3/17/56 **And The Angels Sing** *Three Chuckles*
7/14/58 **Angel Baby** *Dean Martin*
8/3/59 **Angel Face** *Jimmy Darren*
4/7/56 **Angel Pie (Postillon!)** *Peggy King*
1/27/58 **Angel Smile** *Nat "King" Cole*
12/10/55 **Angels In The Sky** *Crew Cuts*
8/17/59 **Angels Listened In** *Crests*
9/16/57 **Angry** *Frank Pizani*
2/3/58 **Anna Marie** *Jim Reeves*
5/5/58 **Another Time, Another Place** *Patti Page*
3/2/59 **Answer To A Maiden's Prayer** *June Valli*
2/16/59 **Anthony Boy** *Chuck Berry*
11/3/56 **Anyway You Want Me (That's How I Will Be)** *Elvis Presley*
7/28/56 **Ape Call** *Nervous Norvus*
Apple Blossom Time ..see: (I'll Be With You In)
April In Paris
1/14/56 *Count Basie*
3/31/56 *Modernaires*
10/28/57 **April Love** *Pat Boone*
2/9/59 **Are You Lonesome Tonight** *Jaye P. Morgan*
8/4/58 **Are You Really Mine** *Jimmie Rodgers*
Are You Satisfied?
12/17/55 *Rusty Draper*
12/17/55 *Sheb Wooley*
2/4/56 *Toni Arden*
2/17/58 **Are You Sincere** *Andy Williams*
Armen's Theme
12/8/56 *Joe Reisman*
12/15/56 *David Seville*
Around The World In 80 Days
5/20/57 *Victor Young (Main Theme)*
6/10/57 *Mantovani*
6/17/57 *Bing Crosby*
8/19/57 *McGuire Sisters*
Arrivederci, Roma
12/3/55 *Georgia Gibbs*
4/14/58 *Roger Williams*
5/26/58 *Mario Lanza*
7/29/57 **Arrow Of Love** *Six Teens*
3/16/59 **As Time Goes By** *Johnny Nash*
2/11/56 **Ask Me** *Nat "King" Cole*
At My Front Door
10/15/55 *El Dorados*
10/29/55 *Pat Boone*
At The Hop
12/9/57 *Danny & The Juniors*
12/30/57 *Nick Todd*
Auctioneer
11/24/56 *Leroy VanDyke*
12/22/56 *Chuck Miller*
Autumn Leaves
8/20/55 *Roger Williams*
11/12/55 *Steve Allen with George Cates*
11/12/55 *Ray Charles Singers*
11/12/55 *Jackie Gleason*
11/12/55 *Mitch Miller*
11/12/55 *Victor Young*
11/10/56 **Autumn Waltz** *Tony Bennett*
8/18/56 **Away All Boats** *Al Hibbler*

B

3/17/58 **Baby, Baby** *Billy Williams Quartet*
12/8/56 **Baby Doll** *Andy Williams*
9/15/58 **Baby Face** *Little Richard*
8/3/59 **Baby Talk** *Jan & Dean*
12/21/59 **Baciare Baciare (Kissing Kissing)** *Dorothy Collins*
6/22/59 **Back In The U.S.A.** *Chuck Berry*
10/7/57 **Back To School Again** *Timmie "Oh Yeah!" Rogers*
2/2/57 **Bad Boy** *Jive Bombers*
3/16/57 **(Bad Donkey) Pum-Pa-Lum** *Steve Lawrence*
10/5/59 **Bad Girl** *Miracles*
3/3/58 **Bad Motorcycle** *Storey Sisters*
3/30/57 **Bahama Mama** *Four Aces*
3/9/59 **Ballad Of A Girl And Boy** *Graduates*
2/3/58 **Ballad Of A Teenage Queen** *Johnny Cash*
Ballad Of Davy Crockett
2/26/55 *Bill Hayes*
3/12/55 *Fess Parker*
3/19/55 *"Tennessee" Ernie Ford*
4/9/55 *Voices of Walter Schumann*
9/8/58 **Ballad Of Thunder Road** *Robert Mitchum*
2/9/57 **Ballerina** *Nat "King" Cole*
Banana Boat (Day-O)
1/12/57 *Harry Belafonte*
4/13/57 *Stan Freberg*
Banana Boat Song
12/22/56 *Tarriers*
12/29/56 *Fontane Sisters*
12/29/56 *Sarah Vaughan*
1/12/57 *Steve Lawrence*
Band Of Gold
11/19/55 *Kit Carson*
12/3/55 *Don Cherry*
2/18/56 *Hi-Fi Four*
7/16/55 **Bandit (O'Cangaceiro)** *Eddie Barclay*
7/30/55 **Banjo's Back In Town** *Teresa Brewer*
Barefoot Contessa ..see: Song Of
Barefoot Mailman ..see: Song Of
9/7/59 **Battle Hymn Of The Republic** *Mormon Tabernacle Choir*
9/7/59 **Battle Of Kookamonga** *Homer & Jethro*
Battle Of New Orleans
4/27/59 *Johnny Horton*
5/25/59 *Vaughn Monroe*
7/28/58 **Baubles, Bangles And Beads** *Kirby Stone Four*
6/16/56 **Be-Bop-A-Lula** *Gene Vincent*
10/7/57 **Be-Bop Baby** *Ricky Nelson*
7/22/57 **Be Careful With A Fool** *B.B. King*
10/26/59 **Be My Guest** *Fats Domino*
6/29/59 **Beach Time** *Roger Smith*
3/23/59 **Beat, The** *Rockin R's*
7/28/58 **Beautiful Delilah** *Chuck Berry*
7/28/56 **Beautiful Friendship** *Ella Fitzgerald*
3/9/59 **Because You're Young** *Jimmie Rodgers*
3/3/58 **Been So Long** *Pastels*
11/3/58 **Beep Beep** *Playmates*
7/6/59 **Bei Mir Bist Du Schon** *Louis Prima & Keely Smith*
10/26/59 **Believe Me** *Royal Teens*
4/7/58 **Believe What You Say** *Ricky Nelson*
7/13/59 **Bells, Bells, Bells (The Bell Song)** *Billie & Lillie*
2/3/58 **Belonging To Someone** *Patti Page*
5/6/57 **Bernardine** *Pat Boone*
1/27/58 **Bertha Lou** *Clint Miller*
11/16/59 **Best Of Everything** *Johnny Mathis*
2/3/58 **Betty And Dupree** *Chuck Willis*
8/4/58 **Betty Lou Got A New Pair Of Shoes** *Bobby Freeman*
8/31/59 **Betty My Angel** *Jerry Fuller*
6/16/58 **Bewildered** *Mickey & Sylvia*
6/30/58 **Bewitched** *Betty Smith Group*
Beyond The Sea ..see: La Mer
11/30/59 **Beyond The Sunset** *Pat Boone*
Bible Tells Me So
8/20/55 *Nick Noble*
9/10/55 *Don Cornell*
3/16/57 **Big Beat** *Dick Jacobs*
12/23/57 **Big Beat** *Fats Domino*
12/8/58 **Big Bopper's Wedding** *Big Bopper*
9/15/58 **Big Brown Eyes** *Redjacks*
8/25/58 **Big Daddy** *Jill Corey*
3/3/58 **Big Guitar** *Owen Bradley Quintet*
7/6/59 **Big Hunk O' Love** *Elvis Presley*
11/16/59 **Big Hurt** *Miss Toni Fisher*
5/5/58 **Big Man** *Four Preps*
3/17/58 **Big River** *Johnny Cash*
3/17/58 **Billy** *Kathy Linden*
12/8/58 **Billy Bayou** *Jim Reeves*
(Billy Goat) ..see: You Hit The Wrong Note
11/10/58 **Bimbombey** *Jimmie Rodgers*
8/4/58 **Bird Dog** *Everly Brothers*
7/7/58 **Bird On My Head** *David Seville*
3/19/55 **Birth Of The Boogie** *Bill Haley*
2/16/57 **Birthday Party** *Sil Austin*
3/10/56 **Bitter With The Sweet** *Billy Eckstine*
Black Denim Trousers
9/24/55 *Cheers*
11/12/55 *Vaughn Monroe*
8/26/57 **Black Slacks** *Joe Bennett*
2/9/59 **Blah, Blah, Blah** *Nicola Paone*
8/4/58 **Blip Blop** *Bill Doggett*
10/6/58 **Blob, The** *Five Blobs*
5/7/55 **Blossom Fell** *Nat "King" Cole*
6/30/58 **Blue Blue Day** *Don Gibson*
8/4/58 **Blue Boy** *Jim Reeves*
12/29/58 **Blue Hawaii** *Billy Vaughn*
1/5/57 **Blue Monday** *Fats Domino*
9/29/56 **Blue Moon** *Elvis Presley*
9/1/58 **Blue Ribbon Baby** *Tommy Sands*
Blue Star
4/30/55 *Les Baxter*
5/28/55 *Felicia Sanders*
Blue Suede Shoes
3/3/56 *Carl Perkins*
4/7/56 *Elvis Presley*
4/14/56 *Boyd Bennett*
10/13/58 **Bluebell** *Mitch Miller*
Blueberry Hill
10/6/56 *Fats Domino*
11/3/56 *Louis Armstrong & Gordon Jenkins*
12/29/58 **Bluebird, The Buzzard & The Oriole** *Bobby Day*
4/28/58 **Bluebirds Over The Mountain** *Ersel Hickey*
Bo Weevil
3/3/56 *Teresa Brewer*
3/3/56 *Fats Domino*

5/25/59 **Bobby Sox To Stockings**
Frankie Avalon
9/2/57 **Bon Voyage** *Janice Harper*
4/13/59 **Bonaparte's Retreat** *Billy Grammer*
5/18/59 **Bongo Rock** *Preston Epps*
11/12/55 **Bonnie Blue Gal** *Mitch Miller*
12/28/59 **Bonnie Came Back** *Duane Eddy*
11/11/57 **Bony Moronie** *Larry Williams*
9/28/59 **Boo Boo Stick Beat** *Chet Atkins*
9/21/59 **Boogie Bear** *Boyd Bennett*
3/24/58 **Book Of Love** *Monotones*
3/30/59 **Boom-A-Dip-Dip** *Stan Robinson*
5/7/55 **Boom Boom Boomerang**
DeCastro Sisters
3/10/58 **Bop-A-Lena** *Ronnie Self*
7/14/56 **Boppin' The Blues** *Carl Perkins*
6/2/56 **Born To Be With You** *Chordettes*
7/21/58 **Born Too Late** *Poni-Tails*
8/18/58 **Borrowed Dreams** *Bobby Helms*
5/25/59 **Boy Without A Girl** *Frankie Avalon*
9/15/58 **Break-Up** *Jerry Lee Lewis*
9/7/59 **Breaking Up Is Hard To Do** *Jivin' Gene*
3/3/58 **Breathless** *Jerry Lee Lewis*
4/9/55 **Breeze And I** *Caterina Valente*
7/20/59 **Broken-Hearted Melody** *Sarah Vaughan*
11/17/56 **Buchanan and Goodman On Trial**
Buchanan & Goodman
7/22/57 **Build Your Love (On A Strong Foundation)** *Johnnie Ray*
9/29/58 **Bullwhip Rock** *Cyclones*
2/23/59 **Bunny Hop** *Applejacks*
Burn That Candle
11/12/55 *Bill Haley*
11/19/55 *Cues*
8/25/56 **Bus Stop Song (A Paper Of Pins)**
Four Lads
6/17/57 **(But As They Say) That's Life** *Jack Pleis*
Butterfly
2/16/57 *Charlie Gracie*
2/23/57 *Andy Williams*
3/2/57 *Bob Carroll*
3/10/56 **Butternut** *Jimmy Heap*
11/25/57 **Buzz-Buzz-Buzz** *Hollywood Flames*
7/28/58 **By The Light Of The Silvery Moon**
Jimmy Bowen
1/5/57 **By You, By You, By You** *Jim Lowe*
Bye Bye Love
5/20/57 *Everly Brothers*
6/3/57 *Webb Pierce*

C

4/20/57 **C.C. Rider** *Chuck Willis*
C'est La Vie
11/19/55 *Sarah Vaughan*
11/26/55 *DeJohn Sisters*
11/26/55 *Sunny Gale*
11/18/57 **Ca, C'est L'amour** *Tony Bennett*
9/29/58 **Call Me** *Johnny Mathis*
3/23/57 **Calypso Melody** *David Rose*
7/8/57 **Can I Come Over Tonight** *Velours*
1/19/57 **Can I Steal A Little Love** *Frank Sinatra*
4/14/56 **Can You Find It In Your Heart**
Tony Bennett
5/27/57 **Can't Wait For Summer** *Steve Lawrence*
Canadian Sunset
6/23/56 *Hugo Winterhalter/Eddie Heywood*
8/11/56 *Andy Williams*
12/14/59 **Candy Apple Red** *Bonnie Guitar*
11/3/58 **Cannonball** *Duane Eddy*
6/15/59 **Cap And Gown** *Marty Robbins*
1/8/55* **Cara Mia** *David Whitfield with Mantovani*
8/3/59 **Caribbean** *Mitchell Torok*
8/25/58 **Carol** *Chuck Berry*
4/27/59 **Castin' My Spell** *Johnny Otis Show*
7/14/56 **Casual Look** *Six Teens*
1/13/58 **Catch A Falling Star** *Perry Como*
8/31/59 **Caterpillar Crawl** *Strangers*
Cattle Call
7/16/55 *Eddy Arnold*
6/17/57 *Dinah Shore*
6/30/58 **Certain Smile** *Johnny Mathis*
8/11/58 **Cerveza** *Boots Brown*
Cha-Hua-Hua
6/2/58 *Pets*
6/9/58 *Eddie Platt*

Chain Gang
1/14/56 *Bobby Scott*
2/18/56 *Len Dresslar*
9/15/56 **Chains Of Love** *Pat Boone*
9/16/57 **Chances Are** *Johnny Mathis*
Chanson d'Amour (Song Of Love)
4/14/58 *Art & Dotty Todd*
4/28/58 *Fontane Sisters*
2/9/57 **Chantez-Chantez** *Dinah Shore*
8/4/58 **Chantilly Lace** *Big Bopper*
8/24/59 **Chapel Of Dreams** *Dubs*
8/11/58 **Chariot Rock** *Champs*
2/2/59 **Charlie Brown** *Coasters*
12/10/55 **Charmaine** *Four Freshmen*
12/8/56 **Cheat, A** *Sanford Clark*
6/11/55 **Chee Chee-Oo-Chee (Sang the Little Bird)** *Perry Como & Jaye P. Morgan*
5/19/58 **Cherie, I Love You** *Pat Boone*
Cherry Pink And Apple Blossom White
3/5/55 *Perez "Prez" Prado*
4/30/55 *Alan Dale*
6/1/59 **Cherrystone** *Addrisi Brothers*
10/28/57 **Chicago** *Frank Sinatra*
3/30/59 **Chick, The** *Lee & Paul*
9/2/57 **Chicken, Baby, Chicken** *Tony Harris*
Chihuahua ..see: Cha-Hua-Hua
Children's Marching Song
1/12/59 *Mitch Miller*
1/12/59 *Cyril Stapleton*
11/10/56 **Chincherinchee** *Perry Como*
4/7/56 **Chinese Rock And Egg Roll**
Buddy Hackett
3/9/59 **Chip Off The Old Block** *Eddy Arnold*
Chipmunk Song
12/1/58 *Chipmunks*
12/14/59 *Chipmunks*
4/30/55 **Chop Chop Boom** *Crew-Cuts*
Church Bells May Ring
4/7/56 *Willows*
4/21/56 *Diamonds*
Ciao, Ciao Bambina
3/9/59 *Domenico Modugno*
6/22/59 *Jacky Noguez*
10/20/58 **Cimarron (Roll On)** *Billy Vaughn*
Cinco Robles (Five Oaks)
1/12/57 *Russell Arms*
1/12/57 *Les Paul & Mary Ford*
11/17/58 **Cinderella** *Four Preps*
Cindy, Oh Cindy
10/13/56 *Vince Martin With The Tarriers*
10/20/56 *Eddie Fisher*
City Lights
8/25/58 *Ray Price*
3/2/59 *Ivory Joe Hunter*
10/20/56 **City Of Angels** *Highlights*
5/18/59 **Class, The** *Chubby Checker*
3/16/59 **Class Cutter (Yeah Yeah)** *Dale Hawkins*
5/5/58 **Claudette** *Everly Brothers*
8/18/56 **Clay Idol** *Betty Johnson*
2/10/58 **Click-Clack** *Dickey Doo & The Don'ts*
12/21/59 **Climb Every Mountain** *Tony Bennett*
10/19/59 **Clouds, The** *Spacemen*
C'mon ..see: Come On
6/3/57 **Cocoanut Woman** *Harry Belafonte*
3/10/58 **College Man** *Bill Justis*
7/21/58 **Come Closer To Me** *Nat "King" Cole*
2/16/57 **Come Go With Me** *Dell-Vikings*
11/12/55 **Come Home** *Bubber Johnson*
6/2/58 **Come In Stranger** *Johnny Cash*
10/26/59 **Come Into My Heart** *Lloyd Price*
9/7/59 **Come On And Get Me** *Fabian*
11/24/58 **C'mon Everybody** *Eddie Cochran*
(Come On Home) ..see: True Love Gone
9/22/58 **Come On Let's Go** *Ritchie Valens*
Come Prima
12/8/58 *Tony Dallara*
12/15/58 *Polly Bergen*
Come Softly To Me
3/9/59 *Fleetwoods*
3/23/59 *Ronnie Height*
2/10/58 **Come To Me** *Johnny Mathis*
3/16/59 **Come To Me** *Marv Johnson*
5/12/58 **Come What May** *Clyde McPhatter*
11/24/56 **Confession Of A Sinner** *Stylers*
11/17/56 **Confidential** *Sonny Knight*
12/14/59 **CooCoo-U** *Kingston Trio*

7/15/57 **Cool Shake** *Del Vikings*
11/17/58 **Coquette** *Fats Domino*
5/12/56 **Corinna, Corinna** *Joe Turner*
11/4/57 **Could This Be Magic** *Dubs*
8/25/58 **Count Every Star** *Rivieras*
1/1/55* **Count Your Blessings** *Eddie Fisher*
7/6/59 **Crackin Up** *Bo Diddley*
12/16/57 **Crazy** *Hollywood Flames*
11/10/58 **Crazy Country Hop** *Johnny Otis*
8/4/58 **Crazy Eyes For You** *Bobby Hamilton*
(Crazy Little Mama) ..see: At My Fron Door
4/7/56 **Crazy Little Palace (That's My Home)**
Billy Williams Quartet
4/27/57 **Crazy Love** *Frank Sinatra*
4/21/58 **Crazy Love** *Paul Anka*
2/5/55 **Crazy Otto (medley)** *Johnny Maddox*
Crazy With Love
11/10/56 *Guy Mitchell*
11/24/56 *Teresa Brewer*
12/9/57 **Creature, The** *Buchanan & Ancell*
Croce Di Oro (Cross Of Gold)
11/12/55 *Patti Page*
11/12/55 *Joan Regan*
4/27/59 **Crossfire** *Johnny & The Hurricanes*
7/20/59 **Cry** *Knightsbridge Strings*
2/18/56 **Cry Baby** *Bonnie Sisters*
11/12/55 **Cry Me A River** *Julie London*

D

1/20/58 **Daddy Cool** *Rays*
Daddy-O
11/12/55 *Bonnie Lou*
11/12/55 *Fontane Sisters*
8/18/58 **Dance Everyone Dance** *Betty Madiga*
5/5/58 **Dance Only With Me** *Perry Como*
12/9/57 **Dance To The Bop** *Gene Vincent*
10/12/59 **Dance With Me** *Drifters*
3/26/55 **Dance With Me Henry (Wallflower)**
Georgia Gibbs
Dance With The Teacher ..see: (I Wanna)
9/2/57 **Dancin'** *Perry Como*
12/22/56 **Dancing Chandelier** *Sylvia Syms*
3/24/58 **Dancing With My Shadow** *Four Voic*
3/12/55 **Danger! Heartbreak Ahead**
Jaye P. Morgan
Danny Boy
6/1/59 *Sil Austin*
9/28/59 *Conway Twitty*
Dark Moon
4/13/57 *Bonnie Guitar*
4/20/57 *Gale Storm*
9/28/59 **Darling, I Love You** *Al Martino*
8/19/57 **Darling It's Wonderful** *Lovers*
3/5/55 **Darling Je Vous Aime Beaucoup**
Nat "King" Cole
12/28/59 **Darling Lorraine** *Knockouts*
8/26/57 **Date With The Blues** *Billy Williams*
Davy Crockett ..see: Ballad Of
8/13/55 **Day By Day** *Four Freshmen*
9/29/58 **Day I Died** *Playmates*
(Day-O) ..see: Banana Boat
Day The Rains Came
9/22/58 *Jane Morgan*
10/27/58 *Raymond Lefevre*
7/7/56 **Daydreams** *Art Mooney*
(Dead Or Alive) ..see: Ninety Nine Ye
9/22/56 **Dear Elvis** *Audrey*
7/1/57 **Dearest** *Mickey & Sylvia*
9/14/59 **Deck Of Cards** *Wink Martindale*
1/20/58 **Dede Dinah** *Frankie Avalon*
7/13/59 **Dedicated To The One I Love** *Shirel*
10/14/57 **Deep Blue Sea** *Jimmy Dean*
9/30/57 **Deep Purple** *Billy Ward & His Domin*
7/14/58 **Delicious!** *Jim Bakus & Friend*
Delilah Jones ..see: Man With The Golden Arm
7/15/57 **Deserie** *Charts*
12/30/57 **Desire Me** *Sam Cooke*
8/11/58 **Devoted To You** *Everly Brothers*
8/18/58 **Devotion** *Janice Harper*
12/8/58 **Diamond Ring** *Jerry Wallace*
7/15/57 **Diana** *Paul Anka*

12/8/58 **Diary, The** *Neil Sedaka*
1/1/55* **Dim, Dim The Lights (I Want Some Atmosphere)** *Bill Haley*
6/9/58 **Ding Dong** *McGuire Sisters*
3/10/58 **Dinner With Drac** *John Zacherle*
4/16/55 **Dixie Danny** *Laurie Sisters*
4/14/58 **Dizzy, Miss Lizzy** *Larry Williams*
4/14/58 **Do I Like It** *Nat "King" Cole*
Do I Love You (Because You're Beautiful)
4/13/57 *Vic Damone*
4/20/57 *Tony Martin*
Do-Re-Mi
12/14/59 *Mitch Miller*
12/28/59 *Anita Bryant*
1/13/58 **Do What You Did** *Thurston Harris*
5/12/58 **Do You Want To Dance** *Bobby Freeman*
4/16/55 **Doesn't Anybody Love Me?** *McGuire Sisters*
11/12/55 **Dogface Soldier** *Russ Morgan*
7/23/55 **Domani (Tomorrow)** *Julius LaRosa*
1/27/58 **Don't** *Elvis Presley*
7/15/57 **Don't Ask Me (To Be Lonely)** *Dubs*
7/7/58 **Don't Ask Me Why** *Elvis Presley*
Don't Be Angry
4/30/55 *Nappy Brown*
4/30/55 *Crew-Cuts*
8/11/56 **Don't Be Cruel** *Elvis Presley*
6/3/57 **Don't Call Me Sweetie (Cause I'm Bitter)** *Eileen Rodgers*
Don't Cha ..see: Doncha'
7/7/56 **Don't Cry** *Frankie Laine with Paul Weston*
5/6/57 **Don't Cry My Love** *Vera Lynn*
(also see: Faithful Hussar)
11/9/59 **Don't Destroy Me** *Crash Craddock*
4/20/57 **Don't Ever Love Me** *Harry Belafonte*
2/22/56 **Don't Forbid Me** *Pat Boone*
3/30/57 **Don't Get Around Much Anymore** *Tab Hunter*
6/9/58 **Don't Go Home** *Playmates*
1/21/56 **Don't Go To Strangers** *Vaughn Monroe*
1/13/58 **Don't Let Go** *Roy Hamilton*
2/22/58 **Don't Pity Me** *Dion & The Belmonts*
9/3/55 **Don't Stay Away Too Long** *Eddie Fisher*
0/19/59 **Don't Take The Stars** *Mystics*
1/19/59 **Don't Take Your Guns To Town** *Johnny Cash*
3/10/56 **Don't Tell Me Not To Love You** *Joni James*
8/10/59 **Don't Tell Me Your Troubles** *Don Gibson*
3/24/58 **Don't You Just Know It** *Huey (Piano) Smith*
9/21/59 **Don't You Know** *Della Reese*
12/8/58 **Don't You Know Yockomo** *Huey "Piano" Smith*
4/21/58 **Doncha' Think It's Time** *Elvis Presley*
2/15/58 **Donde Esta Santa Claus?** *Augie Rios*
1/24/58 **Donna** *Ritchie Valens*
5/21/55 **Door Is Still Open To My Heart** *Don Cornell*
6/23/58 **Dottie** *Danny & The Juniors*
2/28/59 **Down By The Station** *Four Preps*
3/11/58 **Down In Virginia** *Jimmy Reed*
3/18/58 **Down The Aisle Of Love** *Quin-Tones*
6/16/58 **Dream** *Betty Johnson*
7/28/56 **Dream Along With Me (I'm On My Way To A Star)** *Perry Como*
4/20/59 **Dream Lover** *Bobby Darin*
7/14/56 **Dreamer** *Four Aces*
(also see: Song Of)
11/3/58 **Dreamy Eyes** *Johnny Tillotson*
2/22/56 **Dreamy Eyes** *Four Preps*
/11/58 **Drip Drop** *Drifters*
/16/57 **Drive In Show** *Eddie Cochran*
Dumplin's
/23/57 *Ernie Freeman*
/30/57 *Doc Bagby*
2/17/55 **Dungaree Doll** *Eddie Fisher*
7/15/57 **Dynamite** *Brenda Lee*

E

Early In The Morning
7/28/58 *Rinky-Dinks*
8/4/58 *Buddy Holly*
Earth Angel
1/1/55* *Penguins*
2/5/55 *Crew-Cuts*
2/12/55 *Gloria Mann*
Earthbound
9/8/56 *Sammy Davis, Jr.*
9/15/56 *Mario Lanza*
East Of Eden ..see: Theme From
12/14/59 **Ebb Tide** *Bobby Freeman*
Eddie My Love
3/3/56 *Teen Queens*
3/10/56 *Chordettes*
3/10/56 *Fontane Sisters*
11/9/59 **El Paso** *Marty Robbins*
5/26/58 **El Rancho Rock** *Champs*
11th Hour Melody
2/4/56 *Al Hibbler*
2/25/56 *Lou Busch*
3/10/56 **Eloise** *Kay Thompson*
Empty Arms
4/6/57 *Teresa Brewer*
4/13/57 *Ivory Joe Hunter*
3/23/59 **Enchanted** *Platters*
6/30/58 **Enchanted Island** *Four Lads*
Enchanted Sea
9/28/59 *Islanders*
10/26/59 *Martin Denny*
9/15/58 **End, The** *Earl Grant*
9/22/56 **Endless** *McGuire Sisters*
5/19/58 **Endless Sleep** *Jody Reynolds*
4/20/59 **Endlessly** *Brook Benton*
8/11/56 **English Muffins And Irish Stew** *Sylvia Syms*
5/11/59 **Eternally** *Thomas Wayne*
1/26/59 **Evening Rain** *Earl Grant*
3/9/57 **Ever Lovin' Fingers** *Jimmy Bowen*
9/22/56 **Every Day Of My Life** *McGuire Sisters*
9/14/59 **Every Little Thing I Do** *Dion & The Belmonts*
3/31/58 **Every Night (I Pray)** *Chantels*
11/24/56 **Every Time (I Feel His Spirit)** *Patti Page*
3/9/59 **Everybody Likes To Cha Cha Cha** *Sam Cooke*
7/21/58 **Everybody Loves A Lover** *Doris Day*
Everybody's Got A Home But Me
12/17/55 *Eddie Fisher*
12/24/55 *Roy Hamilton*
7/15/57 **Everybody's Somebody's Fool** *Heartbeats*
11/17/58 **Everyone Was There** *Bob Kayli*
7/1/57 **Everyone's Laughing** *Spaniels*
7/16/55 **Experience Unnecessary** *Sarah Vaughan*
8/25/56 **Experiments With Mice** *Johnny Dankworth*

F

Fabulous
5/6/57 *Charlie Gracie*
5/27/57 *Steve Lawrence*
7/14/56 **Fabulous Character** *Sarah Vaughan*
12/1/56 **Faded Summer Love** *Georgie Shaw*
10/13/56 **Faithful Hussar** *Ted Heath*
(also see: Don't Cry My Love)
Fallen Star
6/10/57 *Jimmy Newman*
7/8/57 *Ferlin Husky*
7/15/57 *Hilltoppers*
7/15/57 *Nick Noble*
10/13/58 **Fallin'** *Connie Francis*
11/2/59 **Fancy Nancy** *Skip & Flip*
8/5/57 **Farther Up The Road** *Bobby Bland*
Fascination
8/26/57 *Jane Morgan*
9/2/57 *David Carroll*
9/2/57 *Dick Jacobs*
9/9/57 *Dinah Shore*
Fever
7/7/56 *Little Willie John*
7/14/58 *Peggy Lee*
9/22/58 **Fibbin'** *Patti Page*
8/18/58 **Fire Of Love** *Jody Reynolds*
9/8/58 **Firefly** *Tony Bennett*
1/26/59 **First Anniversary** *Cathy Carr*
11/3/56 **First Born** *"Tennessee" Ernie Ford*
3/30/57 **First Date, First Kiss, First Love** *Sonny James*
8/12/57 **First Kiss** *Norman Petty Trio*
9/28/59 **First Love, First Tears** *Duane Eddy*
10/26/59 **First Name Initial** *Annette*
7/14/56 **Five** *Sammy Davis, Jr.*
8/24/59 **Five Feet High And Rising** *Johnny Cash*
6/2/56 **Five Hundred Guys** *Frank Sinatra*
(Five Oaks) ..see: Cinco Robles
6/29/59 **Five Pennies** *Dodie Stevens*
11/10/58 **Flamingo l'Amore** *Gaylords*
4/28/58 **Flip Flop And Bop** *Floyd Cramer*
6/9/58 **Flip Top Box** *Dicky Doo & The Don'ts*
6/8/59 **Flower Of Love** *Crests*
2/25/56 **Flowers Mean Forgiveness** *Frank Sinatra*
8/4/56 **Flying Saucer** *Buchanan & Goodman*
7/22/57 **Flying Saucer The 2nd** *Buchanan & Goodman*
9/14/59 **Fog Cutter** *Frantics*
Fool, The
7/28/56 *Sanford Clark*
8/18/56 *Gallahads*
12/8/58 **Fool And The Angel** *Bobby Helms*
Fool Such As I ..see: (Now and Then There's)
8/13/55 **Fooled** *Perry Como*
3/9/57 **Fools Fall In Love** *Drifters*
9/14/59 **Fools Hall Of Fame** *Pat Boone*
8/4/58 **Fool's Paradise** *Crickets*
3/23/59 **For A Penny** *Pat Boone*
9/22/58 **For My Good Fortune** *Pat Boone*
For Sentimental Reasons ..see: (I Love You)
4/21/58 **For Your Love** *Ed Townsend*
6/16/58 **For Your Precious Love** *Jerry Butler & The Impressions*
12/23/57 **Forever** *Sam Cooke*
2/25/56 **Forever Darling** *Ames Brothers*
9/29/58 **Forget Me Not** *Kalin Twins*
10/22/55 **Forgive My Heart** *Nat "King" Cole*
4/6/57 **Forty Cups Of Coffee** *Bill Haley*
6/8/59 **Forty Days** *Ronnie Hawkins*
6/15/59 **Forty Miles Of Bad Road** *Duane Eddy*
9/8/56 **49 Shades Of Green** *Ames Brothers*
5/4/59 **Fountain Of Youth** *Four Lads*
Four Walls
4/29/57 *Jim Reeves*
5/6/57 *Jim Lowe*
5/6/57 **1492** *Betty Johnson*
5/18/59 **Frankie** *Connie Francis*
4/27/59 **Frankie And Johnny** *Johnny Cash*
Fraulein
7/15/57 *Bobby Helms*
10/28/57 *Steve Lawrence*
6/9/56 **Free** *Tommy Leonetti*
7/21/58 **Freeze, The** *Tony & Joe*
Freight Train
5/20/57 *Rusty Draper*
5/27/57 *Chas. McDevitt Skiffle Group*
3/30/59 **French Foreign Legion** *Frank Sinatra*
3/23/59 **Fried Eggs** *Intruders*
10/6/58 **Fried Onions** *Lord Rockingham's XI*
Friendly Persuasion (Thee I Love)
9/15/56 *Pat Boone*
9/22/56 *Four Aces*
9/22/56 **From A School Ring To A Wedding Ring** *Rover Boys*
8/18/56 **From The Candy Store On The Corner To The Chapel On The Hill** *Tony Bennett*
12/29/58 **Funny** *Jesse Belvin*
8/10/59 **Furry Murray** *Tradewinds*

G

3/24/56 **Gal With The Yaller Shoes** *Four Aces*

10/20/56 **Garden Of Eden** *Joe Valino*
8/18/58 **Gas Money** *Jan & Arnie*
1/5/59 **Gazachstahagen** *Wild-Cats*
8/3/59 **Gee** *George Hamilton IV*
9/22/58 **Gee, But It's Lonely** *Pat Boone*
12/17/55 **Gee Whittakers!** *Pat Boone*
12/30/57 **Geisha Girl** *Hank Locklin*
10/13/58 **Geraldine** *Jack Scott*
Get A Job
1/20/58 *Silhouettes*
3/3/58 *Mills Brothers*
7/14/56 **Get Me To The Church On Time** *Julius LaRosa*
3/31/56 **Get Up! Get Up! (You Sleepyhead)** *Jaye P. Morgan*
7/14/56 **Ghost Town** *Don Cherry*
Giant
10/20/56 *Les Baxter*
10/20/56 *Jack Pleis*
11/3/56 *Art Mooney*
4/27/59 **Gidget** *Jimmy Darren*
5/5/58 **Gigi** *Vic Damone*
11/16/59 **Gilee** *Sonny Spencer*
7/21/58 **Ginger Bread** *Frankie Avalon*
Girl And Boy ..see: Ballad Of
1/26/57 **Girl Can't Help It** *Little Richard*
5/19/56 **Girl In My Dreams** *Cliques*
7/20/59 **Girl Like You** *Gary Stites*
1/5/59 **Girl On Page 44** *Four Lads*
5/20/57 **Girl With The Golden Braids** *Perry Como*
8/17/59 **Girl's Work Is Never Done** *Chordettes*
12/15/56 **Give Me** *Eileen Rodgers*
9/10/55 **Give Me Love** *McGuire Sisters*
2/2/59 **Give Me Your Love** *Nat "King" Cole*
9/29/58 **Give Myself A Party** *Don Gibson*
8/4/56 **Give Us This Day** *Joni James*
3/5/55 **Glad Rag Doll** *Crazy Otto*
2/23/59 **Glad Rags** *Tennessee Ernie Ford*
6/9/56 **Glendora** *Perry Como*
10/13/58 **Go Chase A Moonbeam** *Jerry Vale*
12/7/59 **Go, Jimmy, Go** *Jimmy Clanton*
Go On With The Wedding
1/7/56 *Kitty Kallen & Georgie Shaw*
1/7/56 *Patti Page*
11/16/59 **God Bless America** *Connie Francis*
5/20/57 **Goin' Steady** *Tommy Sands*
8/18/58 **Going To Chicago Blues** *Count Basie*
3/2/57 **Gone** *Ferlin Husky*
Gonna Find Me A Bluebird
5/20/57 *Marvin Rainwater*
6/3/57 *Eddy Arnold*
6/3/57 *Joyce Hahn*
12/1/56 **Gonna Get Along Without Ya Now** *Patience & Prudence*
8/6/55 **Good And Lonesome** *Kay Starr*
9/8/56 **Good Book** *Kay Starr*
2/17/58 **Good Golly, Miss Molly** *Little Richard*
1/12/59 **Good Rockin' Tonight** *Pat Boone*
12/15/58 **Goodbye Baby** *Jack Scott*
10/12/59 **Goodbye Charlie** *Patti Page*
4/13/59 **Goodbye Jimmy, Goodbye** *Kathy Linden*
4/20/59 **Goodnight Irene** *Billy Williams*
Goodnight My Love
12/8/56 *McGuire Sisters*
11/16/59 *Ray Peterson*
7/22/57 **Goody Goody** *Frankie Lymon & his Teenagers*
11/11/57 **Got A Date With An Angel** *Billy Williams*
Got A Match?
6/16/58 *Daddy-O's*
6/23/58 *Frank Gallup*
9/21/59 **Got The Feeling** *Fabian*
9/9/57 **Gotta Get To Your House** *David Seville*
8/4/58 **Gotta Have Rain** *Eydie Gorme*
6/22/59 **Gotta New Girl** *Bobby Day*
11/24/58 **Gotta Travel On** *Billy Grammer*
Graduation Day
5/12/56 *Four Freshmen*
5/12/56 *Rover Boys*
5/18/59 **Graduation's Here** *Fleetwoods*
11/25/57 **Great Balls Of Fire** *Jerry Lee Lewis*
12/17/55 **Great Pretender** *Platters*
12/29/58 **Green Chritma** *Stan Freberg*
9/22/56 **Green Door** *Jim Lowe*
8/25/58 **Green Mosquito** *Tune Rockers*

12/29/56 **Greensleeves** *Beverly Sisters*
10/13/58 **Guaglione** *Perez Prado*
9/8/58 **Guess I've Been Around Too Long** *Carl Smith*
6/2/58 **Guess Things Happen That Way** *Johnny Cash*
3/30/59 **Guess Who** *Jesse Belvin*
3/9/59 **Guitar Boogie Shuffle** *Virtues*
8/27/55 **Gum Drop** *Crew-Cuts*

H

12/9/57 **Ha! Ha! Ha! (Chella Lla!)** *Kay Armen*
1/1/55* **Haji Baba (Persian Lament)** *Nat "King" Cole*
7/27/59 **Half-Breed** *Marvin Rainwater*
5/18/59 **Hallelujah, I Love Him So** *Peggy Lee*
Hand Jive ..see: Willie And The Hand Jive
12/28/59 **Handy Man** *Jimmy Jones*
4/28/58 **Hang Up My Rock And Roll Shoes** *Chuck Willis*
2/2/59 **Hanging Tree** *Marty Robbins*
5/5/58 **Happiness** *Billy & Lillie*
Happiness Street
8/18/56 *Tony Bennett*
8/18/56 *Georgia Gibbs*
Happy Anniversary
11/9/59 *Four Lads*
11/9/59 *Jane Morgan*
9/16/57 **Happy, Happy Birthday Baby** *Tune Weavers*
3/16/59 **Happy Organ** *Dave 'Baby' Cortez*
12/7/59 **Happy Reindeer** *Dancer, Prancer & Nervous*
6/29/59 **Happy Vacation** *Jackie Lee*
4/28/56 **Happy Whistler** *Don Robertson*
8/4/58 **Happy Years** *Diamonds*
6/30/58 **Hard Headed Woman** *Elvis Presley*
12/23/57 **Hard Times (The Slop)** *Noble "Thin Man" Watts*
6/4/55 **Hard To Get** *Gisele MacKenzie*
4/29/57 **Harem Dance** *Armenian Jazz Sextet*
(also see: Shish-Kebab)
12/28/59 **Harlem Nocturne** *Viscounts*
8/11/58 **Harvey's Got A Girl Friend** *Royal Teens*
5/5/58 **Have Faith** *Gene Allison*
10/7/57 **Have I Told You Lately That I Love You?** *Ricky Nelson*
3/30/59 **Hawaiian War Chant** *Billy Vaughn*
12/29/58 **Hawaiian Wedding Song** *Andy Williams*
9/10/55 **Hawk-Eye** *Frankie Laine*
He
10/15/55 *Al Hibbler*
10/29/55 *McGuire Sisters*
12/28/59 **He'll Have To Go** *Jim Reeves*
9/30/57 **He's Gone** *Chantels*
He's Got The Whole World (In His Hands)
3/24/58 *Laurie London*
4/28/58 *Mahalia Jackson*
4/6/57 **He's Mine** *Platters*
Heart
5/14/55 *Eddie Fisher*
5/28/55 *Four Aces*
10/6/56 **Heart And Soul** *Johnny Maddox*
7/28/56 **Heart Hideaway** *Cathy Carr*
10/6/56 **Heart Without A Sweetheart** *Gale Storm*
9/8/56 **Heartaches** *Somethin' Smith & The Redheads*
10/5/59 **Heartaches By The Number** *Guy Mitchell*
12/29/58 **Heartbeat** *Buddy Holly*
Heartbreak Hotel
3/3/56 *Elvis Presley*
7/21/56 *Stan Freberg*
12/10/55 **Heartless** *Tommy Leonetti*
Hearts Of Stone
1/1/55* *Charms*
1/1/55* *Fontane Sisters*
7/14/56 **Heaven On Earth** *Platters*
3/16/59 **Heavenly Lover** *Teresa Brewer*
4/7/56 **Held For Questioning** *Rusty Draper*
2/3/58 **Helpless** *Platters*
1/6/58 **Henrietta** *Jimmy Dee*
6/29/59 **Here Comes Summer** *Jerry Keller*

12/22/58 **Here I Stand** *Wade Flemons*
8/4/58 **Hey Girl - Hey Boy** *Oscar McLollie & Jeanette Baker*
10/27/56 **Hey! Jealous Lover** *Frank Sinatra*
11/18/57 **Hey! Little Girl** *Techniques*
8/24/59 **Hey Little Girl** *Dee Clark*
5/18/59 **Hey Little Lucy! (Don'tcha Put No Lipstick On)** *Conway Twitty*
5/21/55 **Hey, Mr. Banjo** *Sunnysiders*
12/23/57 **Hey, Schoolgirl** *Tom & Jerry*
1/1/55* **Hey There** *Rosemary Clooney*
Hi-Lili, Hi-Lo
4/21/56 *Dick Hyman Trio*
5/26/56 *Roger Williams*
9/22/58 **Hideaway** *Four Esquires*
6/15/59 **High Hopes** *Frank Sinatra*
6/2/58 **High School Confidential** *Jerry Lee Lewis*
8/12/57 **High School Dance** *Larry Williams*
8/19/57 **High School Romance** *George Hamilton IV*
10/19/59 **High School U.S.A.** *Tommy Facenda*
4/14/58 **High Sign** *Diamonds*
3/9/57 **Hold 'Em Joe** *Harry Belafonte*
11/10/58 **Hold It** *Bill Doggett*
1/1/55* **Hold My Hand** *Don Cornell*
2/2/57 **Holiday For Trombones** *David Rose*
1/1/55* **Home For The Holidays** *Perry Como*
10/14/57 **Home Of The Blues** *Johnny Cash*
9/30/57 **Honest I Do** *Jimmy Reed*
11/2/59 **Honestly And Truly** *Tommy Edward*
4/23/55 **Honey-Babe** *Art Mooney*
12/28/59 **Honey Hush** *Joe Turner*
9/16/57 **Honey Rock** *Ricky Nelson (Barney Kessel Orch.)*
8/12/57 **Honeycomb** *Jimmie Rodgers*
8/18/56 **Honky Tonk (Parts 1 & 2)** *Bill Dogge*
10/6/58 **Hoopa Hoola** *Betty Johnson*
6/9/56 **Hot And Cold Running Tears** *Sarah Vaughan*
3/10/56 **Hot Diggity (Dog Ziggity Boom)** *Perry Como*
6/16/56 **Hot Dog Buddy Buddy** *Bill Haley*
8/4/56 **Hound Dog** *Elvis Presley*
11/16/59 **Hound Dog Man** *Fabian*
House, A Car And A Wedding Ring
11/10/58 *Dale Hawkins*
12/1/58 *Mike Preston*
6/18/55 **House Of Blue Lights** *Chuck Miller*
3/30/59 **House Of Love** *Scott Garrett*
9/1/56 **House With Love In It** *Four Lads*
12/7/59 **How About That** *Dee Clark*
5/12/58 **How Are Ya' Fixed For Love?** *Frank Sinatra & Keely Smith*
How Important Can It Be?
2/19/55 *Joni James*
2/26/55 *Sarah Vaughan*
5/7/55 *Teresa Brewer*
5/19/56 **(How Little It Matters) How Little We Know** *Frank Sinatra*
12/30/57 **How Lovely Is Christmas** *Bing Cros*
7/21/56 **How Lucky You Are** *Joni James*
8/18/58 **How The Time Flies** *Jerry Wallace*
Hula Hoop Song
10/6/58 *Teresa Brewer*
10/6/58 *Georgia Gibbs*
9/2/57 **Hula Love** *Buddy Knox*
Hummingbird
7/9/55 *Les Paul & Mary Ford*
9/3/55 *Frankie Laine*
9/16/57 **Humpty Dumpty Heart** *LaVern Bak*
Hunch, The
10/26/59 *Paul Gayten*
10/26/59 *Bobby Peterson Quintet*
2/23/59 **Hurtin' Inside** *Brook Benton*
5/25/59 **Hushabye** *Mystics*
7/1/57 **Hypnotized** *Drifters*

I

I Ain't Never
8/10/59 *Webb Pierce*
9/14/59 *Four Preps*
6/2/56 **I Almost Lost My Mind** *Pat Boone*
8/19/57 **I Am** *Tony Bennett*

(I Am The Japanese Sandman) ..see: Rang Tang Ding Dong
1/27/58 I Beg Of You *Elvis Presley*
8/4/58 I Believe In You *Robert & Johnny*
5/18/59 I Can't Get You Out Of My Heart *Al Martino*
3/10/58 I Can't Help It (If I'm Still In Love With You) *Margaret Whiting*
10/6/56 I Can't Love You Enough *LaVern Baker*
3/9/59 I Can't Sit Down *Marie & Rex*
2/24/58 I Can't Stop Loving You *Don Gibson*
I Could Have Danced All Night
4/28/56 *Dinah Shore*
5/12/56 *Sylvia Syms*
5/19/56 *Rosemary Clooney*
8/31/59 I Cried *Joe Damiano*
12/8/58 I Cried A Tear *LaVern Baker*
10/12/59 I Dig Girls *Bobby Rydell*
10/13/56 I Don't Care If The Sun Don't Shine *Elvis Presley*
5/18/59 (I Don't Care) Only Love Me *Steve Lawrence*
10/12/59 I Don't Know *Ruth Brown*
12/14/59 I Don't Know What It Is *Bluenotes*
2/16/59 I Don't Need You Anymore *Teddy Bears*
8/18/56 I Don't Want Nobody (To Have My Love But You) *Woody Herman*
11/24/56 I Dreamed *Betty Johnson*
12/15/56 I Feel Good *Shirley & Lee*
1/19/57 I Feel The Beat *Jim Lowe*
3/9/59 I Go Ape *Neil Sedaka*
10/13/58 I Got A Feeling *Ricky Nelson*
1/26/59 I Got A Wife *Mark IV*
8/3/59 I Got Stripes *Johnny Cash*
11/3/58 I Got Stung *Elvis Presley*
10/22/55 I Hear You Knocking *Gale Storm*
5/6/57 I Just Don't Know *Four Lads*
12/15/58 I Just Thought You'd Like To Know *Johnny Cash*
I Kissed You ..see: ('Til)
3/9/59 I Kneel At Your Throne *Joe Medlin*
6/8/59 I Know *Perry Como*
6/9/58 I Know Where I'm Goin' *George Hamilton IV*
5/20/57 I Like Your Kind Of Love *Andy Williams*
6/23/56 I Look At You *Lassies*
8/24/59 I Looked At Heaven *Tommy Edwards*
6/22/59 I Love An Angel *Little Bill & The Bluenotes*
9/22/56 I Love Mickey *Mickey Mantle & Teresa Brewer*
12/22/56 I Love My Baby (My Baby Loves Me) *Jill Corey*
I Love My Girl
4/27/57 *Hilltoppers*
5/6/57 *Cozy Morley*
12/16/57 I Love You, Baby *Paul Anka*
12/30/57 (I Love You) For Sentimental Reasons *Sam Cooke*
1/15/55 I Love You Madly *Four Coins*
6/16/58 I Love You So *Chantels*
(also see: Ko Ko Mo, and That's Why)
8/12/57 I Love You So Much It Hurts *Charlie Gracie*
8/3/59 I Loves You, Porgy *Nina Simone*
4/21/58 I Met Him On A Sunday *Shirelles*
I Miss You So
10/27/56 *Chris Connor*
3/30/59 *Paul Anka*
5/25/59 I Must Be Dreaming *Nat "King" Cole*
1/1/55* I Need You Now *Eddie Fisher*
1/18/57 I Need You So Bad *B.B. King*
3/30/59 I Need Your Love Tonight *Elvis Presley*
5/20/57 I Need Your Lovin' *Conway Twitty*
4/20/59 I Need Your Lovin' *Roy Hamilton*
4/6/59 I Never Felt Like This *Jack Scott*
6/1/59 I Only Have Eyes For You *Flamingos*
7/28/56 I Only Know I Love You *Four Aces*
(I Pray) ..see: Every Night
7/28/56 I Promise To Remember *Frankie Lymon & The Teenagers*
1/24/56 I Saw Esau *Ames Brothers*
4/13/59 I Still Get A Thrill (Thinking Of You) *Joni James*
7/13/59 I Still Get Jealous *Joni James*
10/28/57 I Still Love You *Fats Domino*
1/5/59 I Talk To The Trees *Edmundo Ros*

4/13/59 I Think I'm Gonna Kill Myself *Buddy Knox*
4/20/59 I Told Myself A Lie *Clyde McPhatter*
4/20/59 I Waited Too Long *LaVern Baker*
I Walk The Line
9/15/56 *Johnny Cash*
11/16/59 *Don Costa*
7/15/57 I Wanna *Platters*
11/30/59 I Wanna Be Loved *Ricky Nelson*
12/8/58 (I Wanna) Dance With The Teacher *Olympics*
11/12/55 I Wanna Go Where You Go *Eddie Fisher*
I Want To Be Happy Cha Cha
11/10/58 *Enoch Light*
12/1/58 *Tommy Dorsey Orchestra*
8/10/59 I Want To Walk You Home *Fats Domino*
5/26/56 I Want You, I Need You, I Love You *Elvis Presley*
I Want You To Be My Baby
9/17/55 *Lillian Briggs*
9/17/55 *Georgia Gibbs*
4/28/56 I Want You To Be My Girl *Frankie Lymon & The Teenagers*
12/30/57 I Want You To Know *Fats Domino*
3/10/56 I Was The One *Elvis Presley*
9/15/58 I Wish *Platters*
4/28/56 I Woke Up Crying *Joni James*
7/8/57 I Wonder If I Care As Much *Everly Brothers*
5/19/58 I Wonder Why *Dion & The Belmonts*
11/24/56 I Wouldn't Know Where To Begin *Eddy Arnold*
12/8/56 I'll Always Be In Love With You *Jack Pleis*
8/25/56 I'll Be Around *Don Cherry*
2/4/56 I'll Be Home *Pat Boone*
6/22/59 I'll Be Satisfied *Jackie Wilson*
I'll Be Seeing You
9/28/59 *Tommy Sands*
10/26/59 *Poni-Tails*
2/2/59 (I'll Be With You In) Apple Blossom Time *Tab Hunter*
12/23/57 I'll Come Running Back To You *Sam Cooke*
7/28/58 I'll Get By (As Long As I Have You) *Billy Williams*
11/26/55 I'll Know *Sammy Davis, Jr.*
9/8/58 I'll Make It All Up To You *Jerry Lee Lewis*
9/14/59 I'll Never Fall In Love Again *Johnnie Ray*
2/25/56 I'll Never Know *Four Lads*
12/2/57 I'll Never Say "Never Again" Again *Dinah Shore*
7/23/55 I'll Never Stop Loving You *Doris Day*
10/28/57 I'll Remember Today *Patti Page*
10/27/58 I'll Remember Tonight *Pat Boone*
1/19/59 I'll Sail My Ship Alone *Jerry Lee Lewis*
4/13/57 I'll Take Romance *Eydie Gorme*
9/16/57 I'll Take You Home Again Kathleen *Slim Whitman*
3/3/56 I'll Wait *Betty Johnson*
10/13/58 I'll Wait For You *Frankie Avalon*
I'll Walk The Line ..see: I Walk The Line
9/7/59 I'm A Hog For You *Coasters*
1/12/59 I'm A Man *Fabian*
4/2/55 (I'm Always Hearing) Wedding Bells *Eddie Fisher*
10/28/57 I'm Available *Margie Rayburn*
7/13/59 I'm Coming Home *Marv Johnson*
(I'm Gettin') Nuttin' For Christmas ..see: Nuttin' For Christmas
7/27/59 I'm Gonna Be A Wheel Some Day *Fats Domino*
6/8/59 I'm Gonna Change Him *Cathy Carr*
8/10/59 I'm Gonna Get Married *Lloyd Price*
1/14/56 I'm Gonna Laugh You Right Out Of My Life *Nat "King" Cole*
3/3/56 I'm Gonna Love You *Ames Brothers*
6/3/57 I'm Gonna Sit Right Down And Write Myself A Letter *Billy Williams*
5/12/58 I'm Happy *Four Dates*
I'm In Love Again
4/28/56 *Fats Domino*
5/26/56 *Fontane Sisters*
6/9/56 I'm In Love With You *Pat Boone*
2/11/56 I'm Just A Dancing Partner *Platters*

11/9/59 I'm Movin' On *Ray Charles*
2/23/59 I'm Never Gonna Tell *Jimmie Rodgers*
5/11/59 I'm Ready *Fats Domino*
4/29/57 I'm Serious *Hilltoppers*
3/23/57 I'm Sorry *Platters*
5/12/58 I'm Sorry I Made You Cry *Connie Francis*
I'm Stickin' With You
2/23/57 *Jimmy Bowen*
5/6/57 *Fontane Sisters*
4/21/56 I'm Still A King To You *Don Cherry*
3/16/57 I'm Waiting Just For You *Pat Boone*
I'm Walkin'
3/9/57 *Fats Domino*
5/6/57 *Ricky Nelson*
6/3/57 I'm Walking The Floor Over You *Georgia Gibbs*
10/26/59 I've Been Around *Fats Domino*
8/10/59 I've Been There *Tommy Edwards*
2/4/56 I've Changed My Mind A Thousand Times *Kay Starr*
4/13/59 I've Come Of Age *Billy Storm*
6/30/56 I've Got Love *Julius LaRosa*
2/23/59 I've Got You Under My Skin *Louis Prima & Keely Smith*
I've Grown Accustomed To Your Face
5/12/56 *Gordon MacRae*
5/26/56 *Rosemary Clooney*
1/26/59 I've Had It *Bell Notes*
10/21/57 Idol With The Golden Head *Coasters*
7/14/58 If Dreams Came True *Pat Boone*
3/2/59 If I Didn't Care *Connie Francis*
If I Give My Heart To You
1/1/55* *Doris Day*
10/5/59 *Kitty Kallen*
12/21/59 If I Had A Girl *Rod Lauren*
5/21/55 If I May *Nat "King" Cole/Four Knights*
2/18/56 If You Can Dream *Four Aces*
11/2/59 (If You Cry) True Love, True Love *Drifters*
11/12/55 If You Don't Want My Love *Jaye P. Morgan*
10/12/59 If You Don't Want My Lovin' *Carl Dobkins, Jr.*
8/17/59 If You Love Me *LaVern Baker*
6/30/56 If You Wanna See Mamie Tonight *Ames Brothers*
10/19/59 Igmoo (The Pride Of South Central High) *Stonewall Jackson*
4/7/56 In A Little Spanish Town ('Twas On A Night Like This) *Bing Crosby*
6/2/56 In A Shanty In Old Shanty Town *Somethin' Smith & The Redheads*
8/4/56 In The Alps *Lawrence Welk & The McGuire Sisters*
In The Middle Of An Island
8/5/57 *Tony Bennett*
8/26/57 *Tennessee Ernie Ford*
In The Middle Of The House
9/1/56 *Rusty Draper*
9/1/56 *Vaughn Monroe*
9/21/59 In The Mood *Ernie Fields*
9/8/56 In The Still Of The Nite *Five Satins*
6/16/58 Indian Love Call *Ernie Freeman*
Innamorata
3/10/56 *Dean Martin*
3/10/56 *Jerry Vale*
11/24/58 Intermission Riff *Bernie Lowe Orchestra*
3/10/56 Into The Night *Dream Weavers*
9/8/58 Invitation To The Blues *Ray Price*
7/29/57 Is It Wrong (For Loving You) *Warner Mack*
5/19/56 Is There Somebody Else *Dream Weavers*
6/3/57 Island In The Sun *Harry Belafonte*
4/27/57 It All Depends On You *Jerry Lewis*
2/23/59 It Doesn't Matter Anymore *Buddy Holly*
11/10/58 It Don't Hurt No More *Nappy Brown*
10/6/56 It Happened Again *Sarah Vaughan*
9/28/59 It Happened Today *Skyliners*
7/8/57 It Hurts To Be In Love *Annie Laurie*
9/29/56 It Isn't Right *Platters*
3/26/55 It May Sound Silly *McGuire Sisters*
5/5/56 It Only Hurts For A Little While *Ames Brothers*
6/22/59 It Was I *Skip & Flip*

4/2/55 **It's A Sin To Tell A Lie**
Somethin' Smith & The Redheads
8/18/58 **It's All In The Game** *Tommy Edwards*
It's Almost Tomorrow
11/12/55 *Dream Weavers*
11/12/55 *Snooky Lanson*
11/26/55 *David Carroll*
11/26/55 *Jo Stafford*
5/19/58 **(It's Been A Long Time) Pretty Baby**
Gino & Gina
9/1/56 **It's Better In The Dark** *Tony Martin*
1/26/59 **It's Just A Matter Of Time** *Brook Benton*
12/15/58 **It's Just About Time** *Johnny Cash*
3/2/59 **It's Late** *Ricky Nelson*
4/29/57 **It's Not For Me To Say** *Johnny Mathis*
11/12/55 **It's Obdacious** *Buddy Johnson*
9/15/58 **It's Only Make Believe** *Conway Twitty*
1/12/59 **It's Only The Beginning** *Kalin Twins*
6/1/59 **It's Only The Good Times**
Tommy Edwards
10/6/58 **It's Raining Outside** *Platters*
11/23/59 **It's Time To Cry** *Paul Anka*
2/17/58 **It's Too Soon To Know** *Pat Boone*
5/27/57 **It's You I Love** *Fats Domino*
10/20/56 **It's Yours** *DeCastro Sisters*
9/1/56 **Italian Theme** *Cyril Stapleton*
Itchy Twitchy Feeling
8/4/58 *Bobby Hendricks*
9/22/58 *Swallows*
Ivory Tower
3/17/56 *Cathy Carr*
3/31/56 *Charms*
4/28/56 *Gale Storm*
10/21/57 **Ivy Rose** *Perry Como*

J

6/1/59 **Jack O'Diamonds** *Ruth Brown*
5/12/58 **Jacqueline** *Bobby Helms*
10/14/57 **Jailhouse Rock** *Elvis Presley*
10/20/56 **Jamaica Farewell** *Harry Belafonte*
4/20/57 **Jamie Boy** *Kay Starr*
12/3/55 **Japanese Farewell Song**
Kay Cee Jones
8/26/57 **Jay-Dee's Boogie Woogie**
Jimmy Dorsey
Jealous Heart
10/20/58 *Tab Hunter*
11/10/58 *Fontane Sisters*
7/14/58 **Jealousy** *Kitty Wells*
3/10/58 **Jeannie Jeannie Jeannie**
Eddie Cochran
Jennie Lee
5/19/58 *Jan & Arnie*
6/2/58 *Billy Ward & His Dominoes*
6/17/57 **Jenny, Jenny** *Little Richard*
12/29/56 **Jim Dandy** *LaVern Baker*
7/1/57 **Jim Dandy Got Married** *LaVern Baker*
3/23/59 **Jimmy Kiss And Run** *Diane Maxwell*
Jingle Bell Rock
12/23/57 *Bobby Helms*
12/22/58 *Bobby Helms*
12/30/57 **Jingle Bells** *Perry Como*
1/20/58 **Jo-Ann** *Playmates*
4/13/59 **Jo-Jo The Dog-Faced Boy** *Annette*
11/17/58 **Joe Joe Gun** *Chuck Berry*
5/5/56 **Joey, Joey, Joey** *Peggy Lee*
10/5/59 **Joey's Song** *Bill Haley*
11/12/55 **Johnnie's Comin' Home** *Johnnie Ray*
4/28/58 **Johnny B. Goode** *Chuck Berry*
7/21/56 **Johnny Casanova** *Jaye P. Morgan*
7/28/56 **Johnny Concho Theme (Wait For Me)**
Frank Sinatra
8/24/59 **Johnny Reb** *Johnny Horton*
Joker (That's What They Call Me)
11/18/57 *Billy Myles*
11/25/57 *Hilltoppers*
7/28/58 **Judy** *Frankie Vaughan*
5/18/59 **Judy** *David Seville*
3/10/56 **Juke Box Baby** *Perry Como*
10/20/56 **Julie** *Doris Day*
(also see: Oh Julie)
8/19/57 **June Night** *Jimmy Dorsey*
2/9/59 **Jupiter-C** *Pat & the Satellites*
7/14/58 **Just A Dream** *Jimmy Clanton*
6/29/59 **Just A Little Too Much** *Ricky Nelson*
4/28/56 **Just As Long As I'm With You**
Pat Boone
8/10/59 **Just As Much As Ever** *Bob Beckham*
8/31/59 **Just Ask Your Heart** *Frankie Avalon*
3/2/57 **Just Because** *Lloyd Price*
9/9/57 **Just Between You And Me** *Chordettes*
10/14/57 **Just Born (To Be Your Baby)**
Perry Como
12/14/59 **Just Come Home** *Hugo & Luigi*
11/10/56 **Just In Time** *Tony Bennett*
5/4/59 **Just Keep It Up** *Dee Clark*
8/4/58 **Just Like In The Movies** *Upbeats*
10/27/56 **Just Love Me** *Jaye P. Morgan*
4/14/58 **Just Married** *Marty Robbins*
10/5/59 **Just To Be With You** *Passions*
5/20/57 **Just To Hold My Hand** *Clyde McPhatter*
9/1/56 **Just Walking In The Rain** *Johnnie Ray*
Just Young
10/6/58 *Paul Anka*
10/6/58 *Andy Rose*

K

Ka-Ding Dong
7/28/56 *G-Clefs*
9/8/56 *Diamonds*
9/15/56 *Hilltoppers*
Kansas City
4/13/59 *Wilbert Harrison*
5/4/59 *Hank Ballard*
5/4/59 *Rocky Olson*
5/11/59 *Little Richard*
7/28/58 **Kathy-O** *Diamonds*
7/13/59 **Katy Too** *Johnny Cash*
9/30/57 **Keep A Knockin'** *Little Richard*
7/30/55 **Kentuckian Song** *Hilltoppers*
4/14/58 **Kewpie Doll** *Perry Como*
1/21/56 **Key To My Heart** *Rosemary Clooney*
3/3/56 **Kiss And Run** *Peggy King*
5/12/56 **Kiss Me Another** *Georgia Gibbs*
11/18/57 **Kisses Sweeter Than Wine**
Jimmie Rodgers
6/29/59 **Kissin' Time** *Bobby Rydell*
(Kissing Kissing) ..see: Baciare Baciare
4/13/59 **Kissing Tree** *Billy Grammer*
1/19/57 **Knee Deep In The Blues** *Guy Mitchell*
Ko Ko Mo (I Love You So)
1/29/55 *Crew-Cuts*
2/5/55 *Perry Como*
4/20/59 **Kookie, Kookie (Lend Me Your Comb)**
Edward Byrnes & Connie Stevens

L

12/29/58 **La Bamba** *Ritchie Valens*
1/6/58 **La Dee Dah** *Billy & Lillie*
9/1/58 **La-Do-Dada** *Dale Hawkins*
3/3/56 **La Mer (Beyond The Sea)** *Roger Williams*
8/11/58 **La Paloma** *Billy Vaughn*
6/8/59 **La Plume De Ma Tante** *Hugo & Luigi*
3/17/56 **Large Large House** *Mike Pedicin Quintet*
9/9/57 **Lasting Love** *Sal Mineo*
6/22/59 **Lavender-Blue** *Sammy Turner*
Lay Down Your Arms
9/29/56 *Chordettes*
9/29/56 *Anne Shelton*
3/10/58 **Lazy Mary** *Lou Monte*
6/9/56 **Lazy River** *Roberta Sherwood*
8/18/58 **Lazy Summer Night** *Four Preps*
8/11/58 **Lean Jean** *Bill Haley*
4/29/57 **Leap Frog** *Chuck Alaimo Quartet*
5/7/55 **Learnin' The Blues** *Frank Sinatra*
11/12/55 **Learning To Love** *Peggy King*
3/2/57 **Leave It To Love** *Sarah Vaughan*
9/29/58 **Leave Me Alone (Let Me Cry)**
Dicky Doo & The Don'ts
8/3/59 **Leave My Kitten Alone** *Little Willie John*
12/22/56 **Left Arm Of Buddha** *Les Baxter*
6/30/58 **Left Right Out Of Your Heart** *Patti Page*
6/9/58 **Leroy** *Jack Scott*
4/20/57 **Let It Be Me** *Jill Corey*
1/7/56 **Let It Ring** *Doris Day*
6/24/57 **(Let Me Be Your) Teddy Bear**
Elvis Presley
Let Me Go, Lover!
1/1/55* *Teresa Brewer*
1/1/55* *Patti Page*
1/1/55* *Joan Weber*
1/8/55 *Sunny Gale*
4/21/58 **Let The Bells Keep Ringing** *Paul*
7/1/57 **Let The Four Winds Blow** *Roy Bro*
8/11/56 **Let The Good Times Roll** *Shirley &*
3/30/57 **Let There Be You** *Five Keys*
4/21/58 **Let's Be Lovers** *Playmates*
2/23/57 **Let's Go Calypso** *Rusty Draper*
8/4/58 **Let's Go Steady For The Summer**
Three G's
12/2/57 **Let's Light The Christmas Tree**
Ruby Wright
1/5/59 **Let's Love** *Johnny Mathis*
12/21/59 **Let's Try Again** *Clyde McPhatter*
10/20/58 **Letter To An Angel** *Jimmy Clantor*
Liechtensteiner Polka
11/18/57 *Will Glahe*
12/2/57 *Lawrence Welk*
11/3/58 **Light Of Love** *Peggy Lee*
8/10/59 **Like I Love You** *Edward Byrnes*
6/1/59 **Like Young**
Andre Previn With David Rose
7/20/59 **Linda Lu** *Ray Sharpe*
1/15/55 **Ling, Ting, Tong** *Charms*
9/23/57 **Lips Of Wine** *Andy Williams*
2/11/56 **Lipstick And Candy And Rubbers Shoes** *Julius LaRosa*
5/18/59 **Lipstick On Your Collar** *Connie F*
Lisbon Antigua
12/10/55 *Nelson Riddle*
2/4/56 *Mitch Miller*
Little Bitty Pretty One
10/21/57 *Thurston Harris*
11/18/57 *Bobby Day*
2/24/58 **Little Blue Man** *Betty Johnson*
2/11/56 **Little Boy Blue** *Billy Vaughn*
6/15/59 **Little Boy Blue** *Huelyn Duvall*
8/25/58 **Little Brass Band** *David Seville*
Little By Little
1/19/57 *Nappy Brown*
2/16/57 *Micki Marlo*
Little Child
2/18/56 *Eddie Albert & Sondra Lee*
2/18/56 *Lael & Cab Calloway*
Little Darlin'
3/16/57 *Diamonds*
4/6/57 *Gladiolas*
5/11/59 **Little Dipper** *Mickey Mozart Quin*
Little Drummer Boy
12/22/58 *Harry Simeone Chorale*
12/14/59 *Harry Simeone Chorale*
12/21/59 *Johnny Cash*
(Little Flower) ..see: Petite Fleur
7/13/59 **Little Girl** *Ritchie Valens*
4/28/56 **Little Girl Of Mine** *Cleftones*
2/24/58 **Little Gypsy** *Ames Brothers*
4/27/57 **Little Loneliness** *Kay Starr*
5/5/56 **Little Love Can Go A Long, Long**
Dream Weavers
7/7/58 **Little Mary** *Fats Domino*
4/7/56 **Little Musicians** *Hugo Winterhalt*
1/27/58 **Little Pigeon** *Sal Mineo*
6/23/58 **Little Pixie** *Moe Koffman Quartet*
4/13/59 **Little Queenie** *Chuck Berry*
12/1/58 **Little Red Riding Hood** *Big Bopp*
12/23/57 **Little Sandy Sleighfoot** *Jimmy D*
Little Serenade
7/21/58 *Teddy Randazzo*
8/4/58 *Ames Brothers*
1/5/59 **Little Space Girl** *Jesse Lee Turn*
7/21/58 **Little Star** *Elegants*
12/28/59 **Little Things Mean A Lot** *Joni Ja*
5/5/58 **Little Train** *Marianne Vasel & Eri*
4/29/57 **Little White Lies** *Betty Johnson*
Living Doll
9/28/59 *Cliff Richard*
10/19/59 *David Hill*
Lola's Theme
8/4/56 *Muir Mathieson*
8/18/56 *Steve Allen*

Lollipop
3/10/58 *Chordettes*
3/17/58 *Ronald & Ruby*
2/28/59 **Lonely Blue Boy** *Conway Twitty*
6/1/59 **Lonely Boy** *Paul Anka*
9/30/57 **Lonely Chair** *Lloyd Price*
4/13/59 **Lonely For You** *Gary Stites*
7/6/59 **Lonely Guitar** *Annette*
3/17/58 **Lonely Island** *Sam Cooke*
/19/59 **Lonely One** *Duane Eddy*
/25/59 **Lonely Saturday Night** *Don French*
9/7/59 **Lonely Street** *Andy Williams*
/24/58 **Lonely Teardrops** *Jackie Wilson*
/11/56 **Lonesome Lover Blues** *Fontane Sisters*
5/4/59 **Lonesome Old House** *Don Gibson*
/20/58 **Lonesome Town** *Ricky Nelson*
5/5/58 **Long Hot Summer** *Jimmie Rodgers*
Long Lonely Nights
/12/57 *Lee Andrews & The Hearts*
/12/57 *Clyde McPhatter*
Long Tall Sally
4/7/56 *Little Richard*
/14/56 *Pat Boone*
/20/55 **Longest Walk** *Jaye P. Morgan*
Look Homeward Angel
5/5/56 *Four Esquires*
/26/57 *Johnnie Ray*
/29/58 **Look Who's Blue** *Don Gibson*
/14/58 **Looking Back** *Nat "King" Cole*
/26/56 **Lost In The Shuffle** *Jaye P. Morgan*
6/9/56 **Lost John** *Lonnie Donegan*
/19/57 **Lotta Lovin'** *Gene Vincent*
/24/57 **Love Affair** *Sal Mineo*
/11/56 **Love Ain't Right** *Kay Starr*
Love And Marriage
1/5/55 *Frank Sinatra*
/12/55 *Dinah Shore*
/20/58 **Love Bug Crawl** *Jimmy Edwards*
/20/56 **Love In A Home** *Doris Day*
/30/57 **Love Is A Golden Ring** *Frankie Laine*
Love Is A Many-Splendored Thing
/27/55 *Four Aces*
12/55 *Don Cornell*
12/55 *Woody Herman*
12/55 *David Rose*
2/3/55 *Don, Dick N' Jimmy*
/27/58 **Love Is All We Need** *Tommy Edwards*
/5/57 **Love Is Strange** *Mickey & Sylvia*
10/55 **(Love Is) The Tender Trap** *Frank Sinatra*
/6/57 **Love Letters In The Sand** *Pat Boone*
Love, Love, Love
23/56 *Clovers*
23/56 *Diamonds*
13/58 **Love Makes The World Go 'Round**
Perry Como
17/56 **Love Me** *Elvis Presley*
Love Me Forever
18/57 *Four Esquires*
16/57 *Eydie Gorme*
17/56 **Love Me Good** *Jo Stafford*
11/59 **Love Me In The Daytime** *Doris Day*
Love Me Or Leave Me
28/55 *Sammy Davis, Jr.*
/9/55 *Lena Horne*
Love Me Tender
20/56 *Elvis Presley*
/8/56 *Henri Rene*
/5/57 **Love Me To Pieces** *Jill Corey*
24/58 **Love Of My Life** *Everly Brothers*
14/59 **Love Potion Number Nine** *Clovers*
/5/59 **Love Walked In** *Flamingos*
7/58 **Love You Most Of All** *Sam Cooke*
0/56 **Lovely One** *Four Voices*
9/59 **Lover's Prayer** *Dion & The Belmonts*
/6/58 **Lover's Question** *Clyde McPhatter*
9/59 **Lovers Never Say Goodbye** *Flamingos*
/6/59 **Lovey Dovey** *Clyde McPhatter*
24/57 **Loving You** *Elvis Presley*
23/57 **Lucille** *Little Richard*
7/59 **Lucky Devil** *Carl Dobkins, Jr.*
2/58 **Lucky Ladybug** *Billy & Lillie*
Lucky Lips
23/57 *Ruth Brown*
6/57 *Gale Storm*
7/55 **Lullaby Of Birdland** *Blue Stars*

M

6/15/59 **M.T.A.** *Kingston Trio*
8/18/58 **Ma Ma Ma Marie** *Gaylords*
Mack The Knife
1/21/56 *Dick Hyman Trio*
2/4/56 *Richard Hayman & Jan August*
2/4/56 *Billy Vaughn*
2/11/56 *Louis Armstrong*
2/11/56 *Les Paul*
2/18/56 *Lawrence Welk*
8/24/59 *Bobby Darin*
3/10/56 **Madeira** *Mitch Miller*
2/2/59 **Madrid** *Nat "King" Cole*
11/12/55 **Magic Fingers** *Eddie Fisher*
11/12/55 **Magic Melody** *Les Paul & Mary Ford*
1/20/58 **Magic Moments** *Perry Como*
Magic Touch ..see: (You've Got)
(Main Theme) ..see: Around The World In 80 Days
Main Title And Molly-O ..see: Man With The Golden Arm
12/2/57 **Majesty Of Love**
Marvin Rainwater & Connie Franics
4/29/57 **Make Like A Bunny, Honey** *Jill Corey*
5/19/58 **Make Me A Miracle** *Jimmie Rodgers*
3/24/58 **(Make With) The Shake** *Mark IV*
Make Yourself Comfortable
1/1/55* *Sarah Vaughan*
2/5/55 *Peggy King*
4/2/55 *Andy Griffith*
7/20/59 **Makin' Love** *Floyd Robinson*
10/27/56 **Mama From The Train** *Patti Page*
Mama Guitar
4/27/57 *Don Cornell*
4/27/57 *Julius LaRosa*
3/23/57 **Mama Look At Bubu** *Harry Belafonte*
7/28/56 **Mama, Teach Me To Dance**
Eydie Gorme
1/1/55* **Mambo Italiano** *Rosemary Clooney*
3/5/55 **Mambo Rock** *Bill Haley*
3/5/55 **Man Chases A Girl** *Eddie Fisher*
Man In The Raincoat
6/25/55 *Priscilla Wright*
7/16/55 *Marion Marlowe*
Man With The Golden Arm (Main Title/Molly-O/Delilah Jones)
3/17/56 *Elmer Bernstein*
3/17/56 *Richard Maltby*
3/24/56 *Dick Jacobs*
3/24/56 *Billy May*
4/7/56 *Les Elgart*
4/21/56 *Buddy Morrow*
5/5/56 *McGuire Sisters*
10/27/58 **Mandolins In The Moonlight**
Perry Como
3/16/57 **Mangos** *Rosemary Clooney*
12/8/58 **Manhattan Spiritual** *Reg Owen*
9/22/58 **Many A Time** *Steve Lawrence*
March From The River Kwai and Colonel Bogey
1/13/58 *Mitch Miller*
2/10/58 *Edmundo Ros*
2/24/58 *Art Mooney*
5/11/59 **Margie** *Fats Domino*
Marianne
2/2/57 *Terry Gilkyson & The Easy Riders*
2/9/57 *Hilltoppers*
3/2/57 *Burl Ives*
3/9/57 *Lane Brothers*
7/14/56 **Marimba Charleston** *Marimba Chiapas*
Marina
11/9/59 *Rocco Granata*
11/16/59 *Jacky Noguez*
11/30/59 *Willy Alberti*
11/10/56 **Married I Can Always Get** *Teddi King*
7/20/59 **Martinique** *Martin Denny*
6/1/59 **Mary Ann Thomas** *Bobby Freeman*
12/28/59 **Mary Don't You Weep**
Stonewall Jackson
8/17/59 **Mary Lou** *Ronnie Hawkins*
12/22/56 **Mary's Boy Child** *Harry Belafonte*
1/19/59 **Matilda** *Cookie & His Cupcakes*
8/17/59 **Mau-Mau** *Wailers*
1/5/59 **May You Always** *McGuire Sisters*
1/20/58 **Maybe** *Chantels*
3/3/58 **Maybe Baby** *Crickets*
8/20/55 **Maybellene** *Chuck Berry*
'Medic' Theme ..see: Blue Star
10/7/57 **Melodie D'Amour** *Ames Brothers*
Melody Of Love
1/1/55* *Billy Vaughn*
1/8/55 *David Carroll*
1/15/55 *Four Aces*
1/22/55 *Frank Sinatra & Ray Anthony*
2/19/55 *Leo Diamond*
Memories Are Made Of This
12/3/55 *Dean Martin*
12/17/55 *Mindy Carson*
12/24/55 *Gale Storm*
Memories Of You
11/26/55 *Four Coins*
1/28/56 *Benny Goodman Trio/Rosemary Clooney*
1/28/56 *Hugo Winterhalter*
12/15/58 **Merry Christmas Baby** *Chuck Berry*
10/6/58 **Mexican Hat Rock** *Applejacks*
3/9/57 **Mi Casa, Su Casa** *Perry Como*
8/3/59 **Miami** *Eugene Church*
7/28/58 **Midnight** *Paul Anka*
8/3/59 **Midnight Flyer** *Nat "King" Cole*
2/9/59 **Midnight Oil** *Charlie Blackwell*
10/19/59 **Midnight Stroll** *Revels*
8/11/58 **Midnighter** *Champs*
11/30/59 **Mighty Good** *Ricky Nelson*
3/10/58 **Million Miles From Nowhere**
Brook Benton
Miracle Of Love
8/18/56 *Eileen Rodgers*
11/3/56 *Ginny Gibson*
7/1/57 **Miss Ann** *Little Richard*
2/16/59 **Miss You** *Jaye P. Morgan*
7/29/57 **Miss You So** *Lillian Offitt*
3/10/56 **Missing** *McGuire Sisters*
Mister ..see: Mr.
10/5/59 **Misty** *Johnny Mathis*
Mocking Bird, The
5/19/56 *Four Lads*
11/3/58 *Four Lads*
Molly-O ..see: Man With The Golden Arm
9/3/55 **Moments To Remember** *Four Lads*
Mona Lisa
6/1/59 *Carl Mann*
7/20/59 *Conway Twitty*
5/12/56 **Money Honey** *Elvis Presley*
Money Tree
12/8/56 *Patience & Prudence*
12/8/56 *Margaret Whiting*
7/28/58 **Moon Talk** *Perry Como*
Moonglow And Theme From "Picnic"
4/14/56 *George Cates*
4/14/56 *Morris Stoloff*
5/5/56 *McGuire Sisters (Picnic)*
5/19/56 *Ralph Marterie (Picnic)*
6/23/58 **Moonlight Bay** *Drifters*
12/1/56 **Moonlight Gambler** *Frankie Laine*
11/3/56 **Moonlight Love** *Perry Como*
2/9/59 **Moonlight Serenade** *Rivieras*
Moonlight Swim
9/9/57 *Nick Noble*
10/7/57 *Tony Perkins*
3/17/58 **Moovin' N' Groovin'** *Duane Eddy*
6/16/56 **More** *Perry Como*
Morgen
8/17/59 *Ivo Robic*
9/14/59 *Leslie Uggams (One More Sunrise)*
Moritat ..see: Mack The Knife
3/2/59 **Morning Side Of The Mountain**
Tommy Edwards
5/14/55 **Most Of All** *Don Cornell*
12/24/55 **Mostly Martha** *Crew Cuts*
Movin' ..see: Moovin'
9/7/59 **Mr. Blue** *Fleetwoods*
10/28/57 **Mr. Fire Eyes** *Bonnie Guitar*
8/5/57 **Mr. Lee** *Bobbettes*
Mr. Sandman
1/1/55* *Chordettes*
1/1/55* *Four Aces*
10/27/58 **Mr. Success** *Frank Sinatra*

Mr. Wonderful
2/11/56 *Sarah Vaughan*
2/18/56 *Teddi King*
3/3/56 *Peggy Lee*
8/24/59 **Mummy, The** *Bob McFadden & Dor*
Mutual Admiration Society
11/10/56 *Teresa Brewer*
12/1/56 *Eddy Arnold & Jaye P. Morgan*
5/26/56 **My Baby Left Me** *Elvis Presley*
12/10/55 **My Believing Heart** *Joni James*
4/28/56 **My Blue Heaven** *Fats Domino*
9/24/55 **My Bonnie Lassie** *Ames Brothers*
My Boy - Flat Top
11/12/55 *Boyd Bennett*
11/12/55 *Dorothy Collins*
3/31/58 **My Bucket's Got A Hole In It**
Ricky Nelson
5/27/57 **My Dream** *Platters*
7/7/56 **My Dream Sonata** *Nat "King" Cole*
3/31/56 **My First Formal Gown** *Patti Page*
12/8/58 **My Happiness** *Connie Francis*
10/26/59 **My Heart Became Of Age** *Annette*
4/13/59 **My Heart Is An Open Book**
Carl Dobkins, Jr.
My Heart Sings ..see: (All of a Sudden)
8/18/58 **My Life** *Chuck Willis*
4/28/56 **My Little Angel** *Four Lads*
5/27/57 **My Little Baby** *Perry Como*
4/27/57 **My Love Song** *Tommy Sands*
9/8/58 **My Lucky Love**
Doug Franklin with the Bluenotes
1/19/59 **My Man** *Peggy Lee*
5/18/59 **My Melancholy Baby** *Tommy Edwards*
My One Sin
7/16/55 *Nat "King" Cole*
9/23/57 *Four Coins*
8/3/59 **My Own True Love** *Jimmy Clanton*
6/17/57 **My Personal Possession**
Nat "King" Cole/Four Knights
7/7/56 **My Prayer** *Platters*
10/14/57 **My Shoes Keep Walking Back To You**
Ray Price
10/14/57 **My Special Angel** *Bobby Helms*
12/31/55 **My Treasure** *Hilltoppers*
6/30/58 **My True Love** *Jack Scott*
7/13/59 **My Wish Came True** *Elvis Presley*

N

10/6/56 **Namely You** *Don Cherry*
Naughty Lady Of Shady Lane
1/1/55* *Ames Brothers*
1/1/55* *Archie Bleyer*
8/18/58 **Near You** *Roger Williams*
5/5/58 **Nee Nee Na Na Na Na Nu Nu**
Dicky Doo & The Don'ts
10/6/58 **Need You** *Donnie Owens*
11/24/58 **Need Your Love** *Bobby Freeman*
(Nel Blu Dipinto Di Blu) ..see: Volare
12/2/57 **Nervous Boogie** *Paul Gayten*
2/23/59 **Never Be Anyone Else But You**
Ricky Nelson
4/21/56 **Never Let Me Go** *Nat "King" Cole*
6/16/56 **Never Turn Back** *Al Hibbler*
11/16/59 **(New In) The Ways Of Love**
Tommy Edwards
11/17/56 **New York's My Home** *Sammy Davis, Jr.*
7/1/57 **Next In Line** *Johnny Cash*
2/4/56 **Next Time It Happens** *Carmen McRae*
7/8/57 **Next Time You See Me**
Little Junior Parker
10/27/56 **Night Lights** *Nat "King" Cole*
2/9/59 **Night Time Is The Right Time**
Ray Charles
9/22/58 **Nine More Miles** *Georgie Young*
3/23/57 **Ninety-Nine Ways** *Tab Hunter*
1/21/56 **Ninety Nine Years (Dead Or Alive)**
Guy Mitchell
No Arms Can Ever Hold You
11/12/55 *Pat Boone*
11/12/55 *Gaylords*
11/12/55 *Georgie Shaw*
6/9/58 **No Chemise, Please** *Gerry Granahan*
12/16/57 **No Love (But Your Love)** *Johnny Mathis*
12/28/59 **No Love Have I** *Webb Pierce*

No More
1/1/55* *DeJohn Sisters*
1/29/55 *McGuire Sisters*
5/5/58 **No, No** *Fats Domino*
1/21/56 **No, Not Much!** *Four Lads*
9/29/58 **No One But You (In My Heart)**
Ames Brothers
8/25/58 **No One Knows** *Dion & The Belmonts*
No Other Arms ..see: No Arms Can Ever Hold You
No Other Arms, No Other Lips
3/2/59 *Chordettes*
3/2/59 *Four Aces*
4/14/56 **No Other One** *Eddie Fisher*
3/9/59 **No Regrets** *Jimmy Barnes*
12/1/58 **Nobody But You** *Dee Clark*
Nola
1/12/59 *Billy Williams*
2/9/59 *Morgan Brothers*
10/13/58 **Non Dimenticar (Don't Forget)**
Nat "King" Cole
12/24/55 **Not One Goodbye** *Jaye P. Morgan*
12/14/59 **Not One Minute More** *Della Reese*
9/22/58 **Nothin' Shakin'** *Eddie Fontaine*
2/25/56 **Nothing Ever Changes My Love For You** *Nat "King" Cole*
8/11/58 **Nothing In The World** *Nat "King" Cole*
3/9/57 **Nothing Is Too Good For You**
Harvey Boys
3/31/58 **Now And For Always**
George Hamilton IV
9/15/56 **Now Is The Hour** *Gale Storm*
3/23/59 **(Now and Then There's) A Fool Such As I** *Elvis Presley*
10/13/56 **Now You Has Jazz**
Bing Crosby & Louis Armstrong
2/18/56 **Nuevo Laredo** *Les Paul & Mary Ford*
11/19/55 **Number One Street** *Bob Corley*
Nuttin' For Christmas
12/17/55 *Fontane Sisters*
12/17/55 *Art Mooney/Barry Gordon*
12/17/55 *Joe Ward*
12/17/55 *Ricky Zahnd*
12/24/55 *Stan Freberg*

O

1/12/59 **O' Falling Star** *Four Knights*
11/12/55 **Occasional Man** *Jeri Southern*
12/3/55 **Of This I'm Sure** *Four Aces*
7/29/57 **Oh Baby Doll** *Chuck Berry*
11/25/57 **Oh, Boy!** *Crickets*
10/12/59 **Oh! Carol** *Neil Sedaka*
Oh Julie
1/6/58 *Crescendos*
2/10/58 *Sammy Salvo*
3/10/58 **Oh Lonesome Me** *Don Gibson*
9/8/56 **Oh My Maria** *Eddie Fisher*
2/17/58 **Oh-Oh, I'm Falling In Love Again**
Jimmie Rodgers
12/10/55 **Oh! Susanna** *Singing Dogs*
6/22/59 **Oh, What A Fool** *Impalas*
3/9/59 **Oh Why** *Teddy Bears*
8/24/59 **Okefenokee** *Freddie Cannon*
5/20/57 **Old Cape Cod** *Patti Page*
9/1/58 **Old MacDonald** *Chargers*
8/11/56 **Old Philosopher** *Eddie Lawrence*
Old Shep
12/29/56 *Elvis Presley*
11/9/59 *Ralph DeMarco*
5/4/59 **Old Spanish Town** *Bell Notes*
7/13/59 **On An Evening In Roma** *Dean Martin*
11/24/56 **On London Bridge** *Jo Stafford*
12/29/56 **On My Word Of Honor** *Platters*
On The Street Where You Live
4/21/56 *Vic Damone*
6/9/56 *Eddie Fisher*
6/23/56 *Lawrence Welk*
3/16/57 **On Treasure Island** *Gale Storm*
5/20/57 **One For My Baby** *Tony Bennett*
12/22/56 **One In A Million** *Platters*
9/22/56 **One Kiss Led To Another** *Coasters*
6/8/59 **One Love, One Heart** *Four Coins*
11/9/59 **One More Chance** *Rod Bernard*
One More Sunrise ..see: Morgen

11/10/58 **One Night** *Elvis Presley*
1/5/59 **One Rose (That's Left In My Heart)**
Teresa Brewer
3/2/57 **One Step At A Time** *Brenda Lee*
3/9/57 **One Suit** *"Tennessee" Ernie Ford*
6/30/58 **One Summer Night** *Danleers*
10/28/57 **Only Because** *Platters*
Only Love Me ..see: (I Don't Care)
2/16/57 **Only One Love** *George Hamilton IV*
6/8/59 **Only Sixteen** *Sam Cooke*
Only You
10/1/55 *Platters*
11/12/55 *Hilltoppers*
4/6/59 *Franck Pourcel's French Fiddles*
6/16/56 **Ooby Dooby** *Roy Orbison*
11/26/55 **Ooh Bang Jiggilly Jang** *Doris Day*
6/9/58 **Ooh! My Soul** *Little Richard*
7/28/58 **Op** *Honeycones*
1/1/55 **Open Up Your Heart (And Let The Sunshine In)**
Cowboy Church Sunday School
8/4/56 **Other Woman** *Sarah Vaughan*
2/11/56 **Our Love Affair** *Tommy Charles*
(also see: Affair To Remember)
9/15/56 **Out Of Sight, Out Of Mind** *Five Key*
Over And Over
8/4/58 *Bobby Day*
8/4/58 *Thurston Harris*
5/13/57 **Over The Mountain; Across The Se**
Johnnie & Joe
9/1/58 **Over The Weekend** *Playboys*

P

5/26/58 **Padre** *Toni Arden*
3/23/57 **Pamela Throws A Party** *Joe Reism*
1/1/55* **Papa Loves Mambo** *Perry Como*
(Paper Of Pins) ..see: Bus Stop So
11/12/55 **Paper Roses** *Lola Dee*
12/29/56 **Paralyzed** *Elvis Presley*
10/20/58 **Paris** *Perez Prado*
11/3/58 **Part Of Me** *Jimmy Clanton*
Party Doll
2/23/57 *Buddy Knox*
2/23/57 *Steve Lawrence*
3/30/57 *Wingy Manone*
4/29/57 *Roy Brown*
11/11/57 **Party Time** *Sal Mineo*
12/22/56 **Party's Over** *Doris Day*
7/29/57 **Passing Strangers**
Sarah Vaughan & Billy Eckstine
6/16/58 **Patricia** *Perez Prado*
5/4/59 **Peace** *McGuire Sisters*
Peace In The Valley ..see: (There'll
9/30/57 **Peanuts** *Little Joe & The Thrillers*
12/8/58 **Peek-A-Boo** *Cadillacs*
11/11/57 **Peggy Sue** *Buddy Holly*
12/23/57 **Penny Loafers And Bobby Socks**
Joe Bennett
Pepper-Hot Baby
11/12/55 *Jaye P. Morgan*
11/19/55 *Gisele MacKenzie*
4/27/59 **Personality** *Lloyd Price*
11/12/55 **Pet Me, Poppa** *Rosemary Clooney*
1/5/59 **Peter Gunn** *Ray Anthony*
1/12/59 **Petite Fleur** *Chris Barber's Jazz Ba*
Petticoats Of Portugal
10/27/56 *Dick Jacobs*
12/15/56 *Billy Vaughn*
Philadelphia U.S.A.
11/17/58 *Nu Tornados*
12/15/58 *Art Lund*
9/1/58 **Pickle Up A Doodle** *Teresa Brewe*
Picnic ..see: Moonglow
3/23/57 **Pied Piper** *Billy Williams*
5/26/58 **Pink Pedal Pushers** *Carl Perkins*
2/16/59 **Pink Shoe Laces** *Dodie Stevens*
Piove ..see: Ciao, Ciao Bambina
4/20/59 **Pipe Dreams** *Jimmy Beck*
1/26/59 **Plain Jane** *Bobby Darin*
2/12/55 **Plantation Boogie** *Lenny Dee*
5/26/56 **Play For Keeps** *Jaye P. Morgan*
3/26/55 **Play Me Hearts And Flowers (I Wa Cry)** *Johnny Desmond*
2/2/57 **Playing For Keeps** *Elvis Presley*
6/18/55 **Playmates** *Fontane Sisters*

Plaything
9/30/57 *Ted Newman*
10/21/57 *Nick Todd*
3/3/58 **Plea, The** *Jesters*
9/1/58 **Please Don't Do It** *Dale Wright*
10/13/56 **Please Don't Leave Me** *Fontane Sisters*
10/20/58 **Please Love Me Forever** *Tommy Edwards*
2/16/59 **Please Mr. Sun** *Tommy Edwards*
7/8/57 **Please Send Me Someone To Love** *Moonglows*
Pledge Of Love
4/6/57 *Ken Copeland*
4/13/57 *Mitchell Torok*
4/20/57 *Dick Contino*
4/29/57 *Johnny Janis*
Pledging My Love
2/19/55 *Johnny Ace*
3/19/55 *Teresa Brewer*
11/17/58 *Roy Hamilton*
9/21/59 **Plenty Good Lovin'** *Connie Francis*
8/24/59 **Poco-Loco** *Gene & Eunice*
6/1/59 **Pointed Toe Shoes** *Carl Perkins*
8/24/59 **Poison Ivy** *Coasters*
12/29/56 **Poor Boy** *Elvis Presley*
10/20/58 **Poor Boy** *Royaltones*
3/30/59 **Poor Jenny** *Everly Brothers*
7/7/58 **Poor Little Fool** *Ricky Nelson*
3/2/57 **Poor Man's Roses (Or A Rich Man's Gold)** *Patti Page*
Poor People Of Paris
2/11/56 *Les Baxter*
2/25/56 *Chet Atkins*
3/3/56 *Russ Morgan*
3/17/56 *Lawrence Welk*
8/13/55 **Popcorn Song** *Cliffie Stone*
11/19/55 **Por Favor** *Vic Damone*
3/24/56 **Port Au Prince** *Nelson Riddle*
5/19/56 **Portuguese Washerwomen** *Joe "Fingers" Carr*
6/15/59 **Prayer And A Juke Box** *Little Anthony & The Imperials*
7/21/56 **President On The Dollar** *Mitch Miller*
Pretend
3/30/57 *Tab Smith*
10/26/59 *Carl Mann*
11/25/57 **Pretend You Don't See Her** *Jerry Vale*
Pretty Baby ..see: (It's Been A Long Time)
11/23/59 **Pretty Blue Eyes** *Steve Lawrence*
12/15/58 **Pretty Girls Everywhere** *Eugene Church*
(Pride Of South Central High) ..see: Igmoo
8/17/59 **Primrose Lane** *Jerry Wallace*
10/27/56 **Priscilla** *Eddie Cooley*
8/25/58 **Prisoner's Song** *Warren Storm*
9/14/59 **Private Eye** *Olympics*
11/10/58 **Problems** *Everly Brothers*
12/28/59 **Promise Me A Rose (A Slight Detail)** *Anita Bryant*
9/1/58 **Promise Me, Love** *Andy Williams*
Proud Ones ..see: Theme From
Pum-Pa-Lum ..see: (Bad Donkey)
6/2/58 **Purple People Eater** *Sheb Wooley*
7/28/58 **Purple People Eater Meets The Witch Doctor** *Joe South*
9/29/58 **Pussy Cat** *Ames Brothers*
12/9/57 **Put A Light In The Window** *Four Lads*
8/18/58 **Put A Ring On My Finger** *Les Paul & Mary Ford*
8/31/59 **Put Your Head On My Shoulder** *Paul Anka*

Q

6/23/56 **Que Sera, Sera (Whatever Will Be, Will Be)** *Doris Day*
10/6/58 **Queen Of The Hop** *Bobby Darin*
5/27/57 **Queen Of The Senior Prom** *Mills Brothers*
6/29/59 **Quiet Three** *Duane Eddy*
4/13/59 **Quiet Village** *Martin Denny*

R

10/20/56 **Race With The Devil** *Gene Vincent*
7/6/59 **Ragtime Cowboy Joe** *Chipmunks*
6/17/57 **Rainbow** *Russ Hamilton*
3/30/59 **Raining In My Heart** *Buddy Holly*
2/16/57 **Ram-Bunk-Shush** *Bill Doggett*
8/25/58 **Ramrod** *Duane Eddy*
5/27/57 **Rang Tang Ding Dong (I Am The Japanese Sandman)** *Cellos*
1/12/59 **Raspberries, Strawberries** *Kingston Trio*
Raunchy
11/18/57 *Ernie Freeman*
11/18/57 *Bill Justis*
12/2/57 *Billy Vaughn*
5/26/58 **Rave On** *Buddy Holly*
1/26/59 **Raw-Hide** *Link Wray*
7/23/55 **Razzle-Dazzle** *Bill Haley*
7/7/56 **Ready Teddy** *Little Richard*
9/22/58 **Real Wild Child** *Ivan*
12/22/58 **Reason, The** *5 Chanels*
9/2/57 **Rebel** *Carol Jarvis*
6/30/58 **Rebel-'Rouser** *Duane Eddy*
3/23/59 **Record Hop Blues** *Quarter Notes*
8/3/59 **Red River Rock** *Johnny & The Hurricanes*
12/29/58 **Red River Rose** *Ames Brothers*
2/2/57 **Red Sails In The Sunset** *Tab Hunter*
11/4/57 **Reet Petite (The Finest Girl You Ever Want To Meet)** *Jackie Wilson*
11/12/55 **Rememb'ring** *Peter Lind Hayes & Mary Healy*
3/17/58 **Remember** *Velours*
6/22/59 **Remember When** *Platters*
8/12/57 **Remember You're Mine** *Pat Boone*
2/2/57 **Repeat After Me** *Patti Page*
4/7/58 **Return To Me** *Dean Martin*
11/2/59 **Reveille Rock** *Johnny & The Hurricanes*
6/4/55 **Rhythm 'N' Blues (Mama's Got The Rhythm - Papa's Got The Blues)** *McGuire Sisters*
12/10/55 **Richest Man (In the World)** *Eddy Arnold*
4/20/57 **Ring-A-Ding-A-Ding** *Tommy Sands*
6/1/59 **Ring-A-Ling-A-Lario** *Jimmie Rodgers*
6/24/57 **Ring My Phone** *Tommy Sands*
Rip It Up
7/7/56 *Little Richard*
8/11/56 *Bill Haley*
4/27/59 **Robbin' The Cradle** *Tony Bellus*
1/20/58 **Roc-A-Chicka** *Warner Mack*
4/7/56 **R-O-C-K** *Bill Haley*
11/12/55 **Rock-A-Beatin' Boogie** *Bill Haley*
4/6/57 **Rock-A-Billy** *Guy Mitchell*
11/24/56 **Rock-A-Bye Your Baby With A Dixie Melody** *Jerry Lewis*
12/2/57 **Rock And Cry** *Clyde McPhatter*
3/3/58 **Rock And Roll Is Here To Stay** *Danny & The Juniors*
11/11/57 **Rock And Roll Music** *Chuck Berry*
3/24/58 **Rock And Roll Rhapsody** *Four Aces*
12/31/55 **Rock And Roll Waltz** *Kay Starr*
4/21/56 **Rock And Roll Wedding** *Sunny Gale*
2/11/56 **Rock Around Mother Goose** *Barry Gordon*
5/14/55 **Rock Around The Clock** *Bill Haley*
Rock Island Line
3/17/56 *Lonnie Donegan*
4/14/56 *Don Cornell*
2/26/55 **Rock Love** *Fontane Sisters*
3/17/56 **Rock Right** *Georgia Gibbs*
5/13/57 **Rock Your Little Baby To Sleep** *Buddy Knox*
12/22/58 **Rocka-Conga** *Applejacks*
12/22/58 **Rockhouse** *Ray Charles*
3/30/59 **Rockin' Crickets** *Hot-Toddys*
6/30/56 **Rockin' Ghost** *Archie Bleyer*
7/13/59 **Rockin' In The Jungle** *Eternals*
8/12/57 **Rockin' Pneumonia And The Boogie Woogie Flu** *Huey Smith & The Clowns*
8/4/58 **Rockin' Robin** *Bobby Day*
6/10/57 **Rockin' Shoes** *Ames Brothers*
7/14/56 **Rockin' Through The Rye** *Bill Haley*
(Roll On) ..see: Cimarron
6/30/56 **Roll Over Beethoven** *Chuck Berry*
6/4/55 **Rollin' Stone** *Fontane Sisters*
11/3/56 **Rose And A Baby Ruth** *George Hamilton IV*
11/12/55 **Rose Tattoo** *Perry Como*
5/13/57 **Rosie Lee** *Mello-Tones*
2/23/57 **Round And Round** *Perry Como*
5/19/56 **Rovin' Gambler** *"Tennessee" Ernie Ford*
12/30/57 **Rudolph The Red-Nosed Reindeer** *Gene Autry*
11/3/56 **Rudy's Rock** *Bill Haley*
4/28/58 **Rumble** *Link Wray*
12/21/59 **Run Red Run** *Coasters*
12/15/58 **Run Rudolph Run** *Chuck Berry*
1/1/55* **Runaround** *Three Chuckles*
10/12/59 **Running Bear** *Johnny Preston*
5/18/59 **Russian Band Stand** *Spencer & Spencer*

S

3/16/57 **'S Wonderful** *Ray Conniff*
9/22/56 **Sadie's Shawl** *Bob Sharples*
12/23/57 **Sail Along Silvery Moon** *Billy Vaughn*
Saint ..see: St.
Saints Rock 'N Roll ..see: When The Saints Go Marching In
8/17/59 **Sal's Got A Sugar Lip** *Johnny Horton*
9/24/55 **Same Old Saturday Night** *Frank Sinatra*
3/5/55 **Sand And The Sea** *Nat "King" Cole*
11/23/59 **Sandy** *Larry Hall*
12/23/57 **Santa And The Satellite** *Buchanan & Goodman*
(Santa Catalina) ..see: 26 Miles
1/1/55* **Santo Natale** *David Whitfield*
12/29/58 **Save My Soul** *Jack Scott*
5/6/57 **Say It Isn't So** *Teddi King*
9/21/59 **Say Man** *Bo Diddley*
11/2/59 **Scarlet Ribbons (For Her Hair)** *Browns*
4/6/57 **School Day** *Chuck Berry*
2/9/59 **Sea Cruise** *Frankie Ford*
7/6/59 **Sea Of Love** *Phil Phillips*
3/2/59 **Search, The** *Dean Reed*
5/13/57 **Searchin'** *Coasters*
11/12/55 **Searching** *Hilltoppers*
6/9/56 **Second Fiddle** *Kay Starr*
9/15/58 **Secret, The** *Gordon MacRae*
5/5/58 **Secretly** *Jimmie Rodgers*
See Saw
9/1/56 *Moonglows*
11/10/56 *Don Cornell*
6/29/59 **See You In September** *Tempos*
1/14/56 **See You Later, Alligator** *Bill Haley*
6/17/57 **Send For Me** *Nat "King" Cole*
4/6/57 **Send Me Some Lovin'** *Little Richard*
6/2/58 **Send Me The Pillow You Dream On** *Hank Locklin*
5/4/59 **Separate Ways** *Sarah Vaughan*
1/5/59 **Sermonette** *Della Reese*
Seven Days
1/28/56 *Dorothy Collins*
2/4/56 *Crew Cuts*
2/4/56 *Clyde McPhatter*
2/24/58 **"7-11" (Mambo No. 5)** *Gone All Stars*
9/14/59 **Seven Little Girls Sitting In The Back Seat** *Paul Evans*
12/1/58 **Seven Minutes In Heaven** *Poni-Tails*
Seventeen
7/9/55 *Boyd Bennett*
8/20/55 *Rusty Draper*
8/20/55 *Fontane Sisters*
4/6/59 **77 Sunset Strip** *Don Ralke*
11/30/59 **Shadows** *5 Satins*
1/26/59 **Shag (Is Totally Cool)** *Billy Graves*
Shake, The ..see: (Make With)
2/10/58 **Shake A Hand** *Mike Pedicin Quintet*
1/1/55* **Shake, Rattle, And Roll** *Bill Haley*
5/27/57 **Shangri-La** *Four Coins*
9/7/59 **Shape I'm In** *Johnny Restivo*
1/26/59 **She Say (Oom Dooby Doom)** *Diamonds*
8/4/58 **She Was Only Seventeen (He Was One Year More)** *Marty Robbins*
1/13/58 **She's Neat** *Dale Wright*
6/30/58 **Sheik Of Araby (Italian Style)** *Lou Monte*
Shifting Whispering Sands
9/24/55 *Billy Vaughn*
10/1/55 *Rusty Draper*

12/7/59 **Shimmy, Shimmy, Ko-Ko-Bop**
Little Anthony & The Imperials
Ship That Never Sailed
3/23/57 *David Carroll*
4/13/57 *Billy Vaughn*
2/16/57 **Shirley** *Schoolboys*
2/23/59 **Shirley** *John Fred*
4/29/57 **Shish-Kebab** *Ralph Marterie*
(also see: Harem Dance)
11/19/55 **Shoot It Again** *Teresa Brewer*
6/24/57 **Short Fat Fannie** *Larry Williams*
1/27/58 **Short Shorts** *Royal Teens*
3/17/58 **Should We Tell Him** *Everly Brothers*
9/21/59 **Shout** *Isley Brothers*
6/3/57 **Shrine Of St. Cecilia** *Faron Young*
5/5/58 **Sick And Tired** *Fats Domino*
3/16/57 **Silent Lips** *Georgia Gibbs*
12/30/57 **Silent Night** *Bing Crosby*
Silhouettes
10/14/57 *Rays*
10/21/57 *Steve Gibson*
11/4/57 *Diamonds*
12/30/57 **Silver Bells**
Bing Crosby & Carol Richards
6/4/55 **Silver Dollar** *Teresa Brewer*
2/16/59 **Since I Don't Have You** *Skyliners*
Since I Met You Baby
11/17/56 *Ivory Joe Hunter*
12/8/56 *Mindy Carson*
6/15/59 **Since You've Been Gone**
Clyde McPhatter
Sincerely
1/8/55 *McGuire Sisters*
3/26/55 *Moonglow's*
2/17/58 **Sing Boy Sing** *Tommy Sands*
11/24/58 **Sing Sing Sing** *Bernie Lowe Orchestra*
6/30/58 **Singing Hills** *Billy Vaughn*
Singing The Blues
10/27/56 *Guy Mitchell*
11/3/56 *Marty Robbins*
6/30/56 **Sinner Man** *Les Baxter*
Sittin' In The Balcony
3/16/57 *Johnny Dee*
3/23/57 *Eddie Cochran*
9/21/59 **Six Boys And Seven Girls** *Anita Bryant*
3/23/59 **Six Nights A Week** *Crests*
11/24/58 **16 Candles** *Crests*
Sixteen Tons
11/12/55 *"Tennessee" Ernie Ford*
11/19/55 *Johnny Desmond*
9/21/59 **Ski King** *E.C. Beatty*
4/14/58 **Skinny Minnie** *Bill Haley*
3/2/57 **Skyliner** *Carmen McRae*
7/27/59 **Sleep Walk** *Santo & Johnny*
4/21/56 **Slipin' And Slidin'** *Little Richard*
(Slop, The) ..see: Hard Times
Slow Walk
11/10/56 *Sil Austin*
11/24/56 *Bill Doggett*
6/15/59 **Small World** *Johnny Mathis*
8/17/59 **Smile** *Tony Bennett*
2/26/55 **Smiles** *Crazy Otto*
Smoke Gets In Your Eyes
4/28/58 *Richard Barrett*
11/17/58 *Platters*
12/10/55 **Smokey Joe's Cafe** *Robins*
11/30/59 **Smokie** *Bill Black's Combo*
11/2/59 **Smooth Operator** *Sarah Vaughan*
12/31/55 **Snowbound For Christmas**
DeCastro Sisters
5/18/59 **So Close** *Brook Benton*
4/6/59 **So Fine** *Fiestas*
7/27/59 **So High So Low** *LaVern Baker*
7/28/56 **So-Long** *Fats Domino*
6/10/57 **So Long I'm Gone** *Warren Smith*
4/27/57 **So Long, My Love** *Frank Sinatra*
10/19/59 **So Many Ways** *Brook Benton*
12/22/58 **So Much** *Little Anthony & The Imperials*
2/23/57 **So Rare** *Jimmy Dorsey*
7/15/57 **So Strange** *Jesters*
So Tough
2/24/58 *Original Casuals*
3/3/58 *Kuf-Linx*
So Young
6/17/57 *Clyde Stacy*
11/16/59 *Clyde Stacy*
11/4/57 **Soft** *Bill Doggett*
9/23/57 **Soft Sands** *Chordettes*
Soft Summer Breeze
6/30/56 *Eddie Heywood*
9/22/56 *Diamonds*
4/19/55 **Softly, Softly** *Jaye P. Morgan*
8/3/59 **Soldier's Joy** *Hawkshaw Hawkins*
1/26/57 **Some Day Soon** *Eddie Fisher*
10/27/58 **Someday You'll Want Me To Want You**
Jodie Sands
10/5/59 **Some Kind-A Earthquake** *Duane Eddy*
8/4/58 **Somebody Touched Me** *Buddy Knox*
7/28/56 **Somebody Up There Likes Me**
Perry Como
Someday ..see: Some Day
3/23/59 **Someone** *Johnny Mathis*
11/19/55 **Someone On Your Mind**
Champ Butler with George Cates
5/18/59 **Someone To Come Home To**
Ames Brothers
12/1/56 **Someone To Love** *Four Aces*
10/22/55 **Someone You Love** *Nat "King" Cole*
8/31/59 **Somethin Else** *Eddie Cochran*
Something's Gotta Give
6/4/55 *Sammy Davis, Jr.*
6/4/55 *McGuire Sisters*
8/4/56 **Song For A Summer Night** *Mitch Miller*
(Song Of Love) ..see: Chanson d'Amour
11/11/57 **Song Of Raintree County**
Nat "King" Cole
1/22/55* **Song Of The Barefoot Contessa**
Hugo Winterhalter
9/16/57 **Song Of The Barefoot Mailman**
Billy Leach
8/27/55 **Song Of The Dreamer** *Eddie Fisher*
(also see: Dreamer)
12/1/56 **Song Of The Sparrow** *Mitch Miller*
3/16/59 **Sorry (I Ran All the Way Home)** *Impalas*
12/28/59 **Sound Of Music** *Patti Page*
Sparrow ..see: Song Of
12/10/55 **Speedoo** *Cadillacs*
6/23/58 **Splish Splash** *Bobby Darin*
8/11/56 **St. Therese Of The Roses**
Billy Ward & The Dominoes
12/8/58 **Stagger Lee** *Lloyd Price*
4/28/58 **Stairway Of Love** *Marty Robbins*
Standing On The Corner
4/28/56 *Four Lads*
5/19/56 *Dean Martin*
5/26/56 *Mills Brothers*
3/30/59 **Star Love** *Playmates*
11/10/56 **Star You Wished Upon Last Night**
Gisele MacKenzie
Stardust
5/6/57 *Nat "King" Cole*
6/17/57 *Billy Ward & His Dominoes*
11/2/59 **Starry Eyed** *Gary Stites*
5/20/57 **Start Movin' (In My Direction)** *Sal Mineo*
8/4/58 **Stay** *Ames Brothers*
Still
10/13/56 *Fontane Sisters*
1/5/57 *LaVern Baker*
2/11/56 **Stolen Love** *Dinah Shore*
12/30/57 **Stood Up** *Ricky Nelson*
11/11/57 **Story Of My Life** *Marty Robbins*
1/26/59 **Story Of My Love** *Conway Twitty*
10/12/59 **Story Of Our Love** *Johnny Mathis*
6/25/55 **Story Untold** *Crew-Cuts*
5/25/59 **Straight Flush** *Frantics*
8/18/58 **Straighten Up & Fly Right**
DeJohn Sisters
Stranded In The Jungle
6/30/56 *Jayhawks*
7/14/56 *Cadets*
7/21/56 *Gadabouts*
8/25/58 **Strange Are The Ways Of Love**
Gogi Grant
7/7/56 **Strangest Romance** *Patti Page*
4/27/59 **String Of Trumpets** *Trumpeteers*
12/30/57 **Stroll, The** *Diamonds*
7/28/58 **Stupid Cupid** *Connie Francis*
Such A Day
2/18/56 *Rita Raines*
3/3/56 *Vera Lynn*
Suddenly There's A Valley
10/1/55 *Gogi Grant*
10/8/55 *Julius LaRosa*
10/15/55 *Jo Stafford*
11/12/55 *Patty Andrews*
11/12/55 *Mills Brothers*
3/10/58 **Sugah Wooga** *Three Playmates*
5/5/58 **Sugar Moon** *Pat Boone*
7/20/59 **Sugaree** *Rusty York*
12/30/57 **Sugartime** *McGuire Sisters*
4/27/59 **Summer Dreams** *McGuire Sisters*
7/15/57 **Summer Love** *Joni James*
Summer Night ..see: Song For A
9/8/56 **Summer Sweetheart** *Ames Brothers*
7/20/59 **Summer's Love**
Richard Barrett/Chantels
11/4/57 **Summertime** *Sam Cooke*
8/4/58 **Summertime Blues** *Eddie Cochran*
9/1/58 **Summertime Lies** *Four Preps*
8/18/58 **Summertime, Summertime** *Jamies*
7/8/57 **Sun Is Shining** *Jimmy Reed*
8/11/58 **Sunday Barbecue**
Tennessee Ernie Ford
6/10/57 **Sunshine Girl** *Eddie Fisher*
8/11/58 **Susie Darlin'** *Robin Luke*
8/31/59 **Suzie Baby** *Bobby Vee*
6/10/57 **Suzie-Q** *Dale Hawkins*
10/8/55 **Swanee** *Jaye P. Morgan*
10/28/57 **Swanee River Rock (Talkin' 'Bout T River)** *Ray Charles*
Sweet And Gentle
7/2/55 *Alan Dale*
7/9/55 *Georgia Gibbs*
3/23/59 **Sweet Annie Laurie** *Sammy Turner*
8/31/59 **Sweet Bird Of Youth** *Nat "King" Col*
6/1/59 **Sweet Chile** *Sheb Wooley*
4/7/58 **Sweet Elizabeth** *Will Glahe*
6/2/56 **Sweet Heartaches** *Eddie Fisher*
11/12/55 **Sweet Kentucky Rose** *Kitty Kallen*
3/24/56 **Sweet Lips** *Jaye P. Morgan*
11/10/58 **Sweet Little Rock And Roll** *Chuck B*
2/17/58 **Sweet Little Sixteen** *Chuck Berry*
12/21/59 **Sweet Nothin's** *Brenda Lee*
6/9/56 **Sweet Old Fashioned Girl**
Teresa Brewer
6/29/59 **Sweet Someone** *Eddie & Betty*
6/17/57 **Sweet Stuff** *Guy Mitchell*
7/6/59 **Sweet Sugar Lips** *Kalin Twins*
7/6/59 **Sweeter Than You** *Ricky Nelson*
7/15/57 **Sweetest One** *Crest's*
11/24/58 **Sweetheart** *Peggy Lee*
2/10/58 **Swingin' Daddy** *Buddy Knox*
12/21/59 **Swingin' On A Rainbow** *Frankie Av*
Swinging Shepherd Blues
1/27/58 *Johnny Pate Quintet*
2/3/58 *Moe Koffman Quartette*
2/24/58 *David Rose*
9/9/57 **Swinging Sweethearts** *Ron Goodw*
11/30/59 **Symphony** *Sammy Turner*

T

6/15/59 **Taboo** *Arthur Lyman*
3/30/59 **Take A Message To Mary**
Everly Brothers
2/2/57 **Take Me Back Baby** *Guy Mitchell*
12/31/55 **Take Me Back To Toyland**
Nat "King" Cole
5/4/59 **Talk Of The School** *Sonny James*
11/23/59 **Talk That Talk** *Jackie Wilson*
10/19/59 **Talk To Me** *Frank Sinatra*
4/7/58 **Talk To Me, Talk To Me** *Little Willie*
5/6/57 **Talkin' To The Blues** *Jim Lowe*
5/18/59 **Tall Cool One** *Wailers*
1/5/59 **Tall Paul** *Annette*
5/11/59 **Tallahassee Lassie** *Freddy Canno*
Tammy
7/1/57 *Ames Brothers*
7/22/57 *Debbie Reynolds*
5/19/56 **Tango Of The Drums** *Les Baxter*
7/7/56 **Te Amo** *Dick Jacobs*
9/1/58 **Tea For Two Cha Cha** *Tommy Dor*
11/30/59 **Teach Me Tiger** *April Stevens*

Teach Me Tonight
1/1/55* *DeCastro Sisters*
1/1/55* *Jo Stafford*
1/5/59 *DeCastro Sisters (Cha Cha)*
5/5/58 **Teacher, Teacher** *Johnny Mathis*
4/21/58 **Teacher's Pet** *Doris Day*
11/30/59 **Tear Drop** *Santo & Johnny*
11/25/57 **Tear Drops** *Lee Andrews & the Hearts*
6/17/57 **Teardrops In My Heart** *Teresa Brewer*
3/9/59 **Teardrops On Your Letter** *Hank Ballard*
2/2/59 **Teardrops Will Fall** *Dicky Doo & The Don'ts*
2/25/56 **Tear Fell** *Teresa Brewer*
8/11/58 **Tears On My Pillow** *Little Anthony & The Imperials*
1/19/59 **Teasable, Pleasable You** *Buddy Knox*
2/22/58 **Teasin'** *Quaker City Boys*
Teddy Bear ..see: (Let Me Be Your)
2/23/57 **Teen-Age Crush** *Tommy Sands*
5/19/58 **Teen-Age Doll** *Tommy Sands*
0/20/56 **Teen Age Goodnight** *Chordettes*
3/16/59 **Teenage Heaven** *Eddie Cochran*
2/18/56 **Teenage Meeting (Gonna Rock It Up Right)** *Don Cornell*
Teen Age Prayer
2/10/55 *Gloria Mann*
2/24/55 *Gale Storm*
2/31/55 *Kitty White*
Teenage Queen ..see: Ballad Of
4/20/59 **Teenager In Love** *Dion & The Belmonts*
8/25/56 **Teenager's Mother (Are You Right?)** *Bill Haley*
5/13/57 **Teenager's Romance** *Ricky Nelson*
2/17/55 **Teen-Ager's Waltz** *Eddy Howard*
2/21/59 **Teen Angel** *Mark Dinning*
9/7/59 **Teen Beat** *Sandy Nelson*
12/1/58 **Teen Commandments** *Paul Anka-Geo. Hamilton IV-Johnny Nash*
Tell Him No
3/23/59 *Dean & Marc*
3/23/59 *Travis & Bob*
Tell Me Why
6/30/56 *Crew Cuts*
6/30/56 *Gale Storm*
2/16/59 **Telling Lies** *Fats Domino*
9/15/58 **Ten Commandments Of Love** *Harvey & The Moonglows*
7/6/59 **Ten Thousand Drums** *Carl Smith*
Tender Trap ..see: (Love Is)
7/13/59 **Tennessee Stud** *Eddy Arnold*
Tennessee Waltz
0/19/59 *Jerry Fuller*
0/26/59 *Bobby Comstock*
Tequila
2/24/58 *Champs*
3/3/58 *Eddie Platt*
1/28/56 **Texas Lady** *Les Paul & Mary Ford*
7/13/59 **Thank You Pretty Baby** *Brook Benton*
That Old Black Magic
7/2/55 *Sammy Davis, Jr.*
11/3/58 *Louis Prima & Keely Smith*
8/12/57 **That'll Be The Day** *Crickets*
2/25/56 **That's All** *"Tennessee" Ernie Ford*
4/20/59 **That's All I Want** *Bobby Day*
That's All I Want From You
1/1/55* *Jaye P. Morgan*
2/16/57 *Silva-Tones*
7/7/56 **That's All There Is To That** *Nat "King" Cole/Four Knights*
1/27/58 **That's Alright** *Little Junior Parker*
7/14/58 **That's How Much I Love You** *Pat Boone*
That's Life ..see: (But As They Say)
4/6/59 **That's My Little Suzie** *Ritchie Valens*
4/13/57 **That's When Your Heartaches Begin** *Elvis Presley*
1/5/59 **That's Why I Cry** *Buddy Knox*
3/23/59 **That's Why (I Love You So)** *Jackie Wilson*
2/16/57 **That's Why I Was Born** *Janice Harper*
1/28/56 **That's Your Mistake** *Otis Williams*
10/6/56 **Theme From East Of Eden** *Dick Jacobs*
Theme From Picnic ..see: Moonglow
Theme From The Man With The Golden Arm ..see: Man With The Golden Arm
Theme From The Proud Ones
7/14/56 *Nelson Riddle*
8/4/56 *Lionel Newman*
8/11/56 *Leroy Holmes*
Theme From The Three Penny Opera ..see: Mack The Knife
10/12/59 **There Comes A Time** *Jack Scott*
6/1/59 **There Goes My Baby** *Drifters*
9/15/58 **There Goes My Heart** *Joni James*
11/9/59 **There, I've Said It Again** *Sam Cooke*
1/19/59 **There Must Be A Way** *Joni James*
4/20/57 **There Oughta Be A Law** *Mickey & Sylvia*
11/19/55 **There Should Be Rules (Protecting Fools Who Fall In Love)** *Betty Madigan*
4/13/57 **(There'll Be) Peace In The Valley (For Me)** *Elvis Presley*
10/26/59 **There's A Girl** *Jan & Dean*
8/19/57 **There's A Gold Mine In The Sky** *Pat Boone*
4/27/59 **There's No Fool Like A Young Fool** *Tab Hunter*
4/7/58 **There's Only One Of You** *Four Lads*
10/28/57 **There's Only You** *Don Rondo*
5/25/59 **There's Something On Your Mind** *Big Jay McNeely & Band*
2/18/56 **These Hands** *Len Dresslar*
6/9/58 **Things I Love** *Fidelity's*
9/8/56 **Things I Never Had** *Kay Starr*
8/5/57 **Think** *"5" Royales*
7/21/58 **Think It Over** *Crickets*
9/16/57 **Third Finger - Left Hand** *Eileen Rodgers*
11/23/59 **This Friendly World** *Fabian*
6/1/59 **This I Swear** *Skyliners*
12/30/57 **This Is The Nite** *Valiants*
2/10/58 **This Little Girl Of Mine** *Everly Brothers*
9/22/58 **This Little Girl's Gone Rockin'** *Ruth Brown*
This Old Man ..see: Children's Marching Song
This Ole House
1/1/55* *Rosemary Clooney*
1/15/55* *Stuart Hamblen*
3/9/59 **This Should Go On Forever** *Rod Bernard*
12/21/59 **This Time Of The Year** *Brook Benton*
12/22/56 **Thousand Miles Away** *Heartbeats*
Three Bells
7/27/59 *Browns*
8/31/59 *Dick Flood*
Three Penny Opera ..see: Mack The Knife
Three Stars
3/30/59 *Tommy Dee*
5/4/59 *Ruby Wright*
Thunder Road ..see: Ballad Of
9/29/58 **Tic Toc** *Lee Allen*
6/15/59 **Tiger** *Fabian*
2/16/57 **Tiger Lily** *Rusty Draper*
3/23/59 **Tijuana Jail** *Kingston Trio*
8/17/59 **('Til) I Kissed You** *Everly Brothers*
Till
4/13/57 *Percy Faith*
10/28/57 *Roger Williams*
6/29/59 **Till There Was You** *Anita Bryant*
8/3/59 **Time Marches On** *Roy Hamilton*
11/12/55 **Times Two, I Love You** *Three Chuckles*
5/27/57 **Tina** *Easy Riders*
8/13/55 **Tina Marie** *Perry Como*
11/2/59 **Tiny Tim** *LaVern Baker*
7/13/59 **To A Soldier Boy** *Tassels*
4/14/58 **To Be Loved** *Jackie Wilson*
4/20/57 **To Be With You** *Highlights*
9/22/58 **To Know Him Is To Love Him** *Teddy Bears*
5/5/56 **To Love Again** *Four Aces*
7/22/57 **To The Aisle** *Five Satins*
10/27/56 **To The Ends Of The Earth** *Nat "King" Cole*
To You, My Love
2/25/56 *Nick Noble*
4/21/56 *Georgie Shaw*
9/29/58 **Tom Dooley** *Kingston Trio*
2/23/59 **Tomboy** *Perry Como*
(Tomorrow) ..see: Domani
4/20/57 **Tonight My Heart Will Be Crying** *Eddie Fisher*
Tonight You Belong To Me
8/4/56 *Patience & Prudence*
9/22/56 *Lawrence Welk with The Lennon Sisters*
9/29/56 *Karen Chandler & Jimmy Wakely*
8/19/57 **Tonite, Tonite** *Mello-Kings*
4/21/56 **Too Close For Comfort** *Eydie Gorme*
5/27/57 **Too Late** *Gene Austin*
12/17/55 **Too Late Now** *DeCastro Sisters*
1/26/57 **Too Much** *Elvis Presley*
Too Young To Go Steady
4/7/56 *Nat "King" Cole*
4/14/56 *Patti Page*
9/15/58 **Topsy I** *Cozy Cole*
8/25/58 **Topsy II** *Cozy Cole*
Torero
5/5/58 *Renato Carosone*
6/16/58 *Julius LaRosa*
9/28/59 **Torquay** *Fireballs*
4/20/59 **Touch Of Pink** *Jerry Wallace*
3/9/57 **Tower's Trot (And Then You Do That Step)** *Dick Jacobs*
Tra La La
12/8/56 *Georgia Gibbs*
12/15/56 *LaVern Baker*
1/26/59 **Tragedy** *Thomas Wayne*
6/2/56 **Transfusion** *Nervous Norvus*
5/26/56 **Treasure Of Love** *Clyde McPhatter*
8/25/58 **Treasure Of Your Love** *Eileen Rodgers*
10/14/57 **Treat Me Nice** *Elvis Presley*
2/2/57 **Trees** *Al Hibbler*
Tricky
12/1/56 *Gus Jinkins*
3/9/57 *Ralph Marterie*
Trouble With Harry
1/28/56 *Alfi & Harry*
2/11/56 *Les Baxter*
6/30/58 **True, Fine Mama** *Little Richard*
True Love
8/25/56 *Jane Powell*
9/8/56 *Bing Crosby & Grace Kelly*
4/20/57 **True Love Gone (Come On Home)** *Betty Madigan*
True Love, True Love ..see: (If You Cry)
8/24/59 **True True Happiness** *Johnny Tillotson*
Trust In Me
6/10/57 *Chris Connor*
1/12/59 *Patti Page*
12/15/58 **Try Me** *James Brown*
6/2/58 **Try The Impossible** *Lee Andrews*
4/14/58 **Trying** *Billy Vaughn*
9/21/59 **Tucumcari** *Jimmie Rodgers*
Tumbling Tumbleweeds
8/25/56 *Roger Williams*
4/7/58 *Billy Vaughn*
10/27/58 **Tunnel Of Love** *Doris Day*
3/30/59 **Turn Me Loose** *Fabian*
12/1/58 **Turvy II** *Cozy Cole*
Tutti-Frutti
1/14/56 *Little Richard*
1/28/56 *Pat Boone*
Tweedlee Dee
1/15/55 *LaVern Baker*
1/29/55 *Georgia Gibbs*
10/14/57 **Twelfth Of Never** *Johnny Mathis*
4/20/57 **Twelve O'Clock Tonight** *Doris Day*
12/10/55 **24 Hours A Day (365 A Year)** *Georgia Gibbs*
1/20/58 **26 Miles (Santa Catalina)** *Four Preps*
8/24/59 **Twice As Nice** *Clyde McPhatter*
4/7/58 **Twilight Time** *Platters*
6/15/59 **Twixt Twelve And Twenty** *Pat Boone*
4/20/59 **Two Brothers** *David Hill*
Two Different Worlds
10/27/56 *Don Rondo*
11/10/56 *Roger Williams Jane Morgan*
12/29/56 *Dick Haymes*
9/21/59 **Two Fools** *Frankie Avalon*
4/2/55 **Two Hearts** *Pat Boone*
7/23/55 **Two Hound Dogs** *Bill Haley*
6/25/55 **Two Lost Souls** *Perry Como & Jaye P. Morgan*

U

12/30/57 **Uh-Huh--mm** *Sonny James*

3/17/58 **Uh-Huh, Oh Yeah** *Steve Lawrence*
Uh! Oh!
11/9/59 *Nutty Squirrels (Part 2)*
12/7/59 *Nutty Squirrels (Part 1)*
Unchained Melody
4/9/55 *Les Baxter*
4/9/55 *Al Hibbler*
4/23/55 *Roy Hamilton*
5/14/55 *June Valli*
10/5/59 **Unforgettable** *Dinah Washington*
9/1/58 **Up Until Now** *Johnnie Ray*

V

5/13/57 **Valley Of Tears** *Fats Domino*
2/18/56 **Valley Valparaiso** *Percy Faith*
6/1/59 **Velvet Waters** *Megatrons*
2/9/59 **Venus** *Frankie Avalon*
3/31/58 **Very Precious Love** *Ames Brothers*
Very Special Love
3/2/57 *Mitch Miller*
12/30/57 *Johnny Nash*
1/20/58 *Debbie Reynolds*
12/14/59 **Village Of St. Bernadette** *Andy Williams*
12/29/58 **Voice In My Heart** *Eydie Gorme*
7/28/56 **Voices** *Fontane Sisters*
Volare (Nel Blu Dipinto Di Blu)
8/4/58 *Dean Martin*
8/4/58 *Domenico Modugno*
9/1/58 *McGuire Sisters*

W

10/21/57 **Wait And See** *Fats Domino*
(Wait For Me) ..see: Johnny Concho Theme
12/30/57 **Waitin' In School** *Ricky Nelson*
Wake The Town And Tell The People
8/13/55 *Les Baxter*
8/27/55 *Mindy Carson*
9/30/57 **Wake Up Little Susie** *Everly Brothers*
2/24/58 **Walk, The** *Jimmy McCracklin*
Walk Hand In Hand
4/21/56 *Tony Martin*
4/21/56 *Andy Williams*
5/19/56 *Denny Vaughn*
2/23/57 **Walkin' After Midnight** *Patsy Cline*
4/20/59 **Walkin' To Mother's** *Ray Anthony*
1/13/58 **Walkin' With Mr. Lee** *Lee Allen*
10/27/58 **Walking Along** *Diamonds*
Wall, The
3/16/57 *Patti Page*
4/6/57 *Eileen Rodgers*
(Wallflower) ..see: Dance With Me Henry
4/13/59 **Walls Have Ears** *Patti Page*
4/20/59 **Wang Dang Taffy-Apple Tango** *Pat Boone*
12/10/55 **Wanting You** *Roger Williams*
9/22/56 **War And Peace** *Vic Damone*
5/20/57 **Warm Up To Me Baby** *Jimmy Bowen*
6/2/56 **Watching The World Go By** *Dean Martin*
5/25/59 **Waterloo** *Stonewall Jackson*
3/9/57 **Watermelon Song** *"Tennessee" Ernie Ford*
11/23/59 **Way Down Yonder In New Orleans** *Freddie Cannon*
6/29/59 **Way I Walk** *Jack Scott*
8/25/58 **Ways Of A Woman In Love** *Johnny Cash*
Ways Of Love ..see: (New In)
Wayward Wind
4/28/56 *Gogi Grant*
6/30/56 *Tex Ritter*
4/14/56 **We All Need Love** *Percy Faith*
2/24/58 **We Belong Together** *Robert & Johnny*
10/12/59 **We Got Love** *Bobby Rydell*
9/22/58 **We Have Love** *Jackie Wilson*
11/23/59 **We Told You Not To Marry** *Titus Turner*
(We're Gonna) Rock Around The Clock ..see: Rock Around The Clock
9/23/57 **Wear My Ring** *Gene Vincent*
4/21/58 **Wear My Ring Around Your Neck** *Elvis Presley*
7/28/56 **Weary Blues** *McGuire Sisters & Lawrence Welk*
Wedding, The
1/14/56 *Chordettes*
11/24/58 *June Valli*
Wedding Bells ..see: (I'm Always Hearing)
9/1/58 **Week End** *Kingsmen*
9/22/56 **Well Did You Evah?** *Bing Crosby & Frank Sinatra*
10/6/58 **Well I'm Your Man** *Johnny Tillotson*
9/22/58 **Wendy, Wendy** *Four Coins*
7/21/58 **Western Movies** *Olympics*
5/25/59 **What A Diff'rence A Day Makes** *Dinah Washington*
12/7/59 **What About Us** *Coasters*
4/28/58 **What Am I Living For** *Chuck Willis*
7/8/57 **What Can I Do** *Donnie Elbert*
10/20/58 **What Do I Care** *Johnny Cash*
2/9/57 **What Is A Teenage Boy?** *Tom Edwards*
2/2/57 **What Is A Teenage Girl?** *Tom Edwards*
12/17/55 **What Is A Wife** *Steve Allen*
7/6/59 **What Is Love?** *Playmates*
10/13/58 **What Little Girl** *Frankie Avalon*
8/12/57 **What Will I Tell My Heart** *Fats Domino*
7/6/59 **What'd I Say** *Ray Charles*
1/12/57 **What's The Reason I'm Not Pleasing You** *Fats Domino*
Whatever Lola Wants
4/23/55 *Sarah Vaughan*
5/14/55 *Dinah Shore*
(Whatever Will Be, Will Be) ..see: Que Sera, Sera
11/2/59 **Wheel Of Fortune** *Knightsbridge Strings*
6/23/58 **When** *Kalin Twins*
11/12/55 **When All The Streets Are Dark** *Somethin' Smith & The Redheads*
9/29/58 **When I Grow Too Old To Dream** *Ed Townsend*
8/12/57 **When I See You** *Fats Domino*
12/1/56 **When My Blue Moon Turns To Gold Again** *Elvis Presley*
7/28/56 **When My Dreamboat Comes Home** *Fats Domino*
4/29/57 **When Rock And Roll Come To Trinidad** *Nat "King" Cole*
6/9/58 **When The Boys Talk About The Girls** *Valerie Carr*
When The Saints Go Marching In
4/7/56 *Bill Haley*
2/16/59 *Fats Domino*
11/4/57 **When The Swallows Come Back To Capistrano** *Pat Boone*
9/15/56 **When The Tide Is High** *Gogi Grant*
When The White Lilacs Bloom Again
9/1/56 *Florian Zabach*
9/1/56 *Helmut Zacharias*
9/8/56 *Leroy Holmes*
9/8/56 *Billy Vaughn*
9/15/56 *Lawrence Welk*
8/25/58 **When Will I Know** *George Hamilton IV*
11/12/55 **When You Dance** *Turbans*
2/4/56 **When You Lose The One You Love** *David Whitfield with Mantovani*
(When Your Heart's On Fire) ..see: Smoke Gets In Your Eyes
9/7/59 **Where** *Platters*
12/28/59 **Where Or When** *Dion & The Belmonts*
8/18/58 **Where The Blue Of The Night** *Tommy Mara*
9/15/56 **Where There's Life** *George Cates*
3/2/59 **Where Were You (On Our Wedding Day)?** *Lloyd Price*
7/8/57 **Whispering Bells** *Dell-Vikings*
6/8/59 **Whistling Organ** *Dave 'Baby' Cortez*
11/10/58 **White Bucks And Saddle Shoes** *Bobby Pedrick, Jr.*
White Christmas
1/1/55* *Bing Crosby*
12/24/55 *Bing Crosby*
12/31/55 *Drifters*
12/29/56 *Bing Crosby*
12/16/57 *Bing Crosby*
12/22/58 *Bing Crosby*
12/28/59 *Bing Crosby*
5/4/59 **White Lightning** *George Jones*
White Silver Sands
7/15/57 *Dave Gardner*
7/15/57 *Don Rondo*
7/29/57 *Owen Bradley Quintet*
White Sport Coat (And A Pink Carnation)
4/13/57 *Marty Robbins*
5/27/57 *Johnny Desmond*
8/18/58 **Who Are They To Say** *DeCastro Siste*
2/4/56 **Who Are We** *Gogi Grant*
1/19/59 **Who Cares** *Don Gibson*
1/26/57 **Who Needs You** *Four Lads*
7/27/59 **Who Shot Sam** *George Jones*
2/24/58 **Who's Sorry Now** *Connie Francis*
3/30/59 **Who's That Knocking** *Genies*
6/24/57 **Whole Lot Of Shakin' Going On** *Jerry Lee Lewis*
11/17/58 **Whole Lotta Loving** *Fats Domino*
3/31/58 **Whole Lotta Woman** *Marvin Rainwate*
1/19/57 **Why** *Cues*
11/23/59 **Why** *Frankie Avalon*
3/16/57 **Why Baby Why** *Pat Boone*
Why Do Fools Fall In Love
2/11/56 *Frankie Lymon & The Teenagers*
2/18/56 *Diamonds*
3/3/56 *Gale Storm*
3/10/56 *Gloria Mann*
12/2/57 **Why Don't They Understand** *George Hamilton IV*
11/12/55 **Why Don't You Write Me** *Jacks*
1/26/59 **Wicked Ruby** *Danny Zella*
12/22/58 **Wiggle, Wiggle** *Accents*
4/7/56 **Wild Cherry** *Don Cherry*
12/16/57 **Wild Is The Wind** *Johnny Mathis*
6/23/58 **Willie And The Hand Jive** *Johnny Otis Show*
8/4/58 **Win Your Love For Me** *Sam Cooke*
3/23/57 **Wind In The Willow** *Jo Stafford*
7/21/58 **Windy** *Paul Gayten*
4/7/56 **Winner Take All** *Platters*
12/15/56 **Wisdom Of A Fool** *Five Keys*
9/14/59 **Wish It Were Me** *Platters*
3/23/59 **Wishful Thinking** *Little Anthony & The Imperials*
4/14/58 **Wishing For Your Love** *Voxpoppers*
4/14/58 **Witch Doctor** *David Seville*
1/20/58 **Witchcraft** *Frank Sinatra*
With A Little Bit Of Luck
7/21/56 *Percy Faith*
8/4/56 *Jo Stafford*
With All My Heart
5/20/57 *Judy Scott*
5/27/57 *Jodie Sands*
7/20/59 **With All Of My Heart** *Brook Benton*
With My Eyes Wide Open I'm Dream
6/15/59 *Enoch Light*
6/15/59 *Patti Page*
7/27/59 **With Open Arms** *Jane Morgan*
1/12/59 **With The Wind And The Rain In You Hair** *Pat Boone*
9/23/57 **With You On My Mind** *Nat "King" Co*
9/29/58 **With Your Love** *Jack Scott*
11/26/55 **Without A Song** *Roy Hamilton*
2/2/57 **Without Love (There Is Nothing)** *Clyde McPhatter*
4/7/56 **Without You** *Eddie Fisher*
8/11/58 **Wizard, The** *Jimmie Rodgers*
Woman In Love
11/19/55 *Four Aces*
11/26/55 *Frankie Laine*
5/18/59 **Wonder Of You** *Ray Peterson*
2/17/58 **Wonderful Time Up There** *Pat Boon*
2/9/57 **Wonderful! Wonderful!** *Johnny Mat*
(also see: Wun'erful, Wun'erful!)
6/15/59 **Wonderful You** *Jimmie Rodgers*
6/3/57 **Wondering** *Patti Page*
11/9/59 **Wont'cha Come Home** *Lloyd Price*
10/5/59 **Woo-Hoo** *Rock-A-Teens*
6/2/58 **Woodchopper's Ball** *Hutch Davie*
6/24/57 **Words Of Love** *Diamonds*
World Outside
11/10/58 *Four Coins*
11/24/58 *Four Aces*
12/8/58 *Roger Williams*
9/14/59 **Worried Man** *Kingston Trio*
12/29/58 **Worryin' Kind** *Tommy Sands*

Wringle, Wrangle
1/26/57 *Bill Hayes*
1/26/57 *Fess Parker*
12/15/56 **Written On The Wind** *Four Aces*
11/11/57 **Wun'erful, Wun'erful!** *Stan Freberg*

Y

6/2/58 **Yakety Yak** *Coasters*
3/24/58 **Yea, Yea** *Kendall Sisters*
12/7/59 **Year Ago Tonight** *Crests*
1/5/59 **Yellow Bird** *Mills Brothers*
Yellow Dog Blues
1/27/58 *Joe Darensbourg*
1/27/58 *Johnny Maddox*
Yellow Rose Of Texas
8/6/55 *Mitch Miller*
8/13/55 *Johnny Desmond*
10/22/55 *Stan Freberg*
3/30/59 **"Yep!"** *Duane Eddy*
9/8/58 **Yes I Want You** *Ivory Joe Hunter*
3/17/58 **Yes, My Darling** *Fats Domino*
4/20/57 **Yes Tonight, Josephine** *Johnnie Ray*
6/1/59 **Yes-Sir-ee** *Dodie Stevens*
4/28/58 **You** *Aquatones*
1/5/59 **You Are Beautiful** *Johnny Mathis*
1/20/58 **You Are My Destiny** *Paul Anka*
2/9/57 **You Are My First Love** *Nat "King" Cole*
10/22/55 **You Are My Love** *Joni James*
2/18/56 **You Baby You** *Cleftones*
9/7/59 **You Better Know It** *Jackie Wilson*
11/11/57 **You Bug Me, Baby** *Larry Williams*
12/16/57 **You Can Make It If You Try** *Gene Allison*
4/13/59 **You Can't Be True Dear** *Mary Kaye Trio*
1/12/59 **You Can't Get To Heaven On Roller Skates** *Betty Johnson*
10/20/56 **You Can't Run Away From It** *Four Aces*
You Cheated
8/4/58 *Slades*
8/25/58 *Shields*
1/21/56 **You Don't Have To Be A Baby To Cry** *"Tennessee" Ernie Ford*
7/27/59 **You Don't Know Girls** *Kathy Linden*
7/7/56 **You Don't Know Me** *Jerry Vale*
1/12/57 **You Don't Owe Me A Thing** *Johnnie Ray*
4/14/58 **You Excite Me** *Frankie Avalon*
9/22/58 **You Got That Touch** *Sonny James*
11/2/59 **You Got What It Takes** *Marv Johnson*
6/10/57 **(You Hit The Wrong Note) Billy Goat** *Bill Haley*
5/4/59 **You Made Me Love You** *Nat "King" Cole*
10/26/59 **You Mean Everything To Me** *Fleetwoods*
5/26/58 **You Need Hands** *Eydie Gorme*
You Send Me
10/21/57 *Sam Cooke*
11/11/57 *Teresa Brewer*
9/30/57 **You Shouldn't Do That** *Sal Mineo*
12/10/55 **You Tickle Me Baby** *Royal Jokers*
11/2/59 **You Went Back On Your Word** *Clyde McPhatter*
3/24/58 **You Were Made For Me** *Sam Cooke*
9/7/59 **You Were Mine** *Fireflies*
You Win Again
11/19/55 *Paulette Sisters*
2/17/58 *Jerry Lee Lewis*
6/9/58 **You'd Be Surprised** *Kathy Linden*
3/3/56 **You'll Get Yours** *Frank Sinatra*
9/29/56 **You'll Never Never Know** *Platters*
8/11/58 **You're A Sweetheart** *Little Willie John*
7/22/57 **You're Cheatin' Yourself (If You're Cheatin' On Me)** *Frank Sinatra*
8/31/59 **You're Gonna Miss Me** *Connie Francis*
9/15/56 **You're In Love** *Gogi Grant*
6/30/58 **You're Making A Mistake** *Platters*
You're Mine
4/7/56 *Dream Weavers*
3/30/57 *Four Aces*
8/26/57 **You're My One And Only Love** *Ricky Nelson*
7/14/56 **You're Sensational** *Frank Sinatra*
4/20/59 **You're So Fine** *Falcons*
11/12/55 **You're So Nice To Be Near** *Loreleis*
5/26/56 **You're The Apple Of My Eye** *Four Lovers*
1/13/58 **You're The Greatest** *Billy Scott*
9/8/58 **You're The Nearest Thing To Heaven** *Johnny Cash*
3/24/56 **(You've Got) The Magic Touch** *Platters*
Young Abe Lincoln
11/12/55 *Don Cornell*
12/10/55 *Hugo & Luigi*
6/23/58 **Young And Warm And Wonderful** *Tony Bennett*
5/6/57 **Young Blood** *Coasters*
5/4/59 **Young Ideas** *Chico Holiday*
Young Love
12/29/56 *Sonny James*
1/12/57 *Crew-Cuts*
1/12/57 *Tab Hunter*
9/22/58 **Young School Girl** *Fats Domino*
Your Cheatin' Heart
9/8/58 *George Hamilton IV*
4/27/59 *Billy Vaughn*
6/17/57 **Your Kisses Kill Me** *Eydie Gorme*
1/19/57 **Your Love For Me** *Frank Sinatra*
3/24/58 **Your Name Is Beautiful** *Carl Smith*
3/23/57 **Your True Love** *Carl Perkins*
2/16/57 **Your Wild Heart** *Joy Layne*

Z

12/24/55 **Zambezi** *Lou Busch*
8/26/57 **Zip Zip** *Diamonds*
5/19/58 **Zorro** *Chordettes*

The RECORD RESEARCH *Collection*

	BOOK TITLE	Quantity	Price	Total
1.	Billboard Pop Charts 1955-1959 (hardcover)	______	$95	______
2.	Billboard Hot 100 Charts — The Sixties (hardcover)	______	$95	______
3.	Billboard Hot 100 Charts — The Seventies (hardcover)	______	$95	______
4.	Billboard Hot 100 Charts — The Eighties (hardcover)	______	$95	______
5.	Top Pop Albums 1955-1992 (hardcover)* *Anticipated publication date: December, 1992	______	$95	______
6.	Top Pop Singles 1955-1990 (hardcover)	______	$70	______
7.	Top Pop Singles 1955-1990 (softcover)	______	$60	______
8.	Pop Singles Annual 1955-1990 (hardcover)	______	$70	______
9.	Pop Singles Annual 1955-1990 (softcover)	______	$60	______
10.	Top Country Singles 1944-1988 (hardcover)	______	$60	______
11.	Top Country Singles 1944-1988 (softcover)	______	$50	______
12.	Top R&B Singles 1942-1988 (hardcover)	______	$60	______
13.	Top R&B Singles 1942-1988 (softcover)	______	$50	______
14.	Pop Memories 1890-1954 (hardcover)	______	$60	______
15.	Top 10 Charts 1958-1988 (softcover)	______	$50	______
16.	Bubbling Under The Hot 100 1959-1985 (hardcover)	______	$45	______
17.	Billboard #1s 1950-1991 (softcover)	______	$35	______
18.	Top 3000+ 1955-1990 (softcover)	______	$25	______
19.	Yearbooks (all softcover) ☐ 1991 ☐ 1990 ☐ 1989 ☐ 1988 ☐ 1987 ☐ 1986 ☐ 1985 ☐ 1984 ☐ 1983		$35 each	______

Subtotal....................$ ______

Shipping & Handling....................$ ______

All U.S. orders add $5 for the first book ordered and $2 for each additional book.

All Canadian and foreign orders add $6 for the first book ordered and $3 for each additional book. Canadian and foreign orders are shipped via surface mail and must be paid in **U.S. dollars**. Call or write for air mail shipping rates.

Total Payment...........$ ______

Payment Method ☐ Check ☐ Money Order ☐ MasterCard ☐ VISA

MasterCard or VISA # _ _ _ _ _ _ _ _ _ _ _ _ _ _ _ _

Expiration Date ______ / ______
Mo. Yr.

Signature ______________________________

To Charge Your Order By Phone, Call 414-251-5408 or
Fax 414-251-9452 (office hours: 8AM-5PM CST)

Name ______________________________

Company Name ______________________________

Address ______________________________ Apt/Suite # __________

City ______________________ State/Province __________

ZIP/Postal Code __________________ Country __________________

For complete book descriptions and ordering information, call write or fax today.

Record Research

The World's Leading Authority On Recorded Entertainment

Record Research Inc.
P.O. Box 200
Menomonee Falls, WI 53052-0200
U.S.A.

Phone: 414-251-5408
Fax: 414-251-9452